# LONGMAN Study Dictionary of American English

PEARSON
Longman

2ND EDITION

Pearson Education Limited
Edinburgh Gate
Harlow
Essex CM20 2JE, England, UK
and associated Companies throughout the world

Visit our website: http://www.pearsonlongman.com/dictionaries



First edition published 2006

Second edition 2011



| | | | |
|---|---|---|---|
| ISBN | Paperback | 978-1-4082-4531-6 | 1 2 3 4 5 6 V011 15 14 13 12 11 10 |
| | Paperback and Online Access | 978-1-4082-4532-3 | 1 2 3 4 5 6 V011 15 14 13 12 11 10 |
| | Hardcover | 978-1-4082-4529-3 | 1 2 3 4 5 6 V011 15 14 13 12 11 10 |
| | Hardcover and Online Access | 978-1-4082-4530-9 | 1 2 3 4 5 6 V011 15 14 13 12 11 10 |

Set in Frutiger and Whitney by Letterpart, UK

Printed by Courier, U.S.

## Acknowledgements

**Editorial Director**
Michael Mayor

**Publishing Manager**
Laurence Delacroix

**Managing Editor**
Chris Fox

**Senior Editor**
Karen Cleveland-Marwick

**Editors**
Evadne Adrian-Vallance
Elizabeth Beizai
Stephen Handorf
Elizabeth Manning
Michael Murphy
Dr Martin Stark

**Project Management**
Alan Savill

**Workbook Section**
Linda Butler
Eudie Pak (2nd edition)

**Production**
Keeley Everitt
Susan Braund

**Editorial Manager**
Paola Rocchetti

**Production Editor**
Anna Bardong

**Pronunciation Editor**
Dinah Jackson

**Proofreaders**
Karin Fischer-Buder
Isabel Griffiths
Ruth Hillmore

**Design**
Matthew Dickin

**Computational Linguist**
Allan Ørsnes

**Project and Databases Administrator**
Denise McKeough

**Picture Research**
Sandra Hilsdon

**Illustrations**
Chris Pavely
Mark Turner (Beehive Illustration)
Laszlo Veres (Beehive Illustration)
Jo Blake (Beehive Illustration)
John Schriener (Debora Wolfe)
Bob Kayganich (Debora Wolfe)

**The publishers would like to express their gratitude to** their special adviser **Dr Kate Kinsella**, Teacher Trainer and School Consultant, San Francisco State University, Department of Secondary Education, for her keen interest, highly informed and focused guidance, and continued support throughout the development of this dictionary.

**The publishers and editorial team would like to thank** the lexicographic team who worked on the Longman Study Dictionary of American English (first edition) and the many people who have contributed advice to making this latest edition.

**The publishers would also like to thank** all the dedicated teachers who have attended focus groups and given their informed feedback on sample text, in particular:

J. J. Lee Gilbert, Cuba Munsay, Karen Ball, Veronica Fern-McElarney, Margaret Klee, Dolores T. Andrews, Adriana Bo, Claire Trepanier, Nancy Rodriguez, Pilar Meija, Wayne Miller, Lorie Johnson, Trudie Heney, Susanna Cawley, Ms Barlow, Kelly Taggart, Sue Bolender, Jane Ardell, Cathy Personius, Steven Kirk, Marlene Churgel, David Roberts, Patricia Armendariz, Ann Ly, Kristien Evans, Donna Minick, Janet Ennis, Sarah Windes, Christina Park, Joyce Gordon, Doris Noriega, Lauri Buehler, Lisa Barnes, Shelly De Simone, Catherine Bunch, Devra Miller, Kim Shults, Ann Pappas, Ann Sokolovskaya, Marty Roberts, Adele Alvarez, Ross Russell, Jim Ybarra, Vanessa Henson, Ryan Coy, Courtney Gonzalez, Xavier Haase, Toni Costantino, Dorothea Jordan, Liane Cismowski, Laura Hill, Corinne Christiansen, Kevin Feldman, Lyndi Stauffer, John F. Fox, Lisa Visendi.

# Table of Contents

What teachers say about the

# Longman Study Dictionary of American English

***The new dictionary looks enchanting and I believe that non native-speakers at various levels of competency in the English language, as well as under-achieving native-speakers who are below standards will benefit from it.***

***The definitions are clear, the example sentences help to learn the meaning of the word, and the Thesaurus, Word Family, and Usage boxes are certainly a good solution that makes the layout much more user-friendly.***

J.J. Lee-Gilbert
ESL Department
Menlo-Atherton High School, California

***Impressive, high access – the word families boxes I especially appreciate – I will be recommending this dictionary in my seminars!***

Dr. Kevin Feldman
Educational Consultant
Healdsburg, California

***Language minority students, struggling adolescent readers, and mixed-ability classrooms pose so many unique challenges and I've been impressed with the consideration Longman has shown to their needs.***

Marty Roberts
Hillsdale High School, San Mateo
California

# Introduction

by **Kate Kinsella,**
Ed.D., San Francisco State University
Department of Secondary Education

A dictionary can be an invaluable resource for young language learners as they tackle the vocabulary demands of challenging reading curricula and academic writing tasks.

Unfortunately, the curricular mainstay of U.S. upper-elementary and secondary classrooms is a collegiate desk dictionary, and as the root word "college" suggests, this lexical tool was designed for a mature adult reader with a highly literate command of English. As a consequence, definitions are overly precise and concise at the expense of clarity, and often include another form of the target word or even more sophisticated words.

Standard desk dictionaries also fail to provide familiar synonyms within a school-aged youth's "personal thesaurus" and illustrative examples drawn from commonplace experiential realms. Students in grades 4-9 are generally too mature for the junior picture dictionary that served them well in the primary grades but far too immature for the comprehensive dictionary that they will need in advanced high school and collegiate coursework. When students find themselves more confused and frustrated than illuminated by a vocabulary resource, they are bound to rely upon unproductive coping strategies like rote copying or abandoning any independent study efforts in hopes of an eventual teacher explanation. Repeated unsuccessful forays into a dictionary have a long-lasting negative impact on struggling learners who internalize their disappointing endeavors as a personal failure rather than a glaring curricular mismatch.

I teach and coach instruction throughout the U.S. in highly diverse 4-12 classrooms, including striving readers and English learners who are woefully under-prepared for the language demands of their grade level curricula. The teachers need a potent lesson-planning tool that will aid them in effectively and efficiently preparing to teach the most critical terms to a linguistically vulnerable class. Likewise, the learners need a non-intimidating resource that won't leave them utterly bewildered and paralyzed with confusion when they are assigned independent vocabulary work.

I am elated to be able to wholeheartedly recommend an appropriate dictionary for the mixed-ability intermediate or secondary classroom. The **Longman Study Dictionary** meets all of my criteria for a "considerate" vocabulary development resource for younger learners. The visual impact of the page spread is appealing for a neophyte academic dictionary user while not appearing juvenile, and the judicious use of color and graphics all make page navigation more manageable.

Furthermore, the meticulously crafted definitions are conscientious explanations written using familiar language within a school-aged youth's daily register rather than the arguably precise yet elusive synonyms and syntax characteristic of the academic lexicon. These accessible explanations are complemented by evocative, familiar examples that help a less experienced young learner build a powerful mental anchor, increasing the odds of word comprehension and successful application.

Equally valuably, the **Longman Study Dictionary** highlights high-incidence academic vocabulary in striking word family boxes, drawing students' attention to critical words for academic endeavors. Knowledge of the most commonly used academic word families across grade levels and subject areas can significantly boost a student's comprehension level of school-based reading material and performance on high stakes writing assignments. These academic "tool kit" words are given lexical status in this learners' dictionary, which should facilitate lesson planning for teachers and independent word study for developing English language users. The embedded thesaurus will also serve as a practical and manageable tool for student writers searching for precise word substitutes for everyday words.

A considerate, developmentally appropriate dictionary should be an educational civil right at every grade level. I sincerely hope the **Longman Study Dictionary** makes its way into as many school libraries, classrooms and backpacks as possible to support young aspiring learners in making the academic language and literacy strides that underlie educational success.

# Guide to the Dictionary

Different meanings are shown clearly, with the most common meaning first.

Definitions explaining the meaning of a word are written in clear simple language, using the 2000-word Longman Defining Vocabulary.

Words with the same or opposite meaning are shown after the definition.

Irregular forms of verbs are shown at the beginning of an entry.

Simple examples show you how to use a word and help to explain its meaning.

Phrasal Verbs are shown in alphabetical order at the end of an entry.

The dictionary contains words that are often used in science lessons and text books.

Pronunciation

A label before a definition shows that a word is formal or informal.

Derived words are shown at the end of an entry. These words can be easily understood from the meaning of the main word.

Different spellings are shown at the beginning of an entry.

Words that are spelled the same but have different parts of speech have separate entries.

**con·clude** Ac /kən'klud/ *verb* (*formal*)

**1** to decide that something is true from the information you have: *He didn't apologize so I concluded that he wasn't sorry for what he did.*

**2** to end or finish something: *She concluded the meeting by thanking everyone.* | *The show concluded with a dance performance by the younger children.* **SYNONYMS: finish, end**; **ANTONYMS: begin, start**

**eat** /it/ *verb* (**ate** /eɪt/, **eaten** /'itn/)

**1** to put food in your mouth and swallow it: *She was eating an apple.* | *I'm still eating my dinner.* | *Do you want something to eat?*

**2** to have a meal: *We usually eat at about 6.*

**PHRASAL VERBS**

**eat out**

to eat in a restaurant: *They usually eat out once a week.*

**eat something up**

**1** to finish eating all of something: *Eat up your breakfast! We're late!*

**2** to use too much of something: *Homework eats up a lot of my free time.*

**en·zyme** /'enzaɪm/ *noun*

a chemical that is produced in plants and animals, and that makes a chemical process start: *Enzymes in the stomach change food so that it can be digested.*

**e·rupt** /ɪ'rʌpt/ *verb*

**1** (*formal*) if violence erupts, it suddenly happens: *In this war-torn country, fighting could erupt again at any time.*

**2** if a VOLCANO erupts, it sends out smoke, fire, and rock into the sky: *More than 800 people died when the volcano erupted.*

—**eruption** /ɪ'rʌpʃən/ *noun* an occasion when a VOLCANO erupts: *The eruption sent a cloud of ash high into the sky.*

[**ORIGIN:** 1600-1700 From the Latin word *eruptus*, a form of the verb *erumpere*, which means "to burst out."]

**judg·ment** (*also* **judgement**) /'dʒʌdʒmənt/ *noun*

**jump**[1] /dʒʌmp/ *verb*

**jump**[2] *noun*

**globe** Ac /gloub/ *noun*
**1 the globe** = the world: *Our company has offices all over the globe.*
**2** a round object that has a map of the Earth on it: *The teacher used a globe to show how the ships sailed from England to America.*
[ORIGIN: 1500-1600 From the Latin word *globus*, which means "something in the shape of a ball."]

**WORD FAMILY: globe**
**globe** *noun* | **global** *adjective* | **globally** *adverb*

**hap·py** /ˈhæpi/ *adjective* (**happier, happiest**)
**1** feeling pleased, for example because your life is good, or something good has happened: *Pete is happy at his new school.* | *I was really happy to hear your good news!*

**THESAURUS: happy**
**cheerful** someone who is cheerful seems happy and smiles a lot: *Tom is a very cheerful little boy.*
**pleased** happy because someone has done something good, or something good has happened: *Her parents were pleased that she had done so well in her classes.*
**glad** happy because something good has happened: *I'm really glad you can come to the party.*
**delighted** very happy because something good has happened: *She will be delighted when she hears the news.*

**inhale**

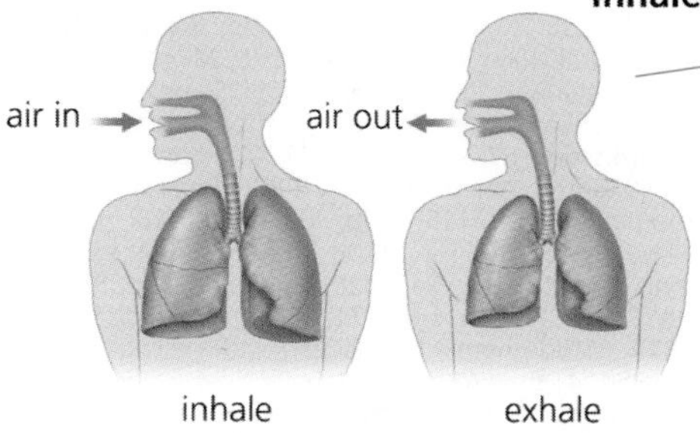


**in·hale** /ɪnˈheɪl/ *verb* (*formal*)
to breathe in air, smoke, or gas: *Some of the people rescued from the fire had inhaled a lot of smoke.* **ANTONYM: exhale**

The Ac label shows that a word is in the Academic Word List. These are important words which students need to learn and use in academic assignments.

Common phrases have their own definition, and the meaning of the whole phrase is explained.

Word Origin notes have interesting facts explaining where a word comes from and where it started to be used.

Word Family boxes have lists of words that are from the same family.

Comparative and superlative forms of adjectives are shown at the beginning of an entry.

Part of speech

The 3,000 most common words in English are highlighted in red.

Thesaurus boxes explain words with similar meanings to the word you are looking up, helping to increase your vocabulary.

Pictures help you to understand the meaning of a word.

# Photo Credits

The publisher would like to thank the following for their kind permission to reproduce their photographs:

(Key: b-bottom; c-centre; l-left; r-right; t-top)

**Alamy Images:** 90, Adrian Brockwell A21 (viola ), Allan Ivy A26 (motor home), Amar and Isabelle Guillen - Guillen Photography A26 (motorcycle), Andre Jenny A27 (ship), artpartner-images.com 235r, Blend Images A17 (florist), Cristina Fumi 689 (sneakers), Culligan Photo A26 (crosswalk), Danita Delimont A25 (volleyball), David Grossman 656t, David Lyons 342, David R Frazier Photography A26 (bus), David R. Frazier Photolibrary, Inc A16 (bank teller), David Robertson 249, Dennis MacDonald / Tresham College of Further and Higher Education A17 (judge and lawyer), Derek Payne 231r, EK Aviation A27 (plane), Eye-Stock 525, Gary K Smith 330, Georgios Kalidas 235l, Glow Asia RF 271, Image Source 184, A16 (doctor and nurse), A17 (counter worker), imagebroker 322, James Davis 369, Joanna Szycik 437tr, Joe Fox New York A26 (cab/taxi), Mark J. Barrett A25 (soccer), Marshall Ikonography 606, MBI 169, Mode Images Ltd 139r, Nikreates 689 (sandals), PCL A26 (subway), Peter Arnold, inc. 771, Peter Horee A27 (truck), PetStockBoys 92, pm 503tl, Scott Hortop A17 (fitness trainer), Sofia Pereira 254, Swerve A25 (rollerblading), Thomas Peterson A26 (train), Tom Carter 55, Vadim Ponomarenko 689 (boots), vario images GmbH & Co.Ka 261, Vicki Beaver 519, Westend61GmbH 373; **Corbis:** Ariel Skelley A27 (rowboat), Bettmann A25 (boxing), Charles & Josette Lenars 164, cultura 790, Dream Pictures / Shannon Faulk / Blend Images A16 (firefighter), Ghislain & Marie David de Lossy. Cultura 864, Joseph Sohm / Visions of America A27 (fire engine), Juice Images A16 (sales person), moodboard 325t, Philip James Corwin 622, Reuters A27 (police car), Tom Bean 613; **DK Images:** 13, 646, A27 (ferry), A13 (blackberries), A13 (blueberries), A13 (dates), A13 (figs), A13 (mango), A13 (rhubarb), A13 (tangerine), A15 (chop), A15 (grate), A15 (mash), A15 (pour), A15 (sprinkle), A15 (strain), A26 (tractor), A27 (ambulance), A27 (helicopter), Andy Crawford 414, Colin Keates 294 , Dave King 196tl, A14 (bear), Dave King / Jeremy Hunt-model maker 685, A14 (shark), Gary Ombler 455, Geoff Brightling 23tr, Jerry Young 23bl, Peter Anderson A14 (bison), Philip Gatward 65, Suzanne Porter 517; **Dreamstime.com:** 505cr, Angelo Gilardelli 344, Rafa Irusta 196bl, William Higgins 196tr; **FLPA Images of Nature:** Mike Parry / Minden Pictures A14 (whale); **Getty Images:** Burazin 110br, Dave King / Dorling Kindersley 485, Fat Chance Productions / iconica A25 (running), For DAGOC A24 (martial arts), hana. Datacroft 831, Heath Korvola A25 (surfing), Jeremy Woodhouse A26 (bicycle), Photographers choice A27 (pickup truck), Tom Bean / Stone 190; **Hemera Photo Objects:** 88tl, 88tc, 88tr, 91l, 339, 340br, 444bl, 570, 655, 671tc, 671tr, 671br, 778, 814, 843, 848, 877; **iStockphoto:** 49bl, 49br, 214, 444tc, 444bc, 558tl, 558tr, 643tr, 643br, 709r, 757, 808r, 811, 825cr, 878, A14 (cardina), 244 , 340 bl, 349 r, A12 (onion), A24 (baseball), A24 (golf), A25 (snowboarding), Adam Kazmierski 54, Allan Mueller A14 (bluejay), Andrea Incalza 74, Andrew Brown 277 t, Antonio D'Albore 485r, Bart Sadowski 582, Chanyut Sribua-Rawd A14 (crocodile), Cheryl Bowman 417 (gauze), Christi Tolbert 498b, Claudiaveja A17 (journalist/ reporter), Craig Veltri 417 (cotton balls), Dmitriy Buyanskiy 438b, Eduardo Jose Bernardino 564, EEI_Tony 809, ej59 848r, Eric Isselee A14 (cougar), A14 (owl), filo 769, Ilda Masa A25 (skiing), iofoto A16 (teacher), Jabejon A25 (swimming), Jared DeCinque 147, Jeffrey Smith 515, Jerry Callaghan 871, juanmorino 437bl, Kaliq A17 (waitress), Ken Canning 491, King Wu 852t, Kris Hollingsworth 467l, Kristina Castagnaa 430l, Lachlan Currie 430r, laughing mango 875l, Lawrence Sawyer 874, Levgenia Tikhonova 572, Lisa F. Young A16 (electrician), Lisa Turay 278, lise gagne 736tl, Luis Carlos Torres 608, Martin Bowker 808l, Martin McCarthy 24, meadowmouse 362, micropic 303, Nico Smit 505b, Paulina Monika Walter 503tr, Quavondo A16 (receptionist), Raoul Vernede 203l, Rebekah Lane 23tl, Roksana Bashyrora 564t, Rudyanto Wijaya A17 (baker ), rypson 735, Sean Locke A16 (pharmacist), A16 (veterinarian), Simon Phipps A14 (beaver), Sisoje 838, Studio ceja 864b, Summer Derrick 729t, technotr A24 (cycling), Tiago Estima 667, Tim Mclean A17 (hairdresser), Tony Campbell A14 (white-tailed deer), Torsten Karock A14 (wolf), Vasiliki Varvaki 196 br, Vikram Raghuvanshi A17 (chef/ cook), Viorika Prikodko A16 (professor); **Pearson Education Ltd:** 49tr, Brand X Picture / Joe Atlas 104tr, 104bl, 127, C Squared Studios / Tony Gable 7tl, 80 (violin and bow), Comstock Images 172r, Eyewire A21 (cello), Gareth Boden 624, KPT PowerPhotos 302, Photodisc 129, 145tr, 281, 432b, 475t, 475b, 104, 145, 172l, 275, 503cr, 505cl, 658, A15 (kitchen verbs), A12 , A13 , A15, A24-A25 , A26 (sailboat); **PhotoDisc:** Musical Instruments 21; **Photolibrary.com:** 110bc, Image Source 746l, Photodisc 671bl; **PunchStock:** A27 (van ), valueline 17tr; **Shutterstock:** 104tl, 703, 862, Alistair Scott 652, Andreja Donko 547, ARENA Creative 406t, Awe Inspiring Images 468tr, Baloncici 653t, Bierchen 600, Bomshtein 80 (toolbox), Boris Djuranovic 334 , Brent Pizzato 736tr, Celso Diniz 177, Christopher Elwell 80 (jewelry box), Costin Cojocaru 358, Dallas Events Inc 793, Daniel Rajszczak A17 (optometrist), danilo ducak 751, David Hughes 653b, Diego Cervo A16 (mechanic), dragon_fang 401r, 682, Egypix 461, Firespots A14 (snake), Fotocrisis 80 (bow and arrow), Galina Barskaya 411t, Greg Perkins 405, James DeBoer 23br, Jonathan Larsen 438, Joy Brown 428c, Katja Kodba 493, Lisa F. Young 266, Margo Harrison 110bl, Michael C. Gray 406b, Michael Shake 576, Mighty Sequoia A14 (alligator), Miss Louise worth 408br, Muellek Josef 417tr, Pavlova Elena 237, Perov Stanislav 409l, Sergey Rusakov 361, Simon Krzic 231l, Stephen Coburn 333, Steve Snowden 61br, Tischenko Irina 41, TooHes 409r, tororo reaction 32, Vakhrushnev Pavel 145tl, Valzan 776, Vishnevskiy Vasily 505t; **Thinkstock:** 67, 91r, 340tr, 403, 417 (bandage), 417 (lotion), 417 (scissors), 428r, 444r, 503, 503bl, 558bl, 558br, 709l, 759, 340 tl, Ablestock.com 57, 876, Barry Austin 805, BrandXimages 80 (lunchbox), 329, 417 (first-aid kit), 468tl, Comstock Images 40tr, 115, 277b, 335, 344tr, 428l, 432l, 755, 774, 834, Creatas 852b, A16 (dentist), Goodshoot A24 (basketball ), Hemera 7tr, 110tc, 110tr, 179, 276, 344c, 344br, 387, 408tl, 408tr, 408cr, 441, 656b, 683, 746r, iStock 17cl, 29l, 49tl, 61t, 61bl, 88c, 94, 132l, 139tc, 253, 306, 325b, 344tl, 347tl, 347tr, 385, 389, 408cl, 408bl, 418t, 420r, 432r, 437tc, 537, 611, 652t, 664, 671tl, 687t, 689 (high heels), 689 (shoes), 689 (slippers), 689 (soccer boots), 689 (thongs), 762, 849c, iStockphoto A17 (painter), Jack Hollingsworth 58l, James Woodson 296, 849l, John Foxx 171, Jupiter images 132r, 354, 418b, 420l, 661, 729b, 743, 849r, Juptier Images 85, 99, 617, Mario Teijeiro 80 (hair bow), Martin Poole 320tl, Medioimages / Photodisc 29r, 58r, Photodisc 875r, A16 (police officer), Photoobjects.net 110tl, 349bl, Pixland 839, Ryan McVay 437br, Siri Stafford 58c, Siri strafford 820, Stockbyte 199cl, 320tr, Stockbyte / Tom Brakefield 29c, Stockxpert 27t, 100, 203r, 27 b, 424, 489, 498t, 539, 541, 687b, 832, 854, Thomas Northcut 437tl, Tom Brakefield 227, A14 (eagle)

# Aa

**a** /ə; *strong* eɪ/ (*also* **an**) *indefinite article*
**1** used when you are mentioning or describing someone or something: *He wants to buy a car.* | *Her mother's a teacher.*
**2** used with "hundred," "thousand," etc. to mean "one": *a thousand dollars* (=$1,000)
**3** each: *The candy costs 75 cents a bag, so two bags cost $1.50.* **SYNONYM: per**

**A** /eɪ/ *noun*
**1** the best GRADE that you can get on a test or in a class: *I did a really good job on my book report, and I got an A.*
**2** the sixth note in the musical SCALE of C, or the musical KEY based on this note

**a·ban·don** Ac /əˈbændən/ *verb* (*formal*)
**1** to leave a person, place, or vehicle and not go back: *The thieves abandoned the car beside the road.*
**2** to stop trying to do something because of problems: *The rescue workers abandoned the search when it became too dark to see.*
—**abandonment** *noun* the action of abandoning someone or something

**ab·bre·vi·a·tion** /əˌbriviˈeɪʃən/ *noun*
the short way of writing a word: *"Mr." is the abbreviation for "Mister."*
[**ORIGIN:** 1400-1500 From the Latin word *brevis*, which means "short."]

**ABCs** /ˌeɪbiˈsiz/ *plural noun*
the letters of the English alphabet: *My little sister is learning her ABCs and can recognize most of the letters.*

**ab·do·men** /ˈæbdəmən/ *noun* (*formal*)
**1** the front part of your body between your chest and your legs
**2** the third part of an insect's body, furthest from its head
—**abdominal** /æbˈdɑmənəl/ *adjective* (*formal*) relating to the abdomen

**ab·duct** /əbˈdʌkt/ *verb* (*formal*)
to take someone away by force in order to keep him or her as your prisoner: *The terrorists abducted him and kept him in the basement of a house.* **SYNONYM: kidnap**
—**abduction** /əbˈdʌkʃən/ *noun* the act of abducting someone: *the abduction of a child*

**a·bil·i·ty** /əˈbɪləti/ *noun* (plural **abilities**)
**1** if you have the ability to do something, you can do it: *Her ability to speak Spanish was very useful when she was in Mexico.*
**2** skill at doing something: *He has a lot of athletic ability and plays many sports well.*
[**ORIGIN:** 1400-1500 From the Latin word *habilis*, which means "skillful."]

**THESAURUS: ability**

**skill** something that you do very well because you have learned and practiced it: *This class will help you improve your writing skills.*

**talent** a natural ability to do something well: *Kate has a lot of musical talent and plays the guitar really well.*

**knack** a natural ability to do something well: *He has a real knack for writing catchy pop songs.*

**a·ble** /ˈeɪbəl/ *adjective*
**1** **able to do something** = if you are able to do something, you can do it: *Marcia is able to play the piano and the violin.*
**2** good at doing something: *All his teachers say that he is a very able student.*

**WORD FAMILY: able**

**able** *adjective* | **unable** *adjective* | **ability** *noun* | **inability** *noun* | **enable** *verb*

**ab·nor·mal** Ac /æbˈnɔrməl/ *adjective* (*formal*)
not normal compared to what is usual: *The doctor said her breathing was abnormal and he sent her to the hospital for tests.*
**ANTONYM: normal**
—**abnormally** *adverb* in an abnormal way: *The weather was abnormally cold that year and a lot of plants died.*
—**abnormality** /ˌæbnɔrˈmæləti/ *noun* something that is abnormal

**a·board** /əˈbɔrd/ *adverb, preposition*
on a ship, airplane, or train: *There were over a thousand passengers aboard the ship.*

A

**a·bol·ish** /əˈbɑlɪʃ/ *verb (formal)*
to officially end a law or system: *The country recently abolished the death penalty.*
—**abolition** /ˌæbəˈlɪʃən/ *noun* the act of abolishing something: *the abolition of slavery*

**ab·o·li·tion·ist** /ˌæbəˈlɪʃənɪst/ *noun*
someone who worked to abolish SLAVERY during the 1800s

**a·bor·tion** /əˈbɔrʃən/ *noun*
an operation to end a PREGNANCY: *She decided not to have an abortion because she wanted to keep the baby.*

**a·bout** /əˈbaʊt/ *adverb, preposition*
**1** used to say what the subject of something is: *She was reading a book about horses.* | *He was worried about the math test.*
**2** used when saying that a number or amount is not exact: *The sun sets at about six o'clock.* | *There were about 50 students at the meeting.* **SYNONYMS: around, approximately**

**THESAURUS: about**

**around** means the same as **about**: *"What time will you get home?" "Around nine, I think."*

**approximately** means the same as **about**. It is often used with measurements: *He is approximately six feet tall.*

**roughly** means the same as **about**. You use it when you are saying a number you know is not exact: *Roughly 7,000 cars cross the border every day.*

**or so** used when you are not sure and cannot be exact about a number, amount, or period of time: *It takes ten minutes or so to drive there, depending on traffic.*

**3 be about to do something** = if you are about to do something, you will do it very soon: *Can I call you back later? We're about to have dinner.*
**4 what about/how about** = **a)** used to suggest doing something: *How about going to a movie?* **b)** used to ask a question relating to something or someone: *What about the food? Was it good?*
**5** concerning someone or something: *There's something weird about that guy – he never looks at me when he's talking to me.*

**a·bove** /əˈbʌv/ *adverb, preposition*
**1** in a higher position than something: *Raise your arm above your head.* | *He heard a noise in the room above.* **ANTONYM: below**
**2** more than a number, amount, or level: *Temperatures rose above freezing today, to 35 degrees.* | *The program is for kids age 8 and above.* **ANTONYM: below**
**3** before, in the same piece of writing: *Look at the picture above and answer these questions.* **ANTONYM: below**
**4 above all** (*formal*) = most importantly, or more than anything else: *Above all, children want to feel safe and loved.*

**a·bridged** /əˈbrɪdʒd/ *adjective*
an abridged book or play has been made shorter than the original one

**a·broad** /əˈbrɔd/ *adverb*
in or to a foreign country: *In college, you can go abroad to study for a year, for example to Spain or England.*

**a·brupt** /əˈbrʌpt/ *adjective*
**1** sudden and unexpected: *There was an abrupt knock at the door.*
**2** speaking with few words in a way that seems rude or unfriendly: *She was very abrupt on the phone, and I thought she must be angry.*
—**abruptly** *adverb* suddenly and unexpectedly: *The train stopped abruptly and I almost fell down.*

**ab·sence** /ˈæbsəns/ *noun*
a time when you are not at school or work: *If children miss school, the school needs to know the reason for their absence.*

**ab·sent** /ˈæbsənt/ *adjective*
not at work, school, or a meeting when other people expect you to be there: *Ten children were absent from class today because of colds.* **ANTONYM: present**
—**absentee** *noun* someone who is absent: *Most people were at the meeting. There were only three absentees.*
[**ORIGIN:** 1300-1400 From the Latin word *absentem*, a form of the verb *abesse*, which means "to be away."]

**ab·so·lute** /ˈæbsəlut/ *adjective*
complete or total: *I have absolute confidence in you and I am sure you will succeed.*

**ab·so·lute·ly** /ˌæbsəˈlutli/ *adverb*
**1** completely or totally: *Are you absolutely sure this is the right way?*
**2** used to emphasize what you are saying: *There's absolutely nothing wrong with the car – it works perfectly.*
**3** used to say that you strongly agree: *"Do you think she's right?" "Absolutely."*

**ab·sorb** /əbˈsɔrb/ *verb* (*formal*)
**1** if something absorbs liquid, gas, or energy, it takes it in and holds it: *The towel absorbed most of the water. | Plants absorb nutrients from the soil.*
**2** to learn and completely understand new information: *There was too much information in the article – I couldn't absorb it all.*
**3 be absorbed in something** = to be very interested in something you are doing or watching so that you do not pay attention to other things: *Daniel was absorbed in his book, and he didn't see me come in the room.*
—**absorbent** *adjective* able to absorb liquid: *Paper towels are useful in the kitchen because they are so absorbent.*
[**ORIGIN:** 1400-1500 From the Latin words *ab* and *sorbere*, which mean "away" and "to suck up."]

**ab·sorb·ing** /əbˈsɔrbɪŋ/ *adjective*
an absorbing book or movie is very interesting, so that you read or watch it with a lot of attention

**ab·stain** /əbˈsteɪn/ *verb*
to not vote when the other people in your group are voting: *Four committee members voted in favor of the plan, two voted against it, and one member abstained.*

**ab·stract** Ac /æbˈstrækt/ *adjective*
**1** relating to ideas rather than things you can see, hear, touch, or taste: *Happiness is an abstract idea. You cannot see it or touch it.*
**2** abstract art consists of shapes and patterns that do not look like real things or people

**ab·surd** /əbˈsɚd/ *adjective*
completely silly: *That's an absurd idea! You can't pretend to be Mom. No one would believe you!*
—**absurdly** *adverb* in an absurd way

**a·bun·dance** /əˈbʌndəns/ *noun* (*formal*)
a lot of something: *There is an abundance of information about this subject on the Internet. You can easily find out more.*

**a·bun·dant** /əˈbʌndənt/ *adjective* (*formal*)
more than enough: *In summer, there is an abundant supply of fresh vegetables, and we are able to store some for the winter.*
**SYNONYM: plentiful**

**a·buse¹** /əˈbyus/ *noun*
**1** cruel or violent treatment of someone: *He was accused of child abuse when he broke his daughter's arm.*
**2** the use of something in a wrong or harmful way: *Alcohol abuse is a problem for some teenagers and can harm their health.*

**a·buse²** /əˈbyuz/ *verb*
**1** to do cruel or violent things to someone: *He admitted that he abused his wife by hitting her.*
**2** to use something in a wrong or harmful way: *Did the senator abuse his power by giving jobs to his friends?*
—**abusive** *adjective* using very unkind words or physical violence: *Abusive behavior such as bullying will be punished.*

**AC** *noun*
**1** (**alternating current**) the type of electric current used in buildings for electrical equipment
**2** (*informal*) another word for AIR CONDITIONING

**ac·a·dem·ic** Ac /ˌækəˈdemɪk/ *adjective*
relating to education in a school, college, or university: *The college has high academic standards and you have to be smart to go there.*

**a·cad·e·my** Ac /əˈkædəmi/ *noun* (plural **academies**)
**1** a school that you pay for: *Many of the students at the academy have wealthy parents.*
**2** a school that teaches a special subject or skill: *His father trained to be a soldier at a military academy.*
**3** an organization whose aim is to encourage art, science, literature, or other subjects: *the National Academy of Sciences*
[**ORIGIN:** 1500-1600 From the Akademeia, the

A

place near Athens where the ancient Greek thinker Plato taught.]

**ac·cel·er·ate** /əkˈseləˌreɪt/ *verb*
if a vehicle or its driver accelerates, the vehicle moves faster: *The car accelerated down the hill and it was going very fast by the time it reached the bottom.*

**ac·cent** /ˈæksent/ *noun*
**1** a way of pronouncing words used by people who live in a place or country: *I guessed he was from Russia because he had a strong Russian accent.*
**2** a mark above a letter that shows how to pronounce that letter: *There is an accent over the "e" in "café."*

**ac·cept** /əkˈsept/ *verb*
**1** to take something that someone offers you: *Are you going to accept their offer? | He wouldn't accept any money from us.* **ANTONYM: refuse**
**2** to agree to go somewhere, when someone has invited you there: *She asked me to come for a visit, and I accepted her invitation gladly.*
**3** to admit that something is true: *She refused to accept that her grandfather had lied to her.*
**4** to let someone join a university or other organization: *My sister has been accepted to Harvard.* **ANTONYM: reject**

**ac·cept·a·ble** /əkˈseptəbəl/ *adjective*
good enough: *Coming to class late is not acceptable. Please get here on time.*
→ see Thesaurus box at **satisfactory**

**ac·cept·ance** /əkˈseptəns/ *noun*
**1** agreement to an offer or suggestion: *His acceptance of the job offer meant the family had to move to Texas.*
**2** agreement that something is true or cannot be changed: *There is acceptance among most scientists that the climate is changing.*

**ac·cept·ed** /əkˈseptɪd/ *adjective*
accepted ideas are considered true or right by most people: *It is an accepted fact that too much sugar is bad for your health.*

**ac·cess¹** Ac /ˈækses/ *noun*
**1** a way that you can have or use something: *The library allows anyone to have access to the Internet.*
**2** a way of getting into a place: *Stores must improve access for customers in wheelchairs.*

**access²** Ac *verb*
to find and use information on a computer: *You can access information about classes and fees on the college website.*

**ac·ces·si·ble** Ac /əkˈsesəbəl/ *adjective*
if something is accessible, you can get to it or find it: *The building has ramps so it is accessible to people in wheelchairs.*

**ac·ces·so·ry** /əkˈsesəri/ *noun* (plural **accessories**)
something that you wear or carry because it is looks good: *The store sells accessories such as jewelry and purses.*

**ac·ci·dent** /ˈæksədənt/ *noun*
**1** something bad that happens by chance and hurts someone or damages something: *Her parents were killed in a car accident. | I'm sorry I broke the glass. It was an accident. | He had an accident and broke his leg.*
**2 by accident** = if something happens by accident, it is not intended or planned: *I found the information by accident – I wasn't even looking for it.* **SYNONYM: accidentally**; **ANTONYM: on purpose**
[**ORIGIN:** 1300-1400 From the Latin word *accidere*, which means "to happen."]

**ac·ci·den·tal** /ˌæksəˈdentəl/ *adjective*
not intended or planned: *The girl's injuries were accidental – she just slipped and fell.* **ANTONYM: deliberate**

**ac·ci·den·tal·ly** /ˌæksəˈdentəli/ *adverb*
if you do something accidentally, you do it without intending to: *I accidentally left my lunch at home.* **ANTONYM: deliberately**

**ac·com·mo·date** Ac /əˈkɑməˌdeɪt/ *verb* (*formal*)
**1** to have enough space for a number of people or things: *The room can accommodate 300 people.*
**2** to do what someone wants or needs: *The education program is designed to accommodate the needs of students at all levels.*

**ac·com·mo·da·tions** /əˌkɑməˈdeɪʃənz/ *plural noun*
a place to live or stay: *The cost of the vacation includes hotel accommodations.*

**ac·com·pa·ny** Ac /əˈkʌmpəni/ *verb* (**accompanied**, **accompanying**, **accompanies**)
**1** (*formal*) to go somewhere with someone: *Her parents accompanied her to the hospital.*
**2** to play music while someone is playing or singing the main tune: *We'll sing and you can accompany us on the piano.*

**ac·com·plish** /əˈkɑmplɪʃ/ *verb*
to succeed in doing something: *We accomplished our goal of raising $45,000.*
—**accomplishment** *noun* something that you have succeeded in doing: *His biggest accomplishment was winning the New York City Marathon.*

**ac·cord** /əˈkɔrd/ *noun*
**of your own accord** = if you do something of your own accord, you do it without being asked or forced to do it: *He never does his homework of his own accord – Mom has to tell him to do it.*

**ac·cord·ing·ly** /əˈkɔrdɪŋli/ *adverb*
**1** in a way that is suitable for the situation, or for what people want: *We listened to students' ideas and made changes accordingly.*
**2** as a result of something: *We don't have as much money as before. Accordingly, we are spending less on things such as eating in restaurants.* SYNONYM: **therefore**

**acˈcording to** *preposition*
**1** used when saying what another person has said, or to say where your information comes from: *According to the weather forecast, it's going to rain tomorrow.* | *According to Sam, there's a concert in the park on Saturday.*
**2** in a way that obeys a rule or follows a plan: *Each student is put into an English class according to his or her level of English.* | *Everything went according to plan and we arrived at the airport on time.*

**ac·cor·di·on** /əˈkɔrdiən/ *noun*
a musical instrument that you play by moving the sides apart and together and pressing buttons and KEYs → see picture on page **A21**

**ac·count¹** /əˈkaʊnt/ *noun*
**1** (*also* **bank account**) an arrangement with a bank to keep your money for you: *The money I earn is deposited directly into my account.* | *It's a good idea to open a savings account and save a little money in it each month.* | *You can write a check to pay for things, using your checking account.*
**2** a description of something that has happened: *His book gives an account of his time in the army.*
**3** **take something into account** = to consider something when you make a decision: *The judges will take your age into account when they are judging the competition.*
**4** **on account of something** = because of something: *He couldn't lift anything heavy on account of his bad back.*
**5** **accounts** = a record of the money that a company has received and spent

**account²** *verb*
PHRASAL VERB
**account for something**
**1** to explain the reason for something that has happened: *No one was able to account for the strange lights in the sky.*
**2** to be a part of an amount: *In California, Asian Americans account for over 12 percent of the population.*

**ac·count·a·ble** /əˈkaʊntəbəl/ *adjective*
responsible for what you do or make happen, and having a duty to explain it: *Teachers are accountable for their students' test scores, so they want their students to do well.*

**ac·count·ant** /əˈkaʊntənt/ *noun*
someone whose job is to keep records of how much money a business has received and spent

**ac·count·ing** /əˈkaʊntɪŋ/ *noun*
the job of being an accountant

**ac·cu·mu·late** Ac /əˈkyumyəˌleɪt/ *verb* (*formal*)
**1** to gradually get more and more of something: *During his life he accumulated a huge amount of money.*
**2** if something accumulates, it gradually increases in amount: *Dust had accumulated in the corners of the room because he never cleaned anything.*
—**accumulation** /əˌkyumyəˈleɪʃən/ *noun* (*formal*) a large amount of something that has increased gradually

**ac·cu·ra·cy** Ac /ˈækyərəsi/ *noun*
**1** the quality of being correct or true: *Check the accuracy of your answers before you give the teacher your test.*

**2** the ability to hit the thing that you are trying to hit: *He can throw the football with amazing accuracy.*

**ac·cu·rate** Ac /ˈækyərɪt/ *adjective*
**1** exactly correct: *I checked the totals with a calculator to see if they were accurate.* **ANTONYM: inaccurate**
**2** an accurate shot or throw hits the thing that you are trying to hit: *He made an accurate throw to first base.*
—**accurately** *adverb* in a way that is exactly correct
→ see Thesaurus box at **right**[1]

| WORD FAMILY: accurate |
|---|
| **accurate** *adjective* \| **inaccurate** *adjective* \| **accurately** *adverb* \| **accuracy** *noun* |

**ac·cu·sa·tion** /ˌækyəˈzeɪʃən/ *noun*
a statement saying that someone has done something wrong: *She was very upset by his accusation that she was lying because it wasn't true.*

**ac·cuse** /əˈkyuz/ *verb*
to say that someone has done something wrong: *Terry accused her of cheating.* | *He was accused of murder.*

| WORD FAMILY: accuse |
|---|
| **accuse** *verb* \| **accusation** *noun* |

**ac·cus·tomed** /əˈkʌstəmd/ *adjective* (*formal*)
**be accustomed to (doing) something** = if you are accustomed to something, it is not strange or unusual for you: *She has to get up at six every day and she is accustomed to getting up early.* **SYNONYM: be used to**

**ace** /eɪs/ *noun*
a PLAYING CARD with one symbol on it. An ace has the highest or lowest value in a game: *the ace of hearts*

**ache**[1] /eɪk/ *verb*
if part of your body aches, it hurts for a long time: *My legs were aching after walking all day.*
→ see Thesaurus box at **hurt**[1]
[**ORIGIN:** From the old English word *acan.*]

**ache**[2] *noun*
a continuous pain: *I've had an ache in my shoulder for a few weeks, so I'm going to go to the doctor.*

**a·chieve** Ac /əˈtʃiv/ *verb*
to succeed in doing or getting something you want: *She always wanted to be a lawyer and she was very proud when she achieved her goal.*
—**achievable** *adjective* able to be achieved: *an achievable goal*

| WORD FAMILY: achieve |
|---|
| **achieve** *verb* \| **achievable** *adjective* \| **achievement** *noun* |

**a·chieve·ment** Ac /əˈtʃivmənt/ *noun*
something important or difficult that you do successfully: *One of his greatest achievements was to win a gold medal at the Olympic Games.*

**ac·id** /ˈæsɪd/ *noun*
a liquid chemical substance that can burn things: *The acid burned a hole in the metal.*
—**acidic** /əˈsɪdɪk/ *adjective* containing acid: *Some plants will not grow in acidic soil.*
[**ORIGIN:** 1600-1700 From the Latin word *acere*, which means "to be sour."]

**ˌacid ˈrain** *noun*
rain that contains POLLUTION and that damages plants, trees, and rivers

**ac·knowl·edge** Ac /əkˈnɑlɪdʒ/ *verb*
**1** to accept or admit that something is true or correct: *Angie acknowledged that she had made a mistake, and apologized.*
**2** to show someone that you have seen or heard him or her: *He didn't even acknowledge me when I said "hi."*
**3** to let someone know that you have received something from him or her: *She never acknowledged my letter, so I don't know if she got it.*
—**acknowledgement** *noun* the act of acknowledging someone or something

**ac·ne** /ˈækni/ *noun*
a skin problem that makes a lot of red spots appear on your face, and is common among young people: *Teenage girls who have acne sometimes use makeup to cover it up.*

**a·corn** /ˈeɪkɔrn/ *noun*
the nut of an OAK tree

**acoustic**

**a·cous·tic** /əˈkustɪk/ *adjective*
an acoustic musical instrument does not use electronic equipment to produce its sound, or make it sound louder: *I have an acoustic guitar. I've never played an electric guitar.*
[ORIGIN: 1700-1800 From the Greek word *akoustikos*, which means "relating to hearing," from *akouein*, which means "to hear."]

**ac·quaint·ance** /əˈkweɪntəns/ *noun*
someone you have met, but do not know well: *He's just an acquaintance – I've only met him a few times at church.*

**ac·quaint·ed** /əˈkweɪntɪd/ *adjective (formal)*
if you are acquainted with someone, you know him or her, or you have met each other: *Are you acquainted with Professor Green?* | *On the first day, we played a game that made us talk to each other and get acquainted.*

**ac·quire** Ac /əˈkwaɪɚ/ *verb (formal)*
to get or buy something: *The state acquired the land to create a wildlife preserve.*
—**acquisition** /ˌækwəˈzɪʃən/ *noun (formal)*
something that you have acquired: *The painting is a new acquisition for the museum.*
→ see Thesaurus box at **buy**

**a·cre** /ˈeɪkɚ/ *noun*
a unit for measuring an area of land, equal to 4,840 square yards or about 4,047 square meters: *a 40-acre farm*

**ac·ro·bat** /ˈækrəˌbæt/ *noun*
someone who entertains people by jumping through the air, walking on his or her hands, or walking on a high rope
[ORIGIN: 1800-1900 From the Greek word *akrobatos*, which means "walking on the ends of the toes."]

**ac·ro·nym** /ˈækrəˌnɪm/ *noun*
a word made from the first letters of each word in something's name: *NASA is an acronym for the National Aeronautics and Space Administration.*
[ORIGIN: 1900-2000 From the Greek words *akros* and *onyma*, which mean "top" and "name."]

**a·cross** /əˈkrɔs/ *adverb, preposition*
**1** from one side of something to the other: *A boy suddenly ran across the road.* | *They are building a bridge across the river.* | *At its widest point, the river is 2 miles across.*
**2** on the opposite side of something: *Ben lives across the street from us.*

**act**[1] /ækt/ *verb*
**1** to do something: *When someone has a heart attack, you need to act fast.*
**2** to behave in a particular way: *Nick's been acting strange recently – is there something worrying him?* | *Stop acting like a child!*
**3** to perform in a play or movie: *She acted in several Hollywood movies.*
**4** to have an effect or use: *Sugar and salt both act as preservatives for food.*

> **WORD FAMILY: act**
> **act** *noun* | **act** *verb* | **action** *noun* | **activity** *noun* | **active** *adjective*

**act**[2] *noun*
**1** something that you do: *He carried the old lady's bags as an act of kindness.*
**2** (*also* **Act**) a law that the government has made: *the Civil Rights Act*
**3** (*also* **Act**) one of the main parts of a play: *In Act II, Ross and Diane get married.*
**4** a short performance that is part of a television or theater show: *They did a great comedy act and we couldn't stop laughing.*
**5** behavior that is not sincere: *He said he loved me, but he didn't. It was just an act.*

**act·ing** /ˈæktɪŋ/ *noun*
the activity of performing in plays or movies: *Naomi was good at acting, so she signed up for drama classes.*

**ac·tion** /ˈækʃən/ *noun*
**1** something that you do: *Alan's quick actions saved Sarah's life after the car accident.* |

A

*People in the neighborhood called a meeting in order to decide the best course of action.*
**2** **take action** = to do something to deal with a situation: *The problem will not just go away. We need to take action.*
**3** the effect that something has on an object or substance: *The rocks are worn away by the action of the waves.*

**ac·ti·vate** /ˈæktəˌveɪt/ *verb* (*formal*)
to make something start working: *If you press this button, it activates the alarm.*

**ac·tive** /ˈæktɪv/ *adjective*
**1** an active person does a lot of different things and has a lot of energy: *Although Bob is over 70, he's still very active and goes for a long walk every day.* **ANTONYM: inactive**
**2** in grammar, if a verb or sentence is active, the SUBJECT of the verb does the action: *In the sentence "The boy kicked the ball," the verb "kick" is active.* **ANTONYM: passive**

**ac·tiv·i·ty** /ækˈtɪvəti/ *noun* (plural **activities**)
**1** something that you do for enjoyment in an organized way: *She enjoys outdoor activities such as hiking and bike riding.*
**2** things that people do because they want to achieve a particular aim: *He became involved in illegal activities and was later arrested.*
**3** a situation in which a lot of things are happening: *Sally loved the noise and activity of the city.*

**ac·tor** /ˈæktɚ/ *noun*
someone who performs in plays, movies, or television shows: *He wanted to go to Hollywood and become a movie actor.*

**ac·tress** /ˈæktrɪs/ *noun*
a woman who performs in plays, movies, or television shows

**ac·tu·al** /ˈæktʃuəl/ *adjective*
real or exact: *Were those his actual words or are you changing it a little? | I know the White Sox won the game, but I don't remember the actual score.*

**ac·tu·al·ly** /ˈæktʃuəli/ *adverb*
**1** used when saying that something is really true or really happened, especially something surprising: *David looks younger than Andy, but actually he's three years older. | When I won the competition, at first I couldn't believe it had actually happened.* **SYNONYM: really**
**2** used when giving your opinion or giving more information: *Actually, I don't really like country music.*

**a·cute** /əˈkyut/ *adjective*
**1** very serious or severe: *There is an acute shortage of food in some parts of the country and people are starving. | She had to take medication for her acute back pain.* **SYNONYM: extreme**
**2** if you have an acute sense of smell, hearing, etc., you can notice things that most people cannot notice: *Dogs have an acute sense of smell and they can use this for finding people in the snow.*
**3** an acute angle is less than 90°

**a·cute·ly** /əˈkyutli/ *adverb*
feeling or noticing something very strongly: *We are acutely aware of the problem and are trying to fix it.* **SYNONYM: extremely**

**ad** /æd/ *noun* (*informal*)
another word for an advertisement: *She put an ad in the newspaper to sell her bike.*
→ see Thesaurus box at **advertisement**

**A.D.**
used to show that a year came after the birth of Jesus Christ: *He became emperor of Rome in 161 A.D.*

**a·dapt** [Ac] /əˈdæpt/ *verb*
**1** to change because you are in a new situation: *In order to survive, animals need to be able to adapt to different conditions.*
**2** to change something so that you can use it in a different way: *The book was turned into a play and adapted for the stage.*
→ see Thesaurus box at **change**[1]

**WORD FAMILY: adapt**
**adapt** *verb* | **adaptable** *adjective*

**a·dapt·a·ble** [Ac] /əˈdæptəbəl/ *adjective*
able to change and deal with new situations: *For this job, you need to be adaptable and able to deal with unexpected situations.*

**ad·ap·ta·tion** [Ac] /ˌædæpˈteɪʃən/ *noun*
**1** a movie, play, or television program that is made from a book: *The play is a stage adaptation of John Grisham's first novel.*
**2** the process of changing to become suitable for a new situation: *The animal evolved*

*through a process of adaptation to the environment.*

**add** /æd/ *verb*
**1** to put numbers together to get the total: *If you add 5 and 3, you get 8.* **ANTONYM: subtract**
**2** to put or mix something with another thing: *Can I add your name to the list? | If the paint is too thick, add a little water.*
**3** to say one more thing: *"Bye! Don't forget to take your jacket," Mom added.*
**4** to increase the amount or cost of something: *Meals in restaurants add to the cost of a vacation.*
→ see Thesaurus box at **say**[1]
[**ORIGIN:** 1300-1400 From the Latin words *ad* and *dare*, which mean "to" and "to give."]

**WORD FAMILY: add**
**add** *verb* | **addition** *noun* | **additional** *adjective*

**PHRASAL VERB**
**add up**
**1** to put numbers together to get the total: *Can you add up these numbers to find out how many points we got?*
**2** to seem true or reasonable: *I don't believe what she said. Her explanation doesn't add up.*

**ad·dict** /ˈædɪkt/ *noun*
**1** someone who cannot stop taking harmful drugs: *She was a drug addict and had lost her job, home, and friends.*
**2** someone who likes using or doing something a lot: *Shelly's a real TV addict. She watches it for hours.*
—**addicted** /əˈdɪktɪd/ *adjective* not able to stop taking a harmful drug: *He was addicted to heroin and it almost killed him.*
—**addiction** /əˈdɪkʃən/ *noun* the problem someone has when they cannot stop taking a harmful drug: *Her addiction to alcohol ruined her life.*

**ad·dic·tive** /əˈdɪktɪv/ *adjective*
very hard to stop doing or using: *Smoking is very addictive.*

**ad·di·tion** /əˈdɪʃən/ *noun*
**1** the process of adding numbers together to get a total: *Most children learn addition in first grade.* **ANTONYM: subtraction**
**2 in addition** = used to add another piece of information: *She's good at sports and music, and in addition to that she gets good grades in everything.*
**3** a person or thing that is added to something, especially to improve it: *This product is a new addition to the company's range of software.*

**ad·di·tion·al** /əˈdɪʃənəl/ *adjective*
more than you already have, or more than was agreed: *Additional information is available on our website.* **SYNONYM: extra**
→ see Thesaurus box at **more**[2]

**ad·dress**[1] /ˈædres/ *noun*
**1** the number of the building and the name of the street and town of someone's home or business: *Write your name and address at the top of the form.*
**2** the letters or numbers you use to send an email to someone, or that you use to get to a website: *Can you give me your email address?*
**3** /əˈdres/ a formal speech: *We all watched the president's address to the nation on TV.*

**ad·dress**[2] /əˈdres/ *verb*
**1** to write a name and address on an envelope or package: *The letter is addressed to you.*
**2** (*formal*) to speak to a group of people: *The senator addressed a large crowd of people.*
**3** (*formal*) to start trying to solve a problem: *Crime is a serious problem and we all need to do more to address it.*

**ad·e·quate** Ac /ˈædɪkwət/ *adjective* (*formal*)
enough or good enough: *The size of this apartment is adequate for one person, but not for a family of five people.* **ANTONYM: inadequate**
—**adequately** *adverb* in an adequate way: *You must work hard so that you are adequately prepared for the test.*
→ see Thesaurus box at **enough**

**WORD FAMILY: adequate**
**adequate** *adjective* | **inadequate** *adjective* | **adequately** *adverb* | **inadequately** *adverb*

**ad·ja·cent** Ac /əˈdʒeɪsənt/ *adjective*
next to something: *The field is adjacent to the gym.*

A

**ad·jec·tive** /ˈædʒɪktɪv/ *noun*
in grammar, a word that describes a noun. In the sentence "I bought a new car," "new" is an adjective.

**ad·just** Ac /əˈdʒʌst/ *verb*
**1** to change something a little to make it better: *How do you adjust the color on the TV? It's too bright.*
**2** to gradually become more familiar with a situation: *The kids are slowly adjusting to their new school – they're making more friends and their grades are improving.*
→ see Thesaurus box at **change**[1]

**WORD FAMILY: adjust**
**adjust** *verb* | **adjustable** *adjective* | **adjustment** *noun*

**ad·just·a·ble** /əˈdʒʌstəbəl/ *adjective*
something that is adjustable can be changed or moved a little to make it better or more suitable for something: *The height of your chair is adjustable – you just press this lever.*

**ad·just·ment** Ac /əˈdʒʌstmənt/ *noun*
**1** a small change you make to something: *The picture is almost finished – I just need to make a couple of small adjustments.*
**2** a change in the way you live, behave, or think: *Moving to the city from the farm was a difficult adjustment for us.*

**ad·min·is·tra·tion** Ac /ədˌmɪnəˈstreɪʃən/ *noun*
**1** the U.S. president and the people who work for him or her: *After the election, we may have a new administration with different policies.*
**2** the job of organizing or managing the work in a company or organization: *We're looking for someone with experience in administration.*
→ see Thesaurus box at **government**

**WORD FAMILY: administration**
**administration** *noun* | **administrator** *noun* | **administrative** *adjective*

**ad·min·is·tra·tive** Ac /ədˈmɪnəˌstreɪtɪv/ *adjective*
relating to organizing or managing the work in a company or organization: *The new computer system will save a lot of money in administrative costs.*

**ad·min·is·tra·tor** Ac /ədˈmɪnəˌstreɪtɚ/ *noun*
someone whose job is organizing an area of work in a company or organization: *Talk to the customer service administrator to get more information.*

**ad·mi·ra·ble** /ˈædmərəbəl/ *adjective*
good in a way that people admire: *He had many admirable qualities, especially honesty.*

**ad·mi·ral** /ˈædmərəl/ *noun*
an officer who has a very high rank in the navy or Coast Guard

**ad·mi·ra·tion** /ˌædməˈreɪʃən/ *noun*
the feeling of respect you have when you think someone or something is very good, beautiful, or intelligent: *I have great admiration for his work – it's the best I've seen.*

**ad·mire** /ədˈmaɪɚ/ *verb*
to think someone or something is very good, beautiful, or intelligent: *Her kids are always well behaved – I really admire the way she's raising them.* | *We admired the view of New York that we could see from his window.*
[**ORIGIN:** 1500-1600 From the Latin word *admirari*, which means "to be amazed at something."]

**WORD FAMILY: admire**
**admire** *verb* | **admiration** *noun* | **admirable** *adjective*

**THESAURUS: admire**
**respect** to admire someone because of his or her knowledge, skill, or good qualities, and treat him or her politely because of this: *She's a good teacher, and the students respect her.*
**look up to someone** to admire and respect someone who is older than you, and to want to be like him or her: *He is an experienced player, and the younger guys look up to him.*

**ad·mis·sion** /ədˈmɪʃən/ *noun*
**1** the price you pay to go to something, for example a movie or sports event: *Admission to the museum is $8.* | *an admission fee*

2 the right to become a student at a college or school: *Tom has applied for admission to City College.*
3 something you say or do that shows you have done something bad: *Running away from the police seems like an admission of guilt.*

**ad·mit** /əd'mɪt/ *verb* (**admitted**, **admitting**)
1 to say that you have done something wrong, or that something bad is true: *In court, the boy admitted stealing the car.* | *She refused to admit (that) she had lied.*
2 to allow someone to enter a place: *No one will be admitted to the game without a ticket.*

**ad·o·les·cent** /ˌædl'esənt/ *noun*
a young person between 12 and 17 years old, when his or her body is changing to become more adult: *At fifteen, Bill was a shy adolescent.*
—**adolescence** *noun* the time of your life when you are an adolescent: *Adolescence can be a difficult time because your body is changing and so are your responsibilities.*
→ see Thesaurus box at **child**

**a·dopt** /ə'dɑpt/ *verb*
1 to legally make someone else's child become your own son or daughter: *The boy was adopted by a couple who could not have their own children.*
2 to begin to use a new way of doing something: *The city has adopted a new method for reducing crime.*
—**adoption** *noun* the act of adopting a child

**a·dor·a·ble** /ə'dɔːrəbəl/ *adjective*
very pretty or easy to love: *Amber was an adorable little girl with big brown eyes and curly hair.*

**a·dore** /ə'dɔr/ *verb*
to love someone or something very much: *She adores her sons and is willing to do anything for them.*

**a·dult** Ac /ə'dʌlt/ *noun*
a person who is not a child: *The tickets are $8 for adults and $5 for children.*
—**adulthood** *noun* the time of your life when you are an adult
[**ORIGIN:** 1500-1600 From the Latin word *adultus*, which means "having grown up." *Adultus* is the past participle of the verb *adolescere*, from which we get the word "adolescent."]

**ad·vance**[1] /əd'væns/ *noun*
1 **in advance** = before something happens or before you go somewhere: *It's a good idea to get tickets in advance. They're selling quickly.*
2 a change that brings progress: *Advances in medicine mean that many people are living longer.*
3 a movement forward to a new position, especially by soldiers: *In class, we studied the map and the advance of the army across Europe.*

**advance**[2] *verb*
1 if technology or knowledge about something advances, it gets better: *Technology has advanced greatly in the past few years. Computers, for example, are faster, more powerful, and cheaper.*
2 to move forward to a new position: *The soldiers advanced steadily across the valley.* **ANTONYM: retreat**

**ad·vanced** /əd'vænst/ *adjective*
1 using technology or methods that are very modern or developed to a very high level: *Our company uses the most advanced computer systems, so we are confident we can do the best job.* | *an advanced nation*
2 studying a subject at a difficult level: *This class is for advanced students who have taken at least three years of English.*

**ad·van·tage** /əd'væntɪdʒ/ *noun*
1 something that helps you to be successful: *In this area, speaking Spanish as well as English is an advantage, because a lot of the people here are Spanish-speaking.* **ANTONYM: disadvantage**
2 something that is good about a place or situation: *We live close to the kids' school, which is an advantage.* **ANTONYM: disadvantage**
3 **take advantage of something** = to use an opportunity: *If you get the opportunity to go to New York, you should take advantage of it.*
4 **take advantage of someone** = to use a person in a way that is not fair: *Some workers feel that their employers take advantage of them, asking them to work extra hours without extra pay.*

A

**ad·ven·ture** /əd'ventʃɚ/ *noun*
an exciting thing that you do, when new things happen to you: *Our trip to Africa was a real adventure.*

**ad·verb** /'ædvɚb/ *noun*
in grammar, a word that describes a verb, an adjective, or another adverb: *In the sentence "He walked slowly," "slowly" is an adverb.*

**ad·ver·sar·y** /'ædvɚˌseri/ *noun* (plural **adversaries**)
someone you are fighting or competing against: *His political adversaries could not find a way to defeat him.*

**ad·ver·tise** /'ædvɚˌtaɪz/ *verb*
**1** to try to make people buy a product or use a service by telling them good things about it, especially using pictures or short movies: *All the stores advertise kids' toys on TV during the holiday season.*
**2** to try to find someone to do a job or share an apartment by putting a notice somewhere, especially in a newspaper or magazine: *The restaurant is advertising for a new chef.*
—**advertising** *noun* the business of advertising products and services: *My dad works in advertising – he makes fashion commercials.*

**WORD FAMILY: advertise**

**advertise** *verb* | **advertisement** *noun* | **advertising** *noun*

**ad·ver·tise·ment** /ˌædvɚ'taɪzmənt/ *noun*
**1** a picture or short movie which tries to make people buy a product or use a service: *The advertisement for this shampoo on TV says it makes your hair shiny.* **SYNONYM: ad**

**THESAURUS: advertisement**

**ad** (*informal*) an advertisement: *The magazine is full of ads for new cars.*

**commercial** an advertisement on TV or radio: *There are always lots of television commercials for toys just before Christmas.*

**billboard** a very large sign at the side of a road or on a building, used as an advertisement: *Billboards lined the streets, advertising cars and movies.*

**poster** an advertisement printed on a large piece of paper, often with a picture on it: *a movie poster outside the theater*

**flier** a piece of paper with an advertisement on it: *They were handing out fliers for the restaurant.*

**junk mail** mail that companies send to your house in order to advertise their products, which you receive even when you have not asked for it: *We get a lot of junk mail from credit card companies.*

**spam** emails that are advertising something, that you receive but do not want to read: *Is there a way to stop spam from getting in my inbox?*

**2** a notice that you put in a newspaper or magazine when you are trying to find someone to do a job or share an apartment: *There are lots of advertisements for computer programmers in the paper.*

**ad·vice** /əd'vaɪs/ *noun*
ideas that other people tell you, that help you to decide what you should do: *My teacher gave me some good advice on how to plan my essay.*
[**ORIGIN:** 1200-1300 From the French word *avis*, which means "opinion."]

**WORD FAMILY: advice**

**advice** *noun* | **advise** *verb* | **adviser** (*also* **advisor**) *noun*

**USAGE: advice, advise**

**Advice** is a noun: *He got a lot of advice from his friends.*

**Advise** is a verb: *His friends advised him to wait.*

**ad·vise** /əd'vaɪz/ *verb*
to tell someone what you think he or she should do: *His doctor advised him to stop smoking.*
—**adviser** (*also* **advisor**) *noun* someone whose job is to advise people, for example about money, the law, or jobs: *I went to see an academic adviser about what subjects I should study to become a doctor.*

**ae·ro·bics** /e'roʊbɪks/ *noun*
exercise that you do with music: *I do aerobics in a class at the gym once a week.*

A

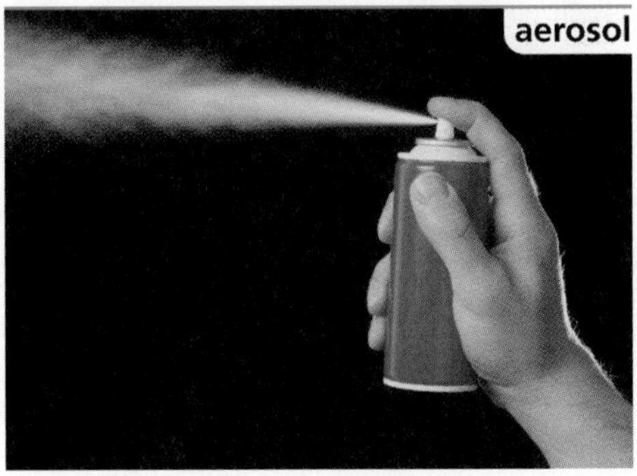


**aer·o·sol** /ˈerəˌsɔl/ *noun*
a container with liquid inside. When you press a button on the container, the liquid is forced out at high pressure.

**af·fair** /əˈfer/ *noun*
**1** a sexual relationship between two people who are not married to each other: *He was having an affair with another man's wife.*
**2** a special event such as a party or wedding: *Thanksgiving is usually a family affair.*
**3 affairs** = events and activities relating to a particular subject: *He's a reporter who writes about foreign affairs; he often writes about China and Japan.*

**af·fect** Ac /əˈfekt/ *verb*
to make someone or something change, especially in a bad way: *The increase in temperature is going to affect the lives of millions of people around the world.*
[ORIGIN: 1300-1400 From the Latin word *affectus*, which means "having been put into a particular state."]

**WORD FAMILY: affect**
**affect** *verb* | **effect** *noun*

**USAGE: affect, effect**
**Affect** is a verb: *How does your illness affect your life?*
**Effect** is usually a noun: *What effect does the illness have on your life?*

**af·fec·tion** /əˈfekʃən/ *noun*
a feeling that you like or love someone you know well: *He had great affection for her – they'd been friends for years.*
—**affectionate** *adjective* showing that you like or love someone: *My father was never very affectionate and we did not have a close relationship.*
—**affectionately** *adverb* in an affectionate way: *She smiled at him affectionately.*

**af·flu·ent** /ˈæfluənt/ *adjective* (*formal*)
having a lot of money: *The kids are from affluent families, so they never worry about money.* SYNONYMS: **rich**, **wealthy**
—**affluence** *noun* the state of being rich

**af·ford** /əˈfɔrd/ *verb*
to have enough money to buy or do something: *We can't afford to buy a new car because Dad isn't working right now.*

**af·ford·a·ble** /əˈfɔrdəbəl/ *adjective*
affordable prices are not too expensive for ordinary people: *The restaurant serves fresh food at affordable prices, so it's always very busy.*

**Af·ghan** /ˈæfgæn/ *noun*
someone from Afghanistan
—**Afghan** *adjective* relating to Afghanistan

**a·fraid** /əˈfreɪd/ *adjective*
**1** frightened of something that may hurt you or be dangerous: *A lot of people are afraid of spiders.* | *Mary is afraid to walk home alone at night.* SYNONYMS: **scared**, **frightened** → see picture on page **A23**
**2** worried about something that may happen in the future: *She loved him and she was afraid of losing him.* | *Joey is afraid that if he wears glasses, the other kids will make fun of him.*
**3 I'm afraid** = used when politely saying something that may disappoint, annoy, or upset someone: *I'm afraid (that) there are no more tickets left.*
→ see Thesaurus box at **frightened**
[ORIGIN: 1300-1400 From the old English word *affray*, which means "to frighten."]

**Af·ri·can** /ˈæfrɪkən/ *adjective*
relating to Africa: *African art*
—**African** *noun* someone from Africa

**ˌAfrican Aˈmerican** *noun*
an American with dark skin, whose family first came to the U.S. from Africa
—**African-American** *adjective* relating to African Americans

**af·ter** /ˈæftɚ/ *preposition, conjunction, adverb*
**1** later than something else: *Let's get some*

A

*pizza after the movie.* | *I went straight home after I left the party.* | *I can come tomorrow or the day after.*

**THESAURUS: after**

**afterward** after an event or time: *He said afterward that it had been the scariest experience of his life.*

**next** after now, or after you have done something else: *I have taken out the trash. What do you want me to do next?*

**later** after the present time, or after the time you are talking about: *Leave those dishes for now – we can clean up later.*

**subsequently** after an event in the past: *He went to law school and subsequently became a lawyer.*

**2** following and trying to stop or catch someone or something: *"Stop!" he shouted, running after the man.*

**3** **five/ten/a quarter, etc. after** = used to say how many minutes past the hour it is: *"What time is it?" "It's quarter after two* (=2:15).*"* **SYNONYM: past**; **ANTONYM: to**

**4** **after all** = used to say that something you expected to happen did not happen: *We'd planned to go to the beach but it was raining so we didn't go after all.*

**af·ter·noon** /ˌæftɚˈnun/ *noun*
the time between 12 NOON and the evening: *I have swimming lessons in the afternoon, but I'm free until noon.* | *Would you like to come to my house this afternoon?*

**af·ter·shave** /ˈæftɚˌʃeɪv/ *noun*
a liquid with a nice smell that a man puts on his face after he SHAVEs

**af·ter·shock** /ˈæftɚˌʃɑk/ *noun*
a small EARTHQUAKE that comes after a stronger earthquake: *The aftershocks brought more buildings down.*

**af·ter·ward** /ˈæftɚwɚd/ (*also* **afterwards**) *adverb*
after an event or time: *They met in 1983 and got married soon afterward.*
→ see Thesaurus box at **after**

**a·gain** /əˈgen/ *adverb*
**1** one more time: *Could you say that again? I didn't hear you.* | *My computer crashed so I had to write the letter all over again.*
**2** **again and again** = many times: *I've tried calling her again and again but she's never there.*

**a·gainst** /əˈgenst/ *preposition*
**1** next to the surface of something, and touching it: *I put my bicycle against the wall.*
**2** if you are against an idea or plan, you do not agree with it and you do not want it to happen: *John was against the idea of selling the house – he wanted to keep it.* **ANTONYM: for**
**3** if you play against another player or team in a game, you try to defeat the other player or team: *The team will play against the Cowboys on Saturday.*
**4** if soldiers fight against another group of soldiers in a war, they try to defeat the other soldiers: *The two armies are fighting against each other in the war.*
**5** if you fight against something bad, you try to stop it from happening: *the fight against crime*
**6** **against the law/the rules** = not allowed by the law or the rules: *Stealing is against the law.*

**age** /eɪdʒ/ *noun*
**1** the number of years that someone has lived: *Children usually start school at the age of five.* | *Paul's younger than I am, but Patrick is the same age as me.*
**2** a time in someone's life: *She has spent her old age taking care of her grandchildren.*
**3** a period of time in history: *We live in the age of computers and the Internet.*
**4** **ages** (*informal*) = a long time: *I've lived in this town for ages.*
**5** the state of being old: *The photograph was brown with age.*

**a·gen·cy** /ˈeɪdʒənsi/ *noun* (plural **agencies**)
**1** a business that provides a service to people: *The travel agency arranged the hotel and the airline tickets for us.*
**2** a part of a government that does a special job: *NASA is the name of the U.S. space agency.*

**a·gen·da** /əˈdʒendə/ *noun*
**1** a list of the subjects that the people at a meeting will discuss: *The first thing on the*

*agenda is to choose a new class president.*
**2** a list of things that an organization is planning to do: *Helping children improve their test scores is high on the agenda.*
[ORIGIN: 1600-1700 From the Latin word for "things to be done," from *agere*, which means "to do."]

**a·gent** /ˈeɪdʒənt/ *noun*
**1** someone whose job is to get secret information about another country, organization, or person: *an FBI agent*
**2** a person or company that arranges things or does work for other people: *A travel agent found the hotel for us.*
[ORIGIN: 1400-1500 From the Latin word *agere*, which means "to do."]

**ag·gra·vate** /ˈægrəˌveɪt/ *verb*
**1** (*formal*) to make an illness, injury, or bad situation worse: *Exercise may aggravate your injury, so wait until it is healed before exercising.*
**2** to annoy someone: *Sometimes my sister really aggravates me. She talks too much.* SYNONYM: **irritate**

**ag·gres·sive** /əˈgresɪv/ *adjective*
**1** behaving in a way that shows you want to fight or argue with someone: *Our dog is very aggressive and he's always growling at people in the street.*
**2** behaving in a way that shows you are determined to succeed: *The company started an aggressive campaign against its rivals.*
—**aggression** *noun* angry feelings that show you want to fight or argue with another person: *His voice was loud and full of aggression.*

**ag·ile** /ˈædʒəl/ *adjective*
able to move quickly and easily: *He was young and agile, and climbed the fence easily.*

**ag·i·tat·ed** /ˈædʒəˌteɪtɪd/ *adjective*
very worried or upset: *The little boy was alone and becoming agitated, so I tried to calm him down.*

**a·go** /əˈgoʊ/ *adverb*
**five minutes/an hour/two years, etc. ago** = five minutes, one hour, etc. before now: *The show started ten minutes ago, so you've missed a little bit.* | *I visited New York a long time ago, when I was only five years old.*

**USAGE: ago, for, since**

**Ago**, **for**, and **since** are all used to talk about time.

**Ago** is used to say how far back in the past something happened. You use **ago** after the amount of time: *My grandfather died two years ago.*

**For** is used to say how long a situation or activity has lasted. You use **for** before the amount of time: *My aunt has been here for three days.*

**Since** is used to say when something started. You use **since** before a day, date, or time: *He's been sick since Sunday.* | *I've been going to school here since 2010.*

**ag·o·ny** /ˈægəni/ *noun* (plural **agonies**)
very bad pain or worry: *I was in agony because my tooth was hurting really badly.*
—**agonizing** /ˈægəˌnaɪzɪŋ/ *adjective* very painful or worrying: *After an agonizing wait, I finally got the news that I had passed my test.*

**a·gree** /əˈgri/ *verb*
**1** to have the same opinion as someone else: *I totally agree with everything you say.* | *Most scientists agree (that) climate change is a serious problem.* ANTONYM: **disagree**
**2** to think that something is right or true: *I don't agree with hitting kids as a punishment.* ANTONYM: **disagree**
**3** to say that you will do something: *My friend agreed to give us a ride to the movie theater.* ANTONYM: **refuse**
**4** to decide something together: *Can we all agree on a date for the next meeting?*

**WORD FAMILY: agree**

**agree** *verb* | **disagree** *verb* | **agreement** *noun* | **disagreement** *noun* | **agreeable** *adjective*

**a·gree·a·ble** /əˈgriəbəl/ *adjective*
**1** (*old-fashioned*) pleasant and nice to be with: *He was an agreeable old man, and people enjoyed talking with him.*
**2** acceptable: *The solution was agreeable to both groups.*

**a·gree·ment** /əˈgrimənt/ *noun*
**1** an arrangement or promise between

organizations, countries, or people: *The war ended and the two countries signed a peace agreement.* | *We made an agreement not to talk about the subject again.*
**2** a situation in which people agree about an idea: *All of us were in agreement about what we should do next.* **ANTONYM: disagreement**

**ag·ri·cul·ture** /ˈægrɪˌkʌltʃɚ/ *noun*
the activity of growing crops and raising animals for people to eat: *The land is mainly used for agriculture and the farmers grow wheat and corn.* **SYNONYM: farming**
—**agricultural** /ˌægrɪˈkʌltʃərəl/ *adjective*
relating to agriculture
[**ORIGIN:** 1400-1500 From the Latin words *ager* and *cultura*, which mean "field" and "taking care of."]

**a·head** /əˈhed/ *adverb*
**1** in front of someone or something: *My friends were walking ahead of me.* | *If you look straight ahead, you can see the ocean.*
**2** in the future: *No one knows what will happen in the years ahead.* | *I always try to plan ahead and think about what I'm going to do next.*
**3** **get ahead** (*informal*) = to be successful in your work or life: *You need to work hard if you want to get ahead.*
**4** **ahead of schedule/time** = earlier than people had planned: *Everything was ready ahead of schedule, so we were able to relax before everyone arrived.*
**5** **go ahead** (*informal*) = used to tell someone that he or she can do something: *"Can I use your phone?" "Go ahead."*

**aid¹** Ac /eɪd/ *noun*
money, food, medicine, or equipment that is sent to people in a difficult situation to help them: *The U.S. is sending aid to the victims of the earthquake.*

**aid²** Ac *verb* (*formal*)
to help someone to do something: *Eating fruit after a meal can aid your digestion.*

**AIDS** /eɪdz/ *noun*
(**Acquired Immune Deficiency Syndrome**) a very serious disease that makes your body unable to fight other diseases. AIDS is caused by the HIV VIRUS.

**aim¹** /eɪm/ *noun*
**1** something that you are trying to achieve: *My aim is to work hard and go to college to study engineering.* **SYNONYM: goal**
**2** **take aim** = to point a gun, ball, arrow, etc. at someone and get ready to fire it or throw it: *Joe took aim at the target.*
→ see Thesaurus box at **purpose**

**aim²** *verb*
**1** to plan or intend to do something: *We aim to finish the work by Friday.*
**2** to point a weapon or ball at someone or something and get ready to fire the weapon or throw the ball: *The man aimed his gun at the target.*
**3** **be aimed at someone** = to be made or intended for a type of person: *The magazine is aimed at teenagers.*

aim

**air¹** /er/ *noun*
**1** the gases around the Earth, which we breathe: *I went outside to get some fresh air.*
**2** if something goes up in the air, it goes up into the sky: *The balloon went up into the air.*
**3** **by air** = using an airplane: *The quickest way to get there is by air.*
**4** **be on the air** = to be broadcasting on television or radio: *The attack happened when the news show was on the air.*

**air²** *verb*
**1** to broadcast a program on television or radio: *The show will air at 9:00 tomorrow night.*
**2** **air your views/opinions** = to tell people what you think about something: *Everyone will have a chance to air his or her views and ask questions.*

**ˈair conˌditioner** *noun*
a machine that makes the air in a room, car, or building stay cool

**ˈair conˌditioning** *noun* (*abbreviation*: **AC**)
a system that makes the air in a room, car, or building stay cool: *It's very hot here in the summer, so it's good to have a car with air conditioning.*

—**air-conditioned** *adjective* having air conditioning: *an air-conditioned office*

**air·craft** /ˈerkræft/ *noun* (plural **aircraft**)
an airplane or other vehicle that can fly: *The aircraft can carry 600 passengers.*

**air·fare** /ˈerfer/ *noun*
the price of an airplane ticket

**ˈair force** *noun*
the part of a country's military that uses airplanes to fight: *He learned to fly planes while he was in the air force.*

**air·line** /ˈerlaɪn/ *noun*
a company that takes passengers and goods to different places by airplane: *I choose the airline that has the cheapest tickets.*

**air·mail** /ˈermeɪl/ *noun*
the system of sending letters and packages by airplane
—**airmail** *adjective*, *adverb* using airmail: *She sent the book airmail.*

**air·plane** /ˈerpleɪn/ *noun*
a vehicle that flies through the air: *From the airplane, I could see the clouds below us.*
**SYNONYM: plane**

**air·port** /ˈerpɔrt/ *noun*
a place where airplanes take off and land, that has buildings for passengers to wait in: *The plane landed at Los Angeles airport.*

**ˈair raid** *noun*
an attack in which bombs are dropped from airplanes

**air·tight** /ˈerˌtaɪt/ *adjective*
if something is airtight, air cannot get into it: *Store the crackers in an airtight container so they don't go soft.*

**air·y** /ˈeri/ *adjective*
an airy room or building has a lot of space and fresh air: *The house is bright and airy with lots of windows.*

**aisle** /aɪl/ *noun*
**1** a long passage between rows of seats in a theater, airplane, or church: *The bride and her father walked down the aisle to the front of the church.*
**2** a long passage between rows of shelves in a store: *Which aisle are the cans of tomatoes in?*

**a·jar** /əˈdʒɑr/ *adjective*
a door or window that is ajar is open a little bit: *He left the door ajar so that he could hear the phone.*

**a·larm**[1] /əˈlɑrm/ *noun*
**1** a piece of equipment that makes a noise to warn people of danger: *a fire alarm* | *If anyone tries to steal the car, it will set off the alarm.*
**2** the part of an alarm clock that makes a noise to wake you up: *The alarm went off at 6:00 and woke me up.*
**3** a feeling of fear when something bad happens: *I realized with alarm that I didn't know the way home.*
[**ORIGIN:** 1500-1600 From the Italian phrase *all' arme*, which means "to the weapon." This phrase was shouted as a warning that danger was near and you might have to fight.]

**alarm**[2] *verb*
to make someone feel very worried or

A

frightened: *I don't want to alarm you, but there's some smoke coming from the kitchen.*
—**alarmed** *adjective* worried or frightened: *She was alarmed by the news.*

**a'larm clock** *noun*
a clock that will make a noise when you want it to wake you up: *I set the alarm clock for 7:00.* → see picture on page **A10**

**al·bum** /ˈælbəm/ *noun*
**1** a group of songs or pieces of music on a CD: *Have you heard the band's new album?*
**2** a book in which you put things that you want to keep, especially photographs or stamps: *a photo album*

**al·co·hol** /ˈælkəˌhɔl/ *noun*
drinks such as beer or wine that can make you drunk: *You're not allowed to drink alcohol unless you're over 21.*

**al·co·hol·ic¹** /ˌælkəˈhɔlɪk/ *adjective*
**1** an alcoholic drink contains alcohol: *Stores are not allowed to sell alcoholic drinks to teenagers.*
**2** used to describe someone who drinks a lot of alcohol and cannot stop drinking it: *Her alcoholic husband could not keep a job.*

**alcoholic²** *noun*
someone who drinks a lot of alcohol and cannot stop drinking it
—**alcoholism** /ˈælkəhɔlˌɪzəm/ *noun* the serious medical problem that people have if they drink too much alcohol and cannot stop drinking it

**a·lert** /əˈlɚt/ *adjective*
always watching and ready to notice anything unusual or dangerous: *It's important to stay alert when you're driving.*

**al·gae** /ˈældʒi/ *noun*
a type of plant that does not have roots, stems, or leaves. Algae grows on the surface of water and rocks.

**al·ge·bra** /ˈældʒəbrə/ *noun*
a type of mathematics that uses letters and symbols to represent numbers and amounts, for example $x^2 + y^2 = 5$
[**ORIGIN:** 1500-1600 From the Arabic phrase *al-jabr*, which means "the act of putting parts together again." Algebra involves numbers and symbols put together in equations.]

**al·i·bi** /ˈæləbaɪ/ *noun*
something that proves that someone was not where a crime happened and is therefore not guilty of the crime: *The man had an alibi because he was at home with his family when the robbery took place.*
[**ORIGIN:** 1600-1700 From the Latin word for "somewhere else."]

**a·li·en** /ˈeɪliən/ *noun*
**1** someone who is working or living in a country, but who comes from a different country: *Every year, thousands of illegal aliens cross the border into the U.S.*
**2** a creature from another PLANET or another part of the UNIVERSE: *In the movie, the aliens try to take over the Earth.*
[**ORIGIN:** 1300-1400 From the Latin word *alienus*, which means "belonging to another person or place."]

**a·li·en·ate** /ˈeɪliəˌneɪt/ *verb*
to do something that makes someone dislike you or not want to support you: *High ticket prices for football games have alienated many fans.*

**a·like** /əˈlaɪk/ *adjective, adverb*
very similar: *Sarah and her sister look alike and they both have the same hairstyle.*
→ see Thesaurus box at **similar**

**al·i·mo·ny** /ˈæləˌmoʊni/ *noun*
money that someone has to pay regularly to his or her former wife or husband after a DIVORCE

**a·live** /əˈlaɪv/ *adjective*
living and not dead: *It was a very bad car accident and he was lucky to be alive.*

**all¹** /ɔl/ *adjective, pronoun*
**1** the whole amount of something: *Have you finished all your homework?* | *I've spent all of the money, and I don't have any left.*
**2** every one of a group of things or people: *Someone has eaten all the cookies.* | *My grandfather is older than all of us – he's over 90 years old.*

**USAGE: all, each, every**

**All**, **each**, and **every** are all used to talk about every person or thing in a group.
When you are thinking about the whole group together, use **all**: *All the children were given balloons.*

When you are thinking about the people or things in the group separately, use **every** or **each**: *Every child at the party was given a balloon.* | *Each child at the party was given a balloon.*

**3** the only thing or things: *All you need to bring is something to drink.* | *All I want to do is sleep.*
**4** **not at all** = used to emphasize a negative sentence: *He's not like you at all.* | *I haven't gotten any email at all today.*
**5** **all kinds/sorts** = a lot of different types of things or people: *Students come here to study English for all kinds of reasons.*

**all²** *adverb*
**1** completely: *The house is all clean and neat so don't make it messy.*
**2** used when saying that two teams or people have an equal number of points in a game: *The score was nine all at halftime.*
**3** **all over** = everywhere: *I've been looking all over for you. Where were you?*
→ **after all** at **after**, **all of a sudden** at **sudden**

**Al·lah** /ˈælə/
the Muslim name for God

**al·lege** /əˈledʒ/ *verb*
to say that someone has done something wrong, although it has not been proved: *He alleged that police officers punched and beat him.*

**al·le·giance** /əˈlidʒəns/ *noun*
loyalty to a leader or country: *We pledge allegiance to the flag of the United States of America.*

**al·ler·gy** /ˈælɚdʒi/ *noun* (plural **allergies**)
a condition that makes you sick when you eat, touch, or breathe in something: *He has an allergy to cats and he can't be in the same room with them.*
—**allergic** /əˈlɚdʒɪk/ *adjective* having an allergy: *I'm allergic to nuts, and if I eat one, I can't breathe and my mouth swells up.*

**al·ley** /ˈæli/ (*also* **al·ley·way** /ˈæliˌweɪ/) *noun*
a narrow street or passage between buildings

**al·li·ance** /əˈlaɪəns/ *noun*
an agreement between countries, groups, or people to work together or fight together: *The alliance between the United States and Britain is strong and has lasted through several wars.*

**al·li·ga·tor** /ˈæləˌgeɪtɚ/ *noun*
a large animal with a long body and a big mouth with sharp teeth: *Alligators live in hot wet places, for example in Florida.*
[**ORIGIN:** 1500-1600 From the Spanish phrase *el lagarto*, which means "the lizard."]

**al·lo·cate** Ac /ˈæləˌkeɪt/ *verb* (*formal*)
to decide to use something such as time or money for a purpose, or give it to a person: *The city has allocated money to build a new swimming pool.*
—**allocation** /ˌæləˈkeɪʃən/ *noun* the action of allocating something, or an amount that is allocated

**al·low** /əˈlaʊ/ *verb*
to say that someone can do something: *Smoking is not allowed in public buildings.* | *Her parents don't allow her to stay out late.*
**ANTONYM: forbid**

**THESAURUS: allow**

**Allow** is used in both formal and informal English: *You're not allowed to use a calculator during the test.*

**Let** is informal and is used a lot in spoken English: *Will your mom let you come to the party?*

**Permit** is formal and is mainly used in written English: *Smoking is not permitted in this building.*

**al·low·ance** /əˈlaʊəns/ *noun*
money that your parents give you regularly: *The kids get an allowance of five dollars every week.*

**all ˈright** *adjective, adverb*
**1** used to say "yes," when someone asks or suggests something: *"Can I borrow your pen?" "All right."* **SYNONYM: OK**
**2** fairly good, but not excellent: *"How was the movie?" "It was all right, but it could have been better."* **SYNONYM: OK**
**3** not sick, in pain, or upset: *"Do you feel all right?" "I'm fine, thanks."* **SYNONYM: OK**
**4** **it's all right** = used when telling someone not to be afraid or worried: *It's all right now. Mommy's here.*

A

**5 Is it all right ... ?** = used when asking if you can do something: *Is it all right if I close the window?*
**6 that's all right** = used in order to tell someone that you are not angry when they say they are sorry to you: *"Sorry, I'm late!" "That's all right."*
**7** used in order to say you are happy about something: *"I got the job!" "All right!"*

**al·ly** /əˈlaɪ/ *noun* (plural **allies**)
a country or person that helps another, especially in a war: *The U.S. and Canada were allies in World War II.*
[ORIGIN: 1300-1400 From the Latin word *alligare*, which means "to tie." The idea is that allies are joined together as if they are tied together.]

**al·mond** /ˈɑmənd/ *noun*
a flat white nut with pale brown skin and a slightly sweet taste → see picture on page **A13**

**al·most** /ˈɔlmoʊst/ *adverb*
nearly but not quite: *The house is almost finished. We just have to paint it.* | *He ate almost all the cake – there was only a little piece left.* | *We see each other almost every day.*

**a·lone** /əˈloʊn/ *adjective, adverb*
**1** without any other people: *The old man lived alone and had no one to talk to.* | *They leave the dog alone in the house all day.*

**THESAURUS: alone**

**on your own** without anyone helping you: *Did you make this on your own?*
**(all) by yourself** without anyone helping you: *The bag was so heavy I could not lift it by myself.*
**solo** done alone, without anyone else helping you: *This is his first solo album after leaving the band.*

**2** (*formal*) only that person or thing: *She alone knows the truth about what happened, because only she was there.*
→ **leave someone alone/leave something alone** at **leave**[1]

**a·long** /əˈlɔŋ/ *adverb, preposition*
**1** moving forward, especially on a road or path: *We walked along the path by the river.* | *They were driving along at 40 miles an hour.*
**2** next to something long: *She planted rose bushes along the fence.* **SYNONYM: beside**
**3** with you or with someone: *Can I bring a friend along to the party?*

**a·long·side** /əˌlɔŋˈsaɪd/ *adverb, preposition*
next to the side of something: *A big ship came alongside our boat.*

**a·loud** /əˈlaʊd/ *adverb*
using your voice: *His mother reads a story aloud to him every night.*

**al·pha·bet** /ˈælfəˌbet/ *noun*
the letters of a language: *The last letter of the English alphabet is "Z."*
—**alphabetical** /ˌælfəˈbetɪkəl/ *adjective* in the order of the letters of the alphabet: *The names of the students are listed in alphabetical order.*
[ORIGIN: 1500-1600 From *alpha* and *beta*, which are the first two letters of the Greek alphabet.]

**al·read·y** /ɔlˈredi/ *adverb*
**1** before now: *I've seen that movie twice already.*
**2** before the time when something happens: *By the time we arrived, the plane had already left.*
**3** used when you are surprised because something happens sooner than you expected: *Is it 5:30 already? I thought it was only about 4:00.*

**USAGE: already, all ready**

**Already** is used in order to talk about something that has happened: *I've already read the book we're studying in my English class.*
**All ready** is used in order to say that someone is ready to do something, or that something is completely prepared: *I'm all ready to go now.* | *Dinner is all ready.*

**al·so** /ˈɔlsoʊ/ *adverb*
used when you mention another thing: *Mike speaks French. He can also speak a little Spanish.* | *The food is not only delicious, but also inexpensive.* **SYNONYM: too**

**USAGE: also, too, as well**

**Also**, **too**, and **as well** mean the same thing, but you use them in different ways.

**Also** is more formal than **too**, and is used more often in writing than in speech: *Tom was very tired, and he was also hungry.*

**Too** and **as well** are less formal and you use them more often in spoken English: *Tom's hungry, and I am too.* | *Oh, are you coming as well?*

In sentences with "not," use **either** rather than **also** or **too**. Do not say "Tom was also not hungry" or "Tom was not hungry too." Say "Tom was not hungry either."

**GRAMMAR: also**

Use **also** before a verb, unless the verb is "be": *Dave also plays baseball.*

Use **also** after the verb "be": *His sister is also tall.*

If there are two or more verbs together, **also** comes after the first one: *Gina can also play the piano.*

**al·tar** /ˈɔltɚ/ *noun*
a table used by the priest in religious ceremonies

**al·ter** Ac /ˈɔltɚ/ *verb*
**1** to change something: *We had to alter our plans for the picnic because of the rain.*
**2** to become different: *My hometown has not altered very much in the last ten years.*
→ see Thesaurus box at **change**[1]

**al·ter·nate**[1] Ac /ˈɔltɚˌneɪt/ *verb*
to do one thing first, then a different thing, and then the first thing again, etc.: *She alternated between feeling happy and feeling sad.*

**al·ter·nate**[2] Ac /ˈɔltɚnɪt/ *adjective*
**1** an alternate plan, way of doing something, etc. can be used instead of another one: *The road was closed and so we had to take an alternate route.* **SYNONYM: alternative**
**2 alternate days/weeks/weekends, etc.** = if you do something on alternate days, you do it on one day, but not the next day, and then do it on the day after that, etc.: *I see my dad on alternate weekends.*

**al·ter·na·tive**[1] Ac /ɔlˈtɚnətɪv/ *adjective*
**1** an alternative plan, way of doing something, etc. can be used instead of another one: *There may be an alternative way of dealing with the problem.* **SYNONYM: alternate**
**2** different from the usual type: *She believes in alternative medicine, and takes herbs instead of regular medicine.*
—**alternatively** *adverb* used for suggesting a different possibility: *You could visit one of the city's museums. Alternatively, you could spend the day in Central Park.*

**alternative**[2] Ac *noun*
something you can choose to do or use instead of something else: *There are a lot of alternatives to going by car: you can take the bus or ride a bicycle.*

**al·though** /ɔlˈðoʊ/ *conjunction*
**1** used when mentioning a fact that makes something surprising: *Although he's over 60, he still goes running every day.*
**2** used instead of saying "but": *I've heard it's a good movie, although I haven't seen it yet myself.*

**al·ti·tude** /ˈæltəˌtud/ *noun*
the height of something above sea level: *The plane was flying at an altitude of 30,000 feet.*

**al·to·geth·er** /ˌɔltəˈgeðɚ/ *adverb*
**1** including everyone or everything: *The trip cost $2,000 altogether.*
**2** completely – used when you want to emphasize what you are saying: *She wants to stop working altogether and just stay at home with the baby.*

**a·lu·mi·num** /əˈlumənəm/ *noun*
a very light silver-gray metal, used to make cans

**al·ways** /ˈɔlweɪz/ *adverb*
**1** every time, or at all times: *He always goes to bed before ten.* | *It's always very cold in the Arctic.*

**USAGE: always, still, yet**

**Always** means "every time" or "at all times": *I always see him on Tuesdays.* | *She is always happy.*

**Still** is used to say that a situation that began in the past has not changed and is continuing: *He still plays basketball twice a week.*

A

**Yet** is used when you ask about something that is expected to happen or say that it has not happened: *Is Mark back from school yet? | I haven't finished the book yet.*

**THESAURUS: always**

**permanently** forever or for a very long time: *His eyesight may be permanently damaged.*

**forever** for all time in the future: *It's so nice here that I'd like to stay forever.*

**for good** used to say that a change is permanent: *They decided to move back to Chicago for good.*

**2** for a very long time: *I've always wanted to go to New York – ever since I was really little.*
**3 you can/could always ...** = used when suggesting that someone should do something: *You could always ask your mom for some help.*

**Alz·heim·er's dis·ease** /ˈɑltshaɪmɚz dɪˌsiz/ *noun*
a serious disease that damages people's brains and makes them unable to remember things. Alzheimer's disease usually affects old people.

**am** /əm; *strong* æm/ *verb*
the present form of the verb BE, that is used with "I." "I am" is often shortened to "I'm": *I am so proud of you.*

**a.m.** /ˌeɪ ˈem/
used to show that a time is in the morning: *I get up at 7:00 a.m.*

**am·a·teur** /ˈæmətʃɚ/ *adjective*
doing something for enjoyment, not for money and not as a job: *The competition is for amateur athletes, not professionals.*
**ANTONYM: professional**
—**amateur** *noun* someone who plays a sport, paints pictures, etc. for enjoyment, not for money or as a job

**a·maze** /əˈmeɪz/ *verb*
to make someone very surprised: *It amazes me that they're still married – they argue all the time.*
—**amazed** *adjective* very surprised: *I was amazed at how much it all cost.*
—**amazing** *adjective* very good in a surprising way: *The movie was amazing – the special effects were so good.*

**WORD FAMILY: amaze**

**amazed** *adjective* | **amazing** *adjective* | **amaze** *verb* | **amazement** *noun*

**a·maze·ment** /əˈmeɪzmənt/ *noun*
the feeling of being very surprised: *I looked up in amazement when they announced that I was the winner of the competition.*

**am·bas·sa·dor** /æmˈbæsədɚ/ *noun*
an important person whose job is to represent his or her country in another country: *He is the U.S. ambassador to France.*

**am·big·u·ous** Ac /æmˈbɪgyuəs/ *adjective*
something that is ambiguous is not clear because it can be understood in more than one way: *The word "soon" is ambiguous because it can mean "in a few minutes," "in a few days," or "in a few weeks."*

**am·bi·tion** /æmˈbɪʃən/ *noun*
**1** something that you want to achieve in the future: *My ambition is to become a writer someday.*
**2** a strong feeling of wanting to be successful: *Craig has a lot of ambition, and I'm sure he'll be very successful in his career.*

**am·bi·tious** /æmˈbɪʃəs/ *adjective*
wanting very much to be successful: *She was very ambitious and decided to start her own company.*

**am·bu·lance** /ˈæmbyələns/ *noun*
a special vehicle for taking sick or injured people to the hospital: *Can someone call an ambulance? I think this man is really sick.* → see picture on page A27
[**ORIGIN:** 1800-1900 From the French word *ambulant*, which means "traveling" and was used about an army hospital that could be moved. "Ambulance" was later used for a vehicle that carried wounded soldiers away.]

**am·bush** /ˈæmbʊʃ/ *noun*
a sudden attack by someone who has been secretly waiting in a hidden place: *Three U.S. soldiers were killed in an ambush.*
—**ambush** *verb* to suddenly attack someone after secretly waiting in a hidden place
[**ORIGIN:** 1300-1400 From the French words *en* and *busche*, which mean "in" and "wood."

People could hide in woods before attacking someone.]

**a·mend** Ac /əˈmend/ *verb*
to make a change to a law or to an important document: *The law needs to be amended so that it helps more people.*
—**amendment** *noun* a change made to a law or important document: *The First Amendment to the Constitution protects freedom of speech.*
→ see Thesaurus box at **change**[1]

**a·men·i·ties** /əˈmenətiz/ *plural noun*
things in a place that make it nice to live in or stay in: *The neighborhood has good schools, a park, and other amenities.*

**A·mer·i·can** /əˈmerɪkən/ *adjective*
from or in the U.S.: *My wife is American.*
—**American** *noun* someone from the U.S.

**AˌmericanˈDream** *noun*
**the American Dream** = the idea that everyone in the U.S. has the opportunity to become successful if he or she works hard

**am·mu·ni·tion** /ˌæmyəˈnɪʃən/ *noun*
things such as bullets that are fired from guns: *He loaded the gun with ammunition.*

**am·nes·ty** /ˈæmnəsti/ *noun* (plural **amnesties**)
an official order that allows prisoners to leave prison, or says that people will not be punished for a crime

**a·moe·ba** /əˈmibə/ *noun*
a very small creature that has only one cell

**a·mong** /əˈmʌŋ/ (*also* **a·mongst** /əˈmʌŋst/) *preposition*
**1** included in a larger group of people or things: *Brad was among the ten students who received the award.*
**2** in the middle of a lot of people or things: *The rabbit disappeared among some trees.*

**USAGE: among, between**

**Among** and **between** are both used to talk about where someone or something is.

Use **among** when someone or something is surrounded by people or things: *Denise was among a group of her friends.*

Use **between** when there is one person or thing on each side of someone or something: *I sat between Alex and Sarah.*

**3** happening to or relating to a group of people: *Acne is a skin problem that is common among teenagers.*

**a·mount**[1] /əˈmaʊnt/ *noun*
a quantity of something: *$80,000 is a very large amount of money.*

**GRAMMAR: amount, number**

Use **amount** with nouns such as "money" and "bread" that do not have plurals: *a large amount of water*

Use **number** with plural forms of nouns: *a large number of cars*

**amount**[2] *verb*
**PHRASAL VERB**
**amount to something**
to make a total: *The money they collected for the charity amounted to $620.*

**amp** /æmp/ (*also* **am·pere** /ˈæmpɪr/) *noun*
a unit for measuring an electric current

**amphibian**

**am·phib·i·an** /æmˈfɪbiən/ *noun*
an animal such as a FROG that begins its life in water and later lives on land
[**ORIGIN:** 1600-1700 From the Greek words *amphis* and *bios*, which mean "on both sides" and "life." Amphibians live both in water and on land.]

**am·phi·the·a·ter** /ˈæmfəˌθiətɚ/ *noun*
a large theater that has no roof, in which the seats go around the stage in a circle or half a circle

**am·ple** /ˈæmpəl/ *adjective*
more than enough: *The car has ample room for five people. Our family fits easily in it.*

A

**am·pu·tate** /ˈæmpyəˌteɪt/ *verb*
to cut off a part of someone's body for medical reasons: *His left leg was badly injured, and the doctors had to amputate it.*
—**amputation** /ˌæmpyəˈteɪʃən/ *noun* the act of cutting off part of someone's body

**a·muse** /əˈmyuz/ *verb*
**1** to make someone laugh or smile: *My joke seemed to amuse him.*
**2 amuse yourself** = to do things so that you do not get bored: *While we waited for the flight, we amused ourselves by doing puzzles.*
—**amused** *adjective* if you are amused, you think that something is funny: *The children laughed, but the teacher did not look amused.*

**WORD FAMILY: amuse**
**amuse** *verb* | **amused** *adjective* | **amusing** *adjective* | **amusement** *noun*

**a·muse·ment** /əˈmyuzmənt/ *noun*
the feeling you have when you think something is funny: *When I asked where the cookies were, she looked at me with amusement and said, "What cookies?"*

**aˈmusement ˌpark** *noun*
a place where people go to enjoy themselves by riding on large machines: *We went for a ride on the roller coaster at the amusement park.*

**a·mus·ing** /əˈmyuzɪŋ/ *adjective*
funny and entertaining: *He told them an amusing story about a man who thinks he can fly.*
→ see Thesaurus box at **funny**

**an** /ən; *strong* æn/ *indefinite article*
used instead of "a" before a word that begins with a vowel sound: *an animal* | *an X-ray* | *an hour*

**a·nal·o·gy** Ac /əˈnælədʒi/ *noun* (plural **analogies**)
**make/draw an analogy** = if you make an analogy between two situations, you say that they are similar in some ways: *We can make an analogy between a brain and a computer – both take in information and deal with it.*

**a·nal·y·sis** Ac /əˈnæləsɪs/ *noun* (plural **analyses**)
careful examination of something in order to understand it or to find out what it contains: *The analysis showed that he had too much sugar in his blood.*
[**ORIGIN:** 1500-1600 From the Greek word *analyein*, which means "to break up." The idea is that you divide something up and examine each part.]

**an·a·lyst** Ac /ˈænl-ɪst/ *noun*
**1** someone whose job is to analyze things: *Some financial analysts think the economy is improving.*
**2** another word for a PSYCHOANALYST

**an·al·yze** Ac /ˈænlˌaɪz/ *verb*
to examine something carefully in order to understand it or to find out what it contains: *We can analyze water from the river and see what chemicals it contains.*

**WORD FAMILY: analyze**
**analyze** *verb* | **analysis** *noun* | **analyst** *noun*

**a·nat·o·my** /əˈnætəmi/ *noun*
**1** the scientific study of the structure of the body: *The biology class contains a section on anatomy.*
**2** the structure of the body of a person or animal: *The anatomy of men and women is slightly different.*
—**anatomical** /ˌænəˈtɑmɪkəl/ *adjective* relating to anatomy
[**ORIGIN:** 1300-1400 From the Greek word *anatome*, which means "cutting up." Scientists cut up the bodies of people and animals to see what their structure is.]

**an·ces·tor** /ˈænˌsestɚ/ *noun*
a member of your family who lived a long time before you were born: *His ancestors came to the U.S. from Germany over a hundred years ago.*
→ see Thesaurus box at **family**
[**ORIGIN:** 1300-1400 From the Latin word *antecessor*, which means "someone who goes before."]

**an·chor** /ˈæŋkɚ/ *noun*

**1** a heavy metal object that is put into the water on a chain to prevent a ship or boat from moving
**2** someone who reads the news on television or radio and introduces news reports: *He is the news anchor on the six o'clock news.*

**an·cient** /ˈeɪnʃənt/ *adjective*
thousands of years old: *The statue was made in ancient Egypt, over five thousand years ago.*
→ see Thesaurus box at **old**

**and** /ən, ənd; *strong* ænd/ *conjunction*
**1** used for connecting two words or parts of a sentence: *They have a cat and a dog.* | *We saw a movie, and then we went to a restaurant.*
**2** used when one number is added to another: *13 and 9 is 22.* **SYNONYM: plus**

**an·ec·dote** /ˈænɪkˌdoʊt/ *noun*
a short story that you tell people, about something interesting or funny that happened to you: *The book is full of anecdotes about his life in Canada.*

**a·ne·mi·a** /əˈnimiə/ *noun*
a medical condition in which there are not enough red cells in your blood, so that you do not have enough energy: *Sometimes teenagers get anemia because they don't eat enough healthy food.*
—**anemic** *adjective* having anemia

**an·es·thet·ic** /ˌænəsˈθetɪk/ *noun*
a drug that stops you from feeling pain during a medical operation: *The doctor gave her a general anesthetic, so she wasn't awake during the operation.*
—**anesthesia** /ˌænəsˈθiZə/ *noun* the use of drugs to stop someone from feeling pain during a medical operation
[**ORIGIN:** 1700-1800 From the Greek word *anaisthetos*, which means "without feeling," from *an-*, meaning "without," and *aisthesis*, meaning "feeling."]

**an·gel** /ˈeɪndʒəl/ *noun*
a spirit who lives with God in heaven, usually shown in pictures as a person with wings
—**angelic** /ænˈdʒelɪk/ *adjective* like an angel, or relating to angels: *The little boy had an angelic face.*
[**ORIGIN:** From the Greek word *angelos*, which means "messenger." Angels brought messages from God to people on Earth.]

**an·ger[1]** /ˈæŋgɚ/ *noun*
a strong feeling that you have when you think someone has behaved very badly or a situation is very unfair: *His voice was full of anger.*

**anger[2]** *verb* (*formal*)
to make someone angry: *His rudeness angered me.*

**angle**

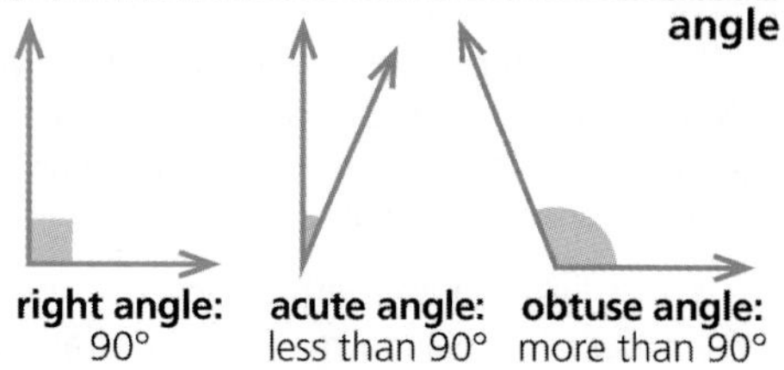


**an·gle** /ˈæŋgəl/ *noun*
**1** the shape that is formed when two straight lines meet each other: *A square has four angles of 90 degrees.*
**2** a way of thinking about a situation: *Let's look at the problem from a different angle.*

**an·gry** /ˈæŋgri/ *adjective* (**angrier**, **angriest**)
feeling a strong emotion because you think someone has behaved very badly or a situation is very unfair: *I was angry at him for treating me like a child.* | *The man suddenly got angry and started yelling.* → see picture on page **A23**
—**angrily** *adverb* in an angry way: *"I don't need any more advice from you," he said angrily.*
[**ORIGIN:** 1200-1300 From the Norse word *angr*, which means "great sorrow."]

**WORD FAMILY: angry**

**angry** *adjective* | **angrily** *adverb* | **anger** *noun* | **anger** *verb*

**THESAURUS: angry**

**annoyed** a little angry: *My mom gets annoyed with me if I come home late.*

**irritated** feeling annoyed and not patient with people or things: *Everyone was talking at once, and I started to feel irritated.*

**furious** very angry: *I was furious with my sister for wearing my new jeans without asking.*

**mad** angry: *She got really mad when he wouldn't listen to her.*

**in a bad mood** behaving in an unfriendly way and becoming angry easily: *The bus was late, which put him in a bad mood.*

**an·guish** /ˈæŋgwɪʃ/ *noun*
a very strong feeling of unhappiness: *He caused a lot of anguish to his family when he did not write home.*

A

**an·i·mal** /ˈænəməl/ *noun*
a living creature that breathes and moves: *Dogs are my favorite animals.*
[**ORIGIN:** 1300-1400 From the Latin word *anima*, which means "life or soul."]

**an·i·ma·tion** /ˌænəˈmeɪʃən/ *noun*
the process of making movies with drawings or models, rather than filming actors: *They use computer animation in the movie to make it look like the house is flying.*
—**animated** *adjective* made using animation: *The kids love watching animated movies.*

**an·kle** /ˈæŋkəl/ *noun*
the joint between your foot and your leg: *My foot twisted to one side and I hurt my ankle.*
→ see picture on page **A2**

**an·ni·ver·sa·ry** /ˌænəˈvɚsəri/ *noun* (plural **anniversaries**)
the day when you remember something important that happened on the same date in a previous year: *My parents' wedding anniversary is in June.*
[**ORIGIN:** 1200-1300 From the Latin words *annus* and *vertere*, which mean "year" and "to turn." An anniversary is a date that returns each year.]

**an·nounce** /əˈnaʊns/ *verb*
to tell people about an important plan or decision: *The coach announced that he was leaving the team.*

**an·nounce·ment** /əˈnaʊnsmənt/ *noun*
an official public statement that tells people some important news: *The principal will make an important announcement about the school this afternoon.*

**an·noy** /əˈnɔɪ/ *verb*
to make someone feel a little angry: *His singing was really bad, and it was starting to annoy me.* **SYNONYM: irritate**
—**annoying** *adjective* something that is annoying makes you feel a little angry: *The woman had an annoying high voice.*
[**ORIGIN:** 1200-1300 From the Latin word *inodiare*, which means "to make someone or something hated."]

**WORD FAMILY: annoy**

**annoy** *verb* | **annoyed** *adjective* | **annoying** *adjective* | **annoyance** *noun*

**an·noy·ance** /əˈnɔɪəns/ *noun*
the feeling of being a little angry: *To his mother's annoyance, John hadn't put away any of his clothes for weeks.* **SYNONYM: irritation**

**an·noyed** /əˈnɔɪd/ *adjective*
a little angry: *My Dad gets annoyed with us when we don't listen.* **SYNONYM: irritated**
→ see Thesaurus box at **angry**

**an·nu·al** Ac /ˈænyuəl/ *adjective*
happening once a year: *Next week, the club will have its annual meeting.*
—**annually** *adverb* once a year
[**ORIGIN:** 1300-1400 From the Latin word *annus*, which means "year."]

**a·non·y·mous** /əˈnɑnəməs/ *adjective*
someone who is anonymous does not tell you his or her name: *An anonymous caller told the police there was going to be a robbery.*
—**anonymously** *adverb* in an anonymous way
[**ORIGIN:** 1600-1700 From the Greek words *an-* and *onyma*, which mean "without" and "name."]

**a·no·rex·i·a** /ˌænəˈreksiə/ *noun*
a medical condition in which someone stops wanting to eat. People with anorexia are often very thin.
—**anorexic** *adjective* having anorexia

**an·oth·er** /əˈnʌðɚ/ *adjective, pronoun*
**1** one more person, thing, or amount of the same kind: *Do you want another cookie?* | *Let's wait another ten minutes – I'm sure he'll be here soon.*
**2** a different person or thing: *Is there another chair I could use? This one is broken.*
→ see Thesaurus box at **more²**

**an·swer¹** /ˈænsɚ/ *verb*
**1** to say or write something after you have been asked a question or given a test: *"Did you see anyone else?" "No," she answered.* | *I couldn't answer all the questions on the test.*

**THESAURUS: answer**

**reply** to answer someone – used especially in written English: *"Are you coming?" "Yes," she replied.* | *He did not reply to my letter.*
**respond** to answer someone, especially in

a way that gives a lot of details: *The speaker will respond to questions at the end of his talk.*

**2 answer the phone** = to speak into a telephone when it rings: *The phone was ringing and Maddy answered it.*
**3 answer the door** = to go to the door when someone knocks or rings a bell: *She heard someone knocking and she went downstairs to answer the door.*

**answer²** *noun*
**1** something that you say or write when someone asks you a question: *His answer to my question was "No." | Can you give me an answer about whether you can come as soon as possible? | What was the answer to question number 3 on the math test?*
**2** something that solves a problem: *There are no easy answers to the problem of crime.* **SYNONYM: solution**

**ˈanswering maˌchine** *noun*
a machine that records messages from the people that call you when you cannot answer your telephone

**ant** /ænt/ *noun*
a common small black or red insect that lives in large groups

**an·tac·id** /ˌæntˈæsɪd/ *noun*
a medicine that stops the burning feeling in your stomach when you have eaten too much

**Ant·arc·tic** /ænˈtɑrktɪk/ *noun*
**the Antarctic** (*also* **Antarctica**) = the very cold, most southern part of the world around the South Pole

**an·te·lope** /ˈæntəlˌoʊp/ *noun*
an animal that has long horns, can run very fast, and is very graceful

**an·ten·na** /ænˈtenə/ *noun*
**1** a piece of equipment for receiving radio or television signals, that is on a car, roof, etc. → see picture on page **A28**
**2** (plural **antennae** /-ni/) one of two long thin things on an insect's head that it uses to feel things
[**ORIGIN:** 1600-1700 From the Latin word *antenna*, which means "pole that holds up a sail."]

**an·them** /ˈænθəm/ *noun*
a song that people sing on special occasions. The national anthem is a country's national song: *The band played the national anthem before the game.*

**an·thro·pol·o·gy** /ˌænθrəˈpɑlədʒi/ *noun*
the study of people in different places around the world and how they live
—**anthropologist** *noun* someone who studies people

**an·ti·bi·ot·ic** /ˌæntɪbaɪˈɑtɪk/ *noun*
a medicine that kills BACTERIA and cures infections

**an·tic·i·pate** [Ac] /ænˈtɪsəˌpeɪt/ *verb* (*formal*)
to expect that something will happen: *The team has practiced hard for the game tomorrow, so I do not anticipate any problems.*
—**anticipation** /ænˌtɪsəˈpeɪʃən/ *noun* the idea or feeling you have when you expect something to happen: *The audience waited for the singer with great anticipation.*

**an·ti·freeze** /ˈæntɪˌfriz/ *noun*
a substance that you put in the water in a car RADIATOR to stop it from freezing in cold weather

**an·ti·his·ta·mine** /ˌæntɪˈhɪstəˌmin/ *noun*
a medicine that is used to treat an ALLERGY: *I take antihistamines to help me stop sneezing when I get hay fever.*

**an·ti·per·spi·rant** /ˌæntɪˈpɚspərənt/ *noun*
a substance that you put under your arms to stop yourself from SWEATing

**antique**

an antique desk

a modern desk

**an·tique** /ˌænˈtik/ *noun*
an old piece of furniture or other old object that is usually valuable: *His house was full of beautiful antiques and old paintings.*

A

—**antique** *adjective* antique objects are old and valuable: *antique furniture*
→ see Thesaurus box at **old**

**an·ti·sep·tic** /ˌæntɪˈseptɪk/ *noun*
a chemical substance that is put on a wound to prevent it from becoming infected: *The nurse put antiseptic on the cut.*
—**antiseptic** *adjective* helping to prevent infection: *an antiseptic cream*

**an·ti·so·cial** /ˌæntɪˈsoʊʃəl/ *adjective*
behaving in a way that annoys or causes problems for other people: *Some antisocial teenagers had painted graffiti on the walls.*

**ant·ler** /ˈæntlɚ/ *noun*
one of the horns that look like tree branches, which animals such as DEER have

**an·to·nym** /ˈæntəˌnɪm/ *noun*
a word that means the opposite of another word: *"Long" is an antonym of "short."*
**ANTONYM: synonym**
[**ORIGIN:** 1800-1900 From the Greek words *anti* and *onyma*, which mean "opposite" and "name or word."]

**anx·i·e·ty** /æŋˈzaɪəti/ *noun*
a strong feeling of worry about something: *I waited with anxiety to find out the results of my tests.* **SYNONYM: worry**

**anx·ious** /ˈæŋkʃəs/ *adjective*
**1** very worried about something: *She was anxious about the health of her baby.*
**SYNONYM: worried**
**2** feeling strongly that you want to do something or want something to happen: *I was anxious to know if she had won the race.*
**SYNONYM: eager**
—**anxiously** *adverb* in an anxious way: *They waited anxiously for news.*
→ see Thesaurus box at **worried**

**an·y¹** /ˈeni/ *adjective, pronoun*
**1** some – used in questions: *Is there any ice cream left?*
**2** **not ... any** = none at all: *I haven't read any of his books.* | *I don't have any friends at school. No one talks to me.*

**GRAMMAR: any, a**

In questions and in sentences with "not," use **any** with nouns such as "money" and "bread" that do not have plurals, and with plural forms of nouns: *Do you have any money?* | *There weren't any books that I wanted to read.*

Use **a** when you are talking about one thing: *Do you have a car?*

**3** used when something is true about every thing or person in a group: *You can buy it at any book store.* | *Any of the contestants could win – they're all good.*

**any²** *adverb*
even a small amount – used in questions and negative statements: *Are you feeling any better?* | *She couldn't walk any farther.*

**an·y·bod·y** /ˈeniˌbɑdi/ *pronoun* (*informal*)
another word for ANYONE

**an·y·how** /ˈeniˌhaʊ/ *adverb* (*informal*)
another word for ANYWAY

**an·y·more** (*also* **any more**) /ˌeniˈmɔr/ *adverb*
if something does not happen anymore, it has stopped happening: *He doesn't play baseball any more because he hurt his leg.*

**an·y·one** /ˈeniˌwʌn/ *pronoun*
**1** someone or a person – used in questions and negative statements: *There wasn't anyone in the room.* | *Is anyone else coming to the party?*

**GRAMMAR: anyone, someone**

In questions and in sentences with "not" in them, we usually use **anyone** and not **someone**: *Have you told anyone about this?* | *I didn't see anyone there.*

In other sentences, we use **someone**: *There's someone here to see you.*

**2** any person, it does not matter who: *The game is so simple that anyone can play it.*

**an·y·place** /ˈeniˌpleɪs/ *adverb* (*informal*)
another word for ANYWHERE

**an·y·thing** /ˈeniˌθɪŋ/ *pronoun*
**1** something or a thing – used in questions and negative statements: *We don't know anything about her, not even her name.* | *Do you need anything else?*

**GRAMMAR: anything, something**

In questions and in sentences with "not" in them, we usually use **anything** and not

**something**: *Did you see anything you liked? | I didn't have anything to eat.*

If you are offering someone some food, a drink, etc., it sounds more polite to use **something**: *Would you like something to eat?*

**2** used when you are saying that it does not matter which thing: *My dog will eat anything – he even tries to eat my slippers.*

**3 or anything** (*informal*) = or something else of the same kind: *I hope it isn't the flu or anything.*

**an·y·time** (*also* **any time**) /ˈeniˌtaɪm/ *adverb*
at any time: *You can call me anytime, even in the middle of the night.*

**an·y·way** /ˈeniˌweɪ/ *adverb*
**1** even though something else is true: *It's probably not a serious injury, but you should see a doctor anyway.*
**2** used to change the subject of a conversation, or to return to the main subject or story: *Anyway, do you want to come over to my house after school?*
**3** used when you are mentioning a more important fact: *I wasn't invited to the party, but I didn't want to go anyway.*
**4** used when you are adding something that limits what you have said: *I can't help you. Not right now, anyway.*

**an·y·where** /ˈeniˌwer/ *adverb*
**1** in or to any place: *I can't find my keys anywhere – I've looked all over the house. | Come home right away. Don't go anywhere else first. | You can go anywhere you want in the building.*

**GRAMMAR: anywhere, somewhere**

In questions and in sentences with "not" in them, we usually use **anywhere** and not **somewhere**: *I can't find my keys anywhere. | Have you seen my book anywhere?*

In other sentences, we use **somewhere**: *My keys must to be in my room somewhere.*

**2** used when you are not sure of the exact number: *His business trip will last anywhere from one to three days.*

**a·part** /əˈpɑrt/ *adverb*
**1** used when saying the distance or time between two places or events: *The two cities are six miles apart. | Our birthdays are only two days apart.*
**2** into many pieces or parts: *He had to take the camera apart to fix it. | The old book came apart in my hands when I tried to pick it up.*
→ **fall apart** at fall[1]
**3 apart from someone or something** = except for someone or something: *Apart from him, everyone else enjoyed the movie.*

**a·part·ment** /əˈpɑrtmənt/ *noun*
a place to live that consists of a set of rooms in a large building: *She lives in a one-bedroom apartment. | a large apartment building*

**ap·a·thy** /ˈæpəθi/ *noun*
the feeling that you are not interested in something and that it does not matter: *There is a lot of apathy among young people about the election – no one really cares.*
—**apathetic** /ˌæpəˈθətɪk/ *adjective* not interested in something and not caring about it

**ape**

gorilla chimpanzee orangutan

**ape** /eɪp/ *noun*
a large animal like a monkey but with no tail or a very short tail: *Gorillas and chimpanzees are apes.*

**a·piece** /əˈpis/ *adverb*
for each one: *The apples are 25 cents apiece.*
**SYNONYM: each**

**a·pol·o·gize** /əˈpɑləˌdʒaɪz/ *verb*
to say that you are sorry about something that you have done: *He apologized for being late.*
—**apologetic** /əˌpɑləˈdʒetɪk/ *adjective* saying or showing that you are sorry about something: *When I showed them the mistake, they were very apologetic.*

A

**a·pol·o·gy** /ə'pɑlədʒi/ *noun* (plural **apologies**)
something that you say or write to show that you are sorry about something that you have done: *She lied to me. I think she owes me an apology.*

**WORD FAMILY: apology**
**apology** *noun* | **apologize** *verb* | **apologetic** *adjective*

**a·pos·tro·phe** /ə'pɑstrəfi/ *noun*
**1** the mark ('), which is used in writing to show that letters have been left out of a word or numbers have been left out of a date, as in "don't" (=do not), '09 (=1909/2009, etc.)
**2** the mark ('), which is used in writing before an "s" to show that something belongs to someone, as in "Sarah's book" (=the book that belongs to Sarah)

**app** /æp/ *noun*
a piece of computer software that does a particular job: *You can download apps from their website.*

**ap·palled** /ə'pɔld/ *adjective*
very shocked: *I am appalled by the amount of violence in some computer games.*

**ap·pa·rat·us** /ˌæpə'rætəs/ *noun* (plural **apparatus** *or* **apparatuses**) (*formal*)
equipment or tools used for something, especially something scientific or technical: *The divers are using a new apparatus for breathing under water.*

**ap·par·ent** Ac /ə'pærənt/ *adjective*
**1** easy to see or understand: *My mom sometimes criticizes me for no apparent reason.* | *It soon became apparent that the man didn't know what he was talking about.*
**SYNONYMS: clear, obvious**
**2** seeming to be true or real: *I was surprised by his apparent lack of interest in his schoolwork.*

**ap·par·ent·ly** Ac /ə'pærəntli/ *adverb*
used when mentioning something that other people say is true: *He was late for school today. Apparently, he overslept.*

**ap·peal**[1] /ə'pil/ *verb*
**1** to ask people, especially the public, for something such as money or help: *The organization is appealing for money to help the earthquake victims.*
**2** to formally ask a court to change a decision that a less important court made: *His lawyers are going to appeal the court's decision.*
**PHRASAL VERB**
**appeal to someone**
to seem attractive or interesting to someone: *The idea of going to college did not appeal to him. He wanted to get a job instead.*

**appeal**[2] *noun*
**1** a strong request to the public for something such as money or help: *The teachers made an appeal to parents for money and help.*
**2** the act of asking a court to change a decision that a less important court made: *He was convicted of murder, and the court rejected his appeal.*
**3** the quality that makes you like something: *The band's music has a lot of appeal for young people.*

**ap·peal·ing** /ə'pilɪŋ/ *adjective*
attractive or interesting: *The company tries to make its products appealing to kids by using cartoon characters and bright colors.*

**ap·pear** /ə'pɪr/ *verb*
**1** to seem: *She appeared nervous.* | *The man appeared to be asleep.*
**2** to begin to be seen: *A face appeared at the window.*
**3** to take part in a movie, television program, or play: *He appeared in several horror movies.*
→ see Thesaurus box at **seem**

**WORD FAMILY: appear**
**appear** *verb* | **disappear** *verb* | **appearance** *noun* | **disappearance** *noun*

**ap·pear·ance** /ə'pɪrəns/ *noun*
**1** the way someone or something looks: *She dyed her hair black and it really changed her appearance.*
**2** a time when someone or something arrives somewhere or can be seen somewhere: *This was his first appearance in court.*

**ap·pen·di·ci·tis** /əˌpendə'saɪtɪs/ *noun*
an illness in which your appendix gets bigger,

becomes painful, and often has to be taken out in an operation

**ap·pen·dix** Ac /əˈpendɪks/ *noun*
**1** a small closed tube that is part of your BOWEL: *He had an operation to take out his appendix.*
**2** (plural **appendixes** *or* **appendices** /-dɪsiz/) a part at the end of a book that has additional information: *There is an appendix at the back of the book with a list of other books on this subject.*

**ap·pe·tite** /ˈæpəˌtaɪt/ *noun*
the feeling that you want to eat: *When I was sick, I lost my appetite and I hardly ate anything.*

**ap·pe·tiz·er** /ˈæpəˌtaɪzɚ/ *noun*
a small amount of food that you eat before the main part of a meal: *He ordered garlic bread as an appetizer.*

**ap·plaud** /əˈplɔd/ *verb*
to hit your hands together many times, for example to show that you enjoyed something such as a play: *When she finished the song, the audience applauded for a long time.* **SYNONYM: clap** → see picture on page **A3**

**ap·plause** /əˈplɔz/ *noun*
the sound of people hitting their hands together many times to show that they enjoyed something or think someone is good: *When he ended his speech, there was loud applause.*

**ap·ple** /ˈæpəl/ *noun*
a hard round red or green fruit that is white inside: *apple pie* | *an apple tree* → see picture on page **A13**

**ap·ple·sauce** /ˈæpəlˌsɔs/ *noun*
a thick smooth food made from cooked apples

**ap·pli·ance** /əˈplaɪəns/ *noun*
a machine that is used in someone's home, such as a REFRIGERATOR or a DISHWASHER: *kitchen appliances*
→ see Thesaurus box at **machine**

**ap·pli·ca·tion** /ˌæplɪˈkeɪʃən/ *noun*
**1** a form that you write on when you are asking for something, for example a job or to join an organization: *a job application* | *Please fill out an application if you are interested in the class.* | *I had forgotten to sign the application form.*
**2** an APP

**ap·ply** /əˈplaɪ/ *verb* (**applied**, **applies**)
**1** to formally ask for something in writing, for example a job or a chance to go to a college: *Fifteen people applied for the job.* | *He applied to law school.*
**2** to affect, or be true for, a particular person or thing: *The rules apply to every student at this school.*
**3** (*formal*) to spread something on a surface, for example paint: *She applied her lipstick.*
—**applicant** /ˈæplɪkənt/ *noun* someone who is applying for something such as a job or college

| WORD FAMILY: apply |
|---|
| **apply** *verb* \| **application** *noun* \| **applicant** *noun* |

**ap·point** /əˈpɔɪnt/ *verb*
to choose someone for a job or position: *She was appointed to the position by the president.* | *He was appointed coach in May.*

**ap·point·ment** /əˈpɔɪntmənt/ *noun*
**1** a meeting that has been arranged for a time and place: *I'd like to make an appointment with Dr. Hanson on Tuesday.* | *I have an appointment at six.*
**2** the act of choosing someone for a job or position: *The appointment of a new principal takes a long time.*

**ap·pre·ci·ate** Ac /əˈpriʃiˌeɪt/ *verb*
**1** to feel grateful for something: *We really appreciate your help.* | *Thanks for meeting with me. I appreciate it.*
**2** (*formal*) to understand a situation or problem: *I appreciate that learning a new language is very difficult.*

| WORD FAMILY: appreciate |
|---|
| **appreciate** *verb* \| **appreciation** *noun* |

**ap·pre·ci·a·tion** Ac /əˌpriʃiˈeɪʃən/ *noun*
the feeling of being grateful for something: *They showed their appreciation for her support by giving her a gift.*

**ap·pren·tice** /əprˈentis/ *noun*
someone who is learning how to do a job by working with someone who can do the job,

A

for example a MECHANIC or a PLUMBER: *He started as an apprentice and in time became a skilled mechanic.*

**ap·proach¹** Ac /əˈproʊtʃ/ *verb*
**1** to move closer to someone or something: *A woman approached me in the street and asked for directions.*
**2** if something is approaching, it will happen soon: *Winter was approaching and the weather was getting colder.*

**approach²** Ac *noun*
a way of doing something or dealing with a problem: *My first attempts to lose weight were unsuccessful, so I decided to try a different approach and do lots of exercise.*

**ap·pro·pri·ate** Ac /əˈproʊpriɪt/ *adjective*
correct or good for a person, situation, or time: *The movie is very violent and is not appropriate for young children.* **ANTONYM: inappropriate**
—**appropriately** *adverb* in an appropriate way

**ap·prov·al** /əˈpruvəl/ *noun*
**1** words or actions that show you think someone or something is good or is doing something right: *Children always want their parents' approval.*
**2** official permission: *The teacher gave his approval to the students' science project and told them to get started.*

**ap·prove** /əˈpruv/ *verb*
**1** to think that something or someone is good or right: *Do her parents approve of her new boyfriend?* **ANTONYM: disapprove**
**2** to give official permission for something: *The plan was approved by California voters.*

**WORD FAMILY: approve**
**approve** *verb* | **disapprove** *verb* | **approval** *noun* | **disapproval** *noun*

**ap·prox·i·mate·ly** Ac /əˈprɑksəmətli/ *adverb*
used when saying that a number or amount is not exact: *The plane will land in approximately 20 minutes.*
—**approximate** *adjective* not exact: *When I say a cup of butter, that's only an approximate amount; you can use a little more if you want.*
→ see Thesaurus box at **about**

**ap·ri·cot** /ˈeɪprɪˌkɑt/ *noun*
a small soft fruit with yellow-orange skin and a PIT (=large hard seed) inside → see picture on page **A13**

**A·pril** /ˈeɪprəl/ *noun* (*written abbreviation*: **Apr.**)
the fourth month of the year, between March and May: *Lucy's birthday is on April 5th.* | *The flowers start to bloom in April.* | *We went to California last April.* | *We're going to see my aunt next April.*
[**ORIGIN:** probably 1200-1300 Possibly from the Latin word *aperire*, which means "to open," because flowers and leaves start to open in April. Also possibly from Aphrodite, the Greek goddess of love.]

**a·pron** /ˈeɪprən/ *noun*
a piece of clothing that you wear over your other clothes in order to keep them clean, especially when you are cooking or painting

**ap·ti·tude** /ˈæptəˌtud/ *noun*
a natural ability that makes it easy for you to learn to do something: *He has an aptitude for sports and he plays baseball and basketball really well.*

aquarium

**a·quar·i·um** /əˈkweriəm/ *noun*
**1** a glass container for keeping fish in
**2** a building where people go to look at fish or other water animals
[**ORIGIN:** 1800-1900 From the Latin word *aqua*, which means "water."]

**A·quar·i·us** /əˈkweriəs/ *noun*
**1** the 11th sign of the ZODIAC, represented by someone carrying water

**2** someone born between January 20 and February 18

**Ar·ab** /ˈærəb/ *adjective*
from the Middle East or North Africa: *Arab women often cover their hair with a headscarf.*
—**Arab** *noun* someone from the Middle East or North Africa: *The Arabs made many important discoveries in mathematics and astronomy.*

**Ar·a·bic** /ˈærəbɪk/ *noun*
the language spoken in many countries in the Middle East and North Africa, such as Egypt and Saudi Arabia

**ar·a·ble** /ˈærəbəl/ *adjective*
arable land is used for growing crops

**ar·bi·trar·y** Ac /ˈɑrbəˌtreri/ *adjective*
arbitrary decisions or rules seem unfair because there are no good reasons for them: *Juan is a really good player but he didn't get on the team – the coach's decision seemed arbitrary.*

**arc** /ɑrk/ *noun*
a curved line, especially one that forms part of a circle: *The Sun appears to move in a big arc across the sky, rising in the east and going down in the west.*
[**ORIGIN:** 1300-1400 From the Latin word *arcus*, which means "bow or arch."]

**ar·cade** /ɑrˈkeɪd/ *noun*
a special room or small building where people pay to play VIDEO GAMEs

**arch** /ɑrtʃ/ *noun* (plural **arches**)
a curved shape at the top of a door or window, or a supporting part of a building or bridge: *The roof of the church was supported by huge arches.*

**ar·chae·ol·o·gy** (*also* **archeology**) /ˌɑrkiˈɑlədʒi/ *noun*
the study of ancient societies, which people do by carefully digging to find old buildings and old objects that have been under the ground for a long time, and then examining them
—**archaeologist** *noun* someone who studies archaeology: *Archaeologists found the remains of an ancient temple.*
—**archaeological** /ˌɑrkiəˈlɑdʒɪkəl/ *adjective* relating to archaeology
[**ORIGIN:** 1600-1700 From the Greek words *archaios* and *-logia*, which mean "ancient" and "study."]

**ar·chi·tect** /ˈɑrkəˌtekt/ *noun*
someone whose job is to design buildings
[**ORIGIN:** 1500-1600 From the Greek word *architekton*, which means "chief builder."]

**ar·chi·tec·ture** /ˈɑrkəˌtektʃɚ/ *noun*
the style and design of buildings: *The city is famous for its architecture and has many beautiful buildings.*

**Arc·tic** /ˈɑrktɪk/ *noun*
**the Arctic** = the most northern part of the Earth, around the North Pole, that includes parts of Alaska and Greenland and the Arctic Ocean

**are** /ɚ; *strong* ɑr/ *verb*
the present form of the verb BE, that is used with plurals and "you"

**ar·e·a** Ac /ˈeriə/ *noun*
**1** a part of a place: *Have you always lived in this area of town?* | *The kitchen has a small dining area.*

**THESAURUS: area**

**region** a large area of a country or the world: *the northwest region of Russia*
**zone** an area where a particular thing happens or where there are special rules: *We can't park here – it's a no-parking zone.*
**district** an area of a city or country: *My dad works downtown in the business district.*
**neighborhood** a small area of a town or city where people live: *We live in a quiet neighborhood.*
**suburb** an area where people live, that is outside the center of a city: *They moved to a quiet suburb of Boston.*

**2** a subject or part of a subject: *Hundreds of scientists are involved in this area of research.*
**3** the size of a flat surface or shape: *You can measure the area of the floor by multiplying the length by the width.*

**ˈarea ˌcode** *noun*
the three numbers before a telephone number that you use to call someone who lives outside your local area

**a·re·na** /əˈrinə/ *noun*
a large building where people go to watch sports games or other events, or listen to concerts: *Hundreds of people were waiting to enter the sports arena for the game.*

**aren't** /ˈɑrənt/ *verb*
**1** the short form of "are not": *They aren't coming to the party.*
**2** the short form of "am not," used in questions: *I'm next, aren't I?*

**ar·gue** /ˈɑrgyu/ *verb*
**1** if people argue, they shout or say angry things because they do not agree with each other: *My parents are always arguing with each other about money.* | *My sister and I argue about everything.*

**THESAURUS: argue**

**argue** (*or* **have an argument**): *My parents were arguing about money.* | *We had an argument about whose turn it was to do the dishes.*

**fight** (*or* **have a fight**) (*informal*) to argue with someone: *My brothers share a room, and they are always fighting.* | *I could hear the neighbors having a fight.*

**2** to explain why you think something is true: *She argued that it wasn't fair to punish her because she didn't know she was breaking the rules.*

**WORD FAMILY: argue**

**argue** *verb* | **argument** *noun* | **argumentative** *adjective*

**ar·gu·ment** /ˈɑrgyəmənt/ *noun*
**1** if people have an argument, they shout or say angry things because they do not agree with each other: *I had a big argument with my mom last night after I came home late.*
**2** a reason that you give to show why something is right or wrong: *We had to write an essay about the arguments for and against the death penalty.*

**ar·gu·men·ta·tive** /ˌɑrgyəˈmentətɪv/ *adjective*
someone who is argumentative often argues with people: *He is very argumentative in class and he always questions what the teacher says.*

**ar·id** /ˈærɪd/ *adjective*
getting very little rain, and therefore very dry: *the hot, arid regions of Central Africa*

**Ar·ies** /ˈeriz/ *noun*
**1** the first sign of the ZODIAC, represented by a RAM
**2** someone born between March 21 and April 19

**a·rise** /əˈraɪz/ *verb* (**arose** /əˈroʊz/, **arisen** /əˈrɪzən/, **arising**) (*formal*)
to happen: *Call me if any problems arise.*

**a·rith·me·tic** /əˈrɪθmətɪk/ *noun*
the activity of adding, SUBTRACTing, dividing, or multiplying numbers
[**ORIGIN:** 1200-1300 From the Greek word *arithmein*, which means "to count."]

**arm¹** /ɑrm/ *noun*
**1** the part of your body between your shoulder and your hand: *She held the baby in her arms.* | *The nurse stuck the needle into his arm.* → see picture on page **A2**
**2** the part of a chair or SOFA that you rest your arm on: *I put my drink on the arm of the chair.*
**3** **arms** = weapons such as guns and bombs: *He ordered the men to put down their arms.*

**arm²** *verb*
to provide someone with weapons: *The money is being used to arm terrorist groups.*

**ar·ma·dil·lo** /ˌɑrməˈdɪloʊ/ *noun*
a small animal with a pointed nose and a hard shell, that lives in hot dry parts of North and South America
[**ORIGIN:** 1500-1600 From the Spanish word *armado*, which means "person wearing armor." The ending *-illo* means "little."]

**arm·chair** /ˈɑrmtʃer/ *noun*
a chair with sides that you can rest your arms on

**armed** /ɑrmd/ *adjective*
having a weapon: *An armed policeman guarded the door.*

**armed ˈforces** *plural noun*
a country's army, navy, air force, etc.

**ar·mor** /ˈɑrmɚ/ *noun*
clothing that will protect your body if you are

attacked because it is made of a strong material, for example metal: *The police are wearing body armor because they are expecting trouble.*

**armored** /ˈɑrmɚd/ *adjective*
an armored vehicle is protected with very strong metal so that it is not easily damaged: *The soldiers travel in armored vehicles to protect them from attacks.*

**arm·pit** /ˈɑrmˌpɪt/ *noun*
the place under your arm where it joins your body

**ar·my** /ˈɑrmi/ *noun* (plural **armies**)
a military force that fights wars on land: *My father fought in Iraq when he was in the army.* | *After high school, she joined the army.*
[**ORIGIN:** 1300-1400 From the Latin word *armata*, which means "a group of armed people or military ships."]

**a·ro·ma** /əˈroʊmə/ *noun*
a strong pleasant smell: *I can smell the aroma of fresh coffee.*
—**aromatic** /ˌærəˈmætɪk/ *adjective* (*formal*) having a strong pleasant smell
→ see Thesaurus box at **smell**[1]

**a·rose** /əˈroʊz/ *verb*
the past tense of ARISE

**a·round** /əˈraʊnd/ *adverb, preposition*
**1** surrounding something or someone: *He put his arms around her.* | *There is a high fence all around the prison.*
**2** in or to many parts of a place: *They walked around the old part of the city.*
**3** in or near a particular place: *Is there a bank around here?*
**4** turning or moving in a circle: *The Earth goes around the Sun.*
**5** used when saying that a number, amount, or time is not exact: *We got back home around 10 o'clock.* **SYNONYM: about**
**6** in the opposite direction: *I turned around and walked back to the car.*
→ see Thesaurus box at **about**

**a·rouse** /əˈraʊz/ *verb* (*formal*)
to make someone have a particular feeling: *Her strange behavior aroused the suspicions of the police.*

**ar·range** /əˈreɪndʒ/ *verb*
**1** to put a group of things in a particular order or position: *She arranged the flowers in the vase.*
**2** to make plans for something to happen: *We arranged to meet outside the restaurant.* | *The doctor arranged for me to have some tests.*

**ar·range·ment** /əˈreɪndʒmənt/ *noun*
something that you do so that something will happen in the way you want: *She is busy making all the arrangements for the wedding and inviting the guests.*

**ar·rest** /əˈrest/ *verb*
if the police arrest someone, they take the person away because they think that he or she has done something illegal: *The police arrested the man and charged him with murder.*
—**arrest** *noun* a situation in which the police arrest someone: *After his arrest, the officers took him to the police station.*

**ar·riv·al** /əˈraɪvəl/ *noun*
**1** the act of arriving somewhere: *Soon after his arrival in New York, he got a job at a newspaper.* **ANTONYM: departure**
**2** a person or thing that has arrived recently: *The teacher welcomed the new arrivals to the class.*

**ar·rive** /əˈraɪv/ *verb*
to get to a place: *What time does the plane arrive in Chicago?* | *The letter arrived yesterday and I read it immediately.*
[**ORIGIN:** 1100-1200 From the Latin word *arripare*, which means "to come to shore."]

**THESAURUS: arrive**

**get to** to arrive somewhere: *What time will you get to Atlanta?*

**reach** to arrive somewhere, especially after a long or difficult trip: *When the climbers finally reached the top of the mountain, they were exhausted.*

**turn up** (*also* **show up**) to arrive somewhere, especially at the place where someone is waiting for you: *Lee turned up an hour late for class.*

**land** to arrive somewhere in an airplane or boat: *Marie's flight landed at 10:15.*

**ar·ro·gance** /ˈærəgəns/ *noun*
a rude and unfriendly attitude that shows that a person thinks that he or she is better or

A

more important than other people: *Her voice was full of arrogance and she seemed to think she was much better than the other students.*

**ar·ro·gant** /ˈærəgənt/ *adjective*
behaving in a rude and unfriendly way because you think that you are better or more important than other people: *He was an arrogant young man who never listened to other people's advice.*
—**arrogantly** *adverb* in an arrogant way
→ see Thesaurus box at **proud**

**ar·row** /ˈæroʊ/ *noun*
**1** a long thin piece of wood or metal, with a point at one end and feathers at the other end. You fire the arrow through the air using a BOW.
**2** a mark or shape like a simple arrow (→) that tells you where to go: *The arrow was pointing in this direction.*

**ar·son** /ˈɑrsən/ *noun*
the crime of deliberately making a building start burning
—**arsonist** *noun* someone who deliberately sets fire to buildings

**art** /ɑrt/ *noun*
**1** things such as paintings, drawings, or photographs that are made for people to look at and enjoy: *There are over 100 works of art in the exhibit at the museum.* | *Do you like modern art?*

**THESAURUS: art**

**Types of Art:**

**painting** a picture that you make using paint

**drawing** a picture that you make using a pen or pencil

**photograph** a picture that you take using a camera

**sculpture** an object that you make out of stone, wood, or clay

**2** the activity of making paintings, drawings, or other things for people to look at and enjoy: *My sister is good at drawing and she wants to study art in college.*
**3 the arts** = the group of subjects that includes painting, music, dance, and literature

**WORD FAMILY: art**
**art** *noun* | **artist** *noun* | **artistic** *adjective*

**ar·ter·y** /ˈɑrtəri/ *noun* (plural **arteries**)
one of the tubes that carries blood from your heart to the rest of your body: *The artery that carries blood to your lungs is called the pulmonary artery.*

**ar·thri·tis** /ɑrˈθraɪtɪs/ *noun*
a disease that causes pain and swelling in people's joints: *My grandmother has arthritis in her knees, and she finds it hard to walk.*

**ar·ti·choke** /ˈɑrtɪˌtʃoʊk/ *noun*
a round green vegetable covered with short thick pointed leaves → see picture on page **A12**

**ar·ti·cle** /ˈɑrtɪkəl/ *noun*
**1** a piece of writing in a newspaper or magazine: *I read an article on President Obama in "Time Magazine."*
**2** (*formal*) a thing, especially one of a group of things: *I picked up every article of clothing on my bedroom floor.*
**3** in grammar, the word "the" is called the DEFINITE ARTICLE, and "a" or "an" are called the INDEFINITE ARTICLE
→ see Thesaurus box at **thing**

**ar·ti·fact** /ˈɑrtɪˌfækt/ *noun*
an object such a tool or weapon that was made a long time ago and is historically important: *There are many interesting artifacts in the museum, including some stone age tools.*

**ar·ti·fi·cial** /ˌɑrtəˈfɪʃəl/ *adjective*
not real or natural, but made by people: *The candies contain artificial coloring.* | *She has an artificial leg.*
—**artificially** *adverb* in an artificial way
[**ORIGIN:** 1300-1400 From the Latin word *artificium*, which means "the work of a skilled craftsman."]

**ˌartificial inˈtelligence** *noun*
the use of computer technology to make computers think and make decisions like humans

**art·ist** /ˈɑrtɪst/ *noun*
someone who produces art: *Picasso was an amazing painter and one of the world's greatest artists.*

**ar·tis·tic** /ɑrˈtɪstɪk/ *adjective*
**1** good at art: *My sister's very artistic – she is especially good at drawing.*
**2** relating to art: *We have the same artistic tastes and we both like paintings by Van Gogh.*

**as** /əz; *strong* æz/ *adverb, preposition, conjunction*
**1 as ... as** = used to compare people or things: *I'm not as old as you.* | *Our team is just as good as theirs.*
**2** used to say what someone's job is: *She works as a teacher.*
**3** used to say what something is used for: *We can use this box as a table.*
**4** while something is happening: *The phone rang just as I was leaving.*
**5 as if/as though** = used when you are saying how someone or something seems: *Her eyes were red and she looked as if she had been crying.*
**6** (*formal*) because: *He decided not to go out, as it was already late.* **SYNONYM: since**

**ASAP** (*also* **a.s.a.p.**) *adverb* (*informal*)
ASAP is short for "as soon as possible": *Finish your classwork ASAP.*

**as·cend** /əˈsend/ *verb* (*formal*)
to go up higher: *The plane ascended into the clouds.* **SYNONYM: rise**; **ANTONYM: descend**
—**ascent** *noun* the act of going up higher: *The ascent of the mountain took six hours.*

**ash** /æʃ/ *noun*
the gray powder that is left after something has burned: *The hillside was covered with ash after the fire.*

**a·shamed** /əˈʃeɪmd/ *adjective*
if you are ashamed, you feel guilty about something you have done: *I felt ashamed that I had been so mean to my friends.* | *Ben had lied to her, and he was ashamed of himself.*

**a·shore** /əˈʃɔr/ *adverb*
onto the land beside the ocean or a lake: *The ship stopped in Miami, and we all went ashore.*

**ash·tray** /ˈæʃtreɪ/ *noun*
a small dish that people use for cigarette ASHes when they are smoking

**A·sia** /ˈeɪʒə/ *noun*
one of the seven CONTINENTs, with countries such as China, Russia, India, Pakistan, and Saudi Arabia in it

**A·sian** /ˈeɪʒən/ *adjective*
from Asia, especially East Asia: *There are several Asian children in my class. They come from China and Japan.*
—**Asian** *noun* someone from Asia

**a·side** /əˈsaɪd/ *adverb*
to one side: *Jack stepped aside so I could pass.* | *Remove the meat from the pan and set it aside.*

**ask** /æsk/ *verb*
**1** to say something that is a question, for example in order to get information or help: *"What's your name?" she asked.* | *Can I ask a question?* | *Why don't you ask your teacher for help?* | *If you need anything, just ask.*

**THESAURUS: ask**

**order** to ask for food or drinks in a restaurant: *Dave ordered a hamburger.*

**demand** to ask for something in a firm or angry way: *My dad demanded to see my report card.*

**request** to ask for something officially or in a polite way: *I called them to request information about dancing classes.*

**beg** to ask for something in a way that shows you want or need it very much: *"Please can I have a puppy?" she begged.*

**question** to ask someone questions about something, especially about a crime: *Police are questioning two men about the robbery.*

**inquire** to ask someone for information: *"What are you doing here?" he inquired.* | *I inquired about the price of tickets.*

**2** to invite someone to go somewhere: *If I ask Tracy to the party, do you think she'll go with me?*

**a·sleep** /əˈsliːp/ *adjective*
sleeping: *The baby is asleep, so don't make a lot of noise.* | *My eyes started to close and I started to fall asleep.* **ANTONYM: awake**

**as·par·a·gus** /əˈspærəgəs/ *noun*
a long thin green vegetable with a pointed top → see picture on page **A12**

**as·pect** [Ac] /ˈæspekt/ *noun* (*formal*)
one of the parts of something such as a situation, problem, or activity: *His illness*

*affects every aspect of his life.*

**as·phalt** /ˈæsˌfɔlt/ *noun*
a hard black substance used to cover roads

**as·pi·rin** /ˈæsprɪn/ *noun* (plural **aspirins** *or* **aspirin**)
a medicine that makes you feel less pain: *If you have a headache, take an aspirin.*

**ass** /æs/ *noun*
a type of DONKEY

**as·sas·sin** /əˈsæsən/ *noun*
someone who kills an important person

**as·sas·si·nate** /əˈsæsəˌneɪt/ *verb*
to kill an important person: *President Lincoln was assassinated in 1865.*
—**assassination** /əˌsæsəˈneɪʃən/ *noun* the act of killing an important person: *the assassination of Martin Luther King, Jr.*

**as·sault** /əˈsɔlt/ *verb*
to attack and hurt someone: *He kicked and hit the policeman and he was later charged with assaulting a police officer.* **SYNONYM: attack**
—**assault** *noun* an act of assaulting someone: *She had to go to the hospital after she was injured in an assault.*
→ see Thesaurus box at **crime**

**assemble**

**as·sem·ble** Ac /əˈsembəl/ *verb*
**1** to put the different parts of something together: *The picture shows you how to assemble the dresser.* **SYNONYM: put together**
**2** if people assemble, they come together in a group: *During a fire drill, all the students assemble in the field.*

**as·sem·bly** Ac /əˈsembli/ *noun* (plural **assemblies**)
**1** a meeting of a large group of people, sometimes to make laws: *He is a member of the State Assembly.*
**2** the process of putting something together: *The instructions make assembly of the table easy.*

**as·ser·tive** /əˈsɚtɪv/ *adjective*
if you are assertive, you act in a confident way and say what you think: *You must be more assertive, and not be afraid to give your opinion.*
—**assertively** *adverb* in an assertive way
—**assertiveness** *noun* the quality of being assertive

**as·sess** Ac /əˈses/ *verb*
to judge how good or bad a person or situation is: *The teacher assesses each student's work and gives the student a grade.*
—**assessment** *noun* the judgment that you make about a person or situation: *What's your assessment of the situation?*

**as·set** /ˈæset/ *noun*
someone or something that helps you to be successful: *He's a great player, and is definitely an asset to the team.*

**as·sign** Ac /əˈsaɪn/ *verb*
to give someone a job to do: *The soldiers were assigned to guard the bank.* | *The teacher assigned us 25 math problems for homework.*

**as·sign·ment** Ac /əˈsaɪnmənt/ *noun*
a piece of work that someone has told you to do: *For your homework assignment, I want you to write an essay.*

**as·sist** Ac /əˈsɪst/ *verb* (*formal*)
to help someone do something: *I will need someone to assist me with this experiment.* **SYNONYM: help**

**as·sist·ance** Ac /əˈsɪstəns/ *noun* (*formal*)
help: *Ask one of your parents for assistance if you're having trouble with the homework.*

**as·sist·ant** Ac /əˈsɪstənt/ *noun*
someone whose job is to help a more important person with his or her work: *The magician's assistant brings him the things he needs to do the tricks.*

**as·so·ci·ate¹** /əˈsoʊʃiˌeɪt/ *verb*
**1** to think of two things as connected with each other: *Many health problems are associated with eating foods full of fat and sugar.*
**2** to spend time with someone such as a friend or someone you work with: *When he went to New York, he began associating with artists and writers.*
[ORIGIN: 1300-1400 From the Latin word *associare*, which means "to join with someone or something."]

**as·so·ci·ate²** /əˈsoʊʃiɪt/ *noun*
someone that you work with: *The research was done by Professor Gray and his associates.* | *a business associate*

**asˌsociate deˈgree** *noun*
a DEGREE that you can get after two years of study at a COMMUNITY COLLEGE in the U.S.

**as·so·ci·a·tion** /əˌsoʊsiˈeɪʃən/ *noun*
an organization of people who do the same type of work or activity: *The Parent-Teacher Association helps to raise money for the school.*

**as·sort·ed** /əˈsɔrtɪd/ *adjective*
of different types: *I bought a bag of assorted nuts, with peanuts and other types of nuts in it.*

**as·sume** [Ac] /əˈsum/ *verb*
to think that something is probably true: *I assumed that they were sisters because they looked so much alike.*
—**assumption** /əˈsʌmpʃən/ *noun* something that you think is probably true: *He made the assumption that Mike and Lisa were married to each other, but actually they were brother and sister.*

**as·sure** [Ac] /əˈʃʊr/ *verb*
to tell someone something in order to stop him or her from worrying: *The doctor assured me that I was fine and that I didn't need to worry.*
—**assurance** *noun* something that you tell someone in order to stop him or her from worrying

**as·ter·isk** /ˈæstərɪsk/ *noun*
a mark like a star (*), used in writing. It usually shows that there is more information at the bottom of the page or in another place.

**as·te·roid** /ˈæstəˌrɔɪd/ *noun*
a rocky object like a small PLANET that moves around the Sun: *The biggest asteroids are almost 600 miles in diameter and the smallest are less than half a mile across.*
[ORIGIN: 1800-1900 From the Greek word *asteroeides*, which means "like a star."]

**asth·ma** /ˈæzmə/ *noun*
a medical problem that sometimes makes it difficult for someone to breathe: *My brother has asthma and last week he had to miss his gym class because his breathing was so bad.*
—**asthmatic** /æzˈmætɪk/ *adjective* having asthma or relating to asthma
[ORIGIN: 1300-1400 From the Greek word *asthma*, which means "breathing hard."]

**as·ton·ish** /əˈstɑnɪʃ/ *verb*
to surprise someone very much: *The team astonished everyone by winning the game 56-0.*
—**astonished** *adjective* very surprised: *They were astonished by the news.*
—**astonishing** *adjective* very surprising: *He He got an A on the test, which was an astonishing achievement.*
[ORIGIN: 1500-1600 From the Latin word *tonare*, which means "to thunder." If something astonishes you, you are as surprised as if you had been struck by lightning during a thunderstorm.]

**as·ton·ish·ment** /əˈstɑnɪʃmənt/ *noun*
great surprise: *Ken looked at her in astonishment when she said that she was getting married.*

**as·trol·o·gy** /əˈstrɑlədʒi/ *noun*
the study of how the position of the stars and PLANETs may affect people's lives
—**astrologer** *noun* someone who tells people how astrology might affect their lives

**as·tro·naut** /ˈæstrəˌnɔt/ *noun*
someone who travels in space: *There were three astronauts living on the space station.*

**as·tron·o·my** /əˈstrɑnəmi/ *noun*
the science that studies stars and PLANETs and other things in space: *An important discovery in astronomy was that the Earth moves around the Sun, not the other way around.*
—**astronomer** *noun* a scientist who studies astronomy
[ORIGIN: 1200-1300 From the Greek words *astron* and *-nomia*, which mean "star" and "arranging."]

A

A

**as·tute** /əˈstut/ *adjective (formal)*
smart and able to understand things quickly: *He is a very astute businessman and he is good at finding ways to make money.*
—**astutely** *adverb* in an astute way

**at** /ət; *strong* æt/ *preposition*
**1** in a particular place: *Meet me at my house.* | *John's at school right now.* | *Write your name at the top of the page.*
**2** used for saying the time when something happens: *The movie starts at 8:00.* | *At night, the streets are empty.*
**3** toward someone or something: *All the children were looking at the teacher.* | *Jake smiled at me.*
**4** used when talking about someone's age: *I started school at age five.*
**5** **good/bad, etc. at something** = able to do something well or badly: *Debbie is good at math – she always gets good grades.*
**6** **at lunch/dinner** = not working because you are eating LUNCH or dinner: *I didn't answer the phone because I was at lunch when you called.*

**ate** /eɪt/ *verb*
the past tense of EAT

**a·the·ist** /ˈeɪθiɪst/ *noun*
someone who does not believe that there is a god
—**atheism** *noun* the belief that there is no god

**ath·lete** /ˈæθlit/ *noun*
someone who is good at sports and often plays sports: *The athletes are getting ready for the start of the race.*
[**ORIGIN:** 1400-1500 From the Greek word *athletes*, which means "someone who takes part in a contest."]

**ath·let·ic** /æθˈletɪk/ *adjective*
**1** relating to sports: *Basketball is part of the school's athletic program.*
**2** an athletic person has a strong body and is good at playing sports: *Bobby was very athletic and played football, basketball, and baseball.*

**ath·let·ics** /æθˈletɪks/ *noun*
sports and other activities you do to keep your body healthy: *Most of the girls I know are involved in athletics, usually either soccer or softball.*

**At·lan·tic** /ətˈlæntɪk/ *noun*
**the Atlantic** = the ocean that is between America and Europe: *The ship sailed across the Atlantic from England to America.*

**at·las** /ˈætləs/ *noun*
a book with maps in it: *a world atlas*
[**ORIGIN:** From Atlas, a giant in an ancient Greek story who had to hold up the sky, or from the mythical King Atlas, who is said to have made the first globe. The name Atlas was used in the title of a 16th-century book of maps.]

**ATM** *noun*
(**Automated Teller Machine**) a machine, usually in a wall, that you put your bank card in to get money from your bank

**at·mos·phere** /ˈætməsˌfɪr/ *noun*
**1** the feeling that a place or situation gives you: *The hotel has a friendly atmosphere.* | *Before the game, there was an atmosphere of excitement.*
**2** the air around the Earth or other PLANETs: *Most of the Earth's atmosphere is nitrogen and oxygen.*
—**atmospheric** /ˌætməsˈferɪk/ *adjective* relating to the atmosphere
[**ORIGIN:** 1600-1700 From the Greek words *atmos* and *sphaira*, which mean "drops of liquid in the air" and "ball."]

**at·om** /ˈætəm/ *noun*
the smallest possible amount of an ELEMENT (=chemical substance) that can exist alone and still have all the qualities of that element: *Water is made of two atoms of hydrogen and one atom of oxygen.*
[**ORIGIN:** 1500-1600 From the Greek word *atomos*, which means "not able to be cut or divided."]

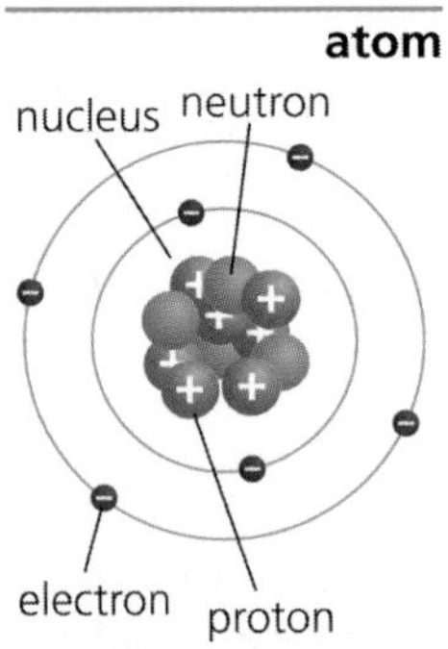


**a·tom·ic** /əˈtɑmɪk/ *adjective*
**1** relating to atoms: *The two substances have a very different atomic structure.*

**2** using the power that comes from dividing atoms: *Atomic bombs are very powerful and can kill large numbers of people.*

**aˌtomic ˈenergy** (*also* **atomic power**) *noun*
the power that comes from dividing atoms, and is used to make electricity

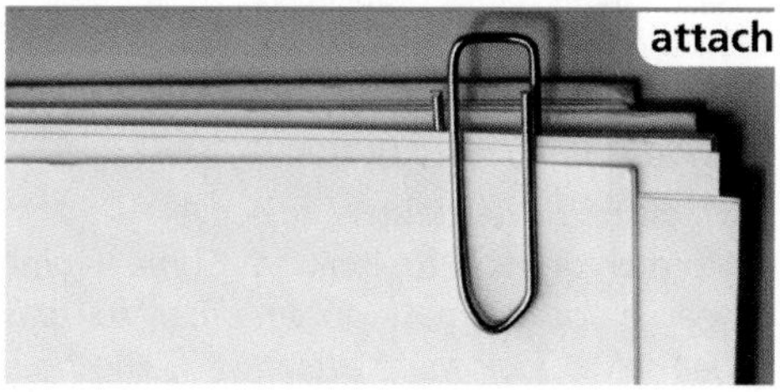


**at·tach** Ac /əˈtætʃ/ *verb*
**1** to fasten one thing to another: *Please attach a photograph to your application form.*
**2** to put a computer FILE with an email in order to send them together: *I've attached a report of the meeting in an email.*
**3 be attached to someone/something** = to like or love a person, animal, home, or other thing that you have known or had for a long time: *The little girl is very attached to her teddy bear.*
→ see Thesaurus box at **fasten**

**WORD FAMILY: attach**
**attach** *verb* | **attachment** *noun* | **detach** *verb*

**at·tach·ment** Ac /əˈtætʃmənt/ *noun*
**1** a computer FILE that you put with an email in order to send them together: *I sent the pictures as an attachment.*
**2** a strong feeling that you like or love someone or something: *She felt a strong attachment to her youngest sister and was very protective of her.*

**at·tack¹** /əˈtæk/ *noun*
**1** an attempt to hurt another person: *There were two attacks on policemen in the neighborhood.*
**2** an attempt to defeat enemy soldiers or damage a place in a war: *The planes started their attack at dawn and began dropping bombs on the town.*
**3** a time when you suddenly get sick: *The smoke made it hard for her to breathe and caused an asthma attack.*
—**attacker** *noun* someone who attacks another person

**attack²** *verb*
**1** to try to hurt someone: *The man attacked him with a knife.*
**2** if a group such as an army attacks a place, it fights the people in it and damages buildings: *The army attacked the city from the south.*
**3** to say bad things about someone or something: *All the newspapers attacked the president.* **SYNONYM: criticize**

**at·tain** Ac /əˈteɪn/ *verb* (*formal*)
to achieve something: *He finally attained his dream of becoming the world's best tennis player.*
—**attainment** *noun* something you achieve

**at·tempt¹** /əˈtempt/ *verb*
to try to do something: *A prisoner had attempted to escape by climbing the wall.*
→ see Thesaurus box at **try¹**

**attempt²** *noun*
the act of trying to do something: *Several people had made an attempt to climb the mountain and failed. | My first attempt at skiing did not go very well.*

**at·tend** /əˈtend/ *verb*
**1** to be at a meeting, class, or special event: *Over a hundred people attended the ceremony.*
**2 attend school/college** = to be a student at a school or college: *My daughter plans to attend college next fall.*
**3** (*formal*) to deal with someone or something: *The doctor will attend to you in a few minutes.*

**at·tend·ance** /əˈtendəns/ *noun*
the activity of going to school, a class, or a meeting: *She has a very good attendance record and has never missed a class.*

**at·tend·ant** /əˈtendənt/ *noun*
someone whose job is to help customers, passengers, or people who are in a place: *The flight attendants were serving drinks to the passengers on the plane.*

**at·ten·tion** /əˈtenʃən/ *noun*
**1** the activity of listening or looking carefully: *Now, class, I want you all to pay attention* (=listen or look carefully) *to the story. | I waved my arm to get the kids' attention so that they would look at me.*

A

**2** care or treatment that you give to someone or something: *Some of the people injured in the accident needed medical attention from a doctor.*

**at·ten·tive** /əˈtentɪv/ *adjective*
an attentive person listens and looks carefully: *Students who are attentive have higher test scores.*
—**attentively** *adverb* in an attentive way: *The children were listening attentively to the teacher.*

**at·tic** /ˈætɪk/ *noun*
a space or room under the roof of a house: *There are a lot of old toys up in the attic.*

**at·ti·tude** Ac /ˈætəˌtud/ *noun*
the way you think or feel about someone or something: *Later, my attitude toward him changed, and I began to like him more.* | *In school, he has a good attitude and works very hard.*

**at·tor·ney** /əˈtəni/ *noun* (plural **attorneys**)
someone whose job is to give people advice about the law, or to represent someone in a court of law: *His attorney advised him not to sign the contract.* **SYNONYM: lawyer**

**at·tract** /əˈtrækt/ *verb*
**1** to make someone feel interested in something: *The TV networks are trying to attract more viewers to the show.* | *I didn't want to attract attention, so I stayed very quiet.*
**2** if a place or thing attracts people or animals, they go to it because it is interesting or good: *The zoo attracts many visitors every year.*
**3 be attracted to someone** = to feel that you like someone and want to have a relationship with that person: *I was attracted to him because he was good-looking and very intelligent.*
**4** if something attracts an object, it pulls the object toward itself: *The needle is attracted by the magnet and moves toward it.* **ANTONYM: repel**

**WORD FAMILY: attract**
**attract** *verb* | **attraction** *noun* | **attractive** *adjective* | **unattractive** *adjective*

**at·trac·tion** /əˈtrækʃən/ *noun*
**1** the feeling of liking someone or something very much: *She felt a strong attraction to the handsome young man who had helped her.*
**2** something that is interesting or fun to see or do: *The Statue of Liberty is one of New York's main tourist attractions.*
**3** a quality or feature that makes you like something: *For me, the main attraction of sailing is the feeling of freedom.*

**at·trac·tive** /əˈtræktɪv/ *adjective*
**1** pretty or nice to look at: *Some women wear a lot of make-up in order to make themselves look more attractive.* | *The house is in an attractive location, next to the ocean.*
**ANTONYM: unattractive**
**2** if something is attractive, you want to have it or do it: *It's a very attractive offer, and I think I will probably accept it.* **ANTONYM: unattractive**
→ see Thesaurus box at **beautiful**

**a·typ·i·cal** /eɪˈtɪpɪkəl/ *adjective*
not typical or usual: *He was an atypical teenager who loved listening to classical music.* **SYNONYM: unusual**; **ANTONYM: typical**

**auc·tion** /ˈɔkʃən/ *noun*
an event at which things are sold to the person who offers the most money: *The painting was sold at an auction for over $15,000.*
—**auction** *verb* to sell something at an auction
—**auctioneer** /ˌɔkʃəˈnɪr/ *noun* a person whose job is to sell things at auctions

**au·di·ble** /ˈɔdəbəl/ *adjective*
loud enough to be heard: *The music is too loud if it is audible to other people when you use earphones.* **ANTONYM: inaudible**

**au·di·ence** /ˈɔdiəns/ *noun*
the people who are watching or listening to a play, movie, concert, or speech: *The audience stood up and clapped after she sang.* | *Four million people watch the show, so it reaches a large audience.*
[**ORIGIN:** 1300-1400 From the Latin word *audire*, which means "to listen."]

**au·di·o** /ˈɔdioʊ/ *adjective*
relating to recording and playing sound: *The audio equipment on the film projector wasn't working and we couldn't hear anything.*

**au·di·o·vis·u·al** /ˌɔdioʊˈvɪʒuəl/ *adjective*
showing and playing recorded pictures and sound: *The teacher uses audiovisual aids such as pictures and tape recordings during the class.*

**au·dit** /ˈɔdɪt/ *verb*
to officially examine a company's financial records to check that they are correct: *The company's accounts are audited at the end of the financial year.*
—**audit** *noun* an official examination of a company's financial records to check that they are correct
—**auditor** *noun* someone who audits companies

**au·di·tion** /ɔˈdɪʃən/ *noun*
a short performance that you do, so that someone can decide if you are good enough to be in a play, movie, or show: *She had an audition for a part in a movie.*
—**audition** *verb* to do a short performance, so that someone can decide if you are good enough to be in a play, movie, or show: *He is auditioning for a part in the school play.*

**au·di·to·ri·um** /ˌɔdɪˈtɔriəm/ *noun*
a large building or room used for concerts or public meetings: *The auditorium is full of people and the concert is about to begin.*

**Au·gust** /ˈɔgəst/ *noun* (*written abbreviation*: **Aug.**)
the eighth month of the year, between July and September: *My birthday is on August 19th.* | *They sold their house in August.* | *It was very hot here last August.* | *Next August, we're going to Mexico.*
[**ORIGIN:** Probably 1000-1100 From Augustus Caesar (63 B.C.-14 A.D.), the first Roman emperor.]

**aunt** /ænt/ *noun*
the sister of your mother or father, or the wife of your uncle: *Aunt Grace is my mom's younger sister.*
[**ORIGIN:** 1200-1300 From the Latin word *amita*, which means "your father's sister."]

**Aus·tra·lian** /ɔˈstreɪlyən/ *noun*
someone from Australia
—**Australian** *adjective* relating to Australia: *Canberra is the Australian capital city.*

**Aus·tri·an** /ˈɔstriən/ *noun*
someone from Austria
—**Austrian** *adjective* relating to Austria: *an Austrian city*

**au·then·tic** /ɔˈθentɪk/ *adjective*
if something is authentic, it really is what people say it is: *The restaurant is owned by Mexicans and serves authentic Mexican food.*
**SYNONYM: genuine**
—**authenticity** /ˌɔθənˈtɪsəti/ *noun* the quality of being authentic

**au·thor** Ac /ˈɔθɚ/ *noun*
someone who writes books: *He is the author of three books on American history.*

**au·thor·i·tar·i·an** /ɔrˌθɔrəˈteriən/ *adjective*
forcing people to obey strict rules: *The government is very authoritarian and they control everything that people do.*

**au·thor·i·ta·tive** Ac /əˈθɔrəˌteɪtɪv/ *adjective*
an authoritative piece of writing is respected because the person who wrote it knows a lot about the subject: *He wrote an authoritative book on the American legal system, which is used by many university students.*

**au·thor·i·ty** Ac /əˈθɔrəti/ *noun*
**1** the power to make official decisions and tell people what to do: *Congress has the authority to raise taxes.* | *I need to speak to someone in a position of authority, for example the manager.*
**2 the authorities** = an organization or government department that controls something: *If you know anything about the accident, please report it to the authorities.*
**3** someone who knows a lot about a subject: *Dr. Ballard is an authority on politics in Russia.*

**WORD FAMILY: authority**
**authority** *noun* | **authoritarian** *adjective* | **authorize** *verb* | **authorization** *noun* | **authoritative** *adjective*

**au·thor·ize** /ˈɔθəˌraɪz/ *verb*
to give official permission for something: *The money for the program has been authorized by Congress.*
—**authorization** /ˌɔθərəˈzeɪʃən/ *noun* official permission to do something: *You need special authorization to park here.*

A

**au·tism** /ˈɔˌtɪzəm/ *noun*
a medical condition in the brain that makes it difficult for someone to communicate and have relationships with other people
—**autistic** /ɔˈtɪstɪk/ *adjective* having autism

**au·to** /ˈɔtoʊ/ *adjective*
relating to cars: *Ford is one of the biggest auto companies in the world.*

**au·to·bi·og·ra·phy** /ˌɔtəbaɪˈɑgrəfi/ *noun* (plural **autobiographies**)
a book that someone writes about his or her own life: *She described her unhappy childhood in her autobiography.*
—**autobiographical** /ˌɔtəbaɪəˈgræfɪkəl/ *adjective* relating to autobiographies

**au·to·graph** /ˈɔtəˌgræf/ *noun*
a famous person's name, written by him or her: *A fan came up and asked for the singer's autograph.*
—**autograph** *verb* to write your autograph on something
[**ORIGIN:** 1600-1700 From the Greek words *autos* and *graphein*, which mean "self" and "to write."]

**au·to·mat·ed** Ac /ˈɔtəˌmeɪtɪd/ *adjective*
using machines to do a job, rather than people: *The factory is almost completely automated, and there are not many people working there now.*
—**automation** /ˌɔtəˈmeɪʃən/ *noun* the use of machines to do a job, rather than people

**au·to·mat·ic** Ac /ˌɔtəˈmætɪk/ *adjective*
**1** an automatic machine works by itself, without people operating it: *an automatic washing machine*
**2** done without thinking: *She jumped back when she saw the snake – it was an automatic reaction.*
[**ORIGIN:** 1700-1800 From the Greek word *automatos*, which means "acting by itself."]

**au·to·mat·i·cally** /ˌɔtəˈmætɪkli/ *adverb*
**1** if a machine does something automatically, it does it without being operated by someone: *The doors open automatically when you go into the building.*
**2** if you do something automatically, you do it without thinking: *I automatically assumed that the man and the woman were married.*

**au·to·mo·bile** /ˌɔtəməˈbil/ *noun* (*formal*)
a car
[**ORIGIN:** 1800-1900 From the Greek word *autos*, which means "self," and the French word *mobile*, which means "moving."]

**au·top·sy** /ˈɔˌtɑpsi/ *noun* (plural **autopsies**)
an official examination of a dead body in order to find out how the person died: *An autopsy showed that she had died of a heart attack.*

**au·tumn** /ˈɔtəm/ *noun* (*formal*)
the season before winter, when the leaves fall off the trees: *The leaves turn red in the autumn.* **SYNONYM: fall**

**a·vail·a·ble** Ac /əˈveɪləbəl/ *adjective*
if something is available, you can have it, buy it, or use it: *There is a lot of information available on the Internet.* | *I called the hotel and asked if they had any rooms available.*
—**availability** /əˌveɪləˈbɪləti/ *noun* the state of being available: *You can check the availability of the store's products on the website.*

**av·a·lanche** /ˈævəˌlæntʃ/ *noun*
a large amount of snow or rocks that falls down a mountain

**av·e·nue** /ˈævənu/ *noun* (*written abbreviation*: **Ave.**)
a wide street in a town or city: *He lives on Melrose Avenue.*
→ see Thesaurus box at **road**

**av·erage¹** /ˈævrɪdʒ/ *adjective*
**1** calculated by adding a group of numbers together, then dividing the total by the number of things in the group: *Three of the students are 12 years old and three are 14, so the average age is 13.*
**2** typical or ordinary: *The average person doesn't understand how computers work.*
→ see Thesaurus box at **normal**
[**ORIGIN:** 1700-1800 From the French word *avarie*, which means "damage to a ship or its cargo." "Average" used to mean the fair sharing out of the costs that had to be paid because of the damage.]

**average²** *noun*
**1** the amount that you get by adding a group of numbers together, then dividing the total by the number of things in the group: *The average of 2, 9, and 10 is 7.*
**2 on average** = usually: *On average, women live longer than men.*
**3 above/below average** = higher or lower

than the usual number or level: *The temperature is below average for this time of year – usually it's 20 degrees, but it's now only 8 degrees.*
—**average** *verb* to be or have a particular number as an average: *He is averaging 17 points a game.*

**a·vi·a·tion** /ˌeɪviˈeɪʃən/ *noun*
the activity of flying aircraft or making aircraft: *The plane crash was one of the worst accidents in the history of aviation.*
[**ORIGIN:** 1800-1900 From the Latin word *avis*, which means "bird."]

**av·id** /ˈævɪd/ *adjective*
showing a lot of interest in something, and eagerness to do it: *She is an avid reader, and she loves reading crime stories.*

**av·o·ca·do** /ˌævəˈkɑdoʊ/ *noun* (plural **avocados**)
a fruit with a green or dark purple skin and a large seed in the middle

**a·void** /əˈvɔɪd/ *verb*
**1** to prevent something from happening: *I wanted to avoid having an argument.*
**2** to try not do something: *He's very lazy and he always tries to avoid doing any work.*
**3** to stay away from someone or something: *Paul's been avoiding me all day – I think he's mad at me.*
**4** to prevent yourself from hitting someone or something: *The driver braked suddenly to avoid a woman who was crossing the road.*
—**avoidable** *adjective* if something is avoidable, you can avoid it: *an avoidable mistake*
—**avoidance** *noun* the act of avoiding something

**a·wait** /əˈweɪt/ *verb* (*formal*)
**1** to wait for something: *The soldiers made a camp and awaited their orders.*
**2** if a situation awaits you, it is going to happen to you: *A surprise awaited him when he arrived home.*

**a·wake**[1] /əˈweɪk/ *verb* (**awoke** /əˈwoʊk/, **awoken** /əˈwoʊkən/) (*formal*)
to wake up: *She awoke as usual at 6 a.m.*

**awake**[2] *adjective*
not asleep: *I have trouble staying awake in class if I go to bed too late the night before.*

**a·ward**[1] /əˈwɔrd/ *noun*
a prize given to someone or something: *The movie has won many awards.* **SYNONYM: prize**

**award**[2] *verb*
to give someone an award: *He was awarded the Nobel Prize for physics, for his discovery of X-rays.*

**a·ware** [Ac] /əˈwer/ *adjective*
if you are aware of a fact or situation, you know about it: *Most people are aware of the dangers of smoking.* | *He was aware (that) someone was following him, and he started to walk faster.* **ANTONYM: unaware**
—**awareness** *noun* knowledge that something exists or that something is happening: *Doctors want to raise public awareness about the disease through advertisements and TV programs.*

**a·way** /əˈweɪ/ *adverb*
**1** further from a person, place, or thing: *Jack was annoying me so I told him to go away.* | *He moved away from the window so that nobody would see him.*
**2** used when saying how far it is to a place, person, or thing: *The nearest city is five miles away.* | *I was standing about ten feet away from him.*
**3** used when saying how much time will pass before something happens: *My birthday is only three days away.*
**4** not at home, at work, or in school: *I'm sorry, Ms. Parker is away this week.*
**5** into the place where you keep something: *The teacher asked the students to put their books away.*

**awe** /ɔ/ *noun*
a feeling of great respect or admiration: *We looked at him with awe when he said that he had climbed the mountain on his own.*

**awe·some** /ˈɔsəm/ *adjective*
**1** (*informal*) very good: *The party was awesome! We had so much fun.*
**2** very impressive, big, or difficult, so that you feel great respect or fear: *The huge volcano was an awesome sight.*

**aw·ful** /ˈɔfəl/ *adjective*
**1** very bad: *It was an awful movie – I didn't like it at all.* | *My head hurts and I feel awful.* |

*The weather was awful and we had to stay inside the whole week.*

**2 an awful lot** (*informal*) = very much or a very great amount: *The shoes cost an awful lot of money, and I didn't have enough money to buy them.*

→ see Thesaurus box at **bad**

**aw·fully** /ˈɔfli/ *adverb* (*informal*)
very: *She looked awfully tired.*

**a·while** /əˈwaɪl/ *adverb*
for a short time: *I waited awhile before ringing the doorbell again.*

**awk·ward** /ˈɔkwɚd/ *adjective*

**1** embarrassing or difficult: *It's an awkward situation because I can't tell him that I don't want him to be here.*

**2** difficult to use or hold: *The room is an awkward shape and it is difficult to fit more than one table in it.*

**3** not able to relax and talk to people easily: *I felt shy and awkward because I didn't know anyone at the party.*

**4** moving in a way that does not seem relaxed or comfortable: *The old man moved slowly with awkward steps, using a stick to keep from falling over.*

—**awkwardly** *adverb* in an awkward way: *"I'm sorry – I forgot your name," she said awkwardly.*

—**awkwardness** *noun* an awkward quality: *After some awkwardness when they first met, the two girls soon started playing happily together.*

[**ORIGIN:** 1500-1600 From the old English word *awk*, which means "turned the wrong way," and the ending "-ward," which means "in the direction of something."]

**awn·ing** /ˈɔnɪŋ/ *noun*
a sheet of material that sticks out like a small roof over a door or window, to keep the sun or the rain off it

**a·woke** /əˈwoʊk/ *verb*
the past tense of AWAKE

**ax** (*also* **axe**) /æks/ *noun*
a tool for cutting wood. An ax has a metal blade on a long handle: *He was chopping up logs with an ax.*

**ax·is** /ˈæksɪs/ *noun* (plural **axes** /ˈæksiz/)

**1** a line at the side or bottom of a GRAPH, where you put a series of numbers. The line that goes from top to bottom is the vertical or "y" axis, and the line that goes across from side to side is the horizontal or "x" axis.

**2** an imaginary line through the middle of something that is turning, for example the Earth

**ax·le** /ˈæksəl/ *noun*
a long bar that connects two wheels on a vehicle

# Bb

**B** /bi/ *noun*
**1** a GRADE that you get on a test or in a class for doing work that is good, but not excellent: *I got a B on the quiz, but I know I can get an A next time.*
**2** the seventh note in the musical SCALE of C, or the musical KEY based on this note

**B.A.** *noun*
(**Bachelor of Arts**) a university degree in a subject such as history, a language, or art: *He has a B.A. in English Literature.* **SYNONYM: bachelor's degree**

**ba·boon** /bæˈbun/ *noun*
a large monkey that lives in Africa and south Asia
[**ORIGIN:** 1400-1500 From the French word *babouin*, from *baboue*, which means "ugly face."]

**ba·by** /ˈbeɪbi/ *noun* (plural **babies**)
a very young child: *The baby is crying.* | *She had a baby last year.* | *a baby girl*
→ see Thesaurus box at **child**

**ˈbaby ˌcarriage** (*also* **ˈbaby ˌbuggy**) *noun*
a thing with wheels that a baby lies in to be pushed from one place to another

**ba·by·sit** /ˈbeɪbiˌsɪt/ *verb*
(**babysat** /ˈbeɪbiˌsæt/, **babysitting**) to take care of a child while his or her parents are not at home: *Jane babysits when the children's parents go out in the evening.*
—**babysitting** *noun* the activity of taking care of a child while his or her parents are not at home: *Babysitting is a good way for teenagers to earn money.*

**ba·by·sit·ter** /ˈbeɪbiˌsɪtɚ/ *noun*
someone who is paid to babysit a child: *The children have a babysitter when their mom and dad go out.*

**bach·e·lor** /ˈbætʃəlɚ/ *noun*
a man who has never been married: *He was 42, and still a bachelor.*

**ˈbachelor's deˌgree** *noun*
a degree you get from a college or university after completing all your classes: *I got my bachelor's degree from Hunter College.*

**back¹** /bæk/ *noun*
**1** the part of your body between your neck and your waist, on the opposite side from your chest and stomach: *His back was hurting from lifting boxes all morning.* | *I lay on my back, looking up at the clouds.*
**2** the part of something that is farthest from the front: *The answers to the questions are in the back of the book.* **ANTONYM: front**
**3** **behind someone's back** = if you do something bad or unkind behind someone's back, you do it without him or her knowing: *You shouldn't say mean things about her behind her back.*
**4** **in the back of your mind** = a thought or feeling in the back of your mind is one that affects you, even though you are not thinking about it all the time: *In the back of his mind, he was always afraid that something bad was going to happen.*

**back²** *adverb*
**1** in the place where someone or something was before: *I'll be back home in an hour.* | *Put the milk back in the refrigerator when you're done with it.*
**2** into the condition that someone or something was in before: *I woke up at 5 a.m. and couldn't get back to sleep.*
**3** in the direction that is behind you: *I looked back over my shoulder.*
**4** doing the same thing to someone that he or she has done to you: *Sarah smiled, and the boy smiled back.*
**5** away from someone or something: *She pulled back the curtains to let the sun in.*
**6** **back and forth** = in one direction and then in the opposite direction several times: *He walked back and forth across the floor.*

**back³** *verb*
**1** (*also* **back up**) to move backward: *We backed away from the barking dog.* | *She backed the car into the garage.*
**2** to support someone or something: *Several environmental groups backed the new law.*
**PHRASAL VERBS**
**back down**
to admit that you are wrong about something

B

and stop arguing: *Everyone disagreed with her, but she refused to back down.*

**back off** (*informal*)

to stop telling someone what to do: *Back off! I don't need your advice.*

**back out**

to decide not to do something you promised to do: *She was going to run for student body president, but backed out.*

**back someone or something up**

to show that what someone is saying is true: *There is no evidence to back up what he says.*

**back**[4] *adjective*

**1** in or on the back of something: *The back door was open.* **SYNONYM: rear**; **ANTONYM: front**

**2** **a back street/road** = a street or road that is not a main one

**back·ache** /ˈbækeɪk/ *noun*

a pain in your back: *She had a backache from moving furniture.*

**back·bone** /ˈbækboʊn/ *noun*

the line of bones down the middle of your back **SYNONYM: spine** → see picture on page A2

**back·break·ing** /ˈbækˌbreɪkɪŋ/ *adjective*

backbreaking work is very difficult physical work

**back·fire** /ˈbækfaɪɚ/ *verb*

if a plan backfires, it does not have the result you wanted it to have: *I pretended to be too sick to go to school, but my plan backfired when Mom said I had to stay in bed all day.*

**back·ground** /ˈbækgraʊnd/ *noun*

**1** the part of a picture that is behind the main part: *Here's a picture of Mary, with our house in the background.*

**2** someone's family, education, and past experience: *They come from very different backgrounds. His family was wealthy and hers was poor.*

**3** the conditions or past events that relate to something: *I'll tell you a little more about the background of the problem, so you'll understand it better.*

**back·log** /ˈbæklɔg/ *noun*

the things that you have not yet been able to deal with: *The company has a huge backlog of orders, and customers have to wait months to receive their goods.*

**back·pack** /ˈbækpæk/ *noun*

a bag that you carry on your back

**back·pack·ing** /ˈbækˌpækɪŋ/ *noun*

the activity of walking and camping while carrying a backpack: *We went backpacking in the Rockies.*

—**backpacker** *noun* someone who walks and camps using a backpack

**back·stage** /ˌbækˈsteɪdʒ/ *adverb*

behind the stage in a theater: *He was allowed to go backstage after the concert to meet the band.*

**back·stroke** /ˈbækstroʊk/ *noun*

a way of swimming on your back. You move one arm up and over your head and then the other.

**back·up** /ˈbækʌp/ *noun*

**1** a person or thing that replaces someone or something that does not work or is lost: *They signed Moon as a backup to their star quarterback, in case he gets injured.* | *Do you have a backup plan?*

**2** a copy of a computer document or program that you can use if the original is lost or damaged: *Make a backup of your work so you don't lose it if the computer crashes.*

**back·ward**[1] /ˈbækwɚd/ (*also* **backwards**) *adverb*

**1** in the direction that is behind you: *She took a step backward, away from me.* **ANTONYM: forward**

**2** toward the beginning: *Count backward from 10 to 1.* **ANTONYM: forward**

**3** with the back part in front: *You have your T-shirt on backward – turn it around.*

**backward**[2] *adjective*

**1** toward the direction that is behind you: *She stopped at the door and took a backward look at her family behind her.* **ANTONYM: forward**

**2** developing more slowly than others: *It was a backward area with no running water or telephones.*

**back·yard** (*also* **back yard**) /ˈbækˌyɑrd/ *noun*

the area of land behind a house: *He was playing in the backyard.*

**ba·con** /ˈbeɪkən/ *noun*
salted or smoked meat from the back or sides of a pig. Bacon is usually served in thin narrow pieces: *We had bacon and eggs for breakfast.*
→ see Thesaurus box at **meat**
[**ORIGIN:** 1300-1400 From an old German word meaning "back." Some bacon comes from the back of a pig.]

**bac·te·ri·a** /bækˈtɪriə/ *noun* (singular **bacterium**)
living things that are too small to see but are all around you. Some kinds of bacteria cause disease: *Cook meat well to kill any bacteria.*
[**ORIGIN:** 1800-1900 From the Greek word *bakterion*, which means "stick or rod." The first bacteria scientists looked at were shaped like rods.]

**bad** /bæd/ *adjective* (**worse** /wɚs/, **worst** /wɚst/)
**1** not nice or enjoyable: *I'm sorry, but I have some bad news.* | *The weather was bad. It rained every day.* **ANTONYM: good**

> **THESAURUS: bad**
>
> **awful** very bad: *The weather was awful. It was windy and rainy the whole time.*
>
> **terrible** very bad or serious: *The food was terrible.* | *a terrible accident*
>
> **horrible** very bad or upsetting: *I had a horrible weekend. Everything went wrong.*
>
> **disgusting** very bad, wrong, or unpleasant: *The smell of rotting fish was disgusting.* | *Their behavior was disgusting.*

**2** not able to do something well: *He's a bad driver who has had many accidents.* | *Brian is bad at sports – he can't catch a ball.* **ANTONYM: good**
**3** of low quality: *Her handwriting is so bad I can't read it.* **ANTONYM: good**
**4** harmful to your health: *Smoking is bad for you.* **ANTONYM: good**
**5** serious or severe: *He didn't go to school because he had a bad cold.* | *The problem is getting worse.*
**6** morally wrong or evil: *A bad man locked the princess in a tower.* **ANTONYM: good**
**7 feel bad** = to feel ashamed or sorry about something: *I feel bad about lying to him.*
**8 too bad** (*informal*) = used for saying that you are sorry about a sad or unpleasant situation: *It's too bad you can't stay longer.*
**9 not bad** (*informal*) = fairly good, but not very good: *The movie wasn't bad, but I wouldn't want to see it again.*
**10 a bad time** = a time that is not appropriate or convenient: *Is this a bad time to call?*
**11** food that is bad is not safe to eat because it is not fresh: *The milk has gone bad.*

**badge** /bædʒ/ *noun*
a small piece of metal or plastic with words or a picture on it, that you wear or carry to show who you are or who you work for: *Workers have a security badge that they must wear at all times.* | *a police badge*

**bad·ly** /ˈbædli/ *adverb* (**worse** /wɚs/, **worst** /wɚst/)
**1** in a way that is not good: *The book is badly written, so it is difficult to understand.* | *The team played very badly and lost the game.* **ANTONYM: well**
**2** very severely: *The houses were badly damaged during the storm.*

**ˈbad·min·ton** /ˈbædˌmɪntən/ *noun*
a game in which two or four players use RACKETs to hit a small object with feathers on it over a net: *Let's play a game of badminton.*
[**ORIGIN:** 1800-1900 From Badminton, an important house in Gloucestershire, England, where the game was first played.]

**baf·fled** /ˈbæfəld/ *adjective*
if you are baffled by something, you cannot understand it: *The code baffled the enemy and they could not solve it.*

**bag**

**bag** /bæg/ *noun*
a container that you carry things in, that is made of paper, plastic, cloth, or leather: *a bag*

*of candy | She was carrying two shopping bags full of clothes.*

**ba·gel** /ˈbeɪgəl/ *noun*
a type of bread that is round with a hole in the center
[**ORIGIN:** 1900-2000 From the Yiddish word *beygel*, which comes from an old German word *boug*, meaning "ring." Yiddish was the language spoken by Jewish people in Europe.]

**bag·gage** /ˈbægɪdʒ/ *noun*
the bags or suitcases that you take with you when you travel on an airplane, train, or bus: *The baggage was taken off the plane.*
[**ORIGIN:** 1400-1500 From the French word *bagage*, from *bague*, which means "bundle."]

**bag·gy** /ˈbægi/ *adjective*
baggy clothes are big and loose **ANTONYM: tight**

**bail[1]** /beɪl/ *noun*
money that someone pays to leave prison until his or her TRIAL. If he or she does not come to trial, the court keeps the money: *He was released from jail on bail.*

**bail[2]** *verb*
**PHRASAL VERB**
**bail someone out**
to help a person or organization get out of trouble: *The government bailed out some of the big banks when it looked like they might fail.*

**bait** /beɪt/ *noun*
a small amount of food that you use to make fish or animals come near so that you can catch them: *We used worms for bait when we were fishing.*

**bake** /beɪk/ *verb*
to cook something such as bread or cake in an OVEN: *Bake the rolls for 15 minutes.*
→ see Thesaurus box at **cook[1]**

**bak·er·y** /ˈbeɪkəri/ *noun* (plural **bakeries**)
a place where bread, cakes, and cookies are made or sold
—**baker** *noun* someone whose job is making bread or cakes → see picture on page **A17**

**bal·ance[1]** /ˈbæləns/ *noun*
**1** the ability to stand or walk steadily, without falling: *She was walking on top of the wall when she lost her balance and fell.*
**2** a situation in which different things are in the right amounts or have the right amount of importance: *A lot of dads want to find a balance between their work and family life.*
**3** the amount of money that someone has in his or her bank account at a particular time: *After all the bills were paid, he had a balance of $170 in his account.*
**4 on balance** = used when telling someone your opinion after considering all the facts: *On balance, I'd say it was a fair decision.*
[**ORIGIN:** 1200-1300 From the Latin word *bilanx*, which means "having two pans," like an old-fashioned scale for weighing things.]

**balance[2]** *verb*
**1** to stay in a steady position, without falling: *He balanced on the tightrope and began to walk across.*
**2** to keep something in a steady position so that it does not fall: *She was balancing a plate of food on her knees.*
**3** to make sure that different things are in the right amounts or have the right amount of importance: *The movie balances fun with a serious message.*
**4 balance a budget** = to make sure that the amount of money that is spent equals the amount of money that is earned

**bal·anced** /ˈbælənst/ *adjective*
including different things in the right amounts: *You should eat a healthy balanced diet with plenty of protein, fruits, and vegetables.*

**bal·co·ny** /ˈbælkəni/ *noun* (plural **balconies**)
**1** a small floor that sticks out from the outside of a building, where you can stand or sit: *The apartments on the second floor have small balconies.*
**2** the seats upstairs in a theater

**bald** /bɔld/ *adjective*
if you are bald, you have little or no hair on your head: *He is going bald on the top of his head.*

**ˈbald ˌeagle** *noun*
a large North American bird with a white head and neck: *The bald eagle is a symbol of the United States.*

**bale** /beɪl/ *noun*
a large amount of something such as paper or HAY that is tied tightly together: *a bale of hay*

**ball** /bɔl/ *noun*
**1** a round object that you throw, hit, or kick

in some games: *He threw the ball to Michael.*
**2** something made into a round shape: *a ball of string*
**3** in baseball, a time when a ball is thrown and the hitter does not try to hit it because it is not in the correct area
**4** **be on the ball** (*informal*) = to be able to think or act quickly: *If he had been more on the ball, he would have bought a ticket before they sold out.*
**5** a large formal party at which people dance
[**ORIGIN:** 1600-1700 Sense 5 is from the Latin word *ballare*, which means "to dance."]

**bal·le·ri·na** /ˌbæləˈrinə/ *noun*
a woman who dances in ballets: *She stood on her toes like a ballerina.*

**bal·let** /bæˈleɪ/ *noun*
**1** a type of dancing which is used to tell a story: *a ballet class*
**2** a performance in which dancing and music are used to tell a story: *We went to see the ballet "Swan Lake."*
[**ORIGIN:** 1600-1700 From the Italian word *balletto*, which means "little dance," from the Latin word *ballare*, which means "to dance."]

**bal·loon** /bəˈlun/ *noun*
a colored rubber bag that you fill with air or gas, and that is often used at parties as a decoration: *We blew up balloons before the party to decorate the house.*

**bal·lot** /ˈbælət/ *noun*
**1** a piece of paper that you mark to vote for someone or something: *They are counting the ballots to see who has won the election.*
**2** a system in which people vote: *We have a ballot to choose the leader.*
[**ORIGIN:** 1500-1600 From the Italian word *ballotta*, which means "small ball." Small balls were dropped into pots as a way of voting.]

**ball·park** /ˈbɔlˌpɑrk/ *noun* (*informal*)
a place for playing baseball

**ball·point pen** /ˌbɔlpɔɪnt ˈpen/ *noun*
a pen with a small ball at the end that rolls ink onto the paper

**ball·room** /ˈbɔlrum/ *noun*
a large room for formal dances: *A band was playing in the ballroom.*

**bam·boo** /ˌbæmˈbu/ *noun*
a tall plant with hard hollow stems that is often used to make things such as furniture, especially in Asia

**ban**[1] /bæn/ *noun*
an official order saying that something is not allowed: *The school has put a ban on candy machines and only sells healthy snacks.*

**ban**[2] *verb* (**banned**, **banning**)
to say officially that something is not allowed: *Students are banned from running inside school buildings to prevent accidents.*
→ see Thesaurus box at **forbid**

**ba·nan·a** /bəˈnænə/ *noun*
a long curved fruit with a yellow skin → see picture on page **A13**
[**ORIGIN:** 1500-1600 Borrowed by the Spanish or Portuguese from an African language.]

**band** /bænd/ *noun*
**1** a group of musicians that plays popular music: *He used to play in a rock band.*
**2** a small group of people who do something together: *The band of explorers crossed North America.* **SYNONYM: group**
**3** a narrow STRIPE or flat piece of material which goes around something else to hold it or decorate it: *The letters were held together with a rubber band.* | *The bird has a band of yellow on its wing.*

**ban·dage** /ˈbændɪdʒ/ *noun*
a long piece of cloth that you put around a wound: *After the accident, her head was wrapped in a bandage.*
—**bandage** *verb* to put a bandage around a wound: *A nurse bandaged my injured leg.*

**ˈBand-Aid** *noun* (*trademark*)
a small piece of material that you stick over a small cut on your skin

**ban·dan·na** (*also* **bandana**) /bænˈdænə/ *noun*
a square piece of colored cloth that you wear around your head or neck
[**ORIGIN:** 1700-1800 From the Hindi word *badhnu*, which means "cloth tied and then colored," from *badhna*, which means "to tie."]

**ban·dit** /ˈbændɪt/ *noun*
someone who robs people who are traveling: *The train was attacked by bandits.*
[**ORIGIN:** 1500-1600 From the Italian word *bandito*, from *bandire*, which means "to officially say that someone, such as a criminal, is not allowed to be in a place."]

B

**bang**[1] /bæŋ/ *verb*
**1** to make a loud noise by hitting something: *He banged on the door with his hands.*
**2** to hit a part of your body on something by accident: *I banged my knee on the corner of the bed.*
→ see Thesaurus box at **hit**[1]

**bang**[2] *noun*
a sudden loud noise: *The door slammed shut with a bang.* → see picture on page **A22**

**bangs** /bæŋz/ *plural noun*
the part of your hair that is cut so that it covers your FOREHEAD

**ban·is·ter** /ˈbænəstɚ/ *noun*
a bar that you hold on to when you go up or down stairs

**ban·jo** /ˈbændʒoʊ/ *noun* (plural **banjos**)
a musical instrument with strings and a round body → see picture on page **A21**

**bank**[1] /bæŋk/ *noun*
**1** the company or place where you can keep your money or borrow money: *I have some savings in the bank.*
**2** the land along the side of a river or lake: *The city is on the banks of the Hudson River.*
**3** a place where a lot of something is stored for people to use: *The food bank gives food to people in need.* | *a blood bank*
→ see Thesaurus box at **shore**
[**ORIGIN:** 1400-1500 From the Italian word *banca*, which means "long seat or table." People who exchanged money put the money on a table.]

**bank**[2] *verb*
to use a particular bank: *She banks with First National.*

**ˈbank acˌcount** *noun*
if you have a bank account, you can keep money in the bank and take some out: *How much money do you have in your bank account?* **SYNONYM: account**

**bank·er** /ˈbæŋkɚ/ *noun*
someone who has an important job in a bank

**bank·ing** /ˈbæŋkɪŋ/ *noun*
the business of banks, for example lending money

**bank·rupt** /ˈbæŋkrʌpt/ *adjective*
not able to pay the money you owe to other people or companies: *The company didn't make enough money to pay its bills and went bankrupt.*
—**bankruptcy** *noun* a situation in which a person or company cannot pay the money they owe to other people or companies
[**ORIGIN:** 1500-1600 From the Italian words *banca* and *rotta*, which mean "bank" and "broken."]

**ban·ner** /ˈbænɚ/ *noun*
a long piece of cloth with writing on it: *The banner over the door said, "Happy Birthday!"*

**ban·quet** /ˈbæŋkwɪt/ *noun*
a big formal meal for many people: *The mayor invited city leaders to the banquet.*

**bap·tism** /ˈbæptɪzəm/ *noun*
a religious ceremony in which water is put on someone to make him or her a member of the Christian religion
—**baptize** *verb* to put water on someone in a religious ceremony, so that he or she becomes a member of the Christian religion

**bar**[1] /bɑr/ *noun*
**1** a small block of something: *He was eating a candy bar.* | *a bar of soap*
**2** a place where people can buy and drink alcohol: *The men were drinking in a bar.*
**3** a COUNTER where alcoholic drinks are served: *He was standing at the bar getting a beer.*
**4** a long thin stick of metal: *The fence was made with iron bars.*
**5** **behind bars** = in prison
**6** a group of notes in music: *He played the first bars of the song.*

**bar**[2] *verb* (**barred**, **barring**)
**1** to officially stop someone from doing something: *Photographers are barred from taking pictures inside the courtroom.*
**2** to put a piece of wood or metal across a door or window to stop people from going in or out: *He locked and barred the gate.*
→ see Thesaurus box at **forbid**

**bar·be·cue** /ˈbɑrbɪˌkyu/ *noun*
**1** a meal or party where you cook food outside: *We're having a barbecue on Saturday with hotdogs and hamburgers.*
**2** a piece of equipment you use to cook food outside: *There were hamburgers cooking on the barbecue.*
→ see Thesaurus box at **meal**
[**ORIGIN:** 1600-1700 From the American Spanish

word *barbacoa*, which probably came from a word meaning "frame of sticks" in a Caribbean language.]

**ˌbarbed ˈwire** *noun*
wire with short sharp points on it: *The cattle were in a field surrounded by a barbed wire fence.*

**bar·ber** /ˈbɑrbɚ/ *noun*
a man whose job is to cut men's hair
—**barbershop** *noun* a store where men's hair is cut
[**ORIGIN:** 1200-1300 From the Latin word *barba*, which means "beard."]

**ˈbar code** *noun*
a row of black lines on something that is sold in a store. The bar code gives a computer information about the thing being sold, for example how much it costs.

**bare** /ber/ *adjective*
**1** not covered by clothes: *The children were running around in bare feet.*
**2** if a room or cupboard is bare, it has nothing in it: *The cupboard was bare so there was nothing to eat.* **SYNONYM: empty**
**3** without any decoration: *They hadn't put up any pictures yet, so the walls were bare.* **SYNONYM: plain**
**4** basic and with nothing extra: *Take only the bare necessities – a toothbrush and change of underwear.*

**bare·foot** /ˈberfʊt/ *adjective, adverb*
not wearing any shoes or socks: *We walked barefoot in the sand.*

**bare·ly** /ˈberli/ *adverb*
almost not: *Her voice was so quiet I could barely hear her.*

**bar·gain¹** /ˈbɑrgən/ *noun*
something that is sold for much less than its usual price: *The jeans were a bargain at $17.00.*

**bargain²** *verb*
to discuss an agreement or a price with someone, so that each side gets something that it wants: *The union is bargaining with the company's management for higher pay.*

**barge** /bɑrdʒ/ *noun*
a large boat with a flat bottom, used for carrying goods on a CANAL or river: *The coal was taken up the river by barge.*

**bar graph**

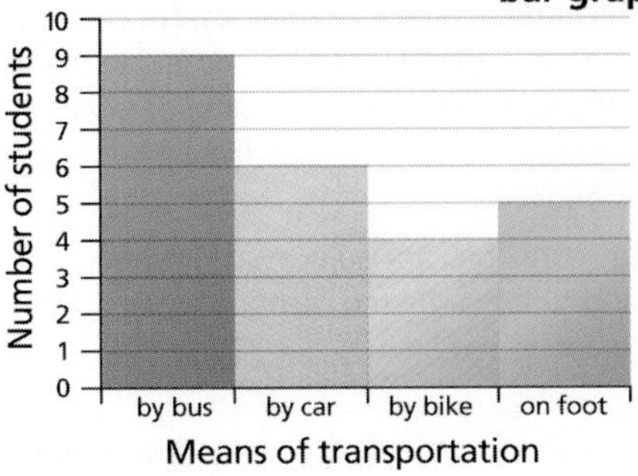


**ˈbar graph** (*also* **bar chart**) *noun*
a GRAPH that uses a series of boxes to show different amounts, so that a tall box represents a larger amount than a short box: *The bar graph shows that the number of cars on the freeway has increased every year for the last ten years.*

**bark¹** /bɑrk/ *verb*
if a dog barks, it makes a short loud sound: *The dog barked at us as we walked past.*

**bark²** *noun*
**1** the sound a dog makes: *The dog gave a loud bark.*
**2** the part that covers the outside of a tree

**bar·ley** /ˈbɑrli/ *noun*
a grain used in making some foods

**bar mitz·vah** /ˌbɑr ˈmɪtsvə/ *noun*
a religious ceremony that takes place when a Jewish boy is 13 years old, that allows him to take part in his religion as an adult. There is a similar ceremony for Jewish girls, called a BAT MITZVAH.

**barn** /bɑrn/ *noun*
a large building on a farm for storing crops or keeping animals in
[**ORIGIN:** From the old English words *bere* and *ærn*, which mean "barley" and "place."]

**ba·rom·e·ter** /bəˈrɑmətɚ/ *noun*
an instrument that measures the pressure of the air around us and shows what the weather will be like. When the air pressure is low, the weather will be rainy. When the air pressure is high, the weather will be fine.
[**ORIGIN:** 1600-1700 From the Greek words *baros* and *metron*, which mean "weight or pressure" and "measure."]

**bar·racks** /ˈbærəks/ *plural noun*
a group of buildings where soldiers live

**bar·rel** /ˈbærəl/ *noun*
**1** a large container for liquids, for example oil or beer. A barrel is like a very large tube with a flat top and bottom: *a barrel of beer*
**2** the part of a gun that the bullets are shot through

**bar·ren** /ˈbærən/ *adjective* (*formal*)
land that is barren cannot grow plants: *a barren desert*

**bar·rette** /bəˈret/ *noun*
a small metal or plastic object that a girl uses to keep her hair in place

**bar·ri·cade** /ˈbærəˌkeɪd/ *noun*
something that is put across a road to prevent people from going past: *Police set up barricades on all the roads to try to catch the men.*
**[ORIGIN:** 1500-1600 From the French word *barrique*, which means "barrel." Early barricades were made from barrels.**]**

**bar·ri·er** /ˈbæriɚ/ *noun*
**1** a fence or wall that stops people from entering a place: *The police put up barriers to hold back the crowds.*
**2** a problem that stops people from doing something: *A lack of education is a barrier to many good jobs.*

**bar·ri·o** /ˈbæriˌoʊ/ *noun* (plural **barrios**)
an area in a city where many Spanish-speaking people live

**bar·tend·er** /ˈbɑrˌtendɚ/ *noun*
someone whose job is to make and serve drinks in a bar

**base¹** /beɪs/ *noun*
**1** the lowest part of something: *At the base of the cliff was a sandy beach.* | *The base of the glass was cracked.*
**2** one of the four places that a baseball player must run to in order to score a point: *She hit the ball and ran to first base.*
**3** the main place used by a company or person: *The company's base is in Atlanta.*
**4** a place where soldiers live and work: *an army base*
**5** a substance that will form a salt if it is combined with an acid: *Bases have a pH higher than 7, so they will turn litmus paper blue.*
**6** the number that a mathematical system is built on: *The decimal system uses a base of 10.*
**[ORIGIN:** 1300-1400 From the Latin word *bassus*, which means "short or low."**]**

**base²** *verb*
to have your main office or home in a place: *The company is based in New York.*
**PHRASAL VERB**
**base something on something**
to use an idea or fact as a start for making something new: *The movie is based on a true story.*

**base·ball** /ˈbeɪsbɔl/ *noun*
**1** a game played by two teams of nine players. The players try to get points by hitting a ball with a BAT and running around four bases: *A group of kids were playing baseball in the park.*
**2** the ball used in the game of baseball

**base·ment** /ˈbeɪsmənt/ *noun*
the part of a building that is below the level of the ground: *They turned their basement into a playroom.*

**bas·es** /ˈbeɪsiz/ *noun*
the plural of BASIS

**bash¹** /bæʃ/ *verb*
to hit something hard: *I bashed my head when I fell down.*

**bash²** *noun* (*informal*)
a party: *We're having a big bash for his birthday.*
→ see Thesaurus box at **party**

**bash·ful** /ˈbæʃfəl/ *adjective*
shy and embarrassed: *When she asked him to dance, he gave her a bashful smile.*
**SYNONYM: shy**
—**bashfully** *adverb* in a bashful way
→ see Thesaurus box at **shy**

**ba·sic** /ˈbeɪsɪk/ *adjective*
**1** simple but important and necessary: *The basic problem is that we don't have enough money.* | *Adding and subtracting are basic mathematics.*

**2** very simple and not advanced: *The computers are old and fairly basic.* → **basics**

**WORD FAMILY: basic**
**basic** *adjective* | **base** *verb* | **base** *noun* | **basis** *noun* | **basically** *adverb* | **the basics** *plural noun*

**ba·si·cally** /ˈbeɪsɪkli/ *adverb*
**1** (*informal*) used when you are giving the most important reason or fact about something: *Basically, you have to study if you want to do well in school.*
**2** in the most important ways: *The two pictures are basically the same, and I had to look carefully to see the differences.*

**basics** /ˈbeɪsɪks/ *plural noun*
**the basics** = the most important facts or things that you need to know: *My mom is teaching me the basics of cooking.*

**ba·sil** /ˈbeɪzəl/ *noun*
a plant with leaves that are used in cooking

**ba·sin** /ˈbeɪsən/ *noun*
**1** a large area of land around a river. The water from the land in the basin goes into the river: *the Amazon basin*
**2** a large bowl, especially one for water: *She poured the water into a basin and washed her face.*

**ba·sis** /ˈbeɪsəs/ *noun* (plural **bases** /ˈbeɪsiz/)
**1** the idea or reason that something comes from: *The students used the picture as the basis for writing a story.*
**2** the most important part of something: *In China, rice forms the basis of most meals.*
**3 on a daily/weekly/monthly/regular, etc. basis** = every day, week, month, etc.: *The classes meet on a daily basis, for an hour each.*
**4 on the basis of something** = because of a particular fact or situation: *He did not get the job on the basis of his age – he was too young.*

**bas·ket** /ˈbæskɪt/ *noun*
**1** a container that you can carry or hold things in, that is made of thin pieces of wood, plastic, or wire: *They took the food to the park in a picnic basket.* | *a shopping basket*
**2** a round metal ring with a net hanging from it, used when playing basketball: *Try to shoot the ball through the basket.*
**3** an occasion when the ball goes through the basket in basketball, so that you score points: *She made eight baskets in the first half of the game.*

**bas·ket·ball** /ˈbæskɪtˌbɔl/ *noun*
**1** a game played by two teams of five players, who try to get points by throwing a ball into a high net at each end of the court
**2** the ball used in this game

basketball

**bass** /beɪs/ *noun*
**1** (*also* **bass guitar**) a GUITAR that plays low notes
**2** another word for a DOUBLE BASS → see picture on page **A21**

**bas·soon** /bəˈsun/ *noun*
a very long wooden musical instrument that is shaped like a tube and has a low sound. You play it by blowing into it and pressing keys. → see picture on page **A21**

**bat¹** /bæt/ *noun*
**1** a long wooden stick that you use to hit the ball in baseball
**2** a small animal that flies at night and looks like a mouse with wings

**bat²** *verb* (**batted**, **batting**)
to hit the ball with a bat in baseball, or to try to hit the ball: *You're the next person to bat, so get ready.*

**batch** /bætʃ/ *noun*
**1** a group of things that are made at the same time: *I baked a batch of cookies.*
**2** a group of things or people that arrive or are dealt with at the same time: *The mailman delivered a big batch of letters.*

**bath** /bæθ/ *noun* (plural **baths** /bæðz/)
**1** if you take a bath, you wash your body while sitting in a bathtub: *I take a bath almost every day.*
**2** the water that you sit in to wash yourself: *I ran a nice hot bath and got in.*

B

**bathe** /beɪð/ *verb* (*formal*)
to wash yourself or someone else in a bathtub

**bathing suit** /ˈbeɪðɪŋ ˌsut/ *noun*
a piece of clothing that you wear for swimming

**bath·robe** /ˈbæθroʊb/ *noun*
a long loose piece of clothing with a belt, that you wear after you take a bath

**bath·room** /ˈbæθrum/ *noun*
**1** a room where there is a toilet and sink. In a house or apartment, there is also a bathtub or a SHOWER: *I washed my hands in the bathroom.*
**2 go to the bathroom** = to use a toilet: *I need to go to the bathroom.*

**bath·tub** /ˈbæθtʌb/ *noun*
a long container that you fill with water and sit in to wash yourself

**bat mitz·vah** /ˌbɑt˺ ˈmɪtsvə/ *noun*
a religious ceremony that takes place when a Jewish girl is 13 years old, that allows her to take part in her religion as an adult. There is a similar ceremony for Jewish boys, called a BAR MITZVAH.

**ba·ton** /bəˈtɑn/ *noun*
**1** a small stick that is used by the CONDUCTOR of a group of musicians to show them what to do
**2** a stick that a MAJORETTE spins and throws into the air
**3** a stick that runners pass to each other during a RELAY

**bat·ter**[1] /ˈbætɚ/ *noun*
**1** a mixture of flour, eggs, and milk, used for making cakes and similar things: *Mix the pancake batter with a spoon.*
**2** the person who is trying to hit the ball in baseball

**batter**[2] *verb*
to hit someone or something very hard many times: *The waves battered against the rocks during the storm.*

**bat·tered** /ˈbætɚd/ *adjective*
old and damaged from being used many times: *He learned to play on his father's battered old guitar.*

**bat·ter·y** /ˈbætəri/ *noun* (plural **batteries**)
an object that provides electricity, for example for a radio, camera, or toy: *My cell phone isn't working because I need to charge the battery.*
→ see picture on page A28

**bat·tle**[1] /ˈbætl/ *noun*
**1** a fight between two armies or groups of people, especially during a war: *The Battle of Gettysburg was fought between the Union and Confederate Armies in the Civil War.*
**2** a situation in which people are trying hard to do something, or to stop something from happening: *He finally won his case after a long legal battle.* | *She died last year after a long battle with cancer.*
[**ORIGIN:** 1200-1300 From the Latin word *battuere*, which means "to hit."]

**battle**[2] *verb*
to try hard to achieve something or deal with something: *He was badly injured and doctors battled for six hours to save his life.*

**bat·tle·ship** /ˈbætlˌʃɪp/ *noun*
a very large ship used in wars

**bawl** /bɔl/ *verb* (*informal*)
to cry loudly: *The baby was bawling in the back of the car.*
**PHRASAL VERB**
**bawl out**
to shout at someone because he or she has done something bad: *The coach bawled me out for not coming to baseball practice yesterday.*

**bay** /beɪ/ *noun*
a part of an ocean or lake that is partly surrounded by a curve in the land: *A ship was anchored in the calm waters of the bay.*

**bay·ou** /ˈbaɪu/ *noun*
a large area of water that moves very slowly and has many water plants, in the southeast U.S.

**ba·zaar** /bəˈzɑr/ *noun*
a market in Asian and Middle Eastern countries

**B.C.**
(**before Christ**) used to show that a year came before the birth of Jesus Christ: *The temple dates from 217 B.C.*

**be** /bi/ (**was**, **were**, **been**) *verb*
**1** used to describe and give information about people or things: *My mother is a teacher.* | *The room was blue and white.*

**2** used with the -ing form of another verb to say that something is happening now, or was happening in the past when something else happened: *It's raining.* | *I was leaving the house when the phone rang.*
**3** used with the -ing form of another verb to say that you have made plans to do something in the future: *We are going to Hawaii on vacation next month.*
**4** used with the past participle of verbs to say what has happened to someone or something: *My grandfather was killed in the war.* | *The old house has been pulled down.*
**5** used when saying that someone or something is in a place: *There are some apples in the kitchen.* | *Is Don here?* | *"Where's my coat?" "It's in the closet."*
**6** used when saying how someone should behave, or how someone is behaving: *Be careful! The knife's very sharp.* | *He is being so mean to me!*
**7** **someone is to do something** (*formal*) = used to say strongly that someone must do something: *You are to be home by 8 o'clock.*

beach

**beach** /bitʃ/ *noun*
an area of sand or small stones at the edge of an ocean or a lake: *We spent the day at the beach swimming and lying in the sun.*
→ see Thesaurus box at **shore**

**bea·con** /ˈbikən/ *noun*
a light or electronic signal used to guide people, boats, or airplanes

**bead** /bid/ *noun*
a small ball of plastic, wood, or glass with a hole in the middle, used for making jewelry: *The necklace was made of colored glass beads.*
[**ORIGIN:** From the old English word *bed*, which means "prayer." People counted beads while saying their prayers.]

**beak** /bik/ *noun*
the hard pointed mouth of a bird: *The bird held a worm in its beak.*

**beak·er** /ˈbikɚ/ *noun*
a glass or plastic cup with straight sides, used in chemistry for measuring liquids

**beam**[1] /bim/ *noun*
**1** a line of light or energy: *A beam of light from the street lamp was shining into the room.*
**2** a long piece of wood or metal used for building things such as houses and bridges: *The roof was supported by thick wooden beams.*

**beam**[2] *verb*
**1** to smile in a happy way: *He beamed proudly when his son scored the goal.*
**2** to send out a line of light or energy: *A bright light was beaming onto the center of the stage.*
**3** to send radio or television signals through the air: *News reports are beamed across the world by satellite, so we get the news very fast.*
→ see Thesaurus box at **smile**[1]

**bean** /bin/ *noun*
**1** a plant that produces seeds that can be cooked and eaten as a vegetable: *We planted beans in the vegetable garden.*
**2** the seeds of the bean plant, or the seed and its cover which can also be eaten: *green beans* | *The tacos came with rice and beans.*
**3** a seed from some other types of plants, used to make drinks or in foods: *He ground fresh coffee beans to make a pot of coffee.* | *cocoa beans*

**bear**[1] /ber/ *noun*
a large strong animal with thick fur and sharp CLAWs: *Black bears live in the forest, but polar bears live near the North Pole.*

**bear**[2] *verb* (**bore** /bɔr/, **borne** /bɔrn/)
**1** to accept something that is very painful or very difficult: *She didn't think she could bear the pain any longer.* **SYNONYM: stand**
**2** **bear the responsibility/blame for something** (*formal*) = to be responsible for something bad that has happened: *He was driving too fast so he bears responsibility for the accident.*
**3** **bear left/right** = to turn toward the left or right when you are driving or walking: *Bear left at the traffic lights.*
**4** **bear in mind** = to consider a fact when you

are deciding what to do or when making a judgment: *Bear in mind that he is only 8 years old, so he is actually reading very well.* **SYNONYM: remember**

**5** **bear the weight of something** = to support the weight of something: *The ice isn't thick enough to bear your weight.* **SYNONYM: hold**

**6** to produce fruit or flowers: *The tree will not bear fruit until it is a few years old.*

**7** (*formal*) to bring or carry something: *In the Bible story, three kings came bearing gifts.*

**bear·a·ble** /ˈberəbəl/ *adjective*
if a situation is bearable, it is difficult but you can accept it: *The doctor gave him medicine which made the pain more bearable.*

**beard**

beard mustache stubble

**beard** /bɪrd/ *noun*
the hair that grows on a man's chin: *The old man had a long white beard.*

**beast** /bist/ *noun* (*formal*)
an animal, especially one that is dangerous or strange: *Jungles are full of all kinds of wild beasts.*

**beat[1]** /bit/ *verb* (**beat**, **beaten** /ˈbitn/)

**1** to get more points or votes than other people in a game or competition: *New York beat Boston 4-1.* | *Carlos beat all the other candidates to become student body president.*

**2** to hit someone or something many times: *He tried beating the door but still no one answered.* | *The waves were beating against the rocks.*

**3** to make a regular sound or movement: *I was nervous and I could feel my heart beating fast.*

**4** to mix foods together quickly using a fork or a kitchen tool: *Beat the eggs.* → see picture on page **A15**

**5** **Beat it!** (*informal*) = an impolite way to tell someone to leave immediately

→ see Thesaurus box at **hit[1]**, **mix[1]**, **win[1]**

**beat[2]** *noun*

**1** the regular pattern of sounds in a piece of music: *When you're dancing you have to move to the beat of the music.*

**2** one of a series of regular movements or sounds: *He had a fever and his heart rate went up to 120 beats a minute.*

**beau·ti·ful** /ˈbyutəfəl/ *adjective*

**1** very nice to look at. You use beautiful especially about a woman, a place, or an object: *She is a very beautiful woman.* | *The views from the top of the mountain were beautiful.* | *a beautiful Chinese vase*

**THESAURUS: beautiful**

**beautiful** used about a woman, girl, or baby who is very nice to look at: *Elena looked beautiful in her blue dress.*

**attractive** used about a man or woman who is nice to look at: *She's a very attractive woman.*

**good-looking** used about a man or woman who is nice to look at: *a tall good-looking man*

**pretty** used about a girl or woman who is nice to look at: *a pretty girl with long brown hair*

**handsome** used about a man or boy who is nice to look at: *Dad looked really handsome in his suit.*

**cute** used about a baby, child, or young person who is nice to look at: *I think Todd is really cute.* | *What a cute baby!*

**gorgeous** extremely attractive: *My sister thinks Robert Pattinson is gorgeous.*

**2** a beautiful song, book, or poem gives you a lot of pleasure: *Listen to this song – it's really beautiful.*

—**beautifully** *adverb* in a way that looks or sounds very good: *He plays the piano beautifully.*

**beau·ty** /ˈbyuti/ *noun* (plural **beauties**)

**1** the quality of being beautiful to look at: *The mountains in Yosemite are famous for their beauty.*

**2** the quality that a very good song, book, or

poem has when it gives you a lot of pleasure: *the beauty of his music*
[**ORIGIN:** 1200-1300 From the Latin word *bellitas*, from *bellus*, which means "pretty or handsome."]

**bea·ver** /ˈbivɚ/ *noun*
a North American animal that has thick fur and a wide flat tail, and that lives in houses made of sticks in the water: *The beavers are building a dam in the stream.*

**be·came** /bɪˈkeɪm/ *verb*
the past tense of BECOME

**be·cause** /bɪˈkɔz/ *conjunction*
used when you are giving the reason for something: *She was tired because she had been standing up all day.* | *The game was canceled because of the rain.*

**be·come** /bɪˈkʌm/ *verb* (**became**, **become**)
**1** to begin to be something: *When fall begins, the weather becomes cooler.* | *The questions were easy at first but then they became more difficult.*

**USAGE: become, get, go**

**Become**, **get**, and **go** can all mean "to begin to be something," but they are used in different ways.

**Become** is used in both written and spoken English: *He's becoming a very good tennis player.* | *The area has become popular with mountain bikers.*

**Get** and **go** are less formal than **become**, and are used more often in spoken English: *I got very hungry.* | *Have you gone crazy?*

**Become** can be used in front of an adjective or a noun: *He became angry and started yelling at me.* | *The noise from the airport is becoming a problem.*

**Get** and **go** are used only in front of an adjective: *It's getting dark.* | *Beethoven went deaf when he was 40 years old.*

**2** to start to have a job or position: *She wants to become a doctor.*

**bed** /bed/ *noun*
**1** a piece of furniture for sleeping on: *The kids are asleep in bed.* | *I usually go to bed around ten o'clock.* | *Straighten up your room and make your bed – the blankets are all over the floor!* → see picture on page **A10**
**2** the ground at the bottom of the ocean, a river, or a lake: *The water was clear and I could see the river bed below our boat.*
**3** an area of ground where you plant flowers or vegetables, but not grass: *The flowerbeds are full of roses.*

**bed·room** /ˈbedrum/ *noun*
a room for sleeping in: *This is Mark's bedroom.* | *a three-bedroom house*

**bed·spread** /ˈbedspred/ *noun*
a large cover that goes on top of a bed, over the sheets and BLANKETs → see picture on page **A10**

**bed·time** /ˈbedtaɪm/ *noun*
the time when you usually go to bed: *It's past your bedtime! Go get your pajamas on.*

**bee** /bi/ *noun*
a yellow and black insect that flies, makes HONEY, and can sting you: *The bees were buzzing around from flower to flower.*

**beech** /bitʃ/ *noun*
a large tree with smooth gray BARK (=the outside covering of the tree) and small nuts

**beef** /bif/ *noun*
meat from a cow: *a slice of roast beef*
→ see Thesaurus box at **meat**
[**ORIGIN:** 1100-1200 From the old French word *buef*, which means "ox."]

**bee·hive** /ˈbihaɪv/ *noun*
a place where bees live **SYNONYM: hive**

**been** /bɪn/ *verb*
**1** the past participle of BE
**2 have been to** = to have visited a place in the past: *Have you ever been to Mexico?*

**USAGE: been, gone**

**Been** and **gone** are past participles of **go**. A past participle is the form of a verb that you use when talking about things that have happened.

**Has been** and **have been** are used to say that someone went to a place and came back: *The Macleans have been to Hawaii. They say they had a great time there.*

**Has gone** and **have gone** are used to say that someone recently went to a place and is still there: *The Macleans have gone to Hawaii. They won't be back for two weeks.*

B

**beep** /bip/ *verb*
if an electronic machine or a car horn beeps, it makes a sound: *The computer beeps when you press the wrong key.*
—**beep** *noun* the sound that an electronic machine or a car horn makes

**beer** /bɪr/ *noun*
a yellow or brown alcoholic drink: *a glass of beer* | *Dad drank a beer after work.*

**beet** /bit/ *noun*
a round dark red vegetable that grows under the ground

**bee·tle** /ˈbitl/ *noun*
an insect with a hard round back that covers its wings

**be·fore¹** /bɪˈfɔr/ *preposition, conjunction*
**1** earlier than something or someone: *I take a shower before breakfast.* | *The other students finished the test before me.* | *It's Wednesday today, so the day before yesterday was Monday.* **ANTONYM: after**

> **THESAURUS: before**
>
> **earlier** near the beginning of a period of time, an event, or a process: *I saw Kim earlier today.*
>
> **previously** before now, or before a particular time: *I had seen him in the music store, about ten minutes previously.*
>
> **prior to something** (*formal*) before: *Please be at the gate at least 30 minutes prior to the plane's departure.*

**2** in front of someone or something else on a list or in an order: *S comes before T in the alphabet.* | *Our house is on the right, just before the church.* **ANTONYM: after**
**3** (*formal*) in front of and facing someone or something: *The governor was standing before a large crowd.*

**before²** *adverb*
at an earlier time: *I'm sure I've seen her somewhere before – she looks very familiar.* | *We didn't go shopping on Saturday because we went the day before – on Friday.*

**be·fore·hand** /bɪˈfɔrˌhænd/ *adverb*
before something happens: *The teacher had warned us beforehand that the test was going to be difficult.*

**beg** /beg/ *verb* (**begged**, **begging**)
**1** to ask someone for food or money because you are very poor: *Some people had no jobs and no homes and had to beg for food.*
**2** to ask for something in a way which shows you want it very much: *I begged my parents to let me go to the concert with my friends.*
**3 I beg your pardon** (*formal*) = **a)** used to ask someone politely to say something again: *"It's 5 dollars." "I beg your pardon?" "I said it's 5 dollars."* **SYNONYM: excuse me**
**b)** used to say you are sorry: *Oh, I beg your pardon, did I hurt you?* **SYNONYM: sorry**
→ see Thesaurus box at **ask**

**be·gan** /bɪˈgæn/ *verb*
the past tense of BEGIN

**beg·gar** /ˈbegɚ/ *noun*
someone who asks people for food and money in order to live: *There are beggars on the streets who stop you and ask you for money.*

**be·gin** /bɪˈgɪn/ *verb* (**began** /bɪˈgæn/, **begun** /bɪˈgʌn/, **beginning**)
**1** to start: *The concert will begin at 8:00.* | *The musicians began playing.* | *It's beginning to rain.* | *Let's begin with exercise 5.* | *The word "psychology" begins with a "p."* **ANTONYMS: end, stop, finish**
**2 to begin with** = used to talk about when you start doing something: *She wasn't very good at the game to begin with, but she soon got better at it.*

**be·gin·ner** /bɪˈgɪnɚ/ *noun*
someone who is starting to do something or learn something: *a guitar class for beginners*

**be·gin·ning** /bɪˈgɪnɪŋ/ *noun*
the start or first part of something: *The beginning of the movie is really exciting, but I didn't like the end.* | *In the beginning, I didn't like him very much, but now I think he's great.* **SYNONYM: start**; **ANTONYM: end**

**be·gun** /bɪˈgʌn/ *verb*
the past participle of BEGIN

**be·half** Ac /bɪˈhæf/ *noun* (*formal*)
**on behalf of someone/on someone's behalf** = if you speak or do something on someone's behalf, you do it instead of that person because you have been asked to do it: *Her lawyer spoke on her behalf.* **SYNONYM: for**

**be·have** /bɪˈheɪv/ *verb*
**1** to do or say things in a particular way: *Lions in a zoo do not behave like lions in the wild.*
**2 behave (yourself)** = to be polite and not cause trouble: *His mother told him to behave.* | *If you behave yourself, you can stay up late.* **ANTONYM: misbehave**

**WORD FAMILY: behave**
**behave** *verb* | **behavior** *noun* | **well-behaved** *adjective*

**be·hav·ior** /bɪˈheɪvyɚ/ *noun*
the way that a person or animal behaves: *His behavior became strange, but I could not understand why.* | *It's important to reward children for good behavior in class.*

**be·hind** /bɪˈhaɪnd/ *preposition, adverb*
**1** at the back of someone or something: *The drugstore is behind the supermarket.* | *I sit behind Jordan in class.*
**2** not doing as well at something as another person or team: *The score was 34-28, so we were behind by six points.*
**3** supporting a person or idea: *Parents are behind the school's efforts to improve. They agree to read with their kids.*
**4** late in doing the things that you have to do: *The doctor was running behind so we had to wait half an hour to see him.*
**5** responsible for causing something: *The police believe a local gang is behind the robberies.*

**beige** /beɪʒ/ *adjective, noun*
a pale brown color: *a beige sweater*

**be·ing**[1] /ˈbi-ɪŋ/ *verb*
the present participle of BE

**being**[2] *noun*
**1** a living thing: *The movie is about strange beings from outer space.*
**2 come into being** (*formal*) = to start to exist: *No one is sure exactly when life on Earth first came into being.*

**be·lief** /bəˈlif/ *noun*
a strong feeling that something is definitely true or right: *It is important to respect other people's religious beliefs.* | *We have a strong belief in the importance of education.*
→ see Thesaurus box at **religion**

**be·lieve** /bəˈliv/ *verb*
**1** to feel sure that something is true or that someone is telling the truth: *She says she's eighteen but I don't believe her. She only looks fifteen.*
**2** to feel sure that something or someone exists: *Do you believe in God?*
**3** to feel sure that something is good or right: *We believe in freedom of speech, which allows everyone to express an opinion.*
**4** to think that something is true, although you are not completely sure: *I believe she will be back on Monday, but I could be wrong.*
—**believer** *noun* someone who believes in God or believes in something
→ see Thesaurus box at **think**

**bell**

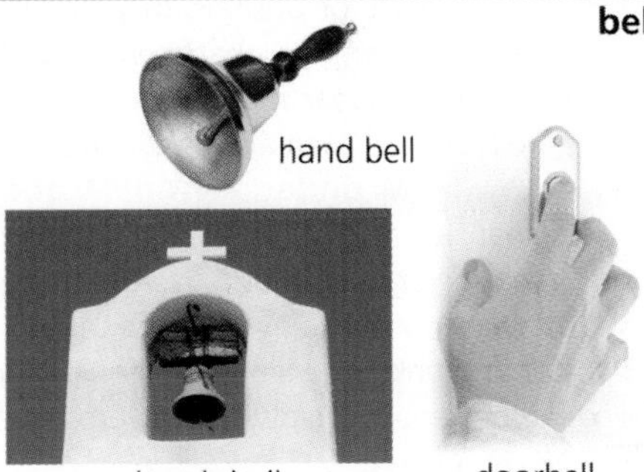


**bell** /bel/ *noun*
**1** a metal object that makes a ringing sound when you hit it or shake it: *The church bells were ringing.*
**2** a piece of electrical equipment that makes a ringing sound: *Someone's ringing the door bell – can you see who it is?*

**bel·ly** /ˈbeli/ *noun* (plural **bellies**) (*informal*)
your stomach: *He had a big belly that hung over his belt.*

**ˈbelly ˌbutton** *noun* (*informal*)
the small hollow place in the middle of your stomach **SYNONYM: navel**

**be·long** /bɪˈlɔŋ/ *verb*
if something belongs somewhere, that is where it is usually kept: *The plates don't belong in this cupboard. They should be over there.*
**PHRASAL VERB**
**belong to**
**1 belong to someone** = if something belongs to you, you own it: *Who does this*

*book belong to? Is it yours, Katie?*
**2 belong to something** = to be a member of a group or organization: *She belongs to the Baptist church on Sixth Street.*

**be·long·ings** /bɪˈlɔŋɪŋz/ *plural noun*
the things that you own, especially the ones you carry with you, for example coats, pens, or books: *Remember to take all your personal belongings with you when you leave the plane.*
→ see Thesaurus box at **property**

**be·loved** /bɪˈlʌvɪd/ *adjective*
used about someone whom you love very much: *His beloved wife had died many years earlier.*

**be·low** /bɪˈloʊ/ *adverb, preposition*
**1** in a lower place or position than someone or something else: *Her apartment is below mine, so she can hear me walking around.* | *Read the story and then answer the questions below.* **SYNONYM: under**; **ANTONYM: above**
**2** less than a particular number or amount: *It's ten degrees below zero outside!* **ANTONYM: above**
**3** lower in rank: *A manager should know what the people below them are doing.* **ANTONYM: above**

**belt** /elt/ *noun*
**1** a band of leather or cloth that you wear around your waist and that holds up your pants: *a brown leather belt* | *He buckled his belt.* → see picture on page **A6**
**2** a circular band of material that moves parts of a machine, and is often made of rubber: *The fan belt in a car's engine makes the fan work.*

**bench** /bentʃ/ *noun*
a long seat for two or more people, often one that does not have a back: *The players wait on the bench, hoping they'll get a chance to go on court.*

**bend¹** /bend/ *verb* (**bent** /bent/)
**1** to move the top part of your body and your head down: *He bent down to stroke the cat.*
**2** to move a part of your body so that it is not straight: *Bend your knees, but keep your back straight.*
**3** to push or press something so that it is no longer flat or straight: *He bent his bike wheel when he ran into the fence.*
**4** if a road bends, it changes direction: *Go slowly – the road suddenly bends to the right here.*

**bend²** *noun*
a curve in something such as a road or river: *There was a sharp bend in the road and we had to slow down.*

**be·neath** /bɪˈniθ/ *adverb, preposition*
under or below something: *She could feel the warm sand beneath her feet.* **SYNONYM: under**

**ben·e·fi·cial** Ac /ˌbenəˈfɪʃəl/ *adjective*
if something is beneficial, it has a good or helpful effect: *More exercise will be beneficial for your health.*

**ben·e·fit¹** Ac /ˈbenəfɪt/ *noun*
**1** an advantage or useful thing that you get from something: *One of the benefits of the Internet is that we can get information very quickly.*
**2** money or insurance that you get from the government or the company you work for: *The company provides medical benefits for all its workers.*
[**ORIGIN:** 1300-1400 From the Latin phrase *bene facere*, which means "to do a good action."]

| **WORD FAMILY: benefit** |
| --- |
| **benefit** *noun* \| **benefit** *verb* \| **beneficial** *adjective* |

**benefit²** Ac *verb* (**benefitted** *or* **benefited**, **benefitting** *or* **benefiting**)
if you benefit from something or if it benefits you, it helps you: *You will benefit from a college education because it should help you get a better job.*

**bent¹** /bent/ *verb*
the past tense and past participle of BEND

**bent**

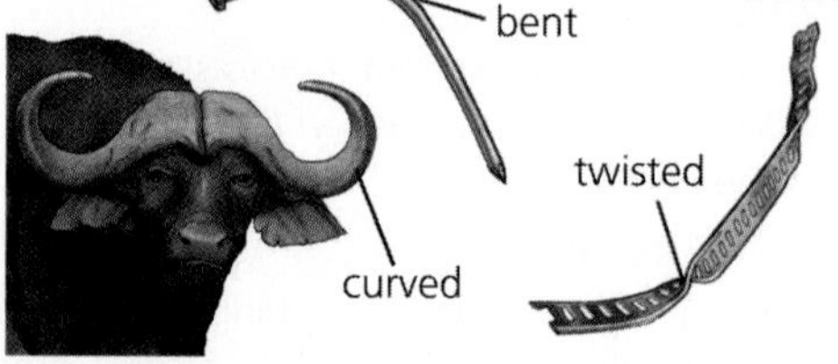


**bent²** *adjective*
not straight – use this about things that are usually straight: *The rails at the side of the*

*road are bent because a car ran into them.* | *a bent nail*

**ber·ry** /ˈberi/ *noun* (plural **berries**)
a type of small soft fruit with very small seeds: *Berries such as strawberries and blackberries are very good for you.*

**ber·serk** /bɚˈsɚk/ *adjective*
**go berserk** (*informal*) = to suddenly become very angry or violent: *The man went berserk and started hitting her.*
[ORIGIN: 1800-1900 From the Norse word *berserkr*, which means "wild fighter." *Berserkr* comes from *björn* and *serkr*, meaning "bear" and "shirt," because these fighters wore bear skins.]

**be·side** /bɪˈsaɪd/ *preposition*
**1** next to or very close to someone or something: *He sat down beside her and started talking to her.*
**2** used when you are comparing two people or things: *So many bad things had happened to her that my problems seemed small beside hers.*
**3 be beside the point** = to not be important compared to something else: *"He's very good-looking." "That's beside the point – we need someone who can do the job!"*

**be·sides** /bɪˈsaɪdz/ *preposition, adverb*
**1** in addition to something or someone: *Besides going to college, she works 15 hours a week.* | *Who's going to be there besides David and me?*
**2** (*informal*) used when giving another reason: *It doesn't take long to walk to my house. Besides, I need the exercise.*

**best¹** /best/ *adjective*
better than anyone or anything else: *He's the best player on the team – no one else is as good.* | *This is the best ice cream I've ever eaten.* | *I like Shannon – she's my best friend.* **ANTONYM: worst**

**best²** *adverb*
**1** in a way that is better than any other: *We won the game because our team played best.* | *I think this shampoo works best.*
**2 like someone or something best** = to like someone or something more than anyone else or anything else: *Which song do you like best?*

**best³** *noun*
**1 the best** = someone or something that is better than all the others: *The teacher said that my essay was the best.* | *There are a lot of good players on the team, but he is the best.*
**2 do your best** = to try as hard as you can to do something: *I did my best on the test, but I don't know if I passed.*
**3 at best** = the most that you can expect: *At best, he will get a C on the test.*

**ˌbest ˈman** *noun*
a male friend who stands next to the man who is getting married during the wedding

**bet¹** /bet/ *verb* (**bet**, **betting**)
**1** to try to win money by guessing who will win a race, game, or competition: *He bet on a horse race, but the horse came last so he lost his money.* **SYNONYM: gamble**
**2 I bet ...** (*informal*) = used when saying that you think something is true or likely to happen: *I bet he'll be late – he always is.*
**3 You bet!** (*informal*) = used in order to emphasize that you really mean "yes" when someone asks you a question: *"Is the prize really $20,000?" "You bet it is!"*

**bet²** *noun*
if you make or place a bet, you try to win money by guessing who will win a race, game, or competition: *He made a bet on the winner of the Super Bowl.*

**be·tray** /bɪˈtreɪ/ *verb*
**1** to not be loyal to your country or group in a way that will harm it: *He betrayed his country by giving secret information to the enemy.*
**2** to behave dishonestly toward someone who trusts you or loves you: *Her husband betrayed her by having an affair with another woman.*

**bet·ter¹** /ˈbetɚ/ *adjective*
**1** more useful, skilled, or of a higher quality than someone or something else: *His computer is much better than mine, but it cost a lot more too.* | *She's better at tennis than I am, so she always wins.* | *Your English is getting better and you can move to a higher class.* **ANTONYM: worse**
**2** less sick than before: *He had a sore throat yesterday, but he is better today.* **ANTONYM: worse**
→ see Thesaurus box at **healthy**

B

**better²** *adverb*
**1** in a way that is more skillful than someone or something else: *My sister can sing much better than me.*
**2 like someone or something better** = to like someone or something more than someone or something else: *I like the blue shirt better, but the green one's okay too.*
**3 had better do something** = used when saying that someone should do something: *You'd better go home now – your mom is probably worried.*
**4 be better off** = to have more money now than you had before: *Dad got a job that paid more so we were much better off.*

**be·tween** /bɪˈtwin/ *preposition, adverb*
**1** with one person or thing on each side: *At lunch, I was sitting between Ethan and Beth.*

> **USAGE: between, among**
>
> **Between** and **among** are both used to talk about where someone or something is.
>
> Use **between** when there is one person or thing on each side of someone or something: *I sat between Alex and Sarah.*
>
> Use **among** when someone or something is surrounded by people or things: *Denise was among a group of her friends.*

**2** after one time, age, or event and before another: *The library is open between 9 and 5 o'clock.* | *The children are between 7 and 13.*
**3** used to show a range of amounts, from the smallest amount to the largest amount: *There were between 30 and 40 people at the party.*
**4** used when you have two choices and you must choose one of them: *She had to choose between studying Spanish or French.*

**bev·er·age** /ˈbevərɪdʒ/ *noun (formal)*
a drink: *Beverages such as soft drinks are often full of sugar.*
[**ORIGIN:** 1300-1400 From the old French word *beivre*, which means "to drink."]

**be·ware** /bɪˈwer/ *verb*
used when you are warning someone to be careful about something: *The sign on the gate said, "Beware of the dog!"*
[**ORIGIN:** 1200-1300 From "be" and the old English word *ware*, which means "careful."]

**be·wil·dered** /bɪˈwɪldəd/ *adjective*
very confused and not sure what to do or think: *It was her first time in the city, and she felt lost and bewildered.*
—**bewildering** *adjective* making you feel confused and not sure what to do or think
[**ORIGIN:** 1600-1700 From the old English word *wilder*, which means "to lead the wrong way or confuse."]

**be·yond** /bɪˈyɑnd/ *preposition, adverb*
**1** on the other side of something: *Beyond the river, I could see the woods.*
**2** later than a time or date: *We need to plan beyond the end of this year.*
**3** more than an amount, level, or limit: *The price was beyond the amount that they could afford.*
**4 be beyond someone** = to be too difficult for someone to understand: *He tried to explain the math problem, but it was beyond me.*

**bi·as** /ˈbaɪəs/ *noun*
an unfair opinion about a person, group, or idea, that makes you treat them differently: *If they will not hire someone who is fat, they are showing a bias against fat people.*
—**bias** *verb* to influence someone or something in an unfair way: *I don't want to bias you by telling you my opinion of his work.*
—**biased** *adjective* thinking that one person, group, or idea is better than another, and treating them differently: *She was biased toward her own son, and didn't believe what I said.*

> **WORD FAMILY: bias**
>
> **bias** *noun* | **bias** *verb* | **biased** *adjective* | **unbiased** *adjective*

**bib** /bɪb/ *noun*
a piece of cloth or plastic that you put around a baby's neck to stop food from getting on his or her clothes

**Bi·ble** /ˈbaɪbəl/ *noun*
**the Bible** = the holy book of the Christian religion. Some parts of the Bible are also a holy book in the Jewish religion: *Genesis is the first book of the Bible.*
—**biblical** *adjective* relating to the Bible
[**ORIGIN:** 1300-1400 From the Greek word *biblia*, which means "books."]

**bib·li·og·ra·phy** /ˌbɪbliˈɑgrəfi/ *noun* (plural **bibliographies**)
a list of books on a subject: *At the end of the book, there's a bibliography that lists more books about the Civil War.*

**bi·cy·cle** /ˈbaɪsɪkəl/ *noun*
a vehicle with two wheels that you ride by pushing the PEDALs with your feet: *She usually rides her bicycle to school.* **SYNONYM: bike**
[**ORIGIN:** 1800-1900 From the Latin word *bi-*, which means "two," and the Greek word *kuklos*, which means "wheel."]

**bid¹** /bɪd/ *noun*
**1** an offer to pay a price for something that several people want to buy: *The painting was sold to the man who made the highest bid.*
**2** an offer to do work for a particular price. Someone offers a bid when several people or companies want to do the work: *Several companies were asked to put in a bid to build the city's new library.*
**3** an attempt to achieve or gain something: *His first bid to reach the top of the mountain was not successful.*

**bid²** *verb* (**bid**, **bidding**)
**1** to offer to pay a price for something that several people want to buy: *He bid $150,000 for the painting, but someone bid even higher.*
**2** to offer to do work for someone for a particular price: *Three companies bid for the contract to clean the offices.*
—**bidder** *noun* someone who makes a bid: *At an auction, houses sell to the highest bidder.*

**big** /bɪg/ *adjective* (**bigger**, **biggest**)
**1** large: *She lives in a big house with six bedrooms.* **ANTONYM: small**

**THESAURUS: big**

**large** big or bigger than usual in size or amount: *New York is the largest city in America.* | *Large numbers of people watched the game on TV.*

**huge** very big: *He ate a huge piece of pie.* | *They live in a huge house with eight bedrooms.*

**enormous** very big: *His car is enormous.* | *The park has several enormous trees.*

**gigantic** extremely tall: *The Empire State Building is gigantic.* | *a gigantic wave*

**Big** and **large** mean the same thing, but **large** is slightly more formal: *That's a big piece of cake!* | *It's the largest building in Chicago.*

Use **large**, not **big**, to describe amounts: *Kelly gets large amounts of homework.*

Use **big**, not **large**, to describe something that is important: *This is a big opportunity for me.*

**bicycle**

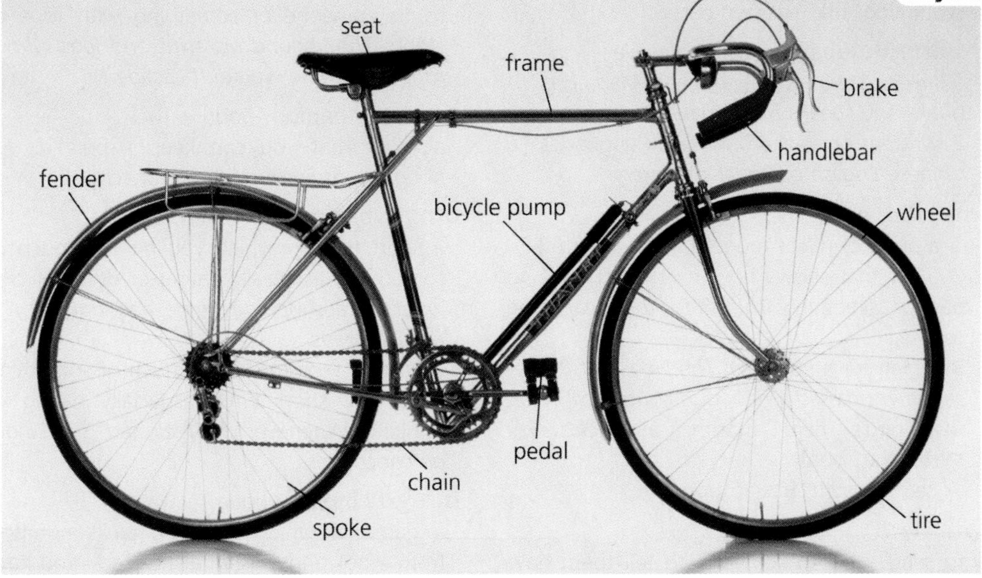

2 important or serious: *They didn't have enough money, which was a big problem.* | *I quit school, and it was the biggest mistake of my life.* **ANTONYM: small**

3 successful or popular: *His last movie was a big hit and earned millions of dollars.*

**ˌbig-ˈheaded** *adjective* (*informal*)
someone who is big-headed thinks that they are better than other people: *Don't keep telling him he's smart – he'll get big-headed.*
→ see Thesaurus box at **proud**

**big·ot** /ˈbɪgət/ *noun*
someone who thinks that people who belong to a different race, religion, or political group are not as good as his or her own group: *I don't like him – he's a racist bigot who thinks that white people are better than other people.*
—**bigoted** *adjective* someone who is bigoted is a bigot: *My father is very bigoted about people from other countries.*
—**bigotry** *noun* behavior that is typical of a bigot

**bike** /baɪk/ *noun* (*informal*)
1 a bicycle: *The kids were riding their bikes around the neighborhood.*
2 a MOTORCYCLE
—**biker** *noun* someone who rides a bike or a MOTORCYCLE

**bi·ki·ni** /bɪˈkini/ *noun*
a piece of clothing that women wear for swimming, that has two parts

**bi·lin·gual** /baɪˈlɪŋgwəl/ *adjective*
1 able to speak two languages: *Maria is bilingual – she speaks both Spanish and English.*
2 written or spoken in two languages: *a Chinese-English bilingual dictionary*

**bill¹** /bɪl/ *noun*
1 a piece of paper money: *a ten-dollar bill*
2 a list that shows how much you have to pay for something: *The bill for the meal came to $42.*
3 a plan for a new law: *The House of Representatives passed a new gun-control bill.*
4 a bird's hard mouth: *a duck's bill* **SYNONYM: beak**
→ see Thesaurus box at **money**

**bill²** *verb*
to send a bill to someone to tell them how much money they must pay: *The company will bill them for the repairs later.*

**bill·board** /ˈbɪlbɔrd/ *noun*
a big sign next to a road, used for advertising something
→ see Thesaurus box at **advertisement**

**bil·lion** /ˈbɪlyən/ *number*
1 1,000,000,000: *$7 billion*

**GRAMMAR: billion, billions**

Use the singular form **billion** after a number: *The company owes eight billion dollars.*

Use the plural form **billions** before "of": *There are billions of stars in the universe.*

2 (*also* **billions**) (*informal*) a very large number of people or things: *There were billions of people at the baseball game last night.*
—**billionth** *number* 1,000,000,000th or 1/1,000,000,000

**ˌBill of ˈRights, the** *noun*
a written statement of the most important rights that citizens of the U.S. have. It is part of the U.S. Constitution: *The Bill of Rights gives people the freedom to follow whatever religion they choose.*

**bin** /bɪn/ *noun*
a large container for storing things: *Put the bottles in the recycling bin.*

**bind** /baɪnd/ *verb* (**bound** /baʊnd/)
to tie someone or something with rope or string: *They bound his arms and legs with a rope so that he wouldn't escape.*

**bind·er** /ˈbaɪndɚ/ *noun*
a cover that you can keep papers in: *He bought a three-ring binder for school.*

**binge** /bɪndʒ/ *noun* (*informal*)
a short time in which you do too much of something, especially eating or drinking: *She went on a shopping binge and bought five pairs of jeans.*
—**binge** *verb* to do too much of something in a very short time, especially eating or drinking: *Whenever she feels sad, she binges on chocolate.*

**bin·go** /ˈbɪŋgoʊ/ *noun*
a game in which someone picks numbers from a box and says what they are. You have

a paper with numbers on it, and if you have the right numbers in a line, you win.

**bin·oc·u·lars** /bɪˈnɑkyələ˞z/ *plural noun*
an object that you look through with both eyes to see things that are far away: *Use a pair of binoculars to see the birds feeding their babies in the nest.*
[ORIGIN: 1800-1900 From the Latin words *bini* and *oculus*, which mean "two" and "eye."]

**binoculars**

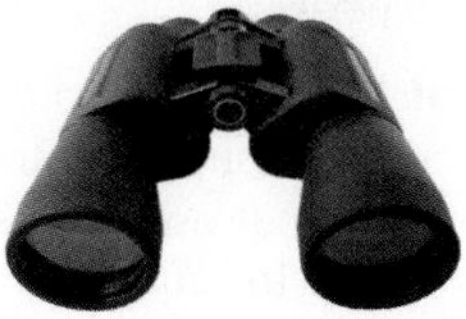

**bi·o·de·grad·a·ble** /ˌbaɪoʊdɪˈgreɪdəbəl/ *adjective*
if something is biodegradable, when you put it into the ground it is destroyed by natural processes in a way that does not harm the environment: *Paper is biodegradable, but plastic isn't.* ANTONYM: **non-biodegradable**

**bi·og·ra·phy** /baɪˈɑgrəfi/ *noun* (plural **biographies**)
a book about a person's life: *He wrote a biography of Abraham Lincoln.*
—**biographer** *noun* someone who writes a book about a person's life
[ORIGIN: 1600-1700 From the Greek words *bios* and *graphein*, which mean "life" and "to write."]

**bi·ol·o·gy** /baɪˈɑlədʒi/ *noun*
the scientific study of living things: *We're learning about cells in biology.*
—**biologist** *noun* someone whose job involves studying biology
—**biological** *adjective* relating to biology or living things
[ORIGIN: 1800-1900 From the Greek words *bios* and *-logia*, which mean "life" and "study."]

**bi·ome** /ˈbaɪoʊm/ *noun*
all the plants and animals that live in an area which has its own type of weather and environment. A forest or an ocean can be a biome: *Each biome is home to many different animals and plants.*

**birch** /bə˞tʃ/ *noun*
a tree with smooth BARK like paper, or the wood of this tree

**bird** /bə˞d/ *noun*
an animal with wings and feathers. Most birds can fly and female birds produce eggs: *In the spring, birds start to build nests.*
[ORIGIN: From the old English word *bridd.*]

**bird·ie** /ˈbə˞di/ *noun*
the small object that you hit across the net in a game of BADMINTON

**birth** /bə˞θ/ *noun*
**1 give birth** = if a woman gives birth, she produces a baby from her body: *Sue gave birth to a healthy baby girl on Tuesday.*
**2** the time when a baby comes out of its mother's body: *The baby weighed seven pounds at birth.*
**3** the nationality or the social position that you have because of the country or the family you come from: *Her father was Mexican by birth but later became a U.S. citizen.*
**4 the birth of something** = the time when something new starts: *The birth of jazz was in New Orleans in the nineteenth century.*

**ˈbirth cerˌtificate** *noun*
an official document that shows when and where you were born

**ˈbirth conˌtrol** *noun*
ways of stopping a woman from becoming PREGNANT SYNONYM: **contraception**

**birth·day** /ˈbə˞θdeɪ/ *noun*
the date of the day when you were born: *My birthday is April 10. | Happy Birthday! How old are you today? | I got ten birthday cards.*

**birth·place** /ˈbə˞θpleɪs/ *noun*
the place where someone was born: *Westmoreland County, Virginia, is the birthplace of George Washington.*

**bis·cuit** /ˈbɪskɪt/ *noun*
a type of bread that you bake in small round shapes

**bi·sect** /ˈbaɪsekt/ *verb* (*formal*)
to divide something into two parts, especially two parts that are the same size: *The city is bisected by a freeway.*

**bish·op** /ˈbɪʃəp/ *noun*
a Christian priest with a high rank who is in charge of all the churches and priests in a large area

**bi·son** /ˈbaɪsən/ *noun* (plural **bison** *or* **bisons**)
a North American wild animal that looks like a large cow with a big head. It has thick brown hair on its neck and shoulders.

B

**bit¹** /bɪt/ *noun*
**1** a small piece or amount of something: *The floor was covered with bits of broken glass.*
**2 a (little) bit** = slightly: *I was a little bit tired after the game.*
**3 quite a bit** = a large amount: *He got quite a bit of help from his brother on the project.*
**4** the smallest unit of information that a computer uses
**5** a metal bar that you put inside a horse's mouth. The bit is attached to the REINS, so that you can make the horse stop or turn.
[**ORIGIN:** From the old English word *bita*, which means "piece that has been bitten off."]

**bit²** *verb*
the past tense of BITE

**bite¹** /baɪt/ *verb* (**bit** /bɪt/, **bitten** /ˈbɪtn/, **biting**)
**1** to cut or crush something with your teeth: *The dog bit him when he tried to pet it.* | *Jim bit into the apple.*
**2** if an insect bites you, it hurts you by making a small hole in your skin: *A mosquito bit me and it is so itchy.*

**bite²** *noun*
**1** if you take a bite of something, you use your teeth to cut a small piece from it: *He took a bite of the cake.*
**2** a wound made when an animal or insect bites you: *a mosquito bite*
**3 a bite (to eat)** (*informal*) = a quick meal: *We can grab a bite before we leave.*

**bit·ten** /ˈbɪtn/ *verb*
the past participle of BITE

**bit·ter** /ˈbɪtɚ/ *adjective*
**1** angry for a long time because you feel something bad or unfair has happened to you: *She felt very bitter about losing her job.*
**2** having a strong taste that is not sweet, like strong coffee without sugar: *The apple tasted bitter, so I threw it out.*
**3** making you feel very unhappy and upset: *Losing the game was a bitter disappointment.*
**4** bitter weather is extremely cold: *a bitter wind*
—**bitterly** *adverb* in a way that shows you are very angry, upset, or unhappy: *Fans were bitterly disappointed by the team's loss.*
—**bitterness** *noun* a bitter quality
→ see Thesaurus box at **taste¹**

**bi·week·ly** /baɪˈwikli/ *adjective, adverb*
happening or done every two weeks: *a biweekly meeting* | *The magazine is published biweekly.*

**bi·zarre** /bɪˈzɑr/ *adjective*
very unusual and strange: *He wore a bizarre green hat with stuff sticking out all over it.*
→ see Thesaurus box at **strange**

**black¹** /blæk/ *adjective*
**1** having a color that is darker than every other color, like the sky at night: *He was wearing a black suit and a white shirt.*
**2** having dark brown skin – used about people whose families originally came from Africa: *In our school, about 50% of the kids are black.*
—**blackness** *noun* the quality of being black or very dark

**black²** *noun*
**1** the darkest color, like the color of the sky at night: *She was wearing black.*
**2 blacks** (*also* **Blacks**) = people with dark brown skin whose families originally came from Africa

**black·ber·ry** /ˈblækˌberi/ *noun* (plural **blackberries**)
a small sweet dark purple fruit that grows on a bush → see picture on page **A13**

**black·bird** /ˈblækbɚd/ *noun*
a common bird in the U.S. and Europe. The male blackbird is completely black.

**black·board** /ˈblækˌbɔrd/ *noun*
a dark smooth board that you write on with CHALK: *The teacher wrote the date on the blackboard.*

**black·mail** /ˈblækmeɪl/ *noun*
the crime of trying to make someone do what you want by threatening to tell that person's secrets: *"Give me the money, or I'll tell your wife what you have done." "This is blackmail!"*
—**blackmail** *verb* to use blackmail: *He tried to blackmail her by threatening to tell the police that she had stolen the jewelry.*
—**blackmailer** *noun* someone who uses blackmail

**ˌblack ˈmarket** *noun*
the system in which people buy and sell

things illegally: *If thieves steal famous paintings, the only way they can sell them is on the black market.*

**black·out** /ˈblækaʊt/ *noun*
**1** a time when electricity stops reaching an area, so that all the lights and other equipment stop working: *There was a blackout last night so we couldn't watch TV.*
**2** if you have a blackout, you are unconscious for a short time because you are sick or have hit your head: *Since the accident, Sam has suffered from blackouts, and he can't remember later what happened.*

**black·smith** /ˈblæksmɪθ/ *noun*
someone who makes HORSESHOEs and other things made of iron

**black·top** /ˈblæktɑp/ *noun*
a black substance used for making the surface of roads, PLAYGROUNDs, and PARKING LOTs: *The children play on the blacktop at recess.*

**blad·der** /ˈblædɚ/ *noun*
the part of your body that holds URINE before it leaves your body → see picture on page A2

**blade** /bleɪd/ *noun*
**1** the flat cutting part of a knife, tool, or weapon: *The blade on this knife is very sharp.*
**2** one piece of grass: *a blade of grass*

**blame¹** /bleɪm/ *verb*
**1** if you blame someone, you say or think that he or she is responsible for something bad that has happened: *The fans blamed the coach for the team's defeat.* | *He's blaming all his problems on me.*
**2 I don't blame you/her/them, etc.** = you say this when you think that what someone does or thinks is reasonable: *"She got really mad at him for being so late again." "I don't blame her!"*

**blame²** *noun*
if you get the blame for something bad that has happened, other people say you are responsible for it: *I always get the blame when things go wrong.* | *Don't put the blame on me if this is the wrong road – you have the map.*

**bland** /blænd/ *adjective*
**1** bland food has very little taste: *I thought the food would be spicy, but it was bland and flavorless.*
**2** without any interesting or exciting qualities: *The group's latest CD is pretty bland; all the songs sound the same.*
→ see Thesaurus box at **taste¹**

**blank¹** /blæŋk/ *adjective*
**1** a blank sheet of paper or a blank space has nothing written on it: *She started writing on a blank page.* | *Can you fill in the blank spaces in the story below?*
**2** a blank DISK has nothing recorded on it: *Do we have any blank CDs? I want to download some music.*
**3 go blank** = if your mind goes blank, you suddenly cannot remember something: *I was so nervous that my mind went blank when I stood up to speak.*
**4** a blank expression or look shows no emotion, understanding, or interest: *I said hello, but she just gave me a blank look as if she did not know me.*
—**blankly** *adverb* if you look at someone or something blankly, you do not show any emotion, understanding, or interest: *I asked the boy where his mother was, but he stared at me blankly.*
[**ORIGIN:** 1200-1300 From the French word *blanc*, which means "white." A blank sheet of paper is plain white.]

**blank²** *noun*
an empty space on a piece of paper, where you must write a word or letter: *Answer the test questions by filling in the blanks.*

**blan·ket** /ˈblæŋkɪt/ *noun*
**1** a thick cover that keeps you warm in bed: *I put another blanket on the bed because I was cold.* → see picture on page A10
**2 a blanket of fog/cloud/snow** = a thick layer of FOG, cloud, or snow: *The ground was covered in a thick blanket of snow.*
[**ORIGIN:** 1300-1400 From the old French word *blankete*, which means "white cloth," from *blanc*, meaning "white."]

**blare** /bler/ *verb*
to make a very loud unpleasant noise: *Music was blaring from the car radio and everyone nearby could hear it.*

**blast¹** /blæst/ *noun*
**1** an explosion: *The blast destroyed several buildings.*
**2** a sudden strong movement of hot or cold air: *I opened the oven door and a blast of hot air came out.*

B

**blast²** *verb*
**1** to break something into pieces using bombs or explosions: *They blasted through solid rock to make the tunnel.*
**2** if music or another sound blasts, it makes a very loud noise: *Music was blasting from two huge speakers, and it hurt my ears.*
**PHRASAL VERB**
**blast off**
if a spacecraft blasts off, it leaves the ground: *Everyone was waiting to see the rocket blast off.*

**bla·tant** /ˈbleɪtənt/ *adjective*
very easy to notice, and shocking: *She told a blatant lie that we all knew wasn't true.* **SYNONYM: obvious**

**blaze¹** /bleɪz/ *verb*
to burn or shine very brightly and strongly: *A fire was blazing in the room.*
[**ORIGIN:** From the old English word *blæse*, which means "torch."]

**blaze²** *noun*
**1** a big fire that spreads and is difficult to control: *The blaze destroyed several buildings and caused thousands of dollars of damage.*
**2** a very bright light or color: *They walked out of the house into a blaze of sunshine.*
→ see Thesaurus box at **fire¹**

**bleach** /blitʃ/ *noun*
a strong chemical used to make clothes white, or to kill GERMs
—**bleach** *verb* to make something lighter in color: *Her hair isn't naturally blonde – she bleaches it.*

**bleach·ers** /ˈblitʃɚz/ *plural noun*
rows of long flat seats where people sit to watch sports. Each row is higher than the row in front of it.

**bleak** /blik/ *adjective*
**1** seeming bad and without anything to make you feel happy or hopeful: *She had no job, and her future seemed bleak.* **ANTONYM: bright**
**2** a bleak day is cold, gray, and often cold: *a bleak day in the middle of winter* **ANTONYM: bright**

**blear·y** /ˈblɪri/ *adjective*
unable to see clearly because you are tired or have been crying: *My eyes were bleary from lack of sleep.*

**bleed** /blid/ *verb* (**bled** /bled/)

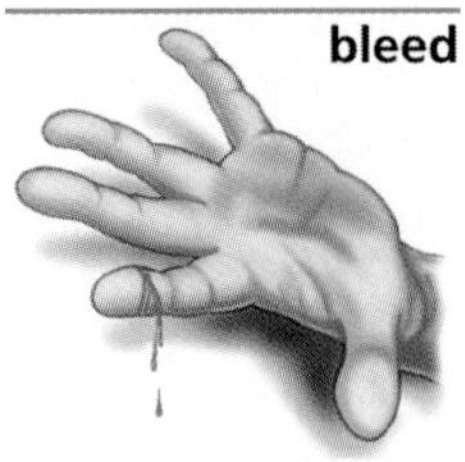


**1** if part of your body bleeds, blood comes out of it: *His finger was bleeding from where he'd cut it on some glass.*
**2** if a color bleeds when it gets wet, it spreads from where it is onto other things: *Wash brightly colored clothes separately, in case the colors bleed.*
[**ORIGIN:** From the old English word *bledan*, from *blod*, which means "blood."]

**WORD FAMILY: bleed**
**bleed** *verb* | **blood** *noun* | **bloody** *adjective*

**blem·ish** /ˈblemɪʃ/ *noun*
a small mark on something or someone, that makes it not look as nice: *The makeup is good for covering up blemishes on your skin.*
→ see Thesaurus box at **mark²**

**blend¹** /blend/ *verb*
to mix things together, especially foods: *Blend the milk and the eggs together until they are completely mixed.*
→ see Thesaurus box at **mix¹**

**blend²** *noun*
a mixture of two or more things or people: *The city has an interesting blend of old and new buildings.*

**blend·er** /ˈblendɚ/ *noun*
a small electric machine that you use to mix liquids or foods together

**bless** /bles/ *verb*
**1** **Bless you!** = you say this when someone SNEEZEs
**2** if God blesses someone, He helps and protects that person: *May God bless you and keep you safe.*
**3** to make something holy: *The priest blessed the bread and the wine.*

**bless·ing** /ˈblesɪŋ/ *noun*
**1** something good that you feel happy about because it makes a situation better: *The cool breeze was a blessing on such a hot day.*
**2** someone's approval and good wishes for the future: *She got married with her parents' blessing – they were very happy for her.*

3 protection and help from God, or a prayer asking for this: *They asked for God's blessing on their child.*

**blew** /blu/ *verb*
the past tense of BLOW

**blimp** /blɪmp/ *noun*
an aircraft without wings that is filled with gas and looks like a very large BALLOON

**blind¹** /blaɪnd/ *adjective*
not able to see: *A dog was leading a blind man across the street. | She wasn't born blind, she went blind when she was two.*
—**blindness** *noun* the state of being blind

**blind²** *verb*
to make someone unable to see, sometimes only for a short time: *He was blinded by the bright lights of the car for a few seconds.*

**blind³** *noun*
a piece of material that you pull down to cover a window: *Can I close the blinds? The sun is so bright.* → see picture on page **A11**

**blind·fold** /ˈblaɪndfoʊld/ *noun*
a piece of cloth that is used to cover someone's eyes so that she or he cannot see
—**blindfold** *verb* to cover someone's eyes with a blindfold

**blink** /blɪŋk/ *verb*
1 to open and close your eyes very quickly: *The dog leaped up and I blinked in surprise.*
2 if a light blinks, it quickly goes on and off: *Why does this light on my computer keep blinking?*

**blink·er** /ˈblɪŋkɚ/ *noun*
a light on a car that goes on and off to show that the car is turning left or right → see picture on page **A28**

**bliss** /blɪs/ *noun*
perfect happiness: *I love swimming in the ocean on a hot day – it's bliss.*
—**blissful** *adjective* very happy
—**blissfully** *adverb* in a very happy way

**blis·ter** /ˈblɪstɚ/ *noun*
a sore area of skin that is filled with liquid. Blisters are caused by something rubbing or burning your skin: *New shoes always give me blisters.*

**bliz·zard** /ˈblɪzɚd/ *noun*
a very bad storm with a lot of snow and wind
→ see Thesaurus box at **snow¹**, **wind¹**

**bloat·ed** /ˈbloʊtɪd/ *adjective*
a body or body part that is bloated is too full of air or liquid: *The bloated body of a dead fish lay on the beach.*

**blob** /blɑb/ *noun*
a small drop of a thick liquid such as paint or ice cream: *Don't use too much glue – you only need a little blob.*

**block¹** /blɑk/ *noun*
1 a square area of buildings in a city, with streets on all four sides: *Let's take the dog for a walk around the block before dinner.*
2 the distance from one street to another in a city: *If you go straight on for two or three blocks, you'll see the park.*
3 a solid piece of something hard, for example wood, stone, or ice. Blocks are usually square or RECTANGULAR: *The statue was made using a huge block of stone.*
4 a small piece of wood or plastic that children build things with. Blocks are usually shaped like cubes: *My little sister was building a tower with her blocks.*
5 a group of things of the same kind that you consider as a single unit: *We bought a block of tickets for the concert so that we could all sit together.*

**block²** *verb*
1 to stop people or vehicles from moving through or along something: *There was a long line of cars because a big truck was blocking the road.*
2 **block someone's view** = if something blocks your view, it is in front of you and you cannot see around or over it: *A tall man in front of me was blocking my view of the movie screen.*
3 to stop something from happening, developing, or succeeding: *People in the neighborhood are trying to block the plan to build a new road.*

**block·age** /ˈblɑkɪdʒ/ *noun*
something that stops other things from moving through a pipe or tube: *There's a blockage in the pipe under the sink – the water's not going down.*

**blog** /blɑg/ *noun*
a WEB page in which you write about your opinions and what you have been doing: *He writes a blog about movies and books that he likes.*
—**blogger** *noun* someone who writes a blog

**blond** (*also* **blonde**) /blɑnd/ *adjective*
blond hair is light yellow in color: *She had long blond hair.*
—**blonde** *noun* a woman who has pale yellow hair

**blood** /blʌd/ *noun*
the red liquid in your body, that comes out if you cut yourself: *After the accident, her face was covered in blood.*

**ˈblood ˌpressure** *noun*
the force with which blood moves around your body. If your blood pressure is high, it can make you have a heart attack: *My father has high blood pressure, so he takes medicine every day.*

**blood·shed** /ˈblʌdʃed/ *noun*
the killing of people in fighting or a war: *The agreement will bring an end to the bloodshed.*

**blood·stream** /ˈblʌdstrim/ *noun*
blood that is flowing around the body: *Sugar from food that you eat is quickly absorbed into the bloodstream.*

**blood·thirst·y** /ˈblʌdˌθɚsti/ *adjective*
enjoying killing and violence: *He was a bloodthirsty leader and the people of the country were afraid of him.*

**ˈblood ˌvessel** *noun*
one of the tubes that blood flows through in your body

**blood·y** /ˈblʌdi/ *adjective*
**1** covered in blood: *He had a bloody nose because someone hit him.*
**2** with a lot of killing and violence: *The battle was long and bloody.*

**bloom¹** /blu:m/ *verb*
if a plant blooms, its flowers open: *The spring flowers were blooming in the park.*

**bloom²** *noun*
**1** **be in bloom** = if a plant is in bloom, its flowers are open: *The sunflowers are in bloom at this time of year.*
**2** a flower: *The rose has beautiful pink blooms.* **SYNONYM: blossom**

**blos·som¹** /ˈblɑsəm/ *noun*
a flower on a tree or bush: *In April, the cherry trees are covered in blossoms.*

**blossom²** *verb*
if a tree or a bush blossoms, it produces flowers: *The apple trees are already starting to blossom.*

**blot¹** /blɑt/ *verb* (**blotted**, **blotting**)
**PHRASAL VERB**
**blot something out**
**1** to cover or hide something completely: *Dark clouds blotted out the sun.*
**2** to forget something, often deliberately: *I tried to blot out the memory of that awful night.*

**blot²** *noun*
a mark or spot that spoils something or makes it dirty: *The letter was covered in ink blots.*

**blouse** /blaʊs/ *noun*
a shirt for a woman or girl: *She is wearing a white blouse and a blue skirt.* → see picture on page **A6**

**blow¹** /bloʊ/ *verb* (**blew** /blu/, **blown** /bloʊn/)
**1** if the wind blows, it makes the air move: *A cold wind was blowing from the east.* | *The wind blew the leaves off the trees.*
**2** to send out air through your mouth: *She blew on her soup to cool it.*
**3** to make a whistle or car horn make a sound: *The football coach blew his whistle to make us stop playing.*
**4** **blow your nose** = to clear your nose by blowing air through it into a piece of cloth or TISSUE
**5** **blow it** (*informal*) = to not succeed in doing something because you make a mistake: *I should have gotten an A on the test, but I blew it and got a D.*
**PHRASAL VERBS**
**blow something out**
to blow air on a flame and make it stop burning: *She blew out all the candles on her birthday cake.*

**blow up**

**1 blow (something) up** = to destroy something in an explosion: *The soldiers blew up the bridge using dynamite.*

**2 blow something up** = to fill something with air or gas, especially a BALLOON: *We blew up the balloons for the party.*

**blow²** *noun*

**1** something very sad and shocking that happens to you: *Her grandfather's death was a terrible blow to her.*

**2** a hard hit with a hand, tool, or weapon: *The boxer took a blow to his face.*

**ˈblow dry** *verb* (**blow dries**, **blow dried**)

to dry hair using a blow dryer

**ˈblow ˌdryer** *noun*

a piece of equipment that blows hot air, which you hold in your hand and use to dry your wet hair

**blown** /bloʊn/ *verb*

the past participle of BLOW

**blue¹** /bluː/ *adjective*

**1** having the same color as the sky on a clear day: *She has beautiful blue eyes.*

**2** (*informal*) sad: *Why are you feeling blue? Did something bad happen?*

**blue²** *noun*

**1** the color of the sky on a clear day: *She was dressed in blue.*

**2 blues** (*also* **the blues**) = a style of music that came from the African-American culture in the southern U.S. Blues songs often tell about the sad or difficult things in someone's life.

**blue·ber·ry** /ˈbluˌberi/ *noun* (plural **blueberries**)

a small dark blue round berry that has a sweet taste: *blueberry muffins* → see picture on page **A13**

**ˌblue-ˈcollar** *adjective*

blue-collar workers do physical work, rather than working in offices

**bluff¹** /blʌf/ *verb*

to pretend that something is true, in order to get an advantage for yourself: *I think he's bluffing. He doesn't really know your secret.*

**bluff²** *noun*

if something is a bluff, it is not true and is done to try to get an advantage for yourself: *It's a bluff. She won't really quit her job; she just hopes they'll pay her more to get her to stay.*

**blunt** /blʌnt/ *adjective*

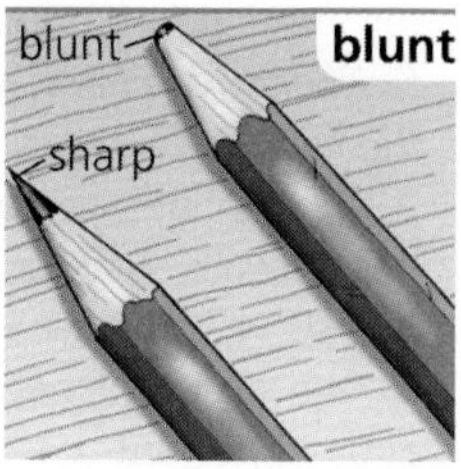


**1** speaking in a very direct and honest way which may upset people: *The coach made some blunt comments about people not playing well, which upset some of the players.*

**2** a blunt object is not sharp: *The knife was too blunt to cut the rope.*

—**bluntly** *adverb* in a blunt way: *"He's not coming with us because I don't like him," she replied bluntly.*

**blur** /blɚ/ *noun*

if something is a blur, you cannot see or remember it clearly: *The accident happened so fast that it's all a blur when I try to remember it.*

**blurred** /blɚd/ *adjective*

**1** (*also* **blurry**) having or showing a shape that is not clear: *a blurry old photograph of his grandmother*

**2** if your EYESIGHT is blurred, you cannot see clearly

**blurt** /blɚt/ *verb*

(*also* **blurt out**) to say something suddenly and without thinking, usually because you are nervous or excited: *Another student blurted out the answer before I could say anything.*

**blush** /blʌʃ/ *verb*

if you blush, your face becomes red, usually because you are embarrassed: *She blushed when he told her she was beautiful.*

[**ORIGIN:** From the old English word *blyscan*, which means "to become red." *Blyscan* is related to the word *blysa,* which means "flame."]

**Blvd.**

the written abbreviation of **boulevard**

**boa con·stric·tor** /ˈboʊə kənˌstrɪktɚ/ *noun*

a very large snake that kills animals by crushing them

**boar** /bɔr/ *noun*

**1** a male pig **ANTONYM: sow**

**2** a wild pig

**board**[1] /bɔrd/ *noun*

**1** a flat piece of wood or plastic that you use for writing or doing things on: *The new teacher wrote her name on the board.* | *Chop the carrots on a cutting board.* | *a chess board*

**2** a long flat piece of wood used for making floors, walls, fences, etc.: *He cut two six-foot boards in half with a saw.*

**3** the group of people who make the rules and important decisions for a school or organization: *The school board is discussing pay with the teachers' union.*

**4 on board** = on an airplane, ship, train, or bus: *There were over 500 passengers on board when the boat sank.*

**5** the meals that are provided for you when you pay to stay somewhere: *College students have to pay for room and board to stay in the dormitories.*

**board**[2] *verb*

to get on an airplane, ship, train, or bus in order to travel somewhere: *The passengers were waiting to board the plane.* **SYNONYM: get on**

**PHRASAL VERB**

**board something up**

to cover a window or door with wooden boards: *They boarded up all the doors to stop people from getting into the building.*

**boast** /boʊst/ *verb*

to talk about how smart or skilled you are, or about how much money you have, in a way that is not polite: *Scott kept boasting about winning the game, and it was starting to annoy us.* **SYNONYM: brag**

—**boastful** *adjective* talking too proudly about the things you have done or own in a way that is not polite

**boat** /boʊt/ *noun*

a vehicle that people travel across water in: *You can only get to the island by boat.*

**bob** /bɑb/ *verb* (**bobbed**, **bobbing**)

to move up and down quickly on water: *Boats were bobbing up and down on the waves.*

**bob·cat** /ˈbɑbkæt/ *noun*

a wild cat that has a short tail and lives in North America

**bod·y** /ˈbɑdi/ *noun* (plural **bodies**)

**1** the physical structure of a person or animal, such as the head, arms, stomach, etc.: *Exercise is good for your body.* | *The drawing of the human body had the names of all the parts written on it.*

**2** the main part of a person or animal, from the shoulders to the HIPs, but not the head, arms, or legs: *She has a short body and long legs.*

**3** a dead person: *They found a body in the woods and called the police.* **SYNONYM: corpse**

**4** the main part of something: *The body of the airplane was not damaged in the crash.*

**[ORIGIN:** From the old English word *bodig.***]**

**ˈbody ˌbuilding** *noun*

hard exercise, such as lifting heavy things, that some people do to get big muscles

—**body builder** *noun* someone who does body building

**bod·y·guard** /ˈbɑdiˌgɑrd/ *noun*

someone whose job is to protect another person from being attacked: *The president's bodyguards go with him wherever he goes.*

**bo·gus** /ˈboʊgəs/ *adjective*

not real, true, or honest: *His claim to be a millionaire turned out to be bogus.*

**boil**[1] /bɔɪl/ *verb*

**1** if a liquid boils, it gets very hot and produces BUBBLEs and steam: *Water boils at 100 degrees Celsius.* | *I boiled some water and added the spaghetti.* → see picture on page **A15**

**2** to cook food in very hot water: *Boil the potatoes for 25 minutes.*

→ see Thesaurus box at **cook**[1]

**boil**[2] *noun*

**1** the state of boiling: *Bring the water to a boil.*

**2** a big sore lump on your skin, where there is an infection

**[ORIGIN:** 1200-1300 From the Latin word *bulla*, which means "bubble."**]**

**boil·er** /ˈbɔɪlɚ/ *noun*
a big container that heats the water for a building

**ˈboiling point** *noun*
the temperature at which a liquid begins to boil

**bois·ter·ous** /ˈbɔɪstərəs/ *adjective*
noisy and full of energy: *A boisterous crowd was yelling as they watched the game.*

**bold** /boʊld/ *adjective*
**1** showing that you are confident and not afraid to do something dangerous or new: *It was a bold move for the coach to put in a new player in such a close game.*
**2** bold colors, shapes, and letters are very strong and clear: *She painted her bedroom in bright bold colors.*

**bo·lo·gna** (*also* **baloney**) /bəˈloʊni/ *noun*
a type of SAUSAGE used for making sandwiches

**bolt¹** /boʊlt/ *noun*
**1** a piece of metal that you slide across to lock a door
**2** a type of screw that goes inside a NUT (=round circle of metal) and is used for holding two things together
**3** **a bolt of lightning/a lightning bolt** = a sudden flash of bright light in the sky during a storm

**bolt²** *verb*
to lock a door with a bolt: *She closed the door and bolted it so no one could get in.*

**bolt³** *adverb*
**sit/stand bolt upright** = to sit or stand with your back very straight: *She heard a noise and sat bolt upright in bed.*

**bomb¹** /bɑm/ *noun*
a weapon that explodes and causes damage: *The bomb went off near the airport and damaged some buildings.*

**bomb²** *verb*
**1** to attack a place with bombs: *Enemy aircraft bombed the city, destroying many homes.*
**2** (*informal*) if a play, movie, or performance bombs, it is not successful: *His second movie bombed – almost no one went to see it.*

**bom·bard** /bɑmˈbɑrd/ *verb*
to attack a place for a long time with guns and bombs: *For three days, the army bombarded the city until much of it was destroyed.*
—**bombardment** *noun* the act of bombarding a place

**bomb·er** /ˈbɑmɚ/ *noun*
**1** an airplane that drops bombs on a place
**2** someone who puts a bomb somewhere

**bond** [Ac] /bɑnd/ *noun*
a strong feeling of love or trust that people have for each other: *There was a special bond between Carlos and his younger brother.*

**bone** /boʊn/ *noun*
one of the hard white parts inside your body that form the structure of your body: *Sam fell and broke a bone in his arm.*

**bon·fire** /ˈbɑnˌfaɪɚ/ *noun*
a large outdoor fire: *They made a bonfire with the branches.*
[**ORIGIN:** 1500-1600 "Bonfire" originally meant "a fire in which bones are burned."]

**bon·net** /ˈbɑnɪt/ *noun*
a hat for a baby, that ties under the chin. Bonnets were also worn by women in the past.

**bo·nus** /ˈboʊnəs/ *noun*
**1** extra money that someone is paid, separately from his or her regular pay: *If employees work hard, they get a bonus at the end of the year.*
**2** an extra good thing that you get, which you did not expect: *He's very nice, and he's good-looking, which is a bonus!*

**bon·y** /ˈboʊni/ *adjective*
**1** very thin, so that you can see the shape of the bones under the skin: *He had long bony fingers.*
**2** a bony fish has a lot of small bones in it

**boo¹** /bu/ *verb*
to shout "boo" to show that you do not like someone or something: *The crowd booed when he announced that the game had been canceled.* **ANTONYM: cheer**

**boo²** *noun*
**1** a word people shout to show that they do not like someone or something: *There were*

*boos from the audience when the singer forgot the words to the song.*
**2** a word you shout to surprise someone who does not know you are there: *Tammy hid behind the door, ready to yell "Boo!"*

**book**[1] /bʊk/ *noun*
**1** something that you read that has a lot of pages inside a cover: *Have you read any books by Roald Dahl?* | *a book about sharks*

**THESAURUS: book**

**Types of Books:**

**nonfiction** books or writing about real facts, people, or events: *I like reading nonfiction, especially history and science.*

**fiction** books and stories about imaginary people and events: *It's fiction, but it gives you an idea about what life as a slave was like.*

**novel** a book in which the story, characters, and events are not real: *All three novels are about the same characters.*

**literature** fiction that people think is important: *My American Literature class is reading "Huckleberry Finn."*

**reference book** a book such as a dictionary or encyclopedia that you look at to find information: *I checked a reference book to see when the Civil War ended.*

**textbook** a book that is used for a class at school: *a science textbook*

**2** pages inside a cover, that you use for writing on: *I'll write your address down in my address book.*
**3 a book of stamps/tickets** = a number of stamps or tickets inside a cover
[**ORIGIN:** From the old English word *boc*. It is related to an old word for "beech tree," and people used to write on beech bark or wood.]

**book**[2] *verb*
**1** to arrange to do or have something at a particular time, for example a seat on an airplane: *He booked a flight to Houston.* **SYNONYM: reserve**
**2** if the police book someone, they write a formal statement saying that he or she may be guilty of a crime: *Newton was arrested and booked for robbery.*

**book·case** /ˈbʊk-keɪs/ *noun*
a piece of furniture with shelves for books

**book·keep·er** /ˈbʊkˌkipɚ/ *noun*
someone whose job is keeping a record of the money that a business receives and spends **SYNONYM: accountant**

**book·keep·ing** /ˈbʊkˌkipɪŋ/ *noun*
the job of keeping a record of the money that a business receives and spends **SYNONYM: accounting**

**book·let** /ˈbʊklət/ *noun*
a very short book that has information about something: *The eight-page booklet is full of advice for travelers.*

**book·mark**[1] /ˈbʊkmɑrk/ *noun*
a piece of paper, leather, or plastic that you put in a book to show you the last page you read

**bookmark**[2] *verb*
to put a website in your list of favorite websites: *It is a useful website, so I bookmarked it.*

**book·shelf** /ˈbʊkʃelf/ *noun* (plural **bookshelves** /ˈbʊkʃelvz/)
a shelf that you keep books on → see picture on page **A10**

**book·store** /ˈbʊkstɔr/ *noun*
a store that sells books

**book·worm** /ˈbʊkwɚm/ *noun*
someone who enjoys reading and reads a lot of books: *He's a real bookworm, and gets books from the library every week.*

**boom**[1] /bum/ *noun*
**1** a deep loud sound, like the sound of a big drum or gun: *I heard a big boom and thought it was a bomb going off.*
**2** a sudden increase in something, especially business: *Recently, there has been a boom in tourism as more and more people travel.*

**boom**[2] *verb*
**1** to make a deep loud sound: *His loud voice boomed in the empty hall.*
**2** to increase suddenly: *The city's population boomed from 8,000 to 30,000 in three years.*

**boo·mer·ang** /ˈbuməˌræŋ/ *noun*
a flat curved piece of wood that flies in a circle and comes back to you when you throw

it: *Boomerangs were originally used for hunting birds and animals in Australia.*

**boost** /bust/ *verb*
**1** to increase or improve something: *If we practice hard, we boost our chances of winning.*
**2** to help someone reach a higher place by lifting him or her: *I can climb over the wall if you boost me up.*
—**boost** *noun* an act of increasing or improving something: *The movie's success gave his career a boost.*

**boot¹** /but/ *noun*
a shoe that covers your ANKLE and sometimes part of your leg: *It's snowing outside; you should wear your boots.*

**boot²** *verb*
(*also* **boot up**) when a computer boots, it starts its basic programs: *I waited for my computer to boot up.*

**booth** /buθ/ *noun*
**1** a small place where one person goes to do something. Booths usually have thin walls that separate them from other booths or from a bigger area: *a voting booth | a phone booth*
**2** a small place, especially outdoors, where you can buy something or get information, for example at a FAIR: *I bought a pin at one of the souvenir booths.* **SYNONYM: stall**
**3** a place in a restaurant that has a table between two long seats with high backs

**bor·der** /ˈbɔrdɚ/ *noun*

**1** the line between two states or countries: *We crossed the border between the U.S. and Mexico.*
**2** a narrow area of a different color around the edge of something: *She was wearing a black skirt with a red border.*

**bore¹** /bɔr/ *verb*
the past tense of BEAR

**bore²** *verb*
if something bores you, you are not interested in it: *The movie really bored me, so I left.*

**WORD FAMILY: bore**
**bore** *noun* | **bore** *verb* | **bored** *adjective* | **boring** *adjective* | **boredom** *noun*



**bore³** *noun*
someone or something that is not interesting: *This homework is a bore!*

**bored** /bɔrd/ *adjective*
if you are bored, you feel that what you are doing, watching, or hearing is not interesting: *The game was for little kids, and I got bored with it fast.* → see picture on page **A23**
—**boredom** *noun* the state of feeling bored

**bor·ing** /ˈbɔrɪŋ/ *adjective*
not interesting: *We watched a boring show on TV and I almost fell asleep.*

**THESAURUS: boring**
**dull** not interesting or exciting: *The movie is really dull. Nothing happens.*
**tedious** boring, and continuing for a long time: *Typing the lists was tedious work.*
**monotonous** boring because the same thing keeps happening, and nothing changes: *I don't want a monotonous job in a factory where I have to do the same thing every day.*

**born¹** /bɔrn/ *verb*
**be born** = to come out of your mother's body: *I was born in Guatemala in 1999.*

**born²** *adjective*
naturally good at doing something: *Michelle is a born leader that the other kids seem to look up to.*

**borne** /bɔrn/ *verb*
the past participle of BEAR

**bor·ough** /ˈbɚoʊ/ *noun*
an area of a large city that has its own government, which is responsible for the schools, hospitals, roads, and other public services in the area: *There are five boroughs in New York City.*
[**ORIGIN:** From the old English word *burg*, which means "castle or town protected by a wall."]

B

**bor·row** /ˈbɑroʊ/ *verb*
**1** to use something that belongs to another person and give it back later: *Can I borrow your bike this afternoon?*

**USAGE: borrow, lend**

If you **borrow** something from someone, he or she lets you have it or use it for a short time: *Can I borrow your pen?*

You cannot say "Can I lend your pen?"

If you **lend** something to someone, you let him or her have it or use it for a short time: *I lent that DVD to Rick.* | *Mom, could you lend me some money?*

You cannot say "Could you borrow me some money?"

**2** if you borrow money from a bank, the bank gives you the money and you promise to pay it back over a period of time: *Ellen borrowed $5,000 to pay for the car.*

**bor·row·er** /ˈbɑroʊə/ *noun*
someone who borrows money from a bank

**boss**[1] /bɔs/ *noun*
someone who is in charge of a group of people at work: *Danny asked his boss if he could leave work early.*

**boss**[2] *verb*
**boss someone around** = to tell someone what to do in an annoying way: *My brother is always bossing me around, and he won't play with me unless I do things his way.*

**boss·y** /ˈbɔsi/ *adjective*
someone who is bossy often tells other people what to do in an annoying way: *Her big sister was very bossy and always chose which game to play.*

**bot·a·ny** /ˈbɑtn-i/ *noun*
the study of plants
—**botanist** *noun* a scientist who studies plants
[**ORIGIN:** 1600-1700 From the Greek word *botane*, which means "a plant, especially grass that animals eat."]

**both** /boʊθ/ *adjective, pronoun*
used for talking about two people or things: *John and Reggie are both very tall.* | *Both of my parents are teachers.* | *Hold the bowl in both hands.*

**GRAMMAR: both**

Do not say "The both men were from Los Angeles." Say *Both men were from Los Angeles* or *Both the men were from Los Angeles.* Do not say "his both sisters." Say *both of his sisters* or *both his sisters.*

**both·er**[1] /ˈbɑðə/ *verb*
**1** to annoy someone by wanting attention when he or she is busy: *Don't bother your dad; he's working.*
**2** to make someone feel worried or upset: *When I get bad grades, it really bothers me.*
**3** to make an effort to do something: *He didn't bother to count the money – he just put it in his pocket.*
**4** if a part of your body bothers you, it hurts a little: *My ankle's bothering me. Maybe I should go to the doctor.*

**bother**[2] *noun*
something or someone that annoys or upsets you: *I don't want to be a bother, but do you think you could help me?*

**bot·tle** /ˈbɑtl/ *noun*
a container for liquids that has a narrow top, and that is usually made of glass or plastic: *I bought a bottle of soda.*
—**bottled** *adjective* bottled drinks are sold in bottles: *She only drinks bottled water.*
[**ORIGIN:** 1300-1400 From the Latin word *buttis*, which means "wooden container for liquid."]

**bot·tom**[1] /ˈbɑtəm/ *noun*
**1** the lowest part or side of something: *Look at the picture at the bottom of the screen.* | *There's some mud on the bottom of your shoe.* **ANTONYM: top**
**2** the ground under an ocean or river: *The ship sank and is now lying on the bottom of the ocean.*
**3** (*informal*) the part of your body that you sit on
**4** the lowest position in a class or organization: *He started at the bottom of the company and worked his way up to a manager's job.* **ANTONYM: top**
**5** **bottoms** = the part of PAJAMAS or a BIKINI that you wear on the bottom half of your body **ANTONYM: top**

**bottom**[2] *adjective*
the bottom shelf, drawer, step, etc. is the

lowest one: *We keep the toys on the bottom shelf so the kids can reach them.*

**bought** /bɔt/ *verb*
the past tense and past participle of BUY

**boul·der** /ˈboʊldɚ/ *noun*
a large rock: *A huge boulder rolled down the mountain.*

**bou·le·vard** /ˈbʊləvɑrd/ *noun* (*written abbreviation*: **Blvd.**)
a wide road in a city: *We drove down Sunset Boulevard.*
→ see Thesaurus box at **road**

**bounce¹** /baʊns/ *verb*
**1** if a ball bounces, it hits something such as the ground or a wall and moves up or away again: *The ball bounced off the wall and hit me in the head.* | *A boy was bouncing a basketball on his driveway.*
**2** to jump or move up and down on something such as a bed or a TRAMPOLINE: *Stop bouncing on the bed!*

**bounce²** *noun*
an act of bouncing: *Catch the ball on its first bounce.*

**bounc·er** /ˈbaʊnsɚ/ *noun*
someone whose job is making people leave clubs and bars if they are too noisy or violent

**bounc·y** /ˈbaʊnsi/ *adjective*
**1** a bouncy ball moves quickly up and away after it hits something
**2** full of energy: *His walk was quick and bouncy.*

**bound¹** /baʊnd/ *verb*
the past tense and past participle of BIND

**bound²** *adjective*
**1 be bound to do something** = to be sure to do something: *You've studied hard. You're bound to pass the test.*
**2** going toward a place: *The plane was bound for Miami.*
**3** (*formal*) having to obey something, or having a duty to do something: *He is bound by the same laws as everyone else.*

**bound³** *verb*
**1** to move or jump with a lot of energy: *George bounded down the stairs and ran out the door.*
**2 be bounded by something** (*formal*) = if a place is bounded by roads, walls, hills, etc., they are around it: *The playing field is bounded by white lines.*

**bound⁴** *noun*
**1** a big jump into or over something: *With one bound, he was over the gate.*
**2 out of bounds** = **a)** outside the playing area in a sport: *He missed the pass and the ball went out of bounds.* **b)** if a place is out of bounds, you are not allowed to go there: *The skier who was hurt was out of bounds, not on a marked ski run.*

**bound·a·ry** /ˈbaʊndəri/ *noun* (plural **boundaries**)
**1** the line that separates two areas of land: *The river forms the boundary between the two countries.*
**2** the limit of what is possible or acceptable: *Swearing in class is outside the boundaries of what the school says is acceptable.*

**bound·less** /ˈbaʊndlɪs/ *adjective*
something that is boundless seems to have no limit: *She was a woman of boundless energy and was always busy doing something.*

**boun·ti·ful** /ˈbaʊntəfəl/ *adjective* (*formal*)
if something is bountiful, there is a lot of it: *There was a bountiful crop of rice that year and everyone had enough to eat.*

**bou·quet** /boʊˈkeɪ/ *noun*
some flowers that are tied together, so they can be given as a present or carried: *The bride carried a bouquet of roses.*
[**ORIGIN:** 1700-1800 From the old French word *bosquet*, which means "plants growing thickly together."]

**bout** /baʊt/ *noun*
**1** a short period of illness or activity: *I had a bout of the flu.*
**2** a BOXING or WRESTLING match

**bou·tique** /buˈtik/ *noun*
a small store that sells fashionable clothes, jewelry, or gifts

**bow¹** /baʊ/ *verb*
to bend your head or the top part of your body forward, in order to show respect or thank an AUDIENCE: *The musicians bowed as the audience applauded.* | *David bowed his head in prayer.*

**bow²** /baʊ/ *noun*
**1** an act of bowing: *At the end of the show, the actors took a bow as people clapped.*
**2** the front part of a ship or boat: *He sat in the bow of the boat.*

**bow**

**bow³** /boʊ/ *noun*
**1** a piece of cloth or string tied in a knot with two LOOPs and two free ends: *The girl had a pretty pink bow in her hair.*
**2** a weapon used to shoot ARROWs, that is made of a long thin piece of wood held in a curve by a tight string: *Native Americans hunted with bows and arrows.*
**3** an object used for playing string instruments such as the VIOLIN, that is made of a long thin piece of wood with hair stretched from one end to the other

**bow·el** /ˈbaʊəl/ *noun*
the long tube inside your body, through which food goes after it leaves your stomach
**SYNONYM: intestine**
[**ORIGIN:** 1200-1300 From the Latin word *botellus*, which means "little sausage." The bowels, or intestines, of animals are cleaned and sausage meat is put inside them.]

**bowl** /boʊl/ *noun*
a deep round dish or container: *He ate a bowl of cereal.*
[**ORIGIN:** From the old English word *bolla*.]

**bowl·ing** /ˈboʊlɪŋ/ *noun*
an indoor game in which you try to knock down a group of objects called pins by rolling a heavy ball at them: *I went bowling with my friends yesterday.*

**bow tie** /ˈboʊ taɪ/ *noun*
a man's tie which has a knot with two LOOPs and two short ends

**box**

**box¹** /bɑks/ *noun*
**1** a container with four sides, usually made of thick stiff paper or wood: *My old toys are in a box in the garage.* | *a box of chocolates*
**2** a small area on an official form, for people to write information in: *Write your name in the box at the top of the form.*
[**ORIGIN:** 900-1000 From the Latin word *buxus*, which is the name of a type of tree whose wood was used for making boxes.]

**box²** *verb*
to fight someone as a sport while wearing big leather GLOVEs

**box·car** /ˈbɑkskɑr/ *noun*
a type of railroad car with a large sliding door, used for carrying goods

**box·er** /ˈbɑksɚ/ *noun*
someone who boxes

**box·ing** /ˈbɑksɪŋ/ *noun*
the sport of fighting while wearing big leather GLOVEs: *The two fighters went into the boxing ring.* → see picture on page **A25**

**ˈbox ˌoffice** *noun*
a place in a theater or concert hall where you can buy tickets: *Tickets are on sale now at the box office.*

**boy** /bɔɪ/ *noun*
a male child: *He likes most of the boys in his class.* | *How old is your little boy?*
—**boyish** *adjective* looking or behaving like a boy: *He's 30 but still has a boyish face.*
—**boyhood** *noun* the time when someone is a boy: *He spent his boyhood in Grand Rapids, Michigan.* | *He never forgot his boyhood friend.*

**boy·cott** /ˈbɔɪkɑt/ *verb*
to refuse to buy something, use something, or do something, as a way of protesting:

*Several countries will boycott the competition because they believe it is unfair.*
—**boycott** *noun* the act of boycotting something as a protest: *The group organized a boycott of the company's products to try to make them treat their workers better.*

**boy·friend** /ˈbɔɪfrend/ *noun*
a boy or man that someone has a romantic relationship with: *Carol and her boyfriend went to a movie on Friday.*

**bra** /brɑ/ *noun*
a piece of underwear that a woman wears to support her breasts

**brace·let** /ˈbreɪslət/ *noun*
a piece of jewelry that you wear around your wrist → see picture on page **A6**

**brac·es** /ˈbreɪsɪz/ *plural noun*
wires that a DENTIST puts on your teeth to make them straight

**brack·et** /ˈbrækɪt/ *noun*
**1** one of the pair of marks [ ] that are put around extra information: *In the sentence "¿Cómo estás? [How are you?]," the English words are in brackets.*
**2 age/income/tax, etc. bracket** (*formal*) = a particular group of ages, incomes, or other set of numbers: *Children in the 12–16 age bracket will like this book.*

**brag** /bræg/ *verb* (**bragged**, **bragging**)
to tell other people how smart or good at something you are, or about how much you have of something such as money, in a way that is not good manners: *He was bragging about the cool things he got for his birthday and trying to make us jealous.* **SYNONYM: boast**

**braid¹** /breɪd/ *verb*
to twist together three amounts of hair, rope, or cloth so that they form one piece: *Her mother was braiding her long hair.*

**braid²** *noun*
three amounts of hair twisted together to form one piece: *She wears her hair in braids.*

**Braille** /breɪl/ *noun*
an alphabet that is written as raised round marks that blind people can read by touching: *The labels on the medicines are in Braille so blind people can read them.*
[**ORIGIN:** From Louis Braille (1809-1852), the blind Frenchman who invented this system of writing.]

**brain** /breɪn/ *noun*
**1** the part inside your head that controls how you think, feel, and move: *Part of her brain was damaged and now she can't remember things.* → see picture on page **A2**
**2 brains** (*informal*) = the ability to think well: *You have brains, but you still need to work hard.*

**brain·storm** /ˈbreɪnˌstɔrm/ *verb*
if a group of people brainstorms, they try to think of many different ways of doing something in order to solve a problem: *They were brainstorming names for the school newspaper.*

**brain·wash** /ˈbreɪnwɑʃ/ *verb*
to make someone believe something that is not true, by repeating it many times and making him or her unable to think clearly: *The article says that the group brainwashes its members to get money from them.*

**brain·y** /ˈbreɪni/ *adjective* (*informal*)
able to think well and learn quickly: *He's brainy enough to go to college by the time he's 15.*

**brake¹** /breɪk/ *noun*
the part of a bicycle, car, or other vehicle that you press on to make it go more slowly or stop: *Bike brakes work by rubbing on the tires.*

**brake²** *verb*
to make a bicycle, car, or other vehicle go more slowly or stop by using its brakes: *She braked suddenly when a dog ran into the road in front of her.*

**bran** /bræn/ *noun*
the crushed outer skin of wheat or another grain

**branch¹** /bræntʃ/ *noun*
**1** a part of a tree that grows out from the main part: *He climbed up into the lowest branches of the tree.*
**2** if a store, bank, or group has branches, it has stores or offices in many different places: *The bank has branches all over the country.*
**3** one part of a large subject of study or knowledge: *Geometry is a branch of mathematics.*
[**ORIGIN:** 1200-1300 From the old French word

*branche*, from the Latin word *branca*, which means "animal's foot." A branch of a tree was thought to look like an animal's foot.]

B

**branch²** *verb*

**PHRASAL VERB**

**branch out**

to do something new in addition to what you usually do: *She designs clothes for women, but she has recently branched out into men's clothing.*

**brand¹** /brænd/ *noun*

**1** a type of product made by a company: *What brand of soap do you use?*

**2** a mark that is made on a cow or a horse to show who it belongs to

→ see Thesaurus box at **type¹**

**brand²** *verb*

to burn a mark onto the skin of a cow or horse to show who it belongs to

**bran·dish** /ˈbrændɪʃ/ *verb (formal)*

to wave something in a threatening way: *He brandished a knife at the cashier and demanded money.*

**ˌbrand-ˈnew** *adjective*

new and never used before: *My parents couldn't afford to buy me a brand-new bicycle.*

**bran·dy** /ˈbrændi/ *noun* (plural **brandies**)

a strong alcoholic drink made from wine

**brash** /bræʃ/ *adjective*

behaving and talking too confidently: *He was a brash young salesman who sometimes offended customers.*

**brass** /bræs/ *noun*

**1** a very hard bright yellow metal that is a mixture of COPPER and ZINC: *The buttons on his coat were made of brass.*

**2 the brass (section)** = the people in an ORCHESTRA or band who play musical instruments such as the TRUMPET or TROMBONE

**brat** /bræt/ *noun (informal)*

a child who behaves badly: *Stop acting like a spoiled brat and help me.*

**brave** /breɪv/ *adjective*

not afraid or not showing fear: *A brave soldier rescued his friend.*

—**bravely** *adverb* in a brave way

[**ORIGIN:** 1400-1500 From the old Italian word *bravo*, which means "wild or brave."]

**brav·er·y** /ˈbreɪvəri/ *noun*

brave behavior, or the quality of being brave: *He showed great bravery in the battle and saved many other men.* **SYNONYM: courage**; **ANTONYM: cowardice**

**bread** /bred/ *noun*

a food made by mixing flour, water, and YEAST, and then baking it: *white bread | She cut me a slice of bread. | He will buy a loaf of bread.*

**breadth** /bredθ/ *noun (formal)*

**1** the distance from one side of something to the other: *He can swim the breadth of the pool, but not the whole length.* **SYNONYM: width**

**2** the breadth of someone's knowledge or experience is how many different things they know about or have done: *The teacher has an impressive breadth of knowledge about music.*

**break¹** /breɪk/ *verb* (**broke** /broʊk/, **broken** /ˈbroʊkən/)

**1** if something breaks, or if you break it, it separates into pieces, especially when it is hit or dropped: *The plate fell on the floor and broke. | If you sit on that old chair, you'll break it. | I fell off my bike and broke my leg.*

**THESAURUS: break**

**smash** to break into a lot of pieces because of being hit with a lot of force – used about plates, glasses, or windows: *The baseball hit the window and smashed it.*

**shatter** to break into a lot of small pieces – used about plates or glass: *I dropped a glass, and it shattered everywhere.*

**crack** to be broken so that there is a line between two parts of something – used about plates, glasses, ice, pieces of rock, etc.: *This cup is cracked.*

**snap** to break into two pieces, making a loud noise: *The stick snapped in two.*

**burst** to break – used about something with liquid inside it: *Our pipes had burst in the freezing weather.*

**pop** to break – used about bubbles or balloons: *In the game, you pop the balloons by sitting on them.*

**2** to damage a machine so that it does not work: *Jimmy broke the DVD player.*
**3** **break a law/rule** = to do something that a law or rule says you must not do: *Students who break the rules will have to stay after school.* **ANTONYM: obey**
**4** **break a promise** = to not do what you promised to do: *I said I wouldn't tell anyone her secret, but I broke my promise.*
**5** **break a record** = to do something faster or better than it has ever been done before: *He broke the world record in the 400 meters.*
**6** **break the news to someone** = to tell someone about something bad that has happened: *She began to cry as the police broke the news to her.*
**7** **break for lunch/coffee, etc.** = to stop working in order to eat or drink something
**8** **break free** = to escape from a person who is holding you or from a situation: *She managed to break free from the man and run away.*
**9** **break even** = to neither make a profit nor lose money: *The company broke even in its first year of business.*
→ see Thesaurus box at **hurt**[1], **stop**[1]

**PHRASAL VERBS**

**break down**
**1** if a car or a large machine breaks down, it stops working: *Our car broke down on the highway.*
**2** to be unable to stop yourself from crying: *She broke down during the funeral.*

**break in/break into something**
to use force to get into a building, usually in order to steal things: *They broke into the house through the back window.*

**break something off**
to end a relationship or discussion: *They've broken off their engagement.*

**break out**
**1** if something bad such as a fire, war, or disease breaks out, it begins to happen: *The fire broke out at two o'clock in the morning.*
**2** to begin to have red spots on your skin, either from ACNE or because of an illness: *The girl had broken out in a rash.*

**break up**
**1** to end a relationship with a boyfriend or girlfriend: *She'd just broken up with Joe.*
**2** **break something up** = to stop a fight or a protest: *Come on, guys, break it up!*

B

**break**[2] *noun*
**1** a period of time when you stop working or studying: *I'm tired. Let's take a break.* | *She's on her lunch break.* | *He was getting ready to go back to college after spring break.*
**2** a period of time when something stops for a while and then starts again: *There was a break in the conversation, and then Anna started talking again.*
**3** **give someone a break** (*informal*) = to stop annoying or criticizing someone: *Give me a break! I've heard enough jokes about me today.*
**4** a chance to become successful: *The band's big break came when they sang on a national TV show.*
**5** a space between two parts of something: *They could see the moon through a break in the clouds.*
→ see Thesaurus box at **vacation**

**break·danc·ing** /ˈbreɪkˌdænsɪŋ/ *noun*
a kind of dancing in which the dancers often stand on their hands or their heads and turn around: *Breakdancing is done to hip-hop music.*

**break·down** /ˈbreɪkdaʊn/ *noun*
**1** if a car or a piece of machinery has a breakdown, it stops working: *We had a breakdown on the freeway and had to be towed to a mechanic.*
**2** an occasion when a relationship or system fails: *There was a breakdown in the peace talks and the fighting began again.*
**3** another word for a NERVOUS BREAKDOWN: *My father had a breakdown when I was eleven and had to spend time in a hospital.*

**break·fast** /ˈbrekfəst/ *noun*
the first meal of the day: *I had bacon and eggs for breakfast.*
→ see Thesaurus box at **meal**
[**ORIGIN:** 1400-1500 From "break" and the noun "fast," which means "a period of time when you choose not to eat." When you have breakfast, you put an end to the period at night when you do not eat.]

**ˈbreak-in** *noun*
an occasion when someone uses force to get into a building in order to steal things: *There was a break-in at the school and several computers were stolen.*

B

**break·through** /ˈbreɪkθru/ *noun*
an important achievement by someone who is trying to make, find, or do something new: *Scientists have made an important breakthrough in the treatment of heart disease.*

**break·up** /ˈbreɪkʌp/ *noun*
the ending of a marriage or other relationship: *He was very unhappy after the breakup of his marriage.*

**breast** /brest/ *noun*
**1** one of the two soft round parts on a woman's chest that can produce milk
**2** the part of a bird's or person's body between the neck and the stomach: *a chicken breast*

**breast·stroke** /ˈbrestˌstroʊk/ *noun*
a way of swimming in which you push your arms forward and then move them around to your sides

**breath** /breθ/ *noun*
**1** the air that you take in and let out when you breathe: *Joe took a deep breath and dived into the water.* | *He has bad breath because he doesn't brush his teeth.*
**2 hold your breath** = to deliberately not breathe for a while, after breathing in: *I stayed under water until I couldn't hold my breath anymore.*
**3 be out of breath** = to be having difficulty breathing because you have been running or exercising: *I was out of breath from climbing so many stairs.*
**4 catch your breath** = to begin breathing normally again after you have been running or exercising: *I had to sit down to catch my breath.*
**5 under your breath** = in a quiet voice: *"Not again," he whispered under his breath.*

**USAGE: breath, breathe**

**Breath** is a noun: *He took a deep breath.*

**Breathe** is a verb: *Breathe deeply.*

**breathe** /brið/ *verb*
to take air into your body through your nose or mouth and let it out again: *He was asleep and breathing quietly.* | *Breathe in through your nose, and then breathe out through your mouth.*
—**breathing** *noun* the action of breathing air in and out: *His breathing was very loud.*

**WORD FAMILY: breathe**

**breathe** *verb* | **breath** *noun* | **breathing** *noun* | **breathless** *adjective*

**THESAURUS: breathe**

**pant** to breathe quickly with short breaths, especially after exercising: *He was panting when he reached the top of the hill.*

**be out of breath** to have difficulty breathing because you have been running or exercising: *She was out of breath after running to catch the bus.*

**gasp** to breathe quickly because you are having difficulty breathing: *She rode the bike as fast as she could, until she was gasping for breath.*

**wheeze** to breathe with difficulty because you are sick, making a sound in your chest: *He has the flu and is wheezing and coughing.*

**breath·less** /ˈbreθləs/ *adjective*
if you are breathless, you are having trouble breathing: *I was breathless from running.*

**breath·tak·ing** /ˈbreθˌteɪkɪŋ/ *adjective*
extremely beautiful, impressive, or surprising: *Our hotel room had a breathtaking view of the mountains.*

**breed¹** /brid/ *noun*
one type of an animal that is kept as a pet or on a farm: *What is your favorite breed of dog? I like poodles.*

**breed²** *verb* (**bred** /bred/)
**1** if animals breed, they have babies
**2** to keep animals so that they will produce young ones: *He breeds horses.*

**breeze** /briz/ *noun*
a light gentle wind: *There was a cool breeze blowing through the window.*
—**breezy** *adjective* with the wind blowing: *a breezy day*
→ see Thesaurus box at **wind¹**

**brew** /bru/ *verb*
**1** to make a drink by leaving tea leaves or crushed coffee beans in boiling water: *She brewed a pot of coffee.*
**2** to make beer
**3 be brewing** = if something bad is brewing, it will happen soon: *Trouble is brewing in Congress over the new bill, and it may not pass.*
—**brewery** *noun* a place where beer is made

**bribe** /braɪb/ *verb*
to give money or a gift to someone so that they will do something you want, especially something illegal: *He bribed the guard to leave the door unlocked so he could escape.*
—**bribe** *noun* money or a gift that is used to bribe someone: *Three police officers have been accused of taking bribes.*
—**bribery** *noun* the action of bribing someone
[**ORIGIN:** 1300-1400 From an old French word meaning "bread given to a beggar."]

**brick** /brɪk/ *noun*
a hard block of baked clay, used for building

**bride** /braɪd/ *noun*
a woman who is getting married or who has just gotten married: *The bride and groom were just leaving the church.*
—**bridal** *adjective* relating to a bride or a wedding: *a bridal gown*

**bride·groom** /ˈbraɪdgrum/ *noun*
another word for GROOM

**brides·maid** /ˈbraɪdzmeɪd/ *noun*
a girl or woman who stands beside a bride at her wedding

**bridge**

**bridge** /brɪdʒ/ *noun*
**1** a structure built over a river or road so that people or vehicles can cross from one side to the other: *We looked down at the water as we drove across the Golden Gate Bridge.*
**2** a card game for four people

**brief** [Ac] /brif/ *adjective*
**1** continuing for a short time: *After a brief period without work, he found another job.* **ANTONYM: long**
**2** using only a few words: *He gave a brief description of the man we were looking for.*
—**briefly** *adverb* in a brief way: *She paused briefly in front of a store window, and then walked on.*
[**ORIGIN:** 1200-1300 From the Latin word *brevis*, which means "short."]

**brief·case** /ˈbrifkeɪs/ *noun*
a flat bag with a handle, used for carrying papers

**brief·ing** [Ac] /ˈbrifɪŋ/ *noun*
an occasion when someone gives you all the information you need about a situation: *A White House spokesman explained the situation to reporters at a press briefing.*

**bright** /braɪt/ *adjective*
**1** having or producing a lot of light: *a bright sunny day* | *The bright lights in the football stadium lit up the field.*
**2** bright colors are strong and easy to see: *a bright red sweater*
**3** quick at learning things: *Susan is a bright child and does well at school.* **SYNONYM: intelligent**
—**brightly** *adverb* in a bright way: *The sun was shining brightly.* | *brightly colored ribbons*
—**brightness** *noun* the quality of being bright
→ see Thesaurus box at **intelligent**
[**ORIGIN:** From the old English word *beorht.*]

**bright·en** /ˈbraɪtn/ (*also* **brighten up**) *verb*
**1** to become brighter or lighter: *It was dawn. The sky was brightening.*
**2** to make something look more colorful and attractive: *Flowers would brighten up this room.*
**3** to become or look happier: *His face brightened when he heard the good news.*

**bril·liant** /ˈbrɪlyənt/ *adjective*
**1** very intelligent or good at your work: *The discovery was made by a brilliant young scientist.*
**2** a brilliant light or color is very bright: *The sky was a brilliant blue.*

—**brilliantly** *adverb* in a brilliant way
—**brilliance** *noun* the quality of being brilliant
→ see Thesaurus box at **intelligent**
[ORIGIN: 1600-1700 From the French word *briller*, which means "to shine."]

B

**brim**[1] /brɪm/ *noun*
**1** the part of a hat that sticks out around your head: *a hat with a wide brim*
**2 the brim** = the top of a container, such as a glass: *The cup was filled to the brim with coffee.*

**brim**[2] *verb*
**be brimming with something** = to be full of something: *She was brimming with confidence after her win.*

**bring** /brɪŋ/ *verb* (**brought** /brɔt/)
**1** to take someone or something with you to a place or person: *Will you bring me a glass of water? | Can I bring a friend to the party? | My father brought this doll back from Japan.*

**THESAURUS: bring**

**bring** to take something or someone to a place: *You should bring her some flowers. | Elise brought her friend with her to the party.*

**take** to move something from one place to another, or help someone go from one place to another: *You'd better take your jacket – it's getting cold. | I can take you home after the concert.*

**get** to go to another place and come back with something or someone: *Just a minute while I get my jacket.*

**2** to make something happen or come: *Every change brings new problems. | Her songs have brought pleasure to millions of people.*
**3** to cause something to be in a particular position or state: *The injury brought his career in baseball to an end. | The store brought their prices down during the sale.*
**4 cannot bring yourself to do something** = to not be able to make yourself do something: *I couldn't bring myself to talk about the bullying for a long time.*

PHRASAL VERBS
**bring something about**
to make something happen: *How can we bring about these changes?*
**bring someone in**
to ask someone to help or become involved in a situation: *The local police brought in the FBI to help with the case.*
**bring something on**
to make something bad begin, for example an illness: *Stress can bring on a heart attack.*
**bring something out**
**1** to make something easier to see or taste: *The color of the shirt brings out the blue in your eyes. | The salt brings out the flavor of the meat.*
**2 bring out the best/worst in someone** = to make someone behave in the best or worst way that he or she can: *Becoming a father has brought out the best in Dan.*
**bring up**
**1 bring someone up** = to care for and educate a child: *She brought up three children by herself.* SYNONYM: **raise**
**2 bring something up** = to mention a particular subject in a conversation or discussion: *That's a good idea. I'll bring it up at the class meeting.* SYNONYM: **raise**

**brink** /brɪŋk/ *noun*
**the brink (of something)** = if you are on the brink of something, it may happen soon: *She is a good actress who is on the brink of becoming a star.*

**brisk** /brɪsk/ *adjective*
quick and full of energy: *A brisk walk is a good way to exercise.*
—**briskly** *adverb* in a quick way that is full of energy

**bris·tle** /ˈbrɪsəl/ *noun*
a short stiff hair or wire: *a brush with short bristles*

**Brit·ish**[1] /ˈbrɪtɪʃ/ *adjective*
from Great Britain: *the British government*

**British**[2] *noun*
**the British** = people from Great Britain: *The British love soccer.*

**brit·tle** /ˈbrɪtl/ *adjective*
hard but easily broken: *She is old and her*

*bones are very brittle, so her hip broke when she fell.*

**broad** /brɔd/ *adjective*
**1** wide: *He has very broad shoulders and looks very strong.* | *The broad Mississippi River separates the two states.* | *a broad smile* **ANTONYM: narrow**
**2** including many different kinds of things or people: *The college offers a broad range of classes, from cooking to literature.* **ANTONYM: narrow**
**3 in broad daylight** = during the day when it is light: *He was attacked in broad daylight.*

**broad·cast** /ˈbrɔdˌkæst/ *verb* (**broadcast**)
to send out a radio or television program: *The music awards will be broadcast on national television.*
—**broadcast** *noun* a program on the radio or television: *a news broadcast*
—**broadcaster** *noun* someone who speaks on radio or television programs, or someone who is in the radio or television business

**broad·ly** /ˈbrɔdli/ *adverb*
**1** in a general way: *I know broadly what to expect, but I would like to know more specific details.* **SYNONYM: generally**
**2 smile/grin broadly** = to have a big smile on your face

**Broad·way** /ˈbrɔdweɪ/ *noun*
an area of New York City where there are many theaters: *The show opens on Broadway next month.*

**broc·co·li** /ˈbrɑkəli/ *noun*
a vegetable with groups of small green flower BUDs on thick stems → see picture on page A12

**bro·chure** /broʊˈʃʊr/ *noun*
a thin book that gives information or advertises something: *We looked through travel brochures, trying to decide where to go for our vacation.*

**broil** /brɔɪl/ *verb*
to cook food by putting it directly over or under flames or heat: *Broil the chicken for 8 minutes on each side.*
→ see Thesaurus box at **cook**[1]
[**ORIGIN:** 1300-1400 From the French word *bruler*, which means "to burn."]

**broil·er** /ˈbrɔɪlɚ/ *noun*
the part of an OVEN where you cook food under heat: *Put the chicken breasts under the broiler.*

**broke**[1] /broʊk/ *verb*
the past tense of BREAK

**broke**[2] *adjective*
**1** if you are broke, you have no money at all: *I can't give you any money, because I'm broke.*
**2 go broke** (*informal*) = if a business goes broke, it can no longer continue because it has no money
→ see Thesaurus box at **poor**

**bro·ken**[1] /ˈbroʊkən/ *verb*
the past participle of BREAK

**broken**[2] *adjective*
**1** damaged or in pieces because of being hit, dropped, etc.: *Don't move him – I think his leg is broken.* | *There was broken glass from the window on the floor.*
**2** not working correctly: *What time is it? My watch is broken.*

**bronze** /brɑnz/ *noun*
a brown-red metal made by mixing COPPER and TIN: *a bronze statue*

**brooch** /broʊtʃ/ *noun*
a piece of jewelry with a pin on the back, that women fasten to their clothes: *She pinned a gold brooch to her coat.*

**brook** /brʊk/ *noun*
a small stream

**broom** /brum/ *noun*
a brush with a long handle, used for sweeping floors

**broth** /brɔθ/ *noun*
a clear soup: *chicken broth*

**broth·er** /ˈbrʌðɚ/ *noun*
a boy or man who has the same parents as you: *This is my little brother Charlie.*
—**brotherly** *adjective* kind, helpful, and loyal, like the behavior of a brother should be: *brotherly love*

**ˈbrother-in-law** *noun*
**1** the brother of your husband or wife
**2** the husband of your sister

**brought** /brɔt/ *verb*
the past tense and past participle of BRING

B

**brow** /braʊ/ *noun (formal)*
the part of your face above your eyes and below your hair: *She wiped the sweat off her brow.* **SYNONYM: forehead**

**brown** /braʊn/ *adjective, noun*
the color of coffee, wood, or dirt: *She has dark brown hair.*

**browse** /braʊz/ *verb*
**1** to look at things in a store or at pages of a magazine, when you do not plan to buy anything or read carefully: *She likes browsing through fashion magazines to see what's in style.*
**2** to look for information on the Internet: *She was browsing the Internet, looking for information on George Washington.*

**brows·er** /ˈbraʊzɚ/ *noun*
a computer program that lets you find and use information on the Internet

**bruise** /bruz/ *noun*
a dark mark on your skin where it has been hit: *She had a big bruise on her arm where she had bumped into the door.*

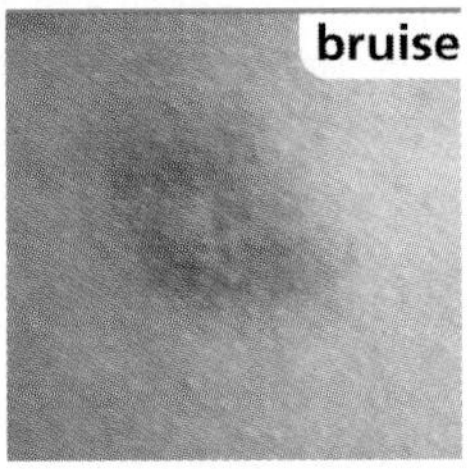


—**bruised** *adjective* having one or more bruises: *He was bruised but not badly hurt in the accident.*
—**bruise** *verb* to get a bruise: *He bruised his knee in this afternoon's game.*
→ see Thesaurus box at **injury**, **mark²**
[**ORIGIN:** From the old English word *brysan*, which means "to crush," and also the old French word *bruisier*, which means "to break."]

**brunch** /brʌntʃ/ *noun*
a meal that you eat in the late morning, as a combination of breakfast and LUNCH: *Let's meet at the restaurant and have brunch at about 11:00.*
→ see Thesaurus box at **meal**

**bru·nette** /bruˈnet/ *noun*
a woman with brown hair

**brunt** /brʌnt/ *noun*
**bear/take the brunt of something** = to be affected most severely by something: *The front part of the truck bore the brunt of the collision.*

**brush¹** /brʌʃ/ *noun*
**1** an object consisting of strong hairs fastened to a handle, used for cleaning, painting, or making something neat: *When you finish painting, wash your brushes in the sink.*
**2** small bushes and trees that cover an area of land: *The cabin is surrounded by brush.*

**brush²** *verb*
**1** to clean your teeth or make your hair look neat using a brush: *Have you brushed your teeth today? | She was brushing her hair.*
**2** to use your hand or a brush to move something off a surface: *She brushed the crumbs off her lap.*
**3** to touch someone or something lightly as you go past: *Her sleeve brushed my arm as she walked past.*
→ see Thesaurus box at **clean²**, **touch¹**

**bru·tal** /ˈbrutl/ *adjective*
very cruel or violent: *The talks may help end ten years of brutal civil war.*
—**brutally** *adverb* in a brutal way
—**brutality** /bruˈtæləti/ *noun* the quality of being brutal

**B.S.** *noun*
(**Bachelor of Science**) a university degree in a science subject

**bub·ble¹** /ˈbʌbəl/ *noun*
a ball of air in a liquid, or a ball of air in something soft such as GUM: *soap bubbles | the bubbles in a glass of soda*

**bubble²** *verb*
if a liquid bubbles, it produces bubbles, usually because it is boiling: *Heat the sauce until it starts to bubble.*

**buck** /bʌk/ *noun*
**1** *(informal)* a dollar: *It costs 75 bucks.*
**2** a male DEER or rabbit

**buck·et** /ˈbʌkɪt/ *noun*
a deep container with a handle over the top, used for carrying and holding liquids: *He put*

*the fire out with a bucket of water.* **SYNONYM: pail**

[**ORIGIN:** 1200-1300 From the old English word *buc*, which means "container for pouring liquid, or belly."]

**buck·le** /ˈbʌkəl/ *noun*
a metal object used to fasten a belt, shoe, bag, etc.
—**buckle** *verb* to fasten something using a buckle: *He got into the car and buckled his seat belt.*

[**ORIGIN:** 1300-1400 From the Latin word *buccula*, which means "cheek strap of a helmet."]

**bud** /bʌd/ *noun*
a young flower or leaf that has not yet opened: *It was spring, and there were buds on the rose bushes, but no flowers yet.*

**Bud·dhis·m** /ˈbudɪzəm/ *noun*
a religion based on the teachings of Buddha, who lived in India 2,500 years ago. Buddhists believe that if people stop wanting things, they will no longer have pain or problems.
—**Buddhist** *noun* someone whose religion is Buddhism

**bud·dy** /ˈbʌdi/ *noun* (plural **buddies**) (*informal*)
a friend: *He is one of Mike's buddies from school.*

**budge** /bʌdʒ/ *verb*
**not budge** = if people or things do not budge, they do not move at all when someone wants them to move: *I pulled, but the dog wouldn't budge.*

**budg·et**[1] /ˈbʌdʒɪt/ *noun*
an amount of money that a person or organization can spend: *We have a budget of $300 to spend on redecorating your room.*

[**ORIGIN:** 1400-1500 From the old French word *bougette*, which means "small leather bag." The idea is that money or spending plans are kept in a bag.]

**budget**[2] *verb*
to plan how much money you can spend: *We budgeted $1,500 for our vacation.*

**buf·fa·lo** /ˈbʌfəˌloʊ/ *noun* (plural **buffaloes** or **buffalo**)
a North American wild animal that looks like a large cow with a big head and thick hair on its neck and shoulders **SYNONYM: bison**

**buf·fet** /bəˈfeɪ/ *noun*
a meal where all of the dishes are on a table and you go and take what you want: *There was a lunch buffet with lots of salads, pasta, and sandwiches.*

**bug**[1] /bʌg/ *noun*
**1** (*informal*) an insect
**2** (*informal*) an illness that passes from one person to another easily: *Three people in my class had a stomach bug and stayed home from school.*
**3** a small fault in a computer program, that stops it from working well: *There must be a bug in the software – it's not working right.*

**bug**[2] *verb* (**bugged**, **bugging**) (*informal*)
to annoy someone: *That music is really bugging me. Can you turn it off?*

**build** /bɪld/ *verb* (**built** /bɪlt/)
**1** to make a building, a bridge, or another structure: *My grandfather built this house himself.* | *The church was built of wood.*
**2** (*also* **build up**) to make something get bigger and stronger: *Exercise will help to build up your muscles.*

**WORD FAMILY: build**
**build** *verb* | **builder** *noun* | **building** *noun*

**build·er** /ˈbɪldɚ/ *noun*
a company or person whose job is building things: *The company is the nation's largest home builder.*

**build·ing** /ˈbɪldɪŋ/ *noun*
**1** a house, school, or anything with a roof and walls: *Dad's office is in a tall building on Main Street.* | *Our apartment is on the seventh floor of the apartment building.*
**2** the process of making a house, school, road, or other structure: *The building of the new hospital is nearly finished.* **SYNONYM: construction**

**build·up** /ˈbɪldʌp/ *noun*
a gradual increase: *There was a buildup of troops along the border before the war began.*

**built** /bɪlt/ *verb*
the past tense and past participle of BUILD

**bulb** /bʌlb/ *noun*
the glass part of an electric light, where the light shines from: *The bulb in the bedroom isn't working – do you have a new one?* **SYNONYM: light bulb**

**bulge** /bʌldʒ/ *verb*
if something bulges, it curves out because there is something inside or under it: *His pockets were bulging with some little toy cars.*
—**bulge** *noun* the curved shape something makes when it bulges

**bulk** Ac /bʌlk/ *noun*
**1 the bulk (of something)** = most of something: *The bulk of the work has been done – there's just some painting to do now.*
**2** the large size of something or someone: *The largest dinosaurs moved slowly because of their bulk.*

**bulk·y** Ac /ˈbʌlki/ *adjective*
big and heavy: *He was wearing a bulky black sweater to keep warm.*

**bull** /bʊl/ *noun*
a male cow, or the male of some other big animals

**bull·dog** /ˈbʊldɔg/ *noun*
a type of dog with a strong body and chest and short fur

**bull·doz·er** /ˈbʊlˌdoʊzɚ/ *noun*
a powerful vehicle used for moving dirt and rocks

**bul·let** /ˈbʊlɪt/ *noun*
a small piece of metal that comes out of a gun when you fire it: *He fired two bullets but failed to hit the target.*

**bul·le·tin** /ˈbʊlətɪn/ *noun*
**1** a short news program on television or radio: *We heard about the plane crash on a news bulletin.*
**2** a short report or letter that gives information: *The church gives out a weekly bulletin to all its members.*
[**ORIGIN:** 1700-1800 From the Latin word *bulla*, which means "official announcement by the pope."]

**ˈbulletin ˌboard** *noun*
**1** a board on a wall where people put information: *There's more information on the bulletin board in the cafeteria.* → see picture on page **A18**
**2** a place on a system of computers where you can leave messages for other people to read: *I posted a message on the bulletin board on the company's website.*

**bul·let·proof** /ˈbʊlɪtˌpruf/ *adjective*
something that is bulletproof is made of material that stops bullets passing through it: *The windows in the bank were made of bulletproof glass.*

**ˈbull's-eye** *noun*
the center of a TARGET, that you aim at when you shoot

**bul·ly** /ˈbʊli/ *noun* (plural **bullies**)
someone who frightens or hurts people in order to make them do things
—**bully** *verb* to frighten or hurt people in order to make them do things: *One of the bigger boys at school bullied me into giving him my money.*
—**bullying** *noun* the activity of frightening or hurting people in order to make them do things: *The school works hard to stop any bullying quickly.*

**bum·ble** /ˈbʌmbəl/ (*also* **bumble around**) *verb*
to move around in a way that is not steady: *Josh was bumbling around in the dark, trying to find the light switch.*

**bum·ble·bee** /ˈbʌmbəlˌbi/ *noun*
a large BEE

**bump¹** /bʌmp/ *verb*
to hit something by accident: *Joey fell and bumped his head on the table.* | *I hurt my arm when I bumped into the door.*
**PHRASAL VERB**
**bump into someone** (*informal*)
to meet someone you know when you are not expecting it: *I bumped into a friend whom I hadn't seen in five years.*

**bump²** *noun*
**1** a raised area on your skin where you hit it on something: *The ball hit him on the head and now he has a big bump there.*
**2** a raised area on the ground: *There were a*

*lot of bumps in the road, so we drove slowly.*
→ see Thesaurus box at **injury**

**bump·er** /ˈbʌmpɚ/ *noun*
the part at the front and back of a car that protects it if it hits anything → see picture on page **A28**

**bump·y** /ˈbʌmpi/ *adjective*
a bumpy road is not smooth to drive on: *Their ranch was at the end of a bumpy dirt road.*

**bun** /bʌn/ *noun*
**1** a small round piece of bread for one person: *a hamburger bun*
**2** if a woman's hair is in a bun, it is tied in a round shape at the back of her head: *The old lady had gray hair in a bun.*

**bunch**

**bunch** /bʌntʃ/ *noun*
**1** a group of things that grow together or are tied together, especially BANANAs, GRAPEs, flowers, or keys: *He gave me a bunch of roses.*
**2** (*informal*) a lot of something: *The doctor asked me a whole bunch of questions.*
**3** (*informal*) a group of people: *I went to the mall with a bunch of my friends.*
→ see Thesaurus box at **group**[1]

**bun·dle** /ˈbʌndl/ *noun*
a group of things that are usually tied together, especially papers, letters, clothes, or sticks: *She went to her desk and took out a bundle of old letters.*
→ see Thesaurus box at **group**[1]

**bun·gle** /ˈbʌŋgəl/ *verb*
to do something badly: *He bungled a kick early in the game, and they lost by one point.*

**bunk** /bʌŋk/ *noun*
**1** (*also* **bunk bed**) one of two beds that are attached together, one on top of the other: *At camp, I slept on the top bunk.*
**2** a narrow bed on a ship or train, that is attached to the wall

**bun·ny** /ˈbʌni/ (*also* **ˈbunny ˌrabbit**) *noun* (plural **bunnies**)
a word used by children to mean "rabbit"

**buoy** /ˈbui/ *noun*
an object that floats on water, used for showing which parts of an area of water are safe or dangerous: *Boats must not go to the right of the buoys because there are rocks there.*

**bur·den** /ˈbɚdn/ *noun*
something you are responsible for that is difficult or that worries you: *My father's long illness was a burden on my mother.*
—**burdensome** *adjective* (*formal*) difficult or worrying to deal with: *For some children, writing letters is burdensome.*

**bu·reau** /ˈbyʊroʊ/ *noun*
**1** a government department: *the Federal Bureau of Investigation*
**2** an organization that collects or provides information: *We went to the visitors' bureau to get some information about the best places to visit in the city.*
[**ORIGIN:** 1600-1700 From the French word for "desk or office." *Bureau* originally meant "cloth used for covering desks."]

**bu·reauc·ra·cy** /byʊˈrɑkrəsi/ *noun*
official systems that are annoying because there are a lot of rules and it takes a long time to do things: *It took three months to get a visa because of all the bureaucracy.*
—**bureaucratic** /ˌbyʊrəˈkrætɪk/ *adjective* relating to bureaucracy: *a bureaucratic government department*

**burg·er** /ˈbɚgɚ/ *noun*
a flat round piece of cooked BEEF, usually eaten inside a BUN: *Could I get a burger and fries, please?* **SYNONYM: hamburger**

**bur·glar** /ˈbɚglɚ/ *noun*
someone who goes into a building to steal things: *Burglars broke into their house and stole the TV.*
—**burglary** *noun* an occasion when someone steals things from a building: *There have been several burglaries in our neighborhood recently.*
—**burglarize** *verb* to go into a building and steal things
[**ORIGIN:** 1500-1600 From the Latin word *burgare*, which means "to break in and steal," from *burgus*, which means "castle or defended place."]

B

**bur·i·al** /ˈberiəl/ *noun*
the act of putting a dead person into the ground: *The pyramids were used for the burial of Egyptian kings.*

**burn¹** /bɚn/ *verb* (**burned** *or* **burnt** /bɚnt/)
**1** to destroy or damage something with fire: *We burned all the dead leaves from the trees. | The fire has caused a lot of damage and many buildings are still burning.*
**2** to hurt your body with fire or something hot: *Ricky burned his hand on the stove.*
**3** if a fire or wood burns, it is producing flames and heat: *A warm fire was burning in the fireplace.*
**PHRASAL VERBS**
**burn something down**
if a building burns down, fire destroys it: *The hotel burned down after a fire started in the kitchen. | Two men used a can of gas to burn the building down.*
**burn up**
to be destroyed by great heat: *The satellite will burn up as it falls back to Earth.*

**burn²** *noun*
an injury or mark caused by fire or heat: *The girl spilled boiling water on her arm, and she was taken to the hospital and treated for burns.*

**burn·out** /ˈbɚnaʊt/ *noun*
the state of being extremely tired and unable to work any longer, because you have been working very hard for a long time: *He stopped coaching in 2003 because of burnout.*

**burnt** /bɚnt/ *verb*
a past tense and past participle of BURN

**burp** /bɚp/ *verb*
if you burp, gas comes up from your stomach through your mouth and makes a noise: *It is not polite to burp when you're sitting at the dinner table.*
—**burp** *noun* the noise you make when you burp

**bur·row** /ˈbɚoʊ/ *noun*
a hole in the ground that a rabbit or another small animal digs and lives in
—**burrow** *verb* if an animal burrows, it digs a hole in the ground

**burst¹** /bɚst/ *verb* (**burst**)
**1** to break open suddenly because of pressure from air, water, or something heavy inside: *One of the pipes in the basement burst and there was water everywhere.*
**2 burst into tears** = to start crying suddenly: *"I hate you!" she shouted, and burst into tears.*
**3 burst out laughing** = to start laughing suddenly: *"Look at his big ears," she said, and burst out laughing.*
→ see Thesaurus box at **break¹**

**burst²** *noun*
**a burst of something** = a short period when there is suddenly more activity or noise than before: *He won the race in a final burst of speed.*

**bur·y** /ˈberi/ *verb* (**buried**, **buries**)
**1** to put a dead person into the ground: *My grandfather died and he was buried in the graveyard.*
**2** to hide something by putting it in the ground or covering it with something: *The pirates buried their treasure on this island.*

**bus** /bʌs/ *noun* (plural **buses**)
a large vehicle that people pay to travel on: *Are you going to go by bus? | Five people got on the bus.* → see picture on page **A26**
[**ORIGIN:** 1800-1900 From the Latin word *omnibus*, which means "for everyone." Buses were originally called "omnibuses," because they were vehicles that everyone could travel in.]

**bush** /bʊʃ/ *noun*
a big plant with a lot of thin branches: *A bird has made its nest in the bush by the fence.*

**bush·el** /ˈbʊʃəl/ *noun*
a unit for measuring dry food, equal to 8 gallons or 36.4 liters

**bush·y** /ˈbʊʃi/ *adjective*
bushy hair or fur is thick and strong and sticks out: *The man had a large nose and big bushy eyebrows.*

**bus·i·ly** /ˈbɪzəli/ *adverb*
in a busy way: *Dad was in the kitchen, busily cooking breakfast.*

**busi·ness** /ˈbɪznɪs/ *noun*
**1** the work of buying and selling goods or providing services: *The company is very successful and it does business all over the*

*world.* | *My father's an engineer and he often travels abroad on business.*
**2** a company that earns money by selling things or providing services: *My brother started his own business repairing computers.*
**3 mind your own business** (*informal*) = used when telling someone in a rude way that they should not ask you about something because it is private: *"Do you love Craig?" "Mind your own business!"*
**4 none of your business** (*informal*) = if something is none of your business, you should not expect to know about it: *It's none of his business how much money you earn.*
→ see Thesaurus box at **company**
[**ORIGIN:** 1300-1400 From "busy." "Business" used to mean "the state of being anxious about something."]

**busi·ness·man** /ˈbɪznɪsˌmæn/ *noun* (plural **businessmen** /ˈbɪznɪsˌmen/)
someone who works in business or who owns a business: *Perry was a very successful businessman and owned his own company.*

**busi·ness·wom·an** /ˈbɪznɪsˌwʊmən/ *noun* (plural **businesswomen** /ˈbɪznɪsˌwɪmɪn/)
a woman who works in business or who owns a business

**ˈbus ˌstation** *noun*
a place where buses start and finish their trips

**ˈbus stop** *noun*
a place where buses stop so people can get on and off: *I'm getting off at the next bus stop.* **SYNONYM: stop** → see picture on page **A26**

**bust¹** /bʌst/ *noun*
**1** a model of someone's head, shoulders, and upper chest: *There was a bust of Abraham Lincoln in the museum.*
**2** a woman's chest area: *This style of dress is good for women with a large bust.*

**bust²** *adjective* (*informal*)
**go bust** = a business that goes bust stops working because it does not make enough money: *The economy was bad, and a lot of small businesses went bust.*

**bus·tle** /ˈbʌsəl/ *verb*
**1** if a place is bustling with activity, people, or life, it is full of people and activity: *Before Christmas, the stores are bustling with people.*
**2** to move around in a busy way: *I could hear Mom bustling around downstairs, making breakfast.*

**bus·y** /ˈbɪzi/ *adjective* (**busier**, **busiest**)
**1** someone who is busy is working or has a lot to do: *Can we talk later? I'm busy right now.*
**2** if a telephone line is busy, someone is talking on it when you try to call them: *I tried to call her earlier, but her line was busy.*
**3** a busy place or time is full of things happening and people working hard: *There are 900 students in the school, so it's a pretty busy place.* **ANTONYM: quiet**

**bus·y·bod·y** /ˈbɪziˌbɑdi/ *noun* (plural **busybodies**)
someone who wants to know about other people's private lives, in a way that is annoying: *She's such a busybody – she's always watching the neighbors over the fence.*

**but¹** /bət; *strong* bʌt/ *conjunction*
**1** used before you say something that is different from or unexpected after what you have just said: *At the end of the day, we were all tired but happy.* | *Dan's smart but he never does well on tests.*
**2** used before you give the reason why you cannot do something: *I'd love to come to your house, but I have homework to do.*
**3** used after "excuse me" and "I'm sorry": *Excuse me, but I didn't hear what you said.*

**but²** *preposition*
except for someone or something: *There's nobody here but me.*

**butch·er¹** /ˈbʊtʃɚ/ *noun*
a person who cuts and sells meat
[**ORIGIN:** 1200-1300 From the old French word *bouchier*, from *bouc*, which means "male goat."]

**butcher²** *verb*
to kill animals in order to use or sell the meat

**butt¹** /bʌt/ *noun*
**1** (*informal*) the part of your body that you sit on **SYNONYM: buttocks**
**2** the end of a cigarette after most of it has been smoked: *The ashtray was full of cigarette butts.*

**butt²** *verb*
PHRASAL VERB
**butt in**
to interrupt someone when he or she is speaking, or try to get involved in what someone is doing: *Julie kept butting in as I was trying to tell my story and it was really annoying.*

**but·ter** /ˈbʌtɚ/ *noun*
a yellow substance made from milk, that you spread on bread or use in cooking: *Do you want some butter on your bread?*
[ORIGIN: From the Greek word *boutyron*, from *bous* and *tyros*, which mean "cow" and "cheese."]

**but·ter·fly** /ˈbʌtɚˌflaɪ/ *noun* (plural **butterflies**)
an insect with large wings that often have beautiful colors on them

**butterfly**

**but·ter·milk** /ˈbʌtɚˌmɪlk/ *noun*
the liquid that is left after butter has been made, which you can drink or use in cooking

**but·ter·scotch** /ˈbʌtɚˌskɑtʃ/ *noun*
a type of candy made from butter and sugar boiled together

**but·tocks** /ˈbʌtəks/ *plural noun* (*formal*)
the part of your body that you sit on SYNONYM: **butt**

**but·ton** /ˈbʌtn/ *noun*
**1** a small round object on a piece of clothing, that you push through a hole to fasten it: *He's only five but he can do up the buttons on his shirt.* → see picture on page **A6**
**2** a small part of a machine that you press to make it work: *She pushed a button on the DVD player and the movie started.*
**3** a small metal or plastic pin with words or a picture on it: *She was wearing a button with "Save the whales" on it.*
—**button** *verb* to fasten clothing using buttons: *She buttoned her jacket and went outside.*
→ see Thesaurus box at **fasten**
[ORIGIN: 1300-1400 From the old French word *boton*, from *boter*, which means "to push."]

**buy** /baɪ/ *verb* (**bought** /bɔt/)
to get something by paying money for it: *Her parents bought her a puppy for her birthday.* | *I bought a nice sweater from that store.*
—**buyer** *noun* someone who wants to buy something from another person: *He has found a buyer for his boat.*

**THESAURUS: buy**

**purchase** to buy something: *You can purchase tickets by phone or online.*

**acquire** (*formal*) to buy a company or property: *The state acquired the land to protect the plants and animals on it.*

**get** to buy or obtain something: *I never know what to get Dad for his birthday.*

**buzz¹** /bʌz/ *verb*
**1** to make a continuous noise like the sound of a BEE: *There was a fly buzzing around my room and I couldn't sleep.*
**2** if a group of people or a place is buzzing with activity or excitement, the people are very busy or excited about something: *The crowd was buzzing with excitement before the band came on stage.*

**buzz²** *noun*
a noise like the sound of a BEE: *I could hear the buzz of voices in the next room.* → see picture on page **A22**

**buz·zard** /ˈbʌzɚd/ *noun*
a large wild bird that eats dead animals SYNONYM: **vulture**

**buzz·er** /ˈbʌzɚ/ *noun*
a button that makes a buzzing sound when you press it: *On the game show, the first person to press the buzzer is allowed to answer the question.*

**by¹** /baɪ/ *preposition*
**1** near or beside: *He was standing by the window and looking out.*
**2** past: *She walked by me but she didn't look at me or say hello.*
**3** used for showing who or what does something: *Her cat was hit by a truck.* | *I'm reading a book written by J.K. Rowling.*
**4** used for saying what someone uses to do something, or how someone achieves something: *Your tickets will be delivered by mail.* | *We came back by bus.* | *You can save*

*money by eating more meals at home.*

**5** not later than a time: *I have to be back home by 6:00.*

**6** used for saying which part of something someone holds: *She grabbed him by the arm.*

**7** used for giving the two different parts of a measurement: *The room is 24 feet wide by 36 feet long.*

**8** **(all) by yourself** = alone or without help: *I was scared to go there by myself.*

→ **by the way** at way

**by²** *adverb*

**1** past: *We sat on the grass in the park and watched the people go by.*

**2** **by and large** = used when talking generally about something: *By and large, the new system is working well, but there are a few small problems.*

**bye** /baɪ/ (*also* **bye-bye**) (*informal*)
another word for GOODBYE

**by·pass** /ˈbaɪpæs/ *noun*
an operation that doctors do on someone's heart because a tube carrying blood is getting blocked. They put in another tube so that blood can flow through it instead: *a heart bypass operation*

**by·stand·er** /ˈbaɪˌstændɚ/ *noun*
someone who is in a place when something happens: *Two innocent bystanders were hurt when a fight started in the street.*

**byte** /baɪt/ *noun*
a unit for measuring the amount of information a computer can use. A byte is equal to eight BITs: *There are one million bytes in a megabyte.*

# Cc

**C¹**
the written abbreviation of **Celsius** or **Centigrade**: *Water boils at 100°C.*

**C²** /si/ *noun*
**1** a GRADE that you get on a test or in a class for doing average work: *Carol got a C in math.*
**2** the first note in the musical SCALE of C, or the musical KEY based on this note

**cab** /kæb/ *noun*
**1** a car with a driver who you pay to take you somewhere: *We'll leave our car at home and take a cab to the airport.* **SYNONYM: taxi** → see picture on page **A26**
**2** the part of a truck or train where the driver sits

**cab·bage** /ˈkæbɪdʒ/ *noun*
a large round vegetable with thick green or purple leaves → see picture on page **A12**
[**ORIGIN:** 1400-1500 From the French word *caboche*, which means "head." A cabbage is round like a person's head.]

**cab·in** /ˈkæbɪn/ *noun*
**1** a small house made of wood, usually in a forest or the mountains: *On weekends, he often goes to his log cabin in the mountains.*
**2** a small room in which you sleep on a ship
**3** the area inside an airplane where the passengers sit

**cab·i·net** /ˈkæbənɪt/ *noun*
**1** a piece of furniture with shelves covered by a door or drawers: *He looked in the kitchen cabinets for something to eat.* → see picture on page **A9**
**2** an important group of politicians who help the leader of a government: *The members of the cabinet discussed the problem with the president.*

**ca·ble** /ˈkeɪbəl/ *noun*
**1** a tube containing wires that carry electricity, telephone signals, or television signals: *I connected my computer to my printer with a cable.* → see picture on page **A20**
**2** a system of broadcasting television using cables: *We have cable mainly because my dad wants to see all the football games.*
**3** a thick strong metal rope: *The bridge is supported by steel cables.*

**cac·tus** /ˈkæktəs/ *noun* (plural **cacti** /ˈkæktaɪ/ *or* **cactuses**)
a plant that has thick stems and leaves covered with sharp points, and that grows in hot dry places such as deserts

**ca·fe** (*also* **café**) /kæˈfeɪ/ *noun*
a restaurant where you can buy drinks and simple meals: *It was a long trip so we stopped for lunch in a cafe.*

**caf·e·te·ri·a** /ˌkæfəˈtɪriə/ *noun*
a restaurant in a school, office, or factory where people take food from a COUNTER and then sit down: *In the school cafeteria, the children can choose hot or cold lunches.*
[**ORIGIN:** 1800-1900 From the Spanish word for "coffee store."]

**caf·feine** /kæˈfin/ *noun*
a substance in coffee, tea, and some other drinks that makes people feel more awake

**cage** /keɪdʒ/ *noun*
a container made of wires or bars, used for keeping birds or animals in: *I didn't like seeing the monkeys in a cage. They should be free and climbing trees.*
[**ORIGIN:** 1100-1200 From the Latin word *cavea*, which means "hollow place, or cage."]

**cake** /keɪk/ *noun*
**1** a sweet food made by baking a mixture of flour, fat, sugar, and eggs: *Do you want a piece of cake? | She made him a birthday cake with 11 candles on it.*
**2** a flat round piece of food made from fish, rice, or potato: *We had salmon cakes for dinner.*
**3** **be a piece of cake** (*informal*) = to be very easy: *"Was the test difficult?" "No, it was a piece of cake."*

**cal·ci·um** /ˈkælsiəm/ *noun*
a chemical ELEMENT. Calcium is a white-gray color and it is necessary for strong teeth and bones: *You get calcium from milk.*

**cal·cu·late** /ˈkælkyəˌleɪt/ *verb*
to find out a number or amount using mathematics: *Calculate how many oranges you can buy with $8 if they cost 50 cents each.*

[**ORIGIN:** 1500-1600 From the Latin word *calculare*, from *calculus*, which means "small stone." Small stones were used for counting.]

**WORD FAMILY: calculate**

**calculate** *verb* | **calculation** *noun* | **calculator** *noun*

**cal·cu·la·tion** /ˌkælkyəˈleɪʃən/ *noun*
if you do a calculation, you use mathematics to find a number or amount: *Can you do this calculation? What's 100 multiplied by 560?*

**cal·cu·la·tor** /ˈkælkyəˌleɪtɚ/ *noun*
a small machine that you can use to find the answer to mathematical problems → see picture on page **A19**

**cal·en·dar** /ˈkæləndɚ/ *noun*
a set of pages that show all the days in a year: *I looked at the calendar and noticed that it was only two weeks until Dad's birthday.* → see picture on page **A19**

[**ORIGIN:** 1100-1200 From the Latin word *kalendae*, which means "the first day of the month."]

**calf** /kæf/ *noun* (plural **calves** /kævz/)
**1** a young cow or BULL
**2** the back of your leg between your knee and your foot → see picture on page **A2**

**call**[1] /kɔl/ *verb*
**1** to telephone someone: *If you are going to be late, don't forget to call me.* | *Why don't you call them and explain the problem?*
**2** to give someone or something a name or description: *We decided to call the puppy Micky.* | *New York is sometimes called The Big Apple.*
**3** to say or shout something loudly: *"I'm coming!" Paula called.* | *I called out his name.*
**4** to ask or order someone to come to you: *The principal called me into her office.* | *Call an ambulance!*
**5** to ask publicly for something to be done: *Many people are calling for new laws to protect the environment.*
**6** **call the shots** (*informal*) = to be the person who decides what will be done in a situation: *My brother was older than me, so he always called the shots.*
→ see Thesaurus box at **shout**[1]

**PHRASAL VERBS**

**call (someone) back**
to telephone someone who has telephoned you: *Can I call you back later? Dinner's ready.*

**call someone in**
to ask or order someone to come and help you with a difficult situation: *The country's leader called in the army to stop the violence.*

**call something off**
to decide that an event will not happen or will not continue: *The game was called off because of the rain.*

**call on someone**
to publicly ask someone to do something: *The teacher called on Jake to answer the question.*

**call**[2] *noun*
**1** if you make a call, you talk to someone by telephone: *Can I use the phone now? I need to make a call.* | *If she wants some advice, ask her to give me a call.*
**2** the high sound that a bird or animal makes: *I could hear the call of an owl in the trees outside my window.*
**3** a request or demand for someone to do something: *There have been calls for the military to withdraw from the area.*
**4** **be on call** = if people such as doctors or nurses are on call, they must be ready to go to work if they are needed: *The doctors are on call 24 hours a day.*
**5** (*informal*) a decision: *No one knows what to do for sure. It's a tough call.*

**call·er** /ˈkɔlɚ/ *noun*
someone who is making a telephone call: *Several callers said they really liked the new radio show.*

**calm**[1] /kɑm/ *adjective*
**1** not angry or upset: *Try to stay calm, even if other people are getting angry.*
**2** if the water in the ocean or in a lake is calm, there are no big waves: *The wind stopped and the lake was calm again.*
**3** peaceful or without any fighting: *Reports from the city say there is no more fighting and the situation is calm.*
**4** not windy: *We were glad of the calm weather after the storm.*
—**calmly** *adverb* in a calm way
—**calmness** *noun* a calm quality

[**ORIGIN:** 1300-1400 From the Latin word *cauma*, which means "heat." Everything is quiet and still in the heat of the middle of the day.]

**calm²** *verb*
**PHRASAL VERB**
**calm down**
to stop being angry or upset: *Calm down. I'm sure she didn't mean to be unkind.*



**cal·o·rie** /ˈkæləri/ *noun*
a unit for measuring the amount of energy food will produce: *A potato has about 90 calories.*
[**ORIGIN:** 1800-1900 From the Latin word *calor*, which means "heat." Calories provide the energy that your body uses to stay warm and do activities.]

**calves** /kævz/ *noun*
the plural of CALF

**cam·cord·er** /ˈkæmˌkɔrdɚ/ *noun*
a small piece of equipment like a camera, that you use to record moving pictures and sound

**came** /keɪm/ *verb*
the past tense of COME

**cam·el** /ˈkæməl/ *noun*
a large animal with one or two HUMPs on its back, that lives in very hot dry places and is used to carry goods or people: *Camels can go without water for days in the desert.*

**cam·er·a** /ˈkæmərə/ *noun*
a piece of equipment used for taking photographs, or for making movies or television programs: *I'll bring my camera with me so I can take some pictures of the trip.*
[**ORIGIN:** 1700-1800 From the Latin phrase *camera obscura*, which literally means "dark room." A camera obscura was a room or box with a hole that light came through, making an image appear on the inside.]

**cam·er·a·man** /ˈkæmərəmæn/ (plural **cameramen**) *noun*
someone whose job is to use a movie or television camera

**cam·ou·flage** /ˈkæməˌflɑːʒ/ *noun*
clothes or colors that hide people, animals, or things by making them look like the things around them: *Soldiers wear camouflage because it makes it more difficult for the enemy to see them.*
—**camouflage** *verb* to hide something using camouflage: *Snakes that live in trees camouflage themselves by having brown or green skin.*
[**ORIGIN:** 1900-2000 From the French word *camoufler*, which means "to change the appearance of something,"]

**camp¹** /kæmp/ *noun*
**1** a place where people stay in tents or in temporary buildings for a short time: *We hiked back to camp. | a refugee camp*
**2** a place where children stay and do activities during their vacation: *At summer camp the kids can be outdoors and active all day.*
[**ORIGIN:** 1500-1600 From the Latin word *campus*, which means "field."]

**camp²** *verb*
to live in a tent for a short time, usually on vacation: *We camped on the shore of the lake.*

**cam·paign¹** /kæmˈpeɪn/ *noun*
a series of things that you do in order to persuade people to do something: *He started a campaign to get kids to eat more fruit in school lunches. | the presidential campaign*
[**ORIGIN:** 1600-1700 From the French word *campagne*, which means "open country." Soldiers went out into the country to fight or to practice fighting, and "campaign" was originally used about military actions.]

**campaign²** *verb*
to try to persuade politicians to do something, or the public to vote for you: *The governor is campaigning for reelection, but I don't know if he will get enough votes.*

**camp·er** /ˈkæmpɚ/ *noun*
**1** a vehicle which you can live in while you are on vacation
**2** someone who is staying in a tent on vacation: *Yellowstone National Park is popular with hikers and campers.*

**camp·ground** /ˈkæmpgraʊnd/ *noun*
a place where there are many small areas for people to camp in: *The largest campground in Yosemite Valley has 238 campsites.*

**camp·ing** /ˈkæmpɪŋ/ *noun*
the activity of living in a tent for a short time: *Do you want to go camping in the mountains this weekend?*

**camp·site** /ˈkæmpsaɪt/ *noun*
a small area in a campground where people can camp: *There are around 60 campsites in the Lower Pines campground.*

**cam·pus** /ˈkæmpəs/ *noun* (plural **campuses**)
the land or buildings of a college: *Many*

*students live on campus, but some live in nearby apartment buildings.*

**can**[1] /kən; *strong* kæn/ *verb*
**1** to be able to do something: *She can speak French because she lived in France.*
**2** to be allowed to do something: *You can leave when you finish your work.*
**3 Can you ...?** = used for asking someone to do something for you: *Can you pass me the salt?*

**can**[2] /kæn/ *noun*
a metal container that you buy food or liquid in: *I opened up a can of soup.*

**Ca·na·di·an** /kəˈneɪdiən/ *adjective*
from Canada
—**Canadian** *noun* someone from Canada

**ca·nal** /kəˈnæl/ *noun*
a kind of river that people have made, so that boats or water can go from one place to another: *The Panama Canal connects the Atlantic and Pacific Oceans.*

**ca·nar·y** /kəˈneri/ *noun* (plural **canaries**)
a small yellow bird that sings and is often kept as a pet

**can·cel** /ˈkænsəl/ *verb*
to stop something that you had planned from happening: *We had to cancel our trip, because Jen got sick.*
—**cancellation** /ˌkænsəˈleɪʃən/ *noun* the act of canceling something: *Snow caused the cancellation of many flights.*

**can·cer** /ˈkænsɚ/ *noun*
a serious illness that makes the cells in a part of the body grow in a way that is not normal: *Smoking is dangerous because it can cause lung cancer.*

**Can·cer** /ˈkænsɚ/ *noun*
**1** the fourth sign of the ZODIAC, represented by a CRAB
**2** someone born between June 22 and July 22

**can·di·date** /ˈkændəˌdeɪt/ *noun*
**1** someone who is trying to win an election: *The Republican candidate for president did not get enough votes to win the election.*
**2** someone who wants to be chosen for a job: *A lot of people applied for the job, but she was the best candidate.*
[**ORIGIN:** 1600-1700 From the Latin word *candidatus*, which means "dressed in white." In ancient Rome, people who were trying to get elected wore white clothes.]

**can·dle** /ˈkændl/ *noun*
a thing that you burn to produce light, made of a piece of WAX with string through the middle: *I lit some candles when the lights went out.* → see picture on page **A8**
[**ORIGIN:** 600-700 From the Latin word *candela*, from *candere*, which means "to shine."]

**can·dle·stick** /ˈkændlˌstɪk/ *noun*
a specially shaped metal or wooden object used to hold a candle

**can·dy** /ˈkændi/ *noun* (plural **candies**)
a sweet food made of sugar or chocolate: *I gave her a piece of candy.*
[**ORIGIN:** 1200-1300 From the Arabic word *qandi*, which means "covered with sugar."]

**ˈcandy bar** *noun*
a long narrow piece of candy, usually covered with chocolate

**cane** /keɪn/ *noun*
**1** a thin stick that you use to help you walk: *My grandfather uses a cane to walk because he's not as strong as he used to be.*
**2** (*also* **sugar cane**) a plant that farmers grow to produce sugar

**canned** /kænd/ *adjective*
canned food is food that you buy in a can: *canned tomatoes*

**can·ni·bal** /ˈkænəbəl/ *noun*
a person who eats human flesh

**can·non** /ˈkænən/ *noun*
a large gun, usually on wheels, that fires a big round metal ball. Cannons were used in the past: *They attacked the fort with cannons.*

**can·not** /ˈkænɑt/ *verb*
can not: *We cannot accept this change in the rules.* **SYNONYM: can't**

**ca·noe** /kəˈnu/ *noun*
a light narrow boat which you move through

the water using a short piece of wood with a flat end, called a PADDLE: *They paddled up the river in their canoe.*

—**canoeing** *noun* the activity of traveling in a canoe

**can·o·py** /ˈkænəpi/ *noun* (plural **canopies**)

**1** a cloth cover above something, for example a bed or door

**2** if trees form a canopy, the branches and leaves of different trees are touching or very close together: *Birds flew from branch to branch beneath the forest canopy.*

**can·ta·loupe** /ˈkæntəlˌoʊp/ *noun*

a large sweet fruit that is a type of MELON and is orange inside → see picture on page **A13**

**can·vas** /ˈkænvəs/ *noun*

**1** a type of strong cloth that is used to make tents, sails, bags, and light shoes: *The tent was made out of canvas.* | *a canvas bag*

**2** a piece of canvas on which a picture is painted

**can·yon** /ˈkænjən/ *noun*

a deep valley with very steep sides: *The Colorado River flows through the Grand Canyon.*

[**ORIGIN:** 1800-1900 From the Spanish word *cañón*, which means "tube or deep valley."]

**can't** /kænt/ *verb*

the short form of "cannot": *I know you told me his name, but I can't remember it.*

**cap** /kæp/ *noun*

**1** a cloth hat with a curved part sticking out at the front: *a baseball cap* → see picture on page **A6**

**2** a cover that closes a bottle or tube, or goes on the end of a pen: *I can't get the cap on this bottle off. Can you try?*

**ca·pa·ble** Ac /ˈkeɪpəbəl/ *adjective*

**1 be capable of (doing) something** = to be able to do something because you have the abilities or qualities that are needed: *He's very fast – I think he's capable of winning a gold medal.* **ANTONYM: incapable**

**2** able to do something well: *She's a very capable lawyer and she wins most of her cases.* **SYNONYM: able**

—**capability** /ˌkeɪpəˈbɪləti/ *noun* the ability to do something: *Do the armed forces have the capability to win the war?*

[**ORIGIN:** 1500-1600 From the Latin word *capabilis*, which means "able to take things in."]

**WORD FAMILY: capable**

**capable** *adjective* | **incapable** *adjective* | **capability** *noun*

**ca·pac·i·ty** Ac /kəˈpæsəti/ *noun* (plural **capacities**) (*formal*)

**1** the amount that something can contain: *The tank has a capacity of 20 gallons.*

**2** the ability to do or produce something: *Children have a great capacity for learning.*

**cape** /keɪp/ *noun*

**1** a long loose piece of clothing without SLEEVEs that fastens around your neck: *Batman wears a black cape.*

**2** a large area of land that has the ocean on three sides of it: *She has a beach house on Cape Cod, on the coast of Massachusetts.*

**cap·i·tal** /ˈkæpətl/ *noun*

**1** the city where a country's or state's main government is: *Rome is the capital of Italy.*

**2** (*also* **capital letter**) the large form of a letter, for example B rather than b: *Begin every new sentence with a capital letter.* | *Please write your name in capitals.*

**3** money you have available to start a business or to make more money: *She started up the company with her own capital and a loan from the bank.*

[**ORIGIN:** 1100-1200 From the Latin word *capitalis*, from *caput*, which means "head." A capital is where the leader, or head, of a country or state stays.]

**cap·i·tal·ism** /ˈkæpətlˌɪzəm/ *noun*

a system in which most businesses belong to private owners, not to the government: *Capitalism is a system that encourages companies to compete with each other.*

—**capitalist** *adjective* based on capitalism:

*The U.S. is the world's greatest capitalist country.*

**cap·i·tal·ize** /ˈkæpətlˌaɪz/ *verb*
to put a capital letter at the beginning of a word or sentence: *The names of countries must be capitalized.*

**ˌcapital ˈpunishment** *noun* (*formal*)
the punishment of legally killing someone for a crime: *The state doesn't have capital punishment, so he won't be executed.* **SYNONYM: death penalty**

**cap·i·tol** /ˈkæpətl/ *noun*
**1 the Capitol** = the building in Washington, D.C. where the U.S. Congress meets
**2** the building in each U.S. state where the people who make state laws meet: *the Virginia state capitol*

**cap·puc·ci·no** /ˌkæpəˈtʃinoʊ/ *noun* (plural **cappuccinos**)
coffee made with hot milk with bubbles

**Cap·ri·corn** /ˈkæprɪˌkɔrn/ *noun*
**1** the tenth sign of the ZODIAC, represented by a goat
**2** someone born between December 22 and January 19

capsize

**cap·size** /ˈkæpsaɪz/ *verb*
if a boat capsizes, it turns over in the water: *Fourteen people died when the boat capsized in freezing water.*

**cap·sule** /ˈkæpsəl/ *noun*
**1** a very small object with medicine in it, that you swallow
**2** the part of a spacecraft that people live and work in
→ see Thesaurus box at **medicine**

**cap·tain** /ˈkæptən/ *noun* (*written abbreviation*: **Capt.**)
**1** someone who is in charge of a ship or airplane: *The captain of the ship was waiting to greet the new passengers.*
**2** the leader of a sports team: *Troy was chosen to be the captain of the football team.*
**3** an officer in the army, air force, or Marines: *My brother is a captain in the army.*
[**ORIGIN:** 1300-1400 From the Latin word *capitaneus*, which means "chief," from *caput*, which means "head."]

**cap·tion** /ˈkæpʃən/ *noun*
words above or below a picture or photograph that give information about it: *The caption under the photograph said "A winter's day in New York."*

**cap·tive** /ˈkæptɪv/ *noun*
someone who is a prisoner, especially in a war: *The enemy soldiers refused to free their captives.*

**cap·tiv·i·ty** /kæpˈtɪvəti/ *noun*
if a person or animal is in captivity, they are kept somewhere and are not free: *The elephants were born in captivity in the zoo, so they have never been in the wild.*

**cap·ture** /ˈkæptʃɚ/ *verb*
**1** to catch a person or animal that you intend to keep somewhere: *Police have captured one of the thieves, but the other escaped.* **SYNONYM: catch**
**2** to get control of a place during a war: *The town was captured by enemy soldiers.*
**3** to get someone's attention: *Her beauty soon captured the attention of the world and she became a star.*
—**capture** *noun* the act of capturing someone or something: *We heard about the capture of the terrorists on the radio.*

**car** /kɑr/ *noun*
**1** a vehicle with four wheels and an engine, that carries a small number of people: *She got into the car and drove away.*
**2** a part of a train that carries passengers or goods: *Most of the cars on the train were completely full.* | *the dining car*

**car·a·mel** /ˈkærəməl/ *noun*
**1** candy made of cooked sugar, butter, and milk
**2** a flavor used in cakes and sweet food, made from burned sugar: *caramel ice cream*

**car·bo·hy·drate** /ˌkɑrboʊˈhaɪdreɪt/ *noun*
a substance in foods such as sugar, rice, bread, or potatoes that gives your body energy: *For your main meal you should have some carbohydrates, as well as protein.*

C

**car·bon** /ˈkɑrbən/ *noun*
a chemical ELEMENT that is in all living things, and in coal and DIAMONDs

**carbon di·ox·ide** /ˌkɑrbən daɪˈɑksaɪd/ *noun*
a gas that is a mixture of carbon and oxygen, and that people breathe out: *Plants take in carbon dioxide from the air.*

**ˌcarbon ˈfootprint** *noun*
the amount of carbon dioxide produced by the activities of a person or organization: *People try to reduce their carbon footprint because carbon dioxide helps to cause global warming.*

**carbon mo·nox·ide** /ˌkɑrbən məˈnɑksaɪd/ *noun*
a poisonous gas that is produced when engines burn gasoline

**card** /kɑrd/ *noun*
**1** a folded piece of stiff paper with a picture on the front, that you send to people at special times: *I have to buy a birthday card for my sister.*
**2** a small flat piece of plastic that you can use to pay for something: *Mom usually pays by card rather than using cash.*
**3** a small piece of plastic or stiff paper that has information about someone or something: *His phone number and email address are on his business card.*
**4** one of a set of 52 pieces of stiff paper that are used for playing games: *There are four players so deal 13 cards to each player.* | *a deck of cards*
**5 cards** = a game in which people use a set of cards: *Let's play cards.*
[**ORIGIN:** 1400-1500 From the Latin word *charta*, which means "sheet of paper."]

**card·board** /ˈkɑrdbɔrd/ *noun*
very thick stiff paper: *When we moved to a new house, we had to pack all our things in cardboard boxes.*

**car·di·nal** /ˈkɑrdənəl/ *noun*
**1** a priest of very high rank in the Roman Catholic Church
**2** a bright red bird

**care¹** /ker/ *verb*
**1** if you care about someone or something, that person or thing is important to you: *He cares deeply about his children.* | *I don't care if it's raining. I'm going to go out anyway.*
**2 who cares?** = used for saying that you do not think something is important: *"It's pretty expensive." "Who cares? It'll be fun!"*

**PHRASAL VERB**

**care for someone or something**
**1** to do things for someone who is old or sick, or for a young child: *She took time off work to care for her sick mother.*
**2 not care for someone or something** = to not like someone or something: *I don't really care for indoor sports. I prefer to be outdoors.*

**care²** *noun*
**1** the things you do to help someone who is old, sick, or very young: *He is old and sick and will need constant medical care.*
**2 take care of something** = **a)** to watch someone or something and make sure it is safe, or to give it the things it needs: *Can you take care of my cat while I'm on vacation?* **b)** to deal with something and do what needs to be done: *She takes care of the paperwork for her husband's business.*
**3** careful attention so that you do not make a mistake or damage something: *They checked the measurements with great care to make sure they were correct.*
**4 take care** (*informal*) = used when saying "goodbye" to someone you know: *"OK, I'll talk to you soon." "Yeah, take care."*

**WORD FAMILY: care**
**care** *noun* | **careful** *adjective* | **carefully** *adverb* | **careless** *adjective* | **carelessly** *adverb* | **carelessness** *noun* | **carefree** *adjective*

**ca·reer** /kəˈrɪr/ *noun*
a job that you know a lot about and that you do for a long time: *During her career as an actress, she appeared in 42 movies.*
→ see Thesaurus box at **job**
[**ORIGIN:** 1500-1600 From the French word *carrière*, which means "road or racetrack." Someone's working life is like a trip along a road.]

**care·free** /ˈkerfri/ *adjective*
without any problems or worries: *The summer was a carefree time, when we didn't have to get up for school and could play all day.*

**care·ful** /ˈkerfəl/ *adjective*
thinking about what you are doing, so that you do not cause something bad to happen:

*Rosy's a careful driver. She's never had an accident.* | *Be careful with that hot pan or you'll get burned!* **ANTONYM: careless**
—**carefully** *adverb* in a careful way: *This is important so please listen carefully.*

**care·less** /ˈkerləs/ *adjective*
not thinking about what you are doing so that you make mistakes or damage things: *The players got a little careless and let the other team score.* | *He knows how to spell these words; he just doesn't think and makes careless mistakes.* **ANTONYM: careful**
—**carelessly** *adverb* in a careless way
—**carelessness** *noun* careless behavior

**ca·ress** /kəˈres/ *verb*
to gently touch or kiss someone in a way that shows love: *She caressed the baby's face.*
—**caress** *noun* an act of caressing someone

**car·go** /ˈkɑrgoʊ/ *noun* (plural **cargoes**)
the things that a ship or airplane is carrying: *The ship was carrying a cargo of oil.*

**Car·ib·be·an** /ˌkærəˈbiən/ *adjective*
from the islands in the Caribbean Sea, such as the Bahamas and Jamaica

**car·i·bou** /ˈkærəbu/ *noun* (plural **caribou**)
a large DEER with horns called ANTLERs that look like tree branches, that lives in the cold parts of North America **SYNONYM: reindeer**

**car·ni·val** /ˈkɑrnəvəl/ *noun*
**1** an outdoor event where people can ride on special machines and play games for prizes: *The kids had fun on the rides at the carnival.* **SYNONYM: fair**
**2** a public event at which people play music, wear special clothes, and dance in the streets: *At the carnival in Rio de Janeiro, people dress in costumes and parade through the streets.*
[**ORIGIN:** 1500-1600 From the Italian word *carnevale*, from *carne* and *levare*, which mean "meat" and "to remove." A carnival was originally an event several weeks before Easter, after which people stopped eating meat until Easter.]

**car·ni·vore** /ˈkɑrnəˌvɔr/ *noun*
an animal that eats meat: *Dogs are carnivores.*
—**carnivorous** /kɑrˈnɪvərəs/ *adjective* carnivorous animals eat meat
[**ORIGIN:** 1800-1900 From the Latin words *carnis*, a form of the word for "meat," and *vorare*, which means "to eat."]

**WORD FAMILY: carnivore**
**carnivore** *noun* | **herbivore** *noun* | **omnivore** *noun*

**car·ol** /ˈkærəl/ *noun*
a song that people sing at Christmas: *On Christmas Eve, we go to church and sing Christmas carols.*

**car·pen·ter** /ˈkɑrpəntɚ/ *noun*
someone whose job is making things from wood: *The carpenter was making some shelves.*
—**carpentry** /ˈkɑrpəntri/ *noun* the activity of making things from wood
[**ORIGIN:** 1100-1200 From the Latin word *carpentarius*, which means "carriage-maker."]

**car·pet** /ˈkɑrpɪt/ *noun*
a thick material for covering the floor of a room: *The carpet in my bedroom is blue.*

**ˈcar pool** *noun*
a group of people who ride together to school or work in one car
—**carpool** *verb* if people carpool, they ride together to school or work in one car

**car·riage** /ˈkærɪdʒ/ *noun*
a vehicle with wheels that is pulled by horses, for people to ride in

**car·rot** /ˈkærət/ *noun*
a long orange vegetable that grows under the ground → see picture on page **A12**

**car·ry** /ˈkæri/ *verb* (**carried**, **carries**)
**1** to have something in your hands or arms, or in your clothes as you go somewhere: *They carried the boxes out of the house.* | *She was carrying a grocery bag.* → see picture on page **A4**
**2** if a vehicle, pipe, or wire carries something, it takes it from one place to another: *The bus was carrying 25 passengers.* | *This wire carries the electricity from the battery to the light.*
**3** if you carry a disease, you can pass it to other people: *You can carry the virus and spread it to other people by sneezing.*
**4** if a store carries something, it has it for sale: *It's a store that carries children's clothes.*
**5 be/get carried away** = to be so excited that you do something that is not sensible: *Joseph got a little carried away, and jumped*

*up screaming "We've won!"*

**6** to have or involve something: *A job in a hospital carries some risks because you are around sick people all the time.*

[**ORIGIN:** 1300-1400 From the old French word *carier*, which means "to take in a vehicle."]



**PHRASAL VERBS**

**carry on**

to continue doing something: *Some of the children were finished, but others carried on working.*

**carry out something**

to do something in a planned and organized way: *Investigators are carrying out more research into the cause of the plane crash.*

**cart** /kɑrt/ *noun*

**1** a metal basket or table on wheels: *I pushed the shopping cart to the checkout counter.*

**2** a vehicle pulled by a horse, used for carrying heavy things: *The farmer loaded the hay into the cart.*

**car·ton** /ˈkɑrtn/ *noun*

a small CARDBOARD box that contains liquid, for example juice, milk, or soup: *a carton of milk*

**car·toon** /kɑrˈtun/ *noun*

**1** a movie or television program with characters that are drawn and not real: *It was Saturday morning, and the kids were watching cartoons.*

**2** a funny drawing in a newspaper

—**cartoonist** *noun* someone who draws cartoons

→ see Thesaurus box at **picture**[1], **program**[1]

[**ORIGIN:** 1500-1600 From the Italian word *cartone*, which means "stiff paper, or a drawing on stiff paper," from *carta*, which means "sheet of paper."]

**car·tridge** /ˈkɑrtrɪdʒ/ *noun*

a small container that you put inside a machine or gun to make it work: *The printer needs a new ink cartridge.*

**cart·wheel** /ˈkɑrtˌwil/ *noun*

a movement in which you turn completely over sideways by putting each hand on the floor so that your legs and feet move across in the air: *He was so happy about winning the race that he did a cartwheel.*

**carve** /kɑrv/ *verb*

**1** to cut a piece of wood or stone into a shape: *He carved a little statue out of wood.*

**2** to cut a large piece of cooked meat into smaller pieces: *Dad always carves the turkey.*

→ see picture on page **A15**

—**carving** *noun* an object or decoration made by carving wood or stone: *a carving of an owl*

→ see Thesaurus box at **cut**[1]

**ˈcar wash** *noun*

a place where you can take your car to be washed

**case**

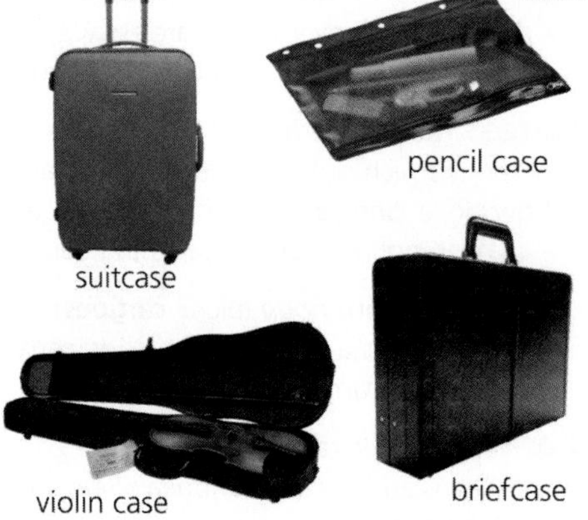


**case** /keɪs/ *noun*

**1** a particular example of a situation, event, or thing: *In most cases, the male and the female birds both help to feed their chicks.* | *He has a case of chickenpox.*

**2** the situation that exists: *"I'll be home late tonight." "Well, in that case, I won't cook dinner."*

**3** **(just) in case** = in order to be prepared for something that might happen: *I'll take an umbrella in case it rains.*

**4** a container for storing something: *Always put your guitar back in its case.*

**5** a crime that the police are trying to find out the truth about: *The police are trying to solve a murder case.*

**6** a TRIAL or a question that a court of law deals with: *The case was brought before the Supreme Court.*

**7** **in any case** = used when mentioning a more important fact: *He won't listen to our advice. In any case, it's too late now.*

**SYNONYM: anyway**

**8** the facts and reasons that show whether something is good or bad, for example in a discussion: *There is a good case for changing the rule, so I think we should do it.*

**cash¹** /kæʃ/ *noun*
the coins and paper money that you use for buying things: *I don't have any cash – I'll have to use my credit card.*
→ see Thesaurus box at **money**

**cash²** *verb*
**cash a check** = to exchange a check for paper money: *I need to cash this check at the bank.*

**cash·ier** /kæˈʃɪr/ *noun*
someone whose job is taking the money that customers pay: *Bill works as a cashier at the gas station.*

**ˈcash ˌregister** *noun*
a machine in a store that shows how much you must pay, and is used to keep the money in

**ca·si·no** /kəˈsinoʊ/ *noun* (plural **casinos**)
a place where people try to win money by playing games, especially card games or DICE games: *the casinos of Las Vegas*

**cas·ket** /ˈkæslɪt/ *noun*
a box in which a dead body is buried **SYNONYM: coffin**

**cas·se·role** /ˈkæsəˌroʊl/ *noun*
food that is cooked slowly in liquid in an OVEN, especially meat or fish with vegetables: *The recipe is for a fish casserole made with potatoes and other vegetables.*
[**ORIGIN:** 1700-1800 From the French word for "cooking pan."]

**cas·sette** /kəˈset/ *noun*
a small plastic case with tape inside, used for playing or recording music or movies: *He recorded all his favorite movies on video cassettes.* **SYNONYM: tape**

**cast¹** /kæst/ *verb* (**cast**)
**1** to choose someone for a part in a movie or play: *She was cast in the leading role in the school play.*
**2 cast your ballot/vote** = to vote in an election: *In some states, voters cast their ballots electronically.*
**3** to throw your fishing line or net into the water, in order to catch fish: *Fishermen go out to cast their nets in the ocean.*
**4** to make an object by pouring hot metal, plastic, or PLASTER into a container: *The sculpture was cast in bronze.*

**cast²** *noun*
**1** a hard cover that doctors put around a broken bone until it gets better: *His left arm was in a cast for six weeks after he broke it.*
**2** all the actors in a play, movie, or television show: *There was a party after the play was over for all the cast members.*

**cas·tle** /ˈkæsəl/ *noun*
a large building with high walls, that was built to protect the people inside from attack: *The castle was built on a hill above the city.*
[**ORIGIN:** 1000-1100 From the Latin word *castellum*, which means "building protected by a wall."]

**cas·u·al** /ˈkæʒuəl/ *adjective*
**1** casual clothes are not formal, and you usually wear them when you are not working: *The store sells casual clothes like jeans and sweatshirts.*
**2** relaxed and not worried about things: *Andy has important tests to do soon, but he seems pretty casual about it.*
—**casually** *adverb* in a casual way: *Jon was casually dressed in a T-shirt and jeans.*

**cas·ual·ty** /ˈkæʒuəlti/ *noun* (plural **casualties**)
someone who is hurt or killed in an accident or war: *After the accident, the casualties were rushed to Boston City hospital.*

**cat** /kæt/ *noun*
**1** a small animal with soft fur and pointed ears, that people often keep as a pet: *Our cat goes out at night and hunts mice.*
**2** any large wild animal that is related to cats: *Big cats such as lions often live in groups.*

**cat·a·log** (*also* **catalogue**) /ˈkætlˌɔg/ *noun*
a book with pictures and information about things you can buy from a company: *Mom buys clothes from a mail-order catalog.*

**ca·tas·tro·phe** /kəˈtæstrəfi/ *noun*
a terrible event that causes a lot of damage or suffering: *The earthquake was the worst catastrophe in the history of the country.* **SYNONYM: disaster**
—**catastrophic** /ˌkætəˈstrɑfɪk/ *adjective* causing a lot of damage or suffering: *The whole area was hit by catastrophic floods, and much of the city was destroyed.*

**catch¹** /kætʃ/ *verb* (**caught** /kɔt/)
**1** to use your hands to stop and hold something that is moving through the air: *Sammy*

*caught the ball and passed it to me.* **ANTONYM: drop** → see picture on page **A5**
**2** to stop a person or animal that wants to escape from you: *A police officer chased after the thief and caught him.*
**3** to get a fish or animal by using a net, hook, or trap: *We went down to the river to try and catch some fish.*
**4** **catch a train/plane/bus** = to get on a train, plane, or bus to go somewhere: *The kids catch the bus to school at 7:30.*
**5** to get an illness from someone else: *If you catch a cold, you should stay at home.*
**6** to see something on television or at the movie theater: *I want to catch the baseball game on TV tonight.*
**7** to see someone doing something bad or wrong: *One of the teachers caught the boys smoking cigarettes.*
**8** to get stuck on something by mistake: *His shirt caught on the fence and got a hole in it.*
**9** **catch your breath** = to begin to breathe normally again after you have been breathing faster than usual: *It was a steep climb, so we stopped to catch our breath.*
**PHRASAL VERBS**
**catch on**
**1** to understand something: *Some of the kids in the class catch on fast, but others have more trouble learning.*
**2** to become a popular idea or thing to do: *Texting people with a cell phone caught on quickly because it is an easy way to send someone a message.*
**catch up**
**1** to reach the same place as a person or car that was in front of you: *She was walking fast and I had to run to catch up with her.*
**2** to reach the same standard as other people: *When children are sick and miss school, it can be hard for them to catch up.*

**catch²** *noun*
**1** the act of catching a ball: *That was a great catch! Did you see how high he jumped?*
**2** a hook for fastening something: *The catch on my necklace broke.*
**3** a hidden problem in a situation that seems to be very good: *If clothes are very cheap, there's usually a catch – often they don't last very long.*
**4** **play catch** = to play a game of throwing a ball between people: *The kids were in the yard playing catch.*

**catch·er** /ˈkætʃɚ/ *noun*
the baseball player who stays behind the BATTER, to catch the balls that the batter misses

**catch·y** /ˈkætʃi/ *adjective*
a catchy tune is easy to remember: *That song's really catchy – I've been singing it all day.*

**cat·e·go·ry** Ac /ˈkætəˌgɔri/ *noun* (plural **categories**)
a group of people or things that are like each other in some way: *They divided the books into two categories: picture books and books for reading.*
—**categorize** /ˈkætəgəˌraɪz/ *verb* to put people or things into groups by deciding that they are like each other in some way: *The students are categorized according to their ability.*
→ see Thesaurus box at **type¹**

**ca·ter·ing** /ˈkeɪtərɪŋ/ *noun*
the job of providing and serving food and drinks at events such as parties: *Who is doing the catering for the wedding?*

**cat·er·pil·lar** /ˈkætɚˌpɪlɚ/ *noun*
a small creature with a long soft body and many small legs. It is the young form of a BUTTERFLY or MOTH: *Soon the caterpillar will turn into a butterfly.*
[**ORIGIN:** 1400-1500 Probably from an old French word *catepelose*, which means "hairy cat."]

**cat·fish** /ˈkætfɪʃ/ *noun*
a fish with long hairs around its mouth, that lives mainly in rivers and lakes

**ca·the·dral** /kəˈθiːdrəl/ *noun*
a big important church: *We visited some beautiful old cathedrals in Europe.*

**Cath·o·lic** /ˈkæθlɪk/ *adjective*
belonging to the part of the Christian religion that has the Pope as its leader: *a Catholic priest* **SYNONYM: Roman Catholic**
—**Catholic** *noun* someone who believes in the Catholic religion
—**Catholicism** /kəˈθɑləˌsɪzəm/ *noun* the Catholic religion

**cat·sup** /ˈketʃəp/ *noun*
another spelling of KETCHUP

**cat·tle** /ˈkætl/ *plural noun*
cows and BULLs that are kept on a farm: *In the field, there was a herd of cattle.*

**Cau·ca·sian** /kɔˈkeɪʒən/ *noun* (*formal*)
a person who belongs to a race of people with pale skin
—**Caucasian** *adjective* having pale skin: *a Caucasian man with blond hair and blue eyes*
SYNONYM: **white**

**cau·cus** /ˈkɔkəs/ (plural **caucuses**) *noun*
a meeting of the members of a political party, to choose a representative or decide on their plans

**caught** /kɔt/ *verb*
the past tense and past participle of CATCH

**cau·li·flow·er** /ˈkɔlɪˌflaʊɚ/ *noun*
a round white vegetable with green leaves around the outside

**cause¹** /kɔz/ *noun*
**1** the thing that makes something happen: *It seems likely that a bomb was the cause of the plane crash.*
**2** a reason for doing or feeling something: *She had some medical tests and was told there was no cause for concern.*
**3** an organization or an idea that a group of people support or do things for: *They are raising money for a good cause – medical help for people in poor countries.*

**cause²** *verb*
to make something happen, especially something bad: *Headaches can be caused by stress.*

**cau·tion** /ˈkɔʃən/ *noun*
if you do something with caution, you are careful because it could be dangerous: *Dogs can bite you, so you should only go near them with caution.*

**cau·tious** /ˈkɔʃəs/ *adjective*
careful about something that could be dangerous or unpleasant: *Young children are often cautious about trying new foods.*
—**cautiously** *adverb* in a cautious way: *Lizzy cautiously put one foot in the water.*
—**cautiousness** *noun* the state of being cautious

**WORD FAMILY: cautious**
**cautious** *adjective* | **cautiously** *adverb* | **cautiousness** *noun* | **caution** *noun*

**cav·al·ry** /ˈkævəlri/ *noun*
soldiers in the past who fought on horses

**cave** /keɪv/ *noun*
a big hole in the side of a cliff or under the ground: *The cave goes 500 feet into the side of the mountain.*
[**ORIGIN:** 1200-1300 From the Latin word *cavus*, which means "hollow."]

**cav·ern** /ˈkævɚn/ *noun*
a big cave, often under the ground

**cav·i·ty** /ˈkævəti/ *noun* (plural **cavities**)
a hole inside something: *The dentist told me that I have a cavity in my tooth that needs to be filled.*
→ see Thesaurus box at **hole**

**cc**
**1** (**cubic centimeter**) used to show the VOLUME of something: *The car has a 2,000cc engine.*
**2** used in emails or business letters to show that you are sending a copy to someone else: *To: Adam Fisher cc: Emma Goldman.*

**CD** *noun*
(**compact disc**) a small round piece of plastic with music or computer information stored on it: *Do you want to listen to my new CD?* → see picture on page **A8**

**CˈD ˌplayer** *noun*
a piece of equipment used for playing music on CDs

**CD-ROM** /ˌsi di ˈrɑm/ *noun*
a CD that stores a large amount of computer information: *You can buy the dictionary as a book, or you can buy it on CD-ROM.*

**cease** [Ac] /sis/ *verb* (*formal*)
to stop: *By noon, the rain had ceased.*
[**ORIGIN:** 1300-1400 From the Latin word *cessare*, which means "to stop."]

**cease·fire** /ˈsisˌfaɪɚ/ *noun*
a time during a war when the enemies agree to stop fighting: *Both sides agreed to a ceasefire during the peace talks.*

**ce·dar** /ˈsidɚ/ *noun*
a tall tree with thin leaves like needles, or the wood from this tree: *She kept extra blankets in a cedar chest.*

**ceil·ing** /ˈsilɪŋ/ *noun*
the top part of a room above your head: *It's a*

*big old house with high ceilings.* → see picture on page **A8**

**cel·e·brate** /ˈseləˌbreɪt/ *verb*
to do something special because it is a special occasion: *We're having a party to celebrate my mom's 40th birthday.*

**WORD FAMILY: celebrate**
**celebrate** *verb* | **celebration** *noun*

**cel·e·brat·ed** /ˈseləˌbreɪtɪd/ *adjective*
famous: *His father was a celebrated pianist.*

**cel·e·bra·tion** /ˌseləˈbreɪʃən/ *noun*
a party, meal, or event that you have for a special occasion: *We were all invited to his 21st birthday celebration.*
→ see Thesaurus box at **party**

**ce·leb·ri·ty** /səˈlebrəti/ *noun* (plural **celebrities**)
a famous person: *The magazine has stories about the lives of actors and other celebrities.*

**cel·er·y** /ˈseləri/ *noun*
a vegetable with long green stems that you can eat uncooked → see picture on page **A12**

**cell** /sel/ *noun*
**1** the smallest part that forms an animal or plant: *The human body is made up of billions of cells.* | *brain cells*
**2** a small room where a prisoner is kept: *The prisoners spend most of the day in their cells.*
[**ORIGIN:** 1100-1200 From the Latin word *cella*, which means "small room."]

**cel·lar** /ˈselɚ/ *noun*
a room under the ground, usually under a building, where things are stored: *There are some old chairs down in the cellar.*

**cel·lo** /ˈtʃeloʊ/ *noun*
a big musical instrument with strings, that you hold between your knees and play by moving a BOW (=type of stick) over the strings → see picture on page **A21**
—**cellist** *noun* someone who plays the cello

**ˈcell phone** (*also* **cellular phone** /ˌselyələ ˈfoʊn/) *noun*
a small telephone that you carry with you: *The man next to me was talking on his cell phone.*

**cel·lu·lar** [Ac] /ˈselyəlɚ/ *adjective*
**1** relating to the cells of plants or animals: *Cellular biology is the study of cells.*
**2** relating to the telephone system that provides signals to cell phones: *Customers generally pay about $35 a month for cellular service, including a free phone.*

**Cel·si·us** /ˈselsiəs/ *noun* (*written abbreviation*: **C**)
a temperature scale in which water freezes at 0° and boils at 100°: *In summer, temperatures reach 40 degrees Celsius.* **SYNONYM: Centigrade**
[**ORIGIN:** From Anders Celsius (1701-44), the Swedish scientist who invented the temperature scale.]

**ce·ment** /sɪˈment/ *noun*
a material used for building, made of a mixture of a powder, water, and sand that becomes hard when it is dry: *The floors of the building were made of cement.*

**cem·e·ter·y** /ˈseməˌteri/ *noun* (plural **cemeteries**)
an area of land where dead people are buried: *My father's grave was in the middle of the cemetery.*
[**ORIGIN:** 1300-1400 From the Greek word *koimeterion*, which means "sleeping room."]

**cen·sor** /ˈsensɚ/ *verb*
if people in authority censor newspapers, books, or movies, they take out any parts that they do not want people to see: *In some countries, newspapers are censored, and no criticism of the government is allowed.*
—**censorship** *noun* the act of censoring something: *Censorship is difficult on the Internet.*

**cen·sus** /ˈsensəs/ *noun* (plural **censuses**)
an official act of counting all the people in a country and collecting information about them: *According to the census, 97% of all homes have telephones.*

**cent** /sent/ *noun*
an amount of money that is worth 1/100 of a dollar: *The card cost only 50 cents.*
[**ORIGIN:** 1300-1400 From the Latin word *centum*, which means "hundred."]

**cen·taur** /ˈsentɔr/ *noun*
a creature in old Greek stories that has the head, chest, and arms of a man, and the body and legs of a horse

**cen·ten·ni·al** /senˈteniəl/ (*also* **cen·ten·a·ry** /senˈtenəri/) *noun*
a special day or year that is 100 years after

something happened or began: *In 2001 the university celebrated its centennial – it was founded in 1901.*

**cen·ter** /ˈsentɚ/ *noun*
**1** the middle of something: *There was a table in the center of the room with chairs around it.*
**2** a big building where people go to do a particular activity, for example shopping: *Why don't we look for some new clothes for you at the shopping center?*
**3** a place that is important for a particular activity: *Montreal is an important business center.*
**4** the player in basketball who plays near the basket: *Sophie was tall and usually played center on the basketball team.*

**WORD FAMILY: center**
**center** *noun* | **central** *adjective* | **centrally** *adverb*

**Cen·ti·grade** /ˈsentəˌgreɪd/ *noun*
another word for CELSIUS

**cen·ti·me·ter** /ˈsentəˌmitɚ/ *noun* (*written abbreviation*: **cm**)
a unit for measuring length, equal to 1/100 of a meter or 0.39 inches: *He was 182 centimeters tall.*

**cen·ti·pede** /ˈsentəˌpid/ *noun*
a small creature with a long soft body and many small legs
[ORIGIN: 1600-1700 From the Latin words *centum* and *pedes*, which mean "hundred" and "feet."]

**cen·tral** /ˈsentrəl/ *adjective*
**1** in the center of an area: *Our apartment is in a central location and it's easy to get anywhere in the city.*
**2** most important: *Harry Potter is the book's central character.* SYNONYM: **main**
—**centrally** *adverb* in a central place: *The hotel is centrally located.*

**cen·tu·ry** /ˈsentʃəri/ *noun* (plural **centuries**)
a period of 100 years: *There were huge changes in technology during the last century.* | *the 21st century*
[ORIGIN: 1300-1400 From the Latin word *centum*, which means "hundred."]

**ce·ram·ics** /səˈræmɪks/ *plural noun*
pots, plates, and other things made from clay
—**ceramic** *adjective* made of clay: *They used ceramic tiles for the kitchen floor.*

**ce·re·al** /ˈsɪriəl/ *noun*
**1** food made from grain that people eat for breakfast with milk: *A bowl of cereal, such as cornflakes, is a good breakfast.*
**2** a plant such as wheat that is grown to produce grain for food: *The farmers grow cereals such as wheat, barley, and corn.*
[ORIGIN: 1800-1900 From Ceres, the ancient Roman goddess of grain and farming.]

**cer·e·mo·ny** /ˈserəˌmoʊni/ *noun* (plural **ceremonies**)
an important public or religious event that involves special words and actions: *It was a beautiful wedding ceremony.*
—**ceremonial** /ˌserəˈmoʊniəl/ *adjective* relating to a ceremony: *the ceremonial opening of the Olympic Games*

**cer·tain** /ˈsɚtn/ *adjective*
**1** if you are certain about something, you have no doubts about it: *I'm certain (that) I've seen that man before.* | *He was born in 1984 – I'm certain about that.* SYNONYM: **sure**
**2** **make certain** = to do what is necessary in order to be sure that something important is done correctly: *Just make certain that you spell everyone's name correctly.*
**3** if something is certain to happen, it is definitely going to happen: *It's almost certain to rain again tomorrow.*
—**certainty** *noun* the quality of being certain

**WORD FAMILY: certain**
**certain** *adjective* | **uncertain** *adjective* | **certainly** *adverb* | **uncertainly** *adverb* | **certainty** *noun* | **uncertainty** *noun*

**cer·tain·ly** /ˈsɚtnli/ *adverb*
**1** without any doubt: *He's certainly taller than he was when I saw him last year!* | *I'm certainly not going to let you go on your own.* SYNONYM: **definitely**
**2** (*formal*) of course: *"Could you get us some water, please?" "Certainly."*

**cer·tif·i·cate** /sɚˈtɪfəkət/ *noun*
an official document showing that something has happened or is acceptable: *You may need your birth certificate in order to get a visa.*

**cer·ti·fy** /ˈsɚtəˌfaɪ/ *verb* (**certified**, **certifies**)
to officially say that something is true: *Two doctors certified that the patient was dead.*

**ce·sar·e·an** /sɪˈzeriən/ (*also* **ceˌsarean ˈsection**) *noun*
an operation to help a baby be born, in which doctors cut open the mother's body and take the baby out: *With her first baby, she had a cesarean.*
[**ORIGIN:** 1600-1700 From Julius Caesar (100-44 B.C.), a Roman soldier and political leader, who is said to have been born in this way.]

**chain¹** /tʃeɪn/ *noun*
**1** a line of metal rings joined together: *Maria wore a silver chain around her neck.*
**2** a number of stores, hotels, or other businesses owned by the same person or company: *The company owns a chain of clothing stores around the world.*
**3** **chain of events** = a series of related events: *The last link in the chain of events that led to the plane crash was the stormy weather.*

**chain²** *verb*
to tie people or things together, using a metal chain: *The prisoners were chained together.*

**chain·saw** /ˈtʃeɪnsɔ/ *noun*
a tool used for cutting wood, that works using a motor

**ˈchain store** *noun*
a store that is one of a number of stores owned by a big company

**chair**

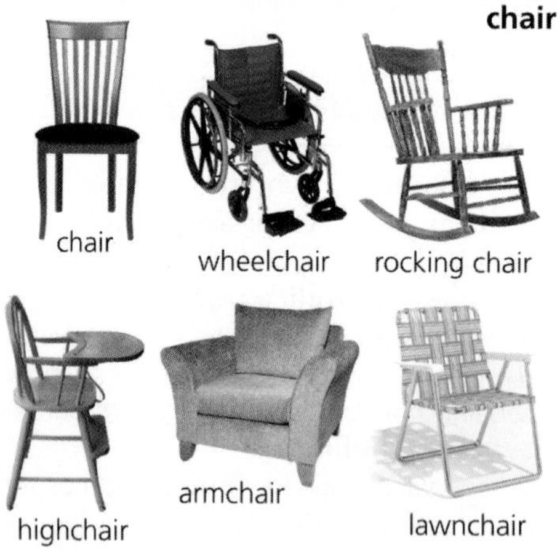


**chair** /tʃer/ *noun*
**1** a piece of furniture for one person to sit on: *There were six chairs around the table.*
**2** another word for a CHAIRPERSON
[**ORIGIN:** 1200-1300 From the old French word *chaiere*, from the Greek word *kathedra*, which means "seat."]

**chair·man** /ˈtʃermən/ *noun* (plural **chairmen** /ˈtʃermən/)
someone who controls a meeting, organization, or university department: *Randall became the new chairman of the committee.*
—**chairmanship** *noun* the position of being a chairman: *He took over the chairmanship in May.*

**chair·per·son** /ˈtʃerˌpɚsən/ *noun* (plural **chairpersons**)
someone who controls a meeting, organization, or university department: *Ann Wright is chairperson of the technology committee.* **SYNONYM: chair**

**chair·wom·an** /ˈtʃerˌwʊmən/ *noun* (plural **chairwomen** /ˈtʃerˌwɪmɪn/)
a woman who controls a meeting, organization, or university department

**chalk** /tʃɔk/ *noun*
**1** a white or colored stick of soft rock that you use for writing or drawing: *Nick did a drawing on black paper using chalk.*
**2** soft white rock that is used to make chalk for writing: *chalk cliffs*
[**ORIGIN:** From the Latin word *calx*, which means "limestone." Limestone is a type of rock that contains calcium, and chalk is a soft kind of limestone.]

**chalk·board** /ˈtʃɔkbɔrd/ *noun*
a hard smooth dark surface that you write on with chalk **SYNONYM: blackboard**

**chal·lenge¹** [Ac] /ˈtʃæləndʒ/ *noun*
**1** something difficult that needs skill or effort to do well: *I'm not looking for an easy job – I want something that will be a challenge.*
**2** the act of asking questions about whether something is right, fair, or legal: *There will be legal challenges to the new law by groups who believe it is unfair to poor families.*

**WORD FAMILY: challenge**
**challenge** *noun* | **challenge** *verb* | **challenging** *adjective*

**challenge²** [Ac] *verb*
**1** to ask someone to play a game or to fight against you: *They challenged us to a game of basketball.*

2 to say that you think something may not be right, and ask for proof: *He enjoys challenging people's assumptions.*

**chal·leng·er** Ac /ˈtʃæləndʒɚ/ *noun*
someone who is competing against another person to win a game, competition, or election: *He still has a big lead over his closest challenger.*

**chal·leng·ing** Ac /ˈtʃæləndʒɪŋ/ *adjective*
difficult in an interesting way: *Why don't you stop reading comics and read something more challenging?*

**champ** /tʃæmp/ *noun (informal)*
another word for a CHAMPION: *He was the school swimming champ every year.*

**cham·pagne** /ʃæmˈpeɪn/ *noun*
a type of wine with a lot of BUBBLEs in it: *They served champagne at the wedding.*

**cham·pi·on** /ˈtʃæmpiən/ *noun*
a person or team that has won a sports competition: *She was the world champion in gymnastics three times in the last ten years.*

**cham·pi·on·ship** /ˈtʃæmpiənˌʃɪp/ *noun* (*also* **championships** *plural noun*)
a competition to find the best player or team in a sport: *Under his coaching, they have won their third world championship.*
→ see Thesaurus box at **competition**

**chance** /tʃæns/ *noun*
1 an opportunity to do something: *I hope I get the chance to travel after I finish college.* SYNONYM: **opportunity**
2 a possibility that something will happen: *Do you think there's a chance that I'll be chosen for the team?*
3 **take a chance** = to do something that is a risk: *Always look carefully before crossing the street – don't take any chances.*
4 the way that something surprising happens without anyone planning it: *By chance, we met again two years later outside a movie theater.*

**chan·cel·lor** /ˈtʃænsələ/ *noun*
1 the most important person in some universities
2 the leader of the government in some countries: *the Chancellor of Germany*

**chan·de·lier** /ˌʃændəˈlɪr/ *noun*
a type of lamp that hangs from the ceiling, holds many small lights, and is decorated with pieces of glass: *A heavy chandelier hung over the dining table.*

**change**[1] /tʃeɪndʒ/ *verb*
1 to become different, or to make something different: *My father changed after Ricky died.* | *The leaves change color in the fall.* | *My mother changed her last name when she got married, from Wilson to Becker.*

**THESAURUS: change**

**alter** to change something, or to make something change: *I altered my schedule so that I could take the advanced Spanish class.* | *My opinion had not altered.*

**adapt** to change something so that you can use it in a different way: *The room has been adapted so that people in wheelchairs can use it.*

**adjust** to change something a little to make it better: *She adjusted the volume on the TV, to make it a little bit louder.*

**amend** to make a change to a law or to an important document: *The law needs to be amended so that it helps more people.*

**reform** to change a law, system, or organization in order to make it better: *the president's plans to reform health care*

**transform** to change completely the way something looks or does things: *The downtown area used to be dirty and run-down, but now it has been completely transformed.*

**convert** to change something so that it can be used for something else: *The old factory was converted into apartments.*

2 to replace something that is old, used, or not working correctly: *Do you know how to change a car tire?* | *I change the sheets on my bed every week.*
3 to put on different clothes: *Remember to change your shirt before you go out.* | *I got changed for soccer practice.*
4 **change your mind** = to decide to use a different idea about something, instead of your first idea: *He decided to call the puppy*

C

*Billy, but then he changed his mind and called it Bobby.*

**5 change a $10/$20, etc. bill** = to give someone coins or smaller bills in exchange for a $10, $20, etc. bill: *Can you change a twenty-dollar bill?*

**6** to exchange money from one country for money from another: *Where can I change my dollars into pesos?*

[**ORIGIN:** 1100-1200 From the old French word *changier*, from the Latin word *cambiare*, which means "to exchange."]

**change²** *noun*

**1** if there is a change, something becomes different: *I noticed a change in his behavior. He was more confident.* | *They have made some changes to the software to improve the way it runs.*

**2 for a change** = if something happens for a change, it is good and different from what normally happens: *It's your turn to listen to me, for a change.*

**3** the money you get back in a store, when you pay more than something costs: *She paid for the groceries, and the cashier gave her 57 cents change.*

**4** coins, not bills: *Do you have any change on you?*

→ see Thesaurus box at **money**

**chan·nel** [Ac] /ˈtʃænl/ *noun*

**1** a television station: *There's a good show on channel 2.*

**2** a long area of water between two areas of land: *The English Channel is between England and France.*

**chant** /tʃænt/ *verb*

to say the same word or phrase many times: *People marched through the city chanting "Victory!"*

—**chant** *noun* something people say or sing many times: *Everyone joined in the chant – "Go Wildcats! Go Wildcats!"*

**cha·os** /ˈkeɪɑs/ *noun*

a very confused situation: *Five bombs exploded, and the city was in chaos.*

—**chaotic** /keɪˈɑtɪk/ *adjective* (*formal*) without any order: *We have six children, so the house is pretty chaotic.*

**chap·el** /ˈtʃæpəl/ *noun*

a small church, or part of a church

[**ORIGIN:** 1100-1200 From the old French word *chapele*, from the Latin word *cappella*, which means "little cloak." The cloak of St. Martin of Tours was kept in a holy place called a chapel, and the word was then used for other similar places.]

**chap·e·rone** /ˈʃæpəˌroʊn/ *noun*

someone who goes somewhere with a young person to make sure they behave well: *Sara went to the dance as a chaperone to her younger sister.*

—**chaperone** *verb* to go with someone as a chaperone

**chap·ter** [Ac] /ˈtʃæptɚ/ *noun*

a part of a book: *There are ten chapters in the book, and I'm reading Chapter 5 now.*

→ see Thesaurus box at **part¹**

**char·ac·ter** /ˈkærɪktɚ/ *noun*

**1** a person's qualities: *"How would you describe Lily's character?" "She's very kind and thoughtful."*

**2** a person in a book, play, movie, etc.: *Huckleberry Finn is the main character in the book.*

**3** good or interesting qualities that a person or place has: *The old hotel had a lot of character, with its marble floors, dark wood furniture, and fancy chandeliers.*

**4** a written sign such as a letter: *He didn't know what the Chinese characters on the T-shirt meant.*

[**ORIGIN:** 1300-1400 From the Greek word *kharakter*, which means "mark made on something, like a label."]

| **WORD FAMILY: character** |
| --- |
| **character** *noun* \| **characteristic** *noun* \| **characteristic** *adjective* |

**char·ac·ter·is·tic** /ˌkærɪktəˈrɪstɪk/ *noun*

a quality that is typical of someone or something: *"What are the characteristics of a good leader?" "He or she should be honest, intelligent, and strong."*

—**characteristic** *adjective* typical of someone or something: *Sleeping late on weekends is characteristic of many teenagers.*

**char·coal** /ˈtʃɑrkoʊl/ *noun*

a substance made of burned wood that is used as FUEL, or for drawing: *Charcoal is the best fuel for barbecues.*

**charge**[1] /tʃɑrdʒ/ *noun*
**1** the amount of money you pay to do something: *There's no charge for entry to the museum.*
**2 be in charge of something** = to be the person who organizes or controls something: *Mr. Taylor is in charge of the school newspaper.*
**3** a formal statement made by the police that someone has done something wrong: *He was tried on charges of theft and kidnapping.*
**4** the amount of electricity there is in something: *There's no charge left in the battery – you'll have to buy a new one.*
→ see Thesaurus box at **cost**[1]

**charge**[2] *verb*
**1** to ask people to pay a particular amount of money for something: *The health club charges $150 for membership.*
**2** to buy something with a CREDIT CARD: *"How would you like to pay?" "I'll charge it."*
**3** if the police charge someone, they say formally that he or she has done something wrong: *Police charged the boy with burglary when they found him with a stolen laptop.*
**4** to move forward very fast in an angry way: *The bull turned and charged toward us.*
**5** to fill a BATTERY with electricity: *It takes three hours to charge the battery in the cell phone.*
→ see Thesaurus box at **run**[1]

**cha·ris·ma** /kəˈrɪzmə/ *noun*
a special natural quality that makes a lot of people like you and that helps you influence them: *He had a lot of charisma and was a natural leader.*
—**charismatic** /ˌkærɪzˈmætɪk/ *adjective* a charismatic person has charisma

**char·i·ta·ble** /ˈtʃærətəbəl/ *adjective*
relating to charities: *Many young people volunteer to do charitable work to help people in their communities.*

**char·i·ty** /ˈtʃærəti/ *noun* (plural **charities**)
an organization that gives money or help to people who need it: *The charity raises money to provide clean drinking water in poor countries.*
[**ORIGIN:** 1100-1200 From the Latin word *caritas*, which means "love."]

**charm**[1] /tʃɑrm/ *noun*
**1** an attractive quality or way of acting with other people that makes them like you: *She had a lot of charm and many friends.*
**2** an object that you believe brings you good luck: *I always get an A when I use this pen – it's my lucky charm.*
[**ORIGIN:** 1200-1300 From the Latin word *carmen*, which means "song." A charm was originally a magic spell that was said or sung.]

**charm**[2] *verb*
to make people like you a lot, by the way you act: *José was good-looking and charmed all the girls.*

**charm·ing** /ˈtʃɑrmɪŋ/ *adjective*
very pleasing or attractive: *Everyone liked her and said she was a charming woman.*

**chart** Ac /tʃɑrt/ *noun*
**1** a drawing that shows information about different amounts: *We made a chart showing the heights of everyone in the class.*
**2 the charts** = a list of the most popular songs, produced each week: *The song reached number two on the charts.*
**3** a map, especially of oceans or stars: *Long ago, sailors used these charts to find their way across the oceans.*
[**ORIGIN:** 1500-1600 From the Latin word *charta*, which means "sheet of paper, or document," from the Greek word *chartes*, meaning "piece of paper."]

**chase** /tʃeɪs/ *verb*
to follow someone or something quickly, because you want to catch him, her, or it: *A police officer chased after the man, but he escaped.*
—**chase** *noun* the act of chasing someone or something: *The best part of the movie is the car chase through New York.*

**chat** /tʃæt/ *verb* (**chatted**, **chatting**)
**1** to talk with friends or in a friendly way: *All the girls were chatting about the party on Saturday night.*
**2** to send and receive messages in a chat room on the Internet
—**chat** *noun* a friendly talk
→ see Thesaurus box at **talk**[1]

**ˈchat room** *noun*
a place on the Internet where you talk to

people by writing messages to them, and they can reply immediately

**chat·ter** /ˈtʃætɚ/ *verb*
to talk a lot about unimportant things: *She chattered about the weather and her clothes.* —**chatter** *noun* a lot of talk about unimportant things

**chauf·feur** /ˈʃoʊfɚ/ *noun*
someone whose job is to drive a car for someone else: *The star's chauffeur opened the door of the limousine for her.*
[**ORIGIN:** 1800-1900 From the French word for "person who looks after the fire of a steam engine."]

**cheap** /tʃip/ *adjective*
**1** not costing a lot of money: *I bought two pairs of jeans because they were really cheap.* **ANTONYM: expensive**
**2** not charging a lot of money: *It's a cheap restaurant, but the food's pretty good.* **ANTONYM: expensive**
**3** low in price and not well made: *Cheap shoes wear out quickly.* **ANTONYM: expensive**
**4** not liking to spend money: *He was too cheap to get her a birthday gift.* **ANTONYM: generous**
[**ORIGIN:** 1500-1600 From the old phrase "good cheap," which means "at a good price, or cheaply," from the old English word *ceap*, which means "price or bargain."]

**cheap·ly** /ˈtʃipli/ (*also* **cheap** (*informal*)) *adverb*
for a low price: *They sell computers really cheaply.*

**cheat¹** /tʃit/ *verb*
**1** to do something that is not honest because you think it will help you succeed: *Molly cheated on the history test by copying from John, but the teacher caught her.*
**2** to get something from someone by doing something that is not honest: *He cheated me out of $50 by not sending me the CDs I had paid for.*
**PHRASAL VERB**
**cheat on someone**
to secretly have another romantic relationship when you have a husband, wife, boyfriend, or girlfriend: *She thinks her husband is cheating on her.*

**cheat²** (*also* **cheat·er** /ˈtʃitɚ/) *noun*
someone who does things that are not honest: *He said the ball was out when it wasn't. He's such a cheat.*

**check¹** /tʃek/ *verb*
**1** to look carefully at something to see if it is correct or the way it should be: *When you finish the test, check your answers.*
**2** to ask someone about something: *If you're worried, check with your doctor.*
**PHRASAL VERBS**
**check in**
to go to the desk at a hotel or airport to say that you have arrived: *We got to the hotel, checked in, and went out to eat.*
**check something off**
to put a mark (✓) next to something on a list: *Check the kids' names off as they get on the bus.*
**check out**
**1** to pay the bill and leave a hotel: *You must check out before 12 o'clock.*
**2** **check something out** = to look at something, especially in order to find out if it is good: *I decided to check out the band's website.*
**3** **check something out** = to borrow a book from a library: *I went to the library and checked out a book on Japan.*

**check**

sign a check

**check²** *noun*
**1** a small printed form that you use to pay for things, using the money in your bank account. Your write the amount of money, the date, and the name of the person you are paying on the check, and then sign it: *Can I pay by check? | He wrote a check for $250.*
**2** a careful look at something to see if it is correct or the way it should be: *I did a quick check to make sure all the doors were locked.*
**3** a piece of paper you get in a restaurant or hotel that shows how much you must pay: *Can I have the check, please?* **SYNONYM: bill**
**4** a mark (✓) that you put next to an answer

to show that it is correct, or that you put next to something on a list to show it has been done or included: *My teacher put a check by each right answer.*
**5** a pattern of squares on something: *He was wearing a shirt with blue and white checks.*

**check·book** /ˈtʃekbʊk/ *noun*
a book of checks that you use to pay for things

**check·er** /ˈtʃekɚ/ *noun*
**1** a program you can use on a computer to check something: *The software includes a spell checker and a grammar checker.*
**2 checkers** = a game for two people, who each move 12 round pieces on a board with a pattern of squares: *Let's play a game of checkers.*

**check·ered** /ˈtʃekɚd/ *adjective*
having a pattern of squares in two different colors: *It was a little Italian restaurant with red and white checkered tablecloths.*

**ˈcheck-in** *noun*
**1** the process of telling someone at a hotel or airport that you have arrived: *Please allow at least an hour for check-in before your flight.*
**2** a place at a hotel or airport where you go to say that you have arrived: *When she got to the check-in counter, she couldn't find her plane ticket.*

**ˈchecking acˌcount** *noun*
a bank account that you can use to write checks

**check·list** /ˈtʃekˌlɪst/ *noun*
a list of things you have to do or remember: *I made a checklist of things I need to do before the trip.*

**check·out** /ˈtʃek-aʊt/ *noun*
**1** (*also* **checkout counter**) a place in a store where you pay for things: *The store was busy and there was a long line at the checkout.*
**2** the time by which you must leave a hotel room: *Checkout is at noon.*

**check·up** (*also* **check-up**) /ˈtʃek-ʌp/ *noun*
an examination by a doctor or DENTIST to see if you are healthy: *I'm fine, the appointment is just for my yearly checkup.*

**ched·dar** /ˈtʃedɚ/ *noun*
a firm yellow cheese

**cheek** /tʃik/ *noun*
the soft round part of your face under each eye: *She had bright blue eyes and pink cheeks.* → see picture on page **A2**
—**cheekbone** *noun* the bone in your cheek, or the top part of your cheek

C

cheer

**cheer¹** /tʃɪr/ *verb*
to shout as a way of showing that you support or like someone or something: *He scored, and everyone cheered loudly.*
**ANTONYM: boo**
→ see Thesaurus box at **shout¹**
**PHRASAL VERB**
**cheer up**
**1** to feel happier: *Cheer up – you'll do better next time.*
**2 cheer someone up** = to make someone feel happier: *I bought Mom some flowers to cheer her up.*

**cheer²** *noun*
a shout that shows that you support or like someone or something: *Everyone gave a loud cheer when the band came on stage.*
**ANTONYM: boo**

**cheer·ful** /ˈtʃɪrfəl/ *adjective*
happy or seeming happy: *I like Sandra – she's always cheerful.*
—**cheerfully** *adverb* in a cheerful way: *"Hi guys," Joey said cheerfully.*
—**cheerfulness** *noun* the state of being cheerful
→ see Thesaurus box at **happy**

**cheer·lead·er** /ˈtʃɪrˌlidɚ/ *noun*
a member of a team of people who encourage the crowd to cheer at sports events

**cheese** /tʃiz/ *noun*
a solid food made from milk: *The type of*

*cheese used on a pizza is called mozzarella.*
[ORIGIN: From the old English word *cese.*]

**cheese·cake** /ˈtʃizkeɪk/ *noun*
a sweet food made with soft white cheese

**chees·y** /ˈtʃizi/ *adjective (informal)*
a cheesy movie, show, song, etc. is silly and not new or interesting: *Dad was watching a really cheesy game show on TV.*

**chee·tah** /ˈtʃitə/ *noun*
an African wild cat with black spots that can run very fast

**chef** /ʃef/ *noun*
someone whose job is cooking in a restaurant: *He works as a chef in a big restaurant.* → see picture on page **A17**

**chem·i·cal¹** Ac /ˈkemɪkəl/ *noun*
a substance used in chemistry, or used for doing something such as cleaning: *The river was full of dangerous chemicals from the factory.*

**WORD FAMILY: chemical**
**chemical** *noun* | **chemical** *adjective* | **chemistry** *noun*

**chemical²** Ac *adjective*
relating to substances or to the ways that substances change or combine with each other: *The chemical reaction between the two substances produces carbon dioxide.*

**chem·ist** /ˈkemɪst/ *noun*
a scientist who does work related to chemistry

**chem·is·try** /ˈkeməstri/ *noun*
the science in which you study substances and the ways that they change or combine with each other: *We did a chemistry experiment to see what happens if you put acid on various metals.*

**che·mo·ther·a·py** /ˌkimoʊˈθerəpi/ (*also* **chemo** /ˈkimoʊ/ *(informal)*) *noun*
the treatment of CANCER using special drugs

**cher·ish** /ˈtʃerɪʃ/ *verb*
if you cherish something, it is very important to you: *I cherish my friends and my family.*

**cher·ry** /ˈtʃeri/ *noun* (plural **cherries**)
a small round fruit with dark red skin and a long stem → see picture on page **A13**

**chess** /tʃes/ *noun*
a game for two players in which you move pieces on a board with black and white squares. The aim of the game is to trap the piece called the king that belongs to the other player: *Do you want to play a game of chess?*

**chest** /tʃest/ *noun*
**1** the front part of your body between your neck and stomach: *She felt a sudden pain in her chest and was afraid she was having a heart attack.* → see picture on page **A2**
**2** a large strong box that you keep things in: *The pirates put the coins in a large chest.*
[ORIGIN: From the Latin word *cista*, which means "box or basket."]

**chest·nut** /ˈtʃesnʌt/ *noun*
a type of nut that is red-brown on the outside and pale yellow on the inside, which you can cook and eat: *a chestnut tree*

**ˌchest of ˈdrawers** *noun* (plural **chests of drawers**)
a piece of furniture with drawers that clothes can be kept in **SYNONYM: dresser**

**chew** /tʃu/ *verb*
to bite food or GUM several times with your back teeth: *Chew your food or you'll choke!*
—**chewy** *adjective* food that is chewy has to be chewed a lot before it is soft enough to eat: *The meat was chewy and hard to eat.*

**ˈchewing gum** *noun*
another word for GUM

**chic** /ʃik/ *adjective*
fashionable and attractive to look at: *They stayed at a chic hotel in Manhattan.*

**Chi·ca·no** /tʃɪˈkɑnoʊ/ *noun*
someone living in the U.S. who was born in Mexico or whose family came from Mexico
—**Chicana** *noun* a woman living in the U.S. who was born in Mexico or whose family came from Mexico

**chick** /tʃɪk/ *noun*
a baby bird: *a hen and her chicks*

**chick·en¹** /ˈtʃɪkən/ *noun*
**1** a farm bird that is kept for its eggs and meat
**2** the meat from this bird: *His favorite food is fried chicken.*
**3** *(informal)* someone who does not have

any courage: *Don't be such a chicken! You can do it.*
—**chicken** *adjective* (*informal*) afraid to do something: *He was so chicken, he wouldn't even get in the water.*

**chicken²** *verb*
PHRASAL VERB
**chicken out**
to decide not to do something that you have said you will do, because you are too afraid: *He said he wanted to go skiing with us, but then he chickened out at the last minute.*

**ˈchicken pox** (*also* **chick·en·pox**) /ˈtʃɪkən ˌpɑks/ *noun*
a disease that children often get, which causes ITCHY red spots on the skin and a fever

**chief¹** /tʃif/ *noun*
1 the leader of a group or organization: *the chief of police*
2 the leader of a tribe: *an Indian chief*
[ORIGIN: 1200-1300 From the Latin word *caput*, which means "head."]

**chief²** *adjective*
most important: *Coffee is one of the country's chief exports.* SYNONYM: **main**

**ˌchief ˈjustice** *noun*
the most important judge in a court of law that has more than one judge, especially in the U.S. Supreme Court

**chief·ly** /ˈtʃifli/ *adverb*
mainly: *The disease chiefly affects women, but some men also get it.*

**child** /tʃaɪld/ *noun* (plural **children** /ˈtʃɪldrən/)
1 a young person who is not yet fully grown: *By law, children must go to school until they are 18 years old.* | *Dad lived in Iowa when he was a child.* SYNONYM: **kid**

**THESAURUS: child**

**Child** is a word that you can use to talk about **young children** and **teenagers**. You do not normally use child to mean a **baby**.

**Kid** is an informal word for a **child**.

You are a **baby** when you are first born. A very young baby who cannot walk or talk yet is called an **infant**.

You are a **teenager** between 13 and 19.

An **adolescent** is a child between about 11 and 17, when he or she is developing into an adult.

2 a son or daughter: *They have three children: a daughter and two sons.* SYNONYM: **kid**

**child·birth** /ˈtʃaɪldbɚθ/ *noun*
the act of having a baby: *Many women want their husbands with them during childbirth.*

**child·care** /ˈtʃaɪldˌker/ *noun*
an arrangement in which someone takes care of children while their parents are at work: *Both of her children are in childcare since she works full time.*

**child·hood** /ˈtʃaɪldhʊd/ *noun*
the time when you are a child: *We've been friends since childhood – we went to elementary school together.*

**child·ish** /ˈtʃaɪldɪʃ/ *adjective*
1 behaving in a silly way that makes you seem younger than you really are: *"I don't want to eat my vegetables." "Don't be so childish!"* SYNONYM: **immature**
2 relating to or typical of young children: *He had the usual childish fascination with colors and shapes.*
—**childishness** *noun* behavior that is silly and makes you seem younger than you really are

**child·less** /ˈtʃaɪldləs/ *adjective*
having no children: *a childless couple*

**chil·dren** /ˈtʃɪldrən/ *noun*
the plural of CHILD

**chil·i** /ˈtʃɪli/ *noun* (plural **chilies**)
1 (*also* **ˈchili ˌpepper**) a small thin red or green pepper with a very hot taste
2 a dish made with beans, chili peppers, and usually meat
[ORIGIN: 1600-1700 From the Nahuatl word *chilli*. Nahuatl was the language used by the Aztecs in Mexico.]

**chill¹** /tʃɪl/ *verb*
1 to make something cold: *Chill the dessert before you serve it.*
2 (*also* **chill out**) (*informal*) to relax: *We were just chilling in front of the TV.*

**chill²** *noun*
1 a feeling of being frightened: *The ghost*

*story was so scary it made a chill run down my spine.*
**2** slight coldness outside or in a building: *Take a sweater – there's a chill in the air.*
**3 chills** = a feeling of being cold that makes you shake, when you are sick: *First I had chills and then a fever.*

C

**chill·y** /ˈtʃɪli/ *adjective*
feeling slightly cold, or making you feel slightly cold: *It was a gray, chilly day in March.*
→ see Thesaurus box at **cold**[1]

**chime** /tʃaɪm/ *verb*
if a clock or bell chimes, it makes a ringing sound: *The clock chimes every hour.*
—**chime** *noun* the ringing sound of a clock or bell

**chim·ney** /ˈtʃɪmni/ *noun* (plural **chimneys**)
a tall pipe that takes smoke from a fire out through the roof of a building
[**ORIGIN:** 1200-1300 From the French word *cheminée*, from the Greek word *kaminos*, which means "fireplace or oven."]

**chim·pan·zee** /ˌtʃɪmpænˈzi/ (*also* **chimp** /tʃɪmp/ (*informal*)) *noun*
an African animal that is like a monkey without a tail: *Chimpanzees are very intelligent animals and can make simple tools.*

**chin** /tʃɪn/ *noun*
the front part of your face below your mouth: *She rested her chin on her hands.* → see picture on page **A2**

**chi·na** /ˈtʃaɪnə/ *noun*
plates, cups, bowls, etc. that are made from white clay of good quality: *a china teacup*

**Chi·nese**[1] /ˌtʃaɪˈniz/ *adjective*
from China: *a Chinese vase*

**Chinese**[2] *noun*
**1** any of the languages spoken in China, such as Mandarin or Cantonese
**2 the Chinese** = people from China

**chip**[1] /tʃɪp/ *noun*
**1** a thin flat piece of potato or TORTILLA that has been cooked until it is hard: *a bag of potato chips*
**2** a small object with electronic connections on it. Chips are used in computers to store information or make the computer work.
**3** a small piece of something such as wood, stone, or chocolate: *You can use the wood chips to make a fire.*
**4** a place on a plate, cup, etc. where a small piece has broken off: *This plate has a chip in it.*
**5** a small flat colored piece of plastic used in games instead of money: *a gambling chip*
[**ORIGIN:** From the old English word *cipp*, which means "small piece of wood."]

**chip**[2] *verb* (**chipped**, **chipping**)
to break a small piece off something: *I chipped one of my fingernails opening the can.*
—**chipped** *adjective* with a piece broken off: *a chipped tooth*

**chip·munk** /ˈtʃɪpmʌŋk/ *noun*
a small brown furry animal with black and white lines on its back: *Chipmunks live in holes in the ground.*

**chi·ro·prac·tor** /ˈkaɪrəˌpræktɚ/ *noun*
someone who treats medical problems such as back pain by moving and pressing people's muscles and bones

**chirp** /tʃɚp/ *verb*
if a bird or insect chirps, it makes short high sounds: *The birds were chirping in the trees.*

**chis·el** /ˈtʃɪzəl/ *noun*
a metal tool with a sharp flat end that you use to cut wood or stone

**chlo·rine** /ˈklɔrin/ *noun*
a gas with a strong smell that is added to the water in swimming pools to keep it clean
[**ORIGIN:** 1800-1900 From the Greek word *chloros*, which means "green." Chlorine is green in color.]

**chlo·ro·phyll** /ˈklɔrəˌfɪl/ *noun*
the green substance in plants, which helps them get energy from sunlight in order to make the food they need
[**ORIGIN:** 1800-1900 From the Greek words *chloros* and *phyllon*, which mean "green" and "leaf."]

**choco·late** /ˈtʃɑklɪt/ *noun*
**1** a sweet brown food that is eaten as candy and used in cooking: *Would you like a piece of chocolate? | a chocolate cake*
**2** a small candy that is made of or covered with chocolate: *a box of chocolates*
[**ORIGIN:** 1600-1700 From the Nahuatl word *xocoatl*, which means "bitter water." Chocolate

was first used as a drink, and not sweetened. Nahuatl was the language used by the Aztecs in Mexico.]

**ˌchocolate ˈchip** *noun*
a small piece of chocolate put in cookies, cakes, and ice cream: *chocolate chip cookies*

**choice** /tʃɔɪs/ *noun*
**1** the chance to choose between two or more things or people, or the action of choosing: *You have a choice between going swimming or going bowling.* | *I think you made the right choice.*
**2** a number of things that someone can choose from: *The bookstore has a wide choice of magazines.*
**3** the person or thing that someone has chosen: *Tom was a good choice as captain.*

**choir** /kwaɪɚ/ *noun*
a group of people who sing together: *She sings in the church choir.*

**choke** /tʃoʊk/ *verb*
**1** to have difficulty breathing because your throat is blocked or there is not enough air: *He choked on a piece of bread.*
**2** to press your hands around someone's throat so that he or she cannot breathe: *Let go of her throat! You're choking her!*

**chol·er·a** /ˈkɑlərə/ *noun*
a very serious disease that affects the BOWEL. People usually catch it by drinking dirty water, especially in tropical countries.

**cho·les·ter·ol** /kəˈlestəˌrɔl/ *noun*
a substance in your blood, and in some foods, that may cause heart disease: *Foods such as steak and eggs contain a lot of cholesterol.*
[**ORIGIN:** 1800-1900 From the Greek words *chole-* and *stereos*, which mean "bile" and "solid." Bile is a liquid produced by your liver that helps you digest fat.]

**choose** /tʃuz/ *verb* (**chose** /tʃoʊz/, **chosen** /ˈtʃoʊzən/, **choosing**)
**1** to decide which one of a group of things or people you want: *She chose the black dress instead of the red one.* | *There are so many books to choose from.*

**THESAURUS: choose**

**pick** to choose someone or something from a group of people or things: *The coach is in charge and he picks the team.*

**select** to choose something or someone by thinking carefully about which is the best: *The judges will select the winner from three finalists.*

**elect** to choose a leader or a representative by voting: *We elected a new president in 2008.*

**decide on something** to choose one thing from many possible choices: *Have you decided on a name for the baby?*

**opt for something** (*formal*) to choose one thing instead of another: *Students in this area can opt for one of three schools.*

**2** to decide to do something: *Why did you choose to study German rather than Spanish?*
→ see Thesaurus box at **decide**

**chop¹** /tʃɑp/ (*also* **chop up**) *verb* (**chopped**, **chopping**)
to cut food up with a knife, or cut wood up with an AX: *Peel and chop the onions.* → see picture on page **A15**
→ see Thesaurus box at **cut¹**
**PHRASAL VERBS**
**chop something down**
to cut down a tree with an AX
**chop something off**
to remove something by cutting it with a knife, AX, or sword: *We chopped off the branches that were too close to the house.*

**chop²** *noun*
a small flat piece of meat on a bone: *a pork chop*

**chop·sticks** /ˈtʃɑpstɪks/ *plural noun*
a pair of thin sticks that people in parts of Asia use for eating food

**chord** /kɔrd/ *noun*
three or more musical notes played at the same time: *I can play a few chords on the guitar.*

**chore** /tʃɔr/ *noun*
a job that you have to do, especially one that you regularly do in your home: *One of my chores is to dust the living room.*

**cho·re·og·ra·phy** /ˌkɔriˈɑgrəfi/ *noun*
the activity of planning movements for dancers, and telling the dancers what to do
[**ORIGIN:** 1700-1800 From the Greek words

*choreia* and *graphein*, which mean "dance" and "to write."]

**cho·rus** /ˈkɔrəs/ *noun*
**1** the part of a song that is repeated after each VERSE: *I don't know all the words of the song. I only know the chorus.*
**2** a large group of people who sing together: *She used to sing in the school chorus.*
**SYNONYM: choir**

C

**chose** /tʃouz/ *verb*
the past tense of CHOOSE

**chos·en** /ˈtʒouzən/ *verb*
the past participle of CHOOSE

**chow·der** /ˈtʃaudɚ/ *noun*
a thick soup made with milk, potatoes, and often fish: *clam chowder*

**Christ** /kraɪst/
Jesus, who Christians believe is the son of God

**chris·ten** /ˈkrɪsən/ *verb*
to officially give a child its name at a Christian religious ceremony: *She was christened Mary Louise.*
—**christening** *noun* a Christian religious ceremony at which a child is given its name and becomes a member of the Christian Church

**Chris·tian** /ˈkrɪstʃən/ *adjective*
relating to the religion that is based on the teaching of Jesus Christ: *Christian beliefs*
—**Christian** *noun* someone who believes in the Christian religion: *His parents are both Christians and go to church every Sunday.*

**Chris·ti·an·i·ty** /ˌkrɪstiˈænəti/ *noun*
the religion that is based on the teaching of Jesus Christ

**Christ·mas** /ˈkrɪsməs/ *noun*
**1** December 25, the day when Christians celebrate the birth of Jesus Christ: *I still have to buy Christmas presents for my family.*
**2** the time around December 25: *My grandparents are coming to stay for Christmas.*
[**ORIGIN:** From "Christ" and "mass (a Christian religious ceremony)."]

**ˌChristmas ˈDay** *noun*
December 25, the day when Christians celebrate the birth of Jesus Christ

**ˌChristmas ˈEve** *noun*
December 24, the day before Christmas

**chrome** /kroum/ (*also* **chro·mi·um** /ˈkroumiəm/) *noun*
a shiny silver-colored metal that is put onto other metals using a special process: *The table was made of chrome and glass.*

**chro·mo·some** /ˈkrouməˌsoum/ *noun*
a part of each cell in a living thing, that contains GENEs. Genes control the size, shape, color, etc. of living things.
[**ORIGIN:** 1800-1900 From the Greek words *chroma* and *soma*, which mean "color" and "body." Scientists chose this name because the body, or main part, of a chromosome easily takes in a substance that colors it.]

**chron·ic** /ˈkrɑnɪk/ *adjective*
a chronic illness, condition, or problem is one that continues for a long time and cannot be cured: *She has chronic back pain and is never comfortable.*

**chron·o·log·i·cal** /ˌkrɑnlˈɑdʒɪkəl/ *adjective*
with things arranged according to the order in which they happened: *Make a list of presidents in chronological order, starting with George Washington.*

**chrys·a·lis** /ˈkrɪsəlɪs/ *noun*
a BUTTERFLY or MOTH at the time when it has a hard covering and is changing from a CATERPILLAR into an adult

**chry·san·the·mum** /krɪˈsænθəməm/ *noun*
a garden plant with large brightly colored flowers

**chub·by** /ˈtʃʌbi/ *adjective*
slightly fat: *He was a chubby little boy, but now he's very thin.*
→ see Thesaurus box at **fat**[1]

**chuck·le** /ˈtʃʌkəl/ *verb*
to laugh quietly: *She chuckled at the memory of Jim falling into the pond.*
—**chuckle** *noun* a quiet laugh
→ see Thesaurus box at **laugh**[1]

**chunk** /tʃʌŋk/ *noun*
a thick piece of something that does not have an even shape: *He broke a chunk off the chocolate bar.*
→ see Thesaurus box at **piece**

**chunk·y** /ˈtʃʌŋki/ *adjective*
**1** thick: *a chunky sweater*

2 chunky food has big pieces in it: *chunky peanut butter*

**church** /tʃɚtʃ/ *noun*
1 a building where Christians go to have religious services: *She goes to church every Sunday.*
2 (*also* **Church**) one of the separate groups within the Christian religion: *the Catholic Church*
[**ORIGIN:** From the old English word *cirice*, from the Greek word *kyriakos*, which means "of the Lord."]

**chute** /ʃut/ *noun*
a tube or sloping surface that things or people can slide down: *The old laundry chute leads to the basement.*

**ci·der** /ˈsaɪdɚ/ (*also* **ˈapple ˌcider**) *noun*
a drink made from apples

**ci·gar** /sɪˈgɑr/ *noun*
a thick tube of rolled tobacco leaves that people smoke: *He was smoking a smelly cigar.*

**cig·a·rette** /ˈsɪgəˌret/ *noun*
a paper tube filled with tobacco that people smoke: *a pack of cigarettes*

**cin·e·ma** /ˈsɪnəmə/ *noun* (*formal*)
movies in general: *The event was a celebration of women in cinema.*

**cin·na·mon** /ˈsɪnəmən/ *noun*
a sweet-smelling brown spice used in baking: *Sprinkle cinnamon and sugar on top of the cookies.*

**cir·cle¹** /ˈsɚkəl/ *noun*
1 a round shape like the letter O: *They sat in a circle around the fire.*
2 a group of people who know each other: *She has a large circle of friends.*

**WORD FAMILY: circle**
**circle** *noun* | **circle** *verb* | **circular** *adjective* | **semicircle** *noun*

**circle²** *verb*
1 to draw a circle around something: *Circle the correct answer.*
2 to move in a circle: *The plane circled the airport before landing.*

**ˈcircle graph** *noun*
a drawing of a circle divided into different parts by lines coming from the center. A circle graph is used to show the sizes of different amounts compared with each other. **SYNONYM: pie chart**

**cir·cuit** /ˈsɚkɪt/ *noun*
the complete path that an electric current travels around: *When the wires meet to complete the circuit, the bulb lights up.*

**circuit**

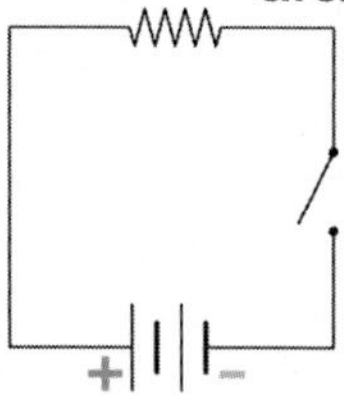


**cir·cu·lar** /ˈsɚkjəlɚ/ *adjective*
shaped like a circle: *They sat around a circular table.*

**cir·cu·late** /ˈsɚkjəˌleɪt/ *verb*
1 to go around inside something: *Blood circulates around the body.*
2 to send information to a group of people: *The results of the survey were circulated to everyone.*

**cir·cu·la·tion** /ˌsɚkjəˈleɪʃən/ *noun*
1 the movement of blood around your body: *Exercise can improve your circulation.*
2 the number of copies of a newspaper or magazine that are sold each time it is printed: *The magazine has increased its circulation to almost 2 million.*

**cir·cum·ference** /sɚˈkʌmfrəns/ *noun*
the distance around the outside of a circle or a round object: *Doctors measure the circumference of a baby's head to check that it is growing well.*
[**ORIGIN:** 1300-1400 From the Latin word *circumferre*, which means "to carry around."]

**cir·cum·stan·ces** Ac /ˈsɚkəmˌstænsɪz/ *plural noun*
1 the conditions or facts that are involved in an event or situation: *She had not been told about the circumstances of his death, and she wanted to know what had happened.*
2 **under no circumstances** = used for saying that something will or should never happen: *Under no circumstances should you lend him money. He'll never pay you back.*
[**ORIGIN:** 1100-1200 From the Latin word *circumstare*, which means "to stand around or surround."]

**cir·cus** /ˈsɚkəs/ *noun*
a show, often in a large tent, given by a group of performers and sometimes animals that

travel from one town to another: *We saw clowns and a trapeze act at the circus.*
[**ORIGIN:** 1300-1400 From a Latin word for "circle." The Romans used this word for large circular buildings where people went to watch races and shows.]

C

**cite** Ac /saɪt/ *verb* (*formal*)
to mention something as an example, a reason, proof, etc.: *The airport cited security reasons for not allowing people without tickets into the waiting areas.*

**cit·i·zen** /ˈsɪtəzən/ *noun*
someone who lives in a particular town, state, or country and has legal rights there: *She is a citizen of Canada.*
—**citizenship** *noun* the state of legally belonging to a particular country, and having rights and duties there: *She has applied for U.S. citizenship.*
[**ORIGIN:** 1200-1300 From the French word *citezein*, from *cité*, which means "city."]

**cit·rus** /ˈsɪtrəs/ *noun*
fruits such as oranges or LEMONS, or the trees they grow on: *The drink had a citrus flavor.*

**cit·y** /ˈsɪti/ *noun* (plural **cities**)
a very large town: *I've always lived in big cities like New York and Los Angeles.*
[**ORIGIN:** 1100-1200 From the Latin word *civitas*, which means "citizenship or state."]

**ˌcity ˈhall** (*also* **City Hall**) *noun*
the local government of a city, or the building it uses as its offices: *The mayor held a news conference at City Hall yesterday.*

**civ·ic** /ˈsɪvɪk/ *adjective*
relating to a city or the people who live in it: *It is a civic duty to serve on a jury.*

**civ·ics** /ˈsɪvɪks/ *noun*
the study of the rights and duties of citizens and the way government works: *We learned about elections in civics class.*

**civ·il** Ac /ˈsɪvəl/ *adjective*
**1** relating to laws about business, property, etc. rather than laws about crimes: *The jury in a civil court agreed that the man's neighbor had damaged the tree and should pay for it.*
**2** relating to the government or people of a country, not a military or religious organization: *We were married in a civil ceremony, not in church.*
**3** polite but not very friendly: *I was civil to him, even though I didn't like him.*
—**civility** /səˈvɪləti/ *noun* (*formal*) behavior that is polite but not very friendly

**ˌcivil engiˈneering** *noun*
the activity of building roads, bridges, and other large structures

**ci·vil·ian** /səˈvɪlyən/ *noun*
anyone who is not in the army, navy, or another military group: *Many innocent civilians were killed in the attack.*

**civ·i·li·za·tion** /ˌsɪvələˈzeɪʃən/ *noun*
a society that is well organized and developed: *The Mayans created a complex civilization that existed long before Europeans arrived in Central America.*

**civ·i·lized** /ˈsɪvəˌlaɪzd/ *adjective*
**1** a civilized society is well organized, and has good laws and ways of living: *All civilized societies have some form of government.*
**2** behaving in a polite and sensible way: *Let's discuss this in a civilized way, without yelling at each other.*

**ˌcivil ˈliberties** *plural noun*
the right of citizens to do whatever they want if it does not harm the rights of other people

**ˌcivil ˈrights** *plural noun*
the legal rights that every citizen of a country has: *The civil rights movement of the 1960s worked for an end to unfair treatment of African-Americans.*

**ˌcivil ˈwar** *noun*
a war between groups of people who live in the same country: *The Civil War between the people from the north and the south of the United States lasted four years.*

**claim¹** /kleɪm/ *verb*
**1** to say that something is true, even though it might not be: *He claims (that) he's 19, but he only looks about 16 to me.*
**2** to ask for something that belongs to you or that you have a right to have: *Lost items can be claimed between 10 a.m. and 4 p.m.*

**claim²** *noun*
**1** a statement that something is true, even though it might not be: *The company made false claims about the safety of its products.*
**2** an official request for something that you think you have a right to have: *He made an*

*insurance claim after his house was destroyed in the storm.*

**clam** /klæm/ *noun*
a small SHELLFISH with two round shells that are joined in one place and tightly closed. You can eat the meat inside the shell: *We dug in the mud for clams.*

**clamp¹** /klæmp/ *verb*
to hold or put something firmly in a particular position so that it cannot move: *Clamp the two pieces of wood tightly together until the glue dries.*
**PHRASAL VERB**
**clamp down**
to become very strict about a rule or law, so that people will stop doing something: *The courts are clamping down on drunk drivers and giving very severe punishments.*

**clamp²** *noun*
a tool used for holding things together tightly

**clan·des·tine** /klænˈdestɪn/ *adjective (formal)*
secret and sometimes illegal: *U.S. officials had a clandestine meeting with the spy.*

**clang** /klæŋ/ *verb*
if a piece of metal clangs, it makes a loud sound when it hits something: *The gate clanged shut behind him.*
—**clang** *noun* a loud sound made by metal hitting something

**clap** /klæp/ *verb* (**clapped**, **clapping**)
to hit your hands together loudly to show that you like something: *The audience was clapping for the band.* **SYNONYM: applaud**
→ see picture on page **A3**

**clar·i·fy** Ac /ˈklærəˌfaɪ/ *verb* (**clarified**, **clarifies**) *(formal)*
to make something easier to understand: *Can you clarify your question? I don't understand exactly what you mean.*
—**clarification** /ˌklærəfəˈkeɪʃən/ *noun* an explanation that makes something clearer

**clar·i·net** /ˌklærəˈnet/ *noun*
a wooden musical instrument like a long black tube, that you play by blowing into it, pressing keys, and covering holes with your fingers → see picture on page **A21**

**clar·i·ty** Ac /ˈklærəti/ *noun (formal)*
the quality of being clear and easy to understand: *The clarity of the instructions makes them easy to follow.*
[**ORIGIN:** 1600-1700 From the Latin word *claritas*, which means "clearness or brightness."]

**clash¹** /klæʃ/ *verb*
**1** to fight or argue with someone: *The police clashed with the angry crowd.*
**2** if colors or patterns clash, they look bad together: *The orange curtains clashed with the purple carpet.*

**clash²** *noun*
a fight or argument: *There were violent clashes between government troops and rebel soldiers.*

**clasp¹** /klæsp/ *verb*
to hold something tightly: *She clasped her hands tightly together as if she were praying.*

**clasp²** *noun*
a small metal object used for fastening a bag or a piece of jewelry: *She undid the clasp of her necklace and took it off.*

**class** /klæs/ *noun*
**1** a group of students who are taught together: *How many students are in your class?*
**2** a period of time during which students are taught: *I enjoy all my science classes.* | *Bob wasn't in class today.*
**3** a group of people in a society that have similar types of jobs, money, or education: *Rich people pay higher taxes than the middle class.*
**4** a group of things that are similar in some way: *To drive some classes of vehicle, such as buses or trucks, you need to have a special license.*

**clas·sic¹** Ac /ˈklæsɪk/ *adjective*
**1** very good and known by a lot of people: *a classic rock song*
**2** very typical: *The building is a classic example of Greek architecture.*

**classic²** Ac *noun*
a book, movie, or song which is very good and which people have liked for a long time: *"Moby Dick" is a classic of American literature.*

**clas·si·cal** Ac /ˈklæsɪkəl/ *adjective*
**1** relating to classical music: *a classical pianist*

C

**2** relating to ancient Greece and Rome: *stories from classical mythology*

**ˌclassical ˈmusic** *noun*
music by people such as Mozart and Beethoven that is considered to be serious and important

C

**clas·si·fied** /ˈklæsəˌfaɪd/ *adjective*
relating to information or documents that the government keeps secret from most people: *He was caught passing classified documents to the enemy.*

**ˌclassified ˈad** *noun*
a small advertisement that you put in a newspaper, for example offering to sell something or offering a job: *He looked in the classified ads every day to find an apartment.*

**clas·si·fy** /ˈklæsəˌfaɪ/ *verb* (**classified**, **classifies**)
to decide which group something belongs to: *His movies are classified as comedy, but I don't find them very funny.*
—**classification** /ˌklæsəfəˈkeɪʃən/ *noun* the process or result of classifying things

**class·mate** /ˈklæsmeɪt/ *noun*
someone who is in the same class as you at school or college: *I'm younger than most of my classmates.*

**class·room** /ˈklæsrum/ *noun*
a room in a school where students are taught

**class·y** /ˈklæsi/ *adjective* (*informal*)
stylish and extremely good in quality: *It's a classy restaurant and the prices are high.*

**clat·ter** /ˈklætɚ/ *verb*
if something clatters, it makes a loud unpleasant noise when it hits another thing: *The pans clattered to the floor.*
—**clatter** *noun* the loud noise made by things hitting together

**clause** Ac /klɔːz/ *noun*
**1** in grammar, a group of words that contains a subject and a verb: *The sentence "I'll do it if I can" contains two clauses: "I'll do it" and "if I can."*
**2** a part of a legal document: *I read every clause in the contract very carefully.*

**claus·tro·pho·bi·a** /ˌklɔstrəˈfoʊbiə/ *noun*
a strong fear of being in a small enclosed place
—**claustrophobic** *adjective* having a feeling of claustrophobia: *I get claustrophobic in elevators.*
[**ORIGIN:** 1800-1900 From the Latin word *claustrum*, which means "bar keeping a door closed" and the Greek word *phobos*, which means "fear."]

**claw** /klɔ/ *noun*
a sharp curved nail on the foot of an animal or bird: *The cat dug its claws into the carpet.*
—**claw** *verb* if an animal claws something, it tears it with its claws

**clay** /kleɪ/ *noun*
sticky soil that is used for making pots or bricks: *a clay pot*

**clean¹** /klin/ *adjective*
**1** not dirty: *Are your hands clean?* | *He put on a clean shirt.* **ANTONYM: dirty**
**2** not involving sex, drugs, alcohol, or anything illegal: *The movie is good clean fun and suitable for small children.*
**3 come clean** (*informal*) = to tell the truth about something after keeping it a secret: *I finally came clean and told my parents I had cheated on the test.*
—**cleanliness** /ˈklenlinɪs/ *noun* the state of being clean

**WORD FAMILY: clean**
**clean** *adjective* | **clean** *verb* | **cleaning** *noun* | **cleaner** *noun* | **cleanse** *verb* | **cleanser** *noun*

**clean²** (*also* **clean up**) *verb*
to make something clean or neat: *I need to clean the bathtub.* | *She's cleaning up her room.*
—**cleaning** *noun* the process of making something clean or neat: *We all help with the cleaning.*

**THESAURUS: clean**
**do the dishes/wash the dishes** to wash plates and pans after a meal: *It's Becky's turn to wash the dishes!*
**scrub** to clean something by rubbing it hard: *The floor was so dirty I had to scrub it with a brush.*
**do the housework** to clean the house: *My mom and dad work all week, so we all help do the housework on Saturday.*

**dust** to clean small light pieces of dirt off of furniture: *I dusted the bedroom furniture.*

**vacuum** to clean a carpet or floor with a machine that sucks up dirt: *Irma was vacuuming the living room.*

**sweep** to clean the dirt from the floor using a brush: *I swept the kitchen floor.*

**mop** to clean the floor with water and a mop (=soft material on a long handle): *Kenny spilled some juice, so I had to mop the floor.*

**do the laundry** to wash clothes: *Mom does a load of laundry every day.*

**brush** to clean something using a brush: *I brush my teeth twice a day.*

**PHRASAL VERB**

**clean something out**

to make the inside of something such as a room or cupboard clean or neat, especially by taking things out of it: *We cleaned out the garage last Sunday.*

**clean·er** /ˈklinɚ/ *noun*

**1** a machine or substance that is used to clean things: *a vacuum cleaner | a bottle of glass cleaner*

**2** someone whose job is to clean houses or other buildings

**3 the cleaners** = a place where you take clothes to be cleaned: *Could you pick up my suit from the cleaners?* **SYNONYM: dry cleaners**

**cleanse** /klenz/ *verb* (*formal*)

to make something completely clean: *Cleanse the cut with soap and water.* **SYNONYM: clean**

**cleans·er** /ˈklenzɚ/ *noun*

**1** a substance used for cleaning your skin

**2** a substance used for cleaning surfaces in a room or building

**clear¹** /klɪr/ *adjective*

**1** easy to understand, hear, or read: *I gave him clear instructions on what to do. | She spoke in a clear voice.*

**2** easy to notice, and impossible to doubt or make a mistake about: *It was clear (that) he was angry. | He made it clear (that) he wasn't interested.*

**THESAURUS: clear**

**noticeable** easy to notice: *There has been a noticeable improvement in her work.*

**obvious** very easy to notice: *It was obvious that Sally was upset.*

**conspicuous** very easy to notice, especially because of being different from other things: *I felt conspicuous in my red coat.*

**striking** unusual or interesting enough to be noticed: *There is a striking resemblance between Paul and his father.*

**3** if a substance is clear, you can see through it: *clear glass bottles* **SYNONYM: transparent**

**4** if a photograph or image is clear, the details are easy to see: *The TV has a very clear picture.* **ANTONYM: fuzzy**

**5** a clear sky has no clouds: *The sky was clear and the sun was shining.* **ANTONYM: cloudy**

**6** not blocked by anything: *No one sat in front of me, so I had a clear view of the screen.*

**7 be clear about something** = if you are clear about something, you understand it completely: *Are you clear about what I expect you to do?*

[**ORIGIN:** 1200-1300 From the Latin word *clarus*, which means "clear or bright."]

**clear²** *verb*

**1** to move things from a place, so that it is neat or empty: *They cleared the land so that they could grow crops. | Patty helped to clear the table and put the dishes in the dishwasher.*

**2** to say officially that someone has not committed a crime or done anything wrong: *The jury cleared Johnson of the murder charge.*

**3** to give or get official permission to do something: *I can maybe turn in the essay late, but I need to clear it with my teacher first.*

**4 clear the air** = to talk about a problem or disagreement, so that bad feeling does not continue: *You should talk to your father and clear the air.*

PHRASAL VERB

**clear up**

**1 clear something up** = to explain something or make it clearer: *I want the teacher to clear up a few details before I start on the project.*

**2** if the sky clears up, the clouds go away

C

**clear·ance** /ˈklɪrəns/ *noun*

**1** official permission to do something: *The pilot was given clearance to land the plane.*
SYNONYM: **permission**

**2** a sale in which a store wants to sell all its older goods to make room for new goods: *Stores have clearance sales after Christmas.*

**clear·ing** /ˈklɪrɪŋ/ *noun*

a small area in a forest where there are no trees

**clear·ly** /ˈklɪrli/ *adverb*

**1** without any doubt: *There's clearly a problem with the engine if the car won't start.*
SYNONYM: **obviously**

**2** in a way that is easy to hear, see, or understand: *Please speak more clearly. I can't understand you.*

**3** if you cannot think clearly, you are confused: *There was so much noise that I couldn't think clearly.*

**clench** /klentʃ/ *verb*

if you clench your hand or teeth, you close your hand or mouth tightly: *He clenched his fist like he wanted to hit me.*

**cler·gy** /ˈklɚdʒi/ *plural noun*

official religious leaders, such as priests: *Priests and other members of the clergy attended the meeting.*

**cler·i·cal** /ˈklerɪkəl/ *adjective*

relating to office work: *A clerical worker typed the report.*

**clerk** /klɚk/ *noun*

**1** someone whose job is to keep records or deal with documents in an office or bank

**2** someone who deals with people arriving at a hotel: *Please return your room key to the clerk at the front desk when you leave.*

[**ORIGIN:** 1000-1100 From the Latin word *clericus*, which means "priest." In medieval times, priests were some of the few people who could read and write. In businesses in the past, clerks were the people who wrote down information about the business.]

**clev·er** /ˈklevɚ/ *adjective*

intelligent and good at thinking of ideas or ways of doing things: *He came up with a clever plan to make lots of money.*

—**cleverly** *adverb* in a clever way

→ see Thesaurus box at **intelligent**

**cli·ché** /kliˈʃei/ *noun*

a phrase or idea that has been used many times before, and so is now boring: *I didn't want to hear clichés like "Time heals all wounds" after my boyfriend left me.*

→ see Thesaurus box at **phrase**

**click** /klɪk/ *verb*

**1** to make a short hard sound: *The door clicked shut.* → see picture on page **A22**

**2** if you click on something on a computer screen, you press a button on the MOUSE to make the computer do something: *Click on the button at the bottom of the screen to open a new page.*

—**click** *noun* a clicking sound: *I heard the click of a light switch.*

**cli·ent** /ˈklaɪənt/ *noun*

someone who pays to have work done by a professional person or a company: *Mr. Johnson is one of the law firm's most important clients.*

**cli·en·tele** /ˌklaɪənˈtel/ *noun* (*formal*)

the people who go to a particular store, restaurant. health club, etc.: *It's a clothes store with a young clientele.*

**cliff** /klɪf/ *noun*

an area of high rock with steep sides: *We walked along the cliff above the beach.*

**cli·mate** /ˈklaɪmət/ *noun*

the type of weather that a place usually has: *In the south of the country, the climate is hot and dry.*

[**ORIGIN:** 1300-1400 From the Greek word *klima*, which means "slope, or area of the world." "Climate" was used to mean an area of the world, or the weather in a particular area.]

**cli·max** /ˈklaɪmæks/ *noun*

the most important or exciting thing that happens: *Winning the gold medal was the climax of his sports career.*

**climb¹** /klaɪm/ *verb*

**1** if you climb a tree, a mountain, or some stairs, you go up toward the top: *It took them*

*five days to climb the mountain.* → see picture on page **A24**
**2** to use your hands and feet to move somewhere: *He climbed through the window to get into the house.*
**3** to increase in amount or level: *During the day, the temperature climbed to 90 degrees.*

**climb²** *noun*
an act of going up toward the top of a tree, hill, or mountain: *It was a steep climb to the top of the hill.*

**climb·er** /ˈklaɪmɚ/ *noun*
someone who climbs mountains or large rocks as a sport: *a rock climber*

**climb·ing** /ˈklaɪmɪŋ/ *noun*
the sport of climbing mountains or large rocks: *We often go climbing in the Rocky Mountains.*

**cling** /klɪŋ/ *verb* (**clung** /klʌŋ/)
to hold onto someone or something tightly: *The boy was frightened and clung to his mother.*

**clin·ic** /ˈklɪnɪk/ *noun*
a place where people can get medical treatment or advice: *I made an appointment at the clinic to see Dr. James.*
[**ORIGIN:** 1800-1900 From the Greek word *klinike*, which means "work done by the bed (of a sick person)."]

**clin·i·cal** /ˈklɪnɪkəl/ *adjective*
relating to treating people who are sick: *In clinical studies of the medicine, patients showed some improvement.*

**clip¹** /klɪp/ *noun*
a small object used for holding things together, especially pieces of paper or hair: *He fastened the pages together with a paper clip.*

**clip²** *verb*
**1** to hold things together with a clip, especially pieces of paper or hair: *Please clip your photo to the front of the form.*
**2** to cut small pieces off something to make it look neater: *He should clip the hedge before it gets too high.*
→ see Thesaurus box at **fasten**

**clip·board** /ˈklɪpbɔrd/ *noun*
a flat board with a clip at the top that holds paper onto it, so that people can write when they are standing up

**clip·pers** /ˈklɪpɚz/ *plural noun*
a tool for cutting small pieces off something: *I used the nail clippers to cut my fingernails.*

**cloak** /kloʊk/ *noun*
a piece of clothing like a big coat with no sleeves

**clock** /klɑk/ *noun*
**1** an instrument that shows the time: *She looked at the clock and saw that it was 3:15.* | *I set my alarm clock to wake me at 7 o'clock.*

**clock**

**2** **around the clock** = all day and all night: *I worked around the clock to finish my essay.*
[**ORIGIN:** 1300-1400 From the Latin word *clocca*, which means "bell." Some clocks have bells that ring to tell you the time.]

**clock·wise** /ˈklɑk-waɪz/ *adverb*
moving in the same direction as the hands of a clock: *We were told to run clockwise around the track.* **ANTONYM: counterclockwise**

**clog** /klɑg/ *noun*
a shoe that covers your toes but is open in the back

**clone** /kloʊn/ *noun*
an exact copy of a plant or animal that a scientist produces from one of its cells: *Dr. Campbell created a clone from just one cell of the sheep.*
—**clone** *verb* to produce a clone from a plant or animal: *Scientists have managed to clone several different animals.*

**close¹** /kloʊz/ *verb*
**1** to shut something: *Don't forget to close the back door when you leave.* **SYNONYM: shut**; **ANTONYM: open**
**2** if a business closes, it stops doing business until the next day: *"What time does the mall close tonight?" "9:00 p.m."* **ANTONYM: open**
**3** (*also* **close down**) if a business closes, it stops doing business permanently: *The factory closed down six months ago.* **ANTONYM: open**
**4** to end something such as a speech, movie, or book in a particular way: *The book opens before the war and closes 30 years later.* **ANTONYM: open**

C

**WORD FAMILY: close**

**close** *verb* | **closed** *adjective* | **closure** *noun*

→ see Thesaurus box at **near**[1]

**close**[2] /klous/ *adjective*
**1** near someone or something: *Our house is close to the beach.* **SYNONYM: near**
**2** likely to happen soon: *We haven't found the answer yet, but we're getting closer.* **SYNONYM: near**
**3 close to** = near a particular time or number: *It was close to midnight by the time we got home. | The Grand Canyon has close to one million visitors each year.*
**4** people who are close like each other a lot and talk to each other often: *We are close friends and see each other almost every day.*
**5** looking at or thinking about something very carefully: *She held the coin up to the light to take a closer look at the date.*
**6** if something such as a game or an election is close, it ends with each side being almost equal: *It was a close game, with the Red Sox losing by just a single run.*
**7 a close call** = a situation in which something dangerous or bad almost happens: *We had a close call driving to school when a van almost hit us.*
—**closeness** *noun* the quality of being close

**close**[3] /klouz/ *noun*
the end of an activity or period of time: *The 20th century was coming to a close.*

**closed** /klouzd/ *adjective*
**1** not open: *Make sure all the windows are closed so the rain doesn't get in.* **SYNONYM: shut**
**2** not doing business: *The store is closed on Sundays.*

**ˌclosed ˌcircuit ˈtelevision** *noun*
a system of cameras placed in public areas and buildings to help prevent crime: *The bank robbers were filmed on closed circuit television.*

**close-knit** /ˌklous ˈnɪt/ *adjective*
a close-knit family or group of people know each other well, live near each other, and help each other: *The town is a close-knit community, and your neighbors are always willing to help you.*

**close·ly** /ˈklousli/ *adverb*
if you look at someone or something closely, you look very carefully: *She was watching him closely because she didn't trust him.*

**clos·et** /ˈklɑzɪt/ *noun*
a place in a room where you hang your clothes, which is built into the wall of the room and has doors: *Let me hang your coat up in the closet.* → see picture on page **A10**

**close-up** /ˈklous ʌp/ *noun*
a photograph or a picture in a movie that is taken very close to someone or something: *There is a close-up of the actress at the end of the movie – her face fills the whole screen.*

**clos·ing** /ˈklouzɪŋ/ *noun*
the last words written in a letter: *"Lots of love" is not a suitable closing for a formal letter.*

**clo·sure** /ˈklouʒɚ/ *noun*
the act of closing a factory, school, or public building permanently: *The closure of the school upset many parents.*

**clot** /klɑt/ *noun*
some blood that has become solid: *The blood forms a clot over the cut, so that it does not keep bleeding.*
—**clot** *verb* if blood clots, it becomes solid

**cloth** /klɔθ/ *noun*
**1** material used for making clothes and other things: *Her dress was made of silk cloth.*
**2** a piece of material that you use for doing something: *Wipe the kitchen counters with a damp cloth.*

**clothe** /klouð/ *verb*
**1** to provide clothes for someone to wear: *We were poor and it was hard for my parents to feed and clothe five children.*
**2 fully/partly clothed** = wearing all of your clothes or wearing only some of your clothes: *Mike jumped into the pool fully-clothed!*

**clothes** /klouðz/ *plural noun*
the things that you wear, for example pants, dresses, underwear, and coats: *I need some new clothes.* → see picture on page **A10**

**GRAMMAR: clothes**

**Clothes** is a plural noun and does not have a singular form: *His clothes are always so nice.*

Do not say "a clothe." If you want to talk about one thing that you can wear, you have to say **a piece of clothing**, **an article of clothing** (*formal*), or **an item of clothing** (*formal*): *She picked up each piece of clothing and folded it carefully.*

You can also just say the name of the piece of clothing, such as **pants**, **a shirt**, or **a dress**.

**clothes·line** /ˈkloʊðzˌlaɪn/ *noun*
a rope that you hang wet clothes on so they will dry

**clothes·pin** /ˈkloʊðzpɪn/ *noun*
something you use to fasten wet clothes to a rope so they will dry

**cloth·ing** /ˈkloʊðɪŋ/ *noun*
clothes: *If you're going skiing, you'll need warm clothing.*

**cloud¹** /klaʊd/ *noun*
**1** a white or gray thing in the sky, that rain sometimes falls from. Clouds are made of many small drops of water: *The sun went behind a cloud.*
**2** a lot of smoke, dust, or steam in the air, in the shape of a cloud: *The fire sent up a huge cloud of smoke.*
[**ORIGIN:** From the old English word *clud*, which means "rock or hill." Some clouds look like rocks.]

**cloud²** *verb*
**PHRASAL VERB**
**cloud up/over**
to become cloudy: *It started to cloud up and looked like it might rain.*

**cloud·y** /ˈklaʊdi/ *adjective*
if it is cloudy, there are a lot of clouds in the sky: *Tomorrow will be cloudy with some rain.*

**clove** /kloʊv/ *noun*
**1** a piece of GARLIC
**2** a strong sweet spice: *The cake has cinnamon and cloves in it.*

**clo·ver** /ˈkloʊvɚ/ *noun*
a small green plant with three round leaves. People often say that finding a clover with four leaves brings you good luck.

**clown** /klaʊn/ *noun*
a person who makes people laugh by wearing funny clothes and a big red nose, and doing silly things: *The funniest part was when one of the clowns jumped into a tub of water.*

**club** /klʌb/ *noun*
**1** a group of people who meet because they share an interest: *Kim joined the art club at school.* | *Are you a member of the drama club?*
**2** a place where people go to dance, listen to music, or enjoy themselves: *All the movie stars go to that club to dance.* | *a comedy club*
**3** a card used in card games. The cards have a picture on them which looks like this (♣): *the king of clubs*
**4** a heavy stick used as a weapon
**5** a metal stick that you use to hit a golf ball

**club·bing** /ˈklʌbɪŋ/ *noun*
the activity of going to clubs to dance and meet people: *They went to a party and then went clubbing.*

**ˌclub ˈsoda** *noun*
water with a lot of bubbles in it, that you can mix with other drinks

**cluck** /klʌk/ *verb*
if a chicken clucks, it makes short low sounds

**clue** /klu/ *noun*
some information that helps you find the truth or the right answer: *Police are still searching for clues to why she disappeared.*
[**ORIGIN:** 1500-1600 From the old English word *clew*, which means "ball of yarn." If you unroll a ball of yarn as you go into a maze, it helps you find your way out again. In the same way, a clue helps you find the answer to a puzzle.]

**clump** /klʌmp/ *noun*
a group of trees or plants growing closely together: *The soldiers were hiding in a clump of trees.*

**clum·sy** /ˈklʌmzi/ *adjective*
someone who is clumsy drops things and falls a lot: *I'm pretty clumsy. I'm always tripping or dropping things.*
—**clumsily** *adverb* in a clumsy way: *Mina stood up, clumsily knocking over a glass of water.*

—**clumsiness** *noun* clumsy behavior or movements

**clung** /klʌŋ/ *verb*
the past tense and past participle of CLING

**clus·ter** /ˈklʌstɚ/ *noun*
a group of things that are close together: *Each branch had a small cluster of red berries growing on it.*

**clutch** /klʌtʃ/ *verb*
to hold something tightly: *"Don't go," she said, clutching his arm.*
→ see Thesaurus box at **hold**[1]

**clut·tered** /ˈklʌtɚd/ *adjective*
if a place is cluttered, it is messy because it is full of things: *His desk is always cluttered with pieces of paper and books.*
—**clutter** *noun* a lot of things that fill a place and make it messy: *The room was so full of clutter that you could hardly get in.*

**cm**
the written abbreviation of **centimeter**: *The plant's leaves are around 5 cm long.*

**Co.**
the written abbreviation of **Company**: *the Ford Motor Co.*

**c/o**
you write **c/o** on a letter that you send to an address where someone is staying, which is not the place where he or she usually lives. **c/o** is short for **in care of**: *Send the letter to me c/o Anne Miller, 868 Brown St., Anytown, IL.*

**coach**[1] /koʊtʃ/ *noun*
**1** someone who helps people get better at a sport, activity, or subject: *The football coach made the players go to extra practices before the big game.*
**2** the cheapest type of seats on an airplane or a train: *We flew coach to Atlanta because it was the cheapest way to go.* **SYNONYM: economy**

**coach**[2] *verb*
to help people get better at a sport, activity, or subject: *Mr. Davis coaches our soccer team.*

**coal** /koʊl/ *noun*
a hard black substance from below the ground that people burn to produce heat: *The coal comes from mines underground.*

**coarse** /kɔrs/ *adjective*
rough and thick, not smooth or fine: *The jeans are made of coarse cloth that feels rough against the skin.* **ANTONYM: fine**

**coast** /koʊst/ *noun*
the land next to the ocean: *The road goes along the coast, so it has good views of the ocean.*
—**coastal** *adjective* near the coast: *Many coastal areas were flooded after the hurricane.*
→ see Thesaurus box at **shore**
[**ORIGIN:** 1300-1400 From the Latin word *costa*, which means "rib or side."]

**ˈCoast Guard** *noun*
**the Coast Guard** = the organization whose job is helping ships and protecting the country's coast. It is part of the U.S. armed forces.

**coast·line** /ˈkoʊstlaɪn/ *noun*
the land at the edge of the ocean: *From the ship, we could see the rocky coastline.*

**coat** /koʊt/ *noun*
**1** something that you wear over other clothes to keep you warm outdoors: *It was a snowy day, so I put on my winter coat.* → see picture on page **A6**
**2** an animal's hair or fur: *The dog had mud all over its coat.*
**3** a thin layer of something that you put on a surface, for example paint: *The walls really need another coat of paint.*

**ˈcoat ˌhanger** *noun*
another word for a HANGER

**coax** /koʊks/ *verb*
to try to get someone to do something by talking to them gently and kindly: *He said he wasn't hungry, but I coaxed him into eating something.*
→ see Thesaurus box at **persuade**

**cob** /kɑb/ *noun*
the long hard part of a corn plant that the yellow seeds grow on

**co·bra** /ˈkoʊbrə/ *noun*
a large poisonous snake that lives in Africa and Asia. Before a cobra bites, it raises its body up and spreads the skin around its head wide.

**cob·web** /ˈkɑbweb/ *noun*
a net of fine threads that a SPIDER makes, used especially about old WEBs that make a

place look dirty: *The old house was dirty and full of cobwebs.*

**cock·pit** /ˈkɑkˌpɪt/ *noun*
the part of an airplane or race car where the pilot or driver sits

**cock·roach** /ˈkɑk-roʊtʃ/ *noun*
a large brown insect that lives in dark or dirty places

**cock·tail** /ˈkɑkteɪl/ *noun*
a drink made by mixing alcohol with other types of drinks

**co·coa** /ˈkoʊkoʊ/ *noun*
**1** a hot chocolate drink: *Do you want a cup of cocoa?*
**2** a brown powder that tastes like chocolate and is used in cooking: *Add four tablespoons of cocoa to the cake mix.*

**co·co·nut** /ˈkoʊkəˌnʌt/ *noun*
a very large brown nut which has liquid inside and white flesh that people eat: *Coconuts grow on palm trees.* → see picture on page A13
[**ORIGIN:** 1600-1700 From the Portuguese word *coco*, which means "grinning face." The bottom of a coconut, with its three spots, looks like a face.]

**co·coon** /kəˈkun/ *noun*
a covering of threads that a CATERPILLAR makes to protect itself while it is changing into a MOTH or BUTTERFLY

**cod** /kɑd/ *noun* (plural **cod**)
an ocean fish that people eat

**code** Ac /koʊd/ *noun*
**1** a way of using words, numbers, or symbols to send secret messages: *The enemy could not understand the messages that were sent in code.*
**2** a set of rules or laws that people must obey: *The school has a code of conduct that says students and teachers must not use racist language.*

**co·erce** /koʊˈɚs/ *verb (formal)*
to force someone to do something by threatening to hurt him or her: *The army is accused of coercing people into leaving the area.* **SYNONYM: force**
→ see Thesaurus box at **force¹**

**cof·fee** /ˈkɔfi/ *noun*
**1** a hot brown drink that is made from the brown beans of the coffee plant: *Let's have a cup of coffee!*
**2** the brown beans of a plant, which are heated and crushed to make a powder, and then mixed with water to make a hot drink: *I bought a jar of coffee.*
[**ORIGIN:** 1500-1600 From the Italian word *caffè*, from the Arabic word *qahwa*. The Arabic word may come from "Kaffa," which is the place in Ethiopia where coffee plants were first found, or it may first have meant "wine."]

**ˈcoffee shop** *noun*
a small restaurant that serves coffee and cheap meals: *I'll get a sandwich from the coffee shop for lunch.*

**cof·fin** /ˈkɔfɪn/ *noun*
the box in which a dead person is buried **SYNONYM: casket**
[**ORIGIN:** 1300-1400 From the Latin word *cophinus*, which means "basket."]

**co·her·ent** Ac /koʊˈhɪrənt/ *adjective (formal)*
clear and easy to understand, especially because there is clear organization: *A coherent story has a clear beginning, middle, and end.* **ANTONYM: incoherent**
—**coherently** *adverb* in a coherent way: *She could not speak coherently enough to tell us what was wrong.*

**coil¹** /kɔɪl/ (*also* **coil up**) *verb*
to wind something long and thin into the shape of a circle: *She coiled some hair around her finger.*

**coil²** *noun*
a piece of rope, wire, or hair that is wound around in a circle: *There was a big coil of rope in the bottom of the boat.*

**coin** /kɔɪn/ *noun*
a piece of money made of metal: *Andy took a few coins from his pocket to pay for the candy.*
→ see Thesaurus box at **money**

**co·in·ci·dence** Ac /koʊˈɪnsədəns/ *noun*
two things that happen at the same time and seem to be related, even though they happen by chance: *By coincidence, his best friend is also called William.*
—**coincide** /ˌkoʊɪnˈsaɪd/ *verb* if two things coincide, they happen at the same time: *The*

C

*movie's release coincided with the start of the summer vacation.*

**co·la** /ˈkoʊlə/ *noun*
a sweet brown drink with a lot of bubbles in it: *a can of cola*

C

**cold[1]** /koʊld/ *adjective*
**1** having a low temperature: *It's very cold in Canada during the wintertime.* | *Drink your hot chocolate before it gets cold.* **ANTONYMS: hot, warm**

**THESAURUS: cold**

**cool** cold in a pleasant way, especially after it has been hot: *It's very hot during the day, but cooler at night.*

**chilly** cold, but not very cold: *The water in the pool felt chilly.*

**frosty** very cold, with the ground covered in frost (=ice that looks white and powdery): *It was a bright, frosty morning.*

**freezing** very cold, so that water outside becomes ice: *It was freezing cold last night.*

**icy** very cold: *An icy wind cut through his jacket.*

**2** if you are cold, you feel uncomfortable, because you are not warm enough: *Shut the window if you feel cold.* **ANTONYM: hot**
**3** cold food has been cooked, but is not warm when you eat it: *For lunch, we had cold chicken and a salad.* **ANTONYM: hot**
**4** not friendly to people: *I met him once, and he seemed cold and formal.*

**cold[2]** *noun*
**1** a common illness that blocks your nose and makes your throat sore: *I had a cold and felt pretty awful.* | *If your clothes get wet, you'll catch a cold.*
**2 the cold** = cold weather: *Don't stand out there in the cold!*

**ˌcold-ˈblooded** *adjective*
a cold-blooded animal, such as a snake, has a body temperature that goes up or down depending on the temperature of the air or ground around it

**ˈcold cuts** *plural noun*
thin pieces of different kinds of cooked meat that you eat cold

**cold·ly** /ˈkoʊldli/ *adverb*
in an unfriendly way: *"I'm busy. Don't bother me," Sarah said coldly.*

**cold·ness** /ˌkoʊldnɪs/ *noun*
**1** unfriendly behavior: *He was upset by his sister's coldness toward him.*
**2** cold in temperature: *The icy coldness of the water shocked him.*

**cole slaw** /ˈkoʊl slɔ/ *noun*
a SALAD made of thinly cut raw CABBAGE

**col·lage** /kəˈlɑʒ/ *noun*
a picture made by sticking many pieces of cloth or paper, photographs, or other things onto a piece of paper: *I made a collage of a face, using pieces of colored paper.*

**col·lapse[1]** Ac /kəˈlæps/ *verb*
**1** if a building, wall, or bridge collapses, it suddenly falls down and is destroyed: *The building collapsed during the fire.*
**2** to suddenly fall down or become unconscious because you are sick or very weak: *He collapsed at the end of the race and he was taken to the hospital.*
**3** if a system collapses, it suddenly fails and cannot continue: *The economy collapsed when banks stopped lending money to small businesses.*
→ see Thesaurus box at **fall[1]**

**collapse[2]** Ac *noun*
**1** a sudden failure in the way a business or system works, so that it cannot continue: *Most Eastern European countries became democracies after the collapse of communism.*
**2** a situation in which a structure such as a building, wall, or bridge falls down
**3** a situation in which a person falls down because he or she is sick or very weak

**collar**

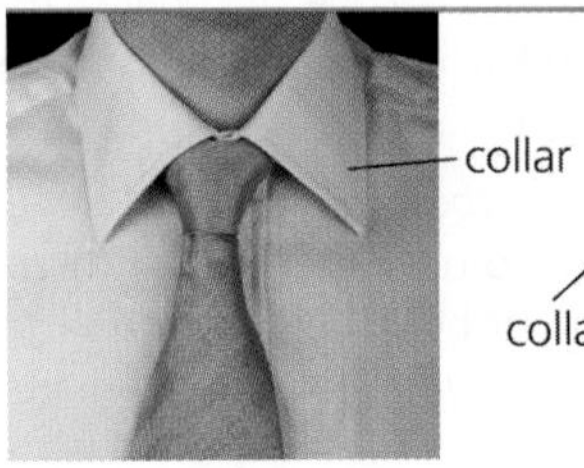

**col·lar** /ˈkɑlɚ/ *noun*
**1** the part of a shirt, coat, or dress that fits around your neck: *The collar of his shirt felt*

*too tight, so he took off his tie and opened the top button.*
**2** a narrow band of leather or plastic put around the neck of a dog or cat: *The dog's collar has its name on it.*
[**ORIGIN:** 1300-1400 From the Latin word *collum*, which means "neck."]

**col·lar·bone** /ˈkɑlɚˌboʊn/ *noun*
one of the pair of bones on your chest that go from the base of your neck to your shoulders
→ see picture on page **A2**

**col·league** Ac /ˈkɑlig/ *noun*
someone who works with you in the same office or organization: *She showed the letter to one of her colleagues.*

**col·lect¹** /kəˈlekt/ *verb*
**1** to get things and bring them together: *The teacher collected all the tests from the students.*
**2** to get and keep objects of the same type because you like them or hope they will become valuable: *She collects old coins.*
**3** if something collects in a place, it gradually increases in amount: *Dust had collected under the sofa.* **SYNONYM: gather**
[**ORIGIN:** 1500-1600 From the Latin words *com-* and *legere*, which mean "together" and "to gather."]

**WORD FAMILY: collect**
**collect** *verb* | **collection** *noun* | **collector** *noun*

**collect²** *adverb*
**call collect** = if you call someone collect, the person who receives the phone call pays for it

**col·lec·tion** /kəˈlekʃən/ *noun*
a group of similar things that have been gathered together: *The museum has a good collection of modern art.*
→ see Thesaurus box at **group¹**

**col·lege** /ˈkɑlɪdʒ/ *noun*
**1** a large school where you can study after high school: *I'm planning to go to college in the fall to study biology.*
**2** the part of a university that teaches a particular subject: *the College of Medicine* **SYNONYM: school**
—**collegiate** /kəˈlidʒɪt/ *adjective* relating to college: *collegiate sports*
[**ORIGIN:** 1300-1400 From the Latin word *collegium*, which means "society."]

**collide**

**col·lide** /kəˈlaɪd/ *verb*
to crash into something or someone with a lot of force: *His car collided with a bus, but luckily no one was hurt.* **SYNONYM: crash**

**col·li·sion** /kəˈlɪʒən/ *noun*
an occasion when one thing crashes into another, especially cars or planes: *The collision closed the northbound lanes of Highway 62.* **SYNONYM: crash**

**co·logne** /kəˈloʊn/ *noun*
a liquid with a pleasant smell that you put on your skin

**co·lon** /ˈkoʊlən/ *noun*
**1** the mark (:) used in writing before a list or before giving an example
**2** a part inside your body where food turns into waste that will leave your body. The colon is the bottom part of a long tube called the INTESTINE.

**colo·nel** /ˈkɚnl/ *noun* (*written abbreviation*: **Col.**)
an officer who has a high rank in the army, air force, or Marines

**co·lo·ni·al** /kəˈloʊniəl/ *adjective*
relating to the control of a place by a more powerful country: *We learned about life in colonial America, when the country was ruled by Britain.*

**col·o·nist** /ˈkɑlənɪst/ *noun*
someone who comes to live in a new colony: *The first colonists came to America in the 1600s.*

**col·o·nize** /ˈkɑləˌnaɪz/ *verb*
to begin to control another country or area, and send people from your own country to live there: *Argentina was colonized by Spain.*
—**colonization** /ˌkɑlənəˈzeɪʃən/ *noun* the process of colonizing a place

C

**col·o·ny** /ˈkɑləni/ *noun* (plural **colonies**)
a country or area that is ruled by a more powerful country, usually one that is far away: *The island used to be a French colony but it is now independent.*
→ see Thesaurus box at **country**
[ORIGIN: 1300-1400 From the Latin word *colonia*, which means "farm, or land on which people have settled."]

C

**col·or¹** /ˈkʌlɚ/ *noun*
**1** red, blue, yellow, green, orange, etc.: *"What color is your new car?" "Blue." | My favorite color is orange. | The room was decorated in bright colors.*
**2 people/men/women, etc. of color** = people who are not white: *We want more people of color to be elected to Congress.*

**color²** *verb*
**1** to add colors to a picture on a piece of paper using colored pencils, pens, or paint: *The little girl sat at the table coloring in a picture.*
**2** if you color your hair, you make it a different color from its natural color **SYNONYM: dye**

**col·or·blind** /ˈkʌlɚˌblaɪnd/ *adjective*
**1** not able to see the difference between particular colors: *My brother is colorblind. He can't tell the difference between red and green.*
**2** treating all races of people fairly and equally: *We want a colorblind society, where everyone is treated equally.*

**col·or·ful** /ˈkʌlɚfəl/ *adjective*
having a lot of bright colors: *The dancers wore colorful clothes.*

**col·or·ing** /ˈkʌlərɪŋ/ *noun*
**1** the color of something, especially someone's hair, skin, or eyes: *Their children all have the same coloring, the same blue eyes and blond hair.*
**2** a substance used for giving a particular color to food: *We put green food coloring into the cake we made for St. Patrick's Day.*

**col·or·less** /ˈkʌlɚlɪs/ *adjective*
not having any color: *Water is a colorless liquid.*

**colt** /koʊlt/ *noun*
a young male horse

**col·umn** /ˈkɑləm/ *noun*
**1** a tall stone post used to support a building: *There were two big columns on either side of the entrance to the temple.*
**2** an article by someone who writes regularly in a newspaper or magazine: *He writes a sports column for the "Los Angeles Times."*
**3** a row of words or numbers that goes down a page: *This dictionary has two columns on each page.*

**co·ma** /ˈkoʊmə/ *noun*
a serious medical condition in which someone is not conscious for a long time, usually after an accident or illness: *After the accident, he was in a coma for six days.*

**comb** /koʊm/ *noun*
an object you use to make your hair neat. A comb is a flat piece of plastic with a row of thin sticks on one side. → see picture on page **A11**
—**comb** *verb* to make your hair neat with a comb: *He brushed his teeth, combed his hair, and got dressed for school.*

**com·bat** /ˈkɑmbæt/ *noun*
fighting during a war: *Her husband was killed in combat.*
→ see Thesaurus box at **war**
[ORIGIN: 1500-1600 From the Latin words *com-* and *batteure*, which mean "together" and "to hit."]

**com·bi·na·tion** /ˌkɑmbəˈneɪʃən/ *noun*
two or more different things that are used together or that happen together: *A combination of talent and hard work helps a player to be successful.*

**com·bine** /kəmˈbaɪn/ *verb*
to join or mix two or more things together: *When hydrogen and oxygen combine, they form water. | The movie combines comedy and excitement.*
→ see Thesaurus box at **mix¹**

**come** /kʌm/ *verb* (**came** /keɪm/, **come**)
**1** to move toward a place: *There was a big truck coming straight toward us, so we jumped to one side.*
**2** to arrive at a place: *The letter came yesterday. | What time did she come home last night?*
**3** to go somewhere with someone: *We're*

*going to see a movie tonight. Do you want to come?*
**4** to happen: *Spring seems to come earlier every year.*
**5** to be in a position or place in a list of things: *P comes before Q in the alphabet.*
**6** to reach a point or level: *The water came up to my knees.*
**7** if a product comes in a particular size or with particular features, you can buy it in that size or with that thing: *The shoes come in all sizes.*
**8 come open/loose/undone, etc.** = to become open or loose: *The door had come open in the wind.*
**9 come as a surprise/a shock/a relief, etc.** = to make someone feel surprised, shocked, etc.: *The news came as a surprise to everyone.*
**10 how come?** (*informal*) = used in order to ask someone why something happened or is true: *How come it always rains when we go for a bike ride?* **SYNONYM: why**
**11 for years to come** = for many years in the future: *People will remember this day for years to come.*
[**ORIGIN:** From the old English word *cuman.*]
**PHRASAL VERBS**
**come along**
to go somewhere with someone: *You're welcome to come along to the meeting.*
**come apart**
to split into pieces: *The book was wet, and it came apart in my hands.*
**come around**
to change your opinion so that you begin to agree with someone or are no longer angry with someone: *I know she's mad at you right now, but she'll come around.*
**come back**
to return from a place: *When is your sister coming back from Seattle?*
**come down**
if a price, level, or amount comes down, it gets lower: *The price of gas went up and then came down a little bit.*
**come down with something**
to get an illness: *I think I'm coming down with the flu.*
**come from**
**1 come from somewhere** = if you come from a place, you were born there: *"Where do you come from?" "Cincinnati."*
**2 come from something** = used when saying where or when something began or was first made or produced: *The word "biology" comes from Greek.*
**come in**
to enter the room or house: *Come in and sit down.*
**come off**
to become separated from the main part of something: *The door handle came off in my hand.*
**come on**
**1** if a light or machine comes on, it starts working: *She pressed the button, and the lights came on.*
**2** used when telling someone to hurry or try something: *Come on! We're late!*
**come out**
**1** if a book, movie, record, or game comes out, it becomes available for people to buy or see: *Her new movie comes out early next year.*
**2** if information about something comes out, people find out about it: *It was several months before the truth came out.*
**come over**
to visit someone at his or her house: *Do you want to come over on Friday night?*
**come through something**
to get to the end of a dangerous or difficult situation without being harmed or damaged: *She came through all her problems and is now happily married.* **SYNONYM: survive**
**come to**
**come to $20/$3, etc.** = used when saying what the total cost of something is: *The meal came to $50 for two people.*
**come up**
**1** to move near to you, especially in order to speak to you: *A man came up to me and asked me what time it was.*
**2** if a problem comes up, it happens: *Please let me know if any problems come up.*
**3 be coming up** = to be happening soon: *My mom's birthday is coming up, and I need to get her a present.*
**come up with something**
to think of an idea, answer, or name: *They still haven't come up with a name for the baby.*

C

**come·back** /ˈkʌmbæk/ *noun*
if someone or something makes a comeback, they become popular or successful again: *The singer is hoping to make a comeback with her first CD in eight years.*

**co·me·di·an** /kəˈmidiən/ *noun*
someone whose job is to tell jokes and make people laugh **SYNONYM: comic**

**com·e·dy** /ˈkɑmədi/ *noun* (plural **comedies**)
a funny movie, play, or television program that makes people laugh: *The movie is a comedy about three guys who get lost in the forest.*
→ see Thesaurus box at **movie**
[**ORIGIN:** 1300-1400 From the Greek words *komos* and *aeidein*, which mean "a party or festival" and "to sing."]

**com·et** /ˈkɑmɪt/ *noun*
an object in the sky that looks like a very bright ball with a tail, that moves through space around the Sun
[**ORIGIN:** 1100-1200 From the Greek word *kometes*, which means "long-haired." *Kometes* was used by the Greeks as the word for a comet because comets look like they have long-haired tails.]

**com·fort¹** /ˈkʌmfət/ *noun*
**1** a feeling of being physically relaxed, and not being in pain or feeling too hot or cold: *I wanted to stay in the comfort of my bed, not get up and go out into the cold.* **ANTONYM: discomfort**
**2** something that makes you feel less upset or worried: *It was a comfort to know that my parents were nearby.*
[**ORIGIN:** 1100-1200 From the Latin word *confortare*, which means "to strengthen," from *fortis*, which means "strong." A comfort makes you feel mentally stronger.]

**WORD FAMILY: comfort**
**comfort** *noun* | **comfortable** *adjective* | **uncomfortable** *adjective* | **discomfort** *noun*

**comfort²** *verb*
to make someone feel less worried or unhappy: *He held the baby close and rocked her to comfort her.*

**com·fort·a·ble** /ˈkʌmftəbəl/ *adjective*
**1** things that are comfortable such as chairs or clothes make you feel physically relaxed: *The bed was very comfortable, and I slept well.*
**2** if you are comfortable, you feel physically relaxed: *Are you comfortable? Would you like another pillow?*
—**comfortably** *adverb* in a comfortable way: *We sat comfortably on the sofa watching TV.*

**com·ic¹** /ˈkɑmɪk/ *adjective*
funny and making you laugh: *I think he's the funniest comic actor around.*

**comic²** *noun*
**1 the comics** = the part of a newspaper that has comic strips in it
**2** a magazine that tells a story using a series of drawings **SYNONYM: comic book**
**3** someone whose job is to tell jokes and make people laugh **SYNONYM: comedian**

**com·i·cal** /ˈkɑmɪkəl/ *adjective*
funny, especially in a strange or unexpected way: *The team played so badly it was almost comical.*

**ˈcomic book** *noun*
a magazine that tells a story using a series of drawings: *Some old Superman comic books are worth a lot of money.*

**ˈcomic strip** *noun*
a series of pictures that are drawn inside boxes and tell a story: *Charlie Brown and Snoopy are characters in the "Peanuts" comic strip.*

**com·ma** /ˈkɑmə/ *noun*
the written mark (,) used in a sentence to show a short pause or to separate words in a list

**com·mand¹** /kəˈmænd/ *noun*
**1** an order from an important person to do something: *The general gave the command to attack.* **SYNONYM: order**
**2** if you are in command, you have control over a group of soldiers or a ship: *The general was in command of more than a thousand soldiers.*
**3** knowledge of something, especially a language: *She has a good command of English.*

**command²** *verb*
**1** to officially tell someone who is less important than you that he or she must do

something: *The police officer commanded him to stop.*
**2** to be the leader of a group of soldiers: *General Eisenhower commanded the U.S. forces in Europe during World War II.*

**com·mand·er** (*also* **Commander**) /kəˈmændɚ/ *noun*
an important officer who is in charge of an army or a group of soldiers: *Military commanders gave the order for their troops to attack the enemy.*

**com·mem·o·rate** /kəˈmeməˌreɪt/ *verb*
to do something in order to remember an important person or event from the past: *The statue commemorates the soldiers who died during the war.*
[**ORIGIN:** 1600-1700 From the Latin word *commemorare*, which means "to remind someone of something."]

**com·mence** Ac /kəˈmens/ *verb* (*formal*)
to begin: *The work will commence in January and end in July.* **SYNONYM: start**

**com·mence·ment** /kəˈmensmənt/ *noun*
**1** (*formal*) the beginning of something: *The two armies prepared for the commencement of the battle.* **SYNONYM: start**
**2** an event at which students get their DIPLOMAs to show they have finished high school or college: *Two students gave speeches at commencement.* **SYNONYM: graduation**

**com·ment¹** Ac /ˈkɑment/ *noun*
something you say which shows your opinion about someone or something: *The other team's coach made some negative comments about our team.*

**comment²** Ac *verb*
to give an opinion about someone or something: *The police have refused to comment on the case.*

**com·men·tar·y** Ac /ˈkɑmənˌteri/ *noun* (plural **commentaries**)
if someone gives a commentary, he or she tells about what is happening during an event such as a game: *He does football commentary.*

**com·men·ta·tor** Ac /ˈkɑmənˌteɪtɚ/ *noun*
someone on television or radio who tells about an event or game as it is happening, or who gives his or her opinions about a subject: *a sports commentator*

**com·merce** /ˈkɑmɚs/ *noun*
the activity of buying and selling things: *The agency is trying to create jobs and increase commerce.* **SYNONYM: trade**
[**ORIGIN:** 1500-1600 From the Latin word *commercium*, from *com-* and *merx*, which mean "together" and "things to be sold."]

**com·mer·cial¹** /kəˈmɚʃəl/ *noun*
an advertisement on television or radio: *There are always lots of television commercials for toys just before Christmas.* **SYNONYMS: ad, advertisement**
→ see Thesaurus box at **advertisement**

**commercial²** *adjective*
**1** relating to business and the buying and selling of things: *This area is all commercial. There are lots of stores but no houses.*
**2** relating to making money or a profit: *The CD was a commercial success, selling millions of copies.*
—**commercially** *adverb* in a commercial way

**com·mis·sion** Ac /kəˈmɪʃən/ *noun*
**1** a group of people who have the official job of finding out about something or controlling something: *The president set up a commission to look at the causes of the disaster.*
**2** an amount of money that is paid to someone for selling a product as part of his or her job: *Employees can earn a 30% commission on each car they sell.*

**com·mit** Ac /kəˈmɪt/ *verb* (**committed, committing**)
**1** to do something wrong or illegal: *Are the police sure that Rogers committed the crime?*
**2 commit suicide** = to kill yourself deliberately
**3 commit yourself (to doing something)** = to say that you will definitely do something: *If you want to be on the team, you have to commit yourself to coming to practice.*

| WORD FAMILY: commit |
| --- |
| **commit** *verb* \| **commitment** *noun* |

**com·mit·ment** Ac /kəˈmɪtmənt/ *noun*
**1** a promise to do something: *When you marry someone, you make a commitment to*

*stay with that person for the rest of your life.*
**2** the hard work and effort that you give to something such as your job or an activity which is important to you: *She shows a lot of commitment to her job. She always comes in early and works late.*

C

**com·mit·tee** /kəˈmɪti/ *noun*
a group of people who have been chosen to do a particular job, for example to make decisions about something: *Jess is on the decorations committee for the spring dance.*

**com·mon** /ˈkɑmən/ *adjective*
**1** something that is common is often seen or often happens: *"Smith" is a very common last name in the U.S.* **ANTONYM: rare**
**2** belonging to or shared by two or more people or things: *We have a lot of common interests, such as reading and music.*
—**commonly** *adverb* often or usually: *Aspirin is commonly used to get rid of headaches.*

**ˌcommon deˈnominator** *noun*
a number that all the numbers below the line in a set of FRACTIONs can be divided into exactly: *The common denominator for $\frac{1}{3}$ + $\frac{1}{2}$ + $\frac{1}{6}$ is 6 because 3, 2 and 6 all divide into 6 exactly.*

**ˌcommon ˈsense** *noun*
the ability to think and behave in a sensible way and not do stupid things: *Locking your door at night is just plain common sense.*

**com·mu·ni·cate** [Ac] /kəˈmyunəˌkeɪt/ *verb*
to talk or write to someone and tell them something: *We communicate with each other mostly by email and phone.*
[**ORIGIN:** 1500-1600 From the Latin word *communicare*, which means "to share, or to give information," from *communis*, which means "shared."]

**WORD FAMILY: communicate**
**communicate** *verb* | **communication** *noun*

**com·mu·ni·ca·tion** [Ac]
/kəˌmyunəˈkeɪʃən/ *noun*
**1** the action of speaking or writing to someone and being understood by him or her: *Communication was difficult because we did not speak the same language.*
**2 communications** = ways of sending information using computers, telephones, or radios: *Modern communications such as email make it possible for people to work from their homes.*

**com·mu·nism** /ˈkɑmyəˌnɪzəm/ *noun*
a political system in which the government of a country owns all the businesses, land, and property
—**communist** *noun* someone who believes that communism is the best political system
—**communist** *adjective* relating to communism: *North Korea is a communist country.*

**com·mu·ni·ty** [Ac] /kəˈmyunəti/ *noun*
(plural **communities**)
**1** all of the people who live in the same town or area: *All the children in our community go to the same school.*
**2** a group of people in an area who belong to the same religion, come from the same country, or do the same activity: *Miami has a large Cuban community.*
[**ORIGIN:** 1300-1400 From the Latin word *communitas*, from *communis*, which means "shared." A community of people all share a place or connection.]

**comˈmunity ˌcollege** *noun*
a college that people can go to, usually for two years, in order to learn a skill or to prepare to go to another college or university
**SYNONYM: junior college**

**com·mute** /kəˈmyut/ *verb*
to travel to work regularly in a car, train, or bus: *He commutes to work by car.*
—**commute** *noun* the trip that someone makes regularly to get to work: *Her commute to the office takes a half hour if she drives.*
—**commuter** *noun* someone who travels to work regularly: *The roads are full of commuters during rush hour.*

**com·pact¹** /ˈkɑmpækt/ *adjective*
small and made to take up very little space: *Compact cars are easy to park and don't use as much gas as bigger cars.*

**compact²** *noun*
**1** (*also* **compact car**) a small car: *The parking space was only big enough for a compact.*
**2** a small flat container with a mirror and powder for a woman's face

**ˌcompact ˈdisc** *noun*
a CD

**com·pan·ion** /kəmˈpænyən/ *noun*
someone you spend a lot of time with: *My dog is my constant companion and goes everywhere with me.*
[**ORIGIN:** 1200-1300 From the Latin words *com-* and *panis*, which mean "with" and "bread." A companion was someone you ate with.]

**com·pa·ny** /ˈkʌmpəni/ *noun* (plural **companies**)
**1** a business that makes or sells things: *I work for a computer company.*

**THESAURUS: company**

**firm** a company, especially one that does something for you rather than one that makes things: *She works for a law firm.*

**business** a company that makes or sells things or that does something for you: *She started her own advertising business.*

**corporation** a large company that often includes several smaller companies: *He works for a large entertainment corporation, in the music division.*

**2** if you have company, there are friends with you at your home: *Don't forget, we have company tonight – Bob and his wife are coming for dinner.*
**3** a group of 100 or 200 soldiers: *Our company was attacked by enemy planes.*

**com·par·a·tive** /kəmˈpærətɪv/ *noun*
**the comparative** = the form of an adjective or adverb you use when comparing someone or something with other people or things, for example when saying that someone is taller, younger, or older than someone else

**com·pare** /kəmˈper/ *verb*
to think about how two or more people or things are different or the same: *We compared the prices of different computers, and this one was the cheapest.*
[**ORIGIN:** 1400-1500 From the Latin word *compar*, which means "like or equal to."]

**WORD FAMILY: compare**
**compare** *verb* | **comparison** *noun* | **comparative** *noun*

**com·par·i·son** /kəmˈpærəsən/ *noun*
**1 in comparison/by comparison** = used when you are comparing two people or things: *Our house is small in comparison with theirs. Ours has two bedrooms, and theirs has six.*
**2** if you make a comparison between two things, you say how you think they are the same or different: *The police took his fingerprints for comparison with the prints found at the crime scene.*

**com·part·ment** /kəmˈpɑrtmənt/ *noun*
a container inside something large or inside a larger container: *He keeps a flashlight in the glove compartment of the car.*

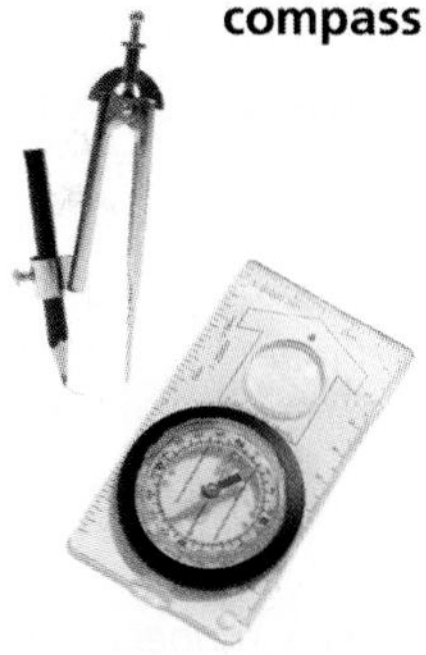

**compass**

**com·pass** /ˈkʌmpəs/ *noun*
**1** an instrument with a needle that always points north, used for showing directions
**2** an instrument shaped like a V that you use for drawing circles

**com·pas·sion** /kəmˈpæʃən/ *noun*
a feeling of being sorry for people who are in a bad situation, and wanting to help them: *He had great compassion for the poor people of the city and often brought food to them.*
—**compassionate** *adjective* feeling or showing compassion

**com·pat·i·ble** Ac /kəmˈpætəbəl/ *adjective*
**1** if two things are compatible, they can exist or be used together without problems: *You won't have any trouble using the software – it's compatible with your computer.*
**2** (*formal*) if two people are compatible, they can have a good relationship because they like the same things or think in the same ways: *My parents are very compatible – they never argue.* **ANTONYM: incompatible**
—**compatibility** /kəmˌpætəˈbɪləti/ *noun* the quality of being compatible

**WORD FAMILY: compatible**
**compatible** *adjective* | **incompatible** *adjective* | **compatibility** *noun* | **incompatibility** *noun*

C

**com·pel** /kəmˈpel/ *verb* (**compelled, compelling**) (*formal*)
to force someone to do something: *He was compelled to give up his job because he had to take care of his son.*
→ see Thesaurus box at **force**[1]

C

**com·pen·sate** Ac /ˈkɑmpənˌseɪt/ *verb* (*formal*)
**1** to pay someone money because something bad has happened to them or to something they own: *He had to compensate the woman for damaging her car.*
**2** to make something bad have a smaller effect on a situation: *He is very smart, and that compensates for his lack of experience.*

**com·pen·sation** Ac /ˌkɑmpənˈseɪʃən/ *noun* (*formal*)
money that is paid to someone because something bad has happened to them or to something they own: *She received over $1 million in compensation for her injuries.*

**com·pete** /kəmˈpit/ *verb*
to take part in a race or competition: *How many runners will be competing in the race?*

**WORD FAMILY: compete**
**compete** *verb* | **competition** *noun* | **competitor** *noun* | **competitive** *adjective*

**com·pe·tent** /ˈkɑmpətənt/ *adjective*
having enough skill or knowledge to do something to a satisfactory standard: *The car has some problems, but a competent mechanic can fix them easily.*
—**competently** *adverb* in a way that shows you have skill or knowledge
—**competence** *noun* the ability to do something to a satisfactory standard

**com·pe·ti·tion** /ˌkɑmpəˈtɪʃən/ *noun*
**1** an organized event in which people or teams try to be the best at doing something: *He wrote a poem and entered it for the poetry competition.*

**THESAURUS: competition**
**contest** a competition in which a judge or group of judges decides the winner: *The school held a contest for the best poster about healthy eating.*
**race** a competition in which people try to run, drive, swim, or ride faster than each other: *He won the race in a time of 21.9 seconds.*
**championship** a competition to find the best player or team in a sport: *the Iowa State Girls' Basketball Championships*
**tournament** a competition in which many players or teams play against each other until there is one winner: *We're playing in a volleyball tournament at the beach this weekend.*
**league** a group of sports teams that play against each other: *Our high school baseball team finished second in the league.*

**2** a situation in which people are all trying to get the same thing, and not everyone will be able to succeed: *There is a lot of competition for roles in the school play, but you're really good at acting so you should get a part.*

**com·pet·i·tive** /kəmˈpetətɪv/ *adjective*
**1** wanting to be more successful than other people: *Steve is very competitive. He hates to lose.*
**2** a competitive activity is done by people or companies who are all trying hard to win or be successful: *Fashion is a very competitive business. You have to work hard to succeed.*

**com·pet·i·tor** /kəmˈpetɪtɚ/ *noun*
a person, team, or company that is competing with another one: *All the competitors lined up for the race.*

**com·plain** /kəmˈpleɪn/ *verb*
to say that you are annoyed about something or not happy with something: *The food tasted awful, so she complained about it to the manager.*

**com·plaint** /kəmˈpleɪnt/ *noun*
a statement in which someone complains about something: *There have been a lot of complaints about the noise.*

**com·plete**[1] /kəmˈpliːt/ *adjective*
**1** including everything or everyone: *This is a complete list of all the people in the class.*
**ANTONYM: incomplete**
**2** in every way: *That meeting was a complete*

*waste of time. We didn't get anything done.* **SYNONYM: total**

**3** finished: *Our project is almost complete. We will be finished this week.*

→ see Thesaurus box at **done**²

**[ORIGIN:** 1300-1400 From the Latin word *complere*, which means "to fill up."**]**

**complete²** *verb*
to finish doing or making something: *The book took five years to complete.*

**com·plete·ly** /kəmˈplitli/ *adverb*
in every way: *I'd never been skiing before, so it was a completely new experience for me.* **SYNONYM: totally**

**com·plex¹** Ac /kəmˈpleks/ *adjective*
something that is complex has a lot of different parts and is difficult to understand or deal with: *The human brain is very complex. Scientists don't fully understand it yet.* **SYNONYM: complicated**

—**complexity** /kəmˈpleksəti/ *noun* the quality of being complex

**[ORIGIN:** 1600-1700 From the Latin word *complexus*, a form of the verb *complecti*, which means "to surround or include." Something that is complex includes many parts or things.**]**

**com·plex²** Ac /ˈkampleks/ *noun*
a group of buildings or one large building that is used for something: *My grandmother lives in an apartment complex for older people.*

**com·plex·ion** /kəmˈplekʃən/ *noun*
the color and appearance of the skin on your face: *She has blond hair and a pale complexion.*

**com·pli·cate** /ˈkampləˌkeɪt/ *verb*
to make a problem or situation more difficult: *The attempt to rescue the climbers was complicated by bad weather.*

**com·pli·cat·ed** /ˈkampləˌkeɪtɪd/ *adjective*
having a lot of different parts, and difficult to understand or deal with: *The instructions were too complicated for a child to understand.* **SYNONYM: complex**; **ANTONYM: simple**

**com·pli·ca·tion** /ˌkampləˈkeɪʃən/ *noun*
something that makes a situation more difficult: *It's a love story, but there are a lot of complications. For one thing, she thinks he's in love with someone else!*

**com·pli·ment¹** /ˈkampləmənt/ *noun*
something nice that someone says to you about your appearance, achievements, or abilities: *Paula got a lot of compliments on her new dress. She looked great in it.*

**com·pli·ment²** /ˈkampləˌment/ *verb*
to say something nice to someone about his or her appearance, achievements, or abilities: *They complimented him on his excellent French.*

**com·ply** /kəmˈplaɪ/ *verb* (**complied, complies**) (*formal*)
to obey a law or rule, or do what someone in authority asks you to do: *If you do not comply with the law, you will have to pay a fine.*

**com·po·nent** Ac /kəmˈpoʊnənt/ *noun* (*formal*)
a part of a machine: *The factory produces components that are used in cars.*

**com·pose** /kəmˈpoʊz/ *verb*
**1 be composed of something** (*formal*) = to be made of two or more things: *Water is composed of hydrogen and oxygen.*

**2** to write a piece of music: *Who composed the music for the movie?*

—**composer** *noun* someone who writes music

**com·po·si·tion** /ˌkampəˈzɪʃən/ *noun* (*formal*)
a piece of music, a poem, or an ESSAY that someone writes: *The song is one of her early compositions.*

→ see Thesaurus box at **music**

**com·post** /ˈkampoʊst/ *noun*
a mixture of decayed leaves and plants that you put on the soil to make it better for growing new plants

**com·pound** Ac /ˈkampaʊnd/ *noun*
**1** a substance that is made of two or more different substances: *The chemical compound is made of two elements.*

**2** an area that contains a group of buildings and is surrounded by a fence or wall: *a prison compound*

**3** (*also* **compound noun**) two or more words that are used together as a noun. For example, the noun "ice cream" is a compound.

**[ORIGIN:** 1500-1600 From the Latin words *com-* and *ponere*, which mean "together" and "to put."**]**

C

**ˌcompound ˈsentence** *noun*
a sentence that has two or more shorter sentences in it. The shorter sentences are joined together by a word such as "and" or "but": *"The dog ran away and the boy ran after him" is a compound sentence.*

C

**ˌcompound ˈword** *noun*
a word made from two or more words that are joined together: *"Ice cream" is a compound word.*

**com·pre·hend** /ˌkamprɪˈhend/ *verb* (*formal*)
to understand something: *It is difficult to comprehend what it is like to be in a war zone if you've never experienced it.* **SYNONYM: understand**
—**comprehension** *noun* (*formal*) someone's ability to understand something: *We were tested on our comprehension of the poem.*
[**ORIGIN:** 1300-1400 From the Latin word *comprehendere*, which means "to take hold of completely."]

**com·pre·hen·sive** Ac /ˌkamprɪˈhensɪv/ *adjective*
including everything that is necessary: *The city has a comprehensive plan for dealing with an earthquake. It includes rules and advice for everyone living and working here.*

**com·prise** Ac /kəmˈpraɪz/ *verb* (*formal*)
to include or be formed of something: *The crew of the space shuttle comprises two women and five men.*

**com·pro·mise¹** /ˈkamprəˌmaɪz/ *noun*
an agreement in which both people or groups accept something different from what they wanted at the beginning: *The company and its employees finally reached a compromise. Employees agreed to work more hours, and the company will pay them more.*

**compromise²** *verb*
to make an agreement by accepting something that is different from what you wanted at the beginning: *Neither side wanted to compromise, so they never made a deal.*

**com·pul·so·ry** /kəmˈpʌlsəri/ *adjective*
if something is compulsory, it must be done because of a rule or law: *School is compulsory until you finish 12th grade.* **SYNONYM: mandatory**; **ANTONYM: voluntary**

**com·put·er** Ac /kəmˈpyutɚ/ *noun*
an electronic machine that stores information and can be used for writing, playing games, and using the Internet: *I do most of my school work on my computer.* | *a computer program*

**con¹** /kan/ *noun*
a disadvantage of something: *List the pros and cons of each plan to help you decide what to do. For example, pro: it will save you time. Con: it's expensive.* **ANTONYM: pro**

**con²** *verb* (**conned**, **conning**) (*informal*)
to trick someone, especially to make him or her believe something that is not true: *He conned me out of $20 by telling me he'd lost his wallet and needed money to get home.*

**con·ceal** /kənˈsil/ *verb* (*formal*)
to hide something: *He concealed the package inside his coat.*
—**concealment** *noun* the act of hiding something
[**ORIGIN:** 1200-1300 From the Latin word *celare*, which means "to hide."]

**con·ceit·ed** /kənˈsitɪd/ *adjective*
too proud of what you can do or how you look: *She's kind of conceited; she thinks she's so pretty.*
→ see Thesaurus box at **proud**

**con·ceive** Ac /kənˈsiv/ *verb* (*formal*)
**1** to imagine or think of something: *It is impossible to conceive of the size of the universe.*
**2** to become PREGNANT: *At 45 years old, she may be too old to conceive.*
—**conceivable** *adjective* possible, or able to be imagined: *The baseball book covers every conceivable aspect of the game, from famous players to different kinds of pitches.*

**WORD FAMILY: conceive**
**conceive** *verb* | **conception** *noun* | **conceivable** *adjective*

**con·cen·trate** Ac /ˈkansənˌtreɪt/ *verb*
to think very carefully about what you are doing: *Quiet! I'm trying to concentrate on my homework.*

**con·cen·tra·tion** Ac /ˌkansənˈtreɪʃən/ *noun*
the act of thinking very carefully about what

you are doing: *I lost concentration when I was counting the money, and had to start again.*

**con·cept** Ac /ˈkɑnsept/ *noun (formal)*
a general idea of something: *It is sometimes difficult for young children to understand the concepts of right and wrong.*
—**conceptual** /kənˈseptʃuəl/ *adjective*
relating to concepts

**con·cep·tion** Ac /kənˈsepʃən/ *noun (formal)*
**1** the idea that one person has about something in his or her mind: *Different people have different conceptions of beauty.*
**2** the act of becoming PREGNANT, so that a baby starts to develop: *A baby is born about 40 weeks after conception.*

**con·cern**¹ /kənˈsɚn/ *noun*
**1** a feeling of worry about something important, or the fact of caring about it: *There is growing concern about the amount of traffic in the city. | We understand your concern for your children's safety.*
**2** something that you feel worried about or care about: *His main concern was the cost of fixing the car.*

**concern**² *verb*
**1** *(formal)* to be about something or someone: *The story concerns a man who lives in Russia.*
**2** to involve someone or be important to someone: *My argument is with your sister – it doesn't concern you.*
**3** to make someone feel worried: *Her daughter's problems at school concerned her greatly.*

**con·cerned** /kənˈsɚnd/ *adjective*
**1** worried about something important: *We're all concerned about her health – she's been so sick lately.*
**2** thinking that something is important: *He seems more concerned about his business than about his family.*
**3** involved in something: *It is important that everyone concerned agrees with the arrangement.*
**4 as far as I'm concerned** = used to show you are giving your opinion: *As far as I'm concerned, the whole idea is crazy.*
→ see Thesaurus box at **worried**

**con·cern·ing** /kənˈsɚnɪŋ/ *preposition (formal)*
about: *Does anyone have any questions concerning the trip?*

**con·cert** /ˈkɑnsɚt/ *noun*
a performance given by musicians or singers: *We went to a concert last night.*
[**ORIGIN:** 1500-1600 Probably from the Italian word *concertare*, which means "to bring into agreement."]

**con·cise** /kənˈsaɪs/ *adjective (formal)*
short and not containing too many words: *His answers were clear and concise.*
[**ORIGIN:** 1500-1600 From the Latin word *concisus*, a form of the verb *concidere*, which means "to cut off."]

**con·clude** Ac /kənˈklud/ *verb (formal)*
**1** to decide that something is true from the information you have: *He didn't apologize so I concluded that he wasn't sorry for what he did.*
**2** to end or finish something: *She concluded the meeting by thanking everyone. | The show concluded with a dance performance by the younger children.* **SYNONYMS: finish, end; ANTONYMS: begin, start**
→ see Thesaurus box at **decide**

| **WORD FAMILY: conclude** |
| --- |
| **conclude** *verb* \| **conclusion** *noun* |

**con·clu·sion** Ac /kənˈkluʒən/ *noun*
**1** a decision that something is true, which you make after thinking about it a lot: *His conclusion was that both students had cheated on the test. | We've come to the conclusion that the book is too difficult for our students.*
**2** *(formal)* the end or last part of something: *At the conclusion of the lecture, everyone applauded.*
[**ORIGIN:** 1300-1400 From the Latin word *concludere*, which means "to close or end."]

**con·clu·sive** Ac /kənˈklusɪv/ *adjective (formal)*
proving that something is true: *There is no conclusive evidence that he is guilty, but many people think that he is.*

**con·crete** /ˈkɑŋkrit/ *noun*
a substance used for making buildings. It is a

C

mixture of a gray powder with sand and water, which becomes hard when it dries: *The bridge is made of concrete and steel.*

**con·cus·sion** /kənˈkʌʃən/ *noun*
a small amount of damage to the brain, caused by hitting your head: *One player had a concussion after he fell.*

C

**con·demn** /kənˈdem/ *verb*
**1** to say very strongly that you do not approve of someone or something: *Local people condemned plans to enlarge the airport.*
**2** to give someone a severe punishment for a crime: *The murderer was condemned to death by the court.*
—**condemnation** /ˌkandəmˈneɪʃən/ *noun*
the act of condemning something

**con·den·sa·tion** /ˌkandənˈseɪʃən/ *noun*
small drops of water that appear on a cold surface when warm air touches it: *There was a lot of condensation on the window, which made it difficult to see out.*

**con·dense** /kənˈdens/ *verb*
**1** to make a speech or piece of writing shorter: *Try to condense your essay onto just one page.*
**2** to make a liquid thicker by removing some of the water from it: *condensed soup*
**3** if gas or warm air condenses, it becomes a liquid as it becomes cooler

**con·de·scend·ing** /ˌkandɪˈsendɪŋ/ *adjective*
showing that you think you are better than someone else: *I didn't like his condescending tone of voice. It made me feel stupid.*

**con·di·tion** /kənˈdɪʃən/ *noun*
**1** the state of something, or of someone's body or mind: *The car is in very good condition – it looks brand new. | He has been very sick, but now his physical condition has improved.*
**2 conditions** = the situation in which someone lives, or in which something happens: *Their living conditions are terrible – there is not enough light, and everything is very dirty. | Bad weather conditions are making driving dangerous.*
**3** a medical problem, especially one that affects someone for a long time: *My father has a heart condition.*
**4** something that you must agree to, or that must happen, before you can do or have something: *I'll tell you on one condition – you must promise not to tell anyone else.*

**con·di·tion·er** /kənˈdɪʃənɚ/ *noun*
a liquid that you put on your hair when you wash it in order to make it softer and easier to comb: *I use conditioner as well as shampoo.*

**con·do·min·i·um** /ˌkandəˈmɪniəm/ (*also* **con·do** /ˈkandoʊ/ (*informal*)) *noun*
a building that consists of a number of apartments with different owners, or one of these apartments

**con·done** /kənˈdoʊn/ *verb* (*formal*)
to say that it is acceptable to do something that other people think is wrong: *He does not condone any kind of drug use, and reports anyone he sees using drugs.*

**con·duct**[1] Ac /kənˈdʌkt/ *verb*
**1** (*formal*) to do something in an organized way: *The police are conducting an investigation into the incident.*
**2** if something conducts electricity or heat, it allows electricity or heat to go through it: *Copper is good at conducting electricity, so it is used in the electrical wiring in houses.*
**3** to stand in front of the musicians in an ORCHESTRA and move your hands to show them when and how to play: *The Boston Pops Orchestra was conducted by John Williams.*
[**ORIGIN:** 1400-1500 From the Latin word *conductus*, a form of the verb *conducere*, which means "to lead or bring together."]

**con·duct**[2] Ac /ˈkandʌkt/ *noun* (*formal*)
the way someone behaves: *He was fired because of his unprofessional conduct.*
**SYNONYM: behavior**

**con·duc·tiv·i·ty** /ˌkandʌkˈtɪvəti/ *noun*
how easily electricity or heat goes through a particular substance: *We did experiments to test the conductivity of different materials.*

**con·duc·tor** /kənˈdʌktɚ/ *noun*
**1** someone who conducts the musicians in an ORCHESTRA
**2** a person who sells and checks tickets on a train

**cone** /koʊn/ *noun*
**1** an object with sloping sides which is round at one end and pointed at the other: *an ice cream cone*
**2** the hard brown fruit of a PINE or FIR tree

**Con·fed·er·a·cy** /kənˈfɛdərəsi/ *noun*
**the Confederacy** = the southern states of the U.S. that fought against the northern states in the Civil War **ANTONYM: the Union**
—**Confederate** *adjective* relating to the Confederacy: *the Confederate army*

**con·fer** Ac /kənˈfɚ/ *verb* (**conferred**, **conferring**) (*formal*)
to discuss something with other people, in order to get their opinion: *You should confer with the other team members before you decide.*

**con·ference** Ac /ˈkɑnfrəns/ *noun*
**1** a large formal meeting where people can listen to talks on a subject and discuss ideas, that usually continues for several days: *The report was presented at a conference on climate change.*
**2** a meeting at which a small number of people discuss something: *Andy's parents had a conference with the teacher to talk about Andy's behavior.*

**con·fess** /kənˈfes/ *verb*
to tell someone that you have done something wrong: *He has confessed to the crime and will have to go to prison.*

**con·fes·sion** /kənˈfeʃən/ *noun*
a statement that you have done something wrong: *He made a full confession at the police station.*

**con·fide** /kənˈfaɪd/ *verb*
to tell someone about something personal and private: *He had confided to friends that he was unhappy.*

**WORD FAMILY: confide**
**confide** *verb* | **confidential** *adjective* | **confidentially** *adverb*

**con·fi·dence** /ˈkɑnfədəns/ *noun*
**1** the feeling that you are able to do things well: *She's been dancing for years, and she has a lot of confidence on stage.* | *He was shy, and lacked confidence.*
**2** the feeling that you can trust someone or something to be good or successful: *The coach has confidence in me. He knows I'll do my best.*
**3 in confidence** = if you tell someone something in confidence, you do not want him or her to tell anyone else

**con·fi·dent** /ˈkɑnfədənt/ *adjective*
**1** someone who is confident believes he or she can do something well and does not feel nervous: *Are you feeling confident about the test or do you need to study more?*
**2** sure that something will happen: *I'm confident (that) the problem can be solved if we try hard.*
—**confidently** *adverb* in a confident way

**con·fi·den·tial** /ˌkɑnfəˈdenʃəl/ *adjective*
if information is confidential, you must not show it or talk about it to other people: *Doctors should not show patients' records to other people because the information in them is confidential.*
—**confidentially** *adverb* in a confidential way

**con·fined** Ac /kənˈfaɪnd/ *adjective*
**1 be confined to someone or something** (*formal*) = to affect only one group of people, or to happen only in one place: *Luckily the fire was confined to one floor of the building.*
**2** a confined space or area is very small: *He disliked confined spaces like elevators.*

**con·firm** Ac /kənˈfɚm/ *verb*
**1** to say or show that something is definitely true: *The doctors confirmed that she had cancer.*
**2** to tell someone that an arrangement is now definite: *Confirm your flight reservation at least two days before you leave.*

**WORD FAMILY: confirm**
**confirm** *verb* | **confirmation** *noun*

**con·fir·ma·tion** [Ac] /ˌkɑnfɚˈmeɪʃən/ *noun*
a statement or letter saying that something is definitely true or will definitely happen: *The school sent a confirmation of the test scores to each student.*

C

**con·fis·cate** /ˈkɑnfəˌskeɪt/ *verb*
if people in authority confiscate something that belongs to you, they take it away from you: *The police confiscated his camera for taking pictures where he wasn't supposed to.*
—**confiscation** /ˌkɑnfəˈskeɪʃən/ *noun* the act of confiscating something

**con·flict¹** [Ac] /ˈkɑnˌflɪkt/ *noun*
**1** a serious disagreement or argument about something: *The teacher helped the students resolve their conflict quickly.*
**2** a war or a period of fighting: *To date, 536 soldiers have died in the conflict.*
→ see Thesaurus box at **war**
[**ORIGIN:** 1400-1500 From the Latin word *conflictus*, a form of the verb *confligere*, which means "to hit things together."]

**con·flict²** [Ac] /kənˈflɪkt/ *verb*
if two ideas or statements conflict with each other, they are completely different: *During the trial, the two witnesses told stories that conflicted with each other.*

**con·form** [Ac] /kənˈfɔrm/ *verb*
to behave in the way that most people behave: *There's always pressure on kids to conform.*

**con·front** /kənˈfrʌnt/ *verb*
**1** to think about and try to deal with a difficult problem, situation, or feeling: *The program helps people confront their fear of flying.* | *When President Obama took office, he was confronted with a bad economy.*
**2** to speak to someone strongly about something serious and bad: *Her mother confronted her about her smoking.*

**con·fron·ta·tion** /ˌkɑnfrənˈteɪʃən/ *noun*
an angry argument or fight: *There have been confrontations between police and protesters.*

**con·fuse** /kənˈfyuz/ *verb*
**1** to make you feel that you do not understand something or do not know what to do: *His directions really confused me, and it took me a long time to find his house.*
**2** to think wrongly that a person or thing is someone or something else: *It's easy to confuse Sue with her sister – they look so similar.*
—**confusing** *adjective* something that is confusing is difficult to understand because it is complicated and not clear: *The instructions in the book were really confusing, and none of the students understood what to do.*

**WORD FAMILY: confuse**
**confuse** *verb* | **confusion** *noun* | **confusing** *adjective* | **confused** *adjective*

**con·fused** /kənˈfyuzd/ *adjective*
someone who is confused does not understand something clearly: *We're a little confused about what we're supposed to be doing.* → see picture on page **A23**

**con·fu·sion** /kənˈfyuʒən/ *noun*
the feeling that you do not understand something or do not know what to do: *There was a lot of confusion about the new rules at first.*

**con·ges·tion** /kənˈdʒestʃən/ *noun*
**1** a situation in which the roads are too full of cars, trucks, etc.: *An accident is causing congestion where the two freeways meet.*
**2** a situation in which your nose is full of a thick liquid: *He has a cold that's causing congestion and a cough.*
—**congested** *adjective* having congestion: *a congested street*

**con·grat·u·late** /kənˈgrætʃəˌleɪt/ *verb*
to tell someone that you are pleased about his or her success or about something good that has happened: *I congratulated them on the birth of their daughter.*

**con·grat·u·la·tions** /kənˌgrætʃəˈleɪʃənz/ *interjection*
used when congratulating someone: *You won? Congratulations!* | *Congratulations on your graduation from high school.*

**con·gre·ga·tion** /ˌkɑŋgrəˈgeɪʃən/ *noun*
the people who are in a church during a service: *The minister asked the congregation to stand.*

**Con·gress** /ˈkɑŋgrɪs/ *noun*
the group of people who have been chosen to make the laws in some countries. In the

U.S., Congress is divided into the Senate and the House of Representatives: *The bill has been approved by both houses of Congress.*

[**ORIGIN:** 1400-1500 From the Latin word *congressus*, which means "meeting," from *congredi*, which means "to come together."]

**con·gress·man** /ˈkɑŋgrɪsmən/ *noun* (plural **congressmen** /ˈkɑŋgrɪsmən/)
a man who is a member of the House of Representatives

**con·gress·wom·an** /ˈkɑŋgrɪsˌwʊmən/ *noun* (plural **congresswomen** /ˈkɑŋgrɪsˌwɪmɪn/)
a woman who is a member of the House of Representatives

**con·gru·ent** /kənˈgruənt/ *adjective*
congruent TRIANGLEs are the same size and shape

**con·i·fer** /ˈkɑnəfɚ/ *noun*
a tree that has leaves that look like needles. Conifers do not lose their leaves in winter, and produce CONEs containing their seeds.
—**coniferous** /kəˈnɪfərəs/ *adjective* containing conifers: *the coniferous forests of the Northwest*

**con·ju·gate** /ˈkɑndʒəˌgeɪt/ *verb*
to give the different forms of a verb, for example the present tense, past tense, and past participle: *We learned to conjugate verbs in Spanish.*

**con·junc·tion** /kənˈdʒʌŋkʃən/ *noun*
**1** a word such as "but," "and," or "while" that connects parts of sentences
**2 in conjunction with someone or something** = with someone or something else: *The school worked out a new way of dealing with bullying, in conjunction with parents.*

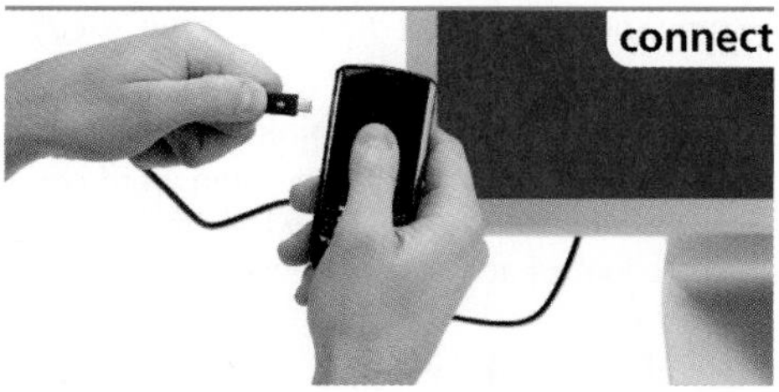


**con·nect** /kəˈnekt/ *verb*
**1** to join one thing to another: *Connect the printer to the computer using this cable.* **ANTONYM: disconnect**
**2** to show or think that a thing or person is related to or involved in something: *There is no evidence to connect him with the crime.*

[**ORIGIN:** 1400-1500 From the Latin words *com-* and *nectere*, which mean "together" and "to tie."]

**con·nect·ed** /kəˈnektɪd/ *adjective*
**1** if two things or events are connected, there is some kind of relationship between them: *The police think that the two murders may be connected with each other.* **SYNONYM: related**
**2** joined to something: *All the computers are connected to the Internet.*

**con·nec·tion** /kəˈnekʃən/ *noun*
**1** a relationship between things or people: *There is a direct connection between smoking and lung disease.* | *He said he had no connection with the organization.*
**2** the state of being joined to something electrical: *Do you have an Internet connection?*
**3** an airplane, bus, or train that people can change to and continue their trip quickly: *The plane I was on was late, so I missed my connection at the airport.*

**con·nois·seur** /ˌkɑnəˈsɚ/ *noun* (*formal*)
someone who knows a lot about something such as art or food: *a connoisseur of fine wines*

**con·quer** /ˈkɑŋkɚ/ *verb*
to defeat people in a war and take their land: *The Romans conquered much of Europe.*
—**conqueror** *noun* a leader or nation that conquers a country or group of people
→ see Thesaurus box at **win**[1]

**con·quest** /ˈkɑŋkwest/ *noun*
the defeat and control of a country or group of people: *The Spanish conquest of Central America took place in the 16th century.*

**con·science** /ˈkɑnʃəns/ *noun*
the feeling inside you that tells you whether it is right or wrong to do something: *I had a guilty conscience about lying to my mother.*

**con·sci·en·tious** /ˌkɑnʃiˈenʃəs/ *adjective*
taking care to do things very well: *He was a conscientious student who spent a lot of time on his homework.*
—**conscientiously** *adverb* in a conscientious way

**con·scious** /ˈkɑnʃəs/ *adjective*
**1** awake and able to understand what is happening: *He was still conscious when he arrived at the hospital, and was able to answer the doctors' questions.* **ANTONYM: unconscious**
**2** knowing about a situation or realizing something: *I was conscious of people staring at me.* **SYNONYM: aware**

C

**WORD FAMILY: conscious**
**conscious** *adjective* | **unconscious** *adjective* | **consciously** *adverb* | **unconsciously** *adverb* | **consciousness** *noun* | **unconsciousness** *noun*

**con·scious·ly** /ˈkɑnʃəsli/ *adverb*
if you do something consciously, you know that you are doing it and you deliberately make an effort to do it: *She consciously chose to wear her best skirt for the date.* **ANTONYM: unconsciously**

**con·scious·ness** /ˈkɑnʃəsnəs/ *noun*
the state of being awake and able to understand what is happening: *Charlie hit his head and lost consciousness.*

**con·sec·u·tive** /kənˈsekjətɪv/ *adjective* (*formal*)
consecutive things happen one after the other: *It rained for three consecutive days.*

**con·sen·sus** Ac /kənˈsensəs/ *noun* (*formal*)
agreement among everyone in a group: *We failed to reach a consensus on what should be done.*

**con·sent** Ac /kənˈsent/ *noun* (*formal*)
permission to do something: *We need your parents' written consent before you can go on the school trip.*
—**consent** *verb* (*formal*) to agree to do something or say that you will allow something to be done: *She consented to give an interview to "Time Magazine."*

**con·se·quence** Ac /ˈkɑnsəˌkwens/ *noun*
something that happens as a result of an action: *He broke the law, and now he must face the consequences.*

**WORD FAMILY: consequence**
**consequence** *noun* | **consequently** *adverb*

**con·se·quent·ly** Ac /ˈkɑnsəˌkwentli/ *adverb* (*formal*)
as a result of something: *The winter was very cold, and consequently many animals died.*

**con·ser·va·tion** /ˌkɑnsəˈveɪʃən/ *noun*
**1** the activity of protecting wild plants and animals: *National Parks help conservation by giving wild animals a safe place to live.*
**2** the activity of using energy, water, or FUEL carefully and not wasting any: *To help with energy conservation, turn off lights when you leave a room.*

**con·ser·va·tion·ist** /ˌkɒnsəˈveɪʃənɪst/ *noun*
someone whose work involves protecting wild plants and animals

**con·serv·a·tive** /kənˈsəvətɪv/ *adjective*
**1** believing in the political ideas that the government should not be too involved in people's lives and that society should not change too much: *Republicans are more conservative than Democrats.* **SYNONYM: right-wing**
**2** believing that the old ways of doing things are best: *Their church is fairly conservative, and they don't want a woman as their minister.*

**con·serve** /kənˈsəv/ *verb* (*formal*)
**1** to use energy, water, or FUEL carefully and not waste any: *People should conserve energy by turning off lights and computers.*
**2** to stop wild plants and animals from being destroyed: *If we do not conserve the rainforests, they will disappear.*

**con·sid·er** /kənˈsɪdə/ *verb* (*formal*)
**1** to think about something carefully: *She's considering joining the softball team.*
**2** to have an opinion about something or someone: *I considered her to be an excellent teacher.*
→ see Thesaurus box at **think**
[**ORIGIN:** 1300-1400 From the Latin word *considerare*, probably from *sidus*, which means "star." People looked at the stars to find their way, or for astrology.]

**con·sid·er·a·ble** Ac /kənˈsɪdərəbəl/ *adjective* (*formal*)
a considerable amount is a lot: *He earns a considerable amount of money, so he buys a lot of expensive things.*

**con·sid·er·a·bly** Ac /kənˈsɪdərəbli/ *adverb (formal)*
by a large amount: *The blue dress is considerably more expensive than the others.*

**con·sid·er·ate** /kənˈsɪdərət/ *adjective*
a considerate person thinks about what other people feel or need: *It was considerate of them to keep quiet while I was trying to sleep.*
—**considerately** *adverb (formal)* in a considerate way
→ see Thesaurus box at **kind**[2]

**con·sid·e·ra·tion** /kənˌsɪdəˈreɪʃən/ *noun*
**1** careful thought about something: *It's an interesting idea, and it needs careful consideration.*
**2** one of the things you think about when trying to make a decision: *When choosing a computer, the price is an important consideration.*

**con·sid·er·ing** /kənˈsɪdərɪŋ/ *preposition, conjunction*
used when mentioning an important fact you thought about when giving your opinion: *She did well on the test, considering that she'd been sick.*

**con·sist** Ac /kənˈsɪst/ *verb (formal)*
**PHRASAL VERB**
**consist of something**
to be formed of something: *The audience consisted largely of teenagers.*

**con·sist·ent** Ac /kənˈsɪstənt/ *adjective*
**1** always doing something in the same way: *Ben is the team's most consistent player – he always plays well.* **ANTONYM: inconsistent**
**2** matching something such as an explanation or a fact: *His explanation of what happened was consistent with the evidence, so it is probably true.*
—**consistently** *adverb* in a consistent way: *Zoe has earned consistently good grades this semester – she's gotten A's and B's on everything.*
—**consistency** *noun* the quality of always doing something in the same way: *The restaurant's food lacks consistency – sometimes it is good, but not always.*

**con·sole** /kənˈsoʊl/ *verb*
to help someone to feel less sad: *When her dog died, we tried to console her.*
—**consolation** *noun* something that makes you feel less sad

**con·sol·i·date** /kənˈsɑləˌdeɪt/ *verb*
to combine two or more things to form a single thing that is more effective or easier to deal with: *She consolidated all her debts into one loan.*
—**consolidation** /kənˌsɑləˈdeɪʃən/ *noun* the act of consolidating something

**con·so·nant** /ˈkɑnsənənt/ *noun*
any letter of the alphabet except a, e, i, o, and u: *The word "bird" begins and ends with a consonant.* **ANTONYM: vowel**
[**ORIGIN:** 1300-1400 From the Latin word *consonare*, which means "to make sounds together." A consonant sound is usually used together with a vowel sound.]

**con·spic·u·ous** /kənˈspɪkyuəs/ *adjective (formal)*
very easy to notice: *Put the sign in a conspicuous place so that lots of people see it.* **SYNONYM: noticeable**
—**conspicuously** *adverb (formal)* in a way that is very easy to notice: *Dave was conspicuously absent from the class.*
→ see Thesaurus box at **clear**[1]

**con·spir·a·cy** /kənˈspɪrəsi/ *noun* (plural **conspiracies**)
a secret plan that people make together to do something bad: *Ten people were involved in the conspiracy to assassinate the president.*
—**conspirator** *noun (formal)* someone who is part of a group that is planning a conspiracy

**con·stant** Ac /ˈkɑnstənt/ *adjective*
**1** happening all the time: *Tiny babies need constant attention.*
**2** staying at the same level: *While she's sick, keep her room at a constant temperature.*
—**constantly** *adverb* all the time: *Technology is constantly changing.*

**con·stel·la·tion** /ˌkɑnstəˈleɪʃən/ *noun*
a group of stars that has a name: *He pointed out the constellation of Orion in the night sky.*

**con·sti·pa·tion** /ˌkɑnstəˈpeɪʃən/ *noun*
difficulty in moving solid waste out of your body: *Eating fruit and vegetables helps to prevent constipation.*
—**constipated** /ˈkɑnstəˌpeɪtɪd/ *adjective* having constipation

C

**con·sti·tute** [Ac] /ˈkɑnstəˌtut/ *verb (formal)*
to form part of something: *Women constitute 51% of the population.*
—**constituent** /kənˈstɪtʃuənt/ *noun* one of the parts that form something

**con·sti·tu·tion** [Ac] (*also* **Constitution**) /ˌkɑnstəˈtuʃən/ *noun*
the basic laws and ideas of a country, state, or organization: *The Constitution says how the American government should be organized, with a president and a congress.*
—**constitutional** *adjective* relating to a constitution: *the constitutional rights of the people*

C

**con·struct** [Ac] /kənˈstrʌkt/ *verb (formal)*
to build something: *The college is planning to construct a new library.*

**WORD FAMILY: construct**
**construct** *verb* | **construction** *noun* | **reconstruction** *noun*

**con·struc·tion** [Ac] /kənˈstrʌkʃən/ *noun*
the process of building something: *A new airport is now under construction and will be finished next year.*

**con·sul** /ˈkɑnsəl/ *noun*
a person whose job is to live in a foreign city and help people from his or her country who also live there: *He was the U.S. consul in Tunis for several years.*

**con·sult** [Ac] /kənˈsʌlt/ *verb (formal)*
to ask someone such as a doctor or a lawyer for advice or information: *She consulted her doctor before starting the diet.*
—**consultation** /ˌkɑnsəlˈteɪʃən/ *noun* a discussion that you have, to get advice or information: *The decision was reached after consultation with parents and teachers.*

**WORD FAMILY: consult**
**consult** *verb* | **consultation** *noun* | **consultant** *noun*

**con·sult·ant** [Ac] /kənˈsʌltənt/ *noun*
someone whose job is to give advice about something: *He's a successful business consultant and works with many different companies.*

**con·sume** [Ac] /kənˈsum/ *verb (formal)*
**1** to use FUEL, energy, water, or time: *Small cars consume less gas.*
**2** to eat or drink something: *You should try to reduce the amount of salt you consume.*

**WORD FAMILY: consume**
**consume** *verb* | **consumer** *noun* | **consumption** *noun*

**con·sum·er** [Ac] /kənˈsumɚ/ *noun*
anyone who buys things or uses services: *Consumers will buy more if the prices are lower.*

**con·sump·tion** [Ac] /kənˈsʌmpʃən/ *noun (formal)*
**1** the amount of FUEL, energy, or water someone or something uses: *Driving more slowly reduces the car's fuel consumption.*
**2** the act of eating or drinking something: *Children need to increase their consumption of fruit and vegetables.*

**con·tact¹** [Ac] /ˈkɑntækt/ *noun*
**1** the act of talking or writing to someone: *I don't have much contact with John since he moved away.*
**2** someone you talk or write to: *Did you add his email address to your list of contacts?*
**3 be/keep/stay in contact with someone** = to talk or write to someone who you do not see often: *Jane lives in Canada now, but I keep in contact with her by email.*
**4** the state of touching: *These two electrical wires should not come into contact or they may start a fire.*

**contact²** [Ac] *verb*
to telephone or write to someone: *I tried to contact her by phone and by email.*

**ˈcontact ˌlens** *noun*
a small round piece of plastic you put in your eye to help you see clearly

**con·ta·gious** /kənˈteɪdʒəs/ *adjective*
if a disease is contagious, you can easily get it from another person: *Diseases such as chickenpox are highly contagious, so if one child gets sick, many others will also get the disease.*

**con·tain** /kənˈteɪn/ *verb*
**1** to have something inside: *His wallet contained $50.*

2 if a piece of writing, a movie, or a television program contains something, that thing is part of it: *The book contains some useful information.*

[ORIGIN: 1200-1300 From the Latin word *continere*, which means "to hold together or surround."]

**con·tain·er** /kənˈteɪnɚ/ *noun*
something you keep things in: *She put the cookies in a plastic container with a tight lid.*

**con·tam·i·nate** /kənˈtæməˌneɪt/ *verb*
to make water, food, or a place dirty or dangerous: *Some of these chemicals contaminate our rivers.*
—**contamination** /kənˌtæməˈneɪʃən/ *noun* the act of contaminating water, food, or a place: *the contamination of the city's water supply*

**con·tem·plate** /ˈkɑntəmˌpleɪt/ *verb (formal)*
to think about doing something important: *She has contemplated joining the army when she's old enough.*
—**contemplation** /ˌkɑntəmˈpleɪʃən/ *noun* the act of thinking about something important

**con·tem·po·ra·ry**[1] [Ac] /kənˈtempəˌreri/ *adjective*
contemporary art, music, dance, or literature belongs to the present time: *I like contemporary art more than 19th century art.*

**contemporary**[2] *noun* (plural **contemporaries**)
someone who lives at the same time as another person: *Many of the scientist's contemporaries did not agree with his theories.*

[ORIGIN: 1600-1700 From the Latin words *com-* and *tempus*, which mean "together" and "time."]

**con·tempt** /kənˈtempt/ *noun*
a complete lack of respect for someone or something: *"You'll never be able to do it," he said with contempt.*
—**contemptuous** *adjective* without any respect: *She gave him a contemptuous look when he made the mistake.*

**con·tend** /kənˈtend/ *verb (formal)*
to compete to get something: *Their team is contending for the national championship.*
—**contender** *noun* someone who is competing to get something: *He's a top contender for the gold medal.*

**con·tent**[1] /kənˈtent/ *adjective*
happy and satisfied: *Are you content with your life or are there changes you want to make?*

**con·tent**[2] /ˈkɑntent/ *noun*
1 **contents** (*formal*) = the things inside something such as a box or bag: *The guard looked through the contents of her purse.*
2 **contents** = a list at the front of a book that tells you what is in it: *The contents page lists all the chapters of the book.*
3 the ideas in something such as a book, speech, television program, or movie: *The content of the book is not appropriate for children.*

**con·tent·ed** /kənˈtentɪd/ *adjective*
happy and satisfied: *They seem like a very contented family. They don't argue much.*

**con·test** /ˈkɑntest/ *noun*
a competition: *At the fair, there was a contest to see who could eat the most hot dogs.*
→ see Thesaurus box at **competition**

[ORIGIN: 1500-1600 From the Latin word *contestari*, which means "to call a witness or take legal action against someone."]

**con·test·ant** /kənˈtestənt/ *noun*
someone who competes in a contest: *She beat all the other contestants on the game show.*

**con·text** [Ac] /ˈkɑntekst/ *noun*
1 the situation in which something happens, that helps you to understand it: *We have to look at the historical context of the laws about who was allowed to vote. What was society like then?*
2 the words before and after a word or sentence: *The context helps you understand the meaning of the word.*

**con·ti·nent** /ˈkɑntənənt/ *noun*
one of the large areas of land on the Earth, such as Africa, Europe, and Asia: *the African continent*
—**continental** /ˌkɑntəˈnentl/ *adjective* relating to a continent, but not its islands: *a map of the continental United States*

[ORIGIN: 1500-1600 From the Latin phrase *terra continens*, which means "continuous area of land."]

**con·tin·u·al** /kənˈtɪnyuəl/ *adjective*
happening a lot or all the time: *My parents' continual arguing upset me.*
—**continually** *adverb* a lot or all the time: *He continually asked questions, until I told him to be quiet.*

C

**con·tin·u·a·tion** /kənˌtɪnyuˈeɪʃən/ *noun* (*formal*)
a situation in which something continues to happen: *No one wants a continuation of this violence.*

**con·tin·ue** /kənˈtɪnyuː/ *verb*
**1** to not stop: *Maya has continued to study hard at school this year.* | *The bad weather is expected to continue.*
**2** to start again after a pause: *We will continue our search tomorrow.* | *After the interruption, the speaker continued.*
—**continuity** /ˌkɑntəˈnuəti/ *noun* (*formal*) a situation in which something continues without stopping or changing: *Traditions such as Thanksgiving give a society a sense of continuity between the past and the present.*

**WORD FAMILY: continue**
**continue** *verb* | **continuity** *noun* | **continual** *adjective* | **continuous** *adjective* | **continuously** *adverb* | **discontinue** *verb*

**conˌtinuing eduˈcation** *noun*
classes for adults who want to study something

**con·tin·u·ous** /kənˈtɪnyuəs/ *adjective*
happening without stopping: *The continuous noise of the ship's engine kept her awake.*
—**continuously** *adverb* without stopping: *It rained continuously for two days.*

**con·tour** /ˈkɑntʊr/ *noun*
**1** the curved shape or edge of something: *The seat fits the contours of your body.*
**2** a line on a map that shows places of the same height: *If contours are close together, it means there is a steep slope there.*

**con·tra·cep·tion** /ˌkɑntrəˈsepʃən/ *noun*
ways of stopping a woman from becoming PREGNANT **SYNONYM: birth control**

**con·tra·cep·tive** /ˌkɑntrəˈseptɪv/ *noun*
something people use to stop a woman from becoming PREGNANT: *She didn't want to have a baby, so she wanted information about contraceptives.*
—**contraceptive** *adjective* relating to the things that stop a woman from becoming pregnant: *the contraceptive pill*

**con·tract¹** Ac /ˈkɑntrækt/ *noun*
a written agreement to work for someone, buy something, etc.: *Dave signed a three-year contract with an oil company.*

**con·tract²** Ac /kənˈtrækt/ *verb*
**1** (*formal*) to get a serious disease: *Thousands of people contracted the disease and died.*
**2** to become smaller: *Metal contracts as it cools.* **ANTONYM: expand**

**con·trac·tion** /kənˈtrækʃən/ *noun*
a short form of a word or words: *"Don't" is a contraction of "do not."*

**con·trac·tor** Ac /ˈkɑnˌtræktɚ/ *noun*
a company or person that does work for other companies, especially building work: *Her father was a building contractor.*

**con·tra·dict** Ac /ˌkɑntrəˈdɪkt/ *verb*
**1** if one statement or fact contradicts another one, they are different and both cannot be true: *The two boys' stories about the fight contradicted each other.*
**2** to say that what someone has just said is wrong: *I knew he was wrong, but I didn't contradict him.*
—**contradiction** /ˌkɑntrəˈdɪkʃən/ *noun* a difference between two statements or facts that cannot both be true
—**contradictory** /ˌkɑntrəˈdɪktəri/ *adjective* contradictory statements or facts are different, and both cannot be true: *The two witnesses gave contradictory statements in court, and it was not clear who was telling the truth.*
[**ORIGIN:** 1500-1600 From the Latin words *contra* and *dicere*, which mean "against" and "to say."]

**con·tra·ry¹** Ac /ˈkɑnˌtreri/ *adverb*
**contrary to something** = different from something that people think or say: *Contrary to what most people think, a little fat is good for you.*

**contrary²** Ac *noun* (*formal*)
**on the contrary** = used when saying that the opposite is true: *He didn't seem disappointed. On the contrary, he seemed pleased.*

—**contrary** *adjective* (*formal*) different from or not agreeing with something: *contrary opinions*

**con·trast¹** Ac /ˈkɑntræst/ *noun*
a big difference between people or things: *The contrast between the rich and poor areas of the city made a big impression on her.*
[**ORIGIN:** 1600-1700 From the Latin words *contra* and *stare*, which mean "against" and "to stand."]

**con·trast²** Ac /kənˈtræst/ *verb*
**1** if two things contrast, they are or look very different: *I like the way the red walls contrast with the wood floors.*
**2** to show how two things are different: *The teacher told us to compare and contrast these two poems.*

**con·trib·ute** Ac /kənˈtrɪbyut/ *verb* (*formal*)
**1** to give money or help for something: *He contributes a lot of money to the church.*
**2** to take part in a class or discussion by saying something: *All the students contributed to the discussion.*
—**contributor** *noun* someone who gives money or help for something: *He was a major contributor to the Republican Party.*

**WORD FAMILY: contribute**
**contribute** *verb* | **contribution** *noun* | **contributor** *noun*

**con·tri·bu·tion** Ac /ˌkɑntrəˈbyuʃən/ *noun* (*formal*)
**1** some money that you give to help pay for something: *Everyone made a contribution of $3 to buy Elsa a present.*
**2** something you do that helps something be successful: *Her work here made a great contribution to the school.*

**con·trol¹** /kənˈtroʊl/ *noun*
**1** the ability to make someone or something do what you want: *Some parents don't have any control over their kids.*
**2 under control** = if a situation is under control, it is happening the way you want: *The school dance was really busy, but the teachers had everything under control.*
**3 out of control** = if something is out of control, you cannot make it do what you want: *The car went out of control and hit a tree.*
**4** the power to decide what happens in a country or organization: *At the moment, the Republicans are in control of Congress.*
**5** the ability to stay calm when you are angry or upset: *I just lost control and ended up screaming at him!*
**6 controls** = the things that you move to make a vehicle or machine work: *The pilot was already at the plane's controls.*

**control²** *verb* (**controlled**, **controlling**)
**1** to make someone or something do what you want: *I couldn't control the horse, and it began to run.*
**2** to have the power in a country or organization: *Nicholls was the man who controlled the company.*

**con·tro·ver·sy** Ac /ˈkɑntrəˌvɚsi/ *noun* (plural **controversies**)
a lot of disagreement among people: *There was a lot of controversy over who should pay to fix the bridge.*
—**controversial** /ˌkɑntrəˈvɚʃəl/ *adjective* causing a lot of disagreement among people: *Using animals for scientific experiments is a controversial issue – many people oppose it, but others say it is necessary.*

**con·vec·tion** /kənˈvekʃən/ *noun*
the movement of a gas or liquid that happens because different parts of it are at different temperatures: *Warm air rises by convection.*

**con·ven·ience** /kənˈvinyəns/ *noun*
the quality of being easy to use: *I like the convenience of foods I can just heat up in the microwave.* **ANTONYM: inconvenience**

**conˈvenience ˌstore** *noun*
a store where you buy food, newspapers, and other things. Many convenience stores are open 24 hours each day.

**con·ven·ient** /kənˈvinyənt/ *adjective*
**1** easy to use or get to: *Using the Internet is a convenient way to shop.* **ANTONYM: inconvenient**
**2** a convenient time is good for you to do something, because you are not busy then: *Is 2 o'clock convenient for you?* **ANTONYM: inconvenient**

**con·vent** /ˈkɑnvent/ *noun*
a place where NUNs (=women who follow a religious life) live together

C

**con·ven·tion** [Ac] /kən'venʃən/ *noun*
a large meeting of people who belong to the same organization, do the same work, or are interested in the same thing: *He gave a speech at the Democratic Convention.*

**con·ven·tion·al** [Ac] /kən'venʃənəl/ *adjective*
belonging to the type that has been used for a long time: *Microwave ovens cook food faster than conventional ovens.*

**con·ver·sa·tion** /ˌkɑnvə'seɪʃən/ *noun*
**1** a talk between two or more people: *I had an interesting conversation with your teacher.*
**2 make conversation** = to talk to someone to be polite: *Everyone stood around, making conversation.*
[ORIGIN: 1300-1400 From the Latin word *conversari*, which means "to live with or spend time with someone."]

**con·verse¹** [Ac] /kən'vəs/ *verb (formal)*
to have a conversation with someone: *He stood in the middle of the room conversing with his guests.* SYNONYM: talk

**con·verse²** [Ac] /'kɑnvəs/ *noun*
**the converse** (*formal*) = the opposite of something: *Clearly, if x = y, the converse is also true: y = x.*
—**conversely** *adverb* used when one situation is the opposite of another: *What do you like most about your job, and conversely, what do you like least?*

**con·ver·sion** [Ac] /kən'vəʒən/ *noun*
the act of changing from one thing to a different one: *his conversion from Islam to Christianity*

**con·vert** [Ac] /kən'vət/ *verb*
**1** to change something into something else: *The old barn was converted into a house.*
**2** to change your religion: *When she married, she converted to Islam.*
→ see Thesaurus box at change¹

**con·ver·ti·ble** [Ac] /kən'vətəbəl/ *noun*
a car with a roof that you can fold back or remove

**con·vey** /kən'veɪ/ *verb (formal)*
to express feelings or ideas to someone: *It's hard to convey in words how I felt.*

**con·vey·or belt** /kən'veɪə bɛlt/ *noun*
a long moving band of rubber or metal, used for moving things from one place to another: *The bags move through the airport on a conveyor belt.*

**con·vict¹** /kən'vɪkt/ *verb*
to decide that someone is guilty of a crime in a court of law: *The man was convicted of murder and sent to prison.*

**con·vict²** /'kɑnvɪkt/ *noun*
a criminal who has been sent to prison: *In the past, all the convicts were sent to a prison on the island.*

**con·vic·tion** /kən'vɪkʃən/ *noun*
**1** a decision made in a court of law that someone is guilty of a crime: *He already has two convictions for burglary.*
**2** (*formal*) a strong belief: *Her mother doesn't drink alcohol because of her strong religious convictions.*

**con·vince** [Ac] /kən'vɪns/ *verb*
**1** to make someone believe something: *He convinced me that he was telling the truth.*
**2** to persuade someone to do something: *I convinced Kate to stay at the party with me.*
—**convincing** *adjective* making you believe that something is true: *The reason she gave for being late was very convincing.*
→ see Thesaurus box at persuade
[ORIGIN: 1500-1600 From the Latin word *convincere*, which means "to prove that something is wrong or that someone is guilty," from *vincere*, which means "to defeat."]

**con·vinced** [Ac] /kən'vɪnst/ *adjective*
certain that something is true: *I'm convinced (that) I saw him at the party.* SYNONYM: sure

**con·voy** /'kɑnvɔɪ/ *noun*
a group of vehicles traveling together: *A convoy of military trucks drove into town.*

**cook¹** /kʊk/ *verb*
to make food ready to eat, for example by heating it: *I'll cook dinner tonight.*

**THESAURUS: cook**

**bake** to cook food such as bread in the oven: *Jeanie baked some cookies.*

**fry** to cook food in hot oil on the top part of the stove: *I fried an egg for breakfast.*

**roast** to cook meat or vegetables in an oven: *The beef needs to roast for three hours.*

**boil** to cook food in boiling water on the top part of the stove: *Boil the potatoes until they are tender.*

**grill** to cook food on a metal frame over a fire: *Dad grilled a steak on the barbecue.*

**broil** to cook food under heat in a special part of the stove: *Broil the fish in the broiler.*

**poach** to cook eggs or fish in a small amount of boiling water: *Poach the eggs in boiling water for 4 minutes.*

**steam** to cook vegetables in a container over boiling water, so that the steam from the water cooks them: *Steaming the broccoli keeps in more of the vitamins.*

**cook²** *noun*
someone who makes food ready to eat: *Kevin works as a cook at the college.* → see picture on page **A17**
[ORIGIN: From the old English word *coc*, from the Latin word *coquus*, from *coquere*, which means "to cook."]

**cook·book** /ˈkʊkbʊk/ *noun*
a book that tells you how to make different foods: *There is a good recipe for making apple pie in the cookbook.*

**cook·ie** /ˈkʊki/ *noun*
a small flat sweet cake: *She's making chocolate chip cookies.*
[ORIGIN: 1700-1800 From the Dutch word *koekje*, which means "little cake."]

**cook·ing** /ˈkʊkɪŋ/ *noun*
the activity of making food ready to eat: *I do most of the cooking at our house.*

**cook·out** /ˈkʊkaʊt/ *noun*
an occasion when a meal is cooked outdoors: *We're going to have hamburgers and hot dogs at the cookout.*

**cool¹** /kul/ *adjective*
**1** (*informal*) used to show that you like or admire someone or something: *Everyone wants to be his friend because he's such a cool guy.*
**2** (*informal*) acceptable to you: *"Do you mind if I bring my sister?" "No, that's cool."*
SYNONYMS: **OK**, **fine**
**3** a little cold, especially in a pleasant way: *A cool breeze came from the ocean.*
**4** calm: *Stay cool – don't let him make you mad.*
—**coolly** /ˈkul-li/ *adverb* in a calm or unfriendly way: *"Can I come with you?" "I don't care what you do," she said coolly.*
→ see Thesaurus box at **cold¹**

**cool²** (*also* **cool down**) *verb*
to become colder: *When you take the cake out of the oven, let it cool for a while.*
PHRASAL VERB
**cool off** (*also* **cool down**)
**1** to make yourself less hot, or to become colder: *We went swimming to cool off.* | *It's hot during the day, but it cools off at night.*
**2** to stop being angry: *Don't talk to him until he cools off.*

**cool³** *noun*
**1** **keep your cool** = to stay calm in a difficult situation: *The players kept their cool and started scoring.*
**2** **lose your cool** = to become angry or upset in a difficult situation: *Be polite, and try not to lose your cool.*

**cool·er** /ˈkulɚ/ *noun*
a box in which you can keep food or drinks cool

**cooped up** /ˌkupt ˈʌp/ *adjective* (*informal*)
if you are cooped up in a small place, you have to stay there for a long period of time, and you feel very uncomfortable: *Let's go out. I've been cooped up in this apartment all day.*

**co·op·er·ate** [Ac] /koʊˈɑpəˌreɪt/ *verb*
to work together with someone else, or do what someone asks you to do: *He may cooperate with the police and tell them where the stolen money is.*
[ORIGIN: 1500-1600 From the Latin word *cooperari*, which means "to work with someone," from *operari*, which means "to work."]

**WORD FAMILY: cooperate**
**cooperate** *verb* | **cooperation** *noun* | **cooperative** *adjective*

**co·op·er·a·tion** [Ac] /koʊˌɑpəˈreɪʃən/ *noun*
the act of working together with someone else or doing what someone asks you to do: *Teachers can't teach without the cooperation of the students.*

C

**co·op·er·a·tive** Ac /koʊˈɑpərətɪv/ *adjective*
someone who is cooperative does what he or she is asked to do: *Most of the kids were cooperative and joined in with the song, but Jamie wouldn't do it.*

**co·or·di·nate** Ac /koʊˈɔrdnˌeɪt/ *verb*
to organize something complicated, so that everyone does the right thing at the right time: *Sam is coordinating the campaign, so if you have questions about what to do, ask him.*
—**coordinator** *noun* someone who coordinates an activity

**WORD FAMILY: coordinate**
**coordinate** *verb* | **coordination** *noun* | **coordinator** *noun*

**co·or·di·na·tion** Ac /koʊˌɔrdəˈneɪʃən/ *noun*
**1** the ability to use the different parts of your body together well: *It takes good eye-hand coordination to catch a ball.*
**2** (*formal*) the act of coordinating an activity

**cop** /kɑp/ *noun* (*informal*)
a police officer: *The cops came into the bar and stopped the fight.*
[**ORIGIN:** 1800-1900 From an English word "cop," which means "to arrest or catch someone."]

**cope** /koʊp/ *verb*
to be able to deal with a difficult situation, especially without becoming too upset: *I started getting a lot of homework, and it was hard to cope.*

**cop·i·er** /ˈkɑpiɚ/ *noun*
a machine for copying pieces of writing or pictures on paper **SYNONYM: photocopier**

**co-pi·lot** /ˈkoʊˌpaɪlət/ *noun*
a pilot who helps the main pilot fly an airplane

**cop·per** /ˈkɑpɚ/ *noun*
an orange-brown metal: *Electrical wires are often made of copper.*
[**ORIGIN:** From the Latin phrase *Cyprium aes*, which means "metal from the island of Cyprus."]

**cop·y**[1] /ˈkɑpi/ *verb* (**copied**, **copies**)
**1** to make or write something that is the same as something else: *He copied his friend's answers on the test.* | *Do you know how to copy a file on your computer?*
**2** to deliberately do what someone else has done: *Other bands have copied their music.*
**PHRASAL VERB**
**copy something down**
to write down the exact words that are said by someone or written somewhere: *She copied down the homework assignment.*

**copy**[2] *noun* (plural **copies**)
**1** something that is made to look exactly the same as something else: *She made a copy of the letter to send to her lawyer.*
**2** one of many books, magazines, or newspapers that are exactly the same: *Do you have another copy of this book?*

**cop·y·right** /ˈkɑpiˌraɪt/ *noun*
the legal right to produce and sell a book, play, movie, or recording: *The software is under copyright, and you can't install it onto another computer.*

**cor·al** /ˈkɔrəl/ *noun*
a hard substance under the ocean that is formed from the bodies of small sea creatures. A long structure of coral is called a REEF.

**cord** /kɔrd/ *noun*
**1** a piece of wire covered with plastic, used for connecting electrical or electronic equipment: *She unplugged the phone cord.*
**2** thin rope: *Put the beads onto a piece of nylon cord to make a bracelet.*

**cor·du·roy** /ˈkɔrdəˌrɔɪ/ *noun*
thick strong cotton cloth with raised lines: *brown corduroy pants*

**core**[1] Ac /kɔr/ *noun*
**1** the central or most important part of something: *These four players are the core of the team. We would not win without them.*
**2** the hard central part of a fruit such as an apple: *He ate the apple and threw the core away.*
**3** the central part of the Earth or any PLANET: *The Earth's core is very hot.*
[**ORIGIN:** 1300-1400 From the Latin word *cor*, which means "heart."]

**core**[2] Ac *adjective*
core things are the most important and basic ones: *All the students take four core classes. They must take these classes to graduate.*

**cork** /kɔrk/ *noun*
**1** the light outer part of a type of tree, which is used for making things: *The bulletin board was covered in cork.*
**2** a piece of this material that is put in the top of a wine bottle to close it

**cork·screw** /ˈkɔrkˌskru/ *noun*
a tool used for pulling corks out of bottles

**corn** /kɔrn/ *noun*
**1** a tall plant with yellow seeds that you can cook and eat: *a field of corn* → see picture on page **A12**
**2** **corn on the cob** = the part of a corn plant with yellow seeds on it, that you cook

**corn·bread** /ˈkɔrnbred/ *noun*
bread made from small pieces of dried corn

**corned beef** /ˌkɔrnd ˈbif/ *noun*
BEEF that has been put in salt water and spices to preserve it

**cor·ner** /ˈkɔrnɚ/ *noun*
**1** the point at which two roads, walls, or edges meet: *Meet me on the corner of Main Street and Elm Street.* | *There was a TV in the corner of the room.*
**2** **see/watch something out of the corner of your eye** = to see or watch something that is to the side, without turning your head: *Suddenly, out of the corner of my eye, I saw something coming toward me.*

**corn·flakes** /ˈkɔrnfleɪks/ *plural noun*
a breakfast food consisting of flat pieces made from corn, which is eaten with milk

**corn·meal** /ˈkɔrnmil/ *noun*
a type of flour made from dried corn

**corn·y** /ˈkɔrni/ *adjective* (*informal*)
corny jokes, songs, movies, etc. are silly and very familiar: *Why do you keep playing those corny old love songs?*

**cor·po·ral** /ˈkɔrpərəl/ *noun* (*written abbreviation*: **Cpl.**)
an officer with a low rank in the army or Marines

**cor·po·rate** Ac /ˈkɔrpərɪt/ *adjective*
belonging to or relating to a corporation: *The company has moved its corporate headquarters to Houston.*

**cor·po·ra·tion** Ac /ˌkɔrpəˈreɪʃən/ *noun*
a large business: *Large corporations can sell their products at lower prices than small businesses.*
→ see Thesaurus box at **company**

**corpse** /kɔrps/ *noun*
a dead human body: *The police found a corpse in the park and are now looking for the killer.* **SYNONYM: body**

**cor·ral** /kəˈræl/ *noun*
an area with a fence around it where cattle or horses are kept

**cor·rect¹** /kəˈrekt/ *adjective*
right or without any mistakes: *He showed me the correct way to hold the baseball bat.* | *"Your name is Ives?" "Yes, that's correct."* **SYNONYM: right**; **ANTONYMS: incorrect, wrong**
—**correctly** *adverb* in a correct way: *Did I say your name correctly?*
→ see Thesaurus box at **right¹**
[**ORIGIN:** 1300-1400 From the Latin word *correctus*, a form of the verb *corrigere*, which means "to make straight or make better."]

| WORD FAMILY: correct |
| --- |
| **correct** *adjective* \| **correct** *verb* \| **correction** *noun* |

**correct²** *verb*
**1** to make something better or make it work in the right way: *Your eyesight can be corrected with glasses.*
**2** to change a piece of writing so that there are no mistakes in it: *I read through my essay carefully and corrected the spelling mistakes.*
**3** to tell someone when he or she says or does something wrong, and tell him or her what is right: *Some of the things he said weren't true, but I didn't want to correct him.*

**cor·rec·tion** /kəˈrekʃən/ *noun*
a change that makes something right or better: *He made a few corrections to his test before he turned it in.*

**cor·re·spond** Ac /ˌkɔrəˈspɑnd/ *verb* (*formal*)
**1** if two people correspond, they write letters to each other: *They've been corresponding since they met on vacation last year.* **SYNONYM: write**
**2** to be like something else or be related to something else: *Each number corresponds to a particular square on the map.*

**cor·re·spond·ence** Ac /ˌkɔrəˈspɑndəns/ *noun (formal)*
**1** a relationship or connection between two things: *There is a correspondence between each letter of the alphabet and the sounds it represents.*
**2** letters or emails that people send and receive: *He had a lot of correspondence to deal with after his vacation.*

**cor·re·spond·ent** /ˌkɔrəˈspɑndənt/ *noun (formal)*
someone whose job is to report news for a newspaper or television station: *She is the political correspondent for the "Washington Post."*

**cor·re·spond·ing** Ac /ˌkɔrəˈspɑndɪŋ/ *adjective (formal)*
relating to or similar to something: *They gave her a more important job and a corresponding increase in pay.*
—**correspondingly** *adverb* in a way that is similar to something else

**cor·ri·dor** /ˈkɔrədə˞/ *noun*
a long hall between two rows of rooms in a large building: *He walked down the corridors of the old hospital.* **SYNONYM: hall**
[**ORIGIN:** 1500-1600 From the Italian word *corridore*, from *correre*, which means "to run."]

**cor·rupt¹** /kəˈrʌpt/ *adjective*
a corrupt official uses his or her power in a way that is wrong, in order to get money or more power: *Corrupt police officers were being paid to help the gang.*
—**corruption** *noun* corrupt behavior: *The country's new president promised an end to government corruption.*

**corrupt²** *verb*
to make someone dishonest or bad: *Power often corrupts people.*

**cos·met·ics** /kɑzˈmetɪks/ *plural noun*
substances that people use to make their faces more attractive: *She bought some lipstick and other cosmetics.*

**cos·met·ic sur·ger·y** /kɑzˌmetɪk ˈsə˞dʒəri/ *noun*
medical operations that some people have to make themselves look more attractive: *She had cosmetic surgery on her nose to make it smaller.*

**cost¹** /kɔst/ *noun*
**1** the amount of money you have to pay for something: *The high cost of health care is a problem for many families.* | *The new runway will be built, but at a cost of over $85 million to the taxpayer.*

**THESAURUS: cost**

**expense** the amount of money that you spend on something: *His medical expenses are high, but the insurance pays for them.*

**price** the amount of money you must pay for something: *House prices keep going up.*

**charge** the amount of money that you have to pay to use or do something: *The books cost $49.50, and there's a mailing charge of $6.75.*

**fee** the amount of money you have to pay to go to some schools, join a club, or have a meeting with a lawyer or doctor: *The membership fee is $325 a year.* | *Tuition fees have gone up again.*

**fare** the amount of money you have to pay to travel somewhere by bus, airplane, or train: *We got a good deal on the air fare.*

**rent** the amount of money you have to pay each month to live in or use a place that you do not own: *My rent is $1,200 a month.*

**2** something that you lose, damage, or give away in order to achieve something: *The cost of the war has been very high – thousands of people have died.*
**3 at all costs/at any cost** = whatever might be damaged or lost, or whatever effort is needed: *He likes to win at all costs, even if he has to cheat to do it.*

**cost²** *verb* (**cost**)
**1** to have a price: *The book costs $15.* | *How much did your new bag cost?*
**2** to make someone lose something important: *One mistake cost us the game.*

**co-star** /ˈkoʊ stɑr/ *noun*
one of the two or more actors who have the main parts in the same movie, play, or television program: *Clooney's co-star in the movie is Jennifer Lopez.*
—**co-star** *verb* to be one of the main actors that work in a movie, play, or television

program: *He co-starred with Jack Nicholson in the movie "The Departed."*

**cost·ly** /ˈkɔstli/ *adjective* (*formal*)
**1** costing a lot of money: *The medical treatment is very costly, and few people can afford it.* **SYNONYM: expensive**
**2** causing a lot of problems: *The team made some costly mistakes, and they lost by three runs.*

**ˌcost of ˈliving** *noun*
the amount of money people must spend in order to buy food, clothes, and a place to live: *The cost of living is much higher in California than in Iowa.*

**cos·tume** /ˈkɑstum/ *noun*
**1** special clothes that someone wears in order to look like someone else: *He wore a clown costume to the Halloween party.*
**2** the special clothes that actors wear: *Backstage, members of the cast were getting into their costumes.*

**cot** /kɑt/ *noun*
a small bed that you can fold up and put away in a small space
[**ORIGIN:** 1600-1700 From the Hindi word *khat*, which means "bed."]

**cot·tage** /ˈkɑtɪdʒ/ *noun*
a small house in the country

**ˈcottage ˌcheese** *noun*
a very soft wet white cheese that has small solid lumps in it

**cot·ton** /ˈkɑtn/ *noun*
**1** cloth made from the white threads around the seeds of the cotton plant: *a cotton shirt* | *The dress was made of cotton.*
**2** the plant used for making this cloth: *Cotton was an important crop in the South.*

**ˈcotton ball** *noun*
a small soft ball made from cotton, used for cleaning skin, especially on your face

**ˈcotton ˌcandy** *noun*
sticky candy that you buy as a big soft ball on a stick. Cotton candy is usually pink: *The kids bought cotton candy at the fair.*

**ˈcotton gin** *noun*
a machine for separating cotton threads from the seeds of the cotton plant

**couch** /kaʊtʃ/ *noun*
a long comfortable seat for two or more people: *She was lying on the couch, watching TV.* **SYNONYM: sofa** → see picture on page **A8**

**ˈcouch poˌtato** *noun* (*informal*)
someone who spends a lot of time sitting and watching television

**cou·gar** /ˈkugɚ/ *noun*
a large brown wild cat. Cougars live in the mountains of northwest and southwest America. **SYNONYM: mountain lion**
[**ORIGIN:** 1700-1800 From the Tupi word *suasuarana*, from *suasu* and *rana*, which mean "deer" and "like." A cougar might be like a deer because of its color or speed. Tupi is a language used in South America.]

**cough¹** /kɔf/ *verb*
if you cough, air suddenly comes out of your throat with a short rough sound: *The smoke made him cough.*

**cough**

**cough²** *noun*
**1** an illness that makes you cough a lot: *I had a slight cough and a runny nose but nothing too serious.*
**2** the sound made when you cough, or the action of coughing: *She gave a nervous cough before she spoke.*

**could** /kəd; *strong* kʊd/ *verb*
**1** used when saying what someone was able to do or was allowed to do: *I could hear children laughing.* | *He said I could borrow his bike.*
**2** used when saying that something is possible or might happen: *He could be a great player if he tried harder.* | *It could be weeks before we see him again.*
**3 could have** = used when saying that something was possible, but did not actually happen: *It was a bad accident, and she could have been killed.*
**4** used when asking someone for something politely: *Could I ask you a couple of questions?*

5 used when suggesting something: *We could have a barbecue.*

**could·n't** /ˈkʊdnt/ *verb*
the short form of "could not": *It was so funny! We couldn't stop laughing.*



**could've** /ˈkʊdəv/ *verb*
the short form of "could have": *He could've called and told me he was going to be late.*

**coun·cil** /ˈkaʊnsəl/ *noun*
a group of people who have been chosen to make laws or decisions for a town or organization: *The city council has approved plans for the new football stadium.*
[**ORIGIN:** 1100-1200 From the Latin word *concilium*, which means "gathering of people."]

**coun·sel** /ˈkaʊnsəl/ *verb*
to listen to someone who has a problem and give him or her advice: *He counsels students with personal problems.*
—**counseling** *noun* advice and support given by a counselor to someone with a problem: *The center offers counseling to anyone with drug or alcohol problems.*

**coun·sel·or** /ˈkaʊnsələ˞/ *noun*
1 someone whose job is to listen to people who have problems and give them advice: *He went to see a counselor after his parents got divorced.*
2 someone who takes care of a group of children at a camp

**count**[1] /kaʊnt/ *verb*
1 to find out how many things there are in a group: *We counted all the votes, and Maria is the new class president.*
2 to say numbers in the right order: *He's only three, but he can count to 50.*
3 to be important: *We won, and that's all that counts.* | *I felt my opinion didn't count for anything.*
4 **count me in/out** (*informal*) = used for saying that you want to do something with other people, or that you do not want to do something with them: *Count me out – I'm too tired to go out tonight.*
[**ORIGIN:** 1300-1400 From the Latin word *computare*, which means "to calculate."]
**PHRASAL VERB**
**count on someone or something**
to depend on someone or something: *He's very nice. You can always count on him to help.*

**count**[2] *noun*
1 the process of counting something: *The teachers made a count of all the children as they got on the bus.*
2 the total that you get when you finish counting something: *At last count, he's seen the movie six times.*
3 **lose count** = to forget how many things you have counted, because there are so many of them: *I've lost count of how many times she's asked me for help.*
4 one of the crimes that the police say someone has done: *He was found guilty on two counts of robbery.*

**count·down** /ˈkaʊntdaʊn/ *noun*
the act of counting from a number down to zero before an event happens, for example before a spacecraft takes off: *The countdown to the launch of the space shuttle has begun.*

**coun·ter** /ˈkaʊntə˞/ *noun*
1 a flat surface in a kitchen where you can prepare food: *She washed the dishes and cleaned the kitchen counters.* → see picture on page A9
2 the place where you pay or are served in a restaurant, store, or bank: *The girl behind the counter took my order.*

**coun·ter·act** /ˌkaʊntə˞ˈækt/ *verb*
to reduce the bad effect of something, by having the opposite effect: *Sunscreen helps to counteract the harmful effects of the sun on your skin.*

**coun·ter·at·tack** /ˈkaʊntə˞əˌtæk/ *noun*
an attack that you make against someone who has attacked you
—**counterattack** *verb* to attack someone who has attacked you

**coun·ter·clock·wise** /ˌkaʊntə˞ˈklɑk-waɪz/ *adjective, adverb*
moving in the opposite direction to the hands of a clock: *Turn the lid counterclockwise.*
**ANTONYM: clockwise**

**coun·ter·feit** /ˈkaʊntə˞fɪt/ *adjective*
made to look exactly like something else in order to trick people: *The woman was*

*arrested when she tried to use a counterfeit $50 bill to pay for the goods.*
→ see Thesaurus box at **fake**

**count·less** /ˈkaʊntlɪs/ *adjective* (*formal*)
very many: *I had seen the movie countless times before, and I didn't need to see it again.*

**coun·try** /ˈkʌntri/ *noun* (plural **countries**)
**1** a large area of land with its own government or ruler: *China is a huge country.* | *She has traveled to many foreign countries.*

**THESAURUS: country**

**nation** a country, its people, and its government: *Rich nations should do more to help poor nations.*

**state** a country that has a government – used to talk about a country as a political organization: *All the farms were owned by the state, rather than by the people who worked on them.*

**colony** a country or area that is ruled by a more powerful country, usually one that is far away: *The island used to be a French colony but it is now independent.*

**land** a country or place – used mostly in writing and stories: *The people of America came from many lands.*

**2 the country** = areas that are not near towns and cities: *He had a house in the country.*

**ˈcountry ˌmusic** (*also* **ˌcountry and ˈwestern**) *noun*
a type of music that is most popular in the southern and western U.S.: *The country music singers Garth Brooks and Loretta Lynn will be performing at the awards ceremony in Nashville.*

**coun·try·side** /ˈkʌntriˌsaɪd/ *noun*
land that is not near towns and cities: *We went for a drive through the Virginia countryside.*

**coun·ty** /ˈkaʊnti/ *noun* (plural **counties**)
a part of a state that has its own government: *Orange County is one of the 58 counties in the state of California.*

**coup** /ku/ *noun* (*formal*)
**1** (*also* **coup d'état** /ˌku deɪˈtɑ/) an action in which a group of people suddenly take control of their country by force: *The president was forced out of office in a military coup.*
**2** an achievement that is impressive because it was difficult: *Winning the scholarship to Yale was quite a coup.*

**cou·ple** Ac /ˈkʌpəl/ *noun*
**1 a couple** (*informal*) = two, or a small number: *I waited for a couple of hours and then tried calling again.*
**2** two people who are married or have a romantic relationship: *There was a young couple with a baby standing next to me.*

**cou·pon** /ˈkupɑn/ *noun*
a piece of paper you can use at a store so that you pay less money for something: *The coupon gives you 50 cents off a box of cereal.*

**cour·age** /ˈkɚɪdʒ/ *noun*
the quality of being brave: *I didn't have the courage to ask my boss for a raise.* **SYNONYM: bravery**
—**courageous** /kəˈreɪdʒəs/ *adjective* brave: *his courageous battle against the disease*
—**courageously** *adverb* in a brave way: *The soldiers defended the town courageously.*
[**ORIGIN:** 1200-1300 From the Latin word *cor*, which means "heart."]

**cou·ri·er** /ˈkʊriɚ/ *noun*
someone whose job is to take documents and packages directly to people

**course** /kɔrs/ *noun*
**1 of course** = **a)** used when saying that something is not surprising: *Of course, she was really upset when she found out he'd been hurt.* **b)** used when saying "yes" in a strong way: *"Are you going to watch the game?" "Of course!"*
**2 of course not** = used when saying "no" in a strong way: *"Do you mind if my sister comes along too?" "Of course not."*
**3** a class in a particular subject: *I'm taking a computer course at night school.*
**4** one of the parts of a meal: *For $25, you get three courses: an appetizer, a main course, and dessert.*
**5** an area of land where golf is played or horse races take place: *Does the hotel have a golf course?*
**6** the planned direction taken by a boat or airplane to reach a place: *The plane changed*

*course to fly around the storm.* | *Their boat was blown off course and heading in the wrong direction.*

**7 a course of action** (*formal*) = a series of things you do in order to deal with a situation: *If you've been threatened, the best course of action is to tell the police.*

**8 in/during/over the course of something** (*formal*) = during a period of time or while something happens: *During the course of the conversation, I learned that Bob had been to college in Chicago.*

**court** /kɔrt/ *noun*

**1** a place where a trial takes place and people decide whether someone is guilty of a crime: *The case will be heard in a court of law.* | *He appeared in court charged with robbery.*

**2** an area made for playing a game such as tennis or basketball: *The players were practicing on the court.*

**3** the place where a king or queen lives and works, or the people there

[**ORIGIN:** 1200-1300 From the Latin word *cohors*, which means "enclosed place."]

**cour·te·ous** /ˈkɚtiəs/ *adjective* (*formal*)

polite: *The salespeople at the store are always very courteous to customers.*

—**courteously** *adverb* in a polite way

**cour·te·sy** /ˈkɚtəsi/ *noun* (plural **courtesies**)

polite behavior: *She didn't have the courtesy to apologize, even though it was her fault.*

**court·house** /ˈkɔrthaʊs/ *noun*

a building containing courts of law and government offices

**ˌcourt-ˈmartial** *noun*

a TRIAL in which a military court decides whether a soldier has done something wrong: *The soldier is facing a court-martial for being drunk while on duty.*

—**court-martial** *verb* if a soldier is court-martialed, he or she has a TRIAL in a military court

**court·room** /ˈkɔrtrum/ *noun*

a room where a law case is decided: *Everyone in the courtroom waited to hear the jury's verdict.*

**court·yard** /ˈkɔrtyɑrd/ *noun*

an open area with walls or buildings all around it: *There are four houses built around a courtyard.*

**cous·in** /ˈkʌzən/ *noun*

a child of your aunt or uncle: *We visited my aunt and I got to see my cousins.*

**cov·er**[1] /ˈkʌvɚ/ *verb*

**1** (*also* **cover up**) to put something over something else: *She covered the child with a blanket.*

**2** if something covers a surface, it forms a layer over all of it: *The ground was covered with snow.*

**3** to include or deal with something: *My literature class covered all the major writers.*

**4** to report an event for a newspaper or a television or radio program: *A team of reporters will be covering the event.*

**WORD FAMILY: cover**

**cover** *verb* | **cover** *noun* | **covering** *noun*

**PHRASAL VERBS**

**cover for someone**

**1** to do someone's work because he or she is sick or is somewhere else: *Brian will be covering for Sandra next week while she's on vacation.*

**2** to stop someone from getting into trouble by lying for them: *Can you cover for me? Just say I had an appointment.*

**cover something up**

to prevent people from discovering something bad: *She tried to cover up her mistake by lying about it.*

**cover**[2] *noun*

**1** the outside of a book or magazine: *Her picture is on the cover of all the fashion magazines.*

**2** protection from attack or bad weather: *The soldiers ran for cover when the shooting started.* | *As the rain started, we took cover under a tree.*

**3** something that is used to cover and protect something else: *There's a plastic cover on the sofa to keep it clean.*

**4 covers** = the sheets and BLANKETs on a bed: *She lay in bed and pulled the covers up.*

**THESAURUS: cover**

**lid** a cover for a box, pot, or other container: *The water will boil faster if you put the lid on the pan.*

**top** the cover for a container or a pen: *I can't get the top off this jar.*

**wrapper** paper or plastic that is around something you buy: *Don't throw the candy wrapper on the ground! Put it in the trash can.*

**cov·er·age** /ˈkʌvərɪdʒ/ *noun*
1 reports in newspapers, on television, etc. about an event: *The trial received a lot of media coverage, including nightly reports on the television news.*
2 the protection your insurance gives you, so that you get money if you are injured or if something is stolen or damaged: *Some families have no health coverage and cannot afford to visit a doctor.*

**cov·er·ing** /ˈkʌvərɪŋ/ *noun*
something that covers something else: *carpets and other types of floor covering*

ˈ**cover-up** *noun*
an attempt to prevent the public from discovering the truth about something: *She claims that the government is involved in a cover-up of the true story.*

**cow** /kaʊ/ *noun*
a large animal that is kept on farms for its milk or meat: *a herd of cows in the pasture*
[**ORIGIN:** From the old English word *cu*.]

**cow·ard** /ˈkaʊɚd/ *noun*
someone who is not brave at all: *The boys called him a coward because he wouldn't fight.*
—**cowardly** *adjective* not brave: *He was too cowardly to complain.*
—**cowardice** *noun* behavior that is not brave

**cow·boy** /ˈkaʊbɔɪ/ *noun*
a man whose job is to take care of cattle: *Two cowboys rode up to the ranch on their horses.*

**cow·girl** /ˈkaʊgɚl/ *noun*
a woman whose job is to take care of cattle

**coy·o·te** /kaɪˈoʊti/ *noun*
a wild animal that looks like a dog and lives in western North America: *We heard the howl of a coyote.*

**co·zy** /ˈkoʊzi/ *adjective*
a cozy place is small, warm, and comfortable: *He lit the fire and the room was soon warm and cozy.*
—**cozily** *adverb* in a cozy way
—**coziness** *noun* the quality of being cozy

**crab** /kræb/ *noun*
a sea animal with ten legs and a round flat shell around its body, or the meat from this animal

**crack¹** /kræk/ *verb*
to break or damage something so that it has a line on its surface: *I dropped my favorite coffee mug and cracked it.* | *The ice started to crack as soon as I stepped onto it.*
—**cracked** *adjective* something that is cracked has a thin line in it where it has broken: *a cracked mirror*
→ see Thesaurus box at **break¹**

**PHRASAL VERBS**

**crack down**
to start dealing with a type of crime or problem more severely: *Police are cracking down on drunk drivers and making lots of arrests.*

**crack someone up** (*informal*)
to make someone laugh a lot: *She tells the funniest stories. She cracks me up.*

**crack**

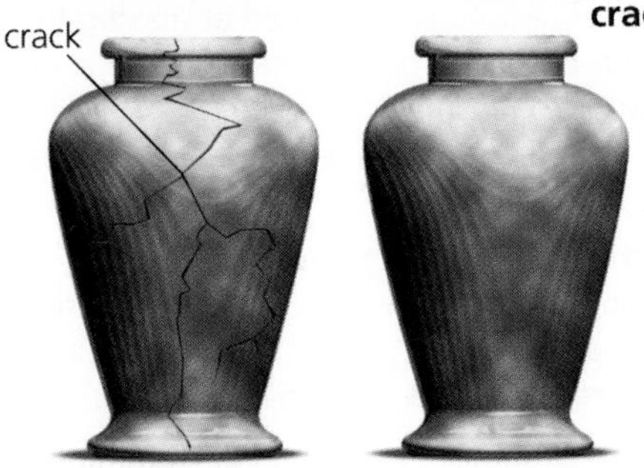


**crack²** *noun*
1 a thin line where something is broken: *There were several small cracks in the vase.*
2 a very narrow space between two things or two parts of something: *The letter had fallen through a crack between the floorboards.* **SYNONYM: gap**
3 a sudden short loud noise: *I heard the crack of the bat as the hitter connected with the ball.*
4 **take a crack at (doing) something** (*informal*) = to try to do something: *I thought I'd take a crack at writing some songs.*
→ see Thesaurus box at **hole**

**crack·down** /ˈkrækdaʊn/ *noun*
actions that are done to deal with a type of

crime or a problem more severely: *Most people support the police crackdown on drug dealing.*

**crack·er** /ˈkrækɚ/ *noun*
a small flat hard piece of bread: *Do you want some cheese and crackers?*

**crack·le** /ˈkrækəl/ *verb*
to make a lot of short sharp noises like something burning in a fire: *The logs were crackling in the fire.*
—**crackle** *noun* a series of short sharp noises: *the crackle of gunfire* → see picture on page A22

**cra·dle** /ˈkreɪdl/ *noun*
a small bed for a baby, which can move from side to side: *She gently rocked the cradle until the baby fell asleep.*

**craft** /kræft/ *noun*
a skilled activity in which you make something using your hands: *You can learn crafts such as sewing and woodworking.*
[**ORIGIN:** From the old English word *cræft*, which means "strength or skill."]

**crafts·man** /ˈkræftsmən/ *noun* (plural **craftsmen** /ˈkræftsmən/)
someone who is very skilled at making things with his or her hands: *The furniture is made by local craftsmen.*
—**craftsmanship** *noun* the skill of a craftsman

**craft·y** /ˈkræfti/ *adjective*
good at getting what you want by tricking people
—**craftily** *adverb* in a crafty way

**cram** /kræm/ *verb* (**crammed**, **cramming**)
**1** to put a lot of things or people into a small space: *I managed to cram all my stuff into the tiny closet.*
**2** **be crammed with something** = to be very full of things or people: *The garage was crammed with junk.*

**cramp** /kræmp/ *noun*
a bad pain that you get when a muscle suddenly becomes too tight: *One runner got leg cramps and had to leave the race.*

**cramped** /kræmpt/ *adjective*
a cramped room or building is too small and does not have enough space for all the things in it: *She wanted to move out of her cramped apartment to a bigger place.*

**cran·ber·ry** /ˈkrænˌberi/ *noun* (plural **cranberries**)
a small sour red fruit that grows on a bush: *We always have cranberry sauce with the turkey on Thanksgiving.* → see picture on page A13

**crane** /kreɪn/ *noun*
**1** a tall machine with a long metal arm for lifting heavy things: *There were two cranes at the construction site moving heavy metal beams.*
**2** a bird with very long legs that lives near water

**crash¹** /kræʃ/ *verb*
**1** if a vehicle crashes, it has an accident and hits something hard: *The plane crashed in the mountains.* | *He crashed his car into a tree.*
**2** to hit something hard, making a loud noise: *A baseball crashed through our living room window.*
**3** if a computer crashes, it suddenly stops working: *My computer crashed and I lost all of my homework.*
**4** (*also* **crash out**) (*informal*) to fall asleep quickly because you are very tired: *I was so tired, I came home at 8:30 and crashed.*

**crash²** *noun*
**1** an accident in which a vehicle hits something hard: *He was killed in a plane crash.*
**2** a sudden loud noise made by something falling or breaking: *The plate fell to the ground with a crash.*
**3** an occasion when the value of STOCKs suddenly falls by a large amount: *a stock market crash*

**crate** /kreɪt/ *noun*
a large wooden or plastic box used for carrying things, especially in a vehicle: *There were crates of strawberries in the back of his truck.*

crater

**cra·ter** /ˈkreɪtɚ/ *noun*
**1** a large round hole in the ground made by a bomb or a METEORITE that has fallen from

space: *There are large round craters on the Moon that you can see from Earth.*
**2** the round hole at the top of a VOLCANO
→ see Thesaurus box at **hole**
[**ORIGIN:** 1600-1700 From the Greek word *krater*, which means "bowl for mixing things."]

**crawl¹** /krɔl/ *verb*
**1** to move along on your hands and knees: *The baby crawled toward his father.* → see picture on page **A4**
**2** if an insect crawls somewhere, it moves there: *There were ants crawling all over the food.*
**3** if vehicles crawl, they move forward very slowly: *Traffic was crawling along at walking pace.*

**crawl²** *noun*
**the crawl** = a way of swimming with your face down in which you move one arm up beside your head, and then the other

**cray·on** /ˈkreɪɑn/ *noun*
a stick of colored WAX that children use to draw pictures

**craze** /kreɪz/ *noun*
something that is very popular for a short time: *Plastic bracelets are the latest craze. Who knows what will be next?* **SYNONYM: fad**

**cra·zy** /ˈkreɪzi/ *adjective* (**crazier**, **craziest**) (*informal*)
**1** not thinking or behaving in a sensible way: *He took all my money. I was crazy to trust him.* | *Whose crazy idea was it to go hiking in a snowstorm?*
**2 be crazy about someone or something** = to like or love someone or something very much: *He's crazy about his new girlfriend.*
**3 like crazy** = very much or very quickly: *We've been working like crazy to get the job done.*
**4** mentally ill: *She went crazy and started hearing voices that weren't really there.*
—**craziness** *noun* behavior or ideas that are crazy

**creak** /krik/ *verb*
if something such as a door or wooden floor creaks, it makes a long high noise when it is moved or pressed: *The old door creaked as it opened.*
—**creak** *noun* a long high noise that something makes when it is moved or pressed → see picture on page **A22**
—**creaky** *adjective* if a door, floor, etc. is creaky, it creaks when you open it, walk on it, etc.: *the creaky wooden stairs*

**cream** /krim/ *noun*
**1** a thick liquid that is part of milk. Cream rises to the top of milk and it is often removed from the milk we drink: *Does she take cream in her coffee?*
**2** a yellowish-white color: *The room had been painted cream.*
**3** a thick smooth substance that you put on your skin: *a jar of face cream*
—**cream** *adjective* having a yellowish-white color

**ˈcream cheese** *noun*
a type of soft white cheese: *I'll have a bagel with cream cheese, please.*

**creamy** /ˈkrimi/ *adjective*
**1** thick and smooth like cream, or containing cream: *I had pasta in a rich creamy sauce.*
**2** having a yellowish-white color: *a creamy white shirt*

**crease** /kris/ *noun*
a deep line in clothes, paper, or someone's skin: *There were deep creases in the old woman's face.*
—**creased** *adjective* having creases

**cre·ate** Ac /kriˈeɪt/ *verb*
to make something new: *How do I create a new file on my computer?* | *The changes to the system created a lot of problems.*
—**creator** *noun* the person who created something: *the creator of the TV series*

**WORD FAMILY: create**
**create** *verb* | **creator** *noun* | **creative** *adjective* | **creation** *noun* | **creativity** *noun* | **creatively** *adverb*

→ see Thesaurus box at **invent**

**cre·a·tion** Ac /kriˈeɪʃən/ *noun*
**1** the act of creating something: *This project will lead to the creation of 300 new jobs.*
**2** something that has been created: *This dish is my own creation – I didn't have a recipe.*

**cre·a·tive** Ac /kriˈeɪtɪv/ *adjective*
good at thinking of new ideas or making new

C

things: *She's very creative. She designs all her own clothes.*
—**creatively** *adverb* in a creative way
—**creativity** /ˌkrieɪˈtɪvəti/ *noun* the quality of being creative: *There is a lack of creativity in his later paintings.*

C

**crea·ture** /ˈkritʃɚ/ *noun*
an animal, fish, or insect: *Wild creatures such as beavers and bears live in the national parks.*

**cre·den·tials** /krəˈdenʃəlz/ *plural noun*
someone's achievements, which prove that he or she has the ability to do something: *Only students with excellent academic credentials are accepted.*

**cred·it**[1] Ac /ˈkredɪt/ *noun*
**1** praise given to someone for doing something: *I can't take all the credit – Nick helped a lot too.*
**2** a way of buying things in which you pay for them later: *My parents bought the new TV on credit, and must pay the money back over the next two years.*
**3** a unit used to measure the amount of work completed at a college or university: *She needs 30 more credits to graduate.*
**4** an amount of money that is put into someone's bank account: *A credit of $65 has been added to your account.* **ANTONYM: debit**
**5 the credits** = a list of all the people involved in making a television program or movie
[**ORIGIN:** 1500-1600 From the Latin word *creditum*, which means "something you have lent to someone."]

**credit**[2] Ac *verb*
**1** to add money to a bank account: *The refund will be credited to his account by the end of the month.* **ANTONYM: debit**
**2 credit someone with (doing) something** = to say that someone achieved something or has an ability: *James Watt is credited with inventing the steam engine.*

**ˈcredit card** *noun*
a small plastic card that you use to buy things and pay for them later: *Can I pay with a credit card?*

**cred·i·tor** Ac /ˈkredɪtɚ/ *noun*
a person or organization that you owe money to

**creed** /krid/ *noun*
a set of beliefs: *There are students of all races and creeds at the school: Muslims, Hindus, and Christians.*

**creek** /krik/ *noun*
a small river: *The boys went fishing in the creek.*

**creep** /krip/ *verb* (**crept** /krept/)
to move slowly and quietly: *I got up during the night and crept downstairs, trying not to wake anyone up.*

**creep·y** /ˈkripi/ *adjective* (*informal*)
making you feel a little frightened: *I don't like spiders – they're creepy.*

**cre·ma·to·ri·um** /ˌkriməˈtɔriəm/ *noun* (plural **crematoriums** *or* **crematoria** /ˌkriːməˈtɔriə/)
a building where the bodies of dead people are burned
—**cremate** /ˈkrimeɪt/ *verb* to burn the dead body of a person
—**cremation** /krɪˈmeɪʃən/ *noun* the act or ceremony of burning a dead body

**cre·ole** /ˈkrioʊl/ *noun*
a language that is a mixture of a European language and another language: *The language that they speak is a creole. It's a mixture of French and African languages.*

**crept** /krept/ *verb*
the past tense and past participle of CREEP

**cres·cent** /ˈkresənt/ *noun* (*formal*)
a curved shape that is wide in the middle and pointed at each end, like a thin moon: *The beach was a crescent of white sand.*

**crest** /krest/ *noun* (*formal*)
the top of a hill or a wave: *The crests of the waves were bright white in the sun.*

**crev·ice** /ˈkrevɪs/ *noun* (*formal*)
a deep narrow crack in rock, the ground, or a wall: *His foot got stuck in a crevice as he was climbing the mountain.*

**crew** /kru/ *noun*
**1** the people who work on a ship or airplane: *The flight crew welcomed us onto the plane.*
**2 a film/camera/TV, etc. crew** = a group of people who make a movie or television program: *A television camera crew was waiting outside the courthouse.*
→ see Thesaurus box at **group**[1]

**[ORIGIN:** 1500-1600 From the old French word *creue*, which means "increase in the number of soldiers."**]**

**crib** /krɪb/ *noun*
a small bed for a baby, that has high sides made of bars: *Timmy slept in a crib until he was two.*

**crick** /krɪk/ *noun*
a sharp pain in your neck or back: *I have a crick in my neck and it hurts when I turn my head.*

**crick·et** /ˈkrɪkɪt/ *noun*
**1** a small brown insect that jumps and makes a short high noise by rubbing its wings together: *Outside at night, I could hear the crickets chirping.*
**2** a game in which you hit a ball and run between two sets of sticks

**cried** /kraɪd/ *verb*
the past tense and past participle of CRY

**cries[1]** /kraɪz/ *noun*
the plural of CRY

**cries[2]** *verb*
the third person singular, present tense of CRY

**crime** /kraɪm/ *noun*
**1** an action that the law does not allow: *Stealing is a crime. | You may go to jail if you commit a crime.*

**THESAURUS: crime**

**Crimes That Involve Stealing Things:**

**theft** the crime of stealing things: *Car theft is a serious problem in this area.*

**robbery** the crime of stealing something from a person, bank, or store: *He went to prison for a bank robbery.*

**burglary** the crime of going into someone's home or a building in order to steal money or valuable things: *They stole all my grandmother's jewelry in the burglary.*

**shoplifting** the crime of taking things from a store without paying for them: *She was caught shoplifting in the grocery store.*

**Crimes That Involve Attacking People:**

**assault** the crime of physically attacking someone: *After the fight, he was arrested for assault.*

**mugging** the crime of attacking and robbing someone in a public place: *Muggings are common, so you shouldn't walk by yourself.*

**murder** the crime of deliberately killing someone: *He is being tried for murder.*

**manslaughter** the crime of killing someone when you did not plan to do it: *The man who started the fire that killed two people was charged with manslaughter.*

**2** illegal activity in general: *We moved to this area because it has very little crime.*
**3 it's a crime** (*informal*) = said when you think something is wrong, and someone should not do it: *It's a crime to throw away all that good food.*

**crim·i·nal[1]** /ˈkrɪmənəl/ *adjective*
relating to crime: *He faces criminal charges for selling drugs.*

**criminal[2]** *noun*
someone who has broken the law: *Dangerous criminals should not be let out of jail.*

**crim·son** /ˈkrɪmzən/ *adjective, noun*
a dark red color: *The plant has crimson flowers.*

**cringe** /krɪndʒ/ *verb*
**1** to feel embarrassed by something that someone says or does: *Seeing my dad dancing made me cringe with embarrassment.*
**2** to move away from someone or something because you are frightened: *He raised his hand to hit the dog, and the dog cringed.*

**crip·ple** /ˈkrɪpəl/ *verb*
to injure someone so that he or she cannot walk anymore: *He fell off a horse, and it crippled him for life.*

**cri·sis** /ˈkraɪsɪs/ *noun* (plural **crises** /ˈkraɪsiz/)
a bad situation with problems that must be dealt with quickly or the situation will get much worse: *The country is in an economic crisis: prices are rising and there are not many jobs.*

**crisp** /krɪsp/ *adjective*
**1** crisp food feels firm and makes a noise when you bite it: *I like crisp green apples.*

C

2 crisp air or weather is cold and dry: *In the mountains, the air was fresh and crisp.*
—**crispness** *noun* the quality of being crisp

**crisp·y** /ˈkrɪspi/ *adjective*
crispy food is pleasantly hard because it has been cooked or dried: *The chicken was crispy on the outside.*

C

**cri·te·ri·a** Ac /kraɪˈtɪriə/ *plural noun* (singular **criterion** /kraɪˈtɪriən/)
rules or standards that you use when making a decision or judgment: *The criteria for being able to vote are that you must be 18 years old and a citizen of the U.S.*

**crit·ic** /ˈkrɪtɪk/ *noun*
1 someone whose job is writing about music, movies, books, etc. and saying whether they are good or bad: *The critics loved the band's last CD, praising it as their best record so far.*
2 someone who says that someone or something is bad or wrong: *He is a leading critic of the war.*
[ORIGIN: 1500-1600 From the Greek word *kritikos*, which means "able to make judgments."]

**crit·i·cal** /ˈkrɪtɪkəl/ *adjective*
1 if you are critical of something, you think or say that it is bad: *Mrs. Watts is always really critical of my work – she finds every mistake.*
2 something that is critical is very important and serious because it affects what happens in the future: *The last year of high school is a critical time because students are preparing for college or work.*
3 **in critical condition** = very sick or very badly hurt, and likely to die: *She was taken to the hospital in critical condition.*

**crit·i·cally** /ˈkrɪtɪkli/ *adverb*
1 in a way that shows you think something is bad: *"I don't think that shirt suits you," she said critically.*
2 **critically injured/wounded** = very badly injured and likely to die: *Two men were critically injured in the attack.*
3 having an important effect on whether a situation goes well or badly: *It's critically important to get food and medicine to the victims of the earthquake as quickly as possible.*

**crit·i·cism** /ˈkrɪtəˌsɪzəm/ *noun*
1 a statement saying what you think is bad about someone or something: *Her criticism of my singing really hurt my feelings.*
2 writing that judges what is good or bad about a book, a piece of music, a movie, etc.: *a book of literary criticism*

**crit·i·cize** /ˈkrɪtəˌsaɪz/ *verb*
to say that someone or something is bad: *Everyone criticized the movie because it was not like the book.* ANTONYM: **praise**

**WORD FAMILY: criticize**
**criticize** *verb* | **criticism** *noun* | **critical** *adjective* | **critic** *noun*

**croak** /kroʊk/ *verb*
1 when a FROG croaks, it makes a low sound
2 to speak in a low rough voice: *"I've got a sore throat," he croaked.*

**croc·o·dile** /ˈkrɑkəˌdaɪl/ *noun*
an animal with a big mouth full of sharp teeth, a long body, and hard thick skin. Crocodiles are REPTILEs and live in or near water.
[ORIGIN: 1200-1300 From the Greek words *kroke* and *drilos*, which mean "small stone" and "worm." Crocodiles like lying on stones in the sunshine.]

**cro·cus** /ˈkroʊkəs/ *noun* (plural **crocuses**)
a small purple, yellow, or white flower that appears in early spring

**crois·sant** /krwɑˈsɑnt/ *noun*
a type of small soft bread in a curved shape, that people eat for breakfast

**crook** /krʊk/ *noun* (*informal*)
a dishonest person or criminal: *The crooks were caught trying to cross the border in a stolen car.*

**crook·ed** /ˈkrʊkɪd/ *adjective*
1 not straight: *Your tie is crooked. Let me straighten it for you.*
2 not honest, or doing criminal things: *In the movie, he plays a crooked cop who passes information to the mob.*

**crop** /krɑp/ *noun*
1 a plant such as corn, wheat, vegetables, etc. that farmers grow: *Most of the land is used for growing crops.*
2 **a good/big/bumper crop** = a large amount of corn, wheat, fruit, etc. that is produced in one year

**cross[1]** /krɔs/ *verb*
**1** to go from one side of something to the other: *Look both ways before you cross the street.* | *He crossed the room to talk to me.*
**2** if roads or lines cross, they go across each other: *The car was parked on the corner of Lowell St., where it crosses Highland Ave.*
**3 cross your legs/arms** = to put one leg or arm over the other one: *Jack sat down on the floor and crossed his legs.*
**4 cross your mind** = if something crosses your mind, you think about it: *It suddenly crossed my mind that she might be sick or hurt, and I started to worry.*
**5 cross your heart** = used when you promise to do something, or when you promise that something is true: *I'll bring your bike back tomorrow, cross my heart.*
**PHRASAL VERBS**
**cross something off (something)**
to draw a line through something on a list because you have bought it, done it, or dealt with it: *I got bananas yesterday, so cross them off the list.*
**cross something out**
to draw a line through something you have written because it is not correct: *If you make a mistake, cross it out.*

**cross[2]** *noun*
**1** an object that is the symbol of the Christian religion, that looks like (†): *There was a gold cross on her necklace.*
**2** the shape (x) or (+): *I've put a cross on the map to mark where our street is.*
**3 a cross between something and something** = something that is a mixture of one thing and another: *Her expression was a cross between pain and anger.*

**ˌcross-exˈamine** *verb*
to ask someone questions in a court of law after another lawyer has already asked that person questions: *The defense lawyer cross-examined the first witness.*

**cross·ing** /ˈkrɔsɪŋ/ *noun*
**1** a place where a railroad crosses a road: *Every railroad crossing is marked by lights and a warning bell.*
**2** a place where you can cross a road or river safely: *Cars must stop for children using a school crossing.*
**3** a place where a road crosses a border between two countries or states: *the border crossing between California and Mexico*

**cross-leg·ged** /ˈkrɔs ˌlegɪd/ *adjective, adverb*
if you sit cross-legged, you sit on the ground with your knees apart and with one foot crossing over your other foot: *We sat cross-legged on the floor.*

**cross-legged**

**ˌcross-ˈreference** *noun*
a note in a book telling you to look on another page for more information

**cross·roads** /ˈkrɔsroudz/ *noun* (plural **crossroads**)
a place where one road goes across another: *We stopped at the crossroads, unsure of which way to turn.*

**ˌcross ˈsection** (*also* **cross-section**) *noun*
a group that includes a wide variety of people or things, which makes it typical of a much larger group: *Our research was based on a cross section of people of all ages.*

**cross·walk** /ˈkrɔswɔk/ *noun*
a place on a street that is marked with lines, so cars stop to let people cross: *Stay in the crosswalk when you cross the street.* → see picture on page **A26**

**cross·word puz·zle** /ˈkrɔswɚd ˌpʌzəl/ (*also* **crossword**) *noun*
a game where you write the answers to a set of questions into numbered squares that go across and down a page: *Are you doing the crossword puzzle? What's the answer to question 4 down?*

**crouch** /krautʃ/ (*also* **crouch down**) *verb*
to bend your knees and lean forward, so your body is close to the ground: *Tom crouched down behind a bush and hoped they would not see him.* → see picture on page **A5**

**crow[1]** /krou/ *noun*
a large black bird that has a loud cry

**crow[2]** *verb*
if a ROOSTER crows, it makes a loud sound

C

**crowd** /kraʊd/ *noun*
**1** a large group of people: *A crowd gathered to watch the parade.*
**2** (*informal*) a group of friends: *I went to the party with Brian and the rest of our crowd.*
—**crowd** *verb* to come together in a large group: *Thousands of baseball fans crowded into the stadium.*
→ see Thesaurus box at **group**[1]

C

**crowd·ed** /ˈkraʊdɪd/ *adjective*
full of people, cars, or things: *a crowded room*

**crown** /kraʊn/ *noun*
a circle of gold and jewels that a king or queen wears on his or her head: *The king wore a gold crown.*
—**crown** *verb* to put a crown on the head of a new king or queen in a special ceremony: *Louis was crowned king of France.*
[**ORIGIN:** 1100-1200 From the Greek word *korone*, which means "circle made of leaves or flowers."]

**cru·cial** Ac /ˈkruʃəl/ *adjective* (*formal*)
very important: *Eating fruits and vegetables is crucial to staying healthy.*
—**crucially** *adverb* (*formal*) in a crucial way
→ see Thesaurus box at **important**

**cru·ci·fix** /ˈkrusəˌfɪks/ *noun*
an object that shows Jesus Christ hanging on a cross: *There was a large crucifix at the front of the church.*

**crude**[1] /krud/ *adjective*
**1** crude words or actions are offensive or rude, often because they deal with sex in an unpleasant way: *His jokes are always so crude.*
**2** made in a simple way that is not very good: *The farm workers sat down to eat at a crude wooden table.* **ANTONYM: sophisticated**
—**crudely** *adverb* in a crude way: *The houses in the village were crudely built.*

**crude**[2] (*also* **crude oil**) *noun*
oil that is in its natural condition, as it comes out of the ground and before it is treated with chemicals

**cru·el** /ˈkruəl/ *adjective*
**1** a cruel person is very unkind, and sometimes hurts people or animals: *He made the dogs fight, and he was later arrested for being cruel to animals.*
**2** making someone suffer or feel very unhappy: *It was a cruel war in which millions of people died.*
—**cruelly** *adverb* in a cruel way: *The dog was beaten and treated cruelly.*
—**cruelty** *noun* the act of hurting people or animals

**cruise**[1] /kruz/ *noun*
a vacation on a large boat that travels on the ocean to different places: *Have you ever been on a cruise around the Caribbean?*

**cruise**[2] *verb*
to move at a steady speed in a car, airplane, or boat: *We cruised along at 65 miles per hour.*

**crumb** /krʌm/ *noun*
a very small piece of bread or cake: *She finished the cake and brushed the crumbs off her skirt.*
→ see Thesaurus box at **piece**

**crum·ble** /ˈkrʌmbəl/ *verb*
if something very old or dry crumbles, it breaks into pieces: *Many of the old stone walls are crumbling.*
—**crumbly** *adjective* breaking into small pieces easily: *The cookies were crumbly.*

**crum·ple** /ˈkrʌmpəl/ (*also* **crumple up**) *verb*
to crush a piece of paper and make it smaller: *Charlie crumpled the letter into a ball and threw it away.*

**crunch**[1] /krʌntʃ/ *noun*
**1** the sound of something being crushed, bitten, or chewed: *She bit into the carrot with a loud crunch.* → see picture on page **A22**
**2** an important period of time, during which you must try hard to achieve something or you will fail to achieve it: *The crunch will come at the end of the semester, when we have to prepare for the final exams.*

**crunch**[2] *verb*
**1** to crush, bite, or chew something in a noisy way: *Rob crunched an apple.*
**2** to make a noise like someone walking on snow or rocks: *I heard boots crunching on the snow.*
—**crunchy** *adjective* crunchy food is firm and makes a noise when you bite it: *Vegetables should be fresh and crunchy.*

**crush** /krʌʃ/ *verb*
to push down hard on something and break or damage it: *The tree fell and crushed the car.* → see picture on page **A15**
→ see Thesaurus box at **press[1]**

**crust** /krʌst/ *noun*
**1** the outer part of bread or PIE, or the bottom part of a PIZZA: *Do you like pizza with a thick or thin crust?*
**2 the Earth's crust** = the hard layer on the surface of the Earth

**crutch** /krʌtʃ/ *noun*
a special stick that you put under your arm to help you walk: *He has been on crutches since breaking his leg.*

**cry[1]** /kraɪ/ *verb* (**cried, cries**)
**1** if you cry, tears come out of your eyes because you are hurt or unhappy: *Sad movies always make me cry.*

> **THESAURUS: cry**
>
> **sob** to cry a lot in a noisy way: *When my grandmother died, my dad just sobbed.*
>
> **be in tears** to be crying: *We were all in tears as we said goodbye.*
>
> **weep** (*formal*) to cry a lot because you feel very sad: *My mother wept quietly as we drove away.*

**2** if a baby cries, it makes a loud sound: *The baby started crying again.*
**3** (*also* **cry out**) to shout something loudly: *"Wait for me!" she cried.* | *The boy cried out for help.*

**cry[2]** *noun* (plural **cries**)
**1** a loud sound you make when you are hurt, frightened, or very happy: *She gave a sudden cry of pain.*
**2** a loud shout: *There was a cry of "Stop, thief!"*
**3** a sound that some animals or birds make: *Outside, I could hear the cry of seagulls.*

**cryp·tic** /ˈkrɪptɪk/ *adjective*
having a meaning that is hard to understand: *He left a cryptic message and we can't figure out what it means.*

**crys·tal** /ˈkrɪstl/ *noun*
**1** glass that is very good quality: *The best wine glasses are made of crystal.*
**2** a small shape that forms when a liquid becomes solid: *It was so cold that there were ice crystals on the window.*
[**ORIGIN:** 1000-1100 From the Greek word *krystallos*, which means "ice or crystal."]

**cub** /kʌb/ *noun*
the baby of some wild animals, for example a lion: *The tiger cubs followed closely behind their mother.*

**cube** /kyub/ *noun*
**1** an object with six square sides: *He put an ice cube in each glass.*
**2 the cube of 2/7/15, etc.** = the number you get when you multiply a number by itself twice: *The cube of 3 is 27* (=3 x 3 x 3 = 27).

**cubed** /kyubd/ *adjective*
a number that is cubed is multiplied by itself twice: *3 cubed is 27* (=3 x 3 x 3 = 27).

**cu·bic** /ˈkyubɪk/ *adjective*
**a cubic inch/centimeter/yard, etc.** = a measurement of the amount of space inside something, which you get by multiplying its length by its height by its width: *The box is two feet high by three feet long by four feet wide, so it measures 24 cubic feet* (=2 x 3 x 4 = 24).

**cu·bi·cle** /ˈkyubɪkəl/ *noun*
a small area which is separated from the rest of a room by thin walls: *The office was divided into small cubicles, with a desk in each one.*

**cu·cum·ber** /ˈkyuˌkʌmbɚ/ *noun*
a long thin round green vegetable that you usually eat uncooked: *a tomato and cucumber salad* → see picture on page **A12**

**cud·dle** /ˈkʌdl/ *verb*
to hold someone close to you, because you love him or her: *Robbie's mom cuddled him on the couch.*
—**cuddly** *adjective* soft, warm, and nice to hold: *a cuddly puppy*

**cuddle**

**cue** /kyu/ *noun*
a signal that it is time for someone to do something: *The actors were waiting for their cue to come on stage.*

C

**cuff¹** /kʌf/ *noun*
**1** the end of a sleeve, where it fastens around the wrist: *The button on my cuff has fallen off.*
**2** a narrow piece of cloth that is turned up at the bottom of your pants
**3** **cuffs** (*informal*) = another word for HANDCUFFS

**cuff²** *verb* (*informal*)
to put HANDCUFFS on someone's hands: *Police cuffed the man's hands behind his back and put him in the police car.*

**cul·prit** /ˈkʌlprɪt/ *noun* (*formal*)
someone who has done something wrong: *There was a burglary last night, and police are still looking for the culprit.*

**cult¹** /kʌlt/ *noun*
a small religious group with strange or extreme ideas and a strong leader who controls the group: *The members of the cult are not allowed to speak to outsiders.*

**cult²** *adjective*
very popular among a small group of people – used about something such as a movie, band, or book: *The strange movie quickly became a cult favorite.*

**cul·ti·vate** /ˈkʌltəˌveɪt/ *verb* (*formal*)
**1** to grow crops and plants by preparing the land for them: *Most of the farmers cultivate rice.*
**2** **cultivate a skill/relationship/reputation** = to work hard to develop something such as a skill or relationship: *He tries to cultivate relationships with professors who can help him in his career.*
—**cultivation** /ˌkʌltəˈveɪʃən/ *noun* the act of growing crops by preparing the land for them: *The wet black soil is perfect for cultivation of many crops.*

**cul·tur·al** Ac /ˈkʌltʃərəl/ *adjective*
**1** relating to a society and its way of life: *There are big cultural differences between the U.S. and Japan.*
**2** relating to art, literature, or music: *With its many art galleries, theaters and museums, New York has a rich and varied cultural life.*

**cul·ture** Ac /ˈkʌltʃɚ/ *noun*
**1** the ideas and way of life of a society: *I love traveling and meeting people from different cultures.*
**2** art, literature, music, etc.: *If you like culture, you should live in the city.*
[**ORIGIN:** 1200-1300 From the Latin word *cultura*, which means "looking after." This word was used about helping plants to grow, and art, literature, etc. are ways of helping your mind to grow.]

**WORD FAMILY: culture**
**culture** *noun* | **cultural** *adjective*

**ˈculture ˌshock** *noun*
a feeling you sometimes get when you visit a foreign country and everything seems strange and confusing: *After growing up in Kansas, living in Japan was quite a culture shock, because it is so different.*

**cun·ning** /ˈkʌnɪŋ/ *adjective*
good at getting what you want, especially by tricking people: *My cunning opponent had made it impossible for me to win.*

**cup**

cup mug

**cup** /kʌp/ *noun*
**1** a small round container with a handle, that you use for drinking tea or coffee: *Would you like a cup of coffee?*
**2** a container that holds eight FLUID OUNCEs. You use a cup to measure foods in cooking: *Stir in a cup of flour.*
**3** (*also* **Cup**) a prize for winning a competition, that is shaped like a bowl and often has two handles: *The team won the Championship Cup.*

**cup·board** /ˈkʌbɚd/ *noun*
a piece of furniture for keeping things in, that has a door and shelves: *There wasn't much food in the kitchen cupboard.* **SYNONYM: cabinet** → see picture on page **A9**
[**ORIGIN:** 1500-1600 This word originally meant "shelf or table for cups."]

**cup·cake** /ˈkʌpkeɪk/ *noun*
a small cake for one person

**curb** /kɚb/ *noun*
the edge of a SIDEWALK, where it joins the road: *A big black car was parked at the curb.*

**cure** /kyʊr/ *verb*
**1** to make an illness better, so that someone is well again: *Many types of cancer can be cured.*
**2** to find a way to stop something bad from happening: *It is impossible to cure the traffic problems in the downtown area.*
—**cure** *noun* a way of making an illness go away: *Scientists have still not found a cure for the disease.*
—**curable** *adjective* if an illness is curable, it is possible to make it go away: *The infection is curable.*

**cur·few** /ˈkɚfyu/ *noun*
**1** the time by which parents tell their children they must be home at night: *My curfew is 9:00 on school nights.*
**2** the time after which the government makes people stay indoors: *There was more fighting, and the army imposed a curfew from 10 p.m. to 5 a.m.*
[**ORIGIN:** 1200-1300 From the old French word *covrefeu*, which means "signal to put out fires," from *covrir* and *feu*, which mean "to cover" and "fire." A bell used to ring to tell people to put out their fires before going to sleep.]

**cu·ri·ous** /ˈkjʊriəs/ *adjective*
**1** wanting to know or learn about something: *Children are naturally curious about the world and eager to learn.*
**2** strange or unusual: *It's a curious fact that chocolate is dangerous for dogs.*
—**curiously** *adverb* in a curious way: *"What do you mean?" she asked, looking at him curiously.*
—**curiosity** /ˌkyʊriˈɑsəti/ *noun* the feeling of being curious: *When he saw the dinosaur bones, Jack's eyes became wide with curiosity.*
[**ORIGIN:** 1300-1400 From the Latin word *curiosus*, which means "doing something with a lot of care, or trying hard to find out something."]

**WORD FAMILY: curious**
**curious** *adjective* | **curiously** *adverb* | **curiosity** *noun*

**curl¹** /kɚl/ *noun*
a piece of hair that grows in the shape of a circle: *The little girl had long blond curls.*
—**curly** *adjective* curly hair grows in curls: *My hair's straight, but Rosa's is curly.*

**curl²** *verb*
to form curves, rather than being straight: *Ivy had curled around the tree.* | *Should I curl my hair for the party?*
**PHRASAL VERB**
**curl up**
to lie or sit with your arms and legs close to your body: *She curled up under a blanket to watch TV.*

**curl·er** /ˈkɚlɚ/ *noun*
a small metal or plastic tube for making hair curl

**cur·ren·cy** [Ac] /ˈkɚənsi/ *noun* (plural **currencies**)
the type of money that a country uses: *The U.S. currency is the dollar.*
→ see Thesaurus box at **money**
[**ORIGIN:** 1600-1700 From the Latin word *currere*, which means "to flow or run." Money moves or flows between people.]

**cur·rent¹** /ˈkɚənt/ *adjective*
happening or existing now: *Who is the current president of the United States?*

**current²** *noun*
**1** a continuous movement of air or water in a particular direction: *The strong current took the boats quickly down the river.*
**2** a flow of electricity through a wire: *The electric current makes the light come on when you press the switch.*

**cur·rent·ly** /ˈkɚəntli/ *adverb*
at this time: *The school currently has about 2,000 students, an increase from last year.*
**SYNONYM: now**
→ see Thesaurus box at **now**

**cur·ric·u·lum** /kəˈrɪkyələm/ *noun* (plural **curricula** /kəˈrɪkyələ/ *or* **curriculums**)
all of the subjects that are taught at a school or college: *Science is an important part of the school's curriculum.*

**curse¹** /kɚs/ *verb*
**1** to say bad words that show you are angry: *The computer crashed again, and Kate cursed.* **SYNONYM: swear**
**2** to say or think bad things about someone or something because they have made you

angry: *I waited for the cars ahead of me to move, and cursed the heavy traffic.*

**curse²** *noun*
**1** magic words that are used to bring someone bad luck: *In the story, the witch puts a curse on the girl and says she will always be poor.*
**2** a bad word or words that you say when you are angry: *Tom dropped his glass and whispered a curse.*

**cur·sor** /ˈkɚsɚ/ *noun*
a shape you can move on a computer screen that shows where you are working: *Place the cursor at the place on the screen where you want to type.*

**cur·tain** /ˈkɚtn/ *noun*
a piece of cloth that you can pull across a window or stage: *It was getting dark outside, so I closed the bedroom curtains.* → see picture on page A8

**curve¹** /kɚv/ *noun*
a line that bends like part of a circle: *The driver was going too fast when he came to a curve in the road, and the car rolled over.*

**curve²** *verb*
to bend or move in a curve: *The road curves around to the right.* **SYNONYM: bend**
—**curved** *adjective* bending in a curve: *Buffaloes have curved horns.*

**cush·ion** /ˈkʊʃən/ *noun*
a bag filled with soft material that you sit on or rest against: *I found a quarter under the sofa cushions.* → see picture on page A8

**cus·to·di·an** /kəˈstoʊdiən/ *noun*
someone whose job is taking care of a public building: *The school custodian came in to fix the window.* **SYNONYM: janitor**

**cus·to·dy** /ˈkʌstədi/ *noun*
**1** the legal right to take care of a child: *The couple divorced, and the mother got custody of the kids.*
**2 in/into custody** = if someone is in custody, they are in prison until they go to court: *The police took two men into custody after the robbery.*

**cus·tom** /ˈkʌstəm/ *noun*
**1** something traditional that people in a society do: *It's the custom to shake someone's hand when you meet him or her for the first time.*
**2 customs** = a place where officials can search your bags when you leave or enter a country: *After the plane lands, you have to go through customs before you can leave the airport.*
[**ORIGIN:** 1100-1200 From the Latin word *consuetudo*, from *consuescere*, which means "to make someone used to something."]

**cus·tom·er** /ˈkʌstəmɚ/ *noun*
someone who buys things from a store or company: *Every day, the store serves about 800 customers.*

**cus·tom·ize** /ˈkʌstəˌmaɪz/ *verb*
to change something to make it more suitable for you, or to make it different from other things of the same type: *You can customize the T-shirt by adding your own picture.*

**cut¹** /kʌt/ *verb* (**cut**, **cutting**)
**1** to divide something using a knife or scissors: *Do you want me to cut the cake? | First, cut the paper into four pieces. | The kids were cutting pictures out of magazines.*

**THESAURUS: cut**

**Cutting Food:**

**chop** to cut meat or vegetables into pieces: *Chop the onion and add it to the pan.*

**slice** to cut bread, meat, or vegetables into thin pieces: *She sliced some tomatoes for the salad.*

**carve** to cut pieces from a large piece of cooked meat: *Dad started carving the turkey.*

**peel** to cut the outside part off fruit or vegetables: *Peel the potatoes and boil them.*

**Cutting Other Things:**

**saw** to cut wood, using a saw (=a tool with a row of sharp points): *I sawed the board in half.*

**chop** to cut something such as a tree into pieces, using an ax: *Joe was chopping wood for the fire.*

**mow** to cut grass using a special machine: *I need to mow the lawn.*

**trim** to cut off a small amount of something to make it look neater, for example hair or a bush: *I got my hair trimmed on Saturday.*

**2** to hurt yourself with a knife or something sharp: *I cut my finger on some broken glass.*
**3** to make hair or grass shorter: *I'm going to the hairdresser to get my hair cut.*
**4** to reduce the number or amount of something: *The company was forced to cut jobs.*
**5** **cut and paste** = to move writing or a picture in a computer document from one place to another
→ see Thesaurus box at **reduce**

**PHRASAL VERBS**

**cut back**
to save money by spending less than you did before: *Our food bills are pretty high, and we're trying to cut back on how much we spend.*

**cut down**
**1** to eat, drink, or use less of something than before: *Try to cut down on foods that contain a lot of fat.* | *People can cut down the amount of gas they use by driving a smaller car.*
**2** **cut something down** = to cut a tree and make it fall to the ground: *Too many trees are being cut down.*

**cut something off**
**1** to stop the supply of something such as electricity or water to a building: *For three days our electricity was cut off because of a storm.*
**2** to remove something from the main part with a knife or scissors: *Cut off all the dead flowers.*
**3** if you are cut off when you are on the telephone, the telephone stops working: *I was talking to Mom on the phone, and I got cut off.*
**4** **be cut off** = a place that is cut off is very difficult to get to because of bad roads or weather: *In the winter, the farm sometimes gets cut off by snow.*

**cut something out**
**Cut it out!/Cut that out!** (*informal*) = used for telling someone to stop doing something that is annoying you: *You're making too much noise. Cut it out!*

**cut something up**
to cut something into smaller pieces: *Cut up an onion and fry it in a pan.* **SYNONYM: chop up**

**cut²** *noun*
**1** an injury you get if something sharp cuts your skin: *She had a deep cut on her arm.*
**2** a hole in something that you make with scissors or a knife: *Make a cut in the paper.*
**3** a reduction in the amount or price of something: *Everyone had to take a cut in pay, because the company was losing money.*
→ see Thesaurus box at **injury**

**cute** /kyut/ *adjective*
**1** if a baby, small child, or animal is cute, they are attractive to look at: *a cute little boy with big brown eyes*
**2** sexually attractive: *That girl is really cute. Are you going to talk to her?*
—**cuteness** *noun* the state of being attractive
→ see Thesaurus box at **beautiful**

**cut·ler·y** /ˈkʌtləri/ *noun* (*formal*)
knives, forks, and spoons **SYNONYM: silverware**

**cy·ber·space** /ˈsaɪbɚˌspeɪs/ *noun*
the name that people use to describe where computer messages go to when they travel between computers: *I sent Chris an email, but he didn't receive it so it must have gotten lost in cyberspace.*

**cy·cle** Ac /ˈsaɪkəl/ *noun*
a set of events that happen again and again in a pattern: *We are studying the life cycle of butterflies.*
—**cyclic** /ˈsɪklɪk/ (*also* **cyclical**) *adjective* happening again and again in a pattern: *The seasons are cyclical: spring always follows winter.*
[**ORIGIN:** 1300-1400 From the Greek word *kyklos*, which means "circle or wheel."]

**cy·cling** /ˈsaɪklɪŋ/ *noun*
the activity or sport of riding a bicycle: *Unlike driving a car, cycling does not cause pollution.*
→ see picture on page **A24**

**cy·clist** /ˈsaɪklɪst/ *noun*
someone who rides a bicycle: *More than 800*

*cyclists will compete in the 100 mile race.*

**cy·clone** /ˈsaɪkloʊn/ *noun*
a very strong wind that moves fast in a circle: *The cyclone destroyed many homes.*
**SYNONYM: tornado**



**cyl·in·der** /ˈsɪləndɚ/ *noun*
**1** a shape like a tube with flat circular ends: *Cans are cylinders.* → see picture on page **A28**
**2** a part in an engine that is shaped like a tube: *The engine has six cylinders.*
—**cylindrical** /səˈlɪndrɪkəl/ *adjective* having a long round shape like a tube: *A pipe has a cylindrical shape.*
[**ORIGIN:** 1500-1600 From the Greek word *kylindros*, from *kylindein*, which means "to roll."]

**cym·bal** /ˈsɪmbəl/ *noun*
a metal musical instrument in the shape of a plate, which you hit with a stick or another cymbal to make a sound → see picture on page **A21**

**cyn·ic** /ˈsɪnɪk/ *noun*
someone who never believes that people are good or that good things will happen: *Some cynics say that people only care about money.*
—**cynical** *adjective* a cynical person never believes that people are good or that good things will happen: *Since her divorce she's been very cynical about men.*

# Dd

**D** /di/ *noun*
**1** a GRADE that you get on a test or in a class for doing work that is not very good: *You got a D on the test – you'll have to study harder.*
**2** the second note in the musical SCALE of C, or the musical KEY based on this note

**'d** /d/ *verb*
**1** the short form of "had": *He'd eaten all the cake before anyone else had a piece.*
**2** the short form of "would": *I'd love to come to the party.*

**dab** *verb*
**1** (*also* **dab at**) to lightly touch something several times, especially with a cloth: *She started to cry and dabbed at her eyes with a tissue.*
**2** to put a small amount of something on something else: *She dabbed some sunscreen on her cheeks.*

**dachs·hund** /ˈdɑkshʊnt/ *noun*
a small dog with short legs and a long body

**dad** /dæd/ *noun* (*informal*)
another word for FATHER: *My mom and dad bought me a new computer. | Dad, can I borrow $20?*

**dad·dy** /ˈdædi/ *noun* (plural **daddies**) (*informal*)
a word for FATHER used by small children: *Where's Daddy?*

**daf·fo·dil** /ˈdæfəˌdɪl/ *noun*
a yellow flower that opens in the spring

**dag·ger** /ˈdægɚ/ *noun*
a short knife used as a weapon

**dai·ly** /ˈdeɪli/ *adverb, adjective*
every day: *Try to exercise daily. | Do you get a daily newspaper?*

**dair·y** /ˈderi/ *noun*
**1** (*also* **dairy products**) foods made from milk, such as butter, cheese, and YOGURT: *She doesn't eat butter or other dairy products because they make her sick.*
**2** (plural **dairies**) a place where milk is put into bottles, and where milk is made into other foods, such as butter and cheese: *The dairy produces several types of cheese.*

**dai·sy** /ˈdeɪzi/ *noun* (plural **daisies**)
a small white flower with a yellow circle in the middle: *The field was covered with daisies.*
[**ORIGIN:** From the old English word *dægeseage*, which means "day's eye." Daisies open when the sun appears and the day starts. ]

**dal·ma·tian** /dælˈmeɪʃən/ *noun*
a large white dog with black or brown spots

**dam**

**dam** /dæm/ *noun*
a wall that is built to keep back the water in a river: *The dam broke and water from the river flooded the town.*
—**dam** *verb* to stop a river from flowing by building a dam

**dam·age**[1] /ˈdæmɪdʒ/ *noun*
if something causes damage, it breaks or destroys something: *The fire caused a lot of damage; several buildings burned down.*

**damage**[2] *verb*
to harm something, so that it is broken or destroyed: *Her car was badly damaged in the accident and she had to get a new one.*
—**damaging** *adjective* causing harm to something: *The chemicals have had damaging effects on the rivers, causing fish and plants to die.*

**damp** /dæmp/ *adjective*
a little wet: *His hair was still damp from the shower.*
—**dampness** *noun* the quality of being damp

**damp·en** /ˈdæmpən/ *verb*
to make something a little wet: *She went to the sink to dampen the cloth.*

**dance**[1] /dæns/ *verb*
to move your body to music: *Tom was dancing with a pretty girl.*
—**dancer** *noun* someone who dances: *She's a famous ballet dancer.*

**dance**[2] *noun*
**1** a set of movements that you do to music: *We did a dance in which everyone holds hands in a circle.*
**2** a party where people dance: *Are you going to the school dance?*

D

**dan·de·li·on** /ˈdændəˌlaɪən/ *noun*
a small wild plant with a yellow flower
[ORIGIN: 1400-1500 From the French word *dent de lion*, which means "lion's tooth." The leaves of dandelions have points along the edge, like a row of teeth.]

**dan·druff** /ˈdændrəf/ *noun*
dry skin that comes off your head in very small white pieces: *She bought a new shampoo to stop her dandruff.*

**dan·ger** /ˈdeɪndʒɚ/ *noun*
**1** a situation in which someone or something may be harmed or something bad may happen: *Claire knew she was in danger when she saw the snake.*

**THESAURUS: danger**
**risk** the chance that something bad may happen: *Smoking increases the risk of lung cancer.*
**hazard** something that may be dangerous or cause accidents: *Ice on the roads is a safety hazard, so drivers must be careful.*

**2** something or someone that may harm you: *Falling rocks are a danger to climbers.*

**WORD FAMILY: danger**
**danger** *noun* | **dangerous** *adjective* | **dangerously** *adverb* | **endanger** *verb*

**dan·ger·ous** /ˈdeɪndʒərəs/ *adjective*
likely to harm someone: *Police say that the man has a gun and is dangerous.*
—**dangerously** *adverb* in a way that is dangerous: *She was driving dangerously fast, and we were scared that she would crash.*

**dan·gle** /ˈdæŋgəl/ *verb*
to hang down and swing from side to side: *A bunch of keys dangled from his belt.*

**Dan·ish**[1] /ˈdeɪnɪʃ/ *adjective*
from Denmark: *a Danish scientist*
—**Dane** *noun* someone from Denmark

**Danish**[2] *noun*
the language spoken in Denmark

**dare** /der/ *verb*
**1** to be brave enough to do something: *Craig didn't dare tell his father that he had broken the window.*
**2** **dare someone to do something** = to say that someone must do something to show they are not afraid: *I dare you to jump off the roof!*
**3** **don't you dare (do something)** (*informal*) = said when telling someone that they must not do something: *Don't you dare be late!*

**dar·ing** /ˈderɪŋ/ *adjective*
if something you do is daring, it is brave or dangerous: *They made a daring escape over the walls of the prison.*

**dark**[1] /dɑrk/ *adjective*
**1** without light: *The room was dark, so I switched on the light.* ANTONYM: **light**
**2** not light in color: *My favorite color is dark blue.* | *She has dark hair.*

**WORD FAMILY: dark**
**dark** *adjective* | **dark** *noun* | **darken** *verb* | **darkness** *noun*

**dark**[2] *noun*
**1** somewhere with no light: *A lot of kids are scared of the dark, so they sleep with a light on.*
**2** the time in the evening when it stops being light: *Dad is hardly ever home before dark.*

**dark·en** /ˈdɑrkən/ *verb*
to become dark: *Clouds appeared, the sky darkened, and rain began to fall.*

**dark·ness** /ˈdɑrknəs/ *noun*
if you are in darkness, there is no light: *The lamp suddenly went out, leaving us in darkness.*

**dar·ling** /ˈdɑrlɪŋ/ *adjective*
loved a lot, or easy to love: *He is a darling little boy, always smiling.*
—**darling** *noun* used when speaking to someone you love: *Welcome home, darling.*

**dart**[1] /dɑrt/ *verb*
to move suddenly and quickly: *A cat darted across the road.*

**dart**[2] /dɑrt/ *noun*
**1** the pointed object that you throw at the board in a game of darts
**2 darts** = a game you play by throwing darts at a board with numbers on it: *They played a game of darts in the basement.*

**dash**[1] /dæʃ/ *verb*
to go somewhere very quickly: *She dashed into the bank just before it closed.*
→ see Thesaurus box at **run**[1]

**dash**[2] *noun*
**1** a short fast run: *I made a dash for the house to get my umbrella when it started to rain.*
**2** a short running race: *He won the 50-yard dash.*
**3** a mark (–) used in writing to show a pause
**4** a small amount of something, especially something that you add to food: *Add just a dash of lemon to the sauce.*

**dash·board** /ˈdæʃbɔrd/ *noun*
the part of a car with the instruments and controls on it, that is in front of the driver → see picture on page **A28**
[**ORIGIN:** 1800-1900 From an old meaning of "dash" - "to splash something." A dashboard was originally a board to stop mud splashing into a vehicle.]

**da·ta** Ac /ˈdeɪtə/ *noun* (singular **datum**)
information or facts: *Scientists are collecting data for their report on wildlife in the local area.*
[**ORIGIN:** 1600-1700 From the Latin word for "things that have been given."]

**da·ta·base** /ˈdeɪtəˌbeɪs/ *noun*
a large amount of information stored in a computer system: *The company keeps a database of customers' names, addresses, and orders.*

**date**[1] /deɪt/ *noun*
**1** a day of the month or year, shown by a number: *"What's today's date?" "It's August 11." | What's the date of the next meeting?*
**2** an arrangement to meet someone, especially a boyfriend or girlfriend, and do something together such as see a movie or go to a restaurant: *Alison went out on a date with Mark on Saturday night.*
**3 date of birth** = the day, month, and year you were born: *My date of birth is June 16, 1998.*
**4 to date** = until now: *The movie has made $16.8 million to date.*
**5 at a later date** = at a time in the future: *You will be given more details at a later date.*
**6** a small sweet sticky brown fruit → see picture on page **A13**
[**ORIGIN:** 1200-1300 Sense 6 is from the Greek word *daktylos*, which means "finger." A date is shaped like a finger.]

**date**[2] *verb*
**1** to write today's date on something: *He dated the letter May 14, 2010.*
**2** to have a boyfriend or girlfriend: *How long have you been dating Mary?*
**PHRASAL VERB**
**date from something** (*also* **date back to something**)
to have existed since a particular time: *The law dates back to the 17th century.*

**dat·ed** /ˈdeɪtɪd/ *adjective*
no longer fashionable or modern: *She bought the dress ten years ago, and it looks dated now.* **SYNONYM: old-fashioned**

**daugh·ter** /ˈdɔtɚ/ *noun*
someone's female child: *She has two daughters and one son.*

**ˈdaughter-in-law** *noun* (plural **daughters-in-law**)
the wife of someone's son: *This is my daughter-in-law, Kim – she's my son Peter's wife.*

**daunt·ed** /ˈdɔntɪd/ *adjective* (*formal*)
afraid or worried about something you have to do: *He felt daunted by all the work he had to do.*

**daunt·ing** /ˈdɔntɪŋ/ *adjective* (*formal*)
if something is daunting, it frightens or worries you because you think it will be difficult:

D

*Being captain of the team can be daunting. There's a lot of responsibility.*

**daw·dle** /ˈdɔdl/ *verb*
to do something slowly, and waste time: *Stop dawdling and get dressed – you'll be late for school!*

**dawn** /dɔn/ *noun*
the time of day when light first appears as the sun comes up: *We got up at dawn, just as it was becoming light.* **SYNONYMS: daybreak, sunrise; ANTONYM: dusk**
[**ORIGIN:** From the old English word *dagian*, which means "to become day." First used, 1200-1300.]

**day** /deɪ/ *noun*
**1** a period of 24 hours, that starts at 12 o'clock at night. There are seven days in a week: *We spent three days in Paris.* | *The letter arrived two days ago.* | *"What day is it today?" "Tuesday."* | *I saw her the day before yesterday.*
**2** the time when it is light, between morning and night: *In the summer, it gets very hot during the day.* **ANTONYM: night**
**3** the part of the day that you spend at school or at work: *The school day finishes at 3:00.*
**4 the other day** = a few days before now: *I saw Tim the other day.*
[**ORIGIN:** From the old English word *dæg*.]

**WORD FAMILY: day**
**day** *noun* | **daily** *adjective* | **daily** *adverb* | **midday** *noun*

**day·break** /ˈdeɪbreɪk/ *noun*
the time of day when light first appears **SYNONYMS: dawn, sunrise; ANTONYM: dusk**

**day·care** /ˈdeɪker/ *noun*
a place where people take care of young children during the day when their parents are at work: *Her kids are in daycare three days a week while she works.*

**day·dream** /ˈdeɪdrim/ *verb*
to think about nice things so that you forget what you should be doing: *She was day-dreaming about her boyfriend when the teacher called her name.*
—**daydream** *noun* thoughts about nice things that make you forget what you should be doing
—**daydreamer** *noun* someone who day-dreams when he or she should be working

**day·light** /ˈdeɪlaɪt/ *noun*
**1** the light that comes from the sun during the day: *He opened the curtains to let the daylight into the room.*
**2** the time in the day when it is light and easy to see: *We started our trip as soon as it was daylight.*

**ˌdaylight-ˈsavings time** *noun*
the time in spring when clocks are set one hour ahead of standard time

**day·time** /ˈdeɪtaɪm/ *noun*
the part of the day when it is light: *I can't sleep in the daytime – the sun and noise outside keep me awake.* **ANTONYM: night-time**

**daze** /deɪz/ *noun*
**in a daze** = unable to think clearly, for exam-ple because you are hurt or very surprised: *When I heard I'd won the $100,000 prize, I just sat there in a daze.*

**dazed** /deɪzd/ *adjective*
unable to think clearly, for example because you are hurt or very surprised: *He had fallen off his bike, and he looked a little dazed.*

**daz·zle** /ˈdæzəl/ *verb*
**1** to make you admire someone or something a lot: *We were dazzled by her talent and charm.*
**2** if a bright light dazzles you, it makes it difficult for you to see clearly: *The lights suddenly came on, dazzling us.*

**daz·zling** /ˈdæzlɪŋ/ *adjective*
**1** very impressive or attractive: *The dancers gave a dazzling performance.*
**2** a dazzling light is so bright that you cannot see clearly for a short time: *We walked out of the dark movie theater into the dazzling sun-shine.*

**DC** *noun*
(**direct current**) a flow of electricity that moves in one direction only. It is the type of electric current that comes from BATTERIES.

**D.C.**
(**District of Columbia**) the area containing the city of Washington, the capital of the U.S.

**dead**[1] /ded/ *adjective*

**1** no longer alive: *Her mother is dead. She died about five years ago.*

**2** a machine or piece of equipment that is dead is not working because there is no power: *The car won't start – the battery is completely dead.*

**3** complete or exact: *Everyone stopped talking at once, and there was dead silence.* | *He hit the target dead center.*

**4** with nothing happening: *The town is dead after 9 o'clock – nothing is open.*

**dead**[2] *adverb* (*informal*)

very: *I was dead tired after going for a long run.*

**dead**[3] *noun*

**1** **the dead** = people who are dead: *Among the dead was the driver of the truck involved in the accident.* **ANTONYM: the living**

**2** **in the dead of winter/night** = in the middle of winter or in the middle of the night

**ˈdead end** *noun*

**1** a street with no way out at one end: *The street is a dead end, with the river at the bottom.*

**2** a situation from which no progress is possible: *The discussions reached a dead end because the two groups couldn't agree.*

**dead·line** /ˈdedlaɪn/ *noun*

the date or time by which you must do something or finish something: *The deadline for the homework is Wednesday, but I'm going to finish before then.*

**dead·ly** /ˈdedli/ *adjective* (**deadlier**, **deadliest**)

something that is deadly can kill you: *Deadly weapons such as guns and knives are commonly carried by gang members.*

**deaf** /def/ *adjective*

**1** not able to hear: *He was born deaf and learned sign language as a child.*

**2** **the deaf** = people who are deaf

—**deafness** *noun* the state of not being able to hear

**deaf·en** /ˈdefən/ *verb*

if a loud noise deafens you, it makes it difficult for you to hear: *The noise of the explosion deafened us.*

—**deafening** *adjective* very loud: *When the team scored, the shouts of the crowd were deafening.*

**deal**[1] /dil/ *noun*

**1** an agreement: *The company made a deal to open 30 stores in China.*

**2** **a great deal/a good deal** = a lot: *The students have learned a great deal this year.*

**3** **make a big deal out of something** (*informal*) = to make something seem more important than it really is: *He had a tiny cut on his arm, but he was making a big deal out of it.*

**4** **no big deal** (*informal*) = not very important: *So you lost one game. That's no big deal.*

**5** if it is your deal, it is your turn to give out cards to players in a card game: *It's your deal, John.*

**6** the way someone is treated: *Girls wanted a fair deal. They wanted to have the same opportunities to play sports that boys had.*

**deal**[2] *verb* (**dealt** /delt/)

to give cards to each player in a card game: *Deal three cards to each player.*

**PHRASAL VERBS**

**deal in something**

to buy and sell a product: *The store deals in jewelry.*

**deal with someone/something**

**1** if you deal with a problem, you do something to stop it: *We have to find new ways to deal with the problem of pollution.*

**2** to be about a subject: *The movie deals with the friendship of three boys.*

**3** to do business with someone: *We've been dealing with their company for ten years.*

**deal·er** /ˈdilɚ/ *noun*

**1** the person who gives out the cards in a card game: *The dealer gives each player five cards.*

**2** someone who buys and sells things: *He is an art dealer who sells mainly paintings and sculptures by Mexican artists.*

—**dealership** *noun* a business that sells a company's product, especially cars: *He owns a used car dealership.*

**dealt** /delt/ *verb*

the past tense and past participle of DEAL

**dean** /din/ *noun*

a university or college official with a high rank

**dear**[1] /dɪr/ *interjection*
**oh dear** = you say this when something bad happens: *Oh dear! We're going to be late.*

**dear**[2] *noun*
you say this to someone you like or love: *Thank you, dear.*

**dear**[3] *adjective*
**1 Dear** = used to begin a letter, before someone's name or title: *Dear Sue, Thank you for the present.*
**2** a dear friend or relative is very important to you and you love him or her very much: *Mark became a dear friend.*

D

**death** /deθ/ *noun*
**1** the end of someone's life: *The sudden death of his mother was a terrible shock.* **ANTONYM: birth**
**2 scared to death/bored to death** = very frightened or bored: *She was scared to death when she saw the snake.*

**'death ˌpenalty** *noun*
the legal punishment of killing someone who is guilty of a serious crime: *He got the death penalty for killing a police officer.*

**de·bat·a·ble** [Ac] /dɪˈbeɪtəbəl/ *adjective*
something that is debatable is not certain because people have different opinions about it: *It's debatable whether this book is as good as the last one she wrote.*

**de·bate**[1] [Ac] /dɪˈbeɪt/ *noun*
**1** discussion of a subject, that often continues for a long time and in which people express different opinions: *There has been a lot of debate in the newspapers about the new law – a lot of people support it, but many also oppose it.*
**2** a formal discussion of a subject, in which people take turns expressing different opinions: *He took part in a college debate on healthcare.*
[**ORIGIN:** 1200-1300 From the old French word *batre*, which means "to hit."]

**debate**[2] [Ac] *verb*
**1** to think about something carefully before making a decision: *I'm still debating what to do. I just can't decide.*
**2** to discuss a subject formally so that you can make a decision or solve a problem: *The Senate will debate the bill on Monday before taking a vote.*

**deb·it** /ˈdebɪt/ *noun*
an amount of money that is taken out of your bank account: *Your bank statement shows all your debits and credits.* **ANTONYM: credit**
—**debit** *verb* to take money out of your bank account: *$25 has been debited from your account.*

**de·bris** /dɪˈbri/ *noun*
the pieces of something that are left after an accident or explosion: *The streets were full of debris after the bombing.*

**debt** /det/ *noun*
**1** money that you owe: *She borrowed money from her parents, but she paid back all her debts within two years.*
**2** if you are in debt, you owe money to people: *When he lost his job, he got in debt very quickly.*
[**ORIGIN:** 1200-1300 From the Latin word *debitum*, from *debere*, which means "to owe."]

**debt·or** /ˈdetɚ/ *noun*
someone who owes money

**de·but** /deɪˈbyu/ *noun*
the first time that someone performs in public: *He made his debut as a movie actor in 1995, and he has appeared in many movies since then.*
[**ORIGIN:** 1700-1800 From the French word *début*, which means "start."]

**dec·ade** [Ac] /ˈdekeɪd/ *noun*
a period of ten years: *My grandparents came to the U.S. four decades ago.*
[**ORIGIN:** 1400-1500 From the Greek word *deka*, which means "ten."]

**de·caf·fein·at·ed** /diˈkæfəˌneɪtəd/ (*also* **de·caf** /ˈdikæf/ (*informal*)) *adjective*
decaffeinated drinks do not contain CAFFEINE: *decaffeinated coffee*

**de·cay**[1] /dɪˈkeɪ/ *verb*
**1** if something decays, natural chemical processes slowly destroy it: *As the dead leaves decay, they put nutrients back into the soil.*
**2** if buildings, structures, or areas decay, their condition slowly becomes worse: *The old hospital has been empty for years and is starting to decay.*
[**ORIGIN:** 1400-1500 From the Latin word *decadere*, which means "to fall or sink."]

**decay**[2] *noun*
**1** a natural process in which something

slowly becomes destroyed: *Brushing your teeth helps prevent tooth decay.*
**2** a process in which the condition of something slowly becomes worse: *Over the years, the area fell into decay and many abandoned houses were burnt down.*

**de·ceased** /dɪˈsist/ *adjective* (*formal*)
dead: *She still spoke often about her deceased husband.*

**de·ceit** /dɪˈsit/ *noun*
behavior that is not honest, especially saying things that are not true: *She suspected him of deceit, but could not understand why he would lie to her.*
—**deceitful** *adjective* not honest
—**deceitfully** *adverb* in a dishonest way

**de·ceive** /dɪˈsiv/ *verb*
to make someone believe something that is not true: *You cannot deceive me; I know that you did not write the essay you turned in.*
→ see Thesaurus box at **lie**[2]

**WORD FAMILY: deceive**
**deceive** *verb* | **deception** *noun* | **deceit** *noun* | **deceitful** *adjective* | **deceptive** *adjective*

**De·cem·ber** /dɪˈsembɚ/ *noun* (*written abbreviation*: **Dec.**)
the 12th month of the year, between November and January: *Her birthday is on December 6.* | *They got married in December.* | *We went to Mexico last December.*
[**ORIGIN:** probably 1000-1100 From the Latin word *decem*, which means "ten." December was the tenth and last month of the old Roman calendar.]

**de·cen·cy** /ˈdisənsi/ *noun*
polite and morally good behavior that shows respect for other people: *It's common decency to answer when you have been asked a question.*

**de·cent** /ˈdisənt/ *adjective*
**1** acceptable and good enough: *The food at the restaurant is decent, and it's not too expensive.*
**2** decent people are good and honest: *He is a decent man who cares about other people.*

**de·cent·ly** /ˈdisəntli/ *adverb*
**1** in a way that is acceptable and good enough: *I don't need a lot of money, just a decently paid job.*
**2** in a way that treats people fairly and kindly: *He's always treated me decently, so I can't complain.*

**de·cep·tion** /dɪˈsepʃən/ *noun*
dishonest behavior, especially saying things that are not true: *She thought he was lying, and his deception made her angry.*

**de·cep·tive** /dɪˈseptɪv/ *adjective* (*formal*)
something that is deceptive makes people believe something that is not true: *The ad is deceptive because the toy doesn't come with all the things pictured.*
—**deceptively** *adverb* in a deceptive way

**dec·i·bel** /ˈdesəˌbel/ *noun*
a unit for measuring how loud something is: *The music was being played at more than 100 decibels.*

**de·cide** /dɪˈsaɪd/ *verb*
**1** to choose what you are going to do, after thinking about it: *I decided to stay home instead of going to the movie.* | *Ted decided (that) the car would cost too much.*

**THESAURUS: decide**
**make up your mind** to decide what to do, after thinking about it for a long time: *Have you made up your mind about which college you want to go to?*
**choose** to decide what you want out of a number of things: *We each chose a different kind of ice cream.*
**resolve** (*formal*) to decide that you will definitely do something in the future: *She resolved to work hard and not disappoint her parents.*
**rule** to make an official decision about something: *The judge ruled that he was guilty.*
**conclude** to decide that something is true, based on the facts that you know: *When he refused to answer questions, detectives concluded that he was hiding something.*

**2** to be the reason why something has a particular result: *One goal decided the game, and we won by a point.*

PHRASAL VERB
**decide on something**
to choose one thing from many possible choices: *Have you decided on a name for the baby?*

**WORD FAMILY: decide**
**decide** *verb* | **decision** *noun* | **decisive** *adjective* | **indecisive** *adjective*

D

**de·cid·u·ous** /dɪˈsɪdʒuəs/ *adjective*
a deciduous tree loses its leaves in winter: *Maple trees are deciduous.* **ANTONYM: evergreen**

**dec·i·mal¹** /ˈdesəməl/ *noun*
a number such as 0.8 or 2.63. A decimal can be a FRACTION, or a whole number and a fraction, written with a decimal point.
[**ORIGIN:** 1600-1700 From the Latin word *decem*, which means "ten."]

**decimal²** *adjective*
the decimal system is based on the number ten

**ˌdecimal ˈpoint** *noun*
a mark (.) used in decimal numbers. The numbers after this mark are tenths, hundredths, etc.

**de·ci·sion** /dɪˈsɪʒən/ *noun*
a choice that you make: *He made the decision to study biology in college.*

**de·ci·sive** /dɪˈsaɪsɪv/ *adjective*
**1** good at making decisions quickly: *As a manager, you need to be decisive and get things done.* **ANTONYM: indecisive**
**2** an action or event that is decisive has a big effect on the way that something develops: *They won a decisive victory that led to the end of the war.*
—**decisively** *adverb* in a decisive way

**deck** /dek/ *noun*
**1** a wooden floor built outside at the back of a house: *In the summer, we often eat dinner on the deck.*
**2** a set of playing cards that you play games with: *a deck of cards*
**3** one of the levels on a ship: *Here's a picture of my father standing on deck in his navy uniform.*

**dec·la·ra·tion** /ˌdekləˈreɪʃən/ *noun*
an important announcement that says you intend to do something: *Congress has the power to make a declaration of war.*

**de·clare** /dɪˈkler/ *verb*
to say officially what will happen or what you have decided: *The U.S. declared war on England in 1812.*
[**ORIGIN:** 1300-1400 From the Latin word *clarare*, which means "to make clear."]

**de·cline¹** Ac /dɪˈklaɪn/ *verb*
**1** to become fewer in number: *The number of new cars sold declined by 5% last year.*
**2** to become worse: *Her health declined rapidly, and she died two weeks later.*
**3** (*formal*) to say no to an invitation, offer, or request, usually politely: *Mary declined Jay's invitation to dinner.*
→ see Thesaurus box at **decrease¹**, **reject**

**decline²** Ac *noun* (*formal*)
a situation in which something becomes fewer, less, or worse: *There has been a decline in the company's profits since last year, and the company is going to lay off workers.*

**de·com·pose** /ˌdikəmˈpoʊz/ *verb*
to be slowly destroyed by a natural process: *A dead fish was decomposing on the beach.*
—**decomposition** /ˌdikɑmpəˈzɪʃən/ *noun* the process of decomposing

**de·con·tam·i·nate** /ˌdikənˈtæməˌneɪt/ *verb*
to remove a dangerous substance from somewhere: *After an attack using chemical weapons, the army had to decontaminate the area.*
—**decontamination** /ˌdikənˈtæməˌneɪʃən/ *noun* the process of decontaminating something

**dec·o·rate** /ˈdekəˌreɪt/ *verb*
**1** to make something look more attractive by adding pretty things to it: *We decorated the room with balloons for the birthday party.*
**2** (*formal*) to give someone an official sign of honor, such as a MEDAL: *The soldiers were decorated for their bravery.*

**decorate**

**—decorative** /ˈdekərətɪv/ *adjective* (*formal*) pretty and used to make something look more attractive: *a decorative frame on the mirror*

**dec·o·ra·tion** /ˌdekəˈreɪʃən/ *noun*
**1** a pretty thing that you use to make something look more attractive: *We use the same decorations every Christmas – this Santa statue was my grandma's.*
**2** something such as a MEDAL that is given to someone as an official sign of honor: *He received a decoration for bravery in the war.*

**de·crease¹** /dɪˈkris/ *verb*
to become fewer or less: *The number of tigers in the wild has decreased steadily.* **ANTONYM: increase**

**THESAURUS: decrease**

**go down** to become lower or less in level, amount, size, quality, etc.: *The price of computers has gone down.*

**drop** to become lower in level or amount: *His grades have dropped from A's and B's to mainly C's.*

**fall** to decrease to a lower level or amount: *Temperatures fell below zero last night.*

**plummet** to suddenly and quickly become lower: *Sales of the car have plummeted.*

**diminish** (*formal*) to become smaller or less important: *The number of accidents has diminished since the new lights were put in.*

**decline** (*formal*) to become smaller or weaker: *Sales of the product declined 3 percent last year.*

→ see Thesaurus box at **reduce**

**[ORIGIN:** 1300-1400 From the Latin words *de* and *crescere*, which mean "down" and "to grow."**]**

**de·crease²** /ˈdikris/ *noun*
the process of becoming less, or the amount by which something becomes less: *There has been a recent decrease in crime, with fewer thefts being reported than last year.* **ANTONYM: increase**

**de·crep·it** /dɪˈkrepɪt/ *adjective*
old and in bad condition: *The buildings were old and decrepit and needed repair.*

**ded·i·cate** /ˈdedəˌkeɪt/ *verb*
**1** to say publicly that you wrote a book or song for someone you love or respect: *She dedicated the book to her husband.*
**2** if you dedicate yourself to something, you give it a lot of time and effort: *She dedicated her life to God and became a nun.*

**ded·i·cat·ed** /ˈdedəˌkeɪtɪd/ *adjective*
someone who is dedicated works very hard at something because it is important to them: *The school has many dedicated teachers who want to help the children succeed.*

**ded·i·ca·tion** /ˌdedəˈkeɪʃən/ *noun*
**1** a situation in which you work very hard because you believe that what you are doing is important: *Professional musicians practice for many hours every day, so that job really takes dedication.*
**2** the words used to show that something has been written, performed, or built for a particular person: *The dedication at the front of the book says, "To my wife, Mary."*

**de·duce** /dɪˈdus/ *verb*
to decide that something is true, using the information you have: *From the fossil shells, you can deduce that these mountains were once under water.*

**de·duct** Ac /dɪˈdʌkt/ *verb* (*formal*)
to take an amount away from a larger amount: *Income tax payments are deducted from your salary.*
**—deductible** *adjective* if an amount of money is deductible, you can take that amount of money away from the amount of tax you have to pay, so that you pay less tax

**de·duc·tion** /dɪˈdʌkʃən/ *noun*
**1** an amount that is taken away from a larger amount: *After deductions for tax, his salary is about $2,500 a month.*
**2** the process of finding the truth, using the information you have: *A detective solves crimes by looking at the clues and using deduction.*

**deed** /did/ *noun*
**1** (*formal*) an action, especially if it is very good or very bad: *A Boy Scout is supposed to do a good deed every day, such as helping someone.*
**2** a legal document that says who owns a

house or land: *She holds the deed to the land, so it belongs to her.*

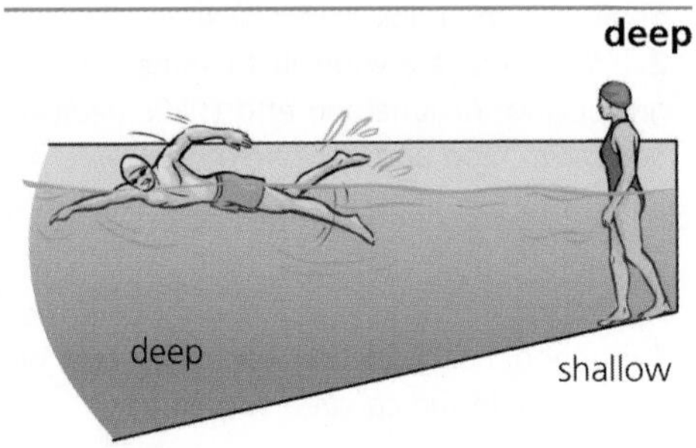


**deep**[1] /dip/ *adjective*
**1** something that is deep goes down a long way: *The path was covered in deep snow that went up to my knees.* | *a deep lake* **ANTONYM: shallow**
**2** used for talking about the distance from the top to the bottom of something: *The pool is eight feet deep.*
**3** going far in from the outside or from the front edge of something: *Terry had a deep cut in his forehead.*
**4** a deep feeling or belief is very strong: *He felt a deep love for his children and would do anything for them.*
**5** a deep sound is very low: *She had a deep voice, almost as low as a man's.*
**6** a deep color is dark and strong: *The bush has red berries and deep green leaves.* **ANTONYMS: light, pale**
**7** serious and often difficult to understand: *The two professors were having a deep conversation about philosophy.*
**8** **deep sleep** = if someone is in a deep sleep, it is difficult to wake him or her
**9** **be in deep trouble** (*informal*) = to be in serious trouble or in an extremely difficult situation: *You're going to be in deep trouble when I tell Mom what you did.*
**10** **deep in thought/conversation** = thinking or talking so much that you do not notice anything else: *I was deep in thought and didn't hear her when she said "hello."*
**11** **take a deep breath** = to breathe a lot of air into your body: *She took a deep breath and began to sing.*

**deep**[2] *adverb*
a long way into or below the surface of something: *Joe shoved his hands deep into his pockets.*

**deep·en** /ˈdipən/ *verb* (*formal*)
**1** to become deeper: *The pool deepens at one end.* | *My love for her has deepened over the years.*
**2** if a serious situation deepens, it becomes worse: *The country's economic problems deepened and the number of people without jobs increased.*

**ˈdeep-fry** (*also* **deep fry**) *verb*
to cook food in a lot of hot oil: *Cut the potatoes into slices and deep-fry them.*
—**deep-fried** *adjective* cooked in a lot of hot oil: *deep-fried chicken*

**deep·ly** /ˈdipli/ *adverb*
extremely or very much: *I was deeply sorry to hear that your sister had died.*

**deer** /dɪr/ *noun* (plural **deer**)
a large wild animal with thin legs and a short tail. Deer live in forests, eat plants, and run fast: *Male deer have large horns called antlers.*
[**ORIGIN:** From the old English word *deor*, which means "animal."]

**de·fault**[1] /dɪˈfɔlt/ *noun*
**1** **by default** = if you win a game or competition by default, you win because your opponent did not play or there were no other competitors: *The other team didn't show up, so we won by default.*
**2** the thing or things your computer will use unless you tell it to use something else: *Blue is the default for the screen background, but you can change the color if you want.*
**3** the action of not paying back money that you owe, or not doing something that a legal agreement says you must do: *The default of a loan can lead to legal problems.*

**default**[2] *verb*
to not pay back money that you owe or to not do something you are legally supposed to do: *He defaulted on his loan payments, and the bank took his car.*

**de·feat**[1] /dɪˈfit/ *verb*
to beat someone in a game, war, or election: *Our soccer team was defeated by 3 goals to 2.*
→ see Thesaurus box at **win**[1]

**defeat²** *noun*
a time when you do not win or succeed: *The team suffered a 7–0 defeat in their most recent game.* **SYNONYM: loss**; **ANTONYM: victory**

**de·fect¹** /ˈdifekt/ *noun (formal)*
a problem in the way something is made, so that it does not work correctly or it looks wrong: *A defect in the way the bed is made means that a child's head could get caught between the bars.*

**de·fect²** /dɪˈfekt/ *verb*
to leave your own country or group and go to an opposing one: *His parents defected to the U.S. from Russia.*
—**defector** *noun* someone who defects
—**defection** /dɪˈfekʃən/ *noun* the act of defecting

**de·fec·tive** /dɪˈfektɪv/ *adjective*
a defective machine or product is not made correctly or does not work correctly: *The car's brakes were defective and caused a terrible accident.*

**de·fend** /dɪˈfend/ *verb*
**1** to protect someone or something from attack: *The soldiers were defending the town from attack by the enemy.*
**2** to say something to support an idea or action that other people do not like: *The coach defended his decision not to let the boy play after he had been caught smoking.*
**3** to try to stop the other team from scoring points: *The main job of the goalie is to defend the goal.*
—**defender** *noun* someone who defends someone or something
[**ORIGIN:** 1200-1300 From the Latin words *de* and *fendere*, which mean "off" and "to hit."]

**WORD FAMILY: defend**
**defend** *verb* | **defense** *noun* | **defender** *noun* | **defenseless** *adjective* | **defensive** *adjective* | **defensive** *noun*

**de·fend·ant** /dɪˈfendənt/ *noun*
the person in a court of law who has been ACCUSEd of a crime: *The defendant says that he is innocent and did not steal the money.*

**de·fense** /dɪˈfens/ *noun*
**1** something that protects someone or something from attack or criticism: *The body has natural defenses against illnesses, but some viruses will still get through.* | *The senator spoke in defense of the health care bill.*
**2** the weapons, people, and systems that a country uses to protect itself from attack: *Modern weapons and a well-trained army and navy provide us with a good defense.*
**3** /ˈdifens/ the players on a sports team whose job is to try to prevent the other team from scoring points: *Our defense did a good job – the other team only scored 12 points.*
**4 the defense** = the lawyers in a court of law who try to show that someone is not guilty of a crime: *The defense tried to prove that the woman is innocent of the crime.*

**de·fense·less** /dɪˈfenslɪs/ *adjective*
unable to protect yourself: *The ship was defenseless against the attack by submarines.*

**de·fen·sive¹** /dɪˈfensɪv/ *adjective*
**1** trying to defend yourself because you think someone is criticizing you: *She got really defensive when I asked her why she was late.*
**2** used for defending someone or something: *The rockets are defensive weapons which will only be used if we are attacked.*
—**defensively** *adverb* in a defensive way
—**defensiveness** *noun* the state of defending someone or something

**defensive²** *noun*
**on the defensive** = behaving in a way that shows that you think that someone is criticizing you, even if they are not: *I knew she'd be mad, so I was on the defensive before she even said anything.*

**de·fer** /dɪˈfɚ/ *verb* (**deferred**, **deferring**) *(formal)*
to delay something until a later date: *The committee has deferred its decision until next week.*

**de·fi·ant** /dɪˈfaɪənt/ *adjective*
refusing to obey someone: *The man was defiant and refused to cooperate with the police.*
—**defiantly** *adverb* in a defiant way
—**defiance** *noun* behavior in which you refuse to obey someone: *The students were told to leave the school because of their defiance of the rules.*

**de·fi·cient** /dɪˈfɪʃənt/ *adjective* (*formal*)
not having or containing enough of something: *The judge was found to be deficient in his knowledge of the law, and he lost his position.*
—**deficiency** *noun* the state of not having enough of something: *Vitamin deficiencies can cause serious illness.*

D

**def·i·cit** /ˈdefəsɪt/ *noun*
the difference between the amount of money that you have and the higher amount that you need: *The government wants to increase taxes to reduce the budget deficit.* **ANTONYM: surplus**

**de·fine** Ac /dɪˈfaɪn/ *verb*
**1** to explain the exact meaning of a word: *A "lie" can be defined as "something that you say that is not true."*
**2** to say exactly what something is: *The school curriculum defines what teachers ought to teach and what students should learn.*
[**ORIGIN:** 1300-1400 From the Latin word *finire*, which means "to put a limit or set a boundary."]

**def·i·nite** Ac /ˈdefɪnət/ *adjective*
**1** certain and not likely to change: *I asked her if she wanted to see him, and her answer was a definite "no."*
**2** clear and noticeable: *His English is showing definite signs of improvement, and he can speak it quite well now.*

**ˌdefinite ˈarticle** *noun*
the word "the"

**def·i·nite·ly** Ac /ˈdefɪnətli/ *adverb*
certainly or without any doubt: *There's definitely something wrong with the car – the engine won't start.* | *"Are you going to be there?" "Definitely."*

**def·i·ni·tion** Ac /ˌdefəˈnɪʃən/ *noun*
an explanation of what a word means, especially one in a dictionary: *Look up the definition of "insect" in the dictionary.*

**de·fin·i·tive** Ac /dɪˈfɪnətɪv/ *adjective* (*formal*)
a definitive thing, such as a book or a description, is so good that there cannot be a better one: *He wrote the definitive book on the Civil War. All other researchers rely on his work.*

**de·for·es·ta·tion** /diˌfɔrəˈsteɪʃən/ *noun*
the action of cutting down or burning down all the trees in an area: *The deforestation occurred because people wanted to clear the land for farming.*
—**deforest** /diˈfɔrɪst/ *verb* to cut down or burn down all the trees in an area

**de·formed** /dɪˈfɔrmd/ *adjective*
if part of someone's body is deformed, it has the wrong shape: *He was born with a deformed foot and had to wear a special shoe.*
—**deformity** *noun* (*formal*) a condition in which part of your body is deformed: *people with physical deformities*

**de·fraud** /dɪˈfrɔd/ *verb* (*formal*)
to trick someone in order to get money from them: *The businessman defrauded his clients of over $5 million before he was arrested.*

**de·frost** /dɪˈfrɔst/ *verb*
to put frozen food in a warmer place, until it is not frozen anymore: *It is safest to defrost food in the refrigerator because it will stay cold enough to kill bacteria.*

**de·fy** /dɪˈfaɪ/ *verb* (**defies**, **defied**)
to refuse to obey someone or something: *He defied his parents and went to the party even though they had said he could not go.*
→ see Thesaurus box at **disobey**

**de·grade** /diˈgreɪd/ *verb* (*formal*)
to treat people or animals very badly, in a way that shows no respect for them: *Treating prisoners like animals degrades them.*

**de·grad·ing** /dɪˈgreɪdɪŋ/ *adjective*
treating someone badly and making that person lose respect for himself or herself: *Magazines with nude pictures of women are degrading.*

**de·gree** /dɪˈgri/ *noun*
**1** a unit for measuring temperature: *It's very cold today. The temperature is only about 20 degrees Fahrenheit.*
**2** a unit for measuring an angle: *The angles of a triangle add up to 180 degrees.*
**3** an official statement that says you have successfully completed all your studies at a university or college: *Ryan has a degree in chemistry.*
**4** the level or amount of something: *The two musicians showed a high degree of talent.*
[**ORIGIN:** 1200-1300 From the old French word *degré*, from the Latin word *gradus*, which means "step."]

**de·hy·drat·ed** /diˈhaɪˌdreɪtɪd/ *adjective*
if you are dehydrated, you do not have enough water in your body: *Some of the runners had not drunk enough and were becoming dehydrated.*
—**dehydration** /ˌdihaɪˈdreɪʃən/ *noun* the state of being dehydrated

**de·lay**[1] /dɪˈleɪ/ *verb* (**delayed**, **delays**)
**1** to make someone or something late: *Our flight was delayed by bad weather, and we arrived in New York one hour late.*
**2** to wait until a later time to do something: *The meeting has been delayed until next week.*

**delay**[2] *noun* (plural **delays**)
if there is a delay, something happens later than you planned or expected: *After three months' delay, work finally began on the new building.*

**del·e·gate**[1] /ˈdeləgət/ *noun*
someone who represents a country or group at a meeting: *Delegates from each college meet once a year at a conference.*

**delegate**[2] *verb*
to give part of your work to someone: *When you delegate work, you expect that it will be done.*

**del·e·ga·tion** /ˌdeləˈgeɪʃən/ *noun*
a group of people that represents an organization and goes somewhere to take part in discussions: *A delegation of American business leaders is visiting China to try to increase trade between the two countries.*

**de·lete** /dɪˈlit/ *verb*
to remove parts of a piece of writing, or to remove a whole computer document: *Some files had been deleted from my computer, and I lost some of my work.*
—**deletion** /dɪˈliʃən/ *noun* the act of deleting something
[**ORIGIN:** 1400-1500 From the Latin word *deletus*, a form of the verb *delere*, which means "to destroy."]

**del·i** /ˈdeli/ *noun*
a small store that sells food such as cheese, cooked meat, and bread, and sometimes sandwiches **SYNONYM: delicatessen**

**de·lib·er·ate**[1] /dɪˈlɪbərət/ *adjective*
planned and intended: *He ignored me, and it felt like a deliberate attempt to insult me.*
[**ORIGIN:** 1400-1500 From the Latin word *deliberare*, which means "to weigh up in the mind," from *libra*, the word for a "scale."]

**de·lib·e·rate**[2] /dɪˈlɪbəˌreɪt/ *verb* (*formal*)
to think about something very carefully or talk about it carefully with other people: *The jury has been deliberating for two days about whether she is guilty.*

**de·lib·er·ate·ly** /dɪˈlɪbərətli/ *adverb*
if you did something deliberately, you intended to do it, and it was not an accident: *He deliberately tripped the other runner, so that he could win.* **SYNONYM: on purpose**

**del·i·ca·cy** /ˈdelɪkəsi/ *noun* (plural **delicacies**)
something good to eat that is expensive or rare: *In France, snails are considered a delicacy.*

**del·i·cate** /ˈdelɪkət/ *adjective*
**1** easily damaged or broken: *Some of the glass ornaments were old and delicate.*
**2** needing great care in order not to upset people: *The situation is delicate – I don't want to upset his parents, but I'm worried that he is becoming depressed.*
**3** small and beautiful: *She had a delicate face and pretty green eyes.*

**del·i·ca·tes·sen** /ˌdelɪkəˈtesən/ *noun*
a small store that sells food such as cheese, cooked meat, and bread, and sometimes sandwiches **SYNONYM: deli**

**de·li·cious** /dɪˈlɪʃəs/ *adjective*
delicious food tastes very good: *This pie is delicious! Can I have another slice?*
→ see Thesaurus box at **taste**[1]
[**ORIGIN:** 1200-1300 From the Latin word *delicere*, which means "to attract."]

**de·light**[1] /dɪˈlaɪt/ *noun*
**1** great pleasure: *She laughed with delight when she opened her birthday present.*
**2** something that is very enjoyable: *Her grandchildren are a delight to her.*

**delight**[2] *verb* (*formal*)
to give someone great pleasure: *Her books delight readers all over the world.*

**de·light·ed** /dɪˈlaɪtɪd/ *adjective* (*formal*)
very happy or pleased: *His parents are delighted with his progress at school.*
→ see Thesaurus box at **happy**

D

**de·light·ful** /dɪˈlaɪtfəl/ *adjective*
very nice: *The park was a delightful place, full of flowers.*
—**delightfully** *adverb* in a very nice way

**de·lin·quent** /dɪˈlɪŋkwənt/ *adjective*
a delinquent child or young person behaves very badly or does illegal things
—**delinquent** *noun* a child or young person who behaves very badly or does illegal things: *a school for juvenile delinquents*

D

**de·lir·i·ous** /dɪˈlɪriəs/ *adjective*
confused and having strange ideas because you are very sick: *He was delirious with fever and did not recognize me.*

**de·liv·er** /dɪˈlɪvɚ/ *verb*
1 to take a letter or package somewhere: *Every morning, the mailman delivers letters to the houses.*
2 **deliver a speech/lecture** = to make a speech to a group of people: *The president will deliver the speech on television tomorrow evening.*
3 **deliver a baby** = to give birth to a baby or to help a woman give birth to a baby: *They rushed her to the hospital where she delivered her baby.*
4 to do what you have promised to do: *Will he deliver on his promise to help us?*
→ see Thesaurus box at **take**
[ORIGIN: 1200-1300 From the Latin word *liberare*, which means "to set free."]

**de·liv·er·y** /dɪˈlɪvəri/ *noun* (plural **deliveries**)
1 the act of bringing something to a place or person, or something that is brought: *Delivery of a package usually takes two days.* | *The supermarket is expecting a delivery of frozen food this afternoon.*
2 the process of a baby being born

**del·ta** /ˈdeltə/ *noun*
a place where a large river spreads out and often divides into smaller rivers, before the water flows into the ocean: *The Mississippi River delta is on the Gulf of Mexico.*

**del·uge¹** /ˈdelyudʒ/ *noun* (*formal*)
1 a large amount of things that someone gets at the same time, and has to deal with: *The company received a deluge of applications for the job – about 5,000 emails and letters.*
2 very heavy rain or a flood: *Several homes were flooded in the country's worst deluge for many years.*

**deluge²** *verb* (*formal*)
to send a lot of things to someone which they have to deal with: *The radio station was deluged with complaints about the program.*

**de·luxe** /dɪˈlʌks/ *adjective*
very good and expensive: *The winner of the competition will get two nights in a deluxe hotel in Los Angeles.*

**delve** /delv/ *verb*
PHRASAL VERB
**delve into something**
to search for more information about someone or something: *When he suddenly became famous, reporters began delving into his past to find out more about him.*

**de·mand¹** /dɪˈmænd/ *noun*
1 if there is a demand for something, people want to buy it: *Tickets for the concert are in great demand – everyone wants them.*
2 a strong request: *In 1920, politicians listened to women's demands and gave them the right to vote.*
[ORIGIN: 1300-1400 From the Latin word *mandare*, which means "to order."]

**demand²** *verb*
1 to ask for something in a strong way: *The man pulled out a gun and demanded money.*
2 to need a skill or quality: *Learning a language demands a lot of effort.*
→ see Thesaurus box at **ask**

**de·mand·ing** /dɪˈmændɪŋ/ *adjective*
1 needing a lot of time, skill, or effort: *She has a demanding job as a nurse and has to work long hours.*
2 wanting good work or a lot of attention: *The coach was very demanding. We started practice every day at 7:00 a.m.*

**de·mands** /dɪˈmændz/ *plural noun*
the things that you need to do, that are difficult or take up your time: *The demands of schoolwork increase as you get older.*

**de·moc·ra·cy** /dɪˈmɑkrəsi/ *noun* (plural **democracies**)
**1** a system in which the people of a country can choose the government by voting: *The protesters want to get rid of the dictator and bring democracy to the country.*
**2** a country which has democracy: *We live in a democracy.*
→ see Thesaurus box at **government**
[ORIGIN: 1500-1600 From the Greek words *demos* and *kratos*, which mean "people" and "power or rule."]

**WORD FAMILY: democracy**
**democracy** *noun* | **democrat** *noun* | **democratic** *adjective* | **democratically** *adverb*

**Dem·o·crat** /ˈdeməˌkræt/ *noun*
a member of the Democratic Party: *Most Democrats support the bill.*

**dem·o·crat·ic** /ˌdeməˈkrætɪk/ *adjective*
**1** a democratic country or system is one in which everyone has the right to vote in order to choose the government or make decisions: *Education is important in a democratic society. People need to be informed to vote.*
**2 Democratic** = relating or belonging to the Democratic Party: *the Democratic presidential candidate*
—**democratically** *adverb* in a democratic way: *a democratically elected government*

**Demoˈcratic ˌParty** *noun*
**the Democratic Party** = one of the two main political parties of the U.S.

**de·mol·ish** /dɪˈmɑlɪʃ/ *verb*
to completely destroy a building or other structure: *Ten houses were demolished to make space for a new park.*
—**demolition** /ˌdeməˈlɪʃən/ *noun* the act of demolishing something
[ORIGIN: 1500-1600 From the Latin word *moliri*, which means "to build." *De-* shows that the opposite happens.]

**de·mon** /ˈdimən/ *noun*
an evil creature or spirit

**dem·on·strate** Ac /ˈdemənˌstreɪt/ *verb*
**1** to show someone how to use or do something: *He demonstrated how to use the machine.*
**2** to show clearly that something is true: *The research demonstrates that pollution is killing the trees.*
**3** to protest or show support for something in public with a lot of other people: *A crowd of people were demonstrating against the war.*
—**demonstrator** *noun* someone who is protesting or showing support for something: *Demonstrators marched through the streets holding "NO WAR" signs.*
→ see Thesaurus box at **explain**

**dem·on·stra·tion** Ac /ˌdemənˈstreɪʃən/ *noun*
**1** if you give a demonstration, you show people how to do something: *The chemistry teacher gave the students a demonstration of how to do the experiment.*
**2** an event at which a lot of people protest or show support for something in public: *Students at the university held a peaceful demonstration to protest the new rules.*

**de·mor·al·ized** /dɪˈmɔrəˌlaɪzd/ *adjective*
unhappier, less confident, and less willing than before to make an effort: *We lost three games in a row, and we were feeling demoralized.*
—**demoralizing** *adjective* making someone feel demoralized: *Failing a test is demoralizing.*

**de·mote** /dɪˈmoʊt/ *verb*
to change someone's rank or position to a lower one: *He was demoted from sergeant to private.* **ANTONYM: promote**
—**demotion** /dɪˈmoʊʃən/ *noun* when someone is demoted

**den** /den/ *noun*
**1** a room in a house where you relax
**2** the home of a wild animal such as a lion or FOX

**de·ni·al** Ac /dɪˈnaɪəl/ *noun*
**1** a statement saying that something is not true: *He repeated his denial, saying, "I did not take the money!"* **ANTONYM: admission**
**2** if you are in denial about something bad, you refuse to believe that it is true: *She's in*

D

*denial about her illness. She won't even say the word "cancer."*

**den·im** /ˈdenəm/ *noun*
a strong cotton cloth, usually blue, used to make JEANS and other clothes: *a denim jacket*
**[ORIGIN:** 1600-1700 From the French phrase *serge de Nîmes*, which means "cloth from Nîmes." Nîmes is a French city where denim was first made.**]**

D

**de·nom·i·na·tion** /dɪˌnɑməˈneɪʃən/ *noun*
a religious group that is part of one of the main world religions. Each denomination has slightly different beliefs: *The Catholic Church is the largest Christian denomination in the U.S.*

**de·nom·i·na·tor** /dɪˈnɑməˌneɪtɚ/ *noun*
the number below the line in a FRACTION

**de·note** Ac /dɪˈnoʊt/ *verb* (*formal*)
to represent or mean something: *The symbol $ denotes "dollars."*

**dense** /dens/ *adjective*
**1** with a lot of things or people that are close together: *The island is covered by a dense forest that is difficult to walk through.*
**2** dense mist or smoke is thick and difficult to see through: *The airport was closed because of dense fog.*
**3** (*informal*) not intelligent: *Don't be so dense – the answer is obvious.*
—**densely** *adverb* in a way that has a lot of people or things close together: *In this densely populated city, many people live in tall apartment buildings.*

**den·si·ty** /ˈdensəti/ *noun*
how heavy something is in comparison to its size: *If you add salt to water, you increase its density, because the water becomes heavier but its volume does not increase.*

**dent** /dent/ *noun*
a bent part of a surface, where something has hit it: *There was a big dent in the car door where the baseball hit it.*
—**dent** *verb* to make a dent in something: *Dad hit a tree and dented the car.*

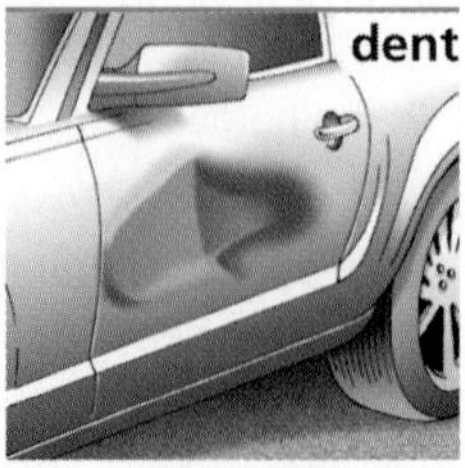


**den·tal** /ˈdentl/ *adjective*
relating to your teeth: *Brushing your teeth every day helps to prevent dental problems.*
**[ORIGIN:** 1500-1600 From the Latin word *dentes*, which means "teeth."**]**

**den·tist** /ˈdentɪst/ *noun*
someone whose job is to do work on people's teeth: *I went to the dentist to have my teeth cleaned and checked.* → see picture on page **A16**
→ see Thesaurus box at **doctor**

**den·tures** /ˈdentʃɚz/ *plural noun*
false teeth worn by people who have lost their real teeth: *He takes his dentures out of his mouth at night.*

**de·ny** Ac /dɪˈnaɪ/ *verb* (**denied**, **denies**)
**1** to say that something is not true: *He denied cheating on the test.* **ANTONYM: admit**
**2** (*formal*) to not let someone have or do something: *In the past, women were denied the right to vote.*

| WORD FAMILY: deny |
| --- |
| **deny** *verb* \| **denial** *noun* \| **undeniable** *adjective* \| **undeniably** *adverb* |

**de·o·dor·ant** /diˈoʊdərənt/ *noun*
a substance that you put under your arms so that you do not smell bad

**de·part** /dɪˈpɑrt/ *verb* (*formal*)
to leave: *The train for Boston will depart from track 9.* **ANTONYM: arrive**

**de·part·ment** /dɪˈpɑrtmənt/ *noun*
a part of a large organization such as a business, college, or government: *I called the English Department to find out about summer classes.*
→ see Thesaurus box at **part**[1]

**deˈpartment ˌstore** *noun*
a large store that sells many different kinds of things including clothes

**de·par·ture** /dɪˈpɑrtʃɚ/ *noun* (*formal*)
the action of leaving a place: *The flight's departure was delayed because of the snow storm.* **ANTONYM: arrival**

**de·pend** /dɪˈpend/ *verb*
**it/that depends** = said when you are not sure about something because you do not know what will happen: *"Are you coming to my*

*house later?" "It depends. I might have homework to do."*
[**ORIGIN:** 1400-1500 From the Latin words *de* and *pendere*, which mean "from" and "to hang."]
**PHRASAL VERB**
**depend on someone/something**
**1** to need the help or support of someone or something: *We all depend on our families and our friends when things get tough.*
**2** to be affected by something that is not certain: *We might go to the game. It depends on whether we can get tickets.*

**de·pend·a·ble** /dɪˈpendəbəl/ *adjective*
someone or something that is dependable will always do what is needed or wanted: *He is a dependable student who always finishes his assignments on time.* | *a dependable car*
**SYNONYM: reliable**

**de·pend·ent¹** /dɪˈpendənt/ *adjective*
needing someone or something in order to live or continue: *For the first few weeks of their lives, kittens are completely dependent on their mother.* **ANTONYM: independent**
—**dependence** *noun* the state of being dependent on someone or something

**dependent²** *noun*
if you have a dependent, you have a child or other family member for whom you buy the things he or she needs because he or she cannot work: *He is not married and has no dependents.*

**de·port** /dɪˈpɔrt/ *verb*
to make someone from a foreign country return to that country: *The illegal immigrants will be deported back to their home country.*
—**deportation** /ˌdipɔrˈteɪʃən/ *noun* the act of deporting someone

**de·pos·it¹** /dɪˈpɑzɪt/ *noun*
**1** an amount of money that is put into a bank account: *I'd like to make a deposit of $250.* **ANTONYM: withdrawal**
**2** a payment that you give a store when you arrange to buy something. You pay the rest later when you get the thing you are buying: *We put down a deposit of $1,000 on the car; we'll pay the rest when the dealer says it's ready.*
**3** an additional amount of money that you pay when you rent something such as an apartment or a car. You get the deposit back if you do not cause any damage: *The apartment costs $900 a month to rent, plus a deposit of $1,000.*

**deposit²** *verb*
to put money into a bank account: *She immediately deposited the money into her savings account.* **ANTONYM: withdraw**

**de·pot** /ˈdipoʊ/ *noun*
**1** a place where a large quantity of things are stored: *They drove to the storage depot to pick up supplies.*
**2** a small train station or bus station

**de·pre·ci·ate** /dɪˈpriʃiˌeɪt/ *verb (formal)*
to go down in value: *New cars depreciate quickly in the first year, often by thousands of dollars.*
—**depreciation** /dɪˌpriʃiˈeɪʃən/ *noun* the process of losing value

**de·press** Ac /dɪˈpres/ *verb*
to make someone feel very sad: *I hate it when I get a bad grade – it depresses me.*

**de·pressed** Ac /dɪˈprest/ *adjective*
very sad: *When people argue, it makes me feel depressed.*
→ see Thesaurus box at **sad**

**WORD FAMILY: depressed**
**depressed** *adjective* | **depressing** *adjective* | **depress** *verb* | **depression** *noun*

**de·press·ing** Ac /dɪˈpresɪŋ/ *adjective*
making you feel sad: *Nothing good happens in the book. It's very depressing.*

**de·pres·sion** Ac /dɪˈpreʃən/ *noun*
**1** a feeling of great sadness that sometimes makes you unable to live normally: *She visited the doctor because she was suffering from depression, and unable to work.*
**2** a long period when the economy is doing badly and many people do not have jobs: *During the Great Depression of the 1930s, a lot of businesses closed because they could not make enough money.*

D

**de·prive** /dɪˈpraɪv/ *verb*

PHRASAL VERB

**deprive someone of something**
to stop someone from having something that he or she needs or should have: *They deprived the prisoners of food and sleep to punish them.*

**de·prived** /dɪˈpraɪvd/ *adjective*
not having the things that you need for a comfortable or happy life: *He had a deprived childhood; his family was very poor and often did not have enough to eat.*
—**deprivation** /ˌdeprəˈveɪʃən/ *noun* (*formal*) the state of being deprived
→ see Thesaurus box at **poor**

**depth** /depθ/ *noun*
**1** the distance from the top to the bottom of something such as a river or a hole: *The depth of the river is about 30 feet.*
**2** the distance from the front to the back of an object: *The height of the bookcase is four feet, the width is three feet, and the depth of the shelves is ten inches.*
**3** how strong or serious something is: *You only had to look at his face to see the depth of his sadness.*
**4 in depth** = if you write or talk about something in depth, you give a lot of details about it: *The book covers the Civil War in depth.*

**dep·u·ty** /ˈdepjəti/ *noun* (plural **deputies**)
**1 a deputy director/superintendent/chief, etc.** = someone who has the second most important job in an organization: *She is the deputy editor of the magazine; her boss is the editor.*
**2** a police officer whose job is to help a SHERIFF

**der·e·lict** /ˈderəˌlɪkt/ *adjective* (*formal*)
a derelict building or vehicle is in bad condition because no one has used it in a long time: *They are knocking down the derelict factory buildings.*

**de·rive** [Ac] /dɪˈraɪv/ *verb*

PHRASAL VERB

**derive from something** (*also* **be derived from something**)
to develop or come from something else: *Our word "science" derives from the Latin word "scientia," meaning "knowledge."*

**de·scend** /dɪˈsend/ *verb*
**1** (*formal*) to go down: *We got in the elevator on the fifth floor and descended to the first floor.* ANTONYM: **ascend**
**2 be descended from someone** = to be related to a person who lived a long time ago: *He is descended from a Native American chief.*
[ORIGIN: 1300-1400 From the Latin words *de* and *scandere*, which mean "down" and "to climb."]

**de·scend·ant** /dɪˈsendənt/ *noun*
someone who is related to a person who lived a long time ago: *Queen Elizabeth II is a direct descendant of Queen Victoria.*
→ see Thesaurus box at **family**

**de·scent** /dɪˈsent/ *noun* (*formal*)
**1** the action of going down: *The plane began its descent to the airport.*
**2** if you are of Mexican, Italian, etc. descent, your family originally came from Mexico, Italy, etc.: *He is of Spanish descent, but he has never been to Spain.*

**de·scribe** /dɪˈskraɪb/ *verb*
to say what someone or something is like: *Can you describe the man who took your purse? | It's hard to describe how I feel.*
[ORIGIN: 1400-1500 From the Latin word *scribere*, which means "to write."]

| WORD FAMILY: describe |
| --- |
| **describe** *verb* \| **description** *noun* |

**de·scrip·tion** /dɪˈskrɪpʃən/ *noun*
a written or spoken statement that says what someone or something is like: *Kate gave us a description of her new house: it is yellow and has three bedrooms and a big yard.*

**de·seg·re·gate** /diˈsegrəˌgeɪt/ *verb*
to stop keeping people of different races separate in schools, restaurants, buses, and other places: *When the schools desegregated, black and white children started going to school together.*
—**desegregation** /diˌsegrəˈgeɪʃən/ *noun* the process of desegregating

**des·ert¹** /ˈdezɚt/ *noun*
a large area of hot dry land where few plants grow: *The Sahara desert in northern Africa is the largest desert in the world.*

**desert²** /dɪˈzɚt/ *verb*
**1** to leave people who love you or need you, and not go back: *He deserted his wife and children and moved to a different state.*
**2** to leave the army without permission: *Some soldiers desert because they do not want to fight.*
—**desertion** /dɪˈzɚʃən/ *noun* the action of deserting

**de·sert·ed** /dɪˈzɚtɪd/ *adjective*
if a place which usually has people in it is deserted, there are no people there: *During the day the town is busy, but at night the streets are deserted.* **SYNONYM: empty**

**de·sert·er** /dɪˈzɚtɚ/ *noun*
a soldier who has left the army without permission

**de·serve** /dɪˈzɚv/ *verb*
if you deserve something, you should get it because of what you have done: *After working so hard, you deserve a rest.*

**de·sign¹** Ac /dɪˈzaɪn/ *noun*
**1** the shape or structure of something, and the way it looks: *I like the design of the car; it's beautiful.*
**2** a drawing of something new that will be made: *Have you seen the designs for the new shopping mall in town?*
**3** a pattern used for decorating something: *The T-shirt has a nice design on the front.*
**4** the process of making a drawing of something new that will be made: *He studied design in college.*

**design²** Ac *verb*
to draw or plan something that is going to be made: *He is an architect, so he designed his house himself.*
—**designer** *noun* someone who designs new things: *a fashion designer*

**de·signed** Ac /dɪˈzaɪnd/ *adjective*
made or planned for a particular purpose or type of person: *This game is designed for younger children.*

**de·sir·a·ble** /dɪˈzaɪrəbəl/ *adjective (formal)*
if something is desirable, people want it because it is good or useful: *The house is in a desirable area where crime is low and schools are good.*
—**desirability** /dɪˌzaɪrəˈbɪləti/ *noun* the quality of being desirable

**de·sire¹** /dɪˈzaɪɚ/ *noun (formal)*
a strong feeling of wanting something: *I had a sudden desire for some chocolate, so I went and got some.*

**desire²** *verb (formal)*
to want something: *The witch said to the girl, "I will give you what you desire most, but you must help me first."*

**desk** /desk/ *noun*
a table that you can sit at to write and work: *Marie was sitting at her desk doing work on the computer.* → see picture on page **A10**

**des·o·late** /ˈdesəlɪt/ *adjective (formal)*
a place that is desolate is empty and makes you feel sad and lonely: *We drove along a desolate stretch of road without trees, grass, or buildings.*

**de·spair** /dɪˈsper/ *noun (formal)*
a very sad feeling, when you have no hope at all: *Many families were in despair after losing their homes in the floods.*
—**despair** *verb* to feel despair
[**ORIGIN:** 1200-1300 From the Latin word *sperare*, which means "to hope." *De-* shows that the opposite happens.]

**des·per·ate** /ˈdespərət/ *adjective*
wanting something very much, and willing to do anything to get it or do it: *He had almost no money, and he was desperate for a job.*
—**desperately** *adverb* in a desperate way: *The doctors tried desperately to save her life.*
—**desperation** /ˌdespəˈreɪʃən/ *noun (formal)* the state of feeling desperate: *Finally, in desperation, she asked a lawyer for advice.*

**de·spise** /dɪˈspaɪz/ *verb (formal)*
to hate someone or something and have no respect for them: *She despised him for hitting her.* **SYNONYM: hate**
→ see Thesaurus box at **hate¹**

**de·spite** Ac /dɪˈspaɪt/ *preposition*
although something happens or exists: *Despite the bad weather, we enjoyed our trip.*

D

**dessert**

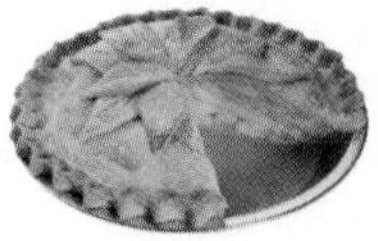
apple pie

chocolate cake

ice cream sundae

strawberry cake

**des·sert** /dɪˈzɚt/ *noun*
sweet food that you eat after the main part of a meal: *There's apple pie or cheesecake for dessert.*
[**ORIGIN:** 1500-1600 From the French word *desservir*, which means "to clear the table." It is the opposite of *servir*, which means "to serve food."]

**des·ti·na·tion** /ˌdestəˈneɪʃən/ *noun* (*formal*)
the place that you are traveling to: *After driving for eight hours, we reached our destination.*

**des·tined** /ˈdestənd/ *adjective*
if you are destined to do something, you will do it in the future: *When he was a boy, he felt he was destined to become famous.*

**des·ti·ny** /ˈdestəni/ *noun* (plural **destinies**)
the things that will happen to someone in the future: *We cannot see the future or know our own destinies.* **SYNONYM: fate**
[**ORIGIN:** 1300-1400 From the Latin word *destinare*, which means "to fix." The idea is that your destiny is the future that is fixed for you.]

**de·stroy** /dɪˈstrɔɪ/ *verb*
to damage something very badly, so that it no longer exists or cannot be repaired: *The building was destroyed by fire.*
[**ORIGIN:** 1100-1200 From the Latin word *struere*, which means "to build." *De-* shows that the opposite happens.]

**WORD FAMILY: destroy**
**destroy** *verb* | **destruction** *noun* | **destructive** *adjective*

**de·stroy·er** /dɪˈstrɔɪɚ/ *noun*
a small fast military ship with guns

**de·struc·tion** /dɪˈstrʌkʃən/ *noun*
the act of destroying something: *The environmental group wants to stop the destruction of the forests.*

**de·struc·tive** /dɪˈstrʌktɪv/ *adjective*
causing a lot of damage: *The computer virus is very destructive; it can make you lose all your files.*

**de·tach** /dɪˈtætʃ/ *verb* (*formal*)
to remove something from the thing that it is attached to: *You can detach the hood from the jacket.*

**de·tached** /dɪˈtætʃt/ *adjective* (*formal*)
not having an emotional feeling about something: *During the funeral, he seemed detached; he did not cry at all.*
—**detachment** *noun* the state of being detached

**de·tail** /ˈditeɪl/ *noun*
**1** a small fact or piece of information about something: *She wanted to know every detail of the trip, including where we had dinner and how much everything cost.*
**2 in detail** = in a way that includes a lot of details: *She described the dress in detail; she said it was light green with white flowers, and had short sleeves.*

**de·tailed** /dɪˈteɪld/ *adjective*
including a lot of details: *It is a detailed map, showing every house on the street.*

**de·tain** /dɪˈteɪn/ *verb* (*formal*)
to officially stop someone from leaving a place: *Police detained one of the men at the police station.* **SYNONYM: hold**

**de·tect** Ac /dɪˈtekt/ *verb* (*formal*)
to find or notice something that is not easy to notice: *He tried to hide his feelings, but I detected a look of disappointment in his eyes.*
**SYNONYM: notice**
—**detector** *noun* a piece of equipment that detects something: *We had to walk through a metal detector at the airport.*
—**detection** /dɪˈtekʃən/ *noun* (*formal*) the act of detecting something

**WORD FAMILY: detect**
**detect** *verb* | **detection** *noun* | **detector** *noun*

**de·tec·tive** Ac /dɪˈtektɪv/ *noun*
a police officer whose job is to find out who has committed a crime

**de·ten·tion** /dɪˈtenʃən/ *noun*
a punishment in which a student has to stay at school after the other students have gone home: *I got detention for talking too much in class.*

**de·ter** /dɪˈtɚ/ *verb* (**deterred**, **deterring**) (*formal*)
to stop someone from doing something by making it difficult: *Do you think higher cigarette prices would deter people from smoking?*
[**ORIGIN:** 1500-1600 From the Latin word *terrere*, which means "to frighten."]

**de·ter·gent** /dɪˈtɚdʒənt/ *noun*
a liquid or powder that works like soap and is used for washing clothes or dishes: *You only need a little detergent for washing clothes.*
[**ORIGIN:** 1600-1700 From the Latin word *tergere*, which means "to clean by rubbing."]

**de·te·ri·o·rate** /dɪˈtɪriəˌreɪt/ *verb* (*formal*)
to become worse: *Her health deteriorated until she could not take care of herself anymore.*
—**deterioration** /dɪˌtɪriəˈreɪʃən/ *noun* (*formal*) the process of deteriorating

**de·ter·mi·na·tion** /dɪˌtɚməˈneɪʃən/ *noun*
a strong desire to do something, even when it will be difficult: *He has been working hard, and the coaches are impressed with his determination.*

**de·ter·mine** /dɪˈtɚmɪn/ *verb* (*formal*)
**1** to find out the facts about something: *Police are trying to determine if his death was an accident.*
**2** to directly affect or control what something will be like or what will happen: *Grades are determined by how good a student's work is.*

**de·ter·mined** /dɪˈtɚmɪnd/ *adjective*
having a strong desire to do something, even when it will be difficult: *She was determined to become a doctor, so she worked hard to earn the money to go to medical school.*

**de·test** /dɪˈtest/ *verb* (*formal*)
to hate someone or something very much: *I detest cigarettes; I will not go into a room when someone is smoking.* **SYNONYM: hate**
→ see Thesaurus box at **hate**[1]

**det·o·nate** /ˈdetnˌeɪt/ *verb*
if someone detonates a bomb, it explodes: *The terrorist tried to detonate the bomb but luckily it did not explode.*
[**ORIGIN:** 1700-1800 From the Latin word *tonare*, which means "to thunder."]

**de·tour** /ˈditʊr/ *noun*
a way of going from one place to another that is longer than the usual way: *We had to take a detour because the road was blocked by a fallen tree.*

**dev·as·tate** /ˈdevəˌsteɪt/ *verb* (*formal*)
to damage something very badly: *The city was devastated by an earthquake.*
—**devastation** /ˌdevəˈsteɪʃən/ *noun* (*formal*) great damage

**WORD FAMILY: devastate**
**devastate** *verb* | **devastating** *adjective* | **devastated** *adjective* | **devastation** *noun*

**dev·as·tat·ed** /ˈdevəˌsteɪtɪd/ *adjective* (*formal*)
extremely upset: *She was devastated when her parents got divorced.*

**dev·as·tat·ing** /ˈdevəˌsteɪtɪŋ/ *adjective* (*formal*)
**1** making someone feel extremely upset: *The news of her sister's sudden death was devastating.*
**2** causing a lot of damage: *The city was hit by a devastating hurricane that destroyed many buildings.*

**de·vel·op** /dɪˈveləp/ *verb*
**1** to change into something bigger, better, or more important: *Caterpillars develop into butterflies.* | *She wants to develop her career as a singer.*
**2** to begin to have an illness, problem, or quality: *Her baby developed a fever during the night.*
**3** to design and produce something new: *The company is developing a new type of plane.*
**4** to make pictures out of film from a camera

**WORD FAMILY: develop**
**develop** *verb* | **developed** *adjective* | **developing** *adjective* | **development** *noun*

**de·vel·oped** /dɪˈveləpt/ *adjective*
**1** a developed country is rich and has a lot of industry
**2** if something is developed, it has become big or effective: *His muscles are well developed because he lifts weights.*

D

**de·vel·op·ing** /dɪˈveləpɪŋ/ *adjective*
**developing countries/nations** = poor countries that are trying to increase their industry and trade

**de·vel·op·ment** /dɪˈveləpmənt/ *noun*
**1** the process of growing: *A healthy diet is necessary for a child's physical development.*
**2** a new event or piece of work that changes a situation: *The magazine tells you about the latest developments in science.*
**3** a group of new buildings, or the work of building them: *They have started building a new housing development where the farm used to be.*

**de·vi·ate** Ac /ˈdiviˌeɪt/ *verb* (*formal*)
to do something different from what has been planned or what is normal: *Everyone must do exactly what we agreed and not deviate from the plan.*
—**deviation** /ˌdiviˈeɪʃən/ *noun* the act of deviating

**de·vice** Ac /dɪˈvaɪs/ *noun*
a machine or small object that is used to do a particular thing: *A corkscrew is a device for opening wine bottles.*
→ see Thesaurus box at **machine**

**dev·il** /ˈdevəl/ *noun*
**the devil** = the most powerful evil spirit in some religions, such as Christianity

**de·vi·ous** /ˈdiviəs/ *adjective* (*formal*)
using tricks or lies to get what you want: *A devious salesman tricked her into paying a lot more for the car than it was worth.*

**de·vise** /dɪˈvaɪz/ *verb* (*formal*)
to think of a way of doing something: *The teacher devised a game to make math more fun.*
→ see Thesaurus box at **invent**

**de·vote** Ac /dɪˈvoʊt/ *verb*
**devote yourself/your time/your life to something** = to spend all your time doing something: *She devoted her life to helping poor people in India.* **SYNONYM: dedicate**

**WORD FAMILY: devote**
**devote** *verb* | **devotion** *noun* | **devoted** *adjective*

**de·vot·ed** Ac /dɪˈvoʊtɪd/ *adjective*
**1** loving and caring about someone a lot: *His girlfriend was completely devoted to him, and spent all her time with him.*
**2 be devoted to something** = to deal with only one thing: *One chapter of the book is devoted to snakes.*

**de·vo·tion** Ac /dɪˈvoʊʃən/ *noun*
the love and care that you have for someone or something: *His devotion to his family is easy to see; he spends all his time with his wife and kids.*

**de·vour** /dɪˈvaʊə/ *verb* (*formal*)
to eat something quickly because you are very hungry: *Dinner was ready at last and the boys soon devoured everything on the table.*

**de·vout** /dɪˈvaʊt/ *adjective*
very religious: *a devout Hindu*

**dew** /du/ *noun*
the small drops of water that form on things outdoors during the night: *In the morning, the grass outside was wet with dew.*

**di·a·be·tes** /ˌdaɪəˈbitiz/ *noun*
a medical condition in which you have too much sugar in your blood
—**diabetic** /ˌdaɪəˈbetɪk/ *adjective* someone who is diabetic has diabetes
—**diabetic** *noun* someone with diabetes

**di·ag·nose** /ˌdaɪəgˈnoʊs/ *verb*
to find out and say what illness someone has: *Luke was covered with red spots and the doctor diagnosed measles.*

**di·ag·no·sis** /ˌdaɪəgˈnoʊsəs/ *noun* (plural **diagnoses** /ˌdaɪəgˈnoʊsiz/)
if a doctor makes a diagnosis, he or she says what illness someone has: *The doctor made a diagnosis of heart disease.*

**di·ag·o·nal** /daɪˈægənəl/ *adjective*
a diagonal line is a straight line that goes from one corner of a shape or area, through the middle, and to the opposite corner: *Draw a diagonal line across the square.*
—**diagonal** *noun* a diagonal line
—**diagonally** *adverb* from one corner to the opposite corner: *Fold the piece of paper diagonally.*

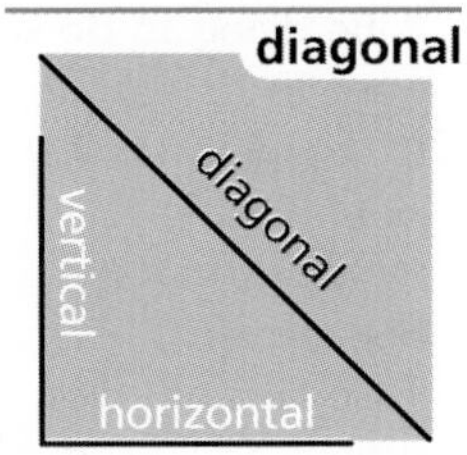


**di·a·gram** /ˈdaɪəˌgræm/ *noun*
a drawing that you make to show the shape or structure of something, or how it works: *The diagram of the engine shows all of its parts.*
**[ORIGIN:** 1600-1700 From the Greek word *diagramma*, from *diagraphein*, which means "to mark out with lines."**]**

**di·al**[1] /daɪəl/ *verb*
to press the buttons on a telephone in order to make a call: *I dialed her number twice, but nobody answered the phone.* **SYNONYM: call**

**dial**[2] *noun*
**1** a round part of a radio or other piece of equipment that you turn in order to change something: *If you want to listen to a different station, turn the dial on the radio.*
**2** a flat thing with numbers on it, on a clock, telephone, or machine. A dial is usually round and often has a thin part that moves to point to the numbers: *The speedometer is a dial in a car that shows how fast you are driving.*

**di·a·lect** /ˈdaɪəˌlekt/ *noun*
a form of a language that is spoken in one area: *In the north of the country, they speak a different dialect from people in the south.*
→ see Thesaurus box at **language**

**di·a·logue** (*also* **dialog**) /ˈdaɪəˌlɔg/ *noun*
conversation in a book, play, or movie: *I like movies with a lot of action, not a lot of dialogue.*
**[ORIGIN:** 1100-1200 From the Greek word *dialogos*, which means "conversation," from *logos*, which means "word or speech."**]**

**ˈdial tone** *noun*
the sound you hear when you pick up a telephone before making a call

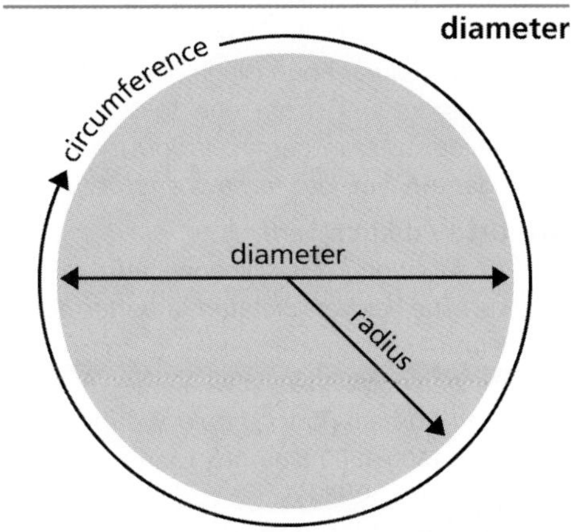


**di·am·e·ter** /daɪˈæmətɚ/ *noun*
a line or measurement from one side of a circle to the other, through the center: *The round table is five feet in diameter.*
**[ORIGIN:** 1300-1400 From the Greek words *dia* and *metron*, which mean "across or through" and "measurement."**]**

**di·a·mond** /ˈdaɪəmənd/ *noun*
**1** a very hard clear expensive stone, used in jewelry: *He bought her a diamond engagement ring.*
**2** a shape with four equal sloping sides, with its points at the top, bottom, and sides
**3** a card used in card games. The cards have a picture on them which looks like this (♦): *the three of diamonds*
**4** the area in a baseball field that is inside the four BASEs
**[ORIGIN:** 1200-1300 From the Greek word *adamas*, which probably means "not able to be tamed or broken."**]**

**di·a·per** /ˈdaɪpɚ/ *noun*
a piece of cloth or paper that is put around a baby's bottom to hold its waste: *I think we need to change the baby's diaper.*

D

**di·ar·rhe·a** /ˌdaɪəˈriə/ *noun*
an illness that causes the solid waste in your body to become liquid, and to come out of your body often: *I had diarrhea after eating some bad meat.*

**di·a·ry** /ˈdaɪəri/ *noun* (plural **diaries**)
a book in which you write about the things that happen to you each day: *I decided to keep a diary during the trip so that I would remember exactly what we did.*
[**ORIGIN:** 1500-1600 From the Latin word *diarium*, from *dies*, which means "day."]

D

**dice** /daɪs/ *plural noun* (singular **die** /daɪ/)
small blocks with from one to six spots on each side, used in games: *If you roll the dice and get a 6, you get to have another turn.*

**dic·tate** /ˈdɪkteɪt/ *verb*
**1** to say words for someone else to write down: *The lawyer dictated a letter to her secretary.*
**2** to tell people exactly what they must do: *You can't dictate how I should live my life!*
[**ORIGIN:** 1500-1600 From the Latin word *dicere*, which means "to say."]

**dic·ta·tion** /dɪkˈteɪʃən/ *noun*
the act of saying words so that someone can write them down exactly as you say them

**dic·ta·tor** /ˈdɪkteɪtɚ/ *noun*
a leader of a country who has complete power: *Dictators often put people who oppose them in prison.*
—**dictatorship** /dɪkˈteɪtɚˌʃɪp/ *noun* a country that is ruled by a dictator

**dic·tion·ar·y** /ˈdɪkʃəˌneri/ *noun* (plural **dictionaries**)
a book that shows words in ALPHABETICAL order and explains what they mean: *If you don't know what a word means, look it up in a dictionary.*
[**ORIGIN:** 1500-1600 From the Latin word *dictio*, which means "word."]

**did** /dɪd/ *verb*
the past tense of DO

**did·n't** /ˈdɪdnt/ *verb*
the short form of "did not": *She didn't get up early because it was Saturday.*

**die**[1] /daɪ/ *verb* (**died**, **dying**)
**1** to stop living: *My grandmother died last year but my grandfather is still alive.* | *He died of cancer.*
**2** **be dying to do something** (*informal*) = to want to do something very much: *I'm dying to know what happened, but my parents won't tell me.*

PHRASAL VERBS

**die down**
if something dies down, it becomes less strong: *The wind died down and the rain stopped.*

**die out**
if a type of animal or thing dies out, it disappears completely: *Scientists have different ideas about why dinosaurs died out.*

**die**[2] *noun*
the singular of DICE

**die·sel** /ˈdizəl/ (*also* ˌ**diesel** ˈ**fuel**) *noun*
a type of FUEL used in some engines, for example in big trucks
[**ORIGIN:** From Rudolph Diesel (1858-1913), a German engineer who invented a type of engine for motor vehicles.]

**di·et** /ˈdaɪət/ *noun*
**1** the type of food that you eat each day: *Fruit and vegetables are part of a healthy diet.*
**2** a plan to eat less food or eat a particular type of food: *I'm on a diet because I want to lose weight.*
—**diet** *verb* to try to eat less food or eat a particular type of food: *You look thinner. Have you been dieting?*
—**dietician** *noun* someone who studies food and advises people on what to eat

**dif·fer** /ˈdɪfɚ/ *verb* (*formal*)
to be different: *How does the movie differ from the book?*

**dif·ference** /ˈdɪfərəns/ *noun*
**1** a way in which one thing is not the same as something else: *One of the differences between baseball and softball is that the ball in softball is bigger and softer.* | *The twins look the same to me – I can't tell the difference.* **ANTONYM: similarity**
**2** **make a difference** = to have an important effect on a situation: *Exercise can make a big difference to how healthy you feel.*
**3** **make no difference** = to be unimportant or to have no effect: *It makes no difference to me what you think. I want to do it so I will.*

**dif·ferent** /ˈdɪfərənt/ *adjective*
not the same: *My sister and I like different*

*kinds of music.* | *Skiing and snowboarding are different from each other in many ways.* **ANTONYM: the same**
—**differently** *adverb* in a different way

**WORD FAMILY: different**
**different** *adjective* | **differently** *adverb* | **differ** *verb* | **difference** *noun*

**dif·fer·en·ti·ate** [Ac] /ˌdɪfəˈrenʃiˌeɪt/ *verb* (*formal*)
to know that two things are different from each other: *I can't differentiate between the colors red and green; the two colors look the same to me.*

**dif·fi·cult** /ˈdɪfɪˌkəlt/ *adjective*
not easy to do, understand, or deal with: *The first question on the test was very difficult, and I got it wrong.* | *No one is sure what to do next – it is a difficult situation.* **SYNONYM: hard**; **ANTONYM: easy**

**dif·fi·cul·ty** /ˈdɪfɪˌkəlti/ *noun* (plural **difficulties**)
**1** if you have difficulty doing something, it is not easy for you to do: *People often have difficulty getting to sleep when they are worried about something.* | *She walks with difficulty because she hurt her knees.*
**2** a problem: *Since he lost his job, he has had financial difficulties.*
**3** the quality of being difficult: *The difficulty of the test means that not many people pass it.*

**dig** /dɪg/ *verb* (**dug** /dʌg/, **digging**)
to make a hole in the ground by moving earth: *We had fun digging in the sand.* | *I dug a hole and put the plant in it.*
**PHRASAL VERBS**
**dig something into something**
to push something hard into something else: *He dug his hand into his pocket and pulled out some candy.*
**dig something up**
to take something out of the ground: *The dog dug up a bone in the backyard.*

**di·gest** /daɪˈdʒest/ *verb*
when you digest food, it changes in your stomach into a form your body can use: *Some people can't digest milk.*
—**digestible** *adjective* easy to digest

**di·ges·tion** /daɪˈdʒestʃən/ *noun*
the process of digesting food
—**digestive** *adjective* relating to digestion

**dig·it** /ˈdɪdʒɪt/ *noun* (*formal*)
any of the numbers from 0 to 9: *a four-digit number such as 9723*
[**ORIGIN:** 1300-1400 From the Latin word *digitus*, which means "finger." People often use their fingers for counting.]

**dig·i·tal** /ˈdɪdʒɪtl/ *adjective*
**1** using a system in which sounds, writing, or pictures are stored as a set of the numbers 1 and 0: *You can put pictures from a digital camera onto your computer.*
**2** giving information in the form of numbers: *On a digital clock, a quarter after ten is shown as 10:15.*

**dig·ni·fied** /ˈdɪgnəˌfaɪd/ *adjective*
calm, serious, and making people feel respect: *The professor was a tall, dignified old man.*

**dig·ni·ty** /ˈdɪgnəti/ *noun*
calm and controlled behavior that makes people respect you: *Everyone respected her because she always behaved with great dignity.*

**dike** /daɪk/ *noun*
a wall or bank that people build to keep back water and prevent flooding

**di·lap·i·dat·ed** /dəˈlæpəˌdeɪtɪd/ *adjective*
a dilapidated building, vehicle, or piece of furniture is old and in bad condition: *The house was dilapidated when he bought it, so he had to do a lot of repairs.*

**di·lem·ma** /dəˈlemə/ *noun*
a situation in which you have to make a difficult choice between two actions: *I'm in a dilemma – I don't want to go to the party, but I don't want to be rude and say "no."*

**dil·i·gent** /ˈdɪlədʒənt/ *adjective* (*formal*)
someone who is diligent works hard and carefully: *Connie is a diligent student and always does extra work.*
—**diligently** *adverb* in a diligent way
—**diligence** *noun* the quality of being diligent

**di·lute** /dɪˈlut/ *verb*
to make a liquid weaker by adding water or another liquid: *You can dilute the orange juice with water.*

D

—**dilution** /daɪˈluʃən/ *noun* the act of diluting something
[**ORIGIN:** 1500-1600 From the Latin word *dilutus*, a form of the verb *diluere*, which means "to wash away."]

**dim** /dɪm/ *adjective* (**dimmer**, **dimmest**)
not bright, so that you cannot see well: *I couldn't read the sign because the light was too dim.*
—**dimness** *noun* the state of not being bright

**dime** /daɪm/ *noun*
a coin that is worth ten cents
→ see Thesaurus box at **money**

**di·men·sion** Ac /dɪˈmenʃən/ *noun*
the length, height, or width of something: *The dimensions of the room are 10 feet by 12 feet.*
[**ORIGIN:** 1300-1400 From the Latin word *dimetiri*, which means "to measure out."]

**di·min·ish** Ac /dɪˈmɪnɪʃ/ *verb* (*formal*)
to become smaller or weaker: *Her anger had diminished, and she felt calmer.*
→ see Thesaurus box at **decrease¹**

**dim·ple** /ˈdɪmpəl/ *noun*
a small hollow place on your cheek or chin: *When my baby sister smiles, she has dimples in her cheeks.*

**din** /dɪn/ *noun*
a loud, continuous, and annoying noise: *I could not hear him because of the din of the crowd.*

**dine** /daɪn/ *verb* (*formal*)
to have dinner: *He had been invited to dine with the president.*

**din·er** /ˈdaɪnɚ/ *noun*
**1** a small restaurant that serves cheap meals
**2** (*formal*) someone who is eating in a restaurant: *The other diners did not look up when we came in.*

**ˈdining room** *noun*
a room in a house where you sit down at a table to eat meals

**ˈdining ˌtable** (*also* **dining room table**, **dinner table**) *noun*
a table at which you eat meals at home

**din·ner** /ˈdɪnɚ/ *noun*
the main meal of the day, usually eaten in the evening: *We usually have dinner around 6:30. | We had fish for dinner.*
→ see Thesaurus box at **meal**
[**ORIGIN:** 1200-1300 From the French word *diner*, which means "to eat" and originally meant "to have breakfast."]

**di·no·saur** /ˈdaɪnəˌsɔr/ *noun*
a large animal that lived millions of years ago and no longer exists: *Tyrannosaurus rex was a large dinosaur that ate other animals.*
[**ORIGIN:** 1800-1900 From the Greek words *deinos* and *sauros*, which mean "terrible" and "lizard."]

**dip¹** /dɪp/ *verb* (**dipped**, **dipping**)
to put something into a liquid and quickly take it out again: *I dipped my toe into the water to feel if it was cold.* → see picture on page **A15**

**dip²** *noun*
a thick mixture that you can dip CHIPs or raw vegetables into, before you eat them: *There was a cheese dip for the potato chips.*

**di·plo·ma** /dɪˈploʊmə/ *noun*
a document that you get when you have successfully completed high school or college: *He earned his high school diploma in 2010.*
[**ORIGIN:** 1600-1700 From the Latin word for "official letter or document," from the Greek word for "folded paper."]

**dip·lo·mat** /ˈdɪpləˌmæt/ *noun*
someone who officially represents his or her government in a foreign country and helps to solve problems between the countries

**dip·lo·mat·ic** /ˌdɪpləˈmætɪk/ *adjective*
**1** relating to the work of diplomats: *We must use diplomatic efforts to end the war.*
**2** if you are diplomatic, you are good at dealing with people politely and not upsetting them: *I tried to be diplomatic when I told her she had made a mistake.*
—**diplomacy** /dɪˈploʊməsi/ *noun* the work of diplomats: *Diplomacy failed and the relationship between the two countries became even worse.*
—**diplomatically** *adverb* in a way that does not upset people: *"You're both right in a way," she said diplomatically.*

**di·rect¹** /dəˈrekt/ *adjective*
**1** going straight from one place to another: *What's the most direct route to the airport?*
**2** with no other person, thing, or event

involved: *The flooding is a direct result of the storm.* **ANTONYM: indirect**

**3** saying exactly what you mean in an honest and clear way: *She's always very direct, so you know what she's thinking.* **ANTONYM: indirect**

—**directness** *noun* the quality that a direct person has

**direct²** *verb*

**1** to tell the actors in a movie or play what to do: *The movie was directed by Joel Coen.*

**2** (*formal*) to tell someone the way to a place: *Another student directed me to the library.*

**3** (*formal*) to aim something at a particular person, place, or thing: *I didn't think the question was directed at me, so I didn't answer.*

**di·rec·tion** /dəˈrekʃən/ *noun*

**1** the way that someone or something is moving, looking, or pointing: *I think we're going in the wrong direction – we should be heading north, not east.* | *He looked in the direction of the house.*

**2 directions** = information about how to get to a place, or about how to do something: *I gave them directions to my house.* | *If you're taking medicine, always follow the directions.*

**di·rect·ly** /dəˈrektli/ *adverb*

**1** with no other person, thing, or event involved: *He was driving the car that hit the boys; he is directly responsible for their deaths.*

**2** exactly in a particular position or direction: *Lucas sat directly behind us.*

**di·rec·tor** /dəˈrektɚ/ *noun*

**1** the person who tells the actors what to do in a movie or play

**2** someone who controls an organization or one of its activities: *The director of the museum is in charge of all the employees.*

**di·rec·to·ry** /daɪˈrektəri/ *noun* (plural **directories**)

**1** a book containing a list of people or businesses and their addresses or telephone numbers: *Is his phone number in the telephone directory?*

**2** a sign in a building that tells you where to find someone or something: *I checked the directory and the doctor's office is on the third floor.*

**3** a list of FILEs on part of a computer: *How do I create a new directory on the C drive?*

**dirt** /dɚt/ *noun*

soil from the ground: *He was digging a hole and had dirt all over his clothes.* **SYNONYM: soil**

**dirty**

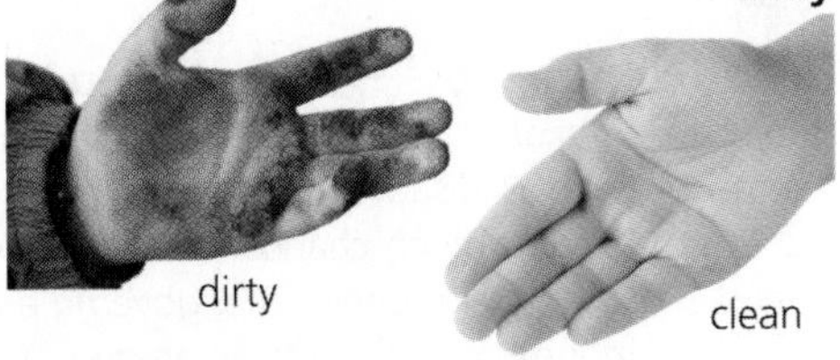


**dirt·y** /ˈdɚti/ *adjective* (**dirtier**, **dirtiest**)

**1** not clean: *My hands were dirty because I had been planting some seeds.*

> **THESAURUS: dirty**
>
> **filthy** very dirty: *The carpet was filthy.*
>
> **dusty** covered with dust: *The shelves in the basement were really dusty.*
>
> **muddy** covered in mud: *My boots were all muddy after walking by the river.*
>
> **greasy** covered with a lot of oil or grease (=an oily substance): *His hair is greasy because he hasn't washed it for a week.*
>
> **polluted** polluted air or water has a lot of harmful chemicals in it: *It is one of the country's most polluted cities, with lots of cars that produce smog.*

**2** unfair or not honest: *He lied to us – it was a really dirty trick.*

**3** relating to sex in a way that people think is bad: *The teacher was angry because Jake was telling dirty jokes to the other kids.*

**dis·a·bil·i·ty** /ˌdɪsəˈbɪləti/ *noun* (plural **disabilities**)

a physical or mental condition that makes it difficult for someone to do things: *The school has ramps and other things to help students with physical disabilities.*

**dis·a·bled** /dɪsˈeɪbəld/ *adjective*

someone who is disabled cannot use a part of his or her body in the way that most people can: *Disabled people in wheelchairs can get into the building easily because there are no steps.*

**dis·ad·van·tage** /ˌdɪsədˈvæntɪdʒ/ *noun*
**1** something that may make someone less successful than other people: *Because I didn't speak Spanish and everyone else did, I was at a disadvantage.*
**2** a bad feature of something: *One disadvantage of this medicine is that it makes you feel sleepy.*

D

**dis·ad·van·taged** /ˌdɪsədˈvæntɪdʒd/ *adjective (formal)*
someone who is disadvantaged is poor and does not have as much chance to succeed as people with more money: *The government provides money to help disadvantaged students.*
→ see Thesaurus box at **poor**

**dis·a·gree** /ˌdɪsəˈgri/ *verb*
to have a different opinion from someone else: *I liked the red dress best, but Alex disagreed with me and preferred the blue one.* **ANTONYM: agree**

**dis·a·gree·a·ble** /ˌdɪsəˈgriəbəl/ *adjective (formal)*
not pleasant or nice: *He's a disagreeable man, and I don't want to see him again.*

**dis·a·gree·ment** /ˌdɪsəˈgrimənt/ *noun*
a situation in which people disagree or argue: *We had a disagreement about the rules of the game, and in the end we stopped playing.*

**dis·ap·pear** /ˌdɪsəˈpɪr/ *verb*
**1** to become impossible to see or find: *My watch has disappeared – it was on the table and now it's gone.*
**2** to stop existing: *Large parts of the forest have disappeared since logging began.*
—**disappearance** *noun* the act of disappearing: *What caused the disappearance of the dinosaurs 65 million years ago?*

**dis·ap·point** /ˌdɪsəˈpɔɪnt/ *verb*
to make someone sad because something does not happen or is not as good as expected: *I'm sorry to disappoint you, but the trip has been canceled.*
—**disappointed** *adjective* sad because something does not happen or is not as good as expected: *I'm disappointed that I didn't win.*
—**disappointing** *adjective* making you feel disappointed: *The high school football team had a disappointing season and only won two games.*

**WORD FAMILY: disappoint**

**disappoint** *verb* | **disappointed** *adjective* | **disappointing** *adjective* | **disappointment** *noun*

**dis·ap·point·ment** /ˌdɪsəˈpɔɪntmənt/ *noun*
**1** a feeling of sadness because something has not happened or is not as good as you expected: *She tried to hide her disappointment at not winning.*
**2** someone or something that is not as good as you hoped or expected: *Their second album was a disappointment because it was not as good as their first.*

**dis·ap·prov·al** /ˌdɪsəˈpruvəl/ *noun*
the opinion that someone or something is bad or wrong: *Mom frowned to show her disapproval of the way I was dressed.* **ANTONYM: approval**

**dis·ap·prove** /ˌdɪsəˈpruv/ *verb*
to think that someone or something is bad or wrong: *Most adults disapprove of teenagers smoking.* **ANTONYM: approve**

**dis·arm** /dɪsˈɑrm/ *verb*
if a country or group disarms, it reduces the number of weapons and soldiers it has: *Both sides must disarm before they can discuss peace.*
—**disarmament** *noun* the process of disarming

**dis·as·ter** /dɪˈzæstɚ/ *noun*
**1** a sudden event that causes great harm or damage, such as an accident or a flood: *In the last two years the country has been hit by three natural disasters – floods, a tornado, and an earthquake.*
**2** a complete failure: *The party was a total disaster and everyone went home early.*
—**disastrous** /dɪˈzæstrəs/ *adjective* very bad: *The candle set fire to the curtains, with disastrous results.*
[**ORIGIN:** 1500-1600 From the Italian word *disastro*, from *dis-* and *astro*, which mean "not" and "star." People thought that luck depended on the position of the stars.]

**dis·be·lief** /ˌdɪsbəˈlif/ *noun* (*formal*)
a feeling that something is not true: *When they told him he had won $1,000,000, he shook his head in disbelief.*

**disc** /dɪsk/ *noun*
another spelling of DISK

**dis·card** /dɪˈskɑrd/ *verb* (*formal*)
to get rid of something because you do not need it: *Take the meat off the chicken and discard the skin and bones.* **SYNONYMS: get rid of, throw out**

**dis·cern** /dɪˈsɚn/ *verb* (*formal*)
to see or understand something that is not easy to see or understand: *In the dark, I could just discern the figure of a man.*
—**discernible** *adjective* able to be seen

**dis·charge** /dɪsˈtʃɑrdʒ/ *verb*
**1** to officially allow or tell someone to leave an organization or a place such as a hospital: *He was discharged from the hospital last night.*
**2** (*formal*) to send out or let out a substance: *The factory was discharging chemicals into the river.*
—**discharge** /ˈdɪstʃɑrdʒ/ *noun* the action of discharging someone or something, or something that is discharged

**dis·ci·ple** /dɪˈsaɪpəl/ *noun*
someone who believes in the ideas of a religious leader or teacher: *Peter was one of Jesus's 12 disciples.*

**dis·ci·pline**[1] /ˈdɪsəplɪn/ *noun*
a situation in which you obey rules and orders, or control your own behavior: *There was no discipline in the classroom. Students were talking and nobody was working.*
[**ORIGIN:** 1200-1300 From the Latin word *disciplina*, which means "teaching."]

**discipline**[2] *verb*
to punish someone who has not obeyed a rule or order: *How should parents discipline their children if they behave badly?*

**dis·close** /dɪsˈkloʊz/ *verb* (*formal*)
to let people know a fact that was a secret: *She refused to disclose her age.* **SYNONYM: reveal**
—**disclosure** *noun* the act of letting people know something that was a secret

**dis·co** /ˈdɪskoʊ/ *noun* (plural **discos**)
a place where people dance to music on CDs or records

**dis·com·fort** /dɪsˈkʌmfɚt/ *noun* (*formal*)
slight pain or a feeling of not being relaxed: *If your bed is causing you discomfort, you might need a different mattress.* **ANTONYM: comfort**

**dis·con·nect** /ˌdɪskəˈnekt/ *verb*
to separate something from the thing it is connected to: *Disconnect the computer from the power supply.* **ANTONYM: connect**

**dis·con·tin·ue** /ˌdɪskənˈtɪnyu/ *verb* (*formal*)
to stop doing something, or stop making something that people buy: *That color of paint has been discontinued – you can't buy it any more.* **ANTONYM: continue**

**dis·count** /ˈdɪskaʊnt/ *noun*
a reduction in the usual price of something: *I get a 10% discount on everything I buy from the store because I'm a student.*

**dis·cour·age** /dɪˈskɚɪdʒ/ *verb*
**1** to persuade someone not to do something: *The teacher discouraged the students from smoking by showing them pictures of someone with lung cancer.* **ANTONYM: encourage**
**2** to make someone feel less confident: *I got a C on the first test, but I tried not to let that discourage me.*
—**discouraged** *adjective* feeling less confident because of something that has happened: *Don't be discouraged. You'll do better next time!*
—**discouraging** *adjective* making you feel less confident: *The beginning of the game was discouraging because the other team scored 15 points in the first six minutes.*

**dis·cov·er** /dɪˈskʌvɚ/ *verb*
**1** to find out a fact: *She discovered that her boyfriend was dating another girl.*
**2** to find something that was hidden or not known about before: *He discovered an old map in a drawer of the desk.* | *Scientists have discovered a new insect.*
→ see Thesaurus box at **find**

**USAGE: discover, invent**

People **discover** a place, force, animal, or plant that was not known about before:

*Herschel discovered the planet Uranus in 1781.*

People **invent** a new machine or a new way of doing something: *Who invented the light bulb?*

**dis·cov·er·y** /dɪˈskʌvəri/ *noun* (plural **discoveries**)

**1** the act of finding out a fact: *Scientists have recently made many discoveries about how genes work.*

**2** the act of finding something that was hidden or not known about before: *The discovery of a new planet caused great excitement.*

**dis·creet** /dɪˈskrit/ *adjective*

careful not to let too many people know something: *She asked me to be discreet because she didn't want everyone to know she was sick.*

**—discreetly** *adverb* in a discreet way

**dis·cre·tion** Ac /dɪˈskreʃən/ *noun* (*formal*)

**1** the right to decide what should be done in a particular situation: *The judge has some discretion when deciding how long someone should go to prison for.*

**2** the quality of being discreet: *You can rely on my discretion – I won't tell anyone your secret.*

**dis·crim·i·nate** Ac /dɪˈskrɪməˌneɪt/ *verb*

**1** to unfairly treat one person or group differently from another: *We do not discriminate against people because of their race.*

**2** (*formal*) to know that two things are different from each other: *Babies can discriminate between a man's voice and a woman's voice.* **SYNONYM: differentiate**

**—discrimination** /dɪˌskrɪməˈneɪʃən/ *noun* the act of discriminating against someone: *They accused the company of racial discrimination for hiring a white man who had less experience than a black man who wanted the job.*

**—discriminatory** /dɪˈskrɪmənəˌtɔri/ *adjective* (*formal*) discriminating against someone: *These discriminatory laws stop women from getting paid as well as men.*

[**ORIGIN:** 1600-1700 From the Latin word *discriminare*, which means "to divide."]

**dis·cuss** /dɪˈskʌs/ *verb*

to talk about something in a serious way: *You should discuss the problem with your teacher.*

→ see Thesaurus box at **talk**[1]

[**ORIGIN:** 1300-1400 From the Latin word *discussus*, a form of the verb *discutere*, which means "to shake to pieces." When you discuss something, you talk about all the pieces, or parts, of it.]

**dis·cus·sion** /dɪˈskʌʃən/ *noun*

a talk in which people give their ideas about something: *We all read the book and then had a class discussion about it.*

**dis·ease** /dɪˈziz/ *noun*

a serious illness: *There is no cure for this disease yet and many people die from it.*

**dis·fig·ure** /dɪsˈfɪgjɚ/ *verb* (*formal*)

if a part of a person's body is disfigured, it has been damaged and looks bad: *The woman's face had been disfigured in the attack.*

**dis·grace** /dɪsˈgreɪs/ *noun*

**1** something or someone that makes people feel ashamed: *After he was caught stealing, his father told him that he was a disgrace to the family.*

**2 in disgrace** = if you are in disgrace, you have done something bad and people are ashamed of you: *He left the school in disgrace after hitting a teacher.*

**dis·grace·ful** /dɪsˈgreɪsfəl/ *adjective* (*formal*)

very bad and wrong: *The salesperson was very rude; his behavior was disgraceful.*

**—disgracefully** *adverb* very badly

**dis·guise**[1] /dɪsˈgaɪz/ *verb*

**1** to make yourself look different, because you want to hide who you are: *She disguised herself as a man.*

**2** to hide your feelings or the truth about something: *Dan likes Katie, but he disguises his feelings so that he won't be teased.*

[**ORIGIN:** 1300-1400 From the old French word *desguiser*, from *guise*, which means "appearance."]

**disguise**[2] *noun*

unusual clothes that you wear to hide who you are: *The movie star went out in disguise to avoid reporters.*

**dis·gust** /dɪsˈgʌst/ *verb*

if something bad disgusts you, you feel

strongly that it is very bad or unpleasant: *His cruel treatment of the dog disgusted me.*
—**disgusted** *adjective* feeling strongly that something is very bad or unpleasant: *I knew that she was lying, and I was disgusted with her.*
—**disgust** *noun* a strong feeling that something is very bad or unpleasant: *She looked around the dirty room in disgust.*

**WORD FAMILY: disgust**
**disgust** *verb* | **disgust** *noun* | **disgusted** *adjective* | **disgusting** *adjective*

**dis·gust·ing** /dɪsˈgʌstɪŋ/ *adjective*
very bad or unpleasant: *This medicine tastes disgusting!*
→ see Thesaurus box at **bad**

**dish** /dɪʃ/ *noun*
**1** a container used for cooking or holding food: *Mom came in with a dish of spaghetti.*
**2** **the dishes** = all the plates, cups, and bowls that you use for a meal: *It's your turn to wash the dishes.*
**3** food that you prepare in a particular way: *She made a delicious dish with mushrooms, garlic, and cheese.*
[**ORIGIN:** From the old English word *disc*, from the Latin word *discus*, which means "flat round object, or plate."]

**dish·cloth** /ˈdɪʃklɔθ/ *noun*
a cloth used for washing dishes

**dis·hon·est** /dɪsˈɑnɪst/ *adjective*
not honest: *It's dishonest to cheat on a test.*
—**dishonesty** *noun* the quality of not being honest

**dis·hon·or** /dɪsˈɑnɚ/ *noun* (*formal*)
the situation you are in when people do not respect you because you have done something bad: *Now he faced the dishonor of going to prison.*
—**dishonor** *verb* to do something that shows you do not respect someone or something: *He thought that if men refused to fight in a war, they dishonored their country.*

**dish·tow·el** /ˈdɪʃˌtaʊəl/ *noun*
a cloth used for drying dishes

**dish·wash·er** /ˈdɪʃˌwɑʃɚ/ *noun*
**1** a machine that washes dishes: *After dinner, would you please load the dishwasher and start it?* → see picture on page **A9**
**2** someone whose job is washing dishes in a restaurant

**dis·il·lu·sioned** /ˌdɪsəˈluʒənd/ *adjective*
no longer believing that someone or something is good or interesting: *He studied law, but he became disillusioned with it when he realized that many lawyers just want to make a lot of money.*
—**disillusionment** *noun* the state of being disillusioned

**dis·in·fect** /ˌdɪsɪnˈfekt/ *verb*
to clean something with a chemical that kills BACTERIA: *Hospital rooms are regularly cleaned and disinfected.*

**dis·in·fect·ant** /ˌdɪsɪnˈfektənt/ *noun*
a chemical that kills BACTERIA, used to clean something

**dis·in·te·grate** /dɪsˈɪntəˌgreɪt/ *verb* (*formal*)
to break up into small pieces: *The pages of the book were old and brown and disintegrated in my hands.*
—**disintegration** /dɪsˌɪntəˈgreɪʃən/ *noun* the process of disintegrating

**disk** (*also* **disc**) /dɪsk/ *noun*
**1** a flat round piece of plastic or metal used for storing computer information, music, or a movie: *I finished my homework assignment and saved it on a disk.*
**2** a flat round object: *People used to think that the Earth was a disk.*

**ˈdisk drive** *noun*
the part of a computer that you put a disk into

**dis·like¹** /dɪsˈlaɪk/ *verb* (*formal*)
to not like someone or something: *A lot of kids dislike vegetables.*
→ see Thesaurus box at **hate¹**

**dislike²** *noun* (*formal*)
a feeling of not liking someone or something: *Maria couldn't hide her dislike for Joe. She wouldn't even talk to him.* **ANTONYM: liking**

**dis·lo·cate** /dɪsˈloʊkeɪt/ *verb*
to make a bone move out of its normal position at a joint in your body: *Pete dislocated his shoulder playing football.*

**dis·loy·al** /dɪsˈlɔɪəl/ *adjective* (*formal*)
doing or saying things that do not support

D

your friends, your country, or the group of people you belong to: *It would be disloyal of me to criticize my friend.* **ANTONYM: loyal**
—**disloyalty** /dɪsˈlɔɪəlti/ *noun* disloyal behavior

**dis·mal** /ˈdɪzməl/ *adjective (formal)*
making you feel unhappy and without hope: *It was a dismal gray afternoon.*

D

**dis·may** /dɪsˈmeɪ/ *noun (formal)*
a feeling of being worried or upset: *Suzy realized with dismay that she'd missed her bus and that she would be late.*
—**dismayed** *adjective* feeling worried or upset: *We were dismayed to find that the car had been stolen.*

**dis·miss** /dɪsˈmɪs/ *verb (formal)*
**1** to tell someone that he or she can leave: *Mrs. Burrows dismissed the class, and they went outside.*
**2** to refuse to think about an idea: *Think about it for a few days – don't just dismiss the idea.*
**3** if your employer dismisses you, you have to leave your job: *The man had been dismissed from his job for stealing.* **SYNONYM: fire**
—**dismissal** *noun* the act of dismissing someone

**dis·o·be·di·ent** /ˌdɪsəˈbidiənt/ *adjective*
refusing to obey someone: *My dog is very disobedient. He never comes when I call him.* **ANTONYM: obedient**
—**disobedience** *noun* disobedient behavior: *The soldier was punished for disobedience.*
—**disobediently** *adverb* in a disobedient way

**dis·o·bey** /ˌdɪsəˈbeɪ/ *verb*
to not obey a person or a rule: *You must not disobey the school rules.*

**THESAURUS: disobey**

**break a rule/law** to disobey a rule or law: *If you drink alcohol and then drive, you're breaking the law.*

**rebel** to disobey or fight against someone who has power over you: *Hannah rebelled against her parents' strict rules.*

**defy** *(formal)* to refuse to obey someone or something: *Mark had never defied his father before.*

**violate** *(formal)* to do something that does not obey a law, rule, or agreement: *The army crossed the border without permission, which violated international law.*

**dis·or·der** /dɪsˈɔrdɚ/ *noun (formal)*
**1** a situation in which things are not organized or neat: *The room was in complete disorder. There were clothes and books all over the floor.* **ANTONYM: order**
**2** an illness: *The doctor said her strange behavior was caused by a mental disorder.*

**dis·or·der·ly** /dɪsˈɔrdɚli/ *adjective (formal)*
**1** not organized or neat: *Disorderly piles of clothes lay on the floor.* **ANTONYM: orderly**
**2** showing bad or violent behavior: *The children were loud and disorderly, and the teacher could not control them.*

**dis·or·ga·nized** /dɪsˈɔrgəˌnaɪzd/ *adjective*
not arranged or organized well: *The meeting was completely disorganized and we didn't decide anything.* **ANTONYM: organized**

**dis·o·ri·ent·ed** /dɪsˈɔriˌəntɪd/ *adjective*
confused about what is happening or where you are: *I fell and hit my head, and when I stood up I felt a little disoriented.*

**dis·patch** /dɪˈspætʃ/ *verb (formal)*
to send a person or thing somewhere: *A new spacecraft will soon be dispatched to Mars.*

**dis·pense** /dɪˈspens/ *verb (formal)*
to give advice or help to people: *The organization dispenses legal advice to the public.*

**dis·pens·er** /dɪˈspensɚ/ *noun*
a machine or piece of equipment that gives you something when you push a button: *There was a soap dispenser next to the sink.*
→ see picture on page **A9**

**dis·place** Ac /dɪsˈpleɪs/ *verb (formal)*
to take the place of someone or something that is not wanted or needed any more: *Computers have displaced typewriters.*
—**displacement** *noun* the act of displacing someone or something

**dis·play¹** Ac /dɪˈspleɪ/ *noun*
**1** an arrangement or show of things for

people to come and see: *There is a display of all the students' work in the hall.*

**2 on display** = in a public place for people to see: *Some of my paintings were on display in the art show.*

**3** a part of an electronic machine that shows you information: *The number you are calling is shown on the phone's display.*

**display²** Ac *verb*

**1** to put things in a place where people can see them: *The students' work is displayed on the board in the classroom.*

**2** to show a feeling or quality: *Her face clearly displayed her anger.*

**dis·pos·a·ble** Ac /dɪˈspoʊzəbəl/ *adjective*
made for someone to use once and then throw away: *Most parents buy disposable diapers for their babies, so there is less laundry to do.*

**dis·pose** Ac /dɪˈspoʊz/ *verb* (*formal*)
**PHRASAL VERB**
**dispose of something**
to throw away or destroy something: *We need better ways to dispose of waste so that it does not harm the environment.* **SYNONYM: get rid of something**
—**disposal** *noun* the act of disposing of something: *The garbage is taken away for disposal.*

**WORD FAMILY: dispose**
**dispose** *verb* | **disposal** *noun* | **disposable** *adjective*

**dis·prove** /dɪsˈpruv/ *verb* (*formal*)
to show that an idea or statement is not true: *Recent research has disproved this idea, but some people still believe it.* **ANTONYM: prove**

**dis·pute** /dɪˈspjut/ *noun* (*formal*)
a serious argument: *The two men got into a dispute over money.*
—**dispute** *verb* to say that you think something is not true: *Some people dispute the idea that pollution is causing the climate to change.*
[**ORIGIN:** 1500-1600 From the Latin word *disputare*, which means "to discuss."]

**dis·qual·i·fy** /dɪsˈkwɑləˌfaɪ/ *verb* (**disqualified, disqualifies**)
to stop someone from taking part in a race, game, or competition because he or she has done something wrong: *He was disqualified for pushing another player.*
—**disqualification** /dɪsˌkwɑləfəˈkeɪʃən/ *noun* the act of disqualifying someone

**dis·re·spect** /ˌdɪsrɪˈspekt/ *noun*
a lack of respect for someone or something: *Criminals show a disrespect for the law.*
—**disrespect** *verb* (*informal*) to show a lack of respect for someone or something: *Don't disrespect me by lying to me.*

D

**dis·re·spect·ful** /ˌdɪsrɪˈspektfəl/ *adjective*
showing no respect for someone or something: *Don't be disrespectful to your mother – listen when she's talking to you.*
**ANTONYM: respectful**

**dis·rupt** /dɪsˈrʌpt/ *verb* (*formal*)
to stop something from happening in a normal way by causing problems: *Bad weather disrupted flights into the airport.*
—**disruption** /dɪsˈrʌpʃən/ *noun* (*formal*) the action of disrupting something: *Cell phones should be turned off so there will be no disruptions during the movie.*
—**disruptive** /dɪsˈrʌptɪv/ *adjective* causing problems by acting badly: *The boy was very disruptive in class, making funny noises when the teacher wasn't looking.*
[**ORIGIN:** 1400-1500 From the Latin word *disruptus*, a form of the verb *disrumpere*, which means "to break."]

**dis·sat·is·fied** /dɪˈsætəsˌfaɪd/ *adjective*
unhappy about something because you do not think it is good enough: *Some teenage girls are dissatisfied with the way they look, and they want to be taller or thinner.*
**ANTONYM: satisfied**
—**dissatisfaction** /dɪˌsætɪsˈfækʃən/ *noun* the feeling of being dissatisfied: *A number of customers expressed dissatisfaction, so the company tried hard to improve its service.*

**dis·sent** /dɪˈsent/ *noun*
an opinion that does not agree with an idea, belief, or law that most people accept: *In some countries you can be jailed for political dissent.*

**dis·si·dent** /ˈdɪsədənt/ *noun*
someone who criticizes the government in a country where this is a crime: *Several political dissidents have been put in jail.*

**dis·sim·i·lar** Ac /dɪˌsɪmələ/ *adjective* (*formal*)
not the same: *The twins look alike, but they are dissimilar in other ways.* **ANTONYM: similar**

**dis·solve** /dɪˈzɑlv/ *verb*
if a substance dissolves in a liquid, it becomes part of the liquid and you cannot see it anymore: *Stir the milk and sugar until the sugar dissolves.*

D

**dis·tance** /ˈdɪstəns/ *noun*
**1** the amount of space between two places: *My house is just a short distance from here.* | *Measure the distance between the two points on the line.*
**2** **in the distance** = far away from you, but near enough to see: *From the mountain, we could see the ocean in the distance.*
**3** **keep your distance** = to stay away from someone or something: *The dogs looked mean, so I kept my distance.*

**dis·tant** /ˈdɪstənt/ *adjective* (*formal*)
**1** far away: *People had come from distant parts of the country, traveling for many days.*
**2** not friendly or not caring: *Jonas listened to me, but he seemed distant.*
**3** a distant relative is a member of your family who is not closely related to you **ANTONYM: close**

**dis·tilled** /dɪˈstɪld/ *adjective*
distilled water or alcohol has been heated until it is a gas and then left to cool into a liquid again, in order to make it more pure
—**distill** *verb* to heat a liquid until it is gas and then let it cool into a liquid again, in order to make it more pure
—**distillation** /ˌdɪstəˈleɪʃən/ *noun* the process of distilling a liquid

**dis·tinct** Ac /dɪˈstɪŋkt/ *adjective*
**1** a distinct feeling, possibility, etc. is clear and definite: *I had the distinct feeling that he didn't like me.*
**2** if two things are distinct, they are clearly different from each other: *There are two distinct types of elephants – Asian and African.*

**dis·tinc·tion** Ac /dɪˈstɪŋkʃən/ *noun*
**1** a clear difference: *One distinction between a horse and a zebra is that a zebra has stripes.*
**2** the quality of doing something very well: *He served with distinction in the war.*
**3** **have the distinction of doing something** = to do something special that everyone admires: *He has the distinction of being the first black president of the United States.*

**dis·tinc·tive** Ac /dɪˈstɪŋktɪv/ *adjective* (*formal*)
different from others and easy to recognize: *Everyone's fingerprints have a distinctive pattern that makes them different from other people's.*

**dis·tinct·ly** Ac /dɪˈstɪŋktli/ *adverb*
very clearly: *I distinctly remember switching off the light, so someone else must have turned it on again.*

**dis·tin·guish** /dɪˈstɪŋgwɪʃ/ *verb* (*formal*)
**1** to see the difference between things: *My parents taught me to distinguish between right and wrong.*
**2** to make something clearly different from something else: *The male bird's bright feathers distinguish it from the female.*

**dis·tin·guished** /dɪˈstɪŋgwɪʃt/ *adjective* (*formal*)
very good and admired by a lot of people: *He had a distinguished career as a scientist.*

**dis·tort** Ac /dɪˈstɔrt/ *verb*
to change something and make it look or sound different from normal: *The funny mirrors distorted our reflections.*
—**distortion** /dɪˈstɔrʃən/ *noun* the act of distorting something
[**ORIGIN:** 1400-1500 From the Latin word *distortus*, a form of the verb *distorquere*, which means "to twist out of shape."]

**dis·tract** /dɪˈstrækt/ *verb*
to make someone stop paying attention to something: *Her music was distracting me from my homework.*
—**distraction** /dɪˈstrækʃən/ *noun* something that makes you stop paying attention: *I can't work at home – there are too many distractions.*

**dis·tress**[1] /dɪˈstres/ *noun* (*formal*)
**1** a feeling of great sadness or worry: *You could see the distress in the child's eyes as she said goodbye to her parents.*
**2** **in distress** = in a very difficult situation and needing help: *Our organization tries to help*

*children in distress in the poorest areas of the world.*

**distress²** *verb* (*formal*)
to make someone sad or worried: *The awful news distressed us all.*
—**distressed** *adjective* feeling very sad or worried: *She was crying and very distressed about her parents' divorce.*
—**distressing** *adjective* making you feel very sad or worried: *It was distressing to see her so sick.*

**dis·trib·ute** [Ac] /dɪˈstrɪbyət/ *verb* (*formal*)
**1** to give something to the people in a group: *The money was distributed among the poorest people.*
**2** to take goods to stores and companies for them to sell: *The company makes and distributes building materials.*

**WORD FAMILY: distribute**
**distribute** *verb* | **distribution** *noun* | **distributor** *noun*

→ see Thesaurus box at **give**

**dis·tri·bu·tion** [Ac] /ˌdɪstrəˈbyuʃən/ *noun*
**1** the act of giving things to a large group of people: *The army helped with the distribution of food to victims of the earthquake.*
**2** the act of taking goods to stores and companies for them to sell: *The company uses trucks for the distribution of its goods.*
—**distributor** /dɪˈstrɪbyətɚ/ *noun* a company that supplies goods to shops or other companies: *The company is a distributor of cell phones.*

**dis·trict** /ˈdɪstrɪkt/ *noun*
an area of a city or country: *She works in the financial district of the city.*
→ see Thesaurus box at **area**

**ˌdistrict atˈtorney** (*also* **D.A.**) *noun*
a lawyer for the government of an area in the U.S.: *He's the D.A. for Harris County.*

**dis·trust** /dɪsˈtrʌst/ *noun* (*formal*)
a feeling that you cannot trust someone: *He had a distrust of politicians; he thought they were all liars.*
—**distrust** *verb* to not trust someone or something
—**distrustful** *adjective* not trusting someone or something: *Kim was distrustful of strangers.*

**dis·turb** /dɪˈstɚb/ *verb*
**1** to interrupt what someone is doing: *Don't disturb Dad – he's working.*
**2** (*formal*) to make someone feel worried or upset: *The strange way she acted had disturbed him.*
—**disturbing** *adjective* making you feel worried or upset: *The news about the war was very disturbing.*

**dis·turb·ance** /dɪˈstɚbəns/ *noun* (*formal*)
**1** something that interrupts what you are doing: *I really need to work without any disturbance.*
**2** a situation in which people fight or cause trouble in public: *Three men were arrested for causing a disturbance.*

**ditch** /dɪtʃ/ *noun*
a long narrow hole dug at the side of a field or road for water to flow away: *I jumped across the ditch and into the field.*

**dive** /daɪv/ *verb* (**dived** *or* **dove** /doʊv/, **dived**)
**1** to jump into water with your head and arms going in first: *Jack dived into the swimming pool.*
**2** to go down suddenly: *The plane began to dive.*
→ see Thesaurus box at **jump¹**

**div·er** /ˈdaɪvɚ/ *noun*
**1** someone who swims under water using equipment for breathing: *The divers found the wreck of an old ship.*
**2** someone who dives into water as a sport

**di·verse** [Ac] /dəˈvɚs/ *adjective* (*formal*)
containing many different types of people or things: *We are a very diverse group. We have students from over 50 countries.*

**WORD FAMILY: diverse**
**diverse** *adjective* | **diversity** *noun*

**di·ver·si·ty** [Ac] /dəˈvɚsəti/ *noun* (*formal*)
if there is diversity in a place, there are many different people or things there: *There is a huge diversity of plants and animals in the rainforest.* **SYNONYM: variety**

**di·vert** /dəˈvɝt/ *verb (formal)*
if cars, airplanes, etc. are diverted, they have to change their direction: *The plane going to Atlanta was diverted to Memphis.*

**di·vide** /dɪˈvaɪd/ *verb*
**1** (*also* **divide up**) to separate something into parts or groups: *The teacher divided the class into groups.*
**2** (*also* **divide up**) to share money, time, etc. between people or activities: *Most students divide their time between school, family, and friends.*
**3** to find how many times a number will go into a bigger number: *15 divided by 3 is 5.* **ANTONYM: multiply**
**4** to make people disagree: *The war divided the nation: some people supported it and others did not.*

| **WORD FAMILY: divide** |
|---|
| **divide** *verb* \| **division** *noun* |

**di·vine** /dɪˈvaɪn/ *adjective*
relating to a god: *the divine power of God*

**ˈdiving board** *noun*
a board that you can stand on before jumping into water: *He jumped off the diving board, and dived into the pool.*

**di·vis·i·ble** /dəˈvɪzəbəl/ *adjective*
if one number is divisible by another number, it can be divided by it: *The number 15 is divisible by 3.*

**di·vi·sion** /dɪˈvɪʒən/ *noun*
**1** the act of finding how many times a number will go into a larger number: *The kids are learning to do division.* | *Who can tell me the answer to the division problem 21 ÷ 3?* **ANTONYM: multiplication**
**2** a part of a company, army, or organization: *"Which part of the company do you work for?" "The sales division."*

**di·vorce¹** /dɪˈvɔrs/ *noun*
a legal agreement to end a marriage: *His wife wants to get a divorce.*
**[ORIGIN:** 1300-1400 From the Latin word *divertere*, which means "to turn aside, or to leave your husband."**]**

**divorce²** *verb*
to end a marriage by law: *My parents got divorced when I was six.*
→ see Thesaurus box at **married**

**di·vulge** /dəˈvʌldʒ/ *verb (formal)*
to give information about something secret: *He always refused to divulge how much money he earned.* **SYNONYMS: disclose, reveal**

**diz·zy** /ˈdɪzi/ *adjective*
feeling unable to stand up steadily because you are sick, or you have been turning around in circles: *I feel a little dizzy, so I think I'll lie down.*
—**dizziness** *noun* a feeling of being dizzy
**[ORIGIN:** From the old English word *dysig*, which means "stupid." If you are dizzy, you sometimes cannot think clearly.**]**

**DJ** /ˈdi dʒeɪ/ *noun*
(**disk jockey**) someone whose job is to play the music on the radio or in a place where people can dance

**DNA** *noun*
a substance in the cells of your body that carries GENETIC information

**do¹** /du/ *auxiliary verb* (**did** /dɪd/, **does** /dʌz/)
**1** used with "not" and another verb to make a negative sentence: *She does not have a car.* | *I didn't understand him.*
**2** used with another verb to ask a question: *Do you know where he lives?*
**3** used with "not" and another verb to tell someone not to do something: *Do not walk on the grass.* | *Don't hit me!*
**4** used to emphasize what you are saying: *I did clean the bathroom – I just forgot to tell you.*

**do²** *verb* (**did** /dɪd/, **done** /dʌn/, **does** /dʌz/)
**1** to perform an action or deal with some work: *I'm going to do my homework now.* | *"What are you doing?" "I'm just making lunch."* | *I've done the ironing.*
**2 What do you do (for a living)?** = used when asking someone what their job is: *"What do you do for a living?" "I'm a teacher."*
**3 What is someone or something doing?** = used when asking the reason why someone is doing something, especially because you are

surprised or annoyed: *What is the dog doing on my desk?*
**4 do well/badly** = to be successful or unsuccessful: *He's doing very well in his new job.* | *William did badly on the test.*
**5 do someone good** = to make someone feel better or more healthy: *The vacation did us all good.*
**6 something will do** = used when saying that something is good enough: *This shirt's a little small, but it will do.*
**7 do your hair/nails/makeup** = to brush your hair, paint your nails, or put on MAKEUP: *Wait a second while I do my hair.*
**8** (*informal*) to travel at a particular speed, or to travel a particular distance: *He was doing 60 miles per hour when he hit the other car.* | *We did almost 200 miles the first day when we drove to Oregon.*
**9 do your own thing** (*informal*) = to do what you enjoy doing: *On the weekend, I like to do my own thing.*

**PHRASAL VERBS**

**do something over**
to do something again, especially because you did it badly: *If you mess up on the test, you can do it over.*

**do with something**
**1 What did you do with something?** = used when asking where someone has put something: *What did you do with those pictures?*
**2 I could do with something** (*informal*) = used when saying that you need or want something: *I could do with some help.*
**3 have something to do with something** = to be related to something: *Her work has something to do with the environment.*

**do without something**
to live or continue without something: *It's difficult to do without a car in Los Angeles.*

**do·a·ble** /ˈduəbəl/ *adjective* (*informal*)
possible to do: *It's a difficult task, but I think it's doable.*

**d.o.b.**
the written abbreviation of **date of birth**

**dock$^1$** /dɑk/ *noun*
a place where a ship or boat stops, so that people can get on or off, or things can be put on or taken off: *The ship was sitting at the dock.*

**dock$^2$** *verb*
if a ship docks, it sails into a dock: *The ship docked in Brooklyn.*

**doc·tor** /ˈdɑktɚ/ *noun*
**1** someone whose job is treating people who are sick: *If you're still sick tomorrow, you should go to the doctor.* → see picture on page **A16**

**THESAURUS: doctor**

**physician** (*formal*) a doctor: *Dr. Meadows is our family physician.*
**surgeon** a doctor who cuts open someone's body in order to fix or replace something: *Surgeons operated on his knee.*
**specialist** a doctor who knows a lot about a particular type of illness or injury: *He is one of the world's leading heart specialists.*
**psychiatrist** a doctor who treats mental illness: *The psychiatrist treated her for depression.*
**pediatrician** a doctor who treats sick children: *She took her son to a pediatrician when he had a high fever.*
**dentist** someone whose job is to take care of people's teeth: *You should see a dentist every six months.*

**2** someone who has the highest type of university degree: *He's a Doctor of Philosophy.*
[**ORIGIN:** 1300-1400 From the Latin word *doctor*, which means "teacher."]

**doc·tor·ate** /ˈdɑktərɪt/ *noun*
the highest type of university degree: *She earned a doctorate in biology.* **SYNONYM: Ph.D.**

**doc·u·ment** [Ac] /ˈdɑkyəmənt/ *noun*
**1** a piece of paper with official information on it: *Keep important documents such as your birth certificate in a safe place.*
**2** a piece of work that you write and keep on a computer: *Don't forget to save your document before you close the program.*
[**ORIGIN:** 1400-1500 From the Latin word *documentum*, which means "lesson, or piece of evidence," from *docere*, which means "to teach."]

D

**doc·u·men·tary** /ˌdɑkyəˈmentri/ *noun* (plural **documentaries**)
a movie or television program that gives you information about a subject: *Did you see that documentary on insects?*
→ see Thesaurus box at **program**[1]

**doc·u·men·ta·tion** Ac /ˌdɑkyəmənˈteɪʃən/ *noun (formal)*
documents which show that something is true or correct: *The documentation gives details of your order and the price you paid for each item.*

D

**dodge** /dɑdʒ/ *verb*
**1** to move quickly in order to avoid someone or something: *I dodged past him and kicked the ball.*
**2** to avoid talking about something or doing something: *Answer me – don't try to dodge the question!*

**doe** /doʊ/ *noun*
a female DEER

**does** /dəz; *strong* dʌz/ *verb*
the third person singular of the present tense of DO

**does·n't** /ˈdʌzənt/ *verb*
the short form of "does not": *The baby doesn't have any teeth yet.*

**dog** /dɔg/ *noun*
an animal that people often keep as a pet or use for guarding buildings: *My dog barks when he hears a strange noise.*
[**ORIGIN:** From the old English word *docga*.]

**doll** /dɑl/ *noun*
a toy that looks like a baby or small person: *Katy loves playing with her dolls.*
[**ORIGIN:** 1500-1600 From the girl's name Doll, a short form of Dorothy.]

**dol·lar** /ˈdɑlɚ/ *noun*
the money used in the U.S. and some other countries, shown by the sign ($): *These pants cost 40 dollars.* | *Can you lend me ten dollars until tomorrow?*
[**ORIGIN:** 1500-1600 From the German word *joachimstaler*, from Joachimsthal, a German town. Silver from a mine near this town was used to make coins.]

**ˈdollar sign** *noun*
the sign ($), used to mean a dollar

dolphin

**dol·phin** /ˈdɑlfɪn/ *noun*
a very intelligent gray ocean animal with a long pointed nose: *We saw a group of dolphins playing in the waves.*

**do·main** Ac /doʊˈmeɪn/ *noun (formal)*
**1** a type of work, activity, or knowledge that one person deals with or is responsible for: *Cooking is my domain – I don't let anyone else in the kitchen.*
**2** an area of land that is controlled by one person, group, or government

**dome** /doʊm/ *noun*
a round curved roof: *If you look across the city, you can see the dome of the cathedral.*

**do·mes·tic** Ac /dəˈmestɪk/ *adjective (formal)*
**1** relating to things that happen inside a country, rather than things that happen in other countries: *The president's speech is about taxes and other domestic policies.*
**2** relating to life at home: *Men still do not do as many domestic chores, such as cleaning and cooking.*
—**domestically** *adverb* inside one country: *Most of these goods are made domestically.*
[**ORIGIN:** 1400-1500 From the Latin word *domus*, which means "house."]

**dom·i·nant** Ac /ˈdɑmənənt/ *adjective*
the most important or powerful: *The Lakers were the dominant team in the NBA for many years.*
—**dominance** *noun* the state of being dominant

**dom·i·nate** Ac /ˈdɑməˌneɪt/ *verb*
to have the most influence or the most important position: *Men still dominate the field of movie directing, but more and more women are making movies.*

—**domination** /ˌdɑməˈneɪʃən/ *noun* the position of dominating something

**WORD FAMILY: dominate**

**dominate** *verb* | **domination** *noun* | **dominant** *adjective* | **dominance** *noun*

**dom·i·no** /ˈdɑməˌnoʊ/ *noun* (plural **dominoes**)
**1 dominoes** = a game played with small pieces of wood or plastic with spots on one side
**2** one of the pieces of wood or plastic that are used to play dominoes

**do·nate** /ˈdoʊneɪt/ *verb*
**1** to give money to an organization that needs help: *Our school donated $500 to the Red Cross.*
**2** to give some of your blood or a part of your body to help someone who is sick: *Hospitals are asking more people to donate blood.*
—**donation** /doʊˈneɪʃən/ *noun* money that you give to help an organization: *Do you want to make a donation to charity?*
[**ORIGIN:** 1400-1500 From the Latin word *donare*, which means "to give."]

**WORD FAMILY: donate**

**donate** *verb* | **donation** *noun* | **donor** *noun*

**done**[1] /dʌn/ *verb*
the past participle of DO

**done**[2] *adjective*
**1** finished: *"Are you finished?" "Not yet, I'll be done in a minute."* | *Put the scissors back when you're done with them.*

**THESAURUS: done**

**finished** if you are finished, you have come to the end of doing something: *Are you finished with your homework?*

**complete** finished, and having all the parts you need: *My history report is almost complete.*

**over** if an event, activity, or period of time is over, it has ended: *The game was over by 10 o'clock.*

**through** if you are through with something, you have finished using it or doing it: *Are you through with those scissors?*

**2** cooked enough to be eaten: *Is the chicken done yet?*

**don·key** /ˈdɑŋki/ *noun*
an animal like a small horse with long ears

**do·nor** /ˈdoʊnɚ/ *noun*
**1 a blood/organ donor** = someone who gives blood or a part of his or her body to help someone who is sick: *The hospital needs more blood donors.*
**2** someone who gives something, especially money, to an organization: *He is a generous donor to the Democratic Party.*

**don't** /doʊnt/ *verb*
the short form of "do not": *I don't know.*

**do·nut** /ˈdoʊnʌt/ *noun*
another spelling of DOUGHNUT

**doo·dle** /ˈdudl/ *verb*
to draw pictures, shapes, or patterns while you are thinking about something else: *He was doodling on a piece of paper while he talked on the phone.*

**doom** /dum/ *noun*
something bad that is certain to happen: *I had a sense of doom before the test – I knew I would do badly.*

**doomed** /dumd/ *adjective*
certain to fail, die, or be destroyed: *Our vacation seemed doomed from the start when we missed the flight.*

**door** /dɔr/ *noun*
**1** the thing that you open to get into a house, room, or car: *I opened the door and went inside.* | *Go out the door and turn right.*
→ see picture on page **A9**
**2 get/answer the door** = to open the door when someone knocks or rings the bell: *Can you get the door, Jody? I'm on the phone.*
**3 next door** = in the room, house, or building next to where you are or where you live: *A very nice family lives next door.*
**4 at the door** = waiting outside the door of a house or apartment: *There's someone at the door who wants to talk to you.*
[**ORIGIN:** From two old English words, *duru*, which means "door," and *dor*, which means "gate."]

D

D

**door·bell** /ˈdɔrbel/ *noun*
a button by a door of a house, that you push to make a sound inside a building: *I went up to the door and rang the doorbell.*

**door·knob** /ˈdɔrnɑb/ *noun*
a round handle that you turn to open a door: *There was no sound inside, so I turned the doorknob.*

**door·mat** /ˈdɔrmæt/ *noun*
a thick piece of material beside a door for you to clean your shoes on: *Ted wiped his muddy boots on the doormat before he went into the house.*

**door·step** /ˈdɔrstep/ *noun*
a step in front of the door of a house: *The dog was standing on the doorstep, wanting to come inside.*

**door·way** /ˈdɔrweɪ/ *noun*
an opening into a room or building, where there is a door: *Cindy stood in the doorway and watched the people in the street.*

**dor·mi·to·ry** /ˈdɔrməˌtɔri/ (*also* **dorm**) (plural **dormitories**) *noun*
a large building at a college where students live: *She lived in my dorm during freshman year.*

**dos·age** /ˈdoʊsɪdʒ/ *noun*
the amount of medicine that you should take at one time: *The correct dosage is one pill, taken thre times a day.*
→ see Thesaurus box at **medicine**

**dose** /doʊs/ *noun*
an amount of medicine: *One spoonful is the right dose for a child.*
→ see Thesaurus box at **medicine**

**dot** /dɑt/ *noun*
**1** a small round mark or spot: *She was wearing a black skirt with white dots.*
**2 on the dot** (*informal*) = exactly at the right time: *Mark arrived at 6:00 on the dot.*

**doub·le¹** /ˈdʌbəl/ *adjective*
**1** having two parts that are the same: *Double doors open onto the porch.*
**2** twice the usual amount or size: *I'm really hungry – I'll have a double cheeseburger with fries.*
**3 a double bed** = a bed for two people
**4 double digits** = the numbers from 10 to 99: *The best three players scored in double digits.*
[**ORIGIN:** 1100-1200 From the Latin word *duplus*, from *duo* and *-plus*, which mean "two" and "multiplied by."]

**double²** *verb*
to become twice as big: *In 30 years, San Francisco doubled in size.*
→ see Thesaurus box at **increase¹**

**double³** *noun*
**1** an amount that is twice as big as another amount: *"He offered me $200." "OK, I'll give you double."*
**2** someone who looks like someone else: *He earned a lot of money working as a double for Tom Cruise.*
**3** a hit in baseball that goes far enough for the BATTER to reach second base

**ˌdouble ˈbass** *noun*
a very big musical instrument like a VIOLIN, that you play while you are standing up **SYNONYM: bass** → see picture on page **A21**

**ˌdouble-ˈcheck** *verb*
to check something again, so you are sure about it: *I think I locked the door, but I'll double-check.*

**ˌdouble ˈnegative** *noun*
the use of two negative words when it is correct to use only one: *The sentence "I don't want nobody to help me" has a double negative. You should say, "I don't want anybody to help me."*

**doubt¹** /daʊt/ *verb*
to think that something may not happen or be true: *Kate might come, but I doubt it. She said she was tired.* | *He doubted that anyone would believe him.*

**WORD FAMILY: doubt**
**doubt** *noun* | **doubt** *verb* | **doubtful** *adjective* | **doubtless** *adverb*

**doubt²** *noun*
**1** a feeling that something is not right or true: *Don't get married if you have any doubts.*
**2 there's no doubt about it** (*also* **without (a) doubt**) = used when saying that something is definitely true: *Without a doubt, this is their best CD yet.*

3 **beyond (a) doubt** = if information is beyond doubt, it is definitely correct: *All the evidence proved beyond a doubt that he was guilty.*

**doubt·ful** /ˈdaʊtfəl/ *adjective*
1 probably not likely to happen, or not true: *He injured his leg and it's doubtful that he'll be able to play in the game.*
2 not sure about something: *I'm still doubtful about whether I should trust him.*

**doubt·less** /ˈdaʊtləs/ *adverb*
used when saying that something is very likely: *The hotel will doubtless be very expensive because it's right in the middle of the city.*
**SYNONYMS: definitely, undoubtedly**

**dough** /doʊ/ *noun*
a soft mixture of flour, butter, water, or other things, that you bake to make bread or cookies
—**doughy** *adjective* soft, like dough: *The bread was a little doughy inside because it hadn't been baked long enough.*

**dough·nut** /ˈdoʊnʌt/ *noun*
a small round cake that is shaped like a ring

**dove¹** /dʌv/ *noun*
a small white bird often used as a sign of peace

**dove²** /doʊv/ *verb*
a past tense of DIVE

**down¹** /daʊn/ *adverb, preposition*
1 toward a lower place: *The kids ran down the hill. | A tree fell down during the night.* **ANTONYM: up**
2 further along a road or path: *I saw George walking down the street.*
3 toward a lower level: *Can you turn the TV down?* **ANTONYM: up**
4 **write/note/take something down** = to write something on paper: *He wrote down my phone number.*
5 toward the south of a country: *We're going to drive down to Texas.* **ANTONYM: up**
→ **come down with** at **come**

**down²** *adjective*
1 sad: *You look down. Are you okay?*
2 lower in amount than before: *The number of students at the school is down this year.* **ANTONYM: up**
3 a computer system that is down is not working: *All the computers in the office are down.*
→ see Thesaurus box at **sad**

**down³** *noun*
the soft feathers of a bird: *The pillow was filled with down.*

**down·fall** /ˈdaʊnfɔl/ *noun*
the complete loss of your money or position in society: *His greed led to his downfall.*

**downhill**

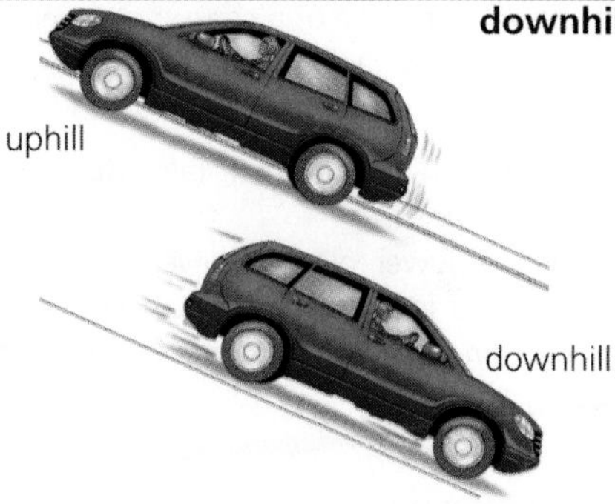


**down·hill** /ˌdaʊnˈhɪl/ *adverb, adjective*
toward a lower level of land: *The land slopes downhill to the river.* **ANTONYM: uphill**

**down·load** /ˈdaʊnloʊd/ *verb*
to move information, programs, etc. to your computer from the Internet or another piece of equipment: *The software can be downloaded from the Internet.*

**ˌdown ˈpayment** *noun*
the first payment that you make on something you are buying, with the rest to be paid later: *My parents put a down payment on a house in Oakland.*

**down·pour** /ˈdaʊnpɔr/ *noun*
a lot of rain that falls in a short time: *We got very wet in a sudden downpour on the way home.*
→ see Thesaurus box at **rain¹**

**down·right** /ˈdaʊnraɪt/ *adverb* (*informal*)
completely or extremely, used especially to emphasize how bad someone or something is: *He's downright lazy – he never helps me do anything at home.*

**down·size** /ˈdaʊnsaɪz/ *verb*
to reduce the number of people who work for a company: *Many people lost their jobs when the company downsized.*

D

**down·stairs** /ˌdaʊnˈsterz/ *adverb, adjective*
down the steps in a building to or on a lower floor: *I went downstairs and opened the front door.* **ANTONYM: upstairs**

**Down syn·drome** /ˈdaʊn ˌsɪndroʊm/ *noun*
a medical condition that someone is born with, which can affect that person's physical and mental development

D

**down·town** /ˌdaʊnˈtaʊn/ *adverb, adjective*
to or in the middle of a city, where there are a lot of stores and businesses: *She works downtown.* | *The hotel is in downtown L.A.*

**down·ward** /ˈdaʊnwərd/ (*also* **downwards**) *adverb, adjective*
toward a lower place or level: *The path led downward to the edge of the lake.* | *a downward movement in prices* **ANTONYM: upward**

**doze** /doʊz/ *verb*
to sleep for a short time: *I was dozing on the couch.*
→ see Thesaurus box at **sleep**[1]
**PHRASAL VERB**
**doze off**
to start sleeping when you do not intend to: *Grandpa dozed off watching TV.*

**doz·en** /ˈdʌzən/ *number*
**1** a group of 12 things: *You can either buy six eggs or a dozen.*
**2** (*informal*) a lot: *I've heard this story dozens of times – he tells it at every party.*
**[ORIGIN:** 1200-1300 From the old French word *doze*, which means "twelve."**]**

**Dr.**
the written abbreviation of **Doctor**

**drab** /dræb/ *adjective*
not colorful or interesting: *The room was drab, with gray walls and a brown carpet.*
**[ORIGIN:** 1500-1600 From the old French word *drap*, which means "cloth." Cloth that has not been dyed is a dull color.**]**

**draft**[1] Ac /dræft/ *noun*
**1** a piece of writing that you plan to make changes to before it is finished: *Can I show you the first draft of my history paper?*
**2** cold air blowing into a room: *There's a draft in here. Is the window open?*
**3 the draft** = a system in which people are ordered to join the military: *Men who were sick avoided the draft.*
**4** a system in which professional sports teams choose players from colleges to join them: *He was one of the first picks in the NBA draft of college players.*

**draft**[2] Ac *verb*
**1** to write something that you plan to make changes to later, until it is the way you want it to be: *I drafted a letter to the newspaper and then asked Mom if it needed any changes.*
**2** to tell someone that he or she must join the military for a period of time: *He was drafted during the Vietnam War, and fought there for several years.*
—**draft** *adjective* a draft letter, report, etc. is one that you will make changes to later: *I gave the draft report to my teacher for comments.*

**draft·y** /ˈdræfti/ *adjective*
a drafty room or building has cold air blowing through it: *Old houses are often drafty.*

**drag** /dræg/ *verb* (**dragged**, **dragging**)
**1** to pull something heavy along the ground: *The boys dragged the boat onto the beach.*
→ see picture on page **A5**
**2** to pull someone in a strong or violent way: *Two men dragged him out of his car.*
→ see Thesaurus box at **pull**[1]
**PHRASAL VERB**
**drag on**
to continue for too long: *The war dragged on and no one knew when it would end.*

**drag·on** /ˈdrægən/ *noun*
a fierce animal in stories, that can fly and breathe out fire

**drag·on·fly** /ˈdrægənˌflaɪ/ *noun* (plural **dragonflies**)
a large insect with a long thin body and two pairs of wings, which lives near lakes and streams

**drain**[1] /dreɪn/ *noun*
**1** a pipe or hole that carries away dirty water: *Leaves had blocked the drains in the streets.*
**2 down the drain** (*informal*) = if something goes down the drain, it is unsuccessful or it is wasted: *Since then, his career has gone down the drain; he hasn't made a single movie.*
**3 a drain on something** = something that

uses a lot of time, money, energy, etc.: *Filling out all these forms is a drain on our time.*

**drain²** *verb*
**1** if a liquid drains, it flows away: *The bath water slowly drained away.*
**2** to make the liquid flow away from something: *When the pasta is cooked, drain it.*

**dra·ma** [Ac] /ˈdrɑmə/ *noun*
**1** a play, television program, or serious movie that tells a story: *She appeared in a medical drama on TV earlier this year.*
**2** acting and plays in general: *Ben loves drama and wants to be an actor.*
**3** exciting things that happen: *It was an exciting game, with plenty of drama.*
—**dramatist** /ˈdræmətɪst/ *noun* (*formal*) someone who writes plays
→ see Thesaurus box at **movie**
[**ORIGIN:** 1500-1600 From the Greek word for "action, or theater plays," from *dran*, which means "to do."]

**WORD FAMILY: drama**
**drama** *noun* | **dramatic** *adjective* | **dramatize** *verb* | **dramatist** *noun* | **dramatization** *noun*

**dra·mat·ic** [Ac] /drəˈmætɪk/ *adjective*
**1** very sudden, exciting, or noticeable: *There has been a dramatic improvement in his work; he was getting C's and D's, and now he's getting A's.*
**2** showing a lot of emotion in a noticeable way: *Stop being so dramatic – you're embarrassing me.*
**3** related to plays and the theater: *His first dramatic role was as Biff in Arthur Miller's play "Death of a Salesman."*
—**dramatically** *adverb* in a very sudden, exciting, or noticeable way: *When she won the singing contest, her life changed dramatically.*

**dram·a·tize** [Ac] /ˈdræməˌtaɪz/ *verb*
to use a real event or a book as the story for a movie, television program, or play: *They are dramatizing her life story for TV.*
—**dramatization** /ˌdræmətəˈzeɪʃən/ *noun* a play, movie, or television program that is based on a real event or a book

**drank** /dræŋk/ *verb*
the past tense of DRINK

**drape** /dreɪp/ *verb*
to put cloth or clothing over or around something: *He draped his coat over a chair.*

**drapes** /dreɪps/ *plural noun*
heavy curtains

**dras·tic** /ˈdræstɪk/ *adjective*
drastic actions or changes have a big effect: *The new law required drastic cuts in the amount of pollution that cars produce.*
—**drastically** *adverb* in a drastic way: *The number of workers was drastically reduced from 800 to 300.*

**draw¹** /drɔ/ *verb* (**drew** /dru/, **drawn** /drɔn/)
**1** to use a pen or pencil to make a picture of something: *She was drawing a picture of a tree.* | *I'll draw you a map of how to get there.*
**2** to pull something or someone: *He drew a piece of paper from his pocket.* | *It was getting dark so she drew the curtains.*
**3** **draw near/closer** = to become closer: *The end of summer is drawing near.*
**4** to attract or interest someone: *The band draws big crowds.*
**5** **draw the line (at something)** = to refuse to do something because you do not approve of it, although you are willing to do other things: *I will help you, but I draw the line at telling lies for you.*
**6** **draw blood** = to make someone bleed: *The dog bit her so hard that it drew blood.*

**PHRASAL VERBS**

**draw back**
to move back from something: *The crowd drew back to let the police get to the injured man.*

**draw something up**
**1** to think of and write a list, plan, or agreement: *The teachers drew up a list of equipment they needed.*
**2** if a car draws up somewhere, it stops there: *A car drew up outside the house.*

**draw²** *noun*
**1** something that attracts people to see it: *The town's new museum will be a big draw for visitors.*
**2** one player's turn to take a card in a game

of cards: *It was my draw, and I picked the ten of hearts.*

**draw·back** /ˈdrɔbæk/ *noun*
something that might be a problem or disadvantage: *The main drawback to living in New York is that the cost of apartments is so high.*

D

**drawer** /drɔr/ *noun*
a part of a piece of furniture which is shaped like a box and slides in and out: *The pens are in the top drawer of my desk.* → see picture on page **A19**

**draw·ing** /ˈdrɔɪŋ/ *noun*
**1** a picture you make with a pen or pencil: *He did a drawing of a cat.*
**2** the art or skill of making pictures with a pen or pencil: *I am not very good at drawing.*
**3** an event in which someone's name is picked by chance from many names, and he or she wins a prize: *There will be a drawing today, and some lucky person will win a new car.*
→ see Thesaurus box at **art**, **picture**[1]

**drawn** /drɔn/ *verb*
the past participle of DRAW

**dread**[1] /dred/ *verb*
to feel very worried about something that is going to happen: *I have a test tomorrow, and I'm dreading it.*

**dread**[2] *noun*
a strong fear of something that is going to happen or may happen: *Flying always fills her with dread.*

**dread·ful** /ˈdredfəl/ *adjective*
very bad or unpleasant: *The performance was dreadful – I just wanted it to end.*
—**dreadfully** *adverb* very badly

**dream**[1] /drim/ *noun*
**1** the images that you see in your mind when you are asleep: *I had a dream about my dog last night.*
**2** something that you hope will happen: *Her dream was to become a drummer in a band.*

**dream**[2] *verb* (**dreamed** *or* **dreamt** /dremt/)
**1** to see images in your mind while you are asleep: *I dreamed that I was flying.*
**2** to think about something that you hope will happen: *She dreamed of becoming a pilot.*

**dream·er** /ˈdrimɚ/ *noun*
someone who has dreams or ideas that are not likely to happen: *The inventor was often accused of being a dreamer.*

**dreamt** /dremt/ *verb*
a past tense and past participle of DREAM

**dream·y** /ˈdrimi/ *adjective*
**1** a dreamy look or smile shows that you are thinking about something pleasant rather than about what is happening around you: *Whenever he talks about his girlfriend he gets a dreamy look on his face.*
**2** pleasant, peaceful, and relaxing: *They play dreamy music in my dentist's office to try to make people relax.*
—**dreamily** *adverb* thinking about pleasant things rather than about what is happening around you: *She looked dreamily at the sky.*

**drear·y** /ˈdrɪri/ *adjective*
not exciting, and making you feel sad or bored: *I was sick of the dreary rainy weather and wanted some sunshine.*

**drench** /drentʃ/ *verb*
to make something completely wet: *The rain drenched us.*
—**drenched** *adjective* completely wet: *I forgot my umbrella and got drenched.*

**dress**[1] /dres/ *verb*
to put clothes on someone or on yourself: *Can you dress the kids while I make breakfast? | He got dressed.*
**PHRASAL VERB**
**dress up**
**1** to wear your best clothes for a special occasion: *Everybody dressed up for the party.*
**2** to wear special clothes that make you look like someone or something else: *I dressed up as a robot for Halloween.*

**dress**[2] *noun*
**1** a piece of clothing for a woman or girl which covers her body and part of her legs: *She was wearing a long red dress.* → see picture on page **A6**
**2** (*formal*) clothes of a particular type: *Everyone at the wedding was in formal dress.*
**3** **dress shirt/dress shoes** = a shirt or shoes that you wear with formal clothes such as a suit

**ˈdress code** *noun*
a set of rules about what you should wear in a place or situation: *The restaurant has a strict dress code. Men have to wear a suit and tie.*

**dress·er** /ˈdresɚ/ *noun*
a piece of furniture with drawers, used for keeping clothes in: *All my T-shirts are in the top drawer of that dresser.* → see picture on page **A10**

**dress·ing** /ˈdresɪŋ/ *noun*
**1** a mixture of oil and other things that you pour over SALAD: *What kind of salad dressing would you like?*
**2** another word for STUFFING: *I'm making dressing for the turkey.*
**3** a piece of material used to cover an injury

**ˈdressing room** *noun*
a room where an actor or performer gets ready before going on stage or television

**dress·mak·er** /ˈdresˌmeɪkɚ/ *noun*
a person whose job is to make clothes for women

**dress·y** /ˈdresi/ *adjective*
dressy clothes are ones you wear for special or formal occasions: *I bought some dressy shoes for the wedding.*

**drew** /dru/ *verb*
the past tense of DRAW

**drib·ble** /ˈdrɪbəl/ *verb*
**1** in SOCCER or basketball, to move a ball toward the goal or basket by kicking or BOUNCING it again and again
**2** if a liquid dribbles somewhere, it flows in a slow thin stream: *Blood from a cut dribbled down the side of his face.*
**3** if you dribble, liquid comes out of your mouth: *The baby's dribbling on your shirt!*
**SYNONYM: drool**

**dried** /draɪd/ *verb*
the past tense and past participle of DRY

**dri·er** /ˈdraɪɚ/ *noun*
another spelling of DRYER

**drift¹** /drɪft/ *verb*
to move along slowly in the air or water: *The leaves drifted slowly down from the trees.*
**PHRASAL VERB**
**drift apart**
if people drift apart, they gradually stop having a close relationship: *Over the years, Marie and her college friends drifted apart.*

**drift²** *noun*
a deep pile of snow that the wind has blown into one place: *The car was buried under a drift of snow.*

**drill¹** /drɪl/ *noun*
**1** a tool or machine used for making holes in something hard: *He used an electric drill to make a hole in the wall.*
**2** a method of teaching something by making people repeat the same thing many times: *The teacher was doing a pronunciation drill with his class.*

**drill²** *verb*
**1** to make a hole with a drill: *The dentist drilled a hole in my tooth.*
**2** to teach people something by making them repeat the same thing many times: *The teacher was drilling the students in pronunciation.*
→ see Thesaurus box at **practice²**

**drink¹** /drɪŋk/ *noun*
**1** an amount of a liquid such as water or juice that you can drink: *Are you thirsty? Would you like a drink of water?*
**2** an alcoholic drink: *The men went to a bar after work for a drink.*

**drink²** *verb* (**drank** /dræŋk/, **drunk** /drʌŋk/)
**1** to take liquid into your mouth and swallow it: *She drank two cups of coffee.* | *Do you want something to drink?*
**2** to drink alcohol, especially regularly: *Don't drink and drive.*
[**ORIGIN:** From the old English word *drincan.*]

**drink·a·ble** /ˈdrɪŋkəbəl/ *adjective*
water that is drinkable is safe to drink

**drink·er** /ˈdrɪŋkɚ/ *noun*
someone who often drinks alcohol: *Greg is a heavy drinker, and his doctor has told him to drink less.*

**ˈdrinking ˌfountain** *noun*
a piece of equipment in a public place that gives you water to drink when you push a button or turn a handle

D

**drip** /drɪp/ *verb* (**dripped**, **dripping**)
1 if a liquid drips from something, it falls in drops: *Water was dripping from the ceiling, and I knew something was wrong.*
2 if something is dripping, drops of a liquid are falling from it: *My nose is dripping – do you have a tissue?*
—**drip** *noun* a small amount of liquid that falls from something
→ see Thesaurus box at **pour**

**drip**

The faucet is dripping.

**drive¹** /draɪv/ *verb* (**drove** /droʊv/, **driven** /ˈdrɪvən/, **driving**)
1 to make a vehicle move in the direction you want: *He was driving a red car.* | *She's learning to drive.*
2 if you drive someone somewhere, you take him or her there in a car: *Many parents drive their children to school.*
3 **drive someone crazy/nuts/insane** (*informal*) = to make someone feel very annoyed or angry: *Stop making that noise! You're driving me crazy!*
4 to hit something hard using a tool, BAT, golf club, etc.: *She drove the ball 100 yards down the hill.* | *He drove a nail into the board.*
→ see Thesaurus box at **take**

**drive²** *noun*
1 a trip in a car: *Let's go for a drive.* | *It's a three-hour drive to the lake.*
2 a part of a computer that can read or store information: *The files are stored on the C drive.* | *the computer's hard drive*
3 used in the names of roads: *We live at the end of Maple Drive.*
4 a planned effort to achieve something, especially by an organization: *The program is part of a drive to reduce gun crime.*
5 determination and energy to succeed: *Greg has the drive to become a successful lawyer.*
6 a hard hit that sends a ball a long way: *He hit a line drive to center field.*

**driv·en** /ˈdrɪvən/ *verb*
the past participle of DRIVE

**driv·er** /ˈdraɪvɚ/ *noun*
someone who drives: *A truck driver stopped and asked us if we needed help with the car.*
→ see picture on page **A26**

**ˈdriver's ˌlicense** *noun*
an official card with your name and picture on it that says you are legally allowed to drive: *He passed the test and got his driver's license.*

**ˈdrive-through** *noun*
a restaurant or bank that you can use without getting out of your car

**drive·way** /ˈdraɪvweɪ/ *noun*
the road or area for cars between a house and the street: *Park your car in the driveway.*

**driz·zle** /ˈdrɪzəl/ *verb*
if it is drizzling, it is raining very lightly: *The rain isn't too bad. It's just drizzling.*
—**drizzle** *noun* a light rain
→ see Thesaurus box at **rain¹**

**drool** /drul/ *verb*
if you drool, liquid comes out of your mouth: *The dog began to drool when it saw the food.*
—**drool** *noun* liquid that comes out of your mouth: *He wiped the drool from the baby's mouth.*

**droop** /drup/ *verb*
if something droops, it hangs down because it is old or weak: *The flowers had started to droop because there had been no rain.*

**drop¹** /drɑp/ *verb* (**dropped**, **dropping**)
1 if you drop something you are holding, you let it fall, often by accident: *She dropped a glass when she was drying the dishes.* → see picture on page **A4**
2 to fall: *Several apples had dropped from the tree.*
3 to become lower in level or amount: *The price of gas has dropped again.* **SYNONYMS: fall, go down**
4 to let someone out of your car when you are driving somewhere: *You can just drop me at the corner.*
5 to stop doing something: *I dropped basketball after school so that I'd have more time to study.*
6 to not keep a player on a team: *Coach Higgs threatened to drop me from the team if I miss practice again.*
→ see Thesaurus box at **decrease¹**

**PHRASAL VERBS**

**drop by** (*also* **drop in**)
to visit someone who does not know you are coming: *Ed dropped by yesterday.*

**drop off**
**1 drop someone off** = to take someone to a place in a car, before going to another place: *Can you drop the kids off at my sister's house on your way to work?*
**2** to begin to sleep: *The baby dropped off to sleep.*
**3** to become less in level or amount: *The number of kids playing hockey has dropped off recently.*

**drop out**
to stop going to school or college, or stop taking part in something, before you have finished: *She dropped out of high school two months before graduation.* | *The injury forced him to drop out of the race.*

**drop²** *noun*
**1** a very small amount of liquid: *Put a drop of oil on the wheel.*
**2** a situation in which the amount or level of something becomes lower: *There has been a drop in the price of computers – you can get a good one now for 400 dollars less than last year.*
**3** a small piece of hard candy or chocolate: *She was sucking on a lemon drop.*

**ˈdrop-in** *adjective*
a drop-in place is a place where you can go and get a service or advice without having to make arrangements first: *The drop-in clinic provides medical services for homeless people.*

**drop·out** /ˈdrɑp-aʊt/ *noun*
someone who leaves school or college without finishing it: *Many high-school dropouts have trouble finding jobs.*

**drought** /draʊt/ *noun*
a long period of dry weather when there is not enough rain: *Crops are dying because of the drought.*

**drove** /droʊv/ *verb*
the past tense of DRIVE

**drown** /draʊn/ *verb*
to die from being under water for too long: *Many people drowned when the ship sank.*

**drows·y** /ˈdraʊzi/ *adjective*
feeling that you want to sleep: *The room was so hot that I began to feel drowsy.* **SYNONYM: sleepy**
—**drowsiness** *noun* a feeling of wanting to sleep: *This medicine can cause drowsiness, so take it before you go to bed.*

**drug¹** /drʌg/ *noun*
**1** an illegal substance that some people take for pleasure: *He has never taken drugs.*
**2** a medicine: *A new drug is being used to treat cancer.*
→ see Thesaurus box at **medicine**

**drug²** *verb*
to give someone drugs, usually to make him or her sleep: *The thieves drugged him and stole his money.*

**drug·store** /ˈdrʌgstɔr/ *noun*
a store where you can buy medicine, soap, TOOTHPASTE, etc.

**drum¹** /drʌm/ *noun*
**1** a round musical instrument which you hit with your hand or a stick: *Johnny plays the drums in a band.* → see picture on page **A21**
**2** a large round container for storing liquids such as oil or chemicals: *an oil drum*

**drum²** *verb* (**drummed**, **drumming**)
**1** to hit something quickly many times, making a sound like a drum: *He drummed his fingers impatiently on the table.*
**2** to play a drum

**drum·stick** /ˈdrʌmˌstɪk/ *noun*
**1** the leg of a chicken or TURKEY that you eat: *We had chicken drumsticks at the barbecue.*
**2** a stick that you use to hit a drum

**drunk¹** /drʌŋk/ *adjective*
if someone is drunk, he or she has drunk too much alcohol and cannot think or act normally: *He got drunk and ran his car into a tree.*

**drunk²** *verb*
the past participle of DRINK

**drunk³** *noun*
someone who is drunk or who often gets drunk

D

**drunk·en** /ˈdrʌŋkən/ *adjective (formal)*
drunk: *A drunken crowd of people came out of the bar.*
—**drunkenness** *noun* drunken behavior

**dry¹** /draɪ/ *adjective* (**drier** *or* **dryer**, **driest** *or* **dryest**)
**1** something that is dry has no water in it or on it: *I got wet in the rain, so I went home to put on dry clothes.* | *The soil in the pot was dry, and the plant was dying.* **ANTONYM: wet**
**2** if the weather is dry, there is no rain: *It's been a very dry summer. We haven't had rain for a month.* **ANTONYM: wet**
**3** if your skin or hair is dry, it does not have enough natural oil in it

D

**dry²** *verb* (**dried**, **dries**)
**1** to make something have no water in it or on it: *He dried his hands on a towel.*
**2** if something dries, it no longer has water in it or on it: *Julia hung the wet clothes outside to dry.*

**ˈdry-clean** *verb*
to clean clothes with chemicals, not water and soap: *It's a wool suit, so it has to be dry-cleaned.*

**ˌdry ˈcleaners** *noun*
a business that dry-cleans clothes

**dry·er** (*also* **drier**) /ˈdraɪɚ/ *noun*
a machine that dries things, especially clothes or hair: *Can you put the wet clothes in the dryer?*

**du·al** /ˈduəl/ *adjective*
having two of something, or two parts: *She plays a dual role in the movie – the main character and her mother.*

**du·bi·ous** /ˈdubiəs/ *adjective (formal)*
**1** if you are dubious about something, you are not sure whether it is good or true: *Anna's parents were dubious about her new boyfriend. They thought he was too old for her.* **SYNONYM: doubtful**
**2** probably not true or honest: *Howells thinks the plan is dubious. It may not even be legal.*

**duck¹** /dʌk/ *noun*
**1** a common bird that swims on water and has short legs and a wide beak: *We went to the pond to feed the ducks.*
**2** the meat from a duck

**duck²** *verb*
to lower your body or head very quickly to avoid something: *He threw a book at me, and I ducked.*

**duck**

**duck·ling** /ˈdʌklɪŋ/ *noun*
a young duck

**duct** /dʌkt/ *noun*
**1** a tube in a building for carrying air or electric wires: *There was no warm air coming from the heating duct.*
**2** a narrow tube inside your body that liquid goes through: *Tears go through your tear ducts.*

**dude** /dud/ *noun (informal)*
a man or boy. This is often used to talk to someone instead of using his name: *Hey dude, what are you doing?*

**due** /du/ *adjective*
**1** expected to happen or arrive at a particular time: *The flight from Chicago is due to arrive at 7 p.m.* | *The baby is due in March.*
**2** if something is due on a particular date, it should be given to someone on or before that date: *Your English papers are due on Friday.*
**3** **due to something** = happening as a result of something: *Her success was due to hard work.*

**du·el** /ˈduəl/ *noun*
a fight in past times between two people with guns or swords: *He was killed in a duel.*
—**duel** *verb* to fight with guns or swords

**dues** /duz/ *plural noun*
money that you pay regularly to be a member of an organization: *Do you have to pay dues to be a member of the club?*

**du·et** /duˈet/ *noun*
a piece of music that is played or sung by two people: *He wrote a duet for flute and violin.*

**dug** /dʌg/ *verb*
the past tense and past participle of DIG

**dull¹** /dʌl/ *adjective*
**1** not interesting or exciting: *The book was so dull that I fell asleep reading it.* **SYNONYM: boring**

**2** a dull pain is not strong: *I had a dull ache in my shoulder.*
**3** not bright or shiny: *The wall was painted a dull gray color.*
**4** not sharp: *The knife was too dull to cut the string.*
**5** a dull sound is not clear or loud: *I heard a dull thud, and I realized that my sister had fallen out of bed.*
→ see Thesaurus box at **boring**

**dull²** *verb (formal)*
to make a pain or feeling less noticeable: *The drug dulled the pain, so that she was able to sleep.*

**du·ly** /ˈduli/ *adverb (formal)*
done in a way that is correct or expected, or that follows the rules: *An employee noticed the problem and duly reported it to her boss.*

**dumb** /dʌm/ *adjective (informal)*
stupid: *I felt really dumb when I couldn't get the box open.* **ANTONYM: smart**

**dum·my** /ˈdʌmi/ *noun* (plural **dummies**)
**1** (*informal*) someone who is stupid: *I forgot her name and felt like such a dummy.* **SYNONYM: idiot**
**2** a large plastic figure of a person: *They crash the cars with dummies inside to see if they become damaged.*

**dump¹** /dʌmp/ *verb*
**1** to drop or put something somewhere in a careless way: *She dumped her suitcase in the middle of the room and left it there.*
**2** to leave something somewhere because you do not want it: *It is illegal to dump garbage here.*
**3** (*informal*) to end a relationship with someone: *Tammy dumped her boyfriend because she likes someone else.*

**dump²** *noun*
**1** a place where you can leave unwanted waste or things you do not want: *We took two bags of garbage and a broken chair to the dump.*
**2** (*informal*) a place that is unpleasant because it is dirty and ugly: *Your apartment's a dump. Do you ever clean it?*

**dune** /dun/ *noun*
a hill made of sand: *We walked over the sand dunes to the beach.*

**dun·geon** /ˈdʌndʒən/ *noun*
a dark prison under a building such as a castle, used in past times: *He was kept in the dungeon of the castle for two years.*

**dunk** /dʌŋk/ *verb*
**1** to quickly put something into a liquid and then take it out again: *He dunked his cookie in his coffee.*
**2** in basketball, to jump up by the basket and throw the ball down through it

**du·o** /ˈduoʊ/ *noun*
two people who do something together: *a singing duo*

**du·plex** /ˈdupleks/ *noun*
a house that is divided into two separate places for people to live

**du·pli·cate¹** /ˈdupləkɪt/ *noun (formal)*
an exact copy of something that you can use in the same way: *He made a duplicate of the house key to give to his sister.* **SYNONYM: copy**
—**duplicate** *adjective* made as an exact copy of something: *a duplicate key*

**du·pli·cate²** /ˈdupləˌkeɪt/ *verb (formal)*
**1** to make an exact copy of something: *You can duplicate digital photographs easily on your computer.*
**2** to repeat something in exactly the same way: *He hopes to duplicate the success he had at the last Olympics by winning another gold medal.*

**du·pli·ca·tion** /ˌdupləˈkeɪʃən/ *noun (formal)*
**1** the process of making an exact copy of something: *Duplication of this software is a crime.*
**2** the act of repeating what someone or something else has done: *The duplication of the experiment showed that the first results were correct.*

**dur·a·ble** /ˈdʊrəbəl/ *adjective*
staying in good condition for a long time: *The sofa is made of a durable material that will last for many years.*
—**durability** /ˌdʊrəˈbɪləti/ *noun* the quality of being durable: *Steel is used in large buildings because of its strength and durability.*

**dur·ing** /ˈdʊrɪŋ/ *preposition*
**1** all through a period of time: *During the day*

D

*when my mom is at work, my little sister stays at my grandmother's house.*

**2** at some point in a period of time: *Henry died during the night.*

[**ORIGIN:** 1300-1400 From the Latin word *durare*, which means "to last or continue."]

**dusk** /dʌsk/ *noun*
the time when it starts to become dark at the end of the day: *The street lights go on at dusk.* **SYNONYM: twilight**; **ANTONYM: dawn**

D

**dust¹** /dʌst/ *noun*
very small pieces of dirt that look like a powder: *She never cleans her house; there is dust on all the furniture.*

**dust²** *verb*
to clean the dust from something with a cloth: *I dusted the shelves in my bedroom.*
→ see Thesaurus box at **clean²**

**dust·pan** /ˈdʌstpæn/ *noun*
a flat container with a handle that you use with a brush to remove dust and waste from the floor

**dust·y** /ˈdʌsti/ *adjective* (**dustier**, **dustiest**)
covered with dust: *I found some dusty old books that nobody had touched for years.*
→ see Thesaurus box at **dirty**

**Dutch¹** /dʌtʃ/ *adjective*
from the Netherlands: *She's Dutch, and she lives in Amsterdam.* | *a Dutch company*

**Dutch²** *noun*
**1** the language used in the Netherlands
**2 the Dutch** = the people of the Netherlands

**du·ti·ful** /ˈdutɪfəl/ *adjective*
a dutiful person does what other people expect him or her to do: *He was a dutiful son who always obeyed his parents.*
—**dutifully** *adverb* in a dutiful way: *Every Sunday she dutifully went to church.*

**du·ty** /ˈduti/ *noun* (plural **duties**)
**1** something that you should do because it is right or it is part of your job: *Parents have a duty to protect their children.*
**2 on duty** = if someone such as a police officer is on duty, he or she is working: *There were two lifeguards on duty at the beach.*

**DVD** *noun*
(**digital video disc**) a flat round object like a CD that has a movie, computer game, television program, or information stored on it: *I was watching a DVD on my laptop.*

**dwarf** /dwɔrf/ *noun* (plural **dwarf** *or* **dwarves**)
**1** an imaginary creature that looks like a small man: *the story of Snow White and the Seven Dwarfs*
**2** a person who is much shorter than usual. Many people think this use is offensive.

**dwell** /dwel/ *verb* (**dwelled** *or* **dwelt** /dwelt/) (*formal*)
to live in a particular place: *The story is about some tiny creatures that dwell in the forest.*
**PHRASAL VERB**
**dwell on/upon something**
to think or talk for too long about something unpleasant: *I tried not to dwell on my mistake; I tried to think about how to fix it instead.*

**dwell·ing** /ˈdwelɪŋ/ *noun* (*formal*)
a house or other building where people live

**dye¹** /daɪ/ *noun*
a substance you use to change the color of cloth or your hair: *She bought some black hair dye.*

**dye²** *verb*
to change the color of something using a dye: *She decided to dye her blond hair black.*

**dy·nam·ic** Ac /daɪˈnæmɪk/ *adjective*
full of energy and ideas: *Our teacher is very dynamic. She's always thinking of new ways to make the class interesting.*

[**ORIGIN:** 1800-1900 From the Greek word *dynamikos*, which means "powerful."]

**dy·na·mite** /ˈdaɪnəˌmaɪt/ *noun*
a substance that is used to make a powerful explosion: *They blew up the building with dynamite.*

**dys·lex·i·a** /dɪsˈleksiə/ *noun*
a condition in the brain that makes you have difficulty reading, writing, and spelling because your brain cannot process written words correctly
—**dyslexic** *adjective* having dyslexia

# Ee

**E** /i/ *noun*
the third note in the musical SCALE of C, or the musical KEY based on this note

**each** /itʃ/ *adjective, pronoun, adverb*
both or every one: *She had a bag in each hand.* | *The kids were given $5 each.* | *Each of her friends gave her a different present.* | *Twelve guests came to the party, and they each brought something to eat.*

**USAGE: each, every, all**

**Each**, **every**, and **all** are all used to talk about every person or thing in a group.

When you are thinking about the people or things in the group separately, use **each** or **every**: *Each child at the party was given a balloon.* | *Every child at the party was given a balloon.*

When you are thinking about the whole group together, use **all**: *All the children were given balloons.*

**ˌeach ˈother** *pronoun*
**1** if people do something to each other, each one does the same thing to the other person or other people: *Sarah and Rob love each other and want to get married.*
**2** used when talking about the position of two people or things: *Our houses are next to each other, so we're neighbors.*

**ea·ger** /ˈigɚ/ *adjective*
wanting to do something very much: *He was eager to meet his new teacher.*
—**eagerly** *adverb* in an eager way: *She opened the letter eagerly.*
—**eagerness** *noun* a feeling of wanting to do something very much: *We were surprised by his eagerness to do the work; he seemed really excited.*

**ea·gle** /ˈigəl/ *noun*
a big wild bird with a beak like a hook. Eagles eat small animals and live in high places.

**ear** /ɪr/ *noun*
one of the two parts of your body that you hear with: *Mark whispered something in her ear.* → see picture on page **A2**

**ear·ache** /ˈɪreɪk/ *noun*
a pain inside your ear: *I had an earache and couldn't sleep.*

**ear·drum** /ˈɪrˌdrʌm/ *noun*
a part inside your ear that moves when sound reaches it. The eardrum sends signals to your brain so that you hear the sound.

**ear·ly¹** /ˈɚli/ *adjective* (**earlier**, **earliest**)
**1** before the usual or expected time: *I was early for my appointment, so I had to wait.* | *We can have an early dinner at about 5:00.* **ANTONYM: late**
**2** near the beginning of the day: *It was early in the morning, about 5:00 a.m.* **ANTONYM: late**
**3** near the beginning of a period of time: *We're leaving in the early afternoon, around 1:00.* **ANTONYM: late**

**early²** *adverb*
**1** before the usual or expected time: *She came to the party early to help me get ready.* **ANTONYM: late**
**2** near the beginning of the day: *He got up very early, at about 5:30 in the morning.* **ANTONYM: late**
**3** near the beginning of a period of time: *He'll be back early in January, probably on the 3rd.* **ANTONYM: late**

**earn** /ɚn/ *verb*
**1** to get money for the work you do: *Alan earns $40,000 a year.* | *I'd like to earn some extra money. Do you have any work I could do for you?*

E

**THESAURUS: earn**

**make** to earn or get money: *Debbie makes a little money by babysitting.*

**get** (*informal*) to receive money for doing work or selling something: *How much did you get for mowing their lawns?*

**be paid/get paid** to be given money for doing a job: *She is paid $7.50 an hour.*

**2** to deserve or get something good because you have worked hard or done something well: *You've earned a rest after all that hard work!*

**ear·nest** /ˈɚnɪst/ *adjective* (*formal*)
serious about what you are saying or doing: *He made an earnest effort to do better in school.*

**earn·ings** /ˈɚnɪŋz/ *plural noun*
money that you get from working: *We spend most of our earnings on basic things like food.*
→ see Thesaurus box at **pay**[2]

**ear·phones** /ˈɪrfoʊnz/ *plural noun*
the things you put into your ear and use for listening to music or the radio. You connect them to a radio, an MP3 PLAYER, etc.

**ear·ring** /ˈɪrɪŋ/ *noun*
a piece of jewelry that you fasten to your ear: *She was wearing a pair of gold earrings.* → see picture on page **A6**

**earth** (*also* **Earth**) /ɚθ/ *noun*
**1** the PLANET that we live on: *The Earth moves around the Sun.*

**THESAURUS: earth**

**Earth** the planet we live on: *The Earth moves around the Sun.*

**world** the planet we live on – used when you are thinking of the Earth as a place where there are people and countries, mountains and oceans, etc.: *This has to be one of the most beautiful places in the world.*

You can use **Earth** to mean "the world": *It's the highest mountain on Earth.* | *It's the highest mountain in the world.*

When you compare the Earth's surface to the ocean, use **land**: *Five weeks after sailing from Ireland, they saw land.*

When you compare the Earth's surface to the sky, use **Earth**: *The space shuttle returned to Earth safely.*

**2** soil or dirt: *He took the shovel and began to dig in the earth.*

**earth·quake** /ˈɚθkweɪk/ *noun*
a sudden shaking of the ground, caused when parts of the Earth's surface move: *The earthquake damaged thousands of buildings.*

**earth·worm** /ˈɚθwɚm/ *noun*
a long thin creature with a soft body and no legs that lives in the ground **SYNONYM: worm**

**ease**[1] /iz/ *noun*
**1 with ease** = if you do something with ease, you do it very easily: *He won the race with ease.*
**2 at ease** = feeling comfortable and relaxed: *The teacher used games to make the new students feel at ease.*

**ease**[2] *verb*
to become less bad or unpleasant: *The doctor gave me drugs to ease the pain.*
→ see Thesaurus box at **reduce**

**ea·sel** /ˈizəl/ *noun*
a frame that you put a drawing or painting on while you are making it
[**ORIGIN:** 1500-1600 From the Dutch word *ezel*, which means "donkey." An easel carries a painting like a donkey carries a person or load.]

**eas·i·ly** /ˈizəli/ *adverb*
**1** without difficulty: *You can find information easily on the Internet.*
**2 easily the best/easily the biggest, etc.** (*informal*) = much better, bigger, etc. than the others: *She is easily the most intelligent girl in the class.*

**east**[1] (*also* **East**) /ist/ *noun*
**1** the direction from which the sun rises: *Which way is east?*
**2 the east** = the eastern part of a country or area: *We live in the east of the city.*

3 **the East** = **a)** the eastern part of the U.S., especially the states north of Washington D.C.: *She was born in the East but later moved to California.* **b)** the countries in Asia, especially China, Korea, and Japan: *I would love to travel in the East.*

**east²** *adjective*
1 in, to, or facing the east: *Our hotel was on the east coast of the island.*
2 **east wind** = a wind that comes from the east

**east³** *adverb*
toward the east: *We drove east along Atlantic Avenue.* | *The window faces east.*

**Eas·ter** /ˈistɚ/ *noun*
a religious holiday in March or April, when Christians remember Jesus Christ's return to life after dying on the cross

**ˈEaster egg** *noun*
an egg that has been colored and decorated for Easter: *At Easter we look for Easter eggs that are hidden around the house.*

**east·ern** /ˈistɚn/ *adjective*
in or from the east: *Several eastern states, such as New York and Massachusetts, have passed the law.*

**ˌEastern ˈDaylight Time** *noun* (*written abbreviation*: **EDT**)
the time that is used in the eastern U.S. for over half the year, including the summer. Eastern Daylight Time is one hour ahead of Eastern Standard Time.

**east·ern·er** /ˈistɚnɚ/ *noun*
someone who comes from the eastern part of a country

**ˌEastern ˈStandard Time** *noun* (*written abbreviation* **EST**)
the time that is used in the eastern U.S. for almost half the year, including the winter

**east·ward** /ˈistwɚd/ *adverb, adjective*
toward the east: *The plane was traveling eastward, from Chicago to New York.*

**eas·y¹** /ˈizi/ *adjective* (**easier**, **easiest**)
1 not difficult: *The test was easy – I knew all the answers.* | *The book is easy to read because it has short sentences.* **ANTONYM: hard**
2 relaxing because you have no problems or worries: *She has an easy life, with a big house and lots of money.*
[**ORIGIN:** 1100-1200 From the old French word *aisié*, which means "having been made comfortable."]

**WORD FAMILY: easy**
**easy** *adjective* | **easily** *adverb* | **ease** *noun*

**easy²** *adverb*
1 **take it easy** = **a)** to relax and not do very much: *I've been working so hard lately, I need to take it easy for a while.* **b)** used to tell someone to become less angry or upset: *OK, you don't need to yell – just take it easy.*
2 **go easy on someone** (*informal*) = to not punish someone too severely or not become too angry with him or her: *He's very upset about his mistake, so go easy on him.*
3 **go easy on something** (*informal*) = to not use or eat too much of something: *I have to go easy on the desserts because I'm getting fat.*
4 **that's easier said than done** = you say this when someone has suggested something that sounds simple but is not: *I should just ask her to be quiet, but that's easier said than done.*

**eas·y·go·ing** /ˌiziˈgoʊɪŋ/ *adjective*
an easygoing person is not easily worried or annoyed: *Her parents are really easygoing; they never yell at her.*

**eat** /it/ *verb* (**ate** /eɪt/, **eaten** /ˈitn/)
1 to put food in your mouth and swallow it: *She was eating an apple.* | *I'm still eating my dinner.* | *Do you want something to eat?*
2 to have a meal: *We usually eat at about 6.*
[**ORIGIN:** From the old English word *etan.*]
**PHRASAL VERBS**
**eat out**
to eat in a restaurant: *They usually eat out once a week.*
**eat something up**
1 to finish eating all of something: *Eat up your breakfast! We're late!*
2 to use too much of something: *Homework eats up a lot of my free time.*

**eat·en** /ˈitn/ *verb*
the past participle of EAT

**eaves·drop** /ˈivzdrɑp/ *verb* (**eavesdropped**, **eavesdropping**)
to listen secretly to other people's conversation: *He stood outside the door so that he could eavesdrop on their conversation.*

**ec·cen·tric** /ɪkˈsentrɪk/ *adjective*
behaving in a way that is unusual and different from most people: *He was an eccentric man who took his pet rat everywhere with him.*
—**eccentric** *noun* an eccentric person
→ see Thesaurus box at **strange**
[**ORIGIN:** 1500-1600 From the Greek word *ekkentros*, which means "out of the center."]

**ech·o[1]** /ˈekoʊ/ *noun* (plural **echoes**)
a sound that is repeated because it comes back off a wall or other surface: *I could hear the echo of my voice from the other side of the cave.*

**echo[2]** *verb* (**echoed**, **echoes**)
if a sound echoes, you hear it again because it comes back off a wall or other surface: *When he shouted, his voice echoed from across the valley.*

**e·clipse** /ɪˈklɪps/ *noun*
an occasion when you cannot see the sun because the moon is in front of it, or when you cannot see the moon because it is covered by the Earth's shadow: *an eclipse of the moon*
[**ORIGIN:** 1200-1300 From the Greek word *ekleipsis*, which means "the act of leaving or disappearing."]

**e·col·o·gy** /ɪˈkɑlədʒi/ *noun*
the study of the environment and the relationship between the environment and all the plants, animals, and people living there
—**ecologist** *noun* someone who studies ecology
—**ecological** /ˌikəˈlɑdʒɪkəl/ *adjective* relating to ecology
[**ORIGIN:** 1800-1900 From the Greek words *oikos* and *-logia*, which mean "home" and "study." The environment is the home of plants and animals.]

**ec·o·nom·ic** Ac /ˌekəˈnɑmɪk/ *adjective*
relating to business, industry, and money in a country or area: *The economic situation in the U.S. is improving; there are more jobs, and people are spending more.*
—**economically** *adverb* in a way that relates to business, industry, and money in a country or area: *Japan grew economically by selling cars and electronic equipment.*

**ec·o·nom·i·cal** Ac /ˌekəˈnɑmɪkəl/ *adjective*
not costing a lot of money to buy or use: *I drive an economical car that doesn't use much gas.*

**ec·o·nom·ics** Ac /ˌekəˈnɑmɪks/ *noun*
the study of business and the ways in which money and goods are produced and used: *It's a basic rule of economics: if you lower the price, people buy more. If you raise the price, they buy less.*
—**economist** /ɪˈkɑnəmɪst/ *noun* someone who knows a lot about economics and advises people about this: *Some economists say that we need higher taxes.*

**e·con·o·mize** /ɪˈkɑnəˌmaɪz/ *verb*
to spend less money or use less of something: *My father economizes by taking his lunch to work, instead of buying it.*

**e·con·o·my** Ac /ɪˈkɑnəmi/ *noun* (plural **economies**)
the system of trade and industry in a country or area: *China's economy is growing rapidly.*
[**ORIGIN:** 1400-1500 From the Greek words *oikos* and *-nomia*, which mean "home" and "managing." This word first meant "running a home" and was later used about managing the money and trade of a country.]

**WORD FAMILY: economy**
**economy** *noun* | **economist** *noun* | **economic** *adjective* | **economics** *noun*

**e·co·sys·tem** /ˈikoʊˌsɪstəm/ *noun*
the environment and all the plants and animals in a place, that are all connected with each other and have an effect on each other:

*The chemicals kill the fish and damage the ecosystem in the river.*

**ec·stat·ic** /ɪkˈstætɪk/ *adjective*
feeling extremely happy and excited: *I was ecstatic when I got an A on my English test!*

**ec·ze·ma** /ˈeksəmə/ *noun*
a medical condition that makes your skin dry, red, and ITCHY

**edge** /edʒ/ *noun*
**1** the part of something that is farthest from the center: *She was leaning on the edge of the table.*
**2** the area beside a steep slope: *We looked over the edge of the cliff, down to the ocean.*
**3** the thin sharp part of a tool used for cutting: *You will need a knife with a sharp edge.*
**4 on edge** = nervous and worried: *Everyone was on edge, because we were worried about our final exams.*

**edg·y** /ˈedʒi/ *adjective*
nervous and easily upset: *He is always tense and edgy before a race.*

**ed·i·ble** /ˈedəbəl/ *adjective*
safe to eat or good enough to eat: *I didn't pick the berries because I wasn't sure if they were edible.* **ANTONYM: inedible**
[**ORIGIN:** 1600-1700 From the Latin word *edibilis*, from *edere*, which means "to eat."]

**ed·it** Ac /ˈedɪt/ *verb*
to make a book, newspaper, magazine, or movie ready for people to read or see, by removing mistakes and deciding what to include: *When he edited the book, he shortened some of the stories in it.*

**e·di·tion** Ac /ɪˈdɪʃən/ *noun*
all the copies of a book, newspaper, or magazine that are produced at the same time: *There are two editions of the newspaper: one in the morning and one in the evening.*

**ed·i·tor** Ac /ˈedətə˞/ *noun*
the person who decides what should be included in a newspaper, magazine, or book: *The editor of the newspaper decided not to print the story.*

**ed·i·to·ri·al**[1] Ac /ˌedəˈtɔriəl/ *noun*
a piece of writing in a newspaper that gives the opinion of the editor, rather than reporting facts: *There was an editorial on the president's new energy policy in yesterday's paper.*

**editorial**[2] Ac *adjective*
relating to editing: *the editorial staff of the newspaper*

**ed·u·cate** /ˈedʒəˌkeɪt/ *verb* (*formal*)
to teach someone: *He was educated at Stanford University.*
—**educator** *noun* a teacher at a school, college, or university
[**ORIGIN:** 1400-1500 From the Latin word *educare*, which means "to bring up or educate."]

**WORD FAMILY: educate**
**educate** *verb* | **educated** *adjective* | **education** *noun* | **educator** *noun*

**ed·u·cat·ed** /ˈedʒəˌkeɪtɪd/ *adjective*
an educated person has had a good education and has read a lot of books: *My grandmother was an educated woman who had a college degree.*

**ed·u·ca·tion** /ˌedʒəˈkeɪʃən/ *noun*
the activities of teaching and learning: *They want their children to get a good education.*
—**educational** *adjective* relating to education

**eel** /il/ *noun*
a long thin fish that looks like a snake

**ef·fect** /ɪˈfekt/ *noun*
**1** a change caused by something: *Smoking has a very bad effect on your health.*
**2 take effect** = if something takes effect, it starts to work: *The pain medicine should take effect in about ten minutes.*
**3 in effect** = used to say what you think the real facts of a situation are: *By not telling him the full story, in effect she had lied.*

**USAGE: effect, affect**
**Effect** is usually a noun: *What effect does the illness have on your life?*

**Affect** is a verb: *How does your illness affect your life?*

**ef·fec·tive** /ɪˈfektɪv/ *adjective*
producing the result that you want: *He is an effective teacher who really makes his students think.* **ANTONYM: ineffective**
—**effectively** *adverb* in an effective way: *The new heating system is not working effectively; the rooms are still too cold.*
—**effectiveness** *noun* the quality of being effective

E

**ef·fi·cient** /ɪˈfɪʃənt/ *adjective*
working well, in a way that does not waste time, money, or energy: *The car's engine is efficient and uses very little gas.* **ANTONYM: inefficient**
—**efficiency** *noun* the quality of being efficient: *The company needs to improve the efficiency of its factories because they waste too much energy.*
—**efficiently** *adverb* in an efficient way

**ef·fort** /ˈefɚt/ *noun*
**1** the physical or mental energy that you use to do something: *Moving a piano takes a lot of effort.* | *You need to put more effort into your homework.*
**2** an attempt to do something: *She started riding her bicycle to school, in an effort to get more exercise.*

**ef·fort·less** /ˈefɚtləs/ *adjective (formal)*
if someone does something in an effortless way, it seems to be easy for him or her: *It's a very hard song to sing, but she makes it look effortless.*
—**effortlessly** *adverb (formal)* in an effortless way

**EFL** *noun*
(**English as a Foreign Language**) the activity of teaching English to people whose first language is not English, and who do not live in an English-speaking country

**e.g.**
the abbreviation of **for example**: *He enjoys studying science, e.g. chemistry and physics.*

**egg** /eg/ *noun*
**1** a round object that contains a baby bird, snake, fish, etc. before it is born: *The bird lays its eggs in the spring.*
**2** an egg from a chicken, eaten as food: *I had scrambled eggs for breakfast.*
**3** a cell in the body of a woman or a female animal that can grow into a baby if it is FERTILIZEd

**egg·plant** /ˈegplænt/ *noun*
a large vegetable with a shiny dark purple skin → see picture on page **A12**

**egg·shell** /ˈegʃel/ *noun*
the hard outside part of an egg

**e·go** /ˈigoʊ/ *noun*
the opinion that you have about yourself: *He has a big ego and is always talking about how great he is.*

**eight** /eɪt/ *number*
**1** 8: *A spider has eight legs.*
**2** eight O'CLOCK: *Dinner will be at eight.*
**3** eight years old: *Annie's brother is eight.*

**eight·een** /ˌeɪˈtin/ *number*
**1** 18: *I've been awake for eighteen hours.*
**2** eighteen years old: *I'm planning on having a big party when I'm eighteen.*
—**eighteenth** *number* 18th or 1/18

**eighth** /eɪtθ/ *number*
**1** 8th
**2** 1/8

**eight·y** /ˈeɪti/ *number*
**1** 80: *A drink costs eighty cents.*
**2** eighty years old: *He is almost eighty.*
**3** **the eighties** (*also* **the '80s**) = the years between 1980 and 1989: *My dad graduated from high school in the eighties.*
**4** **in your eighties** = between 80 and 89 years old: *My grandfather is in his eighties.*
**5** **in the eighties** = between 80 and 89 degrees FAHRENHEIT in temperature: *The temperature was in the eighties all week.*
—**eightieth** /ˈeɪt̬iɪθ/ *number* 80th or 1/80

**ei·ther¹** /ˈiðɚ/ *conjunction*
**either ... or** = used when saying that there are two or more possibilities: *We can either take the bus, or we can fly.*

**either²** *pronoun, adjective*
**1** one or the other of two people or things: *"Do you want chocolate or strawberry ice cream?" "Either is fine!"* | *Either team could win.*
**2** used in negative sentences, when saying that something is true about both of two

things or people: *"Which one of these dresses do you like best?" "I don't like either of them."*

**3 either side/end/hand, etc.** = both sides, ends, etc.: *He stood in the door with a policeman on either side of him.*

**either³** *adverb*
used in negative sentences to mean "also": *"I can't swim." "I can't either."*

**e·lab·o·rate** /ɪˈlæbərət/ *adjective* (*formal*)
having a lot of small details or parts that are connected together in a complicated way: *The carpet had a very elaborate design.* **ANTONYM: simple**
—**elaborately** *adverb* in an elaborate way

**e·las·tic** /ɪˈlæstɪk/ *noun*
a type of rubber material that can stretch and then return to its usual size
—**elastic** *adjective* made of elastic: *The pants have an elastic waist, so they are easy to put on.*

**el·bow** /ˈelboʊ/ *noun*
the joint where your arm bends → see picture on page **A2**
[**ORIGIN:** From the old English word *elboga.*]

**el·der** /ˈeldɚ/ *adjective* (*formal*)
an elder sister or brother is older than you: *My elder sister is a nurse.*

**el·der·ly** /ˈeldɚli/ *adjective*
old: *an elderly woman with white hair*

**el·ders** /ˈeldɚz/ *plural noun* (*formal*)
your elders are people who are older than you are: *Young people should have more respect for their elders.*

**el·dest** /ˈeldəst/ *adjective* (*formal*)
the eldest son or daughter was born first: *Their eldest daughter is 17.*

**e·lect** /ɪˈlekt/ *verb*
to choose someone for an official position by voting: *She was elected to Congress in 2000.* → see Thesaurus box at **choose**
[**ORIGIN:** 1400-1500 From the Latin word *electus*, a form of the verb *eligere*, which means "to choose."]

**e·lec·tion** /ɪˈlekʃən/ *noun*
an event in which people vote to choose someone for an official position: *Who do you think will win the next presidential election?*

—**electoral** /ɪˈlektərəl/ *adjective* relating to elections

**e,lectoral 'college** *noun*
the group of people who officially elect the U.S. president. The people in the state vote, and in most states the winner of the vote gets all the electoral college votes from that state.

**e·lec·tric** /ɪˈlektrɪk/ *adjective*
**1** needing electricity in order to work: *an electric guitar*
**2** relating to electricity: *When the electric current flows through the wire, the light comes on.*

**WORD FAMILY: electric**
**electric** *adjective* | **electricity** *noun* | **electrical** *adjective* | **electrician** *noun*

**e·lec·tri·cal** /ɪˈlektrɪkəl/ *adjective*
**1** relating to electricity: *The machine uses electrical power.*
**2** using electricity: *The store sells electrical goods like televisions and kitchen appliances.*

**e·lec·tri·cian** /ɪˌlekˈtrɪʃən/ *noun*
someone whose job is to put in electrical wires and repair electrical equipment: *We need an electrician to fix the light switch.* → see picture on page **A16**

**e·lec·tric·i·ty** /ɪˌlekˈtrɪsəti/ *noun*
a type of energy that is used to make lights, televisions, etc. work, and is carried through wires: *The new light bulbs use less electricity than the old ones.*
[**ORIGIN:** 1600-1700 From the Greek word *elektron*, which means "amber." Amber is a yellowish substance that came out of trees and then hardened a long time ago. Electricity was first made by rubbing amber.]

**e·lec·tron** /ɪˈlektrɑn/ *noun*
a very small piece of matter that moves around the NUCLEUS (=central part) of an atom

**e·lec·tron·ic** /ɪˌlekˈtrɑnɪk/ *adjective*
**1** electronic equipment has small parts inside it that control the electricity that the equipment uses to do complicated things: *The store sells electronic equipment such as computers, cell phones, TVs, and MP3 players.*
**2** made or done using electronic equipment: *The band plays electronic music.*

—**electronically** *adverb* using electronic equipment

**e·lec·tron·ics** /ɪˌlekˈtrɑnɪks/ *noun*
the technology used for making electronic equipment such as computers and televisions

**el·e·gant** /ˈeləgənt/ *adjective*
very beautiful and graceful: *She was a tall elegant woman who always dressed in beautiful clothes.*
—**elegance** *noun* the quality of being elegant: *I love the elegance of the city's old buildings.*
[ORIGIN: 1400-1500 From the Latin word *elegans*, which means "specially chosen as being of good quality," from *eligere*, which means "to choose."]

**el·e·ment** Ac /ˈeləmənt/ *noun*
1 (*formal*) one part of something: *The most important element in any movie is the story.*
2 (*formal*) a small but important amount of something, for example danger, truth, or risk: *There is always an element of risk when you're climbing a mountain.*
3 a basic chemical substance, for example oxygen or HYDROGEN, that consists of only one type of atom

**el·e·men·ta·ry** /ˌeləˈmentri/ *adjective*
basic and simple: *The youngest students are learning elementary mathematics.*

**eleˈmentary ˌschool** *noun*
a school that children go to for the first five or seven years of their education: *Our elementary school has kindergarten through sixth grade.* SYNONYM: **grade school**

**el·e·phant** /ˈeləfənt/ *noun*
a very large gray animal with big ears, a TRUNK (=a long nose that it can use to pick things up), and TUSKs (=long teeth): *Elephants live in parts of Africa and Asia.*

**el·e·va·tion** /ˌeləˈveɪʃən/ *noun*
the height of a place, measured from the level of the ocean: *The city is in the mountains at an elevation of 7,000 feet.*

**el·e·va·tor** /ˈeləˌveɪṭə/ *noun*
a machine like a small room that takes people from one level to another in a building: *I took the elevator to the 26th floor.*

**e·lev·en** /ɪˈlevən/ *number*
1 11: *There are eleven players on a soccer team.*
2 eleven O'CLOCK
3 eleven years old: *I was eleven when my sister was born.*

**e·lev·enth** /ɪˈlevənθ/ *number*
1 11th
2 1/11

**elf** /elf/ *noun* (plural **elves** /elvz/)
a small imaginary person with pointed ears, who appears in stories

**el·i·gi·ble** /ˈelədʒəbəl/ *adjective* (*formal*)
officially allowed to do or have something: *People are eligible to vote at the age of 18.*
—**eligibility** /ˌelədʒəˈbɪləti/ *noun* the official right to do something

**e·lim·i·nate** Ac /ɪˈlɪməˌneɪt/ *verb* (*formal*)
1 to get rid of something completely: *We want to eliminate bullying at this school.*
2 **be eliminated** = to be defeated in a sports competition, so that you can no longer take part in it: *The New England Patriots were eliminated in the playoffs.*
[ORIGIN: 1500-1600 From the Latin word *eliminare*, which means "to put out of doors."]

**e·lite¹** /eɪˈlit/ *adjective*
an elite group has the best people or things in it: *an elite college*

**elite²** *noun*
a small group of people who are powerful or important: *He was a member of the powerful political elite in Washington, D.C.*

**elk** /elk/ *noun* (plural **elk** *or* **elks**)
a type of large DEER. Male elk have large horns called ANTLERs, that look like tree branches.

**el·lipse** /ɪˈlɪps/ *noun*
a shape like a circle, but longer than it is wide: *A football is in the shape of an ellipse.* SYNONYM: **oval**

**elm** /elm/ *noun*
a large tall tree

**e·lope** /ɪˈloʊp/ *verb*
if two people elope, they go away secretly to get married

**el·o·quent** /ˈeləkwənt/ *adjective* (*formal*)
able to express your ideas and opinions in a clear way that is beautiful to listen to or read: *The president is a very eloquent and persuasive speaker.*

—**eloquently** *adverb* in an eloquent way
—**eloquence** *noun* the quality of being eloquent

**else** /els/ *adverb*
**1** another thing or person: *Do you want anything else to eat? | Someone else must have taken the money – I didn't take it. | We have tried everything to make it work; there's nothing else we can do.*
**2 or else** = used when saying that there will be a bad result if someone does not do something: *Hurry up, or else you'll be late for school!*

**else·where** /ˈelswer/ *adverb (formal)*
in or to another place: *She didn't know anyone at college; her friends from high school had gone elsewhere.*

**ELT** /ˌiː el ˈtiː/ *noun*
(**English Language Teaching**) the activity of teaching English to people whose first language is not English

**elves** /elvz/ *noun*
the plural of ELF

**e·mail** (*also* **e-mail**) /ˈi meɪl/ *noun*
**1** a written message that is sent from one computer to another: *I got an email from her yesterday.* → see picture on page **A20**
**2** a system that allows you to send and receive messages by computer: *I'll send the pictures by email. | What's your email address?*
—**email** (*also* **e-mail**) *verb* to send a message to someone's computer using email: *He emailed them to tell them when he was arriving.*

**e·man·ci·pate** /ɪˈmænsəˌpeɪt/ *verb (formal)*
to make someone free and able to have the same rights as other people in society: *American slaves were emancipated after the Civil War.*
—**emancipation** /ɪˌmænsəˈpeɪʃən/ *noun* the act of emancipating someone: *the emancipation of women*
[**ORIGIN:** 1600-1700 From the Latin word *emancipare*, which means "to give up ownership or power."]

**em·bark** /ɪmˈbɑrk/ *verb (formal)*
to go onto a large ship or airplane
[**ORIGIN:** 1500-1600 From the French word *embarquer*, from *barque*, which means "ship."]

**PHRASAL VERB**
**embark on something**
to start something new and exciting: *He embarked on a new career as a teacher.*

**em·bar·rass** /ɪmˈbærəs/ *verb*
to make someone feel embarrassed: *I didn't want to embarrass her by talking about her problems in front of her friends.*
—**embarrassing** *adjective* making someone feel embarrassed: *Mom showed everyone embarrassing photos of me as a baby.*

**em·bar·rassed** /ɪmˈbærəst/ *adjective*
feeling worried and unhappy about what other people will think of you: *I was embarrassed because I had made such a stupid mistake.* → see picture on page **A23**

**WORD FAMILY: embarrassed**
**embarrassed** *adjective* | **embarrassing** *adjective* | **embarrass** *verb* | **embarrassment** *noun*

**em·bar·rass·ment** /ɪmˈbærəsmənt/ *noun*
the feeling of being embarrassed: *She tried to hide her embarrassment, but her face was all red.*

**em·bas·sy** /ˈembəsi/ *noun* (plural **embassies**)
the office used by officials who work for their country's government in a foreign country: *He works at the Mexican Embassy in Washington, D.C.*

**emblem**

national emblem of Canada

Olympic emblem

**em·blem** /ˈembləm/ *noun*
a picture, shape, or object that represents something such as a country or a company: *The national emblem of Canada is the maple leaf.*

**em·brace** /ɪmˈbreɪs/ *verb (formal)*
to put your arms around someone and hold him or her in a caring way: *They embraced each other and said goodbye.* **SYNONYM: hug**

E

—**embrace** *noun* the action of embracing someone

**em·broi·der·y** /ɪmˈbrɔɪdəri/ *noun*
**1** patterns or pictures that you sew on cloth as a decoration: *The dress had beautiful silk embroidery.*
**2** the skill of sewing patterns on cloth as a decoration
—**embroider** *verb* to sew patterns on cloth as a decoration

E

**em·bry·o** /ˈembriˌoʊ/ *noun*
an animal or human that has not yet been born and has just begun to develop

**em·er·ald** /ˈemərəld/ *noun*
a valuable bright green jewel: *an emerald ring*

**e·merge** Ac /ɪˈmɚdʒ/ *verb* (*formal*)
**1** to appear after being covered or hidden: *The sun emerged from behind the clouds.*
**2** to become known: *He was fired when it emerged that he had lied on his job application.*

**e·mer·gen·cy** /ɪˈmɚdʒənsi/ *noun* (plural **emergencies**)
a very serious and dangerous situation that you must deal with immediately: *Call an ambulance! This is an emergency!*
—**emergency** *adjective* relating to or used for emergencies: *If there is a fire, please use the emergency exit.*
[**ORIGIN:** 1600-1700 From "emerge." An emergency is something that happens suddenly, like something appearing suddenly.]

**eˈmergency ˌroom** *noun*
the part of a hospital that treats people who have been seriously hurt or have suddenly become seriously ill: *They took him to the emergency room after he was hit by a car.*

**em·i·grate** /ˈeməˌgreɪt/ *verb*
to leave your own country in order to live in another: *His family had emigrated from France to Canada.*
—**emigration** /ˌeməˈgreɪʃən/ *noun* the action of emigrating

**WORD FAMILY: emigrate**
**emigrate** *verb* | **emigration** *noun* | **immigrate** *verb* | **immigration** *noun* | **immigrant** *noun*

**e·mis·sions** /ɪˈmɪʃənz/ *plural noun* (*formal*)
smoke and chemicals that are sent into the air by cars, factories, etc.: *Emissions from cars are causing a lot of damage to the environment.*

**Em·my** /ˈemi/ *noun* (plural **Emmies**)
a prize given every year to the best program, actor, etc. on U.S. television

**e·mo·tion** /ɪˈmoʊʃən/ *noun*
a strong feeling such as love, hate, or sadness: *My only emotion was a feeling of deep relief.* | *Her voice was full of emotion.*
[**ORIGIN:** 1500-1600 From the French word *émotion*, from *émouvoir*, which means "to stir up or shake."]

**e·mo·tion·al** /ɪˈmoʊʃənəl/ *adjective*
**1** showing strong feelings to other people, especially by crying: *Everyone was very emotional because it was sad to say goodbye.*
**2** relating to someone's feelings: *He talked about his emotional problems with a counselor.*
—**emotionally** *adverb* in a way that relates to someone's feelings

**em·pa·thize** /ˈempəˌθaɪz/ *verb* (*formal*)
to understand someone else's feelings and problems, because you have been in the same situation yourself: *I empathized with the book's main character because he was exactly my age.*
—**empathy** *noun* (*formal*) the ability to empathize: *I felt a lot of empathy for him because his family was very similar to mine.*
—**empathetic** /ˌempəˈθetɪk/ *adjective* (*formal*) able to empathize

**em·per·or** /ˈempərɚ/ *noun*
the ruler of an empire: *a Roman emperor*
[**ORIGIN:** 1100-1200 From the old French word *empereor*, from the Latin word *imperare*, which means "to command."]

**em·pha·sis** Ac /ˈemfəsɪs/ *noun* (plural **emphases** /ˈemfəsiz/)
**1** special importance that is given to something: *In our drama group, the emphasis is on having fun.*
**2** special importance that is given to part of a word or phrase by saying it louder or higher, or by printing it in a special way: *In "hotel," the emphasis is on the second syllable.*
**SYNONYM: stress**

**WORD FAMILY: emphasis**
**emphasis** *noun* | **emphasize** *verb*

**em·pha·size** Ac /ˈemfəˌsaɪz/ *verb*
to say or show that something is important: *He emphasized the need for students to learn grammar when they study a foreign language.*

**em·pire** /ˈempaɪɚ/ *noun*
**1** a group of countries that are all controlled by one ruler or government: *The Roman Empire included many parts of Europe and North Africa.*
**2** a large group of companies that are all controlled by one person: *He runs a huge media empire that includes newspapers, magazines, and television companies.*

**em·ploy** /ɪmˈplɔɪ/ *verb*
**1** to pay someone to work for you: *The company employs over 5,000 people.*
**2** (*formal*) to use something: *The police employ the latest technology to find criminals.*
—**employable** *adjective* having the skills that you need to get a job with a company: *He had no experience, so he wasn't very employable.*

**WORD FAMILY: employ**
**employ** *verb* | **employer** *noun* | **employee** *noun* | **employment** *noun* | **unemployed** *adjective* | **unemployment** *noun*

**em·ploy·ee** /ɪmˈplɔɪ-i/ *noun*
someone who is paid to work for a person, company, or organization: *a government employee* **SYNONYM: worker**

**em·ploy·er** /ɪmˈplɔɪɚ/ *noun*
a person, company, or organization that pays people to work for them: *Employers are looking for people who have experience doing the job.*

**em·ploy·ment** /ɪmˈplɔɪmənt/ *noun* (*formal*)
work that you do to earn money: *He's still looking for employment, but there are not many jobs right now.* **SYNONYM: work**

**em·pow·er** /ɪmˈpaʊɚ/ *verb* (*formal*)
to give someone the confidence, power, or right to do something: *Teachers should empower children to make decisions for themselves.*

**em·press** /ˈemprɪs/ *noun*
the female ruler of an EMPIRE, or the wife of an EMPEROR

**empty**

empty full

**emp·ty**[1] /ˈempti/ *adjective* (**emptier**, **emptiest**)
**1** having nothing inside: *He drank until his glass was empty.* | *an empty box* **ANTONYM: full**
**2** having no one inside: *The house was empty; no one was home.* **ANTONYM: full**
**3** if your life feels empty, it seems to have no purpose and you feel unhappy because nothing interesting is happening: *When all my kids were away at college, my life felt empty.*

**empty**[2] *verb* (**emptied**, **empties**)
**1** to take out everything that is inside something: *Can you empty the dishwasher?*
**2** if a place empties, the people inside it leave: *After the show, the theater began to empty.*

**en·a·ble** Ac /ɪˈneɪbəl/ *verb* (*formal*)
to make it possible for someone or something to do something: *The Internet enables you to find out information about almost anything.*

**en·act** /ɪˈnækt/ *verb* (*formal*)
to make a new law: *Congress enacted a new law to cut taxes.*

**e·nam·el** /ɪˈnæməl/ *noun*
the hard white material on the outside of your teeth: *Sugar damages the enamel on your teeth.*

**en·chant·ed** /ɪnˈtʃæntɪd/ *adjective*
changed by magic: *The frog told her he was an enchanted prince.*
—**enchantment** *noun* magic that is used to change something: *He didn't know how to*

E

*free the sleeping princess from the witch's enchantment.*

**en·close** /ɪnˈkloʊz/ *verb*
**1** to put something inside an envelope with a letter: *I enclosed a picture of our house with the letter.*
**2 be enclosed by something** = to be surrounded by something, for example a fence or wall: *The yard was enclosed by a high wall.*

**en·clo·sure** /ɪnˈkloʊʒɚ/ *noun*
an area that is surrounded by something such as a wall or fence: *The animals are kept in a large enclosure.*

E

**en·coun·ter¹** Ac /ɪnˈkaʊntɚ/ *noun (formal)*
**1** an occasion when you experience something, especially something bad: *My first encounter with bullying was in the park.*
**2** an occasion when you meet a person or animal: *In the book, he describes his encounter with a huge bear.*

**encounter²** Ac *verb (formal)*
**1** to experience something, especially problems: *Did you encounter any problems?*
**2** to meet a person or animal: *He was the most unusual man I had ever encountered.*

**en·cour·age** /ɪnˈkɚɪdʒ/ *verb*
**1** to try to persuade someone to do something: *My parents encourage me to study hard, and help me whenever I need it.* **ANTONYM: discourage**
**2** to make someone feel more hopeful and more confident: *He encouraged me by saying that I had a good chance of winning.* **ANTONYM: discourage**
—**encouraging** *adjective* making you feel more hopeful and more confident: *The latest test scores are encouraging, because they mean that students are getting better at math.*
—**encouragement** *noun* things that you say in order to try to persuade someone to do something or make him or her feel more confident: *The coach said a few words of encouragement to the team.*
→ see Thesaurus box at **persuade**

**en·cy·clo·pe·di·a** /ɪnˌsaɪkləˈpidiə/ *noun*
a large book or set of books that has a lot of facts about many subjects or about one subject: *I looked in the encyclopedia for information about spiders.*
[ORIGIN: 1500-1600 From the Greek phrase *enkyklios paideia*, which means "general education."]

**end¹** /end/ *noun*
**1** the last part of something: *At the end of the story, the boy finds his father. | My birthday is at the end of July, on the 29th. | I was sad when my uncle's visit came to an end.* **ANTONYM: beginning**
**2** the part of something that is farthest from its beginning or from its center: *We live at the far end of the street.*

> **THESAURUS: end**
>
> **point** the sharp end of something: *the point of a pencil*
>
> **tip** the end of something long, narrow, and pointed: *the tip of your nose*

**3 in the end** = after thinking about something for a long time, or after a lot of other things have happened: *We couldn't decide between going to Florida or Mexico, but in the end, we chose Mexico.* **SYNONYM: finally**
**4 make ends meet** = to have just enough money to buy what you need: *My father had to do two jobs in order to make ends meet.*

**end²** *verb*
to stop happening, or to make something stop happening: *World War II ended in 1945. | I tried to end the conversation.* **ANTONYM: begin**
**PHRASAL VERBS**
**end in something**
to have a particular result, or to finish in a particular way: *Their marriage ended in divorce.*
**end up**
to arrive somewhere after many other things have happened, when you did not plan to arrive in that place: *We went out to eat and then to a movie, and ended up at Joe's house.*

**en·dan·ger** /ɪnˈdeɪndʒɚ/ *verb (formal)*
to put someone or something in a dangerous or harmful situation: *Smoking seriously endangers your health.*

**enˌdangered ˈspecies** *noun*
a type of animal or plant that soon might not exist anymore because there are very few left:

*The Siberian tiger is now an endangered species.*

**end·ing** /ˈendɪŋ/ *noun*
the end of a story, movie, or play: *She finds her lost dog, so the show has a happy ending.*

**end·less** /ˈendləs/ *adjective*
continuing for a very long time: *They asked me endless questions, until I got tired of answering them.*

**en·dorse** /ɪnˈdɔrs/ *verb*
**1** to officially say that you support or approve of someone or something: *The mayor endorsed the plan today, saying, "I believe it will be a very good thing for our city."*
**2** to sign your name on the back of a check: *You need to endorse the check to get cash for it.*
—**endorsement** *noun* a statement in which you officially say that you support or approve of someone or something

**en·dur·ance** /ɪnˈdurəns/ *noun* (*formal*)
the ability to continue doing something difficult or painful for a long time: *The 26 mile race is a test of the runners' endurance.*

**en·dure** /ɪnˈdur/ *verb* (*formal*)
**1** to suffer pain or deal with a very difficult situation for a long time: *People have endured months of fighting.*
**2** to continue for a long time: *Their marriage has endured for over 50 years.*

**en·e·my** /ˈenəmi/ *noun* (plural **enemies**)
**1** someone who hates you and wants to harm you or prevent you from being successful: *She is not a nice person and has made a lot of enemies during her career.*
**ANTONYM: friend**
**2** the people that you are fighting in a war: *The enemy started firing rockets at us.* | *enemy soldiers* **ANTONYM: ally**
[**ORIGIN:** 1200-1300 From the Latin word *inimicus*, from *in-* and *amicus*, which mean "not" and "friend."]

**en·er·get·ic** Ac /ˌenɚˈdʒetɪk/ *adjective*
very active and doing things with a lot of energy: *He was an energetic coach, who often ran up and down the court with the players.*
—**energetically** *adverb* in an energetic way

**en·er·gize** /ˈenɚˌdʒaɪz/ *verb*
to make someone feel more determined and full of energy: *The president's speech energized us, and made us want to work hard for our country.*

**en·er·gy** Ac /ˈenɚdʒi/ *noun*
**1** the physical and mental strength that makes you able to do things: *She was young and full of energy.*
**2** power that is used to produce light and heat, make machines work, etc.: *The U.S. gets most of its energy from oil, coal, and natural gas.*

**WORD FAMILY: energy**
**energy** *noun* | **energetic** *adjective* | **energetically** *adverb* | **energize** *verb*

**en·force** Ac /ɪnˈfɔrs/ *verb*
to make people obey a rule or law: *The police have the job of enforcing the law.*
—**enforcement** *noun* the process of making people obey a rule or law: *law enforcement*

**en·gage** /ɪnˈgeɪdʒ/ *verb* (*formal*)
**engage someone in conversation** = to begin talking to someone: *A woman sat down next to me and engaged me in conversation.*
**PHRASAL VERB**
**engage in something**
to do an activity: *Only 10% of Americans engage in regular exercise.*

**en·gaged** /ɪnˈgeɪdʒd/ *adjective*
two people who are engaged have agreed to marry each other: *They got engaged in May, and they got married a year later.*
→ see Thesaurus box at **married**

**en·gage·ment** /ɪnˈgeɪdʒmənt/ *noun*
an agreement to marry someone: *The couple announced their engagement in March.*

**en·gine** /ˈendʒɪn/ *noun*
**1** the part of a vehicle or machine that produces power to make it move: *The car's engine made a funny sound when it started.*
→ see picture on page **A28**
**2** the part of a train that pulls the rest of it along **SYNONYM: locomotive**
[**ORIGIN:** 1300-1400 From the Latin word *ingenium*, which means "skill or cleverness you are born with." An engine is a machine or part of a machine that is cleverly designed.]

E

**en·gi·neer** /ˌendʒəˈnɪr/ *noun*
**1** someone whose job is to design and build machines, roads, and bridges: *The engineers developed a new, very fast computer.*
**2** the person who drives a train

**en·gi·neer·ing** /ˌendʒəˈnɪrɪŋ/ *noun*
the job of designing and building machines, roads, and bridges

**En·glish¹** /ˈɪŋglɪʃ/ *noun*
**1** the language used in places such as the U.S., Canada, and Great Britain: *She speaks very good English.*
**2 the English** = the people of England: *The English love soccer.*

**English²** *adjective*
from England: *Her husband is English.* | *the English language*
—**Englishman** *noun* a man from England
—**Englishwoman** *noun* a woman from England

**en·grossed** /ɪnˈgroʊst/ *adjective* (*formal*)
so interested in something that you do not notice anything else: *He was engrossed in his book and didn't see me leave the room.*

**en·joy** /ɪnˈdʒɔɪ/ *verb*
**1** to like doing something or watching something: *Did you enjoy the movie?* | *I enjoyed watching the game.*

> **THESAURUS: enjoy**
>
> **like** to enjoy something, or think that it is nice or good: *I liked the movie a lot; it was really good.*
>
> **love** to enjoy doing something very much: *My daughter loves to read.*
>
> **have a good/great time** to enjoy doing something or going somewhere, usually with other people: *Did you have a good time at the party?*
>
> **have fun** to enjoy doing an activity: *We were having fun in the pool.*

**2 enjoy yourself** = to be happy and have fun in a situation: *I enjoyed myself at the party.*
—**enjoyment** *noun* pleasure that you get from doing something
[ORIGIN: 1300-1400 From the Latin word *gaudere*, which means "to feel very happy."]

> **WORD FAMILY: enjoy**
>
> **enjoy** *verb* | **enjoyment** *noun* | **enjoyable** *adjective*

**en·joy·a·ble** /ɪnˈdʒɔɪəbəl/ *adjective* (*formal*)
giving you pleasure: *We had an enjoyable afternoon playing in the water at the beach.*
SYNONYM: **fun**
→ see Thesaurus box at **nice**

**en·large** /ɪnˈlɑrdʒ/ *verb*
to make something become bigger, for example a picture or a photograph: *I'm going to enlarge these two pictures on my computer.*
—**enlargement** *noun* a picture or photograph that is a bigger copy of another one

**en·light·en·ing** /ɪnˈlaɪtnɪŋ/ *adjective* (*formal*)
making someone learn or understand something better: *The movie was enlightening. It explained global warming really clearly.*

**en·list** /ɪnˈlɪst/ *verb*
to join the army, navy, etc.: *Her son has enlisted in the army.*
—**enlistment** *noun* the action of enlisting

**e·nor·mous** [Ac] /ɪˈnɔrməs/ *adjective*
extremely large: *Their house is enormous – it has eight bedrooms!* SYNONYM: **huge**
—**enormously** *adverb* very, or very much: *The book was enormously successful.*
→ see Thesaurus box at **big**
[ORIGIN: 1500-1600 From the Latin word *enormis*, which means "unusual or unusually large," from *ex* and *norma*, which mean "out of" and "standard or rule."]

**e·nough** /ɪˈnʌf/ *adverb, adjective, pronoun*
**1** as much, as many, or as big as you need: *He doesn't have enough money to buy a new car.* | *Is this room big enough for both of you?*

> **THESAURUS: enough**
>
> **plenty** a large amount that is enough or more than enough: *Try to eat plenty of fruits and vegetables.*
>
> **sufficient** (*formal*) as much as you need for a particular purpose: *We weren't given sufficient time to finish the test.*
>
> **adequate** (*formal*) enough for a particular purpose: *The light was not adequate for reading.*

**2 have had enough** (*informal*) = to want a situation to stop because it is making you annoyed or tired and impatient: *I have had enough of winter and can't wait until spring.*

**en·roll** /ɪnˈroʊl/ *verb*
to join a school, class, university, or club: *He enrolled at the local community college.*

**en·sure** [Ac] /ɪnˈʃʊr/ *verb* (*formal*)
to make certain that something happens: *Please ensure that you have all your luggage with you when you get off the plane.*

**en·ter** /ˈentɚ/ *verb*
**1** to go or come into a place: *He entered the room quietly and sat down.*

**THESAURUS: enter**

**go in** to enter a place: *Frank opened the door, and we went in.*

**come in** to enter the room where you are: *Come in and sit down.*

**get in** to enter a place, especially when this is difficult: *"How did the burglars get in?" "Through the window."*

**trespass** (*formal*) to go onto someone's land without permission: *The sign said, "No Trespassing."*

**2** to start studying or working somewhere: *Many older students are now entering college.*
**3** to take part in a competition, race, or election: *Over 100 athletes entered the race.*
**4** to put information into a computer or write it on an official document: *Enter your name and address.*
**5 enter into an agreement/a contract** (*formal*) = to officially make an agreement

**WORD FAMILY: enter**

**enter** *verb* | **entry** *noun* | **entrance** *noun*

**en·ter·prise** /ˈentɚpraɪz/ *noun* (*formal*)
**1** a company or business: *a successful business enterprise*
**2** the ability to think of and try new things, especially in business: *She showed enterprise by making bracelets and selling them to her friends.*

**en·ter·tain** /ˌentɚˈteɪn/ *verb*
**1** to do something that interests people or makes them laugh: *He entertained them with funny stories about his life in Hong Kong.*
**2** to treat someone as a guest by providing food and drink for him or her: *The company spends a lot of money on entertaining business clients.*
—**entertaining** *adjective* interesting and enjoyable: *an entertaining movie*

**WORD FAMILY: entertain**

**entertain** *verb* | **entertaining** *adjective* | **entertainment** *noun* | **entertainer** *noun*

**en·ter·tain·er** /ˌentɚˈteɪnɚ/ *noun*
someone whose job is to do something such as tell jokes or sing for people: *a popular TV entertainer*

**en·ter·tain·ment** /ˌentɚˈteɪnmənt/ *noun*
things for people to watch and do in order to enjoy themselves: *For most people, television is the main form of entertainment.*

**en·thrall·ing** /ɪnˈθrɔlɪŋ/ *adjective* (*formal*)
something that is enthralling is so interesting, exciting, or enjoyable that you give it all your attention: *The audience was silent through the whole enthralling performance.*
—**enthralled** *adjective* if you are enthralled by something, you enjoy it so much that you give it all your attention

**en·thu·si·as·m** /ɪnˈθuziˌæzəm/ *noun*
a strong feeling of interest and excitement: *The students were full of enthusiasm and were ready to work hard.*
[**ORIGIN:** 1500-1600 From the Greek word *enthousiasmos*, which means "having been filled with abilities or ideas by a god," from *theos*, which means "a god."]

**WORD FAMILY: enthusiasm**

**enthusiasm** *noun* | **enthusiastic** *adjective* | **enthusiastically** *adverb* | **enthusiast** *noun*

**en·thu·si·ast** /ɪnˈθuziˌæst/ *noun* (*formal*)
someone who likes and is very interested in something: *My father is a baseball enthusiast; he watches every game he can.* **SYNONYM: fan**

**en·thu·si·as·tic** /ɪnˌθuziˈæstɪk/ *adjective*
showing a lot of interest and excitement

E

about something: *My sister was enthusiastic about the idea of a costume party.*
—**enthusiastically** *adverb* in an enthusiastic way

**en·tire** /ɪnˈtaɪɚ/ *adjective*
all of something: *Mom spent the entire day cooking for the party.*
—**entirely** *adverb* completely: *She looks entirely different when she wears glasses.*

**en·ti·tle** /ɪnˈtaɪtl/ *verb* (*formal*)
**1** to give someone the right to have or do something: *Membership at the YMCA entitles you to use the gym and pool.*
**2** if a book, play, poem, or movie is entitled something, that is its name: *He read out a poem by Walt Whitman entitled "To a Stranger."*
—**entitlement** *noun* the amount of something that you are allowed to have according to the rules

**en·trance** /ˈentrəns/ *noun*
**1** a door, gate, or other opening that you go through to enter a place: *He walked into the building through the main entrance.* **ANTONYM: exit**
**2** the right or ability to go into a place: *Entrance to the museum costs $10.00.*

**en·trée** /ˈɑntreɪ/ *noun*
the main food that you eat at a meal: *The entrée was a chicken dish, served with potatoes and vegetables.*

**en·tre·pre·neur** /ˌɑntrəprəˈnɚ/ *noun*
someone who starts a company and arranges business deals in order to make money: *The company was started by a couple of young entrepreneurs in 2005.*

**en·try** /ˈentri/ *noun* (plural **entries**)
**1** the right or ability to go into a place: *People traveling without a visa will be refused entry into the United States.*
**2** the act of becoming involved in doing something: *The entry of the US into World War II meant defeat for Germany.*
**3** something you write, draw, or do in order to try to win a competition: *The winning entry in this year's essay competition was written by Roberto Bolano.*
**4** (*also* **entryway**) a door, gate, or opening that you go through to go into a place: *The entry is in the back of the building.* **SYNONYM: entrance**
**5** a word and the explanation of what it means in a dictionary: *The dictionary has over 15,000 entries.*

**ˈentry-ˌlevel** *adjective*
an entry-level job is for people who have never done that type of job before, and who are starting at the lowest level: *After college, she found an entry-level job in a software company.*

**en·vel·op** /ɪnˈveləp/ *verb* (*formal*)
to cover something completely: *The building was quickly enveloped in smoke from the fire.*

**en·ve·lope** /ˈenvəˌloʊp/ *noun*
a paper cover that you put a letter in: *She wrote the address on the envelope.*
[**ORIGIN:** 1700-1800 From the French word *enveloper*, which means "to wrap."]

**en·vi·ous** /ˈenviəs/ *adjective*
wishing that you had something that someone else has: *Jackie was envious of her sister's success.*
—**enviously** *adverb* in an envious way: *He looked enviously at John's new car.*

**en·vi·ron·ment** Ac /ɪnˈvaɪɚnmənt/ *noun*
**1 the environment** = the natural world, including water, air, land, and plants. The environment can be harmed by the way we live: *To protect the environment, companies must stop polluting the air and water.*
**2** the people and things around you that affect your life: *A police officer's work environment is sometimes very dangerous.*
—**environmental** /ɪnˌvaɪɚnˈmentl/ *adjective* relating to the environment: *The oil spill caused environmental damage to the coastline.*
—**environmentally** *adverb* in a way that relates to the environment: *Solar power is an environmentally safe source of energy.*
[**ORIGIN:** 1600-1700 From the French word *environner*, which means "to surround."]

**enˌvironmentally ˈfriendly** *adjective*
not damaging the environment: *Bicycles are environmentally friendly because they do not produce any pollution.*

**en·vy[1]** /ˈenvi/ *noun*
the feeling of wanting something that someone else has: *She looked with envy at Ben's new computer.*
[**ORIGIN:** 1200-1300 From the Latin word *invidere*, which means "to look at with bad feelings."]

**envy[2]** *verb* (**envied**, **envies**)
if you envy someone, you wish you had something that he or she has: *I envy Meg – her parents buy her anything she wants.*

**en·zyme** /ˈenzaɪm/ *noun*
a chemical that is produced in plants and animals, and that makes a chemical process start: *Enzymes in the stomach change food so that it can be digested.*

**ep·ic[1]** /ˈepɪk/ *adjective*
an epic story or trip is very long, exciting, or impressive: *Lewis and Clark's epic trip to the Pacific Coast took two years.*

**epic[2]** *noun*
a book, poem, or movie that tells a long story about brave actions and exciting events: *Homer's poem "The Odyssey" is an epic about a Greek hero's ten-year journey home after the Trojan War.*

**ep·i·dem·ic** /ˌepəˈdemɪk/ *noun*
if there is an epidemic, a lot of people get a disease at the same time: *The swine flu epidemic spread quickly around the world.*
[**ORIGIN:** 1600-1700 From the Greek word *epidemos*, which means "among the people, or visiting people," from *demos*, which means "people."]

**ep·i·lep·sy** /ˈepəˌlepsi/ *noun*
a medical condition in the brain, that can make someone suddenly become unconscious or unable to control body movements for a short time
—**epileptic** /ˌepəˈleptɪk/ *noun* someone who has epilepsy
—**epileptic** *adjective* related to epilepsy: *She had an epileptic fit.*

**ep·i·sode** /ˈepəˌsoʊd/ *noun*
**1** a television or radio program that is one of a series of programs that tell a story: *I watched an old episode of "The Simpsons" last night.*
**2** an event or a short period of time during which something happened: *The death of his wife was a sad episode in his life.*
→ see Thesaurus box at **part[1]**

**e·qual[1]** /ˈiːkwəl/ *adjective*
**1** the same in size, value, or amount: *She cut the cake into eight equal parts.* | *The two towns are equal in size.* | *A dime is equal to ten pennies.*
**2** having the same rights and opportunities as everyone else: *Women had to fight for equal rights, such as the right to vote.*

**equal[2]** *verb* (**equaled** *or* **equalled**, **equaling** *or* **equalling**)
**1** to be the same as something else: *Four plus four equals eight.*
**2** to do something as well as another person: *He equaled the world record for the 200 meters.*

**equal[3]** *noun*
someone who is as important or intelligent as you are, or who has the same rights that you have: *Young people want adults to treat them as equals.*

**e·qual·i·ty** /ɪˈkwɑləti/ *noun*
a situation in which people from different groups have the same rights and opportunities: *Women want equality with men and are demanding equal pay for the same job.* **ANTONYM: inequality**

**e·qual·ly** /ˈikwəli/ *adverb*
**1** just as much, or to the same degree: *Jim and his sister are equally intelligent.*
**2** in equal parts or amounts: *We divided the money equally among the four of us.*

**ˈequal sign** *noun*
the sign (=) that you use in mathematics to show that two things are the same size, number, or amount

**e·qua·tion** [Ac] /ɪˈkweɪʒən/ *noun*
a statement in mathematics showing that two quantities are equal, for example 2 x 3 = 6: *What number is missing in this mathematical equation: 4 + __ = 12?*

**e·qua·tor** (*also* **Equator**) /ɪˈkweɪtɚ/ *noun*
**the equator** = an imaginary line around the Earth that divides it equally into its northern and southern halves: *The island is 80 miles north of the equator.*
—**equatorial** /ˌekwəˈtɔriəl/ *adjective* near

the equator, or relating to the equator: *the rainforests of equatorial Africa*

**e·qui·lat·er·al tri·an·gle** /ˌikwəˌlætərəl ˈtraɪˌæŋgəl/ *noun*
a TRIANGLE with three sides that are all the same length and three angles of 60 degrees

**equilateral triangle**

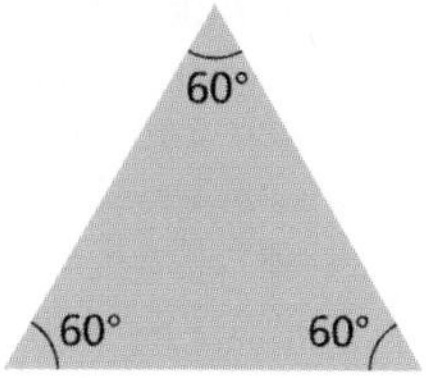


**e·qui·nox** /ˈikwəˌnɑks/ *noun*
one of the two times each year when day and night are equal in length everywhere on earth: *The spring equinox is on March 20.*

**e·quip** Ac /ɪˈkwɪp/ *verb* (**equipped**, **equipping**)
to provide the tools or equipment that someone needs to do something: *The city has equipped all the schools with new computers.*

**equipment**

sports equipment

**e·quip·ment** Ac /ɪˈkwɪpmənt/ *noun*
the tools, machines, or clothes that you need to do something: *I don't have the right equipment to change the tire.* | *The store sells sports equipment, like tennis rackets.*

**GRAMMAR: equipment**

Do not say "an equipment" or "equipments." Say, for example, **some equipment** or **a piece of equipment**: *We'll need to borrow some equipment.* | *It's an expensive piece of equipment.*

**eq·ui·ty** /ˈekwəti/ *noun*
the amount of money that you would have left if you sold your house and paid off the money you borrowed to buy it: *People who have owned their home for a long time will have a lot of equity in the property.*

**e·quiv·a·lent¹** Ac /ɪˈkwɪvələnt/ *adjective*
the same in amount, value, or importance as something else: *The certificate is equivalent to a high school diploma.*

**equivalent²** Ac *noun*
something that is equal in amount, value, or importance to something else: *The car cost the equivalent of six months' pay.*

**e·ra** /ˈɪrə/ *noun* (*formal*)
a period of time in history: *The end of the war brought an era of peace to the region.*

**e·rad·i·cate** /ɪˈrædəˌkeɪt/ *verb* (*formal*)
to destroy or remove something completely: *The school is trying hard to eradicate bullying.*
—**eradication** /ɪˌrædəˈkeɪʃən/ *noun* the complete removal or destruction of something
[**ORIGIN:** 1400-1500 From the Latin word *eradicare*, which means "to pull out by the root," from *radix*, meaning "root."]

**erase**

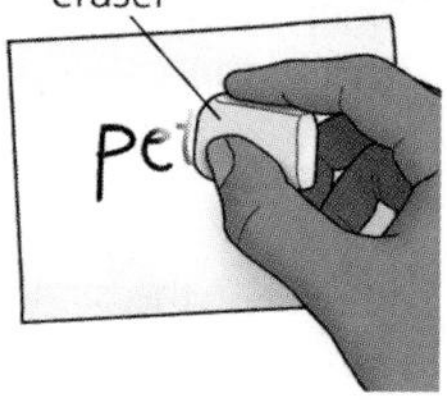


**e·rase** /ɪˈreɪs/ *verb*
**1** to remove writing or drawing with an eraser: *Use a pencil, so that you can erase any mistakes.*
**2** to remove information, a movie, or music from a computer or disk: *I erased the file from the computer by mistake.*
[**ORIGIN:** 1500-1600 From the Latin word *erasus*, a form of the verb *eradere*, which means "to scrape off."]

**e·ras·er** /ɪˈreɪsɚ/ *noun*
**1** a piece of rubber that you use to remove pencil marks from paper
**2** an object that you use to clean marks from a BLACKBOARD or WHITEBOARD

**e·rect¹** /ɪˈrekt/ *adjective*
in a straight upright position: *The rabbit stopped to listen, with its ears erect.*

**erect²** *verb* (*formal*)
to build something: *The town hall was erected in 1892.*

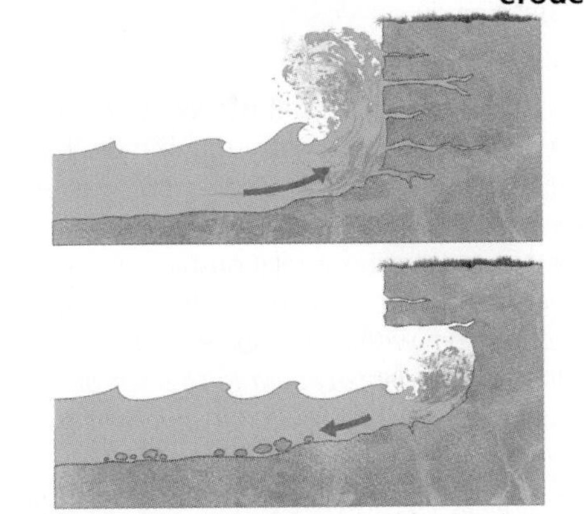


The shore is being damaged by erosion.

**e·rode** Ac /ɪˈroʊd/ *verb*
if land, rock, or soil is eroded, it is gradually destroyed by wind, rain, or water: *Acid rain has eroded the faces on the stone statues.*
—**erosion** /ɪˈroʊʒən/ *noun* the gradual destruction of land by wind, rain, or water: *Planting trees will help to prevent soil erosion.*

**e·rot·ic** /ɪˈrɑtɪk/ *adjective*
involving or producing sexual feelings: *an erotic painting of a nude woman*
—**erotically** *adverb* in an erotic way

**er·rand** /ˈerənd/ *noun*
if you do an errand, you go somewhere to buy, get, or deliver something: *She gets her son to run errands, such as buying milk on the way home from school.*

**er·rat·ic** /ɪˈrætɪk/ *adjective* (*formal*)
not following a regular pattern: *The team has been erratic, losing one week and winning the next.*
—**erratically** *adverb* in an erratic way: *He was seen driving erratically just before the crash.*

**er·ror** Ac /ˈerɚ/ *noun*
a mistake: *There are a lot of grammatical errors in your essay.*
[**ORIGIN:** 1200-1300 From Latin, from *errare*, which means "to wander, or to make a mistake."]

**e·rupt** /ɪˈrʌpt/ *verb*
**1** (*formal*) if violence erupts, it suddenly happens: *In this war-torn country, fighting could erupt again at any time.*
**2** if a VOLCANO erupts, it sends out smoke, fire, and rock into the sky: *More than 800 people died when the volcano erupted.*
—**eruption** /ɪˈrʌpʃən/ *noun* an occasion when a VOLCANO erupts: *The eruption sent a cloud of ash high into the sky.*
[**ORIGIN:** 1600-1700 From the Latin word *eruptus*, a form of the verb *erumpere*, which means "to burst out."]

**es·ca·late** /ˈeskəˌleɪt/ *verb* (*formal*)
**1** if an argument or fight escalates, it quickly becomes worse: *The argument escalated into a violent fight.*
**2** to become higher, or increase: *The price of gas continues to escalate.*
—**escalation** /ˌeskəˈleɪʃən/ *noun* an increase in something, or a process in which something becomes worse: *Sending more troops will lead to an escalation of the war.*

**es·ca·la·tor** /ˈeskəˌleɪtɚ/ *noun*
moving stairs that carry people from one level of a building to another: *We took the escalator to the first floor of the store.*

**es·cape¹** /ɪˈskeɪp/ *verb*
**1** to get away from a place or person, when it is dangerous or when someone is trying to stop you: *The girl climbed through a window to escape the fire.* | *He escaped from prison by digging a tunnel.*

**2** if you escape something bad, it does not happen to you: *The two boys escaped punishment by blaming another child.*
—**escaped** *adjective* an escaped prisoner or animal has gotten away from a place

**escape²** *noun*
**1** the act of getting away from a place or a bad situation: *They made their escape from the jail while the guards were not looking.*
**2** a way of forgetting about a bad or boring situation for a short time: *Movies are a form of escape, because you can forget about your problems for a while.*

**es·cort¹** /ɪˈskɔrt/ *verb*
to go somewhere with someone, in order to make sure that he or she gets there safely or does not escape: *Guards escorted the prisoners to the courthouse.*

E

**es·cort²** /ˈeskɔrt/ *noun*
the person or group of people that goes somewhere with someone in order to protect them: *The governor always travels with a police escort.*

**ESL** *noun*
(**English as a Second Language**) the activity of teaching English to students whose first language is not English, but who live in an English-speaking country: *an ESL student*

E

**e·soph·a·gus** /ɪˈsɑfəgəs/ *noun*
the tube that food goes down from your throat to your stomach

**es·pe·cial·ly** /ɪˈspeʃəli/ *adverb*
**1** more than other people or things: *I like all of their albums, especially the last one.* | *He is especially good at math.* **SYNONYM: particularly**
**2** for a particular person or reason: *She bought new clothes especially for the trip.*

**es·pi·o·nage** /ˈespiəˌnɑʒ/ *noun*
the activity of finding out secret information about a country or company and giving it to your own country or company

**es·pres·so** /eˈspresoʊ/ *noun*
very strong coffee that you drink in a small cup

**es·say** /ˈeseɪ/ *noun*
a short piece of writing about a subject: *I had to write an essay about Abraham Lincoln for history class.* **SYNONYM: paper**
[**ORIGIN:** 1400-1500 From the old French word *essai*, which means "attempt." Essay may have come to mean a piece of writing because in an essay you attempt to write down your thoughts and reasons.]

**es·sence** /ˈesəns/ *noun* (*formal*)
the most basic and important quality of something: *The essence of the problem is that many of the students cannot afford to buy computers.*
[**ORIGIN:** 1300-1400 From the Latin word *essentia*, from *esse*, which means "to be."]

**es·sen·tial** /ɪˈsenʃəl/ *adjective*
important and necessary: *A car is essential out here in the country where there aren't any buses.*
→ see Thesaurus box at **important**

**es·sen·tial·ly** /ɪˈsenʃəli/ *adverb*
relating to the most basic and important facts about something: *The story is essentially true, although the writer changed the names of some of the people in it.*

**es·tab·lish** Ac /ɪˈstæblɪʃ/ *verb* (*formal*)
**1** to start a company or organization that will exist for a long time: *The school was established in 1922.*
**2** to start having a relationship with another person, group, or country: *We established a connection with a school in Guatemala, so that the students can write to each other.*
[**ORIGIN:** 1300-1400 From the Latin word *stabilire*, which means "to make firm."]

**es·tab·lish·ment** Ac /ɪˈstæblɪʃmənt/ *noun* (*formal*)
**1** an organization: *Harvard University is one of the most famous educational establishments in the world.*
**2** the act of starting an organization, relationship, or system: *The U.S. supported the establishment of a Jewish state in the Middle East.*

**es·tate** Ac /ɪˈsteɪt/ *noun*
**1** the property and money that someone leaves after he or she dies: *She left her estate to her three children when she died.*
**2** a large area of land in the country with a large house on it, that is owned by one person or organization

**es·teem** /ɪˈstim/ *noun* (*formal*)
respect and admiration for someone: *She is held in high esteem by her fellow teachers and her students.*

**es·ti·mate¹** Ac /ˈestəmeɪt/ *verb*
to calculate a number or amount approximately: *I estimate that it will take about thirty minutes to walk there.*

**es·ti·mate²** Ac /ˈestəmɪt/ *noun*
**1** a guess about the number or amount of something: *The project should take you about five hours of work, but that's just an estimate. Some of you will finish sooner.*
**2** a statement of how much it will probably cost to build or repair something: *Did the garage gave you an estimate for fixing the car?*

**etc.** /et ˈsetrə/ *adverb*
(**et cetera**) used at the end of a list to show that you could add similar things: *He's been to many European countries: France, Germany, Spain, etc.*

**e·ter·nal** /ɪˈtɚnl/ *adjective*
continuing forever: *The possibility of eternal life is an important idea in some religions.*
—**eternally** *adverb* forever: *Christians believe that the soul lives eternally.*

**e·ter·ni·ty** /ɪˈtɚnəti/ *noun*
**1** the whole of time, without any end: *Although Shakespeare is dead, his works will live on for eternity.*
**2 an eternity** = a period of time that seems very long: *We waited for an eternity, and the bus still didn't come.*

**eth·ic** Ac /ˈeθɪk/ *noun*
**1 ethics** = rules that people use to decide what is right and wrong: *Doctors must follow a strict code of ethics when treating a patient.*
**2** an idea or belief that influences people's behavior and attitudes: *My family were hard-working farmers who passed a strong work ethic on to all their children.*

**eth·i·cal** Ac /ˈeθɪkəl/ *adjective*
**1** involving beliefs about what is right and wrong: *It is a difficult ethical decision to use animals in scientific tests, but it often helps develop medical treatments for people.*
**2** morally good or correct: *Is it ethical for doctors to use drugs to control people's behavior?*
—**ethically** *adverb* in an ethical way

**eth·nic** Ac /ˈeθnɪk/ *adjective*
relating to a group of people who have the same religion or culture or who come from the same country: *Although the college has students of all races, Asian Americans form the largest ethnic group.*
—**ethnicity** /eθˈnɪsəti/ *noun* (*formal*) the race or nationality that someone belongs to: *Treating people unfairly because of their ethnicity is both wrong and illegal.*
[**ORIGIN:** 1300-1400 From the Greek word *ethnos*, which means "nation or people."]

**et·i·quette** /ˈetɪkət/ *noun* (*formal*)
the rules of how to behave politely: *It is very bad etiquette to talk while chewing your food.*

**et·y·mol·o·gy** /ˌetəˈmɑlədʒi/ (plural **etymologies**) *noun*
the history of words, or a description of the origin or changing meaning of a word: *Do you know the etymology of the word "camp?" It comes from the Latin word for "field."*

**Eu·rope** /ˈyʊrəp/ *noun*
the CONTINENT that has England, France, Germany, and other countries in it. Europe is north of the Mediterranean Sea and west of the Ural mountains: *He visited Poland and other countries in Eastern Europe.*

**Eu·ro·pe·an** /ˌyʊrəˈpiən/ *adjective*
from Europe: *He speaks several European languages, including French and Italian.*
—**European** *noun* someone from Europe: *The Portuguese may have been the first Europeans to visit Australia.*

**e·vac·u·ate** /ɪˈvækjueɪt/ *verb*
to move people from a dangerous place to a safe place: *The building was evacuated when the fire started.*
—**evacuation** /ɪˌvækyuˈeɪʃən/ *noun* the action of moving people from a dangerous place to a safe place: *As the hurricane came closer, the mayor ordered the evacuation of the city.*
[**ORIGIN:** 1300-1400 From the Latin word *evacuare*, which means "to empty."]

**e·vade** /ɪˈveɪd/ *verb* (*formal*)
**1** to avoid doing something you should do, or avoid talking about something: *The senator is evading the question because he does not know the answer.*
**2** to avoid being caught by someone who is trying to catch you: *The escaped prisoner evaded capture for three days before the police caught him again.*

**e·val·u·ate** Ac /ɪˈvælyuˌeɪt/ *verb* (*formal*)
to judge how good, useful, or successful someone or something is: *We put cars through a crash test and evaluate the results.*
—**evaluation** /ɪˌvælyuˈeɪʃən/ *noun* a judgment about how good, useful, or successful someone or something is: *The evaluation of the new computer system found that there were many problems.*

**e·vap·o·rate** /ɪˈvæpəˌreɪt/ *verb*
if a liquid evaporates, it changes into steam or a gas: *When sea water evaporates, it leaves salt behind.*
—**evaporation** /ɪˌvæpəˈreɪʃən/ *noun* the process of evaporating: *In warm weather,*

*evaporation causes the water level of the lake to drop.*

**e·va·sion** /ɪˈveɪʒən/ *noun* (*formal*)

**1** the act of avoiding doing something that you should do: *If you do not pay tax on your income, you could go to prison for tax evasion.*

**2** the act of deliberately avoiding talking about something or answering a question: *His answer was full of lies and evasions, but she kept asking until he finally told her the truth.*

E

**e·va·sive** /ɪˈveɪsɪv/ *adjective* (*formal*)

not willing to answer questions directly: *He was very evasive when I asked him where he had been. "Just out," he said.*

**eve** /iv/ *noun*

the night or day before a religious day or a holiday: *We're going to a big party on New Year's Eve.* | *Christmas Eve*

**e·ven¹** /ˈivən/ *adverb*

**1** used when adding something surprising: *He keeps everything, even old bus tickets.* | *The mountains always have snow on them, even in summer.*

**2** used when you want to emphasize that someone or something is bigger, better, stronger, etc. than another person or thing: *There will be heavy snow today, and an even bigger storm on Friday.*

**3** **even if** = used to say that something will still be true if another thing happens: *I'll finish the job even if I have to work all night.*

**even²** *adjective*

**1** flat, level, or smooth: *The sidewalk is nice and even, good for skateboarding on.*

**2** an even rate, speed, or temperature is steady and does not change much: *Store the chemicals at an even temperature.*

**3** divided equally, so that there is the same amount of something in each: *Divide the children into six even groups.*

**4** an even number can be divided exactly by two: *2, 4, 6, and 8 are even numbers.*

**ANTONYM: odd**

**5** **be even** (*informal*) = to no longer owe someone something, especially money: *I paid for the movies, so if you pay for the pizza, we'll be even.*

**6** a game or competition that is even is one where the teams are equal and as good as each other: *It was an even contest in the first half, which ended 1–1.*

—**evenly** *adverb* in an even way: *Spread the frosting evenly over the cake.* | *The two teams were evenly matched.*

→ see Thesaurus box at **flat¹**

**even³** *verb*

**PHRASAL VERBS**

**even (something) out**

if things even out, the differences between them become smaller: *Girls often learn to talk earlier than boys, but the difference in speech soon evens out.*

**even something up**

to make something become equal or the same: *O'Malley hit a home run to even up the score.*

**eve·ning** /ˈivnɪŋ/ *noun*

**1** the end of the day and the early part of the night: *We usually eat at around 6:00 in the evening.* | *Do you want to come to my house tomorrow evening?*

**2** **(good) evening** = said in order to greet someone in the evening: *Good evening, ladies and gentlemen, and welcome to our performance.*

**e·vent** /ɪˈvent/ *noun*

**1** something that happens, especially something important, interesting, or unusual: *The election of a black president was a historic event.*

**2** something that has been organized, such as a party, sports game, or show: *The Super Bowl is one of the most important sports events of the year.*

[**ORIGIN:** 1500-1600 From the Latin word *eventus*, a form of the verb *evenire*, which means "to happen."]

**e·vent·ful** /ɪˈventfəl/ *adjective*

full of interesting or important events: *The trip was very eventful – we saw and did a lot of exciting things.*

**e·ven·tu·al** Ac /ɪˈventʃuəl/ *adjective*

happening at the end of a long period of time, or after a lot of other things have happened: *The eventual winner of the election will take office in January.*

—**eventually** *adverb* after a long time or after a lot of things have happened: *We* *eventually arrived at my sister's house, over three hours late.*

**ev·er** /ˈevɚ/ *adverb*

**1** at any time: *Have you ever been to New York? | Nothing ever makes Paul angry. | That was one of the best meals I've ever had.*

**2 ever since** = all the time since something happened: *He went to college in Colorado and has lived there ever since.*

**GRAMMAR: ever**

You use **ever** when you ask a question, but not when you answer a question: *"Have you ever been to San Francisco?" "Yes, I have been there."*

**ever-** /ˈevɚ-/

always: *I looked out at the ever-changing view from the bus window.*

**ev·er·green** /ˈevɚˌgrin/ *adjective*

an evergreen tree or plant does not lose its leaves in winter

—**evergreen** *noun* an evergreen tree or plant

evergreen

**ev·ery** /ˈevri/ *adjective*

**1** each of the people or things in a group: *Every student will receive a certificate. | They cut down every single tree in the yard; there is not one tree left.*

**USAGE: every, each, all**

**Every**, **each**, and **all** are all used to talk about every person or thing in a group.

When you are thinking about the people or things in the group separately, use **every** or **each**: *Every child at the party was given a balloon. | Each child at the party was given a balloon.*

When you are thinking about the whole group together, use **all**: *All the children were given balloons.*

**2** all the days, times, distances, etc.: *He calls his girlfriend every day. | I had to stop and rest every hundred yards.*

**3 every so often** (*also* **every now and then**) = sometimes, but not often: *We still go to a game every so often, maybe twice a year. | I still see her every now and then, usually around Christmas.*

**ev·ery·bod·y** /ˈevriˌbɑdi/ *pronoun*

another word for EVERYONE

**ev·ery·day** /ˈevriˌdeɪ/ *adjective*

ordinary, usual, or happening every day: *Going to school is part of everyday life for most children.*

**ev·ery·one** /ˈevriˌwʌn/ *pronoun*

every person: *She knew everyone at the party.* **SYNONYM: everybody**; **ANTONYMS: no one, nobody**

**USAGE: everyone, every one**

**Everyone** means all the people in a group: *Everyone had a book to read.*

**Every one** is used to emphasize that you mean each person or each thing in a group. You can use "of" after **every one**: *I have read every one of his books.*

**ev·ery·thing** /ˈevriˌθɪŋ/ *pronoun*

**1** each thing or all things: *I've put everything we need into the car. | Can you wash the dishes? I've done everything else.* **ANTONYM: nothing**

**2** used when you are talking in general about your life or about a situation: *Everything's going wrong today: I was late for school, and now I've lost my keys.* **ANTONYM: nothing**

**3 be everything** = to be more important than anything else: *Money isn't everything; your family, friends, and your health are more important.*

**ev·ery·where** /ˈevriˌwer/ *adverb*

in every place or to every place: *I've looked everywhere for my keys, but I can't find them. | He's been everywhere in California.*

**e·vict** /ɪˈvɪkt/ *verb*

to legally force someone to leave the house he or she is living in: *Frank was evicted from his apartment because he did not pay the rent.*

—**eviction** /ɪˈvɪkʃən/ *noun* the act of evicting someone: *The evictions came after the building was found to be unsafe.*

E

**ev·i·dence** [Ac] /ˈevədəns/ *noun*
**1** things that you see, hear, or learn that make you believe that something exists or is true: *There is clear evidence that eating too much fat can lead to heart disease.*
**2** the facts and objects that a lawyer shows to a court in order to prove that something is true: *The new evidence helped to convict Hayes of the crime.*

**ev·i·dent** [Ac] /ˈevədənt/ *adjective* (*formal*)
clear and easily seen: *It was evident that she was unhappy because she was crying.*
—**evidently** *adverb* in a way that is clear and easy to see: *The crowd was cheering, evidently excited by the close game.*

E

**e·vil** /ˈivəl/ *adjective*
very cruel or bad: *He was an evil person.*
—**evil** *noun* something that is very cruel or bad: *Poverty is one of the greatest evils of our time.*

**ev·o·lu·tion** [Ac] /ˌevəˈluʃən/ *noun*
the scientific idea that plants and animals develop and change gradually over a very long period of time
—**evolutionary** *adjective* related to evolution: *She is studying the evolutionary development of birds.*

**e·volve** [Ac] /ɪˈvɑlv/ *verb*
**1** to develop gradually: *Their small family store evolved into a chain of supermarkets.*
**2** if a plant or animal evolves, it develops and changes physically over a long period of time: *Fish evolved from prehistoric sea creatures.*

**ewe** /yu/ *noun*
a female sheep

**ex** /eks/ *noun* (*informal*)
the person who used to be someone's wife, husband, GIRLFRIEND, or BOYFRIEND

**ex-** /eks/
used at the beginning of words to show that someone used to be something: *Jake is my ex-boyfriend – I was going out with him last year.* **SYNONYM: former**

**ex·act** /ɪgˈzækt/ *adjective*
**1** completely correct: *The exact time is 11:27 a.m.* | *I can't remember the exact date that we moved here, but it was in early July.*
**2 the exact opposite** = something that is as different as possible from another thing: *I thought I'd hate my new school, but it's the exact opposite – I love it.*

**ex·act·ly** /ɪgˈzæktli/ *adverb*
**1** completely correct: *We got home at exactly six o'clock.* **SYNONYM: precisely**
**2** in every way: *The twins look exactly alike to me.* **SYNONYM: just**
**3** said when you agree with someone: *"So you're saying all the money has gone?" "Exactly!"*
**4 not exactly** = used when saying that something is not at all true: *The meal was not exactly cheap – it cost $75 per person!*

**ex·ag·ger·ate** /ɪgˈzædʒəˌreɪt/ *verb*
to make something seem bigger, better, worse, etc. than it really is: *Oh, stop exaggerating! His hair is shorter, but he's not bald like you said!*
—**exaggeration** /ɪgˌzædʒəˈreɪʃən/ *noun* a statement in which you exaggerate: *Everyone likes her. That's not an exaggeration; everyone who meets her really likes her.*

**ex·am** /ɪgˈzæm/ *noun*
**1** an important test at the end of a class in school or college: *When do you take your history exam?*
**2** a set of medical tests to see if your body is healthy: *I had an eye exam yesterday.*

**ex·am·i·na·tion** /ɪgˌzæməˈneɪʃən/ *noun*
**1** the process of looking at something carefully: *The police made a careful examination of the room where the murder happened.*
**2** (*formal*) an exam

**ex·am·ine** /ɪgˈzæmɪn/ *verb*
to look at something carefully in order to find out or decide something: *The doctor examined me and said I was very healthy.*
[**ORIGIN:** 1300-1400 From the Latin word *examinare*, which means "to weigh or test."]

**ex·am·ple** /ɪgˈzæmpəl/ *noun*
**1** something that you mention to show the kind of thing you mean, or to show that something is true: *"Can anyone give me an example of a verb?" "Give is a verb."* | *The car is a good example of an invention that changed people's lives.*
**2 for example** = used when giving an example: *Many countries, for example Mexico and Japan, have a lot of earthquakes.*
**3 set an example** = if you set an example,

you do something good that should be copied by other people: *Try to share your toys and set a good example for your sister.*
[ORIGIN: 1300-1400 From the Latin word *exemplum*, from *eximere*, which means "to take out." An example is one thing that you have taken out from a group of similar things.]

**ex·as·per·at·ed** /ɪgˈzæspəˌreɪtɪd/ *adjective* feeling very annoyed: *He never listens to me, and I get so exasperated with him.*
—**exasperating** *adjective* something that is exasperating makes you feel very annoyed
—**exasperation** /ɪgˌzæspəˈreɪʃən/ *noun* a very annoyed feeling

**ex·ceed** Ac /ɪkˈsiːd/ *verb* (*formal*)
to be more than a particular amount: *The total cost was $110, so it exceeded $100.*

**ex·cel** /ɪkˈsel/ *verb* (**excelled**, **excelling**) (*formal*)
to do something very well: *He excelled in baseball in high school and now plays for a major league team.*

**ex·cel·lent** /ˈeksələnt/ *adjective*
extremely good: *You should definitely go to the restaurant – the food was excellent.*
—**excellence** /ˈeksələns/ *noun* (*formal*) the quality of being excellent: *The university is famous for the excellence of its teachers.*
→ see Thesaurus box at **good**[1]

**WORD FAMILY: excellent**
**excellent** *adjective* | **excellence** *noun* | **excel** *verb*

**ex·cept**[1] /ɪkˈsept/ *preposition*
not including someone or something: *The store is open every day except Monday.* | *Everyone went to the show, except for Scott and Danny.*

**except**[2] *conjunction*
used when adding something that shows why your statement is not completely true or exact: *I have earrings like those, except they're silver not gold.*

**ex·cep·tion** /ɪkˈsepʃən/ *noun*
someone or something that is different and that cannot be included in a group of things or people: *It has been very cold, but today is an exception.* | *We all laughed, with the exception of Joey, who looked annoyed.*

**ex·cep·tion·al** /ɪkˈsepʃənəl/ *adjective* (*formal*)
**1** very good in a way that is unusual: *She is an exceptional student who always has the best grades in the class.*
**2** unusual and not happening often: *The tar on the roads had melted in the exceptional heat.*
—**exceptionally** *adverb* in an exceptional way: *an exceptionally cold winter*
→ see Thesaurus box at **good**[1]

**ex·cess**[1] /ˈekses/ *adjective* (*formal*)
more than is needed or allowed: *Cut the excess fat off the meat.*

**excess**[2] *noun*
**in excess of something** (*formal*) = more than something: *He earns in excess of $200,000 a year.*

**ex·ces·sive** /ɪkˈsesɪv/ *adjective*
too large or too much: *Paying $80 for a T-shirt seems excessive.*
—**excessively** *adverb* too: *There are excessively high levels of salt in some frozen meals.*

**ex·change**[1] /ɪksˈtʃeɪndʒ/ *noun*
the act of giving someone something and getting something similar from him or her: *I gave him the book in exchange for a CD.*

**exchange**[2] *verb*
to give someone something and get something similar from him or her: *This skirt is too small; can I exchange it for a larger one?*

**exˈchange rate** *noun*
the value of the money of one country compared to the money of another country: *The exchange rate was 120 yen to the dollar.*

**ex·cite** /ɪkˈsaɪt/ *verb*
to make someone feel happy and eager or interested: *Teachers have found great ways to excite the students about science.*
—**excitable** /ɪkˈsaɪtəbəl/ *adjective* becoming excited very easily: *The puppies are now starting to get really excitable.*
[ORIGIN: 1300-1400 From the Latin word *excitare*, which means "to wake someone or make them move."]

**ex·cit·ed** /ɪkˈsaɪtɪd/ *adjective*
happy and eager or interested: *The kids are really excited about going camping this weekend.* → see picture on page **A23**

E

**WORD FAMILY: excited**

**excited** *adjective* | **exciting** *adjective* | **excitement** *noun* | **excite** *verb* | **excitable** *adverb*

**ex·cite·ment** /ɪkˈsaɪtmənt/ *noun*
the feeling you have when you are excited: *Stella was filled with excitement on her birthday.*

**ex·ci·ting** /ɪkˈsaɪtɪŋ/ *adjective*
something that is exciting makes you feel excited: *an exciting movie about pirates and battles at sea*

**ex·claim** /ɪkˈskleɪm/ *verb (formal)*
to say something loudly and suddenly because you are surprised, excited, or angry: *"I didn't expect to see you here!" exclaimed Laura.*
—**exclamation** /ˌekskləˈmeɪʃən/ *noun* something that someone exclaims: *There were exclamations of joy from the children watching the fireworks display.*

**exclaˈmation ˌpoint** *noun*
the sign (!), used in writing to show that someone is angry, surprised, or excited: *Use an exclamation point when someone shouts something: "Come here!"*

**ex·clude** Ac /ɪkˈsklud/ *verb*
**1** to not allow someone or something to enter a place or to do an activity: *The club is very old-fashioned and excludes women.* ANTONYM: **include**
**2** to not include something: *Some important facts seem to have been excluded from the report.* SYNONYM: **leave out**
—**excluding** *preposition* not including: *The store is open every day excluding Sundays.*
—**exclusion** *noun (formal)* the act of excluding someone or something

**WORD FAMILY: exclude**

**exclude** *verb* | **include** *verb* | **excluding** *preposition* | **including** *preposition* | **exclusive** *adjective* | **inclusive** *adjective* | **exclusion** *noun* | **inclusion** *noun*

**ex·clu·sive** Ac /ɪkˈsklusɪv/ *adjective (formal)*
**1** exclusive places are for people who have a lot of money or belong to a high social class: *They bought an expensive house in an exclusive neighborhood.*
**2** used by only one person or group, and not shared: *The pool is for the exclusive use of the hotel's guests.*

**ex·clu·sive·ly** Ac /ɪkˈsklusɪvli/ *adverb*
only: *The gym is exclusively for members of the health club.*

**ex·crete** /ɪkˈskrit/ *verb*
to get rid of waste material from your body: *Urine is stored in the bladder before it is excreted from the body.*

**ex·cur·sion** /ɪkˈskɚʒən/ *noun (formal)*
a short trip made for pleasure: *They took the children on an excursion to the zoo.*

**ex·cuse¹** /ɪkˈskyuz/ *verb*
**1 excuse me = a)** said when asking a question politely, especially when you ask someone you do not know well: *Excuse me, is this the way to the train station?* **b)** said when you are sorry for doing something rude: *She burped and said, "Excuse me."*
**2 excuse me? =** said when you want someone to repeat what he or she has said: *"What time is it?" "Excuse me?" "I asked the time ."*
**3** to forgive someone for something: *Please excuse my bad handwriting.*
**4** to allow someone to leave a place or not to do something: *The teacher excused her from class so that she could go to the nurse's office.*

**ex·cuse²** /ɪkˈskyus/ *noun*
a reason that you give for doing something that you should not do: *His excuse for being late was that his alarm clock didn't go off.*
→ see Thesaurus box at **reason¹**

**ex·e·cute** /ˈeksəˌkyut/ *verb*
to kill someone as an official punishment: *He was found guilty of murder, and executed.*
—**execution** /ˌeksəˈkyuʃən/ *noun* the act of killing someone as an official punishment: *His execution will take place on November 14.*

**ex·ec·u·tive¹** /ɪgˈzekjətɪv/ *noun*
an important manager in an organization or company: *He became a successful business executive, leading a large company.*

**executive²** *adjective*
**1** relating to making decisions in a company

or organization: *The executive committee of the charity wanted to try a new way to raise money.*
**2 the executive branch** = the part of a government that approves decisions and laws and is responsible for making them work

**ex·empt** /ɪgˈzempt/ *verb (formal)*
to give someone special permission not to do something: *One student was exempted from the test because he was in the hospital.*
—**exempt** *adjective* not having to do something: *Men over the age of 45 were exempt from military service during the war.*
—**exemption** /ɪgˈzempʃən/ *noun* official permission not to do something

**ex·er·cise**[1] /ˈeksɚˌsaɪz/ *noun*
**1** physical activity that you do in order to stay strong and healthy: *He watches too much TV and doesn't get much exercise.* | *Do some stretching exercises before you start jogging.*
**2** a set of questions in a book that you do in order to learn or practice something: *For homework, do exercises 1 and 2 in your math book.*
[**ORIGIN:** 1300-1400 From the Latin word *exercere*, which means "to drive someone or something on, or to keep busy."]

**exercise**[2] *verb*
to do physical activity so that you stay strong and healthy: *I exercise three times a week, usually by swimming.*

**THESAURUS: exercise**

**run/go running** to move quickly using your legs: *He runs about three miles every day.* | *I try to go running three times a week.*

**jog/go jogging** to run at a slow steady speed: *She was jogging in the park.* | *Sam and I go jogging together.*

**swim/go swimming** to move through water using your legs and arms: *Kate swam 30 laps of the pool.* | *Let's go swimming this afternoon.*

**lift weights** to lift heavy pieces of metal in order to make your muscles stronger: *Members of the football team were lifting weights.*

**work out** to do exercises that make your body stronger or fitter: *Sue works out in the gym twice a week.*

**warm up** to do gentle exercises that prepare your body for an activity: *Always warm up before playing any sport.*

**ex·er·tion** /ɪgˈzɚʃən/ *noun (formal)*
a lot of physical effort: *The doctor said that too much exertion could lead to another heart attack.*

**ex·hale** /eksˈheɪl/ *verb*
to breathe air out of your nose or mouth: *Take a deep breath, then exhale slowly.*
**ANTONYM: inhale**

**ex·haust**[1] /ɪgˈzɔst/ *verb*
to make someone very tired: *The long walk exhausted her.*
—**exhausting** *adjective* making you feel extremely tired: *It was a long and exhausting trip.*

**WORD FAMILY: exhaust**
**exhaust** *verb* | **exhausted** *adjective* | **exhausting** *adjective* | **exhaustion** *noun*

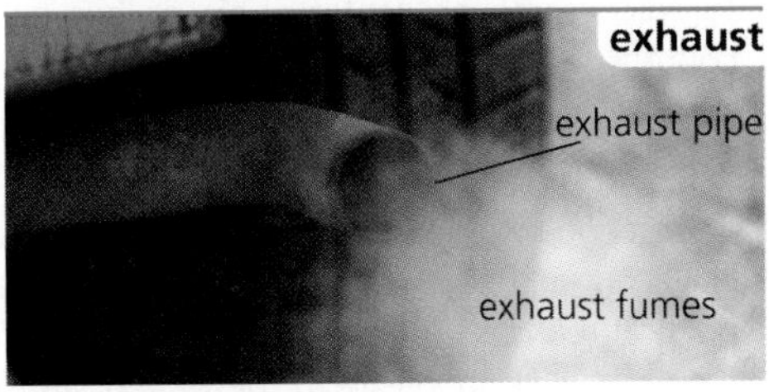


**exhaust**[2] *noun*
**1** the gas that is produced when a machine such as a car is working: *It was a bad traffic jam, and you could smell the exhaust fumes.*
**2** (*also* **exhaust pipe**) a pipe at the back of a car that exhaust comes out of: *Black smoke was coming out of the exhaust.*

**ex·haust·ed** /ɪgˈzɔstɪd/ *adjective*
extremely tired: *They were exhausted from the tough game.*
—**exhaustion** /ɪgˈzɔstʃən/ *noun* the state of being exhausted: *It is a long race, and two runners were taken to the hospital suffering from exhaustion.*

**ex·hib·it**[1] Ac /ɪgˈzɪbɪt/ *verb*
to show something such as art in a public

place: *Her paintings have been exhibited at several galleries.*
—**exhibitor** *noun* someone who is exhibiting his or her work or products

**WORD FAMILY: exhibit**
**exhibit** *verb* | **exhibit** *noun* | **exhibition** *noun* | **exhibitor** *noun*

exhibit
an exhibition

**exhibit²** Ac (*also* **exhibition**) /ˌeksəˈbɪʃən/ *noun*
a public show of something such as art: *a photographic exhibition*

**ex·ile¹** /ˈegzaɪl/ *verb* (*formal*)
to force someone to leave his or her own country, especially for political reasons: *The king exiled his enemies from the kingdom.*

**exile²** *noun*
**1** someone who is in exile has been forced to leave his or her own country, especially for political reasons: *The Cuban writer has spent many years living in exile in the United States.*
**2** someone who has been exiled: *Her parents were Russian exiles who were forced to leave Russia during the revolution.*

**ex·ist** /ɪgˈzɪst/ *verb*
to be present in the world: *The building no longer exists – it was destroyed in a fire.*

**ex·ist·ence** /ɪgˈzɪstəns/ *noun*
the state of existing: *She believes in the existence of ghosts.*

**ex·ist·ing** /ɪgˈzɪstɪŋ/ *adjective*
an existing thing is one that exists now or that you have now: *The company sends catalogs to both new and existing customers.*

**ex·it** /ˈegzɪt/ *noun*
**1** a door that you go through to get out of a place: *There are two exits at the back of the plane.* **ANTONYM: entrance**
**2** a place where vehicles can leave a large road: *From the expressway, take Exit 41.*
[**ORIGIN:** 1500-1600 From the Latin word *exire*, which means "to go out."]

**ex·ot·ic** /ɪgˈzɑtɪk/ *adjective*
something that is exotic is unusual and exciting because it is foreign: *They went on vacations to exotic places like Thailand.*

**ex·pand** Ac /ɪkˈspænd/ *verb*
to become larger: *When you blow air into a balloon, it expands.* | *The business expanded by opening a new store.* **ANTONYM: contract**
[**ORIGIN:** 1400-1500 From the Latin word *expandere*, which means "to spread out."]

**ex·pan·sion** Ac /ɪkˈspænʃən/ *noun*
the process of expanding: *After the expansion of the airport is finished, it will be twice as big.*

**ex·pect** /ɪkˈspekt/ *verb*
**1** to think that something will happen: *I didn't expect to win the race.* | *The movie was better than I expected.*
**2** to be waiting for someone or something to arrive: *I'm expecting a package in the mail.*
**3** to demand that someone do something: *Students are expected to return their homework on Friday.*
**4** **be expecting (a baby)** = if a woman is expecting, she is going to have a baby: *She's expecting her first child in September.*
—**expectation** /ˌekspekˈteɪʃən/ *noun* a belief or strong hope that something will happen: *He has high expectations for his daughter, and hopes that she will one day become a lawyer.*

**ex·pe·di·tion** /ˌekspəˈdɪʃən/ *noun*
a long and carefully organized trip, especially to a dangerous place: *They are planning an expedition to the North Pole.*

**ex·pel** /ɪkˈspel/ *verb* (**expelled**, **expelling**)
to officially make someone leave a school, organization, or country: *He was expelled from school for hitting a teacher.*

**ex·pend·i·ture** /ɪkˈspendətʃɚ/ *noun* (*formal*)
the total amount of money that a person or organization spends: *The state's expenditure on education needs to increase.*

**ex·pense** /ɪkˈspens/ *noun*
money that you have to spend on something: *The insurance helps to pay her medical expenses.*
→ see Thesaurus box at **cost**[1]

**ex·pen·sive** /ɪkˈspensɪv/ *adjective*
something that is expensive costs a lot of money: *She owns a lot of expensive jewelry, such as diamond rings and a pearl necklace.* | *At $500, the jacket is far too expensive.*
ANTONYMS: **cheap**, **inexpensive**
—**expensively** *adverb* in a way that costs a lot of money

**WORD FAMILY: expensive**

**expensive** *adjective* | **inexpensive** *adjective* | **expensively** *adverb* | **expense** *noun*

**USAGE: expensive, high**

Use **expensive** about things: *She likes buying expensive clothes.*

Use **high** about prices and costs: *They charge high prices for their clothes.*

Do not say "expensive prices."

**ex·pe·ri·ence**[1] /ɪkˈspɪriəns/ *noun*
**1** something that happens to you: *Seeing the whales in the ocean was an amazing experience.*
**2** knowledge or skill that you get from doing a job or activity: *Our English teacher has 20 years of teaching experience.*

**experience**[2] *verb*
if you experience something, it happens to you: *Have you ever experienced an earthquake?*

**ex·pe·ri·enced** /ɪkˈspɪriənst/ *adjective*
good at doing something because you have been doing it for a long time: *We felt safer flying with such an experienced pilot.*
ANTONYM: **inexperienced**

**ex·per·i·ment**[1] /ɪkˈsperəmənt/ *noun*
a scientific test that you do to learn about something or show something: *We did an experiment in class to find out what materials a magnet will attract.*
[ORIGIN: 1300-1400 From the Latin word *experimentum*, from *experiri*, which means "to try out."]

**experiment**[2] *verb*
**1** to try using things in order to find out what the results are: *She's a good cook, and she likes to experiment with new foods.*
**2** to do a scientific test in order to find out or show something: *The company does not test its products by experimenting on animals.*
—**experimentation** /ɪkˌsperəmənˈteɪʃən/ *noun* the act of experimenting

**ex·pert** [Ac] /ˈekspɚt/ *noun*
someone with special skills or knowledge of a subject: *I am going to ask Dr. Patel, who is an expert on this disease, for his opinion.* | *I can't fix your computer; you need an expert.*
—**expert** *adjective* having or showing the skills of an expert: *Get some expert advice from a lawyer before signing a contract.*
—**expertly** *adverb* in a skillful way

**ex·per·tise** [Ac] /ˌekspɚˈtiz/ *noun* (*formal*)
special skills or knowledge: *A teacher with expertise in teaching young children helped write the book.*

**ex·pire** /ɪkˈspaɪɚ/ *verb*
if a document expires, it is no longer legal: *When my passport expires in September, I'll have to apply for a new one.*
—**expiration** /ˌekspəˈreɪʃən/ *noun* the act of expiring: *The expiration date on my credit card is November 2014.*

**ex·plain** /ɪkˈspleɪn/ *verb*
**1** to tell someone about something so that he or she can understand it: *Don explained the rules of the game to me.* | *Could you explain how the camera works?*

**THESAURUS: explain**

**tell** to give someone facts or information about something: *Can you tell me how to get to the Empire State Building?*

**show** to teach someone how to do something: *Ellen showed me how to turn on the dishwasher.*

**demonstrate** to show someone how to use or do something: *The coach demonstrated the correct way to shoot the ball toward the basket.*

**go through something** to explain something carefully, especially one step at a

E

time: *Mrs. Riddell went through the homework assignment.*

**2** to give a reason for something, or be the reason for it: *He explained that he was late because his car had a flat tire.*

**WORD FAMILY: explain**
**explain** *verb* | **explanation** *noun*

**ex·pla·na·tion** /ˌekspləˈneɪʃən/ *noun*
**1** a reason why something happened: *He gave no explanation for his strange actions.*
**2** something you say or write to help someone understand something: *Mrs. Reed gave a quick explanation of the rules of the game.*
→ see Thesaurus box at **reason**[1]

E

**explicit** Ac /ɪkˈsplɪsɪt/ *adjective*
said or written in a way that is very clear: *The teacher gave her class explicit instructions not to leave their seats while she was out of the room.*
—**explicitly** *adverb* clearly

**ex·plode** /ɪkˈsploʊd/ *verb*
to burst into small pieces with a loud noise and a lot of force: *The bomb exploded at 6:16.*
[**ORIGIN:** 1500-1600 From the Latin word *explodere*, which means "to force an actor to leave the stage by clapping." The word changed from describing people making a lot of noise to a thing bursting and making a lot of noise.]

**WORD FAMILY: explode**
**explode** *verb* | **explosion** *noun* | **explosive** *adjective* | **explosive** *noun*

**ex·ploit** Ac /ɪkˈsplɔɪt/ *verb*
to use someone or something in an unfair way: *The company exploits its workers by paying them less than the minimum wage.*
—**exploitative** *adjective* treating people unfairly
—**exploitation** /ˌeksplɔɪˈteɪʃən/ *noun* the act of exploiting someone or something

**ex·plore** /ɪkˈsplɔr/ *verb*
**1** to travel around an area in order to find out what it is like: *They wanted to explore the island, so they rented bikes.*
**2** to think carefully about all the parts or results of something: *He was exploring the possibility of going to college.*
—**explorer** *noun* someone who explores unknown places: *Columbus, the famous explorer*
—**exploration** /ˌeksplәˈreɪʃәn/ *noun* the activity of traveling to unknown places, to find out more about them: *space exploration*

**ex·plo·sion** /ɪkˈsploʊʒən/ *noun*
an occasion when something such as a bomb explodes: *The soldier was injured in an explosion caused by a car bomb.*

**ex·plo·sive**[1] /ɪkˈsploʊsɪv/ *adjective*
**1** able or likely to explode: *The chemical is highly explosive, so we have to handle it carefully.*
**2** an explosive situation is likely to become violent very quickly: *The situation in the country was explosive, and fighting could begin any time.*

**explosive**[2] *noun*
a substance that can cause an explosion: *Dynamite is a type of explosive.*

**ex·port**[1] Ac /ekˈspɔrt/ *verb*
to sell things to another country: *The company exports computer equipment to Russia.* **ANTONYM: import**
—**exporter** *noun* a person, company, or country that exports things
[**ORIGIN:** 1400-1500 From the Latin words *ex* and *portare*, which mean "out" and "to carry."]

**export**[2] Ac *noun*
**1** something that one country sells to another country: *The country's main export is coffee.* **ANTONYM: import**
**2** the business of selling and sending things to another country: *The company makes computers for export.* **ANTONYM: import**

**WORD FAMILY: export**
**export** *verb* | **export** *noun* | **exporter** *noun*

**ex·pose** Ac /ɪkˈspoʊz/ *verb* (*formal*)
**1** to show something that has been covered or hidden: *He pulled up his shirt and exposed his stomach.*
**2** to put someone in a situation or place where something bad could affect them: *Doctors and nurses are exposed to diseases every day.*

**ex·po·sure** Ac /ɪkˈspoʊʒɚ/ *noun* (*formal*)
**1** the state of being in a bad or harmful

situation with nothing to protect you: *Exposure to cigarette smoke can harm children.*
**2** the harmful effect of very cold weather on someone's body: *The climbers survived the snow storm but were suffering from exposure.*

**ex·press¹** /ɪkˈspres/ *verb*
to tell or show people what you think or feel: *The kids express their feelings easily, telling us when they are happy or sad.* | *He's shy, and it's hard for him to express himself.*
→ see Thesaurus box at **say¹**

**express²** *adjective*
**1 an express train/bus** = a train or bus that does not stop at many places and travels very quickly: *I took the express train to Baltimore.*
**2 express mail** = mail that arrives more quickly than normal: *The package was sent by express mail.*

**ex·pres·sion** /ɪkˈspreʃən/ *noun*
**1** the look on someone's face: *He had a sad expression on his face as we said goodbye.*
**2** a word or words with a particular meaning: *The expression "what's up?" means "what is happening?" or "what are you doing?"*
**3** in math, a group of signs and numbers that represent an amount or idea, and that does not have an equal sign: *A car is traveling at 60 mph. Write an expression that shows how far it has traveled in x hours. Answer: 60x.*
**4** (*formal*) something you do that shows what you think or feel: *I sent her some flowers as an expression of my thanks.*
→ see Thesaurus box at **phrase**

**ex·pres·sive** /ɪkˈspresɪv/ *adjective*
showing your thoughts or feelings: *I always know what she feels because she has very expressive eyes.*
—**expressively** *adverb* in an expressive way: *Poets use words expressively.*

**ex·press·ly** /ɪkˈsprɛsli/ *adverb* (*formal*)
**1** in a clear and firm way: *I went to the party even though I had been expressly told that I was not allowed to go.*
**2** for a particular purpose or reason: *The school was started expressly to give poor children a better education.*

**ex·press·way** /ɪkˈspresˌweɪ/ *noun*
a wide road that lets cars travel quickly through a city: *The truck was traveling north on the expressway.* **SYNONYM: freeway**
→ see Thesaurus box at **road**

**ex·pul·sion** /ɪkˈspʌlʃən/ *noun* (*formal*)
an act of ordering someone to leave a school, an organization, or a country permanently: *Expulsion from school is a very severe punishment.*

**ex·quis·ite** /ɪkˈskwɪzɪt/ *adjective* (*formal*)
very beautiful: *She wore an exquisite diamond necklace.*

E

**ex·tend** /ɪkˈstend/ *verb*
**1** to make something bigger or longer: *The road has been extended so that it meets the highway.*
**2** to make something include more things or time: *We decided to extend our visit to Mexico for another week.*
**3** to continue for a particular distance or period of time: *The fire extended for 15 miles across the plain.*

**exˌtended ˈfamily** *noun*
a family group that includes parents, children, grandparents, and other family members: *In the summer, we had a big party for our extended family and friends.*

**ex·ten·sion** /ɪkˈstenʃən/ *noun*
**1** more time that you are given to finish doing something: *If students are sick, they can ask for an extension to finish their work.*
**2** one of the telephones in a building that are all part of one telephone system. Each extension has its own number: *Call the office and ask for extension 3658.*
**3** (*formal*) the process of making something longer or bigger: *The extension of the railroad to the West Coast took many years.*

**ex·ten·sive** /ɪkˈstensɪv/ *adjective*
**1** affecting or covering a large area: *The storm caused extensive damage to the town, destroying many of the houses.*
**2** containing a lot of something, especially information: *The story received extensive coverage in the news media.*
—**extensively** *adverb* a lot: *He has traveled extensively in the Far East, especially in China.*

**ex·tent** /ɪkˈstent/ *noun*
**1** how big or important something is: *We did*

*not realize the extent of the problem until hundreds of people complained.*

**2 to some extent** = partly: *I agree with him to some extent, but I think his last point is wrong.*

**ex·te·ri·or¹** /ɪkˈstɪriɚ/ *noun*
the outside of something: *The exterior of the house was painted blue.* **ANTONYM: interior**

**exterior²** *adjective*
on the outside of something: *The exterior lights of the house come on when someone comes up to the front door.* **ANTONYM: interior**

E

**ex·ter·mi·nate** /ɪkˈstɚməˌneɪt/ *verb* (*formal*)
to kill all of a particular group of living things: *They use chemicals to exterminate the insects that get into buildings.*
—**exterminator** *noun* someone whose job is to kill insects and small animals, such as rats, in people's houses
—**extermination** /ɪkˌstɚməˈneɪʃən/ *noun* (*formal*) the act of exterminating living things: *Pollution has caused the extermination of fish in the river.*

**ex·ter·nal** Ac /ɪkˈstɚnl/ *adjective*
relating to the outside of something: *The external walls of the building were painted white.* **ANTONYM: internal**
—**externally** *adverb* in a way that relates to the outside of something

**ex·tinct** /ɪkˈstɪŋkt/ *adjective*
an extinct type of plant or animal does not exist now: *Why did dinosaurs become extinct?*
—**extinction** /ɪkˈstɪŋkʃən/ *noun* the state of being extinct: *Several types of plants are near extinction and could die out completely.*

**ex·tin·guish** /ɪkˈstɪŋgwɪʃ/ *verb* (*formal*)
to make a fire stop burning: *Finally, the forest fires were extinguished.* **SYNONYM: put out**

**ex·tin·guish·er** /ɪkˈstɪŋgwɪʃɚ/ *noun*
another word for a FIRE EXTINGUISHER

**ex·tra¹** /ˈekstrə/ *adjective, adverb*
**1** more than the usual amount or price: *Can I have a pizza with extra cheese?* | *If you want air conditioning, you have to pay extra.*
**2** in addition to what you need or are using: *We have an extra room for guests.*
→ see Thesaurus box at **more²**

**extra²** *noun*
**1** something you get in addition to the usual product or service: *For an additional $500, the car comes with extras such as a sun roof and cruise control.*
**2** an actor in a TV program or movie who does not say anything but is part of a crowd: *The director needs hundreds of extras for the battle scenes.*

**ex·tract** Ac /ɪkˈstrækt/ *verb* (*formal*)
to remove something from a place: *The dentist extracted one of my teeth.*
[**ORIGIN:** 1400-1500 From the Latin word *extractus*, a form of the verb *extrahere*, which means "to pull out."]

**ex·tra·cur·ric·u·lar** /ˌekstrəkəˈrɪkjəlɚ/ *adjective*
extracurricular activities are sports or other activities that are not part of a student's usual classes

**ex·traor·di·nar·y** /ɪkˈstrɔrdnˌeri/ *adjective*
very unusual or surprising: *Winning four Olympic gold medals was an extraordinary achievement.*
[**ORIGIN:** 1400-1500 From the Latin phrase *extra ordinem*, which means "out of the usual order or group."]

**ex·tra·ter·res·tri·al** /ˌekstrətəˈrestriəl/ *adjective*
from space or from another PLANET: *The movie is about extraterrestrial beings that visit Earth in spaceships.*
—**extraterrestrial** *noun* a creature that may exist on another PLANET

**ex·trav·a·gant** /ɪkˈstrævəgənt/ *adjective* (*formal*)
spending too much money or using too many things, in a way that seems wasteful: *They had extravagant parties with live music and champagne.*
—**extravagance** *noun* (*formal*) the act of spending too much money: *Her extravagance resulted in serious money problems.*
[**ORIGIN:** 1300-1400 From the Latin words *extra* and *vagari*, which mean "outside" and "to wander." The idea is that when you are extravagant, you go outside the limits of what you should spend.]

**ex·treme** /ɪkˈstrim/ *adjective*
**1** very great in degree: *Martha got bad burns in the fire and was in extreme pain.*

2 **an extreme case/example** = very unusual and bad: *In extreme cases, the spider's bite can kill a person.*
3 extreme opinions are very unusual and often not sensible: *The group has extreme views, including the idea that the world will end in 2012.*
4 extreme sports are dangerous and exciting: *Your vacation insurance does not cover extreme sports like white water rafting.*

**ex·treme·ly** /ɪkˈstrimli/ *adverb*
very: *The test was extremely difficult.*

**ex·tro·vert·ed** /ˈekstrəˌvɚtɪd/ *adjective*
an extroverted person is confident and likes being with people **ANTONYM: introverted**
—**extrovert** *noun* someone who is confident and likes being with people.
→ see Thesaurus box at **shy**

**eye**

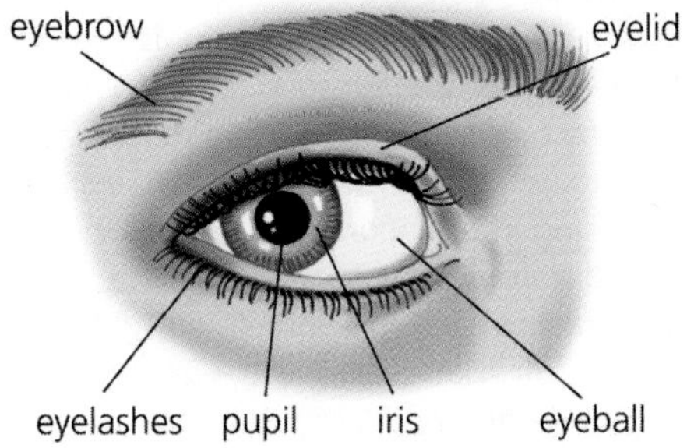


**eye** /aɪ/ *noun*
1 the part of your face that you see with: *Gina has blue eyes.*
2 **keep an eye on someone or something** = to watch someone or something to make sure they are safe: *Can you keep an eye on the baby while I go to the store?*
3 **in someone's eyes** = in someone's opinion: *In Joey's eyes, she's perfect.*
4 **catch someone's eye** = to get someone's attention: *A beautiful red dress caught my eye, so I went into the store to look at it.*
5 **see eye to eye** = to agree with someone: *I don't always see eye to eye with my parents.*
6 the hole in a needle that you put thread through
7 **the eye of a storm/hurricane/tornado** = the center of a big storm
[**ORIGIN:** From the old English word *eage*.]

**eye·ball** /ˈaɪbɔl/ *noun*
the whole of your eye, including the part inside your head → see picture at **eye**

**eye·brow** /ˈaɪbraʊ/ *noun*
the line of short hairs above your eye: *He had black eyebrows.* → see picture at **eye**

**ˈeye ˌcontact** *noun*
the action of looking directly at someone's eyes: *She was shy, and she usually did not like to make eye contact with other people.*

**eye·glass·es** /ˈaɪˌglæsɪz/ *plural noun*
another word for GLASSES

**eye·lash** /ˈaɪlæʃ/ *noun*
one of the small hairs that grow on your eyelids → see picture at **eye**

**eye·lid** /ˈaɪlɪd/ *noun*
the piece of skin that covers your eye when it is closed → see picture at **eye**

**eye·shad·ow** /ˈaɪˌʃædoʊ/ *noun*
color that women put on their eyelids to make their eyes look more attractive

**eye·sight** /ˈaɪsaɪt/ *noun*
the ability to see: *My eyesight is good.*

**eye·wit·ness** /ˌaɪˈwɪtnɪs/ *noun*
someone who sees a crime or an accident happen: *Eyewitnesses said the car was going very fast before it hit the tree.*

E

# Ff

**F¹** /ef/ *noun*

**1** a GRADE that you get when you fail a test or a class: *Jill got an F in biology.*

**2** the fourth note in the musical SCALE of C, or the musical KEY based on this note

**F²**

the written abbreviation of FAHRENHEIT: *The temperature will drop to 32°F tonight, so it'll be icy on the roads.*

**fa·ble** /ˈfeɪbəl/ *noun*

a story, especially one with animals, that teaches us something: *The fable teaches that it is important to work slowly and carefully.*

→ see Thesaurus box at **story**

**fab·ric** /ˈfæbrɪk/ *noun*

cloth: *She made the curtains out of a thick cotton fabric.* **SYNONYM: material**

**[ORIGIN:** 1400-1500 From the Latin word *fabrica*, which means "place where things are made, or something that has been made." Fabric is cloth that has been made especially in a factory.**]**

**fab·u·lous** /ˈfæbjələs/ *adjective*

extremely good: *We had a fabulous time in New York City.*

**face¹** /feɪs/ *noun*

**1** the front of your head, where your eyes, nose, and mouth are: *She has a pretty face.*

**2** the part of a clock or watch that you look at to see the time: *The face of the watch has large numbers for children who are learning to tell time.* → see picture at **watch**

**3** the expression on someone's face: *I could tell by the children's happy faces that they were having a great time.*

**4** a side of a mountain, cliff, or tall building: *They climbed the north face of the mountain.*

**face²** *verb*

**1** to be looking or pointing toward someone or something: *Mom turned to face me. | Our house faces the park.*

**2** if you cannot face something, you do not want to do it because it will be difficult: *I knew Dad would be mad, and I couldn't face seeing him.*

**3** to accept that something bad is true: *She couldn't face the fact that her son was dying.*

**ˈface-lift** *noun*

an operation on your face to make you look younger

**fa·cial¹** /ˈfeɪʃəl/ *adjective*

relating to the face: *a man with facial hair*

**facial²** *noun*

a treatment to clean the skin on your face and make it softer

**fa·cil·i·tate** Ac /fəˈsɪləˌteɪt/ *verb* (*formal*)

to make something happen more easily: *A good math game on the computer can facilitate learning.*

**fa·cil·i·ty** Ac /fəˈsɪləti/ *noun* (plural **facilities**) (*formal*)

a building or piece of equipment you can use for doing something: *The university has very good sports facilities, including a new gym.*

**fact** /fækt/ *noun*

**1** a piece of information that is true: *The book has lots of interesting facts about plants.*

**2 in fact** = used when adding more information to what you have just said, especially surprising information: *The puzzle looks difficult, but in fact it's fairly easy.*

**3 a fact of life** = something difficult or unpleasant that everyone has to accept: *For kids, tests at school are just a fact of life.*

**—factual** /ˈfæktʃuəl/ *adjective* relating to facts: *You can find more factual information about dinosaurs on our website.*

**[ORIGIN:** 1400-1500 From the Latin word *factum*, which means "thing that is done," from *facere*, meaning "to do."**]**

**fac·tion** /ˈfækʃən/ *noun*

a small group of people within a larger group, who have different ideas than the larger group: *The different factions began to fight, causing a civil war in the country.*

**fac·tor** Ac /ˈfæktɚ/ *noun*

**1** one of many things that affects a situation: *The weather could be an important factor in tomorrow's game – if it snows, our team will have the advantage.*

**2** a number that you can divide into another number exactly: *3 is a factor of 15 because 3 × 5 = 15.*

**[ORIGIN:** 1400-1500 From the Latin word *factor*, which means "person who does or makes something," from *facere*, meaning "to do or make."

"Factor" was first used to mean a person, and later to mean a thing.]

factory

**fac·to·ry** /ˈfæktəri/ *noun* (plural **factories**)
a building where goods are made: *Skilled workers at the factory earn good money.*

**fac·ul·ty** /ˈfækəlti/ *noun* (plural **faculties**)
the teachers in a school, college, or university: *The school has 45 faculty members.*

**fad** /fæd/ *noun*
something that is popular for a short time: *The stickers were a fad among the girls.*

**fade** /feɪd/ *verb*
to become less bright in color: *If you wash these jeans a lot, they will fade.*

**Fahr·en·heit** /ˈfærənˌhaɪt/ *noun* (*written abbreviation*: **F**)
a system of measuring temperature in which water freezes at 32° and boils at 212°
[**ORIGIN:** From Gabriel Fahrenheit (1686-1736), the German scientist who invented the temperature scale.]

**fail** /feɪl/ *verb*
1 to not succeed at something: *The doctors tried everything, but they failed to save the man's life.* **ANTONYM: succeed**
2 (*formal*) to not do something: *The flight failed to arrive on time; it was an hour late.*
3 if you fail a test, you do not pass it: *I failed the math test because I didn't understand some of the questions.* **ANTONYM: pass**
4 if part of a machine or your body fails, it stops working: *When he tried to stop the car, the brakes failed and he hit a tree.*
5 if a business fails, it cannot continue working because it has no money
[**ORIGIN:** 1200-1300 From the Latin word *fallere*, which means "to deceive or disappoint."]

**WORD FAMILY: fail**
**fail** *verb* | **failure** *noun*

**fail·ing** /ˈfeɪlɪŋ/ *noun*
a problem or weakness that a person or system has: *One of his failings is that he doesn't do what he promises to do.*

**fail·ure** /ˈfeɪljɚ/ *noun*
1 someone or something that is not successful: *The movie was a total failure – no one went to see it.* **ANTONYM: success**
2 a situation when something stops working correctly: *He died from heart failure.* | *There was a mechanical failure, so the plane had to go back to the airport.*
3 a situation when someone does not do what he or she should do or does not succeed in doing something: *Mike's teacher called his parents about his failure to do his homework.*

**faint¹** /feɪnt/ *adjective*
1 a faint sound, smell, light, etc. is not strong or clear: *I heard a faint sound downstairs.*
2 feeling weak and as if you are about to become unconscious: *He was faint with hunger.*

**faint²** *verb*
to become unconscious for a short time: *When they told her the bad news, she fainted.*

**fair¹** /fer/ *adjective*
1 treating people in an equal way: *Why can Danny go, but not me? It's not fair!* | *All prisoners have the right to a fair trial.* **ANTONYM: unfair**
2 **fair hair/skin** = hair or skin that is light in color **ANTONYM: dark**
3 **a fair price** = a price that is not too much: *It is a good car at a fair price.*
4 good enough, but not very good: *Her test scores in science were fair but not great.* **SYNONYM: average**
5 if the weather is fair, it is bright and pleasant, with no wind or rain **SYNONYM: fine**
—**fairness** *noun* the quality of treating people in an equal way

**fair²** *noun*
1 an outdoor event where you can ride on exciting machines, and play games to win prizes. Sometimes farmers show their animals and crops at a fair: *the Ohio state fair*

F

2 an event at which businesses or other organizations show or sell things: *the school science fair*

**fair·ly** /ˈferli/ *adverb*

1 more than a little, but much less than very: *He speaks Spanish fairly well, but not perfectly.*

2 in an equal way: *Divide the candy fairly, so that everyone gets the same amount.*

**fair·y** /ˈferi/ *noun* (plural **fairies**)

in stories, a fairy is a very small person with wings who can do magic

[ORIGIN: 1300-1400 From the Latin word *fatum*, which means "fate." Fate was sometimes seen as a being that had a magic power over people's lives, and fairies also had magic powers.]

F

**ˈfairy tale** *noun*

a story for children in which magic things happen

**faith** /feɪθ/ *noun*

1 a strong belief that someone or something will succeed or will help you: *I didn't do well in school, but my parents always had faith in me.*

2 belief in God: *My faith in God helped me through the bad times.*

3 a religion: *We have people of all faiths at our school.* | *the Christian faith*

→ see Thesaurus box at **religion**

**faith·ful** /ˈfeɪθfəl/ *adjective*

1 loyal to someone or something: *The coach thanked the team's faithful fans for their continued support.*

2 someone who is faithful to his or her wife, husband, or partner does not have a sexual relationship with anyone else: *At their wedding, they promised to be faithful to each other.* **ANTONYM: unfaithful**

3 describing or showing something exactly, without changing it: *The movie is faithful to the book – the director has not changed the story at all.*

**faith·ful·ly** /ˈfeɪθfəli/ *adverb*

1 in a loyal way: *He served the king faithfully.*

2 in an exact way: *The book faithfully records their trip, giving details about every town they went to.*

**fake** *adjective* /feɪk/

not real, but made to look like something real: *He was arrested for making fake passports.*

**THESAURUS: fake**

**false** not real, but made to look real: *Grandpa has false teeth.*

**imitation** made to look like something real – used about materials that look expensive, but are made of something cheaper: *an imitation leather jacket*

**counterfeit** counterfeit money is made to look like real money in order to trick people: *a counterfeit $10 bill*

**phony** (*informal*) not real, and intended to trick people: *He used a phony driver's license as ID.*

**forged** a forged document, check, signature, etc. has been copied illegally: *The two men used forged passports to try to enter the U.S.*

—**fake** *noun* a copy of something, which is intended to trick people: *The experts decided that the painting was a fake.*

**fall¹** /fɔl/ *verb* (**fell** /fel/, **fallen** /ˈfɔlən/)

1 (*also* **fall down**) to accidentally drop down onto the ground: *Be careful you don't fall!* | *Chris fell down and hurt his knee.* → see picture on page **A5**

**THESAURUS: fall**

**trip** to hit your foot against something, so that you fall or almost fall: *I'm always tripping over that cat!*

**slip** to slide on something that is wet or icy, so that you fall or almost fall: *She slipped on the ice and broke her leg.*

**stumble** to fall or almost fall when you are walking, usually because you hit something with your foot: *Megan stumbled over the rug as she left the room.*

**lose your balance** to start to fall because you are standing on something high or narrow: *She was walking on top of the wall when she lost her balance and fell.*

**collapse** to suddenly fall down because you are very weak or sick: *He collapsed during the race and was taken to the hospital.*

**2** to move down toward the ground: *Snow was falling heavily.* | *The leaves on the trees were beginning to fall.*
**3** if a price, amount, or temperature falls, it becomes less: *The price of computers has fallen.* | *The temperature fell to 10 degrees below zero.* **ANTONYM: rise**
**4** **fall asleep** = to start to sleep: *Tommy was so tired he fell asleep on the couch.*
**5** **fall in love** (*also* **fall for someone**) = to begin to love someone: *As soon as I saw her, I fell in love with her.*
**6** **fall ill/silent** = to become ill or silent: *Suddenly, everyone in the room fell silent.*
→ see Thesaurus box at **decrease**[1]
[**ORIGIN:** From the old English word *feallan.*]
**PHRASAL VERBS**
**fall apart**
**1** to break into pieces: *My old shoes are falling apart – they have holes in them.*
**2** to stop working well, or stop being successful: *The economy is falling apart; prices are rising and there are no jobs.*
**fall back on something**
to use something if it becomes necessary: *Make sure you keep some extra money to fall back on.*
**fall behind**
to make less progress than other people or than you planned: *Going up the hill, Anna had fallen behind the other runners.* | *Don't fall behind in your schoolwork.*
**fall for something**
to believe that something you are told is true, when it is not: *I told him a complete lie, and he fell for it.*
**fall through**
if a plan or deal falls through, it is not completed successfully: *My parents were planning to buy a new house, but the deal fell through.*

**fall**[2] *noun*
**1** the season before winter, when the leaves fall off the trees in cool countries: *My brother's starting college in the fall.* **SYNONYM: autumn**
**2** the act of accidentally dropping down onto the ground: *He had a bad fall from a ladder.*
**3** if there is a fall in a price, amount, or temperature, it becomes less: *There's been a fall in the number of students who study nursing.* **SYNONYM: drop**; **ANTONYM: rise**

**fall·en** /ˈfɔlən/ *verb*
the past participle of FALL

**false** /fɔls/ *adjective*
**1** not true: *Read the paragraph and say whether these statements are true or false.* **ANTONYM: true**
**2** not real, but made to look real: *Grandpa has false teeth.*
→ see Thesaurus box at **fake**, **wrong**
[**ORIGIN:** 900-1000 From the Latin word *falsus*, a form of the verb *fallere*, which means "to deceive."]

**ˌfalse aˈlarm** *noun*
a situation when people think that something bad is happening, but it is not: *Everyone thought the building was on fire, but it was a false alarm.*

**fal·si·fy** /ˈfɔlsəˌfaɪ/ *verb* (**falsified**, **falsifies**) (*formal*)
to change information so that it is not true: *He went to jail for falsifying the company's financial records.*

**fame** /feɪm/ *noun*
the state of being known and admired by a lot of people: *He won fame when he sang on a popular TV series.*

**fa·mil·iar** /fəˈmɪljɚ/ *adjective*
**1** **be familiar with something** = to know something well: *I lived in New York for a year, so I'm familiar with the city.*
**2** a familiar person or thing is one that you recognize: *Her face is familiar, but I can't remember her name.*
—**familiarity** /fəˌmɪliˈærəti/ *noun* knowledge of something: *Many children have greater familiarity with computers than their parents.*
—**familiarize** *verb* to get to know something well: *Read the story so that you familiarize yourself with the characters.*

**fam·i·ly** /ˈfæməli/ *noun* (plural **families**)
**1** a group of people who are related to each other, especially parents and their children: *My family and I are going skiing in Colorado.*

**THESAURUS: family**

**relative** a member of your family: *Most of my relatives are in California.*

**relation** a member of your family – used about people such as aunts, uncles, and cousins, but not your parents, brothers, or sisters: *There are some relations in Montana that I've never met.*

**ancestor** a member of your family who lived a long time before you were born: *His ancestors came to the U.S. from Germany over a hundred years ago.*

**descendant** someone who is related to a person who lived a long time ago: *She is a descendant of Christopher Columbus.*

F

**2** someone's children: *He didn't like being away from his wife and family.*

[**ORIGIN:** 1400-1500 From the Latin word *familia*, which means "people living in a house," from *famulus*, which means "servant."]

**ˈfamily ˌname** *noun*
the name that you share with the other people in your family, which in English comes after your other names: *Todd's family name is Dyson.*

**ˌfamily ˈtree** *noun*
a drawing that shows how all the people in a family are related to each other

**fam·ine** /ˈfæmɪn/ *noun*
a very bad situation when a lot of people do not have enough food to eat: *Thousands of people died in the famine.*

[**ORIGIN:** 1300-1400 From the Latin word *fames*, which means "condition of being hungry."]

**fa·mous** /ˈfeɪməs/ *adjective*
known and admired by a lot of people: *She's a famous writer.* | *San Francisco is famous for its great food.*

[**ORIGIN:** 1300-1400 From the Latin word *fama*, which means "report or fame."]

**WORD FAMILY: famous**

**famous** *adjective* | **infamous** *adjective* | **fame** *noun*

**fan[1]** /fæn/ *noun*
**1** someone who likes a person or thing very much: *She's a big fan of the band.* | *Gary's a sports fan.*
**2** a machine or object you can use to make the air move and cool you: *It was hot, so I turned on the fan.* → see picture on page **A8**

**fan[2]** *verb* (**fanned**, **fanning**)
to make yourself feel cool by waving something that makes the air move: *She fanned her face with a newspaper.*

**fa·nat·ic** /fəˈnætɪk/ *noun*
**1** someone who has extreme political or religious ideas, which makes that person dangerous: *Some of the terrorists are religious fanatics.*
**2** someone who likes a thing or activity very much: *He's a fanatic about health and goes running every day.*
—**fanatical** *adjective* a fanatical person has extreme ideas, or likes something very much
—**fanaticism** /fəˈnætəˌsɪzəm/ *noun* a belief in extreme religious or political ideas, which make someone dangerous

**fan·cy** /ˈfænsi/ *adjective* (**fancier**, **fanciest**)
**1** special and expensive: *We had dinner at a fancy restaurant on Mom's birthday.*
**2** not plain or simple: *I don't like fancy wallpaper; I want a simple pattern.*

**fang** /fæŋ/ *noun*
one of the long sharp teeth that an animal such as a dog or snake has: *The big dog growled, and I saw its fangs.*

**fan·ny pack** /ˈfæni pæk/ *noun*
a small bag for carrying money, keys, etc., that you wear around your waist

**fan·ta·size** /ˈfæntəˌsaɪz/ *verb*
to think about doing or having something exciting, even though it is very unlikely to happen: *I sometimes fantasize about winning millions of dollars.*

**fan·tas·tic** /fænˈtæstɪk/ *adjective*
**1** very good or attractive: *You look fantastic in that dress!* | *That's a fantastic idea.*
**2** strange or imaginary: *The movie is about fantastic creatures from another world.*
→ see Thesaurus box at **good[1]**, **nice**

**fan·ta·sy** /ˈfæntəsi/ *noun* (plural **fantasies**)
**1** something that you imagine happening, but that is not real: *I used to have fantasies about becoming a movie star.*
**2** a story or movie about strange imaginary

events or creatures: *The book is a fantasy about a world with dragons.*
[**ORIGIN:** 1300-1400 From the Greek word *phantasia*, which means "imagination."]

**far**[1] /fɑr/ *adverb* (**farther** /ˈfɑrðɚ/ *or* **further** /ˈfɚðɚ/, **farthest** /ˈfɑrðɪst/ *or* **furthest** /ˈfɚðɪst/)
**1** a long distance: *Did you have to walk far to get to the subway? | Which of you can swim the farthest?* → see picture at **near**

> **GRAMMAR: far**
>
> When you are talking about distances, you can use **far** in questions and in sentences with "not": *How far is it to the stadium? | It's not very far.*
>
> You can also use **far** after "too," "as," and "so": *It's too far to walk. | I ran as far as I could. | I wish he didn't live so far away.*
>
> But do not use **far** in other kinds of sentence. For example, do not say "It's far to Boston from here." Say: *It's a long way to Boston from here.*

**2 How far ...?** = used when asking about a distance: *"How far is it to the ocean?" "Only about ten miles."*
**3 as far as something** = to a particular place or point: *We walked as far as the river.*
**4 so far** = until now: *There haven't been any problems so far.*
**5 by far the largest/the best, etc.** = much larger, better, etc. than any others: *I think they are by far the best new band.*
**6 far bigger/better/smarter, etc.** (*formal*) = much bigger, better, smarter, etc.: *She did a far better job than I could have.*
**7 go too far** = to do something bad that people cannot accept: *He's always been mean, but this time he went too far.*
**8 far off/away** = a long way from where you are: *Far off, we could hear shouting.* **ANTONYMS: close by, nearby**
**9 so far, so good** (*informal*) = used when saying that things have been good until now: *"How's your new school?" "So far, so good."*
**10 as far as I know ...** = used when saying that you think something is true, but you are not sure: *As far as I know, they still live in Washington, but I could be wrong.*
→ **as far as I'm concerned** at **concerned**

**far**[2] *adjective* (**farther**, **farthest**)
a long distance away: *We can walk to the store from here – it's not far. | They live at the far end of the street.* **ANTONYMS: close, near**

**farce** /fɑrs/ *noun*
**1** a funny play or movie in which a lot of silly things happen
**2** a situation in which things seem too silly to be true: *The class was a farce – we didn't learn anything.*
[**ORIGIN:** 1500-1600 From the Latin word *farcire*, which means "to fill something by putting things into it." Early religious plays often had funny parts put into them.]

**fare** /fer/ *noun*
the price you pay to travel by bus, train, airplane, etc.: *How much is the bus fare to get downtown?*
→ see Thesaurus box at **cost**[1]

**ˌFar ˈEast** *noun*
**the Far East** = the countries of east Asia, such as China and Japan

**fare·well** /ferˈwel/ *noun* (*formal*)
goodbye: *We said farewell to our friends.*
—**farewell** *adjective* relating to the time when someone leaves a place: *Everyone came to his farewell party.*

**farm** /fɑrm/ *noun*
an area of land used for growing food or raising animals: *We drove past lots of farms with corn growing in the fields.*
—**farmer** *noun* a person who works on a farm
—**farming** *noun* the work of growing food or raising animals

**farm·house** /ˈfɑrmhaʊs/ *noun*
the main house on a farm, where the farmer lives

**farm·land** /ˈfɑrmlænd/ *noun*
land used for farming: *This is good farmland, so corn grows very well here.*

**farm·yard** /ˈfɑrmyɑrd/ *noun*
an area with farm buildings around it: *There were goats and chickens in the farmyard.*

**far·sight·ed** /ˈfɑrˌsaɪtɪd/ *adjective*
a farsighted person cannot see things that are

near to him or her clearly: *I can't read without glasses because I'm farsighted.* **ANTONYM: nearsighted**

**far·ther** /ˈfɑrðɚ/ *adjective, adverb*
the comparative of FAR: *The school was farther away than I thought.*

**USAGE: farther, further**

Use **farther** to talk about distance: *Room 211 is just a little farther down the hall.*

Use **further** to talk about amounts, levels, or time: *Your grades cannot drop further, or you won't be able to play on the soccer team.* | *I don't want to discuss this any further.*

Many people use **further** in spoken English to talk about distance, but many teachers think that this is not correct.

F

**far·thest** /ˈfɑrðɪst/ *adjective, adverb*
the superlative of FAR: *The small planet Pluto is farthest from the sun.* **ANTONYM: closest**

**fas·ci·nate** /ˈfæsəˌneɪt/ *verb*
to interest someone very much: *Stories about magic fascinate children.*
—**fascinated** *adjective* very interested
—**fascinating** *adjective* very interesting: *History is a fascinating subject.*
[**ORIGIN:** 1500-1600 From the Latin word *fascinare*, which means "to use magic on someone."]

**fas·ci·na·tion** /ˌfæsəˈneɪʃən/ *noun*
a very strong interest in something or someone: *She has a fascination with famous movie stars.*

**fash·ion** /ˈfæʃən/ *noun*
**1** something that is popular at a particular time, especially a style of clothes: *The magazine has pictures of the latest fashions.*
**2 in fashion** = liked or worn by a lot of people now: *Long skirts are in fashion again.* **SYNONYM: fashionable**
**3 out of fashion** = not liked or worn by people now: *My old coat is completely out of fashion now.* **SYNONYM: unfashionable**
[**ORIGIN:** 1300-1400 From the French word *façon*, which means "appearance or way of doing something," from the Latin word *factio*, which means "the act of making or doing something."]

**fash·ion·a·ble** /ˈfæʃənəbəl/ *adjective*
**1** in the style that is popular now: *Short jackets are fashionable this year.*
**2** a fashionable place is expensive, and rich people go there or live there: *She lived in a fashionable part of Manhattan.*

**fast[1]** /fæst/ *adjective*
**1** moving or doing something quickly: *Jake's a fast runner – he always beats me in races.* | *She's a fast learner.* **ANTONYM: slow**
**2** if a clock or watch is fast, it shows a time that is later than the real time: *My watch is fast – it says it's 5:30, but it's only 5:15.* **ANTONYM: slow**

**fast[2]** *adverb*
**1** moving quickly: *Don't drive so fast!* **ANTONYM: slowly**

**THESAURUS: fast**

**quickly** moving fast or done in a very short amount of time: *I ran quickly down the stairs.* | *She showered and dressed quickly.*

**rapidly** increasing, happening, or changing very quickly: *A child's body changes rapidly during the teenage years.*

**swiftly** moving very quickly or happening immediately: *She walked swiftly away.*

**2 fast asleep** = sleeping very well: *By 10 o'clock, he was already fast asleep.*

**fast[3]** *verb*
to eat little or no food for a period of time, especially for religious reasons: *During the religious celebration of Ramadan, Muslims fast during the daytime.*

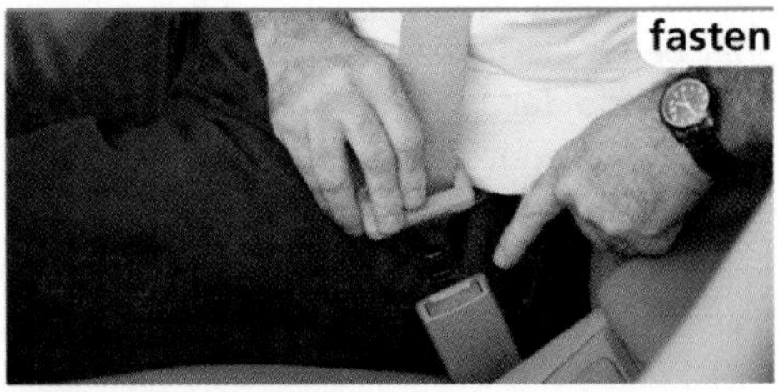
fasten

**fas·ten** /ˈfæsən/ *verb*
**1** to join together the two sides of something: *Fasten your seat belts.*
**2** to attach something to another thing: *We can fasten the cloth to the paper with a staple.*

**THESAURUS: fasten**

**tie** to fasten something such as a tie or shoelaces by making a knot: *Tie your shoelaces; you'll trip!*

**button** to fasten the buttons on a shirt, coat, etc.: *Craig buttoned up his jacket.*

**zip** to fasten clothes, bags, etc. with a zipper: *I can't zip up these jeans; they're too tight.*

**attach** to fasten something firmly to another object or surface: *Please attach two photographs to your passport application form.*

**glue** to fasten things together using glue: *The children glued shapes onto the paper to make pictures.*

**tape** to fasten something using tape: *Michelle taped a card to the present.*

**staple** to fasten something using staples (=small pieces of bent wire that go through paper): *The paper was stapled together in the left corner.*

**clip** to fasten things together using a clip (=a small object that goes over paper to hold it together): *The pages were clipped together.*

**fas·ten·er** /ˈfæsənɚ/ *noun*
a button, pin, etc. that you use to attach things to each other: *There was a small fastener, like a hook, at the top of the zipper.*

**ˈfast food** *noun*
food that comes from a restaurant where they make and serve food quickly: *We bought hamburgers at a fast food restaurant.*

**fat¹** /fæt/ *adjective*
having too much flesh on your body: *You'll get fat if you eat all that chocolate!* **ANTONYM: thin**

**THESAURUS: fat**

You can call yourself **fat**, but it is not polite to tell someone else that they are fat: *I'm getting really fat.*

**overweight** weighing more than you should: *He's a little overweight.*

**heavy** fat – it is more polite to say that someone is heavy than to say he or she is fat: *She is a heavy woman in her late fifties.*

**obese** very fat in a way that is dangerous to your health: *Obese people often have heart disease and other health problems.*

**chubby** slightly fat – used especially about a baby or child: *He is such a cute, chubby baby.*

**plump** slightly fat in a pleasant way: *Mrs. Wilson was a plump, kind-looking woman.*

**fat²** *noun*
**1** an oily substance in food such as milk, cheese, or butter: *Pizza contains a lot of fat, so you shouldn't eat it too often.*
**2** the soft substance under the skin of people and animals: *I don't like meat that has too much fat on it.*

**fa·tal** /ˈfeɪtl/ *adjective*
a fatal accident, disease, etc. causes someone to die: *There have been several fatal accidents on this road.*
—**fatally** *adverb* in a way that causes death: *He was fatally wounded in the attack and died two days later.*

**fa·tal·i·ty** /fəˈtæləti/ *noun* (plural **fatalities**) (*formal*)
a death in an accident or an attack: *Several people were hurt, but there were no fatalities.*

**fate** /feɪt/ *noun*
**1** a power that some people think controls what happens to you in your life: *I knew it was fate that I met her, and I knew I wanted to marry her.* **SYNONYM: destiny**
**2** the things that will happen to someone or something: *The fate of the earthquake victims depends on us sending them help.*
[**ORIGIN:** 1300-1400 From the Latin word *fatum*, from *fari*, which means "to speak." The idea is that your fate is what the gods have said will happen to you.]

**fa·ther** /ˈfɑðɚ/ *noun*
**1** your male parent: *My father is a doctor.* **SYNONYM: dad**
**2** (*also* **Father**) a priest in some Christian churches: *Do you know Father Vernon?*

F

—**fatherhood** /ˈfɑðɚhʊd/ *noun* the state of being a father
—**fatherly** *adjective* typical of a good father: *fatherly advice*

**ˈfather-in-law** *noun* (plural **fathers-in-law**) the father of someone's husband or wife

**ˈFather's Day** *noun*
the third Sunday in June, when people give cards and gifts to their fathers

**fa·tigue** /fəˈtig/ *noun* (*formal*)
extreme tiredness: *He had not slept, and fatigue caused him to make mistakes.*
—**fatigued** *adjective* very tired

F

**fat·ten** /ˈfætn/ (*also* **fatten up**) *verb*
to make a person or animal fatter: *The good grass fattens up the cattle.*

**fat·ty** /ˈfæti/ *adjective*
containing a lot of fat: *Too much fatty food is bad for you.*

**fau·cet** /ˈfɔsɪt/ *noun*
the thing that you turn on and off to control the water coming from a pipe: *I filled my glass with water and turned off the faucet.* → see picture on page **A9**

**fault** /fɔlt/ *noun*
**1 be someone's fault** = if something bad is your fault, you caused it to happen: *It's my fault we're late – I should have gotten up earlier.*
**2 be at fault** = to be responsible for something bad that has happened: *The report on the accident said the pilot was at fault.*
**3** something that is bad about someone's character: *Her worst fault is that she is lazy.*
**4** a problem with a machine or piece of equipment that stops it from working correctly: *The repairman came to fix a fault in the washing machine.*
**5** a large crack in the rocks that form the Earth. Earthquakes happen along a fault: *There have been many earthquakes along the San Andreas fault in California.*
**6 find fault with someone or something** = to criticize someone or something: *My English teacher is always finding fault with my work.*
—**faultless** *adjective* having no mistakes
[**ORIGIN:** 1200-1300 From the old French word *faute*, from the Latin word *fallere*, which means "to deceive or disappoint."]

**fault·y** /ˈfɔlti/ *adjective*
not working correctly: *The accident happened because the truck had faulty brakes.*

**fa·vor¹** /ˈfeɪvɚ/ *noun*
**1** something helpful you do for someone: *Can you do me a favor and give me your notes from history class?*
**2 be in favor of something** = to support or agree with something: *Most of the people at the meeting were in favor of the plan.*

**favor²** *verb*
to like someone or something better than other things, or to treat someone better than other people: *Mrs. Adams clearly favors her daughter and ignores her son.*

**fa·vor·able** /ˈfeɪvərəbəl/ *adjective* (*formal*)
**1** showing that people think someone or something is good: *The movie's had a lot of favorable reviews, so I think I'll go and see it.*
**2** likely to make someone or something succeed: *They waited for favorable weather before starting to climb the mountain.*
—**favorably** *adverb* (*formal*) in a way that shows you think someone or something is good: *Everyone reacted favorably to the plan and said they would help.*

**fa·vor·ite¹** /ˈfeɪvərɪt/ *adjective*
your favorite person or thing is the one you like most: *My favorite sport is baseball.*

**favorite²** *noun*
**someone's favorite** = something that someone likes more than any others: *I like all her books, but this one is my favorite.*

**fawn** /fɔn/ *noun*
a young DEER

**fax** /fæks/ *noun*
**1** a copy of a document that is sent through a telephone line and then printed on paper: *He sent a fax with all the information.*
**2** (*also* **fax machine**) a machine used for sending and receiving faxes
—**fax** *verb* to send a fax: *The company faxed him a copy of the report.*

**fear¹** /fɪr/ *noun*
**1** the feeling you have when you are afraid: *When he heard the dragon coming, he trembled with fear. | She has a fear of flying.*
**2** a feeling of great worry: *There are fears that hundreds of people may have been hurt.*

[ORIGIN: From the old English word *fær*, which means "danger." Fear is the feeling that danger causes.]

**WORD FAMILY: fear**
**fear** *noun* | **fear** *verb* | **fearful** *adjective* | **fearless** *adjective* | **fearlessly** *adverb*

**fear²** *verb (formal)*
**1** to feel worried that something bad could happen: *I got lost once, and feared that I would never find the way home.*
**2** to be afraid of someone or something: *Many children fear dogs because they sometimes bite.*

**fear·ful** /ˈfɪrfəl/ *adjective (formal)*
afraid: *Doctors are fearful of getting the disease because it passes so easily from person to person.*

**fear·less** /ˈfɪrləs/ *adjective*
not afraid of anything: *As a boy, he was a fearless climber who we often saw at the tops of trees.*
—**fearlessly** *adverb* without any fear

**feast¹** /fist/ *noun*
a large meal for many people: *Everyone was invited to the wedding feast.*
[ORIGIN: 1100-1200 From the Latin word *festum*, which means "holiday or festival."]

**feast²** *verb*
**PHRASAL VERB**
**feast on something** *(formal)*
to eat a lot of food with great enjoyment: *We feasted on chicken and potatoes.*

**feat** /fit/ *noun*
an impressive achievement needing a lot of skill, effort, or strength: *The bridge is an amazing feat of engineering.*

**feath·er** /ˈfeðɚ/ *noun*
one of the light soft things that cover a bird's body: *a bird with beautiful green feathers*

**fea·ture¹** Ac /ˈfitʃɚ/ *noun*
**1** an important, interesting, or typical part of something: *The cell phone has a lot of useful features, such as a camera and a calendar.*
**2** a part of your face, for example your mouth or nose: *He has strong features.*
**3** a piece of writing about a subject in a newspaper or a magazine, or a special report on television or on the radio: *There is a big feature on Brad Pitt in this week's magazine.*
[ORIGIN: 1300-1400 From the old French word *feture*, which means "shape or form," from the Latin word *facere*, which means "to do or make."]

**feature²** Ac *verb*
if something features a person or thing, that person or thing has an important part in it: *The movie features Julia Roberts.*

**Feb·ru·ar·y** /ˈfebyuˌeri/ *noun (written abbreviation*: **Feb.**)
the second month of the year, between January and March: *My birthday is in February.*
[ORIGIN: probably 1100-1200 From *Februa*, which was a Roman religious ceremony to make things pure that took place in this month.]

**fe·ces** /ˈfisiz/ *plural noun*
the solid waste that comes out of someone's body

**fed** /fed/ *verb*
the past tense and past participle of FEED

**fed·er·al** Ac /ˈfedərəl/ *adjective*
relating to the central government of a country that consists of several states: *Workers pay both federal and state income tax.*
—**federally** *adverb* by the central government of a country: *His research is federally funded.*
[ORIGIN: 1600-1700 From the Latin word *foedus*, which means "formal agreement, or joining together."]

**fed·er·a·tion** /ˌfedəˈreɪʃən/ *noun*
an official group of organizations or states: *the U.S. Gymnastics Federation*

**ˌfed ˈup** *adjective (informal)*
annoyed or bored, and wanting change: *I'm fed up with the way he treats me.*

**fee** Ac /fi/ *noun*
**1** an amount of money that you pay to do something: *The museum entrance fee is $10.*
**2** an amount of money that you pay someone such as a lawyer or doctor for their work: *She used the money to pay her legal fees.*
→ see Thesaurus box at **cost¹**
[ORIGIN: 1300-1400 From the old French word *fief*, which means "land given in return for service," and the old English word *feoh*, which means "cattle, possessions, or money."]

F

**fee·ble** /ˈfibəl/ *adjective*
**1** extremely weak: *"I don't feel very good," she said in a feeble voice.*
**2** not good or effective: *His feeble excuse was that the dog ate his homework.*
—**feebly** *adverb* in a feeble way

**feed** /fid/ *verb* (**fed** /fed/)
**1** to give food to a person or animal: *Did you feed the dog?*
**2** if animals feed on something, they eat it: *Cows feed on grass.*
**3** to put small amounts of something into a machine, especially one after another: *He fed three quarters into the parking meter.*

F

**feed·back** /ˈfidbæk/ *noun*
things people say about how well someone has done something, and usually how it can be improved: *My English teacher gave me some helpful feedback on my essay.*

**feel[1]** /fil/ *verb* (**felt** /felt/)
**1** to experience a physical feeling such as coldness or tiredness, or an emotion such as sadness or happiness: *She was feeling tired, and she wanted to go to bed.* | *"How do you feel?" "I feel a lot better today."*
**2** used to say how something seems to you when you touch it or are in it: *The kitten's fur felt soft.* | *It feels very hot in here.*
**3** if a situation feels good, bad, exciting, etc., it gives you that emotion: *It feels good to be home.*
**4** to touch something with your hand or fingers in order to find out about it: *Feel my forehead. Does it seem hot to you?*
**5** to notice something that is touching you: *She felt a bug crawling up her leg.*
**6** to have a particular opinion: *He feels that the teacher treated him unfairly.*
**7** **feel like (doing) something** = to want to do something or have something: *I feel like going out tonight – do you want to go to a movie?*
**8** **feel free** = used when offering something to someone or when giving someone permission to do something: *Feel free to ask questions.*
→ see Thesaurus box at **touch[1]**
**PHRASAL VERB**
**feel for someone**
to feel sympathy for someone: *I really felt for her when she said she had been crying all night.*

**feel[2]** *noun*
**1** the way that something feels when you touch it: *The coat has a nice soft feel.*
**2** the ability to do something well because you have a natural skill or because you have done it many times before: *Surfers have a feel for the waves, and know which ones will be good to ride.*

**feel·ing** /ˈfilɪŋ/ *noun*
**1** an emotion that you have in your mind, such as happiness, excitement, or love: *There's always a great feeling of excitement before the race starts.*
**2** something you feel in your body, such as pain or cold, or the ability to feel things in your body: *He has no feeling in his legs.* **SYNONYM: sensation**
**3** a belief or opinion about something: *My feeling is that we could have won if we had tried harder.* **SYNONYM: opinion**
**4** **someone's feelings** = the way someone feels at a particular time, for example whether he or she feels sad, happy, etc.: *I lied and said I liked the present because I didn't want to hurt her feelings.*

**feet** /fit/ *noun*
the plural of FOOT

**feist·y** /ˈfaɪsti/ *adjective*
having a strong determined character and a lot of energy: *He's a feisty player who never gives up.*

**fe·line** /ˈfilaɪn/ *adjective*
relating to cats

**fell** /fel/ *verb*
the past tense of FALL

**fel·low[1]** /ˈfeloʊ/ *adjective*
belonging to the same class, school, or group as you: *She is popular with her fellow students.*

**fellow[2]** *noun*
an old-fashioned word for a man

**fel·o·ny** /ˈfeləni/ *noun* (plural **felonies**)
a serious crime that is punished by more than a year in prison, for example murder: *They charged him with a felony.*

**felt¹** /felt/ *verb*
the past tense and past participle of FEEL

**felt²** *noun*
a thick soft material made from threads that have been pressed together, especially wool threads: *a felt hat*

**ˌfelt tip ˈpen** *noun*
a pen that has a hard piece of felt at the end that the ink comes through

**fe·male¹** /ˈfimeɪl/ *noun*
a person or animal that belongs to the sex that can have babies or produce eggs: *The female is brown in color, but the male is red.* **ANTONYM: male**
[**ORIGIN:** 1300-1400 From the Latin word *femella*, which means "girl." The spelling was changed to make it like "male," although the words are not related.]

**female²** *adjective*
belonging to the sex that can have babies or produce eggs: *A female horse carries her baby for about 340 days before it is born.* **ANTONYM: male**

**fem·i·nine** /ˈfemənɪn/ *adjective*
**1** having qualities that are considered to be typical of women: *Most people think of pink as a feminine color.* **ANTONYM: masculine**
**2** in English, a feminine noun or PRONOUN is used to talk about women or girls: *"She" is a feminine pronoun. | "Waiter" is the masculine form; "waitress" is the feminine form.* **ANTONYM: masculine**
**3** in other languages, some nouns and adjectives are feminine, and others are MASCULINE: *In French, the noun "rose" is feminine.* **ANTONYM: masculine**
—**femininity** /ˌfeməˈnɪnəti/ *noun* the quality of being feminine

**fem·i·nism** /ˈfeməˌnɪzəm/ *noun*
the belief that women should have the same rights and opportunities as men
—**feminist** *noun* someone who believes strongly that women should have the same rights and opportunities as men
—**feminist** *adjective* relating to feminism: *feminist literature*

**fence** /fens/ *noun*
**1** a structure made of wood or metal that surrounds a piece of land and keeps people or animals in or out: *There is a high fence all around the prison.*
**2 on the fence** (*informal*) = trying to avoid saying which side of an argument you agree with: *I wish she'd stop sitting on the fence and tell me what she really thinks!*

**fenc·ing** /ˈfensɪŋ/ *noun*
a sport in which two people fight each other with light thin swords

**fend·er** /ˈfendɚ/ *noun*
**1** the part of a car on the side that is over and around one of the wheels: *There was a scratch on the rear left fender of the car.*
**2** a curved piece of metal over the wheel of a bicycle, that prevents mud or water from hitting you → see picture at **bicycle**

**fern** /fɚn/ *noun*
a plant with green leaves shaped like large feathers and no flowers

**fe·ro·cious** /fəˈroʊʃəs/ *adjective*
**1** extremely violent and likely to attack: *Tigers are ferocious hunters.*
**2** very strong or severe: *A ferocious storm left 2 feet of snow in just 6 hours.*
—**ferociously** *adverb* in a ferocious way
—**ferocity** /fəˈrɑsəti/ *noun* the quality of being ferocious
[**ORIGIN:** 1600-1700 From the Latin word *ferox*, which means "wild or fierce."]

**Fer·ris wheel** /ˈferɪs wil/ *noun*
a big wheel with chairs that go up into the air for people to ride on at an AMUSEMENT PARK

**fer·ry** /ˈferi/ *noun* (plural **ferries**)
a boat that regularly carries people and cars across a narrow area of water: *We took the ferry from Manhattan to Staten Island.* → see picture on page **A27**

**fer·tile** /ˈfɚtl/ *adjective*
**1** able to produce good crops: *The land next to the river is very fertile.*

F

2 able to produce children: *The test showed that she was still fertile, so they decided to try to have a baby.*
—**fertility** /fə'tɪləti/ *noun* the state of being fertile

**fer·til·ize** /'fətl,aɪz/ *verb*
1 to add substances to the soil to help plants grow: *Some farmers fertilize their land with chemicals.*
2 to make a new animal or plant start to develop: *The eggs laid by the female fish are fertilized by the male.*

**fer·til·iz·er** /'fətl,aɪzə/ *noun*
a substance that is put on the soil to help plants grow: *Waste from farm animals is often used as fertilizer.*

F

**fes·ti·val** /'festəvəl/ *noun*
1 a special occasion when people celebrate something: *There will be food, music, and dancing at the festival.*
2 an event at which many films, plays, pieces of music, etc. are shown or performed: *the Cannes film festival*

**fes·tive** /'festɪv/ *adjective*
1 happy because you are celebrating something: *A festive crowd cheered during the parade.*
2 relating to a celebration: *Families often get together on festive occasions such as Thanksgiving.*

**fetch** /fetʃ/ *verb*
to go and get something and bring it back: *The dog fetched the stick.*

**fe·tus** /'fitəs/ *noun*
a baby before it is born: *Smoking can cause damage to the fetus.*

**feud** /fyud/ *noun*
an angry argument between two people or groups that continues for a long time: *The feud between the two families lasted for years.*
—**feud** *verb* to have a feud with someone

**fe·ver** /'fivə/ *noun*
an illness or medical condition in which you have a very high temperature: *She feels very hot – I think she has a fever.*
—**feverish** *adjective* having a fever

**few** /fyu/ *pronoun, adjective*
1 **a few** = a small number of things or people: *I only had a few coins in my pocket. | "How many people know about this?" "Only a few."*
2 not many: *There are few things as exciting as traveling to a new place on vacation.*

**GRAMMAR: fewer, less**

Use **fewer** before plural forms of nouns: *There were fewer cars on the roads in the 1950s. | Fewer people than I expected were at the game.*

Use **less** before nouns such as "money" and "bread" that do not have plurals: *Add less salt to your food. | This book has less information than the other one.*

3 **quite a few** = a fairly large number of people or things: *Quite a few people came to the meeting.*
4 **be few and far between** = to be rare: *Jobs are few and far between these days.*

**fi·an·cé** /,fiɑn'seɪ/ *noun*
the man that a woman is going to marry: *Her fiancé bought her an engagement ring.*

**fi·an·cée** /,fiɑn'seɪ/ *noun*
the woman that a man is going to marry: *Ron and his fiancée were at the party.*

**fi·as·co** /fi'æskoʊ/ *noun* (plural **fiascoes** *or* **fiascos**)
an event that is not successful at all, in a way that is very embarrassing or disappointing: *The food was burned and the ice cream had melted, so the dinner was a complete fiasco.*

**fib** /fɪb/ *noun* (*informal*)
a small, unimportant lie: *You shouldn't tell fibs because then people won't believe you when you tell the truth.* **ANTONYM: the truth**
—**fib** *verb* (*informal*) to tell a small lie to someone **SYNONYM: lie**
→ see Thesaurus box at lie[2]

**fi·ber** /'faɪbə/ *noun*
1 parts of plants that you eat but cannot DIGEST. Fiber is good for you because it helps food to move through your body: *My doctor says that I need to eat more fiber.*

2 a type of thread or cloth: *The dress is made from some kind of artificial fiber.*

**fic·tion** /ˈfɪkʃən/ *noun*
1 books and stories about imaginary people and events: *I write fiction because I like making up stories.* **ANTONYM: nonfiction**
2 something that is not true: *The singer says that the newspaper stories about her are complete fiction.*
→ see Thesaurus box at **book**[1]
[**ORIGIN:** 1300-1400 From the Latin word *fictio*, which means "the act of making something," from *fingere*, which means "to shape or make."]

**fid·dle**[1] /ˈfɪdl/ *noun* (*informal*)
a VIOLIN

**fiddle**[2] *verb*
to keep moving and touching something because you are bored or nervous: *She started fiddling with her hair.*

**fidg·et** /ˈfɪdʒɪt/ *verb*
to keep moving your hands or feet because you are bored or nervous: *The children fidgeted in their seats because they were bored.*

**field** /fild/ *noun*
1 an area of land in the country where crops are grown or animals feed on grass: *There were fields of wheat for mile after mile.*
2 an area of ground where sports are played: *a baseball field | The team ran out on the field.*
3 a subject that people study, or a type of work: *Professor Kramer is an expert in the field of biology.*
4 **oil/gas/coal field** = an area where there is a lot of oil, gas, or coal under the ground

**field·er** /ˈfildɚ/ *noun*
one of the players in baseball who plays farthest away from the BATTER and tries to catch the ball after the batter has hit it: *The center fielder caught the ball.*

**ˈfield trip** *noun*
a trip that students go on to a place, such as a MUSEUM or park, in order to see and learn about things

**fierce** /fɪrs/ *adjective*
1 a fierce animal or person looks angry or ready to attack: *The house was guarded by a fierce dog.*
2 involving a lot of energy and strong feelings: *The two football teams are in a fierce battle for first place.*
3 fierce heat, cold, weather, etc. is very extreme or severe: *The heat was fierce, so we stayed inside where it was cool.*
—**fiercely** *adverb* in a fierce way

**fi·er·y** /ˈfaɪəri/ *adjective*
1 full of strong or angry emotion: *She gave a fiery speech that got our attention.*
2 very bright, with red or yellow colors like a fire: *a fiery sunset*
3 having a lot of flames: *The plane was destroyed in a fiery explosion.*

**fi·es·ta** /fiˈestə/ *noun*
a party or religious holiday with dancing, music, etc., in places where people who speak Spanish live: *At fiesta time, the streets are full of people singing and dancing.*

**fif·teen** /ˌfɪfˈtin/ *number*
1 15: *There are fifteen steps up to the door.*
2 fifteen years old: *Her brother's fifteen.*
—**fifteenth** *number* 15th or 1/15

**fifth** /fɪfθ/ *number*
1 5th
2 1/5

**fif·ty** /ˈfɪfti/ *number*
1 50: *A ticket to the concert costs $50.*
2 fifty years old: *He is almost fifty.*
3 **the fifties** (*also* **the '50s**) = the years between 1950 and 1959: *The city was built in the fifties.*
4 **in your fifties** = between 50 and 59 years old: *My mother is in her fifties.*
5 **in the fiftees** = between 50 and 59 degrees FAHRENHEIT in temperature: *The temperature will be in the fifties with a cool wind.*
—**fiftieth** *number* 50th or 1/50

**fig** /fɪg/ *noun*
a small soft sweet fruit with red-brown flesh, that is often eaten dried → see picture on page **A13**

**fig.**
the written abbreviation of **figure** (=a numbered drawing in a book): *See fig. 3.1 on page 45.*

**fight**[1] /faɪt/ *verb* (**fought** /fɔt/)
1 to use physical force or weapons to try to

hurt someone: *Boxers fight with gloves on.* | *My brother fought in the Iraq War.*

**2** to argue: *My parents sometimes fight about money.*

**3** to try hard to do or get something: *Parents are fighting to keep the school open.*

**4** to try hard to stop something: *Martin Luther King spent his whole life fighting against racism.*

→ see Thesaurus box at **argue**

[**ORIGIN:** From the old English word *feohtan*.]

**PHRASAL VERB**

**fight back**

**1** to try hard to win when you are losing: *Lewis fought back to win the match.*

**2** to begin arguing or fighting with someone who attacks or insults you, instead of doing nothing: *If they say mean things to you, don't just stand there – fight back!*

**3** to try hard not to have or show a feeling: *She fought back her tears.*

**fight²** *noun*

**1** a situation in which two people or groups attack each other and try to hurt each other using physical force: *I got into a fight with another boy, and he hit me in the face.*

**2** an argument: *My dad and I had a fight about keeping my room clean.*

**3** the process of trying very hard to achieve something or prevent something: *The country had a long fight for independence.* | *the fight against crime*

**fight·er** /ˈfaɪtɚ/ *noun*

**1** someone who continues to try to do something although it is difficult: *She has cancer, but she's a fighter and I know she'll get better.*

**2** someone who fights as a sport **SYNONYM: boxer**

**3** (*also* **fighter plane**) a small fast military airplane that can destroy other airplanes

**fig·u·ra·tive** /ˈfɪgyərətɪv/ *adjective*

if a word or expression is used in a figurative way, it does not have its usual meaning, but describes something in an interesting way: *"A mountain of debt" is a figurative way of saying "a large amount of debt."*

—**figuratively** *adverb* (*formal*) in a figurative way

**fig·ure¹** /ˈfɪgjɚ/ *noun*

**1** a number: *Add up these two figures.* | *a six-figure salary*

**2** an important or famous person: *Thomas Jefferson was one of the most important figures in American history.*

**3** the shape of a woman's body: *My sister has a great figure.*

**4** a shape of a person, when it is difficult to see the shape: *I could see a dark figure in the distance, but I couldn't see who it was.*

**5** a shape in mathematics: *A cube is a six-sided figure.*

**6** (*written abbreviation*: **fig.**) a numbered drawing in a book: *See Figure 2.1, page 20.*

**7** a person in a painting or photograph, or a STATUE of a person: *The figures in the background are not painted in great detail.*

[**ORIGIN:** 1200-1300 From the Latin word *figura*, which means "shape," from *fingere*, which means "to shape or make."]

**figure²** *verb*

**1** to think that something is probably true: *We figured that you might need some help.*

**2 that figures/it figures** (*informal*) = used when you are not surprised or disappointed because a situation is the way you expected it to be: *"Sarah's not going to Brandon's party." "That figures. She can't stand him."*

**3 go figure** (*informal*) = used when saying that something seems strange and you cannot understand it: *She says she's a vegetarian, but she eats bacon. Go figure.*

**PHRASAL VERBS**

**figure on something** (*informal*)

to expect something or include it in your plans: *"How much do you want to pay for the car?" "We figured on paying about $5,000."*

**figure out**

**1 figure someone or something out** = to understand someone or something: *I still can't figure out why she lied to me.*

**2 figure something out** = to find an answer to a problem: *Let's figure out a way to help her.*

**ˈfigure ˌskating** *noun*

a type of skating (SKATE) in which you move in patterns on the ice

—**figure skater** *noun* someone who does this type of skating

**file**[1] Ac /faɪl/ *noun*

**1** a set of papers that contain information about a person or subject: *The school keeps files on each student.*
**2** information that is stored on a computer under a particular name: *I pressed the wrong button and accidentally deleted the file.*
**3** a box or thick paper cover where you can keep loose papers together: *They keep their old bank statements in a file.*
**4** a tool with a rough surface that you rub on something to make it smooth: *Use a nail file to shape your nails.*
**5 in single file** = moving in a line, with one person behind another: *We walked in single file along the narrow trail.*

**file**[2] Ac *verb*
**1** to store papers or information in a particular order or a particular place: *The papers are filed in alphabetical order.*
**2** to ask for something to be dealt with by a court of law or other official organization: *The couple has filed for divorce.*
**3** if people file somewhere, they walk in a line, with one person behind another: *The students filed out of the classroom.*
**4** to make something smooth by rubbing it with a special tool: *She filed her nails.*

**ˈfile ˌcabinet** *noun*
a tall piece of furniture with drawers in which you store pieces of paper → see picture on page **A18**

**fil·et** /fɪˈleɪ/ *noun*
another spelling of FILLET

**fill** /fɪl/ *verb*
**1** (*also* **fill up**) to put something in a container or space so that it becomes full: *She filled the bowls with soup.*
**2** (*also* **fill up**) to become full of something: *Her eyes filled with tears.*
**3** if something fills a place, it uses all of the space, and there is none left: *Smoke filled the room.*

**PHRASAL VERBS**

**fill in**
**1 fill something in** = to write something in a space on a piece of paper: *Fill in the blanks in these sentences.*
**2 fill someone in** = to tell someone about things that have happened recently: *I'll fill you in on all the news later.*
**3** to do someone's job because he or she is not there: *Could you fill in for Bob while he's sick?*

**fill something out**
to write the necessary information on an official piece of paper: *You have to fill out this form.* **SYNONYM: complete**

**fil·let** (*also* **filet**) /fɪˈleɪ/ *noun*
a piece of meat or fish without bones: *a salmon fillet*

**fill·ing** /ˈfɪlɪŋ/ *noun*
**1** a small amount of metal that a DENTIST puts into a hole in your tooth: *He had a gold filling.*
**2** the food that you put in a PIE, SANDWICH, etc.

**film**[1] /fɪlm/ *noun*
**1** the plastic material that you put in older cameras to take pictures: *He used three rolls of film and took over a hundred pictures.*
**2** a movie: *The film is based on a true story.*
**3** a very thin layer of liquid or powder: *A thin film of grease covered everything in the kitchen.*
—**filmmaker** *noun* someone who makes movies
→ see Thesaurus box at **movie**

[**ORIGIN:** From the old English word *filmen*, which means "thin skin." The material used for making photographs or movies had a thin layer of a chemical substance on it.]

**film**[2] *verb*
to use a camera to make a movie or a television program: *He is currently filming an action movie.*

**fil·ter**[1] /ˈfɪltɚ/ *noun*
something that you put a gas or liquid through in order to remove unwanted substances: *The water filter cleans chemicals out of the water you drink.*

[**ORIGIN:** 1300-1400 From the Latin word *filtrum*, which means "piece of felt." Felt is a type of thick cloth that was used to filter liquids.]

**filter²** *verb*
**1** to clean a liquid or gas using a filter: *Filter the water until it is clear.*
**2** if light filters into a place, only some of it comes in: *Sunshine filtered through the curtains.*

**filth** /fɪlθ/ *noun* (*formal*)
a lot of dirt: *Look at the filth in this place – it's disgusting!*

**filth·y** /ˈfɪlθi/ *adjective* (**filthier**, **filthiest**)
very dirty: *I didn't want to go into the bathroom because it was filthy.*
→ see Thesaurus box at **dirty**

F

**fin** /fɪn/ *noun*
one of the flat parts of a fish's body, that it uses to swim

**fin**

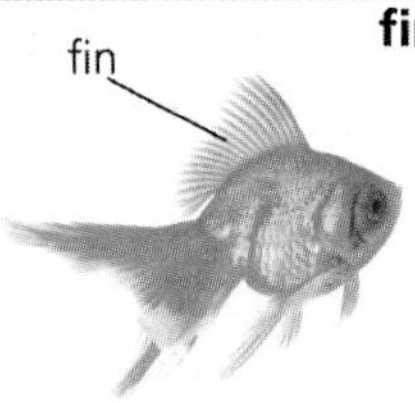


**fi·nal¹** Ac /ˈfaɪnl/ *adjective*
**1** last: *The final page of the book was missing.*
**2** a final decision or offer cannot or will not be changed: *You don't have to make a final decision yet.*
[**ORIGIN:** 1300-1400 From the Latin word *finalis*, from *finis*, which means "end."]

**final²** Ac *noun*
**1** the last and most important game, race, or stage in a competition: *The team is very excited to have reached the finals.*
**2** an important test that students take at the end of a SEMESTER: *How did your finals go?*
—**finalist** *noun* someone who is in the final of a competition

**fi·nal·ly** Ac /ˈfaɪnl-i/ *adverb*
**1** after a long time: *I finally read that book you gave me last year.*
**2** used before saying the last of a series of things: *And finally, I'd like to thank my teachers for all the help they gave me.*

**fi·nance¹** Ac /fəˈnæns/ *noun*
**1** the control of money, especially for a company or a government: *She's an accountant in the Finance Department.*
**2 finances** = the money that a person or organization has, and how it is used: *The company's finances were a mess, so they hired an accountant.*
[**ORIGIN:** 1300-1400 From the old French word *finer*, which means "to end, or to settle a debt by making a payment."]

**WORD FAMILY: finance**
**finance** *noun* | **finance** *verb* | **financial** *adjective* | **financially** *adverb*

**finance²** Ac *verb*
to provide a lot of money to pay for something: *Who will finance the project?*

**fi·nan·cial** Ac /fəˈnænʃəl/ *adjective*
relating to money: *He has financial problems and is looking for a second job.*
—**financially** *adverb* in a way that relates to money: *A lot of college students are supported financially by their parents.*

**find** /faɪnd/ *verb* (**found** /faʊnd/)
**1** to see or get something after looking for it, or by chance: *I can't find my keys.* | *She's hoping to find a job soon.* | *He found a dollar bill on the street.*

**THESAURUS: find**
**discover** to find something that was hidden or that people did not know about before: *Scientists believe that they have discovered a cure for the disease.*
**trace** to find someone or something that has disappeared: *The police are trying to trace a man who was seen near the house that night.*
**locate** (*formal*) to find the exact place where someone or something is: *The pirates could not locate the spot where they had buried the treasure.*
**track someone/something down** to find someone or something after searching in different places: *Detectives finally tracked her down in California.*

**2** to learn new information as a result of tests or experience: *Researchers have found that people who have pets stay healthier.*
**3** to have an opinion about someone or something: *She finds history very interesting.* | *I found it difficult to understand her.*
**4 be found somewhere** = to live or exist somewhere: *Pandas are found only in China.*
**5 find your way (somewhere)** = to arrive at

a place without being told how to get there: *I found my way home using a map.*

**6** **find someone guilty/not guilty** = to officially decide that someone is guilty or not guilty of a crime: *He was found guilty of murder.*

**PHRASAL VERB**

**find out something**

to get knowledge of a fact: *I'll find out what time the movie starts.* | *If Dad ever finds out, he'll be really mad.*

**fine¹** /faɪn/ *adjective*

**1** good enough or acceptable: *Your work is fine.* | *"I'll give the book back to you tomorrow." "That's fine."* **SYNONYMS: okay, all right**

**2** healthy and happy: *"How are you?" "Fine, thanks."*

**3** very thin or made of very small pieces: *The desk was covered with a fine layer of dust.*

**4** very good: *You're doing a fine job and I'm really pleased with you.*

**5** if the weather is fine, it is sunny and pleasant, with no rain: *It was a fine morning, so we decided to go for a walk along the beach.* **SYNONYM: fair**

—**fine** *adverb* in an acceptable way: *He fixed the vacuum and now it's working fine.*

—**finely** *adverb* into very small pieces: *Chop the onions finely.*

→ see Thesaurus box at **healthy**

**fine²** *noun*

money that you have to pay as a punishment for breaking a law or rule: *The company had to pay a fine for polluting the river.*

**fine³** *verb*

to make someone pay money as a punishment: *He was fined $50 for driving too fast.*

**fin·ger** /ˈfɪŋgɚ/ *noun*

**1** one of the long parts at the end of your hand: *He pointed his finger at the house.* → see picture on page **A2**

**2** **keep/have your fingers crossed** = to hope that something will happen the way you want: *We get our grades today, so I'm keeping my fingers crossed that I get an "A."*

**fin·ger·nail** /ˈfɪŋgɚˌneɪl/ *noun*

the hard flat part at the end of your finger: *Don't bite your fingernails.* → see picture at **hand**

**fin·ger·print** /ˈfɪŋgɚˌprɪnt/ *noun*

a mark that a finger makes. Fingerprints have a pattern of lines, and every person's fingerprints are different: *Did the thief leave any fingerprints?*

**fingerprint**

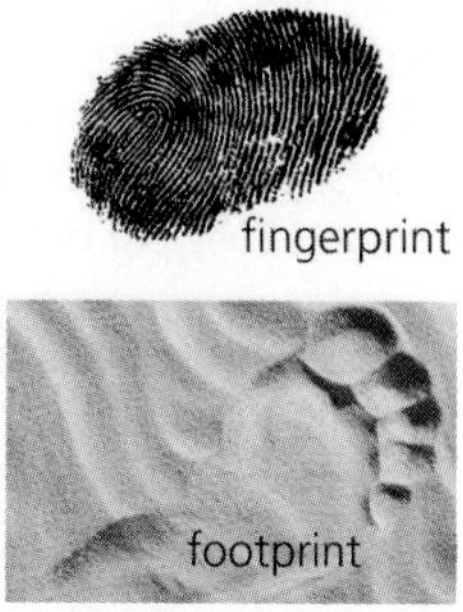


**fin·ger·tip** /ˈfɪŋgɚˌtɪp/ *noun*

the end of a finger: *She touched the flower with her fingertips.*

**fin·ish¹** /ˈfɪnɪʃ/ *verb*

**1** to come to the end of doing or making something: *Can I go out after I finish my homework?* | *She finished second in the race.* **ANTONYMS: start, begin**

**2** (*also* **finish off**) to eat or drink the rest of something: *Who finished off the cake?*

[**ORIGIN:** 1300-1400 From the Latin word *finire*, from *finis*, which means "end."]

**finish²** *noun*

**1** the end of an event: *The race had an exciting finish.* | *I enjoyed the show from start to finish.*

**2** the way that the surface of an object looks: *The table had a shiny finish.*

**fin·ished** /ˈfɪnɪʃt/ *adjective*

**1** if you are finished, you have come to the end of doing something: *I waited until he was finished talking, and then I spoke.* **SYNONYM: done**

**2** **be finished with something** = to no longer need to use something: *Are you finished with the scissors?* **SYNONYM: done**

→ see Thesaurus box at **done²**

**ˈfinish line** *noun*

the line that you cross at the end of a race: *The winner is the first person who crosses the finish line.*

**fi·nite** Ac /ˈfaɪnaɪt/ *adjective*

something that is finite has an end or limit: *There is a finite amount of oil in the ground.* **ANTONYM: infinite**

F

**fir** /fɚ/ *noun*
a tree with leaves shaped like needles that do not fall off in winter: *Our Christmas tree is a fir.*

**fire¹** /faɪɚ/ *noun*
**1** flames and heat that burn things: *The forest fires are still burning in parts of the state.* | *They put out the fire with water.*

> **THESAURUS: fire**
>
> **flame** the bright part of a fire that you see burning in the air: *There were flames coming from the roof of the building.* | *a candle flame*
>
> **blaze** the flames from a fire, or a large and dangerous fire: *Firemen fought to keep the blaze under control.*



**2 be on fire** = to be burning: *The house must be on fire. There's smoke coming out of the window.*
**3 catch fire** = to start burning: *The curtains caught fire when a candle fell over.*
**4 set fire to something** = to make something start burning that should not burn: *The police are looking for the person who set fire to the empty building.*
**5** a pile of burning wood or coal that provides heat: *When we were camping, we lit a fire and toasted marshmallows.*
**6** shooting with guns: *The soldiers opened fire on the people who were attacking them.*

**fire²** *verb*
**1** to make someone leave his or her job: *She was fired from her job for being always late.*
**2** to use a gun: *He raised his gun and fired several shots at the target.*

**ˈfire aˌlarm** *noun*
a piece of equipment that makes a loud noise to warn people of a fire in a building: *We all left the building when the fire alarm went off* (=made a noise).

**fire·arm** /ˈfaɪɚɑrm/ *noun*
a gun: *The police arrested a man for carrying an illegal firearm.*

**fire·crack·er** /ˈfaɪɚˌkrækɚ/ *noun*
an object that explodes with a loud noise when you light it. Firecrackers are used at parties and special celebrations.

**ˈfire deˌpartment** *noun*
an organization whose job is to stop fires: *The person who noticed the fire called the fire department.*

**ˈfire drill** *noun*
an occasion when people practice how to leave a building safely if there is a fire

**ˈfire ˌengine** *noun*
a large vehicle that carries people and equipment to stop fires → see picture on page **A27**

**ˈfire esˌcape** *noun*
metal stairs on the outside of a building, that people can use to escape from a fire

**ˈfire exˌtinguisher** *noun*
a metal container with water or chemicals in it, used to stop small fires

**fire·fight·er** /ˈfaɪɚˌfaɪtɚ/ *noun*
someone whose job is to stop fires → see picture on page **A16**

**ˈfire ˌhydrant** *noun*
a metal object in the street, from which FIREFIGHTERs can get water to stop fires

**fire·man** /ˈfaɪɚmən/ *noun* (plural **firemen** /ˈfaɪɚmən/)
a man whose job is to stop fires

**fire·place** /ˈfaɪɚˌpleɪs/ *noun*
an open place in the wall of a room, where you can have a fire: *A fire was burning in the fireplace.*

**fire·proof** /ˈfaɪɚˌpruf/ *adjective*
something that is fireproof cannot be damaged by fire: *They keep their records in a fireproof file cabinet.*

**ˈfire ˌstation** *noun*
a building where FIREFIGHTERs and their vehicles stay until they are needed

**fire·wood** /ˈfaɪɚwʊd/ *noun*
wood for burning on a fire

**fire·work** /ˈfaɪɚˌwɚk/ *noun*
an object that explodes and produces bright lights in the sky, which people use to celebrate special days: *People were watching the Fourth of July fireworks display.*

**firm**[1] /fɚm/ *adjective*

**1** something that is firm does not bend much when you press it: *I need a firm bed to sleep on – mine is too soft.* | *The tomatoes are firm because they're not ripe.* **ANTONYM: soft**

**2** definite and not likely to change: *I think I want to be a doctor, but I haven't made a firm decision yet.*

**3** strong and in control: *If you're firm with your dog, he will learn to obey you.*

**4** holding something strongly: *I kept a firm grip on my purse so nobody would steal it.*

—**firmly** *adverb* in a firm way: *She told him firmly that he had to wait.*

→ see Thesaurus box at **hard**[1]

**firm**[2] *noun*

a business or small company: *a law firm*

→ see Thesaurus box at **company**

**first**[1] /fɚst/ *number, pronoun*

**1** 1st; coming before the other things or people: *April 1st* | *I've only read the first chapter of the book.* | *The second week of our vacation was better than the first.*

**2 at first** = in the beginning, before there is a change: *At first I thought he was weird, but now I really like him.*

**3 in the first place** = at the beginning of something that happened: *Don't blame me – it was your idea in the first place.*

**4 first thing** = as soon as you get out of bed: *I'll call him first thing in the morning.*

**5 at first glance** = the first time you look at something, when you do not notice details: *At first glance, the twins look exactly the same, but their eyes are a different color.*

**first**[2] *adverb*

**1** before the other things or people: *Andy arrived at the house first, and his friends arrived ten minutes later.* | *First of all, cut the onions and carrots into pieces.*

**2** before doing something: *I'd like to come over, but I have to finish my homework first.*

**3** for the first time: *I first saw the movie when I was seven.*

**first**[3] *noun*

**a first** = something that has never happened before: *"Dad actually washed the dishes tonight." "That's a first."*

**ˌfirst ˈaid** *noun*

simple medical treatment that you give quickly to someone who is injured or sick: *The injured driver was given first aid and then taken to a hospital.*

**ˌfirst-ˈclass** *adjective*

of the best kind: *It's a first-class hotel with beautiful rooms and a great restaurant.*

—**first class** *adverb* if you travel first class, you travel in one of the best seats: *He always flies first class.*

**ˌfirst ˈfloor** *noun*

the part of a building that is on the same level as the ground: *Her office is on the first floor of the building.* **SYNONYM: ground floor**

**ˌfirst-geneˈration** *adjective*

**first-generation American/Canadian, etc.** = an American, Canadian, etc. whose parents came to live in America, Canada, etc. from another country

**ˌfirst ˈlady** *noun*

the wife of the president of the U.S.: *The first lady will give a speech about education.*

**first·ly** /ˈfɚstli/ *adverb* (*formal*)

used before saying the first of several things: *Firstly, I thank you all for coming.*

**ˈfirst name** *noun*

the first of your names that your parents choose for you: *Mrs. Green's first name is Caroline.*

**ˌfirst ˈperson** *noun*

**the first person** = "I" and "we," and the verb forms you use with them: *The sentence "I live in Boston." is written in the first person.*

**ˌfirst-ˈrate** *adjective*

extremely good: *She is a first-rate writer whose books have won many awards.*

**fish**[1] /fɪʃ/ *noun* (plural **fish** *or* **fishes**)

an animal without legs that lives in water, or the meat of this animal: *How many fish did you catch?* | *We had fish for dinner.*

[**ORIGIN:** From the old English word *fisc.*]

**fish**[2] *verb*

to try to catch fish: *Dad's fishing for trout.*

—**fishing** *noun* the activity of trying to catch fish: *Let's go fishing this weekend.*

**fish·bowl** /ˈfɪʃboʊl/ *noun*

a round glass container for pet fish

**fish·er·man** /ˈfɪʃəmən/ *noun* (plural **fishermen** /-mən/)
a man who catches fish as a job or a sport

**ˈfishing ˌrod** *noun*
a long stick with a long string at the end, used to catch fish

**ˈfish stick** *noun*
a piece of fish covered in little pieces of bread

**fish·y** /ˈfɪʃi/ *adjective*
**1** (*informal*) seeming bad or dishonest: *There was something fishy about his story, and I didn't trust him.*
**2** tasting or smelling like fish

F

**fist** /fɪst/ *noun*
a hand with the fingers closed tightly together: *He hit me with his fist.*

**fit¹** /fɪt/ *verb* (**fit**, **fitting**)
**1** to be the right size and shape for someone or something: *My old jeans still fit me.*
**2** if something fits in a place or container, there is enough space for it and it is not too big to go in: *We can't fit any more people into the car.*
**3** to have the qualities that match a description or a list of things someone needs: *He fits the description of the man the police are looking for.*
**4** to be appropriate for something: *The punishment should fit the crime.*
**PHRASAL VERB**
**fit in**
to be accepted by the other people in a group: *She hoped she would fit in at her new school.*

**fit²** *adjective*
**1** healthy and strong: *Playing basketball keeps me physically fit.* **ANTONYM: unfit**
**2** good enough for someone or something: *The bread was so old that it wasn't fit to eat.* **ANTONYM: unfit**

**fit³** *noun*
**1 have/throw a fit** (*informal*) = to become very angry and shout a lot: *Mom's going to have a fit when she sees that you broke this.*
**2** a short period of time when you are sick or angry, in a way that you cannot control: *I had a coughing fit while we were eating dinner.* | *In a fit of rage, he kicked the TV.*
**3 be a good/perfect fit** = to fit well or be suitable: *The skirt was a perfect fit, so I bought it.*

**fit·ness** /ˈfɪtnəs/ *noun*
the condition of being healthy and strong: *Running will improve your fitness.*

**five¹** /faɪv/ *number*
**1** 5: *There are five apples left in the bag.*
**2** five O'CLOCK
**3** five years old: *Mary was five when she started kindergarten.*

**five²** *noun*
a piece of paper money worth $5: *I paid with a five.*

**fix** /fɪks/ *verb*
**1** to repair something: *Don't ride your bike until I fix the brakes.*
**2** to prepare a meal or drink: *Mom was fixing dinner in the kitchen.* **SYNONYM: make**
**3** to decide on a date or time for something: *Have you fixed a date for the wedding?*
→ see Thesaurus box at **repair²**
**PHRASAL VERB**
**fix something up**
to decorate or repair a room or building: *We fixed up the guest bedroom, so now it has new curtains.*

**fix·ture** /ˈfɪkstʃə/ *noun*
a piece of equipment that is attached inside a house, for example an electric light or a FAUCET: *There are new light fixtures in all the bedrooms.*

**fizz** /fɪz/ *noun*
the bubbles of gas in some types of drinks: *The soda has lost its fizz.* → see picture on page **A22**
—**fizz** *verb* if a liquid fizzes, the gas bubbles in it rise to the surface and burst
—**fizzy** *adjective* a fizzy drink has bubbles of gas in it
[**ORIGIN:** 1600-1700 From the sound.]

**flab·by** /ˈflæbi/ *adjective* (**flabbier**, **flabbiest**) (*informal*)
if a part of your body is flabby, it is too fat and not firm: *a flabby stomach*
—**flab** *noun* (*informal*) soft fat on a person's body

**flag** /flæg/ *noun*
a piece of cloth with a picture or pattern on it. Flags are used as the symbol of a country or

group, or as a signal: *The American flag is red, white, and blue.*

**flag·pole** /ˈflægpoʊl/ *noun*
a tall pole for a flag

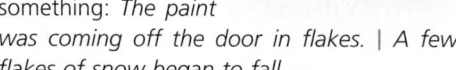

**flair** /fler/ *noun*
a natural ability to do something very well: *He has a flair for foreign languages – he can speak six.*

**flake** /fleɪk/ *noun*
**1** a flat thin piece of something: *The paint was coming off the door in flakes.* | *A few flakes of snow began to fall.*
**2** (*informal*) someone who does not do what he or she says he will do: *Carla is such a flake – she'll probably forget that the party's tonight.*

**flak·y** /ˈfleɪki/ *adjective*
**1** easily breaking into flat thin pieces: *The crust of the pie is nice and flaky.*
**2** (*informal*) someone who is flaky easily forgets things or does strange things: *You can't rely on her – she's pretty flaky.*

**flame** /fleɪm/ *noun*
**1** a hot bright light that you see when something is burning: *a candle flame*
**2 in flames** = if a building or area is in flames, a fire is destroying it: *A fire started, and within minutes the whole house was in flames.*
→ see Thesaurus box at **fire**[1]

**fla·min·go** /fləˈmɪŋgoʊ/ *noun* (plural **flamingos** *or* **flamingoes**)
a tall pink water bird with long thin legs and a long curved neck
[**ORIGIN:** 1500-1600 From the Portuguese word *flamengo*, from the Latin word *flamma*, which means "fire or flame." The bird's feathers are a reddish-pink, almost like a flame.]

**flam·ma·ble** /ˈflæməbəl/ *adjective*
something that is flammable burns very easily: *Gasoline is a flammable liquid.*

**flan·nel** /ˈflænl/ *noun*
soft cotton or wool cloth used for making warm clothes: *It was cold, so he put on a flannel shirt.*

**flap**[1] /flæp/ *verb* (**flapped**, **flapping**)
**1** if a bird flaps its wings, it moves them up and down: *The bird flapped its wings and flew away.*
**2** if something such as a piece of cloth flaps, it moves in one direction and then the other: *The ship's sails flapped in the wind.*

**flap**[2] *noun*
a thin flat piece of cloth or paper that is attached at one side to something: *He licked the flap of the envelope and closed it.*

**flare**[1] /fler/ (*also* **flare up**) *verb*
**1** to suddenly begin to burn very brightly: *The fire flared up, and we could see the people around us for a minute.*
**2** if tempers flare, people suddenly become angry or violent: *Tempers flared during the game, and some players started fighting.*

**flare**[2] *noun*
an object that you use as a signal. You light a flare and it burns with a very bright light: *A police officer was lighting warning flares along the highway near the accident.*

**flared** /flerd/ *adjective*
flared pants or skirts are wider toward the bottom

**flash**[1] /flæʃ/ *verb*
**1** to shine brightly for a short time: *Lightning flashed in the sky.* | *They saw the flashing lights of the ambulance.*
**2** to move very quickly: *The race cars flashed past.*
→ see Thesaurus box at **shine**

**flash**[2] *noun*
**1** a sudden quick bright light: *We saw a flash of lightning.*
**2** a bright light on a camera, that you use when taking photographs inside a building: *The flash always makes me blink.*
**3 in a flash** = very quickly or suddenly: *It was fun, so the day went by in a flash.*

**ˈflash card** *noun*
a card with a word or picture on it that you use to practice and remember things you are trying to learn

**flash·light** /ˈflæʃlaɪt/ *noun*
a small electric light that you carry in your hand: *He was shining his flashlight on my face.*
→ see picture at **light**

**flash·y** /ˈflæʃi/ *adjective* (*informal*)
flashy clothes, cars, etc. are too big, bright, or expensive, and are intended to make people to notice you: *She wears flashy jewelry.*

**flat¹** /flæt/ *adjective* (**flatter**, **flattest**)
**1** smooth and level, with no slopes or raised parts: *There are no hills in this road; it's flat for the next 50 miles.*

**THESAURUS: flat**

**level** flat, with no part higher than the rest: *Make sure the shelves are level.*

**even** flat, level, and smooth: *The surface has to be even or it's no good for skateboarding.*

**horizontal** a horizontal line goes straight across without sloping up or down: *A horizontal stripe was painted across the wall about halfway up.*

**smooth** having an even surface, without any holes or raised areas: *a smooth round stone | a baby's smooth skin*

**2** a flat tire does not have enough air inside it: *I have to fix the flat tire on my bike before I can ride it again.*
**3** **E flat/B flat, etc.** = a musical note that is slightly lower than E, B, etc., and is shown by the sign (♭)
**4** a drink that is flat has no bubbles in it when it should have bubbles: *This cola is flat.*
—**flatness** *noun* the quality of being flat: *The flatness of the land makes biking easy.*

**flat²** *adverb*
**1** with every part touching a surface, and no parts raised: *He was lying flat on his back looking at the ceiling.*
**2** **in ten seconds/two minutes, etc. flat** (*informal*) = very quickly, in exactly ten seconds, two minutes, etc.: *I was out of the house in 10 minutes flat.*
**3** if you sing or play music flat, you sing or play slightly lower than the correct note
**ANTONYM: sharp**

**flat·ly** /ˈflætli/ *adverb*
in a firm way: *The bank flatly refused to lend him the money.*

**flat·ten** /ˈflætn/ *verb*
to make something flat: *The heavy rain flattened the plants.*

**flat·ter** /ˈflætɚ/ *verb*
**1** **be/feel flattered** = to feel happy because someone likes or admires you: *When they asked me to join their club, I felt flattered.*
**2** to say nice things to someone, sometimes when you do not really mean it: *I flattered her by saying her performance was wonderful.*
—**flattery** *noun* nice things you say when you are flattering someone: *She tried using flattery to get me to do her work.*

**fla·vor¹** /ˈfleɪvɚ/ *noun*
the taste of a food or drink: *The Mexican soup has a spicy flavor. | My favorite flavor of ice cream is chocolate.*
—**flavorful** /ˈfleɪvɚfʊl/ *adjective* having a good strong taste: *a flavorful stew*

**flavor²** *verb*
to give food or drink a particular taste: *He flavored the sauce with lemon and herbs.*

**fla·vor·ing** /ˈfleɪvərɪŋ/ *noun*
a substance used to give food or drink a particular taste: *This yogurt contains no artificial flavorings.*

**flaw** /flɔ/ *noun*
a mark or weakness that stops something from being perfect: *The model plane kept crashing because of a flaw in its design.*
**SYNONYM: weakness**
—**flawed** *adjective* having one or more flaws: *The experiment was flawed and so the results were not correct.*

**flax** /flæks/ *noun*
a plant used for making cloth and oil

**flea** /fli/ *noun*
a very small jumping insect that bites animals to drink their blood: *Their dog has fleas.*

**ˈflea ˌmarket** *noun*
a market where old or used things are sold

**flee** /fli/ *verb* (**fled** /fled/) (*formal*)
to leave a place very quickly in order to escape from danger: *Many people have fled the country since the war started.*

**fleet** /flit/ *noun*
**1** a group of vehicles that are controlled by

one company: *The company owns a fleet of trucks.*

**2** a group of ships: *The navy attacked the enemy fleet.*

[**ORIGIN:** From the old English word *fleot*, which means "ship," from *fleotan*, which means "to float."]

**flesh** /fleʃ/ *noun*

**1** the soft part of a person's or animal's body: *The lion bit into the zebra's flesh.*

**2** the soft part inside a fruit or vegetable: *the sweet yellow flesh of a mango*

**3 in the flesh** = if you see someone in the flesh, you see someone who you have only seen in pictures, in movies, or on television: *I saw Brad Pitt in the flesh, on the street!*

—**fleshy** *adjective* having a lot of fat: *He was a heavy man with fleshy arms and a big stomach.*

**flew** /flu/ *verb*

the past tense of FLY

**flex·i·ble** Ac /ˈfleksəbəl/ *adjective*

**1** able to change easily: *She has flexible work hours, so she can work at times that suit her.*

**2** easy to bend: *Shoes with a flexible rubber sole are comfortable for walking.*

—**flexibility** /ˌfleksəˈbɪləti/ *noun* the quality of being flexible

[**ORIGIN:** 1400-1500 From the Latin word *flexus*, a form of the verb *flectere*, which means "to bend."]

**flick** /flɪk/ *verb*

**1** to move something with a quick movement of your finger: *He flicked the ball of paper into the trash.* → see picture on page **A3**

**2** if you flick a switch, you quickly change its position: *I flicked the switch from "off" to "on."*

—**flick** *noun* a quick movement of your finger or wrist: *I brushed the fly away with a flick of my wrist.*

**flick·er** /ˈflɪkɚ/ *verb*

to burn or shine with a light that is not steady: *The candles flickered in the wind.*

→ see Thesaurus box at **shine**

**fli·er** /ˈflaɪɚ/ *noun*

**1** a sheet of paper advertising something: *They handed out fliers advertising the restaurant to people on the street.*

**2** someone who flies an airplane or travels in an airplane: *He's a nervous flier, so he avoids traveling by plane.*

→ see Thesaurus box at **advertisement**

**flight** /flaɪt/ *noun*

**1** a trip on an airplane, or the airplane making a particular trip: *She was tired after the long flight.* | *When is the next flight to Miami?*

**2** the act of flying through the air: *The book has beautiful photographs of birds in flight.*

**3 a flight of stairs** = a set of stairs between one floor and the next: *I had to walk up six flights of stairs.*

**4 take flight** = to run away: *The robbers took flight when the police arrived.*

**ˈflight atˌtendant** *noun*

someone whose job is to take care of the passengers on a plane

**flim·sy** /ˈflɪmzi/ *adjective*

**1** a flimsy object is not strong or thick: *I was sitting in a flimsy plastic chair, and it broke.*

**2** a flimsy argument or excuse is not good enough to accept or believe: *Martha said she couldn't go, and gave me a flimsy excuse about her dog being sick.*

**fling**[1] /flɪŋ/ *verb* (**flung** /flʌŋ/)

to throw or move something quickly with a lot of force: *He flung the covers back and jumped out of bed.*

→ see Thesaurus box at **throw**[1]

**fling**[2] *noun* (*informal*)

a short romantic relationship that is not serious: *We went out for a few months, but it was just a fling.*

**flip** /flɪp/ *verb* (**flipped**, **flipping**)

**1** (*also* **flip over**) to turn over quickly: *The car went off the road and flipped over.* | *Flip the hamburger over to cook the other side.*

**2** if you flip a switch, you quickly change its position: *I flipped the switch, and the music came on.*

**3 flip a coin** = to throw a coin up in the air, and see which side is showing when it lands. You flip a coin in order to choose something: *We flipped a coin to decide who would start.*

**PHRASAL VERB**

**flip through something**

to look quickly at the pages of a book or magazine: *I flipped through a magazine while I waited for her to get ready.*

F

**flip·per** /ˈflɪpɚ/ *noun*
**1** a sea animal's flippers are the flat parts of its body that it uses to swim: *Seals and whales have flippers.*
**2** a large flat rubber shoe that you wear in order to swim faster

**flirt** /flɚt/ *verb*
to behave as if you are sexually attracted to someone, but not in a serious way: *You were flirting with her at the dance!*
—**flirtatious** /flɚˈteɪʃəs/ *adjective* someone who is flirtatious likes to flirt or flirts a lot

F

**float** /floʊt/ *verb*
**1** to stay on the surface of a liquid: *The tiny boat floated on the pond.* **ANTONYM: sink**
**2** to stay in the air or move slowly through the air: *Her balloon floated up into the sky.*

**flock** /flɑk/ *noun*
a group of sheep, goats, or birds: *A flock of geese was flying south.*
→ see Thesaurus box at **group**[1]
[**ORIGIN:** From the old English word *flocc*, which means "crowd."]

**flood**[1] /flʌd/ *noun*
a very large amount of water that flows onto and covers land that is usually dry: *The floods destroyed many homes.*

**flood**[2] *verb*
**1** to cover an area with water: *The river flooded the fields.* | *The basement flooded, and all our books and clothes got wet.*
**2** **be flooded with something** = to receive so many letters or calls that you cannot deal with them all: *The radio station was flooded with complaints when they changed the type of music they played.*
—**flooding** *noun* a situation in which a place is flooded: *The heavy rain could cause flooding.*

**flood·light** /ˈflʌdlaɪt/ *noun*
a very bright light that is used to light a sports field or the outside of a building at night

**floor** /flɔr/ *noun*
**1** the surface that you stand on in a building: *Don't leave your clothes on the floor.* → see picture on page **A11**

**USAGE: floor, ground**

The **floor** is the surface that you stand on in a building: *There was a thick rug on the floor.*
The **ground** is the surface that you stand on outdoors: *There was snow on the ground.*

**2** one of the levels in a building: *We live on the third floor of our apartment building.*

**floor·board** /ˈflɔrbɔrd/ *noun*
a long flat piece of wood that is part of a floor: *The old floorboards made a noise when I stepped on them.*

**flop** /flɑp/ *verb* (**flopped**, **flopping**)
**1** to sit down or fall in a loose heavy way: *I was so tired that I flopped onto the bed and fell asleep right away.*
**2** (*informal*) if a play, movie, or product flops, it is not successful: *The movie flopped, and the producers lost a lot of money.*
—**flop** *noun* (*informal*) something that is not successful: *The play was a flop; audiences hated it.*

**flop·py** /ˈflɑpi/ *adjective*
soft and hanging loosely down: *The dog had long floppy ears.*

**flo·ral** /ˈflɔrəl/ *adjective* (*formal*)
made of flowers or decorated with pictures of flowers: *The dress had a pretty floral pattern.*

**flo·rist** /ˈflɔrɪst/ *noun*
someone who works in a store that sells flowers → see picture on page **A17**

**floss** /flɔs/ *verb*
to clean between your teeth with special string: *I floss regularly.*
—**floss** (*also* **dental floss**) *noun* special string that you use to clean between your teeth

**floun·der** /ˈflaʊndɚ/ *noun*
a flat ocean fish, or the meat from this fish

**flour** /flaʊɚ/ *noun*
a powder made from wheat, that is used to make bread, cookies, and cakes
[**ORIGIN:** From an old meaning of "flower" - "the best part of something." Flour is the best part of crushed wheat. "Flour" became the spelling in about 1830.]

**flour·ish** /ˈflɚɪʃ/ *verb* (*formal*)
to grow well or to develop and be successful: *These plants flourish in damp soil.* | *His business flourished and he became a rich man.*
[**ORIGIN:** 1200-1300 From the Latin word *florere*, which means "to produce flowers," from *flos*, the word for "flower."]

**flow¹** /floʊ/ *verb*
if a liquid flows, it moves along steadily: *The river flows through a wide valley to the ocean.*
→ see Thesaurus box at **pour**

**flow²** *noun*
a steady movement of liquid: *Doctors tried to stop the flow of blood from her leg.*

**ˈflow chart** *noun*
a drawing that uses shapes and ARROWs to show how the parts of a process are connected to each other: *The flow chart shows how clouds, rain, and water are connected.*

**flow·er** /ˈflaʊɚ/ *noun*
**1** a pretty colored part on a plant: *This plant has yellow flowers in the spring.*
**2** a small plant that produces flowers: *I planted these flowers myself.*
—**flower** *verb* (*formal*) to produce flowers: *The plant flowers in early summer.*
—**flowered** *adjective* decorated with pictures of flowers: *flowered wallpaper*

**flow·er·bed** /ˈflaʊɚˌbed/ *noun*
a garden area in which flowers are grown

**flown** /floʊn/ *verb*
the past participle of FLY

**flu** /flu/ *noun*
an illness that is like a bad cold but is more serious. The flu gives you a fever and makes you feel very tired and weak: *If you have the flu, stay in bed and drink plenty of water.*

**fluc·tu·ate** Ac /ˈflʌktʃuˌeɪt/ *verb*
if an amount or number fluctuates, it goes up and down more than once: *Her weight fluctuated between 120 and 150 pounds.*
—**fluctuation** /ˌflʌktʃuˈeɪʃən/ *noun* a change up and down: *Fluctuations in temperature will harm the plant.*
[**ORIGIN:** 1600-1700 From the Latin word *fluctuare*, which means "to move like waves."]

**flu·ent** /ˈfluənt/ *adjective*
able to speak a language or read well: *She is fluent in French.* | *He spoke fluent English.*
—**fluently** *adverb* in a fluent way: *She speaks Spanish fluently.*
—**fluency** *noun* the ability to speak a language or read very well
[**ORIGIN:** 1500-1600 From the Latin word *fluere*, which means "to flow." If you speak a language well, the words come out of your mouth smoothly, like water flowing.]

**fluff** /flʌf/ *noun*
soft light pieces that come off wool, fur, etc.: *There's a piece of fluff on your skirt.*

**fluff·y** /ˈflʌfi/ *adjective*
soft and light, or with soft fur: *a fluffy baby rabbit*

**flu·id** /ˈfluɪd/ *noun* (*formal*)
a liquid: *My doctor told me to drink lots of fluids to help me get better.*
—**fluid** *adjective* able to flow or move like a liquid

**ˌfluid ˈounce** *noun*
a unit for measuring liquids, equal to 1/16 of a PINT or 0.0296 liters

**flung** /flʌŋ/ *verb*
the past tense and past participle of FLING

**flunk** /flʌŋk/ *verb* (*informal*)
to fail a test or class: *I flunked my history exam because I didn't study at all.*
**PHRASAL VERB**
**flunk out** (*informal*)
to have to leave a college because your work is not good enough: *He flunked out of college and had to find a job.*

**fluo·res·cent** /flʊˈresənt/ *adjective*
**1** a fluorescent light is a very bright electric light, produced in a glass tube filled with gas
**2** fluorescent colors are very bright: *The workers wear fluorescent yellow jackets so that car drivers can see them easily.*

**fluor·ide** /ˈflɔraɪd/ *noun*
a chemical that helps to protect your teeth from decay, that is put in TOOTHPASTE and sometimes in water

**flur·ry** /ˈflɚi/ *noun* (plural **flurries**)
**1** a sudden increase in activity for a short time: *There was a flurry of activity as we got ready for the party to start.*

2 a small amount of snow that falls and blows around: *There were snow flurries, but the snow didn't even stick to the ground.*

**flush** /flʌʃ/ *verb*
1 if you flush a toilet, you make water go through it to clean it
2 (*formal*) if you flush, your face becomes red because you are embarrassed or angry: *She felt her cheeks flush with embarrassment.*

**flushed** /flʌʃt/ *adjective*
if someone's face is flushed, it is red: *His face was flushed because he had been running.*

F

**flus·tered** /ˈflʌstɚd/ *adjective*
feeling nervous and confused: *She got flustered and forgot what she wanted to say.*

**flute** /flut/ *noun*
a musical instrument like a pipe that you hold across your lips and blow → see picture on page A21
—**flutist** *noun* someone who plays the flute

**flut·ter** /ˈflʌtɚ/ *verb*
1 to make small movements in the air: *The flags fluttered in the wind.*
2 if a small bird or an insect flutters somewhere, it flies there: *Butterflies fluttered over the fields.*

**fly**[1] /flaɪ/ *verb* (**flew** /flu/, **flown** /floʊn/, **flies**)
1 to move through the air: *The bird flew away.*
2 to travel by airplane: *We flew to Phoenix, Arizona to visit my family.*
3 to control an airplane: *Kathy is learning to fly a plane.*
4 if a flag is flying, it is being shown on a pole
5 to suddenly move very quickly: *I flew down the stairs to see what was making the noise.*

**WORD FAMILY: fly**
**fly** *verb* | **flight** *noun*

**fly**[2] *noun* (plural **flies**)
1 a common small flying insect: *There were flies all over the food.*
2 the part at the front of a pair of pants that you can open: *Your fly is unzipped.*

**fly·er** /ˈflaɪɚ/ *noun*
another spelling of FLIER

**ˌflying ˈsaucer** *noun*
a spacecraft shaped like a plate, which comes from another PLANET. Some people believe they have seen flying saucers. **SYNONYM: UFO**

**foal** /foʊl/ *noun*
a very young horse

**foam** /foʊm/ *noun*
1 a lot of very small bubbles on the top of a liquid: *The soap bubbles made a white foam in the sink.*
2 a very light but solid substance that changes shape easily when it is pressed: *a foam mattress* | *The box has foam inside to keep the glasses from breaking.*

**fo·cus**[1] [Ac] /ˈfoʊkəs/ *verb*
1 to give your attention to a particular thing: *You need to focus on your schoolwork, and not watch so much TV.*
2 to move part of a camera, TELESCOPE, etc. so that you can see something clearly: *She focused the camera on the baby's face.*
3 if your eyes focus, you start seeing clearly: *I tried to read the sign, but my eyes would not focus because I was so tired.*
—**focused** *adjective* giving your attention to a particular thing: *If we don't stay focused, we could lose this game.*
[**ORIGIN:** 1600-1700 From the Latin word for "fireplace." It is not known why this word has its modern meanings, but it may be because the fireplace was what people gave most attention to in a house.]

**focus**[2] [Ac] *noun*
1 the thing that is given most attention: *The focus of this book is the history of the city.*
2 attention that you give to a particular thing: *At the kids' club, the focus is on fun.*
3 **in focus/out of focus** = if a photograph or something seen through a TELESCOPE is in focus, it is clear and easy to see. If it is out of focus, it is not clear.

**foe** /foʊ/ *noun* (*formal*)
an enemy: *He finally defeated his old foe.* **ANTONYMS: ally, friend**

**fog** /fɑg/ *noun*
cloudy air near the ground that is difficult to see through: *We got lost in the thick fog.*
—**foggy** *adjective* if it is foggy, there is fog in

the air: *People were driving slowly because it was foggy.*

**foil** /fɔɪl/ *noun*
very thin metal, used for covering food: *Cover the pan with aluminum foil, and put it in the oven.*

**fold[1]** /fould/ *verb*
**1** to bend a piece of paper or cloth so that one part covers another part: *Could you fold those towels for me? | Fold the paper in half.*
**2** (*also* **fold up**) to make something such as a table smaller by bending parts of it: *Fold up the ironing board when you are done.*
**3 fold your arms** = to bend your arms so that they are resting across your chest, with one arm crossing the other
—**folding** *adjective* able to be folded: *The group sat on metal folding chairs in the middle of the room.*

**fold[2]** *noun*
a line or area where paper or cloth is bent: *Make a fold in the paper, and cut along it.*

**fold·er** /ˈfouldɚ/ *noun*
**1** a large folded piece of strong paper, in which you keep documents: *Put all your homework in this folder and put it in your backpack.* → see picture on page **A18**
**2** a group of FILEs that are stored together on a computer: *You can move files from one folder to another.*

**fo·li·age** /ˈfouli-ɪdʒ/ *noun* (*formal*)
the leaves of a plant or tree: *This bush has dark green foliage.*
**[ORIGIN:** 1400-1500 From the Latin word *folium*, which means "leaf."**]**

**folk** /fouk/ *adjective*
traditional and done by the ordinary people who live in a country: *a folk song | He read her a story from a book of Russian folk tales.*
**[ORIGIN:** From the old English word *folc*.**]**

**folk·lore** /ˈfouk-lɔr/ *noun*
the stories, beliefs, and customs that the ordinary people in a country pass along to their children: *American folklore is full of stories about people who cross the wilderness to make a new life for themselves.*

**folks** /fouks/ *plural noun* (*informal*)
**1** people in general: *Some folks might not like the idea.*
**2** your parents: *Have you told your folks that you're getting married?*

**ˈfolk tale** *noun*
a very old story that people tell their children: *"The Little Red Hen" is a folk tale that teaches us about helping other people.*

**fol·low** /ˈfɑlou/ *verb*
**1** to move along behind someone else: *I followed him up the steps. | The patrol car followed the speeding car for several miles.*
**2** to happen immediately after something else: *I heard a yell, followed by a loud crash.*
**3** to continue on a road, or go in the same direction as a river: *Follow this road to the coast.*
**4** to do what a person, rule, or instruction tells you to do: *Follow the safety rules when doing science experiments at school. | I followed my dad's advice, and put my money in the bank.*
**5** to understand something such as an explanation or story: *The movie was hard to follow because the plot was so complicated.*
**6** to do what someone else has already done: *He followed in his father's footsteps and became a doctor.*

**PHRASAL VERBS**

**follow through**
to do what you have promised to do or started doing: *He followed through on his promise and quit smoking.*

**follow (something) up**
to find out more about something, or to do more about something: *The students should follow up on what they have learned in class by looking on the Internet.*

**fol·low·er** /ˈfɑlouɚ/ *noun*
someone who believes in someone's ideas or supports them: *Buddha told his followers to help others.*

**fol·low·ing[1]** /ˈfɑlouɪŋ/ *adjective*
**the following day/year/afternoon, etc.** = the next day, year, etc.: *I was born in 1992, and my sister was born the following year.*

**following[2]** *preposition*
after something or as a result of something: *He missed three games following the injury to his leg.*

**fond** /fɑnd/ *adjective*
**be fond of someone or something** = to like

someone or something: *She was very fond of her aunt.*
—**fondly** *adverb* in a way that shows that you like someone or something
—**fondness** *noun* love for a person or thing: *She has a special fondness for cats.*
[ORIGIN: From the old English word *fonne*, which means "silly person." "Fond" used to mean "silly," and then meant "liking someone too much, in a silly way." First used with its modern meaning, 1300-1400.]

**food** /fud/ *noun*
things that people, animals, and plants eat: *We went to the grocery store to buy food.* | *I love Chinese food.* | *dog food*
[ORIGIN: From the old English word *foda*.]

**food chain**

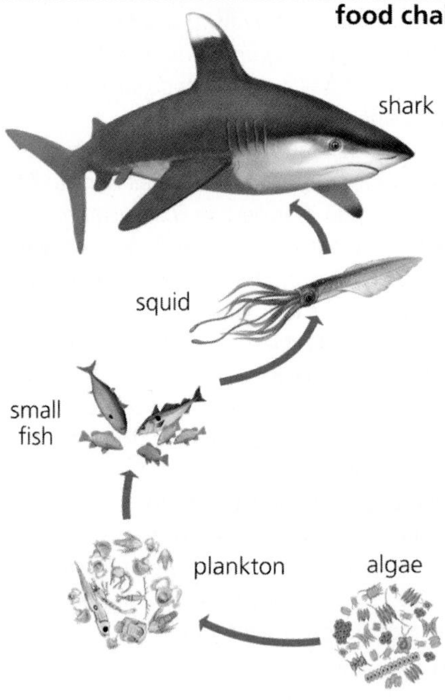


**ˈfood chain** *noun*
a food chain shows which animals eat other animals or plants. For example, a FOX eats rabbits and rabbits eat grass, so the food chain is grass → rabbits → fox.

**ˈfood ˌprocessor** *noun*
a piece of electrical equipment that cuts or mixes food very quickly

**ˈfood stamps** *plural noun*
special pieces of paper that the U.S. government gives to poor people so that they can buy food

**ˈfood web** *noun*
a food web shows how animals and plants are connected by what they eat. For example, a tree has seeds that mice, birds, and insects eat. The birds also eat the insects and some birds and animals eat the mice.

**fool[1]** /ful/ *noun*
**1** a stupid person: *Don't be a fool – it's a great job, so take it.* SYNONYM: **idiot**
**2 make a fool of yourself** = to do something silly or embarrassing, which other people can see: *I don't dance at parties because I don't want to make a fool of myself.*
[ORIGIN: 1200-1300 From the Latin word *follis*, which first meant "bag for blowing air, or ball full of air," and later meant "empty-headed person."]

**fool[2]** *verb*
to make someone believe something that is not true: *She fooled her parents into thinking she was sick.*
PHRASAL VERB
**fool around**
**1** to spend time having fun: *We spent the day fooling around at the beach.*
**2** to behave in a silly way or waste time: *Stop fooling around and start studying!*

**fool·ish** /ˈfulɪʃ/ *adjective*
silly or not sensible: *It's foolish to go to school if the doctor told you to stay home.* SYNONYM: **stupid**
—**foolishly** *adverb* in a foolish way: *She foolishly agreed to lend him some money.*
—**foolishness** *noun* foolish behavior

**WORD FAMILY: foolish**
**foolish** *adjective* | **foolishly** *adverb* | **foolishness** *noun* | **fool** *noun* | **fool** *verb*

**fool·proof** /ˈfulpruːf/ *adjective*
a foolproof idea is sure to be successful: *This plan is foolproof. There's no way we can fail.*

**foot** /fʊt/ *noun*
**1** (plural **feet** /fit/) the part of your body at the end of your leg, which you stand on: *My brother has big feet.* | *Waitresses are on their feet all day at work.*
**2** (plural **feet** *or* **foot**) (*abbreviation:* **ft.**) a length equal to 12 inches or 30.5 centimeters, used for measuring things: *Craig is six feet tall.*
**3 on foot** = if you go somewhere on foot,

you walk there: *We parked at the edge of the forest and went the rest of the way on foot.*
4 **the foot of something** = the bottom of something tall or high such as a mountain, tree, or set of stairs: *They camped at the foot of the mountain.*
5 **put your foot down** = to say very firmly what someone must do or must not do: *My mother put her foot down and said I could not go.*
6 **get/rise/jump, etc. to your feet** = to stand up after you have been sitting
7 **set foot in something** = to go into a place: *I left home to go to college, and I never set foot in that town again.*

**foot·ball** /ˈfʊtbɔl/ *noun*
1 a game in which two teams of 11 players throw, catch, and run with a ball toward the area at the end of field, in order to win points: *I'm going to a football game tonight.* → see picture on page **A24**
2 the ball that you use in this game

**foot·print** /ˈfʊtˌprɪnt/ *noun*
a mark made by a foot or shoe: *There were footprints in the snow.* → see picture at **fingerprint**

**foot·step** /ˈfʊtstep/ *noun*
the sound of each step when someone is walking: *I heard footsteps behind me.*

**foot·wear** /ˈfʊtwer/ *noun* (*formal*)
things such as shoes or boots that you wear on your feet: *Choose comfortable footwear for hiking.*

**for¹** /fɚ; *strong* fɔr/ *preposition*
1 intended to be given to someone or used by someone: *I have a present for you.* | *It's a movie for kids, not adults.*
2 with a particular purpose: *Do you have a knife for cutting bread?* | *They had to fight for their freedom.* | *What did you do that for?*
3 used when saying how long something continues or lasts: *I've known her for five years.*

**USAGE: for, since, ago**

**For**, **since**, and **ago** are all used to talk about time.

**For** is used to say how long a situation or activity has lasted. You use **for** before the amount of time: *My aunt has been here for three days.*

**Since** is used to say when something started. You use **since** before a day, date, or time: *He's been sick since Sunday.* | *I've been going to school here since 2010.*

**Ago** is used to say how far back in the past something happened. You use **ago** after the amount of time: *My grandfather died two years ago.*

4 in order to help someone: *Let me lift that box for you.*
5 because of something or as a result of something: *He got a ticket for speeding.*
6 used when saying where a person or vehicle is going: *She was just leaving for school when the phone rang.*
7 used when saying how far someone or something goes: *We walked for 6 miles.*
8 used when talking about the price of something: *I got this jacket for $70.*
9 used when saying what you eat at a meal: *We had steak for dinner last night.* | *"What's for lunch?" "Pasta."*
10 used when saying that someone is part of a team or company: *He used to play for the Boston Red Sox.* | *My brother works for a software company.*
11 used when saying that you support someone or something: *Who did you vote for in the election?* **ANTONYM: against**
12 with a particular meaning: *What's the Spanish word for "oil?"*

**for²** *conjunction* (*formal*)
because: *We left quickly, for we knew we were in great danger.*

**for·bid** /fɚˈbɪd/ *verb* (**forbade** /fɚˈbæd/, **forbidden** /fɚˈbɪdn/) (*formal*)
to order someone not to do something: *I forbid you to see him again.* **ANTONYM: permit**
—**forbidden** *adjective* not allowed: *Alcohol is forbidden for Muslims.*

**THESAURUS: forbid**

**not allow, not permit, not let** to say that someone must not do something, and stop him or her doing it: *His parents don't allow* *him to go out on school nights. | Smoking is not permitted inside the hospital.*

**ban** to say officially that people must not do something or that something is not allowed: *Fires are banned in the campground.*

**prohibit** (*formal*) if something is prohibited, a law or rule does not allow it: *The law prohibits people from owning these rare birds as pets.*

**bar** to officially stop someone from doing something: *Reporters were barred from the courtroom.*

F

**force[1]** /fɔrs/ *verb*

**1** to make someone do something that he or she does not want to do: *You can't force me to be a doctor if I don't want to be one.*

**THESAURUS: force**

**make** to force someone to do something: *You can't make her come if she doesn't want to.*

**coerce** (*formal*) to make someone do something by threatening to hurt or punish that person if he or she does not do it: *He claims that the police coerced him into saying that he committed the crime.*

**compel** (*formal*) to force someone to do something: *The law will compel employers to provide health insurance.*

**pressure** to try to make someone feel that he or she must do something, when he or she does not really want to: *Don't let your friends pressure you into trying alcohol.*

**2** to use your strength to move something: *The police had to force open the door.*

**force[2]** *noun*

**1** a group of people who do military or police work: *The U.S. is withdrawing its military forces.*

**2** violence that someone uses to achieve something: *The government says it will use force to stop the protesters.*

**3** the physical power that something has: *The force of the explosion threw me to the ground. | Waves were hitting the rocks with great force.*

**4** something that moves things or has an effect on them, although it cannot be seen: *The force of gravity pulls everything downward.*

**5** **join forces** = if people join forces, they start working together: *Several groups have joined forces to raise money for the charity.*

**6** **in force** = if a law or rule is in force, it exists and must be obeyed

[**ORIGIN:** 1200-1300 From the Latin word *fortis*, which means "strong."]

**WORD FAMILY: force**

**force** *noun* | **force** *verb* | **forceful** *adjective* | **forcefully** *adverb*

**forced** /fɔrst/ *adjective*

**1** not natural or sincere: *She had a forced smile on her face, but she wasn't happy.*

**2** done suddenly and quickly because a situation makes it necessary: *The plane lost power and had to make a forced landing in a field.*

**force·ful** /ˈfɔrsfəl/ *adjective*

powerful and strong: *She had a forceful way of speaking that convinced people to do things.*

—**forcefully** *adverb* in a powerful way: *He argued forcefully against the plan.*

**ford** /fɔrd/ *noun*

a place where a river is not deep, so that you can cross it without a bridge: *The horses and wagons crossed the ford in the river.*

**fore·arm** /ˈfɔrɑrm/ *noun*

the part of your arm between your hand and your elbow → see picture on page **A2**

**fore·cast** /ˈfɔrkæst/ *noun*

a description of what is likely to happen: *The weather forecast said that it would be sunny.*

—**forecast** *verb* to say what is likely to happen: *They are forecasting that the summer will be very dry.*

**fore·fa·thers** /ˈfɔrˌfɑðɚz/ *plural noun* (*formal*)

**1** the members of your family who lived a long time ago: *Our forefathers fished in these lakes five hundred years ago.* **SYNONYM: ancestors**

**2** the people in the past who helped to start something such as a country or religion: *Our* *nation's forefathers wrote the constitution that we use today.*

**fore·front** /ˈfɔrfrʌnt/ *noun*
**in/at the forefront of something** = doing the most or doing the newest things in an area of activity: *Scientists at the university are at the forefront of research into the disease.*

**fore·head** /ˈfɔrhed/ *noun*
the part of your face above your eyes: *He wiped the sweat from his forehead.* → see picture on page **A2**

**for·eign** /ˈfɑrɪn/ *adjective*
from or relating to a country that is not your own: *Can you speak a foreign language?*
[**ORIGIN:** 1200-1300 From the old French word *forein*, from the Latin word *foris*, which means "outside."]

**for·eign·er** /ˈfɑrənɚ/ *noun*
someone who comes from a country that is not your country

**fore·man** /ˈfɔrmən/ *noun* (plural **foremen** /ˈfɔrmən/)
**1** someone who is in charge of a group of workers: *The factory foreman has twenty people working under him.*
**2** the leader of a JURY: *The foreman of the jury said, "We find the defendant not guilty."*

**fore·most** /ˈfɔrmoʊst/ *adjective* (*formal*)
the best or most important: *The country's foremost writers came to the White House for a special dinner.*

**fore·see** /fɔrˈsi/ *verb* (**foresaw** /fɔrˈsɔ/, **foreseen** /fɔrˈsin/) (*formal*)
to know that something will happen in the future: *He foresaw the war that began two years later.* **SYNONYM: predict**

**for·est** /ˈfɔrɪst/ *noun*
a large area of land covered with trees: *The animal lives in trees in the forest.* **SYNONYM: woods**
→ see Thesaurus box at **tree**
[**ORIGIN:** 1200-1300 From the Latin word *foris*, which means "outside." The forest was outside the main fenced area of woods.]

**for·ev·er** /fəˈrevɚ/ *adverb*
**1** for all of the future: *You can't live forever.* | *I wanted the vacation to last forever.* **SYNONYM: always**
**2** (*informal*) a very long time: *It'll take forever to walk to Amy's house.*
**3 go on forever** (*informal*) = to be extremely long or large: *The road seemed to go on forever.*
→ see Thesaurus box at **always**

**fore·word** /ˈfɔrwɚd/ *noun*
a short piece of writing at the beginning of a book that gives information about the book or its writer

**for·gave** /fɚˈgeɪv/ *verb*
the past tense of FORGIVE

**forge** /fɔrdʒ/ *verb*
to illegally copy a document, a painting, or paper money in order to make people think it is real: *He was arrested for using a forged passport to try to get into the country.*
—**forger** *noun* someone who illegally copies documents, paintings, or paper money

**WORD FAMILY: forge**
**forge** *verb* | **forgery** *noun* | **forger** *noun*

**for·ger·y** /ˈfɔrdʒəri/ *noun* (plural **forgeries**)
**1** a document, painting, or piece of paper money that someone has illegally copied: *The police discovered that her passport was a forgery and arrested her.* **SYNONYM: fake**
**2** the crime of illegally copying something

**for·get** /fɚˈget/ *verb* (**forgot** /fɚˈgɑt/, **forgotten** /fɚˈgɑtn/, **forgetting**)
**1** to not be able to remember a fact or something that happened: *I forgot where I hid the money, and couldn't find it.* | *I've forgotten her name – do you know it?*
**2** to not remember to do something that you should do: *I forgot to lock the door.*
**3** to not remember to bring something with you: *I forgot my book. I left it in my room.*

**USAGE: forget, leave**
You can say "I forgot my homework."
You cannot say "I forgot my homework at home."
When you want to say where you left something by mistake, you must use **leave**: *I left my homework at home.*

**4** to stop thinking or worrying about someone or something: *When I listen to music, I forget about my problems.*
**5 forget it** (*informal*) = **a)** used in order to

tell someone that something is not important: *"I'm sorry, I shouldn't have yelled at you." "Forget it."* **b)** used in order to tell someone to stop asking or talking about something because it is annoying you: *I'm not buying you that bike, so just forget it.*

**WORD FAMILY: forget**

**forget** *verb* | **forgetful** *adjective* | **forgetfulness** *noun*

**for·get·ful** /fɚˈgetfəl/ *adjective*
if you are forgetful, you often forget things that you should remember: *Many old people become forgetful.*
—**forgetfulness** *noun* forgetful behavior

F

**for·give** /fɚˈgɪv/ *verb* (**forgave** /fɚˈgeɪv/, **forgiven** /fɚˈgɪvən/)
to stop being angry with someone who has done something wrong: *I can't forgive him for the terrible things he said.*
—**forgiveness** *noun* the act of forgiving someone: *He was really sorry for what he'd done and asked for forgiveness.*

**fork¹** /fɔrk/ *noun*
**1** a small tool with points at the end that you use for picking up food when you eat: *He picked up a piece of meat with his fork.* → see picture on page **A9**
**2** a place where a road or river divides into two parts: *Go left when you come to the fork in the road.*

**fork²** *verb*
if a road or river forks, it divides into two parts: *When the road forks, follow the signs for Newark.*

**forked** /fɔrkt/ *adjective*
divided at the end, in the shape of a letter "y": *The snake has a forked tongue.*

**form¹** /fɔrm/ *noun*
**1** one type of something: *You'll need two forms of ID, like a passport and a driver's license.* **SYNONYM: kind**
**2** the way in which something exists or appears: *The data on a computer is stored in digital form.*
**3** an official document with spaces where you have to write information: *Please fill out the form in black ink.* | *a job application form*
**4** (*formal*) a shape: *The dark form in the trees was a bear.*

**form²** *verb*
**1** to start to exist: *Winter is coming, and ice is forming on the lake.* **SYNONYM: develop**
**2** to make a particular shape: *He formed a circle with his thumb and finger.*
**3** to start a new organization or group: *We formed the company back in 1990.* **SYNONYM: create**
**4** to make something by combining two or more parts: *You can form an adverb by adding "ly" to the end of an adjective.*
**5** to be part of something: *Rice forms a basic part of Chinese meals.*

**for·mal** /ˈfɔrməl/ *adjective*
**1** formal language, clothes, or behavior are used in important or official situations: *Use formal language in your school essays, not slang.* **ANTONYM: informal**
**2** a formal occasion is an important event, such as a wedding or a GRADUATION ceremony: *The dinner was a formal occasion, so everyone was wearing their best clothes.*
**3** official and public: *The head of the company made a formal announcement that he was going to resign.* **ANTONYM: informal**
**4 formal education/training/qualifications** = education in a subject or skill, that you receive in school, not from experience
—**formally** *adverb* in a formal way: *The winner of the competition will be formally announced this afternoon.*

**WORD FAMILY: formal**

**formal** *adjective* | **informal** *adjective* | **formally** *adverb* | **informally** *adverb* | **formality** *noun* | **informality** *noun*

**for·mal·i·ty** /fɔrˈmæləti/ *noun* (plural **formalities**)
something that you must do as part of an official activity: *The agreement has been made, so your signature on it is a formality.*

**for·mat** Ac /ˈfɔrmæt/ *noun*
the way in which something is organized or arranged: *The talk show is a popular format on daytime TV.* | *The interview was written in a question-and-answer format.*
[**ORIGIN:** 1800-1900 From the Latin word *formare*, which means "to form."]

**for·ma·tion** /fɔrˈmeɪʃən/ *noun*
**1** the process of making a new organization: *I was involved in the formation of the club.*
**2** something that has been formed into a particular shape: *The rock formations in the desert were beautiful.*

**for·mer¹** /ˈfɔrmɚ/ *adjective*
**1** having a particular job or position in the past, but not now: *Two former U.S. presidents, Bill Clinton and George W. Bush, were at the ceremony.*
**2** existing in the past, but not now: *The Ukraine was part of the former Soviet Union.*

**former²** *noun*
**the former** (*formal*) = the first of two people or things that are mentioned: *She likes both the red dress and the blue one, but the former costs $125 and the latter $85.*
**ANTONYM: latter**

**for·mer·ly** /ˈfɔrmɚli/ *adverb*
in the past, not now: *New York was formerly called New Amsterdam.*

**for·mi·da·ble** /ˈfɔrmədəbəl/ *adjective*
**1** very difficult to deal with and needing a lot of effort or skill: *Firefighters faced formidable problems putting out the blaze.*
**2** very powerful or impressive: *He is a player with formidable talents.*

**for·mu·la** [Ac] /ˈfɔrmyələ/ *noun* (plural **formulas** *or* **formulae** /-li/)
**1** a series of numbers or letters that represent a mathematical or scientific rule: *The formula for figuring out the perimeter of a rectangle is P = 2L + 2W, where P is the perimeter, L is the length, and W is the width.*
**2** a liquid food for babies that is similar to a mother's milk: *She gave the baby formula in a bottle.*
[**ORIGIN:** 1600-1700 From the Latin word for "small mold, or rule to follow."]

**fort** /fɔrt/ *noun*
**1** a strong building used by soldiers for defending an important place: *The soldiers were in a fort on the hill.*
**2** a place where an army lives and trains
[**ORIGIN:** 1400-1500 From the Latin word *fortis*, which means "strong."]

**forth** /fɔrθ/ *adverb* (*formal*)
toward a place that is in front of you: *The soldiers went forth into battle.*
→ **back and forth** at **back¹**

**for·tress** /ˈfɔrtrɪs/ *noun*
a large strong building that soldiers use for defending an important place

**for·tu·nate** /ˈfɔrtʃənət/ *adjective* (*formal*)
in a good situation because of luck: *It's fortunate that we arrived before it started snowing.*
**SYNONYM: lucky; ANTONYM: unfortunate**

**WORD FAMILY: fortunate**
**fortunate** *adjective* | **unfortunate** *adjective* | **fortunately** *adverb* | **unfortunately** *adverb* | **fortune** *noun* | **misfortune** *noun*

**for·tu·nate·ly** /ˈfɔrtʃənətli/ *adverb*
happening because of good luck: *We got stuck in traffic on the way to the airport, but fortunately we didn't miss our flight.*
**ANTONYM: unfortunately**

**for·tune** /ˈfɔrtʃən/ *noun*
**1** a very large amount of money: *It cost Jim a fortune to get the car fixed.*
**2** luck: *I had the good fortune to find a job as soon as I got to St. Louis.*
**3** the good or bad things that happen to you: *A year later, his fortunes changed when he met Karen.*
**4 tell someone's fortune** = to tell someone what will happen to him or her in the future, for example by using special cards

**ˈfortune ˌteller** *noun*
someone who uses special cards or looks at your hands in order to tell you what is going to happen to you in the future

**for·ty** /ˈfɔrti/ *number*
**1** 40: *The shoes cost forty dollars.*
**2** forty years old: *He will be forty next July.*
**3 the forties** (*also* **the '40s**) = the years between 1940 and 1949: *My grandfather came to live here in the forties.*
**4 in your forties** = between 40 and 49 years old: *Police are looking for a tall man in his forties.*
**5 in the forties** = between 40 and 49

F

degrees FAHRENHEIT in temperature: *Night-time temperatures are in the forties, so bring a warm jacket.*
—**fortieth** *number* 40th or 1/40

**fo·rum** /ˈfɔrəm/ *noun*
a place or meeting where people can discuss things: *Is there a forum on the Internet where you can get advice about keeping pets?*

**for·ward¹** /ˈfɔrwəd/ *adverb*
**1** (*also* **forwards**) toward a place that is in front of you: *When the gates opened, the crowd moved forward into the stadium.*
**ANTONYM: backward**
**2** toward a situation that develops and becomes better: *You have to forget about the mistakes you made and move forward.*
→ **look forward to something** at **look¹**

**forward²** *adjective*
**1** toward a place that is in front of you: *The bus jolted into slow forward movement.*
**2 forward thinking/planning** = plans or ideas that help you to prepare for the future: *If we do some forward planning now, we will be ready if an emergency happens.*

**forward³** *verb*
to send a letter or email that has been sent to you to another person: *I'll forward the email I got from Kristen to you.*

**forward⁴** *noun*
a player on some sports teams such as basketball whose job is to score points or goals

**fossil**

**fos·sil** /ˈfɑsəl/ *noun*
a rock that shows part of an animal or plant that lived thousands or millions of years ago: *Scientists found fossils of dinosaurs in the rocks.*
[**ORIGIN:** 1500-1600 From the Latin word *fossilis*, which means "dug up."]

**ˈfossil ˌfuel** *noun*
a substance such as coal, gas, or oil that can be burned for energy. Fossil fuels are formed from plants and animals that died millions of years ago.

**fos·ter¹** /ˈfɑstə/ *verb*
to take care of someone else's child for a period of time, without becoming the child's legal parent: *The girls were fostered from the age of six.*

**foster²** *adjective*
relating to an arrangement in which a child is taken care of by someone who is not his or her parent: *He lived with foster parents for three years before he was adopted.*

**fought** /fɔt/ *verb*
the past tense and past participle of FIGHT

**foul¹** /faʊl/ *adjective*
**1** tasting or smelling very unpleasant: *A foul smell was coming from the garbage.*
**2 foul language** = rude and offensive words: *Students are not allowed to use foul language in class.*
**3** relating to an action in a sport that is not allowed by the rules: *He hit two foul balls before striking out.*
**4 foul weather** = bad weather, with strong winds, rain, or snow: *We canceled the trip because of the foul weather.*
**5 in a foul mood** = in a very bad mood and likely to get angry: *I was in a foul mood and didn't want to talk to anyone.*

**foul²** *noun*
an action in a sport that is not allowed by the rules: *Jess pushed another player, and the referee called a foul.*

**foul³** *verb*
to do something that is not allowed by the rules of a sport: *He turned to shoot the ball, and Bailey fouled him.*

**found¹** Ac /faʊnd/ *verb*
the past tense and past participle of FIND

**found²** Ac *verb*
to start a business, organization, or school: *The college was founded in 1701.*
[**ORIGIN:** 1300-1400 From the old French word *fonder*, from the Latin word *fundus*, which means "bottom." The idea is of putting the bottom part of something in place, so that you can build the rest of it.]

**foun·da·tion** Ac /faʊnˈdeɪʃən/ *noun*
**1** a solid base that is built below the ground

to support the building that is on top of it: *The men were laying the foundation for a new office building.*

**2** an important basic idea, fact, or system that something is based on or develops from: *Elementary school gives students a foundation in reading, writing, and math.*

**3** an organization that gives money to be used for special purposes: *The foundation that Bill Gates started has helped improve health care for children in India.*

**found·er** [Ac] /ˈfaʊndɚ/ *noun*
someone who starts a business, organization, or school

**foun·tain** /ˈfaʊntən/ *noun*

**1** an object that makes water go up into the air or pour down its sides, and is used as a decoration outside: *There is a big fountain in the middle of the park.*

**2** an object that you drink from by putting your mouth over the stream of water that comes up: *You can get a drink from the water fountain in the hall.*

[**ORIGIN:** 1300-1400 From the Latin word *fontana*, from *fons*, which means "place where water comes out of the ground."]

**four** /fɔr/ *number*

**1** 4: *Our house has four bedrooms.* | *She is going to meet four of her friends at the mall.*

**2** four O'CLOCK: *I'll meet you at four.*

**3** four years old: *She'll be four next week.*

**four·teen** /ˌfɔrˈtin/ *number*

**1** 14: *The journey took fourteen hours.*

**2** fourteen years old: *She is fourteen and in 9th grade.*

—**fourteenth** *number* 14th or 1/14

**fourth** /fɔrθ/ *number, noun*

**1** 4th

**2** 1/4 **SYNONYM: quarter**

**ˌFourth of Juˈly** *noun*
a national holiday in the U.S. to celebrate the time when the U.S. first became an independent nation **SYNONYM: Independence Day**

**fowl** /faʊl/ *noun* (plural **fowl** *or* **fowls**)
a bird such as a chicken or a TURKEY that is used as food

**fox** /fɑks/ *noun*
a wild animal like a small dog with dark red fur and a thick tail

**foy·er** /ˈfɔɪɚ/ *noun*
a room at the entrance of a house or large public building such as a hotel or theater

**frac·tion** /ˈfrækʃən/ *noun*

**1** a number that is smaller than 1, for example 3/4 or 1/2, and that shows you how many parts of a whole there are: *When you are adding fractions, the denominator (bottom number) needs to be the same.*

**2** a very small amount of something: *For a fraction of a second it was quiet, and then someone laughed.*

—**fractionally** *adverb* by a very small amount

[**ORIGIN:** 1300-1400 From the Latin word *fractio*, which means "the act of breaking something," from *frangere*, which means "to break."]

**frac·ture¹** /ˈfræktʃɚ/ *noun*
a crack or break in a bone or rock: *Many older people suffer hip fractures if they fall.*

**fracture²** *verb*
to crack or break a bone in your body: *He fractured his arm when he fell off the ladder.*

**frag·ile** /ˈfrædʒəl/ *adjective*
easily broken or damaged: *The wine glasses are fragile because they are thin glass.*

—**fragility** /frəˈdʒɪləti/ *noun* the quality of being fragile

[**ORIGIN:** 1400-1500 From the Latin word *fragilis*, from *frangere*, which means "to break."]

**frag·ment** /ˈfrægmənt/ *noun*
a small piece that has broken off a larger object: *The scientists found fragments of broken pottery in the ground.*

→ see Thesaurus box at **piece**

**fra·grance** /ˈfreɪgrəns/ *noun*

**1** a nice smell: *The plant's leaves have a spicy, sweet fragrance.* **SYNONYM: smell**

**2** another word for a PERFUME

→ see Thesaurus box at **smell¹**

**fra·grant** /ˈfreɪgrənt/ *adjective*
having a nice smell: *The apple tree has fragrant blossoms in the spring.*

—**fragrantly** *adverb* in a fragrant way

**frail** /freɪl/ *adjective*
someone who is frail is thin and weak: *Grandpa looked old and frail.*

—**frailty** *noun* the condition of being frail

[**ORIGIN:** 1300-1400 From the Latin word *fragilis*, from *frangere*, which means "to break."]

F

**frame¹** /freɪm/ *noun*
**1** a structure made of wood or metal, that surrounds a picture, door, window or mirror: *a picture frame | a door frame* → see picture on page **A8**
**2** the main structure of a house, piece of furniture, or vehicle, which gives it a shape and supports it: *The tires fit onto the bike frame.*
**3** **frames** = the part of a pair of GLASSES that holds the glass LENSes: *The glasses come with red, blue, or black frames.*
**4** **frame of mind** = the way you are feeling at a particular time: *Melissa was in a good frame of mind; she talked about the future in a positive way.*



**frame²** *verb*
**1** to put a picture in a frame: *I'll get the photograph framed and give it Mom for her birthday.*
**2** to try to make someone seem guilty of a crime by giving false information: *His lawyer claims that the police officers framed him for the theft.*

**frame·work** Ac /ˈfreɪmwɚk/ *noun*
**1** the basic structure of a building or vehicle, which gives it a shape and supports the rest of it: *The skyscraper is supported by a steel framework.*
**2** a plan or system that other details can be added to: *Decide on your main points, and use them as a framework for your essay.*

**frank** /fræŋk/ *adjective*
someone who is frank says things in an honest and direct way: *To be frank with you, Mr. Lee, you don't have enough experience for the job.*
—**frankly** *adverb* in an honest and direct way: *He spoke frankly about his problems at school.*
—**frankness** *noun* the quality of being honest and direct
[**ORIGIN:** 1300-1400 From the old French word *franc*, which means "free or generous." This word came from the name of the Franks, a German people who took over the land now called France.]

**frank·fur·ter** /ˈfræŋkˌfɚt̬ɚ/ *noun*
a type of SAUSAGE **SYNONYM: hot dog**

**fran·tic** /ˈfræntɪk/ *adjective*
**1** extremely hurried and not organized: *We were late, and there was a frantic rush to get to the airport.*
**2** very worried and upset: *He didn't come home from school, and his mother is frantic with worry.*
—**frantically** *adverb* in a frantic way

**fraud** /frɔd/ *noun*
**1** the crime of deceiving people in order to get money, goods, or something else you want: *There were accusations of fraud after the election because votes from some areas were not counted.*
**2** someone who pretends to be someone else in order to deceive people: *I wasn't really qualified for the job, and I felt like a fraud.*

**fraud·u·lent** /ˈfrɔdʒələnt/ *adjective*
intended to trick people: *She tried to get a Social Security card using a fraudulent birth certificate.*
—**fraudulently** *adverb* in a way that is intended to trick people

**fray** /freɪ/ *verb*
if a cloth or rope frays, its threads become loose at the edge because it is old or torn: *The blanket was fraying around the edges.*
—**frayed** *adjective* with loose threads at the edge

**freak¹** /frik/ *noun* (*informal*)
**1** someone who is very interested in a subject or activity, in a way that other people think is too much: *He is a computer freak who spends all day in front of his computer.*
**2** someone who looks very strange or behaves in a very unusual way: *Everyone stared at me in my old-fashioned dress. I felt like a freak.*

**freak²** *adjective*
a freak accident or storm is very unusual and strange: *A wall fell down in a freak accident and injured two people.*

**freck·le** /ˈfrekəl/ *noun*
a small light brown spot on someone's skin, especially on the face: *The little girl had red hair and freckles.*

—**freckled** *adjective* having freckles: *A freckled young man said hello to me.*
→ see Thesaurus box at **mark**[2]

**free**[1] /fri/ *adjective*
**1** not costing any money: *I won free tickets to the concert in a competition.*
**2** able to do what you want, and not controlled by someone else: *You're free to play after you've done your homework.* | *After two years in jail, he was a free man again.*
**3** not busy doing other things: *Are you free on Saturday to go to a movie?* | *free time*
**4** not being used: *Excuse me, is this seat free?*
**5** not containing something: *sugar-free bubble gum*
→ **feel free** at **feel**[1]

| WORD FAMILY: free |
| --- |
| **free** *adjective* \| **freedom** *noun* \| **freely** *adverb* |

**free**[2] *adverb*
**1** (*also* **for free**) without having to pay any money: *Children under four can travel free on the buses.*
**2** moving without being controlled or kept in one place: *The horses were running free in the field.*

**free**[3] *verb*
to let someone leave a place where he or she has been forced to stay: *She was freed from prison last week.*

**free·bie** /ˈfribi/ *noun* (*informal*)
something that a store or business gives you, that you do not have to pay for: *The bank was giving away a radio as a freebie to new customers.*

**free·dom** /ˈfridəm/ *noun*
**1** the state of being free and allowed to do what you want: *The prisoner was given his freedom after spending five years in jail.*
**2** the legal right to do something, without the government stopping you: *Everyone in this country has the freedom to vote for the candidate they choose.*

**free·ly** /ˈfrili/ *adverb*
without anyone or anything controlling or stopping something: *People can travel freely across the border of the two countries.*

**ˌfree ˈmarket** *noun*
an economic system in which the government does not control prices or control who can buy and sell things

**free·way** /ˈfriweɪ/ *noun*
a very wide road on which cars can go very fast: *We took the freeway to downtown Los Angeles.*
→ see Thesaurus box at **road**

**freeze** /friz/ *verb* (**froze** /froʊz/, **frozen** /ˈfroʊzən/)
**1** if water freezes, it becomes solid and hard because it is so cold: *The water in the bucket froze during the night.* **ANTONYM: thaw**
**2** if you freeze food, you put it in a freezer to get cold and hard so that you can keep it longer: *Buy two packs of chicken and freeze one.* **ANTONYM: thaw**
**3 be freezing** (*informal*) = to feel very cold: *It's freezing in here; can we turn up the heat?* | *I forgot my coat and I'm freezing.*
**4** to suddenly stop moving and stay very still: *The police officer pointed his gun at the robber and shouted, "Freeze!"*

**freez·er** /ˈfrizɚ/ *noun*
a large piece of electrical equipment that makes food very cold and hard, so that you can keep it for a long time: *Put the ice cream in the freezer.* → see picture on page **A9**

**freez·ing** /ˈfrizɪŋ/ *noun*
**above/below freezing** = if the weather is above freezing or below freezing, the temperature is above or below the point at which water freezes (32°F or 0°C): *It was below freezing all day.*
→ see Thesaurus box at **cold**[1]

**freight** /freɪt/ *noun*
things that trucks, airplanes, or ships take from one place to another: *Trucks take freight from the warehouse to the stores.*

**French**[1] /frentʃ/ *adjective*
from France
—**Frenchman** *noun* a man from France
—**Frenchwoman** *noun* a woman from France

**French**[2] *noun*
**1** the language spoken in France, some other

countries, and some parts of Switzerland and Canada: *Can you speak French?*

**2 the French** = the people of France

**French fries** /ˌfrentʃ ˈfraɪz/ *plural noun*
potatoes cut into long thin pieces and cooked in hot oil: *I ordered a hamburger and French fries.*

**ˌFrench ˈhorn** *noun*
a metal instrument shaped like a circle, that you play by blowing into it and pressing keys

**French toast** /ˌfrentʃ ˈtoʊst/ *noun*
bread that you put into a mixture of eggs and milk and then cook in a pan: *Do you want French toast for breakfast?*

F

**fren·zy** /ˈfrenzi/ *noun*
if people or animals are in a frenzy, they are very worried or excited and cannot control their behavior: *The dogs go into a frenzy of barking when someone comes to the door.*
—**frenzied** *adjective* feeling very worried and excited

**fre·quen·cy** /ˈfrikwənsi/ *noun* (plural **frequencies**)
**1** the number of times that something happens: *The new traffic lights should lower the frequency of accidents.*
**2** the rate at which a sound or light WAVE pattern is repeated, which affects how high the sound is or what color a light is: *Dogs can hear higher frequencies than humans can.*

**fre·quent** /ˈfrikwənt/ *adjective*
happening very often: *They make frequent trips to New York, at least once a month.* **ANTONYM: infrequent**
—**frequently** *adverb* very often: *He's frequently late for school.*

**WORD FAMILY: frequent**
**frequent** *adjective* | **infrequent** *adjective* | **frequently** *adverb* | **infrequently** *adverb* | **frequency** *noun*

**fresh** /freʃ/ *adjective*
**1** fresh food or flowers have been picked or made only a short time ago: *Eat lots of fresh fruit and vegetables to stay healthy.*
**2** new or clean, and replacing what was there before: *I put on some fresh clothes and put the others in the wash.*
**3** new and different from what has been done before: *We need some fresh ideas to encourage people to recycle.* **ANTONYM: old**
**4 fresh air** = clean air that you breathe when you are outdoors: *I'm going for a walk to get some fresh air.*
**5** fresh water has no salt and comes from rivers and lakes
—**freshly** *adverb* recently: *They sell freshly baked bread, straight from the oven.*
—**freshness** *noun* a fresh quality: *Flowers quickly lose their freshness after they are picked.*
→ see Thesaurus box at **new**

**fresh·en** /ˈfreʃən/ (*also* **freshen up**) *verb*
to change or clean something so that it seems newer: *Abby freshened up her makeup.*

**fresh·man** /ˈfreʃmən/ *noun*
a student in the first year of high school or college: *He'll be a freshman in high school this fall; he's going into ninth grade.*

**fret** /fret/ *verb*
to worry about things that are not very important: *Kelly was fretting about being late for the party.*

**fric·tion** /ˈfrɪkʃən/ *noun*
**1** if there is friction between people, they disagree and argue: *Dad and I argue about everything, so there is always a lot of friction between us.*
**2** a force that makes something move more slowly because it is rubbing against another thing: *The brakes on the bike work by friction, because the brake pad rubs against the tire.*
[**ORIGIN:** 1500-1600 From the Latin word *frictio*, which means "the act of rubbing," from *fricare*, which means "to rub."]

**Fri·day** /ˈfraɪdi/ *noun* (*written abbreviation*: **Fri.**)
the sixth day of the week: *Diane won't be here Friday.* | *I have school on Friday.* | *Next Friday is my birthday.* | *I talked to Jim last Friday.* | *Do you have plans for Friday night?*
[**ORIGIN:** From Frigg, who was the goddess of love and the most important goddess in the religion of some peoples in Northern Europe before Christianity.]

**fridge** /frɪdʒ/ *noun*
a short word for a REFRIGERATOR: *Put the milk back in the fridge.* → see picture on page **A9**

**fried**[1] /fraɪd/ *verb*
the past tense and past participle of the verb FRY

**fried**[2] *adjective*
cooked in hot oil: *Jim ate a fried egg with toast.*

**friend** /frend/ *noun*
**1** someone whom you like very much and enjoy spending time with: *I'm meeting a friend for lunch.* | *Tony has been my best friend since second grade.* **ANTONYM: enemy**
**2 make friends** = to start having someone as a friend: *It can be hard to make friends at a new school.*
**3 be friends** = to be someone's friend: *Eve and Ellie are friends.*
**—friendship** *noun* the relationship that friends have: *The two girls have formed a close friendship.*

**friend·ly** /ˈfrendli/ *adjective* (**friendlier**, **friendliest**)
**1** wanting to talk to and be nice to people you do not know: *He's a friendly man who always says hello when we go past his house.*
**2** if you are friendly with someone, the two of you are friends: *I became friendly with Jane after we met on vacation.*
**—friendliness** *noun* the quality of being friendly

**fries** /fraɪz/ *plural noun*
a short word for FRENCH FRIES

**fright** /fraɪt/ *noun*
a sudden feeling of fear: *The boy saw the gun and started shaking with fright.*

**WORD FAMILY: fright**
**fright** *noun* | **frighten** *verb* | **frightened** *adjective* | **frightening** *adjective* | **frighteningly** *adverb*

**fright·en** /ˈfraɪtn/ *verb*
to make someone feel afraid: *The loud noise of the fireworks frightened the dog.* **SYNONYM: scare**

**fright·ened** /ˈfraɪtnd/ *adjective*
feeling afraid: *It was dark and I was alone and frightened.*

**THESAURUS: frightened**
**afraid** frightened of something that may hurt you or be dangerous: *She was afraid to go by herself, so she asked her friend to go with her.*
**scared** afraid and nervous about something: *I've always been scared of dogs.*
**terrified** very frightened: *I'm terrified of heights.*
**petrified** very frightened: *He's petrified of snakes.*

**fright·en·ing** /ˈfraɪtn-ɪŋ/ *adjective*
making you feel afraid: *Being lost in the woods was a frightening experience.* **SYNONYM: scary**
**—frighteningly** *adverb* in a frightening way

**frill** /frɪl/ *noun*
**1** a piece of cloth with many small folds in it, that you use to decorate clothes or other things made of cloth: *The frills on the dress made it hard to iron.*
**2** something that is nice but not really needed, that can be added to something you buy: *The car has no frills – no air conditioning, no sunroof, and no electric windows.*
**—frilly** *adjective* having a lot of frills as decoration: *a frilly blouse*

**fringe** /frɪndʒ/ *noun*
**1** a lot of thick threads that hang from something such as a curtain or piece of clothing as a decoration: *He was wearing a cowboy jacket with leather fringe.*
**2** the area that is furthest from the center of something: *New homes are being built on the fringe of the city.* **SYNONYM: outskirts**

**Fris·bee** /ˈfrɪzbi/ *noun* (*trademark*)
a piece of plastic shaped like a plate that people throw and catch as a game

**frisk** /frɪsk/ *verb*
to move your hands over someone's clothes to see if he or she has a hidden weapon: *Police officers frisked the man for weapons.*

**frisk·y** /ˈfrɪski/ *adjective*
full of energy, happiness, and fun: *The kitten was frisky and playful.*

**frog** /frɔg/ *noun*
a small green or brown animal that lives in or near water and has long legs for jumping: *A frog jumped out of the pond.* → see picture at **amphibian**

**from** /frəm; *strong* frʌm/ *preposition*
**1** used when saying where someone was born, lives, or works: *My grandfather came from Mexico.* | *I'm from New York and have lived there all my life.* | *Someone from the library is going to talk to the class.*
**2** used when saying where something starts or used to be: *He drove all the way from Colorado to Florida.* | *Mike brought his report card home from school.* | *I got the scissors from the drawer.*
**3** used when saying what time something starts: *The class is from 9:00 to 11:00.* | *Twenty years from now you'll probably be married and have kids yourself.*
**4** used when saying who has given or sent something: *Who is the present from?* | *This watch was a birthday gift from my sister.*
**5** used when talking about the distance between two places: *I live about a mile from the school.*
**6** as a result of something: *He got sick from drinking dirty water.*
**7** used when saying what something is made of: *Ice cream is made from milk and sugar.*
**8** used to say where you are when you see or do something: *From the top of the mountain, you can see the ocean.*

F

**front¹** /frʌnt/ *noun*
**1** the part of something that is furthest forward: *The front of the store is painted blue.* | *Good students usually sit near the front of the room.* **ANTONYM: back**
**2** the most important side of something, that you look at first: *The book had a picture of a lion on the front.* | *The front of your T-shirt has ketchup on it.* **ANTONYM: back**
**3 in front of someone or something** = **a)** ahead of someone or something: *There's a big tree in front of their house.* | *Two girls were standing in front of me in line.* **b)** facing someone or something: *They ate dinner in front of the TV.* **ANTONYM: behind**
**4 in front of someone** = when someone is with you: *Her parents never argue in front of their kids.*
**5 out front** = in the area near the entrance to the building that you are in: *The car is parked out front, not in the driveway.*
**6** the place where there is fighting in a war: *There was heavy fighting at the front.*
**7** the edge of an area of warm or cold air, that makes the weather change: *A cold front is moving in from the north, bringing sleet and snow.*

**front²** *adjective*
at, on, or in the front of something: *The front door was locked.* | *He got into the front seat of the car.* **ANTONYM: back**

**fron·tier** /frʌnˈtɪr/ *noun*
**1 the frontier** = the part of country or area that is furthest away from the area where most people live, and where people are just beginning to travel to or live: *In the 1880s, the land that is now Colorado and Utah was still the frontier.*
**2** the place where two countries meet: *The Pakistan-Afghanistan frontier is mountainous.* **SYNONYM: border**

**frost** /frɔst/ *noun*
a white powder of ice that covers things that are outside when it is very cold: *It was a freezing morning and there was frost on the grass.*
—**frosty** *adjective* very cold and covered with frost
→ see Thesaurus box at **snow¹**

**frost·bite** /ˈfrɔstbaɪt/ *noun*
if you get frostbite, parts of your body freeze and are badly damaged: *The hikers were caught in a snowstorm, and they suffered frostbite in their hands and feet.*

**frost·ing** /ˈfrɔstɪŋ/ *noun*
a mixture made with sugar, that you put on a cake: *a cake with chocolate frosting* **SYNONYM: icing**

**frown** /fraʊn/ *verb*
to move your EYEBROWs together and turn the corners of your mouth down when you are angry, unhappy, or thinking hard: *The coach frowned as Steve missed the shot.*
—**frown** *noun* an angry or unhappy expression you make when you frown

**froze** /froʊz/ *verb*
the past tense of FREEZE

**fro·zen**[1] /ˈfroʊzən/ *verb*
the past participle of FREEZE

**frozen**[2] *adjective*
**1** food that is frozen has been kept in a very cold place so that it freezes and becomes hard: *She took a frozen pizza out of the freezer and put it in the oven to cook.*
**2** made into ice because of the cold: *People were skating on the frozen lake.*

**fruit** /frut/ *noun*
**1** a type of food that grows on trees and plants, and often tastes sweet, for example apples and oranges: *Bananas are my favorite fruit.* | *a piece of fruit*
**2** the part of a plant that contains the seeds, and which develops from the flower
[**ORIGIN:** 1100-1200 From the Latin word *fructus*, which means "useful result or product."]

**fruit·ful** /ˈfrutfəl/ *adjective* (*formal*)
producing something that is good or useful: *I spent a fruitful morning in the library and got a lot of information.*

**frus·trate** /ˈfrʌstreɪt/ *verb*
**1** if something frustrates you, it makes you feel annoyed or angry because you cannot do or have what you want: *It frustrates me when my parents don't listen to me.*
**2** (*formal*) to stop someone from being able to do something: *Computer problems frustrated their effort to finish the work on time.*
—**frustrated** *adjective* annoyed and angry because you cannot do or have what you want: *David got frustrated because he couldn't understand the math homework.*
—**frustrating** *adjective* making you feel frustrated: *It's so frustrating when we play really well but still lose.*
—**frustration** /frʌˈstreɪʃən/ *noun* the feeling of being frustrated: *The little boy started crying in frustration when he couldn't do the puzzle.*

**fry** /fraɪ/ *verb* (**fried**)
to cook something in hot oil or butter: *I fried some bacon for breakfast.*
→ see Thesaurus box at **cook**[1]

**ˈfrying ˌpan** *noun*
a round flat pan with a handle, used for frying food → see picture on page **A9**

**ft.**
the written abbreviation of **foot**

**fudge** /fʌdʒ/ *noun*
a kind of soft candy, made with butter, sugar, milk, and usually chocolate

**fu·el** /ˈfyuəl/ *noun*
a substance such as coal, gas, or oil that you can burn to make heat or power: *The plane has enough fuel to fly from Chicago to Los Angeles.*
—**fuel** *verb* to put fuel in something such as a car or an airplane
[**ORIGIN:** 1100-1200 From the old French word *fouaille*, from the Latin word *focus*, which means "fireplace." You would burn fuel in a fireplace.]

**fu·gi·tive** /ˈfyudʒətɪv/ *noun*
someone who is trying to avoid being caught by the police: *He is a fugitive whom the police have been looking for for months.*
[**ORIGIN:** 1300-1400 From the Latin word *fugere*, which means "to run away."]

**ful·fill** /fʊlˈfɪl/ *verb* (*formal*)
to do something you wanted or promised to do: *Mr. Jackson fulfilled his promise and gave Robert a job.*
—**fulfillment** *noun* the act of doing something you wanted or promised to do

**full** /fʊl/ *adjective*
**1** something that is full contains so many things or people that no more will fit in it: *This suitcase is full, so I can't get any more clothes into it.* | *a full carton of milk* **ANTONYM: empty** → see picture at **empty**[1]

**THESAURUS: full**

**filled with something** full of something: *The bucket was filled with water.*

**packed** so full of people or things that no more can get in: *The stadium was packed with fans.*

**crammed** completely full of people or things: *The book is crammed with information.*

**overflowing** so full that liquid or other things come over the top: *Her shopping cart was overflowing with groceries.*

**2 be full of something** = to contain many things of the same kind: *Eric's essay is full of*

*spelling mistakes.* | *The room was full of people.*
**3** if you are full, you have eaten a lot and cannot eat any more: *"Would you like some more soup?" "No thanks. I'm full."*
**4** complete or whole: *What is your full name and address?* | *It was a full year before she was able to get a job.*
**5** the highest level or biggest amount of something that is possible: *The ship was moving at full speed.* | *I didn't pay full price for the dress; it was on sale.*

**ˌfull-ˈlength** *adjective*
**1** not shorter than the usual length: *"Snow White" was the first cartoon to be made into a full-length movie.*
**2** showing all of a person: *a full-length mirror*
**3** a full-length skirt or dress reaches the ground

full moon

**ˌfull ˈmoon** *noun*
the moon when it looks completely round

**ˌfull-ˈtime** *adverb*
if you work or study full-time, you work or study for the usual number of hours that people are expected to: *Angela works full-time, from 9 to 5 every weekday.* **ANTONYM: part-time**
—**ˈfull-time** *adjective* working or studying full-time: *a full-time student*

**ful·ly** /ˈfʊli/ *adverb*
completely: *The snake can be six feet long when it is fully grown.*

**fum·ble** /ˈfʌmbəl/ *verb*
**1** to try to hold, move, or find something with your hands in an awkward way: *Gary fumbled for the light switch in the dark.*
**2** to drop a ball after catching it, especially a football: *He caught the pass, but then fumbled the ball as he fell.*
—**fumble** *noun* the act of dropping a ball

**fumes** /fuumz/ *plural noun*
gas or smoke that has an unpleasant smell: *The fumes from car exhausts cause air pollution.*

**fun¹** /fʌn/ *noun*
**1** enjoyment or pleasure that you get from an activity: *All the kids were having fun at the party.* | *He began running for fun, and now he's on the track team.*

**USAGE: fun, funny**
Use **fun** to talk about situations or activities that you enjoy: *This game is a lot of fun.*
Use **funny** to describe someone or something that makes you laugh: *The movie was so funny we couldn't stop laughing.*

**2 make fun of someone or something** = to make unkind jokes about someone or something: *Some girls made fun of her because her dress was too small.*

**fun²** *adjective*
enjoyable: *There are lots of fun things to do at the beach.*

**func·tion¹** Ac /ˈfʌŋkʃən/ *noun*
**1** the purpose that something has, or the job that something or someone does: *The function of the kidneys is to remove waste from your body.*
**2** a large party or social event: *The room is available for weddings and other functions.*
—**functional** *adjective* designed to be useful or to do a particular job, rather than to look attractive
[**ORIGIN:** 1500-1600 From the Latin word *functio*, from *fungi*, which means "to perform an action."]

**WORD FAMILY: function**
**function** *noun* | **function** *verb* | **functional** *adjective*

**function²** Ac *verb*
if something functions, it does what it should do: *The alarm system was not functioning when the paintings were stolen.* **SYNONYM: work**

PHRASAL VERB
**function as something**
to be used in a particular way: *The sofa can also function as a bed.*

**fund[1]** Ac /fʌnd/ *noun*
**1** an amount of money that is collected for a purpose: *My parents save money in a pension fund for their retirement.*
**2 funds** = the money that an organization needs or has: *The school needs funds for new computer equipment.*

**fund[2]** Ac *verb*
to give the money that is needed for an activity or piece of work: *She took out a loan to fund her college education.* SYNONYM: **pay for**

**fun·da·men·tal** Ac /ˌfʌndəˈmentl/ *adjective*
**1** relating to the most basic and important parts of something: *When their parents divorce, there is a fundamental change in the way children live.* SYNONYM: **basic**
**2** necessary for something to exist or develop: *Water is fundamental to life.* SYNONYM: **necessary**
—**fundamentally** *adverb* in the most basic and important way: *He believes that men and women are fundamentally different.*
[ORIGIN: 1400-1500 From the Latin word *fundus*, which means "the bottom of something." The idea is that the ideas or things that are at the bottom of something are the most basic or important parts of it.]

**fu·ner·al** /ˈfyunərəl/ *noun*
a ceremony for a dead person before their body is buried or burned: *There will be a funeral service at the Baptist church.*

**fun·gus** /ˈfʌŋgəs/ *noun* (plural **fungi** /ˈfʌndʒaɪ/ *or* **funguses**)
a type of plant such as a mushroom or mold, that usually grows on decaying things or in damp places: *Mildew is a type of fungus that grows in warm, damp places, for example in the bathroom.*
—**fungal** *adjective* caused by a fungus

**funk·y** /ˈfʌŋki/ *adjective* (*informal*)
**1** fashionable and interesting in an unusual way: *She was wearing funky purple pants.*
**2** funky music has a strong RHYTHM that is easy to dance to

**fun·nel** /ˈfʌnl/ *noun*
a tube that is wide at the top and narrow at the bottom, used for pouring liquids or powders into a container

**fun·ny** /ˈfʌni/ *adjective* (**funnier**, **funniest**)
**1** if something is funny, it makes you laugh: *She told a funny story about forgetting to bring her shoes to the wedding.* | *I thought the show was very funny.*

**USAGE: funny, fun**

Use **funny** to describe someone or something that makes you laugh: *The movie was so funny we couldn't stop laughing.*

Use **fun** to talk about situations or activities that you enjoy: *This game is a lot of fun.*

**THESAURUS: funny**

**hilarious** very funny in a way that makes you laugh a lot: *The book is hilarious. I laughed out loud while reading it.*

**amusing** funny in a way that makes you smile: *The movie is full of amusing surprises.*

**humorous** funny: *There's a humorous story in the newspaper about a dog that flies kites.*

**witty** saying interesting things in an amusing and intelligent way: *She's a smart, witty woman who always has something interesting to say.*

**2** strange and difficult to understand or explain: *Your voice sounds funny. Do you have a cold?* | *The meat was bad and had a funny smell.*
**3 feel funny** = to feel slightly sick
→ see Thesaurus box at **strange**

**fur** /fɚ/ *noun*
the thick soft hair that covers an animal's

F

body: *The dog's fur was thick and soft.*
—**fur** *adjective* made of fur: *a fur coat*
[ORIGIN: 1300-1400 From the old French word *forrer*, which means "to cover the inside of a piece of clothing." Fur was sometimes put inside clothes to make them warmer.]

**fu·ri·ous** /ˈfyʊriəs/ *adjective*
**1** very angry: *She is furious with Jack because he lied to her.*
**2** happening very quickly or done with a lot of energy or anger: *They worked at a furious pace and finished earlier than planned.*
—**furiously** *adverb* in a furious way
→ see Thesaurus box at **angry**

F

**fur·nace** /ˈfɚnɪs/ *noun*
a large container with a fire inside it, used to heat a building or to melt metal

**fur·nish** /ˈfɚnɪʃ/ *verb*
**1** to put furniture and other things into a room or house: *We furnished the room with two beds and a dresser.*
**2** (*formal*) to give or provide something: *The U.S. embassy can furnish you with a visa application form.*
—**furnished** *adjective* a furnished room or building already has furniture in it: *a furnished apartment*

**fur·nish·ings** /ˈfɚnɪʃɪŋz/ *plural noun* (*formal*)
the furniture and other things in a room, such as curtains and lights

**fur·ni·ture** /ˈfɚnɪtʃɚ/ *noun*
things such as chairs, tables, and beds that you use in a room: *The only piece of furniture in the room was an old sofa.* | *office furniture*
[ORIGIN: 1500-1600 From the old French word *furnir*, which means "to provide equipment."]

**GRAMMAR: furniture**

Do not say "furnitures" or "a furniture." You can say, for example, **some furniture**, **any furniture**, or **a piece of furniture**: *When they got married, they didn't have any furniture at all.* | *a comfortable piece of furniture*

**fur·ry** /ˈfɚi/ *adjective*
**1** a furry animal has a body that is covered in fur
**2** covered with fur or covered in a material that looks like fur: *furry slippers*

**fur·ther¹** /ˈfɚðɚ/ *adverb*
**1** more: *I have told you everything, and I have nothing further to say.*
**2 go further/get further** = to do more, or make more progress: *The team went further than last year, finishing in third place as compared to last year's sixth place.*
**3 take something further** = to continue doing something at higher or more serious levels: *He decided to take his education further and get a master's degree.*
**4** a greater distance: *The library was further away than I'd thought, and it took half an hour to walk there.*
**5** more time into the future or the past: *We have to look further ahead, beyond the next ten years.*

**USAGE: further, farther**

Use **further** to talk about amounts, levels, or time: *Your grades cannot drop further, or you won't be able to play on the soccer team.* | *I don't want to discuss this any further.*

Use **farther** to talk about distance: *Room 211 is just a little farther down the hall.*

Many people use **further** in spoken English to talk about distance, but many teachers think that this is not correct.

**further²** *adjective* (*formal*)
additional or more: *Further information is available on the website.* **SYNONYM: more**
→ see Thesaurus box at **more²**

**fur·ther·more** Ac /ˈfɚðɚˌmɔr/ *adverb* (*formal*)
used when adding another piece of information: *He handed in his homework late. Furthermore, it was full of careless mistakes.*

**fur·thest** /ˈfɚðɪst/ *adjective, adverb*
**1** at the greatest distance from a place or person: *Of my three friends, Rob lives furthest away from the school.* **SYNONYM: farthest**
**2** to the greatest degree or amount: *Smith's book has probably gone furthest to explain these events.*

**fu·ry** /ˈfyʊri/ *noun*
a feeling of very strong anger: *Her face was red with fury as she shouted at him.*

**fuse** /fyuz/ *noun*

**1** a thin wire inside a piece of electrical equipment, that breaks if too much electricity passes through it, so that the electricity does not damage the equipment: *The lights went out when a fuse blew.*

**2** a long string connected to a bomb or a FIREWORK, used to make it explode: *Light the fuse of the firework and then move away from it.*

**3** **have a short fuse** = used for saying that someone becomes angry very easily: *Mom has a short fuse when she's tired.*

**fu·sion** /ˈfyuʒən/ *noun*

**1** a process in which different substances become joined or mixed together: *Energy is produced by the fusion of hydrogen atoms.*

**2** a combination of separate things: *The restaurant's food is a fusion of Japanese and Californian cooking.*

[**ORIGIN:** 1500-1600 From the Latin word *fusio*, from *fundere*, which means "to pour or melt." The idea is that you pour or melt things together so that they mix.]

**fuss**[1] /fʌs/ *noun*

**1** unnecessary attention, excitement, or activity: *I wanted a quiet birthday without any fuss.*

**2** **make a fuss/kick up a fuss** = to complain loudly or become angry about something, especially something unimportant: *Joe was making a fuss about having to eat the vegetables.*

**3** **make a fuss over someone** = to give too much attention to someone: *The women made a big fuss over the baby.*

**fuss**[2] *verb*

if a baby fusses, it cries a little: *The baby started fussing because it was hungry.*

**PHRASAL VERBS**

**fuss over someone**

to give a lot of attention to someone, especially a child: *The women started fussing over Kate's baby.*

**fuss with something**

to continuously move or touch something in a way that shows you are nervous: *Stop fussing with your clothes; you look great!*

**fuss·y** /ˈfʌsi/ *adjective* (**fussier**, **fussiest**)

**1** if you are fussy, you only accept a few particular things or things that are exactly right: *He's fussy about his clothes and will only wear things that are comfortable.* **SYNONYM: picky**

**2** a fussy baby cries a lot

—**fussily** *adverb* in a fussy way

**fu·tile** /ˈfyutl/ *adjective* (*formal*)

futile actions have no chance of being successful, and are not worth doing: *I made a futile attempt to calm her down, but she just kept crying.*

—**futility** *noun* the fact that something you do is futile

**fu·ture**[1] /ˈfyutʃɚ/ *noun*

**1** **the future** = the time after the present: *He talked about his plans for the future.* **ANTONYM: past**

**2** the things that will happen to someone or something in the time after the present: *He's a smart kid who has a great future ahead of him.* | *They are meeting to discuss the future of the company, which is having financial problems.*

**3** **the future** = the FUTURE TENSE: *The future of "do" is "will do."*

[**ORIGIN:** 1300-1400 From the Latin word *futurus*, which means "going to be."]

**future**[2] *adjective*

relating to or happening in the future: *We need to take care of the planet for future generations.* **ANTONYM: past**

**ˈfuture ˌtense** *noun*

the form of a verb that you use when you are talking about the future. In English, "I will go" is in the future tense.

**fuzz·y** /ˈfʌzi/ *adjective* (*informal*)

**1** covered with short soft hair or fur: *fuzzy slippers*

**2** unclear and confusing: *It happened a long time ago and my memory is fuzzy now.*

**3** if a sound or picture is fuzzy, it is not clear: *Unfortunately, a lot of the photographs are fuzzy.*

# Gg

**g**
the written abbreviation of **gram**

**G** /dʒi/ *noun*
the fifth note in the musical SCALE of C, or the musical KEY based on this note

**gadg·et** /ˈgædʒɪt/ *noun*
a small tool or machine, especially a new one: *He has a new gadget for opening jars.*
→ see Thesaurus box at **machine**



**gag**[1] /gæg/ *noun*
**1** a joke: *I didn't think many of the gags were very funny.*
**2** a piece of cloth that someone ties over your mouth so that you cannot speak

**gag**[2] *verb* (**gagged**, **gagging**)
**1** to tie a piece of cloth over someone's mouth: *The robbers gagged her so that she couldn't shout for help.*
**2** to almost bring up food from your stomach: *The food was so bad that it made me gag.*

**gain** /geɪn/ *verb*
**1** to get something important or useful: *Firefighters finally gained control of the fire.* | *The class lets students gain the confidence to give a speech.* **ANTONYM: lose**
**2** to get more of something over a period of time: *The bike gained speed as it went down the hill.* **ANTONYM: lose**
—**gain** *noun* the act of gaining something: *What is the reason for his weight gain?*

**gait** /geɪt/ *noun*
the way that someone walks: *He walked with an unsteady gait.*

**gal·ax·y** /ˈgæləksi/ *noun* (plural **galaxies**)
a very large group of stars: *Our solar system is part of the Milky Way galaxy.*
—**galactic** /gəˈlæktɪk/ *adjective* relating to a galaxy
[**ORIGIN:** 1300-1400 From the Latin word *galaxias*, from the Greek word *gala*, which means "milk." The stars far away in our galaxy look like a milky white stripe from the Earth.]

**gale** /geɪl/ *noun*
a very strong wind: *Several trees blew down in the gale.*
→ see Thesaurus box at **wind**[1]

**gal·ler·y** /ˈgæləri/ *noun* (plural **galleries**)
a room or building where people can look at or buy art

**gal·lon** /ˈgælən/ *noun*
a unit for measuring liquid, equal to four QUARTs or 3.785 LITERs: *Josh put five gallons of gas in the car.*
[**ORIGIN:** 1200-1300 From the Latin word *galeta*, which means "container for liquid."]

gallop

**gal·lop** /ˈgæləp/ *verb*
if a horse gallops, it runs very fast
—**gallop** *noun* the fastest speed that a horse can run: *He was riding at a gallop.*

**gam·ble**[1] /ˈgæmbəl/ *verb*
to try to win money, for example by playing cards or guessing the result of a race or game: *He gambled and lost all his money.*
—**gambler** *noun* someone who gambles
—**gambling** *noun* the activity of gambling

**gamble**[2] *noun*
an action that might not have a successful result: *The coach took a gamble by using a rookie, but it paid off when he scored.*

**game** /geɪm/ *noun*
**1** a sport or enjoyable activity in which you try to win or score points: *Soccer is a good game.* | *My brother likes to play computer games.* | *When it rains, we play board games like chess and checkers.*

**THESAURUS: game**

**sport** a physical activity in which people or teams play against each other and try to win: *Her favorite sport is basketball.*
**recreation** activities that you do for fun: *Sports are a great form of recreation.*

**puzzle** a game in which you have to think hard to find the correct answer: *The book has puzzles such as codes and crosswords.*

**hobby** an activity that you enjoy doing in your free time: *Her hobbies are reading and music.*

**2** an occasion when people play a game: *We won the basketball game.* | *Would you like to play a game of chess?*

**3 play games (with someone)** = to behave dishonestly toward someone: *I thought he liked me but he was just playing games.*

**4** wild animals and birds that people hunt: *He hunts deer and other game.*

**ˈgame show** *noun*
a television program in which people play games in order to win prizes

**gang¹** /gæŋ/ *noun*
**1** an organized group of young people in a city, who may be involved in crime or violence: *He tries to help youngsters stay off drugs and keep out of gangs.*
**2** a group of people who do something together: *Gangs of teenage girls hang out at the mall.*
→ see Thesaurus box at **group¹**

**gang²** *verb*
**PHRASAL VERB**
**gang up on someone**
if a group of people gangs up on someone, they all criticize, attack, or make jokes about him or her: *My brothers gang up on me and tease me.*

**gang·ster** /ˈgæŋstɚ/ *noun*
a member of a group of violent criminals

**gap** /gæp/ *noun*
**1** an empty space between two things or two parts of something: *I squeezed through a gap in the fence.*
**2** a difference between two people, things, or groups: *The gap between the rich and the poor is getting wider all the time.*
**3** something that is missing, so that something else is not good or complete: *New scientific discoveries fill gaps in our knowledge.*
→ see Thesaurus box at **hole**

**gap·ing** /ˈgeɪpɪŋ/ *adjective*
a gaping hole is very wide: *The bomb left a gaping hole in the wall of the building.*

**ga·rage** /gəˈrɑʒ/ *noun*
**1** a building at your house where you keep your car: *She must be home. Her car's in the garage.*
**2** a place where cars are repaired: *The guy at the garage said he could fix the car today.*
**3** a building or underground area where people can park their cars
[**ORIGIN:** 1900-2000 From the French word *garer*, which means "to shelter."]

**gaˈrage ˌsale** *noun*
a sale of things that you no longer want, that you sell outside your house, usually in front of your garage: *My parents bought a lot of our toys at garage sales.*

**gar·bage** /ˈgɑrbɪdʒ/ *noun*
**1** waste food, paper, and other things you throw away, or the container you put it in: *Throw the wrapper in the garbage.* | *Put the paper in with the rest of the garbage.*

**THESAURUS: garbage**

**trash** things that you do not want and throw away, such as old food and dirty paper: *Six bags were full of trash.* | *Can you take out the trash, please?*

**refuse** (*formal*) things that people throw away, such as old food and dirty paper: *The city buries the refuse it collects.*

**litter** things such as papers, cans, or food containers that people leave on the ground in public places: *The Scouts picked up litter in the park.*

**waste** (*formal*) unwanted materials or substances that are left after you have used something: *Is there a way to safely get rid of waste from nuclear power stations?* | *I try to recycle most of my household waste.*

**2** (*informal*) something that is very bad, silly, or low quality: *I thought the TV show was garbage.*

**ˈgarbage ˌcan** *noun*
a large container for waste **SYNONYM: trash can** → see picture on page **A9**

G

**'garbage col,lector** (*also* **'garbage ,man**) *noun*
someone whose job is to take away the things inside garbage cans

**'garbage ,truck** *noun*
a large vehicle that carries away things from garbage cans

**gar·den** /ˈgardn/ *noun*
a piece of land where you grow flowers or vegetables: *I planted some sunflower seeds in the garden.*

**gar·den·ing** /ˈgardnɪŋ/ *noun*
the work of growing plants in a garden: *He mows the lawn and does the gardening.*
—**gardener** *noun* someone who works in a garden, especially as a job

G

**gar·gle** /ˈgargəl/ *verb*
to clean your throat by breathing out while you have a liquid in the back of your mouth: *If you have a sore throat, try gargling with salt water.*

**gar·lic** /ˈgarlɪk/ *noun*
a small plant like an onion that gives a strong taste to food → see picture on page **A12**
—**garlicky** *adjective* tasting or smelling of garlic

**gar·ment** /ˈgarmənt/ *noun* (*formal*)
a piece of clothing: *The women wore simple black garments.*

**gas** /gæs/ *noun* (plural **gases**)
**1** a liquid that you put in a car to make it go: *Most cars use unleaded gas.* **SYNONYM: gasoline**
**2** a substance like air that is not a liquid or a solid: *Oxygen is a gas that you cannot see.*
**3** a type of gas that people burn to heat their houses or cook food: *Many power stations burn natural gas to produce energy.*
**4 the gas** = the PEDAL that you use to make a car go faster: *He started the car, stepped on the gas, and pulled away from the curb.*
[**ORIGIN:** 1600-1700 From the Greek word *khaos*, which means "empty space." The word "gas" was invented by a Dutch scientist.]

**gas·e·ous** /ˈgæsiəs/ *adjective*
in a form like air: *gaseous fuels*

**gash** /gæʃ/ *noun*
a deep cut: *She had a gash in her leg that was bleeding.*
—**gash** *verb* to make a deep cut in something: *He fell and gashed his chin.*

**gas·o·line** /ˌgæsəˈlin/ *noun*
a liquid that you put in a car to make it go
**SYNONYM: gas**

**gasp** /gæsp/ *verb*
to breathe in quickly and loudly, once or several times: *People gasped with surprise when the jury said he was innocent.* | *She put her head above the water and gasped for air.*
—**gasp** *noun* a quick breath in: *The runners were breathing in quick gasps.*
→ see Thesaurus box at **breathe**

**'gas ,station** *noun*
a place where you can buy gas for your car

**gate** /geɪt/ *noun*
**1** a door in a fence or outside wall: *Who left the gate open?*
**2** a place where you leave an airport building to get on a plane: *Passengers for Flight 186 should go to Gate 7.*

**gate·way** /ˈgeɪtweɪ/ *noun*
a place from which you can reach another place: *St. Louis was once the gateway to the western part of the U.S.*

**gath·er** /ˈgæðɚ/ *verb*
**1** to come together in a group: *A crowd gathered to watch the fight.*
**2** to bring things from different places together: *She gathered the dirty clothes and put them in the washing machine.*
**3** to think something because of what you have heard: *I heard her talking to her friend, and I gather (that) they are moving to Chicago.*

**gath·er·ing** /ˈgæðərɪŋ/ *noun*
a meeting of a group of people: *We have a family gathering every summer, when all my aunts and uncles come to our house.*

**gauge¹** /geɪdʒ/ *noun*
an instrument that measures something: *The gas gauge showed that the car needed more gas.* → see picture on page **A28**

**gauge²** *verb*
to judge or measure something by using the information you have: *How do teachers gauge the progress a student has made?*

**gauze** /gɔz/ *noun*
a type of thin cloth used to cover wounds and make clothes → see picture at **kit**

**gave** /geɪv/ *verb*
the past tense of GIVE

**gay** /geɪ/ *adjective*
**1** sexually attracted to people of the same sex **SYNONYM: homosexual**; **ANTONYM: straight**
**2** an old-fashioned word meaning bright or happy: *The room was painted in gay colors.*
—**gay** *noun* a gay person

**gaze** /geɪz/ *verb*
to look at someone or something for a long time: *He gazed at his reflection in the mirror.*
—**gaze** *noun* a long steady look: *She turned her gaze back to the TV.*
→ see Thesaurus box at **look**[1]

**gear** /gɪr/ *noun*
**1** part of a car, bicycle, or other machine that makes it move well at different speeds: *She shifted into first gear, and the car moved forward slowly.*
**2** special equipment or clothes that you need for an activity: *We put our tent and the rest of the camping gear into the car.*

**gear·shift** /ˈgɪrˌʃɪft/ *noun*
a stick that you move to change gears when driving a car → see picture on page **A28**

**GED** *noun*
(**General Equivalency Diploma**) an official piece of paper that people who did not finish HIGH SCHOOL can get by taking a test

**gee** /dʒi/ *interjection*
something you say when you are surprised, pleased, or excited: *Gee, that pie smells good!*

**geese** /gis/ *noun*
the plural of GOOSE

**gel** /dʒel/ *noun*
a thick clear wet substance: *He uses hair gel to make his hair stick up.*

**gel·a·tin** /ˈdʒelətən/ *noun*
a clear substance that is used to make foods such as Jell-O more solid

**gem** /dʒem/ *noun*
**1** a valuable stone that has been cut into a particular shape: *diamonds and other gems* **SYNONYM: jewel**
**2** (*informal*) something that is very good or special: *This book is a gem that every teenager should read.*

**Gem·i·ni** /ˈdʒeməˌnaɪ/ *noun*
**1** the third sign of the ZODIAC, represented by TWINs
**2** someone born between May 21 and June 21

**gem·stone** /ˈdʒemˌstoʊn/ *noun*
a valuable stone

**gen·der** [Ac] /ˈdʒendɚ/ *noun*
**1** the fact of being male or female: *You cannot choose the gender of a baby.* **SYNONYM: sex**
**2** in grammar, the three groups that words are divided into in some languages. The three groups are called MASCULINE, FEMININE, and NEUTER: *In some languages, like Spanish, nouns have different genders.*
[**ORIGIN:** 1300-1400 From the Latin word *genus*, which means "race or type."]

**gene** /dʒin/ *noun*
a part of a cell in a living thing that controls what the living thing is like, for example what color someone's eyes are, how tall a plant is, etc.
[**ORIGIN:** 1900-2000 From the Greek word *genos*, which means "birth, or group of related people."]

**gen·er·al**[1] /ˈdʒenərəl/ *adjective*
**1** relating to the whole of something or to the main parts: *Except for one cold, my general health has been good. | The class is a general introduction to computers.*
**2 in general** = **a)** usually or mostly: *In general, I am happier than I used to be.* **b)** used when talking about all things or people of one type: *I like animals in general, and dogs in particular.*
**3** including or relating to most people or things: *There was general agreement that we need to improve our defense.*
[**ORIGIN:** 1100-1200 From the Latin word *generalis*, which means "of the whole type," from *genus*, meaning "type."]

**WORD FAMILY: general**
**general** *adjective* | **generally** *adverb* | **generalize** *verb* | **generalization** *noun*

**general²** *noun*
an officer with a very high rank in the army, air force, or Marines

**gen·er·al·ize** /ˈdʒenərəˌlaɪz/ *verb*
to say something about people or things of a particular kind which may not be true about all of them: *You shouldn't generalize about women by saying that they are all bad drivers.*
—**generalization** /ˌdʒenərələˈzeɪʃən/ *noun* a statement in which someone generalizes

**gen·er·al·ly** /ˈdʒenərəli/ *adverb*
**1** usually or mostly: *I generally go to bed at about 11, but sometimes later.* | *Her school work is generally very good.*
**2** by most people: *He is generally believed to be one of the best quarterbacks in the NFL.*

G

**gen·er·ate** Ac /ˈdʒenəˌreɪt/ *verb*
**1** to make electricity: *We burn coal to generate electricity.*
**2** to make something happen: *The team's success in the World Cup generated a lot of interest in soccer.*

**WORD FAMILY: generate**
**generate** *verb* | **generator** *noun*

**gen·er·a·tion** Ac /ˌdʒenəˈreɪʃən/ *noun*
**1** the people in a society or family who are about the same age: *Three generations of the family live in the same house: grandparents, parents, and children.*
**2** a period of about 25 years, which is the time between two generations of a family: *A generation ago, video games were simple.*

**gen·er·a·tor** /ˈdʒenəˌreɪtɚ/ *noun*
a machine that makes electricity

**gen·er·os·i·ty** /ˌdʒenəˈrɑsəti/ *noun*
generous behavior: *Thank you for your generosity; the money you gave us was a great help.*

**gen·er·ous** /ˈdʒenərəs/ *adjective*
someone who is generous gives people a lot of money, things, or help: *It was very generous of Tommy to lend you his bike.*
—**generously** *adverb* in a generous way
→ see Thesaurus box at **kind²**
[**ORIGIN:** 1500-1600 From the Latin word *generosus*, which means "born into an upper-class family."]

**ge·net·ics** /dʒəˈnetɪks/ *noun*
the study of GENEs
—**genetic** *adjective* relating to genes or caused by genes: *He was born with a genetic disease that caused problems with his heart.*
—**genetically** *adverb* in a way that relates to genes: *The two viruses are genetically related.*

**ge·nie** /ˈdʒini/ *noun*
a magical creature in old Arab stories, who can make wishes come true: *When Aladdin rubbed the lamp, a genie appeared and asked him what he wished for.*

**ge·nius** /ˈdʒiniəs/ *noun*
someone who has much more intelligence, ability, or skill than is usual: *Mozart was a musical genius who was writing music when he was five years old.*
[**ORIGIN:** 1300-1400 From a Latin word which means "spirit who looks after a person from birth." This word was also sometimes used to mean "natural ability or intelligence."]

**gen·o·cide** /ˈdʒenəˌsaɪd/ *noun*
an attempt to kill a whole race of people
[**ORIGIN:** 1900-2000 From the Greek word *genos*, which means "race of people" and the Latin word *caedere*, which means "to kill."]

**gen·re** /ˈʒɑnrə/ *noun*
a particular type of writing, music, art, or movie: *Science fiction is my favorite genre of literature.*

**gen·tle** /ˈdʒentl/ *adjective*
**1** careful not to hurt anyone or anything: *Be gentle with the baby – don't hurt her.*
**2** not strong, loud, or extreme: *She sang in a gentle voice, and I fell asleep.* | *The gentle breeze was just enough to keep us cool.*
—**gently** *adverb* in a gentle way: *His mother gently wiped away his tears.*
—**gentleness** *noun* the quality of being gentle

**gen·tle·man** /ˈdʒentlmən/ *noun* (plural **gentlemen** /ˈdʒentlmən/)
**1** a polite word for a man you do not know: *Can you show this gentleman to his seat?* | *Thank you, ladies and gentlemen.*
**2** a man who is polite and behaves well: *He was always a gentleman around my parents.*

**gen·u·ine** /ˈdʒenyuɪn/ *adjective*
real, not pretended or false: *Her surprise was*

*genuine – she really didn't know about the party.* | *Is the stone a genuine diamond?*

—**genuinely** *adverb* really: *He seemed genuinely sorry.*

**ge·og·ra·phy** /dʒiˈɑgrəfi/ *noun*
the study of the Earth's surface and the countries of the world: *In geography, we are learning about rainforests.*

—**geographical** /ˌdʒiəˈgræfɪkəl/ (*also* **geographic**) *adjective* relating to the Earth's surface and the countries of the world: *geographical features such as rivers*

[**ORIGIN:** 1400-1500 From the Greek words *ge* and *graphein*, which mean "earth" and "to write or to draw."]

**ge·ol·o·gy** /dʒiˈɑlədʒi/ *noun*
the study of rocks and soil

—**geologist** *noun* someone who studies rocks and soil

—**geological** /ˌdʒiəˈlɑdʒɪkəl/ *adjective* relating to rocks and soil: *the geological processes that form rocks*

[**ORIGIN:** 1700-1800 From the Greek words *ge* and *-logia*, which mean "earth" and "study."]

**ge·om·e·try** /dʒiˈɑmətri/ *noun*
the study of shapes, lines, and angles, and the mathematics relating to them

—**geometric** /ˌdʒiˈmetrɪk/ *adjective* relating to or made of shapes or lines: *The Olympic symbol is a geometric pattern of circles.*

[**ORIGIN:** 1300-1400 From the Greek words *ge* and *metrein*, which mean "earth" and "to measure."]

**ger·bil** /ˈdʒɚbəl/ *noun*
a small furry animal with a long tail, often kept as a pet

**germ** /dʒɚm/ *noun*
a living thing that can make you sick, which is too small to see: *Sneezing spreads germs.*

[**ORIGIN:** 1400-1500 From the Latin word *germen*, which means "seed or bud." A germ is the thing that produces a disease, like a seed is the thing that produces a plant.]

**German¹** /ˈdʒɚmən/ *noun*
**1** someone from Germany
**2** the language spoken in Germany, Austria, and parts of Switzerland

**German²** *adjective*
from Germany: *a German passport*

**ˌGerman ˈmeasles** *noun*
a disease that causes red spots on your body. German measles is not usually serious, but it can be dangerous for a PREGNANT woman's unborn baby.

**ˌGerman ˈshepherd** *noun*
a large strong dog that looks like a WOLF, used especially by the police or for guarding property

**ger·mi·nate** /ˈdʒɚməˌneɪt/ *verb*
if a seed germinates, it begins to grow: *It takes a week for the seeds to germinate.*

**ges·ture¹** /ˈdʒestʃɚ/ *noun*
**1** a movement of your hand, arms, or head that shows what you mean or how you feel: *He made a gesture with his hands to show that he didn't understand what I was saying.*
**2** something you do to show your feelings toward someone, usually feelings of friendship: *"She sent me a card when I was sick." "That was a nice gesture."*

**gesture²** *verb*
to move your hand, arms, or head, in order to tell someone something: *He gestured for the waiter to come over to their table.*

**get** /get/ *verb* (**got** /gɑt/, **gotten** /ˈgɑtn/, **getting**)
**1** to receive or be given something: *Did you get my email?* | *I got an A in Spanish.* | *She got lots of presents for her birthday from her friends.*
**2** to obtain or buy something: *Where did you get those shoes?*
→ see Thesaurus box at **buy**
**3** to receive money for working: *Jennifer gets $19 an hour at her new job.*
→ see Thesaurus box at **earn**
**4** **have got** = to have something. "Have got" is used in spoken English. We usually shorten it to "I've/you've/they've/we've got," and "she's/he's got": *I've got a lot of work to do.*
**5** to become: *It gets hot in the summer.*

**USAGE: get, go, become**

**Get**, **go**, and **become** can all mean "to begin to be something," but they are used in different ways.

**Get** and **go** are less formal than **become**, and are used more often in spoken English: *I got very hungry.* | *Have you gone crazy?*

G

**Become** is used in both written and spoken English: *He's becoming a very good tennis player.* | *The area has become popular with mountain bikers.*

**Get** and **go** are used only in front of an adjective: *It's getting dark.* | *Beethoven went deaf when he was 40 years old.*

**Become** can be used in front of an adjective or a noun: *He became angry and started yelling at me.* | *The noise from the airport is becoming a problem.*

**6** to move somewhere: *Get down on the floor!* | *They couldn't get out of the building.*
**7** to arrive or reach somewhere: *We got home very late.* **SYNONYM: arrive**
**8** to catch an illness: *I'm getting a cold.*
**9** to go onto a bus, plane, train, etc.: *He got the next plane to New York.* **SYNONYM: catch**
**10** to bring someone or something back from somewhere: *She's gone to get the kids from school.* **SYNONYM: pick up**

**THESAURUS: get**

**get** to go to another place and come back with something or someone: *Just a minute while I get my jacket.*

**bring** to take something or someone to a place: *You should bring her some flowers.* | *Elise brought her friend to the party.*

**take** to move something from one place to another, or help someone go from one place to another: *You'd better take your jacket – it's getting cold.* | *I can take you home after the concert.*

**11** to arrange for something to be done: *I'm going to get my hair cut later today.*
**12 get to do something** = if you get to do something, you are able to do it: *We got to see a lot of famous places.*
**13 get someone to do something** = to persuade someone to do something: *We couldn't get him to change his mind.* **SYNONYM: persuade**
**14** to reach a particular stage in a process: *I started reading the book, but I never got to the end.*
**15** to understand something: *I didn't get the joke.*

**PHRASAL VERBS**

**get ahead**
to be successful in your work and make progress in your career: *Do you need a college education to get ahead?*

**get along (with someone)**
to have a friendly relationship with someone: *The two boys get along well with each other.*

**get around something**
to avoid something that will cause problems: *I'm sure there is a way of getting around the problem.*

**get around to doing something**
to do something you have been intending to do for a long time: *I still haven't gotten around to calling her – I've been too busy.*

**get away**
to escape: *The police tried to stop the man, but he got away.*

**get back**
**1** to return: *When do you get back from your vacation?*
**2** to reply to someone at a later time: *Thanks for your call. I'll get back to you soon.*

**get in**
**1** when a plane, train, or bus gets in, it arrives somewhere: *What time does your flight get in?*
**2 get something in** = to give something to someone, especially written work: *Make sure that you get your assignment in on time.* **SYNONYM: turn in**

**get into something**
**1** to be allowed to go to a school, college, or university: *She is hoping to get into Harvard.*
**2** to start to be in a situation, especially one that involves trouble or problems: *He was always getting into trouble with the police.*

**get off (something)**
**1** to leave a bus, train, plane, etc.: *She got off at the next bus stop.* | *We had to get off the plane because of problems with the engine.*
**2** to finish work: *What time do you get off work?*

**get on (something)**
**1** to go onto a bus, train, plane, etc.: *She*

*couldn't get on because the bus was full.* | *We had to run to get on the train.*
**2** **get on with something** = to continue or to make progress with something: *I need to get on with my work, or I won't finish it on time.*
**get out**
**1** to leave: *The professor kept talking, and we finally got out of class at 5 o'clock.*
**2** **get something out** = to remove something, especially a mark on cloth: *The ink stain was hard to get out.*
**get out of (doing) something**
to avoid doing something that you should do: *He's lazy, and he always tries to get out of doing any work.*
**get over**
**1** to feel better after a bad experience or an illness: *She never got over her son's death.*
**2** **can't get over something** = used when you feel very surprised by something: *I can't get over how tall you are – you've grown about three inches since I last saw you!*
**get through**
**1** to succeed in calling someone on the telephone: *I finally got through to him, after trying four times.*
**2** **get through something** = to succeed in dealing with a bad experience: *It was a bad time, but my mom helped me get through it.*
**3** **get through something** = to finish doing something: *I have so much work to get through.*
**get up**
**1** to get out of bed after you have been sleeping: *She usually gets up at 6:00.*
**2** to stand up: *He got up and left.*

**get·a·way** /ˈgetəˌweɪ/ *noun*
**make your getaway** (*informal*) = to escape from somewhere: *The robbers made their getaway in a car parked outside the store.*

**ˈget-toˌgether** *noun*
a small informal party or meeting: *We're having a get-together with some friends. Do you want to come?*
→ see Thesaurus box at **party**

**gey·ser** /ˈgaɪzɚ/ *noun*
hot water and steam that come up from a hole in the ground into the air in a natural process: *In Yellowstone Park, the geyser called Old Faithful erupts 100 feet into the air.*

**ghet·to** /ˈgetoʊ/ *noun* (plural **ghettos** *or* **ghettoes**)
a part of a city where poor people live in bad conditions, especially people of one particular race: *He grew up in the ghetto, in one of the poorest areas of Chicago.*

**ghost** /goʊst/ *noun*
the spirit of a dead person that stays in a place: *The owner says she saw the ghost of a young girl in the old house.*
—**ghostly** *adjective* frightening and making you think of ghosts: *a ghostly sound*

**gi·ant¹** /ˈdʒaɪənt/ *adjective*
very big, and much bigger than other things of the same type: *There was a giant screen in the baseball stadium.*

**giant²** *noun*
a very tall strong man or woman, in children's stories

**gift** /gɪft/ *noun*
**1** something that you give someone on a special occasion: *The bike was a birthday gift from my parents.* **SYNONYM: present**
**2** a natural ability to do something well: *She is a good teacher with a gift for explaining things in a simple way.* **SYNONYM: talent**

**gift·ed** /ˈgɪftɪd/ *adjective*
having the natural ability to do something very well: *She is a gifted dancer.* **SYNONYM: talented**

**gig** /gɪg/ *noun*
a performance by rock, POP, or JAZZ musicians: *The band has played gigs in Las Vegas.*

**gig·a·byte** /ˈgɪgəˌbaɪt/ *noun*
a unit for measuring computer information, equal to 1,024 MEGABYTEs

**gi·gan·tic** /dʒaɪˈgæntɪk/ *adjective*
extremely large: *Sequoias are gigantic trees that can grow up to 300 feet tall.*
→ see Thesaurus box at **big**

**gig·gle** /ˈgɪgəl/ *verb*
to laugh quickly and in a high voice: *The girls giggled as they tried on the silly hats.*
—**giggle** *noun* a quick high laugh
→ see Thesaurus box at **laugh¹**

G

**gill** /gɪl/ *noun*
one of the parts at the sides of a fish's head with which it breathes

**gim·mick** /ˈgɪmɪk/ *noun* (*informal*)
something that a company does or gives you to make you want to buy something: *The free software is a gimmick that gets you to try more of the company's products.*

**gin** /dʒɪn/ *noun*
a strong clear alcoholic drink made from grain and berries

**gin·ger** /ˈdʒɪndʒɚ/ *noun*
a light brown root with a strong taste, which is used in cooking

**ˈginger ˌale** *noun*
a sweet gold-colored drink with bubbles

G

**gin·ger·bread** /ˈdʒɪndʒɚˌbred/ *noun*
a type of cookie or cake with ginger in it: *We baked gingerbread men for the holidays.*

**gi·raffe** /dʒəˈræf/ *noun*
a very tall African animal with a long neck and long legs, and dark spots on its yellow-brown fur: *Giraffes have long necks so that they can eat the leaves off trees.*

**girl** /gɚl/ *noun*
a female child: *She is a pretty little girl.* | *They have two boys and a girl.*
—**girlish** *adjective* like a little girl: *She has a girlish laugh.*
[**ORIGIN:** From the old English word *gurle* or *girle*, which meant "child or young person." First used with its modern meaning, 1300-1400]

**girl·friend** /ˈgɚlfrend/ *noun*
**1** a girl or woman with whom you have a romantic relationship: *He's had a lot of girlfriends.*
**2** a woman's or girl's female friend: *My sister is always talking to her girlfriends on the phone.*

**give** /gIv/ *verb* (**gave** /geɪv/, **given** /ˈgɪvən/)
**1** to let someone have something as a present: *She gave him a watch for his birthday.*
**2** to put something in someone's hand: *Give that bag to me – I'll carry it.*
**3** to provide something for someone: *Can I give you some help?* | *Sugar gives you energy quickly.*
**4** to tell someone something: *I gave her my phone number.* | *I asked John why he had lied, but he wouldn't give me an answer.*
**5** to allow someone to do something: *The teacher gave me permission to miss the class.*
**6** to do an action: *She gave a big smile.* | *Give me a call tonight – here's my number.*
**7** to do a performance or talk: *The singer is giving a concert in New York.* | *I have to give a speech at the wedding.*
**8** to cause someone to have something: *I don't want to give you my cold.* | *My computer has been giving me problems.*
**9** to make someone have a punishment: *The judge gave him five years in prison.*
**10 give way** = if something gives way, it breaks or falls down suddenly because there is too much weight or pressure on it: *The branch gave way because he was too heavy for it.*
**11 give or take** = used when saying that a number or amount is not exact: *The show lasts about an hour, give or take five minutes.*
[**ORIGIN:** From the old English word *giefan*.]

**PHRASAL VERBS**

**give something away**
to give someone something without asking for money: *I gave my old clothes away.*

**give something back**
to return something to its owner: *I'll give the money back to you next week.*

**give in**
to finally agree to do something that you did not want to do: *The kids kept asking for candy, and finally she gave in and bought them some.*

**give off something**
to produce a smell, light, heat, sound, etc.: *The old meat gave off a terrible smell.*

**give something out**
to give something to each person in a group: *The teacher gave out the tests to the students.*

**THESAURUS: give out**

**pass** to take something and put it in someone's hand: *Could you pass me the salt?*

**hand** to pass something to someone: *He handed me a card with his phone number on it.*

**hand out/pass around** to give something to each of the people in a group: *Mr. Goodman handed out the tests.* | *Pass those cookies around, please.*

**distribute** (*formal*) to give things to a large number of people: *The money will be distributed to schools in the area.*

**give up**

**1** to stop trying to do something because it is too difficult: *You have almost reached the top – don't give up now!* **SYNONYM: quit**

**2 give up something** = to stop doing something that you have done a lot: *My dad gave up smoking about 10 years ago.* **SYNONYMS: stop, quit**

**3 give yourself up** = to allow yourself to be caught by the police or enemy soldiers: *The man threw down his weapon and gave himself up to the police.*

**giv·en**[1] /ˈgɪvən/ *verb*

the past participle of GIVE

**given**[2] *adjective*

**any given/a given ...** = used when saying that any particular time or situation could be used as an example: *In any given year, half of all accidents happen in the home.*

**given**[3] *preposition*

taking something into account: *Given his age, my grandfather is healthy and strong.*

**ˈgiven name** *noun*

your first name: *His given name is Michael and his last name is Johnson.*

**gla·cier** /ˈgleɪʃɚ/ *noun*

a large amount of ice that moves very slowly forward over the land: *The glaciers in these mountains slowly carved out the valleys.*

[**ORIGIN:** 1700-1800 From the Latin word *glacies*, which means "ice."]

**glad** /glæd/ *adjective*

**1** happy about something: *I'm so glad that you're feeling better.* | *She was glad to be home again.*

**2 be glad to do something** = to be willing and happy to do something: *I would be glad to help you.*

→ see Thesaurus box at **happy**

[**ORIGIN:** From the old English word *glæd*, which means "bright, shining, or happy."]

**glad·ly** /ˈglædli/ *adverb*

in a way that shows that you are pleased: *I gladly accepted his offer.*

**glam·or·ous** /ˈglæmərəs/ *adjective*

attractive and exciting because of being rich and successful: *My sister looked very glamorous in her prom dress.*

**glam·our** (*also* **glamor**) /ˈglæmɚ/ *noun*

the quality of being glamorous: *People are fascinated by the glamour of Hollywood.*

[**ORIGIN:** 1700-1800 From the Scottish English word for "magic," from "grammar." "Grammar" used to mean "knowledge" and was used about knowledge of magic.]

**glance**[1] /glæns/ *verb*

**1** to look at someone or something quickly and then look away: *He glanced at his watch.*

**2** to read something very quickly: *He glanced at the menu and ordered a hamburger.*

→ see Thesaurus box at **look**[1]

**glance**[2] *noun*

**1** a quick look: *Mom took one glance at me and said "Go get cleaned up."*

**2 at a glance** = immediately and by looking very quickly: *I knew at a glance that something was wrong.*

→ **at first glance** at **first**[1]

**gland** /glænd/ *noun*

a part of your body that produces a substance such as SWEAT or SALIVA: *Sweat glands help to keep your body cool when it is very hot.*

**glare**[1] /gler/ *verb*

**1** to look angrily at someone or something for a long time: *She glared at me, then asked me why I had lied to her.*

**2** to shine with a strong bright light that hurts your eyes: *The sun glared down on us all afternoon on the beach.*

**glare**[2] *noun*

**1** a strong bright light that hurts your eyes: *He wore dark glasses to protect his eyes from the glare of the sun.*

**2** a long angry look: *She gave him an angry glare.*

**glass** /glæs/ *noun*

**1** a hard clear material that is used to make windows, bottles, etc.: *The windows of the car are made of very strong glass.*

**2** a glass container used for drinking: *a wine*

*glass | a glass of milk* → see picture on page **A9**
**3 glasses** = two pieces of special glass in a frame that you wear in order to see better: *She has to wear glasses for reading. | I need a new pair of glasses.*

**glaze** /gleɪz/ (*also* **glaze over**) *verb*
if your eyes glaze, they show no expression because you are bored or tired: *Her eyes glaze over when I talk about baseball.*

**gleam¹** /glim/ *verb*
**1** to shine because of being very clean: *He washed the windows until they gleamed.*
**2** if your eyes gleam, they are bright and show that you are excited: *Her eyes gleamed with excitement when she saw the present he had brought her.*



**gleam²** *noun*
**1** a look in someone's eyes that shows feelings, especially of happiness or interest: *There was a gleam of happiness in her eyes as she read his letter.*
**2** a shiny quality: *I spotted the gleam of polished metal in the distance.*

**glee** /gli/ *noun*
a feeling of excitement and satisfaction: *We shouted with glee when our team scored the winning goal.*

**glide** /glaɪd/ *verb*
to move smoothly and quietly: *We watched the sailboats glide across the lake.*

**glid·er** /ˈglaɪdɚ/ *noun*
a light airplane that flies without an engine

**glim·mer¹** /ˈglɪmɚ/ *noun*
**1** a slight feeling: *There is still a glimmer of hope that the men might be found alive.*
**2** a light that is not very bright or steady: *the glimmer of a candle flame*

**glimmer²** *verb*
to shine with a light that is not very bright or steady: *A light glimmered across the lake.*

**glimpse** /glɪmps/ *noun*
if you catch a glimpse of someone or something, you are able to see that person or thing for a very short time: *The fans hoped to catch a glimpse of the singer at her hotel.*
—**glimpse** *verb* to see someone or something, but only for a very short time: *I thought I glimpsed Cindy in the crowd as we drove by.*

**glis·ten** /ˈglɪsən/ *verb*
to shine and look wet or oily: *Her eyes glistened with tears.*

**glitch** /glɪtʃ/ *noun*
a small problem with a machine or system that stops it from working correctly: *The plane took off late because of a glitch in the computer system.*

**glit·ter¹** /ˈglɪtɚ/ *verb*
if something glitters, you see a lot of small flashes of light when the sun or a light shines on it: *Snow glittered in the sunlight.*

**glitter²** *noun*
**1** small shiny pieces of metal or paper that are used to decorate something: *They glued glitter onto the Christmas cards they made.*
**2** the flashes of light that come off something: *the glitter of her diamond ring*
→ see Thesaurus box at **shine**

**gloat** /gloʊt/ *verb*
to behave in a way that shows that you are happy that you have succeeded and that another person has failed: *The fans are still gloating over their team's victory.*

**glob·al** Ac /ˈgloʊbəl/ *adjective*
including or affecting the whole world: *Climate change is a global problem that affects every country.* SYNONYM: **worldwide**
—**globally** *adverb* all over the world, or affecting the whole world

**ˌglobal ˈwarming** *noun*
an increase in world temperatures, caused by an increase of CARBON DIOXIDE around the Earth: *Global warming is mainly caused by pollution from cars, planes, and factories.*

**globe**

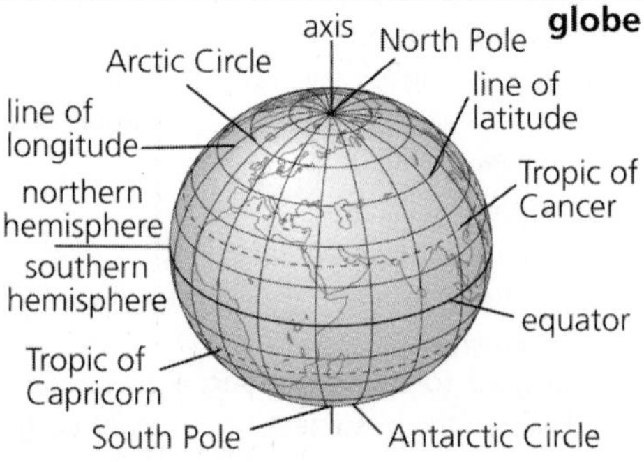


**globe** Ac /gloʊb/ *noun*
**1 the globe** = the world: *Our company has offices all over the globe.*

**2** a round object that has a map of the Earth on it: *The teacher used a globe to show how the ships sailed from England to America.*
[**ORIGIN:** 1500-1600 From the Latin word *globus*, which means "something in the shape of a ball."]

**WORD FAMILY: globe**
**globe** *noun* | **global** *adjective* | **globally** *adverb*

**gloom** /glum/ *noun*
**1** a feeling of sadness, when you have no hope: *The country was full of gloom after President Kennedy's death.*
**2** darkness that makes it difficult for you to see: *Nobody was outside in the cold winter gloom.*

**gloom·y** /glumi/ *adjective*
**1** sad, or making you feel sad: *Watching the news on TV always makes me gloomy.*
**2** dark, especially in a way that makes you feel sad: *The basement was damp and gloomy.*

**glo·ri·fy** /ˈglɔrəˌfaɪ/ *verb* (**glorified**, **glorifies**)
**1** to make someone or something seem better or more important than they really are: *Too many movies glorify violence by making it seem exciting.*
**2** to praise someone or something, especially God

**glo·ri·ous** /ˈglɔriəs/ *adjective*
**1** very beautiful or impressive: *It was a glorious day, and there wasn't a cloud in the sky.*
**2** very good and deserving praise and honor: *The country has a glorious history.*
—**gloriously** *adverb* in a very good or impressive way

**glo·ry** /ˈglɔri/ *noun* (plural **glories**)
**1** praise and honor that someone gets for achieving something: *The victory brought the team glory.*
**2** the beautiful and impressive appearance that something has: *Ahead of us we saw the Grand Canyon, in all its glory.*
**3** an achievement that is greatly admired or respected: *The singer matches his past glories on this great album.*

**glos·sa·ry** /ˈglɑsəri/ *noun* (plural **glossaries**)
a list of words with an explanation of their meaning, usually printed at the end of a book

**gloss·y** /ˈglɔsi/ *adjective*
**1** shiny and smooth: *She had long glossy black hair.*
**2** a glossy magazine, book, or photograph is printed on good quality shiny paper: *I saw a picture of the hotel in a glossy magazine.*
—**gloss** *noun* a shiny attractive appearance: *The dog was sick, and its fur had lost its gloss.*

**glove** /glʌv/ *noun*
a piece of clothing that you wear on your hand, that has a separate part for each finger: *Do you have a warm pair of gloves?* → see picture on page **A6**

**glow¹** /gloʊ/ *verb*
to shine with a soft steady light: *The harbor lights glowed in the distance.*
→ see Thesaurus box at **shine**

**glow²** *noun*
**1** a soft steady light: *I saw the man in the glow of the street lights.*
**2** if your face has a glow, it has a bright color and you look healthy, warm, or happy: *His face has a healthy glow.*

**glu·cose** /ˈglukoʊs/ *noun*
a natural form of sugar that is found in many types of foods, especially bread, rice, potatoes, etc.

**glue¹** /glu/ *noun*
a sticky substance used for attaching one thing to another: *I stuck the two pieces of wood together with glue.*

**glue²** *verb*
**1** to stick things together using glue: *Glue the colored shapes to the paper.*
**2** **be glued to something** (*informal*) = to look at something such as the television with all your attention because you are very interested in it: *My sister was glued to the TV, watching cartoons.*
→ see Thesaurus box at **fasten**

**gnaw** /nɔ/ *verb*
to keep biting at something: *The dog was gnawing on a bone.* **SYNONYM: chew**

**GNP** *noun*
(**gross national product**) the total value of the goods and services produced by a country: *Government spending is more than 15 percent of the GNP.*

**go**[1] /goʊ/ *verb* (**went** /went/, **gone** /gɔn/, **been** /bɪn/, **goes** /goʊz/)

**1** to move or travel to a place: *He went home at 5 o'clock.* | *"Where's Maria?" "She had to go to the library."* | *I usually go to school by bus.* | *Have you ever been to Paris?*

**USAGE: gone, been**

**Gone** and **been** are past participles of **go**. A past participle is the form of a verb that you use when talking about things that have happened.

**Has gone** and **have gone** are used to say that someone recently went to a place and is still there: *The Macleans have gone to Hawaii. They won't be back for two weeks.*

**Has been** and **have been** are used to say that someone went to a place and came back: *The Macleans have been to Hawaii. They say they had a great time there.*

G

**2** to leave: *It's time for us to go.*

**3 be going to do something** = used when saying that something will happen, or that you intend to do something: *It looks like it is going to rain.* | *I'm going to stay with my grandparents in New York.*

**4** to do an activity in a different place from where you are now: *I want to go shopping tomorrow.* | *Do you want to go for a walk?*

**5** to regularly attend school, a church, etc.: *Which college did you go to?*

**6** to change, especially by becoming worse than before: *I'll go crazy if I have to stay here another week!* | *Her hair is starting to go gray.*

**USAGE: go, get, become**

**Go**, **get**, and **become** can all mean "to begin to be something," but they are used in different ways.

**Go** and **get** are less formal than **become**, and are used more often in spoken English: *Have you gone crazy?* | *I got very hungry.*

**Become** is used in both written and spoken English: *He's becoming a very good tennis player.* | *The area has become popular with mountain bikers.*

**Go** and **get** are used only in front of an adjective: *Beethoven went deaf when he was 40 years old.* | *It's getting dark.*

**Become** can be used in front of an adjective or a noun: *He became angry and started yelling at me.* | *The noise from the airport is becoming a problem.*

**7** to happen in a particular way: *The party went well, and everyone had a good time.*

**8** used to say where a road or path leads: *This road goes south to Dallas.*

**9** if something goes somewhere, it should be put there: *"Where does this pan go?" "On the top shelf."*

**10 to go** = **a)** used when saying how much time there is before something happens: *Only two more days to go before our vacation!* **b)** food that is to go is bought from a restaurant and taken away to be eaten: *I'll have two large fries to go.*

**11 How's it going?/How are things going?** = used when you meet someone, to ask how he or she is: *"Hey, Jimmy, how's it going?" "I'm good. And you?"*

**12 go to sleep** = to start to sleep: *I went to sleep at about 11:00.*

**13 go (to the bathroom)** = to use the toilet: *Mommy, I have to go!*

[**ORIGIN:** From the old English word *gan*.]

**PHRASAL VERBS**

**go after someone or something**

to try to catch or get someone or something: *The police went after the robber.*

**go ahead**

**1** used when giving someone permission to do something or to start speaking: *"Can I sit here?" "Go ahead!"*

**2** to do something that you were planning to do: *They decided to go ahead and get married.*

**go along with someone or something**

to agree with or support someone or something: *You'll never get Mom to go along with your idea.*

**go away**

to leave a place or a person: *We're going away for two weeks in June.* | *Go away, and leave me alone!*

**go back**
**1** to return to a place: *I never want to go back there again.*
**2** to have existed for a long time: *The town goes back to the 19th century.*

**go by**
if time goes by, it passes: *The days went by, and he still didn't call me.*

**go down**
**1** to become less: *The temperature went down to 15 degrees below zero.*
**2** when the sun goes down, it appears to move down until you cannot see it anymore and night begins
**3** if a computer system goes down, it stops working for a short time

**go for**
**1** **go for something** = to try to get or win something: *He's going for his fifth gold medal at the Winter Olympics.*
**2** **Go for it!** (*informal*) = used when you want to encourage someone to do something: *If you really want to be an actor, then go for it!*
**3** **go for someone or something** (*informal*) = to usually like a particular type of person or thing: *I don't usually go for pink clothes.*

**go into something**
to describe or explain something thoroughly: *I don't want to go into details, but it was awful.*

**go off**
**1** to explode: *A bomb went off in the street.*
**2** if an alarm goes off, it makes a loud noise: *My alarm clock didn't go off, and I slept until 10 o'clock.*
**3** if a light or the power supply goes off, it stops working: *Suddenly, the lights went off.*

**go on**
**1** to continue: *He stopped for a few minutes and then went on with his work.*
**2** to happen – used especially when you think something bad or unusual is happening: *I heard a strange noise downstairs, and I wondered what was going on.*
**3** if a machine or light goes on, it starts working or starts shining: *The lights went on in the yard, and we saw a deer.*

**go out**
**1** to leave your house, especially in order to do something you enjoy: *We're going out for dinner. Do you want to come?*
**2** to have a romantic relationship with someone: *She has been going out with David for over a year.*
**3** if the TIDE goes out, the water moves away from the land **ANTONYM: come in**
**4** if a light or fire goes out, it stops shining or burning: *The lights went out, and we couldn't find a candle.*

**go through something**
**1** to have a very upsetting or difficult experience: *She has been through a lot in her life – her parents died when she was ten.*
**2** to look at, read, or explain something carefully: *The teacher went through all the questions so that we understood them.*

**go through with something**
to do something you had planned or promised to do: *I'm not sure if I can go through with the wedding – I'm so scared.*

**go together**
if two things go together, they look good or taste good together: *Do you think these colors go together?*

**go up**
to increase: *Our rent has gone up by almost 20%.* **SYNONYM: rise**

**go with something**
**1** to look good or taste good with something: *That blue dress goes well with your blonde hair.*
**2** to accept someone's idea or plan: *I'm happy to go with that idea, if you agree.*

**go**$^2$ *noun*
**1** **give it a go** (*informal*) = to try doing something: *I'd never ice skated before, but I thought I'd give it a go.* **SYNONYM: give it a try**
**2** **on the go** (*informal*) = very busy doing a lot of things, and not stopping for a rest: *I've been on the go all day, so I need to sit down.*

**ˈgo-aˌhead** *noun*
**give the go-ahead/get the go-ahead** (*informal*) = to give or be given official permission to start doing something: *The school has been given the go-ahead to build a new library.*

G

**goal** Ac /goʊl/ *noun*
**1** something that you hope to achieve in the future: *My ultimate goal is to win a medal at the Olympics.*
**2** the place where you send the ball or PUCK to score a point in sports, for example football, SOCCER, or HOCKEY: *She kicked the ball into the goal.*
**3** the action of scoring a point in a sport, or the point that you get: *All the fans cheered when Boselli scored a goal.*
→ see Thesaurus box at **purpose**

**goal·ie** /ˈgoʊli/ *noun* (*informal*)
a goalkeeper

**goal·keep·er** /ˈgoʊlˌkipɚ/ (*also* **goal·tend·er** /ˈgoʊlˌtendɚ/) *noun*
the player whose job is to stop the ball from going into the goal in sports such as SOCCER



**goat** /goʊt/ *noun*
a farm animal that has horns and long hair under its chin

**gob·ble** /ˈgɑbəl/ (*also* **gobble up/down**) *verb* (*informal*)
to eat something very quickly: *The kids gobbled up the cake and then asked for more.*

**gob·lin** /ˈgɑblɪn/ *noun*
a small ugly creature in children's stories that likes to trick people

**god** /gɑd/ *noun*
**1 God** = the maker and ruler of the universe, according to the Christian, Jewish, and Muslim religions: *Do you believe in God?*
**2** one of many male spirits who have special powers, in some religions: *Mars was the Roman god of war.*

**god·child** /ˈgɑdtʃaɪld/ *noun* (plural **godchildren** /ˈgɑdˌtʃɪldrən/)
a child that a godparent promises to help

**god·daugh·ter** /ˈgɑdˌdɔtɚ/ *noun*
a female godchild

**god·dess** /ˈgɑdɪs/ *noun*
one of many female spirits who have special powers, in some religions: *Athena was the Greek goddess of wisdom.*

**god·fa·ther** /ˈgɑdˌfɑðɚ/ *noun*
a male godparent

**god·moth·er** /ˈgɑdˌmʌðɚ/ *noun*
a female godparent

**god·par·ent** /ˈgɑdˌperənt/ *noun*
someone who promises at a BAPTISM to help a child, and to teach him or her Christian values

**god·son** /ˈgɑdsʌn/ *noun*
a male GODCHILD

**goggles**

swim goggles — safety goggles

**gog·gles** /ˈgɑgəlz/ *plural noun*
special glasses that fit close to your face, so that things cannot go into your eyes: *I wear goggles when I go swimming, so that the water doesn't get into my eyes.*

**gold** /goʊld/ *noun*
a valuable yellow metal that is used to make things such as jewelry or coins: *The necklace is made of pure gold.*
—**gold** *adjective* made of gold: *a gold ring*

**gold·en** /ˈgoʊldən/ *adjective*
**1** having a bright shiny yellow color: *golden hair*
**2** made of gold: *The king was wearing a golden crown.*
**3 a golden opportunity** = a good chance to be very successful or to get something important: *The team missed a golden opportunity to win the game in the last quarter.*

**gold·fish** /ˈgoʊldˌfɪʃ/ *noun* (plural **goldfish**)
a small orange fish that people often keep as a pet

**ˈgold ˌmine** *noun*
**1** a place below the ground where gold is dug out from rocks
**2** (*informal*) a business or activity that makes you a lot of money: *The restaurant turned out to be a real gold mine.*

**golf** /gɑlf/ *noun*
a game in which you hit a small white ball into holes in the ground with a special stick

called a golf club: *Dad plays golf every weekend.* → see picture on page **A24**
—**golfer** *noun* someone who plays golf

**gone** /gɔn/ *verb*
the past participle of GO

**good[1]** /gʊd/ *adjective* (**better**, **best**)
**1** of a high standard: *His last album was really good. | His work just isn't good enough.* ANTONYM: **bad**

**USAGE: good, well**

Use **good** to talk about the quality of something or someone: *Was the movie good? | a good teacher*

Use **well** to talk about the way someone does something: *He plays tennis very well.*

**THESAURUS: good**

**great** very good or very enjoyable: *We had a really great time at camp.*

**excellent** very good and of a high standard: *It was an excellent concert.*

**wonderful** very good or enjoyable, in a way that makes you feel happy: *It was wonderful to be back home again.*

**fantastic** very good, in a way that makes you feel happy or excited: *The movie's special effects were fantastic.*

**outstanding** better than anyone or anything else: *Her work this year has been outstanding.*

**exceptional** (*formal*) very good in a way that is unusual: *She is an exceptional athlete.*

**2** useful or appropriate: *It was a good day for going to the beach.* ANTONYM: **bad**
**3** likely to be successful: *That's a good idea. | We have a good chance of winning.* ANTONYM: **bad**
**4** if you are good at something, you can do it well: *I'm not a very good swimmer. | Andrea is very good at her job.*
**5** enjoyable and pleasant: *good weather | It's good to see you again.*
**6** likely to make you healthy: *Fresh fruit and vegetables are good for you.* ANTONYM: **bad**
**7** if a child is good, he or she is behaving well: *Wait for me here, and be a good girl.*
**8** kind and helpful: *All the nurses at the hospital were very good to me.*
**9** **as good as** = almost: *The work is as good as finished.*
**10** **good luck** = used to tell someone that you hope he or she will be successful: *Good luck! I know you can do it!*

**good[2]** *noun*
**1** **not any/much good** = bad in quality: *The movie wasn't any good.*
**2** **no good/not much good** = not useful or not successful: *It's no good trying to explain it to her – she won't listen.*
**3** **do someone good** = to have a good effect on someone: *A vacation would do you good.*
**4** **for good** = permanently: *I'd like to live in Denver for good.*
**5** behavior or actions that are morally right: *the struggle between good and evil*
**6** **goods** (*formal*) = things that are produced and sold: *The store sells furniture and other goods for the home.*

**good ˌafterˈnoon** *interjection* (*formal*)
something you say when you meet someone in the afternoon: *Good afternoon, sir. Can I help you?*

**good·bye** /gʊdˈbaɪ/ *interjection*
something you say when you are leaving, or when someone is leaving: *Goodbye, John, see you tomorrow.*
[ORIGIN: 1500-1600 From the phrase "God be with you."]

**good ˈevening** *interjection* (*formal*)
something you say when you meet someone in the evening: *Good evening, ladies and gentlemen.*

**ˌGood ˈFriday** *noun*
the Friday before the Christian holiday of EASTER

**ˌgood-ˈhearted** *adjective*
someone who is good-hearted is kind and willing to help people: *My aunt was a good-hearted woman who often took care of us.*

**ˌgood-ˈlooking** *adjective*
someone who is good-looking is attractive: *Brad Pitt is a really good-looking guy.*
→ see Thesaurus box at **beautiful**

**good ˈmorning** *interjection*
something you say when you meet someone in the morning: *Good morning, Debbie – how are you?*

**good·ness** /ˈgʊdnɪs/ *noun*
**1** (*also* **my goodness**) you say this when you are surprised about something: *My goodness, you've gotten so tall!*
**2** **for goodness sake** = you say this when you are annoyed about something: *For goodness sake, stop yelling.*
**3** the quality of being good and kind to other people: *Everyone loved her for her goodness and generosity.*

**good ˈnight** *interjection*
something you say when someone is leaving at night, or when someone is going to bed: *Good night. See you tomorrow.*



**good·will** /gʊdˈwɪl/ *noun*
kind feelings between people and a feeling of wanting to be helpful: *The principal has the goodwill and respect of the teachers.*

**goo·ey** /ˈgui/ *adjective* (*informal*)
sticky and soft: *The fudge was gooey and stuck to my fingers.*

**goof**[1] /guf/ (*also* **goof up**) *verb* (*informal*)
to make a silly mistake: *I goofed and sent the letter to the wrong address.*
**PHRASAL VERBS**
**goof around**
to spend time doing silly or unimportant things: *Stop goofing around, and clean your room.*
**goof off**
to not do any work: *She goofed off in college and never got her degree.*

**goof**[2] *noun* (*informal*)
someone who is silly: *He's such a big goof – he makes me laugh.*

**goof·y** /ˈgufi/ *adjective* (*informal*)
stupid or silly: *a goofy smile*

**goose** /gus/ *noun* (plural **geese** /gis/)
a large white bird that looks like a duck, but is bigger

**goose·bumps** (*also* **goose bumps**) /ˈgusbʌmps/ *plural noun*
small raised spots on your skin that you get because you are cold, afraid, or excited: *I was so cold – I had goosebumps.*

**GOP** *noun*
**the GOP** (**the Grand Old Party**) = another name for the Republican Party

**go·pher** /ˈgoʊfɚ/ *noun*
a North American animal with light brown fur, fat cheeks, and a short tail, that lives in holes in the ground

**gorge** /gɔrdʒ/ *noun*
a narrow valley with high straight sides: *We looked down into the deep gorge.*
[**ORIGIN:** 1300-1400 From the French word for "throat," from the Latin word *gurges*. Perhaps the idea is that water runs through a gorge like water goes through your throat.]

**gor·geous** /ˈgɔrdʒəs/ *adjective* (*informal*)
very beautiful: *You look gorgeous with your new haircut!* | *gorgeous mountains*
→ see Thesaurus box at **beautiful**

**go·ril·la** /gəˈrɪlə/ *noun*
a large animal that looks like a monkey. Gorillas are the largest type of APE → see picture at **ape**
[**ORIGIN:** 1800-1900 From the word *Gorillai*, used as the name of an African tribe of hairy women in a Greek translation of a book by an ancient explorer.]

**gor·y** /ˈgɔri/ *adjective*
involving or showing a lot of violence: *Horror movies are too gory and scary.*

**gosh** /gɑʃ/ *interjection*
something you say when you are surprised: *Gosh! I never expected the pool to be so big.*

**gos·ling** /ˈgɑzlɪŋ/ *noun*
a baby GOOSE

**gos·pel** /ˈgɑspəl/ *noun*
**1** (*also* **Gospel**) one of the four books of the Christian Bible that tell the story of Jesus's life

**2** the ideas that Jesus taught: *They wanted to spread the gospel.*

**3** (*also* **gospel truth**) something that is completely true: *You can't take what he says as gospel because he loves to trick people.*

[ORIGIN: From the old English words *god* and *spell*, which mean "good" and "news."]

**gos·sip¹** /ˈgɑsəp/ *noun*

things that people say about other people's behavior and lives, especially things that are unkind or untrue: *It's not just Hollywood gossip; this story is really true.*

[ORIGIN: From the old English word *godsibb*, which means "godparent or close friend." The word was later used to refer to someone who talks about the unimportant things that happen each day, and then to the things that person says. First used in English with its modern meaning, 1800-1900]

**gossip²** *verb*

to talk about other people's behavior and lives, often saying things that are unkind or untrue: *Everyone started gossiping about them because we all thought they were secretly dating.*

→ see Thesaurus box at **talk¹**

**got** /gɑt/ *verb*

**1** the past tense of GET

**2** a past participle of GET

**got·ten** /ˈgɑtn/ *verb*

the usual past participle of GET

**gourd** /gɔrd/ *noun*

a large round fruit with a hard shell that was used as a bowl or cup in the past

**gour·met¹** /gʊrˈmeɪ/ *adjective*

relating to food and drink that is very good quality: *a gourmet meal*

**gourmet²** *noun*

someone who enjoys food and drink that is good quality, and knows a lot about them

**gov·ern** /ˈgʌvən/ *verb*

**1** to legally control a country, state, or city and make all the decisions about taxes, laws, etc.: *The President must work with Congress to govern the country.*

**2** (*formal*) if laws or rules govern something, they say what should happen: *The school's dress code governs what clothes you are allowed to wear to school.*

[ORIGIN: 1200-1300 From the Latin word *gubernare*, from the Greek word *kybernan*, which means "to steer a ship." The idea is that controlling a country is like steering a ship.]

**WORD FAMILY: govern**

**govern** *verb* | **government** *noun* | **governmental** *adjective* | **governor** *noun* | **governorship** *noun*

**gov·ern·ment** /ˈgʌvəmənt/ *noun*

**1** (*also* **Government**) the group of people who govern a country or state: *The federal government provides the money, not the state government.* | *government officials*

**THESAURUS: government**

**administration** the U.S. president and the people who work for the president: *Most Americans think that the administration is doing a good job.*

**democracy** a political system in which the people of a country can choose the government by voting: *In a move toward democracy, the country held elections for the first time.*

**republic** a country that elects its government and does not have a king or queen: *The United States and France are both republics.*

**monarchy** the system in which a country is ruled by a king or queen, or in which a king or queen is the head of state: *Britain is a monarchy, but it also has an elected government.*

**regime** a government, especially one that is strict or has not been elected fairly: *The regime sent its opponents to jail.*

**dictatorship** a country that is ruled by a leader with complete power, who has not been elected: *When Saddam Hussein led Iraq, the country was a dictatorship.*

**2** the process of governing a place: *The candidate does not have much experience in government.*

**3** a system for governing a place: *In a democratic government, people elect their leaders.*

—**governmental** /ˌgʌvənˈmentl/ *adjective* relating to government

G

**gov·er·nor** (*also* **Governor**) /ˈgʌvənɚ/ *noun*
the person in charge of a state in the U.S.: *the Governor of California*

**gown** /gaʊn/ *noun*
**1** a long dress worn by a woman on formal occasions: *She wore a red silk evening gown.*
**2** a long loose piece of clothing worn for formal ceremonies by people such as judges or students at GRADUATION: *The students walked across the stage in their black graduation gowns.*
**3** a loose piece of clothing worn in a hospital by a doctor or a patient during an operation: *a hospital gown*

**GPA** *noun*
(**grade point average**) the average of all the grades that a student gets. An A is 4 points, a B is 3 points, a C is 2 points, a D is 1 point, and an F is 0: *He graduated in 2000 with a GPA of 3.3.*

**grab** /græb/ *verb* (**grabbed**, **grabbing**)
to take hold of someone or something in a rough or violent way: *Rob grabbed my arm and pulled me away.*
→ see Thesaurus box at **hold**[1]

**grace** /greɪs/ *noun*
**1** a smooth way of moving that appears natural, relaxed, and attractive: *She moves with the grace of a dancer.*
**2** polite behavior: *She accepted her punishment with grace; she did not cry or get angry.*
**3** the kindness and love that God shows to people: *By the grace of God, I was able to walk again.*
**4** a short prayer said before a meal: *Before we eat – Tom, can you please say grace?*
[**ORIGIN:** 1100-1200 From the Latin word *gratia*, which means "pleasing quality."]

**grace·ful** /ˈgreɪsfəl/ *adjective*
moving in a way that is smooth and attractive: *The ballet dancer's movements were graceful.*
—**gracefully** *adverb* in a graceful way: *The dolphins swam gracefully through the ocean.*

**gra·cious** /ˈgreɪʃəs/ *adjective*
behaving in a polite and kind way: *She was gracious as she thanked the people who had helped her win the election.*
—**graciously** *adverb* in a polite and kind way: *Mr. Allen graciously thanked us all for coming.*
—**graciousness** *noun* behavior that is polite and kind

**grade**[1] Ac /greɪd/ *noun*
**1** one of the 12 years that students are in school in the U.S.: *My brother is in third grade.* | *a fourth-grade class*
**2** a letter or number that shows how good a student's work is: *His grades are improving, and he now has mostly B's.* | *Paul has to get good grades to get into college.*
**3** a level of quality that shows you how good a product, material, etc. is: *The farm produces high grade eggs and milk.*
**4 make the grade** = to succeed or be as good as a particular standard: *Only a few young athletes will make the grade in professional sports.*
[**ORIGIN:** 1500-1600 From the Latin word *gradus*, which means "step."]

**grade**[2] Ac *verb*
to give a grade to a test or to a piece of school work: *The teacher is grading the papers tonight.*

**ˈgrade point ˌaverage** *noun*
GPA

**ˈgrade ˌschool** *noun*
ELEMENTARY SCHOOL

**grad·u·al** /ˈgrædʒuəl/ *adjective*
happening slowly over a long period of time: *Over the last few weeks, there has been a gradual improvement in his health.*
**ANTONYM: sudden**
—**gradually** *adverb* slowly, over a long period of time: *Spring was coming, and the temperature was gradually getting warmer.*

**grad·u·ate**[1] /ˈgrædʒˌuət/ *noun*
someone who has finished studying at a school, college, or university and has a DIPLOMA or a degree: *high school graduates* | *a graduate of MIT*

**WORD FAMILY: graduate**
**graduate** *verb* | **graduate** *noun* | **graduation** *noun*

**grad·u·ate²** /ˈgrædʒueɪt/ *verb*
to finish studying at a school, college, or university and get a DIPLOMA or a degree: *My sister graduated from college last year.*

graduate

**grad·u·ate³** /ˈgrædʒuɪt/ *adjective*
relating to a student who is studying to get a MASTER'S DEGREE or a PH.D.: *After getting his college degree, he did graduate work at Columbia University.* | *a graduate student*

**ˈgraduate ˌschool** *noun*
a college or university where you can study for a MASTER'S DEGREE or a PH.D. after finishing your first degree

**grad·u·a·tion** /ˌgrædʒuˈeɪʃən/ *noun*
a ceremony when students receive their DIPLOMA or degree: *We went to Bobby's graduation yesterday.*

graffiti

**graf·fi·ti** /grəˈfiti/ *noun*
writing and pictures that people draw illegally on buildings, fences, signs, etc.: *The doors and walls were covered with graffiti.*
[ORIGIN: 1800-1900 From the Italian word *graffiare*, which means "to make marks in a surface."]

**grain** /greɪn/ *noun*
**1** the seeds of crops such as wheat, BARLEY, or rice that are eaten as food: *Most of the grain that we grow is used to feed cattle.*
**2** a very small piece of sand, salt, or sugar: *It was windy at the beach, and grains of sand kept blowing into my eyes.*
**3 the grain** = the natural lines or patterns you can see in wood: *Split the wood along the grain.*
**4 a grain of something** = a very small amount of something: *There is a grain of truth in his story, but most of it is a lie.*
**5 take something with a grain of salt** = to realize that part of what someone says may not be true: *He sometimes lies, so take what he says with a grain of salt.*
[ORIGIN: 1200-1300 From the Latin word *granum*, which means "seed."]

**gram** /græm/ *noun* (*written abbreviation*: **gm**)
a unit for measuring weight. There are 1,000 grams in a kilogram.

**gram·mar** /ˈgræmɚ/ *noun*
the rules of a language, which control how words change tense and how sentences are formed: *There are some mistakes in your spelling and grammar.*
—**grammatical** /grəˈmætɪkəl/ *adjective*
relating to grammar: *a grammatical error*
[ORIGIN: 1300-1400 From the Greek word *gramma*, which means "letter."]

**grand** /grænd/ *adjective*
**1** big and impressive: *We drove through a rich neighborhood past some grand old buildings.*
**2 grand total** = the total you get when you add up several numbers or amounts: *We added up all the money everyone had given, and the grand total was $580.*
**3 grand opening** = a special event on the day that a business opens for the first time: *The store had its grand opening yesterday, with a band playing and balloons for the kids.*
[ORIGIN: 1500-1600 From the Latin word *grandis*, which means "big or great."]

**grand·child** /ˈgræntʃaɪld/ *noun* (plural **grandchildren** /ˈgrænˌtʃɪldrən/)
the child of your son or daughter

**grand·daugh·ter** /ˈgrænˌdɔtɚ/ *noun*
the daughter of your son or daughter

**grand·fa·ther** /ˈgrændˌfɑðɚ/ *noun*
the father of your mother or father

**ˈgrandfather ˌclock** *noun*
a clock in a tall wooden case that stands on the floor

**grand·ly** /ˈgrændli/ *adverb*
in a way that is impressive or intended to attract attention: *Jessie walked grandly into the room, hoping everyone would look at her.*

**grand·ma** /ˈgrændmɑ/ *noun* (*informal*)
another word for GRANDMOTHER

G

**grand·moth·er** /ˈgrændˌmʌðɚ/ *noun*
the mother of your mother or father

**grand·pa** /ˈgrændpɑ/ *noun (informal)*
another word for GRANDFATHER

**grand·par·ent** /ˈgrændˌperənt/ *noun*
the parent of your mother or father

**grand·son** /ˈgrændsʌn/ *noun*
the son of your son or daughter: *I have a grandson who is two years old.*

**grand·stand** /ˈgrændstænd/ *noun*
rows of seats outdoors where people sit to watch sports: *We watched the race from the grandstand.*

**gran·ite** /ˈgrænɪt/ *noun*
a type of hard gray rock

G

**gra·no·la** /grəˈnoʊlə/ *noun*
a breakfast food made of OATS, nuts, seeds, and sometimes fruit

**grant¹** Ac /grænt/ *noun*
money that an organization gives to people for a special purpose: *He got a grant for his research from the government.*

**grant²** Ac *verb*
**1 take it for granted (that)** = to think that something is definitely true, although it may not be true: *His parents took it for granted that he would go to college, but he did not want to.* **SYNONYM: assume**
**2** *(formal)* to allow someone to do or have something: *She granted them permission to take photographs of her house.*

**grape** /greɪp/ *noun*
a small round green or red fruit. Grapes can be eaten or used to make wine: *I bought a bunch of grapes at the grocery store.* → see picture on page **A13**
**[ORIGIN:** 1200-1300 From an old French word meaning "hook." Grapes were picked using a hook.**]**

**grape·fruit** /ˈgreɪpfrut/ *noun*
a big round yellow fruit with a thick skin, that looks like a large orange but is not as sweet → see picture on page **A13**
**[ORIGIN:** 1800-1900 From the words "grape" and "fruit," because grapefruits grow in bunches, like grapes.**]**

**grape·vine** /ˈgreɪpvaɪn/ *noun*
the plant that grapes grow on **SYNONYM: vine**

**graph**

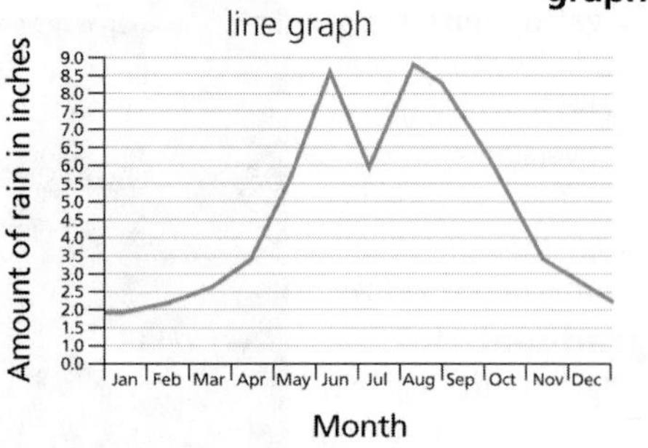


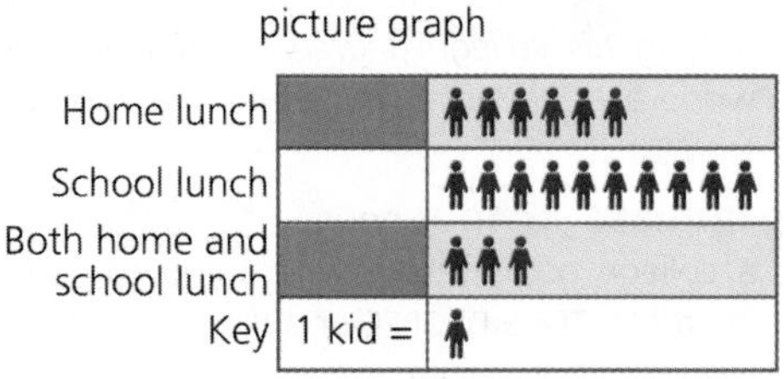


**graph** /græf/ *noun*
a drawing that uses bars or lines to show different numbers or amounts: *This graph shows the amount of rain in Miami for every month of the year.*
**[ORIGIN:** 1800-1900 From the Greek word *graphein*, which means "to draw or write."**]**

**graph·ic** /ˈgræfɪk/ *adjective*
**1** describing or showing something very clearly or with a lot of details, especially something unpleasant: *He gave a graphic description of the train crash.*
**2** relating to drawing and design, especially for magazines, advertisements, or websites: *A graphic artist designed the book's cover.*
—**graphically** *adverb* very clearly: *The TV program graphically showed the results of the earthquake.*

**graph·ics** /ˈgræfɪks/ *plural noun*
the images on a computer screen or in a computer game: *The video game's graphics are so good that the places and characters seem almost real.*

**grasp** /græsp/ *verb*
**1** to hold something firmly: *Grasp the rope with both hands, so that you don't drop it.*
**2** to understand something: *At first, I didn't grasp what she was saying to me, but then I understood.*

**grass** /græs/ *noun*
a plant with thin green leaves that covers the ground in yards, parks, and fields: *The grass in the backyard needs cutting.*

**grass·hop·per** /ˈgræsˌhɑpɚ/ *noun*
a green or brown insect with long back legs that lives in the grass, can jump high, and makes a short loud noise

**gras·sy** /ˈgræsi/ *adjective*
covered with grass: *There are some grassy areas around the school where the kids play.*

**grate¹** /greɪt/ *verb*
to cut food into small thin pieces by rubbing it against a tool called a grater: *Grate the cheese over the pasta.* → see picture on page A15
—**grater** *noun* a metal kitchen tool with many sharp holes in its surface, used for cutting food into small thin pieces

**grate²** *noun*
**1** a metal frame with bars across it, over a hole in the street or in front of a window: *Iron grates covered the prison windows.* **SYNONYM: grating**
**2** the metal frame that holds the wood in a FIREPLACE

**grate·ful** /ˈgreɪtfəl/ *adjective*
wanting to thank someone who has been kind or helpful: *I was grateful for all his help.*
—**gratefully** *adverb* in a grateful way: *She gratefully accepted his offer of a ride home.*

**WORD FAMILY: grateful**
**grateful** *adjective* | **ungrateful** *adjective* | **gratefully** *adverb* | **gratitude** *noun*

**grat·i·fy** /ˈgrætəˌfaɪ/ *verb* (**gratified, gratifies**) (*formal*)
if you are gratified by something, it makes you feel happy and satisfied: *The actors were gratified that the audience loved the play.*
—**gratification** /ˌgrætəfəˈkeɪʃən/ *noun* pleasure and satisfaction that you get from something: *Teachers get a lot of gratification from seeing students learn and develop.*

**grat·ing** /ˈgreɪtɪŋ/ *noun*
another word for a GRATE

**grat·i·tude** /ˈgrætəˌtud/ *noun*
the feeling you have when you want to thank someone because he or she has been kind or helpful to you: *Maria was full of gratitude for his support.*

**gra·tu·i·tous** /grəˈtuətəs/ *adjective* (*formal*)
unnecessary and likely to upset people: *Why do so many movies contain scenes of gratuitous violence?*

**gra·tu·i·ty** /grəˈtuəti/ *noun* (plural **gratuities**) (*formal*)
an additional amount of money that you give to a worker who has done something for you **SYNONYM: tip**

**grave¹** /greɪv/ *noun*
a hole in the ground where a dead person is buried: *We visited my grandma's grave at the cemetery.*

**grave²** *adjective* (*formal*)
very serious and making people worry: *The fire was big and put the houses next door in grave danger.*
—**gravely** *adverb* seriously: *She was gravely ill and almost died.*

**grav·el** /ˈgrævəl/ *noun*
small stones that are used to make the surface of a path or road: *I heard the sound of footsteps on the gravel outside.*

**grave·stone** /ˈgreɪvstoʊn/ *noun*
a stone on a grave that shows the name of the person buried there, and the date he or she was born and died

**grave·yard** /ˈgreɪvyɑrd/ *noun*
an area of land where dead people are buried: *There was an old graveyard next to the church.*

**grav·i·ty** /ˈgrævəti/ *noun*
**1** the force that makes things fall to the ground: *An apple falls down from a tree because of the Earth's gravity.*
**2** (*formal*) how bad a situation is: *Photographs of the damage caused by the hurricane show the full gravity of the situation.*
[**ORIGIN:** 1400-1500 From the Latin word *gravitas*, which means "heaviness."]

**gra·vy** /ˈgreɪvi/ *noun*
a liquid made from the juice of cooked meat, that you serve with the meat: *We had roast beef and potatoes with gravy.*

**gray¹** /greɪ/ *adjective*
**1** having the color of black mixed with white: *My dad is getting older, and he has gray hair.* |

G

*He was wearing a gray suit.*
**2** cloudy and with no sun: *It was a gray day in winter.*

**gray²** *noun*
the color that you get when you mix black with white: *The shoes come in gray or red.*

**graze** /greɪz/ *verb*
**1** if an animal grazes, it eats grass: *Some cows were grazing in the field.*
**2** to slightly damage the skin on part of your body: *Billy fell and grazed his knee, but it didn't bleed much.*

**grease¹** /gris/ *noun*
**1** soft fat from cooked meat: *The pan was full of hot grease.*
**2** a thick oil that you put on the moving parts of a machine to help them move smoothly: *His hands were covered in grease from fixing the bike.*
[**ORIGIN:** 1200-1300 From the old French *craisse* or *graisse*, from the Latin word *crassus*, which means "thick or fat."]

**grease²** *verb*
to put fat or oil on something: *Grease the pan with butter.*

**greas·y** /ˈgrisi/ *adjective*
**1** cooked in too much oil: *Greasy food is bad for you.*
**2** greasy hair is very dirty and looks like there is too much oil in it: *His hair was greasy, and he needed a bath.* **SYNONYM: oily**; **ANTONYM: dry**
→ see Thesaurus box at **dirty**

**great** /greɪt/ *adjective*
**1** very good or enjoyable: *We saw a great movie last night. | It's great to see you again! | This pasta dish is great for a quick dinner.* **SYNONYM: excellent**
**2** very important or famous: *Abraham Lincoln was a great American president.*
**3** very big or very large in amount: *She had great big brown eyes. | Professional players spend a great deal of time practicing.*
**4 great-grandmother/great-grandfather** = the mother or father of one of your grand-parents
**5 great-granddaughter/great-grandson** = the daughter or son of your GRANDCHILD
→ see Thesaurus box at **good¹**, **nice**

**great·ly** /ˈgreɪtli/ *adverb* (*formal*)
very much: *If you practice a lot, it will greatly increase your chances of winning.*

**greed·y** /ˈgridi/ *adjective* (**greedier, greediest**)
wanting much more of something than you need, especially more money or food: *Some greedy companies want to make more money even if it harms the environment.*
—**greed** *noun* the feeling you have when you want much more of something than you need: *He didn't need the money – he stole it from his company out of greed.*
—**greedily** *adverb* in a greedy way: *Jake greedily ate all the chocolate cake.*

**Greek** /grik/ *noun*
**1** someone from Greece
**2** the language spoken in Greece
—**Greek** *adjective* from Greece: *a Greek woman*

**green¹** /grin/ *adjective*
**1** having the color of grass: *She has green eyes.*
**2** covered with grass and trees: *Cities need more green areas.*

**green²** *noun*
the color of grass: *Green is my favorite color.*

**ˌgreen ˈcard** *noun*
an official card that allows someone from a different country to live and work in the U.S.

**green·house** /ˈgrinhaʊs/ *noun*
**1** a glass building for growing plants that need a warm light place
**2 greenhouse gas** = a gas such as CARBON DIOXIDE that stops heat from escaping from the Earth
**3 the greenhouse effect** = the process in which the air around the Earth is getting slowly warmer because greenhouse gases stop the heat from escaping

**greet** /grit/ *verb*
**1** to welcome or say hello to someone: *He greeted her with a hug.*
**2** to react to a suggestion or something that happens: *My plan was greeted with laughter.*

**greet·ing** /ˈgritɪŋ/ *noun*
**1** something you say or do when you meet someone: *Kissing someone's cheeks is a common greeting in France.*

**2** a message that you send to someone on a special occasion: *Sara got lots of birthday greetings from all her friends.* | *a holiday greeting card*

**gre·nade** /grəˈneɪd/ *noun*
a small bomb that someone can throw or fire from a gun: *One soldier threw a grenade through the door.*

**grew** /gru/ *verb*
the past tense of GROW

**grey** /greɪ/ *adjective, noun*
another spelling of GRAY

**grey·hound** /ˈgreɪhaʊnd/ *noun*
a thin dog that can run very fast.

**grid** /grɪd/ *noun*
a pattern of straight lines that cross each other and form squares: *The puzzle consists of a grid of nine squares, and you have to fit the numbers into the grid.*

**grief** /grif/ *noun*
great sadness: *Her feelings of grief lasted for months after her husband died.*
[**ORIGIN:** 1200-1300 From the old French word *gref*, from the Latin word *gravis*, which means "heavy or unpleasant."]

**griev·ance** /ˈgrivəns/ *noun (formal)*
something that you want to complain about because you think it is unfair to you: *The people who lost their jobs met to discuss their grievances.*

**grieve** /griv/ *verb*
to feel very sad because someone you love has died: *The family is still grieving for their son, who died in the crash.*

**griev·ous** /ˈgrivəs/ *adjective (formal)*
very bad or serious: *The surgeon made a grievous mistake and operated on the wrong leg.*

**grill[1]** /grɪl/ *verb*
to cook food on a frame over a fire: *Grill the chicken for fifteen minutes.*
→ see Thesaurus box at **cook[1]**

**grill[2]** *noun*
a metal frame that you put food on to cook it over a fire: *He put the steaks on the grill.*

**grim** /grɪm/ *adjective*
**1** making you feel worried and unhappy: *The news that day was grim; it was all about war.*
**2** looking very serious and sad: *The policeman looked grim as he explained how the accident had happened.*
—**grimly** *adverb* in a very serious way: *"I lost my job," he said grimly.*

**grim·ace** /ˈgrɪməs/ *verb*
to twist your face because you feel pain or do not like something: *Lou grimaced with pain when the baseball hit him on the shoulder.*
—**grimace** *noun* a look on your face that shows you feel pain or do not like something: *She swallowed the medicine with a grimace.*

**grin** /grɪn/ *noun*
a big smile: *He opened the door with a big grin on his face and hugged me.*
—**grin** *verb* to give a big smile: *"It's great to see you," she said, grinning.*
→ see Thesaurus box at **smile[1]**

**grind** /graɪnd/ *verb* (**ground** /graʊnd/)
to crush or cut something into small pieces or powder: *This machine grinds the coffee beans.*

**grind·er** /ˈgraɪndɚ/ *noun*
a machine that crushes or cuts something into small pieces or powder: *Put the coffee beans in the grinder.*

**grip[1]** /grɪp/ *noun*
**1** a strong hold on something: *He had a firm grip on my arm as he pushed me through the door.*
**2** control of your feelings or of a situation: *Oh, stop crying! Get a grip on yourself!*

**grip[2]** *verb* (**gripped**, **gripping**)
to hold something very firmly: *She gripped the rail to stop herself from falling.*
→ see Thesaurus box at **hold[1]**

**grit** /grɪt/ *noun*
very small pieces of dirt or stone: *Wash the vegetables to remove any grit.*

**griz·zly bear** /ˈgrɪzli ˌber/ (*also* **grizzly**) *noun*
a large brown bear that lives in parts of North America

G

**groan** /groʊn/ *verb*
to make a long deep sound because you are in pain or not happy: *One of the players was on the ground, holding his leg and groaning.*
—**groan** *noun* a long deep sound that you make when you are in pain or not happy: *Mom read the bad news and gave a groan.*

**gro·cer** /ˈgroʊsɚ/ *noun*
someone who owns or works in a grocery store
[**ORIGIN:** 1200-1300 From the old French word *grossier*, which means "person who sells in large quantities," from *gros* meaning "big."]

**gro·cer·ies** /ˈgroʊsəriz/ *plural noun*
the food and things you use in the home that you buy in a store: *I put the groceries away in the refrigerator.*

**gro·cer·y store** /ˈgroʊsəri ˌstɔr/ (*also* **grocery**) *noun*
a store that sells food and things you use in the home: *I went to the grocery store to get some milk.*

**groom** /grum/ *noun*
a man who is getting married: *The groom arrived at the church first.* **SYNONYM: bridegroom**

**groove** /gruv/ *noun*
a thin line that goes into the surface of something: *Make some grooves in the soil and plant the seeds about six inches apart.*

**grope** /groʊp/ *verb*
to use your hands to find something, when you cannot see it: *It was dark, and Mark groped for the light switch.*

**gross** /groʊs/ *adjective*
**1** (*informal*) very unpleasant: *The smell from the garbage truck was really gross.*
**2** very serious or wrong: *That's a gross exaggeration. It costs much less than that.*
**3** before tax or other amounts have been taken away: *He earns a gross income of $45,000.*
[**ORIGIN:** 1300-1400 From the French word *gros*, which means "big or thick."]

**ˌgross ˌnational ˈproduct** *noun*
another word for GNP

**gro·tesque** /groʊˈtesk/ *adjective*
ugly and very strange in a way that is frightening: *Some of the people in his paintings are grotesque.*
[**ORIGIN:** 1500-1600 From French, from the old Italian phrase *pittura grottesca*, which means "cave painting." This probably comes from paintings of strange creatures and scenes on the walls of Roman ruins.]

**grouch·y** /ˈgraʊtʃi/ *adjective* (*informal*)
likely to get angry with people and complain about things: *The long drive home made him feel tired and grouchy.*

**ground[1]** /graʊnd/ *noun*
**1** the surface of the Earth: *A tree had fallen to the ground.*

> **USAGE: ground, floor**
> The **ground** is the surface that you stand on outdoors: *There was snow on the ground.*
> The **floor** is the surface that you stand on in a building: *There was a thick rug on the floor.*

**2** soil or land: *It was winter, and the ground was hard.*
**3** a wire that connects electrical equipment to the ground, so you can use it safely
**4 grounds** = **a)** an area of land or sea that is used for a particular purpose: *The tribe refused to leave their hunting grounds.* | *fishing grounds* **b)** the land or gardens that surround a large building: *You are not allowed to leave the school grounds during lunch.* **c)** a good reason for doing something: *Did the police have legal grounds to arrest him?*

**ground[2]** *verb*
the past tense and past participle of GRIND

**ground[3]** *adjective*
**1 ground beef/pork, etc.** = meat that is cut up into very small pieces: *You make hamburgers with ground beef.*
**2** ground coffee or pepper has been crushed into a powder: *Add some ground pepper.*

**ˌground ˈfloor** *noun*
the part of a building that is on the same level as the ground: *My office is on the ground floor.* **SYNONYM: first floor**

**ground·hog** /ˈgraʊndhɔg/ *noun*
a small animal with thick brown fur and big front teeth: *Groundhogs live in holes in the ground.*

**Ground·hog Day** /ˈgraʊndhɔg ˌdeɪ/ *noun*
February 2; in American stories, a GROUNDHOG comes out of its hole on this day. If it sees its shadow, there will be six more weeks of winter. If it does not see its shadow, good weather will come early.

**group**[1] /grup/ *noun*
**1** several people or things that are together in the same place: *An argument started between two groups of men.* | *We sat in the shade, under a group of trees.*

**THESAURUS: group**

**Group of People:**

**crowd** a large group of people in a public place: *A crowd of people were watching the parade.*

**team** a group of people who play a sport or game together: *Ryan is trying out for the football team.*

**crew** the group of people who work on a ship or airplane: *The fishing boat had a small crew.*

**gang** a group of young people in a city, who may be involved in crime: *There is a problem with gangs in some neighborhoods.*

**mob** a large noisy group of people, especially one that is angry and violent: *An angry mob was gathering outside the courtroom.*

**bunch** (*informal*) a group of people: *They are a nice bunch of kids.*

**Group of Animals:**

**herd** a group of large animals such as cows or elephants: *The herd of elephants had come to the watering hole to drink.*

**flock** a group of sheep, goats, or birds: *I could see a flock of geese flying south.*

**school/shoal** a group of fish: *A school of dolphin swam right next to the boat.*

**pack** a group of animals such as dogs that hunt together: *Wolves hunt together in packs.*

**swarm** a large group of flying insects: *The swarm of locusts had eaten all the crops.*

**Group of Things:**

**bunch** a group of fruit or flowers: *Dad gave Mom a bunch of roses on their anniversary.*

**collection** a group of similar things that have been gathered together: *The gallery has a fine collection of modern art.*

**set** a group of similar things, which you use together: *Dad keeps a set of tools in the basement.* | *a chess set*

**bundle** a collection of things tied together: *Bundles of newspapers were stacked on the curb.*

**2** several people or things that are similar or connected in some way: *You must find a new group of friends.*
**3** several musicians who play and sing popular music together: *They formed a rock group.* **SYNONYM: band**

**group**[2] *verb*
**1** to arrange things in a group: *Books can be grouped into two basic types: fiction and nonfiction.*
**2** to come together and form a group: *The cows had grouped together under the trees.*

**grove** /groʊv/ *noun*
a group of trees, especially trees of the same type: *an orange grove*

**grov·el** /ˈgrɑvəl/ *verb*
to try hard to please someone or to get him or her to do something for you, in a way that makes you not respect yourself: *He doesn't want the job if he has to grovel for it.*

**grow** /groʊ/ *verb* (**grew** /gru/, **grown** /groʊn/)
**1** to get bigger in size or amount: *Babies grow quickly in their first year.* | *The number of students grew by 5% last year.*
**2** if a plant grows somewhere, it exists there:

*Trees will not grow that far up the mountain.*
**3** to plant crops and take care of them: *We grow our own vegetables.*
**4** to become something, especially gradually: *Grandad is growing old and becoming forgetful.* | *By March, the days were growing longer.*
→ see Thesaurus box at **increase**[1]

**WORD FAMILY: grow**
**grow** *verb* | **grown** *adjective* | **growth** *noun*

**PHRASAL VERBS**
**grow out of something**
**1** if a child grows out of clothes, he or she becomes too big to wear them: *I grew out of my shoes in just four months.*
**2** if you grow out of a habit, you stop doing it as you become older: *I used to suck my thumb, but I grew out of it.*
**grow up**
to gradually change from being a child to being an adult: *Dad grew up in San Diego.*

**growl** /graʊl/ *verb*
if an animal such as a dog or bear growls, it makes a deep angry sound: *The dog usually growls at visitors.*
—**growl** *noun* a deep angry sound made by an animal such as a dog or bear: *The bear gave a loud growl.*

**grown**[1] /groʊn/ *adjective*
**grown man/woman** = an adult – used about an adult who is behaving more like a child: *I had never seen a grown man cry before.*

**grown**[2] *verb*
the past participle of GROW

**grown-up**[1] /ˈgroʊnʌp/ *noun* (*informal*)
an adult: *My brother and I listened while the grown-ups talked.*

ˈ**grown-up**[2] *adjective*
someone who is grown-up is an adult: *She has two grown-up daughters – one is 25 and the other is 22.*

**growth** /groʊθ/ *noun*
**1** an increase in amount, number, or size: *The growth of the Internet has happened very quickly.*
**2** the increase in the physical size and strength of a person, animal, or plant over a period of time: *The milk has everything a baby needs for healthy growth.*

**grub·by** /ˈgrʌbi/ *adjective* (*informal*)
dirty: *Her hands were grubby from cleaning the mud off her bike.*

**grudge** /grʌdʒ/ *noun*
an unfriendly feeling toward someone because he or she did something bad to you in the past: *He still has a grudge against me because I tripped him in a race last year.*

**gru·el·ing** /ˈgruəlɪŋ/ *adjective*
very difficult and tiring: *It was a grueling five-hour climb to the top of the mountain.*
[**ORIGIN:** 1800-1900 From "gruel," which was a kind of food made from grain that was given to people as a punishment. A grueling experience is like a punishment.]

**grue·some** /ˈgrusəm/ *adjective*
very unpleasant or shocking, and usually involving death or injury: *Several drivers were injured in the gruesome accident.*
[**ORIGIN:** 1500-1600 From the old English word *grue*, which means "to shake with fear."]

**grum·ble** /ˈgrʌmbəl/ *verb*
to keep complaining about something, especially something that is not very important: *He's always grumbling about how expensive everything is.*

**grump·y** /ˈgrʌmpi/ *adjective* (**grumpier**, **grumpiest**)
a grumpy person gets annoyed easily and does not seem happy: *He's grumpy because he's tired.*
—**grumpily** *adverb* in a grumpy way: *"Leave me alone," she said grumpily.*

**grun·gy** /ˈgrʌndʒi/ *adjective* (*informal*)
dirty and sometimes smelling bad: *a pair of grungy jeans*

**grunt** /grʌnt/ *verb*
**1** to make a short low sound instead of talking: *I told him to get out of bed, but he just grunted and went back to sleep.*
**2** if a pig grunts, it makes a low rough sound
—**grunt** *noun* a short low sound that you make in your throat, or a similar sound that a pig makes: *Alex answered with a grunt.*

**gua·ca·mo·le** /ˌgwɑkəˈmoʊleɪ/ *noun*
a cold Mexican food made with crushed AVOCADO
[**ORIGIN:** 1900-2000 From the Nahuatl words

G

*ahuacatl* and *molli*, which mean "avocado" and "sauce." Nahuatl was the language used by the Aztecs in Mexico.]

**guar·an·tee¹** Ac /ˌgærənˈti/ *verb*
to promise to do something, or to promise that something will happen: *We guarantee we will repair your computer within 48 hours.* | *I guarantee that you'll love this movie.*
**SYNONYM: promise**
→ see Thesaurus box at **promise¹**

**guarantee²** Ac *noun*
**1** a promise by a company to repair or replace a product if it breaks or stops working: *The TV has a two-year guarantee.*
**2** something that makes sure that something else happens: *Working hard is usually the best guarantee of success.*

**guard¹** /gɑrd/ *noun*
**1** someone whose job is to protect a person or place: *A security guard was standing outside the jewelry store.*
**2** someone whose job is to prevent a prisoner from escaping: *The guards took him back to his prison cell.*
**3** the act of protecting a person or place, or preventing a prisoner from escaping: *Soldiers are always on guard outside the embassy.*

**guard²** *verb*
**1** to protect someone or something from being attacked or stolen: *Two large dogs guard the building at night.*
**2** to prevent a prisoner from escaping: *The prisoners are guarded 24 hours a day.*

→ see Thesaurus box at **protect**
**PHRASAL VERB**
**guard against something**
to prevent something bad from happening: *Wash your hands regularly to guard against illnesses such as flu.*

**ˈguard dog** *noun*
a dog that protects someone's home or property

**guard·ed** /ˈgɑrdɪd/ *adjective*
careful not to show your emotions or give away information: *The Senator gave a guarded answer to the reporter's question, saying "I'm not sure I can tell you anything more now."*

**guard·i·an** /ˈgɑrdiən/ *noun*
someone who is legally responsible for a child, but who is not the child's parent: *His parents died, and his aunt is his legal guardian.*

**guer·ril·la** (*also* **guerilla**) /gəˈrɪlə/ *noun*
a member of a group of fighters who are not part of an official army: *The guerillas made a surprise attack on a government building.*
[**ORIGIN:** 1800-1900 From the Spanish word *guerra*, which means "war."]

**guess¹** /ges/ *verb*
**1** to answer a question or decide something when you are not sure if you are right: *I think he's about 40, but I'm just guessing.* | *"Guess how much this dress cost?" "I don't know, about $50? $75?"* | *Can you guess my age?*
**2 keep someone guessing** = to make someone feel excited or not sure about what will happen next: *The movie is a mystery that really keeps the audience guessing.*
**3 I guess** = **a)** used to say that you think something is probably true: *He's not here yet, but I guess he'll be coming later.* | *"Does she make a lot of money?" "I guess so."* **b)** used to say that you will do something, even though you do not really want to: *I'm tired, so I guess I'll stay home tonight.*

**guess²** *noun*
an attempt to answer a question or decide something when you are not sure if you are right: *I couldn't decide which answer was right, so I had to make a guess.*

**guest** /gest/ *noun*
**1** someone who you invite to stay in your home or invite to an event: *How many guests are coming to your party?*
**2** someone who is staying in a hotel: *Use of the swimming pool is free to hotel guests.*
[**ORIGIN:** 1200-1300 From the Norse word *gestr*. Norse was a language used in Scandinavian countries.]

**guid·ance** /ˈgaɪdns/ *noun*
helpful advice: *Your teacher can give you guidance on choosing a career.*

**guide¹** /gaɪd/ *noun*
**1** someone whose job is to show a place to

tourists: *The tour guide was taking a group of tourists around the museum.*

**2** a book that gives information about a particular subject or explains how to do something: *I bought him a beginner's guide to using the Internet.*

**3** something that helps you make a decision: *Use your nose as a guide – if the fish is fresh, it will smell fresh.*

**guide²** *verb*

**1** to help someone to go somewhere, for example by showing them the right direction: *He took the old lady's hand and guided her across the road.*

**2** to help someone manage a difficult situation: *The school staff can guide you when you apply for colleges.*

G

**guide·book** /ˈgaɪdbʊk/ *noun*

a book that gives visitors information about a city, area, or country: *The guidebook gives the hotel three stars and says it has a good restaurant.*

guide dog

**ˈguide dog** *noun*

a dog that has been trained to help blind people travel to places: *Joanna's guide dog helps her to cross the road safely.* **SYNONYM: seeing-eye dog**

**guide·lines** [Ac] /ˈgaɪdlaɪnz/ *plural noun*

rules or instructions about the best way to do something: *The teacher gave the class some guidelines on writing essays for the exam.*

**guilt** /gɪlt/ *noun*

**1** a sad feeling you have when you have done something wrong: *She felt a sense of guilt about lying to her parents.*

**2** the fact that someone has broken a law: *They were sure that he had stolen the money, but they couldn't prove his guilt.* **ANTONYM: innocence**

**3 a guilt trip** (*informal*) = a feeling of being sorry for doing something, that you feel because of what someone else says: *My parents are giving me a guilt trip for scratching the car.*

**guilt·y** /ˈgɪlti/ *adjective*

**1** unhappy and ashamed because you have done something that you know is wrong: *Rob felt guilty about stealing the book.*

**2 find someone guilty (of something)** = if a court of law finds someone guilty of a crime, it decides that he or she committed that crime: *The jury found him guilty of robbery.* **ANTONYM: innocent**

—**guiltily** *adverb* in an ashamed way because you have done something that you know is wrong: *"Yes, I took it," she said guiltily.*

**guin·ea pig** /ˈgɪni ˌpɪg/ *noun*

**1** a small furry animal with no tail that is often kept as a pet

**2** someone who is used in a scientific test to see how successful or safe a new product or system is: *The scientists are looking for guinea pigs to try out a new diet.*

**gui·tar** /gɪˈtɑr/ *noun*

a wooden musical instrument with strings and a long neck, which you play by pulling the strings: *He began learning how to play the guitar when he was ten.* → see picture on page **A21**

—**guitarist** *noun* someone who plays the guitar

[**ORIGIN:** 1600-1700 From the Spanish word *guitarra*, from the Greek word *kithara*, which was the name of a type of stringed instrument.]

**gulf** /gʌlf/ *noun*

**1** a large area of ocean that is partly surrounded by land: *The Gulf of Mexico is to the west of Florida.*

**2** a big difference between two groups of people: *The gulf between rich people and poor people is wider than ever.*

**gull** /gʌl/ *noun*

a SEAGULL

**gul·li·ble** /ˈgʌləbəl/ *adjective*

a gullible person is easy to trick because he or she always believes what other people say:

*"He said his mother needed the money and I believed him." "You are so gullible!"*

**gulp¹** /gʌlp/ *verb*
**1** (*also* **gulp down**) to swallow food or drink quickly: *She gulped down her breakfast and ran for the bus.*
**2** to swallow suddenly because you are surprised or nervous: *Ed gulped when he saw how hard the test questions were.*

**gulp²** *noun*
the action of swallowing a lot of a drink or air quickly: *He took a gulp of his lemonade.*

**gum** /gʌm/ *noun*
**1** (*also* **chewing gum**) a sweet type of candy that you chew for a long time, but do not swallow
**2** the pink parts inside your mouth that your teeth grow out of

**gun** /gʌn/ *noun*
**1** a weapon that fires bullets: *The man was carrying a gun. | Someone fired a gun at the President.*
**2** a tool that forces out small objects or a liquid by pressure: *He used a spray gun to paint the car.*

**gun·fire** /ˈgʌnfaɪɚ/ *noun*
shots fired from a gun: *The soldiers could hear gunfire in the distance.*

**gun·man** /ˈgʌnmən/ *noun* (plural **gunmen** /ˈgʌnmən/)
a criminal who uses a gun: *The gunman walked into the bank and demanded money.*

**gun·point** /ˈgʌnpɔɪnt/ *noun*
**at gunpoint** = while threatening someone or being threatened with a gun: *They were held at gunpoint while the man stole their car.*

**gun·pow·der** /ˈgʌnˌpaʊdɚ/ *noun*
an explosive substance used in bombs and FIREWORKs

**gun·shot** /ˈgʌnʃɑt/ *noun*
**1** the sound made by a gun: *We heard a gunshot and a loud scream.*
**2** the bullets that are shot from a gun: *He died from a gunshot wound.*

**gur·gle** /ˈgɚgəl/ *verb*
**1** if water gurgles, it makes a sound as it moves along: *A small stream gurgled over the rocks.*
**2** if a baby gurgles, the baby makes a pleasant low sound in its throat: *The baby smiled and gurgled with pleasure.*

**gu·ru** /ˈgʊru/ *noun*
**1** (*informal*) someone who knows a lot about a subject, and who gives advice to other people: *The magazine has tips from fashion gurus on what to wear this fall.*
**2** a Hindu religious teacher

**gush** /gʌʃ/ *verb*
if liquid gushes somewhere, a large amount of it flows there: *Blood gushed from a cut in his arm.*
→ see Thesaurus box at **pour**

**gust** /gʌst/ *noun*
a sudden strong wind: *A gust of wind blew our tent down.*
→ see Thesaurus box at **wind¹**

**gut¹** /gʌt/ *adjective*
**gut feeling/gut reaction/gut instinct** (*informal*) = a feeling or idea that you are sure is right, although you cannot give a reason for it: *My gut reaction is that this is a bad idea.*

**gut²** *noun* (*informal*)
**1** (*also* **guts**) your stomach and the tubes in your body that food passes through: *My guts were aching after eating too much at dinner. | The ball hit him right in the gut.*
**2** **guts** = courage and determination to do something difficult: *She didn't have the guts to tell her father he was wrong.*

**gut³** *verb* (**gutted**, **gutting**)
to destroy the inside of a building completely: *The house was gutted by fire.*

**gut·ter** /ˈgʌtɚ/ *noun*
**1** an open pipe at the edge of a roof for carrying away rainwater: *The gutter was blocked by leaves.*
**2** the low place along the edge of a road where water collects and flows away

G

**guy** /gaɪ/ *noun* (*informal*)
a man: *He's a really nice guy.*
[ORIGIN: From Guy Fawkes (1570-1606), who tried to blow up the English parliament. In Britain, figures of Guy Fawkes are made and burned on bonfires on the anniversary of that event, and the word "guy" came to be used for a man wearing old or strange clothes. First used with its modern meaning, 1800-1900.]

**guz·zle** /ˈgʌzəl/ *verb* (*informal*)
to drink a lot of something very quickly: *My brother and his friends were eating pizza and guzzling soda.*

**gym** /dʒɪm/ *noun*
a building or room that has equipment for doing physical exercise: *I go to the gym three times a week.*
[ORIGIN: 1500-1600 From the Greek word *gymnasion*, from *gymnos*, which means "naked." Greek men used to train and do physical exercises with no clothes on.]

G

**gym·na·si·um** /dʒɪmˈneɪziəm/ *noun*
a GYM

**gym·nas·tics** /dʒɪmˈnæstɪks/ *noun*
a sport involving skillful physical exercises and movements → see picture on page **A24**
—**gymnast** /ˈdʒɪmnæst/ *noun* someone who performs gymnastics: *an Olympic gymnast*

**gy·ne·col·o·gy** /ˌgaɪnəˈkɑlədʒi/ *noun*
the study and treatment of medical conditions relating to women's ability to have children
—**gynecologist** *noun* someone who studies gynecology
—**gynecological** /ˌgaɪnəkəˈlɑdʒɪkəl/ *adjective* relating to gynecology

**gyp·sy** /ˈdʒɪpsi/ *noun* (plural **gypsies**)
a member of a group of people who travel around rather than live in one place. Gypsies originally came from northern India.

# Hh

**ha** /hɑ/ *interjection*
said when you are surprised or pleased about something: *Ha! I knew I was right.*

**hab·it** /ˈhæbɪt/ *noun*
something that you do often or regularly: *We got in the habit of staying up very late.* | *Smoking is a very bad habit.*

**hab·i·tat** /ˈhæbəˌtæt/ *noun*
the place in which a plant or animal lives: *The woods are the natural habitat of foxes.*
[**ORIGIN:** 1700-1800 From the Latin word *habitare*, which means "to live in a place."]

**hack** /hæk/ *verb*
**1** to cut something roughly or violently: *Tom hacked the branches off the tree.*
**2** to use a computer to enter someone else's computer system in order to damage it or get secret information: *The criminals hacked into the bank's computer system and moved money into their bank accounts.*

**hack·er** /ˈhækɚ/ *noun* (*informal*)
someone who secretly uses or changes the information in other people's computer systems: *A hacker stole some information from the company's computer system.*
—**hacking** *noun* the activity of secretly using or changing information in other people's computer systems

**hack·saw** /ˈhæksɔ/ *noun*
a type of cutting tool with small teeth on its blade, used especially for cutting metal
—**hacksaw** *verb* to cut something with a hacksaw

**had** /əd; *strong* hæd/ *verb*
the past tense and past participle of HAVE

**had·n't** /ˈhædnt/ *verb*
the short form of "had not": *I hadn't eaten anything all day.*

**hai·ku** /ˈhaɪku/ *noun* (plural **haiku** *or* **haikus**)
a short poem with three lines. The first line has five SYLLABLEs, the second line has seven syllables, and the third line has five syllables. Haikus came from Japan.

**hail¹** /heɪl/ *verb*
if it hails, small hard pieces of frozen rain fall from the sky: *It was hailing when we left school.*

**hail²** *noun*
small hard pieces of frozen rain that fall from the sky: *There will be some hail later today.*
→ see Thesaurus box at **rain¹**, **snow¹**

**hail·stone** /ˈheɪlˌstoʊn/ *noun*
a small ball of frozen rain: *Most hailstones are about the size of peas.*

**hair** /her/ *noun*
**1** the thin things that grow on your head: *Tim has brown hair.* | *She was brushing her hair.* → see picture on page **A2**

> **GRAMMAR: hair**
> In this meaning, **hair** does not have a plural. Do not say "She has long hairs." Say *She has long hair.*

**2** one of the thin things that grow on the skin of a person or animal: *There are cat hairs all over this chair.*

**hair·brush** /ˈherbrʌʃ/ *noun*
a brush that you use to make your hair look neat → see picture at **brush**

**hair·cut** /ˈherkʌt/ *noun*
**1** if you have a haircut, someone cuts your hair: *My hair's too long, so I'm going to get a haircut.*
**2** the way your hair is cut: *Do you like my new haircut?*

**hair·do** /ˈherdu/ *noun* (plural **hairdos**) (*informal*)
the style in which a woman's hair is cut or arranged: *Mom came home with a new hairdo.* **SYNONYM: hairstyle**

**hair·dress·er** /ˈherˌdresɚ/ *noun*
someone whose job is to cut and arrange people's hair: *Marie's always been good at cutting hair, so she's training to be a hairdresser.* → see picture on page **A17**

**hair·dry·er** /ˈherˌdraɪɚ/ *noun*
a machine that you use to dry your hair

**hair·style** /ˈherstaɪl/ *noun*
the style in which your hair is cut and arranged: *She has a short hairstyle.*

**hair·y** /ˈheri/ *adjective*
hairy arms, legs, etc. have a lot of hair on them: *a big man with a hairy chest*

**Haj** (*also* **Hajj**) /hɑdʒ/ *noun*
a trip to Mecca that all Muslims try to make for religious reasons
—**Haji** (*also* **Hajji** /ˈhɑdʒi/) *noun* a Muslim who has made the trip to Mecca

**ha·lal** /həˈlɑl/ *adjective*
halal meat is from animals that were killed in a way that Muslim law approves

**half¹** /hæf/ *noun* (plural **halves** /hævz/), *pronoun*
**1** one of two equal parts of something: *Half of 10 is 5.* | *Half the students spoke Spanish, and the other half spoke English.* | *I cut the sandwich in half* (=in two equal pieces). | *My brother is two and a half* (=two years and six months old).
**2** one of two parts of a game in some sports: *Alan scored a goal at the end of the first half.*
**3** **half an hour** = thirty minutes: *I'll be there in half an hour.*
**4** **half a dozen** = six: *half a dozen eggs*

**half²** *adverb*
partly but not completely: *A half-empty coffee cup was on the table.*

**ˈhalf-ˌbrother** *noun*
a boy or man who has the same mother or father as you

**ˌhalf-ˈhearted** *adjective*
if you do something in a half-hearted way, you do it without trying very hard or caring about the result: *She was very upset, but she made a half-hearted attempt to smile.*

**ˌhalf-ˈhour** *noun*
thirty minutes: *The cake is not done – it needs another half-hour in the oven.*
—**half-hour** *adjective* continuing for thirty minutes: *a half-hour TV show*

**ˌhalf-ˈmast** *noun*
**at half-mast** = if a flag is at half-mast, it is in the middle of the pole and not at the top because someone important has died: *The flag flew at half-mast for a week after the governor died.*

**ˈhalf-ˌsister** *noun*
a girl or woman who has the same mother or father as you

**half·time** /ˈhæftaɪm/ *noun*
the short period of time between the two parts of a game such as football: *Our team was winning at halftime, but the other team scored twice in the second half.*

**half·way** /ˌhæfˈweɪ/ *adjective, adverb*
**1** in the middle between two places or things: *The boat was halfway across the lake.*
**2** in the middle of a period of time or an event: *Dad fell asleep halfway through the movie.*

**hall** /hɔl/ *noun*
**1** a narrow area in a house or building, with doors that lead to other rooms: *Go down the hall and turn right, and you'll see the bathroom.* **SYNONYM: hallway**
**2** a room that you go through when you enter a house, with doors that lead to other rooms: *You can hang your coats in the front hall.* **SYNONYM: hallway**
**3** a big room or building that people use for public meetings, concerts, etc.: *The audience was coming into the concert hall.*

**hal·le·lu·jah** /ˌhæləˈluyə/
a word people say to praise God

**Hal·low·een** /ˌhæləˈwin/ *noun*
the night of October 31, when children dress as WITCHES,GHOSTS, etc., and go to people's houses asking for candy by saying, "trick or treat!"
[**ORIGIN:** From the old English word *Allhallow-even*, which means "the day before the day of all saints." November 1 is the day on which all Christian saints are honored.]

**hal·lu·ci·nate** /həˈlusəˌneɪt/ *verb*
to see or hear something that is not really there: *The patient started hallucinating and saying he could see tigers around his bed.*
—**hallucination** /həˌlusəˈneɪʃən/ *noun* something you see or hear that is not really there: *His wife wasn't really in the room. He was just having a hallucination.*
[**ORIGIN:** 1800-1900 From the Latin word *hallucinari*, which means "to dream."]

**hall·way** /ˈhɔlweɪ/ *noun*
**1** a small area near the front door inside a house, that has doors that lead to other rooms: *I came into the house and found Sam standing in the hallway.* **SYNONYM: hall**
**2** a narrow area in a house or building, with

H

doors that lead to other rooms: *The long hallway had doors leading to six classrooms.* **SYNONYM: hall**

**ha·lo** /ˈheɪloʊ/ *noun* (plural **halos**)
a bright circle drawn around the heads of ANGELs and holy people in paintings

**halt**[1] /hɔlt/ *verb* (*formal*)
to stop: *Our taxi halted outside the airport.*

**halt**[2] *noun* (*formal*)
a stop: *Cars suddenly came to a halt because children were crossing the road.*

**halve** /hæv/ *verb*
**1** to cut something into two equal parts: *Halve the tomato, and remove the seeds.*
**2** to make an amount half as big: *The museum halved the price of its tickets to attract more visitors.*

**halves** /hævz/ *noun*
the plural of HALF

**ham** /hæm/ *noun*
the meat from a pig with salt added to it to keep it fresh: *I put two slices of ham in the sandwich.*
→ see Thesaurus box at **meat**

**ham·burg·er** /ˈhæmˌbɚgɚ/ *noun*
**1** a flat round piece of cooked BEEF, usually eaten inside a BUN: *He was eating a hamburger and fries.*
**2** BEEF that is cut into very small pieces, used for making hamburgers and other dishes: *I bought a pound of hamburger.* **SYNONYM: ground beef**
[**ORIGIN:** 1800-1900 From the German words for "Hamburg steak," named after the German city of Hamburg.]

**ham·mer**[1] /ˈhæmɚ/ *noun*
a tool you use for hitting nails into wood

**hammer**[2] *verb*
**1** to hit something with a hammer: *He hammered a nail into the fence.*
**2** to hit something many times, making a loud noise: *The rain was hammering on the roof of the tent.*

**ham·mock** /ˈhæmək/ *noun*
a piece of net or other material that hangs between two trees or poles that you use for sleeping in
[**ORIGIN:** 1500-1600 From the Spanish word *hamaca*, from a Taino word. Taino was a language used by the people of some Caribbean islands.]

**ham·per** /ˈhæmpɚ/ *noun*
**1** a large basket that you put dirty clothes in
**2** a basket for carrying food: *a picnic hamper*

**ham·ster** /ˈhæmstɚ/ *noun*
a small soft animal like a mouse with no tail, that children often keep as a pet → see picture at **pet**

**hand**

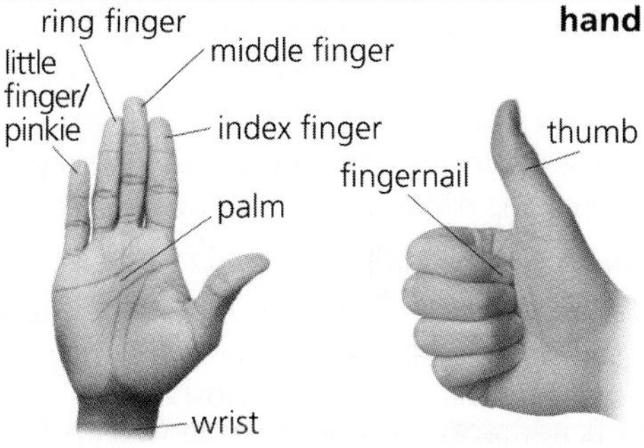


**hand**[1] /hænd/ *noun*
**1** the part of your body at the end of your arm, that you use to hold things: *Go and wash your hands.* | *I write with my right hand.* | *Raise your hand if you know the answer.*
**2 give/lend someone a hand** = to help someone: *Can you give me a hand with this box? It's really heavy.*
**3 on the other hand** = used when mentioning a very different fact or idea: *The work was hard, but on the other hand I learned a lot.*
**4 by hand** = done or made by a person, not a machine: *The rug was made by hand.*
**5** one of the parts on a clock that move to show the time: *The hands on the clock moved slowly toward noon.*
**6 be/get out of hand** = to be or become impossible to control: *The party was beginning to get out of hand, so Dad told everyone to leave.*
**7 on hand** = near and ready if needed: *A teacher is always on hand to help.*
**8** the cards that you are holding in a game: *Tom held the winning hand.*

**hand**[2] *verb*
to give something to someone else using your hand: *Can you hand me a towel?*
→ see Thesaurus box at **give**

PHRASAL VERBS

**hand something down**
to give something to a younger member of your family: *This necklace was handed down from my grandmother to me.*

**hand something in**
to give something to a teacher, the police, or someone in authority: *Hand in your homework, please.*

**hand something out**
to give something to everyone in a group: *The teacher handed out the tests.*

**hand something over**
to give something to someone else using your hand: *She handed the phone over to me.*

**hand·bag** /ˈhændbæg/ *noun*
a bag in which a woman carries money, keys, and other small things: *She was carrying a brown leather handbag.* SYNONYM: **purse** → see picture on page A6

H

**hand·book** /ˈhændbʊk/ *noun*
a small book with useful information about something: *A photography handbook will give you tips on taking good pictures.*

**hand·cuffs** /ˈhændkʌfs/ *plural noun*
two metal rings joined by a chain, that hold a prisoner's wrists together: *The police took him away in handcuffs.*
—**handcuff** *verb* to put handcuffs on someone: *An officer handcuffed him.*

**hand·ful** /ˈhændfʊl/ *noun*
**1** an amount that you can hold in your hand: *She took a handful of nuts from the bowl.*
**2 a handful of something** = a small number of people or things: *Only a handful of people came to the meeting – I think there were five people there.*

**hand·gun** /ˈhændgʌn/ *noun*
a small gun you can hold in one hand

**hand·i·cap** /ˈhændiˌkæp/ *noun*
**1** something that is permanently wrong with a part of your body or mind: *Some people are born with physical handicaps that make them unable to walk.* SYNONYM: **disability**
**2** something that makes it difficult for you to do something: *If you don't speak Spanish, it will be a handicap when you travel in South America.* SYNONYM: **disadvantage**

**hand·i·capped** /ˈhændiˌkæpt/ *adjective*
not able to use a part of your body or mind because there is something permanently wrong with it: *The school is good for physically handicapped children because there are no stairs.* SYNONYM: **disabled**

> **USAGE: handicapped**
> The word **handicapped** is old-fashioned and may offend some people. It is better to use the word **disabled**: *The hotel has rooms on the ground floor for disabled people.*

**hand·ker·chief** /ˈhæŋkɚtʃɪf/ *noun*
a piece of cloth that you use for drying your nose or eyes

**han·dle¹** /ˈhændl/ *verb*
**1** to deal with something: *If there are any problems, I'll handle them.*
**2** to pick up or touch something: *If you are handling food, wash your hands first.*

**handle**

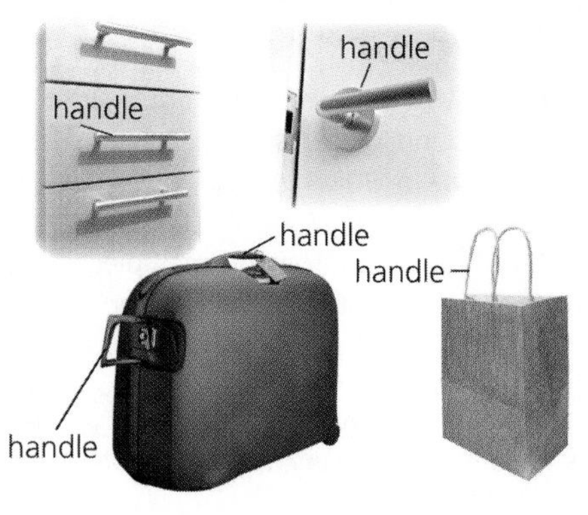


**handle²** *noun*
the part of something that you have in your hand when you hold or open it: *The handle of my suitcase is broken.* | *a door handle*

**han·dle·bars** /ˈhændlˌbɑrz/ *plural noun*
the part of a bicycle or MOTORCYCLE that you hold with your hands when you are riding it

**hand·made** /ˌhændˈmeɪd/ *adjective*
made by a person, not a machine: *She bought a handmade rug for the bedroom.*

**hand·out** /ˈhændaʊt/ *noun*
**1** a piece of paper with information on it, that you give to people in a class or meeting:

*The teacher gave us a handout with our math homework on it.*
**2** money or food that people receive because they need help: *There are many poor people living on government handouts.*

**hand·shake** /ˈhændʃeɪk/ *noun*
the act of taking someone's right hand in your right hand and moving it up and down. You do this when you meet someone or make an agreement: *People welcomed us with smiles and handshakes.*

**hand·some** /ˈhænsəm/ *adjective*
a handsome man is attractive: *He was a handsome young man, and he worked as a model for a while.* **SYNONYM: good-looking**; **ANTONYM: ugly**
→ see Thesaurus box at **beautiful**
[**ORIGIN:** "Handsome" used to mean "easy to handle," and later meant "of a good size" and "having a good appearance." First used in English with its modern meaning, 1500-1600.]

**hand·stand** /ˈhændstænd/ *noun*
a movement in which you put your hands on the ground and hold your legs up in the air

**hand·writ·ing** /ˈhændˌraɪtɪŋ/ *noun*
the way someone writes with a pen or a pencil: *She has very neat handwriting, which is easy to read.*

**hand·writ·ten** /ˈhændˌrɪtn/ *adjective*
written with a pen or pencil, not printed or written on a computer: *A handwritten sign said "Puppies for sale."*

**hand·y** /ˈhændi/ *adjective*
**1** useful: *The string came in handy when my shoelaces broke.*
**2** near and easy to reach: *Do you have a pen handy?*

**hand·y·man** /ˈhændiˌmæn/ *noun* (plural **handymen** /ˈhændiˌmen/)
someone who is good at making and repairing things

**hang¹** /hæŋ/ *verb*
**1** (**hung** /hʌŋ/) to put something somewhere so that its top part is firmly fastened but its bottom part is free to move: *I hung my coat on a hook in the hall. | The swing hangs from a tree branch.*
**2** (**hung** /hʌŋ/) to fasten a picture, photograph, mirror, etc. to a wall: *We could hang the mirror in the hall.*
**3** (**hanged**) to kill someone by putting a rope around the person's neck and letting him or her drop down toward the ground: *In the past, people were hanged as a punishment.*
**PHRASAL VERBS**
**hang around** (*informal*)
to stay in one place and not do much: *On Saturdays, kids hang around downtown.*
**hang on**
**1** to hold something tightly in order to keep it or yourself safe: *The little boy hung on to his mother's hand as they crossed the street.* **SYNONYM: hold on**
**2** (*informal*) you say this when you want someone to wait for you: *Hang on – I'm almost ready to go.* **SYNONYM: hold on**
**hang out** (*informal*)
to spend a lot of time somewhere with friends and not do much: *I'm going to hang out at the beach all summer.*
**hang up**
to finish speaking on the telephone by putting the telephone down: *She said goodbye and hung up.*

**hang²** *noun* (*informal*)
**get the hang of something** = to learn how to do or use something: *He falls off his bike a lot, but he'll get the hang of it soon.*

**hang·er** /ˈhæŋɚ/ *noun*
a curved piece of wood, plastic, or metal with a hook at the top, on which you hang clothes

**Ha·nuk·kah** /ˈhɑnəkə/ *noun*
an eight-day Jewish holiday in November or December during which people light CANDLEs to remember the time in 165 B.C. when a Jewish army regained control of the Holy TEMPLE in Jerusalem

**hap·haz·ard** /ˌhæpˈhæzɚd/ *adjective*
not organized, neat, or planned: *Brian's books were all over his desk in a haphazard way.*
—**haphazardly** *adverb* in a haphazard way: *She threw her clothes haphazardly onto the bed.*

**hap·pen** /ˈhæpən/ *verb*
**1** when something happens, there is an event that no one planned or expected: *The accident happened outside my house. | You're covered in mud! What happened to you?*

**THESAURUS: happen**

**happen** if something happens, you usually did not plan or expect it: *A strange thing happened on my way to school.*

**take place** if an event takes place, it is planned or arranged to happen: *The next meeting will take place on Thursday.*

**occur** (*formal*) if an event occurs, it happens in a particular place or at a particular time: *The robbery occurred around 9 p.m.*

**2 happen to do something** = to do something by chance: *I happened to meet Greg at the mall yesterday.*

[ORIGIN: 1300-1400 From the old English word *hap*, which means "chance or luck."]

H

**hap·pi·ness** /ˈhæpinəs/ *noun*
the state of being happy: *Her happiness was easy to see from the big smile on her face.*

**hap·py** /ˈhæpi/ *adjective* (**happier**, **happiest**)
**1** feeling pleased, for example because your life is good, or something good has happened: *Pete is happy at his new school.* | *I was really happy to hear your good news!* **ANTONYM: sad** → see picture on page **A23**

**THESAURUS: happy**

**cheerful** someone who is cheerful seems happy and smiles a lot: *Tom is a very cheerful little boy.*

**pleased** happy because someone has done something good, or something good has happened: *Her parents were pleased that she had done so well in her classes.*

**glad** happy because something good has happened: *I'm really glad you can come to the party.*

**delighted** very happy because something good has happened: *She will be delighted when she hears the news.*

**2 Happy Birthday/New Year, etc.** = you say this to someone on a special occasion to show that you hope they have a nice time
—**happily** *adverb* in a happy way: *They laughed happily.*

**ha·rass** /həˈræs/ *verb*
to keep doing things to someone that make him or her feel upset or threatened: *The man harassed her by calling her several times every night.*
—**harassment** *noun* behavior in which someone harasses someone else: *The cases of harassment were reported to the supervisor.*
[ORIGIN: 1600-1700 From the French word *harasser*, from the old French word *harer*, which means "to make a dog chase an animal."]

harbor

**har·bor** /ˈhɑrbɚ/ *noun*
an area of water next to the land, where ships can stay safely

**hard¹** /hɑrd/ *adjective*
**1** not soft, and difficult to bend, break, or cut: *I didn't sleep well because the bed was so hard.* | *Diamonds are the hardest substance in the world.* **ANTONYM: soft**

**THESAURUS: hard**

**firm** not bending easily when you press it, but not completely hard either: *Bake the cake until it is firm when you touch it.*

**stiff** difficult to bend: *The students used stiff cardboard to make models of their homes.*

**solid** something that is solid is very hard and does not bend or move when you touch it: *solid rock* | *It was winter and the lake was frozen solid.*

**2** difficult to do or understand: *Some of the test questions were hard.* **ANTONYM: easy**
**3** needing a lot of effort or work: *There is a lot of hard work to do on a farm.* **ANTONYM: easy**
**4 be hard on someone** (*informal*) = to criticize someone or be unfair to him or her: *His*

*parents are too hard on him. They punish him when he doesn't get good grades.*
—**hardness** *noun* the quality of being difficult to press down, break, or cut: *The hardness of the soil made it difficult to dig.*

**hard**[2] *adverb*
with a lot of effort or force: *He worked hard and saved his money.* | *It was raining hard.*

**hard·cov·er** /ˈhardˌkʌvɚ/ (*also* **hardback** /ˈhardbæk/) *noun*
a book that has a strong stiff cover

**ˌhard ˈdisk** (*also* **ˌhard ˈdrive**) *noun*
the part of a computer where information and programs can be stored permanently: *You can install the software on your hard disk.*

**hard·en** /ˈhardn/ *verb*
to become firm or stiff: *The glue takes about an hour to harden.*

**hard·ly** /ˈhardli/ *adverb*
almost none, or almost not at all: *When my family moved to this area, we hardly knew anyone.* | *I hardly ever watch that show on TV because I don't really like it.*

**USAGE: hardly**
Do not use **hardly** as the adverb of **hard**. The adverb of **hard** is also **hard**: *The teacher made us work very hard.*
Do not say "The teacher made us work very hardly."

**hard·ship** /ˈhardˌʃɪp/ *noun*
something that makes life difficult, such as not having enough food or money: *There was a lot of hardship during those years and many people didn't have enough to eat.*

**hard·ware** /ˈhardwer/ *noun*
**1** computer machinery and equipment: *A computer's hardware includes the hard drive and the keyboard.*
**2** tools you use to build and fix things: *He stopped by the hardware store to buy some nails.*

**ˌhard-ˈworking** *adjective*
someone who is hard-working works using a lot of effort: *He gets good grades because he's very hard-working.* ANTONYM: **lazy**

**hare** /her/ *noun*
an animal like a large rabbit, with longer ears and longer back legs

**harm**[1] /harm/ *noun*
damage, injury, or trouble: *The boys were just having fun – they didn't mean any harm.*

**WORD FAMILY: harm**
**harm** *noun* | **harm** *verb* | **harmful** *adjective* | **harmless** *adjective* | **harmlessly** *adverb*

**harm**[2] *verb*
to hurt or damage something: *Too much sun will harm your skin.* SYNONYM: **damage**

**harm·ful** /ˈharmfəl/ *adjective*
causing harm: *These chemicals are harmful to the environment.*

**harm·less** /ˈharmləs/ *adjective*
something that is harmless will not hurt someone or damage something: *The snake is harmless – it will not bite you.*
—**harmlessly** *adverb* in a harmless way

**har·mon·i·ca** /harˈmanɪkə/ *noun*
a small metal musical instrument that fits in your hand. You play a harmonica by blowing into the holes along its side. → see picture on page **A21**

**har·mo·ny** /ˈharməni/ *noun* (plural **harmonies**)
**1** a situation in which people do not argue with each other: *Why can't people live in harmony and be happy?*
**2** musical notes sung or played at the same time, that sound good together: *The song has beautiful harmonies.*

**har·ness** /ˈharnɪs/ *verb*
to control and use the energy from a natural force: *The machine harnesses the energy of ocean waves to produce electricity.*

**harp** /harp/ *noun*
a musical instrument like a frame with three corners, with strings stretched from the top to the bottom of the frame. You play the strings with your hands. → see picture on page **A21**
—**harpist** *noun* someone who plays the harp

H

**harsh** /hɑrʃ/ *adjective*
**1** severe or unpleasant, in a way that is not nice to experience: *Many plants died in the harsh winter.* | *The lighting in the living room was too bright and harsh.*
**2** unkind or too strict: *I think describing her work as terrible is too harsh.*
—**harshly** *adverb* in a harsh way
—**harshness** *noun* the quality of being harsh

**har·vest¹** /ˈhɑrvɪst/ *noun*
the work of collecting crops that have grown, or the amount that is collected: *The wheat harvest has begun.* | *This year, most farms have had a good harvest.*

**harvest²** *verb*
to collect crops: *They will harvest the corn later in the year.*

H

**has** /əz; *strong* hæz/ *verb*
the third person singular of the present tense of HAVE: *She has three sisters.*

**hash** /hæʃ/ *noun*
a dish made with cooked meat and potatoes mixed together

**ˌhash ˈbrowns** *plural noun*
small pieces of potato, cooked in oil

**has·n't** /ˈhæznt/ *verb*
the short form of "has not": *He hasn't come home yet.*

**has·sle** /ˈhæsəl/ *noun*
something that is annoying to do or deal with: *He eats takeout because he thinks it's too much hassle to cook for himself.*

**haste** /heɪst/ *noun* (*formal*)
if you do something in haste, you do it very quickly because you are in a hurry: *In her haste to get to the airport, Pam forgot the tickets.*

**hast·y** /ˈheɪsti/ *adjective* (*formal*)
done too quickly or without thinking carefully enough: *I made a hasty decision, and now I wish I could change it.* **SYNONYM: quick**
—**hastily** *adverb* quickly: *She was upset so I hastily apologized.* **SYNONYM: quickly**

**hat**

**hat** /hæt/ *noun*
a piece of clothing that you wear on your head: *Wear a wool hat to keep your head warm.*

**hatch** /hætʃ/ *verb*
if an egg hatches, a baby bird, fish, or insect comes out of it

**hatch·et** /ˈhætʃɪt/ *noun*
a small AX

**hate¹** /heɪt/ *verb*
to dislike someone or something very much: *I hate really cold weather.* | *She hated the boy for laughing at her.* **ANTONYM: love**

**THESAURUS: hate**

**dislike** to not like someone or something: *The only food I dislike is peanut butter.*

**can't stand** to dislike someone or something very much: *I can't stand being late.*

**detest** (*formal*) to hate someone or something very much: *He detests people who cheat or lie.*

**despise** (*formal*) to hate someone very much and not respect him or her at all: *She despised him for being such a coward.*

**hate²** *noun*
a very strong feeling of dislike: *She felt hate for the men who had hurt her brother.* **SYNONYM: hatred**; **ANTONYM: love**

**hate·ful** /ˈheɪtfəl/ *adjective*
very unpleasant and bad: *It was a mean and hateful thing to say to her.*

**ha·tred** /ˈheɪtrəd/ *noun*
a very strong feeling of dislike: *He would not fight in the war because of his hatred of violence.* **SYNONYM: hate**; **ANTONYM: love**

**haul** /hɔl/ *verb*
to pull or carry something heavy: *They hauled the boat up onto the beach.*
→ see Thesaurus box at **pull**[1]

**haunt** /hɔnt/ *verb*
**1** if the spirit of a dead person haunts a place, it sometimes appears there: *People say that the ghost of a soldier haunts the old house.*
**2** if something haunts you, you keep thinking and worrying about it: *He was a pilot in the war, and the things he saw haunted him all his life.*
—**haunted** *adjective* a haunted building is one where the spirits of dead people are believed to appear: *Would you spend the night in a haunted house?*

**haunt·ing** /ˈhɔntɪŋ/ *adjective*
a haunting song, story, idea, etc. is beautiful and a little sad, and stays in your thoughts for a long time: *The haunting tune made me want to cry.*

**have**[1] /həv; *strong* hæv/ *auxiliary verb* (**had**, **has**)
used before the past participle of a verb to form the PRESENT PERFECT tense, when talking about the period of time up to the present: *She has never been on a plane before.* | *"Have you seen the new movie?" "No, I haven't."*
[**ORIGIN:** From the old English word *habban.*]

**have**[2] *verb* (**had**, **has**)
**1** to own, possess, or include something: *Do you have a car?* | *She had beautiful brown eyes.* | *The school has over 1,000 students.*
→ see Thesaurus box at **own**[2]
**2** to eat, drink, or smoke something: *What time do you usually have breakfast?* | *Can I have another cup of coffee?*
**3** to experience something: *I often have problems with my computer.* | *Did you have a good time at the party?*
**4** to be sick with an illness, or affected by an injury: *She has a cold.* | *He has a broken leg.*
**5** to be carrying something with you: *Do you have your wallet with you?*
**6** to be allowed a particular amount of time to do something: *You have 30 minutes to finish the test.*
**7** to think of something: *I have an idea!*
**8** if a woman has a baby, the baby is born: *When is she going to have the baby?*
**9 had better do something** = if you had better do something, you should do it: *You had better tell her that you're sorry.*
**10 have your hair cut/your car fixed, etc.** = to pay someone to do something for you, for example to cut your hair, or fix your car: *You need to have your hair cut.*
**11 have your eyes closed/your mouth open, etc.** = to keep part of your body in a particular position: *He had his eyes closed, and he looked like he was asleep.*
**PHRASAL VERB**
**have something on**
to be wearing something: *She had a long white dress on and she looked wonderful.*

H

**have·n't** /ˈhævənt/ *verb*
the short form of "have not": *I haven't seen him in a long time – does he still live here?*

**have to** /ˈhæftə; *strong* ˈhæftu/ (*also* **have ˈgot to**) *verb*
**1** if you have to do something, you must do it: *I have to go now. I'm already late!* | *You've got to make a decision by tomorrow.*

**USAGE: have to, must, have got to**

**have to** – used when a rule, law, situation, etc. forces you to do something and you do not have a choice about it: *You have to pass a test before you are allowed to drive.* | *I have to get this essay finished by tomorrow.*

**must** – used especially in more formal writing when a law or someone who is in charge of something forces you to do something: *All students must have shorts and a T-shirt for P.E.* | *Motorcycle riders must wear helmets.*

**must** – used when you make yourself do something because you think it is a good idea or necessary: *We must visit Grandma on Sunday. We haven't seen her for weeks.* | *I must study for tomorrow's test.*

**have got to** – used in spoken English

instead of **have to** or **must** to show how important it is to do something: *I've got to talk to him.*

**2** used when saying that you are sure that something is true or will happen: *This letter has to be a joke – they can't really expect me to pay them $500.*

**hawk** /hɔk/ *noun*
a large bird that eats small birds and animals

**hay** /heɪ/ *noun*
dry grass that is used for feeding farm animals: *In winter, we give the horses hay.*

**ˈhay ˌfever** *noun*
a condition like a bad cold that some people get from breathing in POLLEN from plants

**haz·ard** /ˈhæzɚd/ *noun*
something that may be dangerous: *Loose wires are a hazard because people may trip over them.*
—**hazardous** *adjective* dangerous: *Snow is making the roads hazardous.*
→ see Thesaurus box at **danger**
[**ORIGIN:** 1200-1300 From the old French word *hasard*, which was a game of chance played with dice. A game of chance involves the risk of losing, and the word was later used for other risks.]

**haze** /heɪz/ *noun*
smoke or dust in the air that is difficult to see through: *Smoke from the forest fires has made a haze over the city.*

**ha·zel·nut** /ˈheɪzəlˌnʌt/ *noun*
a small round nut that tastes sweet

**haz·y** /ˈheɪzi/ *adjective*
**1** air that is hazy has smoke or dust in it: *The mountains looked hazy in the early morning sun.* **ANTONYM: clear**
**2** a hazy memory or idea is not clear: *I was very young, so my memories of that night are a little hazy.*

**he** /i; *strong* hi/ *pronoun*
used when talking about a man, boy, or male animal: *"That's my brother." "How old is he?"*

**head¹** /hed/ *noun*
**1** the top part of your body, where your eyes, mouth, and ears are: *She wrapped a scarf around her head to keep warm. | Mom shook her head in disagreement. | He was covered in mud from head to toe.* → see picture on page **A2**
**2** your mind: *I can't get that song out of my head. | Come on, use your head. You must be able to think of a plan.* **SYNONYM: brain**
**3** the person who is in charge of a group or organization: *Who's the head of the biology department?*
**4** the top or front of something, or the most important part of it: *His mother sat at the head of the table. | Our band was at the head of the parade.*
**5 heads** = the side of a coin that has a picture of someone's head on it: *I called heads when she tossed the coin, but I lost because it landed with tails facing up.* **ANTONYM: tails**
**6 keep your head** = to stay calm in a difficult situation: *He fell through the ice on the lake, but he kept his head and pulled himself out.*
**7 lose your head** = to behave stupidly in a difficult situation: *When all the lights went out, she lost her head and started screaming.*
**8 go to someone's head** = to make someone feel more important than he or she really is: *Don't let your success go to your head.*
**9 laugh/yell/scream your head off** (*informal*) = to laugh or shout a lot: *The movie was so funny – we laughed our heads off.*

**head²** *verb*
**1** to go in a particular direction: *We traveled south, heading for Mexico.*
**2** to be in charge of a group or organization: *The company is headed by David Marshall.*
**3 be heading/headed for something** = if you are heading for something, it is likely to happen to you: *The team has to learn how to work together, or they'll be headed for trouble when the season starts.*

**head·ache** /ˈhedeɪk/ *noun*
a pain in your head: *I had a bad headache from being out in the sun all day.*

**head·ing** /ˈhedɪŋ/ *noun*
a word or words at the beginning of a piece of writing that tells you what it is about: *The heading of the next chapter was "Secrets."*

**head·light** /ˈhedlaɪt/ *noun*
one of the two large lights on the front of a car: *It was getting dark and cars had their headlights on.* → see picture on page **A28**

**head·line** /ˈhedlaɪn/ *noun*
the title of a report in a newspaper: *"President Flies Home," said the headline.*

**headphones**

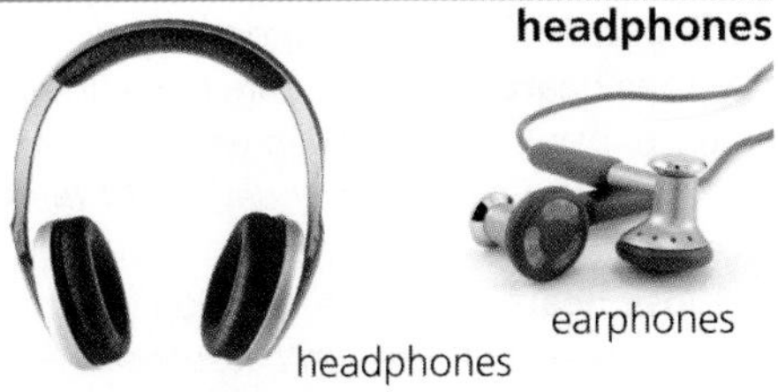


**head·phones** /ˈhedfoʊnz/ *plural noun*
a piece of equipment that you wear over your ears to listen to music

**head·quar·ters** /ˈhedˌkwɔtɚz/ *noun* (*abbreviation*: **HQ**)
the place from which people run a large organization or control military activities: *The company's headquarters are in New York.*

**ˌhead ˈstart** *noun*
the advantage you get by starting before other people: *We gave the younger kids a head start in the race, so that they had a chance to win.*

**head·way** /ˈhedweɪ/ *noun*
**make headway** = to succeed in achieving part of something that is difficult: *The officers trying to solve the crime have not made much headway.* **SYNONYM: make progress**

**heal** /hil/ *verb*
**1** if a wound heals, the skin or flesh grows back together and becomes healthy again: *The cut on her finger healed quickly.*
**2** to make a sick person or a wound get better: *The cream will heal the cut faster.*
—**healer** *noun* someone who makes sick people get better, but not with ordinary medical treatment: *a religious healer*

**health** /helθ/ *noun*
the condition of your body and your mind: *Smoking is bad for your health.* | *My mother had a lot of mental health problems.*
[**ORIGIN:** From the old English word *hal*, which means "whole or healthy."]

**ˈhealth care** (*also* **health·care**) /ˈhelθker/ *noun*
medical treatment and care: *Many people cannot afford to pay for health care when they get sick.*

**ˈhealth food** *noun*
food that contains only natural substances that are good for you: *I buy pure fruit juice from a health food store.*

**health·ful** /ˈhelθfəl/ *adjective* (*formal*)
good for your body: *Try to eat plenty of fruit, vegetables, and other healthful food.* **SYNONYM: healthy**

**health·y** /ˈhelθi/ *adjective* (**healthier, healthiest**)
**1** physically well and strong: *The best way to stay healthy is to eat well and exercise.* **ANTONYM: sick**

**THESAURUS: healthy**

**well** healthy – used for saying how someone feels or looks: *Aren't you feeling well?*

**fine** healthy – used when someone has asked you how you feel and you are replying that you feel well: *"Hi, Tom, how are you?" "Fine, thanks."*

**better** less sick than you were, or no longer sick: *I'm feeling a lot better now.*

**in shape** healthy and physically strong because you do a lot of exercise: *He keeps in shape by running.*

**physically fit** having a strong healthy body because you exercise regularly: *Even kids need daily exercise to be physically fit.*

**2** good for your body or your mind: *I try to eat a healthy diet and get plenty of fresh air.* | *It's not healthy to be alone so much.* **ANTONYM: unhealthy**

**heap¹** /hip/ *noun*
a large messy pile of things: *There was a heap of clothes on the floor.*

**heap²** *verb*
to put a lot of things on top of each other in a messy way: *He heaped his plate with food.*

**hear** /hɪr/ *verb* (**heard** /hɚd/)
**1** to notice a sound with your ears: *He heard footsteps and turned to see who it was.* | *I could hear my parents yelling downstairs.*
**2** to be told some news or information: *Have you heard the news? Jen had her baby.* | *I heard that he was sick.*

H

**3** **have heard of someone/something** = to recognize the name of someone or something that is mentioned to you: *I've heard of the book, but I've never read it.*

PHRASAL VERB

**hear from someone**

to get news or information from someone: *I heard from John. He sent me an email.*

**hear·ing** /ˈhɪrɪŋ/ *noun*

**1** your ability to hear: *My hearing is not very good, so you'll have to speak louder.*

**2** an official meeting to find out the facts about something: *The Senate began hearings on airline safety this week.*

**ˈhearing aid** *noun*

a small object that you put in your ear if you cannot hear well, to make sounds louder

**heart**

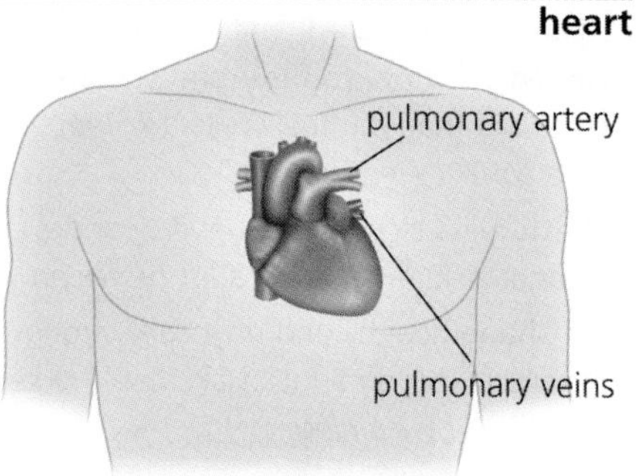


**heart** /hɑrt/ *noun*

**1** the body part inside your chest that makes blood move through your body: *Running makes your heart beat faster.*

**2** the part of you which has strong feelings such as love: *I loved her with all my heart.*

**3** a shape that is used to mean love, which looks like this (♥): *He sent her a card with pink hearts on it.*

**4** **the heart of something** = **a)** the middle of an area or thing: *The hotel is in the heart of the city so it is easy to get everywhere.* **b)** the most important part of something: *We need to get to the heart of the problem so that we can fix it.*

**5** a card used in card games. The cards have a picture on them which looks like this (♥): *I had the king of hearts.*

**6** **know/learn something by heart** = if you know a poem or song by heart, you know it so well that you can say it or sing it without reading it: *All the students learned the poem by heart.*

**7** **break someone's heart** = to make someone very unhappy: *It breaks my heart to see this beautiful forest being destroyed.*

**8** **take heart** = to have more hope and confidence than before: *Though we didn't win, the team played really well today, and I think we can take heart from that.*

**9** **lose heart** = to have less hope and confidence than before: *Don't lose heart – we'll find an answer to the problem!*

**10** **someone's heart sinks** = used when saying that someone suddenly loses hope or becomes very sad: *My heart sank when I saw how difficult the test questions were.*

**11** **at heart** = used when saying what type of person someone is, especially when this is different from how the person seems: *Grandma's seventy but she's young at heart.*

[ORIGIN: From the old English word *heorte.*]

**ˈheart atˌtack** *noun*

a time when someone's heart suddenly stops working normally: *He had a heart attack and was rushed to the hospital.*

**heart·beat** /ˈhɑrtbit/ *noun*

the movement or sound that your heart makes: *The doctor listened to the baby's heartbeat and said that it was normal.*

**heart·break** /ˈhɑrtbreɪk/ *noun*

a strong feeling of sadness that you feel when something happens: *When a family pet dies, it can cause heartbreak for the children.*

—**heartbroken** *adjective* very sad because of something that has happened: *He was heartbroken when his girlfriend ended their relationship.*

**heart·less** /ˈhɑrtləs/ *adjective*

cruel or unkind: *The thieves were so heartless that they even stole the Christmas presents from under the tree.*

**heart·y** /ˈhɑrti/ *adjective* (*formal*)

a hearty meal is very big: *Everyone was hungry, and ate a hearty dinner.*

**heat¹** /hit/ *noun*

**1** the warmth from something hot: *She felt the heat from the sun on her face.*

**2** very hot weather: *I can't work in this heat.*

**3** **the heat** = the system in a building that

keeps it warm: *It's cold in here – I'll turn the heat on.*
**4** one part of a race or competition. The winners of each heat compete against each other in the next part: *Burns won his heat so he's still in the competition.*

**heat²** (*also* **heat up**) *verb*
to make something warm or hot: *I'll heat up some soup for dinner.*

**heat·ed** /ˈhitɪd/ *adjective*
if an object is heated, a heater makes it warm: *The hotel has a heated pool.*

**heat·er** /ˈhitɚ/ *noun*
a machine for heating air or water: *He lived in a small room with one electric heater to keep him warm.*

**ˈheat wave** *noun*
some days or weeks when the weather is very hot: *In August, there was a heat wave when the temperature was over 95° Fahrenheit for a week.*

**heave** /hiv/ *verb*
to lift or pull something heavy: *Three men heaved the big box into the house.*
→ see Thesaurus box at **pull¹**

**heav·en** /ˈhevən/ *noun*
in some religions, the place where God is, and good people go after they die: *Do you think you'll go to heaven?* **ANTONYM: hell**

**heav·en·ly** /ˈhevənli/ *adjective*
**1** relating to heaven: *She prayed to her Heavenly Father.*
**2** very good: *a heavenly chocolate cake*

**heavy**

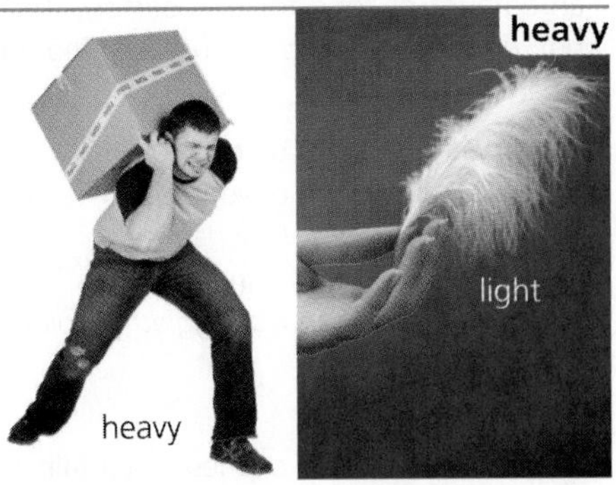


**heav·y** /ˈhevi/ *adjective* (**heavier**, **heaviest**)
**1** weighing a lot: *I couldn't lift the box – it was too heavy.* **ANTONYM: light**
**2** large in amount: *There was heavy snow and some roads were closed.* | *He was late because of heavy traffic on the freeway.*
**ANTONYM: light**
**3 a heavy smoker/drinker** = someone who smokes a lot, or drinks a lot of alcohol: *Lung cancer is more common if you are a heavy smoker.*
**4 a heavy sleeper** = someone who is difficult to wake when he or she is sleeping: *I'm a heavy sleeper, so I didn't hear the storm.*
—**heavily** *adverb* a lot: *It was snowing heavily.*
—**heaviness** *noun* the state of being heavy
→ see Thesaurus box at **fat¹**

**ˌheavy-ˈduty** *adjective*
very strong and not easily damaged: *The workmen need to wear heavy-duty boots to protect their feet.*

**heav·y·weight** /ˈheviˌweɪt/ *noun*
in BOXING, someone who belongs in the group of people who weigh the most

**He·brew** /ˈhibru/ *noun*
**1** the language spoken in Israel
**2** a member of the Jewish people who lived long ago in the past
—**Hebrew** *adjective* relating to Hebrews or their language: *the letters of the Hebrew alphabet*

**hec·tic** /ˈhektɪk/ *adjective*
very busy, with a lot of different things happening: *I had a hectic week, with three exams and a paper due on Friday.*

**hedge** /hedʒ/ *noun*
a row of small bushes or trees growing close together, used as a border around a yard or between two yards

**heel** /hi:l/ *noun*
**1** the round part in the back of your foot
**2** the part on the bottom of a shoe in the back: *She likes shoes with high heels for parties.* → see picture at **shoe**

**heft·y** /ˈhefti/ *adjective* (*informal*)
**1** a hefty amount of money is very large: *They paid him a hefty salary – over two million dollars.*
**2** someone who is hefty is large and heavy: *The police officer was a hefty guy.*

H

**height** /haɪt/ *noun*

**1** how tall someone or something is: *First, the doctor measured her height.*

**2** the level something is above the ground: *You can change the height of your chair and make it lower if that is more comfortable.*

**3** the time when something is busiest or most successful: *July is the height of the tourist season, and thousands of people come here every day.*

**heir** /er/ *noun*

someone who gets money or other things from a person who has died: *She chose her nephew as her heir, and all her money went to him when she died.*

**held** /held/ *verb*

the past tense and past participle of HOLD

**hel·i·cop·ter** /ˈhelɪˌkɑptɚ/ *noun*

an aircraft with long metal parts on top that spin around to make it fly. A helicopter can go straight up into the air: *A police helicopter landed on top of the building.* → see picture on page **A27**

[**ORIGIN:** 1800-1900 From the Greek words *helikos*, a form of the word for "spiral," and *pteron*, which means "wing."]

**he·li·um** /ˈhiliəm/ *noun* (*written abbreviation*: **HE**)

a gas that is lighter than air: *A balloon filled with helium will float up into the sky.*

[**ORIGIN:** 1800-1900 From the Greek word *helios*, which means "the Sun." Helium was discovered to be on the Sun before it was found on Earth.]

**hell** /hel/ *noun*

in some religions, the place where bad people go when they die **ANTONYM: heaven**

**hel·lo** /həˈloʊ/ *interjection*

a word you say when you meet someone, or talk on the telephone: *Hello Paul, how are you?*

[**ORIGIN:** From the old word *hollo*, which was shouted to get someone's attention. First used in the modern way, 1800-1900.]

**hel·met** /ˈhelmət/ *noun*

a hard hat that covers and protects your head: *Don't forget to wear your bicycle helmet.* → see picture on page **A26**

**help¹** /help/ *verb*

**1** to do something that makes it easier for another person to do something: *"This box is really heavy." "Let me help."* | *Mom, can you help me with my homework?*

**2** to make something bad or unpleasant better: *If you have a headache, lying down helps.*

**3 can't help doing something** = used to say that you cannot stop yourself from doing something: *She looked so funny – I couldn't help laughing.*

**4 help yourself** = used to tell someone to take as much food or drink as he or she wants to: *There's plenty of food, so help yourself.*

**5 Help!** = a word you shout when you are in danger, and you need someone to come

—**helper** *noun* someone who helps another person: *We had plenty of helpers, so we were able to do the work quickly.*

**WORD FAMILY: help**

**help** *verb* | **help** *noun* | **helpful** *adjective* | **helpfully** *adverb* | **helper** *noun*

**help²** *noun*

something that makes it easier for another person to do something: *Do you need any help with the cooking?* | *If you don't understand, ask your teacher for help.*

**help·ful** /ˈhelpfəl/ *adjective*

**1** useful: *The website is full of helpful information about the college.*

**2** willing to help: *The librarian was very helpful and found exactly the book I wanted.*

—**helpfully** *adverb* in a helpful way: *"If you need anything, just ask me," he said helpfully.*

**help·ing** /ˈhelpɪŋ/ *noun*

an amount of food for one person, that you put on a plate: *I had a big helping of ice cream.*

**help·less** /ˈhelpləs/ *adjective*

not able to take care of yourself: *When babies are born, they are totally helpless.*

—**helplessly** *adverb* in a helpless way: *He could not swim, and struggled helplessly in the water.*

**hem** /hem/ *noun*

the bottom edge of clothes or curtains, that you make by folding the edge and sewing it: *I shortened the skirt, and sewed up the hem.*

**hem·i·sphere** /ˈheməˌsfɪr/ *noun*

one half of the Earth, especially one of the

halves above and below the EQUATOR: *Australia is in the southern hemisphere.* → see picture at **globe**

[ORIGIN: 1500-1600 From the Greek words *hemi-* and *sphaira*, which mean "half" and "ball."]

**hen** /hen/ *noun*
a female chicken: *Hens usually lay eggs in the same place every day.*

**hep·a·ti·tis** /ˌhepəˈtaɪtɪs/ *noun*
a serious disease of the LIVER

**her** /ɚ; *strong* hɚ/ *pronoun*
a woman or girl: *I gave her $20.*
—**her** *adjective* belonging to a woman or girl: *Mom lost her purse.*

**herb** /ɚb/ *noun*
a plant that you use in order to give more taste to food, or to make medicine: *Cook the chicken with some fresh herbs.*
[ORIGIN: 1200-1300 From the Latin word *herba*, which means "grass or herb."]

**herb·i·vore** /ˈhɚbəˌvɔr/ *noun*
an animal that only eats plants: *Sheep are herbivores and eat mainly grass.*
[ORIGIN: 1800-1900 From the Latin words *herba* and *vorare*, which mean "herb" and "to eat."]

**herd**[1] /hɚd/ *noun*
a group of big animals of the same kind that live together: *There was a herd of cattle in the field.*
→ see Thesaurus box at **group**[1]

**herd**[2] *verb*
to make a large group of people or animals move somewhere: *The teacher herded the children into the museum.*

**here** /hɪr/ *adverb*
**1** in or to the place where you are: *How long have you lived here? | Come here, and stand next to me.*
**2** if a period of time is here, it has begun: *Winter is gone and spring is here!*
**3 here/here you go/here you are** = said when you are giving something to someone: *"Can I see your pictures?" "Sure, here you go."*
**4 here and there** = in different places: *Boats were sailing here and there on the water.*

**her·it·age** /ˈherətɪdʒ/ *noun*
the traditional customs, CULTURE, and other things that connect you to the people of your country or to a group who lived before you: *My family is proud of our Chinese heritage.*
[ORIGIN: 1200-1300 From the old French word *heriter*, which means "to inherit," from the Latin word *hereditas*, meaning "inheritance."]

**he·ro** /ˈhɪroʊ/ *noun* (plural **heroes**)
**1** someone who people admire for doing something very brave or good: *When he came back from the war, he was welcomed as a hero.*
**2** a man who is the most important character in a book, play, or movie: *The hero marries the heroine at the end of the movie.*
—**heroism** /ˈheroʊˌɪzəm/ *noun* a lot of courage and brave actions: *My father received a medal for his heroism.*

**he·ro·ic** /hɪˈroʊɪk/ *adjective*
very determined or brave: *Firefighters made a heroic effort to save the burning building.*

**her·o·ine** /ˈheroʊɪn/ *noun*
a woman who is the most important character in a book, play, or movie: *In movies, the heroine is usually beautiful.*

**her·on** /ˈherən/ *noun*
a big bird with very long legs and a long beak, that lives near water and eats fish

**her·ring** /ˈherɪŋ/ *noun* (plural **herring** *or* **herrings**)
a long thin silver fish that lives in the ocean

**hers** /hɚz/ *pronoun*
something that belongs to a woman or girl: *That's not my bag – it's hers.*

**her·self** /ɚˈself; *strong* hɚˈself/ *pronoun*
**1** the woman or girl who you have just mentioned: *Anna looked at herself in the mirror.*
**2** used with "she" or a woman's name to emphasize that she did something: *I know it's true because she told me herself.*
**3 (all) by herself** = alone or without help: *She painted the house by herself.*

**hes·i·tate** /ˈhezəˌteɪt/ *verb*
to wait for a moment before you do or say something, because you are thinking about what to do or say: *She hesitated for a second before she picked up the phone.*
—**hesitation** /ˌhezəˈteɪʃən/ *noun* an act of hesitating: *He asked her to marry him, and she said "yes" without hesitation.*
[ORIGIN: 1600-1700 From the Latin word *haesitare*, which means "to be uncertain."]

**het·er·o·sex·u·al** /ˌhetərəˈsekʃuəl/ *adjective*
someone who is heterosexual is attracted to people of the opposite sex

**hex·a·gon** /ˈheksəˌgɑn/ *noun*
a flat shape with six sides
—**hexagonal** /hekˈsægənl/ *adjective* a hexagonal shape has six sides

**hexagon**

**hey** /heɪ/ *interjection*
you say this to get someone's attention: *Hey, what are you doing with my jacket?*

**he'd** /id; *strong* hid/
**1** the short form of "he had": *He'd met her before.*
**2** the short form of "he would": *George said he'd be late.*

H

**he'll** /il; *strong* hil/
the short form of "he will": *He'll call us when he gets there.*

**he's** /iz; *strong* hiz/
**1** the short form of "he is": *He's a doctor.*
**2** the short form of "he has": *He's already finished the book.*

**hi** /haɪ/ *interjection* (*informal*)
another word for HELLO: *Hi Jen! How are you?*

**hi·ber·nate** /ˈhaɪbɚˌneɪt/ *verb*
if an animal hibernates, it sleeps all through the winter: *Some bears hibernate and wake up in the spring.*
—**hibernation** /ˌhaɪbɚˈneɪʃən/ *noun* the time when an animal is sleeping because it is winter
[**ORIGIN:** 1800-1900 From the Latin word *hibernare*, which means "to spend the winter somewhere," from *hibernus*, which means "relating to winter."]

**hic·cups** /ˈhɪkʌps/ *plural noun*
if you get the hiccups, you start making short sounds in your throat that you cannot control: *I suddenly got the hiccups, and had to drink some water to make them go away.*

**hide¹** /haɪd/ *verb* (**hid** /hɪd/, **hidden** /ˈhɪdn/)
**1** to put something where people cannot see it or find it: *She didn't want him to see the letter, so she hid it in a drawer.*
**2** to go somewhere where people cannot see you or find you: *Jake hid from his mom because he thought she would be mad.*
**3** to stop other people from knowing the truth, or seeing how you feel: *Mark couldn't hide the fact that he liked Kim a lot.*

**hide²** *noun*
the skin of an animal, that people use for leather

**ˌhide-and-ˈseek** *noun*
a game in which one child tries to find all the other children, who are hiding in different places: *The kids were in the yard, playing hide-and-seek.*

**hid·e·ous** /ˈhɪdiəs/ *adjective*
very ugly: *The story is about a hideous monster with a big green face and hairy ears.*
[**ORIGIN:** 1300-1400 From the old French word *hidous*, from *hide*, which means "terror." Something that is very ugly might make you frightened.]

**hi·er·ar·chy** Ac /ˈhaɪəˌrɑrki/ *noun* (plural **hierarchies**)
a system of organizing people in which some people are more important and powerful than others: *The president is at the top of the hierarchy.*
[**ORIGIN:** 1300-1400 From the Greek word *hierarchia*, which means "rule by a chief priest."]

**hier·o·glyph·ics** /ˌhaɪrəˈglɪfɪks/ *noun*
a system of writing used by the ancient Egyptians, in which pictures represent words

**high¹** /haɪ/ *adjective* (**higher**, **highest**)
**1** high mountains and walls are tall: *Mount Everest is the highest mountain in the world.* | *There was a high wall around the house.* **ANTONYM: low**
**2** high windows, cupboards, and shelves are a long way above the ground: *Keep medicine in a high cupboard that children cannot reach.* **ANTONYM: low**

**USAGE: high, tall**
Use **high** about mountains, walls, fences, etc.: *The highest mountain in the U.S.A. is Mount McKinley.*

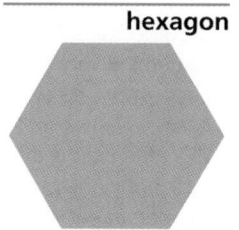

Use **high** to talk about how far something is above the ground: *The shelf is too high for the kids to reach.*

Use **tall** about people, trees, and other narrow things: *She was tall and slim.* | *The bird's nest was at the top of a tall tree.* | *a tall flagpole*

When describing buildings, we usually use **tall**, not **high**: *the tall buildings in the downtown area*

**3** used for asking or talking about how tall something is: *How high is the wall?* | *The fence was only two feet high.*
**4** a high amount or number is big: *I got a really high score on my math test; it was the best score in the whole class!* **ANTONYM: low**

**USAGE: high, expensive**

Use **high** about prices and costs: *They charge high prices for their clothes.*

Use **expensive** about things: *She likes buying expensive clothes.*

Do not say "expensive prices."

**5** of a very good quality or standard: *The food in that store is expensive but it is very high quality.* **ANTONYM: low**
**6** a high sound is near the top of the sounds that people can hear, like a whistle or a child's voice: *Some of the notes in this song are so high that I can't sing them.* **ANTONYM: low**
**7 be high in something** = to have a lot of a substance: *Candy bars are not healthy because they are very high in fat.*

**WORD FAMILY: high**

**high** *adjective* | **height** *noun*

**high²** *adverb*
a long way above the ground: *I saw an eagle flying high in the sky above us.* | *Can't you jump any higher?* **ANTONYM: low**

**ˌhigher eduˈcation** *noun*
education at a college or university: *The school encourages its students to go on to higher education.*

**ˈhigh jump** *noun*
**the high jump** = a sport in which you jump as high as you can over a bar

**high·light¹** [Ac] /ˈhaɪlaɪt/ *verb*
**1** to mark important words on paper or on a computer, using a color that is easy to see: *Use a colored pen to highlight information that you want to remember.*
**2** to make people pay attention to something you think is important: *In his speech, the president highlighted the issue of crime.*

**highlight²** [Ac] *noun*
**1** the best or most important part of something: *We can watch the highlights of the game on TV later tonight.*
**2 highlights** = parts of someone's hair that have been made a lighter color than the rest: *She asked the hairdresser to put some blond highlights in her hair.*

**high·ly** /ˈhaɪli/ *adverb*
very, very much, or very well: *The movie was highly successful – millions of people went to see it.* | *He is a highly respected writer.*

**High·ness** /ˈhaɪnɪs/ *noun*
**Your/His/Her Highness** = a title for a king or queen, and some other royal people

**ˌhigh-ˈpitched** *adjective*
a high-pitched sound is not low like a man's voice: *I could hear the high-pitched laughter of the girls upstairs.*

**ˈhigh school** *noun*
a school in the U.S. and Canada for students over the age of 14: *Wendy and I were good friends in high school.* | *high school students*

**high-tech** (*also* **hi-tech**) /ˌhaɪ ˈtek/ *adjective*
using very modern equipment and methods: *In Japan, there are a lot of high-tech companies that produce electronic goods.*

**ˌhigh ˈtide** *noun*
the time when the ocean comes a long way up the beach: *At high tide, the water covers the whole beach.*

**high·way** /ˈhaɪweɪ/ *noun*
a big fast road between cities: *The highway between Los Angeles and Santa Barbara is very busy.*
→ see Thesaurus box at **road**

H

**hi·jack** /ˈhaɪdʒæk/ *verb*
to use violence or threats to take control of an airplane, vehicle, or ship: *The terrorists hijacked a plane flying from London to the U.S.*
—**hijacker** *noun* someone who hijacks an airplane, vehicle, or ship: *A hijacker in Miami took a school bus and left the children by the side of the road.*
—**hijacking** *noun* the act of hijacking an airplane, vehicle, or ship: *Two people were shot in the hijacking.*

**hike** /haɪk/ *noun*
a long walk in the country: *On Sunday, we took a hike in the mountains.*
—**hike** *verb* to walk a long way in the country: *A lot of people hike the mountain trail that runs from New Hampshire to Georgia.*
—**hiking** *noun* the activity of taking long walks in the country

H

**hi·lar·i·ous** /hɪˈleriəs/ *adjective*
very funny: *His jokes were hilarious – I couldn't stop laughing.*
→ see Thesaurus box at **funny**
[**ORIGIN:** 1800-1900 From the Latin word *hilarus*, which means "cheerful."]

**hill** /hɪl/ *noun*
an area of high land, like a small mountain: *Why don't we climb to the top of the hill?*
—**hilly** *adjective* having a lot of hills: *San Francisco is a hilly city.*

**him** /ɪm; *strong* hɪm/ *pronoun*
a man or boy: *I gave him the letter.*

**him·self** /ɪmˈself; *strong* hɪmˈself/ *pronoun*
**1** the man or boy who you have just mentioned: *Pete fell and hurt himself.*
**2** used with "he" or a man's name to emphasize that he did something: *Dad made the boat himself.*
**3 (all) by himself** = alone or without help: *He likes working by himself, rather than with other people.*

**hin·der** /ˈhɪndɚ/ *verb* (*formal*)
to make it difficult for someone to do something: *The bad weather hindered their efforts to save the men.*

**hind·sight** /ˈhaɪndsaɪt/ *noun*
the ability to understand a situation, that you can only get after it has happened: *In hindsight, I realize that he was lying to me, but at the time I believed him.*

**Hin·du·ism** /ˈhɪnduˌɪzəm/ *noun*
the main religion in India
—**Hindu** *noun* someone whose religion is Hinduism
—**Hindu** *adjective* relating to Hinduism: *a Hindu temple*

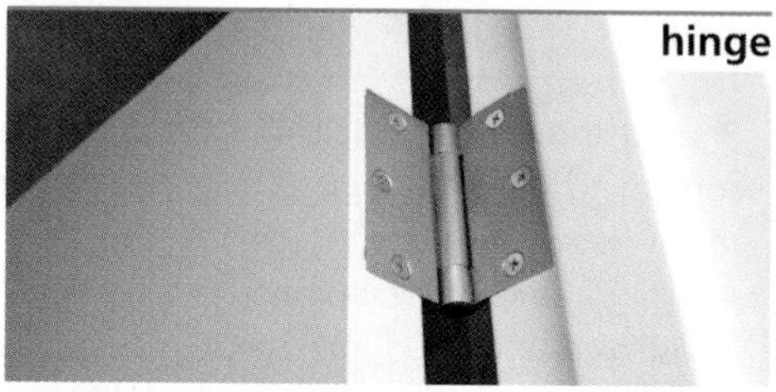
**hinge**

**hinge** /hɪndʒ/ *noun*
a piece of metal that is used to join a door to its frame or a lid to a box, so that it can open and shut: *The door's hinges squeak every time it opens.*

**hint** /hɪnt/ *noun*
**1** something you say that helps someone guess something: *I don't know the answer. Can you give me a hint?* | *I gave Mom a couple of hints about what I'd like for my birthday.*
**2** a piece of useful advice: *The book is full of hints on how to make easy healthy meals.*
—**hint** *verb* to say something that helps someone guess something

**hip** /hɪp/ *noun*
the part of your body where your legs join your body: *The woman was holding a baby on her hip.* → see picture on page **A2**

**ˈhip-hop** *noun*
a type of popular music with a strong beat and spoken words, that people dance to

**hip·pie** (*also* **hippy**) /ˈhɪpi/ *noun*
someone from the 1960s and 1970s who had long hair and unusual clothes and who did not want war or a traditional way of living

**hip·po·pot·a·mus** /ˌhɪpəˈpɑtəməs/ (*also* **hip·po** /ˈhɪpoʊ/) *noun* (plural **hippopotamuses**)
a large African animal with a fat body and thick gray skin, that lives in and near water
[**ORIGIN:** 1500-1600 From the Greek words *hippos* and *potamos*, which mean "horse" and "river."]

**hire** /haɪɚ/ *verb*
to pay someone to work for you: *Most hotels hire more people during the summer when it is busy.* **SYNONYM: employ**

**his¹** /ɪz; *strong* hɪz/ *adjective*
belonging to a man or boy: *Did he do his homework?*

**his²** *pronoun*
something that belongs to a man or boy: *That's not my jacket – it's his.*

**His·pan·ic** /hɪˈspænɪk/ *noun*
someone from a country where the people speak Spanish
—**Hispanic** *adjective* from a country where the people speak Spanish: *Hispanic students*
[**ORIGIN:** 1500-1600 From *Hispania*, the word that the Romans used for the area that is now Spain and Portugal.]

**hiss** /hɪs/ *verb*
**1** to make a sound like "ssss": *The snake hissed at me.* → see picture on page **A22**
**2** to say something quietly, in an angry or firm way: *"Stay where you are," he hissed, "and keep quiet."*
**3** to make a sound like "ssss" when you do not like a performer or speaker: *His jokes were not funny and the audience started to hiss at him.*
—**hiss** *noun* a sound like "ssss": *The elevator doors opened with a hiss.*
[**ORIGIN:** 1300-1400 From the sound.]

**his·to·ri·an** /hɪˈstɔriən/ *noun*
someone who studies or writes about history: *She is a famous historian who knows a lot about early American history.*

**his·tor·ic** /hɪˈstɔrɪk/ *adjective*
important in history: *It was a historic moment when the two countries signed the peace agreement.*

**his·to·ry** /ˈhɪstəri/ *noun*
**1** the study of things that happened in the past: *My favorite subject at school is history.*
**2** all the things that happened in the past: *The Civil War was the most difficult time in the history of our nation.*
—**historical** /hɪˈstɔrɪkəl/ *adjective* relating to things that have happened in the past: *I like reading historical novels, especially ones that are set in the 19th century.*
[**ORIGIN:** 1400-1500 From the Latin word *historia*, which means "story of events in the past," from the Greek word *historia*, which means "knowledge, or the activity of asking questions to find things out."]

**WORD FAMILY: history**

**history** *noun* | **historic** *adjective* | **historical** *adjective* | **historian** *noun* | **prehistoric** *adjective*

**hit¹** /hɪt/ *verb* (**hit**, **hitting**)
**1** to move your hand quickly, so that you touch something with a lot of force: *One boy hit me on the arm really hard.* | *I picked up the bat and got ready to hit the ball.* → see picture on page **A5**

**THESAURUS: hit**

**punch** to hit someone hard with your closed hand: *One of the boys punched him in the stomach.*

**slap** to hit someone with the flat part of your hand: *Did your parents ever slap you?*

**beat** to hit someone or something many times: *He had been robbed and beaten.*

**smack** to hit someone or something, usually with your open hand: *The ball smacked him in the face.*

**strike** (*formal*) to hit someone or something very hard: *She fell and struck her head on a table.*

**knock** to hit a door with your closed hand so that the people inside can hear you: *Someone was knocking on the door.*

**bang** to hit something hard, making a loud noise: *A policeman was banging on the door.*

**tap** to gently hit your fingers or foot against something: *I tapped him on the shoulder and said "Hi."*

**pound** to knock very hard, making a lot of noise: *Scott pounded on the table with his fist.*

**2** if something hits something else, it touches it with a lot of force: *Ann's car went off the road and hit a tree.* | *The bullet hit his shoulder.*
**3** to affect someone or something very badly:

H

*The increase in prices will hit poor families.*

**4 hit the roof/ceiling** (*informal*) = to become very angry: *Dad hit the roof when I got home late.*

**5 hit it off** = if two people hit it off, they like each other as soon as they meet: *Alice and I hit it off on our very first day of school, and we've been friends ever since.*

[**ORIGIN:** 1000-1100 From the Norse word *hitta*, which means "to find or hit." Norse was a language used in Scandinavian countries.]

**PHRASAL VERB**

**hit on something**

to have a good idea about something: *She hit on the idea of starting a children's party business, and it has been a success.*

**hit²** *noun*

**1** a movie, song, or play that is very successful: *The band's first song was a big hit and reached number one in the charts.*

**2** the act of hitting the ball in a game such as baseball: *Michael played really well – he had four hits.*

**hitch·hike** /ˈhɪtʃhaɪk/ *verb*

to travel by asking for free rides from people who are driving past you: *I hitchhiked around Europe because I didn't have enough money for the trains.*

—**hitchhiker** *noun* someone who is hitchhiking: *I picked up a hitchhiker when I was driving home.*

**hi-tech** /ˌhaɪ ˈtek/ *adjective*

another spelling of HIGH-TECH

**HIV** *noun*

(**Human Immunodeficiency Virus**) a VIRUS people get that can cause AIDS

**hive** /haɪv/ *noun*

**1** (*also* **beehive**) a place where BEEs live

**2 hives** = a medical condition in which someone's skin swells and becomes red. It usually happens because you are ALLERGIC to something.

**HMO** *noun*

(**Health Maintenance Organization**) a type of insurance organization that pays for your health care if you use doctors and hospitals that are part of the organization

**hoard¹** /hɔrd/ *verb*

to collect or hide a lot of something you will use in the future: *Animals such as squirrels hoard food for the winter.*

**hoard²** *noun*

a large amount of something that someone has hidden to keep it safe: *People say there is a hoard of gold buried somewhere on the island.*

**hoarse** /hɔrs/ *adjective*

if you are hoarse, your voice sounds low and is not clear: *I talked so much that I was hoarse by the end of the day.*

—**hoarsely** *adverb* if you speak hoarsely, your voice sounds hoarse: *"I have a sore throat so I can't talk very well," he said hoarsely.*

—**hoarseness** *noun* the quality of sounding hoarse

**hoax** /hoʊks/ *noun*

a trick that makes a lot of people believe something that is not true: *The caller said there was a bomb in the store, but it was a hoax.*

[**ORIGIN:** 1700-1800 Probably from *hocus pocus*, a fake Latin phrase used by people doing magic tricks.]

**hob·ble** /ˈhɑbəl/ *verb*

to walk with difficulty, taking small steps because your foot or leg is injured: *His leg was hurting badly, but he managed to hobble home.*

**hob·by** /ˈhɑbi/ *noun* (plural **hobbies**)

an activity that you enjoy doing in your free time: *My hobbies are swimming and playing the piano.*

→ see Thesaurus box at **game**

[**ORIGIN:** The word "hobby" was used to refer to a horse, and then to a toy horse that a child would pretend to ride. It later came to be used for any activity that you do for fun. First used with its modern meaning, 1800-1900.]

**hock·ey** /ˈhɑki/ *noun*

(*also* **ice hockey**) a sport that two teams play on ice, using curved sticks to hit a hard flat object → see picture on page **A24**

**hoe** /hoʊ/ *noun*

a garden tool with a long handle, used to make the soil loose

**hog¹** /hɔg/ *noun*

**1** a large pig: *a hog farm*

**2** someone who takes more than his or her

share of something: *Don't be a ball hog – pass the ball to your teammates.*

**hog²** *verb* (**hogged, hogging**) (*informal*)
to use something a lot, so it is difficult for other people to use it: *My sister always hogs the bathroom.*

**ho·gan** /ˈhoʊgən/ *noun*
a traditional Navajo house made of branches covered with mud or soil

**hoist** /hɔɪst/ *verb*
to lift something or someone up, often using ropes: *The soldiers hoisted a flag over the fort.*

**hold¹** /hoʊld/ *verb* (**held** /held/)
1 to have something in your hands or arms: *The boy was holding a $10 bill.* | *Hold my hand when we cross the street.* → see picture on page A5

**THESAURUS: hold**

**grip** to hold something firmly: *I gripped the rail and tried not to look down at the street far below.*

**take/keep/grab hold of something** to take something in your hands and hold it tightly: *Doug took hold of my hand and pulled me away from the crowd.*

**grab** to take hold of someone or something suddenly or violently: *Vince grabbed his coat and ran out of the house.*

**seize** (*formal*) to take hold of something or someone suddenly and using force: *The soldiers seized him and quickly moved him away from the scene.*

**clutch** to hold something tightly: *a child clutching a bag of candy*

2 to keep something in a position: *He held the picture up so we could see it.* | *She held the door open for me.*
3 to have a formal meeting or party: *The school is holding a meeting for parents and teachers next week.*
4 to have space for a number or amount of something: *The theater holds 800 people.* | *The container holds one gallon of liquid.*
5 (*formal*) to have a position, job, or level of achievement: *He held the position of governor for four years.* | *She holds a degree in computer science.*
6 **Hold it!** (*informal*) = you say this when you are telling someone to wait or stop doing something: *"Hold it!" said the policeman. "Stay right there."*
7 **hold your breath** = to breathe in and not breathe out again for a short time: *I held my breath, and jumped into the water.*
→ **hold your breath** at **breath**
[**ORIGIN:** From the old English word *healdan.*]

**PHRASAL VERBS**

**hold something against someone**
to blame or dislike someone for something he or she did: *He didn't mean to upset you, so don't hold it against him.*

**hold something back**
to stop something or someone from moving forward: *The police were trying to hold the crowds back, but they kept on pushing toward the stage door.*

**hold on**
1 **Hold on!** (*informal*) = used when asking someone to wait, while you do or say something: *Hold on a minute – I need to find my keys.*
2 **hold on to something** = to keep something carefully or tightly in your hand: *If you go out at night, hold on to your wallet.*

**hold someone or something up**
to make someone or something late: *Bad weather held us up, and we got home an hour late.*

**hold²** *noun*
1 **take/grab/keep hold of something** = to take something in your hand and keep it there: *Mom took hold of the handle and pulled hard.*
2 **get (a) hold of someone or something** = to find someone or something that you need or want: *I need to get hold of Mike to ask him a question.*
3 **on hold** = if you are on hold, you are waiting to speak to someone on the telephone: *Every time I call the company, they put me on hold for about half an hour.*
4 **the hold** = the bottom part of a ship, where you store goods

**hold·er** /ˈhoʊldɚ/ *noun*

**1** someone who has or owns something: *Only ticket holders can go into the stadium.*

**2** something that holds or contains another thing: *I put my can of soda in the car's cup holder.*

**hold·up** /ˈhoʊldʌp/ *noun*

**1** a delay: *There was a holdup on the freeway because of an accident.*

**2** if there is a holdup, people try to rob a store or bank using guns or other weapons: *Three men took part in a holdup at the store, and got away with thousands of dollars.*

**hole** /hoʊl/ *noun*

**1** an empty space, especially where something is broken or torn: *There's a hole in my sweater.*

**THESAURUS: hole**

**space** the empty area between two things, into which you can put something: *There's a space for that box on the shelf over there.*

**gap** an empty space between two things or two parts of something: *She has a gap between her two front teeth.*

**leak** a small hole that lets liquid or gas flow into or out of something: *There is a leak in the gas tank, which is why you are losing fuel.*

**crack** a very narrow space between two things or two parts of something: *He pushed the letter through the crack under the door.*

**slot** a narrow hole in a machine where you put money: *Put the coins in the slot and pick up the candy bar at the bottom of the machine.*

**crater** a round hole in the ground, made by something falling, or by an explosion: *The surface of the Moon is covered in craters.*

**cavity** a hole in a tooth, made by decay: *Brushing your teeth twice a day helps to prevent cavities.*

**2** a space in the ground where an animal lives: *a rabbit hole*

**hol·i·day** /ˈhɑləˌdeɪ/ *noun* (plural **holidays**)

an official day when people do not have to go to school or work: *Many of the stores were closed because it was a national holiday.*

→ see Thesaurus box at **vacation**

[**ORIGIN:** From the old English word *haligdæg*, which means "holy day." The word was first used for days that were important in the Christian religion, such as Christmas.]

**hol·low** /ˈhɑloʊ/ *adjective*

having an empty space inside: *The kids hid in the old tree, which was hollow inside.*

a hollow tree

**hol·ly** /ˈhɑli/ *noun*

a small tree with dark green pointed leaves and small red fruits: *At Christmas, we decorate the house with holly leaves.*

**ho·ly** /ˈhoʊli/ *adjective* (**holier**, **holiest**)

**1** relating to God or religion: *Jerusalem is a holy city for Christians, Muslims, and Jews.* **SYNONYM: sacred**

**2** a holy person is very good and close to God: *The priest was a very holy man.*

—**holiness** *noun* the quality of being very good and close to God

**home**[1] /hoʊm/ *noun*

**1** the place where you live: *On Monday, Mia felt sick, so she stayed at home.*

**THESAURUS: home**

**house** the house or apartment where someone lives: *Her house is always really clean.*

**place** (*informal*) the house, apartment, or room where someone lives: *We went back to my place after the movie.*

**residence** (*formal*) the place where someone lives: *The White House is the president's official residence.*

**2** a place where people live if they need someone to take care of them: *That building is now a home for elderly people.*

**3 be/feel at home** = to feel happy and confident somewhere, because you know it well:

*I feel at home in the city because I've lived here all my life.*

**[ORIGIN:** From the old English word *ham*, which means "village or house."**]**

**home²** *adverb*
to or at the place where you live: *I was tired, and I wanted to go home.* | *Hi Mom, I'm home.*

**home³** *adjective*
**1** relating to the place where you were born or where you live: *My home town is Chicago.* | *Most students have a home computer that they can use for studying after school.*
**2** playing on your team's sports field, not the field of another team: *The team has won all its home games.* **ANTONYM: away**

**home·land** /ˈhoʊmlænd/ *noun*
the country where you were born: *When the war started, many people left their homeland to escape the fighting.*

**home·less** /ˈhoʊmləs/ *adjective*
without a place to live: *There were terrible floods, and a lot of people became homeless.*
**—the homeless** *plural noun* people who do not have a place to live: *The money will be used to buy food and clothing for the homeless.*

**home·made** /ˌhoʊmˈmeɪd/ *adjective*
homemade food has been made at home, rather than bought from a store: *I love my mom's homemade cookies.*

**ˈhome page** (*also* **homepage**) /ˈhoʊmpeɪdʒ/ *noun*
the first page of a website, that gives you general information about the website: *This arrow will take you back to the homepage.*

**ˈhome plate** *noun*
the place where you stand to hit the ball in baseball. The home plate is also the last place the player who is running must touch in order to get a point.

**home·room** /ˈhoʊmrum/ *noun*
a room where students go at the beginning of each day or SEMESTER, so they can get information: *Carrie and I sit next to each other in homeroom.*

**ˌhome ˈrun** *noun*
a good hit in baseball, that gives the player time to run all the way around, and get a point: *Johnny's a good baseball player – he hit a home run in our last game.*

**home·sick** /ˈhoʊmˌsɪk/ *adjective*
sad because you are away from your home: *When Jessie went to camp for three weeks, she was really homesick.*
**—homesickness** *noun* the feeling you have when you are homesick
→ see Thesaurus box at **sad**

**home·stead** /ˈhoʊmsted/ *noun*
**1** a farmhouse and the area of land around it
**2** a piece of farming land that was given to people by the U.S. government under the Homestead Act, a law that was passed in 1862

**home·work** /ˈhoʊmwɚk/ *noun*
work for school that students do at home: *After dinner, I did my math homework.*

**hom·i·cide** /ˈhɑməˌsaɪd/ *noun*
the crime of murder: *The police charged the man with homicide for killing two people.*

**[ORIGIN:** 1200-1300 From the Latin words *homo* and *caedere*, which mean "man" and "to kill."**]**

**hom·o·graph** /ˈhɑməgrɑf/ *noun*
a word that is spelled the same way as another, but has a different meaning or part of speech. For example, the noun "record" is a homograph of the verb "record."

**hom·o·nym** /ˈhɑməˌnɪm/ *noun*
a word that is spelled the same and sounds the same as another, but has a different meaning. For example, the noun "bear" and the verb "bear" are homonyms.

**hom·o·phone** /ˈhɑməˌfoʊn/ *noun*
a word that sounds the same as another but has a different meaning. For example, the verb "knew" and the adjective "new" are homophones.

**ho·mo·sex·u·al** /ˌhoʊməˈsekʃuəl/ *adjective*
sexually attracted to people of the same sex **SYNONYM: gay**; **ANTONYM: heterosexual**
**—homosexuality** /ˌhoʊməˌsekʃuˈæləti/ *noun* the state of being homosexual

**hon·est** /ˈɑnɪst/ *adjective*
an honest person is good, and does not lie or steal: *He is an honest man and I trust him completely.* | *Be honest – do I look good in this dress?* **ANTONYM: dishonest**
**—honestly** *adverb* behaving in an honest

way: *Please answer these questions honestly.*
[ORIGIN: 1200-1300 From the Latin word *honestus*, which means "respected or deserving respect."]

**WORD FAMILY: honest**
**honest** *adjective* | **honestly** *adverb* | **honesty** *noun* | **dishonest** *adjective* | **dishonestly** *adverb* | **dishonesty** *noun*

**hon·es·ty** /ˈɑnɪsti/ *noun*
the quality of being good and not lying or stealing: *Thank you for telling me the truth – I admire your honesty.* **ANTONYM: dishonesty**

**hon·ey** /ˈhʌni/ *noun*
a sweet sticky liquid that BEEs make, and that people eat

**hon·ey·moon** /ˈhʌniˌmun/ *noun*
a vacation that people take after they get married: *Two days after the wedding, they went to Greece on their honeymoon.*
→ see Thesaurus box at **vacation**

**honk** /hɑŋk/ *verb*
to use the horn in a car, so that it makes a loud noise: *I crossed the road in front of a cab, and the driver honked his horn.*

**hon·or¹** /ˈɑnɚ/ *noun*
**1** something that makes you feel proud: *It was an honor to play for this great team.*
**2 in honor of someone or something** = in order to show respect for someone or something important: *They built a memorial in honor of the soldiers who died in the war.*
**3** something that is officially given to someone as a sign of praise and respect for something good he or she has done: *The medal is the highest honor that the president can give to someone.*
**4** the respect that someone or something receives from people: *His brave actions brought honor to his family and country.*

**honor²** *verb*
**1** to do something to show that someone is admired and respected, for example giving that person a special title or prize: *The team will be honored with a parade.*
**2 be/feel honored** = to feel very proud: *I am honored to have been chosen as team captain.*

**hon·or·a·ble** /ˈɑnərəbəl/ *adjective*
behaving in a way that is morally good or honest and deserves people's respect: *The honorable thing to do would be to admit you made a mistake.*

**hood** /hʊd/ *noun*
**1** the part of a jacket, coat, or SWEATER that you pull up to cover your head: *It started to rain, so I pulled up my hood.* → see picture on page **A6**
**2** the metal cover over the engine of a car: *I lifted the hood of the car to look at the engine.*

**hoof** /hʊf/ *noun* (plural **hoofs** *or* **hooves** /huvz/)
the hard foot of an animal such as a horse or a cow

**hook** /hʊk/ *noun*
**1** a curved piece of metal, wood, or plastic that you hang things on: *Kate took off her coat and hung it on a hook behind the door.*
**2** a thin curved piece of metal that you tie on the end of a long piece of string and use for catching fish: *a fish hook*
**3 off the hook** = if a telephone is off the hook, the part that you speak into is not on its base, so nobody can call you

**hooked** /hʊkt/ *adjective* (*informal*)
if you are hooked on something, you like it so much that you want to do it as often as possible: *My brother is hooked on computer games and he sometimes plays them all night.*

**hoop** /hu:p/ *noun*
a piece of wood, metal, or plastic that is shaped like a ring: *To score points in basketball, you throw the ball through a hoop.*

**hoo·ray** /hʊˈreɪ/ *interjection*
you shout this when you are very happy about something: *Hooray! We won!*

**hoot¹** /hut/ *verb*
**1** if an OWL hoots, it makes a loud noise: *That night, I heard an owl hooting outside.*
**2** to laugh loudly because you think something is funny or stupid: *The home fans hooted and cheered when Trent missed the field goal.*
—**hoot** *noun* the loud noise that an owl makes

**hoot²** *noun*
**1** the sound that an owl makes
**2** a loud laugh or shout that shows you think something is funny or stupid: *The joke brought hoots of laughter from the audience.*

**hooves** /huvz/ *noun*
a plural of HOOF

**hop** /hɑp/ *verb* (**hopped**, **hopping**)
**1** if a bird or animal hops, it moves with short quick jumps: *The bird hopped across the grass and ate the bread.*
**2** if people hop, they jump on one leg: *Can you hop from one side of the yard to the other?* → see picture at **jump**
**3** **hop in/hop out** (*informal*) = to get into or out of a car: *Hop in, and I'll give you a ride to your house.*
—**hop** *noun* a short jump
→ see Thesaurus box at **jump¹**

**hope¹** /hoʊp/ *verb*
to want something to happen or be true: *I hope that you feel better soon.* | *Bill is hoping to play on the soccer team this year.* | *"Do you think we'll win?" "I hope so."*

**WORD FAMILY: hope**
**hope** *verb* | **hope** *noun* | **hopeful** *adjective* | **hopeless** *adjective* | **hopelessness** *noun*

**hope²** *noun*
**1** the feeling that something good may happen: *My family was poor, but we always had hope for the future.*
**2** a chance that you will succeed in doing something: *We have been playing so badly that we have no hope of winning the game.*
**3** something that you hope will happen: *He talked about his hopes and dreams for the future.*

**hope·ful** /ˈhoʊpfəl/ *adjective*
believing that what you want will happen: *Scientists are hopeful that they will find a cure for the disease.*

**hope·ful·ly** /ˈhoʊpfəli/ *adverb*
**1** used when saying what you hope will happen: *Hopefully, I'll be home early.*
**2** in a hopeful way: *"Can I have some ice cream?" Kayla asked hopefully.*

**hope·less** /ˈhoʊpləs/ *adjective*
**1** a hopeless situation is very bad and unlikely to improve: *The climbers were lost on the mountain, and the situation seemed hopeless.*
**2** feeling no hope that something good will happen: *When Toni lost her job, she felt depressed and hopeless.*
—**hopelessness** *noun* a feeling of having no hope

**ho·ri·zon** /həˈraɪzən/ *noun*
**the horizon** = the line where the land or ocean seems to meet the sky: *We looked out at the ocean and saw a ship on the horizon.*
[**ORIGIN:** 1300-1400 From the Greek word *horizein*, which means "to limit." The horizon is the limit of what you can see in the distance.]

**hor·i·zon·tal** /ˌhɔrəˈzɑntl/ *adjective*
flat and level: *The American flag has horizontal red and white stripes going across it.* → see picture at **diagonal**
—**horizontally** *adverb* flat, or level with a flat surface such as the floor: *Hold both arms out horizontally.*
→ see Thesaurus box at **flat¹**

**hor·mone** /ˈhɔrmoʊn/ *noun*
a chemical that your body produces, and that makes your body grow and change
[**ORIGIN:** 1900-2000 From the Greek word *hormon*, from *horman*, which means "to cause to move around."]

**horn** /hɔrn/ *noun*
**1** a hard pointed part that grows on the heads of some animals: *Cows often have horns.*
**2** the thing in a car, bus, etc. that makes a loud sound when you push a button: *The driver behind us was honking his horn.* → see picture on page **A28**

H

**3** a musical instrument that you play by blowing into it

**hor·net** /ˈhɔrnɪt/ *noun*
a large black and yellow flying insect that can sting you

**hor·o·scope** /ˈhɔrəˌskoʊp/ *noun*
a description of the things that will happen to you during your life, which is based on the position of the stars when you were born: *My horoscope says I will have good luck today.*
[**ORIGIN:** 1000-1100 From the Greek words *hora* and *skopein*, which mean "hour" and "to look at." Someone who does your horoscope looks at the hour of your birth.]

**hor·ri·ble** /ˈhɔrəbəl/ *adjective*
very bad or frightening: *I had a horrible dream last night.* | *The food in the school cafeteria is horrible – I won't eat it.* **SYNONYMS: terrible, awful**
—**horribly** *adverb* very badly: *I got horribly sunburned.*
→ see Thesaurus box at **bad**
[**ORIGIN:** 1200-1300 From the Latin word *horribilis*, from *horrere*, which means "to have your hair standing on end or to shake with fear."]

**hor·ri·fied** /ˈhɔrəˌfaɪd/ *adjective*
feeling very shocked or upset: *We were horrified to hear that she had died so young.*
—**horrify** *verb* to make someone feel horrified: *The pictures of the crash horrified me.*

**hor·ror** /ˈhɔrɚ/ *noun*
**1** a feeling of great shock or fear: *I watched in horror as the car rolled into the lake.*
**2** **horror movie/story** = a movie or story in which strange and frightening things happen
[**ORIGIN:** 1300-1400 From the Latin word *horror*, from *horrere*, which means "to have your hair standing on end or to shake with fear."]

**horse** /hɔrs/ *noun*
a large animal that people ride: *The cowboys were riding horses.*

**horse·back** /ˈhɔrsbæk/ *noun*
**on horseback** = riding a horse: *We passed two girls on horseback.*

**ˈhorseback ˌriding** *noun*
the activity of riding horses: *On weekends, I go horseback riding.*

**horse·shoe** /ˈhɔrʃ-ʃu/ *noun*
a curved piece of iron that is attached to the bottom of a horse's foot to protect it

**hor·ti·cul·ture** /ˈhɔrtəˌkʌltʃɚ/ *noun*
the activity or science of growing plants
[**ORIGIN:** 1600-1700 From the Latin words *hortus* and *cultura*, which mean "garden" and "taking care of."]

**hose** /hoʊz/ *noun*
a long tube that water or air can travel through: *Dad was watering the yard with the hose.*
[**ORIGIN:** From the old English word *hosa*, which means "covering for the leg." The word "hose" was used for clothing that covered the legs tightly, and later came to be used for a tube.]

**hos·pi·ta·ble** /hɑˈspɪtəbəl/ *adjective* (*formal*)
willing to welcome people who visit your home or country: *I traveled all over Europe, and the people were very hospitable.*

**hos·pi·tal** /ˈhɑspɪtl/ *noun*
a building where doctors and nurses help people who are sick or hurt: *Eric's dad is in the hospital because he had an accident.*
[**ORIGIN:** 1200-1300 From the Latin word *hospitale*, which means "place where people can stay," from *hospes*, which means "guest."]

**hos·pi·tal·i·ty** /ˌhɑspəˈtæləti/ *noun* (*formal*)
friendly behavior toward people who visit you: *They welcomed us into their home with great hospitality.*

**host** /hoʊst/ *noun*
**1** a person who organizes a party and invites people to it: *Our host greeted us at the door.*
**2** the person who introduces the guests on a television or radio show: *a game show host*

**hos·tage** /ˈhɑstɪdʒ/ *noun*
someone who is kept as a prisoner by an enemy, until other people do what the enemy asks: *The terrorists are still holding five hostages and demanding money from the U.S.*

**host·ess** /ˈhoʊstɪs/ *noun*
**1** a woman who organizes a party and invites

H

people to it: *Our hostess asked if we would like a soft drink.*
**2** a woman whose job is to take people to their seats in a restaurant

**hos·tile** /ˈhɑstl/ *adjective*
very unfriendly: *The fans can be pretty hostile to the opposing team.*
—**hostility** /hɑˈstɪləti/ *noun* very unfriendly feelings or behavior: *The hostility between the two countries continued for years after the war had ended.*
[**ORIGIN:** 1500-1600 From the Latin word *hostis*, which means "enemy."]

**hot** /hɑt/ *adjective* (**hotter**, **hottest**)
**1** having a lot of heat: *Don't touch the iron – it's hot.* | *It was summer, and the weather was hot.* **ANTONYM: cold**

**THESAURUS: hot**

**warm** slightly hot, especially in a pleasant way: *a warm summer evening* | *The bread was still warm from the oven.*

**humid** if the weather is humid, the air feels hot and wet: *It can be very humid in Florida in the summer.*

**lukewarm** a lukewarm liquid is only slightly warm – used especially about liquids that are not as hot as they should be: *The soup was only lukewarm.*

**scalding** a scalding liquid is hot enough to burn your skin: *He spilt a cup of scalding coffee on his hand, burning it quite badly.*

**2** hot food has a burning taste: *I like pizza with hot peppers.*

**hot-ˈair balˌloon** *noun*
a large BALLOON filled with hot air or gas, with a basket under it that people can travel in

**ˈhot dog** (*also* **hot·dog**) /ˈhɑtdɔg/ *noun*
a long SAUSAGE that you eat in a piece of bread

**ho·tel** /hoʊˈtel/ *noun*
a building where you pay to stay when you are traveling or on vacation: *In Jamaica, we stayed in a hotel right next to the ocean.*

**ˈhot plate** (*also* **hot·plate**) /ˈhɑtpleɪt/ *noun*
a piece of equipment with a flat top that is heated by electricity and that you use for cooking food

**hour** /aʊɚ/ *noun*
**1** a time of 60 minutes: *The show lasted an hour.* | *I'll be home in an hour.* | *It's a ten-hour trip by car to Chicago.*
**2** a particular time during the day or night: *Call me at any hour of the day or night.* | *Their office hours are 9 to 5.*
**3 hours** (*informal*) = a long time: *I've been waiting for him to get here for hours.*
**4 on the hour** = at exactly one o'clock, two o'clock, three o'clock, etc.: *Classes begin on the hour.*
**5 at this hour** = at a time that is so late: *I'm sorry to call you at this hour, but I didn't know what else to do.*

**ˈhour ˌhand** *noun*
the short thin piece of metal that points to the hours on a clock or watch: *If the hour hand is pointing to 12 and the minute hand is pointing to 9, the time is 12:45.*

**hour·ly** /ˈaʊɚli/ *adjective, adverb*
happening every hour: *The bus leaves hourly from outside the airport.*

**house** /haʊs/ *noun* (plural **houses** /ˈhaʊzɪz/)
**1** a building that you live in, especially with your family: *Come over to my house after school.*
**2** all the people who live in a house: *Be quiet, or you'll wake up the whole house!*
→ see Thesaurus box at **home**[1]

**house·hold** /ˈhaʊshoʊld/ *noun*
the people who are living together in a house or apartment: *Most households have at least one computer.*
—**household** *adjective* relating to a house and the people who live in it: *He didn't like doing household chores.*

**ˌHouse of Repreˈsentatives** *noun*
the larger of the two parts of the government in the U.S., Australia, and New Zealand

**house·wife** /ˈhaʊswaɪf/ *noun* (plural **housewives** /ˈhaʊswaɪvz/)
a married woman who works at home doing the cooking and cleaning for her family: *When her son was born, she quit her job and became a housewife.*

H

**house·work** /ˈhaʊswɚk/ *noun*
the work that you do to keep a house clean: *On Saturday, we all help to do the housework. My job is to clean my bedroom.*

**hous·ing** /ˈhaʊzɪŋ/ *noun (formal)*
houses and apartments that people live in: *They are building new housing downtown.*

**hov·er** /ˈhʌvɚ/ *verb*
to stay in one place in the air: *A helicopter hovered above the crowd.*

**how** /haʊ/ *adverb, conjunction*
**1** used in order to ask or talk about the way something is done: *How do you spell your name? | My dad taught me how to swim.*
**2 How much/How long/How old, etc. ...?** = used in order to ask about the amount of something or the age of someone or something: *How much did your jeans cost? | How long have you lived here? | How old are you?*
**3** used in order to ask if someone is well and happy: *How are you? | How's your mother?*
**4 How about ...?** (*informal*) = used in order to suggest something: *I can't come tonight, but how about tomorrow?*
**5 How come?** (*informal*) = why?: *How come you were so late?*
**6** used when asking someone for their opinion: *"How do I look in this dress?" "Great!"*
**7 how strange/how pretty/how interesting, etc.** = used in order to give your opinion: *"Nina's not back yet." "How strange!"*
**8 How do you do?** (*formal*) = you say this when you meet someone for the first time

**how·dy** /ˈhaʊdi/ (*informal*)
you can use this to say "hello" in a very informal way

**how·ev·er** /haʊˈevɚ/ *adverb*
**1** you use this to mean "but," before saying something a little surprising: *It was a very hard test; however, everyone passed.*
**2 however long/difficult, etc. ...** = even if something is very long, difficult, etc.: *She goes swimming every day, however cold the weather is.*

**howl** /haʊl/ *verb*
to make a long loud sound like a dog crying: *A wild dog howled, and another one answered.*
—**howl** *noun* a sound like a dog crying

**ˈhow-to** *adjective*
a how-to book or DVD tells you the way to do something: *a how-to book on fixing a bicycle*

**hud·dle** /ˈhʌdl/ *verb*
(*also* **huddle together**) to move very close to the other people in a small group: *We huddled around the fire to keep warm.*

**hug** /hʌg/ *verb* (**hugged**, **hugging**)
to put your arms around someone to show love or friendship: *My grandmother hugged me and gave me a kiss.*
—**hug** *noun* the act of hugging someone: *Come here and give me a hug!*

**huge** /hyudʒ/ *adjective*
very big: *Their house is huge – it has six bedrooms and a big playroom.*
→ see Thesaurus box at **big**

**huge·ly** /ˈhyudʒli/ *adverb*
very: *The TV show was hugely popular for years.*

**hum** /hʌm/ *verb* (**hummed**, **humming**)
**1** to sing a tune with your mouth closed: *Dad was humming as he worked.*
**2** to make a low steady sound like a BEE: *High in the sky, an airplane hummed.*

**hu·man** /ˈhyumən/ *adjective*
belonging or relating to people: *Through most of human history, people have only lived for 30 or 40 years. | the human body*

**ˌhuman ˈbe·ing** (*also* **human**) *noun*
a person, not an animal: *They have not tested the drug on human beings yet.*

**hu·mane** /hyuˈmeɪn/ *adjective (formal)*
not cruel: *Farm animals should have humane treatment.* **ANTONYM: inhumane**
—**humanely** *adverb* in a humane way

**hu·man·i·tar·i·an** /hyuˌmænəˈteriən/ *adjective*
relating to helping people who are suffering in a war or from the effects of an event such as an EARTHQUAKE: *The U.S. sent humanitarian aid to the people affected by the earthquake.*

**hu·man·i·ty** /hyuˈmænəti/ *noun (formal)*
**1** all the people in the world: *He thought he*

H

*was different from the rest of humanity.*

**2** kindness and respect toward other people: *We should treat prisoners with humanity.*

**3 humanities** = subjects such as literature, history, art, and philosophy that are not science subjects

**hu·man·ly** /ˈhyumənli/ *adverb*

**humanly possible** = able to be done by someone who is trying very hard: *The doctors did everything humanly possible to save his life.*

**ˌhuman ˈrace** *noun*

**the human race** = people considered as a group: *The human race must learn to live in peace.*

**ˌhuman ˈrights** *plural noun*

the basic rights that everyone has to be treated well, especially by the government: *The country has a bad record on human rights; many people have been unfairly put in prison.*

**hum·ble** /ˈhʌmbəl/ *adjective*

**1** someone who is humble does not think that he or she should be treated in a special or important way: *The great scientist was a humble man who did not want praise.* **ANTONYM: proud**

**2** poor and of a low social rank: *Abe Lincoln rose from his humble beginnings to become president of the United States.*

—**humbly** *adverb* in a humble way: *I humbly begged her forgiveness.*

[**ORIGIN:** 1200-1300 From the Latin word *humilis*, which means "low or humble," from *humus*, meaning "the ground."]

**hu·mid** /ˈhyumɪd/ *adjective*

if the weather is humid, the air feels warm and wet: *Summers here are hot and humid.*

—**humidity** /hyuˈmɪdəti/ *noun* the amount of water contained in the air: *The heat and humidity made me feel tired.*

→ see Thesaurus box at **hot**

**hu·mil·i·ate** /hyuˈmɪliˌeɪt/ *verb*

to make someone feel or seem stupid or weak, in an upsetting way: *His father humiliated him by laughing at his idea.*

—**humiliated** *adjective* upset because you have been made to seem stupid or weak

—**humiliating** *adjective* making someone seem stupid or weak

—**humiliation** /hyuˌmɪliˈeɪʃən/ *noun* the feeling of being humiliated: *The team lost badly and could hardly face the fans after their humiliation.*

**hum·ming·bird** /ˈhʌmɪŋˌbɚd/ *noun*

a very small brightly colored bird whose wings move very quickly

**hu·mor** /ˈhyumɚ/ *noun*

**1 sense of humor** = the ability to be funny and to understand things that are funny: *She has a great sense of humor and is always saying funny things.*

**2** funny things that someone says or writes: *There's a lot of humor in the book, and it often made me smile.*

**hu·mor·ous** /ˈhyumərəs/ *adjective* (*formal*)

funny: *His humorous stories about his family made everybody laugh.*

—**humorously** *adverb* in a funny way

→ see Thesaurus box at **funny**

**hump** /hʌmp/ *noun*

a round part of something that is higher than the surface around it: *Some camels have one hump on their backs and some have two.*

**hunch** /hʌntʃ/ *noun*

a feeling that something is true or will happen, which is not based on any facts: *My hunch is that things will improve soon.*

**hunched** /hʌntʃt/ *adjective*

bending forward so that your back forms a curve: *He sat hunched over his desk.*

**hun·dred** /ˈhʌndrɪd/ *number*

100: *They invited two hundred people to their wedding.*

**GRAMMAR: hundred**

Use the singular form **hundred** after a number: *This city was built three hundred years ago.*

Use the plural form **hundreds** before "of": *He lives hundreds of miles away.*

—**hundredth** *number* 100th or 1/100

**hung** /hʌŋ/ *verb*

a past tense and past participle of HANG

**Hun·ga·ri·an** /hʌŋˈgeriən/ *noun*

**1** someone from Hungary

**2** the language spoken in Hungary

—**Hungarian** *adjective* from Hungary: *Hungarian folk music*

H

**hun·ger** /ˈhʌŋgɚ/ *noun*
the state of needing or wanting to eat: *There has been no food in this town for weeks, and people are dying of hunger.*

**hun·gry** /ˈhʌŋgri/ *adjective* (**hungrier**, **hungriest**)
**1** needing or wanting to eat something: *When's dinner? I'm hungry.*
**2 go hungry** = to not have enough food to eat: *My family was poor, but we never went hungry.*

**hunk** /hʌŋk/ *noun*
a thick piece of something with a shape that is not regular: *He tore a hunk of bread off the loaf.*

**hunt** /hʌnt/ *verb*
**1** to chase wild animals in order to kill them: *They hunted deer in the woods.*
**2** to look for something or someone very carefully: *She hunted for her keys all around the house.* **SYNONYM: search**
—**hunting** *noun* the activity of chasing wild animals in order to kill them: *We're going hunting in the White Mountains this week-end.*
—**hunt** *noun* an attempt to catch or find someone or something: *The hunt for the terrorists could last for years, and we may never find them.*

**hunt·er** /ˈhʌntɚ/ *noun*
someone who hunts wild animals: *a deer hunter*

**hur·dle** /ˈhɚdl/ *noun*
**1** a small fence that a person or a horse jumps over during a race: *Sally won the 100 meter hurdles race.*
**2** something difficult that you have to do: *The biggest hurdle is raising the money for the project.*

**hurl** /hɚl/ *verb*
to throw something with a lot of force: *He hurled a brick through the window.*
→ see Thesaurus box at **throw[1]**

**hur·ri·cane** /ˈhɚɪˌkeɪn/ *noun*
a storm with very strong fast winds that comes from the ocean: *The hurricane destroyed many buildings.*
→ see Thesaurus box at **wind[1]**
[**ORIGIN:** 1500-1600 From the Spanish word *huracán*, from a Taino word. Taino was a language used by the people of some Caribbean islands.]

**hur·ry[1]** /ˈhɚi/ *verb* (**hurried**, **hurries**)
to do something or go somewhere quickly: *We have to hurry or we'll miss the plane.* | *The girls hurried home to tell their parents.*
**SYNONYM: rush**
**PHRASAL VERB**
**hurry up**
to do something or move somewhere more quickly than before: *Hurry up! We're going to be late!*

**hurry[2]** *noun*
**1 be in a hurry** = to need to do something or go somewhere very quickly: *He was in a hurry and couldn't stop to talk.*
**2 (there's) no hurry** = used when telling someone that he or she does not have to do something immediately: *You can give me the CD back any time – there's no hurry.*

**hurt[1]** /hɚt/ *verb* (**hurt**)
**1** to injure yourself or someone else: *She fell and hurt her knee.* | *No one was hurt in the explosion.*

**THESAURUS: hurt**

**To Injure Someone:**

**Hurt** and **injure** can mean the same, but **hurt** is usually used when the damage to your body is not very serious: *Alex fell and hurt his knee.*

**injure** to damage someone's body, especially in an accident: *Three people were seriously injured in the crash.*

**wound** to injure someone using a weapon such as a gun or knife: *The policeman was wounded by a bullet as he got out of the patrol car.*

**break** to hurt a part of your body by breaking a bone in it: *Rob broke his arm when he was skateboarding.*

**sprain** to hurt part of your body by suddenly twisting it: *I sprained my ankle playing football.*

**To Feel Pain:**

**ache** to feel a continuous pain: *My back was aching.*

**sting** to cause a sudden sharp pain in your eyes, throat, or skin: *The soap got in my eyes and stung a lot.*

**be tender** if a part of your body is tender, it is painful if you touch it: *The bruise on her leg was very tender.*

**be stiff** if a part of your body is stiff, your muscles hurt and it is difficult to move, usually because you have exercised too much or you are sick: *My legs are so stiff!*

**be sore** to be painful as a result of a wound, infection, or too much exercise: *My ankle was really sore where I'd twisted it. | She had a sore throat and fever.*

**2** if a part of your body hurts, it is painful: *My stomach hurts.*
**3** if an action hurts, it makes you feel pain: *My throat is sore, and it hurts to swallow.*
**4** to make someone feel upset: *He said some terrible things that really hurt my feelings.*

**hurt**[2] *adjective*
**1** injured: *Is he badly hurt?*
**2** upset: *I felt hurt when they didn't invite me to the party.*

**hurt·ful** /ˈhɚtfəl/ *adjective*
making you feel upset: *That's a hurtful thing to say – you should say you're sorry.*

**hus·band** /ˈhʌzbənd/ *noun*
the man that a woman is married to: *She and her husband Bob have lived here for 12 years.*
[**ORIGIN:** From the Norse words *hus* and *bondi*, which mean "house" and "someone who lives in a house." First used in English with its modern meaning, probably 1100-1200.]

**hush**[1] /hʌʃ/ *verb*
said in order to tell someone, especially a child, to be quiet or stop crying: *Hush now. It's time to go to sleep.*

**hush**[2] *noun (formal)*
a peaceful silence: *When the president stood up to speak, a hush fell over the crowd.*

**hus·ky** /ˈhʌski/ *adjective*
**1** a husky voice sounds low and a little rough: *I have a cold and that's why my voice is husky.*
**2** a husky person has big bones and muscles and is sometimes a little fat: *a husky little boy*

**hut** /hʌt/ *noun*
a small simple house or building: *The village is a group of mud huts.*

**hy·brid** /ˈhaɪbrɪd/ *noun*
**1** an animal or plant produced from parents that are GENETICALLY different: *A mule is a hybrid of a donkey and a horse.*
**2** a car that uses both gasoline and electricity

**hy·dro·e·lec·tric** /ˌhaɪdroʊɪˈlektrɪk/ *adjective*
hydroelectric power is electricity that is produced by the force of water

**hy·dro·gen** /ˈhaɪdrədʒən/ *noun*
a light gas that is an ELEMENT
[**ORIGIN:** 1700-1800 From the Greek word *hydro-*, which means "water" and the French ending *-gène*, which means "producing." Hydrogen produces water when it is burned.]

**hy·giene** /ˈhaɪdʒin/ *noun*
things you do to keep people and things clean in order to prevent diseases: *Personal hygiene is important, so take a bath or shower regularly.*
—**hygienic** /haɪˈdʒenɪk/ *adjective* clean, so that people will not get diseases: *Restaurants must have hygienic kitchens, so that customers do not get sick.*
[**ORIGIN:** 1600-1700 From the Greek word *hygies*, which means "healthy."]

**hy·gien·ist** /haɪˈdʒinɪst/ *noun*
someone who works with a DENTIST and cleans people's teeth or gives advice about how to care for teeth

**hymn** /hɪm/ *noun*
a song that people sing in Christian churches
[**ORIGIN:** 800-900 From the Greek word *hymnos*, which means "song praising a god or hero."]

**hype** /haɪp/ *noun (informal)*
attempts to make people think something is good or important by talking about it a lot on television and on the radio: *There was a lot of media hype about the movie, but it wasn't really very good.*

**hy·per·ac·tive** /ˌhaɪpɚˈæktɪv/ *adjective*
someone, especially a child, who is hyperactive is too active and is not able to keep quiet or be still for very long

**hy·per·bo·le** /hɪˈpɚbəli/ *noun*
a way of describing something, in which you

say that it is much bigger, better, more exciting, etc. than it really is: *Movie trailers are full of hyperbole like "the greatest film ever made!"*

**hy·phen** /ˈhaɪfən/ *noun*
a mark (-) that you use to join two words or parts of a word: *The word "four-legged" has a hyphen in it.*

**hyp·no·sis** /hɪpˈnoʊsɪs/ *noun*
a relaxed state that is similar to being asleep, during which another person can control or affect your thoughts: *Hypnosis can help some people quit smoking.*
—**hypnotize** /ˈhɪpnəˌtaɪz/ *verb* to put someone in a state of hypnosis
—**hypnotist** /ˈhɪpnətɪst/ *noun* someone who hypnotizes people
**[ORIGIN:** 1600-1700 From the Greek word *hypnos*, which means "sleep."**]**

H

**hyp·o·crite** /ˈhɪpəˌkrɪt/ *noun*
someone who tells people to behave in a particular way, but who does not behave in that way himself or herself: *You're such a hypocrite – you told me never to lie, but now you're lying!*
—**hypocritical** /ˌhɪpəˈkrɪtɪkəl/ *adjective* someone who is hypocritical is a hypocrite
—**hypocrisy** /hɪˈpɑkrəsi/ *noun* the behavior of a hypocrite
**[ORIGIN:** 1100-1200 From the Greek word *hypokrites*, which means "actor."**]**

**hy·pot·e·nuse** /haɪˈpɑtn-us/ *noun*
the longest side in a RIGHT TRIANGLE, opposite the RIGHT ANGLE

**hy·poth·e·sis** Ac /haɪˈpɑθəsɪs/ *noun* (plural **hypotheses** /haɪˈpɑθəsiz/)
an idea that no one has proved to be true yet: *The scientist did an experiment to test his hypothesis.* **SYNONYM: theory**
**[ORIGIN:** 1500-1600 From a Greek word meaning "base." A hypothesis is an idea that you take as the basis for an experiment or discussion.**]**

**hy·po·thet·i·cal** Ac /ˌhaɪpəˈθetɪkəl/ *adjective*
a hypothetical situation is not real, but might happen: *I'm going to give you a hypothetical situation, and you tell me how you would deal with it if it really happened.*

**hys·ter·i·cal** /hɪˈsterəkəl/ *adjective*
**1** so upset or excited that you cannot control yourself: *When she was told her daughter had been in a car accident, she became hysterical.*
**2** very funny: *The movie was hysterical – I couldn't stop laughing!*
—**hysteria** /hɪˈsteriə/ *noun* a situation in which someone feels fear, anger, or excitement: *There was public hysteria when the paper reported that the disease was spreading.*
**[ORIGIN:** 1800-1900 From the Greek word *hystera*, which means "uterus." The uterus is the part inside a woman where a baby develops, and it was believed that hysteria was caused by this part.**]**

# Ii

**I¹** /aɪ/ *pronoun*
used as the subject of a verb when you are talking about yourself: *I saw Mike yesterday.*

**I²**
the number 1 in the system of ROMAN NUMERALs

**ice** /aɪs/ *noun*
water that has frozen: *Do you want some ice in your drink? | Ice began to cover the lake.*

**ice·berg** /ˈaɪsbɚg/ *noun*
a very large piece of ice floating in the ocean
[**ORIGIN:** 1700-1800 From the Dutch word *ijsberg*, which means "ice mountain."]

**ˈice cap** *noun*
an area of thick ice that covers the North and South Poles

**ˈice cream** *noun*
a sweet frozen food made from milk or cream: *chocolate ice cream*

**ˈice cream ˌcone** *noun*
a hard thin cookie shaped like a CONE, with ice cream in it → see picture at **cone**

**ˈice cube** *noun*
a small square piece of ice that you put in a drink

**ˌiced ˈtea** *noun*
cold tea served with ice and often LEMON or sugar

**ˈice skate** *verb*
to move along on ice wearing special boots
—**ice skate** *noun* a special boot with a blade attached under it that you wear for moving on ice
—**ice skater** *noun* someone who ice skates

**i·ci·cle** /ˈaɪsɪkəl/ *noun*
a long pointed piece of ice that hangs down from something: *It was freezing cold and there were icicles hanging from the roof.*

**ic·ing** /ˈaɪsɪŋ/ *noun*
a sweet substance that you put on top of a cake **SYNONYM: frosting**

**i·con** /ˈaɪkɑn/ *noun*
**1** a small picture on a computer screen that you can choose with your mouse to make the computer do something: *Click on that icon to check your email.*
**2** someone who is famous and admired by many people: *Elvis Presley is a pop icon.*
[**ORIGIN:** From the Greek word *eikon*, which means "image or figure," from *eikenai*, which means "to be like someone or something." First used with its modern meanings in English, 1900-2000.]

**ic·y** /ˈaɪsi/ *adjective* (**icier**, **iciest**)
**1** very cold: *An icy wind was blowing from the north.*
**2** covered in ice: *Cars were sliding on the icy road.*
→ see Thesaurus box at **cold¹**

**ID** *noun*
an official document that shows who you are. It has information such as your name and date of birth on it, and usually your picture: *The police officer asked to see his ID.*

**I'd** /aɪd/
**1** the short form of "I had": *I'd never seen her before.*
**2** the short form of "I would": *I'd love to come!*

**i·de·a** /aɪˈdɪə/ *noun*
**1** something that you think of, especially a plan or suggestion that you tell someone about: *"Let's ask Jim what to do." "That's a good idea." | I like the idea of getting a dog.*
**2** understanding or knowledge of something: *I was lost – I had no idea where I was. | Can you give me an idea of the cost?*
**3** an opinion or belief: *He has old-fashioned ideas about how women should behave.*
**4 the idea** = the aim of an action or plan: *The idea is to use games to teach children math.*
[**ORIGIN:** 1300-1400 From the Greek word for "form or appearance," from *idein*, which means "to see."]

I

**i·de·al¹** /ˌaɪˈdɪəl/ *adjective*
the best possible: *With its great beaches and warm weather, California is an ideal place for a vacation.* **SYNONYM: perfect**
—**ideally** *adverb* used when saying what would be the best thing to happen: *Ideally, you should start learning to play soccer at the age of about five.*

**ideal²** *noun*
a standard or a way of behaving that is the very best and that you would like to achieve: *We believe strongly in the American ideals of freedom and democracy.*

**i·de·al·ism** /aɪˈdiəˌlɪzəm/ *noun*
the belief that a good world and good behavior are possible: *His youthful idealism made him decide to join the Peace Corps.*
—**idealistic** /ˌaɪdiəˈlɪstɪk/ *adjective* believing that a good world and good behavior are possible: *an idealistic young teacher*
—**idealist** /aɪˈdiəlɪst/ *noun* someone who is idealistic

**i·de·al·ize** /aɪˈdiəˌlaɪz/ *verb* (*formal*)
to think or try to show that something is much better than it really is: *The show idealizes family life by showing a "perfect" family in a "perfect" house.*

**i·den·ti·cal** Ac /aɪˈdentɪkəl/ *adjective*
exactly the same: *Your dress is identical to mine.* | *Daniel and his brother Justin are identical twins.*
→ see Thesaurus box at **similar**
[**ORIGIN:** 1500-1600 From the Latin word *idem*, which means "same."]

**i·den·ti·fi·ca·tion** Ac /aɪˌdentəfəˈkeɪʃən/ *noun*
an official document that proves who you are. It has information such as your name and date of birth on it, and usually your picture: *You can use a passport as identification.* **SYNONYM: ID**

**i·den·ti·fy** Ac /aɪˈdentəfaɪ/ *verb* (**identified, identifies**)
to say who someone is or what something is: *Our teacher could identify all the plants we saw.*
**PHRASAL VERB**
**identify with someone**
to feel that someone is similar to you, so that you can understand his or her feelings: *I could identify with the main character in the book because he was the same age as me.*

**WORD FAMILY: identify**
**identify** *verb* | **identification** *noun* | **identity** *noun*

**i·den·ti·ty** Ac /aɪˈdentəti/ *noun* (plural **identities**)
**1** someone's name: *The police do not know the identity of the dead man.*
**2** the qualities that make one person or group different from others: *My Italian family background is an important part of my identity.*

**i·de·ol·o·gy** Ac /ˌaɪdiˈɑlədʒi/ *noun* (plural **ideologies**)
a set of political beliefs or ideas: *Communist ideology*
—**ideological** /ˌaɪdiəˈlɑdʒɪkəl/ *adjective* relating to ideologies: *The two men have ideological differences.*

**id·i·om** /ˈɪdiəm/ *noun*
a group of words which have a special meaning when they are used together: *"To get cold feet" is an idiom which means "to suddenly feel worried about doing something."*
—**idiomatic** /ˌɪdiəˈmætɪk/ *adjective* being an idiom, or containing idioms
→ see Thesaurus box at **phrase**
[**ORIGIN:** 1500-1600 From the Greek word *idioma*, which means "personal way of expressing yourself," from *idios*, which means "personal."]

**id·i·ot** /ˈɪdiət/ *noun*
a stupid person: *Don't drive so fast, you idiot!*
—**idiotic** /ˌɪdiˈɑtɪk/ *adjective* stupid: *Don't ask such idiotic questions.*

**i·dle** /ˈaɪdl/ *adjective*
**1** not working or being used: *Machines are sitting idle because there is no one to operate them.*
**2** an old-fashioned word meaning "lazy"
—**idleness** *noun* the state of not working or doing anything useful

**i·dol** /ˈaɪdl/ *noun*
**1** someone, especially someone famous, who you admire very much: *The skateboarder Tony Hawk is his idol.*
**2** a STATUE of a god: *People worshiped the idol in the temple.*

—**idolize** *verb* to admire someone very much: *He idolizes his father and says he wants to be just like him.*

**i.e.** /ˌaɪ ˈi/
used before explaining exactly what you mean: *The movie is for adults only, i.e. people over the age of 18.*

**if** /ɪf/ *conjunction*
**1** used when talking about something that might happen or that might have happened: *If I get any news, I'll call you.* | *If we hadn't taken him to the hospital, he would have died.*
**2** whether: *I don't know if I'll be able to come.*
**3** whenever: *If I drink milk, I get a stomachache.*
**4 if I were you** = used when giving advice: *If I were you, I'd wear something warmer because it's getting really cold.*
→ **even if** at **even**[1], **as if/though** at **as**, **if only** at **only**[1]

**ig·loo** /ˈɪglu/ *noun*
a round house made out of blocks of hard snow by Inuit people
[**ORIGIN:** 1800-1900 From the Inuit word *iglu*, which means "house." Inuit people live in cold northern parts of the world.]

**ig·ne·ous** /ˈɪgniəs/ *adjective*
igneous rock is formed when the hot melted rock from a VOLCANO cools and becomes solid

**ig·nite** /ɪgˈnaɪt/ *verb* (*formal*)
to make something start burning: *A cigarette ignited the gas, and the gas exploded.*

**ig·ni·tion** /ɪgˈnɪʃən/ *noun*
the part of a car where you put a key to start the engine: *He turned the key in the ignition.*
→ see picture on page **A28**

**ig·no·rance** Ac /ˈɪgnərəns/ *noun*
the state of not knowing something, especially something you should know: *Ignorance of the rule is not a good excuse for breaking it.*

**ig·no·rant** Ac /ˈɪgnərənt/ *adjective*
not knowing something, especially something you should know: *She had just come to this country and was ignorant of her rights as a U.S. citizen.*

**ig·nore** Ac /ɪgˈnɔr/ *verb*
to not pay any attention to someone or something: *I tried to talk to her, but she ignored me.*
[**ORIGIN:** 1600-1700 From the Latin word *ignorare*, which means "not to know something."]

**ill** /ɪl/ *adjective*
someone who is ill has a disease or does not feel well: *She can't go to work because she's ill.* | *He is mentally ill.*
→ see Thesaurus box at **sick**

**I'll** /aɪl/
the short form of "I will": *I'll be back soon.*

**il·le·gal** Ac /ɪˈligəl/ *adjective*
not allowed by the law: *It's illegal to drive without a license.* | *Police searched the house for illegal weapons.* **ANTONYM: legal**
—**illegally** *adverb* in an illegal way: *They had entered the country illegally, so they were sent back to their own country.*

**il·leg·i·ble** /ɪˈledʒəbəl/ *adjective*
impossible to read: *I couldn't read the letter because his writing was illegible.* **ANTONYM: legible**

**il·le·git·i·mate** /ˌɪləˈdʒɪtəmət/ *adjective*
if a child is illegitimate, his or her parents were not married when he or she was born: *He has an illegitimate son.*
—**illegitimacy** /ˌɪləˈdʒɪtəməsi/ *noun* the state of being illegitimate

**il·lit·er·ate** /ɪˈlɪtərət/ *adjective*
not able to read or write: *She did not know what the letter said because she was illiterate.*
—**illiteracy** /ɪˈlɪtərəsi/ *noun* the fact of not being able to read or write

**ill·ness** /ˈɪlnəs/ *noun*
a disease, or a period of being ill: *She has cancer, which is a very serious illness.*

**il·log·i·cal** Ac /ɪˈlɑdʒɪkəl/ *adjective*
an illogical idea or action is not based on good thinking: *It is illogical to hit your computer when it does something that you do not like.* **ANTONYM: logical**

**il·lu·mi·nate** /ɪˈluməˌneɪt/ *verb* (*formal*)
if a light illuminates something, it makes it bright: *The fire illuminated her face, and I could see that she was crying.*
—**illumination** /ɪˌluməˈneɪʃən/ *noun* the act of making a place bright

I

**il·lu·sion** /ɪˈluʒən/ *noun*
**1** something that seems to be real or true but is not: *One line looks longer than the other, but that is an optical illusion; they are actually the same length.*
**2** a false belief: *She has no illusions about her chances of winning – she knows it is unlikely.*

**il·lus·trate** Ac /ˈɪləˌstreɪt/ *verb*
**1** to give or be an example that makes something clearer: *This story illustrates how important it is to tell the truth.*
**2** to add pictures to a book: *She illustrates children's books.*
—**illustrator** *noun* someone who draws pictures for books
[**ORIGIN:** 1500-1600 From the Latin word *illustrare*, which means "to make bright or clear."]

**WORD FAMILY: illustrate**
**illustrate** *verb* | **illustration** *noun* | **illustrator** *noun*

I

**il·lus·tra·tion** Ac /ˌɪləˈstreɪʃən/ *noun*
**1** a picture in a book: *The book has beautiful color illustrations.*
**2** an example that shows something: *His success is a good illustration of how much you can achieve if you do not give up.*
→ see Thesaurus box at picture[1]

**IM** *verb*
(**instant message**) to send messages to someone using the Internet, using a program that lets him or her reply immediately: *IM me later.*

**I'm** /aɪm/
the short form of "I am": *I'm hungry.*

**im·age** Ac /ˈɪmɪdʒ/ *noun*
**1** a picture that you can see on a television, in a mirror, or in a photograph: *We watched the images on TV of the destruction caused by the flood.*
**2** the way that someone or something seems to people: *She decided to change her image, so she cut her hair and bought new clothes.*
**3** a picture that you have in your mind: *I have a clear image of the kind of house I want to live in.*
[**ORIGIN:** 1100-1200 From the Latin word *imago*, which means "picture or statue."]

**im·age·ry** Ac /ˈɪmɪdʒri/ *noun*
the things described or shown in poems, books, movies, etc.: *The song's violent imagery upset many people.*

**i·mag·i·nar·y** /ɪˈmædʒəˌneri/ *adjective*
something that is imaginary is not real and only exists in your mind: *Dragons are imaginary animals that exist only in stories, not in real life.*

**i·mag·i·na·tion** /ɪˌmædʒəˈneɪʃən/ *noun*
the ability to think of new things or form pictures in your mind: *She has a vivid imagination and makes up wonderful stories.*
—**imaginative** /ɪˈmædʒənətɪv/ *adjective* having or showing a lot of imagination: *The story is told in a very imaginative way, using acting and dancing.*

**i·mag·ine** /ɪˈmædʒɪn/ *verb*
**1** to think about what something could be like or what it must have been like: *Imagine that you have lots of money, and you can do anything you want.* | *I can imagine how you felt – you must have been really mad.*
**2** to think that something will probably happen or is probably true: *I imagine she was pretty upset.*

**WORD FAMILY: imagine**
**imagine** *verb* | **imagination** *noun* | **imaginative** *adjective* | **imaginary** *adjective*

**im·i·tate** /ˈɪməˌteɪt/ *verb*
**1** to copy the way a person or animal speaks or moves to entertain other people: *He imitated the teacher to make the other kids laugh.*
**2** to copy something because you think it is good: *His way of playing the guitar was imitated by other musicians.* **SYNONYM: copy**

**im·i·ta·tion**[1] /ˌɪməˈteɪʃən/ *noun*
the act of copying the way someone speaks or moves: *My sister can do a really funny imitation of our aunt.*

**imitation**[2] *adjective*
made to look like something real: *The necklace was made of imitation pearls, not real ones.*
→ see Thesaurus box at fake

**im·ma·ture** Ac /ˌɪməˈtʃʊr/ *adjective*
an immature person behaves in a silly way that seems much younger than his or her real age: *I think Jim is too immature to babysit for other people.* **SYNONYM: childish**; **ANTONYM: mature**
—**immaturity** /ˌɪməˈtʃʊrəti/ *noun* the quality of being immature

**im·me·di·ate** /ɪˈmidiət/ *adjective*
**1** happening or coming very soon after something: *I wrote them an email, and I got an immediate reply.*
**2 someone's immediate family** = someone's parents, children, brothers, and sisters: *Rob and Sarah only invited their immediate families to the wedding.*

**im·me·di·ate·ly** /ɪˈmidiətli/ *adverb*
very quickly and with no delay: *I knew immediately that something was wrong, when I saw that she had been crying.*

**THESAURUS: immediately**

**instantly** immediately – used when something happens at almost the same time as something else: *As soon as she saw his face, she knew instantly that something was wrong.*

**at once** immediately or without waiting: *I realized at once that I had said the wrong thing.*

**right away** immediately, without waiting: *When Jill got the message, she called him right away.*

**right now** at this time, not later: *Ben! Stop that right now!*

**im·mense** /ɪˈmens/ *adjective*
very large: *We have an immense amount of work to do, so we had better get started.* **SYNONYMS: enormous, huge**
[**ORIGIN:** 1400-1500 From the Latin word *immensus*, from *im-* and *mensus*, which mean "not" and "measured."]

**im·mense·ly** /ɪˈmensli/ *adverb*
very or very much: *The show is immensely popular.*

**im·merse** /ɪˈmɚs/ *verb*
**1** to put something into a liquid so that the liquid covers it completely: *Do not immerse this equipment in water.*
**2 immerse yourself in something** (*formal*) = to give all your attention to something: *She immersed herself in her school work because she didn't want to think about her problems.*
—**immersion** /ɪˈmɚʒən/ *noun* the act of putting something into a liquid so that the liquid covers it completely

**immerse**

The egg is immersed in water.

**im·mi·grant** Ac /ˈɪməgrənt/ *noun*
someone who comes to live in a country: *His grandparents were Chinese immigrants who moved to the United States in 1962.*
[**ORIGIN:** 1600-1700 From the Latin word *immigrare*, which means "to go into a place."]

**im·mi·gra·tion** Ac /ˌɪməˈgreɪʃən/ *noun*
the act of coming to live in a country: *People on the border are trying to stop illegal immigration.*
—**immigrate** /ˈɪməˌgreɪt/ *verb* to come to live in a country: *He immigrated to the United States from Poland.*

**WORD FAMILY: immigration**

**immigration** *noun* | **immigrate** *verb* | **immigrant** *noun* | **emigration** *noun* | **emigrate** *verb*

**im·mor·al** /ɪˈmɔrəl/ *adjective*
bad and wrong: *Religions teach us that killing and stealing are immoral.*
—**immorality** /ˌɪməˈræləti/ *noun* immoral behavior

**im·mor·tal** /ɪˈmɔrtl/ *adjective*
living forever or remembered forever: *Some people believe the soul is immortal and lives after the body dies.* **ANTONYM: mortal**
—**immortality** /ˌɪmɔrˈtæləti/ *noun* the state of living or being remembered forever: *George Washington has achieved a kind of immortality by being the first president of the United States.*

**im·mune** /ɪˈmyun/ *adjective*
not able to be affected by something bad, especially a disease: *A small group of people are immune to the virus and have not gotten sick at all.*
—**immunity** /ɪˈmyunəti/ *noun* the state of being immune to something: *The children do not have immunity to the disease.*

**imˈmune ˌsystem** *noun*
the system by which your body protects itself against disease: *People with weakened immune systems are at risk from the disease.*

**im·mu·nize** /ˈɪmyəˌnaɪz/ *verb*
to protect someone from a disease by giving him or her a VACCINE (=a weak form of the disease): *Children can be immunized against diseases such as measles.*
—**immunization** /ˌɪmyənəˈzeɪʃən/ *noun* the act of immunizing someone

**im·pact** Ac /ˈɪmpækt/ *noun*
the effect that something has: *Global warming could have a major impact on the weather.*
—**impact** /ɪmˈpækt/ *verb* to affect something: *How does the disease impact on your life?*

**im·pair** /ɪmˈper/ *verb*
to make something less good or useful, especially something such as an ability: *The injury to her brain impaired her ability to talk.*
—**impairment** *noun* the state of being less good or useful: *He has a hearing impairment, so you have to speak louder.*

**im·par·tial** /ɪmˈpɑrʃəl/ *adjective*
not supporting any person or group: *The judge's decision must be impartial and based only on the evidence.* **SYNONYM: objective**; **ANTONYM: biased**
—**impartiality** /ɪmˌpɑrʃiˈæləti/ *noun* the quality of being impartial

**im·pa·tient** /ɪmˈpeɪʃənt/ *adjective*
**1** annoyed because something has not been done immediately: *We started to get impatient when the pizza did not arrive after 30 minutes.*
**2 impatient to do something** = wanting to do something immediately: *Juan was impatient to leave because he had to meet his friend.*
—**impatience** *noun* a feeling of being impatient
—**impatiently** *adverb* in an impatient way

**im·peach** /ɪmˈpitʃ/ *verb*
to say officially that a public official has committed a serious crime
—**impeachment** *noun* when someone is impeached

**im·per·a·tive¹** /ɪmˈperətɪv/ *noun*
the form of a verb that you use when you tell someone to do something: *In the sentence "Come here!" the verb "come" is in the imperative.*
[ORIGIN: 1400-1500 From the Latin word *imperare*, which means "to command."]

**imperative²** *adjective* (*formal*)
something that is imperative is very important and must be done: *It is imperative that we win this game.*

**im·per·fect** /ɪmˈpɚfɪkt/ *adjective* (*formal*)
not perfect: *This solution is imperfect, but it is the best I can do.*
—**imperfection** /ˌɪmpɚˈfekʃən/ *noun* a fault or mark that stops something from being perfect: *There were some imperfections in the cloth, so they lowered the price.*

**im·pe·ri·al·ism** /ɪmˈpɪriəˌlɪzəm/ *noun*
a political system in which one country controls a lot of other countries
—**imperialist** (*also* **imperialistic** /ɪmˌpɪriəˈlɪstɪk/) *adjective* wanting to control a lot of other countries

**im·per·son·al** /ɪmˈpɚsənəl/ *adjective*
not showing any feelings of friendliness or interest: *The company sent me an impersonal letter in reply to my complaint.*

**im·per·so·nate** /ɪmˈpɚsəˌneɪt/ *verb*
to copy someone's voice and behavior in order to entertain or trick people: *He impersonates many famous people on his show.*
—**impersonator** *noun* someone who impersonates someone else: *an Elvis impersonator*
—**impersonation** /ɪmˌpɚsəˈneɪʃən/ *noun* the act of impersonating someone: *He does a good impersonation of the president.*

**im·ple·ment¹** Ac /ˈɪmpləˌment/ *verb* (*formal*)
to make a plan or process start happening:

*The president hopes to implement his proposals as soon as possible.*

—**implementation** /ˌɪmpləmənˈteɪʃən/ *noun* the act of implementing a plan

**implement²** Ac *noun* (*formal*)
a simple tool: *The museum had old plows and other farm implements.*

**im·pli·ca·tion** Ac /ˌɪmpləˈkeɪʃən/ *noun*
a possible result or effect of something: *If oil prices rise, one of the implications is that other prices will have to rise as well.*

**im·plic·it** Ac /ɪmˈplɪsɪt/ *adjective*
an implicit meaning can be understood from something someone says, but is not said directly: *She didn't say I had done the wrong thing, but her words contained an implicit criticism.*

—**implicitly** *adverb* in a way that is not direct

**im·ply** Ac /ɪmˈplaɪ/ *verb* (**implied, implies**)
to suggest that something is true, without saying this directly: *Are you implying that the accident was my fault?*

→ see Thesaurus box at **say¹**

**im·po·lite** /ˌɪmpəˈlaɪt/ *adjective*
not polite: *It's impolite to yawn when someone is talking.*

→ see Thesaurus box at **rude**

**im·port¹** /ɪmˈpɔrt/ *verb*
to bring things into a country to sell or use: *We import a lot of oil from other countries.* **ANTONYM: export**

—**importer** *noun* a person or company that imports things

[**ORIGIN:** 1400-1500 From the Latin word *importare*, which means "to carry or bring into a place."]

**import²** *noun*
**1** something that is brought into a country to be sold or used: *The stores are full of cheap imports.* **ANTONYM: export**
**2** the action of bringing things into a country to sell or use: *The government stopped the import of weapons.* **ANTONYM: export**

**WORD FAMILY: import**

**import** *noun* | **import** *verb* | **importer** *noun*

**im·por·tance** /ɪmˈpɔrtns/ *noun*
the quality of being important: *I understand the importance of a good education because my parents did not have one.*

**im·por·tant** /ɪmˈpɔrtnt/ *adjective*
**1** if something is important, you care about it a lot or should care about it a lot: *This is the most important part of the class.* | *My family is very important to me.*

**THESAURUS: important**

**crucial** very important: *It is crucial that you study hard if you want to go to college.*

**vital** very important or necessary: *She gave the police some vital clues that helped them catch the robber.*

**essential** very important and necessary: *Water is essential in order for plants and animals to live.*

**major** very large or important, especially when compared to other things: *The airline flies to all the major European cities, including London, Paris, and Rome.*

**significant** noticeable or important: *His music has had a significant influence on other musicians.*

**key** very important and needed for success: *One of the team's key players is injured and won't be playing this Friday.*

**2** an important person has power or influence: *The quarterback is the most important player on a football team.*

—**importantly** *adverb* used when mentioning something important: *The restaurant is beautiful and, more importantly, the food is excellent.*

[**ORIGIN:** 1400-1500 From the old Italian word *importante*, which means "carrying a meaning," from the Latin word *importare*, which means "to carry in."]

**WORD FAMILY: important**

**important** *adjective* | **unimportant** *adjective* | **importance** *noun* | **importantly** *adverb*

**im·pose** Ac /ɪmˈpoʊz/ *verb* (*formal*)
to force people to have a law, punishment, etc.: *The principal imposed a new rule to stop students from wearing jewelry in school.*

I

—**imposition** /ˌɪmpəˈzɪʃən/ *noun* the act of imposing something

[**ORIGIN:** 1400-1500 From the Latin word *imponere*, which means "to put something on something else."]

**im·pos·ing** Ac /ɪmˈpoʊzɪŋ/ *adjective*
large and impressive: *The White House is an imposing building.*

**im·pos·si·ble** /ɪmˈpɑsəbəl/ *adjective*
not able to be done or to happen: *I could not do it – it was an impossible job.* | *It was so hot that it was impossible to sleep.*
—**impossibility** /ɪmˌpɑsəˈbɪləti/ *noun* the fact that something is impossible, or something that is impossible: *We knew that keeping the dog hidden from our parents would be an impossibility.*

**im·pos·ter** /ɪmˈpɑstɚ/ *noun*
someone who pretends to be someone else in order to trick people: *He wasn't a real police officer; he was an imposter.*

**im·prac·ti·cal** /ɪmˈpræktɪkəl/ *adjective*
an impractical plan or way of doing something is too difficult or expensive, or will not work: *It would be impractical to ask every person what he or she thinks.*

**im·pre·cise** Ac /ˌɪmprɪˈsaɪs/ *adjective* (*formal*)
not exact: *I believe there were about 1,500 people there, but that is an imprecise number.*

**im·press** /ɪmˈpres/ *verb*
to make someone think you are good or important: *He rented a nice car to impress his girlfriend.*
—**impressed** *adjective* thinking that someone or something is good or important: *The coach said that she was very impressed with my attitude.*

**WORD FAMILY: impress**
**impress** *verb* | **impressed** *adjective* | **impressive** *adjective*

**im·pres·sion** /ɪmˈpreʃən/ *noun*
**1** the opinion or feeling you have about someone or something because of what you see or hear: *I got the impression that he didn't like me.* | *I wanted to make a good impression on our new teacher.*
**2** **be under the impression that** = to think that something is true when it is not: *I was under the impression that they were married, but they are not.*
**3** the act of copying the voice or behavior of a famous person in order to entertain people: *Erin does a great impression of Britney Spears.*
**SYNONYM: impersonation**

**im·pres·sive** /ɪmˈpresɪv/ *adjective*
if something is impressive, it is very good and you admire it: *Winning five gold medals is an impressive achievement.*

**im·pris·on** /ɪmˈprɪzən/ *verb* (*formal*)
to put someone in prison: *The new leader imprisoned anyone who disagreed with him.*
—**imprisonment** *noun* the state of being in prison: *He was sentenced to six years' imprisonment for robbing a store.*

**im·prob·a·ble** /ɪmˈprɑbəbəl/ *adjective* (*formal*)
not likely to happen or to be true: *We might win the lottery, but it is highly improbable.*
**SYNONYM: unlikely**; **ANTONYM: probable**

**im·prop·er** /ɪmˈprɑpɚ/ *adjective* (*formal*)
wrong or unacceptable: *He was sent off the field for improper behavior after swearing at an umpire.*
—**improperly** *adverb* in a way that is wrong: *The judge said that the police had improperly obtained the evidence.*

**im·prove** /ɪmˈpruv/ *verb*
to become better, or to make something better: *Her health improved when she stopped smoking.* | *I want to improve my language skills.*

[**ORIGIN:** 1500-1600 From the old French word *emprouer*, which means "to make a profit out of something." You can make a profit from something that you have made better, so that it is worth more.]

**im·prove·ment** /ɪmˈpruvmənt/ *noun*
**1** when something becomes better: *I'm pleased to say there has been an improvement in his behavior.*
**2** a change that makes something better: *If you revise an essay, you make improvements to it.*

**im·pro·vise** /ˈɪmprəvaɪz/ *verb*
**1** to do or make something from the things you have available, without preparing first: *I*

*didn't have a screwdriver, so I improvised and used a coin.*
**2** to act or play music without preparing, making it up as you perform: *It is usual for jazz musicians to improvise during a performance.*
—**improvisation** /ɪmˌprɑvəˈzeɪʃən/ *noun* the act of improvising

**im·pulse** /ˈɪmpʌls/ *noun*
a sudden desire to do something: *I had the impulse to laugh when I saw his new haircut, but I managed to stop myself.*
[**ORIGIN:** 1600-1700 From the Latin word *impulsus*, a form of the verb *impellere*, which means "to drive forward."]

**im·pul·sive** /ɪmˈpʌlsɪv/ *adjective*
someone who is impulsive does things suddenly, without thinking about the results: *Small children are impulsive; they will do or say anything that they think of.*
—**impulsively** *adverb* suddenly, without thinking about the results: *Impulsively, he kissed her.*

**im·pure** /ɪmˈpyʊr/ *adjective*
**1** containing another substance that is unwanted: *The water is impure and not fit to drink.* **ANTONYM: pure**
**2** (*formal*) bad, according to a religion: *He was ashamed of his impure thoughts.* **ANTONYM: pure**
—**impurity** /ɪmˈpyʊrəti/ *noun* an unwanted substance that another substance contains: *We can remove some of the impurities from the water to make it taste better.*

**in** /ɪn/ *preposition, adverb*
**1** inside a container or building, or surrounded by a place: *She had a pencil in her pocket.* | *Put the knives and forks in the drawer.* | *He lives in Denver.* | *Come in!*
**2** during a month, year, etc.: *We moved here in September.* | *I was born in 1990.*
**3** after a period of time: *Gerry should be home in an hour.*
**4** using a particular language or way of speaking: *He said something in Italian.* | *They spoke in whispers.*
**5** wearing: *Who's the woman in the black dress?*
**6** if you are in something, you are part of it or involved in it: *I talked to the other people in the group.* | *He has appeared in several movies.* | *the best team in the competition*
**7** (*informal*) fashionable now: *Long hair is in again.* **ANTONYM: out**
**8 be in for something** = if you are in for something, it is about to happen to you: *If you think this game is going to be easy, you're in for a shock.*
**9 be in on something** = to be involved in something secret, or know about it: *Do you think he was in on the robbery?*
**10 in all** = used when mentioning a total amount: *There were 20 of us in all.*

**in.**
the written abbreviation of **inch**

**in·a·bil·i·ty** /ˌɪnəˈbɪləti/ *noun* (*formal*)
the fact of not being able to do something: *He was embarrassed about his inability to read.* **ANTONYM: ability**

**in·ac·ces·si·ble** [Ac] /ˌɪnəkˈsesəbəl/ *adjective* (*formal*)
difficult or impossible to reach: *The house is inaccessible in winter because snow blocks the road.* **ANTONYM: accessible**

**in·ac·cu·rate** [Ac] /ɪnˈækjərət/ *adjective* (*formal*)
not completely correct: *He gave an inaccurate description of the house, so we did not recognize it when we saw it.* **ANTONYM: accurate**
—**inaccuracy** *noun* the quality of being inaccurate
→ see Thesaurus box at **wrong**

**in·ac·tive** /ɪnˈæktɪv/ *adjective* (*formal*)
not doing anything: *Most fish are inactive at night.* **ANTONYM: active**
—**inactivity** /ˌɪnækˈtɪvəti/ *noun* the state of not doing anything

**in·ad·e·quate** [Ac] /ɪnˈædəkwət/ *adjective* (*formal*)
not good enough: *His thin coat was inadequate for the freezing weather.* **ANTONYM: adequate**
—**inadequately** *adverb* in a way that is not good enough

**in·an·i·mate** /ɪnˈænəmɪt/ *adjective*
something that is inanimate is not alive: *The pictures were of inanimate objects, such as cars and washing machines, not people.*

I

**in·ap·pro·pri·ate** [Ac] /ˌɪnəˈproʊpri-ət/ *adjective*
not right for a particular situation or person: *The movie is scary and inappropriate for young children.* **ANTONYM: appropriate**
—**inappropriately** *adverb* in an inappropriate way

**in·au·di·ble** /ɪnˈɔdəbəl/ *adjective (formal)*
too quiet to hear: *Her reply was almost inaudible, so I asked her to say it again.* **ANTONYM: audible**

**in·au·gu·rate** /ɪˈnɔgyəˌreɪt/ *verb*
to have a ceremony when someone begins an important job: *The president is inaugurated in January.*
—**inaugural** /ɪˈnɔgyərəl/ *adjective* relating to an inauguration: *the president's inaugural speech*
—**inauguration** /ɪˌnɔgyəˈreɪʃən/ *noun* the process of being inaugurated

**in·bound** /ˈɪnbaʊnd/ *adjective*
inbound planes, trains, cars, etc. are coming toward or into a place: *Traffic is slow on the inbound lanes of the freeway.* **ANTONYM: outbound**

**Inc.**
the written abbreviation of **incorporated**, used after the name of a big company: *General Motors Inc.*

**in·ca·pa·ble** [Ac] /ɪnˈkeɪpəbəl/ *adjective (formal)*
**incapable of (doing) something** = not able to do something: *Since the accident, she has been incapable of moving her legs.*

**in·car·cer·ate** /ɪnˈkɑrsəˌreɪt/ *verb (formal)*
to put or keep someone in a prison: *He has been incarcerated in jail for ten years.*

**in·censed** /ɪnˈsenst/ *adjective (formal)*
very angry: *She was incensed at his rudeness.*
[ORIGIN: 1400-1500 From the Latin word *incensus*, a form of the verb *incendere*, which means "to make something start burning." The idea is that being angry is like burning uncontrollably.]

**in·cen·tive** [Ac] /ɪnˈsentɪv/ *noun*
something that makes you want to do something: *Money is a good incentive to make people work hard.*

**inch** /ɪntʃ/ *noun* (plural **inches**)
(*written abbreviation*: **in.**) a unit for measuring length, equal to 2.54 centimeters: *There are 12 inches in a foot.* | *The insect is about 1.5 inches long.*
[ORIGIN: 1000-1100 From the Latin word *uncia*, which means "one twelfth."]

**in·ci·dent** [Ac] /ˈɪnsədənt/ *noun (formal)*
something unusual, serious, or violent that happens: *You should report the incident to the police.*

**in·ci·den·tally** [Ac] /ˌɪnsəˈdentli/ *adverb*
used when giving more information or starting to talk about something new: *He's an excellent player. Incidentally, he's also my cousin.*

**in·cin·er·ate** /ɪnˈsɪnəˌreɪt/ *verb (formal)*
to burn something in order to destroy it: *We incinerate a lot of our garbage.*
—**incineration** /ɪnˌsɪnəˈreɪʃən/ *noun* the act of incinerating something
—**incinerator** *noun* a machine in which you incinerate things

**in·cli·na·tion** [Ac] /ˌɪnkləˈneɪʃən/ *noun*
a feeling that you want to do something: *He showed no inclination to go to college.*

**in·clined** [Ac] /ɪnˈklaɪnd/ *adjective*
**be inclined to do something** = **a)** to feel that you want to do something, but not strongly: *I'm inclined to trust him because he's always been honest with me.* **b)** to often do something in a particular situation: *He's inclined to get upset over small things.*

**in·clude** /ɪnˈklud/ *verb*
**1** if one thing includes another, the second thing is part of the first: *The trip includes a visit to the Grand Canyon.*
**2** to make someone or something part of a larger group: *Did you include my name on the list?* **ANTONYM: exclude**
—**inclusion** /ɪnˈkluʒən/ *noun* the act of including something

**WORD FAMILY: include**
**include** *verb* | **exclude** *verb* | **including** *preposition* | **excluding** *preposition* | **inclusive** *adjective* | **exclusive** *adjective* | **inclusion** *noun* | **exclusion** *noun*

**in·clud·ing** /ɪnˈkludɪŋ/ *preposition*
used when saying that someone or something is part of the group you are talking about:

*There were 20 people in the room, including the teacher.* **ANTONYM: excluding**

**in·clu·sive** /ɪnˈklusɪv/ *adjective (formal)*
including many different people or things: *The price for the vacation is inclusive of flight, hotel, and all taxes.*

**in·co·her·ent** [Ac] /ˌɪnkoʊˈhɪrənt/ *adjective (formal)*
speaking or writing in a way that is unclear and does not make sense: *She was drunk and incoherent.*
—**incoherently** *adverb* in a way that is very unclear
—**incoherence** *noun* the quality of being incoherent

**in·come** [Ac] /ˈɪŋkʌm/ *noun*
the money that you get, for example for working: *She has an income of $50,000 per year.*
→ see Thesaurus box at **pay**[2]

**ˈincome tax** *noun*
money that you must give the government when you earn money

**in·com·pat·i·ble** [Ac] /ˌɪnkəmˈpætəbəl/ *adjective*
too different to be able to work together well or have a good relationship: *The software is incompatible with the software I already have.* **ANTONYM: compatible**
—**incompatibility** /ˌɪnkəmˌpætəˈbɪləti/ *noun* the quality of being incompatible: *My parents' incompatibility led to their divorce.*

**in·com·pe·tent** /ɪnˈkɑmpətənt/ *adjective*
not able to do your job well: *He was fired for being incompetent.* **ANTONYM: competent**
—**incompetence** *noun* the quality of being incompetent: *The police lost some of the evidence and were criticized for their incompetence.*

**in·com·plete** /ˌɪnkəmˈplit/ *adjective*
not having all its parts or not finished yet: *The bridge is incomplete, but it will be finished later this year.* **ANTONYM: complete**

**in·com·pre·hen·si·ble** /ˌɪnkɑmpriˈhensəbəl/ *adjective (formal)*
impossible to understand: *The song is incomprehensible to me because I don't speak Spanish.*

**in·con·clu·sive** [Ac] /ˌɪnkənˈklusɪv/ *adjective (formal)*
not resulting in clear information or a clear situation: *The medical tests were inconclusive; they did not show what was causing her pain.*

**in·con·sid·er·ate** /ˌɪncənˈsɪdərɪt/ *adjective (formal)*
not thinking or caring about what other people feel or need: *You never call to say you are going to be late, and that's inconsiderate.* **ANTONYM: considerate**

**in·con·sist·ent** [Ac] /ˌɪnkənˈsɪstənt/ *adjective*
not always the same or not the same as others: *He's an inconsistent player – sometimes good, sometimes terrible.*

**in·con·ven·ient** /ˌɪnkənˈviniənt/ *adjective*
causing problems or difficulties: *If this is an inconvenient time to talk, I'll call you back later.*
—**inconvenience** *noun* problems, or something that causes problems: *We are sorry for the inconvenience caused by this delay.*

**in·cor·po·rate** [Ac] /ɪnˈkɔrpəˌreɪt/ *verb (formal)*
to include something as part of something else: *I tried to incorporate the changes that my teacher suggested into my report.*

**in·cor·rect** /ˌɪnkəˈrekt/ *adjective (formal)*
not right: *That answer is incorrect.* **SYNONYM: wrong; ANTONYM: correct**
—**incorrectly** *adverb* in a way that is not right
→ see Thesaurus box at **wrong**

**in·crease**[1] /ɪnˈkris/ *verb*
if an amount increases, or if something increases it, it becomes larger: *My weight had increased by five pounds so I decided to get more exercise.* | *Smoking increases your chances of getting cancer.* **ANTONYM: decrease**
[**ORIGIN:** 1300-1400 From the Latin word *increscere*, from *crescere*, which means "to grow."]

**THESAURUS: increase**

**go up** to increase in number, amount, or value: *Prices have gone up 2%.*

I

**rise** to increase in number, amount, quality, or value: *The city's population has risen to over 10 million people.*

**grow** to get bigger in size or amount over a period of time: *The number of students at the school has grown in the last five years from 200 to over 300.*

**double** to become twice as big: *The company doubled in size in ten years.*

**shoot up** (*informal*) to quickly increase in number, size, or amount: *House prices in the area shot up by 30% last year.*

**raise** to make prices, taxes, or standards increase: *The landlord is planning to raise the rent.*

**increase**

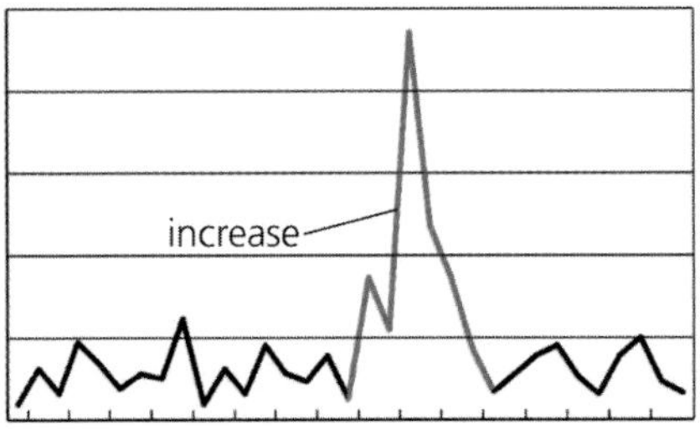


The graph shows an increase in temperature

**increase²** *noun*
a rise in the amount of something: *The principal was worried about the increase in bullying.*
**ANTONYM: decrease**

**in·creas·ing·ly** /ɪnˈkrisɪŋli/ *adverb*
more and more: *He wasn't home by midnight and his parents were becoming increasingly worried.*

**in·cred·i·ble** /ɪnˈkredəbəl/ *adjective*
**1** very good: *I love the food at this restaurant; it's incredible!*
**2** very large or extreme: *When I broke my leg, the pain was incredible.*
**3** very hard to believe: *It's incredible that he survived the fall from the third floor.*
—**incredibly** *adverb* very: *She works incredibly hard.*

**in·crim·i·nate** /ɪnˈkrɪməˌneɪt/ *verb* (*formal*)
to make someone seem guilty of a crime: *He didn't say anything because he didn't want to incriminate himself.*
—**incriminating** *adjective* making someone seem guilty of a crime: *They found the gun and other incriminating evidence in his house.*

**in·cu·ba·tor** /ˈɪŋkyəˌbeɪtɚ/ *noun*
a special container in a hospital, where very small or weak babies are put so that they stay alive

**in·cur** /ɪnˈkɚ/ *verb* (**incurred**, **incurring**) (*formal*)
if you incur something bad, it happens to you, especially because of something you do: *He incurred huge debts by using his credit card.*

**in·cur·a·ble** /ɪnˈkyʊrəbəl/ *adjective*
an incurable disease cannot be cured

**in·debt·ed** /ɪnˈdetɪd/ *adjective*
**be indebted to someone** (*formal*) = to be very grateful to someone for his or her help: *We are indebted to everyone who helped us write this magazine.*

**in·de·cent** /ɪnˈdisənt/ *adjective*
likely to shock people: *You can't wear a skirt that short – it's indecent!*
—**indecency** *noun* indecent behavior

**in·de·ci·sive** /ˌɪndɪˈsaɪsɪv/ *adjective*
not able to make decisions quickly: *As a quarterback, you can't be indecisive about who you're going to throw the ball to.*
**ANTONYM: decisive**

**in·deed** /ɪnˈdid/ *adverb* (*formal*)
**1** used in order to emphasize what you are saying: *The tests proved that he did indeed fire the gun.*
**2** used when adding information: *He liked the book. Indeed, he said it was the best one he had ever read.*

**in·def·i·nite** [Ac] /ɪnˈdefənət/ *adjective*
an indefinite period of time has no fixed end: *The painting is on loan to the museum for an indefinite period.*
—**indefinitely** *adverb* for a period of time that has no fixed end: *The store will stay closed indefinitely.*

**inˌdefinite ˈarticle** *noun*
"a" and "an"

**inˌdefinite ˈpronoun** *noun*
a word such as "someone" or "anything,"

which does not refer to a particular person or thing

**in·dent** /ɪnˈdent/ *verb*
to leave a space at the beginning of a line of writing: *Indent the first line of each paragraph.*

**in·de·pend·ence** /ˌɪndəˈpendəns/ *noun*
**1** the freedom to do what you want to do and take care of yourself: *Having a job gives you financial independence.*
**2** freedom from control by another country: *Nigeria gained independence from Britain in 1960.*

**Indeˈpendence ˌDay** *noun*
a U.S. national holiday on July 4, when Americans celebrate the time when their country became independent from Britain

**in·de·pend·ent** /ˌɪndəˈpendənt/ *adjective*
**1** doing what you want to do and taking care of yourself: *He wanted to move out of his parents' home and be independent.* **ANTONYM: dependent**
**2** not controlled by another country, organization, or group: *India became independent in 1947.*
—**independently** *adverb* in an independent way

**WORD FAMILY: independent**
**independent** *adjective* | **dependent** *adjective* | **independence** *noun* | **dependence** *noun* | **independently** *adverb*

**ˈin-depth** *adjective*
considering or dealing with all the details of something: *The program took an in-depth look at the problem of racism.*

**in·de·scrib·a·ble** /ˌɪndɪˈskraɪbəbəl/ *adjective*
not possible to describe: *The joy I felt when I saw my mother again was indescribable.*

**in·dex** Ac /ˈɪndeks/ *noun* (plural **indexes** *or* **indices** /ˈɪndəˌsiz/)
a list at the end of a book that tells you the page where each thing in the book is mentioned: *Subjects in the index are in alphabetical order.*
[**ORIGIN:** 1500-1600 From the Latin word for "first finger, or something that points out," from *indicare*, which means "to show or to make something known."]

**ˈindex ˌfinger** *noun*
the finger next to your thumb

**In·di·an¹** /ˈɪndiən/ *adjective*
**1** from India
**2** a word meaning NATIVE AMERICAN, which some people think is offensive

**Indian²** *noun*
**1** someone from India
**2** a word for a NATIVE AMERICAN, which some people think is offensive

**in·di·cate** Ac /ˈɪndəˌkeɪt/ *verb* (*formal*)
**1** to show that something is likely to be true: *All the evidence indicates that our planet is getting warmer.*
**2** to say something in a way that is not direct: *She nodded several times to indicate that she agreed.*
—**indicator** *noun* something that shows something else: *Most doctors think that your weight is an important indicator of how healthy you are.*
—**indicative** /ɪnˈdɪkətɪv/ *adjective* showing something: *The team's loss last night is indicative of how bad the season has been for them.*
[**ORIGIN:** 1600-1700 From the Latin word *indicare*, which means "to show or to make something known."]

**WORD FAMILY: indicate**
**indicate** *verb* | **indication** *noun* | **indicative** *adjective* | **indicator** *noun*

**in·di·ca·tion** Ac /ˌɪndəˈkeɪʃən/ *noun*
a sign that something exists or is likely to be true: *There are some indications that the fire was started deliberately.*

**in·di·ces** /ˈɪndəˌsiz/ *noun*
a plural of INDEX

**in·dict** /ɪnˈdaɪt/ *verb* (*formal*)
to officially say that someone may have committed a crime: *He was indicted for taking bribes, and put on trial.*
—**indictment** *noun* an official written statement saying that someone may have committed a crime

**in·dif·ferent** /ɪnˈdɪfərənt/ *adjective*
not at all interested in something, or not caring about something: *He was indifferent to their opinions.*
—**indifference** *noun* no interest in something

**in·di·ges·tion** /ˌɪndɪˈdʒestʃən/ *noun*
an unpleasant feeling that you get when your stomach cannot deal with the food you have eaten: *I ate too much, and now I have indigestion.*

**in·dig·nant** /ɪnˈdɪgnənt/ *adjective* (*formal*)
angry because you feel that someone has treated you in a rude or unfair way: *She was indignant at the man's offensive questions.*
—**indignantly** *adverb* in an indignant way
—**indignation** /ˌɪndɪgˈneɪʃən/ *noun* an indignant feeling: *Students protested to show their indignation at the high cost of a college education.*

**in·di·rect** /ˌɪndəˈrekt/ *adjective*
**1** not directly caused by or relating to something: *The accident was an indirect result of the heavy rain, which had created a hole in the road.* **ANTONYM: direct**
**2** an indirect way of showing what you think or feel is not very clear: *His silence was an indirect way of showing his anger.* **ANTONYM: direct**
**3** (*formal*) an indirect way of getting to a place is not the straightest one: *We took an indirect route through the country.* **ANTONYM: direct**
—**indirectly** *adverb* in an indirect way: *I was indirectly responsible for her mistake because I forgot to check her work.*

**ˌindirect ˈobject** *noun*
a word or phrase referring to the person or thing that receives something: *In the sentence "Pete gave me the money," "me" is the indirect object.*

**in·dis·creet** /ˌɪndɪˈskrit/ *adjective*
someone who is indiscreet talks about things that should be kept secret

**in·dis·pu·ta·ble** /ˌɪndɪˈspyutəbəl/ *adjective* (*formal*)
definitely true: *I have indisputable evidence that he has been lying.*
—**indisputably** *adverb* used to emphasize that something is definitely true

**in·dis·tin·guish·a·ble** /ˌɪndɪˈstɪŋgwɪʃəbəl/ *adjective* (*formal*)
things that are indistinguishable are so similar that you cannot see any difference between them: *This material is indistinguishable from real silk.*

**in·di·vid·u·al¹** Ac /ˌɪndəˈvɪdʒuəl/ *adjective*
**1** used when talking about each person or thing, rather than the whole group: *We have to think about the needs of the individual student.*
**2** for one person rather than a group: *The children had individual desks.*
—**individually** *adverb* separately: *The teacher spoke to the students individually.*
[**ORIGIN:** 1400-1500 From the Latin word *individuus*, which means "unable to be divided." A group can be divided into smaller groups, but a group with only one person or thing in it cannot be divided.]

**WORD FAMILY: individual**
**individual** *adjective* | **individual** *noun* | **individually** *adverb* | **individualized** *adjective*

**individual²** Ac *noun* (*formal*)
a person, not a group: *Every individual is different.*

**in·di·vid·u·al·ism** Ac /ˌɪndəˈvɪdʒuəˌlɪzəm/ *noun*
the practice of allowing people to do what they want, alone, and in their own way
—**individualist** *noun* someone who believes in individualism
—**individualistic** /ˌɪndəˌvɪdʒuəˈlɪstɪk/ *adjective* doing what you want, alone, and in your own way

**in·di·vid·u·al·i·ty** /ˌɪndəˌvɪdʒuˈæləti/ *noun*
the quality that makes someone different from other people: *People can show their individuality by the clothes they choose.*

**in·di·vid·u·al·ized** /ˌɪndəˈvɪdʒuəˌlaɪzd/ *adjective* (*formal*)
made or designed for a particular person: *Each person who joins the gym receives an individualized exercise program.*

**in·di·vis·i·ble** /ˌɪndəˈvɪzəbəl/ *adjective*
if something is indivisible, you cannot divide it

or separate it into parts: *Electrons are tiny, indivisible particles.*

**in·door** /ˈɪndɔr/ *adjective*
inside a building: *an indoor swimming pool*
**ANTONYM: outdoor**

**in·doors** /ˌɪnˈdɔrz/ *adverb*
into or inside a building: *It's raining – let's stay indoors.* **SYNONYM: inside**; **ANTONYM: outdoors**

**in·dulge** /ɪnˈdʌldʒ/ *verb*
**1** to do something that you enjoy, which you do not usually do or should not do: *I had a little extra time, so I indulged in an afternoon nap.*
**2** to let someone do or have whatever he or she wants, even if it is not needed: *Her parents indulge her, giving her toys whenever she asks for them.*
—**indulgent** *adjective* letting someone do or have whatever he or she wants: *Some parents are too indulgent and let their kids do anything they want.*
—**indulgence** *noun* something that you do or have because you enjoy it, not because you need it

**in·dus·tri·al** /ɪnˈdʌstriəl/ *adjective*
relating to industry, or having a lot of industries: *The river has been polluted by industrial waste.*

**in·dus·tri·al·ized** /ɪnˈdʌstriəˌlaɪzd/ *adjective*
an industrialized country has a lot of industries
—**industrialization** /ɪnˌdʌstriələˈzeɪʃən/ *noun* the process of developing a lot of industries: *Industrialization meant that more people worked in factories instead of on farms.*

**in·dus·tri·ous** /ɪnˈdʌstriəs/ *adjective* (*formal*)
an industrious person works hard
—**industriously** *adverb* in an industrious way

**in·dus·try** /ˈɪndəstri/ *noun* (plural **industries**)
**1** the making of things in factories: *He wanted a job in industry.*
**2** all the businesses that make or do a particular type of thing: *She has friends in the music industry.*
[**ORIGIN:** 1400-1500 From the Latin word *industria*, which means "willingness to work hard."]

**WORD FAMILY: industry**
**industry** *noun* | **industrial** *adjective* | **industrialized** *adjective* | **industrialization** *noun*

**in·ed·i·ble** /ɪnˈedəbəl/ *adjective* (*formal*)
dangerous to eat or tasting too bad to eat: *The cookies were so burned they were inedible.* **ANTONYM: edible**

**in·ef·fec·tive** /ˌɪnəˈfektɪv/ *adjective*
something that is ineffective does not achieve what you want: *The medicine was ineffective, so the pain did not go away.* **ANTONYM: effective**

**in·ef·fi·cient** /ˌɪnəˈfɪʃənt/ *adjective*
working or done in a way that wastes time, money, or energy: *The engine is inefficient and uses a lot of fuel.* **ANTONYM: efficient**
—**inefficiently** *adverb* in an inefficient way
—**inefficiency** *noun* the quality of being inefficient

**in·el·i·gi·ble** /ɪnˈelədʒəbəl/ *adjective*
not allowed to do or have something, according to a rule: *He is ineligible for money from the government because he earns too much money.* **ANTONYM: eligible**

**in·e·qual·i·ty** /ˌɪnɪˈkwɑləti/ *noun* (plural **inequalities**)
an unfair situation in which some people in society have more money or opportunities than other people: *There is still inequality in the amount of pay women and men receive for the same work.* **ANTONYM: equality**

**in·ev·i·ta·ble** [Ac] /ɪˈnevətəbəl/ *adjective*
certain to happen and impossible to avoid: *He drives so fast that it was inevitable he would get a speeding ticket some day.*
—**inevitably** *adverb* if something will inevitably happen, it will definitely happen

**in·ex·pen·sive** /ˌɪnɪkˈspensɪv/ *adjective*
cheap: *The food is simple and inexpensive.*
**ANTONYM: expensive**
—**inexpensively** *adverb* cheaply

**in·ex·pe·ri·enced** /ˌɪnɪkˈspɪriənst/ *adjective*
not having much experience: *Inexperienced drivers have more accidents than people who*

*have driven for many years.* **ANTONYM: experienced**
—**inexperience** *noun* lack of experience

**in·fa·mous** /ˈɪnfəməs/ *adjective*
well known for being bad or evil: *He was involved in the infamous attack on the World Trade Center.* **SYNONYM: notorious**
—**infamy** *noun* the state of being infamous

**in·fant** /ˈɪnfənt/ *noun* (*formal*)
a baby: *The class is for mothers and infants.*
—**infancy** /ˈɪnfənsi/ *noun* the period when someone is a baby: *Their son died in infancy.*
→ see Thesaurus box at **child**
[**ORIGIN:** 1300-1400 From the Latin word *infans*, which means "unable to speak."]

**in·fan·try** /ˈɪnfəntri/ *noun*
soldiers who fight on foot: *The infantry followed the tanks into the area.*

**in·fat·u·at·ed** /ɪnˈfætʃuˌeɪtɪd/ *adjective*
having a feeling of love for someone that is too strong or not sensible: *He's infatuated with her, so he can't see any of her faults.*
—**infatuation** /ɪnˌfætʃuˈeɪʃən/ *noun* a feeling of love for someone that is too strong or not sensible

I

**in·fect** /ɪnˈfekt/ *verb*
to give someone a disease: *People with the flu can easily infect others.*
—**infected** *adjective* having caught a disease, or having harmful BACTERIA: *Keep the cut clean or it will get infected.*
[**ORIGIN:** 1300-1400 From the Latin word *infectus*, a form of the verb *inficere*, which means "to stain or spoil."]

**WORD FAMILY: infect**
**infect** *verb* | **infection** *noun* | **infectious** *adjective* | **infected** *adjective*

**in·fec·tion** /ɪnˈfekʃən/ *noun*
a disease affecting a part of your body. An infection is caused by BACTERIA or a VIRUS: *I have an ear infection, so the doctor gave me some drops to put in my ear.*

**in·fec·tious** /ɪnˈfekʃəs/ *adjective*
an infectious disease can be passed from one person to another, often through the air you breathe: *Infectious diseases like the flu can spread quickly.*

**in·fer** Ac /ɪnˈfɚ/ *verb* (**inferred**, **inferring**) (*formal*)
to decide that something is probably true because of what you see or hear: *They inferred from his refusal to answer that he was guilty.*

**in·fe·ri·or** /ɪnˈfɪriɚ/ *adjective*
not as good as someone or something else: *The new gym is inferior to the old one, and no one is happy with it.* **ANTONYM: superior**
—**inferiority** /ɪnˌfɪriˈɑrəti/ *noun* the state of being inferior to someone or something else: *He had failed twice, and his feeling of inferiority was growing.*
[**ORIGIN:** 1400-1500 From the Latin word for "lower," from *inferus*, which means "below."]

**in·fest** /ɪnˈfest/ *verb*
if insects, mice, or rats infest a place, there are a lot of them there: *The old hotel was infested with rats.*

**in·field** /ˈɪnfild/ *noun*
the part of a baseball field that is inside the four bases

**in·fi·nite** Ac /ˈɪnfənət/ *adjective*
without a limit or end: *Is the universe infinite, or does it have an edge?* **ANTONYM: finite**
[**ORIGIN:** 1300-1400 From the Latin word *infinitus*, from *in-* meaning "not" and *finis*, which means "end or limit."]

**in·fi·nite·ly** Ac /ˈɪnfənɪtli/ *adverb* (*formal*)
very much: *Their first album was infinitely better than this one. I don't like this one at all.*

**in·fin·i·tive** /ɪnˈfɪnətɪv/ *noun*
the basic form of a verb, used with "to": *In the sentence "I want to go," "to go" is an infinitive.*

**in·fin·i·ty** /ɪnˈfɪnəti/ *noun*
**1** a space or distance without a limit or end: *The road seemed to go on to infinity.*
**2** a number or quantity that cannot be counted or measured, because it has no end: *It is impossible to count to infinity.*

**in·flamed** /ɪnˈfleɪmd/ *verb* (*formal*)
red, swollen, and painful: *Her throat was inflamed because of an infection.*

**in·flam·ma·ble** /ɪnˈflæməbəl/ *adjective*
something that is inflammable burns very easily: *Gasoline is highly inflammable, so you*

*should never smoke near it.* **SYNONYM: flammable**

**in·flam·ma·tion** /ˌɪnfləˈmeɪʃən/ *noun (formal)*
the state of being red, swollen, and painful: *There was some inflammation around the cut on her arm.*

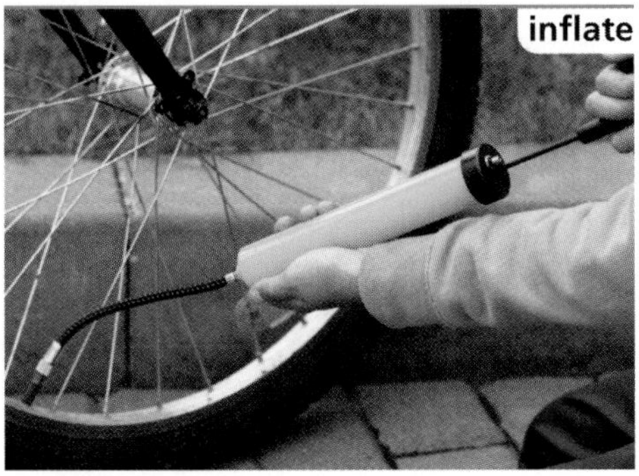


**in·flate** /ɪnˈfleɪt/ *verb*
to fill something with air or gas, so that it becomes larger: *Inflate the bicycle's tires.*
—**inflatable** *adjective* something that is inflatable can be inflated: *an inflatable boat made of rubber*

**in·fla·tion** /ɪnˈfleɪʃən/ *noun*
a continuing increase in prices: *Because of inflation, a loaf of bread costs more now than it did ten years ago.*
—**inflationary** /ɪnˈfleɪʃəˌneri/ *adjective* causing inflation

**in·flict** /ɪnˈflɪkt/ *verb (formal)*
to make someone suffer something bad: *He seemed to enjoy inflicting pain on his younger brother.*

**in·flu·ence¹** /ˈɪnfluəns/ *noun*
**1** the power to affect what someone does or thinks: *Television has a lot of influence on young people. They often behave like people they see on TV.*
**2** someone or something that affects what someone does or thinks: *He's a bad influence. I want you to stop being friends with him.*
**3 under the influence of alcohol/drugs** *(formal)* = drunk or affected by drugs: *He was arrested for driving under the influence of alcohol.*
—**influential** /ˌɪnfluˈenʃəl/ *adjective* having a lot of influence: *He was an influential thinker, whose ideas have changed the world.*

**influence²** *verb*
to affect what someone does or thinks: *If I tell you which college I like best, I might influence your decision, and I don't want to do that.*

**in·form** /ɪnˈfɔrm/ *verb (formal)*
to tell someone something: *I informed them that I would be arriving on June 24.*

**WORD FAMILY: inform**
**inform** *verb* | **information** *noun* | **informative** *adjective*

**in·for·mal** /ɪnˈfɔrməl/ *adjective*
**1** relaxed, and not done in an official way or according to rules: *It was an informal meeting, and no one bothered to take notes.* **ANTONYM: formal**
**2** appropriate for ordinary situations rather than formal ones: *"See you!" is an informal way of saying "goodbye."* **ANTONYM: formal**
—**informally** *adverb* in an informal way
—**informality** /ˌɪnfɔrˈmæləti/ *noun* the quality of being informal

**in·for·ma·tion** /ˌɪnfɚˈmeɪʃən/ *noun*
facts about something: *An encyclopedia contains information about many subjects.*

**GRAMMAR: information**
Do not say "an information" or "informations." Say, for example, *some information, a lot of information*, or *a piece of information*: *Do you have any information about tickets?* | *I need a couple more pieces of information before I can finish my report.*

**in·form·a·tive** /ɪnˈfɔrmətɪv/ *adjective*
giving many facts: *It was a very informative program – I learned a lot.*

**in·fra·red** /ˌɪnfrəˈred/ *adjective*
infrared light produces heat but cannot be seen. It does this because the light WAVEs being produced are longer than the waves of light that we can see: *In an infrared photograph, you can see which parts of something are warmest.*

**in·fra·struc·ture** Ac /ˈɪnfrəˌstrʌktʃɚ/ *noun (formal)*
the basic systems and structures that a country needs, for example roads, hospitals, and

telephone systems: *The earthquake damaged a lot of the country's infrastructure, so travel is difficult.*

**in·fre·quent** /ɪnˈfrikwənt/ *adjective (formal)*
not happening often: *We enjoy her infrequent visits and wish she would come more often.*
**SYNONYM: rare**
—**infrequently** *adverb* not often

**in·fu·ri·ate** /ɪnˈfjʊriˌeɪt/ *verb (formal)*
to make someone very angry: *He was lazy, which infuriated his parents.*
—**infuriating** *adjective* making you feel angry or annoyed: *He always interrupts – it's infuriating.*

**in·ge·nious** /ɪnˈdʒiniəs/ *adjective*
**1** an ingenious plan, method, or machine is the result of new and intelligent ideas: *These ingenious computer games teach math in a fun way.*
**2** good at thinking of new ideas or making new things: *Thomas Edison was an ingenious man who came up with many new inventions.*
—**ingenuity** /ˌɪndʒəˈnuəti/ *noun* the quality of being ingenious
**[ORIGIN:** 1400-1500 From the Latin word *ingenium*, which means "natural ability."**]**

**in·gre·di·ent** /ɪnˈgridiənt/ *noun*
one of the things that you use to make a particular food: *Mix the egg with the other ingredients and pour the mixture into a cake pan.*
**[ORIGIN:** 1400-1500 From the Latin word *ingredi*, which means "to go in." An ingredient is something that goes into a mixture.**]**

**in·hab·it** /ɪnˈhæbɪt/ *verb (formal)*
if people or animals inhabit a place, they live there: *These people have inhabited the region for 800 years.*
—**inhabited** *adjective* if a place is inhabited, people live there: *They did not know if the island was inhabited because they didn't see any houses.*

**WORD FAMILY: inhabit**
**inhabit** *verb* | **inhabited** *adjective* | **inhabitant** *noun*

**in·hab·it·ant** /ɪnˈhæbətənt/ *noun (formal)*
one of the people who live in a place: *It is a small town with only 250 inhabitants.*

**inhale**

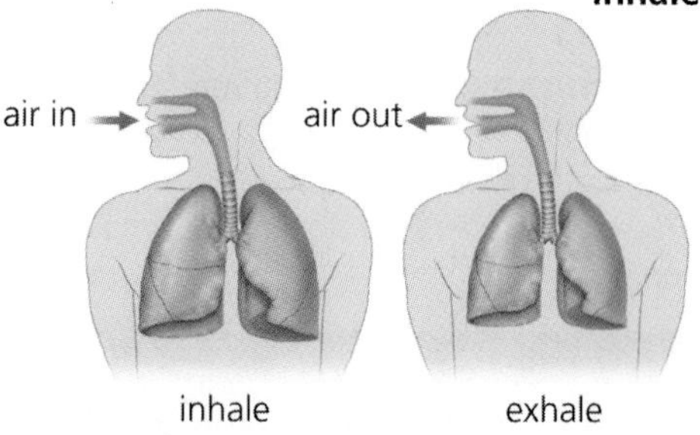


**in·hale** /ɪnˈheɪl/ *verb (formal)*
to breathe in air, smoke, or gas: *Some of the people rescued from the fire had inhaled a lot of smoke.* **ANTONYM: exhale**

**in·hal·er** /ɪnˈheɪlɚ/ *noun*
an object that you use to breathe in medicine through your mouth. Inhalers are used by people who have problems with their breathing.

**in·her·ent** Ac /ɪnˈhɪrənt/ *adjective (formal)*
a quality or feature that is inherent in something is a basic and permanent part of it, so that it cannot be changed: *The problem is inherent in the system, so we have to change the system to fix the problem.*
—**inherently** *adverb* because of the basic qualities of something: *Being a firefighter is an inherently dangerous job.*

**in·her·it** /ɪnˈherɪt/ *verb*
**1** to get something from someone after he or she has died: *I inherited the house from my uncle when he died.*
**2** to get a quality or feature from one of your parents: *Anna inherited her mother's good looks.*
—**inheritance** *noun* money or things that you get from someone after he or she has died: *He spent all his inheritance on expensive cars.*

**in·hu·mane** /ˌɪnhyuˈmeɪn/ *adjective (formal)*
an inhumane action is cruel: *We are trying to end the inhumane treatment of prisoners.*
**ANTONYM: humane**
—**inhumanity** /ˌɪnhyuˈmænəti/ *noun* cruel actions

**i·ni·tial¹** /ɪˈnɪʃəl/ *noun*
the first letter of a name: *His name is John Smith, so his initials are J.S.*

[**ORIGIN:** 1500-1600 From the Latin word *initialis*, from *initium*, which means "beginning."]

**initial**[2] *adjective*
happening at the beginning: *My initial reaction was shock. But then I was angry.* **SYNONYM: first**

**in·i·tial·ly** Ac /ɪˈnɪʃəli/ *adverb* (*formal*)
at first: *Initially, my new job seemed very difficult, but after a few weeks it became easier.*

**i·ni·ti·ate** Ac /ɪˈnɪʃiˌeɪt/ *verb* (*formal*)
to start something: *I initiated the conversation by asking him what his name was.*

**i·ni·ti·a·tion** Ac /ɪˌnɪʃiˈeɪʃən/ *noun*
the action of making someone a member of a group, usually with a ceremony: *The club has an initiation ceremony for new members once a year.*

**i·ni·tia·tive** Ac /ɪˈnɪʃətɪv/ *noun*
**1** the ability to do things without waiting for someone to tell you what to do: *The boy showed initiative by organizing a bike ride as a way to raise money to help the earthquake victims.*
**2** an important plan or way of solving a problem: *The initiative to reduce crime in the area has been a success.*
**3 take the initiative** = to do something rather than waiting for other people to do something: *She knew Mike was shy, so she decided to take the initiative and ask him out.*

**in·ject** /ɪnˈdʒekt/ *verb*
to put a drug into someone's body using a special needle: *The doctor injected the patient with the new drug.*
—**injection** /ɪnˈdʒekʃən/ *noun* if you have an injection, a drug is injected into your body: *The nurse gave me an injection of penicillin.*

**inject**

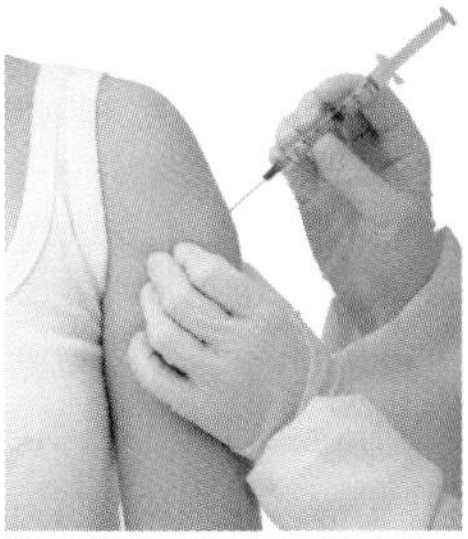

[**ORIGIN:** 1500-1600 From the Latin word *injectus*, a form of the verb *inicere*, which means "to throw or put in."]

**in·jure** Ac /ˈɪndʒɚ/ *verb*
to damage someone's body: *Her father was seriously injured in a car accident.* | *I injured my knee playing football.*
—**injured** *adjective* if you are injured, part of your body is damaged
→ see Thesaurus box at **hurt**[1]

| **WORD FAMILY: injure** |
|---|
| **injure** *verb* \| **injured** *adjective* \| **injury** *noun* |

**in·ju·ry** Ac /ˈɪndʒəri/ *noun* (plural **injuries**)
physical damage to someone's body: *He suffered a serious injury to his leg and couldn't use it for months.*

**THESAURUS: injury**

**wound** an injury, especially a deep cut made in your skin, for example by a knife or bullet: *The soldier was being treated for a bullet wound in his leg.*

**cut** a wound you get if a sharp object cuts your skin: *Kate had some cuts and bruises from falling off her bike.*

**scratch** a long thin cut on your skin: *Her legs and arms were covered in scratches from where she'd pushed through the bushes.*

**bruise** a dark mark on your skin that you get when you fall or get hit: *The ball hit him on the cheek and left a bruise.*

**bump** a raised area of skin that you get if you fall or get hit: *"How did you get that bump on your forehead?" "I hit my head on the car door!"*

**sprain** an injury to a joint in your body, caused by suddenly twisting it: *He missed the race because of an ankle sprain.*

**in·jus·tice** /ɪnˈdʒʌstɪs/ *noun*
a situation in which someone is treated unfairly: *He fought against the injustice of innocent people being sent to prison for crimes they were not involved in.* **ANTONYM: justice**

**ink** /ɪŋk/ *noun*
a colored liquid used for writing or printing

**ˈin-laws** *plural noun*
the parents of your husband or wife: *We're spending the weekend with my in-laws.*

I

**ˌin-line ˈskating** *noun*
the activity of moving along while wearing special boots with a line of wheels under them
—**in-line skates** *plural noun* special boots with a line of wheels under them

**in·mate** /ˈɪnmeɪt/ *noun*
someone who is kept in a prison or a mental hospital: *Two of the inmates got into a fight and were sent back to their prison cells.*

**inn** /ɪn/ *noun*
a small hotel, usually not in a city

**in·ner** /ˈɪnɚ/ *adjective*
**1** inside or close to the middle of something: *The front door of the building was open, but all the inner doors were locked.* **ANTONYM: outer**
**2** relating to your private thoughts or feelings: *Her faith gives her inner strength.*

**ˌinner ˈcity** *noun* (plural **inner cities**)
an area that is close to the middle of a city, where many poor people live: *The program is designed to help kids from the inner city whose families do not have a lot of money.*
—**inner-city** *adjective* existing in the inner city: *inner-city schools*

**in·ner·most** /ˈɪnɚˌmoʊst/ *adjective*
your innermost feelings or thoughts are your most private ones: *He did not tell anyone his innermost thoughts.*
→ see Thesaurus box at **private**[1]

**in·ning** /ˈɪnɪŋ/ *noun*
one of the nine playing periods in a game of baseball

**in·no·cent** /ˈɪnəsənt/ *adjective*
**1** not guilty of a crime: *They cannot send an innocent man to jail. | He was freed after the jury found him innocent.* **ANTONYM: guilty**
**2** someone who is innocent does not have much experience of the bad things in life, and believes that everyone is good and honest: *I was young and innocent, and I trusted everyone.*
**3** **innocent victim/bystander/civilian, etc.** = someone who gets hurt or killed in a war or during a crime, though he or she is not involved in it: *Dozens of innocent civilians were hurt in the blast.*
—**innocently** *adverb* in an innocent way
—**innocence** *noun* the quality of being innocent
[**ORIGIN:** 1300-1400 From the Latin words *in-* meaning "not" and *nocere*, which means "to harm."]

**in·no·vate** [Ac] /ˈɪnəˌveɪt/ *verb* (*formal*)
to start to use a new idea, invention, or way of doing something: *We try not to repeat what we did in the past – we want to innovate.*
—**innovative** *adjective* new and better than in the past: *The company has been successful by developing innovative new products.*

**WORD FAMILY: innovate**
**innovate** *verb* | **innovation** *noun* | **innovative** *adjective*

**in·no·va·tion** [Ac] /ˌɪnəˈveɪʃən/ *noun*
a new idea, invention, or way of doing something: *We are constantly seeing new innovations in medicine, that can improve health.*

**in·oc·u·late** /ɪˈnɑkyəˌleɪt/ *verb* (*formal*)
to protect someone against a disease by putting a weak form of the disease into his or her body using a needle: *Doctors are inoculating every child in the village to stop the disease.*
—**inoculation** /ɪˌnɑkyəˈleɪʃən/ *noun* the act of inoculating someone

**in·of·fen·sive** /ˌɪnəˈfensɪv/ *adjective*
not likely to make people upset: *His jokes are gentle and inoffensive, and he never swears.* **ANTONYM: offensive**

**in·pa·tient** /ˈɪnˌpeɪʃənt/ *adjective*
relating to someone who stays in hospital while he or she is being given medical treatment: *Inpatient care is usually much more expensive than outpatient treatment.*

**in·put** [Ac] /ˈɪnpʊt/ *noun*
**1** ideas that you have or things that you do to help make something succeed: *We want to get input from all the students in the class so that we can make the changes that they want.*
**2** information that is put into a computer **ANTONYM: output**

**in·quire** /ɪnˈkwaɪɚ/ *verb* (*formal*)
to ask someone for information: *"Do you live*

*here?" he inquired.* | *A man called me to inquire whether my car was still for sale.*
—**inquirer** *noun* someone who inquires about something
→ see Thesaurus box at **ask**
[**ORIGIN:** 1200-1300 From the Latin word *inquirere*, which means "to look for."]

**in·quir·y** /ɪnˈkwaɪəri/ *noun* (plural **inquiries**) (*formal*)
**1** a question you ask in order to get information: *You should make inquiries about the area before you decide to move there.*
**2** an official process to try to find out why something bad happened: *Relatives of the dead woman have asked for an inquiry into the crash.*

**in·quis·i·tive** /ɪnˈkwɪzətɪv/ *adjective*
interested in finding out about things: *Jake's an inquisitive boy; he asks questions about everything.*

**in·sane** /ɪnˈseɪn/ *adjective*
**1** (*informal*) very stupid, and often dangerous: *It's insane to try to cross the ocean in such a small boat.*
**2** someone who is insane has a severe mental illness: *a hospital for the criminally insane*
—**insanity** /ɪnˈsænəti/ *noun* severe mental illness
→ see Thesaurus box at **crazy**

**in·sect** /ˈɪnsekt/ *noun*
a small creature such as an ANT or a fly, with six legs and a body divided into three parts. Some insects also have wings.
[**ORIGIN:** 1600-1700 From the Latin word *insectum*, from *insecare*, which means "to cut into." Insects have a body that is divided into three parts.]

**in·sec·ti·cide** /ɪnˈsektəˌsaɪd/ *noun*
a chemical substance used for killing insects

**in·se·cure** Ac /ˌɪnsɪˈkjʊr/ *adjective*
not feeling confident, for example about your appearance, your abilities, or your future: *Many teenagers feel insecure about their looks; they worry about being too fat or not having the right clothes.* **ANTONYM: confident**
—**insecurity** *noun* the feeling of not being confident

**in·sen·si·tive** /ɪnˈsensətɪv/ *adjective* (*formal*)
not noticing or caring whether you upset someone: *Some of the children made insensitive remarks about her weight.*

**in·sep·a·ra·ble** /ɪnˈsepərəbəl/ *adjective*
**1** people who are inseparable are always together because they like each other a lot: *The kids became inseparable, playing together every day.*
**2** things that are inseparable cannot be considered separately: *The problems of hunger and poverty are inseparable in this area; we cannot end hunger unless we also end poverty.*

**in·sert** Ac /ɪnˈsɚt/ *verb* (*formal*)
to put something inside or into something else: *Insert a CD into the CD player.*
—**insertion** /ɪnˈsɚʃən/ *noun* the action of putting something inside something else

**in·side**[1] /ɪnˈsaɪd/ *adverb, preposition*
in a container, room, building, etc.: *Her keys were locked inside the car.* | *It's raining – let's go inside.* **ANTONYM: outside**

**inside**[2] *noun*
**1 the inside** = the inner part of something: *The skin on the inside of my ear was red and sore.* | *The door was locked from the inside and I couldn't get in.*
**2 inside out** = if clothing is inside out, the part that is usually on the outside is on the inside: *One of her socks was inside out.*

**inside**[3] *adjective*
on the inside of something: *He took a pen from the inside pocket of his jacket.*

**in·sid·er** /ɪnˈsaɪdɚ/ *noun*
someone who works for an organization and knows a lot about it: *Some insiders believe the company is having trouble, but there have been no public announcements.*

**in·sight** Ac /ˈɪnsaɪt/ *noun*
the ability to understand what people and situations are really like: *Living in Paris really*

*gave me insight into the way the French people live.*

—**insightful** *adjective* able to understand what people and situations are really like

**in·sig·ni·a** /ɪnˈsɪgniə/ *noun* (plural **insignia**)
a small design or symbol that shows someone's rank or the organization he or she works for. It is usually worn on a shirt or jacket: *His shirt had a navy insignia on the arm.*

**in·sig·nif·i·cant** Ac /ˌɪnsɪgˈnɪfɪkənt/ *adjective* (*formal*)
too small or unimportant to think or worry about: *Our problems seem insignificant compared to the problems of the people whose houses were destroyed.*

—**insignificance** *noun* the fact that something is insignificant

**in·sin·cere** /ˌɪnsɪnˈsɪr/ *adjective*
pretending to think or feel something that you do not really think or feel: *He said he was sorry, but his apology sounded insincere.*

—**insincerity** /ˌɪnsɪnˈserəti/ *noun* insincere feelings or behavior

**in·sist** /ɪnˈsɪst/ *verb*
**1** to keep saying firmly that something is true, even when other people think you may not be telling the truth: *He kept insisting that Mike was driving when the accident happened.*
**2** to say firmly that you will do something or that something must happen: *He insisted on going to work even though he was sick.*

—**insistence** *noun* the act of saying firmly that something is true or must happen

[**ORIGIN:** 1500-1600 From the Latin word *insistere*, which means "to continue in a determined way."]

**in·som·ni·a** /ɪnˈsɑmniə/ *noun*
if you have insomnia, you are not able to sleep

—**insomniac** /ɪnˈsɑmniˌæk/ *noun* someone who regularly has difficulty sleeping

**in·spect** Ac /ɪnˈspekt/ *verb*
to examine something carefully, especially as part of an official activity: *The bags will be inspected by a customs official.*

—**inspector** *noun* someone whose job is to check that something is being done correctly and that rules are being obeyed: *Building inspectors checked the new building.*

**in·spec·tion** Ac /ɪnˈspekʃən/ *noun*
a careful examination of something, to make sure that something is in good condition or that something has been done correctly: *a safety inspection | Engineers do an inspection of the engines before the plane takes off.*

**in·spi·ra·tion** /ˌɪnspəˈreɪʃən/ *noun*
**1** something or someone that makes you want to achieve something: *I want to be a famous singer, and Mariah Carey is my inspiration.*
**2** something or someone that you gives you new ideas: *The author said that his children were the inspiration for many of his stories.*

—**inspirational** *adjective* making you want to achieve something: *He gave an inspirational speech that made everyone want to try harder.*

**in·spire** /ɪnˈspaɪə/ *verb*
**1** to make you feel that you want to do or achieve something: *His love for the young woman inspired him to write the song.*
**2** to make someone have a particular feeling: *The coach's attitude inspired confidence in the players.*

**in·stall** /ɪnˈstɔl/ *verb*
**1** (*formal*) to put a piece of equipment somewhere and connect it so that it is ready to be used: *It took me two hours to install the new light in the bedroom ceiling.*
**2** to add new computer software onto a computer: *Download the software, and install it on your computer.*

—**installation** /ˌɪnstəˈleɪʃən/ *noun* the act of putting a new piece of equipment somewhere

**in·stall·ment** /ɪnˈstɔlmənt/ *noun*
**1** one of a number of regular payments that you make in order to pay for something: *You can pay for the laptop in twelve monthly installments.*
**2** one part of a story in a magazine or one part of a television series: *The first installment of the new series was watched by over 12 million viewers.*

**in·stance** Ac /ˈɪnstəns/ *noun*
**1 for instance** = for example: *In some states, for instance Nevada, gambling is legal.*

2 (*formal*) an example of something, especially something bad: *There are too many instances of people being cruel to animals.*

**in·stant¹** /ˈɪnstənt/ *adjective*
1 happening immediately: *The movie was an instant success.*
2 instant coffee or food can be prepared very quickly by adding hot water: *instant noodles*

**instant²** *noun*
1 a very short period of time: *I saw her for an instant, and then she was gone.* **SYNONYM: moment**
2 **the instant (that)** = as soon as: *I knew something was wrong the instant I picked up the phone.*

**in·stan·ta·ne·ous** /ˌɪnstənˈteɪniəs/ *adjective*
happening immediately: *With email, communication is almost instantaneous.*
—**instantaneously** *adverb* immediately

**in·stant·ly** /ˈɪnstəntli/ *adverb*
immediately: *He still looked exactly the same, and I recognized him instantly.*
→ see Thesaurus box at **immediately**

**ˌinstant ˈmessaging** *noun*
(*abbreviation:* **IM**) a service on the Internet that makes it possible to have conversations with people by sending and receiving written messages immediately

**ˌinstant ˈreplay** *noun*
an occasion when the action in a sports game on television is shown again, immediately after it happens: *You could see from the instant replay that his foot was in the end zone when he caught the football.*

**in·stead** /ɪnˈsted/ *adverb*
rather than something else: *If you don't want chicken, you can have beef instead.* | *I think I'll ride my bike to school instead of walking.*

**in·stinct** /ˈɪnstɪŋkt/ *noun*
a way of behaving that is natural, not learned or thought about carefully: *I was very scared, and my instinct was to run to a safe place.*
—**instinctive** *adjective* based on instinct: *Most children have an instinctive fear of the dark.*
—**instinctively** *adverb* in a way that is based on instinct: *I knew instinctively that he wasn't guilty.*
[**ORIGIN:** 1400-1500 From the Latin word *instinctus*, a form of the verb *instinguere*, which means "to make someone want to do something."]

**in·sti·tute** Ac /ˈɪnstəˌtut/ *noun*
an organization where people work on a subject related to education, especially a science: *the Massachusetts Institute of Technology*

**in·sti·tu·tion** Ac /ˌɪnstəˈtuʃən/ *noun*
1 a large important organization, such as a bank, hospital, or university: *Banks and other financial institutions took too many risks.*
2 a system that has been in a society for a very long time: *People still respect the institution of marriage.*
—**institutional** *adjective* relating to an institution

**in·struct** Ac /ɪnˈstrʌkt/ *verb* (*formal*)
1 to officially tell someone to do something: *Employees were instructed not to talk to the media.*
2 to teach someone something: *The program instructs students in English grammar.*
—**instructor** *noun* someone who teaches a skill or activity: *a swimming instructor*

**WORD FAMILY: instruct**
**instruct** *verb* | **instructor** *noun* | **instruction** *noun*

**in·struc·tion** Ac /ɪnˈstrʌkʃən/ *noun*
1 a statement telling someone what they must do: *He gave instructions that I should deliver the package to you.*
2 (*formal*) lessons in a particular skill or subject: *She had received some instruction in drawing.*
3 **instructions** = information that tells you how to do something: *To install the software, follow the on-line instructions.* | *The invitation came with a map and instructions on how to get to the party.* **SYNONYM: directions**

**in·stru·ment** /ˈɪnstrəmənt/ *noun*
1 something such as a piano, VIOLIN, or GUITAR that you play to make music: *Can you play any musical instruments?*
2 a piece of scientific equipment or a medical tool: *The doctor had his surgical instruments laid out for the operation.*

**in·stru·men·tal** /ˌɪnstrəˈmentl/ *adjective*
**1** instrumental music is played on instruments, without any singing
**2 be instrumental in doing something** (*formal*) = to be one of the people that make something happen: *John's father was instrumental in getting the teacher to change her decision.*

**in·sub·stan·tial** /ˌɪnsəbˈstænʃəl/ *adjective* (*formal*)
not large or definite enough to have an important effect: *The evidence against him was insubstantial and did not convince the jury.*

**in·suf·fi·cient** Ac /ˌɪnsəˈfɪʃənt/ *adjective* (*formal*)
not enough: *We had insufficient time to see all the paintings, so we only looked at some of them.* **ANTONYM: sufficient**
—**insufficiently** *adverb* not enough

**in·su·late** /ˈɪnsəˌleɪt/ *verb*
**1** to cover something with a material that stops electricity, sound, or heat from getting in or out: *Insulate the pipes to stop them from freezing.*
**2** to protect someone from bad experiences: *Kids from wealthy families are insulated from the problems that poor kids have.*
—**insulation** /ˌɪnsəˈleɪʃən/ *noun* material used to insulate something, for example walls or water pipes
[**ORIGIN:** 1500-1600 From the Latin word *insulatus*, which means "made into an island," from *insula*, meaning "island." If something is insulated, it is separated from other things by something that will protect it.]

**in·su·lin** /ˈɪnsələn/ *noun*
a substance which your body makes naturally in order to change sugar into energy. People with DIABETES do not have enough insulin.

**in·sult¹** /ɪnˈsʌlt/ *verb*
**1** to say something unkind, rude, or offensive about someone: *You insulted him when you said he didn't have enough skill to do the job himself.*
**2 be insulted** = to feel upset because someone has said or done something unkind, rude, or offensive: *She might be insulted if we don't come to her party.*
[**ORIGIN:** 1500-1600 From the Latin word *insultare*, which means "to jump on."]

**insult²** *noun*
a rude or offensive remark or action: *The man and woman were yelling nasty insults at each other.*

**WORD FAMILY: insult**
**insult** *noun* | **insult** *verb* | **insulting** *adjective*

**in·sult·ing** /ɪnˈsʌltɪŋ/ *adjective*
very rude or offensive to someone: *His jokes are insulting to women.* | *insulting remarks*
→ see Thesaurus box at **rude**

**in·sur·ance** /ɪnˈʃʊrəns/ *noun*
an arrangement in which you pay money to a company regularly, and the company pays you money if anything bad happens to you or something you own: *If you don't have health insurance, how will you pay for medical treatment?* | *car insurance*

**inˈsurance ˌpolicy** *noun* (plural **insurance policies**)
a legal written agreement with an insurance company so that you have insurance: *If I die, my life insurance policy will pay my wife a large amount of money.*

**in·sure** /ɪnˈʃʊr/ *verb*
**1** to buy or provide insurance for something or someone: *This painting is insured for $5,000 in case it is stolen or damaged.*
**2** to make certain that something happens: *The gift of $200,000 dollars will insure that the school has enough money to build a new library.*
—**insurer** *noun* a company that provides insurance

**WORD FAMILY: insure**
**insure** *verb* | **insurance** *noun* | **insurer** *noun*

**in·tact** /ɪnˈtækt/ *adjective*
not harmed or damaged: *The storm destroyed many of the wooden buildings, but the hotel was still intact.*

**in·te·ger** /ˈɪntədʒɚ/ *noun*
a whole number, not a FRACTION such as ½ or ¾: *6, -2, and 0 are all integers.*

**in·te·gral** Ac /ˈɪntəgrəl/ *adjective* (*formal*)
forming an important and necessary part of something: *Women are now an integral part of our military; we could not fight a war without them.*

**in·te·grate** Ac /ˈɪntəgreɪt/ *verb*

**1** to become part of a group or society and be accepted by them: *It takes some time for immigrants to integrate into American life.*

**2** to end the practice of separating people of different races in schools or institutions: *The Supreme Court's decision to integrate public schools allowed black children and white children to go the same schools across the U.S.*

—**integrated** *adjective* having people from different places or of different types living together: *We live in an integrated community with people of all races and religions.*

—**integration** /ɪntəˈgreɪʃən/ *noun* the process of becoming part of a group or society and being accepted by them

[ORIGIN: 1600-1700 From the Latin word *integrare*, which means "to make something whole," from *integer*, which means "whole."]

**in·teg·ri·ty** Ac /ɪnˈtegrəti/ *noun*

the quality of being honest and doing what you believe is right: *I admire his integrity; I have known him for 20 years, and I have never heard him lie.*

**in·tel·lect** /ˈɪntəˌlekt/ *noun*

the ability to understand things and think intelligently: *My professor is a woman of great intellect.*

**in·tel·lec·tu·al¹** /ˌɪntəˈlektʃuəl/ *adjective*

**1** relating to your ability to think and understand ideas and information: *Solving the puzzle needs a lot of intellectual effort.*

**2** intelligent and interested in serious ideas and complicated subjects: *Mark is very intellectual, and his interests include literature and politics.*

**intellectual²** *noun*

an intelligent person who is interested in serious subjects or complicated ideas: *Many intellectuals went to the poetry reading.*

**in·tel·li·gence** Ac /ɪnˈtelədʒəns/ *noun*

**1** the ability to learn, understand, and think about things: *He was a child of average intelligence, who got Bs and Cs at school.*

**2** information about the secret activities of foreign governments or military groups: *According to our intelligence, further terrorist attacks are likely.*

**WORD FAMILY: intelligence**

**intelligence** *noun* | **intelligent** *adjective* | **intelligently** *adverb*

**in·tel·li·gent** Ac /ɪnˈtelədʒənt/ *adjective*

able to learn and understand things quickly: *My dog is intelligent and quickly learned to obey me.* | *She's a good student who asks intelligent questions.* **ANTONYM: stupid**

—**intelligently** *adverb* in an intelligent way

[ORIGIN: 1500-1600 From the Latin word *intellegere*, which means "to understand."]

**THESAURUS: intelligent**

**smart** intelligent: *He's a really smart guy and he studies really hard.*

**bright** quick at learning things – used especially about children and young people: *Their daughter is very bright; she is only four and she has already learned to read.*

**brilliant** very intelligent and good at the work you do: *a brilliant scientist*

**clever** intelligent and good at thinking of ways of doing things: *He's clever, and can usually figure out a way to get what he wants.*

**wise** able to make good decisions and give sensible advice because you have a lot of experience of life: *My grandmother is a wise woman and I always talk to her if I need advice.*

**in·tend** /ɪnˈtend/ *verb*

**1** to plan to do something: *The work took three months longer than we intended.* | *Bob never intended to hurt me; it was an accident.* **SYNONYM: mean**

**2 be intended for someone/something** = made for a particular person or designed for a particular purpose: *It's a movie for kids – it's not intended for adults.*

[ORIGIN: 1300-1400 From the Latin word *intendere*, which means "to stretch toward something or to turn your attention to something."]

**WORD FAMILY: intend**

**intend** *verb* | **intention** *noun* | **intentional** *adjective* | **intentionally** *adverb* | **intent** *noun*

I

**in·tense** Ac /ɪnˈtens/ *adjective*
having a very strong effect or felt very strongly: *The heat from the burning building was intense.* | *intense pain*
—**intensely** *adverb* in an intense way: *Bill disliked her intensely.*

**in·ten·si·fy** Ac /ɪnˈtensəˌfaɪ/ *verb* (**intensified**, **intensifies**) (*formal*)
to increase, for example in size, strength, or effort: *The pain intensified, until it was so bad that I went to the hospital.* | *Officials have intensified the search for the missing children.*

**in·ten·si·ty** Ac /ɪnˈtensəti/ *noun*
when something is felt very strongly or has a very strong effect: *You could see the intensity of the love he felt for his children in the gentle way he took care of them.*

**in·ten·sive** Ac /ɪnˈtensɪv/ *adjective*
involving a lot of work in a short period of time: *The team did two months of intensive training before the Olympics.*
—**intensively** *adverb* in an intensive way

I

**in·tent** /ɪnˈtent/ *noun* (*formal*)
what you want or plan to do: *It was never my intent to hurt anybody – the bad things that happened were an accident.* **SYNONYM: intention**

**in·ten·tion** /ɪnˈtenʃən/ *noun*
something that you plan to do: *I have no intention of retiring – I'm going to continue working as long as possible.*

**in·ten·tion·al** /ɪnˈtenʃənəl/ *adjective*
done deliberately: *He broke the rules, but I'm sure it wasn't intentional.*
—**intentionally** *adverb* deliberately

**in·ter·act** Ac /ˌɪntəˈrækt/ *verb* (*formal*)
to talk or do something with someone: *He interacts well with other children in the class.*
—**interaction** /ˌɪntəˈrækʃən/ *noun* the activity of talking or doing things with other people

**in·ter·ac·tive** Ac /ˌɪntəˈræktɪv/ *adjective*
if something such as a piece of equipment or software is interactive, you can make it do things: *You can design your own city of the future using this interactive software.*

**in·ter·cept** /ˌɪntɚˈsept/ *verb*
to stop something that is going from one place to another before it gets there: *He threw the ball to a teammate, but a member of the other team intercepted it.*
—**interception** /ˌɪntɚˈsepʃən/ *noun* the action of stopping something before it gets somewhere

**in·ter·change·a·ble** Ac /ˌɪntɚˈtʃeɪndʒəbəl/ *adjective*
if things are interchangeable, they can be used instead of each other: *These sports sunglasses have interchangeable lenses for different light conditions.*

**in·ter·com** /ˈɪntɚˌkɑm/ *noun*
a system that lets people in different parts of a building, aircraft, or ship speak to each other: *The pilot spoke to us over the intercom, welcoming us aboard the flight.*

**in·ter·con·nect·ed** /ˌɪntɚkəˈnektɪd/ *adjective* (*formal*)
if two or more things are interconnected, they are related to each other or connected to each other: *Computers have thousands of interconnected parts.*

**in·ter·de·pend·ent** /ˌɪntɚdɪˈpendənt/ *adjective* (*formal*)
if people, animals, or things are interdependent, they cannot exist or work without each other: *The plants and wildlife in the rainforest are interdependent.*
—**interdependence** *noun* a situation in which people, animals, or things cannot exist or work without each other

**in·terest**[1] /ˈɪntrəst/ *noun*
**1** the feeling that you want to know more about a subject or person, or do more of an activity: *My sister has started to show an interest in fashion.* | *I lost interest and stopped reading when the book got really technical.*
**2** a subject or activity that you enjoy studying or doing: *My interests are music, soccer, and riding horses.*
**3** money that you must pay a bank when you borrow money, or money that a bank pays you if you save money: *He was having difficulty paying the interest on the loan.*

**interest**[2] *verb*
if a subject, activity, or person interests you, you want to know more about them: *The idea of studying journalism interests me and I want to learn more about it.*

**in·terest·ed** /ˈɪntrəstɪd/ *adjective*
**1** if you are interested in something, you want to learn more about it because you enjoy it: *Most girls who are my age are interested in music, clothes, and boys.*
**2** if you are interested in doing something, you want to do it: *I'm interested in buying your truck. How much money do you want for it?*

**in·terest·ing** /ˈɪntrəstɪŋ/ *adjective*
if something is interesting, it keeps your attention or makes you want to know more: *I saw an interesting program about dinosaurs yesterday.*

**WORD FAMILY: interesting**
**interesting** *adjective* | **interested** *adjective* | **interest** *verb* | **interest** *noun*

**in·ter·fere** /ˌɪntɚˈfɪr/ *verb*
to get involved in a situation when other people do not want you to: *It's better not to interfere in their arguments. They need to solve their problems themselves.*
—**interference** *noun* an act of interfering
[**ORIGIN:** 1400-1500 From the old French word *entreferir*, which means "to hit each other."]
**PHRASAL VERB**
**interfere with something**
to prevent something from happening in the way that is planned: *Her family problems began to interfere with her work and her boss had to talk to her about it.*

**in·te·ri·or** /ɪnˈtɪriɚ/ *noun* (*formal*)
the inside of something: *The interior of the church was cool and dark.* **ANTONYM: exterior**
—**interior** *adjective* inside: *The outside of the house needs painting, but the interior walls are fine.*

**in·ter·jec·tion** /ˌɪntɚˈdʒekʃən/ *noun*
a word or phrase that is used to express surprise, shock, pain, etc. In the sentence "Ouch, that hurt!" "Ouch" is an interjection.

**in·ter·me·di·ate** [Ac] /ˌɪntɚˈmidiət/ *adjective*
done or happening between two other stages or levels: *First you take the beginning English class, then the intermediate class, and then the advanced class.*

**in·ter·mis·sion** /ˌɪntɚˈmɪʃən/ *noun*
a break in the middle of a play or concert, when the performance stops before starting again a short time later: *The show lasts 85 minutes with a short intermission in the middle.*

**in·tern**[1] /ˈɪntɚn/ *noun*
**1** a student who works without pay so that he or she can learn how to do a job
**2** someone who has almost finished training as a doctor and is working in a hospital

**in·tern**[2] /ɪnˈtɚn/ *verb*
**1** to work at an organization as an intern: *Scott's interning at a law firm during summer vacation from law school.*
**2** to put someone in prison for political reasons or during a war, without charging him or her with a crime: *Thousands of people were interned at labor camps and forced to build roads.*
—**internment** *noun* the practice of keeping people in prison for political reasons or during a war, without charging them with a crime

**in·ter·nal** [Ac] /ɪnˈtɚnl/ *adjective*
**1** existing or happening within a company, organization, or country: *The bank began an internal investigation into the illegal actions of its employees.*
**2** inside your body: *In this picture, you can see the internal organs, such as the heart and lungs.* **ANTONYM: external**
—**internally** *adverb* within an organization or country, or inside someone's body

**in·ter·na·tion·al** /ˌɪntɚˈnæʃənəl/ *adjective*
involving or existing in more than one country: *They asked the United Nations and other international organizations for help.* | *international flights*
—**internationally** *adverb* in more than one country
[**ORIGIN:** 1700-1800 From the Latin word *inter-* meaning "between" and the word "nation."]

**In·ter·net** /ˈɪntɚˌnet/ *noun*
**the Internet** = a computer system that allows millions of computer users around the world to send and receive information: *You can buy airline tickets on the Internet.* **SYNONYMS: the Net, the Web**

I

**in·ter·pret** Ac /ɪnˈtɚprɪt/ *verb*
**1** to change what someone is saying in one language into another language: *Gina speaks Spanish, so she interpreted for me when we were in Mexico.*
**2** (*formal*) to believe that something has a particular meaning: *I interpreted his silence as a sign of guilt.*
—**interpreter** *noun* someone who changes what someone is saying in one language into another language

**in·ter·pre·ta·tion** Ac /ɪnˌtɚprəˈteɪʃən/ *noun* (*formal*)
the way in which someone understands or explains something: *What is your interpretation of the end of the story? Do you think the characters are happy?*

**in·ter·ra·cial** /ˌɪntɚˈreɪʃəl/ *adjective*
happening or existing between different races of people: *Interracial marriage is more common now than it used to be.*

**in·ter·ro·gate** /ɪnˈterəˌgeɪt/ *verb*
to ask someone questions for a long time in order to get information: *The police interrogated the men for more than three hours, trying to find out exactly what happened.*
—**interrogator** *noun* a police officer or other official who asks someone questions in order to get information
—**interrogation** /ɪnˌterəˈgeɪʃən/ *noun* the act of asking someone questions for a long time in order to get information

**in·ter·rupt** /ˌɪntəˈrʌpt/ *verb*
**1** to say or do something that stops someone else from speaking: *He got mad at me for interrupting his conversation.*
**2** to make a process or activity stop for a short time: *The rain interrupted our barbecue.*
—**interruption** /ˌɪntɚˈrʌpʃən/ *noun* something that makes an activity stop for a short time
[**ORIGIN:** 1300-1400 From the Latin word *interruptus*, a form of the verb *interrumpere*, which means "to break."]

**in·ter·sect** /ˌɪntɚˈsekt/ *verb*
if roads or lines intersect, they meet or cross each other: *Where the two paths intersect, you should turn left.*

**in·ter·sec·tion** /ˌɪntəˈsekʃən/ *noun*
a place where two or more roads meet and cross each other, often where there is a traffic light: *Turn left at the next intersection.*

**in·ter·state**[1] /ˈɪntɚˌsteɪt/ *noun*
a wide road that goes between states, on which cars can travel very fast: *The car was going south on Interstate 93.*
→ see Thesaurus box at **road**

**interstate**[2] *adjective*
between different states in the U.S.: *interstate transportation*

**in·ter·val** Ac /ˈɪntəvəl/ *noun*
**1** a period of time or a distance between two things: *There was a short interval of good weather between the storms.*
**2** **at regular intervals** = with equal amounts of time or space between them: *The trees were planted at regular intervals, thirty feet apart.*
[**ORIGIN:** 1300-1400 From the Latin word *intervallum*, which means "space between castle walls, or space between things."]

**in·ter·vene** Ac /ˌɪntɚˈvin/ *verb* (*formal*)
to try to stop an argument, problem, or fight involving other people: *Their mother could hear them arguing, but she decided not to intervene.*
—**intervention** /ˌɪntɚˈvenʃən/ *noun* the act of intervening in something: *They oppose U.S. military intervention in the area.*

**in·ter·ven·ing** Ac /ˌɪntɚˈvinɪŋ/ *adjective*
**the intervening months/years, etc.** (*formal*) = the time that has passed between two events: *I hadn't visited my school in a long time, and a lot had changed in the intervening years.*

**in·ter·view**[1] /ˈɪntɚˌvyu/ *noun*
**1** an occasion when a famous person is asked questions about his or her life and opinions for a newspaper, magazine, or television program: *In an interview, Jack said that he planned to get married in the fall.*
**2** a formal meeting in which you are asked questions by someone at a place where you want to work or study: *I have an interview at Dartmouth College tomorrow.* | *a job interview*
[**ORIGIN:** 1500-1600 From the old French word *entrevue*, from *entrevoir*, which means "to see each other."]

**interview**[2] *verb*
to ask someone questions during an

interview: *Kelly was interviewed on the radio after the game.* | *We are interviewing 15 people for the job.*
—**interviewer** *noun* the person who asks someone questions during an interview

**in·tes·tine** /ɪnˈtestɪn/ *noun*
the long tube in your body that food passes through after it leaves your stomach and before it leaves your body → see picture on page A2
—**intestinal** *adjective* related to the intestine: *intestinal infection*

**in·ti·mate** /ˈɪntəmət/ *adjective*
**1** having a very close relationship with someone: *a small party for intimate friends*
**2** relating to very private or personal matters: *He told his new wife everything, even his most intimate secrets.*
**3 intimate knowledge of something** = very detailed and thorough knowledge of something, gained through experience or study: *During his four years in Mexico City, he gained an intimate knowledge of Mexican life.*
—**intimately** *adverb* in an intimate way
—**intimacy** /ˈɪntəməsi/ *noun* the fact of having a close personal relationship with someone

**in·tim·i·date** /ɪnˈtɪməˌdeɪt/ *verb*
to deliberately make someone feel frightened of you, so that he or she does what you want: *The gang members intimidated witnesses into not giving evidence in court.*
—**intimidating** *adjective* making you feel worried or not confident: *He finds long books intimidating.*
—**intimidation** /ɪnˌtɪməˈdeɪʃən/ *noun* the act of intimidating someone

**in·to** /ˈɪntə; *before vowels* ˈɪntʊ; *strong* ˈɪntu/ *preposition*
**1** inside a container or place: *When she saw his car coming, Ruth ran into the house.* | *I can't get any more clothes into my suitcase.*
**2** becoming involved in a situation or activity: *After college, he decided to go into teaching.* | *Those boys are always getting into trouble.*
**3** becoming a different thing: *Caterpillars turn into butterflies.* | *They are going to make the book into a movie.*
**4** hitting something, usually by accident: *Dick drove his dad's car into a tree and wrecked it.*
**5 be into something** (*informal*) = to like something very much: *I'm totally into sports, especially football.*
**6** in a particular direction: *She held my face and looked into my eyes.*
**7** used when dividing one number by another number: *Five goes into ten two times.*

**in·tol·er·a·ble** /ɪnˈtɑlərəbəl/ *adjective* (*formal*)
more difficult, bad, or painful than you can deal with: *The pain became intolerable, so I went to the hospital.*

**in·tol·er·ant** /ɪnˈtɑlərənt/ *adjective*
not willing to accept a way of behaving or a belief that is different from your own: *He is intolerant of other people's political beliefs.*
—**intolerance** /ɪnˈtɑlərəns/ *noun* unwillingness to accept a way of behaving or a belief that is different from your own: *They had to leave their country because of the religious intolerance there.*

**in·tox·i·cat·ed** /ɪnˈtɑksəˌkeɪtɪd/ *adjective* (*formal*)
**1** drunk: *He was arrested for driving while intoxicated.*
**2** very happy and excited by something, so that you stop thinking clearly: *He became intoxicated by dreams of winning lots of money in Las Vegas.*
—**intoxicating** *adjective* making you drunk: *intoxicating liquor*
—**intoxication** /ɪnˌtɑksəˈkeɪʃən/ *noun* the state of being drunk

**in·tran·si·tive** /ɪnˈtrænsətɪv/ *adjective*
an intransitive verb does not have an object. In the sentence "They arrived early," "arrive" is an intransitive verb.

**in·tri·cate** /ˈɪntrɪkət/ *adjective*
containing many small parts or details: *the intricate patterns of an Oriental rug*

**in·trigue** /ɪnˈtrig/ *verb* (*formal*)
if something intrigues you, it interests you because it seems strange or mysterious: *The title of the book intrigued me because it was so unusual.*
—**intriguing** *adjective* interesting and slightly strange or mysterious: *The experiment*

*produced some intriguing results, and scientists are investigating them further.*
—**intrigued** *adjective* interested in something because it seems strange or mysterious

**in·trin·sic** Ac /ɪnˈtrɪnzɪk/ *adjective* (*formal*)
if a quality is intrinsic, something has that quality because of what it is like or what it is made of: *This plastic bracelet has little intrinsic value, but it's precious to me because my friend gave it to me.*
—**intrinsically** *adverb* because of a basic quality in something: *Sports like mountain climbing are intrinsically dangerous.*

**in·tro·duce** /ˌɪntrəˈdus/ *verb*
**1** if you introduce someone, you tell people his or her name when they first meet: *She took me home and introduced me to her parents.* | *Let me introduce myself. My name is Mark Wright.*
**2** to start selling or using something new: *The store introduced a new range of sports wear for children.*
**3** to show someone something new or help someone experience something for the first time: *My brother introduced me to fishing when I was seven.*
[**ORIGIN:** 1400-1500 From the Latin word *introducere*, which means "to lead or bring into a place," from *ducere*, which means "to lead."]

**WORD FAMILY: introduce**
**introduce** *verb* | **introduction** *noun* | **introductory** *adjective*

**in·tro·duc·tion** /ˌɪntrəˈdʌkʃən/ *noun*
**1** (*formal*) the act of starting to sell something new or have a new system: *Every year we see the introduction of new, more powerful computers.*
**2** the act of telling people someone's name when they first meet: *Wade greeted his guests and made the introductions.*
**3** a short explanation at the beginning of a book or speech: *In the introduction, the author explains why he wrote the book.*
**4** the act of showing someone something new or helping someone experience something for the first time: *The class is an introduction to American literature.*
—**introductory** /ˌɪntrəˈdʌktəri/ *adjective* done as an introduction: *Write an introductory paragraph to your essay stating your main ideas.*

**in·tro·vert·ed** /ˈɪntrəˌvɚtɪd/ *adjective*
an introverted person is quiet and shy, and does not enjoy being with other people: *At 15 years old, she was quiet and introverted.*
**ANTONYM: extroverted**
—**introvert** *noun* someone who is introverted
→ see Thesaurus box at **shy**

**in·trude** /ɪnˈtrud/ *verb* (*formal*)
to go into a private place or ask about something private, when someone does not want you to: *"I hope I'm not intruding," she said, walking into his room.*
—**intrusion** /ɪnˈtruʒən/ *noun* an occasion when someone intrudes

**in·trud·er** /ɪnˈtrudɚ/ *noun*
**1** someone who illegally enters a building or area in order to steal something: *The intruders entered the school building through a window.*
**2** someone who is in a place where he or she is not wanted: *When my mom remarried, I felt like an intruder in my own home.*

**in·tu·i·tion** /ˌɪntuˈɪʃən/ *noun*
the feeling that you know something is true or correct without having definite facts: *My intuition told me not to trust him, but I wasn't sure why.*
—**intuitive** /ɪnˈtuətɪv/ *adjective* based on feelings, not facts or knowledge

**In·u·it** /ˈɪnuɪt/ *noun*
**the Inuit** = a race of people who live in the very cold parts of North America

**in·un·date** /ˈɪnənˌdeɪt/ *verb*
**be inundated with/by something** = to receive too much of something, so that you cannot deal with all of it: *We were inundated with phone calls from people who wanted tickets.*
[**ORIGIN:** 1500-1600 From the Latin word *inundare*, which means "to flow over or flood," from *unda*, which means "wave."]

**in·vade** /ɪnˈveɪd/ *verb*
to enter a country with an army in order to

take control of it: *Iraqi troops invaded Kuwait in 1990.*
—**invader** *noun* a country or army that invades another country

**in·va·lid¹** /ˈɪnvələd/ *noun*
someone who is sick, injured, or old and needs other people to do things for him or her

**in·va·lid²** [Ac] /ɪnˈvælɪd/ *adjective*
something that is invalid is not legally acceptable because it breaks a rule: *If the credit card doesn't have a signature, it is invalid and cannot be used.* **ANTONYM: valid**
—**invalidate** *verb* to make something invalid

**in·val·ua·ble** /ɪnˈvælyəbəl/ *adjective* (*formal*)
very useful: *His experience was invaluable to the younger players on the team.* **SYNONYM: valuable**

**in·va·sion** /ɪnˈveɪʒən/ *noun*
an occasion when an army enters a country in order to take control of it: *The invasion of Poland marked the beginning of World War II.*

**in·vent** /ɪnˈvent/ *verb*
**1** to make, design, or think of something that is completely new and different: *Alexander Graham Bell invented the telephone in 1876.*

**USAGE: invent, discover**

People **invent** a new machine or a new way of doing something: *Who invented the light bulb?*

People **discover** a place, force, animal, or plant that was not known about before: *Herschel discovered the planet Uranus in 1781.*

**THESAURUS: invent**

**create** to make or design something new: *Each student has to create his or her own website.*

**think up something** to produce an idea or plan that is completely new: *Teachers constantly have to think up ways to keep the students interested.*

**come up with something** to think of a new idea or plan: *Carson said he came up with the idea for the book about five years ago.*

**devise** (*formal*) to invent a way of doing something: *The teacher devised the game as a way of making math fun.*

**make up something** to invent a new story, song, or excuse: *Grandpa made up stories for us at bedtime.*

**2** to think of a reason, story, etc. that is not true and tell it to people: *She invented a reason not to go to the party.*
—**inventive** *adjective* able to think of new, different, or interesting ideas
→ see Thesaurus box at **lie²**
[**ORIGIN:** 1400-1500 From the Latin word *inventus*, a form of the verb *invenire*, which means "to find."]

**WORD FAMILY: invent**

**invent** *verb* | **inventor** *noun* | **invention** *noun* | **inventive** *adjective*

**in·ven·tion** /ɪnˈvenʃən/ *noun*
something that has been invented, or the act of inventing something: *The computer industry is constantly coming up with new inventions.* | *The invention of television changed the world.*

**in·ven·tor** /ɪnˈventɚ/ *noun*
someone who thinks of or makes something completely new and different

**in·ven·to·ry** /ˈɪnvənˌtɔri/ *noun* (plural **inventories**)
**1** all the things that are for sale in a store
**2** a list of all the things in a place

**in·ver·te·brate** /ɪnˈvɚtəbrɪt/ *noun*
a creature that does not have a BACKBONE: *Worms are invertebrates.*

**in·vest** [Ac] /ɪnˈvest/ *verb*
**1** to buy property, shares, or other things because you hope their value will increase and you will make a profit: *He decided to invest the money in land.*
**2** to use a lot of time, effort, or money to improve something and make it succeed: *The government has invested heavily in education.*

I

—**investor** *noun* someone who buys property, shares, or other things in order to make a profit

**WORD FAMILY: invest**
**invest** *verb* | **investment** *noun* | **investor** *noun*

**in·ves·ti·gate** Ac /ɪnˈvestəˌgeɪt/ *verb*
to try to find out the reasons why something happened, especially a crime: *After investigating the case, the police arrested two men.* | *I heard a strange noise and went downstairs to investigate.*
—**investigator** *noun* someone who investigates a crime or accident
[**ORIGIN:** 1500-1600 From the Latin word *investigare*, which means "to follow the track of something," from *vestigium*, meaning "track."]

**WORD FAMILY: investigate**
**investigate** *verb* | **investigation** *noun* | **investigator** *noun*

I

**in·ves·ti·ga·tion** Ac /ɪnˌvestəˈgeɪʃən/ *noun*
an attempt to find out the reasons why something happened, especially to find out who committed a crime or why an accident happened: *They are carrying out an investigation into the cause of the plane crash.*

**in·vest·ment** Ac /ɪnˈvestmənt/ *noun*
**1** the act of buying property, shares, or other things in order to make a profit: *Buying that house was a good investment because it is now worth much more.*
**2** something that you buy or do because it will be valuable or useful later: *Going to college is a good investment.*

**in·vis·i·ble** Ac /ɪnˈvɪzəbəl/ *adjective*
something that is invisible cannot be seen: *Oxygen is a gas that has no color and is invisible.*
—**invisibility** /ɪnˌvɪzəˈbɪləti/ *noun* the fact that something is invisible

**in·vi·ta·tion** /ˌɪnvəˈteɪʃən/ *noun*
**1** a request inviting someone to go somewhere or do something: *I decided to accept Andrea's invitation to visit her.*
**2** a piece of paper that someone sends you to ask you to come to a party or event: *You have to bring the invitation with you to get into the party.*

**in·vite** /ɪnˈvaɪt/ *verb*
to ask someone to come to an event such as a party, wedding, or meal: *"Why weren't you at Eva's party?" "I wasn't invited."* | *She invited the Rosens to dinner.*
**PHRASAL VERBS**
**invite someone in**
to ask someone to come into your home: *We stood on the front porch for a while, but she didn't invite us in.*
**invite someone over**
to ask someone to come to your home, especially for a meal: *They invited us over for a barbecue.*

**in·vit·ing** /ɪnˈvaɪtɪŋ/ *adjective*
something that is inviting is attractive and makes you want to enjoy it: *The swimming pool looked inviting, so I went for a swim.*
—**invitingly** *adverb* in an inviting way

**in·voice** /ˈɪnvɔɪs/ *noun*
a list that shows how much you must pay for things you have bought or work that has been done **SYNONYM: bill**
—**invoice** *verb* to send someone an invoice

**in·voke** Ac /ɪnˈvoʊk/ *verb* (*formal*)
to use a law, principle, etc. to support your ideas or actions: *Stern invoked his rights and refused to answer questions in court* (=he used his right to not answer questions).

**in·vol·un·tar·y** /ɪnˈvɑlənˌteri/ *adjective*
an involuntary movement or sound is one that you make suddenly in a way that you cannot control: *Eve gave an involuntary cry when she fell.*
—**involuntarily** /ɪnˌvɑlənˈterəli/ *adverb* in an uncontrolled way: *My left eye began to twitch involuntarily.*

**in·volve** Ac /ɪnˈvɑlv/ *verb*
**1** to include or affect someone or something: *His car was involved in an accident.*
**2** to encourage or allow someone to take part in something, for example a game or a discussion: *It's important to involve children in making decisions.*
**3** if an activity or situation involves something, that thing is part of it or is the result of it: *Taking the job involves moving to Texas.* |

*They all knew the risks involved in trying to climb the mountain.*

[**ORIGIN:** 1300-1400 From the Latin word *involvere*, which means "to wrap." The things that are involved in something are like things wrapped up together in a piece of cloth.]

**in·volved** Ac /ɪnˈvɑlvd/ *adjective*
if you are involved in an activity or event, you take part in it: *I don't want to get involved in anything that's illegal.*
—**involvement** *noun* the act of taking part in something: *They want to increase the involvement of young people in politics.*

**inward**

inward outward

**in·ward** /ˈɪnwɚd/ (*also* **inwards**) *adverb*
toward the inside or center of something: *The door opens inward.* **ANTONYM: outward**
—**inward** *adjective* toward the inside or center of something

**in·ward·ly** /ˈɪnwɚdli/ *adverb*
in a way that is not seen or noticed by other people: *I laughed inwardly, but said nothing.*

**IOU** *noun*
(**I owe you**) a piece of paper that you sign to say that you owe someone some money

**IPA** *noun*
(**International Phonetic Alphabet**) a system of symbols that represent the sounds made when speaking

**IQ** *noun*
(**intelligence quotient**) the level of someone's intelligence. It is shown as a number, with 100 being the average: *He's extremely intelligent. He has an IQ of 130.*

**I·ra·ni·an** /ɪˈreɪniən/ *noun*
someone from Iran
—**Iranian** *adjective* relating to Iran

**I·ra·qi** /ɪˈrɑki/ *noun*
someone from Iraq
—**Iraqi** *adjective* relating to Iraq

**I·rish¹** /ˈaɪrɪʃ/ *adjective*
coming from Ireland or relating to Ireland

**Irish²** *noun*
**the Irish** = the people of Ireland

**iron**

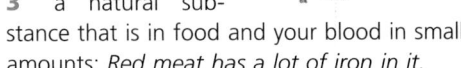

**i·ron¹** /ˈaɪɚn/ *noun*
**1** a piece of electrical equipment used for making clothes smooth: *Be careful – the iron is still hot!*
**2** a common hard metal that is used to make steel: *The old fence was made of iron.*
**3** a natural substance that is in food and your blood in small amounts: *Red meat has a lot of iron in it.*

**iron²** *verb*
to make your clothes smooth using an iron: *Thanks for ironing my shirt – it looks a lot better now.*
**PHRASAL VERB**
**iron something out** (*informal*)
to solve a small problem: *The embassy helped me iron out some problems with my visa.*

**iron³** *adjective*
made of iron: *an iron gate*

**i·ron·ic** /aɪˈrɑnɪk/ *adjective*
**1** funny or sad because something happens that is the opposite of what you expect: *It's ironic that his car was stolen from right outside the police station.*
**2** saying the opposite of what you really mean: *You could tell by the way he said "great!" that he was being ironic, and that really the movie was awful.*

**i·ron·ing** /ˈaɪɚnɪŋ/ *noun*
the activity of making clothes smooth using an iron: *I usually do the ironing while I watch TV.*

**ˈironing ˌboard** *noun*
a tall narrow table used for ironing clothes → see picture at **iron**

**i·ro·ny** /ˈaɪrəni/ *noun* (plural **ironies**)
**1** a situation that is funny or sad because something strange happens, or because something happens that is the opposite of

I

what you expect: *The irony is that their attempts to solve the problem only made it worse.*

**2** a form of humor in which you say the opposite of what you really mean

[**ORIGIN:** 1500-1600 From the Greek word *eironeia*, which means "not being truthful, especially pretending not to know something."]

**ir·ra·tion·al** Ac /ɪˈræʃənəl/ *adjective*
not based on sensible thinking or good reasons: *I know my fear of dogs is irrational, but I can't stop being afraid.* **ANTONYM: rational**
—**irrationally** *adverb* in an irrational way: *He was behaving irrationally and refused to calm down.*

**ir·reg·u·lar** /ɪˈregyələ/ *adjective* (*formal*)
**1** happening at times that are not an equal time apart: *The test showed that she had an irregular heartbeat and needed medical treatment.*
**2** not happening at the normal time: *Actors work irregular hours; often a movie will be filmed in the middle of the night.*
**3** having a shape or surface that is not even or smooth: *the irregular edges of a piece of broken glass*
**4** an irregular verb, noun, or adjective has forms that are not made in the normal way: *"Go" is an irregular verb. Its past tense is "went" and its past participle is "gone."* **ANTONYM: regular**

**ir·reg·u·lar·i·ty** /ɪˌregyəˈlærəti/ *noun* (plural **irregularities**) (*formal*)
**1** something that is not done according to a law or rule: *There were some voting irregularities, so that some people may have been allowed to vote twice.*
**2** a situation in which there is not an equal amount of time between things: *The doctors discovered an irregularity in her heartbeat.*

**ir·rel·e·vant** Ac /ɪˈreləvənt/ *adjective*
not useful or not relating to a particular situation, and therefore not important: *If he can do the job, his age is irrelevant.* **ANTONYM: relevant**
—**irrelevance** *noun* the quality of being irrelevant

**ir·re·sist·i·ble** /ˌɪrɪˈzɪstəbəl/ *adjective*
**1** if something is irresistible, it is so attractive or nice that you cannot stop yourself from wanting it: *We were full, but the desserts were irresistible and we all had one.*
**2** too strong or powerful to be stopped: *She suddenly felt an irresistible urge to cry.*
—**irresistibly** *adverb* in an irresistible way

**ir·re·spon·si·ble** /ˌɪrɪˈspɑnsəbəl/ *adjective*
behaving in a careless way, without thinking about the bad results that might happen: *It was irresponsible to go out without telling us.* **ANTONYM: responsible**
—**irresponsibly** *adverb* in an irresponsible way
—**irresponsibility** /ˌɪrɪˌspɑnsəˈbɪləti/ *noun* the quality of being irresponsible

**ir·ri·gate** /ˈɪrəˌgeɪt/ *verb*
to supply water to land or crops: *Egyptian farmers used water from the Nile to irrigate their land.*
—**irrigation** /ˌɪrəˈgeɪʃən/ *noun* the process of supplying land or crops with water

**ir·ri·ta·ble** /ˈɪrətəbəl/ *adjective*
an irritable person gets annoyed or angry very easily: *He's always irritable in the morning, so it's best not to talk to him then.*
—**irritably** *adverb* in an irritable way
—**irritability** /ˌɪrət̬əˈbɪləti/ *noun* the fact that someone is irritable

**ir·ri·tate** /ˈɪrəˌteɪt/ *verb*
**1** to make someone angry or annoyed: *His bad jokes are starting to irritate me.*
**2** to make a part of your body painful and sore: *Cigarette smoke irritates your lungs, making you cough.*
—**irritating** *adjective* making you feel angry or annoyed
—**irritated** *adjective* feeling angry or annoyed
—**irritant** *noun* something that keeps you angry or annoyed for a long period of time
—**irritation** /ˌɪrəˈteɪʃən/ *noun* the feeling of being angry or annoyed

**IRS** *noun*
**the IRS** (**the Internal Revenue Service**) = the government organization in the U.S. that deals with taxes

**is** /z, s, əz; *strong* ɪz/ *verb*
the third person singular of the present tense of BE

**Is·lam** /ˈɪzlɑm/ *noun*
the Muslim religion, which was started by Muhammad and whose holy book is the Koran
—**Islamic** /ɪzˈlɑmɪk/ *adjective* relating to the religion of Islam or to Muslim people and countries: *Their system is based on Islamic law.*

**is·land** /ˈaɪlənd/ *noun*
a piece of land completely surrounded by water: *a small island off the coast of Florida | You can take the ferry to Staten Island.*

[**ORIGIN:** From the old English word *igland*, from *ig*, which means "island" and the word "land."]

**isle** /aɪl/ *noun*
an island: *a desert isle | the Isle of Skye*

**is·n't** /ˈɪzənt/ *verb*
the short form of "is not": *He isn't here right now, but he'll be back in an hour.*

**i·so·late** Ac /ˈaɪsəˌleɪt/ *verb*
to keep one person or thing separate from others: *The heavy snow has completely isolated the mountain town.*

**i·so·lat·ed** Ac /ˈaɪsəˌleɪtɪd/ *adjective*
**1** far away from other things: *They lived on an isolated farm and had no neighbors.*
**2** feeling alone or unable to meet or speak to other people: *She did not know anyone and felt isolated at school.*
**3** an isolated action or event happens only once and is not likely to happen again: *The attack is not an isolated incident – there were two other attacks earlier this week.*

**i·sos·ce·les** /aɪˌsɑsəliz/ *adjective*
an isosceles TRIANGLE has two sides that are the same length and one side that is a different length → see picture at **triangle**

**Is·rae·li** /ɪzˈreɪli/ *noun*
someone from Israel
—**Israeli** *adjective* relating to Israel

**is·sue¹** Ac /ˈɪʃu/ *noun*
**1** a subject or problem that people discuss: *The cost of health care is an issue that affects everyone. | They will discuss this issue at the meeting.*
**2** a magazine or newspaper that is sold on a particular day or in a particular week or month: *The article is in this month's issue of the magazine.*

**issue²** Ac *verb* (*formal*)
**1** to make an official statement, or to give an order or a warning: *The mayor issued a statement saying that the school would close.*
**2** to officially provide someone with documents or equipment: *The U.S. will not issue a visa to people with a criminal record.*

**isth·mus** /ˈɪsməs/ *noun*
a narrow piece of land, with water on both sides, that connects two larger pieces of land: *The Panama Canal cuts through the Isthmus of Panama to connect the Atlantic and Pacific Oceans.*

**it** /ɪt/ *pronoun*
**1** used to talk about something you have already mentioned or something that people already know about: *"Did you bring your umbrella?" "No, I left it at home." | Don't get angry with me. It wasn't my fault.*
**2** used to talk about the situation that someone is in now: *I can't stand it any longer. I'm leaving.*
**3** used as the subject or object of a sentence when the real subject or object is later in the sentence: *It costs less to drive than to take the bus.*
**4** used with the verb "be" to talk about the weather, time, or distance: *It's cold today. | It was late by the time we got home. | It's not far to the beach from here.*
**5** used to talk about a child or animal when you do not know whether it is male or female: *"Marilyn had a baby." "Is it a boy or girl?"*

**IT** *noun*
(**information technology**) the study or use of computers and other electronic equipment to store and use information

**I·tal·ian** /ɪˈtælyən/ *noun*
**1** someone from Italy
**2** the language spoken in Italy
—**Italian** *adjective* relating to Italy: *Italian food | Paola's grandmother is Italian.*

**i·tal·ics** /ɪˈtælɪks/ *plural noun*
a style of printed letters that lean to the right: *The examples in this dictionary are written in italics.*
—**italic** *adjective* printed in italics: *Italic characters lean to the right.*
[ORIGIN: From the Latin word *italicus*, which means "Italian." These letters were introduced by an Italian printer in 1501.]

**itch** /ɪtʃ/ *noun*
**1** an unpleasant feeling on your skin that makes you want to rub it with your nails: *I have an itch on my back – can you scratch it for me?*
**2** (*informal*) a strong desire to do or have something: *I've got this itch to go to Australia. I think it would be a lot of fun.*
—**itch** *verb* to feel an itch: *My arms itched where the wool touched them.*

**itch·y** /ˈɪtʃi/ *adjective*
if your skin is itchy, it feels unpleasant in a way that makes you want to rub your nails across it: *My skin felt dry and itchy.*

I

**it'd** /ˈɪtəd/
**1** the short form of "it would": *It'd be more fun if we both went.*
**2** the short form of "it had": *It'd been a warm summer, but now it was growing cooler.*

**i·tem** Ac /ˈaɪtəm/ *noun*
**1** a single thing in a set, group, or list: *There were several items of clothing on the floor. | I checked every item on the list.*
**2** a single piece of news in a newspaper, on television, or on the radio: *I heard a news item about his arrest on the radio.*
→ see Thesaurus box at **thing**
[ORIGIN: 1500-1600 From a Latin word for "also." This word was used before each thing in a list.]

**i·tin·er·ar·y** /aɪˈtɪnəˌreri/ *noun* (plural **itineraries**)
a list of the places you will visit on a trip: *The first place on our itinerary is Las Vegas, and after that we go to the Grand Canyon.*

**it'll** /ˈɪtl/
the short form of "it will": *It'll be fun, I promise.*

**its** /ɪts/ *adjective*
belonging to a thing, animal, or baby that has been mentioned: *The dog was barking and wagging its tail. | The school has had some problems with its computer systems.*

**it's** /ɪts/
**1** the short form of "it is": *It's snowing!*
**2** the short form of "it has": *It's been so hot all week.*

**USAGE: it's, its**

**It's** means "it is" or "it has": *I like this poem because it's funny. | I love history – it's always been my favorite subject.*

**Its** means "belonging to it": *He put the game back in its box.*

"Tom's" can mean "belonging to Tom," but "it's" does not mean "belonging to it."

**it·self** /ɪtˈself/ *pronoun*
**1** used to show that a thing, animal, or baby is affected by its own action: *Our country has the right to defend itself. | The cat was licking itself. | A baby cannot look after itself.*
**2** **in itself** = only the thing mentioned, and not anything else: *You finished the race, and that in itself is fantastic, even if you didn't win.*
**3** used to emphasize a particular thing: *The acting is good, but the movie itself is a little slow.*

**I've** /aɪv/
the short form of "I have": *I've never been to New York.*

**i·vo·ry** /ˈaɪvəri/ *noun*
the hard smooth white substance that an ELEPHANT's long teeth are made of
—**ivory** *adjective* made of ivory: *an ivory bracelet*

**i·vy** /ˈaɪvi/ *noun*
a plant with dark green shiny leaves that grows up the walls of buildings: *They lived in a old house, with ivy covering the walls.*

**ˈIvy ˌLeague** *adjective*
relating to a group of eight important and respected colleges in the northeast of the U.S.: *an Ivy League school*

# Jj

**jab¹** /dʒæb/ *verb* (**jabbed**, **jabbing**)
to quickly push something pointed into someone or something: *Mom, Laurie just jabbed her finger in my eye!*

**jab²** *noun*
a sudden hard push or hit: *I gave him a jab in the ribs with my finger to get his attention.*

**jack** /dʒæk/ *noun*
**1** a piece of equipment used for lifting a car off the ground: *She got the jack out of the car and started to change the flat tire.*
**2** a card used in card games, which has a picture of a young man on it: *the jack of clubs*

**jack·al** /ˈdʒækəl/ *noun*
a wild animal like a dog that lives in Africa and Asia

**jack·et** /ˈdʒækɪt/ *noun*
a short light coat: *a black leather jacket* → see picture on page **A6**
[**ORIGIN:** 1400-1500 From the French word *jaque*, which means "short coat." This may come from the first name Jacques, used to refer to a poor farmer, or from the Spanish word *jaco*, which means "armor covering the chest and back."]

**jack·ham·mer** /ˈdʒækˌhæmɚ/ *noun*
a large powerful tool used for breaking up rock or the surface of a road

**ˈjack-in-the-ˌbox** *noun*
a box with a toy person or animal inside that jumps up when you open the lid of the box

**jack·knife** /ˈdʒæknaɪf/ *noun* (plural **jackknives** /ˈdʒæknaɪvz/)
a knife with a blade that folds into its handle

**jack-o'-lan·tern** /ˈdʒæk ə ˌlæntən/ *noun*
a PUMPKIN with holes cut into it to make it look like a face. It usually has a light inside it and is used at HALLOWEEN.

**jack·pot** /ˈdʒækpɑt/ *noun*
**1** a very large amount of money that you can win in a game: *If you win the jackpot, you get $55 million.*
**2 hit the jackpot** = to win a lot of money or be very lucky: *He hit the jackpot when he married Kim – she's just right for him.*

**Ja·cuz·zi** /dʒəˈkuzi/ *noun* (*trademark*)
a large heated bathtub for several people to sit in. It makes bubbles that help to relax your muscles.

**jade** /dʒeɪd/ *noun*
a green stone used especially for jewelry
[**ORIGIN:** 1500-1600 From French, from the Spanish phrase *piedra de la ijada*, which means "stone of the lower back." It was believed that jade cures pain in the kidneys.]

**jag·ged** /ˈdʒægɪd/ *adjective*
having a rough uneven edge with a lot of sharp points: *The jagged rocks along the coast are a danger to ships.*

**jag·uar** /ˈdʒægwɑr/ *noun*
a large wild cat with yellow fur and black spots that lives mainly in Central and South America
[**ORIGIN:** 1600-1700 From Portuguese, from the Guarani word *yaguara* and the Tupi word *jaguara*, which probably meant "large animal that eats meat." Guarani and Tupi are languages used by the native people of Paraguay and Brazil.]

**jail** /dʒeɪl/ *noun*
a place where criminals are sent as a punishment for a crime: *He was sentenced to 10 years in jail for stealing.* | *You could go to jail for doing that.* **SYNONYM: prison**
—**jail** *verb* to put someone in prison: *The judge jailed him for stealing cars.*
[**ORIGIN:** 1200-1300 From the old French word *jaiole*, from the Latin word *caveola*, from *cavea*, which means "cage."]

**jam¹** /dʒæm/ *verb* (**jammed**, **jamming**)
**1** to push something into a small space using a lot of force: *I jammed all the books I needed into my backpack.*

J

2 if a machine jams, it stops working because a part of it is stuck: *The copy machine kept jamming, so she got someone to repair it.*
3 if a lot of people or things jam a place, they completely fill it and it is difficult for them to move: *It was 5:00 p.m. and the freeway was jammed with cars.*
4 if a door jams, it becomes stuck and will not open or close: *The bathroom door had jammed, trapping her inside.*

**jam²** *noun*
1 a thick sticky sweet food made from fruit that you eat on bread. Jam has small pieces of fruit in it: *toast with butter and jam*
2 **be in a jam/get into a jam** (*informal*) = to be or become involved in a difficult or bad situation: *Sarah, I'm in a jam – could you help me out?*
3 a situation in which something is stuck somewhere: *There is a paper jam in the fax machine.*
4 a TRAFFIC JAM

**ˌjam-ˈpacked** *adjective* (*informal*)
completely full of people or things: *The mall was jam-packed with people.*

**jan·gle** /ˈdʒæŋgəl/ *verb*
if metal objects jangle, they make a noise when they hit each other: *The keys jangled in his pocket.*

**jan·i·tor** /ˈdʒænətɚ/ *noun*
someone whose job is to clean and take care of a large building: *the school janitor*
**SYNONYM: custodian**

**Jan·u·ar·y** /ˈdʒænyuˌeri/ *noun* (*written abbreviation*: **Jan.**)
the first month of the year, between December and February: *We got married on January 12, 2000.* | *It's very cold here in January.* | *We moved to Texas last January.*
[**ORIGIN:** probably 1100-1200 From Janus, the Roman god of doorways. January is the first month, which is like a doorway into a new year.]

**Jap·a·nese¹** /ˌdʒæpəˈniz/ *adjective*
from Japan: *Japanese students*

**Japanese²** *noun*
1 the language used in Japan
2 **the Japanese** = the people of Japan

**jar** /dʒɑr/ *noun*
a round glass container with a lid, used in order to store food: *a jar of peanut butter*
[**ORIGIN:** 1500-1600 From the old French word *jarra*, from the Arabic word *jarrah*, which means "pot for carrying water."]

**jar·gon** /ˈdʒɑrgən/ *noun*
technical words and phrases that people doing the same type of work use, which other people find difficult to understand: *Legal jargon can be confusing.*
→ see Thesaurus box at **language**

**jav·e·lin** /ˈdʒævəlɪn/ *noun*
1 **the javelin** = a sport in which you throw a long pointed stick as far as you can
2 the long pointed stick used in this sport

**jaw** /dʒɔ/ *noun*
1 the bottom part of your face: *He had been hit in the jaw while playing hockey.* → see picture on page **A2**
2 one of the parts that contain an animal's or a person's teeth: *The crocodile opened its jaws and we could see all its teeth.*

**jay** /dʒeɪ/ *noun*
a type of bird that is noisy and bright in color

**jay·walk·ing** /ˈdʒeɪˌwɔkɪŋ/ *noun*
the act of walking across a street at a place where it is dangerous to cross: *The police officer fined me for jaywalking and told me to cross at the corner.*
—**jaywalk** *verb* to cross a street at a place where it is dangerous to cross
—**jaywalker** *noun* someone who jaywalks

J

**jazz** /dʒæz/ *noun*
a type of popular music. Jazz musicians often change the music or add notes as they play

**jeal·ous** /ˈdʒeləs/ *adjective*
**1** feeling unhappy because someone else has something that you wish you had: *He was jealous of his brother's nice car.* **SYNONYM: envious**
**2** feeling angry or unhappy because the person you love likes another person, or another person likes the person you love: *It makes me jealous when my boyfriend dances with other women.* → see picture on page **A23**
—**jealousy** *noun* a feeling of being jealous

**jeans** /dʒinz/ *noun*
pants made from DENIM (=a strong, usually blue, cotton cloth): *She was wearing a pair of jeans and a T-shirt.* → see picture on page **A6**
[**ORIGIN:** 1800-1900 From the French phrase *jean fustian*, which means "strong cloth from Genoa." Genoa is an Italian city.]

**Jeep** /dʒip/ *noun* (*trademark*)
a type of car made for traveling over rough ground

**jeer** /dʒɪr/ *verb*
to laugh and shout rude things at someone in order to show that you do not respect him or her: *The crowd began to jeer at the soldiers and throw rocks.*
—**jeer** *noun* something rude that you shout at someone

**Jell-O** /ˈdʒeloʊ/ *noun* (*trademark*)
a soft sweet food made from fruit juice, that shakes when you move it

**jel·ly** /ˈdʒeli/ *noun*
a thick sticky sweet food made from fruit that you eat on bread: *a peanut butter and jelly sandwich*
[**ORIGIN:** 1300-1400 From the French word *gelee*, from *geler*, which means "to freeze."]

**jel·ly·bean** /ˈdʒeliˌbin/ *noun*
a small soft candy that is shaped like a bean

**jel·ly·fish** /ˈdʒeliˌfɪʃ/ *noun*
a sea animal that has a round transparent body with parts hanging down that can sting you

**jeop·ard·ize** /ˈdʒepɚˌdaɪz/ *verb* (*formal*)
to risk losing or destroying something that is valuable or important: *The injury could jeopardize his career in football.*

**jerk¹** /dʒɚk/ *verb*
to move with a sudden quick movement: *"Don't touch me," she said, jerking her arm away.*

**jerk²** *noun*
**1** (*informal*) someone, especially a man, who does stupid or annoying things: *Your brother's a real jerk – he says such rude things!*
**2** a sudden quick movement: *The car stopped with a jerk, and I hit my forehead on the windshield.*
—**jerky** *adjective* stopping and starting suddenly and roughly: *The elevator's jerky movements frightened me.*

**jer·sey** /ˈdʒɚzi/ *noun* (plural **jerseys**)
a shirt worn as part of a sports uniform: *The team was wearing red and white jerseys.*

**Je·sus** /ˈdʒizəs/ (*also* ˌ**Jesus** ˈ**Christ**)
the person who Christians believe was the son of God, and whose life and ideas Christianity is based on

**jet** /dʒet/ *noun*
**1** a fast airplane with a special type of engine that pushes out hot gases: *Military jets flew overhead.*
**2** a thin stream of liquid or gas that comes out of a small hole very quickly: *The fountain sends a jet of water up into the air.*

ˈ**jet lag** *noun*
the feeling of being very tired after traveling a long distance in an airplane to a part of the world where the time is different
—**jet-lagged** *adjective* feeling the effects of jet lag

**jew·el** /ˈdʒuəl/ *noun*
a small valuable stone, such as a DIAMOND

> **WORD FAMILY: jewel**
> **jewel** *noun* | **jewels** *plural noun* | **jewelry** *noun* | **jeweler** *noun*

**jew·el·er** /ˈdʒuəlɚ/ *noun*
someone who buys, sells, makes, or repairs jewelry

J

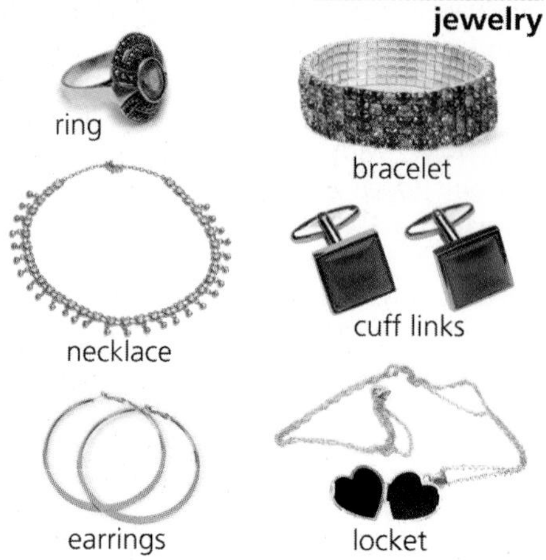


**jew·el·ry** /ˈdʒuəlri/ *noun*
small things that you wear for decoration, such as rings and NECKLACEs: *She was wearing a gold necklace and other expensive jewelry.*

**jew·els** /ˈdʒuəlz/ *plural noun*
another word for jewelry

**Jew·ish** /ˈdʒuɪʃ/ *adjective*
relating to Judaism
—**Jew** *noun* someone whose religion is Judaism

J

**jig·gle** /ˈdʒɪgəl/ *verb (informal)*
to move from side to side with short quick movements: *I jiggled the baby up and down on my knee.*

**jig·saw puz·zle** /ˈdʒɪgsɔ ˌpʌzəl/ (*also* **puzzle**) *noun*
a picture that has been cut into many pieces. You put the pieces together to make the whole picture.

**jin·gle** /ˈdʒɪŋgəl/ *verb*
to shake small metal objects together so that they produce a noise: *I could hear coins jingling in his pocket.*

**jinx¹** /dʒɪŋks/ *noun*
someone or something that brings bad luck

**jinx²** *verb*
to make someone have bad luck: *I don't want to talk about winning – I'm afraid I'll jinx myself.*
—**jinxed** *adjective* having a lot of bad luck

**job** Ac /dʒɑb/ *noun*
**1** work that you do regularly in order to earn money: *Dad's always telling me to get a job and earn some money.* | *He applied for a job at the bank.*

**USAGE: job**

Do not say "What is your job?" or "What is your work?" Say *"What do you do?"* or *"What kind of work do you do?"*

**THESAURUS: job**

Your **job** is the work you do regularly to earn money: *I got a job in a music store.*

**Work** is used in a more general way to talk about the job you do: *What kind of work do you do?*

**Position** is a more formal word for a job in a particular organization: *He was offered a teaching position at the college.*

**Occupation** is a word used mainly on official forms to mean your job: *Please give your name, age, and occupation.*

A **profession** is a job for which you need special education and training: *the legal profession*

Your **career** is the work you do for most of your life: *I'm interested in a career in journalism.*

A **vocation** is a job that you do because you feel you are the right type of person to do it: *For me, nursing is a vocation, not just a job.*

**2 on the job** = while at work, or while doing your job: *He was injured on the job, so his employer paid for his treatment.*
**3** something that you are responsible for doing: *It's my job to watch my little brother.*
**4** something that you have to do without being paid: *I have a lot of little jobs to do at home this weekend, like cleaning out the garage.* SYNONYM: **task**
**5 do a good/great/bad, etc. job** = to do something well or badly: *You did a great job on the picture – it really looks like Sarah.*

**jock·ey** /ˈdʒɑki/ *noun*
someone who rides horses in races

**jog** /dʒɑg/ *verb* (**jogged**, **jogging**)
to run at a slow steady speed for exercise:

*Julie jogs in the park every morning.* → see picture on page **A4**

—**jog** *noun* a slow steady run

—**jogging** *noun* the activity of running at a slow steady speed: *I went jogging.*

—**jogger** *noun* someone who jogs

**join** /dʒɔɪn/ *verb*

**1** to become a member of an organization, society, or group: *He joined the army when he was nineteen.*

**2** (*also* **join in**) to begin to take part in an activity that other people are involved in: *Other kids started to join in the laughter.* | *More police arrived to join the search.*

**3** to go somewhere in order to do something with someone else: *Why don't you join us for dinner?*

**4** to do something with other people, as a group: *Please join with me in welcoming tonight's speaker.*

**5** to be connected or fastened together: *This is where the two rivers join to form the Ohio River.*

**joint¹** /dʒɔɪnt/ *adjective*

involving two or more people, or owned or shared by two or more people: *The two senators had a joint news conference.* | *My husband and I have a joint bank account.*

—**jointly** *adverb* in a way that involves two or more people: *The company is jointly owned.*

**joint**

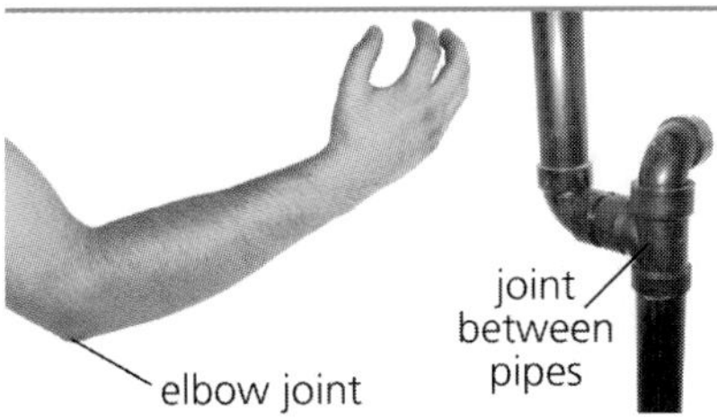


**joint²** *noun*

**1** a part of the body where two bones meet, that can bend: *the elbow joint*

**2** (*informal*) a cheap restaurant or club: *She works in a hamburger joint.*

**3** a place where two parts of something are connected or joined together: *One of the pipe joints was leaking.*

**joke¹** /dʒoʊk/ *noun*

**1** something funny that you say to make people laugh: *We laughed and told jokes all night.* | *Don't make jokes about your mother!*

**2 be a joke** (*informal*) = to be completely stupid or unreasonable: *I thought his idea was a joke, but the teacher loved it.*

**WORD FAMILY: joke**

**joke** *noun* | **joke** *verb* | **joker** *noun* | **jokingly** *adverb*

**joke²** *verb*

to say things that are intended to be funny: *I saw him in the hall talking and joking with my girlfriend.*

—**jokingly** *adverb* as a joke: *She jokingly said her brother was a lot like Bart Simpson, the cartoon character.*

—**joker** *noun* someone who likes to tell jokes and make people laugh

**jol·ly** /ˈdʒɑli/ *adjective* (**jollier**, **jolliest**)

happy and friendly: *Santa Claus is a jolly old man with a long white beard.*

**jolt¹** /dʒoʊlt/ *noun*

**1** a sudden surprise or shock: *The news came as a jolt to the whole family.*

**2** a sudden rough or violent movement: *He fell and hit the ground with a jolt.*

**jolt²** *verb*

**1** to make something move suddenly and roughly: *The earthquake jolted southern California.*

**2** to give someone a sudden shock: *She was jolted awake by a loud bang.*

**jos·tle** /ˈdʒɑsəl/ *verb*

to push roughly against other people in a crowd, usually so that you can get somewhere or do something before them: *People in the crowd jostled for a better view of the field.*

**jot** /dʒɑt/ *verb* (**jotted**, **jotting**)

**PHRASAL VERB**

**jot something down**

to write something quickly on a piece of paper: *I jotted down her address and phone number.*

**jour·nal** Ac /ˈdʒɚnl/ *noun*

**1** a book in which you write about your thoughts and feelings or the things that happen to you each day: *He wrote several pages in his journal that night to record everything that had happened.* **SYNONYM: diary**

**2** a serious magazine or newspaper produced

for professional people, such as doctors: *They wrote about their discovery in a scientific journal.*

**jour·nal·ist** /ˈdʒɚnlɪst/ *noun*
someone who writes reports for newspapers, magazines, television, or radio: *Several journalists asked the president the same question.* **SYNONYM: reporter** → see picture on page **A17**
—**journalism** *noun* the job or activity of writing reports for newspapers, magazines, television, or radio: *During his career in journalism, he has worked for newspapers and on television.*

**jour·ney** /ˈdʒɚni/ *noun*
a trip from one place to another, especially over a long distance: *The book is about the two men's journey across North America.*
→ see Thesaurus box at **travel²**
[**ORIGIN:** 1100-1200 From the old French word *journee*, which means "a day's journey," from *jour*, meaning "day."]

**joy** /dʒɔɪ/ *noun*
**1** a feeling of great happiness and pleasure: *You could see the joy on the kids' faces when they saw the puppies.*
**2** something or someone that gives you happiness or pleasure: *The car is a joy to drive.*
—**joyful** *adjective* very happy or likely to make people happy: *The birth of a child is a joyful experience.*
—**joyous** *adjective* very happy or likely to make people happy: *The day she came home from the hospital was a joyous occasion for the family.*
[**ORIGIN:** 1100-1200 From the French word *joie*, from the Latin word *gaudia*.]

**joy·stick** /ˈdʒɔɪˌstɪk/ *noun*
a handle that you use to control an aircraft or a computer game

**Jr.**
the written abbreviation of **Junior**

**Ju·da·ism** /ˈdʒudiˌɪzəm/ *noun*
the Jewish religion. Judaism is based on books called the Hebrew Scriptures, which include many of the books that are in the Old Testament of the Christian BIBLE.

**judge¹** /dʒʌdʒ/ *noun*
**1** the person in control of a court who decides how criminals should be punished: *The judge gave Simmons six years in jail for the crime.* → see picture on page **A17**
**2** someone who decides the result of a competition: *The judges gave her high scores for her ice skating performance.*
**3 a good/bad judge of something** = someone whose opinion about something is usually right or wrong: *My father is a good judge of character and he thinks you're a fool.*

**judge²** *verb*
**1** to decide something or form an opinion about someone or something: *Judging from her expression, I'd say she was angry.* | *You will be judged on how many correct answers you give.*
**2** to decide the result of a competition: *Kim and I will be judging the writing competition.*

**judg·ment** (*also* **judgement**) /ˈdʒʌdʒmənt/ *noun*
**1** an opinion that you reach after thinking about something: *It's too early to make a judgment; we need more information.*
**2** the ability to make good decisions about situations or people: *I trust your judgment, and I know you will make the right decision.*
**3** an official decision made by a judge or a court of law: *Justice Reynolds listened to all the evidence before announcing the court's final judgment.*

**ju·di·cial** /dʒuˈdɪʃəl/ *adjective*
**1** relating to a court of law or a judge: *He thinks that the judicial process is affected by having cameras in courts.*
**2 the judicial branch** = the part of a government that consists of all the judges in a country
—**judiciary** *noun* the judicial branch

**ju·do** /ˈdʒudoʊ/ *noun*
a sport, originally from Japan, in which you try to throw your opponent onto the ground
[**ORIGIN:** 1800-1900 A Japanese word meaning "gentle way."]

**jug** /dʒʌg/ *noun*
a large container for liquids that has a small opening at the top and a handle on the side: *She bought a gallon jug of milk.*

**jug·gle** /ˈdʒʌgəl/ *verb*

**1** to keep three or more objects moving through the air by throwing them up and catching them: *He could juggle three tennis balls.*

**2** to try to do two or more jobs or activities at the same time: *He has to juggle three jobs to support his family.*

—**juggler** *noun* someone who juggles objects in the air

**[ORIGIN:** 1300-1400 From the old French word *jogleour*, which means "joker or entertainer," from the Latin word *jocus*, meaning "joke."**]**

**juice** /dʒus/ *noun*

**1** the liquid that comes from fruit and vegetables, or a drink made from this: *a glass of orange juice*

**2** the liquid that comes out of meat when it is cooked

**juic·y** /ˈdʒusi/ *adjective* (**juicier**, **juiciest**)

containing a lot of juice: *a juicy peach*

—**juiciness** *noun* the fact of containing a lot of juice

**juke·box** /ˈdʒukˌbɑks/ *noun*

a machine that plays music when you put money in it. Jukeboxes are usually in places such as bars and restaurants.

**Ju·ly** /dʒʊˈlaɪ/ *noun* (*written abbreviation*: **Jul.**)

the seventh month of the year, between June and August: *Her birthday is on July 9.* | *Henry started working here in July.* | *Next July is my mom's 40th birthday.*

**[ORIGIN:** probably 1000-1100 From Julius Caesar (100-44 B.C.), a Roman political leader, whose birthday was in this month.**]**

**jum·ble** /ˈdʒʌmbəl/ *noun*

a group of things mixed together in a messy way: *There was a jumble of books and magazines next to his bed.*

—**jumble** *verb* to mix things together in a messy way

**jum·bo** /ˈdʒʌmboʊ/ *adjective*

larger than other things of the same type: *I ordered a plate of jumbo shrimp.*

**jump**[1] /dʒʌmp/ *verb*

**1** to push yourself up into the air or over something using your legs: *Her horse jumped over the fence easily.* | *Some fans tried to jump onto the stage with the band.* | *Karen was waving her arms and jumping up and down with excitement.*

**THESAURUS: jump**

**skip** to move forward with little jumps from one foot to the other: *Tammy skipped along ahead of her mother.*

**hop** to move by jumping on one leg or by making short quick jumps on both legs: *A frog hopped into the pool.*

**leap** to jump high into the air or to jump over something: *The dog leaped over the fence.*

**dive** to jump into water with your head and arms going in first: *The swimmers dived into the water.*

**spring** to jump or move somewhere suddenly and quickly: *He sprang out of bed and ran downstairs.*

**2** to drop down from a place that is above the ground: *The cat jumped down and came to meet us.* | *Kids were jumping off the wall.*
**3** to move somewhere quickly or suddenly: *Paul jumped up from his chair to help me with the grocery bags.*
**4** if an amount jumps, it increases suddenly and by a large amount: *The population of Arizona has jumped 500% since 1950.*
**5 make someone jump** = if something makes you jump, it frightens you and your body makes a sudden movement: *A branch touched my arm in the dark and made me jump.*
**6 jump to conclusions** = to form an opinion about something before you have all the facts: *Don't jump to conclusions – we don't have all the information yet.*

**PHRASAL VERB**

**jump at something**
to eagerly accept the chance to do something: *Heidi jumped at the chance to go to Harvard.*

**jump²** *noun*
**1** a movement in which you push yourself up into the air using your legs
**2** a movement in which you drop from a place that is above the ground: *a parachute jump*
**3** a sudden large increase in an amount: *There's been another big jump in gas prices; they went up by 20 cents.*

**jump·er** /ˈdʒʌmpɚ/ *noun*
a dress with no sleeves that is worn over a shirt

**ˈjump rope** *noun*
a piece of rope that you turn and jump over as a game or for exercise

**jump·y** /ˈdʒʌmpi/ *adjective*
worried or nervous because you are expecting something bad to happen: *We'd heard that there might be an attack, and everyone was jumpy.* **SYNONYM: nervous**

**junc·tion** /ˈdʒʌŋkʃən/ *noun*
a place where two roads or railroad tracks meet: *The bakery is near the junction of Highland Avenue and Lowell Street.* **SYNONYM: intersection**

**June** /dʒun/ *noun* (*written abbreviation*: **Jun.**)
the sixth month of the year, between May and July: *Can you come to our party on June 24?* | *Janet was born in June.* | *Last June I got my driver's license.*
[**ORIGIN:** probably 1100-1200 From Juno, the Roman queen of the gods.]

**jun·gle** /ˈdʒʌŋgəl/ *noun*
a tropical forest with many trees and large plants growing very close together: *the Amazon jungle*
→ see Thesaurus box at **tree**
[**ORIGIN:** 1700-1800 From the Hindi word *jangal*, which means "forest."]

**ˈjungle ˌgym** *noun*
a metal or wooden structure that children climb and play on

**jun·ior¹** /ˈdʒunyɚ/ *noun*
a student in the third year of HIGH SCHOOL or college: *I'm a junior at Van Nuys High School.*
[**ORIGIN:** 1200-1300 From the Latin word for "younger."]

**junior²** *adjective*
**1 Junior** (*written abbreviation*: **Jr.**) = used after the name of a man who has the same name as his father: *Martin Luther King, Jr.*
**2** lower in rank or younger: *Junior army officers receive their orders from the senior officer.* | *Children under 12 can join the junior basketball team.* **ANTONYM: senior**

**ˌjunior ˈcollege** *noun*
a college that people can go to, usually for two years, in order to learn a skill or to prepare to go to another college or university SYNONYM: **community college**

**ˌjunior ˈhigh school** (*also* **ˌjunior ˈhigh**) *noun*
a school in the U.S. and Canada for students who are between 12 and 14 or 15 years old

**junk** /dʒʌŋk/ *noun*
old or unwanted things that have no use or value: *Let's have a yard sale and sell all that junk in the garage.*

**ˈjunk food** *noun* (*informal*)
food that is not healthy because it has a lot of fat or sugar: *He just eats junk food like French fries and hamburgers.*

**ˈjunk mail** *noun*
mail that companies send to your house in order to advertise a product

**Ju·pi·ter** /ˈdʒupətɚ/ *noun*
the fifth PLANET from the Sun. Jupiter is the largest planet in our SOLAR SYSTEM.

**ju·ror** /ˈdʒʊrɚ/ *noun*
a member of a jury: *The jurors decided he was innocent.*

**ju·ry** /ˈdʒʊri/ *noun* (plural **juries**)
a group of 12 people who listen to a case in court and decide whether someone is guilty of a crime

**just[1]** /dʒʌst/ *adverb*
**1** exactly: *Jack's twin brother looks just like him.* | *These pants fit just right. They're perfect.* | *Just then the bus came around the corner.*
**2** only: *You can't blame him, he's just a kid.* | *I'll be okay – I just need a good night's sleep.* | *He's making just enough money to pay his rent and bills, with nothing left over.*
**3** if something has just happened, it happened only a short time ago: *I just got back from Maria's house two minutes ago.* | *He just left, but he should be back soon.*
→ see Thesaurus box at **recently**
**4 just before/after** = only a short time before or after something else: *Theresa got home just before us.*
**5 just about** (*informal*) = almost: *I go to the gym just about every day.*
**6 be just about to do something** = if you are just about to do something, you are going to do it soon: *I was just about to call you.*
**7 just (barely)** = if something just happens, it does happen, but it almost did not: *Kurt just barely made it home before the storm.*
**8 just a minute/second/moment** = used in order to ask someone to wait for a short time while you do something: *Just a second – I'm on the phone.*
**9** used for emphasizing something you are saying: *I just knew he was going to be late again.* | *Just be quiet, will you?*

**just[2]** *adjective* (*formal*)
morally right and fair: *He received a just punishment for his crimes.* ANTONYM: **unjust**

**jus·tice** /ˈdʒʌstɪs/ *noun*
**1** the action of treating people in a way that is fair and right: *He murdered their daughter, and they want justice.* ANTONYM: **injustice**
**2** the laws of a country and the way they are used: *the criminal justice system*
**3** a judge in a court of law: *a Supreme Court justice*

**ˌjustice of the ˈpeace** *noun*
someone who judges law cases that are not serious, and who can perform marriages

**jus·ti·fy** Ac /ˈdʒʌstəˌfaɪ/ *verb* (**justified, justifies**)
to give a reason for doing something, when other people think what you have done is wrong: *How can she justify spending money on shoes, when she can't pay the rent?*
—**justifiable** *adjective* an action that is justifiable is done for good reasons: *Can killing someone ever be justifiable?*
—**justification** *noun* a reason you give for doing something, when other people think what you have done is wrong: *Her justification for taking the money was that the people she stole it from were rich.*

**ju·ve·nile** /ˈdʒuvənl/ *adjective*
relating to children younger than 16. This word is used only in legal language: *There has been an increase in juvenile crime.*
—**juvenile** *noun* a child younger than 16

**ˌjuvenile deˈlinquent** *noun*
a person under the age of 18 who breaks rules or laws

J

# Kk

**K** /keɪ/
**1** (*informal*) 1,000: *He earns $50K* (=$50,000) *a year.*
**2** the written abbreviation of **kilometer**: *a 10K race*
**3** the written abbreviation of **kilobyte**

**ka·leid·o·scope** /kəˈlaɪdəˌskoʊp/ *noun*
a tube with mirrors and pieces of colored glass in it, which you look into and turn to make different patterns
**[ORIGIN:** 1800-1900 From the Greek words *kalos*, *eidos*, and *skopein*, which mean "beautiful," "form," and "to look at."**]**

**kan·ga·roo** /ˌkæŋgəˈru/ *noun*
an Australian animal with strong back legs that it uses for jumping. A mother kangaroo carries her baby in a POUCH on her stomach after it is born.

karate

**ka·ra·te** /kəˈrɑti/ *noun*
a sport from Japan, in which you fight using your hands and feet to hit and kick your opponent
**[ORIGIN:** 1900-2000 A Japanese word meaning "empty hand."**]**

**kay·ak** /ˈkaɪæk/ *noun*
a small boat for one or two people, that has pointed ends and is covered so that water cannot get inside. You use a long PADDLE with two flat ends to move a kayak through the water.
**[ORIGIN:** 1700-1800 From the Inuit word *qajaq*.**]**

**keen** /kin/ *adjective*
very interested in something or wanting to do it: *He said he was keen to help.*
—**keenly** *adverb* with a lot of interest

**keep** /kip/ *verb* (**kept** /kept/)
**1** to continue to have something and not give it away or throw it out: *You can keep that sweater – it's too small for me.* | *I kept all his old letters.*
**2** to make someone or something continue to be in a place or situation: *The doctors kept him in the hospital for three days.* | *Put your coat on to keep warm.*
**3 keep (on) doing something** = to continue doing something: *He keeps making spelling mistakes.* | *It was noisy, but she kept on reading.*
**4** to store something in a place: *We keep the glasses in that cupboard there.*
**5 keep a record/diary/journal** = to write down information regularly: *The teacher keeps a record of who was in class each day.*
**6 keep your promise** = to do what you have promised to do: *He said he'd meet her at the restaurant, but he didn't keep his promise.*
**7 keep a secret** = to not tell anyone a secret: *"Can you keep a secret?" "Yes." "Well, Lisa told me she really likes Danny."*
**8** if food keeps, it stays fresh enough to be eaten: *Eggs keep better in the refrigerator.*
**9 Keep Out!** = used on signs to tell people that they are not allowed to go into a place

**PHRASAL VERB**

**keep up**
**1** to do something as fast or as well as someone else: *The little boy had to run to keep up with his sisters.*
**2 keep something up** = to continue to do something: *Keep up the good work!*

**keep·er** /ˈkipɚ/ *noun*
someone whose job is to take care of something: *The keepers at the zoo had to feed the baby penguins by hand.* | *a lighthouse keeper*

**ken·nel** /ˈkenl/ *noun*
a place where you can take your dog, so that someone will take care of it while you are away
**[ORIGIN:** 1300-1400 From the Latin word *canile*, from *canis*, which means "dog."**]**

**kept** /kept/ *verb*
the past tense and past participle of KEEP

**ker·nel** /ˈkɚnl/ *noun*
a seed that you can eat: *corn kernels*

**ker·o·sene** /ˈkerəˌsin/ *noun*
a type of oil that people burn for heat and light

**ketch·up** /ˈketʃəp/ *noun*
a red sauce made from tomatoes, that you can put on different foods, for example HAMBURGERs: *Do you want ketchup on your fries?*
**[ORIGIN:** 1600-1700 From the Malay word *kechap*, which was used for a spicy sauce made from fish.**]**

**ket·tle** /ˈketl/ *noun*
a metal container used for boiling and pouring water → see picture on page **A9**

**key¹** /ki/ *noun*
**1** a shaped piece of metal that you use to open or close a lock or to start the engine of a car: *She couldn't find her car keys.* | *Do you have a key to the front door?*
**2** one of the parts you press on something such as a computer keyboard: *Use the Control and S keys to save your work.* → see picture on page **A20**
**3** one of the parts you press on a musical instrument, such as a piano, to make a sound: *A piano has black and white keys.*
**4** a set of musical notes with a particular base note: *The song was in the key of C.*
**5 the key** = the most important thing that helps you do something: *Exercise is the key to a healthy life.*

**key²** *adjective*
very important and needed for success: *She's a key player on the basketball team. We couldn't win without her.*
→ see Thesaurus box at **important**

**key·board** /ˈkibɔrd/ *noun*
**1** a piece of computer equipment with parts that you press to do work on the computer → see picture on page **A20**
**2** the row of keys on a musical instrument, such as a piano, that you press to make a sound
**3** a musical instrument that is like a small electric piano. A keyboard can make the sounds of many different musical instruments.

**key·hole** /ˈkihoʊl/ *noun*
the hole in a lock that you put a key in

**ˈkey ring** *noun*
a metal ring that you keep keys on

**kg**
the written abbreviation of **kilogram**

**kha·ki** /ˈkæki/ *adjective, noun*
a light brown color
**[ORIGIN:** 1800-1900 From a Hindi word meaning "dusty or dust-colored," from *khak*, which means "dust."**]**

**kha·kis** /ˈkækiz/ *plural noun*
pants that are a light brown color

**kick¹** /kɪk/ *verb*
**1** to hit something with your foot: *Juan kicked the ball into the goal.* → see picture on page **A5**
**2** to move your legs in the air: *The baby was kicking his legs.*
**PHRASAL VERBS**
**kick off** (*informal*)
to start an event: *The Cubs kicked off the baseball season with a win against the Cincinnati Reds.*
**kick someone out** (*informal*)
to make someone leave a place: *Sean was kicked out of school for cheating.*

**kick²** *noun*
**1** an act of hitting something with your foot: *Evan's kick was good, and we scored the extra point.*
**2** (*informal*) a strong feeling of excitement or pleasure: *He gets a kick out of hearing the kids laugh at his jokes.*

**kick·off** /ˈkɪk-ɔf/ *noun*
**1** the time when a game of football or SOCCER starts: *The stadium opens at 2:00 and kickoff is at 3:00.*
**2** the first kick in a game of football or SOCCER

**kid¹** /kɪd/ *noun*
**1** a child: *The kids were playing outside.* | *"Do you have any kids?" "Yes, I have two sons."*
**2** a young goat
→ see Thesaurus box at **child**
**[ORIGIN:** 1100-1200 From the Norse word *kith*, which means "young goat." Norse was a language used in Scandinavian countries.**]**

**kid²** *verb* (**kidded, kidding**) (*informal*)
**1** to say something that is not true, as a joke: *"Did you really eat all those cookies?" "No, I was just kidding!"* | *"The bear came right into our campsite!" "You're kidding!"*

**2 no kidding** = **a)** used when you agree with what someone says: *"He's always late." "No kidding!"* **b)** used when you are slightly surprised by what someone says: *"Her dad's an actor." "No kidding?"*

**kid·nap** /ˈkɪdnæp/ *verb* (**kidnapped, kidnapping** *also* **kidnaped, kidnaping**)
to take someone away using force: *The group kidnapped the son of a rich man and asked for money.*
—**kidnapper** *noun* someone who kidnaps people
—**kidnapping** *noun* the crime of kidnapping people
[ORIGIN: 1600-1700 From "kid," meaning "child," and the old word "nap," which meant "to take."]

**kid·ney** /ˈkɪdni/ *noun*
an organ in your body that cleans waste liquid from your blood and makes URINE. You have two kidneys. → see picture on page **A2**

**kill** /kɪl/ *verb*
**1** to make a person, plant, or animal die: *Her son was killed in the war.* | *If you don't water the plants, you'll kill them.*
**2** (*informal*) to be very angry at someone: *My mom will kill me if I'm late again.*

K

**kill·er** /ˈkɪlɚ/ *noun*
a person, animal, or thing that kills: *Police are still looking for the girl's killer.*

**ki·lo** /ˈkiloʊ/ *noun* (plural **kilos**)
an abbreviation of **kilogram**

**ki·lo·byte** /ˈkɪləˌbaɪt/ *noun* (*abbreviation*: **k**)
a unit for measuring computer information, which is around 1,000 BYTEs

**kil·o·gram** /ˈkɪləˌgræm/ (*also* **kilo**) *noun*, (*written abbreviation*: **kg**)
a unit for measuring weight, equal to 1,000 grams

**ki·lom·e·ter** /kɪˈlɑmətɚ/ *noun* (*written abbreviation*: **km**)
a unit for measuring length, equal to 1,000 meters
[ORIGIN: 1800-1900 From the Greek words *chilioi* and *metron*, which mean "thousand" and "measure."]

**kil·o·watt** /ˈkɪləˌwɑt/ *noun* (*written abbreviation*: **kW**)
a unit for measuring electrical power, equal to 1,000 WATTs

**kin** /kɪn/ *noun*
your family: *The police are trying to find the dead man's next of kin* (=closest relative).

**kind**[1] /kaɪnd/ *noun*
**1** a type of person or thing: *"What kind of dog is that?" "It's an English Sheepdog."* | *I like all kinds of music – hip hop, rock, jazz, country, and other kinds too.* **SYNONYMS: sort, type**
**2 kind of** (*informal*) = a little bit: *I felt kind of scared.* | *It's kind of hard to explain the story.* **SYNONYM: slightly**

**kind**[2] *adjective*
helpful, friendly, and nice to other people: *Our neighbors were very kind to us when we moved into our new house; they even made us dinner!*

**THESAURUS: kind**

**nice** friendly and kind: *My English teacher is really nice and gives us extra help if we need it.*

**considerate** (*formal*) a considerate person thinks about what other people feel or need: *Our neighbors are very considerate; they don't play their music too loud.*

**thoughtful** thinking of things you can do to make other people happy: *He brought her flowers when she wasn't feeling well, which was really thoughtful.*

**generous** kind because you give people money or presents: *It was very generous of Grandma to buy me a computer.*

—**kindly** *adverb* in a kind way: *She kindly drove me home.*
—**kindness** *noun* kind behavior toward someone: *She showed kindness to anyone who needed help.*

**kin·der·gar·ten** /ˈkɪndɚˌgɑrtn/ *noun*
a class in school for children who are about five years old. Children go to kindergarten before they start ELEMENTARY SCHOOL.

**[ORIGIN:** 1800-1900 A German word meaning "children's garden." The word was invented by a German teacher who believed that young children learn best by playing.**]**

**ki·net·ic** /kɪˈnetɪk/ *adjective*
caused by movement, or relating to movement: *Kinetic energy is the energy created by an object that is moving.*

**king** /kɪŋ/ *noun*
**1** a man who is the ruler of a country because he is from a royal family: *King George III was king of England during the American Revolution.*
**2** a card used in card games, which has a picture of a king on it

**king·dom** /ˈkɪŋdəm/ *noun*
a country that has a king or queen

**ˈking-size** (*also* **ˈking-sized**) *adjective*
a king-size bed is the largest size: *All the hotel rooms have a king-size bed.*

**kiss** /kɪs/ *verb*
to touch someone with your lips to show that you love him or her, or to do this when you say hello or goodbye to someone: *Roseanne and her boyfriend started kissing.* | *Grandma kissed me on the cheek.*
—**kiss** *noun* a touch with your lips: *Her mother gave her a kiss on the forehead.*
**[ORIGIN:** From the old English word *cyssan.***]**

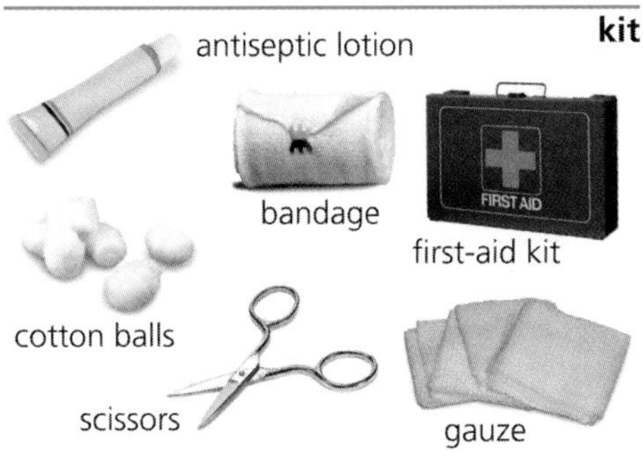


**kit** /kɪt/ *noun*
**1** a set of tools or equipment that you use to do something: *There are some bandages in the first-aid kit.*
**2** a set of parts that you buy and put together to make something: *a model airplane kit*

**kitch·en** /ˈkɪtʃən/ *noun*
the room where you cook food: *Jay's in the kitchen washing the dishes.*
**[ORIGIN:** From the old English word *cycene.***]**

**kite** /kaɪt/ *noun*
a toy that you fly in the air on the end of a long string

**kit·ten** /ˈkɪtn/ *noun*
a young cat
**[ORIGIN:** 1300-1400 Probably from an old French word *caton,* meaning "little cat."**]**

**kit·ty** /ˈkɪti/ (*also* **kit·ty·cat** /ˈkɪtiˌkæt/) *noun* (plural **kitties**) (*informal*)
a cat: *Here, kitty kitty! Here's your food.*

**ki·wi** /ˈkiwi/ (*also* **ˈkiwi fruit**) *noun*
a soft green fruit with small black seeds and a thin brown skin → see picture on page **A13**

**Kleen·ex** /ˈklineks/ *noun* (*trademark*)
a piece of soft thin paper, that you use to clean your nose or dry your eyes: *She was crying, so I handed her a Kleenex.* **SYNONYM: tissue**

**klutz** /klʌts/ *noun* (*informal*)
someone who often drops things or falls easily: *I looked like a real klutz when I tripped over the dog.*
**[ORIGIN:** 1900-2000 From the Yiddish word *klotz,* from the German word for "block of wood or lump of something." Yiddish was the language spoken by Jewish people in Europe.**]**

**km**
the written abbreviation of **kilometer**

**knack** /næk/ *noun* (*informal*)
the ability to do something well: *Kelly has a knack for learning languages – she speaks Chinese, Greek, and French.*
→ see Thesaurus box at **ability**

**knead** /nid/ *verb*
to press a bread mixture with your hands to make it ready to cook: *Knead the dough for ten minutes.* → see picture on page **A15**

**knee** /ni/ *noun*
**1** the middle part of your leg, where it can bend: *Sally cut her knee climbing over the gate.* | *I got down on my knees to look under the bed.* → see picture on page **A2**

K

**2** the part of your pants that covers your knee: *Billy's jeans had holes in both knees.*

**knee·cap** /ˈnikæp/ *noun*
the bone at the front of your knee → see picture on page **A12**

ˌ**knee-ˈdeep** *adjective*
deep enough to reach your knees: *The water was knee-deep.*

**kneel** /nil/ (*also* **kneel down**) *verb* (**knelt** /nelt/ *or* **kneeled**)
to put your knees on the ground, so that they are supporting your body: *She knelt down beside the bed to pray.* → see picture on page **A5**

**knew** /nu/ *verb*
the past tense of KNOW

**knife** /naɪf/ *noun* (plural **knives** /naɪvz/)
a tool used to cut things or as a weapon. It has a sharp metal part and a handle: *Mom cut up the chicken with a knife.* → see picture on page **A9**

**knight** /naɪt/ *noun*
a soldier who had a high position in society in MEDIEVAL times. Knights wore ARMOR and fought while riding horses.

**knit** /nɪt/ *verb* (**knit** *or* **knitted**, **knitting**)
to make clothes out of thick thread using long pointed sticks: *Grandma is knitting a sweater.*
—**knitting** *noun* the activity of making clothes out of thick thread, or something that is being knitted: *We learned sewing and knitting from our mother.* | *She put her knitting away.*

**knob** /nɑb/ *noun*
**1** a round handle on a door or drawer: *I turned the knob, but the door was locked and wouldn't open.*
**2** a round part that you turn to control something, for example a radio: *The volume knob on the stereo was turned all the way up.*

**knock**[1] /nɑk/ *verb*
**1** to hit a door or window with your closed hand so that people inside will hear you: *I knocked on the door for five minutes, but nobody answered.*
**2** to hit something hard so that it moves or falls down: *The dog knocked the phone off the table.*
**3** **knock it off** (*informal*) = used to tell someone to stop doing something that is annoying you: *Hey you two, knock it off! I'm on the phone.*
→ see Thesaurus box at **hit**[1]

He is knocking on the door.

**PHRASAL VERBS**
**knock something down**
to hit or push something so that it falls to the ground: *The wind was so strong it knocked down trees.*
**knock someone out**
to hit someone hard so that he or she falls down and cannot get up: *The boxer knocked his opponent out in the fifth round.*

**knock**[2] *noun*
the sound that is made by hitting something hard: *There was a loud knock on the door.*

**knock·out** /ˈnɑk-aʊt/ *noun*
an act of hitting someone so hard in the sport of BOXING that he falls down and cannot get up again

**knot** /nɑt/ *noun*
**1** a place on a rope or piece of string where it is tied to another rope or string: *We learned how to tie knots for rock climbing.*
**2** a unit for measuring the speed of a ship or aircraft, that is equal to about 1,853 meters in an hour
—**knot** *verb* to tie something in a knot: *She knotted the scarf around her neck.*
[**ORIGIN:** From the old English word *cnotta.*]

**know** /noʊ/ *verb* (**knew** /nu/, **known** /noʊn/)
**1** to have information or a fact about something in your mind: *Do you know the answer?* | *Doctors don't really know much about the disease.* | *We don't know what we're supposed to be doing.* | *I knew that*

K

*Andy would help us.* | *"Is Bob coming?" "I don't know."*

**2** **know how to do something** = to be able to do something: *By age six, most kids know how to tie their shoes.*

**3** to have met someone before, or to have been to a place before, so that you have information about them in your mind: *I've known Ben since I was three years old.* | *She's been to New York many times and knows the city well.*

**4** **you know** = **a)** said by someone when he or she is thinking of what to say next: *Then I said, you know, let's go to the movies on Friday.* **b)** used to make sure that someone understands what you are saying or that he or she is listening: *She just seems so angry all the time, you know?*

**5** **I know (what you mean)** = used to say that you agree with or understand what someone is saying: *"Science was so boring today!" "I know."*

**6** **as far as I know** = said when you think something is true, but you are not sure: *Tom's never been married, as far as I know.*

**7** **know better** = to be old enough or understand a situation enough not to do something bad or wrong: *You know better than to play ball in the house!*

**WORD FAMILY: know**

**know** *verb* | **knowledge** *noun* | **knowledgeable** *adjective* | **known** *adjective* | **unknown** *adjective*

**ˈknow-how** *noun* (*informal*)
the knowledge or ability you need to do something: *He has the technical know-how to keep the computers working.*

**knowl·edge** /ˈnɑlɪdʒ/ *noun*
**1** all the information you have learned about something: *Laura's knowledge of Spanish helped her get a job.*
**2** the state of knowing about a situation or event: *She went to the concert without her parents' knowledge.*
—**knowledgeable** *adjective* knowing a lot about something: *He's very knowledgeable about cars and knows how to fix them.*

**known**[1] /noʊn/ *verb*
the past participle of KNOW

**known**[2] *adjective*
if someone or something is known, many people know about them: *Ansel Adams is known for his photographs of Yosemite National Park.* **SYNONYM: famous**

**knuck·le** /ˈnʌkəl/ *noun*
one of the places where your fingers can bend, including the places where they join your hand

**ko·a·la** /koʊˈɑlə/ (*also* **koˈala bear**) *noun*
an Australian animal that looks like a small bear and that lives in trees and eats leaves

**Ko·ran** /kəˈræn/ *noun*
**the Koran** = the holy book of the Muslim religion

**Ko·re·an**[1] /kəˈriən/ *adjective*
from Korea

**Korean**[2] *noun*
**1** someone from Korea
**2** the language spoken in Korea

**ko·sher** /ˈkoʊʃɚ/ *adjective*
kosher food is prepared according to Jewish law

**ku·dos** /ˈkudoʊs/ *noun*
praise for doing something well: *The newspaper gave kudos to Jim Carrey for an excellent performance.*

**kung fu** /ˌkʌŋ ˈfu/ *noun*
a sport from China in which you fight using your hands and feet to hit and kick your opponent

**kW**
the written abbreviation of **kilowatt**

# Ll

**lab** /læb/ *noun* (*informal*)
a LABORATORY

label

**la·bel¹** Ac /ˈleɪbəl/ *noun*
a piece of paper or cloth that is attached to something and has information about it: *Always read the instructions on the label before taking any medicine.*
[ORIGIN: 1200-1300 From an old French word for "long narrow piece of cloth."]

**label²** Ac *verb*
**1** to put a label on something or write information on it: *We labeled each toy box with what was inside it: cars, blocks, dolls.*
**2** to always use a particular word to describe someone even if it is not a true or fair way to describe him or her: *The other kids labeled him a nerd.*

**la·bor¹** Ac /ˈleɪbɚ/ *noun*
**1** hard work that you do using your body and hands: *The prisoners had to do hard labor, such as digging ditches.*
**2** people who work for a company or in a country: *The car industry needs skilled labor.*
**3** if a woman is in labor, she is pushing a baby out of her body

**labor²** Ac *verb* (*formal*)
to work very hard: *They labored in the fields from early morning until late in the evening.*

**lab·ora·to·ry** /ˈlæbrəˌtɔri/ *noun* (plural **laboratories**)
a room where scientists work and do EXPERIMENTs: *The blood sample has been sent to the laboratory for testing.* SYNONYM: **lab**
[ORIGIN: 1600-1700 From the Latin word *laborare*, which means "to work."]

**ˈLabor Day** *noun*
a holiday on the first Monday in September, that shows respect for people who work

**ˈlabor ˌunion** *noun*
an organization that helps a group of workers get better pay, health insurance, etc.: *The labor union wants to make sure employees receive better health care.* SYNONYM: **union**

**lab·y·rinth** /ˈlæbəˌrɪnθ/ *noun*
another word for a MAZE

**lace¹** /leɪs/ *noun*
**1** a type of cloth that has a pattern made of very small holes in it: *The wedding dress was covered with lace.*
**2** a string that you tie your shoes with: *His laces were untied.* SYNONYM: **shoelace**

**lace²** (*also* **lace up**) *verb*
to fasten something by tying a lace: *Paul put on his boots and laced them up.*

**lack¹** /læk/ *noun*
the state of not having something, or of not having enough of something: *A lack of money meant they did not have enough to eat.*

**lack²** *verb* (*formal*)
to not have something, or to not have enough of it: *Workers at these low-paid jobs often lack an education.*

**lad·der** /ˈlædɚ/ *noun*
**1** a piece of equipment that you use to climb up to high places. It is made of two long pieces of metal or wood with bars between them that you step on: *The painter climbed up the ladder to reach the top of the wall.*
**2** a series of levels in a company, organization, or society, in which each level is better than the one before it: *Nelson worked hard to climb the company ladder and get a job in management.*

**ˈladies' room** *noun*
a room in a public building with toilets for women

**la·dle** /ˈleɪdl/ *noun*
a deep spoon with a long handle, that you use to put soup into bowls
—**ladle** *verb* to use a ladle to put food into or onto something: *Mom ladled the soup into each bowl.*

L

**la·dy** /ˈleɪdi/ *noun* (plural **ladies**)
**1** a polite word for a woman: *Ladies and gentlemen, thank you for coming.*
**2** (*informal*) used to speak rudely to a woman you do not know: *Hey, lady, hurry up!*
[**ORIGIN:** From the old English word *hlæfdige*, from *hlaf* and *-dige*, which mean "bread" and "person who kneads dough."]

**la·dy·bug** /ˈleɪdiˌbʌg/ *noun*
a small insect that has red or orange wings with black spots on them

**lag** /læg/ *verb* (**lagged**, **lagging**)
to move or develop more slowly than other things or people: *Jonathan lagged behind the rest of the kids climbing the hill.*

**la·goon** /ləˈgun/ *noun*
a pool of sea water that is separated from the ocean by a low narrow piece of land

**laid** /leɪd/ *verb*
the past tense and past participle of LAY

**ˌlaid-ˈback** *adjective*
relaxed and not worried about anything: *My teacher is pretty laid-back. He likes to have fun in class.*

**lain** /leɪn/ *verb*
the past participle of LIE

**lake** /leɪk/ *noun*
a large area of water with land all around it: *We're going swimming in the lake.* | *Lake Michigan*

**lake·front** /ˈleɪkfrʌnt/ *noun*
the land next to a lake: *They built a house on the lakefront so they could go boating and fishing whenever they wanted to.*

**lamb** /læm/ *noun*
a young sheep, or the meat of a young sheep

**lame** /leɪm/ *adjective*
**1** (*informal*) silly or not very good: *The jokes were lame, and no one laughed.*
**2** (*formal*) not able to walk easily because your leg or foot is hurt: *The horse was lame; it had cut its leg on a fence.*

**lamp** /læmp/ *noun*
a type of light that you can put on a table or stand on the floor: *She turned on the lamp to read.* → see picture at **light**
[**ORIGIN:** 1100-1200 From the Latin word *lampas*, from the Greek word *lampein*, which means "to shine."]

**lamp·shade** /ˈlæmpʃeɪd/ *noun*
a cover over a LIGHT BULB

**land¹** /lænd/ *noun*
**1** an area of ground, especially one used for farming or building: *Mr. Peterson owns the land near the river and grows crops there.*
**2** the part of the Earth that is not covered by water: *Frogs live on land and in the water.*
**3** (*formal*) a country: *People came to America from many lands.*
→ see Thesaurus box at **country**, **earth**

**land**

land

take off

**land²** *verb*
**1** to arrive somewhere in an airplane or boat: *We will be landing in 30 minutes.*
**2** if an airplane or a bird lands, it moves down onto something and stops flying: *Airplanes land and take off from the airport every few minutes.*
**3** to fall onto a surface after moving through the air: *The ball went over the fence and landed in our neighbor's yard.* | *Chris slipped and landed on his back.*
→ see Thesaurus box at **arrive**

**land·fill** /ˈlændfɪl/ *noun*
a place where waste from houses is buried under the ground: *The trash is taken to a landfill.*

**land·ing** /ˈlændɪŋ/ *noun*
the action of bringing an airplane down to the ground: *The pilot made a perfect landing.*
**ANTONYM: takeoff**

**land·la·dy** /ˈlændˌleɪdi/ *noun* (plural **landladies**)
a woman who owns a house or apartment and rents it to other people

L

**land·lord** /ˈlændlɔrd/ *noun*
someone who owns a house or apartment and rents it to other people

**land·mark** /ˈlændmɑrk/ *noun*
**1** a building or place that is easy to recognize and helps you know where you are: *The Empire State Building is a famous landmark in New York.*
**2** an important event: *The discovery of penicillin was a landmark in medicine.*

**land·own·er** /ˈlændˌoʊnɚ/ *noun*
someone who owns a lot of land

**land·scape** /ˈlændskeɪp/ *noun*
a view across an area of land: *The snow changed the landscape, making it seem soft and beautiful.*

**land·slide** /ˈlændslaɪd/ *noun*
**1** a sudden fall of a lot of dirt and rocks down the side of a mountain: *Part of the highway is blocked by a landslide.*
**2** a victory in which someone wins an election by a very large number of votes: *Wilson won in a landslide – he had twice as many votes as his closest opponent.*

**lane** /leɪn/ *noun*
**1** one of the parts that a wide road is divided into, so that people can drive along next to each other: *Three lanes of the freeway were closed because of an accident.*
**2** one of the parts that a race track or swimming pool is divided into, and along which people swim or run: *Johnson will be running in lane 4.*
→ see Thesaurus box at **road**

**lan·guage** /ˈlæŋgwɪdʒ/ *noun*
**1** the words and grammar that people living in a country use: *the English language* | *"Do you speak any foreign languages?" "Yes, I speak Arabic."*

**THESAURUS: language**

**dialect** a form of a language that is spoken in one area of a country, which is different from the way it is spoken in other areas: *Cantonese and Mandarin are only two of many Chinese dialects.*

**slang** very informal spoken words or phrases: *"Wicked" is a slang word that means "good."*

**jargon** technical words and phrases used by people doing a particular job: *The computer manual was full of technical jargon that I could not understand.*

**tongue** (*formal*) a language: *Juan was born in Mexico, so his mother tongue is Spanish.* | *They were speaking in a foreign tongue.*

**2** words of a particular type: *The book uses scientific language that is hard to understand.*
**3** a system used to give instructions to a computer: *Java is a computer programming language often used in making websites.*
[**ORIGIN:** 1200-1300 From the Latin word *lingua*, which means "tongue or language."]

**ˈlanguage ˌarts** *noun*
a subject in school that includes reading, writing, spelling, and grammar

**lan·tern** /ˈlæntɚn/ *noun*
a type of lamp you can carry, that has a metal frame and glass sides: *He used the lantern to find his way to the tent.* → see picture at **light**

**lap¹** /læp/ *noun*
**1** the flat area formed by the tops of your legs when you are sitting down: *The little girl was sitting on her mother's lap.*
**2** one trip around a race track, or a trip from one end of a swimming pool to the other: *Patty swims 30 laps every day.*
[**ORIGIN:** 1200-1300 From the old English word *læppa*, which means "flap or folded piece of cloth." The word "lap" came to be used for the bottom part of a shirt or skirt, and then for the part of the body it covered.]

**lap²** (*also* **lap up**) *verb* (**lapped, lapping**)
if an animal laps a drink, it drinks it by touching it with its tongue: *The cat lapped up the milk.*

**la·pel** /ləˈpel/ *noun*
a part at the front of a coat or jacket which is folded back: *The doctor wore a name tag on his lapel.*

**lapse** /læps/ *noun* (*formal*)
a short period of time when you forget something or do not do something you should: *There was a lapse in security at the airport, and a man with a gun got on the plane.*

**lap·top** /ˈlæptɑp/ *noun*
a small computer that you can carry with you
→ see picture on page A19

**lar·ce·ny** /ˈlɑrsəni/ *noun* (*formal*)
the crime of stealing something

**lard** /lɑrd/ *noun*
a thick white fat from pigs, used in cooking

**large** /lɑrdʒ/ *adjective*
**1** big in size, number, or amount: *a large pizza | The high school has 1,500 students, so it is much larger than the middle school.*
**ANTONYM: small**
**2 by and large** = used when talking generally about something: *By and large, the new system is working well, but there are a few small problems.*
→ see Thesaurus box at big

**large·ly** /ˈlɑrdʒli/ *adverb*
mostly or mainly: *Grizzly bears largely eat fruit and plants, but will also eat meat.*

**lark** /lɑrk/ *noun*
a small wild brown bird that sings and has long pointed wings

**lar·va** /ˈlɑrvə/ *noun* (plural **larvae** /ˈlɑrvi/)
a young insect with a soft body and no wings, that will become an insect with wings later in its life
[**ORIGIN:** 1600-1700 From the Latin word for "ghost, or mask." The word "larva" was chosen by the Swedish scientist Carl Linnaeus because he thought that the larva stage was like a mask that hid what the young insect would become.]

**lar·yn·gi·tis** /ˌlærənˈdʒaɪtɪs/ *noun*
an illness that makes it difficult for you to speak because your larynx is swollen and painful: *The singer has had to cancel the concert because she has laryngitis.*

**lar·ynx** /ˈlærɪŋks/ *noun* (*formal*)
the part of your throat where your voice is produced **SYNONYM: voice box**

**la·ser** /ˈleɪzɚ/ *noun*
a piece of equipment that produces a powerful narrow beam of light: *Doctors can use lasers to correct your eyesight.*
[**ORIGIN:** 1900-2000 From the first letters of the phrase "light amplification by stimulated emission of radiation." "Amplification" means "making something more powerful." "Emission" means "producing."]

**lash** /læʃ/ *noun*
an EYELASH

**las·so** /ˈlæsoʊ/ *noun*
a long rope with one end tied in a circle, which you throw over the head of a cow or horse to catch it
—**lasso** *verb* to catch a cow or horse using a lasso
[**ORIGIN:** 1700-1800 From Spanish, from the Latin word *laqueus*, which means "trap."]

**last¹** /læst/ *adjective*
**1** most recent: *The last time we played tennis, you won. | I saw Tim last week.*

> **USAGE: last, latest**
>
> Use **last** to mean "the one before the present one or the present time": *I didn't like his last movie, but this one is better.*
>
> Use **latest** to mean "happening now or very recently": *He is about to publish the results of his latest research.*

**2** at the end, after everyone or everything else: *We were last in line for tickets. | When is the last day of school? | the last chapter*
**3** the last one is the only one left: *Do you want the last piece of cake?*
**4 the last person/thing** = a person or thing that you do not expect or want at all: *He's the last person I'd want to go on a date with!*

**last²** *verb*
**1** to happen for a period of time: *The meeting lasted only ten minutes.*
**2** to continue to exist or stay in good condition: *The weather has been good, but I don't think it will last. | Lemons may last six weeks in a refrigerator.*

**last³** *adverb*
**1** most recently: *"When did you see her last?" "Three days ago."*
**2** after everything or everyone else: *I run as fast as I can, but I always finish last.*
**3 last but not least** = used to say that the last person or thing in a list is as important as the others: *Last but not least, I'd like to thank my mother for all the help she has given me.*

**last⁴** *noun*
**1 at last** = after a long time: *The rain stopped at last.*

**2 the last** = the person or thing that is after all the others: *Joe was the last to go to bed.*

**last·ing** /ˈlæstɪŋ/ *adjective*
continuing for a long time: *We have a lasting friendship – we met 25 years. ago*

**last·ly** /ˈlæstli/ *adverb* (*formal*)
used when telling someone the last thing you want to say: *Lastly, I'd like to thank you all for coming.*

**ˈlast-ˌminute** *adjective*
happening just before it is too late, or just before something happens: *Lucas made some last-minute changes to his test before he gave it to the teacher.*

**ˈlast name** *noun*
your family's name, which in English comes after your other names: *I think Julio's last name is Martinez.*

**latch** /lætʃ/ *noun*
a small metal object that keeps a door, gate, or window closed

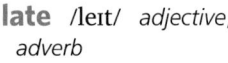

**late** /leɪt/ *adjective*, *adverb*
**1** after the usual or expected time: *She was late for school and got in trouble again.* | *Our flight got to Houston two hours late, so we missed our next flight.*
**2** near the end of a period of time: *The house was built in the late 19th century.* | *The team finally scored late in the game.*
**3** at night, or near the end of the day: *It's late and I'm tired.* | *the late show on TV*

**late·ly** /ˈleɪtli/ *adverb*
recently: *"Have you seen Barbara lately?" "No, not for several months."* | *Lately, I've been really busy.*
→ see Thesaurus box at **recently**

**lat·er**[1] /ˈleɪtɚ/ *adverb*
**1** after the present time, or after the time you are talking about: *I'll see you later.* | *They met in July, and only two months later they got married.*
**2 later on** = at some time in the future, or after something else: *She said she would meet you later on this evening.*
→ see Thesaurus box at **after**

**later**[2] *adjective*
**1** coming in the future, or after something else: *You can freeze the soup and use it at a later time.*
**2** more recent: *Later models of the car are much improved.*

**lat·est** /ˈleɪtəst/ *adjective*
most recent: *The paper gives you the latest news.*
→ see Thesaurus box at **new**

**USAGE: latest, last**

Use **latest** to mean "happening now or very recently": *He is about to publish the results of his latest research.*

Use **last** to mean "the one before the present one or the present time": *I didn't like his last movie, but this is much better.*

**La·tin** /ˈlætn/ *noun*
the language used by the ancient Romans. Many Latin words are still used in science, law, and medicine: *The names of each plant are given in Latin.*

**La·ti·na** /ləˈtinə/ *noun*
a woman in the U.S. whose family came from a country in Latin America

**ˌLatin Aˈmerica** *noun*
Mexico, Central America, and South America
—**Latin American** *adjective* from or in Latin America: *Latin American art*

**La·ti·no** /ləˈtinoʊ/ *noun*
a man in the U.S. whose family came from a country in Latin America. In the plural, Latinos can mean a group of men and women: *Many Latinos live in the southwestern United States.*
—**Latino** *adjective* belonging to or relating to Latinos: *a Latino neighborhood*

**lat·i·tude** /ˈlætəˌtud/ *noun*
the distance north or south of the EQUATOR (=an imaginary line around the middle of the Earth): *New York City is on the same latitude as Naples, Italy.*

**lat·ter** /ˈlætɚ/ *noun*
**the latter** (*formal*) = the second of two people or things that someone talks about: *When the students could choose between juice or cola, most of them chose the latter.*

L

**laugh**[1] /læf/ *verb*
to make a sound with your voice because you think something is funny: *No one laughed at my jokes.* | *We made her laugh by telling funny stories.*

> **THESAURUS: laugh**
>
> **giggle** to laugh quickly in a high voice: *The girls were giggling about something that had happened at school.*
>
> **chuckle** to laugh quietly: *Jimmy chuckled to himself as he read the funnies.*
>
> **snicker** to laugh quietly in a way that is not nice: *As Pam read out her poem, some of the kids started snickering.*
>
> **roar with laughter** to laugh very loudly: *When he finished the joke, the audience roared with laughter.*

PHRASAL VERB
**laugh at someone**
to laugh or make jokes about someone in an unkind way: *Other kids laughed at him because he couldn't read.*

**laugh**[2] *noun*
the sound you make when you laugh: *"That's funny!" he said, with a laugh.*

> **WORD FAMILY: laugh**
>
> **laugh** *noun* | **laugh** *verb* | **laughter** *noun*

**laugh·ter** /ˈlæftɚ/ *noun*
the sound of people laughing: *I could hear laughter coming from her bedroom.*

**launch** /lɔntʃ/ *verb*
1 to start something new and important: *The school launched a healthy eating campaign.*
2 to send a spacecraft or MISSILE into the sky: *They launched the space shuttle from Cape Canaveral.*
3 to put a boat or ship into the water: *The ship was launched in 1911.*
[ORIGIN: 1300-1400 From the old French word *lancher*, from the Latin word *lanceare*, which means "to throw a spear."]

**laun·dro·mat** /ˈlɔndrəˌmæt/ *noun*
a place where you pay to wash your clothes in a machine

**laun·dry** /ˈlɔndri/ *noun*
1 clothes and sheets that you need to wash: *Put your dirty laundry in the washing machine.* → see picture on page **A10**
2 clothes and sheets that you have washed: *I folded the laundry and put it away.*
3 **do the laundry** = to wash clothes and sheets
[ORIGIN: 1500-1600 From the old French word *lavanderie*, from the Latin word *lavare*, which means "to wash."]

**la·va** /ˈlɑvə/ *noun*
hot liquid rock that comes out of the top of a mountain → see picture at **volcano**

**lav·a·to·ry** /ˈlævəˌtɔri/ *noun* (plural **lavatories**) (*formal*)
a room with a toilet, in a public building or airplane
[ORIGIN: 1300-1400 From the Latin word *lavatorium*, which means "bowl for washing in," from *lavare*, which means "to wash."]

**lav·en·der** /ˈlævəndɚ/ *noun*
a plant with purple flowers that have a pleasant smell

**law** /lɔ/ *noun*
1 **the law** = the system of rules in a country: *Driving without a seat belt on is against the law.* | *People who break the law should be punished.*
2 a rule that everyone in a country must obey: *There is a law against driving too fast.*
3 the study of legal systems: *I'd like to study law.*
4 a statement in math or science that explains how or why something happens: *The law of gravity explains why things fall down to the ground.*
→ see Thesaurus box at **rule**[1]

**ˈlaw-aˌbiding** *adjective*
a law-abiding person always obeys the law: *I am a law-abiding citizen – I have never gotten into trouble with the police.*

**law·ful** /ˈlɔfəl/ *adjective* (*formal*)
allowed or recognized by the law: *Do you take this woman to be your lawful wedded wife?* SYNONYM: **legal**; ANTONYM: **illegal**

**lawn** /lɔn/ *noun*
an area of grass around a house or building: *We need to mow the lawn* (=cut the grass).
[ORIGIN: 1500-1600 From the old French word *launde*, which means "open space between woods."]

L

**ˈlawn ˌmower** *noun*
a machine that cuts grass

**law·suit** /ˈlɔsut/ *noun*
a problem that someone takes to a court of law so that a judge can decide who is right and who is wrong: *They filed a lawsuit against the building company when it did not complete its work.*

**law·yer** /ˈlɔyɚ/ *noun*
someone whose job is to advise people about the law, and speak for them in court: *My lawyer told me not to give them any money until they sign the papers.* **SYNONYM: attorney** → see picture on page **A17**

**lay¹** /leɪ/ *verb* (**laid** /leɪd/)
**1** to put something down in a flat position: *He laid the baby on the bed.* | *She stopped reading and laid down her book.*

> **USAGE: lay, lie**
>
> **Lay** means to put something down in a flat position. The past tense for this is **laid**: *She laid the newspaper down and picked up the phone.*
>
> **Lie** has two different meanings:
>
> 1) to be in, or move into, a flat position on the floor, a bed, etc.: *Lie down on the sofa.*
>
> The past tense for this meaning of **lie** is **lay**: *He lay on the bed.*
>
> 2) to say something that is not true: *Why did you lie to me?*
>
> The past tense for this meaning of **lie** is **lied**: *The police think that he lied.*

**2** to put something on the floor or in the ground, where it will stay: *They plan to lay a new carpet in the living room.*
**3** if a bird or insect lays eggs, eggs come out of its body: *The hen laid an egg.*

**PHRASAL VERBS**

**lay someone off**
if a company lays off workers, it stops employing them because it does not have enough work for them: *The company laid off 25 workers because sales were down.*

**lay something out**
**1** to spread something out so that it is lying flat: *Pam laid out her dress on the bed.*
**2** to explain or describe an idea with all the details: *The mayor laid out her plans for building two new parks downtown.*

**lay²** *verb*
the past tense of LIE

**lay·er** [Ac] /ˈleɪɚ/ *noun*
**1** an amount of something that covers a surface: *The house was empty, and there was a thick layer of dust on the table.*
**2** something that you put on or between other things: *It was cold, so we wore several layers of clothing.*

**lay·off** /ˈleɪɔf/ *noun*
the act of ending someone's employment because there is not enough work for them: *The factory closed down, and there were about 100 layoffs.*

**lay·out** /ˈleɪaʊt/ *noun*
**1** the way things are arranged in a place: *I wanted to change the layout of my bedroom, and put the bed under the window.*
**2** the way writing and pictures are arranged on a page: *The newspaper's page layout makes it easy to read.*

**la·zy** /ˈleɪzi/ *adjective* (**lazier**, **laziest**)
**1** not wanting to work or make any effort: *Tom is so lazy; he never helps with the housework.*
**2** a lazy time is spent relaxing and not doing any work: *We spent a lazy day at the pool.*
**ANTONYM: busy**
—**laziness** *noun* the quality of being lazy: *She complained about his laziness, saying all he did was watch TV.*

**lb.**
the written abbreviation of **pound**: *I weigh 140 lbs.*
[**ORIGIN:** 1300-1400 From the Latin word *libra*, which means "pound."]

**lead¹** /lid/ *verb* (**led** /led/)
**1** to show someone the way somewhere, by walking in front of him or her: *You lead, and we'll follow.* | *He led his horse to the barn.*
**ANTONYM: follow**
**2** to go in front of a group of people or vehicles: *Our town's high school band is leading the parade.*
**3** if a road, path, or door leads to a place, you can get there by using it: *This road leads to Springfield.*

L

**4** to be winning a game or competition: *Our team was leading 8-0.*
**5** to be in charge of an activity or a group of people: *Who is leading the investigation?*
**6** to be more successful at an activity than other companies, countries, or people: *The U.S. leads the world in this type of research.*
**7 lead a ... life** = to have a particular kind of life: *It's hard to lead a normal life when you're famous.*

**PHRASAL VERBS**

**lead to something**
to cause something to happen or exist: *This research led to new treatments for cancer.*

**lead up to something**
to come before something: *In the days leading up to her operation she was very nervous.*
**ANTONYM: follow**

**WORD FAMILY: lead**
**lead** *verb* | **leader** *noun* | **leadership** *noun*

**lead²** *noun*
**1** the position in front of everyone else in a competition or race: *Barron is still in the lead, but the race is only half finished.*
**2** the amount by which one person is ahead of another during a competition or race: *We are in first place with a lead of ten points.*
**3** a piece of information that may help you discover something: *The police got an important lead when someone reported seeing a tall man near the murder scene.*

**lead³** /led/ *noun*
**1** a heavy gray metal: *lead pipes*
**2** the gray substance in a pencil that makes marks when you write: *The lead on my pencil broke.*

**lead·er** /ˈlidɚ/ *noun*
**1** the person who is in charge of a country or group of people: *The meeting will be attended by many world leaders, including the president.*
**2** the person or team that is winning a race or competition: *She was the leader for the first half of the race.*
—**leadership** *noun* the quality of being good at leading people

**lead·ing** /ˈlidɪŋ/ *adjective*
**1** most important or most successful: *He got a leading part in the play.*
**2 leading lady/man** = the actor who has the most important female or male part in a movie: *The leading man needs to have star quality.*

**leaf** /lif/ *noun* (plural **leaves** /livz/)
one of the flat green parts of a plant or tree, that grow from its stem or branches: *There are still some leaves on the trees, but most of them have fallen off.*

**leaf·let** /ˈliflɪt/ *noun*
a piece of paper with information or an advertisement printed on it: *They gave out leaflets in the street for the restaurant.*

**league** /lig/ *noun*
**1** a group of sports teams that play against each other in order to see who is best: *How many teams are in the National Football League?*
**2** a group of people or countries that have joined together to achieve something: *the League of Women Voters*
→ see Thesaurus box at **competition**
[**ORIGIN:** 1400-1500 From the French word *ligue*, which means "agreement to act together," from the Latin word *ligare*, which means "to tie."]

**leak¹** /lik/ *verb*
**1** if something leaks, liquid or gas comes out of a hole in it where it is broken or damaged: *The roof leaks when it rains.*
**2** to give secret information to a newspaper or television company, so that people find out about something: *Details of the president's speech were leaked to reporters.*
—**leakage** *noun* liquid or gas that leaks from something
—**leaky** *adjective* something that is leaky is leaking
→ see Thesaurus box at **pour**

**leak²** *noun*

**1** a hole that liquid or gas comes out of, where something is broken or damaged: *There is a leak in the pipe under the sink. Can you fix it?*
**2** a situation in which someone gives secret information to a newspaper or television company, so that people find out about

something: *No one knew about the deal until there was a leak from the White House.*
→ see Thesaurus box at **hole**

**lean**[1] /lin/ *verb*
**1** to bend your body forward, backward, or to the side: *She leaned forward to kiss him.*
**2** to stand or sit with part of your body resting against something: *She leaned on her cane as she walked.*
**3** to put something in a sloping position against something else: *He leaned the ladder against the wall.*
**PHRASAL VERB**
**lean toward something**
to slightly prefer one thing when you are trying to choose from several things: *She's leaning toward majoring in history, but she hasn't decided for sure yet.*

**lean**[2] *adjective*
**1** thin in a healthy way: *His body was lean and athletic.* **ANTONYM: fat**
**2** lean meat does not have much fat on it **ANTONYM: fatty**
→ see Thesaurus box at **thin**

**leap** /lip/ *verb* (**leaped** *or* **leapt** /lept/)
to jump into the air or to jump over something: *The dog leaped over the fence.* | *Jon leapt up from the chair to answer the phone.* → see picture at **jump**
→ see Thesaurus box at **jump**[1]
—**leap** *noun* an act of leaping: *With one leap, she crossed the stream.*

**leap·frog** /ˈlipfrɑg/ *noun*
a children's game in which one child bends down so that another child can jump over him or her

**ˈleap year** *noun*
a year when February has 29 days instead of 28, which happens every four years

**learn** /lɚn/ *verb*
**1** to study or practice a subject or activity so that you know about it or know how to do it: *The students learn new skills.* | *We learned about electricity in school.*

**USAGE: learn, teach**

You **learn** a subject or skill when you study or practice it: *I want to learn English.* | *Jo is learning to drive.*

If you **teach** someone a subject or skill, you help him or her learn it: *Dad is teaching me to play the guitar.*

You cannot say "Dad learned me to play the guitar."

**2** to practice a poem, a piece of music, etc. many times, so that you can remember it exactly: *She learned the poem and said it in front of the class.*
**3** to receive information or news: *He was delighted to learn that he had been accepted at Harvard.*
[**ORIGIN:** From the old English word *leornian.*]

**learn·ing** /ˈlɚnɪŋ/ *noun*
the process of getting knowledge or skills: *Learning is fun if new information is taught correctly.*

**lease** /lis/ *noun*
a legal agreement that allows you to live in or use a building or car for a period of time: *The company signed a five-year lease on their new offices.*
—**lease** *verb* to use a building or car by having a lease for it, or to allow someone to use a building or car by having a lease
[**ORIGIN:** 1300-1400 From the old French word *laissier*, which means "to let go," from the Latin word *laxare*, which means "to loosen or open."]

**leash** /liʃ/ *noun*
a piece of rope, leather, or chain that you attach to a dog's collar and hold when you take the dog for a walk: *Please keep your dog on a leash.*

**least** /list/ *pronoun, adverb, adjective*
**1** less than anything or anyone else: *She*

L

*doesn't have much money, so she bought the least expensive computer.* **ANTONYM: most**

**2 at least** = **a)** used to say something good about a bad situation: *It's not good news, but at least we know now what the problem is.* **b)** not less than a number or amount: *He's tall – at least six feet.*

**3 least of all** = especially not: *I don't like vegetables, least of all carrots.*

**4 not in the least** = not at all: *It was a gray and windy morning, and I wasn't in the least surprised when it started raining.*

**5 the least** = the smallest number or amount: *$10,000 is the least we'll need to repair the roof.*

**leath·er** /ˈleðɚ/ *noun*

a strong material made from the skin of an animal, used for making shoes, bags, belts, etc. Most leather comes from cow skins: *a leather jacket*

—**leathery** *adjective* like leather: *Her skin was leathery from spending years in the sun.*

**leave**[1] /liv/ *verb* (**left** /left/)

**1** to go away from a place: *The bus leaves in five minutes – you'd better get on.* | *I leave school at 3:00 and I'm home by 3:30.* **ANTONYM: arrive**

**2** to put something somewhere and go away without it: *We left the car at the airport.* | *Leave the keys on the table.*

**USAGE: leave, forget**

When you want to talk about the place where you left something by mistake, you must use **leave**, not **forget**: *I left my homework at home.*

You can say "*I forgot my homework*" but do not say "I forgot my homework at home."

**3 leave a message** = to tell someone something by asking someone else to tell him or her or by writing a note: *Pete was out, so I left a message with his mom.*

**4** to let something stay the way it is: *Leave your coat on – we're going out again.*

**5** to stop living with your husband, wife, or partner because you no longer love him or her: *He left his wife after three years of marriage.*

**6** to stop doing a job or going to a school or college and not return to it: *He left school and got a job.* **SYNONYM: quit; ANTONYM: start**

**7 leave someone alone** = used to tell someone to stop annoying or upsetting someone: *Go away and leave me alone!*

**8 leave something alone** = used for telling someone to stop touching something: *Leave those glasses alone, or you'll break them.*

**9** if something is left, it is still there after everything else has gone: *There wasn't much food left at the end of dinner.*

**10** to not do something until later: *Let's leave the dishes until the morning.*

**11** to arrange for someone to have something you own after you die: *She left a lot of money to her son in her will.*

**PHRASAL VERBS**

**leave something behind**

to not take something with you when you go somewhere: *When we moved to the U.S., we had to leave our dog behind in Mexico.*

**leave out**

**1 leave something out** = to not include something: *Tell me everything that Colleen said, and don't leave out any details.*

**2 be/feel left out** = to feel as if you are not accepted or welcome in a particular group of people: *I feel left out when my older sisters do things without me.*

**leave something to someone**

to let someone make a decision or be responsible for something and not do it yourself: *It's your money, so I'll leave the decision to you.*

**leave**[2] *noun*

time that you are allowed to spend away from work, for example because you are sick or on vacation: *She took sick leave when she had the flu.*

→ see Thesaurus box at **vacation**

**leaves** /livz/ *noun*

the plural of LEAF

**lec·ture**[1] Ac /ˈlektʃɚ/ *noun*

**1** a formal talk to a group of people about a subject: *The professor gave a lecture on modern art.*

2 a long serious conversation in which someone tells you how you should behave: *Dad gave me a lecture about my schoolwork.*
[ORIGIN: 1200-1300 From the Latin word *lectura*, which means "the act of reading," from *legere*, meaning "to read." Someone who gives a lecture often reads from his or her notes.]

**lecture²** Ac *verb*
1 to talk to someone in a serious way about how he or she should behave: *Mom is always lecturing me about doing my homework.*
2 to give a formal talk about a subject to a group of people: *She lectures on art history at the museum.*
—**lecturer** *noun* someone who gives lectures that teach people about a subject

**led** /lɛd/ *verb*
the past tense and past participle of LEAD

**ledge** /lɛdʒ/ *noun*
a narrow flat surface like a shelf, that sticks out from the side of a building or cliff: *A bird landed on the window ledge.*

**ledg·er** /ˈlɛdʒɚ/ *noun*
a book in which a business records the money it receives and spends

**leek** /lik/ *noun*
a long vegetable with straight green leaves that tastes like an onion → see picture on page A12

**left¹** /lɛft/ *verb*
the past tense and past participle of LEAVE

**left²** *noun*
1 the side from which you start reading a line of writing in English: *The school is up ahead on the left.* ANTONYM: right
2 **the left** = in politics, people who think the government should use taxes to pay for important things people need, and that business should have less power: *Many people on the left support the idea of government health care for everyone.* ANTONYM: the right

**left³** *adjective*
on or toward the left side: *He writes with his left hand.* | *The store is on the left side of the street.* ANTONYM: right
[ORIGIN: From the old English word for "weak." The left hand is the weaker hand for most people.]

**left⁴** *adverb*
toward the left side: *Turn left at the next street.* ANTONYM: right

**ˌleft-ˈhanded** *adjective*
someone who is left-handed uses his or her left hand to write, throw a ball, etc. ANTONYM: right-handed
—**left-hander** *noun* someone who is left-handed

**left·ist** /ˈlɛftɪst/ *adjective*
another word for LEFT-WING: *The military did not like the leftist government.*

**left·o·vers** /ˈlɛftˌoʊvɚz/ *noun*
food that remains at the end of a meal, that you can keep and eat later: *They gave the leftovers from dinner to the dog.*

**ˌleft-ˈwing** *adjective*
people who are left-wing believe that the government should pay for the important things that people need and that business should not have too much power: *My brother is more left-wing than I am.* ANTONYM: right-wing

**leg** /lɛg/ *noun*
1 one of the two long parts of your body that you use for standing and walking: *Dogs have four legs.* | *She fell and broke her leg.* → see picture on page A2
2 one of the long parts that support a piece of furniture such as a table or chair: *One of the table legs is too short.*
3 the part of a pair of pants that covers your leg: *I got paint all over the leg of my jeans.*

**leg·a·cy** /ˈlɛgəsi/ *noun* (plural **legacies**)
1 money or property that you receive from someone after he or she dies SYNONYM: inheritance
2 a situation that exists because of things

that happened at an earlier time: *The country's debt is a legacy of the war.*

**le·gal** [Ac] /ˈligəl/ *adjective*
**1** relating to laws: *Is the legal system fair? | He should go and get legal advice from his lawyer.*
**2** allowed by the law: *Is it legal to copy a DVD?* **ANTONYM: illegal**
—**legally** *adverb* according to the law: *You can't legally buy alcohol until you're 21.*
—**legalize** *verb* to make something legal: *a plan to legalize gambling*
—**legality** /lɪˈgæləti/ *noun* the state of being legal: *His lawyer questioned the legality of the evidence.*
[ORIGIN: 1400-1500 From the Latin word *leges*, which means "laws."]

**WORD FAMILY: legal**
**legal** *adjective* | **illegal** *adjective* | **legally** *adverb* | **illegally** *adverb* | **legalize** *verb*

**ˌlegal ˈholiday** *noun*
a holiday on which government offices, schools, and banks are officially closed: *Christmas Day is a legal holiday.*

**leg·end** /ˈledʒənd/ *noun*
**1** an old well-known story about people who lived long ago, that is usually not true: *According to the legend, King Arthur had a magic sword called Excalibur.*
**2** someone who is famous for a long time because he or she is very good at doing something: *Peyton Manning is already a football legend.*
→ see Thesaurus box at **story**
[ORIGIN: 1300-1400 From the Latin word *legenda*, which means "things to be read," from *legere*, meaning "to read."]

**leg·end·ar·y** /ˈledʒənˌderi/ *adjective*
famous and admired: *the legendary baseball player, Babe Ruth*

**leg·gings** /ˈlɛgɪŋz/ *plural noun*
tight pants for girls or women, that stretch and fit very closely to the legs: *I wear leggings and a T-shirt for my dance class.*

**leg·i·ble** /ˈledʒəbəl/ *adjective*
written or printed clearly enough for you to read: *The teacher gave my paper back because my writing was not legible.* **ANTONYM: illegible**

**le·gion** /ˈlidʒən/ *noun (formal)*
a large number of people or things: *The singer has legions of fans around the world.*

**leg·is·late** [Ac] /ˈledʒəˌsleɪt/ *verb (formal)*
to make a law about something: *Congress will try to legislate new health care changes.*
—**legislator** *noun* someone who has the power to make new laws: *A group of legislators will discuss the bill.*
[ORIGIN: 1400-1500 From the Latin phrase *legis lator*, which means "suggester of a law."]

**leg·is·la·tion** [Ac] /ˌledʒəˈsleɪʃən/ *noun*
a law or set of laws: *Congress wants to pass new legislation to reduce pollution.*

**leg·is·la·tive** [Ac] /ˈledʒəˌsleɪtɪv/ *adjective (formal)*
**1** relating to laws or to making laws: *Congress's legislative powers*
**2** **the legislative branch** = the part of a government that makes laws

**leg·is·la·ture** [Ac] /ˈledʒəˌsleɪtʃə/ *noun*
a group of people who make or change laws in a government: *The state legislature will vote on the bill tomorrow.*

**le·git·i·mate** /ləˈdʒɪtəmət/ *adjective*
**1** reasonable or acceptable: *She has a legitimate reason for not coming to school – her mother is very sick.*
**2** allowed by law or done according to the law: *It is only legitimate to use the software if you have paid for it.* **ANTONYM: illegal**
—**legitimacy** *noun* the state of being legitimate: *We have questions about the legitimacy of the election because too many people were not allowed to vote.*
—**legitimize** *verb* to make something legitimate: *Nothing can legitimize the killing of innocent people.*

**lei·sure** /ˈliʒə/ *noun*
the time when you are not at school or working and can do things that you enjoy: *I like to play soccer in my leisure time.*
[ORIGIN: 1200-1300 From the old French word *leisir*, which means "to be allowed," from the Latin word *licere*.]

**lei·sure·ly** /ˈliʒəli/ *adjective*
done in a slow and relaxed way: *They took a leisurely walk around the park.*

**lem·on** /ˈlemən/ *noun*
a yellow fruit with a juice that tastes sour:

*There was a slice of lemon with each piece of fish.* | *lemon juice* → see picture on page **A13**
—**lemony** *adjective* tasting or smelling of lemon
**[ORIGIN:** 1300-1400 From the French word *limon*, from the Arabic word *laymun*.**]**

**lem·on·ade** /ˌleməˈneɪd/ *noun*
a drink made with lemon juice, sugar, and water: *a nice cold glass of lemonade*

**lend** /lend/ *verb* (**lent** /lent/)
**1** to let someone have some money or something that belongs to you for a short time: *Could you lend me your bike tonight?*

**USAGE: lend, borrow**

If you **lend** something to someone, you let him or her have it or use it for a short time: *I lent that DVD to Rick.* | *Mom, could you lend me some money?*

You cannot say "Could you borrow me some money?"

If you **borrow** something from someone, he or she lets you have it or use it for a short time: *Can I borrow your pen?*

You cannot say "Can I lend your pen?"

**2** if a bank lends you money, it gives it to you but you must pay it back within a certain time and pay an additional amount of money called "interest": *The bank lends money to people who want to start a business.*



**length** /leŋθ/ *noun*
**1** the distance from one end of something to the other end: *The length of the room is ten feet.* | *The pole was about seven feet in length.*
**2** the amount of time during which something happens or continues: *The length of summer vacation is about ten weeks.*

**length·en** /ˈleŋθən/ *verb*
to make something longer: *There are new plans to lengthen the school day from six and a half to seven hours.* **ANTONYM: shorten**

**length·wise** /ˈleŋkθwaɪz/ (*also* **length·ways** /ˈleŋkθweɪz/) *adverb*
in the direction or position of something's longest side: *Fold the cloth lengthwise.*

**length·y** /ˈleŋθi/ *adjective* (*formal*)
continuing for a long time: *We had a lengthy discussion that took over an hour.*

**le·ni·ent** /ˈliniənt/ *adjective* (*formal*)
not strict in the way that you punish someone who has broken a rule: *I think judges are too lenient with drunk drivers; they should take the drunk driver's license away the first time.*
—**leniently** *adverb* in a lenient way
—**leniency** *noun* lenient behavior or a lenient attitude

**lens**

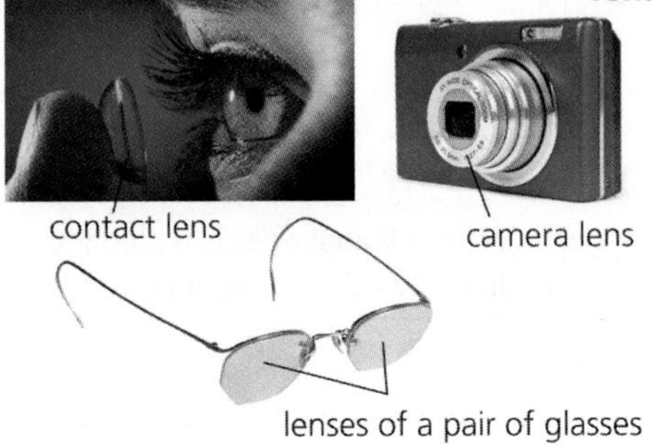


**lens** /lenz/ *noun*
**1** a piece of curved glass or plastic that makes things look bigger, smaller, or clearer: *His glasses had thick lenses.* | *a camera lens*
**2** the part inside your eye that bends light so that an image is formed on the back of your eye
**[ORIGIN:** 1600-1700 From the Latin word for "lentil." Some lenses are shaped like lentils, with a surface that curves outward on both sides.**]**

**lent** /lent/ *verb*
the past tense and past participle of LEND

**len·til** /ˈlentəl/ *noun*
a small round seed which has been dried and can be cooked

**Le·o** /ˈlioʊ/ *noun*
**1** the fifth sign of the ZODIAC, represented by a lion
**2** someone born between July 23 and August 22

**leop·ard** /ˈlepɚd/ *noun*
a large wild cat with yellow fur and black spots, that lives in Africa and southern Asia
**[ORIGIN:** 1200-1300 From the Greek words *leon* and *pardos*, which mean "lion" and "panther."**]**

**le·o·tard** /ˈliəˌtɑrd/ *noun*
a piece of clothing that fits the body tightly

from the neck to the tops of the legs: *The ballet dancers wore black leotards.*

**les·bi·an** /ˈlezbiən/ *noun*
a woman who is sexually attracted to other women
—**lesbian** *adjective* relating to lesbians

**less¹** /les/ *adverb*
**1 less important/likely/busy, etc.** = not as important, likely, busy, etc.: *This hotel is less expensive than the other one, but it's not as nice.* | *People who exercise are less likely to develop heart disease.* **ANTONYM: more**
**2** fewer times or for a shorter time: *I see him much less than I used to.* **ANTONYM: more**
**3 less and less** = used to say that an amount keeps getting smaller: *It seemed less and less likely that we could win the game.*

**less²** *adjective, pronoun*
a smaller amount: *I'm trying to exercise more and eat less to lose weight.* | *He earns less money than some of his friends.* | *She spends less of her time studying now that she has a job.* **ANTONYM: more**

**GRAMMAR: less, fewer**

Use **less** before nouns such as "money" and "bread" that do not have plurals: *Add less salt to your food.* | *This book has less information than the other one.*

Use **fewer** before plural forms of nouns: *There were fewer cars on the roads in the 1950s.* | *Fewer people than I expected were at the game.*

**less·en** /ˈlesən/ *verb*
to become less, or to make something become less: *If you wear a seat belt, you lessen the chances that you will be hurt in a car accident.* **ANTONYM: increase**
→ see Thesaurus box at **reduce**

**less·er** /ˈlesɚ/ *adjective (formal)*
not as large, as important, or as much as something else: *These wounds would have killed a lesser man* (=someone not as strong).

**les·son** /ˈlesən/ *noun*
**1** a period of time when someone teaches you something: *I have a guitar lesson today.* | *Hannah is taking swimming lessons.*
**2** an experience you learn something from, or the thing that you learn: *If you don't study, and fail the test, you have learned the valuable lesson that studying is necessary.*
[**ORIGIN:** 1100-1200 From the French word *leçon*, from the Latin word *lectio*, which means "the act of reading." In churches, parts of the Bible were read aloud so that people could learn from them.]

**let** /let/ *verb* (**let**, **letting**)
**1** to allow someone to do something, or allow something to happen: *I wanted to go, but my mom wouldn't let me.* | *Let me finish this, and then we can go.*
**2** to allow someone or something to come into or go out of a place: *Security guards refused to let reporters into the building.* | *He opened the door to let the dog out.*
**3 let go** = to stop holding someone or something: *You can let go of my hand after we cross the street.*
**4 let someone go** = to allow someone to go, after you have been keeping them somewhere: *The police let him go after asking him some questions.* **SYNONYM: release**
**5 let someone know** = to tell someone something: *I'll let you know when dinner is ready.*
**6 let me do something** = said when you are offering to help someone: *Let me carry that for you.*
→ see Thesaurus box at **allow**

**PHRASAL VERB**

**let someone down**
to make someone feel disappointed because you have not done what he or she wanted or expected you to do: *She had promised them a dog, and she didn't want to let them down.*

**let·down** /ˈletdaʊn/ *noun*
something that makes you feel disappointed because it is not as good as you expected: *Our hotel was a big letdown – the rooms were very small and not very clean.* **SYNONYM: disappointment**

**le·thal** /ˈliθəl/ *adjective*
lethal weapons or substances can kill someone: *The snake's bite can be lethal if you don't get treatment immediately.*
[**ORIGIN:** 1500-1600 From the Latin word *letum* or *lethum*, which means "death."]

**le·thar·gic** /ləˈθɑrdʒɪk/ *adjective*
having no energy and feeling tired or lazy: *The heat was making me feel lethargic.*

**let's** /lets/
the short form of "let us," used when you want to suggest that someone or a group of people do something with you: *I'm hungry – let's eat.* | *Let's not talk about this right now.*

**let·ter** /ˈletɚ/ *noun*
**1** a written message that you put into an envelope and send to someone by mail: *I wrote a letter to my mother telling her that I was coming to visit.* | *Can you mail this letter on your way to work?*
**2** one of the signs in writing that represents a sound in speech: *There are 26 letters in the English alphabet.*

**let·tuce** /ˈletɪs/ *noun*
a green vegetable with large leaves that you eat raw in SALADs → see picture on page **A12**
[**ORIGIN:** 1200-1300 From the Latin word *lactuca*, from *lac*, which means "milk." A milky liquid comes from the stem of a lettuce when you break it.]

**let·up** /ˈletʌp/ *noun*
a pause or a reduction in something unpleasant or difficult: *There's no letup in the rain – it's supposed to continue all weekend.*

**leu·ke·mia** /luˈkimiə/ *noun*
a serious disease that makes your body produce too many white blood cells. Leukemia is a CANCER of the blood: *Her son had leukemia and died last year.*
[**ORIGIN:** 1800-1900 From the Greek words *leukos* and *haima*, which mean "white" and "blood."]

L

**lev·ee** /ˈlevi/ *noun*
a wall that is built to stop a river from flooding

**lev·el¹** /ˈlevəl/ *noun*
**1** the amount or degree of something: *Will the price of gas stay at this level?*
**2** the height or position of something in relation to the ground or to another thing: *The water level in the lake is very high and houses near the shore have flooded.*
**3** a standard of skill or ability in something: *Rick played football at the highest level – the NFL.*
**4** a floor in a building with several floors: *The entrance to the parking lot is on Level 2.*

**level²** *adjective*
**1** flat and not sloping, with no part higher than any other part: *The floor isn't level so the furniture doesn't sit straight.*
**2** at the same height as something else: *The top of my head was level with his chin.*
→ see Thesaurus box at **flat¹**

**level³** *verb*
**1** to knock down or completely destroy a building or area: *An earthquake leveled several buildings in the city.*
**2** to make a surface flat and smooth: *Level the ground before putting the brick sidewalk down.*

**lev·er** /ˈlevɚ/ *noun*
**1** a long handle that you pull or push to make a machine start
**2** a long piece of metal used for lifting something heavy. You put one end under the object and push down on the other end.
[**ORIGIN:** 1200-1300 From the French word *lever*, which means "to raise," from the Latin word *levare*.]

**lev·er·age** /ˈlevərɪdʒ/ *noun* (*formal*)
influence that you can use to make people do what you want: *The United States used its political leverage to bring the leaders to the peace talks.*

**li·a·ble** /ˈlaɪəbəl/ *adjective*
**1 be liable to do something** = to be likely to do something: *Remind me to call her because I'm liable to forget.*
**2** legally responsible for the cost of something: *When you rent the equipment, you become liable for any damage caused.*
—**liability** /ˌlaɪˈbɪləti/ *noun* legal responsibility for the cost of something: *The airline tried to deny liability for the accident.*

**li·ar** /ˈlaɪɚ/ *noun*
someone who deliberately says something that is not true: *You're a liar! I didn't say that.*

**li·bel** /ˈlaɪbəl/ *noun*
the illegal act of writing or printing things about someone that are not true: *He is suing the magazine for libel after it said that he had spent time in jail.*

**lib·eral¹** Ac /ˈlɪbərəl/ *adjective*
willing to accept or respect other people's ideas and behavior even if they are different from your own: *a liberal church that welcomes people of other religions* **ANTONYM: conservative**

**liberal²** Ac *noun*
someone with liberal opinions or principles: *Political liberals want to spend more on education.* **ANTONYM: conservative**
—**liberalism** *noun* the attitude or behavior of liberals

**ˌliberal ˈarts** *plural noun*
subjects that develop someone's general knowledge and ability to think, rather than practical skills: *He enjoys liberal arts subjects such as history and sociology.*

**lib·eral·ize** Ac /ˈlɪbrəˌlaɪz/ *verb* (*formal*)
to make rules or laws less strict so that people have more freedom: *The state government plans to liberalize gambling laws.*

**lib·er·ate** Ac /ˈlɪbəˌreɪt/ *verb* (*formal*)
**1** to free people or a place from someone's control: *The U.S. army liberated the town from the Nazis in 1945.*
**2** to free someone from feelings or situations that make his or her life difficult: *Machines such as dishwashers have liberated us from a lot of hard work at home.*
—**liberator** *noun* someone who liberates people or a place: *The foreign soldiers were seen as liberators who would remove the dictator.*
—**liberation** /ˌlɪbəˈreɪʃən/ *noun* the act of liberating people or a place: *the liberation of Eastern Europe*

**lib·er·ty** /ˈlɪbəti/ *noun* (plural **liberties**)
**1** the freedom to do what you want without too much control from a government or authority: *The people of this country fought for liberty and democracy.*
**2** a particular legal right: *The new law will protect religious liberties so that all people can worship as they choose.*
**[ORIGIN:** 1300-1400 From the Latin word *libertas*, from *liber*, which means "free."**]**

**Li·bra** /ˈlibrə/ *noun*
**1** the seventh sign of the ZODIAC, represented by a SCALE
**2** someone born between September 23 and October 23

**li·brar·y** /ˈlaɪˌbreri/ *noun* (plural **libraries**)
a room or building containing books that you can borrow or read there: *He borrowed a book from the school library.* | *library books*
—**librarian** /laɪˈbreriən/ *noun* someone who works in a library
**[ORIGIN:** 1300-1400 From the Latin word *libri*, which means "books."**]**

**lice** /laɪs/ *noun*
the plural of LOUSE

**li·cense¹** Ac /ˈlaɪsəns/ *noun*
an official document that gives you permission to own something or do something: *He has a driver's license so he can drive.*

**license²** Ac *verb*
to give official permission for someone to own or do something: *Williams is not licensed to practice law in New York.*

**ˈlicense plate** *noun*
one of the signs with numbers and letters on it on the back or front of a car → see picture on page **A28**

**lick** /lɪk/ *verb*
to move your tongue across the surface of something: *The dog jumped up and licked her face.*

**lic·o·rice** /ˈlɪkərɪʃ/ *noun*
a type of black or red candy with a strong taste
**[ORIGIN:** 1100-1200 From the Greek word *glycyrrhiza*, which means "sweet root." The flavor for licorice used to come from the root of a plant.**]**

**lid** /lɪd/ *noun*
a cover for a pot, box, or other container: *He carefully lifted the lid of the box to see what was inside.*
→ see Thesaurus box at **cover²**

**lie¹** /laɪ/ *verb* (**lay** /leɪ/, **lain** /leɪn/, **lying**)
**1** to be or move into a position in which your body is flat on something: *We lay on the beach all day.* | *I'm going upstairs to lie down.*
**2** to be in a flat position on a surface: *His dirty clothes were lying all over the floor.*

**lie²** *verb* (**lied** /laɪd/, **lying**)
to deliberately tell someone something that is not true: *She lied about her age and said she was 30, when she was really 35.*

**USAGE: lie, lay**

**Lie** has two different meanings:
1) to be or move into a flat position on the floor, a bed, etc.: *Lie down on the sofa.*

L

The past tense for this meaning of **lie** is **lay**: *He lay on the bed.*

2) to say something that is not true: *Why did you lie to me?*

The past tense for this meaning of **lie** is **lied**: *The police think that he lied.*

**Lay** means to put something down in a flat position. The past tense for this is **laid**: *She laid the newspaper down and picked up the phone.*

**THESAURUS: lie**

**make something up** to think of a story that is not true, and tell it to someone: *"What will you tell your mother?" "I'll make something up."*

**fib** (*informal*) to tell someone a lie about something that is not important: *Were you fibbing when you said you didn't see what happened?*

**tell a lie** to say something that you know is not true: *I didn't want to tell a lie, but I didn't want to get Brian in trouble, either.*

**invent** to think of an idea or story that is not true: *John invented some excuse about having a headache.*

**mislead** (*formal*) to make someone believe something that is not true, by not giving all the information or by giving false information: *The ads mislead people by saying the drink contains extra vitamins, when it doesn't.*

**deceive** (*formal*) to make someone believe something that is not true: *She deceived her parents by saying that she was studying at a friend's house, when really she was meeting her boyfriend.*

**lie³** *noun*
something that you say which you know is not true: *He's telling lies – he said he was at school, when I know he wasn't.*

**lieu·ten·ant** /luˈtenənt/ *noun* (*written abbreviation*: **Lt.** *or* **Lieut.**)
an officer who has a middle rank in the armed forces or the police: *He's a lieutenant in the army.* | *Lieutenant Patrick Smith*

**life** /laɪf/ *noun* (plural **lives** /laɪvz/)
**1** the period of time between someone's birth and death: *Tim lived in New York all his life.* | *She spent her life helping others.*
**2** the state of being alive: *Wearing a helmet when you ride a motorcycle could save your life.* | *Firemen risked their lives to save him.*
**3** all the experiences and activities that are typical of a particular job, place, society, or way of living: *Life in the city is very exciting.*
**4** the type of experience that someone has during his or her life: *Grandma had a full and happy life.* | *Most teenagers should have busy social lives, seeing friends and being active.*
**5** living things such as people, animals, or plants: *Do you think there is life on other planets?*
**6** activity or movement: *The house looked empty, and there were no signs of life.* | *Katie was young and full of life.*
**7** human existence, and all the things that can happen during someone's life: *Life can be hard sometimes.*
**8** **real life** = things that really happen, rather than things that happen in a story or in someone's imagination: *TV shows are fun, but real life isn't like that.*

**life·boat** /ˈlaɪfboʊt/ *noun*
a small boat carried on a ship, that people can use if the ship sinks: *The ship has lifeboats in case of an emergency.*

**ˈlife ˌcycle** *noun*
all the stages in the life of an animal or plant, as it develops and changes into different forms: *In biology class, we learned about the life cycle of the butterfly.*

**ˈlife guard** *noun*
someone whose job is to help swimmers who are in danger: *The life guard was standing on the edge of the pool watching the swimmers.*

**ˈlife inˌsurance** *noun*
a type of insurance that pays money to your family when you die

**ˈlife ˌjacket** *noun*
a special jacket that fills with air and stops you from sinking if you fall into water

**life·less** /ˈlaɪflɪs/ *adjective*
**1** not exciting or interesting: *a lifeless, boring party*

2 dead or seeming to be dead: *They pulled her lifeless body from the river.*

**life·like** /ˈlaɪflaɪk/ *adjective*
very much like a real person or thing: *The statue was so lifelike that I thought it was a real person.*

**life·long** /ˈlaɪflɔŋ/ *adjective*
continuing all through your life: *My mom and Mrs. Evans have been lifelong friends.*

**ˈlife ˌpreserver** *noun*
a LIFE JACKET or a special ring filled with air, that you wear to stop yourself from sinking if you fall into water

**ˈlife raft** *noun*
a small rubber boat filled with air, that can be used by passengers if their ship sinks

**ˌlife ˈsentence** *noun*
the punishment of sending someone to prison for the rest of his or her life: *The judge gave him a life sentence for the murder.*

**life·style** /ˈlaɪfstaɪl/ *noun*
the way in which you live your life, including the kind of activities you do, where you live, and how much money you have: *She has a healthy lifestyle: she eats well and exercises.*

**life·time** /ˈlaɪftaɪm/ *noun*
the period of time during which someone is alive: *I never thought that there would be another big war in my lifetime.*

**lift**[1] /lɪft/ *verb*
1 (*also* **lift up**) to raise something or someone up into the air: *Lift up your feet so I can sweep the floor.* → see picture on page A4
2 to go up into the air: *The fog started to lift and the sun came out.*
3 to end a rule or a law that says that something is not allowed: *Will the government lift the ban on traveling to Cuba?*
4 (*informal*) to take someone else's words or ideas and use them in your own work: *She lifted parts of her essay directly from the Internet.* SYNONYM: **copy**

**lift**[2] *noun*
1 something that makes something more successful, or that makes people happier: *I got a good grade on the test, and that gave me a real lift.*
2 a piece of equipment for carrying people or heavy objects to a higher place: *We rode the ski lift to the top of the mountain.*
3 an occasion when you take someone somewhere in your car: *Can I give you a lift to school?* SYNONYM: **ride**

**ˈlift-off** *noun*
the moment when a space vehicle leaves the ground and rises up into the air: *After lift-off, the rocket shot up into the sky.*

**lig·a·ment** /ˈlɪgəmənt/ *noun*
a band of strong white material in your body that holds your bones together at a joint: *He damaged a ligament in his knee, so he can't play football for a while.*

**light**

**light**[1] /laɪt/ *noun*
1 the brightness from the sun, a lamp, or a flame, that allows you to see things: *The room has big windows and there's a lot of light.* ANTONYM: **dark**
2 something that produces light, for example an electric lamp: *Don't forget to turn off the lights.*
3 a set of red, green, and yellow lights used to control traffic: *Turn left at the light.*
4 **a different/new light** = a different or new opinion that you have about someone or something: *I thought he was lazy, but I began to think of him in a different light when I saw how hard he was trying.*
[ORIGIN: From the old English word *leoht*.]

**light**[2] *adjective*
1 not weighing very much: *The box was very light and easy to carry.* ANTONYM: **heavy** → see picture at heavy
2 a light color is not dark and seems to have

a lot of white mixed into it: *Tammy was wearing a light blue dress.* **SYNONYM: pale**; **ANTONYM: dark**

**3** if it is light, the sky or a place is not dark and there is brightness from the sun or a lamp: *It gets light at about 5 a.m. in the summer.* | *The room was nice and light.*

**4** light clothes are thin and not very warm: *She put on a light sweater when it got cooler in the evening.* **ANTONYM: thick**

**5** a light wind is not strong: *A light breeze blew through her hair.* **SYNONYM: gentle**; **ANTONYM: strong**

**6** if something is light, there is only a small amount of it: *light rain* | *The traffic was light on the freeway.* **ANTONYM: heavy**

**7** gentle and soft: *She gave him a light kiss on the cheek.*

**8 make light of something** = to joke about something that is serious or to treat it as if it were not important: *She tried to make light of the problem, but deep down it worried her.*

—**lightness** *noun* the quality of being light

**light³** *verb* (**lit** /lɪt/ *or* **lighted**)

**1** to make something start burning or producing light: *We lit a fire for warmth.*

**2** to provide light in a place: *The room is lit by candles.*

**PHRASAL VERB**

**light up**

**1 light something up** = to make something become bright: *Fireworks lit up the night sky.*

**2** if your face or eyes light up, you show that you are happy or excited: *Paula's eyes lit up when she saw all of her presents.*

**ˈlight bulb** *noun*

the round glass part of an electric lamp

**light·en** /ˈlaɪtn/ *verb*

**1** (*formal*) to become brighter: *The sky started to lighten and the sun came out.* **ANTONYM: darken**

**2** to make something less heavy: *I took some boxes out of the car to lighten the load.*

**PHRASAL VERB**

**lighten up**

to stop being so serious: *He needs to lighten up and stop worrying.*

**light·er** /ˈlaɪtɚ/ *noun*

a small object that produces a flame, used to light something such as a cigarette

**ˌlight-ˈheaded** *adjective*

unable to think clearly or move steadily, for example because you have drunk alcohol or you are sick: *She had a fever and felt light-headed.* **SYNONYM: dizzy**

**light·house** /ˈlaɪthaʊs/ *noun*

a tall building by the ocean, with a very bright light at the top that turns on and off to warn ships that they are near rocks or the coast

**light·ing** /ˈlaɪtɪŋ/ *noun*

the lights in a building or street, or how bright the lights are: *The lighting in the bedroom is so bad that it's impossible to read.*

**light·ly** /ˈlaɪtli/ *adverb*

gently: *I tapped her lightly on the shoulder so as not to scare her.*

**light·ning** /ˈlaɪtnɪŋ/ *noun*

a bright flash of light in the sky, that happens during a storm: *The tree was hit by lightning and split in two.*

**light·weight** /ˈlaɪtweɪt/ *noun*

a BOXER who weighs between 126 and 135 pounds

**ˈlight year** *noun*

the distance that light travels in one year: *The star is millions of light years away from the Earth.*

**lik·a·ble** (*also* **likeable**) /ˈlaɪkəbəl/ *adjective*

a likable person is nice and easy to like: *She's funny and likable and has lots of friends.*

**like¹** /laɪk/ *preposition, conjunction*

**1** similar to another person or thing: *Ken looks like his brother.* | *The Earth is round like a ball.* **ANTONYM: unlike**

**2** typical of a person or thing, or what they usually do: *It's not like Nancy to be late.*

**3** (*informal*) used when you are describing someone or something: *He acts like he knows everything.* | *"What was the movie like?" "It was good."*

**4** *(informal)* used to give an example of something. Many teachers think that this use of "like" is incorrect, and use "such as" or "for example" instead: *Vegetables like broccoli and carrots are very good for you.*
→ see Thesaurus box at **similar**

**like²** *verb*
**1** to think that someone or something is nice or good, or to enjoy doing something: *I never liked her brother very much.* | *She likes swimming.* | *He doesn't like to talk about himself.* **ANTONYM: dislike**

**GRAMMAR: like**

Do not say "I am liking bananas" or "I am liking to read." Say "*I like bananas*" or "*I like to read.*"
Do not say "I am liking Anna very much." Say "*I like Anna very much.*"

**2** to think that someone is nice and attractive: *"Do you like Jeff?" "Yeah, he's really cute."*
**3** to want something or want to do something: *I'd like a slice of pizza.* | *Would you like to come to the movies?*
→ see Thesaurus box at **enjoy**

**like·ly** /ˈlaɪkli/ *adjective*
if something is likely, it will probably happen or is probably true: *It's likely to rain tomorrow.*
—**likelihood** *noun* the state of being likely: *What is the likelihood of getting the disease?*

**like·ness** /ˈlaɪknəs/ *noun*
a picture or image of someone: *The stamp had a likeness of President Lincoln on it.*

**ˈlikes** *plural noun*
**likes and dislikes** = the things that you like and do not like: *Children have strong likes and dislikes about food.*

**like·wise** Ac /ˈlaɪk-waɪz/ *adverb*
**1** *(formal)* in the same way: *The boss stood up, and everyone else did likewise.*
**2** used when saying that you feel the same as the other person: *"It's great to see you." "Likewise."*

**lik·ing** /ˈlaɪkɪŋ/ *noun*
the feeling when you like someone or something: *He's always had a liking for ice cream and usually orders it for dessert.*

**li·lac** /ˈlaɪlək/ *noun*
**1** a small tree with purple or white flowers, which has a nice smell
**2** a light purple color
—**lilac** *adjective* having a light purple color
[**ORIGIN:** 1600-1700 From the Arabic word *lilak*. This comes from the Persian word *nilak*, which means "bluish in color," from *nil*, meaning "blue."]

**lil·y** /ˈlɪli/ *noun* (plural **lilies**)
a plant with large flowers, which are usually white or yellow: *There was a beautiful bunch of lilies in a vase.*

**limb** /lɪm/ *noun* *(formal)*
**1** an arm or leg: *He had a fever and all his limbs were shaking.*
**2** a large branch of a tree: *The cat climbed the tree and sat on one of the limbs.*

**lime** /laɪm/ *noun*
a small round green fruit that has a sour taste: *a lime tree* → see picture on page **A13**
[**ORIGIN:** 1600-1700 From French, from the Arabic word *limah*, which is related to the Arabic word for "lemon."]

**lim·er·ick** /ˈlɪmərɪk/ *noun*
a short funny poem with five lines, in which the first, second, and last lines RHYME, and the third and fourth lines have a different rhyme

**lim·it¹** /ˈlɪmɪt/ *noun*
**1** the greatest amount, number, or distance that is allowed or is possible: *The speed limit is 65 miles per hour.* | *There is a limit on how much money you can take out of the bank at one time.*
**2** the edge or border of something: *There are farms outside the city limits.*
**3** **be off limits** = if a place is off limits, you are not allowed to go there: *The military base is off limits to the public.*

**limit²** *verb*
to stop an amount or number from getting bigger than a particular amount: *Class size is limited to 30.* | *I limit the amount of TV my kids watch.*
—**limited** *adjective* small in number or amount: *There are a limited number of tickets, so get yours early.*

**lim·it·less** /ˈlɪmɪtlɪs/ *adjective*
without a limit or end: *There is an almost limitless number of books to read.*

**lim·o** /ˈlɪmoʊ/ *noun (informal)*
a LIMOUSINE

**lim·ou·sine** /ˈlɪməˌzin/ *noun*
a very large expensive car that is driven by someone who is paid to drive: *The band arrived at the concert in a limousine.*
**[ORIGIN:** 1900-2000 From Limousin, an area of France. The type of car that was originally called a limousine had a roof like the hood of a cloak worn in that area, or the driver wore this type of cloak.**]**

**limp¹** /lɪmp/ *adjective*
not stiff or firm: *Her legs went limp and she fell to the ground.*
—**limply** *adverb* in a limp way: *Her weak arm hung limply at her side.*

**limp²** *verb*
to walk with difficulty because your leg or foot is hurt: *He limped off the soccer field after he was knocked down.*
—**limp** *noun* a way of walking with difficulty because your leg or foot is hurt: *After the accident, he always walked with a limp.*
→ see Thesaurus box at **walk¹**

**line¹** /laɪn/ *noun*
**1** a long thin mark on a surface, especially a straight mark: *She drew a line across the page.* | *He reached the finish line at the end of the race.*
**2** a row of people or things: *A long line of cars was waiting to buy gas.* | *Mia stood in line at the cafeteria to get her food.*
**3** a long piece of string or rope: *I hung the wet clothes on the line.* | *a fishing line*
**4** a border between two states or countries: *I crossed the state line into Kansas.*
**5** the direction something travels, or the imaginary path between two points in space: *Light travels in a straight line – it doesn't curve.*
**6** a single row of words in a poem, play, song, or book: *I only know the first three lines of the poem.*
**7** a wire or connection, for example for electricity or the telephone: *The strong winds blew the power lines down.* | *I tried to call him, but the line was busy.*
**8 out of line** *(informal)* = not acceptable in a particular situation: *You're out of line! Don't swear at your mother!*
**[ORIGIN:** 1200-1300 From the Latin word *linea*, which means "thread or string," from *linum*, which means "flax (=a plant that is grown to make thread for cloth)."**]**

**line²** *verb*
**1** to cover the inside of something with something else: *We lined the box with old cloths to make it soft for the kittens.*
**2** to form a line along the edge of something: *Trees line the streets.*
**PHRASAL VERB**
**line up**
to form a line of people or things: *The fans lined up outside the stadium.*

**ˈline graph** *noun*
a GRAPH that uses a line to show how amounts change over time: *The line graph showed the amount of rain in different months of the year.* → see picture at **graph**

**lin·en** /ˈlɪnən/ *noun*
**1** a kind of cloth made from a plant called FLAX, used to make clothes, sheets, TABLECLOTHs, etc.: *a cool linen shirt*
**2 bed/table linen** *(formal)* = sheets or TABLECLOTHs

**lin·er** /ˈlaɪnɚ/ *noun*
a large ship for carrying people: *They sailed to Hawaii on an ocean liner.*

**line·up** /ˈlaɪnʌp/ *noun*
**1** the players on a sports team who are playing in a game: *He won't be in the lineup for tonight's game because of an injury.*
**2** a set of events, performers, or television programs that have been arranged to happen one after the other: *Friday night's TV lineup includes three comedy shows.*

**lin·ger** /ˈlɪŋgɚ/ (*also* **linger on**) *verb (formal)*
to stay somewhere for a long time: *The smell of onions lingered in the kitchen.*

**lin·ge·rie** /ˌlɑnʒəˈreɪ/ *noun (formal)*
women's underwear

**lin·guis·tics** /lɪŋˈgwɪstɪks/ *noun*
the study of languages, including their grammar and history

**lin·ing** /ˈlaɪnɪŋ/ *noun*
a piece of material covering the inside of

something such as a coat or box: *a jacket with a red lining*

**link¹** Ac /lɪŋk/ *verb*
**1** to say or show that two things are related, so that one thing causes or affects the other: *Smoking is linked to cancer.*
**2** to connect two things or places together: *The interstate highway links the two major cities. | You'll need a modem in order to link your computer to the Internet.*

**link²** Ac *noun*
**1** a relationship or connection between two or more things or people: *The police think that there is a link between the two burglaries.*

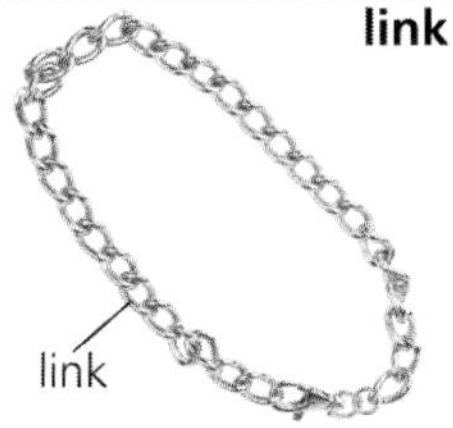


**2** one of the rings in a chain: *One of the links on my necklace has broken.*
**3** a connection between two websites that you CLICK on to move from one website to the other: *If you click on the link, it will take you to a site where you can buy the CD.*
**4 a satellite/telephone/rail, etc. link** = something that makes it possible to communicate or travel between different places: *The reporters sent the pictures back to the TV studio using a satellite link.*

**li·no·le·um** /lɪˈnoʊliəm/ *noun*
smooth material that is used to cover a floor: *The linoleum on the kitchen floor is easy to keep clean.*

**lint** /lɪnt/ *noun*
soft small pieces of thread that come off cotton, wool, or other material

**li·on** /ˈlaɪən/ *noun*
a large wild cat that lives in Africa: *Male lions have long thick hair around their necks.*

**li·on·ess** /ˈlaɪənɪs/ *noun*
a female lion

**lip** /lɪp/ *noun*
**1** your lips are the two outer parts of your mouth where the skin is redder or darker: *She kissed him on the lips.* → see picture on page A2
**2** the top edge of a container such as a cup or a bowl: *Soup had spilled over the lip of the bowl.*

**lip·stick** /ˈlɪpˌstɪk/ *noun*
a substance that women use to put color on their lips: *I wear lipstick if I'm going out.*

**liq·ue·fy** /ˈlɪkwəˌfaɪ/ *verb* (**liquefied, liquefies**) (*formal*)
to change into a liquid: *The gas liquefies when it is cooled to a low temperature.*

**liq·uid** /ˈlɪkwɪd/ *noun*
a substance such as water that is not a solid or a gas: *There was still some liquid in the bottle.*
—**liquid** *adjective* not a solid or a gas: *a bottle of liquid soap*

**liq·uor** /ˈlɪkɚ/ *noun*
a strong alcoholic drink such as WHISKEY: *The bar sells whiskey and other kinds of liquor.*
[**ORIGIN:** 1200-1300 From a Latin word for "liquid," from *liquere*, which means "to flow."]

**ˈliquor store** *noun*
a store where alcohol is sold

**lisp** /lɪsp/ *noun*
if someone has a lisp, he or she pronounces "s" sounds as "th" when speaking

**list¹** /lɪst/ *noun*
a set of things that you write one below the other: *Make a list of the things you'll need. | Is my name on the list?*

**list²** *verb*
to write or say a list of things: *List your ten favorite movies, starting with the one you like the best.*

**lis·ten** /ˈlɪsən/ *verb*
**1** to pay attention to what someone is saying or to a sound such as music: *Listen carefully – this is important. | He was listening to a CD.*
**2** (*informal*) used when you want someone to pay attention to what you are saying: *Listen, Amanda, it's time to clean up your room.*
**3 Listen up!** (*informal*) = said in order to get a group of people's attention when you are going to say something important: *Okay, class, listen up! Turn to page 33.*
—**listener** *noun* someone who listens to what people are saying, or to a radio station: *Do you want to talk about it? I'm a good listener.*

**list·ing** /ˈlɪstɪŋ/ *noun*
a list, or something that is on a list: *She*

L

*checked the TV listings to see if there was anything good on TV.*

**lit**[1] /lɪt/ *verb*
the past tense and past participle of LIGHT

**lit**[2] *adjective*
**1** if a room is brightly lit, it has a lot of light. If a room is badly lit, it has very little light: *The room was brightly lit and I could see everyone's face clearly.*
**2** if something is lit, it is burning: *The candles were all lit.*

**lite** /laɪt/ *adjective*
used in the names of food and drink products that have less fat, sugar, or alcohol than normal

**li·ter** /ˈlitɚ/ *noun* (*written abbreviation*: **l**)
a unit for measuring liquids, equal to 0.26 gallons: *a liter of water*
[**ORIGIN:** 1700-1800 From the Greek word *litra*, a unit of weight.]

**lit·er·a·cy** /ˈlɪtərəsi/ *noun*
the ability to read and write: *The literacy program helps adults improve their reading and writing skills.*

**lit·er·al** /ˈlɪtərəl/ *adjective*
the literal meaning of a word is its basic or first meaning: *The fight against crime is not a literal fight – we are not using our fists against criminals.* **ANTONYM: metaphorical**

**lit·er·al·ly** /ˈlɪtərəli/ *adverb*
**1** used to emphasize that something is really true: *There are literally hundreds of birds in the tree.*
**2** according to the original meaning of the word: *The word "telephone" literally means "far sound."*

**lit·er·ar·y** /ˈlɪtəˌreri/ *adjective*
relating to literature: *He writes poems and other literary works.*

**lit·er·ate** /ˈlɪtərɪt/ *adjective*
able to read and write: *People who are not literate cannot read job application forms.* **ANTONYM: illiterate**

**lit·er·a·ture** /ˈlɪtərətʃɚ/ *noun*
books, plays, and poems that people think are good or important: *I studied Mark Twain's "Adventures of Huckleberry Finn" in my American literature class.*
→ see Thesaurus box at **book**[1]
[**ORIGIN:** 1300-1400 From the Latin word *litteratura*, which means "writing or learning," from *littera*, meaning "letter."]

**lit·ter** /ˈlɪtɚ/ *noun*
**1** waste paper, cans, etc. that people have left on the ground in a public place: *People have picnics in the park and then just leave their litter on the ground instead of putting it in the trash cans.*
**2** a group of baby animals born to one mother at the same time: *Our cat just had a litter of five kittens!*
—**litter** *verb* if things litter a place, they are there and make it look messy: *The floor was littered with toys.*
→ see Thesaurus box at **garbage**

**lit·tle**[1] /ˈlɪtl/ *adjective, pronoun*
**1** small: *The dog had cute little ears.* | *The mother was carrying her little girl.*
**2** (**less**, **least**) a small amount: *I only know a little Spanish – just the basics.* | *"Would you like some gravy?" "Just a little."* | *Can I have a little bit of milk in my coffee, please?* | *Little is known about the disease, but scientists are trying to learn more.*

> **GRAMMAR: little, a little**
>
> Use **little** when you mean "not much": *I have very little money left.*
>
> Use **a little** when you mean "a small amount": *I accidentally spilled a little milk on the carpet.*
>
> **Little** and **a little** are always used with nouns such as "money" and "bread" that do not have plurals.

**3** short in time or distance: *I'll wait a little while and then call again.* | *Anna walked a little way down the road with him.*
**4** not important: *He gets angry over little things.*
→ see Thesaurus box at **small**

**little**[2] *adverb*
**1** **a little** = slightly: *I was a little nervous at first, but then I calmed down.*
**2** not much: *I slept very little last night and I'm very tired today.*

**liv·a·ble** (*also* **liveable**) /ˈlɪvəbəl/ *adjective*
good enough to live in: *We could make the*

L

*neighborhood more livable by giving children a safe place to play.*

**live¹** /lɪv/ *verb*
1 to be alive: *Grandma lived until she was 88.* | *He was the best athlete who ever lived.*
2 to have your home in a particular place: *I live in Atlanta.*
3 to have a particular kind of life: *I just want to live a normal life.*
PHRASAL VERBS
**live on/off something**
1 to eat only one kind of food: *These animals live on insects.*
2 to have an amount of money to spend on things you need: *We were living on $1,500 a month.*
**live up to something**
to be as good as someone expects: *The movie didn't live up to my expectations.*
**live with someone**
to share your home with someone, especially a boyfriend or girlfriend: *Tim's living with a girl he met in college.*

**WORD FAMILY: live**
**live** *verb* | **life** *noun* | **living** *adjective* | **alive** *adjective* | **live** *adjective*

**live²** /laɪv/ *adjective*
1 live animals are not dead: *The snake eats live mice.* ANTONYM: **dead**
2 a live broadcast on television or the radio lets people see or hear an event as it happens: *I listened to a live broadcast of the president's speech from the White House.*
3 live music is performed in front of a group of people who are watching and listening: *The club has live music three nights a week, with a different band each night.*
—**live** *adverb* broadcast as something is actually happening: *The ceremony will be broadcast live on television.*

**live-in** /ˈlɪv ɪn/ *adjective*
living in the same home as the person you work for, or living in the same home as your boyfriend or girlfriend: *a live-in cook*

**live·li·hood** /ˈlaɪvliˌhʊd/ *noun*
the way you earn money in order to live: *Farming is their livelihood, so when crops are bad, they have no money.*

**live·ly** /ˈlaɪvli/ *adjective* (**livelier**, **liveliest**)
full of energy, activity, or excitement: *Our dog is very lively and he's always running.* | *The discussion was lively with lots of shouting.*

**liv·er** /ˈlɪvɚ/ *noun*
1 a large organ inside your body which cleans your blood → see picture on page A2
2 the liver of an animal, eaten as meat

**lives** /laɪvz/ *noun*
the plural of LIFE

**live·stock** /ˈlaɪvstɑk/ *noun*
animals that are kept on a farm: *They keep cows and other livestock.*

**liv·ing¹** /ˈlɪvɪŋ/ *adjective*
alive: *The ocean is full of fish and other living things.* ANTONYM: **dead**

**living²** *noun*
1 money for things that you need in order to live, or a way of making money: *"What does he do for a living?" "He's a doctor."* | *He makes a living by doing odd jobs.*
2 **the living** (*formal*) = the people who are alive: *We must help the living before burying the dead.*

**ˈliving room** *noun*
the main room in a house, where you sit and relax: *Jack was lying on the sofa in the living room, reading.*

**liz·ard** /ˈlɪzɚd/ *noun*
an animal that has rough skin, short legs, and a long tail: *Lizards are a kind of reptile.*
[ORIGIN: 1300-1400 From the old French word *lesard*, from the Latin word *lacerta*.]

**'ll** /l, əl/ *verb*
the short form of "will": *She'll do it tomorrow.*

**load¹** /loʊd/ *noun*
1 a large amount of something that is carried by a vehicle or person: *The truck was carrying a load of fruit.*
2 the amount of work that someone has to do or that a machine can do: *Some teachers have a heavy teaching load.* | *I put a load of laundry in the washing machine.*
3 **loads of something** (*informal*) = a lot of something: *If he can afford to live in Manhattan, he must have loads of money.*

**load²** *verb*
1 (*also* **load up**) to put heavy things into a

vehicle: *We loaded the van with boxes to take to the new apartment.*

**2** to put bullets into a gun, or film into a camera: *He loaded the gun and aimed at the target.*

**3** to put a program into a computer: *It doesn't take long to load the software.*

**loaf** /loʊf/ *noun* (plural **loaves** /loʊvz/)
bread that has been cooked in one large piece: *I bought a loaf of bread.*
**[ORIGIN:** From the old English word *hlaf.***]**

**loan[1]** /loʊn/ *noun*
an amount of money that you borrow, especially from a bank: *He had to get a loan from the bank to buy the car.*

**loan[2]** *verb*
**1** to lend someone money: *I loaned him $20.*
**SYNONYM: lend**
**2** to let someone borrow something you own: *He loaned me his bike on Saturday.*
**SYNONYM: lend**

**loaves** /loʊvz/ *noun*
the plural of LOAF

**lob·by** /ˈlɑbi/ *noun* (plural **lobbies**)
**1** a large hall inside the entrance of a building: *Wait for me in the hotel lobby.*
**2** a group of people who try to persuade the government to do something: *The environmental lobby wants the government to make laws that protect the environment.*
—**lobby** *verb* to try to persuade the government to do something
—**lobbyist** *noun* someone who tries to persuade the government to do something
**[ORIGIN:** 1500-1600 From the Latin word *lobium*, which means "covered area for walking along."**]**

**lobster**

**lob·ster** /ˈlɑbstɚ/ *noun*
a sea animal which has a hard body and ten legs. The two front legs have large CLAWs.

**lo·cal** /ˈloʊkəl/ *adjective*
in or relating to the area where someone lives: *We borrowed books from the local library.*
—**locally** *adverb* in the area where someone lives: *Most of the fruit we buy is grown locally.*
—**local** *noun* someone who lives in the place you are talking about: *I asked one of the locals how to get to the highway.*
→ see Thesaurus box at **near[1]**
**[ORIGIN:** 1300-1400 From the Latin word *locus*, which means "place."**]**

**ˈlocal time** *noun*
the time in a particular part of the world: *We'll arrive in Denver at four o'clock local time.*

**lo·cate** [Ac] /ˈloʊkeɪt/ *verb* (*formal*)
**1 be located** = to be in a particular place: *The hotel is located near the airport, so it's easy to get to.*
**2** to find the place where something is: *The police have located the hidden bomb.*
→ see Thesaurus box at **find**
**[ORIGIN:** 1500-1600 From the Latin word *locare*, which means "to put or place," from *locus*, meaning "place."**]**

**lo·ca·tion** [Ac] /loʊˈkeɪʃən/ *noun*
the place where something is, or where something happens: *The map shows the exact location of the island.*
→ see Thesaurus box at **place[1]**

**lock[1]** /lɑk/ *noun*
a metal object that you open or close with a key. A lock prevents other people from opening a door, drawer, or container: *He turned the key in the lock and opened the door.*

**lock[2]** *verb*
to close a door, drawer, or container with a lock: *Did you remember to lock the door when you left this morning? | The prisoners are locked in their cells.* **ANTONYM: unlock**
**PHRASAL VERB**
**lock up**
**1 lock someone up** (*also* **lock someone away**) = to put someone in prison: *They*

L

*should lock up criminals like that and never let them out.*
**2** to lock all the doors of a building: *Don't forget to lock up when you leave.*

**lock·er** /ˈlɑkɚ/ *noun*
a small cupboard where you leave things you own, especially at school or when you are playing sports

**ˈlocker room** *noun*
a room with lockers in it, where people change their clothes before playing sports

**lock·et** /ˈlɑkɪt/ *noun*
a piece of jewelry that you wear around your neck on a chain, with a small metal case in which you can put a picture → see picture at **jewelry**

**lo·co·mo·tive** /ˌloʊkəˈmoʊtɪv/ *noun*
the part of a train that pulls the other parts along **SYNONYM: engine**

**lodge¹** /lɑdʒ/ *verb*
**1** to become stuck somewhere: *A fish bone was lodged in his throat.*
**2 lodge a complaint/protest** (*formal*) = to officially complain about something: *I would like to lodge a complaint with management about the bad service we received.*

**lodge²** *noun*
**1** a simple building or hotel in the country where people can stay for a short time: *a ski lodge*
**2** the home of a BEAVER

**lodg·ing** /ˈlɑdʒɪŋ/ *noun*
a place to stay: *The tourist office will help you find lodging when you arrive.*

**loft** /lɔft/ *noun*
an area with a floor that is above a room or in a BARN: *The farmer stored hay in the loft.*

**log¹** /lɔg/ *noun*
**1** a thick piece of wood that has fallen off or been cut off a tree: *Put another log on the fire so the flames don't go out.*
**2** an official record of things that have happened or been done, especially on a ship: *The ship's captain wrote about the problems with the sails in the log.*

**log²** *verb* (**logged**, **logging**)
**PHRASAL VERBS**
**log off/out**
to stop using a computer or computer program that you have entered a PASSWORD to use: *Log off and switch off the computer when you're finished.*
**log on/in**
to enter information to start using a computer: *I can't log on because I've forgotten my password.*

**log·ging** /ˈlɔgɪŋ/ *noun*
the activity of cutting down trees in a forest

**log·ic** [Ac] /ˈlɑdʒɪk/ *noun*
a way of thinking about something carefully, in which you examine facts and see if they are connected to each other in a reasonable or sensible way: *If the lights are on, logic tells us that someone must have turned them on.*
[**ORIGIN:** 1300-1400 From the Greek word *logike*, from *logos*, which means "reasoning."]

**WORD FAMILY: logic**
**logic** *noun* | **logical** *adjective* | **illogical** *adjective* | **logically** *adverb*

**log·i·cal** [Ac] /ˈlɑdʒɪkəl/ *adjective*
sensible and based on good thinking: *It doesn't seem logical to blame someone who wasn't even there.* **ANTONYM: illogical**
—**logically** *adverb* in a logical way

**lo·go** /ˈloʊgoʊ/ *noun* (plural **logos**)
a picture that is the official sign of a company or organization: *The players have the team logo on their helmets.*

**lol·li·pop** /ˈlɑliˌpɑp/ *noun*
a hard candy on the end of a stick

**lone** /loʊn/ *adjective* (*formal*)
used to talk about the only person or thing in a place or the only one doing something: *The lone survivor of the crash was the driver.*

**lone·ly** /ˈloʊnli/ *adjective*
**1** unhappy because you are alone: *He is lonely without his wife.*
**2** a long way from where people live: *a lonely country road*
—**loneliness** *noun* the feeling you have when you are lonely

**lone·some** /ˈloʊnsəm/ *adjective*
lonely: *I felt so lonesome when she left.*

**long**[1] /lɔŋ/ *adjective*
**1** measuring a large distance from one end to the other: *Julie has long hair. | The line for food was really long.* **ANTONYM: short**
**2** continuing for a large amount of time: *I had a long talk with him. | It happened a long time ago – back in 1853.* **ANTONYM: short**
**3 in the long run** = in the future, not immediately: *Good shoes are expensive, but they save you money in the long run because they don't fall apart.*
**4** used to ask or talk about how much time or distance something has or continues for: *"How long is the movie?" "About 2 hours." | The snake was three feet long.*
**5** containing a lot of words, names, or pages: *The book was so long – 750 pages! | a long list of names* **ANTONYM: short**

**long**[2] *adverb*
**1** (*also* **for long**) for a large amount of time: *Have you been waiting long? | He didn't stay angry for long. The next day he was fine.*
**2 long before/after** = a time that is many days, years, etc. before or after an event: *He died long before you were born.*
**3 as long as** (*also* **so long as**) = if: *You can go as long as you're back by four o'clock.*
**4 no longer** (*also* **not any longer**) = used about something that used to happen or be true in the past, but does not happen or is not true now: *She no longer teaches at this school – she's now at Hansen Middle School.*
**5 before long** = soon: *Before long, we arrived at the station.*
**6 so long** (*informal*) = goodbye

**long**[3] *verb*
to want something very much: *She longed to go home and thought about it every day.*

**ˌlong-ˈdistance** *adjective*
**1** a long-distance telephone call is one you make to someone who lives far away: *I made a long-distance call to my sister in Hawaii.* **ANTONYM: local**
**2** traveling between places that are far away from each other: *long-distance truck drivers*
—**long-distance** *adverb* speaking by telephone to someone who is far away: *She called her boyfriend long-distance every night while she was on vacation.*

**long·house** /ˈlɔŋhaʊs/ *noun*
a type of house that was used by some Native American tribes: *A typical longhouse was about 80 feet long by 18 feet wide.*

**long·ing** /ˈlɔŋɪŋ/ *noun*
a strong feeling of wanting someone or something very much: *He was filled with longing to be back home.*
—**longingly** *adverb* in a way that shows you want someone or something very much: *The boy looked longingly at the cookies in the jar, but his mother said "no."*

**lon·gi·tude** /ˈlɑndʒəˌtud/ *noun*
the distance east or west of an imaginary line going from the top of the Earth to the bottom. Longitude is used to show the position of a place, measured in degrees: *The island is at longitude 21° west.*

**ˈlong jump** *noun*
**the long jump** = a sport in which you jump as far as possible

**ˌlong-ˈrunning** *adjective*
happening continuously for a long time: *The long-running legal battle has lasted for five years.*

**ˌlong-ˈterm** *adjective*
relating to what will happen a long time in the future: *My long-term goal is to go to law school, and eventually to become a lawyer.* **ANTONYM: short-term**

**look**[1] /lʊk/ *verb*
**1** to move your eyes toward something or someone so that you can see them: *David took $5 from her purse when she wasn't looking. | She looked at me and smiled.* → see picture at **see**

**USAGE: look at, see, watch**

You **look at** a picture, person, thing, etc. because you want to do this: *Hey, look at the hat that man is wearing. | Maria was looking at a picture book.*

You **see** something without planning to do this: *Two people saw him take the woman's purse. | I saw a big black dog in the park.*

You **watch** TV, a movie, or something that happens for a period of time: *My parents*

L

*always come to watch me play basketball.* | *The kids are watching TV.*

You can also say that you **saw** a movie, a program, etc., but you cannot say "see television": *I saw a great movie on TV last night.*

**THESAURUS: look**

**Look at Something:**

**watch** to look at something that is moving, or to look at a sport, television show, or movie: *I watched her leave.* | *Dad is watching a baseball game on TV.*

**glance** to look at someone or something for a short time and then look quickly away: *Kevin glanced at the clock.*

**peek** to quickly look at something, especially something you are not supposed to see: *Close your eyes and don't peek – I'm going to bring you a surprise.*

**peer** to look very carefully, especially because you cannot see something well: *Hansen peered through the screen door but could not see anyone in the kitchen.*

**stare** to look at someone or something for a long time without moving your eyes: *That man is staring at me!*

**gaze** to look at someone or something for a long time, often while thinking about something else: *Helen gazed out the window at the lake.*

**Look for Someone/Something:**

**search** to look carefully for someone or something: *We searched the whole house for the keys.*

**try to find someone/something** to look for someone or something, especially when this is difficult: *My brother has been trying to find a job for six months.*

**seek** (*formal*) to try to find or get something, especially help or advice: *If the cough does not go away, you should seek advice from your doctor.*

**2** to try to find someone or something that is hidden or lost: *I looked everywhere for my car keys but I couldn't find them.* | *"Is there any orange juice?" "Look in the refrigerator."*

**3** to try to find someone or something that you need: *He says he wants a new job, but he's not looking very hard.* | *My band is looking for somebody who can play the drums.*

**4** to seem or appear to be something: *Mom's eyes were closed and she looked tired.* | *The movie looks like it will be good.*

→ see Thesaurus box at **seem**

**5 strange-looking/odd-looking/tough-looking etc.** = having a particular appearance: *That's a strange-looking dog!*

**6 Look ...** = said when you are annoyed and you want to emphasize what you are saying: *Look, I'm not giving you any money, so don't ask me again!*

**PHRASAL VERBS**

**look after someone**

to take care of someone or something: *Sarah asked me to look after her dog while she was on vacation.*

**look ahead**

to think about what will happen in the future: *You need to look ahead and make plans for when you graduate.*

**look around (something)**

to look at what is in a building, store, or place while you are walking: *We have about three hours to look around the mall.*

**look forward to something**

to be excited and happy about something that is going to happen: *I'm looking forward to seeing my dad when he comes home.*

**look into something**

to try to find out the truth about a crime or problem: *The police are looking into the cause of the fire.*

**look on**

**1** to watch something happening, without being involved in it: *A truck pulled the car out of the mud while several people looked on.*

**2 look on/upon something** (*formal*) = to think about something in a particular way: *There are some problems that I have to solve, but I look on them as challenges.*

L

**look out**
**Look out!** = use this to tell someone to pay attention because something dangerous is happening: *Look out! There's a car coming.*

**look something over** (*informal*)
to examine something quickly: *Can you look over my homework before I turn it in?*

**look up**
1 **look something up** = to try to find information in a book: *I had to look the word up in the dictionary to find out what it means.*
2 **look someone up** = to go to see someone you know when you are visiting the place where he or she lives: *I looked up an old friend when I went to Seattle on business.*

**look up to someone**
to admire and respect someone: *He looks up to his older brothers and wants to be just like them.*

**look²** *noun*
1 an act of looking at something: *We decided to take a look around the museum at the paintings and sculptures.*
2 an expression that you make with your eyes or face to show how you feel: *There was a look of surprise on her face.* | *Jon gave me an angry look.*
3 **looks** = how attractive someone is: *He has the looks to become a model.*

L

**look·out** /ˈlʊk-aʊt/ *noun*
1 **be on the lookout (for something)** (*informal*) = to watch everything that is happening around you in order to find something you want or to be ready for problems: *Be on the lookout for snakes – they hide in the grass.*
2 someone whose job is to watch carefully for danger

**loom** /lum/ *verb* (*formal*)
1 to appear as a large unclear shape that seems dangerous or frightening: *The huge house loomed over him in the darkness.*
2 if a problem or difficult situation is looming, it is likely to happen very soon: *The deadline for finishing our science project was looming.*

**loop¹** /lup/ *noun*
a shape like a circle in a piece of string or wire: *The keys were hanging from a loop of string.*

**loop²** *verb*
to tie string or wire around something in the shape of a circle: *I looped the rope around the tree and tied a knot.*

**loop·hole** /ˈluphoʊl/ *noun*
a small mistake in a law that people use to avoid doing what the law intended: *Congress closed this loophole in the law so that all businesses now have to pay the tax.*

**loose** /lus/ *adjective*
1 not firmly attached to something: *I have two loose teeth, and they'll probably fall out soon.* | *One of the buttons on my shirt is coming loose – I need to sew it back on.*
2 loose clothes do not fit tightly on your body: *My jeans are loose and comfortable.*
SYNONYM: **baggy**
3 free to move around, and not in a CAGE or prison: *The dogs got loose and started chasing the horses.*
4 if your hair is loose, it is not tied or kept firmly in place: *Her hair was loose and hung down her back.*
—**loosely** *adverb* not tied firmly or tightly: *He wrapped the towel loosely around his waist.*

**USAGE: loose, lose**

**Loose** is an adjective: *Tighten the loose screw with a screwdriver.*

**Lose** is a verb: *I didn't want to lose the game.*

**ˌloose-ˈleaf** *adjective*
having pages that can be put in or removed easily: *You can add pages to a loose-leaf binder.*

**loos·en** /ˈlusən/ *verb*
to make something less tight or less firmly fastened: *He took off his shoes and loosened his tie.*

**loot** /lut/ *verb*
to steal things from stores or houses during a war or RIOT: *The mob started looting stores and setting fire to cars.*
—**loot** *noun* money or things that have been stolen, especially during a war

—**looting** *noun* the act of stealing things during a war or RIOT
—**looter** *noun* someone who loots

**lop·sid·ed** /ˌlɑpˈsaɪdɪd/ *adjective* (*informal*)
1 having one side that is heavier, larger, or lower than the other side: *a lopsided smile*
2 not equal or fair: *The Red Sox beat Baltimore 10-0 in a lopsided game.*

**Lord** /lɔrd/ *noun*
1 a title used for God or Jesus Christ, used especially when praying: *Let us give thanks to the Lord our God.*
2 a man who belongs to the highest social class in Britain, and can use the word "Lord" before his name: *the poet Lord Byron*
[ORIGIN: From the old English word *hlaford*, from *hlaf* and *weard*, which mean "bread" and "keeper."]

**lose** /luz/ *verb* (**lost** /lɔst/)
1 to stop having something that is important to you or that you need: *Michelle lost her job and needs to get another one quickly.* | *Her family lost everything they owned in the storm.*
2 to be unable to find someone or something: *I think I lost my wallet – I can't find it anywhere.*
3 to not win a game, war, or argument: *Napoleon's army was defeated, and France lost the war.* | *We played well, but we still lost the game by 2 points.*
4 to have less of something than before: *I need to lose weight.* | *Many people lost money when the company went bankrupt.*
5 to stop having an ability, quality, or attitude: *Grandpa's getting old and losing his hearing.* | *Marie lost interest in going to college and decided to get a job instead.*
6 **lose your temper** = to become angry: *Jake lost his temper and started yelling at everyone.*
7 if you lose a member of your family, that person dies: *Mrs. Keenan lost two sons in the war.*
8 **lose your life** = to die: *More than 2,000 people lost their lives in the earthquake.*
9 **lose someone** (*informal*) = to confuse someone when you are trying to explain something: *You lost me. Can you explain it again, please?*

[ORIGIN: From the old English word *losian*, which means "to destroy or be destroyed."]

**WORD FAMILY: lose**

**lose** *verb* | **lost** *adjective* | **loser** *noun* | **loss** *noun*

**USAGE: lose, loose**

**Lose** is a verb: *I didn't want to lose the game.*

**Loose** is an adjective: *Tighten the loose screw with a screwdriver.*

**los·er** /ˈluzɚ/ *noun*
1 someone who loses a competition or game: *The losers of this game will get the silver medal, and the winners will get the gold medal.* ANTONYM: **winner**
2 (*informal*) you use this about someone who you do not like or respect: *Don't go to the dance with him – he's such a loser.*

**loss** /lɔs/ *noun*
1 the fact of no longer having something: *weight loss* | *The factory is closing, and there will be many job losses.*
2 if a business has a loss, it spends more money than it earns: *The company had huge losses last year, and investors were not happy.*
3 an occasion when you do not win a game: *The team has three wins and four losses this season.*
4 the death of someone: *We are all very sad at the loss of a dear friend.*

**lost**[1] /lɔst/ *adjective*
1 if you get lost, you do not know where you are or how to get somewhere: *It's easy to get lost in a city this big.* | *We were lost, so we asked a policeman for directions.*
2 if something is lost, you cannot find it: *I'm calling to report a lost credit card.*
3 **Get lost!** (*informal*) = used to tell someone rudely to go away or to stop annoying you

**lost**[2] *verb*
the past tense and past participle of LOSE

**ˌlost-and-ˈfound** *noun*
a place where things that people have lost are kept until someone comes to get them

**lot** /lɑt/ *noun*
1 **a lot** = **a)** (*also* **lots** (*informal*)) a large amount or number: *A million dollars is a lot of*

L

money. | The police asked me lots of questions, but I couldn't answer them all. **b)** very much: *I like her a lot – she's a very good friend.* | *We'll get there a lot faster if we drive.*

**GRAMMAR: a lot of, much, many**

You can use **much** or **many** instead of **a lot of**.

**Much** is used with nouns such as "money" and "bread" that do not have plurals: *"How much money does a ticket cost?"* **Much** is used in sentences with "not" and in questions: *There isn't much milk left.*

**Many** is used with the plural forms of nouns: *I didn't see many people there that I knew.*

**A lot of** can be used with both types of noun: *We're going to need a lot of paint.* | *She doesn't have a lot of friends.*

**2** a small area of land in a town or city, that is used for a particular purpose, especially for building houses: *We bought the empty lot next to our house.*

**lo·tion** /ˈloʊʃən/ *noun*
a liquid that you put on your skin in order to make it soft or to protect it: *I put hand lotion on my dry hands.*
[**ORIGIN:** 1300-1400 From the Latin word *lotio*, which means "the act of washing."]

L

**lot·ter·y** /ˈlɑtəri/ *noun* (plural **lotteries**)
a game in which you buy tickets with a series of numbers on them. If your number is picked, you can win a lot of money: *Maybe I'll win the lottery and never have to work again!* | *a lottery ticket*

**lot·to** /ˈlɑtoʊ/ *noun*
a lottery: *He won $10.5 million in the New York Lotto.*

**loud** /laʊd/ *adjective*
making a lot of noise: *The music was so loud that I didn't hear the phone.* | *There was a loud cheer.* **ANTONYM: quiet**
—**loudly** *adverb* in a loud way
—**loudness** *noun* the quality of being loud

**loud·speak·er** /ˈlaʊdˌspikɚ/ *noun*
a piece of equipment that makes sounds louder: *A voice on the loudspeaker told us that the flight was delayed.*

**lounge**[1] /laʊndʒ/ *noun*
a room in a hotel, an airport, or other public building where people can relax, sit down, or have a drink: *We sat and waited for the taxi in the hotel lounge.*

**lounge**[2] *verb*
to sit or lie in a place in a very relaxed way without doing much: *My brother and his friends were lounging in front of the TV.*

**louse** /laʊs/ *noun* (plural **lice** /laɪs/)
a very small insect that can live on the skin and hair of animals and people

**lous·y** /ˈlaʊzi/ *adjective* (*informal*)
very bad: *I lied to her, and now I feel lousy.* | *We had lousy seats, way in the back.*

**lov·a·ble** /ˈlʌvəbəl/ *adjective*
easy to love: *a sweet, lovable child*

**love**[1] /lʌv/ *verb*
**1** to care very much about someone, especially a member of your family or a close friend: *Mom loves us, feeds us, and takes care of us.*
**2** to like someone very much in a romantic way: *I love you, Amy, and I want to marry you.*
**3** to enjoy doing something very much: *Tom loves to read.* | *I love playing hockey.*
→ see Thesaurus box at **enjoy**

**love**[2] *noun*
**1** a strong romantic feeling for someone: *He is in love with Laura.* | *We fell in love, got married, and had children.*
**2** the strong feeling of caring very much about someone or something: *a mother's love for her child*
**3** something that you like or enjoy doing very much: *My sister and I both have a love of books.*
**4** someone you love romantically: *Mike was my first love.*
**5 love/lots of love/all my love** (*informal*) = written at the end of a letter to a friend, parent, husband, etc.: *Take care. Lots of love, Dad.*
[**ORIGIN:** From the old English word *lufu.*]

**ˈlove afˌfair** *noun*
a romantic sexual relationship between two people who are not married to each other: *His*

*wife divorced him when she found out about his love affair.*

**love·ly** /ˈlʌvli/ *adjective*
**1** attractive: *She was lovely, with beautiful black hair and big brown eyes.*
**2** very enjoyable: *Everyone had a lovely time at the beach.*

**lov·er** /ˈlʌvɚ/ *noun*
**1** someone's lover is the person he or she is having a sexual relationship with but is not married to
**2** someone who enjoys something very much: *The park was full of dog lovers walking their dogs.*

**lov·ing** /ˈlʌvɪŋ/ *adjective*
behaving in a gentle and caring way toward the people you love: *She has a wonderful loving husband and three great kids.*

**low¹** /loʊ/ *adjective*
**1** not high, or not far above the ground: *The dog jumped over the low wall easily.* | *The shelf was low enough for me to reach.* **ANTONYM: high**
**2** small in amount, or less than the usual amount: *The work is hard and the pay is low.* | *That restaurant serves good food at low prices.* **ANTONYM: high**
**3** bad, or below the usual standard: *Kim got a low grade on the test because she didn't study.* **ANTONYM: high**
**4** containing very little of something: *Fish is good for you because it is low in fat.* **ANTONYM: high**
**5** not having much of something because you have used most of it: *We're running low on milk – can you get some at the store?*
**6** unhappy: *I've been feeling low ever since my best friend moved away.* **SYNONYM: depressed**
**7** a low sound is quiet or deep: *"I am leaving now," she said in a low voice that I could barely hear.* **ANTONYM: loud**
→ see Thesaurus box at **sad**

**low²** *adverb*
in a low position or at a low level: *It was getting late, and the sun had sunk low in the sky.* | *low-flying aircraft* **ANTONYM: high**

**low³** *noun*
a low level: *The temperature tonight will reach a low of 23 degrees.* **ANTONYM: high**

**low·er¹** /ˈloʊɚ/ *verb*
**1** to reduce something: *Most stores lower their prices in January to try to increase sales.*
**2** to move something down: *The flag is lowered every evening and put away.*
**3** to make something less loud: *She lowered her voice so that no one else could hear her.*
→ see Thesaurus box at **reduce**

**lower²** *adjective*
**1** below something else of the same kind: *He cut his lower lip when he fell.* | *I picked an apple from one of the lower branches of the tree.* **ANTONYM: upper**
**2** smaller in amount or level than something else: *That store has lower prices than the supermarket.* | *Temperatures will be lower than yesterday.* **ANTONYM: higher**

**low·er·case** /ˈloʊɚˌkeɪs/ *noun*
letters written in their small form, such as a, b, and c: *Use a capital letter for the first word in the sentence and write the rest in lowercase.* **ANTONYM: uppercase**
—**lowercase** *adjective* lowercase letters are written in their small form: *a lowercase m*

**ˌlower ˈclass** *noun*
**the lower class** = the people in a country who do not have much money or power
—**lower-class** *adjective* relating to the lower class: *a lower-class neighborhood*

**ˌlow ˈtide** *noun*
the time when the ocean is at its lowest level and far away from the shore

**loy·al** /ˈlɔɪəl/ *adjective*
always supporting a person, group, country, or idea: *The team has loyal fans that come to every game.* | *He is loyal to his friends and will always help them.*
—**loyalty** *noun* the quality of being loyal: *Most people have a sense of loyalty to their country.*
[**ORIGIN:** 1500-1600 From the old French word *leial*, from the Latin word *legalis*, which means "relating to the law." A person who is loyal to his or her country obeys all the laws.]

**lu·bri·cate** /ˈlubrəˌkeɪt/ *verb* (*formal*)
to put a substance such as oil on something in order to make it move smoothly: *If you lubricate the door with some oil, it won't squeak.*

—**lubrication** /ˌlubrəˈkeɪʃən/ *noun* the act of lubricating something
—**lubricant** /ˈlubrəkənt/ *noun* a substance that is put on something to make it move smoothly

**luck** /lʌk/ *noun*
1 (*also* **good luck**) good things that happen to people by chance: *I never have any luck playing board games. Someone else always wins.* | *People throw rice at the married couple for good luck.*
2 **bad luck** = bad things that happen to people by chance: *We've had a lot of bad luck – first Mom got sick and then I broke my arm.*
3 **Good luck!** = used to tell someone that you hope that he or she will be successful: *Good luck on your test!*
4 **be in luck/be out of luck** = to get or not get something that you want: *You're in luck – there's one ticket left!*

**luck·y** /ˈlʌki/ *adjective* (**luckier**, **luckiest**)
1 if you are lucky, good things happen to you by chance: *The prize was $100 so I was very lucky to win.* | *We were lucky that the plane was delayed because we got to the airport late.* SYNONYM: **fortunate**; ANTONYM: **unlucky**
2 a lucky number or object makes you have good luck: *I chose the number 7 because it is my lucky number.*
—**luckily** *adverb* used for saying that it is good that something has happened: *Luckily, no one was hurt in the accident.*

**lug** /lʌg/ *verb* (**lugged**, **lugging**) (*informal*)
to carry something with difficulty because it is very heavy: *We had to lug our bags up to the 5th floor.*

**lug·gage** /ˈlʌgɪdʒ/ *noun*
the bags that you carry when you are traveling: *She helped us carry our luggage to our hotel room.*

**luke·warm** /ˌlukˈwɔrm/ *adjective*
1 liquid or food that is lukewarm is slightly warm, often when it should be hot: *The soup was only lukewarm, so it didn't taste that good.*
2 not showing very much interest or excitement: *Writers gave the movie lukewarm reviews.*
→ see Thesaurus box at **hot**

**lul·la·by** /ˈlʌləˌbaɪ/ *noun* (plural **lullabies**)
a quiet slow song that you sing to small children to make them go to sleep: *Maria sat by her son's bed and sang him a lullaby.*
[ORIGIN: 1500-1600 From words used to make a child calm or sleepy.]

**lum·ber** /ˈlʌmbɚ/ *noun*
wood that is used for building: *The lumber is taken from the forest in big trucks.*

**lum·ber·jack** /ˈlʌmbɚˌdʒæk/ *noun*
someone whose job is cutting down trees for wood

**lump** /lʌmp/ *noun*
1 a small piece of something that does not have a regular shape: *Stir the mixture until all the lumps are gone.* | *a lump of wet clay*
2 a small hard swollen area under the surface of your skin, caused by an injury or illness: *If a woman feels a lump in her breast, she should see a doctor.*
→ see Thesaurus box at **piece**

**lump·y** /ˈlʌmpi/ *adjective* (**lumpier**, **lumpiest**) (*informal*)
something that is lumpy has a lot of lumps in it: *A lumpy mattress is hard to sleep on.*

**lu·nar** /ˈlunɚ/ *adjective* (*formal*)
relating to the moon: *The spacecraft landed on the lunar surface.*
[ORIGIN: 1400-1500 From the Latin word *luna*, which means "the moon."]

**lu·na·tic** /ˈlunətɪk/ *noun* (*informal*)
someone who is crazy or behaves in a very stupid way: *He was running down the road after the bus like a lunatic.*
[ORIGIN: 1200-1300 From the Latin word *luna*, which means "the moon." People thought mental illness was caused by the moon.]

**lunch** /lʌntʃ/ *noun*
a meal that you eat in the middle of the day: *I had a sandwich for lunch.* | *We usually eat lunch at noon.* | *Let's have lunch together.*
→ see Thesaurus box at **meal**

**lunch·time** /ˈlʌntʃtaɪm/ *noun*
the time in the middle of the day when people eat lunch: *I usually just have a sandwich at lunchtime.*

**lung** /lʌŋ/ *noun*
one of the two parts inside your chest that you use for breathing: *Smoking is bad for your lungs.* → see picture on page **A2**

L

**lunge** /lʌndʒ/ *verb*
to move toward someone or something quickly and strongly, often in order to attack: *The dog suddenly lunged forward and bit me.*
—**lunge** *noun* a sudden strong movement toward someone or something

**lurch** /lɚtʃ/ *verb*
to move in an uncontrolled or unsteady way: *The train lurched forward, making some people fall.*
—**lurch** *noun* an uncontrolled movement forward

**lush** /lʌʃ/ *adjective*
lush plants are healthy and have a lot of green leaves: *a lush green lawn*

**lux·u·ry** /ˈlʌkʃəri/ *noun* (plural **luxuries**)
**1** the comfort and pleasure that you get from expensive things: *They live in luxury in a huge house.* | *a luxury car with leather seats*
**2** something expensive that you want to have but do not need: *Vacations abroad are a luxury for most families.*
—**luxurious** /lʌgˈʒʊriəs/ *adjective* very expensive, beautiful, and comfortable: *They have a luxurious home with thick carpet and beautiful furniture.*
[**ORIGIN:** 1300-1400 From the Latin word *luxuria*, which means "having or spending too much."]

**ly·ing** /ˈlaɪ-ɪŋ/ *verb*
the present participle of LIE

**lynch** /lɪntʃ/ *verb*
if a crowd of people lynches someone, they kill that person by HANGing him or her illegally: *A crowd of angry men lynched him before the trial could start.*
—**lynching** *noun* an occasion when someone is lynched

**lyr·ics** /ˈlɪrɪks/ *plural noun*
the words of a popular song: *I love the lyrics to this song, but I don't really like the tune.*
—**lyricist** /ˈlɪrəsɪst/ *noun* someone who writes the words of a song

L

# Mm

**m**
the written abbreviation of **meter**

**'m** *verb*
the short form of "am": *I'm late for school.*

**M.A.** *noun*
(**Master of Arts**) a university degree in a subject such as History or Art, which is more advanced than a B.A.

**ma'am** /mæm/ *noun*
used to speak politely to a woman when you do not know her name: *May I help you, ma'am?*

**mac·a·ro·ni** /ˌmækəˈroʊni/ *noun*
a type of PASTA in the shape of small tubes: *macaroni and cheese*

**ma·chine** /məˈʃin/ *noun*
a piece of equipment that is used to do a job, and that uses power to make it work: *We need a new washing machine.*
[ORIGIN: 1500-1600 From the Greek word *mechane*, which means "way of doing something, or object made for lifting things."]

**WORD FAMILY: machine**
**machine** *noun* | **machinery** *noun* | **mechanical** *adjective*

**THESAURUS: machine**
**appliance** a machine that is used in the home: *kitchen appliances such as refrigerators*
**device** a piece of equipment that is usually small and usually electronic, that does a special job: *A memory card is a useful device for storing digital pictures.*
**gadget** a small piece of equipment that makes a job easier to do: *a new gadget for opening the garage door*

**maˈchine gun** *noun*
a gun that fires a lot of bullets very quickly

**ma·chin·er·y** /məˈʃinəri/ *noun*
large machines: *This piece of machinery rolls the paper flat and dries it.*

**ma·cho** /ˈmɑtʃoʊ/ *adjective* (*informal*)
a man who is macho wants to show people that he is strong and brave, and never shows that he feels sad or frightened: *He's a macho guy who thinks he has to be tough.*
[ORIGIN: 1900-2000 From the Spanish word for "male."]

**mad** /mæd/ *adjective* (**madder**, **maddest**)
1 (*informal*) angry: *Mom is still mad at me for breaking the vase.* | *It makes me so mad when he doesn't listen!* → see picture on page A23
2 **do something like mad** (*informal*) = to do something as quickly as you can: *I've been working like mad to get this essay finished on time.*
3 mentally ill: *He was afraid that he was going mad because he kept hearing voices in his head.* SYNONYMS: **crazy**, **insane**
→ see Thesaurus box at **angry**

**mad·am** /ˈmædəm/ *noun* (*formal*)
used when you do not know a woman's name: *Dear Sir or Madam: I am writing about the job you advertised in the paper.*
[ORIGIN: 1200-1300 From the French phrase *ma dame*, which means "my lady."]

**made** /meɪd/ *verb*
the past tense and past participle of MAKE

**mad·ly** /ˈmædli/ *adverb*
1 **madly in love (with someone)** = very much in love: *They were young and madly in love with each other.*
2 in a fast uncontrolled way: *The kids ran madly out of the school gates.*

**mad·man** /ˈmædmən/ *noun* (plural **madmen**)
a man who is mentally ill

**mad·ness** /ˈmædnəs/ *noun*
1 very stupid or dangerous behavior: *It's madness to spend so much money on a dress you'll only wear once.*
2 mental illness: *There's a history of madness in their family – her aunt was put in an institution.* SYNONYM: **insanity**

**mad·wom·an** /ˈmædˌwʊmən/ *noun* (plural **madwomen** /ˈmædˌwɪmɪn/)
a woman who is mentally ill

**mag·a·zine** /ˈmægəˌzin/ *noun*
a big thin book with a paper cover that you can buy every week or every month. Magazines have news, stories, games, or pictures in

them: *a sports magazine for kids* → see picture on page A8

[ORIGIN: 1500-1600 From the French word *magasin*, which means "store or warehouse," from the Arabic word *makhazin*. A magazine is like a warehouse because it contains a lot of things.]

**mag·ic¹** /ˈmædʒɪk/ *noun*

1 a special power that makes strange or impossible things happen in stories: *The witch turned the prince into a frog by magic.*

2 the skill of doing tricks that look like magic in order to entertain people: *The magician did some magic and took a rabbit out of a hat.*

3 a quality that makes something seem exciting and special: *There's something special about the magic of Paris in the spring.*

[ORIGIN: 1300-1400 From the Greek word *magike*, from *magos*, which means "person with magic powers."]

**magic²** *adjective*

1 a magic word or object has a special power that makes strange or impossible things happen in stories: *The witch said some magic words and turned the frog into a prince.*

2 relating to the skill of doing tricks that look like magic in order to entertain people: *My favorite magic trick is the one where they saw a woman in half.*

3 **the magic word** = a phrase that adults use when they want children to say "please": *"Mom, I want a piece of cake." "What's the magic word?" "Please, Mom."*

**mag·i·cal** /ˈmædʒɪkəl/ *adjective*

1 very enjoyable and exciting, in a strange or special way: *There's something magical about these beautiful mountains.*

2 relating to magic, or done using magic: *The wizard used his magical powers to make the monster disappear.*

**ma·gi·cian** /məˈdʒɪʃən/ *noun*

someone who does magic tricks in order to entertain people: *The magician did some amazing tricks with cards.*

**ma·gis·trate** /ˈmædʒəˌstreɪt/ *noun*

a government official who decides if someone is guilty in a court that deals with less serious crimes

**mag·ma** /ˈmægmə/ *noun*

hot melted rock below the surface of the Earth → see picture at volcano

**mag·ne·si·um** /mægˈniziəm/ *noun*

(*abbreviation:* **Mg**) a common silver-white metal

**mag·net** /ˈmægnət/ *noun*

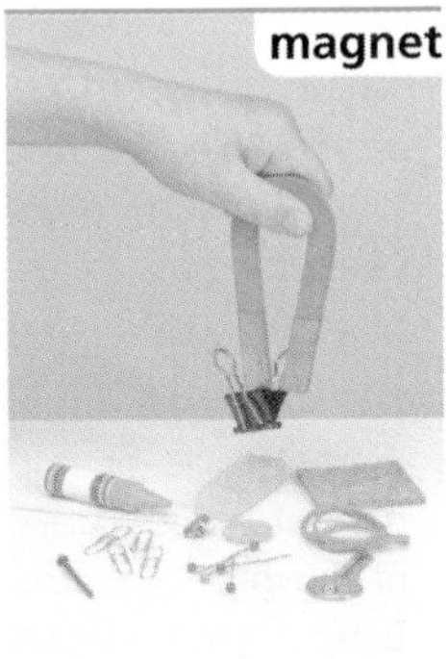


1 a piece of iron or steel that makes other metal objects move toward it: *I use little magnets to hold photographs on the refrigerator door.*

2 a person or place that attracts many other people or things: *Hollywood is a magnet for young actors.*

—**magnetize** /ˈmægnəˌtaɪz/ *verb* to make a piece of iron or steel able to pull other pieces of metal toward it

[ORIGIN: 1400-1500 From the Greek phrase *magnes lithos*, which means "stone of Magnesia." Magnesia was a place in Greece.]

**mag·net·ic** /mægˈnetɪk/ *adjective*

relating to the way a magnet can pull metal objects toward it: *Some rocks are magnetic and can attract metal.*

—**magnetism** /ˈmægnəˌtɪzəm/ *noun* the physical force that makes metal objects move toward each other

**mag·nif·i·cent** /mægˈnɪfəsənt/ *adjective*

very good or beautiful, and very impressive: *We had a magnificent view of the Grand Canyon.*

—**magnificence** *noun* the fact that something is magnificent

[ORIGIN: 1400-1500 From the Latin word *magnificus*, from *magnus*, which means "big or large."]

**mag·ni·fy** /ˈmægnəˌfaɪ/ *verb* (**magnified**, **magnifies**)

to make something look larger than it really is: *The microscope magnifies the drop of water so that you can see the tiny living things in it.*

M

—**magnification** /ˌmæɡnəfəˈkeɪʃən/ *noun* the process of magnifying something, or the amount to which something is magnified

ˈ**magnifying ˌglass** *noun*
a round piece of glass with a handle, that you look through to make things seem bigger: *Grandpa has to use a magnifying glass to read the paper.*

**mag·ni·tude** /ˈmæɡnəˌtud/ *noun* (*formal*)
**1** how large or important something is: *We need to understand the magnitude of the problem of global warming.*
**2** how strong an EARTHQUAKE is

**mag·pie** /ˈmæɡpaɪ/ *noun*
a wild bird with black and white feathers that makes a loud sound

**ma·hog·a·ny** /məˈhɑɡəni/ *noun*
a hard dark wood used to make furniture
—**mahogany** *adjective* made of mahogany: *a mahogany table*

**maid** /meɪd/ *noun*
a woman whose job is to clean a house or the rooms in a hotel

**maid·en**[1] /ˈmeɪdn/ *noun*
a girl or young woman who is not married: *In the story, the prince meets a beautiful maiden.*

**maiden**[2] *adjective*
**maiden flight/voyage** = the first trip a plane or ship makes

**maid·en name** /ˈmeɪdn ˌneɪm/ *noun*
the family name that a woman has before she gets married and uses her husband's family name: *Mom's maiden name was Anne Jackson before she met Dad and became Mrs. Anne Brown.*

ˌ**maid of ˈhonor** *noun*
the most important BRIDESMAID at a wedding

**mail**[1] /meɪl/ *noun*
**1** the system of collecting and delivering letters and packages: *I got a letter in the mail from Jo.* | *Your tickets will be delivered by mail.*
**2** the letters and packages that are delivered to your house or office: *"Is there any mail for me?" "Just a postcard from Frank."*
**3** messages that you send and receive on a computer: *I checked my computer to see if I had any mail.* **SYNONYM: email**
[**ORIGIN:** 1200-1300 From the old French word *male*, which means "bag." Letters and packages were carried in a bag.]

**mail**[2] *verb*
**1** to send a letter or package to someone: *I'll mail the book to you tomorrow.*
**2** to send something to someone using a computer: *I'll mail the photo to you as an attachment.* **SYNONYM: email**

**mail·box** /ˈmeɪlbɑks/ *noun*
**1** a box outside your house where letters are put when they are delivered to your house: *There were some letters in the mailbox.*
**2** a special box in the street or at a POST OFFICE where you put the letters you are sending: *There's a mailbox on the corner for letters.*
**3** the part of a computer's memory where email messages are kept: *You should get rid of all the old messages from your mailbox.*

ˈ**mail ˌcarrier** *noun*
someone whose job is delivering mail to people's houses

**mail·man** /ˈmeɪlmæn/ *noun* (plural **mailmen** /meilmen/)
a man whose job is delivering mail to people's houses

ˌ**mail ˈorder** *noun*
a way of buying things in which the company sends you the things by mail: *You can order the jeans from a mail order catalog.*

**maim** /meɪm/ *verb* (*formal*)
to injure someone very badly: *The bomb maimed hundreds of people and killed 12.*

**main** /meɪn/ *adjective*
bigger and more important than other things of the same kind: *The main character in the book is a ten-year-old girl.* | *My main worry is that I'll forget what I'm going to say.*

ˈ**main clause** *noun*
in a sentence, a group of words with a noun and a verb that can be a complete sentence on its own. In the sentence "At four o'clock, I walked home," "I walked home" is the main clause.

# Picture Dictionary

## Body

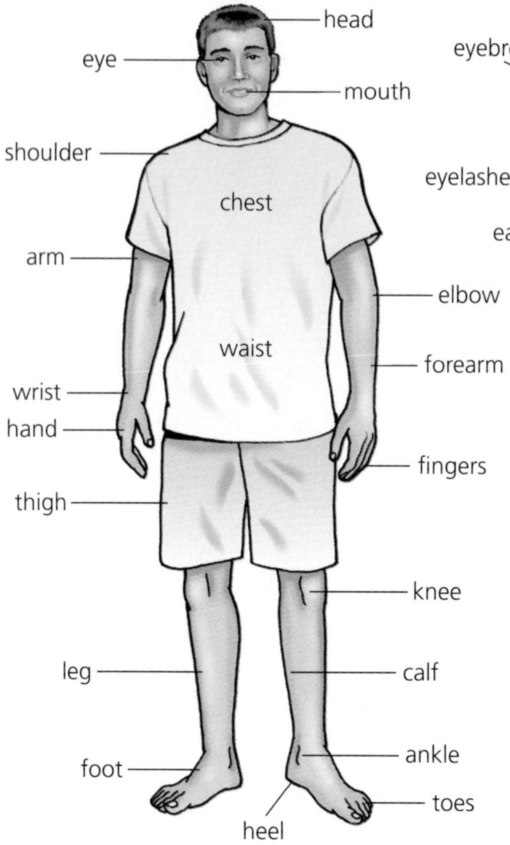
head
eye
mouth
shoulder
chest
arm
elbow
waist
forearm
wrist
hand
fingers
thigh
knee
leg
calf
foot
ankle
toes
heel

## Face

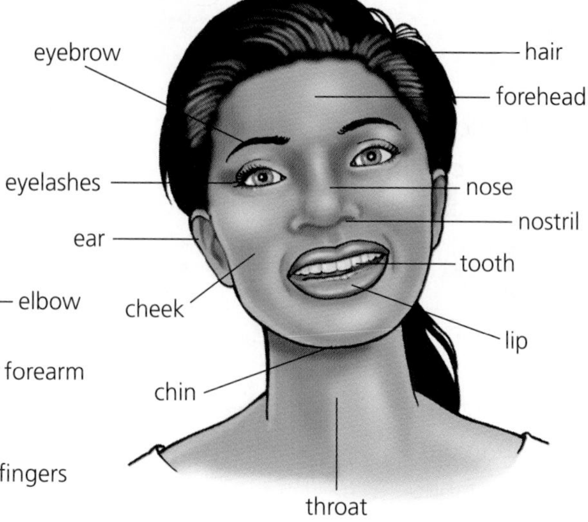
eyebrow
hair
forehead
eyelashes
nose
nostril
ear
tooth
cheek
lip
chin
throat

## Skeleton

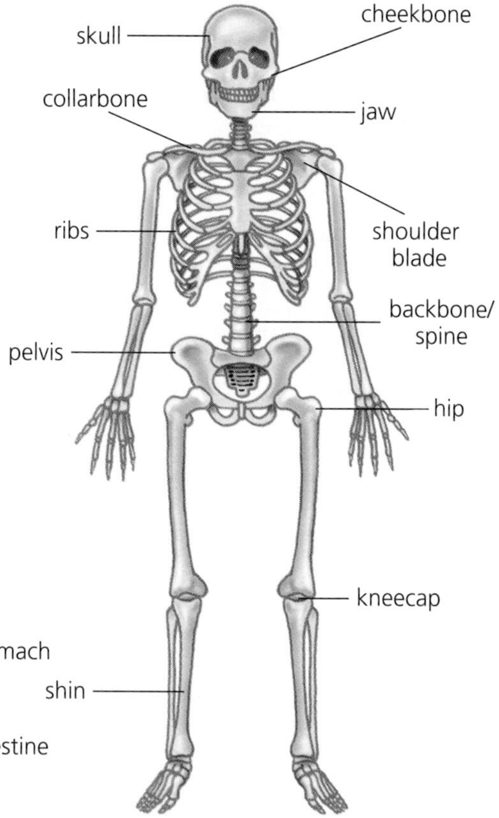
skull
cheekbone
collarbone
jaw
ribs
shoulder
blade
backbone/
spine
pelvis
hip
kneecap
shin

## Internal Organs

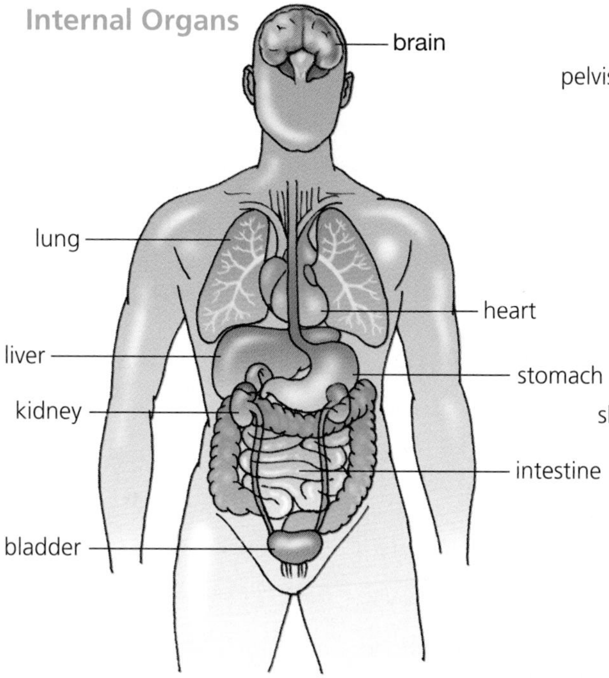
brain
lung
heart
liver
stomach
kidney
intestine
bladder

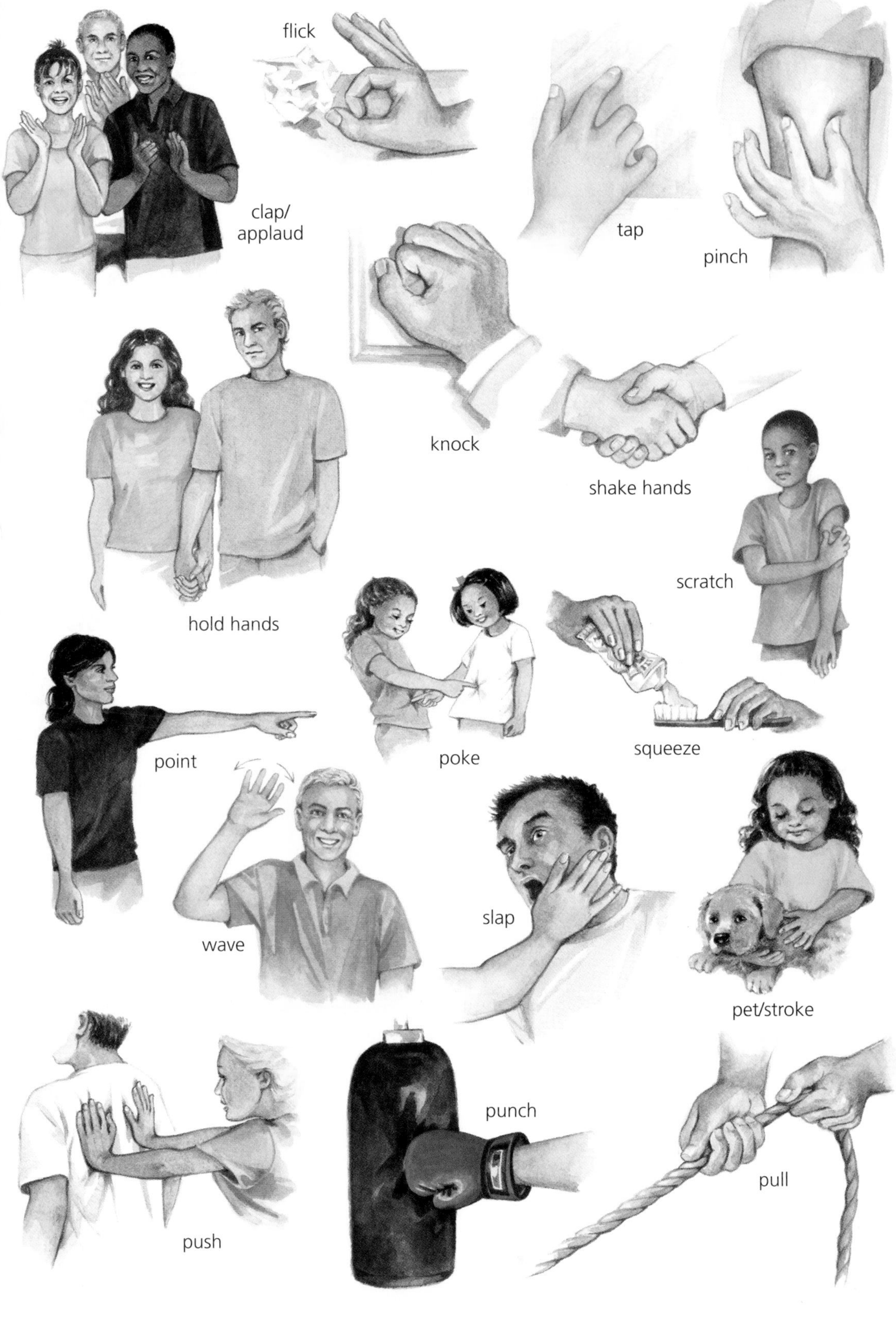
flick
clap/
applaud
tap
pinch
knock
shake hands
hold hands
scratch
point
poke
squeeze
wave
slap
pet/stroke
punch
pull
push

# Verbs of Movement (body) A4

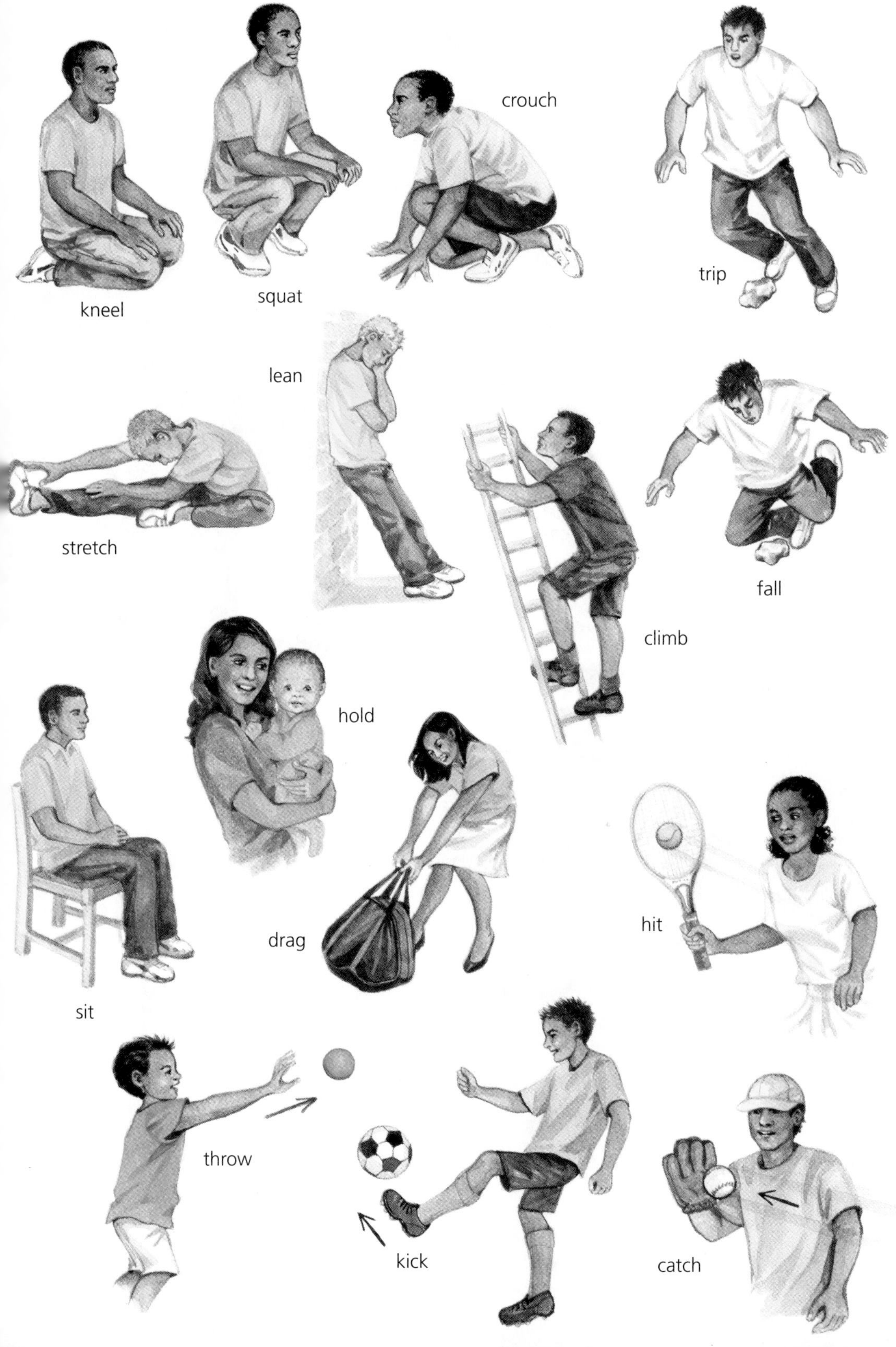
kneel
squat
crouch
trip
lean
stretch
climb
fall
hold
sit
drag
hit
throw
kick
catch

hat
earring
necklace
sleeve
bracelet
purse/
handbag
dress
sandals
scarf
blouse
coat
skirt
stockings/
pantyhose
high heels
sports bag
shirt
collar
tie
belt
suit
briefcase
pants
hard
hat
jacket/
raincoat
sweater
button
overalls
glove
toolbox
workboots
jeans
umbrella
hood
sweatshirt
sweat
suit
sock
sneakers
cap
T-shirt
shorts

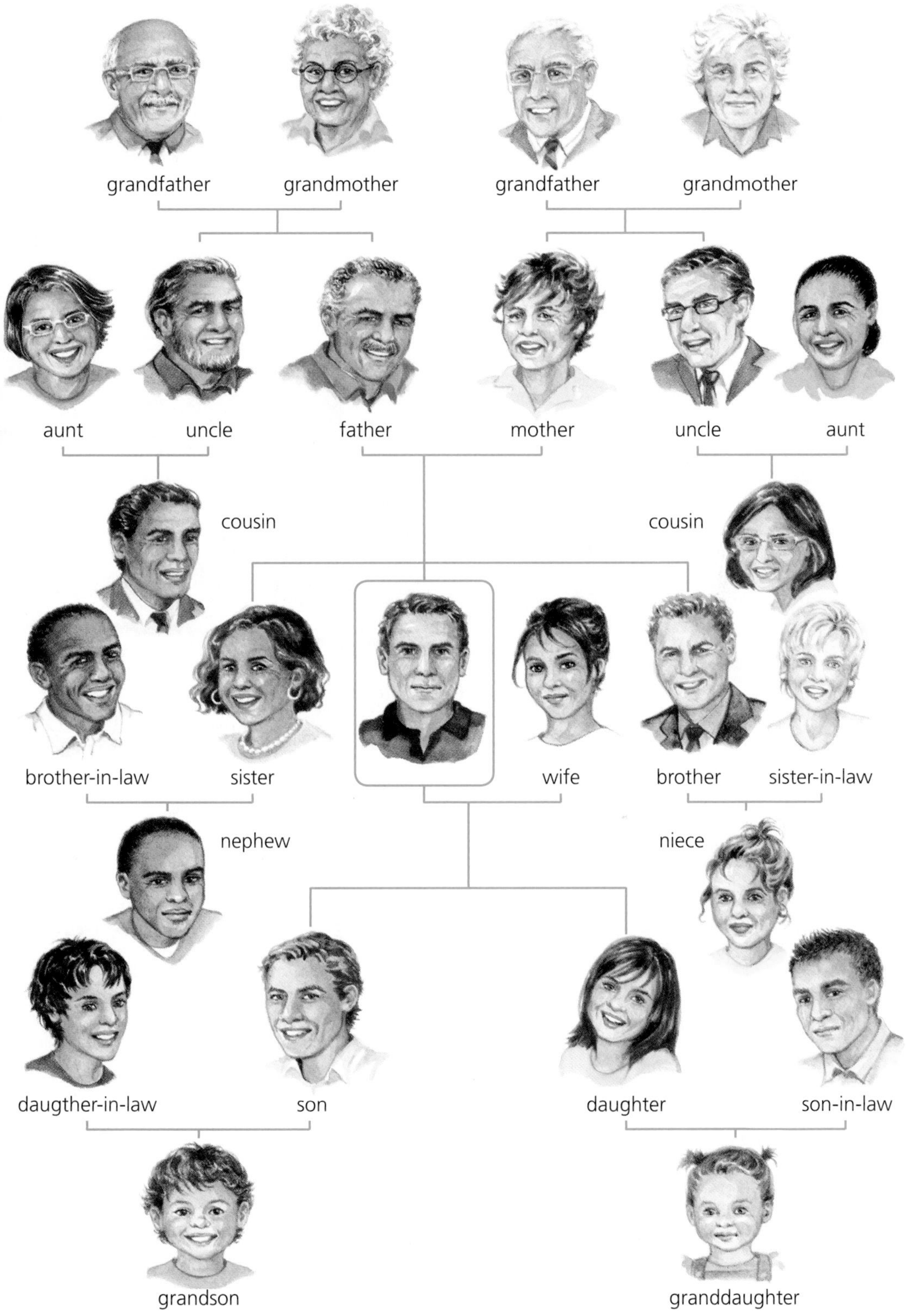
grandfather
grandmother
grandfather
grandmother
aunt
uncle
father
mother
uncle
aunt
cousin
cousin
brother-in-law
sister
wife
brother
sister-in-law
nephew
niece
daugther-in-law
son
daughter
son-in-law
grandson
granddaughter

# Living Room



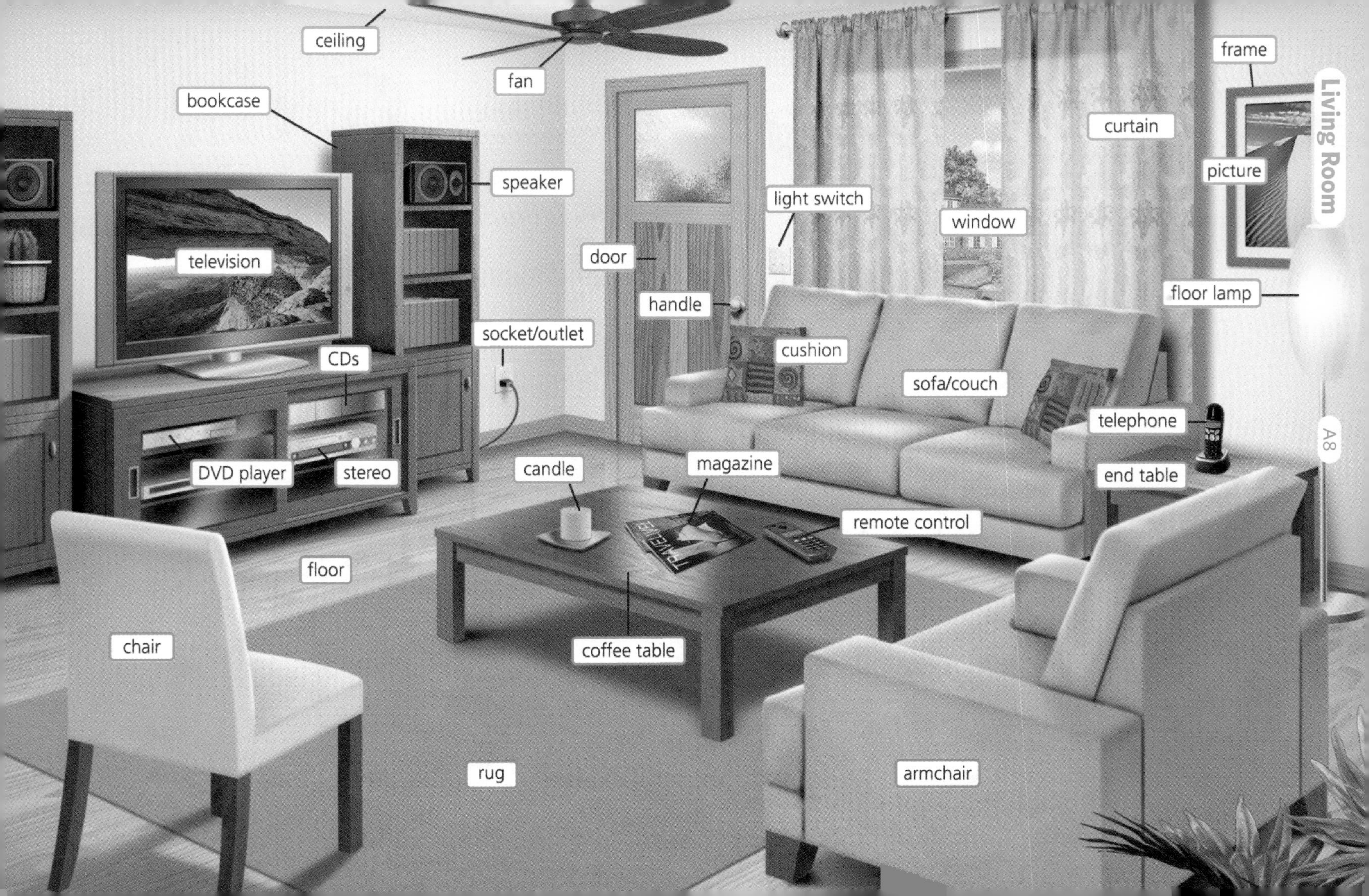
ceiling
fan
bookcase
speaker
television
socket/outlet
CDs
DVD player
stereo
candle
floor
chair
rug
coffee table
door
handle
light switch
cushion
sofa/couch
magazine
remote control
window
curtain
frame
picture
floor lamp
telephone
end table
armchair

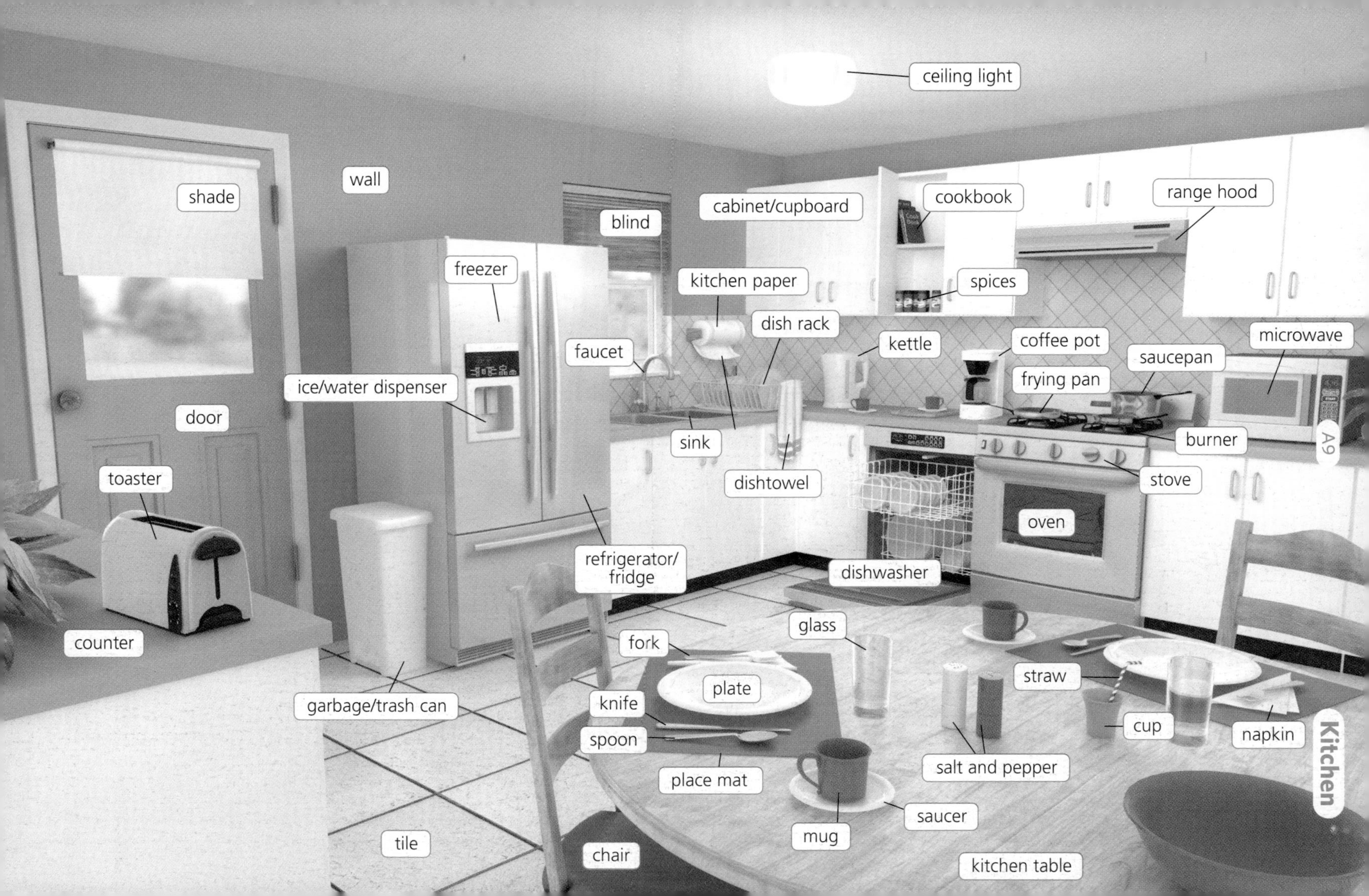
ceiling light
wall
shade
blind
cabinet/cupboard
cookbook
range hood
freezer
kitchen paper
spices
dish rack
kettle
coffee pot
microwave
saucepan
frying pan
faucet
ice/water dispenser
door
sink
burner
dishtowel
stove
toaster
oven
refrigerator/
fridge
dishwasher
glass
counter
fork
plate
straw
knife
garbage/trash can
spoon
cup
napkin
salt and pepper
place mat
saucer
mug
tile
chair
kitchen table

Bedroom
A10
shade
poster
wardrobe/closet
bookshelf
curtain
lamp
clothes
mirror
window
alarm clock
stereo
pillow
blanket
bedspread
night table
chest of drawers/dresser
racket
sheet
bed
laundry
laundry basket
rug
computer
chair
ice skates
book
MP3 player
shoes
keyboard
mouse
carpet

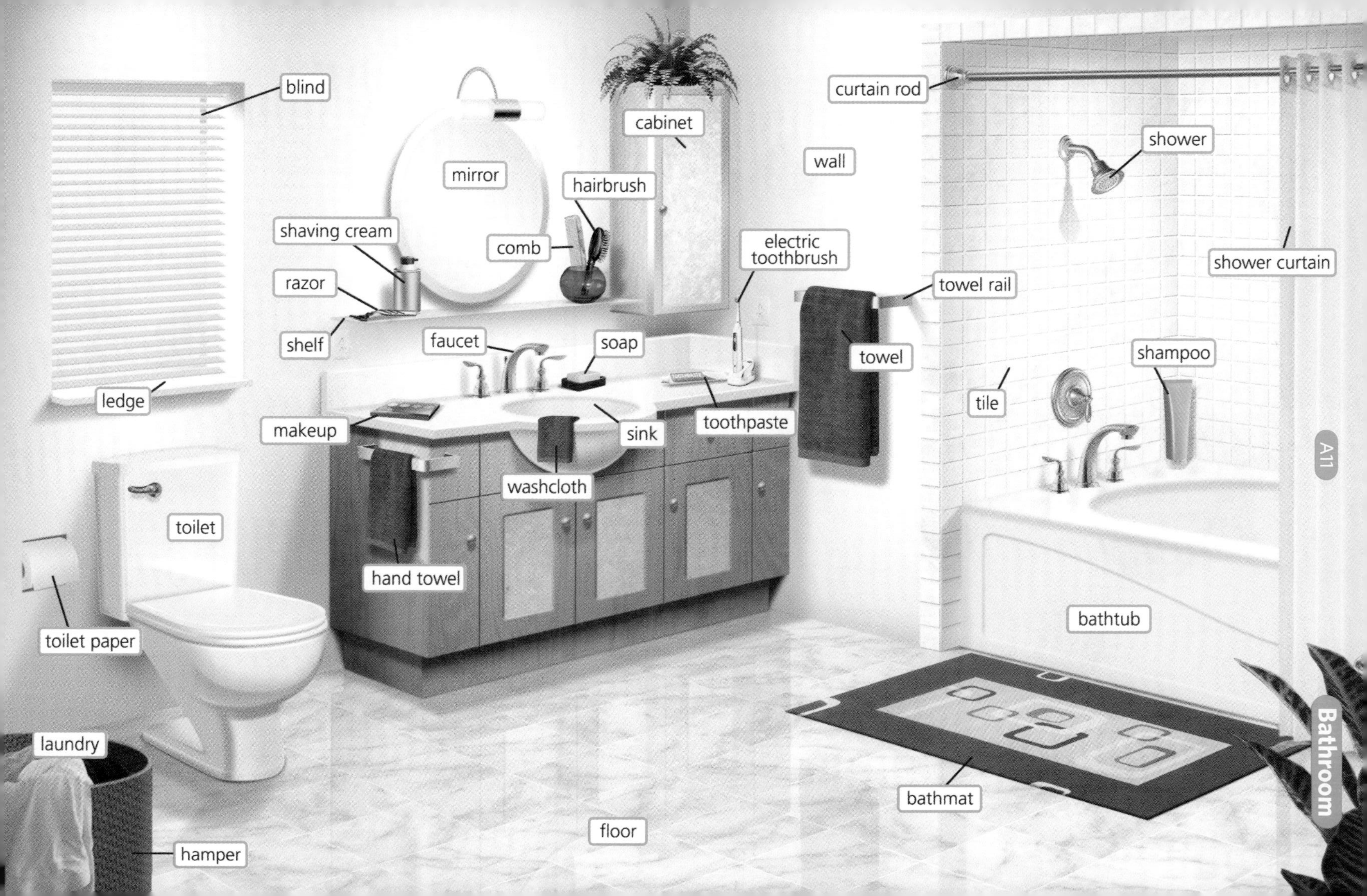
blind
mirror
cabinet
curtain rod
shower
wall
hairbrush
shaving cream
comb
electric toothbrush
shower curtain
razor
towel rail
shelf
faucet
soap
towel
shampoo
ledge
tile
makeup
sink
toothpaste
washcloth
toilet
hand towel
toilet paper
bathtub
laundry
bathmat
floor
hamper

# Vegetables



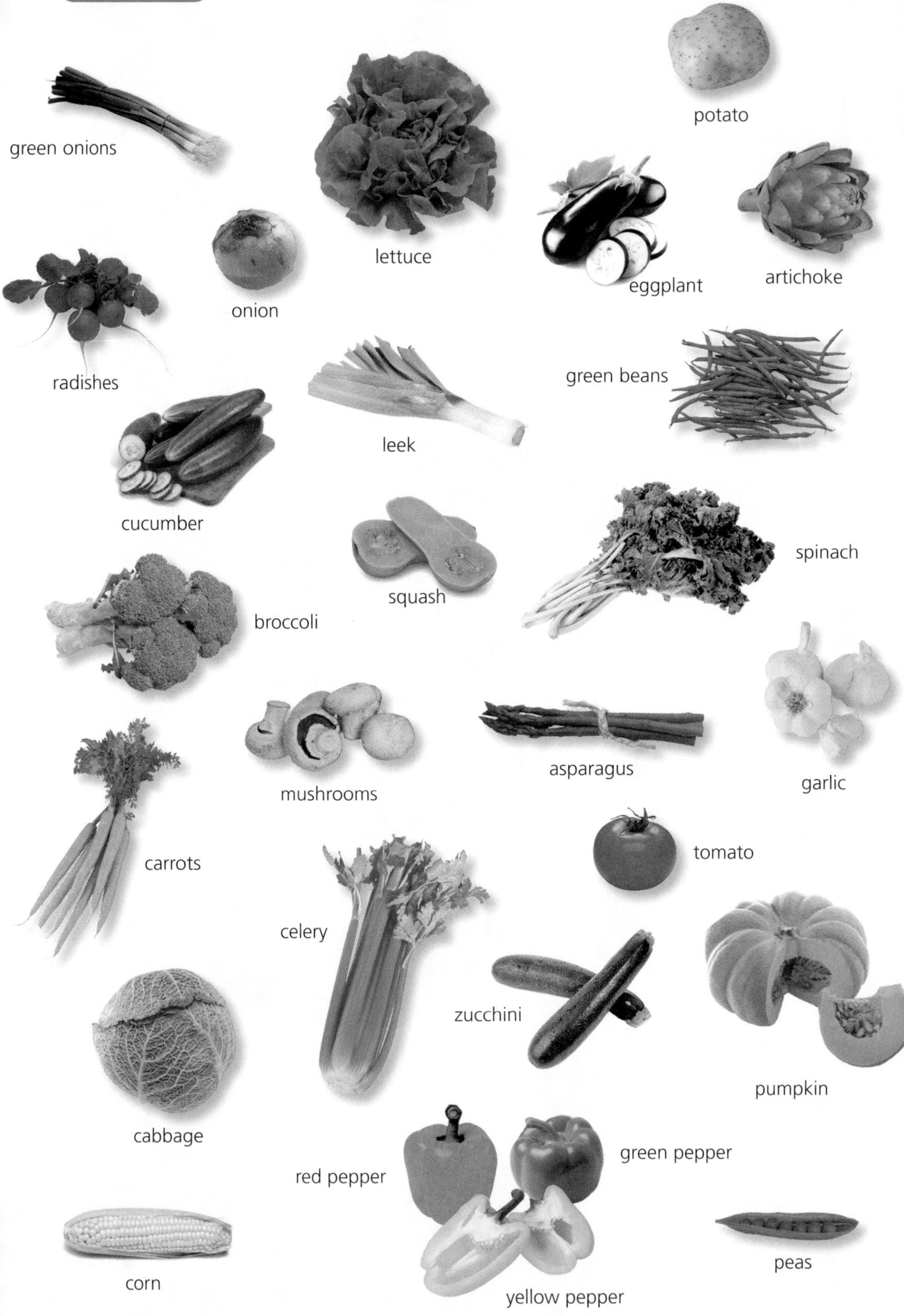
green onions
potato
lettuce
eggplant
artichoke
onion
radishes
green beans
leek
cucumber
spinach
squash
broccoli
garlic
asparagus
mushrooms
tomato
carrots
celery
pumpkin
zucchini
cabbage
green pepper
red pepper
peas
corn
yellow pepper

apple
pear
tangerine
lemon
lime
kiwi
grapes
melon
pineapple
peach
nectarine
plum
apricot (fresh)
cherries
banana
figs (fresh)
orange
grapefruit
watermelon
cantaloupe
rhubarb
mango
strawberries
raspberries
blueberries
blackberries
cranberries
dried prunes
dried apricots
dried figs
raisins
coconut
peanuts
almonds
pecans
dates
walnut

# Animals

eagle

blue jay

cardinal

owl

alligator

crocodile

snake

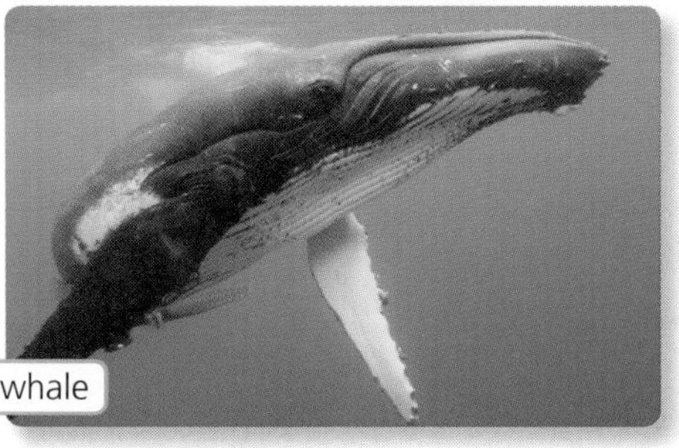
whale

shark

white-tailed deer

wolf

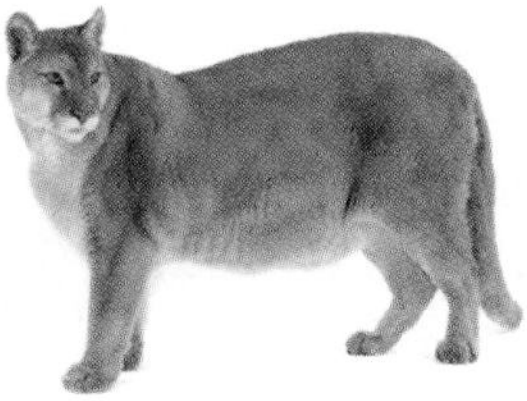
cougar

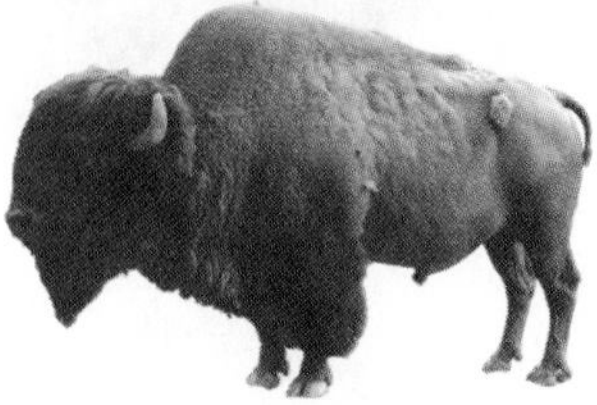
bison

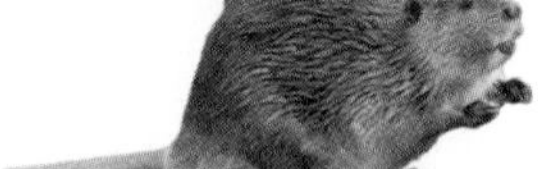
beaver

bear

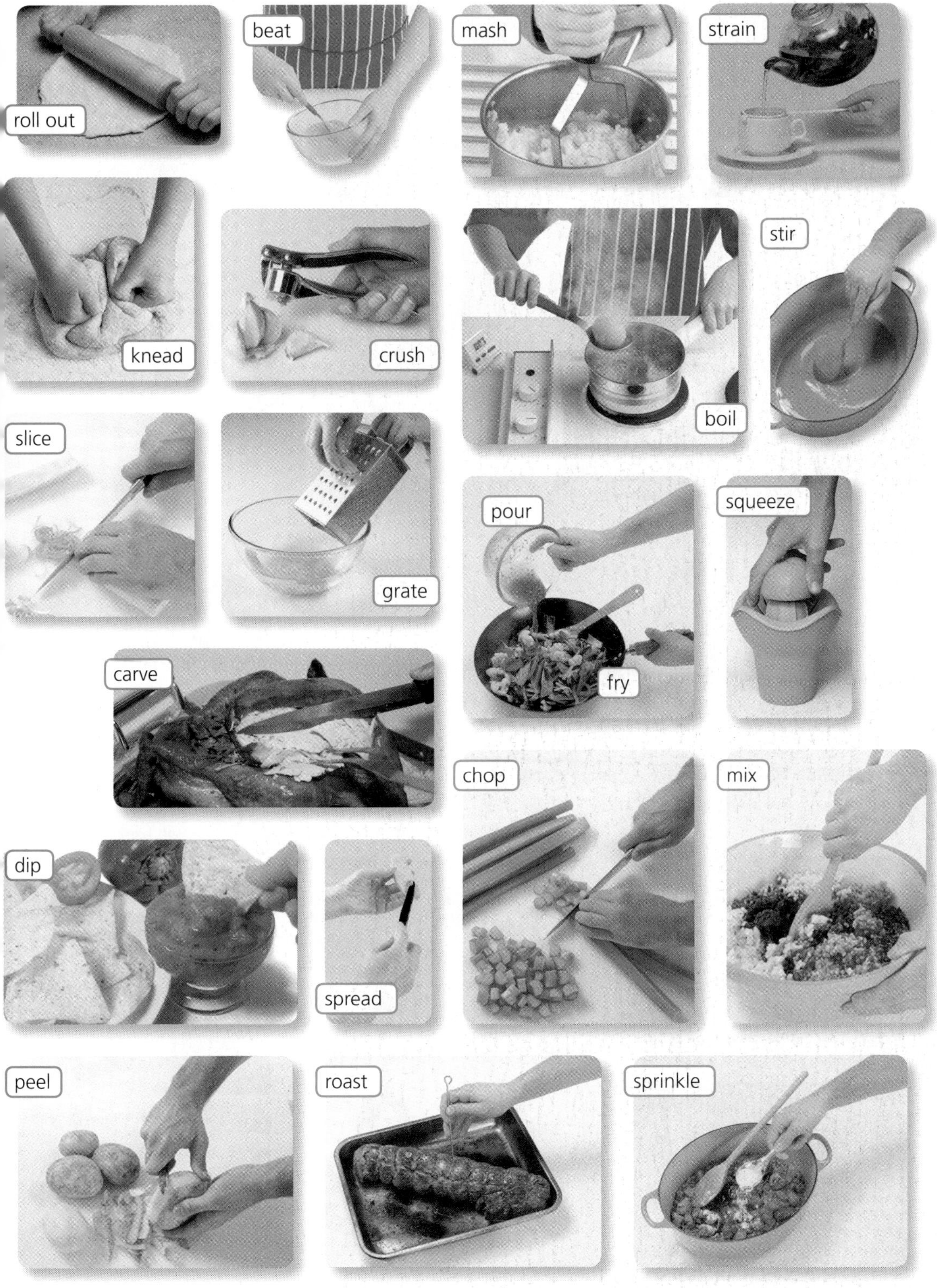
roll out
beat
mash
strain
knead
crush
boil
stir
slice
grate
pour
fry
squeeze
carve
chop
mix
dip
spread
peel
roast
sprinkle

# Jobs

mechanic

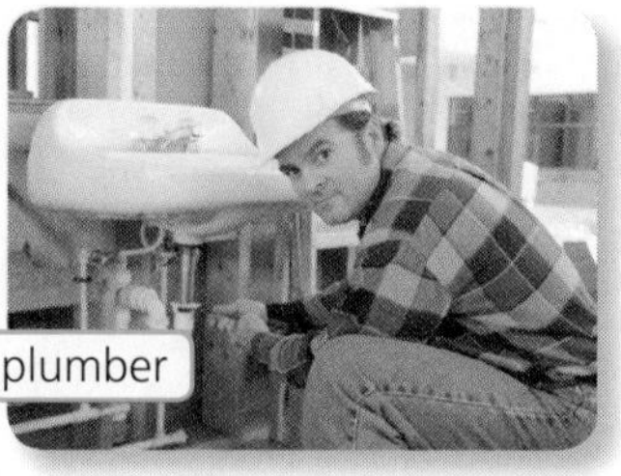
plumber

electrician

fire fighter

police officer

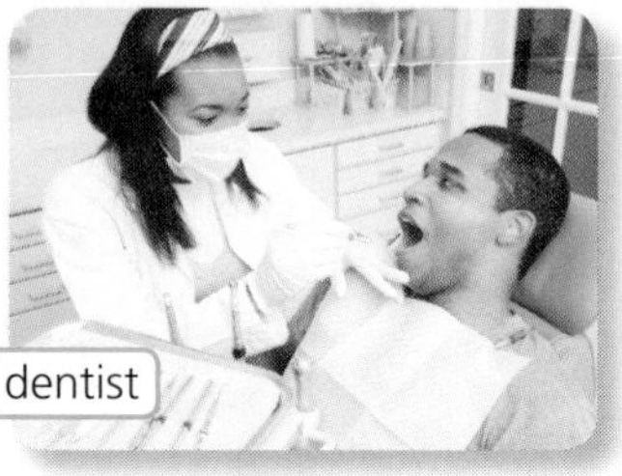
dentist

nurse

doctor

veterinarian

pharmacist

receptionist

bank teller

sales person

professor

teacher

florist

waitress

counter worker

chef/cook

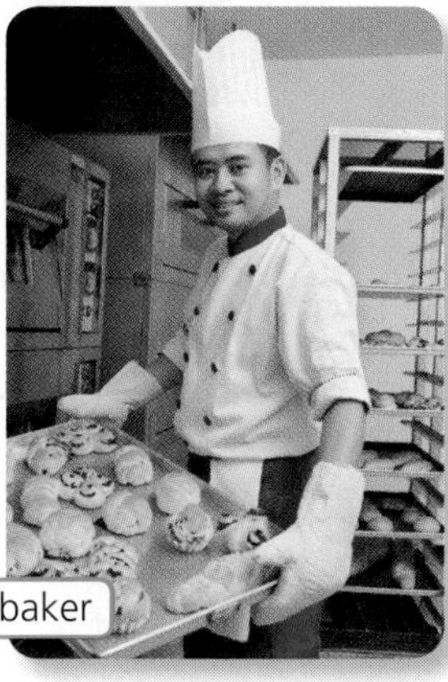

baker

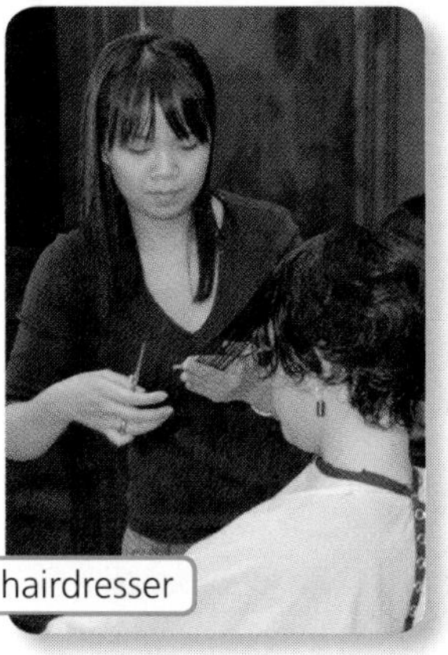

hairdresser

judge

lawyer

fitness trainer

painter

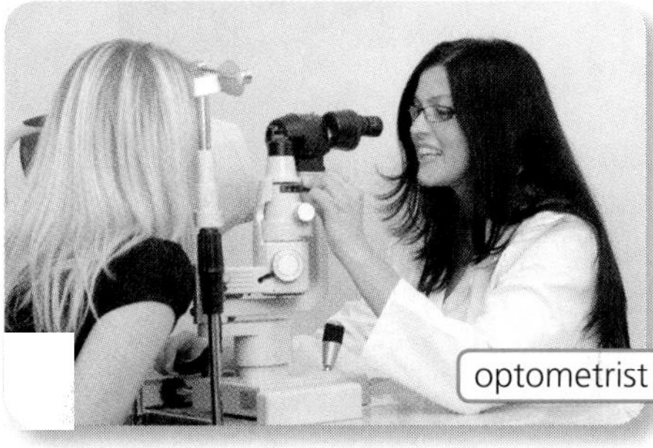

optometrist

journalist/reporter

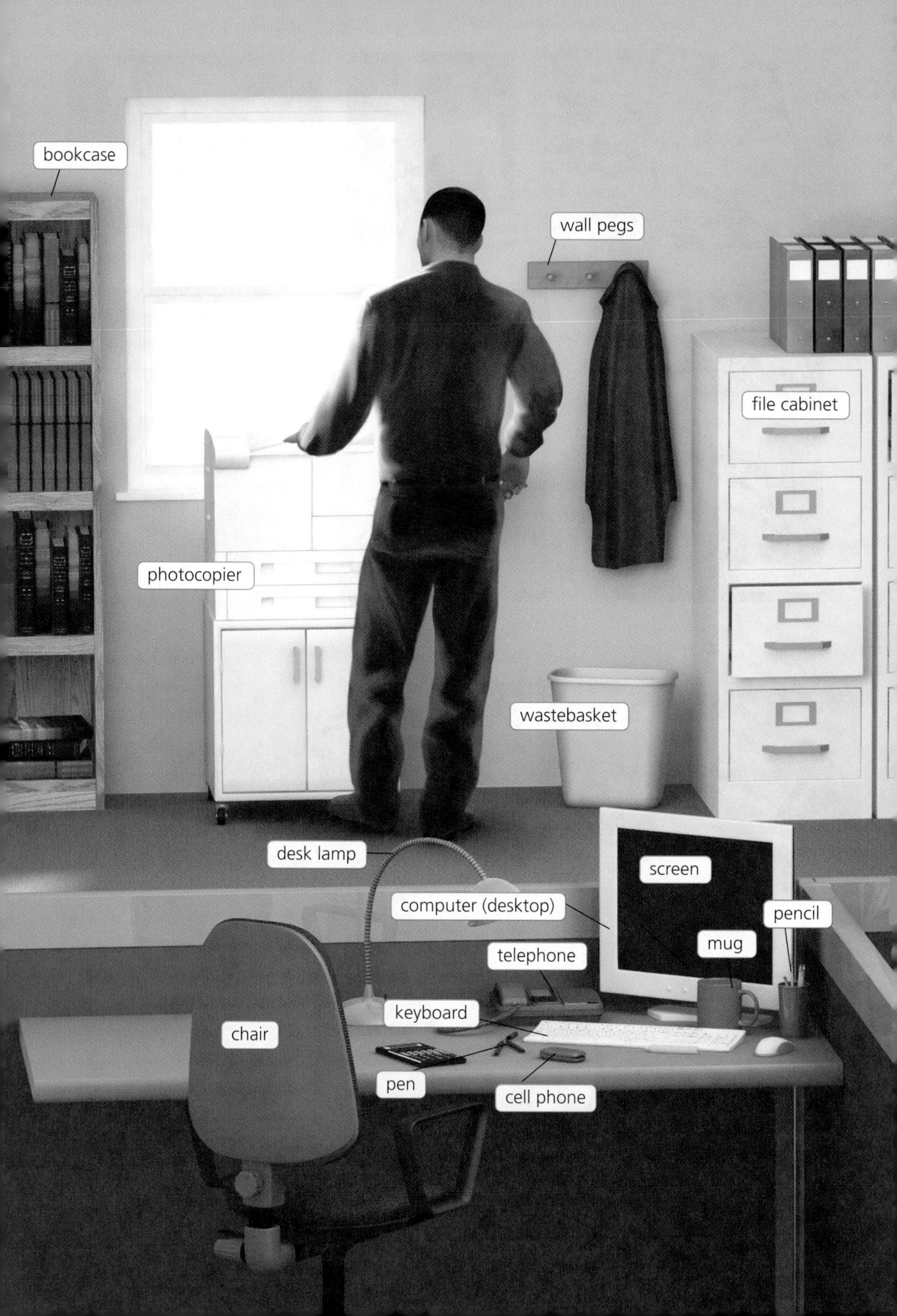
bookcase
wall pegs
file cabinet
photocopier
wastebasket
desk lamp
screen
computer (desktop)
pencil
mug
telephone
keyboard
chair
pen
cell phone

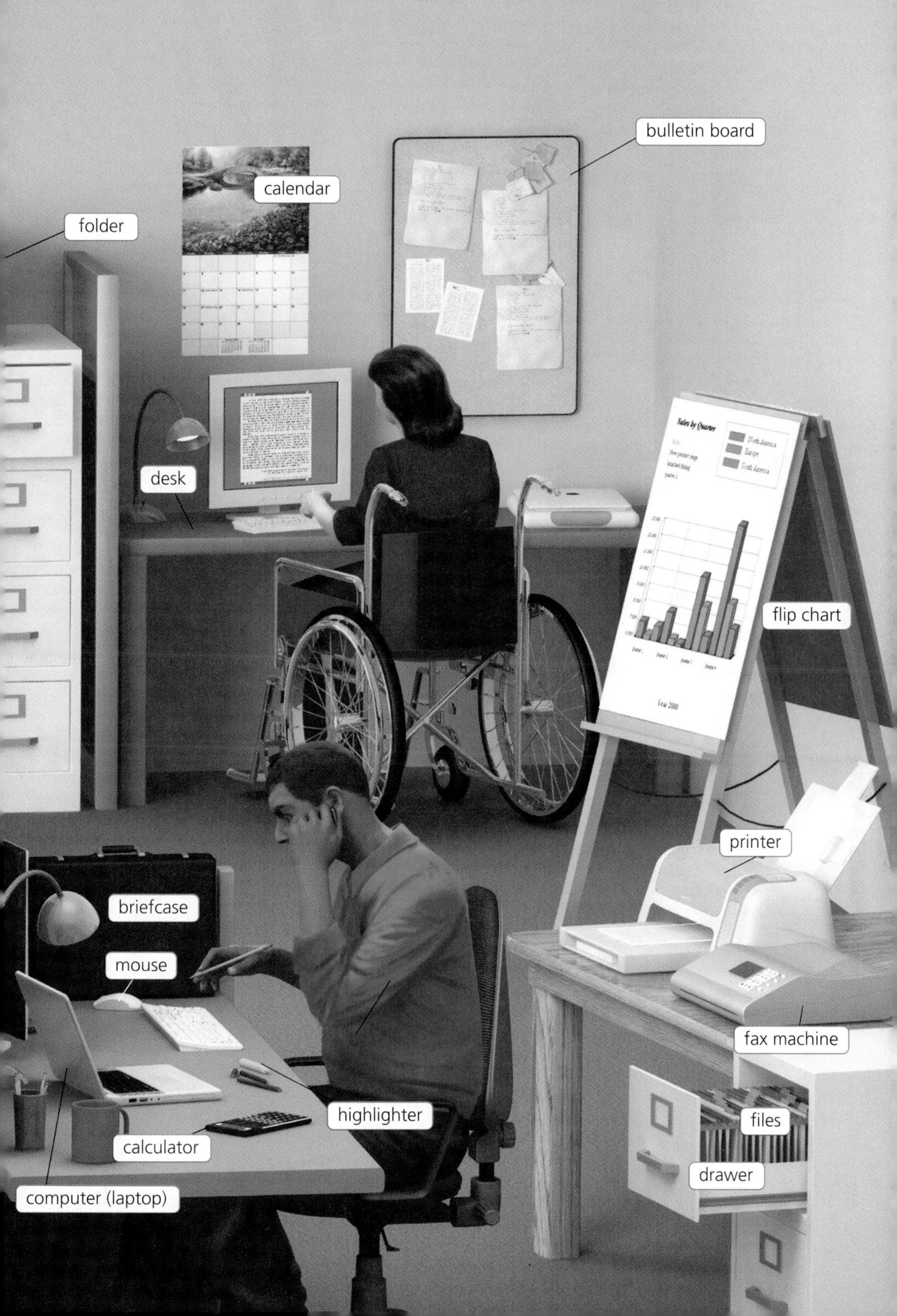
bulletin board
calendar
folder
desk
flip chart
Sales by Quarter
North America
Europe
South America
Year 2000
printer
briefcase
mouse
fax machine
files
highlighter
calculator
drawer
computer (laptop)

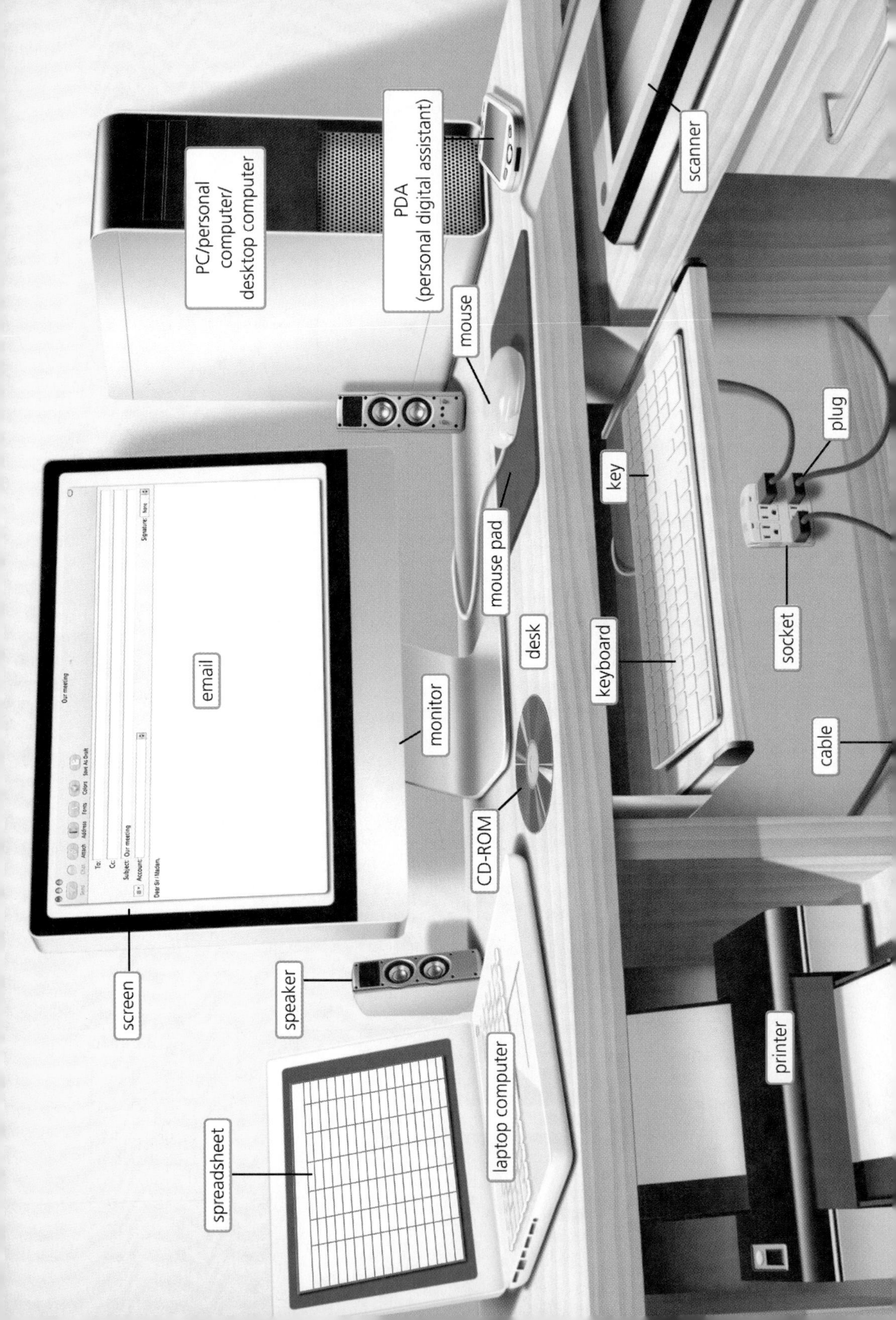
PC/personal computer/ desktop computer
PDA (personal digital assistant)
scanner
mouse
plug
key
mouse pad
socket
desk
keyboard
email
monitor
cable
CD-ROM
screen
speaker
laptop computer
printer
spreadsheet

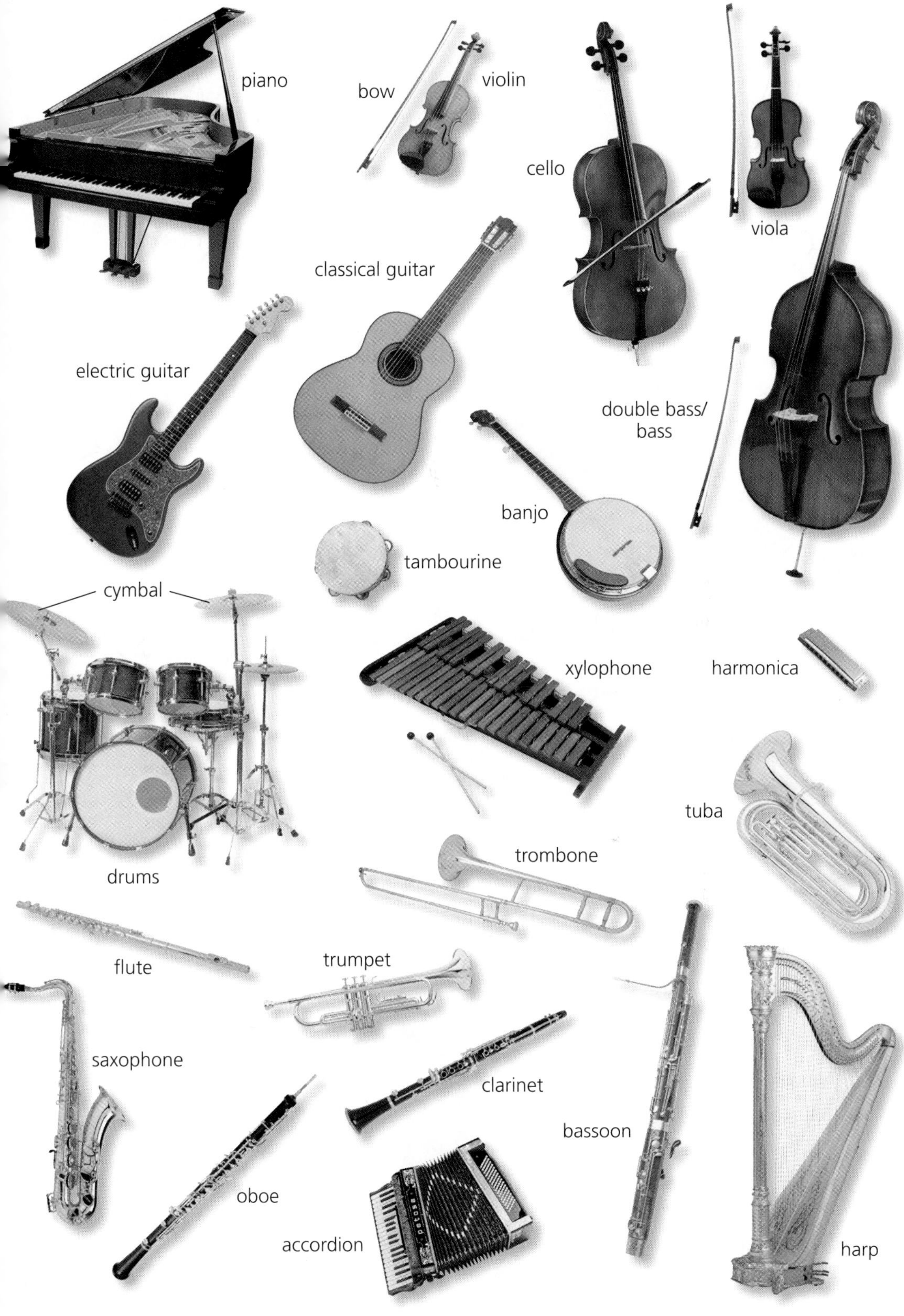
piano
bow
violin
cello
viola
classical guitar
electric guitar
double bass/
bass
banjo
tambourine
cymbal
xylophone
harmonica
tuba
trombone
drums
flute
trumpet
saxophone
clarinet
bassoon
oboe
accordion
harp

click
rustle
ring
splash
buzz
rattle
tick
crackle
snap
crunch
creak
fizz
sizzle
squeak
bang
hiss
smash
slam

sad
stressed/
nervous
mad/angry
surprised
bored
happy
scared/afraid
jealous
worried
tired
embarrassed
excited
confused

## Sports

ice hockey

basketball

sailing

martial arts

tennis

football

golf

climbing

fencing

gymnastics

baseball

cycling

surfing

riding

swimming

volleyball

boxing

skiing

snowboarding

water skiing

rollerblading

soccer

running

traffic lights
crosswalk
car

train
railroad tracks

sailboat
sailor

cab/taxi

motorcycle
helmet

bus stop
3 KING DRIVE
driver
passenger
cta 4875
bus

station
subway
Main Street Flushing
5 Avenue Times Square
platform

tractor

bicycle

motor home

van

police car
CHICAGO POLICE

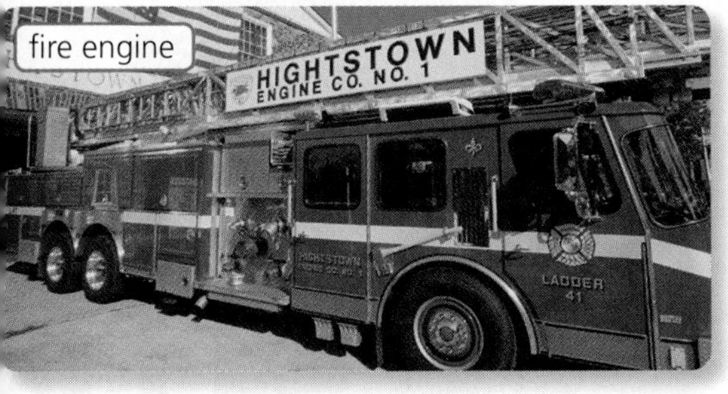
fire engine
HIGHTSTOWN
ENGINE CO. NO. 1
LADDER
41

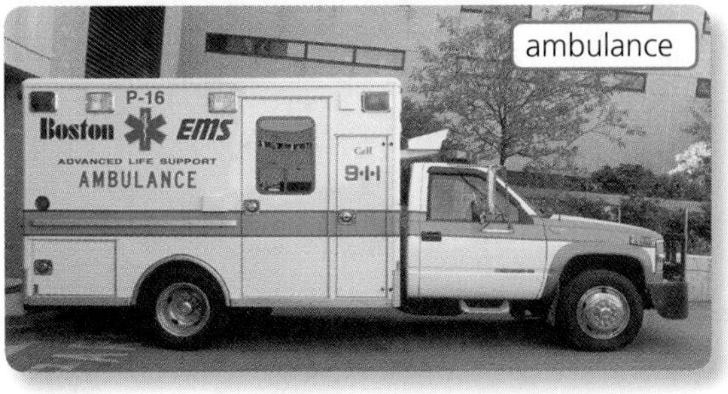
ambulance
P-16
Boston EMS
ADVANCED LIFE SUPPORT
AMBULANCE
9-1-1

plane
runway

pickup truck

rowboat

ship

ferry

N22CP
helicopter

truck

# Car



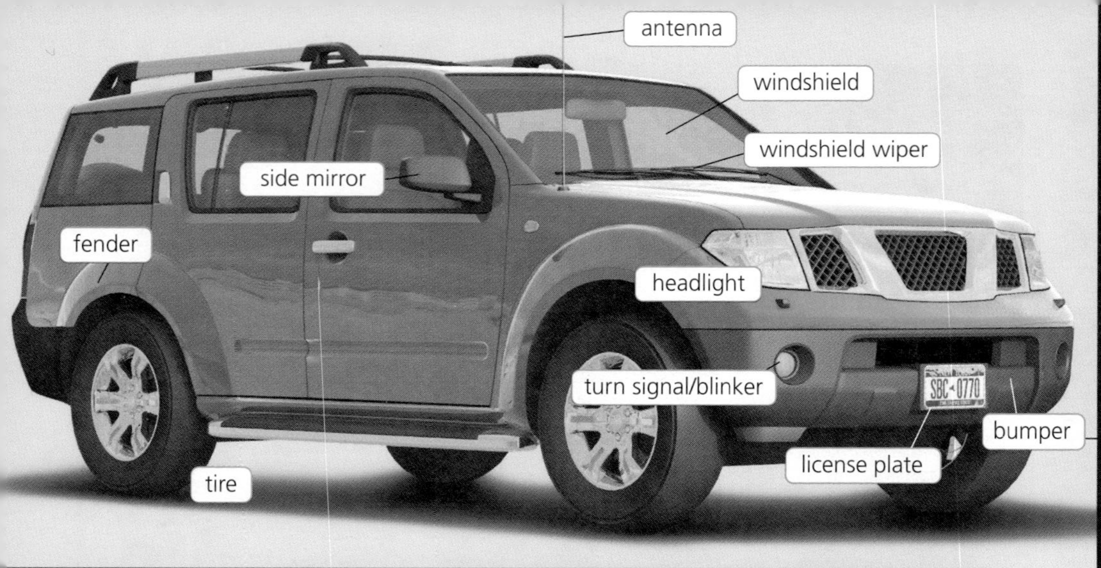
antenna
windshield
windshield wiper
side mirror
fender
headlight
turn signal/blinker
license plate
bumper
tire

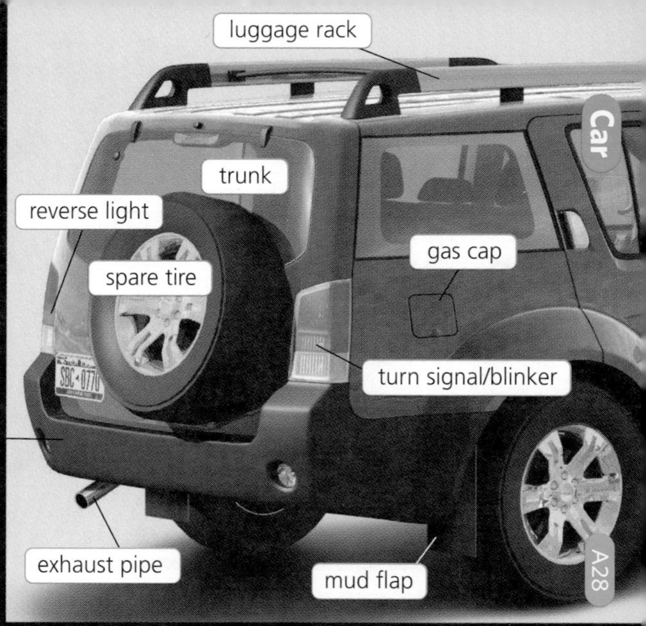
luggage rack
trunk
reverse light
spare tire
gas cap
turn signal/blinker
exhaust pipe
mud flap

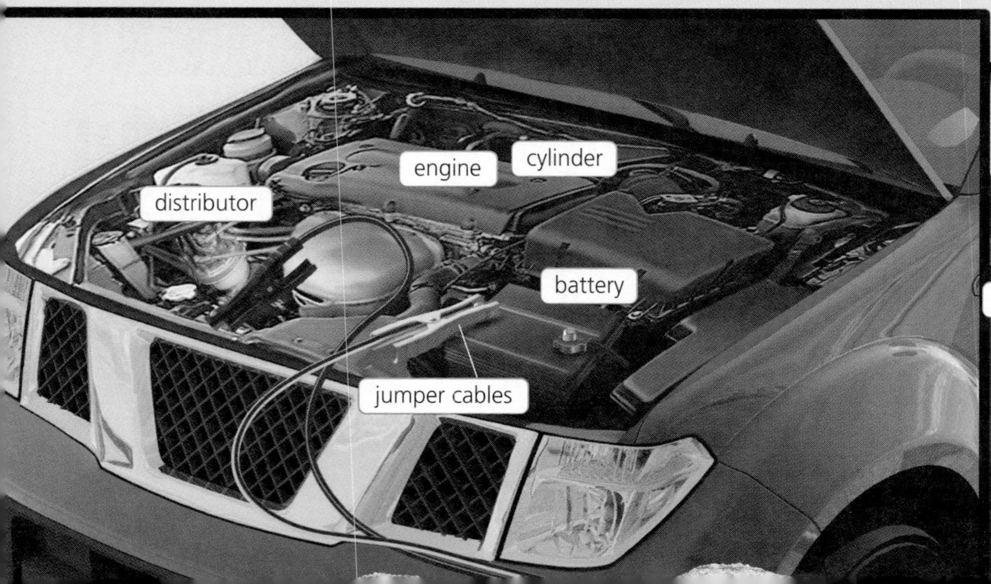
engine
cylinder
distributor
battery
jumper cables

rearview mirror
speedometer
steering wheel
glove compartment
dashboard
gas gauge
horn
turn signal
airbag
headrest
ignition
radio
clutch pedal
CD player
brake pedal
gas pedal
gearshift
passenger seat
seat belt
emergency brake

(see also page 900)

## Height

**Metric system**
m = meter
dm = decimeter
cm = centimeter
mm = millimeter

**U.S. customary system**
yd = yard
ft = foot
in = inch

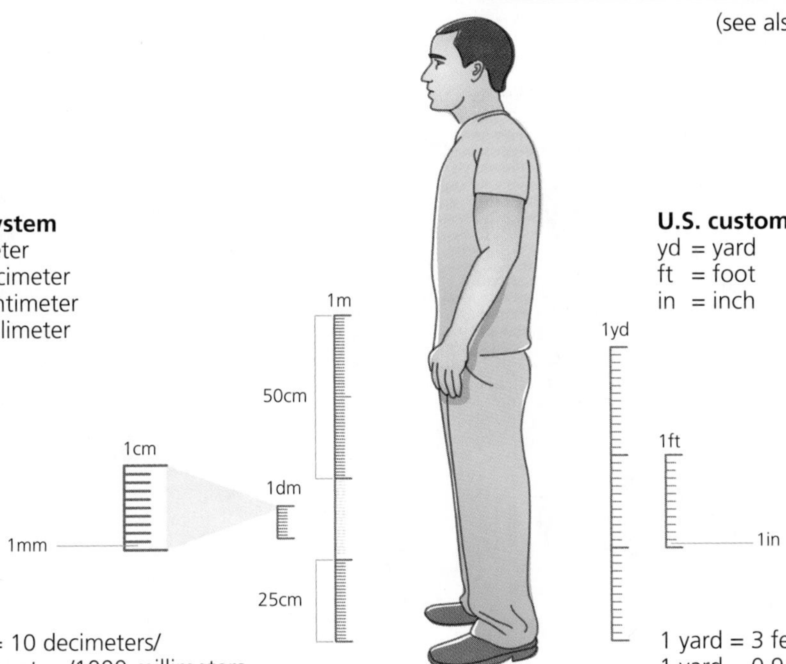


1 meter = 10 decimeters/
100 centimeters/1000 millimeters

1 yard = 0.9144 meter

1 yard = 3 feet/36 inches
1 yard = 0.9144 meter

## Temperature

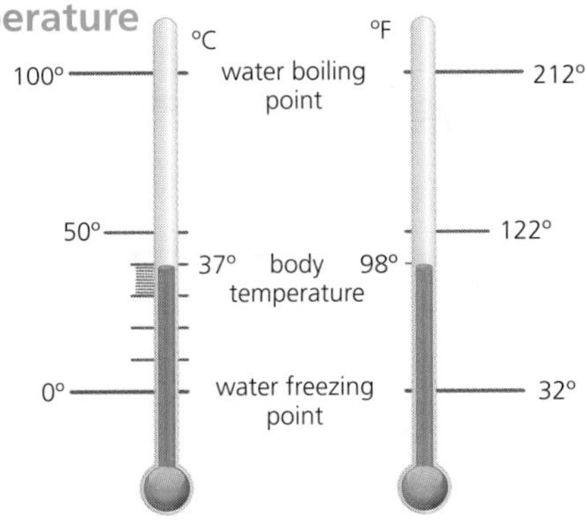


Celsius/
Centigrade

Fahrenheit

## Speed

km/h = kilometers per hour
mph = miles per hour

1kilometer = 1000 meters
1 mile = 1,760 yards/1,609 meters

## Weight

kg = kilogram
lb = pound
1 kilogram = 2.205 pounds

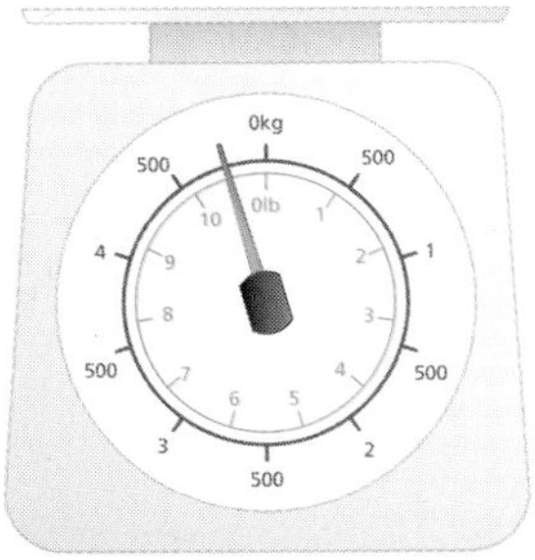


## Volume

**Metric system**
l = liter
dl = deciliter
cl = centiliter
ml = milliliter

1 liter = 1.06 quarts
1 pint = 0.4732 liters

**US customary system**
pt = pint
qt = quart
fl oz = fluid ounce

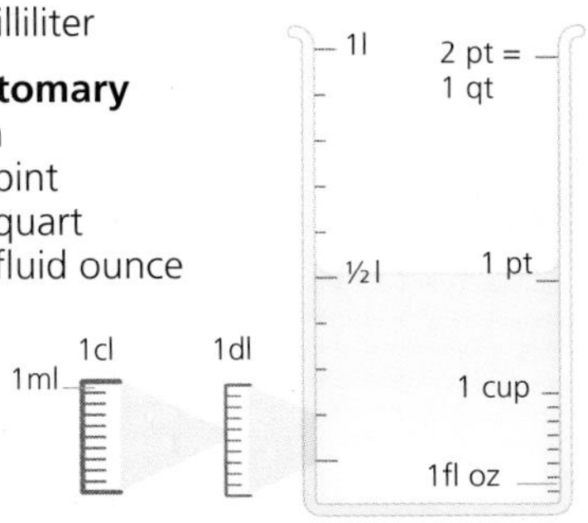


## Charts

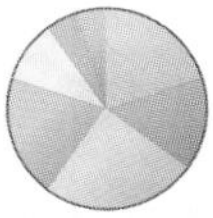

pie chart

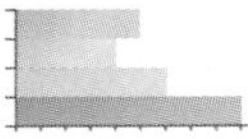

bar chart

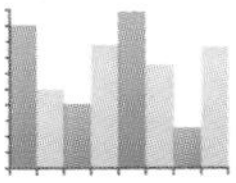

column chart

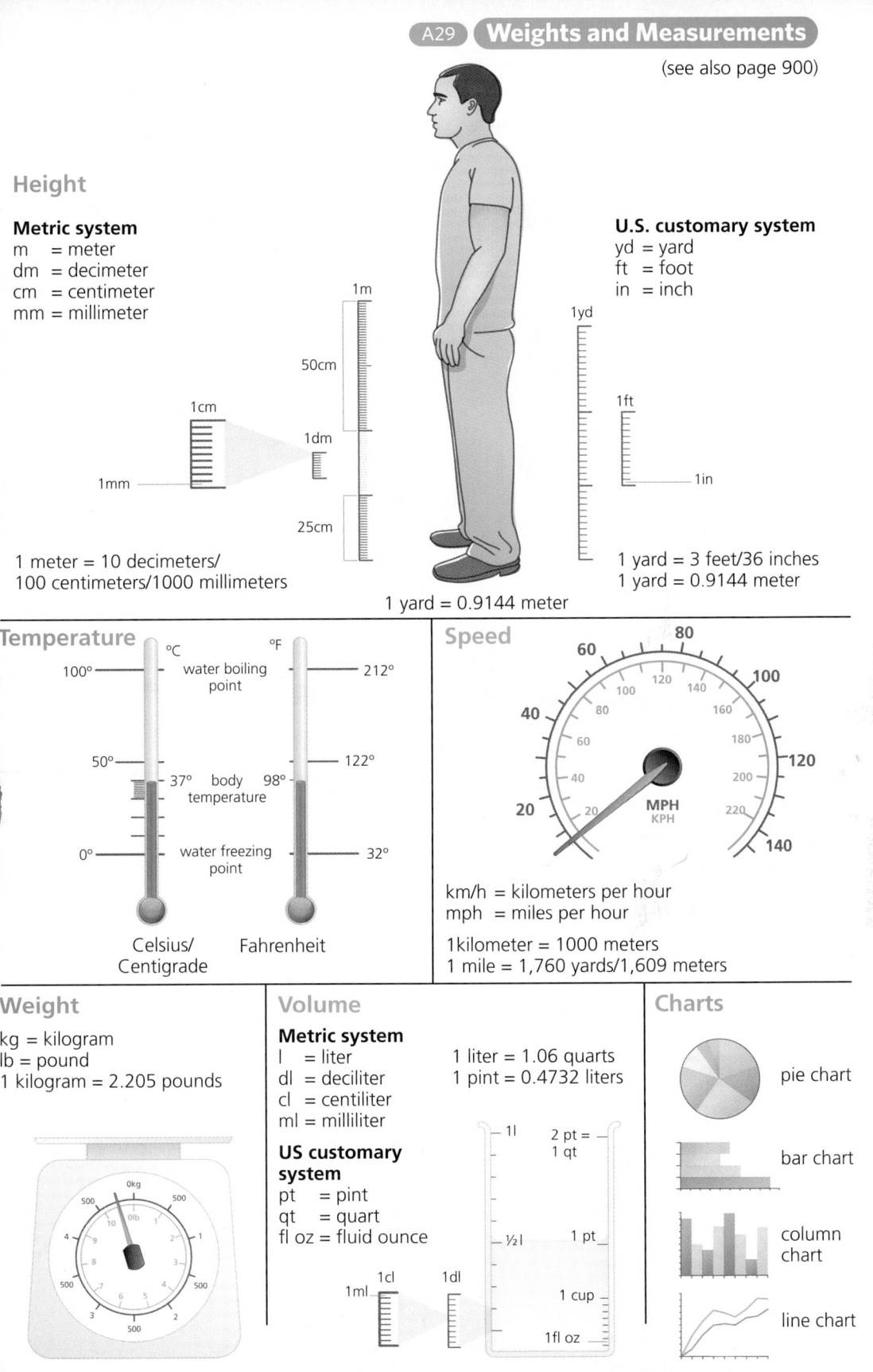

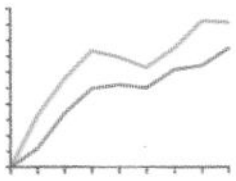

line chart

1 entrance

2 departures

3 security

4 departure lounge

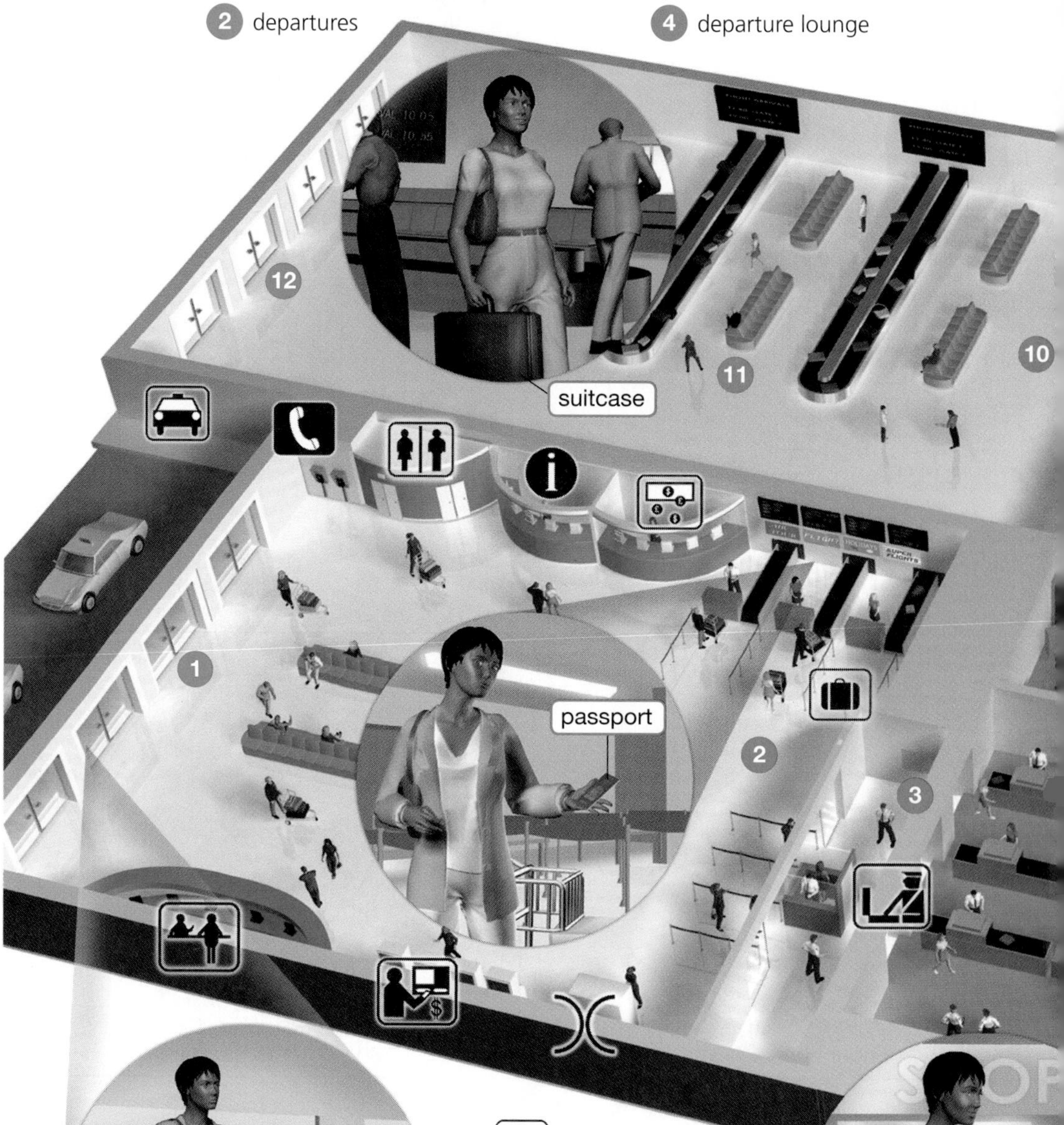


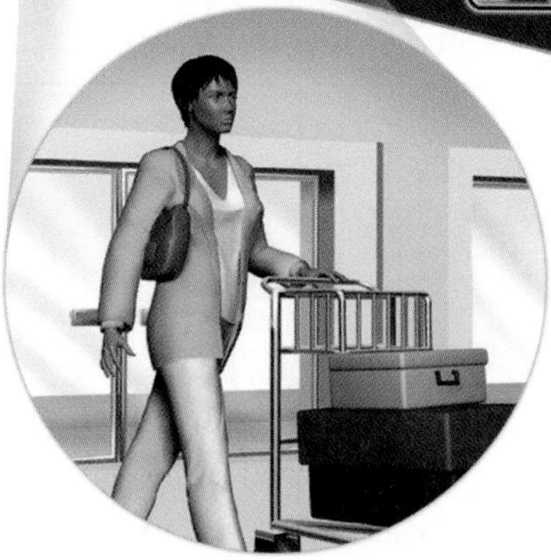

- taxi/car
- telephone
- restroom
- information
- currency exchange
- check-in
- ATM
- ticket desk

5 boarding gates
6 shops
7 seating area
8 information screen
9 café/restaurant
10 arrivals
11 baggage reclaim
12 exit

customs
internet point
café/restaurant
baggage carts

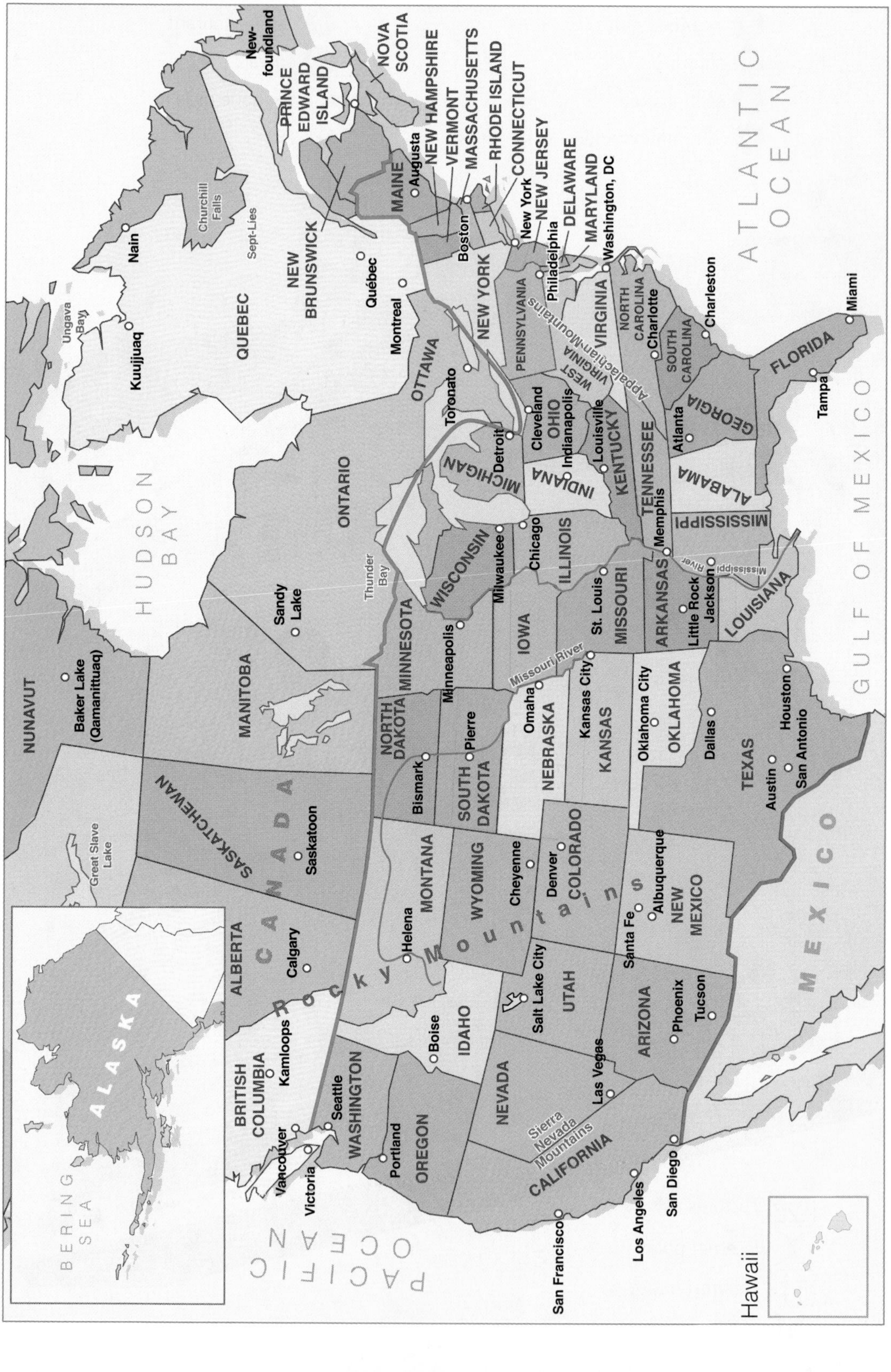
NUNAVUT
Baker Lake (Qamanittuaq)
Great Slave Lake
ALBERTA
BRITISH COLUMBIA
SASKATCHEWAN
MANITOBA
ONTARIO
QUEBEC
NEW BRUNSWICK
PRINCE EDWARD ISLAND
NOVA SCOTIA
New-foundland
Nain
Churchill Falls
Sept-Lies
Ungava Bay
Kuujjuaq
Québec
Montreal
OTTAWA
Toronato
Sandy Lake
Thunder Bay
Saskatoon
Calgary
Kamloops
Vancouver
Victoria
CANADA
HUDSON BAY
ALASKA
BERING SEA
PACIFIC OCEAN
ATLANTIC OCEAN
GULF OF MEXICO
MEXICO
Hawaii
Rocky Mountains
Sierra Nevada Mountains
Appalachian Mountains
Missouri River
Mississippi River
WASHINGTON
OREGON
CALIFORNIA
NEVADA
IDAHO
MONTANA
WYOMING
UTAH
COLORADO
ARIZONA
NEW MEXICO
NORTH DAKOTA
SOUTH DAKOTA
NEBRASKA
KANSAS
OKLAHOMA
TEXAS
MINNESOTA
IOWA
MISSOURI
ARKANSAS
LOUISIANA
WISCONSIN
ILLINOIS
MICHIGAN
INDIANA
OHIO
KENTUCKY
TENNESSEE
MISSISSIPPI
ALABAMA
GEORGIA
FLORIDA
SOUTH CAROLINA
NORTH CAROLINA
VIRGINIA
WEST VIRGINIA
PENNSYLVANIA
NEW YORK
MAINE
NEW HAMPSHIRE
VERMONT
MASSACHUSETTS
RHODE ISLAND
CONNECTICUT
NEW JERSEY
DELAWARE
MARYLAND
Washington, DC
Seattle
Portland
San Francisco
Los Angeles
San Diego
Las Vegas
Boise
Helena
Salt Lake City
Phoenix
Tucson
Santa Fe
Albuquerque
Denver
Cheyenne
Bismark
Pierre
Minneapolis
Omaha
Kansas City
Oklahoma City
Dallas
Houston
Austin
San Antonio
St. Louis
Little Rock
Jackson
Memphis
Milwaukee
Chicago
Detroit
Indianapolis
Louisville
Cleveland
Atlanta
Tampa
Miami
Charleston
Charlotte
Philadelphia
New York
Boston
Augusta

# Workbook

## LESSON 1

**Objective:** Introducing the dictionary

**Dictionary Skill:** Find words in the dictionary

**Tasks:** Putting words in alphabetical order, Using guidewords, Recognizing key words

### EXERCISE 1

The dictionary lists words in alphabetical order. These are called main words. It does not matter if the word begins with a capital letter (*English*) or if it is a compound word (*ice cream* or *man-made*) or an abbreviation (*Dr.*).

➤ Number these groups of words in alphabetical order.

| Group 1 | | Group 2 | | Group 3 | | Group 4 | | Group 5 | |
|---|---|---|---|---|---|---|---|---|---|
| bacon | 2 | finish | ☐ | bulldog | ☐ | heel | ☐ | parrot | ☐ |
| apron | 1 | monk | ☐ | bright | ☐ | hello | ☐ | parking lot | ☐ |
| pot | ☐ | captain | ☐ | bell | ☐ | half-brother | ☐ | parent | ☐ |
| day | ☐ | health | ☐ | bath | ☐ | how | ☐ | party | ☐ |
| face | ☐ | VIP | ☐ | black | ☐ | howl | ☐ | partner | ☐ |

### EXERCISE 2

Guidewords show you the first word on the left page and the last word on the right page. ➤ Look at these guidewords for pages in the dictionary. Which word will you find on those pages? Circle it.

1 Pages 194–195: *deprive* to *despite* a departure b detonate c desolate
2 Pages 616–617: *rating* to *real* a read b rate c reason
3 Pages 582–583: *prairie* to *preference* a prelude b president c preconception
4 Pages 72–73: *blog* to *boar* a blow b border c bogus
5 Pages 248–249: *evasion* to *evict* a evil b evacuate c every
6 Pages 350–351: *height* to *hesitate* a hate b hierarchy c heroic

### EXERCISE 3

The most common main words in the dictionary look like this: **happy**. These are called key words, and they are very important words to learn. ➤ The words in each group have similar meanings, but only one is a key word. Work with a partner and use your dictionaries to find the key word in each group. Circle it.

1 heavy plump fat chubby
2 gifted brilliant bright genius
3 accomplish conquer fulfill succeed
4 scent aroma smell odor
5 grip hold clutch seize

## LESSON 2

**Objective:** Develop accuracy in spelling

**Dictionary Skill:** Find how to spell a word

**Tasks:** Using the dictionary to check spelling, Checking spelling changes in inflected words

### EXERCISE 1

Use the dictionary when you are not sure how to spell a word. ➤ Each word is missing one letter. Write the correct spelling on the line.

1 begining ___beginning___
2 exitement ______________
3 diffrent ______________
4 saden ______________
5 finaly ______________
6 libary ______________
7 Artic ______________
8 suprise ______________

### EXERCISE 2

Some words change their spelling when you add an ending (to make a noun plural or to change a verb to the simple past tense, for example). The dictionary shows those spelling changes. ➤ Complete each sentence with the word in parentheses plus the ending. Make other necessary spelling changes. Check your answers in the dictionary.

1 (thief + -s) The ___thieves___ wanted the jewelry from my house.
2 (bounce + -ing) Sandra is ______________ the ball.
3 (pretty + -est) That red dress was the ______________ in the store.
4 (supply + -s) The new school ______________ can be found in the bottom cabinet.
5 (day + -ly) Eric likes to read the ______________ newspaper.
6 (plan + -ed) The boy ______________ to play baseball after school.

### EXERCISE 3

You must know the first few letters of a word to find it in the dictionary. If you cannot find a word, you might have the wrong spelling. Then you need to think about other possible ways to spell the word. ➤ These words have errors in the first few letters. Working with a partner, find the correct spelling and write it on the line.

1 kemistry ___chemistry___
2 nife ______________
3 seel ______________
4 pithon ______________
5 reck ______________
6 jiraffe ______________
7 farmacy ______________
8 ourly ______________

Workbook

## LESSON 3

**Objective:** Develop learner understanding of grammatical functions of words

**Dictionary Skill:** Find what part of speech a word is

**Tasks:** Locating information about parts of speech, Recognizing words that can be more than one part of speech, Analyzing words for their function in sentences

### EXERCISE 1

The dictionary tells you what **part of speech** a word is. That is, it tells you how the word functions in a sentence. ➤ Draw a line to match each word with its part of speech.

| | | | |
|---|---|---|---|
| 1 embarrass | a noun | 5 now | e adjective |
| 2 her | b pronoun | 6 beautiful | f adverb |
| 3 doctor | c verb | 7 but | g modal verb |
| 4 with | d preposition | 8 shall | h conjunction |

### EXERCISE 2

Some words can be more than one part of speech. When you see a small, raised number after a main word, like **call**[1], look for other entries for that word. ➤ Check (✓) the words that can be more than one part of speech. Write the parts of speech on the line.

1 ☐ with ___preposition___

2 ☑ damage ___noun, verb___

3 ☐ budget ______

4 ☐ honey ______

5 ☐ monitor ______

6 ☐ party ______

7 ☐ advance ______

8 ☐ elite ______

### EXERCISE 3

Sometimes a word can be two different parts of speech. The second part of speech is sometimes shown at the end of the entry for the word. For example, look at the entry for *fur*. ➤ Find the entries for these words. Write both parts of speech shown in the entry.

1 fur a ___noun___ b ___adjective___

2 pink a ______ b ______

3 dispute a ______ b ______

4 lobby a ______ b ______

5 shove a ______ b ______

6 inward a ______ b ______

7 despair a ______ b ______

8 growl a ______ b ______

## EXERCISE 4

➤ Read the sentences. What part of speech is the word in **bold** letters? Circle your answer.

| | | |
|---|---|---|
| 1 | My dog **escaped** from the house. | verb / noun |
| 2 | Movies can be a great **escape** from stress. | verb / noun |
| 3 | Studying math **interests** me. | verb / noun |
| 4 | I lost **interest** in the book. | verb / noun |
| 5 | The farmer **milked** the cows. | verb / noun |
| 6 | She poured **milk** in the cup. | verb / noun |
| 7 | My dad likes to drive **fast**. | adjective / adverb |
| 8 | Are you a **fast** reader? | adjective / adverb |
| 9 | He knows the **answer** to the question. | verb / noun |
| 10 | Please **answer** the door. | verb / noun |

## EXERCISE 5

➤ Play this game with a partner. Tell your partner a number between 1 and 878. Write down the number your partner gives you. (It must be the number of a full page in the dictionary.) Find words on that page to write in the chart. They must be the right parts of speech. The first person to complete his or her chart is the winner.

| | **Page _____** |
|---|---|
| a noun | |
| a verb | |
| an adjective | |
| a word that can be more than one part of speech | |

| | **Page _____** |
|---|---|
| a noun | |
| a verb | |
| an adjective | |
| a word that can be more than one part of speech | |

## LESSON 4

**Objective:** Develop learner awareness of multiple senses of words

**Dictionary Skill:** Understand definitions, Recognize words with multiple senses, Distinguish among definitions

**Tasks:** Understanding definitions, Finding the number of senses, Recognizing the more common meanings, Choosing the appropriate definition

### EXERCISE 1

➤ Match each word with its meaning. Write the word next to the definition.

| | | | | | |
|---|---|---|---|---|---|
| currency | penalize | parameter | tolerate | attention | scold |

1 a limit or rule that controls the way that something should be done ___parameter___

2 the state of listening or looking carefully ________

3 the type of money that a country uses ________

4 to punish someone for not obeying a rule ________

5 to tell someone in an angry way that he or she has done something wrong ________

6 to accept behavior or a situation that you do not like and not do anything about it ________

### EXERCISE 2

Some words have more than one meaning. Different meanings are listed after the blue numbers 1, 2, and so on. ➤ How many meanings does each of these words have in the dictionary? Write the number of meanings on the line. (Remember to count all the meanings of words that can be more than one part of speech.)

1 quick __2__

2 certain ____

3 issue ____

4 hook ____

5 pleasant ____

6 flash ____

7 schedule ____

8 term ____

## EXERCISE 3

Each word in **bold blue** letters has more than one meaning in the dictionary.
➤ Find the right meaning of the word as it is used in the sentence. The small numbers indicate which entry you need to look at, for example **kind**[1] – *noun*. Circle the number of the meaning.

1 What **kind**[1] of car do you have? 1 2

2 The dogs **guard**[2] the house. 1 2

3 Compare and **contrast**[2] the two horror movies. 1 2

4 The family went on a picnic to enjoy the **fine**[1] weather. 1 2 3 4 5

5 The bicyclist was in a **minor**[1] accident. 1 2

6 He might **equal**[2] the world record. 1 2

## EXERCISE 4

When a word has more than one meaning, the dictionary shows the most common meaning first. That is the meaning most often used, but you should read the other definitions, too. ➤ Read each pair of sentences. The words in **bold blue** letters have different meanings. Check (✓) the sentence that uses the more common meaning of the word.

1 ☐ a Nobody liked the old lady. She was a **cold** person.
☑ b My apartment is so **cold**! I have to wear a sweater when I go to sleep.

2 ☐ a You should not leave your dog **alone** in the car.
☐ b He **alone** knows how to fix that car.

3 ☐ a The clown tried to **juggle** six balls at the same time.
☐ b She **juggled** two jobs to help her family.

4 ☐ a The U.S.'s **occupation** of South Korean began in the 1950s.
☐ b What is your father's **occupation**?

5 ☐ a There will be a **review** to make sure the plan is still working well.
☐ b The positive **review** made me want to read the book immediately.

6 ☐ a Wow, you lost an **unbelievable** amount of weight!
☐ b Ted's reason for being late to class is **unbelievable**.

## LESSON 5

**Objective:** Develop learner understanding of word usage

**Dictionary Skill:** Use the dictionary to find word forms and usage information

**Tasks:** Finding irregular plurals, Finding irregular verb forms, Distinguishing levels of formality, Identifying academic vocabulary

### EXERCISE 1

Most plural nouns end in *-s*. A few nouns do not. They have irregular plurals.
➤ Write the irregular plural form of each noun.

1 one wife, two ___wives___
2 one sheep, two ________
3 one half, two ________
4 one tomato, two ________
5 one goose, two ________
6 one cactus, two ________
7 one man, two ________
8 one ox, two ________

### EXERCISE 2

A regular verb ends in *-ed* in the simple past and past participle, for example:

Base form: Tell them to listen.
Simple past: I listened to the weather report last night.
Past participle: I have listened to Latin music all my life.

An irregular verb is different. The dictionary tells you its simple past form and its past participle. You can find this information in the entry for the verb and also in the chart on pages 879–881. ➤ Complete the sentences. Use (a) the simple past and (b) the past participle of the bold blue verb.

1 He likes to **bring** his lunch every day. He (a) ________ a ham sandwich last Friday. He has (b) ________ peanut butter and jelly sandwiches before.

2 The bird will **fly** south during the cold winter months. It (a) ________ to the Florida Keys last December. It has (b) ________ as far south as the Caribbean.

3 Do you like to **swim**? Marcy (a) ________ with Jake last week. I haven't (b) ________ in a really long time!

4 My mom will **pay** for your ticket. She (a) ________ online, and then printed the receipt for proof. My older sister has (b) ________ for her own ticket.

5 Do you like to **wear** big floppy hats in the summer? My friend Casey (a) ________ one the other day at the beach. I have always (b) ________ them on sunny days to keep me cool.

6 Can you **take** a look at Britney's cell phone? She (a) ________ it to the store the other day to get it repaired, but there seems to be a problem with it again. This is the third time she has (b) ________ it to get it fixed.

## EXERCISE 3

Most words can be used in both spoken and written English, but not all. **Formal** words are usually used in writing but not in conversation. **Informal** words are fine for conversation but not for academic writing. The dictionary tells you when a word is formal or informal. ➤ The two words in parentheses have similar meanings. Circle the less formal word. Then ask a partner the questions, using the less formal words. Check (✓) your partner's answers.

| | always | usually | sometimes | never |
|---|---|---|---|---|
| 1 Do you spend Saturdays with your (friends/buddies)? | ☐ | ☐ | ☐ | ☐ |
| 2 Do you have a big (bash/party) for your birthday? | ☐ | ☐ | ☐ | ☐ |
| 3 Do your brothers and sisters (bug/annoy) you? | ☐ | ☐ | ☐ | ☐ |
| 4 Do you (purchase/buy) new clothes at the start of the school year? | ☐ | ☐ | ☐ | ☐ |
| 5 Do you like to watch (stupid/dumb) movies? | ☐ | ☐ | ☐ | ☐ |
| 6 How often do you eat (exotic/weird) food when you're on vacation? | ☐ | ☐ | ☐ | ☐ |
| 7 Do you exercise to strengthen the muscles in your (stomach/abdomen)? | ☐ | ☐ | ☐ | ☐ |
| 8 Do you (assist/help) your friends with their homework? | ☐ | ☐ | ☐ | ☐ |

## EXERCISE 4

Words labeled [Ac] in the dictionary are academic words. They often occur in textbooks. These are important words to learn for the reading and writing you do in school. ➤ Choose the academic word and use it to complete the sentence.

1 (compensate/pay) Most medical professions ___*compensate*___ better than those in the publishing field.

2 (components/parts) Airplanes are made from many different ____________ .

3 (end/outcome) Do you know the ____________ of the story of the Trojan War?

4 (restrictions/rules) Some parents place many ____________ on their children when they're young in hopes that they'll become responsible adults.

5 (fight/debate) There was a big ____________ over healthcare reform in the United States.

6 (aware/mindful) You need to be ____________ of your surroundings when you walk home after dark.

7 (transfer/send) Do you prefer to ____________ your money electronically to your bank or receive a pay check in the mail?

8 (laws/legislation) Congress should pass stronger ____________ to help prevent more illegal drugs from coming into the country.

## LESSON 6

**Objective:** Develop learner understanding of idiomatic language

**Dictionary Skill:** Locate and interpret information about phrasal verbs and idioms

**Tasks:** Finding phrasal verb entries, Recognizing phrasal verb meanings, Matching particles to verbs to form phrasal verbs, Identifying and interpreting idiomatic expressions

### EXERCISE 1

A **phrasal verb** is a special verb. It is a verb followed by one or two other words (adverbs or prepositions). The meaning of a phrasal verb can be very different from the meaning of the verb alone. ➤ Look for phrasal verbs at the end of verb entries in the dictionary. Complete the phrasal verbs in the sentences. Use a verb from the box.

| run | look | talk | back | eat | hold |
|---|---|---|---|---|---|

1 I ___run___ **into** my classmates all the time at the shopping mall.
2 Do you think you can ____________ him **into** joining the science club for next semester?
3 Tell her what you really think, and don't ____________ **down**.
4 You can ____________ **up** the meaning of the word in the dictionary.
5 I should not ____________ **out** so often, but I don't have time to cook.
6 I didn't tell her your secrets, so don't ____________ it **against** me.

### EXERCISE 2

➤ Write each phrasal verb from Exercise 1 next to its meaning.

1 to meet someone when you were not expecting to: ___run into___
2 to admit that you are wrong about something and stop arguing: ____________
3 to try to find information in a book: ____________
4 to persuade someone to do something: ____________
5 to eat in a restaurant: ____________
6 to blame or dislike someone for something he or she did: ____________

### EXERCISE 3

The words in **bold blue** letters are parts of phrasal verbs. ➤ Complete the phrasal verb in each question with the correct word from the box. The words can be used more than once. Then find a partner and ask the questions. Circle your partner's answers.

| in | off | on | out of | up | up to |
|---|---|---|---|---|---|

1 Do you **stand** ___up to___ people who are being mean to you? Yes, I do. / No, I don't.
2 Can you **drop** the dog ________ at the veterinarian for me? Yes, I can. / No, I can't.

3 Have you ever **taken** ________ a new hobby or sport? Yes, I have. / No, I haven't.

4 Does your mother remember to **pass** ________ messages to you? Yes, she does. / No, she doesn't.

5 Have you ever **run** ________ time on a test? Yes, I have. / No, I haven't.

6 Do your grades **go** ________ when you study hard? Yes, they do. / No, they don't.

7 Have you ever **mixed** ________ your schedule and gone to the wrong class? Yes, I have. / No, I haven't.

8 Do you always remember to **turn** ________ your homework on time? Yes, I do. / No, I don't.

## EXERCISE 4

An **idiom** is a group of words with a special meaning. The meaning of the group is different from the meanings of the individual words put together. Many idioms are used mostly in informal English. ➤ Look up each word in **bold blue** letters in the dictionary. In the entry for that word, find the idiom and underline it in the sentence below. Then match the definition (a–f) to the idiom by writing the correct letter on the line.

1 __c__ She talked quite a **bit** during the meeting.

2 _____ The party was getting out of **hand**, so the neighbors called the police.

3 _____ Do you think you can **fall** in love with someone you just met?

4 _____ My sister borrows my clothes without asking. She's a **pain** in the neck.

5 _____ I read your history report, but it doesn't make **sense**.

6 _____ You might not get another chance to try this, so make the **most** of it!

a to begin to love someone

b to have a clear meaning and be easy to understand

c a large amount

d to use a good opportunity well

e to be or become impossible to control

f to be very annoying

## EXERCISE 5

➤ Work with a partner. Guess if each statement is true or false, and circle your answer. Then check your answer by looking up the idioms under the words in **bold blue**. Underline the idioms.

| | Your guess |
|---|---|
| 1 If you visit someone **now** and then, you see them all the time. | True / False |
| 2 If you **flip** a coin, you throw it to choose something. | True / False |
| 3 If politicians **air** their views, that means they need a fan. | True / False |
| 4 If you **count** me in, I want to do something with you. | True / False |
| 5 If you **pull** someone's leg, you're just joking around. | True / False |
| 6 If you **break** even in a card game, you've lost a lot of money. | True / False |

## LESSON 7

**Objective:** Expand learner vocabulary through learning words from the same family

**Dictionary Skill:** Find words not listed as main words, Find words related to main words, Use Word Family Boxes

**Tasks:** Finding related words within the same entry, Finding related words in separate entries, Using Word Family Boxes

## EXERCISE 1

Words belong to families. For example, the words *whaler* and *whaling* are related. In this dictionary, you can find them in the entry for the main word *whale* because they are less common than *whale*. ➤ The words in the list are not main words in the dictionary. Write the related main word where you can find each word.

1 courageous ___courage___
2 jealousy ______
3 feverish ______
4 dependence ______
5 librarian ______
6 recognizable ______

## EXERCISE 2

The words in the chart are main words in the dictionary. ➤ Look in the entries for these words and find other words from the same family. Use the related words to complete the chart.

| Nouns | Verbs | Adjectives | Adverbs |
|---|---|---|---|
| 1 | | defiant | |
| 2 | whisper | | |
| 3 pleasure | | | |
| 4 | | bright | |
| 5 father | | | |
| 6 | recruit | | |

## EXERCISE 3

Sometimes two or more main words are related. Look at the nearby entries for members of the same word family. Read the definitions to see if the words are related. For an example, see the entries for *assist*, *assistance*, and *assistant*.
➤ Work with a partner. Complete the word family chart.

| Nouns | Verbs | Adjectives | Adverbs |
|---|---|---|---|
| fear \| fearlessness | fear | fearful \| fearless | fearfully \| fearlessly |
| | delight | | |
| | | | openly |
| weakling | | | |
| | criticize | | |

## EXERCISE 4

The dictionary has Word Family Boxes that show words with the same root. ➤ Find the Word Family Box for each word in **bold blue** letters. Complete each sentence with the correct word from the box.

1 a Please **inform** the school if you are sick.
  b Look in this book for more ___information___ about African animals.
  c History books are ___informative___ . They teach us about our past.

2 a I spilled soda on the couch. Please don't be **angry**!
  b You should not be late. You will ______________ the boss.
  c "I don't want to see you ever again!" she said ______________ .

3 a Don't put yourself in **danger** by flying kites in stormy weather.
  b It is very ______________ to text on a cell phone while driving a car.
  c The little girl was ______________ close to the edge of the cliff and could have fallen.

4 a Do you **know** the answer to the question?
  b Her ______________ of Spanish helped her get a job.
  c New York is ______________ for being the biggest city in the U.S.

5 a I don't understand her explanations, they are very **confusing**.
  b The changes at school have caused a lot of ______________ .
  c I got ______________ when I read the directions and I did not know which way to go.

Workbook

## LESSON 8

**Objective:** Expand learner vocabulary through learning synonyms, antonyms, and related words

**Dictionary Skill:** Locate synonyms and antonyms, Use Thesaurus Boxes

**Tasks:** Finding synonyms and antonyms, Determining word relationships, Comparing related words in Thesaurus Boxes

### EXERCISE 1

Sometimes the entry for a word reads "another word for … ." For example, the entry for *watchdog* says, "another word for a GUARD DOG." *Watchdog* and *guard dog* are **synonyms** — words with the same meaning — but *guard dog* is more commonly used. ➤ Find synonyms for the words in this list. Write them on the line.

| | | | |
|---|---|---|---|
| 1 service station | gas station | 5 puma | ______ |
| 2 everybody | ______ | 6 skillet | ______ |
| 3 navel | ______ | 7 fragrance | ______ |
| 4 dad | ______ | 8 register | ______ |

### EXERCISE 2

A synonym can sometimes be found at the end of an entry. ➤ Find synonyms for these words. Write them on the lines.

| | | | |
|---|---|---|---|
| 1 costly | expensive | 5 terrific | ______ |
| 2 autumn | ______ | 6 shriek | ______ |
| 3 nicely | ______ | 7 courage | ______ |
| 4 jail | ______ | 8 untrue | ______ |

### EXERCISE 3

An **antonym** is a word with the opposite meaning. An antonym can sometimes be found at the end of an entry. ➤ Look at these pairs of words. Are they **synonyms** (do they have the same meaning)? Or are they **antonyms** (do they have a different meaning? Underline your answers. Use your dictionary to check them.

| | |
|---|---|
| 1 least – most | synonyms / <u>antonyms</u> |
| 2 accept – reject | synonyms / antonyms |
| 3 tactful – tactless | synonyms / antonyms |
| 4 weaken – strengthen | synonyms / antonyms |
| 5 credit – debit | synonyms / antonyms |
| 6 applaud – clap | synonyms / antonyms |
| 7 slender – slim | synonyms / antonyms |
| 8 amateur – professional | synonyms / antonyms |

## EXERCISE 4

The **Thesaurus Boxes** in the dictionary group together words with similar meanings or words that all relate to a particular topic. ➤ Go to the Thesaurus Box at each word in **bold** letters. Read the definitions for the other words. Notice how they are used in sentences. Then complete the exercise.

1 meal: barbecue picnic snack
  a An apple is a healthy ___snack___ in the middle of the afternoon.
  b It was sunny, so we had a ______________ on Saturday, with hot dogs and hamburgers.
  c She made sandwiches for the ______________ in the park on Sunday.

2 reject: decline say no refuse
  a Thank you for inviting me to your wedding, but I must ______________ the invitation.
  b He wanted her to go with him, but she ______________ because she didn't like him.
  c My brother ______________ when I asked him to pick up his toys.

3 smell: perfume odor aroma
  a My mother smells nice. She is wearing her favorite ______________.
  b The ______________ from the cookies that were baking made me hungry.
  c What is that terrible ______________ coming from your refrigerator?

## EXERCISE 5

➤ Work with a partner. Each of you chooses a list of words. Look for synonyms for the words in your list. If there is a synonym, write it in the chart. If there is no synonym, mark an *X*. When you finish, check each other's answers.

| List 1 | | List 2 | |
|---|---|---|---|
| 1 hall | hallway | 1 great | excellent |
| 2 desire | | 2 embrace | |
| 3 dull | | 3 beverage | |
| 4 misplace | | 4 global | |
| 5 commence | | 5 afraid | |
| 6 confession | | 6 noble | |
| 7 sign | | 7 flaw | |
| 8 expressway | | 8 assist | |

## LESSON 9

**Objective:** Develop learner ability to understand information on word origins

**Dictionary Skill:** Locate and use word origin information

**Tasks:** Matching words to their original meanings and locating appropriate information to fill in the blanks.

Word Origin information tells you what language a word comes from, and the original meaning of this word.

### EXERCISE 1

➤ What is the language of origin of each of these words?

| | | | |
|---|---|---|---|
| 1 pizza | Italian | 7 hospital | ______ |
| 2 bagel | ______ | 8 hurricane | ______ |
| 3 beef | ______ | 9 ketchup | ______ |
| 4 chocolate | ______ | 10 octopus | ______ |
| 5 coffee | ______ | 11 pretzel | ______ |
| 6 cookie | ______ | 12 tea | ______ |

### EXERCISE 2

➤ Locate the English words in your dictionary and find their Word Origin information. Draw a line to their original meaning.

| | |
|---|---|
| 1 cafeteria | a road or racetrack |
| 2 neat | b to owe |
| 3 career | c coffee store |
| 4 ecology | d bright or beautiful |
| 5 generous | e home + study |
| 6 debt | f born into an upper class family |

### EXERCISE 3

Locate the English words and find their Word Origin information. Fill in the blanks.

| English word | Language origin | Original word(s) | Original meaning |
|---|---|---|---|
| 1 rank | French | renc | line or row |
| 2 biography | Greek | ______ | ______ |
| 3 phobia | ______ | ______ | fear |
| 4 mistake | ______ | mistaka | ______ |
| 5 reflect | ______ | reflectere | ______ |
| 6 prohibit | ______ | ______ | ______ |

## EXERCISE 4

➤ Look up the origins of the words in the box:

| | | | | | |
|---|---|---|---|---|---|
| biology | carnivore | lunar | transportation | century | minor |

Use the information about these word origins to guess the meanings of the words below. Match each word to its correct definition. Then check your ideas in the dictionary.

1 psychology
2 omnivore
3 lunatic
4 translation
5 centipede
6 minority

a someone who is crazy or behaves in a very stupid way
b the study of the mind
c something that has been changed from one language to another
d a small group of people or things that are part of a larger group
e a small creature with a long soft body and many small legs
f an animal that eats meat and plants

## EXERCISE 5

Guess the answers to the questions and tick the correct answers. Check in your dictionary.

1 The word "grocer" comes from an Old French word meaning someone who:
 a ☐ sells things in large quantities
 b ☐ owns a vegetable garden
 c ☐ owns a farm and grows crops on it

2 The word "academy" comes from the name for a school in
 a ☐ Athens  b ☐ Rome  c ☐ Alexandria

3 The word "acid" comes from a Latin word meaning:
 a ☐ hot  b ☐ sweet  c ☐ sour

4 The word "chlorine" comes from a Greek word meaning:
 a ☐ yellow  b ☐ green  c ☐ blue

## LESSON 10

**Objective:** Familiarize the learner with the dictionary's other resources

**Dictionary Skill:** Use all sections of the dictionary

**Tasks:** Locating special sections of the dictionary, Looking up information in special sections of the dictionary, Reviewing past sections of the dictionary

### EXERCISE 1

In addition to the A to Z pages, the dictionary has several sections with specialized information. ➤ Write the page number where you can find each section.

1 Guide to the Dictionary ____
2 Picture Dictionary ____
3 Irregular Verbs ____
4 Table of Weights and Measures ____
5 School Content Vocabulary ____
6 Map of the United States ____
7 Geographical Names ____

### EXERCISE 2

In which class/subject would you probably hear and read these words? ➤ Write your answers on the lines. Then go to the section "School Content Vocabulary" and check your answers.

| biology | chemistry | computers | sports | politics |
|---|---|---|---|---|

1 element, nitrogen, purify, chemist, dilute, radioactive: ______________
2 ambassador, conservative, liberal, parliament, courthouse, petition: ______________
3 carnivore, antibiotic, DNA, thyroid, mental illness, surgery: ______________
4 PC, megabyte, attachment, laptop, upload, virus: ______________
5 tennis, bat, leader, goal, workout, opponent: ______________

### EXERCISE 3

➤ Work with a partner. Find the answers to these questions in the special sections of the dictionary. Write the answer and the page number where you found it.

1 What is the past tense of freeze? ______________ (page _____ )
2 Which is more, a quart or a gallon? ______________ (page _____ )
3 Write down the names of three types of jobs. ______________ (page _____ )
4 Which word is a measure for volume – hectare or liter?
______________ (page _____ )
5 Which state is south of Virginia? ______________ (page _____ )
6 Name three things that you find in a kitchen. ____________________ (page _____ )
7 What do you call a person from Nepal? ______________ (page _____ )

M

**main·frame** /ˈmeɪnfreɪm/ *noun*
a large powerful computer that has a lot of smaller computers connected to it

**main·land** /ˈmeɪnlənd/ *noun*
**the mainland** = the land that forms the main part of a country, not including any islands near it: *A bridge connects the island to the mainland.*
—**mainland** *adjective* relating to the main part of a country, not including any islands: *mainland China*

**main·ly** /ˈmeɪnli/ *adverb*
mostly or almost all: *The students here are mainly from California and Oregon, but there are several from other states.*

**main·stream** /ˈmeɪnstrim/ *noun*
**the mainstream** = the usual ideas or ways of doing something: *His paintings are outside the mainstream of American art, so many people think that they are strange.*
—**mainstream** *adjective* relating to the usual ideas or ways of doing something: *In the U.S., the mainstream political parties are the Republicans and the Democrats.*

**main·tain** [Ac] /meɪnˈteɪn/ *verb*
**1** to keep something in good condition by taking care of it: *The city pays to maintain the roads and keep them in good condition.*
**2** to make something continue in the same way as before: *Students have to maintain their grades to play on the school teams.*
**3** to say that something is true or correct, especially when other people disagree: *He is in prison, but he maintains that he is innocent.*

**main·te·nance** [Ac] /ˈmeɪntənəns/ *noun*
work that is done to keep something in good condition and working correctly: *The class teaches people about car maintenance, such as checking the oil and changing a tire.*

**ma·jes·tic** /məˈdʒestɪk/ *adjective*
very big and impressive: *majestic mountains*
—**majestically** *adverb* in an impressive way

**maj·es·ty** /ˈmædʒəsti/ *noun*
**1** the quality of being impressive and beautiful: *The photograph showed the majesty of the snow-covered mountains.*
**2 Your/His/Her Majesty** (*formal*) = used when you are talking to a king or queen, or talking about a king or queen

**ma·jor¹** /ˈmeɪdʒɚ/ *adjective*
**1** very large or important: *Heavy traffic is a major problem in most cities.* **ANTONYM: minor**
**2** based on a particular type of musical SCALE **ANTONYM: minor**
→ see Thesaurus box at **important**
**[ORIGIN:** 1200-1300 From the Latin word for "bigger."**]**

**major²** [Ac] *noun*
**1** the main subject that you study in college: *His major in college was history.* | *She's a math major.*
**2** (*written abbreviation*: **Maj.**) an officer who has a middle rank in the army, air force, or Marines: *Major Arnold was in charge of the soldiers who attacked the enemy camp.*

**major³** [Ac] *verb*
**PHRASAL VERB**
**major in something**
to study something as your main subject in college: *Stewart majored in biology at Stanford.*

**ma·jor·ette** /ˌmeɪdʒəˈret/ *noun*
a girl who spins a BATON (=thin stick) while marching in a PARADE

**ma·jor·i·ty** [Ac] /məˈdʒɔrəti/ *noun* (plural **majorities**)
**1** most of the people or things in a group: *The majority of Americans support the president, but of course not all of them do.* **ANTONYM: minority**
**2** more votes than other people or groups in an election: *The senator won the election with a large majority.*

**ˌmajor ˈleagues** *noun*
the group of teams that form the highest level of professional baseball: *Schmidt pitched in the major leagues for ten years.*
—**major-league** *adjective* relating to the major leagues: *a major-league baseball team*

**make** /meɪk/ *verb* (**made** /meɪd/)
**1** to produce or build something: *The birds made a nest in the tree.* | *Do you want to make some cookies with me?* | *It's Dad's turn to make dinner.*
**2** to do something: *It's easy to make a mistake, so be careful.* | *Everyone was making*

M

*too much noise.* | *I need to make an appointment to see the doctor.*

**3** to cause something to happen, or someone to do or feel something: *He makes me so mad sometimes!* | *Winning an award makes you feel good.* | *The disease can make it difficult for the patient to walk.*

**4** to force someone to do something: *My parents used to make me take piano lessons even though I didn't enjoy them.* | *The math teacher makes us work hard by giving us a lot of homework.*

**5** to equal a number or amount when you add things together: *2 and 2 make 4.*

**6** to earn money: *He makes $8 an hour at his job.* | *I want a job where I can make a lot of money.*

**7** to have the qualities that you need for a job or purpose: *Jane will make a good nurse – she's very kind and patient.* | *The book would make a good movie because it's exciting and has a lot of action in it.*

**8 be made of/from something** = to be made from a particular substance or material: *The table is made of solid wood and is very heavy.*

**9** if you make the team, you win a place on it: *She's pretty good so I think she'll make the basketball team.*

**10 make it** = **a)** to arrive somewhere or go to an event: *Did you make it to school on time?* | *I'm sorry, but I can't make it to your birthday party. I'm going to be away on vacation.* **b)** to be successful at something: *Do you think Deon is good enough to make it in basketball?*

→ **make a difference** at **difference**, **make friends** at **friend**, **make fun of someone or something** at **fun**, **make sure** at **sure**, **make sense** at **sense**, **make up your mind** at **mind**[1]

→ see Thesaurus box at **earn**, **force**[1]

**[ORIGIN:** From the old English word *macian*.**]**

**PHRASAL VERBS**

**make out**

**make something out** = to be able to hear, see, or understand something: *I couldn't make out what he was saying because he was speaking too quietly.*

**make up**

**1 make something up** = to think of and tell someone a story that is not true: *She made up an excuse for why she was late.* | *The children made up stories and drew pictures.*

**2 make up** = to become friends with someone again, after you have had an argument: *Katie and Maria are always fighting and then making up.*

**ˈmake-beˌlieve** *adjective*

not real, but imagined or pretended: *The boys were flying around the room in make-believe airplanes.*

—**make-believe** *noun* the act of imagining something

—**make believe** *verb* to imagine something

**make·up** /ˈmeɪk-ʌp/ *noun*

colored powder and creams that some women put on their faces to look prettier: *I don't usually wear makeup unless I'm going somewhere special.*

**ma·lar·i·a** /məˈleriə/ *noun*

a serious disease that people get when a MOSQUITO with the disease bites them

**[ORIGIN:** 1700-1800 From the Italian phrase *mala aria*, which means "bad air." It was believed that the disease came from gases that came out of wet land.**]**

**male**[1] /meɪl/ *adjective*

**1** a male person or animal is the type that cannot have babies or lay eggs: *a male lion* | *She has many male friends.* **ANTONYM: female**

**2** relating to men: *a male voice* **ANTONYM: female**

**male**[2] *noun*

**1** a man or boy: *Young males are more likely to have car accidents than any other group of people.* **ANTONYM: female**

**2** a male animal: *The males have brightly colored feathers, while the female bird is brown.* **ANTONYM: female**

**mal·ice** /ˈmælɪs/ *noun*

a feeling of wanting to hurt or upset someone: *My sisters teased me, but they did it without malice – they weren't really mean.*

—**malicious** /məˈlɪʃəs/ *adjective* intended to hurt or upset someone

**mall** /mɔl/ *noun*

a very large building with a lot of stores in it: *I'll meet you at the mall and we can go shopping.* **SYNONYM: shopping mall**

**[ORIGIN:** In the 17th to 19th centuries, a mall was

a long area of grass used for playing a game called "pall-mall," and then a long area for walking along. First used with its modern meaning, 1900-2000.]

**mal·nu·tri·tion** /ˌmælnuˈtrɪʃən/ *noun*
illness that is caused by not having enough food to eat, or by not eating healthy food: *Malnutrition is common in poor countries where there isn't enough food.*

**mal·prac·tice** /ˌmælˈpræktɪs/ *noun*
actions by a professional person that are very careless or criminal, which could cause that person to lose his or her job: *The doctor operated on the wrong knee, so he was guilty of malpractice.*

**ma·ma** (*also* **momma**) /ˈmɑmə/ *noun* (*informal*)
a word meaning MOTHER, used especially by children: *Happy birthday, Mama.*
[**ORIGIN:** 1500-1600 From the "ma" sounds made by a baby.]

**mam·mal** /ˈmæməl/ *noun*
an animal that drinks its mother's milk when it is young, for example a cow, lion, or person. A mammal gives birth to baby animals, not eggs.
[**ORIGIN:** 1800-1900 From the Latin *mamma*, which means "breast." Female mammals feed their babies with milk from their bodies.]

**mam·moth¹** /ˈmæməθ/ *adjective*
very big: *mammoth redwood trees* **SYNONYM: huge**

**mammoth²** *noun*
an animal that lived on Earth thousands of years ago. A mammoth looked like a big hairy ELEPHANT with long TUSKs.

**man¹** /mæn/ *noun* (plural **men** /men/)
**1** an adult male person: *Chris is an intelligent young man. | The room was full of men watching the football game.*
**2** all people, both men and women, considered as a group: *This is one of the worst diseases known to man.*
**3** (*informal*) used to emphasize what you are saying: *Oh, man! I'm going to be really late.*

**man²** *verb* (**manned**, **manning**)
**1** to operate a machine: *The helicopters were manned by American pilots.*
**2** to work at or guard a place: *At night, five guards manned the bridge.*

**man·age** /ˈmænɪdʒ/ *verb*
**1** to succeed in doing something difficult: *Rick managed to run the whole 10 miles!*
**2** to be in charge of a business or store and the people who work there: *He owns and manages a restaurant.*

**man·age·a·ble** /ˈmænɪdʒəbəl/ *adjective*
able to be done or controlled: *Teachers should give a manageable amount of homework so that students don't become frustrated.*

**man·age·ment** /ˈmænɪdʒmənt/ *noun*
**1** the job of controlling and organizing the work of a company or store: *He is responsible for the management of the department, and 25 employees report to him.*
**2** the people who control and organize the work of a company or store: *The store has new management, so maybe it will improve.*

**man·ag·er** /ˈmænɪdʒɚ/ *noun*
someone who is in charge of a business, store, or group of people: *He's the manager of a bookstore.*
—**managerial** /ˌmænəˈdʒɪriəl/ *adjective* relating to the job of a manager

**man·da·to·ry** /ˈmændəˌtɔri/ *adjective*
if something is mandatory, a law or rule says that it must be done: *It is mandatory for people riding motorcycles to wear a helmet.*

**mane** /meɪn/ *noun*
the long hair on the neck of a horse or male lion

**ma·neu·ver** /məˈnuvɚ/ *verb*
to move something into a different position, using your skill: *She maneuvered the car into a small parking space.*
—**maneuver** *noun* a movement in which you maneuver something

**man·go** /ˈmæŋgoʊ/ *noun* (plural **mangos** *or* **mangoes**)
a sweet juicy tropical fruit that is orange inside and has a large seed → see picture on page **A13**

**ma·ni·ac** /ˈmeɪniˌæk/ *noun* (*informal*)
someone who behaves in a crazy or dangerous way: *He was driving like a maniac and scared all of us in the car.*

**man·i·cure** /ˈmænɪˌkyʊr/ *noun*
a treatment for your hands that includes cutting and painting your FINGERNAILs

M

—**manicurist** *noun* someone whose job is giving people a manicure
[**ORIGIN:** 1800-1900 From the Latin words *manus* and *cura*, which mean "hand" and "care."]

**ma·nip·u·late** Ac /məˈnɪpyəˌleɪt/ *verb* (*formal*)
**1** to move things into different positions: *The computer program lets you manipulate writing and pictures.*
**2** to secretly make someone do what you want, without that person realizing that you are doing this: *She's trying to manipulate you into doing the work for her.*
—**manipulation** /məˌnɪpyəˈleɪʃən/ *noun* the act of manipulating someone
—**manipulative** /məˈnɪpyˌleɪtɪv/ *adjective* good at manipulating people

**man·kind** /ˌmænˈkaɪnd/ *noun*
all people, considered as a group: *A cure for cancer would be good for all mankind.*

**man·ly** /ˈmænli/ *adjective*
having qualities that people think a man has, such as strength and courage: *He had a deep manly voice.*
—**manliness** *noun* qualities such as strength and courage, that men are considered to have

**ˌman-ˈmade** *adjective*
man-made things, such as plastic, are made by people, rather than being produced from animals, plants, or the Earth: *The jacket is 80% wool and 20% man-made material.*
**ANTONYM: natural**

**man·ner** /ˈmænɚ/ *noun* (*formal*)
**1** the way in which something is done or happens: *They greeted us in a very friendly manner.*
**2** the way in which you behave with other people: *She has a calm, happy manner.*

**man·ner·ism** /ˈmænəˌrɪzəm/ *noun*
a way of speaking or moving that a person often uses: *He and his father have some of the same mannerisms – they both close their eyes when they're thinking.*

**man·ners** /ˈmænɚz/ *plural noun*
polite ways of behaving: *Her children have good manners. They always say "please" and "thank you."*

**man·sion** /ˈmænʃən/ *noun*
a very large house: *He's a millionaire who lives in a mansion.*

**man·slaugh·ter** /ˈmænˌslɔtɚ/ *noun*
the crime of killing someone when you did not plan to do it: *The drunk driver who killed the woman was arrested for manslaughter.*
→ see Thesaurus box at **crime**

**man·tel** /ˈmæntl/ (*also* **man·tel·piece** /ˈmæntlˌpis/) *noun*
the shelf above a FIREPLACE

**man·u·al**[1] Ac /ˈmænyuəl/ *adjective*
**1** manual work is done using your hands or your strength: *He earns a little money doing manual labor such as gardening.*
**2** operated by hand: *The car has a manual gear shift, rather than an automatic one.*
—**manually** *adverb* using your hands
[**ORIGIN:** 1400-1500 From the Latin word *manus*, which means "hand."]

**manual**[2] Ac *noun*
a book that gives instructions about how to do something: *What does the computer manual say to do?*

**man·u·fac·ture** /ˌmænyəˈfæktʃɚ/ *verb*
to use machines to make things in large amounts: *The company manufactures jet engines.*
—**manufacture** *noun* the process of manufacturing goods
—**manufacturer** *noun* a company that manufactures things
[**ORIGIN:** 1500-1600 From the Latin phrase *manu factus*, which means "made by hand."]

**ma·nure** /məˈnʊr/ *noun*
waste that animals produce, that people put into the earth to make plants grow better

**man·u·script** /ˈmænyəˌskrɪpt/ *noun*
**1** a piece of writing before it is printed as a book or before it is printed in a magazine or newspaper: *Writers send publishers hundreds of manuscripts every week.*
**2** a very old book or document that was written by hand
[**ORIGIN:** 1500-1600 From the Latin phrase *manu scriptus*, which means "written by hand."]

**man·y** /ˈmeni/ *adjective, pronoun* (**more** /mɔr/, **most** /moʊst/)
**1** a large number of people or things: *We lived in New Hampshire for many years.* |

*There aren't many cookies left – only about three.* | *Many of the students did very well on the test.* **ANTONYM: few**

**GRAMMAR: much, many, a lot of**

**Many** is used with the plural forms of nouns: *I didn't see many people there that I knew.*

**Much** is used with nouns such as "money" and "bread" that do not have plurals, especially in questions and negative sentences: *There isn't much milk left.*

**A lot of** can be used with both types of noun: *She doesn't have a lot of friends.* | *We're going to need a lot of paint.*

**THESAURUS: many**

**a large number**: *A large number of people came to the meeting.*

**a lot, lots** a large amount, quantity, or number of something: *She has written lots of really good books.* | *He has a lot of money.*

**plenty** a large amount, which is as much as you need: *Make sure you eat plenty of fruit and vegetables.*

**several** more than a few, but not a large number: *We lived in Boston for several years before moving to New York.*

**2 how many** = used for asking about the number of people or things: *How many people are coming to the party?*

**map** /mæp/ *noun*
a drawing of an area that shows things such as the roads, rivers, cities, mountains, or countries: *You can see on the map that Boston is north of New York.*

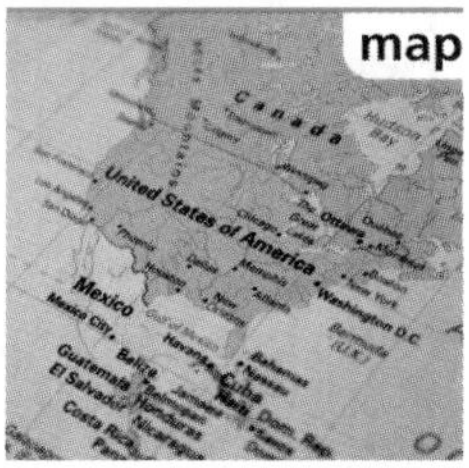


[**ORIGIN:** 1500-1600 From the Latin word *mappa*, which means "cloth." Maps were drawn on pieces of cloth.]

**ma·ple** /ˈmeɪpəl/ *noun*
a tree that grows in northern countries. It has leaves with five points that turn red and yellow in the fall.

**mar** /mɑr/ *verb* (**marred, marring**)
to spoil something and make it less attractive or enjoyable: *His handsome face is marred by a large scar running across his cheek.*

**mar·a·thon** /ˈmærəˌθɑn/ *noun*
a race in which people run 26 miles and 385 yards: *She ran the Boston Marathon in just over three hours.*
[**ORIGIN:** From Marathon, a place in Greece where there was a battle in 490 B.C. There is a story that a Greek soldier ran about 25 miles from Marathon to Athens, to tell people that the Athenians had beaten the Persians. This story gave the race its name in the first modern Olympic games in 1896.]

**mar·ble** /ˈmɑrbəl/ *noun*
**1** a type of hard rock that people can cut and POLISH, and that is often used to make floors, buildings, and STATUEs: *The statue was made out of marble.*
**2** a small colored glass ball that children roll along the ground as part of a game: *Does anyone want to play marbles?*

**march**[1] /mɑrtʃ/ *verb*
**1** to walk with regular steps and lift your knees up, like a soldier: *The band marched onto the field.* → see picture on page **A4**
**2** to walk somewhere with a large group of people in order to protest about something: *Hundreds of people marched to protest against the war.*
**3** to walk quickly because you are angry or determined: *My mother stood up angrily and marched out of the room.*
—**marcher** *noun* someone who walks somewhere with a large group of people in order to protest about something
→ see Thesaurus box at **walk**[1]
[**ORIGIN:** 1300-1400 From the old French word *marchier*, which means "to step heavily."]

**march**[2] *noun*
**1** an event in which many people walk together in order to protest about something: *Thousands of people took part in civil rights marches during the 1960s.*
**2** an occasion when soldiers march somewhere: *The soldiers were tired at the end of the day's march.*
**3** a piece of music with a regular beat for soldiers to march to: *Bands played marches in the parade.*

M

**March** /mɑrtʃ/ *noun* (*written abbreviation*: **Mar.**)
the third month of the year, between February and April: *We have an appointment on March 15.* | *I might be going to California in March.* | *Julia had her baby last March.* | *The movie will open next March.*
[**ORIGIN:** probably 1100-1200 From Mars, the Roman god of war.]

**mare** /mer/ *noun*
a female horse or DONKEY

**mar·ga·rine** /ˈmɑrdʒərɪn/ *noun*
a yellow food that is like butter, but is made from vegetable oil
[**ORIGIN:** 1800-1900 From the Greek word *margaron*, which means "pearl." A substance used to make margarine was thought to shine like a pearl.]

**mar·gin** Ac /ˈmɑrdʒɪn/ *noun*
**1** the empty space at the side of a page of writing: *In the margin, my teacher had written "Good work."*
**2** the amount by which someone wins an election, competition, or game: *They won the game by a small margin of 4 points.*
[**ORIGIN:** 1300-1400 From the Latin word *margo*, which means "border."]

**mar·gin·al** Ac /ˈmɑrdʒənl/ *adjective* (*formal*)
small in importance or amount: *There has been a marginal improvement in his work, but he could still do better.*
—**marginally** *adverb* a little bit

**ma·rine** /məˈrin/ *adjective*
**1** relating to the ocean and the animals and plants that live there: *This part of the ocean is full of fish and other marine life.*
**2** relating to ships or the navy
[**ORIGIN:** 1300-1400 From the Latin word *marinus*, from *mare*, which means "sea."]

**Maˈrine Corps** /məˈrin kɔr/ *noun*
**the Marine Corps** (*also* **the Marines**) = a part of the U.S. armed forces in which soldiers are trained to fight on land and on ships
—**Marine** *noun* a soldier in the Marine Corps

**mark¹** /mɑrk/ *verb*
**1** to write a word or draw a sign on something: *The box was marked "toys."*
**2** to show where something is: *Lights marked the entrance to the harbor.*
**3** to be a sign of an important event: *The ceremonies marked the 50th anniversary of the end of World War II.*
**4** to make a mark on something in a way that spoils or damages it: *The rubber heels of his boots had marked the floor.*
**PHRASAL VERB**
**mark something down**
to make the price of something lower: *These shoes were marked down to $10!* **SYNONYM: reduce**

**mark²** *noun*
**1** a spot or dirty area on something that spoils how it looks: *Who made these black marks on the couch?*

**THESAURUS: mark**

**Types of Dirty Marks:**

**stain** a mark that is difficult to remove: *There was an ink stain on his shirt pocket.*

**spot** a small mark on something: *Spots of paint covered the floor.*

**smudge** a dirty mark, made when something is rubbed against a surface: *The kids touch the walls when they go upstairs, leaving smudges.*

**Types of Marks on Someone's Skin:**

**bruise** a purple or brown mark on your skin that you get because you have fallen or been hit: *His legs are covered in bruises from falling off his bike.*

**scar** a permanent mark on your skin, caused by a cut or by something that burns you: *She has a scar under her chin, from when she fell and cut it open.*

**blemish** a mark on your skin that spoils the way it looks: *She wears makeup to cover a blemish on her cheek.*

**pimple** (*also* **zit** (*informal*)) a small raised red mark or lump on your skin that teenagers often have: *Most teenagers get pimples; it's nothing to worry about.*

**freckle** one of several small light brown marks on someone's skin: *Toby has red hair and freckles.*

M

**mole** a small usually brown mark on the skin that is often slightly higher than the skin around it: *Some moles can be a sign of cancer, so get a doctor to check them.*

**2** a cut or damaged area on someone or something: *She had scratch marks on her hand from the cat.*
**3** a sign or shape that is written or printed: *Put a question mark by her name – I don't know if she's coming.*

**mar·ket** /ˈmɑrkɪt/ *noun*
**1** a place where people buy and sell goods and food: *I bought peaches at the market.*
**2 on the market** = available for someone to buy: *Our house is on the market now.*
**3** all the people who want to buy something: *The market for online games is still growing.*
**4 the job/labor market** = the number of jobs available or the number of people looking for work
**[ORIGIN:** 1100-1200 From the Latin word *mercatus*, which means "buying and selling, or market," from *mercari*, which means "to buy and sell."**]**

**mar·ket·place** /ˈmɑrkɪtˌpleɪs/ *noun*
**1 the marketplace** = the business of buying and selling things in competition with other companies: *A good quality product helps a company do well in the marketplace.*
**2** an open area where there is a market

**ma·roon** /məˈrun/ *adjective, noun*
a very dark red-brown color: *a maroon T-shirt*

**mar·riage** /ˈmærɪdʒ/ *noun*
**1** the relationship between two people who are married: *Their long and happy marriage lasted 60 years.*
**2** the ceremony in which two people get married: *The marriage will take place in St. Augustine's Church next Saturday.* **SYNONYM: wedding**

**mar·ried** /ˈmærid/ *adjective*
if you are married, you have a husband or a wife: *Is Sam married or single?* | *Helen is married to a lawyer.*

**THESAURUS: married**

If someone is **single**, he or she is not married.

If someone is **engaged**, he or she has agreed to marry someone.

If a husband and wife are **separated**, they are living apart because they are having problems in their marriage.

If a husband and wife get **divorced**, they legally end their marriage.

If two people **live with** each other, they are in a romantic relationship and share a home together, but are not married.

A **widow** is a woman whose husband has died.

A **widower** is a man whose wife has died.

**mar·ry** /ˈmæri/ *verb* (**married, marries**)
**1** to become someone's husband or wife: *He asked Linda to marry him.* | *They got married last July.*
**2** to perform the ceremony at which two people get married: *The priest has agreed to marry them at St. Peter's Church.*
**[ORIGIN:** 1200-1300 From the Latin word *maritare*, from *maritus*, which means "husband."**]**

**WORD FAMILY: marry**

**marry** *verb* | **married** *adjective* | **unmarried** *adjective* | **marriage** *noun*

**Mars** /mɑrz/ *noun*
the fourth PLANET from the Sun. Mars is the nearest planet to the Earth and it looks red in the sky.

**marsh** /mɑrʃ/ *noun*
an area of ground that is soft and wet: *Many animals and birds live in these marshes.*

**mar·shal** /ˈmɑrʃəl/ *noun*
**1** a police officer in the U.S. whose job is to make sure that people do what a court of law has ordered them to do: *He was arrested by federal marshals and taken back to Chicago.*
**2** the officer in charge of a city's fire department: *The fire marshal can close a building if it does not have enough fire exits.*

**marsh·mal·low** /ˈmɑrʃˌmeloʊ/ *noun*
a very soft white or colored candy: *We toasted marshmallows on the fire.*

**mar·su·pi·al** /mɑrˈsupiəl/ *noun*
a type of animal that carries its babies in a pocket on the front of its body. The pocket is called a POUCH: *Kangaroos and koala bears are marsupials.*

M

**mar·tial** /ˈmɑrʃəl/ *adjective*
relating to the army, war, and fighting: *The country is under martial law, so the army is controlling the government.*
**[ORIGIN:** 1300-1400 From the Latin word *martialis*, which means "belonging to Mars." Mars was the Roman god of war.**]**

**ˌmartial ˈarts** *plural noun*
sports such as JUDO or KARATE, in which you fight with your hands and feet: *A martial arts class will teach you to protect yourself.* → see picture on page **A24**

**mar·vel·ous** /ˈmɑrvələs/ *adjective*
very good or enjoyable: *We had a great time, and the weather was marvelous.*

**mas·car·a** /mæˈskærə/ *noun*
a dark substance that a woman puts on her EYELASHes to make them look darker and thicker

**mas·cot** /ˈmæskɑt/ *noun*
an animal or toy that a team or organization has because they believe it brings them good luck: *The team's mascot is an eagle.*
**[ORIGIN:** 1800-1900 From the French *mascotte*, which means "magic object," from *masco*, which means "witch."**]**

**mas·cu·line** /ˈmæskjələn/ *adjective*
**1** like a man or how a man behaves: *He has a deep, masculine voice.* **ANTONYM: feminine**
**2** in English, a masculine noun or PRONOUN is used to talk about men or boys: *"He" is a masculine pronoun.* | *"Waiter" is the masculine form; "waitress" is the feminine form.* **ANTONYM: feminine**
**3** in other languages, some nouns and adjectives are masculine, and others are FEMININE: *The Spanish word for day ("el día") is masculine.* **ANTONYM: feminine**

**mash** /mæʃ/ *verb*
to crush food until it is soft: *Mash the potatoes until they are smooth.* → see picture on page **A15**
→ see Thesaurus box at **press[1]**

**mask** /mæsk/ *noun*
something you wear over your face to hide or protect it: *He is wearing a clown mask for the Halloween party.* | *The workers wear masks to protect them from the fumes.*

**mas·quer·ade** /ˌmæskəˈreɪd/ *verb (formal)*
to pretend to be someone or something else, in order to trick people: *The thief masqueraded as a police officer so he could get into the building.*

**mass** /mæs/ *noun*
**1** a large amount of something: *The volcano sent a mass of ash and smoke up into the air.*
**2** in science, the amount of matter that an object contains: *How do scientists measure the mass of a star?*
**3** (*also* **Mass**) the main religious ceremony in some Christian churches, especially the Roman Catholic Church: *I go to Mass every Sunday at St. Mary's.*

**mas·sa·cre** /ˈmæsəkɚ/ *verb*
to kill a lot of people, especially people who cannot defend themselves: *Terrorists massacred hundreds of innocent people.*
—**massacre** *noun* an occasion when a lot of people are massacred

**mas·sage** /məˈsɑʒ/ *noun*
the action of pressing and rubbing someone's body with your hands, in order to make pain better or help him or her relax: *Can you give my back a massage, please?*
—**massage** *verb* to give someone a massage
**[ORIGIN:** 1800-1900 From the French word *masser*, from the Arabic word *massa*, which means "to stroke."**]**

**mas·sive** /ˈmæsɪv/ *adjective*
very large or powerful: *There was a massive earthquake in Japan that killed 5,000 people.*

**ˌmass ˈmedia** *noun*
all the organizations, such as television, radio, and newspapers, that give news and information to people: *The trial was reported in the mass media.*

**mast** /mæst/ *noun*
**1** a tall pole that the sails of a ship hang from
**2** a tall pole that a flag hangs from

**mas·ter[1]** /ˈmæstɚ/ *noun*
**1** the owner of a dog: *The dog stood by its master's side.*
**2** someone who is very skilled at doing something: *J. K. Rowling is a master of storytelling and children love her books.*
**3** a man who is in charge of servants or SLAVEs
**[ORIGIN:** 1000-1100 From the Latin word *magister*, which means "chief or teacher."**]**

M

**master²** *verb*
to learn a skill or language so well that you can do it easily: *He mastered French after living in France for only a year.*

**ˌmaster of ˈceremonies** *noun*
(*abbreviation*: **M.C.**)
someone who introduces speakers or performers at an event: *He was the master of ceremonies at the awards ceremony.*

**mas·ter·piece** /ˈmæstɚˌpis/ *noun*
a piece of art, literature, or music that is the best that someone has produced, or that is one of the best in the world: *Shakespeare's plays are masterpieces.*

**mas·ter's** /ˈmæstɚz/ *noun* (*informal*)
a master's degree

**ˈmaster's deˌgree** *noun*
a university degree that you get by studying for one or two years after your first degree: *a master's degree in history*

**mat** /mæt/ *noun*
**1** a piece of thick material that covers part of a floor: *Please wipe your feet on the mat when you come in.*
**2** a small piece of material that you put under a plate or glass to protect the surface of a table: *She put the hot plates down onto place mats.*
**3** a piece of thick soft material used in some sports for people to fall onto: *Wrestling matches take place on a gym mat.*

**match¹** /mætʃ/ *noun*
**1** a small wooden or paper stick that you use to light a fire because it makes a flame when you rub it against a special surface: *a box of matches | She struck a match and lit the fire.*
→ see picture at **light**
**2** something that looks good or goes well with another thing: *The job is a good match for her interests and skills.*
**3** a game or competition between two people or teams, in BOXING, SOCCER, tennis, and some other sports: *Are you going to watch the boxing match tonight?*

**match²** *verb*
**1** if two things match, they look good or go well together, often because they are similar: *The slippers are pink and match the bathrobe.*
**2** to put two things together in a suitable way: *Match the pictures on the right with the words on the left.*
**3** to be equal to something in size, value, or quality: *He won five races, matching the record set by his brother two years ago.*
—**matching** *adjective* similar to something else, especially because it is the same color or made of the same material: *Her two sons wore matching T-shirts.*

**mate¹** /meɪt/ *noun*
**1** the sexual partner of an animal: *In spring, the male bears try to find a mate.*
**2** a husband or wife: *He's dated a lot of women, but he's still searching for the perfect mate.*

**mate²** *verb*
if animals mate, they come together to make babies: *The birds mate in the spring.*

**ma·te·ri·al** /məˈtɪriəl/ *noun*
**1** cloth used for making things such as clothes and curtains: *She chose some material to make a skirt.*
**2** a solid substance such as wood, plastic, or metal: *The students were testing different materials to see if they would float on water.*
**3** (*also* **materials**) the things that you use in order to do a job or activity: *For the art class, you'll need drawing materials such as paper and pencils.*
**4** information or ideas used in books and movies: *He walked the trail from Mexico to Washington, which gave him the material for his new book.*
[**ORIGIN:** 1300-1400 From the Latin word *materia*, which means "substance or stuff."]

**ma·ter·ni·ty** /məˈtɚnəti/ *adjective*
relating to women who are going to have a baby or who have just had a baby: *She started wearing maternity clothes when she was five months pregnant.*
[**ORIGIN:** 1600-1700 From the Latin word *mater*, which means "mother."]

**math** /mæθ/ *noun*
the short form of the word mathematics: *The math test covered adding and subtracting.*

**math·e·mat·ics** /ˌmæθəˈmætɪks/ *noun*
the study of numbers and shapes: *He teaches mathematics, and is really good at explaining algebra and geometry.* **SYNONYM: math**

M

—**mathematical** *adjective* relating to mathematics: *a mathematical calculation*
—**mathematician** /ˌmæθməˈtɪʃən/ *noun* someone who has studied mathematics to a high level or who teaches mathematics
[**ORIGIN:** 1500-1600 From the Greek word *mathema*, which means "learning."]

**mat·i·née** /ˌmætnˈeɪ/ *noun*
a performance of a play or movie in the afternoon: *The matinée starts at 2:30 p.m.*

**mat·ter**[1] /ˈmætɚ/ *noun*
**1** a subject or situation that you have to think about or deal with: *Bullying is a serious matter, the school deals with it quickly.*
**2** the material everything is made of: *Matter can be solid, liquid, or gas.*
**3 what's the matter?** = used to ask why someone is upset or why something is not working: *What's the matter? Why are you crying?*
**4 something is the matter/nothing is the matter** = used to say that there is a problem, or that there is no problem: *There's something the matter with the engine – it won't start.*
**5 no matter how/where/what, etc.** = used to say that something does not change: *No matter how hard she tried, she couldn't get the door open.*
**6 as a matter of fact** (*informal*) = used when you are telling someone something that is surprising: *"Did you just get here?" "No, as a matter of fact I got here an hour ago."*

**matter**[2] *verb*
to be important: *She is the only person that really matters to him.* | *It doesn't matter how long it takes, as long as the work gets done.*

**mat·tress** /ˈmætrəs/ *noun*
the soft part of a bed that you lie on

**ma·ture**[1] Ac /məˈtʃʊr/ *adjective*
**1** behaving in a sensible and responsible way, like an adult: *He is mature enough to lose a game without getting upset.* **ANTONYM: immature**
**2** a mature animal or plant has grown to its full size: *The park has many mature trees.*
—**maturity** /məˈtʃʊrəti, -ˈtʊr-/ *noun* the quality or state of being mature: *Rabbits reach maturity in only five weeks.*

**mature**[2] Ac *verb*
**1** to begin to behave in a sensible and responsible way, like an adult: *She has matured a lot since going to college.*
**2** to become fully grown or developed: *These fish mature in three months.*

**max·i·mize** Ac /ˈmæksəˌmaɪz/ *verb*
to make something as large in amount or size as possible: *You can maximize your chances of winning the race by practicing every day.*
**ANTONYM: minimize**

**max·i·mum** Ac /ˌmæksəmən/ *noun*
the largest number or amount that is possible or allowed: *There is a maximum of 20 students in each class.* **ANTONYM: minimum**
—**maximum** *adjective* biggest or greatest: *a maximum speed of 130 miles per hour*
[**ORIGIN:** 1500-1600 From the Latin word *maximus*, which means "biggest."]

**may** /meɪ/ *verb*
**1** used for saying that something is possible: *I may need your help later.* | *I don't know where they are. They may have gotten lost.*
**2** used for asking or giving permission: *May I speak with Anne, please?* | *You may ask questions at the end of the class.*

**May** /meɪ/ *noun*
the fifth month of the year, between April and June: *My birthday is on May 1.* | *We might be going to Texas in May.* | *We haven't seen Tania since last May.*
[**ORIGIN:** probably 1100-1200 From Maia, a Roman goddess of the earth.]

**may·be** /ˈmeɪbi/ *adverb*
**1** used for saying that something may be true or may happen: *Maybe her phone's not working.* | *"Will you be there tomorrow night?" "Maybe."* **SYNONYM: perhaps**
**2** used when making a suggestion: *Maybe Jeff could help you. Why don't you ask him?*

**may·on·naise** /ˈmeɪəˌneɪz/ *noun*
a thick white sauce made of egg and oil: *He mixed the tuna with the mayonnaise and spread it on the bread.*

**may·or** /ˈmeɪɚ/ *noun*
someone who is elected to lead the government of a town or city: *the mayor of Chicago*
[**ORIGIN:** 1200-1300 From the old French word *maire*, from the Latin word *major*, which means "bigger."]

**maze** /meɪz/ *noun*
**1** a place that has many confusing paths that are difficult to find your way through: *He led us through a maze of streets.*
**2** a special system of paths surrounded by tall plants, usually in a park. Many of the paths do not lead anywhere, making it difficult to find your way through.
**3** a game in which you have to draw a line through a confusing set of lines, without crossing any of them: *The book had mazes and other kinds of puzzles.*
[ORIGIN: 1200-1300 Related to "amaze," which used to mean "to confuse."]

**M.C.**
the abbreviation of **master of ceremonies**

**M.D.**
the abbreviation of **Doctor of Medicine**: *Karen Johnson, M.D.*

**me** /mi/ *pronoun*
**1** used after a verb or PREPOSITION when you are talking about yourself: *He doesn't like me.* | *Listen to me.*
**2 me too** = used when saying that you are like the person you are talking to: *"I'm hungry!" "Me too. Let's eat."*

**mead·ow** /ˈmedoʊ/ *noun*
a field with wild grass and flowers

**meal** /mil/ *noun*
the food that you eat at a particular time: *We had a nice meal at that new restaurant.* | *Most people eat three meals a day.*
[ORIGIN: From the old English word *mæl*, which means "fixed time or meal time."]

**THESAURUS: meal**

**Types of Meals:**

**breakfast** a meal that you eat in the morning: *It's important to eat breakfast before you go to school.*

**lunch** a meal that you eat in the middle of the day: *I had a sandwich for lunch.*

**brunch** a meal that you eat in the late morning, instead of breakfast or lunch: *We went to a nice restaurant for brunch.*

**dinner/supper** a meal that you eat in the evening: *I had dinner with my family.* | *What's for supper, Mom?*

**snack** a small amount of food that you eat between meals, for example cookies or an apple: *I had a quick snack before I left the house.*

**picnic** a meal that you eat outdoors, with food that you make earlier: *We took a picnic to the park.*

**barbecue** a meal that you cook and eat outdoors: *It was a warm evening, so we had a barbecue.*

**meal·time** /ˈmiltaɪm/ *noun*
a time when you have a meal: *At mealtimes we all sit down together to eat.*

**mean¹** /min/ *verb* (**meant** /ment/)
**1** to have a particular meaning: *In Spanish, the word "rojo" means "red."* | *The red light means "stop."*
**2** to want to do something: *Sorry, I didn't mean to scare you.* | *It was meant to be a joke!*
SYNONYM: **intend**
**3** to have a particular result: *This injury means that he won't play Saturday.*
**4** used when you want to give or ask for an explanation: *"He isn't coming back." "What do you mean?"*
**5 means a lot to someone** = to be very important to someone: *This award means a lot to me.*
**6 I mean** = **a)** used when explaining what you have just said or giving an example: *It is unfair to punish him. I mean, he hasn't done anything wrong.* **b)** used when you have just said something wrong: *She plays the violin, I mean the viola.*

**mean²** *adjective*
not kind or nice: *He's a mean man who yells at you if you step on his grass.*

M

**mean·ing** /ˈminɪŋ/ *noun*
**1** the idea or information that a word or sign gives you: *Look up the meaning of the word in a dictionary.*
**2** the quality of being important or having a purpose: *He wanted to help people to give his life meaning so he became a doctor.*
—**meaningful** *adjective* having some importance or purpose, or giving information: *In class, we had a meaningful discussion about what we can do to protect the environment.*
—**meaningless** *adjective* without any purpose or not giving any information: *He couldn't read the letter so it was meaningless to him.*

**means** /minz/ *noun* (plural **means**)
**1** a method or thing that you use to do something: *Cars are the most common means of transportation.* | *This drug is the only effective means of controlling the disease.*
**2 by all means** (*formal*) = used for saying in a strong way that someone may do something: *"May I borrow your pencil?" "By all means."*
**3 by no means** (*formal*) = not at all: *It is by no means easy to solve this problem, but we must try.*
**4** (*formal*) the money that you have and can use: *These houses are beyond the means of most people because they are very expensive.*

**meant** /ment/ *verb*
the past tense and past participle of MEAN

**mean·time** /ˈmintaɪm/ *noun*
**in the meantime** = in the time before something happens: *John will be here soon. In the meantime, I'll get things ready.*

**mean·while** /ˈminwaɪl/ *adverb*
while something is happening, or before something happens: *I did my homework. Meanwhile, my brother practiced the guitar.*

**mea·sles** /ˈmizəlz/ (*also* **the measles**) *noun*
an illness in which you have small red spots on your body: *Now, fewer children get the measles because there is a vaccine.*

**meas·ure¹** /ˈmeʒɚ/ *verb*
**1** to find out the size or amount of something, using a piece of equipment: *She measured the piece of wood with a ruler.*
**2** to be a particular size: *The table measures four feet by six feet.*
—**measurable** *adjective* able to be measured

**PHRASAL VERB**
**measure up**
to be good enough: *He is afraid he won't measure up.*

**measure²** *noun*
**1** an official action that someone does to deal with a problem: *The teachers have taken measures to stop bullying at school.*
**2 a measure of something** = something that shows what the size or amount of something is: *Test scores are a measure of a student's progress.*

**meas·ure·ment** /ˈmeʒɚmənt/ *noun*
the length, width, height, or amount of something: *He wrote down their height and weight measurements.*

**meat** /mit/ *noun*
the flesh of animals and birds eaten as food: *Vegetarians don't eat meat.* | *Eating too much red meat, such as beef, is not good for you.*
[**ORIGIN:** From the old English word *mete*, which means "food."]

**THESAURUS: meat**

**Types of Meat:**
**beef** the meat from a cow
**veal** the meat from a young cow
**pork** the meat from a pig
**ham** meat from a pig's leg, which has salt added to it to keep it fresh
**bacon** meat from a pig's back or side, cut into long thin pieces. Bacon has salt or smoke added to it to keep it fresh.

The meat from lamb, birds, or fish is called by the name of the animal: *We had chicken for dinner.* | *a tuna sandwich*

**meat·ball** /ˈmitbɔl/ *noun*
a small round ball made from very small pieces of meat: *We had spaghetti and meatballs for dinner.*

**me·chan·ic** /mɪˈkænɪk/ *noun*
someone whose job is to repair cars, airplanes, or other kinds of machines: *What did the mechanic say was wrong with the car?* → see picture on page **A16**

**me·chan·i·cal** /mɪˈkænɪkəl/ *adjective*
relating to machines: *The plane could not fly because of a mechanical problem.*
—**mechanically** *adverb* like a machine

**mech·a·nism** Ac /ˈmekəˌnɪzəm/ *noun*
the part of a machine that does a particular job: *The car's steering mechanism is broken, so it is impossible to steer the car.*

**WORD FAMILY: mechanism**
**mechanism** *noun* | **mechanical** *adjective* | **mechanically** *adverb* | **mechanic** *noun*

**med·al** /ˈmedl/ *noun*
a piece of metal that someone gets as a prize or gets for doing something brave: *The swimmer won a gold medal in the competition.*
—**medalist** *noun* someone who has won a medal

**me·di·a** Ac /ˈmidiə/ *plural noun*
**the media** = television, radio, and newspapers: *The event was widely reported in the media.* | *The trial got a lot of media attention.*

**me·di·an** Ac /ˈmidiən/ *noun*
(*also* **ˈmedian ˌstrip**) a narrow piece of land or a fence that divides a road or HIGHWAY

**med·ic** /ˈmedɪk/ *noun*
someone in the army who is trained to give medical treatment

**med·i·cal** Ac /ˈmedɪkəl/ *adjective*
relating to illnesses and injuries, and ways of treating them: *He was taken to the hospital for medical treatment.*
—**medically** *adverb* in a way that relates to illnesses or injuries, and ways of treating them
[ORIGIN: 1600-1700 From the Latin word *medicus*, which means "doctor," from *mederi*, meaning "to heal."]

**WORD FAMILY: medical**
**medical** *adjective* | **medically** *adverb* | **medication** *noun* | **medicine** *noun* | **medicinal** *adjective*

**med·i·ca·tion** /ˌmedəˈkeɪʃən/ *noun*
medicine, especially medicine that you take regularly: *Grandpa is on medication for his heart.*
→ see Thesaurus box at **medicine**

**med·i·cine** /ˈmedəsən/ *noun*
**1** something that you drink or take when you are sick, for example a drug, to help you get better: *Remember to take your medicine.*

**THESAURUS: medicine**
**pill/tablet** a small hard piece of medicine that you swallow: *The doctor gave her pills for the pain.* | *a vitamin tablet*
**capsule** a small object with medicine inside that you swallow whole: *She took two capsules of aspirin for her headache.*
**eye/ear drops** liquid medicine that you put into your eyes or ears because they are sore or infected: *The ear drops will get rid of the infection.*
**drug** a substance that is put in medicines to treat illnesses: *The drug is used to treat some types of cancer.*
**medication** medicine that someone takes regularly for a health problem: *He's on medication for his heart.*
**dosage/dose** the amount of medicine that you should take: *The usual dosage is 25 to 50 mg.* | *Never take more than the recommended dose of two pills every four hours.*

**2** the study and treatment of illnesses and injuries: *She wanted to study medicine.*
—**medicinal** /məˈdɪsənəl/ *adjective* used for treating illnesses and injuries: *medicinal herbs*

M

**me·di·e·val** /ˌmɪdˈivəl/ *adjective*
relating to the time between the 5th and 15th centuries A.D.: *a medieval castle*
[ORIGIN: 1800-1900 From the Latin phrase *medium aevum*, which means "middle age." Medieval times are in the middle between ancient times and modern times.]

**me·di·o·cre** /ˌmidiˈoʊkɚ/ *adjective*
not very good, but not really bad: *My grades were mediocre – mostly Cs and one D.*
[ORIGIN: 1500-1600 From the Latin word *mediocris*, which means "halfway up a mountain," from *medius*, which means "middle" and *ocris*, which means "stony mountain."]

**Med·i·ter·ra·ne·an** /ˌmedɪtəˈreɪniən/ *noun*
**the Mediterranean** = the sea between northern Africa and southern Europe, and the land around it
—**Mediterranean** *adjective* in or relating to the Mediterranean

**me·di·um** Ac /ˈmidiəm/ *adjective*
not big or small: *She is of medium height – about the same height as most of her classmates.* | *"What size T-shirt do you wear?" "Medium."*

**meet**[1] /mit/ *verb* (**met** /met/)
**1** (*also* **meet up (with someone)**) to come to the same place as someone else because you have planned this: *My mom will meet us in front of the school.*
**2** to see and talk to someone for the first time: *"Paul, this is Jack." "Nice to meet you."*
**3** to see and talk to someone without planning to do this: *Guess who I met at the store: Diane, from softball!*
**4** to do or be what people need or want: *A school should meet the needs of all its students.* | *We've met our goal of raising $5,000.*
**5** if things meet, they join or touch: *The two trails meet at the lake.*
PHRASAL VERB
**meet with someone**
to have a meeting with someone: *My parents met with my teacher to discuss my progress.*

**meet**[2] *noun*
a sports competition with races: *a swim meet*

**meet·ing** /ˈmitɪŋ/ *noun*
a time when people come together to discuss something: *The coach had a meeting with the team yesterday.* | *Mr. Dexter is in a meeting right now.*

**meg·a·byte** /ˈmegəˌbaɪt/ *noun* (*written abbreviation*: **MB**)
a unit for measuring computer information, equal to a million BYTEs

**mel·an·chol·y** /ˈmelənˌkɑli/ *adjective* (*formal*)
sad: *I felt melancholy when she had gone.*
—**melancholy** *noun* sadness

**mel·low** /ˈmeloʊ/ *adjective*
**1** relaxed and calm: *He's become a little more mellow. He doesn't get angry as often.*
**2** sounding or tasting smooth and pleasant: *His mellow voice put me to sleep.*

**me·lod·ic** /məˈlɑdɪk/ *adjective*
having a pleasant tune or a pleasant sound: *Their earlier songs are more melodic and easier to sing.*

**mel·o·dra·mat·ic** /ˌmelədrəˈmætɪk/ *adjective*
showing feelings that are extreme and not reasonable: *"My life is ruined!" "Stop being so melodramatic."*

**mel·o·dy** /ˈmelədi/ *noun* (plural **melodies**)
the main set of musical notes in a song or piece of music: *The song has a really pretty melody.* SYNONYM: **tune**
→ see Thesaurus box at **music**
[ORIGIN: 1100-1200 From the Greek word *meloidia*, which means "singing."]

**mel·on** /ˈmelən/ *noun*
a large juicy fruit with a thick yellow or green skin and a lot of seeds: *Cantaloupes and watermelons are both types of melon.* → see picture on page **A13**

**melt** /melt/ *verb*
if something solid melts, or if you melt it, it changes to a liquid when it becomes warmer: *The snowman's melting.* | *Melt some butter in a pan.*

**ˈmelting pot** *noun*
a place where people from different countries, with different religions or customs, all live together and start to share ideas and beliefs: *The U.S. is often called a melting pot because people came from all over the world and became Americans.*

**mem·ber** /ˈmembɚ/ *noun*
someone who belongs to a group or organization: *a member of the Boy Scouts*
[ORIGIN: 1300-1400 From the Latin word *membrum*, which means "limb or part." A member of a group is part of that group.]

**mem·ber·ship** /ˈmembɚˌʃɪp/ *noun*
**1** the state of being a member of a group or organization: *She applied for membership in the health club.* | *The membership fee is $25.*
**2** the members of a group or organization: *The group's membership is around 400.*

**mem·o** /ˈmemoʊ/ (*also* **mem·o·ran·dum** /ˌmeməˈrændəm/) *noun* (plural **memos**)
a short note to another person in the same organization: *The principal sent a memo about the changes to all the teachers.*

**mem·o·ra·bil·i·a** /ˌmemərəˈbɪliə/ *noun*
things that people collect because they are related to a famous person or event: *The museum has a large collection of Civil War memorabilia.*

**mem·ora·ble** /ˈmemərəbəl/ *adjective*
likely to be remembered: *The day I learned to ride a bike was the most memorable day of my childhood.*

**me·mo·ri·al** /məˈmɔriəl/ *noun*
something that is built to remind people of someone who has died: *All the soldiers' names are carved on the war memorial.*
—**memorial** *adjective* done or built to remind people of someone who has died: *There will be a memorial service for the people who died in the plane crash.*

**mem·o·rize** /ˈmeməˌraɪz/ *verb*
to learn words, music, or facts so that you can remember them: *She memorized her speech so she wouldn't have to read it when she spoke.*

**mem·o·ry** /ˈheməri/ *noun* (plural **memories**)
**1** the ability to remember things: *I have a good memory and I was able to remember the car's license plate.*
**2** something in the past that you remember: *I have a lot of good memories of our family's vacations.*
**3** the amount of space that a computer has for keeping information: *The computer has 256 megabytes of memory.*
**4** **from memory** = using what you remember, and without needing to read something or look at something: *She played the song from memory, without music.*
**5** **in memory of someone** = as a way of remembering someone who has died: *They lit candles in memory of those who died.*
[ORIGIN: 1200-1300 From the Latin word *memoria*, from *memor*, which means "remembering."]

**WORD FAMILY: memory**
**memory** *noun* | **memorize** *verb* | **memorable** *adjective* | **memorial** *noun*

**men** /men/ *noun*
the plural of MAN

**men·ace** /ˈmenɪs/ *noun*
something or someone that is dangerous or very annoying: *This disease is a menace to people everywhere.*

**mend** /mend/ *verb*
to repair a damaged piece of clothing: *Your shirt is torn – let me mend it for you.*
→ see Thesaurus box at **repair**[1]

**men·o·pause** /ˈmenəˌpɔz/ *noun*
the time when a woman stops being able to have a baby

**me·no·rah** /məˈnɔrə/ *noun*
a special CANDLESTICK that holds seven CANDLEs, used in Jewish ceremonies

**ˈmen's room** *noun*
a room in a public place with toilets for men

**men·stru·ate** /ˈmenstruˌeɪt/ *verb*
if a woman menstruates, blood flows out of her body every month
—**menstruation** /ˌmenstruˈeɪʃən/ *noun* when blood flows out of a woman's body
—**menstrual** *adjective* relating to menstruation

**men·tal** [Ac] /ˈmentl/ *adjective*
**1** relating to your thoughts or imagination: *I have a mental picture of what the house will be like.*
**2** relating to the health or state of someone's mind: *He has mental problems and sometimes behaves strangely.*
—**mentally** *adverb* in a way that relates to the mind: *She has prepared herself mentally and physically for the race.*
[ORIGIN: 1400-1500 From the Latin word *mentalis*, from *mens*, which means "mind."]

**men·tal·i·ty** Ac /menˈtæləti/ *noun* (plural **mentalities**) (*formal*)
a particular attitude or way of thinking: *It's hard to understand the mentality of these terrorists. What are they thinking?*

**ˌmentally ˈill** *adjective*
having an illness of the mind that affects the way you behave: *She works in a hospital, taking care of people who are mentally ill.*
—**mental illness** *noun* the state of being mentally ill

**men·tion** /ˈmenʃən/ *verb*
**1** to say something, without giving a lot of information: *I mentioned to Dad that the TV wasn't working.*
**2 not to mention someone or something** = used when adding something to what you have said, usually something more important: *He didn't want to disappoint his teacher, not to mention his parents.*
—**mention** *noun* the act of mentioning someone or something: *He made no mention of his family, and talked only about his work.*
→ see Thesaurus box at **say**[1]

**men·u** /ˈmenyu/ *noun*
**1** a list of the food that you can eat in a restaurant: *There was no fish on the menu, so I ordered chicken.*
**2** a list of things that you can ask your computer to do: *Go to the Edit menu and select "Copy."*

**me·ow** /miˈaʊ/ *verb*
if a cat meows, it makes a sound
—**meow** *noun* the sound that a cat makes

**mer·chan·dise** /ˈmɚtʃənˌdaɪz/ *noun* (*formal*)
things that are for sale: *The stores are full of cheap merchandise.*

**mer·chan·dis·ing** /ˈmɚtʃənˌdaɪzɪŋ/ *noun*
the activity of trying to sell things: *The new movie is a great merchandising opportunity – kids will want to buy the toys.*

**mer·chant** /ˈmɚtʃənt/ *noun* (*formal*)
someone who buys and sells things: *a wine merchant*

**mer·ci·ful** /ˈmɚsɪfəl/ *adjective* (*formal*)
kind and forgiving: *The king was merciful and did not punish the man.*

**mer·ci·less** /ˈmɚsɪlɪs/ *adjective*
not at all kind or forgiving: *He was merciless to his enemies.*
—**mercilessly** *adverb* in a merciless way

**mer·cu·ry** /ˈmɚkyəri/ *noun*
a liquid silver-colored metal: *In some thermometers, a line of mercury shows what the temperature is.*

**Mer·cu·ry** /ˈmɚkyəri/ *noun*
the first PLANET from the Sun. Mercury is the smallest planet.

**mer·cy** /ˈmɚsi/ *noun*
kindness and a willingness to forgive people: *He said he was guilty, but begged the judge for mercy.*

**mere·ly** /ˈmɪrli/ *adverb* (*formal*)
only: *Ken merely smiled in reply to her question and did not say anything.* **SYNONYM: just**
—**mere** *adjective* only: *The house took a mere two weeks to build.*

**merge** /mɚdʒ/ *verb*
to join together to form one thing: *The school later merged with two others to form the largest school in the county.*

**me·rid·i·an** /məˈrɪdiən/ *noun*
a line drawn from the North Pole to the South Pole on a map: *The zero meridian goes through Greenwich, England.*

**me·ringue** /məˈræŋ/ *noun*
a light sweet food made by mixing sugar and the white part of eggs: *lemon meringue pie*

**mer·it**[1] /ˈmerɪt/ *noun*
a good quality of something: *One of the merits of this book is that it is written very clearly.*

**merit**[2] *verb* (*formal*)
to deserve something: *It's a good idea which merits more discussion.*

**mer·maid** /ˈmɚmeɪd/ *noun*
a woman in stories who has a fish's tail instead of legs
[**ORIGIN:** 1300-1400 From the old English word *mere*, which means "sea or lake," and the word "maid," which used to mean "girl or young woman."]

**mer·ry** /ˈmeri/ *adjective* (**merrier**, **merriest**)
happy: *People wish each other Merry Christmas at Christmas time.*

**ˈmerry-go-ˌround** *noun*
a machine that turns around and around, and has wooden animals for children to sit on and ride on for fun

**mess¹** /mes/ *noun*
**1** a place or a group of things that is not organized or neat and may be dirty: *The room was a mess, with books, newspapers, and clothes everywhere.* | *We made a mess in the kitchen when we baked cookies.*
**2** a situation in which there are a lot of problems: *She didn't pay her credit card bills and got into a real mess.*

**mess²** *verb*
**PHRASAL VERBS**
**mess around** (*informal*)
to play or do silly things when you should be working or paying attention: *Stop messing around in class or you're going to get a bad grade.*
**mess up** (*informal*)
**1 mess something up** = to spoil or ruin something: *I hope I haven't messed up your plans by not coming.*
**2 mess something up** = to make something dirty or messy: *The wind had messed her hair up.*
**3 mess (something) up** = to make a mistake or do something badly: *I know I messed up the test – I just hope I don't get an F.*
**mess with something** (*informal*)
to change or get involved with something, in a way that results in problems: *If something works, don't mess with it.*

**mes·sage** /ˈmesɪdʒ/ *noun*
information that you leave for someone or send to him or her: *Mike left a message saying he would be late.* | *If Tony calls when I'm out, could you take a message?*
[**ORIGIN:** 1200-1300 From old French, from the Latin word *missaticum*, from *mittere*, which means "to send."]

**mes·sen·ger** /ˈmesəndʒɚ/ *noun*
someone who takes packages or messages to other people: *The note was delivered by messenger.*

**mess·y** /ˈmesi/ *adjective* (**messier, messiest**)
**1** dirty or not neat: *Your bedroom is very messy – you'd better clean it up.* | *His hands were getting messy working on the car.*
**2** a messy person or activity makes things dirty or leaves things in a way that is not neat: *Cleaning the oven can be a messy job.* | *He's a very messy person and doesn't like to clean.*
**3** a messy situation is complicated and hard to deal with: *She's just been through a messy divorce and is still very upset.*

**met** /met/ *verb*
the past tense and past participle of MEET

**me·tab·o·lism** /məˈtæbəˌlɪzəm/ *noun*
the chemical process in your body which changes food into the energy that you need to do things: *Exercise speeds up your metabolism and helps you to lose weight.*

**met·al** /ˈmetl/ *noun*
a hard substance such as iron, gold, or steel: *Coins are made of metal.* | *a metal spoon*
—**metallic** /məˈtælɪk/ *adjective* made of metal or similar to metal
[**ORIGIN:** 1200-1300 From the Greek word *metallon*, which means "a mine, or something that comes from a mine."]

**met·a·morph·ic** /ˌmetəˈmɔrfɪk/ *adjective*
metamorphic rock is formed when heat and pressure change the structure of other types of rock deep inside the Earth: *Marble is a metamorphic rock that forms from limestone.*

**metamorphosis**

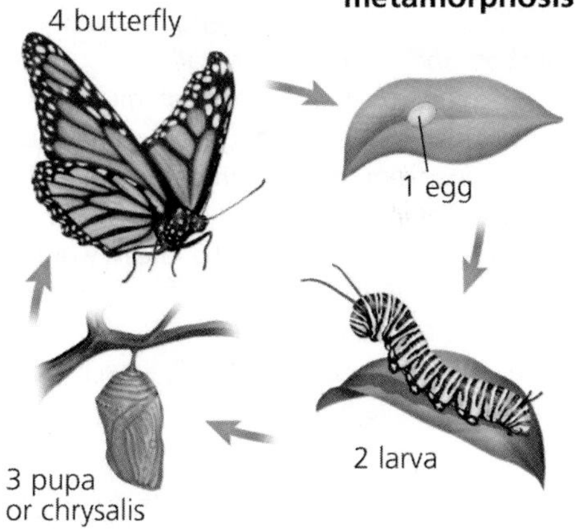


**met·a·morph·o·sis** /ˌmetəˈmɔrfəsɪs/ *noun*
the changes that some types of animals go through as they develop: *A caterpillar goes through a metamorphosis when it changes into a butterfly.*

**met·a·phor** /ˈmetəˌfɔr/ *noun*
a way of describing something by comparing

it to something else that has similar qualities, without using the words "like" or "as": *The sentence "She cried a river of tears" uses a metaphor. It means that she cried a lot.*
—**metaphorical** /ˌmetəˈfɔrɪkəl/ *adjective* being or relating to a metaphor
[ORIGIN: 1400-1500 From the Greek word *metaphora*, from *meta-*, which indicates change, and *pherein*, which means "to carry." The idea is that a meaning is carried over from one word to another.]

**me·te·or** /ˈmitiɚ/ *noun*
a piece of rock or metal that burns very brightly when it falls from space into the air around the Earth
[ORIGIN: 1500-1600 From the Greek word *meteoron*, which means "something high up in the sky."]

**me·te·or·ite** /ˈmitiəˌraɪt/ *noun*
a piece of rock or metal from space that has landed on the Earth's surface

**me·te·or·ol·o·gy** /ˌmitiəˈrɑlədʒi/ *noun*
the scientific study of the weather
—**meteorologist** *noun* someone whose job is to study the weather, especially in order to say what it will be like in the next days or weeks

**meter** /ˈmitɚ/ *noun*
**1** (*written abbreviation*: **m**) a unit for measuring length, equal to 100 centimeters or 39.37 inches: *She is 1.68 meters tall.*
**2** a piece of equipment that measures the amount of gas, electricity, etc. you have used: *Someone from the gas company came to look at the meter.*
[ORIGIN: 1800-1900 From the Greek word *metron*, which means "measure."]

**meth·ane** /ˈmeθeɪn/ *noun*
a gas with no color or smell, which can be burned to give heat

**meth·od** Ac /ˈmeθəd/ *noun*
a way of doing something: *There are different methods for sticking papers together: glue, tape, and staples.* | *I think email is a good method of communication.*

**me·thod·i·cal** Ac /məˈθɑdɪkəl/ *adjective*
doing things in a careful and organized way: *The police made a methodical search of the area, making sure not to miss anything.*
—**methodically** *adverb* in a careful and organized way

**meth·od·ol·o·gy** Ac /ˌmeθəˈdɑlədʒi/
*noun* (plural **methodologies**)
the set of methods and rules you use when you are studying something or doing a particular type of work: *The students learn a methodology for simple science experiments.*
—**methodological** /ˌmeθədəˈlɑdʒɪkəl/ *adjective* relating to methodology

**me·tic·u·lous** /məˈtɪkyələs/ *adjective*
extremely careful to make sure that every small detail is right: *The business keeps meticulous financial records.*
—**meticulously** *adverb* in a meticulous way: *Their trip was meticulously planned.*

**met·ric sys·tem** /ˈmetrɪk ˌsɪstəm/ *noun*
the system of measuring that is based on meters, grams, and liters
—**metric** *adjective* using the metric system

**met·ro·pol·i·tan** /ˌmetrəˈpɑlətn/ *adjective*
in or relating to a big city: *Pollution is a big problem in metropolitan areas such as Los Angeles or Denver.*

**Mex·i·can** /ˈmeksɪkən/ *adjective*
from Mexico: *Mexican food*
—**Mexican** *noun* someone from Mexico

**mg**
the written abbreviation of **milligram**

**mice** /maɪs/ *noun*
the plural of MOUSE

**mi·crobe** /ˈmaɪkroʊb/ *noun*
a very small living thing that you cannot see without a MICROSCOPE

**mi·cro·chip** /ˈmaɪkroʊˌtʃɪp/ *noun*
a small part in a computer, which stores information or controls what the computer does **SYNONYM: chip**

**mi·cro·film** /ˈmaɪkrəˌfɪlm/ *noun*
film on which there are very small photographs of documents, which you can read using a special machine: *Images of the old newspapers are stored on reels of microfilm.*

**mi·cro·org·an·ism**
/ˌmaɪkroʊˈɔrgəˌnɪzəm/ *noun*
a living thing that is so small that it cannot be seen without a microscope: *Germs and bacteria are microorganisms.* **SYNONYM: microbe**

M

**mi·cro·phone** /ˈmaɪkrəˌfoʊn/ *noun*
a piece of equipment that you speak into to make your voice sound louder or to record it: *Please speak into the microphone so we can hear you.*
[ORIGIN: 1600-1700 From the Greek words *mikros* and *phone*, which mean "small" and "sound."]

microphone

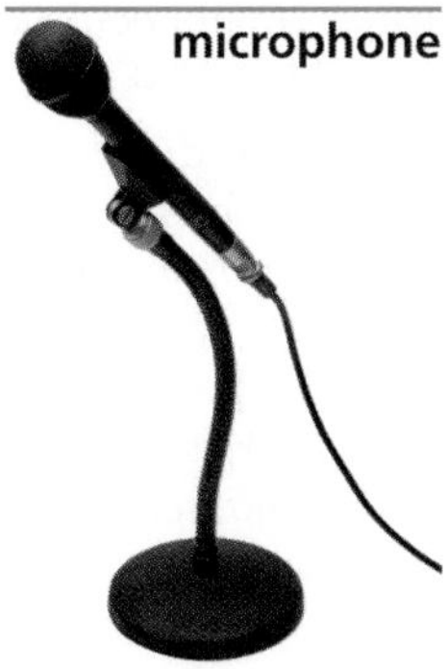

**mi·cro·scope** /ˈmaɪkrəˌskoʊp/ *noun*
a scientific instrument that helps you to see very small things by making them look bigger: *We looked at the pond water under a microscope, and saw lots of tiny insects in it.*
[ORIGIN: 1600-1700 From the Greek words *mikros* and *skopein*, which mean "small" and "to look at."]

microscope

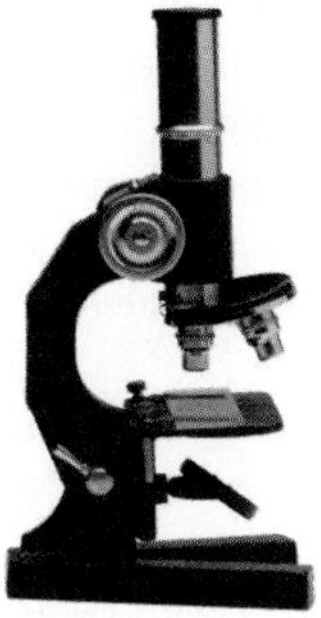

**mi·cro·scop·ic** /ˌmaɪkrəˈskɑpɪk/ *adjective*
extremely small: *Water has microscopic creatures living in it.*
→ see Thesaurus box at **small**

**mi·cro·wave** /ˈmaɪkrəˌweɪv/ (*also* **microwave oven**) *noun*
a type of machine that cooks food very quickly: *Cook the vegetables in the microwave for three minutes.* → see picture on page **A9**
—**microwave** *verb* to cook something in a microwave

**mid** (*also* **mid-**) /mɪd/
used before other words to talk about the middle of a period of time: *It was mid-morning and the sun was starting to get hotter.* | *The weather was warm for mid December.*

**mid·air** /ˌmɪdˈer/ *noun*
**in midair** = in the air or sky: *The balloon was floating in midair, high above the trees.*

**mid·day** /ˈmɪd-deɪ/ *noun* (*formal*)
the middle of the day, around 12:00 p.m.: *At midday, lunch was on the table.* **SYNONYM: noon**

**mid·dle¹** /ˈmɪdl/ *noun*
**1 the middle** = the part that is closest to the center of something: *The lake is very deep in the middle.* | *There was a big table in the middle of the room.* **SYNONYM: center**
**2 the middle** = the part that is between the beginning and the end of a period of time or an event: *He woke up in the middle of the night and couldn't get back to sleep.*

**middle²** *adjective*
closest to the center of something: *The socks are in the middle drawer, not the top drawer.*

**ˌmiddle ˈclass** *noun*
**the middle class** = the group of people in a country who are not rich but not poor either: *Most teachers belong to the middle class.*
—**middle-class** *adjective* belonging or relating to the middle class: *middle-class families*

**ˌMiddle ˈEast** *noun*
**the Middle East** = the part of Asia that is between the Mediterranean Sea and the Arabian Sea, and includes countries such as Egypt and Iran

**ˈmiddle school** *noun*
a school in the U.S. for students between the ages of 10 and 14, or in GRADEs 5 or 6 through 8: *She's a science teacher at Rockridge Middle School.*

**midg·et** /ˈmɪdʒɪt/ *noun*
a rude word for someone who is very short

**mid·night** /ˈmɪdnaɪt/ *noun*
12 o'clock at night: *The party ended at midnight.*

**midst** /mɪdst/ *noun*
**in the midst of** = in the middle of something: *She was in the midst of the huge crowd.*

**mid·way** /ˌmɪdˈweɪ/ *adjective, adverb*
**1** at the middle point between two places: *There's a gas station midway between here and Fresno.*
**2** in the middle of a period of time or an event: *I left midway through the show because I wasn't feeling well.*

**Mid·west** /ˌmɪdˈwest/ *noun*
**the Midwest** = the central area of the U.S.:

M

*The Midwest is known mainly for its farms.*
—**Midwesterner** *noun* someone who comes from the Midwest

**mid·wife** /ˈmɪdwaɪf/ *noun* (plural **midwives** /ˈmɪdwaɪvz/)
a nurse whose job is to help women when they are having a baby

**might**[1] /maɪt/ *verb*
**1** used for talking about what was or is possible: *I might be able to get free tickets – let me check.* | *I don't know what happened to the bike. Someone might have taken it.*
**2** used for giving advice or making a suggestion: *You might want to see a doctor if you're still sick.*

**might**[2] *noun*
**1** power, especially a country's military or economic power: *China's economic might has been growing.*
**2** **with all your might** = using all your strength: *She pulled on the rope with all her might.*

**might·y** /ˈmaɪti/ *adjective*
strong and powerful: *Many trees fell down in the mighty wind.*

**mi·graine** /ˈmaɪgreɪn/ *noun*
a very bad HEADACHE: *Emma had a migraine and had to go to bed.*

**mi·grant** [Ac] /ˈmaɪgrənt/ *noun*
someone who goes to another area or country in order to find work: *200,000 migrant workers will enter Canada this year to look for jobs.*

**mi·grate** [Ac] /ˈmaɪgreɪt/ *verb*
**1** if birds or animals migrate, they travel to a warmer part of the world in winter and return in spring: *Ducks migrate south every fall.*
**2** if people migrate, they move to another area or country in order to find work: *People migrated from the countryside to the cities.*
—**migration** /maɪˈgreɪʃən/ *noun* the act of migrating somewhere
—**migratory** /ˈmaɪgrəˌtɔri/ *adjective* migratory birds or animals migrate

**WORD FAMILY: migrate**
**migrate** *verb* | **migration** *noun* | **migrant** *noun* | **migratory** *adjective*

**mike** /maɪk/ *noun* (*informal*)
a MICROPHONE

**mild** /maɪld/ *adjective*
**1** not very severe or serious: *Children often have mild illnesses such as colds.* **SYNONYM: slight**
**2** having a taste that is not strong or spicy: *Young kids usually like foods with a mild flavor, not really spicy things.*
**3** mild weather is not too hot and not too cold: *The weather was mild enough to go out without a coat.*

**mile** /maɪl/ *noun*
**1** a unit for measuring distance, equal to 5,280 feet or about 1,609 meters: *Mark jogs five miles a day.*
**2** **miles** (*informal*) = a very long distance: *We walked for miles without seeing anyone.*
[**ORIGIN:** From the Latin phrase *mille passuum* or *milia passuum*, which means "a thousand paces."]

**mile·age** /ˈmaɪlɪdʒ/ *noun*
**1** the number of miles that a car has traveled since it was new: *He wants to buy a used car with low mileage, not one that's been driven a lot.*
**2** the number of miles a car can travel using one gallon of gasoline: *Does the car get good gas mileage?*

**mile·stone** /ˈmaɪlstoʊn/ *noun*
a very important event in the development or progress of something: *Winning the match was a milestone in his tennis career.*

**mil·i·tant** /ˈmɪlətənt/ *adjective*
willing to do violent or extreme things in order to change a government or political system: *A militant group made the attack against government buildings.*
—**militant** *noun* someone who is militant

**mil·i·tar·y** [Ac] /ˈmɪləˌteri/ *adjective*
relating to the army, navy, or air force: *Five military aircraft took part in the attack.* **ANTONYM: civilian**
—**military** *noun* a country's army, navy, or air force: *Both my brothers are in the military.*
[**ORIGIN:** 1400-1500 From the Latin word *militaris*, from *miles*, which means "soldier."]

**mi·li·tia** /məˈlɪʃə/ *noun*
a group of ordinary people who have weapons and have been trained as soldiers, but

who are not part of the permanent army: *The president has the authority to use the militia to repel invasion of the U.S.*

**milk**[1] /mɪlk/ *noun*

**1** the white liquid that people drink, that comes from a cow: *He put milk on his cereal.*
**2** a white liquid that female animals produce to feed their babies
—**milky** *adjective* containing milk
[**ORIGIN:** From the old English word *meolc.*]

**milk**[2] *verb*

to take milk from a cow or goat: *The farmer was milking the cows.*

**milk·shake** /ˈmɪlkʃeɪk/ *noun*

a thick drink made from milk and ICE CREAM: *a chocolate milkshake*

**ˌMilky ˈWay** *noun*

**the Milky Way** = the pale white band of stars that you can see across the sky at night

**mill** /mɪl/ *noun*

**1** a factory where materials such as paper, steel, or cotton cloth are made: *He worked in a steel mill.*
**2 coffee/pepper mill** = a small machine for crushing coffee beans or pepper
**3** a building containing a large machine for crushing grain into flour, or the machine itself: *The farmer took his wheat to the flour mill.*

**mil·li·gram** /ˈmɪləˌɡræm/ *noun* (*written abbreviation*: **mg**)

a unit for measuring weight. There are 1,000 milligrams in a gram.

**mil·li·li·ter** /ˈmɪləˌlitɚ/ *noun* (*written abbreviation*: **ml**)

a unit for measuring liquids. There are 1,000 milliliters in a liter.

**mil·li·me·ter** /ˈmɪləˌmitɚ/ *noun* (*written abbreviation*: **mm**)

a unit for measuring length. There are 1,000 millimeters in a meter.
[**ORIGIN:** 1800-1900 From the Latin word *mille*, which means "thousand," and the Greek word *metron*, which means "measure."]

**mil·lion** /ˈmɪlyən/ *number*

**1** 1,000,000: *It cost $350 million.*

**GRAMMAR: million**

Use the singular form **million** after a number: *a city of eight million people*

Use the plural form **millions** before "of": *Millions of Americans now use the Internet.*

**2** (*also* **millions**) (*informal*) a very large number of people or things: *I've heard that excuse a million times.*
**3 not/never in a million years** (*informal*) = used when saying that something is impossible: *I never would have guessed in a million years.*
—**millionth** /ˈmɪlyənθ/ *number* 1,000,000th or 1/1,000,000

**mil·lion·aire** /ˌmɪlyəˈner/ *noun*

someone who is very rich and has more than one million dollars: *He's a millionaire with houses all over the world.*

**mim·ic** /ˈmɪmɪk/ *verb* (**mimicked**, **mimicking**) (*formal*)

to copy the way someone talks or moves in order to make people laugh: *Lily mimicked Sue's Southern accent.*
—**mimic** *noun* someone who mimics other people: *He was a good mimic and could speak just like she did.*

**mind**[1] /maɪnd/ *noun*

**1** your thoughts, or the part of your brain you use for thinking and imagining things: *His mind was full of ideas for stories.* | *What do you have in mind for your birthday party?*
**2 change your mind** = to change your opinion or decision about something: *If you change your mind and want to come, just let me know.*
**3 make up your mind** = to decide something: *Have you made up your mind which college you want to go to?*
**4 be out of your mind** (*informal*) = to be crazy: *You want an alligator as a pet? Are you out of your mind?*
**5 on your mind** = if something is on your mind, you are thinking or worrying about it a lot: *Sorry I didn't call, but I've had a lot on my mind lately.*

**mind**[2] *verb*

**1** to feel annoyed or angry about something: *Do you think she'd mind if I borrowed this book?* | *I don't mind helping you.*
**2 do you mind?/would you mind?** = used to ask politely if you can do something or if someone will do something: *Do you mind if I*

M

*use your phone? | Would you mind waiting here a minute?*

**3 I wouldn't mind (doing) something** = used when saying you would like to do something: *I wouldn't mind learning to surf. I think it might be fun.*

**mind·ful** /ˈmaɪndfəl/ *adjective (formal)*
remembering a fact or information when you are deciding what to do: *They were mindful of what their mother said, and came home before dark.*

**mine**[1] /maɪn/ *pronoun*
the thing that belongs to the person who is speaking: *Theresa's coat is black. Mine is blue. | He doesn't have a skateboard so I let him borrow mine.*

**mine**[2] *noun*
**1** a deep hole in the ground from which people dig something such as coal or gold: *a coal mine*
**2** a type of bomb under the ground or in the ocean, that explodes when someone or something touches it: *Three soldiers were hurt when their car hit a land mine.*

**mine**[3] *verb*
**1** to dig something such as coal or gold out of the ground: *They were mining for gold.*
**2** to hide bombs under the ground or in the ocean: *The area had been mined to stop the enemy from crossing it.*

**mine·field** /ˈmaɪnfild/ *noun*
an area of land that has mines hidden in it

**min·er** /ˈmaɪnɚ/ *noun*
someone who digs something such as coal or gold out of the ground: *a coal miner*

**min·er·al** /ˈmɪnərəl/ *noun*
a natural substance such as iron, coal, or salt that is in the earth and also in some foods: *Milk is full of vitamins and minerals that you need to stay healthy.*

**ˈmineral ˌwater** *noun*
water that comes from under the ground and has minerals in it, which you can buy in bottles

**min·gle** /ˈmɪŋgəl/ *verb*
**1** to meet and talk with a lot of different people, for example at a party: *The school fair gives parents a chance to mingle with students and teachers.*
**2** if smells, sounds, or feelings mingle, they mix together: *He felt anger mingled with disappointment.*

**min·i** /ˈmɪni/ *noun*
another word for a MINISKIRT

**min·i·a·ture** /ˈmɪniətʃɚ/ *adjective*
smaller than other things of the same kind: *The miniature camera fits in your pocket.*
—**miniaturized** *adjective* made to be miniature
→ see Thesaurus box at **small**
[**ORIGIN:** 1500-1600 From the Italian word *miniatura*, which means "the art of drawing small pictures." This comes from the Latin word *miniare*, which means "to color with minium (a red substance)."]

**min·i·mal** Ac /ˈmɪnəməl/ *adjective*
very small in amount: *Luckily, the fire caused minimal damage.*

**min·i·mize** Ac /ˈmɪnəˌmaɪz/ *verb (formal)*
**1** to make the amount of something as small as possible: *You can minimize your risk of catching the flu by washing your hands regularly.* **ANTONYM: maximize**
**2** if you minimize a program that you are using on the computer, it becomes very small, so that the program is still open but it is not on the screen **ANTONYM: maximize**

**min·i·mum** Ac /ˈmɪnəməm/ *noun*
the smallest possible number, amount, or size: *You should spend a minimum of 30 minutes on your homework.* **ANTONYM: maximum**
—**minimum** *adjective* smallest or lowest: *The minimum age for voting is eighteen.*
[**ORIGIN:** 1600-1700 From the Latin word *minimus*, which means "smallest."]

**WORD FAMILY: minimum**
**minimum** *noun* | **minimum** *adjective* | **minimize** *verb* | **minimal** *adjective*

**ˌminimum ˈwage** *noun*
the lowest amount of money that the person you work for can legally pay you for one hour of work: *Jobs that pay the minimum wage are usually not very good.*

**min·ing** /ˈmaɪnɪŋ/ *noun*
the job or industry of digging substances such as gold and coal out of the ground: *The main industry in the state is coal mining.*

**min·i·skirt** /ˈmɪniˌskɚt/ *noun*
a very short skirt

**min·is·ter** /ˈmɪnəstɚ/ *noun*
**1** a religious leader in some Christian churches: *The minister prayed for peace.*
**2** a politician who is in charge of a government department in some countries: *the British Education Minister*

**min·is·try** Ac /ˈmɪnəstri/ *noun* (plural **ministries**)
**1 the ministry** = the work of being a church leader: *He was very religious and decided to enter the ministry.*
**2** a government department in some countries: *She worked for the Ministry of Agriculture.*

**mi·nor¹** Ac /ˈmaɪnɚ/ *adjective*
**1** small or not very important: *They had minor injuries such as cuts and bruises.* **ANTONYM: major**
**2** based on a particular type of musical SCALE **ANTONYM: major**
[**ORIGIN:** 1200-1300 From the Latin word for "smaller."]

**minor²** Ac *noun*
**1** (*formal*) someone who is younger than 18, and is not allowed by law to do things such as drink alcohol or vote: *It's illegal to sell cigarettes to minors.* **ANTONYM: adult**
**2** the second main subject that you study for your college degree: *She has a major in physics and a minor in history.*

**minor³** *verb*
**PHRASAL VERB**
**minor in something**
to study a second main subject as part of your college degree: *She minored in English in college, but history was her main subject.*

**mi·nor·i·ty** Ac /məˈnɔrəti/ *noun* (plural **minorities**)
**1** a group of people whose race or religion is different from that of most people in a country: *Our organization helps African Americans and other minorities.*
**2** a small group of people or things that are part of a larger group: *A minority of students failed the test, but more than 75% passed.* **ANTONYM: majority**

**mint** /mɪnt/ *noun*
**1** a candy with a strong fresh taste
**2** a plant whose leaves have a strong fresh taste and are used in cooking
—**minty** *adjective* tasting like mint: *a minty flavor*

**mi·nus¹** /ˈmaɪnəs/ *preposition*
used in mathematics to show that you SUBTRACT one number from another: *10 minus 2 equals 8 is written as 10 – 2 = 8.* **ANTONYM: plus**
[**ORIGIN:** 1400-1500 From the Latin word for "less."]

**minus²** *noun*
**1** a minus sign (-): *Negative numbers have a minus in front of them, for example -6.* **ANTONYM: plus**
**2** something bad about a situation: *One of the minuses of living near an airport is the noise.* **ANTONYM: plus**

**minus³** *adjective*
**1 A minus/B minus, etc.** (*also* **A-/B-, etc.**) = a GRADE for a piece of work that is slightly lower than a grade A, grade B, etc.: *I was hoping to get an A- but I only got a B+.*
**2 minus 5/20/30, etc.** = 5, 20, 30, etc. degrees less than zero in temperature: *The temperature dropped to minus 10.*

**ˈminus sign** *noun*
a sign (-) showing that a number is less than zero, or that the second of two numbers should be SUBTRACTed from the first **ANTONYM: plus sign**

**min·ute¹** /ˈmɪnɪt/ *noun*
**1** a measure of time equal to 60 seconds: *The plane will be landing in ten minutes.* | *I looked at my watch. It was three minutes to four.*
**2** a very short period of time: *For a minute I thought he was serious, but then I realized he was joking.* | *It will only take a minute to drive over there.* | *I'll come and help you in a minute.* **SYNONYM: moment**
**3 any minute (now)** = used when saying that you expect something to happen very soon: *She should be here any minute now.*
**4 at the last minute** = at the last possible time, just before you have to do something: *Frank changed his mind at the last minute and decided to come with us.*
**5 just a minute** = used when asking someone to wait for a short time until you have

M

done something: *"Are you coming?" "Yes, just a minute – I need to get some money."*

**6 this minute** = used when telling someone to do something immediately: *Come here this minute!*

**7 minutes** = a written record of the things people say at a meeting: *We will send a copy of the minutes to everyone.*

[ORIGIN: 1300-1400 From the Latin phrase *pars minuta prima*, which means "first small part" and was used by the mathematician Ptolemy for one-sixtieth of a circle. It was later used about the minutes on a clock.]

**mi·nute²** /maɪˈnut/ *adjective*
very small: *I could hardly read the minute writing.* **SYNONYM: tiny**
→ see Thesaurus box at **small**

**min·ute hand** /ˈmɪnɪt ˌhænd/ *noun*
the long thin piece of metal that points to the minutes on a clock or watch: *The minute hand pointed to the three, and the hour hand pointed to the one, so it was 1:15.*

**min·ute·man** /ˈmɪnɪtˌmæn/ *noun*
one of a group of men who were not soldiers but who were ready to fight at any time during the Revolutionary War in the U.S.

**mir·a·cle** /ˈmɪrəkəl/ *noun*
**1** something lucky that happens, which you did not think was possible: *It's a miracle that you weren't killed!*
**2** a surprising event that people believe God caused: *The statue cried tears of blood and people said it was a miracle.*
—**miraculous** /mɪˈrækyələs/ *adjective* like a miracle: *He has made a miraculous recovery after the accident, and is walking again.*

**mi·rage** /mɪˈrɑʒ/ *noun*
something that you think you can see, but is not really there. Mirages are caused by hot air, especially in the desert.

**mir·ror** /ˈmɪrɚ/ *noun*
a piece of special flat glass that you look at when you want to see yourself: *She looked in the mirror as she brushed her hair.* → see picture on page **A11**

[ORIGIN: 1200-1300 From the old French word *mirer*, which means "to look at," from the Latin word *mirare*, which means "to admire."]

**mis-** /mɪs/
used at the beginning of words to mean "bad" or "wrong": *misspell* (=spell something wrong)

**mis·be·have** /ˌmɪsbɪˈheɪv/ *verb*
if children misbehave, they behave badly: *If the kids misbehave, teachers make them stay late after school.*
—**misbehavior** /ˌmɪsbɪˈheɪvyɚ/ *noun* bad behavior

**mis·car·riage** /ˈmɪsˌkærɪdʒ/ *noun*
if a PREGNANT woman has a miscarriage, the baby is born before it is fully developed and it dies: *She had a miscarriage last year and lost the baby.*
—**miscarry** /mɪsˈkæri/ *verb* to have a miscarriage

**mis·cel·la·ne·ous** /ˌmɪsəˈleɪniəs/ *adjective*
including many different kinds of things or people: *The box contained a doll, some pens, a telephone, and other miscellaneous objects.*

**mis·chief** /ˈmɪstʃɪf/ *noun*
bad behavior by children that causes no serious harm: *He likes to make mischief and is always hiding his friends' stuff.*
—**mischievous** /ˈmɪstʃəvəs/ *adjective* regularly making mischief: *He's a naughty, mischievous child.*

**mis·con·duct** /ˌmɪsˈkɑndʌkt/ *noun* (*formal*)
bad or dishonest behavior by someone in his or her job: *The officer was fired for misconduct after he hit the prisoner.*

**mis·er·a·ble** /ˈmɪzərəbəl/ *adjective*
**1** very unhappy: *She's been miserable since she broke up with her boyfriend.*
**2** very bad or unpleasant: *It was a miserable night: cold, wet, and windy.*
—**miserably** *adverb* in a miserable way: *"I've made a terrible mistake," she thought miserably.*
→ see Thesaurus box at **sad**

**mis·er·y** /ˈmɪzəri/ *noun* (plural **miseries**)
great unhappiness or suffering: *He told us about the misery of life in prison.*

**mis·for·tune** /mɪsˈfɔrtʃən/ *noun* (*formal*)
bad luck or something that happens as a result of bad luck: *We had the misfortune of being in an airport when the snowstorm hit.*

**mis·in·ter·pret** Ac /ˌmɪsɪnˈtɚprɪt/ *verb* (*formal*)
to think what someone says or does means

something different from what it really means: *She misinterpreted my joke and thought I was criticizing her.*

**—misinterpretation** /ˌmɪsɪnˌtɚprəˈteɪʃən/ *noun* the act of misinterpreting something

**mis·lead** /mɪsˈlid/ *verb* (**misled** /mɪsˈled/) (*formal*)

to make someone believe something that is not true by not giving all the information or by giving wrong information: *He misled Rachel by not telling her he was married.*

**—misleading** *adjective* likely to make someone believe something that is not true: *The information was misleading even if it wasn't actually dishonest.*

→ see Thesaurus box at **lie**[2]

**mis·place** /ˌmɪsˈpleɪs/ *verb* (*formal*)

to put something somewhere and then forget where you put it: *The teacher had misplaced her pen again and spent several minutes looking for it.* **SYNONYM: lose**

**mis·print** /ˈmɪsˌprɪnt/ *noun*

a word in a book or magazine that is printed with a mistake: *"Coal" is a misprint and should read "coral."*

**mis·rep·re·sent** /ˌmɪsreprɪˈzent/ *verb* (*formal*)

to deliberately give a false description of something: *He claims that the newspaper misrepresented what he said and made it sound worse than it was.*

**miss**

She missed the bus.
He missed the basket.
21

**miss**[1] /mɪs/ *verb*

**1** to not do something because you forget about it or are doing something else: *I missed the party because I was on vacation.*

**2** to arrive too late to get on a train, bus, or plane: *Hurry or we'll miss the flight.*

**3** to feel sad because someone is not with you, or because you are away from a place where you feel happy: *Did you miss me while I was gone?*

**4** to not hit or catch something: *He threw the ball to me, but I missed it.*

**5** to not see, hear, or notice something: *Did you hear what he said? I missed it.* | *It's a big red house – you can't miss it.*

**6 miss the point** = to not understand the main idea of what someone is saying: *You're missing the point – taking the money is not just a bad idea, it's illegal.*

**PHRASAL VERB**

**miss out (on something)**

to not have the chance to do something that you enjoy: *You'll be missing out on a good time if you don't come to our party.*

**miss**[2] *noun*

**1 Miss** = used in front of the family name of a girl or a woman who is not married: *My teacher's name is Miss Harris.*

**2** an action in which you try to hit or catch something but fail: *He hit ten balls without a miss.*

**mis·sile** /ˈmɪsəl/ *noun*

a weapon that flies a long way and explodes when it hits something: *The plane fired a missile at the enemy camp.*

**miss·ing** /ˈmɪsɪŋ/ *adjective*

something that is missing is not in the correct place and you cannot find it: *Some money is missing from my purse. Did you take it?* | *Police are looking for a missing child.*

**mis·sion** /ˈmɪʃən/ *noun*

**1** something important that an organization or person wants to achieve: *The principal's mission was to improve the test scores.*

**2** an important job that someone has been given to do or sent somewhere to do: *They were sent on a mission to help people affected by the floods.*

**3** a trip in a space vehicle or military plane: *The spacecraft went on a mission to Mars.*

**4** a church that was started by missionaries

[ORIGIN: 1500-1600 From the Latin word *missio*,

M

which means "the act of sending," from *mittere*, which means "to send."]

**mis·sion·ar·y** /ˈmɪʃəˌneri/ *noun* (plural **missionaries**)
someone who goes to another country in order to teach people about his or her religion: *He went to Africa as a missionary to teach about Christianity.*

**mis·spell** /ˌmɪsˈspel/ *verb*
to spell a word incorrectly: *She misspelled the word "friend" as "freind."*
—**misspelling** *noun* a word that is spelled incorrectly

**mist** /mɪst/ *noun*
a light low cloud close to the ground: *We couldn't see through the mist over the field.*

**mis·take¹** /mɪˈsteɪk/ *noun*
**1** something that is not correct: *You made a mistake: this 3 should be a 5.* | *His work is full of spelling mistakes.* SYNONYM: **error**
**2** something you do that you later realize was not the right thing to do: *Marrying him was a big mistake.* | *I made the mistake of giving her my phone number, and now she calls me all the time.*
**3 by mistake** = without intending to do something: *I brought the wrong book home by mistake.* SYNONYM: **accidentally**; ANTONYMS: **on purpose**, **deliberately**
[ORIGIN: 1300-1400 From the Norse word *mistaka*, which means "to take wrongly."]

**mistake²** *verb* (**mistook** /mɪˈstʊk/, **mistaken** /mɪˈsteɪkən/)
PHRASAL VERB
**mistake something for something**
to think that one person or thing is someone or something else because they are very similar: *I'm sorry – I mistook you for someone I know.*

**mis·tak·en** /mɪˈsteɪkən/ *adjective*
wrong about something: *I was mistaken when I said she was a teacher. She is a doctor.*
—**mistakenly** *adverb* wrongly: *They mistakenly believed the Earth was flat.*

**mis·treat** /ˌmɪsˈtrit/ *verb* (*formal*)
to treat someone in a cruel way: *The guards mistreated the prisoners by hitting them.*

**mis·tress** /ˈmɪstrɪs/ *noun*
a woman who a man regularly has sex with while he is married to someone else

**mis·trust** /mɪsˈtrʌst/ *noun* (*formal*)
the feeling that you cannot trust someone: *He has a deep mistrust of politicians – he thinks they are all liars.*
—**mistrust** *verb* to not trust someone

**mist·y** /ˈmɪsti/ *adjective*
if it is misty, there is a lot of mist in the air, making it hard to see far: *It was misty, and we could only just see across the lake.*

**mis·un·der·stand** /ˌmɪsʌndɚˈstænd/ *verb* (**misunderstood** /ˌmɪsʌndɚˈstʊd/)
to not understand something correctly: *She wanted water, but the waiter misunderstood and gave her wine.*

**mis·un·der·stand·ing** /ˌmɪsʌndɚˈstændɪŋ/ *noun*
**1** a problem caused by someone not understanding a question, situation, or instruction correctly: *There's been a misunderstanding – this house isn't for sale.*
**2** a disagreement that is not very serious: *They had a slight misunderstanding about how much money Jerry owed him.*

**mitt** /mɪt/ *noun*
a big leather GLOVE that you use to catch a ball in baseball

**mit·ten** /ˈmɪtn/ *noun*
a piece of clothing that keeps your hand warm, with one part for your four fingers together and one part for your thumb

**mix¹** /mɪks/ *verb*
**1** to put different substances together to make something new: *Mix the butter and flour together.* | *Mix blue and yellow paint to get green.* → see picture on page **A15**

**THESAURUS: mix**

**combine** to join two or more things together: *Combine the flour and milk and beat until smooth.*

**stir** to mix a liquid or food by moving a spoon around in it: *Stir the mixture over a low heat.*

**blend** to mix together soft or liquid foods to form a single smooth substance: *Blend the yogurt with fruit for a wonderful drink.*

**beat** to mix food together quickly and thoroughly using a fork or kitchen tool: *Beat the eggs and add to the sugar mixture.*

**2** to put different feelings, activities, ideas, or groups together: *I felt excitement mixed with fear.* | *The two classes mix for music lessons.*

**PHRASAL VERB**

**mix up**

**1 mix someone/something up** = to think wrongly that a person or thing is someone or something else: *I keep mixing him up with his brother because they look so much alike.* **SYNONYM: confuse**

**2 mix something up** = to move things around so that they are in the wrong order: *Don't mix up those papers, or we'll never find the ones we need.*

**mix²** *noun*
different things or people together in a place: *There was a good mix of people – young and old, men and women.*

**ˌmixed ˈup** *adjective*
if you are mixed up, you are confused, so you do the wrong thing: *I got mixed up and went to the wrong classroom.* **SYNONYM: confused**

**mix·ture** /ˈmɪkstʃɚ/ *noun*
**1** a substance you make by mixing different things together: *Pour the mixture into a pan.*
**2** several different things, feelings, ideas, etc. together: *I felt a mixture of fear and excitement.*

**ˈmix-up** *noun*
a situation in which someone is confused about something, so that the wrong thing happens: *There was a mix-up, and Tyra got on the wrong bus.*

**ml**
the written abbreviation of **milliliter**

**mm**
the written abbreviation of **millimeter**

**moan** /moʊn/ *verb*
**1** to make a low sound because part of your body hurts or because you are unhappy: *A man was lying on the floor moaning in pain.* **SYNONYM: groan**
**2** to complain about something in an annoying way: *Stop moaning about your problems and get to work!*
—**moan** *noun* a long low sound that you make because part of your body hurts or because you are unhappy

**moat** /moʊt/ *noun*
a deep hole that was dug around a castle and filled with water, to help protect the castle from people attacking it

**mob** /mɑb/ *noun*
a large group of people who are noisy or angry: *He was attacked by a mob of angry young men.*
→ see Thesaurus box at **group¹**

**mo·bile** /ˈmoʊbəl/ *adjective*
able to move or be moved easily from place to place: *I'll be more mobile when I have a car.* | *a mobile library*
—**mobility** /moʊˈbɪləti/ *noun* how mobile someone is: *The new wheelchair is smaller, so I have much better mobility.*
[**ORIGIN:** 1400-1500 From the Latin word *mobilis*, which means "able to be moved."]

**ˌmobile ˈhome** *noun*
a small metal house built in a factory that a vehicle takes to the place where it will stay: *Several mobile homes were destroyed by a tornado.*

**moc·ca·sin** /ˈmɑkəsɪn/ *noun*
a flat comfortable shoe made of soft leather. Native Americans wore moccasins.
[**ORIGIN:** 1600-1700 From the Algonquian word *mockasin*. Algonquian is a Native American language.]

**mock** /mɑk/ *verb* (*formal*)
to laugh at someone in a way that is not nice: *The other boys mocked him because he wore strange clothes.*

**mock·ing·bird** /ˈmɑkɪŋˌbɚd/ *noun*
a gray and white bird in North and South America that copies the songs of other birds

**mo·dal verb** /ˈmoʊdl vɚb/ (*also* **modal auxiliary** /ˌmoʊdl ɔgˈzɪlyəri/) *noun*
a word such as "can," "may," or "might" that comes before another verb: *In the sentence "I might go to the party," "might" is a modal verb.*

**mod·el¹** /ˈmɑdl/ *noun*
**1** a small copy of something that you build or make: *I'm building a model of a ship.*
**2** a beautiful person who wears new clothes

M

in fashion shows and magazines: *She works as a model for Tommy Hilfiger.*
**3** one type of vehicle or machine that a company makes: *The car maker has several new models this year.*
**4** someone who lets an artist draw, paint, or photograph him or her: *They're looking for models for their art class.*
**5** a description that a scientist uses to explain how something works or happens: *Using this climate model, we can predict future weather patterns.*
→ see Thesaurus box at **type**[1]

**model**[2] *adjective*
**1** **model airplane/train/castle, etc.** = a small copy of an airplane, train, etc., especially one that you put together from separate parts
**2** **model student/employee/citizen, etc.** = a very good student, employee, etc.: *Joe is a model student and always works hard.* **SYNONYM: perfect**

**model**[3] *verb*
**1** to wear new clothes in fashion shows or magazines in order to show them to people: *She modeled for Vogue magazine.*
**2** to let an artist draw or paint you: *An artist asked if I would model for him.*
**PHRASAL VERB**
**model something on something**
to copy the way another thing is done: *The author modeled the main character on her own son.*

**mo·dem** /ˈmoʊdəm/ *noun*
a piece of equipment that connects your computer to the Internet using a telephone line

**mod·er·ate** /ˈmɑdərət/ *adjective*
not extreme, so that something is not too much or too little: *Cook the mixture over moderate heat, making sure that the pan is hot enough, but not too hot.* **SYNONYM: medium**

**mod·ern** /ˈmɑdɚn/ *adjective*
**1** belonging to the present time: *The modern world is very different from the world that people lived in 100 years ago.*
**2** using the most recent designs, methods, and ideas: *The old buildings are gone, and the area is now much more modern.* **ANTONYMS: old-fashioned, traditional** → see picture at **antique**
→ see Thesaurus box at **new**
**[ORIGIN:** 1500-1600 From the Latin word *modernus*, from *modo*, which means "just now."**]**

**WORD FAMILY: modern**
**modern** *adjective* | **modernize** *verb* | **modernization** *noun*

**mod·ern·ize** /ˈmɑdɚˌnaɪz/ *verb*
to make something less old-fashioned: *We're modernizing the house, starting with a new kitchen.*
—**modernization** /ˌmɑdɚnəˈzeɪʃən/ *noun* the process of modernizing something

**mod·est** /ˈmɑdɪst/ *adjective*
**1** not talking too proudly about your abilities or the things you do well: *She is very modest about her success – she doesn't like to brag.* **ANTONYM: conceited**
**2** not very big: *They are not rich and live in a modest house.*
—**modestly** *adverb* in a modest way

**mod·i·fi·er** /ˈmɑdəˌfaɪɚ/ *noun*
a word that gives extra information about another word in a sentence: *In the sentence "He walked slowly," "slowly" is a modifier.*

**mod·i·fy** Ac /ˈmɑdəˌfaɪ/ *verb* (**modified**, **modifies**) (*formal*)
**1** to make small changes to something: *The car had been modified for a disabled driver.*
**2** if one word in a sentence modifies another, it gives more information about it: *In the sentence, "I'm reading a good book," "good" modifies "book."*
—**modification** *noun* a small change to something

**mod·ule** /ˈmɑdʒul/ *noun*
a part of something that can be separated from the main part and used for a particular purpose, for example part of a spacecraft or machine: *When did the Apollo lunar module land on the Moon?*

**moist** /mɔɪst/ *adjective*
a little wet: *Her eyes were moist with tears.*
—**moisten** /ˈmɔɪsən/ *verb* to make something moist
**[ORIGIN:** 1300-1400 From the Latin word *mucidus*, which means "wet and slippery."**]**

**mois·ture** /ˈmɔɪstʃɚ/ *noun*
small amounts of water that make something a little wet: *Plants use their roots to absorb moisture from the soil.*

**mois·tur·ize** /ˈmɔɪstʃəˌraɪz/ *verb*
to put a substance on your skin to make it soft and not dry: *This cream is good for moisturizing your skin.*
—**moisturizer** *noun* a substance that you put on your skin to make it soft

**mo·lar** /ˈmoʊlɚ/ *noun*
one of the large teeth in the back of your mouth

**mo·las·ses** /məˈlæsɪz/ *noun*
a thick sweet brown liquid that you use in cooking

**mold¹** /moʊld/ *noun*
**1** a substance that grows on old food and on things that are warm and wet: *The bathroom tiles were covered in green mold.*
**2** a container that you pour liquid into, so that when the liquid becomes solid, it has the shape of the container: *She poured the Jell-O into the ring-shaped mold.*
—**moldy** *adjective* covered in mold: *moldy bread*

**mold²** *verb*
**1** to give a shape to a substance by pressing it or putting it in a mold: *We molded the clay with our fingers.*
**2** to have a big effect on the type of person someone becomes: *The training molds the men into soldiers.*

**mole** /moʊl/ *noun*
**1** a small dark brown spot on someone's skin: *The doctor said the dark mole on my shoulder should be removed.*
**2** a small animal with black fur that lives in holes in the ground
→ see Thesaurus box at **mark²**

**mol·e·cule** /ˈmɑləˌkyul/ *noun*
the smallest amount of a substance that can exist separately. Molecules are made of atoms: *A molecule of water has two hydrogen atoms and one oxygen atom.*
—**molecular** /məˈlekyəlɚ/ *adjective* relating to molecules
[**ORIGIN:** 1700-1800 From the Latin word *molecula*, which means "a small amount," from *moles*, which means "mass or amount."]

**mo·lest** /məˈlest/ *verb*
to harm someone in a sexual way

**mol·lusk** /ˈmɑləsk/ *noun*
a creature with a soft body, which usually has a shell. SNAILs and CLAMs are mollusks.

**molt** /moʊlt/ *verb*
if a bird or animal molts, its feathers, hair, or skin come off so that new feathers, hair, or skin can grow: *Moose molt after the winter and lose their thick coats.*

**mol·ten** /ˈmoʊltn/ *adjective*
molten metal or rock is liquid because it is very hot: *Molten rock flowed out of the volcano.*

**mom** /mɑm/ *noun*
mother: *Do you think your mom will let you go to the movie?* | *Is dinner ready, Mom?*

**mo·ment** /ˈmoʊmənt/ *noun*
**1** a particular point in time: *Just at that moment, Shelly came in.* | *From the moment we met, we've been friends.*
**2** **at the moment** = now: *Japanese food is popular at the moment.*
**3** (*formal*) a very short period of time: *Jacob stopped talking for a moment and then started again.* | *Where did he go? He was here a moment ago.* **SYNONYM: minute**
**4** **for the moment** = now, although the situation might change: *The rain has stopped for the moment.*
**5** **any moment (now)** (*formal*) = used when saying that you expect something to happen very soon: *Susan will be here any moment now.*

**mo·men·tar·i·ly** /ˌmoʊmənˈterəli/ *adverb* (*formal*)
**1** for a very short time: *I was momentarily blinded by the sunlight when I stepped outside.* **SYNONYM: briefly**
**2** very soon: *I'll be back momentarily.*

—**momentary** *adjective* lasting only a short time: *He felt a momentary panic, then realized his wallet was in the other pocket.*

**mo·men·tous** /moʊˈmentəs/ *adjective* (*formal*)
a momentous event or change is very important: *When did Columbus set off on his momentous voyage?*

**mo·men·tum** /moʊˈmentəm/ *noun*
the force that makes something continue to move: *If you roll a ball down a hill, it goes faster as it gains momentum.*
[**ORIGIN:** 1600-1700 From the Latin word for "movement."]

**mom·my** /ˈmɑmi/ *noun* (plural **mommies**) (*informal*)
used by children to mean "mother": *"I want my mommy," the little girl cried.*

**mon·arch** /ˈmɑnɚk/ *noun* (*formal*)
a king or queen: *The British monarch is Queen Elizabeth II.*
[**ORIGIN:** 1400-1500 From the Greek words *monos* and *archein*, which mean "alone" and "to rule."]

**mon·arch·y** /ˈmɑnɚki/ *noun* (plural **monarchies**)
the system of having a king or queen as the leader of a country: *In Norway, they have a monarchy as well as an elected government.*
→ see Thesaurus box at **government**

**mon·as·ter·y** /ˈmɑnəsˌteri/ *noun* (plural **monasteries**)
a place where MONKs (=men who follow a religious life) live together
[**ORIGIN:** 1300-1400 From the Greek word *monazein*, which means "to live alone," from *monos*, meaning "alone." Monks live apart from other people.]

**Mon·day** /ˈmʌndi/ *noun* (*written abbreviation*: **Mon.**)
the second day of the week, between Sunday and Tuesday: *The results were announced Monday.* | *It snowed on Monday.* | *Kelly came last Monday.* | *I'll call you first thing Monday morning.*
[**ORIGIN:** From an old English word meaning "day of the moon."]

**mon·ey** /ˈmʌni/ *noun*
**1** coins and pieces of paper that you use to buy things: *Mom went to the bank to get some money.* | *He started a business and made a lot of money.*

**THESAURUS: money**

**Types of Money:**

**bill** paper money: *a $20 bill*

**coin** metal money: *She gave each child a few coins to buy candy with.*

**penny** a coin worth 1 cent

**nickel** a coin worth 5 cents

**dime** a coin worth 10 cents

**quarter** a coin worth 25 cents

**cash** the coins and paper money that you use for buying things: *I didn't have enough cash, so I paid by credit card.*

**change** coins, not paper money: *Do you have any change for the phone?*

**change** the coins or bills you get back when you have paid for something with more money than it costs: *I paid for the meal with a $20 bill and the waitress gave me my change.*

**currency** the type of money used in a particular country: *He had $500 worth of Japanese currency.*

**2 get your money's worth** = to get enough use or enjoyment from something you buy, for the price you pay: *These running shoes are expensive but they're good – you'll get your money's worth.*
**3 for my money** (*informal*) = in my opinion: *For my money, Williams is the best player.*
[**ORIGIN:** 1200-1300 From Moneta, a name given to the Roman goddess Juno. The ancient Romans produced money in or near the temple of this goddess, and used the word *moneta* to mean "coins."]

**mon·i·tor**[1] /ˈmɑnətɚ/ *noun*
**1** the part of a computer that shows information or pictures: *Your eyes should be on the same level as your computer monitor.* → see picture on page **A20**
**2** a machine that shows you information about something: *The heart monitor shows how fast the patient's heart is beating.*
**3** a student who does a particular job at

school: *The hall monitor told them to get to class.*

**monitor²** [Ac] *verb*
to carefully watch or measure something to see if it changes: *Your teacher will monitor your work during the year to make sure that you understand everything.*

**monk** /mʌŋk/ *noun*
a man who belongs to a religious group of men who live together

**mon·key** /ˈmʌŋki/ *noun*
an animal that climbs trees, and that has a long tail and can hang onto things with its feet and hands

**mon·o·lin·gual** /ˌmɑnoʊˈlɪŋgwəl/ *adjective*
using only one language: *Most of the people there were monolingual and couldn't even say hello in another language.*

**mon·o·logue** (*also* **monolog**) /ˈmɑnlˌɔg/ *noun*
a long speech by one person in a play or movie: *There is a five-minute monologue in the play where the main character talks about his feelings.*
[ORIGIN: 1600-1700 From the Greek words *monos* and *logos*, which mean "alone" and "speech."]

**mon·o·nu·cle·o·sis** /ˌmɑnoʊˌnukliˈoʊsɪs/ *noun*
a disease that makes you feel weak for a long time, and gives you a fever and a sore throat. Mononucleosis most often affects teenagers.

**mo·nop·o·ly** /məˈnɑpəli/ *noun* (plural **monopolies**)
if a company has a monopoly on a business activity, it has complete control of it and other companies cannot compete: *If these two oil companies join together, they will have a monopoly on the country's oil industry.*
—**monopolize** *verb* to have complete control of a business activity: *The company has monopolized the music industry.*

**mo·not·o·nous** /məˈnɑtnəs/ *adjective*
boring and always the same: *I don't want a monotonous job in a factory where I have to do the same thing every day.*
—**monotony** *noun* when something is boring and always the same: *It was a long trip, so we played a game to break the monotony.*
→ see Thesaurus box at **boring**

**mon·soon** /ˌmɑnˈsun/ *noun*
the time when it rains a lot in India and other parts of Asia
[ORIGIN: 1500-1600 From the old Dutch word *monssoen*, from the Arabic word *mawsim*, which means "time or season."]

**mon·ster** /ˈmɑnstɚ/ *noun*
**1** a frightening creature in stories or dreams: *The monster had two heads and six legs.*
**2** a very bad cruel person: *He was a monster who was cruel to animals.*
[ORIGIN: 1200-1300 From the Latin word *monstrum*, which means "warning sign, or monster." Strange creatures that were born or seen were thought to be warning signs from God.]

**month** /mʌnθ/ *noun*
**1** one of the 12 parts of a year: *January is the first month of the year.*
**2** a period of about 30 days: *I haven't been to the gym for a month.*
[ORIGIN: From the old English word *monath*, from the word for Moon. The Moon takes 28 days, or a month, to go around the Earth. ]

**month·ly** /ˈmʌnθli/ *adjective, adverb*
happening every month: *Every teacher has to write a monthly report.* | *The magazine is published monthly, so I get 12 issues a year.*

**mon·u·ment** /ˈmɑnyəmənt/ *noun*
something that is built so people will remember an important event or person: *The statue is a monument to the men who died in the war.*
[ORIGIN: 1200-1300 From the Latin word *monumentum*, from *monere*, which means "to remind."]

**mon·u·men·tal** /ˌmɑnyəˈmentl/ *adjective* (*formal*)
very big or important: *Exploring space is a monumental challenge.*

**moo** /mu/ *noun*
the sound that a cow makes
—**moo** *verb* to make the sound that a cow makes

**mood** /mud/ *noun*
the way you feel at a particular time, for example whether you are happy or sad: *Dad's in a good mood because he got a raise.* | *She was in a bad mood and shouted at me.*
—**moody** *adjective* if you are moody, your

M

feelings change often: *She is really moody. One minute she's happy, the next minute she's sad.*

**moon** /mun/ *noun*
**1 the Moon** = the round object that moves around the Earth once each month, and shines at night: *Men first landed on the Moon in 1969. | The night was clear and the moon was shining brightly.*
**2** a round object that moves around another PLANET: *Saturn has several moons.*

**moon·light¹** /ˈmunlaɪt/ *noun*
the light from the Moon: *The water looked silver in the moonlight .*

**moonlight²** *verb (informal)*
to do a second job, when you are not doing your main job: *He's a firefighter, but he moonlights as a waiter to earn extra money.*

**moose** /mus/ *noun*
a wild animal like a very big DEER that has big flat ANTLERs (=horns)

**mop¹** /mɑp/ *noun*
a thing that you use to wash floors, that is made of a long stick with soft material on the end: *I washed the floor with a mop.*

**mop²** *verb* (**mopped**, **mopping**)
to wash a floor with a mop: *There was a man in the kitchen, mopping the floor.*
→ see Thesaurus box at **clean²**
**PHRASAL VERB**
**mop something up**
to get liquid off something using a mop or cloth: *I got a paper towel to mop up the juice I spilled.*

**mope** /moʊp/ *verb*
to be unhappy, and not want to do anything: *Since his girlfriend left him, he's been moping around the house all day.*

**mor·al¹** /ˈmɔrəl/ *adjective*
**1** relating to what is right and wrong: *Many people did not agree with the war for moral reasons.*
**2** a moral action is good and right: *The moral thing to do would be to tell your friend the truth.* **ANTONYM: immoral**
—**morally** *adverb* according to what is right and wrong: *It is morally wrong to cheat on a test.*

[**ORIGIN:** 1300-1400 From the Latin word *mores*, which means "customs."]

**WORD FAMILY: moral**
**moral** *adjective* | **moral** *noun* | **morally** *adverb* | **immoral** *adjective* | **morality** *noun*

**moral²** *noun*
**1** a lesson about life that you learn from a story or something that happens: *The moral of the story is that money doesn't make you happy.*
**2 morals** = someone's ideas about what is right and wrong: *My father was a man with very strong morals – he never lied.*

**mo·rale** /məˈræl/ *noun*
the happiness and confidence that a group of people feel: *The morale of the team is high because they have won the last three games.*

**mo·ral·i·ty** /məˈræləti/ *noun*
ideas about what is right and wrong and how people should behave: *Some people think changes in morality have led to more crime.*

**more¹** /mɔr/ *adverb*
**1 more important/difficult/beautiful, etc.** = having a greater amount of importance, etc.: *The second test was more difficult, and I did not do as well. | I think history is more interesting than math.* **ANTONYM: less**
**2** a larger amount, a greater number of times, or for longer: *We need to practice more if we want to improve.* **ANTONYM: less**
**3 more and more** = used to say that a quality or amount keeps increasing: *He got more and more angry, until he started yelling at me.*
**4 more or less** = about or almost: *My parents have lived here for twenty years, more or less. | Their scores were all more or less the same.* **SYNONYMS: approximately, roughly**

**more²** *adjective, pronoun*
**1** an additional amount of something: *Would you like some more lemonade? | Could I have a little more? I'm still hungry.*

**THESAURUS: more**
**another** one more person or thing of the same kind: *Do you want another cup of coffee?*

**extra** more than the usual or expected amount of something: *I gave her an extra five dollars, since she'd helped wash the car.*

**additional** more than you already have, or more than was agreed or expected: *You can find additional information on our website.*

**further** (*formal*) more, used especially when something happens again or is done again: *Further research is needed to make sure that the medicine is completely safe.*

**2** a greater amount or number: *She's won more prizes than any other student.* | *We spend more of our money on food than we used to.* | *These jeans are nicer than those, but they cost more.* **ANTONYMS: less, fewer**

**3 more and more** = used to say that an amount keeps increasing: *He is spending more and more time at the gym. Now he's there for a couple of hours every day.*

**more·o·ver** /mɔrˈoʊvɚ/ *adverb* (*formal*)
you use this to mean "also" when you are giving more information: *This house is much bigger; moreover, it has a big yard.* **SYNONYM: furthermore**

**morgue** /mɔrg/ *noun*
a building or room for keeping dead bodies, before burying or burning them

**morn·ing** /ˈmɔrnɪŋ/ *noun*
**1** the time from when the sun rises until the middle of the day: *Classes start at 8 o'clock in the morning.* | *I have an appointment this morning.* | *See you tomorrow morning.*
**2** (*also* **good morning**) you say this when you meet someone in the morning: *Morning, Kim. You're up early today!*

**Morse code** /ˌmɔrs ˈkoʊd/ *noun*
a way of sending messages using short and long signals of sound or light: *In Morse code, three short flashes of light means "S."*

**mor·tal** /ˈmɔrtl/ *adjective* (*formal*)
not living forever: *All humans are mortal. We will all eventually die.* **ANTONYM: immortal**
—**mortally** *adverb* in a way that causes death: *He was mortally wounded in the battle and died the next day.* **SYNONYM: fatally**
—**mortality** /mɔrˈtæləti/ *noun* the fact that you will die one day
[**ORIGIN:** 1300-1400 From the Latin word *mortalis*, from *mors*, which means "death."]

**mort·gage** /ˈmɔrgɪdʒ/ *noun*
money that you borrow from a bank to buy a house, and pay back over a long time: *The bank agreed to give them a mortgage, so they were able to buy the house.*
—**mortgage** *verb* if your house is mortgaged, you bought it with a mortgage and you have not paid the money back yet

**mo·sa·ic** /moʊˈzeɪ-ɪk/ *noun*
a pattern or picture made of small pieces of stone, glass, or POTTERY

**Mos·lem** /ˈmɑzləm/ *noun*
another spelling of MUSLIM, which many Muslims do not like

**mosque** /mɑsk/ *noun*
a building where Muslims go to pray

**mos·qui·to** /məˈskitoʊ/ *noun* (plural **mosquitoes** *or* **mosquitos**)
a small flying insect that bites people, drinks blood, and spreads disease

**mosquito**

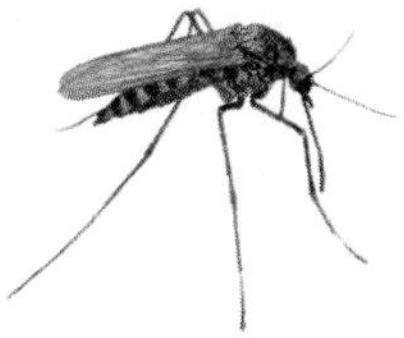

**moss** /mɔs/ *noun*
a soft green plant that grows on wet ground, trees, and rocks
—**mossy** *adjective* covered with moss: *a mossy bank beside the river*

**most¹** /moʊst/ *adverb*
**1 most powerful/popular/important, etc.** = having the largest amount of power, etc.: *The president is the most powerful man in the U.S.* **ANTONYM: least**
**2** more than anything or anyone else: *Which of these three shirts do you like most?* | *Sean worried most of all about money.*

**most²** *adjective, pronoun*
**1** almost all: *Most birds can fly, but a few can only walk or run.* | *We've already eaten most of the cake, but there's still a little bit left.*

**GRAMMAR: most**

When you are talking about a type of thing, use **most** before the plural form of a

M

noun or before a noun such as "money" and "bread" that does not have a plural: *I like most animals.* | *He thinks most poetry is boring.*

When you are talking about a particular group or thing, use **most of** before "the," "this," "my," etc. and a noun: *I got most of the answers right.* | *He does most of his work at home.*

**2** the largest amount or number of something: *Of all my family, I like my sister the most.* | *The team that scores the most points wins the game.*

**3 at most/at the most** = not more than: *The test will take one hour at the most.*

**4 make the most of something** = to use a good opportunity well, so that you get a lot from it: *You're only young once, so make the most of it!*

**5 for the most part** = in almost all ways or parts: *The meal was disappointing, for the most part – I only liked the dessert.*

**most·ly** /ˈmoʊstli/ *adverb*
**1** usually: *Mostly, we visit my grandparents on the weekend.*
**2** almost all: *My friends are mostly in the same class as me. I don't know many other kids.*

**mo·tel** /moʊˈtel/ *noun*
a hotel you stay in when you are traveling by car, with a place for your car near your room

**moth** /mɔθ/ *noun*
an insect with wings that flies at night

**moth·er** /ˈmʌðɚ/ *noun*
your female parent: *I asked my mother if I could go to the party.*
—**motherly** *adjective* kind and loving, like a good mother
—**motherhood** /ˈmʌðɚhʊd/ *noun* the state of being a mother

**ˈmother-in-ˌlaw** *noun* (plural **mothers-in-law**)
the mother of someone's husband or wife

**ˈMother's Day** *noun*
the second Sunday of May, when people give cards and gifts to their mothers

**ˈmother ˌtongue** *noun*
the first language that you learn, when you are a child: *I was born in Mexico, so my mother tongue is Spanish.*

**mo·tion** /ˈmoʊʃən/ *noun*
movement: *Scientists study the motion of the planets around the Sun.* | *Please stay in your seats while the bus is in motion.*

**mo·tion·less** /moʊʃənləs/ *adjective* (*formal*)
not moving: *After falling from the ladder, he lay motionless on the ground.*

**ˌmotion ˈpicture** *noun*
a movie: *The book was made into a major motion picture.*

**mo·ti·vate** Ac /ˈmoʊt̬əˌveɪt/ *verb*
to make you want to do something: *If classes are interesting, it motivates students to learn.*
—**motivation** /ˌmoʊt̬əˈveɪʃən/ *noun* a reason for wanting to do something: *What is your motivation for wanting to be an actor?*
**SYNONYM: reason**

**WORD FAMILY: motivate**
**motivate** *verb* | **motivation** *noun* | **motive** *noun*

**mo·tive** Ac /ˈmoʊt̬ɪv/ *noun*
the reason why someone does something, usually something bad: *Police are unsure about the motive for the attack.*
→ see Thesaurus box at **reason**[1]

**mo·tor** /ˈmoʊt̬ɚ/ *noun*
the part of a machine that makes it work or move: *This toy works using a small electric motor.*
[**ORIGIN:** 1400-1500 From the Latin word *motus*, a form of the verb *movere*, which means "to move."]

**mo·tor·boat** /ˈmoʊt̬ɚˌboʊt/ *noun*
a small fast boat with an engine

**mo·tor·cade** /ˈmoʊt̬ɚˌkeɪd/ *noun*
a group of cars and vehicles that travel together with a very important person's car: *The president's motorcade has just left the airport.*

**mo·tor·cy·cle** /ˈmoʊt̬ɚˌsaɪkəl/ *noun*
a fast vehicle with two wheels and an engine
→ see picture on page **A26**

**ˈmotor home** *noun*
a big vehicle with beds and a kitchen in it,

M

that people use for traveling and living in on vacation → see picture on page **A26**

**mo·tor·ist** /ˈmoʊtərɪst/ *noun* (*formal*)
someone who drives a car: *Snow is causing problems for motorists.* **SYNONYM: driver**

**ˈmotor ˌvehicle** *noun* (*formal*)
a car, bus, truck, etc.: *There's been an accident involving five motor vehicles.* **SYNONYM: vehicle**

**mot·to** /ˈmɑtoʊ/ *noun* (plural **mottos** *or* **mottoes**)
a few words that show the main aim, belief, or rule of a person, school, or organization: *The motto of the Boy Scouts is "Be Prepared."*
[**ORIGIN:** 1500-1600 From the Italian word for "word."]

**mound** /maʊnd/ *noun*
**1** a pile of something, especially earth: *There was a mound of dirt next to a deep hole.*
**2** **the mound** = the small hill that you stand on to throw the ball toward the BATTER in baseball

**mount[1]** /maʊnt/ *verb*
**1** to attach something to a wall, board, or piece of paper: *A large screen was mounted on the wall of the classroom.*
**2** (*also* **mount up**) to increase over a period of time: *Dad had no job, and our debts were mounting up.* **SYNONYMS: grow, increase**
**3** (*formal*) to get on a horse or bicycle
[**ORIGIN:** 1200-1300 From the French word *monter*, which means "to go up," from the Latin word *mons*, which means "mountain."]

**mount[2]** *noun*
**Mount** = used before the name of a mountain: *Mount Everest*

**moun·tain** /ˈmaʊntən/ *noun*
**1** a very high hill: *It took us five hours to climb the mountain.* | *the Rocky Mountains*
**2** a large amount of something: *I have a mountain of work to do so I'll be busy all weekend.*
—**mountainous** *adjective* having a lot of very high hills

**mountain**

**ˈmountain ˌbike** *noun*
a bicycle with a strong frame and thick tires, that you can ride over rough ground

**ˈmountain ˌlion** *noun*
another word for a COUGAR

**ˈmountain ˌrange** *noun*
a group of mountains in one area

**mourn** /mɔrn/ *verb* (*formal*)
to feel very sad because someone has died: *She is still mourning her son's death.*
—**mourning** *noun* when you feel and show great sadness because someone has died: *The president died, and the whole nation was in mourning.*

**mourn·er** /ˈmɔrnɚ/ *noun* (*formal*)
someone who is at a funeral: *Hundreds of mourners came to the church for the funeral.*

**mourn·ful** /ˈmɔrnfəl/ *adjective* (*formal*)
very sad: *He could hear the mournful howling of a lonely dog.*

**mouse** /maʊs/ *noun*
**1** (plural **mice** /maɪs/) a small animal with a long tail that lives in buildings or fields: *The cat has caught a mouse again.*
**2** (plural **mouses** *or* **mice**) the thing that you use to control a computer, by moving it with your hand: *Press the left mouse button to select a file.* → see picture on page **A20**

**ˈmouse pad** *noun*
a flat piece of plastic or rubber on which you move a computer mouse

**mouse·trap** /ˈmaʊstræp/ *noun*
a small trap that you use in a house to catch mice

**mousse** /mus/ *noun*
**1** a cold sweet food made by mixing cream, eggs, and fruit or chocolate: *chocolate mousse*
**2** a substance that you put in your hair to keep it in a particular style: *Use this mousse to make your hair look thicker.*

**mouth** /maʊθ/ *noun* (plural **mouths** /maʊðz/)
**1** the part of your face that you use for speaking and eating: *She opened her mouth to say something and then stopped.* → see picture on page **A2**
**2** the part of a river where it joins the ocean:

M

*New Orleans is at the mouth of the Mississippi, where it flows into the Gulf of Mexico.*
**3** the entrance to a CAVE or HARBOR
**4 keep your mouth shut** (*informal*) = to not say what you are thinking, or not tell someone a secret: *I was getting really mad, but I kept my mouth shut.*
**5 big mouth** (*informal*) = used about someone who often says things that he or she should not say: *Don't tell Maya any secrets – she has a very big mouth.*

**mouth·ful** /ˈmaʊθfʊl/ *noun*
an amount of food or drink that you put in your mouth: *He took another mouthful of salad and started to chew.*

**mouth·wash** /ˈmaʊθwɑʃ/ *noun*
a liquid you use to clean your mouth and make it smell nice

**mov·a·ble** /ˈmuvəbəl/ *adjective*
able to be moved: *The doll's arms and legs are movable.*

**move¹** /muv/ *verb*
**1** to go from one place or position to another: *I could hear Mom moving around downstairs.* | *I moved closer to the door.*
**2** to put something in a different place or position: *Could you move your car, please?*
**3** (*also* **move away**) to go to live in a different place: *We moved to Texas from Arizona when I was five.* | *Carla moved away, and I never saw her again.*
**4** to make someone feel a strong emotion: *People were moved by the pictures from after the earthquake, and sent money to help.*

**PHRASAL VERBS**

**move in**
to start living in a new home: *Has your new neighbor moved in yet, or is the house still empty?*

**move out**
to leave the house where you are living, and go to live somewhere else: *He said he would move out after he graduated from college.*

**move over**
to move to the left or right of where you are sitting or standing, so that there is more space for someone else: *Could you move over, so I can sit next to Dan?*

**move²** *noun*
**1** a movement that someone makes: *Becky made a move toward the door as she got ready to leave.*
**2** the act of leaving your home and going to live somewhere else: *Our move to Seattle was very hard because my brother didn't want to go.*
**3** something that you do in order to achieve something: *The team is practicing more this year, and that's a good move.*
**4** the action of moving an object in a game such as CHESS: *It's your move now.*

**move·ment** /ˈmuvmənt/ *noun*
**1** the action of moving from one position to another: *The rocking movement of the boat was making me sleepy.* | *He watched the dancer's graceful movements.*
**2** a group of people who want to change something in society: *The environmental movement is fighting to stop the rainforest from being cut down.*

**mov·er** /ˈmuvɚ/ *noun*
someone whose job is helping people move from one house to another: *The movers came and packed up all our things to take to the new house.*

**mov·ie** /ˈmuvi/ *noun*
**1** a story that is told using moving pictures: *Do you want to see a movie tonight?* | *"The Wizard of Oz" is a great movie.*

**THESAURUS: movie**

**film** a movie, especially one that people think is very good or important: *It won an Oscar as the Best Film in a Foreign Language.*

**motion picture** a movie that you see in a movie theater: *The book was made into a major motion picture.*

**comedy** a funny movie that makes people laugh: *It's a comedy about three guys from the city who get lost in the forest.*

**drama** a serious movie, especially one about the relationships that people have with each other: *The movie is a drama that shows what happens to a family when one of the sons dies.*

**romantic comedy** a funny movie about two people who are in love: *Romantic comedies often feature a couple who don't realize they are in love.*

**thriller** a movie about crime or spies that is exciting because you never know what will happen next: *The "Mission Impossible" movies have been pretty good thrillers.*

**horror movie** a movie in which strange and frightening things happen: *I can't watch horror movies; they give me bad dreams.*

**science fiction movie** a movie about events that happen in the future or about other worlds: *"Star Wars" is one of my favorite science fiction movies.*

**action movie** an exciting movie that has lots of fighting and explosions: *It has the most exciting car chase I've ever seen in an action movie.*

**western** a movie with cowboys in it: *I watched an old western on TV.*

**musical** a movie that has songs and dancing in it: *"High School Musical" helped make musicals popular with kids again.*

**animated movie** a movie that uses drawings, models, or computer pictures, rather than real actors: *"Toy Story" was one of the first animated movies to use computer animation.*

**2 the movies** = the theater where you go to see a movie: *How often do you go to the movies?*

**'movie star** *noun*
a famous movie actor or actress: *Will Smith is my favorite movie star.*

**'movie ˌtheater** *noun*
a building where you go to see movies

**mov·ing** /ˈmuvɪŋ/ *adjective*
**1** making you feel strong emotions: *The book tells a moving story about love and death.*
**2** changing from one position to another: *the moving parts of an engine*

**mow** /moʊ/ *verb* (**mowed** *or* **mown** /moʊn/)
to cut grass with a machine: *Dad usually mows the lawn on Sunday.*
—**mower** *noun* a machine that you use to cut grass
→ see Thesaurus box at **cut**[1]

**MP3** *noun*
a type of computer FILE that contains music: *He was listening to some songs on his MP3 player.*

**mph**
the written abbreviation of **miles per hour**: *The car was going at 60 mph.*

**Mr.** /ˈmɪstɚ/
a word you use before a man's family name: *This is Mr. Brown.*

**Mrs.** /ˈmɪsɪz/
a word you use before the family name of a married woman: *Mrs. Brown is on the telephone.*

**Ms.** /mɪz/
a word you can use before a woman's family name, that does not show if she is married or not: *Ms. Aitkins is the head of the department.*

**M.S.** (*also* **M.Sc.**) *noun*
(**Master of Science**) a university degree in a science subject, which is more advanced than a B.S.

**much**[1] /mʌtʃ/ *adverb*
**1** a lot: *Alaska is much bigger than California.* | *This T-shirt is much too big.* | *Thank you very much. I really liked the gift.* | *"Did you like the movie?" "No, not very much."*
**2 so much** = used to say that you feel something very strongly: *My brother left home a year ago, and I miss him so much.*

**much**[2] *adjective, pronoun*
**1** a lot of something: *Hurry up – we don't have much time.*

M

**GRAMMAR: much, many, a lot of**

**Much** is used with nouns such as "money" and "bread" that do not have plurals: *There isn't much milk left.*

**Many** is used with the plural forms of nouns: *I didn't see many people there that I knew.*

**A lot of** can be used with both types of noun: *We're going to need a lot of paint.* | *She doesn't have a lot of friends.*

In sentences that do not have "not" in them, use **a lot of** rather than **much**: *There was a lot of traffic.*

Do not say "There was much traffic."

**2 how much** = used when asking about the amount or cost of something: *How much water is left in the bottle?* | *"How much were those jeans?" "About $30."*

**3 too much** = more than you need or want: *I ate too much, and I feel sick.*

**4 not much** = used when saying that something is not important or interesting: *"What did you do on Saturday?" "Not much – just hung around with my brothers."*

**5 as much as** = the same amount as: *I've done as much work as I can today. I can't do any more.*

**mud** /mʌd/ *noun*
wet earth that is soft and sticky: *Take your boots off – they're covered in mud!*
—**muddy** *adjective* covered with mud: *After the rain, the path was muddy.*

**muf·fin** /ˈmʌfən/ *noun*
a sweet type of bread that often has fruit in it, and that has a round shape: *I had a blueberry muffin for breakfast.*

**mug¹** /mʌg/ *noun*
a large cup with straight sides and a handle: *a mug of coffee* → see picture at **cup**

**mug²** *verb* (**mugged**, **mugging**)
to attack and rob someone: *She was mugged outside her apartment by a man with a gun.*
—**mugger** *noun* someone who attacks and robs people
—**mugging** *noun* an act of mugging someone: *The mugging happened Saturday night.*

**mug·gy** /ˈmʌgi/ *adjective* (*informal*)
if it is muggy, the weather is hot and there is a lot of water in the air, making you feel uncomfortable: *It was a muggy night, and I couldn't sleep.* **SYNONYM: humid**

**Mu·ham·mad** /muˈhæməd/
the man who started the religion of Islam in the 7th century A.D.

**mule** /myul/ *noun*
an animal that has a DONKEY and a horse as parents

**multi-** /mʌlti/
many: *multicolored* (=having many colors)

**mul·ti·cul·tur·al** /ˌmʌltiˈkʌltʃərəl/ *adjective*
including people or things from many different cultures: *We live in a multicultural society where people of all nationalities live together.*

**mul·ti·me·di·a** /ˌmʌltɪˈmidiə/ *adjective*
using pictures, sounds, and words to give information on a computer: *The multimedia learning software teaches kids with pictures, video, songs, and games.*

**mul·ti·ple¹** /ˈmʌltəpəl/ *adjective* (*formal*)
many: *He suffered multiple injuries to his arms, legs, and head in the accident.*

**multiple²** *noun*
a number that can be divided by a smaller number an exact number of times: *42 is a multiple of 6 because 6 x 7 = 42.*

**ˌmultiple-ˈchoice** *adjective*
a multiple-choice test or question shows you a number of answers, and you must choose the right one

**ˌmultipliˈcation ˌtable** *noun*
a list that shows the results when you multiply a number by another number. For example, the multiplication table for 3 is 1 x 3 = 3, 2 x 3 = 6, 3 x 3 = 9, etc. **SYNONYM: times table**

**mul·ti·ply** /ˈmʌltəˌplaɪ/ *verb* (**multiplied**, **multiplies**)
**1** if you multiply a number, you add it to itself a number of times: *4 multiplied by 5 is 20* (=4 x 5 = 20).
**2** to increase a lot: *Bacteria multiply very quickly in warm conditions.*
—**multiplication** /ˌmʌltəpləˈkeɪʃən/ *noun* the act of multiplying a number

**mul·ti·ra·cial** /ˌmʌltiˈreɪʃəl/ *adjective*
including people of many different races: *We live in a multiracial society with people from all over the world.*

**mum·ble** /ˈmʌmbəl/ *verb*
to say something very quietly, in a way that is not clear: *If you mumble, the rest of the class can't hear or understand you.*
→ see Thesaurus box at **say**[1]

**mum·my** /ˈmʌmi/ *noun* (plural **mummies**)
a dead body that is wrapped in cloth and treated with special chemicals, in order to preserve it. This method of preserving bodies was popular in ancient Egypt.

**mumps** /mʌmps/ *noun*
an illness that makes your throat and neck swell and become painful

**munch** /mʌntʃ/ (*also* **munch on**) *verb*
to eat something in a steady or noisy way: *We munched on popcorn as we watched the movie.*

**mu·nic·i·pal** /myuˈnɪsəpəl/ *adjective*
relating to the government of a town or city: *He is running for mayor in the municipal elections.*

**mu·ral** /ˈmjʊrəl/ *noun*
a large painting that someone has done on a wall: *The school has murals on the walls that the students painted.*

**mur·der**[1] /ˈmɚdɚ/ *noun*
the crime of killing someone on purpose: *Wilson was 23 when he committed the murder.*
→ see Thesaurus box at **crime**

**murder**[2] *verb*
to kill someone on purpose: *The police still do not know who murdered the girl.*
—**murderer** *noun* a person who murders someone: *The murderer spent the rest of his life in prison.* **SYNONYM: killer**

**mur·mur** /ˈmɚmɚ/ *verb*
to say something in a quiet gentle voice: *"Goodnight, dear," she murmured.*
—**murmur** *noun* a quiet voice or a quiet continuous sound: *I lay in bed listening to the murmur of voices downstairs.*
→ see Thesaurus box at **say**[1]

**mus·cle** /ˈmʌsəl/ *noun*
a part of your body under your skin that you use to move: *Running will make your leg muscles stronger.*
[**ORIGIN:** 1300-1400 From the Latin word *musculus*, which means "little mouse," from *mus*, meaning "mouse." A muscle moving was thought to look like a mouse under your skin.]

**mus·cu·lar** /ˈmʌskjəlɚ/ *adjective*
**1** having big strong muscles: *He had muscular arms from lifting weights.*
**2** relating to the muscles: *It is a muscular disease that affects your ability to move.*

**mu·se·um** /myuˈziəm/ *noun*
a building where people can go and see art or other important or valuable objects: *We saw some interesting paintings at the Museum of Modern Art.*
[**ORIGIN:** 1600-1700 From the Greek word *Mouseion*, which means "place of the Muses, or place for learning." The Muses were nine Greek goddesses of music, poetry, and learning.]

**mush** /mʌʃ/ *noun*
something that is soft and wet, in way that is unpleasant: *The fruit was old and had turned to mush.*
—**mushy** *adjective* soft and wet, in a way that is unpleasant: *The vegetables were overcooked and too mushy.*

**mush·room** /ˈmʌʃrum/ *noun*
a type of FUNGUS with a stem and a round top. Some kinds of mushroom can be eaten.
→ see picture on page **A12**

**mu·sic** /ˈmyuzɪk/ *noun*
**1** the sounds that people make when they play instruments or sing: *Ben's in his room, listening to music on his iPod.*

**THESAURUS: music**

**tune** a series of musical notes that are nice to listen to: *Suzy was humming a tune.*

**melody** the main set of musical notes in a tune or piece of music: *It's a good song with a beautiful melody.*

**song** a short piece of music with words: *I heard a great song on the radio.*

**piece/piece of music** music that someone has written: *Learn these three pieces for your next lesson.*

M

**composition** a piece of music that someone has written: *She played one of Schubert's compositions.*

**2** the marks on paper that tell you what music to play or sing: *He can play songs he has heard, but he can't read music.*

[ORIGIN: 1200-1300 From the Greek word *mousike*, which means "art or skill of the Muses." The Muses were nine Greek goddesses of music, poetry, and learning.]

**mu·si·cal¹** /ˈmjuːzɪkəl/ *adjective*

**1** relating to music: *"Do you play a musical instrument?" "Yes, I play the piano."*

**2** good at playing music or singing: *My family is very musical. Everyone sings and plays an instrument.*

**musical²** *noun*

a play or movie that has songs and dancing in it: *"High School Musical" helped make musicals popular with kids again.*

→ see Thesaurus box at **movie**

**mu·si·cian** /mjuːˈzɪʃən/ *noun*

someone who plays or sings music well, or as a job: *He's a well-known jazz musician.*

**Mus·lim** /ˈmʊzləm/ *noun*

someone whose religion is Islam

—**Muslim** *adjective* relating to Islam: *Iraq is mainly a Muslim country.*

**mus·sel** /ˈmʌsəl/ *noun*

a small sea animal with a black shell and a soft body that you can eat

**must¹** /məst; *strong* mʌst/ *verb*

**1** if you must do something, it is very important that you do it: *Everyone must give me their homework by 9 o'clock tomorrow.*

**USAGE: must, have to, have got to**

**must** – used especially in more formal writing when a law or someone who is in charge of something forces you to do something: *All students must have shorts and a T-shirt for P.E.* | *Motorcycle riders must wear helmets.*

**must** – used when you make yourself do something because you think it is a good idea or necessary: *We must visit Grandma on Sunday. We haven't seen her for weeks.* | *I must study for tomorrow's test.*

**have to** – used when a rule, law, situation, etc. forces you to do something and you do not have a choice about it: *You have to pass a test before you are allowed to drive.* | *I have to get this essay finished by tomorrow.*

**have got to** – used in spoken English instead of **have to** or **must** to show how important it is to do something: *I've got to talk to him.*

**2** used to say that you think something is true or probably happened: *The door's open, so she must be at home.* | *There's no more cake – Dad must have eaten it.*

**must²** /mʌst/ *noun*

**be a must** (*informal*) = to be something that you must do, see, or have: *A warm coat is a must if you are going out in the snow.*

**mus·tache** /ˈmʌstæʃ/ *noun*

hair that grows above a man's mouth: *He has a beard and a mustache.* → see picture at **beard**

**mus·tard** /ˈmʌstɚd/ *noun*

a yellow sauce with a hot taste, that is made from the seeds of a plant: *I had a hamburger with mustard and ketchup.*

**mu·ti·ny** /ˈmyutəni/ *noun* (plural **mutinies**)

a situation in which soldiers or SAILORs refuse to obey their leader or captain: *There was a mutiny on the ship, and the sailors took control of it.*

**mut·ter** /ˈmʌtɚ/ *verb*

to say something quietly because you are annoyed or do not want people to hear: *"That's a lie," Lisa muttered, so no one would hear.*

→ see Thesaurus box at **say¹**

**mu·tu·al** [Ac] /ˈmyutʃuəl/ *adjective*

**1** if a feeling is mutual, two people have the same feeling toward each another: *I really like him, and I hope the feeling is mutual.*

**2 a mutual friend/interest** = a friend or interest that two people share: *We discovered we have a mutual friend – we both know Carrie Richards.*

**my** /maɪ/ *adjective*

belonging to me: *It's my birthday tomorrow.*

M

**my·self** /maɪˈself/ *pronoun*
**1** used after "I" and a verb to mean the person who is speaking or writing: *I looked at myself in the mirror.* | *I think I'll make myself a sandwich.*
**2** yourself and no one else: *I chose this dress myself.*
**3 (all) by myself** = alone or without help: *Look, Mommy – I tied my shoelacess all by myself!*

**mys·te·ri·ous** /mɪˈstɪriəs/ *adjective*
strange and difficult to explain or understand: *A lot of people saw the mysterious light in the sky, but no one knew what it was.*
—**mysteriously** *adverb* in a mysterious way: *The money mysteriously disappeared while the room was locked.*
→ see Thesaurus box at **strange**

**mys·ter·y** /ˈmɪstəri/ *noun* (plural **mysteries**)
**1** something that is difficult to explain or understand: *The reason why the ship sank in calm weather is still a mystery.*
**2** a story about a murder or other crime, in which you do not know who COMMITted the crime until the end: *I love reading murder mysteries, but I don't often guess the murderer correctly.*

**mys·ti·fy** /ˈmɪstəˌfaɪ/ *verb* (**mystified, mystifies**)
if something mystifies you, it is very difficult to explain or understand: *Her death has mystified the police, and there are few clues.*

**myth** /mɪθ/ *noun*
**1** an old story about gods, brave men, strange creatures, or events at the beginning of the world: *In Greek myths, the gods lived in a palace on Mount Olympus.*
**2** an idea that many people believe, but that is not true: *It's a myth that men are better drivers than women. They just think they are.*
—**mythical** *adjective* existing in myths, but not real: *The mythical hero Hercules had great physical strength.*
→ see Thesaurus box at **story**
[**ORIGIN:** 1800-1900 From the Greek word *mythos*, which means "story."]

**my·thol·o·gy** /mɪˈθɑlədʒi/ *noun*
old stories about gods, brave men, strange creatures, or events at the beginning of the world: *Cerberus, the three-headed dog of Greek mythology, guarded the entrance to Hades.*
—**mythological** /ˌmɪθəˈlɑdʒɪkəl/ *adjective* existing in myths, but not real: *dragons and other mythological creatures*

# Nn

**nag** /næg/ *verb* (**nagged**, **nagging**)
to keep asking someone to do something, in an annoying way: *Mom's been nagging me to clean up my room, but I don't want to do it.*

**nail¹** /neɪl/ *noun*
**1** the hard flat part at the end of each of your fingers and toes: *Maria had painted her nails red.*
**2** a thin pointed piece of metal that you hit into a piece of wood or a wall with a hammer: *I'll need a few nails to fix this chair.*

**nail**

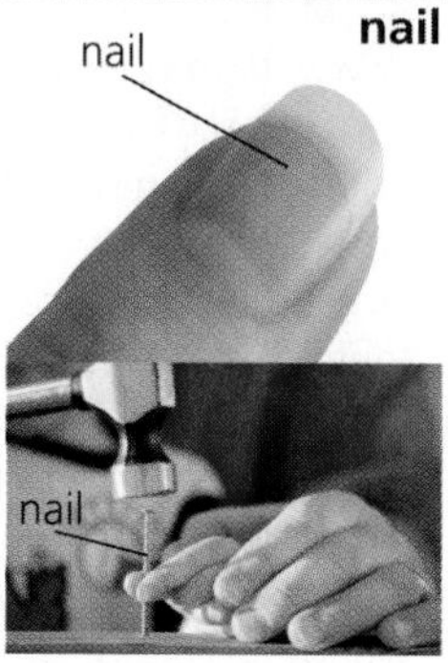


**nail²** *verb*
to join things by hitting nails into them: *We made a boat by nailing old pieces of wood together.*

**ˈnail ˌclipper** *noun*
a small metal tool for cutting the nails on your fingers or toes

**ˈnail file** *noun*
a thin piece of metal with a rough surface that you use for shaping your nails

**ˈnail ˌpolish** *noun*
liquid that a woman paints on her nails to make them look attractive

**na·ïve** /nɑˈiv/ *adjective*
believing that people are nicer and things are easier than they really are because you do not have much experience of life: *She was young and naïve, and trusted people too easily.*
—**naïvely** *adverb* in a naïve way: *He said he loved me, and I naïvely believed him.*
—**naïvete** /nɑˌivˈteɪ/ *noun* the quality of being naïve

**na·ked** /ˈneɪkɪd/ *adjective*
**1** not wearing any clothes: *He had just gotten out of the shower and he was still naked.* **SYNONYM: nude**
**2** **the naked eye** = if something can be seen with the naked eye, it can be seen without using a TELESCOPE or a MICROSCOPE: *These creatures are so small they are invisible to the naked eye.*

**name¹** /neɪm/ *noun*
**1** the word that someone or something is called: *"What's your name?" "Carlos."* | *I can't remember the name of the hotel.*

**THESAURUS: name**

**first name** for example "Bret" in the name Bret Stern

**last name, family name, surname** for example "Potter" in the name Harry Potter

**middle name** the name between your first and last names, for example "Ann" in Lisa Ann Smith

**full name** your complete name: *She wrote her full name, Mary Louise Johnson, in the space on the form.*

**maiden name** a woman's last name before she marries and begins to use her husband's name: *Mrs. Robertson's maiden name was Hansen.*

**nickname** a name your friends and family use for you instead of your real name: *He runs so fast that his nickname is "Flash."*

**pen name, pseudonym** a name a writer uses instead of his or her real name: *Mark Twain is a pen name; his real name was Samuel Clemens.*

**2** **a big/household name** = a famous or important person: *The movie made him a big name in Hollywood.*
**3** **a good/bad name** = if you have a good or bad name, people think you are good or bad: *The company has a very good name.* **SYNONYM: reputation**

**name²** *verb*
**1** to give a name to someone or something: *They named their son Jacob.*

2 to say what the name of someone or something is: *"Name animals that live in Africa." "Lions, elephants, and giraffes."*

**name·ly** /ˈneɪmli/ *adverb* (*formal*)
used for giving more exact information about something you have mentioned: *They both speak the same language, namely Korean.*

**nan·ny** /ˈnæni/ *noun* (plural **nannies**)
a woman that people pay to take care of their children in their home: *The couple hired a nanny to take care of the kids while they were at work.*

**nap** /næp/ *noun*
a short sleep during the day: *Joe's two, so he still takes a nap after lunch.*

**nap·kin** /ˈnæpkɪn/ *noun*
a piece of cloth or paper that you use to clean your mouth or hands when you are eating: *He wiped his mouth with a paper napkin.* → see picture on page **A9**
[**ORIGIN:** 1600-1700 From the old French word *nape*, which means "tablecloth," from the Latin word *mappa*, which means "cloth." The ending "-kin" means "little."]

**nar·cot·ic** /nɑrˈkɑtɪk/ *noun*
a drug that stops pain and usually makes people sleep: *Some narcotics are used in hospitals, but others are illegal.*
—**narcotic** *adjective* relating to a narcotic: *The drug has a narcotic effect, so you will probably fall asleep.*

**nar·rate** /ˈnæreɪt/ *verb*
to describe what is happening in a movie, a television program, or a story: *A well-known actor narrates the documentary.*
—**narration** /næˈreɪʃən/ *noun* a description of what is happening in a movie, television program, or story
—**narrator** *noun* the person who narrates a movie, television program, or story: *The narrator of the story is a young girl.*

**nar·ra·tive** /ˈnærətɪv/ *noun*
the description of events in a story: *The writer based the narrative on events from his own childhood.*

**narrow**

a narrow path a wide path

**nar·row** /ˈnæroʊ/ *adjective*
**1** measuring only a small distance from one side to the other: *In the old part of the town, the streets were very narrow, and cars could not drive down them.* **ANTONYM: wide**
**2 a narrow escape** = an occasion when something bad almost happens to you: *I had a narrow escape when a falling rock nearly hit me.*
—**narrowly** *adverb* by only a small amount: *The driver narrowly escaped injury when a tree fell on her car.*

**ˌnarrow-ˈminded** *adjective*
not willing to accept ideas that are new or different: *People in very small towns are sometimes narrow-minded and unaccepting of new ideas or people.*

**na·sal** /ˈneɪzəl/ *adjective*
relating to the nose: *He couldn't breathe through his nose because his nasal passages were blocked.*

**nas·ty** /ˈnæsti/ *adjective* (**nastier**, **nastiest**)
**1** very bad or severe: *It was a nasty accident and several people were hurt.*
**2** having an unpleasant taste, smell, or appearance: *That medicine has a nasty taste.*
**3** not kind or nice: *She wrote him a nasty letter when she was angry.*

**na·tion** /ˈneɪʃən/ *noun*
**1** all the people living in a country: *The president will give a speech to the nation.*
**2** a country with its own government: *He declared the republic an independent nation.*
→ see Thesaurus box at **country**, **race**[1]
[**ORIGIN:** 1200-1300 From the Latin word *natio*, from *natus*, which means "born." A nation was originally a group of people who were born in the same place or from the same group of families.]

**WORD FAMILY: nation**

**nation** *noun* | **national** *adjective* | **nationally** *adverb* | **nationality** *noun* | **nationalism** *noun* | **nationalist** *noun* | **nationalistic** *adjective*

**na·tion·al** /ˈnæʃənəl/ *adjective*
relating to the whole of a nation: *Today is a national holiday, so no one has to go to work.* | *national elections for president*

**ˌnational ˈanthem** *noun*
the official song of a nation, that people sing or play on special occasions

**na·tion·al·ism** /ˈnæʃənəlˌɪzəm/ *noun*
the belief that your country is good, or better than any other country
—**nationalist** *noun* someone who is very proud of his or her country
—**nationalistic** /ˌnæʃənlˈɪstɪk/ *adjective* relating to nationalism: *a nationalistic speech*

**na·tion·al·i·ty** /ˌnæʃəˈnæləti/ *noun* (plural **nationalities**)
the fact of being a citizen of a particular country: *He has Canadian nationality but he lives in the U.S.* **SYNONYM: citizenship**

**na·tion·al·ly** /ˈnæʃənəli/ *adverb*
everywhere in a country: *The Super Bowl is broadcast nationally.*

**ˌnational ˈpark** *noun*
a large area of natural land that the government protects, and allows people to visit: *Yellowstone National Park*

**na·tion·wide** /ˌneɪʃənˈwaɪd/ *adjective, adverb*
in every part of a country: *The band went on a nationwide tour from California to Maine.*

**na·tive**¹ /ˈneɪtɪv/ *adjective*
**1** **native language/tongue** = the first language you spoke: *She speaks English well, but her native language is Japanese.*
**2** (*formal*) used for talking about the place where you were born: *Two years later, he returned from Japan to his native South Africa.*
**3** native plants or animals grow or live naturally in a place: *This type of tree is not native to America – it was brought here from Europe.*

**native**² *noun* (*formal*)
someone who was born in a particular country: *Andrea is a native of Brazil, but she moved to the U.S. with her parents.*

**ˌNative Aˈmerican** *noun*
someone who belongs to one of the tribes that lived in North America before Europeans arrived
—**Native American** *adjective* relating to Native Americans: *the Native American languages*

**ˌnative ˈspeaker** *noun*
someone who speaks a language as his or her first language: *He was born in Rome and is a native speaker of Italian.*

**nat·u·ral** /ˈnætʃərəl/ *adjective*
**1** existing in nature, and not made by people: *I love the natural beauty of the mountains.* | *earthquakes and other natural disasters* **ANTONYM: man-made**
**2** normal or usual: *It's natural to feel nervous before you start at a new school.* **ANTONYM: unnatural**
**3** **a natural leader/athlete, etc.** = someone who is born with an ability to lead people, play sports, etc.: *He was tall and slim and a natural athlete.*

**nat·u·ral·ize** /ˈnætʃərəlaɪz/ *verb*
**be naturalized** = to become a citizen of a different country: *He was born in Lebanon, but was naturalized as a U.S. citizen in 1994.*
—**naturalized** *adjective* having been naturalized: *a naturalized U.S. citizen*
—**naturalization** /ˌnætʃərələˈzeɪʃən/ *noun* the process of being naturalized

**nat·u·ral·ly** /ˈnætʃərəli/ *adverb*
**1** happening or existing on its own, without people doing anything to make it happen or exist: *Alison's hair is naturally curly – she doesn't have to curl it.*
**2** in a way that is normal or not surprising: *Naturally, we wanted to win.*

**na·ture** /ˈneɪtʃɚ/ *noun*
**1** the world and everything in it that people have not made, such as plants, animals, or the weather: *I grew up in the country, surrounded by nature.*
**2** what someone's character is like: *Jenny has a cheerful nature, which means she's fun to be around.*

**naugh·ty** /ˈnɔti/ *adjective*
**1** a naughty child behaves badly, for example by being rude or not obeying a parent or teacher: *When Anthony was naughty, his parents made him go to his room.*
**2** a naughty word is a bad word that you should not say

**nau·se·a** /ˈnɔziə/ *noun* (*formal*)
the feeling you have when you think you are going to VOMIT: *Some people feel nausea when they travel on a boat over rough waves.*
[**ORIGIN:** 1400-1500 From the Greek word *nausia*, which means "seasickness," from *naus*, meaning "ship."]

**na·val** /ˈneɪvəl/ *adjective*
relating to the navy: *a naval officer*

**na·vel** /ˈneɪvəl/ *noun* (*formal*)
another word for a BELLY BUTTON

**nav·i·gate** /ˈnævəˌgeɪt/ *verb*
**1** to decide which direction a car, ship, or airplane should travel: *Sailors used to navigate using the stars.*
**2** to move around a website or from one website to another: *The university's website is easy to navigate.*
**3** to sail along a river or area of water: *In some places, the river is too narrow to navigate.*
—**navigator** *noun* a person on a ship or airplane who decides which direction to travel
—**navigation** /ˌnævəˈgeɪʃən/ *noun* the act of deciding which direction to travel: *GPS equipment makes navigation easy – you just turn when it tells you to turn.*
[**ORIGIN:** 1500-1600 From the Latin word *navigare*, which means "to sail," from *navis*, meaning "ship."]

**na·vy** /ˈneɪvi/ *noun* (plural **navies**)
the organization that a country's ships and sailors belong to: *Frank is in the navy and sails around the world.* | *After high school, I joined the navy.*
[**ORIGIN:** 1300-1400 From the Old French word *navie*, which means "group of ships," from the Latin word *navis*, which means "ship."]

**ˌnavy ˈblue** (*also* **navy**) *adjective, noun*
a very dark blue color: *a navy blue jacket*

**near¹** /nɪr/ *adverb, preposition*
**1** close to someone or something: *The hotel was near the beach.* | *Is there a bank near here?*

**THESAURUS: near**

**close** not far from someone or something: *He sat close to his mom.*

**not far/not far away** not a long distance away: *The park's not far away.*

**nearby** near here or near a particular place: *Is there a grocery store nearby?* | *I lived in Boston for a year and then moved to the nearby town of Newton.*

**within walking distance** easy to walk to from somewhere: *The school is within walking distance of their house.*

**local** local stores, schools, and other things are in the area where you live: *She teaches at one of the local schools.*

**neighboring** a neighboring country, state, or town is next to another country, state, or town: *The storm affected Florida and the neighboring states of Georgia and Alabama.*

**2** close to a time or event: *Near the end of the game, a lot of people started to leave because it was clear who was going to win.*

**near²** *adjective*
**1** only a short distance from you: *We quickly drove to the nearest hospital.*
**2 in the near future** = soon: *I will visit you again in the near future.*
**3** used for describing something bad that almost happens: *There was a near disaster in the kitchen when I almost dropped the turkey.*

**near·by** /ˌnɪrˈbaɪ/ *adverb, adjective*
only a short distance from you or your home: *My friend Amy lives nearby, so we see each*

*other often.* | *The kids rode their bikes to a nearby pool to go swimming.*
→ see Thesaurus box at **near¹**



**near·ly** /ˈnɪrli/ *adverb*
**1** almost: *He's nearly ten years old. His birthday is next month.*
**2 not nearly** = much less than you need: *I've saved $50, but that's not nearly enough to buy a good bicycle.*

**near·sight·ed** /ˈnɪrˌsaɪtɪd/ *adjective*
unable to see things that are far away from you: *I'm nearsighted, so I wear glasses to see what the teacher writes on the board.* **ANTONYM: farsighted**

**neat** /nit/ *adjective*
**1** clean and in good order: *They keep their house neat and clean, and it always looks great when I visit.*
**2** (*informal*) you use this to say that you like something or someone a lot: *Todd's new computer is really neat. It has a lot of great features.* **SYNONYM: great**
**3** a neat way of doing something is simple and works well: *That's a neat way of solving the problem. It's really clever.*
—**neatly** *adverb* in a way that is clean and in good order: *The young women were neatly dressed in white uniforms.*
—**neatness** *noun* the state of being clean and in good order
[**ORIGIN:** 1500-1600 From the French word *net*, from the Latin word *nitidus*, which means "bright or beautiful."]

**nec·es·sar·i·ly** /ˌnesəˈserəli/ *adverb*
**not necessarily** = used for saying that something may not always be true: *Having a lot of money does not necessarily make you happy.*

**nec·es·sar·y** /ˈnesəˌseri/ *adjective*
if something is necessary, you need to have it or do it: *A good tent is necessary for camping outdoors.* | *It's necessary to study hard if you want to get good grades.*

**WORD FAMILY: necessary**
**necessary** *adjective* | **necessity** *noun*

**ne·ces·si·ty** /nəˈsesəti/ *noun* (plural **necessities**) (*formal*)
something you need to have or do: *Light is a necessity for plants to grow.*

**neck** /nek/ *noun*
**1** the part of your body between your head and your shoulders: *She was wearing a gold chain around her neck.* | *Swans are large white water birds with long necks.*
**2** the narrow part at the end of something such as a bottle: *He held the bottle of soda by its neck.*
**3 neck and neck** (*informal*) = having an equal chance of winning in a competition or race: *It was an exciting race, with two of the horses running neck and neck.*
[**ORIGIN:** From the old English word *hnecca.*]

**neck·lace** /ˈnek-ləs/ *noun*
a piece of jewelry that you wear around your neck: *Sue was wearing a silver necklace.* → see picture on page **A6**

**neck·tie** /ˈnektaɪ/ *noun*
another word for a TIE: *He put on a white shirt and a purple necktie.*

**nec·tar** /ˈnektɚ/ *noun*
the sweet liquid that BEEs collect from flowers: *Bees use nectar to make honey.*

**nec·ta·rine** /ˌnektəˈrin/ *noun*
a juicy fruit that has a smooth yellow and red skin and a big seed inside → see picture on page **A13**

**need¹** /nid/ *verb*
**1** if you need something, you must have it in order to do something: *You need flour to make pancakes.* | *I'm too hot – I need some fresh air.*
**2 need to do something** = to have to do something: *I need to write my English paper tonight.* | *There's something I need to tell you.*

**need²** *noun*
**1** if there is a need for something, it is necessary and you must have it: *There's a need for more nurses in our hospitals.* | *The boys are safe now, so there is no need to worry.*
**2** something that you want to have or must have: *A small baby's needs are simple: food, sleep, and love.*
**3 in need of something** (*formal*) = needing to have something: *The house is in need of repairs.*
**4 in need** = not having enough food or money: *We're collecting money for children in need.*

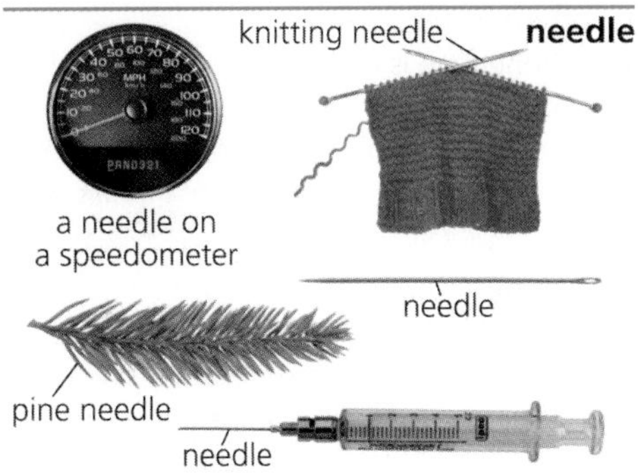


**nee·dle** /ˈnidl/ *noun*
**1** a thin pointed piece of metal with a hole at one end for thread, that you use for sewing: *a needle and thread*
**2** a thin hollow sharp piece of metal that a doctor or nurse uses to put medicine into your body or take blood out: *The nurse used a needle to take a blood sample from my arm.*
**3** (*also* **knitting needle**) one of two pointed sticks used for KNITting
**4** a thin pointed leaf from a tree such as a PINE tree: *There were dry needles all over the carpet from the Christmas tree.*
**5** a long thin part on a piece of electrical equipment, that points to measurements or directions: *The needle on the car's gas gauge was pointing to "empty."*
[**ORIGIN:** From the old English word *nædl.*]

**need·less** /ˈnidləs/ *adjective* (*formal*)
**1** not necessary: *It would have saved needless worry if you had just called to tell me where you were.*
**2** **needless to say** = used when you say something that someone already knows or expects: *Needless to say, her four kids keep her very busy.*
—**needlessly** *adverb* in a way that is not necessary: *People are suffering needlessly because of poor health care.*

**need·y** /ˈnidi/ *adjective*
not having enough money or food: *They collect food and give it to needy families.*
→ see Thesaurus box at **poor**

**neg·a·tive**[1] Ac /ˈnegətɪv/ *adjective*
**1** bad or harmful: *Too much TV can have a negative effect on kids.* **ANTONYM: positive**
**2** thinking only about what is bad or wrong with a situation or person: *Don't be so negative! We can do this! | a negative attitude* **ANTONYM: positive**
**3** meaning "no" or containing a word such as "not" or "never": *"They do not eat meat" is a negative sentence.*
**4** a negative number is less than zero: *A negative number is shown by a minus sign, for example -3.*
**5** a medical test that is negative shows that someone does not have a disease or condition: *The tests were negative – I'm fine.* **ANTONYM: positive**
—**negatively** *adverb* in a way that shows dislike of something: *A lot of people reacted negatively to the idea of a new airport.*

**negative**[2] Ac *noun*
**1** a piece of film from which you print a photograph
**2** something bad about a plan, idea, or situation: *I think it's a good idea, and I can't see any negatives.* **ANTONYM: positive**
**3** (*formal*) a word or expression that is used to say no: *"Do you need help?" "Negative."*

**ne·glect**[1] /nɪˈglekt/ *verb*
**1** to not give someone or something enough care or attention: *Martin was working too hard and neglecting his family.*
**2** **neglect to do something** (*formal*) = to not do something that you should do: *He neglected to tell his mother that he had to stay after school, so she didn't know he would be late.*
—**neglected** *adjective* not cared for well: *The organization helps neglected children.*

**neglect**[2] *noun*
when someone or something is not cared for well: *I saw a lot of young kids suffering from neglect because their parents took drugs.*

**ne·go·ti·ate** /nɪˈgoʊʃiˌeɪt/ *verb* (*formal*)
to talk about something in order to get an agreement: *Leaders from both countries met to try and negotiate an end to the war.*
—**negotiator** *noun* someone who negotiates
—**negotiation** /nɪˌgoʊʃiˈeɪʃən/ *noun* the act of negotiating: *The plan is still under negotiation – nothing has been agreed yet.*
[**ORIGIN:** 1500-1600 From the Latin word *negotiari,* which means "to do business," from

*negotium*, meaning "business." *Negotium* comes from *neg-* and *otium*, which mean "not" and "time for relaxing."]



**neigh** /neɪ/ *verb*
if a horse neighs, it makes a long loud sound
—**neigh** *noun* the sound that a horse makes

**neigh·bor** /ˈneɪbɚ/ *noun*
**1** someone who lives in the house next to your house, or very near you: *The neighbor came over to borrow a ladder.* | *John is my next-door neighbor.*
**2** a country that is next to another country: *Canada and Mexico are neighbors of the U.S.*
**3** someone who is sitting next to you: *His teacher saw him pass a note to his neighbor.*
—**neighboring** *adjective* next to a place: *We went to Indiana and the neighboring states of Ohio and Illinois.*
[**ORIGIN:** From the old English word *neahgebur*, from *neah* and *gebur*, which mean "near" and "someone living somewhere."]

**neigh·bor·hood** /ˈneɪbɚˌhʊd/ *noun*
a small area of a town, where there are places to live rather than a lot of businesses: *I know all the kids in my neighborhood.*
→ see Thesaurus box at **area**

**nei·ther¹** /ˈniðɚ/ *adjective, pronoun*
not one and not the other of two people or things: *It was a boring game, and neither team played well.* | *We both started laughing, and then neither of us could stop.*

**neither²** *adverb*
you use this for agreeing with a negative statement: *"I don't like coffee." "Neither do I."* | *"Tom can't swim yet." "Neither can Sam."*

**neither³** *conjunction*
**neither ... nor ...** = not one and not the other: *Neither his mother nor his father speaks English.*

**ne·on** /ˈniɑn/ *noun*
a gas used in electric lights and signs, that shines very brightly when electricity goes through it: *the bright neon lights of Las Vegas*

**neph·ew** /ˈnefju/ *noun*
**1** the son of your brother or sister
**2** the son of the brother or sister of your husband or wife

**Nep·tune** /ˈneptun/ *noun*
the eighth PLANET from the Sun

**nerd** /nɚd/ *noun* (*informal*)
someone who is boring, and is interested only in boring things: *Alex didn't play sports, and the guys at school thought he was a nerd.*
—**nerdy** *adjective* being a nerd: *Mark was a nerdy engineer.*

**nerve** /nɚv/ *noun*
**1** the ability to do something difficult or brave: *I wanted to jump from the bridge into the river, but I didn't have the nerve.*
**2** a part in your body like a long thin thread that sends information between your brain and other parts of your body: *When we want to move, our nerves send a message to our muscles.*
**3 have the nerve to do something** (*informal*) = to do something that seems rude or unreasonable: *He had the nerve to ask me for more money!*
**4 nerves** = the feeling of being nervous: *I do some breathing exercises to calm my nerves before going on stage.*
**5 get on someone's nerves** = to annoy someone: *Stop complaining. You're getting on my nerves.*

**ˈnerve-ˌracking** (*also* **nerve-wracking**) *adjective*
very worrying or frightening: *Taking tests is always nerve-racking.*

**nerv·ous** /ˈnɚvəs/ *adjective*
**1** worried or frightened: *I get really nervous before going to the dentist.* → see picture on page **A23**
**2** a nervous person gets worried or upset easily: *My mother's a nervous person, so she doesn't like driving alone.*
**3** relating to the nerves in your body: *The human body's nervous system is what allows us to feel heat, pressure, and pain.*
—**nervously** *adverb* in a worried or frightened way: *"I thought I heard a noise downstairs," she said nervously.*
—**nervousness** *noun* the state of being worried or frightened
→ see Thesaurus box at **worried**

**ˌnervous ˈbreakdown** *noun*
a mental illness in which someone is very worried and upset all the time, and cannot live normally: *He got really stressed out at work and had a nervous breakdown.*

**nest** /nest/ *noun*
**1** a place that a bird makes to lay its eggs in: *A bird is building a nest in that tree.*
**2** a place where some small animals or insects live: *a wasps' nest*

**net** /net/ *noun*
**1** material made of string or wire tied together with spaces in between, used for catching fish, insects, or animals: *a fishing net*
**2** a thing made of string that you throw a basketball through
**3** a thing made of string that goes in the middle of a tennis, VOLLEYBALL, or BADMINTON court
**4 the Net** = another word for the INTERNET: *You can find a lot of useful information on the Net.*

**net·work** [Ac] /ˈnetwɚk/ *noun*
**1** a system of things such as roads, wires, or computers that are connected to each other: *the university's computer network* | *The city has a complicated network of streets.*
**2** a radio or television company that shows the same programs across the country: *the ABC television network*

**neu·rot·ic** /nʊˈrɑtɪk/ *adjective*
worried or frightened about something in a way that is not normal: *Some people are neurotic about their health and always believe they are sick.*

**neut·er** /ˈnutɚ/ *adjective*
**1** in English, a neuter noun or PRONOUN is used to talk about things: *"It" is a neuter pronoun.*
**2** in other languages, a noun or adjective that is not MASCULINE or FEMININE: *In the Norwegian language, the word for "house" is neuter, but the word for "chair" is masculine.*

**neu·tral** [Ac] /ˈnutrəl/ *adjective*
**1** not supporting any country, person, or group in a war or argument: *Switzerland was neutral during World War II.*
**2** a neutral color is not strong or bright: *Gray is a neutral color.*
—**neutrality** /nuˈtræləti/ *noun* the state of not supporting any country, person, or group in a war or argument
[**ORIGIN:** 1400-1500 From the Latin word *neuter*, which means "neither of two things."]

**neu·tral·ize** [Ac] /ˈnutrəˌlaɪz/ *verb* (*formal*)
to stop something from having an effect: *The spray helps neutralize pet smells and keeps your home smelling fresh.*

**neu·tron** /ˈnutrɑn/ *noun*
a very small part in the NUCLEUS of an atom: *Neutrons have no electrical charge.* → see picture at **atom**

**nev·er** /ˈnevɚ/ *adverb*
**1** at no time: *I've never been to Europe, but I hope to go there one day.* | *She'll never forgive him for saying that.*
**2 never mind** = you use this for telling someone that something is not important: *"Oh no, we missed the bus!" "Never mind, it's not too far to walk."*

**nev·er·the·less** [Ac] /ˌnevɚðəˈles/ *adverb* (*formal*)
in spite of that: *He spotted a small but nevertheless important mistake in the letter.*

**new** /nu/ *adjective*
**1** if something is new, it was made or produced recently: *The city is building a new football stadium.* | *New technology is making our lives easier.* **ANTONYM: old**

**THESAURUS: new**

**recent** used about something that was new or that happened a short time ago: *This is a recent photograph of him, taken about a month ago.*

N

N

**modern** used about things belonging to the present time, that are different from earlier things of the same kind: *There are a few old buildings, but most of them are modern.*

**original** new and different from anything that has been done or thought of before: *The book is interesting and has some original ideas.*

**fresh** used about food that was made, picked, or prepared only a short time ago: *I love the smell of fresh bread.*

**latest** newest and most recent, used especially about movies, books, or fashion: *We're going to see his latest movie.*

**2** not owned or used by anyone before: *He bought a brand new car.* **ANTONYM: used**
**3** not one that you had, used, or experienced before: *Do you like your new teacher?* | *Learning a new language is always hard.*
**4** if something is new, people have only just discovered it: *Scientists are always discovering new creatures at the bottom of the sea.*
**5** if you are new to a place, you started living, studying, or working there recently: *I'm new to the area – I've only been here a couple of weeks.* | *Could you show the new students around the school?*
—**newness** *noun* the state of being new

**new·born** /ˈnubɔrn/ *adjective*
born very recently: *Newborn babies sleep a lot.*

**new·com·er** /ˈnuˌkʌmɚ/ *noun*
someone who has recently arrived somewhere: *Are you a newcomer to San Diego or have you lived here for a while?*

**new·ly** /ˈnuli/ *adverb*
**newly arrived/discovered, etc.** = very recently arrived, discovered, etc.: *I just bought the band's newly released CD.*
→ see Thesaurus box at **recently**

**new·ly·wed** /ˈnuliˌwed/ *noun*
a person who has recently gotten married: *The newlyweds are on their honeymoon.*

**ˌnew ˈmoon** *noun*
the moon when it first appears in the sky as a thin curved shape

**news** /nuz/ *noun*
**1** reports in the newspapers or on television or the radio about things that are happening in the world: *I like reading the sports news in the newspaper.* | *Dad turned on the TV to watch the news.*
**2** information about things that have happened in someone's life recently: *My friend Diane called me to tell me all her news.*

**GRAMMAR: news**

**News** looks like a plural, but it is not a plural. It is followed by a singular verb form such as "is" or "has": *The news about the field trip was very exciting.*

You can say **some news**, **any news**, etc., or **a piece of news**: *Is there any interesting news in the paper?*

**news·cast** /ˈnuzkæst/ *noun*
a news program on television or the radio: *the evening newscast*
—**newscaster** *noun* someone who reads the news on television **SYNONYM: anchor**

**news·pa·per** /ˈnuzˌpeɪpɚ/ *noun*
pieces of thin paper that have news printed on them, that you can buy and read every day or every week: *I read about the football game in the newspaper.* **SYNONYM: paper**

**news·stand** /ˈnuzˌstænd/ *noun*
a place on a street where you can buy newspapers and magazines

**ˌnew ˈyear** *noun*
the year that will start soon: *We're moving to a different house in the new year.*

**ˌNew Year's ˈDay** *noun*
January 1: *Most offices are closed on New Year's Day.*

**ˌNew Year's ˈEve** *noun*
December 31: *Are you going to a party on New Year's Eve?*

**next**[1] /nekst/ *adjective, pronoun*
**1** the next one is the one after this one: *School starts next Monday.* | *I'll see you next week.* | *Be more careful next time.*
**2** the person or thing that is after the present one: *What's next on the shopping list?*

3 closest to where you are now: *Turn left at the next street.*
→ see Thesaurus box at **after**

**next²** *adverb*
1 after now, or after you have done something else: *We're almost finished. What do you want to do next?* | *Next, I'm going to show you how to make cookies.*
2 **next to someone or something** = close to someone or something, with no other person or thing in between: *I sat next to Danny on the bus so we could talk.* **SYNONYM: beside**
3 **next to nothing** = very little: *She was feeling sick and ate next to nothing.*

**next 'door** *adverb*
in the room or building that is next to another room or building: *My friend's apartment is next door.*

**ˌnext-door 'neighbor** *noun*
someone who lives in the house or apartment next to yours: *Our next-door neighbors will take care of the cats when we are on vacation.*

**nib·ble** /ˈnɪbəl/ *verb*
to eat food by taking small bites: *I wasn't very hungry, so I just nibbled on some potato chips.*

**nice** /naɪs/ *adjective*
1 pleasant, attractive, or enjoyable: *Michael looks nice in a suit.* | *Did you have a nice time at the party?*

**THESAURUS: nice**

**enjoyable** something enjoyable makes you have fun and be happy because it is interesting or exciting: *It's an enjoyable movie.*

**pleasant** something pleasant is peaceful or relaxing and you enjoy it: *It had been a pleasant evening.*

**great/fantastic/wonderful** something great, fantastic, or wonderful is very good or enjoyable and you like it a lot: *"How was your vacation?" "Wonderful!"* | *We had a great time at the beach.*

2 friendly or kind: *She's a nice old lady and fun to visit.* | *Everyone was very nice to me.*
3 used to say that you think something is good or is what you want to do: *It was nice to be back home again.* | *It would be nice to learn to play the guitar.*
4 **nice to meet you** = used when you are meeting someone for the first time: *"Hi, I'm Joe." "Hi, I'm Steve. Nice to meet you."*
—**niceness** *noun* the quality of being nice
→ see Thesaurus box at **kind²**
[ORIGIN: 1200-1300 From an old French word meaning "stupid," from the Latin word *nescius*, which means "not knowing something." This word has gone through many changes in meaning, and has meant "fussy" and "delicate."]

**nice·ly** /ˈnaɪsli/ *adverb*
1 in a pleasant, attractive, or satisfactory way: *The girls were nicely dressed.* | *Brian's broken leg is healing nicely.* **SYNONYM: well**
2 in a polite or friendly way: *I'm sure he'll help if you ask him nicely.*

**nick·el** /ˈnɪkəl/ *noun*
1 a coin used in the U.S. and Canada, that is worth five cents
2 a hard silver colored metal
→ see Thesaurus box at **money**
[ORIGIN: 1700-1800 From the German word *Kupfernickel*, which referred to a substance from which people could get the metal nickel. This word was formed from *Kupfer*, meaning "copper" and *Nickel*, meaning "spirit that plays tricks" because the substance contains no copper, even though it looks like copper.]

**nick·name** /ˈnɪkneɪm/ *noun*
a name that your friends or family use instead of your real name: *His nickname was "Tiny" because he was very short.*
—**nickname** *verb* to give someone another name
→ see Thesaurus box at **name¹**
[ORIGIN: 1400-1500 From the old English word *eke*, which means "also," and the word "name." The phrase "an ekename" became "a nekename" and then "a nickname."]

**nic·o·tine** /ˈnɪkəˌtin/ *noun*
a substance in tobacco, that makes it difficult for people to stop smoking: *Smokers are addicted to the nicotine in cigarettes.*

**niece** /nis/ *noun*
the daughter of your brother or sister, or the daughter of your husband's or wife's brother or sister: *This is my niece, Kelli. She's my sister's daughter.*

**night** /naɪt/ *noun*
**1** the part of the day when it is dark and most people are sleeping: *It was a hot night and I couldn't sleep. | We went out at night to look at the stars.*
**2** the evening: *We have dinner together as a family almost every night.*
**3 night and day** (*also* **day and night**) = all the time: *It rained day and night.*

N

**night·club** /ˈnaɪtklʌb/ *noun*
a place where people go to drink and dance that is open late at night

**night·fall** /ˈnaɪtfɔl/ *noun*
the time when it begins to get dark in the evening: *We drove until nightfall and then we stopped at a motel.* **SYNONYM: dusk**

**night·gown** /ˈnaɪtgaʊn/ *noun*
a piece of loose clothing, like a dress, that a woman wears in bed: *She put on her night-gown, brushed her teeth, and went to bed.*

**night·in·gale** /ˈnaɪtɪŋˌgeɪl/ *noun*
a small wild bird that sings very beautifully, especially at night

**night·life** /ˈnaɪtlaɪf/ *noun*
all the entertainment that people can take part in during the evening in towns and cities, for example dancing and going to restaurants: *Restaurants, clubs, and shows give New York City an exciting nightlife.*

**night·ly** /ˈnaɪtli/ *adjective, adverb*
happening every night: *The report was on the nightly TV news.*

**night·mare** /ˈnaɪtmer/ *noun*
**1** a very frightening dream: *He still has night-mares about the accident.*
**2 be a nightmare** (*informal*) = if a situation is a nightmare, it is difficult, bad, or frightening: *The freeway can be a nightmare at rush hour because there is so much traffic.*
[**ORIGIN:** 1200-1300 From "night" and the old English word *mare*, which means "evil spirit."]

**ˈnight school** *noun*
classes taught at night, for people who work during the day: *After work, Juan goes to night school to study English.*

**ˈnight shift** *noun*
**1** a period of time at night when people work: *My mother works the night shift as a nurse at the hospital.*
**2** the group of people who work on the night shift: *The night shift starts to arrive about 9:45 p.m.*

**night·time** /ˈnaɪt-taɪm/ *noun*
the time during the night when the sky is dark: *The desert is hot during the day, but cold at nighttime.* **ANTONYM: daytime**

**nine** /naɪn/ *number*
**1** 9: *I rode nine miles on my bicycle today.*
**2** nine O'CLOCK: *I have to be in school by nine.*
**3** nine years old: *I'll be nine next Tuesday.*

**nine·teen** /ˌnaɪnˈtin/ *number*
**1** 19: *My parents have been married for nineteen years.*
**2** nineteen years old: *He's nineteen, but he looks older.*
—**nineteenth** /ˌnaɪnˈtinθ/ *number* 19th or 1/19

**nine·ty** /ˈnaɪnti/ *number*
**1** 90: *A soccer game lasts ninety minutes.*
**2** ninety years old: *Grandpa is ninety.*
**3 the nineties** (*also* **the '90s**) = the years between 1990 and 1999: *They won the World Series four times in the nineties.*
**4 in your nineties** = between 90 and 99 years old: *My grandmother is in her nineties.*
**5 in the nineties** = between 90 and 99 FAHRENHEIT in temperature: *It was hot, with temperatures in the nineties.*
—**ninetieth** /ˈnaɪntiɪθ/ *number* 90th or 1/90

**ninth** /naɪnθ/ *number*
**1** 9th
**2** 1/9

**nip** /nɪp/ *verb* (**nipped**, **nipping**)
to bite someone or something with small sharp bites: *The puppy kept nipping my ankle.*

**nip·ple** /ˈnɪpəl/ *noun*
**1** the dark raised circle in the middle of a woman's breast that a baby sucks in order to get milk
**2** one of the two dark raised circles on a man's chest
**3** the small piece of rubber on the end of a baby's bottle

**ni·tro·gen** /ˈnaɪtrədʒən/ *noun* (*written abbreviation*: **N**)
a gas that is the main part of the Earth's air

**nit·ty-grit·ty** /ˈnɪti ˌgrɪti/ *noun (informal)*
the important details of how an agreement or activity can be done: *Let's get down to the nitty-gritty and talk about the cost.*

**no**[1] /noʊ/ *adverb*
**1** used to answer a question when something is not true or when you do not want something: *"Is your sister married?" "No, she's not. She's still single." | "Do you need a ride home?" "No, thanks. I'm going to walk."*
**ANTONYM: yes**
**2** used when you do not agree with something someone says: *"You and your sister are very alike." "No, we're not!"* **ANTONYM: yes**

**no**[2] *adjective*
**1** not any: *There are no chocolates left in the box.*
**2 No Parking/No Smoking, etc.** = used on signs that say something is not allowed in a place

**no·bil·i·ty** /noʊˈbɪləti/ *noun*
the group of people in some countries who have the highest social class: *His grandfather was a Duke in the Russian nobility.*

**no·ble** /ˈnoʊbəl/ *adjective*
**1** for the good of other people, not yourself: *The group raises money for noble causes, such as helping the poor in Africa.*
**2** belonging to the richest or most respected social group, in some countries: *He was born into a noble family.*
—**nobly** *adverb* in a noble way

**no·bod·y**[1] /ˈnoʊˌbɑdi/ *pronoun*
no person: *I knocked, but nobody was home.*
**SYNONYM: no one**

**nobody**[2] *noun* (plural **nobodies**)
someone who is not important, successful, or famous: *When his first movie was a hit, he went from being a nobody to being a star.*

**noc·tur·nal** /nɑkˈtɚnl/ *adjective*
nocturnal animals sleep during the day and are awake at night: *Mice are nocturnal so you don't often see them in the daytime.*

**nod** /nɑd/ *verb* (**nodded**, **nodding**)
**1** to move your head up and down, to show that you agree with something or understand something: *"Yes," he said, nodding his head.*
**2** to move your head up and down once in order to greet someone or to give someone instructions to do something: *"Sally's in there," Jim said, nodding toward the door.*
—**nod** *noun* an act of nodding: *He gave a nod of agreement.*

**PHRASAL VERB**
**nod off** *(informal)*
to begin to sleep when you do not plan to: *I keep nodding off in front of the TV.*

**noise** /nɔɪz/ *noun*
a loud or annoying sound: *The noise of the police siren woke the baby. | Why are the kids making so much noise?*

**nois·y** /ˈnɔɪzi/ *adjective* (**noisier**, **noisiest**)
**1** making a lot of noise: *A noisy crowd of hockey fans watched the game. | Jet engines are really noisy.*
**2** filled with noise: *The restaurant was crowded and noisy.*
—**noisily** *adverb* in a noisy way: *They talked and laughed noisily.*

**no·mad** /ˈnoʊmæd/ *noun*
a member of a group of people that move from place to place to find food: *Nomads traveled the plains hunting and looking for food.*
—**nomadic** /noʊˈmædɪk/ *adjective* relating to nomads
[**ORIGIN:** 1500-1600 From the Greek word *Nomades*, which means "people who move around to find grass for their animals," from *nomos*, which means "place where animals can eat grass."]

**nom·i·nate** /ˈnɑməˌneɪt/ *verb*
to officially suggest someone or something for an important job or prize: *The movie has been nominated for three Academy Awards.*
—**nomination** /ˌnɑməˈneɪʃən/ *noun* the act of nominating someone or something for a job or prize
[**ORIGIN:** 1500-1600 From the Latin word *nominare*, from *nomen*, which means "name."]

**none** /nʌn/ *pronoun*
**1** not any of something: *"Can I have some more pie?" "Sorry, there's none left." | None of the information they gave us was correct.*
**2** not one person or thing in a group: *None of my friends like baseball.*

**none·the·less** [Ac] /ˌnʌnðəˈles/ *adverb* (*formal*)
used when saying something that is surprising, after what you have just said: *Everyone in the family works, but nonetheless they are still poor.* **SYNONYMS: however, nevertheless**

**non·ex·ist·ent** /ˌnɑnɪgˈzɪstənt/ *adjective*
not present in a particular place: *In this small town, traffic accidents are almost nonexistent.*

**non·fic·tion** /ˈnɑnˈfɪkʃən/ *noun*
books or writing about real facts or events, not imagined ones: *I like reading nonfiction, especially books about animals or history.* **ANTONYM: fiction**
—**nonfiction** *adjective* relating to a book or a piece of writing that deals with real facts or events: *a nonfiction book about the rainforest*
→ see Thesaurus box at **book**[1]

**non·sense** /ˈnɑnsens/ *noun*
**1** something false or stupid that someone says: *"Mom hates me." "That's nonsense!"*
**2** bad behavior: *The teacher won't take any nonsense from the kids in her class.*
**3** speech or writing that has no meaning: *The letter was nonsense. I couldn't figure out what she was trying to say.*

**non·stick** /ˌnɑnˈstɪk/ *adjective*
nonstick pans have a special surface inside that food will not stick to

**non·stop** /ˌnɑnˈstɑp/ *adjective, adverb*
without stopping: *It's been raining nonstop since we got here, and I just want to see the sun.* | *a nonstop flight from New York to L.A.*

**noo·dles** /ˈnudlz/ *plural noun*
food made from flour, eggs, and water, cut into long flat thin pieces and cooked in boiling water: *Add the noodles to the chicken soup.*

**noon** /nun/ *noun*
12 O'CLOCK in the middle of the day: *We ate lunch at noon.*
[**ORIGIN:** From the old English word *non*, which means "the ninth hour from sunrise," from the Latin word *nonus*, meaning "ninth." Prayers were said at the ninth hour, which was 3 o'clock. This time for prayers was later moved to 12 o'clock. ]

**ˈno one** *pronoun*
not anyone: *I rang the doorbell, but no one came to the door.* **SYNONYM: nobody**

**nope** /noʊp/ *adverb* (*informal*)
no: *"Do you want to go to the movies?" "Nope, I'm too tired."*

**nor** /nɚ; *strong* nɔr/ *conjunction* (*formal*)
**1 neither ... nor** = used to say that two things are not true or possible: *My mother's family was neither rich nor poor.*
**2** and not: *I didn't tell Dad, nor did John. So Dad never knew.*

**norm** [Ac] /nɔrm/ *noun* (*formal*)
**1** the usual or normal way of doing something: *Working during your lunch break is becoming the norm for many people.*
**2 norms** = accepted ways of behaving in society: *In school, there are norms of behavior that children must follow.*

**nor·mal** [Ac] /ˈnɔrməl/ *adjective*
usual, typical, or expected: *Since the accident, he has not been able to lead a normal life.* | *It's normal to feel nervous before an exam.*
—**normality** /nɔrˈmæləti/ *noun* a state in which something is normal
[**ORIGIN:** 1400-1500 From the Latin word *norma*, which means "tool for checking straight lines and angles." The Latin word *normalis* was used to describe something that matched a straight edge, and something that is normal matches what is expected.]

**WORD FAMILY: normal**
**normal** *adjective* | **abnormal** *adjective* | **normally** *adverb* | **normality** *noun* | **normalize** *verb*

**THESAURUS: normal**
**ordinary** not special, unusual, or different in any way: *It's just an ordinary watch. It doesn't have an alarm or anything extra.*
**regular** ordinary, with no special features or qualities: *He's a star on the football field, but his friends still treat him like a regular guy.*
**average** typical of a normal person or thing, and not special or unusual: *The average family has two kids.*

**standard** usual – used about sizes, shapes, prices, or ways of doing things: *The shoes only come in standard sizes.*

**routine** normal and done regularly, not for any special or unusual reason: *The ground crew made a routine check of the plane.*

**nor·mal·ize** Ac /ˈnɔrməˌlaɪz/ *verb (formal)*
to become normal again: *After all the problems caused by the storm, things have begun to normalize again.*

**nor·mal·ly** Ac /ˈnɔrməli/ *adverb*
usually or in the expected way: *I normally bike to school, but today I took the bus.*

**Norse** /nɔrs/ *noun*
the language spoken in Scandinavian countries in the past
—**Norse** *adjective* relating to Scandinavian countries in the past, or to the language people in those countries spoke: *Thor was one of the Norse gods.*

**north**

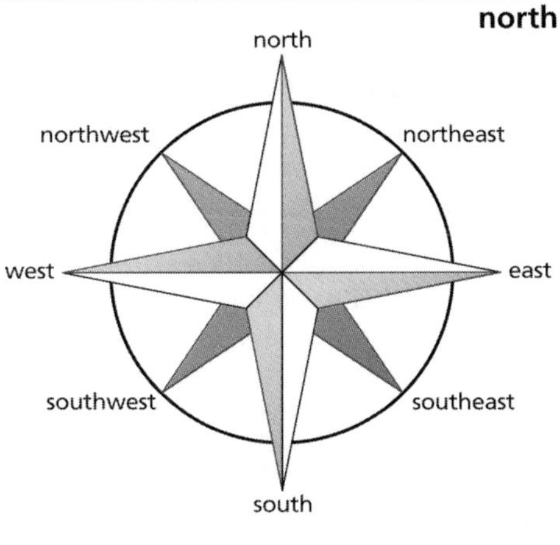


**north**[1] (*also* **North**) /nɔrθ/ *noun*
**1** the direction toward the top of a map of the world: *Which way is north?*
**2 the north** = the northern part of a country or area: *My family came from the north of Ireland.*
**3 the North** = the part of the U.S. east of the Mississippi River and north of Washington, D.C.

**north**[2] *adjective*
**1** in, to, or facing north: *We live in a town 20 miles north of Salem.* | *My uncle lives on the north side of Chicago.*
**2 north wind** = a wind that comes from the north: *a cold north wind*

**north**[3] *adverb*
toward the north: *Drive north on the highway.*

**north·east**[1] /ˌnɔrθˈist/ *noun*
**1** the direction that is exactly between north and east → see picture at **north**
**2 the Northeast** = the northeast part of a country or area: *Boston is the largest city in the Northeast.*
—**northeastern** /ˌnɔrθˈistən/ *adjective* in or from the northeast

**northeast**[2] *adverb, adjective*
in, from, or toward the northeast: *a northeast wind*

**north·ern** /ˈnɔrðən/ *adjective*
in or from the north: *the giant redwood trees in northern California*

**northerner** /ˈnɔrðənə/ *noun*
someone who comes from the northern part of a country

**ˌNorth ˈPole** *noun*
**the North Pole** = the most northern place on the surface of the earth: *Scientists at the North Pole are studying the effects of global warming on the ice.* → see picture at **globe**

**northward** /ˈnɔrθwəd/ *adverb, adjective*
toward the north: *The ship sailed northward.*

**north·west**[1] /ˌnɔrθˈwest/ *noun*
**1** the direction that is exactly between north and west: *The weather report said that a storm would arrive from the northwest.* → see picture at **north**
**2 the Northwest** = the northwest part of a country or area: *The state of Washington is in the Northwest.*
—**northwestern** /ˌnɔrθˈwestən/ *adjective* in or from the northwest: *the northwestern states of the U.S.*

**northwest**[2] *adverb, adjective*
in, from, or toward the northwest: *We drove northwest through the Rockies.*

**Nor·we·gian** /nɔrˈwidʒən/ *noun*
**1** someone from Norway
**2** the language spoken in Norway
—**Norwegian** *adjective* relating to Norway: *a Norwegian skier*

N

**nose** /noʊz/ *noun*
**1** the part of a person's or animal's face that they use for smelling and breathing: *The man had a big nose.* | *He took out a tissue and blew his nose.* → see picture on page A2
**2** the pointed front end of an airplane, boat, or ROCKET
**3** **(right) under someone's nose** (*informal*) = so close to someone that he or she should notice, but does not: *The lost key was on the table all the time, right under my nose!*

**nose·bleed** /ˈnoʊzblid/ *noun*
if you have a nosebleed, blood starts coming out of your nose: *He hit me on the nose and gave me a nosebleed.*

**nos·tal·gia** /nɑˈstældʒə/ *noun*
the feeling that you get when you remember a happy time in the past and wish that things had not changed: *He was full of nostalgia as he watched old home movies of the kids.*
—**nostalgic** *adjective* feeling slightly sad about a happy time you remember from the past that you wish had not changed
[**ORIGIN:** 1700-1800 From the Greek words *nostos* and *algos*, which mean "return to your home" and "pain." The idea is that you feel unhappy because you want to return to a time in the past.]

**nos·tril** /ˈnɑstrəl/ *noun*
one of the two holes at the end of your nose, through which you breathe → see picture on page A2
[**ORIGIN:** From the old English word *nosthyrl*, which means "nose-hole."]

**nos·y** /ˈnoʊzi/ *adjective*
always trying to find out information about other people's lives: *My nosy little sister was reading my journal!*
—**nosiness** *noun* the act of being nosy

**not** /nɑt/ *adverb*
**1** used when you want to give the opposite meaning to a word, statement, or question: *She's not very tall, and she can't reach the top shelf.* | *There isn't much traffic at night.* | *"Can you help me?" "Not right now, I'm busy."*
**2** **not only** = used to say that someone has one quality and also another quality: *She's not only funny, she's also smart.*

**note¹** /noʊt/ *noun*
**1** a very short letter: *I wrote Grandma a note thanking her for the present.*
**2** something that you write down to help you remember it: *Let me make a note of your new address so I don't forget it.*
**3** a musical sound, or the sign for that sound: *I can sing the low notes, but I can't reach the high notes.*
**4** **take note (of something)** = to pay careful attention to something: *The coach took note of who was playing well during practice.*

**note²** *verb*
**1** (*formal*) to notice or pay careful attention to something: *Please note that the museum is closed on Mondays.*
**2** (*also* **note down**) to write something down so that you will remember it: *I carefully noted down the train times.*

**note·book** /ˈnoʊtbʊk/ *noun*
**1** a book in which you write notes: *I wrote the answers to the math problems in my notebook.*
**2** a small computer that you can carry

**note·pa·per** /ˈnoʊtˌpeɪpɚ/ *noun*
paper used for writing letters or notes

**notes** /noʊts/ *plural noun*
information that a student writes down from a class or book: *I take notes during class and use them when I study for a test.*

**noth·ing¹** /ˈnʌθɪŋ/ *pronoun*
**1** not anything or no thing: *There was nothing in the room except a chair.* | *My sister knows nothing about football so she never knows who's winning or losing.*
**2** something that you do not think is important or interesting: *There's nothing on TV tonight. Let's go see a movie.*
**3** (*informal*) zero: *We won the game three nothing.*
**4** **for nothing** (*informal*) = **a)** without paying or being paid: *You can't ask people to work for nothing.* **b)** without getting what you expected or wanted: *"I'm sorry, he left an hour ago." "You mean, we drove all the way over here for nothing?"*
**5** **have nothing to do with someone or something** = to not be related or involved with a situation or person: *His bad mood had nothing to do with us. He was upset because he got a bad grade on the test.*
**6** **nothing but ...** (*informal*) = only: *I've had*

*nothing but bad luck today. Everything keeps going wrong!*
[ORIGIN: From the Old English phrase *nan thing*, which means "not one thing."]

**nothing²** *adverb*
**be nothing like someone or something** (*informal*) = to not be at all similar to someone or something else: *Tommy is nothing like his father. They're completely different.*

**no·tice¹** /ˈnoʊtɪs/ *verb*
to see, feel, or hear someone or something: *He noticed that it had started raining.* | *Did you notice how tired Jean looked?*
—**noticeable** *adjective* easy to notice: *There's been a noticeable change in his schoolwork.*
→ see Thesaurus box at **see**

**notice²** *noun*
**1** a piece of paper with information, which someone has put on a wall or door in a public place: *The notice on the door said the library was closed.*
**2** information or a warning about something that will happen: *In most jobs, you have to give two weeks' notice if you want to quit.*
**3 take notice (of someone or something)** = to listen to what someone tells you and do what he or she wants: *I told him to stop, but he didn't take any notice.*

**no·ti·fy** /ˈnoʊtəˌfaɪ/ *verb* (**notified**, **notifies**) (*formal*)
to tell someone officially about something: *Please notify the school if you will be absent because you are sick.* **SYNONYM: inform**

**no·tion** [Ac] /ˈnoʊʃən/ *noun* (*formal*)
an idea, belief, or opinion about something: *She had no notion what he meant and couldn't understand a word he had said.*

**no·to·ri·ous** /noʊˈtɔriəs/ *adjective*
famous for something bad: *Mrs. Green is notorious for giving a lot of homework.*
—**notoriously** *adverb* in a notorious way

**not·with·stand·ing** [Ac] /ˌnɑtwɪθˈstændɪŋ/ *preposition*, *adverb* (*formal*)
in spite of something: *The weather notwithstanding, we had a good vacation.*

**noun** /naʊn/ *noun*
a word that is the name of a person, place, thing, quality, action, or idea: *In the sentence "Joe parked his car outside the store," "Joe," "car," and "store" are nouns.*
[ORIGIN: 1300-1400 From the Latin word *nomen*, which means "name."]

**nour·ish** /ˈnɚɪʃ/ *verb* (*formal*)
to give a person, plant, or animal the food they need in order to live, grow, and be healthy: *Fertilizer nourishes the soil and helps to produce strong plants.*
—**nourishing** *adjective* nourishing food makes you strong and healthy.

**nour·ish·ment** /ˈnɚɪʃmənt/ *noun* (*formal*)
food that people and other living things need in order to live and be healthy: *Fresh fruit and vegetables provide nourishment for your body.*

**nov·el¹** /ˈnɑvəl/ *noun*
a book in which the story, characters, and events are not real: *"The Grapes of Wrath" is a famous novel by John Steinbeck.*
—**novelist** *noun* someone who writes novels
→ see Thesaurus box at **book¹**
[ORIGIN: 1500-1600 From the Italian word *novella*, which means "new story," from the Latin word *novus*, meaning "new."]

**novel²** *adjective* (*formal*)
new and unusual: *We need a novel solution to the problem – the old ways aren't working.*

**nov·el·ty** /ˈnɑvəlti/ *noun* (plural **novelties**)
**1** something new and unusual: *In the 1990s, cell phones were a novelty, but now everyone has them.*
**2** the quality of being new and unusual: *Going to the gym was fun at first, but the novelty wore off and I became bored with it.*

**No·vem·ber** /noʊˈvembɚ/ *noun* (*written abbreviation*: **Nov.**)
the 11th month of the year, between October and December: *His birthday is on November 6.* | *Thanksgiving is in November.* | *We plan to get married next November.*
[ORIGIN: probably 1100-1200 From the Latin word *novem*, which means "nine." November was the ninth month of the old Roman calendar.]

**nov·ice** /ˈnɑvɪs/ *noun*
someone who has just begun learning a skill or activity: *The basic class is for computer novices.*

**now** /naʊ/ *adverb*
**1** at the present time: *I was sick yesterday, but I feel better now.*

N

**THESAURUS: now**

**at the moment** now: *The TV isn't working at the moment.*

**for the moment** happening now but likely to change in the future: *I'll just leave these things here for the moment.*

**at present** (*formal*) happening or existing now: *Mrs. Smith is in a meeting at present.*

**currently** happening or existing now: *I'm currently a student, but I will graduate in June.*

**2 for now** = for a short time: *Leave your coat on the sofa for now, and I'll hang it up later.*
**3** immediately: *You'd better go now or you'll miss the bus.* **ANTONYM: later**
**4 now and then** (*also* **now and again**) = used to say that something happens sometimes but not very often: *My grandson writes me letters now and then, but he never visits.*
**5 now that** = as a result of something: *Now that I have my own room, I'm a lot happier.* **SYNONYM: since**

**now·a·days** /ˈnaʊəˌdeɪz/ *adverb*
now – used when comparing the present time with a time in the past: *Computers used to be huge but nowadays some are small enough to carry.*

**no ˈway** *adverb* (*informal*)
used to say that you will not agree to do something: *"You should tell your parents." "No way, they won't listen!"*

**no·where** /ˈnoʊwer/ *adverb*
**1** not any place: *There was nowhere to sit down.* | *Some of the island plants only grow there and nowhere else.*
**2 get/go nowhere** (*informal*) = to have no success, or make no progress: *I tried to explain, but I got nowhere. He wouldn't listen.*

**nu·cle·ar** Ac /ˈnukliə˞/ *adjective*
**1** using or relating to nuclear energy: *The nuclear power plant produces electricity.*
**2** involving the use of nuclear weapons: *People were afraid there would be a nuclear war.*

**ˌnuclear ˈenergy** *noun*
the power produced by splitting an atom or joining two atoms together: *The main use of nuclear energy is to produce electricity.*

**ˌnuclear ˈfamily** *noun*
a family that includes parents and children and no other relatives

**ˌnuclear ˈweapon** *noun*
a very powerful bomb or other weapon that uses nuclear energy

**nu·cle·us** /ˈnukliəs/ *noun* (plural **nuclei** /ˈnukliaɪ/)
**1** the central part of an atom: *The nucleus of an atom is surrounded by electrons.*
**2** the central part of a cell: *The nucleus of a cell contains genetic information.*
[**ORIGIN:** 1700-1800 From the Latin word for "the center of a nut," from *nux*, which means "nut."]

**nude**[1] /nud/ *adjective, adverb*
not wearing any clothes: *There's a special beach for people who like to sunbathe nude.* **SYNONYM: naked**
—**nudity** /ˈnudəti/ *noun* the state of not wearing any clothes

**nude**[2] *noun*
**1** a painting or STATUE of someone without any clothes: *Most of his paintings are nudes.*
**2 in the nude** = not wearing any clothes

**nudge** /nʌdʒ/ *verb*
to push someone gently, especially with your elbow, in order to get his or her attention: *Ken nudged me with his elbow and said, "Let's go."*
—**nudge** *noun* a gentle push
→ see Thesaurus box at **push**[1]

**nug·get** /ˈnʌgɪt/ *noun*
a small rough piece of a valuable metal found in the earth: *a gold nugget*

**nui·sance** /ˈnusəns/ *noun*
someone or something that annoys you or causes problems: *Jon kept phoning, and his calls were becoming a nuisance.*
[**ORIGIN:** 1400-1500 From the old French word *nuisir*, which means "to harm."]

**numb** /nʌm/ *adjective*
**1** if a part of your body is numb, you are not

able to feel anything in it: *His feet were numb from the cold.*

**2** not able to react or show emotion in the normal way: *I was so shocked by the news of his death that I just felt numb.*

—**numbness** *noun* the feeling of being numb

**num·ber**[1] /ˈnʌmbɚ/ *noun*

**1** a word or sign that shows a quantity: *Add the numbers 7, 4, and 3.*

**2** a telephone number: *Give me your number and I'll call you.*

**3** a number showing the position of something on a list: *Try to answer question number five.*

**4** a set of numbers that show who someone is: *What's your Social Security number?*

**5** an amount of something that you can count: *We have been friends for a number of years.* | *There have been a large number of accidents on this road.*

**WORD FAMILY: number**

**number** *noun* | **numerical** *adjective*

**GRAMMAR: number, amount**

Use **number** with plural forms of nouns: *a large number of cars*

Use **amount** with nouns such as "money" and "bread" that do not have plurals: *a large amount of water*

**number**[2] *verb*

**1** to give a number to something that is part of a set or list: *He numbered the pages one through six.*

**2** if people or things number a particular amount, there are that many people or things: *General Lee's army numbered about 50,000 men.*

**ˈnumber line** *noun*

a line with numbers written along it in order. Students can use a number line to help them add or take away numbers.

**ˌnumber ˈone** *adjective*

the best or most important: *He is currently the number one tennis player in the world.*

**ˈnumber sentence** *noun*

a way of writing a calculation using numbers and signs such as (+), (-), and (=): *1 + 2 = 3 is a number sentence.*

**nu·mer·al** /ˈnumərəl/ *noun*

a written sign that represents a number: *10, 89, and 323 are all numerals.*

**nu·me·ra·tor** /ˈnuməˌreɪtɚ/ *noun*

the number that appears above the line in a FRACTION: *5 is the numerator in the fraction 5/6.*

**nu·mer·i·cal** /nuˈmerɪkəl/ *adjective*

expressed in numbers, or consisting of numbers: *Make sure that the pages are in numerical order, with page 1 first, 2 second, and so on.*

—**numerically** *adverb* in a way that relates to numbers

**num·er·ous** /ˈnumərəs/ *adjective* (*formal*)

many: *I've been to Chicago numerous times, so I know the city fairly well.*

[**ORIGIN:** 1400-1500 From the Latin word *numerosus*, from *numerus*, which means "number."]

**nun** /nʌn/ *noun*

a woman who is a member of a group of religious women who live together

**nurse**[1] /nɚs/ *noun*

someone whose job is to take care of people who are sick or injured: *The nurse gave him his medication and asked how he was feeling.* → see picture on page **A16**

[**ORIGIN:** 1200-1300 From the old French word *nurice*, from the Latin word *nutricia*, which means "someone who feeds or takes care of a child."]

**nurse**

**nurse**[2] *verb*

**1** to take care of people who are sick or injured: *Michael nursed his wife through a long illness.*

**2** if a woman nurses a baby, she feeds it with milk from her breasts: *I nursed my son until he was about nine months old.*

**nurs·er·y** /ˈnɚsəri/ *noun* (plural **nurseries**)

**1** a place where you can buy plants and trees: *We went to the nursery to buy some plants.*

N

**2** a bedroom for a baby: *They got the nursery ready before the baby was born.*

**ˈnursery rhyme** *noun*
a short well-known poem or song for children: *She read the children nursery rhymes before they went to bed.*

**ˈnursery ˌschool** *noun*
a school for children from three to five years old

**nurs·ing** /ˈnɚsɪŋ/ *noun*
the job of taking care of people who are sick, injured, or very old: *She chose a career in nursing because she likes helping people.*

**ˈnursing home** *noun*
a place where people who are too old or sick to take care of themselves can live: *Grandpa's very old now, and he might have to go to live in a nursing home.*

**nur·ture** /ˈnɚtʃɚ/ *verb*
to help someone or something to grow and develop: *Her parents nurtured her musical talent by giving her piano lessons.*

**nut** /nʌt/ *noun*
**1** a large seed that you can eat, that usually grows in a hard brown shell: *a bowl of cashew nuts*
**2** a small piece of metal with a hole in the middle. You screw it onto a BOLT to fasten things together: *Use a wrench to loosen the nut.*
**3** (*informal*) someone who is silly or crazy: *Some nut was driving on the wrong side of the road.*

**nu·tri·ent** /ˈnutriənt/ *noun*
a chemical or food that helps plants, animals, or people to live and grow: *These plants need soil with a lot of nutrients.*
[**ORIGIN:** 1600-1700 From the Latin word *nutrire*, which means "to feed someone or help something to grow."]

**nu·tri·tion** /nuˈtrɪʃən/ *noun*
the process of eating the right types of food for good health and growth: *Make sure you eat different foods for good nutrition.*
—**nutritional** *adjective* relating to the substances in food that help you to stay healthy and grow well: *Potato chips have little nutritional value.*
—**nutritionist** *noun* someone who gives people advice about nutrition

**WORD FAMILY: nutrition**
**nutrition** *noun* | **nutritious** *adjective* | **nutritional** *adjective* | **nutritionist** *noun*

**nu·tri·tious** // *adjective*
full of the natural substances that your body needs to stay healthy and grow well: *Peanut butter is a nutritious food.*

**nuts** /nʌts/ *adjective* (*informal*)
crazy or very angry: *I think anyone who jumps out of a plane must be nuts!* | *The kids have been so noisy they're driving me nuts* (=making me annoyed).

**nut·shell** /ˈnʌtʃel/ *noun*
**1** **(to put it) in a nutshell** (*informal*) = used when you are telling someone the main facts about something in a short clear way: *In a nutshell, I think you should study harder so that you get better grades.*
**2** the hard outer part of a nut

**nut·ty** /ˈnʌti/ *adjective*
**1** tasting like nuts: *Almonds give the cake a nutty flavor.*
**2** (*informal*) crazy: *We want to take a train across the country, but Mom thinks it's a nutty idea.*

**ny·lon** /ˈnaɪlɑn/ *noun*
a strong material that is used for making plastic, cloth, and rope: *Some guitar strings are made of nylon.*

**ny·lons** /ˈnaɪlɑnz/ *plural noun*
a piece of clothing that women wear on their legs, that is very thin and made of nylon **SYNONYM: pantyhose**

# Oo

**O** /oʊ/ *number*
used for saying the number zero: *She lives in apartment two 0 four* (=204).

**oak** /oʊk/ *noun*
a large tree that is common in northern countries, or the hard wood of this tree

**oar** /ɔr/ *noun*
a long pole with a wide blade at one end, used for rowing a boat → see picture at **boat**

oasis

**o·a·sis** /oʊˈeɪsɪs/ *noun* (plural **oases** /oʊˈeɪsiz/)
a place with trees and water in a desert

**oath** /oʊθ/ *noun* (plural **oaths** /oʊðz/)
**1** a formal and serious promise: *He took an oath to defend the United States when he joined the army.*
**2 be under oath** = to have made an official promise to tell the truth in a court of law: *All witnesses in court are under oath, so they have to tell the truth.*

**oat·meal** /ˈoʊtmil/ *noun*
crushed oats that you cook and eat for breakfast or use in cooking: *I ate a bowl of oatmeal for breakfast.*

**oats** /oʊts/ *plural noun*
a grain that is used as food
—**oat** *adjective* made of oats: *oat cereal*

**o·be·di·ent** /əˈbidiənt/ *adjective*
always doing what a rule or someone in authority tells you to do: *Teach your dog to be obedient, so that he sits when you tell him to.* **ANTONYM: disobedient**
—**obedience** *noun* obedient behavior
—**obediently** *adverb* in an obedient way

**o·bese** /oʊˈbis/ *adjective*
very fat in a way that is unhealthy: *Her doctor told her she was obese and needed to lose weight.*
—**obesity** *noun* the condition of being very fat
→ see Thesaurus box at **fat**[1]
[**ORIGIN:** 1600-1700 From the Latin word *obesus*, a form of the verb *obedere*, which means "to eat up."]

**o·bey** /əˈbeɪ/ *verb* (**obeyed**, **obeys**)
to do what a law, rule, or person in authority tells you: *If you do not obey the law, then you will be punished.* **ANTONYM: disobey**
[**ORIGIN:** 1200-1300 From the Latin word *oboedire*, from *audire*, which means "to hear."]

**WORD FAMILY: obey**

**obey** *verb* | **disobey** *verb* | **obedient** *adjective* | **disobedient** *adjective* | **obedience** *noun* | **disobedience** *noun*

**THESAURUS: obey**

**do what someone says/do what someone tells you**: *You'd better do what the coach says if you want to stay on the team.*

**do what you are told/do as you are told**: *We expect our students to be polite and do what they are told.*

**follow someone's orders/instructions**: *Follow the instructions at the top of the test.* | *You must follow your doctor's orders.*

**ob·ject**[1] /ˈɑbdʒɪkt/ *noun*
**1** a thing that you can see and touch: *Keep your back straight when you lift heavy objects.*
**2** the purpose of a plan, action, or activity: *The object of the game is to score points by throwing the basketball through the hoop.*
**3** in grammar, the person or thing that is affected by the action of the verb: *"Book" is the object in the sentence "I read the book."*
→ see Thesaurus box at **thing**

**ob·ject**[2] /əbˈdʒekt/ *verb*
to say that you do not like or approve of

O

something: *A lot of the kids objected to the idea of wearing a uniform to school.*

**ob·jec·tion** /əbˈdʒekʃən/ *noun*
the reason someone gives for not approving of an idea or plan: *My main objection to your idea is that it would cost too much money.*



**ob·jec·tive¹** [Ac] /əbˈdʒektɪv/ *noun*
something that you are working hard to achieve: *My objective is to win the game.*
→ see Thesaurus box at **purpose**

**objective²** *adjective*
based on facts rather than your feelings or beliefs: *Scientists need to be objective when doing research.* **ANTONYM: subjective**

**ob·li·gat·ed** /ˈɑbləˌgeɪtɪd/ *adjective*
**be/feel obligated to do something** = to have to do something because of a rule or law or because you feel it is your duty: *You are obligated to pay your rent on time.* **SYNONYM: obliged**

**ob·li·ga·tion** /ˌɑbləˈgeɪʃən/ *noun*
something that you must do because it is the law or your duty: *Schools have an obligation to provide a safe place for students to learn.*

**o·blig·a·to·ry** /əˈblɪgəˌtɔri/ *adjective* (*formal*)
something that is obligatory must be done because of a law or rule: *P.E. is obligatory for all students.* **SYNONYM: mandatory**

> **WORD FAMILY: obligatory**
> **obligatory** *adjective* | **obliged** *adjective* | **obligated** *adjective* | **obligation** *noun*

**o·bliged** /əˈblaɪdʒd/ *adjective*
**be/feel obliged to do something** (*formal*) = to have to do something because of a rule or law or because you feel it is your duty: *All the people in the car are obliged to wear seat belts.* **SYNONYM: obligated**
[**ORIGIN:** 1200-1300 From the Latin word *obligare*, from *ligare*, which means "to tie." If you are obliged to do something, it is as though you were tied by a rope to that thing.]

**o·blique** /əˈblik/ *adjective*
said in a way that is not direct or clear: *The letter contained oblique references to their argument, but didn't mention it directly.*

**ob·liv·i·ous** /əˈblɪviəs/ *adjective*
not knowing about or not noticing something that is happening around you: *The boys were oblivious to danger as they started climbing down the cliff.* **SYNONYM: unaware**
[**ORIGIN:** 1400-1500 From the Latin word *oblivio*, which means "the state of forgetting or being forgotten."]

**ob·long** /ˈɑblɔŋ/ *adjective*
having a shape that is longer than it is wide: *This oblong table is 58 inches long by 36 inches wide.*
[**ORIGIN:** 1400-1500 From the Latin word *oblongus*, which means "fairly long."]

**ob·nox·ious** /əbˈnɑkʃəs/ *adjective*
very offensive or rude: *Some of the boys were so loud and obnoxious that they were asked to leave the dance.*
[**ORIGIN:** 1500-1600 From Latin word *noxa*, which means "harm."]

**o·boe** /ˈoʊboʊ/ *noun*
a long thin wooden musical instrument that you play by blowing and covering holes in it with your fingers → see picture on page **A21**
[**ORIGIN:** 1600-1700 From the French word *hautbois*, from *haut* and *bois*, which mean "high" and "wood."]

**ob·scene** /əbˈsin/ *adjective*
showing or talking about sex in a way that is offensive or shocking: *Students who use obscene language in class will be suspended.*

**ob·scure¹** /əbˈskjʊr/ *adjective*
**1** not well known and not very important: *The paintings were done by an obscure French artist that few people have heard of.*
**2** unclear or difficult to understand: *The library was closed at lunchtime for some obscure reason that no one could explain.*

**obscure²** *verb* (*formal*)
to make something difficult to see or hear: *Clouds obscured the top of the mountain.*

**ob·serv·ant** /əbˈzɚvənt/ *adjective*
good at noticing the things that happen around you: *Police officers are trained to be observant.*

**ob·ser·va·tion** /ˌɑbzɚˈveɪʃən/ *noun*
**1** the process of watching someone or something carefully for a long time: *After his heart attack, he was in the hospital under observation for two days.*
**2** a remark about something that you have

noticed: *He made some funny observations about the other students in the class.*

**ob·serv·a·to·ry** /əbˈzɚvəˌtɔri/ *noun* (plural **observatories**)
a special building with TELESCOPEs that scientists use to study the stars, PLANETs, and sky

**ob·serve** /əbˈzɚv/ *verb* (*formal*)
**1** to notice something: *Mr. Davis told police that he had observed the woman entering the building at 9:18.*
**2** to watch someone or something carefully: *One student does the experiment while his partner observes.*
—**observer** *noun* someone who watches someone or something carefully
[**ORIGIN:** 1300-1400 From the Latin word *observare*, which means "to guard or watch."]

**WORD FAMILY: observe**
**observe** *verb* | **observer** *noun* | **observant** *adjective* | **observation** *noun*

**ob·sessed** /əbˈsest/ *adjective*
if you are obsessed with someone or something, you think about them all the time and cannot think about anything else: *Jake is obsessed with baseball. That's all he talks about.*

**ob·ses·sion** /əbˈseʃən/ *noun*
something that you think about too much, in a way that is not normal: *Young girls often have an unhealthy obsession with being thin.*

**ob·so·lete** /ˌɑbsəˈlit/ *adjective*
no longer used or needed because something newer and better has been made: *Videotapes are becoming obsolete.*
[**ORIGIN:** 1500-1600 From the Latin word *obsoletus*, which means "having become old and no longer used."]

**ob·sta·cle** /ˈɑbstɪkəl/ *noun*
**1** something that stops you from doing or achieving something successfully: *The biggest obstacle to getting a good job is not having a high school diploma.*
**2** something that blocks a road or path so that you must go around it: *They had to drive around obstacles in the road.*
[**ORIGIN:** 1300-1400 From the Latin word *obstaculum*, from *obstare*, which means "to stand in the way."]

**ob·sti·nate** /ˈɑbstənɪt/ *adjective*
refusing to change your opinions or behavior: *Why are you being so obstinate? Why won't you change you mind?*

**ob·struct** /əbˈstrʌkt/ *verb* (*formal*)
to block a road, passage, etc. so that nothing can get past: *The truck was on its side and obstructed two lanes of traffic.*
[**ORIGIN:** 1600-1700 From the Latin word *obstructum*, a form of the verb *obstruere*, which means "to build in the way."]

obstruction

**ob·struc·tion** /əbˈstrʌkʃən/ *noun* (*formal*)
something that blocks something such as a road or passage: *A tree had fallen on the road, causing an obstruction.*

**ob·tain** Ac /əbˈteɪn/ *verb* (*formal*)
to get something that you want: *You need to obtain a visa to visit Australia.*
—**obtainable** *adjective* (*formal*) able to be obtained

**ob·vi·ous** Ac /ˈɑbviəs/ *adjective*
easy to notice or understand: *It was obvious (that) he was sick from the way he looked.*
—**obviously** *adverb* in an obvious way: *He's obviously nervous. He keeps biting his nails.*
→ see Thesaurus box at **clear**[1]
[**ORIGIN:** 1500-1600 From the Latin word *obvius*, which means "easy to meet or often met," from *obviam*, which means "in the way, or within reach."]

**oc·ca·sion** /əˈkeɪʒən/ *noun*
**1** a time when something happens: *I met with him on several occasions.*
**2** an important event or ceremony: *We only use the good plates at Christmas and other special occasions.*

**oc·ca·sion·al** /əˈkeɪʒənəl/ *adjective*
happening sometimes but not often: *Her English is good, but she makes the occasional mistake.*
—**occasionally** *adverb* sometimes, but not often: *I occasionally eat fish, maybe once a month.*

**oc·cu·pa·tion** Ac /ˌɑkjəˈpeɪʃən/ *noun*
**1** a job or profession: *Write your name and occupation at the top of the form.*
**2** the act of entering a place and getting control of it, using military force: *The enemy's occupation of the city lasted several months.*
**3** something you do in your free time, for enjoyment: *Donna's favorite occupation is shopping.*
—**occupational** *adjective* related to or caused by your job: *Injuries are an occupational risk for athletes.*
→ see Thesaurus box at **job**

**oc·cu·py** Ac /ˈɑkjəˌpaɪ/ *verb* (**occupied**, **occupies**) (*formal*)
**1** to live in or use a building: *The same family has occupied the apartment for 20 years.*
**2** to enter a place and get control of it, usually by force: *Soldiers have occupied the town.*
**3** to fill a space: *Family photos occupied the entire wall.*
**4** to keep someone busy: *We played games to occupy the time.*
—**occupant** *noun* (*formal*) someone who lives or stays in a house, room, or vehicle

**oc·cur** Ac /əˈkɚ/ *verb* (**occurred**, **occurring**) (*formal*)
to happen without being expected: *Earthquakes occur without any warning signs.*
—**occurrence** *noun* (*formal*) something that happens: *Forest fires are a common occurrence in the summer.*
→ see Thesaurus box at **happen**
[**ORIGIN:** 1500-1600 From the Latin word *occurrere*, which means "to run towards or appear."]
**PHRASAL VERB**
**occur to someone** (*formal*)
if a thought or idea occurs to you, you suddenly think of it: *It never occurred to me (that) she might be married. I just assumed she was single.*

**o·cean** /ˈoʊʃən/ *noun*
**1** **the ocean** = the large amount of salt water that covers most of the Earth's surface: *We went swimming in the ocean.*
**2** one of the large areas of salt water in a particular part of the world, which together make up the whole ocean: *The islands of Hawaii are in the Pacific Ocean.*
—**oceanic** /ˌoʊʃiˈænɪk/ *adjective* related to the ocean: *oceanic currents*
[**ORIGIN:** 1200-1300 From the Greek word *Okeanos*, which was the name of a river believed to flow around the edge of the world.]

**o'clock** /əˈklɑk/ *adverb*
**one/two/three, etc. o'clock** = one of the times when the clock shows the exact hour as a number from 1 to 12: *I'll meet you at one o'clock for lunch.*
[**ORIGIN:** 1400-1500 From the phrase "of the clock."]

**oc·ta·gon** /ˈɑktəˌgɑn/ *noun*
a flat shape with eight sides
—**octagonal** *adjective* having eight sides

**Oc·to·ber** /ɑkˈtoʊbɚ/ *noun* (*written abbreviation*: **Oct.**)
the tenth month of the year, between September and November: *The group will be performing on October 22.* | *Clare's going to be two in October.*
[**ORIGIN:** Probably 1000-1100 From the Latin word *octo*, which means "eight." October was the eighth month of the old Roman calendar.]

**oc·to·pus** /ˈɑktəpəs/ *noun* (plural **octopuses** or **octopi** /ˈɑktəpaɪ/)
an ocean creature with a soft round body and eight arms
[**ORIGIN:** 1700-1800 From the Greek words *okto* and *pous*, which mean "eight" and "foot."]

**odd** Ac /ɑd/ *adjective*
**1** strange or different from normal: *He always calls if he's going to be late, so it's odd (that) he hasn't called by now.*
**2** an odd number cannot be divided by two: *1, 3, 5, and 7 are all odd numbers.*
→ see Thesaurus box at **strange**

**odd·i·ty** /ˈɑdəti/ *noun* (plural **oddities**) (*formal*)
a strange or unusual person or thing: *In the 1960s, foreign cars were an oddity in the U.S. Everyone had an American car.*

**ˈodd jobs** *plural noun*
small jobs of different types, for example fixing things: *I earned extra money doing odd jobs, like painting and fixing fences.*

**odds** Ac /ɑdz/ *plural noun*
**the odds** = how likely it is that something will

or will not happen: *The team's odds of reaching the championships are not good because they have lost their last five games.*

**ˌodds and ˈends** *plural noun (informal)*
various small things that have little value: *I need to stop at the store to pick up a few odds and ends.*

**o·dor** /ˈoʊdɚ/ *noun (formal)*
a bad smell: *There's an unpleasant odor coming from the drain.*
→ see Thesaurus box at **smell**[1]

**of** /əv; *strong* ʌv/ *preposition*
**1** used when something has a feature or quality: *Did you see the color of her eyes? | I was surprised by the size of the building.*
**2** used for showing what type of people or things are in a group: *A group of students was studying in the library. | a pack of dogs*
**3** used for showing what something is a part of: *I really liked the first scene of the movie.*
**4** belonging to someone or something: *She is the daughter of a famous actor.*
**5** used for showing what something contains: *Do you want a glass of milk?*
**6** showing or describing someone or something: *This is a picture of my family.*
**7** made or produced by someone: *The novels of Mark Twain are still popular.*
**8** used when giving the time, to mean "before": *It's ten of five means that it is ten minutes before five o'clock.* **SYNONYM: to**
**9** used in dates when the number of the day is given before the name of the month: *I'll see you on the 23rd of January.*
**10** because of something: *She died of cancer.*
→ **of course** at **course**

**off** /ɔf/ *adverb, preposition, adjective*
**1** not on something, or removed from something: *Get your feet off the couch! | He took his shoes off. | He fell off his chair.* **ANTONYM: on**
**2** away from a place: *She waved and drove off.*
**3** out of a bus, airplane, train, or boat: *The bus stopped, and she got off.* **ANTONYM: on**
**4** if a machine or light is off, someone has made it stop working for a time: *Turn the lights off when you leave.* **ANTONYM: on**
**5** a distance away, or in the future: *Off in the distance, we could see the mountains. | Summer is a long way off.*
**6** not at work or school: *We're off tomorrow because of the winter holidays. | Dad is going to take a day off and take us to the zoo.*
**7** if a planned event is off, it will not now take place: *The wedding's off. Brad and Kim aren't even speaking to each other.* **ANTONYM: on**
**8** if there is money off something, it is being sold at a lower price than before: *The dress was 20% off, so I bought it.*
**9 off and on/on and off** = for short periods of time during a longer period: *It rained off and on all morning.*

**of·fend** /əˈfend/ *verb*
to make someone angry and upset: *I offended him by laughing at his haircut.*

**WORD FAMILY: offend**
**offend** *verb* | **offense** *noun* | **offensive** *adjective* | **inoffensive** *adjective*

**of·fend·er** /əˈfendɚ/ *noun*
someone who is guilty of a crime: *Offenders must pay a fine of $125.*

**of·fense**[1] /əˈfens/ *noun*
**1** an action that is against the law: *He has committed a serious offense and will probably be sent to prison.*
**2 take offense** = to feel angry and upset because of what someone has said or done: *She took offense when I asked how old she was.*

**of·fense**[2] /ˈɔfens/ *noun*
**1** a group of players who try to score points in a sports game: *The team's offense scored 14 points in the first half.*
**2** the action of trying to score points in a sports game: *The team needs to improve its offense if it wants to win more games.*

**of·fen·sive** /əˈfensɪv/ *adjective*
**1** very impolite and likely to upset people: *You may not use swear words or any other offensive language in school.* **SYNONYM: rude**; **ANTONYM: inoffensive**
**2** used for attacking a person or place: *Airlines do not allow offensive weapons to be taken onto planes.* **ANTONYM: defensive**
**3** relating to the players who try to score

points in a sports game: *Henderson is a good offensive player.*
→ see Thesaurus box at **rude**

**of·fer¹** /ˈɔfɚ/ *verb*
**1** to ask someone if he or she would like to have something: *I offered him a slice of pizza.*
**2** to say that you will do something for someone: *She offered to help me.*
**3** to say that you are willing to pay a particular amount for something: *They offered us $325,000 for the house.*
[**ORIGIN:** 1200-1300 From the Latin word *offerre*, from *ferre*, which means "to carry." If you offer to do something, it is as though you were carrying that thing.]

**offer²** *noun*
a statement that you are willing to do something for someone or give someone something: *He refused all offers of help.* | *He got a job offer at the supermarket.*

**of·fice** /ˈɔfɪs/ *noun*
**1** a building where people work at desks, or a room in this building: *Is the principal in his office?* | *I called the doctor's office.*
**2** an important job, especially in government: *The president has just finished his first year in office.* | *The mayor took office in December after the election.*
[**ORIGIN:** 1200-1300 From the Latin word *officium*, which means "service or duty."]

**of·fi·cer** /ˈɔfəsɚ/ *noun*
**1** someone who has an important position in the army, navy, or air force: *The soldiers must obey the officer's orders.*
**2** a POLICE OFFICER: *Officer Johnson arrested him for drunk driving.*
**3** someone who has an important position in an organization: *He is the chief financial officer of the company.*

**of·fi·cial¹** /əˈfɪʃəl/ *adjective*
done or produced by someone who has an important position in the government or in an organization: *The president was on an official visit to Mexico.*
—**officially** *adverb* in an official way: *Ed was officially warned about being late.*

**official²** *noun*
someone who has an important position in an organization: *Government officials say the problem is getting worse.*

**ˈoff-ˌseason** *noun*
the time in the year when a sport is not usually played: *The football player wanted to wait until the off-season to have surgery.*

**off·set** Ac /ˌɔfˈset/ *verb* (**offset**, **offsetting**)
if something offsets another thing, it has an opposite effect: *Higher fuel prices will offset the savings people make by driving less.*

**off·shore** /ˌɔfˈʃɔr/ *adjective, adverb*
in the ocean, at a distance from the coast: *an offshore oil rig*

**off·spring** /ˈɔfˌsprɪŋ/ *noun* (plural **offspring**)
**1** an animal's baby or babies: *The male and female bird both collect food to feed their hungry offspring.*
**2** a person's child or children: *The young mother seemed unable to control her offspring, who kept running around the store.*

**of·ten** /ˈɔfən/ *adverb*
**1** many times: *She often goes swimming on weekends.* **ANTONYM: rarely**

**THESAURUS: often**

**a lot** (*informal*) a large amount or number: *We go to the beach a lot in the summer.*

**frequently** very often: *He's frequently late for school.*

**regularly** often and at regular times, for example every day, every week, or every month: *You should exercise regularly.*

**constantly** all the time, used especially about something that is annoying or causes problems: *She talked constantly about herself.*

**continuously** without stopping: *It's been raining continuously since we got here.*

**again and again/over and over (again)** many times, and more often than you would expect: *They keep making the same mistakes again and again.* | *I get bored doing the same thing over and over again.*

**2 how often** = used to ask how many times something happens during a period of time: *"How often do you go to the dentist?" "Twice a year."*
**3 every so often** = sometimes, but not regularly: *We go to the movies every so often.*

**o·gre** /ˈoʊgɚ/ *noun*
in children's stories, a large ugly creature who eats people

**oh** /oʊ/
**1** said when you are surprised, happy, upset, etc.: *Oh, no! My wallet is gone!*
**2** said before you answer someone: *"Why?" "Oh, I don't know."*

**ohm** /oʊm/ *noun*
a unit for measuring how hard it is for electricity to flow through something
[ORIGIN: From Georg Simon Ohm (1787-1854), a German scientist who discovered things about electricity.]

**oil**[1] /ɔɪl/ *noun*
**1** a thick liquid from under the ground which people use for making gasoline, for heating, or for making machines work smoothly: *The company wants to start drilling for oil in Alaska.*
**2** a thick liquid from a plant which you use in cooking: *Fry the vegetables in olive oil.*
[ORIGIN: 1100-1200 From the Latin word *oleum*, which means "olive oil," from the Greek word *elaia*, which means "olive."]

**oil**[2] *verb*
to put oil into or onto something: *He oiled the hinges of the door to stop them squeaking.*

**ˈoil rig** *noun*
a large structure with equipment for digging into the ground or under the ocean to get oil

**ˈoil well** *noun*
a deep hole that people dig so that they can get oil out from under the ground

**oil·y** /ˈɔɪli/ *adjective*
covered with oil, or containing a lot of oil: *The car mechanic wiped his hands on an oily rag.*

**oint·ment** /ˈɔɪntmənt/ *noun*
a substance that you rub into your skin as a medicine

**o·kay** (*also* **OK**) /oʊˈkeɪ/ *adjective* (*informal*)
**1** used for saying yes: *"Can I come too?" "Okay."* **SYNONYM: all right**
**2** used to get people's attention before saying something: *OK, let's get started.*
**3** acceptable: *"I don't want to go out tonight." "That's okay."* **SYNONYM: all right**
**4** not sick, hurt, or unhappy: *Are you okay? Did you hurt yourself?* **SYNONYM: all right**
**5** fairly good: *"Was the movie good?" "It was OK, but nothing special."* **SYNONYM: all right**
—**okay** (*also* **OK**) *adverb* fairly well: *She's doing okay in school, but she's not getting A's.*
[ORIGIN: 1800-1900 From the first letters of "oll korrect," a funny spelling of "all correct."]

**old** /oʊld/ *adjective*
**1** having lived for a long time: *My grandmother is very old.* **ANTONYM: young**
**2** having existed for a long time: *The old building needed repairs.* **ANTONYM: new**

**THESAURUS: old**

**ancient** from a time thousands of years ago – used about buildings, cities, or languages: *ancient history* | *the ancient city of Rome*

**antique** antique furniture, jewelry, or toys are old and valuable: *an antique rug*

**used** cars or other things that are used are not new, but people sell them: *a used car dealer*

**stale** stale bread, cake, or cookies are no longer fresh or good to eat

**3** used for asking or talking about the age of someone or something: *How old are you?* | *Our dog is three years old.*
**4** **an old friend** = a friend that you have known for a long time
**5** **someone's old house/job/teacher, etc.** = the house, etc. that someone had before, but does not have now: *Our old house was smaller than this one.*
**6** **the old** = people who are old: *The old and the sick were taken care of.*
[ORIGIN: From the old English word *eald*.]

**old ˈage** *noun*
the time when you are old: *He took care of his parents in their old age.*

**ˌold-ˈfashioned** *adjective*
not modern or popular now, but used in the past: *There was an old-fashioned telephone with a dial on the desk.*

**ol·ive** /ˈɑlɪv/ *noun*
a small green or black fruit that you can eat or use for making oil: *I asked for olives on my pizza.*

O

**O·lym·pic Games** /əˌlɪmpɪk ˈgeɪmz/ *plural noun*
**the Olympic Games** (*also* **the Olympics**) = a sports competition that happens every four years, in which people from many different countries take part
—**Olympic** *adjective* relating to the Olympic Games

**ome·let** (*also* **omelette**) /ˈɑmlɪt/ *noun*
eggs mixed together and cooked in a pan without STIRring. You usually put cheese or vegetables in an omelet and then fold it over
[ORIGIN: 1600-1700 From the French word *omelette*, from the Latin word *lamella*, which means "thin plate." An omelet is flat, like a plate.]

**om·i·nous** /ˈɑmənəs/ *adjective*
making you feel worried that something bad is going to happen: *There were ominous black clouds in the sky, and we were sure it would start raining soon.*
—**ominously** *adverb* in a way that makes you feel worried

**o·mit** /oʊˈmɪt/ *verb* (**omitted**, **omitting**) (*formal*)
to not include something: *His name was omitted from the list of players because he was injured.* SYNONYM: **leave out**
—**omission** /oʊˈmɪʃən/ *noun* the act of omitting something

**om·ni·vore** /ˈɑmnɪˌvɔr/ *noun*
an animal that eats meat and plants: *Humans are omnivores.*

**on** /ɔn/ *preposition, adjective, adverb*
**1** supported by a surface, or covering part of a surface: *a magazine on the table | I have mud on my shoes.* ANTONYM: **off**
**2** wearing something: *Put your coat on. It's cold outside.*
**3** in a particular place: *The answer is on page 44. | I grew up on a farm.*
**4** in or into a bus, airplane, train, or boat: *Did you sleep on the plane? | When the bus came, I got on.* ANTONYM: **off**
**5** at the side of a road, river, lake, or sea: *The store is on Main Street.*
**6** during a particular day: *The next game is on March 12.*
**7** if a machine or light is on, someone has made it start working: *The TV was on and I could hear it upstairs. | Turn on the light if you're going to read.* ANTONYM: **off**
**8** being broadcast by a television or radio station: *What's on TV tonight? | The news will be on at 6:00.*
**9** about a particular subject: *I'm reading a book on China.*
**10** used when saying that someone or something continues: *We drove on to the next town. | Go on, Cheryl. What happened next?*
**11** using something: *I talked to him on the phone. | She played a tune on the piano.*
**12** taking part or included in something: *Is he on the soccer team?*
**13** if you are on a trip or a visit, you are going somewhere or have come from somewhere: *They met on a trip to Spain.*
**14** used when showing who or what is affected by something: *Should people do experiments on animals?*
**15** if a planned event is on, it is going to happen: *Is the party still on? Someone said it might be canceled.* ANTONYM: **off**
→ **later on** at later[1], **on and off** at off

**once**[1] /wʌns/ *adverb*
**1** one time: *I've only met her once. | She goes to the gym once a week.*
**2** at a time in the past: *They were once good friends, but they had an argument and now they don't talk to each other any more.*
**3** **(every) once in a while** = sometimes, but not often: *We go fishing every once in a while.*
**4** **at once** = **a)** at the same time: *I can't do two things at once!* **b)** immediately: *He still looks the same, and I recognized him at once.*
**5** **all at once** = suddenly: *All at once, I felt a pain in my leg.*
**6** **once again/more** = again: *I tried once more to persuade him not to go.*
**7** **for once** = used when something that happens is unusual: *For once, he was right.*
**8** **once and for all** = completely and finally: *Let's settle this once and for all so we don't keep fighting about it.*
**9** **once upon a time** = a long time ago. This is used at the beginning of children's stories

**once**[2] *conjunction*
after or when: *It's easy to ride a bicycle once you learn how to do it.*

**one¹** /wʌn/ *number*
**1** 1: *I have one brother and two sisters.* | *One of the windows was broken.*
**2** one O'CLOCK: *I'll have to leave at one.*
**3** one year old: *Katie's almost one.*
**4** in math, a unit which is equal to 1: *In the number 365, the 5 is in the ones place.*
**5** **one or two** (*informal*) = a few: *I have one or two things to do.*

**one²** *pronoun*
**1** used instead of a noun when it is clear what kind of thing you mean: *"Do you have a bike?" "No, but I'm getting one for my birthday."* | *"Which candy bar do you want?" "That one."*
**2** **one by one/one after the other/one after another** = first one person or thing, then the next, etc.: *One by one, people got off the bus.*
**3** (*formal*) people in general: *One does not usually talk about one's health to strangers.*

**one³** *adjective*
**1** **one day/afternoon, etc.** = **a)** on a particular day, etc. in the past: *One day, I got a call from my brother.* **b)** on some day, etc. in the future: *We should get together one evening.*
**2** only: *My one goal is to do better in school.*

**one·self** /wʌnˈself/ *pronoun* (*formal*)
used when saying that people in general do something to themselves: *One must protect oneself.*

**ˌone-ˈway** *adjective*
**1** moving or allowing movement in only one direction: *a one-way street*
**2** a one-way ticket is for going from one place to another, but not back again

**on·go·ing** [Ac] /ˈɔnˌgoʊɪŋ/ *adjective* (*formal*)
continuing: *They are doing an ongoing study of children's health.*

**on·ion** /ˈʌnjən/ *noun*
a round vegetable with many white layers inside which has a strong taste and smell → see picture on page A12

**on·line** (*also* **on-line**) /ˈɔnlaɪn/ *adjective, adverb*
using the Internet: *online shopping*

**on·ly¹** /ˈoʊnli/ *adverb*
**1** used when a number or amount seems small: *Only five people came to the party.*
**2** not anyone or anything else: *She eats only vegetables.* | *This room is for teachers only. Students aren't allowed.* **SYNONYM: just**
**3** not in any other way or not in any other situation: *You can only get there by boat. There are no roads to the area.* | *Eat only when you are hungry.* **SYNONYM: just**
**4** used for saying that something is not very important or serious: *Don't get upset about losing. It's only a game.* **SYNONYM: just**
**5** **if only** = I wish: *If only I'd kept a copy of the letter! I'd love to read it again.*

**only²** *adjective*
**1** used for saying that there is not more than one person or thing of a particular kind: *You're the only person I can trust.*
**2** **an only child** = someone who has no brothers or sisters

**only³** *conjunction* (*informal*)
but: *I'd help, only I'm really busy that day.*

**ˈon-the-job** *adjective*
on-the-job training is training you get while you are working

**on·to** /ˈɔntə; *before vowels* ˈɔntʊ; *strong* ˈɔntu/ *preposition*
to a place which is on something: *He climbed onto the roof.*

**on·ward** /ˈɔnwɚd/ (*also* **onwards**) *adverb* (*formal*)
**1** **from ... onward** = beginning at a particular time: *From the 1980s onward, the town got bigger.*
**2** forward: *The ship sailed onward.*

**ooh** /u/ *interjection*
said when you like something or are excited: *Ooh, look at those cool shoes!*

**oops** /ʊps/ *interjection*
said when someone has fallen, dropped something, or made a small mistake: *Oops! I spilled some milk.*

**ooze** /uz/ *verb*
to flow from something very slowly: *Blood oozed from the cut.*
→ see Thesaurus box at **pour**

**ooze**
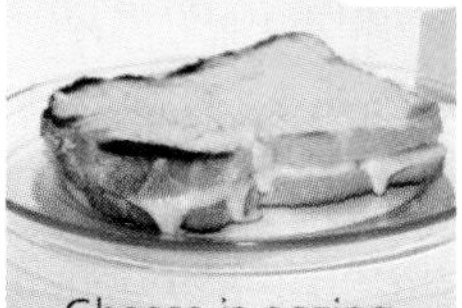
Cheese is oozing out of the sandwich.

**o·paque** /oʊˈpeɪk/ *adjective*
not letting light through: *The glass in the door*

O

*is transparent, but the wood around it is opaque.* **ANTONYMS: clear, transparent**
[**ORIGIN:** 1400-1500 From the Latin word *opacus*, which means "dark."]

**o·pen[1]** /ˈoʊpən/ *adjective*
**1** not closed: *Who left the window open? | I'm so tired I can't keep my eyes open.* → see picture at **ajar**
**2** if a place such as store or a library is open, people can come in: *Is the library open today?*
**3** an open area is not surrounded by things or does not have many buildings or trees on it: *The park is a green open space in the middle of the city.*
**4** honest and not hiding anything: *Some parents are open with their children when they are having money problems.*
**5** if something is open to people of a particular kind, they can take part in it: *The competition is open to children aged 7 to 14.*

**open[2]** *verb*
**1** to move something so that it is open, or to become open: *I opened my eyes and looked around. | The door opened, and Frank came in.* **ANTONYMS: close, shut**
**2** when something such as a store, library, or public place opens, people can go in: *What time does the bookstore open on Sundays?* **ANTONYM: close**
**3** to start something: *The principal opened the meeting by thanking us for coming.*
**4** **open an account** = to start having a bank account

**PHRASAL VERB**
**open up**
**1** **open (something) up** = to make something available, or to become available: *Education opens up the chance for college or a better job.*
**2** to stop being shy and talk about your feelings: *After she got to know me better, she started to open up.*

**o·pen·er** /ˈoʊpənɚ/ *noun*
a tool used for opening things: *a can opener*

**o·pen·ing[1]** /ˈoʊpənɪŋ/ *noun*
**1** the time when a place such as a new store or a MUSEUM opens for the first time: *The opening of the new restaurant is on May 6.*
**2** a hole in something that a person or thing can go through: *He went through a narrow opening in the fence.*
**3** a chance, especially for a job: *There are a few openings for part-time jobs at the store.*

**opening[2]** *adjective*
coming at the start of something: *The opening chapter of the book introduces all of the main characters.*

**o·pen·ly** /ˈoʊpənli/ *adverb*
not trying to hide anything: *They talk openly about their problems.*

**op·er·a** /ˈɑprə/ *noun*
a play in which the actors sing all the words: *Mozart wrote many famous operas.*
[**ORIGIN:** 1600-1700 From the Latin word for "work or works."]

**op·er·ate** /ˈɑpəˌreɪt/ *verb*
**1** (*formal*) to use a machine: *Do you know how to operate the washing machine?*
**2** to work: *The company operates from offices in Seattle.*
**3** to cut into someone's body in order to repair or remove a part that is damaged: *The doctors operated on her stomach.*

**op·er·a·tion** /ˌɑpəˈreɪʃən/ *noun*
**1** the process of cutting into someone's body to repair or remove a part that is damaged: *He needs to have an operation on his knee.*
**2** an organized set of actions by a number of people in order to achieve something: *The rescue operation was successful and all the people were saved.*

**op·er·a·tor** /ˈɑpəˌreɪtɚ/ *noun*
**1** someone whose job is to connect telephone calls: *The hotel operator can connect your call.*
**2** someone whose job is to use a machine or piece of equipment: *a crane operator*

**o·pin·ion** /əˈpɪnyən/ *noun*
your ideas about something, for example whether you think it is good or right: *What's your opinion about school uniforms? | You did the right thing, in my opinion.*

**o·pin·ion·at·ed** /əˈpɪnyəˌneɪtɪd/ *adjective*
expressing very strong opinions, and sure that your opinions are right: *He's very opinionated and thinks that everyone else is wrong.*

**o·pos·sum** /əˈpɑsəm/ *noun*
an American animal that looks like a large rat and can climb trees

**op·po·nent** /əˈpoʊnənt/ *noun*
**1** someone who tries to defeat someone else in a competition, game, or election: *The Dallas Cowboys easily beat their opponents.*
**2** someone who disagrees with an idea or action: *Opponents of the plan spoke against it at the meeting.*

**op·por·tu·ni·ty** /ˌɑpɚˈtunəti/ *noun* (plural **opportunities**)
a chance to do something: *I was glad to have the opportunity to be in the play.*

**op·pose** /əˈpoʊz/ *verb*
to disagree with an idea or action: *They oppose the plan because they think it will cost too much money.*

**WORD FAMILY: oppose**
**oppose** *verb* | **opposed** *adjective* | **opposition** *noun* | **opposing** *adjective* | **opponent** *noun*

**op·posed** /əˈpoʊzd/ *adjective*
**be opposed to something** = to disagree with an idea or action: *He was opposed to the war.*

**op·pos·ing** /əˈpoʊzɪŋ/ *adjective*
opposing teams or groups are trying to defeat each other: *I think our team played better than the opposing team.*

**op·po·site¹** /ˈɑpəzɪt/ *adjective*
**1** as different as possible from something else: *The cars went in opposite directions. One went west and the other went east.* | *Short and tall have opposite meanings.*
**2** on the other side of something: *They crossed to the opposite side of the river.* **SYNONYM: other**

**opposite²** *noun*
someone or something that is as different as possible from someone or something else: *Hot is the opposite of cold.*

**op·po·si·tion** /ˌɑpəˈzɪʃən/ *noun*
**1** strong disagreement with or protest against something: *There has been opposition to the plan to close the school.*
**2** the person or team you are competing against: *The opposition played well.*

**op·press** /əˈpres/ *verb*
if people with power oppress other people, they treat them badly or do not let them do what they want: *The king oppressed the poor farmers and took their crops.*
—**oppressive** *adjective* treating people badly and not letting them do what they want: *He was an oppressive ruler.*
—**oppressed** *adjective* being badly treated and not allowed to do what you want: *The slaves were oppressed.*
—**oppression** /əˈpreʃən/ *noun* if there is oppression, people are treated badly and not allowed to do what they want

**opt** /ɑpt/ *verb*
to choose to do or have one thing instead of another: *I opted for the apple pie instead of the cake.*

**op·ti·cal** /ˈɑptɪkəl/ *adjective*
relating to seeing things: *The store sells mostly optical equipment such as cameras and telescopes.*
[**ORIGIN:** 1500-1600 From the Greek word *optikos*, which means "relating to sight" and is related to *ops*, a word for "eye."]

**op·ti·cian** /ɑpˈtɪʃən/ *noun*
someone who makes or sells glasses

**op·ti·mism** /ˈɑptəˌmɪzəm/ *noun*
a belief that good things will happen: *Because of her optimism, she was sure that things would get better.* **ANTONYM: pessimism**
[**ORIGIN:** 1700-1800 From the Latin word *optimus*, which means "best."]

**op·ti·mist** /ˈɑptəˌmɪst/ *noun*
someone who believes that good things will happen: *I'm an optimist, so I'm not worried about the future.* **ANTONYM: pessimist**

**op·ti·mist·ic** /ˌɑptəˈmɪstɪk/ *adjective*
believing that good things will happen: *I'm optimistic about our chances of winning today.*
**ANTONYM: pessimistic**

**op·tion** Ac /ˈɑpʃən/ *noun*
something that you can choose to do: *You have two options: you can come with us or stay here on your own.*
[**ORIGIN:** 1500-1600 From the Latin word *optio*, which means "the ability to choose."]

**op·tion·al** Ac /ˈɑpʃənl/ *adjective*
if something is optional, you do not have to do it or have it: *Attendance at the meeting is*

*optional, so you don't have to go if you don't want to.* **ANTONYM: compulsory**

**op·tom·e·trist** /ɑpˈtɑmətrɪst/ *noun*
someone who tests people's eyes and orders glasses for them
—**optometry** /ɑpˈtɑmətri/ *noun* the work of an optometrist → see picture on page **A17**
[**ORIGIN:** 1800-1900 From the Greek words *opto-* and *metron*, which mean "seeing" and "measure."]

**or** /ɚ; *strong* ɔr/ *conjunction*
**1** used when mentioning another possible thing: *On weekends, I usually play computer games or go to the park.*
**2** used when mentioning another thing after "not," "never," etc.: *I don't like broccoli or peas.*
**3** used when mentioning something bad that will happen if someone does not do something: *Hurry, or you'll be late!*

**o·ral** /ˈɔrəl/ *adjective* (*formal*)
**1** spoken, not written: *In French class, you will take an oral test as well as a written test.*
**2** relating to the mouth: *oral cancer*
—**orally** *adverb* through the mouth: *The medicine is taken orally.*
[**ORIGIN:** 1600-1700 From the Latin word *oralis*, from *oris*, a form of *os*, which means "mouth."]

**or·ange** /ˈɔrɪndʒ/ *noun*
**1** a round juicy fruit that is a color between red and yellow and has a thick skin: *orange juice* → see picture on page **A13**
**2** a color that is a mix of red and yellow
—**orange** *adjective* having a color that is a mix of red and yellow: *The sun was bright orange before it set.*
[**ORIGIN:** 1300-1400 From the Arabic word *naranj*, from the Sanskrit word *naranga*, which means "orange tree." Sanskrit is an old language that was used in India.]

**o·rang·u·tan** /əˈræŋəˌtæn/ *noun*
a large APE that has long arms and orange-brown hair → see picture at **ape**
[**ORIGIN:** 1600-1700 From the Malay phrase *orang hutan*, which means "man of the forest."]

**or·bit¹** /ˈɔrbɪt/ *noun*
the path of an object that is moving around another object in space: *the Moon's orbit around the Earth*
[**ORIGIN:** 1500-1600 From the Latin word *orbita*, which means "wheel track," from *orbis*, meaning "something with the shape of a circle."]

**orbit**

**orbit²** *verb*
to move around an object in space: *Many satellites now orbit the Earth.*

**or·chard** /ˈɔrtʃɚd/ *noun*
a place where fruit trees are grown

**or·ches·tra** /ˈɔrkɪstrə/ *noun*
a large group of musicians who play CLASSICAL MUSIC: *She plays violin in the orchestra.*
[**ORIGIN:** 1600-1700 From the Greek word for a space in a theater where dancers performed, from *orcheisthai*, which means "to dance." When "orchestra" was first used in English, it meant this space. Later, it began to be used about a group of musicians, perhaps because musicians played for dancers.]

**or·deal** /ɔrˈdil/ *noun* (*formal*)
a very bad or difficult experience: *He was badly injured, and spent a long time recovering from the ordeal.*
[**ORIGIN:** From the old English word *ordal*, which means "trial or judgment." People who were accused of a crime used to have to experience painful things to prove that they were innocent.]

**or·der¹** /ˈɔrdɚ/ *noun*
**1 in order to do something** = so that you can do something: *I came in order to see you.*
**2** the way that you arrange things or put them on a list: *Write the names in alphabetical order, starting with names that begin with A.*
**3** something that you ask for from a business or in a restaurant: *Your order will be sent by mail.* | *The waiter came and took our order.*
**4** something that someone in authority tells you to do: *Soldiers must obey orders.* **SYNONYM: command**
**5 out of order** = if a machine is out of order, it is not working: *The elevator was out of order, so we had to use the stairs.*

6 a situation in which people obey rules and do not behave violently: *Children learn best when the teacher keeps order.*

**order²** *verb*
1 to ask for something from a business or in a restaurant: *My parents ordered a new carpet for the bedroom.*
2 to tell someone to do something: *The police officer ordered the driver to stop.*
→ see Thesaurus box at **ask**

**or·der·ly** /ˈɔrdəli/ *adjective*
1 arranged or organized in a neat way: *We moved the seats into orderly rows.*
2 sensible and calm: *Students should leave the classroom in an orderly way and not all rush for the door.*

**or·di·nal num·ber** /ˌɔrdn-əl ˈnʌmbə/ *noun*
a word that shows where something comes in a series: *"First," "second," "third," etc. are ordinal numbers.*

**or·di·nar·i·ly** /ˌɔrdnˈerəli/ *adverb*
usually: *Ordinarily, I leave the house at 8:00, but today I left at 9:00.*

**or·di·nar·y** /ˈɔrdnˌeri/ *adjective*
1 not different or special in any way: *It was just an ordinary day – nothing unusual happened.*
2 **out of the ordinary** = unusual: *Did you notice anything out of the ordinary?*
→ see Thesaurus box at **normal**

**ore** /ɔr/ *noun*
rock or earth that people can get metal from: *The country exports iron ore.*

**or·gan** /ˈɔrgən/ *noun*
1 a part of your body that has a particular purpose: *The heart is the organ that makes blood move around your body.*
2 a musical instrument like a piano but with long pipes, or an electric instrument that makes similar sounds: *She plays the organ for the church.*
—**organist** *noun* someone who plays the organ
[**ORIGIN:** 1200-1300 From the Greek word *organon*, which means "tool or instrument."]

**or·gan·ic** /ɔrˈgænɪk/ *adjective*
1 grown or produced without using chemicals: *organic vegetables*
2 relating to living things: *You can improve your soil by adding organic matter such as leaves and grass.*
—**organically** *adverb* without using chemicals: *The restaurant only uses organically grown vegetables.*

**or·ga·nism** /ˈɔrgəˌnɪzəm/ *noun*
a living thing, especially a very small one: *Pond water contains many organisms.*

**or·ga·ni·za·tion** /ˌɔrgənəˈzeɪʃən/ *noun*
1 a group of people such as a club or business: *The United Nations is an international organization.*
2 the way in which something is organized: *Good organization makes your work easier.*
3 the job of organizing something: *The school concert needs a lot of organization before it can be performed.*

**or·ga·nize** /ˈɔrgəˌnaɪz/ *verb*
1 to put people or things into an order or system: *The books are organized alphabetically so that you can find what you want.*
2 to plan an activity or event: *Who is organizing the party?*
—**organizer** *noun* someone who organizes something

**WORD FAMILY: organize**
**organize** *verb* | **organizer** *noun* | **organized** *adjective* | **disorganized** *adjective* | **organization** *noun*

**or·ga·nized** /ˈɔrgəˌnaɪzd/ *adjective*
1 planned or arranged carefully: *The book is well organized – it's easy to find the information you need.* **ANTONYM: disorganized**
2 an organized person plans and arranges things carefully: *Debbie always does a good job. She's very organized.* **ANTONYM: disorganized**
3 involving a group of people doing something together: *organized religion*

**o·ri·ent·ed** Ac /ˈɔriˌentɪd/ *adjective*
**family-oriented / customer-oriented / goal-oriented, etc.** = caring most about families, customers, etc.: *He's very goal-oriented and is always thinking about his future.*

**or·i·gin** /ˈɔrədʒɪn/ *noun*
1 the start of something: *There are different*

*ideas about the origin of the universe, but no one knows for sure how it started.*
**2** the place or group of people that someone comes from: *Many of the students are of Hispanic origin and speak Spanish at home.*

**WORD FAMILY: origin**
**origin** *noun* | **original** *adjective* | **originally** *adverb*

**o·rig·i·nal** /əˈrɪdʒɪnəl/ *adjective*
**1** first: *Our original plan was to go to Florida, but then we decided to go to Yellowstone.*
**2** new and different: *The book is very interesting and contains a lot of original ideas.*
**3** not copied: *an original painting*
→ see Thesaurus box at **new**

**o·rig·i·nal·ly** /əˈrɪdʒɪnəli/ *adverb*
in the beginning: *I'm originally from Texas, but I've lived in Oregon for 10 years.*

**or·na·ment** /ˈɔrnəmənt/ *noun*
a beautiful object that you show in your home or use to decorate something: *We hung the ornaments on the Christmas tree.*

**or·phan** /ˈɔrfən/ *noun*
a child whose parents are dead

**or·phan·age** /ˈɔrfənɪdʒ/ *noun*
a home for children whose parents are dead

**orth·o·don·tist** /ˌɔrθəˈdɑntɪst/ *noun*
someone whose job is to make people's teeth straight: *The orthodontist said I needed braces.*

**or·tho·dox** /ˈɔrθəˌdɑks/ *adjective*
**1 Orthodox** = following the traditional beliefs of a religion: *an Orthodox Jew*
**2** accepted by most people as correct or normal: *He tried acupuncture before going to the doctor for orthodox medical treatment.*
[**ORIGIN:** 1500-1600 From the Greek words *orthos* and *doxa*, which mean "correct" and "opinion."]

**os·trich** /ˈɑstrɪtʃ/ *noun*
a very large African bird with long legs that runs fast but cannot fly

**oth·er** /ˈʌðɚ/ *adjective, pronoun*
**1** the second of two things: *Here's one sock, where's the other?* | *His left hand was empty, but there was something in his other hand.*
**2** the rest of a group: *We're the only ones here. All the others have left.*
**3** different things or people of the same kind: *Does anyone have any other questions?* | *Some computers are better than others.*
**4 the other day/week** = the days or weeks just before this one: *I saw Rosie the other day.*
**5 other than** = except for something: *Was there anything other than lettuce in your salad?* **SYNONYM: besides**
**6 every other day/week, etc.** = every two days, weeks, etc.: *The class meets every other Thursday.*
**7 someone/something/somewhere, etc. or other** = used when you are not certain about something: *We'll get the money somehow or other.*

**oth·er·wise** /ˈʌðɚˌwaɪz/ *adverb*
**1** used when mentioning something bad that will happen if someone does not do something: *You have to put the fish back in the water; otherwise, it'll die.*
**2** if the situation had been different: *Our flight was delayed. Otherwise, we would have gotten here sooner.*
**3** except for what has just been mentioned: *The sleeves are too long, but otherwise the dress fits.*

**ot·ter** /ˈɑtɚ/ *noun*
a small animal with brown fur that eats fish and can swim

**ouch** /aʊtʃ/ *interjection*
said when you suddenly feel pain: *Ouch! That hurt!*

**ought to** /ˈɔtə; *strong* ˈɔtu/ *verb*
**1** used for saying that someone should do something: *It's a great place – you ought to go there.* **SYNONYM: should**
**2** used for saying that you expect something to happen or be true: *He's smart – he ought to pass easily.* **SYNONYM: should**

**ounce** /aʊns/ *noun* (*written abbreviation*: **oz.**)
**1** a unit for measuring weight, equal to 28.35 grams: *There are 16 ounces in a pound.*
**2** (*also* **fluid ounce**) a unit for measuring liquid, equal to 1/16 of a pint or 0.0296 LITERs

**our** /aʊɚ/ *adjective*
belonging to us: *Our house is very small.*

**ours** /aʊɚz/ *pronoun*
something that belongs to us: *"Whose car is that?" "It's ours."*

**our·selves** /aʊɚˈselvz/ *pronoun*
**1** the people, including yourself, that you have just mentioned: *It was strange seeing ourselves on television.*
**2** used with "we" to emphasize that we did something: *We did all the work ourselves.*
**3 (all) by ourselves** = alone or without help: *Amy and I made supper all by ourselves.*

**out** /aʊt/ *adverb, adjective, preposition*
**1** away from the inside of a place or container: *She went out into the yard. | The keys must have fallen out of my pocket. | He put his head out the window and looked around.* **ANTONYM: in**
**2** not at home or in the office where you work: *Did anyone call while I was out?* **ANTONYM: in**
**3** not shining or burning: *The lights are out. I don't think anyone's home.*
**4** away from the main part or center of something: *Several roads lead out from the center of the town.*
**5** able to be seen in the sky: *The rain stopped and the sun came out.*
**6** a player who is out cannot play anymore in that game: *I caught the ball, so you're out.*
**7** available to buy: *His new CD will be out next week.*
**8** if you read or shout something out, you say it in a voice that is loud enough for others to hear: *She read out the names of the students chosen to play in the game.*
**9 out of something** = if you are out of something, you do not have any of it left: *The car is almost out of gas.*
**10 two out of three/three out of four, etc.** = used for talking about part of a group: *Three out of four students think the test is too hard.*

**out·bound** /ˈaʊtbaʊnd/ *adjective*
outbound planes, trains, or cars are going away from a place: *All the outbound flights did not leave because of the snow.* **ANTONYM: inbound**

**out·break** /ˈaʊtbreɪk/ *noun (formal)*
the start of something bad such as a war or disease: *People left the country quickly at the outbreak of war.*

**out·burst** /ˈaʊtbɚst/ *noun*
a sudden expression of a strong emotion: *She found her father's angry outbursts very frightening.*

**out·come** Ac /ˈaʊtkʌm/ *noun*
the final result of something: *Did his injury change the outcome of the game?*
→ see Thesaurus box at **result**[1]

**out·dat·ed** /ˌaʊtˈdeɪtɪd/ *adjective*
old and no longer useful: *The textbooks are outdated and need to be replaced.*

**out·do** /aʊtˈdu/ *verb* (**outdid** /aʊtˈdɪd/, **outdone** /aʊtˈdʌn/, **outdoes** /aʊtˈdʌz/)
to be better or more successful than someone else: *The skaters were trying to outdo each other by doing more and more difficult turns.*

**out·door** /ˈaʊtdɔr/ *adjective*
happening or used outside: *The motel has an outdoor swimming pool.* **ANTONYM: indoor**

**out·doors** /ˌaʊtˈdɔrz/ *adverb*
outside, not in a building: *It's a nice day – let's play outdoors.* **ANTONYM: indoors**

**out·er** /ˈaʊtɚ/ *adjective*
on or near the outside of something: *Take off the cabbage's outer leaves before you cook it.* **ANTONYM: inner**

**ˌouter ˈspace** *noun*
the area outside the Earth's air, where the stars and PLANETs are: *The movie is about creatures from outer space that attack the Earth.*

**out·field** /ˈaʊtfild/ *noun*
the part of a baseball field that is farthest from the player who is BATting

**out·fit** /ˈaʊtˌfɪt/ *noun*
a set of clothes that you wear together: *She bought a new outfit for the party.*

**out·go·ing** /ˈaʊtˌgoʊɪŋ/ *adjective*
someone who is outgoing enjoys meeting and talking to people: *Sally is really outgoing and easy to talk to.* **SYNONYM: friendly**
→ see Thesaurus box at **shy**

**out·grow** /aʊtˈgroʊ/ *verb* (**outgrew** /aʊtˈgru/, **outgrown** /aʊtˈgroʊn/)
if children outgrow their clothes, they grow too big for them: *Kara's already outgrown her shoes. We'll have to buy her a new pair.*

**out·ing** /ˈaʊtɪŋ/ *noun*
a short trip in which you go somewhere for fun: *a family outing to the beach*

O

**out·last** /aʊtˈlæst/ *verb*
to continue to exist or do something longer than something or someone else: *Plastic bags do not rot, so they outlast the other things we throw away.*

**out·law¹** /ˈaʊtlɔ/ *verb*
to say that something is illegal or not allowed: *The new law would outlaw cigarette machines.*

**outlaw²** *noun*
used in the past to mean a criminal who is hiding from the police: *the outlaws of the Wild West*

**out·let** /ˈaʊtlet/ *noun*
**1** a place on a wall where you can connect things to the electricity supply: *We plugged the TV into the electrical outlet.* → see picture on page **A8**
**2** (*also* **outlet store**) a store that sells things for less than the usual price: *I got these jeans at an outlet store for $20.*
**3** a way of using your energy or expressing your feelings: *Painting is fun and a good outlet for expressing your creativity.*

**out·line** /ˈaʊtlaɪn/ *noun*
**1** the main ideas or facts: *Write an outline of your essay first, so that you organize your ideas.*
**2** if you can see the outline of something, you can see its shape, but you cannot clearly see other parts of it: *The outline of the Statue of Liberty showed against the sky.*

**out·look** /ˈaʊtlʊk/ *noun*
**1** what people expect to happen in the future: *The outlook for people with this disease is good, as they will get better with treatment.*
**2** the way you think about life and what happens to you: *Neil has a positive outlook; he tries to see the good things in life.*

**out·num·ber** /aʊtˈnʌmbɚ/ *verb*
to be more in number than another group: *In this class, girls outnumber boys. There are 15 girls and 10 boys.*

**ˌout-of-ˈdate** *adjective*
another word for OUTDATED

**out·pa·tient** /ˈaʊtˌpeɪʃənt/ *adjective*
relating to someone who goes to the hospital for treatment from a doctor, but does not stay there for very long: *She went to an outpatient clinic for treatment for her fever.*
—**outpatient** *noun* someone who goes to the hospital for treatment from a doctor, but does not stay there for very long

**out·put** [Ac] /ˈaʊtpʊt/ *noun*
the amount of goods or work that a company or country produces: *The company has increased its output by 15% this year.* **SYNONYM: production**

**out·rage** /ˈaʊtreɪdʒ/ *noun*
**1** a strong feeling of anger or shock: *The plan to close the school caused outrage in the community.*
**2** something that causes a strong feeling of anger and shock: *It is an outrage that people in some countries do not have enough to eat.*

**out·ra·geous** /aʊtˈreɪdʒəs/ *adjective*
**1** something that is outrageous is very wrong, and makes you feel very shocked and angry: *He told some outrageous lies that really made me angry.*
**2** very unusual or strange, but in a way that people like: *She wears outrageous clothes, like purple velvet pants, but she looks great.*
—**outrageously** *adverb* in a way that makes you feel shocked or angry: *The shoes were outrageously expensive.*

**out·right¹** /ˈaʊtraɪt/ *adjective*
complete and very clear: *He told me an outright lie. He said he went to school when I know he did not.*

**out·right²** /aʊtˈraɪt/ *adverb*
**1** clearly and directly: *She asked me outright if I agreed with her.*
**2** **buy/own something outright** = to own something such as a house completely because you have paid the full price with your own money

**out·set** /ˈaʊtset/ *noun*
**at/from the outset** = at or from the beginning: *It was clear from the outset of the game that the other team would win.*

**out·side¹** /ˌaʊtˈsaɪd/ (*also* **out'side of**) *adverb, preposition*
**1** not inside a building or room, but near it: *Mom, can I go outside and play? | She waited outside of his classroom.* **ANTONYM: inside**

2 not in a city or country, but near it: *They live just outside Seattle.*
3 not in a group or organization: *Don't talk about this to anyone outside the family.*

**outside²** *adjective*
not inside a building: *We turned off the outside lights when we went to bed.* **ANTONYM: inside**

**outside³** *noun*
**the outside** = the outer part or surface of something: *They painted the outside of the building pink.* **ANTONYM: inside**

**out·sid·er** /aʊtˈsaɪdɚ/ *noun*
someone who does not belong to a particular group or organization: *Lisa was new at the school and felt like an outsider.*

**out·skirts** /ˈaʊtskɚts/ *plural noun*
**the outskirts** = the parts of a city or town that are far away from the center: *The restaurant is on the outskirts of town.*

**out·spo·ken** /aʊtˈspoʊkən/ *adjective*
an outspoken person says what he or she thinks, even when it may shock people or make them angry: *She is confident and outspoken, and not afraid to give her opinion.*

**out·stand·ing** /aʊtˈstændɪŋ/ *adjective*
better than anyone or anything else: *Nikki is an outstanding basketball player.* **SYNONYM: excellent**
→ see Thesaurus box at **good¹**

**out·ward¹** /ˈaʊtwɚd/ *adjective*
1 relating to how someone seems to feel or think, when this might be different from what that person really feels or thinks: *I waited for his expression to change, but there were no outward signs that he was upset.* **ANTONYM: inward**
2 going away from a place or toward the outside: *The outward flight was bumpy, but the trip back was fine.* **SYNONYM: outbound**

**outward²** (*also* **outwards**) *adverb*
toward the outside of something, or away from the middle: *He was standing with his hands on his hips, so his elbows pointed outwards.* **ANTONYM: inward** → see picture at **inward**

**out·weigh** /aʊtˈweɪ/ *verb*
to be more important or have more effect than something else: *The benefits of the new cancer drug outweigh the risks.*

**o·val** /ˈoʊvəl/ *noun*
a shape that is like a circle, but longer than it is wide → see picture at **shape**
—**oval** *adjective* in the shape of an oval: *an oval table*
[**ORIGIN:** 1500-1600 From the Latin word *ovum*, which means "egg."]

**ˌOval ˈOffice** *noun*
**the Oval Office** = the office where the president of the U.S. works, in the White House in Washington, D.C.

**o·va·ry** /ˈoʊvəri/ *noun* (plural **ovaries**)
1 the part of a woman's body or a female animal's body that produces eggs
2 the part of a female plant that produces seeds

**ov·en** /ˈʌvən/ *noun*
a piece of equipment that you cook food inside, shaped like a metal box with a door on it. An oven is usually part of a STOVE: *Bake the cake in the oven for 30 minutes.* → see picture on page **A9**

**o·ver¹** /ˈoʊvɚ/ *preposition*
1 above or higher than something: *I leaned over the desk. | The sign over the door said "Exit."* **ANTONYM: under**
2 moving across the top of something, or from one side of it to the other: *We walked over the hill. | The dog jumped over the fence.* **ANTONYM: under**
3 covering someone or something: *I put the blanket over the baby.* **ANTONYM: under**
4 more than an amount, number, or age: *Over a hundred people came to the school play. | The game is for children over seven years old.* **ANTONYM: under**
5 during: *Where did you go over summer vacation?*
6 **all over** = everywhere in a place: *Why are your clothes all over the floor?*
7 **be/get over something** = to feel better after being sick, upset, or angry: *I can't seem to get over this cold.*

**over²** *adverb*
1 down from an upright position: *Do you remember when that big tree fell over? | I knocked over a glass.*

**2** used for showing where someone or something is, when you can point to it: *I'm over here! | There's a mailbox over on the corner.*
**3** to or in a place: *Can I go over to Scott's house to play?*
**4** again: *I got confused when I was counting the money and had to start over.*
**5** so that another side is showing: *Turn the test over and start writing. | He rolled over in bed and faced the wall.*
**6 think/read/talk something over** = to think, read, or talk about something carefully before deciding what to do: *I might go to summer school, but I need to talk it over with my mom first.*
**7** above: *A helicopter flew over.*
**8** more than a particular amount, number, or age: *The game is for children ages six and over.* **ANTONYM: under**

**over**[3] *adjective*
**1** finished: *The game's over – Dallas won.* **SYNONYM: done**
**2 get something over with** (*informal*) = to do something that you do not want to do, so that it is finished: *You have to tell her you're sorry, so call her and get it over with.*
→ see Thesaurus box at **done**[2]

**o·ver·all** Ac /ˌoʊvɚˌɔl/ *adjective*
including everything: *The overall cost of the trip is $500, including food, hotel, and transportation.*

**o·ver·alls** /ˈoʊvɚˌɔlz/ *plural noun*
heavy cotton pants with a square piece covering your chest and two STRAPs (=thin pieces of cloth) that go over your shoulders to hold them up → see picture on page **A6**

**o·ver·board** /ˈoʊvɚˌbɔrd/ *adverb*
**1** over the side of a boat into the water: *He fell overboard into the lake during the storm.*
**2 go overboard** = to do or say something that is too extreme for the situation: *Don't go overboard with your makeup. Just a little is enough.*

**o·ver·cast** /ˈoʊvɚˌkæst/ *adjective*
if the sky is overcast, it is dark and cloudy

**o·ver·charge** /ˌoʊvɚˈtʃɑrdʒ/ *verb*
to make someone pay too much money for something: *I think the restaurant overcharged us – the bill seems way too high.*

**o·ver·coat** /ˈoʊvɚˌkoʊt/ *noun*
a long warm coat that you wear over other clothes

**o·ver·come** /ˌoʊvɚˈkʌm/ *verb* (**overcame** /ˌoʊvɚˈkeɪm/, **overcome**) (*formal*)
**1** to succeed in controlling a feeling or solving a problem: *He has overcome his fear of flying. | The city has to overcome some serious transportation problems.*
**2** if you are overcome by a feeling, you feel it very strongly: *She was overcome with shyness when she went into the new class.*

**o·ver·crowd·ed** /ˌoʊvɚˈkraʊdɪd/ *adjective*
a place that is overcrowded has too many people or things in it: *The room was overcrowded, and I couldn't find a chair to sit in.*

**o·ver·do** /ˌoʊvɚˈdu/ *verb* (**overdid** /ˌoʊvɚˈdɪd/, **overdone** /ˌoʊvɚˈdʌn/, **overdoes** /ˌoʊvɚˈdʌz/)
to do or use too much of something: *It's good to exercise, but don't overdo it or you might hurt yourself.*

**o·ver·dose** /ˈoʊvɚˌdoʊs/ *noun*
too much of a drug taken at one time: *He died from a heroin overdose.*
—**overdose** *verb* to take too much of a drug at one time

**o·ver·due** /ˌoʊvɚˈdu/ *adjective*
late in arriving or late in being done: *My library books are overdue; I was supposed to return them last week.* **SYNONYM: late**

**o·ver·es·ti·mate** Ac /ˌoʊvɚˈestəˌmeɪt/ *verb*
to think that something is bigger, longer, more important, etc. than it really is: *I overestimated the distance to the school; it was only a mile, not three miles.*

**o·ver·flow** /ˌəʊvəˈfloʊ/ *verb*
if something overflows, liquid or objects fill it completely and come over its edge: *It had rained so much that the river had overflowed its banks.*

**o·ver·grown** /ˌoʊvɚˈgroʊn/ *adjective*
covered with plants that have grown without being cut: *Their yard was overgrown with weeds.*

**o·ver·hand** /ˈoʊvɚˌhænd/ *adjective, adverb*
if you throw a ball overhand, your arm is higher than your shoulder when you throw: *In*

*baseball, you throw the ball overhand to the batter.* **ANTONYM: underhand**

**o·ver·head** /ˌoʊvɚˈhed/ *adjective, adverb*
above your head: *A plane flew overhead, and we looked up. | an overhead light*

**o·ver·hear** /ˌoʊvɚˈhɪr/ *verb* (**overheard** /ˌoʊvɚˈhɚd/)
to hear what other people are saying by accident, when they do not know that you are listening: *I overheard my parents arguing.*

**o·ver·lap** Ac /ˌoʊvɚˈlæp/ *verb* (**overlapped, overlapping**)
if two or more things overlap, part of one thing covers part of another thing: *Draw two circles that overlap, and color in the area that they share.*

**o·ver·load·ed** /ˌoʊvɚˈloʊdɪd/ *adjective*
if someone is overloaded, he or she has too many things to do or think about: *Our teachers are already overloaded; they don't need more work to do.*
—**overload** *verb* to give someone or something too many things to do

**o·ver·look** /ˌoʊvɚˈlʊk/ *verb*
**1** to have a view of something from above: *Three of the windows overlook the street.*
**2** to not see or notice something: *It's easy to overlook mistakes in your own writing.*

**o·ver·night** /ˌoʊvɚˈnaɪt/ *adverb*
**1** for or during the night: *She's staying overnight at a friend's house.*
**2** very quickly and suddenly: *He won the lottery and became a millionaire overnight.*
**3** an overnight bag is one you use on short trips

**o·ver·pass** /ˈoʊvɚˌpæs/ *noun*
a part of a road that is like a bridge that goes over another road or a railroad: *The overpass crosses Market Street.*

**o·ver·pop·u·la·tion** /ˌoʊvɚˌpɑpyəˈleɪʃən/ *noun*
if there is overpopulation, too many people are living in a place: *Overpopulation is a problem in this city because so many people have moved here.*
—**overpopulated** /ˌoʊvɚˈpɑpyəˌleɪtɪd/ *adjective* an overpopulated area has too many people living in it

**o·ver·pow·er·ing** /ˌoʊvɚˈpaʊərɪŋ/ *adjective*
very strong: *The smell of garbage was overpowering, and made me feel sick.*

**o·ver·rat·ed** /ˌoʊvɚˈreɪtɪd/ *adjective*
not as good as some people say: *I think he's overrated as a player. He's not that great.*

**o·ver·seas** Ac /ˌoʊvɚˈsiz/ *adjective, adverb*
to or in a country that is across the ocean: *Her dad got a job overseas, so they're moving to Europe.*

**o·ver·shad·ow** /ˌoʊvɚˈʃædoʊ/ *verb*
to make someone seem less important: *Lori's older sister had always overshadowed her at school; she got better grades and was better at sports than Lori was.*

**o·ver·sleep** /ˌoʊvɚˈslip/ *verb* (**overslept** /ˌoʊvɚˈslept/)
to sleep for longer than you planned to: *I overslept and was late for class.*
→ see Thesaurus box at **sleep**[1]

**ˌover-the-ˈcounter** *adjective*
over-the-counter medicines are ones that you can buy in a store without needing to see a doctor first: *You can buy over-the-counter pain relievers without a prescription.*

**o·ver·throw** /ˌoʊvɚˈθroʊ/ *verb* (**overthrew** /ˌoʊvɚˈθru/, **overthrown** /ˌoʊvɚˈθroʊn/)
to remove a leader or government from power by using force: *Rebels are trying to overthrow the government.*

**o·ver·time** /ˈoʊvɚˌtaɪm/ *noun*
**1** extra hours that someone works at a job, in addition to the normal number of hours he or she works in a week: *Dad had to work overtime to fix the computer problems.*
**2** a period of extra playing time at the end of a sports game, so that one of the two teams has a chance to win: *The two teams were tied, so the game went into overtime.*

**o·ver·turn** /ˌoʊvɚˈtɚn/ *verb* (*formal*)
**1** to turn upside down or onto one side: *The bottle overturned and the juice spilled.*
**2** to change an official decision: *The judge overturned the court's original decision and ordered the man to be released from prison.*

**o·ver·view** /ˈoʊvɚˌvyu/ *noun*
a short description of something, that gives the main ideas but not the details: *The article*

*gave an overview of the history of the sport.*

**o·ver·weight** /ˌoʊvɚˈweɪt/ *adjective*
too fat: *He was 20 pounds overweight and the doctor told him to eat less and start exercising.*
→ see Thesaurus box at **fat**[1]



**o·ver·whelmed** /ˌoʊvɚˈwelmd/ *adjective*
if you are overwhelmed by something, it has a very strong effect on your feelings: *I was so overwhelmed by their kindness that I cried.*
[ORIGIN: 1300-1400 From the old English word *whelm*, which means "to turn over or cover up."]

**o·ver·whelm·ing** /ˌoʊvɚˈwelmɪŋ/ *adjective*
1 very big in amount or number: *There was overwhelming evidence that he was guilty of the crime.*
2 an overwhelming feeling is very strong: *When he held his baby sister, Jon felt overwhelming love.*
—**overwhelmingly** *adverb* in an overwhelming way

**owe** /oʊ/ *verb*
1 to have to give money back to someone because you borrowed it from him or her: *Bob still owes me the $20 that he borrowed from me last month.*
2 to feel that you should do something for someone because he or she has done something for you: *My mother helped me a lot. I owe everything to her.*

**owl** /aʊl/ *noun*
a bird that hunts at night and has large eyes

**own**[1] /oʊn/ *adjective, pronoun*
1 belonging to a particular person: *I want to buy my own car when I'm sixteen.* | *You must make your own decision.*
2 **(all) on your own** = without anyone with you or helping you: *Did you write this story on your own?* | *You can't leave young kids on their own. It's not safe.*

**own**[2] *verb*
if you own something, it belongs to you: *The city owns the buildings.*

**THESAURUS: own**

**have** to own something: *Do you have a bike?*

**belong to someone** if something belongs to you, you own it: *This ring belonged to my grandmother.*

**possess** (*formal*) to own or have something: *He was arrested for possessing explosives.*

PHRASAL VERB
**own up**
to admit that you did something wrong: *He'll never own up to his mistakes.*

**own·er** /ˈoʊnɚ/ *noun*
someone who owns something: *Dog owners need to clean up after their dogs.*
—**ownership** *noun* the fact of owning something: *home ownership*

**ox** /ɑks/ *noun* (plural **oxen** /ˈɑksən/)
a male cow that farmers use for farm work: *The two oxen pulled the plow.*

**ox·y·gen** /ˈɑksɪdʒən/ *noun* (*written abbreviation*: **O**)
a gas in the air that all plants and animals need in order to live: *As you breathe, your lungs send the oxygen into your blood.*
[ORIGIN: 1700-1800 From the Greek word *oxys*, which means "acid," and the French ending *-gène*, which means "producing." It was believed that oxygen forms part of all acids.]

**oys·ter** /ˈɔɪstɚ/ *noun*
a small sea animal that has a shell and can produce a jewel called a PEARL

**oz.**
the written abbreviation of **ounce**

**o·zone lay·er** /ˈoʊzoʊn ˌleɪɚ/ *noun*
a layer of gases around the Earth that stops harmful RADIATION from the sun from reaching the Earth

# Pp

**pace**[1] /peɪs/ *noun*
**1** the speed at which you do something: *Older people tend to walk at a slower pace than younger ones.*
**2** a step that you make when you are walking: *He took a pace toward the door.*

**pace**[2] *verb*
to walk first in one direction and then in another, when you are waiting or worried about something: *Darren paced back and forth in the hospital waiting room.*

**Pa·cif·ic O·cean** /pəˌsɪfɪk ˈoʊʃən/ *noun*
**the Pacific Ocean** (**the Pacific**) = the large ocean between Asia and Australia in the west, and North and South America in the east

**pac·i·fi·er** /ˈpæsəˌfaɪɚ/ *noun*
a plastic or rubber object that a baby sucks on so that he or she does not cry

**pac·i·fist** /ˈpæsəfɪst/ *noun*
someone who believes that wars and violence are wrong
—**pacifism** *noun* the belief that wars and violence are wrong

**pack**[1] /pæk/ *verb*
**1** (*also* **pack up**) to put things into boxes or bags so you can take them somewhere: *Mr. Levy packed his suitcase and left for the airport.*
**2** if a crowd of people packs a place, there are so many people that the place is full: *50,000 fans packed the stadium.*
—**packing** *noun* the act of putting things into boxes or bags so that you can take them somewhere: *Have you done your packing yet?*

**WORD FAMILY: pack**
**pack** *verb* | **pack** *noun* | **package** *noun* | **packaging** *noun*

**PHRASAL VERB**
**pack up**
(*informal*) to put things into boxes or bags and get ready to leave: *In the morning I packed up my things.*

**pack**[2] *noun*
**1** a small box or paper that holds a set of things: *a pack of gum*
**2** a set of things that are put or tied together, to make them easy to carry or sell: *a six-pack of soda*
**3** a group of wild animals that live and hunt together: *a wolf pack*
**4** a BACKPACK
→ see Thesaurus box at **group**[1]

**package**

**pack·age** /ˈpækɪdʒ/ *noun*
**1** something that you have wrapped in paper or put in a box or bag so that you can mail it: *Did you mail that package at the post office?*
**2** a box or bag that holds food or other things so they can be sold: *I bought two packages of cookies.*
**3** a group of things or services that are being sold or given together: *The cable TV company offers a 31-channel package.*
—**package** *verb* to put something into a box or bag, ready to be sold or sent somewhere

**pack·ag·ing** /ˈpækɪdʒɪŋ/ *noun*
the box or paper that something is sold in: *The toys are sold in colorful packaging.*

**packed** /pækt/ *adjective*
full of people or things: *The theater was packed and we couldn't find seats.*
→ see Thesaurus box at **full**

**pack·et** /ˈpækɪt/ *noun*
an envelope that holds something: *a packet of seeds*

**pact** /pækt/ *noun* (*formal*)
an agreement between two groups, countries, or people: *The two boys made a pact that they would always be friends.*
[**ORIGIN:** 1400-1500 From the Latin word *pactum*, a form of the verb *pacisci*, which means "to agree."]

**pad** /pæd/ *noun*
**1** a lot of sheets of paper fastened together

at one edge: *He wrote the message on a pad of paper near the phone.*
**2** a thick piece of soft material that protects something or makes it more comfortable: *A football player was putting his shoulder pads on.*
**3** a place from which a ROCKET is sent up into the sky: *The rocket was ready on the launch pad.*

P

**pad·ded** /ˈpædɪd/ *adjective*
covered or filled with a soft material: *a soft padded chair*
—**pad** *verb* to cover or fill something with a soft material
—**padding** *noun* material that fills or covers something to make it softer or more comfortable

**pad·dle¹** /ˈpædl/ *noun*
**1** a short pole with a wide flat end, that you use to move a small boat across water
**2** a small round board with a handle, for hitting the ball in PING-PONG

**paddle²** *verb*
to move a small boat across water, using a paddle: *They paddled up the river in their canoes.*

**pad·lock** /ˈpædlɑk/ *noun*
a lock with a curved bar at the top, that you can put on something such as a door or a bicycle: *He unlocked the padlock on the gate.*
→ see picture at **lock¹**

**page** /peɪdʒ/ *noun*
**1** one side of a sheet of paper in a book, magazine, or newspaper: *The book has 147 pages. | Do the questions on page 10 for homework.*
**2** all the writing and pictures that you see on a computer screen when you visit a website: *a web page*

**pag·eant** /ˈpædʒənt/ *noun*
a competition for women in which people judge them by how beautiful they are: *She is beautiful and has won a beauty pageant.*

**paid** /peɪd/ *verb*
the past tense and past participle of PAY

**pail** /peɪl/ *noun*
**1** a deep container with a handle over the top, used especially for carrying water: *He had a pail of water to wash the car with.* **SYNONYM: bucket**
**2** a container you use to carry or hold something: *a garbage pail*

**pain** /peɪn/ *noun*
**1** the feeling you have when part of your body hurts: *He was badly injured and in terrible pain. | I felt a sharp pain in my chest.*
**2** a feeling of unhappiness when something bad has happened: *Parents can help children deal with the pain of divorce.*
**3 be a pain (in the neck/butt)** (*informal*) = to be very annoying: *My brother's a real pain.*
[**ORIGIN:** 1200-1300 From the Greek word *poine*, which means "payment or punishment."]

**WORD FAMILY: pain**
**pain** *noun* | **painful** *adjective* | **painless** *adjective* | **painfully** *adverb*

**pain·ful** /ˈpeɪnfəl/ *adjective*
**1** making part of your body hurt: *a painful injury | After I fell on the ice, it was painful to walk.* **ANTONYM: painless**
**2** making you feel unhappy: *The memories were too painful to talk about.*
—**painfully** *adverb* in a way that is upsetting or very difficult: *Their progress through the thick jungle was painfully slow.*

**pain·kill·er** /ˈpeɪnˌkɪlɚ/ *noun*
a medicine that stops you from feeling too much pain

**pain·less** /ˈpeɪnləs/ *adjective*
causing no pain: *Dentists try to make fixing your teeth as painless as possible.* **ANTONYM: painful**

**pains·tak·ing** /ˈpeɪnzˌteɪkɪŋ/ *adjective*
done very carefully: *Repairing the old paintings is painstaking work.*
—**painstakingly** *adverb* very carefully

**paint¹** /peɪnt/ *noun*
a colored liquid that you use to cover surfaces or make pictures: *Mix yellow and blue paint to make green paint. | The walls need another coat of paint – you can still see the old color.*

**paint²** *verb*
**1** to put paint on a surface: *They should finish painting the house tomorrow.*
**2** to make a picture using paint: *The children painted pictures of their own faces.*

**paint·brush** /ˈpeɪntbrʌʃ/ *noun*
a special brush used for painting → see picture at **brush**

**paint·er** /ˈpeɪntɚ/ *noun*
**1** someone who paints pictures: *Picasso was a famous painter.* **SYNONYM: artist** → see picture on page **A17**
**2** someone whose job is painting the walls of houses or rooms: *The painters are coming Tuesday to paint the garage.*

**paint·ing** /ˈpeɪntɪŋ/ *noun*
a painted picture: *There was a painting of some mountains on the wall.*
→ see Thesaurus box at **art**, **picture**[1]

**pair** /per/ *noun* (plural **pairs** *or* **pair**)
**1** two things of the same kind that are used together: *a pair of socks*
**2** something made of two parts that are joined together: *Are you wearing a new pair of glasses? | I have two pairs of jeans.*
**3** two people who are standing or doing something together: *We worked in pairs – I worked with Jacob.*
[**ORIGIN:** 1200-1300 From the Latin word *paria*, which means "things that are equal."]

**pa·ja·mas** /pəˈdʒɑməz/ *plural noun*
soft pants and a shirt that you wear in bed: *He put on his pajamas and got into bed.*
[**ORIGIN:** 1800-1900 From the Hindi word *pajama*, from the Persian words *pa* and *jama*, which mean "leg" and "piece of clothing."]

**pal** /pæl/ *noun* (*informal*)
a friend: *Okay, pal. See you later.*
[**ORIGIN:** 1600-1700 From the Romany word for "brother." Romany is a language used by gypsies.]

**pal·ace** /ˈpælɪs/ *noun*
a large house where a king or queen lives: *Buckingham Palace is the home of the British queen.*
—**palatial** /pəˈleɪʃəl/ *adjective* a palatial house or building is very large
[**ORIGIN:** 1200-1300 From Palatium, the Latin name of a hill in Rome where the emperor's palace was.]

**pal·ate** /ˈpælɪt/ *noun*
the hard top part inside your mouth

**pale** /peɪl/ *adjective*
**1** someone who is pale looks white because he or she is sick or frightened: *Ellie has a fever and is very pale.*
**2** a pale color is very light: *a pale blue shirt*

**pa·le·on·tol·o·gy** /ˌpeɪliənˈtɑlədʒi/ *noun*
the study of FOSSILs (=rocks showing the forms of animals or plants that lived a very long time ago)

**pal·ette** /ˈpælɪt/ *noun*
**1** the curved board that an artist mixes paints on
**2** the set of colors that an artist uses: *I like this artist's palette of strong reds and oranges.*

**palm** /pɑm/ *noun*
**1** the flat part of your hand, which your fingers bend toward: *She held the little bird in the palm of her hand.* → see picture at **hand**
**2** another word for a PALM TREE

**ˈpalm tree** *noun*
a tree that grows in warm places. It has a long straight trunk and big pointed leaves at the top: *Tall palm trees grow near the beach.*

**palm tree**

**pam·per** /ˈpæmpɚ/ *verb*
to give someone a lot of attention and do a lot of things for that person, which may be bad for him or her: *Some owners pamper their dogs by buying them clothes!*

**pam·phlet** /ˈpæmflɪt/ *noun*
a very thin book with a paper cover, that gives information about something: *a pamphlet about the dangers of using drugs*

**pan**[1] /pæn/ *noun*
**1** a metal container that you cook food in, that often has a handle: *a large pan of boiling water | Heat the oil in the frying pan.*
**2** a container with low sides, used for holding liquids: *a car's oil pan*

**pan**[2] *verb*
to wash sand and small stones from a river in a pan in order to find gold: *Miners came to this area in the 19th century to pan for gold.*

**pan·cake** /ˈpænkeɪk/ *noun*
a flat round bread that is made from flour, milk, and eggs and cooked in a pan on top of

the STOVE: *Do you want pancakes with maple syrup for breakfast?*

**pan·cre·as** /ˈpæŋkriəs/ *noun*
an organ in your body that produces a liquid that helps your body DIGEST food. It also produces INSULIN, which helps your body use sugar for energy.

**pan·da** /ˈpændə/ *noun*
a large black and white animal, similar to a bear, that lives in China

P

**pane** /peɪn/ *noun*
a piece of glass in a window or door: *The ball broke a window pane.*

**pan·el** Ac /ˈpænl/ *noun*
**1** a group of people who are chosen to talk about or decide something: *A panel of judges will choose the winner of the competition.*
**2** a flat sheet of wood, glass, etc. that forms part of a door, wall, or ceiling: *a door with three wooden panels*
**3 instrument/control panel** = the place in an airplane, boat, or spacecraft that has the controls and instruments that give you information about things such as your speed: *The pilot looked at his instrument panel to check the speed of the plane.*

**pan·ic¹** /ˈpænɪk/ *noun*
a sudden strong feeling of fear and worry that makes you do things without thinking carefully: *The bomb warning caused panic, and people started to run in all directions.*
[**ORIGIN:** 1600-1700 From the Greek word *panikos*, which means "relating to the god Pan." Pan was the Greek god of nature, who sometimes frightened people.]

**panic²** *verb* (**panicked**, **panicking**)
to suddenly feel so frightened that you do things without thinking carefully first: *If there is a fire, don't panic, and walk slowly out of the building.*
—**panicky** *adjective* feeling panic

**pan·o·ram·a** /ˌpænəˈræmə/ *noun*
a view over a wide area of land: *From the plane they could see a panorama of the Rocky Mountains.*
—**panoramic** *adjective* a panoramic view or picture shows a wide area of land
[**ORIGIN:** 1700-1800 From the Greek words *pan* and *horama*, which mean "all" and "sight."]

**pant** /pænt/ *verb*
to breathe quickly with short breaths because you have been exercising or because it is hot: *He was panting when he reached the top of the hill.*
→ see Thesaurus box at **breathe**

**pan·ther** /ˈpænθɚ/ *noun*
**1** a black LEOPARD (=large wild African or Asian cat)
**2** another word for a COUGAR or a JAGUAR

**pant·ies** /ˈpæntiz/ *plural noun*
a piece of underwear that girls or women wear on their bottoms

**pan·try** /ˈpæntri/ *noun* (plural **pantries**)
a large cupboard or small room in a kitchen, where you can keep food and dishes

**pants** /pænts/ *plural noun*
a piece of clothing that covers you from your waist to your feet, and that has a separate part for each leg: *Joe was wearing a new pair of pants.* → see picture on page **A6**
[**ORIGIN:** 1800-1900 From Pantaloon, a character in a funny play who wore tight pants.]

**pan·ty·hose** /ˈpæntiˌhoʊz/ *noun*
a very thin, tight piece of clothing that covers the legs from the waist to the feet. Women often wear pantyhose instead of socks under dresses or skirts. → see picture on page **A6**

**pa·pa** /ˈpɑpə/ *noun*
a name that some children call their father: *Where are you going, Papa?*

**pa·pa·ya** /pəˈpaɪə/ *noun*
a big yellow-green tropical fruit that has sweet orange flesh and a lot of small black seeds inside

**pa·per** /ˈpeɪpɚ/ *noun*
**1** thin sheets that you write or draw on, use to wrap gifts, etc.: *Write your name at the top of a piece of paper.* | *a brown paper bag*

**GRAMMAR: paper**

Do not say "a paper." Say **a piece of paper** or **a sheet of paper**: *I need a piece of paper to write on.* | *a blank sheet of paper*

**2** a newspaper: *There's an article in the paper about the school football team.*
**3** a piece of writing that you do for a class:

*Your paper should be three pages long.*

**4 papers** = official documents, such as your PASSPORT: *The border guards looked at my papers.*

[ORIGIN: 1300-1400 From the French word *papier*, from the Latin word *papyrus*. Papyrus is a plant from which paper was made by the Egyptians, Greeks, and Romans.]

**pa·per·back** /ˈpeɪpɚˌbæk/ *noun*
a book with a thick paper cover: *I take a lot of paperbacks to read on vacation.*

**ˈpaper clip** *noun*
a small piece of curved wire that you use to hold sheets of paper together

**pa·per·work** /ˈpeɪpɚˌwɚk/ *noun*
**1** official pieces of paper that you must write information on in order to do something or get something: *We had to fill out a lot of paperwork before we could get the dog from the animal shelter.*
**2** work such as writing letters or reports: *Dad says he has a lot of paperwork to do this weekend.*

**pap·ier-mâ·ché** /ˌpeɪpɚ məˈʃeɪ/ *noun*
a mixture of paper, water, and glue that becomes hard when it dries. You use papier-mâché for making things: *We made the puppets' heads out of papier-mâché.*

**par·a·chute** /ˈpærəˌʃut/ *noun*
a large piece of cloth that you attach to your back so that you can jump out of an airplane and fall slowly and safely to the ground: *He jumped from the plane and opened his parachute.*

parachute

[ORIGIN: 1700-1800 From the French words *para-* and *chute*, which mean "defense against" and "fall."]

**pa·rade¹** /pəˈreɪd/ *noun*
a celebration in which musical bands, decorated trucks, etc. move in a long line along a street: *The school band got to march in the parade.*

**parade²** *verb*
to walk or march together to celebrate or protest something: *The protesters paraded in front of City Hall.*

**par·a·dise** /ˈpærəˌdaɪs/ *noun*
**1** a place that is very beautiful and enjoyable: *The island seemed like paradise, with its white beaches and blue water.*
**2 a)** another word for HEAVEN **b)** the place where Adam and Eve first lived, according to the Bible

[ORIGIN: 1100-1200 From the Greek word *paradeisos*, from the old Iranian word *pairidaeza*, which means "park or garden surrounded by a wall."]

**par·a·dox** /ˈpærəˌdɑks/ *noun*
a statement or situation that seems strange because it contains two ideas or things that are very different but are both true: *It's a paradox that such a rich country has so many poor people.*
—**paradoxical** /ˌpærəˈdɑksɪkəl/ *adjective* involving a paradox
—**paradoxically** *adverb* used when talking about a paradoxical situation: *Paradoxically, the more locks they put on their doors, the less safe they feel.*

**par·a·graph** [Ac] /ˈpærəˌgræf/ *noun*
a part of a piece of writing that contains several sentences, starts on a new line, and deals with one idea: *The first paragraph of your essay should say what your main point is.*

[ORIGIN: 1400-1500 From the Greek word *paragraphos*, which means "mark or note beside part of a piece of writing."]

**par·a·keet** /ˈpærəˌkit/ *noun*
a small bird with brightly colored feathers and a long tail, that some people keep as a pet

**par·a·le·gal** /ˌpærəˈligəl/ *noun*
someone whose job is to help a lawyer do his or her work

**par·al·lel¹** [Ac] /ˈpærəlel/ *adjective*
lines that are parallel go in the same direction and are the same distance apart along their whole length: *The street runs parallel to the train tracks.*

[ORIGIN: 1500-1600 From the Greek word *parallelos*, from *para* and *allelon*, which mean "beside" and "each other."]

**parallel²** [Ac] *noun*
**1** if there is a parallel between people, events, or situations, they are like each other in some way: *There are many parallels between the two men. Both, for example,*

P

*grew up without a mother on small farms.*
**2** an imaginary line around the Earth that is north or south of the EQUATOR: *Not many icebergs float as far south as the 40th parallel.*
—**parallel** *verb* if something parallels something else, it is like it in some way

**par·al·lel·o·gram** /ˌpærəˈleləˌgræm/ *noun*
a flat shape with four straight sides. Each side is the same length as the side parallel to it: *Rectangles and squares are parallelograms.*

**pa·ral·y·sis** /pəˈræləsɪs/ *noun*
the lack of the ability to move or feel part of your body: *The snake's poison causes paralysis, so that the animals it bites cannot move to escape.*

**par·a·lyze** /ˈpærəˌlaɪz/ *verb*
**1** to make someone unable to move part of his or her body, or to feel anything in it: *The disease paralyzed his legs and he could no longer walk.*
**2** to make something or someone unable to work normally: *Heavy snow has paralyzed New York City.*
—**paralyzed** *adjective* unable to move part of your body: *The injury left him paralyzed and unable to take care of himself.*

**par·a·med·ic** /ˌpærəˈmedɪk/ *noun*
someone whose job is to help sick or injured people until they get to a hospital: *Paramedics arrived in an ambulance and tried to help the injured woman.*

**pa·ram·et·er** Ac /pəˈræmətɚ/ *noun* (*formal*)
something that affects the way that something can or should be done: *The dance was outside the normal parameters of ballet because it included some hip-hop movements.*

**par·a·mil·i·tar·y** /ˌpærəˈmɪləˌteri/ *adjective*
a paramilitary group is organized like an army, but is not part of the legal military forces of a country

**par·a·noid** /ˈpærəˌnɔɪd/ *adjective*
believing that you cannot trust other people, or that they are trying to harm you: *He was so paranoid he thought everyone was watching him.*
—**paranoia** /ˌpærəˈnɔɪə/ *noun* the illness or feeling of being paranoid

**par·a·phrase** /ˈpærəˌfreɪz/ *verb*
to say or write what someone else has said, using different words: *Lincoln said, "We hold these truths to be self-evident, that all men are created equal." This can be paraphrased as, "It is clear that everyone is equal."*
—**paraphrase** *noun* something written or said that paraphrases something else

**par·a·site** /ˈpærəˌsaɪt/ *noun*
a plant or animal that lives on or in another plant or animal and gets food from it: *Fleas are parasites that live on animals.*

**par·cel** /ˈpɑrsəl/ *noun*
something that has been wrapped in paper so that it can be sent through the mail: *The mailman left a parcel for you.* SYNONYM: package

**par·don¹** /ˈpɑrdn/ *verb*
**1 pardon me** = **a)** used to politely say you are sorry: *Pardon me, I didn't mean to push you.* | *Pat burped and said, "Pardon me."* SYNONYM: excuse me **b)** (*also* **Pardon?**) used to politely ask someone to say something again: *"Are you and Ken going together?" "Pardon me?" "Are you and Ken going to the party together?"* SYNONYM: excuse me? **c)** used to politely get someone's attention: *Pardon me, do you know what time it is?* SYNONYM: excuse me
**2** to allow someone who is guilty of a crime not to be punished for it: *The men were in jail, but they were later pardoned by the governor.*

**pardon²** *noun*
an official order that allows someone who is guilty of a crime not to be punished for it: *The governor gave him a pardon for his crime.*
→ **I beg your pardon** at beg

**par·ent** /ˈperənt/ *noun*
a father or mother: *I have to call my parents and tell them if I'm going to be out late.*
—**parental** /pəˈrentl/ *adjective* relating to being a parent or to what a parent does
—**parenthood** /ˈperəntˌhʊd/ *noun* the fact of being a parent
[ORIGIN: 1400-1500 From the Latin verb *parere*, which means "to give birth to."]

**pa·ren·the·ses** /pəˈrenθəˌsiz/ *plural noun*
the signs ( ). Parentheses are used around extra information, and are also used around numbers and symbols in mathematics: *The dates in parentheses tell you when the people were born and when they died.*

**park¹** /pɑrk/ *noun*
**1** a large area with grass and trees in a town, where people can walk, play games, have PICNICs, etc.: *The kids were climbing trees in the park.*
**2** a large area of land that has been kept in its natural state to protect the plants and animals there: *Yellowstone is a national park.*

**park²** *verb*
to put your car somewhere and leave it there for a period of time: *We parked outside their house.*

**par·ka** /ˈpɑrkə/ *noun*
a thick warm coat with a HOOD (=part that goes over your head): *It was snowing, and the children had their parkas on.*
[**ORIGIN:** 1700-1800 From a Russian word for "animal skin and fur, or a jacket made from this." This word was also used by the native people of Alaska.]

**ˌpark and ˈride** *noun*
a system in which you leave your car in a special parking lot and take a bus or train to another part of a city

**park·ing** /ˈpɑrkɪŋ/ *noun*
**1** the act of putting your car somewhere and leaving it there for a period of time: *Parking in the red zone is illegal.*
**2** spaces in which you can leave a car: *There is parking behind the store.* | *a parking space*

**ˈparking lot** *noun*
a large area where people can leave their cars: *The parking lot was almost full.*

**ˈparking ˌmeter** *noun*
a machine that you put money into, to pay for parking in the space next to it: *He put fifty cents into the parking meter for an hour.*

**park·way** /ˈpɑrkweɪ/ *noun*
a wide road, with grass and trees in the middle or along the sides: *Traffic was slow on the parkway this morning.*

**par·lia·ment** /ˈpɑrləmənt/ *noun*
a group of people who are elected to make laws, in countries such as Canada or Great Britain
—**parliamentary** /ˌpɑrləˈmentri/ *adjective* relating to what is done in a parliament
[**ORIGIN:** 1200-1300 From the French word *parler*, which means "to speak."]

**par·lor** /ˈpɑrlɚ/ *noun*
**ice cream/beauty/funeral, etc. parlor** = a store or business that sells a particular thing or provides a particular service: *I went to the beauty parlor today to get my hair cut.*

**pa·ro·chi·al school** /pəˈroʊkiəl ˌskul/ *noun*
a school that is run by or connected with a church: *Mary goes to a Catholic parochial school.*

**par·o·dy** /ˈpærədi/ *noun* (plural **parodies**)
a piece of writing, a movie, etc. that copies a particular type of story or movie, in a funny way: *The movie is a parody of horror movies and is funny rather than scary.*
—**parody** *verb* to copy something in a funny way

**pa·role** /pəˈroʊl/ *noun*
if a prisoner gets parole, he or she is allowed to leave prison. If that person does not behave well, he or she will go back to prison: *He is now on parole after being in prison for five years.*
—**parole** *verb* to give someone parole
[**ORIGIN:** 1400-1500 From a French word for "speech or word." A prisoner gives his or her word (=promises) that he or she will behave well.]

**par·rot** /ˈpærət/ *noun*
a tropical bird with colored feathers and a curved beak. You can teach some parrots to say words.

**pars·ley** /ˈpɑrsli/ *noun*
a plant with green curled leaves, that you use in cooking or as a decoration on food

**part¹** /pɑrt/ *noun*
**1** one piece, area, or amount of something: *Which part of town do you live in?* | *The fight was the best part of the whole movie.*

**THESAURUS: part**

**piece** a part of something that is separate from the rest of it: *One of the pieces of the jigsaw puzzle was missing.* | *a piece of pie*

P

**section** one of the parts that something is divided into: *He only reads the sports section of the newspaper.*

**chapter** one of the parts that a book is divided into: *I've read the first two chapters.*

**scene** one of the parts that a play or movie is divided into: *The best scene is when he fights the dragon.*

**episode** one part of a story on the television, which is shown in separate parts: *The final episode of the series was watched by millions of viewers.*

**department** a part of a company, school, or government that is responsible for a particular kind of work: *the history department at the school* | *The contract must be checked by our legal department before we sign it.*

P

**2** one of the pieces that a machine or vehicle is made of: *Do you sell parts for Ford cars?*
**3 take part** = to do an activity with other people: *Twenty runners took part in the race.* **SYNONYM: participate**
**4** a character in a play, movie, or television show, that an actor will play: *She got a big part in a new TV series.* **SYNONYM: role**
**5** the actions of one person in a situation where several people are doing something together: *She was given a medal for her part in the rescue.*
**6** the line on your head that you make when you divide your hair with a comb: *Your part isn't straight.*
**7 for the most part** = mostly or most of the time: *The children get along well, for the most part.*

**part[2]** *verb*
**1** if you part your hair, you comb your hair so that some of it is on one side of a line on your head and some of it is on the other side: *Her hair is parted in the middle.*
**2** to move the two sides of something apart: *He parted the curtains and looked out.*
**PHRASAL VERB**
**part with something**
to give or sell something to someone, when you do not want to: *Someone offered to buy the picture from him, but he did not want to part with it.*

**part[3]** *adverb*
if something is part one thing and part another thing, some of it is the first thing, and some of it is the second thing: *He drew an animal that was part snake and part bird.*

**par·tial** /ˈpɑrʃəl/ *adjective*
not complete: *He cannot see very well because he has only partial vision in one eye.*
**ANTONYM: full**
—**partially** *adverb* partly

**par·tic·i·pant** Ac /pɑrˈtɪsəpənt/ *noun* (*formal*)
someone who does an activity with other people: *Every participant in the race is given a certificate.*

**par·tic·i·pate** Ac /pɑrˈtɪsəˌpeɪt/ *verb* (*formal*)
to do an activity with other people: *I want to thank everyone who participated in the festival.* **SYNONYM: take part**

**par·ti·ci·ple** /ˈpɑrtəˌsɪpəl/ *noun*
the form of a verb that you use to make verb tenses or that you use as an adjective: *The past participle of "sing" is "sung" and the present participle is "singing."*

**par·ti·cle** /ˈpɑrtɪkəl/ *noun* (*formal*)
a very small piece of something: *The air is full of particles of dust.*

**par·tic·u·lar** /pɚˈtɪkjəlɚ/ *adjective*
**1** special or definite: *Did you have a particular reason for coming here today?*
**2** a particular thing is the one you are talking about and not any other: *I've read some Harry Potter books, but not that particular one.*
**3** (*formal*) choosing what you like very carefully, and not accepting anything else: *She's very particular about what she wears, and only buys expensive clothes.* **SYNONYM: picky**
**4 in particular** (*formal*) = more than others: *I like sports, baseball in particular.*

**par·tic·u·lar·ly** /pɚˈtɪkjəlɚli/ *adverb*
**1** (*formal*) more than others, or more than usual: *I like bright colors, particularly red.* | *We have had a particularly cold winter.* **SYNONYM: especially**

**2 not particularly** = not very: *She's not particularly pretty, but she has a lot of charm.*

**part·ly** /ˈpɑrtli/ *adverb*
a little, but not completely: *Her face was partly covered by a scarf, but I could see her eyes.*

**part·ner** Ac /ˈpɑrtnɚ/ *noun*
**1** someone with whom you do an activity that involves two people, such as dancing: *His partner kept stepping on his toes as they danced.*
**2** one of the owners of a business: *She's a partner in a law firm.*
**3** someone's husband, wife, girlfriend, or boyfriend: *He and his partner have just bought a house.*
—**partnership** *noun* a relationship between business partners, or between organizations that work together: *He went into partnership with another lawyer.*

**ˌpart of ˈspeech** *noun* (plural **parts of speech**)
one of the groups that you can divide words into, such as "noun" or "verb"

**ˌpart-ˈtime** *adjective, adverb*
if you work or study part-time, you do it for only part of each day or week: *a part-time student* | *Mom works part-time.*

**par·ty** /ˈpɑrti/ *noun* (plural **parties**)
**1** an occasion when people enjoy themselves by eating, drinking, or dancing together, for example when it is someone's birthday: *We're having a party on Saturday.* | *a birthday party.*

**THESAURUS: party**

**get-together** (*informal*) a small informal party: *I'm having a get-together with some friends on Friday. Want to come?*

**bash** (*informal*) a party: *His wife is planning a big bash for his fiftieth birthday.*

**celebration** a party or other special event to celebrate something: *Please join us for our son's 21st birthday celebration!*

**reception** a large formal party, for example after a wedding: *There were over 200 guests at their wedding reception.*

**baby/wedding/bridal shower** a party for a woman who is going to have a baby or get married, at which people give her presents: *A lot of her friends came to her baby shower.*

**2** a group of people with the same political views, who work to win elections for the CANDIDATE they support: *the Democratic Party*
**3** a group of people who do something together for a period of time: *Lewis and Clark organized a party to find a way across land to the Pacific Ocean.*
[**ORIGIN:** 1200-1300 From the old French word *partie*, which means "part, or separate group of people," from *partir*, which means "to divide."]

**pass**[1] /pæs/ *verb*
**1** to go past someone or something: *She waved at me as she passed our house.*
**2** to take something and put it in someone's hand: *Pass the salt, please.* | *Can you pass me a pen?*
**3** to kick, throw, or hit a ball to someone on your team during a game: *Dad taught me how to pass a football.*
**4** to succeed in a test or class: *Did your brother pass his driving test?* | *You won't pass if you don't study.* **ANTONYM: fail**
**5** to go through or over a place: *We passed through Texas on our way to Mexico.* | *A plane passed over the fields.* **SYNONYM: go**
**6** to officially accept a law by voting: *The new law was passed by 15 votes to 3.*
**7** when time passes, the minutes, hours, etc. go by: *Time passes very slowly when you're waiting.* **SYNONYM: go by**
**8** to end or finish: *The storm soon passed.* | *Ann will be upset for a while, but it'll pass.*
→ see Thesaurus box at **give**, **throw**[1]

**PHRASAL VERBS**

**pass something around**
to give something to each person in a group: *Pass these dictionaries around so everyone has one.*

**pass away**
to die: *He was very old when he passed away.*

**pass something on**
to tell someone information that someone told you: *I will pass the message on to her.*

**pass out**
to suddenly become unconscious: *The pain*

*was so strong that I passed out.* **SYNONYM: faint**

**pass up something**
to not do something you have the chance to do: *I couldn't pass up an opportunity to meet the president!*

**pass²** *noun*
**1** the act of kicking, throwing, or hitting a ball to someone on your team in a game: *Roy caught the pass and scored.*
**2** a special piece of paper that allows you to go somewhere or do something: *You need a pass to use the ski lifts.* | *a bus pass*
**3** a road or path high up in the mountains: *We walked to the other side of the mountain along a narrow mountain pass.*

**pas·sage** /ˈpæsɪdʒ/ *noun*
**1** a short piece of writing or music, that is taken from a longer piece: *He read a passage from the Bible.*
**2** a narrow place in a building, that connects one room with another: *There was a short passage connecting the two rooms.*
**3** a tube in your body that air or liquid passes through: *When you have a cold, the passages in your nose become blocked.*

**pas·sen·ger** /ˈpæsəndʒɚ/ *noun*
someone who is traveling in a car, bus, airplane, etc., but is not driving it: *There were 10 passengers on the bus.* → see picture on page **A26**

**pass·ing** /ˈpæsɪŋ/ *adjective*
**1** going past: *I couldn't hear for a minute because of noise from a passing truck.*
**2** (*formal*) continuing for only a short time: *She had a passing interest in horses when she was ten.*

**pas·sion** /ˈpæʃən/ *noun*
**1** a very strong feeling such as love, hate, or anger: *He spoke with passion about feeding the poor.*
**2** a strong feeling of liking something: *He has a passion for golf and plays often.*
[**ORIGIN:** 1100-1200 From the Latin word *passio*, which means "suffering," from *pati*, meaning "to suffer." Passion was first used about Christ's suffering on the cross. Later, it came to mean strong emotions.]

**pas·sion·ate** /ˈpæʃənət/ *adjective*
showing a very strong feeling such as love, hate, or anger: *a passionate kiss* | *She is passionate about animals and has several pets.*
—**passionately** *adverb* in a passionate way

**pas·sive** Ac /ˈpæsɪv/ *adjective*
**1** a passive person lets things happen to him or her without trying to change them, instead of doing things him or herself: *The children are not passive learners – they do the science experiments and write down their findings.*
**2** in grammar, if a verb or sentence is passive, the subject of the verb is affected by the action: *In the sentence "The ball was kicked by John," "was kicked" is a passive verb.* **ANTONYM: active**
—**passively** *adverb* in a passive way: *She passively accepted all the bad things that happened to her.*
—**passivity** /pæˈsɪvəti/ *noun* passive behavior

**pass·port** /ˈpæspɔrt/ *noun*
a small book with your photograph inside, which you must have to leave one country and go to another: *They checked my passport and let me onto the plane.* → see picture on page **A30**

**pass·word** /ˈpæswɚd/ *noun*
a secret word or group of letters or numbers that you need to get into a place or a computer system: *Type in your password and press Enter.*

**past¹** /pæst/ *noun*
**1 the past** = all the time before now: *Traveling is much easier now than it was in the past.* **ANTONYM: the future**
**2 someone's past** = someone's life before now: *I don't know anything about his past.*

**past²** *adjective*
**1** used when talking about an earlier time that has been happening until now: *He's tired because he's been working hard the past few weeks.* **SYNONYM: last**
**2** past events happened before now: *Our current problems are the result of past mistakes.* **ANTONYM: future**

**past³** *adverb, preposition*
**1** up to and beyond someone or something: *He walked right past me as if he hadn't seen me.* | *Mrs. Carter drove past.*
**2** after a particular time: *The train is due to arrive at three minutes past five.*

**pas·ta** /ˈpɑstə/ *noun*
an Italian food made from flour and water, that you can buy in different shapes: *My favorite kind of pasta is spaghetti.*

**paste¹** /peɪst/ *noun*
**1** a type of thick glue: *We used wallpaper paste to stick the paper to the wall.*
**2** a soft wet mixture that you can spread easily: *Mix the water and the powder into a smooth paste.*

**paste²** *verb*
**1** to put words in a new place on a computer screen after moving or copying them from another place: *Cut and paste your address into a new file.*
**2** to stick one thing to another using thick glue: *The kids were pasting pieces of colored paper together.*

**pas·tel** /pæˈstel/ *noun*
**1** a soft pale color such as pale blue or pale pink: *The baby's room was painted in pastels.*
**2** a small colored stick used for drawing pictures, similar to CHALK
—**pastel** *adjective* pale: *pastel colors*

**pas·time** /ˈpæstaɪm/ *noun* (*formal*)
something that you do to have fun or relax when you are not working: *His pastimes include watching TV and reading.* **SYNONYM: hobby**
[**ORIGIN:** 1400-1500 A pastime is something that you do while time goes by (=passes).]

**pas·tor** /ˈpæstɚ/ *noun*
a minister in a church: *He is a pastor in a Baptist church.*
[**ORIGIN:** 1300-1400 From the Latin word for "someone who takes care of sheep." A pastor is meant to take care of the people who come to his church like a farmer takes care of his sheep.]

**ˌpast ˈparticiple** *noun*
the form of a verb that is used when talking about things that have happened, and in PASSIVE sentences. The past participle of a regular verb is formed by adding "-ed" to the verb: *"Dropped" is the past participle of the verb "drop."*

**pas·tra·mi** /pəˈstrɑmi/ *noun*
smoked BEEF that contains a lot of spices: *a pastrami sandwich*

**pas·try** /ˈpeɪstri/ *noun* (plural **pastries**)
**1** a mixture of flour, butter, and water which is used to make the outer part of a PIE: *Roll out the pastry and put it in a pie pan.*
**2** a small sweet type of cake: *A cinnamon swirl is a kind of pastry in a round shape.*

**ˌpast ˈtense** *noun*
the form of a verb that shows that things happened in the past: *The past tense of the verb "go" is "went."*

**pas·ture** /ˈpæstʃɚ/ *noun*
land covered with grass for cows and sheep to eat: *Cows were in the pasture.*

**pat** /pæt/ *verb* (**patted**, **patting**)
to touch something lightly several times, with your hand flat: *He patted the dog.*
—**pat** *noun* an act of patting something: *"Good job!" he said, and gave me a pat on the back.*
→ see Thesaurus box at **touch¹**

**patch¹** /pætʃ/ *noun*
**1** a small piece of material that covers a hole in clothes: *His pants had patches on the knees where the holes had been.*
**2** a part of an area that is different from the parts around it: *The sky was gray, except for a small patch of blue between the clouds.*

**patch²** *verb*
to put a small piece of material over a hole to cover it: *I patched the bicycle tire with a piece of rubber.*

**pa·tent** /ˈpætnt/ *noun*
if you have a patent on something, only you have the legal right to make it or sell it: *He applied for a patent on his new machine.*
—**patent** *verb* to get a patent on something new

**path** /pæθ/ *noun* (plural **paths** /pæðz/)
**1** a narrow road for walking on: *We walked along the path going through the park.*
**2** the direction in which something is moving: *The hurricane destroyed everything in its path.*
**SYNONYM: way**

**pa·thet·ic** /pəˈθetɪk/ *adjective*
very bad, useless, or weak: *The team is pathetic. They haven't won a single game.*
—**pathetically** *adverb* in a pathetic way

**pa·tience** /ˈpeɪʃəns/ *noun*
the ability to deal with a problem or wait for something without becoming angry or upset: *My little brother wouldn't stop bugging me, and I finally lost my patience with him.*
**ANTONYM: impatience**

P

**pa·tient¹** /ˈpeɪʃənt/ *noun*
someone who is getting medical treatment from a doctor or hospital: *There are 150 patients in the hospital.*
[**ORIGIN:** 1300-1400 From the Latin word *pati*, which means "to suffer."]

**patient²** *adjective*
able to deal with a problem or wait for something without getting angry or upset: *Be patient – the bus will be here soon.*
**ANTONYM: impatient**
—**patiently** *adverb* in a patient way: *She waited patiently for her friend to arrive.*

**WORD FAMILY: patient**
**patient** *adjective* | **patiently** *adverb* | **patience** *noun*

**pat·i·o** /ˈpætiˌoʊ/ *noun* (plural **patios**)
a hard flat area outside of a house, where you can sit or eat: *It was a warm morning, so we had breakfast on the patio.*

**pa·tri·ot** /ˈpeɪtriət/ *noun*
someone who loves his or her country: *These soldiers are patriots who are proud to defend their country.*
[**ORIGIN:** 1500-1600 From the Greek word *patris*, which means "your native country," from *patrios*, which means "of your father or ancestors."]

**pa·tri·ot·ic** /ˌpeɪtriˈɑtɪk/ *adjective*
someone who is patriotic loves his or her country: *He is very patriotic and has the flag outside his house on July 4.*
—**patriotically** *adverb* in a patriotic way

**pa·tri·ot·ism** Ac /ˈpeɪtriəˌtɪzəm/ *noun*
great love of your country: *The president praised the senator's patriotism and devotion to his country.*

**pat·rol¹** /pəˈtroʊl/ *verb* (**patrolled, patrolling**)
to go around a place checking for problems or crime: *The police patrol the area regularly.*

**patrol²** *noun*
**1** the action of going around a place checking for problems or crime: *Guards were on patrol throughout the night.* | *Police carry out regular patrols near the border.*
**2** a group of police officers or soldiers that patrols a place: *The California Highway Patrol reported an accident on Interstate 5.*

**paˈtrol car** *noun*
a police car that drives around the streets of a city

**pa·tron** /ˈpeɪtrən/ *noun* (*formal*)
someone who helps an organization, artist, or performer by giving money: *He is a patron of the arts who has given thousands of dollars to public art galleries.*

**pa·tron·iz·ing** /ˈpeɪtrəˌnaɪzɪŋ/ *adjective*
a patronizing person treats you as though you are less important or less intelligent than him or her: *He is so patronizing. He is always explaining simple things that I already know.*

**pat·ter** /ˈpætɚ/ *noun*
the sound of something that is not heavy hitting a hard surface many times: *I heard the patter of rain on the roof.*

**pat·tern** /ˈpætɚn/ *noun*
**1** an arrangement of shapes, lines, and colors that is used to decorate something: *The dress has a pattern of flowers on it.*
**2** the regular way that something happens: *There is a pattern to his headaches – they usually come in the morning before he eats breakfast.*
**3** shapes that you attach to cloth and cut around to get pieces to make clothing: *She used the pattern to make a skirt.*

**pat·ty** /ˈpæti/ *noun* (plural **patties**)
small pieces of meat or other food pressed together into a round flat shape: *Shape the tuna mixture into patties and then fry them.*

**pause¹** /pɔz/ *verb*
**1** to stop speaking or doing something for a short time: *When he reached the top of the hill, he paused to rest.*
**2** to push a button on a machine to make a

CD, DVD, or tape stop playing for a short time: *Pause the movie while I go get a drink.*
→ see Thesaurus box at **stop**[1]
[**ORIGIN:** 1400-1500 From the Greek word *pausis*, from *pauein*, which means "to stop."]

**pause**[2] *noun*
a short time when you stop speaking or doing something: *After a pause he added, "You could come with us if you want."*

**pave** /peɪv/ *verb*
**1** to cover a road or area with a hard surface such as CONCRETE: *They paved an area in the park for people to play basketball.*
**2 pave the way for something** = to do something that will make something else possible in the future: *My parents worked hard and paved the way for us to go to college.*

**pave·ment** /ˈpeɪvmənt/ *noun*
the hard surface of a road: *She fell off her bike and hit her head on the pavement.*

**paw** /pɔ/ *noun*
the foot of an animal such as a dog or cat: *The cat hurt its paw and is walking strangely.*

**pay**[1] /peɪ/ *verb* (**paid** /peɪd/)
**1** to give money to someone when you buy something or when the person has done work for you: *How much did you pay for those sneakers?* | *He gets paid $10 an hour.* | *Dad pays me to wash his car.*
**2** if something pays, it has a good result for you: *Crime doesn't pay.* | *It pays to get there early because you get the best seats.*
**3 pay attention** = to listen or watch something carefully: *I wasn't paying attention. What did you say?*
**4 pay a visit** = to visit a person or place: *When are you going to pay us a visit?*
**5 pay a compliment** = to say something nice to someone about the way he or she looks or about something he or she has done: *He was always paying her compliments and saying how great she looked.*
**6 pay your way** = to pay for things you need, without asking for money from anyone else: *My friends are rich but I always pay my way.*
[**ORIGIN:** 1100-1200 From the old French word *paier*, from the Latin word *pacere*, which means "to make a person or place calm." The idea is that someone you owe money to is anxious or angry, and you make him or her calm by paying what you owe.]

**PHRASAL VERBS**

**pay someone back**
to give someone the money that you owe him or her: *Can I borrow $10? I'll pay you back tomorrow.* **SYNONYM: repay**

**pay off**
**1** to have a good result: *All her hard work paid off, and she got into law school.*
**2 pay something off** = to pay all the money that you owe for something: *She's paid off all her debts.*

**pay**[2] *noun*
money you get for work you have done: *You will get your pay on Friday.* | *She asked her boss for a pay raise.*

**THESAURUS: pay**

**income** money that you get for working, from an investment, or from the government: *If your family has a low income, you may get free lunches at school.*

**salary** the pay that professional people, such as teachers or managers, earn every month or year: *The president of the company earns a salary of $145,000 a year.*

**wages** the pay that someone earns every hour or every week: *Her wages barely cover the rent.*

**earnings** (*formal*) all the money that you earn by working: *He puts all his earnings in his college savings account.*

**pay·a·ble** /ˈpeɪəbəl/ *adjective*
**1** if an amount of money is payable, you must pay it: *You can pay $50 now, and the rest is payable when your order arrives.*
**2 payable to someone** = if you make a check payable to someone, you write his or her name on it so he or she gets the money

**pay·check** /ˈpeɪtʃek/ *noun*
a check that you get as pay for work you have done: *He gets a paycheck from his employer every week.*

**pay·day** /ˈpeɪdeɪ/ *noun*
the day when you get your money for work you have done: *I can't pay the bill until payday.*

**pay·ment** /ˈpeɪmənt/ *noun*
**1** an amount of money that you pay, often one of many amounts in a series: *Most people make monthly payments for gas and electricity.*
**2** the act of paying: *Late payment of this bill will result in a $10 fine.*

**ˈpay phone** *noun*
a telephone you can use by putting coins or a card into it: *There's a pay phone on the corner of the street where you can make the call.*

**pay·roll** /ˈpeɪroʊl/ *noun*
a list of all the people who work for a company and are paid by the company: *We have 127 employees on the payroll.*

**PC¹** *noun*
(**personal computer**) a type of computer that people have at home: *I do my homework on my PC.* → see picture on page **A20**

**PC²** *adjective*
(**politically correct**) using careful language to avoid upsetting anyone belonging to a particular religion, sex, race, etc.: *It's not PC to call a woman "baby."*

**P.E.** *noun*
(**physical education**) sports and exercise taught as a school subject

**pea** /pi/ *noun*
a very small round green vegetable: *Eat your peas.* → see picture on page **A12**

**peace** /piːs/ *noun*
**1** a time when there is no war or fighting: *We all hope for world peace.*
**2** a situation that is quiet and calm: *I went to the library to work in peace.*
[**ORIGIN:** 1100-1200 From the old French word *pais*, from the Latin word *pax*.]

**WORD FAMILY: peace**
**peace** *noun* | **peaceful** *adjective* | **peacefully** *adverb*

**peace·ful** /ˈpisfəl/ *adjective*
**1** quiet and calm: *The house is peaceful in the early morning, when everyone's still asleep.*
**2** without fighting or violence: *The leaders are trying to find a peaceful solution to the disagreement.*
—**peacefully** *adverb* in a peaceful way: *The baby was sleeping peacefully.*

**peace·keep·ing** /ˈpisˌkipɪŋ/ *noun*
the process of trying to stop people from fighting each other: *The soldiers are being sent on a peacekeeping operation.*
—**peacekeeper** *noun* someone who tries to stop people from fighting each other: *United Nations peacekeepers*

**peach** /pitʃ/ *noun*
a juicy yellow and red fruit with a soft skin and one large rough seed
[**ORIGIN:** 1200-1300 From the French word *peche*, from the Latin word *persicus*, which means "Persian." Peach trees came to Europe from Persia, which is the old name for Iran.]

**pea·cock** /ˈpikɑk/ *noun*
a large bird with a long neck. A male peacock has long blue and green tail feathers that it can spread out.

**peak** /pik/ *noun*
**1** the pointed top of a mountain: *The peak of the mountain was covered in snow.*
**2** the time when something is most successful, best, etc.: *Rob was 45 and at the peak of his career.*

**peal** /pil/ *noun* (*formal*)
a long loud sound of someone laughing, thunder, or church bells ringing: *There was a flash of lightning and then a peal of thunder.*

**pea·nut** /ˈpinʌt/ *noun*
**1** a small light brown nut with a thin soft shell: *He bought a soda and a pack of peanuts.* → see picture on page **A13**
**2** **peanuts** (*informal*) = a very small amount of money: *I'm tired of working for peanuts – I want to make more money.*

**ˈpeanut ˌbutter** *noun*
a soft food made from crushed peanuts, that you eat on bread: *a peanut butter and jelly sandwich*

**pear** /per/ *noun*
a sweet juicy fruit, usually green or yellow, that is round and wide at the bottom and thin at the top → see picture on page **A13**

**pearl** /pɚl/ *noun*
a small round white object that forms inside an OYSTER, and is a valuable jewel: *She wore a necklace of pearls.*

**peas·ant** /ˈpezənt/ *noun*
a poor person who works on the land. This word is used mainly about people in past times.

**peb·ble** /ˈpebəl/ *noun*
a small smooth stone on a beach or in a river: *The boys were throwing pebbles in the water.*

**pe·can** /pɪˈkɑn/ *noun*
a long brown sweet nut: *pecan pie* → see picture on page **A13**

**peck** /pek/ *verb*
if a bird pecks something, it quickly bites it with its beak: *A bird was pecking at the berries on the tree.*

**pe·cu·liar** /pɪˈkjuljɚ/ *adjective*
**1** strange or unusual: *The cheese had a peculiar smell and I didn't want to taste it.*
**2 be peculiar to someone or something** (*formal*) = if something is peculiar to one place or person, only that place or person has it: *Both these animals are peculiar to Alaska – you won't find them anywhere else.*
—**peculiarly** *adverb* in a strange or unusual way: *Ben's been behaving very peculiarly – he won't talk to anyone.*
—**peculiarity** /pɪˌkyuliˈærəti/ *noun* an unusual quality or feature: *One of the peculiarities of this fish is that it has no tail fin.*
→ see Thesaurus box at **strange**

**ped·al¹** /ˈpedl/ *noun*
a part of a bicycle, car, piano, etc. that you push with your foot: *She stepped on the gas pedal, and the car moved forward.* → see picture at **bicycle**
[**ORIGIN:** 1600-1700 From the Latin word *pedalis*, which means "relating to the foot."]

**pedal²** *verb*
to ride a bicycle by pushing the pedals with your feet: *It was hard work pedaling the bike up the hill.*

**pe·des·tri·an** /pəˈdestriən/ *noun*
someone who is walking in a town, rather than traveling in a car or riding a bicycle: *The car stopped and waited for the pedestrians to cross the road.*
[**ORIGIN:** 1700-1800 From the Latin word *pedester*, which means "going on foot," from *pedes*, which means "feet."]

**pe·di·a·tri·cian** /ˌpidiəˈtrɪʃən/ *noun*
a doctor who treats children
→ see Thesaurus box at **doctor**

**ped·i·gree** /ˈpedəˌgri/ *noun*
a list of the parents and other past family members of an animal or person, used especially to show that the person or animal comes from a good family: *We bought the puppy because it has a very good pedigree.*

**peek** /pik/ *verb*
to quickly look at something, especially in a secret or shy way: *He peeked inside her bag.*
—**peek** *noun* a quick look: *I took a quick peek at her diary when she was not at home.*
→ see Thesaurus box at **look¹**

**peek**

He peeks through his fingers.

**peel¹** /pil/ *verb*
to take off the skin of a fruit or vegetable: *I'll peel the potatoes.* → see picture on page **A15**
→ see Thesaurus box at **cut¹**

**peel²** *noun*
the skin of a fruit or vegetable: *a banana peel*

**peep** /piːp/ *verb*
to look somewhere quickly in a secret way: *I saw someone peeping through the window.*

**peer¹** /pɪr/ *noun*
your peers are people who are the same age as you: *Teenagers usually want to spend time with their peers, not adults or little kids.*

**peer²** *verb*
to look very carefully because it is dark or you cannot see well: *The old lady peered at me through her glasses.*
→ see Thesaurus box at **look¹**

**peg** /peg/ *noun*
**1** a short piece of wood or metal attached to a wall, that you hang things on: *All the children have pegs to hang their coats on.* → see picture on page **A18**
**2** (*also* **tent peg**) a pointed piece of wood or metal that you push into the ground to keep a tent in the right place

**pel·i·can** /ˈpelɪkən/ *noun*
a big bird that has a bag of skin under its beak, where it stores fish before it eats them

**pel·let** /ˈpelɪt/ *noun*
a small hard ball made from metal, food, etc.: *The farmer gives the cattle food pellets.*

**pelt¹** /pelt/ *verb*
to throw a lot of things at someone: *Two kids were pelting each other with snowballs.*

P

**pelt²** *noun*
the skin of a dead animal with the fur on it: *Hunters killed the animals and sold their pelts.*

**pel·vis** /ˈpelvɪs/ *noun*
the wide curved bones at the base of your SPINE, and at the top of your legs → see picture on page **A2**
—**pelvic** *adjective* relating to the pelvis: *the pelvic bones*

**pen** /pen/ *noun*
**1** something you use for writing and drawing in ink: *I borrowed a pen to write down her address.* | *Fill out the form in pen.*
**2** a small area with a fence around it where a farmer keeps animals: *The lambs are kept in indoor pens.*
[**ORIGIN:** 1200-1300 From the Latin word *penna*, which means "feather." People used to dip the hard end of feathers in ink and write with them.]

**pe·nal·ize** /ˈpinlˌaɪz/ *verb*
**1** to punish someone for not obeying a rule: *His book report was too short, and his teacher penalized him by giving him a lower grade.*
**2** to punish a player or team in sports by giving an advantage to the other team: *The player was penalized for fouling another player by being sent off the field.*

**pen·al·ty** /ˈpenlti/ *noun* (plural **penalties**)
**1** a punishment for not obeying a rule or law: *The penalty for the crime is five years in prison.*
**2** a disadvantage that a player or team in sports gets for not obeying the rules: *The penalty against the Cowboys made them move back five yards.*
[**ORIGIN:** 1500-1600 From the Latin word *poena*, which means "punishment."]

**pen·cil** /ˈpensəl/ *noun*
a wooden stick that you write or draw with, that has a gray or colored substance inside: *Write in pencil so you can erase it if you make a mistake.* → see picture on page **A18**
[**ORIGIN:** 1300-1400 From the Latin word *penicillus*, which means "paintbrush or pencil," from *peniculus*, which means "little tail." A paintbrush has hairs like a tail.]

**pend·ing** /ˈpendɪŋ/ *preposition* (*formal*)
until something happens or is completed: *Mrs. Green will be in charge, pending the arrival of a new principal.*

**pen·du·lum** /ˈpendʒələm/ *noun*
a long stick with a weight on the end that swings from side to side in a large clock
[**ORIGIN:** 1600-1700 From the Latin word *pendulus*, which means "hanging," from *pendere*, meaning "to hang."]

**pen·e·trate** /ˈpenəˌtreɪt/ *verb* (*formal*)
to pass into or through something that is deep or thick: *This type of bullet can penetrate metal.*
—**penetration** /ˌpenəˈtreɪʃən/ *noun* the act of penetrating something

**pen·guin** /ˈpeŋgwɪn/ *noun*
a big black and white sea bird that swims very quickly under water but cannot fly. Penguins live in cold southern areas of the world, including the Antarctic.

**pen·i·cil·lin** /ˌpenəˈsɪlən/ *noun*
a medicine that cures infections by destroying BACTERIA

**pe·nin·su·la** /pəˈnɪnsələ/ *noun*
a piece of land that has water on most sides, but is joined to a bigger area of land: *Most of the state of Florida is a peninsula.*
[**ORIGIN:** 1500-1600 From the Latin word *paeninsula*, from *paene* and *insula*, which mean "almost" and "island."]

**pen·i·ten·tia·ry** /ˌpenəˈtenʃəri/ *noun* (plural **penitentiaries**)
a prison: *He was found guilty of robbery and sent to the state penitentiary.*

**pen·knife** /ˈpen-naɪf/ *noun* (plural **penknives** /ˈpennaɪvz/)
another word for a POCKET KNIFE

**ˈpen name** *noun*
a name a writer uses instead of his or her real name: *Samuel Clemens wrote his books using "Mark Twain" as his pen name.* **SYNONYM: pseudonym**

**pen·ni·less** /ˈpenɪləs/ *adjective*
having no money: *He had no job and was penniless.*

**pen·ny** /ˈpeni/ *noun* (plural **pennies**)
a coin that is worth 1 cent
→ see Thesaurus box at **money**

**ˈpen pal** *noun*
someone in another country that you write letters to, as a way of becoming friends: *I have a pen pal in Mexico. We write to each other once a month.*

**pen·sion** /ˈpenʃən/ *noun*
the money that a company pays regularly to someone who has stopped working: *He started receiving a pension when he retired.*

**pent·a·gon** /ˈpentəˌgɑn/ *noun*
a flat shape with five sides

**Pen·ta·gon** /ˈpentəˌgɑn/ *noun*
**the Pentagon** = the government building in Washington, D.C. where the people who control the army, navy, etc. work

**pent·house** /ˈpenthaʊs/ *noun*
an expensive apartment on the top floor of a tall building: *She lived in a penthouse on Fifth Avenue.*

**peo·ple** /ˈpipəl/ *noun*
**1** the plural of PERSON: *There were about a hundred people at the party.*

**THESAURUS: people**

**the public** all the people in an area or country: *The museum is open to the public from 10 a.m. to 6 p.m.*

**society** all the people who live in a country, and the way they live: *American society has changed a lot in the past 50 years.*

**the human race/mankind** all the people in the world, considered as a group: *Is mankind harming our environment?*

**population** the number of people who live in an area: *What's the population of Los Angeles?*

**2 the people** = all the ordinary people in a country or a state: *The mayor should remember that he was elected to serve the people.*
**3** a race or nation: *The Statue of Liberty was a gift from the people of France.*
→ see Thesaurus box at **race**[1]

**pep·per** /ˈpepɚ/ *noun*
**1** a powder that tastes a little hot, which you put on food to give it more flavor: *Add some salt and pepper to the soup.*
**2** a hollow red, green, or yellow vegetable that you can cook or eat uncooked → see picture on page **A12**

**pep·per·mint** /ˈpepɚˌmɪnt/ *noun*
**1** a plant with a strong sweet taste and smell, used in candy or TOOTHPASTE or for making tea: *peppermint tea*
**2** a candy that tastes like peppermint: *Would you like a peppermint?*

**pep·pe·ro·ni** /ˌpepəˈroʊni/ *noun*
an Italian SAUSAGE with a strong taste

**per** /pɚ/ *preposition*
for or during each: *Tickets are $10 per person.* | *The park has four million visitors per year.*

**per·ceive** Ac /pɚˈsiv/ *verb* (*formal*)
**1** to have a particular opinion about what someone or something is like: *Many of the children perceived the changes at school as frightening.*
**2** to see or hear something: *Cats cannot perceive as many colors as humans do and mostly see shades of gray.*

**per·cent** Ac /pɚˈsent/ *noun*
**five percent (5%)/10 percent (10%), etc.** = five, ten, etc. in every hundred: *Sixty percent of the students are boys and 40 percent are girls.*

**per·cent·age** Ac /pɚˈsentɪdʒ/ *noun*
an amount that you express as part of 100: *"What percentage of students from this school go to college?" "Sixty percent."*

**per·cep·tion** Ac /pɚˈsepʃən/ *noun* (*formal*)
your belief or opinion about what someone or something is like: *There is a perception that the class is hard, but if you study, you will do fine in it.*

P

**per·cep·tive** /pɚˈseptɪv/ *adjective*
good at noticing and understanding what is happening: *She was only 8, but she was very perceptive and could tell when other people were upset.*

**perch** /pɚtʃ/ *verb*
to sit on something high up, or on the edge of something: *A bird flew down and perched on the branch.*
—**perch** *noun* a branch or stick where a bird sits

**per·cus·sion** /pɚˈkʌʃən/ *noun*
drums and other musical instruments which you play by hitting them
[**ORIGIN:** 1500-1600 From the Latin word *percussio*, which means "the act of hitting," from *percutere*, which means "to hit hard."]

**per·fect¹** /ˈpɚfɪkt/ *adjective*
**1** if something is perfect, it is so good that it could not be better: *Lori wanted a perfect wedding.* | *Your English is perfect.*
**2** exactly right for something: *The weather was perfect for a picnic.*
[**ORIGIN:** 1200-1300 From the Latin word *perfectus*, which means "finished," and is a form of the verb *perficere*, which means "to finish or do completely."]

**WORD FAMILY: perfect**
**perfect** *adjective* | **perfect** *verb* | **perfectly** *adverb* | **perfection** *noun* | **perfectionist** *noun*

**per·fect²** /pɚˈfekt/ *verb*
to make something very good and without any mistakes: *She spent a year in France to perfect her French.*

**per·fec·tion** /pɚˈfekʃən/ *noun*
**1** the state of being perfect and without any mistakes: *Dan's piano teacher expected perfection from him; no mistakes were allowed.*
**2** **to perfection** = in a way that makes something so good that it could not be better: *The food was cooked to perfection.*
—**perfectionist** *noun* someone who wants everything to be perfect

**per·fect·ly** /ˈpɚfɪktli/ *adverb*
**1** without any mistakes or problems: *He lived in Mexico for many years and speaks Spanish perfectly.*
**2** completely or very: *If you feel nervous before your test, that's perfectly normal.*

**per·form** /pɚˈfɔrm/ *verb*
**1** to act in a play, play music, dance, etc. to entertain people: *The drama club is performing a new play next week.*
**2** (*formal*) to do a job or piece of work: *Surgeons wash their hands before performing an operation.*

**per·form·ance** /pɚˈfɔrməns/ *noun*
**1** an occasion when someone performs a play, piece of music, etc.: *The performance begins at 8 o'clock, so let's get to the theater about 7:30.*
**2** **someone's/something's performance** = how well someone or something does something: *Linda's performance at school has gotten much better; she's getting A's and B's instead of C's.*

**per·form·er** /pɚˈfɔrmɚ/ *noun*
someone who acts, plays music, dances, etc. to entertain people: *There were over 50 performers in the show.*

**per·fume** /ˈpɚfyum/ *noun*
**1** a liquid with a pleasant smell that women put on their skin: *She was wearing a lot of perfume, and I could smell it across the room.*
**2** a pleasant sweet smell: *The air was full of the perfume of flowers.*
→ see Thesaurus box at **smell¹**
[**ORIGIN:** 1500-1600 From the Latin word *fumare*, which means "to smoke." A pleasant smell goes through the air like smoke.]

**per·haps** /pɚˈhæps/ *adverb* (*formal*)
**1** possibly: *Perhaps it will snow later today. I hope it does.* **SYNONYM: maybe**
**2** used when suggesting something politely: *Perhaps you should see a doctor.* **SYNONYM: maybe**
[**ORIGIN:** 1500-1600 From the old English words *per* and *hap*, which mean "by" and "chance."]

**per·il** /ˈperəl/ *noun* (*formal*)
great danger: *A storm began, and the ship was in peril.*
—**perilous** *adjective* (*formal*) very dangerous: *They set off on their perilous trip through the mountains.*

**pe·rim·e·ter** /pəˈrɪmətɚ/ *noun*
the length around the edge of an area or shape: *Find the perimeter of the triangle by measuring all its sides.*
[ORIGIN: 1500-1600 From the Greek words *peri* and *metron*, which mean "around" and "measure."]

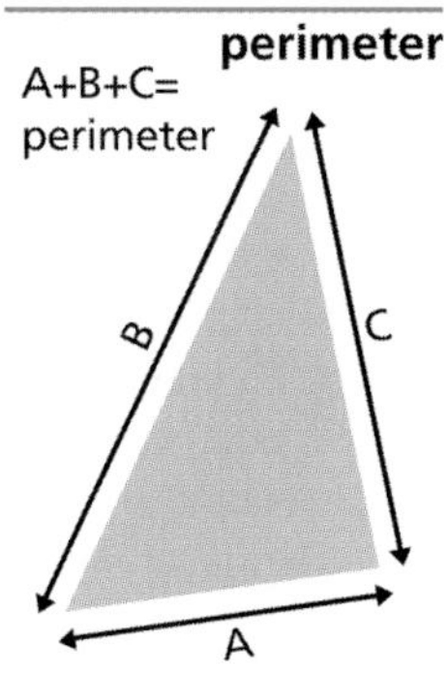


**pe·ri·od** Ac /ˈpɪriəd/ *noun*
**1** a length of time: *The disease usually lasts for a period of two weeks.* | *The stores are very busy during the Christmas period.*
**2** the mark (.) that you use in writing at the end of a sentence, or after an abbreviation
**3** one of the equal parts of a school day: *I have a history test during first period.*
**4** one part of a game in some sports: *They scored four goals in the third period.*
**5** the time when blood comes out of a woman's body once a month

**pe·ri·od·ic** Ac /ˌpɪriˈɑdɪk/ *adjective* (*formal*)
happening again and again, or regularly: *Dave gets periodic headaches, about once a month.*
—**periodically** *adverb* again and again, or regularly: *The river floods periodically – usually every two or three years.*

**pe·ri·od·ic·al** /ˌpɪriˈɑdɪkəl/ *noun*
a magazine, especially one about a serious or technical subject, that comes out at regular times such as once a month

**ˌperiodic ˈtable** *noun*
**the periodic table** = a list showing the ELEMENTs (=simple chemical substances) in a special order, so that similar elements are together

**pe·riph·e·ral** /pəˈrɪfərəl/ *adjective* (*formal*)
less important than others: *He had only a peripheral role in what happened – he was hardly involved at all.* SYNONYM: **minor**

**per·i·scope** /ˈperəˌskoʊp/ *noun*
a long tube with mirrors in it that you use for looking over the top of something, especially in a SUBMARINE
[ORIGIN: 1800-1900 From the Greek words *peri* and *skopein*, which mean "around" and "to look."]

**per·ish** /ˈperɪʃ/ *verb* (*formal*)
to die: *Hundreds perished when the ship sank.*

**per·ju·ry** /ˈpɚdʒəri/ *noun*
the crime of telling a lie in a court of law: *He had committed perjury when he said he had not met her. In fact, he knew her very well.*

**perk·y** /ˈpɚki/ *adjective*
happy and liking to be active: *You seem perky this morning. Did you have a good sleep?*

**perm** /pɚm/ *noun*
a treatment for hair that makes it curly: *I hate my straight hair, so I got a perm.*

**per·ma·nent** /ˈpɚmənənt/ *adjective*
continuing for a long time or for always: *Luckily, the damage to his eyesight isn't permanent – he will be able to see again.* ANTONYM: **temporary**
—**permanence** *noun* the state of being permanent
—**permanently** *adverb* for ever: *The business has closed permanently – it won't reopen.*
[ORIGIN: 1400-1500 From the Latin word *permanere*, which means "to stay till the end."]

**per·mis·si·ble** /pɚˈmɪsəbəl/ *adjective* (*formal*)
allowed by law or the rules: *Smoking in school is not permissible.* ANTONYM: **forbidden**

**per·mis·sion** /pɚˈmɪʃən/ *noun*
if you are given permission to do something, someone allows you to do it: *I asked my teacher for permission to leave class early.*

**per·mit**[1] /pɚˈmɪt/ *verb* (**permitted**, **permitting**) (*formal*)
**1** to allow someone to do something: *You are permitted to bring a dictionary into the examination room.*
**2** **weather permitting/time permitting, etc.** = used to say that you will do something if something allows you to, for example if the weather is good enough or if you have enough time to do it: *Weather permitting, we're planning to eat outside.*
→ see Thesaurus box at **allow**
[ORIGIN: 1400-1500 From the Latin word *permittere*, which means "to let through or allow."]

**WORD FAMILY: permit**
**permit** *verb* | **permit** *noun* | **permission** *noun* | **permissible** *adjective*

**per·mit²** /ˈpɚmɪt/ *noun*
an official piece of paper that allows you to do something: *You can't park here without a permit.*

**per·pen·dic·u·lar** /ˌpɚpənˈdɪkyələ/ *adjective*
if two lines are perpendicular to each other, they form an angle of 90 degrees where they cross: *The wall is perpendicular to the ground.*
—**perpendicular** *noun* an exactly upright position or line: *Draw a line 15 degrees from the perpendicular.*

**per·se·cute** /ˈpɚsɪˌkyut/ *verb (formal)*
to treat someone in a bad way because of his or her ideas: *In Roman times, the rulers persecuted Christians.*
—**persecution** /ˌpɚsɪˈkyuʃən/ *noun* the act of persecuting someone

**per·se·vere** /ˌpɚsəˈvɪr/ *verb (formal)*
to continue trying to do something difficult: *Physics was the hardest class Toni had ever taken, but she persevered.*
—**perseverance** *noun* determination to keep doing something difficult

**per·sist** Ac /pɚˈsɪst/ *verb (formal)*
**1** to continue to do something in a determined way: *He didn't reply to her emails, but she persisted in trying to contact him.*
**2** to continue to happen: *If the pain persists, go to see a doctor.*
—**persistent** *adjective* continuing to do something, or continuing to happen: *He was very persistent, and kept asking her out.* | *He gets these persistent headaches.*
—**persistence** *noun* determination to succeed in doing something, by trying many times: *I admire her persistence – she never gives up.*

**per·son** /ˈpɚsən/ *noun* (plural **people** /ˈpipəl/)
**1** a man, woman, or child: *Diane is a really nice person.* | *In this game, each person has to think of an animal.*
**2** **in person** = if you do something in person, you do it by going to a place, not by writing or using the telephone: *I wanted to thank you in person, rather than just calling you.*
[ORIGIN: 1100-1200 From the Latin word *persona*, which first meant "actor's mask, or character in a play," and then came to mean "person."]

**per·son·al** /ˈpɚsənəl/ *adjective*
**1** belonging or relating to you: *Rich packed all his personal belongings in a small suitcase.*
**2** relating to your private life and relationships: *She's had some personal problems recently. I think she broke up with her boyfriend.*
**3** doing something yourself, instead of asking someone else to do it: *The president made a personal visit to the scene of the disaster.*
→ see Thesaurus box at **private¹**

**ˌpersonal comˈputer** *noun (abbreviation:* **PC**)
a type of computer that people have at home

**per·son·al·i·ty** /ˌpɚsəˈnæləti/ *noun* (plural **personalities**)
**1** someone's character and how he or she behaves toward other people: *She has a great personality – she's very friendly and funny.*
**2** someone who is well known because he or she is often on television or radio: *TV personality Jon Stewart was the host of the show.*

**per·son·al·ly** /ˈpɚsənəli/ *adverb*
**1** used when saying what you think about something, not what anyone else thinks: *Many people like spicy food. Personally, I hate it.*
**2** if you do something personally, you do it and no one else does it for you: *I know she has the letter because I gave it to her personally.*
**3** if you know someone personally, you have met and talked to him or her: *I've seen her around, but I don't know her personally.*
**4** **take something personally** = to get upset by the things other people say because you think they are saying them because they do not like you: *He's mean to everyone, so don't take the things he said personally.*

**ˌpersonal ˈpronoun** *noun*
a word such as "I," "you," "she," or "they"

**per·son·i·fi·ca·tion** /pɚˌsɑnəfəˈkeɪʃən/ *noun*
**1** **the personification of something** = someone who is a perfect example of a particular

quality, especially a very good or very bad quality: *The newspapers said that he was a very bad man, the personification of evil.*
**2** the representation of a thing or quality as a person: *Uncle Sam, with his red, white, and blue hat, is a personification of the United States.*

**per·son·nel** /ˌpɚsəˈnel/ *plural noun*
people who work for an organization: *Military personnel were checking the vehicles using the road.* **SYNONYM: staff**

**per·spec·tive** Ac /pɚˈspektɪv/ *noun (formal)*
**1** a way of thinking about something: *Try to look at the situation from my perspective.* **SYNONYM: viewpoint**
**2** the ability to think about something sensibly, so that it does not seem worse than it is: *You need to keep things in perspective and not get too upset – we lost a football game, that's all.*

**per·spire** /pɚˈspaɪɚ/ *verb (formal)*
if you perspire, SWEAT (=salty liquid) comes out of your skin because you are hot **SYNONYM: sweat**
—**perspiration** /ˌpɚspəˈreɪʃən/ *noun* water from your skin when you perspire **SYNONYM: sweat**

**per·suade** /pɚˈsweɪd/ *verb*
to make someone decide to do something by giving him or her good reasons: *We persuaded him to wear a suit by telling him he looked cool.*

**WORD FAMILY: persuade**
**persuade** *verb* | **persuasion** *noun* | **persuasive** *adjective* | **persuasively** *adverb*

**THESAURUS: persuade**
**talk someone into something** (*informal*) to persuade someone to do something: *He talked her into helping him with his report.*
**get someone to do something** (*informal*) to persuade someone to do something: *She is trying to get the kids to help around the house more.*
**encourage** to persuade someone to do something, especially by telling him or her that it is good for him or her: *My parents encourage me to try new things.*
**convince** to persuade someone that something is true or that something is the right thing to do: *Kim convinced her dad that she was telling the truth.*
**coax** to persuade someone to do something by talking gently and kindly: *"Come for Christmas," Jody coaxed over the phone.*

**per·sua·sion** /pɚˈsweɪʒən/ *noun*
the act of persuading someone to do something: *After a lot of persuasion, she agreed to go.*

**per·sua·sive** /pɚˈsweɪsɪv/ *adjective*
able to persuade people to do things: *She is very persuasive and got Angela to help us.*
—**persuasively** *adverb* in a persuasive way: *He argued persuasively about changing the system and convinced many people.*

**pes·si·mis·m** /ˈpesəˌmɪzəm/ *noun*
the feeling that bad things will happen, not good things: *Some students are sure they will fail, and this pessimism is a problem.* **ANTONYM: optimism**
[**ORIGIN:** 1700-1800 From the Latin word *pessimus*, which means "worst."]

**pes·si·mist** /ˈpesəmɪst/ *noun*
someone who thinks that bad things will happen, not good things: *Ray is a pessimist: every time he gets on a plane, he's sure there will be an accident.* **ANTONYM: optimist**

**pes·si·mis·tic** /ˌpesəˈmɪstɪk/ *adjective*
someone who is pessimistic thinks that bad things will happen, not good things: *I'm pessimistic about the future – I think things will get worse.* **ANTONYM: optimistic**

**pest** /pest/ *noun*
**1** an animal or insect that harms crops or damages places where people live: *Farmers put chemicals on their crops to kill pests.*
**2** (*informal*) someone who annoys you: *That kid is a pest! I wish he would stay at home.*

**pes·ter** /ˈpestə/ *verb*
to ask someone for something many times in an annoying way: *He pestered his mother to buy the game for him.*

**pes·ti·cide** /ˈpestəˌsaɪd/ *noun*
a chemical that kills insects that destroy crops: *Farmers spray pesticides on their crops to kill insects.*

**pet**

**pet¹** /pet/ *noun*
an animal that you keep at home: *I have two pets: a dog and a cat.* | *a pet rabbit*

**pet²** *verb* (**petted**, **petting**)
to move your hand over an animal's fur to show that you like it: *Can I pet your dog?* → see picture on page **A3**
→ see Thesaurus box at **touch¹**

**pet·al** /ˈpetl/ *noun*
one of the brightly colored parts of a flower: *The flower has purple petals.*

**pe·tite** /pəˈtit/ *adjective* (*formal*)
a woman who is petite is short and thin in a nice way **SYNONYM: small**

**pe·ti·tion** /pəˈtɪʃən/ *noun*
a piece of paper that a lot of people sign in order to ask for something or complain about something: *I signed a petition against the closing of the school.*
—**petitioner** *noun* someone who organizes or signs a petition: *Petitioners collected 500 signatures.*

**pet·ri·fied** /ˈpetrəˌfaɪd/ *adjective*
very frightened: *I'm petrified of dogs. When I see one, I can't move.* **SYNONYM: terrified**
—**petrify** *verb* to make someone petrified
→ see Thesaurus box at **frightened**
[**ORIGIN:** 1400-1500 From the French word *pétrifier*, which means "to become rock or become hard," from the Greek word *petra*, meaning "rock." If you are petrified, you are too frightened to move.]

**pe·tro·le·um** /pəˈtroʊliəm/ *noun*
oil from beneath the ground for making gasoline
[**ORIGIN:** 1500-1600 From the Latin words *petra* and *oleum*, which mean "rock" and "oil."]

**pet·ty** /ˈpeti/ *adjective*
caring too much about things that are not important or serious: *They had a petty argument about who had nicer shoes.*

**pew** /pyu/ *noun*
a long wooden seat in a church

**phan·tom** /ˈfæntəm/ *noun* (*formal*)
the spirit of a dead person that some people believe you can see **SYNONYM: ghost**

**pha·raoh** /ˈferoʊ/ *noun*
a ruler of ancient Egypt

**phar·ma·ceu·ti·cal** /ˌfɑrməˈsutɪkəl/ *noun* (*formal*)
a medicine: *The drug company sells pharmaceuticals to hospitals.* **SYNONYM: drug**
—**pharmaceutical** *adjective* relating to medicines: *pharmaceutical companies*

**phar·ma·cist** /ˈfɑrməsɪst/ *noun*
someone whose job is to prepare and sell medicines: *The pharmacist at the drugstore gave me my pills.* → see picture on page **A16**

**phar·ma·cy** /ˈfɑrməsi/ *noun* (plural **pharmacies**)
a store that sells medicines: *I bought some cough medicine from the pharmacy.*
[**ORIGIN:** 1300-1400 From the Greek word *pharmakon*, which means "magic liquid, poison, or drug."]

**phase¹** [Ac] /feɪz/ *noun*
**1** one part of a process in which something develops: *The first phase of the building work will be to clear the ground.* **SYNONYM: stage**
**2** one of the different shapes the moon has in each part of the month, when it is looked at from the Earth
[**ORIGIN:** 1800-1900 From the Greek word *phasis*, which means "appearance of a star or the moon," from *phainein*, which means "to show."]

**phase²** Ac *verb*
PHRASAL VERB
**phase something in**
to gradually start using a new way of doing something: *The changes will be gradually phased in over the next two years.*

**Ph.D.** /ˌpi eɪtʃ ˈdi/ *noun*
the highest possible university degree: *It took her about eight years to complete her Ph.D. in history.* **SYNONYM: doctorate**

**phe·nom·e·nal** Ac /fɪˈnɑmənl/ *adjective*
extremely impressive or good: *His new business was a phenomenal success and he made a lot of money.*
—**phenomenally** *adverb* extremely: *He is phenomenally intelligent and got the highest score ever on the test.*

**phe·nom·e·non** Ac /fɪˈnɑmənən/ *noun* (plural **phenomena** /fɪˈnɑmənə/) (*formal*)
something that happens in society or in nature: *Homelessness is not a new phenomenon – it has always existed.*
[ORIGIN: 1500-1600 From the Greek word *phainomenon*, a form of the verb *phainesthai*, which means "to appear."]

**phi·lan·thro·pist** /fɪˈlænθrəpɪst/ *noun*
a rich person who gives money to help poor people
[ORIGIN: 1600-1700 From the Greek words *philos* and *anthropos*, which mean "loving" and "human being."]

**phi·los·o·pher** Ac /fɪˈlɑsəfɚ/ *noun*
someone who studies or teaches philosophy: *Socrates was a Greek philosopher.*
[ORIGIN: 1300-1400 From the Greek words *philos* and *sophia*, which mean "loving" and "knowledge."]

**phi·los·o·phy** Ac /fɪˈlɑsəfi/ *noun* (plural **philosophies**)
**1** the study of ideas about life and what life means: *She has a degree in philosophy.*
**2** your ideas about how life should be lived: *My philosophy is that you should do things now, and not wait until later.*
—**philosophical** /ˌfɪləˈsɑfɪkəl/ *adjective* relating to philosophy: *They used to have long philosophical discussions about life.*

**WORD FAMILY: philosophy**
**philosophy** *noun* | **philosopher** *noun* | **philosophical** *adjective*

**pho·bi·a** /ˈfoʊbiə/ *noun* (*formal*)
a strong fear of something: *She has a phobia about the dark and sleeps with the light on.*
[ORIGIN: 1700-1800 From the Greek *phobos*, which means "fear."]

**phone¹** /foʊn/ *noun*
a piece of equipment you use to speak to someone in another place: *The phone's ringing.* | *I got up to answer the phone.* | *Karen's been on the phone for hours, talking to Kayla.* **SYNONYM: telephone**

**phone²** *verb*
to talk to someone using a phone: *I'll phone you tomorrow.* **SYNONYM: call**

**ˈphone book** *noun*
a book that has the names, addresses, and telephone numbers of all the people living in an area

**ˈphone booth** *noun*
a small structure with a telephone inside that you pay to use: *She called me from a phone booth on Polk Street.*

**ˈphone ˌnumber** *noun*
a set of numbers that you press on a telephone when you call someone: *What's your phone number?*

**pho·net·ic** /fəˈnetɪk/ *adjective*
relating to the sounds you make when you speak: *The dictionary uses phonetic symbols to show how words are pronounced.*

**pho·net·ics** /fəˈnetɪks/ *noun*
the study of sounds you make when you speak

**phon·ics** /ˈfɑnɪks/ *noun*
a way of teaching people to read by teaching them the sounds of single letters and combinations of letters

**pho·ny** /ˈfoʊni/ *adjective* (*informal*)
false or not real: *He gave the police a phony address so they wouldn't know where he lived.*
→ see Thesaurus box at **fake**

**phos·pho·rus** /ˈfɑsfərəs/ *noun*
a chemical ELEMENT that burns when air touches it

**pho·to** /ˈfoʊtoʊ/ *noun* (plural **photos**)
a photograph: *There was a photo of the man*

P

*and his family in the paper.* | *Who's the girl in the photo?* **SYNONYM: picture**
→ see Thesaurus box at **picture**[1]

**WORD FAMILY: photo**
**photo** *noun* | **photograph** *noun* | **photograph** *verb* | **photographer** *noun* | **photography** *noun*

P

**pho·to·cop·i·er** /ˈfoʊtəˌkɑpiɚ/ *noun*
a machine for copying pieces of writing or pictures: *I made three copies of the letter on the photocopier.* **SYNONYM: copier** → see picture on page **A18**

**pho·to·cop·y**[1] /ˈfoʊtəˌkɑpi/ *noun* (plural **photocopies**)
a copy of a piece of writing or a picture that you make on a photocopier: *I gave him a photocopy of the letter and kept the original.* **SYNONYM: copy**

**photocopy**[2] *verb*
to make a copy of a piece of writing or a picture on a photocopier: *Photocopy your story when you finish it, so you have a copy in case something happens.* **SYNONYM: copy**

**pho·to·graph**[1] /ˈfoʊtəˌgræf/ *noun*
a picture you make using a camera: *I took photographs of everybody at the party.* **SYNONYM: picture**
→ see Thesaurus box at **art**, **picture**[1]
[**ORIGIN:** 1800-1900 From the Greek words *photos*, a form of the word for "light," and *graphein*, which means "to write or draw."]

**photograph**[2] *verb* (*formal*)
to make a picture of someone or something using a camera: *He has photographed many famous people.*

**pho·tog·ra·pher** /fəˈtɑgrəfɚ/ *noun*
someone whose job is to make pictures using a camera: *The wedding photographer took the bride's picture.*

**pho·tog·ra·phy** /fəˈtɑgrəfi/ *noun*
the art or business of making pictures with a camera: *I'm taking a class in photography and learning to use my camera better.*
—**photographic** /ˌfoʊtəˈgræfɪk/ *adjective* relating to photography: *a photographic image*

**pho·ton** /ˈfoʊtɑn/ *noun*
the smallest possible amount of light. A photon has energy but no mass.

**pho·to·syn·the·sis** /ˌfoʊtoʊˈsɪnθəsɪs/ *noun*
the process by which plants use light to change CARBON DIOXIDE and water into CARBOHYDRATEs which plants use as food

**ˌphrasal ˈverb** *noun*
a verb that consists of a verb and a word such as "off," "up," or "down": *"Take off" and "give up" are phrasal verbs.*

**phrase** /freɪz/ *noun*
a group of words that is not a complete sentence: *"Later that day" and "on the way home" are phrases.*

**THESAURUS: phrase**
**expression** a word or phrase that has a particular meaning: *She used the expression "break a leg" to wish me good luck.*
**idiom** a group of words that have a special meaning that is different from the usual meaning of each word: *The phrase "under the weather" is an idiom that means "sick."*
**cliché** a phrase that has been used so often that it is boring: *It's a cliché, but we really do have to take this one day at a time.*
**saying/proverb** a phrase that many people know, that gives advice or information about life: *The old proverb "Don't count your chickens before they hatch" means that you should not make plans that depend on something happening because it might not happen.*

**phys·i·cal**[1] Ac /ˈfɪzɪkəl/ *adjective*
**1** relating to your body, not your mind or soul: *Physical activity such as walking or swimming is good for you.*
**2** relating to things that you can see, touch, smell, or taste: *An emotion like love is not a physical thing.*
—**physically** *adverb* in a physical way: *He was not physically fit and needed to exercise.*
[**ORIGIN:** 1400-1500 From the Latin word *physica*, which means "the study of nature," from the Greek word *physis*, meaning "nature."]

**physical²** Ac *noun*
a medical examination by a doctor to check that you are healthy: *She had a physical before she started running on the track team.*

**ˌphysical ˈtherapy** *noun*
the treatment of injuries and muscle problems with exercises, rubbing, or heat: *After her accident, she had physical therapy to strengthen her ankle.*

**phy·si·cian** /fɪˈzɪʃən/ *noun* (*formal*)
a doctor
→ see Thesaurus box at **doctor**

**phys·ics** /ˈfɪzɪks/ *noun*
the study of natural forces, such as heat, light, and movement: *We're learning about gravity in physics.*
—**physicist** /ˈfɪzəsɪst/ *noun* someone who studies or teaches physics

**phys·i·ol·o·gy** /ˌfɪziˈɑlədʒi/ *noun*
the study of how the bodies of living things work

**phy·sique** /fəˈzik/ *noun* (*formal*)
the shape and size of someone's body: *He has a good physique from playing a lot of sports.*

**pi** /paɪ/ *noun*
a number that is equal to the distance around a circle divided by its width. Pi is represented by the Greek letter (π) and is about 3.1416.

**pi·an·ist** /piˈænɪst/ *noun*
someone who plays the piano

**pi·an·o** /piˈænoʊ/ *noun* (plural **pianos**)
a large musical instrument with a row of black and white keys that play notes when you press them: *She plays the piano really well.* → see picture on page **A21**
[**ORIGIN:** 1800-1900 From the Italian phrase *piano e forte*, which means "quiet and loud." Unlike earlier instruments with keys, the piano could produce quiet and loud notes.]

**pick¹** /pɪk/ *verb*
**1** to choose something: *If you ask kids whether they want fries or vegetables, they pick fries.*
**2** to pull a flower or fruit from a plant or tree: *She picked an apple from the tree.*
**3** to remove small pieces from something with your fingers: *Stop picking your nose! | Don't pick at the scab before the cut has healed completely.*
**4 pick a fight** = to begin an argument or fight with someone: *He's always picking fights with younger kids.*
—**picker** *noun* someone who picks flowers or fruit: *fruit pickers*
→ see Thesaurus box at **choose**

**PHRASAL VERBS**

**pick on someone**
to treat someone in an unfair or unkind way: *Children picked on him by calling him names.*

**pick up**
**1 pick something up** = to lift something up from a surface: *He bent down to pick up his keys.* → see picture on page **A4**
**2 pick someone/something up** = to go somewhere and get someone or something: *Dad came to pick me up from school.*
**3 pick something up** = to learn something by watching or listening to other people: *I picked up a little Spanish when I went to Mexico.*
**4 pick something up** (*informal*) = to buy something: *Will you pick up some bread on the way home?*

**pick up on something**
to notice something about the way someone is feeling or behaving: *I was worried about my grades, but my parents didn't pick up on it.*

**pick²** *noun*
**take your pick** = used when telling someone to choose anything from a group of things: *There are four kinds of cake, so take your pick.*

**pick·et** /ˈpɪkɪt/ *noun*
a group of people who stand outside the place where they work to show they want more money or better work conditions: *He joined the picket line protesting job cuts.*
—**picket** *verb* to take part in a picket: *Workers are threatening to picket for better working conditions.*

**pick·le** /ˈpɪkəl/ *noun*
a small CUCUMBER kept in VINEGAR (=a liquid with a sour taste) or salt water: *Would you like pickles on your hamburger? | a dill pickle*

**pick·pock·et** /ˈpɪkˌpɑkɪt/ *noun*
someone who steals things from people's pockets

**pick·up** /ˈpɪkʌp/ *noun*
a small truck with a part with no roof in the back, used for carrying large things

**pick·y** /ˈpɪki/ *adjective* (**pickier**, **pickiest**)
someone who is picky is difficult to please because there are a lot of things he or she does not like: *I'm not picky about food – I'll eat anything.* SYNONYMS: **fussy**, **particular**

**pic·nic** /ˈpɪknɪk/ *noun*
an occasion when you take food and eat it outdoors: *We made some sandwiches and had a picnic by the lake.*
→ see Thesaurus box at **meal**

P

**pic·to·graph** /ˈpɪktəˌgræf/ (*also* **pic·to·gram** /ˈpɪktəˌgræm/) *noun*
a picture, symbol, or sign that represents a word or idea: *Some languages, such as ancient Egyptian, are written using pictograms.*

**pic·ture¹** /ˈpɪktʃɚ/ *noun*
**1** a drawing, painting, or photograph: *Draw a picture of a tree.* | *When he won an Olympic medal, his picture was in all the newspapers.*
→ see picture on page **A8**

**THESAURUS: picture**

**painting** a picture that someone has painted: *There are many famous paintings in the Museum of Modern Art.*

**drawing** a picture that someone has drawn with a pencil or pen: *We put the children's drawings up on the classroom wall.*

**sketch** a picture that someone draws quickly and that does not have a lot of details: *He drew a sketch of the flower in his notebook.*

**portrait** a painting, drawing, or photograph of a person: *The painting is a portrait of a woman with her baby.*

**cartoon** a funny drawing in a newspaper or magazine: *The cartoon shows the president in a cowboy hat, riding on a horse into the meeting.*

**illustration** a picture in a book: *The illustrations in this children's book are wonderful.*

**photograph/photo** a picture you take using a camera: *This is a photo I took of you and your sister when you were little.* | *wedding photographs*

**2 take a picture** = to take a photograph: *She took a picture of the waterfall.*
**3** an idea or image in your mind of what something is like: *After talking to Lynn, I had a clearer picture of what was going on.*
**4** the image that you see on a television or in a movie: *The picture's not very clear on this TV set.*
[ORIGIN: 1400-1500 From the Latin word *pictura*, from *pictus*, a form of the verb *pingere*, which means "to paint."]

**picture²** *verb*
**1** to imagine something: *I can't picture myself as a mother.*
**2** to show something or someone in a photograph, painting, or drawing: *She was pictured in a magazine standing outside her new home.*

**ˈpicture graph** *noun*
a GRAPH that uses pictures to represent information → see picture at **graph**

**pic·tur·esque** /ˌpɪktʃəˈresk/ *adjective*
a picturesque place is pretty to look at: *It is a picturesque town with a lot of old buildings.*

**pie** /paɪ/ *noun*
a type of food made with fruit baked inside a PASTRY covering: *Would you like some apple pie?*

**piece** /pis/ *noun*
**1** a part of something that is separate from the rest of it: *He took a piece of cake.* | *I dropped a glass and it broke into pieces.* | *You glue the pieces of the airplane together to make the model.*

**THESAURUS: piece**

**scrap** a small piece of paper, cloth, or food: *She wrote her phone number on a scrap of paper.*

**chunk** a thick piece of something that does not have an even shape: *The soup had large chunks of chicken in it.*

**lump** a small piece of something solid that does not have a definite shape: *He put a few lumps of charcoal on the barbecue.*

**fragment** (*formal*) a very small piece that has broken off something hard, such as glass or rock: *Fragments of glass from the car crash were still on the street.*

**slice** a thin flat piece of bread, meat, cake, or cheese cut from a larger piece: *a slice of blueberry pie*

**crumb** a very small piece of bread or cake: *There were crumbs all over the floor.*

**speck** a very small piece of dirt or dust: *She wiped some specks of dirt off her coat.*

**2** a single thing of a particular type: *This is a very expensive piece of equipment.* | *He wrote his phone number on a piece of paper.*
**3** **a piece of writing/music/art, etc.** = something that someone has written, drawn, or made: *I did a piece of writing about our family.*
**4** **a piece of advice/information/news, etc.** = some advice, information, etc.: *She gave me one piece of advice: don't smoke.*
**5** a small object used in a board game such as CHESS: *Each player has sixteen pieces at the start of the game.*
**6** a coin that is worth a particular amount: *a 50-cent piece*
→ see Thesaurus box at **part¹**

**ˈpie ˌchart** *noun*
a drawing of a circle divided into different parts by lines coming from the center. A pie chart is used to show the sizes of different amounts compared with each other. **SYNONYM: circle graph**

**pier** /pɪr/ *noun*
a long structure you can walk along that goes from the land into the ocean: *We stood on the pier watching the boats.*

**pierce** /pɪrs/ *verb*
to make a hole in something with a sharp object: *I want to have my ears pierced so I can wear earrings.* | *The needle pierced her skin.*

**pierc·ing¹** /ˈpɪrsɪŋ/ *adjective*
a piercing sound is loud and high, and not nice: *I heard a piercing scream.*

**piercing²** *noun*
a hole that is made in your body for jewelry: *He has several tattoos and piercings.*

**pig** /pɪg/ *noun*
**1** a fat pink farm animal: *Bacon and pork come from pigs.*
**2** (*informal*) someone who eats too much, is very dirty, or is offensive in some way: *Don't be such a pig – leave some for everyone else.*

**pi·geon** /ˈpɪdʒən/ *noun*
a gray bird that you often see in cities

**ˈpiggy bank** *noun*
a container that children save coins in, that is often in the shape of a pig

**pig·let** /ˈpɪglət/ *noun*
a young pig

**pig·sty** /ˈpɪgstaɪ/ (*also* **pig·pen** /ˈpɪgpen/) *noun* (plural **pigsties**)
**1** a place on a farm where pigs are kept
**2** if a place is a pigsty, it is very dirty and messy: *Your room is a pigsty – go and clean it up!*

**pig·tail** /ˈpɪgteɪl/ *noun*
if a girl has pigtails, her hair is tied together on each side of her head, and it may be BRAIDed: *The little girl had her hair in pigtails.*

**pile¹** /paɪl/ *noun*
**1** a lot of things on top of each other: *There was a pile of books on the table.*
**2** an amount of something in the shape of a small hill: *There were piles of snow by the side of the road.* **SYNONYM: mound**

**pile²** *verb*
**1** (*also* **pile up**) to put a lot of things together in a pile: *They piled the boxes in a corner.* | *Our suitcases were piled up on a cart.*
**2** **be piled with something** = to be filled or covered with a lot of things: *The shelves were piled with toys.*

**pil·grim** /ˈpɪlgrəm/ *noun*
**1** someone who travels a long way to get to a holy place for religious reasons: *Thousands of pilgrims travel to Mecca each year.*
**2** **the Pilgrims** = a group of people who left England and came to America in 1620 because of religious disagreements: *The Pilgrims' ship was called the "Mayflower."*
—**pilgrimage** *noun* a trip by pilgrims: *They went on a pilgrimage to Jerusalem.*
[**ORIGIN:** 1100-1200 From the old French word *peligrin*, from the Latin word *peregrinus*, which means "foreigner."]

**pill** /pɪl/ *noun*
a small hard piece of medicine that you eat: *If*

P

*you have a headache, take a pill.* **SYNONYM: tablet**
→ see Thesaurus box at **medicine**
[**ORIGIN:** 1400-1500 From the Latin word *pilula*, which means "little ball."]

**pil·lar** /ˈpɪlɚ/ *noun*
a tall piece of stone that supports part of a building: *Ten pillars support the roof of the building.* **SYNONYM: column**

P

**pil·low** /ˈpɪloʊ/ *noun*
a soft square thing that you rest your head on in bed → see picture on page **A10**

**pil·low·case** /ˈpɪloʊˌkeɪs/ *noun*
a cover for a pillow: *She changed the sheets and pillowcases.*

**pi·lot** /ˈpaɪlət/ *noun*
someone who flies an aircraft: *The pilot flew the plane very well.*
[**ORIGIN:** 1500-1600 From the old Italian word *pilota* or *pedota*, which means "someone who steers a boat." A pilot was first someone who controlled the direction of a boat, and then someone who controlled the direction of an aircraft.]

**pim·ple** /ˈpɪmpəl/ *noun*
a small raised red spot on your skin: *Teenagers often get pimples on their faces.*
—**pimply** *adjective* covered with pimples
→ see Thesaurus box at **mark²**

**pin¹** /pɪn/ *noun*
**1** a short piece of metal with a sharp point, that you use to fasten pieces of material together: *She turned up the bottom of the skirt and put pins in it.*
**2** a piece of jewelry that you fasten to your clothes: *He wore a pin with a Canadian flag on it.*
**3** one of the things you try to knock down in a game of BOWLING: *He knocked down all ten pins.*

**pin**

**pin²** *verb* (**pinned**, **pinning**)
**1** to use a pin or a THUMBTACK to attach something somewhere: *The teacher pinned the list of names on the board.*
**2** to hold someone so he or she cannot move: *The police officer pinned him against the wall and wouldn't let him go.*

**pi·ña·ta** /piˈnyɑtə/ *noun*
a decorated paper container filled with candy or toys, that you hang up so that children can try to break it open by hitting it with a stick

**pinch¹** /pɪntʃ/ *verb*
to press a piece of someone's skin between your finger and thumb: *My grandmother always pinches my cheeks and kisses me.* → see picture on page **A3**
→ see Thesaurus box at **press¹**

**pinch²** *noun*
**1** the act of pressing someone's skin between your finger and thumb: *I gave her a pinch on the arm, and she yelled "Ouch!"*
**2 a pinch of salt** = a small amount of salt that you can hold between your finger and thumb: *Put a pinch of salt in the soup.*

**pine** /paɪn/ *noun*
**1** (*also* **pine tree**) a tree with long pointed leaves that do not fall off in winter. The seeds of a pine tree are in hard seed containers called CONEs: *Some pine trees are used as Christmas trees.*
**2** a soft light-colored wood from pine trees: *a pine kitchen table*

**pine·ap·ple** /ˈpaɪnˌæpəl/ *noun*
a large yellow fruit that is rough on the outside and grows in hot places

**ˈpine cone** *noun*
the brown seed container of a pine tree → see picture at **cone**

**Ping-Pong** /ˈpɪŋpɑŋ/ *noun* (*trademark*)
a game in which two people hit a small ball across a net on a table

**pink** /pɪŋk/ *adjective*, *noun*
a color that is a mixture of red and white: *pink lipstick*

**pink·ie** /ˈpɪŋki/ *noun* (*informal*)
the smallest finger on your hand → see picture at **hand**

**pin·na·cle** /ˈpɪnəkəl/ *noun* (*formal*)
the most successful part of something: *At 40, she had reached the pinnacle of her law career.*

**pin·point** /ˈpɪnpɔɪnt/ *verb*
to say exactly when, where, or what something is: *I can pinpoint the moment I first met Steve – it was on my 12th birthday.*

**pint** /paɪnt/ *noun*
a unit for measuring liquid, equal to 16 FLUID OUNCEs or 0.47 liters: *a pint of milk | He lost two pints of blood in the accident.*

**pi·o·neer** /ˌpaɪəˈnɪr/ *noun*
**1** one of the first people to do something that later has a big effect on people's lives: *The Wright Brothers, who made the first powered flight in 1903, were aviation pioneers.*
**2** one of the first people to go to a new place and start living there: *The pioneers crossed the plains in wagons.*
—**pioneering** *adjective* using new ideas and better methods for the first time: *a pioneering heart surgeon*
[**ORIGIN:** 1500-1600 From the old French word *peonier*, which means "soldier who travels on foot." Sometimes soldiers would be sent forward to prepare the way for an army, and this is where we got the idea of a pioneer being the first person to go somewhere or do something.]

**pipe¹** /paɪp/ *noun*
**1** a tube for carrying water or gas: *One of the water pipes broke and flooded the basement.*
**2** an object for smoking tobacco. It is made of a narrow tube with a small bowl at the end: *My grandfather smoked a pipe.*

**pipe²** *verb*
to send a liquid or gas through a pipe: *They pipe water into the fields from the river.*

**pipe·line** /ˈpaɪplaɪn/ *noun*
**1** a system of pipes that carry oil or gas over long distances: *The pipeline carries oil from Russia to western Europe.*
**2** **in the pipeline** = if something is in the pipeline, it is still being prepared, but it will happen soon: *He has a new movie in the pipeline, and filming should start next year.*

**pi·rate¹** /ˈpaɪrət/ *noun*
someone who sails on the ocean, attacking other ships and stealing from them: *He was dressed as a pirate, with a patch on his eye.*
[**ORIGIN:** 1200-1300 From the Greek word *peirates*, from *peiran*, which means "to make an attempt or attack."]

**pirate²** *verb*
to copy and sell movies, music, or computer programs in a way that is not legal: *Pirated copies of the movie were being sold illegally.*
—**piracy** *noun* the act of pirating something

**Pis·ces** /ˈpaɪsiz/ *noun*
**1** the 12th sign of the ZODIAC, represented by two fish
**2** someone born between February 19 and March 20

**pis·tol** /ˈpɪstl/ *noun*
a small gun
[**ORIGIN:** 1500-1600 From the Czech word *pist'ala*, which means "pipe or gun."]

**pit** /pɪt/ *noun*
**1** a large hole in the ground: *They dug a pit and buried the garbage in it.*
**2** a large hard seed in some fruits: *a peach pit*
**3** **be the pits** (*informal*) = to be very bad or unpleasant: *This is the pits! I hate having to get up early!*

**pitch¹** /pɪtʃ/ *verb*
**1** to throw the ball for a player to hit in baseball: *Who's pitching in tonight's baseball game?*
**2** **pitch a tent** = to put up a tent so that you can use it: *We pitched our tent near the river.*
→ see Thesaurus box at **throw¹**
**PHRASAL VERB**
**pitch in**
to help other people with a job: *Everyone pitched in so that we could finish the cleaning and go home.*

**pitch²** *noun*
**1** a throw of the ball for a player to hit in baseball: *His next pitch was high, and the batter let it pass.*
**2** the pitch of a musical note is how high or low it is: *Trumpet players use their lips to change the pitch of a note.*

**pitch·er** /ˈpɪtʃɚ/ *noun*
**1** a container used for holding and pouring liquids: *a pitcher of cold water* **SYNONYM: jug**
**2** the baseball player who throws the balls for other players to hit

**pit·fall** /ˈpɪtfɔl/ *noun*
a problem or difficulty that is likely to happen in a particular job, situation, or activity: *One of the pitfalls of being famous is having no privacy.*

**pit·i·ful** /ˈpɪtɪfəl/ *adjective*
very bad, in a way that makes you sad: *Children begging for money is a pitiful sight.*
—**pitifully** *adverb* in a pitiful way: *Their pay is pitifully low.*

**pit·y¹** /ˈpɪti/ *noun*
**1** the sadness you feel when someone is in a bad situation: *I feel pity for people who have nowhere to live.*
**2 take/have pity on someone** = to help someone who is in a bad situation: *When she said she had no money, he took pity on her and gave her $50.*
**3 it's a pity/what a pity** = used to say that you wish a situation was different: *What a pity (that) you can't come with us.*

**pity²** *verb* (**pitied**, **pities**)
to feel sadness for someone because he or she is in a bad situation: *I pity people who have no family.*

**pix·el** /ˈpɪksəl/ *noun*
one of the small areas of light that cover a television or computer screen: *Each picture and word on the screen is formed from many pixels.*

**piz·za** /ˈpitsə/ *noun*
a food made of round flat bread, with tomato, cheese, and other things on top: *We ordered a pepperoni pizza.*
—**pizzeria** /ˌpitsəˈriə/ *noun* a restaurant that sells pizzas
[**ORIGIN:** 1800-1900 From the Italian word for "pie."]

**plac·ard** /ˈplækəd/ *noun*
a sign with writing on that people carry when they are protesting against something: *They carried placards saying, "Stop the War."*

**place¹** /pleɪs/ *noun*
**1** an area, building, city, or country: *He lives in a place called Maple Meadows.* | *This is the place where I first saw her.* | *My cousin needed a place to stay, so he moved in with us.*

**THESAURUS: place**

**position** the exact place where someone or something is, in relation to other things: *The shortstop's position is between second and third base.*

**spot** (*informal*) a place, especially a pleasant one where you spend time: *It's a good spot for a picnic.*

**location** (*formal*) the place where a building is: *The hotel is in a great location, right near the beach.*

**site** a place where something is going to be built, or where something important happened: *Gettysburg is the site of a famous Civil War battle.* | *the site for the new airport*

**point** a particular place on a road or river: *At this point, the two roads cross.*

**2** a space for something or someone: *Put the CD back in its place.* | *He returned to his place at the table.*
**3** (*informal*) someone's home: *Do you want to study at my place?*
**4 all over the place** (*informal*) = everywhere: *I dropped a vase, and pieces of glass went all over the place.*
**5 first/second/last, etc. place** = the position of being first, second, etc. in a race or competition: *Joe finished the race in third place.*
**6 in place** = if something is in place, it is ready if people need it: *We now have a system in place to deal with emergencies.*
**7 out of place** = if something is out of place in a particular situation, it does not belong there: *She felt out of place because all the other people were men.*
**8 in place of** = instead of someone or something: *I use honey in place of sugar in tea.*
**9 take place** = to happen: *The meeting will take place on Friday.*
**10 take someone's place** = to do something instead of someone else: *I took Tommy's place in the team when he got injured.*
→ see Thesaurus box at **home¹**

**place²** *verb* (*formal*)
**1** to put something somewhere carefully: *Rachel placed the box on the table.*
**2 place an order** = to say that you want to buy something that you will get at a later time: *He placed an order for a new computer,*

*and it was delivered one week later.* **SYNONYM: order**

**ˈplace ˌvalue** *noun*
the value of the position that a figure has in a number: *In the number 467, the digit 4 is in the hundred place value, so it is equal to 400.*

**pla·gia·rism** /ˈpleɪdʒəˌrɪzəm/ *noun*
the act of copying someone else's words or ideas and pretending they are your own: *His whole paper was copied from the Internet, and a teacher discovered his plagiarism.*
—**plagiarize** *verb* to copy someone else's words or ideas and pretend they are your own

**plague** /pleɪg/ *noun*
a disease that kills people and spreads quickly: *The plague that killed thousands of people in the 1500s was called "The Black Death."*

**plaid** /plæd/ *noun*
a pattern of squares and lines crossing each other that is on cloth: *a plaid work shirt*

**plain¹** /pleɪn/ *adjective*
**1** something that is plain does not have a pattern on it or anything extra on it: *He wore a plain blue suit. | I wanted plain paper, not paper with lines on.* **ANTONYM: fancy**
**2** easy to see, hear, or understand: *He made it plain (that) he didn't like me. | Try to write your essay in plain English, without too many technical words.* **SYNONYM: clear**
**3** a plain woman or girl is not beautiful: *She was a plain girl with thin brown hair.*
[**ORIGIN:** 1200-1300 From the Latin word *planus*, which means "flat, level, or clear."]

**plain²** *noun*
a large area of flat land: *Farmers grow wheat in the plains of America.*

**plain·ly** /ˈpleɪnli/ *adverb*
**1** in a way that is easy to see, hear, or understand: *He was plainly embarrassed because he was turning bright red.* **SYNONYMS: clearly, obviously**
**2** in a simple way: *She was plainly dressed in jeans and a T-shirt.*

**plan¹** /plæn/ *noun*
**1** something you have decided to do: *Do you have any plans for Friday night?*
**2** an idea for how you can do something, especially one that is written down with details: *The city has a plan for dealing with a big earthquake.*
**3** a drawing showing all the parts of a building, room, machine, etc.: *All the rooms and corridors are shown clearly on this plan.*

**plan²** *verb* (**planned**, **planning**)
**1** to think carefully about how you will do something: *Carla's planning a party for her sixteenth birthday.*
**2** to intend to do something: *Do you plan on staying long? | I plan to become an actor.*

**plane** /pleɪn/ *noun*
**1** a vehicle that flies, that has wings and an engine: *The plane landed at O'Hare Airport.* **SYNONYM: airplane** → see picture on page **A27**
**2** a tool with a blade in the bottom, that you push along wood to make it smooth

**plan·et** /ˈplænət/ *noun*
**1** a large round object in space that moves around a star such as the Sun. The Earth is one of the eight planets that move around our Sun: *Jupiter is the largest planet in the solar system.*
**2 the planet** = the Earth: *Pollution is destroying the planet.*
—**planetary** /ˈplænəˌtɛri/ *adjective* relating to planets: *planetary movements*
[**ORIGIN:** 1100-1200 From the Greek word *planes* or *planetes*, which means "wanderer." The stars do not appear to move in the sky from night to night, but the planets do.]

**plan·e·tar·i·um** /ˌplænəˈteriəm/ *noun*
a building that has a special curved ceiling with lights that show the stars and the movement of the PLANETs

**plank** /plæŋk/ *noun*
a long flat piece of wood used for building something: *He made a table from planks of wood he found in the old house.*

**plank·ton** /ˈplæŋktən/ *noun*
very small plants and animals that float in the ocean and lakes: *Fish eat plankton.*

**plant¹** /plænt/ *noun*
**1** a living thing that has leaves and roots and grows in soil: *I'm going to water the plants. | This plant has yellow flowers in the summer.*
**2** a factory: *The car plant produces thousands of vehicles every year.*

P

**plant²** *verb*
to put plants or seeds in soil to grow: *We have planted an apple tree in our backyard.*

**plan·ta·tion** /plænˈteɪʃən/ *noun*
a large farm in a hot place, where a crop such as tea, cotton, or sugar is grown: *a sugar plantation*



**plaque** /plæk/ *noun*
**1** a flat piece of metal or stone with writing on it: *A plaque on the house said: "Walt Whitman was born here."*
**2** a harmful substance that forms on your teeth: *Brushing your teeth every day helps to remove plaque.*

**plas·ter¹** /ˈplæstɚ/ *noun*
a substance that is put on walls and ceilings to give them a smooth surface: *The plaster was dry so we could paint.*

**plaster²** *verb*
**1** to spread or stick things all over a surface: *The walls of the restaurant were plastered with pictures of movie stars.*
**2** to cover a wall or ceiling with plaster: *They used a mud mixture to plaster their huts.*
—**plasterer** *noun* someone whose job is to plaster walls and ceilings

**plas·tic** /ˈplæstɪk/ *noun*
a light strong substance made from chemicals, that is used for making many things: *Many children's toys are made of plastic.*
—**plastic** *adjective* made of plastic: *a plastic bag | plastic bottles*
[**ORIGIN:** From the Greek word *plastikos*, which means "able to be shaped," from *plassein*, which means "to shape." Plastic can be easily made into many different shapes. First used as a noun in English, 1900-2000.]

**ˌplastic ˈsurgery** *noun*
a medical operation to improve or repair the way you look: *She needed plastic surgery after being attacked by a dog.*

**plate** /pleɪt/ *noun*
**1** a flat dish that you eat from or serve food on: *He put some rice and beans on his plate.* → see picture on page **A9**
**2** (*also* **plateful** /ˈpleɪtfʊl/) the amount of food on a plate: *He was eating a plate of pasta.*
**3** in baseball, the place where you stand to hit the ball

**pla·teau** /plæˈtoʊ/ *noun*
a large area of flat land that is much higher than the land around it

**plat·form** /ˈplætfɔrm/ *noun*
**1** a raised structure for people to stand or work on: *He stood on the platform and began to speak to the crowd.*
**2** the place in a railroad station where you get on and off a train: *The train leaves from platform 9.* → see picture on page **A26**
**3** the main ideas and aims that a political party or politician states before an election: *The party is running on a platform of better education and health care.*

**plat·ing** /ˈpleɪtɪŋ/ *noun*
a thin layer of metal that covers a metal object: *Some of the silver plating on the spoon had worn away.*

**plat·i·num** /ˈplætn-əm/ *noun*
an expensive silver-white metal that is used for making jewelry
—**platinum** *adjective* made of platinum: *a platinum ring*

**plat·ter** /ˈplætɚ/ *noun*
**1** a large plate, used for serving food: *Arrange the lettuce on a serving platter.*
**2** (*also* **platterful** /ˈplætɚfʊl/) the amount of food on a platter: *a platter of sliced cheese*

**play¹** /pleɪ/ *verb*
**1** to take part in a game or sport: *I like playing baseball. | We're playing against a team from Indiana.*

> **GRAMMAR: play**
>
> Do not use the word "the" or a preposition such as "at" after **play** when you are talking about playing a game or sport. Say *They are playing football.*
>
> Do not say "They are playing at football" or "They are playing the football."

**2** if children play, they enjoy themselves with toys and games: *Mom told us to play outside in the yard. | My little sister plays with dolls.*
**3** to perform a piece of music on an instrument: *He plays the violin in an orchestra. | The band will be playing here tomorrow night.*
**4** to act the part of a character in a movie,

play, or television program: *In the movie, Potts plays a high school teacher.*

PHRASAL VERB

**play with something**

to keep touching or moving something: *She told me to sit up straight and stop playing with my hair.*

**play²** *noun*

1 a story that actors perform in a theater or on the radio: *He was a good actor and usually got the main part in the school plays.*

2 the actions of the players in a game or sport: *The first play of the game was very exciting.*

3 the things that children do for fun, such as using toys or playing games: *Children learn through play.*

**play·er** /ˈpleɪɚ/ *noun*

1 someone who plays a game or sport: *a basketball player*

2 someone who plays a musical instrument: *a piano player*

3 **CD/DVD/MP3 player** = a machine that plays music or movies stored on a CD, DVD, or MP3 computer FILE

**play·ful** /ˈpleɪfəl/ *adjective*

1 intended to be fun or friendly rather than serious: *She gave him a playful push.*

2 active and wanting to have fun: *Kittens are usually very playful.*

—**playfully** *adverb* in a playful way

—**playfulness** *noun* the quality of being playful

**play·ground** /ˈpleɪgraʊnd/ *noun*

an outdoor area where children can play, often with equipment to play on: *The playground in the park is a good place for children to run, climb, and swing.*

**ˈplaying card** *noun*

one of a set of 52 cards with numbers or pictures on them that you use for playing games **SYNONYM: card**

**play·mate** /ˈpleɪmeɪt/ *noun*

a friend that a child plays with: *Children will find plenty of playmates at school.*

**play·pen** /ˈpleɪpen/ *noun*

a structure that a very young child can play in safely

**play·wright** /ˈpleɪraɪt/ *noun*

someone who writes plays

**pla·za** /ˈplɑzə/ *noun*

1 a place in a town, where there are a lot of stores: *They have a store in the Horton Plaza.*

2 a wide public area in a town

**plea** /pli/ *noun* (*formal*)

1 if you make a plea for something, you ask for it in a way that shows a lot of strong feelings: *Nobody heard her pleas for help.*

2 a statement someone makes in a court of law saying that he or she is guilty or not guilty of a crime: *The day after the trial started, he changed his plea to "guilty."*

**plead** /plid/ *verb* (*formal*)

1 to ask for something in a way that shows strong feelings: *The woman pleaded for help to find her daughter.* **SYNONYM: beg**

2 to officially say to a court of law whether you are guilty of a crime: *Parker pleaded "not guilty" to four charges of theft.*

**pleas·ant** /ˈplezənt/ *adjective*

1 enjoyable, nice, or good: *We spent a pleasant evening talking and playing card games.* | *a pleasant surprise* **SYNONYM: nice**; **ANTONYM: unpleasant**

2 polite and friendly: *The hotel manager was very pleasant and helpful.* **SYNONYM: nice**; **ANTONYM: unpleasant**

—**pleasantly** *adverb* in a pleasant way: *We were pleasantly surprised by how friendly everyone was.*

→ see Thesaurus box at **nice**

**please¹** /pliz/ *interjection*

1 used when politely asking someone to do something or give you something: *Can I have a cookie, please?*

2 used when politely accepting something that someone offers you: *"Would you like a glass of orange juice?" "Yes, please."*

**please²** *verb*

to make someone feel happy or satisfied: *I've tried to give him things he might like, but he's very hard to please.*

**WORD FAMILY: please**

**please** *verb* | **pleased** *adjective* | **pleasing** *adjective* | **pleasant** *adjective* | **pleasure** *noun*

P

**pleased** /plizd/ *adjective*
happy or satisfied: *Ellen was pleased that he remembered her birthday.*
→ see Thesaurus box at **happy**

**pleas·ing** /ˈplizɪŋ/ *adjective (formal)*
making you feel pleased: *The website has a pleasing design.*

**pleas·ure** /ˈpleʒɚ/ *noun*
**1** a feeling of happiness, satisfaction, or enjoyment: *I get a lot of pleasure from playing the guitar.* | *The baby giggled with pleasure when I tickled him.*
**2** an enjoyable experience: *It was a pleasure to meet you.*
—**pleasurable** *adjective* giving you pleasure: *Schools should make reading a pleasurable experience for children.*

**pleat** /plit/ *noun*
a permanent fold in a piece of clothing
—**pleated** *adjective* a pleated skirt, dress, etc. has pleats in it

**pledge¹** /pledʒ/ *noun*
a formal promise to do something: *The Republicans have made a pledge to cut taxes.*

**pledge²** *verb*
to make a formal promise to do something: *The government pledged to provide help for the people affected by the storm.*
→ see Thesaurus box at **promise¹**

**plen·ti·ful** /ˈplentɪfəl/ *adjective*
more than enough in amount: *The birds come to the area because of the plentiful supply of food.*

**plen·ty** /ˈplenti/ *pronoun*
more than enough: *Make sure you eat plenty of fruit.* | *There's plenty to see in New York City.*
→ see Thesaurus box at **enough**
[**ORIGIN:** 1200-1300 From the Latin word *plenitas*, which means "fullness."]

**pli·ers** /ˈplaɪɚz/ *plural noun*
a small metal tool used for bending or cutting wire: *a pair of pliers*

**pliers**

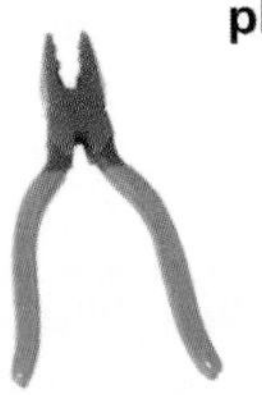

**plot¹** /plɑt/ *noun*
**1** the story that is told in a book, movie, or play: *The plot is simple – boy meets girl and they fall in love.*
**2** a secret plan to do something illegal or bad: *He was involved in a plot to kill the president.*
**3** a piece of land for building or growing things on: *The house is built on a two-acre plot of land.*

**plot²** *verb* (**plotted**, **plotting**)
to make a secret plan to do something illegal or bad: *She was put in jail for plotting to kill her husband.*

**plow¹** /plaʊ/ *noun*
**1** a large piece of equipment used on farms, that cuts up the ground so that seeds can be planted
**2** another word for a SNOWPLOW

**plow²** *verb*
to use a plow in order to cut up the ground so seeds can be planted: *The farmer was plowing the field.*

**pluck** /plʌk/ *verb*
**1** to pull something quickly in order to remove it: *He plucked a flower from the bush.* **SYNONYM: pick**
**2** to pull the feathers off a chicken or other bird before cooking it

**plug¹** /plʌg/ *noun*
**1** the object that you push into a special place on a wall to get electricity for a piece of equipment: *She put the plug in the socket and turned the TV on.* → see picture on page **A20**
**2** a round flat piece of rubber used for blocking the hole in a bathtub or SINK: *He pulled the plug out and the water drained out of the sink.*

**plug²** *verb* (**plugged**, **plugging**)
(*also* **plug up**) to fill a hole in something so that nothing can get through: *We managed to plug the hole in the pipe.*
**PHRASAL VERB**
**plug something in**
to connect a piece of electrical equipment to a supply of electricity: *Is the TV plugged in? It's not working.* **ANTONYM: unplug**

**plum** /plʌm/ *noun*
a soft round red or purple fruit with one large seed: *a plum tree* → see picture on page **A13**

**plumb·er** /ˈplʌmɚ/ *noun*
someone whose job is to put in and repair water pipes, SINKs, toilets, etc. → see picture on page **A16**
[**ORIGIN:** 1300-1400 From the Latin word *plumbus*, which means "lead." Water pipes were originally made of lead.]

**plumb·ing** /ˈplʌmɪŋ/ *noun*
**1** the system of water pipes in a building: *The plumbing in the bathroom leaks and needs to be replaced.*
**2** the job that a plumber does

**plum·met** /ˈplʌmɪt/ *verb*
**1** if a price or amount plummets, it quickly becomes much lower: *House prices have plummeted, and you can buy homes really cheaply now.* **SYNONYM: plunge**
**2** to fall quickly from a high place: *The plane plummeted to the ground.* **SYNONYM: plunge**
→ see Thesaurus box at **decrease**[1]

**plump** /plʌmp/ *adjective*
**1** large and round in an attractive way: *plump juicy strawberries*
**2** a polite way of describing someone who is fat: *He was 67, short, and a little plump.*
→ see Thesaurus box at **fat**[1]

**plunge** /plʌndʒ/ *verb*
**1** to fall quickly from a high place: *The plane caught fire and plunged into the jungle.* **SYNONYM: plummet**
**2** to jump into water: *She jumped off the rock and plunged into the ocean.*
**3** if an amount or level plunges, it quickly becomes much lower: *Profits plunged by 25%, and the company had to lay off workers.* **SYNONYM: plummet**
**PHRASAL VERB**
**plunge something into something**
to quickly push something deep into something else: *She plunged her spoon into the jar of honey.*

**plu·ral** /ˈplʊrəl/ *noun*
the form of a word that you use when talking about more than one person or thing: *"Dogs" is the plural of "dog."*
—**plural** *adjective* used for talking about more than one person or thing: *"They" is a plural pronoun.*
[**ORIGIN:** 1300-1400 From the Latin word *pluralis*, from *plus*, which means "more."]

**plu·ral·ism** /ˈplʊrəˌlɪzəm/ *noun*
a situation in which people of many different races, religions, and beliefs live together successfully in a society: *In this country there is religious pluralism and people are free to belong to any religion they want.*

**plus**[1] Ac /plʌs/ *preposition*
used when one number or amount is added to another: *Three plus six equals nine* (=3 + 6 = 9). | *The jacket costs $49.95 plus tax.*
**ANTONYM: minus**

**plus**[2] Ac *noun*
something good about a situation: *The fact that the campsite is close to the beach is a big plus.* **ANTONYM: minus**

**plus**[3] Ac *adjective*
**A plus/B plus, etc.** (*also* **A+/B+, etc.**) = a grade for a piece of work that is slightly higher than a grade A, a grade B, etc.: *I got a C plus. If I'd answered two more questions right, I would have gotten a B minus.*

**plus**[4] *conjunction*
and also: *You'll need to show them a birth certificate, plus a photo I.D.*
[**ORIGIN:** 1500-1600 From the Latin word for "more."]

**ˈplus sign** *noun*
the sign (+) that is used to show that numbers are being added, or to mean "and"

**Plu·to** /ˈplutoʊ/ *noun*
an object that goes round the Sun and is further away than Neptune. Many scientists now think Pluto is too small to be called a PLANET.

**plu·to·ni·um** /pluˈtoʊniəm/ *noun*
a RADIOACTIVE metal that is used for making NUCLEAR power and nuclear bombs

**ply·wood** /ˈplaɪwʊd/ *noun*
a type of board made from thin pieces of wood that have been stuck together: *They nailed a sheet of plywood over the broken window.*

**p.m.** /ˌpi ˈem/
used when talking about times in the afternoon or evening, from 12 o'clock NOON until 12 o'clock MIDNIGHT: *I got home at 5:30 p.m, just at dinnertime.*

**pneu·mat·ic** /nʊˈmætɪk/ *adjective*
**1** filled with air: *a pneumatic tire*
**2** a pneumatic tool or machine works by using air pressure: *a pneumatic drill*

**pneu·mo·nia** /nʊˈmoʊnjə/ *noun*
a serious illness that affects your lungs and makes it difficult to breathe

**poach** /poʊtʃ/ *verb*
**1** to cook food such as eggs or fish in a small amount of boiling liquid
**2** to catch animals illegally: *They are trying to stop people from poaching deer.*
→ see Thesaurus box at **cook**[1]

**P.O. Box** /pi ˈoʊ ˌbɑks/ *noun*
a numbered box in a post office, where you can receive mail, instead of at your home

**pock·et** /ˈpɑkɪt/ *noun*
the part of a coat, skirt, pair of pants, etc. that you can put things in: *He had a few coins in his pocket.* | *his coat pocket*
[**ORIGIN:** 1400-1500 From the old French word *pokete*, which means "small bag," from *poke*, meaning "bag."]

**pock·et·book** /ˈpɑkɪtˌbʊk/ *noun*
another word for a PURSE

**ˈpocket knife** *noun*
a small knife with a blade that you can fold into its handle **SYNONYM: penknife**

**pod** /pɑd/ *noun*
the long part of plants such as beans and PEAs that the seeds grow in

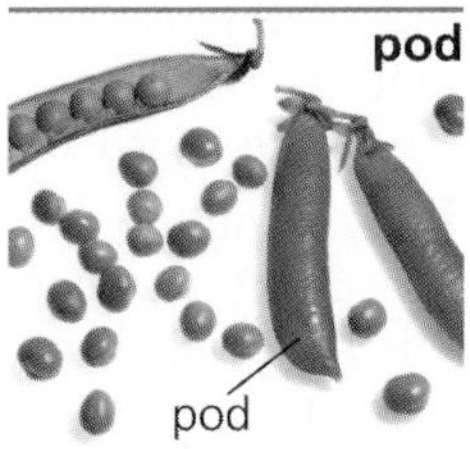


**po·di·um** /ˈpoʊdiəm/ *noun*
**1** a small raised area where someone stands to give a speech or CONDUCT a group of musicians: *She stepped up on the podium to make her speech.*
**2** a tall narrow desk that someone stands behind when giving a speech to a lot of people

**po·em** /ˈpoʊɪm/ *noun*
a piece of writing with short lines, which sometimes RHYME (=end with the same sound): *He read a poem by Robert Frost.*
[**ORIGIN:** 1400-1500 From the Greek word *poiema*, which means "something that is made or written," from *poiein*, meaning "to make or create."]

**WORD FAMILY: poem**
**poem** *noun* | **poet** *noun* | **poetry** *noun* | **poetic** *adjective*

**po·et** /ˈpoʊɪt/ *noun*
someone who writes poems

**po·et·ic** /poʊˈetɪk/ *adjective*
relating to poetry, or typical of poetry: *He used poetic language to describe the sunset.*

**po·et·ry** /ˈpoʊətri/ *noun*
poems: *She writes poetry about her feelings.*

**point**[1] /pɔɪnt/ *noun*
**1** an idea or opinion in an argument or discussion: *You made a lot of good points in your speech.*
**2 the point** = the most important fact or idea: *The point is (that) I don't want to stay here any more.* | *You're missing the point! He wasn't serious – he was joking.*
**3** the purpose or aim of doing something: *The whole point of traveling is to experience new things.* | *There's no point in worrying about things if you can't change them.*
**4** a particular moment or time: *He started yelling, and at that point I decided to leave.* | *She had reached a point in her life when she wanted to do something new.*
**5** a particular position or place: *the point where two lines cross each other*
**6** a unit used for showing the score in a game or sport: *The Rams beat the Giants by six points.*
**7** the way you say the sign (.) before a DECIMAL: *four point five percent* (=4.5%)
**8** the sharp end of something: *the point of a needle*
**9** a quality that someone or something has: *Patience is one of his strong points.*
**10 up to a point** = partly, but not completely: *He believed her story, up to a point.* → **point of view**
→ see Thesaurus box at **end**[1], **place**[1]

**point**[2] *verb*
**1** to show someone something by holding your finger out toward it: *John pointed to the house and said, "That's where I used to live."*
→ see picture on page **A3**
**2** to aim something in a particular direction: *Hundreds of cameras were pointing at the president.*

**PHRASAL VERB**

**point something out**
to tell someone something that he or she does not already know or has not yet noticed: *He pointed out that I had made a mistake.*

**point·ed** /ˈpɔɪntɪd/ *adjective*
having a point at the end: *The shoes had pointed toes.*

**point·er** /ˈpɔɪntɚ/ *noun*
**1** a helpful piece of advice: *Dad gave me some pointers on how to play tennis.* **SYNONYM: tip**
**2** a small ARROW on a computer screen that you use to do things on the computer: *Move the pointer to the picture and click.*
**3** a long stick used for pointing at things such as a map or a board

**point·less** /ˈpɔɪntləs/ *adjective*
having no purpose, or not likely to have any effect: *It's pointless trying to call him – he isn't home.*

**ˌpoint of ˈview** *noun*
**1** your opinion about something: *My parents didn't agree with my point of view and wouldn't let me stay out late.*
**2** a way of thinking about or judging a situation: *The show was not successful from a financial point of view because it did not make any money.*

**poi·son¹** /ˈpɔɪzən/ *noun*
a substance that can kill you or make you sick: *We used poison to kill the rats.*
[**ORIGIN:** 1200-1300 From an old French word for "drink or poison," from the Latin *potio*, which means "drink."]

**WORD FAMILY: poison**
**poison** *noun* | **poisonous** *adjective*

**poison²** *verb*
to kill or harm someone by using poison: *She was put in jail after she tried to poison her husband.*

**ˌpoison ˈivy** *noun*
a plant that makes your skin red and painful when you touch its leaves

**ˌpoison ˈoak** *noun*
a plant that makes your skin red and painful when you touch its leaves

**poi·son·ous** /ˈpɔɪzənəs/ *adjective*
containing poison: *Some wild mushrooms are poisonous.*

**poke** /poʊk/ *verb*
to push your finger or something pointed into something or someone: *Polly poked me in the stomach with her finger.* → see picture on page **A3**
→ see Thesaurus box at **push¹**

**pok·er** /ˈpoʊkɚ/ *noun*
**1** a card game that people play to win money
**2** a metal stick used for moving coal or wood on a fire so that it burns better

**po·lar** /ˈpoʊlɚ/ *adjective*
relating to the North Pole or the South Pole: *polar ice*

**ˈpolar bear** *noun*
a large white bear that lives near the North Pole

**pole** /poʊl/ *noun*
**1** a long post made of wood or metal: *The telephone poles hold up telephone wires along the road.*
**2** the most northern or southern point of the Earth: *There is a lot of snow and ice at the North Pole.*
**3** one of the two ends of a BATTERY or a MAGNET

**Pole** /poʊl/ *noun*
someone from Poland

**ˈpole vault** *noun*
**the pole vault** = a sport in which you jump over a high bar using a long pole

**po·lice** /pəˈlis/ *noun*
the group of people whose job is to catch criminals and make sure that people obey the law: *I saw someone stealing a car and called the police.* | *a police car*
[**ORIGIN:** 1400-1500 From the Greek word *politeia*, which means "a state, or the condition of being a citizen."]

**poˈlice force** *noun*
the group of police in a particular country or place: *Jones joined the Los Angeles police force in 2003.*

**po·lice·man** /pəˈlismən/ *noun* (plural **policemen** /pəˈlismən/)
a male police officer

**po'lice ˌofficer** *noun*
a member of the police: *Police officers arrested the man for stealing a car.* → see picture on page **A16**

**po'lice ˌstation** *noun*
the office of the police in a town or city: *He went to the police station to report the attack.*

P

**po·lice·wom·an** /pəˈlisˌwʊmən/ *noun* (plural **policewomen** /pəˈlisˌwɪmɪn/)
a female police officer

**pol·i·cy** Ac /ˈpɑləsi/ *noun* (plural **policies**)
**1** the way of doing things that has been decided by an organization: *The school has a strict policy on smoking, so no one is allowed to smoke.*
**2** an agreement with an insurance company: *The car insurance policy says that the company will pay if the car is damaged in an accident.*

**po·li·o** /ˈpoʊliˌoʊ/ *noun*
a serious disease that affects the SPINAL CORD and can permanently stop someone from moving the muscles in a part of the body

**pol·ish¹** /ˈpɑlɪʃ/ *verb*
to make something shiny by rubbing it: *He polished his shoes each night.*
—**polished** *adjective* shiny after being polished: *a smooth, polished wooden floor*

**polish²** *noun*
a substance that you rub on something to make it shiny: *shoe polish*

**Po·lish¹** /ˈpoʊlɪʃ/ *adjective*
from Poland

**Polish²** *noun*
the language spoken in Poland

**po·lite** /pəˈlaɪt/ *adjective*
behaving well, in a way that shows you respect other people: *It's not polite to talk with your mouth full of food.* **ANTONYMS: impolite, rude**
—**politely** *adverb* in a polite way
—**politeness** *noun* the quality of being polite

**po·lit·i·cal** /pəˈlɪtɪkəl/ *adjective*
relating to the government or politics of a country: *The U.S. has two main political parties: the Republicans and the Democrats.*
—**politically** *adverb* in a political way

**poˌlitically cor'rect** *adjective* (*abbreviation*: **PC**)
very careful to treat people equally and not to offend or insult anyone: *He made jokes about women that were not politically correct.*

**pol·i·ti·cian** /ˌpɑləˈtɪʃən/ *noun*
someone who was elected as a member of a government, or who wants to be: *Most Democratic politicians voted for the new law.*

**pol·i·tics** /ˈpɑlətɪks/ *noun*
**1** all the ideas and activities that relate to getting and using power in a country, city, office, etc.: *My parents are not very interested in politics, but they do vote.*
**2** the job of being a politician: *Smith went into politics as a young man.*
[**ORIGIN:** 1400-1500 From the Greek word *politika*, which means "things relating to cities or states," from *polis*, meaning "city or state."]

**WORD FAMILY: politics**
**politics** *noun* | **politician** *noun* | **political** *adjective*

**pol·ka** /ˈpoʊlkə/ *noun*
a fast dance for people dancing in pairs

**'polka dot** *noun*
one of a number of round spots on cloth: *The dress was blue with white polka dots.*

**poll** /poʊl/ *noun*
**1** if an organization does a poll, it asks a lot of people questions in order to find out what they think about something: *The opinion poll shows that 63% of people do not like the plan.*
**2 polls** = if people go to the polls, they vote in an election: *Next Tuesday voters go to the polls to elect a new president.*
—**poll** *verb* to do a poll: *They polled over 2,000 people to get their opinions.*

**pol·len** /ˈpɑlən/ *noun*
a powder that flowers produce, which is carried by the wind or insects to other flowers so they can make seeds: *Pollen from some flowers makes me sneeze.*
[**ORIGIN:** 1700-1800 From the Latin word for "fine flour or dust."]

**pol·li·nate** /ˈpɑləˌneɪt/ *verb*
to make a flower produce seeds by giving it pollen from another flower: *Bees and other insects pollinate the flowers.*

—**pollination** /ˌpɑləˈneɪʃən/ *noun* the process of pollinating a flower

**pol·lute** /pəˈlut/ *verb*
to make air, water, or soil dirty and dangerous to people and other living things: *Smoke from the factory pollutes the air.*
—**polluted** *adjective* with a lot of harmful and dirty substances in the air, water, or soil: *It is one of the country's most polluted cities, with lots of cars that produce smog.*
—**pollutant** *noun* something that pollutes air, water, or soil: *We need to reduce the amount of pollutants that cars produce.*

**pollution**

**pol·lu·tion** /pəˈluʃən/ *noun*
**1** substances that make air, water, or soil dirty and dangerous to people and other living things: *Cars can produce a lot of air pollution.*
**2** the process of making air, water, or soil dangerously dirty: *The pollution of lakes and rivers by factories is killing fish.*

**pol·y·es·ter** /ˈpɑliˌestɚ/ *noun*
an artificial type of cloth: *The shirt was made from cotton and polyester.*

**pol·y·gon** Ac /ˈpɑliˌgɑn/ *noun*
a flat shape with three or more straight sides: *Squares and hexagons are polygons.*

**pom·e·gran·ate** /ˈpɑməˌgrænɪt/ *noun*
a round fruit with a thick red skin and many small red seeds inside it that you eat

**pomp·ous** /ˈpɑmpəs/ *adjective*
trying to make people think you are important by using a lot of formal words: *He made a long and pompous speech about his achievements.*

**pon·cho** /ˈpɑntʃoʊ/ *noun* (plural **ponchos**)
a type of coat that is made of a square piece of cloth with a hole in the middle for your head, and no sleeves: *He wore a rain poncho.*
[ORIGIN: 1700-1800 From American Spanish, from the word *pontho*, which means "woolen cloth" in the language of the native people of Chile.]

**pond** /pɑnd/ *noun*
an area of fresh water that is smaller than a lake: *Ducks were swimming on the pond.*

**pon·der** /ˈpɑndɚ/ *verb*
to think carefully about something: *She pondered the question before she gave her answer.*
[ORIGIN: 1300-1400 From the Latin word *ponderare*, which means "to weigh or consider," from *pondus*, meaning "weight."]

**po·ny** /ˈpoʊni/ *noun* (plural **ponies**)
a small horse: *The children were riding ponies.*

**po·ny·tail** /ˈpoʊniˌteɪl/ *noun*
long hair that you tie together at the back of your head: *Chrissy pulled her hair back in a ponytail.*

**poo·dle** /ˈpudl/ *noun*
a dog with thick curly hair
[ORIGIN: 1800-1900 From the German word *Pudelhund*, which means "dog that splashes in water."]

**pool** /pul/ *noun*
**1** (*also* **swimming pool**) a large container that is filled with water for people to swim in: *He was swimming in the pool in their backyard.*
**2** a small amount of a liquid such as blood, water, or oil that is on the ground or another surface: *Underneath the car, there was a pool of oil.*
**3** a game in which you use a stick to hit colored balls into holes in the sides and corners of a table: *Let's play a game of pool.*

**poor** /pʊr/ *adjective*
**1** having very little money: *They were so poor that they couldn't buy new shoes for the children.* | *a poor country* **ANTONYM: rich**

**THESAURUS: poor**

**needy** not having enough food or money: *The program provides health care to needy families.*

**broke** (*informal*) not having any money, usually for a short period of time: *He was broke and hungry.*

**disadvantaged** (*formal*) having social problems, such as a lack of money, that make it difficult to succeed: *Students from disadvantaged groups may need more help in school.*

**underprivileged** (*formal*) very poor and not having the same chances as other people in society: *The center is a place where underprivileged kids can go for help.*

**deprived** (*formal*) not having the things that you need for a comfortable or happy life: *It is a deprived area in the inner city, with a lot of crime.*

**2** not very good: *He is unable to work because of poor health.* | *The workers did a poor job of fixing the roof because water still leaks through it.* **ANTONYM: good**
**3** said in order to show that you feel sorry for someone: *The poor boy looked very tired.*

**poor·ly** /ˈpʊrli/ *adverb*
badly: *The essay was poorly written and had a lot of spelling mistakes.*

**pop[1]** /pɑp/ *verb* (**popped**, **popping**)
**1** to make a short loud sound, for example by bursting: *Jody squeezed the balloon until it popped.*
**2** to go somewhere quickly or suddenly: *I need to pop in to the grocery store to buy some milk.*
→ see Thesaurus box at **break[1]**

**pop[2]** *noun*
**1** (*also* **ˈpop ˌmusic**) modern music that is popular with young people: *a pop concert*
**2** a sweet drink with bubbles that does not contain alcohol: *She drank a can of pop.* **SYNONYM: soda**
**3** a sudden short sound like a small explosion: *The balloon burst with a pop.*

**pop·corn** /ˈpɑpkɔrn/ *noun*
a type of corn that swells and bursts open when you cook it: *They were eating popcorn while they watched the movie.*

**Pope** /poʊp/ *noun*
the leader of the Roman Catholic Church: *Pope Benedict XVI*

**pop·u·lar** /ˈpɑpyələ˞/ *adjective*
liked by a lot of people: *Tom is very popular with women and always has a girlfriend.* **ANTONYM: unpopular**
—**popularize** *verb* to make something become popular
[**ORIGIN:** 1400-1500 From the Latin word *popularis*, which means "belonging to the people," from *populus*, meaning "the people."]

**pop·u·lar·i·ty** /ˌpɑpyəˈlærəti/ *noun*
the quality of being liked by a lot of people: *The growing popularity of Internet shopping is badly affecting many downtown stores.*

**pop·u·lat·ed** /ˈpɑpyəˌleɪtɪd/ *adjective*
a populated area has people living in it: *New York City is one of the most densely populated areas of the country.*
—**populate** *verb* if groups of people populate an area, they live there

**pop·u·la·tion** /ˌpɑpyəˈleɪʃən/ *noun*
the number of people who live in a place: *Chicago has a population of nearly 3 million.*
→ see Thesaurus box at **people**

**pop·u·lous** /ˈpɑpyələs/ *adjective*
a populous place has a lot of people living in it: *China and India are the world's most populous countries.*

**por·ce·lain** /ˈpɔrsəlɪn/ *noun*
a hard shiny white substance that is used for making things such as expensive plates, bowls, and cups

porch

**porch** /pɔrtʃ/ *noun*
a structure with a floor and roof, that is built onto a house at its front or back door: *On summer evenings, he sat on the porch reading a book.*
[**ORIGIN:** 1200-1300 From the old French word *porche*, from the Latin word *porticus*, which means "covered area for walking along."]

**por·cu·pine** /ˈpɔrkyəˌpaɪn/ *noun*
an animal with long sharp needle-like parts growing all over its back and sides

**pore**[1] /pɔr/ *noun*
one of the small holes in your skin that SWEAT comes through

**pore**[2] *verb*
**PHRASAL VERB**
**pore over something**
to read or look at something carefully for a long time: *He spent hours poring over his school books.*

**pork** /pɔrk/ *noun*
the meat from pigs: *The sausage is made from pork.*
→ see Thesaurus box at **meat**
[**ORIGIN:** 1200-1300 From the French word *porc*, from the Latin word *porcus*, which means "pig."]

**por·poise** /ˈpɔrpəs/ *noun*
a large ocean animal, like a DOLPHIN, that breathes air

**por·ridge** /ˈpɔrɪdʒ/ *noun*
OATMEAL cooked in hot water or milk: *I have porridge for breakfast.*

**port** /pɔrt/ *noun*
**1** a place where ships stop and people put goods onto them or take goods off: *The ship was getting ready to leave the port.* → see picture at **boat**
**2** a town or city with a port: *Hong Kong is the world's largest port.*

**port·a·ble** /ˈpɔrtəbəl/ *adjective*
light and easy to move or carry: *Portable computers make it easy for businessmen to take work with them when they travel.*
—**portability** /ˌpɔrtəˈbɪləti/ *noun* the quality of being portable
[**ORIGIN:** 1300-1400 From the Latin word *portabilis*, which means "able to be carried," from *portare*, meaning "to carry."]

**por·ter** /ˈpɔrtɚ/ *noun*
someone whose job is to carry travelers' bags at places such as airports and hotels

**port·fo·li·o** /pɔrtˈfoʊliˌoʊ/ *noun* (plural **portfolios**)
**1** a large flat case for carrying pictures or documents
**2** a collection of paintings, photographs, or pieces of writing that an artist or writer shows people as an example of his or her work: *Art students will have to produce a portfolio of work.*

**por·tion** Ac /ˈpɔrʃən/ *noun*
**1** (*formal*) a part of something larger: *He spent a portion of his birthday money on a game, and put the rest in the bank.* **SYNONYM: part**
**2** an amount of food for one person: *The food at the restaurant was good, but the portions were small.*

**por·trait** /ˈpɔrtrɪt/ *noun*
a painting, drawing, or photograph of someone: *I painted a portrait of my sister.*
→ see Thesaurus box at **picture**[1]

**por·tray** /pɔrˈtreɪ/ *verb* (**portrayed**, **portrays**) (*formal*)
**1** to describe someone or something, or to show someone or something in a picture: *Her paintings portray the city as a very busy place.*
**2** to act the part of a character in a play or movie: *In the movie, he portrays a college professor.* **SYNONYM: play**
—**portrayal** *noun* the way that someone or something is portrayed: *The movie gives a realistic portrayal of life during the Vietnam War.*

**Por·tu·guese**[1] /ˌpɔrtʃəˈgiz/ *adjective*
from Portugal: *I have a Portuguese friend who was born in Lisbon.*

**Portuguese**[2] *noun*
**1** the language spoken in Portugal and Brazil: *Can you speak Portuguese?*
**2** **the Portuguese** = people from Portugal in general: *The Portuguese are very proud of their soccer team.*

**pose**[1] Ac /poʊz/ *verb*
**1** to cause a problem or danger: *Getting back down the mountain posed several problems.*
**2** to sit or stand so that someone can do a painting or photograph of you: *The president posed for photographs before the meeting.*
**3** **pose a question** = to ask a question: *The teacher posed some difficult questions to the class.*
**4** **pose as somebody** = to pretend to be someone in order to deceive people: *The thief posed as a salesman in order to get inside the old lady's house.*

**pose**[2] Ac *noun*
the position that you stand or sit in when someone is doing a painting of you or taking

P

a photograph of you: *She sat in a strange pose, with her head to one side.*

**po·si·tion** /pəˈzɪʃən/ *noun*
**1** the place where someone or something is, in relation to other things: *She changed the position of the furniture by moving the sofa near the window.*
**2** the way someone stands, sits, or lies: *This exercise is done in a sitting position.*
**3** the situation that someone or something is in: *I'm not sure what I would do if I were in your position.* **SYNONYM: situation**
**4** (*formal*) a job: *He gave up his position as coach of the football team.*
**5** someone's official rule or opinion about something: *The school's position is that cell phones must be switched off during class.*
→ see Thesaurus box at **job**, **place**[1]

P

**pos·i·tive** Ac /ˈpɑzətɪv/ *adjective*
**1** very sure that something is right or true: *I'm positive I told her to meet us here at 2:00.*
**2** good or useful: *The club has been a positive experience because she has made new friends.* **ANTONYM: negative**
**3** expressing support, agreement, or approval: *We have had a lot of positive responses to the plan.* **ANTONYM: negative**
**4** hopeful and confident, and thinking about what is good in a situation rather than what is bad: *She has a very positive attitude, even though she has health problems.* **ANTONYM: negative**
**5** a positive number is greater than zero: *When you multiply one positive number by another, the product is always positive.* **ANTONYM: negative**
**6** a medical test that is positive shows that someone has a particular disease or condition: *Her pregnancy test is positive, so she is going to have a baby!* **ANTONYM: negative**
—**positively** *adverb* in a positive way: *They knew they could trust me, and responded positively.*

**pos·sess** /pəˈzes/ *verb* (*formal*)
to own or have something: *They lost everything they possessed in the fire.*
—**possessor** *noun* someone who possesses something
→ see Thesaurus box at **own**[2]

**pos·ses·sion** /pəˈzeʃən/ *noun* (*formal*)
**1** something that you own: *One bag held all his possessions.* **SYNONYM: belongings**
**2** the state of having or owning something: *He was arrested for possession of illegal drugs.*

**pos·ses·sive** /pəˈzesɪv/ *adjective*
**1** not wanting to share someone or something: *Small children can be possessive about their toys.*
**2** in grammar, relating to words that show who something belongs to: *Add "'s" to a noun to make the possessive form: This is John's bike.*
—**possessive** *noun* in grammar, words that show who something belongs to: *Words such as "my" and "theirs" are possessives.*

**pos·si·bil·i·ty** /ˌpɑsəˈbɪləti/ *noun* (plural **possibilities**)
something that might happen or be true: *There's a possibility that Jim won't play in Saturday's game because he hurt his leg.*

**pos·si·ble** /ˈpɑsəbəl/ *adjective*
**1** something that is possible may happen or be true: *It's possible that he is lying.* | *Some math problems have more than one possible answer.*
**2** if something is possible, people can do it: *It is possible to send people to Mars, but no country has done it.* **ANTONYM: impossible**
**3 as soon as possible/as long as possible/as much as possible, etc.** = as soon as you can, as long as you can, etc.: *She needs to see a doctor as soon as possible because she is very sick.*
**[ORIGIN:** 1300-1400 From the Latin word *possibilis*, from *posse*, which means "to be able."**]**

**WORD FAMILY: possible**
**possible** *adjective* | **possibly** *adverb* | **possibility** *noun*

**pos·si·bly** /ˈpɑsəbli/ *adverb*
**1** used when saying that something may be true or may happen: *The rehearsal may take two hours, possibly three.* **SYNONYMS: perhaps, maybe**
**2** used to emphasize what someone can or cannot do. The words "can" and "could" are used with "possibly" in this meaning: *I can't possibly be there by three o'clock because school doesn't finish until then.*

**pos·sum** /ˈpɑsəm/ *noun* (*informal*)
another word for an OPOSSUM

**post¹** /poʊst/ *noun*
**1** a wood or metal pole that you put into the ground to support something: *a fence post*
**2** (*formal*) an important job: *She decided to leave her post at the Justice Department.*
**3** something that you write on a website that allows people to talk about different subjects: *I read some of the posts about her new book.*

**post²** *verb*
to put a message or notice about something on a wall or website: *The school rules are posted on the bulletin board.*

**post·age** /ˈpoʊstɪdʒ/ *noun*
the money that you pay for sending something by mail: *How much was the postage for that package you sent to Dan?*

**ˈpostage stamp** *noun* (*formal*)
another word for a STAMP

**post·al** /ˈpoʊstl/ *adjective* (*formal*)
relating to the organization that takes letters from one place to another: *Postal workers are very busy during the holidays.*

**post·card** /ˈpoʊskɑrd/ *noun*
a card with a picture on the front, that you can send in the mail without an envelope: *Emily sent me a postcard from Yellowstone National Park.*

**post·er** /ˈpoʊstɚ/ *noun*
a large printed notice or picture, that advertises something or that you use as a decoration: *Did you see the poster advertising the school play?* → see picture on page **A10**
→ see Thesaurus box at **advertisement**

**post·man** /ˈpoʊstmən/ *noun* (plural **postmen**)
a man whose job is delivering mail to people's houses **SYNONYM: mailman**

**post·mark** /ˈpoʊstmɑrk/ *noun*
a mark on a letter or package that shows the place and time it was sent: *The letter had a New York postmark, so she must have mailed it when she was there.*
—**postmark** *verb* to put a postmark on a letter or package

**ˈpost ˌoffice** *noun*
a place where you can buy stamps and send letters and packages: *I'm going to the post office to mail this package.*

**ˈpost office ˌbox** *noun* (*abbreviation*: **P.O. Box**)
a numbered box in a post office, where you can receive mail, instead of at your home

**post·pone** /poʊsˈpoʊn/ *verb* (*formal*)
to change the time of an event to a later time or date: *The game was postponed because of rain.* **SYNONYM: put off**
—**postponement** *noun* the act of postponing something
**[ORIGIN:** 1400-1500 From the Latin word *postponere*, which means "to put after."**]**

**pos·ture** /ˈpɑstʃɚ/ *noun*
the way you hold your body when you sit or stand: *Back exercises will help his bad posture.*

**pot** /pɑt/ *noun*
**1** a round container that you cook things in: *Mom made a big pot of chicken soup.*
**2** a container with a handle and a lid, that you use to make and pour coffee or tea: *a coffee pot*
**3** a container that you grow plants in: *She planted some flower seeds in a pot.*

**po·tas·si·um** /pəˈtæsiəm/ *noun*
a silver-white soft metal that is in some types of food in very small amounts. The symbol for potassium is K: *Bananas have potassium in them.*

**po·ta·to** /pəˈteɪtoʊ/ *noun* (plural **potatoes**)
a hard round white vegetable with brown, red, or yellow skin, that grows under the ground: *Peel the potatoes and boil them.* → see picture on page **A12**
**[ORIGIN:** 1500-1600 From the Spanish word *patata*, from *batata*, the Taino word for "sweet potato." Taino was a language used by the people of some Caribbean islands.**]**

**poˈtato chip** *noun*
a thin hard piece of potato that was cooked in oil: *He opened a bag of potato chips.*

**po·ten·tial** [Ac] /pəˈtenʃəl/ *noun*
a quality or an ability that may develop more in the future: *He has the potential to be one of our best players, but he's still very young.*
—**potential** *adjective* possible, but not yet completely developed: *We need to be ready for any potential problems that may occur.*

—**potentially** *adverb* possibly in some situations or in the future
[ORIGIN: 1300-1400 From the Latin word *potentia*, which means "power or ability."]

**pot·hole** /ˈpɑthoʊl/ *noun*
a hole in the surface of a road: *Some men were filling in the potholes in the street.*

**pot·luck** /ˌpɑtˈlʌk/ *noun*
a meal for which everyone brings food to share: *Can you bring a chicken dish for the potluck?*

**pot·ter·y** /ˈpɑtəri/ *noun*
**1** the activity of making objects out of clay and then baking them: *She's taking a pottery class.*
**2** plates, cups, and other objects that are made out of clay that you bake: *Jill makes and sells bowls and other pottery.*
—**potter** *noun* someone who makes pottery

**pouch** /paʊtʃ/ *noun*
a pocket of skin that an animal such as a KANGAROO carries its baby in

**poul·try** /ˈpoʊltri/ *noun* (*formal*)
birds such as chickens and ducks that are kept on farms for their eggs and meat: *At this poultry farm, the chickens are not kept in cages.*

**pounce**

**pounce** /paʊns/ *verb*
to suddenly jump on and catch a person or animal: *The cat pounced on a bird.*

**pound[1]** /paʊnd/ *noun*
**1** (*written abbreviation*: **lb.**) a unit for measuring weight, equal to 16 OUNCEs or 453.6 grams: *Jim weighs 175 pounds.*
**2** the standard unit of money in Great Britain and some other countries
**3** **the pound** = a place where a city keeps lost dogs and cats

**pound[2]** *verb*
**1** to hit something many times: *Someone was pounding on the door, trying to wake the people inside.*
**2** if your heart pounds, it beats very quickly: *I was scared, and my heart was pounding.*
→ see Thesaurus box at **hit[1]**

**pour** /pɔr/ *verb*
**1** to make a liquid or other substance flow out of or into a container: *Will you pour me a glass of apple juice, please? | Pour the batter into a cake pan.* → see picture on page **A15**

**THESAURUS: pour**

**flow** to move in a steady stream: *The river flows into the sea.*

**drip** if a liquid drips or if something drips liquid, the liquid falls in drops: *Water dripped onto the floor.*

**leak** if a liquid leaks or something leaks a liquid, the liquid goes through a hole or crack: *The car is leaking oil.*

**ooze** to flow from something very slowly: *Blood started to ooze from the cut on his knee.*

**gush** if liquid gushes, a lot of liquid flows or pours out quickly: *One of the pipes broke, and water gushed out of it.*

**run** to flow: *Tears ran down her cheeks. | The hot water ran into the tub.*

**2** if a liquid pours somewhere, it flows there quickly: *After running up the hill, I had sweat pouring down my face.*
**3** to rain a lot: *It's been pouring all afternoon.*
**4** to move somewhere quickly and in large numbers: *As soon the gates were opened, people poured into the stadium.*

**pov·er·ty** /ˈpɑvɚti/ *noun*
the state of being poor: *Many people live in poverty and don't have enough money to buy food every day.*

**ˈpoverty-ˌstricken** *adjective* (*formal*)
very poor: *They live in poverty-stricken communities with no running water.*

**pow·der** /ˈpaʊdɚ/ *noun*
a soft dry substance in the form of very small

grains: *Add one teaspoon of chili powder to the meat mixture.*
—**powdery** *adjective* feeling or looking like powder

**pow·er** /ˈpaʊɚ/ *noun*
**1** the ability to control people or control what happens: *The president has a lot of power.*
**2** energy such as electricity that is used to make a machine work, or to give light or heat: *The flashlight went out because there was no power left in the batteries.*
**3** force or strength: *the terrifying power of a tornado*
**4 to the power of 3/4/5, etc.** = if a number is increased to the power of 3, 4, etc., it is multiplied by itself 3 times, 4 times, etc.: *2 to the power of 3 (2 x 2 x 2) equals 8.*

**WORD FAMILY: power**
**power** *noun* | **powerful** *adjective* | **powerfully** *adverb* | **powerless** *adjective*

**pow·er·boat** /ˈpaʊɚˌboʊt/ *noun*
a boat that people use for racing

**pow·er·ful** /ˈpaʊɚfəl/ *adjective*
**1** a powerful person or country is important and has a lot of control over other people or over what happens: *The president is one of the most powerful men in the world.*
**2** something that is powerful is very strong or has a strong effect: *The car has a powerful engine and can go very fast.* | *Television has a powerful influence on our lives.*
—**powerfully** *adverb* in a powerful way

**pow·er·less** /ˈpaʊɚləs/ *adjective*
not having strength or control: *I wanted to help her, but I was powerless to do anything.*

**ˈpower plant** (*also* **ˈpower ˌstation**) *noun*
a building where electricity is made for people to use in their homes or businesses

**prac·ti·cal** /ˈpræktɪkəl/ *adjective*
**1** sensible and likely to work correctly or do something in a way that works well: *A sports car isn't practical for a family with three kids because it isn't big enough.*
**2** relating to doing things rather than thinking or talking about them: *The students do experiments and other practical work in the chemistry lab.*
[**ORIGIN:** 1500-1600 From the Greek word *praktikos*, from *prassein*, which means "to do."]

**ˌpractical ˈjoke** *noun*
a trick that surprises someone and makes other people laugh: *He put a rubber snake in her desk drawer as a practical joke.*

**prac·ti·cally** /ˈpræktɪkli/ *adverb* (*informal*)
almost: *These shoes are practically new – I bought them a month ago.*

**prac·tice**[1] /ˈpræktɪs/ *noun*
**1** the activity of doing something regularly so that you will do it better: *It takes a lot of practice to be a good piano player.* | *What time is baseball practice?*
**2 in practice** = used in order to say what the real situation is rather than what seems to be true: *Jess is listed as the leader of the club, but in practice, Lisa runs everything.*
**3 be out of practice** = to not be able to do something well because you have not done it for a long time: *I used to play the guitar, but I'm really out of practice now.*
**4** the work or business of a doctor or lawyer: *He started his own legal practice when he finished law school.*

**practice**[2] *verb*
**1** to do something regularly in order to improve your skill at it: *Kate practices the piano for half an hour every day.*

**THESAURUS: practice**
**rehearse** to practice something such as a play or concert before people come to see it: *The band was rehearsing for the show.*
**work on something** to practice a skill in order to improve: *Jessie has been working on her tennis serve.*
**train** to prepare for a sports event by exercising and practicing: *Olympic swimmers train for hours every day.*
**drill** to teach people something by making them repeat the same thing many times: *The teacher was drilling the class on their multiplication tables.*

**2** to work as a doctor or lawyer: *Bill is practicing medicine in Ohio now.*

**prag·mat·ic** /prægˈmætɪk/ *adjective*
dealing with situations in a sensible way that

is likely to work: *The article had pragmatic ideas for getting kids to eat vegetables.*
—**pragmatism** /ˈprægməˌtɪzəm/ *noun* the quality of being pragmatic

**prai·rie** /ˈpreri/ *noun*
a large area of land in the middle part of North America that is covered in grass and does not have many trees: *In the 1860s, the family moved to a small farm on the Iowa prairie.*

**praise**[1] /preɪz/ *verb*
**1** to say that someone has done something well, or that something is good: *The coach praised the team for playing so well.*
**2** to give your thanks and respect to God: *They sang songs to praise God.*
[**ORIGIN:** 1200-1300 From the old French word *preisier*, from the Latin word *pretiare*, which means "to value highly," from *pretium*, meaning "price or value."]

**praise**[2] *noun*
**1** words that you say or write to praise someone or something: *The movie has gotten praise from the critics.*
**2** respect or thanks that you give to God: *Let us give praise to the Lord.*

**prank** /præŋk/ *noun*
a joke in which you play a trick on someone in order to make him or her look silly: *We played a prank on her by telling her that everyone had to come to the party dressed as a pirate, even though she'd be the only one.*

**pray** /preɪ/ *verb*
to talk to God or other gods to ask for help or give thanks: *We prayed for Nancy when she was in the hospital.*
[**ORIGIN:** 1200-1300 From the old French word *preier*, from the Latin word *precari*, which means "to ask someone to do something, or to pray."]

**prayer** /prer/ *noun*
the act of praying, or the words that you say when you pray: *He says his prayers before bed.* | *She spent a few minutes in prayer.*

**preach** /pritʃ/ *verb*
to talk about a religious subject in church: *The minister preached about helping other people.*
[**ORIGIN:** 1200-1300 From the old French word *prechier*, from the Latin word *praedicare*, which means "to say publicly."]

**preach·er** /ˈpritʃɚ/ *noun*
someone who talks about religious subjects in a church **SYNONYM: minister**

**pre·car·i·ous** /prɪˈkeriəs/ *adjective*
likely to become worse or dangerous very suddenly: *His health is in a precarious condition and his family is worried.*
—**precariously** *adverb* in a way that may become worse or dangerous very suddenly: *He was sitting precariously on the branch of a tree and looked like he could fall.*

**pre·cau·tion** /prɪˈkɔʃən/ *noun*
something that you do to stop something bad or dangerous from happening: *You should take the precaution of locking the doors to prevent robberies.*
—**precautionary** *adjective* relating to something you do as a precaution

**pre·cede** Ac /prɪˈsid/ *verb* (*formal*)
to be or happen before something else: *A loud explosion preceded the fire.*

**pre·cinct** /ˈprisɪŋkt/ *noun*
one of the parts that a city is divided into: *The voting results have come in from three of the city's twelve precincts.*
[**ORIGIN:** 1400-1500 From the Latin word *praecinctum*, which means "place surrounded by a boundary," from *praecingere*, which means "to put a belt around, or to surround."]

**pre·cious** /ˈpreʃəs/ *adjective*
**1** very valuable and important: *The crown has diamonds and other precious jewels on it.*
**2** very important or special to you: *The doll is precious because it was my grandmother's.*
[**ORIGIN:** 1200-1300 From the Latin word *pretiosus*, from *pretium*, which means "price."]

**pre·cip·i·ta·tion** /prɪˌsɪpəˈteɪʃən/ *noun* (*formal*)
rain or snow

**pre·cise** Ac /prɪˈsaɪs/ *adjective*
exact and correct: *There were more than a hundred people at the concert, but I don't know the precise number.*
—**precisely** *adverb* exactly and correctly: *He arrived precisely at 4:00.*

**WORD FAMILY: precise**
**precise** *adjective* | **imprecise** *adjective* | **precisely** *adverb* | **precision** *noun*

**pre·ci·sion** Ac /prɪˈsɪʒən/ *noun (formal)*
the quality of being very exact and correct: *He sliced the meat with precision into half-inch pieces.*
—**precision** *adjective* made in a very exact way, or doing something in a very exact way: *Scientists use precision instruments that measure things accurately.*

**pre-Co·lum·bi·an** /ˌpri kəˈlʌmbiən/ *adjective*
relating to the time before 1492, when Christopher Columbus came to the Americas: *The museum has a large collection of pre-Columbian art.*

**pre·con·cep·tion** /ˌprikənˈsepʃən/ *noun (formal)*
an idea that you have about something before you know what it is really like: *Many parents have preconceptions of what their children will do at school, but schools have changed a lot.*

**pred·a·tor** /ˈpredətɚ/ *noun*
an animal that kills and eats other animals: *Sharks are predators that eat fish in the ocean.*

**pred·e·ces·sor** /ˈpredəˌsesɚ/ *noun (formal)*
**1** something that existed before the thing that exists now: *This computer is much faster than its predecessors.*
**2** someone that did a job before the person who does that job now: *President Obama's predecessor was George W. Bush.*

**pre·dic·a·ment** /prɪˈdɪkəmənt/ *noun (formal)*
a difficult situation in which you do not know what is the best thing to do: *We were lost in the woods and were frightened about our predicament.*

**pred·i·cate** /ˈpredɪkɪt/ *noun*
in grammar, the part of a sentence that has the main verb, and that tells what the subject is doing or describes the subject. In the sentence "He ran out of the house," "ran out of the house" is the predicate.

**pre·dict** Ac /prɪˈdɪkt/ *verb*
to say what is going to happen before it happens: *The weatherman predicted rain this weekend.*
—**predictable** *adjective* happening in the way that you expect

**pre·dic·tion** Ac /prɪˈdɪkʃən/ *noun*
a statement saying what is going to happen before it happens: *It's too early to make predictions about who will win.*

**pre·dom·i·nant** Ac /prɪˈdɑmənənt/ *adjective (formal)*
most common, most noticeable, or strongest: *Red was the predominant color in the painting, but other colors were used as well.*
—**predominate** *verb* to be predominant

**pre·dom·i·nant·ly** Ac /prɪˈdɑmənəntli/ *adverb (formal)*
mostly or mainly: *They are the only Asian family in a predominantly white neighborhood.*

**pref·ace** /ˈprefəs/ *noun*
a part of a book that comes before the main part, and that tells you about the book or the writer: *The preface to the novel tells the reader a little bit about Mark Twain's life.*

**pre·fer** /prɪˈfɚ/ *verb* (**preferred**, **preferring**)
to like someone or something better than someone or something else: *Which color do you prefer?*

**pref·er·a·ble** /ˈprefərəbəl/ *adjective (formal)*
better or more appropriate: *Classes with only 20 children are preferable to larger ones.*
—**preferably** *adverb* in a way that is better or more appropriate

**pref·er·ence** /ˈprefərəns/ *noun*
if someone has a preference for something, he or she likes it better than another thing: *Even small babies show preferences for some kinds of food – they like some, and dislike others.*

P

**pre·fix** /ˈprifɪks/ *noun*
a group of letters that you add to the beginning of a word in order to make a new word: *If we add the prefix "un" to the word "happy," we make the word "unhappy."*
[**ORIGIN:** 1600-1700 From the Latin word *praefixus*, a form of the verb *praefigere*, which means "to fasten before."]

P

**preg·nan·cy** /ˈpregnənsi/ *noun* (plural **pregnancies**)
the state of having a baby growing inside your body: *Women sometimes feel sick at the start of a pregnancy.*

**preg·nant** /ˈpregnənt/ *adjective*
if a woman is pregnant, she has a baby growing in her body: *She's about five months pregnant.*
[**ORIGIN:** 1400-1500 From the Latin word *praegnans*, from *prae-* and *gnatus*, which mean "before" and "born."]

**pre·his·tor·ic** /ˌprihɪˈstɔrɪk/ *adjective*
relating to the time thousands of years ago, before anything was written down: *In prehistoric times, people lived in caves.*

**prej·u·dice** /ˈpredʒədɪs/ *noun*
an unfair belief that someone who is a different race, sex, or religion is not as good as you are: *Black people still often have to deal with prejudice.*

**THESAURUS: prejudice**

**racism** unfair treatment of people because they belong to a different race: *Because of racism, in the past, black children were not allowed to go to the same schools as white children.*

**sexism** unfair treatment of women: *Sexism kept women out of good jobs.*

**discrimination** the practice of treating one group of people differently from another in an unfair way: *There was discrimination against Jews, so that they were paid less than other people.*

**bigotry** an unreasonable hatred for people of other races, religions, or countries: *His speeches are full of bigotry and hatred.*

**prej·u·diced** /ˈpredʒədɪst/ *adjective*
believing unfairly that someone who is a different race, sex, or religion is not as good as you are: *He is prejudiced and would never hire a woman for an important job.*
[**ORIGIN:** 1200-1300 From the Latin word *praejudicium*, from *prae-* and *judicium*, which mean "before" and "judgment." If you are prejudiced toward people, you have judged them before knowing them.]

**pre·lim·i·nar·y** Ac /prɪˈlɪməˌneri/ *adjective* (*formal*)
done at the beginning of something, to get ready for it: *Joe made a preliminary drawing before starting to paint.*

**prel·ude** /ˈpreɪlud/ *noun* (*formal*)
**be a prelude to something** = to happen just before something else: *The rain was a prelude to a terrible storm.*

**pre·ma·ture** /ˌpriməˈtʃʊr/ *adjective*
happening too early or before the right time: *The baby was six weeks premature and was very small.*
—**prematurely** *adverb* too early or before the right time

**pre·mier**[1] (*also* **Premier**) /prɪˈmɪr/ *noun*
the leader of the government in some countries: *The president is going to meet with the Chinese premier.*

**premier**[2] *adjective* (*formal*)
best or most important: *The Superbowl is football's premier event.*
[**ORIGIN:** 1400-1500 From the French word for "first," from the Latin words *primarius* and *primus*, which mean "first."]

**pre·mi·um** /ˈprimiəm/ *noun*
the money that you pay for insurance every month or year: *Dad pays $1,500 per year in car insurance premiums.*

**pre·oc·cu·pied** /priˈɑkjəˌpaɪd/ *adjective*
thinking about something a lot, so that you do not pay attention to other things: *Dad was preoccupied with work and didn't say much.*
—**preoccupation** /priˌɑkyəˈpeɪʃən/ *noun* the state of being preoccupied

**prep·a·ra·tion** /ˌprepəˈreɪʃən/ *noun*
**1** the act of getting something or someone ready for something: *We cleaned the house in preparation for our cousins' visit.*
**2** **preparations** = the things that you do to get ready for something: *The soldiers made preparations to attack.*

**pre·par·a·to·ry** /prɪˈpærəˌtɔri/ *adjective*
done in order to get ready for something: *She's taking college preparatory classes.*

**pre·pare** /prɪˈper/ *verb (formal)*
**1** to make something ready: *Mom was preparing dinner in the kitchen.*
**2** to make yourself or another person ready to do something: *Angie was studying to prepare for a math test.*

**WORD FAMILY: prepare**
**prepare** *verb* | **preparation** *noun* | **preparatory** *adjective* | **prepared** *adjective* | **unprepared** *adjective*

**pre·pared** /prɪˈperd/ *adjective*
**1** ready to do something or to be used: *He wasn't prepared for their questions and didn't know how to answer them.*
**2 be prepared to do something** = to be willing to do something: *I'm prepared to stay and help if you need me.*
—**preparedness** /prɪˈperɪdnɪs/ *noun* a state of being ready for something

**prep·o·si·tion** /ˌprepəˈzɪʃən/ *noun*
a word such as "to," "for," "on," or "by," which is put in front of a noun to show place, time, or direction: *In the sentence "I'm going to the store," "to" is a preposition.*
—**prepositional** *adjective* relating to prepositions and how they are used: *a prepositional phrase*

**pre·school** /ˈpriskul/ *noun*
a school that children between the ages of two and five can go to, where they learn things that help make them ready to go to a school for older children: *Look at the painting Andy did at preschool.*
—**preschool** *adjective* relating to a preschool: *preschool education*

**pre·scribe** /prɪˈskraɪb/ *verb*
to say what medicine or treatment a sick person should have: *The doctor prescribed pills for the pain.*
[**ORIGIN:** 1400-1500 From the Latin word *praescribere*, which means "to write at the beginning, or to order."]

**pre·scrip·tion** /prɪˈskrɪpʃən/ *noun*
a piece of paper on which a doctor writes what medicine a sick person should have: *The doctor wrote a prescription for antibiotics for her sore throat.*

**pres·ence** /ˈprezəns/ *noun*
**1** the state of being in a particular place at a particular time: *The experiment showed the presence of salt in the liquid.* **ANTONYM: absence**
**2 in someone's presence/in the presence of someone** *(formal)* = with someone, or in the same place as him or her: *He never uses swear words in the presence of his children.*

P

**pres·ent¹** /ˈprezənt/ *adjective*
**1 be present** *(formal)* = to be in a particular place: *All twenty-eight children were present in class.* **ANTONYM: absent**
**2** happening or existing now: *We need to change the present system so that it works better.*

**pres·ent²** *noun*
**1** something that you give someone: *What are you giving Anne as a birthday present?* **SYNONYM: gift**
**2 the present** = the time that is happening now: *The family has lived on the farm from 1901 until the present.*
**3 at present** *(formal)* = at this time: *There are no jobs available at present.*

**pres·ent³** /prɪˈzent/ *verb*
**1** *(formal)* to give something to someone: *He presented a gold cup to the winning team.*
**2** to give or show information: *Students presented their work to the rest of the class.*

**pres·en·ta·tion** /ˌprizənˈteɪʃən/ *noun*
**1** *(formal)* the act of giving someone something in a formal ceremony: *The presentation of the awards will take place after dinner.*
**2** a formal talk about a particular subject: *The students each gave a short presentation about the book they had read.*

**ˌpresent ˈparticiple** *noun*
the form of a verb that ends in "-ing," which you use for showing an action that is continuing, or as an adjective: *In the sentences "The child is sleeping" and "I woke the sleeping child," "sleeping" is a present participle.*

**ˌpresent ˈperfect** *noun*
**the present perfect** = the form of a verb made by adding the verb "have" to the PAST PARTICIPLE of a verb, which you use to talk

about a time up to and including the present time: *In the sentence "I have eaten the cake," "have eaten" is in the present perfect.*

**ˌpresent ˈtense** *noun*
the form of a verb that shows what exists or happens now: *In the sentence, "I leave for school at 7:45," "leave" is in the present tense.*

**pre·serv·a·tive** /prɪˈzɝvətɪv/ *noun*
a chemical that food companies add to food to stop it from going bad: *The bread has preservatives in it to stop it from becoming stale too quickly.*

**pre·serve¹** /prɪˈzɝv/ *verb*
to keep something from being harmed or damaged: *The fish is preserved with salt.* | *The group is working to preserve the rainforests.*
—**preservation** /ˌprezɚˈveɪʃən/ *noun* the act of preserving something
→ see Thesaurus box at **protect**

**preserve²** *noun*
an area of land or water in which the government protects animals, fish, or trees: *The part of the ocean where the seals live is a marine preserve.*

**pres·i·den·cy** /ˈprezədənsi/ *noun* (plural **presidencies**)
the job or time of being a president: *The election for the presidency takes place in November.*

**pres·i·dent** /ˈprezədənt/ *noun*
**1** the leader of the government in some countries, including the U.S.: *President Washington was our first president.* | *He was the president of Mexico.*
**2** someone who is in charge of an organization such as a business, bank, club, or college: *She won the election for president of the student council.*
—**presidential** /ˌprezəˈdenʃəl/ *adjective* relating to a president
[**ORIGIN:** 1300-1400 From the Latin word *praesidere*, which means "to watch over or command."]

**ˈPresident's ˌDay** *noun*
a U.S. holiday that shows respect for two of America's important presidents, George Washington and Abraham Lincoln. The holiday is on the third Monday in February because both presidents were born in February.

**press¹** /pres/ *verb*
**1** to push something with your finger: *Press the blue button to turn the TV on.*

**THESAURUS: press**

**push** to press a button or switch with your finger to make a piece of equipment start or stop working: *Push the red button to start recording.*

**squash** to press something and damage it by making it flat: *Put the tomatoes at the top of the bag, where they won't get squashed.*

**squeeze** to press something from both sides, usually with your fingers: *Squeeze the toothpaste tube from the bottom.* | *The orange juice is freshly squeezed.*

**pinch** to press someone's skin between your finger and thumb: *She pinched my arm and it hurt!*

**crush** to press something very hard so that it breaks or is damaged: *The tree fell onto a car and crushed it.*

**mash** to press fruit or cooked vegetables until they are soft and smooth: *Mash the potatoes well.*

**2** to push something hard against something else: *Mike pressed the phone against his ear.*
**SYNONYM: push**
**3** to make clothes smooth using an iron: *I need to press a shirt for tomorrow.*
**SYNONYM: iron**

**press²** *noun*
**the press** = newspapers and magazines and the people who work for them: *Members of the press were not allowed in the courtroom.*

**press·ing** /ˈpresɪŋ/ *adjective* (*formal*)
a pressing problem or question needs to be dealt with very soon: *The country's most pressing problem is that there is not enough food for everyone.* **SYNONYM: urgent**

**pres·sure** /ˈpreʃɚ/ *noun*
**1** the use of strong words or arguments to try to make someone do something: *Her parents put a lot of pressure on her to do well at school.*
**2** the things that are happening in your life

that make you worry and feel that you have a lot to do: *I've been under pressure at school because of all the tests.*

**3** the force that something causes when it pushes on another thing: *The air pressure in the tires might be low.* | *I could feel the pressure of his hand on my shoulder.*

—**pressure** *verb* to make someone feel that he or she must do something, when he or she does not really want to: *If your friend pressures you to smoke, he's not really a good friend.*

→ see Thesaurus box at **force**[1]

**pres·tige** /preˈstiʒ/ *noun*

if you have prestige, people respect and admire you because of your job or something that you have achieved: *His position as the head of a company gives him prestige.*

—**prestigious** /preˈstɪdʒəs/ *adjective* having prestige: *Being mayor is a prestigious job.*

[**ORIGIN:** 1600-1700 From the old French word for "deceiving, or magic tricks," from the Latin word *praestigiae*, meaning "magic tricks." The idea is that people are very impressed by someone's high position or achievements, as they would be by magic tricks.]

**pre·sum·a·bly** Ac /prɪˈzuməbli/ *adverb*

used when you think that something is probably true: *It's raining so presumably the picnic will be canceled.*

**pre·sume** Ac /prɪˈzum/ *verb* (*formal*)

to think that something is probably true: *I left a message with the man who answered the phone. I presumed it was Tony's father.* **SYNONYM: assume**

—**presumption** /prɪˈzʌmpʃən/ *noun* the belief that something is probably true

**pre·sup·pose** /ˌprisəˈpoʊz/ *verb* (*formal*)

to depend on something you believe may happen or be true: *This math topic presupposes that the children can add and subtract.* **SYNONYM: assume**

**pre·tend** /prɪˈtend/ *verb*

to behave as if something is true or real, when it is not: *Terry pretended to be asleep.* | *The kids are pretending that they are lions.*

—**pretense** /ˈpritens/ *noun* the act of pretending that something is true

**pre·ten·tious** /prɪˈtenʃəs/ *adjective*

trying to seem more important, rich, or smart than you really are: *He used a lot of big words, so he sounded pretentious.*

—**pretension** /prɪˈtenʃən/ *noun* the act of trying to seem more important, rich, or smart than you really are

**pre·text** /ˈpritekst/ *noun*

a false reason that you give for doing something, in order to hide the real reason: *I called Gina on the pretext of asking about the homework, when really I wanted to hear about her date with Ron.*

**pret·ty**[1] /ˈprɪti/ *adjective* (**prettier, prettiest**)

nice to look at or listen to: *Jenny is so pretty she could be a model.* | *That's a pretty song.*

→ see Thesaurus box at **beautiful**

[**ORIGIN:** From the old English word *prættig*, which means "clever," from *prætt*, meaning "trick or skill." The word later meant "skillfully made" and then came to have its modern meaning.]

**pretty**[2] *adverb*

**1** more than usually or normally, but not very: *I thought the test was pretty easy, but a couple of the questions were hard.* | *Dad was pretty angry about the broken window, but he didn't yell or anything.* **SYNONYM: fairly**

**2 pretty much** (*informal*) = almost completely: *I'm pretty much done with my homework. I'll be finished in five minutes.*

**pret·zel** /ˈpretsəl/ *noun*

a type of bread that is baked in the shape of a loose knot and has salt on top

[**ORIGIN:** 1800-1900 From German, probably from the Latin word *bracchium*, which means "arm." A pretzel has the shape of folded arms.]

**pre·vent** /prɪˈvent/ *verb*

to stop something from happening, or stop someone from doing something: *To prevent accidents, don't run near the swimming pool.* | *A knee injury prevented him from playing in the basketball game.*

—**preventable** *adjective* able to be prevented

—**preventive** *adjective* done in order to prevent something

[**ORIGIN:** 1400-1500 From the Latin word *preventus*, a form of the verb *praevenire*, which means "to come before."]

**WORD FAMILY: prevent**

**prevent** *verb* | **prevention** *noun* | **preventable** *adjective* | **preventive** *adjective*

P

**pre·ven·tion** /prɪˈvenʃən/ *noun*
the things you do in order to stop something happening: *Washing your hands is an important step in the prevention of colds and flu.*

**pre·view** /ˈprivyu/ *noun*
an advertisement for a movie or television program, showing short parts from it: *Have you seen the previews for that new science fiction movie?*

P

**pre·vi·ous** Ac /ˈpriviəs/ *adjective*
happening before or earlier: *She has two children from a previous marriage and one child with her current husband.*
[ORIGIN: 1600-1700 From the Latin word *praevius*, which means "going before, or leading the way."]

**pre·vi·ous·ly** Ac /ˈpriːviəsli/ *adverb*
before now: *It isn't as cold today as it was previously.*
→ see Thesaurus box at **before**[1]

**prey** /preɪ/ *noun*
an animal that another animal kills and eats: *A spider catches its prey in its web.*

**price** /praɪs/ *noun*
the amount of money that you must pay in order to buy something: *The price of gas has gone up again.* | *Is there a big difference in price between the two computers?*
→ see Thesaurus box at **cost**[1]

**price·less** /ˈpraɪsləs/ *adjective*
very valuable: *The museum has many priceless works of art.*

**pric·ey** (*also* **pricy**) /ˈpraɪsi/ *adjective* (*informal*)
costing a lot of money, or making you pay a lot of money for something: *The clothes at that store are beautiful but very pricey.* **SYNONYM: expensive**

**prick** /prɪk/ *verb*
to make a small hole in something with a sharp point: *She pricked her finger on the needle.*

**pride** /praɪd/ *noun*
a feeling of happiness and respect for yourself because you have done something well or have something good: *Joey took a lot of pride in the bird house he had made.* | *She looked at her daughter with pride.*

**priest** /prist/ *noun*
someone who performs religious duties and ceremonies in some religions: *a Catholic priest*

**pri·mar·i·ly** Ac /praɪˈmerəli/ *adverb* (*formal*)
mainly: *The children primarily speak English, but they occasionally speak Spanish.*

**pri·mar·y** Ac /ˈpraɪˌmeri/ *adjective* (*formal*)
most important: *The primary aim of any business is to make money.* **SYNONYM: main**
[ORIGIN: 1400-1500 From the Latin word *primarius*, from *primus*, which means "first."]

**ˌprimary ˈcolor** *noun*
one of the three colors – red, yellow, and blue – that you can mix together to make any other color

**prime** Ac /praɪm/ *adjective* (*formal*)
**1** most important: *Smoking is the prime cause of lung disease.* **SYNONYMS: primary, main**
**2** very good: *Soccer is a prime example of a game that girls and boys can play together.*

**ˌprime ˈminister** *noun*
the leader of the government in some countries, for example Great Britain

**ˌprime ˈnumber** *noun*
a number that can only be divided by itself and the number one: *7 is a prime number.*

**prim·i·tive** /ˈprɪmətɪv/ *adjective*
**1** belonging to an early stage in the development of humans or animals: *Some primitive people lived in caves.* **ANTONYM: modern**
**2** very simple and without anything modern: *The houses were primitive, and did not have water or electricity.*

**prince** /prɪns/ *noun*
**1** the son of a king or queen: *In the story, the prince falls in love with Cinderella.*
**2** a male ruler of some countries: *the Prince of Monaco*
[ORIGIN: 1100-1200 From the Latin word *princeps*, which means "leader."]

**prin·cess** /ˈprɪnses/ *noun*
the daughter of a king or queen, or the wife of a prince: *In the story of "Snow White," the princess runs away from the evil queen.*

**prin·ci·pal**[1] Ac /ˈprɪnsəpəl/ *noun*
someone who is in charge of a school: *Helen*

*Davies is the principal of Ferry Elementary School.*

**principal²** Ac *adjective*
most important: *New York is one of America's principal cities.* **SYNONYM: main**

> **USAGE: principal, principle**
>
> **Principal** is an adjective meaning "most important," or a noun meaning "someone who is in charge of a school": *Our principal concern is safety.* | *She is a former school principal.*
>
> **Principle** is a noun meaning "an idea that you believe is right": *The Constitution talks about the principle of equality.*

**prin·ci·ple** Ac /ˈprɪnsəpəl/ *noun*
an idea that you believe is right, and that helps you to decide how to behave: *One of our school's principles is that we treat every child fairly.*
[**ORIGIN:** 1300-1400 From the Latin word *principium*, which means "beginning." The idea is that a principle is the beginning from which you decide how to act.]

**print¹** /prɪnt/ *verb*
**1** to put words, numbers, or pictures on paper, using a machine: *He wrote his report on the computer and printed it.*
**2** to write words without joining the letters together: *Please print your name clearly.*
—**printable** *adjective* able to be printed
[**ORIGIN:** 1200-1300 From the old French verb *preindre*, which means "to press." The simplest way of printing is to put ink on something and then press it onto paper.]
**PHRASAL VERB**
**print something out**
to make a printed copy of something from a computer: *I printed out a picture of a shark from a website.*

**print²** *noun*
**1** the letters and numbers that are printed in books, newspapers, and magazines: *Children's books often have big print.*
**2** a mark that something makes on a surface or in something soft: *The dog had made muddy paw prints on the floor.*
**3** a picture or painting that has been printed on paper: *Do you want extra prints of your photographs?*

**print·er** /ˈprɪntɚ/ *noun*
**1** a machine that puts the words or pictures from a computer onto paper: *a color printer*
→ see picture on page **A20**
**2** a person or business whose work is printing books, magazines, etc.

**print·ing** /ˈprɪntɪŋ/ *noun*
the process of printing words and pictures in a book or magazine using a machine: *Tony works in the printing industry.*

**print·out** /ˈprɪntˌaʊt/ *noun*
a piece of paper with information on it, that you print from a computer: *The teacher gave a printout of the story to each student.*

**pri·or** Ac /ˈpraɪɚ/ *adjective* (*formal*)
**1 prior to something** = before: *The President went back to Washington two days prior to the election.*
**2** done, given, etc. at an earlier time: *The school needs the parents' prior agreement before children can go on the field trip.*

**pri·or·i·ty** Ac /praɪˈɔrəti/ *noun* (plural **priorities**)
the thing that you think is most important and that needs your attention first: *My top priority this week is to study for the test.*
—**prioritize** *verb* to decide what is most important, so that you can do it first: *Try to prioritize your work and deal with the most important things first.*

**prism** Ac /ˈprɪzəm/ *noun*
**1** a block of glass that separates light into different colors. The ends of a prism are in the shape of a TRIANGLE: *If you shine white light through a prism, it will split into the colors of the rainbow.*
**2** a solid figure with ends that are the same size and shape, and sides that are PARALLELOGRAMs

**pris·on** /ˈprɪzən/ *noun*
a building where people must stay as a punishment for a crime: *He attacked an old lady, and spent four years in prison.* **SYNONYM: jail**
[**ORIGIN:** 1100-1200 From French, from the Latin word *prehensio*, which means "the act of taking hold of someone or something," from *prehendere*, meaning "to take hold."]

**pris·on·er** /ˈprɪzənɚ/ *noun*
someone who must stay in a prison as a

punishment for a crime: *Many of the prisoners have been in prison for a very long time.* **SYNONYM: convict**

**ˌprisoner of ˈwar** *noun* (*abbreviation*: **P.O.W.**)
a member of the military who is caught by the enemy during a war and kept as a prisoner

P

**pri·va·cy** /ˈpraɪvəsi/ *noun*
**1** the state of being able to be alone when you want to be: *Teenagers need privacy and a room of their own.*
**2** the state of being able to keep your life secret: *Movie stars have very little privacy. Reporters and photographers are always following them.*

**pri·vate¹** /ˈpraɪvət/ *adjective*
**1** secret and not for other people to know about: *She wrote all her private thoughts in her journal.*

**THESAURUS: private**

**secret** known or felt only by you, and not talked about or shown to anyone else: *Her secret dream was to be a famous singer, but she did not tell anyone because she did not want to be teased.*

**personal** if something is personal, it is about you and private, and other people do not need to know about it: *He asked me personal questions like how much I weigh.*

**innermost** (*formal*) your innermost thoughts or feelings are the ones you feel strongly but keep private: *Collins expressed her innermost feelings in her poetry.*

**be none of your business** (*informal*) if something is none of your business, it is private and you should not ask about it: *I don't know how much money he makes, and really it's none of my business.*

**2** for one person or group, and not for everyone: *The band flew to Miami in a private jet.*
**3** owned by a person or business, and not a government: *The museum is a private organization.* **ANTONYM: public**
**4** quiet and without other people: *Is there a private place where we can talk?*

**private²** *noun*
**1 in private** = without other people listening or watching: *I need to talk to you in private.*
**2** someone who has the lowest position in the army: *He started as a private, and worked his way up to colonel.*

**pri·vate·ly** /ˈpraɪvɪtli/ *adverb*
**1** secretly, so that other people do not know about something: *He told me privately how unhappy he was.*
**2** in a quiet place without other people: *Is there some place we can meet privately?*
**3 privately owned/funded/run, etc.** = owned, etc. by a person or business and not the government: *The company is privately owned.*

**ˈprivate school** *noun*
a school where parents pay for their children's education

**priv·i·lege** /ˈprɪvəlɪdʒ/ *noun*
a special advantage that only one person or group gets: *Students at the school get more privileges as they get older.*

**priv·i·leged** /ˈprɪvəlɪdʒd/ *adjective* (*formal*)
having more advantages than other people, such as more money, opportunities, and better jobs: *Ben comes from a privileged background because his parents are rich.*

**prize** /praɪz/ *noun*
something that you win in a game, competition, or race: *I entered an essay competition, and won first prize!*

**pro¹** /proʊ/ *noun*
**1** (*informal*) someone who is paid to do something, such as play a sport, act, or play music, that other people do for fun: *He is a tennis pro.* **SYNONYM: professional**
**2** (*informal*) someone who has had a lot of experience with a particular type of situation: *The construction guys are pros, so they'll do a good job.*
**3** an advantage of something: *You should consider the pros and cons of the plan before you act.* **ANTONYM: con**

**pro²** *adjective* (*informal*)
paid to do something such as a sport, that other people do for fun: *pro basketball*

*players* **SYNONYM: professional**; **ANTONYM: amateur**

**prob·a·bil·i·ty** /ˌprɑbəˈbɪləti/ *noun*
how likely it is that something will happen: *There is a high probability of rain that day.*

**prob·a·ble** /ˈprɑbəbəl/ *adjective*
likely to happen or be true: *You have studied hard, so it is probable that you will pass the test.*

**prob·a·bly** /ˈprɑbəbli/ *adverb*
likely to happen or be true: *Mom will probably call me later today.*

**WORD FAMILY: probably**
**probably** *adverb* | **probable** *adjective* | **probability** *noun*

**probe**[1] /proʊb/ *verb*
**1** to ask questions in order to find things out: *The reporters probe into the personal lives of movie stars.*
**2** to look for something or examine something, using a long thin instrument
—**probing** *adjective* relating to finding out information by asking questions: *The interviewer asked several probing questions.*

**probe**[2] *noun*
a spacecraft without people in it, that goes into space to get information: *They sent a space probe to Mars.*

**prob·lem** /ˈprɑbləm/ *noun*
**1** a situation that causes difficulties: *Bullying is a serious problem in some schools.* | *I'm having problems with my computer; it keeps crashing.*
**2** a question that you must answer using numbers or other information: *Mom, can you help me solve this math problem?*
**3 no problem** (*informal*) = used for saying that you are willing to do something: *"Can you give me a ride to school?" "Sure, no problem."*
**[ORIGIN:** 1300-1400 From the Greek word *problema*, which means "something put forward for you to deal with," from *proballein*, which means "to put forward."**]**

**prob·lem·at·ic** /ˌprɑbləˈmætɪk/ (*also* **prob·le·mat·i·cal** /ˌprɑbləˈmætɪkəl/) *adjective*
full of problems or causing problems: *Mike and Lisa's relationship was very problematic and they were always arguing.*

**pro·ce·dure** Ac /prəˈsidʒɚ/ *noun* (*formal*)
the correct or normal way of doing something: *You must follow the correct procedure for installing the software or it won't work.*
—**procedural** *adjective* relating to a procedure

**pro·ceed** Ac /prəˈsid/ *verb* (*formal*)
**1** to do something that you have planned to do: *The college will proceed with plans to build a new library.*
**2** to move in a particular direction: *Please proceed to the nearest exit.*
**[ORIGIN:** 1300-1400 From the Latin word *procedere*, which means "to go forward."**]**

**pro·cess**[1] Ac /ˈprɑses/ *noun*
**1** a series of things you do to achieve a particular result: *Education is the process of teaching and learning.*
**2** a series of changes that happen naturally over a period of time: *Growing up is a natural process.*

**process**[2] *verb*
to deal with information or requests in a series of stages: *We are still processing your application.*

**pro·ces·sion** /prəˈseʃən/ *noun*
a line of people or cars moving slowly as part of a ceremony: *A procession of cars went by on the way to a funeral.*

**pro·ces·sor** Ac /ˈprɑsesɚ/ *noun*
the part of a computer that deals with information and controls the other parts of the computer: *Processors are much faster today than they used to be.*

**pro·cras·ti·nate** /prəˈkræstəˌneɪt/ *verb*
to delay doing something that you ought to do: *Just stop procrastinating and do your homework.*
—**procrastinator** *noun* someone who procrastinates
—**procrastination** /prəˌkræstəˈneɪʃən/ *noun* the act of procrastinating
**[ORIGIN:** 1500-1600 From the Latin word *procrastinare*, from *cras*, which means "tomorrow."**]**

P

**pro·duce[1]** /prəˈdus/ *verb*
**1** to make something happen or have a particular effect: *What kind of effects does alcohol produce in the body?*
**2** to make something naturally: *Plants produce oxygen.*
**3** to make or grow something in order to sell it: *Japan produces a lot of electronic goods.*
**4** to make something using a skill or art: *The kids have produced some fantastic paintings.*
**5** to control the making of a movie, play, or television show: *Walt Disney produced the movie "Snow White."*

> **WORD FAMILY: produce**
> **produce** *verb* | **producer** *noun* | **product** *noun* | **production** *noun* | **productive** *adjective*

**prod·uce[2]** /ˈprɑdus/ *noun (formal)*
food that people grow to sell, especially fruits and vegetables: *Good restaurants always use fresh produce.*

**pro·duc·er** /prəˈdusɚ/ *noun*
**1** a person, company, or country that makes or grows something to sell: *The company is a producer of computer equipment.*
**2** someone whose job is to control how a movie, play, or television program is prepared: *He's a Hollywood producer and has made many successful movies.*

**prod·uct** /ˈprɑdʌkt/ *noun*
**1** *(formal)* something that people grow or make in order to sell it: *The price of food products goes up all the time.*
**2** the number you get when you multiply numbers: *The product of 3 x 3 is 9.*

**pro·duc·tion** /prəˈdʌkʃən/ *noun*
**1** the process of making or growing things in order to sell them: *the production of cotton in California*
**2** a movie, play, or show that people go to see: *We went to the theater to see a production of "The Sound of Music."*

**pro·duc·tive** /prəˈdʌktɪv/ *adjective*
producing or achieving a lot: *If people are happy at work, they are more productive.*
—**productively** *adverb* in a way that produces or achieves something useful

**pro·fes·sion** /prəˈfeʃən/ *noun*
a job that needs special education and training: *People in the medical profession have studied for many years before becoming doctors.*
→ see Thesaurus box at **job**

> **WORD FAMILY: profession**
> **profession** *noun* | **professional** *adjective* | **professional** *noun* | **professionalism** *noun*

**pro·fes·sion·al[1]** Ac /prəˈfeʃənəl/ *adjective*
**1** relating to a job that needs special education and training: *A lawyer can give you professional advice.*
**2** doing a sport or activity for money, as a job: *Professional football players earn a lot of money.* **ANTONYM: amateur**

**professional[2]** Ac *noun*
someone who works in a job that needs a lot of education or training: *Trained professionals can earn plenty of money.*
—**professionalism** *noun* the skill that a professional person has

**pro·fes·sor** /prəˈfesɚ/ *noun*
a teacher at a university: *a professor of economics* | *Professor Davis teaches American history.* → see picture on page **A16**

**pro·fi·cient** /prəˈfɪʃənt/ *adjective (formal)*
able to do something very well: *Most young people are proficient at using the Internet.*
—**proficiency** *noun* the state of being able to do something very well: *The tests show each student's proficiency in math and English.*

**pro·file** /ˈproʊfaɪl/ *noun*

**profile**

**1** a view or picture of someone's head from the side: *The painting is of a young girl in profile.*
**2** a short description that gives important details about what someone or something is like: *The students write profiles of themselves to go in the book.*

**prof·it** /ˈprɑfɪt/ *noun*
**1** money that you get when you sell something for more than you paid: *He made a big*

*profit when he sold his house because it had increased a lot in value.*

**2** the money that a company makes by doing business, after paying costs such as WAGEs or rent: *The company's profits rose to $23 million.*

—**profit** *verb* to get money or something useful as a result of something that happens: *The record company profited from the work of these musicians.*

**[ORIGIN:** 1200-1300 From French, from the Latin word *profectus*, which is a form of the verb *proficere*, which means "to make progress or get something done."**]**

**prof·it·a·ble** /ˈprɑfɪtəbəl/ *adjective*
earning a profit: *The restaurant is a profitable business because it is always busy.*

—**profitably** *adverb* in a way that is profitable

**pro·found** /prəˈfaʊnd/ *adjective* (*formal*)
having a very great effect: *The story had a profound influence on me and made me want to become a writer.*

**pro·gram¹** /ˈproʊgræm/ *noun*
**1** a show on television or radio: *What's your favorite TV program? | We watched a program about whales.*

**THESAURUS: program**

**soap opera/soap** a program that is on television regularly, often every day, about the same group of people: *She was watching one of the daytime soap operas.*

**sitcom** a funny program which has the same people in different stories every week: *"Friends" was a popular sitcom about a group of friends in New York City.*

**game show** a program in which people play games in order to win prizes: *He won a trip to Hawaii on a game show.*

**talk show** a program in which famous people answer questions about themselves: *David Letterman's late night talk show*

**cartoon** a program with characters that are drawn and not real: *What's your favorite Saturday morning cartoon?*

**series** a set of programs about the same group of people or about one subject: *a new drama series about cops and lawyers*

**documentary** a program that gives information about a subject: *a documentary about wolves*

**2** a set of instructions for a computer that makes it do something: *The students are learning how to write computer programs.*

**3** a set of organized activities that people do in order to achieve something: *Members of the team have to follow an exercise program.*

**4** a piece of paper or a thin book that gives information about a play, event, or concert you go to: *The program gave the names of all the performers.*

**[ORIGIN:** 1600-1700 From the Greek word *programma*, which means "public notice," from *prographein*, which means "to write before."**]**

**program²** *verb* (**programmed, programming**)
to give a set of instructions to a computer to make it do something: *You can program a computer to play chess.*

—**programming** *noun* the act or job of writing instructions for a computer: *He's studying computer programming.*

**pro·gram·mer** /ˈproʊˌgræmɚ/ *noun*
someone whose job is writing programs for computers: *a computer programmer*

**prog·ress¹** /ˈprɑgrəs/ *noun*
**1** the process of getting better at doing something: *Bob has made good progress in math this year.*

**2** the process of getting closer to achieving something: *There has been progress toward peace in the area.*

**3** movement toward a place: *The traffic was bad, so we made slow progress.*

**4 in progress** = happening now: *Please be quiet – there is a test in progress.*

**prog·ress²** /prəˈgres/ *verb* (*formal*)
**1** to continue to get better and develop: *Technology is progressing all the time.*

**2** to happen or move forward slowly: *I got bored as the meeting progressed.*

**pro·gres·sion** /prəˈgreʃən/ *noun* (*formal*)
a process of changing and developing: *You can see the progression of the artist's work during these years.*

**pro·gres·sive** /prəˈgresɪv/ *adjective* (*formal*)
liking or using modern ideas and ways of doing things: *Our new teacher is very progressive and is always trying new ideas.*
—**progressive** *noun* someone who is progressive

**pro·hib·it** Ac /proʊˈhɪbɪt/ *verb* (*formal*)
if something is prohibited, the law does not allow it: *Smoking is strictly prohibited on board the aircraft.* **ANTONYM: permit**
—**prohibition** /ˌproʊhɪˈbɪʃən/ *noun* the act of not allowing people to do something
→ see Thesaurus box at **forbid**
[**ORIGIN:** 1400-1500 From the Latin word *prohibere*, which means "to hold back or prevent."]

**pro·hib·i·tive** Ac /proʊˈhɪbətɪv/ *adjective* (*formal*)
preventing people from doing or buying something: *The cost of the trip was prohibitive* (=too expensive for people to do).

**proj·ect¹** Ac /ˈprɑdʒekt/ *noun*
some work that you plan carefully, and that often takes a long time: *I'm still working on my school science project.*

**proj·ect²** Ac /prəˈdʒekt/ *verb*
**1** to calculate what the amount or cost of something will be in the future: *The population is projected to increase to 26 million.*
**2** to show a movie or picture on a screen or wall, using a projector: *The movie is projected onto the screen from the projector in the back of the theater.*

**pro·jec·tion** Ac /prəˈdʒekʃən/ *noun* (*formal*)
a statement that says what is likely to happen in the future: *Some projections of future weather show that the ice at the North Pole will melt.*

**pro·jec·tor** /prəˈdʒektɚ/ *noun*
a machine that shows a movie or picture on a screen or wall by shining light through the film or picture: *a movie projector*

**pro·lif·ic** /prəˈlɪfɪk/ *adjective*
a prolific writer or artist produces a lot of books, songs, paintings, etc.: *He's a prolific writer and has published about 20 books.*

**pro·long** /prəˈlɔŋ/ *verb* (*formal*)
to make something continue for longer: *Modern medicine is prolonging our lives.*

**prom** /prɑm/ *noun*
a formal dance party for students in HIGH SCHOOL: *Who are you going to the prom with?*

**prom·i·nent** /ˈprɑmənənt/ *adjective* (*formal*)
famous or important: *A number of prominent politicians, including the Speaker of the House, support the bill.*
—**prominence** *noun* the state of being prominent: *He rose to prominence when he appeared in a very successful TV series.*
[**ORIGIN:** 1400-1500 From the Latin word *prominere*, which means "to stick out."]

**prom·ise¹** /ˈprɑmɪs/ *verb*
**1** to say that you will definitely do something: *Lou promised to give me a ride to the dance.* | *I promise that I'll call you.*

**THESAURUS: promise**

**swear** to make a very serious promise: *Do you swear to tell the truth?*

**take/swear an oath** (*formal*) to make a very serious promise in public: *Every soldier must take an oath of loyalty to his or her country.*

**vow** (*formal*) to promise to do something, in a very definite way: *At their wedding, they vowed to love and take care of each other.*

**guarantee** to promise that something will happen: *I guarantee that you'll love this book.*

**pledge** to make a formal and public promise to do something: *The new governor pledged to increase spending on education.*

**give someone your word** to promise someone very sincerely that you will do something: *He gave us his word that he would pay us back the money he borrowed.*

**2** to seem likely to be good, exciting, etc.: *The game on Saturday promises to be exciting.*

**promise²** *noun*
a statement saying that you will definitely do

something: *Mom made a promise to take me to Disneyland on my birthday.*

**prom·is·ing** /ˈprɑmɪsɪŋ/ *adjective*
likely to be good or successful: *She's a promising young singer and certain to have a great career.*

**pro·mote** Ac /prəˈmoʊt/ *verb*
**1** to give someone a more important job at work: *Her boss promoted her to senior salesperson.*
**2** to help sell something new by telling people about it: *She promoted her new book on the show.*
**3** to help something increase or become more popular: *We hope these visits will promote understanding between our countries.*

**WORD FAMILY: promote**
**promote** *verb* | **promotion** *noun*

**pro·mo·tion** Ac /prəˈmoʊʃən/ *noun*
**1** a move to a better position at work: *Dean got a promotion to manager.*
**2** something you do to make people want to buy or do something: *The music company spends a lot of money on promotion for its bands.*

**prompt** /prɑmpt/ *adjective*
done without delay: *I wrote to the company last week, and received a prompt reply.*
—**promptly** *adverb* without delay: *Callan dealt with the problem promptly before it got any worse.*
—**promptness** *noun* the quality of being prompt

**prone** /proʊn/ *adjective* (*formal*)
likely to do something bad or have something bad happen: *This river is prone to flooding when there is a lot of rain.*

**pro·noun** /ˈproʊnaʊn/ *noun*
a word like "he," "she," "it", etc., which you use instead of using a noun

**pro·nounce** /prəˈnaʊns/ *verb*
to make the sound of a word or letter: *I know how to spell her name but I don't know how to pronounce it.*

**pro·nun·ci·a·tion** /prəˌnʌnsiˈeɪʃən/ *noun*
**1** the way in which a word or letters should sound in a language: *The pronunciation of some words is different in the U.S. and England.*
**2** the way a particular person says a word or letters: *I need to improve my pronunciation in Spanish.*

**proof** /pruf/ *noun*
facts that prove something is true: *There is no proof that humans can get this disease.*

**proof·read** /ˈpruf-rid/ *verb* (**proofread** /ˈprufred/)
to read through a piece of writing in order to correct any mistakes: *A team of people proofread the book to make sure there were no mistakes.*

**prop**[1] /prɑp/ *verb* (**propped**, **propping**)
to make something stay in a particular position, by using something to support it: *He propped his bike against the fence.*

**prop**[2] *noun*
a small object, such as a book or weapon, used by actors in a play or movie

**prop·a·gan·da** /ˌprɑpəˈgændə/ *noun*
information that a government or organization uses to try to make people agree with them. Some propaganda is false: *They did not believe the government propaganda about the enemy.*

**pro·pane** /ˈproʊpeɪn/ *noun*
a gas used for cooking and heating

**pro·pel·ler** /prəˈpelɚ/ *noun*
a piece of equipment with curved parts that turn around to make an airplane or ship move: *The helicopter's propellers began to spin.*

**prop·er** /ˈprɑpɚ/ *adjective* (*formal*)
**1** right or correct: *Our teacher showed us the proper way to throw the ball.*
**2** appropriate: *You can't go skiing without the proper clothes or you'll get wet and cold.*
**3** showing that you know how to behave well: *I wanted a drink, but I didn't think it was proper to ask.*

**prop·er·ly** /ˈprɑpɚli/ *adverb*
in the right way: *My camera isn't working properly. I need to get it fixed.* **SYNONYM: correctly**

**ˌproper ˈnoun** (*also* **ˌproper ˈname**) *noun*
a noun that is the name of a particular

P

person, place, or thing: *"Tom," "Boston," and "January" are proper nouns.*

**prop·er·ty** /ˈprɑpɚti/ *noun* (plural **properties**)
**1** something that someone owns: *The floods caused a lot of damage to personal property.*

**THESAURUS: property**

**possessions** (*formal*) all the things that you own: *The fire destroyed most of their possessions.*

**things** (*informal*) small objects that you own or are carrying: *Just put your things over there.*

**stuff** (*informal*) the personal things that you own, such as clothes or books: *I don't want my little brother to touch my stuff.*

**belongings** things you own, especially things you carry or take with you: *Each child has a drawer to keep their belongings in.*

**2** (*formal*) a piece of land or a building: *They're going to build a house on the property.*
**3** a quality that something has: *In science, children learn about the physical properties of materials, such as whether something is hard or soft.*
[**ORIGIN:** 1200-1300 From the Latin word *proprietas*, which means "ownership," from *proprius*, which means "your own."]

**proph·e·cy** /ˈprɑfəsi/ *noun* (plural **prophecies**)
a statement that says what will happen in the future: *There is a prophecy that the hero will return when his country needs him.*

**proph·et** /ˈprɑfɪt/ *noun*
**1** someone who tells people about God or what will happen in the future: *the prophets in the Bible*
**2 the Prophet** = Muhammad, who began the religion of Islam
—**prophetess** *noun* a woman who tells people about what will happen in the future

**pro·por·tion** [Ac] /prəˈpɔrʃən/ *noun*
**1** an amount or quantity that is part of a whole, used especially when you are talking about the size of that part: *Immigrants form a large proportion of the city's population.*
**2** the relationship between the amount of two different things: *The proportion of older people in the population may rise above 20%.*
**3 proportions** = size or shape: *We are facing a crisis of enormous proportions.*
—**proportional** *adjective* something that is proportional to something else is the right size in relation to it: *The punishment should be proportional to the crime.*

**pro·pos·al** /prəˈpoʊzəl/ *noun*
**1** (*formal*) a plan or suggestion: *The city is considering a proposal to build a stadium.*
**2** the act of asking someone to marry you: *He asked her to marry him and she accepted his proposal.*

**pro·pose** /prəˈpoʊz/ *verb* (*formal*)
**1** to suggest something: *The principal proposed another meeting next week.*
**2** to intend to do something: *I'll explain the problem, and tell you what we propose to do.*
**3** to ask someone to marry you: *Has he proposed to you yet?*

**prop·o·si·tion** /ˌprɑpəˈzɪʃən/ *noun* (*formal*)
**1** a statement in which you express an idea: *Do you agree with the proposition that money can buy you happiness?*
**2** a new law that people in a state or city vote on: *If the proposition passes, there will be more money for building new schools.*

**pro·pri·e·tor** /prəˈpraɪətɚ/ *noun* (*formal*)
an owner of a business: *My uncle was the proprietor of a small hotel.*

**prose** /proʊz/ *noun*
writing that is not poetry: *In his early novels, his prose is simple and clear.*

**pros·e·cute** /ˈprɑsəˌkyut/ *verb*
to say officially that you think someone is guilty of a crime, so that he or she must be judged in a court of law: *The police decided to prosecute him for theft.*
—**prosecutor** /ˈprɑsəˌkyutɚ/ *noun* a lawyer who is trying to show that someone is guilty of a crime
[**ORIGIN:** 1400-1500 From the Latin word *prosecutus*, a form of the verb *prosequi*, which means "to follow and try to catch."]

**pros·e·cu·tion** /ˌprɑsəˈkyuʃən/ *noun*
**the prosecution** = the lawyers in a court of law who are trying to show that someone is guilty of a crime: *The prosecution has to prove that he started the fire deliberately.*
ANTONYM: **the defense**

**pros·pect¹** Ac /ˈprɑspekt/ *noun* (*formal*)
the thought of something that will probably happen in the future: *The prospect of getting married frightened Alice.*

**prospect²** *verb*
to look for gold, silver, oil, etc. under the ground: *They plan to prospect for oil in the Arctic.*
[ORIGIN: 1400-1500 From the Latin word *prospectus*, a form of the verb *prospicere*, which means "to look forward."]

**pro·spec·tive** Ac /prəˈspektɪv/ *adjective* (*formal*)
**prospective customer/buyer, etc.** = someone who may become a customer, a buyer, etc.: *A lot of prospective buyers came to look at the house.*

**pros·per** /ˈprɑspɚ/ *verb* (*formal*)
to be successful or become rich: *Matt worked hard, and his business prospered.*

**pros·per·i·ty** /prɑˈsperəti/ *noun* (*formal*)
the state of having money and being successful: *The country had many years of peace and prosperity.*

**pros·per·ous** /ˈprɑspərəs/ *adjective* (*formal*)
rich and successful: *She was a prosperous businesswoman and drove an expensive car.*
→ see Thesaurus box at **rich**

**pros·ti·tute** /ˈprɑstəˌtut/ *noun*
someone who has sex with people to earn money

**pro·tect** /prəˈtekt/ *verb*
to stop someone or something from being harmed or damaged: *Bike riders should wear helmets to protect their heads.*

**THESAURUS: protect**

**guard** to protect a place or person by staying near them and watching carefully for danger: *Soldiers guarded the camp.*

**shield** to protect someone or something from being damaged or harmed: *She put up her arms to shield her face.*

**give/offer/provide protection** to protect someone from something harmful: *A hat gives some protection from the sun.*

**shelter** (*formal*) to provide a place where someone is protected from the weather or from danger: *A row of trees shelters the house from the wind.*

**preserve** to keep something from being damaged or changed too much: *National Parks help to preserve our wilderness.*

**pro·tec·tion** /prəˈtekʃən/ *noun*
something that protects someone or something: *The trees gave us some protection from the wind.*

**pro·tein** /ˈproʊtin/ *noun*
a substance in food such as meat or eggs that helps your body to grow and be healthy: *Make sure you eat plenty of fruit, vegetables, and protein.*

**pro·test¹** /ˈproʊtest/ *noun*
**1** something that you say or do to show you do not agree with something: *She turned off the TV despite the kids' protests.*
**2** a public event where a large group of people show that they do not agree with something: *There have been protests against the war in all the major cities.*

**pro·test²** /prəˈtest/ *verb*
if a group of people protest, they show in public that they do not agree with something: *Teachers have protested against the larger class sizes.*
—**protester** (*also* **protestor**) *noun* someone who protests about something in public, with a group of other people: *Over 1,000 protesters marched to the Capitol.*

**Prot·es·tant** /ˈprɑtəstənt/ *adjective*
relating to Christian churches that are not Roman Catholic or Orthodox: *There are several Protestant churches in town – a Lutheran one, a Baptist one, and a Methodist one.*
—**Protestant** *noun* someone who belongs to a Protestant church

**pro·to·col** Ac /ˈproʊtəˌkɔl/ *noun*
rules for the correct way to behave: *Any*

P

*organization has its own protocol that members must follow.*

**pro·ton** /ˈproʊtɑn/ *noun*
a very small part in the NUCLEUS of an atom. A proton has a positive charge. → see picture at **atom**

**pro·trac·tor** /proʊˈtræktɚ, prə-/ *noun*
something that you use for measuring and drawing angles. It is in the shape of a half-circle with degrees (0°–180°) marked on it.



**pro·trude** /proʊˈtrud/ *verb* (*formal*)
to stick out from somewhere: *A gun was protruding from his pocket.*
—**protruding** *adjective* sticking out from somewhere: *She had protruding teeth and had to wear braces to correct them.*

proud

**proud** /praʊd/ *adjective*
**1** feeling pleased about something good that was done by you, a member of your family, your country, etc.: *When he graduated, his parents were very proud of him.*

**THESAURUS: proud**

**conceited** (*formal*) very proud of how you look or what you can do, in a way that annoys people: *I don't want to sound conceited, but school was easy for me.*

**vain** very proud of the way you look, in a way that annoys people: *There were a lot of vain guys at the gym who kept looking at themselves in the mirrors.*

**big-headed** (*informal*) behaving in a way that shows you think you are very important or intelligent: *He's a good player, but he is big-headed and the other players don't like him.*

**arrogant** rude and unfriendly because you think that you are more important or intelligent than other people: *He's arrogant and won't listen to anyone else's ideas.*

**2** wanting to do things for yourself so that you get respect from other people: *They were proud people, who wouldn't accept any help from the government.*
—**proudly** *adverb* in a way that shows you feel proud: *Johnny proudly showed me his test score.*

**prove** /pruv/ *verb* (**proved**, **proved** *or* **proven** /ˈpruvən/)
**1** to show that something is true: *The police were able to prove that she was guilty.*
**2** (*formal*) if something proves to be difficult, helpful, effective, etc., you find out that it is difficult, helpful, effective, etc.: *He doesn't have a high school diploma, so getting a job has proved difficult.*

**prov·en** /ˈpruvən/ *adjective*
shown to be good or true: *He is a player of proven ability with an excellent record of scoring touchdowns.*

**prov·erb** /ˈprɑvɚb/ *noun*
a short well-known statement that gives advice about life: *The old proverb "An apple a day keeps the doctor away" tells you that eating apples is good for your health.*
**SYNONYM: saying**
→ see Thesaurus box at **phrase**

**pro·vide** /prəˈvaɪd/ *verb*
to give something that someone needs: *The school provides books for the children.*
**PHRASAL VERB**
**provide for someone**
to be able to buy the food, clothes, and other things that someone needs: *Dad worked hard, but it wasn't easy to provide for five children.*

**pro·vid·ed** /prəˈvaɪdɪd/ (*also* **pro·vid·ing** /prəˈvaɪdɪŋ/) *conjunction*
**provided/provided that** = if something happens: *You'll pass the class, provided that you do the work.*

**prov·ince** /ˈprɑvɪns/ *noun*
a large area of a country, with its own local government: *British Columbia and Alberta are two of the western provinces of Canada.*
—**provincial** /prəˈvɪnʃəl/ *adjective* relating to a province: *the provincial capital*

**pro·vi·sions** /prəˈvɪʒənz/ *plural noun* (*formal*)
food supplies: *We had enough provisions for at least two weeks in the woods.*

**pro·voke** /prəˈvoʊk/ *verb*
to deliberately make someone angry: *She provoked him by kissing another guy.*

**prowl** /praʊl/ *verb*
to move around quietly, especially to hunt: *Cats go out at night to prowl around.*

**pru·dent** /ˈprudənt/ *adjective* (*formal*)
sensible and careful: *It is prudent to save some of your money.*

**prune** /prun/ *noun*
a dried PLUM (=type of fruit)

**pry** /praɪ/ *verb* (**pried**, **pries**)
**1** to open or remove something using force: *Jim used a metal bar to pry the door open.*
**2** to try to find out about someone's life when that person does not want you to: *Movie stars always have people prying into their lives.*

**P.S.**
used before adding something at the end of a letter. P.S. is short for "postscript," which means "written after": *P.S. See you in December!*

**psalm** /sɑm/ *noun*
a song or poem praising God: *a psalm from the Bible*

**pseu·do·nym** /ˈsudnˌɪm/ *noun*
a name that a writer or artist uses instead of his or her real name: *"Mark Twain" is the pseudonym that the writer Samuel Clemens used.*
[**ORIGIN:** 1800-1900 From the Greek words *pseudes* and *onyma*, which mean "false" and "name."]

**psy·chi·a·try** /saɪˈkaɪətri/ *noun*
the study and treatment of mental illness: *He studied psychiatry because he wanted to understand the human mind.*
—**psychiatrist** *noun* a doctor who treats people who have a mental illness
[**ORIGIN:** 1800-1900 From the Greek words *psyche* and *iatreia*, which mean "soul or mind" and "cure."]

**psy·chic**[1] /ˈsaɪkɪk/ *adjective*
someone who is psychic seems to have strange mental abilities such as knowing what other people are thinking: *His followers believe that he has psychic powers and can see into the future.*

**psychic**[2] *noun*
someone who has strange mental abilities such as knowing what other people are thinking

**psy·cho·an·a·lyst** /ˌsaɪkoʊˈænl-ɪst/ *noun*
someone who helps people with problems by listening to them talk about their lives and their feelings **SYNONYM: analyst**

**psy·chol·o·gy** [Ac] /saɪˈkɑlədʒi/ *noun*
the study of the mind and how it affects behavior: *He's interested in child psychology, especially how children learn.*
—**psychological** /ˌsaɪkəˈlɑdʒɪkəl/ *adjective* relating to the mind: *Children who are not loved when they are young may have psychological problems later.*
—**psychologist** *noun* someone who has studied psychology

**psy·cho·path** /ˈsaɪkəˌpæθ/ *noun*
someone who has a mental illness and behaves in a violent way: *Her killer was a psychopath who had killed several times before.*

**PTA** *noun*
(**Parent-Teacher Association**) an organization of the teachers and parents at a particular school

**pu·ber·ty** /ˈpyubəˑti/ *noun*
the time when your body changes from a child to an adult: *Puberty usually takes place from about ages 10 to 15.*

**pub·lic**[1] /ˈpʌblɪk/ *adjective*
**1** relating to all the people in an area or country: *Dirty drinking water is a danger to public health.*
**2** for anyone to use: *A lot of people use cars rather than public transportation.* **ANTONYM: private**
**3** relating to the government and the services it provides for people: *The Republican Party wants to reduce public spending.*

P

4 **make something public** = to tell something to all the people in an area or country: *The White House did not make this information public.*

—**publicly** *adverb* in a way that everyone can see or hear: *The company publicly apologized for its mistake.*

[**ORIGIN:** 1400-1500 From the Latin word *publicus*, from *populus*, which means "the people."]

P

**public²** *noun*

1 **the public** = all the people in an area or country: *The museum is open to the public five days a week.*

2 **in public** = in a place where anyone can see or hear: *They tried not to argue in public.*

**pub·li·ca·tion** Ac /ˌpʌbləˈkeɪʃən/ *noun*

1 the process of printing a book, newspaper, or magazine and sending it to stores for people to read and buy: *She was in New York for the publication of her new book.*

2 a book, magazine, or newspaper: *I read "Sports Illustrated" and some other publications.*

**pub·lic·i·ty** /pʌˈblɪsəti/ *noun*

the attention that newspapers, television, or radio gives to someone or something: *His new movie has received a lot of publicity.*

—**publicize** /ˈpʌbləˌsaɪz/ *verb* to give information about something to as many people as possible: *They publicized the concert by putting a short video on the Internet.*

**ˌpublic ˈschool** *noun*

a school that everyone can go to because the government pays for it

**ˌpublic ˈservice** *noun*

jobs that help people, especially jobs in the government: *She spent many years in public service, serving on the school board and on the city council.*

**pub·lish** Ac /ˈpʌblɪʃ/ *verb*

to print a book, magazine, or newspaper and make it available for people to read and buy: *The book was first published in 1968.*

[**ORIGIN:** 1300-1400 From the Latin word *publicare*, which means "to make something public."]

**WORD FAMILY: publish**

**publish** *verb* | **publisher** *noun* | **publication** *noun*

**pub·lish·er** Ac /ˈpʌblɪʃɚ/ *noun*

a person or company that produces and sells books, newspapers, or magazines

**puck** /pʌk/ *noun*

the flat round thing that the players hit in a game of HOCKEY

**pud·ding** /ˈpʊdɪŋ/ *noun*

a thick sweet food that you make with milk, eggs, and sugar: *chocolate pudding*

[**ORIGIN:** 1200-1300 Probably from the French word *boudin*, from the Latin word *botellus*, which means "sausage." In the past, some kinds of puddings were boiled in a bag, like a sausage being cooked in its skin.]

**pud·dle** /ˈpʌdl/ *noun*

a small pool of water on the ground or road: *The kids splashed in the puddles after it rained.*

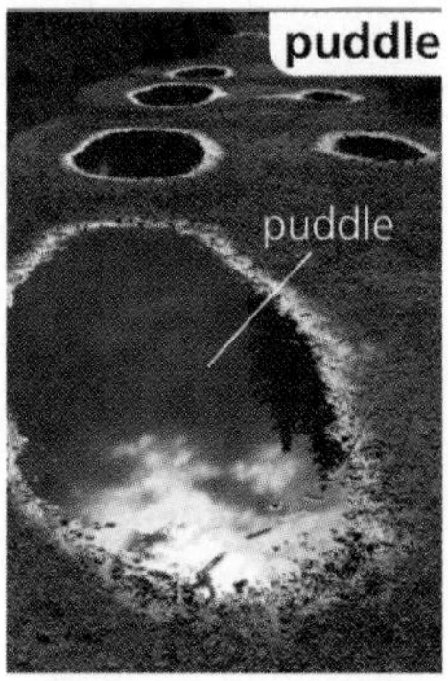


**pueb·lo** /ˈpweblou/ *noun*

1 a small town of Native American homes in the southwest U.S. The homes are made of stone or ADOBE (=earth and STRAW bricks) and are built next to and on top of each other.

2 a small town, especially in the southwest U.S. near Mexico

**puff¹** /pʌf/ *verb*

to breathe quickly and with difficulty, for example because you have been running or carrying something heavy: *Grandpa was puffing after climbing the stairs.*

**puff²** *noun*

a small amount of air, smoke, or wind: *Some puffs of smoke were coming from the chimney.*

**puff·y** /ˈpʌfi/ *adjective*

puffy eyes, cheeks, or faces are swollen: *Her eyes were red and puffy from crying.*

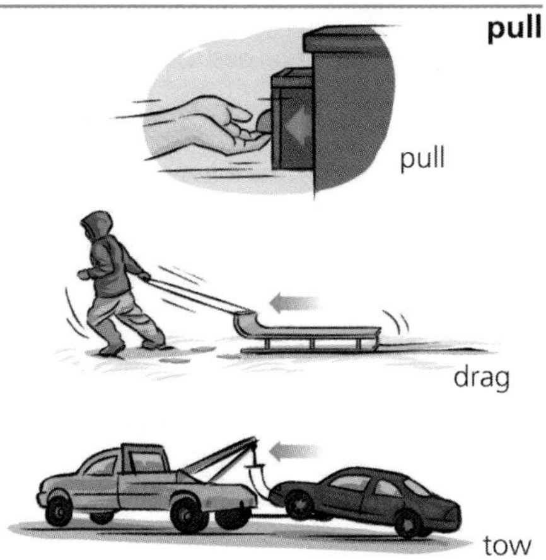


**pull¹** /pʊl/ *verb*

**1** to use your hands to move something toward you: *I pulled the door shut.* | *Stop pulling my hair!* **ANTONYM: push**

**THESAURUS: pull**

**tug** to pull something using sudden short movements: *The little boy was tugging at her sleeve.*

**drag** to pull something heavy along the ground: *She dragged a chair over to their table.*

**haul** to pull something big and heavy somewhere, especially using a rope: *The men hauled all the furniture upstairs.*

**tow** to pull a vehicle along using a rope or chain: *He parked in a red zone, and they towed his car away.*

**heave** to lift or pull something heavy with a lot of effort: *I heaved the toolbox onto the table.*

**2** to make something move behind you in the direction you are moving: *The truck was pulling a trailer.* **ANTONYM: push**

**3** to remove something from its place, especially by using force: *The dentist pulled out the tooth.*

**4** to injure a muscle by stretching it too much when doing a physical activity: *He pulled a muscle in his back picking up a bag of cement.* **SYNONYM: strain**

**5 pull someone's leg** (*informal*) = to tell someone something that is not true, as a joke: *I don't think he was serious – he was just pulling your leg.*

**6 pull a gun/knife (on someone)** = to take out a gun or knife and be ready to use it: *The man suddenly pulled a gun and began shooting.*

**PHRASAL VERBS**

**pull away**
to start to drive away from a place: *She watched the cars slowly pull away.*

**pull back**
if soldiers pull back, they move back from a place: *The general gave the order for his soldiers to pull back.*

**pull for someone** (*informal*)
to want someone to succeed, and encourage them to do this: *The fans were all pulling for their team.*

**pull in (something)**
if a car pulls in, it drives into a place and stops: *I looked out the window just as Reggie was pulling in the driveway.*

**pull off**
**1 pull something off** = to quickly take off some clothes: *He pulled off his wet clothes and put them by the fire.*
**2 pull off (a road)** = to leave a road in order to stop or to turn into another road: *They pulled off the freeway and went to get some lunch.*
**3 pull something off** (*informal*) = to succeed in doing something difficult: *Tom thinks he can win, but I don't think he will pull it off.*

**pull something on**
to quickly put some clothes on: *She pulled on her sweater and ran downstairs.*

**pull out**
**1** to drive onto a road, especially when other cars are driving more quickly than you are: *Another car suddenly pulled out in front of me, and I had to brake.*
**2** to leave a dangerous place or situation: *Firefighters had to pull out because the fire was too dangerous.*

**pull over**
to drive to the side of a road and stop your car: *The police officer told us to pull over.*

P

**pull through** (*informal*)
to stay alive after a serious injury or illness: *He's very weak after his operation, but his doctor says that he will pull through.*

**pull yourself together**
to stop being upset or frightened: *Stop crying and pull yourself together – you're going to be fine.*

**pull up**
**1 pull up** = if a car pulls up, it stops: *The car pulled up at the stop lights.*
**2 pull up a chair/stool, etc.** = to get a chair and sit down near someone who is already sitting

**pull²** *noun*
**1** the action of holding something and using force to make it move toward you: *Give the rope a good pull.* **ANTONYM: push**
**2** (*informal*) power and influence: *He is a very wealthy businessman, and he has a lot of pull in this city.*

**pul·ley** /ˈpʊli/ *noun*
a piece of equipment for lifting things, that has a rope that goes around a wheel. You attach one end of the rope to the object you are lifting, and pull the other end: *They hooked the engine to the pulley and lifted it off the floor.*

**pulp** /pʌlp/ *noun*
**1** the soft inside part of a fruit or vegetable: *The orange juice had a lot of pulp in it.*
**2** a soft substance that is almost liquid: *Mash the bananas to a pulp.*

**pul·pit** /ˈpʊlpɪt/ *noun*
a high place where a priest or minister stands to speak to people in a church

**pulse** /pʌls/ *noun*
the regular beat that you can feel as your heart moves blood around your body: *The nurse took my pulse and said it was a little fast.*

**pu·ma** /ˈpumə/ *noun*
another word for a COUGAR

**pump¹** /pʌmp/ *noun*
a machine that makes liquid or gas go into or out of something: *He filled up the car at the gas pump. | Do you have a bicycle pump? My bike has a flat tire.* → see picture at **bicycle**

**pump²** *verb*
**1** to make liquid or gas move in a particular direction, using a pump: *The farmers pumped water from the river onto their fields.*
**2 pump money into something** = to supply a lot of money for something: *The state pumped money into the research project.*

**pump·kin** /ˈpʌmpkɪn/ *noun*
a very large orange fruit that grows on the ground: *At Halloween, children cut faces in pumpkins and put candles inside.*
[**ORIGIN:** 1600-1700 From the French word *pompon*, which means "melon or pumpkin," from the Greek word *pepon*, which means "ripe."]

**pun** /pʌn/ *noun*
a joke using a word that has two very different meanings: *Here's a good pun: "Why do leopards never escape from the zoo? Because they're always spotted."*

**punch¹** /pʌntʃ/ *verb*
**1** to hit someone hard with your hand closed: *He punched me in the stomach, and I bent over in pain.* → see picture on page **A3**
**2** to make a hole in something, using something sharp: *I punched three holes in the paper so I could put it on the rings in my binder.*
→ see Thesaurus box at **hit¹**

**punch²** *noun*
**1** a hard hit with your hand closed: *I'll give you a punch on the nose!*
**2** a drink made from fruit juice, sugar, and water: *We made a bowl of punch for the party.*

**punc·tu·al** /ˈpʌŋktʃuəl/ *adjective*
someone who is punctual arrives at exactly the right time: *She's very punctual and has never been late for school.*
—**punctually** *adverb* at the right time: *He's a good customer who pays his bills punctually.*
—**punctuality** /ˌpʌŋktʃuˈæləti/ *noun* the quality of being punctual

**punc·tu·ate** /ˈpʌŋktʃuˌeɪt/ *verb*
to use punctuation marks in your writing: *The students are learning how to punctuate a sentence correctly.*

**punc·tu·a·tion** /ˌpʌŋktʃuˈeɪʃən/ *noun*
the use of punctuation marks in your writing:

*Learning the rules of punctuation will make your writing better.*

**ˌpunctuˈation mark** *noun*
a sign, such as a PERIOD (.), COMMA (,), or QUESTION MARK (?), that you use in your writing to make sentences clearer: *A period is the punctuation mark you use at the end of a sentence.*

**punc·ture** /ˈpʌŋktʃɚ/ *verb (formal)*
to make a small hole in something, so that air or liquid comes out: *He punctured the balloon with a pin.*
—**puncture** *noun* a small hole made by something sharp

**pun·ish** /ˈpʌnɪʃ/ *verb*
to make someone suffer because he or she has done something wrong: *I came home late, so my father punished me by not giving me my allowance.*

**pun·ish·ment** /ˈpʌnɪʃmənt/ *noun*
something that is done to punish someone: *The punishment for his crime was four years in prison.*

**punk** /pʌŋk/ *noun (informal)*
a young man who often has fights and does illegal things: *Some punks started a fight in the street.*

**pu·pa** /ˈpyupə/ *noun* (plural **pupae** /-pi/)
a young insect at a stage when it is protected inside a cover before it becomes an adult: *The pupae develop into adult ants.*

**pu·pil** /ˈpyupəl/ *noun*
**1** *(formal)* a child in school: *There are 500 pupils in my school.*
**2** the small black part in the middle of your eye: *In bright light, your pupils get smaller.* → see picture at **eye**
[**ORIGIN:** Sense 1 is from the Latin word *pupillus*, which means "young boy who is taken care of." First used in English, 1300-1400. Sense 2 is from the Latin word *pupilla*, which means "little girl or doll." You can see a little image of yourself in someone else's eye. First used in English, 1300-1400.]

**pup·pet** /ˈpʌpɪt/ *noun*
a toy in the shape of a person or animal. You move a puppet by pulling its strings or by putting your hand inside it: *He had a puppet on each hand and was making them talk to each other.*
—**puppeteer** /ˌpʌpəˈtɪr/ *noun* someone who makes and uses puppets
[**ORIGIN:** 1500-1600 From the French word *poupette*, which means "little doll," from the Latin word *pupa*, which means "doll or girl."]

**pup·py** /ˈpʌpi/ *noun* (plural **puppies**)
a young dog

**pur·chase**[1] [Ac] /ˈpɚtʃəs/ *verb (formal)*
to buy something: *You can purchase tickets over the phone.*
—**purchaser** *noun* someone who purchases something
→ see Thesaurus box at **buy**
[**ORIGIN:** 1200-1300 From the old French word *purchacier*, which means "to try to get," from *chacier*, meaning "to run after and try to catch."]

**purchase**[2] [Ac] *noun (formal)*
**1** the act of buying something: *I made a purchase using my credit card.*
**2** something you bought: *The store will deliver your purchases.*

**pure** /pyʊr/ *adjective*
**1** a pure substance or material is not mixed with anything else: *The ring was made of pure gold.* **ANTONYM: impure**
**2** pure air or water is clean and does not contain anything harmful: *The water is pure, so you can drink it.* **ANTONYM: impure**
**3** **pure joy/pleasure/sorrow, etc.** = a feeling of complete happiness, sadness, etc.: *A smile of pure joy appeared on her face when she read the good news.* **SYNONYM: total**
—**purity** *noun* the quality of being pure: *I love the purity of the air in the mountains.*

**WORD FAMILY: pure**
**pure** *adjective* | **impure** *adjective* | **purify** *verb* | **purity** *noun*

**pure·ly** /ˈpyʊrli/ *adverb (formal)*
in every way: *I found the money purely by accident – someone had dropped it in the street.* **SYNONYMS: completely, totally**

**pu·ri·fy** /ˈpyʊrəˌfaɪ/ *verb* (**purified**, **purifies**)
to remove the dirty parts from something such as water or air: *Purify the water by putting it through a filter.*
—**purification** /ˌpyʊrəfəˈkeɪʃən/ *noun* the process of purifying something

**pur·ple** /ˈpɚpəl/ *noun, adjective*
a dark color that is a mixture of red and blue: *She had a purple bruise on her leg.*

**pur·pose** /ˈpɚpəs/ *noun*
**1** the thing you are trying to achieve by doing something: *The purpose of exercise is to keep you healthy.*

**THESAURUS: purpose**

**aim** something that you want to achieve: *Her aim is to go to college and get a degree.*

**goal** something that you hope to achieve in the future: *My goal is to run in the Olympics.*

**objective** (*formal*) something that you are working hard to achieve: *The state set an objective for schools: every child should be reading by age nine.*

**2 on purpose** = if you do something on purpose, you intend to do it and it is not an accident: *He pushed me on purpose because he was mad at me.* **SYNONYM: deliberately**; **ANTONYM: accidentally**

**pur·pose·ful** /ˈpɚpəsfəl/ *adjective* (*formal*)
having a clear aim or purpose: *Children work harder when their work is purposeful.*

**pur·pose·ly** /ˈpɚpəsli/ *adverb* (*formal*)
if you do something purposely, you plan to do it and it is not an accident: *I purposely closed the door so no one could hear our conversation.* **SYNONYMS: on purpose, deliberately**; **ANTONYM: accidentally**

**purr** /pɚ/ *verb*
if a cat purrs, it makes a soft low sound when it is happy
—**purr** *noun* the sound a cat makes when it is happy

**purse** /pɚs/ *noun*
a bag that women use to carry money and other things: *She took her keys out of her purse.* → see picture at **bag**
**[ORIGIN:** 1200-1300 From the Latin word *bursa*, which means "bag."**]**

**pur·sue** Ac /pɚˈsu/ *verb* (*formal*)
**1** to chase someone in order to catch him or her: *The police pursued the man who had stolen the car.*
**2** to work hard in order to achieve something: *He wanted to pursue a career in acting.* **SYNONYM: follow**

**pur·suit** Ac /pɚˈsut/ *noun* (*formal*)
**1** the act of chasing someone in order to catch him or her: *A truck drove by fast, with a police car in pursuit.*
**2** an activity that you spend a lot of time doing: *She enjoys pursuits such as reading and sewing.*
**3** the act of trying to get something: *He'd spent his adult life in the pursuit of money; he ended up rich, but lonely.*

**pus** /pʌs/ *noun*
a yellow liquid that comes out of an infected part of your body: *The wound had pus in it.*

**push**[1] /pʊʃ/ *verb*
**1** to move something away from you by pressing it with your hand: *We pushed the car out of the garage.* | *She pushed her sister into the swimming pool.* **ANTONYM: pull** → see picture on page **A3**

**THESAURUS: push**

**poke** to push someone or something with your finger or something sharp: *Jill poked Miguel in the arm to get his attention.*

**shove** to push someone or something in a rough way: *He shoved her out of the way.*

**nudge** to push someone gently with your elbow to get his or her attention: *"Move over," she said, nudging my arm.*

**2** to press a button to make a machine start or stop working: *Push the green button to start the engine.*
**3** to go past people by moving them out of your way with your arms or body: *The men pushed their way to the front of the crowd.*
**4** to try hard to persuade someone to do something: *My parents pushed me into going to college.*
**5** to make someone work very hard: *He has been pushing himself too hard in order to make straight A's.*
→ see Thesaurus box at **press**[1]
**[ORIGIN:** 1300-1400 From the Latin word *pulsare*, which means "to hit."**]**

**PHRASAL VERBS**

**push someone around**
(*informal*) to tell someone what to do in a rude or threatening way: *Tell the big kids to stop pushing you around.*

**push something through**
to get a new law or plan accepted quickly, especially when other people oppose it: *The president tried to push his plan through.*

**push something up**
to make something increase: *The high oil prices pushed up the cost of air travel.*

**push²** *noun*
**1** the act of pushing someone or something: *I'm sure that the door will open if you give it a good push.* **ANTONYM: pull**
**2** a situation in which someone works very hard to get or achieve something: *The school is making a big push to get parents to help at the school.*

**ˈpush-up** *noun*
an exercise in which you lie facing the floor, and push yourself up with your arms: *I do push-ups to make my arms and chest stronger.*

**push·y** /ˈpʊʃi/ *adjective*
trying hard to get what you want, in a rude way: *The salesman was pushy, and wouldn't go away when I said I didn't want to buy anything.*

**puss·y·cat** /ˈpʊsiˌkæt/ *noun* (*informal*)
**1** a cat
**2** a kind and gentle person: *He looks tough, but he's a real pussycat.*

**put** /pʊt/ *verb* (**put**, **putting**)
**1** to move something into a place or position: *"Where did you put my shoes?" "They're by the door." | She put the money in the bank.*
**2** to write or print something: *Put your name at the top of your answer sheet.*
**3** to make someone be in a situation or make someone have a feeling: *The sunshine put everyone in a good mood.*
**4** to say something in a particular way: *If you don't understand what I'm saying, I'll put it another way.*
**5 put an end to something/put a stop to something** = to stop an activity that is bad or not acceptable: *The city authorities want to put an end to the violence.*
**6 put something behind you** = to try to forget about a bad experience or a mistake so that it does not affect you now: *I had some problems, but now I have to put them behind me.*
[**ORIGIN:** From the old English word *putian.*]

**PHRASAL VERBS**

**put something away**
to put something in the place where it is usually kept: *Make sure that you put all your clothes away before you go to bed.*

**put something forward**
to suggest a plan or idea: *I wanted to put forward a suggestion.*

**put off**
**1 put something off** = to delay something: *We decided to put off our trip to Europe until next year.* **SYNONYM: postpone**
**2 put someone off (something)** = to make someone dislike something or not want to do something: *The fruit has a strong smell, which puts some people off.*

**put on**
**1 put something on** = to put a piece of clothing on your body: *He put on his best suit for the wedding.* **ANTONYM: take off**
**2 put on weight/five pounds, etc.** = to become fatter and heavier: *She put on a lot of weight after she had the baby.*

**put out**
**1 put out a fire/cigarette** = to make a fire or cigarette stop burning: *It took almost three hours to put out the fire.* **SYNONYM: extinguish**
**2 put out your hand/arm/foot** = to move your hand or foot away from your body: *She put out her hand and touched the baby's face.*

**put someone through something**
to make someone do something that is very bad or difficult: *The soldiers are put through eight weeks of basic training.*

**put together**
**1 put something together** = to make something by joining its different parts together, for example a model: *It took a long time to put the toy together.*
**2 put together** = combined: *He earns more money than the rest of us put together.*

**put up**
**1 put something up** = to build something such as a building, wall, or fence: *We put up a new fence last summer.*
**2 put something up** = to attach a picture, notice, or decorations to a wall, so that people can see them: *Someone had put up a sign on the wall advertising free puppies.*
**3 put someone up** (*informal*) = to let someone stay in your house: *One of his friends offered to put me up while I was in town.*
**put up with someone or something**
to accept an unpleasant situation or person without complaining: *Her brother is so annoying – I don't know how she puts up with him.*

puzzle

**puz·zle¹** /ˈpʌzl/ *noun*
**1** a picture that has been cut into many pieces. You put the pieces together to make the whole picture: *We put together a 100-piece puzzle of a map of the United States.*
**SYNONYM: jigsaw puzzle**
**2** a game in which you have to think hard to solve a problem: *Could you help me do this number puzzle?*
**3** something that is difficult to understand or explain: *The way an engine works is a puzzle to me.*
→ see Thesaurus box at **game**

**puzzle²** *verb*
if something puzzles you, it confuses you because you cannot understand it: *It puzzled me that he hadn't asked for help sooner.*
—**puzzled** *adjective* confused because you cannot understand something: *Adam looked puzzled and said, "Why isn't Kevin here?"*
—**puzzling** *adjective* making you puzzled: *Her decision not to run was puzzling, because she had won all of her races so far that year.*
**PHRASAL VERB**
**puzzle over something**
to think for a long time about something because you do not understand it: *He sat puzzling over his homework.*

**py·lon** /ˈpaɪlɑn/ *noun*
a tall metal structure that supports wires carrying electricity

**pyr·a·mid** /ˈpɪrəmɪd/ *noun*
**1** a solid shape with a flat base and four sides that form a point at the top: *The sides of a pyramid are triangles.* → see picture at **shape**
**2** a very large stone building in the shape of a pyramid, in Mexico or Egypt: *We visited the pyramids near Mexico City.*

**py·thon** /ˈpaɪθɑn/ *noun*
a large snake that kills animals for food by curling around them and pressing them

# Qq

**Q-tip** /ˈkyu tɪp/ *noun (trademark)*
a small thin stick with cotton at each end, that is used for cleaning parts of your body such as your ears

**quack**[1] /kwæk/ *verb*
if a duck quacks, it makes a short loud sound

**quack**[2] *noun*
**1** the sound a duck makes
**2** (*informal*) someone who pretends to be a doctor: *The doctor was a quack and had never been to medical school.*

**quad·ri·lat·er·al** /ˌkwɑdrəˈlætərəl/ *noun*
a flat shape with four straight sides
—**quadrilateral** *adjective* having four straight sides

**quadrilateral**

**quad·ru·ple** /kwɑˈdrupəl/ *verb (formal)*
to become four times as big as before: *The number of children at the school has quadrupled, from 100 to 400.*
—**quadruple** *adjective* four times as big as before: *a quadruple increase in price*
[**ORIGIN:** 1300-1400 From the Latin word *quadruplus*, which means "four times as much," from *quadri-*, meaning "four."]

**quail** /kweɪl/ *noun*
a small bird that people hunt for food or as a sport

**quaint** /kweɪnt/ *adjective*
a quaint place is pretty, in an old-fashioned way: *This quaint little town still looks as it did in the 1950s.*

**quake**[1] /kweɪk/ *verb*
to shake because you are afraid: *"I saw the ghost!" she said, quaking with fear.*
**SYNONYM: tremble**

**quake**[2] *noun (informal)*
a strong and sudden shaking of the ground: *Many buildings were destroyed in the quake.*
**SYNONYM: earthquake**

**qual·i·fi·ca·tion** /ˌkwɑləfəˈkeɪʃən/ *noun*
experience or skills that make you able to do a particular job: *He had all the qualifications that he needed to be a teacher.*

**qual·i·fied** /ˈkwɑləˌfaɪd/ *adjective*
having the right knowledge or skills to do something: *She is qualified to teach drama as well as English.* | *There is a shortage of qualified workers.*

**qual·i·fi·er** /ˈkwɑləˌfaɪɚ/ *noun*
**1** someone who has proved that he or she is good enough to be in a race or competition: *She was the fastest qualifier for the final race.*
**2** a word or phrase that tells you more about another word or phrase: *In the phrase "her new red bike," "new" and "red" are qualifiers.*

**qual·i·fy** /ˈkwɑləˌfaɪ/ *verb* (**qualified, qualifies**)
**1** to have the education or skills that you need to do a particular job: *A high-school diploma qualifies you for a lot of jobs.*
**2** to be able to have or do something because of something you have done or because you are in a particular situation: *Poor children qualify for free school lunches.*

**WORD FAMILY: qualify**
**qualify** *verb* | **qualification** *noun* | **qualified** *adjective* | **unqualified** *adjective* | **disqualify** *verb*

**qual·i·ty** /ˈkwɑləti/ *noun* (plural **qualities**)
**1** how good or bad something is: *The quality of his work is excellent.* | *All the clothes in the store are of the highest quality.* | *They complained about the poor quality of the food.*
**2** something that is part of a person's character or the nature of a thing: *His greatest quality is his kindness.* | *The plant has medicinal qualities.*

**quan·ti·fy** /ˈkwɑntəˌfaɪ/ *verb* (**quantified, quantifies**) (*formal*)
to measure something and say how big it is in numbers: *The damage to the company is difficult to quantify in a dollar amount.*

**quan·ti·ty** /ˈkwɑntəti/ *noun* (plural **quantities**) (*formal*)
an amount of something: *He drank a large quantity of water.*

**quar·an·tine** /ˈkwɔrənˌtin/ *noun*
**in quarantine** = if a person or animal is in quarantine, they must stay in a place away from other people or animals so they do not pass on a dangerous disease: *His dog was kept in quarantine for 120 days after arriving in Hawaii.*
—**quarantine** *verb* (*formal*) to put a person or animal in quarantine
**[ORIGIN:** 1600-1700 From the Italian word *quarantina*, which means "period of forty days," from *quaranta*, meaning "forty." A ship with people who might be carrying a disease would not be allowed to enter a port for forty days.**]**

**quar·rel¹** /ˈkwɔrəl/ *noun*
an angry argument: *We had a quarrel about money.*
**[ORIGIN:** 1300-1400 From the Latin word *querela*, which means "complaint."**]**

**quarrel²** *verb*
to have an angry argument: *The children are always quarreling over something.*

**quar·ry** /ˈkwɔri/ *noun* (plural **quarries**)
a place where vehicles and machines dig stone or sand out of the ground: *The marble comes from a quarry in Colorado.*
**[ORIGIN:** 1300-1400 From the old French word *quarriere*, from the Latin word *quadrare*, which means "to make something square." A quarry was a place where square blocks of stone were cut.**]**

**quart** /kwɔrt/ *noun*
a unit for measuring liquid, equal to two PINTs or 0.95 liters: *There are two pints in one quart.* | *a quart of milk*

**quar·ter** /ˈkwɔrtɚ/ *noun*
**1** one of four equal parts of something: *A quarter of 44 is 11.* | *Cut the sandwiches into quarters.*
**2** a coin worth 25 cents: *He put a quarter in the machine.*
**3** 15 minutes: *I left home at a quarter after 7:00* (=7:15). | *I'll meet you at quarter to three* (=2:45). | *The bus leaves at quarter of ten* (=9:45). | *The baby cried for a quarter of an hour* (=15 minutes). | *Can you be ready to go in three-quarters of an hour* (=45 minutes)*?*
**4** one of the four equal periods that a basketball or football game is divided into: *The score was 66-58 in the third quarter.*
**5** one of the four periods into which a college year is divided: *I'm taking three classes this quarter.*
**6** a period of three months – used when talking about business or financial matters: *The company's profits fell in the first quarter.*
→ see Thesaurus box at **money**
**[ORIGIN:** 1200-1300 From the Latin word *quartus*, which means "fourth."**]**

**quar·ter·back** /ˈkwɔrtɚˌbæk/ *noun*
the player in football who throws the ball and directs the team's attacking play: *The quarterback passed the ball to the receiver.*

**quarter-hour** *noun*
15 minutes: *The break lasts a quarter-hour.*

**ˈquarter inch** *noun*
a unit for measuring length that is equal to 6.35 MILLIMETERs: *There are four quarter inches in an inch.*

**quar·ter·ly** /ˈkwɔrtɚli/ *adjective, adverb*
every three months, or four times a year: *The first quarterly report comes at the end of March.*

**ˈquarter moon** *noun*
the moon when you can only see half of it because it is one quarter or three quarters of the way through its monthly CYCLE

**quar·tet** /kwɔrˈtet/ *noun*
a group of four musicians or singers: *A string quartet has two violin players, one viola player, and one cello player.*

**quartz** /kwɔrts/ *noun*
a hard rock used in electronic watches and clocks

**quartz**

**quay** /keɪ/ *noun*
a place where boats can be tied up, or can be loaded and unloaded: *We went to the quay and got on the boat.* **SYNONYM: dock**

**quea·sy** /ˈkwizi/ *adjective*
feeling that you are going to VOMIT: *The sight of blood makes me queasy.*

**queen** /kwin/ *noun*
**1** the female ruler of a country, or the wife of a king: *Elizabeth I became Queen of England in 1558.*
**2** a card used in card games, which has a

picture of a queen on it: *He put down the queen of diamonds.*
**3** a female BEE, WASP, or ANT that lays eggs
[**ORIGIN:** From the old English word *cwen*, which means "woman or queen."]

**ˈqueen-size** *adjective*
a queen-size bed is a bed for two people that is bigger than the usual size

**queer** /kwɪr/ *adjective*
strange and not normal: *I had this queer feeling, as if I was in someone else's body.* **SYNONYMS: peculiar, odd**

**quench** /kwentʃ/ *verb* (*formal*)
**quench your thirst** = to drink something so that you stop feeling thirsty: *I drank some water to quench my thirst.*

**que·ry** /ˈkwɪri/ *noun* (plural **queries**) (*formal*)
a question asking for more information about something: *Here is your bill – if you have any queries, call me.*
—**query** *verb* to ask a question about something because you want more information: *I queried the price because it seemed too high.*

**ques·tion**[1] /ˈkwestʃən/ *noun*
**1** something you say or write to ask something: *Can I ask you a question – how old are you?* | *You didn't answer my question.* | *She asked some questions about the math homework.* **ANTONYM: answer**
**2** a part of a test that asks you to give information: *The history test had twenty questions.*
**3** a problem that people need to talk about and deal with: *We discussed the question of where Jon should live.* **SYNONYM: issue**
**4 be out of the question** = to not be possible or allowed: *No, you're not going. It's out of the question!*
[**ORIGIN:** 1200-1300 From the Latin word *quaestio*, from *quaestus*, which is a form of the verb *quaerere*, which means "to ask."]

**question**[2] *verb* (*formal*)
**1** to ask someone about something: *Police questioned him about the crime.*
**2** to start to have doubts about something: *I'm not questioning your honesty because I know I can trust you.*
→ see Thesaurus box at **ask**

**ques·tion·a·ble** /ˈkwestʃənəbəl/ *adjective* (*formal*)
not certain: *It's questionable whether she will pass the test because she hasn't done much studying.* **SYNONYM: doubtful**

**ˈquestion mark** *noun*
the sign (?), used in writing at the end of a question

**ques·tion·naire** /ˌkwestʃəˈner/ *noun*
a written set of questions that someone gives to a large number of people in order to collect information: *I filled out a questionnaire about where I buy my clothes.*

**quiche** /kiʃ/ *noun*
a mixture of eggs, cheese, and vegetables cooked in a PIE CRUST

**quick** /kwɪk/ *adjective*
**1** something that is quick takes only a short time: *It was just a quick visit – I was only there for five minutes.* **SYNONYM: brief**; **ANTONYM: long**
**2** someone or something that is quick moves fast or does things fast: *He's a quick worker and always finishes first.* | *a quick sports car* **SYNONYM: fast**; **ANTONYM: slow**
[**ORIGIN:** From the old English word *cwic*, which means "alive." The idea of something being alive changed to the idea of something being lively and active.]

**quick·ly** /ˈkwɪkli/ *adverb*
**1** fast: *He was walking so quickly that she could not keep up with him.*
**2** after a very short time: *I quickly discovered I had made a mistake.* **SYNONYM: soon**
→ see Thesaurus box at **fast**[2]

**quick·sand** /ˈkwɪksænd/ *noun*
wet sand that is very dangerous because you sink down into it if you walk on it: *In the movie, he gets sucked into quicksand.*

**qui·et**[1] /ˈkwaɪət/ *adjective*
**1** without a lot of noise: *Be quiet – I'm on the phone!* | *It's very quiet in the middle of the night.* **ANTONYMS: noisy, loud**
**2** without a lot of activity: *I had a quiet day at home.* **ANTONYM: busy**
**3** someone who is quiet does not talk very much: *Mike's a nice guy, but he's kind of quiet and shy.*
—**quietly** *adverb* without making a lot of noise: *I sat quietly in the armchair, reading.*

**quiet²** *noun*
the state of being quiet: *I love the peace and quiet of the morning.* **ANTONYM: noise**

**quilt** /kwɪlt/ *noun*
a cover for a bed, made by sewing two large pieces of cloth together and putting feathers or cotton inside: *A patchwork quilt is made from squares of material.*
[**ORIGIN:** 1200-1300 From the old French word *cuilte*, from the Latin word *culcita*, which means "mattress."]

Q

**quit** /kwɪt/ *verb* (**quit**, **quitting**) (*informal*)
**1** to stop doing something: *I quit smoking cigarettes last year.* | *Quit hitting your sister!* **ANTONYM: start**

**THESAURUS: quit**

**give up** to stop doing something, or stop trying to do something: *Learning to drive is hard at first, but don't give up.*

**drop out** (*informal*) to stop going to school or doing an activity before you have finished it: *Tucker dropped out of high school when he was 16.*

**resign** to officially leave your job or position: *She decided to resign and look for another job.*

**retire** to stop working at the end of your working life: *Dad plans to retire when he's 65.*

**2** to leave your job: *Betty quit her job to stay home with the kids.* | *I hated my boss, so I quit.* **SYNONYM: resign**

**quite** /kwaɪt/ *adverb*
**1** very, but not extremely: *The house is quite big, but not huge.* **SYNONYM: pretty**
**2 not quite** = not completely: *I'm not quite ready – I still have to brush my teeth.*

**quiv·er** /ˈkwɪvɚ/ *verb*
to shake a little because you are afraid or upset: *The little girl quivered with fear.* **SYNONYM: tremble**

**quiz** /kwɪz/ *noun* (plural **quizzes**)
**1** a short test: *Every week, the teacher gives us a math quiz.*
**2** a set of questions that you answer for fun: *There's a quiz about finding your perfect boyfriend in the magazine.*

**quo·ta** /ˈkwoʊtə/ *noun*
**1** an official limit on the number or amount of something you are allowed to have: *There is a quota on the number of fish that fishermen are allowed to catch.* **SYNONYM: limit**
**2** an amount of something that someone is expected to do or achieve: *Each of us was given a quota of tickets to sell.* **SYNONYM: target**

**quo·ta·tion** Ac /kwoʊˈteɪʃən/ *noun*
words from a book or speech that you repeat in your own speech or writing: *"To be or not to be" is a famous quotation from Shakespeare.* **SYNONYM: quote**

**quoˈtation ˌmarks** *plural noun*
the marks ("..."), which you write before and after what someone says

**quote¹** Ac /kwoʊt/ *verb*
**1** to say or write exactly what someone else has written: *She quoted President Roosevelt, "You have nothing to fear but fear itself."*
**2** to tell someone how much he or she will have to pay you for something: *The airline quoted me $400 for a ticket to New York.*

**WORD FAMILY: quote**
**quote** *verb* | **quote** *noun* | **quotation** *noun*

**quote²** Ac *noun*
another word for QUOTATION

**quo·tient** /ˈkwoʊʃənt/ *noun*
the number you get when you divide one number by another number: *If you divide 15 by 3, the quotient is 5.*

**Qur·'an** /kəˈræn/ *noun*
another spelling of KORAN

# Rr

**R & B** *noun*
(**rhythm and blues**) a type of popular music that is a mixture of BLUES and JAZZ

**rab·bi** /ˈræbaɪ/ *noun* (plural **rabbis**)
a Jewish religious leader and teacher
[**ORIGIN:** 1000-1100 From the Hebrew word for "my master."]

**rab·bit** /ˈræbɪt/ *noun*
a small animal with long ears that lives in holes in the ground, that some people keep as a pet → see picture at **pet**

**rac·coon** /ræˈkun/ *noun*
an animal with black fur around its eyes and black and white lines around its tail: *A raccoon was looking for food in the trash can.*
[**ORIGIN:** 1600-1700 From the Algonquian word *äräkhun*, which means "he scratches with his hands." Raccoons use their front paws like hands. Algonquian is a Native American language.]

**race¹** /reɪs/ *noun*
**1** a competition to find out who can do something fastest, for example running, driving, or swimming: *Who won the race?*
**2** one of the groups that humans can be divided into because of the color of their skin and the way they look: *People of many different races live in America.*

**WORD FAMILY: race**
**race** *noun* | **racial** *adjective* | **racist** *noun* | **racist** *adjective* | **racism** *noun* | **racially** *adverb* | **multiracial** *adjective*

**THESAURUS: race**
**ethnic group** (*formal*) a group of people of the same race, nation, or tribe: *Many different ethnic groups live in New York.*
**people** a race or group of people that live in a particular country. The plural of this meaning of "people" is "peoples": *the native peoples of the United States*
**tribe** a group of people within a country who are the same race, and who have the same language and traditions and the same leader: *The Navajo tribe is the second largest in the U.S.*
**nation** a country and its people: *The leaders of several Western nations are meeting in Paris this week.*

**race²** *verb*
**1** to compete in a race: *She'll be racing against some of the best athletes.*
**2** to go somewhere very quickly: *I raced home to see if the letter had arrived.*
→ see Thesaurus box at **run¹**

**ˈrace car** *noun*
a special car for racing

**race·horse** /ˈreɪsˌhɔrs/ *noun*
a horse that competes in races

**race·track** /ˈreɪs-træk/ *noun*
a special road where horses, cars, or people compete in races: *I went to the racetrack to watch the horse racing.* **SYNONYM: track**

**ra·cial** /ˈreɪʃəl/ *adjective*
relating to someone's race: *Racial discrimination in the workplace is against the law.*
—**racially** *adverb* in a way that relates to someone's race

**rac·ism** /ˈreɪsɪzəm/ *noun*
the act of treating people badly because they belong to a different race: *They accused him of racism when he fired a black woman.*
→ see Thesaurus box at **prejudice**

**rac·ist** /ˈreɪsɪst/ *noun*
someone who believes that his or her own race of people is better than any other
—**racist** *adjective* treating people of other races badly because you think your race is better than theirs: *He made racist remarks about a Chinese student.*

**rack** /ræk/ *noun*
a frame, bar, or shelf that things are put on: *Leave the cookies to cool on a wire rack.* | *She hung her scarf and coat on the coat rack.*

**rack·et** /ˈrækɪt/ *noun*
**1** (*informal*) a loud noise: *The kids were making such a racket I didn't hear the doorbell.*
**2** something you use to hit the ball in

**racket**
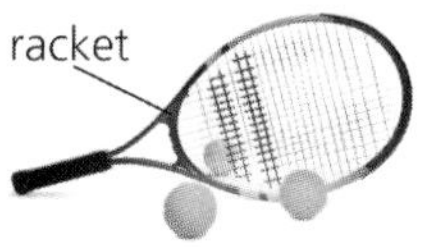

games such as tennis: *One of the strings on his tennis racket broke.*

[ORIGIN: 1500-1600 Sense 2 is from the French word *raquette* and the Italian word *racchetta*, from the Arabic word *rahah*, which means "front of the hand."]

**rack·et·ball** /ˈrækɪtˌbɔl/ *noun*
an indoor game in which two players hit a ball against the walls of a special room

**ra·dar** /ˈreɪdɑr/ *noun*
a system that uses radio waves to find out where ships and planes are, or the equipment used to do this: *The radar showed that two ships were coming.*

R

**ra·di·ant** /ˈreɪdiənt/ *adjective*
looking very happy: *The bride had a radiant smile.*

**ra·di·a·tion** /ˌreɪdiˈeɪʃən/ *noun*
a form of energy that is dangerous to living things if there is too much of it: *Radiation killed many people when the nuclear bomb exploded.*

**ra·di·a·tor** /ˈreɪdiˌeɪtɚ/ *noun*
**1** a flat metal object on a wall, which hot water passes through to make a room warm: *The radiators were turned off, so the house was cold.*
**2** the part of a car that keeps the engine cool: *He put some more water in the radiator to cool the engine.*

**rad·i·cal** [Ac] /ˈrædɪkəl/ *adjective*
**1** changing something completely: *He made a radical change in his life, leaving his job and becoming a priest.* SYNONYM: **big**; ANTONYMS: **slight**, **small**
**2** wanting to change a political system or society completely: *Radical political groups supported the use of violence to get rid of the government.* ANTONYM: **moderate**
—**radically** *adverb* extremely or completely: *Many African countries are radically different from the U.S.A.*

[ORIGIN: 1300-1400 From the Latin word *radicalis*, from *radix*, which means "root or basis." A radical change involves changing the most basic part of something.]

**ra·di·o** /ˈreɪdiˌoʊ/ *noun*
**1** a piece of electrical equipment that you use to listen to music, news, and other programs: *I was listening to the radio in the car.*
**2** the activity of making and broadcasting programs that people listen to on the radio: *He wants to get a job in radio.*
**3** a piece of equipment used for sending and receiving spoken messages, or the system for sending messages in this way: *Ships send messages to each other by radio.*

**ra·di·o·ac·tive** /ˌreɪdioʊˈæktɪv/ *adjective*
radioactive materials have a type of energy which is dangerous to living things if there is too much of it
—**radioactivity** /ˌreɪdioʊækˈtɪvəti/ *noun* the quality of being radioactive

**rad·ish** /ˈrædɪʃ/ *noun*
a small red or white vegetable with a hot taste. A radish grows in the ground and you do not cook it: *Radishes are great in salads.* → see picture on page **A12**

**ra·di·us** /ˈreɪdiəs/ *noun* (plural **radii** /ˈreɪdiaɪ/)
**1** the distance from the center of a circle to the edge → see picture at **diameter**
**2** **within a ten-mile/100-meter, etc. radius** = not more than ten miles, 100 meters, etc. from a place, in any direction: *All the students live within a 15-mile radius of the school.*

**raf·fle** /ˈræfəl/ *noun*
a competition in which people buy tickets with numbers on them in order to try to win prizes: *Kelly won a bike in the raffle the school held to raise money.*

**raft** /ræft/ *noun*
**1** a flat boat made by tying pieces of wood together: *They made a raft and left the island.*
**2** a small flat rubber boat filled with air: *We paddled out to the island in a rubber raft.*

**rag** /ræg/ *noun*
**1** a small piece of old cloth: *He wiped his shoes clean with an old rag.*
**2** **in rags** = wearing old torn clothes: *The children were poor and dressed in rags.*

**rage** /reɪdʒ/ *noun*
very strong anger: *She was filled with rage when she realized Steve had lied to her.* SYNONYM: **fury**

**raid**[1] /reɪd/ *noun*
**1** a sudden visit to a place by the police, so that they can look for something illegal: *Police*

*officers found drugs during a raid on the apartment.*
**2** a sudden attack on a place during a war: *He flew planes on bombing raids during the war.*

**raid²** *verb*
**1** if the police raid a place, they go there suddenly to look for something illegal: *Police found guns when they raided his home.*
**2** to attack a place suddenly, in a war: *Soldiers raided the village.*
—**raider** *noun* someone who raids a place

**rail** /reɪl/ *noun*
**1** a bar that you can hold when going up and down stairs, or a bar that goes around an area to stop you falling over an edge: *I held the rail and looked down at the tiny cars on the street below us.*
**2** one of the two long metal bars that a train moves on: *Snow on the rails stopped the train from leaving.* **SYNONYM: track**
**3** a railroad system: *It is the safest rail system in the country.*

**rail·ing** /ˈreɪlɪŋ/ *noun*
a fence made of metal or wooden bars with a rail on top, for example at the edge of a BALCONY or a set of steps: *The steps were steep, so I held onto the railing.*

**rail·road** /ˈreɪlroʊd/ *noun*
the system of tracks and equipment that trains use: *A train was coming toward them along the railroad tracks.*

**rail·way** /ˈreɪlweɪ/ *noun*
another word for RAILROAD

**rain¹** /reɪn/ *noun*
water that falls from the sky: *The weather forecast said there would be rain.* | *During the night, there was heavy rain.*
**[ORIGIN:** From the old English word *regn.***]**

**THESAURUS: rain**

**drizzle** light rain with very small drops of water: *A light drizzle was falling as I left the apartment.*

**shower** a short period of rain: *Tomorrow, there will be a few heavy showers with sunny periods in between.*

**downpour** a lot of rain that falls in a short period of time: *The downpour made driving difficult.*

**hail** small hard drops of frozen rain that fall from the clouds: *A hail storm flattened crops.*

**sleet** a mixture of snow and rain: *As it got colder the rain turned to sleet and then snow.*

**rain²** *verb*
if it rains, drops of water fall from the sky: *Is it still raining?* | *It started raining hard.*

**rain·bow** /ˈreɪnboʊ/ *noun*
a large curve of different colors in the sky. You see a rainbow when the sun shines while there is still a little rain in the air.

**rain·coat** /ˈreɪnkoʊt/ *noun*
a coat that keeps you dry in the rain → see picture on page **A6**

**rain·drop** /ˈreɪndrɑp/ *noun*
a single drop of rain: *There were raindrops on the window.*

**rain·fall** /ˈreɪnfɔl/ *noun*
the amount of rain that falls somewhere: *Rainfall in the Amazon is around 20 meters a year.*

**rain·forest** /ˈreɪnfɒrɪst/ *noun*
a thick forest in a part of the world that is hot and wet: *The rainforests are being destroyed by people cutting down trees for wood.*

**rain·y** /ˈreɪni/ *adjective*
if it is rainy, there is rain: *On rainy days, Dad drives me to school.*

**raise¹** /reɪz/ *verb*

raise

**1** to move something to a higher position: *He raised his arms above his head.* | *Raise your hand if you know the answer.* **SYNONYM: lift; ANTONYM: lower**
**2** to increase something: *They raised the price from $1.99 to $3.99.* **ANTONYM: lower**
**3** to take care of children, animals, or crops

R

until they are grown: *She raised three sons on her own.*

**4** to collect money to help people: *The kids raised $400 for the school by washing cars.*

**5** to begin to talk or write about something that you want people to think about: *The students raised several questions during the discussion.*

→ see Thesaurus box at **increase**[1]

**raise**[2] *noun*

an increase in the money you earn: *She asked her boss for a raise after a year.*

**USAGE: raise, rise**

A **raise** is an increase in the money you earn: *He's a good worker and deserves a raise.*

A **rise** is an increase in anything: *The rise in the number of cars led to more pollution.*

R

**rai·sin** /ˈreɪzən/ *noun*

a dried GRAPE: *The cookies had raisins in them.*

[ORIGIN: 1300-1400 From the French word for "grape," from the Latin word *racemus*, which means "bunch of grapes."]

**rake**[1] /reɪk/ *noun*

a garden tool that you use for gathering dead leaves together or for making the soil level

**rake**[2] (*also* **rake up**) *verb*

to use a rake to gather dead leaves together or to make the soil level: *He spends hours raking leaves every fall.*

**ral·ly**[1] /ˈræli/ *noun* (plural **rallies**)

**1** a large public meeting to support a political idea or a sports team: *The cheerleaders led a rally before the first football game.*

**2** a car race on public roads

**rally**[2] *verb* (**rallied**, **rallies**)

to join other people in order to support a person or idea: *Republicans rallied to the president after Democrats criticized his leadership.*

**ram**[1] /ræm/ *verb* (**rammed**, **ramming**)

to hit something with a lot of force: *A truck rammed into a line of cars, causing a huge accident.*

**ram**[2] *noun*

a male sheep

**ramp** /ræmp/ *noun*

**1** a road for driving onto or off a main road: *There was a line of cars on the exit ramp.*

**2** a slope that connects two places that are at different levels: *The building has ramps for wheelchair users.*

**ramp·ant** /ˈræmpənt/ *adjective* (*formal*)

if something bad is rampant, there is a lot of it and it is difficult to control: *Violent crime is rampant in the city and no one feels safe.*

**ran** /ræn/ *verb*

the past tense of RUN

**ranch** /ræntʃ/ *noun*

a large farm with cows, horses, or sheep: *He owns a sheep ranch in Australia.*

—**rancher** *noun* someone who owns or works on a ranch

—**ranching** *noun* the job of owning or working on a ranch

[ORIGIN: 1800-1900 From the Mexican Spanish word *rancho*, which means "farm."]

**ran·dom** Ac /ˈrændəm/ *adjective*

happening or chosen without any plan or pattern: *The CDs were arranged in random order, not alphabetically.*

—**randomly** *adverb* in a random way: *The lottery numbers are randomly chosen.*

**rang** /ræŋ/ *verb*

the past tense of RING

**range**[1] Ac /reɪndʒ/ *noun*

**1** a number of things that are all of the same general type, but are all different: *The store sells a wide range of shoes.*

**2** the amounts or numbers between two limits: *The games are good for the 8-12 age range.* | *That car is out of our price range; we'll have to buy a cheaper one.*

**3** a line of mountains or hills: *The Alps are the largest mountain range in Europe.*

**4** the distance that something can reach or travel: *The missiles have a range of 300 miles.*

**5** a place where you can practice shooting: *a rifle range*

**range**[2] *verb*

**1** **range from ... to ...** = to include the numbers or amounts mentioned, and others between them: *The ages of the students ranged from 11 to 14.*

**2** to move over a large area of land: *Bears range freely across this wilderness.*

**rang·er** /ˈreɪndʒɚ/ *noun*
someone whose job is to take care of a forest or park: *The ranger gave a talk about all the animals that live in the park.*

**rank¹** /ræŋk/ *noun*
the position or level that someone has in an organization: *A general is an army officer with a very high rank.*
[**ORIGIN:** 1300-1400 From the old French word *renc*, which means "line or row." The idea is that where you are in a line or row shows how important or powerful you are.]

**rank²** *verb*
to have a particular position in a list that shows how good someone or something is: *The team ranks 12th in the league after losing their last six games.*

**ran·som** /ˈrænsəm/ *noun*
money that is paid to criminals who are keeping someone prisoner, so that the criminals will let that person go: *The kidnappers wanted a $200,000 ransom to release the businessman's wife.*

**rap¹** /ræp/ (*also* **ˈrap music**) *noun*
a type of popular music in which someone speaks words rather than singing them
—**rapper** *noun* someone who performs rap

**rap²** *verb* (**rapped**, **rapping**)
**1** to knock on something quickly several times: *Nina rapped on my door.*
**2** to say the words of a rap song

**rap·id** /ˈræpɪd/ *adjective*
done very quickly, or happening in a short time: *Many children have a period of rapid growth during the teenage years.* **SYNONYMS: fast, quick; ANTONYM: slow**
—**rapidly** *adverb* very quickly: *The number of people using cell phones grew rapidly.*
—**rapidity** /rəˈpɪdəti/ *noun* the quality of being rapid

**rap·ids** /ˈræpɪdz/ *plural noun*
a place in a river where the water is moving very fast over rocks

**rare** /rer/ *adjective*
**1** not happening or seen very often: *These rare birds are found in only two or three places in the world.* **ANTONYM: common**
**2** meat that is rare is cooked on the outside but still red in the middle: *I'd like my steak rare, please.*

**rare·ly** /ˈrerli/ *adverb*
not often: *He's very sick and rarely leaves his home.* **ANTONYM: frequently**

**rash¹** /ræʃ/ *adjective*
done too quickly and without thinking carefully: *I know you're angry with him, but don't do anything rash and get into trouble.*

**rash²** *noun*
red spots on someone's skin, caused by an illness or by something he or she has eaten or touched: *He had a fever, and a rash on his chest.*

**rasp·ber·ry** /ˈræzˌberi/ *noun* (plural **raspberries**)
a soft sweet red BERRY: *Raspberries grow on bushes.* → see picture on page **A13**

**rat** /ræt/ *noun*
an animal that looks like a large mouse with a long tail: *I saw a big rat run across the basement of the old house.*

**rate¹** /reɪt/ *noun*
**1** the speed at which something happens: *Children learn at different rates.*
**2** the number of times that something happens in a period of time: *Utah has one of the lowest crime rates in the U.S.*
**3** a particular amount that someone charges or pays: *The hourly rate of pay for the job is $15. | The interest rate on the loan is 10%.*
**4 at any rate** = used when mentioning a fact that is definitely important or true, when other things may not be: *We'll be there. At any rate, I will be.*

**rate²** *verb*
**1** to decide how good, bad, or important something is when compared to others: *He is rated the best quarterback in the league.*
**2** to give something a rank or level: *The movie is rated G, so all children can see it.*

**rath·er** /ˈræðɚ/ *adverb*
**1 rather than** = instead of: *Let's go out tonight rather than tomorrow night.*
**2 would rather** = used when you would like to do or have one thing more than another: *I*

R

*hate having nothing to do; I'd rather be busy.* | *Dave would rather have a dog than a cat.*
**3** to a fairly great degree: *He was rather tired after his long trip.* **SYNONYMS: fairly, quite, somewhat**
**4 or rather** = used to correct something that you have said: *We stayed at Tony's house, or rather at his parents' house.*

**rat·ing** /ˈreɪtɪŋ/ *noun*
a measurement of how good or popular something is: *The hotel was given a low rating for its food.*

R

**ra·ti·o** Ac /ˈreɪʃiˌoʊ/ *noun* (plural **ratios**)
a relationship between two amounts that shows how much bigger one amount is than another. For example, you write a ratio in the form "3:2." This means that there are three of one thing for each two of the other thing: *There are 20 boys and 10 girls in the class, so the ratio of boys to girls is 2:1 (2 to 1).*

**ra·tion** /ˈræʃən/ *noun*
a limited amount of something such as food or gas that you are allowed to have when there is not much available: *During the war, the weekly meat ration was very small.*
—**ration** *verb* to limit the amount of something that people can have because there is not much available: *When stocks of rice ran low, it had to be rationed.*

**ra·tion·al** Ac /ˈræʃənəl/ *adjective*
based on facts or sensible reasons, not on your feelings: *It's not easy to make a rational decision about when to have a baby.* **ANTONYM: irrational**
—**rationally** *adverb* in a rational way: *We were too shocked to think rationally.*
[**ORIGIN:** 1300-1400 From the Latin word *ratio*, which means "reason."]

**ra·tion·ale** /ˌræʃəˈnæl/ *noun* (*formal*)
the reasons that you use to make a decision: *The judge gave no rationale for his decision, and many people were confused by it.*

**rat·tle¹** /ˈrætl/ *verb*
to shake and make a knocking sound: *There was something rattling around in the trunk.*

**rattle²** *noun*
a baby's toy that makes a noise when you shake it → see picture on page **A22**

**rat·tle·snake** /ˈrætlˌsneɪk/ *noun*
a poisonous American snake that makes a noise like a rattle with its tail

**ra·ven** /ˈreɪvən/ *noun*
a large shiny black bird with a black beak and a loud cry

**ra·vine** /rəˈvin/ *noun*
a deep narrow valley with steep sides **SYNONYM: gorge**

**raw** /rɔ/ *adjective*
not cooked: *Wash your hands after touching raw meat.*

**ˌraw maˈterials** *plural noun*
substances such as coal, oil, or iron that are in their natural state, before people change them so that they can be used

**ray** /reɪ/ *noun*
**1** a narrow beam of light from the sun or a lamp: *A ray of light came through a gap in the curtains.*
**2 a ray of hope** = a small amount of hope: *This new medicine offers a ray of hope to cancer sufferers.*
**3** a large flat ocean fish that has wide FINs that look like wings, and a long pointed tail

**ray·on** /ˈreɪɑn/ *noun*
a smooth artificial cloth used for making clothes

**ra·zor** /ˈreɪzɚ/ *noun*
a sharp tool for removing hair from your body: *He shaved off his beard with an electric razor.* → see picture on page **A11**
[**ORIGIN:** 1200-1300 From the old French word *raseor*, from *raser*, which means "to scrape or shave."]

**ˈrazor blade** *noun*
a small flat sharp piece of metal, used in razors

**Rd.**
the written abbreviation of **road**, used when you are writing someone's address: *John Smith, 5421 Hill Rd.*

**'re** /ɚ/ *verb*
the short form of "are": *We're late.*

**reach**[1] /ritʃ/ *verb*

**1** to move your hand or arm to touch or pick up something: *I can't reach the cans on the top shelf.* | *David reached for his glass.*

**2** to arrive somewhere: *We reached home before it was dark.*

**3** to get to an amount or level: *The temperature will reach 95°F today.*

**4** **reach a decision/conclusion/verdict** = to decide something after thinking carefully: *Have you reached a decision about what to do?*

**5** to be able to talk to someone on the telephone: *I tried calling him at home, but I couldn't reach him.*

→ see Thesaurus box at **arrive**

**reach**[2] *noun*

**1** **out of reach** = too far away for you to touch or get: *The ball rolled under the bed, just out of reach.*

**2** **within reach** = close enough for you to touch or get: *Babies try to grab everything within reach.*

**re·act** Ac /riˈækt/ *verb*

**1** to do something or behave in a particular way because something has happened: *How did she react to the news?*

**2** if a chemical substance reacts with another substance, it changes when they are put together: *Iron reacts with oxygen to form rust.*

**WORD FAMILY: react**

**react** *verb* | **reaction** *noun*

**re·ac·tion** Ac /riˈækʃən/ *noun*

**1** something that you feel or do because of something that has happened: *Crying is a very natural reaction to sad news.*

**2** a chemical change that happens when you put substances together: *When you add an acid to the mixture, a chemical reaction occurs.*

**re·ac·tion·ar·y** Ac /riˈækʃəˌneri/ *adjective*

strongly opposed to social or political change: *Reactionary politicians voted against the new welfare plan.*

**read** /rid/ *verb* (**read** /red/)

**1** to look at words and understand them: *He's only four and he can already read.* | *She was reading a magazine.*

**2** to say written words to other people: *She was reading a story to her kids.*

[**ORIGIN:** From the old English word *rædan.*]

**read·a·ble** /ˈridəbəl/ *adjective*

interesting, enjoyable, or easy to read: *The book is very readable, and I enjoyed it a lot.*

—**readability** /ˌridəˈbɪləti/ *noun* the fact of being easy or enjoyable to read

**read·er** /ˈridɚ/ *noun*

**1** someone who reads something: *The book will appeal to young readers.*

**2** someone who reads a particular book, newspaper, or magazine: *The magazine's readers are mostly women.*

**3** a book for people who are learning to read, or learning to read another language

**read·i·ly** /ˈredəli/ *adverb*

quickly and easily: *The information is readily available on the Internet.*

**read·i·ness** /ˈredinəs/ *noun*

the state of being ready to deal with something that might happen: *The army was waiting in readiness for an attack.*

**read·ing** /ˈridɪŋ/ *noun*

the activity of looking at words and understanding them: *Paula loves reading and is always buying books.*

**read·y** /ˈredi/ *adjective*

**1** if you are ready, you are prepared for what you are going to do: *Aren't you ready yet?* | *We're just about ready to eat.* | *Go get ready for bed.*

**2** something that is ready can be used or eaten immediately: *Is supper ready?* | *Is everything ready for the party?*

**3** willing to do something: *She's always ready to help.*

**real** /rɪəl/ *adjective*

**1** something that is real exists and is not imaginary: *Monsters and ghosts are not real.* | *I think she has a real chance of winning.*

**2** true: *What's the real reason you were*

R

*late?* | *Everyone called him Johnny but his real name was David.*

**3** not false or artificial: *His shoes were real leather.* **ANTONYM: fake**

**4** (*informal*) used to emphasize what you are saying: *You made a real mess in here!*

[**ORIGIN:** 1400-1500 From the Latin word *realis*, which means "relating to things," from *res*, meaning "thing."]

**WORD FAMILY: real**

**real** *adjective* | **unreal** *adjective* | **reality** *noun* | **really** *adverb*

R

**ˈreal esˌtate** *noun*
buildings or land: *She sells houses and other real estate.*

**ˈreal eˌstate ˌagent** *noun*
someone whose job is to sell houses or land

**re·al·is·tic** /rɪəˈlɪstɪk/ *adjective*
**1** someone who is realistic accepts the facts about a situation and understands what is possible or not possible: *You have to be realistic about what kind of job you can get with a high school diploma.*
**2** showing things as they are in real life: *His paintings are so realistic, they look like photographs.*
—**realistically** *adverb* in a realistic way

**re·al·i·ty** /riˈæləti/ *noun* (plural **realities**)
**1** the real or true situation, not what you imagine or would like: *I'd love to be a pro basketball player, but the reality is that I'm not good enough.*
**2 in reality** = used to say what the true situation is: *The color in the newspaper picture looks green, but in reality it is made of tiny blue and yellow dots.*

**re·al·i·za·tion** /ˌrɪələˈzeɪʃən/ *noun* (*formal*)
the act of realizing that something is true: *I finally came to the realization that I would have to study harder to do well at school.*

**re·al·ize** /ˈrɪəˌlaɪz/ *verb*
**1** to know or understand something that you did not know before: *I didn't realize how late it was.* | *I suddenly realized that someone was watching me.*
**2 realize your dream** = to achieve something that you hoped to achieve: *He finally realized his dream of competing in the Olympic Games.*

**real·ly** /ˈrɪəli/ *adverb*
**1** very or very much: *Tom's a really nice guy – everyone likes him.* | *His letter really annoyed me.*
**2** used for saying what is true, rather than what seems to be true: *He's not really angry – he's just pretending.*
**3** used to emphasize that something is definitely true: *It really is the best thing to do.*
**4 really?** = used when you are surprised about or interested in what someone has said: *"Meg's getting married." "Really? When?"*
**5 not really** = used in order to say "no": *"Are you okay?" "Not really, my back hurts."*

**realm** /relm/ *noun*
**1** an area of knowledge, experience, or thought: *Many advances have been made in the realm of medicine.*
**2** (*formal*) a country ruled by a king or queen

**Real·tor** /ˈriltɚ/ *noun* (*trademark*)
someone whose job is to sell houses and land
**SYNONYM: real estate agent**

**rear[1]** /rɪr/ *noun* (*trademark*)
**1** the back part of a car, building, or object: *There is a parking lot at the rear of the restaurant.*
**2** (*also* **rear end** (*informal*)) your bottom: *He got up from the ground and brushed the dirt off his rear end.*

**rear[2]** *adjective*
relating to the back of something: *He got into the rear seat of the taxi.* **ANTONYM: front**

**re·ar·range** /ˌriəˈreɪndʒ/ *verb*
**1** to put things in different positions: *We rearranged the furniture in the living room and put the couch by the window.*
**2** to change the time or day when a meeting or event will happen: *The meeting has been rearranged so that more people can come.*
—**rearrangement** *noun* the act of rearranging things

**rear·view mir·ror** /ˌrɪrvyu ˈmɪrɚ/ *noun*
the mirror in a car that you use to see what is behind you

**rea·son[1]** /ˈrizən/ *noun*
**1** a fact that explains why something happens or why someone does something: *Did he*

*give any reason for quitting? | There are many reasons why people get cancer.*

**THESAURUS: reason**

**explanation** a reason for why something happened or why you did something: *Did she give any explanation for why she went home early?*

**excuse** a reason you use to explain why you did something bad or did not do something you should have done: *I hope she has a good excuse for being late again.*

**motive** (*formal*) a reason that makes someone do something, especially something bad or dishonest: *The police do not know the criminal's motive for the attack.*

**grounds** reasons that make it right or fair to do something: *If he does not go to work, the company has grounds to fire him.*

**2** a fact that makes it right or fair to do something: *I had no reason to think she was lying.*

**3** the ability to think about something in a clear and sensible way and make good judgments: *Students are encouraged to use reason to solve the problem.*

**reason²** *verb*
to decide that something is true by thinking about the facts: *He reasoned that if he did not touch anything in the room, no one would know he had been there.*

**PHRASAL VERB**

**reason with someone**
to try to persuade someone to be more sensible: *I tried reasoning with her, but she wouldn't listen.*

**rea·son·a·ble** /ˈrizənəbəl/ *adjective*
**1** fair and sensible: *The idea sounds perfectly reasonable – let's try it. | He seemed like a reasonable guy who would be easy to work with.* **ANTONYM: unreasonable**
**2** a reasonable amount, number, or price is not too much or too big: *The restaurant serves good food at a reasonable price.*

**rea·son·a·bly** /ˈrizənəbli/ *adverb*
**1** fairly but not very: *I did reasonably well on the test, but I didn't get an A.* **SYNONYMS: fairly, quite**
**2** in a way that is fair or sensible: *"I'm sure we can find an answer," Steve said reasonably.*

**rea·son·ing** /ˈrizənɪŋ/ *noun*
the process of thinking carefully about something in order to find the answer or make a judgment: *Why do you think that? Could you explain your reasoning?*

**re·as·sess** Ac /ˌriəˈses/ *verb*
to think about something again, in order to decide if you should change your opinion or decision: *If this doesn't work, we will have to reassess the situation.*

**re·as·sure** /ˌriəˈʃʊr/ *verb*
to make someone feel less worried about something: *My doctor reassured me that I would be fine after the operation.*
—**reassurance** *noun* something that reassures someone: *Children often need reassurance when they first start school.*

**re·bate** /ˈribeɪt/ *noun*
an amount of money that is paid back to you after you have paid too much rent or tax, or an amount that is taken off a price: *He received a tax rebate of $1,590.*

**reb·el¹** /ˈrebəl/ *noun*
someone who fights against a leader or government: *Rebels have overthrown the government.*
[**ORIGIN:** 1300-1400 From the Latin word *rebellare*, which means "to fight back against someone," from *bellum*, which means "war."]

**re·bel²** /rɪˈbel/ *verb* (**rebelled**, **rebelling**)
to disobey or fight against someone who has power over you, such as parents or the government: *Teenagers sometimes rebel against their parents.*
→ see Thesaurus box at **disobey**

**re·bel·lion** /rɪˈbelyən/ *noun*
an attempt to remove a government or political leader by using violence: *He led an armed rebellion against the government.*

**re·bel·lious** /rɪˈbelyəs/ *adjective*
someone who is rebellious refuses to obey people in authority, such as parents or teachers: *Anne became very rebellious as a*

R

*teenager and refused to do anything her parents asked.*

**re·boot** /riˈbut/ *verb*
if you reboot a computer, you start it again after it has stopped working: *The computer crashed, so I had to reboot it.*

**re·call** /rɪˈkɔl/ *verb*
to remember something from the past: *I recall that he looked very nervous on that day.*

**re·ceipt** /rɪˈsit/ *noun*
a piece of paper that shows you have paid for something: *If you keep the receipt, you can take the shirt back to the store if it doesn't fit.*

R

**re·ceive** /rɪˈsiv/ *verb (formal)*
to get or be given something: *You will receive the tickets in the mail within three days.* | *He received an award.* **SYNONYM: get**
[**ORIGIN:** 1300-1400 From the Latin word *recipere*, which means "to take back or get back."]

**re·ceiv·er** /rɪˈsivɚ/ *noun*
**1** the part of a telephone that you hold next to your mouth and ear: *The phone rang and he picked up the receiver.*
**2** a piece of equipment that receives radio or television signals and changes them into sound and images: *a satellite receiver*

**re·cent** /ˈrisənt/ *adjective*
happening or done a short time ago: *He still hasn't completely recovered from his recent illness.*
→ see Thesaurus box at **new**

**re·cent·ly** /ˈrisəntli/ *adverb*
not long ago: *We recently moved from Ohio.* | *He worked as a teacher until recently.*

**THESAURUS: recently**

**just** only a few minutes, hours, or days ago: *The show just started.* | *He just got home from school.*

**a little while ago** not very long ago: *I talked to Mark a little while ago.*

**lately** in the days or weeks before now: *Have you seen Angie lately?*

**freshly** used about something that was made or done very recently: *I love the smell of freshly baked bread.* | *The room had been freshly painted.*

**newly** used about something that happened or was done recently: *Tom and Laura are newly married.* | *newly built homes*

**re·cep·tion** /rɪˈsepʃən/ *noun*
**1** a large formal party to celebrate something or to welcome someone: *They got married and had the wedding reception at a hotel.*
**2** **reception desk/area** = the desk or area where visitors who are arriving in a hotel or business go first: *He was waiting for me in the reception area.*
**3** the quality of the signal that gives you a picture or sound on a television, radio, or CELL PHONE: *The TV reception was poor, and the picture kept disappearing.*
→ see Thesaurus box at **party**

**re·cep·tion·ist** /rɪˈsepʃənɪst/ *noun*
someone whose job is to answer the phone and welcome people when they arrive at an office or hotel → see picture on page **A16**

**re·cess** /ˈrises/ *noun*
**1** a time in the school day when children go outside to play: *Charlie got into a fight with another kid during recess.*
**2** a time during the day or year when a government or law court does not work: *Congress hopes to pass the bill before the summer recess.*

**re·ces·sion** /rɪˈseʃən/ *noun*
a time when businesses are not very successful and many people do not have a job: *During the last recession, a lot of small companies were forced to close down.*

**re·charge** /ˌriˈtʃɑrdʒ/ *verb*
to put a new supply of electricity into a BATTERY: *I need to recharge my cell phone – the battery is dead.*

**rec·i·pe** /ˈresəpi/ *noun*
a set of instructions that tells you how to cook something: *He gave me a recipe for chocolate cake.*
[**ORIGIN:** 1300-1400 From the Latin word *recipe*, which means "take!" This instruction would be the first word of a medical prescription or a recipe written in Latin.]

**re·cip·i·ent** /rɪˈsɪpiənt/ *noun (formal)*
someone who receives something: *Bauer is the recipient of many awards for his work.*

**re·cite** /rɪˈsaɪt/ *verb*
to say the words of a poem or story that you have learned, without reading it: *She recited a poem at the school concert.*

**reck·less** /ˈrekləs/ *adjective*
doing something in a dangerous way, without thinking about the bad things that could happen: *The accident was caused by his reckless driving.*
—**recklessness** *noun* careless and dangerous behavior

**re·claim** /rɪˈkleɪm/ *verb*
**1** to ask for something to be given back to you: *You can reclaim Canadian sales tax if you are only there on vacation.*
**2** to make an area of land able to be used for farming or building when it could not be used before: *The airport was built on land reclaimed from the ocean.*

**rec·og·ni·tion** /ˌrekəgˈnɪʃən/ *noun*
**1** the act of knowing someone because you have seen him or her before: *She hoped to avoid recognition by wearing dark glasses.*
**2** public praise and thanks for what someone has done: *She was given an award in recognition of her bravery.*

**rec·og·nize** /ˈrekəgˌnaɪz/ *verb*
**1** to know who someone is because you have seen or met that person before: *He had lost so much weight that I didn't recognize him.*
**2** to know something because you have seen, heard, smelled, or tasted it before: *I only recognized one song the band played.*
**3** to realize or accept that something is true: *Sarah refused to recognize that her illness was serious.*
—**recognizable** /ˌrekəgˈnaɪzəbəl/ *adjective* able to be recognized: *The actor's face is instantly recognizable.*
[**ORIGIN:** 1400-1500 From the Latin word *recognoscere*, which means "to know again," from *cognoscere*, which means "to know."]

**rec·ol·lect** /ˌrekəˈlekt/ *verb*
to remember something: *I cannot recollect his name.*
—**recollection** /ˌrekəˈlekʃən/ *noun* a memory: *My recollection of the event is different from his.*

**re·com·mence** /ˌrikəˈmens/ *verb (formal)*
to begin something again after it has stopped: *Work on the building recommenced in June after a short pause.*

**rec·om·mend** /ˌrekəˈmend/ *verb*
**1** to say that someone should do something: *Dentists recommend that you get a new toothbrush every few months.*
**2** to say that you think someone or something is good: *A friend recommended this restaurant to me; I hope it's good.*

**rec·om·men·da·tion** /ˌrekəmenˈdeɪʃən/ *noun*
**1** official advice telling people what they should do: *Doctors have made the recommendation that babies should sleep on their backs.*
**2** a suggestion to choose someone or something because that person or thing is good: *We took the tour on a friend's recommendation – he thought it was great.*

**re·con·sid·er** /ˌrikənˈsɪdɚ/ *verb*
to think again about a decision in order to decide if you should change it: *I wish you'd reconsider your decision to quit the team.*

**re·con·struc·tion** Ac /ˌrikənˈstrʌkʃən/ *noun (formal)*
work that people do to repair a building or place that has been almost destroyed: *He helped in the reconstruction of the city after the war.*

**re·cord¹** /ˈrekɚd/ *noun*
**1** information that you write down or put on a computer and keep: *Keep a record of how much you spend.* | *His medical records showed he'd had a heart attack in 2002.*
**2** the best result that anyone has ever achieved: *She set a new world record for the 1,500 meters, beating the old record by almost a second.*
**3** a round flat piece of black plastic on which music is stored: *She has a huge collection of old records.*
**4** the facts about how good or bad someone or something has been in the past: *The airline has a good safety record. It has never had a major accident.*

**re·cord²** /rɪˈkɔrd/ *verb*
**1** to write down information or put it on a computer so that you can look at it later: *She recorded all the events in her diary.*
**2** to store something such as music or a television program on tape or a DISK so that

people can listen to it or watch it later: *I recorded tonight's show so I can watch it tomorrow.*

[ORIGIN: 1100-1200 From the Latin word *recordari*, which means "to remember," from *cor*, which means "heart." People sometimes talk about the heart as a place where you keep memories of things.]

**re·cord·er** /rɪˈkɔrdɚ/ *noun*

**1** another word for a TAPE RECORDER

**2** a simple wooden or plastic musical instrument that you play by blowing

**re·cord·ing** /rɪˈkɔrdɪŋ/ *noun*

something such as a speech or a piece of music that has been recorded: *We listened to a recording of Mozart's music.*

R

**ˈrecord ˌplayer** *noun*

a piece of equipment for playing music stored on records

**re·cov·er** Ac /rɪˈkʌvɚ/ *verb*

**1** to get better after an illness or injury: *Have you recovered from your cold?*

**2** to get back something that was lost or stolen: *The stolen paintings have been recovered.*

**re·cov·er·y** Ac /rɪˈkʌvəri/ *noun*

the process of getting better after an illness or injury: *Doctors expect Mr. Kelly to make a full recovery from his heart attack.*

**re·cre·ate** Ac /ˌrikriˈeɪt/ *verb*

to make something like it was in the past or like something in another place: *The zoo tries to recreate the places where the animals would live in the wild.*

**rec·re·a·tion** /ˌrekriˈeɪʃən/ *noun*

an activity that you do for fun: *The parks are a great place for outdoor recreation such as soccer games or barbecues.*

→ see Thesaurus box at **game**

**re·cruit¹** /rɪˈkrut/ *verb*

to find new people to work in a company or join an organization: *We need to recruit new police officers.*

—**recruitment** *noun* the process of finding new people to work in a company or join an organization: *The company is trying to improve its recruitment of new lawyers.*

—**recruiter** *noun* someone whose job is to find new people to work in a company or join an organization: *He was an army recruiter.*

**recruit²** *noun*

someone who has recently joined a company or an organization

**rec·tan·gle** /ˈrekˌtæŋgəl/ *noun*

a shape with four straight sides, two of which are longer than the other two → see picture at **shape**

[ORIGIN: 1500-1600 From the Latin words *rectus* and *angulus*, which mean "right" and "angle."]

**rec·tan·gu·lar** /rekˈtæŋgjəlɚ/ *adjective*

having a shape like a rectangle: *a rectangular table*

**rec·ti·fy** /ˈrektəˌfaɪ/ *verb* (**rectified**, **rectifies**) (*formal*)

to correct something that is wrong: *All attempts to rectify the problem have failed.*

**re·cu·per·ate** /rɪˈkyupəˌreɪt/ *verb* (*formal*)

to get better after an illness or injury: *Jan is still recuperating from her operation.*

—**recuperation** /rɪˌkupəˈreɪʃən/ *noun* the process of recuperating

**re·cy·cle** /ˌriˈsaɪkəl/ *verb*

to put things that are not wanted anymore through a special process so that the material can be used again: *The city is recycling glass, plastic bottles, cans, and paper.*

—**recycled** *adjective* having been recycled: *These bags are made from recycled paper.*

**recycle**

[ORIGIN: 1900-2000 From "re-," which means "again," and the Greek word root *cycl*, which means "circle" or "wheel." The idea is that when you recycle something, you move it in a kind of circle from being made, and being used, to being broken down and made again.]

**re·cy·cling** /riˈsaɪklɪŋ/ *noun*

the process of treating glass, plastic bottles, newspapers, etc. so that they can be used again: *The city runs a recycling program.*

**red** /red/ *noun*, *adjective*

**1** the color of blood: *Strawberries are red.* | *a red dress*

**2** red hair is an orange-brown color

**re·deem** /rɪˈdim/ *verb*
to exchange a piece of paper representing an amount of money for that amount of money, or for things that are worth that amount: *You can redeem the coupon for $1 off a pack of diapers.*

**ˌred-ˈhanded** *adjective*
**catch someone red-handed** (*informal*) = to catch someone at the moment when he or she is doing something wrong: *She was caught red-handed stealing money.*

**re·do** /riˈdu/ *verb* (**redid** /riˈdɪd/, **redone** /riˈdʌn/, **redoes** /riˈdʌz/)
to do something again: *The essay wasn't good enough so I had to redo it.*

**ˌred ˈtape** *noun*
official rules that seem unnecessary and that delay something: *We had to deal with a lot of red tape to get the visa.*

**re·duce** /rɪˈdus/ *verb*
to make something smaller or less than it was before: *Eating healthy food reduces your risk of getting cancer.* | *The jacket was reduced from $75 to $35.*
[**ORIGIN:** 1300-1400 From the Latin word *reducere*, which means "to lead back or bring back."]

**THESAURUS: reduce**

**To Reduce Prices, Numbers, or Amounts:**

**lower** to make the amount of something less than it was before: *The store lowered prices for the sale.*

**decrease** to become less or make an amount become less: *The price of a house decreased by 15% last year.*

**cut** to reduce the amount of something: *Stores often cut prices after Christmas.*

**slash** to make a price, amount, or size much lower, especially suddenly: *The school slashed class sizes from 30 to only 20 students in each class.*

**To Reduce Pain:**

**relieve** to make pain less bad: *Aspirin is good for relieving headaches.*

**ease** to make pain less bad and make someone feel more comfortable: *A hot bath can ease the pain from sore muscles.*

**lessen** to make something less bad: *The medicine lessens the pain from the disease, but does not cure it.*

**re·duc·tion** /rɪˈdʌkʃən/ *noun*
if there is a reduction, the amount of something becomes smaller or less than it was before: *After the road signs were improved, there was a reduction in the number of accidents.* | *a 25% price reduction*

**red·wood** /ˈredwʊd/ *noun*
a very tall tree that grows near the coast in Oregon and California: *redwood forests*

**reed** /rid/ *noun*
a tall plant that looks like grass and grows near water

**reef** /rif/ *noun*
a line of sharp rocks or a raised area of sand near the surface of the sea

**reel** /ril/ *noun*
a round object onto which you wind things such as film or string: *Over a thousand reels of movie film are stored in the library.*

**re·e·lect** /ˌriəˈlekt/ *verb*
to choose the same person again to do a job, by voting: *Bush was elected as president in 2000 and then reelected in 2004.*
—**reelection** /ˌriəˈlekʃən/ *noun* the act of reelecting someone

**re·fer** /rɪˈfɚ/ *verb* (**referred**, **referring**)
**PHRASAL VERB**
**refer to**
**1 refer to someone/something** = to mention someone or something: *He referred to Jack in his letter.*
**2 refer to something** = to look at a book or map in order to find information: *Refer to page 14 for instructions.*

**ref·er·ee** /ˌrefəˈri/ *noun*
someone who makes sure that players in a sports game obey the rules: *The referee called a foul.*

**USAGE: referee, umpire**

**Referee** and **umpire** mean the same thing but are used for different sports. Use **referee** when you are talking about football, soccer, ice hockey, basketball, boxing, wrestling, or volleyball. Use **umpire** when you are talking about baseball or tennis.

**ref·er·ence** /ˈrefərəns/ *noun*
**1** the act of looking at something for information: *I keep the dictionary on my desk for reference.*
**2** a mention of someone or something: *Her writing is full of references to her hometown.*
**3** a letter about you, written by someone who knows you well, that you use when trying to get a job or a chance to go to a college: *Your teachers will write references for you when you apply to colleges.*
**4** someone who knows you and can give you a letter about you: *If you do not get an interview, your references will not be contacted.*

R

**ˈreference ˌbook** *noun*
a book such as a dictionary that you look at to find information

**ref·er·en·dum** /ˌrefəˈrendəm/ *noun* (plural **referenda** /ˌrefəˈrendə/ *or* **referendums**)
an occasion when people in a state or country vote in order to make a decision about a particular subject: *Quebec held a referendum on independence from Canada, but it failed.*

**re·fill**[1] /ˌriːˈfɪl/ *verb*
to fill something again: *A waiter refilled our glasses with water.*

**re·fill**[2] /ˈrifɪl/ *noun*
another drink to fill your cup or glass again: *You get free refills for all the soft drinks.*

**re·fine** Ac /rɪˈfaɪn/ *verb*
to remove things from a substance to make it more pure, for example a substance such as oil or sugar: *Oil is refined to make gasoline.*

**re·fin·er·y** /rɪˈfaɪnəri/ *noun* (plural **refineries**)
a factory where things are removed from a substance to make it more pure, for example a substance such as oil or sugar: *an oil refinery*

**re·flect** /rɪˈflekt/ *verb*

**1** if something is reflected in a mirror or water, you can see an image of it: *We could see the mountains reflected in the lake.*
**2** if a surface reflects light, heat, or sound, it sends it back: *The white walls reflect the heat, so the inside of the building stays cool.* | *The sunlight reflected off the shiny car.*
**3** to show or be a sign of something: *His home reflected his love of art and was full of paintings.*
**4** (*formal*) to think carefully: *When I reflect on what I did, I think I made the right decision.*
[**ORIGIN:** 1300-1400 From the Latin word *reflectere*, which means "to bend back." The idea is that light hits something such as a mirror and bends back to where it came from.]

**re·flec·tion** /rɪˈflekʃən/ *noun*
**1** the image you see when you look in a mirror or water: *John was looking at his reflection in the mirror.*
**2** (*formal*) the process of thinking carefully about something: *At first I disagreed with her but, on reflection, I think she's right.*
**3** a sign of something: *The rise in crime is a reflection of a violent society.*
**4** the process of light, heat, or sound being reflected back off a surface

**re·form**[1] /rɪˈfɔrm/ *verb*
to improve an organization, law, or system by making changes to it: *There are plans to reform the way young children are educated.*
→ see Thesaurus box at **change**[1]

**reform**[2] *noun*
a change that improves an organization, law, or system: *There have been calls for a reform of the health care system.*

**re·fresh** /rɪˈfreʃ/ *verb* (*formal*)
to make someone feel less tired or hot: *A shower will refresh you.*
—**refreshed** *adjective* less tired or hot: *I felt refreshed after a good night's sleep.*

**re·fresh·ing** /rɪˈfreʃɪŋ/ *adjective*
**1** making you feel less tired or less hot: *We went for a refreshing swim.*
**2** different from usual, in a good way: *It was a refreshing change to go out for dinner because usually I cook.*

**re·fresh·ments** /rɪˈfreʃmənts/ *plural noun* *(formal)*
food and drinks that you get at a meeting, show, sports game, or party: *During the break, they served refreshments.*

**re·frig·er·ate** /rɪˈfrɪdʒəˌreɪt/ *verb (formal)*
to put food into a refrigerator to keep it cold and fresh: *Milk will go bad if you do not refrigerate it.*
—**refrigeration** /rɪˌfrɪdʒəˈreɪʃən/ *noun*
the process of refrigerating food
[**ORIGIN:** 1500-1600 From the Latin word *refrigerare*, which means "to make something cold," from *frigus*, meaning "coldness."]

**re·frig·er·a·tor** /rɪˈfrɪdʒəˌreɪtɚ/ *noun*
a large piece of kitchen equipment that you put food in to keep it cold and fresh: *I took some cheese out of the refrigerator.* **SYNONYM: fridge** → see picture on page **A9**

**ref·uge** /ˈrefyudʒ/ *noun (formal)*
**1** protection from bad weather or danger: *When the storm started, we took refuge in a store.* **SYNONYM: shelter**
**2** a place where you are protected from danger or bad weather: *a wildlife refuge*
[**ORIGIN:** 1300-1400 From the Latin word *refugium*, from *refugere*, which means "to run away." A refuge is a place where people who run away from danger are safe.]

**ref·u·gee** /ˌrefyʊˈdʒi/ *noun*
someone who has to leave his or her own country because it is dangerous to be there: *During the war, many refugees crossed the border into neighboring countries.*

**re·fund¹** /riˈfʌnd/ *verb*
to give someone back the money he or she paid you for something: *If the toaster breaks within six months, we will refund your money.*

**re·fund²** /ˈrifʌnd/ *noun*
if you get a refund, you get back the money that you paid for something because it is not good enough: *The clock I bought was broken, so I asked for a refund.*

**re·fus·al** /rɪˈfyuzəl/ *noun (formal)*
an act of saying that you will not do something or will not allow something: *His refusal to pay the fine means he may go to jail.* **ANTONYM: agreement**

**re·fuse¹** /rɪˈfyuz/ *verb*
to say that you will not do something or will not allow something: *Steve refused to answer any questions.* **ANTONYM: agree**
→ see Thesaurus box at **reject**

**ref·use²** /ˈrefyus/ *noun (formal)*
things that are thrown away, such as old food and dirty paper: *A truck comes to collect the refuse.* **SYNONYM: garbage**
→ see Thesaurus box at **garbage**

**re·gain** /rɪˈgeɪn/ *verb (formal)*
to get back something that you used to have: *After the accident, she did not regain the use of her legs.*

**re·gard¹** /rɪˈgɑrd/ *verb (formal)*
to think about someone in a particular way: *I regard you as my friend.*

**regard²** *noun (formal)*
**1** respect for someone or something: *Most people have a high regard for doctors and think they do an important job.*
**2 with/in regard to something** = used when saying what you are talking or writing about: *I am writing to you with regard to your son's bad behavior in class.* **SYNONYM: regarding**
**3 regards** = good wishes: *Give my regards to your parents.*

**re·gard·ing** /rɪˈgɑrdɪŋ/ *preposition (formal)*
used when saying what you are talking or writing about: *I wrote a letter regarding my daughter's progress.* **SYNONYM: about**

**re·gard·less** /rɪˈgɑrdlɪs/ *adverb (formal)*
without being affected by something: *He does what he wants regardless of what I say.*

**reg·gae** /ˈregeɪ/ *noun*
a type of popular music from Jamaica: *I love reggae, especially Bob Marley.*

**re·gime** Ac /reɪˈʒim/ *noun (formal)*
a government, especially one that is strict or has not been elected: *Opponents of the regime are put in jail.*
→ see Thesaurus box at **government**

R

**reg·i·ment** /ˈredʒəmənt/ *noun*
a large group of soldiers who are part of an army: *There are 400 soldiers in the regiment.*

**re·gion** Ac /ˈridʒən/ *noun*
a large area of a country or the world: *The Great Lakes region includes eight U.S. states.*
—**regional** *adjective* relating to regions: *There are regional differences in the way Americans talk.*
→ see Thesaurus box at **area**
[ORIGIN: 1300-1400 From the Latin word *regio*, from *regere*, which means "to rule." The idea is that someone would have ruled an area.]

R

**reg·is·ter¹** Ac /ˈredʒəstɚ/ *noun*
**1** an official list or record of something: *The museum is on the Register of Historic Places.*
**2** another word for a CASH REGISTER

**register²** Ac *verb*
**1** to put a name or details on an official list: *The car is registered in my name.* | *How many students registered for the history class?*
**2** (*formal*) if an instrument registers an amount, it shows that amount: *The thermometer registered 74°F.*

**ˌregistered ˈnurse** *noun*
a nurse who has a college degree and has worked in a hospital as part of his or her training **SYNONYM: R.N.**

**reg·is·trar** /ˈredʒəˌstrɑr/ *noun*
someone in a school or college who takes care of official records: *The registrar keeps a record of students' grades.*

**reg·is·tra·tion** Ac /ˌredʒəˈstreɪʃən/ *noun*
**1** the act of putting names or details on an official list: *Registration for classes will take place on Monday.*
**2** a piece of paper that shows you have registered something on an official list: *Can I see your car registration, please?*

**reg·is·try** /ˈredʒəstri/ *noun* (plural **registries**)
a place where there are official records: *The Registry of Motor Vehicles keeps the addresses of car owners.*

**re·gret¹** /rɪˈgret/ *verb* (**regretted**, **regretting**)
**1** to wish that you had not done something: *I regret leaving home because I miss my family.*
**2** (*formal*) to be sorry about a situation: *The letter read, "I regret that I will not be able to attend your wedding."*

**regret²** *noun*
sadness that you feel because you wish you had not done something: *I have no regrets about telling her the truth; it was the right thing to do.*

**re·group** /riˈgrup/ *verb*
to form new groups, or to form a group again: *The team has regrouped after a poor season, with a number of new players.*

**reg·u·lar** /ˈregyəlɚ/ *adjective*
**1** happening or repeated at the same time every second, hour, day, etc.: *His heartbeat is strong and regular.* | *We have a regular meeting every Monday.* **ANTONYM: irregular**
**2** normal or usual, and not special or different: *I saw Dr. Stein because my regular doctor was on vacation.* | *He didn't want a regular job; he wanted something exciting.*
**3** of a standard size: *Do you want a large or regular Cola?*
**4** a regular verb or noun changes its forms in the same way as most verbs or nouns: *The verb "walk" is regular, but the verb "be" is not.* **ANTONYM: irregular**
→ see Thesaurus box at **normal**
[ORIGIN: 1300-1400 From the Latin word *regula*, which means "ruler for drawing straight lines."]

**reg·u·lar·i·ty** /ˌregyəˈlærəti/ *noun* (*formal*)
the fact that something happens or is repeated at the same time every second, hour, day, etc.: *I listened to the regularity of the clock's ticking.*

**reg·u·lar·ly** /ˈregyəlɚli/ *adverb*
**1** at the same time every second, hour, day, etc.: *Take the medicine regularly twice a day.*
**2** often: *When using a computer, save your work regularly.*
→ see Thesaurus box at **often**

**reg·u·late** Ac /ˈregyəˌleɪt/ *verb* (*formal*)
**1** to control activities or people by having rules: *The Medical Board regulates doctors.*
**2** to keep something at the same level: *People sweat to regulate their body heat, so they don't get too hot.*
—**regulatory** /ˈregyələˌtɔri/ *adjective* controlling an activity: *There are regulatory laws controlling nuclear waste.*

**WORD FAMILY: regulate**

**regulate** *verb* | **regulation** *noun* | **regulatory** *adjective*

**reg·u·la·tion** Ac /ˌregyəˈleɪʃən/ *noun* (*formal*)
**1** an official rule: *Fire regulations say that you must not block the exits.*
**2** the act of controlling something, using rules: *The Internet has little regulation, so people can put almost anything they want on it.*
→ see Thesaurus box at **rule**[1]

**re·hears·al** /rɪˈhɚsəl/ *noun*
a practice of a play, show, or concert before people come to see it: *Rehearsals for the play will take place after school.*

**re·hearse** /rɪˈhɚs/ *verb*
to practice for a play, show, or concert before people come to see it: *They rehearsed the song many times before the performance.*
→ see Thesaurus box at **practice**[2]
[**ORIGIN:** 1200-1300 From the old French word *rehercier*, which means "to break up the soil again," from *herce*, a farm tool for breaking up soil. The word came to mean "to repeat."]

**reign** /reɪn/ *noun*
the time when a king or queen rules a country: *The king's reign lasted two years.*
—**reign** *verb* to be the king or queen of a country: *The king reigned for 52 years.*
[**ORIGIN:** 1200-1300 From the Latin word *regnum*, from *rex*, which means "king."]

**re·im·burse** /ˌriɪmˈbɚs/ *verb* (*formal*)
to give someone the amount of money he or she paid for something: *He will pay the hotel bill, and then his company will reimburse him.*

**rein·deer** /ˈreɪndɪr/ *noun* (plural **reindeer**)
a large animal with horns that look like branches on its head. Reindeer live in cold northern parts of the world.

**re·in·force** Ac /ˌriɪnˈfɔrs/ *verb*
**1** to make someone's beliefs, opinions, or behavior stronger and more definite: *Praising your dog when it obeys you reinforces its good behavior.*
**2** to make a part of a building or a piece of clothing stronger: *They reinforced the wall with concrete.* **SYNONYM: strengthen**

**reins** /reɪnz/ *plural noun*
long pieces of leather that you hold to control a horse when you are riding it: *She pulled on the reins, and the horse stopped.*

**re·ject** Ac /rɪˈdʒekt/ *verb* (*formal*)
**1** to say firmly that you do not want something or someone: *She rejected my offer of help.* **ANTONYM: accept**

**THESAURUS: reject**

**refuse** to say firmly that you will not do something someone has asked you to do: *When she asked him to leave, he refused to go.*

**turn down** (*informal*) to say that you do not want something that you have been offered, especially something good: *They offered her a job, but she turned it down.*

**say no** (*informal*) to say that you do not want something, or that you will not do something: *I asked him if he wanted a drink, but he said no.*

**decline** (*formal*) to say politely that you will not do something or accept an offer: *The senator declined to say whether he would vote for the bill.*

**2** to say that you do not like a suggestion or believe an idea: *The proposal was rejected by the committee.* | *Most other scientists rejected his theory, but it was later proven to be true.*
[**ORIGIN:** 1400-1500 From the Latin word *rejectus*, a form of the verb *reicere*, which means "to throw back."]

**re·jec·tion** Ac /rɪˈdʒekʃən/ *noun* (*formal*)
the act of saying or showing that you do not want something or someone: *He was afraid of rejection, and didn't ask her for a date in case she said no.* **ANTONYM: acceptance**

**re·joice** /rɪˈdʒɔɪs/ *verb* (*formal*)
to feel or be very happy: *His parents rejoiced when he came home safely.*

**re·late** /rɪˈleɪt/ *verb*
**1** if two things relate to each other, there is a connection between them: *It is more interesting doing math problems that relate to our own lives.*
**2** to tell someone about something that happened: *He related the whole story to us.*

3 (*formal*) if people relate to each other, they like and understand each other: *He has a hard time relating to other children of his own age.*

**re·lat·ed** /rɪˈleɪtɪd/ *adjective*
1 if two people are related, they are in the same family: *I'm related to John – he's my uncle.*
2 if two things are related, there is a connection between them: *Lung cancer is related to smoking.* | *Politics and economics are closely related.* **SYNONYM: connected**

**WORD FAMILY: related**
**related** *adjective* | **unrelated** *adjective* | **relate** *verb* | **relation** *noun* | **relationship** *noun*

R

**re·la·tion** /rɪˈleɪʃən/ *noun*
1 a connection between things: *There is a direct relation between smoking and cancer.* **SYNONYM: relationship**
2 a member of your family: *All my aunts, uncles, and other relations came to the wedding.* **SYNONYM: relative**
3 **relations** = the way people, groups, or countries behave toward each other: *After my parents' divorce, relations between them were not good.*
→ see Thesaurus box at **family**

**re·la·tion·ship** /rɪˈleɪʃənˌʃɪp/ *noun*
1 the way in which people or groups feel about and behave toward each other: *My mother and I have a good relationship and enjoy spending time together.* | *The relationship between the two countries is friendly.*
2 the way in which events or situations are connected: *The relationship between health and exercise is clear.*
3 a situation in which two people are together because they love each other: *She is not in a relationship with anyone.*

**rel·a·tive¹** /ˈrelətɪv/ *noun*
a member of your family: *Her parents, sister and other close relatives visited her in the hospital.* **SYNONYM: relation**
→ see Thesaurus box at **family**

**relative²** *adjective*
having a particular quality when compared with something else: *The airbed lets you sleep on the ground in relative comfort.*

**ˌrelative ˈclause** *noun*
a part of a sentence that has a verb in it and begins with a word such as "who," "which," or "that": *In the sentence, "The dress that I bought is too small," "that I bought" is a relative clause.*

**rel·a·tive·ly** /ˈrelətɪvli/ *adverb*
when compared with something else: *Compared with some cell phones, this one is relatively cheap.*

**ˌrelative ˈpronoun** *noun*
a word such as "who," "which," or "that," which connects a RELATIVE CLAUSE to the rest of the sentence: *In the sentence, "The dress that I bought is too small," "that" is the relative pronoun.*

**re·lax** [Ac] /rɪˈlæks/ *verb*
1 to rest and not do very much: *After school, I just want to sit down and relax.*
2 to become less worried and more calm: *Don't worry about it. Try to relax.*
3 if your muscles relax, they become less tight or stiff: *He felt his muscles relax as he lay in the bathtub.*
[**ORIGIN:** 1300-1400 From the Latin word *relaxare*, which means "to loosen," from *laxus*, which means "loose."]

**WORD FAMILY: relax**
**relax** *verb* | **relaxed** *adjective* | **relaxing** *adjective* | **relaxation** *noun*

**re·lax·a·tion** [Ac] /ˌrilækˈseɪʃən/ *noun*
the state of being less worried, less busy, or less stiff in your body: *Yoga is good for relaxation.*

**re·laxed** [Ac] /rɪˈlækst/ *adjective*
calm and not worried: *Gail was lying in the sun, looking relaxed.* **ANTONYM: tense**

**re·lax·ing** [Ac] /rɪˈlæksɪŋ/ *adjective*
making you feel calm, or less stiff in your body: *A hot bath is very relaxing.*

**re·lay¹** /ˈrileɪ/ *verb* (*formal*)
to send information from one person or place to another: *The manager relayed the news to the staff.* **SYNONYM: pass**

relay

a relay race

**relay**[2] *noun*
a race in which each member of a team runs or swims part of the distance: *Smith ran the first 400 meters of the relay.*

**re·lease**[1] Ac /rɪˈlis/ *verb*
**1** to let a person or animal go free: *Four prisoners have been released from jail.* | *I released the bird from its cage.*
**2** to let people know about something that has happened: *The police have not released details of the crime.*
**3** to make a movie, song, or CD available for people to buy or see: *The band has just released a new album and it is in stores.*
[**ORIGIN:** 1200-1300 From the old French word *relessier*, from the Latin word *relaxare*, which means "to loosen." If you release something, you have to loosen your hold or control on it so that you can let it go.]

**release**[2] Ac *noun*
**1** the act of letting someone go free: *After his release from prison, he worked as a truck driver.*
**2** a new movie, book, or song that is available for people to see or buy: *The band's new release is on sale now.*

**re·lent·less** /rɪˈlentləs/ *adjective* (*formal*)
if something bad is relentless, it continues without stopping or getting better: *Students take a lot of tests, and the pressure can feel relentless.*

**rel·e·vant** Ac /ˈreləvənt/ *adjective*
directly relating to what you are discussing or doing: *We can't make a decision until we have all the relevant information.* **ANTONYM: irrelevant**
—**relevance** *noun* the fact that something is relevant

**WORD FAMILY: relevant**
**relevant** *adjective* | **irrelevant** *adjective* | **relevance** *noun* | **irrelevance** *noun*

**re·li·a·ble** Ac /rɪˈlaɪəbəl/ *adjective*
**1** reliable people do what they say they will do: *He's a reliable worker who always comes to work on time.* **SYNONYM: dependable**; **ANTONYM: unreliable**
**2** something that is reliable does what it should do: *We need a reliable car that won't break down.* **ANTONYM: unreliable**
—**reliably** *adverb* in a reliable way: *The washing machine has worked reliably for ten years.*
—**reliability** /rɪˌlaɪəˈbɪləti/ *noun* the state of being reliable

**re·li·ant** Ac /rɪˈlaɪənt/ *adjective* (*formal*)
**be reliant on someone** = if you are reliant on someone, you cannot do something without him or her: *She does not have a job, so she's reliant on her parents for money.* **SYNONYM: dependent**
—**reliance** *noun* the state of being reliant on someone

**re·lief** /rɪˈlif/ *noun*
**1** happiness because something bad did not happen or has finished: *I hate tests, and it was a relief when they were over.*
**2** the act of making pain go away: *This medicine is used for pain relief.*
**3** food, clothes, and money that organizations give to people who are suffering because of a war, flood, EARTHQUAKE, etc.: *Victims of the flood are receiving disaster relief, including clean water and food.*

**re·lieve** /rɪˈliv/ *verb*
**1** to make pain or trouble less bad: *The medicine relieved his headache.*
**2** to do a duty that someone else has been doing: *The guard will be relieved at midnight by another soldier.*
→ see Thesaurus box at **reduce**

**re·lieved** /rɪˈlivd/ *adjective*
happy because something bad did not happen or is finished: *We were relieved when Gary called to tell us he was safe.*

**re·li·gion** /rɪˈlɪdʒən/ *noun*
**1** belief in one or more gods: *Religion is very important to me, and I pray every day.*

R

**THESAURUS: religion**

**faith** belief in God, or a particular religion: *Her faith helped her get through a really difficult time.* | *the Jewish faith*

**belief** an idea that you think is true or right: *He has strong religious beliefs.*

**2** a particular set of beliefs in one or more gods: *Hinduism and Buddhism are important religions in India.*

**re·li·gious** /rɪˈlɪdʒəs/ *adjective*
**1** relating to religion: *We have different religious beliefs, I am a Muslim and he is a Christian.*
**2** a religious person believes in a god or gods and obeys the rules of his or her religion: *My mother is very religious, and goes to church.*

**re·li·gious·ly** /rɪˈlɪdʒəsli/ *adverb*
if you do something religiously, you always do it: *I run five miles religiously every day.*

**rel·ish** /ˈrelɪʃ/ *verb*
to enjoy something or like it: *She has five brothers and sisters, so she relished the chance to be alone in the house.*

**re·lo·cate** Ac /riˈloʊˌkeɪt/ *verb*
to move to a new place: *We lived in New York until Dad's company relocated to California.*
—**relocation** /ˌriloʊˈkeɪʃən/ *noun* the act of relocating

**re·luc·tant** Ac /rɪˈlʌktənt/ *adjective*
if you are reluctant to do something, you do not want to do it even though you may have to: *I was reluctant to go to the party because none of my friends would be there.* **ANTONYM: eager**
—**reluctance** *noun* the state of being reluctant
—**reluctantly** *adverb* in a reluctant way: *She reluctantly gave all her money to Mark.*

**re·ly** Ac /rɪˈlaɪ/ *verb* (**relied**, **relies**)
**PHRASAL VERB**
**rely on someone**
**1** to need someone to help you or do something: *The villagers rely on the river for water.*
**2** to know that someone will help you or do something: *Ann is a good friend, and I can rely on her.*

**WORD FAMILY: rely**

**rely** *verb* | **reliable** *adjective* | **unreliable** *adjective* | **reliably** *adverb* | **reliability** *noun*

**re·main** /rɪˈmeɪn/ *verb* (*formal*)
**1** to continue being something: *They met in high school, and remained friends for years.*
**2** to stay in the same place: *The others left while I remained at home.*
**3** to still exist, after other things or parts have gone: *One wall remained after the fire had destroyed the rest of the building.*

**re·main·der** /rɪˈmeɪndɚ/ *noun* (*formal*)
**1** the part of something that is still there after all the other parts are gone: *I'll go with you; the remainder of the group can stay here.* **SYNONYM: rest**
**2** the number that is left when one number cannot be divided exactly by another: *Seventeen divided by three leaves a remainder of two (17 ÷ 3 = 5 remainder 2).*

**re·main·ing** /rɪˈmeɪnɪŋ/ *adjective*
the remaining things or people are the ones that are still there when the others are gone: *I took an apple and put the remaining fruit in the bowl.*

**re·mains** /rɪˈmeɪnz/ *plural noun* (*formal*)
**1** the parts of something that are left after the rest is gone: *The remains of the evening meal were on the table.*
**2** a person's body after he or she has died: *His remains are buried in the graveyard.*

**re·mark¹** /rɪˈmɑrk/ *noun*
something that you say: *He made a rude remark about the woman.* **SYNONYM: comment**

**remark²** *verb*
to say something: *One woman remarked that he was handsome.*

**re·mark·a·ble** /rɪˈmɑrkəbəl/ *adjective*
unusual or surprising, especially in a good way: *She has made remarkable progress in English in just one year.*
—**remarkably** *adverb* in a remarkable way: *Steven is only eight, but he plays the guitar remarkably well.*

**re·mar·ry** /ˌriˈmæri/ *verb* (**remarried**, **remarries**)
to get married again: *After her husband's death, Carol never remarried.*
—**remarriage** *noun* the act of getting married again

**re·me·di·al** /rɪˈmidiəl/ *adjective*
remedial work or classes are for students who need extra help to learn something: *Remedial math is for children who find number work difficult.*

**rem·e·dy** /ˈremədi/ *noun* (plural **remedies**) (*formal*)
**1** a successful way of dealing with a problem: *The best remedy for a bad mood is a good night's sleep.* **SYNONYM: cure**
**2** a medicine or drink that stops pain or makes an illness better: *Honey and lemon is a remedy for colds.* **SYNONYM: cure**
[**ORIGIN:** 1200-1300 From the Latin word *remedium*, from *mederi*, which means "to heal."]

**re·mem·ber** /rɪˈmembɚ/ *verb*
**1** if you remember something, it is in your mind or comes into your mind: *I practiced saying the lines until I could remember the whole poem.* **ANTONYM: forget**
**2** to not forget to do something you need to do: *Did you remember to feed the cat this morning?* **ANTONYM: forget**
[**ORIGIN:** 1300-1400 From the Latin word *rememorari*, from *memor*, which means "remembering."]

**re·mem·brance** /rɪˈmembrəns/ *noun* (*formal*)
the act of remembering and showing respect to someone who has died: *She planted a tree in remembrance of her husband.*

**re·mind** /rɪˈmaɪnd/ *verb*
to make someone remember something that he or she must do: *Remind me to mail that letter tomorrow.*
**PHRASAL VERB**
**remind someone of someone or something**
to make you think of someone or something that is like another person or thing: *Julia reminds me of my sister; they have the same smile.*

**re·mind·er** /rɪˈmaɪndɚ/ *noun*
something that makes you remember something else: *The damaged buildings were a reminder of the recent war.*

**rem·i·nisce** /ˌreməˈnɪs/ *verb*
to think or talk about nice things that happened in the past: *My grandparents were reminiscing about things they did when they were young.*

**rem·nant** /ˈremnənt/ *noun* (*formal*)
a small part of something that is still there after the rest has gone: *These woods are only a remnant of what was once a very big forest.*

**re·morse** /rɪˈmɔrs/ *noun*
a feeling that you are sorry for doing something very bad: *The thief showed no remorse for his crime.*

**re·mote** /rɪˈmoʊt/ *adjective*
**1** far away from other places: *They lived on a remote farm, miles away from town.*
**2** a remote chance or possibility is very unlikely to happen: *The possibility that the team will go to the championships is remote.*
**3** far away in time: *In the remote past, dinosaurs lived on Earth.*
[**ORIGIN:** 1400-1500 From the Latin word *remotus*, a form of the verb *removere*, which means "to move something back or away."]

**reˌmote conˈtrol** (*also* **remote**) *noun*
a thing that you use to control a machine such as a television or DVD player from a distance, for example to turn it on and off: *Where's the remote control for the TV?* → see picture on page **A8**

**re·mote·ly** /rɪˈmoʊtli/ *adverb*
used for emphasizing that someone or something does not have any of the qualities you are talking about: *I'm not even remotely interested in computer games; I never play them.*

**re·mov·al** Ac /rɪˈmuvəl/ *noun*
the act of taking something away: *His mouth hurt from the removal of four teeth.*

**re·move** Ac /rɪˈmuv/ *verb*
**1** to take something away from a place: *Please do not remove these books from the library.*
**2** (*formal*) to take off a piece of clothing: *He removed his hat.*

R

—**removable** *adjective* easy to take away: *The seat has a removable cover.*

**Ren·ais·sance** /ˈrenəˌzɑns/ *noun*
**the Renaissance** = the period in Europe between the 14th and 17th centuries, when there was a lot of new art and scientific progress

**re·new** /rɪˈnu/ *verb*
**1** to do the things you need to do so that you can use something for a longer time: *I need to renew my passport; it expired last month.* | *Do you want to renew your library books for another two weeks?*
**2** (*formal*) to begin to do something again: *The police will renew their search for the missing boy in the morning.* **SYNONYM: resume**

R

**re·new·a·ble** /rɪˈnuəbəl/ *adjective*
**1** if an official document or agreement is renewable, you can make it continue: *Is the visa renewable?*
**2** if something is renewable, you will always be able to get more of it because it continues to be produced all the time: *Wind power is a renewable source of energy.*

**ren·o·vate** /ˈrenəˌveɪt/ *verb*
to fix a building so that it looks new: *The company renovated the hotel.*
—**renovation** /ˌrenəˈveɪʃən/ *noun* the process of fixing a building so that it looks new: *The museum is closed for renovation.*
→ see Thesaurus box at **repair**[1]

**re·nowned** /rɪˈnaʊnd/ *adjective*
famous for something: *The restaurant is renowned for its excellent food.*

**rent**[1] /rent/ *verb*
**1** to pay money to live in a place: *We rent the apartment from my uncle.*
**2** to pay money to use something for a short time: *They're going to rent a car.*
**3** (*also* **rent out**) if you rent something that you own, you allow someone else to use it, and they pay you money: *They rent the house out to tourists in the summer.*
—**renter** *noun* someone who pays money to live in a place: *They have two renters living in the apartment.*

**rent**[2] *noun*
**1** money that you pay to live in a place or use something for a period of time: *The rent for the house is paid each month.*
**2 for rent** = available to be rented: *Do you have any apartments for rent?*
→ see Thesaurus box at **cost**[1]

**rent·al** /ˈrentl/ *noun*
an arrangement in which you pay to use something that belongs to someone else: *a car rental company* | *Ski rental is $14.*

**re·paid** /riˈpeɪd/ *verb*
the past tense and past participle of REPAY

**re·pair**[1] /rɪˈper/ *verb*
to fix something that is damaged or not working: *How much will it cost to repair the TV?* | *Where can I get my shoes repaired?*

**THESAURUS: repair**

**fix** to repair something that is broken or not working correctly: *Someone's coming to fix the washing machine.*

**mend** to repair a hole in a piece of clothing: *She was mending a pair of jeans.*

**renovate** (*formal*) to repair a building, room, or furniture so that it looks new again: *They renovated the kitchen when they moved into the house.*

**restore** (*formal*) to repair something so it is as good as when it was new: *He restores old cars.*

**repair**[2] *noun*
something that you do to fix something that is damaged or not working: *Dad's always doing repairs on his car.* | *The roof is badly in need of repair.*
[**ORIGIN:** 1300-1400 From the Latin word *reparare*, from *parare*, which means "to prepare."]

**re·pair·man** /rɪˈpermæn/ *noun*
someone whose job it is to fix something that is damaged or not working: *a TV repairman*

**re·pay** /rɪˈpeɪ/ *verb* (**repaid** /riˈpeɪd/, **repays**)
**1** to give money back to someone you have borrowed it from: *I'll repay the money you lent me by next week.*
**2** to do something for someone because he or she has helped you: *I'd like to buy him something to repay him for his kindness.*
—**repayment** *noun* the act of giving back

money that you have borrowed: *The repayment of the loan took several years.*

**re·peal** /rɪˈpil/ *verb*
to officially end a law: *In 1933, Congress repealed the law that had stopped alcohol from being sold to anyone.*
—**repeal** *noun* the act of officially ending a law

**re·peat¹** /rɪˈpit/ *verb*
to say or do something again: *Could you repeat what you just said?* | *Repeat the exercises twice a day.*

**WORD FAMILY: repeat**
**repeat** *verb* | **repeat** *noun* | **repetition** *noun* | **repeated** *adjective* | **repeatedly** *adverb* | **repetitive** *adjective*

**repeat²** *noun*
**1** something that happens in exactly the same way as it happened before: *We don't want a repeat of the problems we had last year.*
**2** a television program that is being shown again: *"Is it a repeat?" "No, it's a new episode."*

**re·peat·ed** /rɪˈpitɪd/ *adjective* (*formal*)
done several times: *He made repeated attempts to lose weight, but he only lost a pound or two each time.*
—**repeatedly** *adverb* again and again: *I asked him repeatedly to leave, but he wouldn't go.*

**re·pel** [Ac] /rɪˈpel/ *verb* (**repelling**, **repelled**)
**1** if something repels you, it is so unpleasant that you do not want to be near it, or it makes you feel sick: *The smell of stale cigarettes repelled him.*
**2** if two objects repel each other they push each other away: *This end of the magnet will repel another magnet, so that you cannot make them stay together.* **ANTONYM: attract**

**rep·e·ti·tion** /ˌrepəˈtɪʃən/ *noun*
**1** the act of saying or doing the same thing again, or doing it many times: *Repetition can help you learn your multiplication tables.*
**2** something that happens in exactly the same way as it happened before: *We don't want a repetition of past mistakes.* **SYNONYM: repeat**

**re·pet·i·tive** /rɪˈpetətɪv/ (*also* **rep·e·ti·tious** /ˌrepəˈtɪʃəs/) *adjective*
something that is repetitive is boring because the same thing is done or said many times: *Many factory jobs are very repetitive.*

**re·place** /rɪˈpleɪs/ *verb*
to get or use a new person or thing instead of the one you used before: *When the TV stopped working, we had to replace it.*
—**replaceable** *adjective* able to be replaced

**re·place·ment** /rɪˈpleɪsmənt/ *noun*
a new person or thing that you use instead of the one you had before: *Who will be the boss's replacement when she retires?*

**re·play** /ˈriːpleɪ/ *noun*
an action in a sports game on television that is shown again immediately after it happens: *You can see on the replay that the player dropped the ball.*
—**replay** /riˈpleɪ/ *verb* to show a replay on television

**rep·li·ca** /ˈreplɪkə/ *noun*
an exact copy of something: *The model was an exact replica of the palace.*
[**ORIGIN:** 1800-1900 From the Italian word for "copy or something repeated," from the Latin word *replicare*, which means "to repeat."]

**re·ply¹** /rɪˈplaɪ/ *verb* (**replied** /rɪˈplaɪd/, **replies** /rɪˈplaɪz/)
to answer: *"Yes, that's true," she replied.* | *He didn't reply to my letter.*
→ see Thesaurus box at **answer¹**

**reply²** *noun* (plural **replies**)
something that you say or write as an answer: *I am still waiting for a reply to my letter.* | *I could barely hear her reply because she spoke so quietly.*

**re·port¹** /rɪˈpɔrt/ *noun*
something written or spoken that gives facts about a situation or event: *The students will write a report on their visit to the museum.* | *a newspaper report*

**report²** *verb*
**1** to tell people about something that has happened: *The newspaper reported that Grayson won the election.*
**2** to tell the police that a crime or accident has happened: *She reported the theft to the police.*

R

PHRASAL VERB
**report to someone**
to work for someone: *The salesmen report to Greg Shaw, who is the manager of the sales department.*

**re'port card** *noun*
a piece of paper with a student's grades on it, and statements from teachers about how hard he or she has worked: *He had three A's, two B's, and a C on his report card.*

**re,ported 'speech** *noun*
in grammar, the style of speech or writing that is used for telling people what someone says, without repeating the actual words: *The sentence "She said she didn't feel well" is an example of reported speech.*

R

**re·port·er** /rɪˈpɔrtɚ/ *noun*
someone who writes news stories: *a newspaper reporter* → see picture on page **A17**

**rep·re·sent** /ˌreprɪˈzent/ *verb*
**1** if someone represents you, he or she officially speaks for you or does a job for you because you cannot do it yourself: *Each class elects two students to represent them on the school council.*
**2** to show or mean something: *The red lines on the map represent the railroad.*
—**representation** /ˌreprɪzenˈteɪʃən/ *noun* the state of having someone to represent you: *Each state has equal representation in the Senate.*

**WORD FAMILY: represent**
**represent** *verb* | **representation** *noun* | **representative** *noun*

**rep·re·sent·a·tive** /ˌreprɪˈzentətɪv/ *noun*
**1** someone who people have chosen to do things for them: *Two representatives from each class are going to the meeting.*
**2 Representative** = a member of the House of Representatives in the U.S. Congress: *She is one of California's Representatives.*

**re·prieve** /rɪˈpriv/ *noun*
an official order to change or delay a decision to kill a prisoner as an official punishment: *The governor granted the prisoner a reprieve at the last minute and saved his life.*

**rep·ri·mand** /ˈreprəˌmænd/ *verb* (*formal*)
to tell someone officially that he or she has done something wrong: *The teacher reprimanded him for being late.*
—**reprimand** *noun* the act of reprimanding someone

**re·pris·al** /rɪˈpraɪzəl/ *noun* (*formal*)
something that you do to punish an enemy: *The gang set fire to a police car in reprisal for the arrest of a gang member.*

**re·proach** /rɪˈproʊtʃ/ *verb* (*formal*)
to say something that makes someone feel sorry for what he or she has done: *Ben's daughter reproached him for not telling her the truth.*

**re·pro·duce** /ˌriprəˈdus/ *verb* (*formal*)
**1** if animals or plants reproduce, they make more animals or plants: *Fish reproduce by laying eggs.*
**2** to make a copy of something such as a work of art: *The artist's paintings are reproduced in this book.*

**re·pro·duc·tion** /ˌriprəˈdʌkʃən/ *noun*
**1** the act of producing babies, young animals, or plants: *We learned about human reproduction in biology class.*
**2** a copy of something such as a work of art: *The picture is a reproduction of a painting by Van Gogh.*

**rep·tile** /ˈreptaɪl/ *noun*
an animal such as a snake or a LIZARD: *Reptiles are cold-blooded. Their body temperature changes when the temperature around them changes.*
[**ORIGIN:** 1300-1400 From the Latin word *reptilis*, which means "creeping."]

**re·pub·lic** /rɪˈpʌblɪk/ *noun*
a country that elects its government and does not have a king or queen: *France is a republic.*
→ see Thesaurus box at **government**
[**ORIGIN:** 1500-1600 From the Latin word *respublica*, which means "the state," from *res* and *publica*, which mean "thing" and "public."]

**Re·pub·li·can** /rɪˈpʌblɪkən/ *noun*
a member of the Republican Party: *Most Republicans in the House voted for a change in the law.*
—**Republican** *adjective* relating to the Republican Party: *a Republican politician*

**Re'publican ˌParty** *noun*
one of the two main political parties of the U.S.: *The Republican Party supports laws that help businesses.*

**rep·u·ta·ble** /ˈrepyətəbəl/ *adjective (formal)*
respected for being honest and doing good work: *If you want a used car, go to a reputable dealer.*

**rep·u·ta·tion** /ˌrepyəˈteɪʃən/ *noun*
the opinion that people have of someone or something: *This school has a very good reputation and many parents want to send their children here.*

**re·quest¹** /rɪˈkwest/ *noun (formal)*
the act of asking for something politely or formally: *The school has made a request for fifteen more computers.*

**request²** *verb (formal)*
to ask for something politely or formally: *To request further information, please call this phone number.*
→ see Thesaurus box at **ask**

**re·quire** Ac /rɪˈkwaɪɚ/ *verb*
**1** to need something: *Pets require a lot of care.*
**2** *(formal)* to say officially that someone must do something: *The school requires that students study a foreign language.*

**re·quire·ment** Ac /rɪˈkwaɪɚmənt/ *noun (formal)*
**1** something that you need: *Food, shelter, and clothing meet people's basic requirements.*
**2** something that you must do or have because of a rule: *P.E. is a requirement, so all students must take a P.E. class.*

**re·run** /ˈrirʌn/ *noun*
a television program that is being shown again: *We watched a rerun of "Friends."*
—**rerun** /riˈrʌn/ *verb* to show a television program again

**re·sched·ule** Ac /riˈskedʒəl/ *verb*
to arrange for something to happen at a different time: *We've rescheduled Tuesday's meeting; it will now take place on Friday.*

**res·cue¹** /ˈreskyu/ *verb*
to save someone when he or she is in danger: *The Coast Guard rescued the sailors from the sinking ship.*
—**rescuer** *noun* someone who rescues someone else

**rescue²** *noun*
an act of saving someone from danger: *The newspaper reported on the rescue of a small boy from the river.*

**re·search¹** Ac /ˈrisɚtʃ/ *noun*
a study of a subject in order to find out new information: *Scientists are doing research into the causes of the disease.*
[ORIGIN: 1500-1600 From the old French word *recerchier*, which means "to find out about something thoroughly," from *cerchier*, which means "to go around, examine, or search."]

**re·search²** Ac /rɪˈsɚtʃ/ *verb*
to study a subject so you can find out new facts about it: *Scientists are researching ways of reducing pollution.*
—**researcher** *noun* someone who researches a subject: *Medical researchers have discovered a new treatment for the illness.*

**re·sem·blance** /rɪˈzembləns/ *noun*
if there is a resemblance between things or people, they look similar to each other: *I don't think I look like my mother, but Dad says there's a strong resemblance.*

**re·sem·ble** /rɪˈzembəl/ *verb (formal)*
to look like or be similar to someone or something: *She resembles her mother in many ways; they are both tall with dark hair.*
[ORIGIN: 1300-1400 From the French word *sembler*, which means "to be like something or to seem," from the Latin word *similis*, which means "like."]

R

**re·sent** /rɪˈzent/ *verb*
to feel angry and upset about something unfair that someone has done to you: *She resented having to clean the house while her brother went out to play.*
—**resentful** *adjective* angry and upset about something unfair that someone has done to you: *She was resentful that her sister got more attention than she did.*
[ORIGIN: 1500-1600 From the French word *ressentir*, which means "to feel strongly about something," from *sentir*, which means "to feel."]

**re·sent·ment** /rɪˈzentmənt/ *noun* (*formal*)
a feeling of anger about something that you think is unfair: *He expressed resentment that no one had believed what he said.*

R

**res·er·va·tion** /ˌrezɚˈveɪʃən/ *noun*
**1** if you make a reservation, you ask for something such as a seat or a room to be kept for you: *They made reservations at the restaurant for 6 o'clock.*
**2** (*formal*) a feeling of doubt about something: *The coach has reservations about letting Jessica play after her leg injury.*
**3** an area of land that is kept separate for Native Americans to live on: *a Navajo reservation*

**re·serve¹** /rɪˈzɚv/ *verb*
**1** to arrange for something to be kept for you to use, for example a seat on an airplane or a room in a hotel: *Tom reserved a table for 8:00 at the restaurant.*
**2** to keep something for a special purpose: *This part of the parking lot is reserved for buses only.*

**reserve²** *noun*
**1** a supply of something that you can use if you need it: *We keep some money in reserve for emergencies.* | *the oil reserves in Alaska*
**2** an area of land where wild animals and plants are protected: *The monkeys live on a wildlife reserve.*

**re·served** /rɪˈzɚvd/ *adjective*
not willing to show your emotions or talk about your thoughts and feelings: *He is a quiet, reserved man, who never shows much emotion.*
→ see Thesaurus box at **shy**

**res·er·voir** /ˈrezɚˌvwɑr/ *noun*
a lake that people have made for storing water: *The water is stored in the reservoir before it goes to people's houses.*

**re·side** /rɪˈzaɪd/ *verb* (*formal*)
to live somewhere: *She was born in New York but now resides in Los Angeles.*

**res·i·dence** Ac /ˈrezədəns/ *noun* (*formal*)
**1** a house where someone lives: *The White House is the president's official residence.*
**2** the state of living in a place: *New York is his main place of residence.*
→ see Thesaurus box at **home¹**

**res·i·dent** Ac /ˈrezədənt/ *noun*
someone who lives in a particular place: *Local residents have complained about the noise from the factory.*

**res·i·den·tial** Ac /ˌrezəˈdenʃəl/ *adjective*
a residential area has houses in it, not offices or businesses: *We live in a quiet, residential neighborhood.*

**res·i·due** /ˈrezəˌdu/ *noun*
the part of a substance that is still there after the rest of it has gone: *Soap can leave a residue on your skin.*

**re·sign** /rɪˈzaɪn/ *verb*
to say officially that you are going to leave your job: *He decided to resign and look for a new job.*
→ see Thesaurus box at **quit**

**res·ig·na·tion** /ˌrezɪgˈneɪʃən/ *noun*
the act of officially saying that you are going to leave your job: *Matt handed in his resignation because he wants to travel for a year.*

**re·signed** /rɪˈzaɪnd/ *adjective*
**be resigned to something/be resigned to doing something** = to accept calmly a bad situation that cannot be changed: *We don't really want to move to Chicago, but we're resigned to it now.*

**re·sist** /rɪˈzɪst/ *verb*
**1** to stop yourself doing something you would like to do, but should not: *I couldn't resist eating some chocolate!* | *She resisted the urge to run away.*
**2** to not want to accept something and try to stop it: *When the police tried to arrest him, he resisted.*
**3** to not be changed or harmed by something: *Vitamin C helps you resist colds.*

[ORIGIN: 1300-1400 From the Latin word *resistere*, from *sistere*, which means "to stop, or to stand somewhere and not move."]

**re·sist·ance** /rɪˈzɪstəns/ *noun*
**1** if there is resistance to something, people do not want to accept it and try to stop it: *There was resistance to the idea of making the school day longer.*
**2** the natural ability that your body has to stop diseases from harming you: *Vitamins can build up your body's resistance to illness.*
**3** the way in which wind, air, water, etc. can cause an object that is moving through it to slow down: *The shape of race cars lowers the wind resistance, so they can go faster.*

**res·o·lu·tion** Ac /ˌrezəˈluʃən/ *noun*
**1** a promise that you make to yourself to do something: *I made a New Year's resolution to study harder at school.*
**2** (*formal*) the ending of a problem or difficulty: *After a long discussion, we came up with a resolution to the problem.*

**re·solve** Ac /rɪˈzɑlv/ *verb* (*formal*)
**1** to do something that ends a problem or disagreement: *Another accident could happen unless we resolve these safety problems.*
**2** to decide to do something: *He resolved to work harder.*
→ see Thesaurus box at **decide**

**re·sort** /rɪˈzɔrt/ *noun*
**1** a place where a lot of people go for a vacation: *Acapulco is one of Mexico's most popular resorts.*
**2 as a last resort** = if everything else fails: *The police only use force as a last resort.*

**re·source** Ac /ˈrisɔrs/ *noun*
**1** something that is available for people to use: *The Internet is a useful resource for finding information.*
**2** something that a country has, for example oil, minerals, or land, which it can use to make money: *The country is rich in natural resources such as oil and coal.*
**3 resources** = all the money, people, skills, and things that you have available to use: *The school is doing a good job, though more resources are needed.*

**re·spect**[1] /rɪˈspekt/ *noun*
**1** a good opinion of someone: *He is a good teacher and I have a lot of respect for him.*
**2** a polite way of behaving toward other people: *Children should show respect for older people.*

**respect**[2] *verb*
**1** to have a good opinion of someone: *She respected him for his honesty.*
**2** to behave in a polite way to other people: *Please respect the other people in the library and try to be quiet.*
**3** if you respect a law or rule, you obey it: *It is important to respect the customs and laws in other countries when you are traveling.*
→ see Thesaurus box at **admire**

**re·spect·a·ble** /rɪˈspektəbəl/ *adjective*
**1** someone who is respectable is good and honest: *They are a respectable family and they work hard.*
**2** clean and neatly dressed: *He wore a suit and tie so that he would look respectable.*
—**respectably** *adverb* in a respectable way: *Jane always dressed respectably when she went to church.*
—**respectability** /rɪˌspektəˈbɪləti/ *noun* the quality of being considered respectable

**re·spect·ful** /rɪˈspektfəl/ *adjective* (*formal*) showing respect for someone or something: *The students listened in respectful silence to the teacher.*
—**respectfully** *adverb* in a way that shows respect

**re·spec·tive** /rɪˈspektɪv/ *adjective* (*formal*) belonging with each of the people or things that you have just mentioned: *I asked my sisters, Amy and Colleen, and their respective boyfriends to the party.*
—**respectively** *adverb* (*formal*) in a way that shows which people or things belong with the things you have mentioned: *The shirt and pants cost $30 and $25, respectively.*

**res·pi·ra·tion** /ˌrespəˈreɪʃən/ *noun* breathing: *When you sleep, your respiration becomes slow and regular.*

**res·pira·to·ry** /ˈresprəˌtɔri/ *adjective* (*formal*) relating to breathing and your lungs: *Smoking can cause respiratory illness.*

**re·spond** Ac /rɪˈspɑnd/ *verb*
**1** (*formal*) to answer: *I responded that I did not believe her.* SYNONYM: **reply**

R

2 to do something because of something that has happened: *Police usually respond to a 911 call in less than five minutes.* **SYNONYM: react**

→ see Thesaurus box at **answer**[1]

[**ORIGIN:** 1500-1600 From the Latin word *respondere*, which means "to promise in return, or answer," from *spondere*, meaning "to promise."]

**WORD FAMILY: respond**
**respond** *verb* | **response** *noun* | **responsive** *adjective*

**re·sponse** Ac /rɪˈspɑns/ *noun* (*formal*)
1 something you say or write as a reply to something: *"Okay," he said in response to the suggestion that we go to the movies.*
2 something you do or feel because of something that has happened: *His quick response to the accident saved the child's life.* **SYNONYM: reaction**

**re·spon·si·bil·i·ty** /rɪˌspɑnsəˈbɪləti/ *noun* (plural **responsibilities**)
1 something that you do because it is your duty or your job: *It's your responsibility to take the dog for a walk.*
2 blame for something bad that has happened: *The coach took the responsibility for the team's losing streak.*

**re·spon·si·ble** /rɪˈspɑnsəbəl/ *adjective*
1 if you are responsible for something bad, you caused it to happen: *The person who is responsible for breaking the window will be punished.*
2 if you are responsible for doing something, it is your duty to do it: *Who is responsible for feeding the dog?*
3 a responsible person behaves in a sensible way and can be trusted: *The children are being cared for by responsible adults.*
—**responsibly** *adverb* in a responsible way: *You can trust Lori to act responsibly.*

**WORD FAMILY: responsible**
**responsible** *adjective* | **responsibly** *adverb* | **responsibility** *noun*

**re·spon·sive** Ac /rɪˈspɑnsɪv/ *adjective* (*formal*)
quick to react in a good or helpful way: *Good teachers are responsive to the needs of their students, so they give help quickly.*

**rest**[1] /rest/ *noun*
1 **the rest** = the part of a thing or group that still remains: *Two of the boys moved slowly forward and the rest followed.* | *What would you like to do for the rest of the day?*
2 a period of time when you can relax or sleep: *You've got a busy day tomorrow, so you'd better get some rest.*
[**ORIGIN:** 1400-1500 Sense 1 is from the Latin word *restare*, which means "to remain."]

**rest**[2] *verb*
1 to spend time relaxing or sleeping: *Let your mom rest when she gets home from work because she'll be tired.*
2 to put something on or against something that will support it: *He rested his hand on his knee.*

**res·tau·rant** /ˈresˌtrɑnt/ *noun*
a place where you can buy and eat a meal: *Have you eaten at this restaurant before?*
[**ORIGIN:** 1800-1900 From the French word *restaurer*, which means "to give someone back energy." "Restaurant" was used to mean a kind of food, and then to mean a place where food is served.]

**rest·ful** /ˈrestfəl/ *adjective*
peaceful and quiet: *He was feeling better after a restful night's sleep.*

**rest·less** /ˈrestləs/ *adjective*
unable to relax and keep still because you are nervous or bored: *The children were beginning to get restless after waiting for so long.*

**re·store** Ac /rɪˈstɔr/ *verb* (*formal*)
1 to make something be the way it was before: *There is hope that the talks will restore peace in the region.*
2 to repair something so that it is as good as when it was new: *They're restoring an old house in town, and it looks so much better.*
—**restoration** /ˌrestəˈreɪʃən/ *noun* (*formal*) the act of restoring something
→ see Thesaurus box at **repair**[2]
[**ORIGIN:** 1200-1300 From the Latin word *restaurare*, which means "to renew or to rebuild."]

**re·strain** Ac /rɪˈstreɪn/ *verb*
to prevent someone or something from moving or from doing something: *The thief tried to run away, and it took three police officers to restrain him.*

**re·strained** [Ac] /rɪˈstreɪnd/ *adjective* (*formal*)
calm and controlled, and not showing any strong emotion: *He answered her in a restrained voice, but I knew he was mad.*

**re·straint** [Ac] /rɪˈstreɪnt/ *noun* (*formal*)
calm and controlled behavior in a difficult situation: *She showed restraint by not yelling at him even though she was very angry.*

**re·strict** [Ac] /rɪˈstrɪkt/ *verb* (*formal*)
to control or limit something: *School rules restrict the type of clothes that students are allowed to wear.*
—**restricted** *adjective* limited or controlled by a law or rule: *The restricted parking is for company employees only.*
—**restrictive** *adjective* stopping people from doing something: *The rules are very restrictive.*
[**ORIGIN:** 1400-1500 From the Latin word *restrictus*, a form of the verb *restringere*, which means "to tie tightly or press together."]

**WORD FAMILY: restrict**
**restrict** *verb* | **restricted** *adjective* | **restriction** *noun* | **restrictive** *adjective*

**re·stric·tion** [Ac] /rɪˈstrɪkʃən/ *noun* (*formal*)
a rule that limits what you are allowed to do: *There's a 50 mph speed restriction on this road.*
→ see Thesaurus box at **rule**[1]

**rest·room** /ˈrestruːm/ *noun*
a room with a toilet, in a public place such as a restaurant or a theater: *I need to use the restroom.*

**re·sult**[1] /rɪˈzʌlt/ *noun*
**1** something that happens or exists because of something that has already happened: *The school was closed as a result of the fire.*

**THESAURUS: result**
**consequences** (*formal*) the bad things that happen as a result of someone's actions: *If you bike without a helmet, it could have serious consequences if you are in an accident.*
**outcome** the final result of something such as an election, game, or war: *We were pleased with the outcome of the election.*

**2** information that you get by testing or examining something: *We are waiting for the results of your blood test.*
**3** the answer you get when you add, subtract, multiply, or divide numbers: *When you multiply 3 by 4, the result is 12.*
**4** the final number of points or votes at the end of a competition or election: *The election results will be announced today.*

**result**[2] *verb* (*formal*)
to happen or exist because of something that happened: *The flooding resulted from all the rain last weekend.*
**PHRASAL VERB**
**result in something**
to make something happen: *The fire resulted in the building being destroyed.* **SYNONYM: cause**

**re·sume** /rɪˈzum/ *verb* (*formal*)
to start again after stopping: *We resumed the meeting after lunch.*

**ré·su·mé** /ˈrezəˌmeɪ/ *noun*
a written document that lists your education and previous jobs, that you send to employers when you are looking for a job: *Send your résumé to our Human Resources department.*

**re·tail** /ˈriteɪl/ *verb*
**retail for/at something** (*formal*) = to be sold at a particular price in stores: *The wine retails for $8.95 a bottle.*
—**retail** *noun* the business of selling goods to people in stores
[**ORIGIN:** 1300-1400 From the old French word *retaillier*, which means "to divide into pieces," from *taillier*, meaning "to cut." A person running a store would divide a large amount of something into smaller pieces to sell it.]

**re·tail·er** /ˈriˌteɪlɚ/ *noun*
a person or business that sells goods to people in a store

**re·tain** [Ac] /rɪˈteɪn/ *verb* (*formal*)
to keep something or to continue to have something: *Pine trees retain their leaves all year.*
—**retention** /rɪˈtenʃən/ *noun* (*formal*) the act of keeping something

**re·tal·i·ate** /rɪˈtæliˌeɪt/ *verb* (*formal*)
to do something bad to someone because he or she has done something bad to you: *Joe hit*

R

*his brother, who retaliated by hitting him back.*
—**retaliation** /rɪˌtæliˈeɪʃən/ *noun* (*formal*) the act of retaliating
[**ORIGIN:** 1600-1700 From the Latin word *retaliare*, from *talio*, which means "a suitable and matching punishment."]

**ret·i·na** /ˈretənə/ *noun*
the area at the back of your eye that receives light and sends an image of what you see to your brain

**re·tire** /rɪˈtaɪɚ/ *verb*
to stop working at the end of your working life: *She's going to retire when she's 65.*
—**retiree** /rɪˌtaɪəˈri/ *noun* someone who has retired from work
→ see Thesaurus box at **quit**

**WORD FAMILY: retire**
**retire** *verb* | **retirement** *noun* | **retiree** *noun*

**re·tire·ment** /rɪˈtaɪɚmənt/ *noun*
the period of time after you have retired: *While you're working, you should be saving money for your retirement.*

**re·treat¹** /rɪˈtrit/ *verb*
**1** if an army retreats, it stops fighting and moves away from the enemy: *The soldiers had to retreat when a larger army attacked them.*
**2** to move away to a safer or quieter place: *When she was upset, she would retreat to her room and listen to music.*

**retreat²** *noun*
if an army makes a retreat, it moves away from the enemy: *The battle went badly, and the general called for a retreat.*

**ret·ri·bu·tion** /ˌretrəˈbyuʃən/ *noun* (*formal*)
severe punishment for doing something: *Neighbors were worried about retribution if they told police about the gang members.*

**re·trieve** /rɪˈtriv/ *verb* (*formal*)
to get something back from the place where it is: *The ball went over the fence, so he went next door to retrieve it.*

**re·turn¹** /rɪˈtɚn/ *verb*
**1** to go or come back to a place where you were before: *Kevin has just returned from Texas.* **SYNONYM: come back**
**2** to give something back to someone: *Will you return these books to the library for me?*
**3** if a feeling or situation returns, it starts happening again: *I felt my anger returning when I remembered how Dan had lied to me.* **SYNONYM: come back**
**4 return someone's call** = to call someone after he or she has tried to speak to you on the telephone: *I left a message on Dave's voice mail, but he hasn't returned my call yet.*

**return²** *noun*
**1** the act of giving something back: *She was willing to pay $500 for the return of her stolen necklace.*
**2** (*formal*) the act of going or coming back to a place where you were before: *We were excited about Mom's return from her trip.*
**3 in return** = if you do something in return, you do it as a payment or thanks for what someone has done for you: *The police let him go, in return for the information he gave them.*

**re·un·ion** /riˈyunyən/ *noun*
a meeting of people who have not met for a long time: *The class of 1997 is having a reunion at the school.*

**re·u·nite** /ˌriyuˈnaɪt/ *verb*
to bring people together again after they have been separated: *The mother and her daughter got separated in the crowd, but were reunited with the help of a police officer.*

**re·use** Ac /ˌriˈyuz/ *verb*
to use something again, instead of throwing it away: *Glass jars can be washed and reused.*
—**reusable** *adjective* able to be reused: *Bring a reusable bag with you when you go shopping.*

**Rev.**
the written abbreviation of REVEREND

**re·veal** Ac /rɪˈvil/ *verb* (*formal*)
**1** to tell people information that was secret: *The boy refused to reveal who had stolen the money.* **ANTONYM: conceal**
**2** to show something that could not be seen before: *He opened his shirt to reveal a scar across his chest.* **ANTONYM: conceal**
[**ORIGIN:** 1300-1400 From the Latin *revelare*, which means "to uncover," from *velum*, which means "curtain or veil."]

R

**WORD FAMILY: reveal**
**reveal** *verb* | **revealing** *adjective* | **revelation** *noun*

**re·veal·ing** [Ac] /rɪˈvilɪŋ/ *adjective*
1 showing something about someone's true character, thoughts, or feelings: *The book tells revealing stories about the actress's life.*
2 revealing clothes show parts of your body that you usually keep covered: *a revealing swimsuit*

**rev·e·la·tion** [Ac] /ˌrevəˈleɪʃən/ *noun* (*formal*)
a surprising fact about someone or something, that people are suddenly told about: *Shocking revelations about her private life appeared in the newspapers.*

**re·venge** /rɪˈvendʒ/ *noun*
something you do in order to punish someone who has done something bad to you: *He wanted revenge on the boys who had made fun of him.*

**rev·e·nue** [Ac] /ˈrevəˌnu/ *noun* (*formal*)
money that a company earns or a government receives from tax: *The state will receive revenue from selling the land.*

**Rev·er·end** /ˈrevrənd/ *noun* (*written abbreviation*: **Rev.**)
used in the title of a minister in a Christian church: *The pastor of the church is Reverend Stephen Dyer.*

**re·verse¹** [Ac] /rɪˈvɚs/ *verb* (*formal*)
to change something so that it is the opposite, or so that it goes back to what it was before: *It will take years to reverse the damage done by pollution.*
—**reversal** *noun* a change to the opposite: *In a reversal of his original decision, the referee said the goal would be allowed.*
—**reversible** *adjective* able to be reversed: *The fan turns clockwise, but the direction is reversible.*

**reverse²** [Ac] *noun*
1 the control in a vehicle that makes it go backward: *Tim put the car in reverse to back out of the driveway.*
2 **the reverse** (*formal*) = the opposite: *I didn't mean to upset her – in fact the reverse. I wanted to help her.*

**reverse³** [Ac] *adjective*
the opposite of what is usual, or the opposite of what you expected: *He was trying to help, but his explanation had the reverse effect and made me more confused.*

**re·view¹** /rɪˈvyu/ *noun*
1 an article in a newspaper or magazine that says what is good and bad about a new book, play, or movie: *The movie got good reviews.*
2 the process of thinking carefully about something or examining it again, to see if it needs to be changed: *The review of the computer equipment showed that some of it needed to be replaced.*
[**ORIGIN:** 1400-1500 From the French word *revue*, a form of the verb *revoir*, which means "to see again."]

**review²** *verb*
1 to write an article in a newspaper or magazine saying what is good and bad about a new book, play, or movie: *He reviewed the movie and said it was good.*
2 to prepare for a test by reading and practicing things again: *I reviewed my notes before the test.*
3 to think about something again, so that you can decide whether it needs to be changed: *The judge reviewed the evidence.*
—**reviewer** *noun* someone whose job is reviewing new books, plays, or movies in a newspaper or magazine **SYNONYM: critic**

**re·vise** [Ac] /rɪˈvaɪz/ *verb*
1 to change your opinions, plans, etc. because you have new information or ideas: *We had to revise our vacation plans when Kelly decided not to go.* **SYNONYM: change**
2 to improve a piece of writing by adding new information or removing mistakes: *Revise your paper before you turn it in again.*
—**revision** /rɪˈvɪʒən/ *noun* the process of changing something in order to improve it
[**ORIGIN:** 1500-1600 From the Latin word *revisere*, which means "to look at again."]

**re·vive** /rɪˈvaɪv/ *verb* (*formal*)
1 to make someone conscious or alive again: *He was taken to hospital, where doctors were able to revive him.*
2 to make something successful or popular again: *Older people are teaching classes to children to try to revive old traditions.*

R

—**revival** *noun* a process in which something becomes successful or popular again

**re·volt¹** /rɪˈvoʊlt/ *verb*
**1** to refuse to obey a government, and use violence to try to change it: *Rebel forces in the country revolted against the government.*
SYNONYM: **rebel**
**2** to refuse to obey a rule, law, or someone who is in charge: *When the girl was forced to wear the hated shoes, she revolted.*
SYNONYM: **rebel**
**3** to make you feel sick and shocked: *The thought of drinking sour milk revolted me.*
—**revolting** *adjective* extremely unpleasant, often in a way that makes you feel sick: *There is a revolting smell in the basement.*

**revolt²** *noun*
strong and often violent action by a lot of people against their ruler or government: *Local leaders started a revolt against the central government.*

**rev·o·lu·tion** Ac /ˌrevəˈluʃən/ *noun*
**1** a time when people change a ruler or political system by using force or violence: *During the American Revolution, Americans fought against their British rulers.*
**2** a complete change in the way people think, work, or do something: *In the past 10 years there has been a revolution in the education system and everything has changed.*
**3** one complete circular movement around a central point: *The Earth makes one revolution around the Sun each year.*
[ORIGIN: 1300-1400 From the Latin word *revolutio*, from *revolvere*, which means "to roll back."]

**rev·o·lu·tion·ar·y** Ac /ˌrevəˈluʃəˌneri/ *adjective*
**1** completely new and different in a way that leads to great improvements: *This revolutionary treatment for the disease could save thousands of lives.*
**2** relating to or involved in a political revolution: *In the American Revolutionary War, the Americans fought for independence from Great Britain.*

**rev·o·lu·tion·ize** Ac /ˌrevəˈluʃəˌnaɪz/ *verb*
to completely change the way people think or do something: *The Internet has revolutionized the way people find information.*

The satellite is revolving around the Earth.

**re·volve** /rɪˈvɑlv/ *verb*
to make a circular movement around a central point: *The Earth revolves around the Sun, going completely around it once a year.*

**re·volv·er** /rɪvˈɑlvɚ/ *noun*
a small gun with a container for bullets that moves around

**re·ward¹** /rɪˈwɔrd/ *noun*
**1** something that you are given because you have done something good: *His parents bought him a bike as a reward for getting good grades.*
**2** money that is offered to people for helping the police to solve a crime: *The police are offering a reward for information about the people who stole the cars.*

**reward²** *verb*
to give something to someone because he or she has done something good: *The company rewarded him with a big pay raise.*

**re·ward·ing** /rɪˈwɔrdɪŋ/ *adjective*
a rewarding activity makes you feel happy and satisfied: *Nursing is hard work, but it can be rewarding.*

**re·wind** /riˈwaɪnd/ *verb* (**rewound** /riˈwaʊnd/)
to make a tape go back to the beginning: *Rewind the videotape when you're done.*

**re·write** /ˌriˈraɪt/ *verb* (**rewrote** /riˈroʊt/, **rewritten** /riˈrɪtn/)
to change a piece of writing in order to improve it or make it correct: *I rewrote the letter because I didn't like what I wrote the first time.*
—**rewrite** /ˈriraɪt/ *noun* a piece of writing that has been rewritten

**rhi·noc·er·os** /raɪˈnɑsərəs/ (*also* **rhi·no** /ˈraɪnoʊ/ (*informal*)) *noun* (plural **rhinoceros** *or* **rhinoceroses**)
a large heavy animal with thick rough skin and one or two horns on its nose
[ORIGIN: 1200-1300 From the Greek words *rhinos*, a form of the word for "nose," and *keras*, which means "horn."]

**rhombus**

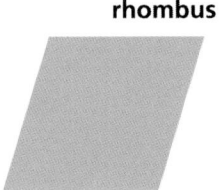

**rhom·bus** /ˈrɑmbəs/ *noun*
a shape with four straight sides that are the same length and four angles that are not 90°

**rhu·barb** /ˈrubɑrb/ *noun*
a plant with long thick red stems that are cooked and eaten as a fruit → see picture on page A13
[ORIGIN: 1300-1400 From the Latin words *rha* and *barbarus*, which mean "rhubarb" and "foreign."]

**rhyme¹** /raɪm/ *verb*
if two words or lines of poetry rhyme, they end with the same sound: *"Door" rhymes with "floor."*

**rhyme²** *noun*
**1** a short children's poem or song that uses words that rhyme
**2** a word that ends with the same sound as another word, such as "big" and "dig"

**rhythm** /ˈrɪðəm/ *noun*
a regular repeated pattern of sounds or movements: *Dancers moved to the rhythm of the drums.*
—**rhythmic** /ˈrɪðmɪk/ *adjective* having a rhythm: *the rhythmic motion of the waves*
[ORIGIN: 1500-1600 From the Greek word *rhythmos*, from *rhein*, which means "to flow."]

**ˌrhythm and ˈblues** *noun*
another word for R & B

**rib** /rɪb/ *noun*
one of the pairs of curved bones in your chest: *She was so thin you could see her ribs under the skin.* → see picture on page A2

**ribbon**

**rib·bon** /ˈrɪbən/ *noun*
**1** a long narrow piece of cloth, used for tying things and making them look pretty: *Karen tied a red ribbon in her daughter's hair.*
**2** a decoration made of colored ribbons, given as a prize in a competition: *Kelli's pony won the blue ribbon at the state fair.*

**ˈrib cage** *noun*
the structure of ribs inside your chest, around your lungs and heart

**rice** /raɪs/ *noun*
a white or brown grain that you boil in water until it becomes soft enough to eat. Rice is produced by plants that are grown in very wet fields: *I always have rice when I eat Chinese food.*
[ORIGIN: 1200-1300 From the Greek word *oryza*, which comes from an old Eastern language.]

**rich** /rɪtʃ/ *adjective*
**1** having a lot of money: *He is one of the richest men in the country.* **ANTONYM: poor**

**THESAURUS: rich**

**wealthy** having a lot of money: *The owner of the company is one of the wealthiest men in the country.*

**well-off** having enough money to have a good life, with all the things you want: *His parents are well-off, so they bought him a car for his 16th birthday.*

**prosperous** (*formal*) rich and successful: *The land is owned by a prosperous family who made their fortune in oil.*

**well-to-do** rich and having a high position in society: *They were dressed in expensive clothes and obviously came from a well-to-do family.*

**2** rich foods contain a lot of butter, cream, or eggs, and make you feel full very quickly: *The cake was rich and tasted great.* **ANTONYM: light**

3 if something is rich in something good, it has a lot of it: *Oranges are rich in Vitamin C.*

**rich·es** /ˈrɪtʃɪz/ *plural noun*
a lot of money or expensive things that someone owns: *Aladdin looked at the riches in the cave, at all the jewels and gold.*

**rich·ly** /ˈrɪtʃli/ *adverb*
in a beautiful or expensive way: *The bedroom was richly decorated with silk and velvet.*

**Rich·ter scale** /ˈrɪktɚ ˌskeɪl/ *noun*
**the Richter scale** = a scale, from 1 up to 10, that shows how powerful an EARTHQUAKE is: *The earthquake measured 6.8 on the Richter scale.*

R

**ric·o·chet** /ˈrɪkəˌʃeɪ/ *verb*
if something flying through the air ricochets, it changes direction when it hits a surface: *The bullet ricocheted off the wall and nearly hit me.*

**rid** /rɪd/ *adjective*
**get rid of something** = to throw away or remove something you do not want: *I got rid of some old books and bought new ones.*

**rid·den** /ˈrɪdn/ *verb*
the past participle of RIDE

**rid·dle** /ˈrɪdl/ *noun*
a question that seems silly or confusing but has a funny or clever answer: *Here's a riddle: What clothing does a house wear? The answer is "Address."*

**ride**[1] /raɪd/ *verb* (**rode** /roʊd/, **ridden** /ˈrɪdn/, **riding**)
1 to sit on a bicycle, MOTORCYCLE, or horse and make it move forward: *She rides her bicycle to school.* | *The cowboys were riding horses.* → see picture on page **A25**
2 to travel in a car, truck, or bus: *We rode the bus into New York City.*

**ride**[2] *noun*
1 a trip in a vehicle or on an animal: *Laura's dad gave me a ride home.*
2 a large machine with moving parts that people sit in at a FAIR or AMUSEMENT PARK: *We went on all the rides except the big roller coaster.*

**rid·er** /ˈraɪdɚ/ *noun*
someone who rides a horse or bicycle: *The rider fell off his horse.*

**ridge** /rɪdʒ/ *noun*
1 a long narrow area of high land along the top of hills or mountains: *He stood on the ridge looking at the valley below.*
2 a long narrow raised area on something: *There was mud between the ridges on the bottom of his shoes.*

**rid·i·cule** /ˈrɪdəˌkyul/ *verb* (*formal*)
to make jokes about someone or something in a way that makes him, her, or it seem stupid: *When I moved to Maine from Alabama, they ridiculed the way I talked and said I had a funny accent.*
—**ridicule** *noun* jokes or remarks that are not nice and are intended to make someone or something seem stupid

**ri·dic·u·lous** /rɪˈdɪkyələs/ *adjective*
very silly: *He looked ridiculous, dressed in women's clothes.*
—**ridiculously** *adverb* in a way that seems very silly
[**ORIGIN:** 1500-1600 From the Latin word *ridiculosus*, from *ridere*, which means "to laugh."]

**rid·ing** /ˈraɪdɪŋ/ *noun*
the sport of riding horses: *Let's go riding.* → see picture on page **A1**

**ri·fle** /ˈraɪfəl/ *noun*
a long gun that you hold up to your shoulder to shoot: *He went hunting with his rifle.*
[**ORIGIN:** 1700-1800 From the old French word *rifler*, which means "to scratch lines in a surface." A rifle has curved lines inside it which make the bullet spin, so it is more accurate.]

**rig**[1] /rɪg/ *verb* (**rigged**, **rigging**)
to dishonestly make a competition or election have the winner you want: *They rigged the election by letting some people vote more than once.*
**PHRASAL VERB**
**rig up**
to make something using the things that you find around you: *We rigged up a tent using an old sheet.*

**rig**[2] *noun*
a large structure that makes a hole for getting oil out of the ground: *an oil rig*

**right**[1] /raɪt/ *adjective*
1 correct: *Did you get the right answer?* | *I thought there was a problem, and I was right.*
**ANTONYM: wrong**

**THESAURUS: right**

**correct** without any mistakes: *Your answer is correct; the Missouri is the longest river in North America.*

**accurate** (*formal*) exactly correct, used especially about measurements or information: *When counting votes, it is important to be accurate.*

**2** on the side of the body that has the hand most people write with: *Take the next right turn.* | *Raise your right hand.* **ANTONYM: left**
**3** if something is right, people should do it because it is good or fair: *It's not right to kill people.* **ANTONYM: wrong**
**4** (*informal*) used when saying that you agree with someone or when asking if someone agrees with you: *You're Steve, right?*
—**rightly** *adverb* in the right way: *He rightly decided to call the police.*
[**ORIGIN:** From the old English word *riht*. This word originally meant "good or correct," and was later also used about the right hand, in place of a word meaning "stronger."]

**right²** *noun*
**1** something that the law says you can do: *In 1920, women got the right to vote.* → **civil rights**, **human rights**
**2** the right side or direction: *My house is the first one on the right.* **ANTONYM: left**
**3** behavior that is good or fair: *We have to teach children the difference between right and wrong.* **ANTONYM: wrong**
**4** **the right** = people who believe that the government should not make too many rules to control businesses and social problems: *Politicians on the right want the government to reduce taxes and cut unemployment benefits.* **ANTONYM: the left**
**5** **the rights to something** = the legal authority to sell a song, publish a book, or show a movie

**right³** *adverb*
**1** exactly in a position or place: *He's right behind you!* | *I left the keys right there.*
**2** correctly: *He has a long name that no one spells right.* **ANTONYM: wrong**
**3** toward the right side: *Turn right at the lights.* **ANTONYM: left**
**4** all the way: *The nail went right through his shoe.*
**5** **I'll/he'll, etc. be right there** = I am, he is, etc. coming now: *Tell Sarah I'll be right there.*
**6** **right away** = without waiting: *When she got his message, she called him back right away.* **SYNONYM: immediately**
**7** **right now** = at this time, not later: *Come here right now!* **SYNONYM: immediately**

**'right ˌangle** *noun*
the shape that two sides of a square make where they meet: *There are 90 degrees in a right angle.* → see picture at **angle**

**right·ful** /ˈraɪtfəl/ *adjective* (*formal*)
correct and fair, or legally correct: *The police returned the stolen painting to its rightful owner.* **SYNONYM: proper**
—**rightfully** *adverb* fairly or legally: *She took back the money that was rightfully hers.*

**ˌright-ˈhanded** *adjective*
someone who is right-handed uses his or her right hand to write or throw a ball: *If you are right-handed, it's hard to throw a ball with your left hand.*

**ˌright ˈtriangle** *noun*
a TRIANGLE that has one RIGHT ANGLE (=angle of 90°)

**ˌright-ˈwing** *adjective*
believing that the government should not make too many rules to control businesses and social problems: *Her father was right-wing and always voted Republican.* **ANTONYM: left-wing**

**rig·id** [Ac] /ˈrɪdʒɪd/ *adjective*
**1** not easy to bend or move: *The box has rigid sides to protect the glasses inside.* **SYNONYM: stiff**; **ANTONYM: flexible**
**2** strict and difficult to change: *Her parents set rigid rules about how much TV she can watch.* **ANTONYM: flexible**
—**rigidly** *adverb* in a rigid way
—**rigidity** /rɪˈdʒɪdəti/ *noun* the quality of being rigid

**rig·or·ous** /ˈrɪgərəs/ *adjective* (*formal*)
involving a lot of work or effort: *Athletes have to do rigorous training, and run for miles every day.* **SYNONYM: strict**
—**rigorously** *adverb* in a rigorous way

**rim** /rɪm/ *noun*
the outside edge of something round: *There was lipstick on the rim of the glass.*

**rind** /raɪnd/ *noun*
the hard outer skin of fruits such as oranges, LEMONs, or MELONs

**ring¹** /rɪŋ/ *noun*
**1** a piece of jewelry that you wear on your finger: *She is wearing a wedding ring.* → see picture at **jewelry**
**2** a circle: *The hot cup made a ring on the table.*
**3** the area where a BOXING or WRESTLING match takes place
**4** the sound that a bell makes: *There was a ring at the door.* → see picture on page **A22**

R

**ring²** *verb* (**rang** /ræŋ/, **rung** /rʌŋ/)
**1** if a bell or telephone rings, it makes a sound: *The telephone's ringing.*
**2** to make a bell make a sound: *I rang the doorbell.*
**3** **ring a bell** (*informal*) = if something rings a bell, you think you have heard it before: *His name rings a bell, but I can't remember what he looks like.*

rink

**rink** /rɪŋk/ *noun*
**1** a flat area of ice that has been specially prepared for SKATING and ICE HOCKEY. It is usually inside a building: *We went skating at the ice rink.*
**2** an area that is made for using ROLLER-SKATEs. It has a smooth surface and is inside a building.

**rinse** /rɪns/ *verb*
to use water to wash soap or dirt off something: *I washed my hands with soap, then rinsed them under the faucet.*

**ri·ot¹** /ˈraɪət/ *noun*
violent behavior by a crowd of people: *During the riot, people set fire to buildings.*
[**ORIGIN:** 1100-1200 From an old French word for "quarrel."]

**riot²** *verb*
if a crowd of people riots, they behave in a violent way: *The crowd rioted, turning over cars and breaking store windows.*

**rip¹** /rɪp/ *verb* (**ripped**, **ripping**)
to tear something quickly: *I ripped my pants on a nail, and now they have a hole in them.*
**PHRASAL VERB**
**rip something up**
to tear something into several pieces: *I ripped up the letter and threw it away.* **SYNONYM: tear up**

**rip²** *noun*
a hole in material where something has torn it: *Oh no! There's a rip in my jeans. That must have happened when I fell over.*

**ripe** /raɪp/ *adjective*
ripe fruit is ready to be eaten: *Bananas turn yellow when they are ripe.*

**rip·en** /ˈraɪpən/ *verb*
if fruit ripens, it becomes softer and ready to eat: *The peaches ripened in the fruit bowl.*

**ˈrip-off** *noun* (*informal*)
a situation in which someone pays more for something than it is worth: *She paid $200 dollars for a pair of sneakers – what a rip-off!*

**rise¹** /raɪz/ *verb* (**rose** /roʊz/, **risen** /ˈrɪzən/, **rising**)
**1** to get bigger in number or amount: *The temperature rose from 70 to 75 degrees F.* **SYNONYMS: increase, go up; ANTONYM: fall**
**2** to go up: *Smoke is rising from the chimney.* **ANTONYM: fall**
**3** if the sun or moon rises, it appears in the sky: *The sun will rise at 7:00 in the morning tomorrow.* **ANTONYM: set**
**4** (*formal*) to stand up: *He got off his chair and rose to his feet.*
→ see Thesaurus box at **increase¹**

**rise²** *noun*
an increase in number or amount: *There was a rise in crime, with more robberies taking place.* **SYNONYM: increase; ANTONYM: fall**

**USAGE: rise, raise**

A **rise** is an increase in anything: *The rise in the number of cars led to more pollution.*

A **raise** is an increase in the money you earn: *He's a good worker and deserves a raise.*

**ris·en** /ˈrɪzən/ *verb*
the past participle of RISE

**risk¹** /rɪsk/ *noun*
**1** the chance that something bad might happen: *Football is a physical game. There's always a risk of injury.*
**2 take a risk** = to do something even though there is a chance that something bad will happen: *She took a risk and started her own business, and it has worked out well.*
→ see Thesaurus box at **danger**
[ORIGIN: 1600-1700 From the old Italian word *risco*, from *rischiare*, which means "to run into danger."]

**risk²** *verb*
to put something in a situation where something could harm it or damage it: *The fireman risked his life by going into a burning building to save a child.*

**risk·y** /ˈrɪski/ *adjective*
if an action is risky, something bad might happen when you do it: *Rock climbing is a risky sport because you could fall, but it's fun.* SYNONYM: **dangerous**; ANTONYM: **safe**

**rit·u·al** /ˈrɪtʃuəl/ *noun*
a set of actions that people do in the same way at an important event or time of year: *Part of the ritual of Christmas is giving presents.*

**ri·val** /ˈraɪvəl/ *noun*
a person, company, or team that tries to do better than another one: *The athlete finished the race two seconds before her closest rival.* SYNONYM: **competitor**
[ORIGIN: 1500-1600 From the Latin word *rivalis*, which means "someone who uses the same stream as another," from *rivus*, meaning "stream." People who lived near a stream might fight over the use of the water.]

**ri·val·ry** /ˈraɪvəlri/ *noun* (plural **rivalries**) (*formal*)
a situation in which two people, companies, or teams are trying to do better than each other: *There's a lot of rivalry between the two teams because both want to be the best.*

**riv·er** /ˈrɪvɚ/ *noun*
a long wide flow of water that goes into the ocean or a lake: *The longest river in Africa is the Nile.*
[ORIGIN: 1200-1300 From the old French word *riviere*. This comes from the Latin word *riparius*, which means "of a river bank," from *ripa*, meaning "bank."]

**R.N.** *noun*
(**registered nurse**) a nurse: *She's an R.N. at a Dallas hospital.*

**roach** /roʊtʃ/ *noun*
a large insect that often lives where there is food: *We used poison to kill the roaches in our kitchen.* SYNONYM: **cockroach**

**road** /roʊd/ *noun*
**1** a hard surface that vehicles travel on: *Find a safe place to cross the road.*

**THESAURUS: road**

**street** a road in a town, with houses or stores on each side: *I crossed the street and walked to the library.*

**avenue** a road in a town – used in street names: *I got a cab on Third Avenue.*

**boulevard** a wide road in a city – used in street names: *We drove down Sunset Boulevard.*

**main road** a large and important road: *Stay on the main road until you get to Las Vegas.*

**highway** a very wide road for traveling fast over long distances: *The highway runs along the coast for most of the way.*

**freeway/expressway** a very wide road in a city or between cities, on which cars can travel very fast without stopping: *Take the freeway downtown.* | *I went north on the expressway.*

**interstate** a wide road that goes between states, on which cars can travel very fast: *The interstate goes from California, through Oregon and Washington, up to the Canadian border.*

**lane** one of the parts of a main road, that are divided by lines to keep traffic apart: *One of the lanes on the freeway was closed because of an accident.*

**2 on the road** = traveling for a long distance in a car or truck: *We've been on the road since 7 a.m.*

[**ORIGIN:** From the old English word *rad*, which means "ride or journey."]

**roam** /roʊm/ *verb*
to walk or travel in a place freely: *Bears and other wild animals roamed through the woods.*

R

**roar[1]** /rɔr/ *verb*
to make a deep loud sound, like a lion or big machine: *Traffic roared along the highway.*

**roar[2]** *noun*
a deep loud noise: *I heard the roar of the race car's engine.*

**roast[1]** /roʊst/ *verb*
to cook meat or vegetables in an OVEN: *We roasted a chicken for dinner.* → see picture on page **A15**
→ see Thesaurus box at **cook[1]**

**roast[2]** *noun*
a large piece of meat that you cook in an OVEN: *We had a pork roast for dinner.*

**roast[3]** *adjective*
roast meat or vegetables have been cooked in an OVEN: *roast beef*

**rob** /rɑb/ *verb* (**robbed**, **robbing**)
to take something that is not yours from a person or place: *They robbed a bank and stole $100,000.*

**WORD FAMILY: rob**
**rob** *verb* | **robber** *noun* | **robbery** *noun*

**rob·ber** /ˈrɑbɚ/ *noun*
someone who goes to a place and takes something that does not belong to him or her: *The robbers stole money and jewelry from the house.* **SYNONYM: thief**

**rob·ber·y** /ˈrɑbəri/ *noun* (plural **robberies**)
a crime in which someone takes something that does not belong to him or her, sometimes using violence: *$500 in cash was stolen from the store during the robbery.*
→ see Thesaurus box at **crime**

**robe** /roʊb/ *noun*
a long loose piece of clothing that covers most of your body: *The judge wore a black robe.*

**rob·in** /ˈrɑbɪn/ *noun*
a bird with a red chest and a dark gray back: *Robins are often the first birds you see in the spring.*

**ro·bot** /ˈroʊbɑt/ *noun*
**1** a machine that can move and do work: *Robots are used in factories for making cars.*
**2** in movies and stories, a machine that can talk, walk, and think like a real person
[**ORIGIN:** 1900-2000 From the Czech word *robotnik*, which means "worker or slave." This word was used in a Czech play about machines that look like people.]

**ro·bust** /roʊˈbʌst/ *adjective* (*formal*)
strong and not likely to have problems: *She was robust and healthy at 65 and still liked to take long walks.* **ANTONYM: weak**
[**ORIGIN:** 1500-1600 From the Latin word *robustus*, which means " strong (like an oak tree)," from *robur*, meaning "oak, or strength."]

**rock[1]** /rɑk/ *noun*
**1** stone that forms part of the Earth's surface. *You can see the different layers of rock in the Grand Canyon.*
**2** a piece of stone lying on the earth's surface: *He sat on a big rock next to the river.*
**3** a type of loud modern music, that uses drums and GUITARS: *Loud rock music with a strong beat came from the speakers.*

**rock[2]** *verb*
to move gently from one side to another: *The boat rocked gently on the water.* | *She rocked the baby until he fell asleep.*

**ˈrock ˌcycle** *noun*
the way in which the Earth's three main rock types change from one type to another over a long period of time: *The rock cycle is a process by which igneous rock can change into sedimentary rock or into metamorphic rock over millions of years.*

**rock·er** /ˈrɑkɚ/ *noun*
a chair that moves backward and forward on

two curved pieces of wood **SYNONYM: rocking chair**

**rock·et** /ˈrɑkɪt/ *noun*

**1** a long tall vehicle that travels into space: *The rocket took the Apollo spacecraft to the Moon.*

**2** a long thin weapon that is fired at things and explodes when it hits them: *The army fired rockets at the enemy.*

**3** a long thin FIREWORK that goes high into the sky and explodes into bright colors

[**ORIGIN:** 1600-1700 From the Italian word *rocchetta*, which means "small stick used in spinning thread." Firework rockets had a similar shape to this stick.]

**ˈrocking chair** *noun*

a chair that moves backward and forward on two curved pieces of wood

**rock 'n' roll** /ˌrɑk ən ˈroʊl/ (*also* **ˌrock and ˈroll**) *noun*

a type of popular music with a strong loud beat, that first became popular in the 1950s

**rock·y** /ˈrɑki/ *adjective*

ground that is rocky has a lot of rocks on it: *The beach was rocky, so I kept my shoes on.*

**rod** /rɑd/ *noun*

a long thin piece of metal or wood: *Men with fishing rods sat by the river.*

**rode** /roʊd/ *verb*

the past tense of RIDE

**ro·dent** /ˈroʊdnt/ *noun*

a type of animal with long sharp front teeth, such as rats and mice: *The snake eats small rodents.*

[**ORIGIN:** 1800-1900 From the Latin word *rodere*, which means "to chew with the front teeth."]

**ro·de·o** /ˈroʊdiˌoʊ, roʊˈdeɪoʊ/ *noun* (plural **rodeos**)

a competition in which people ride horses and catch cows with ropes

[**ORIGIN:** 1800-1900 From the Spanish word *rodear*, which means "to surround." Rodeo was first used to describe how cowboys made cattle move into a large enclosed area, surrounded by fences.]

**role** Ac /roʊl/ *noun*

**1** the job or purpose that someone has in a situation or activity: *The captain's role is to make all the players feel like they are part of the team.* **SYNONYM: part**

**2** a character in a play or movie: *He played the role of the king in the show.* **SYNONYM: part**

**ˈrole ˌmodel** *noun*

someone who other people want to be like because they think he or she is good: *The young athlete says that Usain Bolt, the gold-medal runner, is his role model.*

**roll**[1] /roʊl/ *verb*

**1** to move by turning over and over: *The ball rolled under the couch.*

**2** to move on wheels: *The car rolled down the hill.*

**3** (*also* **roll up**) to make something into the shape of a tube or ball by turning it over and over: *Roll up the carpet so we can carry it.*

**4** (*also* **roll out**) to make something in a ball or tube become flat and straight: *He took his sleeping bag out of its bag, and rolled it out on the floor.* → see picture on page **A15**

**5** if you roll DICE, you throw them as part of a game: *He rolled two sixes.*

**PHRASAL VERB**

**roll over**

to turn your body so you are lying in a different position: *She rolled over so that she was lying on her back.*

**roll**[2] *noun*

**1** a long piece of paper, film, etc. that has been rolled into the shape of a tube: *a roll of toilet paper*

**2** a small round piece of bread: *I put some butter on my roll.*

**3** a list of names of everyone in a class or at a meeting: *The teacher called the roll, and only Bella was absent.*

**Roll·er·blade** /ˈroʊlɚˌbleɪd/ *noun* (*trademark*)

a boot with a row of wheels on the bottom: *She put on a pair of rollerblades and skated away.*

—**rollerblading** *noun* the sport of moving on rollerblades → see picture on page **A25**

**ˈroller ˌcoaster** *noun*

a ride at a FAIR or AMUSEMENT PARK, in which people sit in special cars that move along a track that goes up very high and suddenly down again

R

**roll·er·skate** /ˈroʊləˌskeɪt/ *noun*
a boot with four wheels on the bottom: *He went down the street on rollerskates.*
—**rollerskating** *noun* the sport of moving on rollerskates

**ˈrolling pin** *noun*
a long round wooden tool that you roll over DOUGH to make it flat

**Ro·man** /ˈroʊmən/ *noun*
someone from ancient Rome: *The Romans built many roads and bridges.*
—**Roman** *adjective* relating to ancient Rome: *a Roman soldier*

R

**ˌRoman ˈCatholic** *adjective*
relating to the church whose leader is the Pope: *Roman Catholic priests are not allowed to marry.* **SYNONYM: Catholic**

**ro·mance** /ˈroʊmæns/ *noun*
**1** an exciting relationship between two people who love each other: *The couple's romance began when they were in high school.*
**2** a story about love between two people: *Her latest novel is a romance.*
[**ORIGIN:** 1200-1300 From an old French word meaning "something written in French," from the Latin word *romanicus*, meaning "Roman." French developed from Latin, the Roman language. Romances were originally about knights and their adventures, which sometimes involved love.]

**ˌRoman ˈnumeral** *noun*
a number in a system that people used in ancient Rome, that uses letters instead of numbers: *X is the Roman numeral for 10.*

**ro·man·tic¹** /roʊˈmæntɪk/ *adjective*
showing strong feelings of love: *They had a romantic dinner with candles and flowers on the table.*

**romantic²** *noun*
someone who is not practical and imagines that everything is better or more exciting than it really is: *He's a romantic who thinks that love is all you need in a marriage.*

**ro·man·ti·cize** /roʊˈmæntəˌsaɪz/ *verb*
to make something bad seem good or exciting: *It's easy to romanticize the past and forget about all the problems we've had.*

**roof** /ruf/ *noun*
**1** the top surface of a building or vehicle: *There was a hole in the roof, and rain was coming into the house.*
**2 the roof of your mouth** = the top part of the inside of your mouth: *The peanut butter stuck to the roof of my mouth.*
[**ORIGIN:** From the old English word *hrof.*]

**rook·ie** /ˈrʊki/ *noun* (*informal*)
someone who has just started doing a job or playing a sport and does not know much about it: *He went from being a rookie cop to Chief of Police in only 20 years.*

**room** /rum/ *noun*
**1** one of the areas inside a building that has walls and doors: *There are three rooms upstairs: two bedrooms and a bathroom.*
**2** enough space: *There is only room in the car for five people.*

**ˌroom and ˈboard** *noun*
a room to sleep in and food to eat, that you must pay for: *Room and board at college costs $600 a month.*

**room·mate** /ˈrumˌmeɪt/ *noun*
someone you share a room or house with: *Jo and I are roommates at college.*

**room·y** /ˈrumi/ *adjective* (*informal*)
with plenty of space: *The car is roomy enough for six people.* **SYNONYM: spacious**

**roost** /rust/ *noun*
a branch of a tree or a small building where birds rest and sleep

**roost·er** /ˈrustɚ/ *noun*
a male chicken: *The rooster woke us up early in the morning.*

**root¹** /rut/ *noun*
**1** the part of a plant or tree that grows under the ground: *Some plants have long roots that go deep into the ground.*
**2** the part of a hair or tooth where it is joined to the rest of your body: *Sally dyes her hair blonde, but the roots are brown.*
**3 roots** = your roots are your family and where they come from: *My family's roots can be traced back to Russia.*
**4** the most basic part of a word, that you can add a PREFIX or SUFFIX to: *The word "coldness" is formed from the root "cold" and the suffix "ness."*
**5** the root of a number is a smaller number

which, when it is multiplied by itself a particular number of times, equals that number: *2 is the fourth root of 16 (2 x 2 x 2 x 2 = 16).*

**root²** *verb*

**PHRASAL VERB**

**root for someone**

to want a person or team to win a game or competition, and give them your support and encouragement: *His whole family was there to root for him.*

**ˈroot beer** *noun*

a sweet drink made from the roots of some plants

**rope** /roʊp/ *noun*

**1** a strong thick string: *He used a piece of rope to tie the dog to the fence.*

**2** **the ropes** = the things someone needs to know in order to do something: *Alex showed me the ropes when I first started at the school.*

**rose¹** /roʊz/ *noun*

a flower with a beautiful smell, that grows on a plant with sharp points on the stem: *He sent her a bunch of red roses.*

**rose²** *verb*

the past tense of RISE

**ros·y** /ˈroʊzi/ *adjective* (**rosier**, **rosiest**)

**1** if the skin on someone's face is rosy, it is pink: *Healthy people have rosy cheeks.* **ANTONYM: pale**

**2** successful or happy: *We expect a rosy future – things are going well for us.* **ANTONYM: bleak**

**rot** /rɑt/ *verb* (**rotted**, **rotting**)

**1** to slowly become bad or soft through natural chemical changes: *After a week, the fruit began to rot.* **SYNONYM: decay**

**2** to make something become bad or soft: *Sugar will rot your teeth.* **SYNONYM: decay**

**ro·tate** /ˈroʊteɪt/ *verb* (*formal*)

**1** to go around like a wheel: *The Earth rotates every 24 hours.* | *Rotate the handle to the right.*

**2** to change who does something or which things you use: *The job of handing out the books rotates until every child has had a chance to do it.*

[**ORIGIN:** 1600-1700 From the Latin word *rotare*, from *rota*, which means "wheel."]

**ro·ta·tion** /roʊˈteɪʃən/ *noun* (*formal*)

a movement around something: *I watched the rotation of the fan.*

**rote** /roʊt/ *noun* (*formal*)

**learn something by rote** = to learn something by repeating it until you remember it: *We learned the poem by rote, and I can still remember it.*

**rot·ten** /ˈrɑtn/ *adjective*

**1** rotten food or wood is old and starting to become soft because of natural chemical changes: *The rotten fish smelled terrible.* **ANTONYM: fresh**

**2** (*informal*) very bad: *I had a bad cold and felt rotten.* **ANTONYM: great**

**rough** /rʌf/ *adjective*

**1** not even or smooth: *His hands were hard and rough from hard work.* → see picture at **smooth**

**2** using force or violence: *Don't be too rough with the baby, or you might hurt her.* **ANTONYM: gentle**

**3** not exact: *I can give you a rough idea of the cost, but not an exact number.*

**4** difficult to deal with: *It was rough when my parents got divorced.* **SYNONYM: hard**

—**roughness** *noun* the quality of being rough

**ˌrough ˈdraft** *noun*

a piece of writing or a drawing that you do first and plan to improve later: *I always write a rough draft of my essay first and then change anything I'm not happy with.*

**rough·ly** /ˈrʌfli/ *adverb*

**1** used when giving a number that is not exact: *There's enough food for roughly ten people.* **SYNONYMS: approximately, about; ANTONYM: exactly**

**2** not gently or carefully: *The boys were playing roughly and Jordan got hurt.*

→ see Thesaurus box at **about**

**round¹** /raʊnd/ *adjective*

shaped like a circle or a ball: *The berries were small and round.* | *a round table*

**round²** *noun*

**1** one of the parts of a competition that you must win or finish to get to the next part: *The winners of this round will play against each other tomorrow.*

2 one in a series of events that are connected: *The first round of meetings went well. The next round is in March.*
3 a bullet that is shot from a gun: *He fired several rounds at the target.*
4 **a round of applause** = a time when people clap to show they enjoyed a performance or approve of something: *The singer received a big round of applause.*
5 a song that people start singing at different times, so that different parts of the song are being sung at the same time

**round³** *verb*
1 to go around a bend or the corner of a building: *The car rounded the bend quickly.*
2 if you round a number to the next whole number, next ten, next hundred, etc., you change the number to the nearest whole number or the nearest MULTIPLE of ten, a hundred, etc.: *If you round 5.8 to the nearest whole number, you get 6.*
**PHRASAL VERB**
**round up**
to find and bring together a group of people or animals: *The cowboys rounded up the cattle.*

**ˈround-trip** *adjective*
a round-trip ticket is for taking a trip from one place to another and back again **ANTONYM: one-way**

**route** Ac /rut, raʊt/ *noun*
the way from one place to another: *What is the shortest route from here to the school?*

**rou·tine¹** /ruˈtin/ *noun*
the usual things that someone does every day, every week, etc.: *His morning routine is a shower, breakfast, and then school.*

**routine²** *adjective*
happening regularly, not for any special reason or problem: *The mechanics did a routine check on the plane's engines.* **ANTONYM: special**
→ see Thesaurus box at **normal**

**rou·tin·ely** /ruˈtinli/ *adverb*
happening regularly, not for any special reason or problem: *Doctors routinely test people's blood pressure.* **SYNONYM: normally**

**row¹** /roʊ/ *noun*

1 a line of things or people next to each other: *There was a row of trees along the street. | I like to sit in the front row.*
2 **three/four, etc. in a row** = happening three times, four times, etc. without anything different in between: *We have lost four games in a row, but I think we can win the next one.*

**row²** *verb*
to make a boat move through water using two long sticks with flat ends: *He took the oars and rowed across the lake.*
—**rowing** *noun* the activity of rowing a boat

**row·boat** /ˈroʊboʊt/ *noun*
a small boat that you move through water using long sticks with flat ends: *I watched the rowboats on the lake.*

**row·dy** /ˈraʊdi/ *adjective*
a rowdy group of people is making a lot of noise: *The rowdy fans shouted as Williams scored.* **SYNONYM: noisy**; **ANTONYM: quiet**
—**rowdiness** *noun* the quality of being rowdy

**roy·al** /ˈrɔɪəl/ *adjective*
relating to or belonging to a king or queen: *Prince Charles is a member of the British royal family.*
[**ORIGIN:** 1200-1300 From the old French word *roial*, from the Latin word *regalis*, which comes from *rex*, meaning "king."]

**roy·al·ty** /ˈrɔɪəlti/ *noun*
members of the family of a king or queen: *The palace was built for royalty.*

**RSVP**
used on invitations for asking someone to reply

**rub** /rʌb/ *verb* (**rubbed**, **rubbing**)
to move your hand or a cloth backward and forward over a surface: *She rubbed her sore arm.*
→ see Thesaurus box at **touch**[1]

**rub·ber** /ˈrʌbɚ/ *noun*
a soft substance that comes from a tree and is used for making tires, boots, and other things: *She wears rubber gloves to wash the dishes.*

**ˌrubber ˈband** *noun*
a thin piece of rubber like a circle, that holds things together: *He gave me a pile of dollar bills with a rubber band around it.*

**rub·ble** /ˈrʌbəl/ *noun*
broken stones or bricks from a building or wall that was destroyed: *After the explosion, the building was just a pile of rubble.*

**ru·by** /ˈrubi/ *noun* (plural **rubies**)
a dark red jewel: *The ring had a single ruby.*
[**ORIGIN:** 1300-1400 From the Latin word *rubeus*, which means "reddish."]

**rud·der** /ˈrʌdɚ/ *noun*
a flat part at the back of a boat that helps the boat to change direction when it is moving → see picture at **boat**

**rude** /rud/ *adjective*
speaking or behaving in a way that is not polite: *It's rude not to say thank you for a gift.*

**THESAURUS: rude**

**impolite** (*formal*) not polite: *Eating with your mouth open is very impolite.*

**insulting** saying or doing something rude or offensive to someone, so that he or she feels upset: *His jokes are insulting to women.*

**tactless** saying things that are likely to upset someone because you have not thought carefully about what you are saying: *It was tactless to say that you don't like the coach, when you know the coach is her dad.*

**offensive** very impolite and likely to upset or offend people: *He made an offensive remark about the way she looks.*

—**rudely** *adverb* in an impolite way: *He rudely interrupted me.*

—**rudeness** *noun* behavior or speech that is not polite
[**ORIGIN:** 1200-1300 From the Latin word *rudis*, which means "raw or rough."]

**ruf·fle** /ˈrʌfəl/ *noun*
a piece of cloth with many small folds in it, that you use to decorate clothes or other things made of cloth: *Her party dress was decorated with ruffles and lace.*

**rug** /rʌg/ *noun*
a thick piece of cloth that covers part of a floor: *The rug covered most of the bedroom floor.*

**rug·ged** /ˈrʌgɪd/ *adjective*
rough, uneven, and with a lot of rocks: *The rugged mountains are hard to climb.*

**ru·in** /ˈruɪn/ *verb*
to spoil something completely: *I spilled ink on my dress and ruined it.*

**ruins** /ˈruɪnz/ *plural noun*
**1 ruins** = the part of a building that is left when the rest has been destroyed: *We saw the ruins of an old church.*
**2 in ruins** = very badly damaged: *After the earthquake, the whole city was in ruins.*

**rule**[1] /rul/ *noun*
**1** a statement of what you can or cannot do:

*In soccer, it's against the rules to pick up the ball.*

**THESAURUS: rule**

**law** a rule that people in a particular country, city, or state must obey: *The law says that motorcyclists must wear helmets.*

**regulation** (*formal*) an official rule or order, which is part of a set of rules made by a government or organization: *Safety regulations say that all cars must have seat belts.*

**restriction** (*formal*) a rule or law that limits what you can do or what is allowed to happen: *During the drought, there were restrictions on the amount of water you could use.*

R

**2** a situation in which a particular group of people control a country: *America was under British rule before 1776.* **SYNONYM: control**

[**ORIGIN:** 1200-1300 From the old French word *reule*, from the Latin word *regula*, which means "ruler for drawing straight lines." The idea is that a rule is like a straight line guiding you.]

**rule**[2] *verb*

**1** to control a country: *The king ruled for 30 years.*

**2** to make an official decision about something: *The judge ruled that the company had broken the law.* **SYNONYM: decide**

→ see Thesaurus box at **decide**

**rul·er** /ˈrulɚ/ *noun*

**1** someone who controls a country: *The country had a military ruler who did not want democracy.*

**2** a long piece of wood or plastic that you use for measuring or for drawing straight lines: *Use a ruler to measure how long your book is.*

**rum** /rʌm/ *noun*

a strong drink that contains alcohol and is made from sugar

**rum·ble** /ˈrʌmbəl/ *verb*

to make a long low sound: *Thunder rumbled across the sky.*

**ru·mor** /ˈrumɚ/ *noun*

information that people tell each other, which may not be true: *I heard a rumor that Kathy is having a party – is that true?*

**run**[1] /rʌn/ *verb* (**ran** /ræn/, **run**, **running**)

**1** to move very quickly using your legs: *He ran all the way to school.* | *Who is running in the race?* → see picture on page **A4**

**THESAURUS: run**

**sprint** to run as fast as you can for a short distance: *I sprinted toward the end zone.*

**dash** to run somewhere very quickly: *The kids dashed into the house when it began to rain.*

**jog/go jogging** to run at a slow steady speed for exercise: *She jogs three times a week.*

**race** to go somewhere very quickly, especially because you have to do something: *I raced home from school to see if the package had arrived.*

**charge** to run quickly and with a lot of energy, so that you might knock someone down: *The bull suddenly charged toward us.*

**2** to control a business or other organization: *Dad runs a small computer company.* **SYNONYM: operate**

**3** if a machine runs, it works or operates: *The car's engine was running.*

**4** to go somewhere quickly, either walking or in a car: *Can you run to the store for me?*

**5** if something such as a path, road, or wall runs somewhere, it goes there: *A road runs along the river bank.*

**6** to use a computer program: *You can run this software on any computer.*

**7** to try to get a job or position by winning an election: *She is running for president.*

**8** if your nose runs, liquid comes out of it: *His nose was running because he had a terrible cold.*

**9** if liquid runs somewhere, it goes there in a steady stream: *Tears ran down her face.* **SYNONYM: flow**

→ see Thesaurus box at **pour**

[**ORIGIN:** From the old English word *rinnan*.]

PHRASAL VERBS

**run after someone or something**
to chase someone or something: *He started to leave, but Kim ran after him.*

**run around**
to be busy doing many small jobs: *She's been running around all day getting things ready for the party.*

**run away**
to leave home because you are unhappy: *He ran away from home after an argument with his father.*

**run into**
**1 run into someone** = to meet someone when you were not expecting to: *I ran into Mrs. Miller at the supermarket.*
**2 run into someone or something** = to hit someone or something with the car you are driving: *He lost control and ran into another car.*

**run off**
**1** to leave a person or place when you should stay where you are: *The dog kept running off, so we had to tie it to the fence.*
**2 run something off** = to make copies of something using a machine: *The principal asked his secretary to run off photocopies of the letter.*

**run out (of something)**
to use all of something, so that there is none left: *We ran out of milk at breakfast, so there wasn't any to put on my cereal.*

**run over someone or something**
to hit someone or something with a car and drive over them: *Dad braked quickly so he wouldn't run over a dog.*

**run²** *noun*
**1** the activity of running, or a distance that you run: *I went for a five-mile run.*
**2** a point in a baseball game: *The Jays scored two runs in the first inning.*
**3 make a run for it** = to suddenly start running, in order to escape: *The prisoner made a run for it and escaped.*

**ˈrun-down** *adjective*
a run-down building or area is in very bad condition: *He lives in a run-down part of town where the buildings are old and need to be painted.*

**rung¹** /rʌŋ/ *verb*
the past participle of RING

**rung²** *noun*
one of the steps of a LADDER: *I stood on the bottom rung, to keep the ladder from tipping.*

**rung**

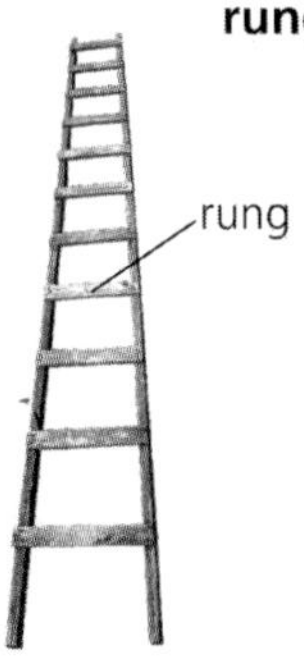


**run·ner** /ˈrʌnɚ/ *noun*
someone who runs as a sport: *The runners have to go around the track twice.*

**ˌrunner-ˈup** *noun* (plural **runners-up**)
the person or team that finishes second in a race or competition: *The winner gets $50 and the runner-up gets $20.*

**run·ning** /ˈrʌnɪŋ/ *noun*
the activity of running as a sport: *I go running every day for exercise.*

**ˈrunning mate** *noun*
the person who will become VICE PRESIDENT if someone is elected president. In some states, people wanting to be elected GOVERNOR also choose running mates: *Joe Biden was Barack Obama's running mate.*

**ˌrunning ˈwater** *noun*
water that comes from a FAUCET: *Some of the houses do not have running water.*

**run·ny** /ˈrʌni/ *adjective*
**1** if you have a runny nose, liquid comes out of it because you are sick: *I had a runny nose and a bad cough.*
**2** a runny liquid is not as thick as it should be: *The paint was runny and got onto the carpet.*

**run·way** /ˈrʌnweɪ/ *noun*
**1** a long wide road that an airplane leaves from and comes down on → see picture on page **A27**
**2** a long narrow part of a stage that goes out into the area where the AUDIENCE sits: *The models walk along the runway to show the clothes.*

**rup·ture** /ˈrʌptʃɚ/ *verb* (*formal*)
if something ruptures, it breaks suddenly so that it has a hole or tear in it: *A water pipe ruptured and flooded the house.*

R

**ru·ral** /ˈrʊrəl/ *adjective*
relating to the country, not the city: *Most people who live in rural areas are farmers.*
**ANTONYM: urban**
[**ORIGIN:** 1400-1500 From the Latin word *ruralis*, from *rus*, which means "open land."]

**rush¹** /rʌʃ/ *verb*
to move or do something quickly because you do not have much time: *Everyone was rushing to catch the last bus.*
**PHRASAL VERB**
**rush into something**
to do something without thinking carefully about it first: *Don't rush into buying the first computer you see.*

R

**rush²** *noun*
**1** a situation in which you need to do things quickly because you do not have much time: *I'm in a rush because the school bus leaves in five minutes.*
**2** a sudden fast movement somewhere by a group of people: *There was a rush for the door, as everyone tried to leave at once.*
**3** a sudden fast movement of air or water: *There was a rush of warm air when I opened the window.*

**ˈrush hour** *noun*
the time of day when there are a lot of vehicles on the road because people are going to and from work: *It was rush hour, so it took us a long time to get home.*

**Rus·sian¹** /ˈrʌʃən/ *adjective*
from Russia: *Russian soldiers*

**Russian²** *noun*
**1** someone from Russia
**2** the language spoken in Russia

**rust¹** /rʌst/ *noun*
the brown substance that forms on metal when it gets wet: *The old car has a lot of rust on it.*

**rust²** *verb*
to become covered with rust: *He painted the gates to stop them from rusting.*

**rus·tle** /ˈrʌsəl/ *verb*
if something such as dry leaves or papers rustle, they make a noise as they rub against each other: *Leaves rustled in the wind.* → see picture on page **A22**
—**rustle** *noun* the sound of something rustling

**rust·y** /ˈrʌsti/ *adjective*
**1** covered with rust: *Some old wood and rusty nails were on the ground near the fence.*
**2** if a skill that you have is rusty, you are not as good at it as you used to be because you have not done it for a long time: *My tennis is a little rusty because I haven't played for a while.*

**rut** /rʌt/ *noun*
**1** a deep narrow hole made by a wheel
**2 in a rut** = living or working in a situation that does not change and is boring: *Try new activities so you don't get stuck in a rut.*

**ruth·less** /ˈruθləs/ *adjective*
not caring if you harm other people to get what you want: *He is a ruthless businessman who has made many enemies.*
[**ORIGIN:** 1300-1400 From the old English word *ruth*, which means "pity." Someone who is ruthless has no pity.]

**Rx** *noun*
a piece of paper that a doctor gives you so that you can get medicine **SYNONYM: prescription**

**rye** /raɪ/ *noun*
**1** the seeds of a crop used for making flour and beer
**2** a type of bread that has a dark color and is made from rye flour: *My favorite sandwich is tuna on rye.*

# Ss

**'s** /z, s/
1 the short form of "is": *What's your name?*
2 the short form of "has": *She's been here before.*
3 the short form of "us": *Let's go, or we'll be late.*
4 used for showing who owns something: *Those are Tom's books.*

**Sab·bath** /ˈsæbəθ/ *noun*
**the Sabbath** = the day of the week when Jews or Christians rest and pray: *They don't work on the Sabbath.*

**sab·o·tage** /ˈsæbəˌtɑʒ/ *verb*
to secretly damage or spoil something: *The soldiers sabotaged the bridge so that the enemy could not use it to cross the river.*
—**sabotage** *noun* the action of sabotaging something

**sack** /sæk/ *noun*
a large bag made of strong material: *The truck carried sacks of rice.*
[ORIGIN: From the Latin word *saccus* and the Greek word *sakkos*, which mean "bag."]

**sa·cred** /ˈseɪkrɪd/ *adjective (formal)*
relating to a god or religion: *A church is a sacred building.* SYNONYM: **holy**

**sac·ri·fice¹** /ˈsækrəˌfaɪs/ *noun*
1 something that you decide not to have or do so that you can have something more important: *My family has made sacrifices, like not eating out or going to movies, so that they can pay for my music lessons.*
2 something that you offer to a god: *They killed a sheep as a sacrifice to God.*
[ORIGIN: 1200-1300 From the Latin word *sacrificium*, from *sacer* and *facere*, which mean "holy" and "to make."]

**sacrifice²** *verb*
to stop having or doing something so that you can have something more important: *She sacrificed her job to take care of her children.*

**sac·ri·lege** /ˈsækrəlɪdʒ/ *noun (formal)*
an occasion when someone treats something holy in a way that does not show respect
—**sacrilegious** /ˌsækrəˈlɪdʒəs/ *adjective* treating something holy in a way that does not show respect: *Some of the jokes were sacrilegious and offended religious people.*

**sad** /sæd/ *adjective* (**sadder**, **saddest**)
not happy because a happy time has ended or something bad has happened: *She's sad because her parents are getting a divorce.* | *I'll be sad to leave all my friends.* ANTONYM: **happy** → see picture on page A23
[ORIGIN: From the old English word *sæd*, which means "having had enough."]

**THESAURUS: sad**

**unhappy** not happy because you are in a bad situation that seems likely to continue: *I was really unhappy about moving and leaving all my friends.*

**miserable** very sad, especially because you are lonely or sick: *My brother was miserable after he broke up with his girlfriend.*

**upset** sad because something bad or disappointing has happened: *She's upset about losing the game.*

**depressed** sad for a long time because things are wrong in your life: *She was really depressed when she lost her job.*

**down/low** (*informal*) a little sad about things in your life: *Whenever I felt down, I'd read the letter from my dad.* | *I guess I've been feeling a little low because of my grandma being sick.*

**homesick** sad because you are away from your home, family, and friends: *I enjoyed camp, but I was homesick, too.*

**sad·den** /ˈsædn/ *verb (formal)*
to make someone feel sad: *We were saddened by her death.*

**sad·dle** /ˈsædl/ *noun*
1 a leather seat that you sit on when riding a horse
2 a seat that you sit on when riding a bicycle or MOTORCYCLE

**sad·ly** /ˈsædli/ *adverb*
1 in a way that shows you are sad: *She watched sadly as he left.* SYNONYM: **unhappily**; ANTONYM: **happily**

2 used when talking about something that you wish were not true: *Sadly, Juan's mother died when he was a baby.* **SYNONYM: unfortunately**; **ANTONYM: happily**

**sad·ness** /ˈsædnɪs/ *noun*
an unhappy feeling: *His sadness grew stronger as he said goodbye to his brother.* **SYNONYM: unhappiness**; **ANTONYM: happiness**

**sa·fa·ri** /səˈfɑri/ *noun*
a trip through a place to watch wild animals, especially in Africa: *We went on safari in Africa and saw elephants and lions.*
[**ORIGIN:** 1800-1900 From the Arabic word *safariy*, which means "relating to a trip."]

S

**safe¹** /seɪf/ *adjective*
**1** if someone or something is safe, no one will harm or destroy him, her, or it: *I don't feel safe walking home alone. | Keep important papers in a safe place.*
**2** not likely to harm you: *Is it safe to cross the street here?* **ANTONYM: dangerous**
—**safely** *adverb*: *Drive safely!*
[**ORIGIN:** 1200-1300 From the old French word *sauf*, from the Latin word *salvus*, which means "safe, unharmed, or healthy."]

**safe²** *noun*
a strong metal box with a lock on it, where you keep money and important things: *You need to know a special number to open the safe.*

**safe·guard** /ˈseɪfgɑrd/ *noun*
a way of protecting someone or something: *Save your computer files regularly as a safeguard against losing information.*
—**safeguard** *verb* to do something that protects someone or something: *We need to reduce the amount of pollution, in order to safeguard the future of our planet.*

**safe·ty** /ˈseɪfti/ *noun*
the state of being safe from danger or harm: *The new traffic lights have improved safety by making it easier to cross the street.*

**ˈsafety belt** *noun*
another word for a SEAT BELT

**ˈsafety pin** *noun*
a pin with a cover that its point fits into, so that it cannot hurt you: *The strap on my dress is broken – do you have a safety pin?*

**sag** /sæg/ *verb* (**sagged, sagging**)
if something sags, it hangs or bends down in the middle because it is old or has been used a lot: *The couch was very old, and it sagged in the middle.*

**sa·ga** /ˈsɑgə/ *noun*
a long story or description of events: *The story is the saga of a family that traveled across America in the 1880s.*

**Sag·it·tar·i·us** /ˌsædʒəˈteriəs/ *noun*
**1** the ninth sign of the ZODIAC, represented by a man with a BOW and ARROWs
**2** someone born between November 22 and December 21

**said** /sed/ *verb*
the past tense and past participle of SAY

sail

**sail¹** /seɪl/ *verb*
to travel on water in a boat or ship: *He got in the boat and sailed across the lake.*
—**sailing** *noun* the activity of traveling on water in boats: *We went sailing.*

**sail²** *noun*
a large cloth that helps to make a boat move along, using the wind

**sail·boat** /ˈseɪlboʊt/ *noun*
a small boat with one or more sails: *A lot of sailboats were out on the lake.* → see picture on page A26

**sail·or** /ˈseɪlɚ/ *noun*
someone who works on a ship → see picture on page A26

**saint** /seɪnt/ *noun*
**1** (*written abbreviation*: **St.**) a good person who lived a religious life. The Christian church decides who will be a saint after he or she has died: *St. Paul helped spread the Christian religion.*
**2** (*informal*) someone who is very good and kind: *Thank you, Gail – you're a saint!*
[**ORIGIN:** 1100-1200 From the Latin word *sanctus*, which means "holy."]

**sake** /seɪk/ *noun*
**1 for someone's sake** = in order to help or

please someone: *I know you don't really want to come, but will you come for my sake?*
**2** **for the sake of something** = in order to try to achieve or improve something: *He needs to do more exercise, for the sake of his health.*
**3** **for goodness'/heaven's sake** (*informal*) = you use this for showing that you are annoyed or surprised: *Why didn't you tell me you would be late, for heaven's sake?*

**sal·ad** /ˈsæləd/ *noun*
a mixture of raw vegetables that you eat cold: *I put three kinds of lettuce in the salad.*
[**ORIGIN:** 1300-1400 From the Latin word *salata*, which means "flavored with salt," from *sal*, meaning "salt." Vegetables flavored with salt water were popular in Roman times.]

**ˈsalad ˌdressing** *noun*
a liquid that you put on a salad to give it more taste

**sa·la·mi** /səˈlɑmi/ *noun*
a type of SAUSAGE that you eat cold in thin pieces

**sal·a·ry** /ˈsæləri/ *noun* (plural **salaries**)
money that you receive every month as payment for the job you do: *He got a new job with a higher salary.*
→ see Thesaurus box at **pay**[2]
[**ORIGIN:** 1200-1300 From the Latin word *salarium*, which means "money given to soldiers to pay for salt," from *sal*, meaning "salt."]

**sale** /seɪl/ *noun*
**1** the act of selling something: *The sale of cigarettes to children is illegal.*
**2** a time when stores sell things at lower prices than usual: *A lot of stores are having sales this week so I'm hoping to buy some cheap shoes.*
**3** the total number of products that are sold: *Sales of cell phones have increased this year.*
**4** **be on sale** = available for people to buy at a lower price than usual: *The sweater was on sale for $8.99 – it usually costs $30!*
**5** **for sale** = if something you own is for sale, you want to sell it: *Their house is for sale because they are moving to California.*
**6** **go on sale** = to become available for people to buy in stores: *The band's new CD went on sale last week.*

**ˈsales clerk** *noun*
someone whose job is to help customers in a store

**sales·person** /ˈseɪlzˌpɚsən/ *noun* (plural **salespeople** /ˈseɪlzˌpipəl/)
someone whose job is to sell things to people: *One of the salespeople helped us choose a car.* → see picture on page **A16**
—**salesman** /ˈseɪlzmən/ *noun* a man whose job is to sell things to people
—**saleswoman** /ˈseɪlzˌwʊmən/ *noun* a woman whose job is to sell things to people

**ˈsales repreˌsentative** (*also* **sales rep** /ˈseɪlz rep/ (*informal*)) *noun*
someone whose job is to travel around and sell a company's products: *He works as a sales rep for a major drug company.*

**ˈsales tax** *noun*
a tax that you pay that is added to the cost of something you are buying: *Sales tax is 8.5% in this city.*

**sa·li·va** /səˈlaɪvə/ *noun* (*formal*)
the liquid that you produce naturally in your mouth: *The smell of food made her mouth fill with saliva.*

**salm·on** /ˈsæmən/ *noun* (plural **salmon**)
a large ocean fish with pink flesh that you can eat

**sa·lon** /səˈlɑn/ *noun*
a place where you can get your hair cut, or have special treatments for your skin or nails: *She went to the salon to get her hair cut.*
[**ORIGIN:** 1600-1700 From French, from the Italian word *salone*, which means "large hall."]

**sal·sa** /ˈsælsə/ *noun*
**1** a strong-tasting Mexican sauce that you make from onions, tomatoes, and PEPPERs: *Buy some chips and salsa for the party.*
**2** a type of Latin American music or dance

**salt** /sɔlt/ *noun*
a white mineral that you add to food to make it taste better: *Put some salt and pepper on the meat before you cook it.*

**salt·y** /ˈsɔlti/ *adjective*
tasting of salt: *I don't like this soup – it's too salty.*
→ see Thesaurus box at **taste**[1]

**sa·lute** /səˈlut/ *verb*
if a soldier salutes, he or she moves the right

hand to the head to show respect to an officer: *The soldier saluted the captain.*
—**salute** *noun* an act of saluting: *He raised his hand in a salute.*
[ORIGIN: 1300-1400 From the Latin word *salutare*, which means "to greet," from *salus*, which means "health," and also means "a greeting," because people wished each other good health as a greeting.]

**sal·vage** /ˈsælvɪdʒ/ *verb (formal)*
to save something after an accident or a situation when other things have been damaged or destroyed: *After the earthquake, people tried to salvage what they could from the damaged houses.*
—**salvage** *noun* the act of salvaging things

S

**same** /seɪm/ *adjective, pronoun*
**1 the same** = **a)** one particular thing, and not a different one: *Kim and I go to the same school.* **b)** exactly like another person or thing: *The two girls were wearing the same blue dress.* | *Thanks for your help! I'll do the same for you one day.* **c)** if someone or something is the same, he, she, or it has not changed: *It was the first time I had seen him in two years, but he is still the same.* **ANTONYM: different**
**2 at the same time** = if two things happen at the same time, they happen together: *We both started to talk at the same time, so I stopped and let him speak.*
—**the same** *adverb* in the same way: *Teachers must treat all the students the same.*

**sam·ple¹** /ˈsæmpəl/ *noun*
a small amount of something that shows you what the rest is like: *The teacher asked if she could see a sample of my work.* **SYNONYM: example**

**sample²** *verb (formal)*
to taste food or drink to see what it is like: *We sampled four different kinds of ice cream.* **SYNONYM: try**

**sanc·tions** /ˈsæŋkʃən/ *plural noun*
laws that stop trade with another country, that are used to punish that country or to persuade the country to do something: *Some people want to end U.S. sanctions against Cuba, and allow U.S. goods to be sold there.*

**sanc·tu·ar·y** /ˈsæŋktʃuˌeri/ *noun* (plural **sanctuaries**)
**1** a safe area for birds or animals where people cannot hunt them: *a wildlife sanctuary*
**2** the part of a religious building that is the most holy part

**sand** /sænd/ *noun*
the very small grains of rock that are on the ground on beaches and in deserts: *The kids wanted to swim in the ocean and play in the sand.*

**san·dal** /ˈsændl/ *noun*
a shoe that does not cover all of the top part of your foot, which you wear in hot weather: *It's hot today, so wear your sandals and a skirt.* → see picture at **shoe**

**sand·box** /ˈsændbɑks/ *noun*
a large box with sand in it, for children to play in

**sand·pa·per** /ˈsændˌpeɪpɚ/ *noun*
strong paper with a rough sand on one side, that you use for rubbing wood to make it smooth

**sand·wich** /ˈsændwɪtʃ/ *noun*
two pieces of bread with something such as cheese or meat between them: *We had ham sandwiches for lunch.*
[ORIGIN: From John Montagu (1718-92), the Earl of Sandwich (a place in England). He ate sandwiches so that he could continue gambling without leaving the table.]

**sand·y** /ˈsændi/ *adjective*
covered with sand: *a sandy beach*

**sane** /seɪn/ *adjective (formal)*
mentally healthy and able to think in a normal way: *Doctors say he was not sane when he killed his wife.* **ANTONYM: insane**

**sang** /sæŋ/ *verb*
the past tense of SING

**san·i·tar·y** /ˈsænəˌteri/ *adjective (formal)*
clean and not likely to make people sick: *The bathrooms are cleaned every night to keep them sanitary.*
—**sanitation** /ˌsænəˈteɪʃən/ *noun* the process of keeping places clean and healthy

**san·i·ty** /ˈsænəti/ *noun (formal)*
the state of having a normal healthy mind: *Sometimes he became violent, and I thought he was losing his sanity.* **ANTONYM: insanity**

**sank** /sæŋk/ *verb*
the past tense of SINK

**San·ta Claus** /ˈsæntə ˌklɔz/ (*also* **Santa**) *noun*
an old man with red clothes and a white BEARD, who children believe brings presents at Christmas

**sap** /sæp/ *noun*
the liquid that carries food through a plant: *Syrup is made of sap from maple trees.*

**sap·phire** /ˈsæfaɪɚ/ *noun*
a bright blue jewel: *a ring with sapphires*

**sar·casm** /ˈsɑrˌkæzəm/ *noun*
a way of speaking in which you say the opposite of what you mean. People use sarcasm when they are criticizing someone or when they are annoyed: *"You're early!" she said with sarcasm, when he came in late.*
—**sarcastic** /sɑrˈkæstɪk/ *adjective* using sarcasm: *"This is fun," she said, in a sarcastic voice, as they walked home in the rain.*
—**sarcastically** *adverb* in a way that uses sarcasm
[**ORIGIN:** 1500-1600 From the Greek word *sarkasmos*, from *sarkazein*, which means "to tear flesh, or bite your lip angrily."]

**sar·dine** /sɑrˈdin/ *noun*
a small silver fish that people eat, that is often packed in flat metal boxes: *a can of sardines*

**sat** /sæt/ *verb*
the past tense and past participle of SIT

**Sa·tan** /ˈseɪtn/ *noun*
another word for the DEVIL, a spirit that some people believe to be the most evil power in the world
—**satanic** /səˈtænɪk/ *adjective* relating to Satan: *a satanic symbol*

satellite

**sat·el·lite** /ˈsætəlˌaɪt/ *noun*
**1** a machine that is sent into space to receive and send radio or television signals and other kinds of signals, as it moves around the Earth: *Television shows can be sent by satellite to anywhere in the world.*
**2** (*formal*) a moon that moves around a PLANET: *The planet Jupiter has four satellites.*
[**ORIGIN:** 1500-1600 From the Latin word *satelles*, which means "personal servant or guard." A satellite stays near to the Earth or another planet, like a personal servant staying near to his master.]

**ˈsatellite ˌdish** *noun*
a piece of equipment that receives radio and television signals sent from a satellite

**sat·in** /ˈsætn/ *noun*
a type of cloth that is very smooth and shiny: *Her dress was made of satin.*

**sat·ire** /ˈsætaɪɚ/ *noun*
something, such as a book or a play, that criticizes someone or something in a funny way: *The book is a satire of American politics.*
—**satirist** *noun* someone who writes satires

**sat·is·fac·tion** /ˌsætɪsˈfækʃən/ *noun*
the feeling you get when you are pleased that you have achieved something: *She had a sense of satisfaction when she finally understood the math problem.*

**sat·is·fac·to·ry** /ˌsætɪsˈfæktəri/ *adjective*
good enough, but not very good: *Stella's progress in science has been satisfactory, but she could do better if she worked harder.*

**THESAURUS: satisfactory**

**good enough** as good as a person or thing needs to be for a purpose or situation: *Is he good enough to play in the major leagues?*

**acceptable** good enough for a particular purpose: *His work is acceptable, though he could do better.*

**adequate** (*formal*) enough in amount or of a good enough quality for a particular purpose: *Plants need adequate sunlight to grow.*

**all right/okay** (*informal*) acceptable, but not very good: *I thought the movie was all right.* | *The food was okay.*

**sat·is·fied** /ˈsætɪsˌfaɪd/ *adjective*
pleased because something is good or because you have achieved something: *I am*

S

*very satisfied with my grades – I got all A's and B's.* **ANTONYM: dissatisfied**

**sat·is·fy** /ˈsætɪsˌfaɪ/ *verb* (**satisfied, satisfies**) to make someone feel happy by doing what he or she wants or giving what is needed: *The sandwich satisfied his hunger.* | *The company works hard to satisfy its customers.*
—**satisfying** *adjective* making you feel happy by giving you what you want or need: *a satisfying meal*
[**ORIGIN:** 1400-1500 From the Latin word *satisfacere*, from *satis* and *facere*, which mean "enough" and "to make."]

**WORD FAMILY: satisfy**
**satisfy** *verb* | **satisfied** *adjective* | **dissatisfied** *adjective* | **satisfying** *adjective* | **satisfactory** *adjective* | **unsatisfactory** *adjective* | **satisfaction** *noun* | **dissatisfaction** *noun*

**sat·u·rat·ed fat** /ˌsætʃəreɪtɪd ˈfæt/ *noun* a type of fat that comes from meat and milk: *Too much saturated fat is not good for you.*

**Sat·ur·day** /ˈsætɚdi/ *noun* (*written abbreviation*: **Sat.**) the seventh day of the week, between Friday and Sunday: *My birthday is Saturday.* | *Jim's going to Phoenix on Saturday.* | *Would next Saturday be a good time for me to visit?* | *What are you doing Saturday night?*
[**ORIGIN:** From Saturn, the Roman god of farming.]

**Sat·urn** /ˈsætɚn/ *noun* the sixth PLANET from the Sun. Saturn is the second largest planet in our SOLAR SYSTEM. It has rings around it and many moons.

**sauce** /sɔs/ *noun* a thick liquid that you serve with food to give it a good taste: *spaghetti with tomato sauce*
[**ORIGIN:** 1300-1400 From the Latin word *salsa*, which means "flavored with salt," from *sal*, meaning "salt."]

**sauce·pan** /ˈsɔspæn/ *noun* a deep metal container with a handle, that you use for cooking: *Heat the soup in a saucepan.* → see picture on page **A9**

**sau·cer** /ˈsɔsɚ/ *noun* a small round plate that you put a cup on: *Some coffee spilled into the saucer when she put the cup down.* → see picture on page **A9**
[**ORIGIN:** 1300-1400 From the old French word *saussier*, which means "plate for sauce."]

**sau·na** /ˈsɔnə/ *noun* a special room that is very hot, where people sit and relax for a short time: *The new health club has a big swimming pool and a sauna.*

**sau·sage** /ˈsɔsɪdʒ/ *noun* meat and spices that are put into a skin shaped like a tube: *A hot dog is a kind of sausage.*
[**ORIGIN:** 1400-1500 From the old French word *saussiche*, from the Latin word *salsicia*, from *salsus*, which means "flavored with salt."]

**sav·age** /ˈsævɪdʒ/ *adjective* very cruel and violent: *She was hurt in a savage attack by a dog.*
—**savagery** /ˈsævɪdʒəri/ *noun* the quality of being savage
[**ORIGIN:** 1200-1300 From the French word *sauvage*, which means "wild." This comes from the Latin word *salvaticus* or *silvaticus*, which means "relating to a forest," from *silva*, meaning "forest."]

**save** /seɪv/ *verb*
**1** to make someone or something safe from danger or harm: *Firefighters saved three children from the fire.* | *The new medical treatment could save his life.*
**2** (*also* **save up**) to keep money, so that you can use it later: *I'm saving up to buy a new computer.*
**3** to use less of something, and not waste it: *It saves electricity if you turn off the lights when you're not using them.*
**4** to keep something, and not use it or throw it away: *She saved all his letters in a box.*
**5** to make a computer keep the work that you have done on it: *Don't forget to save your work before you turn the computer off.*

**sav·ings** /ˈseɪvɪŋz/ *plural noun* all the money you have saved: *I'm going to use my savings to buy a new skateboard.*

**ˈsavings acˌcount** *noun* a bank account that you put money in to save for a later time

**sav·ior** /ˈseɪvyɚ/ *noun*
**1** someone or something that can help you, when you are in a difficult or dangerous situation: *We hope that the new coach will be the savior of the team.*

**2 the/our Savior** = used as a name for Jesus Christ, who Christians believe saves people from evil

**saw**[1] /sɔ/ *verb*
the past tense of SEE

**saw**[2] *noun*
a tool that you use for cutting wood, with a flat blade and a row of sharp points

**saw**[3] *verb* (**sawed**, **sawed** *or* **sawn** /sɔn/)
to cut something using a saw: *He sawed the wood into three pieces.*
→ see Thesaurus box at **cut**[1]

**saw·dust** /ˈsɔdʌst/ *noun*
very small pieces of wood that fall to the ground when you cut wood with a SAW

**saw·mill** /ˈsɔmɪl/ *noun*
a factory where machines cut trees into boards

**sax** /sæks/ *noun* (*informal*)
another word for a SAXOPHONE

**sax·o·phone** /ˈsæksəˌfoʊn/ *noun*
a metal musical instrument that you play by blowing into it and pressing buttons on it → see picture on page **A21**
[**ORIGIN:** From Adolphe Sax (1814-94), the Belgian musician who invented the instrument. *-phone* comes from the Greek word for "sound."]

**say**[1] /seɪ/ *verb* (**said** /sed/, **says** /sez/)
**1** to tell someone something using words: *"I'll see you later," she said.* | *He said that he wasn't feeling well.* | *Did she say where she was going?*

**USAGE: say, tell, talk**

You **say** words **to** someone. You cannot say "Say me." Say: *Did Nick say anything to you?*

You **tell** a person facts or information: *She told me that she was going home.*

You **talk about** a particular subject: *Each student had to talk about his or her family.*

**THESAURUS: say**

**mention** to say something but without giving many details: *He mentioned something about having a party, but he didn't say when.*

**add** to say something more about something: *"We would have to walk. And it's too far," she added.*

**express** to say how you feel about something: *A two-year-old child can't always express what he or she feels.*

**point out** to say something that other people had not noticed or thought of: *Liz pointed out that the picture was hanging upside down.*

**suggest/imply** to say that something is true, in a way that is not direct: *He seemed to be suggesting that I'd stolen it!*

**whisper** to say something very quietly: *"Is the baby asleep?" she whispered.*

**mumble** to say something quietly and without saying the words clearly: *Robbie mumbled an answer, but I couldn't quite hear what it was.*

**mutter** to say something quietly because you are annoyed or do not want anyone to hear: *"It's not fair," she muttered.*

**murmur** to say something in a soft quiet voice: *She held her son close to her. "It's okay, you're going to be all right," she murmured.*

**2** to give information in writing, pictures, or numbers: *The clock said 6:45.* | *What did the newspapers say about the accident?* | *The label says to take one pill before meals.*
[**ORIGIN:** From the old English word *secgan*.]

**say**[2] *noun*
the chance to give an opinion and help decide something: *Everyone in the family should have a say in where we go for our vacation.*

**say·ing** /ˈseɪ-ɪŋ/ *noun*
a phrase that most people know that gives advice or information about life: *The old saying, "An apple a day keeps the doctor away," means that you should eat healthy food.*
→ see Thesaurus box at **phrase**

**scab** /skæb/ *noun*
a hard layer of dried blood that forms over a cut or wound: *The girl had a scab on her knee where she had scraped it.*

**scaf·fold·ing** /ˈskæfəldɪŋ/ *noun*
a structure made of poles and boards that is put on the outside of a building, for people to stand on while they work on the building: *They put up scaffolding so they could paint the building.*

**scald** /skɔld/ *verb*
to burn yourself with hot liquid or steam: *She spilled boiling water and scalded her arm.*
—**scalding** *adjective* extremely hot: *The water in the tub was scalding, so I had to wait for it to cool down.*

**scale¹** /skeɪl/ *noun*
**1** a piece of equipment for weighing people or objects: *I weighed myself on the scale in the bathroom.* → see picture at **weigh**
**2** a system for measuring something: *Your performance will be judged on a scale of 1 to 10, with 1 being very bad and 10 being very good.*
**3** the relationship between a map and the size of the place it represents: *The map has a scale of 1 inch equaling 1 mile.*
**4** a series of musical notes that you play in a set order, so that the notes become gradually higher or lower in sound: *She was playing the scale of C major on the piano.*
**5** a set of marks on a tool or instrument for measuring something: *I need a ruler with a metric scale.*
**6** one of the small flat pieces of hard skin that cover the body of a fish, snake, or other REPTILE
**7** how big or important something is: *At first we didn't understand the scale of the problem or how much work we would have to do.*

**scale²** *adjective*
**scale model/drawing** = a model or drawing of something in which each part has been made smaller or larger by the same amount, so it looks exactly the same as the real thing: *He made a scale model of the building out of cardboard.*

**sca·lene tri·an·gle** /ˌskeɪlin ˈtraɪˌæŋgəl/ *noun*
a TRIANGLE with sides that are all different lengths → see picture at **triangle**

**scal·lop** /ˈskæləp/ *noun*
a small sea animal that you can eat, which has a hard flat shell

**scalp** /skælp/ *noun*
the skin under the hair on your head: *This shampoo is good for your hair and scalp.*

**scal·pel** /ˈskælpəl/ *noun*
a small sharp knife that a doctor uses for doing an operation: *The doctor cut open the patient's stomach with a scalpel.*

**scam** /skæm/ *noun* (*informal*)
a dishonest plan to get money by tricking people: *The scam involved getting people to pay for things without ever sending them the goods.*

**scan¹** /skæn/ *verb* (**scanned**, **scanning**)
**1** (*also* **scan through**) to read something quickly to find the information you want: *He scanned the menu, looking for something he liked.*
**2** to get a picture of what is inside something, or read electronic information using a machine called a SCANNER: *All suitcases are scanned at the airport to find guns or bombs.* | *The salesperson scans the bar codes to see how much you have to pay.*
**3** to copy a picture or piece of writing onto a computer using a machine called a SCANNER: *You can scan the pictures and email them to your brother.*

**scan²** *noun*
a medical test in which a machine produces a picture of something inside your body: *He had a brain scan at the hospital to see if there was something wrong.*

**scan·dal** /ˈskændl/ *noun*
if there is a scandal, people are shocked by something bad that a famous or important person has done: *There was a big scandal when they found out the mayor had taken the money.*

S

—**scandalize** *verb* to do something that shocks someone: *Donna scandalized her father by living with her boyfriend.*

**scan·dal·ous** /ˈskændl-əs/ *adjective*
shocking and involving very bad behavior: *The newspapers printed scandalous stories about the senator's secret girlfriend.*

**Scan·di·na·vi·an** /ˌskændəˈneɪviən/ *adjective*
from Norway, Sweden, Denmark, Finland, or Iceland: *My father is Scandinavian – he was born in Sweden.*
—**Scandinavian** *noun* someone from Norway, Sweden, Denmark, Finland, or Iceland

**scan·ner** /ˈskænɚ/ *noun*
**1** a piece of equipment that copies a picture or piece of writing onto a computer → see picture on page **A20**
**2** a piece of equipment that produces a picture of what is inside something, or reads electronic information: *Your bag is put through a scanner when you go through airport security.*

**scape·goat** /ˈskeɪpgoʊt/ *noun*
someone who people blame for something bad that happens, even if it is not his or her fault: *They made me the scapegoat for their mistakes because they didn't want to admit they had done anything wrong.*

**scar¹** /skɑr/ *noun*
a permanent mark on your skin from a cut or wound: *The burn left a scar on her hand.*
→ see Thesaurus box at **mark²**

**scar²** *verb* (**scarred**, **scarring**)
to leave a permanent mark on your skin from a cut or injury: *The burns scarred his face.*

**scarce** /skers/ *adjective*
if something is scarce, there is not much of it and it is difficult to get: *Fresh fruit was scarce during the winter.*
—**scarcity** *noun* a situation in which something is scarce: *The scarcity of medical supplies was a problem.*

**scarce·ly** /ˈskersli/ *adverb*
almost not at all, or almost none at all: *The town has scarcely changed in the last 20 years.* **SYNONYMS: barely, hardly**

**scare¹** /sker/ *verb*
to make someone feel afraid: *The sudden loud noise scared me.* **SYNONYM: frighten**
[**ORIGIN:** 1100-1200 From the Norse word *skirra*, from *skjarr*, which means "shy or afraid."]

**WORD FAMILY: scare**
**scare** *verb* | **scare** *noun* | **scared** *adjective* | **scary** *adjective*

**scare²** *noun*
**1** a sudden feeling of fear: *The dog gave me a scare when it jumped up at me.*
**2** a situation that frightens or worries people because they think something bad will happen: *There was a bomb scare at the subway station and everyone had to leave.*

**scare·crow** /ˈskerkroʊ/ *noun*
a figure of a person that a farmer puts in a field to frighten away birds that might eat seeds or crops

**scared** /skerd/ *adjective*
afraid or nervous about something: *A lot of people are scared of flying.* | *She was scared that she might slip and fall on the ice.* **SYNONYMS: afraid, frightened** → see picture on page **A23**
→ see Thesaurus box at **frightened**

**scarf** /skɑrf/ *noun* (plural **scarves** /skɑrvz/ or **scarfs**)
a piece of material that you wear around your neck to keep you warm or to make you look attractive: *It was cold, so she put on a hat, scarf, and gloves.* → see picture on page **A6**

**scar·let** /ˈskɑrlɪt/ *adjective, noun*
a very bright red color
[**ORIGIN:** 1200-1300 From the Latin word *scarlata*, which means "scarlet cloth," from *saqalat*, a Persian word for a type of fine cloth.]

**ˌscarlet ˈfever** *noun*
a disease that gives you a sore throat, a red tongue, and red spots on your skin, and that mainly affects children

**scar·y** /ˈskeri/ *adjective* (**scarier**, **scariest**)
making you feel afraid: *It's a scary movie about ghosts.* **SYNONYM: frightening**

**scat·ter** /ˈskætɚ/ *verb*
**1** to throw or drop a lot of things over a

wide area: *Scatter the flower seeds over the soil, and then cover them with the dirt and water them.*
**2** to move away quickly in different directions, usually to escape from danger: *The sound of gunfire made the crowd scatter.*

**sce·nar·i·o** Ac /sɪˈneriˌoʊ/ *noun* (plural **scenarios**)
something that could possibly happen: *The hotel could close down, but the most likely scenario is that it will be sold.*

**scene** /sin/ *noun*
**1** a short part of a play or movie, during which the events happen in the same place: *The main character dies in the last scene of the play.*
**2** the place where an accident or crime happened: *Police are examining the scene of the crime for clues.*
**3** a view or picture of a place: *He painted a beautiful scene of mountains and a lake.*
→ see Thesaurus box at **part**[1]
[ORIGIN: 1500-1600 From the Greek word *skene*, which means "stage where a play is performed."]

**sce·ner·y** /ˈsinəri/ *noun*
**1** the natural things you can see in a place, such as mountains, forests, and fields: *The scenery is very beautiful in this part of Canada.*
**2** the background and furniture on a theater stage: *The scenery for the play is simple: just a chair and a desk.*

**sce·nic** /ˈsinɪk/ *adjective*
with beautiful views of natural things such as mountains, forests, oceans, and lakes: *We took a scenic route along California's coastline, where we could see the ocean.*

**scent** /sent/ *noun*
**1** a pleasant smell: *The scent of flowers filled the room.*
**2** the smell that a person or animal leaves behind: *Police dogs are trained to follow a person's scent.*
—**scented** *adjective* having a pleasant smell: *scented candles*
→ see Thesaurus box at **smell**[1]
[ORIGIN: 1300-1400 From the Latin word *sentire*, which means "to feel, see, hear, etc."]

**sched·ule** Ac /ˈskedʒəl/ *noun*
**1** a plan of what you will do and when you will do it: *She has a busy schedule, with band practice three times a week.*
**2** a list showing the times that buses or trains arrive at and leave a place: *The schedule showed the train was due to arrive at 6:50.*
[ORIGIN: 1300-1400 From the Latin word *schedula* or *scheda*, which means "piece of paper."]

**scheme**[1] Ac /skim/ *noun*
a plan, especially to do something bad or illegal: *He thought of a scheme to avoid paying taxes.*

**scheme**[2] Ac *verb*
to secretly make dishonest plans to get or achieve something: *He had been scheming to steal his uncle's money.* **SYNONYM: plot**
—**schemer** *noun* someone who schemes to do something

**schiz·o·phre·ni·a** /ˌskɪtsəˈfriniə/ *noun*
a serious mental illness in which someone's thoughts and feelings are not connected with what is really happening around him or her: *He had schizophrenia and sometimes heard voices when no one was there.*
—**schizophrenic** /ˌskɪtsəˈfrenɪk/ *adjective* relating to or having schizophrenia
—**schizophrenic** *noun* someone who has schizophrenia

**schol·ar** /ˈskɑlɚ/ *noun*
**1** someone who studies a subject and knows a lot about it: *Legal scholars disagree about the meaning of the law.*
**2** someone who has been given money to study at a school or university: *The university scholars are chosen from the students who get top grades in high school.*
—**scholarly** *adjective* relating to the serious study of a subject: *scholarly research*

**schol·ar·ship** /ˈskɑlɚˌʃɪp/ *noun*
an amount of money that an organization gives someone to help pay for his or her education: *Michael got a scholarship to Harvard University, which will pay for his books and tuition.*

**school** /skul/ *noun*
**1** a place where children go to learn: *Which school do you go to? | I saw her at school.*

S

2 the time you spend at school: *What are you doing after school?*
3 all the students and teachers at a school: *He gave a speech to the whole school.*
4 a university, or a university department that teaches a particular subject: *He was a young lawyer, just out of law school.*
5 a group of fish: *Many fish swim in schools for protection.*
→ see Thesaurus box at **group**[1]
[ORIGIN: From the Greek word *schole*, which meant "leisure," and then later also meant "discussion of ideas for pleasure" and "place for discussing and learning."]

**sci·ence** /ˈsaɪəns/ *noun*
the study of the animals, plants, and the physical world, and the facts about them that have been discovered or proved: *He studied science at Stanford.* | *We have to take science classes such as chemistry and biology.*
[ORIGIN: 1300-1400 From the Latin word *scientia*, which means "knowledge."]

**WORD FAMILY: science**
**science** *noun* | **scientist** *noun* | **scientific** *adjective*

**ˌscience ˈfiction** *noun*
books and stories about the future, for example about traveling in time and space: *I'm reading a science fiction book about a boy living on Mars.*

**sci·en·tif·ic** /ˌsaɪənˈtɪfɪk/ *adjective*
relating to or based on science: *There is no scientific evidence that the drug is safe.*

**sci·en·tist** /ˈsaɪəntɪst/ *noun*
someone who works in science: *Scientists have shown that smoking causes cancer.*

**sci-fi** /ˌsaɪˈfaɪ/ *noun (informal)*
another word for SCIENCE FICTION

**scis·sors** /ˈsɪzɚz/ *plural noun*
a tool for cutting paper or cloth, that has two sharp blades and handles with holes for your finger and thumb: *I need a pair of scissors to cut this package open.*

**scissors**

[ORIGIN: 1300-1400 From the old French word *cisoires*, from the Latin word *cisorium*, meaning "cutting tool," from a form of the verb *caedere*, which means "to cut."]

**scold** /skoʊld/ *verb*
to tell someone in an angry way that he or she has done something wrong: *Mom scolded us for taking the candy without asking first.*

**scoop**[1] /skup/ *noun*
1 a deep spoon for serving food
2 an amount of food that a scoop holds: *I put two scoops of ice cream on my pie.*

**scoop**[2] *verb*
to pick up or remove something using a spoon or your curved hand: *Cut the melon and scoop out the seeds.*

**scoot·er** /ˈskutɚ/ *noun*
1 a children's vehicle with a tall handle on a board with two wheels. You stand on the board with one foot and move by pushing against the ground with your other foot.
2 a type of MOTORCYCLE with two small wheels and a small engine

**scope** Ac /skoʊp/ *noun*
the range of things that a subject, activity, book, etc. deals with: *Limit the scope of your paper to the most important issues.*

**scorch** /skɔrtʃ/ *verb*
to burn the surface of something and make it change color: *Turn down the iron or you'll scorch your shirt.*

**score**[1] /skɔr/ *noun*
1 the number of points that you get in a game or on a test: *He got a score of 85 out of a possible 100 on the math test.* | *The final score of the game was 35 to 17.*
2 **keep score** = to write down how many points each person or team has won in a game: *Who's going to keep score?*
[ORIGIN: 1000-1100 From the Norse word *skor*, which means "a mark cut into a surface." People kept count of things by making marks on a stick, like you keep count of the points in a game. Norse was a language used in Scandinavian countries.]

**score**[2] *verb*
1 to get points in a game or on a test: *How many goals has he scored this year?*
2 to give a particular number of points in a game, competition, or test: *The tests will be scored by computer.*

S

**score·board** /ˈskɔrbɔrd/ *noun*
a sign that shows the latest score in a game, while it is being played

**scorn** /skɔrn/ *noun*
a complete lack of respect for someone or something because you think he, she, or it is not important or good: *He felt scorn for the people who did not understand his ideas.*
—**scorn** *verb* (*formal*) to treat a person or idea as if he, she, or it is stupid and not worth considering: *They scorned her ideas and laughed at her.*

**Scor·pi·o** /ˈskɔrpiˌoʊ/ *noun*
**1** the eighth sign of the ZODIAC, represented by a SCORPION
**2** someone born between October 23 and November 21

S

**scor·pi·on** /ˈskɔrpiən/ *noun*
a small animal that stings with its tail: *Scorpions live in hot countries.*

**Scotch tape** /ˈskɑtʃ teɪp/ *noun* (*trademark*)
a long narrow piece of clear sticky material, used for sticking things together: *She used Scotch tape to fix the tear in the picture.*

**Scot·tish** /ˈskɑtɪʃ/ *adjective*
from Scotland

**scout¹** /skaʊt/ *noun*
**1** a member of the GIRL SCOUTS or BOY SCOUTS
**2** a soldier who is sent to search an area in front of an army and get information about the enemy: *The captain sent out three scouts to check for enemy soldiers.*
**3** someone whose job is to look for good sports players in order to employ them
[**ORIGIN:** 1300-1400 From the old French word *escouter*, which means "to listen," from the Latin word *auscultare*. The idea of getting information by listening changed to the idea of getting information by going to look somewhere.]

**scout²** *verb*
(*also* **scout around**) to look for something in a particular area: *I'll scout around for a place to eat.*

**scowl¹** /skaʊl/ *verb*
to look at someone in an angry or disapproving way: *I took another cookie and Mom scowled at me.*

**scowl²** *noun*
an angry or disapproving look that you give someone: *"That's not true," she said with a scowl.*

**scram·ble** /ˈskræmbəl/ *verb*
**1** to climb up or over something quickly, using your hands to help you: *The kids were scrambling over the rocks.*
**2** to try to do something very quickly: *We're scrambling to finish the project on time.*

**ˈscrambled ˌeggs** *plural noun*
eggs that have been cooked after mixing the white and yellow parts together

**scrap** /skræp/ *noun*
a small piece of paper, cloth, etc.: *He wrote his address on a scrap of paper.*
→ see Thesaurus box at **piece**

**scrap·book** /ˈskræpbʊk/ *noun*
a book with empty pages, in which you can stick pictures, newspaper articles, or other things you want to keep: *He kept a scrapbook of pictures his children had painted.*

**scrape** /skreɪp/ *verb*
**1** to remove something from a surface using the edge of an object such as a knife: *Scrape the mud off your boots before you come into the house.*
**2** to damage something by rubbing it against a rough surface: *She fell and scraped her knee.*

**scratch¹** /skrætʃ/ *verb*
**1** to rub your skin with your FINGERNAILs: *The mosquito bite on her hand itched so much she couldn't stop scratching it.* → see picture on page **A3**
**2** to damage a surface or slightly cut someone's skin by pulling something sharp across it: *Don't drag the chair – you'll scratch the floor.* | *The tree branch scratched her arm.*
→ see Thesaurus box at **touch¹**

**scratch²** *noun*
a long thin cut or mark on the surface of something or on someone's skin: *a scratch on the car door*
→ see Thesaurus box at **injury**

**scratch·y** /ˈskrætʃi/ *adjective*
scratchy clothes or materials have a rough surface and are uncomfortable to wear or

touch: *The sweater was made of scratchy wool and made her skin itch.*

**scream¹** /skrim/ *verb*
to make a loud high noise with your voice because you are afraid, hurt, excited, or angry: *There was a loud bang and people started screaming.* | *She was screaming at her husband.*
→ see Thesaurus box at **shout¹**

**scream²** *noun*
a loud high noise that you make when you are afraid, hurt, excited, or angry: *When people heard the girl's screams, they ran to see what was wrong.*

**screech** /skritʃ/ *verb*
**1** to shout something in a high voice because you are angry or upset: *"Get out of my way!" she screeched.*
**2** if a vehicle screeches, its wheels make a loud high noise when it is moving or stopping: *The car screeched around the corner.*

**screen** /skrin/ *noun*
**1** the flat glass part of a television or a computer: *The computer has an 18-inch screen.* → see picture on page **A20**
**2** a large flat white surface that movies are shown on in a movie theater: *I don't like to sit too close to the screen at the movies.*
**3** a wire net that covers an open door or window, keeping insects out but allowing air to get inside the house: *The screens on the windows keep flies out.*
**4** a piece of material on a frame that you use for dividing one part of a room from another part: *The doctor asked him to undress behind the screen.*

**ˈscreen ˌsaver** *noun*
a moving picture that appears on your computer screen when you are not using the computer

**screw¹** /skru/ *noun*
a thin pointed piece of metal that you push and turn, in order to fasten pieces of wood or metal together: *Tighten the screws in the bookcase with a screwdriver.*

**screw²** *verb*
**1** to fasten one thing to another, using a screw: *Screw the shelf to the wall.*
**2** to fasten or close something by turning it: *Screw the lid back on the jar.*

**screw·driv·er** /ˈskruˌdraɪvɚ/ *noun*
a tool that you use to turn screws: *She used a screwdriver to put the furniture together.*

**scrib·ble** /ˈskrɪbəl/ (*also* **scribble down**) *verb*
to write something quickly in a messy way: *He scribbled down his phone number on a piece of paper.*
[**ORIGIN:** 1400-1500 From the Latin word *scribere*, which means "to write."]

**scrim·mage** /ˈskrɪmɪdʒ/ *noun*
a game played for practice in sports such as football and basketball: *The team played a few scrimmages to prepare for the big game.*

**script** /skrɪpt/ *noun*
the written words of a movie, play, or speech: *He wrote the script and directed the movie.*
[**ORIGIN:** 1300-1400 From the Latin word *scriptum*, which means "something written," from *scribere*, which means "to write."]

**scrip·ture** /ˈskrɪptʃɚ/ *noun*
**1** (*also* **the (Holy) Scriptures**) the Bible
**2** the holy books of any religion: *Buddhist scriptures*

**scroll¹** /skroʊl/ *verb*
to move information up or down a computer screen so that you can read it: *You can scroll up and down using the arrows at the right of the screen.*

**scroll²** *noun*
a long piece of paper that can be written on and rolled up. Scrolls were used in the past

**scrub** /skrʌb/ *verb* (**scrubbed**, **scrubbing**)
to clean something by rubbing it very hard: *Tom was on his knees, scrubbing the floor.*
→ see Thesaurus box at **clean²**

**scru·ple** /ˈskrupəl/ *noun*
a belief about what is right and wrong that prevents you from doing something bad: *He's dishonest and has no scruples about lying.*

**scru·pu·lous** /ˈskrupyələs/ *adjective* (*formal*)
careful to be completely honest, fair, and correct: *He was too scrupulous to cheat on a test.*
—**scrupulously** *adverb* in a scrupulous way

S

**scu·ba div·ing** /ˈskubə ˌdaɪvɪŋ/ *noun*
the sport of swimming under water while breathing from a container of air on your back: *We went scuba diving in Hawaii and saw so many beautiful fish.*
[**ORIGIN:** 1900-2000 The word "scuba" comes from the first letters of the phrase "self-contained underwater breathing apparatus." "Self-contained" means "not needing anything else to work."]

**sculp·tor** /ˈskʌlptɚ/ *noun*
an artist who makes objects from stone, wood, or metal
—**sculpt** *verb* to make objects from stone, wood, or metal as art: *He sculpted the statue of the woman from marble.*

**sculp·ture** /ˈskʌlptʃɚ/ *noun*
**1** an object that someone has made from stone, wood, or metal as art: *There is a bronze sculpture of a lion in front of the library.*
**2** the art of making objects from stone, wood, or metal: *The sculpture class is working on making figures of people out of clay.*
→ see Thesaurus box at **art**
[**ORIGIN:** 1300-1400 From the Latin word *sculptura*, from *sculpere*, which means "to carve."]

**scum** /skʌm/ *noun*
a dirty substance that forms on the top of a liquid: *There was green scum on the surface of the pond.*

**sea** /si/ *noun*
**1** a large area of salty water that is smaller than an ocean: *the Mediterranean Sea*
**2** the ocean: *The boat was heading out to sea.*

**sea·food** /ˈsifud/ *noun*
ocean animals such as fish and SHELLFISH that you can eat: *I love seafood like lobster.*

**sea·gull** /ˈsigʌl/ *noun*
a common gray and white bird that lives near the sea and has a loud cry

**seal**[1] /sil/ *noun*
**1** a large animal that lives near the ocean, swims, has smooth fur, and eats fish
**2** an official mark that is put on documents or objects in order to prove that they are legal or real: *The visa had a government seal on it.*
**3** a piece of plastic or paper that you have to break in order to open a bottle for the first time: *Do not use this medicine if the seal on the bottle is broken.*

**seal**[2] *verb*
**1** (*also* **seal up**) to close an entrance, container, or hole with something that stops air or water from getting in or out: *The medicine bottle is sealed shut, and you have to break the seal to use it.*
**2** to close an envelope or package with something sticky: *She put the letter in the envelope and sealed it.*

**ˈsea ˌlevel** *noun*
the height of the surface of the ocean. Sea level is used when talking about how high or low places are compared to the surface of the ocean: *Mexico City is 7,300 feet above sea level.*

**ˈsea ˌlion** *noun*
a large seal with ears that stick out and long FLIPPERs that it can use to walk on land, that lives mainly in the Pacific Ocean

**seam** /sim/ *noun*
the line where two pieces of cloth have been sewn together: *His shirt was torn along the seam.*

**search**[1] /sɚtʃ/ *noun*
**1** an attempt to find someone or something by looking very carefully: *Police are continuing their search for the missing girl.* | *His family moved to California in search of work.*
**2** an attempt to find information or an answer: *I did a search on the Internet for information about the disease.*

**search**[2] *verb*
**1** to try to find someone or something by looking very carefully: *Police searched the house for weapons.* | *I searched through the papers on my desk, looking for the letter.*
**2** to try to find information or an answer to a problem: *He was searching the Web for cheap flights.*
→ see Thesaurus box at **look**[1]
[**ORIGIN:** 1300-1400 From the old French word *cerchier*, which means "to go around or search," from the Latin word *circare*, which means "to go around."]

**ˈsearch ˌengine** *noun*
a computer program that helps you find information on the Internet: *I used a search engine to find the address of an old friend from high school.*

**search·light** /ˈsɚtʃlaɪt/ *noun*
a large bright light used for finding people or things at night: *The searchlight from the police helicopter lit up the whole field.*

**sea·shell** /ˈsiʃel/ *noun*
an empty shell of a small sea animal: *The kids were collecting seashells on the beach.*

**sea·shore** /ˈsiʃɔr/ *noun*
**the seashore** = the land along the edge of the ocean: *She was looking for shells on the seashore.*
→ see Thesaurus box at **shore**

**sea·sick** /ˈsiˌsɪk/ *adjective*
feeling sick because of the movement of a boat: *I always get seasick on ships if the ocean is rough.*
—**seasickness** *noun* the feeling of being seasick

**sea·son** /ˈsizən/ *noun*
**1** one of the four periods of the year, which each have their own type of weather. The seasons are winter, spring, summer, and fall: *Summer is my favorite season because I like hot weather.*
**2** a time in a year when an activity or type of event happens: *The football season starts next month.*
**3** the time of year when most people take their vacations, or when there is a special holiday: *"Will you be seeing your grandparents during the holiday season?" "Yes, we'll visit them on Christmas Day."*
—**seasonal** *adjective* relating to seasons, or to one season: *There are seasonal changes in temperature – it is hot in summer and cold in winter.*
[**ORIGIN:** 1300-1400 From the French word *saison*, from the Latin word *satio*, which means "the activity of sowing seeds." This word was later used to mean "the time for sowing seeds," and was then used for other times of the year.]

**sea·son·ing** /ˈsizənɪŋ/ *noun*
salt, pepper, or SPICEs that you add to food to make it taste better

**seat**

**seat** /sit/ *noun*
**1** something you can sit on: *He made a speech and then went back to his seat.* | *I was driving and the kids were sitting in the back seat.* → see also picture at **bicycle**
**2** **take a seat/have a seat** = to sit down: *She took a seat next to him on the sofa.*
**3** the part of something that you sit on: *the toilet seat*

**ˈseat belt** *noun*
a belt that holds you in your seat in a car or airplane: *Fasten your seat belt when the plane is taking off.* → see picture on page **A28**

**sea·weed** /ˈsiwid/ *noun*
a green or brown plant that grows in the ocean

**se·cede** /sɪˈsid/ *verb* (*formal*)
to stop being part of a country or group: *The Southern states seceded from the rest of the U.S., and the Civil War began.*

**se·clud·ed** /sɪˈkludɪd/ *adjective* (*formal*)
a secluded place is very private and quiet: *We spent a quiet afternoon on a secluded beach.*
—**seclusion** /sɪˈkluʒən/ *noun* the state of being in a quiet place away from other people

**sec·ond**[1] /ˈsekənd/ *number, pronoun*
2nd; someone or something that is after the first one: *September 2nd* | *Jane's second husband* | *Kara won the race and Jody came in second.*

**second**[2] *noun*
**1** a unit for measuring time. There are 60 seconds in a minute: *He finished the 100-meter race in 10.03 seconds.*

2 (*informal*) a very short period of time: *I'll be ready in a second!*

[ORIGIN: 1300-1400 From the Latin phrase *secunda pars minuta*, which means "second small part." An hour is divided into 60 small parts (minutes) and then divided a second time into seconds.]

**sec·ond·ar·y** /ˈsekənˌderi/ *adjective*
not as important as something else: *For John, school was secondary to his friends.*

**ˈsecondary ˌschool** *noun* (*formal*)
a school for children over 11 or 12 years old, after ELEMENTARY SCHOOL

**ˌsecond-ˈclass** *adjective*
considered to be less important or good than other people or things: *People should not be treated like second-class citizens because of their race or religion.*

S

**ˌsecond-ˈhand** *adjective*
something that is second-hand has already been used by someone before you buy it: *We bought a second-hand car that was two years old.* SYNONYM: **used**; ANTONYM: **new**

**ˌsecond ˈperson** *noun*
**the second person** = "you" and the verb forms that are used with "you," for example "are" or "have"

**ˌsecond-ˈrate** *adjective*
not very good: *He was just a second-rate actor that no one remembers anymore.*

**se·cre·cy** /ˈsikrəsi/ *noun*
a situation in which people keep something secret: *The trial took place in secrecy and no one knew what happened.*

**se·cret¹** /ˈsikrət/ *adjective*
if something is secret, only you or only a few people know about it: *He hid the money in a secret place.* | *He kept the party secret so it would be a surprise.*
—**secretly** *adverb* without other people knowing: *I secretly recorded our conversation.*
→ see Thesaurus box at **private¹**

[ORIGIN: 1300-1400 From the Latin word *secretus*, a form of the verb *secernere*, which means "to separate." The idea is that something secret is separated or kept away from other people.]

**WORD FAMILY: secret**
**secret** *adjective* | **secret** *noun* | **secretly** *adverb* | **secrecy** *noun* | **secretive** *adjective*

**secret²** *noun*
1 an idea, plan, or information that you do not tell other people about: *Don't tell anyone about this. It's a secret.* | *Jane can't keep a secret; she'll tell everyone what happened.*
2 **in secret** = without other people knowing: *They met in secret without telling even their closest friends.*

**ˌsecret ˈagent** *noun*
someone whose job is to find out about other countries' political or military secrets: *No one realized that he was a Russian secret agent.*
SYNONYM: **spy**

**sec·re·tar·y** /ˈsekrəˌteri/ *noun* (plural **secretaries**)
1 someone who works in an office answering the telephone, writing letters, or arranging meetings: *You can talk to my secretary to make an appointment.*
2 an official who is in charge of a large U.S. government department: *the Secretary of Defense*

**se·cre·tive** /ˈsikrətɪv/ *adjective*
not wanting to tell people things: *She is very secretive about her past, so I don't know much about her.*

**ˌsecret ˈservice** *noun*
**the Secret Service** = the U.S. government department whose job is to protect the president

**sect** /sekt/ *noun*
a religious group that has separated from a larger group: *There are many sects of Islam, each of which has slightly different beliefs.*

**sec·tion** Ac /ˈsekʃən/ *noun*
a part of something: *the children's section of the library* | *The rocket is built in sections and then put together later.*
→ see Thesaurus box at **part¹**

[ORIGIN: 1300-1400 From the Latin word *sectio*, from the verb *secare*, which means "to cut."]

**sec·tor** Ac /ˈsektɚ/ *noun*
a part of a country's industry or business: *The country's manufacturing sector has grown.*

**se·cure** Ac /sɪˈkyʊr/ *adjective*
1 not likely to change or be lost: *His job is secure, so he doesn't have to worry about the future.*
2 safe from damage or attack: *People tried to*

*make their houses secure before the storm hit.* **SYNONYM: safe**

**3** firmly fastened: *Make sure the rope is secure before you start climbing.*

**4** a secure person feels confident and safe: *They want their children to feel secure and good about themselves.*

—**securely** *adverb* in a way that is secure: *The door was securely locked.*

[**ORIGIN:** 1500-1600 From the Latin word *securus*, which means "not worried," from *se-*, meaning "without" and *cura*, meaning "worry." This word was later used to mean "safe" because if something is safe, you do not worry about it.]

**WORD FAMILY: secure**

**secure** *adjective* | **securely** *adverb* | **security** *noun*

**se·cu·ri·ty** Ac /sɪˈkyʊrəti/ *noun*

**1** things that a government or organization does to protect people and places from crime or attack: *They increased security at airports after the attack, for example by having more guards and searching more bags.*

**2** the state of being safe from damage or attack: *Terrorism is a threat to world peace and security.* **SYNONYM: safety**

**se·dan** /sɪˈdæn/ *noun*

a car that has four doors, seats for four or more people, and a TRUNK

**sed·a·tive** /ˈsedətɪv/ *noun*

a medicine that makes someone feel calm or go to sleep: *The doctor gave her a sedative to help her relax.*

**sed·i·ment** /ˈsedəmənt/ *noun*

small solid pieces that go to the bottom of a liquid: *Sand and small pieces of rock form layers of sediment at the bottom of the lake.*

—**sedimentary** /ˌsɛdəˈmɛntri, -ˈmɛntəri/ *adjective* sedimentary rock is formed when sand, rocks, mud, etc. left by water or ice are pressed together and become solid

**se·duce** /sɪˈdus/ *verb*

**1** to persuade someone to do something by making it seem very attractive or interesting: *Shoppers are often seduced into buying something by its attractive packaging.*

**2** to persuade someone to have sex with you

**see** /si/ *verb* (**saw** /sɔ/, **seen** /sin/)

**1** to notice someone or something with your eyes: *He saw her go into the house.* | *I can't see anything without my glasses.*

**USAGE: see, look at, watch**

You **see** something without planning to do this: *Two people saw him take the woman's purse.* | *I saw a big black dog in the park.*

You **look at** a picture, person, thing, etc. because you want to do this: *Hey, look at the hat that man is wearing.* | *Maria was looking at a picture book.*

You **watch** TV, a movie, or something that happens for a period of time: *My parents always come to watch me play basketball.* | *The kids are watching TV.*

You can also say that you **saw** a movie, a program, etc., but you cannot say "see television." Say *I saw a great movie on TV last night.*

**THESAURUS: see**

**notice** to see something interesting or unusual: *I noticed a police car outside their house.*

**spot** to notice or recognize someone, especially someone you are looking for: *Mark spotted Carrie standing with her friends at the bus stop.*

**catch a glimpse of someone/something** to see someone or something for only a short time, and not clearly: *I caught a glimpse of his face as he ran past the window.*

**make something out** to see something, when this is difficult to do: *You could hardly make out the cars ahead of you in the fog.*

**witness** to see an accident or a crime happen: *Several people witnessed the attack.*

**2** to understand or realize something: *Do you see what I mean?* | *I could see that she didn't like me.* | *"You have to press this button to switch it on." "Oh, I see."*

**3** to meet or visit someone: *I saw Rob on Saturday.* | *You ought to see a doctor.*

S

4 to find out information or a fact: *Plug the radio in and see if it's working.*
5 to watch a television program, play, or movie: *Have you seen his new movie yet?*
6 **see you (later)** = used in order to say goodbye to someone you will meet again: *I have to go now, Ben; I'll see you later.*
7 **let's see/let me see** = said when you are thinking about something, or trying to remember something: *Let me see, there will be 12 people so we need two more chairs.*
8 **I'll see/we'll see** = said when you do not want to make a decision immediately: *"Can Denise come too?" "We'll see."*

**PHRASAL VERBS**

**see someone off**
to go to an airport, station, etc. to say goodbye to someone who is leaving: *My friends came to see me off at the airport.*

**see to something**
to deal with something or make sure that it happens: *I'll make the food for the party, and you see to the drinks.*

**seed** /sid/ *noun*
a small grain that a new plant grows from: *She was planting sunflower seeds.*

**ˌSeeing ˈEye ˌdog** *noun (trademark)*
a dog that has been trained to guide blind people **SYNONYM: guide dog**

**seek** Ac /sik/ *verb* (**sought** /sɔt/) *(formal)*
to try to find or get something: *He was sick and sought help from a doctor.*
→ see Thesaurus box at **look**[1]

**seem** /sim/ *verb*
used to say what quality you think something or someone has: *It seems strange that he didn't call.* | *She seems to be much happier at her new school.* **SYNONYM: appear**

**THESAURUS: seem**

**appear** to seem to have particular qualities: *Light colors make a room appear bigger than it is.*

**look** to seem to be something, from what you can see with your eyes: *Rick looked very tired.*

**sound** to seem to have a particular quality when you hear or read about it: *The book sounded really interesting.*

—**seemingly** *adverb* used to say that something seems to be true but is not really true: *We spent seemingly endless hours doing homework.*

**seen** /sin/ *verb*
the past participle of SEE

**seep** /sip/ *verb*
if a liquid seeps somewhere, it flows slowly through small holes in something: *Water that splashed out of the bathtub started to seep through the floor.*

**see·saw** /ˈsisɔ/ *noun*
a piece of equipment that two children play on. A seesaw is made of a board that is supported in the middle, so that one end goes up when the other end goes down.

**seg·ment** /ˈsegmənt/ *noun (formal)*
one part of something: *He peeled the orange and offered me a segment.* | *a large segment of the population*
[**ORIGIN:** 1500-1600 From the Latin word *segmentum*, from the verb *secare*, which means "to cut."]

**seg·re·gat·ed** /ˈsegrəˌgeɪtɪd/ *adjective*
if a place is segregated, people of different races, religions, or sexes are not allowed to be there together: *In the 1950s, black and white children went to racially segregated schools.*
—**segregation** /ˌsegrəˈgeɪʃən/ *noun* the practice of keeping people of different races, religions, or sexes apart: *Segregation of students is no longer permitted here.*
[**ORIGIN:** 1500-1600 From the Latin word *segregare*, from *se-*, meaning "apart" and *grex*, meaning "herd." The idea is of one group of animals being separated from the rest of the herd.]

**seize** /siz/ *verb (formal)*
1 to take hold of something quickly and in a forceful way: *Thomas seized her hand and dragged her out of the water.* **SYNONYM: grab**
2 to take control of a place, using military force: *Rebel soldiers have seized control of the city.*
3 if the police seize something illegal, they take it away from someone: *Police seized the*

*illegal DVDs that the men were planning to sell.*
→ see Thesaurus box at **hold**[1]

**sei·zure** /ˈsiʒɚ/ *noun*
**1** (*formal*) the act of taking illegal things away from someone: *The police investigation led to the seizure of the illegal weapons.*
**2** a short time when someone is unconscious and cannot control the movements of his or her body: *She had an epileptic seizure, and fell to the ground with her legs kicking.*

**sel·dom** /ˈseldəm/ *adverb*
not often: *She is old now and seldom travels.* **SYNONYM: rarely**

**se·lect** Ac /sɪˈlekt/ *verb*
to choose something or someone: *The other students selected him to represent them at the meeting.* **SYNONYMS: choose, pick**
→ see Thesaurus box at **choose**
[**ORIGIN:** 1500-1600 From the Latin word *selectus*, a form of the verb *seligere*, from *se-*, meaning "apart," and *legere*, meaning "to gather or choose."]

**WORD FAMILY: select**
**select** *verb* | **selection** *noun* | **selective** *adjective*

**se·lec·tion** Ac /sɪˈlekʃən/ *noun*
**1** the action of choosing someone or something: *Make a selection from the list.* | *the selection of a new captain for the team* **SYNONYM: choice**
**2** a group of things that you can choose from: *The restaurant offers a wide selection of dishes, including some vegetarian food.* **SYNONYMS: choice, range**

**se·lec·tive** Ac /sɪˈlektɪv/ *adjective*
careful about what you choose: *The college is selective and only takes the best students.*

**self** /self/ *noun* (plural **selves** /selvz/)
the type of person you are, including what you feel and think and how you behave: *When he gets angry, he changes from his normal quiet self into a monster.*

**ˌself-ˈcentered** *adjective*
only interested in yourself and not thinking about other people: *You're so self-centered! You don't care how I feel!* **SYNONYM: selfish**

**ˌself-ˈconfident** *adjective*
feeling sure that you can do things well and that people like you: *He came back from college more self-confident than when he left.* **SYNONYM: confident**; **ANTONYM: shy**
—**self-confidence** *noun* a belief that you can do things well and that people like you

**ˌself-ˈconscious** *adjective*
worried and embarrassed about what you look like or what other people think of you: *Lou's very self-conscious about his baldness.*

**ˌself-conˈtrol** *noun*
the ability to control your feelings and behavior even when you are angry, excited, or upset: *She lacks self-control and often shouts at her children.*

**ˌself-deˈfense** *noun*
the use of force to protect yourself when you are attacked: *He attacked her, and she shot him in self-defense.*

**ˌself-emˈployed** *adjective*
working for yourself, not employed by a company: *Self-employed people have to pay for their own health insurance.*
—**self-employment** *noun* the state of being self-employed

**ˌself-esˈteem** *noun*
the feeling that you are a good person and that you deserve to be liked and respected: *Children who don't have many friends often have low self-esteem.*

**ˌself-ˈinterest** *noun*
the feeling of caring about what is best for you instead of what is best for other people: *People often vote for someone out of self-interest because they think that person will help them most.*

**self·ish** /ˈselfɪʃ/ *adjective*
caring only about yourself and not about other people: *Eating all the pie was a very selfish thing to do.* **ANTONYM: unselfish**
—**selfishly** *adverb* in a selfish way
—**selfishness** *noun* selfish behavior

**ˌself-ˈpity** *noun*
the feeling of being sorry for yourself because you have been unlucky or because you think people have treated you badly: *It is easy to become full of self-pity when bad things keep happening to you.*

**ˌself-reˈspect** *noun*
the feeling that you are a good person and that you deserve to be respected: *She lost her job, then her home, and finally her self-respect.*

**ˌself-ˈrighteous** *adjective*
very sure that your beliefs, attitudes, and opinions are right, in a way that annoys other people: *He's one of those self-righteous people who always think they are right.*

**ˌself-ˈservice** (*also* **ˌself ˈserve**) *adjective*
a self-service store or restaurant is one where you get things for yourself, rather than being served by someone else: *He put gas in his car at a self-service gas station.*

S

**ˌself-sufˈficient** *adjective*
able to provide all the things you need without help from other people: *The country is self-sufficient in oil.*
—**self-sufficiency** *noun* the fact that someone or something is self-sufficient

**sell** /sel/ *verb* (**sold** /soʊld/)
to give something to someone in exchange for money: *We sold the house and moved to Florida.* | *I sold my car for $5,000.* | *Does the store sell milk?* **ANTONYM: buy**
**PHRASAL VERB**
**sell out**
if a product sells out, all of it is sold and there is none left: *All the tickets for tonight's concert have sold out.*

**sell·er** /ˈselɚ/ *noun*
a person or company that sells something **ANTONYM: buyer**

**se·man·tics** /səˈmæntɪks/ *noun*
the meaning of words and phrases
—**semantic** *adjective* relating to semantics

**se·mes·ter** /səˈmestɚ/ *noun*
one of two equal periods into which a year at school or college is divided: *I'm taking Algebra I this semester.*
[**ORIGIN:** 1800-1900 From the Latin word *semestris*, which means "relating to a period of six months," from *sex*, meaning "six," and *mensis*, meaning "month."]

**semi-** /ˈsemi/
partly but not completely: *He's semi-retired; he still does some part-time work.* | *I could only just see her in the semi-darkness.*

**sem·i·cir·cle** /ˈsemiˌsɚkəl/ *noun*
half a circle: *Students sat in a semicircle, facing the teacher.*
[**ORIGIN:** 1500-1600 From the Latin word *semi-*, which means "half," and the word "circle."]

**sem·i·co·lon** /ˈsemiˌkoʊlən/ *noun*
the mark (;) that you use in writing to separate different parts of a sentence or list

**sem·i·fi·nal** /ˌsemiˈfaɪnl/ *noun*
one of the two sports games that are played in a competition before the final game. The winners of the two semifinals play each other in the last game to decide the winner of the competition.

**sem·i·nar** /ˈseməˌnɑr/ *noun*
a class in which a small group of students talk about a particular subject: *I went to seminars on creative writing when I was in college.*

**sen·ate** (*also* **Senate**) /ˈsenɪt/ *noun*
the smaller of the two government groups that make laws in the U.S. and in most U.S. states. Some other countries, for example Canada and Australia, also have senates: *The Senate voted 74–22 for the bill.*
[**ORIGIN:** 1100-1200 From the Latin word *senatus*, from *senex*, which means "old man." The Roman senate was a council made up of older men.]

**sen·a·tor** (*also* **Senator**) /ˈsenətɚ/ *noun*
a member of a senate: *a senator from Ohio*

**send** /send/ *verb* (**sent** /sent/)
**1** to arrange for something to go or be taken to another place: *I sent you an email.* | *Do you want me to send the bill to you?*
**2** to make someone go somewhere: *They sent their children to a school in Massachusetts.*
**PHRASAL VERB**
**send for someone or something**
to ask someone to come to you: *He was very sick, so his wife sent for the doctor.*

**se·nile** /ˈsinaɪl/ *adjective*
a senile person is often confused and cannot remember things because he or she is old: *My grandfather is going senile and barely knows who I am.*
—**senility** /sɪˈnɪləti/ *noun* the fact of being senile

**se·nior**[1] /ˈsinyɚ/ *noun*
**1** a student in the last year of HIGH SCHOOL

or college: *The high school seniors are deciding which college to go to.*

**2** another word for SENIOR CITIZEN

**[ORIGIN:** 1300-1400 From the Latin word for "older," from *senis*, which means "old."**]**

**senior²** *adjective*

**1** older or higher in rank: *The case is being looked at by a senior police officer.* **ANTONYM: junior**

**2 Senior** (*written abbreviation*: **Sr.**) = used after the name of a man who has the same name as his son: *After Martin Holmes Sr. died, his son Martin Holmes Jr. took over the family business.*

**ˌsenior ˈcitizen** *noun*

someone who is over 60 years old: *The restaurant has special prices for senior citizens.*

**se·nior·i·ty** /ˌsinˈyɔrəti/ *noun*

if you have seniority in a company or organization, you have worked there for a long time and have some advantages: *Wages are based on seniority, so people who have worked here longer make more money.*

**sen·sa·tion** /senˈseɪʃən/ *noun*

**1** a feeling that you get in your body: *Matt felt a burning sensation in his eyes from the smoke.*

**2** a feeling that is difficult to describe, caused by a particular event, experience, or memory: *I had a strange sensation that I was being watched.*

**3** something people get excited about, or the excitement people feel about something: *She became an overnight sensation after her appearance on "American Idol."*

**sen·sa·tion·al** /senˈseɪʃənəl/ *adjective*

**1** very good, interesting, or exciting: *You look sensational in that dress!*

**2** intended to excite or shock people: *The magazine has sensational stories about movie stars' private lives.*

**sense¹** /sens/ *noun*

**1** the ability to make good decisions and not do stupid things: *I hope he had the sense to lock the door when he left.*

**2** a feeling about something: *We all felt a great sense of relief when the plane landed safely.*

**3 make sense** = **a)** to have a clear meaning and be easy to understand: *These instructions just don't make sense.* **b)** if it makes sense to do something, there is a sensible reason to do it: *It makes sense to call him first, before we drive all the way to his house.*

**4** one of the five natural abilities that people and animals have. The senses are sight, hearing, touch, taste, and smell: *Dogs have a very good sense of smell.*

**5 sense of humor** = the ability to understand and enjoy things that are funny, or the ability to make people laugh: *Jack's got a terrific sense of humor – he's a funny guy.*

**6** the meaning of a word or phrase: *The word "flat" has many senses, which are listed in the dictionary.*

**[ORIGIN:** 1300-1400 From the Latin word *sensus*, from *sentire*, which means "to feel or think."**]**

**sense²** *verb*

to feel or know that something is true without being told or having proof: *I could sense that something was wrong – she just didn't seem happy.*

**sense·less** /ˈsensləs/ *adjective*

**1** happening or done for no good reason or with no purpose: *Building a new spacecraft would be a senseless waste of money.*

**2** unconscious: *The falling rock knocked him senseless.*

**sen·si·ble** /ˈsensəbəl/ *adjective*

**1** showing good judgment and an ability to make practical decisions: *I always get sensible advice from my mother.*

**2** suitable for a particular purpose, and practical rather than fashionable: *It's a long walk, so wear sensible shoes.*

—**sensibly** *adverb* in a way that shows good judgment and an ability to make practical decisions

**sen·si·tive** /ˈsensətɪv/ *adjective*

**1** able to understand other people's feelings and problems: *Good nurses are sensitive to their patients' feelings.* **ANTONYM: insensitive**

**2** easily upset by the things that other people do or say: *Christy is very sensitive about her weight, so don't say anything about how she looks.*

**3** easily hurt or damaged by a substance or by hot or cold temperatures: *My teeth are sensitive to cold water.* | *sensitive skin*

—**sensitively** *adverb* in a way that shows you understand other people's feelings and problems
—**sensitivity** /ˌsensəˈtɪvəti/ *noun* the fact of being sensitive

**sent** /sent/ *verb*
the past tense and past participle of SEND

**sen·tence¹** /ˈsentəns/ *noun*
**1** a group of words with a subject and a verb, that makes a statement or asks a question. In written English, a sentence begins with a capital letter and ends with a PERIOD, QUESTION MARK, or EXCLAMATION POINT: *Please write your answers in complete sentences. For example, do not just write "Twain." Instead, write "The book was written by Mark Twain."*
**2** a punishment that a judge gives to someone who is guilty of a crime: *He is serving a 10-year prison sentence for bank robbery.*
[**ORIGIN:** 1200-1300 From the Latin word *sententia*, which means "feeling, thought, or decision," from *sentire*, which means "to feel or think." The idea is that you express your feelings or thoughts in a sentence.]

S

**sentence²** *verb*
if a judge sentences someone who is guilty of a crime, he or she gives the person an official punishment: *The judge sentenced the burglar to five years in prison.*

**sen·ti·ment** /ˈsentəmənt/ *noun* (*formal*)
an opinion or feeling that you have about something: *I agree with the sentiments he expressed in his speech.*

**sen·ti·men·tal** /ˌsentəˈmentl/ *adjective*
showing emotions such as love, pity, and sadness too strongly: *sentimental love songs*
—**sentimentality** /ˌsentəmenˈtæləti/ *noun* the quality of being sentimental

**sep·a·rate¹** /ˈseprɪt/ *adjective*
**1** different: *Write each list on a separate sheet of paper.*
**2** not joined to or touching something else: *Keep the blue cards separate from the green cards.*
**3** not related to or not affected by something else: *My personal life is separate from my work life.*

**sep·a·rate²** /ˈsepəˌreɪt/ *verb*
**1** to divide something into two or more parts: *Ms. Barker separated the class into four groups.*
**2** to be between two things and keep them apart: *A fence separates the house from the parking lot.*
**3** to stop living with your husband, wife, or partner: *My parents separated last year, but they're not divorced.*
→ see Thesaurus box at **married**

**sep·a·rate·ly** /ˈseprɪtli/ *adverb*
not together with other people or things: *They arrived separately, but they left together.*

**sep·a·ra·tion** /ˌsepəˈreɪʃən/ *noun*
**1** the act of separating something, or the state of being separate: *The separation of church and state means that religion and government should not affect each other.*
**2** a situation in which a husband and wife decide to live apart even though they are still married: *They agreed to a separation and Dan moved out.*

**Sep·tem·ber** /sepˈtembɚ/ *noun* (*written abbreviation*: **Sept.**)
the ninth month of the year, between August and October: *The party is on September 2.* | *School starts in September.* | *They're getting married next September.*
[**ORIGIN:** probably 1000-1100 From the Latin word *septem*, which means "seven." September was the seventh month of the old Roman calendar.]

**se·quel** /ˈsikwəl/ *noun*
a movie or book that continues the story of an earlier one: *I don't think the sequel is as good as the original movie.*

**se·quence** Ac /ˈsikwəns/ *noun*
a series of related things that happen in a particular order: *The book explains the sequence of events that led to the war.*
[**ORIGIN:** 1300-1400 From the Latin word *sequi*, which means "to follow." Things that are in a sequence follow each other.]

**se·quin** /ˈsikwɪn/ *noun*
a small shiny flat circle that is sewn on clothes for decoration: *The sequins on her dress glittered as she danced across the stage.*
[**ORIGIN:** 1500-1600 From the Italian word *zecchino*, which was the name of a gold coin. This word came from *zecca*, which means "place where coins are made," from the Arabic word *sikka*, which means "coin."]

**se·quoi·a** /sɪˈkwɔɪə/ *noun*
another word for a REDWOOD
[ORIGIN: 1800-1900 From Sequoya (about 1770-1843), a Cherokee Indian who invented a way to write down the Cherokee language. This type of tree was named in his honor.]

**se·rene** /səˈrin/ *adjective* (*formal*)
very calm or peaceful: *The view was serene, with the river flowing gently through the valley.*
—**serenely** *adverb* in a serene way

**se·ren·i·ty** /səˈrenəti/ *noun* (*formal*)
calmness and peace: *Her bedroom is a place of serenity away from the noise of the children.*

**ser·geant** /ˈsɑrdʒənt/ *noun* (*written abbreviation*: **Sgt.**)
someone with a fairly low rank in the army, air force, or police
[ORIGIN: 1100-1200 From the old French word *sergent*, which means "servant," from the Latin word *servens*, a form of the verb *servire*, which means "to serve."]

**se·ri·al** /ˈsɪriəl/ *noun*
a story that is shown on television, broadcast on radio, or printed in a newspaper in several separate parts

**se·ries** Ac /ˈsɪriz/ *noun* (plural **series**)
**1 a series of something** = several events, actions, or things of the same kind that happen one after the other: *There have been a series of robberies on this block.*
**2** a set of television programs with the same characters or on the same subject: *What's your favorite comedy series on TV?*
**3** a set of sports games played between the same two teams: *There are seven games in baseball's World Series, so a team has to win four games to win the series.*
→ see Thesaurus box at **program**[1]

**se·ri·ous** /ˈsɪriəs/ *adjective*
**1** a serious problem or situation is very bad or dangerous: *Violent crime is a serious problem in many cities.*
**2** saying what you really mean, and not joking or pretending: *If you are serious about becoming a doctor, you need to study harder.*
**3** important and deserving a lot of attention: *We discussed some serious subjects such as the environment.*
—**seriousness** *noun* the quality of being serious

**se·ri·ous·ly** /ˈsɪriəsli/ *adverb*
**1** in a way that is bad or dangerous: *He got seriously ill and died a few days later.*
**2** in a way that shows that you think something is important: *She takes her running seriously and is always out on the track.*

**ser·mon** /ˈsɚmən/ *noun*
a talk about a religious subject, given by a priest or MINISTER in church
[ORIGIN: 1100-1200 From the Latin word *sermo*, which means "speech or conversation."]

**serv·ant** /ˈsɚvənt/ *noun*
someone who is paid to work in a rich person's house doing cleaning, cooking, or other jobs: *The prince told one of his servants to bring him some fruit.*

**serve** /sɚv/ *verb*
**1** to give someone food or drinks as part of a meal: *We'll serve lunch about noon.*
**2** to be used for a particular purpose: *The sofa can also serve as a bed.*
**3** to work in the army, navy, police force, or other similar organization: *Kelly served in the army for three years.*
**4** to hit a ball over a net to start a game such as tennis or VOLLEYBALL: *It's your turn to serve.*
**5 it serves someone right** (*informal*) = used for saying that someone deserves something unpleasant that happens because he or she has done something bad: *"I failed my test." "It serves you right for not studying."*
—**serve** *noun* an act of hitting a ball over a net to start a game such as tennis

**WORD FAMILY: serve**
**serve** *verb* | **service** *noun* | **server** *noun*

**serv·er** /ˈsɚvɚ/ *noun*
**1** a computer that has information and programs that are used by other computers in a NETWORK: *The server isn't working and we can't look at any of the files.*
**2** someone who brings you food in a restaurant

**serv·ice**[1] /ˈsɚvɪs/ *noun*
**1** the help that people who work in a restaurant, hotel, or store give you: *The service in the restaurant was awful – we had to*

S

*wait 30 minutes for the waiter to take our order.*

**2** the work that you do for a person or organization over a long period of time: *He retired after 20 years of service in the army.*

**3** work or a business that involves helping people or doing jobs for them: *Their delivery service brings the groceries to your door.*

**4** a formal religious ceremony: *The funeral service was held at the Baptist church.*

**5** a regular examination of a car or machine to make sure that it keeps working correctly: *The car needs a service every 10,000 miles.*

**6 the service** = a country's military forces: *He joined the service in 1970 and was sent to Vietnam.*

**service²** *verb*
to examine a car or machine, and fix anything that needs fixing: *A mechanic should service your car regularly.*

**'service ˌstation** *noun*
another word for a GAS STATION

**ses·sion** /ˈseʃən/ *noun*
**1** a period of time when people work or do a particular activity: *a computer training session*
**2** a formal meeting or group of meetings of a court of law or government organization: *The bill will be discussed during the next session of Congress. | The court is now in session.*
[**ORIGIN:** 1300-1400 From the Latin word *sessio*, which means "the act of sitting," from *sedere*, which means "to sit." The idea is that you would sit and discuss something in a session.]

**set¹** /set/ *verb* (**set**, **setting**)
**1** to put something down somewhere carefully: *Just set that bag of groceries down on the table.*
**2** if a movie, story, or play is set in a place or time, the events happen there or at that time: *Science fiction movies are usually set in the future.*
**3** to decide and show how something should be done so that other people can continue doing it that way: *Try to set an example for the younger kids by being polite.*
**4** to move the controls on a clock or a machine so that it will do something at a particular time: *I set my alarm for 6:30.*
**5 set something on fire** (*also* **set fire to something**) = to make something start burning: *The angry crowd set the building on fire.*
**6 set the table** = to put knives, forks, plates, etc. on a table so that you can eat a meal: *Help me set the table – dinner's almost ready.*
**7** when the sun or moon sets, it moves lower in the sky and disappears: *The sun sets about 7:00 this time of year.* **ANTONYM: rise**
**8 set someone or something free** = to let a person or animal go free: *The army set some of the prisoners free.*
**9** if a substance sets, it becomes hard: *Concrete will usually set in less than two hours.*

**PHRASAL VERBS**

**set something off**
to make something start happening or doing something: *When thieves tried to break into his car, they set off the alarm.*

**set something up**
**1** to build or put something somewhere in order to prepare for something: *It took us two hours to set up all of the equipment before the dance.*
**2** to start a company or organization: *His parents set up a small business that became very successful.*

**set²** *noun*
**1** a group of similar things that belong together: *a new set of dishes, with flowers on the plates, bowls, and cups | a chess set*
**2** a television: *Do you have a TV set in your bedroom?*
**3** a place where a movie or television program is filmed: *The two actors met on the set of their last movie.*
**4** one part of a game such as tennis or VOLLEYBALL: *He won the match by 3 sets to 1.*
→ see Thesaurus box at **group¹**

**set³** *adjective*
**1** if something is set, it has been decided and will not change: *I pay a set amount each month to use the gym.*
**2** (*informal*) ready for something: *I'm all set, so we can leave any time.*

**set·back** /ˈsetbæk/ *noun*
a problem that makes progress or success less likely: *The patient suffered a major setback when he had a second heart attack.*

**set·ting** /ˈsetɪŋ/ *noun*
**1** the place where something is or happens,

and the area surrounding it: *The house is in a beautiful mountain setting.*
**2** the place or time in which the events in a book, movie, or play happen: *Mexico is the setting for the story.*
**3** the position that you move the controls to on a machine: *Turn the oven to its lowest setting.*

**set·tle** /ˈsetl/ *verb*
**1** to end an argument or a disagreement: *I hope they can settle their differences and become friends again.* | *Everyone wants to settle the case before it goes to court.*
**2** to decide or choose something: *Have you settled on a name for the baby?*
**3** to begin to live in a place where you live for a long time: *He worked in several cities before he finally settled in Atlanta.*
**4** to move into a comfortable position: *Dave settled back on the sofa and turned on the TV.*
**5** if snow or dust settles, it falls on a surface and stays there: *Dust had settled on the furniture while they were gone.*
**6** (*also* **settle up**) to pay all the money that you owe on a bill: *Please settle your bill before leaving the hotel.*
**PHRASAL VERBS**
**settle down**
**1** to become quiet and calm: *Kids, settle down and eat your dinner.*
**2** to start living a quiet and calm life in one place, especially when you get married: *I think I'm ready to settle down and start a family.*
**settle for something**
to accept something that is not as good as the thing you really wanted: *We couldn't afford to rent a house, so we had to settle for an apartment.*
**settle in** (*also* **settle into something**)
to become happier in a new situation or place than you were at the beginning: *Adam seems to have settled in at his new school. He's made a few friends.*

**set·tled** /ˈsetld/ *adjective*
**feel/be settled** = to feel comfortable in your home or job, and be unlikely to move: *It took a few weeks, but we feel settled at our new school now.*

**set·tle·ment** /ˈsetlmənt/ *noun*
**1** an official agreement or decision that ends an argument: *She was given $2 million as part of the divorce settlement.*
**2** a group of buildings where people live, in a place where no group lived before: *Scientists are studying what is left of a Native American settlement in the hills.*

**set·tler** /ˈsetlɚ/ *noun*
someone who goes to live in a new place where there were few people before: *The early settlers of the American West had to work very hard to stay alive.*

**set·up** /ˈsetʌp/ *noun*
**1** a way of organizing or arranging something: *We moved all the desks to this side of the classroom – do you like the new setup?*
**2** (*informal*) a dishonest plan that is intended to trick someone: *The phone call was part of a setup to get her out of the house, so they could steal the computer.*

**sev·en** /ˈsevən/ *number*
**1** 7: *There are seven days in the week.*
**2** seven O'CLOCK: *The movie starts at seven.*
**3** seven years old: *Janis is seven already.*

**sev·en·teen** /ˌsevənˈtin/ *number*
**1** 17: *There were seventeen books in the pile.*
**2** seventeen years old: *Her brother is seventeen.*
—**seventeenth** /ˌsevənˈtinθ/ *number* 17th or 1/17

**sev·enth** /ˈsevənθ/ *number*
**1** 7th
**2** 1/7

**sev·en·ty** /ˈsevənti/ *number*
**1** 70: *a short seventy-minute flight*
**2** seventy years old: *Your grandpa will be seventy next week.*
**3** **the seventies** (*also* **the '70s**) = the years between 1970 and 1979: *A lot of men had really long hair in the '70s.*
**4** **in your seventies** = between 70 and 79 years old: *Grandma's in her early seventies.*
**5** **in the seventies** = between 70 and 79 degrees FAHRENHEIT in temperature: *Temperatures will be in the seventies tomorrow.*
—**seventieth** /ˈsevəntiɪθ/ *number* 70th or 1/70

**sev·er** /ˈsevɚ/ *verb* (*formal*)
**1** to cut through something completely:

*When he could not undo the knot, he severed the rope with his knife.*

**2** to end a relationship or agreement with someone: *She has severed all ties with her former husband.*

**sev·eral** /ˈsevrəl/ *adjective, pronoun*
three or more people or things, but not a lot: *I've been to Miami several times.* | *Several of my friends offered to help.*
→ see Thesaurus box at **many**

**se·vere** /səˈvɪr/ *adjective*
**1** very bad or serious: *Severe weather, with bad storms, kept the plane from landing.*
**2** very strict or extreme: *People who commit serious crimes deserve severe punishments.*
—**severity** /sɪˈvɛrəti/ *noun* the state of being severe

S

**se·vere·ly** /səˈvɪrli/ *adverb*
**1** very badly or very much: *Fire severely damaged the building.*
**2** in a strict or extreme way: *Prisoners who break the rules will be severely punished.*

**sew** /soʊ/ *verb* (**sewed**, **sewn** /soʊn/ *or* **sewed**)
to use a needle and thread to make or repair clothes: *I learned how to sew from watching my mother.* | *Can you sew a button on this shirt for me?*

**sew·age** /ˈsuɪdʒ/ *noun*
dirty water and waste from toilets that is carried away from buildings by sewers

**sew·er** /ˈsuɚ/ *noun*
a pipe or passage under the ground that carries away dirty water and waste from toilets

**sew·ing** /ˈsoʊɪŋ/ *noun*
the activity of using a needle and thread to make or repair clothes or other things made of cloth: *My sister is very good at sewing. She makes a lot of her own clothes.*

**ˈsewing ˌmachine** *noun*
a machine used for making or repairing clothes or other things made of cloth

**sex** Ac /seks/ *noun*
**1** the fact of being male or female: *Do you know what sex your baby is going to be?*
**2** one of the two groups of people or animals, male and female: *He was always shy around members of the opposite sex.*

**sex·ism** Ac /ˈsekˌsɪzəm/ *noun*
unfair treatment of one sex, usually women, that comes from the belief that one sex is weaker, less intelligent, or less important than the other: *Sue believed that her boss's sexism kept her from getting a better job.*
→ see Thesaurus box at **prejudice**

**sex·u·al** Ac /ˈsekʃuəl/ *adjective*
**1** relating to sex: *They are too young to be having a sexual relationship.*
**2 sexual intercourse** = the physical activity that two people do together, which can produce a baby
—**sexually** *adverb*

**ˌsexual ˈharassment** *noun*
sexual remarks, looks, or touching done to someone who does not want it

**Sgt.**
the written abbreviation of SERGEANT

**shab·by** /ˈʃæbi/ *adjective*
**1** shabby clothes, places, or objects are old and in bad condition: *They lived in a shabby apartment that needed painting.*
**2** unfair or wrong: *I don't deserve this kind of shabby treatment.*
—**shabbily** *adverb* in a shabby way

**shack** /ʃæk/ *noun*
a small building that has not been built very well: *The old man lived in a shack made out of scraps of wood and metal.*

**shack·le¹** /ˈʃækəl/ *noun*
one of a pair of metal rings joined by a chain, used for keeping a prisoner's hands or feet tied together: *The prisoner came to court with shackles on his ankles.*

**shackle²** *verb*
to put shackles on someone: *Guards shackled the prisoners and took them away.*

**shade¹** /ʃeɪd/ *noun*
**1** an area that is cooler and darker because

the light of the sun does not reach it: *We sat in the shade under a tree.*
**2** a particular form of a color: *I like this dark shade of red better than this bright one.*
**3** a piece of material that can be rolled down to cover a window, stopping light from entering a room: *If the sun is in your eyes, pull down the shade.*
**4** a cover over a light: *The bedside lamps have white shades.*
**5** **shades** (*informal*) = another word for SUNGLASSES

**shade²** *verb*
to stop the sun's light from reaching something: *She used her hand to shade her eyes from the sun.*

**shad·ow¹** /ˈʃædoʊ/ *noun*
**1** a dark shape on a surface, made by someone or something blocking the light: *He put his hand in front of the lamp and made a shadow on the wall.*
**2** **without/beyond a shadow of a doubt** = without any doubt at all: *The new evidence proved he was guilty beyond a shadow of a doubt.*
**3** **cast a shadow on/over something** = to make a time less happy or enjoyable: *My grandfather's illness cast a shadow over the holiday celebrations.*

**shadow²** *verb*
to follow someone in order to watch what they are doing: *Two police officers shadowed him when he came out of the casino.*

**shad·ow·y** /ˈʃædoʊi/ *adjective*
mysterious and secret: *He lived in the shadowy world of spies and terrorists.*

**shad·y** /ˈʃeɪdi/ *adjective*
**1** protected from the sun: *Let's find a nice shady spot under the trees for our picnic.*
**2** (*informal*) not honest or legal: *I don't want to be involved in any shady business deals.*

**shaft** /ʃæft/ *noun*
**1** a long narrow passage that goes up through a building or down into the ground: *an elevator shaft*
**2** **a shaft of light/sunlight** = a narrow beam of light
**3** the long narrow part of something such as an ARROW or a golf club: *The shaft of the spear is made of wood.*
**4** an ARROW or SPEAR
**5** a long piece of metal in a machine that turns and makes another part of the machine turn

**shag·gy** /ˈʃægi/ *adjective*
having long rough hair: *a big shaggy dog*

**shake¹** /ʃeɪk/ *verb* (**shook** /ʃʊk/, **shaken** /ˈʃeɪkən/)
**1** to move up and down or from side to side with quick movements: *She was so cold her whole body started to shake.* | *Shake the juice before you pour it.* → see picture on page A3
**2** if you shake your head, you turn your head from side to side as a way of saying no: *"I can't do it," Bill said, shaking his head.*
**3** if you shake someone's hand, you hold it and move it up and down as a greeting or to show that you have agreed on something: *Ron introduced the two women, and they shook hands.*
**4** if your voice shakes, it sounds unsteady because you are upset, nervous, or angry: *Mom's voice started to shake with anger.*
**5** to make someone feel less confident or sure about something: *Losing the first match has really shaken her confidence.*
**PHRASAL VERB**
**shake up**
**1** **shake someone up** = if an unpleasant experience shakes someone up, he or she is shocked or upset by it: *The accident really shook her up.*
**2** **shake something up** = to make a lot of changes to an organization in order to make it more effective: *The new manager has promised to shake up the department.*

**shake²** *noun*
**1** if you give something a shake, you move it up and down or from side to side with quick movements: *Give the juice a shake before you pour it.*

2 a MILKSHAKE: *I had a hamburger and a chocolate shake.*

**shak·en** /ˈʃeɪkən/ *adjective*
**be/look/feel shaken** = to be frightened, shocked, or upset: *Mark looked shaken as he put down the phone. "Dad's been in an accident," he said.*

**shake·up** /ˈʃeɪk-ʌp/ *noun*
a process in which an organization, company, etc. makes a lot of changes in a short time in order to be more effective: *A few employees lost their jobs in the department shakeup.*

**shak·y** /ˈʃeɪki/ *adjective*
**1** weak and unsteady because of illness, old age, or shock: *I was sick yesterday, and I still felt shaky when I got up this morning.*
**2** not very good or strong: *Their relationship is a little shaky.*

S

**shall** /ʃəl; *strong* ʃæl/ *modal verb (formal)*
**1 Shall I/we ...?** = used to make a suggestion or ask someone what to do: *Shall I turn on the air conditioner?*
**2** used to say that something must or will happen, especially in official documents: *No changes shall be made without written permission.*

**shal·low** /ˈʃæloʊ/ *adjective*
**1** measuring only a short distance from the top to the bottom: *Stay in the shallow end of the pool until you can swim better.* **ANTONYM: deep** → see picture at **deep**
**2** not interested in important or serious matters: *She's very shallow and only cares about money.* **ANTONYM: deep**

**sham** /ʃæm/ *noun*
something that tricks people by seeming good, real, or true, when it is not: *Our marriage is a sham – he doesn't really love me.*

**shame** /ʃeɪm/ *noun*
**1** used when a situation makes you feel sad or disappointed: *It's a shame that your brother can't come to your wedding.*
**2** the guilty feeling you have after doing something that is wrong: *She felt a deep sense of shame for stealing from her mother.*
**3 Shame on you!** = said to tell someone that he or she should feel ashamed for doing something that is wrong: *You cheated on the test? Shame on you!*
**4** a loss of respect or honor: *His behavior brought shame on the whole family.*
—**shame** *verb* to make someone feel ashamed: *It shamed her to admit that she had lied.*

**WORD FAMILY: shame**
**shame** *noun* | **shame** *verb* | **ashamed** *adjective* | **shameful** *adjective* | **shamefully** *adverb*

**shame·ful** /ˈʃeɪmfəl/ *adjective*
so bad that someone should be ashamed: *It's shameful that they leave their dogs outside in the cold.*
—**shamefully** *adverb* in a shameful way

**sham·poo** /ʃæmˈpu/ *noun*
a liquid soap used for washing your hair
—**shampoo** *verb* to wash your hair with a liquid soap
[**ORIGIN:** 1700-1800 From the Hindi word *cāpo*, from *cāpna*, which means "to press or massage." When you use shampoo to wash your hair, you have to press on or rub your head.]

**shape**

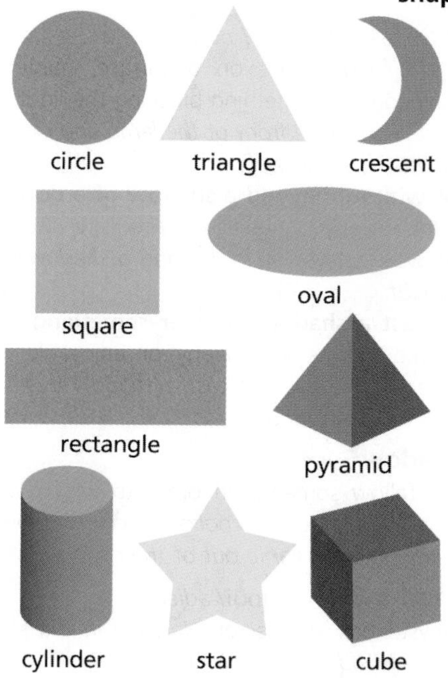


**shape¹** /ʃeɪp/ *noun*
**1** the form of an object, for example round, square, or TRIANGULAR: *She made him a cake in the shape of a football. | A square is a shape with four sides that are all the same length.*

**2 in good/bad shape** = in good or bad condition or health: *Make sure your car is in good shape before starting a long trip.*
**3 in shape/out of shape** = if you are in shape, your body and muscles are healthy and strong. If you are out of shape, your body and muscles are not healthy and strong: *I'm trying to get in shape by going to the gym.*
**4 take shape** = if an idea or plan takes shape, it develops into something clear and definite: *Plans for the party began to take shape; we decided where it would be.*
**5** a person or thing that you cannot see clearly enough to recognize: *A dark shape moved through the fog in front of them.*
**—shaped** *adjective* having a particular shape: *The room was L-shaped.* | *She was wearing a pin shaped like a star.*

**shape²** *verb*
**1** to influence the way something develops or changes: *His mother's early death shaped the rest of his life.*
**2** to make something have a particular shape: *Shape the dough into small balls.*
**PHRASAL VERB**
**shape up** (*informal*)
to improve your behavior or work: *You'd better shape up, Greg, or I'll have to call your parents.*

**share¹** /ʃer/ *verb*
**1** to have or use something with someone else: *There's only one book – we'll have to share.* | *She shared an apartment with her cousin for two years.*
**2** to let someone have or use something that belongs to you: *My sister doesn't like to share her toys with me.*
**3** to be responsible for doing something along with someone else: *They all shared the chores.*
**4** to tell someone else about ideas, information, or problems that you have: *The students are asked to share their ideas with the rest of the class.*
**5** to have the same interest, opinion, name, etc. as someone else: *We share an interest in sports and watch games on TV together.*

**share²** *noun*
**1** the part of something that you own, deserve, or are responsible for: *I paid my share of the bill and left.*
**2** one of the equal parts into which the OWNERSHIP of a company is divided: *He sold 500 shares in the company.*

**share·hold·er** /ˈʃerˌhoʊldɚ/ *noun*
someone who owns STOCK in a company: *a meeting of company shareholders*

**shark** /ʃɑrk/ *noun*
a large ocean fish with very sharp teeth

**shark**

**sharp¹** /ʃɑrp/ *adjective*
**1** with a very thin edge or point that can cut things easily: *You need a sharp knife to cut the meat.* **ANTONYM: dull** → see picture at **blunt**
**2** a sharp pain is sudden and very bad: *I felt a sharp pain in my chest and I had to sit down.* **ANTONYM: dull**
**3** a sharp bend or turn changes direction suddenly: *Slow down. There's a sharp turn in the road ahead.*
**4** a sharp increase or fall is sudden and large: *There has been a sharp increase in traffic accidents because of the bad weather.*
**5** good at noticing things and thinking quickly: *You won't be able to fool her – she's very sharp.*
**6** if an image or picture is sharp, you can see all the details very clearly: *We get a really sharp picture on our new TV.*
**7** attractive and fashionable: *He always has great clothes – he's a very sharp dresser.*
**8 F sharp/C sharp, etc.** = a musical note that is slightly higher than the note F, C, etc., and is shown by the sign (#) **ANTONYM: flat**
**—sharpness** *noun* the quality of being sharp

**sharp²** *adverb*
**at 8 o'clock sharp/at 2:30 sharp, etc.** = at exactly 8 o'clock, 2:30, etc.: *The class starts at 9:00 sharp, so don't be late.*

**sharp·en** /ˈʃɑrpən/ *verb*
to make something sharper: *Can you sharpen this pencil for me?*

**sharp·en·er** /ˈʃɑrpənɚ/ *noun*
a tool that you use to make pencils or knives sharper

**sharp·ly** /ˈʃɑrpli/ *adverb*
**1** suddenly and by a large amount: *Prices have risen sharply.*
**2** in a way that shows a lot of disapproval: *His actions have been sharply criticized.*

**shat·ter** /ˈʃætɚ/ *verb*
**1** to break suddenly into very small pieces: *The plate hit the floor and shattered.*
**2** to completely destroy someone's hopes, beliefs, or confidence: *The accident shattered her dreams of becoming a professional athlete.*
→ see Thesaurus box at **break**[1]

**shave**[1] /ʃeɪv/ *verb*
to cut off hair very close to the skin using a RAZOR: *Aren't you going to shave before you go to work?*

S

**shave**[2] *noun*
an act of shaving: *He rubbed his chin and said, "I need a shave."*

**shav·er** /ˈʃeɪvɚ/ *noun*
a small electrical tool used for shaving

**ˈshaving ˌcream** *noun*
a thick substance made of soap that a man puts on his face when he shaves

**shawl** /ʃɔl/ *noun*
a piece of cloth that a woman wears around her shoulders or head: *She wrapped a wool shawl around her shoulders to keep warm.*

**she** /ʃi/ *pronoun*
a woman or girl, or a female animal. You use "she" instead of someone's name when you have already talked about that person: *Cathy was excited when she heard you were coming.* | *"Where's Kate?" "She went inside."*

**shear** /ʃɪr/ *verb* (**sheared**, **sheared** *or* **shorn** /ʃɔrn/)
to cut the wool off a sheep: *How long does it take to shear a sheep?*
**PHRASAL VERB**
**shear something off**
to cut or separate something from something else: *The tornado sheared off part of the roof.*

**shears** /ʃɪrz/ *plural noun*
a tool like a large pair of scissors: *Use the garden shears to trim the bushes.*

**shed**[1] /ʃed/ *noun*
a small building used especially for storing things: *The tool shed has his saws, hammers, and things in it.*

**shed**[2] *verb* (**shed**, **shedding**)
**1** if a plant sheds its leaves or an animal sheds its hair or skin, they fall off as part of a natural process: *As it grows, a snake regularly sheds its skin.*
**2 shed light on something** = to make something easier to understand: *The investigation should shed light on what started the fire.*
**3 shed tears** (*formal*) = to cry: *She shed a few tears as she said goodbye to her sister.*

**she'd** /ʃid/
**1** the short form of "she had": *She knew she'd seen the man before.*
**2** the short form of "she would": *She said she'd like to come.*

**sheep** /ʃip/ *noun* (plural **sheep**)
a farm animal that is kept for its wool and its meat
[**ORIGIN:** From the old English word *sceap.*]

**sheep·ish** /ˈʃipɪʃ/ *adjective*
embarrassed because you have done something silly or wrong: *Al looked sheepish when he told us he still hadn't finished the work.*
—**sheepishly** *adverb* in a sheepish way

**sheer** /ʃɪr/ *adjective*
**1** complete, with no other quality or feeling mixed in: *It was sheer luck that we saw each other at the airport.* **SYNONYM: pure**
**2** used to emphasize the size or amount of something: *The sheer size of the building impressed us. It was at least 70 stories tall.*
**3** a sheer cliff goes straight down: *It was too dangerous to climb down the sheer cliff, even with ropes.*
**4** sheer material is very thin, so that you can almost see through it: *The sheer curtains did not keep out much sunlight.*

**sheet** /ʃit/ *noun*
**1** a large piece of thin cloth that you put on a bed to lie on or under: *I put some clean sheets on the bed.*
**2** a thin flat piece of paper, metal, glass, or plastic: *Can I borrow a sheet of paper to write this down on?*
**3** a large flat area of ice or water spread over a surface: *The road was covered with a sheet of ice, so driving was very dangerous.*

**shelf** /ʃelf/ *noun* (plural **shelves** /ʃelvz/)
a long flat board for putting things on, that is attached to a wall or is part of a piece of furniture: *the top shelf of the bookcase*

**shell**[1] /ʃel/ *noun*
**1** the hard outside part of a nut or egg: *We took the shells off the walnuts.*
**2** the hard part that protects the body of an animal such as a CRAB, TURTLE, or SNAIL: *A turtle can pull its head inside its shell to protect itself.* | *We looked for shells on the beach.*

**shell**

**3** a metal tube containing a bullet and an explosive substance, which is fired from a gun: *Police found three empty shells where the shooting happened.*
**4** a metal tube containing a bomb, which is fired from a large gun: *The soldiers ran for cover as shells landed all around them.*

**shell**[2] *verb*
**1** to remove nuts from their shells, or beans or PEAs from their PODs, in order to eat them: *Mom was in the kitchen, shelling peas.*
**2** to fire shells from large guns at something: *The army began shelling the town yesterday.*

**she'll** /ʃil/
the short form of "she will": *She says she'll be here at 6:00.*

**shell·fish** /ˈʃelˌfɪʃ/ *noun* (plural **shellfish**)
a small sea or water animal that has a shell, or this animal eaten as a food: *Crabs and shrimp are shellfish.*

**shel·ter**[1] /ˈʃeltɚ/ *noun*
**1** protection from bad weather or danger: *They took shelter from the storm under a big tree.*
**2** a building that protects you from bad weather or danger: *The Scouts learned how to build a shelter out of tree branches.*
**3** a place where people or pet animals can go if they have no home or are being treated badly: *He lived in homeless shelters until he found a job and could afford an apartment.*

**shelter**[2] *verb*
to protect someone or something from bad weather or danger: *A row of trees sheltered the house from the wind.*
→ see Thesaurus box at **protect**

**shelve** /ʃelv/ *verb*
to decide not to continue with a plan, although you might continue with it later: *Plans to build the stadium have been shelved until more money can be found.*

**shelves** /ʃelvz/ *noun*
the plural of SHELF

**shep·herd** /ˈʃepɚd/ *noun*
someone whose job is to take care of sheep

**sher·bet** /ˈʃɚbət/ *noun*
a frozen sweet food made from water, fruit, sugar, and milk
[**ORIGIN:** 1600-1700 From the Persian word *sharbat*, which means "drink made from fruit and sugar," from the Arabic word *sharbah*, which means "drink."]

**sher·iff** /ˈʃerɪf/ *noun*
the chief police officer in a COUNTY. A sheriff is elected.
[**ORIGIN:** From the old English word *scirgerefa*, from *scir*, which means "area with its own government," and *gerefa*, which means "person in charge of an area."]

**she's** /ʃiz/
**1** the short form of "she is": *She's my English teacher.*
**2** the short form of "she has": *She's already seen the movie twice.*

**shh** /ʃʃ/ *interjection*
used when telling someone to be quiet: *Shh! You'll wake the baby!*

**shield**[1] /ʃild/ *noun*
**1** a large piece of metal, wood, or leather that soldiers used in past times to protect themselves in battle: *He blocked the other soldier's sword with his shield.*
**2** something that protects someone or something from being hurt or damaged: *The animal's thick fur is a shield against the cold.*

**shield**[2] *verb*
to protect someone or something from being hurt, damaged, or upset: *Parents cannot shield their children from every danger.*
→ see Thesaurus box at **protect**

**shift**[1] Ac /ʃɪft/ *verb*
**1** to move from one place or position to

S

another: *The wind shifted from the west to the east.*

**2** to change the GEAR when you are driving: *When you slow down, you need to shift into a lower gear.*

**3** if someone's opinion or attitude shifts, it changes: *Public support has shifted away from the president's plan.*

**shift²** Ac *noun*

**1** one of the periods during each day and night when workers in a factory, hospital, etc. are at work: *She doesn't like to work the night shift because it is hard to stay awake.*

**2** a change in the way most people think about something, or in the way something is done: *There has been a shift in spending habits. People now buy things with credit cards rather than with cash.*

S

**shim·mer** /ˈʃɪmɚ/ *verb*

to shine with a soft light that seems to shake slightly: *The lake shimmered in the moonlight.* → see Thesaurus box at **shine**

**shin** /ʃɪn/ *noun*

the front part of your leg between your knee and your foot → see picture on page **A2**

**shine** /ʃaɪn/ *verb*

**1** (**shone** /ʃoʊn/) to produce light: *The sun was shining brightly.*

**THESAURUS: shine**

**flash** to shine brightly for a very short time: *Lightning flashed across the sky.*

**flicker** to shine with a light that is not steady: *The wind made the candle flicker.*

**twinkle** to shine in the dark with a light that keeps changing from bright to less bright: *The stars were twinkling in the sky.*

**sparkle/glitter** to shine brightly with a lot of small flashes of light: *The glasses were so clean they sparkled in the sunlight.*

**glow** to shine with a warm soft light: *From outside, I could see a lamp glowing in the window.*

**shimmer** to shine with a soft light that seems to shake slightly: *As she moved, her silk dress shimmered in the spotlight.*

**2** (**shone** *or* **shined**) to look bright and shiny: *Mom polished the table until it shone.*

**3** (**shone** *or* **shined**) to point a light in a particular direction: *Don't shine the flashlight in my eyes!*

**4** (**shined**) to make something bright by rubbing it: *I need to shine my shoes before the party.*

**shin·gle** /ˈʃɪŋgəl/ *noun*

one of many thin pieces of wood or other material, used for covering the roof or walls of a house

**shin·y** /ˈʃaɪni/ *adjective* (**shinier**, **shiniest**)

having a bright smooth surface that sends back light: *The car was clean and shiny.*

**ship¹** /ʃɪp/ *noun*

**1** a large boat that carries people and things on the ocean: *The ship was sailing to the Bahamas.* | *Supplies came by ship.* → see picture on page **A27**

**2** a large spacecraft

[**ORIGIN:** From the old English word *scip*.]

**ship²** *verb* (**shipped**, **shipping**)

to send or deliver goods to customers: *Your order will be shipped to you the next day.*

**PHRASAL VERB**

**ship out**

to leave on a ship: *The sailors are going to ship out tomorrow.*

**ship·ment** /ˈʃɪpmənt/ *noun*

**1** an amount of goods that are being delivered: *We received a shipment of art supplies this morning.*

**2** an act of sending or delivering goods: *The books are packed and ready for shipment to the customer.*

**ship·ping** /ˈʃɪpɪŋ/ *noun*

**1** the activity or cost of sending or delivering goods: *There is no charge for shipping on orders over $100.*

**2** the business of carrying goods in ships: *The canal has been closed to shipping, so no ships will go through until it reopens.*

**ship·wreck** /ˈʃɪp-rek/ *noun*

an accident in which a ship is destroyed

**ship·wrecked** /ˈʃɪprekt/ *adjective*

if people are shipwrecked, the ship they are traveling in is destroyed, usually in a storm: *The crew of the boat was shipwrecked on a small island.*

**ship·yard** /ˈʃɪpˌyɑrd/ *noun*
a place where ships are built or repaired

**shirt** /ʃɚt/ *noun*
a piece of clothing that covers the top half of your body, and that usually has a collar, sleeves, and buttons down the front: *He was wearing a clean white shirt and a tie.* → see picture on page **A6**

**shiv·er** /ˈʃɪvɚ/ *verb*
to shake slightly because you are cold or frightened: *You're shivering – you should put on a coat.*

**shoal** /ʃoʊl/ *noun*
**1** a large group of fish that swim together: *a shoal of tuna*
**2** a small hill of sand just below the surface of water that is dangerous for boats
→ see Thesaurus box at **group**[1]

**shock**[1] /ʃɑk/ *noun*
**1** if something that happens is a shock, you did not expect it, and it makes you feel very surprised and upset: *It was a big shock to everyone when Chuck was badly hurt in the football game.*
**2** the feeling of surprise you have when something very bad happens that you do not expect: *The team was in shock after the surprise defeat.*
**3** if you are suffering from shock, you are weak and unable to think clearly because you have been injured, frightened, or upset: *After the bus crashed, many people were suffering from shock.*
**4** a sudden painful feeling caused by a flow of electricity passing through your body: *Ow! The light switch gave me a shock.*
[**ORIGIN:** 1500-1600 From the French word *choc*, from *choquer*, which means "to hit against something."]

**shock**[2] *verb*
to make someone feel very surprised and upset: *Mrs. Worth's decision to leave shocked the whole school. No one expected it.*
—**shocked** *adjective* feeling shock: *We were shocked at how poor the people were.*

**shock·ing** /ˈʃɑkɪŋ/ *adjective*
very surprising, upsetting, or offensive: *The pictures of the dead soldiers were shocking.*

**shoes**

**shoe** /ʃu/ *noun*
**1** something that you wear to cover your feet, that is made of leather or some other strong material: *Billy needs a new pair of shoes for school.* | *high-heeled shoes*
**2 be in someone's shoes** = to be in the situation that someone else is in: *She's in so much trouble – I wouldn't want to be in her shoes.*
[**ORIGIN:** From the old English word *scoh*.]

**shoe·lace** /ˈʃuleɪs/ *noun*
a thin piece of string or leather that you use to tie your shoes: *Your shoelaces are untied.*
**SYNONYM: lace**

**shone** /ʃoʊn/ *verb*
a past tense and past participle of SHINE

**shook** /ʃʊk/ *verb*
the past tense of SHAKE

**shoot**[1] /ʃut/ *verb* (**shot** /ʃɑt/)
**1** to make a bullet come out of a gun: *The officer shouted, "Stop or I'll shoot!"* | *They shot at the deer but it ran away.*
**2** to injure or kill someone with a gun: *The man had been shot in the leg.*
**3** to move quickly in a particular direction: *The cat shot across the yard and into the house.*

**4** in sports, to throw, kick, or hit the ball toward the place where you can get points: *He shot the ball at the basket and scored!*
**5** to take photographs or make a movie: *The movie was shot in New Zealand.*
**PHRASAL VERB**
**shoot up**
to increase quickly in number or amount: *Prices shot up by 60% in under a year.*

**shoot²** *noun*
a new part of a plant: *It was early spring, and there were new shoots on the bushes.*

**shoot³**
you say this when you are slightly annoyed because of something you have done: *Shoot! I forgot to call Chris about the party.*

S

**shoot·ing** /ˈʃutɪŋ/ *noun*
a situation in which someone is killed or injured by a gun: *There have been three shootings this week, and two men have died.*

**shop¹** /ʃɑp/ *noun*
**1** a small store that sells only a particular type of goods: *a card shop*
**2** a place or business where things are made or repaired: *The car is in the repair shop for a week.*

**shop²** *verb* (**shopped**, **shopping**)
to go to one or more stores to buy things: *We shopped all day for Christmas presents.*
**PHRASAL VERB**
**shop around**
to compare the prices and quality of different things before you decide which to buy: *It's a good idea to shop around for the best deal when you're buying a computer.*

**shop·lift·ing** /ˈʃɑpˌlɪftɪŋ/ *noun*
the crime of stealing things from a store: *Dina was arrested for shoplifting when she walked out of the store with a dress she hadn't paid for.*
—**shoplifter** *noun* someone who shoplifts
→ see Thesaurus box at **crime**

**shop·per** /ˈʃɑpɚ/ *noun*
someone who is shopping: *The sidewalks were full of Christmas shoppers.*

**shop·ping** /ˈʃɑpɪŋ/ *noun*
the activity of going to stores to buy things: *Let's go shopping at the mall this afternoon.* | *I need to do some grocery shopping.*

**ˈshopping ˌcenter** *noun*
a group of stores built together in one area

**ˈshopping mall** *noun*
another word for a MALL

**shore** /ʃɔr/ *noun*
the land along the edge of an ocean or lake: *The boat sank a few miles from shore.* | *the shores of Lake Michigan*

**THESAURUS: shore**

**coast** the land next to the ocean: *There are many small islands off the coast of Florida.*
**beach** an area of sand or small stones at the edge of an ocean or lake: *We went to the beach and swam in the ocean.*
**seashore** the land at the edge of an ocean, where there is sand, stones, or rocks: *She was looking for shells along the seashore.*
**bank** the land along the edge of a river: *the banks of the Mississippi River*

**shore·line** /ˈʃɔrlaɪn/ *noun*
the edge of a lake or ocean, where the land begins: *We had a cabin on the shoreline of Lake Michigan.*

**short** /ʃɔrt/ *adjective*
**1** measuring only a small distance from one end to the other: *Short hair is a lot easier to take care of.* | *a short skirt* | *The store is only a short distance away.* **ANTONYM: long**
**2** happening for only a little time or for less time than usual: *a short meeting* | *She worked here for a short time, no more than three months.* | *Summer was nearly over and the days were getting shorter.* **ANTONYM: long**
**3** not tall: *Sarah is too short to reach the top shelf.* **ANTONYM: tall**
**4** a short book, letter, or note does not have many words or pages: *He left a short note to tell us where he was.* **ANTONYM: long**
**5** **be short for something** = used to say that part of a word is used instead of the whole word: *The name "Will" is short for "William."*
**6** **in the short run/term** = in the period of time that is not very far into the future: *They may make a little money in the short run, but over time the business will fail.*
**7** **short of breath** = unable to breathe easily:

*Dad was short of breath after climbing the stairs.*

—**shortness** *noun* the fact of being short

**short·age** /ˈʃɔrtɪdʒ/ *noun*
a situation in which there is not enough of something that people need: *There was a shortage of clean drinking water after the hurricane.*

**ˌshort ˈcircuit** *noun*
a problem in a piece of electrical equipment that makes it stop working, caused by two wires touching each other

**short·com·ing** /ˈʃɔrtˌkʌmɪŋ/ *noun*
a bad quality or weakness that someone or something has: *The accident showed some of the shortcomings of our safety rules.*

**short·cut** /ˈʃɔrtkʌt/ *noun*
**1** a quicker more direct way of going somewhere: *We took a shortcut across the field, rather than going around it.*
**2** a quicker way of doing something: *There aren't really any shortcuts to learning English.*

**short·en** /ˈʃɔrtn/ *verb*
to become shorter, or make sth shorter: *In the fall, the days begin to shorten.* | *These pants are too long. How much will it cost to shorten them?* **ANTONYM: lengthen**

**short·fall** /ˈʃɔrtfɔl/ *noun*
the difference between the amount you have and the amount you need or expect: *The city needs $1 million to pay for shortfalls in the budget.*

**short·hand** /ˈʃɔrthænd/ *noun*
a fast way of writing that uses special signs and short forms of words: *She took notes in shorthand, and typed them up after the meeting.*

**ˈshort list** *noun*
a list of the best people or things for a job, prize, etc., who are chosen from a larger group: *The book is on the short list for this year's Pulitzer Prize.*

**short-lived** /ˌʃɔrtˈlɪvd/ *adjective*
existing only a short time: *Our family's problems were short-lived because my father soon found a new job.*

**short·ly** /ˈʃɔrtli/ *adverb*
very soon: *I expect him to come home shortly.* | *We arrived shortly before 5:00.*

**ˌshort-ˈrange** *adjective*
short-range weapons are designed to travel or be used over a short distance: *short-range missiles*

**shorts** /ʃɔrts/ *plural noun*
pants that end at or above the knee: *It's so hot – I'm going to wear shorts.* → see picture on page **A6**

**short·sight·ed** (**short-sighted**) /ˌʃɔrtˈsaɪtɪd/ *adjective*
not considering the future effects of something: *It was very short-sighted to spend the money instead of saving it.*

**short·stop** /ˈʃɔrtstɑp/ *noun*
the baseball player whose position is between second base and third base

**ˌshort ˈstory** *noun* (plural **short stories**)
a short written story about imaginary events: *a book of short stories*

**ˌshort-ˈterm** *adjective*
continuing for only a short time into the future: *This is a short-term solution, but what will we do in the future?* **ANTONYM: long-term**

**short·wave** /ˈʃɔrtˌweɪv/ *noun*
a range of radio waves used for broadcasting around the world

**shot**[1] /ʃɑt/ *verb*
the past tense and past participle of SHOOT

**shot**[2] *noun*
**1** if you fire a shot, you make a bullet come out of a gun: *Where were you when you heard the shot?* | *Police fired shots into the air.*
**2** an attempt to throw, kick, or hit a ball toward the place where you can get points in a sport: *Elliott blocked the shot and stopped the Celtics from scoring.*
**3** a photograph, or a view of something in a movie or television program: *I'd like to get a shot of you with your mother.*
**4** (*informal*) an attempt to do or achieve something: *I've never tried snowboarding before, but I'll give it a shot.*
**5** if you are given a shot, medicine or a VACCINE is put into your body using a needle: *Have you gotten a flu shot this year?*
**6 like a shot** (*informal*) = very quickly: *She ran out of the house like a shot.*

**shot·gun** /ˈʃɑtgʌn/ *noun*
a long gun that fires a lot of small round bullets, used especially for shooting animals and birds

**should** /ʃəd; *strong* ʃʊd/ *modal verb*
**1** used when you say or ask what is the right or sensible thing to do: *You should phone your mom if you are going to be late getting home.* | *What should I do now?* | *They should have called the police sooner.*
**2** used to say what you expect to happen or be true: *We should be done by 5:00.*

**shoul·der** /ˈʃoʊldɚ/ *noun*
**1** one of the two parts of your body on each side of your neck where your arms are connected: *She rested her head on his shoulder and fell asleep.* | *Jane's hair comes down to her shoulders.* → see picture on page **A2**
**2** an area of ground beside a road where drivers can stop their cars if they are having trouble: *He drove the car onto the shoulder to change the tire.*

ˈ**shoulder blade** *noun*
one of the two flat bones on each side of your back, near your shoulders → see picture on page **A2**

**should·n't** /ˈʃʊdnt/ *modal verb*
the short form of "should not": *You shouldn't have lied to me.*

**should've** /ˈʃʊdəv/ *modal verb*
the short form of "should have": *You should've called me – I would have helped you.*

**shout¹** /ʃaʊt/ *verb*
to say something very loudly: *"Help me!" she shouted.* | *Stop shouting at me.*

**THESAURUS: shout**

**yell** to shout something very loudly: *Someone yelled at them to be quiet.*

**call** to shout in order to get someone's attention: *They called for help.*

**scream** to shout in a very loud high voice because you are frightened, hurt, or excited: *She burned her hand and screamed in pain.*

**cry/cry out** to shout something suddenly or loudly: *"There's Grandpa!" the little boy cried.*

**cheer** to shout to show that you like something, for example a team or a performance: *The audience clapped and cheered.*

**PHRASAL VERB**
**shout something out**
to say something suddenly in a loud voice: *Don't shout out the answer – raise your hand.*

**shout²** *noun*
something that someone shouts: *There were shouts of anger from the crowd.*

**shove** /ʃʌv/ *verb*
to push someone or something with your hand or shoulder, using a lot of force: *People were pushing and shoving so that they could see the band.*
—**shove** *noun* a hard push with your hand or shoulder: *We gave the door a shove to open it.*
→ see Thesaurus box at **push¹**

**shov·el¹** /ˈʃʌvəl/ *noun*
a tool that you use for digging earth or moving snow. It has a long handle and a wide piece of metal at the bottom: *He got the shovel and began to dig a hole.*

**shovel²** *verb*
to dig earth or move snow using a shovel: *Dad was outside shoveling snow from the driveway.*

**show¹** /ʃoʊ/ *verb* (**showed**, **shown** /ʃoʊn/)
**1** to let someone see something: *Will you show me your photos?* | *I showed the letter to Ruth.*
**2** to teach someone how to do something by doing it yourself so that he or she can copy you: *Can you show me how to make these cookies?*
**3** to take someone to a place, when that person does not know the way: *I'll show you the way to the cafeteria.*
**4** to provide facts that prove something exists or is true: *Studies show that children are getting less exercise than in the past.*
**5** if you show what you are feeling, other people can see it easily: *Alan tried not to show his disappointment.* | *Her anger showed on her face.*
**6** if a theater shows a movie, people can go

and see it there: *The theater's showing the new James Bond movie.*

**7** if a picture shows something, that thing can be seen in the picture: *The photograph shows a group of children playing baseball.*

→ see Thesaurus box at **explain**

[**ORIGIN:** From the old English word *sceawian*, which means "to look or see."]

**PHRASAL VERBS**

**show off**

to do things to try to make people think you are funny, smart, or attractive: *The boys were showing off in front of the girls.*

**show up** (*informal*)

to arrive somewhere, especially when other people are waiting for you: *Paula finally showed up an hour later.*

**show²** *noun*

**1** a play, performance, or program on television: *What's your favorite TV show?* | *The show starts at 8 p.m.*

**2** a public event where people can see a special group of things: *The art show has paintings, photographs, and sculptures done by the students.* | *a Paris fashion show*

**show biz** /ˈʃoʊ bɪz/ *noun* (*informal*)

another word for SHOW BUSINESS

**ˈshow ˌbusiness** *noun*

the business of making movies, plays, or television programs: *She wanted to be an actress and have a career in show business.*

**show·down** /ˈʃoʊdaʊn/ *noun* (*informal*)

the final argument, fight, or competition between two people or groups that have argued or competed for a long time: *The final showdown between the two armies came three months later.*

**show·er** /ˈʃaʊɚ/ *noun*

**1** a piece of bathroom equipment that you stand under to wash yourself: *The water coming out of the shower was cold.* | *Craig's in the shower now.* → see picture on page **A11**

**2** if you take a shower, you wash yourself by standing under a shower: *I usually take a shower in the morning.*

**3** a short period of rain: *It was sunny in the morning but there were a few showers during the afternoon.*

**4** a party at which people give presents to a woman who is getting married or having a baby: *We're having a baby shower for Karen on Friday.*

—**shower** *verb* to wash yourself by standing under a shower: *Tom showered and put on clean clothes.*

→ see Thesaurus box at **rain¹**

**shown** /ʃoʊn/ *verb*

the past participle of SHOW

**ˈshow-off** *noun* (*informal*)

someone who does things to try to make people think he or she is funny, smart, or attractive: *Dan always wants people to see how smart he is – he's such a show-off!*

**show·room** /ˈʃoʊrum/ *noun*

a large room where you can look at things that are for sale: *a car showroom*

**show·y** /ˈʃoʊi/ *adjective*

very big, bright, or expensive in a way that people notice: *She was wearing a showy diamond ring.*

**shrank** /ʃræŋk/ *verb*

the past tense of SHRINK

**shrap·nel** /ˈʃrapnəl/ *noun*

small pieces of metal from a bomb or bullet that has exploded: *The bomb exploded, and a piece of shrapnel hit his chest.*

[**ORIGIN:** 1800-1900 From Henry Shrapnel (1761-1842), a British army officer who invented a type of bomb that exploded in the air.]

**shred¹** /ʃred/ *noun*

a small thin piece that is torn or cut from something: *Michael tore the letter to shreds and threw the pieces in the trash.*

**shred²** *verb* (**shredded**, **shredding**)

to cut something into small thin pieces: *I shredded some lettuce and added it to the sandwich.*

—**shredder** *noun* a machine used to cut documents into small pieces

**shrewd** /ʃrud/ *adjective*

good at judging situations or people, and able to make good decisions: *He is a shrewd businessman who knows when something is a good idea.*

—**shrewdness** *noun* the quality of being shrewd

**shriek** /ʃrik/ *verb*

to shout in a high voice because you are

frightened, excited, or angry: *"I can't swim," she shrieked.* **SYNONYM: scream**

**shrill** /ʃrɪl/ *adjective*
a shrill voice or noise is high and loud in a way that sounds unpleasant: *"There's a spider in my room," Lucy cried in a shrill voice.*

**shrimp** /ʃrɪmp/ *noun*
a very small sea animal with a soft shell, that you can eat

**shrine** /ʃraɪn/ *noun*
a holy place that people visit for religious reasons: *They traveled for many miles to visit the saint's shrine.*

**shrink** /ʃrɪŋk/ *verb* (**shrank** /ʃræŋk/, **shrunk** /ʃrʌŋk/)
to become smaller: *Oh no! I washed my favorite sweater, and it shrank.* | *In the ocean, the number of fish is shrinking.*

S

**shrink·age** /ˈʃrɪŋkɪdʒ/ *noun*
the act of becoming smaller: *Wash the sweater in cold water to prevent shrinkage.*

**shriv·el** /ˈʃrɪvəl/ (*also* **shrivel up**) *verb*
if something shrivels, it becomes smaller because it is dry or old: *The plants will soon shrivel up if they are not watered.*

**shroud[1]** /ʃraʊd/ *noun*
a cloth that you wrap around a dead person's body before burying it

**shroud[2]** *verb*
**1** to be covered and hidden by something such as clouds or darkness: *The top of the mountain was shrouded in clouds, so we could not see it.*
**2** if something is shrouded in mystery or secrecy, people have not been able to find out anything about it: *His disappearance is shrouded in mystery. No one knows if he died or just left secretly.*

**shrub** /ʃrʌb/ *noun*
a small bush: *The park is full of beautiful trees and shrubs.*
—**shrubbery** *noun* shrubs that are grown close together

**shrug** /ʃrʌg/ *verb* (**shrugged**, **shrugging**)
to move your shoulders up and down to show that you do not know something, or do not care about it: *I asked Dan if he knew the answer, but he just shrugged.*
—**shrug** *noun* a movement of the shoulders that you make to show that you do not know or do not care

**shrunk** /ʃrʌŋk/ *verb*
the past participle of SHRINK

**shud·der** /ˈʃʌdɚ/ *verb*
if you shudder, your body suddenly shakes because you are frightened, shocked, or cold: *Liz shuddered when she saw the dead rat.*
—**shudder** *noun* a shaking movement of your body because you are frightened, shocked, or cold

**shuf·fle** /ˈʃʌfəl/ *verb*
**1** to walk without lifting your feet off the ground: *The old lady stood up and shuffled into the kitchen.*
**2** to mix playing cards or papers into a different order: *Murphy shuffled the cards for a game of poker.*

**shun** /ʃʌn/ *verb* (**shunned**, **shunning**) (*formal*)
to avoid a person, thing, or place deliberately: *The actor lives alone and shuns publicity.*

**shunt** /ʃʌnt/ *verb*
to move someone or something to another place or position, in a way that does not seem fair: *Some of the children were shunted aside into slower classes, even though they had been doing their work.*

**shush** /ʃʌʃ, ʃʊʃ/ *interjection*
used when telling someone to be quiet: *Shush! Let him explain.*

**shut[1]** /ʃʌt/ *verb* (**shut**, **shutting**)
to close something: *Could you shut the window?* | *Shut your eyes and go to sleep.* | *I heard the door shut.* **ANTONYM: open**

**PHRASAL VERBS**

**shut down**
**1 shut (something) down** = if a company or factory shuts down, it stops doing business permanently or for a period of time: *The business lost customers and eventually shut down.* **SYNONYM: close down**
**2 shut something down** = to make a computer or program stop working: *How do I shut down this computer?*

**shut something off**
to make a machine or a piece of equipment stop working, or to stop electricity or water flowing: *She shut off the water and left the*

*glass in the sink.* | *This button shuts off the alarm.*

**shut up** (*informal*)
used to rudely tell someone to stop talking: *Shut up! I'm watching TV.*

**shut²** *adjective*
closed: *Are all the windows shut?* **ANTONYM: open**

**shut·down** /ˈʃʌtdaʊn/ *noun*
a situation in which a company or factory stops doing business permanently or for a period of time: *Many people were sad about the shutdown of the newspaper.*

**shut·ter** /ˈʃʌtɚ/ *noun*
**1** a wood or metal cover on the outside of a window, that you can open and close: *In some countries, houses have shutters to keep out the heat.*
**2** a part of a camera that lets in light

**shut·tle** /ˈʃʌtl/ *noun*
**1** a SPACE SHUTTLE
**2** an airplane, bus, or train that makes regular short trips between two places: *We got the shuttle from the airport into the city.*

**shy** /ʃaɪ/ *adjective*
nervous about meeting people and talking to them: *His brother is shy and never says very much.* | *Don't be shy about asking questions.*

**THESAURUS: shy**

**Shy:**

**timid** shy, and not brave or confident: *She was too timid to raise her hand in class.*

**bashful** shy, and easily embarrassed in social situations: *He was too bashful to talk to any of the girls at the party.*

**reserved** preferring not to show or talk about your feelings or thoughts: *She is a quiet, reserved woman.*

**introverted** (*formal*) quiet and shy, and preferring not to be with other people: *He was an introverted boy who didn't join in with the other children very easily.*

**Not Shy:**

**outgoing** always willing to meet and talk to new people: *Anna is an outgoing, popular girl.*

**extroverted** (*formal*) confident, and enjoying being with other people: *A good salesman is often extroverted and likes to talk to people.*

—**shyness** *noun* the quality of being shy: *Shyness is very common in teenagers.*

**sib·ling** /ˈsɪblɪŋ/ *noun* (*formal*)
a brother or sister: *"Do you have any siblings?" "Yes, I have a brother and two sisters."*
[**ORIGIN:** From an old English word for "relative." First used in its modern meaning, 1900-2000.]

**sick** /sɪk/ *adjective*
**1** having a disease or illness: *His mother's very sick – she has cancer.* | *She got sick and had to stay home.* **ANTONYM: well**

**THESAURUS: sick**

**not feel good/well** to feel sick: *Mommy, I don't feel good. My throat hurts.*

**ill** (*formal*) sick: *His grandmother's very ill and is in the hospital.*

**not very well** a little sick: *You don't look very well; you should try to rest.*

**2 be sick** = to bring food up from your stomach and out of your mouth: *Stop the car – I think I'm going to be sick.* **SYNONYM: vomit**
**3 feel sick** = to feel that you might bring food up from your stomach and out of your mouth: *I feel sick after eating all that candy.* **SYNONYM: queasy**
**4 be sick of something** (*informal*) = **a)** to be angry about something and want it to stop: *I'm sick of the way he treats me.* **b)** to be bored with something: *I'm sick of potatoes – let's have rice instead.*
**5 make me sick** (*informal*) = if something makes you sick, it makes you feel angry because you think it is wrong: *When people tell lies, it makes me sick.*
[**ORIGIN:** From the old English word *seoc.*]

**sick·en** /ˈsɪkən/ *verb*
to make you feel angry and shocked: *Pictures of starving people sickened the whole world.*
—**sickening** *adjective* making you feel angry and shocked: *It's sickening the way some people scream at their kids.*

S

**ˈsick leave** *noun*
the time when you are away from work because you are sick: *I haven't taken any sick leave this year.*

**sick·ness** /ˈsɪknəs/ *noun*
the state or feeling of being sick: *The drinking water was dirty, and there was a lot of sickness.*

**ˈsick pay** *noun*
money that the person or company you work for pays you when you are sick and cannot work

**side** /saɪd/ *noun*
**1** a part of something that is not the front, back, top, or bottom: *There's a bad scratch on the side of the car, near the door.*
**2** one of the flat surfaces of something: *A cube has six sides.* | *Write your name on both sides of the paper.*
**3** one half of a place or thing: *Jim grew up on the east side of the city.* | *He was driving on the wrong side of the road.*
**4** the part of something that is near the edge, not in the middle: *We stood at the side of the road and waited for the bus.*
**5** the left or right part of your body, from your shoulder to the top of your leg: *Turn over, and lie on your right side.*
**6** one of the people, groups, or countries in an argument or fight: *We are hoping to find a solution that both sides will accept.* | *I'm on your side. I think you're right and they're wrong.*
**7** all the people who are related to one of your parents: *My father's side of the family is from Ireland.*
**8 side by side** = next to each other: *The sisters were walking side by side.*

**side·burns** /ˈsaɪdbɚnz/ *plural noun*
hair that grows on the sides of a man's face, in front of his ears
[**ORIGIN:** From Ambrose Burnside (1824-81), a U.S. general who grew his beard down the sides of his face but shaved his chin and upper lip.]

**ˈside efˌfect** *noun*
an unwanted effect that medicine has on your body, in addition to curing pain or an illness: *Headaches are a common side effect of this medicine.*

**side·walk** /ˈsaɪdwɔk/ *noun*
a path with a hard surface, that you walk on next to a street: *A couple of boys were running down the sidewalk.*

**side·ways** /ˈsaɪdweɪz/ *adverb*
toward one side: *He stepped sideways to let me pass.*

**siege** /sidʒ/ *noun*
a situation in which an army surrounds a place, and stops food and weapons from getting to it: *The siege of the city had lasted three months and the people inside were starving.*

**si·es·ta** /siˈestə/ *noun*
a short sleep in the afternoon, especially in warm countries: *In Spain, people take a siesta after lunch.*
[**ORIGIN:** 1600-1700 From Spanish, from the Latin phrase *sexta hora*, which means "sixth hour." Noon was the sixth hour after sunrise, and was when people rested because of the heat.]

**sift** /sɪft/ *verb*
to remove large pieces from a substance such as flour by letting it fall through an object with small holes in it: *Sift the flour and add it to the butter and sugar in the bowl.*

**sigh** /saɪ/ *verb*
to breathe out loudly and slowly because you are sad, happy, bored, etc.: *When the plane landed safely, Jenny sighed with relief.*
—**sigh** *noun* an act of sighing: *"We're home at last," she said with a sigh.*

**sight** /saɪt/ *noun*
**1** the ability to see: *If your sight gets worse, you'll need to wear glasses.* **SYNONYM: eyesight**
**2** the act of seeing something, or something you see: *A lot of people don't like the sight of blood.* | *The piano on the beach was a strange sight.*
**3 in sight** = if something is in sight, you can see it: *There was nobody in sight.*
**4 out of sight** = if something is out of sight, you cannot see it: *I watched the car until it was out of sight.*
**5 catch sight of something** = if you catch sight of something, you suddenly see it: *As he was leaving the house, he caught sight of his reflection in the mirror.*
**6 the sights** = the famous buildings and

interesting places in a city or country, that people go to see: *While he was in San Francisco, he wanted to see the sights.*

**sight·see·ing** /ˈsaɪtˌsiɪŋ/ *noun*
the activity of visiting famous or interesting places: *On our first day in Egypt, we went sightseeing and saw the pyramids.*
—**sightseer** *noun* someone who is visiting a famous or interesting place

**sign¹** /saɪn/ *noun*
**1** a board in a public place that has words or a picture on it giving people information: *The sign says, "No smoking." | It's against the law to drive through a stop sign without stopping.*
**2** a picture or shape that has a particular meaning: *"$" is the dollar sign.* **SYNONYM: symbol**
**3** a movement or action that you use to tell someone something: *He nodded at her as a sign that he understood.*
**4** a fact or information which shows that something is true or is starting to happen: *Her work is showing signs of improvement.*

**sign**

**sign²** *verb*
to write your name, for example at the end of a letter: *Please fill out this form and sign it.*
—**signer** *noun (formal)* someone who signs his or her name on something: *the signers of the Declaration of Independence*

**PHRASAL VERB**

**sign up**
to put your name on a list to show that you want to do something: *If you want to join the drama club, sign up today.*

**sig·nal¹** /ˈsɪgnəl/ *noun*
**1** a sound or action that tells someone to do something: *He blew on a whistle to give the signal for the race to begin.*
**2** a series of light WAVEs, sound waves, or radio waves that travel to a television, telephone, or radio and carry information or pictures: *The spacecraft sent signals back to Earth, with information about the planet.*

**signal²** *verb*
to make a movement or sound that tells someone to do something: *Tom signaled with his hand to the waiter for the check.*

**sig·na·ture** /ˈsɪgnətʃə/ *noun*
your usual way of writing your name, for example at the end of a letter or on a check: *I need your signature on this form.*

**sig·nif·i·cance** Ac /sɪgˈnɪfɪkəns/ *noun*
**1** the importance of something: *We learned about the historical significance of the Bill of Rights in class.*
**2** the meaning of something: *In the poem, the significance of the two roads is that the poet has two things to choose between.*



**sig·nif·i·cant** Ac /sɪgˈnɪfɪkənt/ *adjective (formal)*
**1** a significant amount is fairly large: *The repairs cost a significant amount of money – almost $25,000.* **ANTONYM: insignificant**
**2** important: *There has been a significant change in the way the school deals with bullying.*
→ see Thesaurus box at **important**

**sig·ni·fy** Ac /ˈsɪgnəˌfaɪ/ *verb* (**signified, signifies**) *(formal)*
to mean or be a sign of something: *"X" signifies the number 10 in Roman numerals.*

**ˈsign ˌlanguage** *noun*
a language that uses hand movements and not words, used by people who cannot hear

**sign·post** /ˈsaɪnpoʊst/ *noun*
a tall sign at the side of a road showing the distance or direction to a place

**Sikh** /sik/ *noun*
someone who belongs to a religious group from India that follows the teachings of Guru Nanak. Sikhs believe that there is only one God.
—**Sikhism** /ˈsikˌɪzəm/ *noun* the religion of Sikhs

**si·lence** /ˈsaɪləns/ *noun*
**1** when nobody is talking: *They didn't feel like talking and drove home in silence.*
**2** when there is no sound: *There was a loud bang, and then there was silence.*

**si·lent** /ˈsaɪlənt/ *adjective*
**1** not talking: *As the president started to speak, the crowd fell silent.*
**2** without any sound: *No one was home, and the house was dark and silent.*

**sil·hou·ette** /ˌsɪluˈet/ *noun*
a dark shape that you see in front of a light background: *I took a photo of the silhouette of a tree against the sunset.*
[**ORIGIN:** From Étienne de Silhouette (1709-67), a French politician who was famous for not liking to spend money. This is probably why his name was used for a cheap simple picture that just showed the outline of a person.]

**sil·i·con** /ˈsɪlɪkən/ *noun*
a chemical ELEMENT in sand and rocks that is used for making glass, bricks, and parts for computers: *Computers contain silicon chips on which programs are stored.*

S

**silk** /sɪlk/ *noun*
a soft cloth made from the threads that a type of CATERPILLAR produces: *a silk shirt*

**silk·y** /ˈsɪlki/ *adjective*
soft and smooth like silk: *Sally had silky hair.*

**sill** /sɪl/ *noun*
the narrow shelf at the bottom of a window **SYNONYM: windowsill**

**sil·ly** /ˈsɪli/ *adjective* (**sillier**, **silliest**)
**1** stupid or not sensible: *You're being silly – you can't wear your princess dress to school.* | *I made a silly mistake.*
**2** not serious: *He used to make up silly little songs.*
[**ORIGIN:** From the old English word *sælig*, which means "happy or blessed." This word has had many changes in meaning, and has meant "deserving pity," "harmless," and "weak."]

**silt** /sɪlt/ *noun*
sand or mud that is carried along by a river. Silt settles at a curve in a river or at the point where a river flows into the ocean: *There is a lot of silt at the bottom of the river.*

**sil·ver** /ˈsɪlvɚ/ *noun*
**1** a shiny white metal that people use for making jewelry and other valuable things: *The bracelet is made of silver.*
**2** the color of this metal: *Her new car is silver.*
—**silver** *adjective* made of silver: *a silver necklace*

**ˌsilver anniˈversary** *noun*
the date that is exactly 25 years after someone got married, or after another important event: *It's Mom and Dad's silver anniversary in July.*

**sil·ver·ware** /ˈsɪlvɚˌwer/ *noun*
knives, forks, and spoons that are made of silver or a similar metal: *The table looked pretty, with bright silverware.*

**sim·i·lar** Ac /ˈsɪmələ/ *adjective*
almost the same, but not exactly: *She has blond hair, similar to mine.* | *The bikes are similar in price, with the red one costing only a few dollars more.*
—**similarly** *adverb* in a similar way: *The two men were similarly dressed – they both wore suits and ties.*

**WORD FAMILY: similar**
**similar** *adjective* | **dissimilar** *adjective* | **similarly** *adverb* | **similarity** *noun*

**THESAURUS: similar**
**like** similar in some way to something else: *The Earth is round, like a ball.* | *Stop acting like a baby!*
**alike** very similar in appearance or behavior: *She and her sister look alike.*
**identical** exactly the same: *The two pictures were identical.*

**sim·i·lar·i·ty** Ac /ˌsɪməˈlærəti/ *noun* (plural **similarities**)
something that is the same about two people or things: *There are some similarities between the two men. Both are tall, for example.*

**sim·i·le** /ˈsɪməli/ *noun*
a way of describing something by comparing it to something else, using the word "like" or "as": *If you say "her dress was white as snow," you are using a simile.*

**sim·mer** /ˈsɪmɚ/ *verb*
to boil very gently: *Let the sauce simmer for 20 minutes.*

**sim·ple** /ˈsɪmpəl/ *adjective*
**1** easy to do or understand: *This cake is very simple to make.* **SYNONYM: easy**; **ANTONYM: hard**
**2** not having a lot of details or decoration:

*She wore a simple white dress.* SYNONYM: **plain**

**3** a tense of a verb in English that is formed without "have" or "be": *In "They played chess," the verb "played" is in the simple past.*

—**simplicity** /sɪmˈplɪsəti/ *noun* the quality of being simple: *I was surprised by the simplicity of the math problem.*

**WORD FAMILY: simple**

**simple** *adjective* | **simply** *adverb* | **simplicity** *noun* | **simplify** *verb*

**sim·pli·fy** /ˈsɪmpləˌfaɪ/ *verb* (**simplified, simplifies**) (*formal*)
to make something easier to do or understand: *The book is really long, so they simplified the story for the movie.*

**sim·plis·tic** /sɪmˈplɪstɪk/ *adjective* (*formal*)
dealing with a difficult subject in a way that does not include important details, so that the subject is not dealt with well: *Saying that your genes make you who you are is too simplistic – it is more complicated than that.*

**sim·ply** /ˈsɪmpli/ *adverb*
**1** only: *Don't buy it simply because it's cheap.* SYNONYM: **just**
**2** in a way that is easy to understand or do: *My teacher explains things simply.*
**3** used for emphasizing what you are saying: *The strain on the rope was simply too great, and it broke.*
**4** without a lot of extra things that are not needed: *They live simply and grow all their own food.*

**sim·u·late** Ac /ˈsɪmyəˌleɪt/ *verb* (*formal*)
to make or do something that seems real, but is not real: *The army training simulates the work that soldiers will do in a war.*

—**simulation** /ˌsɪmyəˈleɪʃən/ *noun* a copy of a real situation: *People can learn to fly a plane using a computer simulation.*

[ORIGIN: 1400-1500 From the Latin word *simulare*, which means "to copy," from *similis*, which means "like something else."]

**si·mul·ta·ne·ous** /ˌsaɪməlˈteɪniəs/ *adjective* (*formal*)
happening at the same time: *The two explosions were almost simultaneous. The first was at 6 a.m., and the second only three seconds later.*

—**simultaneously** *adverb* at the same time: *The game is being broadcast simultaneously on TV and radio.*

**sin** /sɪn/ *noun*
something you do that religious rules do not allow: *He confessed his sins to a priest.*

**since** /sɪns/ *preposition, conjunction, adverb*
**1** from a time in the past until now: *I've been waiting for him since 2 o'clock.* | *She met Steve two years ago, and they've been together ever since.*

**USAGE: since, for, ago**

**Since**, **for**, and **ago** are all used to talk about time.

**Since** is used to say when something started. You use **since** before a day, date, or time: *He's been sick since Sunday.* | *I've been going to school here since 2010.*

**For** is used to say how long a situation or activity has lasted. You use **for** before the amount of time: *My aunt has been here for three days.*

**Ago** is used to say how far back in the past something happened. You use **ago** after the amount of time: *My grandfather died two years ago.*

**2** because: *Since it was a sunny day, I decided to walk.* SYNONYM: **as**

**sin·cere** /sɪnˈsɪr/ *adjective*
honest and meaning what you say: *He said he was sorry, and he seemed sincere.* ANTONYM: **insincere**

—**sincerity** /sɪnˈserəti/ *noun* the quality of being sincere: *He apologized with great sincerity.*

[ORIGIN: 1500-1600 From the Latin word *sincerus*, which means "clean or pure."]

**sin·cere·ly** /sɪnˈsɪrli/ *adverb*
**1** in an honest way, and meaning what you say: *I sincerely hope that you succeed.*
**2** **Sincerely** = something you write at the end of a formal letter, before you write your name: *Sincerely, Hilary Walsh.*

**sin·ful** /ˈsɪnfəl/ *adjective* (*formal*)
wrong: *I know that lying is sinful.*

**sing** /sɪŋ/ *verb* (**sang** /sæŋ/, **sung** /sʌŋ/)
to make musical sounds with your voice: *Nick*

*played the guitar and sang a song.* | *I can hear the birds singing.*

**sing·er** /ˈsɪŋɚ/ *noun*
someone who sings: *He's a singer in a band.*

**sin·gle¹** /ˈsɪŋgəl/ *adjective*
**1** only one: *We lost the game by a single point.*
**2** not married: *Is he married or single?*
**3** **every single** = used for emphasizing that you mean every person or thing: *I've read every single book that he has written.*
**4** **a single bed/room** = a bed or room for one person only
**5** **(in) single file** = in a line, with one person walking behind another: *We walked single file along the narrow trail.*
→ see Thesaurus box at **married**

S

**single²** *noun*
**1** one song, which you can buy on a record or CD, or DOWNLOAD: *The band's latest single sold 3 million copies.*
**2** a piece of paper money worth one dollar
**3** **singles** = people who are not married: *The bar is popular with singles.*

**single³** *verb*
**PHRASAL VERB**
**single someone/something out**
to give special attention to one person or thing from a group: *Rachel was singled out for special praise.*

**sin·gu·lar** /ˈsɪŋgyələ˞/ *noun*
**the singular** = the form of a word that you use when talking about only one person or thing: *"Child" is the singular, and "children" is the plural.*
—**singular** *adjective* used for talking about only one person or thing: *If the subject is singular, use a singular verb.*

**sin·is·ter** /ˈsɪnɪstɚ/ *adjective* (*formal*)
frightening, and making you feel that something bad will happen to you: *I noticed a man watching the house, which seemed sinister.*
[**ORIGIN:** 1400-1500 From the Latin word *sinister*, which means "on the left side." The left side was thought by the Romans to be the unlucky or bad side.]

**sink¹** /sɪŋk/ *verb* (**sank** /sæŋk/ *or* **sunk** /sʌŋk/, **sunk**)
**1** if a ship, boat, or other object sinks, it goes down below the surface of water: *The ship hit some rocks, and it sank.* **ANTONYM: float** → see picture at **float**
**2** to move down to a lower level: *The level of water in the lake sank by six feet last summer.*

**sink²** *noun*
the container in a kitchen or bathroom that you fill with water to wash dishes or your hands: *There were some dirty dishes in the sink.* → see picture on page **A11**

**sin·ner** /ˈsɪnɚ/ *noun*
someone who does bad things that religious rules do not allow

**sip** /sɪp/ *verb* (**sipped**, **sipping**)
to drink something slowly in small amounts: *Marcia sipped her hot tea slowly.*
—**sip** *noun* a very small amount of a drink: *Can I have a sip of your lemonade?*

**sir** /sɚ/ *noun*
**1** used for speaking politely to a man: *Can I help you, sir?*
**2** **Dear Sir** = used at the beginning of a formal letter to a man, if you do not know his name
[**ORIGIN:** 1200-1300 From the old French word *sire*, from the Latin word *senior*, which means "older."]

**si·ren** /ˈsaɪrən/ *noun*
a piece of equipment on a police car, fire engine, or AMBULANCE that makes a very loud warning sound: *A police car went past with its siren on.*

**sir·loin** /ˈsɚlɔɪn/ (*also* ˌ**sirloin** ˈ**steak**) *noun*
a good piece of meat from a cow

**sis·ter** /ˈsɪstɚ/ *noun*
**1** a girl or woman who has the same parents as you: *My little sister is five years younger than me.* | *I have one brother and two sisters.*
**2** a NUN: *Sister Frances has been a nun for twenty years.*

ˈ**sister-in-**ˌ**law** *noun* (plural **sisters-in-law**)
**1** the sister of your husband or wife
**2** the wife of your brother

**sit** /sɪt/ *verb* (**sat** /sæt/, **sitting**)
**1** to put your bottom on a chair or the ground, with your body upright: *Can I sit next to you?* | *I usually sit at the front of the class.*
→ see picture on page **A5**
**2** if something is sitting on or in a place, it is

on that surface or in that place: *Her purse was sitting on the kitchen table.*

**3** to take care of children while their parents are not at home: *I need someone to sit for us on Saturday.* **SYNONYM: babysit**

**PHRASAL VERBS**

**sit around**

to sit somewhere, and not do anything useful: *Teenagers spend a lot of time sitting around in their rooms.*

**sit down**

to move so that you are sitting on something, after you have been standing up: *Sam sat down beside me.*

**sit up**

to move so that you are sitting, after you have been lying down: *She heard a noise downstairs, and sat up in bed.*

**sit·com** /ˈsɪtkɑm/ *noun*

a funny television program that has the same people in different situations each week

→ see Thesaurus box at **program**¹

**site** [Ac] /saɪt/ *noun*

**1** a place where something important or interesting happened: *This field is the site of a famous battle.*

**2** an area where people build something: *They're building two new hotels on this site.*

**3** a website

→ see Thesaurus box at **place**¹

**sit·ter** /ˈsɪtɚ/ *noun*

another word for a BABYSITTER

**sit·u·at·ed** /ˈsɪtʃuˌeɪtɪd/ *adjective (formal)*

**be situated** = to be in a particular place: *The college is situated outside the city.*

**sit·u·a·tion** /ˌsɪtʃuˈeɪʃən/ *noun*

the things that are happening at a particular time, or the things that are happening in someone's life: *My friends are arguing, so I'm in a difficult situation because I don't want to take sides.*

**ˈsit-up** *noun*

an exercise in which you lie on your back and raise the top part of your body until you are sitting: *I do sit-ups to strengthen my stomach muscles.*

**six** /sɪks/ *number*

**1** 6: *There should be six eggs in the box.*

**2** six O'CLOCK: *I'll see you at six.*

**3** six years old: *We moved to Houston when I was six.*

**ˈsix-pack** *noun*

six bottles or cans of a drink, that you buy together: *a six-pack of soda*

**six·teen** /ˌsɪkˈstin/ *number*

**1** 16: *There were sixteen fish in the tank.*

**2** sixteen years old: *You can drive a car once you're sixteen.*

—**sixteenth** /ˌsɪksˈtinθ/ *number* 16th or 1/16

**sixth** /sɪksθ/ *number*

**1** 6th

**2** 1/6

**six·ty** /ˈsɪksti/ *number*

**1** 60: *I gave him sixty dollars for his old bike.*

**2** sixty years old: *He is almost sixty.*

**3 the sixties** (*also* **the '60s**) = the years between 1960 and 1969: *My mum and dad got married in the sixties.*

**4 in your sixties** = between 60 and 69 years old: *Your grandfather is in his late sixties now.*

**5 in the sixties** = between 60 and 69 degrees FAHRENHEIT in temperature: *It will be a pleasant day with the temperature in the high sixties.*

—**sixtieth** /ˈsɪkstiɪθ/ *number* 60th or 1/60

**siz·a·ble** (*also* **sizeable**) /ˈsaɪzəbəl/ *adjective*

fairly large: *A sizable number of people – at least fifty – agreed to help.*

**size** /saɪz/ *noun*

**1** how big or small something is: *Your house and mine are around the same size.*

**2** a number or letter that tells you how big or small clothes are: *I wear size 10 shoes.*

**siz·zle** /ˈsɪzəl/ *verb*

to make the sound of food cooking in hot oil: *The sausages were sizzling in the pan.* → see picture on page **A22**

**skate**¹ /skeɪt/ *noun*

a special boot with wheels or a blade on the bottom of it: *roller skates | ice skates*

**skate**² *verb*

to move over ice or along the ground wearing skates: *In the winter, the lake is frozen and you can skate on it.*

**skate·board** /ˈskeɪtbɔrd/ *noun*

a short board with wheels under it that you

stand on and move by pushing with one foot against the ground

—**skateboarding** *noun* the activity of riding on a skateboard: *Let's go skateboarding in the park.*

**skat·ing** /ˈskeɪtɪŋ/ *noun*
the activity or sport of moving over ice or along the ground wearing skates: *Let's go skating at the ice rink tomorrow.*

**skel·e·ton** /ˈskelətən/ *noun*
all the bones in a person or animal: *In the museum, I saw the skeleton of a dinosaur.*
[ORIGIN: 1500-1600 From the Greek word *skeletos*, which means "dried up." In Greek, *skeletos* was used both about the bones and about a mummy, which was a dried-up dead body.]

S

**skep·ti·cal** /ˈskeptɪkəl/ *adjective*
not believing that something is true or right: *Sometimes I'm skeptical about what I read in the newspaper. Reporters don't always get all the facts.*

—**skeptic** *noun* someone who is skeptical
[ORIGIN: 1500-1600 From the Greek word *skeptikos*, which means "thoughtful," from *skeptesthai*, which means "to look or consider."]

**sketch¹** /sketʃ/ *noun*
a quick drawing that does not have a lot of details: *I did a sketch of the bird before it flew away.*
→ see Thesaurus box at **picture¹**

**sketch²** *verb*
to draw a picture quickly and without a lot of details: *Rob quickly sketched the view from the top of the hill.*

**ski¹** /ski/ *noun* (plural **skis**)
a long narrow piece of plastic that you fasten to a special boot so that you can move easily on snow: *a pair of skis*
[ORIGIN: 1700-1800 From Norwegian, from the Norse word *skith*, which means "piece of wood."]

**ski²** *verb*
to move over snow on skis: *She skied down the mountain.*

—**skier** *noun* someone who skis: *He's a good skier.*

**skid** /skɪd/ *verb* (**skidded**, **skidding**)
if a vehicle skids, it suddenly slides sideways: *A car skidded on the ice.* → see picture at **slide**

**ski·ing** /ˈskiːɪŋ/ *noun*
the activity or sport of moving over snow on skis: *We're going skiing in the mountains.* → see picture on page **A25**

**skill** /skɪl/ *noun*
an ability to do something very well because you have learned it: *He was proud of his skill as a basketball player.* | *This test will measure your language skills.*
→ see Thesaurus box at **ability**
[ORIGIN: 1100-1200 From the Norse word *skil*, which means "good judgment or knowledge."]

**skilled** /skɪld/ *adjective*
having the training and ability to do a job well: *Skilled workers earn more money than unskilled workers.* **ANTONYM: unskilled**

**skil·let** /ˈskɪlɪt/ *noun*
another word for a FRYING PAN

**skill·ful** /ˈskɪlfəl/ *adjective*
good at doing something: *He is a very skillful painter who does wonderful paintings of birds.*

**skim** /skɪm/ *verb* (**skimmed**, **skimming**)
**1** to remove oil, cream, etc. that is floating on top of a liquid: *Skim the fat off the soup.*
**2** (*also* **skim through**) to read something very quickly: *I only had time to skim through the newspaper.*

ˈ**skim milk** *noun*
milk without much fat in it

**skin¹** /skɪn/ *noun*
**1** the outer covering of a person's or animal's body: *Maria has beautiful skin.* | *a purse made from snake skin*
**2** the outer layer of some fruits and vegetables: *Bananas have yellow skins.*

**skin²** *verb* (**skinned**, **skinning**)
**1** to hurt your skin by rubbing it against something rough, so that it bleeds: *She fell and skinned her knee.*
**2** to remove the skin from an animal

**skin·ny** /ˈskɪni/ *adjective* (**skinnier**, **skinniest**)
very thin or too thin: *He was a tall, skinny kid.*
→ see Thesaurus box at **thin**

**skip** /skɪp/ *verb* (**skipped**, **skipping**)
**1** to not do something that you would usually do or that you should do: *I was late so I skipped breakfast.* | *Brad got in trouble for skipping school.*

**2** to not do something, and do the next thing instead: *I skipped question four and went on to question five.*
**3** to move forward with small jumps from one foot to the other: *The girls were skipping down the street.* → see picture on page **A4**
→ see Thesaurus box at **jump**[1]

**skirt** /skɚt/ *noun*
a piece of clothing for a girl or woman, that hangs down from her waist over her legs: *She was wearing a short black skirt and a white top.* → see picture on page **A6**
[**ORIGIN:** 1200-1300 From the Norse word *skyrta*, which means "shirt." Norse was a language used in Scandinavian countries.]

**skull** /skʌl/ *noun*
the bones of a person's or animal's head → see picture on page **A2**

**skunk** /skʌŋk/ *noun*
a small black and white animal that makes a very bad smell when it is afraid
[**ORIGIN:** 1600-1700 From an Algonquian word meaning "the fox that urinates." Algonquian is a Native American language.]

**sky** /skaɪ/ *noun* (plural **skies**)
the space above the Earth where the Sun, clouds, and stars are: *The sun was shining and the sky was blue.* | *There were a few clouds in the sky.*
[**ORIGIN:** 1200-1300 From the Norse word for "cloud."]

**sky·div·ing** /ˈskaɪˌdaɪvɪŋ/ *noun*
the sport of jumping from an airplane and falling through the sky before opening a PARACHUTE
—**skydiver** *noun* someone who does sky-diving

**sky·line** /ˈskaɪlaɪn/ *noun*
the shape that tall buildings or hills make against the sky: *From the boat, we could see the New York City skyline.*

**sky·scrap·er** /ˈskaɪˌskreɪpɚ/ *noun*
a very tall building in a city: *He works at the top of a 30-story skyscraper in Manhattan.*

**slab** /slæb/ *noun*
a thick flat piece of something: *She put a big slab of meat on my plate.* | *a slab of rock*

**slack** /slæk/ *adjective*
loose and not pulled tight: *The rope was slack, and the clothes that hung on it almost touched the ground.*

**slacks** /slæks/ *plural noun*
pants made out of good material, which are not part of a suit: *Rob was neatly dressed in blue slacks, a shirt, and a sweater.*

**slam** /slæm/ *verb* (**slammed**, **slamming**)
**1** to shut a door, lid, etc. with a loud noise: *She was angry and slammed the door as she went out.* | *The gate slammed shut.*
**2** to put something somewhere quickly and with a lot of force: *He slammed his fist on the desk angrily.* → see picture on page **A22**

**slan·der** /ˈslændɚ/ *noun*
the crime of saying something that is bad and not true about someone, which could make people have a bad opinion of that person: *He sued the radio station for slander when they claimed he wasn't a qualified doctor.*
—**slander** *verb* to say something about someone that is bad and not true

**slang** /slæŋ/ *noun*
very informal spoken words: *"Wicked" is a slang word that means "good."*
→ see Thesaurus box at **language**

**slant** /slænt/ *verb*
to be at an angle, not straight or flat: *Light from the sun slanted through the window.*
—**slant** *noun* something that is at an angle: *Her writing went on a slant across the page.*

**slap**[1] /slæp/ *verb* (**slapped**, **slapping**)
to hit someone quickly with your hand held flat: *He was rude to her, so she slapped his face.* → see picture on page **A3**
→ see Thesaurus box at **hit**[1]

**slap**[2] *noun*
**1** a quick hit with your hand held flat: *I was so angry that I felt like giving him a slap.*

S

**2 a slap on the wrist** = a punishment that is not strong enough: *He hit somebody with his car and only got a slap on the wrist!*
**3 a slap in the face** = something that insults you: *When she invited everyone to her party except me, it was a real slap in the face.*

**slash** /slæʃ/ *verb*
**1** to cut something in a very violent way: *Someone had slashed the tires of his car.*
**2** (*informal*) to reduce something by a large amount: *Stores have slashed prices in their year-end sales.*
→ see Thesaurus box at **reduce**

**slat** /slæt/ *noun*
a thin flat piece of wood, plastic, or metal that is part of a piece of furniture or a window BLIND: *Sunlight was coming through the slats of the blind.*

S

**slate** /sleɪt/ *verb*
**be slated to do something/be slated for something** = if something is slated to happen, it is planned to happen in the future: *The school was slated to be closed.*

**slaugh·ter** /ˈslɔtɚ/ *verb*
**1** to kill a lot of people in a violent way: *Hundreds of innocent people had been slaughtered by the army.*
**2** to kill an animal for food: *The cows are slaughtered for their meat.*
—**slaughter** *noun* the act of slaughtering people or animals
[**ORIGIN:** 1200-1300 From the Norse word *slatr*, which means "meat, or the act of killing animals for meat."]

**slave¹** /sleɪv/ *noun*
someone who is owned by another person and is forced to work for no money: *In the 18th century, many Africans were taken to America and forced to work as slaves.*
[**ORIGIN:** 1200-1300 From the Latin word *Sclavus*, which means "Slav (a person living in Eastern or Central Europe)." In medieval times, many Slavs were taken as slaves by people who took control of their countries.]

**slave²** (*also* **slave away**) *verb*
to work very hard: *I've been slaving away in the kitchen all day!*

**slav·er·y** /ˈsleɪvəri/ *noun*
the system of having slaves: *The Civil War ended slavery in the United States.*

**slea·zy** /ˈslizi/ *adjective*
**1** not honest, and willing to do things that are illegal or not right: *The sleazy landlord took their rent, but never fixed anything.*
**2** a sleazy place is dirty and is used by people who are not honest or who do things that are not right: *a sleazy motel*

**sled** /sled/ *noun*
something you sit or lie on to slide over snow: *They pulled the sled back up to the top of the hill and slid down again.*

**sleek** /slik/ *adjective*
**1** sleek hair or fur is smooth and shiny: *The cat had sleek black fur.*
**2** having a modern and attractive shape: *a sleek new office building*

**sleep¹** /slip/ *verb* (**slept** /slept/)
**1** to lie down with your eyes closed and your mind and body not active, so that you do not know if anything happens around you: *Did you sleep well? | I couldn't sleep last night because I was so worried.*

**USAGE: sleep**

Use **sleep** when you are talking about something such as how long someone sleeps, or where he or she sleeps: *Young children need to sleep for about 12 hours each night. | We slept on the floor.*

Do not use **sleep** to say that someone starts sleeping. Use **fall asleep** or **go to sleep**: *She fell asleep in front of the TV. | Ben and Adam, stop talking and go to sleep!*

**THESAURUS: sleep**

**be asleep** to be sleeping: *Your father is asleep, so don't make any noise.*

**doze** to sleep lightly for a short time, especially when you did not intend to: *He was dozing in front of the TV when the phone rang.*

**doze off** to fall asleep, especially when you did not intend to: *I tried to read, but I kept dozing off.*

**take a nap** to sleep for a short time during the day: *Young babies need to take two naps a day.*

**oversleep** to sleep for longer than you intended: *I overslept and was late for school.*

**2** to have enough beds or space for a particular number of people to sleep there: *The tent sleeps six people.*
**3 Sleep tight.** = used to tell someone that you hope he or she sleeps well
**PHRASAL VERBS**
**sleep in**
to sleep later than usual in the morning: *I sleep in on Sundays if there is nothing special I need to do.*
**sleep over**
to sleep at someone's house for a night: *Mom, can I sleep over at Ann's tonight?*
**sleep through something**
to continue sleeping while something noisy is happening: *How could you have slept through the earthquake?*

**sleep²** *noun*
**1** the state of being asleep: *I didn't get much sleep last night because of the noise. | Ed sometimes talks in his sleep.*
**2** a period when you are sleeping: *You'll feel better after a good night's sleep.*
**3 go to sleep/get to sleep** = to start sleeping: *Turn the light off and go to sleep. | What time did you get to sleep last night?*

**ˈsleeping bag** *noun*
a large warm bag for sleeping in, especially in a tent

**sleep·less** /ˈslipləs/ *adjective*
**a sleepless night** = a night when you cannot sleep: *He had a sleepless night worrying about the test.*

**sleep·walk·er** /ˈslipˌwɔkɚ/ *noun*
someone who walks around while he or she is sleeping
—**sleepwalking** *noun* the activity of walking around while you are sleeping

**sleep·y** /ˈslipi/ *adjective*
tired and wanting to sleep: *The warmth of the sun made him feel sleepy.*

**sleet** /slit/ *noun*
a mixture of rain and snow
→ see Thesaurus box at **rain¹**, **snow¹**

**sleeve** /sliv/ *noun*
the part of a piece of clothing that covers your arm or part of your arm: *The shirt had short sleeves.* → see picture on page **A6**

**sleigh** /sleɪ/ *noun*
a vehicle with metal bars instead of wheels under it, which horses pull across snow: *We went for a sleigh ride.*

**slen·der** /ˈslendɚ/ *adjective*
thin in a way that looks good: *The ballet dancer was tall and slender. | the swan's long slender neck* **SYNONYM: slim**
→ see Thesaurus box at **thin**

**slept** /slept/ *verb*
the past tense and past participle of SLEEP

**slice¹** /slaɪs/ *noun*
a flat piece of bread, meat, or PIE that is cut from a whole: *He was eating a slice of bread with peanut butter on it. | Cut the tomato into thick slices.*
→ see Thesaurus box at **piece**
[**ORIGIN:** 1400-1500 From the old French word *esclice*, which means "thin piece broken off," from *esclicier*, which means "to break into thin pieces."]

**slice²** (*also* **slice up**) *verb*
to cut meat, bread, etc. into thin flat pieces: *Slice the onion thinly.* → see picture on page **A15**
→ see Thesaurus box at **cut¹**

**slick¹** /slɪk/ *adjective*
**1** good at persuading people, often in a way that does not seem honest: *A slick salesman may get you to buy things you don't need.*
**2** done with a lot of skill and good to look at: *The movie is slick and beautifully filmed.*
**3** smooth and wet or shiny: *His hands were slick with sweat.* **SYNONYM: slippery**

**slick²** *verb*
**PHRASAL VERB**
**slick something back/down**
to make your hair smooth and shiny by putting water or oil on it: *His hair was slicked back from his face.*

**slide**

**slide¹** /slaɪd/ *verb* (**slid** /slɪd/)
**1** to move smoothly over a surface: *The kids were sliding on the ice.* | *She slid the door open.*
**2** to go somewhere quietly without other people noticing: *Jennifer slid quietly out of the room while the others were talking.*

**slide²** *noun*
something for children to play on which has a slope that they slide down

**slight** /slaɪt/ *adjective*
small and not serious or important: *There was a slight problem with the engine, but it was easily fixed.*

**slight·ly** /ˈslaɪtli/ *adverb*
a little: *He moved slightly as I was taking the photo.* | *We painted the room a slightly different color. It's still blue, but it's a little lighter.*

**slim¹** /slɪm/ *adjective* (**slimmer**, **slimmest**)
**1** thin in a way that looks good: *She went on a diet because she wanted to be slimmer.* **SYNONYM: slender**; **ANTONYM: fat**
**2** very small in amount: *We have only a slim chance of winning.*
→ see Thesaurus box at **thin**
[**ORIGIN:** 1600-1700 From a Dutch word for "bad or of low quality."]

**slim²** *verb* (**slimmed**, **slimming**)
**PHRASAL VERB**
**slim down**
to become thinner by eating less and exercising more: *He slimmed down from 194 pounds to 160 pounds.*

**slime** /slaɪm/ *noun*
a thick wet substance that is not nice to touch: *She came out of the pond covered in mud and slime.*
—**slimy** *adjective* covered with slime: *The worm felt slimy.*

**sling** /slɪŋ/ *noun*
a piece of cloth tied around your neck to support your arm or hand when it is hurt: *Emily broke her arm and it was in a sling for six weeks.*

**slip¹** /slɪp/ *verb* (**slipped**, **slipping**)
**1** to accidentally slide on a smooth surface and fall down or almost fall down: *Be careful not to slip on the ice.* → see picture at **slide**
**2** to slide out of the correct position or out of your hand: *The knife slipped and cut her finger.*
**3** to go somewhere without other people noticing: *He slipped away without saying goodbye.*
**4** to put something somewhere or give someone something quietly or secretly: *Someone slipped a note under my door.*
→ see Thesaurus box at **fall¹**
**PHRASAL VERB**
**slip up**
to make a mistake: *They slipped up and sent me the wrong form.*

**slip²** *noun*
**1** a small piece of paper: *She wrote her phone number on a slip of paper.*
**2** a piece of underwear that a woman wears under a dress or skirt
**3** a small mistake: *If we make one slip, we could lose the game.*

**slip·per** /ˈslɪpɚ/ *noun*
a soft shoe that you wear in your house: *The floor was cold, so I put on a pair of slippers.*
→ see picture at **shoe**

**slip·per·y** /ˈslɪpəri/ *adjective*
something that is slippery is difficult to walk on or hold because it is wet or covered with something such as oil or ice: *He had just washed the floor and it was slippery.*

**slit¹** /slɪt/ *noun*
a narrow cut or space in something: *He looked out through a slit in the curtains.*

**slit²** *verb* (**slit**, **slitting**)
to make a narrow cut in something: *He slit the envelope open.*

**slith·er** /ˈslɪðɚ/ *verb*
to slide somewhere in a smooth way, close to the ground: *The snake slithered away into the bushes.*

**slob** /slɑb/ *noun (informal)*
someone who is lazy and messy: *Don't be such a slob! Pick your coat up off the floor.*

**slo·gan** /ˈslouɡən/ *noun*
a short phrase that is easy to remember, used in advertisements and politics: *The posters against smoking had the slogan "Smokers die younger."*
[**ORIGIN:** 1500-1600 From the Gaelic word *sluagh-ghairm*, which means "army cry." Soldiers going into battle would shout out a phrase to encourage themselves to fight bravely. Gaelic is the old language of Scotland.]

**slope¹** /sloup/ *noun*
a piece of ground or a surface that is higher at one end than the other: *People were skiing down the ski slope.*

**slope²** *verb*
if a surface or piece of ground slopes, it is higher at one end than the other: *The field sloped down to the lake.*

**slop·py** /ˈslɑpi/ *adjective*
**1** not done neatly or carefully: *His handwriting is sloppy and hard to read.*
**2** wet and not pleasant: *He gave her a sloppy kiss on the cheek.*
—**sloppily** *adverb* in a sloppy way

**slot** /slɑt/ *noun*
a long narrow hole that you put something in: *Put the coins in the slot and pick up the candy bar at the bottom of the machine.*
→ see Thesaurus box at **hole**

**ˈslot maˌchine** *noun*
a machine in which you put coins so that you can play games or try to win money

**slouch** /slautʃ/ *verb*
to stand, sit, or walk with your shoulders bent forward: *Sit up straight! Don't slouch.*

**slow¹** /slou/ *adjective*
**1** not moving or happening quickly: *The slowest runners had not yet finished the race. | He's a slow learner. | Traffic is slow on the expressway.* **ANTONYM: fast**
**2** if a clock or watch is slow, it shows a time that is earlier than the true time: *My watch is a few minutes slow; it says 13:50 but the real time is 13:56.* **ANTONYM: fast**
—**slowness** *noun* the quality of being slow

**slow²** *verb*
**PHRASAL VERB**
**slow down**
to go less fast than before: *Slow down. You're driving too fast!*

**slow·ly** /ˈslouli/ *adverb*
at a slow speed: *He was walking slowly because his feet hurt.* **ANTONYM: quickly**

**slug** /slʌɡ/ *noun*
a small creature with a soft body and no legs, that moves very slowly: *Slugs eat garden plants.*

**slug·gish** /ˈslʌɡɪʃ/ *adjective*
less good or fast than usual: *The team's performance was sluggish. They couldn't seem to move the ball down the court quickly enough.*

**slum** /slʌm/ *noun*
an area of a city where the houses are in bad condition and many poor people live: *She grew up in the slums of Rio.*

**slum·ber par·ty** /ˈslʌmbɚ ˌpɑrti/ *noun* (plural **slumber parties**)
a party at which a group of children sleep at one child's house
[**ORIGIN:** 1300-1400 "Slumber" is an old word meaning "sleep" that comes from the old English word *sluma*.]

**slump** /slʌmp/ *verb*
**1** to sit with the top part of your body leaning forward and down: *Sit up straight. Don't slump.*
**2** to suddenly go down in value, amount, or price: *Sales have slumped by 30% compared to this time last year.*

**slur** /slɚ/ *verb* (**slurred**, **slurring**)
to speak in a way that is not clear because you are drunk or sick: *After a few drinks, he started to slur his words.*

**slush** /slʌʃ/ *noun*
snow on the ground that has started to melt
→ see Thesaurus box at **snow¹**

**sly** /slaɪ/ *adjective*
good at getting what you want by tricking people or doing unfair things: *Watch out –*

*he's sly and he might be trying to trick you.*
—**slyly** *adverb* in a sly way

**smack** /smæk/ *verb*
to hit someone or something in a way that makes a noise: *Stop it or I'll smack you!*
→ see Thesaurus box at **hit**[1]

**small** /smɔl/ *adjective*
**1** not large in size or amount: *Rhode Island is the smallest state in the U.S.* | *This jacket is too small.* | *Only a small number of people have been to the Moon.* **ANTONYM: big**

**THESAURUS: small**

**little** small in size: *a little piece of cake*

**tiny** very small: *a tiny baby*

**minute** (*formal*) extremely small and difficult to see or notice: *Even in minute amounts, the chemical is harmful.*

**microscopic** extremely small and impossible to see without a microscope: *There were microscopic creatures in the water.*

**miniature** much smaller than the usual size: *The doctors use a miniature camera to see inside the body.*

**2** not important: *We've had a few small problems with the new car.* **SYNONYM: minor**; **ANTONYM: big**
**3** a small child is young: *She was my best friend when I was small.* **SYNONYM: little**

**small·pox** /ˈsmɔlpɑks/ *noun*
a serious disease that causes spots on the skin. Smallpox killed many people in the past, but no one has had it for a long time.

**smart** /smɑrt/ *adjective*
**1** intelligent: *Jill's a smart kid and always gets good grades.* | *He's smart enough not to waste a good opportunity.* **ANTONYM: stupid**
**2** trying to seem intelligent or funny, in a way that annoys someone: *Don't get smart with me, young lady!*
→ see Thesaurus box at **intelligent**

**smarty-pants** /ˈsmɑrti ˌpænts/ *noun* (*informal*)
someone who tries to seem intelligent or funny in a way that you think is annoying: *OK, smarty-pants, if you know all the answers, why are you asking me?*

**smash** /smæʃ/ *verb*
**1** to break into many small pieces: *The plates fell onto the floor and smashed.* | *The ball smashed a window.* → see picture on page **A22**
**2** to hit something with a lot of force: *Murray smashed his fist against the wall.* | *He died when his motorcycle smashed into a car.*
→ see Thesaurus box at **break**[1]

**smear**[1] /smɪr/ *verb*
to spread a liquid or soft substance on something in a messy way: *She smeared the bread with jam.*
[**ORIGIN:** From the old English word *smerian*, which means "to put grease or oil on something."]

**smear**[2] *noun*
a long dirty or oily mark that has been rubbed onto something: *There was a smear of blood on his cheek.*

**smell**[1] /smel/ *noun*
**1** the quality that you recognize by using your nose: *I love the smell of fresh bread.* | *There was a strong smell of gas before the explosion.*

**THESAURUS: smell**

**aroma** (*formal*) a nice smell from coffee or food that is being made: *The aroma of baking cookies was wonderful.*

**scent** a pleasant smell, or the smell left by an animal: *The scent of wood smoke from the campfires filled the air.*

**fragrance/perfume** (*formal*) a nice smell, especially from flowers, plants, or trees: *the fragrance of the roses*

**stink** (*informal*) a very strong bad smell: *The stink of cigarette smoke filled the air.*

**odor** (*formal*) a bad smell: *There's a horrible odor coming from the trash can.*

**2** a bad smell: *What's that smell in the basement?*
**3** the ability to notice or recognize smells: *Dogs have an excellent sense of smell.*

**smell**[2] *verb*
**1** to have a particular smell: *Dinner smells good!* | *The perfume smells like strawberries.*
**2** to have a bad smell: *His feet smelled*

*because he'd been wearing sneakers without socks.* **SYNONYM: stink**

**3** to use your nose to notice something: *Come smell these roses.* | *I can smell something burning.*

**smell·y** /ˈsmeli/ *adjective*
having a bad smell: *Put those smelly socks in the washing machine.*

**smile[1]** /smaɪl/ *verb*
to raise the corners of your mouth because you are happy or being friendly: *Keith smiled at me and said "Hi!"*

> **THESAURUS: smile**
>
> **grin** to smile with a very big smile: *He was grinning with excitement.*
>
> **beam** to smile in a very happy way: *Jenny was beaming with pleasure as she watched her son pick up his award.*

**smile[2]** *noun*
a happy expression on your face: *He had a big smile on his face so I knew he had passed his driving test.*

**smog** /smɑg/ *noun*
dirty air caused by smoke from cars and factories in cities

**smoke[1]** /smoʊk/ *noun*
the white, gray, or black gas that comes from something when it burns: *cigarette smoke* | *The fire sent up a huge cloud of smoke.* → see picture at **volcano**

**smoke[2]** *verb*
**1** to breathe in smoke from a cigarette or pipe: *He went outside to smoke a cigarette.*
**2** to produce smoke: *The fire was still smoking the next morning.*

**smok·er** /ˈsmoʊkɚ/ *noun*
someone who smokes: *She used to be a heavy smoker but now she only smokes occasionally.*

**smok·ing** /ˈsmoʊkɪŋ/ *noun*
the activity of smoking cigarettes or a pipe: *Smoking is bad for your health.*

**smok·y** /ˈsmoʊki/ *adjective*
filled with smoke: *The room was smoky from all the people with cigarettes.*

**smol·der** /ˈsmoʊldɚ/ *verb*
to burn slowly with smoke but no flame: *The factory is still smoldering after last night's fire.*

**smooth**

**smooth** /smuð/ *adjective*
**1** without any LUMPs or rough areas: *Babies have beautiful smooth skin.* | *Mix the butter and sugar together until the mixture is soft and smooth.* **ANTONYM: rough**
**2** with no sudden movements or changes of direction: *Swing the tennis racket in one smooth movement.*
**3** happening without problems: *Women are still usually responsible for the smooth running of the home.*
—**smoothness** *noun* the quality of being smooth
→ see Thesaurus box at **flat[1]**

**smooth·ie** /ˈsmuði/ *noun*
a thick drink that is a mixture of fruit and juice or milk: *a strawberry and banana smoothie*

**smooth·ly** /ˈsmuðli/ *adverb*
well and without problems or difficulties: *Everything went very smoothly on our trip. We didn't have car problems and we didn't get lost.*

**smoth·er** /ˈsmʌðɚ/ *verb*
**1** to put something over someone's face so that he or she cannot breathe: *The blanket had become twisted around the child's head, almost smothering him.*
**2** to cover the whole surface of something with a substance: *The cake was smothered in chocolate.*

**smudge[1]** /smʌdʒ/ *noun*
a dirty mark: *There was a smudge of lipstick on the cup.*
→ see Thesaurus box at **mark[2]**

**smudge[2]** *verb*
to put a dirty mark on a surface by touching it: *The mirror was smudged with dirty fingerprints.*

**smug** /smʌg/ *adjective*
too happy about how smart, lucky, or good you are, in a way that annoys other people:

S

*She had the smug smile of someone who knew she had aced the test.*

—**smugly** *adverb* in a smug way: *"My kids always eat healthy food," she said smugly.*

**smug·gle** /ˈsmʌgəl/ *verb*

to take someone or something illegally from one place to another: *They were trying to smuggle guns into the country.*

—**smuggling** *noun* the activity of taking something illegally from one place to another: *He was jailed for drug smuggling.*

**smug·gler** /ˈsmʌglɚ/ *noun*

someone who takes something illegally from one place to another: *Police caught the drug smugglers.*

S

**snack¹** /snæk/ *noun*

something that you eat between meals: *It's bad to eat too much candy and other sugary snacks.*

→ see Thesaurus box at **meal**

[ORIGIN: 1700-1800 Probably from the old Dutch word *snacken*, which means "to bite at something."]

**snack²** *verb*

to eat food between meals: *You'll get fat if you snack on cookies all the time.*

ˈ**snack bar** *noun*

a place where you can buy drinks, snacks, and small meals: *The theater has a snack bar which serves coffee and sandwiches.*

**snag** /snæg/ *noun* (*informal*)

a small problem: *It's a good job, but the snag is that he has to work at night.*

**snail** /sneɪl/ *noun*

a small soft creature with no legs, that moves very slowly and has a hard shell on its back

**snake** /sneɪk/ *noun*

a long thin animal with no legs, that slides along the ground: *Watch out for snakes; if they bite you, you could die.*

**snap¹** /snæp/ *verb* (**snapped**, **snapping**)

**1** to break with a short loud noise: *Dry branches snapped under their feet. | He snapped the chalk in two.*

**2** to open, close, or join together with a short loud noise: *The pieces just snap together like this. | She snapped her purse shut.*

**3** to suddenly speak to someone in an angry way: *"Don't be stupid," she snapped.*

**4 snap your fingers** = to make a noise by quickly moving your finger against your thumb: *"It could happen this fast," Jake said, snapping his fingers.*

→ see Thesaurus box at **break¹**

**snap²** *noun*

**1** a sudden short loud noise of something breaking: *I heard the snap of a twig behind me.* → see picture on page **A1**

**2 cold snap** = a time when the weather suddenly becomes very cold: *There was an early cold snap and snow in November.*

**snap·shot** /ˈsnæpʃɑt/ *noun*

a photograph that you take quickly: *He showed us some snapshots of his kids.*

**snare** /sner/ *noun*

a trap for catching an animal

—**snare** *verb* to catch an animal using a snare

**snarl** /snɑrl/ *verb*

**1** to say something in an angry way: *"Shut up!" he snarled.*

**2** if an animal snarls, it makes a low angry sound and shows its teeth: *The two dogs snarled at each other and started fighting.*

**snatch¹** /snætʃ/ *verb*

to take something from someone very quickly: *I saw two kids snatch her purse and run off.* SYNONYM: **grab**

**snatch²** *noun*

**a snatch of conversation/song, etc.** = a short part of something that you hear: *I could hear snatches of conversation from across the room.*

**sneak** /snik/ *verb* (**sneaked** *or* **snuck** /snʌk/)

to go somewhere quietly because you do not want people to see or hear you: *She snuck out of the house once her parents were asleep.*

**sneak·er** /ˈsnikɚ/ *noun*

a soft shoe that you wear for playing sports: *She was wearing a pair of white sneakers.* → see picture at **shoe**

**sneak·y** /ˈsniki/ *adjective*

doing things secretly in a way that is not fair or honest: *He made it look like I was the one who cheated, which was a sneaky trick.*

**sneer** /snɪr/ *verb*

to smile or speak in a way that is not nice and

shows you have no respect for someone: *He sneered at her taste in music, saying that country music was silly.*

**sneeze** /sniz/ *verb*
to make air suddenly come out of your nose and mouth, for example because you have a cold: *All the dust in the air made her sneeze.*
—**sneeze** *noun* the act or sound of sneezing

**snick·er** /ˈsnɪkɚ/ *verb*
to laugh quietly in a way that is not nice: *The teacher tripped, and some of the students snickered.*
→ see Thesaurus box at **laugh**[1]

**sniff** /snɪf/ *verb*
**1** to breathe in through your nose in order to smell something: *The dog sniffed the bone.*
**2** to breathe air into your nose with a loud sound, for example when you are crying or when you have a cold: *Stop sniffing and blow your nose!*

**snip** /snɪp/ *verb* (**snipped**, **snipping**)
to cut something quickly with scissors: *She snipped off the dead flowers with some scissors.*
—**snip** *noun* a quick small cut that you make with scissors

**snip·er** /ˈsnaɪpɚ/ *noun*
someone who shoots at people from a hidden place

**snip·pet** /ˈsnɪpɪt/ *noun*
a small piece of news, information, or conversation: *I only heard a few snippets of their conversation, not the whole thing.*

**snob** /snɑb/ *noun*
someone who thinks that he or she is better than other people: *She is a terrible snob who would never wear cheap clothes.*
—**snobbish** (*also* **snobby**) *adjective* behaving like a snob: *Her snobbish parents thought she should marry someone rich.*
—**snobbery** *noun* the attitudes and behavior of snobs
[**ORIGIN:** This word used to mean "shoemaker, or someone of a low social class." It later came to mean "someone who admires people of a higher class too much." First used with its modern meaning, 1800-1900.]

**snoop** /snup/ *verb*
to try to find out about someone's life or activities by secretly looking at his or her things: *I caught her snooping around in my room, looking in my drawers.*
[**ORIGIN:** 1800-1900 From the Dutch word *snoepen*, which means "to eat something secretly."]

**snooze**[1] /snuz/ *verb*
to sleep for a short time: *Dad was snoozing in front of the TV.* **SYNONYM: doze**

**snooze**[2] *noun*
a short sleep: *Grandpa sometimes has a snooze after lunch.* **SYNONYM: nap**

**snore** /snɔr/ *verb*
to make a loud noise each time you breathe when you are sleeping: *She couldn't sleep because her husband was snoring so loudly.*
—**snore** *noun* the sound you make when you snore
[**ORIGIN:** 1300-1400 From the sound that you make when you snore.]

**snor·kel** /ˈsnɔrkəl/ *noun*
a tube that allows a swimmer to breathe air when his or her face is under water
[**ORIGIN:** 1900-2000 From the German word *Schnorchel*, which means "nose."]

**snort** /snɔrt/ *verb*
to make a sudden loud noise through your nose, for example because you are angry or laughing: *He snorted with laughter.*

**snout** /snaʊt/ *noun*
the long nose of a pig or similar animal

**snow**[1] /snoʊ/ *noun*
soft white pieces of frozen water that fall from the sky when it is very cold: *It was winter and snow was falling.* | *High winds and heavy snow caused problems on the roads.*

**THESAURUS: snow**

**snowflakes** pieces of falling snow
**sleet** a mixture of snow and rain
**slush** snow on the ground that has started to melt and is very wet
**blizzard** a storm with a lot of snow and a strong wind
**frost** a white powder of ice that covers the ground when it is cold
**hail** balls of frozen rain

**snow²** *verb*
**1** if it snows, snow falls from the sky: *Look, it's snowing!*
**2 be snowed in** = to not be able to leave a place because so much snow has fallen: *We were snowed in for a week after that last big snowstorm.*

**snow·ball** /ˈsnoʊbɔl/ *noun*
a ball that children make from snow and throw at each other: *The kids were having a snowball fight outside.*

**snow·board** /ˈsnoʊbɔrd/ *noun*
a large board that you stand on with both feet and use to slide down a hill that is covered in snow
—**snowboarding** *noun* the activity of using a snowboard → see picture on page A25

S

**snow·bound** /ˈsnoʊbaʊnd/ *adjective*
surrounded by so much snow that traveling is impossible: *They were trapped in a snow-bound car.*

**snow·drift** /ˈsnoʊˌdrɪft/ *noun*
a deep pile of snow which the wind has blown into one place

**snow·fall** /ˈsnoʊfɔl/ *noun*
a time when snow falls from the sky, or the amount that falls: *We had the first snowfall of winter last night.*

**snow·flake** /ˈsnoʊfleɪk/ *noun*
a soft white piece of frozen water that falls from the sky when it is very cold

**snow·man** /ˈsnoʊmæn/ *noun* (plural **snowmen** /ˈsnoʊmen/)
a simple figure of a person made out of balls of snow: *The kids were building a snowman.*

**snow·plow** /ˈsnoʊplaʊ/ *noun*
a vehicle used for pushing snow off roads

**snow·storm** /ˈsnoʊstɔrm/ *noun*
a storm with strong winds and a lot of snow

**snow·y** /ˈsnoʊi/ *adjective*
covered in snow, or with a lot of snow: *snowy fields* | *It was a snowy January day.*

**snuck** /snʌk/ *verb*
a past tense and past participle of SNEAK

**snug** /snʌg/ *adjective*
warm and comfortable: *The children were safe and snug in their beds.*

**snug·gle** /ˈsnʌgəl/ *verb*
to get into a warm comfortable position: *I snuggled down in my sleeping bag and tried to get warm.*

**so¹** /soʊ/ *adverb*
**1** used for emphasizing what you are saying: *The party was so boring!* | *He was so weak that he could hardly stand up.*
**2** used in place of what has just been said, to avoid repeating it: *If you have not paid yet, please do so now.* | *"Will I need my coat?" "I don't think so."* | *You have to turn the TV off; Mom said so.*
**3 so do I/so is he/so would John, etc.** = used for saying that something is also true about someone else: *"I have a lot to do today." "So do I."* | *Ann was there and so was Mary.*
**4** used for getting someone's attention or before asking someone a question: *So, Lisa, I hear you just got a dog.* | *So you aren't actually leaving until Friday?*
**5 or so** = used when you are not giving an exact number or amount: *He left a week or so ago.* | *The trip takes an hour or so.*
**6 and so on** = used after a list to show that there are other similar things that you have not mentioned: *He does all the cooking, cleaning, and so on.*
**7 So long!** = used in order to say goodbye: *So long, George, and good luck!*
**8 So?/So what?** = used for saying in an impolite way that you do not think something is important: *"I don't like it." "So? Eat it anyway."* | *Yeah, I'm late. So what?*

**so²** *conjunction*
**1** used for showing why something happens: *I got hungry, so I ate a sandwich.*
**2** in order to do something or make something happen: *I put your keys in the drawer so that they wouldn't get lost.* | *We got up early so we could go swimming.*

**soak** /soʊk/ *verb*
**1** to leave something in water for a time: *Soak the beans in water overnight to soften them.* | *I left the dirty pans to soak.*
**2** to make something completely wet: *The rain soaked his shoes.*
**PHRASAL VERB**
**soak something up**
if something soaks up a liquid, it takes the

liquid into itself: *The bread will soak up the milk.* **SYNONYM: absorb**

**soaked** /soʊkt/ *adjective*
very wet: *I got soaked in the rain.*

**soak·ing** /ˈsoʊkɪŋ/ (*also* ˌ**soaking** ˈ**wet**) *adjective*
very wet: *I fell in the pool and my clothes are soaking wet.*

**soap** /soʊp/ *noun*
**1** a substance that you use with water to wash yourself: *a bar of soap | Wash your hands with soap.* → see picture on page **A11**
**2** (*informal*) a SOAP OPERA
[**ORIGIN:** From the old English word *sape.*]

ˈ**soap** ˌ**opera** *noun*
a story on television about the lives of a group of people: *My mom likes to relax by watching soap operas.*

**soap·y** /ˈsoʊpi/ *adjective*
containing soap: *soapy water in the bathtub*

**soar** /sɔr/ *verb*
**1** to go up quickly to a high level: *It was cool at night, but during the day the temperature soared to 97°F.*
**2** to fly high in the air: *They could see an eagle soaring above them.*

**sob** /sɑb/ *verb* (**sobbed**, **sobbing**)
to cry with quick noisy breaths: *She was stroking the dead cat and sobbing.*
—**sob** *noun* a crying noise that you make with quick noisy breaths: *I could still hear my mother's sobs.*
→ see Thesaurus box at **cry**[1]

**so·ber** /ˈsoʊbɚ/ *adjective*
not having drunk too much alcohol: *You're not sober enough to drive.* **ANTONYM: drunk**

ˈ**so-called** *adjective*
used when you think the word for describing someone or something is not suitable or correct: *This so-called expert didn't really know anything.*

**soc·cer** /ˈsɑkɚ/ *noun*
a game in which two teams of 11 players try to kick a ball into a large net at each end of a field → see picture on page **A25**
[**ORIGIN:** 1800-1900 From "soc" in "Association Football," the official name for "soccer."]

**so·cia·ble** /ˈsoʊʃəbəl/ *adjective*
someone who is sociable is friendly and enjoys being with other people: *She was very sociable and loved going to parties.*

**so·cial** /ˈsoʊʃəl/ *adjective*
**1** relating to the people in a society and the way they live: *Social problems such as poverty and crime are difficult to solve.*
**2** relating to spending time with people for fun: *He has a lot of friends and a good social life.*
—**socially** *adverb* in a way that relates to society or spending time with people for fun: *Rude behavior like eating with your mouth open is socially unacceptable.*

**WORD FAMILY: social**
**social** *adjective* | **socially** *adverb* | **sociable** *adjective* | **socialize** *verb* | **society** *noun*

**so·cial·is·m** /ˈsoʊʃəˌlɪzəm/ *noun*
a system of government that tries to make people more equal, and in which many businesses belong to the government
—**socialist** *noun* someone who agrees with socialism

**so·cial·ize** /ˈsoʊʃəˌlaɪz/ *verb*
to spend time with people for fun: *We don't socialize much with our neighbors.*

ˌ**social** ˈ**science** *noun*
a subject such as history, politics, or ECONOMICS, in which you study relationships in society

ˌ**Social Se**ˈ**curity** *noun*
money that the government pays to people who are old or cannot work: *He's 75 and lives on Social Security.*

ˈ**social** ˌ**studies** *noun*
a school subject that includes the study of history, GEOGRAPHY, and government

ˈ**social work** *noun*
the job of helping people who are poor or have problems
—**social worker** *noun* someone who does social work: *A social worker visited her because her kids looked like they'd been hit.*

**so·ci·e·ty** /səˈsaɪəti/ *noun* (plural **societies**)
**1** all the people who live in a country, and the way they live: *There is too much violence in our society.*
**2** an organization of people with the same interest or purpose: *He belongs to the local*

S

*Historical Society, which tries to find information about the history of our area.*
→ see Thesaurus box at **people**

**WORD FAMILY: society**
**society** *noun* | **social** *adjective* | **sociology** *noun* | **sociologist** *noun*

**so·ci·o·ec·o·nom·ic** /ˌsoʊsioʊˌekəˈnɑmɪk/ *adjective*
based on a combination of social and economic conditions: *The researchers studied children from different socioeconomic backgrounds.*

**so·ci·ol·o·gy** /ˌsoʊsiˈɑlədʒi/ *noun*
the study of the way people behave
—**sociologist** *noun* someone who studies the way people behave: *Sociologists have been studying the effect of television on children's behavior.*

S

**sock** /sɑk/ *noun*
a piece of clothing that you wear on your foot inside your shoe: *She took off her shoes and socks.* → see picture on page **A6**
[**ORIGIN:** From the old English word *socc*, from the Latin word *soccus*, which means "light shoe."]

**sock·et** /ˈsɑkɪt/ *noun*
**1** a place in a wall where you can connect a piece of equipment to the supply of electricity **SYNONYM: outlet** → see picture on page **A20**
**2** the place where one thing fits into another: *It felt like the rope was pulling my arm out of its socket.*

**sod** /sɑd/ *noun*
the top layer of soil that has grass growing in it

**so·da** /ˈsoʊdə/ *noun*
a sweet drink with bubbles, that does not contain alcohol **SYNONYMS: soft drink, pop**
[**ORIGIN:** From the Latin name of a plant from which a chemical called "soda" was obtained. This chemical fizzes when mixed with an acid, and the soda you drink also fizzes. First used with its modern meaning, 1800-1900.]

**so·di·um** /ˈsoʊdiəm/ *noun*
a silver-white chemical ELEMENT that you need in small amounts in your body: *Salt is a combination of sodium and chlorine.*

**so·fa** /ˈsoʊfə/ *noun*
a comfortable seat that is wide enough for two or three people: *Her sister was lying on the sofa in the living room.* **SYNONYM: couch**
→ see picture on page **A8**
[**ORIGIN:** 1600-1700 From the Arabic word *suffah*, which means "long seat."]

**soft** /sɔft/ *adjective*
**1** not hard or firm, but easy to press: *a soft pillow* **ANTONYM: hard**
**2** having a surface that is smooth and nice to touch: *She stroked the cat's soft fur.* **ANTONYM: rough**
**3** a soft sound is quiet: *Her voice was soft and gentle.* **ANTONYM: loud**
**4** soft colors or lights are not too bright: *the soft light from the candles* **ANTONYM: harsh**
**5** (*informal*) not strict enough: *He accused the Democrats of being soft on crime.*
—**softness** *noun* the quality of being soft

**soft·ball** /ˈsɔftbɔl/ *noun*
a game similar to baseball, but played with a larger and softer ball: *She played softball in high school.*

**ˈsoft drink** *noun*
a sweet drink with bubbles, that does not contain alcohol: *cola and other soft drinks* **SYNONYM: soda**

**soft·en** /ˈsɔfən/ *verb*
**1** to become less hard, or make something less hard: *Cook until the onions soften.* | *Soften the butter by leaving it at room temperature.* **ANTONYM: harden**
**2** to become gentler or kinder: *His voice softened when he talked to the little girl.*

**soft·ly** /ˈsɔftli/ *adverb*
quietly: *"Are you awake?" she said softly.*

**ˌsoft-ˈspoken** *adjective*
having a quiet gentle voice

**soft·ware** /ˈsɔft-wer/ *noun*
a set of programs that tells a computer to do something: *I installed some new software that lets me compose music on my computer.*

**sog·gy** /ˈsɑgi/ *adjective*
too wet and soft: *The pie crust was kind of soggy and didn't seem cooked.*

**soil** /sɔɪl/ *noun*
the substance in which plants grow: *The plants did not grow well because the soil was too dry.* **SYNONYM: dirt**

**so·lar** /ˈsoʊlɚ/ *adjective*
relating to the Sun: *They use solar energy to heat their water.*
[**ORIGIN:** 1400-1500 From the Latin word *sol*, which means "the sun."]

**ˌsolar ˈenergy** *noun*
energy from the Sun: *Solar energy can be used to provide heat and electricity.*

**ˈsolar ˌsystem** *noun*
**the solar system** = the Sun, and the PLANETs that move around it: *The Earth is part of the solar system.*

**sold** /soʊld/ *verb*
the past tense and past participle of SELL

**sol·dier** /ˈsoʊldʒɚ/ *noun*
someone in the army: *The soldiers fought bravely.*
[**ORIGIN:** 1200-1300 From the old French word *soudier*, from *soulde*, which means "to pay." This came from *solidus*, the Latin word for a gold coin. A soldier was someone who was paid to fight.]

**sole**[1] Ac /soʊl/ *adjective* (*formal*)
only: *Their sole source of heat was the stove.*
[**ORIGIN:** 1200-1300 From the Latin word *solus*, which means "alone."]

**sole**[2] Ac *noun*
the bottom of your foot or shoe: *There was gum stuck to the sole of my shoe.* → see picture at **shoe**
[**ORIGIN:** 1300-1400 From the Latin word *solea*, which means "light shoe."]

**sole·ly** Ac /ˈsoʊli/ *adverb* (*formal*)
only: *He is interested solely in money.*

**sol·emn** /ˈsɑləm/ *adjective*
serious or formal: *The funeral was a solemn event.*
—**solemnly** *adverb* in a solemn way
—**solemnity** /səˈlemnəti/ *noun* the quality of being solemn

**sol·id**[1] /ˈsɑlɪd/ *adjective*
**1** hard or firm, and not a liquid or gas: *He was too sick to eat solid food.* | *The lake was frozen solid.*
**2** having no space or holes inside: *A tennis ball is hollow but a golf ball is solid.*
**ANTONYM: hollow**
**3 solid gold/silver/oak, etc.** = completely made of gold, etc.: *a solid gold necklace*
—**solidify** /səˈlɪdəˌfaɪ/ *verb* if a liquid solidifies, it becomes hard or firm
→ see Thesaurus box at **hard**[1]

**solid**[2] *noun*
a substance that is not a liquid or gas: *Wood is a solid.*

**sol·i·tar·y** /ˈsɑləˌteri/ *adjective* (*formal*)
**1** done or experienced alone: *He enjoys solitary activities like reading and jogging more than group activities.*
**2** only one: *There was one solitary tree in the middle of the field.*

**sol·i·tude** /ˈsɑləˌtud/ *noun* (*formal*)
the state of being alone, usually because you want to be: *He lived in solitude all his adult life, as he never married, and had few friends.*

**so·lo**[1] /ˈsoʊloʊ/ *adjective*
done alone, without anyone else helping you: *This is his first solo album after leaving the band.*
→ see Thesaurus box at **alone**

**solo**[2] *noun*
a piece of music performed by one person: *a violin solo*
—**soloist** /ˈsoʊloʊɪst/ *noun* a musician or singer who performs alone
[**ORIGIN:** 1600-1700 From the Italian word for "alone," from the Latin word *solus*.]

**sol·u·bil·i·ty** /ˌsɑlyəˈbɪləti/ *noun*
the ability of a solid substance to DISSOLVE in a liquid: *We put salt, sand, and flour in water to test their solubility.*

**sol·u·ble** /ˈsɑlyəbəl/ *adjective*
a soluble substance can be mixed with a liquid until it becomes part of the liquid: *Salt is soluble in water.*

**so·lu·tion** /səˈluʃən/ *noun*
**1** a way of stopping a problem: *We must find a solution to this problem.* | *If you cannot control your dog, the only solution is to get rid of it.*
**2** the right answer to a PUZZLE or a difficult question: *The solution to the puzzle is on page 14.*
**3** a liquid which has a substance mixed completely into it: *a solution of sugar and water*

**solve** /sɑlv/ *verb*
**1** to find a successful way of dealing with a

problem: *Mike thinks money will solve all his problems.*
**2** to find the correct answer to a PUZZLE or a difficult question: *Police are still trying to solve the mystery.*

**WORD FAMILY: solve**

**solve** *verb* | **solution** *noun*

**sol·vent** /ˈsɑlvənt/ *noun*
a chemical into which a substance can mix completely: *Some solvents are used for cleaning things because the dirt mixes into the chemical and comes off the surface.*

**some** /səm; *strong* sʌm/ *adjective, pronoun, adverb*
**1** an amount of something, or a number of people or things: *Would you like some ice cream?* | *If you need a pen, there are some in the drawer.*
**2** part of a group or thing: *Some people believe in ghosts.* | *Some of my friends can skate, and some can't.* | *I'd like some of that pie, please.*
**3** used instead of "a" when you do not know who someone is or what something is: *Some guy called while you were out.* | *He doesn't like her, for some reason.*

**some·bod·y** /ˈsʌmˌbɑdi/ *pronoun*
another word for SOMEONE

**some·day** /ˈsʌmdeɪ/ *adverb*
at some time in the future: *Someday, I'm going to have my own boat.*

**some·how** /ˈsʌmhaʊ/ *adverb*
**1** in some way, although you do not know how: *We'll get the money somehow.*
**2** for a reason which you cannot explain clearly: *Somehow it seemed like the right thing to do.*

**some·one** /ˈsʌmwʌn/ *pronoun*
a person: *Be careful! Someone could get hurt.* | *"Is she still going out with Dave?" "No, she's dating someone else."* **SYNONYM: somebody**

**GRAMMAR: someone, anyone**

In questions and in sentences with "not" in them, we usually use **anyone** and not **someone**: *Have you told anyone about this?* | *I didn't see anyone there.*

In other sentences, we use **someone**: *There's someone here to see you.*

**some·place** /ˈsʌmpleɪs/ *adverb* (*informal*)
another word for SOMEWHERE

**som·er·sault** /ˈsʌməˌsɔlt/ *noun*
a movement in which you roll or jump forward, so that your feet go over your head: *We learned how to do somersaults in gymnastics.*
[**ORIGIN:** 1500-1600 From the old French word *sombresaut*, from the Latin words *super* and *saltus*, which mean "over" and "jump."]

**some·thing** /ˈsʌmθɪŋ/ *pronoun*
**1** a thing: *There's something in my eye.* | *Let's talk about something else.* | *Do you want to get something to eat?*

**GRAMMAR: something, anything**

In questions and in sentences with "not" in them, we usually use **anything** and not **something**: *Did you see anything you liked?* | *I didn't have anything to eat.*

If you are offering someone some food, a drink, etc., it sounds more polite to use **something**: *Would you like something to eat?*

**2 or something** (*informal*) = said when you cannot remember or are not sure: *I'm not sure where she is. She might be out shopping or something.*
**3 something like 100/2,000, etc.** = around 100, 2,000, etc.: *He earns something like $80,000 a year.*
→ see Thesaurus box at **thing**

**some·time** /ˈsʌmtaɪm/ *adverb*
at some time in the past or future: *I'll call you sometime next week.*

**some·times** /ˈsʌmtaɪmz/ *adverb*
on some occasions, but not always: *Sometimes I don't go to bed until midnight.*

**THESAURUS: sometimes**

**occasionally** sometimes, but not often: *Let the soup cook for 30 minutes, stirring it occasionally.*

**(every) once in a while/every so often** sometimes, but not regularly: *Every once in a while, we visit my aunt and uncle in Long*

*Beach.* | *We go out for dinner every so often.*

**from time to time** sometimes, but not often or regularly: *I have problems from time to time with my computer, but I don't know why.*

**some·what** Ac /ˈsʌmwʌt/ *adverb*
slightly: *He seemed somewhat confused, so I explained the rules again.*

**some·where** /ˈsʌmwer/ *adverb*
**1** in or to some place: *I still have that book somewhere.* | *Let's go somewhere else.*

**GRAMMAR: somewhere, anywhere**

In questions and in sentences with "not" in them, we usually use **anywhere** and not **somewhere**: *I can't find my keys anywhere.* | *Have you seen my book anywhere?*

In other sentences, we use **somewhere**: *My keys must be in my room somewhere.*

**2 somewhere between 30 and 40/$50 and $80, etc.** = more than 30 but less than 40, etc.: *It'll take somewhere between three and four hours.*

**son** /sʌn/ *noun*
someone's male child: *Her son's name is David.* | *She has two daughters and one son.*

**so·na·ta** /səˈnɑtə/ *noun*
a piece of CLASSICAL MUSIC for one instrument, or for one instrument and a piano: *a violin sonata*

**song** /sɔŋ/ *noun*
a short piece of music with words: *We sang a few songs.*
→ see Thesaurus box at **music**

**ˈson-in-ˌlaw** *noun* (plural **sons-in-law**)
the husband of your daughter: *Their son-in-law, Jenny's husband, is a lawyer.*

**son·net** /ˈsɑnɪt/ *noun*
a poem that has 14 lines that RHYME with each other in a particular pattern: *Shakespeare wrote sonnets as well as plays.*

**soon** /sun/ *adverb*
**1** after a short time: *Dinner will be ready soon.* | *I met her soon after we moved here.* | *Get him to the hospital as soon as possible.*
**2 as soon as** = immediately after something has happened: *I tried to call you as soon as I heard the news.*
**3 sooner or later** = used for saying that something will definitely happen, but you are not sure when: *She's going to find out you lied to her sooner or later.*
**4 no sooner had ... than** = used for saying that something happened almost immediately after something else: *No sooner had I stepped in the shower than the phone rang.*

**soot** /sʊt/ *noun*
the black powder that is left on things by smoke: *After the fire, the walls of the kitchen were covered with soot.*

**soothe** /suð/ *verb*
**1** to make someone feel less worried, angry, or upset: *Lucy soothed the baby by rocking him in her arms.*
**2** to make something less painful: *The medicine soothed my sore throat.*
—**soothing** *adjective* making someone feel less worried, angry, or upset: *Soothing music was playing in the dentist's waiting room.*

**so·phis·ti·cat·ed** /səˈfɪstəˌkeɪtɪd/ *adjective*
**1** confident and knowing a lot about art, fashion, food, etc.: *She admired her rich, sophisticated cousin.*
**2** complicated, and needing a lot of intelligence and skill to make: *The airport now has sophisticated security equipment.*
—**sophistication** /səˌfɪstəˈkeɪʃən/ *noun* the quality of being sophisticated
[**ORIGIN:** From the Greek word *sophistes*, which means "someone who teaches people how to say things cleverly." First used in English with its modern meaning, 1800-1900.]

**soph·o·more** /ˈsɑfmɔr/ *noun*
a student in the second year of high school or college

**so·pra·no** /səˈprænoʊ/ *noun* (plural **sopranos**)
a female singer or boy singer with a very high voice

**sore¹** /sɔr/ *adjective*
painful: *I have a sore throat.*
—**soreness** *noun* the quality of feeling painful

**sore²** *noun*
a place where your skin is painful or infected:

*She was thin and weak, and her body was covered with sores.*

**sore·ly** /ˈsɔrli/ *adverb (formal)*
very much: *He will be sorely missed by everyone.*

**sor·row** /ˈsɑroʊ/ *noun*
**1** a very strong feeling of sadness: *He expressed his sorrow at her mother's death.* **ANTONYM: joy**
**2** an event or situation that makes you feel very unhappy: *He tried to forget his sorrows and go on with his life.* **ANTONYM: joy**

**sor·ry** /ˈsɑri/ *adjective*
**1 sorry/I'm sorry** = used for telling someone that you feel bad about doing something: *"You didn't put the milk back in the refrigerator." "Sorry." | I'm sorry that I lied to you. | I'm sorry to call you so late, but this is important.*
**2** disappointed or sad about something: *I'm sorry that you can't come to the party. | I was sorry to hear you're leaving.* **ANTONYM: glad**
**3 feel sorry for someone** = to feel sad for someone because he or she is in a bad situation: *He was lonely and I felt sorry for him.*
[**ORIGIN:** From the old English word *sarig*, from *sar*, which means "painful."]

**sort¹** /sɔrt/ *noun*
**1** a type of person or thing: *What sort of music do you like?* **SYNONYMS: type, kind**
**2 sort of** (*informal*) = used to say that something is partly true but not totally true: *I feel sort of responsible for him because he's my little brother. | "Do you like him?" "Sort of. He's okay."*
[**ORIGIN:** 1300-1400 From the Latin word *sors*, which means "chance, or what you get by luck."]

**sort²** *verb*
to put things in a particular order or into groups: *I've sorted the dirty clothes into different piles: white, red, and dark.*
**PHRASAL VERBS**
**sort something out**
to find an answer to a problem: *It is a complicated problem that will be difficult to sort out.*
**sort through something**
to look at a lot of things in order to find something: *She sorted through the photos to find one of the wedding.*

**SOS** *noun*
a signal or message that a ship or airplane is in danger and needs help: *The captain sent out an SOS just before the ship sank.*

**ˈso-so** *adjective, adverb (informal)*
neither very good nor very bad: *"How was the movie?" "So-so."*

**sought** [Ac] /sɔt/ *verb*
the past tense and past participle of SEEK

**soul** /soʊl/ *noun*
the part of you that is not your body but contains your most important thoughts and feelings: *When Grandpa died, his soul went to heaven.*

**sound¹** /saʊnd/ *noun*
**1** something that you hear: *I heard the sound of birds singing outside. | She didn't make a sound until she knew the men were gone.*
**2 from/by the sound of something** (*informal*) = judging by what you have heard or read about something: *From the sound of it, it's going to be a pretty big storm.*

**sound²** *verb*
**1** to seem good, bad, exciting, etc. because of what you have read or heard: *Surfing sure sounds like fun. | Mark sounds like a nice guy from what Marcy has told me about him.*
**2** to be pronounced in a particular way: *"Wait" and "weight" sound the same.*
**3** to produce a noise: *Church bells sounded in the distance.*
→ see Thesaurus box at **seem**

**sound³** *adverb*
**sound asleep** = completely asleep: *The children were sound asleep and didn't hear anything.*

**sound⁴** *adjective (formal)*
sensible and likely to produce good results: *She gave her daughters some sound advice about men.*

**sound·ly** /ˈsaʊndli/ *adverb*
**1 sleep soundly** = to sleep well and peacefully: *I slept soundly and woke up rested.*
**2** completely or severely: *We were soundly defeated 24–3 by the other team.*

**sound·proof** /ˈsaʊndpruf/ *adjective*
a soundproof room or building is one that

sound cannot pass into or out of: *The walls of the recording studio must be soundproof.*
—**soundproof** *verb* to make a room or building soundproof

**sound·track** /ˈsaʊndtræk/ *noun*
the music that is played during a movie: *I like a lot of the songs on the soundtrack to the movie.*

**soup** /sup/ *noun*
a hot liquid food that usually has pieces of meat or vegetables in it: *a bowl of chicken noodle soup*
[**ORIGIN:** 1600-1700 From the French word *soupe*, probably from the Latin word *suppa*, which means "piece of bread dipped in liquid."]

**sour** /saʊɚ/ *adjective*
**1** having a strong taste, like the taste of a LEMON: *The apple wasn't ripe and was very sour.*
**2** sour milk is not fresh and has a bad taste and smell: *How old is the milk? I think it's gone sour.*
→ see Thesaurus box at **taste**[1]

**source** Ac /sɔrs/ *noun*
**1** the place or thing that something comes from: *Sunlight is a clean source of energy.*
**2** a person, book, or place that you get information from: *The Internet is a great source of information.*
**3** the cause of something, especially a problem: *The mechanic found the source of the problem – the battery wasn't working.*
[**ORIGIN:** 1300-1400 From the old French word *sourse*, from *sourdre*, which means "to rise or come from something," from the Latin word *surgere*, meaning "to rise."]

**south**[1] /saʊθ/ *noun*
**1** the direction toward the bottom of a map of the world: *Which way is south?*
**2 the south** = the southern part of a country or area: *The south of France is very beautiful.*
**3 the South** = the southeastern part of the U.S.

**south**[2] *adjective*
**1** in, to, or facing the south: *They live in a town 30 miles south of Phoenix.* | *the south side of the island* | *South Dakota*
**2 south wind** = a wind that comes from the south

**south**[3] *adverb*
toward the south: *We left Dallas and flew south to San Antonio.*

**south·east**[1] /ˌsaʊθˈist/ *noun*
**1** the direction that is exactly between south and east → see picture at **north**
**2 the Southeast** = the southeast part of a country or area
—**southeastern** /saʊθˈistɚn/ *adjective* in or from the southeast

**southeast**[2] *adverb, adjective*
in, from, or toward the southeast: *We drove southeast till we reached the ocean.*

**south·ern** /ˈsʌðɚn/ *adjective*
in or from the south: *Los Angeles is in southern California.*

**south·ern·er** /ˈsʌðɚnɚ/ *noun*
someone who comes from the southern part of a country

**ˌSouth ˈPole** *noun*
**the South Pole** = the most southern point on the surface of the Earth → see picture at **globe**

**south·ward** /ˈsaʊθwɚd/ *adverb, adjective*
toward the south: *The ship sailed southward.*

**south·west**[1] /ˌsaʊθˈwest/ *noun*
**1** the direction that is exactly between south and west → see picture at **north**
**2 the Southwest** = the southwest part of a country or area
—**southwestern** /saʊθˈwestɚn/ *adjective* in or from the southwest

**southwest**[2] *adverb, adjective*
in, from, or toward the southwest: *We drove southwest.*

**sou·ve·nir** /ˌsuvəˈnɪr/ *noun*
an object that you buy in order to remember a special occasion or a place that you have visited: *I bought a small Statue of Liberty as a souvenir of New York.*
[**ORIGIN:** 1700-1800 From the French word for "to remember."]

**sov·e·reign**[1] /ˈsɑvərɪn/ *noun* (*formal*)
a king or queen

**sovereign**[2] *adjective*
a sovereign country is independent and governs itself

S

**sow**[1] /soʊ/ *verb* (**sowed**, **sown** /soʊn/ *or* **sowed**)
to put seeds into soil so that they will grow into plants: *He sowed the seeds in the field in the late spring.*

**sow**[2] /saʊ/ *noun*
a female pig

**soy·bean** /ˈsɔɪbin/ *noun*
a bean from which oil and foods are produced

**soy sauce** /ˈsɔɪ sɔs/ *noun*
a dark brown liquid made from soybeans, used in Chinese and Japanese cooking

**spa** /spɑ/ (*also* **health spa**) *noun*
a place that people go to in order to improve their health or beauty
[**ORIGIN:** 1600-1700 From Spa, a Belgian town with a spa. Originally, a spa was a place with a spring (=a place where water flows out of the ground), especially a warm one. People used to bathe in the springs for their health.]

**space**[1] /speɪs/ *noun*
**1** an area that is empty and available to be used: *Now that we have children, we need an apartment with more space.* | *There is space for some more things in my suitcase.* **SYNONYM: room**
**2** an empty area between two things: *The dog squeezed through the space between the fence posts.* | *parking spaces*
**3** the area beyond the Earth, where the stars and PLANETs are: *The astronauts spent several days in space.* **SYNONYM: outer space**
→ see Thesaurus box at **hole**

**space**[2] *verb*
to put objects somewhere with a particular amount of space between them: *Space the tomato plants two feet apart.*

**space·craft** /ˈspeɪs-kræft/ *noun* (plural **spacecraft**)
a vehicle that can travel in space

**space·ship** /ˈspeɪsˌʃɪp/ *noun*
a vehicle that can carry people through space

**ˈspace ˌshuttle** *noun*
a vehicle that can carry people into space and return to Earth more than once

**ˈspace ˌstation** *noun*
a structure in space where people can stay and do scientific work

**space·suit** /ˈspeɪsˌsut/ *noun*
a special piece of clothing covering the whole body that ASTRONAUTs wear in space

**spa·cious** /ˈspeɪʃəs/ *adjective* (*formal*)
a spacious room, apartment, car, etc. is large and has a lot of space inside: *They have three sofas in their spacious living room.*

**spade** /speɪd/ *noun*
**1** a tool used for digging that has a handle and a flat pointed metal end: *She got the spade and dug a hole to plant the tree in.*
**2** a card used in card games. The cards have a picture on them which looks like this (♠): *the king of spades*

**spa·ghet·ti** /spəˈgeti/ *noun*
long thin pieces of PASTA, that look like strings: *spaghetti with tomato sauce and meatballs*
[**ORIGIN:** 1800-1900 From Italian, from *spago*, which means "string."]

**spam** /spæm/ *noun*
email messages and advertisements that you receive but do not want to read: *His mailbox was full of spam.*
→ see Thesaurus box at **advertisement**

**span**[1] /spæn/ *noun*
**1** a length of time: *Many insects have a very short life span – they live only a day or two.*
**2** the distance from one side of something to the other: *The golden eagle has a wing span of seven feet.*

**span**[2] *verb* (**spanned**, **spanning**) (*formal*)
**1** to include all of a length of time: *Her acting career spanned 25 years.*
**2** to go from one side of something to the other: *The bridge spans the river.*

**Span·ish**[1] /ˈspænɪʃ/ *adjective*
from Spain: *Roberto is Spanish. He was born in Valencia.* | *the Spanish soccer team*

**Spanish**[2] *noun*
**1** the language spoken in Spain, Mexico, South America, etc.: *He went to Costa Rica to learn Spanish.*
**2** **the Spanish** = the people of Spain

**spank** /spæŋk/ *verb*
to hit a child on the BUTTOCKS with your open hand: *My parents only spanked me if I did something very bad.*

—**spanking** *noun* an action of spanking someone

**spare¹** /sper/ *adjective*
**1 spare key/clothes, etc.** = an extra key, set of clothes, etc. that you have available for a time when it might be needed: *We've given a spare key to our neighbor in case we lock ourselves out of the house.*
**2** not being used by anyone now, and available to be used: *If you stay, you can sleep in the spare bedroom.*
**3 spare time** = time when you are not working or at school: *She spent her spare time reading.*

**spare²** *verb*
**1** if you have something such as time or money to spare, there is some left in addition to what you have used or need: *We made it to the airport with 10 minutes to spare.*
**2** to be able to give or lend someone something, especially when this is difficult: *"Can you lend me some money?" "I guess I can spare a few dollars if it will help you out."*
**3** (*formal*) to not harm someone when you could hurt or kill them: *In the end, the king spared the prisoners' lives.*

**spark** /spɑrk/ *noun*
a very small piece of burning material that comes from a fire: *He threw a log onto the fire and sparks flew into the air.*

**spar·kle** /ˈspɑrkəl/ *verb*
to shine with small bright lights: *The snow sparkled in the sunlight.*
—**sparkle** *noun* the way something that sparkles looks
→ see Thesaurus box at **shine**

**spar·row** /ˈspæroʊ/ *noun*
a common small brown or gray bird

**sparse** /spɑrs/ *adjective*
existing only in small amounts: *There was only a sparse crowd for the game – 5,000 in a stadium that seats 20,000.*
—**sparsely** *adverb* with only a few things or people: *The room is sparsely furnished with just a desk and two chairs.*

**spat** /spæt/ *verb*
a past tense and past participle of SPIT

**speak** /spik/ *verb* (**spoke** /spoʊk/, **spoken** /ˈspoʊkən/)
**1** to talk to someone about something: *Hello, can I speak to Mr. Sherwood, please? | The principal would like to speak with you after school.*
**2** to use your voice to say words: *He spoke so softly I could hardly hear him.*
**3** to be able to talk in a particular language: *I cannot speak French.*
→ see Thesaurus box at **talk¹**
[**ORIGIN:** From the old English word *sprecan* or *specan.*]
**PHRASAL VERBS**
**speak out**
to say publicly what you think about something: *Many students spoke out against the school's new uniform rules.*
**speak up**
to speak more loudly: *Could you speak up please – I can't hear you.*

**speak·er** /ˈspikɚ/ *noun*
**1** someone who makes a speech: *The main speaker at the conference is Professor Sinclair.*
**2** the part of a radio, television, music system, etc. that the sound comes from → see picture on page **A20**

**spear** /spɪr/ *noun*
a pole with a sharp pointed blade at one end, used as a weapon: *He threw a spear at the deer and killed it.*

**spe·cial¹** /ˈspeʃəl/ *adjective*
**1** different from ordinary things, and better in some way: *I wanted to do something special for your birthday. | Dad only wears a suit on special occasions, like weddings.*
**2** very important and deserving your love and attention: *I invited a few special friends to dinner. | He bought me presents and made me feel special.*
[**ORIGIN:** 1100-1200 From the Latin word *specialis*, which means "particular," from *species*, which means "kind or sort."]

**special²** *noun*
**1** a price for something that is cheaper than usual: *The stores announced a special on a four-pound box of cookies.*
**2** a television show that is only on television once and is not part of a series: *The TV special will be shown on Thanksgiving Day.*

**ˌspecial efˈfects** *plural noun*
images or sounds that have been produced artificially for a movie

**spe·cial·ist** /ˈspeʃəlɪst/ *noun*
someone who knows a lot about a subject, or is skilled at doing something: *Dr. Diaz is a cancer specialist.*
→ see Thesaurus box at **doctor**

**spe·cial·ize** /ˈspeʃəˌlaɪz/ *verb*
to study, sell, or deal with only one particular thing, so that you know a lot about it: *The company specializes in building inexpensive homes.*

**spe·cial·ly** /ˈspeʃəli/ *adverb*
for one particular purpose: *Pilots have to be specially trained to fly the plane.*

S

**spe·cial·ty** /ˈspeʃəlti/ *noun* (plural **specialties**)
a subject that you know a lot about or an activity that you are skilled at doing: *The doctor's specialty is treating sports injuries.*

**spe·cies** /ˈspiʃiz/ *noun* (plural **species**)
a group of animals or plants of the same kind, that breed together to produce young animals or plants: *Three different species of deer live in the forest.*
→ see Thesaurus box at **type**[1]

**spe·cif·ic** Ac /spəˈsɪfɪk/ *adjective*
**1** detailed or exact: *He gave us specific directions to his apartment.*
**2** used when talking about one particular thing, person, time, etc.: *The game is intended for a specific age group: children between six and eight years old.*

**spe·cif·i·cally** Ac /spəˈsɪfɪkli/ *adverb*
**1** for a particular type of person or thing: *The book was written specifically for teenagers.*
**2** in a detailed or exact way: *I specifically asked you to call me when you got to Ramon's house.*

**spe·ci·fy** Ac /ˈspesəˌfaɪ/ *verb* (**specified**, **specifies**) (*formal*)
to state something in an exact and detailed way: *He didn't specify how much he had paid for the house.*

**spec·i·men** /ˈspesəmən/ *noun* (*formal*)
a small amount or piece of something that is taken so that it can be tested or examined: *The doctors need to take a blood specimen.*
**SYNONYM: sample**

**speck** /spek/ *noun*
a very small mark or piece of something: *I brushed some specks of dust off my jacket.*
→ see Thesaurus box at **piece**

**spec·ta·cle** /ˈspektəkəl/ *noun* (*formal*)
a very impressive or unusual thing that you see: *The tornado was an amazing spectacle.*

**spec·tac·u·lar** /spekˈtækyələ˞/ *adjective*
very impressive or exciting: *During the helicopter ride, we had a spectacular view of the Grand Canyon.*

**spec·ta·tor** /ˈspekˌteɪtə˞/ *noun*
someone who watches an event or game: *There were over 50,000 spectators at the football game.*
[**ORIGIN:** 1500-1600 From the Latin word *spectare*, which means "to watch."]

**spec·trum** /ˈspektrəm/ *noun* (plural **spectra** /ˈspektrə/)
**1** the set of different colors that light separates into when it passes through a clear block of glass: *The colors of the spectrum are red, orange, yellow, green, blue, indigo, and violet.*
**2** (*formal*) a wide range of opinions, things, or people: *I felt a wide spectrum of emotions, from happiness to sadness.*

**spec·u·late** /ˈspekyəˌleɪt/ *verb* (*formal*)
to think about what might have caused something or the effects something might have, without knowing all the facts: *The police speculate that the same person carried out all the robberies.*
—**speculation** /ˌspekyəˈleɪʃən/ *noun* (*formal*) the act of speculating about something

**sped** /sped/ *verb*
a past tense and past participle of SPEED

**speech** /spitʃ/ *noun*
**1** a formal talk about a particular subject that someone gives to a group of people: *The class president gave a speech to the whole school.*
**2** the act of speaking words: *A young baby isn't capable of speech.*

**speech·less** /ˈspitʃləs/ *adjective*
unable to speak because you are too

surprised: *It was such a shock to see him that I was speechless for a moment.*

**speed¹** /spid/ *noun*
**1** how fast something moves: *The car was moving at a speed of 60 miles an hour.*
**2** how quickly something happens: *Children learn at different speeds.* | *The city's population is growing at great speed.*
**3 five-speed/ten-speed, etc.** = used to talk about the number of GEARs a car, truck, or bicycle has: *a ten-speed bike*
[**ORIGIN:** From the old English word *sped*, which means "success, or quickness."]

**speed²** *verb* (**sped** /sped/ *or* **speeded**)
**1** to move or happen quickly: *A police car sped past on its way to the accident.*
**2 be speeding** = to be driving faster than the legal limit: *The police officer said she was speeding and gave her a ticket.*
**PHRASAL VERB**
**speed up**
to move or happen faster: *The train began to speed up as we left the station.*

**speed·boat** /ˈspidboʊt/ *noun*
a small boat with a powerful engine that can go very fast

**speed·ing** /ˈspidɪŋ/ *noun*
the crime of driving faster than you are legally allowed to drive: *The police stopped him for speeding because he was going 50 mph in a 35 mph zone.*

**ˈspeed ˌlimit** *noun*
the fastest speed that you are allowed to drive on a particular road: *The speed limit is 40 miles per hour.*

**speed·om·e·ter** /spɪˈdɑmətɚ/ *noun*
an instrument in a vehicle that shows the driver how fast it is going → see picture on page **A28**

**speed·y** /ˈspidi/ *adjective* (**speedier**, **speediest**)
happening quickly or done without any delay: *I hope you have a speedy recovery from your illness.*

**spell¹** /spel/ *verb*
**1** to say or write the letters of a word in the correct order: *"How do you spell your name?" "C-L-A-I-R-E."*
**2** if letters spell a word, they make that word: *C-A-T spells "cat."*

**spell²** *noun*
**1** words or actions that make something magic happen: *In the story, the witch casts a spell on the girl, and turns her into an old woman.*
**2** a period of something, for example a type of weather: *The rain was welcome after the long dry spell.* | *The team went through a spell when they lost five games in a row.*
[**ORIGIN:** From the old English word for "speech or story."]

**spell·ing** /ˈspelɪŋ/ *noun*
**1** the ability to spell words correctly: *I'm not very good at spelling.*
**2** the way that a word is spelled: *What is the correct spelling of the word "Mississippi"?*

S

**spend** /spend/ *verb* (**spent** /spent/)
**1** to use your money to buy or pay for something: *She spends all her money on clothes.*
**2** to do something or stay somewhere for a period of time: *We spent the day relaxing at the beach.*
[**ORIGIN:** 1100-1200 From the Latin word *expendere*, which means "to weigh out money, or pay."]

**spent** /spent/ *verb*
the past tense and past participle of SPEND

**sperm** /spɚm/ *noun* (plural **sperm**)
a male cell that can join with a female egg, so that a new baby or animal starts developing

**sphere** [Ac] /sfɪr/ *noun*
something that has the shape of a ball: *The Earth is a sphere.*
—**spherical** /ˈsfɪrɪkəl/ *adjective* round, like a ball: *a spherical object*
[**ORIGIN:** 1200-1300 From the Greek word *sphaira*, which means "ball."]

**spice** /spaɪs/ *noun*
a seed or powder from plants that you put into food to give it a special taste: *Indian food uses spices such as curry or chili powder.*
—**spicy** *adjective* food that is spicy contains a lot of spices: *The Mexican food was hot and spicy.*

**spi·der** /ˈspaɪdɚ/ *noun*
a small creature with eight legs. Most spiders make WEBs to catch insects.
[**ORIGIN:** From the old English word *spithra*, from

*spinnan*, which means "to spin." Spiders spin webs.]

**spied** /spaɪd/ *verb*
the past tense and past participle of SPY

**spike** /spaɪk/ *noun*
a thin piece of metal with a sharp point: *The wall has spikes on the top to stop people from climbing over.*

**spill** /spɪl/ *verb*
if you spill a liquid, it flows over the edge of a container by accident: *I spilled coffee on my shirt.*
—**spill** *noun* an occasion when a liquid accidentally flows out of something: *The oil spill caused pollution along the coast.*
[ORIGIN: From the old English word *spillan*, which means "to kill or destroy."]

S

**spin** /spɪn/ *verb* (**spun** /spʌn/, **spinning**)
**1** to turn around and around very quickly: *The Earth spins as it moves around the Sun.* | *The wheels of the car kept spinning around in the snow without getting any grip.*
**2** if a spider spins a WEB, it makes it with thread from its body: *Spiders spin webs to catch insects.*
**3** to make cotton or wool into thread by twisting it

**spin·ach** /ˈspɪnɪtʃ/ *noun*
a vegetable with large dark green leaves → see picture on page **A12**

**ˈspinal cord** *noun*
the long string of nerves that goes from your brain down your back, through your spine

**spine** /spaɪn/ *noun*
**1** the long row of bones down the center of your back → see picture on page **A2**
**2** a stiff sharp point on an animal or plant: *cactus spines*
—**spinal** *adjective* relating to your spine: *a spinal injury*

**spi·ral** /ˈspaɪrəl/ *noun*
a curve that goes around a central point many times, for example on a screw
—**spiral** *adjective* in the shape of a spiral: *a spiral staircase*

**spir·it** /ˈspɪrɪt/ *noun*
**1** a person's attitudes, thoughts, and feelings: *My grandma is 85, but she is still young in spirit.*
**2** a creature such as a GHOST or an ANGEL that does not have a physical body: *They were worried that there was some kind of evil spirit in the house.*
**3** courage and determination: *The team showed a lot of spirit today, even when they were losing.*
**4** **spirits** = how happy or sad you are feeling: *The good news lifted our spirits.*

**spir·it·u·al** /ˈspɪrɪtʃuəl/ *adjective*
**1** relating to religion: *The priest at her church gives her spiritual guidance.*
**2** relating to your attitudes, thoughts, and feelings, rather than to your body: *Yoga is not only good for your body, it's good for your spiritual health.*

**spit**[1] /spɪt/ *verb* (**spit** *or* **spat** /spæt/, **spitting**)
to force a small amount of liquid or food from your mouth: *He tasted the drink and immediately spat it out.*

**spit**[2] *noun*
**1** the liquid that you produce naturally in your mouth **SYNONYM: saliva**
**2** a long thin stick that you put through meat so you can turn the meat while it is cooking: *They roasted a pig on a spit.*

**spite** /spaɪt/ *noun*
**1** **in spite of something** = even though something is true or happens: *We had a really good time in spite of the rain.* **SYNONYM: despite**
**2** a feeling of wanting to upset or hurt someone: *He said some very mean things out of spite.*

**spite·ful** /ˈspaɪtfəl/ *adjective*
deliberately unkind to someone in order to upset or hurt him or her: *Cinderella's stepsisters were spiteful and made sure she got the hardest jobs.*

**splash**[1] /splæʃ/ *verb*
**1** if a liquid splashes, it falls noisily on a surface and then goes in different directions: *The water splashed against the rocks.*
**2** to make water move through the air by hitting it or jumping in it: *The children were splashing around in the pool.*

**splash**[2] *noun*
the sound or movement of something hitting

water: *Jerry jumped into the water with a loud splash.* → see picture on page **A22**

**splen·did** /ˈsplendɪd/ *adjective* (*formal*)
excellent or impressive: *There's a splendid view from the top of the building.*
[**ORIGIN:** 1600-1700 From the Latin word *splendere*, which means "to shine."]

**splen·dor** /ˈsplendɚ/ *noun* (*formal*)
impressive beauty: *We were amazed by the splendor of the mountains.*

**splin·ter** /ˈsplɪntɚ/ *noun*
a very small sharp piece of wood, glass, or metal that has broken off a larger piece: *Help me get this splinter out of my finger.*

**split[1]** /splɪt/ *verb* (**split**, **splitting**)
**1** (*also* **split up**) to divide something into groups or parts: *The teacher split the class into two groups.* | *We decided to split the money between us.*
**2** to tear or break apart: *The wood had split in two.*
**PHRASAL VERB**
**split up**
if people split up, they end their marriage or relationship: *Her parents split up when she was three.*

**split[2]** *noun*
**1** a situation in which people disagree and separate into two groups: *The disagreements led to a split in the organization.*
**2** a cut or tear in something: *There was a split in the seat of his pants.*

**spoil** /spɔɪl/ *verb*
**1** to make something less good, attractive, or enjoyable: *I don't want to spoil your enjoyment of the movie, so I won't tell you how it ends.*
**2** to let a child have or do everything he or she wants, which has a bad effect on the child's behavior: *Some parents spoil their kids by buying them too many presents.*
—**spoiled** *adjective* behaving badly because of having been spoiled by your parents: *a spoiled little rich kid*
[**ORIGIN:** 1200-1300 From the Latin word *spoliare*, which means "to rob a place or person."]

**spoke[1]** /spoʊk/ *verb*
the past tense of SPEAK

**spoke[2]** *noun*
one of the thin pieces of metal or wood that connect the outer edge of a wheel to the center → see picture at **bicycle**

**spok·en** /ˈspoʊkən/ *verb*
the past participle of SPEAK

**spokes·per·son** /ˈspoʊksˌpɚsən/ *noun*
someone whose job is to speak to REPORTERs as the representative for a group or organization: *A company spokesperson said that the drug was completely safe.*
—**spokesman** /ˈspoʊksmən/ *noun* a man who speaks for a group or organization
—**spokeswoman** /ˈspoʊksˌwʊmən/ *noun* a woman who speaks for a group or organization

**sponge** /spʌndʒ/ *noun*
**1** an object that is used for washing something, made from a soft substance that is full of small holes: *I used a sponge to wipe the table.*
**2** a sea animal with a soft body

**spon·sor** /ˈspɑnsɚ/ *noun*
a person or company that provides money to help pay for a television show, sports team, sports event, etc.: *The team is looking for a new sponsor.*
—**sponsor** *verb* to provide money to help pay for something: *The show is sponsored by a sportswear company.*
[**ORIGIN:** 1600-1700 From the Latin word *spondere*, which means "to promise." A sponsor was originally someone who promised to help or give money if necessary.]

**spon·ta·ne·ous** /spɑnˈteɪniəs/ *adjective*
if something is spontaneous, people suddenly decide to do it, and it is not planned: *It was a spontaneous decision – we hadn't discussed it at all.*
—**spontaneously** *adverb* suddenly, without planning

**spook·y** /ˈspuki/ *adjective* (*informal*)
strange and frightening: *The kids were afraid to go near the spooky old house.*

**spool** /spul/ *noun*
an object shaped like a small wheel that you wind wire, thread, film, etc. around: *a spool of thread*

**spoon** /spun/ *noun*
a tool used for eating food such as soup or ice cream, that is made of a small bowl on the end of a handle: *I used a spoon to get the*

*honey out of the jar.* → see picture on page A9

[**ORIGIN:** From the old English word *spon*, which means "piece of wood split off."]

**spoon·ful** /ˈspunfʊl/ *noun*
the amount that a spoon can hold: *a spoonful of sugar*

**sport** /spɔrt/ *noun*
a physical activity in which people compete against each other: *Soccer and basketball are team sports.*
→ see Thesaurus box at **game**

[**ORIGIN:** 1300-1400 From the old English word *disport*, which means "to have fun."]

ˈ**sports car** *noun*
a low fast car

ˈ**sports ˌjacket** (*also* ˈ**sports coat**) *noun*
a man's comfortable jacket, worn on informal occasions

**sports·man·ship** /ˈspɔrtsmənˌʃɪp/ *noun*
behavior that is fair and polite in a sport or game: *It's good sportsmanship to shake hands with the opposing team after a game.*

**spot**[1] /spɑt/ *noun*
**1** a place: *We found a good spot for the picnic near the river.*
**2** a small round area of color, that is a different color from the area around it: *a white dog with black spots*
**3** a small mark on something: *There are spots of paint on the floor.*
→ see Thesaurus box at **mark**[2], **place**[1]

**spot**[2] *verb* (**spotted**, **spotting**)
to notice or recognize someone or something: *Someone spotted the criminals at Los Angeles airport.*
→ see Thesaurus box at **see**

**spot·less** /ˈspɑtləs/ *adjective*
completely clean: *Her apartment is spotless – she must spend all her time cleaning.*

**spot·light** /ˈspɑtlaɪt/ *noun*
**1** a powerful light that is pointed at someone or something, for example on the stage in a theater: *He stood alone in the spotlight, in the middle of the stage.*
**2 the spotlight** = the attention someone or something receives in the newspapers or on television: *The spotlight will be on the two quarterbacks as the game approaches.*

**spot·ted** /ˈspɑtɪd/ *adjective*
covered in round spots of color: *a spotted dog*

**spot·ty** /ˈspɑti/ *adjective*
good in some parts, but bad in others: *The team's record is spotty this season, with five wins and four losses.*

**spouse** /spaʊs/ *noun* (*formal*)
a husband or wife: *Employees may bring their spouses to the party.*

[**ORIGIN:** 1100-1200 From the old French word *espous(e)*, from the Latin word *sponsus*, which means "promised (in marriage)," from *spondere*, meaning "to promise."]

**spout** /spaʊt/ *noun*
a small pipe on the side of a container, through which you pour liquid out: *the spout of a coffee pot*

**sprain** /spreɪn/ *verb*
to injure a joint in your body by suddenly twisting it: *He fell down and sprained his ankle.*
—**sprain** *noun* an injury you get in a joint by suddenly twisting it
→ see Thesaurus box at **injury**, **hurt**[1]

**sprang** /spræŋ/ *verb*
a past tense of SPRING

**sprawl** /sprɔl/ (*also* **sprawl out**) *verb*
to lie or sit with your arms or legs stretched out: *They sprawled out on the sofa in front of the TV.*

**spray**[1] /spreɪ/ *verb*
to make a liquid come out of something in very small drops: *She sprayed some perfume on her wrist.*

**spray**[2] *noun*
liquid that comes out of a container in a stream of very small drops: *She uses hair spray to keep her hair in place.*

**spread** /spred/ *verb* (**spread**)
**1** (*also* **spread out**) to open something that is folded, so that it covers a bigger area: *She spread the map out on the floor.* | *The bird spread its wings.*
**2** if something such as a disease spreads, it starts affecting more people: *Scientists are worried that the disease could spread.*
**3** if news spreads, more people find out about it: *The news spread quickly and soon everyone was talking about it.*

**4** to put a soft substance evenly over a surface: *She spread some butter on the bread.* → see picture on page **A15**

**PHRASAL VERB**

**spread out**

if people spread out, they move apart from each other: *OK, everyone, spread out so you all have enough space.*

**spread·sheet** /ˈspredʃit/ *noun*
numbers or information arranged in rows and COLUMNs, usually made using a computer: *The spreadsheet shows the grades of all the students throughout the year.* → see picture on page **A20**

**spree** /spri/ *noun*
a short period in which someone spends a lot of money or drinks a lot of alcohol: *She went on a shopping spree and spent $500.*

**spring¹** /sprɪŋ/ *noun*
**1** the season between winter and summer, when leaves and flowers begin to grow: *The birds make their nests in the spring.*
**2** a strong piece of metal that is twisted around in a circle several times. A spring returns to its original shape after it has been pressed down or pulled apart: *The springs in the old mattress poked me in the back.*
**3** a place where water comes up naturally from the ground: *There are hot springs in Yellowstone National Park.*

**spring²** *verb* (**sprang** /spræŋ/ *or* **sprung** /sprʌŋ/, **sprung**)
**1** to jump or move suddenly and quickly in a particular direction: *He sprang out of bed and ran down the stairs.*
**2** **spring a leak** = if a boat or a container springs a leak, it begins to let liquid in or out through a crack or hole
→ see Thesaurus box at **jump¹**

**PHRASAL VERB**

**spring up**

to suddenly appear or start to exist: *New buildings are springing up everywhere.*

**spring·time** /ˈsprɪŋtaɪm/ *noun*
the time of year when it is spring

**sprin·kle¹** /ˈsprɪŋkəl/ *verb*
**1** to scatter small drops of liquid or small pieces of something onto something else: *We sprinkled cheese on the pizza.* → see picture on page **A15**
**2** if it is sprinkling, it is raining lightly

**sprinkle²** *noun*
**1** a few small pieces or drops of something, especially food: *The cookies have a sprinkle of sugar on them.*
**2** a short period of light rain

**sprin·kler** /ˈsprɪŋklɚ/ *noun*
a piece of equipment used for scattering water on grass

**sprint¹** /sprɪnt/ *noun*
a race in which you run fast for a short distance
—**sprinter** *noun* someone who takes part in a sprint

**sprint²** *verb*
to run quickly for a short distance: *She sprinted up the stairs.*
→ see Thesaurus box at **run¹**

S

**sprout¹** /spraʊt/ *verb*
**1** to start to grow: *The seeds are already sprouting.*
**2** (*also* **sprout up**) to appear suddenly in large numbers: *Lots of new businesses have sprouted up in the area.*

**sprout²** *noun*
a new growth on a plant: *bean sprouts*

**spruce** /sprus/ *noun*
a tree with short leaves shaped like needles

**sprung** /sprʌŋ/ *verb*
a past tense and the past participle of SPRING

**spun** /spʌn/ *verb*
the past tense and past participle of SPIN

**sput·ter** /ˈspʌtɚ/ *verb*
if an engine sputters, it makes sounds like very small explosions because it is not working correctly: *The old truck sputtered as it went up the hill.*

**spy¹** /spaɪ/ *noun* (plural **spies**)
someone who is paid to find out secret information about another country or group: *The spy was passing secret military plans to the enemies of the U.S.*

**spy²** *verb* (**spied**, **spies**)
**1** to secretly watch people or collect information about them: *I think that someone is spying on us through that window.*
**2** to see someone or something: *I spied my brother in the crowd.*

**squad** /skwɑd/ *noun*
**1** a group of police officers or soldiers who do a special job: *The police bomb squad removed the strange package.*
**2** the group of people that make up a sports team: *There are 22 players in the national soccer squad.*

**squan·der** /ˈskwɑndɚ/ *verb*
to carelessly waste money, time, or an opportunity: *He squandered all his money on fancy clothes.*

**square**[1] /skwer/ *adjective*
**1** having four equal straight sides and four RIGHT ANGLEs (=angles of 90 degrees): *Fold a square piece of paper in half.*
**2 a square inch/mile, etc.** = the area of a square with sides an inch, a mile, etc. long. You multiply the length of the area by its width to find the total: *The room measured 10 feet by 20 feet, so its area was 200 square feet.*
[**ORIGIN:** 1200-1300 From the old French word *esquarre*, from the Latin word *exquadrare*, which means "to make square," from *quadr-*, meaning "four."]

**square**[2] *noun*
**1** a shape with four equal straight sides and four RIGHT ANGLEs (=angles of 90 degrees) → see picture at **shape**
**2** an open area with buildings around it in the middle of a town: *Thousands of people marched to the city's main square.*
**3** the result of multiplying a number by itself: *The square of 5 is 25.*

**square**[3] *verb*
to multiply a number by itself: *10 squared is 100.*

ˈ**square root** *noun*
the square root of a number is the number which, when multiplied by itself, equals that number: *5 is the square root of 25.*

**squash**[1] /skwɑʃ/ *verb*
to press something so that it becomes flatter, often damaging it: *Someone sat on the box and squashed all the chocolates.*
→ see Thesaurus box at **press**[1]

**squash**[2] *noun*
a type of large vegetable with solid flesh and a hard skin → see picture on page **A12**
[**ORIGIN:** 1600-1700 From the Narragansett word *askutasquash*, which means "the green things that can be eaten raw." Narragansett is a Native American language.]

**squat** /skwɑt/ (*also* **squat down**) *verb* (**squatted**, **squatting**)
to bend your knees so that your body is near the ground, supported on the backs of your legs: *He squatted down next to the car and checked the tire.* → see picture on page **A5**

**squawk** /skwɔk/ *verb*
if a bird squawks, it makes a loud angry noise
—**squawk** *noun* a loud angry noise made by a bird

**squeak**[1] /skwik/ *verb*
to make a short high sound: *The door squeaks when I open it.*

**squeak**[2] *noun*
a short high sound: *The mouse gave a squeak.* → see picture on page **A22**
—**squeaky** *adjective* making short high sounds: *She had a funny squeaky voice.*

**squeal** /skwil/ *verb*
to make a long loud high sound or cry: *The children squealed with excitement when they saw their presents.*
—**squeal** *noun* a long loud high sound or cry: *a squeal of delight*

**squeeze** /skwiz/ *verb*
**1** to press something firmly together with your fingers or hands: *He squeezed her hand and said that he was glad to meet her.* | *Squeeze some lemon juice onto the salad.* → see picture on page **A15**
**2** to go into or through a small space: *She squeezed past the other people.*
→ see Thesaurus box at **press**[1]
[**ORIGIN:** 1500-1600 From an earlier form *quease*, from the old English word *cwysan*, which means "to press or squeeze."]

**squid** /skwɪd/ *noun* (plural **squid** *or* **squids**)
a sea animal with a long soft body and ten soft arms, or the meat from this creature: *fried squid*

**squint** /skwɪnt/ *verb*
to look at something with your eyes partly closed, in order to see better or because the light is very bright: *He squinted at the tiny writing on the bottle.*

**squirm** /skwɚm/ *verb*
**1** to feel embarrassed or uncomfortable

because of something that you see or hear: *I squirmed when the teacher read out my terrible poem.*
**2** to twist your body around because you are uncomfortable: *The baby was crying and squirming in my arms and I almost dropped her.*

**squir·rel** /ˈskwɚəl/ *noun*
a small animal with a long furry tail that lives in trees and eats nuts
[**ORIGIN:** 1300-1400 From the old French word *esquirel*, from the Greek word *skiouros*. This comes from the words *skia* and *oura*, which mean "shadow" and "tail."]

**squirt** /skwɚt/ *verb*
if liquid squirts out, it comes out of a narrow hole very quickly: *The ketchup squirted out of the bottle.* | *Tommy squirted water at me with the hose.*

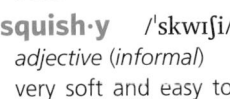

**squish·y** /ˈskwɪʃi/ *adjective* (*informal*)
very soft and easy to press: *The peaches were brown and very squishy.*

**Sr.**
the written abbreviation of **Senior**

**St.**
**1** the written abbreviation of **street**, used when you are writing someone's address: *35 Broad St.*
**2** the written abbreviation of **Saint**: *St. Patrick*

**stab**[1] /stæb/ *verb* (**stabbed**, **stabbing**)
to push a sharp object into someone or something: *Someone tried to stab him with a knife.*

**stab**[2] *noun*
**1** (*informal*) an attempt to do something difficult or new: *I had never cooked before, but I made a good stab at it.*
**2** a sudden strong and unpleasant feeling: *He felt a stab of pain as the nurse pushed the needle into his arm.*

**sta·bi·lize** Ac /ˈsteɪbəˌlaɪz/ *verb*
to become steady and stop changing: *The doctors say that his condition has stabilized and he is no longer in danger.*

**sta·ble**[1] Ac /ˈsteɪbəl/ *adjective*
**1** staying in the same position and not moving: *Be careful – the ladder doesn't look very stable.* **ANTONYM: unstable**
**2** staying the same, with no big changes or problems: *He has a stable marriage and two cute children.* **ANTONYM: unstable**
**3** calm, reasonable, and not easy to upset: *He was a stable person, and she knew she could rely on him.* **ANTONYM: unstable**
—**stability** /stəˈbɪləti/ *noun* conditions in which there is no sudden change
[**ORIGIN:** 1200-1300 From the Latin word *stabilis*, from *stare*, which means "to stand." If something is stable, it stands in the same position without moving.]



**stable**[2] Ac *noun*
a building where horses are kept: *She led the horses back into the stable.*

**stack**[1] /stæk/ *noun*
a group of things that have been placed on top of each other: *There was a stack of magazines on the table.* **SYNONYM: pile**

**stack**[2] (*also* **stack up**) *verb*
to put things into a neat pile: *Can you help me stack the chairs?*

**sta·di·um** /ˈsteɪdiəm/ *noun* (plural **stadiums** or **stadia** /ˈsteɪdiə/)
a building where people watch sports events or concerts, with rows of seats around a field: *The football stadium can hold 55,000 people.*
[**ORIGIN:** 1300-1400 From Latin, from the Greek word *stadion*, which means "a length of about 600 feet." This word was also used to mean "racetrack," because the track at Olympia in Greece was one stadion long.]

**staff**[1] /stæf/ *noun*
**1** the people who work for an organization: *There was a meeting for all the teaching staff at the school.*
**2** a big stick that you carry to help you walk, used mainly in the past: *The shepherd put down his staff and rested on a rock.*
**3** the set of five lines that music is written on

**staff**[2] *verb*
to provide an organization or place with workers: *The school was staffed entirely by female teachers.*

**stage** /steɪdʒ/ *noun*
**1** a time in the development of something: *If the disease is still in its early stages, it will be easier to treat.*
**2** the raised floor in a theater, where people perform: *The crowd cheered when the band came on stage.*
[ORIGIN: 1200-1300 From the old French word *estage*, probably from a Latin word *staticum*, meaning "place to stand," from *stare*, which means "to stand."]

**stage·coach** /ˈsteɪdʒkoʊtʃ/ *noun*
a covered vehicle pulled by horses. A stage-coach carried passengers and mail over long distances in the past.

**stag·ger** /ˈstægɚ/ *verb*
to walk or move in an unsteady way, almost falling over: *He staggered home from the bar.*

**stag·nant** /ˈstægnənt/ *adjective*
stagnant water does not move and often smells bad: *The water in the pond is stagnant and not fit to drink.*

**stain**[1] /steɪn/ *noun*
**1** a mark that is difficult to remove: *The tablecloth was covered with coffee stains.*
**2** a liquid that you use to change the color of wood: *He used a brown stain to make the wood darker.*
→ see Thesaurus box at **mark**[2]

**stain**[2] *verb*
to make a mark on something, that is difficult to remove: *The red wine had stained the carpet.*

**stainless steel** /ˈsteɪnlɪsˌstil/ *noun*
a type of steel that does not RUST: *a stainless steel sink*

**stair·case** /ˈsterkeɪs/ *noun*
a set of stairs inside a building, and the structure that supports it

**stairs** /sterz/ *plural noun*
a set of steps built for going from one level of a building to another: *He ran up the stairs to the second floor.*

**stair·way** /ˈsterweɪ/ *noun*
a set of stairs and the structure that supports it, either inside or outside a building

**stake**[1] /steɪk/ *noun*
**1** a thin pointed piece of wood or metal that you push into the ground, for example to hold a rope or support a fence: *She put stakes in the vegetable garden to mark where she'd planted different seeds.*
**2 be at stake** = if something important is at stake, you could lose it if an action is not successful: *We have to raise the money – the future of the school is at stake.*
**3 have a stake in something** = if you have a stake in a business or plan, you have a share in it and you want it to be successful: *Everyone in the company has a stake in the success of the project.*

**stake**[2] *verb*
**1** to risk money on the result of a race, game, or competition: *He staked all his money on the horse race.*
**2** to risk losing something valuable or important, if a plan or action is not successful: *The governor has staked his reputation on rebuilding the state's economy.*
**3 stake a claim** = to say publicly that you think you have a right to have or own something: *Both countries staked a claim to the islands.*

**stale** /steɪl/ *adjective*
no longer fresh: *This bread is old and stale.*
ANTONYM: **fresh**
→ see Thesaurus box at **old**

**stale·mate** /ˈsteɪlmeɪt/ *noun*
**1** a situation in which progress toward achieving something stops because the people involved cannot agree: *Talks between the union and the company have reached a stalemate, with neither side willing to compromise.*
**2** a position in CHESS in which neither player can win, so the game ends

**stalk**[1] /stɔk/ *noun*
the long narrow part of a plant, that leaves or flowers grow on: *celery stalks*

**stalk**[2] *verb*
to follow a person or animal secretly or quietly in order to kill or harm him, her, or it: *He stalked the actor for two years before he was finally arrested.* | *The tiger slowly stalked its prey.*

**stall**[1] /stɔl/ *noun*
**1** a table or a small store with an open front, especially outdoors, where goods are sold: *At the fair there were lots of stalls selling art.*

**2** a small enclosed area in a room, for washing or using the toilet: *a shower stall*
**3** an enclosed area in a building for an animal such as a horse

**stall²** *verb*
**1** if a car engine stalls, it suddenly stops working: *The car kept stalling so we had to get it fixed.*
**2** to deliberately delay doing something, in order to give yourself more time: *Quit stalling and answer my question!*

**stal·lion** /ˈstæljən/ *noun*
a fully grown male horse

**stam·i·na** /ˈstæmənə/ *noun*
physical or mental strength that lets you continue doing something for a long time without getting tired: *You need a lot of stamina to run 20 miles.*

**stam·mer** /ˈstæmɚ/ *verb*
to speak or say something with a lot of pauses and repeated sounds: *"I, uh, need, uh, I need more time," he stammered.*
—**stammer** *noun* the condition of stammering: *I used to get nervous about talking because I had a stammer.*

**stamp¹** /stæmp/ *noun*
**1** a small piece of paper that you stick onto an envelope or package to show you have paid to mail it: *a 37-cent stamp*
**2** an official mark, or a special tool for making this mark: *They put a stamp in my passport when I crossed the border.*

**stamp²** *verb*
**1** to put your foot down very hard: *The little boy screamed and stamped his feet.*
**2** to put an official mark on a piece of paper using a special tool: *The official stamped her passport.*
PHRASAL VERB
**stamp something out**
to prevent something bad from continuing: *The police are trying to stamp out this new sort of crime.*

**stam·pede** /stæmˈpid/ *noun*
an occasion when a lot of people or animals suddenly start running together: *When the fire started, there was a stampede toward the exit of the building.*
—**stampede** *verb* if a lot of people or animals stampede, they suddenly start running together
[**ORIGIN:** 1800-1900 From the American Spanish word *estampida*, from *estampar*, which means "to stamp."]

**stand¹** /stænd/ *verb* (**stood** /stʊd/)
**1** to be on your feet, in an upright position: *We stood outside the theater and waited to go in.*
**2** (*also* **stand up**) to move so that you are on your feet, after you have been sitting or lying down: *At the end of his speech, everyone stood and clapped.*
**3** to be in a place: *The house stood on top of a hill.*
**4** if you cannot stand something painful or unpleasant, you are not able to deal with it: *He couldn't stand the pain anymore.* SYNONYMS: **bear**, **tolerate**
**5** **can't stand someone or something** = to dislike someone or something very much: *I can't stand the smell of cigarette smoke.*
**6** **stand on your head/hands** = to support yourself on your head or hands in an upright position, with your feet in the air
**7** **stand on your own two feet** (*informal*) = to be independent and not need help from other people: *As kids get older, they need to learn to stand on their own two feet.*
**8** **know where you stand** = to know what people really think about you: *You always know where you stand with Joe – he tells you what he thinks.*
**9** **know where someone stands** = to know what someone's opinion about something is: *Voters need to know where each candidate stands on important issues.*
PHRASAL VERBS
**stand back**
to move back away from someone or something: *Stand back so that the doctor can get through.*
**stand by**
**1** **stand by something** = to continue to believe that something you said or did was right: *I stand by what I said earlier.*
**2** **stand by someone** = to stay loyal to someone and support him or her in a difficult situation: *His friends all stood by him when he was in prison.*
**3** to be waiting, ready to do something:

*Firefighters are standing by in case the fire spreads.*

**stand for something**
**1** to mean something, or be a short way of writing something: *CD stands for "compact disc."*
**2** to support an idea, principle, etc.: *Martin Luther King stood for justice and equality.*

**stand up**
**1** to move so that you are on your feet, after you have been sitting or lying down: *He stood up and walked toward the door.*
**2** if something stands up, it is shown to be true: *His argument doesn't stand up if you look at it carefully.*
**3** **stand someone up** = to not meet someone when you have promised to meet him or her: *My date stood me up last night.*

**stand up for someone or something**
to defend someone or something that is being attacked or criticized: *Don't be afraid to stand up for what you believe in.*

**stand up to someone**
to be brave and refuse to accept criticism or do what someone wants: *He stood up to the older boys and told them he wouldn't help them steal.*

**stand²** *noun*
**1** an object that you put something on: *The cello player put a sheet of music on the music stand.*
**2** a table or CART used for selling things to people: *a hotdog stand*
**3** if you take a stand, you show firmly and publicly what your opinion is about something: *Many people took a stand against the war by marching in the streets.*
**4** **the stands** = the seats where people sit to watch a sports game

**stan·dard¹** /ˈstændɚd/ *noun*
**1** a level that measures how good something is or how good it should be: *The standard of the students' work was very high.*
**2** **by ... standards** = compared to the level that you usually expect: *The house was small by American standards.*

**standard²** *adjective*
normal or usual: *A CD-ROM drive is a standard feature on all computers.*
→ see Thesaurus box at **normal**

**stan·dard·ize** /ˈstændɚˌdaɪz/ *verb*
to make all the things of one type be the same as each other: *The tests of all schools in the area have been standardized.*

**ˌstandard of ˈliving** *noun* (plural **standards of living**)
the kind of life that people have, based on the money they earn and the things they can afford to buy: *Most people in Japan have a high standard of living.*

**stand·by** /ˈstændbaɪ/ *noun* (plural **standbys**)
**1** someone or something that is ready to be used when needed: *The hospital has a generator which can be used as a standby if there is a power failure.*
**2** **on standby** = **a)** if you are on standby for an airplane ticket, you will be allowed to travel if there are any seats that are not being used **b)** ready to be used when needed: *The police are on standby in case of trouble.*

**stand·ing** /ˈstændɪŋ/ *noun*
the opinion that people have about how good someone is: *The issue could damage the president's standing with voters.*

**stand·point** /ˈstændpɔɪnt/ *noun*
one way of thinking about a situation: *Let's look at this from a different standpoint.*
**SYNONYM: point of view**

**stand·still** /ˈstændˌstɪl/ *noun*
a situation in which there is no movement or activity at all: *The traffic came to a standstill because of the accident.*

**stank** /stæŋk/ *verb*
a past tense of STINK

**sta·ple¹** /ˈsteɪpəl/ *noun*
**1** a small thin piece of metal that is pushed through pieces of paper to fasten them together
**2** a basic type of food that people eat a lot: *They buy staples such as bread and rice every week.*

**staple²** *verb*
to fasten pieces of paper together with a

staple: *I stapled my photograph to the application form.*
→ see Thesaurus box at **fasten**

**sta·pler** /ˈsteɪplɚ/ *noun*
a small tool used for putting staples into paper

**star¹** /stɑr/ *noun*
**1** a point of light in the sky at night. Stars are made of burning gases. The Sun is a star: *They looked up at the stars in the night sky.*
**2** a famous actor, musician, or sports player: *The movie star was paid $5 million for his last picture.*
**3** a shape with five or six points, that is supposed to look like a star in the sky: *The stars on the U.S. flag represent the 50 states.*
[**ORIGIN:** From the old English word *steorra.*]

**star²** *verb* (**starred**, **starring**)
to be the main character in a movie, TV program, or play: *He has starred in many Hollywood movies.*

**starch** /stɑrtʃ/ *noun*
**1** a substance in foods such as bread, rice, and potatoes: *His doctor told him to eat less starch and more green vegetables.*
**2** a substance used for making cloth stiff: *He used starch to keep his shirt collars stiff.*
—**starch** *verb* to make cloth stiff by using starch: *These shirts need to be starched.*
—**starchy** *adjective* a starchy food contains a lot of starch

**star·dom** /ˈstɑrdəm/ *noun*
the situation of being a famous actor, musician, or sports player: *Many young actors hope for stardom.*

**stare** /ster/ *verb*
to look at someone or something for a long time without moving your eyes: *It's rude to stare at people.* → see picture at **see**
—**stare** *noun* the act of looking at someone or something for a long time without moving your eyes: *She gave him an angry stare.*
→ see Thesaurus box at **look¹**

**star·fish** /ˈstɑrˌfɪʃ/ *noun* (plural **starfish**)
a flat sea animal that is shaped like a star

**Star-Span·gled Ban·ner** /ˌstɑr ˌspæŋgəld ˈbænɚ/ *noun*
**the Star-Spangled Banner** = the U.S. national song

**start¹** /stɑrt/ *verb*
**1** to begin doing something: *Have you started making dinner? | The little girl started to cry. | Mark's starting college in the fall.*
**ANTONYM: stop**
**2** to begin happening: *What time does the party start?* **ANTONYM: end**
**3** (*also* **start up**) to make a new company or organization: *Brad left his father's company to start a business of his own.*
**4** if a car or an engine starts, it begins to work: *The car wouldn't start this morning, so we had to take the bus.*
[**ORIGIN:** From the old English word *styrtan*, which means "to jump up."]
**PHRASAL VERBS**
**start off**
to begin doing something: *Let's start off by introducing ourselves.*
**start over**
to start doing something again from the beginning: *When I'm drawing, if I make just one mistake, I have to start over.*

**start²** *noun*
the beginning of something: *Hurry – I don't want to miss the start of the movie.*
**ANTONYM: end**

**start·le** /ˈstɑrtl/ *verb*
to surprise someone by suddenly appearing in an unexpected way: *I didn't hear him come into the room and he startled me.*
—**startled** *adjective* surprised because something has suddenly happened: *I was startled to see a woman standing outside my window.*
—**startling** *adjective* very unusual or surprising: *startling news*

**star·va·tion** /stɑrˈveɪʃən/ *noun*
a situation in which someone has little or no food to eat: *People are dying of starvation because there is not enough food for everyone.*

**starve** /stɑrv/ *verb*
to become sick or die because you do not have enough to eat: *He got lost in the desert and starved to death.*
[**ORIGIN:** From the old English word *steorfan*, which means "to die."]

S

**WORD FAMILY: starve**
**starve** *verb* | **starving** *adjective* | **starved** *adjective* | **starvation** *noun*

**starv·ing** /ˈstɑrvɪŋ/ *adjective*
**1** someone who is starving is sick or dying because he or she has not had enough food for a long time: *The country is full of starving people because there is no rain and no food.*
**2** (*also* **starved**) (*informal*) very hungry: *Is dinner ready? I'm starving.*

**state¹** /steɪt/ *noun*
**1** (*also* **State**) one of the parts that the U.S. and some other countries are divided into: *the state of Texas*
**2** (*formal*) a country that has its own government: *They want the region to become an independent state.*
**3** the condition that someone or something is in: *Everyone was in a state of panic.*
**4 the States** (*informal*) = the United States: *How long have you been back in the States?*
→ see Thesaurus box at **country**

**state²** *verb* (*formal*)
to say something publicly or officially: *When the police asked him, he stated that he had never seen the woman before.*

**state·hood** /ˈsteɪthʊd/ *noun*
**1** if an area achieves statehood, it becomes one of the states that make up a nation such as the U.S.: *Kansas achieved statehood in 1861.*
**2** if a country achieves statehood, it becomes an independent nation: *Slovakia achieved independent statehood in 1992.*

**state·ly** /ˈsteɪtli/ *adjective* (*formal*)
impressive in style and size: *The stately old building has been turned into apartments.*

**state·ment** /ˈsteɪtmənt/ *noun*
something that you say or write publicly and officially: *The president is going to make a statement to reporters later today.*

**states·man** /ˈsteɪtsmən/ *noun* (plural **statesmen** /ˈsteɪtsmən/)
an experienced and respected politician: *Lincoln was a great statesman.*

**stat·ic** /ˈstætɪk/ *noun*
**1** the noise that you hear when electricity in the air spoils the sound from a radio or TV: *I couldn't hear the song on the radio because there was too much static.*
**2** (*also* **static electricity**) electricity that is not flowing in a current, but collects on the surface of an object and gives you a small electric shock

**sta·tion¹** /ˈsteɪʃən/ *noun*
**1** a place where trains or buses stop so that people can get on and off: *I'm getting off at the next station.* → see picture on page **A26**
**2** a building where police officers or FIRE-FIGHTERs are based: *a police station* | *a fire station*
**3** a company that broadcasts on radio or television: *He was listening to the local radio station.*
[**ORIGIN:** 1500-1600 From the Latin word *statio*, which means "place for standing or stopping," from *stare*, meaning "to stand."]

**station²** *verb*
to put someone in a particular place in order to do a job or military duty: *Her father was stationed in Germany while he was in the army.*

**sta·tion·a·ry** /ˈsteɪʃəˌneri/ *adjective* (*formal*)
not moving: *The truck hit a stationary vehicle.*

**sta·tion·er·y** /ˈsteɪʃəˌneri/ *noun*
things such as paper and envelopes that you use for writing: *Her desk drawers were filled with stationery.*

**ˈstation ˌwagon** *noun*
a large car with space at the back for carrying things

**sta·tis·tic** Ac /stəˈtɪstɪk/ *noun*
**1** a number that represents a fact or measurement: *These statistics show that the population is still increasing.*
**2 statistics** = the study of numbers that represent facts or measurements: *He's studying statistics at college.*
—**statistical** *adjective* relating to statistics: *The statistical information shows that there are fewer tigers now than fifty years ago.*
—**statistician** /ˌstætəˈstɪʃən/ *noun* someone who works with statistics
[**ORIGIN:** 1700-1800 From the Latin word *statisticus*, which means "relating to a state or country," from *status*, which means "state." Statistics was originally the science of facts relating to a country and its people.]

**stat·ue** /ˈstætʃu/ *noun*
a stone or metal model of a person or animal: *The Statue of Liberty stands on an island in New York Harbor.*
[ORIGIN: 1300-1400 From the Latin word *statua*, from *statuere*, which means "to set up."]

statue

**ˌStatue of ˈLiberty** *noun*
**the Statue of Liberty** = a very large statue of a woman in New York Harbor, which represents the idea of freedom in the U.S.

**sta·tus** Ac /ˈsteɪtəs/ *noun*
**1** someone's position in society or in a job, especially in relation to other people: *The status of women in society has improved and they are treated with more respect.*
**2** the legal and official state or condition of someone or something: *When they ask you your marital status, they want to know whether you are married or single.*

**ˈstatus ˌsymbol** *noun*
something you own that shows you are rich or important: *Expensive cars are seen as status symbols.*

**stat·u·to·ry** /ˈstætʃəˌtɔri/ *adjective (formal)*
set or controlled by law: *The criminal received three years in prison, which is the maximum statutory sentence for the crime.*

**stay¹** /steɪ/ *verb*
**1** to continue to be in the same place and not leave: *Do you want to come with me or stay here? | Donny has the flu, so he's staying home from school today.*
**2** to continue to be in the same condition: *I was very sleepy, and it was hard to stay awake. | We met at college and have stayed friends since then.*
**3** to spend a short time in a place: *He stayed at a hotel while he was in town.*
[ORIGIN: 1400-1500 From the old French word *ester*, which means "to stand or stay," from the Latin word *stare*, which means "to stand."]

PHRASAL VERB
**stay up**
to not go to bed: *We stayed up late last night, and I was very tired this morning.*

**stay²** *noun*
the period of time you spend visiting a place: *We're planning a two-week stay in Florida.*

**stead·fast** /ˈstedfæst/ *adjective*
refusing to change your opinion or actions, especially because you are very loyal to someone: *He was a steadfast supporter of the president and worked with him for many years.*

**stead·i·ly** /ˈstedəli/ *adverb*
at a speed or level that does not change very much: *His work has improved steadily.*

**stead·y¹** /ˈstedi/ *adjective*
**1** something that is steady does not move or shake: *It's important to hold the camera steady when you take a photograph.*
**2** continuing at the same speed or level without stopping or changing: *They drove along at a steady 50 miles per hour. | a steady heartbeat*
**3 a steady relationship/job** = a relationship or job that has continued or is likely to continue for a long time: *His parents want him to find a steady job. | Does he have a steady girlfriend?*

**steady²** *verb* (**steadied**, **steadies**)
**1** to hold something firmly so that it stops moving: *He steadied the boat with his hand as Sarah got into it.*
**2 to steady your nerves** = to make yourself feel calmer: *She took a deep breath to steady her nerves before diving into the water.*

**steak** /steɪk/ *noun*
a thick flat piece of meat or fish, especially BEEF: *a grilled steak*

**steal** /stil/ *verb* (**stole** /stoʊl/, **stolen** /ˈstoʊlən/)
**1** to take something that belongs to someone else: *Someone stole $5 from her purse.*
**2** to run to the next base in baseball before someone hits the ball: *You can help your team by stealing a base.*

**steam¹** /stim/ *noun*
**1** the gas or mist that hot water produces: *She left a pan of boiling water on the stove and the kitchen was full of steam.*
**2 let/blow off steam** = to get rid of your anger or energy by doing something: *Doing physical exercise is a good way of letting off steam.*

**steam²** *verb*
**1** to produce steam: *The cup of coffee was steaming.*
**2** to cook something using steam: *Steam the vegetables over a pan of boiling water.*
—**steaming** *adjective* hot and producing steam
→ see Thesaurus box at **cook¹**

**steel** /stil/ *noun*
a strong metal that is used for making things such as knives, cars, or tall buildings: *The bridge is made of steel.*

**steep** /stip/ *adjective*
a steep road or hill goes up or down very quickly: *The road was too steep for us to ride our bicycles up.*

**stee·ple** /ˈstipəl/ *noun*
a tall pointed tower on the roof of a church: *a church steeple*

**steer¹** /stɪr/ *verb*
to control the way a vehicle goes: *He steered the car into the driveway.*

**steer²** *noun*
a young male cow whose sex organs have been removed

**ˈsteering wheel** *noun*
the round object in a car or other vehicle that you turn to make the vehicle go right or left: *He was driving with one hand on the steering wheel.* → see picture on page **A28**

**stem¹** /stem/ *noun*
the long narrow part of a plant, that leaves or flowers grow on: *The stems of these roses have thorns on them.* **SYNONYM: stalk**

**stem²** *verb* (**stemmed**, **stemming**)
**PHRASAL VERB**
**stem from something**
to happen as a result of something: *All their problems stemmed from their lack of money.*

**sten·cil** /ˈstensəl/ *noun*
a piece of stiff paper or plastic with a design cut out of it. You paint over the holes on the stencil to put the design on something: *She painted a pattern of leaves along the wall using a stencil.*
—**stencil** *verb* to paint a design on something using a stencil

**step¹** /step/ *noun*
**1** the movement of lifting one foot and putting it down in front of the other: *He took a few steps toward the door and then turned around.*
**2** one in a series of things that you do in order to achieve something: *The next step is to mix the eggs with the cream.*
**3** a surface that you put your foot onto so that you can go up or down to another level: *Ellen ran up the steps and knocked on the front door.*
**4 watch your step** = used to tell someone to be careful about what they do or say: *You'd better watch your step – you don't want to make him mad.*

**step²** *verb* (**stepped**, **stepping**)
to move somewhere by lifting your foot and putting it down again: *She stepped carefully over the dog.*
**PHRASAL VERB**
**step out**
to go out for a short time: *Sandy just stepped out – may I take a message?*

**step·broth·er** /ˈstepˌbrʌðɚ/ *noun*
the son of someone who has married one of your parents

**ˌstep-by-ˈstep** *adjective*
step-by-step instructions tell you how to do each part of something in the correct order: *a step-by-step guide to making a birdhouse*

**step·child** /ˈstepˌtʃaɪld/ *noun* (plural **stepchildren** /ˈstepˌtʃɪldrən/)
a STEPSON or STEPDAUGHTER

**step·daugh·ter** /ˈstepˌdɔtɚ/ *noun*
a daughter that someone's husband or wife has from another marriage or relationship

**step·fa·ther** /ˈstepˌfɑðɚ/ *noun*
a man who is married to your mother but who is not your father

**step·lad·der** /ˈstepˌlædɚ/ *noun*
a LADDER with two sloping parts joined at the top: *He climbed up the stepladder to change the light bulb.*

**step·moth·er** /ˈstepˌmʌðɚ/ *noun*
a woman who is married to your father but who is not your mother

**step·par·ent** /ˈstepˌperənt/ *noun*
a STEPFATHER or STEPMOTHER

**step·sis·ter** /ˈstepˌsɪstɚ/ *noun*
the daughter of someone who has married one of your parents

**step·son** /ˈstepsʌn/ *noun*
a son that someone's husband or wife has from another marriage or relationship

**ster·e·o** /ˈsteriˌoʊ/ *noun* (plural **stereos**)
a machine for playing CDs, records, etc. that produces sound from two SPEAKERs

**ster·e·o·type** /ˈsteriəˌtaɪp/ *noun*
a common idea of what a type of person is like, which is often not correct: *The stereotype of a Texan is someone who wears a big cowboy hat and boots.*
—**stereotype** *verb* to think or say that someone has particular qualities, just because he or she belongs to a particular race, sex, social class, etc.: *Some children's books in the past used to stereotype girls as being weak.*

**ster·ile** /ˈsterəl/ *adjective*
**1** completely clean and not containing any BACTERIA: *Put a sterile bandage on the wound.*
**2** unable to have children: *His wife is sterile, so they can't have children.* **ANTONYM: fertile**

**ster·ling sil·ver** /ˌstɚlɪŋ ˈsɪlvɚ/ *noun*
very pure silver: *This ring is made of sterling silver.*

**stern**[1] /stɚn/ *adjective*
very serious or strict: *The teacher gave me a stern look when I got the answer wrong.*
—**sternly** *adverb* in a stern way

**stern**[2] *noun*
the back part of a ship: *The captain stood at the stern of the ship, looking back at the port.*
→ see picture at **boat**

**steth·o·scope** /ˈsteθəˌskoʊp/ *noun*
an instrument that a doctor uses to listen to your heart or breathing: *The doctor put the stethoscope on my chest to listen to my heart.*
[**ORIGIN:** 1800-1900 From the Greek words *stethos* and *skopein*, which mean "chest" and "to look at."]

**stew** /stu/ *noun*
a meal made of pieces of meat and vegetables that you cook slowly in liquid: *beef stew*
—**stew** *verb* to cook pieces of meat and vegetables slowly in liquid

**stew·ard** /ˈstuɚd/ *noun*
a man whose job is to serve food and drinks to people on a ship or airplane: *a ship's steward*

**stew·ard·ess** /ˈstuɚdɪs/ *noun*
a woman whose job is to serve food and drinks to people on a ship or airplane: *The stewardess brought him his drink.*

**stick**[1] /stɪk/ *verb* (**stuck** /stʌk/)
**1** to join one thing to another using glue: *I stuck a label on the bottle.*
**2** if something sticks to a surface, it stays on it because it has glue on it, is wet, etc.: *The wet leaves were sticking to my shoes.*
**3** to push a pointed object into something: *The nurse stuck a needle in my arm.*
**PHRASAL VERBS**
**stick out**
**1** if something sticks out, it comes out from a surface: *Mike's ears stick out.*
**2 stick something out** = to deliberately move part of your body forward: *The boy stuck his tongue out at me.*
**stick to something**
to continue doing something in the way you planned to do it: *I think we should stick to what we decided and not make any changes.*
**stick together** (*informal*)
if people stick together, they continue to support each other when they have problems:

S

*We're a family and we stick together no matter what happens.*

**stick up**

if something sticks up, it is not flat and comes up above a surface: *Your hair is sticking up – you should comb it.*

**stick up for someone**

to defend someone who is being criticized: *Thanks for sticking up for me.*

**stick²** *noun*

**1** a long thin piece of wood from a tree: *They collected sticks to build a fire.*

**2** a long thin piece of wood or plastic that you use for a particular purpose: *She used a walking stick during the hike.*

**3** a long thin piece of something: *a stick of gum*

S

**stick·er** /ˈstɪkɚ/ *noun*

a small piece of paper or plastic with a picture or writing on it, that you can stick onto something: *Kerry put colored stickers all over her notebook.*

**stick·y** /ˈstɪki/ *adjective* (**stickier**, **stickiest**)

**1** covered with or made of a substance that sticks to surfaces: *The floor in the theater was sticky from sodas that people had spilled.*

**2** (*informal*) sticky weather is very hot and the air feels wet: *It was a hot and sticky summer day.* **SYNONYM: humid**

**stiff¹** /stɪf/ *adjective*

**1** if you are stiff, your muscles or joints hurt and it is difficult to move: *My legs are really stiff after exercising so much yesterday.*

**2** difficult to bend or move: *The signs were printed on stiff pieces of cardboard.*

**3** very severe: *There are stiff fines for speeding in this county.*

**4** **stiff competition/opposition** = someone who you will not defeat easily: *The company is facing stiff competition from other computer games companies.*

—**stiffly** *adverb* moving in a stiff way: *The old woman moved stiffly across the room.*

—**stiffness** *noun* the quality of being stiff so that you cannot move easily: *There is still some stiffness in my leg where I broke it.*

→ see Thesaurus box at **hard¹**

**stiff²** *adverb* (*informal*)

**scared/bored/worried stiff** = very frightened, bored, or worried: *I was scared stiff when the doctor told me I had to have an operation.*

**stiff·en** /ˈstɪfən/ *verb*

if you stiffen, your body suddenly becomes firm or still because you are angry, frightened, or worried: *When he touched her, she stiffened.*

**stig·ma** /ˈstɪgmə/ *noun*

a strong feeling in society that a type of behavior or a particular illness or condition is something to be ashamed of: *There is still a stigma in our society about having a mental illness.*

[**ORIGIN:** 1500-1600 From the Greek word for "mark made on something, such as a brand on an animal." The idea is that if you have something to be ashamed of, it is like having a mark on your body.]

**still¹** /ˈstɪl/ *adverb*

**1** used for saying that a situation has not changed and is continuing: *It started snowing an hour ago, and it's still snowing.*

**USAGE: still, always, yet**

**Still** is used to say that a situation that began in the past has not changed and is continuing: *He still plays basketball twice a week.*

**Always** means "every time" or "at all times": *I always see him on Tuesdays.* | *She is always happy.*

**Yet** is used when asking about something that is expected to happen, or saying that it has not happened: *Is Mark back from school yet?* | *I haven't finished the book yet.*

**2** not moving: *When he heard the sound, the dog stood still and listened.*

**3** in spite of what has just been said or done: *I studied hard, but I still failed the test.* **SYNONYMS: nonetheless, nevertheless**

**still²** *adjective*

quiet and calm: *In the early morning, the town was still.*

—**stillness** *noun* a situation in which nothing is moving or making a sound

**stim·u·late** /ˈstɪmyəˌleɪt/ *verb*

**1** to help something begin, develop, or happen more: *The warm sun in the spring stimulates the plants to grow.*

2 to make someone excited about and interested in something: *We hope to stimulate students' interest in art with trips to the museum.*
—**stimulating** *adjective* making you feel excited or interested: *The preschool is a fun and stimulating place for young children.*
—**stimulation** /ˌstɪmyəˈleɪʃən/ *noun* things that make you feel excited or interested

**WORD FAMILY: stimulate**
**stimulate** *verb* | **stimulating** *adjective* | **stimulation** *noun* | **stimulus** *noun*

**stim·u·lus** /ˈstɪmyələs/ *noun* (plural **stimuli** /ˈstɪmyəlaɪ/)
something that causes something else to happen, develop, or react: *Music can be a powerful stimulus to a baby's brain.*
[ORIGIN: 1600-1700 From the Latin word for "sharp stick for making animals move."]

**sting**
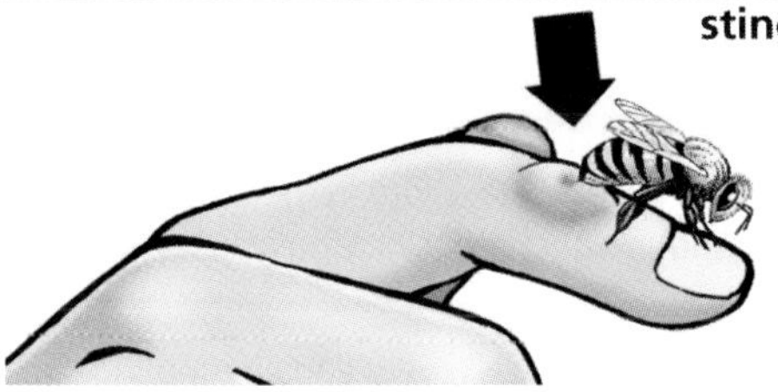

**sting¹** /stɪŋ/ *verb* (**stung** /stʌŋ/)
1 if an insect, JELLYFISH, or plant stings you, it puts poison into your skin and causes a sharp pain: *Ouch! That bee just stung me.*
2 to cause a sudden sharp pain on your skin or in your eyes: *The smoke made my eyes sting.*
→ see Thesaurus box at **hurt¹**

**sting²** *noun*
a wound made when an insect, JELLYFISH, or plant stings you: *a bee sting*

**stin·gy** /ˈstɪndʒi/ *adjective*
not willing to spend money or give someone money: *He was so stingy that he didn't even buy her a birthday present.* **ANTONYM: generous**
—**stinginess** *noun* the quality of being stingy

**stink** /stɪŋk/ *verb* (**stunk** *or* **stank** /stæŋk/, **stunk** /stʌŋk/)
1 to have a very strong bad smell: *His socks really stink after he has been jogging.*
2 (*informal*) to be bad or unfair: *It stinks that I have to do all the work.*
—**stink** *noun* a very strong bad smell: *the stink of rotting vegetables*
—**stinky** *adjective* having a very strong bad smell: *stinky cheese*
→ see Thesaurus box at **smell¹**

**stir** /stɚ/ *verb* (**stirred**, **stirring**)
to mix a liquid or food by moving a spoon around in it: *Stir the sauce until it is smooth.*
→ see picture on page **A15**
→ see Thesaurus box at **mix¹**

**ˈstir-fry** *verb* (**stir-fried**, **stir-fries**)
to cook meat, fish, or vegetables quickly by moving them around in a small amount of hot oil: *Stir-fry the vegetables in a large pan.*
—**stir-fry** *noun* food that has been stir-fried

**stitch¹** /stɪtʃ/ *noun*
1 one of the small lines of thread where a piece of cloth has been sewn: *She sewed the quilt with tiny neat stitches.*
2 a small line of thread where a doctor has sewn together a cut or wound: *Steven had to have three stitches in his chin after he fell down.*
3 one of the small circles of YARN you make around a needle when you are KNITTING: *I dropped a stitch when the yarn fell off the needle.*

**stitch²** *verb*
to sew two pieces of cloth together: *She stitched the lace onto the shirt.*
—**stitching** *noun* a line of stitches on a piece of cloth

**stock¹** /stɑk/ *noun*
1 a supply of something that is kept to be sold or used later: *The hospital keeps large stocks of blood for emergencies.*
2 **in stock/out of stock** = in a store and able to be sold, or not in a store and so not available for sale: *The book is out of stock right now, but we can order a copy for you.*
3 someone who owns stock in a company owns part of the company. Stocks are bought and sold on the stock market: *She sold all her*

S

*stock in the company just before the price dropped.*
**4** a liquid made by boiling meat, bones, or vegetables: *a cup of chicken stock*

**stock²** *verb*
to have a supply of something available to be sold: *Does the store stock camping equipment?*
**PHRASAL VERB**
**stock up**
to buy a lot of something, so that you can use it later: *People stocked up on food before the hurricane came.*

**stock·brok·er** /ˈstɑkˌbroʊkɚ/ *noun*
a person or company whose job is to buy and sell STOCKs in companies for other people

S

**ˈstock exˌchange** *noun*
a place where people buy and sell STOCKs in companies: *The New York Stock Exchange is on Wall Street.*

**stock·ing** /ˈstɑkɪŋ/ *noun*
**1 stockings** = a thin piece of clothing that fits tightly and covers a woman's feet and legs: *She was wearing a black dress and black stockings.* → see picture on page **A6**
**2** a large sock that people hang up before Christmas to be filled with presents: *We hung our stockings by the fireplace on Christmas Eve.*

**ˈstock ˌmarket** *noun*
the business of buying and selling STOCKs in companies, or the value of stocks: *It is risky investing in the stock market.*

**stock·pile** /ˈstɑkpaɪl/ *noun*
a large supply of something that you collect in order to use in the future: *Stockpiles of oil have fallen to their lowest level in ten years.*
—**stockpile** *verb* to collect a large supply of something to use in the future: *People were stockpiling food and supplies before the storm.*

**stock·y** /ˈstɑki/ *adjective*
having a short heavy body that looks strong

**stole** /stoʊl/ *verb*
the past tense of STEAL

**sto·len** /ˈstoʊlən/ *verb*
the past participle of STEAL

**stom·ach** /ˈstʌmək/ *noun*
**1** the organ in your body that DIGESTs the food you eat: *After dinner, I started having pains in my stomach.* → see picture on page **A2**
**2** the front part of your body, below your chest: *He never exercises, and he has a really big stomach.*
[**ORIGIN:** 1300-1400 From the Greek word *stomachos*, which means "throat."]

**stom·ach·ache** /ˈstʌməkˌeɪk/ *noun*
a pain in your stomach: *He had a bad stomachache after eating too much.*

**stomp** /stɑmp/ *verb*
to walk by putting your feet down firmly and noisily, especially because you are angry: *She stomped out of the room and slammed the door behind her.*

**stone** /stoʊn/ *noun*
**1** a hard solid substance that is found in the earth, used for building things: *The wall around the yard is made of stone.* **SYNONYM: rock**
**2** a small rock: *A few of the protesters began throwing stones at the police.* **SYNONYM: rock**
**3** a jewel: *She wore a necklace made of diamonds and other precious stones.*

**ˈStone Age** *noun*
**the Stone Age** = a very early period in human history, when people used stone for making tools and weapons

**stood** /stʊd/ *verb*
the past tense and past participle of STAND

**stool** /stul/ *noun*
a seat that has three or four legs, but no back or arms: *We sat on stools at the counter and ate our sandwiches.* → see picture at **seat**

**stoop** /stup/ *verb*
to bend forward and down: *Tyler stooped to pick up his pencil.*

**stop¹** /stɑp/ *verb* (**stopped**, **stopping**)
**1** to not continue doing something: *He finally stopped smoking.*
**2** to end, or make something not continue: *I wish that noise would stop.* | *The doctor managed to stop the bleeding.*
**3** to not move any farther, or to make something not move any farther: *The car*

*stopped outside our house.* | *You're supposed to stop the car at a red light.*

**4** to prevent someone from doing something: *She stopped me as I was leaving and asked me where I was going.*

**5** to pause during an activity or trip in order to do something: *Let's stop and have lunch before we finish painting the room.*

**THESAURUS: stop**

**have/take a break** to stop doing something for a short time in order to rest: *Okay, everyone, take a break and get a drink of water.*

**break** to stop for a short time in order to rest or eat something: *We broke for lunch about one o'clock.*

**pause** to stop speaking or doing something for a short time before starting again: *He paused for a moment to think.*

**6 Stop it/that!** = said when you want someone to stop annoying or upsetting you: *Stop it! That hurts!*

**7 stop short of something** = to stop before you do or say something extreme: *Tom said she wasn't very honest, but he stopped short of calling her a liar.*

**PHRASAL VERBS**

**stop by/in**
to make a short visit to a person or place, especially when you are going somewhere else: *Carol stopped by to return your CD.*

**stop off**
to make a short visit to a place when you are going somewhere else: *I need to stop off at the post office.*

**stop²** *noun*
**1** if something comes to a stop, it stops: *The taxi came to a stop outside his hotel.*
**2** a place where you stop during a trip, or the short time you spend at that place: *Memphis was the first stop on our trip.*
**3** a place where a bus or train regularly stops for its passengers: *I need to get off the train at the next stop.*

**stop·light** /ˈstɑplaɪt/ *noun*
a set of red, yellow, and green lights used for controlling traffic

**stop·o·ver** /ˈstɑpˌoʊvɚ/ *noun*
a short time between parts of a long airplane trip: *We had a three-hour stopover in Chicago before we flew on to Denver.*

**stop·watch** /ˈstɑpwɑtʃ/ *noun*
a watch used for measuring the exact time taken to do something, for example run a race

**stor·age** /ˈstɔrɪdʒ/ *noun*
**1** if you put something in storage, you put it away somewhere until you need it: *We use the attic for storage.*
**2** the action of keeping something in a place until you need it: *the safe storage of dangerous chemicals*

**store¹** /stɔr/ *noun*
**1** a building where things are sold to the public: *I'm going to the grocery store – is there anything you need?*
**2** a supply of something that you keep to use later: *He keeps a store of canned food in the basement.*
**3 in store (for someone)** = about to happen to someone: *There's a surprise in store for you!*

**store²** *verb*
**1** to put things away and keep them until you need them: *I store all of my winter clothes in these boxes.*
**2** to keep information in a computer or on something such as a CD: *She stored her research papers on CDs.*

**stork** /stɔrk/ *noun*
a tall white bird with long legs and a long beak

**storm¹** /stɔrm/ *noun*
if there is a storm, there is a lot of wind and rain or snow: *Several branches came off the tree in the storm.*
—**stormy** *adjective* stormy weather has a lot of wind and rain or snow: *It's been stormy all week, so we haven't gone outside to play.*
→ see Thesaurus box at **wind¹**

**storm²** *verb*
**1** to attack a place and enter it using force: *Police officers stormed the building and arrested the men inside.*
**2** to go somewhere quickly and in a noisy

way because you are very angry: *Angela got mad and stormed out of the room.*

**sto·ry** /ˈstɔri/ *noun* (plural **stories**)

**1** a description of real or imaginary events that is intended to entertain people: *Juan told us a funny story about his trip to Las Vegas.* | *a love story*

**THESAURUS: story**

**tale** (*formal*) a story about exciting imaginary events that happened in the past: *Many fairy tales begin with the line, "Once upon a time ..."*

**myth** a very old story about gods, magical creatures, or the beginning of the world: *In Greek myths, Poseidon was the god of the ocean.*

**legend** an old story about brave people or magical events: *In the legend of King Arthur, Arthur pulls a sword out of a stone to show that he is the king.*

**fable** a story that teaches us a lesson about life. Fables usually have animals in them: *The fable about the race between the tortoise and the hare shows that steady work can have good results.*

**2** a report in a newspaper or news broadcast about a recent event: *There's a story on the flood in the local paper.*

**3** a level of a building: *Our apartment is on the sixth story of the building.* **SYNONYM: floor**

**4 it's a long story** = said when you think something will take too long to explain: *It's a long story – I'll tell you later.*

**5 to make a long story short** = said when you want to finish explaining something quickly: *To make a long story short, she left the next day.*

**6** an excuse, explanation, or lie: *I don't believe his story about where he was last night.*

[**ORIGIN:** 1200-1300 From the Latin word *historia*, which means "story of events in the past."]

**sto·ry·board** /ˈstɔriˌbɔrd/ *noun*

a set of drawings that show a series of events, especially drawings that show what will happen in a movie: *The students are doing a storyboard first, to plan what will happen in the video.*

**stove** /stoʊv/ *noun*

**1** a large piece of kitchen equipment that you use to cook food. It has a place to cook food on top and an OVEN inside: *The soup is in a pot on the stove.*

**2** a piece of equipment for heating a room, that you burn wood or coal inside: *The cabin has an old wood stove.* → see picture on page **A9**

[**ORIGIN:** 1400-1500 From an old Dutch or German word for "heated room."]

**straight¹** /streɪt/ *adverb*

**1** in a line or direction that is not bent, curved, or at an angle: *Just keep going straight ahead.* | *Stand up straight!* → see picture at **wavy**

**2** immediately: *He got into bed and went straight to sleep.*

**3** happening one after the other in a series: *We drove five hours straight without stopping.*

**4 not think straight** = to not be able to think clearly: *It was so noisy, I could hardly think straight.*

[**ORIGIN:** 1300-1400 From a past participle of the old English verb *streccan*, which means "to stretch."]

**straight²** *adjective*

**1** not bent or curved: *I wish my hair was straight instead of curly.* | *Use your ruler to draw a straight line 3 inches long.*

**2** level or upright, and not leaning at an angle: *The picture on that wall isn't straight. Move the left side down a little.* | *Braces will make your teeth straighter.*

**3** honest and direct: *Just give me a straight answer and stop avoiding the question.*

**4** one after the other: *The team has had three straight wins, with no losses.*

**5 get/keep something straight** (*informal*) = to correctly understand or remember things without being confused: *There are so many kids in the class, I can't keep all their names straight.*

**6 get straight A's, B's, etc.** = to get the GRADE A, B, etc. in all of your school subjects: *Susan studies hard and always gets straight A's.*

**straight·en** /ˈstreɪtn/ *verb*

straighten

**1** (*also* **straighten out**) to make something straight: *She had to wear braces to straighten her teeth.*
**2** (*also* **straighten up**) to clean a room that is messy: *You need to straighten up your room before you go to the mall.*

PHRASAL VERBS

**straighten out**
**1 straighten something out** = to deal successfully with a difficult situation or problem: *I'll talk to your teacher and try to get this mess straightened out.*
**2 straighten someone out** = to deal successfully with someone's bad behavior or personal problems: *A few years in the army will straighten him out.*

**straighten up**
**1** to make your back straight, or to stand up straight after bending down: *The students straightened up in their seats when the principal walked in the room.*
**2** to start behaving well: *You'd better straighten up or you'll be in big trouble.*

**straight·for·ward** Ac /ˌstreɪtˈfɔrwərd/ *adjective*
**1** simple and easy to understand: *The directions are fairly straightforward, so you shouldn't have problems understanding them.*
**2** honest and not hiding what you think: *He is very straightforward and will tell you if you're wrong.*

**strain**[1] /streɪn/ *verb*
**1** to injure part of your body by stretching it or using it too much: *Rob strained his back lifting boxes.*
**2** to try very hard to do something using a lot of effort: *She was straining to hear what they were saying.* → see picture on page **A15**
**3** to separate solid things from a liquid by pouring the liquid through a container with holes
**4** to cause problems or difficulties, especially because something is very difficult to deal with: *The increase in rent will strain their finances.*

**strain**[2] *noun*
**1** a feeling of worry caused by having to work too hard or deal with too many problems: *The strain of working long hours was making him sick.*
**2** an injury to part of your body, caused by stretching it or using it too much: *Lee couldn't play in the game because of a muscle strain.*

**strained** /streɪnd/ *adjective*
**1** unfriendly, not relaxed, and showing a lack of trust: *Our relationship has been strained since I said I would not loan him money.*
**2** looking or sounding worried and tired: *She was very pale and looked strained.*

**strait** /streɪt/ *noun*
a narrow area of water that joins two larger areas of water: *The Florida Strait connects the Gulf of Mexico and the Atlantic Ocean.*

**strand** /strænd/ *noun*
a piece of thread, hair, or wire: *She brushed a few loose strands of hair from her face.*

**strand·ed** /ˈstrændɪd/ *adjective*
not able to leave a place, for example because of bad weather: *After the flight was canceled, we were stranded at the airport.*

**strange** /streɪndʒ/ *adjective*
**1** unusual or surprising, in a way that is difficult to understand: *Strange noises were coming from outside.* | *It was strange to see someone else wearing my clothes.*

**THESAURUS: strange**

**funny** a little strange or unusual: *The washing machine is making a funny noise.*

**weird** strange and different from what you are used to: *She wears weird clothes that never match.*

**odd** strange or different from normal, especially in a way that you do not approve of or cannot understand: *It was odd that she wasn't home because she told me to meet her there.*

**peculiar** (*formal*) slightly strange, and different from what you would expect: *The fish had a peculiar taste.*

S

**mysterious** strange in a way that is hard to explain or understand: *There were mysterious lights in the sky.*

**bizarre** very unusual and strange in a way that is hard to explain or understand: *He kept standing up and sitting down for no reason, and his bizarre behavior was starting to worry me.*

**eccentric** (*formal*) behaving in a way that is very different from how most people behave, and seeming strange or slightly crazy: *She was an eccentric woman who made her dresses out of old curtains.*

**2** not familiar: *I was in a strange neighborhood and didn't know anyone.*

—**strangely** *adverb* in a strange way: *The town was strangely quiet.*

[**ORIGIN:** 1200-1300 From the old French word *estrange*, which means "foreign," from the Latin word *extraneus*, meaning "outside or foreign."]

**strang·er** /ˈstreɪndʒɚ/ *noun*
someone you do not know: *Never talk to strangers in the street.*

**stran·gle** /ˈstræŋgəl/ *verb*
to kill someone by tightly pressing his or her throat with your hands, a rope, etc.: *Someone had strangled the woman to death.*

**strap¹** /stræp/ *noun*
a band of cloth, leather, or plastic that is attached to something. A strap is used to fasten, carry, or hang something up: *a watch strap | People were holding onto the straps on the ceiling of the subway train.* → see picture at **watch**

**strap²** *verb* (**strapped**, **strapping**)
to hold something or someone in place by fastening a strap around them: *He strapped a flashlight to his head so he could keep his hands free. | You must strap yourself in before the plane takes off.*

**stra·te·gic** Ac /strəˈtidʒɪk/ *adjective*
**1** done as part of a plan to achieve something: *The company made a strategic decision to move its factory to a cheaper location.*
**2** strategic weapons are designed to reach an enemy's country from your own country

**strat·e·gy** Ac /ˈstrætədʒi/ *noun* (plural **strategies**)
a planned way of achieving something: *The Colts' strategy in the final quarter was to stop the quarterback from passing the ball.*
[**ORIGIN:** 1800-1900 From the Greek word *strategia*, which means "the art of leading an army," from *strategos*, the word for "general of an army."]

**straw** /strɔ/ *noun*
**1** a thin tube of plastic used for sucking a drink from a bottle or glass → see picture on page **A9**
**2** dried stems of wheat or similar plants, used for animals to sleep on, or for making things such as hats: *The floor of the barn was covered with straw.*
**3** **the last/final straw** = the last problem in a series of problems, that finally makes you get angry or stop trying to achieve something: *When the dog bit the mailman, that was the last straw. We had to get rid of the dog.*

**straw·ber·ry** /ˈstrɔˌberi/ *noun* (plural **strawberries**)
a soft sweet red berry with small pale seeds on its surface → see picture on page **A13**

**stray¹** /streɪ/ *verb*
to move away from the place where you should be, especially without intending to: *The dog had strayed from its neighborhood and was lost.*

**stray²** *adjective*
**1** a stray animal is lost or has no home: *There were stray dogs running around in the street.*
**2** accidentally in a different place from the main part or group: *She brushed a few stray hairs off her jacket.*

**streak¹** /strik/ *noun*
**1** a colored line or thin mark: *There were dirty streaks on the windows.*
**2** a quality you have that seems different from the rest of your character: *Matt has a stubborn streak and he refuses to admit that he is wrong.*
**3** a period of time when you are always successful or always failing: *The team is on a four-game winning streak.*

**streak²** *verb*
**1** to move somewhere very fast: *A jet plane streaked across the sky.*

**2 be streaked with something** = to have lines or long thin marks: *His face was streaked with mud.*

**stream¹** /striːm/ *noun*
**1** a natural flow of water that is smaller than a river: *They drank water from a mountain stream.* → see picture at **river**
**2** a flow of air, water, or smoke: *A stream of hot air blew out of the machine.*
**3** a long line of people or things that are moving in the same direction: *A steady stream of traffic drove by.*

**stream²** *verb*
to move somewhere quickly and steadily, in large numbers or amounts: *Thousands of fans streamed out of the stadium after the game.* | *Tears were streaming down her face.*

**stream·er** /ˈstrimɚ/ *noun*
a long thin piece of colored paper or cloth, used as a decoration: *They decorated the room with streamers and balloons for his birthday.*

**street** /strit/ *noun*
**1** a road in a town or city with houses, stores, or offices along it: *Watch for cars when you cross the street.* | *I live across the street from the park.*
**2 the street/the streets** = the busy public parts of a city, where there is a lot of activity or crime: *He left home at 16 and lived on the street for two years.*
→ see Thesaurus box at **road**

**street·light** /ˈstritlaɪt/ *noun*
a light at the top of a tall pole in a street

**strength** /streŋkθ/ *noun*
**1** the physical power to lift, move, or do things: *I pulled at the rope with all my strength.* | *After his long illness, he barely had the strength to walk.* **ANTONYM: weakness**
**2** the quality of being brave or determined in dealing with difficult situations: *My parents' support gave me the strength to keep trying.*
**3** the power of a country or leader: *The country's military strength helped it win the war.* **ANTONYM: weakness**
**4** how strong a feeling, belief, or relationship is: *Her actions showed the strength of her love for her children.*
**5** a quality or ability that makes someone or something good or successful: *Her intelligence is her greatest strength.* **ANTONYM: weakness**

**strength·en** /ˈstreŋkθən/ *verb*
**1** to make something such as a feeling, belief, or relationship stronger: *Eating together can strengthen family relationships.* | *Her belief in God strengthened as she became older.* **ANTONYM: weaken**
**2** to make something such as your body or a building stronger: *This exercise helps strengthen your arms.* **ANTONYM: weaken**
**3** to improve something, or make something more effective and successful: *Creating jobs will strengthen the nation's economy.* **ANTONYM: weaken**

**stren·u·ous** /ˈstrenyuəs/ *adjective*
**1** needing or using a lot of effort and strength: *The doctor told him not to do any strenuous exercise until he felt stronger.*
**2** determined: *She made a strenuous effort to lose weight.*
—**strenuously** *adverb* in a strenuous way

S

**stress¹** Ac /stres/ *noun*
**1** a continuous feeling of worry about work or your personal life, that prevents you from relaxing: *Students are under a lot of stress before final exams.*
**2** special attention or importance that you give to an idea or activity: *Mom always put stress on having good manners.* **SYNONYM: emphasis**
**3** the physical force or pressure on an object: *The constant traffic put the old bridge under stress until it finally broke.*
**4** special loudness or force when saying a word or part of a word: *In the word "after," the stress is on the first syllable.* **SYNONYM: emphasis**

**WORD FAMILY: stress**
**stress** *noun* | **stress** *verb* | **stressed** *adjective* | **stressful** *adjective*

**stress²** Ac *verb*
**1** to make it very clear that something is true or important: *Ricardo stressed that everyone was welcome to come.* **SYNONYM: emphasize**
**2** to say a word or part of a word louder or

with more force: *"Don't do that," she said, stressing the word "don't."*

PHRASAL VERB

**stress (someone) out**

to feel worried and unable to relax: *I was stressing out before my biology test because I hadn't studied.*

—**stressed (out)** *adjective* worried and unable to relax

**stress·ful** Ac /ˈstresfəl/ *adjective*

making you worry a lot: *He has a very stressful job and finds it hard to relax.*

**stretch**

**stretch¹** /stretʃ/ *verb*

**1** (*also* **stretch out**) to become bigger or looser as a result of being pulled: *The jeans will stretch after you start wearing them.* | *You're too big to wear my sweater – you'll stretch it.*

**2** to spread or reach out your arms or legs as far as possible: *Kim sat up in bed and stretched.*

**3** to spread out over a large area: *The line of people waiting for the store to open stretched down the sidewalk.*

**4** to pull something so it is tight: *They stretched a rope between two trees to hang their wet clothes on.*

**5 stretch your legs** (*informal*) = to stand up and move around, after you have been sitting for a long time: *A few people got off the bus to stretch their legs.*

PHRASAL VERB

**stretch out**

(*informal*) to lie down with your body straight so you can rest or sleep: *He stretched out on the bed.*

**stretch²** *noun*

**1** an area of land or water: *This stretch of the road is steep and dangerous.*

**2** a continuous period of time: *You should not look at a computer screen for a long stretch of time without taking a break.*

**3** an action in which you stretch part of your body: *It's good to do a few stretches before you exercise.*

**stretch·er** /ˈstretʃɚ/ *noun*

something that is used to carry a sick or injured person, that is made of a light frame covered in cloth

**strict** /strɪkt/ *adjective*

**1** making people obey rules or do what you say: *Her parents are very strict – she's not allowed to go out at all during the week.*

**2** a strict rule, order, or law must be obeyed: *The school has strict rules about how students should behave.*

[**ORIGIN:** 1400-1500 From the Latin word *strictus*, a form of the verb *stringere*, which means "to tie tightly or press together." A strict rule stops you from doing things, as if you were tied up.]

**strict·ly** /ˈstrɪktli/ *adverb*

**1** in a way that must be obeyed: *Smoking is strictly forbidden.*

**2** only: *I play the piano strictly for fun. I never perform.*

**stride¹** /straɪd/ *verb* (**strode** /stroʊd/, **stridden** /ˈstrɪdn/)

to walk with quick long steps: *He strode confidently across the room.*

→ see Thesaurus box at **walk¹**

**stride²** *noun*

**1** a long step that you make when you walk: *He reached the door in three long strides.*

**2 take something in stride** = to not be upset by something bad that happens: *She took the defeat in stride and got ready for the next track meet.*

**strike¹** /straɪk/ *verb* (**struck** /strʌk/)

**1** (*formal*) to hit someone or something: *Strike the ball with the flat part of the golf club.* | *She struck him hard across the face.*

**2** if a thought or idea strikes you, you suddenly realize it or think of it: *It suddenly struck me that I hadn't eaten all morning.*

**3 strike someone as something** = to seem to someone to have a particular quality: *She strikes me as a very intelligent woman.*

**4** if workers strike, they stop working for a while because they want more money or better working conditions: *The pilots are striking for higher pay.*

5 to attack quickly and suddenly: *Police fear the killer will strike again.*
6 if something bad strikes, it happens suddenly: *Most people were asleep when the earthquake struck.*
7 when a clock strikes, it makes ringing sounds to show the time: *The clock struck midnight.*
—**striker** *noun* one of a group of workers who have stopped working because they want more money or better working conditions
→ see Thesaurus box at **hit**[1]

**strike**[2] *noun*
1 a time when workers stop working for a while because they want more money or better working conditions: *The hotel workers went on strike for health insurance.*
2 a military attack: *Air strikes have destroyed large parts of the city.*
3 an unsuccessful attempt to hit the ball in baseball

**strik·ing** /ˈstraɪkɪŋ/ *adjective*
1 unusual or interesting enough to be noticed: *He has a striking resemblance to his father.*
2 very attractive, often in an unusual way: *She is a tall striking woman, with long red hair.*
→ see Thesaurus box at **clear**[1]

**string**[1] /strɪŋ/ *noun*
1 a strong thread made of several threads twisted together, used for tying things: *The pen was attached to the desk by a long piece of string.*
2 a number of similar things that happen one after the other: *There has been a string of accidents along this part of the highway.*
3 a set of things such as BEADs or lights that are connected together on a piece of string or wire: *She wore a string of pearls around her neck.* | *They put a string of colored lights on the Christmas tree.*
4 one of the long thin pieces of wire that is stretched across a musical instrument to produce sound: *One of the strings on her guitar broke.* → see picture at **acoustic**
5 **the strings** = the people in an ORCHESTRA who play instruments such as the VIOLIN or CELLO

**string**[2] *verb*
1 to hang or put things on a string or wire: *A woman was stringing the wash out on the line.*
2 to put strings on a musical instrument: *Do you know how to string a guitar?*

**string·y** /ˈstrɪŋi/ *adjective*
1 stringy food has long thin pieces in it that are difficult to eat: *The meat was stringy and hard to chew.*
2 stringy hair is thin, dirty, and unpleasant looking: *He had a messy beard and long stringy hair.*

**strip**[1] /strɪp/ *verb* (**stripped**, **stripping**)
1 to take off your clothes: *He stripped and got into the shower.*
2 to remove something that is covering the surface of something else: *We need to strip off the wallpaper before we start painting.*

**strip**[2] *noun*
1 a long narrow piece of cloth, paper, etc.: *Tear the paper into one-inch strips.*
2 a long narrow area of land: *They own a strip of land by the lake.*

**stripe** /straɪp/ *noun*
a long narrow line of color: *A zebra has black and white stripes on its body.*

**striped** /straɪpt/ *adjective*
having a pattern of stripes: *red and white striped pajamas*

**strive** /straɪv/ *verb* (**strove** /stroʊv/ *or* **strived**, **striven** /ˈstrɪvən/ *or* **strived**) (*formal*)
to try very hard to get or do something: *The school is striving to improve its students' test scores.*

**stroke**[1] /stroʊk/ *noun*
1 if someone has a stroke, one of the tubes that carry blood to the brain bursts or becomes blocked: *After Grandma had a stroke she couldn't move her left arm.*
2 a way of swimming: *We learned the back stroke in swimming lessons today.*
3 a single movement of a pen or brush, or a line made by doing this: *If you look closely at the painting you can see the artist's brush strokes.*
4 **a stroke of luck** = something lucky that happens: *That's a stroke of luck – there are two seats left at the front.*

**5 at the stroke of midnight/9/6, etc.** = at exactly 12 o'clock, 9 o'clock, etc.

**stroke²** *verb*
to move your hand gently over something: *He gently stroked the cat in his lap.* → see picture on page **A3**
→ see Thesaurus box at **touch¹**

**stroll** /stroʊl/ *verb*
to walk in a slow relaxed way: *We strolled along the street and looked in the store windows.*
—**stroll** *noun* a slow relaxed walk: *We went for a stroll after dinner.*
→ see Thesaurus box at **walk¹**

**stroll·er** /ˈstroʊlɚ/ *noun*
a chair on wheels, in which a small child can be pushed as you walk behind it

S

**strong** /strɔŋ/ *adjective*
**1** having a lot of physical power: *He's so strong that he can move the refrigerator by himself.* | *She has strong muscular legs from biking.* **ANTONYM: weak**
**2** not easily broken or damaged: *These plastic bags are stronger than thin paper ones.* | *The tent is made of a strong material that won't tear easily.* **ANTONYM: weak**
**3** determined and able to deal with problems without becoming upset or worried by them: *She's a strong person – she has survived bigger problems than this.*
**4** having a lot of power, influence, or ability: *We need a strong leader that people will listen to.* | *They are a strong team, and they'll be hard to beat.* **ANTONYM: weak**
**5** a strong feeling or belief is one that you feel or believe a lot: *She has a strong belief that people are good.*
**6** a strong argument or strong reason is likely to persuade people that something is true or correct: *There is strong scientific evidence that the drug prevents heart attacks.* **ANTONYM: weak**
**7** a strong relationship or friendship is likely to last a long time: *They have a very strong friendship, so little arguments are not a big problem.*
**8** a strong taste, smell, or color is easy to notice: *The smell of her perfume was so strong it made me feel sick.*
**9** a strong liquid or medicine has a lot of a substance in it: *This coffee is too strong – could you put some more milk in it?* **ANTONYM: weak**
**10** a strong wind blows with a lot of force: *The wind was so strong I could hardly stand up.*
**11** very likely to succeed or happen: *There's a strong chance it will rain, so you'd better take an umbrella.*
—**strongly** *adverb* very much: *I strongly agree with everything he said.*

**WORD FAMILY: strong**
**strong** *adjective* | **strongly** *adverb* | **strength** *noun* | **strengthen** *verb*

**struck** /strʌk/ *verb*
the past tense and past participle of STRIKE

**struc·ture¹** Ac /ˈstrʌktʃɚ/ *noun*
**1** the way that the parts of something are arranged and connect with each other: *The structure of the brain is extremely complex.*
**2** something that has been built: *The museum is a huge structure of steel and glass.*
—**structural** *adjective* relating to the structure of something
[**ORIGIN:** 1400-1500 From the Latin word *structura*, which means "the act of building," from *struere*, meaning "to build."]

**structure²** Ac *verb*
to plan something carefully so that the parts come in a particular order and connect together in a sensible way: *The teacher structured the lesson so that the children would have time to learn about magnets and time to use them.*

**strug·gle¹** /ˈstrʌgəl/ *verb*
**1** to try very hard to do or achieve something difficult: *She's struggling to raise her children alone.*
**2** to fight someone who is attacking you or holding you: *She struggled with her attackers and screamed for help.*
**3** to move somewhere with a lot of difficulty: *The old man struggled up the stairs.*

**struggle²** *noun*
**1** a long hard attempt to get or do something: *King was a leader in the struggle for equal rights.* | *Getting him to do homework is a struggle.*

**2** a fight: *One of the men was injured during the struggle.*

**strut** /strʌt/ *verb* (**strutted**, **strutting**)
to walk in a very proud and confident way, with your head up and your chest pushed forward: *He strutted around as if he was better than everyone else.*

**stub¹** /stʌb/ *noun*
**1** the part of a ticket that is returned to you as proof that you have paid: *You need to show your ticket stub to get back inside.*
**2** the short part of something that is left after the rest has been used: *The stub of the candle was still burning.*

**stub²** *verb* (**stubbed**, **stubbing**)
**stub your toe** = to hurt your toe by hitting it against something

**stub·born** /ˈstʌbɚn/ *adjective*
determined not to do something or change your opinion: *He's so stubborn – there's nothing you can say to change what he thinks.*

**stuck¹** /stʌk/ *verb*
the past tense and past participle of STICK

**stuck²** *adjective*
**1** not able to move: *I can't open the drawer – it's stuck.* | *We got stuck in traffic.*
**2** not able to continue working on something because it is too difficult: *Can you help me with my homework? I'm stuck on question 7.*
**3** not able to get away from a boring or unpleasant situation: *I hate being stuck in the house on a rainy day.*

**stu·dent** /ˈstudnt/ *noun*
someone who is studying at a school, university, etc.: *She has 30 students in her class.* | *high school students*

**stu·di·o** /ˈstudiˌoʊ/ *noun*
**1** a room where television and radio programs are made and broadcast, or where music is recorded: *a recording studio*
**2** a movie company or a place where movies are made: *He works for one of the big Hollywood studios.*
**3** a room where a painter or photographer works: *an art studio*
**4** (*also* **studio apartment**) a small apartment with one main room

**stud·y¹** /ˈstʌdi/ *verb* (**studied**, **studies**)
**1** to spend time going to classes, reading, etc. to learn about a subject: *I need to study for my biology test.* | *She wants to go to college to study psychology.*
**2** to examine something carefully to find out more about it: *Scientists are studying how cars affect the Earth's temperature.*
[**ORIGIN:** 1100-1200 From the Latin word *studere*, which means "to work hard or eagerly at something."]

**study²** *noun* (plural **studies**)
**1** a piece of work that is done to find out more about a particular subject or problem: *a scientific study* | *The study shows the dangerous effects of the drug.*
**2** the activity of learning about a subject: *the study of ancient history*
**3** a room in a house that is used for work or study
**4** **studies** = the work you do in order to learn about something: *After he finished his studies, he got a job with the government.*

**stuff¹** /stʌf/ *noun* (*informal*)
**1** a substance or material of any type: *What's this sticky stuff on the table?*
**2** a number of different things: *Where's the camping stuff?* | *You can put your stuff over here for now.*
**3** activities that someone does: *I have a lot of stuff to do.* | *He likes camping and fishing and stuff like that.*
**4** things that someone says or thinks: *You don't believe all the stuff he says, do you?*
→ see Thesaurus box at **property**, **thing**
[**ORIGIN:** 1300-1400 From the old French word *estoffe*, which means "equipment, supplies, or material," from *estoffer*, which means "to provide a place or group of people with necessary things."]

**stuff²** *verb*
**1** to push things into a small space quickly: *He stuffed some clothes into a bag and left.*
**2** to fill something until it is full: *They stuff the dolls' bodies with cotton.*

**stuff·ing** /ˈstʌfɪŋ/ *noun*
**1** a mixture of bread, rice, or other foods that you put inside a chicken, vegetable, etc. before cooking it
**2** material that is used for filling something such as a PILLOW

**stuff·y** /ˈstʌfi/ *adjective*
if a place is stuffy, there is not enough fresh

air in it: *The room was hot and stuffy, so I opened a window.*

**stum·ble** /ˈstʌmbəl/ *verb*
**1** to almost fall down while you are walking, especially because your foot hits something: *Larry got out of bed and stumbled over a book on the floor.*
**2** to make a mistake when you are reading or speaking to people: *He was nervous and stumbled over the words as he read his speech.*
→ see Thesaurus box at **fall**[1]

**PHRASAL VERB**
**stumble across/on/upon someone or something**
to discover someone or something by chance: *I stumbled across some old pictures while I was cleaning my room.*

**stump**[1] /stʌmp/ *noun*
**1** the part of a tree that is still in the ground after the rest has been cut down: *He sat on a tree stump to rest.*
**2** the part of an arm or leg that remains when the rest has been cut off

**stump**[2] *verb*
if a question stumps you, you cannot think of the correct answer: *This question has stumped scientists for years, but now they have come up with an answer.*

**stun** /stʌn/ *verb* (**stunned**, **stunning**)
**1** to surprise or shock someone so much that he or she cannot react immediately: *My sister stunned the family when she told us she was leaving home.*
**2** to make someone almost unconscious for a short time by hitting him or her on the head: *The blow to his head stunned him for several minutes.*
—**stunned** *adjective* very surprised or shocked

**stung** /stʌŋ/ *verb*
the past tense and past participle of STING

**stunk** /stʌŋk/ *verb*
a past tense and the past participle of STINK

**stun·ning** /ˈstʌnɪŋ/ *adjective*
**1** extremely attractive or beautiful: *You look stunning in that dress.*
**2** very surprising or shocking: *The team's stunning victory surprised everyone.*

**stunt** /stʌnt/ *noun*
a dangerous action that someone does to entertain people, especially in a movie: *In the movie he does a stunt in which his car rolls right over.*

**stu·pid** /ˈstupɪd/ *adjective*
not intelligent or not showing good sense: *It was stupid of me to tell him my secret.* | *Stop asking stupid questions.* **SYNONYM: dumb**; **ANTONYM: smart**
—**stupidity** /stuˈpɪdəti/ *noun* stupid behavior

[**ORIGIN:** 1500-1600 From the Latin word *stupidus*, from *stupere*, which means "to surprise someone very much." The idea is that you are so surprised that you cannot think clearly.]

**stur·dy** /ˈstɚdi/ *adjective* (**sturdier**, **sturdiest**)
strong and not likely to break: *sturdy hiking boots* **ANTONYMS: fragile, delicate**

**stut·ter** /ˈstʌtɚ/ *verb*
to speak with difficulty, repeating the first sound of some words: *"My n-n-n-name is Joe," he stuttered.*
—**stutter** *noun* a way of talking in which you stutter

**style** Ac /staɪl/ *noun*
**1** a particular way of doing something: *Her style of cooking is very simple.*
**2** a design for clothes, hair, furniture, etc.: *I'm tired of my hair – I need a new style.*
**3** if you have style, you dress or do things in a way that people admire: *She dresses with a lot of style, and always looks great.*

[**ORIGIN:** 1200-1300 From the Latin word *stilus*, which means "pointed tool used for writing," and came to mean "writing or way of writing."]

**styl·ish** Ac /ˈstaɪlɪʃ/ *adjective*
stylish people or things look good in a fashionable way: *She was wearing a stylish black dress.*

**styl·ist** /ˈstaɪlɪst/ *noun*
someone whose job is to cut or arrange people's hair

**Sty·ro·foam** /ˈstaɪrəˌfoʊm/ *noun* (*trademark*)
a light plastic material with air in it, used for making containers: *They were drinking coffee out of Styrofoam cups.*

**sub·dued** /səbˈdud/ *adjective* (*formal*)
more quiet than usual: *He seemed subdued,*

*and only spoke when I asked him questions.* **ANTONYM: talkative**

**sub·ject¹** /ˈsʌbdʒɪkt/ *noun*
**1** the thing you are talking or writing about: *The subject of this poem is my cat Rosie. | Whenever I try to talk to you about your grades, you change the subject!*
**2** something that you study at school: *My favorite subject is math.*
**3** the person, thing, or place that a sentence is about. The subject of a sentence usually comes before the verb: *In the sentence "Jane bought some bread," "Jane" is the subject.*

**sub·ject²** /səbˈdʒekt/ *verb* (*formal*)
**PHRASAL VERB**
**subject someone to something**
to make someone experience something bad: *The guards subjected prisoners to beatings.*

**sub·jec·tive** /səbˈdʒektɪv/ *adjective*
based on your feelings or opinions, not on facts: *Judgments about art are subjective. One person might say a painting is good and another person might hate it.* **ANTONYM: objective**

**ˈsubject ˌmatter** *noun* (*formal*)
the subject matter of a book, movie, class, etc. is what it is about: *The subject matter of the movie is not suitable for children.*

**sub·let** /sʌbˈlet/ *verb* (**sublet**, **subletting**)
to rent to someone a property that you are renting from the property's owner: *She moved out of her rented apartment for the summer and sublet it.*

**sub·ma·rine** /ˈsʌbməˌrin/ *noun*
a ship that travels under water
**[ORIGIN:** 1600-1700 From the Latin words *sub* and *marinus*, which mean "under" and "relating to the sea."**]**

**sub·merge** /səbˈmɚdʒ/ *verb* (*formal*)
to go under the surface of water: *Many homes were submerged by the flood.*

**sub·mit** Ac /səbˈmɪt/ *verb* (**submitted**, **submitting**) (*formal*)
**1** to give something such as a plan or a piece of work to someone so that he or she can make a decision about it: *He failed the class because he submitted his work late.*
**2** to agree to obey someone, or allow something to happen to you: *He refused to submit to a breath test to see if he had been drinking.*

**sub·scribe** /səbˈskraɪb/ *verb*
to pay money so that you will get a magazine, newspaper, or service regularly: *I subscribe to a monthly computer magazine.*
—**subscription** /səbˈskrɪpʃən/ *noun* an arrangement to get a magazine, newspaper, or service regularly

**sub·se·quent** Ac /ˈsʌbsəkwənt/ *adjective* (*formal*)
coming after something: *This topic will be discussed again in subsequent chapters.* **SYNONYM: later; ANTONYM: earlier**
—**subsequently** *adverb* later: *He went to medical school and subsequently became a doctor.*

**sub·side** /səbˈsaɪd/ *verb* (*formal*)
to become less strong or loud: *He took a pill, and soon the pain subsided.* **ANTONYM: increase**

**sub·stance** /ˈsʌbstəns/ *noun* (*formal*)
any type of solid or liquid: *Glue is a sticky substance.* **SYNONYM: stuff**

**sub·stan·tial** /səbˈstænʃəl/ *adjective* (*formal*)
large in amount or number: *$100,000 is a substantial amount of money.*

**sub·sti·tute¹** Ac /ˈsʌbstəˌtut/ *noun*
someone or something that does what another person or thing usually does: *Our teacher, Miss Stein, was sick, so we had a substitute.* **SYNONYM: replacement**

**substitute²** Ac *verb*
to use something new or different instead of something else: *You can substitute margarine for butter in this recipe.* **SYNONYM: replace**
—**substitution** /ˌsʌbstəˈtuʃən/ *noun* the act of substituting one thing for another

**sub·ti·tles** /ˈsʌbˌtaɪtlz/ *plural noun*
words written at the bottom of a screen that

S

tell you what is being said by the actors, when the movie is in a foreign language: *We watched a French movie with English subtitles.*

**sub·tle** /ˈsʌtl/ *adjective*
not easy to notice: *There are subtle differences in the way people from different parts of the state talk.* **SYNONYM: small**; **ANTONYM: obvious**
—**subtlety** *noun* the quality of being subtle, or a detail that is not easy to notice: *I didn't understand all the subtleties of the play.*

**sub·to·tal** /ˈsʌbˌtoʊtl/ *noun*
the amount you get when you add some but not all of a set of numbers: *Add up the subtotals to get the total.*

S

**sub·tract** /səbˈtrækt/ *verb*
to take one number or amount from another: *If you subtract 3 from 5, you get 2.* **SYNONYM: take away**; **ANTONYM: add**

**sub·trac·tion** /səbˈtrækʃən/ *noun*
the act of subtracting one number or amount from another: *They worked on subtraction problems such as "15 – 5."* **ANTONYM: addition**

**subˈtraction ˌsign** *noun*
a symbol (–) showing that one number should be taken away from another **SYNONYM: minus sign**

**sub·urb** /ˈsʌbɚb/ *noun*
an area away from the center of a city, where people live: *She lives in a quiet suburb of Chicago.*
—**suburban** /səˈbɚbən/ *adjective* in or relating to a suburb
→ see Thesaurus box at **area**
[**ORIGIN:** 1300-1400 From the Latin word *suburbium*, from *sub* and *urbs*, which mean "near" and "city."]

**sub·way** /ˈsʌbweɪ/ *noun* (plural **subways**)
a railroad that is under the ground in a city: *He rode the subway around New York City.* → see picture on page **A26**

**suc·ceed** /səkˈsid/ *verb*
**1** to do something that you wanted to do or tried to do: *The climbers finally succeeded in reaching the top of the mountain.* **ANTONYM: fail**
**2** to do well at school or in your job: *You don't need a college degree to succeed in business.*

**WORD FAMILY: succeed**
**succeed** *verb* | **success** *noun* | **successful** *adjective* | **unsuccessful** *adjective* | **successfully** *adverb*

**suc·cess** /səkˈses/ *noun*
**1** if you have success, you do what you wanted to do or what you tried to do: *The team has had a lot of success in the league this year, winning 90% of all their games.* **ANTONYM: failure**
**2** someone or something that has the result you wanted: *The party was a big success, and everyone had a good time.* **ANTONYM: failure**

**suc·cess·ful** /səkˈsesfəl/ *adjective*
**1** someone who is successful has done what he or she wanted or tried to do: *She is very successful, and owns her own business.* **ANTONYM: unsuccessful**
**2** giving the result that you wanted: *It was a successful shopping trip because we came back with everything on our list.* **ANTONYM: unsuccessful**
—**successfully** *adverb* in a successful way

**such** /sʌtʃ/ *adverb, adjective*
**1** used when saying that something is very good, very big, very bad, etc.: *She's such a nice person.* | *I had such a bad headache (that) I had to lie down.*
**2** (*formal*) like the thing you have just mentioned: *He hates big parties, so he doesn't go to such events.*
**3** **such as** = used when giving an example of something: *I like team sports such as basketball.* **SYNONYM: for example**

**suck** /sʌk/ *verb*
**1** to hold something in your mouth and pull on it with your lips and tongue: *Lots of kids suck their thumbs.*
**2** to pull liquid into your mouth with your lips: *The baby sucked milk from a bottle.*
**3** to pull air, liquid, or dust somewhere: *A vacuum cleaner sucks up dirt from the floor.*
**4** (*informal*) if something sucks, it is very bad: *The movie sucked.*

**sud·den** /ˈsʌdn/ *adjective*
**1** something that is sudden happens quickly, when you are not expecting it: *A sudden gust of wind blew his hat off.*
**2 all of a sudden** = suddenly: *It was warm and sunny, then all of a sudden, it started to rain.*

**sud·den·ly** /ˈsʌdnli/ *adverb*
if something happens suddenly, it happens quickly, when you are not expecting it: *A dog suddenly ran into the road in front of our car.*

**sue** /su/ *verb*
to try to make someone pay you money in a court of law because he or she has made something bad happen to you: *She sued the man for damaging her car.*

**suede** /sweɪd/ *noun*
soft leather with a slightly rough surface: *a suede jacket*
[**ORIGIN:** 1600-1700 From the French phrase *gants de Suède*, which means "Swedish gloves."]

**suf·fer** /ˈsʌfɚ/ *verb*
**1** to feel a lot of pain or unhappiness: *I hope she didn't suffer much before she died.*
**2** (*formal*) if you suffer an injury or difficult situation, you experience it: *The team suffered a bad defeat.*
**3** to become worse in quality because of something: *He studied less, and his work began to suffer.*
—**sufferer** *noun* someone who has a disease or medical condition: *asthma sufferers*
**PHRASAL VERB**
**suffer from something**
to have a disease or medical condition: *People who suffer from asthma sometimes find it difficult to breathe.*

**suf·fer·ing** /ˈsʌfərɪŋ/ *noun*
a lot of pain or trouble: *It is terrible to see the suffering of people who have no food.*

**suf·fi·cient** Ac /səˈfɪʃənt/ *adjective* (*formal*)
enough: *One chicken is sufficient to feed four people.* **ANTONYM: insufficient**
—**sufficiently** *adverb* enough: *He wasn't sufficiently interested to listen anymore.*
→ see Thesaurus box at **enough**

**suf·fix** /ˈsʌfɪks/ *noun*
a group of letters that you add to the end of a word to make a new word: *You can add the suffix "ness" to the adjective "kind" to make "kindness."*
[**ORIGIN:** 1600-1700 From the Latin word *suffixus*, a form of the verb *suffigere*, which means "to fasten something below or on something."]

**suf·fo·cate** /ˈsʌfəˌkeɪt/ *verb*
to die because there is not enough air to breathe: *The men trapped in the mine underground eventually suffocated.*
—**suffocation** /ˌsʌfəˈkeɪʃən/ *noun* death by suffocating

**suf·frage** /ˈsʌfrɪdʒ/ *noun*
the right to vote in national elections: *The struggle for women's suffrage in America began in the 1820s and lasted until the 1920s.*

**sug·ar** /ˈʃʊgɚ/ *noun*
a sweet white or brown substance used to make food or drinks sweet
—**sugary** *adjective* containing a lot of sugar
[**ORIGIN:** 1200-1300 From the Arabic word *sukkar*, from the Sanskrit word *sarkara*, which originally meant "small pieces of rock." Sanskrit is an old language that was used in India.]

**sug·gest** /səgˈdʒest/ *verb*
**1** to tell someone you think he or she should do something: *I suggest (that) you take the subway – it will be quicker than driving.* | *They suggested meeting at 6.30.*
**2** (*formal*) to seem to show that something is true: *Her red face suggested that she was embarrassed.*
→ see Thesaurus box at **say**[1]

**sug·ges·tion** /səgˈdʒestʃən/ *noun*
an idea about what someone should or could do: *Do you have any suggestions about where we could eat?*

**su·i·cide** /ˈsuəˌsaɪd/ *noun*
the act of killing yourself: *He was very depressed and thought about committing suicide.*

**suit**[1] /sut/ *noun*
**1** a set of clothes made of the same material, including a short coat and pants or a short coat and a skirt: *He wears a suit for work.* → see picture on page **A6**
**2** one of the four types of cards in a set of playing cards. They are called DIAMONDS, HEARTS, SPADES, and CLUBS.
**3** a problem that someone brings to a court of law so that a judge can make a decision about it: *He filed a suit against the company that fired him.* **SYNONYM: lawsuit**

S

**suit**[2] *verb*
**1** to be acceptable to you and not cause any problems: *"Can you come tomorrow?" "That suits me fine."*
**2** if clothes or colors suit you, they make you look attractive because they go well with your skin color, shape, etc.: *Short skirts don't suit people with fat legs.*

**suit·able** /ˈsutəbəl/ *adjective*
right for a person or situation: *Violent movies are not suitable for small children.* **SYNONYM: appropriate**; **ANTONYM: unsuitable**

**suit·case** /ˈsutkeɪs/ *noun*
a large bag with a handle, in which you carry clothes when you travel: *She carried a small suitcase with her onto the plane.* → see picture at **case**

S

**suite** /swit/ *noun*
a group of rooms in a hotel, especially an expensive hotel: *The band was staying in a suite at the best hotel in town.*

**sul·fur** (*also* **sulphur**) /ˈsʌlfɚ/ *noun*
a yellow chemical substance with a strong smell: *Sulfur mixed with hydrogen has a bad smell.*

**sulk** /sʌlk/ *verb*
to show that you are annoyed about something by not saying anything and looking sad: *Her youngest son sulks when he doesn't get what he wants.*

**sul·len** /ˈsʌlən/ *adjective*
not saying anything and seeming slightly angry: *Her sullen face showed she was annoyed.*

**sul·phur** /ˈsʌlfɚ/ *noun*
another spelling of SULFUR

**sum**[1] Ac /sʌm/ *noun*
**1** an amount of money: *$5,000 is a large sum of money.*
**2 the sum of something** = the amount you get when you add two numbers together: *The sum of 4 and 5 is 9.*

**sum**[2] Ac *verb* (**summed**, **summing**)
**PHRASAL VERB**
**sum up**
to repeat the main points made in a speech or document in a short statement at the end: *He spoke for an hour about his father, then summed up by saying, "He was a great man."*

**sum·ma·rize** Ac /ˈsʌməˌraɪz/ *verb*
to give the main information about something, not all the details: *We had to summarize the chapter in five sentences.*

**sum·ma·ry** Ac /ˈsʌməri/ *noun* (plural **summaries**)
a short statement that gives the main information about something, not all the details: *Read the article and write a short summary of it.*

**sum·mer** /ˈsʌmɚ/ *noun*
the season between spring and fall, when the weather is hottest: *The pool is open in the summer.*

**sum·mer·time** /ˈsʌmɚˌtaɪm/ *noun*
the time of year when it is summer: *In summertime, the days are longer.*

**sum·mit** /ˈsʌmɪt/ *noun* (*formal*)
**1** the top of a mountain: *He climbed to the summit of Mount Everest.*
**2** a meeting between the leaders of two or more countries: *Thirty world leaders are planning to attend the summit.*
**[ORIGIN:** 1300-1400 From the Latin word *summus*, which means "highest."**]**

**sum·mon** /ˈsʌmən/ *verb* (*formal*)
to order someone to come to a place: *The principal summoned us to her office.* **SYNONYM: call**

**sun** /sʌn/ *noun*
**1** (*also* **Sun**) the star in the sky that we see during the day, that gives us light and heat: *The sun was shining. | The Earth moves around the Sun.*
**2** the heat and light that come from the Sun: *We went to the beach to lie in the sun.*

**sun·bathe** /ˈsʌnbeɪð/ *verb*
to lie in the sun so that your skin becomes brown: *We sunbathed by the pool.*

**sun·block** /ˈsʌnblɑk/ *noun*
a cream that you put on your skin to stop the sun from burning you

**sun·burn** /ˈsʌnbɚn/ *noun*
if you have a sunburn, your skin is red and sore because you have spent too much time in the sun: *You'd better come inside now, or you'll get a sunburn.*
**—sunburned** (*also* **sunburnt**) *adjective*
having a sunburn

**sun·dae** /ˈsʌndeɪ/ *noun*
ICE CREAM with fruit, nuts, or a sweet liquid on it: *For dessert, I had a chocolate sundae.*

**Sun·day** /ˈsʌndi/ *noun* (*written abbreviation*: **Sun.**)
the first day of the week, between Saturday and Monday: *Anna is coming back Sunday.* | *I have to work on Sunday.* | *We're going to a baseball game next Sunday.* | *She usually wakes up early on Sunday morning.*
[**ORIGIN:** From an old English word meaning "day of the sun."]

**sun·down** /ˈsʌndaʊn/ *noun*
the time when the sun disappears and night begins: *They work all day from sunrise to sundown.* **SYNONYM: sunset**

**sun·flow·er** /ˈsʌnˌflaʊə/ *noun*
a tall plant with a large yellow flower and seeds that you can eat

**sung** /sʌŋ/ *verb*
the past participle of SING

**sun·glass·es** /ˈsʌnˌglæsɪz/ *plural noun*
dark glasses that you wear to protect your eyes when the sun is bright

**sunk** /sʌŋk/ *verb*
a past tense and the past participle of SINK

**sunk·en** /ˈsʌŋkən/ *adjective*
having sunk to the bottom of the ocean: *Divers discovered a sunken ship.*

**sun·light** /ˈsʌnlaɪt/ *noun*
light from the sun: *She opened the curtains, and sunlight filled the room.*

**sun·ny** /ˈsʌni/ *adjective*
if it is sunny, the sun is bright and there are few clouds: *It was a sunny day, and the sky was blue.* **ANTONYM: cloudy**

**sun·rise** /ˈsʌnraɪz/ *noun*
the time in the morning when the sun first appears: *We got up at sunrise and started making breakfast.*

**sun·screen** /ˈsʌnskrin/ *noun*
a cream that you put on your skin to stop the sun from burning you

**sun·set** /ˈsʌnset/ *noun*
the time when the sun disappears and night begins: *We watched the beautiful sunset.*

**sun·shine** /ˈsʌnʃaɪn/ *noun*
the light and heat from the sun: *I left the clothes to dry in the sunshine.*

**sun·tan** /ˈsʌntæn/ *noun*
if you have a suntan, your skin is brown because you have spent time in the sun: *She came back from vacation with a suntan.* **SYNONYM: tan**

**su·per** /ˈsupə/ *adjective* (*informal*)
very good: *You did a super job on your homework – you get an A!* **SYNONYM: great**

**su·perb** /sʊˈpəb/ *adjective*
very good: *The hotel was superb, with big rooms and great food.* **SYNONYM: excellent**

**su·per·fi·cial** /ˌsupəˈfɪʃəl/ *adjective*
**1** only dealing with the most basic parts of something, and not thorough or complete: *My knowledge of medicine is superficial – I'm not a doctor, after all.*
**2** relating to the surface or outside of something, or the appearance of something: *She had some superficial cuts on her arm, but no serious injuries.*
[**ORIGIN:** 1300-1400 From the Latin word *superficies*, which means "surface."]

**su·per·flu·ous** /sʊˈpəfluəs/ *adjective* (*formal*)
not needed or wanted: *Remove superfluous information from your essay to make it shorter.*

**su·per·in·tend·ent** /ˌsupərɪnˈtendənt/ *noun*
**1** someone who is responsible for all the schools in an area: *The superintendent of schools makes decisions for the whole school district.*
**2** (*also* **super** (*informal*)) someone who takes care of an apartment building

**su·pe·ri·or**[1] /səˈpɪriə/ *adjective* (*formal*)
better than other people or things: *The new computers are superior to the old ones and can do much more.* **ANTONYM: inferior**
—**superiority** /səˌpɪriˈɔrəti/ *noun* the quality of being better than other people or things
[**ORIGIN:** 1300-1400 From the Latin word for "further above."]

S

**superior²** *noun* (*formal*)
someone who has a higher position than you in your job: *His superiors told him he needed to work harder.*

**su·per·la·tive** /sʊˈpɚlətɪv/ *noun*
a form of a word that shows that something is the best, worst, biggest, smallest, etc.: *"Fastest" is the superlative of "fast."*

**su·per·mar·ket** /ˈsupɚˌmɑrkɪt/ *noun*
a large store that sells food and things that people need for the house: *Mom bought some bread, meat, and milk at the supermarket.*

**su·per·nat·u·ral** /ˌsupɚˈnætʃərəl/ *adjective*
supernatural things cannot be explained by science and the laws of nature: *The boy in the movie has supernatural powers, and can talk to ghosts.*

S

**sup·er·pow·er** /ˈsupɚˌpaʊɚ/ *noun*
a large powerful country, with a big army

**su·per·son·ic** /ˌsupɚˈsɑnɪk/ *adjective*
faster than the speed of sound: *The planes can fly at supersonic speeds.*

**su·per·sti·tion** /ˌsupɚˈstɪʃən/ *noun*
a belief that some things are lucky and some are not: *There is a superstition that the number 13 is unlucky.*
—**superstitious** *adjective* having many superstitions

**su·per·vise** /ˈsupɚˌvaɪz/ *verb*
to be in charge of a person or activity and make sure that the activity is done correctly or that the person behaves correctly: *The teachers who go on the field trip are responsible for supervising the students.*
—**supervisory** /ˌsupɚˈvaɪzəri/ *adjective* relating to supervising people: *a supervisory job*
[**ORIGIN:** 1500-1600 From the Latin word *supervidere*, from *super* and *videre*, which mean "over" and "to see."]

**su·per·vi·sion** /ˌsupɚˈvɪʒən/ *noun*
the act of being in charge of a person or activity and making sure that things happen correctly: *Some students need a lot of supervision or they don't finish their work.*

**su·per·vis·or** /ˈsupɚˌvaɪzɚ/ *noun*
someone who watches people to make sure they do the right things while they work: *Report any problems with the machines to your supervisor.*

**sup·per** /ˈsʌpɚ/ *noun*
an evening meal: *We had a light supper of soup and salad.* | *What's for supper?*
**SYNONYM: dinner**
→ see Thesaurus box at **meal**
[**ORIGIN:** 1200-1300 From the old French word *souper*, which means "to eat your evening meal," from *soupe*, meaning "soup."]

**sup·ple·ment** Ac /ˈsʌpləˌment/ *verb* (*formal*)
to add something extra that makes something better or larger: *He took a night job to supplement his income.*
—**supplement** /ˈsʌpləmənt/ *noun* something that is added to something else: *People who do not eat the right kind of food may need vitamin supplements.*

**sup·pli·er** /səˈplaɪɚ/ *noun*
a company that provides things for businesses to buy: *The bakery called its supplier to order more flour.*

**sup·ply¹** /səˈplaɪ/ *noun* (plural **supplies**)
**1** an amount of something that you can use when you need it: *We took a week's supply of food with us when we went camping.*
**SYNONYM: store**
**2 supplies** = food and other things that people need: *The truck was carrying food, medicine, and other essential supplies for the soldiers.*

**supply²** *verb* (**supplied**, **supplies**)
to give or sell something to someone who needs it: *The farmers supply milk and vegetables to people in the town.* **SYNONYM: provide**

**sup·port¹** /səˈpɔrt/ *verb*
**1** to hold something so that it does not fall: *Six wooden posts support the roof.*
**2** to say that you agree with a person, group, or idea: *Which candidate do you support?*
**3** to provide the food and other things that someone needs in order to live: *He earns enough money to support his family.*
**4** to help and encourage someone during a difficult time: *She supported me when my mother was very sick.*
[**ORIGIN:** 1300-1400 From the Latin word *supportare*, which means "to carry."]

**support²** *noun*
**1** if you give someone your support, you help

that person or say that you hope he or she will be successful: *They showed their support for the president by clapping and waving flags.*
**2** something that holds something else so that it does not fall: *Metal supports hold up the roof.*

**sup·port·er** /səˈpɔrtɚ/ *noun*
someone who supports a person, group, or plan: *The mayor's supporters hope that he will be re-elected.*

**sup·port·ive** /səˈpɔrtɪv/ *adjective*
a supportive person gives you help and advice during a difficult time in your life: *My parents were very supportive when I broke up with my boyfriend.*

**sup·pose** /səˈpoʊz/ *verb*
**1 be supposed to do something** = used when saying what someone should do, or what should happen: *You're supposed to stop your car at a red light.* | *When is the movie supposed to start?*
**2 be supposed to be something** = if something is supposed to be something, people say that it is like that: *I've never read it, but it's supposed to be a good book.*
**3 I suppose** = used when you think that something is probably true or might happen: *He's not here, so I suppose he went home.*
**4 suppose (that)** = used when talking about what might happen: *Suppose you found some money. What would you do?*

**sup·pos·ed·ly** /səˈpoʊzɪdli/ *adverb*
used when saying what other people say about someone or something, when you do not think they are right: *How could a supposedly intelligent person make so many stupid mistakes?*

**sup·pos·ing** /səˈpoʊzɪŋ/ *conjunction*
used when talking about what might happen or be true: *Supposing it really was a ghost – that would be really scary!*

**sup·press** /səˈpres/ *verb* (*formal*)
to control a feeling, so that you do not show it: *He could not suppress his anger, and started shouting.*
—**suppression** /səˈpreʃən/ *noun* the act of suppressing something

**su·preme** /səˈprim/ *adjective*
highest, best, or most important: *He was the supreme commander of the NATO military forces.*

**Su͵preme ˈCourt** *noun*
the most important court in the country or in a state

**sure¹** /ʃʊr/ *adjective*
**1** certain about something: *Yes, I'm sure (that) he was there. I saw him!* | *I'm not sure what happened, but I can tell you what I heard.*
**2 be sure to do something** = to be certain to do something: *Whatever he decides to do, he's sure to be successful.*
**3 for sure** = if you know something for sure, you know that it is definitely true: *I think he's married, but I don't know for sure.*
**4 make sure (that)** = **a)** to check that something is true or that something has been done: *He called to make sure that we got home okay.* **b)** to do something because it is important: *Make sure you write your name at the top of your answer sheet.*
[**ORIGIN:** 1300-1400 From the old French word *sur*, from the Latin word *securus*, which means "not worried, or safe."]

**sure²** *adverb*
**1** (*informal*) used as a way of saying "yes" to someone: *"Can I borrow your ruler?" "Sure."*
**2** (*informal*) used when emphasizing something you are saying: *It sure is cold today!*
**SYNONYM: certainly**
**3 sure enough** = used when saying that something that you expected to happen happened: *I thought she would be angry, and sure enough, she was.*

**sure·ly** /ˈʃʊrli/ *adverb*
used when you are surprised about something: *Surely you're not leaving so soon?*

surf

**surf¹** /sɚf/ *verb*
**1** to ride on ocean waves while standing on a board
**2 surf the Internet/Net/Web** = to look quickly at different pages on the Internet: *I*

S

*was surfing the Internet and found this really interesting website.*
—**surfing** *noun* the activity of surfing: *We went surfing in Hawaii.*

**surf²** *noun*
white waves that come onto the beach: *The surf wet my feet as I walked along the beach.*

**sur·face¹** /ˈsɚfɪs/ *noun*
**1** the outside or top part of something: *The astronauts left footprints on the surface of the Moon. | Leaves floated on the surface of the lake.*
**2** the qualities that someone or something appears to have, when the other qualities are hidden or not easy to notice: *On the surface, she seems friendly, but when you get to know her better, she can be very mean.*
[**ORIGIN:** 1600-1700 From the French words *sur* and *face*, which mean "on" and "face or side."]

**surface²** *verb*
**1** if something surfaces, people start to know about it: *News reports began to surface that the leader was sick.* **SYNONYM: appear**
**2** to rise to the surface of water: *He went under the water and surfaced a few seconds later.* **SYNONYM: come up**; **ANTONYM: sink**

**surf·board** /ˈsɚfbɔrd/ *noun*
a board that you stand on to ride on ocean waves

**surge¹** /sɚdʒ/ *verb*
to suddenly move very quickly in a particular direction: *The crowd surged forward.* **SYNONYMS: push, press**

**surge²** *noun*
a sudden large increase in something: *There is always a surge in demand for toys at Christmas.*

**sur·geon** /ˈsɚdʒən/ *noun*
a doctor who cuts open someone's body to fix or replace something inside: *Surgeons performed an operation on Mary's heart.*
→ see Thesaurus box at **doctor**
[**ORIGIN:** 1300-1400 From the old French word *cirurgien*, from the Greek word *cheirourgos*, which means "working with your hands," from *cheir*, meaning "hand," and *ergon*, meaning "work."]

**sur·ger·y** /ˈsɚdʒəri/ *noun*
the act of cutting open someone's body to fix or replace something inside: *She had surgery to repair her broken leg.*

**sur·name** /ˈsɚneɪm/ *noun*
your family's name, which in English comes after your other names: *Michael's surname is Baxter.* **SYNONYM: last name**

**sur·plus** /ˈsɚpləs/ *noun*
more of something than you need or can use: *We had a surplus of food, so we gave some of it away.* **SYNONYM: excess**; **ANTONYM: shortage**
—**surplus** *adjective* extra because you already have enough: *The army sells its surplus equipment.*

**sur·prise¹** /sɚˈpraɪz/ *noun*
**1** the feeling you have when something unusual or unexpected happens: *She stepped back in surprise, as a man came out of the women's bathroom.*
**2** something that is unusual or that you did not expect: *I didn't know you were coming. What a surprise!*
**3 take someone by surprise** = if something takes you by surprise, you did not expect it: *The rain took me by surprise, and I didn't have an umbrella.*
—**surprise** *adjective* not expected: *a surprise party*

**WORD FAMILY: surprise**

**surprise** *noun* | **surprise** *verb* | **surprise** *adjective* | **surprised** *adjective* | **surprising** *adjective*

**surprise²** *verb*
to make someone have a feeling of surprise: *His reaction surprised me – I thought he would be pleased, but he was angry.*
—**surprised** *adjective* having a feeling of surprise: *I'm surprised you're here – I thought you were working today.*

**THESAURUS: surprised**

**amazed/astonished** very surprised because something seems unlikely: *Grandma was amazed at how much I'd grown since last year. | We were astonished that nobody was badly hurt in the crash.*

**shocked** feeling surprised, and often upset or offended: *We were all shocked by the news.*

**startled** surprised because something has suddenly happened: *She looked startled, as though she hadn't expected me to be there.*

—**surprising** *adjective* giving you a feeling of surprise: *It's not surprising that the game is so popular – it's really fun.*

**sur·ren·der** /sə'rendə/ *verb*
to stop fighting because you know that you cannot win: *Finally, the army surrendered to the stronger enemy.*
—**surrender** *noun* the act of surrendering

The house is surrounded by a fence.

**sur·round** /sə'raʊnd/ *verb*
to be or go all around something: *The school is surrounded by a fence.* | *Police officers surrounded the house.*
[**ORIGIN:** 1400-1500 From the Latin word *superundare*, which means "to overflow," from *super* and *unda*, which mean "over" and "wave." The idea is probably that water goes around something on all sides, and this meaning was influenced by a similar French word.]

**sur·round·ings** /sə'raʊndɪŋz/ *plural noun*
the place that you are in and all the things in it: *When I moved to the new house, I missed my old surroundings.*

**sur·vey**[1] Ac /'sɚveɪ/ *noun*
a set of questions that you ask a large number of people in order to find out about their opinions or behavior: *They did a survey to see what kind of shampoo people buy.*
[**ORIGIN:** 1400-1500 From the old French word *surveeir*, which means "to look over something."]

**sur·vey**[2] Ac /sɚ'veɪ/ *verb*
to ask a large number of people a set of questions in order to find out about their opinions or behavior: *They surveyed 1,000 students to find out what foods they eat.*

**sur·viv·al** Ac /sɚ'vaɪvəl/ *noun*
the state of continuing to live after a difficult or dangerous time: *He is very sick and his chances of survival are not good.*

**sur·vive** Ac /sɚ'vaɪv/ *verb*
to continue to live after an accident, illness, or war: *Three people survived the car accident.*
—**survivor** *noun* someone who survives something
[**ORIGIN:** 1400-1500 From the Latin word *supervivere*, which means "to live longer than someone else," from *super* and *vivere*, which mean "over or beyond" and "to live."]

**WORD FAMILY: survive**
**survive** *verb* | **survival** *noun* | **survivor** *noun*

**sus·cep·ti·ble** /sə'septəbəl/ *adjective* (*formal*)
if you are susceptible to an illness or problem, you are likely to get it or experience it: *Young children are susceptible to coughs and colds.*

**sus·pect**[1] /sə'spekt/ *verb*
**1** to think that someone may be guilty of a crime: *They suspected her of taking the money, so they told their teacher.*
**2** to think that something is probably true: *I suspect (that) they lost my letter because I never got a reply.* **SYNONYM: think**
→ see Thesaurus box at **think**

**WORD FAMILY: suspect**
**suspect** *verb* | **suspect** *noun* | **suspicion** *noun* | **suspicious** *adjective*

**sus·pect**[2] /'sʌspekt/ *noun*
someone who the police think may have committed a crime: *The police interviewed the murder suspect.*

**sus·pend** Ac /sə'spend/ *verb*
**1** to officially stop someone from going to a school, being on a team, or working for an organization for a period of time, as a punishment: *He was suspended from school for swearing at a teacher.*
**2** (*formal*) to officially stop something from continuing for a short time: *Bad weather caused the airport to suspend flights.*

S

3 (*formal*) if something is suspended somewhere, it hangs there: *They suspended a light from the ceiling.* **SYNONYM: hang**

**sus·pense** /səˈspens/ *noun*
a feeling of not knowing what is going to happen next: *Don't keep us in suspense – what happened?*
—**suspenseful** *adjective* giving you a feeling of suspense

**sus·pen·sion** [Ac] /səˈspenʃən/ *noun*
**1** an official punishment in which someone is not allowed to go to a school, be on a team, or work for an organization for a period of time: *He got a three-day suspension for starting a fight at school.*
**2** (*formal*) the act of officially stopping something for a period of time: *Successful peace talks led to the suspension of fighting.*

S

**sus·pi·cion** /səˈspɪʃən/ *noun*
**1** a belief that something, especially something bad, may be true: *I had a suspicion (that) Joe was lying, but I wasn't sure.*
**2** a feeling that you do not trust someone: *Strangers are viewed with suspicion by the people in the town.*

**sus·pi·cious** /səˈspɪʃəs/ *adjective*
**1** not trusting someone or something: *She wouldn't tell me who gave her the money, and that made me suspicious. | He's suspicious of strangers.*
**2** making you think that something bad or wrong is happening: *There was something suspicious about the way he kept hiding his face.*

**sus·tain** [Ac] /səˈsteɪn/ *verb* (*formal*)
**1** to make something continue to exist or happen: *John is doing well in school now, but will he be able to sustain his progress?* **SYNONYM: maintain**
**2** **sustain an injury/damage** = to be hurt or damaged: *He sustained minor injuries when his car crashed.* **SYNONYM: suffer**

**sus·tain·a·ble** [Ac] /səˈsteɪnəbəl/ *adjective* (*formal*)
if something is sustainable, it can continue for a long time: *Their level of effort was not sustainable, and eventually they stopped working so hard.*

**swal·low**[1] /ˈswɑloʊ/ *verb*
to make food or drink go down your throat: *I put a pill in my mouth and swallowed it.*

**swallow**[2] *noun*
**1** an act of making food or drink go down your throat: *Mike drank his milk in one swallow.*
**2** a small bird with a tail that has two points

**swam** /swæm/ *verb*
the past tense of SWIM

**swamp** /swɑmp/ *noun*
land that is always soft and very wet: *Alligators live in the swamp.*
—**swampy** *adjective* like a swamp: *swampy ground*

**swan** /swɑn/ *noun*
a large white bird with a long neck, that swims on lakes

**swap** /swɑp/ *verb* (**swapped**, **swapping**)
to exchange something you have for something someone else has: *Can I swap seats with you so I can sit next to Ben?* **SYNONYM: trade**
—**swap** *noun* an act of swapping things
[**ORIGIN:** This word used to mean "to put hands loudly together," when agreeing a business deal. First used with its modern meaning, 1500-1600.]

**swarm**[1] /swɔrm/ *noun*
a large group of insects that move together: *A swarm of bees came out of the tree.*
→ see Thesaurus box at **group**[1]

**swarm**[2] *verb*
**1** to move in a large group: *The crowd swarmed into the building.*
**2** if a place is swarming with people, it is full of people moving around: *The beach is swarming with people in July.*

**sway** /sweɪ/ *verb*
**1** to move slowly from one side to the other: *The trees swayed in the wind.*
**2** to influence someone's decision: *She has decided to leave, and nothing you say will sway her.*

**swear** /swer/ *verb* (**swore** /swɔr/, **sworn** /swɔrn/)
**1** to say very rude words: *Don't swear in front of the children; we don't want them to use words like that.*
**2** to promise that you will do something: *At*

*the beginning of a court case, he had to swear to tell the truth.*
→ see Thesaurus box at **promise**[1]
**3** to say firmly that what you are saying is true: *I swear I didn't tell anybody where you were.*
**PHRASAL VERB**
**swear someone in**
to officially give someone an important job in a ceremony: *The new governor was sworn in today.*

**sweat**[1] /swet/ *verb*
if you sweat, liquid comes out of your skin because you are hot: *She was sweating when she reached the top of the hill.* **SYNONYM: perspire**

**sweat**[2] *noun*
**1** liquid that comes out of your skin when you are hot: *Sweat poured down his face as he ran.* **SYNONYM: perspiration**
**2 sweats** = another word for a SWEAT SUIT, or thick pants that you wear when you play sports
—**sweaty** *adjective* covered in sweat: *She wiped her sweaty face with a towel.*

**sweat·er** /ˈswetɚ/ *noun*
a piece of warm clothing for the top part of your body: *She put her sweater on over her shirt.* → see picture on page **A6**

**sweat·shirt** /ˈswet-ʃɚt/ *noun*
a soft thick piece of clothing for the top part of your body → see picture on page **A6**

**ˈsweat suit** *noun*
a set of clothes made of thick soft cotton that you wear when you play sports **SYNONYM: sweats** → see picture on page **A6**

**Swed·ish** /ˈswɪdɪʃ/ *noun*
the language spoken in Sweden
—**Swedish** *adjective* relating to Sweden: *Stockholm is the Swedish capital.*

**sweep** /swip/ *verb* (**swept** /swept/)
**1** to clean dirt from the floor or the ground using a brush: *I sweep the floor with a broom.*
**2** to move quickly or move something quickly: *The fire swept through the hotel.* | *Their car was swept away by floods.*
→ see Thesaurus box at **clean**[2]

**sweep·stakes** /ˈswipsteɪks/ *noun* (plural **sweepstakes**)
a competition in which you have a chance to win a big prize if your name is chosen

**sweet** /swit/ *adjective*
**1** containing sugar or tasting like sugar: *I love sweet foods like chocolate and ice cream.*
**ANTONYM: sour**
**2** pleasant, kind, and friendly: *It was sweet of you to help.* | *She has a sweet smile.*
**SYNONYM: nice**
—**sweeten** *verb* to make something sweet
→ see Thesaurus box at **taste**[1]

**sweet·heart** /ˈswithɑrt/ *noun*
**1** used when talking to someone you love: *Good night, sweetheart.*
**2** a person that you love in a romantic way: *He married his childhood sweetheart.*

**ˈsweet poˌtato** *noun*
a vegetable that looks like a long potato, and is orange or yellow inside **SYNONYM: yam**

**swell** /swel/ (*also* **swell up**) *verb* (**swelled**, **swollen** /ˈswoʊlən/)
to get bigger and rounder, especially because of being hurt: *My ankle swelled up like a balloon after I twisted it playing football.*
—**swelling** *noun* an area on your body that has become larger than usual because of injury or sickness

**swept** /swept/ *verb*
the past tense and past participle of SWEEP

swerve

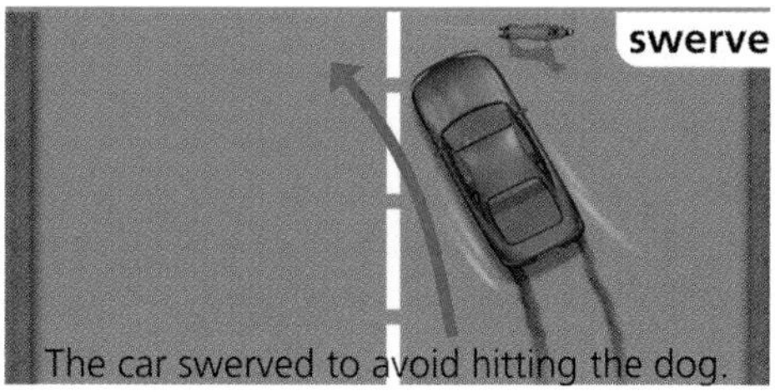

The car swerved to avoid hitting the dog.

**swerve** /swɚv/ *verb*
to move suddenly to the left or right, especially so that you do not hit something: *The car swerved across the road to avoid hitting the boy.*

**swift** /swɪft/ *adjective*
happening or moving very quickly: *My letter received a swift reply.*
—**swiftly** *adverb* very quickly

S

**swim**[1] /swɪm/ *verb* (**swam** /swæm/, **swum** /swʌm/, **swimming**)
to move through the water, using your arms and legs: *We swam in the ocean.*
—**swimming** *noun* the activity of moving through the water using your arms and legs: *Can we go swimming today?*
—**swimmer** *noun* someone who swims: *All the lifeguards are good swimmers.*

S

**swim**[2] *noun*
a time when you swim: *Do you want to go for a swim in the lake?*

**ˈswimming pool** *noun*
a structure that is filled with water for people to swim in **SYNONYM: pool**

**swim·suit** /ˈswɪmsut/ *noun*
a piece of clothing worn for swimming **SYNONYM: bathing suit**

**swin·dle** /ˈswɪndl/ *verb*
to get money from someone by tricking him or her: *He swindled his customers out of millions of dollars by selling them vacation homes that had never been built.*
—**swindle** *noun* the act of getting money from people by tricking them
—**swindler** *noun* someone who gets money from people by tricking them

**swing**[1] /swɪŋ/ *verb* (**swung** /swʌŋ/)
**1** to move backward and forward or from side to side: *The sign was swinging in the wind.* | *The door swung open when he pushed it.* → see picture on page **A4**
**2** to try to hit something: *He swung the bat at the ball, but missed.*

**swing**[2] *noun*
**1** a seat hanging from ropes or chains, which you sit on and make move backward and forward: *The kids were playing on the swings.*
**2** **take a swing at someone or something** = to try to hit someone or something: *The boy took a swing at the ball.*

**swipe** /swaɪp/ *verb*
**1** to pull a plastic card through a machine that can read the electronic information on it: *He swiped his security card in the machine.*
**2** (*informal*) to steal something, especially something small: *He swiped a candy bar from the store and felt guilty about it later.*

**Swiss**[1] /swɪs/ *adjective*
relating to or coming from Switzerland: *a Swiss watch*

**Swiss**[2] *plural noun*
**the Swiss** = people from Switzerland: *The Swiss did well in the skiing competition.*

**switch**[1] /swɪtʃ/ *verb*
**1** to change from one thing to another: *He played soccer at first, and then switched to football.* | *Dad switched channels and started watching something else.*
**2** to exchange something you have for something that someone else has: *Do you want to switch places with me?* **SYNONYMS: swap, trade**

**PHRASAL VERBS**

**switch something off**
to make a light or machine stop working by pressing a switch: *Don't forget to switch off your computer when you're finished.* **SYNONYM: turn off**

**switch something on**
to make a light or machine start working by pressing a switch: *He switched on the car radio to listen to music.* **SYNONYM: turn on**

**switch**[2] *noun*
a thing that you press to make a light or machine start or stop working: *a light switch* → see picture on page **A8**

**switch·board** /ˈswɪtʃbɔrd/ *noun*
a piece of equipment that connects all the telephone calls made to or from a hotel, company, etc.

**swol·len**[1] /ˈswoʊlən/ *verb*
the past participle of SWELL

**swollen**[2] *adjective*
a part of your body that is swollen is bigger than usual because of injury or sickness: *The side of his face was all swollen where he'd been hit by the ball.*

**swoop** /swup/ *verb*
if a bird or aircraft swoops, it flies quickly and

suddenly down through the air, especially in order to catch or attack something: *The bird swooped down to catch a fish.*

**sword** /sɔrd/ *noun*
a weapon with a long sharp blade and a handle, which was used for fighting in past times: *The Roman soldiers marched forward with their swords in their hands.*

**swore** /swɔr/ *verb*
the past tense of SWEAR

**sworn** /swɔrn/ *verb*
the past participle of SWEAR

**swum** /swʌm/ *verb*
the past participle of SWIM

**swung** /swʌŋ/ *verb*
the past tense and past participle of SWING

**syc·a·more** /ˈsɪkəˌmɔr/ *noun*
a tree with wide leaves, and BARK that comes off as the new bark grows

**syl·la·ble** /ˈsɪləbəl/ *noun*
one of the parts that a word can be divided into. Each syllable has a single vowel sound: *"Cat" has one syllable, and "butter" has two syllables.*

**syl·la·bus** /ˈsɪləbəs/ *noun* (plural **syllabi** /ˈsɪləbaɪ/ *or* **syllabuses**)
a plan that shows what students will be studying during a class: *The syllabus covers American literature from 1900 to the present day.*

**sym·bol** Ac /ˈsɪmbəl/ *noun*
a picture, object, or color that represents something else: *The dove is a symbol of peace.*
—**symbolize** *verb* to be the symbol of something: *A heart shape symbolizes love.*
[**ORIGIN:** 1400-1500 From the Greek word *symbolon*, which means "sign or mark for judging something by," from *symballein*, which means "to bring things together or compare things."]

**sym·bol·ism** /ˈsɪmbəˌlɪzəm/ *noun*
the use of pictures, shapes, colors, or words to represent an idea: *The picture is full of religious symbolism – for example, the shepherd taking care of his sheep represents Jesus.*

**sym·met·ri·cal** /sɪˈmetrɪkəl/ *adjective*
having two sides that are exactly the same size and shape: *The plant's leaves are perfectly symmetrical.*
—**symmetry** /ˈsɪmətri/ *noun* the condition of having two sides that are exactly the same

**sym·pa·thet·ic** /ˌsɪmpəˈθetɪk/ *adjective*
kind to someone who has problems or worries, and showing that you understand how he or she feels: *The nurse was very sympathetic and told me that I would soon feel better.* **ANTONYM: unsympathetic**

**sym·pa·thize** /ˈsɪmpəˌθaɪz/ *verb*
to show that you understand someone's problems and feel sorry for him or her: *I can sympathize with anyone who is being bullied because it happened to me.*

**sym·pa·thy** /ˈsɪmpəθi/ *noun* (plural **sympathies**)
a sad and kind feeling you have toward someone when something bad has happened to him or her: *She felt a lot of sympathy for him when his parents died.*
[**ORIGIN:** 1500-1600 From the Greek word *sympatheia*, from *syn* and *pathos*, which mean "together with" and "feeling."]

**WORD FAMILY: sympathy**
**sympathy** *noun* | **sympathetic** *adjective* | **sympathize** *verb*

**sym·pho·ny** /ˈsɪmfəni/ *noun* (plural **symphonies**)
a long piece of music written for an ORCHESTRA
[**ORIGIN:** 1200-1300 From the Greek word *symphonia*, which means "harmony," from *syn* and *phone*, which mean "together with" and "sound."]

**symp·tom** /ˈsɪmptəm/ *noun*
something that shows you may have a disease or sickness: *The usual symptoms of a cold are a sore throat and a runny nose.*
[**ORIGIN:** 1500-1600 From the Greek word *symptoma*, which means "something that happens," from *sympiptein*, which means "to happen."]

**syn·a·gogue** /ˈsɪnəˌgɑg/ *noun*
a building where Jewish people go to have religious services

**syn·di·cate** /ˈsɪndəkət/ *noun*
a group of people or companies that join together to achieve something: *The land was bought by a syndicate of buyers.*

**syn·o·nym** /ˈsɪnəˌnɪm/ *noun*
a word with the same meaning as another word: *"Sad" and "unhappy" are synonyms.*
**ANTONYM: antonym**
[**ORIGIN:** 1400-1500 From the Greek words *syn* and *onyma*, which mean "with" and "name or word."]

**syn·tax** /ˈsɪntæks/ *noun*
the way words are arranged in order to form sentences or phrases

**syn·thet·ic** /sɪnˈθetɪk/ *adjective*
synthetic materials are not natural, but are made by people in factories: *The shoes are made from a synthetic material, not leather.*

S

**sy·ringe** /səˈrɪndʒ/ *noun*
a hollow tube attached to a needle, which is used for giving medicine or taking out liquids through the skin: *The doctor got a syringe and gave me an injection of antibiotics.*

**syr·up** /ˈsɚəp/ *noun*
a thick sweet liquid made from sugar: *Can I have some more syrup on my pancakes?*

**sys·tem** /ˈsɪstəm/ *noun*
**1** a group of things or parts that work together for one purpose: *the city's transportation system | Your stomach is part of your digestive system.*
**2** a group of computers that are connected to each other: *The computer system has crashed, so I cannot look at your records.*
**3** an organized way of doing something, following rules: *The school now has a new system for grading students. | a democratic system of government*

**sys·tem·at·ic** /ˌsɪstəˈmætɪk/ *adjective*
done in a carefully organized way: *The police made a systematic search of the building, starting on the ground floor and working upward.*
—**systematically** *adverb* in a carefully organized way

# Tt

**tab** /tæb/ *noun*
**1** a key that you press on a computer to make the CURSOR move to a new place
**2** a small piece of metal or plastic that you pull to open a container
**3** a bill showing how much you need to pay for food or drink that you have had: *Put those drinks on my tab, and I'll pay you Friday.*

**tab·by** /ˈtæbi/ *noun* (plural **tabbies**)
a cat with light and dark lines on its fur

**ta·ble** /ˈteɪbəl/ *noun*
**1** a piece of furniture with a flat top supported by legs: *We all sat down at the table for dinner.*
**2** a list of numbers or other information, arranged in rows on a page: *The table shows the average height and weight of children at different ages.*
[ORIGIN: 1100-1200 From the Latin word *tabula*, which means "board."]

**ta·ble·cloth** /ˈteɪbəlˌklɔθ/ *noun*
a large piece of cloth used for covering a table

**ˌtable of ˈcontents** *noun*
a list at the beginning of a book that tells you the order and the page numbers of the CHAPTERs

**ta·ble·spoon** /ˈteɪbəlˌspun/ *noun*
**1** a special spoon used for measuring amounts of food in cooking: *Add two tablespoons of sugar.*
**2** a large spoon used for eating food
—**tablespoonful** /ˈteɪbəlspunˌfʊl/ *noun* the amount a tablespoon holds

**tab·let** /ˈtæblɪt/ *noun*
**1** a small round piece of medicine that you swallow: *I have to take two tablets after every meal.* **SYNONYM: pill**
**2** a set of pieces of paper for writing on that are glued together at the top: *a tablet of writing paper*
→ see Thesaurus box at **medicine**

**ˈtable ˌtennis** *noun*
a game in which two people hit a small ball across a net on a table

**tack** /tæk/ *noun*
a small nail with a flat top: *They fixed the carpet down with tacks.*

**tack·le¹** /ˈtækəl/ *verb*
**1** to try to deal with a difficult problem: *What do you think is the best way to tackle the problem of bullying on the playground?*
**2** to make a player fall to the ground in football, so that he or she cannot carry the ball forward: *He was tackled by two players from the other team.*

**tackle²** *noun*
**1** the act of making a player fall to the ground in football: *He made 52 successful tackles this year.*
**2** a football player who tries to make other players fall to the ground
**3** equipment you use for fishing: *The shop sells fishing tackle.*

**tack·y** /ˈtæki/ *adjective*
**1** showing poor judgment about what is socially acceptable: *He left the price tag on the present! That is just so tacky!*
**2** tacky things are badly made and look cheap: *a shop selling tacky souvenirs*

**ta·co** /ˈtɑkoʊ/ *noun* (plural **tacos**)
a TORTILLA that is folded in half and filled with meat, beans, or other food

**tact** /tækt/ *noun*
the ability to say or do things carefully and politely so that you do not upset someone: *You need to use a lot of tact when you're dealing with customers.*

**WORD FAMILY: tact**
**tact** *noun* | **tactful** *adjective* | **tactfully** *adjective* | **tactless** *adjective*

**tact·ful** /ˈtæktfəl/ *adjective*
careful not to say or do something that will upset someone: *Doctors have to be tactful when they are asking people about their personal problems.* **ANTONYM: tactless**
—**tactfully** *adverb* in a tactful way

**tac·tic** /ˈtæktɪk/ *noun*
a plan for doing or achieving something: *We changed tactics in the second half of the game and we did much better.*
[ORIGIN: 1600-1700 From the Greek word

*taktikos*, which means "relating to the arrangement of soldiers or ships," from *tassein*, which means "to arrange things."]

**tact·less** /ˈtæktlɪs/ *adjective*
saying or doing things that are likely to upset someone because you have not thought carefully enough: *It was tactless to say that she needed to lose some weight.* **ANTONYM: tactful**
→ see Thesaurus box at **rude**

**tad·pole** /ˈtædpoʊl/ *noun*
a small creature with a long tail that lives in water and grows into a FROG or TOAD

**tag** /tæg/ *noun*
**1** a small piece of paper, plastic, etc. that is attached to something and gives information about it: *It says $50 on the price tag.* | *Our employees all wear name tags.*
**2** a children's game in which one player chases and tries to touch the others: *The kids were playing tag out on the playground.*

**tail** /teɪl/ *noun*
**1** a part of an animal's body that the animal can move and that sticks out from just above their bottom: *The dog was wagging its tail.*
**2** the back part of an airplane → see picture at **airplane**
**3 tails** = the side of a coin that does not have a picture of someone's head on it: *I'll flip a coin and you call heads or tails.* **ANTONYM: heads**

**tail·light** /ˈteɪl-laɪt/ *noun*
one of the two red lights at the back of a car

**tai·lor** /ˈteɪlɚ/ *noun*
someone whose job is to make clothes, especially men's clothes: *His suits came from a very expensive tailor in New York.*
[**ORIGIN:** 1200-1300 From the old French word *taillier*, which means "to cut."]

**Tai·wan·ese¹** /ˌtaɪwɑˈniz/ *adjective*
relating to or coming from Taiwan

**Taiwanese²** *noun* (plural **Taiwanese**)
someone from Taiwan

**take** /teɪk/ *verb* (**took** /tʊk/, **taken** /ˈteɪkən/)
**1** to move someone or something from one place to another: *The ambulance took him to the hospital.* | *You'd better take your jacket.*

**THESAURUS: take**

**bring** to take something or someone to a place: *You should bring her some flowers.* | *Elise brought her friend with her to the party.*

**drive** to take someone somewhere in a vehicle: *Would you like me to drive you to school today?*

**deliver** to take a letter or package somewhere: *The mailman delivers the mail every morning.*

**2** to remove something from a place: *Can you take the turkey out of the oven for me?*
**3** to get hold of something in your hands: *Let me take your coat.*
**4** to steal or borrow something without asking someone's permission: *The thieves took all her money.*
**5** used with some nouns when saying that someone does something: *Take a look at this!* | *I usually take a shower before breakfast.* | *We had to take a written test.*
**6** used when saying that a quality or an amount of time, money, or effort is needed to do something: *The game takes a lot of skill.* | *It takes about three hours to drive to Los Angeles.*
**7** to accept something that someone has offered you: *Are you going to take the job?*
**8** to drink or swallow some medicine or a drug: *"I have a headache." "Why don't you take an aspirin?"*
**9** to use a car, bus, train, etc.: *I'll take the subway home.*
**10** to study a subject in school or college: *I decided to take French.*
**11** to react to something in a particular way: *"How did she take the news?" "She took it pretty badly."*
**12** (*also* **take down**) to write down information: *He's not here; can I take a message?*
**13** to measure the amount, level, or rate of something, for example someone's temperature: *My mother took my temperature using a thermometer.* | *The scientist took a reading from the device.*

**14** to have enough space to contain a particular number of people or things: *The hall can take up to 300 people.*

**15** to wear a particular size of clothing or shoes: *"What size shoes do you take?" "I take a size 8."*

**16** to subtract a number from another number: *If you take 8 away from 20, you get 12.*

→ **take care, take care of something** at **care**[2], **take effect** at **effect**, **take notice** at **notice**[2], **take part** at **part**[1], **take place** at **place**[1]

→ see Thesaurus box at **bring**, **get**

**PHRASAL VERBS**

**take after someone**

to look or behave like someone in your family who is older than you: *She takes after her mother.*

**take something away**

to remove something: *They delivered a new bed and took the old one away.*

**take something back**

to return something to the store where you bought it because it does not fit, is not what you wanted, etc.: *If you don't like the dress, you can take it back.*

**take in**

**1 take someone/something in** = to give a home to a person or animal who has nowhere to live: *He had nowhere to live, but luckily one of his friends took him in.*

**2 be taken in** = to be deceived by someone who tells lies to you: *I was taken in by her story and gave her $20.*

**take off**

**1 take something off** = to remove something you are wearing: *She took off her coat and sat down in a chair.* **ANTONYM: put on**

**2 take off** = if a plane takes off, it leaves the ground and goes up into the air → see picture at **land**

**3 take off** (*informal*) = to leave a place quickly: *They took off without saying goodbye.*

**4 take time off/take a week off, etc.** = to not go to work for a period of time: *You look tired – you should take some time off.*

**5 take off** = to suddenly become successful: *He died just as his film career was taking off.*

**take out**

**1 take someone out** = to go with someone to a restaurant, movie, etc., and pay for this: *His girlfriend is taking him out for dinner on his birthday.*

**2 take out a loan** = to borrow money from a bank

**take over something**

to take control of something: *His son will take over the business when he retires.*

**take up something**

**1** to begin doing a job or activity: *He took up swimming in order to try to lose weight.*

**2** to fill a particular amount of time or space: *Our new car takes up the whole garage.*

**3** to make a piece of clothing shorter: *Can you take up this dress for me?*

**ˈtake-home ˌpay** *noun*

the amount of money you get for doing your job after taxes have been taken away: *After taxes and Social Security, his take-home pay was less than he expected.*

**tak·en** /ˈteɪkən/ *verb*

the past participle of TAKE

**take·off** /ˈteɪk-ɔf/ *noun*

the time when an airplane leaves the ground and begins to fly: *They served the meal shortly after takeoff.* **ANTONYM: landing**

**take·out** /ˈteɪk-aʊt/ *noun*

food that you buy at a restaurant to eat at home: *I don't feel like cooking tonight – let's get takeout.*

**tale** /teɪl/ *noun* (*formal*)

a story, usually about events that are not real: *The book tells a tale of love and adventure during the war.* **SYNONYM: story**

→ see Thesaurus box at **story**

**tal·ent** /ˈtælənt/ *noun*

an ability to do something well: *Vinny has a real talent for photography.*

—**talented** *adjective* very good at something: *He's a very talented actor; you really believe that he is the character.*

→ see Thesaurus box at **ability**

[**ORIGIN:** 1400-1500 From the Greek word *talanton*, which was a unit of weight or money. The modern meaning comes from a story in the Bible in which a man gives talents to his three servants, and two of them use them well.]

**talk¹** /tɔk/ *verb*
to say things to someone: *We spent the whole evening talking about the trip.* | *Who's he talking to on the phone?*
—**talker** *noun* someone who talks a lot, or talks in a particular way

**WORD FAMILY: talk**
**talk** *verb* | **talk** *noun* | **talkative** *adjective*

**USAGE: talk, tell, say**
You **talk** about a particular subject: *Each student had to talk about his or her family.*
You **tell** a person facts or information: *She told me that she was going home.*
You **say** words to someone. You cannot say "say me": *Did Nick say anything to you?*

**THESAURUS: talk**
**speak** to talk to someone about something: *The coach would like to speak with you after practice.*
**have a conversation** to talk to another person or people: *It's so noisy in here that it's hard to have a conversation.*
**chat** to talk to someone in a friendly way about things that are not very important: *She was chatting to her friends on the school bus.*
**discuss** to talk about something in order to make a decision or make plans: *The teacher will discuss your progress with your parents.*
**gossip** to talk about other people's behavior and lives when they are not there: *My aunts were gossiping about my sister's new boyfriend.*

**PHRASAL VERBS**
**talk back**
to answer a parent, teacher, etc. in a rude way: *Don't talk back to your father!*
**talk someone into doing something**
to persuade someone to do something: *The kids talked us into getting a dog.*
**talk someone out of (doing) something**
to persuade someone not to do something: *His mom talked him out of dropping out of school.*
**talk something over**
to discuss something with someone before deciding what to do: *It sounds like a good idea, but we should talk it over with everyone else before we do anything.*

**WORD FAMILY: talk**
**talk** *verb* | **talk** *noun* | **talkative** *adjective*

**talk²** *noun*
**1** a conversation: *I need to have a talk with Suzanne about the way she's been behaving.*
**2** a speech to a group of people: *Ms. Mason will be giving a talk on how to find a job.*

**talk·a·tive** /ˈtɔkətɪv/ *adjective*
someone who is talkative talks a lot: *He's very talkative and tells me about everything.*

**ˈtalk show** *noun*
a television show in which famous people answer questions about themselves

**tall** /tɔl/ *adjective*
**1** bigger in height than most other people or things: *John is a lot taller than his younger brother.* | *The tallest building in town has 24 floors.* **ANTONYM: short**

**USAGE: tall, high**
Use **tall** about people, trees, and other narrow things: *She was tall and slim.* | *The bird's nest was at the top of a tall tree.* | *a tall flagpole*
Use **high** about mountains, walls, fences, etc.: *The highest mountain in the USA is Mount McKinley.*
Use **high** to talk about how far something is above the ground: *The shelf's too high for the kids to reach.*
When describing buildings, we usually use **tall**, not **high**: *the tall buildings in the downtown area*

**2** having a particular height: *My brother's almost 6 feet tall.*

**ˌtall ˈtale** *noun*
a story that is difficult to believe because the events in it seem too unlikely to be true: *She told us a tall tale about Paul Bunyan, the biggest man who ever lived.*

**tal·ly** /ˈtæli/ *noun* (plural **tallies**)
a record you keep when you are counting something: *Keep a tally of each player's score.*

**tam·bou·rine** /ˌtæmbəˈrin/ *noun*
a musical instrument that you shake or hit with your hand. It looks like a small drum with metal pieces around the edge. → see picture on page **A21**

**tame¹** /teɪm/ *adjective*
a tame animal is one that is not afraid of people because it has been near them a lot: *The bird was very tame, and flew right onto my hand.* **ANTONYM: wild**

**tame²** *verb*
to train a wild animal so that it is not frightened of people and will not hurt them: *They tamed the monkeys.*

**tam·per** /ˈtæmpɚ/ *verb*
**PHRASAL VERB**
**tamper with something**
to touch or change something secretly, in order to cause damage: *Someone has tampered with the lock and now it's broken.*

**tam·pon** /ˈtæmpɑn/ *noun*
a tube-shaped piece of cotton that a woman puts inside herself during her PERIOD to stop blood from coming out

**tan¹** /tæn/ *noun*
**1** the darker skin that you get after you have been in the sun: *Monica got a nice tan during her trip to Hawaii.* **SYNONYM: suntan**
**2** a pale yellow-brown color

**tan²** *adjective*
**1** someone who is tan has darker skin than usual because he or she has been in the sun: *You're really tan – have you been to the beach?* **SYNONYM: tanned**
**2** having a pale yellow-brown color: *He was wearing a pair of tan shoes.*

**tan·ger·ine** /ˌtændʒəˈrin/ *noun*
a sweet fruit that looks like a small orange → see picture on page **A13**
[**ORIGIN:** 1600-1700 From Tangier, a city in Morocco.]

**tan·gi·ble** /ˈtændʒəbəl/ *adjective* (*formal*)
if something is tangible, you can be certain that it exists because you can see it, touch it, or prove it: *His work was starting to produce tangible results that everyone could see.*

**tan·gle** /ˈtæŋgəl/ *verb*
to twist hair, threads, or wire together into messy knots: *The strong wind tangled her long hair.*
—**tangle** *noun* a messy knot of hairs, threads, or wire: *Mom combed the tangles out of my hair.*
—**tangled** *adjective* twisted together into messy knots: *tangled threads*

**tangle**

tangled Christmas lights

**tank** /tæŋk/ *noun*
**1** a large container for holding liquid or gas: *She filled up the car's gas tank.* | *a fish tank*
**2** a heavy military vehicle with guns on it and metal belts over its wheels
[**ORIGIN:** 1600-1700 From the Portuguese word *tanque*, which means "pool."]

**tank·er** /ˈtæŋkɚ/ *noun*
a large ship or truck that carries liquids: *an oil tanker*

**tanned** /tænd/ *adjective*
someone who is tanned has darker skin than usual because he or she has been in the sun: *The girl playing tennis had long, tanned legs.* **SYNONYM: tan**

**tan·trum** /ˈtæntrəm/ (*also* **temper tantrum**) *noun*
a time when a young child suddenly becomes angry and starts shouting and crying: *My little brother had a tantrum in the supermarket because Mom wouldn't buy him any candy.*

**tap¹** /tæp/ *verb* (**tapped, tapping**)
to gently hit your fingers or foot against something: *She tapped her fingers on the table as she listened to the music.*
→ see Thesaurus box at **hit¹**

**tap²** *noun*
**1** an act of hitting something gently: *I felt a tap on my shoulder and turned around.* → see picture on page **A3**
**2** an object that starts and stops the flow of liquid out of a pipe or container **SYNONYM: faucet**

T

**ˈtap ˌdancing** *noun*
a type of dancing in which you wear special shoes that make a sound on the floor as you dance

**tape¹** Ac /teɪp/ *noun*
**1** a material for recording sounds or pictures, made of a long thin band of special plastic in a small case: *Put the tape in the VCR and press the "play" button.*
**2** a long band of sticky clear plastic that you use for sticking things together: *The picture was stuck to the wall with tape.*

**tape²** Ac *verb*
**1** to record sounds or pictures onto a tape: *If we tape the movie, we can watch it later.*
**2** to stick something onto something else using tape: *He has lots of postcards taped to his wall.*
→ see Thesaurus box at **fasten**

T

**ˈtape ˌmeasure** *noun*
a long band of cloth or metal with inches or centimeters marked on it, that you use for measuring things

**ˈtape reˌcorder** *noun*
a machine that records and plays music and other sounds
—**tape recording** *noun* something that has been recorded using a tape recorder: *Police made a tape recording of the interview.*

**tap·es·try** /ˈtæpəstri/ *noun* (plural **tapestries**)
a picture that someone makes by weaving colored threads into heavy cloth: *There were many tapestries hanging on the walls in the palace.*

**tar** /tɑr/ *noun*
a thick sticky black substance used for making roads: *The men had put fresh tar on the road and it was still sticky.*

**ta·ran·tu·la** /təˈræntʃələ/ *noun*
a large hairy SPIDER that lives in hot countries and eats insects or small animals

**tar·get** Ac /ˈtɑrgɪt/ *noun*
**1** an object that you aim at if you are shooting: *Pete shot the arrow and missed the target by two inches.*
**2** an object, person, or place that someone chooses to attack: *The building was the target of a terrorist bomb.*
**3** the aim or result that you try to achieve: *We're raising money for charity and hope to reach our target of $3,000.*
[**ORIGIN:** 1200-1300 From the old French word *targette*, which means "small shield," from *targe*, meaning "shield."]

**tar·iff** /ˈtærɪf/ *noun*
a tax on goods that enter or leave a country: *The government may put new tariffs on imports to protect its own industries.*

**tart** /tɑrt/ *adjective*
having a sharp sour taste: *Add some sugar to the berries if they're too tart.*

**task** Ac /tæsk/ *noun*
something that you have to do: *The competition judges had the task of choosing a winner.*
[**ORIGIN:** 1200-1300 From the Latin word *tasca*, which means "money to be paid or service to be done for a ruler," from *taxare*, which means "to make a judgment about something, or to tax something."]

**taste¹** /teɪst/ *noun*
**1** the feeling that you get when your tongue touches a food or drink: *Chocolate has a sweet taste. | I don't like the taste of garlic.*

**THESAURUS: taste**

**delicious** having a very good taste: *a delicious apple pie | The meal was delicious.*

**disgusting, horrible, awful** having a very bad taste: *The food was disgusting – nothing seemed to be cooked right.*

**sweet** containing a lot of sugar, or tasting like sugar: *He loves sweet foods like chocolate and ice cream.*

**salty** containing a lot of salt: *Potato chips are salty.*

**sour** having a strong taste like a lemon: *Some kinds of apples are very sour.*

**bitter** having a strong bad taste that is not at all sweet: *The coffee was strong and bitter.*

**hot, spicy** containing spices that make your mouth feel very hot: *Some Mexican food can be really spicy.*

**bland** not having very much taste: *The soup was really bland.*

**tasty** having a pleasant taste, but usually not sweet: *The hotdog was covered in a tasty chili sauce.*

**2 sense of taste** = your sense of taste is your ability to notice the different tastes of food and drink
**3** the type of clothes, music, etc. that someone likes: *We have similar taste in clothes.*
**4** a small amount of a food or drink that you put in your mouth to find out what it is like: *Can I have a taste of your ice cream?*
[ORIGIN: 1200-1300 From the old French word *taster*, which means "to test or taste," from the Latin word *taxare*, which means "to make a judgment about something."]

**taste**[2] *verb*
**1** to have a particular taste: *The chicken tastes really good – how did you make it?*
**2** to put a small amount of food or drink in your mouth in order to find out what it is like: *Taste this and see if it needs more salt.*
**3** to be able to recognize the taste of a food or drink: *You can really taste the honey in these cookies.*

**ˈtaste bud** *noun*
one of the parts on your tongue that help you to taste things: *Your taste buds tell you whether a food is sweet, salty, sour, or bitter.*

**taste·ful** /ˈteɪstfəl/ *adjective*
something that is tasteful looks attractive and shows that you have good judgment in choosing things: *He wore a tasteful dark suit.*
—**tastefully** *adverb* in a tasteful way: *The apartment was tastefully decorated.*

**taste·less** /ˈteɪstləs/ *adjective*
slightly offensive and not suitable for the situation: *She made a tasteless joke about a pop star who had just died.*

**tast·y** /ˈteɪsti/ *adjective* (**tastier**, **tastiest**)
having a very good taste: *The fish was tasty.*

**tat·tle·tale** /ˈtætlˌteɪl/ *noun*
someone who tells a teacher or parent that another child has done something bad

**tat·too** /təˈtu/ *noun* (plural **tattoos**)
a permanent picture or word on your skin, done using a needle and ink: *He has a tattoo of a snake on his left arm.*

tattoo

[ORIGIN: 1700-1800 From the Tahitian word for these pictures, *tatau*. Tahiti is one of the Polynesian islands in the South Pacific.]

**taught** /tɔt/ *verb*
the past tense and past participle of TEACH

**taunt** /tɔnt/ *verb* (*formal*)
to try to make someone upset or angry by saying cruel things: *The other kids taunted him about his weight.*

**Tau·rus** /ˈtɔrəs/ *noun*
**1** the second sign of the ZODIAC, represented by a BULL
**2** someone born between April 20 and May 20

**taut** /tɔt/ *adjective*
stretched tight: *The rope should be taut, not loose.*

**tax**[1] /tæks/ *noun*
the money you have to pay the government, based on how much you earn, what you buy, etc.: *There is a tax on gasoline.*
[ORIGIN: 1200-1300 From the Latin word *taxare*, which means "to make a judgment about something, or to tax something."]

**WORD FAMILY: tax**
**tax** *noun* | **tax** *verb* | **taxation** *noun* | **taxable** *adjective*

**tax**[2] *verb*
to make people pay tax: *The government taxes people to pay for schools, roads, and many other things.*
—**taxable** *adjective* if something is taxable, you have to pay tax on it: *taxable income*

**tax·a·tion** /tækˈseɪʃən/ *noun*
the system of charging taxes, or the money a government gets from taxes

**tax·i** /ˈtæksi/ *noun*
a car with a driver that you pay to take you somewhere: *We took a taxi to the airport.* | *a*

*taxi driver* **SYNONYMS: cab, taxicab** → see picture on page **A26**

**tax·i·cab** /ˈtæksiˌkæb/ *noun*
another word for a TAXI

**tea** /ti/ *noun*
a hot drink that you make by pouring boiling water onto dried leaves: *Would you like a cup of tea or coffee?*
**[ORIGIN:** 1600-1700 From the Chinese word *te.***]**

**teach** /tiːtʃ/ *verb* (**taught** /tɔt/)
**1** to give someone lessons in a school or college: *She teaches math at Jackson High School.*
**2** to tell or show someone how to do something: *My dad taught me how to swim.*
**[ORIGIN:** From the old English word *tæcan*, which means "to show or teach."**]**

**USAGE: teach, learn**

If you **teach** someone a subject or skill, you help him or her learn it: *Brad is teaching me to play the guitar.*

You cannot say "Dad learned me to play the guitar."

You **learn** a subject or skill when you study or practice it: *I want to learn English.* | *Jo is learning to drive.*

**teach·er** /ˈtitʃɚ/ *noun*
someone whose job is to teach: *She's a history teacher.* → see picture on page **A16**

**ˌteacher's ˈpet** *noun* (*informal*)
a child who everyone thinks is the teacher's favorite student, so the other children do not like him or her

**teach·ing** /ˈtitʃɪŋ/ *noun*
the job of being a teacher: *He went into teaching after finishing college because he likes working with children.*

**tea·ket·tle** /ˈtiˌketl/ *noun*
a metal container used for boiling and pouring water **SYNONYM: kettle**

**team** [Ac] /tim/ *noun*
**1** a group of people who compete against another group in a sport or game: *Which team is winning?* | *the baseball team*
**2** a group of people who work together to do something: *A team of scientists is searching for a cure for the disease.*
→ see Thesaurus box at **group¹**

**team·mate** /ˈtim-meɪt/ *noun*
someone who plays or works on the same team as you

**team·work** /ˈtimwɚk/ *noun*
the ability of a group of people to work well together: *The children all helped to organize the school fair – it was great teamwork.*

**tea·pot** /ˈtipɑt/ *noun*
a container used for serving tea

**tear¹** /ter/ *verb* (**tore** /tɔr/, **torn** /tɔrn/)
**1** to make a hole in paper or cloth by pulling it apart: *She tore her shirt on a nail.* | *The thin paper tears very easily.* **SYNONYM: rip**
**2** to pull something away from a person or place with a lot of force: *The strong wind tore the door off its hinges.*
**3** to move very quickly: *The cat came tearing out of the house.*

**PHRASAL VERBS**

**tear something down**
to deliberately destroy a building: *The old train station was torn down in 1990.*

**tear something up**
to tear a piece of paper or cloth into small pieces: *He tore up the pictures of his ex-girlfriend.*

**tear²** /ter/ *noun*
a hole in a piece of paper or cloth where someone or something has torn it: *I offered to sew up the tear in his shirt.*

**tear³** /tɪr/ *noun*
a drop of liquid that comes out of your eyes when you cry: *I had tears in my eyes as we said goodbye.*
—**tearful** *adjective* crying, or feeling as if you want to cry: *He said a tearful goodbye to his mother.*

**tear·drop** /ˈtɪrdrɑp/ *noun*
one drop of liquid that has come out of your eyes when you are crying

**tease** /tiz/ *verb*
to make jokes about someone in order to embarrass or annoy him or her: *His friends teased him about his accent.*

**tea·spoon** /ˈtispun/ *noun*
**1** (*written abbreviation*: **tsp.**) a special small

spoon used for measuring food

**2** a small spoon used for eating or for putting sugar in coffee or tea

—**teaspoonful** /ˈtispunˌfʊl/ *noun* the amount a teaspoon holds

**tech·ni·cal** Ac /ˈteknɪkəl/ *adjective* relating to machines or science: *We offer technical support if you are having problems with your computer.*

[ORIGIN: 1600-1700 From the Greek word *technikos*, which means "artistic or skillful," from *techne*, meaning "art or skill."]

**tech·ni·cal·i·ty** /ˌteknɪˈkæləti/ *noun* (plural **technicalities**)

a small detail in a law or rule: *The police believed he was guilty, but they had to let him go because of a technicality.*

**tech·ni·cian** /tekˈnɪʃən/ *noun*

someone whose job involves using special equipment or machines to do something: *a computer technician | Lab technicians were testing all the blood samples.*

**tech·nique** Ac /tekˈnik/ *noun*

a special way of doing something: *Learning some relaxation techniques can help you deal with stress.*

**tech·nol·o·gy** Ac /tekˈnɑlədʒi/ *noun* (plural **technologies**)

scientific knowledge used for making machines, or machines that use advanced scientific knowledge: *New technology has meant that cell phones are much smaller than they used to be.*

—**technological** /ˌteknəˈlɑdʒɪkəl/ *adjective* relating to technology: *Technological developments have allowed more people to work from home.*

**ted·dy bear** /ˈtedi ˌber/ *noun*

a soft toy that looks like a bear

[ORIGIN: From Theodore ("Teddy") Roosevelt (1858-1919), a U.S. president, who liked hunting bears.]

**te·di·ous** /ˈtidiəs/ *adjective* (*formal*)

boring, and continuing for a long time: *I had the tedious job of typing all of the information into the computer.*

→ see Thesaurus box at **boring**

**teen** /tin/ *noun*

**1** another word for a TEENAGER

**2** **teens** = the period of time when you are between 13 and 19 years old: *She got married when she was still in her teens.*

**teen·ag·er** /ˈtiˌneɪdʒɚ/ *noun*

someone who is between 13 and 19 years old: *The mall is full of teenagers after school.*

—**teenage** *adjective* between the ages of 13 and 19: *The magazine is intended for teenage girls.*

→ see Thesaurus box at **child**

**tee·ny** /ˈtini/ *adjective* (*informal*)

very small: *I'll just have a teeny bit of ice cream, please – I'm already pretty full.* **SYNONYM: tiny**

**teeth** /tiθ/ *noun*

the plural of TOOTH

**tel·e·com·mu·ni·ca·tions** /ˌteləkəˌmyunəˈkeɪʃənz/ *noun*

the process of sending and receiving messages by telephone, radio, SATELLITE, etc.: *Telecommunications companies provide telephone services.*

**tel·e·gram** /ˈteləˌgræm/ *noun*

a message that someone sends by telegraph

**tel·e·graph** /ˈteləˌgræf/ *noun*

an old way of sending messages through wires using electrical signals

—**telegraph** *verb* to send a message by telegraph

[ORIGIN: 1700-1800 From the Greek words *tele* and *graphein*, which mean "far away" and "to write."]

**tel·e·phone** /ˈteləˌfoʊn/ *noun*

a piece of equipment that you use to talk to someone in another place: *Can you answer the telephone if it rings?* **SYNONYM: phone**

→ see picture on page **A8**

—**telephone** *verb* (*formal*) to call someone using a telephone

[ORIGIN: 1800-1900 From the Greek words *tele* and *phone*, which mean "far away" and "sound or voice."]

**ˈtelephone diˌrectory** *noun* (plural **telephone directories**) (*formal*)

another word for a PHONE BOOK

**ˈtelephone ˌnumber** *noun*

another word for a PHONE NUMBER

**tel·e·scope** /ˈteləˌskoʊp/ *noun*
a piece of equipment that makes things that are far away look bigger and closer. It is made of a long tube with special curved glass LENSes in it: *You can use a telescope to study the moon.*
[ORIGIN: 1600-1700 From the Greek words *tele* and *skopein*, which mean "far away" and "to look at."]

**telescope**

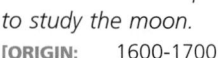

**tel·e·vise** /ˈteləvaɪz/ *verb*
to broadcast something on television: *The concert will be televised, so if you can't get tickets, let's watch it on TV.*

**tel·e·vi·sion** /ˈteləˌvɪʒən/ *noun*
**1** (*also* **television set**) a piece of equipment with a screen that you watch programs on: *Lucy turned on the television to watch the news.* SYNONYM: TV → see picture on page **A8**
**2** the programs that you can watch on a television: *He's been watching television all day.* | *What's on television?* SYNONYM: TV
**3** the activity of making and broadcasting programs on television: *Jean works in television.*
[ORIGIN: 1900-2000 From the Greek word *tele*, which means "far away," and the word "vision."]

**tell** /tel/ *verb* (**told** /toʊld/)
**1** to give someone information by talking or writing to them: *Tell me about your trip to New York.* | *She wrote to tell me that she was getting married.*

> **USAGE: tell, say, talk**
>
> You **tell** a person facts or information: *She told me that she was going home.*
>
> You **say** words to someone. You cannot say "say me": *Did Nick say anything to you?*
>
> You **talk** about a particular subject: *Each student had to talk about his or her family.*

**2** to say that someone should do something: *She told Mike not to call her anymore.* | *His doctor told him to get more exercise.*
**3 can tell** = to know that something is true because you can see something that shows you it is true: *You can tell that they're sisters – they look so much alike.* | *I could tell that she was lying by the guilty look on her face.*
→ see Thesaurus box at **explain**

**tell·er** /ˈtelɚ/ *noun*
someone whose job is to receive and pay out money in a bank: *The bank teller counted out the money and gave it to the customer.*

**temp** /temp/ *noun* (*informal*)
someone who works for different companies for short periods of time: *We'll need a temp while Janet is on vacation.*

**tem·per** /ˈtempɚ/ *noun*
**1** someone who has a temper gets angry easily or suddenly: *Julie has a terrible temper – she often shouts and throws things.*
**2 lose your temper** = to suddenly become very angry: *Al lost his temper and started screaming at us.*

**tem·pera·ment** /ˈtempərəmənt/ *noun*
the type of character you have, for example whether you get angry easily or are usually relaxed: *He has a calm temperament and is easy to be around.*

**tem·pera·men·tal** /ˌtempərəˈmentl/ *adjective*
a temperamental person often changes from being happy to being angry or sad without a good reason: *He is so temperamental, you never know what sort of mood he will be in.*

**tem·perate** /ˈtempərət/ *adjective*
a part of the world that is temperate is never very hot or very cold: *These plants grow best in a temperate climate and cannot survive in extreme temperatures.*

**tem·pera·ture** /ˈtemprətʃɚ/ *noun*
**1** how hot or cold something is: *The temperature at night can drop to as low as 10° F.*
**2 take someone's temperature** = to measure the temperature of someone's body, to find out whether he or she is sick: *The nurse took my temperature with a thermometer.*
**3 have a temperature** = to be hot because you are sick: *He had a temperature and had to stay in bed.*

**ˈtemper ˌtantrum** *noun*
another word for a TANTRUM

**tem·plate** /ˈtempleɪt/ *noun*
something that you can copy when you want to produce a similar thing: *The software has templates for different types of letters, such as formal ones.*

**tem·ple** /ˈtempəl/ *noun*
**1** a building where people in some religions go to pray: *a Buddhist temple*
**2** the area on the side of your head, between your ear and your eye: *His dark hair is gray at the temples.*

**tem·po** /ˈtempoʊ/ *noun* (plural **tempos**)
the speed at which a person or band plays a piece of music: *He played the music at the wrong tempo – it was way too slow.*

**tem·po·rar·y** Ac /ˈtempəˌreri/ *adjective*
existing or happening for a short time only: *Many college students get temporary jobs during the summer.* **ANTONYM: permanent**
—**temporarily** /ˌtempəˈrerəli/ *adverb* for a short time only: *The museum will be temporarily closed for repairs.*
[**ORIGIN:** 1500-1600 From the Latin word *temporarius*, from *tempus*, which means "time."]

**tempt** /tempt/ *verb*
to make you want to have or do something, especially something that will have a bad effect: *I was tempted to tell her what I really thought, but I decided not to.*

**WORD FAMILY: tempt**
**tempt** *verb* | **tempting** *adjective* | **temptation** *noun*

**temp·ta·tion** /tempˈteɪʃən/ *noun*
a strong feeling of wanting to have or do something that you should not: *I wanted another cookie, but I resisted the temptation and didn't take one.*

**tempt·ing** /ˈtemptɪŋ/ *adjective*
something that is tempting seems good and you would like to have it: *During the holidays, there are a lot of tempting foods around, and it's hard to stay on a diet.*

**ten¹** /ten/ *number*
**1** 10: *The book cost ten dollars.*
**2** ten O'CLOCK: *The store closes at ten.*
**3** ten years old: *My brother is ten.*

**ten²** *noun*
a piece of paper money worth $10: *I paid with a ten.*

**ten·ant** /ˈtenənt/ *noun*
someone who pays rent to live in a room or house: *The landlord is looking for new tenants for the apartment.*
[**ORIGIN:** 1300-1400 From the Latin word *tenere*, which means "to hold."]

**tend** /tend/ *verb*
**tend to do something** = to be likely to do something, or to usually do something: *People tend to need less sleep as they become older.*

**WORD FAMILY: tend**
**tend** *verb* | **tendency** *noun*

**tend·en·cy** /ˈtendənsi/ *noun* (plural **tendencies**)
if you have a tendency to do something, you usually do it: *He has a tendency to talk too much, which annoys his friends.*

**ten·der** /ˈtendɚ/ *adjective*
**1** gentle and loving: *She gave her son a tender kiss.*
**2** tender food is soft and easy to cut and eat: *This steak is nice and tender.* **ANTONYM: tough**
**3** painful when touched: *My arm is still tender where I hurt it when I fell off my bicycle.*
—**tenderly** *adverb* in a gentle and loving way: *He kissed her tenderly on the cheek.*
—**tenderness** *noun* a gentle and careful quality that shows love

**ten·don** /ˈtendən/ *noun*
a part of your body that connects muscle to a bone

**ten·nis** /ˈtenɪs/ *noun*
a game in which two or four people use RACKETs to hit a ball to each other across a net → see picture on page A24

**ˈtennis shoe** *noun*
a shoe used for sports: *a pair of tennis shoes*

**ten·or** /ˈtenɚ/ *noun*
a male singer with a high voice

**tense¹** Ac /tens/ *adjective*
**1** nervous and worried: *He felt very tense before the test.* **ANTONYM: calm**
**2** a tense situation makes people feel nervous

T

or worried: *It was a tense game which either team could have won.*

**3** tense muscles feel tight and stiff: *A warm bath will relax your tense muscles.*

[**ORIGIN:** 1600-1700 From the Latin word *tensus*, which means "stretched," and is a form of the verb *tendere*, meaning "to stretch."]

**WORD FAMILY: tense**

**tense** *adjective* | **tension** *noun*

**tense²** Ac *noun*
a form of a verb that shows whether you are talking about the past, the present, or the future. For example, in the sentence "I like dogs," the verb "like" is in the present tense: *She used the past tense when talking about him, saying "he was" and "he had."*
[**ORIGIN:** 1300-1400 From the Latin word *tempus*, which means "time."]

T

**ten·sion** Ac /ˈtenʃən/ *noun*
a nervous feeling that you have when you do not know what is going to happen: *The room was filled with tension as the students waited for the test to begin.*

**tent** /tent/ *noun*
a structure that you sleep in when you are camping, which is made of cloth and held up by poles and ropes: *We put up the tent in the campground.*

[**ORIGIN:** 1200-1300 From the Latin word *tendere*, which means "to stretch." A tent is made from cloth stretched over a frame.]

**ten·ta·cle** /ˈtentəkəl/ *noun*
one of the long soft arms of a sea animal such as an OCTOPUS

**ten·ta·tive** /ˈtentətɪv/ *adjective (formal)*
not definite or certain: *We have tentative plans to go swimming on Tuesday, but we'll make definite plans on Monday.*

**tenth** /tenθ/ *number*
**1** 10th
**2** 1/10

**te·pee** (*also* **teepee** *or* **tipi**) /ˈtipi/ *noun*
a large round tent with a pointed top, used in past times by some Native Americans
[**ORIGIN:** 1700-1800 From the Sioux word *tipi*, from the words *ti* and *pi*, which mean "to live in a place" and "to use for." Sioux is a Native American language.]

**te·qui·la** /təˈkilə/ *noun*
a strong alcoholic drink made in Mexico

**term¹** /tɚm/ *noun*
**1** a word or phrase: *The book contains a lot of difficult scientific terms.*
**2** a period of time during which someone does a job: *The president is hoping to win a second term of office.*
**3** one of the periods that the school or college year is divided into: *She'll graduate after spring term.*
**4 in terms of something** = in relation to something: *"Avatar" has been his most successful movie in terms of money.*
**5 terms** = the things that you accept or agree to do as part of a legal agreement: *Both sides have accepted the terms of the agreement.*
[**ORIGIN:** 1200-1300 From the Latin word *terminus*, which means "boundary, limit, or end." A term is a specific period of time that has an end.]

**term²** *verb (formal)*
to use a word to describe something or give it a name: *Very bad headaches of this type are termed "migraines."*

**ter·min·al¹** Ac /ˈtɚmənəl/ *noun*
**1** a building where people get on airplanes, buses, or ships: *Our plane leaves from Terminal 4.*
**2** a screen and KEYBOARD that are connected to a computer: *She was sitting at a computer terminal, typing a report.*
**3** one of the points at which you can connect wires in an electrical CIRCUIT: *Each battery has a positive and a negative terminal.*

**terminal²** *adjective*
a terminal illness cannot be cured, and causes death: *He has terminal cancer.*

**ter·mi·nate** Ac /ˈtɚməˌneɪt/ *verb (formal)*
to end something: *He terminated his contract with the baseball club and become a free agent.*
—**termination** /ˌtɚməˈneɪʃən/ *noun* the act of ending something

**ter·mite** /ˈtɚmaɪt/ *noun*
an insect that eats wood from trees and buildings, so that they are damaged

**ˈterm ˌpaper** *noun*
a long piece of written work by a student for a particular class: *I'm writing a term paper on the Civil War for my history class.*

**ter·race** /ˈterɪs/ *noun*
a flat area next to a building or on a roof, where you can sit: *They sat on the terrace and watched the sunset.*
[**ORIGIN:** 1500-1600 From the old French word *terrasse*, which means "pile of earth, or platform on a pile of earth," from the Latin word *terra*, which means "earth or land."]

**ter·rain** /təˈreɪn/ *noun (formal)*
a particular type of land: *You need a strong pair of boots when walking over this rocky terrain.*
[**ORIGIN:** 1700-1800 From French, from the Latin word *terra*, which means "earth or land."]

**ter·ri·ble** /ˈterəbəl/ *adjective*
very bad: *He's a terrible cook – he always burns the food.* **SYNONYM: awful**
→ see Thesaurus box at **bad**
[**ORIGIN:** 1300-1400 From the Latin word *terribilis*, which means "frightening," from *terrere*, which means "to frighten."]

**ter·ri·bly** /ˈterəbli/ *adverb*
**1** very badly: *The team played terribly and deserved to lose.*
**2** very: *It's terribly important that I talk to him.*

**ter·rif·ic** /təˈrɪfɪk/ *adjective (informal)*
very good: *That's a terrific idea! Let's get started! | You look terrific in that dress.* **SYNONYM: wonderful**
[**ORIGIN:** 1600-1700 From the Latin word *terrificus*, which means "frightening," from *terrere*, which means "to frighten." "Terrific" later meant "very big" and then "very good."]

**ter·ri·fy** /ˈterəˌfaɪ/ *verb* (**terrified**, **terrifies**)
to make someone very frightened: *Flying terrifies me – I hate airplanes.*
—**terrified** *adjective* very frightened: *She was terrified of the big barking dog.*
—**terrifying** *adjective* making someone very frightened: *Being in jail was terrifying.*

**ter·ri·to·ry** /ˈterəˌtɔri/ *noun* (plural **territories**)
**1** land that is owned or controlled by a particular country: *Hong Kong became Chinese territory in 1997.*
**2** an area of land: *This part of the mountains was unknown territory to me.*
[**ORIGIN:** 1300-1400 From the Latin word *territorium*, which means "land around a town," from *terra*, which means "earth or land."]

**ter·ror** /ˈterɚ/ *noun*
**1** a feeling of great fear: *She ran away in terror when she saw that the man had a gun.*
**2** violent actions that are done to achieve a political purpose: *The president said he was doing everything possible to protect the country from terror.* **SYNONYM: terrorism**

**WORD FAMILY: terror**
**terror** *noun* | **terrorize** *verb* | **terrorist** *noun* | **terrorism** *noun*

**ter·ror·ism** /ˈterəˌrɪzəm/ *noun*
the use of violent actions, usually against ordinary people, to try to force a government to do something: *The bombing was an act of terrorism.*

**ter·ror·ist** /ˈterərɪst/ *noun*
someone who uses violent actions for political reasons, especially actions against ordinary people: *The terrorists tried to take bombs onto the airplanes.*

**ter·ror·ize** /ˈterəˌraɪz/ *verb*
to deliberately frighten people by threatening to hurt them so that they will do what you want: *Some of the older children terrorized the younger kids.*

**test¹** /test/ *noun*
**1** a set of questions or activities that are used to measure your knowledge or skill: *I passed my history test with a C. | She had to take her driving test three times before she passed.*
**2** a medical check on part of your body: *Children should have an eye test every year.*
**3** something that scientists do to examine a substance: *Scientists are doing tests on the water to see if bacteria are present.*
[**ORIGIN:** 1300-1400 From an old French word for a pot used for testing metals, from the Latin word *testum*, which means "clay pot."]

**test²** *verb*
**1** to measure someone's knowledge or skill by asking questions or making him or her do things: *You'll be tested on everything we've learned this semester.*
**2** to use something to find out whether it

works: *The company is testing its new computer software before selling it.*
**3** to do a medical check on part of someone's body: *The doctor tested her for heart disease.*
**4** to check a substance to see what is in it: *They tested the water in the river for pollution.*

**tes·ti·fy** /ˈtestəˌfaɪ/ *verb* (**testified, testifies**)
to say in a law court what you know about something: *She testified that she had seen O'Brien leaving the house where the murder took place.*
[**ORIGIN:** 1300-1400 From the Latin word *testificari*, from *testis*, which means "witness in a court of law."]

**tes·ti·mo·ny** /ˈtestəˌmoʊni/ *noun* (plural **testimonies**)
the things you say in a law court about what you know about a crime: *The mother of the victim will give testimony on Friday.*

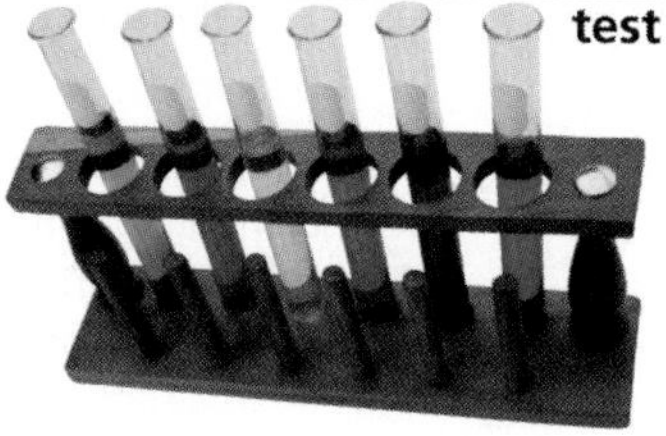

**test tube**

**ˈtest tube** *noun*
a small narrow glass container used in scientific tests: *The scientist poured the liquid into the test tube.*

**tet·a·nus** /ˈtetn-əs/ *noun*
a serious disease that is caused by an infection in a cut on your skin, and that makes the jaw muscles and other muscles stiff

**text¹** Ac /tekst/ *noun*
**1** (*also* **text message**) a written message that you send using a CELL PHONE: *I sent him a text to say "Good luck."*
**2** the writing in a book, magazine, computer document, etc., rather than the pictures: *I found it hard to read the text on the screen.*
**3** a book about a subject which students use: *That novel is one of the texts we have to read for our English class.* **SYNONYM: textbook**
[**ORIGIN:** 1300-1400 From the Latin word *textus*, a form of the verb *texere*, which means "to weave, or to put things together to make something." In texts, words are put together to make meanings.]

**text²** *verb*
to send someone a written message using a CELL PHONE: *I'll text you when I get to the park.*

**text·book** /ˈtekstbʊk/ *noun*
a book about a subject, which students use: *Your science textbook describes the experiment.* **SYNONYM: text**
→ see Thesaurus box at **book¹**

**tex·tile** /ˈtekstaɪl/ *noun*
any material that is made by WEAVING threads (=crossing threads over and under each other), such as cloth or rugs: *The country exports textiles, especially silk and cotton cloth.*

**tex·ture** /ˈtekstʃɚ/ *noun*
the way that something feels when you touch it: *Sandpaper has a rough texture.*

**than** /ðən; *strong* ðæn/ *preposition, conjunction*
used when comparing people or things: *My brother's older than me.* | *These shoes are cheaper than the other ones.*

**thank** /θæŋk/ *verb*
**1** to tell someone that you are pleased about something he or she has done for you or given you: *She thanked the boy for helping her.*
**2** **thank you** = said to thank someone: *Thank you for the birthday present!* | *"Here's your dinner." "Thank you."*

**thank·ful** /ˈθæŋkfəl/ *adjective*
glad about something: *We're thankful (that) nobody was hurt in the accident.*
—**thankfully** *adverb* used for saying that you are glad about something: *Thankfully, it didn't rain during our picnic.*

**thanks¹** /θæŋks/ *interjection*
said to thank someone: *Thanks for taking the time to explain this to me.* | *"What time is it?" "Six o'clock." "Thanks."*

**thanks²** *plural noun*
**1** something that you say or do to thank someone: *I wrote him a letter of thanks.*
**2** **thanks to someone or something** = because of someone or something: *We arrived late, thanks to the traffic.*

**Thanks·giv·ing** /ˌθæŋksˈgɪvɪŋ/ *noun*
a holiday in the U.S. and Canada in the fall when families have a large meal together to show their thanks for food, families, health,

etc.: *My whole family was here for Thanksgiving, and of course we had turkey and pumpkin pie.*

**ˈthank-you** *noun*
something that you say or do to thank someone: *They gave her some flowers as a thank-you.*

**that**[1] /ðæt/ *adjective, pronoun* (plural **those** /ðoʊz/)
**1** used for talking about someone or something that is farther away from you, often in a place you point at: *Do you see that green car?* | *Who are those boys over there?* | *Give me that!* **ANTONYM: this**
**2** used for saying something about a thing or person that has already been mentioned: *I've never seen that movie.* | *"We're going to have a new teacher." "Who told you that?"* | *I'd like to see those photos you were talking about.*
**3** /ðət/ used instead of "who" or "which": *He's the boy that hit me.* | *There are lots of things that I need to do before I leave.*

**that**[2] /ðət; *strong* ðæt/ *conjunction*
**1** used when mentioning something that is said or believed, or when describing a fact, in order to join two parts of a sentence: *He promised that he would be here.* | *Is it true that you're leaving?*
**2** used after a phrase with "so" or "such" to say what the result of something is: *I was so tired that I could hardly walk.* | *They were making so much noise that I didn't hear the phone.*

**that**[3] /ðæt/ *adverb*
**1** so or very: *It won't cost all that much.* | *I didn't realize things were that bad.*
**2** used when showing an amount or size with your hands: *The car missed us by about that much.*

**thaw** /θɔ/ (*also* **thaw out**) *verb*
if something frozen thaws, it becomes warmer until all the ice is gone: *The freezer broke and all the food thawed out.* **ANTONYM: freeze**
—**thaw** *noun* a time when ice or snow thaws

**the** /ðə; *before a vowel* ði; *strong* ði/ *definite article*
**1** used before a noun to show that you are talking about a particular person or thing: *The boy was riding a blue bicycle.* | *That's the dress I want to buy.* | *He went to the store to buy some milk.*
**2** used before the names of rivers, oceans, and groups of mountains: *the Mississippi River* | *the Atlantic Ocean* | *the Alps*
**3** used before the names of some countries: *the Philippines* | *the United States*
**4** used for talking about a group of people: *a school for the deaf* | *He warned people that the British were coming.*
**5** used for talking about a particular date or period of time: *Today is the fifth of May.* | *the music of the 1960s*
**6** used for saying that something is the best or most famous one: *This is the movie to see this year.*

**USAGE: the**

Do not use **the** when you are talking about a type of thing: *I like ice cream.* | *Cats often hunt at night.*

Use **the** when you are talking about a particular thing or group: *I like the ice cream you bought.* | *The cats on our street make a lot of noise.*

Do not use **the** before the names of airports, train stations, or streets: *We arrived at O'Hare.* | *The train leaves from Grand Central.* | *She lives on Carr Avenue.*

Use **the** when you are talking about a particular airport, train station, or street without naming it: *We arrived at the airport.* | *The train was just leaving the station.* | *A car came down the street.*

**the·a·ter** /ˈθiətɚ/ *noun*
**1** a building where actors perform plays: *He has performed in musicals in several Broadway theaters.*
**2** a building where you go to see movies: *There's a good movie showing at the theater.*
**3** the business of writing or performing plays: *I'd love to have a career in theater.*
—**theatrical** /θiˈætrɪkəl/ *adjective* relating to writing and performing plays: *She studied acting and joined a theatrical company.*
[**ORIGIN:** 1300-1400 From the Greek word *theatron*, from *theasthai*, which means "to watch."]

T

**theft** /θeft/ *noun*
the crime of stealing something: *Police caught the boys in the stolen car and arrested them for theft.*
→ see Thesaurus box at **crime**

**their** /ðɚ; *strong* ðer/ *adjective*
belonging to particular people or animals: *My neighbors are selling their house.* | *Parents arrived at the school to take their children home.*

**USAGE: their, they're, there**

**Their** means "belonging to them": *They took off their coats.*

**They're** means "they are": *They're my friends.*

**There** is used when talking about places, or things that happen: *You can sit there, next to Sarah.* | *There was a knock at the door.*

T

**theirs** /ðerz/ *pronoun*
the thing or things that belong to particular people or animals: *Our front door is red and theirs is blue.*

**them** /ðəm; *strong* ðem/ *pronoun*
the people or things that have already been mentioned: *We made some cookies, and then we ate them all.* | *I have looked everywhere for my keys but cannot find them.*

**theme** [Ac] /θim/ *noun*
the main subject or idea in a book, movie, speech, etc.: *Love is the central theme of the book.*
—**thematic** /θiˈmætɪk/ *adjective* relating to a theme: *The two poems have thematic similarities – one is about growing up and the other is about growing old.*
—**thematically** *adverb* in a way that relates to a theme
[**ORIGIN:** 1200-1300 From the Greek word *thema*, which means "something laid down or given as a subject," from *tithenai*, which means "to put or lay down."]

**ˈtheme park** *noun*
an AMUSEMENT PARK where the rides relate to one thing, for example water or space travel

**them·selves** /ðəmˈselvz/ *pronoun*
**1** used when the same people or animals that you have just mentioned do an action: *The elephants were washing themselves in the river.*
**2** used for emphasizing that particular people do something: *Kids should clean their rooms themselves.*
**3 (all) by themselves** = alone or without help: *Many old people live by themselves.*

**then** /ðen/ *adverb*
**1** after that: *I get up at 7:30, and then I have breakfast.*
**2** at a time in the past: *We lived in New York back then.*
**3** used for saying what the result of a situation is: *"My jeans are all dirty!" "Then you'll have to put a clean pair on."*
→ **now and then** at **now**[1]

**the·ol·o·gy** /θiˈɑlədʒi/ *noun*
the study of religion

**the·o·ret·i·cal** [Ac] /ˌθiəˈretɪkəl/ *adjective*
based on ideas, rather than real events or actions: *Life on other planets is only a theoretical possibility – there is no evidence for it.*
—**theoretically** *adverb* according to an idea

**the·o·ry** [Ac] /ˈθiəri/ *noun* (plural **theories**)
an idea or set of ideas that tries to explain why something happens: *According to this theory, all the dinosaurs died because a large asteroid hit the Earth.*
—**theorist** *noun* (*formal*) someone who thinks of theories
—**theorize** *verb* (*formal*) to think of a theory: *Scientists theorize about how the universe began.*
[**ORIGIN:** 1500-1600 From the Greek word *theoria*, which means "the act of looking at something," from *theorein*, meaning "to look at." You come up with a theory after looking at or considering something that needs explaining.]

**WORD FAMILY: theory**

**theory** *noun* | **theoretical** *adjective* | **theoretically** *adverb* | **theorist** *noun* | **theorize** *verb*

**ther·a·py** /ˈθerəpi/ *noun* (plural **therapies**)
**1** treatment of an illness or injury over a long period of time: *He is having therapy for his injured knee, but he won't play football again this year.*
**2** treatment for mental problems that

involves talking to a doctor about your feelings: *After her son died, she had therapy for depression.*
—**therapist** *noun* someone whose job is treating mental or physical problems: *A physical therapist gave me a program of exercises to do.*

**there¹** /ðer/ *pronoun*
**there is/there are, etc.** = used for describing what is in a place, or what happens: *There's a big truck parked outside.* | *Is there a store around here?*

**there²** *adverb*
**1** in or to another place, not the place where you are: *I know Seattle well because I used to live there.* | *Jamie's having a party at 8, so I'm going over there about 8:30.*
**2** **hello there/hi there** (*informal*) = said to greet someone

**USAGE: there, their, they're**

**There** is used when talking about places, or things that happen: *You can sit there, next to Sarah.* | *There was a knock at the door.*

**Their** means "belonging to them": *They took off their coats.*

**They're** means "they are": *They're my friends.*

**there·by** Ac /ðerˈbaɪ/ *adverb* (*formal*)
with the result that something happens: *Cars produce poisonous gas, thereby polluting the air.*

**there·fore** /ˈðerfɔr/ *adverb* (*formal*)
for the reason that you have mentioned: *This house is smaller, and therefore cheaper.*

**ther·mal** /ˈθɚməl/ *adjective*
relating to or caused by heat: *Thermal energy from the sun heats the water.*

**ther·mom·e·ter** /θɚˈmɑmətɚ/ *noun*
an instrument that measures how hot or cold something is, for example your body or the air: *When I was sick, the nurse took my temperature with a thermometer.*
[**ORIGIN:** 1600-1700 From the Greek words *therme* and *metron*, which mean "heat" and "measure."]

**Ther·mos** /ˈθɚməs/ *noun* (*trademark*)
a special type of bottle that keeps drinks hot or cold: *She brought a Thermos of soup for lunch.*

**ther·mo·stat** /ˈθɚməˌstæt/ *noun*
an instrument that controls how hot or cold a room or machine is: *Dad turned the thermostat down to 65° to save energy.*

**the·sau·rus** /θɪˈsɔrəs/ *noun* (plural **thesauruses** *or* **thesauri**) /θɪˈsɔraɪ/
a book which lists groups of words that have similar meanings

**these** /ðiz/ *adjective, pronoun*
the plural of THIS

**the·sis** Ac /ˈθisɪs/ *noun* (plural **theses** /ˈθisiz/)
**1** a long piece of writing that you do in college, especially for a MASTER'S DEGREE: *He wrote his thesis on 18th century literature.*
**2** the main idea in an essay, that the writer gives details about: *Your thesis statement usually comes at the end of your first paragraph.*
[**ORIGIN:** 1300-1400 From the Greek word for "the act of laying down," from *tithenai*, which means "to put or lay down." "Thesis" used to mean "statement put down to be discussed."]

**they** /ðeɪ/ *pronoun*
the people or things that you have just mentioned: *I called Carl and Tammy, but they weren't home.* | *Look at these flowers – aren't they beautiful?*

**they'd** /ðeɪd/
**1** the short form of "they had": *When I arrived, they'd already left.*
**2** the short form of "they would": *They said they'd help us.*

**they'll** /ðeɪl/
the short form of "they will": *If they are late, they'll miss the plane.*

**they're** /ðɚ; *strong* ðer/
the short form of "they are": *I love cats – they're so cute.*

**USAGE: they're, their, there**

**They're** means "they are": *They're my friends.*

**Their** means "belonging to them": *They took off their coats.*

T

**There** is used when talking about places, or things that happen: *You can sit there, next to Sarah.* | *There was a knock at the door.*

**they've** /ðeɪv/
the short form of "they have": *They've lived in this neighborhood for twenty years.*

**thick**

**thick** /θɪk/ *adjective*
**1** a thick object or material has a large distance between one side and the other: *The old building had thick stone walls.* | *Dad cut a thick slice of bread.* **ANTONYM: thin**
**2** if you have thick hair, you have a lot of hair **ANTONYM: thin**
**3** a thick liquid does not have much water in it: *If the paint is too thick, add a little water.* **ANTONYM: thin**
**4** thick FOG or smoke is difficult to see through or breathe in: *The fog was so thick we couldn't see more than five yards ahead.* **SYNONYM: dense**
**5** a thick forest or JUNGLE has trees or plants growing closely together: *They cut their way through the thick jungle.* **SYNONYM: dense**
[**ORIGIN:** From the old English word *thicce.*]

**thick·en** /ˈθɪkən/ *verb*
if a liquid thickens, it becomes more solid, with less water: *Heat the sauce until it thickens.*

**thick·ly** /ˈθɪkli/ *adverb*
in thick pieces, or in a thick layer: *The ham was thickly sliced.* | *He spread the butter thickly on his bread.* **ANTONYM: thinly**

**thick·ness** /ˈθɪknəs/ *noun*
how thick and solid something is: *Cook the meat for 15-20 minutes, depending on its thickness.*

**thief** /θif/ *noun* (plural **thieves** /θivz/)
someone who steals things: *A thief grabbed my purse and ran away with it.* | *a car thief*

**thigh** /θaɪ/ *noun*
the top part of your leg above your knee → see picture on page **A2**

**thin** /θɪn/ *adjective* (**thinner**, **thinnest**)
**1** not having much fat on your body: *He's tall and thin.* **ANTONYM: fat**

**THESAURUS: thin**

**slim** thin in a way that looks good: *a slim young woman*

**slender** thin in a way that looks good, used especially to describe someone who is tall or to describe arms or legs: *The model's legs are long and slender.*

**skinny** very thin in a way that does not look attractive: *He's a tall, skinny kid.*

**lean** thin in a way that looks healthy: *His body was lean and muscular.*

**2** having a small distance between one side and the other: *a thin layer of snow* **ANTONYM: thick** → see picture at **thick**
**3** if you have thin hair, you do not have a lot of hair: *an old man with thin gray hair* **ANTONYM: thick**
**4** a liquid that is thin has a lot of water in it: *This soup's too thin.* **ANTONYM: thick**
—**thinness** *noun* the state of having very little fat on your body: *I was shocked by her thinness.*

**thing** /θɪŋ/ *noun*
**1** an object: *What's that thing on the table?*

**THESAURUS: thing**

**something** a thing, used especially when you do not know its name or what it is: *There's something in my eye.*

**object** a thing you can see or touch: *The children were testing to see which objects would float and which would sink.*

**item** a single thing in a set, group, or list: *He opened the box and took out each item, one by one.*

**stuff** (*informal*) a number of different things: *I keep the painting stuff in the cupboard.*

**article** (*formal*) a thing, especially one of a group of things: *He folded each article of clothing as he took it out of the dryer.*

**2** an event, or something that someone says or does: *A funny thing happened last week.* | *That's a terrible thing to say.* | *The best thing to do if you burn yourself is to put cold water on the burn.*
**3** **things** = the events that are happening in your life: *How are things with you?* | *I hope things will get better soon.*
**4** **someone's things** = the objects that someone owns: *I packed all my things and put them in the car.*
**5** **for one thing** = used for giving one of the reasons for something: *We can't go. For one thing, we don't have the money.*
**6** **first thing** = as soon as you get out of bed and start activities: *I'll clean my room first thing tomorrow.*

**think** /θɪŋk/ *verb* (**thought** /θɔt/)
**1** to use your mind to have ideas or solve problems: *I was thinking about what you said.* | *Think carefully before you answer this question.* | *We need to think of a new plan.*
**2** to have an opinion or belief: *I think that Mr. Anderson is a great teacher.* | *"Will you see Ben this weekend?" "I think so."* | *What do you think of my new haircut?*

**THESAURUS: think**

**believe** to think that something is true: *We believe that freedom of speech is very important.*

**suspect** to think that something, especially something bad, is probably true: *She suspected that he was lying to her.*

**consider** (*formal*) to think about something carefully before deciding what to do: *Have you considered going to a community college?*

**3** to consider the idea of doing something in the future: *I'm thinking about studying to be a teacher.*

[**ORIGIN:** From the old English word *thencan*.]
**PHRASAL VERBS**
**think something over**
to consider something carefully before you decide about it: *When they offered him the job, he asked for some time to think it over.*
**think something up**
to have an idea, plan, etc. that is completely new: *He's always thinking up crazy ideas for making money.*

**think·er** /ˈθɪŋkɚ/ *noun*
someone who uses his or her mind in a particular way: *She's a very creative thinker with some great ideas.*

**thin·ly** /ˈθɪnli/ *adverb*
**1** in thin pieces, or in a thin layer: *Slice the meat thinly.* | *Spread the butter thinly – don't put too much on.* **ANTONYM: thickly**
**2** **thinly populated** = if an area is thinly populated, only a small number of people live there: *The state of Alaska is thinly populated.* **ANTONYM: densely**

**third** /θɚd/ *number*
**1** 3rd; someone or something that is after the second one
**2** 1/3

**ˌthird ˈperson** *noun*
**the third person** = the PRONOUNs "he," "she," "it," and "they," and the forms of the verbs you use with them. For example, in the sentence "He speaks Spanish and English," "speaks" is in the third person singular.

**ˌThird ˈWorld** *noun*
**the Third World** = the poor countries of the world that do not have a lot of industry

**thirst** /θɚst/ *noun*
**1** the feeling of wanting a drink: *If we don't find water soon, we'll die of thirst.*
**2** a strong feeling of wanting to have or do something: *He had a great thirst for knowledge and was interested in many subjects.*

**thirst·y** /ˈθɚsti/ *adjective* (**thirstier**, **thirstiest**)
feeling that you want to drink something: *We were all very thirsty, so we stopped and drank some water.*
—**thirstily** *adverb* in a way that shows that you are thirsty: *Eve drank the water thirstily.*

**thir·teen** /ˌθɚˈtin/ *number*
**1** 13: *It took thirteen hours to get to Miami.*

T

**2** thirteen years old: *Most of the kids in my class are still thirteen.*
—**thirteenth** /ˌθɚˈtinθ/ *number* 13th or 1/13

**thir·ty** /ˈθɚti/ *number*
**1** 30: *There are thirty days in April.*
**2** thirty years old: *He got married when he was thirty.*
**3 the thirties** (*also* **the '30s**) = the years between 1930 and 1939: *The Great Depression happened in the thirties.*
**4 in your thirties** = between 30 and 39 years old: *She's in her early thirties and just had her first baby.*
**5 in the thirties** = between 30 and 39 degrees in temperature: *It was a hot day with temperatures in the high thirties.*
—**thirtieth** /ˈθɚtiɪθ/ *number* 30th or 1/30

T

**this[1]** /ðɪs/ *adjective, pronoun* (plural **these** /ðiz/)
**1** the one that is close to you, or that you are holding: *This is my book, and that's yours.* | *My grandmother gave me this necklace.* | *These are the best shoes I have.* **ANTONYM: that**
**2 this Monday/this week/this month, etc.** = the day, week, etc. that is closest to today: *We're going to see a movie this Friday.*
**3** (*informal*) used for talking about something that someone has just mentioned: *Where is this party you're going to?*

**this[2]** *adverb*
**this big/tall/hard, etc.** = as big, tall, etc. as the one you are talking about: *I've never seen an apple this big before.*

**this·tle** /ˈθɪsəl/ *noun*
a wild plant with leaves that have sharp points and purple or white flowers

**thongs** /θɔŋz/ *plural noun*
a pair of flat shoes that are open at the top. Thongs are held on your feet by a band of material that goes between your toes. → see picture at **shoe**

**tho·rax** /ˈθɔræks/ *noun*
the middle part of an insect's body between its head and its ABDOMEN

**thorn** /θɔrn/ *noun*
a sharp point that grows on a plant such as a rose: *I scratched my hand on the bush's thorns.*

**thorn·y** /ˈθɔrni/ *adjective*
**1 a thorny problem/issue, etc.** = a problem that is very difficult to deal with: *Immigration is a thorny issue in states that border Mexico.*
**2** having a lot of thorns: *a thorny bush*

**thor·ough** /ˈθɚoʊ/ *adjective*
very careful and checking everything: *The police made a thorough search of the house, looking for clues.*
—**thoroughness** *noun* the quality of being thorough: *The doctor impressed me with his thoroughness.*

**thor·ough·bred** /ˈθɚəˌbred/ *noun*
a horse that has both parents of one very good breed

**thor·ough·ly** /ˈθɚoʊli/ *adverb*
**1** completely or very much: *I was thoroughly confused – I didn't understand at all what was going on.*
**2** carefully, so that nothing is missed or forgotten: *Check your answers thoroughly before handing in your test.*

**those** /ðoʊz/ *adjective, pronoun*
the plural of THAT

**though** /ðoʊ/ *conjunction*
**1** used when you mention a fact that makes the other part of your sentence seem surprising: *My family was very happy, though we were poor.*
**2** but: *I think I passed the test, though I'm not completely sure.*
**3 as though** = used when you are saying how someone or something seems: *You look as though you need a vacation.* **SYNONYM: as if**

**thought[1]** /θɔt/ *verb*
the past tense and past participle of THINK

**thought[2]** *noun*
**1** an idea in your mind: *The thought of food was making me hungry.* | *Let me know if you have any other thoughts on this.*
**2** the act of thinking about something, especially carefully: *I'll give your idea some thought.*

**thought·ful** /ˈθɔtfəl/ *adjective*
**1** serious and quiet because you are thinking about something: *Dad was sitting in the*

*kitchen with a thoughtful look on his face.*
**2** kind and thinking how to make other people happy: *It was thoughtful of you to call me on my birthday.*
→ see Thesaurus box at **kind**[2]

**thought·less** /ˈθɔtləs/ *adjective*
not kind and not thinking about the feelings of other people: *He made a thoughtless remark about fat people.*

**thou·sand** /ˈθaʊzənd/ *number*
**1** 1,000

**GRAMMAR: thousand, thousands**

Use the singular form **thousand** after a number: *Five thousand people came to the event.*

Use the plural form **thousands** before "of": *Thousands of homes were damaged by the hurricane.*

**2 thousands** (*informal*) = a lot: *We've received thousands of letters from fans.*
—**thousandth** *number* 1,000th or 1/1,000

**thread**[1] /θred/ *noun*
a long thin string of cotton that you use for sewing cloth: *She got a needle and thread and began sewing the button back on to her coat.*

**thread**[2] *verb*
to put thread through a hole: *Can you thread this needle for me?*

**threat** /θret/ *noun*
a statement in which someone says that he or she will hurt you if you do not do what he or she wants: *They used threats of violence to control the prisoners.* | *a bomb threat*

**threat·en** /ˈθretn/ *verb*
to say that you will do something bad to someone if he or she does not do what you want: *He threatened to tell the teacher if we didn't stop being mean to him.*
—**threatening** *adjective* seeming to threaten someone: *He shook his fist at them in a threatening way.*

**three** /θri/ *number*
**1** 3: *I've got three sisters.* | *They have lost three of their last five games.*
**2** three O'CLOCK: *I'll meet you at three.*
**3** three years old: *My sister is three.*

**ˌthree-diˈmensional** (*also* **3-D** /ˌθri ˈdi/) *adjective*
**1** having length, depth, and height: *A cube is a three-dimensional shape.*
**2** a 3-D movie, computer game, etc. seems to show people and things with length, depth, and height

**threw** /θru/ *verb*
the past tense of THROW

**ˈthrift store** *noun*
a store that sells used things and old clothes at low prices

**thrif·ty** /ˈθrɪfti/ *adjective*
good at using money carefully and not wasting any: *He's hard-working and thrifty and has managed to save a lot of money.*

**thrill**[1] /θrɪl/ *noun*
a strong feeling of excitement and pleasure: *It was a thrill to meet a professional basketball player.*

**thrill**[2] *verb*
to make someone feel great excitement and pleasure: *The idea of studying in Europe thrilled her.*

**thrilled** /θrɪld/ *adjective*
very excited, pleased, or happy: *Her parents were thrilled when she graduated from college.*

**thrill·er** /ˈθrɪlɚ/ *noun*
a movie or book that tells an exciting story about murder or crime
→ see Thesaurus box at **movie**

**thrill·ing** /ˈθrɪlɪŋ/ *adjective*
exciting and interesting: *It was a thrilling game with lots of action!*

**thrive** /θraɪv/ *verb*
**1** to become very successful: *Their business is thriving and they're going to hire more people.*
**2** to become very strong and healthy: *These plants thrive in dry conditions.*

**throat** /θroʊt/ *noun*
**1** the passage at the back of your mouth, where you swallow: *I have a sore throat, and it hurts when I swallow.*
**2** the front part of your neck: *His shirt was buttoned up to his throat.*

**throb** /θrɑb/ *verb* (**throbbed**, **throbbing**)
if part of your body throbs, you keep getting a regular feeling of pain in it: *My sore finger was throbbing.*

**throne** /θroʊn/ *noun*
the special chair on which a king or queen sits

**through¹** /θru/ *preposition, adverb*
**1** in one side of something, and out the other side: *The train went through a tunnel.* | *I managed to open a window and climb through.*
**2** from the beginning to the end of something: *I was so tired I slept through the entire movie.*
**3** across an area to another area: *They drove through Arizona on the way to California.*
**4** until the end of a day or month: *The museum is open Wednesday through Saturday.*
**5** because of someone or something: *He got the job through a friend.*

**through²** *adjective* (*informal*)
**be through with something** = to have finished using something, doing something, etc.: *Are you through with the phone yet?*
→ see Thesaurus box at **done²**

**through·out** /θruˈaʊt/ *preposition, adverb*
**1** in every part of a place: *The band is famous throughout the world.*
**2** during all of a period of time: *She stayed with him in the hospital throughout the day.*

**through·way** (*also* **thruway**) /ˈθruˌweɪ/ *noun*
a big wide road for traffic that is traveling fast: *He took the throughway to get to work faster.*

**throw**

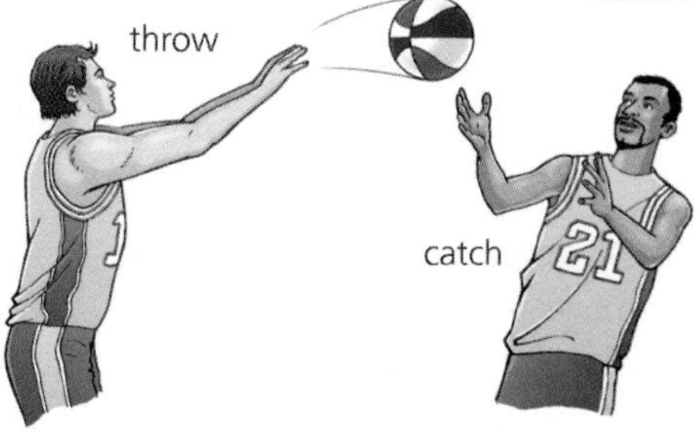


**throw¹** /θroʊ/ *verb* (**threw** /θru/, **thrown** /θroʊn/)
to make something go through the air, by moving your arm and letting it go out of your hand: *He threw the ball to his sister, and she caught it.*

**THESAURUS: throw**

**To Throw Something:**

**toss** to throw something in a careless way: *She tossed her coat onto the bed.*

**hurl** to throw something with a lot of force: *They hurled a brick through his window.*

**fling** to throw something somewhere with a lot of force: *"I hate him," she said, as she flung her engagement ring into the lake.*

**To Throw a Ball in a Sport:**

**pass** to throw a basketball or football to another member of your team: *Rodriguez passed to Johnson, who scored.*

**pitch** to throw the ball for a player to hit in baseball: *Mitchell will pitch in Friday's game.*

PHRASAL VERBS

**throw something away**
to get rid of something by putting it in the GARBAGE: *We used paper plates, so we could throw them away after the party.*

**throw out**
**1 throw something out** = to get rid of something that you do not want or need: *I'm throwing out some of my old clothes.*
**2 throw someone out** = to make someone leave a place quickly, especially because he or she is behaving badly: *Jay got drunk and they threw him out of the restaurant.*

**throw²** *noun*
an action of throwing something such as a ball: *That was a good throw – the ball came right to me!*

**thrown** /θroʊn/ *verb*
the past participle of THROW

**thrust** /θrʌst/ *verb* (**thrust**) (*formal*)
to push something somewhere suddenly or with force: *He thrust his hands into his pockets, and walked away angrily.*

**thud** /θʌd/ *noun*
the low sound of something heavy hitting the ground: *Mark fell off the horse, and landed with a thud.*

**thug** /θʌg/ *noun*
someone who is violent and may attack people: *A gang of thugs attacked the man and stole his money.*
[**ORIGIN:** 1800-1900 From the Hindi word *thag*, which means "thief or robber."]

**thumb** /θʌm/ *noun*
**1** the short thick finger on your hand that helps you hold things: *She held the coin between her finger and thumb.* → see picture at **hand**
**2** **give something the thumbs up** (*informal*) = to say or show that you think something is good: *It's a pretty exciting movie – I'd give it the thumbs up.*

**thumb·tack** /ˈθʌmtæk/ *noun*
a short pin with a round flat top, that you use for attaching papers to walls: *I used thumbtacks to put the sign on the board.*

**thump** /θʌmp/ *verb*
**1** to hit something in a way that makes a low sound: *Someone was outside the house, thumping on the door.*
**2** if your heart is thumping, it is beating very quickly because you are frightened or excited
—**thump** *noun* a low sound made by something hitting something else

**thun·der** /ˈθʌndɚ/ *noun*
the loud noise that you sometimes hear in the sky during a storm, after LIGHTNING has flashed: *There was a storm last night, and the thunder woke me up.*

**thun·der·storm** /ˈθʌndɚˌstɔrm/ *noun*
a storm with THUNDER and LIGHTNING: *I was woken by a thunderstorm in the night.*

**Thurs·day** /ˈθɚzdi/ *noun* (*written abbreviation*: **Thurs.**)
the fifth day of the week, between Wednesday and Friday: *I tried to call you Thursday.* | *Kim is leaving for Chicago on Thursday.* | *He was arrested last Thursday.* | *I made the appointment for next Thursday.*
[**ORIGIN:** From Thor, the god of thunder in the religion of some peoples in Northern Europe before Christianity.]

**thus** /ðʌs/ *adverb* (*formal*)
**1** as a result of what you have just said: *There will be more and more cars, and thus pollution will increase.* **SYNONYM: SO**
**2** **thus far** = until now: *Thus far, the disease has spread slowly, but it is uncertain what will happen in the future.*

**thy·roid** /ˈθaɪrɔɪd/ (*also* **ˈthyroid ˌgland**) *noun*
an organ in your neck that produces HORMONEs (=substances that affect your body and your behavior)

**ti·a·ra** /tiˈɑrə/ *noun*
a piece of jewelry like a small CROWN that a woman wears on formal occasions

**tick**[1] /tɪk/ *noun*
**1** a small creature like an insect that goes into your skin and sucks your blood: *After you go hiking, check your arms and legs for ticks.*
**2** the short sound that a clock or watch makes: *The tick of the clock was the only sound in the room.* → see picture on page **A22**

**tick**[2] *verb*
if a clock or watch ticks, it makes a short sound every second: *In the silence, I could hear the clock ticking.*

**tick·et** /ˈtɪkɪt/ *noun*
**1** a small piece of paper that shows that you have paid to see a movie, travel on a bus, etc.: *Tickets for the concert cost $15.* | *Do you have your plane ticket?* → see picture on page **A31**
**2** a legal note saying that you must pay some money because you drove or parked your car illegally: *He got a parking ticket.*
[**ORIGIN:** 1500-1600 From the old French word *etiquet*, which means "notice attached to something," from *estiquier*, meaning "to attach."]

**ˈticket ˌoffice** *noun*
a place that sells tickets: *She called the airline's ticket office about flying to Minneapolis.*

**tick·le** /ˈtɪkəl/ *verb*
to move your fingers lightly on parts of someone's body to try and make him or her laugh: *Dad tickled us under our arms until we screamed with laughter.*
—**ticklish** *adjective* if you are ticklish, you laugh easily when someone tickles you: *Don't touch my feet – I'm ticklish!*

**tic-tac-toe** /ˌtɪk tæk ˈtoʊ/ *noun*
a children's game in which two players draw either Xs or Os in nine squares and try to get three of the same letter in a row

**ˈtidal wave** *noun*
a very big wave that causes a lot of damage when it comes onto the land: *The tidal wave*

T

*was caused by an earthquake under the ocean.*

**tide** /taɪd/ *noun*
the regular change in the level of the ocean next to the land. Tides are caused by the GRAVITY of the Sun and the Moon on the oceans: *The ocean covers the whole beach at high tide.*

**ti·dy** /ˈtaɪdi/ *adjective*
neat and with everything in the right place: *My room isn't very tidy.*

**tie**[1] /taɪ/ *verb* (**tied**, **tying**)
**1** to fasten something by making a knot in rope, string, etc.: *I tied the dog to a tree so it wouldn't run away.* **ANTONYM: untie**
**2** if two players or teams tie, they have the same number of points at the end of a game, or they finish a race together: *The two runners tied for first place.*
—**tied** *adjective* having the same number of points during a game: *The teams were tied 13–13 at halftime.*
→ see Thesaurus box at **fasten**
**PHRASAL VERB**
**tie up**
**1 tie someone up** = to tie someone's arms or legs so that he or she cannot move: *They tied the prisoners up, and left them.*
**2 tie something up** = to fasten something together using string or rope: *The box broke, so I tied it up with some string.*
**3 be tied up** = to be very busy: *I can't come right now – I'm tied up with something.*

**tie**[2] *noun*
**1** a narrow piece of cloth that men tie around their necks and wear outside their shirts: *He wears a suit and tie in the office.* → see picture on page **A6**
**2** a relationship between two people, groups, or countries: *Their family ties are strong, and they see their grandparents every week.*
**3** the result of a game in which two people or teams get the same number of points: *He finished in a tie for third place.*

**ti·ger** /ˈtaɪgɚ/ *noun*
a large wild cat that has orange fur with black lines: *Tigers live mainly in India and Southeast Asia.*

**tight**[1] /taɪt/ *adjective*
**1** tight clothes fit your body very closely: *If those jeans are too tight, try a bigger size.* **ANTONYM: loose**
**2** firmly in position, and difficult to move: *Make sure the screws are tight.* | *He had a tight grip on her arm.*
**3 air-tight/water-tight** = not allowing air or water to get in: *Keep the cookies in an air-tight container.*

**tight**[2] *adverb*
very firmly: *Hold on tight so you don't fall off.* **SYNONYM: tightly**

**tight·en** /ˈtaɪtn/ *verb*
to fasten something so that it is firmly in position or not loose: *A screw was loose, so I tightened it.*

**tight·ly** /ˈtaɪtli/ *adverb*
very firmly: *He tied the rope tightly around the tree, so it wouldn't become loose.* **SYNONYM: tight**

**tights** /taɪts/ *plural noun*
a piece of clothing for girls or women that fits closely over the feet and legs and goes up to the waist

**tile** /taɪl/ *noun*
a thin square piece of baked clay that is used for covering floors or walls: *We're putting*

*new floor tiles in the kitchen.* → see picture on page **A9**

**till¹** /tɪl/ *preposition, conjunction*
until: *I stayed in the library till 5.* | *Wait there till I get back.*

**till²** *noun*
another word for a CASH REGISTER

**tilt** /tɪlt/ *verb*
to move something so that its position is not straight or upright: *You can tilt this chair back when you want to relax.*

**tim·ber** /ˈtɪmbɚ/ *noun*
trees that people cut down and use for building things **SYNONYM: lumber**

**time¹** /taɪm/ *noun*
**1** the thing that people measure in minutes, hours, years, etc.: *I like to spend time relaxing with my friends.* | *You don't need to hurry – we have plenty of time.*
**2** the exact hour and minute in a day that you can see on a clock: *"What time is it?" "It's 12:15."*
**3** an occasion when you do something: *I remember the first time I saw a bear.* | *Next time I go downtown, I'll take the bus.* | *I go swimming three times a week.*
**4** a period of time: *Learning a new language takes a long time.*
**5** a particular period of history: *Life was not easy during pioneer times.*
**6 on time** = at the right time, and not early or late: *The train arrived on time.*
**7 in time** = early enough to do something: *We got to the stadium in time to see the start of the game.*
**8 all the time** = without stopping or very often: *Todd listens to music in his room all the time.*
**9 have a good/great time** = to enjoy yourself: *Did you have a good time at the party?*
**10 it's time ...** = you use this for saying that something should happen now or soon: *It's time for dinner.* | *It's time to go.*
**11 from time to time** = sometimes, but not very often: *I only see Lou from time to time because he doesn't live nearby.*
**12 in no time** = soon or quickly: *If you help me, we'll be done in no time.*
**13 one/two, etc. ... at a time** = one, two, etc. on the same occasion or at the same moment: *You can borrow three books at a time.*
**14 ahead of time** = before an event or before you need to do something: *We finished ahead of time and got to relax.*
**15 take your time** = to do something slowly or carefully without hurrying: *Take your time – don't make your decision too quickly.*
**16 for the time being** = for a short time, but not permanently: *For the time being, she's living with her father.*

**time²** *verb*
**1** to arrange for something to happen at a particular time: *The heating is timed to come on at 4:00.*
**2** to measure how long it takes someone to do something: *Jill ran one hundred meters, and I timed her.*

**ˌtime and a ˈhalf** *noun*
one and a half times the normal rate of pay: *He gets time and a half for working on Sundays, so instead of making $6 an hour, he makes $9 an hour.*

**ˈtime card** *noun*
a card on which the hours you have worked are recorded by a machine: *At the beginning and end of each day, the workers put their time cards in the machine.*

**ˈtime-conˌsuming** *adjective (formal)*
taking a long time to do: *Buying a house can be a time-consuming process.*

**time·less** /ˈtaɪmləs/ *adjective (formal)*
continuing to be attractive or good, and not affected by changes in fashion: *This is a timeless song that has remained popular for many years.*

**ˈtime ˌlimit** *noun*
the longest time in which you are allowed to do something: *The time limit for the test is three hours.*

**time·line** /ˈtaɪmlaɪn/ *noun*
a line next to which you write different events to show the order in which they happened: *On the classroom wall, we have a timeline of the 20th century showing all the important historical events.*

**time·ly** /ˈtaɪmli/ *adjective (formal)*
done or happening at exactly the right time:

T

*We were saved by the timely arrival of the police.*

**ˌtime ˈoff** *noun*
time when you do not do your usual work: *He asked his boss if he could have some time off.*

**ˌtime ˈout** *noun*
a short break during a sports game to let the players rest or plan how they will play the rest of the game: *The L.A. Lakers took a time out after the other team scored ten points in a row.*

**tim·er** /ˈtaɪmɚ/ *noun*
a part of a machine or system that you use to make it stop or start at a particular time: *You can set the timer to turn the oven on and off to cook food when you aren't at home.*

**times** /taɪmz/ *preposition*
multiplied by: *Two times two equals four (2 x 2 = 4).*

**ˈtime sheet** *noun*
a piece of paper on which you write the hours you have worked during a particular period of time: *Have you filled in your time sheet?*

**ˌtimes ˈtable** *noun*
a list that shows the results when you multiply a number by other numbers. For example, the times table for 3 is 1 x 3 = 3, 2 x 3 = 6, 3 x 3 = 9, etc. **SYNONYM: multiplication table**

**ˈtime zone** *noun*
one of the 24 areas that the world is divided into, each of which has its own time: *When you fly across the U.S. you cross four time zones.*

**tim·id** /ˈtɪmɪd/ *adjective*
shy and nervous: *He was a timid boy who almost never spoke.* **SYNONYM: shy**
—**timidly** *adverb* in a shy and nervous way: *She timidly asked if she could borrow the book.*
→ see Thesaurus box at **shy**

**tin** /tɪn/ *noun*
a soft silver-white metal that is often used to cover and protect iron and steel: *Many cans have a covering of tin.*

**tin·gle** /ˈtɪŋgəl/ *verb*
if a part of your body tingles, the skin feels slightly uncomfortable: *Her face tingled from the cold wind.*

**ti·ny** /ˈtaɪni/ *adjective* (**tinier**, **tiniest**)
very small: *They live in a tiny house, with only three rooms.*
→ see Thesaurus box at **small**

**tip[1]** /tɪp/ *noun*
**1** the end of something long, narrow, and pointed: *He touched the flower with the tip of his finger.*
**2** a useful piece of advice: *He gave me some tips on how to study for tests.*
**3** an additional amount of money that you give to someone who has done a job for you as a way of thanking him or her: *He left a $5 tip for the waitress.*
→ see Thesaurus box at **end[1]**

**tip[2]** *verb* (**tipped**, **tipping**)
**1** to move something so that one part of it is higher than the other: *The dentist told Joe to tip his head back.*
**2** to give an additional amount of money to someone who has done a job for you as a way of thanking him or her: *He tipped the waiter $5.*

**tip·sy** /ˈtɪpsi/ *adjective* (*informal*)
slightly drunk: *The wine had made her tipsy.*

**tip·toe[1]** /ˈtɪptoʊ/ *noun*
**on tiptoe** = if you stand or walk on tiptoe, you stand or walk just on your toes: *Kelli stood on tiptoe to reach the top of the whiteboard.*

She is standing on tiptoe.

**tiptoe[2]** *verb*
to walk quietly and carefully on your toes: *She tiptoed down the stairs, trying not to make any noise.* → see picture on page **A4**

**tire[1]** /taɪɚ/ *noun*
a thick round piece of rubber that fits around the wheel of a car, bicycle, etc.: *We had to stop on the way home because we had a flat tire.* → see picture at **bicycle**

**tire[2]** (*also* **tire out**) *verb*
to make you feel tired: *All that dancing has tired me out.*

**tired** /taɪɚd/ *adjective*
**1** someone who is tired feels that they want to sleep or rest: *I had been working hard all day, and I felt really tired.* → see picture on page **A23**
**2 tired of (doing) something** = bored or annoyed with something: *I'm tired of waiting.*
—**tiredness** *noun* the state of feeling tired

**tir·ing** /ˈtaɪərɪŋ/ *adjective*
making you feel tired: *The long trip was very tiring.*

**tis·sue** /ˈtɪʃu/ *noun*
**1** a piece of soft thin paper that you use to blow your nose: *She used a whole box of tissues when she had a cold.*
**2** a group of cells that form part of an animal or plant: *Scientists looked at the tissue for cancer cells.*

**ti·tle** /ˈtaɪtl/ *noun*
**1** the name given to a book, painting, play, etc.: *The title of the book is "Easy Computing."*
**2** a word such as "Mr.," "Mrs.," or "Dr." that you use before someone's name: *Many women use the title "Ms."*
**3** the position of being the winner of an important sports competition: *This young golfer is trying to win her first title.*
**4** *(formal)* the legal right to own something: *Who has title to this land?*

| WORD FAMILY: title |
| --- |
| **title** *noun* \| **entitle** *verb* |

**to¹** /tə; *before vowels* tʊ; *strong* tu/
**1** used with verbs to make the INFINITIVE: *It's starting to rain.* | *She asked the teacher to help her.* | *Sarah seems to be very happy.*
**2** used when showing the purpose of an action: *I came here to see if you need some help.* SYNONYM: **in order to**

**to²** *preposition*
**1** used to say where someone or something goes: *He ran to the door.* | *We're going on vacation to Hawaii.* | *I went to a party last night.*
**2** used to say who receives something: *I gave my old jacket to my sister.*
**3** used to say who is affected by an action: *Mark is talking to Steve.* | *He was very nice to me.*
**4** used to say when something ends: *The museum is open from 10:30 to 5.*
**5** before a particular hour or event: *It's ten to four.* | *It is two weeks to Mom's birthday.*
**6** used to say who has an idea or opinion: *That seems fair to me.*
**7** used to say where something is fixed: *He tied the rope to a tree.*

**toad** /toʊd/ *noun*
a brown animal like a large FROG: *Toads have dry bumpy skin and live mainly on land.* → see picture at **amphibian**

**toast¹** /toʊst/ *noun*
**1** bread that has been heated until it is brown: *He ate a slice of toast for breakfast.*
**2** if you make a toast, you thank someone, wish someone luck, etc. and then drink something: *They drank a toast to the newly married couple.*

**toast²** *verb*
**1** to heat bread until it is brown: *She toasted a slice of bread.*
**2** to thank someone, wish someone luck, etc. and then drink something: *They toasted the soldiers who had come back from the war.*

**toast·er** /ˈtoʊstɚ/ *noun*
a machine used for making toast: *She put two slices of bread in the toaster.* → see picture on page **A9**

**to·bac·co** /təˈbækoʊ/ *noun*
dried brown leaves that people smoke in cigarettes and pipes: *pipe tobacco*

**to·day¹** /təˈdeɪ/ *adverb*
**1** on this day: *David has his piano lesson today.* | *I'm going swimming today.*
**2** during the present period of time: *Today, half of all marriages end in divorce.*

**today²** *noun*
**1** this day: *What's today's date?* | *Today is Wednesday.*
**2** the present period of time: *Today's computers are very powerful.*

**tod·dler** /ˈtɑdlɚ/ *noun*
a very young child who is just learning to walk

**toe** /toʊ/ *noun*
**1** one of the five parts at the end of your foot: *These shoes hurt my toes.*
**2 on your toes** = ready for anything that

might happen: *Pop quizzes keep the students on their toes.*

**TOEFL** /ˈtoufəl/ *noun*
(**Test of English as a Foreign Language**) a test of English that students can take if their first language is not English

**toe·nail** /ˈtouneɪl/ *noun*
the hard flat part at the end of your toe: *She painted her toenails red.*

**tof·fee** /ˈtɔfi/ *noun*
a sticky brown candy: *The toffee made his teeth stick together.*

**to·geth·er** /təˈgeðɚ/ *adverb*
**1** if two or more people do something together, they do it as a group, not alone: *They wrote all the songs together.* | *We worked together to solve the problem.*
**2** if you put two or more things together, you join or mix them so that they form a single thing: *I glued the pieces of wood together.* | *Mix the eggs and the cream together.*
**3** if people or things are together, they are with or next to each other: *The girls were standing together in a group.* | *I put all the books together in a box.*

**to·geth·er·ness** /təˈgeðɚnɪs/ *noun*
the nice feeling you have when you are part of a group of people who have a close relationship with each other: *Our family has a strong sense of togetherness.*

**toi·let** /ˈtɔɪlɪt/ *noun*
a large bowl that you sit on to get rid of waste substances from your body → see picture on page **A11**
[**ORIGIN:** 1500-1600 From the French word *toilette*, which means "cloth." "Toilet" first meant a cloth or bag used when getting dressed, doing your hair, etc., and then meant a room where you get dressed and wash yourself.]

**ˈtoilet ˌpaper** *noun*
soft thin paper that you use to clean yourself after you have used the toilet: *a roll of toilet paper*

**toi·let·ries** /ˈtɔɪlətriz/ *plural noun* (*formal*)
things such as soap, TOOTHPASTE, etc. that you use to clean yourself

**to·ken** /ˈtoukən/ *noun*
**1** a round piece of metal that you use instead of money in some machines: *a subway token*
**2** (*formal*) something that represents your feelings toward someone: *I gave her a bracelet as a token of our friendship.*

**told** /tould/ *verb*
the past tense and past participle of TELL

**tol·er·ance** /ˈtɑlərəns/ *noun* (*formal*)
**1** willingness to let people do, say, or believe what they want, even if you do not agree with them: *Our teacher has no tolerance for rudeness.*
**2** the degree to which someone or something can suffer pain or difficulty without being harmed: *These plants have a low tolerance for the cold and usually die if it gets too cold in the spring.*

**tol·er·ant** /ˈtɑlərənt/ *adjective*
letting other people do, say, or believe what they want, even if you do not agree with it: *We should be tolerant of other people's beliefs.*

**tol·er·ate** /ˈtɑləˌreɪt/ *verb* (*formal*)
to accept behavior or a situation that you do not like, and not do anything about it: *The teacher will not tolerate bad behavior in class.*
**SYNONYM: put up with**

**WORD FAMILY: tolerate**
**tolerate** *verb* | **tolerant** *adjective* | **tolerance** *noun*

**toll[1]** /toul/ *noun*
**1** the number of people that have been killed by something: *The death toll from the earthquake has risen to 200.*
**2** money that you pay so that you can use a road, bridge, etc.: *The highway toll is $2.*
**3** a bad effect that something has on someone or something over a long period of time: *Smoking has taken a toll on his health; he now has lung cancer.*

**toll[2]** *verb* (*formal*)
if a large bell tolls, or you toll it, it keeps ringing slowly: *The church bell tolled.*

**to·ma·to** /təˈmeɪtou/ *noun* (plural **tomatoes**)
a soft round red fruit, that is eaten as a vegetable: *Do you like tomatoes in your salad?* → see picture on page **A12**
[**ORIGIN:** 1600-1700 From the Spanish word *tomate*, from the Nahuatl word *tomatl*, which

means "swelling fruit." Nahuatl was the language used by the Aztecs in Mexico.]

**tomb** /tum/ *noun*
a large grave or room where a dead person is buried: *They discovered the tomb of an Egyptian king.*

**to·mor·row¹** /tə'mɑroʊ/ *adverb*
on or during the day after today: *He's leaving tomorrow.*
[**ORIGIN:** From the old English words *to* and *morgen*, which mean "at or on" and "morning."]

**tomorrow²** *noun*
the day after today: *Today is Wednesday, and tomorrow is Thursday.* | *Do you have any plans for tomorrow?*

**ton** /tʌn/ *noun*
a unit for measuring weight, equal to 2,000 pounds: *The ship weighs 62,000 tons.*

**tone** /toʊn/ *noun*
**1** the sound of someone's voice, or of a musical instrument: *"Come on in," he said in a friendly tone.*
**2** the general feeling or quality that something has: *People like the humorous tone of the ad.*
**3** one of the sounds that you hear on the telephone: *Please leave a message after the tone.* **SYNONYM: beep**
**4** **muscle tone** = how strong and firm your muscles are: *These exercises will improve your muscle tone.*
**5** the difference in sound between two musical notes that are separated by one key on the piano

**ˌtone-'deaf** *adjective*
unable to hear the difference between different musical notes: *I can't sing at all because I'm tone-deaf.*

**tongs** /tɑŋz/ *plural noun*
a tool for picking things up, which has two thin pieces of metal joined together at the top: *I used a pair of tongs to turn over the steaks on the barbecue.*

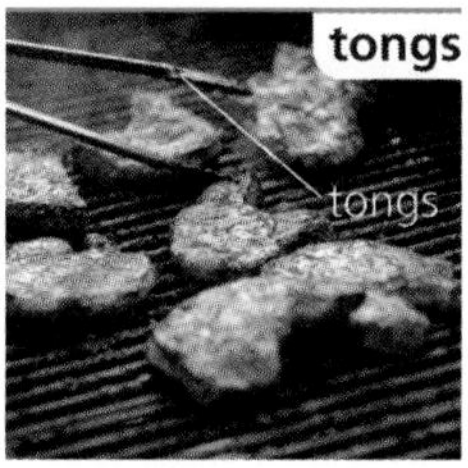


**tongue** /tʌŋ/ *noun*
**1** the soft part inside your mouth that moves when you eat and speak: *She rudely stuck her tongue out at me.*
**2** a language: *They were speaking in a foreign tongue.*
→ see Thesaurus box at **language**

**ˌtongue-in-'cheek** *adjective*
a tongue-in-cheek remark is said as a joke, not seriously: *He made a tongue-in-cheek comment about how excited he was to be going back to work after his vacation.*

**'tongue-tied** *adjective*
unable to speak easily because you are nervous: *I always feel tongue-tied when I have to say something in class.*

**'tongue ˌtwister** *noun*
a word or phrase with many similar sounds that is difficult to say quickly: *"She sells sea shells by the sea shore" is a well-known tongue twister.*

**to·night¹** /tə'naɪt/ *adverb*
during the night of this day: *I think I'll go to bed early tonight.*

**tonight²** *noun*
the night of this day: *Here is tonight's news.*

**ton·sil·li·tis** /ˌtɑnsə'laɪtɪs/ *noun*
an infection of the tonsils that causes a sore throat and a fever

**ton·sils** /'tɑnsəlz/ *plural noun*
the two small round pieces of flesh at the sides of your throat, near the back of your tongue

**too** /tu/ *adverb*
**1** used when saying that something else is also true, or that something is true about another person or thing: *Jan plays the guitar, and she plays the piano too.* | *"I'm really hungry." "Me too."*

**USAGE: too, also, as well**

**Too**, **also**, and **as well** mean the same thing, but you use them in different ways.

**Too** and **as well** are less formal than **also**, and you use them more often in spoken English: *Tom's hungry, and I am too.* | *Oh, are you coming as well?*

**Also** is more formal, and is used more often in writing than in speech: *Tom was very tired, and he was also hungry.*

T

In sentences with "not," use **either** rather than **also** or **too**. Do not say "Tom was also not hungry" or "Tom was not hungry too." Say *Tom was not hungry either.*

**2** more than you want or need, or more than you think is acceptable: *It's too hot in here.* | *He was driving much too fast.* | *This house is too small for six people.*

**USAGE: too, very**

**Too** is usually used to show that you do not like the amount or level of something, or that it makes something impossible: *This cereal is too sweet.* | *The book was too big to fit in my bag.*

**Very** is used to emphasize something which may be good or bad: *It's very hot today.* | *She's always very busy.*

T

**took** /tʊk/ *verb*
the past tense of TAKE

**tool** /tul/ *noun*
any object that you hold in your hand and use for doing a particular job: *Children can be taught to use real tools such as hammers and screwdrivers safely.*

**tool·bar** /ˈtulbɑr/ *noun*
a row of small pictures that a program shows on a computer screen. You CLICK on the pictures in order to make the computer do things.

**tooth** /tuθ/ *noun* (plural **teeth** /tiθ/)
**1** one of the hard white things in your mouth that you use for biting food: *Did you brush your teeth?* → see picture on page **A2**
**2** one of the pointed parts of a comb or saw

**tooth·ache** /ˈtuθeɪk/ *noun*
a pain in a tooth: *I have a toothache – I'll have to go to the dentist.*

**tooth·brush** /ˈtuθbrʌʃ/ *noun*
a small brush for cleaning your teeth → see picture at **brush**

**tooth·paste** /ˈtuθpeɪst/ *noun*
a substance that you use for cleaning your teeth: *a tube of toothpaste*

**tooth·pick** /ˈtuθˌpɪk/ *noun*
a very small pointed stick of wood that you use for removing pieces of food from between your teeth

**top¹** /tɑp/ *noun*
**1** the highest part of something: *The cat climbed to the top of the tree.* | *Write your name at the top of the page.* **ANTONYM: bottom**
**2 the top** = the best or most important position in a group or organization: *I want to get to the top and be the best tennis player in the world.*
**3** a piece of clothing that you wear on the top half of your body: *She was wearing jeans and a pink top.*
**4** the lid or cover for a container or a pen: *I can't get the top off this jar.*
**5 off the top of your head** (*informal*) = if you say something off the top of your head, you say it immediately, without thinking carefully or checking the facts: *Off the top of my head, I'd say it will cost about $50.*
→ see Thesaurus box at **cover²**

**top²** *adjective*
**1** highest: *We took the elevator right up to the top floor.* **ANTONYM: bottom**
**2** best or most successful: *He won the top prize of $500.*

**top·ic** [Ac] /ˈtɑpɪk/ *noun*
a subject that people talk or write about: *The topic we will discuss in class today is why earthquakes happen.*
[**ORIGIN:** 1400-1500 From a Greek book by Aristotle called Topika, from *topos*, which means "place, or part of something written." Topika was about developing an argument from a "place" or idea.]

**top·i·cal** [Ac] /ˈtɑpɪkəl/ *adjective*
related to events that are happening now: *Terrorism is a topical issue that all the newspapers and magazines have articles on.*

**ˈtopic ˌsentence** *noun*
the sentence in a PARAGRAPH that states the main idea you are writing about: *The topic sentence is usually the first sentence in a paragraph.*

**tops** /tɑps/ *adverb* (*informal*)
at the most: *It won't take long to get there – ten minutes, tops.*

**ˌtop-ˈsecret** *adjective*
top-secret documents or information must be

kept completely secret: *a top-secret report to be read only by the president*

**top·sy-tur·vy** /ˌtɑpsi ˈtɚvi/ *adjective* (*informal*)
completely messy or completely out of order: *He left his room topsy-turvy, with the bed not made and clothes all over the floor.*

**To·rah** /ˈtɔrə/ *noun*
**the Torah** = the holy writings of the Jewish religion, which are written in Hebrew. The Torah contains the first five books of the Jewish Bible.

**torch**[1] /tɔrtʃ/ *noun*
a long stick that you burn at one end for light or as a symbol: *The Olympic torch is lit before every Olympic Games.*

**torch**[2] *verb*
to deliberately make a building, vehicle, etc. start to burn: *Protesters torched several government buildings.*

**tore** /tɔr/ *verb*
the past tense of TEAR

**tor·ment** /tɔrˈment/ *verb* (*formal*)
to deliberately keep hurting, upsetting, or annoying someone: *He was always tormenting his little sister by stealing her toys.*
[**ORIGIN:** 1200-1300 From the Latin word *tormentum*, which means "torture," from *torquere*, which means "to twist."]

**torn** /tɔrn/ *verb*
the past participle of TEAR

**tor·na·do** /tɔrˈneɪdoʊ/ *noun* (plural **tornadoes**)
a violent storm with strong winds that go around and around: *A tornado tore the roof off of the building.*
→ see Thesaurus box at **wind**[1]
[**ORIGIN:** 1500-1600 Probably from the Spanish word *tronada*, which means "thunderstorm," but changed so that it is more like the Spanish word *tornar*, which means "to turn."]

**tor·pe·do** /tɔrˈpidoʊ/ *noun* (plural **torpedoes**)
a weapon that travels under the surface of the ocean and explodes when it hits something. A torpedo is fired from a SUBMARINE or a ship: *The ship was hit by a torpedo and blown up.*
[**ORIGIN:** 1700-1800 From the Latin name for a type of fish that can produce electricity to make animals attacking it numb. This comes from the Latin word *torpere*, which means "to be stiff or numb."]

**tor·til·la** /tɔrˈtiyə/ *noun*
a type of thin round Mexican bread made from corn or wheat flour

**tor·toise** /ˈtɔrtəs/ *noun*
a slow-moving animal that can put its legs and head inside the shell that covers its body
[**ORIGIN:** 1400-1500 From the Latin word *tortuca*, probably from an earlier Latin word *tartaruchus*, which means "belonging to Tartarus." Tartarus was the land of the dead in ancient stories, and it used to be thought that tortoises and turtles came from hell.]

**tor·ture**[1] /ˈtɔrtʃɚ/ *verb*
to deliberately hurt someone a lot for a long time: *They tortured him until he told them everything they wanted to know.*

**torture**[2] *noun*
**1** the act of deliberately hurting someone a lot for a long time: *They used torture to make the prisoners give them information.*
**2** mental or physical suffering: *It was torture having to wait for the test results.*

**toss** /tɔs/ *verb*
to throw something somewhere in a careless way: *He tossed the keys to me.*
→ see Thesaurus box at **throw**[1]

**to·tal**[1] /ˈtoʊtl/ *adjective*
**1** complete: *When I said the wrong answer, I felt like a total idiot!*
**2** including everything: *The total cost of the medical treatment will be $8,250.*

**total**[2] *noun*
the number that you get when you have added everything together: *We made a total of $589 dollars from our garage sale.*
—**total** *verb* to be a particular amount when added together: *His debts total over $25,000.*

**to·tal·i·tar·i·an** /toʊˌtæləˈteriən/ *adjective*
a totalitarian country is one in which ordinary people have no power and are completely controlled by the government: *In a totalitarian state, people are not free to say what they think.*
—**totalitarianism** *noun* a political system in which ordinary people have no power and are completely controlled by the government

T

**to·tal·ly** /ˈtoʊtl-i/ *adverb*
completely: *I totally agree.* | *Los Angeles is totally different from New York.*

**to·tem pole** /ˈtoʊtəm poʊl/ *noun*
a tall wooden pole with images of animals or plants on it. Totem poles are made by Native Americans: *An eagle's head was carved into the top of the totem pole.*

**touch**[1] /tʌtʃ/ *verb*
**1** to put your finger or hand onto something or someone for a short time: *She touched his arm gently.*

**THESAURUS: touch**

**feel** to touch something with your fingers in order to find out about it: *Feel this material; it's so soft.*

**stroke** to move your hand gently over something: *Ellie stroked her son's hair gently.*

**rub** to move your hand or fingers over a surface while pressing it: *Bill yawned and rubbed his eyes.*

**scratch** to rub your skin with your fingernails because it itches: *Try not to scratch those mosquito bites.*

**pat** to touch someone or something lightly several times with your hand flat: *Todd patted him on the back and told him he'd done a good job.*

**pet** to move your hand over an animal's fur to show that you like it: *The kitten loves it when you pet her.*

**brush** to touch someone or something lightly as you pass by: *Her hand brushed mine.*

**2** if two things touch, there is no space in between them: *Their legs touched under the table.*
**3** to affect your emotions, especially so that you feel sympathy or sadness for someone: *The boy's sad situation touched the hearts of people around the world.*
—**touching** *adjective* making you feel sympathy or sadness: *One touching moment in the movie is when the little girl tries to comfort her mother.*

**touch**[2] *noun*
**1** the ability to know what something is like when you feel it with your fingers: *We take in information through sight, sound, taste, touch, and smell.*
**2** the action of putting your finger, hand, etc. on someone or something: *Rita felt the touch of his hand on her shoulder.*
**3 get in touch/be in touch** = to write to or call someone: *We've been trying to get in touch with her, but she hasn't been answering her phone.*
**4 keep in touch/stay in touch** = to continue to speak or write to someone who does not live near you: *Jane and I keep in touch by email.*
**5 a touch of something** = a small amount of something: *Add a touch of lemon juice to the salad.*

**touch·down** /ˈtʌtʃdaʊn/ *noun*
**1** if you score a touchdown in football, you take the ball over the other team's line: *Brown scored the first touchdown.*
**2** the moment when a plane or spacecraft lands on the ground: *The spacecraft is three minutes away from touchdown.*

**touch·y** /ˈtʌtʃi/ *adjective*
easily offended or annoyed: *He is touchy about losing, so don't ask him what happened or he'll get upset.*

**tough** /tʌf/ *adjective*
**1** difficult to do or deal with: *It's a tough decision – I'm going to have to think about it.* | *The game will be tough, but I'm sure we can win.* **SYNONYM: hard**; **ANTONYM: easy**
**2** strong, brave, or determined: *You have to be tough if you want to be successful in business.*
**3** very strict: *We need tougher laws to fight crime.*
**4** strong and difficult to damage: *Sails are made of tough cloth.*
**5** tough meat is difficult to cut or bite: *The steak was tough and hard to cut.* **ANTONYM: tender**
—**toughness** *noun* the quality of being tough

**tough·en** /ˈtʌfən/ (*also* **toughen up**) *verb*
**1** to make a rule or law more strict: *The state*

has toughened the laws against drunk driving.

**2** to make someone stronger physically or emotionally: *He made his son play football to toughen him up.*

**tou·pée** /tuˈpeɪ/ *noun*
a piece of artificial hair that a man can wear when he has no hair on part of his head: *You could tell that he was wearing a toupée.*

**tour[1]** /tʊr/ *noun*
**1** a trip to several different places in a country, city, or area: *We went on a tour of Italy, and visited Rome, Naples, and Venice.*
**2** a trip around the different parts of a building: *Would you like a guided tour of the museum?*
**3** a trip to different places to give concerts or performances: *The band is on tour, and will be in Dallas in June.*

**WORD FAMILY: tour**
**tour** *noun* | **tour** *verb* | **tourism** *noun* | **tourist** *noun*

**tour[2]** *verb*
to travel around an area, visiting different places: *We're going to tour New England this summer, and see lots of historical places.*

**tour·ism** /ˈtʊrɪzəm/ *noun*
the business of providing tourists with places to stay and things to do: *The island's main industry is tourism.*

**tour·ist** /ˈtʊrɪst/ *noun*
someone who visits a place for pleasure: *San Francisco is full of tourists from all over the world in the summer.*

**tour·na·ment** /ˈtʊrnəmənt/ *noun*
a competition in which many players or teams compete against each other until there is one winner: *She is playing in a tennis tournament next week.*
→ see Thesaurus box at **competition**

**tow** /toʊ/ *verb*
if one vehicle tows another one, it pulls the other vehicle along behind it: *Our car had to be towed away when it stopped working.* → see picture at **pull**
—**tow** *noun* an act of pulling a vehicle with a rope or chain: *The truck gave the car a tow to the repair shop.*
→ see Thesaurus box at **pull[1]**

**to·ward** /tɔrd/ (*also* **towards**) *preposition*
**1** in a particular direction: *I saw a man coming toward me.*
**2** just before a particular time: *I always feel tired toward the end of the day.*
**3** showing how you behave to someone: *He's always been quite friendly toward me.*

**tow·el** /ˈtaʊəl/ *noun*
a piece of cloth used for drying something: *She dried her hair with a towel.* → see picture on page **A11**

**tow·er** /ˈtaʊɚ/ *noun*
a tall narrow building or part of a building: *There are fire towers on the mountain tops, so that people can watch for forest fires.*

**tow·er·ing** /ˈtaʊərɪŋ/ *adjective*
very tall: *towering mountains*

**town** /taʊn/ *noun*
a place with many buildings and streets, that is smaller than a city: *We live in a small town with only 3,400 people.*
[**ORIGIN:** From the old English word *tun*, which means "buildings inside a wall, or village."]

**ˌtown ˈhall** *noun*
a public building used for a town's local government: *The mayor held a meeting in the town hall.*

**tox·ic** /ˈtɑksɪk/ *adjective*
poisonous: *We must keep toxic chemicals out of our water.*
[**ORIGIN:** 1600-1700 From the Greek word *toxikon*, which means "poison for arrows," from *toxon*, which means "bow used to shoot arrows."]

**tox·in** /ˈtɑksɪn/ *noun* (*formal*)
a poisonous substance

**toy** /tɔɪ/ *noun*
a thing for children to play with: *The children were playing with their toys.* | *a toy car*

**trace[1]** Ac /treɪs/ *verb*
**1** to copy a picture by drawing on a thin piece of paper that you put over it: *I traced the map by using a piece of transparent paper.*
**2** to find someone or something that has

disappeared: *Police are still trying to trace the missing child.*

**3** to find out when something began or where it came from: *They traced their family history back to the 17th century.*

→ see Thesaurus box at **find**

**trace²** Ac *noun*

**1** a sign that someone or something has been in a place: *He has a trace of a Southern accent because he lived in Georgia for a while.*

**2** a very small amount of something that is difficult to notice: *The police found traces of poison in the food.*

**track¹** /træk/ *noun*

**1** **tracks** = marks on the ground that were made by someone or something that was moving: *You could see the tire tracks in the dirt.*

**2** **keep/lose track of something** = to pay attention to something so you know what is happening to it, or to fail to do this: *She quickly lost track of all the money she was spending at the mall, and spent way too much.*

**3** a course with a special surface on which people, cars, horses, etc. race: *The car reached 190 mph on the track.*

**4** the sport of running races on a track: *He ran track in high school.*

**5** (*also* **track and field**) sports such as running, jumping, and throwing things: *She's on the track team; she runs the hurdles.*

**6** the two metal lines that a train travels on: *train tracks*

**7** **be on the right/wrong track** = to think in a way that is likely to lead to the correct or incorrect result: *"A chili pepper?" "Keep guessing – you're on the right track. It's small and red, and you can eat it." "A tomato." "Yes!"*

**track²** *verb*

PHRASAL VERB

**track someone/something down**

to find someone or something by searching or asking questions: *Police were unable to track down the killer.*

**ˈtrack ˌrecord** *noun*

all the things that a person or organization has done in the past that show how well he, she, or it is likely to do in the future: *He has a great track record, so people are expecting his next movie to be good too.*

**trac·tor** /ˈtræktɚ/ *noun*

a strong vehicle with large wheels that is used on farms: *He drove the tractor through the field, pulling a load of hay.* → see picture on page **A26**

[**ORIGIN:** 1700-1800 From the Latin word *tractus*, a form of the verb *trahere*, which means "to pull."]

**trade¹** /treɪd/ *noun*

**1** the business of buying and selling things, especially between countries: *Last year the U.S. increased its trade with Saudi Arabia.*

**2** if you make a trade, you exchange something you have for something that someone else has: *Let's make a trade – my baseball cap for your soccer ball.*

**3** a skilled job that involves working with your hands: *He wanted to learn a trade, so he went to school to become a plumber.*

**trade²** *verb*

**1** to exchange one thing for another: *I'll trade my apple for your candy bar.*

**2** to buy and sell goods and services: *The two countries have traded with each other for hundreds of years, selling and buying everything from cloth to cars.*

PHRASAL VERB

**trade something in**

to give something that you own as part of the payment when you buy something similar: *You can trade your old computer games in for new ones.*

**trade·mark** /ˈtreɪdmɑrk/ *noun*

a special word or picture on a product that shows it is made by a particular company: *"Coca-Cola" is a trademark.*

**trad·er** /ˈtreɪdɚ/ *noun*

someone who buys and sells goods or STOCKs

**tra·di·tion** Ac /trəˈdɪʃən/ *noun*

something that people have done for a long time, and continue to do: *We have a tradition of eating a special meal on Thanksgiving.*

[**ORIGIN:** 1300-1400 From the Latin word *traditio*, which means "the act of handing something over," from *tradere*, meaning "to hand over." The idea is that traditions are customs that people hand over to the people who come after them.]

**WORD FAMILY: tradition**
**tradition** *noun* | **traditional** *adjective* | **traditionally** *adverb*

**tra·di·tion·al** Ac /trəˈdɪʃənəl/ *adjective*
based on ideas and ways of doing things that have existed for a long time: *It is traditional to exchange gifts at Christmas.*
—**traditionally** *adverb* in a traditional way: *In the past, women traditionally stayed at home to look after the children.*

**traf·fic** /ˈtræfɪk/ *noun*
**1** all the vehicles moving along a road: *We left early to avoid the traffic during rush hour.*
**2** the movement of aircraft, ships, or trains from one place to another: *There has been an increase in air traffic as flights have gotten cheaper.*

**ˈtraffic jam** *noun*
a long line of vehicles on the road that are not moving or are moving very slowly: *We were stuck in a traffic jam for two hours.*

**traf·fick·ing** /ˈtræfɪkɪŋ/ *noun*
**drug/arms trafficking** = the activity of buying and selling illegal drugs or weapons
—**trafficker** *noun* someone who buys and sells illegal drugs or weapons: *a drug trafficker*

**ˈtraffic ˌlight** (*also* **ˈtraffic ˌsignal**) *noun*
a set of colored lights at the side of the road that show when cars are allowed to move: *He stopped because the traffic lights turned red.*
→ see picture on page **A26**

**trag·e·dy** /ˈtrædʒədi/ *noun* (plural **tragedies**)
**1** a very sad event: *They suffered a terrible tragedy when their son was killed in a car accident.*
**2** a serious play with a sad ending: *"Romeo and Juliet" is a tragedy because the main characters die at the end of the play.*
[**ORIGIN:** 1300-1400 From the Greek word *tragoidia*. This word was used for a play with a sad ending and it probably comes from the words *tragos* and *aeidein*, which mean "goat" and "to sing," although it is not clear why.]

**tra·gic** /ˈtrædʒɪk/ *adjective*
very sad: *He died in a tragic accident.*
—**tragically** *adverb* in a very sad way: *She tragically lost her husband last year.*

**trail** /treɪl/ *noun*
**1** a dirt path that you walk on through a forest, in the mountains, etc.: *The trail led through the forest to the lake.*
**2** a long line or a series of marks that has been left by someone or something: *The injured animal left a trail of blood on the ground.*

**trail·er** /ˈtreɪlɚ/ *noun*
**1** (*also* **trailer home**) a small metal house on wheels. A trailer can be moved, but people usually live in it permanently.
**2** a vehicle that can be pulled behind a car, used for living in during a vacation: *A car towing a trailer arrived at the campsite.*
**3** a vehicle that can be pulled behind another vehicle, used for carrying something heavy: *They loaded the boat onto the trailer.*

**ˈtrailer ˌpark** *noun*
an area where trailers are parked and used as people's homes: *He lives in a trailer park.*

**train**¹ /treɪn/ *noun*
a line of vehicles that are connected together and travel along a railroad: *I took the train to Baltimore.* | *Should we drive or go by train?* → see picture on page **A26**
[**ORIGIN:** 1400-1500 From the old French word *trainer*, which means "to pull along."]

**train**² *verb*
**1** to teach or learn the skills needed to do something difficult: *The company will train you to use the computer system.* | *He trained to become a teacher.*
**2** to prepare for a sports competition by exercising and practicing: *He is training for the Olympics.*
→ see Thesaurus box at **practice**²

**train·ee** /ˌtreɪˈni/ *noun*
someone who is being trained for a job: *a trainee in the sales department*

**train·ing** /ˈtreɪnɪŋ/ *noun*
activities that help you learn how to do a job or play a sport: *All the employees receive training in how to deal with customers.*

**trai·tor** /ˈtreɪtɚ/ *noun*
someone who helps the enemies of his or her country or group: *He was a traitor to his country who sold secrets to the enemy.*

T

**tramp**[1] /træmp/ *noun*
someone poor who has no home or job and moves from place to place

**tramp**[2] *verb*
to walk somewhere with heavy steps: *The kids were tramping through the snow.*

**tram·ple** /ˈtræmpəl/ *verb*
to step heavily on something and damage it: *Don't trample on the flowers!*

**tram·po·line** /ˌtræmpəˈlin/ *noun*
a piece of sports equipment that you jump up and down on, made of a large piece of material attached by springs to a frame: *She was bouncing up and down on the trampoline.*

**trance** /træns/ *noun*
a state in which you seem to be asleep, but you are still able to hear and understand things: *Listening to the doctor's soft voice, she went into a trance, and he gave her instructions about stopping smoking.*
[**ORIGIN:** 1300-1400 From the old French word *transir*, which means "to die or become unconscious," from the Latin word *transire*, which means "to go across."]

T

**tran·qui·liz·er** /ˈtræŋkwəˌlaɪzɚ/ *noun*
a drug that makes someone calm or sleepy: *The doctor gave him a tranquilizer to help him calm down.*
—**tranquilize** *verb* to make someone calm or sleepy by giving him or her a drug: *They tranquilized the lion before moving him.*

**trans·ac·tion** /trænˈzækʃən/ *noun*
an action in which you buy or sell something: *The company keeps a record of all the financial transactions it makes.*
[**ORIGIN:** 1500-1600 From the Latin word *transactus*, a form of the verb *transigere*, which means "to complete some business."]

**trans·at·lan·tic** /ˌtrænzətˈlæntɪk/ *adjective*
**1** crossing the Atlantic Ocean: *a transatlantic flight from New York to London*
**2** involving countries on both sides of the Atlantic: *a transatlantic agreement between Canada and Great Britain*

**trans·con·ti·nen·tal** /ˌtrænskɑntənˈentl/ *adjective*
crossing a CONTINENT: *The transcontinental railroad went from the Atlantic coast to the Pacific coast.*

**trans·fer**[1] Ac /ˈtrænsfɚ/ *verb* (**transferred, transferring**)
**1** to move someone or something from one place to another: *They transferred the patient to a special children's hospital.* | *She transfers some money from her savings account to her checking account.*
**2** to officially give property or land to someone else: *He transferred ownership of the land to his son.*
—**transferable** /trænsˈfɚəbəl/ *adjective* able to be used by a different person or in a different place: *Air tickets are not transferable. They can only be used by the person named on them.*
[**ORIGIN:** 1300-1400 From the Latin word *transferre*, which means "to carry across."]

**transfer**[2] Ac *noun*
**1** the process of moving someone or something from one place or person to another: *The teacher refused to accept a transfer to another school.* | *the transfer of power from one president to the next*
**2** a ticket that allows a passenger to change from one bus, train, etc. to another without paying more money: *You should ask the bus driver for a transfer because you need to change buses.*

**trans·form** Ac /trænsˈfɔrm/ *verb* (*formal*)
to change someone or something completely: *Technology, such as computers and cell phones, has transformed our lives.*
—**transformation** /ˌtrænsfɚˈmeɪʃən/ *noun* a complete change in someone or something: *The transformation of a caterpillar into a butterfly takes several weeks.*
→ see Thesaurus box at **change**[1]

**tran·sit** Ac /ˈtrænzɪt/ *noun* (*formal*)
**1** a system of buses or trains that people use to travel around a city or area: *He uses public transit – either the bus or the subway – to get to work.*
**2** the process of moving people or goods from one place to another: *The painting was damaged in transit.*
[**ORIGIN:** 1400-1500 From the Latin word *transire*, which means "to go across."]

**tran·si·tion** Ac /trænˈzɪʃən/ *noun* (*formal*)
the process of changing from one form or state to another: *Making the transition from*

*being a child to being an adult can be very difficult.*

—**transitional** *adjective* relating to a period of transition: *A transitional government is running the country until new elections are held.*

**tran·si·tive** /ˈtrænsətɪv/ *adjective*
a transitive verb must have an object. In the sentence "She makes her own clothes," "makes" is a transitive verb.

**trans·late** /trænzleɪt/ *verb*
**1** to change speech or writing from one language to another: *He translated the book from English into German.*
**2** (*formal*) if one thing translates into another, the second thing happens as a result of the first: *They hope that the money spent on the team will translate into wins.*
—**translator** *noun* someone whose job is to translate things from one language into another
[**ORIGIN:** 1300-1400 From the Latin word *translatus*, a form of the verb *transferre*, which means "to carry across." The idea is that the meaning of the words you are translating is carried across into the other language.]

**trans·la·tion** /trænzˈleɪʃən/ *noun*
**1** something that has been changed from one language into another: *This is an English translation of a French poem.*
**2** the process of changing the words of one language into another: *We were given a paragraph in Spanish for translation into English.*

**trans·mit** Ac /trænzˈmɪt/ *verb* (**transmitted, transmitting**) (*formal*)
to send out radio or television signals: *They transmitted the message by radio.*
—**transmitter** *noun* a machine that sends out radio or television signals: *a radio transmitter*
—**transmission** /trænzˈmɪʃən/ *noun* the act of transmitting something
[**ORIGIN:** 1300-1400 From the Latin word *transmittere*, which means "to send across."]

**trans·par·ent** /trænˈspærənt/ *adjective*
if something is transparent, you can see through it: *The box is made of transparent plastic so you can see what is inside.*
[**ORIGIN:** 1400-1500 From the Latin word *transparere*, which means "to show through."]

**trans·plant** /trænsˈplænt/ *verb*
**1** to remove an organ from someone's body and put it in the body of a sick person who needs it: *The doctor transplanted the kidney from the dead man into the patient.*
**2** to move a plant from one place to another
—**transplant** /ˈtrænsplænt/ *noun* an operation to move a body part from one person to another: *He had a heart transplant last year.*
—**transplantation** /ˌtrænsplænˈteɪʃən/ *noun* the act of moving a body part from one person to another

**trans·port** Ac /trænsˈpɔrt/ *verb*
to move things or people from one place to another in a vehicle: *The coal is transported by train to all parts of the country.*
[**ORIGIN:** 1300-1400 From the Latin word *transportare*, which means "to carry across."]

**trans·por·ta·tion** Ac /ˌtrænspɚˈteɪʃən/ *noun*
**1** vehicles that people use to travel from one place to another: *If public transportation, such as buses and subways, was cheaper, more people would use it.*
**2** the activity of moving people or things from one place to another: *There are strict rules about the transportation of dangerous chemicals.*

**trap[1]** /træp/ *noun*
**1** a piece of equipment for catching animals: *a mouse trap*
**2** a trick for catching or harming someone: *The police set a trap for the thieves.*

**trap[2]** *verb* (**trapped**, **trapping**)
**1 be trapped** = to not be able to escape from a bad place or situation: *Three people were trapped in the burning building.*
**2** to catch an animal in a trap

**tra·peze** /træˈpiz/ *noun*
a short bar hanging from two ropes above the ground, that is used in GYMNASTICS or in a CIRCUS

**trap·e·zoid** /ˈtræpəˌzɔɪd/ *noun*
a shape with four sides, two of which are parallel

**trash** /træʃ/ *noun*
**1** waste food, paper, etc., or the container you put it in: *Put that peel in the trash.* | *Will someone take out the trash?* **SYNONYM:**

T

**garbage** → see picture on page **A9**
**2** (*informal*) something of very bad quality: *He spends all day watching trash on TV.*
→ see Thesaurus box at **garbage**

**ˈtrash can** *noun*
a large container outside your house, in which you put waste **SYNONYM: garbage can**

**trash·y** /ˈtræʃi/ *adjective* (*informal*)
of very bad quality: *Why do you read those trashy novels? They aren't worth reading.*

**trau·ma** /ˈtrɔmə/ *noun*
a feeling of being extremely upset, or an extremely upsetting experience: *He never recovered from the trauma of being separated from his parents.*
[**ORIGIN:** 1600-1700 From the Greek word for "wound."]

T

**trau·mat·ic** /trɔˈmætɪk/ *adjective*
extremely upsetting: *She went through many traumatic experiences during the war.*

**trav·el¹** /ˈtrævəl/ *verb*
**1** to go from one place to another: *He hates traveling by bus.* | *The band has traveled the world.*
**2** to move a particular distance or at a particular speed: *Sound travels at 330 meters per second.*
**3** in basketball, to take more than three steps while holding the ball. This is against the rules.
[**ORIGIN:** 1300-1400 From the old French word *travaillier*, which means "to work very hard." In medieval times, travel over long distances was difficult and needed a lot of effort.]

**travel²** *noun*
**1** the activity of traveling: *His job involves a lot of travel. He's already been to Mexico and Brazil this year.*

**THESAURUS: travel**

**trip** an occasion when you travel from one place to another: *My parents are planning a trip to Hawaii.* | *She had to make two trips to the store because she forgot to buy milk.*

**journey** (*formal*) a trip that is long or difficult: *Lewis and Clark's journey across America took many months.*

**travels** (*formal*) trips to places that are far away: *She wrote a book about her travels in South America.*

**voyage** a long trip in a ship or a spacecraft: *We learned about Columbus's voyage across the ocean.*

**2 someone's travels** (*formal*) = someone's trips to places that are far away: *She saw many interesting things on her travels through Asia.*

**ˈtravel ˌagency** *noun* (plural **travel agencies**)
a business that arranges travel and vacations

**ˈtravel ˌagent** *noun*
someone who works in a travel agency: *A travel agent can help you plan your vacation.*

**trav·el·er** /ˈtrævələ·/ *noun*
someone who goes on a trip: *Travelers can now buy plane tickets online.*

**ˈtraveler's ˌcheck** *noun*
a special check for a specific amount that you can use as money when you travel

**tray** /treɪ/ *noun*
a flat piece of plastic, metal, or wood that is used for carrying plates, glasses, etc.: *The waiter brought their drinks on a tray.*

**treach·er·ous** /ˈtretʃərəs/ *adjective*
**1** dangerous: *Ice made the roads treacherous, and there were several accidents.*
**2** (*formal*) someone who is treacherous secretly intends to harm his or her friends: *A treacherous member of the gang had told the police what they were planning.*
—**treachery** *noun* (*formal*) the actions of a treacherous person

**tread** /tred/ *noun*
the lines in the surface of a tire or the bottom of a shoe: *The tread on the tire should be at least a quarter of an inch deep.*

**tread·mill** /ˈtredmɪl/ *noun*
a piece of exercise equipment that you walk or run on, which has a large flat surface that moves: *He ran a mile on the treadmill at the gym.*

**trea·son** /ˈtrizən/ *noun*
the crime of helping your country's enemies: *He committed treason when he sold his government's secrets to other countries.*

**treas·ure¹** /ˈtreʒɚ/ *noun*
a group of valuable things, such as gold, silver, or jewels: *The map shows where the treasure is buried.*

**treasure²** *verb*
to keep or love something that is very important to you: *She treasures the necklace her grandmother gave her.*

**treas·ur·er** /ˈtreʒərɚ/ *noun*
the person who takes care of an organization's money

**treas·ur·y** /ˈtreʒəri/ *noun* (plural **treasuries**)
the government office that controls a country's money: *The Treasury has decided to print more money.*

**treat¹** /trit/ *verb*
**1** to behave toward someone in a particular way: *You should treat people fairly.* | *Stop treating me like an idiot!*
**2** to do something to make a sick or injured person better: *Doctors are treating the people who were hurt in the crash.*
**3** to deal with something in a particular way: *The police are treating the death as murder.*
**4** to buy something special for someone: *We're treating Mom to dinner for her birthday.*

**WORD FAMILY: treat**
**treat** *verb* | **treat** *noun* | **treatment** *noun* | **mistreat** *verb*

**treat²** *noun*
something nice and special: *Mom bought us an ice cream cone as a treat.*

**treat·ment** /ˈtritmənt/ *noun*
**1** a way of making a sick or injured person better: *a new treatment for cancer*
**2** a way of behaving toward someone: *His treatment of his wife was terrible – he used to hit her.*

**trea·ty** /ˈtriti/ *noun* (plural **treaties**)
a formal written agreement between two or more countries: *The countries signed a peace treaty to end the war.*

**tree** /tri/ *noun*
a tall plant that has a wooden TRUNK, branches, and leaves: *an apple tree*
[**ORIGIN:** From the old English word *treow.*]

**THESAURUS: tree**

**the woods** a large area of land with many trees: *We took a walk in the woods on the edge of town.*

**woodland** (*formal*) an area of land that is covered with trees: *The town is surrounded by woodland.*

**forest** a very large area of land with a lot of trees growing closely together: *Large parts of Washington and Oregon are covered in forest.*

**rainforest** a forest with a lot of very tall trees, in an area of the world where it rains a lot and is hot: *Are there monkeys in the rainforest?*

**jungle** a forest with trees and large plants growing close together, in a part of the world where it is hot: *The tribe lives deep in the Amazon jungle.*

T

**trem·ble** /ˈtrembəl/ *verb*
to shake because you are very afraid, excited, etc.: *He began to tremble with fear.*

**tre·men·dous** /trɪˈmendəs/ *adjective*
**1** very large in size, amount, or power: *I have tremendous respect for her.*
**2** very good: *He's a tremendous player.*
—**tremendously** *adverb* very or very much
[**ORIGIN:** 1600-1700 From the Latin word *tremendus*, which means "so frightening that it makes you tremble," from *tremere*, meaning "to tremble."]

**trem·or** /ˈtremɚ/ *noun*
a small EARTHQUAKE in which the ground shakes slightly

**trench** /trentʃ/ *noun*
a long narrow hole that is dug in the ground: *The men were digging a trench for a new gas pipe.*

**trend** Ac /trend/ *noun*
a change that is happening in society, or the way this change is developing: *There is a trend toward smaller families.*

**trend·y** /ˈtrendi/ *adjective* (**trendier**, **trendiest**) (*informal*)
fashionable: *He wanted to impress her so he took her to a trendy restaurant.*

**tres·pass** /ˈtrespæs/ *verb*
to go onto someone's land without permission: *He said we were trespassing and told us to get out of his yard.*
—**trespasser** *noun* someone who trespasses
→ see Thesaurus box at **enter**

**tri·al** /ˈtraɪəl/ *noun*
**1** the process by which a court of law decides whether someone is guilty of a crime: *the murder trial | He is on trial for robbery.*
**2** a test to find out if someone or something is good or effective: *Researchers have begun trials of the new drug.*

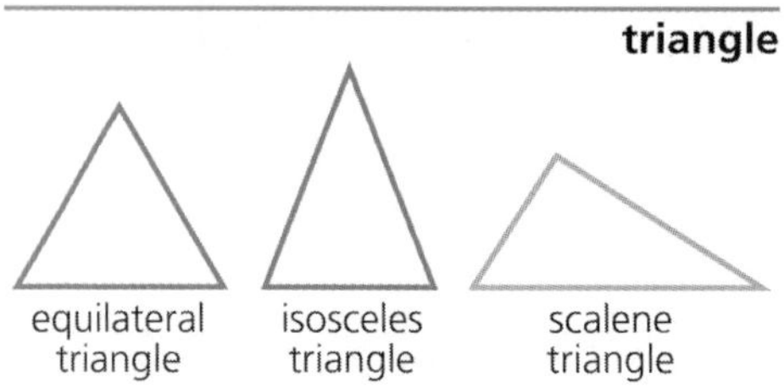


**tri·an·gle** /ˈtraɪˌæŋɡəl/ *noun*
a flat shape with three straight sides: *She cut the sandwich into two triangles.* → see picture at **shape**
—**triangular** /traɪˈæŋɡyəlɚ/ *adjective* shaped like a triangle
**[ORIGIN:** 1300-1400 From the Latin words *tri-* and *angulus*, which mean "three" and "angle."**]**

**tri·ath·lon** /traɪˈæθlɑn/ *noun*
a sports competition in which you run, swim, and ride a bicycle

**trib·al** /ˈtraɪbəl/ *adjective*
relating to a tribe: *We learned about the different tribal customs of Western Africa.*

**tribe** /traɪb/ *noun*
a group of people who live in the same area and have the same language and customs: *He was the chief of a Native American tribe.*
→ see Thesaurus box at **race**¹

**trib·u·ta·ry** /ˈtrɪbyəˌteri/ *noun* (*plural* **tributaries**)
a river or stream that flows into a larger river: *The Gila River is one of the main tributaries of the Colorado River.*

**trib·ute** /ˈtrɪbyut/ *noun*
**1** something that you do to show that you respect and admire someone a lot: *He wrote the song as a tribute to his wife.*
**2 pay tribute to someone** = to say how much you respect and admire someone
**[ORIGIN:** 1300-1400 From the Latin word *tributum*, which means "amount that is given or paid," from *tribuere*, which means "to give or pay." A tribute is now usually something that you do or say, rather than something you give.**]**

**trick¹** /trɪk/ *noun*
**1** something that you do to deceive someone, in order to get something or for fun: *My brother played a trick on me by putting a plastic spider in my bed.*
**2** a skillful action that you do to entertain people: *He did magic tricks, like making coins disappear.*

**trick²** *verb*
to deceive someone in order to make him or her do something: *He tricked me into telling him the secret by pretending he already knew it.*
—**trickery** *noun* actions by which you deceive someone

**trick·le** /ˈtrɪkəl/ *verb*
to flow slowly in a thin line: *Sweat trickled down his face.*
—**trickle** *noun* a small amount of liquid that is flowing slowly: *The trickle of water coming from the hose formed a small puddle on the ground.*

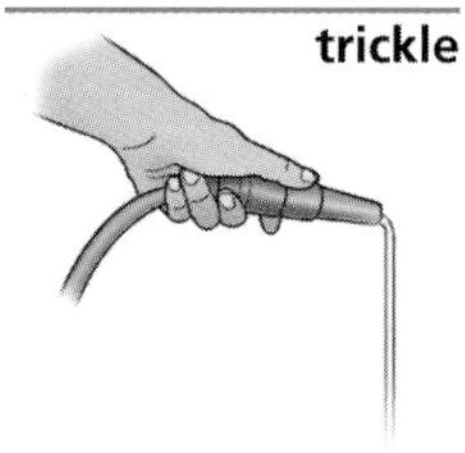


**trick·y** /ˈtrɪki/ *adjective* (**trickier**, **trickiest**) (*informal*)
difficult and needing to be thought about very carefully: *Some of the test questions were very tricky, so I don't know how well I did.*

**tri·cy·cle** /ˈtraɪsɪkəl/ *noun*
a vehicle like a bicycle, but with one wheel at the front and two wheels at the back
**[ORIGIN:** 1900-2000 From the Greek words *tri-* and *kuklos*, which mean "three" and "wheel."**]**

**tried** /traɪd/ *verb*
the past tense and past participle of TRY

**trig·ger¹** Ac /ˈtrɪɡɚ/ *noun*
the part of a gun that you move with your finger to fire it: *Carter aimed the gun and pulled the trigger.*

**trigger²** [Ac] *verb*
to make something happen: *A shocking event can trigger a heart attack.*

**trig·o·nom·e·try** /ˌtrɪgəˈnɑmətri/ *noun*
the study of the relationships between the angles and sides of TRIANGLEs
[**ORIGIN:** 1600-1700 From the Greek words *trigonon* and *metrein*, which mean "triangle" and "to measure."]

**tril·lion** /ˈtrɪlyən/ *number*
1,000,000,000,000

**tril·o·gy** /ˈtrɪlədʒi/ *noun* (plural **trilogies**)
a set of three books, plays, or movies that are about the same characters: *I really like the "Lord of the Rings" trilogy.*
[**ORIGIN:** 1600-1700 From the Greek word *trilogia*, which means "group of three plays," from *tri-*, meaning "three," and *logos*, meaning "story."]

**trim** /trɪm/ *verb* (**trimmed**, **trimming**)
to cut a small amount off something to make it look neater: *Could you trim my hair for me? It's getting too long.*
→ see Thesaurus box at **cut¹**

**tri·o** /ˈtrioʊ/ *noun*
a group of three people, especially musicians: *a jazz trio with a piano player, a clarinet player, and a bass player*

**trip¹** /trɪp/ *noun*
a visit to a place: *We're going on a trip to Florida.* | *He made two trips to Japan last year.*
→ see Thesaurus box at **travel²**

**trip²** *verb* (**tripped**, **tripping**)
**1** to hit your foot against something so that you fall or almost fall: *I tripped on a rock and fell.* → see picture on page **A5**
**2** to make someone fall by putting something in front of his or her foot: *Brian stuck out his foot and tripped Joe.*
→ see Thesaurus box at **fall¹**

**tri·ple¹** /ˈtrɪpəl/ *adjective*
involving three similar things: *a triple gold medal winner*

**triple²** *verb*
to become three times as big: *The city's population has tripled over the last 20 years, from half a million to 1.5 million.*

**tri·umph** /ˈtraɪəmf/ *noun*
a great win or success: *The team is celebrating its 100–88 triumph over Philadelphia.*
**SYNONYMS:** victory, win; **ANTONYM:** defeat
—**triumphant** /traɪˈʌmfənt/ *adjective* very happy and proud because you have won or succeeded

**triv·i·a** /ˈtrɪviə/ *noun*
unimportant facts: *He knows lots of trivia about celebrities.*

**triv·i·al** /ˈtrɪviəl/ *adjective*
not important: *Why are we arguing over something so trivial as whose turn it is to wash the dishes?*
[**ORIGIN:** 1400-1500 From the Latin word *trivialis*, which means "ordinary or found everywhere." This word comes from *trivium*, which means "place where three roads meet," from *tri-* meaning "three" and *via* meaning "road."]

**troll** /troʊl/ *noun*
an imaginary creature in stories who is usually very big or ugly

**trol·ley** /ˈtrɑli/ *noun*
an electric vehicle like a bus that runs along the street on metal tracks

**trom·bone** /trɑmˈboʊn/ *noun*
a metal musical instrument that you play by blowing into it and moving a long sliding part
→ see picture on page **A21**
—**trombonist** *noun* someone who plays the trombone

**troop** /trup/ *noun*
**1 troops** = soldiers: *The U.S. will be sending more troops to the area.*
**2** a group of people or animals: *a Girl Scout troop*

**troop·er** /ˈtrupɚ/ *noun*
a member of a state police force in the U.S.: *A state trooper pulled him over for speeding.*

trophy

**tro·phy** /ˈtroʊfi/ *noun* (plural **trophies**)
a metal cup or other object that someone gets for winning a game or race: *He's won many trophies for tennis.*

T

**trop·i·cal** /ˈtrɑpɪkəl/ *adjective*
in or from the hottest and wettest parts of the world: *tropical fruits such as pineapples and bananas*

**trop·ics** /ˈtrɑpɪks/ *plural noun*
**the tropics** = the hottest and wettest parts of the world: *Some plants grow only in the tropics.*

**trot** /trɑt/ *verb* (**trotted**, **trotting**)
to run with quick short steps: *The horse trotted along.*
—**trot** *noun* the speed of a person or animal that is trotting

**trou·ble¹** /ˈtrʌbəl/ *noun*
**1** problems or difficulty: *She's been having trouble with her computer.* | *My grandpa has heart trouble.*
**2** **the trouble with someone or something** = what is not good about someone or something: *The trouble with you is you don't listen.*
**3** **in trouble** = **a)** if you are in trouble, you have done something wrong and someone in authority knows about it: *He got in trouble at school, and the principal called his parents.* **b)** having a lot of problems: *Their marriage was in trouble and she was afraid that her husband might leave her.*
**4** an effort that you must make to do something: *She took the trouble to explain it to us again.* | *"Could you help me carry this?" "Sure, it's no trouble."*

T

**trouble²** *verb* (*formal*)
to make someone feel worried: *It was clear that something was troubling him because he looked worried.* **SYNONYM: bother**
—**troubling** *adjective* making you feel worried: *His behavior is troubling, because it is so different from before.*

**trou·bled** /ˈtrʌbəld/ *adjective* (*formal*)
**1** worried: *He was troubled about his mother's health problems.*
**2** having a lot of problems: *She had a troubled childhood because her father was an alcoholic.*

**trou·ble·mak·er** /ˈtrʌbəlˌmeɪkɚ/ *noun*
someone who deliberately causes problems: *A teacher needs to know how to deal with troublemakers who try to interrupt the class.*

**trou·ble·shoot** /ˈtrʌbəlˌʃut/ *verb*
to deal with problems in an organization, system, etc.: *His job is to troubleshoot computer problems.*
—**troubleshooter** *noun* someone who troubleshoots problems

**trough** /trɔf/ *noun*
a long narrow open container that holds water or food for animals: *The pigs were all eating at the trough.*

**trou·sers** /ˈtraʊzɚz/ *plural noun*
another word for PANTS

**trout** /traʊt/ *noun*
a common river fish

**tru·ant** /ˈtruənt/ *adjective*
not going to school when you do not have permission to stay away and you are not sick: *If you are truant, the school will talk to your parents to find out why you aren't coming to school.*
—**truancy** *noun* the action of being truant
—**truant** *noun* someone who is truant
[**ORIGIN:** 1300-1400 From an old French word for "wanderer."]

**truce** /trus/ *noun*
an agreement between two enemies to stop fighting or arguing for a time: *The two armies called a truce and said they would not attack each other.*
[**ORIGIN:** 1300-1400 From the plural of the old English word *trewe* or *treow*, which means "agreement or treaty."]

**truck** /trʌk/ *noun*
a large vehicle that people use for carrying things: *They loaded the furniture into the truck.* → see picture on page **A27**

**true** /tru/ *adjective*
**1** correct and based on facts: *Is it true (that) you're changing schools next year?* | *I swear this is a true story.*
**2** real: *A true friend would be completely honest with you.*
**3** **come true** = if a dream or wish comes true, what you hope for happens: *She has always wanted to be a singer, and now her dream has come true.*
[**ORIGIN:** From the old English word *treowe*, which means "faithful or trustworthy."]

**WORD FAMILY: true**

**true** *adjective* | **untrue** *adjective* | **truly** *adverb* | **truth** *noun* | **truthful** *adjective* | **truthfully** *adverb*

**tru·ly** /ˈtruli/ *adverb* (*formal*)
used to emphasize that something is true or real: *I truly believe we can win.* **SYNONYM: really**

**trum·pet** /ˈtrʌmpɪt/ *noun*
a metal musical instrument that you play by blowing into it and pressing three buttons
—**trumpeter** *noun* someone who plays the trumpet

**trunk** /trʌŋk/ *noun*
**1** the thick wooden stem of a tree: *The squirrel ran up the tree trunk.*
**2** a covered space in the back of a car where you can carry things: *Put the suitcases in the trunk.* → see picture on page **A28**
**3** a large box in which you store or carry things: *She kept some blankets in a trunk at the end of her bed.*
**4** the long nose of an ELEPHANT
**5** **trunks** = short pants that men wear when they swim: *He needs a new pair of swimming trunks.*

**trust¹** /trʌst/ *verb*
**1** to believe that someone will do what they say or what is right: *I don't trust her because she lied to me before.*
**2** to believe that something is correct: *I trust his judgment.*

**trust²** *noun*
the belief that you can trust someone or something: *They have a good relationship that is based on trust.* **ANTONYMS: distrust, mistrust**

**WORD FAMILY: trust**

**trust** *noun* | **trust** *verb* | **trustful** *adjective* | **trustworthy** *adjective* | **distrust** *noun* | **mistrust** *noun*

**trust·ful** /ˈtrʌstfəl/ *adjective*
believing that other people are good and honest and will not harm you: *He's too trustful of strangers and should be more careful.*

**trust·wor·thy** /ˈtrʌstˌwɚði/ *adjective*
someone who is trustworthy is honest, and you can trust him or her to do something: *Let John take care of the money; he's trustworthy.*
—**trustworthiness** *noun* the quality of being trustworthy

**truth** /truθ/ *noun*
the true facts about something: *"Do you think he's telling the truth about what happened?" "Yes, he wouldn't lie."*

**truth·ful** /ˈtruθfəl/ *adjective*
giving the true facts about something: *It's better to be truthful about what happened, even if you get into trouble for it.* **SYNONYM: honest**
—**truthfully** *adverb* in an honest and truthful way: *Answer me truthfully – did you scratch the car?*

**try¹** /traɪ/ *verb* (**tried**, **tries**)
**1** to make an effort to do something: *I tried to lift the box, but it was too heavy.* **SYNONYM: attempt**

**THESAURUS: try**

**attempt** to try to do something, especially something difficult: *They're attempting to climb the world's tallest mountain.*

**do your best** to try as hard as you can to do something: *We'll do our best to get the work finished by Friday.*

**make an effort to do something** to try to do something that is difficult to do: *He's been making a real effort to improve his grades.*

**2** to do, use, or taste something in order to find out if it is good or successful: *Try some of this cake – I think it's delicious.* | *If the computer isn't working, try turning it off and turning it on again.*
**3** if someone is tried for a crime, people in a court of law listen to the facts about the crime in order to decide whether that person is guilty: *Three men were tried for the murder.*

**PHRASAL VERBS**

**try something on**
to put on a piece of clothing to find out if it fits or makes you look attractive: *I tried on three dresses, but I didn't like any of them.*

T

**try something out**
to use something in order to find out if it works or is good: *I bought a new bike last week, but I haven't had a chance to try it out yet.*

**try²** *noun* (plural **tries**)
an attempt to do something: *I passed the test on my first try.*

**try·out** /ˈtraɪ-aʊt/ *noun*
a time when people who want to be on a sports team are tested so that the best players can be chosen: *The softball tryouts are after school on Wednesday.*

**T-shirt** /ˈti ʃɚt/ *noun*
a soft cotton shirt, with short sleeves: *He was wearing a T-shirt and jeans.* → see picture on page **A6**

T

**tsu·na·mi** /tsuˈnɑmi/ *noun*
a very large ocean wave that destroys buildings and kills people: *An earthquake under the ocean caused a tsunami that killed nearly 30,000 people.*
**[ORIGIN:** 1800-1900 From Japanese, from *tsu* and *nami*, which mean "harbor" and "wave."**]**

**tub** /tʌb/ *noun*
**1** another word for BATHTUB: *He got in the tub and started to wash himself.* → see picture on page **A11**
**2** a plastic or paper container with a lid, that food is sold in: *He bought a tub of popcorn at the movie theater.*

**tu·ba** /ˈtubə/ *noun*
a large metal musical instrument that makes very low sounds, and that you play by blowing into it → see picture on page **A21**

**tube**

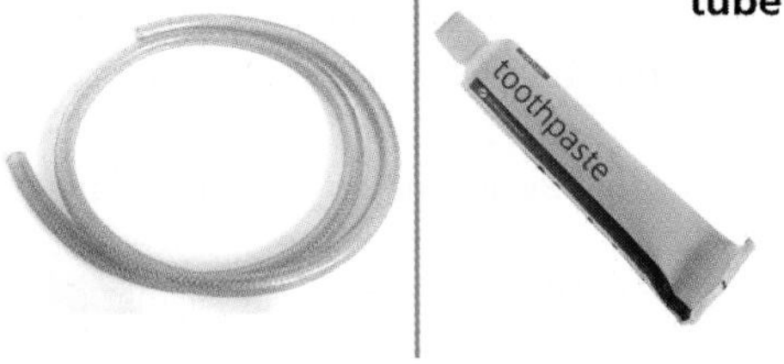


**tube** /tub/ *noun*
**1** a narrow pipe that a liquid or gas can flow through: *The water passes through this rubber tube into the glass jar.*
**2** a round hollow object with ends shaped like circles: *the cardboard tube inside a roll of toilet paper*
**3** a container for a substance such as TOOTHPASTE, that you press to get the substance out: *a tube of toothpaste*

**tu·ber·cu·lo·sis** /tʊˌbɚkyəˈloʊsɪs/ *noun*
a serious infectious disease that affects someone's lungs

**tuck** /tʌk/ *verb*
**1** to push the edge of a piece of cloth or clothing into or under something else: *He tucked his shirt into his pants.*
**2** to put something in a small space or a safe place: *She tucked the money into her pocket.*
**PHRASAL VERB**
**tuck someone in**
to make a child feel comfortable in bed by arranging the covers around him or her: *You go get in bed, and I'll come tuck you in.*

**Tues·day** /ˈtuzdi/ *noun* (*written abbreviation*: **Tues.**)
the third day of the week, between Monday and Wednesday: *He'll be back Tuesday.* | *Martha is going to St. Louis on Tuesday.* | *I'll see you next Tuesday.* | *My grandparents will be arriving Tuesday afternoon.*
**[ORIGIN:** From Tiw, the god of war in the religion of some peoples in Northern Europe before Christianity.**]**

**tug¹** /tʌg/ *verb* (**tugged**, **tugging**)
to pull something suddenly and hard: *Annie tugged at his hand and said, "Look over here, Dad."*
→ see Thesaurus box at **pull¹**

**tug²** *noun*
**1** (*also* **tug boat**) a small powerful boat used for pulling ships
**2** a sudden strong pull: *I gave the rope a tug.*

**ˌtug-of-ˈwar** *noun*
a competition in which two teams pull on the opposite ends of a rope

**tu·i·tion** /tuˈɪʃən/ *noun*
the money you pay for someone to teach you: *Jeff worked while he was in college to help pay his tuition.*

**tu·lip** /ˈtulɪp/ *noun*
a brightly colored garden flower that is shaped like a cup and has a tall stem

[ORIGIN: 1500-1600 From the Turkish word *tülbend*, which means "turban." The flower was thought to be shaped like a turban.]

**tum·ble** /ˈtʌmbəl/ *verb*
to fall with a rolling movement: *Everything tumbled out when I opened the closet door.*

**tum·bler** /ˈtʌmblɚ/ *noun*
a drinking glass with straight sides and no handle

**tum·ble·weed** /ˈtʌmbəlˌwid/ *noun*
a plant with a round shape that grows in the desert areas of North America. Dead tumbleweeds are blown from place to place by the wind.

**tum·my** /ˈtʌmi/ *noun* (plural **tummies**) (*informal*)
your stomach: *Mommy, I have a tummy ache.*

**tu·mor** /ˈtumɚ/ *noun*
a group of unhealthy cells in someone's body that have grown too quickly. Some tumors are caused by CANCER: *He had an operation to remove a brain tumor.*

**tu·na** /ˈtunə/ *noun*
a large common ocean fish, or the meat from this fish: *She opened a can of tuna and made a sandwich.*

**tun·dra** /ˈtʌndrə/ *noun*
the large flat areas of land where it is very cold and there are no trees, in places such as the north of Canada and Russia

**tune¹** /tun/ *noun*
a series of musical notes that are nice to listen to: *He picked up his flute and played a tune.*
→ see Thesaurus box at **music**

**tune²** *verb*
to make small changes to a musical instrument so that it makes the correct sounds: *You tune a guitar by making the strings tighter or looser.*

**PHRASAL VERB**

**tune in**
to watch or listen to a particular television or radio program: *Millions of people tuned in to watch the game.*

**ˈtune-up** *noun*
the small changes made to a vehicle's engine so that it will continue to work well: *He took the car to the service station for a tune-up.*

**tun·nel¹** /ˈtʌnl/ *noun*
a passage through a mountain or under the ground: *The train went through a tunnel in the mountain.*

**tunnel²** *verb*
to dig a passage through a mountain or under the ground: *They tunneled through the mountain to make a road to the other side.*

**tur·ban** /ˈtɚbən/ *noun*
a long piece of cloth that men from some religions wrap around their heads: *Many men in India wear turbans.*

**tur·bu·lent** /ˈtɚbyələnt/ *adjective* (*formal*)
**1** a turbulent time or situation is one that has a lot of sudden changes: *Life was difficult during the turbulent years of the war.*
**2** turbulent water or air has strong currents which change direction: *It was hard to steer the little boat in the turbulent waters of the river.*
—**turbulence** *noun* the quality of being turbulent: *There was a lot of turbulence during the flight so we kept our seat belts on.*

**turf** /tɚf/ *noun*
short grass and the soil under it: *They want to replace the turf on the football field with artificial turf.*

**tur·key** /ˈtɚki/ *noun*
a large bird that is often eaten at Christmas and Thanksgiving, or the meat from this bird: *We have turkey at Thanksgiving.*
[ORIGIN: 1500-1600 From the country Turkey. The word "turkey" was first used for an African bird (the guinea fowl) which was brought into Europe through Turkey. American turkeys were called "turkey" because they looked like this bird.]

**turn¹** /tɚn/ *verb*
**1** to move your body so that you are looking in a different direction: *She turned and looked at me.*
**2** to go in a new direction when you are walking, driving, etc.: *Turn right at the next light.*
**3** to move an object so that it is facing in a

T

different direction: *She turned the key and opened the door.*

**4** to keep going around: *The wheels of the train began to turn slowly.*

**5** to become different from before: *The weather turned colder. | The argument turned into a fight. | They're planning to turn the building into a museum.*

**6** to become a particular age: *He has just turned 40.*

**7** to move a page in a book or magazine so that you can see the next one: *She began to turn the pages of her magazine. | Turn to page 53 in your history book.*

**8 turn your back on someone** = to stop being friendly with someone and refuse to help him or her: *After she became famous, she turned her back on all her old friends.*

**9 turn over a new leaf** = to change the way you behave and become a better person

**10 turn someone or something loose** = to allow a person or animal to be free: *She turned the dogs loose in the yard.*

**PHRASAL VERBS**

**turn someone against someone/something**

to make someone dislike or disagree with someone or something: *He said his ex-wife had tried to turn his son against him.*

**turn someone away**

to refuse to let people into a theater, restaurant, etc., for example because it is too full: *The concert was so popular that they had to turn people away.*

**turn back**

to stop going in a particular direction and start going in the opposite direction: *We had to turn back because of the snow.*

**turn down**

**1 turn something down** = to make a machine such as a television or an OVEN produce less sound or heat: *The TV's very loud. Can you turn it down?* **ANTONYM: turn up**

**2 turn someone/something down** = to refuse someone's offer, request, or invitation: *He didn't ask her for a date because he was worried that she would turn him down.*

**turn in**

**1 turn something in** = to give work that you have done to your teacher: *Have you turned in your homework?*

**2 turn in** (*informal*) = to go to bed: *It's getting late – I think I'll turn in.*

**3 turn someone in** = to tell the police where a criminal is

**turn off**

**1 turn something off** = to make a machine or light stop working: *Don't forget to turn off your computer.* **ANTONYM: turn on**

**2 turn off a road** = to drive off one road and onto another, often a smaller one: *We turned off the highway looking for a place to eat.*

**3 turn someone off (something)** = to make someone not like someone or something: *He kept talking about himself, which really turned me off.*

**turn on**

**turn something on** = to make a machine or light start working: *It was getting dark, so she turned on the light.* **ANTONYM: turn off**

**turn out**

**1 turn out** = to happen in a particular way, or to have a particular result: *Don't worry. I'm sure that everything will turn out fine.*

**2 turn out a light** = to make a light stop working **ANTONYM: turn on**

**3 turn out** = if people turn out for an event, they go to it: *Only about 30 people turned out for the show.*

**turn something over to someone**

to make someone the owner of something, or make someone responsible for dealing with something: *He turned the business over to his children.*

**turn to someone/something**

to try to get help, advice, or sympathy from someone or something: *I turned to my parents for advice.*

**turn up**

**1 turn something up** = to make a machine such as a television or an OVEN produce more sound or heat: *Can you turn up the radio? I can't hear it.* **ANTONYM: turn down**

**2 turn up** (*informal*) = to arrive: *Danny turned up late as usual.*

**3 turn up** = if something you have lost turns up, you find it by chance: *The keys turned up in the kitchen drawer.*

**4 turn up** = if an opportunity turns up, it

T

happens, especially when you are not expecting it: *Don't worry – a job will turn up soon.*

**turn**[2] *noun*

**1** the time when it is your chance or duty to do something that a group of people are doing, one after another: *It's your turn to pick a card.*

**2 take turns** = if a group of people take turns doing something, one person does it, then another person does it, etc.: *Mom and Dad took turns driving.*

**3** a change in the direction you are moving in: *Make a right turn at the end of the road.*

**4** a place where a road joins another road: *Take the second turn on the left.*

**5** the action of moving something around: *Give the wheel another turn.*

**ˈturning ˌpoint** *noun*
the time when an important change starts to happen: *After losing so many times, the win was a turning point in his athletic career.*

**tur·nip** /ˈtɚnɪp/ *noun*
a large round pale yellow or white vegetable that grows under the ground

**turn·pike** /ˈtɚnpaɪk/ *noun*
a large road for fast traffic that drivers have to pay to use: *the New Jersey Turnpike*
[**ORIGIN:** A turnpike was a post with sharp points fixed into it that turned and was used to control movement past it. First used to mean a road, 1700-1800.]

**ˈturn ˌsignal** *noun*
one of the lights on a car that flash to show that the car is going to turn left or right → see picture on page A28

**tur·quoise** /ˈtɚkwɔɪz/ *noun*

**1** a bright blue-green color

**2** a blue-green stone that is used in jewelry

—**turquoise** *adjective* having a bright blue-green color

[**ORIGIN:** 1400-1500 From the old French word *turqueise*, which means "Turkish." The turquoise stone was found in Turkestan.]

**tur·tle** /ˈtɚtl/ *noun*
an animal with a hard shell that covers its body. Some turtles can live on land or in water.

**tur·tle·neck** /ˈtɚtlˌnek/ *noun*
a top or SWEATER with a high collar that folds over and covers most of your neck

**tusk**

**tusk** /tʌsk/ *noun*
one of the two very long teeth that stick out of the mouth of an animal such as an ELEPHANT

**tu·tor**[1] /ˈtutɚ/ *noun*
someone who teaches a subject to one student or only a few students: *Mom hired a math tutor for me.*
[**ORIGIN:** 1300-1400 From the Latin word for "guardian," from *tutus*, a form of the verb *tueri*, which means "to watch or guard."]

**tutor**[2] *verb*
to teach a subject to one student or only a few students: *He's tutoring me in French.*

**tu·to·ri·al**[1] /tuˈtɔriəl/ *noun*
a computer program that tells you how to do something: *There is an online tutorial showing you how to use the software.*

**tutorial**[2] *adjective*
relating to a tutor or the work of a tutor: *They offer an after-school math tutorial program.*

**tu·tu** /ˈtutu/ *noun*
a short skirt that female BALLET dancers wear, made with many layers of stiff material

**tux·e·do** /tʌkˈsiːdoʊ/ *noun* (plural **tuxedos**)
a suit, usually a black one, that a man wears at formal events: *He rented a tuxedo to wear to the prom.*
[**ORIGIN:** 1800-1900 From Tuxedo Park, a town in New York State. A tuxedo was first worn at a club in this town.]

**TV** *noun*
television: *Our new TV is bigger than our old one.* | *I saw a good program on TV last night.* | *The kids were watching TV.* | *a TV show*

**tweez·ers** /ˈtwizɚz/ *plural noun*
a small tool made from two thin metal pieces that are joined at one end, used for holding or pulling very small things: *She was removing hairs from her eyebrows with a pair of tweezers.*

T

**twelfth** /twelfθ/ *number*
**1** 12th
**2** 1/12

**twelve** /twelv/ *number*
**1** 12: *The table had twelve chairs around it.*
**2** twelve O'CLOCK: *I'm going to lunch at twelve.*
**3** twelve years old: *He's twelve.*

**twen·ty¹** /ˈtwenti/ *number*
**1** 20: *The train ticket cost almost twenty dollars.*
**2** twenty years old: *She left home when she was twenty.*
**3 the twenties** (*also* **the '20s**) = the years between 1920 and 1929: *The painter lived in Paris in the twenties.*
**4 in your twenties** = between 20 and 29 years old: *a woman in her early twenties*
**5 in the twenties** = between 20 and 29 degrees in temperature: *The temperature is likely to reach the low twenties today.*
—**twentieth** /ˈtwentiɪθ/ *number* 20th or 1/20

**twenty²** *noun* (plural **twenties**)
a piece of paper money worth $20: *Do you have two ten-dollar bills for a twenty?*

**ˌtwenty-ˈfirst** *noun, adjective*
21st

**ˌtwenty-ˈone** *number*
**1** 21
**2** 21 years old

**twice** /twaɪs/ *adverb*
two times: *I go swimming twice a week.* | *This book costs $10. That one is $20, which is twice as much.*

**twig** /twɪg/ *noun*
a very thin branch that grows on a larger branch of a tree: *Birds gather twigs to make their nests.*

**twi·light** /ˈtwaɪlaɪt/ *noun*
the time between day and night when the sky starts to become dark, or the pale light at this time: *It was twilight, and you could only see the dark outlines of the trees.*

**twin¹** /twɪn/ *noun*
one of two children who are born at the same time to the same mother: *Jenny and Julie are identical twins – they look exactly the same.* | *I have a twin brother.*

**twin²** *adjective*
twin things are two things of the same kind: *a twin-engined aircraft*

**ˈtwin bed** *noun*
a bed for one person

**twin·kle** /ˈtwɪŋkəl/ *verb*
if a star or light twinkles, it shines with a light that keeps changing from bright to less bright: *The stars were twinkling in the sky.*
→ see Thesaurus box at **shine**

**twirl** /twɚl/ *verb*
to turn around several times very quickly: *The dancers were twirling around.*

**twist¹** /twɪst/ *verb*
**1** to bend or wind something around something else several times: *Twist the ends of the wire together.*
**2** to turn something so that it moves around in a circle: *He twisted the lid off the bottle.*
**3** to change the position of your body by turning: *He twisted around to look at me.*
**4** if you twist a part of your body, you injure it by turning it too much or in the wrong way: *I fell and twisted my ankle.*
**5** if a road or river twists, it has a lot of curves in it: *The road twists through the mountains.*

**twist²** *noun*
**1** an unexpected change in a story or situation: *There was a final twist in the movie that surprised everyone.*
**2** a movement in which you turn something in a circle: *He put the key in the lock and gave it a twist.*

**twitch** /twɪtʃ/ *verb*
if a part of your body twitches, it makes a sudden small movement that you cannot control: *His eye twitches when he's tired.*
—**twitch** *noun* a sudden small movement of your body that you cannot control

**two** /tu/ *number*
**1** 2: *Most families in the neighborhood have two cars.* | *Two of my classmates live on my street.*
**2** two O'CLOCK: *The game begins at two.*
**3** two years old: *She'll be two in April.*

**ty·coon** /taɪˈkun/ *noun*
someone who is very successful in business

and has a lot of money and power: *That big house is owned by a billionaire oil tycoon.*

**ty·ing** /ˈtaɪ-ɪŋ/ *verb*
the present participle of TIE

**type¹** /taɪp/ *noun*
a group of people or things that are similar to each other in some way: *"What type of music do you like?" "I like music you can dance to."*

**THESAURUS: type**

**kind, sort** a type of person or thing: *What kind of fish is this? | The store sells all sorts of toys.*

**category** a group of people or things that are all of the same type: *The books are divided into two categories: fiction and nonfiction.*

**brand** a type of product made by a particular company – used about things you use every day, for example foods or cleaning products: *More people buy this brand of coffee than any other.*

**make** a type of product made by a company, especially a machine or a car: *"What make of car do you own?" "A Toyota."*

**model** one particular type of a product, especially a car or machine: *Ford's new models come out in September.*

**species** a group of plants or animals that are all similar and can produce young animals or plants: *This species of spider is only found in the rainforest.*

**type²** *verb*
to write something using a computer or TYPEWRITER: *I need to type my book report.*

**type·writ·er** /ˈtaɪpˌraɪtɚ/ *noun*
a machine that prints letters, numbers, or symbols onto paper when you press the buttons on it

**ty·phoid** /ˈtaɪfɔɪd/ (*also* **ˌtyphoid ˈfever**) *noun*
a serious disease that is caused by BACTERIA in food or water

**ty·phoon** /taɪˈfuːn/ *noun*
a violent tropical storm in the western part of the Pacific Ocean: *A typhoon struck the island, causing a lot of damage.*
→ see Thesaurus box at **wind¹**
[**ORIGIN:** 1800-1900 From the Greek word *typhon*, which means "whirlwind," and the Chinese phrase *daai fong*, which means "big wind."]

**typ·i·cal** /ˈtɪpɪkəl/ *adjective*
having the usual qualities of a particular person, group, or thing: *On a typical day, I leave the house by 8 a.m. | This painting is typical of the artist's work.*
—**typically** *adverb* used to say what is typical: *Typically, students finish the program in two years.*

**ty·po** /ˈtaɪpoʊ/ *noun* (*informal*)
a small mistake in the way something has been TYPEd or printed: *There's a typo on page 3 – it says "frim" instead of "firm."*

**tyr·an·ny** /ˈtɪrəni/ *noun*
government by a cruel ruler who has complete power: *People did not want to live under the tyranny of the king.*
—**tyrant** /ˈtaɪrənt/ *noun* a cruel ruler who has complete power

# Uu

**UFO** *noun*
(**unidentified flying object**) a strange moving object in the sky that some people believe is a spacecraft from another PLANET: *Many people thought the lights in the skies were UFOs.*

**ugh** /ʌg, ʌk, ʌh/ *interjection*
said when you dislike something very much: *Ugh! I hate fish!*

**ug·ly** /ˈʌgli/ *adjective* (**uglier**, **ugliest**)
not nice to look at: *Their dog is so ugly! It looks like its face has been squashed.* **ANTONYM: beautiful**
—**ugliness** *noun* the quality of being ugly
[**ORIGIN:** 1200-1300 From the Norse word *uggligr*, which means "frightening."]

U

**ul·cer** /ˈʌlsɚ/ *noun*
a sore area on your skin or inside your body: *a stomach ulcer*

**ul·ti·mate** Ac /ˈʌltəmət/ *adjective*
**1** most important and last in a process or series: *His ultimate goal is to become a doctor.*
**2** better, bigger, harder, etc. than all other things of the same kind: *The Olympic Games are the ultimate test for any athlete.*
—**ultimately** *adverb* finally, at the end of a process
[**ORIGIN:** 1600-1700 From the Latin word *ultimare*, which means "to come to an end or be last," from *ultimus*, which means "last."]

**ul·ti·ma·tum** /ˌʌltəˈmeɪtəm/ *noun*
a statement saying that if someone does not do what you want, he or she will be punished: *Mom gave me an ultimatum: either improve my grades or quit football.*

**ultra-** /ʌltrə/
extremely or beyond what is usual: *an ultra-fast connection to the Internet*

**ul·tra·vi·o·let** /ˌʌltrəˈvaɪələt/ *adjective* (*abbreviation*: **UV**)
ultraviolet light cannot be seen but makes your skin darker when you are in the sun: *The sunglasses block ultraviolet light.*

**um·brel·la** /ʌmˈbrelə/ *noun*
a piece of cloth or plastic on a metal frame, that you hold above your head to protect yourself from the rain: *He opened his umbrella when it started to rain.*

**umbrella**

[**ORIGIN:** 1600-1700 From the Italian word *ombrella*, which means "object used to shade you from the sun," from the Latin word *umbra*, which means "shade or shadow." In rainy countries such as Britain, the object is used to give protection from rain instead.]

**um·pire** /ˈʌmpaɪɚ/ *noun*
the person who makes sure that the players obey the rules in sports such as baseball and tennis: *The umpire said the runner was out.*
→ see Thesaurus box at **referee**
[**ORIGIN:** 1500-1600 From the old French word *nonper*, which means "not equal or not an even number." If there are two people (an even number), a third person (the umpire) is needed to judge between them. The phrase "a numpire" became "an umpire."]

**un·a·ble** /ʌnˈeɪbəl/ *adjective*
not able to do something: *After the accident, she was unable to walk.* **ANTONYM: able**

**un·ac·cept·a·ble** /ˌʌnəkˈseptəbəl/ *adjective*
something that is unacceptable is wrong or bad and should not be allowed to continue: *Rude behavior in class is unacceptable.* **ANTONYM: acceptable**
—**unacceptably** *adverb* in an unacceptable way: *The level of air pollution is unacceptably high.*

**un·ac·cus·tomed** /ˌʌnəˈkʌstəmd/ *adjective* (*formal*)
not used to something: *He was from the country and unaccustomed to city life.* **ANTONYM: accustomed**

**un·af·fect·ed** Ac /ˌʌnəˈfektɪd/ *adjective*
not changed or influenced by something: *Carla had lots of energy and seemed unaffected by the hot weather.*

**un·af·ford·a·ble** /ˌʌnəˈfɔrdəbəl/ *adjective*
costing too much for someone to be able to buy: *Ticket prices have become unaffordable for most families.* **ANTONYM: affordable**

**un·a·fraid** /ˌʌnəˈfreɪd/ *adjective (formal)*
not afraid: *The horses were big, but she was unafraid.* **ANTONYMS: afraid, scared**

**u·nan·i·mous** /yuˈnænəməs/ *adjective*
a unanimous decision or vote is one on which everyone agrees: *It was a unanimous decision to go to the lake, so we were all happy.*
—**unanimously** *adverb* in a unanimous way: *They voted unanimously to make Juan the class representative.*
[**ORIGIN:** 1600-1700 From the Latin words *unus* and *animus*, which mean "one" and "mind."]

**un·armed** /ˌʌnˈɑrmd/ *adjective*
not carrying any weapons: *The men were unarmed, but the soldiers shot them anyway.* **ANTONYM: armed**

**un·at·trac·tive** /ˌʌnəˈtræktɪv/ *adjective*
not nice to look at: *He had long greasy hair and she thought he was very unattractive.* **SYNONYM: ugly; ANTONYM: attractive**

**un·a·void·a·ble** /ˌʌnəˈvɔɪdəbəl/ *adjective*
impossible to prevent: *Because of an unavoidable delay, we arrived late.*

**un·a·ware** Ac /ˌʌnəˈwer/ *adjective*
not knowing or seeing what is happening: *They are on vacation, so they are unaware their house has been burglarized.* **ANTONYM: aware**

**un·bear·a·ble** /ʌnˈberəbəl/ *adjective*
if something is unbearable, it is so bad or unpleasant that you want it to end: *The pain was becoming unbearable, so she went to the hospital.* **ANTONYM: bearable**
—**unbearably** *adverb* in an unbearable way

**un·be·liev·a·ble** /ˌʌnbəˈlivəbəl/ *adjective*
**1** very difficult to believe and probably not true: *Yvonne's excuse was totally unbelievable. She said her dog ate her homework!* **ANTONYM: believable**
**2** used for emphasizing how good, bad, surprising, etc. something is: *He has unbelievable talent and will be very successful.*
—**unbelievably** *adverb* extremely: *The puppies were unbelievably cute.*

**un·bi·ased** Ac /ʌnˈbaɪəst/ *adjective*
fair and not influenced by someone's personal opinions: *We need unbiased information to make the right decision.* **SYNONYM: impartial; ANTONYM: biased**

**un·born** /ˌʌnˈbɔrn/ *adjective*
not yet born: *The tests show that the woman and her unborn child are healthy.*

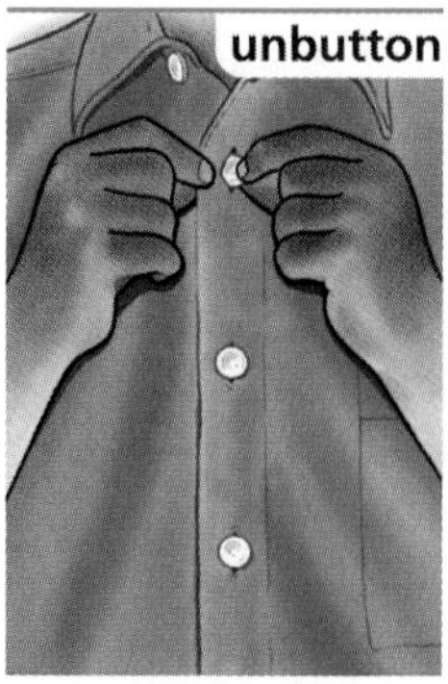


**un·but·ton** /ʌnˈbʌtn/ *verb*
to unfasten a piece of clothing that is closed with buttons: *He unbuttoned his shirt and took it off.* **ANTONYM: button**

**un·cer·tain** /ʌnˈsɚtn/ *adjective*
**1** not sure: *I'm uncertain about what to do, so I called you for some advice.* **ANTONYM: certain**
**2** not clear, definite, or decided: *Because the club keeps losing members, its future is uncertain.*
—**uncertainty** *noun* the quality of being uncertain

**un·changed** /ʌnˈtʃeɪndʒd/ *adjective*
not having changed: *The little town was unchanged; everything was exactly how she remembered it.*

**un·chang·ing** /ʌnˈtʃeɪndʒɪŋ/ *adjective*
always staying the same: *The rhythm of his heartbeat was regular and unchanging.*

**un·cle** /ˈʌŋkəl/ *noun*
the brother of your mother or father, or the husband of your AUNT: *My aunt and uncle came for Thanksgiving.* | *Uncle Bill*
[**ORIGIN:** 1200-1300 From the Latin word *avunculus*, which means "mother's brother" and is related to *avus*, which means "grandfather."]

**un·clean** /ˌʌnˈklin/ *adjective (formal)*
dirty: *Unclean drinking water made a lot of people sick.* **ANTONYM: clean**

**un·clear** /ˌʌnˈklɪr/ *adjective*
difficult to understand or know about: *The directions were unclear and I couldn't understand the assignment.* **ANTONYM: clear**

**Uncle Sam** /ˌʌŋkəl ˈsæm/ *noun (informal)*
a picture of a man with a white BEARD and a tall hat. Uncle Sam represents the U.S., or the U.S. government.

**un·com·fort·a·ble** /ʌnˈkʌmftəbəl/ *adjective*
**1** not nice to wear, sit on, or lie in: *These shoes are uncomfortable. They're too tight.* **ANTONYM: comfortable**
**2** feeling a little bit worried or embarrassed: *I'm a little shy, and I feel uncomfortable talking to strangers.*
—**uncomfortably** *adverb* in a way that feels unpleasant: *The train was uncomfortably crowded.*

**un·com·mon** /ʌnˈkɑmən/ *adjective*
unusual, and not happening or seen very often: *It's pretty uncommon to see someone wearing a shirt and tie at the beach.* **SYNONYM: rare; ANTONYM: common**

**un·con·scious** /ʌnˈkɑnʃəs/ *adjective*
not awake and not knowing what is happening, for example after being injured: *The branch hit him on the head and knocked him unconscious.* **ANTONYM: conscious**
—**unconsciousness** *noun* the state of being unconscious

U

**un·con·scious·ly** /ˌʌnˈkɑnʃəsli/ *adverb*
without noticing or knowing that you are doing something: *She moves her hands a lot when she talks, totally unconsciously.* **ANTONYM: consciously**

**un·con·sti·tu·tion·al** Ac /ˌʌnkɑnstəˈtuʃənəl/ *adjective*
not allowed by the rules of a country or organization: *The Supreme Court said the law was unconstitutional and had to be changed.* **ANTONYM: constitutional**

**un·con·trol·la·ble** /ˌʌnkənˈtroʊləbəl/ *adjective*
impossible to control or stop: *Olivia's body was shaking with uncontrollable laughter.*

**un·con·ven·tion·al** Ac /ˌʌnkənˈvenʃənəl/ *adjective*
very different from the usual way people do things: *Her unconventional style of clothes makes people notice her.* **ANTONYM: conventional**

**un·con·vinced** /ˌʌnkənˈvɪnst/ *adjective*
not certain that something is true or good: *We told Tania that the trip would be fun, but she was unconvinced.* **ANTONYM: convinced**

**un·cool** /ˌʌnˈkul/ *adjective* (*informal*)
not fashionable or acceptable: *My parents are so uncool – they always embarrass me.* **ANTONYM: cool**

**un·co·op·era·tive** /ˌʌnkoʊˈɑprətɪv/ *adjective*
not willing to help people or not willing to do what they ask: *Some people were uncooperative and wouldn't move out of the way.* **ANTONYM: cooperative**

**un·couth** /ʌnˈkuθ/ *adjective* (*formal*)
behaving or speaking in a way that is not polite or acceptable: *Other guests were shocked by his uncouth manners.*

**un·cov·er** /ʌnˈkʌvɚ/ *verb*
**1** to discover something that has been kept secret or hidden: *Police uncovered a secret plan to rob the bank.*
**2** to remove the cover from something: *Uncover the dish and let the food cool.* **ANTONYM: cover**

**un·de·cid·ed** /ˌʌndɪˈsaɪdɪd/ *adjective*
if you are undecided, you have not made a decision about something yet: *I'm still undecided about which shoes to buy – can I try both pairs on again?*

**un·de·ni·a·ble** Ac /ˌʌndɪˈnaɪəbəl/ *adjective*
definitely true or certain: *It is an undeniable fact that the disease is spreading.*
—**undeniably** *adverb* definitely

**un·der** /ˈʌndɚ/ *preposition, adverb*
**1** below something or covered by it: *Your shoes are under the bed. | She's hiding under the blanket.*
**2** less than a particular age, number, amount, or price: *What can I buy for under $20? | The toy is for children six and under.* **ANTONYM: over**
**3** controlled or governed by a particular leader, government, or system: *The country was under communist rule for many years.*
**4 be under discussion/construction/attack, etc.** = being discussed, built, attacked, etc.: *The city is under attack by rebel forces.*
**5** experiencing something, or affected by something: *We're under pressure to finish the work this week. | He found it hard to keep his temper under control.*
**6 under way** = happening or in the process

of being done: *Construction is already under way on the new airport.*

**un·der·class·man** /ˌʌndɚˈklæsmən/ *noun* (plural **underclassmen** /ˌʌndɚˈklæsmən/)
a student in the first two years of HIGH SCHOOL or college

**un·der·cov·er** /ˌʌndɚˈkʌvɚ/ *adjective*
working or done secretly, in order to catch criminals or find out information: *Undercover police officers bought drugs to catch the drug dealers.*

**un·der·de·vel·oped** /ˌʌndɚdɪˈveləpt/ *adjective*
an underdeveloped country or area is poor and does not have a lot of modern industry: *Developed nations have promised to lend money to the underdeveloped world.* **SYNONYM: developing**; **ANTONYM: developed**

**un·der·dog** /ˈʌndɚˌdɔg/ *noun*
the person or team in a competition that is not expected to win: *Everyone was surprised when the underdogs won the game.*

**un·der·es·ti·mate** Ac /ˌʌndɚˈestəˌmeɪt/ *verb*
**1** to think that something is smaller, cheaper, easier, etc. than it really is: *They underestimated the cost of the trip – in the end it cost $300 more than they thought.* **ANTONYM: overestimate**
**2** to think that someone is not as good at something or as intelligent as he or she really is: *Don't underestimate Sheila – she's very smart.*

**un·der·go** Ac /ˌʌndɚˈgoʊ/ *verb* (**underwent** /ˌʌndɚˈwent/, **undergone** /ˌʌndɚˈgɔn/)
to experience a change or something bad or difficult: *He underwent surgery to remove the cancer.*

**un·der·grad·u·ate** /ˌʌndɚˈgrædʒuət/ *noun*
a student in college, who is working for his or her BACHELOR'S DEGREE: *She's an undergraduate at Notre Dame University.*
—**undergraduate** *adjective* relating to undergraduates and the work they do: *undergraduate classes*

**un·der·ground** /ˌʌndɚˈgraʊnd/ *adjective, adverb*
under the earth's surface: *An underground tunnel connects the two buildings.*

**un·der·growth** /ˈʌndɚˌgroʊθ/ *noun*
bushes, small trees, etc. that grow around and under bigger trees: *I couldn't push my way through the dense undergrowth.*

**un·der·hand** /ˈʌndɚˌhænd/ *adjective, adverb*
if you throw a ball underhand, you keep your arm below your shoulder when you throw: *In softball, you throw the ball underhand to the batter.*

**un·der·line** /ˈʌndɚˌlaɪn/ *verb*
to draw a line under a word: *She underlined the important sentences on the page.*

**un·der·ly·ing** Ac /ˈʌndɚˌlaɪ-ɪŋ/ *adjective* (*formal*)
very basic or important, but not easily noticed: *Stress is the underlying cause of the illness.*

**un·der·mine** /ˈʌndɚˌmaɪn/ *verb*
to do or say something that makes someone or something less strong or effective over a period of time: *The bullying began to undermine her confidence.*

**un·der·neath** /ˌʌndɚˈniθ/ *preposition, adverb*
directly below or under something: *He stood underneath the bridge to get out of the rain.*

**un·der·nour·ished** /ˌʌndɚˈnɚɪʃt/ *adjective* (*formal*)
not healthy because you have not eaten enough food or enough of the right type of food: *They were poor and did not have enough food, so the children were undernourished and sick.*

**un·der·paid** /ˌʌndɚˈpeɪd/ *adjective*
earning less money than you should: *Nurses here are underpaid for their hard work.*
—**underpay** /ˌʌndɚˈpeɪ/ *verb* to pay someone less money than he or she deserves

**un·der·pants** /ˈʌndɚˌpænts/ *plural noun*
a piece of clothing that covers your bottom and is worn under your other clothes

**un·der·pass** /ˈʌndɚˌpæs/ *noun*
a road or path that goes under a road or

U

railroad: *We took the underpass to get to the other side of Main Street.*

**un·der·priv·i·leged** /ˌʌndɚˈprɪvəlɪdʒd/ *adjective (formal)*
very poor and not having the same education, health care, safety, etc., that most other people in society have: *The program helps underprivileged children get a good education.* **ANTONYM: privileged**
→ see Thesaurus box at **poor**

**un·der·shirt** /ˈʌndɚˌʃɚt/ *noun*
a soft piece of clothing that you wear under a shirt: *It's cold today; put on an undershirt.*

**un·der·stand** /ˌʌndɚˈstænd/ *verb* (**understood** /ˌʌndɚˈstʊd/)
**1** to know the meaning of what someone is saying: *Do you understand Spanish? | I'm sorry, I didn't understand – could you say that again?*
**2** to know how someone feels and why he or she behaves in a particular way: *I understand how you feel – the same thing happened to me before.*
**3** to know how something works or why something happens: *I don't understand how television works. | Her mother has died, but she's too young to understand why her mother isn't here.*
**4** to believe something because you have heard or read it: *I understand that you're planning to move.*
—**understanding** *noun* knowledge of a subject, or an ability to learn something: *He has a good understanding of what he has read.*

**WORD FAMILY: understand**
**understand** *verb* | **misunderstand** *verb* | **understanding** *noun* | **misunderstanding** *noun* | **understandable** *adjective*

**un·der·stand·a·ble** /ˌʌndɚˈstændəbəl/ *adjective*
reasonable and easy to understand: *It's an important test so your anxiety is understandable.*

**un·der·stand·ing** /ˌɚndɚˈstændɪŋ/ *adjective*
someone who is understanding is kind and knows how you feel when you have problems: *My teacher was understanding when I explained why my homework was late.*

**un·der·state·ment** /ˈʌndɚˌsteɪtmənt/ *noun*
a statement that is not strong enough to show how good or bad something really is: *To say the movie isn't very good is an understatement – it is terrible!*

**un·der·stood** /ˌʌndɚˈstʊd/ *verb*
the past tense and past participle of UNDERSTAND

**un·der·tak·er** /ˈʌndɚˌteɪkɚ/ *noun*
someone whose job is to organize funerals and get dead bodies ready to be buried

**un·der·tak·ing** Ac /ˈʌndɚˌteɪkɪŋ/ *noun*
an important job or piece of work that you agree to do: *Planning the dance was a big undertaking, but the kids did a great job.*

**underwater**

**un·der·wa·ter** /ˌʌndɚˈwɔtɚ/ *adjective, adverb*
below the surface of the water: *I don't like to open my eyes underwater.*

**un·der·wear** /ˈʌndɚˌwer/ *noun*
clothes that you wear next to your body, under your other clothes

**un·der·went** Ac /ˌʌndɚˈwent/ *verb*
the past tense of UNDERGO

**un·der·world** /ˈʌndɚˌwɚld/ *noun*
the criminals in a particular place and the activities they are involved in: *She had become involved in the city's dangerous criminal underworld.*

**un·de·sir·a·ble** /ˌʌndɪˈzaɪrəbəl/ *adjective (formal)*
bad or harmful and not wanted: *The drug can produce undesirable side effects such as headaches.* **ANTONYM: desirable**

**un·do** /ʌnˈdu/ *verb* (**undid** /ʌnˈdɪd/, **undone** /ʌnˈdʌn/, **undoes** /ʌnˈdʌz/)
**1** to open something that is fastened, tied, or

U

wrapped: *He undid his shoelaces and took off his shoes.*
**2** to change something back to the way it was before: *Once you've done something, you can't undo it.*

**un·do·ing** /ʌnˈduɪŋ/ *noun*
**be someone's undoing** = to be the reason why someone is not successful in the end: *He didn't listen to his father's advice, and that was his undoing.*

**un·done** /ˌʌnˈdʌn/ *adjective*
**1** not fastened or tied: *Your zipper's undone.*
**2** not finished: *A lot of the work was still undone when they left.* **ANTONYM: done**

**un·doubt·ed·ly** /ʌnˈdaʊtɪdli/ *adverb*
used to say that something is definitely true: *Your parents will undoubtedly be pleased about how well you've done.*

**un·dress** /ʌnˈdres/ *verb*
to take your clothes off: *Yvonne undressed and got into bed.* **ANTONYM: dress**
—**undressed** *adjective* not wearing any clothes

**un·eas·y** /ʌnˈizi/ *adjective*
worried because you think something bad might happen: *I was uneasy about leaving my little sister by herself.*
—**uneasily** *adverb* in an uneasy way
—**unease** (*also* **uneasiness**) *noun* an uneasy feeling
→ see Thesaurus box at **worried**

**un·ed·u·cat·ed** /ʌnˈdʒəˌkeɪtɪd/ *adjective*
not having a lot of education: *Uneducated people have trouble finding good jobs.* **ANTONYM: educated**

**un·em·ployed** /ˌʌnɪmˈplɔɪd/ *adjective*
without a job: *My father has been unemployed since the factory closed last year.*

**un·em·ploy·ment** /ˌʌnɪmˈplɔɪmənt/ *noun*
**1** the condition of not having a job: *There is a lot of unemployment here because many businesses have closed.* **ANTONYM: employment**
**2** money that the government gives regularly to people who do not have jobs, so that they can buy food and pay for a place to live: *He's been on unemployment since he was laid off from his job.*

**un·e·qual** /ʌnˈikwəl/ *adjective*
not the same or not equal: *The rooms were of unequal size – one was bigger than the other. | The unequal treatment of people because of race is illegal.* **ANTONYM: equal**

**un·e·ven** /ʌnˈivən/ *adjective*
**1** not flat or smooth: *The ground was uneven and hard to walk on.* **ANTONYM: even**
**2** good in some parts and bad in others: *The quality of his work is uneven – some of it is quite good, but some is not.*
—**unevenly** *adverb* in an uneven way

**un·ex·pect·ed** /ˌʌnɪkˈspektɪd/ *adjective*
surprising because of not being expected: *Her victory was unexpected – everyone thought her opponent would win.* **ANTONYM: expected**
—**unexpectedly** *adverb* in an unexpected way: *She arrived unexpectedly.*

**un·fair** /ˌʌnˈfer/ *adjective*
not right or not fair: *It's unfair to punish me for something Eric did.* **ANTONYM: fair**
—**unfairly** *adverb* in an unfair way
—**unfairness** *noun* the quality of being unfair, or unfair actions

**un·faith·ful** /ʌnˈfeɪθfəl/ *adjective*
someone who is unfaithful has sex with someone who is not his or her wife, husband, or usual partner: *She left her husband because he was unfaithful to her and had a secret relationship with his secretary.* **ANTONYM: faithful**

**un·fa·mil·iar** /ˌʌnfəˈmɪlyɚ/ *adjective*
**1** not known to you: *The author's name was unfamiliar to me – I had never heard of her before.* **ANTONYM: familiar**
**2 be unfamiliar with something** = to not have any knowledge of or experience with something: *We were unfamiliar with the neighborhood and didn't know where to eat.* **ANTONYM: be familiar with something**

**un·fash·ion·a·ble** /ʌnˈfæʃənəbəl/ *adjective*
not popular or fashionable at the present time: *Her clothes were old and unfashionable.* **ANTONYM: fashionable**

**un·fas·ten** /ʌnˈfæsən/ *verb*
to open something that is fastened or tied:

*Lewis unfastened his seat belt and got out of the car.* **SYNONYM: undo**; **ANTONYM: fasten**

**un·fa·vor·a·ble** /ʌnˈfeɪvərəbəl/ *adjective* showing that someone does not like or approve of something: *The movie got a lot of unfavorable reviews, so we decided not to go.* **ANTONYM: favorable**

**un·fin·ished** /ʌnˈfɪnɪʃt/ *adjective* not complete or finished: *When she died, the book she was writing was still unfinished.* **ANTONYM: finished**

**un·fit** /ʌnˈfɪt/ *adjective* not good enough to do something or to be used for something: *The judge said she was an unfit mother and took her children away.* **ANTONYM: fit**

**un·fold** /ʌnˈfoʊld/ *verb* to open something that was folded: *She unfolded the map and spread it out on the table.* **ANTONYM: fold**

U

**un·fore·seen** /ˌʌnfɔrˈsin/ *adjective* (*formal*) an unforeseen situation is one that you did not expect to happen: *We had to cancel the trip because of unforeseen problems.*

**un·for·tu·nate** /ʌnˈfɔrtʃənət/ *adjective*
**1** an unfortunate situation is not good and you wish it was different: *It's unfortunate that no one wanted to help us.* **ANTONYM: fortunate**
**2** happening because of bad luck: *Three people were killed in the unfortunate accident.*

**un·for·tu·nate·ly** /ʌnˈfɔrtʃənətli/ *adverb* used when you wish something were not true and you feel sad or disappointed about it: *Unfortunately, I won't be able to come to your birthday party.* **ANTONYM: fortunately**

**un·friend·ly** /ʌnˈfrendli/ *adjective* not kind or friendly: *Most of the neighbors were unfriendly and we did not feel welcome.* **ANTONYM: friendly**

**un·grate·ful** /ʌnˈgreɪtfəl/ *adjective* not thanking someone for something he or she has given to you or done for you: *He's so ungrateful – he didn't even thank us for our help.* **ANTONYM: grateful**

**un·hap·py** /ʌnˈhæpi/ *adjective* (**unhappier, unhappiest**)
**1** not happy: *I was very unhappy when Lora moved away.* | *an unhappy childhood* **SYNONYM: sad**; **ANTONYM: happy**
**2** thinking something is not good enough: *The teacher was unhappy with our test scores and said we should have studied harder.* **ANTONYMS: pleased, satisfied**
—**unhappily** *adverb* in an unhappy way
—**unhappiness** *noun* an unhappy feeling
→ see Thesaurus box at **sad**

**un·health·y** /ʌnˈhelθi/ *adjective*
**1** not physically healthy, and often sick: *He was an unhealthy baby, but now he is fine.* **ANTONYM: healthy**
**2** likely to make you sick: *Eating a lot of junk food is very unhealthy.* **ANTONYM: healthy**

**un·heard-of** /ʌnˈhɚd ʌv/ *adjective* something that is unheard-of is very unusual, or has never happened before: *When my grandfather was little, owning a television was unheard-of.*

**un·help·ful** /ʌnˈhelpfəl/ *adjective* not helping someone: *The sales clerk was pretty unhelpful, so we left without buying anything.* **ANTONYM: helpful**

**u·ni·corn** /ˈyunəˌkɔrn/ *noun* a white horse with a horn on its head, that exists only in stories
[**ORIGIN:** 1200-1300 From the Latin words *unus* and *cornu*, which mean "one" and "horn."]

**u·ni·form¹** /ˈyunəˌfɔrm/ *noun* special clothes that people wear for some jobs, schools, or sports: *One of the men was wearing an army uniform.*
[**ORIGIN:** 1500-1600 From the Latin words *uni-* and *forma*, which mean "one" and "form or shape." People who wear a uniform all have the same appearance.]

**uniform**

**uniform²** Ac *adjective* (*formal*) exactly the same in size, shape, color, etc.: *Make sure all the pieces are a uniform length.*
—**uniformly** *adverb* all or always: *The food at the restaurant is uniformly excellent.*
—**uniformity** /ˌyunəˈfɔrməti/ *noun* the state of being uniform

**u·ni·fy** Ac /ˈyunəˌfaɪ/ *verb* (**unified**, **unifies**)
to join the different parts of a country or organization together: *They signed an agreement that unified Germany.*
—**unification** /ˌyunəfəˈkeɪʃən/ *noun* the act of unifying a country, organization, etc.

**un·i·mag·in·a·ble** /ˌʌnɪˈmædʒənəbəl/ *adjective*
impossible to imagine: *Our modern world would be unimaginable to people who lived 500 years ago.*

**un·im·por·tant** /ˌʌnɪmˈpɔrtnt/ *adjective*
not important: *I'm not going to worry about unimportant details.* **ANTONYM: important**

**un·in·hab·it·ed** /ˌʌnɪnˈhæbɪtɪd/ *adjective*
an uninhabited place has no one living there: *All the people have left the island and it is now uninhabited.* **ANTONYM: inhabited**

**un·in·ter·est·ed** /ʌnˈɪntrəstɪd/ *adjective*
not interested: *Larry was always uninterested in sports.* **ANTONYM: interested**

**un·in·ter·est·ing** /ʌnˈɪntrɪstɪŋ/ *adjective*
not interesting: *He had a very uninteresting job in a factory.* **SYNONYM: boring**; **ANTONYM: interesting**

**un·ion** /ˈyunyən/ *noun*
**1** (*also* **labor union**) an organization that workers form to protect their rights: *The teacher's union is asking for smaller classes and better pay.*
**2** a group of countries or states that have joined together: *Britain, Spain and France are all members of the European Union.*
**3** (*formal*) the act of joining countries, people, etc. together: *Marriage is the union of two people who have decided to spend the rest of their lives together.*
**4 the Union** = the states that stayed loyal to the U.S. government during the Civil War **ANTONYM: the Confederacy**
—**unionized** *adjective* unionized workers have formed or joined a union: *About 50% of workers are unionized.*

**u·nique** Ac /yuˈnik/ *adjective*
**1** very special and good: *He has a unique ability to learn languages very quickly.*
**2** not like anything or anyone else: *It's hard to describe the flavor of the fruit because it's unique.*
—**uniquely** *adverb* in a way that is not like anything or anyone else: *This tradition is uniquely Mexican.*
[**ORIGIN:** 1600-1700 From the Latin word *unicus*, from *unus*, which means "one."]

**u·ni·sex** /ˈyunɪˌseks/ *adjective*
suitable for men and women: *There's a unisex hair salon in Davis Square that cuts men's and women's hair.*

**u·ni·son** /ˈyunəsən/ *noun*
**in unison** = if a number of people do something in unison, they all do it at the same time: *The children stood up and sang the song in unison.*

**u·nit** /ˈyunɪt/ *noun*
**1** one part in something larger: *Our science textbook has ten units, each about a different topic.*
**2** a standard that people use to measure amounts: *A kilowatt is a unit of energy.*

**u·nit·ed** /yunaɪtɪd/ *adjective*
**1** a united country is formed by two or more countries or states joining together: *the United States of America*
**2** if people are united, they have the same aims: *We are all united in our desire to improve the school.*
—**unite** *verb* to join together or work together with other people: *The nation united behind the president.*
—**unity** *noun* when everyone in a group or country has the same aims: *The flag is the symbol of our national unity.*

**UˌnitedˈNations** *noun*
**the United Nations** (*also* **the U.N.**) = an organization of many countries that tries to solve world problems in a peaceful way

**u·ni·ver·sal** /ˌyunəˈvɚsəl/ *adjective* (*formal*)
involving all the people in a group or in the world: *Some countries have universal health care, paid for by taxes.*
—**universally** *adverb* for or by everyone: *Education should be universally available.*

**u·ni·verse** /ˈyunəˌvɚs/ *noun*
**the universe** = all the space, stars, and PLANETs that exist: *There are billions of stars in the universe.*

U

**u·ni·ver·si·ty** /ˌyunəˈvɚsəti/ *noun* (plural **universities**)
a school where you study at a high level to get a DEGREE: *She studied history at the University of Virginia.*
[**ORIGIN:** 1300-1400 From the Latin word *universitas*, which first meant "the whole of something" and later meant "group or society."]

**un·just** /ˌʌnˈdʒʌst/ *adjective* (*formal*)
not fair: *People thought that the new law was unjust.* **ANTONYM: just**
—**unjustly** *adverb* in an unjust way: *Greta felt that she had been unjustly punished, and complained.*

**un·jus·ti·fied** Ac /ˌʌnˈdʒʌstəˌfaɪd/ *adjective* (*formal*)
done without an acceptable reason: *The punishment was unjustified because he had not broken the rules.* **ANTONYM: justified**

**un·kind** /ˌʌnˈkaɪnd/ *adjective*
unpleasant or cruel to other people: *One of the girls said that Sally was fat, which was very unkind.* **SYNONYM: mean**; **ANTONYM: kind**
—**unkindly** *adverb* in an unkind way
—**unkindness** *noun* unkind actions

**un·known** /ˌʌnˈnoʊn/ *adjective* (*formal*)
not known: *The cause of the disease is unknown, which makes it scarier.*

**un·law·ful** /ʌnˈlɔfəl/ *adjective* (*formal*)
against the law: *He was arrested and charged with unlawful possession of a gun.* **SYNONYM: illegal**
—**unlawfully** *adverb* in a way that is against the law

**un·lead·ed** /ʌnˈledɪd/ *adjective*
unleaded gas does not contain any LEAD

**un·less** /ənˈles/ *conjunction*
used when one thing will happen if something else does not happen: *You'll miss your bus unless you leave now.*

**un·like** /ˌʌnˈlaɪk/ *preposition*
**1** different from another person or thing: *Japanese is completely unlike English.* **ANTONYM: like**
**2** not typical of someone: *It's unlike Judy to leave without telling us.* **ANTONYM: like**

**un·like·ly** /ʌnˈlaɪkli/ *adjective*
not likely to happen: *It's a long trip, so it's unlikely that we'll get there before 6:00.*

**un·load** /ʌnˈloʊd/ *verb*
**1** to take things out of a vehicle: *Outside the store, some men were unloading a truck.* **ANTONYM: load**
**2** to take something out of a machine or piece of equipment: *Can you unload the dishwasher and put the clean dishes away?* **ANTONYM: load**

**un·lock** /ʌnˈlɑk/ *verb*
to open a door, box, etc. with a key: *He unlocked the door and went in.* **ANTONYM: lock**

**un·luck·y** /ʌnˈlʌki/ *adjective*
not lucky: *Many people believe that 13 is an unlucky number.* **ANTONYM: lucky**

**un·mar·ried** /ˌʌnˈmærid/ *adjective*
not married: *Maggie was 30 and still unmarried.* **SYNONYM: single**

**un·mis·tak·a·ble** /ˌʌnmɪˈsteɪkəbəl/ *adjective*
easy to recognize: *Garlic has an unmistakable taste – you know what it is when you taste it in food.*
—**unmistakably** *adverb* in a way that is easy to recognize

**un·nat·u·ral** /ˌʌnˈnætʃərəl/ *adjective*
different from what is normal or natural: *It's unnatural for someone his age to sleep so much.* **ANTONYM: natural**

**un·nec·es·sar·y** /ʌnˈnesəˌseri/ *adjective*
not needed: *We already have plenty of juice, so it is unnecessary to buy more.* **ANTONYM: necessary**
—**unnecessarily** /ʌnˌnesəˈserəli/ *adverb* in a way that is not needed: *I try not to spend money unnecessarily on things I don't need.*

**un·of·fi·cial** /ˌʌnəˈfɪʃəl/ *adjective*
not said, done, or approved by someone in authority: *According to unofficial reports, eight people were arrested.* **ANTONYM: official**
—**unofficially** *adverb* in an unofficial way

**un·pack** /ʌnˈpæk/ *verb*
to take everything out of a suitcase or box: *We arrived at our hotel, and unpacked our suitcases.* **ANTONYM: pack**

**un·paid** /ˌʌnˈpeɪd/ *adjective*
not paid: *He was worried about all his unpaid bills.*

**un·pleas·ant** /ʌnˈplezənt/ *adjective*
not nice or enjoyable: *Cleaning the bathroom is an unpleasant job.* **ANTONYM: pleasant**
—**unpleasantly** *adverb* in an unpleasant way: *The water was unpleasantly cold.*

**un·plug** /ʌnˈplʌg/ *verb* (**unplugged, unplugging**)
to remove a PLUG from a wall, and stop something electrical from working: *My computer wasn't working because someone had unplugged it.* **ANTONYM: plug in**

**un·pop·u·lar** /ʌnˈpɑpyələ˞/ *adjective*
not liked by many people: *Difficult subjects are often unpopular with students.* **ANTONYM: popular**
—**unpopularity** /ʌnˌpɑpyəˈlærəti/ *noun* the state of being unpopular

**un·pre·pared** /ˌʌnprɪˈperd/ *adjective*
not ready to deal with something: *I was totally unprepared for the question and didn't know what to say.* **ANTONYMS: prepared, ready**

**un·pro·fes·sion·al** /ˌʌnprəˈfeʃənəl/ *adjective*
not behaving in the way someone doing a particular job should behave: *It is unprofessional to criticize the people that you work with.* **ANTONYM: professional**
—**unprofessionally** *adverb* in an unprofessional way

**un·prof·it·a·ble** /ʌnˈprɑfɪtəbəl/ *adjective* (*formal*)
not making a profit: *Many small businesses became unprofitable and had to close.* **ANTONYM: profitable**

**un·qual·i·fied** /ʌnˈkwɑləˌfaɪd/ *adjective*
not having the knowledge, experience, or education to do something: *Why did they hire him when he's unqualified for the job?* **ANTONYM: qualified**

**un·ques·tion·a·bly** /ʌnˈkwestʃənəbli/ *adverb* (*formal*)
used for emphasizing that something is certainly true: *The team is unquestionably better this year, and we've won a lot more games.*
—**unquestionable** *adjective* completely certain or true

**un·rav·el** /ʌnˈrævəl/ *verb*
**1** if threads unravel, they stop being twisted together: *The sweater is old and is starting to unravel.*
**2** to find out the truth about something very complicated: *Detectives are still trying to unravel the mystery surrounding the woman's death.*

**un·real** /ˌʌnˈril/ *adjective*
**1** not really happening or existing: *While I was on vacation, all my problems back home began to seem unreal.* **ANTONYM: real**
**2** (*informal*) very unusual or special: *We went on a trip to the Andes – it was unreal!*

**un·re·al·is·tic** /ˌʌnriəˈlɪstɪk/ *adjective*
an unrealistic hope or idea is not reasonable, and what you hope or expect is not likely to happen: *It's unrealistic to expect all your school friendships to last.* **ANTONYM: realistic**

U

**un·rea·son·a·ble** /ʌnˈrizənəbəl/ *adjective* (*formal*)
**1** not fair or sensible: *It's unreasonable to expect you to work all weekend.* **ANTONYM: reasonable**
**2** unreasonable prices are too high: *The prices in that store are unreasonable, so I don't shop there.* **ANTONYM: reasonable**
—**unreasonably** *adverb* in a way that is not fair or sensible

**un·re·lat·ed** /ˌʌnrɪˈleɪtɪd/ *adjective*
if events are unrelated, they are not connected with each other: *The two crimes were similar, but probably unrelated.* **ANTONYM: related**

**un·re·li·a·ble** Ac /ˌʌnrɪˈlaɪəbəl/ *adjective*
not possible for you to believe or trust: *Some of the information on the Internet is unreliable, so check it carefully before using it.* **ANTONYM: reliable**

**un·rest** /ʌnˈrest/ *noun* (*formal*)
a situation in which people protest or behave violently: *There was not enough food, which caused unrest across the country.*

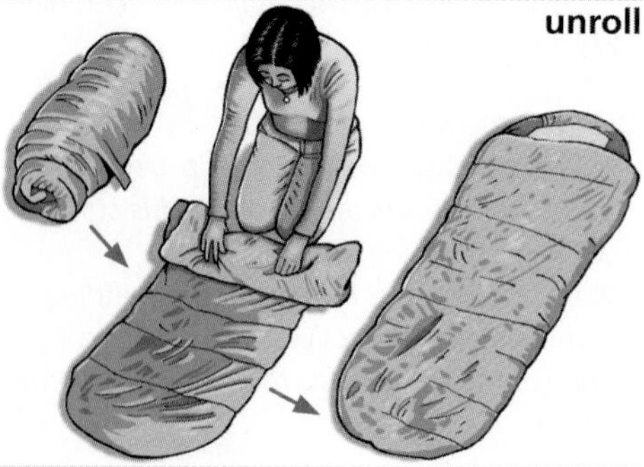


**un·roll** /ʌnˈroʊl/ *verb*
to open something that has been wrapped around itself, and make it flat: *She unrolled the sleeping bag and climbed inside.* **ANTONYM: roll up**

**un·ru·ly** /ʌnˈruli/ *adjective (formal)*
behaving badly or violently, and difficult to control: *Teachers have to learn to deal with unruly children.*

**un·safe** /ˌʌnˈseɪf/ *adjective*
dangerous: *It's unsafe to swim in the river because the current is very strong.* **ANTONYM: safe**

**un·san·i·tar·y** /ʌnˈsænəˌteri/ *adjective (formal)*
dirty and likely to cause disease: *The kitchen had not been cleaned in weeks – it was so unsanitary.* **ANTONYM: sanitary**

**un·sat·is·fac·to·ry** /ˌʌnsætɪsˈfæktəri/ *adjective (formal)*
not good enough: *Your report is unsatisfactory, and you need to rewrite it.* **ANTONYM: satisfactory**

**un·screw** /ʌnˈskru/ *verb*
to remove something by twisting it or taking screws out: *Turn off the light before unscrewing the bulb.*

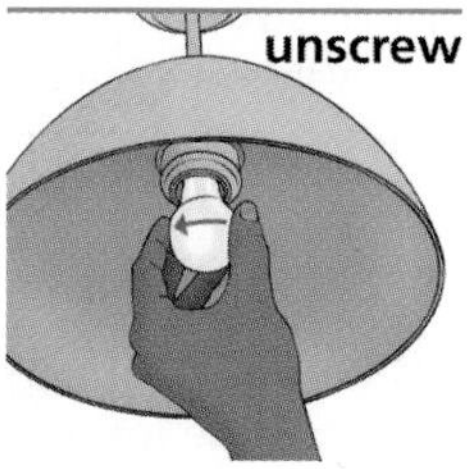


**un·scru·pu·lous** /ʌnˈskrupyələs/ *adjective*
behaving in an unfair or dishonest way: *Some unscrupulous people pretended to have rocks from the moon to sell.*

**un·self·ish** /ʌnˈselfɪʃ/ *adjective*
doing things for other people, rather than just doing things for yourself: *She is an unselfish girl who likes making her friends happy.* **ANTONYM: selfish**

**un·set·tling** /ˌʌnˈsetlɪŋ/ *adjective (formal)*
making you feel worried or nervous: *I got a letter from Amy with some unsettling and disturbing news.*
—**unsettled** /ˌʌnˈsetld/ *adjective (formal)* worried or nervous: *Going to a new school often makes kids feel unsettled.*

**un·skilled** /ˌʌnˈskɪld/ *adjective (formal)*
without any special training for a job: *It's hard for unskilled workers to find a job.* **ANTONYM: skilled**

**un·sta·ble** Ac /ʌnˈsteɪbəl/ *adjective (formal)*
**1** likely to fall or move: *Be careful – the ladder's a little unstable.* **ANTONYM: stable**
**2** not always able to think or behave in a normal controlled way: *The woman was mentally unstable and often started fights with strangers.* **ANTONYM: stable**

**un·stead·y** /ʌnˈstedi/ *adjective*
shaking and likely to fall, drop something, etc.: *A baby's first steps are always a little unsteady.* **ANTONYM: steady**
—**unsteadily** *adverb* in an unsteady way

**un·suc·cess·ful** /ˌʌnsəkˈsesfəl/ *adjective*
not succeeding in doing something: *He made several unsuccessful attempts to climb the mountain before finally succeeding.* **ANTONYM: successful**
—**unsuccessfully** *adverb* in an unsuccessful way: *Joe worked in a restaurant, after trying unsuccessfully to become an actor.*

**un·suit·a·ble** /ʌnˈsutəbəl/ *adjective*
not good for a particular person or purpose: *This movie is unsuitable for young children because it is very frightening.* **SYNONYM: inappropriate**; **ANTONYM: suitable**

**un·sure** /ˌʌnˈʃʊr/ *adjective*
not sure about something: *If you're unsure about anything, ask the teacher.*

**un·sym·pa·thet·ic** /ˌʌnsɪmpəˈθetɪk/ *adjective*
not kind to someone who has problems or worries: *The teacher was unsympathetic when I got a D on the test, and said it was my own fault.* **ANTONYM: sympathetic**

**un·tan·gle** /ʌnˈtæŋgəl/ *verb*
to separate pieces of string, hair, etc. that are twisted together: *Untangle your hair with a comb before you dry it.* **ANTONYM: tangle**

**un·think·a·ble** /ʌnˈθɪŋkəbəl/ *adjective*
impossible to imagine, accept, or do: *It was unthinkable that we would not all go to Grandma's for Thanksgiving.*

**un·tie** /ʌnˈtaɪ/ *verb*
to undo string, rope, etc. that someone has tied in a knot: *I untied the rope and got into the boat.* **ANTONYM: tie**

**un·til** /ʌnˈtɪl/ *preposition, conjunction*
**1** continuing to a particular time and then stopping: *I have classes until 4 p.m. today.*
**2 not until** = not before a particular time or event: *The movie doesn't start until 8 p.m.*

**un·time·ly** /ʌnˈtaɪmli/ *adjective (formal)*
**an untimely death** = the death of someone when he or she is still young: *Bonnie died an untimely death at the age of 19.*

**un·to** /ˈʌntu/ *preposition*
an old word that means "to"

**un·true** /ʌnˈtru/ *adjective*
not true: *He said he loved me, but it was untrue.* **SYNONYM: false; ANTONYM: true**

**un·used** /ˌʌnˈyuzd/ *adjective (formal)*
not used: *The upstairs rooms of the old house were empty and unused.*

**un·u·su·al** /ʌnˈyuʒuəl/ *adjective*
different from what is usual or normal: *It's unusual for Dave to be late.* | *That's an unusual name – how do you spell it?*
—**unusually** *adverb* more than usual: *Ben was unusually tall – 6 feet 7 inches.*

**un·veil** /ʌnˈveɪl/ *verb (formal)*
to tell people about a new plan for the first time: *The mayor unveiled plans for a new park.*

**un·wel·come** /ʌnˈwelkəm/ *adjective (formal)*
not wanted: *All the other people ignored me, and I felt unwelcome.* **ANTONYM: welcome**

**un·will·ing** /ʌnˈwɪlɪŋ/ *adjective (formal)*
not wanting to do something: *Rickie was unwilling to spend any more money, so I had to pay for everything.* **ANTONYM: willing**
—**unwillingly** *adverb* in an unwilling way: *I unwillingly agreed to stay at home and take care of my brother.*
—**unwillingness** *noun* the state of not wanting to do something

**un·wind** /ʌnˈwaɪnd/ *verb* (**unwound** /ʌnˈwaʊnd/)
**1** to relax, especially when you stop working: *Dad watches TV after work to unwind.*
**2** to undo rope, string, etc. that is wrapped around something else: *I unwound the hose and rinsed off the car.* **ANTONYM: wind**

**un·wise** /ˌʌnˈwaɪz/ *adjective (formal)*
not sensible: *It would be unwise to go out in the snow without a coat.* **ANTONYM: wise**
—**unwisely** *adverb* in a way that is not sensible: *I unwisely told her the secret, and she told everyone else.*

**un·wound** /ʌnˈwaʊnd/ *verb*
the past tense and past participle of UNWIND

**un·wrap** /ʌnˈræp/ *verb* (**unwrapped, unwrapping**)
to remove the paper, plastic, etc. that is around something: *Beth was unwrapping her birthday presents.* **ANTONYM: wrap**

**un·zip** /ʌnˈzɪp/ *verb* (**unzipped, unzipping**)
to unfasten clothing, a bag, etc. by opening the ZIPPER on it: *Lucy unzipped her jacket because she was hot.* **ANTONYM: zip up**

**up¹** /ʌp/ *adverb, preposition*
**1** toward or in a higher place: *We rode the elevator up to the fourth floor.* | *The cat ran*

*up the tree.* | *Billy was so excited that he was jumping up and down.* **ANTONYM: down**
**2** to a higher level, amount, or number than before: *Can you turn up the TV? I can barely hear it.* | *The number of children at the school has gone up from 600 to 800.* **ANTONYM: down**
**3** into a more upright position: *The teacher came in and we all sat up straight.*
**4** in or to a place that is further along the road: *Ted lives up the street from me.* **SYNONYM: down**
**5** very close to someone or something: *He came up to me and asked me for some money.*
**6** until something is completely gone: *I've used up all the food in the fridge.* | *The books burned up in the fire.*
**7 it's up to someone** = used for saying who has to make a decision: *You can paint your room any color you want – it's up to you.*
**8 up to 20 people/10 dollars, etc.** = no more than 20 people, 10 dollars, etc.: *We can take up to six people in our car.*
**9 up to now** = until this time: *Up to now, we've always gone to Florida for our vacation, but we may go somewhere new this year.*
**10 be up to something** = to be doing something secret or bad: *He comes home late every day, and I'm sure he's up to something.*

**up²** *adjective*
**1** awake or out of bed: *I'm usually up at 7:00 every day.*
**2** if a period of time is up, it is finished: *I didn't finish the test before the two hours were up.*
**3 what's up?** (*informal*) = used when you meet someone, or used to ask if there is a problem: *You look worried. What's up?*
**4 be up on something** = to know about something: *She reads a lot of magazines, so she's up on all the celebrity gossip.*
**5 be up and running** = to be working and ready to use: *The new computer system is up and running now.*

**ˌup-and-ˈcoming** *adjective*
likely to become successful: *an up-and-coming young singer*

**up·beat** /ˌʌpˈbit/ *adjective*
cheerful and confident that good things will happen: *He is upbeat about the team's chances to win the tournament.*

**up·bring·ing** /ˈʌpˌbrɪŋɪŋ/ *noun*
the way that your parents care for you and teach you to behave: *Mandy had loving parents and a very good upbringing.*

**up·com·ing** /ˈʌpˌkʌmɪŋ/ *adjective*
happening soon: *Here are some details of the museum's upcoming events for the rest of the year.*

**up·date** /ʌpˈdeɪt/ *verb*
to add the most recent information to something: *We need to update our computer records with the new data.*
—**update** *noun* the most recent information about something: *People were kept informed by hourly news updates.*

**up·front** /ʌpˈfrʌnt/ *adverb*
**1** speaking in a direct and honest way and not trying to hide anything: *The doctor was upfront about the operation and said it would be risky.*
**2** paid before someone does any work: *The builder wants $300 upfront before he'll even start working.*
—**ˈup-front** *adjective* up-front payments are ones you make before someone does any work: *He charges an upfront fee of $500.*

**up·grade** /ʌpˈgreɪd/ *verb*
to improve something, or to exchange it for something better: *The company is upgrading its computer system, so in a few weeks everything will be done much faster.*

**up·heav·al** /ʌpˈhivəl/ *noun* (*formal*)
a very big change that may cause problems: *Going to live in a new place can be a big upheaval.*

**up·hill** /ˌʌpˈhɪl/ *adjective, adverb*
toward the top of a hill: *The road began to go uphill.* | *an uphill climb* **ANTONYM: downhill**
→ see picture at **downhill**

**up·hold** /ʌpˈhoʊld/ *verb* (**upheld** /ʌpˈheld/) (*formal*)
to support a law or decision: *The court upheld the other judge's decision.*

**up·hol·ster·y** /əˈpoʊlstəri/ *noun*
material that has been used for covering a chair or seat: *Our car seats have leather upholstery.*

**up·keep** /ˈʌpkip/ *noun*
the process of keeping a building or machine in good condition: *The upkeep of a big house can be very expensive.*

**up·load** /ʌpˈloʊd/ *verb*
to move information from your computer to the Internet or to another piece of equipment: *How do I upload this file to the network?*

**up·on** /əˈpɑn/ *preposition* (*formal*)
on: *The movie is based upon a true story.* | *There was a big castle upon the hill.*

**up·per** /ˈʌpɚ/ *adjective*
in a higher position than another part of something: *His upper lip was bleeding.* **ANTONYM: lower**

**ˌupperˈcase** *noun*
letters written in their large form, such as A, B, D, G, J, etc.: *The names were printed in uppercase.* **SYNONYM: capitals**; **ANTONYM: lowercase**
—**uppercase** *adjective* uppercase letters are written in their large form: *an uppercase M*

**ˌupper ˈclass** *noun*
**the upper class** = the group of people in a country who are very rich or who have a lot of power
—**upper-class** *adjective* belonging or relating to the upper class

**up·per·class·man** /ˌʌpɚˈklæsmən/ *noun* (plural **upperclassmen** /ˌʌpɚˈklæsmən/)
a student in the last two years of HIGH SCHOOL or college

**up·per·most** /ˈʌpɚˌmoʊst/ *adjective* (*formal*)
highest: *The uppermost part of a house is the roof.* **SYNONYM: top**

**up·right** /ˈʌp-raɪt/ *adjective* (*formal*)
**1** straight up, not lying flat or leaning: *Stand the bottle upright on the table.* | *She sat upright to eat her breakfast in bed.*
**2** honest and good: *They were upright people who always obeyed the law.*

**up·ris·ing** /ˈʌpˌraɪzɪŋ/ *noun*
a situation in which people in a country fight against their government because they disagree with it: *The government used the army to end the uprising and stay in power.* **SYNONYM: rebellion**

**up·roar** /ˈʌp-rɔr/ *noun*
if there is uproar, people complain in an angry way about something: *The movie was very violent, and caused uproar among parents.*

**ˌups and ˈdowns** *plural noun*
good things and bad things that happen: *Every marriage has its ups and downs.*

**up·set¹** /ʌpˈset/ *adjective*
sad because something bad has happened: *She was upset because her cat had died.*
→ see Thesaurus box at **sad**

**upset²** *verb* (**upset**, **upsetting**)
**1** to make someone feel sad: *He upset me by saying I was dumb.*
**2** if something upsets a plan, it changes it and causes problems: *The rain upset our plans, and we had to cancel the picnic.* **SYNONYM: spoil**

**up·side down** /ˌʌpsaɪd ˈdaʊn/ *adverb, adjective*
with the top at the bottom, and the bottom at the top: *He turned the bag upside down and shook everything out onto the table.*

**upside down**

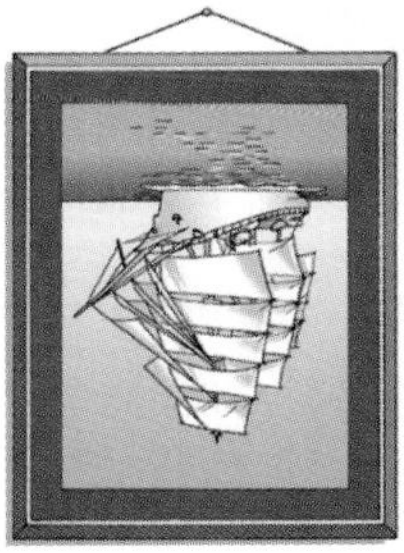

**up·stairs** /ˌʌpˈsterz/ *adjective, adverb*
on or moving to a higher level of a building: *I went upstairs to bed.* **ANTONYM: downstairs**

**up·tight** /ˌʌpˈtaɪt/ *adjective*
nervous and angry: *Dad gets so uptight when I'm late.*

**ˌup to ˈdate** (*also* **up-to-date**) *adjective*
**1** knowing about all the most recent things that have happened: *The president's advisors keep him up to date on events around the world.*

U

**2** including all the newest information, technology, or fashions: *The map is not up-to-date and some new roads aren't on it.* **ANTONYM: out-of-date**

**ˌup-to-the-ˈminute** *adjective*
including the newest information about what has been happening: *up-to-the-minute news*

**up·town** /ˌʌpˈtaʊn/ *adjective, adverb*
in or toward the northern area of a city: *We took an uptown train to get to Yankee Stadium.*

**up·ward** /ˈʌpwɚd/ *adverb, adjective*
toward a higher place or level: *The balloon moved slowly upward into the sky.* **ANTONYM: downward**

**u·ra·ni·um** /yʊˈreɪniəm/ *noun*
a substance used for producing NUCLEAR energy and weapons: *The atomic bomb was made out of uranium.*
[**ORIGIN:** 1700-1800 From the planet Uranus, because the substance was discovered soon after the planet.]

U

**U·ra·nus** /yʊˈreɪnəs/ *noun*
the seventh PLANET from the Sun

**ur·ban** /ˈɚbən/ *adjective*
relating to a town or city: *People moved to urban areas in order to look for work.* **ANTONYM: rural**
—**urbanization** /ˌɚbənəˈzeɪʃən/ *noun* a process in which urban areas get bigger
[**ORIGIN:** 1600-1700 From the Latin word *urbanus*, from *urbs*, which means "city."]

**urge¹** /ɚdʒ/ *verb*
to try hard to persuade someone to do something: *His parents urged him not to join the army, but he did it anyway.*

**urge²** *noun*
a strong feeling that you want to do something very much: *I suddenly felt the urge to go back home.*

**ur·gent** /ˈɚdʒənt/ *adjective*
if something is urgent, it is very important and someone needs to deal with it as soon as possible: *I need to talk to Nick right away – I have an urgent message for him.*
—**urgently** *adverb* as soon as possible: *He needs to see a doctor urgently or he could die.*
—**urgency** /ˈɚdʒənsi/ *noun* the need to do something as soon as possible

**u·rine** /ˈyʊrɪn/ *noun* (*formal*)
liquid that comes out of your body when you go to the toilet
—**urinate** /ˈyʊrəˌneɪt/ *verb* to let urine out of your body

**us** /əs; *strong* ʌs/ *pronoun*
used after a verb or PREPOSITION when you are talking about yourself and one or more other people: *We went to the movies and Jack came with us.*

**U.S.** *noun*
**the U.S.** = the United States of America: *She lives in the U.S.*

**us·a·ble** /ˈyusəbəl/ *adjective* (*formal*)
if something is usable, you can use it: *Some of the damaged houses need only small repairs to be usable.*

**us·age** /ˈyusɪdʒ/ *noun* (*formal*)
**1** the way that people use words in a language: *Many words from other languages have come into English usage.*
**2** the amount of something that is used: *The usage of water increases in the summer because people water their lawns.*

**use¹** /yuz/ *verb*
**1** if you use something, you do something with it: *They used candles to light the room.*
**2** to take something so that some or all of it is gone: *Big cars use a lot of gas.*
**PHRASAL VERB**
**use something up**
to use all of something: *He took a shower and used up all the hot water.*

**use²** /yus/ *noun*
**1** the act of using something: *When will the machine be ready for use?*
**2** a way in which something is used, or what it is used for: *The room's main use is for meetings.*
**3** if you have the use of something, you can use it: *He gave me the use of his car.* | *After the accident, she lost the use of both her legs.*
**4 it's no use** = you say this when you stop doing something because you do not think it will be successful: *It's no use. I can't fix it. We'll have to call the repair man.*

**5 make use of something** (*formal*) = to use something that is there for you to use: *Can you make use of these old clothes?*
**6 in use** = if something is in use, someone is using it: *The computer in the library was already in use when I went in.*

**used**[1] /yuzd/ *adjective*
used things such as cars and clothes are not new and have already had an owner: *We bought a used car because we couldn't afford a new one.* **SYNONYM: second-hand**
→ see Thesaurus box at **old**

**used**[2] *adjective*
**be used to something** = if you are used to something, you have experienced it many times before so it does not seem strange or difficult: *He delivers newspapers, so he's used to getting up early.*

**used to** /ˈyustə; *final or before a vowel* ˈyustu/ *verb*
if something used to happen, it happened in the past, but it does not happen now: *I used to live in New York before I moved to Wisconsin.*

**USAGE: used to, be used to**

**Used to** is used when saying that someone did something regularly or for some time in the past, but does not do it anymore: *I used to play tennis twice a week, but I don't have time now.*

**Be used to** and **get used to** are used to talk about being or becoming more comfortable with something, so that it does not seem strange or difficult anymore: *Are you used to the cold winters yet? | It was hard to get used to being in a different country.*

**use·ful** /ˈyusfəl/ *adjective*
helping you to do or get what you want: *It is useful to write a list of all your homework, so that you don't forget any assignments.* **ANTONYM: useless**
—**usefully** *adverb* in a useful way
—**usefulness** *noun* how useful something is: *Everyone knows the usefulness of the Internet for finding information.*

**use·less** /ˈyusləs/ *adjective*
not helpful or useful: *The flashlight is useless if there aren't any batteries in it.* **ANTONYM: useful**

**us·er** /ˈyuzɚ/ *noun*
someone who uses something such as a product or a service: *The number of Internet users is highest during working hours.*

**ˌuser-ˈfriendly** *adjective*
easy to use: *The software is so user-friendly that even small children can use it.*

**ush·er** /ˈʌʃɚ/ *noun*
someone who shows people to their seats in a place such as a theater or church

**u·su·al** /ˈyuʒuəl/ *adjective*
**1** if something is usual, it is the thing that happens most often, and it happens in the way that you expect it to: *Let's meet at the usual place. | I woke up at 5 a.m., an hour earlier than usual.*
**2 as usual** = in the way that happens most of the time: *They were late, as usual.*

**u·su·al·ly** /ˈyuʒuəli/ *adverb*
used when saying what happens most of the time: *I'm usually at school early, but today I was late.* **SYNONYM: normally**

**u·ten·sil** /yutensəl/ *noun* (*formal*)
a tool or object that you use for preparing and eating food: *Knives, pots, and other kitchen utensils lay on the counter.*
[**ORIGIN:** 1300-1400 From the Latin word *utensilis*, which means "useful," from *uti*, which means "to use."]

**u·ter·us** /ˈyutərəs/ *noun*
the part inside a woman or female MAMMAL where a baby develops before it is born

**u·til·i·ty** Ac /yuˈtɪləti/ *noun* (plural **utilities**)
a service such as gas or electricity: *Is the cost of utilities included in the rent?*

**u·til·ize** Ac /ˈyutlˌaɪz/ *verb* (*formal*)
to use something: *Most schools utilize computers to help children learn.*
—**utilization** /ˌyutl-əˈzeɪʃən/ *noun* the act of utilizing something
[**ORIGIN:** 1800-1900 From the Latin word *utilis*, which means "useful," from *uti*, meaning "to use."]

U

**u·to·pi·a** /yuˈtoʊpiə/ *noun (formal)*
a perfect world where everyone is happy, but that does not really exist: *They dream of a utopia of world peace.*
—**utopian** *adjective* relating to a utopia: *a utopian society*
[**ORIGIN:** From Utopia, an imaginary perfect country in the book Utopia (1516) by Sir Thomas More. The name comes from the Greek words *ou* and *topos*, which mean "not" and "place."]

**ut·ter**[1] /ˈʌtɚ/ *adjective (formal)*
complete or extreme: *We watched the magician's show in utter amazement.* | *After losing her job, she felt like an utter failure.*
—**utterly** *adverb (formal)* completely or extremely: *He felt utterly exhausted after walking all day.*

**utter**[2] *verb (formal)*
to say something: *No one uttered a word of protest.*

**U-turn** /ˈyu tɚn/ *noun*
if you make a U-turn in a vehicle, you turn around and drive in the direction you came from

U

# Vv

**V** /vi/
the number 5 in the system of ROMAN NUMERALs

**va·can·cy** /ˈveɪkənsi/ *noun* (plural **vacancies**)
**1** a room in a hotel that is available for someone to stay in: *The motel had several vacancies, so we stayed there.*
**2** (*formal*) a job that is available for someone to start doing: *The company has a vacancy for a driver.*

**va·cant** /ˈveɪkənt/ *adjective* (*formal*)
empty and available for someone to use: *The building has three vacant apartments for rent.*
[**ORIGIN:** 1200-1300 From the Latin word *vacare*, which means "to be empty or free from something."]

**va·ca·tion** /veɪˈkeɪʃən/ *noun*
a time away from work and school when you can relax: *They're on vacation for the next two weeks.* | *We took a vacation to the Virgin Islands.*
[**ORIGIN:** 1300-1400 From the Latin word *vacatio*, which means "freedom from having to work," from *vacare*, which means "to be empty or free from something."]

**THESAURUS: vacation**

**holiday** a day when no one officially has to go to work or to school: *the Thanksgiving holiday*

**break** a time when you stop working or studying in order to rest, or a short vacation from school: *a ten-minute coffee break* | *We went to Florida for spring break.*

**leave** a time when you are allowed not to work for a special reason: *Paul has been on sick leave since the accident.*

**honeymoon** a vacation that people take after they get married: *We went to Hawaii for our honeymoon.*

**vac·cine** /vækˈsin/ *noun*
a medicine that stops you from getting a disease: *The doctor gave us a flu vaccine.*
—**vaccinate** /ˈvæksəˌneɪt/ *verb* to give someone a vaccine: *Babies are vaccinated against measles.*
—**vaccination** /ˌvæksəˈneɪʃən/ *noun* the act of putting a vaccine into someone
[**ORIGIN:** 1700-1800 From the Latin word *vacca*, which means "cow." The first vaccine was germs of a disease that affected cows, which was given to people to stop them from getting smallpox, a related disease.]

**vac·uum¹** /ˈvækyum/ *noun*
**1** (*also* **vacuum cleaner**) a machine that cleans floors by sucking up dirt
**2** a space that has no air or gas in it: *Sound cannot travel through a vacuum.*
[**ORIGIN:** 1500-1600 From the Latin word *vacuus*, which means "empty."]

**vacuum²** *verb*
to clean a floor or CARPET with a machine that sucks up dirt: *She vacuumed the living room before her friends arrived.*
→ see Thesaurus box at **clean²**

**vague** /veɪg/ *adjective*
not clear in your mind because of not having enough details: *I have only a vague memory of my first day at school.* **SYNONYM: unclear**
—**vaguely** *adverb* not clearly: *His name was vaguely familiar, but I couldn't remember meeting him before.*
—**vagueness** *noun* the quality of being unclear

**vain** /veɪn/ *adjective*
**1** too proud of the way you look or what you can do: *She was very vain and always looking at herself in the mirror.*
**2** without success: *The prisoner was quickly caught after a vain attempt to escape.*
—**vainly** *adverb* without success: *He tried vainly to find a way into the locked house.*
→ see Thesaurus box at **proud**

**Val·en·tine's Day** /ˈvæləntaɪnz ˌdeɪ/ *noun*
February 14, a day when people give cards, candy, or flowers to people they love

—**valentine** *noun* someone you give a card or gift to on Valentine's Day

**val·id** Ac /ˈvælɪd/ *adjective*
**1** if a ticket or official document is valid, you can use it: *You need a valid passport to travel overseas.* **ANTONYM: invalid**
**2** reasonable and likely to be accepted: *There must be a valid reason for you to miss school, for example illness.* **SYNONYM: good**
—**validate** /ˈvæləˌdeɪt/ *verb* to make something valid
—**validity** /vəˈlɪdəti/ *noun* the state of being valid

valley

**val·ley** /ˈvæli/ *noun*
a low area of land between hills or mountains: *A river runs through the bottom of the valley.*

**val·u·a·ble** /ˈvælyəbəl/ *adjective*
**1** worth a lot of money: *Diamonds are very valuable.* **ANTONYM: worthless**
**2** very useful: *He gave me a lot of valuable advice.*
—**valuables** *plural noun* things that are valuable: *Keep valuables in a safe place.*

**val·ue**[1] /ˈvælyu/ *noun*
**1** the amount of money that something is worth: *The value of the house is $1 million.*
**2** the importance or usefulness of something: *Most of the students understand the value of working hard because it helps them succeed.*
**3** **be good/great value** = to be worth the amount you pay for something: *At $20, these coats are great value.*
**4** **values** = your beliefs about what is right and wrong, or about what is important in life: *They have strong religious values, and believe that marriage is very important.*
**5** in math, an amount: *If x + 4 = 10, then what is the value of x? The value of x is 6.*

**WORD FAMILY: value**
**value** *noun* | **value** *verb* | **valuable** *adjective* | **invaluable** *adjective* | **valuables** *plural noun*

**value**[2] *verb*
**1** to think that something is important and useful to you: *I value your friendship.*
**2** to say how much something is worth: *They valued the painting at $5 million.*

**valve** /vælv/ *noun*
a part of a pipe that opens and closes to control the flow of liquid or gas passing through it: *A fuel valve in the engine was leaking.*

**vam·pire** /ˈvæmpaɪɚ/ *noun*
in stories and movies, a person who bites people's necks and sucks their blood

**van** /væn/ *noun*
a small truck with an enclosed back part, used for carrying goods or people: *A van took us from the hotel to the airport.* → see picture on page A27

**van·dal** /ˈvændl/ *noun*
someone who deliberately damages public property: *Vandals had broken store windows.*
—**vandalism** *noun* the crime of deliberately damaging property
—**vandalize** *verb* to deliberately damage property
[**ORIGIN:** From a group of German people called the Vandals who attacked and damaged the city of Rome in 455 A.D. First used in English with its modern meaning, 1600-1700.]

**va·nil·la** /vəˈnɪlə/ *noun*
a substance used to give flavor to foods such as ice cream and cake: *I had some vanilla ice cream.*

**van·ish** /ˈvænɪʃ/ *verb*
to disappear suddenly, in a way that you cannot explain: *He was there, but when I looked again, he'd vanished.*

**van·i·ty** /ˈvænəti/ *noun* (*formal*)
the quality of being too proud of the way you look or what you can do: *He should wear glasses, but his vanity stops him.*

V

**va·por** /ˈveɪpɚ/ *noun*
a gas that comes from a substance that is liquid or solid at normal temperatures. Vapor is produced when the liquid or solid is heated: *When the water vapor cools, it becomes liquid again.*
—**vaporize** *verb* to become vapor

**var·i·a·ble** [Ac] /ˈveriəbəl/ *adjective* (*formal*)
something that is variable changes a lot: *The weather is variable: one day it's raining and the next it's sunny.* **ANTONYM: constant**
—**variability** /ˌveriəˈbɪləti/ *noun* the condition of being variable

**var·i·a·tion** [Ac] /ˌveriˈeɪʃən/ *noun*
a difference between similar things: *There are big variations in height in our class. Some people are very tall and some are quite short.*

**var·ied** [Ac] /ˈverid/ *adjective*
including many different types of things or people: *He eats a varied diet, with many different kinds of food.*

**va·ri·e·ty** /vəˈraɪəti/ *noun* (plural **varieties**)
**1** a type of something that is different from other similar things: *There are many different varieties of apples.*
**2 a variety of something** = a lot of different things: *The shirts come in a variety of colors, including red, green, and blue.*
**3** the differences within something that make it interesting: *The restaurant has introduced more variety into its menu, and now serves everything from burgers to salads.*

**var·i·ous** /ˈveriəs/ *adjective*
several different: *We buy food from various stores, but I prefer the supermarket on 16th Street.*

**var·nish** /ˈvɑrnɪʃ/ *noun*
a clear liquid that you paint onto something made of wood to give it a shiny surface
—**varnish** *verb* to put varnish on something

**var·si·ty** /ˈvɑrsəti/ *noun* (plural **varsities**)
the varsity team at a school or college is its main team

**var·y** [Ac] /ˈveri/ *verb* (**varied**, **varies**)
**1** to change often: *His mood varied: sometimes he was cheerful, sometimes he was miserable.*
**2** to be different from other things of the same type: *The photos vary in quality: some are good and some are bad.*
—**varying** *adjective* different from other things of the same type: *The library has books for children of varying ages, from toddlers to teenagers.*

**WORD FAMILY: vary**
**vary** *verb* | **variety** *noun* | **varied** *adjective* | **varying** *adjective* | **various** *adjective* | **variable** *adjective* | **variation** *noun*

**vase** /veɪs/ *noun*
a container that you put flowers in

**vast** /væst/ *adjective*
extremely large: *The Sahara is a vast desert.* **SYNONYMS: enormous, huge; ANTONYM: tiny**
—**vastly** *adverb* very much, or very: *The two countries are vastly different.*
—**vastness** *noun* the state of being extremely large: *the vastness of outer space*

**vault** /vɔlt/ *noun*
a room with thick walls and a strong door, where money and jewels are kept safely: *The gold is stored in a vault under the bank.*

**VCR** *noun*
a machine used for recording television shows or watching VIDEOTAPES

**'ve** /v, əv/ *verb*
the short form of "have": *I've hurt my leg.* | *We've decided to sell the car.*

**veal** /vil/ *noun*
meat from a young cow: *The veal was very tender.*
→ see Thesaurus box at **meat**

**ve·gan** /ˈvigən/ *noun*
someone who does not eat meat, fish, eggs, or milk: *Vegans will not eat anything that comes from an animal.*

**vege·ta·ble** /ˈvedʒtəbəl/ *noun*
a plant that you can eat, such as a potato, CARROT, or LETTUCE: *The school lunches include vegetables such as green beans or peas.*
[**ORIGIN:** 1300-1400 From the Latin word *vegetabilis*, which means "growing," from *vegetare*, which means "to make something be active."]

V

**veg·e·tar·i·an** /ˌvedʒəˈteriən/ *noun*
someone who does not eat meat: *She's a vegetarian, so she had the bean burger while the rest of us had hamburgers.*

**veg·e·ta·tion** /ˌvedʒəˈteɪʃən/ *noun* (*formal*)
the plants in an area: *Thick green vegetation covers the ground in the jungle.*

**ve·hi·cle** Ac /ˈviɪkəl/ *noun* (*formal*)
something such as a car or bus that carries people or things: *There were a lot of vehicles on the road.*
—**vehicular** /vɪˈhɪkyələ˞/ *adjective* relating to vehicles: *The road is closed to vehicular traffic.*
[**ORIGIN:** 1600-1700 From the Latin word *vehiculum*, from *vehere*, which means "to carry."]

**veil** /veɪl/ *noun*
a thin piece of material that some women wear to cover their faces: *At the wedding, the bride wore a veil over her face.*

**vein** /veɪn/ *noun*
one of the tubes in your body that carry blood to your heart: *Your veins look blue under your skin.*

**Vel·cro** /ˈvelkroʊ/ *noun* (*trademark*)
pieces of special material that are used to fasten things. The small hooks on one piece stick to the other piece.

**ve·loc·i·ty** /vəˈlɑsəti/ *noun* (plural **velocities**) (*formal*)
the speed at which something moves in a particular direction: *During the hurricane, the wind velocity reached 95 miles per hour.*

**vel·vet** /ˈvelvɪt/ *noun*
thick cloth with a soft surface on one side: *A pair of velvet drapes hung at the window.*
—**velvety** *adjective* soft like velvet
[**ORIGIN:** 1300-1400 From the old French word *veluotte*, from the Latin word *villus*, which means "rough hair."]

**vend·ing ma·chine** /ˈvendɪŋ məˌʃin/ *noun*
a machine that you can buy candy, drinks, and other things from: *I put my money in the vending machine and chose a candy bar.*

**Ve·ne·tian blind** /vəˌniʃən ˈblaɪnd/ *noun*
an object that you pull down to cover a window, made from many long wooden or plastic parts

**venge·ance** /ˈvendʒəns/ *noun* (*formal*)
if you want vengeance, you want to do something bad to someone because he or she has done something bad to you: *In the story, a desire for vengeance made the prince go to war.*
**SYNONYM: revenge**
—**vengeful** *adjective* wanting vengeance

**ven·i·son** /ˈvenəsən/ *noun*
meat from a DEER

**ven·om** /ˈvenəm/ *noun*
the poison of an animal such as a snake or SPIDER

**vent** /vent/ *noun*
a hole or pipe through which gas, smoke, or liquid can go in or out: *There's an air vent in the roof of the tent.* → see picture at **volcano**

**ven·ti·la·tion** /ˌventɪlˈeɪʃən/ *noun* (*formal*)
a way of letting fresh air into a room or building: *We opened the windows for ventilation.*
—**ventilate** /ˈventɪlˌeɪt/ *verb* to let fresh air into a room or building
[**ORIGIN:** 1400-1500 From the Latin word *ventilare*, which means "to fan someone to make them cool," from *ventus*, which means "wind."]

**ven·ti·la·tor** /ˈventɪlˌeɪtə˞/ *noun*
a machine that helps a very sick person to breathe: *He's in the hospital on a ventilator.*

**ven·ture** /ˈventʃə˞/ *noun*
a new business activity that someone starts doing: *The new theme park is a joint venture between two companies.*

**ven·ue** /ˈvenyu/ *noun*
a place where an organized event such as a meeting or a concert takes place: *The venue for the concert was the school auditorium.*

**Ve·nus** /ˈvinəs/ *noun*
the second PLANET from the Sun. It is between Mercury and the Earth.

**verb** /vɚb/ *noun*
a word such as "run," "give," or "feel," used for showing that someone does something or experiences something: *In the sentence, "She wrote a letter," "wrote" is the verb.*
[**ORIGIN:** 1300-1400 From the Latin word *verbum*, which means "word."]

**ver·bal** /ˈvɚbəl/ *adjective (formal)*
**1** relating to words or using words: *The game improves the verbal skills of students because they have to describe people and places.*
**2** spoken, not written: *There was no written contract, just a verbal agreement.*
—**verbally** *adverb* using words, especially by speaking to someone: *He accepted the offer verbally.*

**ver·dict** /ˈvɚdɪkt/ *noun*
if a JURY in a court of law reaches a verdict, it decides whether someone is guilty of a crime
[**ORIGIN:** 1200-1300 From the old French words *ver* and *dit*, which mean "true" and "saying or judgment."]

**verge** /vɚdʒ/ *noun*
**be on the verge of (doing) something** = to be going to do something very soon: *She was very upset and on the verge of crying.*

**ver·i·fy** /ˈverəˌfaɪ/ *verb* (**verified**, **verifies**) *(formal)*
to make sure that something is correct or true: *There was no way to verify his story, so we had to trust him.*
—**verification** /ˌverəfəˈkeɪʃən/ *noun* the process of verifying something

**ver·sa·tile** /ˈvɚsətl/ *adjective*
able to do a lot of different things or to be used in a lot of different ways: *He's a versatile actor who is good in both funny and serious movies.*
—**versatility** /ˌvɚsəˈtɪləti/ *noun* the quality of being versatile

**verse** /vɚs/ *noun*
**1** a set of lines that forms one part of a poem or song: *We started singing the first verse of the song.*
**2** poetry: *a book of verse*

**ver·sion** Ac /ˈvɚʒən/ *noun*
**1** a form of something that is slightly different from other forms: *The new version of this video game is much better than the old one.*
**2** one person's description of something that has happened: *Bobby and Steve each told a different version of what happened.*

**ver·sus** /ˈvɚsəs/ *preposition (written abbreviation:* **vs.** *or* **v.***)*
used for showing that two people or teams are against each other in a game or a court case: *Tonight's game is the Dallas Cowboys versus the New York Giants.*

**ver·te·bra** /ˈvɚtəbrə/ *noun* (plural **vertebrae** /-breɪ, -bri/)
one of the small bones down the center of your back

**ver·te·brate** /ˈvɚtəbrət/ *noun*
an animal that has a SPINE: *Birds, fish, and mammals are all vertebrates.*

**ver·ti·cal** /ˈvɚtɪkəl/ *adjective*
pointing straight upward: *He drew a vertical line from the top to the bottom of the paper.*
**ANTONYM: horizontal** → see picture at **diagonal**
—**vertically** *adverb* in a vertical way

**ver·ti·go** /ˈvɚtɪˌgoʊ/ *noun*
a feeling of fear and DIZZINESS because you are looking down from a high place

**ve·ry** /ˈveri/ *adverb*
**1** used for emphasizing another word: *It's a very good book; you should read it.* | *She speaks English very well.*
**2 not very** = not at all: *I'm not very good at basketball.*
**3 very much** = a lot: *It didn't cost very much.* | *I enjoyed my visit very much.*
[**ORIGIN:** 1200-1300 From the old French word *verai*, which means "true or real," from the Latin word *verus*, which means "true."]

**USAGE: very, too**

**Very** is used to emphasize something which may be good or bad: *It's very hot today.* | *She's always very busy.*

**Too** is usually used to show that you do not like the amount or level of something, or that it makes something impossible: *This cereal is too sweet.* | *The book was too big to fit in my bag.*

**ves·sel** /ˈvesəl/ *noun*
**1** a tube in your body that liquid flows through: *a blood vessel*
**2** a ship: *a fishing vessel*

**vest** /vest/ *noun*
**1** a piece of clothing without sleeves that has buttons down the front. You wear a vest over a shirt, often under a JACKET.
**2** a piece of special clothing with no SLEEVEs that you wear to protect your body: *Police officers wear bulletproof vests.*
[**ORIGIN:** 1600-1700 From the Latin word *vestis*, which means "piece of clothing."]

**vet** /vet/ *noun* (*informal*)
**1** another word for a VETERINARIAN
**2** another word for a VETERAN

**vet·er·an** /ˈvetərən/ *noun*
someone who has been a soldier in a war: *My grandfather is a veteran of the Vietnam War.*

**vet·er·i·nar·i·an** /ˌvetərəˈneriən/ *noun*
a doctor for animals: *We are taking the dog to the veterinarian because he is sick.* **SYNONYM: vet** → see picture on page **A16**
—**veterinary** /ˈvetərəˌneri/ *adjective* relating to the work of a veterinarian: *a veterinary clinic*

V

**ve·to** /ˈvitoʊ/ *verb* (**vetoed**, **vetoes**)
if someone in a powerful position vetoes something, he or she refuses to allow it: *The president vetoed the bill that had been passed by Congress.*
—**veto** *noun* the action of vetoing something, or the right to veto something
[**ORIGIN:** 1600-1700 From the Latin word for "I forbid."]

**vi·a** Ac /ˈvaɪə/ *preposition* (*formal*)
**1** by traveling through one place when you are going to a different place: *We went from New York to Miami via Washington.*
**2** by using a method or person to send or receive something: *I sent her a message via email.* **SYNONYM: by**

**vibe** /vaɪb/ *noun*
the general feeling that you get from a person or place: *The club has a good vibe and a lot of young people go there.*

**vi·brate** /ˈvaɪbreɪt/ *verb*
to shake a little bit for a long time: *When you hit the bell, it vibrates, and this makes the sound you hear.*
—**vibration** /vaɪˈbreɪʃən/ *noun* the act of vibrating: *On deck, you could feel the vibration of the boat's engine.*

**vice** /vaɪs/ *noun*
**1** criminal activities that involve sex or drugs
**2** a bad habit: *Her only vice was eating too much candy.* **ANTONYM: virtue**

**ˌvice ˈpresident** *noun*
**1** the person who is next in importance to the president of a country: *If the president dies, the vice president becomes president.*
**2** someone who is responsible for one part of a company: *She's the vice president of the company's sales department.*

**vi·ce ver·sa** /ˌvaɪs ˈvɚsə/ *adverb*
used when the opposite of a situation you have just described is also true: *Sam didn't want to sit next to Bill, and vice versa, Bill didn't want to sit next to Sam.*

**vi·cin·i·ty** /vəˈsɪnəti/ *noun* (*formal*)
**in the vicinity (of something)** = near a place: *The storm damaged 300 buildings in the vicinity of Atlanta.*

**vi·cious** /ˈvɪʃəs/ *adjective* (*formal*)
**1** violent and likely to hurt someone: *The dog is vicious and might bite someone.*
**2** cruel and deliberately trying to upset someone: *He told vicious lies about other people.*
—**viciously** *adverb* in a vicious way
—**viciousness** *noun* the quality of being vicious

**vic·tim** /ˈvɪktɪm/ *noun*
someone who has been hurt or killed by someone or something, or who has been affected by a bad situation: *The organization helps victims of crime.* | *a cancer victim* | *an aid program for earthquake victims*

**vic·tim·ize** /ˈvɪktɪˌmaɪz/ *verb* (*formal*)
to deliberately treat someone in an unfair way: *He believed that the police victimized him because they arrested him for no reason.*

**vic·to·ry** /ˈvɪktəri/ *noun* (plural **victories**) (*formal*)
the act of winning a battle, game, or election: *The team has had five victories in a row.* **ANTONYM: defeat**
—**victorious** /vɪkˈtɔriəs/ *adjective* having

won a battle, game, or election: *a victorious army*

[ORIGIN: 1300-1400 From the Latin word *victoria*, from *victus*, a form of the verb *vincere*, which means "to defeat."]

**vid·e·o** /ˈvɪdioʊ/ *noun* (plural **videos**)

**1** a copy of a movie or television program that is recorded on VIDEOTAPE: *Let's watch a video tonight.*

**2** a short recording of moving images: *My cousin emailed me a funny video.*

**3** a short recording like a movie of a singer or band performing a song: *We watched music videos on MTV.*

**4** the process of recording or showing moving images: *I recorded it on video.*

[ORIGIN: 1900-2000 From the Latin word *videre*, which means "to see."]

**ˈvideo ˌcamera** *noun*

a special camera that can be used to film moving images: *Nick has a video camera, so he agreed to videotape the wedding.*

**ˈvideo ˌgame** *noun*

a game in which you press electronic controls to move pictures on a screen: *My brother just sits at home and plays video games all day.*

**vid·e·o·tape** /ˈvɪdioʊˌteɪp/ *noun*

a thing that you record television programs, movies, and actions onto, made of a long band inside a plastic box: *We have a videotape of my dance show.* **SYNONYM: tape**

—**videotape** *verb* to record something on videotape: *His interview with the police was videotaped.*

**view¹** /vyu/ *noun*

**1** the things that you can see from a place: *The view from the top of the hill was beautiful.*

**2** the ability to see something from a place: *We had a good view of the game from our seats.*

**3** your opinion about something: *The students gave their views on ways to protect the environment.*

[ORIGIN: 1400-1500 From the old French word *veue*, from *veeir*, which means "to see," from the Latin word *videre*.]

**view²** *verb* (*formal*)

**1** to have a particular opinion about something: *He views the changes as necessary.* **SYNONYM: regard**

**2** to look at or watch something: *When viewed from space, the Earth looks mainly blue.*

**view·er** /ˈvyuɚ/ *noun*

someone who watches a television program: *The TV show has more than five million viewers.*

**view·point** /ˈvyupɔɪnt/ *noun*

a particular way of thinking about something: *From an environmental viewpoint, recycling is a very good idea.* **SYNONYM: point of view**

**vig·i·lant** /ˈvɪdʒələnt/ *adjective* (*formal*)

watching carefully, so that you will notice if something bad happens: *The guards must be vigilant, so that no one can get in without them seeing.*

—**vigilance** *noun* vigilant behavior

**vig·or·ous** /ˈvɪgərəs/ *adjective* (*formal*)

**1** using a lot of energy or effort: *Experts recommend 20 minutes of vigorous exercise every day.*

**2** strong and very healthy: *He was a vigorous young man with lots of energy.*

—**vigor** *noun* great energy

—**vigorously** *adverb* in a vigorous way

**vil·lage** /ˈvɪlɪdʒ/ *noun*

a very small town: *My aunt lives in a small village in Mexico.*

—**villager** *noun* someone who lives in a village

[ORIGIN: 1300-1400 From the old French word *ville*, which means "farm or village," from the Latin word *villa*, which means "country home with farmland."]

**vil·lain** /ˈvɪlən/ *noun*

the bad character in a movie, play, or story: *The evil queen is the villain of the story.* **ANTONYM: hero**

**vin·di·cate** /ˈvɪndəˌkeɪt/ *verb* (*formal*)

to show that someone was right, or did not do anything wrong: *He said that the accusations were not true and he would be vindicated in court.*

**vin·dic·tive** /vɪnˈdɪktɪv/ *adjective* (*formal*)

very mean to someone because you think he or she has harmed you: *His ex-wife was a bitter and vindictive woman.*

**vine** /vaɪn/ *noun*
a plant with long stems that attach themselves to other plants, walls, or fences: *The side of the building was covered in vines.*

**vin·e·gar** /ˈvɪnɪgɚ/ *noun*
a very sour liquid that is used in cooking: *He made a salad dressing from olive oil and vinegar.*
[ORIGIN: 1200-1300 From the French word *vinaigre*, from *vin* and *aigre*, which mean "wine" and "sour."]

**vine·yard** /ˈvɪnjɚd/ *noun*
a piece of land where someone grows GRAPEs for making wine

**vin·tage** /ˈvɪntɪdʒ/ *adjective*
old and valuable or interesting: *He drives a vintage car from the 1940s.*



**vi·nyl** /ˈvaɪnl/ *noun*
a type of strong plastic: *We put a vinyl tablecloth on the picnic table.*

**vi·o·la** /viˈoʊlə/ *noun*
a musical instrument that looks like a large VIOLIN but has a lower sound → see picture on page **A21**

**vi·o·late** Ac /ˈvaɪəˌleɪt/ *verb (formal)*
to break a law or rule: *The actions by the military violated international law.*
—**violation** /ˌvaɪəˈleɪʃən/ *noun* an act of breaking a law or rule: *Driving without a seat belt is a traffic violation.*
→ see Thesaurus box at **disobey**

**vi·o·lence** /ˈvaɪələns/ *noun*
**1** behavior that hurts someone in a physical way: *There's too much violence on TV – I'm tired of seeing people get beaten up or killed.*
**2** very great force: *The car was lifted into the air by the violence of the explosion.*

**vi·o·lent** /ˈvaɪələnt/ *adjective*
**1** involving actions that hurt someone physically: *There has been an increase in violent crimes involving guns.*
**2** someone who is violent is likely to attack and hurt other people: *He is a violent man who hit a police officer.*
**3** happening with a lot of force: *The roof blew off during a violent storm.*
—**violently** *adverb* in a violent way: *The waves beat violently against the rocks.*

**WORD FAMILY: violent**
**violent** *adjective* | **violently** *adverb* | **violence** *noun*

**vi·o·let** /ˈvaɪəlɪt/ *noun*
**1** a small purple flower with a sweet smell
**2** a purple color

**vi·o·lin** /ˌvaɪəˈlɪn/ *noun*
a wooden musical instrument with four strings, that you hold under your chin and play by pulling a BOW across the strings: *Sarah plays the violin.* → see picture on page **A21**
—**violinist** *noun* someone who plays a violin

**VIP** *noun*
(**Very Important Person**) someone who is famous or important, and is treated in a special way: *VIPs arrived at the theater in limousines and walked up the red carpet.*

**vi·ral** /ˈvaɪrəl/ *adjective*
relating to or caused by a VIRUS: *A cold is a viral infection.*

**vir·gin** /ˈvɚdʒɪn/ *noun*
someone who has never had sex

**Vir·go** /ˈvɚgoʊ/ *noun*
**1** the sixth sign of the ZODIAC, represented by a young woman
**2** someone born between August 23 and September 22

**vir·tu·al** Ac /ˈvɚtʃuəl/ *adjective*
**1** on a computer, rather than in the real world: *The website allows you to take a virtual tour of the art gallery.*
**2** very close to being something: *They sat together in virtual silence, only speaking once or twice.*
—**virtually** *adverb* almost: *He goes camping virtually every weekend; he's hardly ever home.*

**ˌvirtual reˈality** *noun*
pictures and sounds that a computer produces to make you feel as if you are in a

particular place: *Virtual reality makes video games exciting.*

**vir·tue** /ˈvɚtʃu/ *noun* (*formal*)
a good quality that someone has: *Honesty is one of his virtues – he never lies.* **ANTONYM: vice**

[**ORIGIN:** 1100-1200 From the Latin word *virtus*, which means "strength, courage, or virtue," from *vir*, which means "man." The idea is that a virtue is a good quality that a man should have.]

**vi·rus** /ˈvaɪrəs/ *noun*
**1** a very small living thing that causes infectious illnesses, or the illness caused by this living thing: *The doctor says I have a virus.* | *the AIDS virus*
**2** a program that destroys or damages information on your computer: *Computer viruses are usually spread through the Internet.*

[**ORIGIN:** 1500-1600 From the Latin word for "slime or poison."]

**vi·sa** /ˈvizə/ *noun*
an official document or mark in your PASSPORT, that allows you to enter or leave another country: *He applied for a tourist visa to visit China.*

**vis·i·ble** Ac /ˈvɪzəbəl/ *adjective*
if something is visible, you can see it: *The ocean is visible from the top of the mountain.* **ANTONYM: invisible**
—**visibly** *adverb* in a way that you can see: *She was visibly upset by the news and soon started to cry.*
—**visibility** *noun* the distance that you can see because of the weather: *Visibility was bad because of the fog.*

[**ORIGIN:** 1300-1400 From the Latin word *visibilis*, from *visus*, a form of the verb *videre*, which means "to see."]

**WORD FAMILY: visible**
**visible** *adjective* | **invisible** *adjective* | **visibly** *adverb* | **visibility** *noun*

**vi·sion** Ac /ˈvɪʒən/ *noun*
**1** your ability to see: *She has poor vision and wears glasses all the time.* **SYNONYM: sight**
**2** an idea of what you think something should be like: *He has a clear vision of what he wants to do in the future.*

**vis·it¹** /ˈvɪzɪt/ *verb*
**1** to go somewhere to see a person or place: *Eric went to Seattle to visit his cousins.* | *My aunt is coming to visit next week.* | *I want to visit the Grand Canyon.*

**THESAURUS: visit**

You **go to** a movie, museum, theater, or sports event: *Did you go to the football game on Friday night?*

You **go to see** or **go and see** a person or place: *We went to see my aunt last week.*

If you **go sightseeing**, you visit famous or interesting places: *On our trip to New York, we went sightseeing and saw the Statue of Liberty.*

If someone **comes over**, he or she visits you in your home in a friendly way: *Mom, can Barbara come over and play?*

If someone **drops in** or **stops by**, he or she visits you in your home, especially on the way to another place: *Paul stopped by on his way home from work.*

**2** to look at a website on the Internet: *Over 1,000 people visit the site every week.*
**3** (*informal*) to talk to someone in a friendly way: *We watched TV while Mom visited with Mrs. Levinson.*

**visit²** *noun*
an occasion when someone goes and sees a place or person: *This is my first visit to Atlanta.*

**vis·i·tor** /ˈvɪzətɚ/ *noun*
someone who comes to visit a place or a person: *The park attracts 100,000 visitors a year.* | *a guidebook for visitors to Rio de Janeiro*

**vi·sor** /ˈvaɪzɚ/ *noun*
**1** the part of a hat that sticks out over your eyes
**2** the flat thing above the front window of a car. You pull a visor down to keep the sun out of your eyes.
**3** the part of a HELMET that you pull down over your face

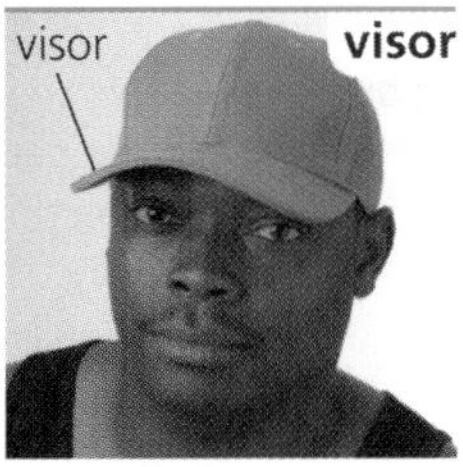

**visor**

**vis·u·al** Ac /ˈvɪʒuəl/ *adjective*
relating to seeing or to your sight: *The movie has some great visual effects.*

V

—**visually** *adverb* in a way that relates to what you can see

**vis·u·al·ize** Ac /ˈvɪʒuəˌlaɪz/ *verb*
to form a picture of someone or something in your mind: *I tried to visualize the house as he described it.* **SYNONYM: imagine**

**vi·tal** /ˈvaɪtl/ *adjective*
extremely important or necessary: *Regular exercise is vital for your health.*
—**vitally** *adverb* in a very important or necessary way: *It is vitally important that you follow the instructions exactly.*
→ see Thesaurus box at **important**
[**ORIGIN:** 1300-1400 From the Latin word *vitalis*, which means "relating to life," from *vita*, meaning "life."]

**vi·ta·min** /ˈvaɪtəmɪn/ *noun*
a natural substance in food, that is important for good health: *Oranges contain vitamin C.*

**viv·id** /ˈvɪvɪd/ *adjective*
**1** giving you a very clear picture in your mind: *I have vivid memories of my first day of school; I can still remember what we did that day.*
**2** **a vivid imagination** = an ability to imagine things very clearly: *Mark used his vivid imagination to write a story about a giant.*
**3** (*formal*) vivid colors are very bright: *The bird's feathers are vivid blue, red, and green.*
—**vividly** *adverb* in a vivid way: *She vividly described her visit to the zoo.*
—**vividness** *noun* the state of being vivid

**vo·cab·u·lar·y** /voʊˈkæbyəˌleri/ *noun* (plural **vocabularies**)
**1** all the words that you know and use: *Reading is one of the best ways to improve your vocabulary.*
**2** the words that people use for talking about a particular subject: *Most technical jobs use a special vocabulary.*
[**ORIGIN:** 1500-1600 From the Latin word *vocabularium*, which means "list of words," from *vocabulum*, which means "word or name."]

**vo·cal** /ˈvoʊkəl/ *adjective*
**1** relating to the voice: *Do you prefer vocal music or instrumental music?*
**2** expressing your opinion strongly: *He's a vocal critic of the president.*
—**vocals** *plural noun* the part of a piece of music that someone sings rather than plays on a musical instrument

**ˈvocal cords** (*also* **vocal chords**) *plural noun*
the thin muscles in your throat that produce sound when you speak or sing

**vo·cal·ist** /ˈvoʊkəlɪst/ *noun*
someone who sings with a band: *The band is looking for a new drummer and vocalist.* **SYNONYM: singer**

**vo·ca·tion** /voʊˈkeɪʃən/ *noun* (*formal*)
a job that you do because you enjoy it and feel you are the right type of person to do it: *Teaching isn't just a job to her – it's her vocation.*
→ see Thesaurus box at **job**

**voˈcational ˌschool** *noun*
a school where you learn skills for doing a job: *She's learning to cut hair at a vocational school.*

**vogue** /voʊg/ *noun*
**be in vogue** = to be fashionable and popular: *Long skirts are back in vogue.*

**voice** /vɔɪs/ *noun*
**1** the sound you make when you speak or sing: *I thought I heard voices downstairs.*
**2** **lose your voice** = to be unable to speak: *He had a cold and had lost his voice.*
**3** **raise your voice** = to speak loudly because you are angry or want someone to hear you: *She raised her voice to interrupt him.*

**ˈvoice box** *noun*
the part of your throat where your voice is produced **SYNONYM: larynx**

**ˈvoice mail** *noun*
a system that records a telephone message from someone so that you can listen to it later: *He wasn't there when I called, so I left a message on his voice mail.*

**void**[1] /vɔɪd/ *noun* (*formal*)
**1** a feeling of great sadness that you have when someone you love dies or when something important is missing from your life: *Work helped to fill the void after his wife died.*
**2** an empty space where nothing exists: *the void between Earth and the Moon*
—**void of** *preposition* (*formal*) without any amount of something: *The presentation was void of any real new ideas.*

V

**void²** *verb*
to officially make something have no legal effect: *If the money is not paid, the contract will be voided.*

**vol·a·tile** /ˈvɑlətl/ *adjective*
**1** a volatile liquid or substance changes easily into gas: *Mercury is volatile at room temperature.*
**2** a volatile situation is likely to change suddenly: *The violence has stopped but the situation is still volatile.*
**3** a volatile person can suddenly become very angry

**volcano**

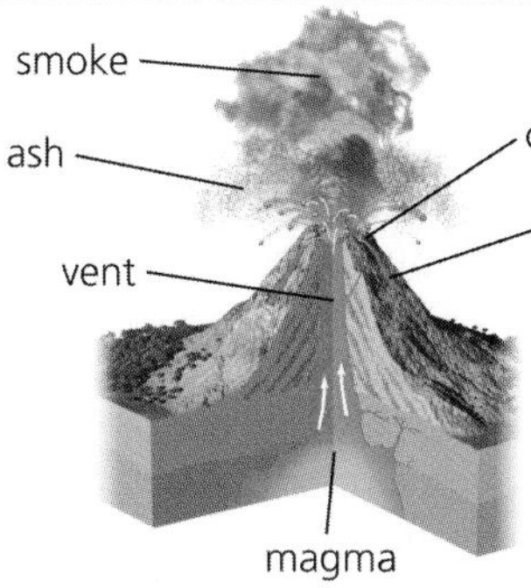


**vol·ca·no** /vɑlˈkeɪnoʊ/ *noun* (plural **volcanoes** *or* **volcanos**)
a mountain with a large hole at the top that burning rocks sometimes come out of: *The volcano erupted and covered the surrounding area in ash.*
—**volcanic** /vɑlˈkænɪk/ *adjective* relating to or coming from volcanoes: *volcanic rocks*
[**ORIGIN:** 1600-1700 From the Italian word *vulcano*, from Vulcan, the Roman god of fire and working with metal.]

**vol·ley** /ˈvɑli/ *noun*
**1** a large number of bullets, ARROWs, etc. that are fired at the same time: *The soldier fired a volley of shots into the air as a warning.*
**2** a movement, for example in tennis or SOCCER, in which a player hits or kicks the ball before it touches the ground

**vol·ley·ball** /ˈvɑliˌbɔl/ *noun*
**1** a game in which two teams hit a ball across a net with their hands, and try not to let it touch the ground: *They were playing volleyball on the beach.* → see picture on page **A25**
**2** the ball used in the game of volleyball

**volt** /voʊlt/ *noun*
a unit for measuring an electric current: *a 9-volt battery*
—**voltage** /ˈvoʊltɪdʒ/ *noun* the amount of power in an electric current: *Both heaters use the same voltage.*

**vol·ume** [Ac] /ˈvɑlyəm/ *noun*
**1** the amount of sound that a television, radio, MP3 player, etc. produces: *I can't hear the TV. Can you turn the volume up, please?*
**2** the total amount of something: *The volume of traffic has increased over the last 20 years.*
**3** a book that is one of a set of books: *This encyclopedia has 12 volumes.*
**4** the amount of space that a substance fills or an object contains: *What is the volume of the gas tank?*

**vol·un·tar·y** [Ac] /ˈvɑlənˌteri/ *adjective*
done because you want to and not because you must: *No one will force you to help. It's completely voluntary.* **ANTONYM: compulsory**
—**voluntarily** /ˌvɑlənˈterəli/ *adverb* because you want to and not because you must

**WORD FAMILY: voluntary**
**voluntary** *adjective* | **voluntarily** *adverb* | **volunteer** *verb* | **volunteer** *noun* | **volunteer** *adjective*

**vol·un·teer** [Ac] /ˌvɑlənˈtɪr/ *noun*
**1** someone who does something to help other people without being paid: *We need volunteers to serve meals at the church.*
**2** someone who offers to do something: *The teacher asked for a volunteer to collect the test papers.*
—**volunteer** *verb* to offer to do something: *He volunteered to help clean up after the party.*
—**volunteer** *adjective* volunteer work is work that you do to help other people, without being paid: *She does volunteer work in a hospital.*

**vom·it** /ˈvɑmɪt/ *verb* (*formal*)
if you vomit, food comes up from your stomach and out through your mouth: *He vomited after eating some bad meat.*

V

—**vomit** *noun* food that someone has vomited

**vote¹** /voʊt/ *verb*
to show which person or plan you choose by marking a piece of paper, pressing a button, or raising your hand: *Vote for Lisa for student body president!* | *Most people voted against the plan.*
—**voter** *noun* someone who votes: *The voters decide who becomes president.*
[**ORIGIN:** 1200-1300 From the Latin word *votum*, which means "promise or wish," from *vovere*, which means "to promise."]

**vote²** *noun*
**1** a choice or decision that you make by voting: *There were 1,079 votes for Swanson, and 766 for Reynolds.*
**2** an act of making a choice or decision by voting: *We couldn't decide, so we took a vote on it.*

**vouch·er** /ˈvaʊtʃɚ/ *noun*
a piece of paper that you can use instead of money to buy a particular thing: *Our flight was canceled, so the airline gave us a voucher to use for a different flight.*

V

**vow** /vaʊ/ *noun* (*formal*)
a serious promise: *She made a vow to herself that she would never go back.* | *marriage vows*
—**vow** *verb* to make a vow
→ see Thesaurus box at **promise¹**

**vow·el** /ˈvaʊəl/ *noun*
one of the letters a, e, i, o, or u, and sometimes y

**voy·age** /ˈvɔɪ-ɪdʒ/ *noun*
a long trip in a ship or a space vehicle: *The voyage from England to Hong Kong took several weeks.*
→ see Thesaurus box at **travel²**

**vs.**
the written abbreviation of VERSUS

**vul·gar** /ˈvʌlgɚ/ *adjective* (*formal*)
dealing with or talking about sex or body waste in a way that people think is rude and offensive: *She was offended by his vulgar jokes.*
—**vulgarity** /vəlˈgærəti/ *noun* the quality of being vulgar
[**ORIGIN:** 1300-1400 From the Latin word *vulgaris*, which means "relating to ordinary people," from *vulgus*, meaning "the ordinary people."]

**vul·ner·a·ble** /ˈvʌlnərəbəl/ *adjective*
easy to harm, hurt, or attack: *Small birds are vulnerable to attack by cats.*
—**vulnerability** /ˌvʌlnərəˈbɪləti/ *noun* the quality of being vulnerable
[**ORIGIN:** 1600-1700 From the Latin word *vulnerare*, which means "to wound," from *vulnus*, meaning "a wound."]

**vul·ture** /ˈvʌltʃɚ/ *noun*
a large wild bird that eats dead animals

# Ww

**wack·y** /ˈwæki/ *adjective (informal)*
unusual in a funny or silly way: *He has some very wacky ideas, and everyone thinks he's a little crazy.*

**wad** /wɑd/ *noun*
a thick pile of papers or paper money: *He had a big wad of dollar bills in his pocket.*

**wad·dle** /ˈwɑdl/ *verb*
to walk with short steps, swinging from side to side: *The duck waddled toward the pond.*

**wade** /weɪd/ *verb*
to walk through water that is not deep: *She waded through the flood water.*
→ see Thesaurus box at **walk¹**

**waf·fle** /ˈwɑfəl/ *noun*
a sweet flat cake with a pattern of deep squares in it, that people eat for breakfast

**waffle**

**wag** /wæg/ *verb* (**wagged**, **wagging**)
if a dog wags its tail, it shakes it from one side to another: *The dog was pleased to see us and was wagging his tail.*

**wage** /weɪdʒ/ *noun*
**1** the amount of money you earn for each hour that you work: *He is paid a wage of $7 per hour.*
**2 wages** = the money that you get each day, week, or month for doing a job: *Poor people often work for very low wages.*

**wag·on** /ˈwægən/ *noun*
**1** a vehicle that horses pull, used for carrying heavy things
**2** a child's toy that is a container on four wheels with a long handle for pulling it

**wail** /weɪl/ *verb (formal)*
to shout or cry with a long high sound because you are in pain or very sad: *"You're hurting me!" she wailed.*
—**wail** *noun* the sound of wailing

**waist** /weɪst/ *noun*
the part in the middle of your body just above your HIPs: *The belt will only fit someone with a small waist.* → see picture on page **A2**

**waist·line** /ˈweɪstlaɪn/ *noun*
the measurement around your waist: *Eating too much candy will put inches on your waistline.*

**wait** /weɪt/ *verb*
**1** to stay somewhere or not do something until something else happens: *There were a lot of people waiting for the bus.* | *Wait right here until I come back.*
**2 wait a minute/second** = used for asking someone to wait for a short time: *Wait a second – I'll get my coat and come with you.*
**3 someone can't wait** = used for saying that someone is very excited about something that is going to happen: *I'm so excited! I can't wait to see her again.*
—**wait** *noun* a time when you wait for something to happen: *We had a long wait for the bus.*
[**ORIGIN:** 1100-1200 From the old French word *waitier*, which means "to watch for someone."]
**PHRASAL VERBS**
**wait on someone**
to serve food to someone in a restaurant: *We sat at the table a long time before anyone waited on us.*
**wait up**
to wait for someone to come home before you go to bed: *I'll be home late so don't wait up for me.*

**wait·er** /ˈweɪtɚ/ *noun*
a man who brings food to the tables in a restaurant: *The waiter took our order.* → see picture on page **A17**

**ˈwaiting room** *noun*
a room for people to wait in, for example to see a doctor

**wait·ress** /ˈweɪtrɪs/ *noun*
a woman who brings food to the tables in a restaurant: *The waitress brought our food very quickly.*

**wake** /weɪk/ (*also* **wake up**) *verb* (**woke** /woʊk/, **woken** /ˈwoʊkən/)
**1** to stop sleeping: *I woke up early this morning.*

2 to make someone stop sleeping: *Try not to wake the baby.*

**walk¹** /wɔk/ *verb*

**1** to move forward by putting one foot in front of the other: *Do you walk to school?* | *John walked into the room and sat down.* → see picture on page **A4**

**THESAURUS: walk**

**march** to walk with regular steps, or in a determined and angry way: *The band marched onto the field.* | *Leon's mother marched into his bedroom and started yelling at him.*

**stride** to walk with quick long steps in a determined way: *A policeman was striding toward us.*

**stroll** to walk slowly in a relaxed way, especially for pleasure: *She strolled down the street, looking in the store windows.*

**wander** to walk slowly around a place, without having a definite idea of where you want to go: *We wandered around the museum for a few hours.*

**creep, sneak** to walk quietly when you do not want to be seen or heard: *Sam crept out of the house when his parents were asleep.* | *The boys tried to sneak into the movie theater.*

**limp** to walk with difficulty because your leg or foot is hurt: *Jess limped off the court after twisting her ankle.*

**wade** to walk through water that is not deep: *The bear waded into the river to catch the fish.*

**hike, go hiking** to take a long walk in the country or mountains: *We hiked to a little lake in the woods.* | *We went hiking in the mountains last weekend.*

**2 walk the dog** = to take your dog for a walk, so that it has exercise

**PHRASAL VERBS**

**walk away**

to leave a bad or difficult situation: *A good coach won't walk away if the team loses.*

**walk in on someone**

to go into a room and see someone doing something that he or she does not want you to see: *He walked in on her while she was taking a shower.*

**walk off**

to leave someone by walking away from him or her: *He turned and walked off.*

**walk out**

to leave a place because you are angry about something: *The movie was so bad that we walked out before it finished.*

**walk²** *noun*

a trip that you make by walking: *Let's go for a walk.* | *I like to take a walk after lunch.* | *The school is a ten-minute walk from here.*

**walk·ie-talk·ie** /ˌwɔki ˈtɔki/ *noun*

a small radio that you carry with you, and use to speak to someone who has the same type of radio

**wall** /wɔl/ *noun*

**1** one of the sides of a room or building: *There were lots of pictures on the walls.* → see picture on page **A9**

**2** a structure made of bricks or stones, that divides one area from another: *There was a brick wall between the two yards.*

**wal·let** /ˈwɑlɪt/ *noun*

a small flat case that you keep paper money or plastic cards in, and carry in your pocket or PURSE: *She put her credit card back in her wallet.*

**wall·pa·per** /ˈwɔlˌpeɪpɚ/ *noun*

**1** paper that you stick onto the walls of a room in order to decorate them

**2** the picture that you have as the background on your computer screen

**ˈWall Street** *noun*

**1** a street in New York City where the New York STOCK EXCHANGE is

**2** the New York STOCK EXCHANGE: *The company's profits were better than Wall Street expected.*

**ˌwall-to-ˈwall** *adjective*

covering the whole floor: *The room has wall-to-wall carpeting.*

**wal·nut** /ˈwɔlnʌt/ *noun*

a nut with a large round shell: *a walnut tree* → see picture on page **A13**

**wal·rus** /ˈwɔlrəs/ *noun*
a large animal that lives in the ocean and has two long teeth that stick out of its mouth

**waltz** /wɔlts/ *noun*
a dance for two people that has a regular pattern of three beats, or the music for this dance
[**ORIGIN:** 1700-1800 From the German word *Walzer*, from *walzen*, which means "to roll or dance."]

**wand** /wɑnd/ *noun*
a thin stick you hold in your hand to do magic tricks: *The magician waved his wand and the rabbit disappeared.*

**wan·der** /ˈwɑndɚ/ *verb*
**1** to walk slowly around somewhere without having a clear idea of where you want to go: *We spent the whole day wandering around the city.*
**2** (*also* **wander off**) to move away from where you are supposed to stay: *The kids got bored and started to wander off.*
**3** if your mind, thoughts, etc. wander, you stop paying attention to something and start thinking about something else: *Class was boring and his mind started to wander.*
—**wanderer** *noun* someone who travels around rather than living in one place
→ see Thesaurus box at **walk**[1]

**wane** /weɪn/ *verb*
when the Moon wanes, you gradually see less of it each night **ANTONYM: wax**

**want**[1] /wʌnt/ *verb*
to feel that you will be happy if you have or do something: *I want a bicycle for my birthday.* | *I want to be a teacher when I grow up.* | *Do you want me to help you?*

**want**[2] *noun* (*formal*)
something that you need or that would make you happy, but that you do not have: *Supermarkets try to satisfy all the needs and wants of shoppers by providing many products.*

**ˈwant ad** *noun*
a small advertisement that you put in a newspaper if you want to buy something or find someone to do a job

**war** /wɔr/ *noun*
a time when countries fight each other: *World War II* | *Many soldiers were killed in the war.* | *The country is preparing to go to war* (=start fighting). **ANTONYM: peace**
—**warring** *adjective* involved in a war: *warring countries*

**WORD FAMILY: war**
**war** *noun* | **warfare** *noun* | **warrior** *noun* | **warring** *adjective*

**THESAURUS: war**
**warfare** (*formal*) the activity of fighting in a war – used especially when talking about particular ways of fighting: *The soldiers get special training in jungle warfare.*
**conflict** (*formal*) a situation in which there is fighting or a war: *The conflict in the Middle East has been going on for many years.*
**combat** fighting during a war: *Soldiers who are wounded in combat are sent home.*

**ward** /wɔrd/ *noun*
a room in a hospital with beds for people to stay in: *She works on the children's ward of the hospital.*

**war·den** /ˈwɔrdn/ *noun*
the person in charge of a prison

**war·drobe** /ˈwɔrdroʊb/ *noun*
**1** the clothes that someone has: *She has a large wardrobe of dresses and shoes.*
**2** a large piece of furniture that holds hanging clothes
[**ORIGIN:** 1300-1400 From the old French words *warder* and *robe*, which mean "to guard or keep" and "piece of clothing."]

**ware·house** /ˈwerhaʊs/ *noun*
a large building where a company stores goods before it sells them: *There are thousands of computers in the warehouse.*

**war·fare** /ˈwɔrfer/ *noun*
the activity of fighting in a war using a particular method or type of weapon: *chemical warfare*
→ see Thesaurus box at **war**
[**ORIGIN:** 1400-1500 From "war" and the old English word *fare*, which means "journey."]

**warm**[1] /wɔrm/ *adjective*
**1** slightly hot: *The water in the pool was nice and warm.* | *We stood close together to keep warm.* **ANTONYM: cool**

**2** warm clothes and buildings keep heat in and stop you from feeling cold: *Put a warm sweater on – it's cold out here.*
**3** friendly: *They gave us a very warm welcome.*
→ see Thesaurus box at **hot**

**warm²** (*also* **warm up**) *verb*
to make someone or something warmer: *Let me warm some soup for you.*
**PHRASAL VERB**
**warm up**
to prepare for an activity or sport by doing gentle exercises or practicing just before the activity or game starts: *The team is warming up before the game.*

**ˌwarm-ˈblooded** *adjective*
warm-blooded animals have a body temperature that stays warm whether the temperature around them is hot or cold: *Mammals are warm-blooded animals, unlike reptiles.*

**warm·ly** /ˈwɔrmli/ *adverb*
**1** in a friendly way: *He greeted us very warmly with a smile and a hug.*
**2** in a way that keeps you warm: *He was warmly dressed in a thick sweater and coat.*

**warmth** /wɔrmθ/ *noun*
**1** the heat that something produces: *The warmth of the sun felt wonderful on her face.*
**2** friendliness: *The warmth of her smile made him feel good.*

**ˈwarm-up** *noun*
**1** a set of exercises that you do just before you do a sport: *We did several stretching exercises as a warm-up.*
**2** something that you do as practice for a more important activity or event: *Thursday's game was a warm-up for the main competition next week.*
—**warm-up** *adjective* done to prepare you for another activity or event: *warm-up exercises*

**warn** /wɔrn/ *verb*
to tell someone that something bad or dangerous may happen, so that he or she can avoid it: *A sign warned drivers of long delays on the freeway.*

**warn·ing** /ˈwɔrnɪŋ/ *noun*
something that tells you that something bad or dangerous might happen, so that you can avoid it: *There are warnings about the dangers of smoking on every pack of cigarettes.* | *The enemy attacked without warning.*

**warped** /wɔrpt/ *adjective*
**1** bent or twisted into the wrong shape: *The door is warped and won't close anymore.*
**2** (*informal*) having ideas or thoughts that most people think are unpleasant or not normal: *He has a warped sense of humor, and sometimes I don't understand him.*

**war·rant** /ˈwɔrənt/ *noun*
an official paper that allows the police to do something: *Officials have issued a warrant for his arrest.*

**war·ran·ty** /ˈwɔrənti/ *noun* (plural **warranties**)
a written promise that a company will fix something if it breaks after you have bought it: *The TV comes with a 3-year warranty, so if it doesn't work right, the company will fix or replace it.* **SYNONYM: guarantee**

**war·ri·or** /ˈwɔriɚ/ *noun*
a soldier from a long time ago who was very brave

**wart** /wɔrt/ *noun*
a small hard lump on your skin: *He had a wart on the bottom of his foot.*

**was** /wəz; *strong* wʌz/ *verb*
the past form of BE that is used after "I," "he," "she," and "it"

**wash¹** /wɑʃ/ *verb*
**1** to clean something using water: *She helped Peggy wash the dishes.*
**2** if a river or the ocean washes something to a place, it pushes that thing there: *Strong waves washed the boat onto the shore.*
—**washable** *adjective* if something is washable, you can wash it without damaging it
[**ORIGIN:** From the old English word *wascan.*]
**PHRASAL VERBS**
**wash off**
if a substance washes off, it comes off the surface of something when you wash it: *Will this paint wash off?*
**wash up**
to wash your hands: *Go wash up for dinner.*

**wash²** *noun*
clothes and sheets that you have washed or

that you need to wash: *He did three loads of wash this morning.* **SYNONYM: laundry**

**wash·cloth** /ˈwɑʃklɔθ/ *noun*
a small square piece of cloth that you use for washing yourself

**wash·er** /ˈwɑʃɚ/ *noun*
another word for a WASHING MACHINE

**ˈwashing maˌchine** *noun*
a machine that washes clothes: *She put the dirty clothes in the washing machine.* **SYNONYM: washer**

**wash·room** /ˈwɑʃrum/ *noun* (*old-fashioned*)
another word for a RESTROOM

**was·n't** /ˈwʌzənt/
the short form of "was not": *He wasn't there.*

**wasp** /wɑsp/ *noun*
a black and yellow flying insect that can sting you

**waste¹** /weɪst/ *verb*
to use something in a way that is silly or useless, or to use too much of it: *It wastes electricity to leave the lights on all the time.*

**waste²** *noun*
**1** the use of something in a way that is silly or useless: *The trip was a waste of time because the museum was closed when we got there.*
**2** things that are left after you have used something: *Waste such as empty cans should be recycled.*
→ see Thesaurus box at **garbage**

**waste·bas·ket** /ˈweɪstˌbæskɪt/ *noun*
a container into which you put paper and other things that you want to get rid of: *She threw the candy wrapper into the wastebasket.* → see picture on page **A18**

**wast·ed** /ˈweɪstɪd/ *adjective*
not used effectively, or not having a useful result: *It was a wasted trip because the store was closed.*

**waste·ful** /ˈweɪstfəl/ *adjective*
using more of something than you need or using it badly, so that it is wasted: *It's wasteful to take more food than you can eat, so that it is thrown away.*
—**wastefulness** *noun* the quality of being wasteful

**waste·land** /ˈweɪstlænd/ *noun*
an area of land that is empty or that cannot be used for anything: *The floods turned parts of the city into a wasteland.*

**waste·pa·per bas·ket** /ˈweɪstˌpeɪpɚ ˌbæskɪt/ *noun*
another word for WASTEBASKET

**watch¹** /wɑtʃ/ *verb*
**1** to look at something and see how it changes or moves: *Steve was watching television.* | *I watched her leave.* → see picture at **see**

**USAGE: watch, look at, see**

You **watch** TV, a movie, or something that happens for a period of time: *My parents always come to watch me play basketball.* | *The kids are watching TV.*

You **look at** a picture, person, thing, etc. because you want to do this: *Hey, look at the hat that man is wearing.* | *Maria was looking at a picture book.*

You **see** something without planning to do this: *Two people saw him take the woman's purse.*

You can also say that you **saw** a movie, a program, etc., but you cannot say "see television": *I saw a great movie on TV last night.*

**2** to be careful not to hurt yourself or to hurt someone else: *Watch that knife – it's sharp.* | *He never watches where he's going, so he's always bumping into things.*
**3 watch your language/mouth** = to be careful not to use rude words or not to talk in a rude way: *Watch your language! I don't want to hear any more bad words!*
**4 watch your weight** = to be careful not to get too fat: *I'm not eating cookies because I'm watching my weight.*
→ see Thesaurus box at **look¹**

**PHRASAL VERBS**

**watch for something**
to pay attention so that you will notice something if it arrives or happens: *Doctors are watching for any signs that the cancer has spread.*

**watch out**
to look for something and be careful, so that you are not hurt: *Watch out for cars when you cross the street.*

**watch over someone**
to guard, protect, or take care of someone: *She watched over her sick son as he slept.*

**watch²** *noun*
**1** a small clock that you wear on your wrist: *I looked at my watch: it was 2:30.*
**2 keep watch** = to look around so that you will see if someone is coming and be able to tell other people: *Jay hid his sister's toys, and I kept watch to tell him if she was coming back.*
**3 keep a watch on something** = to keep looking at something carefully, to see what happens: *Police kept a close watch on the house.*

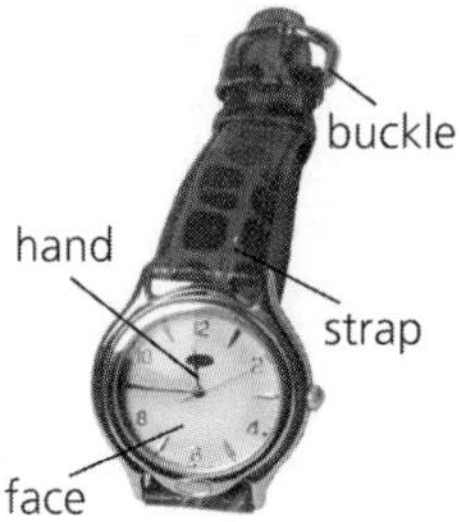


**watch·dog** /ˈwɑtʃdɔg/ *noun*
**1** another word for a GUARD DOG
**2** a person or group that makes sure that other people do not break rules: *The nuclear watchdog agency makes sure that nuclear power is produced safely.*

**watch·ful** /ˈwɑtʃfəl/ *adjective*
**under the watchful eye of someone** = with someone watching you carefully: *She learned to cook under the watchful eye of her mother.*

**wa·ter¹** /ˈwɔtɚ/ *noun*
**1** a clear liquid that you drink and use for washing: *Would you like a glass of water?*
**2 in hot water** = if you are in hot water, you are in a situation in which you have a lot of trouble: *He's in hot water because his mother caught him telling a lie.*

**water²** *verb*
**1** to pour water on a plant or seeds that you are growing: *The plant died because I never watered it.*
**2** if your eyes water, they fill with tears because something is hurting them: *The smoke made my eyes water.*
**3** if your mouth waters, it fills with a liquid called SALIVA because you see or smell something that looks good to eat

**ˈwater ˌbuffalo** *noun* (plural **water buffalo** *or* **water buffalos**)
a large Asian animal that pulls farm vehicles or equipment

**wa·ter·col·or** /ˈwɔtɚˌkʌlɚ/ *noun*
**1** a type of paint that is mixed with water, used for making pictures: *The artist used both oil paints and watercolors.*
**2** a painting made using paint mixed with water: *I painted a watercolor of a group of trees.*

**ˈwater ˌcooler** *noun*
a large container where you can fill a cup with drinking water

**wa·ter·fall** /ˈwɔtɚˌfɔl/ *noun*
water from a river or stream that falls from a high place down to the ground: *The waterfall flows over the edge of the cliff to the valley below.*

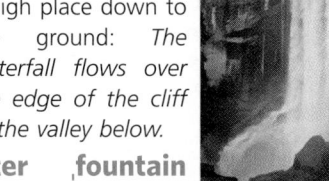

**ˈwater ˌfountain** *noun*
a piece of equipment in a public place that gives you water to drink when you push a button or turn a handle: *I pushed the button on the water fountain and the water shot up and hit me in the face.*
**SYNONYM: drinking fountain**

**wa·ter·front** /ˈwɔtɚˌfrʌnt/ *noun*
land at the edge of a lake, river, or ocean: *There are several restaurants on the waterfront, with great views of the lake.*

**ˈwatering ˌcan** *noun*
a container with a long SPOUT that you use for pouring water on plants

**ˈwater ˌlily** *noun* (plural **water lilies**)
a water plant with large flowers, and round leaves that float on the water: *The water lilies in the pond are blooming.*

**wa·ter·logged** /ˈwɔtɚˌlɔgd/ *adjective*
something, especially ground, that is waterlogged is completely wet: *The heavy rain has left the ground waterlogged.*

W

**ˈwater main** *noun*
a large pipe under the ground that carries water to buildings

**wa·ter·mel·on** /ˈwɔtɚˌmelən/ *noun*
a large round green fruit that is pink inside, with black seeds: *He ate a slice of watermelon.* → see picture on page **A13**

**ˈwater pipe** *noun*
a pipe that carries water: *Copper water pipes carry water around the house.*

**wa·ter·proof** /ˈwɔtɚˌpruf/ *adjective*
if a material is waterproof, water cannot get through it: *It began to rain, but my waterproof clothing kept me dry.*

**ˈwater ˌskiing** *noun*
a sport in which you wear two long narrow pieces of plastic on your feet, as a boat pulls you along the water: *We went water skiing on the lake.* → see picture on page **A25**
—**water ski** *verb* to do water skiing
—**water skier** *noun* someone who does water skiing

**ˈwater supˌply** *noun* (plural **water supplies**)
water that goes to all the buildings in an area or city, through a system of pipes: *Dangerous chemicals got into the water supply.*

**wa·ter·tight** /ˈwɔtɚˌtaɪt/ *adjective*
if an object is watertight, water cannot get into it: *The boat has a watertight storage box.*

**wa·ter·way** /ˈwɔtɚˌweɪ/ *noun* (*formal*)
a river or CANAL that boats can travel along: *The Panama Canal is a waterway that connects two oceans.*

**watt** /wɑt/ *noun*
a unit for measuring electrical power: *Do you have a 60-watt light bulb?*
[**ORIGIN:** 1800-1900 From James Watt (1736-1819), a Scottish engineer who made big improvements to the steam engine.]

**wave¹** /weɪv/ *noun*
**1** high water that moves on the surface of the ocean: *A big wave turned the boat over.*
**2** a movement of your hand from side to side: *She gave us a wave as she drove away.*
**3** a sudden large amount of a feeling or activity: *A wave of sadness passed over him as he thought about his family.* | *During the crime wave, many cars were stolen.*
**4** the form in which some types of energy travel, such as light and sound: *Sound is carried by sound waves, which get weaker as you move away from the source of the sound.*

**wave²** *verb*
**1** to move your hand from side to side, to say hello or goodbye to someone, or to get someone's attention: *We waved goodbye to them as they left.* | *He stopped the car because a man was waving at him and yelling.* → see picture on page **A3**
**2** to move from side to side: *The flag waved in the wind.* | *She waved the letter in front of my face.*

**wave·length** /ˈweɪvleŋkθ/ *noun*
the distance between matching points on one wave of light or sound and the next: *Red light has a longer wavelength than green light.*

**wavy**

wavy straight curly

**wav·y** /ˈweɪvi/ *adjective*
wavy hair has curved shapes in it **ANTONYM: straight**

**wax¹** /wæks/ *noun*
**1** a hard substance used for making CANDLEs
**2** a natural brown substance in your ears

**wax²** *verb*
**1** to put wax on something to protect it or make it shine: *My brother was washing and waxing his car.*
**2** when the moon waxes, you gradually see more of it each night **ANTONYM: wane**

**way¹** /weɪ/ *noun*
**1** the road or path you follow to get somewhere: *Which way should we go?* | *Can you tell me the way to the school?*
**2** a particular direction: *Look both ways before you cross the street.* | *Take two steps this way.*
**3** how something is done or can be done:

*The best way to get in shape is by walking.* | *He has a funny way of talking.*
**4** the distance between two places: *Houston is a long way from New York.* | *He ran all the way home.*
**5 by the way** = used when you want to talk about a new subject: *Oh, by the way, your mom called earlier.*
**6 have your way/get your way** = to do what you want, even if someone else wants you to do something different: *That kid is spoiled – he always gets his way!*
**7 in a way/in some ways** = used when saying that something is partly true: *In a way, I'd like to be old because old people know a lot about life.*
**8 in the way/in your way** = if something is in the way, it is in a position where it is stopping you moving forward or doing something: *I couldn't put my bicycle in the garage because the car was in the way.*
**9 make your way** = to go somewhere slowly or with difficulty: *I made my way toward her through the crowd.*
**10 No way!** (*informal*) = used when you will not do something, or when you are very surprised by something: *"Will you help me clean my room?" "No way!"* | *She's 30? No way – she looks like she's 19!*
**11 on the way/on your way** = while going somewhere: *I went home, and bought some food on the way.*
**12 out of the way/out of your way** = if something moves out of the way, it moves so it is no longer stopping you moving forward or doing something: *I can't get past – get out of the way!*
**13 under way** = happening or moving: *Building work has not started yet, but it will soon be under way.*
**14 way around/up** = used when talking about what position something should be in: *Which way around does this skirt go* (=which part is the front and which part is the back)? | *The boat turned over, and we couldn't get it the right way up.*
**15 Way to go!** (*informal*) = used when you think someone has done something very well: *"I got an A on my science test." "Way to go!"*
**[ORIGIN:** From the old English word *weg.*]

**way**$^2$ *adverb* (*informal*)
much: *He's way smarter than me – he's a genius!*

**ˌway of ˈlife** *noun* (plural **ways of life**)
the way someone lives: *They moved away from the city to have a more relaxed way of life.*

**ˌway-ˈout** *adjective* (*informal*)
new and strange: *I like some jazz, but not the way-out stuff.*

**we** /wi/ *pronoun*
the person who is speaking and one or more other people: *I know John. We are friends.*

**weak** /wik/ *adjective*
**1** not physically strong: *She was too weak to lift the box.* **ANTONYM: strong**
**2** not having much power, influence, or ability: *We must protect the weaker members of our society.* **ANTONYM: strong**
**3** easily persuaded to do something wrong because you cannot make good decisions: *He's so weak – he'll do whatever his friends tell him to do.*
**4** not likely to make people believe that something is true, right, or interesting: *The evidence against him is fairly weak.* **ANTONYM: strong**
**5** a weak liquid or medicine has only a little of a substance in it: *The coffee was weak – it hardly had any taste.* **ANTONYM: strong**

| WORD FAMILY: weak |
| --- |
| **weak** *adjective* \| **weaken** *verb* \| **weakness** *noun* \| **weakling** *noun* |

**weak·en** /ˈwikən/ *verb*
to make someone or something less strong: *The bridge had been weakened by the storm.* **ANTONYM: strengthen**

**weak·ling** /ˈwik-lɪŋ/ *noun*
someone who is not physically strong: *The other kids called him a weakling because he couldn't carry his own suitcase.*

**weak·ness** /ˈwiknəs/ *noun*
**1** a fault in someone or something: *Spending too much money on clothes is her weakness.* **ANTONYM: strength**
**2** the state of not having a lot of strength in your body: *Not eating enough can cause weakness.* **ANTONYM: strength**

W

**wealth** /welθ/ *noun* (*formal*)
**1** a large amount of money that someone has: *The family had great wealth, and owned three homes.*
**2 a wealth of something** = a lot of something useful or good: *There is a wealth of information on the Internet.*
[**ORIGIN:** 1200-1300 From the old English word *wele* or *weal*, which means "the condition of being happy or successful."]

**wealth·y** /ˈwelθi/ *adjective* (**wealthier**, **wealthiest**) (*formal*)
having a lot of money: *A wealthy businessman bought the plane.* **SYNONYM: rich**; **ANTONYM: poor**
→ see Thesaurus box at **rich**

**weap·on** /ˈwepən/ *noun*
something that people fight with, for example a knife or a gun: *A gun is a dangerous weapon.*
—**weaponry** /ˈwepənri/ *noun* weapons

**wear¹** /wer/ *verb* (**wore** /wɔr/, **worn** /wɔrn/)
**1** to have clothes or jewelry on your body: *She wore a pretty dress.*
**2** to make something thinner or weaker by using it or wearing it a lot: *You've worn a hole in your sock.*
**3** to have your hair in a particular style: *He wears his hair short.*
**4 wear well** = to stay in good condition after a period of time: *These shoes have worn well. They still look new.*
**PHRASAL VERBS**
**wear down**
to make something smaller or weaker by using it a lot: *The heels on my shoes are worn down.*
**wear off**
if a feeling or effect wears off, it gradually disappears: *When the pain medicine wears off, your leg may hurt.* **ANTONYM: increase**
**wear something out**
to use something so much that it becomes too weak or damaged to use: *He walks a lot, so he is always wearing his shoes out.*

**wear²** *noun*
**1** a particular kind of clothes, or clothes for a particular activity: *The store sells sports wear and shoes.*
**2** normal damage that something has because it has been used a lot: *The tire was showing signs of wear, so we got a new one.*

**wea·ry** /ˈwɪri/ *adjective* (**wearier**, **weariest**) (*formal*)
very tired: *I felt weary after working all day.*
—**wearily** *adverb* in a very tired way: *He sat down wearily.*
—**weariness** *noun* a feeling of extreme tiredness

**wea·sel** /ˈwizəl/ *noun*
a small animal with a long thin body, short legs, and red-brown fur: *The weasel chased the rabbit into a hole.*

**weath·er** /ˈweðɚ/ *noun*
the weather in a place is how warm or cold it is and whether it is raining, sunny, windy, etc.: *The airport was closed because of bad weather.* | *What's the weather like in Atlanta this time of year?*
—**weathered** *adjective* changed by the weather: *He has a brown, weathered face because he works outdoors all the time.*
[**ORIGIN:** From the old English word *weder.*]

> **USAGE: weather, whether**
> **Weather** is a noun: *The weather stayed warm.*
> **Whether** is a conjunction: *The students were asked whether they enjoyed math.*

**ˈweather ˌforecast** *noun*
a report on the television or radio that says what the weather will be like: *According to the weather forecast, it will rain tomorrow.*

**ˈweather vane** *noun*
a metal object on the top of a building, that moves to show the direction of the wind

**weave** /wiv/ *verb*
**1** (**wove** /woʊv/, **woven** /ˈwoʊvən/) to make cloth, CARPET, or basket by putting threads of material over and under each other: *They used special machines to weave wool into carpets.*
**2** (**weaved**) to move somewhere by turning and changing direction a lot: *The car was weaving in and out of traffic.*
—**weaver** *noun* someone who weaves cloth
—**weaving** *noun* the activity of weaving cloth

**web** /web/ *noun*

**1** a net of threads that a SPIDER makes to catch insects: *A spider was spinning a web.*
**2 the Web** = the system that makes it possible for you to see and use information on the Internet: *You can find out about anything on the Web.* **SYNONYM: World Wide Web**

**web·cam** /ˈwebkæm/ *noun*
a video camera on a computer that you can use to put pictures on the Internet

**web·site** /ˈwebsaɪt/ *noun*
a set of pages on the Internet about a particular subject or belonging to a particular organization: *You will find information about the organization on its website.*

**wed** /wed/ *verb* (**wedded** *or* **wed**) (*formal*)
to marry someone: *She wed Jeremiah Wooton in 1896.*

**we'd** /wid/
**1** the short form of "we had": *We'd forgotten our map.*
**2** the short form of "we would": *We'd love to come to your party.*

**wed·ding** /ˈwedɪŋ/ *noun*
an event at which two people get married: *I've been invited to their wedding in June.*

**wedge** /wedʒ/ *noun*
a piece of something that is thick at one end and pointed at the other end: *They put a wedge under the door to keep it open.*

**Wednes·day** /ˈwenzdi/ *noun* (*written abbreviation*: **Weds.**)
the fourth day of the week, between Tuesday and Thursday: *Classes start Wednesday.* | *What time are you coming on Wednesday?* | *It's my birthday next Wednesday.* | *We're all going out to dinner on Wednesday night.*
[**ORIGIN:** From Woden, the most important god in the religion of some peoples in Northern Europe before Christianity.]

**weed**[1] /wid/ *noun*
a wild plant that grows where you do not want it to grow: *The garden was full of weeds and looked very messy.*

**weed**[2] *verb*
to remove weeds from the ground: *She cut the grass and weeded the flowerbeds.*

**week** /wik/ *noun*
**1** a period of seven days: *We went on vacation for two weeks.* | *I'll see you next week.*
**2** the part of a week when people work or go to school, from Monday to Friday: *I don't have much free time during the week.*

**week·day** /ˈwikdeɪ/ *noun*
any day of the week except Saturday and Sunday: *Most people work on weekdays.*

**week·end** /ˈwikend/ *noun*
Saturday and Sunday: *Do you want to come over to my house this weekend?* | *I play soccer on weekends.*

**week·ly** /ˈwikli/ *adverb, adjective*
once a week, or every week: *The newspaper is printed weekly, on Fridays.* | *The teachers have weekly meetings.*

**week·night** /ˈwiknaɪt/ *noun*
any night except Saturday or Sunday: *I go to bed early on weeknights, but stay up late on weekend nights.*

**weep** /wip/ *verb* (**wept** /wept/)
to cry a lot: *She wept when she heard he had died.*
→ see Thesaurus box at **cry**[1]

**weigh** /weɪ/ *verb*

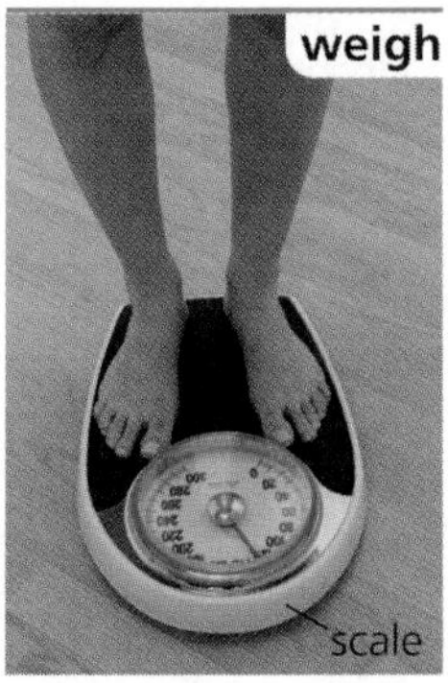


**1** to have a particular weight: *The baby weighs 12 pounds.* | *How much does that suitcase weigh?*
**2** to measure how heavy someone or something is: *I weighed the fish. It was two pounds.*
**3** to think about something carefully: *You have to weigh whether or not you agree with him.*

**weight** /weɪt/ *noun*
**1** how heavy someone or something is: *The baby's weight was 9 pounds.*
**2** a heavy piece of metal that people lift to make their muscles bigger: *He was in the gym lifting weights.*
**3** something that is heavy: *I put a weight on*

*the paper to stop it from blowing away.*

**4** **lose weight** = to become thinner: *If you eat less food, you will lose weight.*

**5** **gain weight/put on weight** = to become fatter: *I gained some weight, and now my clothes don't fit.*

**weight·lift·ing** /ˈweɪtˌlɪftɪŋ/ *noun*
the sport of lifting a bar with heavy metal objects on each end
—**weight-lifter** *noun* someone who does weightlifting

**weird** /wɪrd/ *adjective* (*informal*)
unusual and strange: *I had a weird feeling, like I was in someone else's body.* **SYNONYM: strange**
—**weirdly** *adverb* in a strange way
—**weirdness** *noun* strangeness
→ see Thesaurus box at **strange**
[**ORIGIN:** 1800-1900 From the old English word *wyrd*, which means "fate." The word was later used as an adjective about supernatural things or other strange or mysterious things.]

**weird·o** /ˈwɪrdoʊ/ *noun* (plural **weirdos**) (*informal*)
a strange person who people do not like or are afraid of: *They called him a weirdo because he wore strange clothes and had green hair.*

**wel·come¹** /ˈwelkəm/ *adjective*
**1** if you are welcome in a place, the people there are happy that you have come: *Our new neighbors were very friendly and made us feel welcome.*
**2** **You're welcome!** = used when someone has said thank you to you for something: *"Thanks for the ride." "You're welcome."*
**3** **be welcome to do something** = used when telling someone that he or she can do something: *You're welcome to stay for lunch – there's plenty of food.*
[**ORIGIN:** From the old English word *wilcuma*, which means "person you are glad to have as a guest," from *willa*, meaning "wish or desire" and *cuma*, meaning "someone who comes."]

**welcome²** *verb*
**1** to say hello in a friendly way to someone who has just arrived: *He welcomed his guests at the door.*
**2** (*formal*) to be pleased if something happens because you think it is a good thing: *We welcome customers' comments on how we can improve our service.*

**welcome³** *noun*
the way someone greets you when you arrive somewhere: *They seemed happy to see us and gave us a warm welcome.*

**weld** /weld/ *verb*
to join metal objects to each other by heating them and pressing them together when they are hot: *The parts of the ship are welded together.*
—**welder** *noun* someone who welds metal

**wel·fare** [Ac] /ˈwelfer/ *noun*
**1** money that the government gives to people who are poor, have no job, etc.: *Most people in this poor neighborhood are on welfare.*
**2** (*formal*) someone's health or happiness: *We put the children's welfare first. They must feel safe in school.*

**well¹** /wel/ *adverb* (**better**, **best**)
**1** in a good way: *Did you sleep well?* | *Mary can read very well.* **ANTONYM: badly**

> **USAGE: well, good**
>
> Use **well** to talk about the way someone does something: *He plays tennis very well.*
>
> Use **good** to talk about the quality of something or someone: *a good teacher* | *Was the movie good?*

**2** very much: *It was late – well after 10 o'clock.*
**3** in a thorough way: *Mix the paint well before you use it.* **SYNONYM: thoroughly**
**4** **as well** = also: *I'd like a cup of coffee and some cake as well.* **SYNONYM: too**

> **USAGE: as well, too, also**
>
> **As well**, **too**, and **also** mean the same thing, but you use them in different ways.
>
> **As well** and **too** are less formal than **also** and you use them more often in spoken English: *Oh, are you coming as well?* | *Tom's hungry, and I am too.*
>
> **Also** is more formal and is used more often in writing than in speech: *Tom was very tired, and he was also hungry.*

W

**5 as well as** = if you do one thing as well as another, you do them both: *I'm learning Spanish as well as Chinese.*

**6 well done** (*formal*) = said when someone has done a good thing or done something well: *"I won the competition." "Well done!"*

**well²** *adjective* (**better**)
healthy and not sick: *He's sick, but we hope he will be well again soon.*
→ see Thesaurus box at **healthy**

**well³** *interjection*
**1** used before you say something or when you are surprised: *Well, I suppose we should go now.* | *Well, what a nice surprise!*
**2** (*also* **oh well**) used to show you accept a situation, even though you are disappointed about it: *"I didn't pass the test." "Oh well, better luck next time."*
**3 Well?** = used when asking someone to answer your question or tell you what happened: *Well? What did he say?*

**well⁴** *noun*
a deep hole dug in the ground, from which people get water or oil: *She lowered the bucket into the well.*

**we'll** /wil/
the short form of "we will": *We'll have to leave soon.*

**ˌwell-beˈhaved** *adjective*
behaving in a good or polite way: *She apologized for her son's behavior and said that he was usually well-behaved.* **SYNONYM: good**

**ˌwell-ˈbeing** *noun* (*formal*)
a feeling of being healthy and happy: *Running gives me a feeling of well-being.*

**ˌwell-ˈdone** *adjective*
well-done meat has been cooked thoroughly: *He likes his steak well done, even black on the outside.* **ANTONYM: rare**

**ˌwell-ˈdressed** *adjective*
wearing clothes that look good and are fashionable: *A well-dressed man wearing a suit and tie came into the room.*

**ˌwell-ˈknown** *adjective*
known about by a lot of people: *It's a well-known fact that smoking is bad for your health.* | *You must have heard of her – she's very well known.* **ANTONYM: unknown**

**ˌwell-ˈmeaning** *adjective*
a well-meaning person tries to help, but makes a situation worse: *I didn't want to see Todd, but a well-meaning neighbor told him where to find me.*

**ˌwell-ˈoff** *adjective*
having enough money to have a good life, with all the things you want: *My parents weren't very well-off, so we lived in a small house.* **SYNONYM: rich**; **ANTONYM: poor**
→ see Thesaurus box at **rich**

**ˌwell-ˈpaid** *adjective*
getting a lot of money as pay for the job that you do: *a well-paid job*

**ˌwell-ˈtimed** *adjective* (*formal*)
said or done at the best possible time: *My arrival wasn't very well-timed because Rob and Lisa were arguing.*

**ˌwell-to-ˈdo** *adjective* (*formal*)
having a lot of money: *The big houses are owned by well-to-do families.* **SYNONYM: rich**; **ANTONYM: poor**
→ see Thesaurus box at **rich**

**Welsh¹** /welʃ/ *adjective*
from Wales: *a Welsh singer*

**Welsh²** *noun*
**1** the language spoken in Wales
**2 the Welsh** = the people of Wales

**went** /went/ *verb*
the past tense of GO

**wept** /wept/ *verb*
the past tense and past participle of WEEP

**were** /wɚ/ *verb*
the past tense of BE that is used after "you," "we," and "they"

**we're** /wɪr/
the short form of "we are": *We're almost finished.*

**weren't** /wɚnt/
the short form of "were not": *I tried to call you, but you weren't home.*

W

**were·wolf** /ˈwerwʊlf/ *noun* (plural **werewolves**)
a person in stories who changes into a WOLF
[**ORIGIN:** From the old English words *wer* and *wulf*, which mean "man" and "wolf."]

**west¹** (*also* **West**) /west/ *noun*
**1** the direction in which the sun goes down: *The sun sets in the west.* → see picture at **north**
**2 the west** = the western part of a country or area: *El Paso is in the west of Texas.*
**3 the West** = the countries in North America and the western part of Europe: *He thinks the richer countries of the West should help poorer countries.*
**4 the West** = the part of the U.S. that is west of the Mississippi River: *There are a lot of cattle ranches in the West, especially in Montana and Wyoming.*

**west²** *adjective*
**1** in, to, or facing the west: *Our hotel was west of the river.*
**2 west wind** = a wind that comes from the west

**west³** *adverb*
toward the west: *We left New York and drove west to Virginia.*

**west·ern¹** /ˈwestərn/ *adjective*
**1** in or from the west: *Vancouver is in western Canada.* **ANTONYM: eastern**
**2 Western** = in or from the countries in North America and the western part of Europe: *William Shakespeare is very important in Western literature.*

**western²** *noun*
a movie about life in the western part of the U.S. in the 19th century
→ see Thesaurus box at **movie**

**west·er·ner** /ˈwɛstərnər/ *noun*
**1** someone who comes from the western part of a country
**2 Westerner** = someone who comes from North America or the western part of Europe, rather than from Africa or Asia: *He was one of the first Westerners to spend time in Japan.*

**west·ward** /ˈwestwərd/ *adverb, adjective*
toward the west: *The ship sailed westward.*

**wet¹** /wet/ *adjective* (**wetter**, **wettest**)
**1** covered in or containing liquid: *It had been raining and the ground was wet. | He took off his wet clothes.* **ANTONYM: dry**
**2** not yet dry: *Don't touch the paint – it's still wet.* **ANTONYM: dry**
**3** if the weather is wet, it is raining or it has been raining: *It's been a very wet spring.* **SYNONYM: rainy; ANTONYM: dry**
—**wetness** *noun* the state of being wet

**wet²** *verb* (**wet** *or* **wetted**, **wetting**)
to make something wet: *Wet your hair before you use the shampoo.* **ANTONYM: dry**

**wet·land** /ˈwetlənd/ *noun*
a very wet area of land: *Wetlands have a lot of different birds in them.*

**wet·suit** (*also* **wet suit**) /ˈwetsut/ *noun*
a piece of rubber clothing that keeps you warm when you go swimming or DIVING

**we've** /wiːv/
the short form of "we have": *We've met before, haven't we?*

**whack** /wæk/ *verb*
to hit someone or something hard: *I swung the bat and whacked the ball over the fence.*
—**whack** *noun* a hard hit

**whale** /weɪl/ *noun*
a large animal that lives in the ocean and breathes through a hole in the top of its head. Whales look like fish, but they are MAMMALs.
—**whaling** *noun* the activity of hunting whales
—**whaler** *noun* someone who hunts whales
[**ORIGIN:** From the old English word *hwæl*.]

**wharf** /wɔrf/ *noun* (plural **wharves** /wɔrvz/)
a long structure that sticks out into the water so that boats can stop next to it: *His boat was tied up at the wharf.* **SYNONYM: pier**

**what** /wət; *strong* wʌt/ *pronoun, adjective*
**1** used when asking a question: *What is your name? | What time is it? | "What do you do?" "I'm a mailman."*
**2** used when mentioning something you are not certain about: *I don't know what he wants for his birthday.*
**3** (*informal*) used when you did not hear what someone said: *"Is it hot?" "What?" "I said, is it hot?"* **SYNONYMS: excuse me, pardon**
**4** (*informal*) used when someone has said your name and you are asking what he or she

W

wants: *"Jane!" "What?" "Come and see this."* **SYNONYM: yes**

**5** the thing or things that have been mentioned or described: *Show me what you bought.* | *I believe what he told me.*

**6** used to say strongly what you think: *"Let's go swimming." "What a great idea!"*

**7 What about ...?** = used when mentioning something that should be considered, or to suggest something: *What about the dog? Who's going to look after him?* | *What about New York? I've always wanted to go there.*

**8 What for?** (*informal*) = used when asking about the reason for something or the purpose of something: *"Can I have this cardboard box?" "What for?"* | *What is this button on the camera for?*

**9 What if ...?** = used when asking about something that might happen: *What if he's not home when we get there?*

**what·ev·er** /wət'evɚ/ *pronoun, adjective*

**1** any or all of the things that someone needs or wants: *Take whatever you need.*

**2** used when saying that it is not important what happens because it does not change a situation: *Whatever I say, she always disagrees.*

**3** (*informal*) used as a reply to say that you do not care about something: *"Do you want a pizza?" "Oh, whatever."*

**wheat** /wit/ *noun*

a plant grown by farmers, that is used for making flour

**wheel** /wil/ *noun*

**1** one of the round things under a car, bicycle, etc. that turns and makes it move → see picture at **bicycle**

**2** a round object that you hold and turn to make a car move to the left or right: *He had an accident when he fell asleep at the wheel of his car.* **SYNONYM: steering wheel**

**wheel·bar·row** /'wil,bæroʊ/ *noun*

a large container with a wheel at the front and two handles at the back, that you use outdoors for moving things from one place to another: *He took the dirt away in a wheelbarrow.*

**wheel·chair** /'wil-tʃer/ *noun*

a chair with wheels for someone who cannot walk: *He broke his back, and is now in a wheelchair.*

**wheeze** /wiz/ *verb*

to breathe with difficulty, making a sound in your chest: *He has a lung disease and wheezes when he breathes.*

→ see Thesaurus box at **breathe**

**when** /wen/ *adverb*

**1** at what time: *When are we leaving?* | *I'll tell you when to stop.*

**2** at the time that something happens: *I moved to the U.S. when I was young.* | *He was asleep when the fire started.*

**3** even though something is true: *Why do you want a new computer when this one works fine?*

**4** immediately after something happens: *I'll call you when I get home.*

**when·ev·er** /wen'evɚ/ *adverb*

**1** every time: *Whenever we come here, we see someone we know.*

**2** at any time: *Come and visit whenever you want.*

**where** /wer/ *adverb*

**1** in or to what place: *"Where does he live?" "On 7th Street."* | *"Where are you going?" "To the store."*

**2** used when giving information about a place: *This is the place where I met Gayle.*

**3** used when talking about one part of a story or movie: *I liked the part where the bird finds its mother.*

**4** used when talking about one stage in a process: *Where did it all start to go wrong?*

**where·a·bouts** /'werə,baʊts/ *plural noun* (*formal*)

the place where someone is: *The police want to talk to him, but do not know his whereabouts.*

**where·as** Ac /wer'æz; *weak* werəz/ *conjunction* (*formal*)

used when saying that two situations are very different: *Jane's family is poor, whereas Jason's is rich.*

**where·by** Ac /wer'baɪ/ *adverb* (*formal*)

used when giving the details of a system, plan, process, etc.: *The store has a system whereby you can return empty bottles and get money.*

W

**where·u·pon** /ˌwerəˈpɑn/ *conjunction* (*formal*)
after the thing you have just mentioned: *The president arrived, whereupon everyone started shouting.*

**wher·ev·er** /werˈevɚ/ *adverb*
**1** in any place: *Sit wherever you like.*
**2** in every place: *They followed us wherever we went.*

**wheth·er** /ˈweðɚ/ *conjunction*
**1** used when talking about a choice between different things: *I don't know whether he'll come or not.* **SYNONYM: if**
**2** used when saying that it does not matter what someone wants or decides because something will still happen: *Whether you like it or not, we're going home.*

**USAGE: whether, weather**

**Whether** is a conjunction: *The students were asked whether they enjoyed math.*

**Weather** is a noun: *The weather stayed warm.*

**which** /wɪtʃ/ *pronoun, adjective*
**1** what person or thing from a pair or group: *Which color do you like better – blue or green?* | *Which of you is taller: Mary or Jane?*
**2** used when adding more information about something: *We went to Plano, which is just outside Dallas.* | *They cut down the trees which grew by the river.*

**which·ev·er** /wɪˈtʃevɚ/ *adjective, pronoun*
**1** used when saying that it does not matter which thing is chosen because the result will be the same: *Whichever sport you play, I'm sure you'll try hard.*
**2** any of a pair or group of things: *Use whichever shampoo suits your hair best.*

**whiff** /wɪf/ *noun*
a smell of something that you notice for only a short time: *As she walked past, I caught a whiff of her perfume.*

**while¹** /waɪl/ *conjunction*
**1** during the time that something is happening: *They arrived while we were having dinner.* | *While she works, she listens to music.*
**2** although: *While it was a good school, I was not happy there.*

**while²** *noun*
**a while** = a period of time: *After a while, she fell asleep.* | *I've only been here for a short while.*

**whim** /wɪm/ *noun*
if you do something on a whim, you do it because you suddenly want to do it: *We decided to go camping for the weekend, on a whim.*

**whim·per** /ˈwɪmpɚ/ *verb*
to make low crying sounds: *The dog was whimpering because it had hurt its paw.*

**whine** /waɪn/ *verb*
**1** to complain about something in a sad annoying voice: *She was whining about how hard her life is.*
**2** to make a long high sound because you feel pain or are unhappy: *The dog whines at the door when he wants to come in.*

**whip¹** /wɪp/ *noun*
a long thin piece of leather with a handle, used for hitting a horse to make it go faster

**whip²** *verb* (**whipped**, **whipping**)
**1** to hit a person or animal with a whip: *He whipped the horse to make it run faster.*
**2** (*informal*) to defeat someone easily: *They whipped the other team 35–0.*
**3** to move something suddenly: *He whipped out a pen and signed his name.*
**4** to quickly mix cream or the clear part of an egg until it becomes thick and stiff **SYNONYM: beat**

**whirl** /wɚl/ *verb*
to make someone or something move around quickly: *He whirled her around the dance floor.* **SYNONYM: spin**

**whirl·pool** /ˈwɚlpul/ *noun*
**1** a bathtub that makes currents of water move around your body
**2** water that moves around and down quickly: *There's a whirlpool at the bottom of the waterfall.*

**whirl·wind¹** /ˈwɚlˌwɪnd/ *noun*
a very strong wind that moves quickly around in a circle, causing a lot of damage **SYNONYM: tornado**

**whirlwind²** *adjective*
happening very quickly: *They had a whirlwind*

W

*romance and were married a month after they met.*

**whisk¹** /wɪsk/ *verb*

**1** to mix liquids or soft foods together very quickly: *Whisk the sauce until it is smooth.* SYNONYM: **beat**

**2** to take someone somewhere very quickly: *He was whisked to the hospital.*

**whisk²** *noun*

a kitchen tool used for mixing liquids or soft foods, made of curved pieces of wire

**whisk·ers** /ˈwɪskɚz/ *plural noun*

**1** long hairs that grow near the mouth of an animal such as a cat or a mouse

**2** the hair on a man's face when he needs to cut it off: *His whiskers tickled her face when he kissed her.*

**whis·key** /ˈwɪski/ *noun*

a drink made from grain, that contains a lot of alcohol

**whis·per** /ˈwɪspɚ/ *verb*

to speak very quietly: *She whispered the answer to me because she didn't want anyone to hear.*

—**whisper** *noun* a very quiet voice: *He spoke in a whisper to avoid disturbing the others.*

→ see Thesaurus box at **say¹**

**whis·tle** /ˈwɪsəl/ *noun*

**1** a small object that produces a high sound when you blow into it: *The P.E. teacher blew a whistle to start the race.*

**2** a high sound made with a whistle or by blowing air through your lips: *When he gave a whistle, his dog ran to him.*

—**whistle** *verb* to make a high sound with a whistle or by blowing air through your lips: *He whistled a song for me.*

**white¹** /waɪt/ *adjective*

**1** having the color of milk, salt, or snow: *a white wedding dress*

**2** having light-colored skin: *Her father is white, and her mother is Asian.*

—**whiten** *verb* to make something white: *This toothpaste will whiten your teeth.*

**white²** *noun*

**1** the color of milk, salt, or snow: *The bride was dressed in white.*

**2** **whites** = people who have light-colored skin: *Blacks, whites, Hispanics, and Asians all live together in this city.*

**3** the part of an egg that becomes white when you cook it: *Mix two egg whites together.* → see picture at **yolk**

**white·board** /ˈwaɪtbɔrd/ *noun*

a large board with a smooth white surface that teachers write on with pens

**ˌwhite-ˈcollar** *adjective*

white-collar workers have jobs in offices, banks, etc., rather than working in factories, building houses, etc.

**ˈWhite House** *noun*

**1** **the White House** = the official home of the president of the U.S., in Washington, D.C.: *We took a tour of the White House and the Capitol.*

**2** the president of the U.S. and the people who work with the president: *The White House did not comment on the issue.*

**whit·tle** /ˈwɪtl/ *verb*

**1** (*also* **whittle down**) to gradually make something smaller: *I've whittled down the list of guests from 30 to 16.*

**2** to cut small pieces off a piece of wood: *He whittled a small figure of a man out of the wood with his knife.*

**whiz¹** /wɪz/ *verb* (**whizzed**, **whizzing**, **whizzes**) (*informal*)

to move very quickly: *A motorcycle whizzed by.*

**whiz²** *noun* (*informal*)

someone who is very good at something: *My brother's a math whiz – he can solve any math problem.*

**who** /hu/ *pronoun*

**1** what person or people: *Who locked the door? | I know who sent you that card.*

**2** used for giving information about someone you have mentioned: *That's the girl who lives next door to us. | My uncle, who is a teacher, gave me this book.*

**who·ev·er** /huˈevɚ/ *pronoun*

**1** the person who: *Whoever broke this is going to be in trouble.*

**2** used when saying that it does not matter who does something because it will not change a situation: *Whoever wins, it's going to be a great game.*

W

**whole**[1] /hoʊl/ *adjective*
all of something: *He ate a whole box of candy and got sick.* | *We spent the whole day at the beach.* **SYNONYM: entire**
—**wholly** *adverb* (*formal*) completely: *Young babies are wholly dependent on their parents.*
[**ORIGIN:** From the old English word *hal*, which means "healthy, unhurt, or complete."]

**whole**[2] *noun*
**1 the whole of something** = all of something: *The floods affected the whole of the city.*
**2 on the whole** = generally: *On the whole, I like school, but I don't like everything about it.*
**3 as a whole** = used when you are considering all of something: *Education benefits society as a whole.*

**whole·heart·ed·ly** /ˌhoʊlˈhɑrtɪdli/ *adverb*
if you believe, feel, or support something wholeheartedly, you believe, feel, or support it completely: *You're right – I agree with you wholeheartedly.*

**ˌwhole ˈnumber** *noun*
a number that does not contain a FRACTION or DECIMAL: *4 is a whole number, but 4.5 is not a whole number.*

**whole·sale** /ˈhoʊlseɪl/ *adjective*
relating to selling things in large quantities to stores: *Wholesale prices are cheaper than the retail prices charged in stores.*
—**wholesale** *adverb* if a store buys things wholesale, it buys them in large quantities, and then sells them to customers
—**wholesaler** *noun* a person or company that sells things to stores

**whole·some** /ˈhoʊlsəm/ *adjective*
**1** good for your health: *Cereal and fruit is a good wholesome breakfast.*
**2** having or showing behavior that is right and acceptable: *It's a wholesome family show that is suitable for everyone to watch.*

**ˈwhole wheat** *adjective*
whole wheat flour or bread is made using every part of the grain

**whom** /hum/ *pronoun*
**1** (*formal*) who – used as the object of a verb or PREPOSITION: *To whom am I speaking?*
**2 some/all/one, etc. of whom** = some, all, etc. of the people just mentioned: *He has two sisters, one of whom is in college.*

**whoop** /hup/ *verb*
to shout loudly and in a happy way: *The audience whooped and cheered when the comedian came on stage.*
—**whoop** *noun* a loud happy shout

**whoop·ing cough** /ˈhupɪŋ kɔf/ *noun*
a serious disease that makes you cough and have difficulty breathing, and that mainly affects children

**whose** /huz/ *adjective*, *pronoun*
**1** used for asking or saying who something belongs to: *Whose jacket is this?*
**2** used for giving information about something that belongs to someone: *That's the man whose house burned down.*

**who'd** /hud/
**1** the short form of "who had": *The teacher asked who'd written on the board.*
**2** the short form of "who would": *Do you know anyone who'd be interested in going?*

**who'll** /hul/
the short form of "who will": *Who'll be here tomorrow?*

**who's** /huz/
**1** the short form of "who is": *Who's coming to the party?*
**2** the short form of "who has": *Who's got my math book?*

**USAGE: who's, whose**

**Who's** means "who is" or "who has": *Who's your favorite actor?* | *I think I know who's done this.*

**Whose** means "belonging to whom": *I don't know whose writing this is.*

**who've** /huv/
the short form of "who have": *People who've seen the show say it's fantastic.*

**why** /waɪ/ *adverb*
**1** for what reason: *Why is she crying?* | *I don't know why he left.* | *"I haven't done my homework." "Why not?"*
**2 Why not ...?** (*informal*) = used for making a suggestion: *Why not just ask him to help you?*
**3 Why not?** (*informal*) = used for saying

"yes" to a suggestion or invitation: *"Do you want to come with us?" "OK, why not?"*

**wick** /wɪk/ *noun*
the string in a CANDLE which burns

**wick·ed** /ˈwɪkɪd/ *adjective*
bad or evil: *The wicked witch turned the boy into a frog.*
—**wickedness** *noun* bad or evil actions

**wick·er** /ˈwɪkɚ/ *adjective*
made from thin branches woven together: *a wicker chair*

**wide¹** /waɪd/ *adjective*
**1** measuring a large distance from one side to the other: *The path was wide enough for two bicycles.* **ANTONYM: narrow** → see picture at **narrow**
**2** used for asking or talking about the distance between the two sides of something: *How wide is the door?* | *The bed is five feet wide.*
**3** including a lot of different things or people: *The store has a wide range of clothes.*

**wide²** *adverb*
completely, or as much as possible: *The door was wide open.* | *It was only 5:30 a.m., but I was wide awake.* | *He spread his arms wide.*

W

**wide·ly** /ˈwaɪdli/ *adverb*
**1** in a lot of places or by a lot of people: *The product is widely available; you can buy it at any computer store.* | *a widely used textbook*
**2 vary/differ widely** = to be very different: *Prices of some goods vary widely from store to store.*

**wid·en** /ˈwaɪdn/ *verb*
to become wider, or to make something wider: *The river widens here.* | *They are going to widen the road to add new lanes.*

**wide·spread** Ac /ˈwaɪdspred/ *adjective*
happening in a lot of places: *The widespread use of computers has changed the way we live.*

**wid·ow** /ˈwɪdoʊ/ *noun*
a woman whose husband has died
→ see Thesaurus box at **married**

**wid·ow·er** /ˈwɪdoʊɚ/ *noun*
a man whose wife has died
→ see Thesaurus box at **married**

**width** /wɪdθ/ *noun*
the distance from one side of something to the other: *They measured the width of the window.* | *The table is three feet in width.*

**wife** /waɪf/ *noun* (plural **wives** /waɪvz/)
the woman that a man is married to: *This is a picture of my brother and his wife.*
[**ORIGIN:** From the old English word *wif*, which means "woman or wife."]

**wig** /wɪg/ *noun*
something that has been made for someone to wear as hair: *The actress wore a blond wig.*
[**ORIGIN:** 1600-1700 A short form of "periwig," which was a type of wig. This word came from the old French word *perruque* and the old Italian word *perrucca*, which mean "hair or wig."]

**wig·gle** /ˈwɪgəl/ *verb*
to move something up and down or from side to side, using small movements: *She wiggled her toes inside her shoes.*

**wig·wam** /ˈwɪgwɑm/ *noun*
a type of small house used in the past by some Native American tribes. A wigwam has a curved frame of wooden poles covered with BARK, animal skins, etc.
[**ORIGIN:** 1600-1700 From the Abnaki and Massachusett word *wikwam*, which means "their house." These are Native American languages.]

**wild¹** /waɪld/ *adjective*
**1** wild animals are not kept by people: *A herd of wild horses galloped past.* **ANTONYM: tame**
**2** wild plants are not grown by people: *We picked some wild mushrooms.*
**3** very angry, excited, etc. and not able to control yourself: *The kids were wild with excitement.*
**4** (*informal*) very exciting and enjoyable, and sometimes including events or behavior that are not usually acceptable: *They could hear the sound of a wild party going on in the next apartment.*
**5** not based on any facts: *It was just a wild guess – it may be wrong.*
**6 not wild about something/someone** (*informal*) = not liking something or someone very much: *I'm not wild about Zack's new friend – he seems a little strange.*

**wild²** *noun*
**in the wild** = in an area that is natural and not looked after by people: *Scientists study the behavior of animals in the wild.*

**wil·der·ness** /ˈwɪldənəs/ *noun*
a large natural area of land where there is nothing made by humans: *They got lost in the wilderness.*
[**ORIGIN:** From the old English word *wildeornes*, which means "land where wild animals live," from *wildeor*, meaning "wild animal."]

**wild·flow·er** /ˈwaɪldˌflaʊə/ *noun*
a flower that has not been grown by people

**ˌwild ˈgoose ˌchase** *noun*
a situation in which you waste a lot of time looking for something that cannot be found: *We went on a wild goose chase looking for that book – it isn't in the library.*

**wild·life** /ˈwaɪldlaɪf/ *noun*
animals that are not kept by people: *We must protect the birds and other wildlife of this area.*

**will**[1] /wɪl/ *verb*
**1** used for talking about the future: *It will probably rain tomorrow.* | *I will call you when I hear any news.*
**2 Will you ...?** = used for asking or telling someone to do something: *Will you turn the TV off, please?*
**3** used for saying what is possible: *The stadium will hold 20,000 people.* **SYNONYM: can**
**4** used for saying what someone plans or agrees to do: *I will help you.*
**5 won't/will not** = used for saying that someone does not want to do something: *Julia won't let me play with her doll!*

**will**[2] *noun*
**1** a strong wish to do something or that something should happen: *He does not have the will to live anymore.* | *You can't force him to stay here against his will.*
**2** a legal document in which you say who will have your money and property after you die: *My grandma left me $7,000 in her will.*

**will**[3] *verb*
to try to make something happen by thinking about it very hard: *He willed the ball to go through the hoop.*

**will·ful** (*also* **wilful**) /ˈwɪlfəl/ *adjective*
doing what you want, even though people tell you not to: *How can you control a willful teenager?*
—**willfully** *adverb* in a willful way
—**willfulness** *noun* willful behavior

**will·ing** /ˈwɪlɪŋ/ *adjective*
**1 be willing to do something** = if you are willing to do something, you do not mind doing it: *Are you willing to help?* **ANTONYM: unwilling**
**2** doing something because you want to do it, not because you have to: *We had a lot of willing helpers.*
—**willingly** *adverb* if you do something willingly, you do it because you want to do it: *He willingly shared his food with us.*
—**willingness** *noun* the state of being willing to do something

**wil·low** /ˈwɪloʊ/ *noun*
a tree with long thin branches, that grows near water

**will·pow·er** /ˈwɪlˌpaʊə/ *noun*
the ability to make yourself do something that is difficult or unpleasant: *I don't have the willpower to stay on a diet.*

**wimp** /wɪmp/ *noun* (*informal*)
someone who is afraid to do things: *He's such a wimp that he'll never have the courage to ask her out.*

**win**[1] /wɪn/ *verb* (**won** /wʌn/, **winning**)
**1** to be the best in a competition, game, etc.: *Who won the election?* | *Our team won by 3 points.* **ANTONYM: lose**

**THESAURUS: win**

**beat** to get more points or votes than other people in a game or competition: *New York beat Boston, 4–1.* | *I beat Dad at chess!*

**defeat** to beat someone in a war, sport, or competition: *UCLA defeated Arizona State in Thursday's game.*

**conquer** (*formal*) to defeat a group of people in a war and take their land: *The Spanish conquered most of South America.*

**2** to get money or a prize by doing well in a competition, game, etc.: *She won a gold medal at the Olympics.*
—**winning** *adjective* the winning team or player is the one that has won
[**ORIGIN:** From the old English word *winnan*, which means "to work or fight."]

W

**win²** *noun*
an occasion when you win a competition, game, etc.: *The college is still happy about their 64–57 win over Oregon State.*
SYNONYM: **victory**; ANTONYM: **loss**

**wince** /wɪns/ *verb*
to suddenly change your expression when you see, feel, hear, or remember something unpleasant: *She winced at the sight of the wound.*

**wind¹** /wɪnd/ *noun*
air outside that moves quickly along: *The trees swayed in the wind.* | *A cold wind was blowing.* | *a strong east wind*

**THESAURUS: wind**

**breeze** a light wind: *A nice breeze came off the ocean.*

**gust** a sudden strong wind: *A gust of wind blew open the door.*

**gale** a very strong wind: *Several trees were blown down in the gale.*

**storm** a period of bad weather when there is a lot of wind and rain or snow: *The storm lasted all night.*

**blizzard** a very bad storm with a lot of snow and wind: *The blizzard left two feet of snow on the ground overnight, making it impossible to go anywhere.*

**hurricane** a storm with very strong fast winds. Hurricanes start in the Atlantic Ocean or in the Caribbean Sea: *The hurricane badly damaged the city of New Orleans.*

**typhoon** a storm with very strong fast winds. Typhoons start in the Pacific Ocean: *The typhoon is expected to hit the coast of Japan today.*

**tornado** a violent storm with strong winds that go around and around. Tornadoes start over land: *The wind in the tornado was moving at 200 miles per hour.*

**wind²** /waɪnd/ *verb* (**wound** /waʊnd/)
**1** to put a piece of string, cloth, etc. around and around something: *He wound his scarf around his neck.*
**2** (*also* **wind up**) to turn a handle around and around in order to make a clock or machine able to work: *You wind up the toy car by turning this key, and then it moves forward.*
**3** if a road, path, or river winds somewhere, it has a lot of curves: *The road winds up the hill to the top.*

PHRASAL VERBS

**wind down**
to become less active before ending: *The party is winding down – everyone will go home soon.*

**wind up**
to be in a bad situation or place after a lot has happened: *If you don't drive more slowly, you'll wind up in the hospital.*

**wind·chill fac·tor** /ˈwɪndtʃɪl ˌfæktɚ/ *noun*
the effect that the wind has on cold weather, making it feel even colder: *The temperature tonight will be around freezing, but expect the windchill factor to make it feel even colder.*

**wind·ed** /ˈwɪndɪd/ *adjective*
if you are winded, you are out of breath, usually because you have been running: *I couldn't talk because I was winded from running.*

**wind farm** /ˈwɪnd ˌfɑrm/ *noun*
a place where wind is used to produce electricity: *The wind farm has a lot of wind turbines, which are turned by the wind.*

**wind·ing** /ˈwaɪndɪŋ/ *adjective*
a winding road, path, or river has a lot of curves

**wind in·stru·ment** /ˈwɪnd ˌɪnstrəmənt/ *noun*
a musical instrument that you blow, such as a FLUTE or CLARINET

**wind·mill** /ˈwɪndˌmɪl/ *noun*
a tall structure with parts that are turned by the wind. Windmills are used to produce power or pump water, and in the past they were used to crush grain into flour.

windmill

**win·dow** /ˈwɪndoʊ/ *noun*
**1** an opening with glass across it in a wall of a building or a vehicle: *He opened the window*

*to let some air in.* | *She looked out the window.* → see picture on page **A10**

**2** an area on a computer screen where you can use a particular program: *You can close the window by clicking on the X in the right-hand corner.*

[**ORIGIN:** 1200-1300 From the Norse word *vindauga*, from *vindr* and *auga*, which mean "wind" and "eye." The first windows were just holes in a roof or wall that the wind came through and that you could see out of.]

**ˈwindow ˌshopping** *noun*
the activity of looking at things in store windows without intending to buy them

**win·dow·sill** /ˈwɪndoʊˌsɪl/ *noun*
a shelf at the bottom of a window: *Put the plant on a windowsill so that it gets lots of sunlight.*

**wind·pipe** /ˈwɪndpaɪp/ *noun*
the tube through which air passes from your throat to your lungs

**wind·shield** /ˈwɪndʃild/ *noun*
the large window at the front of a vehicle: *He scraped the ice off his windshield.* → see picture on page **A28**

**ˈwindshield ˌwiper** *noun*
a long thin object that moves across a windshield to remove rain: *It started raining, so I turned on the windshield wipers.*

**wind·surf·ing** /ˈwɪndˌsɚfɪŋ/ *noun*
the sport of moving across water by standing on a board and holding onto a sail
—**windsurfer** *noun* someone who does windsurfing
—**windsurf** *verb* to do windsurfing

**wind tur·bine** /ˈwɪnd ˌtɚbaɪn/ *noun*
a tall structure with parts that are turned by the wind, used for producing electricity **SYNONYM: windmill**

**wind·y** /ˈwɪndi/ *adjective*
if it is windy, there is a lot of wind: *It was a windy day, and leaves were being blown off the trees.*

**wine** /waɪn/ *noun*
an alcoholic drink made from GRAPEs: *a glass of red wine*
—**winery** /ˈwaɪnəri/ *noun* a place where a company makes wine

**wing** /wɪŋ/ *noun*
**1** one of the parts of a bird's or insect's body that it uses to fly: *The duck flapped its wings and flew off.*
**2** one of the two flat parts that stick out of the sides of an airplane → see picture at **airplane**
**3** a part of a large building that is not the main part: *The new wing of the museum is for Asian art.*

**wing·span** /ˈwɪŋspæn/ *noun*
the distance from the end of one wing to the end of the other: *The plane had a wingspan of 80 feet.*

**wink** /wɪŋk/ *verb*
to close and open one eye quickly, usually to show that you are joking or being friendly: *"Don't tell Mom," he said, winking at her.*

**wink**

—**wink** *noun* the movement you make with your eye when you wink: *He gave her a wink to let her know he'd seen her.*

**win·ner** /ˈwɪnɚ/ *noun*
someone who wins a competition, race, or game: *The winner of the race gets a prize of $1,000.* **ANTONYM: loser**

**win·ter** /ˈwɪntɚ/ *noun*
the season between fall and spring, when the weather is coldest: *We get a lot of snow here in the winter.* | *I'm going skiing this winter.*
—**wintry** *adjective* cold: *a wintry day*

**wipe** /waɪp/ *verb*
**1** to remove dirt, water, etc. from something by moving a cloth or your hand across it: *She wiped her eyes with a tissue.* | *Could you wipe off the table?*
**2** to dry or clean something by rubbing it on something soft: *She wiped her wet hands on a towel.*

**PHRASAL VERBS**

**wipe something out**
(*informal*) to destroy or remove something completely: *Entire villages were wiped out by the floods.*

**wipe something up**
to remove liquid from a surface using a cloth: *I wiped up the water I spilled.*

W

**wip·er** /ˈwaɪpɚ/ *noun*
another word for WINDSHIELD WIPER

**wire** /waɪɚ/ *noun*
**1** a long thin piece of metal that carries electricity or electrical signals: *a telephone wire*
**2** a piece of metal that is long and thin like string or thread: *copper wire* | *a wire fence*
—**wiring** *noun* all the electrical wires in a building or machine

**wire·tap** /ˈwaɪɚˌtæp/ *noun*
the act of secretly listening to someone's telephone calls by connecting something to the wires of his or her telephone: *The FBI gathered information about the criminals' plans using wiretaps.*

**wis·dom** /ˈwɪzdəm/ *noun*
good judgment and sensible ideas: *My grandfather is full of wisdom, so we often ask for his advice.*

**ˈwisdom tooth** *noun*
one of the four large teeth at the back of an adult's mouth

**wise** /waɪz/ *adjective*
**1** sensible: *I think you've made a wise decision. I would do the same thing.* **ANTONYMS: stupid, unwise**
**2** able to make good decisions and give good advice: *We need a wise leader who we can trust.*
—**wisely** *adverb* in a sensible way: *He wisely did not say anything while she was yelling at him.*
→ see Thesaurus box at **intelligent**

**wish¹** /wɪʃ/ *verb*
**1** to want something to happen, even though it is unlikely: *I wish (that) I had a million dollars.* | *He wished for a more exciting life.*
**2 wish someone something** = to say that you hope someone will be happy, lucky, etc.: *Wish me luck!* | *He wished me a happy New Year.*
**3 wish to do something** (*formal*) = to want to do something: *I wish to make a complaint.*
[**ORIGIN:** From the old English word *wyscan.*]

**wish²** *noun*
**1** something that you want to have or to happen: *She wanted to be famous, and she got her wish when she won the singing competition.*
**2** (*formal*) the feeling of wanting to have something or wanting something to happen: *He quit school, against his parents' wishes.*
**3** if you make a wish, you ask for something to happen, believing that magic or luck will make it happen: *Blow out your candles and make a wish!*
**4 best wishes** = a friendly phrase that you write before your name in a card or at the end of a letter

**ˌwishful ˈthinking** *noun*
a belief or hope that something will happen, when it is not possible: *I hope he'll be well enough to play in the game next week, but maybe that's just wishful thinking.*

**wish·y-wash·y** /ˈwɪʃi ˌwɑʃi/ *adjective* (*informal*)
a wishy-washy person does not have firm ideas or plans: *He's too wishy-washy to be a good leader.*

**wit** /wɪt/ *noun*
**1** the ability to say things that are funny and smart: *He was famous for his quick wit and always having something funny to say.*
**2 wits** = your ability to think and make good decisions quickly: *He survived on the street by using his wits.*
**3 scare someone out of his or her wits** = to frighten someone very much

**witch** /wɪtʃ/ *noun*
a woman who has magic powers, especially one who does bad things: *The old witch knew many magic spells.*

W

—**witchcraft** /ˈwɪtʃˌkræft/ *noun* the use of magic powers: *Women who knew how to use plants to make medicines were sometimes accused of witchcraft.*

**with** /wɪθ/ *preposition*
**1** used for saying that people or things are together: *She walks to school with her sister.* | *Put this bag with the others.* | *Serve the fish with rice.*
**2** using something: *Stir the sauce with a wooden spoon.*
**3** having or carrying something: *I'd like a room with a nice view.* | *The man with the gun ran off.*
**4** used for saying what covers or fills something: *His hands were covered with blood.*
**5** because of something: *She was shaking with fear.*
**6** used for saying who or what a feeling or attitude is related to: *I was pretty angry with her.*
**7** used for saying who else is involved in an activity: *Have you talked about it with her?* | *He gets into fights with people.*
**8** used for saying how someone does something: *They spoke to the senator with great respect.*
**9** used for talking about the position of someone's body: *He was standing with his hands in his pockets.*
**10** supporting someone: *You're either with me or against me.*

**with·draw** /wɪθˈdrɔ/ *verb* (**withdrew** /wɪθˈdru/, **withdrawn** /wɪθːˈdrɔn/)
**1** to take money out of a bank account: *He withdrew $200 from the bank.* **ANTONYM: deposit**
**2** if soldiers withdraw from an area, they leave it: *U.S. troops withdrew from the south of the country.*
**3** to stop taking part in a competition or race: *She withdrew from the race because she hurt her leg.*

**with·draw·al** /wɪθˈdrɔəl/ *noun*
**1** the act of taking money out of your bank account: *He made a withdrawal of $200 from his savings account.*
**2** when soldiers leave an area: *The U.S. will continue its troop withdrawal from the region.*
**3** the act of stopping taking part in a competition or race: *He announced his withdrawal from the race.*

**with·er** /ˈwɪðɚ/ *verb*
if a plant withers, it becomes dry and it starts to die: *It was very hot, and a lot of the plants withered.*

**with·hold** /wɪθˈhoʊld/ *verb* (**withheld** /wɪθˈheld/) (*formal*)
to refuse to give someone something: *The police accused him of withholding information when he first talked to them.*

**with·in** /wɪˈðɪn/ *preposition, adverb*
**1** before a period of time ends: *Please pay your bill within two weeks.*
**2** less than a particular distance from somewhere: *The hotel is within a mile of the beach, so you can walk between the two.*
**3** inside an organization, group, or country: *He has been offered another job within the same company.*

**with·out** /wɪˈðaʊt/ *preposition*
**1** not having something or someone with you: *I left the house without my gloves.* | *I don't want to go to the party without you.*
**2** **without doing something** = not doing a particular thing: *He left without saying goodbye.*
**3** **go/do without something** = to not have something that you need or want: *I don't like going without enough sleep.*

**with·stand** /wɪθˈstænd/ *verb* (**withstood** /wɪθˈstʊd/) (*formal*)
to not be harmed or affected by something: *This plant can withstand very hot, dry conditions.*

**wit·ness** /ˈwɪtnəs/ *noun*
**1** someone who saw an accident or a crime happen: *Were there any witnesses to the accident who can tell us what happened?*
**2** someone who tells a court of law what he or she knows about a crime: *The lawyer questioned the witness.*
—**witness** *verb* to see an accident or a crime happen
→ see Thesaurus box at **see**

**wit·ty** /ˈwɪti/ *adjective* (**wittier**, **wittiest**)
good at talking in a funny or interesting way:

*Max is really witty and makes everyone laugh.*
→ see Thesaurus box at **funny**

**wives** /waɪvz/ *noun*
the plural of WIFE

**wiz·ard** /ˈwɪzɚd/ *noun*
**1** a man who has magic powers: *It's a story about witches and wizards.*
**2** (*also* **wiz** /wɪz/ (*informal*)) someone who is very good at doing something: *He's a computer wizard and writes computer games in his spare time.*
—**wizardry** /ˈwɪzɚdri/ *noun* great skill at doing something: *Thanks to Tom's technical wizardry, we managed to get the engine working again.*
[**ORIGIN:** 1400-1500 From *wys*, the old spelling of "wise." The ending *-ard* was used to make words referring to a person who had a quality or did something, so "wizard" originally meant "wise person."]

**wob·ble** /ˈwɑbəl/ *verb*
to move from side to side in an unsteady way: *The bicycle wobbled and Freddie fell off.*
—**wobbly** *adjective* moving from side to side in an unsteady way: *Be careful – the chair's a little wobbly.*

**wok** /wɑk/ *noun*
a large round pan that you use for Chinese cooking

W

**woke** /woʊk/ *verb*
the past tense of WAKE

**wo·ken** /ˈwoʊkən/ *verb*
the past participle of WAKE

**wolf** /wʊlf/ *noun* (plural **wolves** /wʊlvz/)
a wild animal that is like a large dog: *The deer was attacked by a pack of wolves.*

**wom·an** /ˈwʊmən/ *noun* (plural **women** /ˈwɪmɪn/)
an adult female person: *His mother is a very kind woman.*
[**ORIGIN:** From the old English word *wifman*, from *wif* and *man*, which mean "woman" and "person."]

**wom·en** /ˈwɪmɪn/ *noun*
the plural of WOMAN

**won** /wʌn/ *verb*
the past tense and past participle of WIN

**won·der**[1] /ˈwʌndɚ/ *verb*
to want to know something that you are not sure about: *I wonder if I passed the test.* | *Molly wondered why he hadn't called her.*

**wonder**[2] *noun*
**1** a feeling of admiration and surprise: *Sam and I looked in wonder at the paintings on the walls.*
**2** **no wonder** = used for saying that something is not surprising: *No wonder you feel sick – you ate too much!*
**3** something that people admire a lot: *Niagara Falls is one of the great wonders of nature.*

**won·der·ful** /ˈwʌndɚfəl/ *adjective*
very good or enjoyable: *It was a wonderful party and we had a great time!* **SYNONYM: great**
—**wonderfully** *adverb* very, or very well: *It is a wonderfully entertaining book.* | *She sang wonderfully.*
→ see Thesaurus box at **good**[1], **nice**

**won't** /woʊnt/ *verb*
the short form of "will not": *I won't tell you what he said.*

**wood** /wʊd/ *noun*
**1** the hard material that trees are made of. Wood is used for making things such as furniture or for burning in a fire: *The door is made of wood.*
**2** **woods** = a small forest: *We saw a deer when we were walking in the woods.*

**wood·en** /ˈwʊdn/ (*also* **wood**) *adjective*
made from wood: *a little wooden table*

**wood·land** /ˈwʊdlənd/ *noun* (*formal*)
land with a lot of trees growing on it: *In the north, there are large areas of woodland.*
→ see Thesaurus box at **tree**

**wood·peck·er** /ˈwʊdˌpekɚ/ *noun*
a bird with a long beak that it uses to make holes in trees to get insects

**wood·winds** /ˈwʊdˌwɪndz/ *plural noun*
the group of musical instruments in an ORCHESTRA that are played by blowing and pressing on keys to cover holes: *The woodwinds include the oboe, the flute, the clarinet, and the bassoon.*

**wood·work** /ˈwʊdwɚk/ *noun*
the parts of a building that are made of wood: *We painted the woodwork around the windows white.*

**wool** /wʊl/ *noun*
the hair on a sheep, that people use for making thread and clothes: *This coat is made of wool.*
—**woolen** (*also* **wool**) *adjective* made of wool: *a warm woolen sweater*
—**wooly** (**woolly**) *adjective* made of wool or like wool

**word** /wɚd/ *noun*
**1** a group of sounds or letters that have a meaning: *You can look up the words you don't know in a dictionary.* | *I have learned all the words to that song.*
**2** a quick talk with someone: *Peter, could I have a word with you?*
**3 give someone your word** = to promise someone something: *I'll do it tomorrow – I give you my word.*
**4 keep your word** = to do what you have promised: *We can trust Jake to keep his word.*
**5** some news or a message that you get: *Andy went to Texas a week ago, but we haven't had any word from him yet.*
**6** a short thing that you say: *Can I give you a word of advice?*
**7 not say/hear/understand/believe a word** = to not say, hear, understand, or believe anything or any part of something: *I can't understand a word of this poem.*
**8 in other words** = used when saying something again in a different or clearer way: *These two pictures are identical. In other words, they are exactly the same.*
**9 in your own words** = describing something in your own way, rather than repeating what you have read or heard: *I want you to listen to the story, and then write it in your own words.*
**10 word for word** = in exactly the same words: *Tell me what he said to you, word for word.*

**ˈword ˌprocessor** (*also* **ˈword ˌprocessing ˌprogram**) *noun*
a computer program that you use for writing
—**word processing** *noun* the activity of writing using a computer

**word·search** /ˈwɚdsɚtʃ/ *noun*
a game in which you look for words that are hidden among other letters

**word·y** /ˈwɚdi/ *adjective*
using more words than is necessary: *Her descriptions are too wordy – they could be a lot shorter.*

**wore** /wɔr/ *verb*
the past tense of WEAR

**work¹** /wɚk/ *verb*
**1** to do a job to earn money: *She works in a bank.* | *My father used to work for a computer company.* | *Lisa works as a nurse.*
**2** to have the effect that you want: *I've tried that diet, but it doesn't work. I didn't lose any weight.*
**3** to use time and effort trying to achieve something: *Kimiko is working hard to improve her English.*
**4** if a machine works, it operates correctly: *The car radio isn't working – it needs to be fixed.*
**5** to operate a machine: *Do you know how to work the printer?*
**6 be/get worked up** (*informal*) = to be upset: *It's only a small problem, so don't get worked up about it.*
→ see Thesaurus box at **job**
[**ORIGIN:** From the old English word *wyrcan.*]
**PHRASAL VERBS**
**work against someone or something**
to not help someone or something to be successful: *If you don't have any experience, it will work against you.*
**work on something**
to try to repair, complete, or improve something: *I need to work on my essay before I give it to the teacher.*
**work out**
**1 work something out** = to find the answer to a question or problem, by thinking about it carefully: *Have you worked out how much the trip will cost?*
**2** to do exercises that make your body stronger or healthier: *Sue works out at the gym twice a week.*
**3** if something works out, it stops being a problem: *I was very worried, but everything worked out in the end.*

**work²** *noun*
**1** a job that you do to earn money: *Rob's still*

*looking for work.* | *What time do you start work in the morning?*

**USAGE: work**

Do not say "What is your work?" or "What is your job?" Say *"What do you do?"* or *"What kind of work do you do?"*

**2 at work** = doing a job, or in the place where you do your job: *At 8 o'clock, the builders were already at work.* | *Dad left his briefcase at work.*

**3** something you do that takes a lot of time and effort: *Taking care of kids can be hard work.*

**4** the things you produce when you are working or studying: *My teacher said that she was pleased with my work.*

**5** a painting, play, piece of music, etc. that an artist, writer, or musician produces: *The museum is full of beautiful works of art.*

**6 out of work** = if you are out of work, you do not have a job, but you want one: *Dad was out of work for six months before he found a job.*

**work·a·ble** /ˈwɚkəbəl/ *adjective*

a workable plan, solution, suggestion, etc. is one that will achieve what you want: *Taking turns to do the housework is a workable solution for us.*

**work·a·hol·ic** /ˌwɚkəˈhɔlɪk/ *noun*

someone who chooses to work all the time: *Tom's still at the office as usual – he's a workaholic.*

**work·book** /ˈwɚkbʊk/ *noun*

a school book with questions and exercises in it: *For homework, please do Exercise 10 in your workbooks.*

**work·er** /ˈwɚkɚ/ *noun*

someone who does a job, but who is not a manager: *Farm workers do not earn a lot of money.*

**work·force** /ˈwɚkfɔrs/ *noun (formal)*

all the people who work in a country or company: *Today, there are many more women in the workforce than 50 years ago.*

**work·ing** /ˈwɚkɪŋ/ *adjective*

**1** having a job: *A lot of families have two working parents.*

**2** relating to work: *The working conditions on the farm were poor, as there was no shade and no time to rest.*

**ˌworking ˈclass** *noun*

**the working class** = the group of people who usually work with their hands, and who do not have much money or power: *Children from the working class have to work harder to be successful.*

—**working-class** *adjective* relating to the working class: *a working-class neighborhood*

**work·ings** /ˈwɚkɪŋz/ *plural noun*

the way something such as a machine or system works: *We still don't understand the workings of the human brain.*

**work·load** /ˈwɚkloʊd/ *noun*

the amount of work that you must do: *Because of her heavy workload, she had little time to spend with her kids.*

**work·man** /ˈwɚkmən/ *noun* (plural **workmen**)

a man who works with his hands building or repairing things: *Some workmen were repairing the road.*

**work·out** /ˈwɚk-aʊt/ *noun*

a series of exercises that you do to keep your body strong or healthy: *Dan does a workout at the gym every morning.*

**work·sheet** /ˈwɚkʃit/ *noun*

a piece of paper with questions for students: *The teacher gave the students some worksheets for homework.*

**work·shop** /ˈwɚkʃɑp/ *noun*

**1** a class where people learn how to do something: *I went to a pottery workshop on Saturday.*

**2** a room or building where people make or repair things: *Dad had a workshop in the garage where he made things out of wood.*

**work·week** /ˈwɚkwik/ *noun*

the number of days or hours in a week that you spend working: *You will be paid for a 40-hour workweek.*

**world** /wɚld/ *noun*

**1 the world** = the PLANET that we live on: *Mount Everest is the highest mountain in the world.* **SYNONYM: Earth**

**2** all the people or countries on Earth: *This terrible event shocked the world.*

W

3 a particular group of countries: *His poems are not well known outside the Arab world.*
4 an area of activity: *He is an influential person in the music world.* | *the glamorous world of fashion*
5 a type of society: *She wants a better world for her kids.*
6 **the animal/plant/insect world** = all animals, plants, or insects as a group: *Elephants are one of the largest creatures in the animal world.*
→ see Thesaurus box at **earth**
[ORIGIN: From the old English word *woruld*, which means "human existence."]

**ˌworld ˈrecord** *noun*
the fastest time, highest jump, etc. that anyone has ever achieved: *He set a new world record for the 400 meters, beating the previous record by almost a second.*

**ˌWorld ˈSeries** *noun*
**the World Series** = the baseball games that decide the best team in the U.S. and Canada each year

**world·wide** /ˌwɚldˈwaɪd/ *adjective, adverb*
everywhere in the world: *The disease affects thousands of people worldwide.*

**ˌWorld Wide ˈWeb** *noun* (*written abbreviation*: **WWW**)
the system that makes it possible for you to see and use information on the Internet
SYNONYM: **Web**

**worm** /wɚm/ *noun*
a long thin creature with a soft body and no legs that lives in the ground: *A bird was eating a worm.*
[ORIGIN: From the old English word *wyrm*, which means "snake or worm."]

**worn¹** /wɔrn/ *verb*
the past participle of WEAR

**worn²** *adjective*
something that is worn has been used a lot and looks old or damaged: *That jacket looks old and worn now.*

**ˌworn ˈout** (*also* **worn-out**) *adjective*
1 very tired: *At the end of the day, I was worn out.* SYNONYM: **exhausted**
2 something that is worn out is old and does not look good any more: *Throw that old sweater away – it's worn out.*

**wor·ried** /ˈwɚid/ *adjective*
unhappy or anxious because you think something bad might happen: *His mother's sick, and he's worried about her.* | *I was worried that you'd had an accident.* → see picture on page **A23**

**THESAURUS: worried**

**anxious** very worried and unable to relax: *She was anxious about her children because they were having problems at school.*

**concerned** worried about a problem, or about someone's health or safety: *Many scientists are concerned about global warming.*

**nervous** worried or frightened about something, so that you cannot relax: *I get really nervous before speaking in front of a group of people.*

**uneasy** worried because you think something bad might happen: *Lois felt uneasy leaving the kids alone, even though Gary was 15 and Hannah was 13.*

**stressed (out)** worried and unable to relax because you have too much work, or have to deal with a difficult problem: *He is getting stressed out about taking the SATs.*

**wor·ry¹** /ˈwɚi/ *verb* (**worried**, **worries**)
to feel unhappy or anxious because you think something bad might happen: *She's always worrying about getting fat.* | *I'm worried that I might fail my tests.*
—**worrying** (*also* **worrisome**) *adjective* making you worry: *Carl's strange behavior was worrying.*
—**worrier** *noun* someone who worries a lot
[ORIGIN: From the old English word *wyrgan*, which means "to strangle."]

**worry²** *noun* (plural **worries**)
1 the feeling of being anxious about something: *Where have you been? I've been sick with worry.*
2 a problem that makes you feel unhappy or anxious: *Just relax for a while and try to forget your worries.*

W

**worse¹** /wɚs/ *adjective*
**1** not as good as something else: *My handwriting is bad, but yours is worse!* **ANTONYM: better**
**2** more unpleasant or severe: *During the night, the storm got worse.* **ANTONYM: better**
**3** sicker than before: *If you're feeling worse, go see the doctor.* **ANTONYM: better**

**worse²** *adverb*
less well or more severely: *They can't play worse than they did last week – they were terrible!* **ANTONYM: better**

**worse³** *noun*
something worse: *The situation was bad, but worse was to come.*

**wors·en** /ˈwɚsən/ *verb (formal)*
to become worse: *The pain worsened, and we called the doctor.*

**ˌworse ˈoff** *adjective*
poorer, or in a worse situation: *Our family was poor, but there were people worse off than us.*

**wor·ship** /ˈwɚʃɪp/ *verb* (**worshiped** *or* **worshipped**, **worshiping** *or* **worshipping**)
to show respect to God or a god by praying or singing: *People come to church to worship God.*
—**worship** *noun* the act of worshiping God or a god: *Praying is an act of worship.*
—**worshiper** (*also* **worshipper**) *noun* someone who worships God or a god
[**ORIGIN:** From the old English word *weorthscipe*, which means "the state of deserving respect or honor."]

W

**worst¹** /wɚst/ *adjective*
worse than all the others, or worse than at any other time: *This is the worst book I've ever read.* | *The traffic is worst in the morning.* **ANTONYM: best**

**worst²** *adverb*
worse than anyone or anything else: *In the areas worst affected by the storm, many homes have been damaged.*

**worst³** *noun*
**1** the one that is worse than all the others: *My painting was the worst and I was embarrassed to have other people see it.*
**2 at worst** = in a situation that is as bad as possible: *The trip will take two hours, or two and a half hours at worst.*

**worth¹** /wɚθ/ *preposition*
**1** if something is worth an amount, it has that value: *This painting is worth $500,000.* | *Each question is worth 4 points.*
**2** if something is worth doing, it is interesting or enjoyable: *The movie was definitely worth seeing.*

**worth²** *noun*
**1** an amount of something that has a particular value: *I bought $5 worth of apples.*
**2** something that takes a particular amount of time to do or use: *There's about a week's worth of work here.*
**3** how important or useful someone or something is: *He has proved his worth by scoring 11 goals.*

**worth·less** /ˈwɚθlɪs/ *adjective*
having no value: *These coins are worthless because they are not used any more.*

**worth·while** /ˌwɚθˈwaɪl/ *adjective*
if something is worthwhile, it is important or useful and deserves the time, effort, or money you give to it: *I think being a nurse is a worthwhile job.*

**wor·thy** /ˈwɚði/ *adjective (formal)*
**1** deserving people's respect or support: *The money is for a worthy cause – it will help victims of the earthquake.*
**2** good enough to deserve something: *The album contains several songs that are worthy of attention.*

**would** /wəd, əd; *strong* wʊd/ *verb*
**1** used instead of "will" when saying what someone said or thought in the past: *She told me she wouldn't come.* | *I didn't think she would marry him.*
**2** used when talking about something that could happen but is unlikely: *If I won the lottery, I would spend the money on a huge house.*
**3 would have** = if something would have happened, it might have happened, but it did not happen: *Dad would have loved this place if he'd still been alive.*
**4 would not/wouldn't** = used when saying that someone refused to do something: *He would not answer my question.*
**5 Would you ...? = a)** used when politely

asking someone to do something: *Would you open the door please?* **b)** used when offering someone something politely: *Would you like something to drink?*
**6** used for saying that something happened regularly in the past: *When I was a little kid, we would visit my grandmother every summer.* **SYNONYM: used to**

**would·n't** /ˈwʊdnt/ *verb*
the short form of "would not": *She wouldn't help me, even though I asked several times.*

**would've** /ˈwʊdəv/ *verb*
the short form of "would have": *You would've enjoyed the movie if you had seen it.*

**wound[1]** /wund/ *noun*
a deep cut made in your skin by something such as a knife or a bullet: *He had a knife wound in his side.*
→ see Thesaurus box at **injury**

**wound[2]** *verb*
**1** to injure someone, especially with a knife or gun: *Several people were wounded in the attack.*
**2** to make someone feel unhappy or upset: *His cruel remarks wounded her.*
—**wounded** *adjective* injured by a weapon: *The wounded soldiers were cared for in the hospital.*
→ see Thesaurus box at **hurt[1]**

**wound[3]** /waʊnd/ *verb*
the past tense and past participle of WIND

**wove** /woʊv/ *verb*
the past tense of WEAVE

**wo·ven** /ˈwoʊvən/ *verb*
the past participle of WEAVE

**wow** /waʊ/ *interjection* (*informal*)
said when you think something is impressive or surprising: *Wow, what a beautiful house!*

**wrap[1]** /ræp/ *verb* (**wrapped**, **wrapping**)
**1** to cover a present with attractive paper: *I haven't wrapped her birthday present yet.*
**2** to put a piece of cloth or paper around something: *She wrapped the baby in a blanket.*
**3 wrap your arms around someone** = to put your arms around someone: *She wrapped her arms around him and squeezed tight.*
—**wrapping** *noun* paper or cloth that is put around something

**wrap[2]** *noun*
**1** thin clear plastic that you put around food to keep it clean: *Cover the plate with plastic wrap and put it in the refrigerator.*
**2** a type of sandwich made with a TORTILLA folded around meat or cheese or other food: *I had a chicken wrap for lunch.*

**wrap·per** /ˈræpɚ/ *noun*
the paper or plastic that covers something you buy: *a candy wrapper*
→ see Thesaurus box at **cover[2]**

**ˈwrapping ˌpaper** *noun*
colored paper that you use to wrap presents: *a roll of wrapping paper*

**wrath** /ræθ/ *noun* (*formal*)
very great anger: *They all hoped to avoid the king's wrath.*
—**wrathful** *adjective* (*formal*) very angry

**wreath**

**wreath** /riθ/ *noun*
a circle of leaves or flowers that you use as a decoration: *They put a wreath on their front door around Christmas.*

**wreck[1]** /rek/ *verb*
to destroy something completely: *The truck was wrecked in the accident.* | *His constant lying wrecked his marriage.*

**wreck[2]** *noun*
**1** a bad accident involving cars or airplanes: *He was killed in a car wreck.* **SYNONYM: crash**
**2** a car, airplane, or ship that has been very badly damaged in an accident: *He was still alive when they pulled him from the wreck.*

**wreck·age** /ˈrekɪdʒ/ *noun*
the broken parts of a vehicle or building that has been destroyed: *After the train crash, several people were trapped in the wreckage.*

**wren** /ren/ *noun*
a very small brown bird

**wrench**[1] /rentʃ/ *verb*
**1** to twist and pull something from somewhere, using force: *Tom wrenched the nail out of the wall.*
**2** to injure a part of your body by twisting it suddenly: *He wrenched his neck when he turned his head suddenly.*

**wrench**[2] *noun*
a metal tool that you use for turning metal parts and making them tighter: *The plumber used a wrench to fix the faucet.*

**wres·tle** /ˈresəl/ *verb*
**1** to fight by holding someone and trying to push him or her to the ground: *The two men wrestled with each other, until Jim forced Mike to the ground.*
**2** to try to solve a very difficult problem or make a very difficult decision: *The school has been wrestling with the problem of bullying for some time.*
—**wrestling** *noun* a sport in which two people wrestle
—**wrestler** *noun* someone who wrestles as a sport

**wretch·ed** /ˈretʃɪd/ *adjective*
**1** very unhappy or in a very bad situation: *These wretched people have lost their homes in the floods.*
**2** (*informal*) very bad: *wretched weather*
[**ORIGIN:** 1100-1200 From the old English word *wrecca*, which means "person who has been made to leave his or her country or community."]

**wrig·gle** /ˈrɪgəl/ *verb*
to twist quickly from side to side: *She wriggled into the tight dress.*

**wring** /rɪŋ/ (*also* **wring out**) *verb* (**wrung** /rʌŋ/)
to twist wet cloth to remove water from it: *Wring out the cloth when you've finished washing the dishes.*

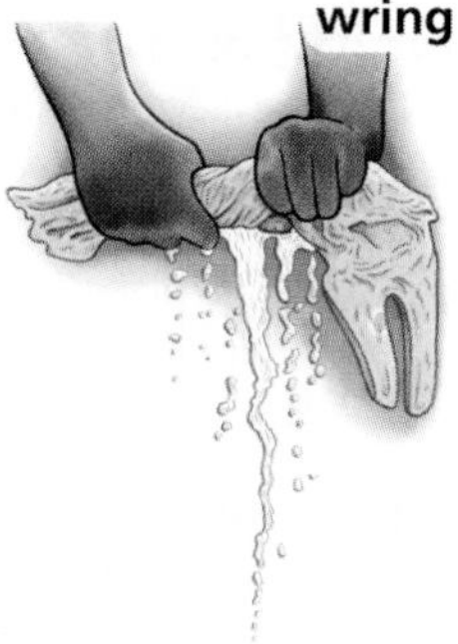


**wrin·kle** /ˈrɪŋkəl/ *noun*
**1** a line on your face that you get when you are old: *The old woman's face was covered with wrinkles.*
**2** a fold in a piece of clothing, that you do not want: *You'll have to iron the shirt to get rid of the wrinkles.*
—**wrinkled** *adjective* covered with wrinkles: *My clothes were wrinkled when I took them out of my suitcase.*

**wrist** /rɪst/ *noun*
the joint between your hand and your arm: *She had a bracelet on her wrist.* → see picture at **hand**

**wrist·watch** /ˈrɪst-wɑtʃ/ *noun*
a watch that you wear on your wrist

**write** /raɪt/ *verb* (**wrote** /roʊt/, **written** /ˈrɪtn/)
**1** to make letters or words on paper, using a pen or pencil: *They teach the children to read and write.* | *Please write your name on this piece of paper.*
**2** to produce a letter to send to someone: *You should write to Aunt Amy to thank her for the present.* | *He wrote me a letter.*
**3** to produce a story, book, song, etc.: *He has written several books about animals.*
[**ORIGIN:** From the old English word *writan*, which means "to scratch pictures or symbols on something, or to draw or write."]
**PHRASAL VERB**
**write something down**
to write something on a piece of paper: *I wrote down her phone number so I wouldn't forget it.*

**writ·er** /ˈraɪtɚ/ *noun*
someone who writes books: *She's a writer of children's books.*

**writ·ing** /ˈraɪtɪŋ/ *noun*
**1** words that are written by hand or printed: *I can't read the writing on the label – it's very small.*
**2** the activity of writing stories, books, poems, etc.: *Writing is fun if you have an interesting story to tell.*
**3** the way someone writes with a pen or pencil: *I recognized Sue's writing on the envelope, so I knew the letter was from her.* **SYNONYM: handwriting**

**writ·ten** /ˈrɪtn/ *verb*
the past participle of WRITE

**wrong** /rɔŋ/ *adjective*
**1** not correct: *You're wrong – I don't live on Northwest Avenue.* | *I'm afraid that's the wrong answer.* **ANTONYM: right**

W

**THESAURUS: wrong**

**incorrect** (*formal*) completely wrong, used especially about facts or answers: *The date given in the book is incorrect – it happened in 1974, not 1977.*

**inaccurate** (*formal*) not completely correct, used especially about facts or information: *The old maps of the area are pretty inaccurate.*

**misleading** (*formal*) likely to make someone believe something that is not true: *The TV commercial is misleading. It makes you think the juice is good for you, when really it is full of sugar.*

**false** not based on true facts: *The rumor that Mrs. Hudson was leaving the school was false.*

**be mistaken** (*formal*) wrong about something, especially because you think that one person or thing is someone or something else: *You're Lisa's cousin, aren't you? Or am I mistaken?*

**2** not morally right: *Some people think it's wrong to kill animals for food.* **ANTONYM: right**

**3** not appropriate: *You're wearing the wrong shoes for an exercise class.* **ANTONYM: right**

**4** if there is something wrong with a machine or a part of your body, it is not working correctly: *There's something wrong with my computer – I can't make it do anything.*

**5** if there is something wrong, something is making you unhappy or worried: *He looked sad so I asked him what was wrong.*

[**ORIGIN:** 1100-1200 From the Norse word *rangr*, which means "not correct or not as planned." Norse was a language used in Scandinavian countries.]

**wrong·do·ing** /ˌrɔŋˈduɪŋ/ *noun* (*formal*)
illegal actions or immoral behavior: *Police are investigating whether there was any actual wrongdoing.*
—**wrongdoer** *noun* someone who does something illegal or immoral: *All wrongdoers will be punished.*

**wrong·ly** /ˈrɔŋli/ *adverb*
in a way that is incorrect, unfair, or immoral: *He was wrongly accused of stealing.*

**wrote** /roʊt/ *verb*
the past tense of WRITE

**wrung** /rʌŋ/ *verb*
the past tense and past participle of WRING

**WWW** *noun*
the abbreviation of WORLD WIDE WEB

# Xx

**X¹**
the number 10 in the system of ROMAN NUMERALs

**X²** *verb*
**PHRASAL VERB**
**X something out**
to put an X on top of something in a piece of writing: *She X'd out the misspelled word and wrote it correctly above the X.* **SYNONYM: cross something out**

**X·mas** /ˈkrɪsməs/ *noun (informal)*
an informal way of writing "Christmas": *Merry Xmas!*

**X-ray¹** /ˈeks reɪ/ *noun*

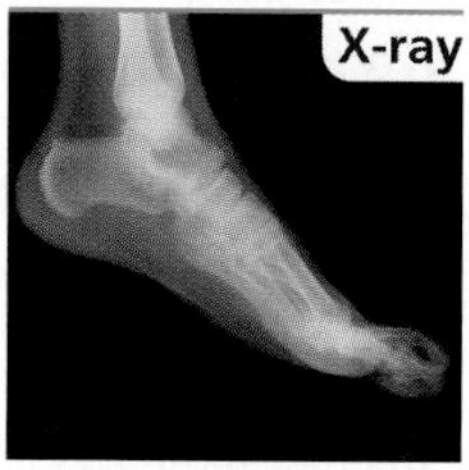


**1** a special beam of light that can go through solid objects, used for taking a photograph of the inside of someone's body: *X-rays can damage human cells.*
**2** a photograph of the inside of someone's body, taken using X-rays: *The X-ray showed that her foot was not broken.*

**X-ray²** *verb*
to photograph part of someone's body using X-rays: *The doctor X-rayed his arm to see if it was broken.*

**xy·lem** /ˈzaɪləm/ *noun*
the part of a plant stem that carries water from the roots to the rest of the plant

**xy·lo·phone** /ˈzaɪləˌfoʊn/ *noun*
a musical instrument with flat metal or wooden bars that you hit with a stick → see picture on page **A21**
[**ORIGIN:** 1800-1900 From the Greek words *xylon* and *phone*, which mean "wood" and "sound."]

# Yy

**yacht** /yɑt/ *noun*
a large expensive boat used for sailing, racing, or traveling for pleasure

**y'all** /yɔl/ *pronoun (informal)*
a word meaning "all of you," used mainly in the southern U.S.: *How are y'all doing?*

**yam** /yæm/ *noun*
another word for a SWEET POTATO

**yank** /yæŋk/ *verb*
to pull something quickly and with force: *One of the boys grabbed her hair and yanked on it.*

**Yan·kee** /ˈyæŋki/ *noun*
**1** a soldier who fought on the side of the Union (=the northern states) during the Civil War
**2** a name for someone from the U.S., used mainly by people from other countries
**3** a name for someone from the northern states of the U.S., used by people from the southern states

**yard** /yɑrd/ *noun*
**1** the land around a house, usually covered with grass: *The kids were playing in the yard.*
**2** (*written abbreviation*: **yd.**) a unit for measuring length, equal to 3 feet or 0.9144 meters: *The beach was only a hundred yards from our back door.*
[**ORIGIN:** Sense 1 is from the old English word *geard*, which means "area surrounded by a wall, fence, etc." Sense 2 is from the old English word *gierd*, which means "stick."]

**ˈyard sale** *noun*
a sale of things that you no longer want that takes place in your yard: *We had a yard sale and sold a lot of our old stuff.*

**yard·stick** /ˈyɑrdˌstɪk/ *noun*
**1** a special stick that is exactly one yard long,

which you use for measuring
**2** a standard that you judge or compare other things with: *The test scores are used as a yardstick for measuring the children's ability.*

**yarn** /yɑrn/ *noun*
thick thread that you use for KNITting: *She is knitting a scarf out of pink yarn.*

**yawn** /yɔn/ *verb*
to open your mouth wide and breathe deeply because you are tired or bored: *He was so tired that he couldn't stop yawning.*
—**yawn** *noun* an act of yawning: *"I'm going to bed," Steve said with a yawn.*

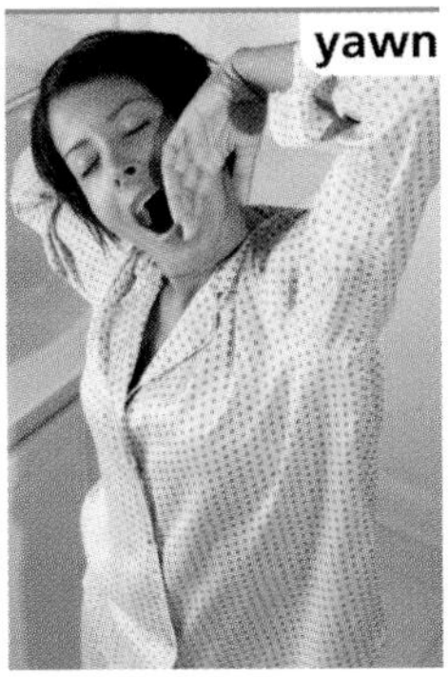


**yd.**
the written abbreviation of YARD

**yeah** /yæ/ *adverb (informal)*
yes: *"Do you want to come with us?" "Yeah, OK."*

**year** /yɪr/ *noun*
**1** a period of 12 months or 365 days: *I have lived here for two years.*
**2** a period from January 1 to December 31: *"What year were you born?" "1985."*
**3** used for talking about someone's age: *I am 12 years old.*
**4 years** = a very long time: *We've been friends for years.* **SYNONYM: ages**

**year·book** /ˈyɪrbʊk/ *noun*
a book that a school produces every year with information about its students and activities: *I showed her my photograph in my high school yearbook.*

**year·ly** /ˈyirli/ *adjective, adverb*
every year: *Every athlete should have a yearly physical.* | *How much do you spend yearly on clothes?*

**ˈyear-round** *adjective, adverb*
continuing through the whole year: *The good weather here allows visitors to play golf year-round.* | *year-round school*

**yeast** /yist/ *noun*
a substance used when making bread. Yeast makes the bread rise and get bigger.

**yell** /yel/ *verb*
to shout something very loudly: *"Come back!" he yelled.* | *Dad sometimes yells at me.*
—**yell** *noun* a loud shout: *He gave a yell when his team scored.*
→ see Thesaurus box at **shout**[1]

**yel·low** /ˈyeloʊ/ *adjective, noun*
the color of a LEMON or a BANANA: *Those yellow flowers are daffodils.* | *Yellow is my favorite color.*

**yes** /yes/ *adverb*
**1** used to say that something is true: *"Are you Ann?" "Yes, I am."* **ANTONYM: no**
**2** used to accept an offer or invitation: *"Would you like some more soup?" "Yes, please."* **ANTONYM: no**
**3** used to say that someone can have or do something: *"Can I have a glass of water, please?" "Yes, of course."* **ANTONYM: no**
**4** used to agree with something: *"This is fun!" "Yes, it is."* **ANTONYM: no**
**5** used to say that the opposite of what someone says is true: *"There isn't any bread left." "Yes, there is. It's on the table."*
**6** said to show that you are excited about something that has happened: *Yes! We won!*

**yes·ter·day** /ˈyestədi/ *adverb, noun*
the day before today: *I went swimming yesterday.*
[**ORIGIN:** From the old English words *giestran* and *dæg*, which mean "yesterday" and "day."]

**yet**[1] /yet/ *adverb*
**1** used to ask about something that you expect to happen or to say that it has not happened: *Have you eaten yet?* | *I don't think she's awake yet; she's still in her bedroom.*

**USAGE: yet, still, always**

**Yet** is used when asking about something that is expected to happen or saying that it has not happened: *Is Mark back from school yet?* | *I haven't finished the book yet.*

**Still** is used to say that a situation that began in the past has not changed and is continuing: *He still plays basketball twice a week.*

**Always** means "every time" or "at all times": *I always see him on Tuesdays.* | *She is always happy.*

**2** in addition to what has already happened: *Bob made yet another mistake – he needs to be more careful.* | *You were late yet again this morning – that's the fourth time this week.*
**3 the best/biggest/most important, etc. yet** = the best, biggest, most important, etc. that has existed up to the present time: *This is his best movie yet.*
**4** (*formal*) used for saying that something could still happen: *The party is not until the weekend, so I may yet get an invitation.*

**yet**[2] *conjunction*
used when what you say next is surprising: *Tanner was a criminal, yet many people admired him.* **SYNONYM: but**

**yield**[1] /yild/ *verb*
**1** (*formal*) to do what someone wants, although you do not want to: *He yielded to pressure from his family to return home.*
**2** (*formal*) to produce something: *Our research has yielded some interesting results.*
**3** to allow cars from another road to go first: *If other cars are coming, you have to yield.*

**yield**[2] *noun* (*formal*)
the amount that something produces: *Scientists are trying to find out how to produce higher yields from crops.*



**yo·ga** /ˈyoʊgə/ *noun*
a set of exercises that relax your mind, keep your muscles strong, and help you to bend your body easily: *She does yoga to stretch her muscles.*
**[ORIGIN:** 1700-1800 From the Sanskrit word for "joining together." Sanskrit was used in India.**]**

**yo·gurt** /ˈyoʊgɚt/ *noun*
a thick liquid food that is made from milk and has a slightly sour taste, and that often has sugar and fruit added to it: *strawberry yogurt*
**[ORIGIN:** 1600-1700 From Turkish.**]**

**yoke** /yoʊk/ *noun*
a wooden bar used for keeping two animals together when they are pulling heavy loads
—**yoke** *verb* to put a yoke on two animals

**yolk** /yoʊk/ *noun*
the yellow part of an egg: *He dipped his toast in the egg yolk.*
**[ORIGIN:** From the old English word *geoloca*, from *geolu*, which means "yellow."**]**

**you** /yə; before vowels yʊ; strong yu/ *pronoun*
**1** the person or people someone is talking to: *Would you like some coffee?* | *I can't hear you.* | *What do you all want to do tonight?*
**2** people in general: *Smoking is bad for you.*

**you'd** /yəd; *strong* yud/
**1** the short form of "you would": *You'd be surprised at how much money she spends.*
**2** the short form of "you had": *If you'd been more careful, the accident would never have happened.*

**you'll** /yəl; *strong* yul/
the short form of "you will": *You'll have to fill out this form.*

**young**[1] /yʌŋ/ *adjective*
a young person or animal has only lived for a short time: *You're too young to get married.* | *a young child* | *My father is 60, but he still looks young.* **ANTONYM: old**

**young**[2] *plural noun*
**1 the young** = young people in general: *The young are often very concerned about the environment.*
**2** an animal's young are its babies: *A mouse can produce 150 young a year.*

**young·ster** /ˈyʌŋstɚ/ *noun*
a child, or a young person who is not an adult: *A lot of youngsters enjoy going to summer camp.*

**your** /yɚ; *strong* yʊr/ *adjective*
belonging to the person or people you are speaking to: *Is this your sweater?* | *I want you to turn in your essays on Friday.*

**USAGE: your, you're**

**Your** means "belonging to you": *Have you brushed your teeth?*

**You're** means "you are": *You're absolutely right.*

**you're** /yɚ; *strong* yʊr/
the short form of "you are": *You're taller than I am.*

**yours** /yɔrz/ *pronoun*
something belonging or relating to you: *Is this bicycle yours? | A friend of yours called this morning.*

**your·self** /yɚˈself/ *pronoun* (plural **yourselves** /yɚˈselvz/)
**1** used to show that the person you are talking to is affected by his or her own action: *Be careful, or you'll hurt yourself. | Make yourself a sandwich.*
**2** used to emphasize "you": *He admitted it – you heard him yourselves.*
**3 by yourself** = alone or without help: *Don't try to lift that box by yourself.*

**youth** /yuθ/ *noun* (plural **youths** /yuðz, yuθs/)
**1** the time when you are young: *In her youth, she played a lot of tennis, but she does not play much now.*
**2** a boy or young man: *A police officer arrested two youths for damaging cars.*
**3 the youth** = young people: *The youth of today have grown up with computers.*

**youth·ful** /ˈyuθfəl/ *adjective*
typical of young people: *The students were full of youthful energy.*

**you've** /yəv; *strong* yuv/
the short form of "you have": *You've eaten all the cake!*

**yo-yo** /ˈyoʊyoʊ/ *noun*
a toy made of two round parts that go up and down on a string that you hold and move

**yuck·y** /ˈyʌki/ *adjective* (*informal*)
very unpleasant: *This juice tastes yucky – I'm not going to drink it.*

**yum·my** /ˈyʌmi/ *adjective* (*informal*)
tasting very good: *These cookies are yummy – can I have another one?*

**yup·pie** /ˈyʌpi/ *noun* (*informal*)
a young person who earns a lot of money and buys expensive things

# Zz

**zeal** /zil/ *noun* (*formal*)
a feeling of being very eager to do something, or great effort with which you do something: *He approached his work with great zeal.*
—**zealous** /ˈzeləs/ *adjective* full of zeal: *She was zealous in doing her job, showing up early and staying late.*

**ze·bra** /ˈzibrə/ *noun*
a wild African animal like a horse, with black and white lines on its body
[**ORIGIN:** 1600-1700 From the Italian word for "wild donkey."]

**ze·ro¹** /ˈzɪroʊ/ *number* (plural **zeros** *or* **zeroes**)
**1** the number 0
**2** 0° in the FAHRENHEIT or CELSIUS systems of measuring temperature: *It was 5° below zero last night.*
**3** the lowest possible amount or level of something: *It's very safe – the risk is almost zero.*

**zero²** *verb*
**PHRASAL VERB**
**zero in on someone or something**
to direct all your attention toward one person or thing: *The teacher looked around the room, and zeroed in on me.*

**zig·zag** /ˈzɪgzæg/ *noun*
a pattern that looks like a line of Zs or Vs joined together: *The road went in a zigzag up the mountain.*

**zil·lion** /ˈzɪlyən/ *number* (*informal*)
an extremely large number: *I've heard that song a zillion times, but I still love it. | There were zillions of mosquitoes in the woods.*

**zinc** /zɪŋk/ *noun*
a white metal that has many uses

**zip** /zɪp/ *verb* (**zipped**, **zipping**)
**1** (*also* **zip up**) to close or fasten something with a ZIPPER: *Zip up your coat; it's cold outside.* **ANTONYM: unzip**
**2** to go somewhere very quickly: *Two police cars zipped past.*
→ see Thesaurus box at **fasten**

**ˈzip code** *noun*
a number that you put below the address on an envelope, which shows the exact area to deliver it to

**zip·per** /ˈzɪpɚ/ *noun*
something you use for fastening clothes or bags, that has two lines of metal or plastic that fit together: *The zipper on my coat is broken, so I can't fasten it.*

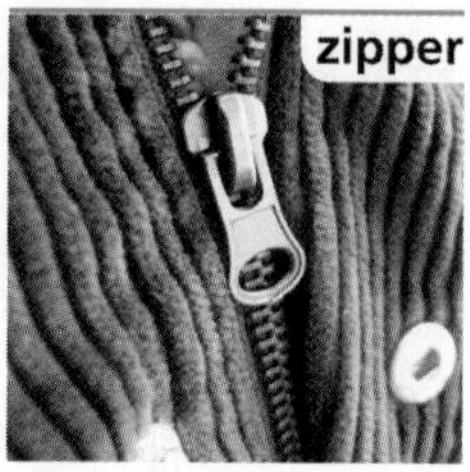


**zit** /zɪt/ *noun* (*informal*)
another word for a PIMPLE: *She says that if she eats chocolate, she gets more zits.*
→ see Thesaurus box at **mark²**

**zo·di·ac** /ˈzoʊdiˌæk/ *noun*
**the zodiac** = a circle of 12 areas in the sky through which the Sun, Moon, and PLANETs appear to travel. Each area has a sign, and some people believe that the sign you were born under affects your personality: *Libra is one of the signs of the zodiac.*

**zom·bie** /ˈzɑmbi/ *noun*
in stories, a dead body that walks around by magic
[**ORIGIN:** 1800-1900 From the Kimbundu word *nzumbi*, which means "spirit of a dead person, or god." Kimbundu is a language used in Angola, in southwest Africa.]

**zone** /zoʊn/ *noun*
an area where a particular thing happens or where there are special rules: *You can't park there – it's a no-parking zone.*
→ see Thesaurus box at **area**

**zoo** /zu/ *noun*
a place where many different animals are kept, so that people can go and see them: *We saw elephants and monkeys at the zoo.*
[**ORIGIN:** From the phrase "zoological garden." The word "zoological" comes from "zoology," from the Greek words *zoion* and *-logia*, which mean "animal" and "study." ]

**zo·ol·o·gy** /zoʊˈɑlədʒi/ *noun*
the study of animals and their behavior

**zoom** /zum/ *verb*
**1** (*informal*) to go somewhere very quickly: *He zoomed down the hill on his bike.*
**2** if a camera zooms in or out, it makes the thing you are taking a picture of seem larger or smaller: *He zoomed in on the deer on the other side of the river.*
—**zoom** (*also* **zoom lens**) *noun* a part of a camera that makes things that are far away look like they are closer

**zuc·chi·ni** /zuˈkini/ *noun*
a long smooth green vegetable

Z

## Irregular Verbs

This chart shows the verbs that have irregular forms for the Past Tense, Past Participle, or Present Participle. When a verb has more than one form that is used, the most common form is given first.

| Verb | Past Tense | Past Participle | Present Participle |
|---|---|---|---|
| **arise** | arose | arisen | arising |
| **awake** | awoke | awoken | awaking |
| **be** | was/were | been | being |
| **bear** | bore | borne | bearing |
| **beat** | beat | beaten | beating |
| **become** | became | become | becoming |
| **begin** | began | begun | beginning |
| **bend** | bent | bent | bending |
| **bet** | bet | bet | betting |
| **bid** | bid | bid | bidding |
| **bind** | bound | bound | binding |
| **bite** | bit | bitten | biting |
| **bleed** | bled | bled | bleeding |
| **blow** | blew | blown | blowing |
| **break** | broke | broken | breaking |
| **breed** | bred | bred | breeding |
| **bring** | brought | brought | bringing |
| **broadcast** | broadcast *or* broadcasted | broadcast *or* broadcasted | broadcasting |
| **build** | built | built | building |
| **burn** | burned *or* burnt | burned *or* burnt | burning |
| **burst** | burst | burst | bursting |
| **buy** | bought | bought | buying |
| **cast** | cast | cast | casting |
| **catch** | caught | caught | catching |
| **choose** | chose | chosen | choosing |
| **cling** | clung | clung | clinging |
| **come** | came | come | coming |
| **cost** | cost | cost | costing |
| **creep** | crept | crept | creeping |
| **cut** | cut | cut | cutting |
| **deal** | dealt | dealt | dealing |
| **dig** | dug | dug | digging |
| **dive** | dived *or* dove | dived | diving |
| **do** | did | done | doing |
| **draw** | drew | drawn | drawing |
| **dream** | dreamed *or* dreamt | dreamed *or* dreamt | dreaming |
| **drink** | drank | drunk | drinking |
| **drive** | drove | driven | driving |
| **dwell** | dwelled *or* dwelt | dwelled *or* dwelt | dwelling |
| **eat** | ate | eaten | eating |
| **fall** | fell | fallen | falling |
| **feed** | fed | fed | feeding |
| **feel** | felt | felt | feeling |
| **fight** | fought | fought | fighting |
| **find** | found | found | finding |
| **fit** | fit *or* fitted | fit *or* fitted | fitting |
| **flee** | fled | fled | fleeing |
| **fling** | flung | flung | flinging |
| **fly** | flew | flown | flying |
| **forbid** | forbid *or* forbade | forbidden | forbidding |
| **foresee** | foresaw | foreseen | foreseeing |
| **forget** | forgot | forgotten | forgetting |
| **forgive** | forgave | forgiven | forgiving |
| **freeze** | froze | frozen | freezing |
| **get** | got | gotten | getting |
| **give** | gave | given | giving |
| **go** | went | gone | going |

| Verb | Past Tense | Past Participle | Present Participle |
|---|---|---|---|
| **grind** | ground | ground | grinding |
| **grow** | grew | grown | growing |
| **hang** | hung | hung | hanging |
| **have** | had | had | having |
| **hear** | heard | heard | hearing |
| **hide** | hid | hidden | hiding |
| **hit** | hit | hit | hitting |
| **hold** | held | held | holding |
| **hurt** | hurt | hurt | hurting |
| **keep** | kept | kept | keeping |
| **kneel** | knelt *or* kneeled | knelt *or* kneeled | kneeling |
| **knit** | knit *or* knitted | knit *or* knitted | knitting |
| **know** | knew | known | knowing |
| **lay** | laid | laid | laying |
| **lead** | led | led | leading |
| **leap** | leaped *or* leapt | leaped *or* leapt | leaping |
| **leave** | left | left | leaving |
| **lend** | lent | lent | lending |
| **let** | let | let | letting |
| **lie**[1] | lay | lain | lying |
| **lie**[2] | lied | lied | lying |
| **light** | lit *or* lighted | lit *or* lighted | lighting |
| **lose** | lost | lost | losing |
| **make** | made | made | making |
| **mean** | meant | meant | meaning |
| **meet** | met | met | meeting |
| **mislead** | misled | misled | misleading |
| **mistake** | mistook | mistaken | mistaking |
| **misunderstand** | misunderstood | misunderstood | misunderstanding |
| **mow** | mowed | mown *or* mowed | mowing |
| **outdo** | outdid | outdone | outdoing |
| **outgrow** | outgrew | outgrown | outgrowing |
| **overcome** | overcame | overcome | overcoming |
| **overdo** | overdid | overdone | overdoing |
| **overhear** | overheard | overheard | overhearing |
| **oversleep** | overslept | overslept | oversleeping |
| **overthrow** | overthrew | overthrown | overthrowing |
| **pay** | paid | paid | paying |
| **prove** | proved | proved *or* proven | proving |
| **put** | put | put | putting |
| **quit** | quit | quit | quitting |
| **read** | read | read | reading |
| **redo** | redid | redone | redoing |
| **repay** | repaid | repaid | repaying |
| **rewind** | rewound | rewound | rewinding |
| **rewrite** | rewrote | rewritten | rewriting |
| **ride** | rode | ridden | riding |
| **ring** | rang | rung | ringing |
| **rise** | rose | risen | rising |
| **run** | ran | run | running |
| **saw** | sawed | sawed *or* sawn | sawing |
| **say** | said | said | saying |
| **see** | saw | seen | seeing |
| **seek** | sought | sought | seeking |
| **sell** | sold | sold | selling |
| **send** | sent | sent | sending |
| **set** | set | set | setting |
| **sew** | sewed | sewn *or* sewed | sewing |
| **shake** | shook | shaken | shaking |
| **shed** | shed | shed | shedding |
| **shine** | shone | shone | shining |
| **shoot** | shot | shot | shooting |
| **show** | showed | shown | showing |

| Verb | Past Tense | Past Participle | Present Participle |
|---|---|---|---|
| **shrink** | shrank | shrunk | shrinking |
| **shut** | shut | shut | shutting |
| **sing** | sang | sung | singing |
| **sink** | sank *or* sunk | sunk | sinking |
| **sit** | sat | sat | sitting |
| **sleep** | slept | slept | sleeping |
| **slide** | slid | slid | sliding |
| **slit** | slit | slit | slitting |
| **sneak** | sneaked *or* snuck | sneaked *or* snuck | sneaking |
| **sow** | sowed | sown *or* sowed | sowing |
| **speak** | spoke | spoken | speaking |
| **speed** | sped *or* speeded | sped *or* speeded | speeding |
| **spend** | spent | spent | spending |
| **spin** | spun | spun | spinning |
| **spit** | spit *or* spat | spit *or* spat | spitting |
| **split** | split | split | splitting |
| **spread** | spread | spread | spreading |
| **spring** | sprang | sprung | springing |
| **stand** | stood | stood | standing |
| **steal** | stole | stolen | stealing |
| **stick** | stuck | stuck | sticking |
| **sting** | stung | stung | stinging |
| **stink** | stank *or* stunk | stunk | stinking |
| **stride** | strode | stridden | striding |
| **strike** | struck | struck *or* stricken | striking |
| **string** | strung | strung | stringing |
| **strive** | strove *or* strived | striven *or* strived | striving |
| **swear** | swore | sworn | swearing |
| **sweep** | swept | swept | sweeping |
| **swell** | swelled | swollen | swelling |
| **swim** | swam | swum | swimming |
| **swing** | swung | swung | swinging |
| **take** | took | taken | taking |
| **teach** | taught | taught | teaching |
| **tear** | tore | torn | tearing |
| **tell** | told | told | telling |
| **think** | thought | thought | thinking |
| **throw** | threw | thrown | throwing |
| **thrust** | thrust | thrust | thrusting |
| **undergo** | underwent | undergone | undergoing |
| **understand** | understood | understood | understanding |
| **undo** | undid | undone | undoing |
| **unwind** | unwound | unwound | unwinding |
| **uphold** | upheld | upheld | upholding |
| **upset** | upset | upset | upsetting |
| **wake** | woke | woken | waking |
| **wear** | wore | worn | wearing |
| **weave** | wove | woven | weaving |
| **weep** | wept | wept | weeping |
| **wet** | wet *or* wetted | wet *or* wetted | wetting |
| **win** | won | won | winning |
| **wind** | wound | wound | winding |
| **withdraw** | withdrew | withdrawn | withdrawing |
| **withhold** | withheld | withheld | withholding |
| **withstand** | withstood | withstood | withstanding |
| **wring** | wrung | wrung | wringing |
| **write** | wrote | written | writing |

# Content Vocabulary

## 1 Art

abstract, *adjective*
architecture, *noun*
art, *noun*
artist, *noun*
artistic, *adjective*
background, *noun*
ceramic, *adjective*
ceramics, *plural noun*
chalk, *noun*
composition, *noun*
craft, *noun*
crayon, *noun*
creative, *adjective*
creatively, *adverb*
creativity, *noun*
criticism, *noun*
design, *noun*
design, *verb*
designer, *noun*
draw, *verb*
drawing, *noun*
easel, *noun*
exhibit, *noun*
exhibit, *verb*
exhibitor, *noun*
genre, *noun*
graphic, *adjective*
graphically, *adverb*
illustrate, *verb*
illustration, *noun*
illustrator, *noun*
imagery, *noun*
landscape, *noun*
nude, *noun*
paint, *noun*
paint, *verb*
painter, *noun*
painting, *noun*
passage, *noun*
pastel, *adjective*
pastel, *noun*
pattern, *noun*
photograph, *noun*
photograph, *verb*
photographic, *adjective*
photography, *noun*
picture, *noun*
picture, *verb*
piece, *noun*
portfolio, *noun*
portrait, *noun*
pose, *noun*
pose, *verb*
potter, *noun*
pottery, *noun*
primary color, *noun*
print, *noun*
produce, *verb*
profile, *noun*
realistic, *adjective*
realistically, *adverb*
reproduction, *noun*
rough draft, *noun*
sculpt, *verb*
sculptor, *noun*
sculpture, *noun*
shade, *noun*
show, *noun*
sketch, *noun*
sketch, *verb*
statue, *noun*
stencil, *noun*
stencil, *verb*
storyboard, *noun*
stroke, *noun*
studio, *noun*
symbol, *noun*
symbolism, *noun*
symbolize, *verb*
tapestry, *noun*
title, *noun*
watercolor, *noun*
weave, *verb*
weaver, *noun*
weaving, *noun*
work, *noun*

## 2 Biology

abdomen, *noun*
abdominal, *adjective*
acute, *adjective*
adaptation, *noun*
adult, *noun*
adulthood, *noun*
AIDS, *noun*
allergic, *adjective*
allergy, *noun*
amoeba, *noun*
amphibian, *noun*
anatomical, *adjective*
anatomy, *noun*
anemia, *noun*
anemic, *adjective*
anesthesia, *noun*
anesthetic, *noun*
animal, *noun*
antenna, *noun*
antibiotic, *noun*
antihistamine, *noun*
appendicitis, *noun*
appendix, *noun*
artery, *noun*
arthritis, *noun*
aspirin, *noun*
asthma, *noun*
asthmatic, *adjective*
backbone, *noun*
bacteria, *plural noun*
beak, *noun*
biological, *adjective*
biologist, *noun*
biology, *noun*
biome, *noun*
bird, *noun*
birth, *noun*
bladder, *noun*
bleed, *verb*
blind, *adjective*
blindness, *noun*
blood, *noun*
blood pressure, *noun*
bloodstream, *noun*
blood vessel, *noun*
body, *noun*
bone, *noun*
botanist, *noun*
botany, *noun*
bowel, *noun*
brain, *noun*
branch, *noun*
breast, *noun*
breathe, *verb*
breathing, *noun*
breed, *noun*
breed, *verb*
bruise, *noun*
bruise, *verb*
bruised, *adjective*
bud, *noun*
bug, *noun*
butterfly, *noun*
calorie, *noun*
cancer, *noun*
carbohydrate, *noun*
cardiovascular, *adjective*
carnivore, *noun*
carnivorous, *adjective*
cat, *noun*
caterpillar, *noun*
cell, *noun*
cellular, *adjective*
cesarean, *noun*
chemotherapy, *noun*
cholesterol, *noun*
chromosome, *noun*
circulate, *verb*
circulation, *noun*
circulatory system, *noun*
citrus, *noun*
claw, *noun*
claw, *verb*
clone, *noun*
clone, *verb*
clot, *noun*
clot, *verb*
cob, *noun*
cold, *noun*
cold-blooded, *adjective*
colon, *noun*
coma, *noun*
conceive, *verb*
conception, *noun*
concussion, *noun*
condition, *noun*
cone, *noun*
conscious, *adjective*
consciousness, *noun*
conservation, *noun*
conservationist, *noun*
conserve, *verb*
constipated, *adjective*
constipation, *noun*
contagious, *adjective*
contract, *verb*
coral, *noun*
core, *noun*
cough, *noun*
cub, *noun*
curable, *adjective*
cure, *noun*
cure, *verb*
cycle, *noun*
cyclic, *adjective*
deaf, *adjective*
deafness, *noun*
death, *noun*
decay, *noun*
decay, *verb*
decompose, *verb*
decomposer, *noun*
decomposition, *noun*
dehydrated, *adjective*
dehydration, *noun*
den, *noun*
dental, *adjective*
develop, *verb*
development, *noun*
diabetes, *noun*
diabetic, *adjective*
diabetic, *noun*
diagnose, *verb*
diagnosis, *noun*
diarrhea, *noun*

diet, *noun*
diet, *verb*
dietician, *noun*
digest, *verb*
digestible, *adjective*
digestion, *noun*
digestive, *adjective*
disease, *noun*
DNA, *noun*
drug, *noun*
duct, *noun*
eardrum, *noun*
ecosystem, *noun*
egg, *noun*
embryo, *noun*
endangered species, *noun*
enzyme, *noun*
epidemic, *noun*
epilepsy, *noun*
epileptic, *adjective*
epileptic, *noun*
esophagus, *noun*
evergreen, *adjective*
evergreen, *noun*
evolution, *noun*
evolutionary, *adjective*
excrete, *verb*
exhale, *verb*
extinct, *adjective*
extinction, *noun*
eyesight, *noun*
farsighted, *adjective*
fat, *noun*
feces, *plural noun*
feline, *adjective*
female, *adjective*
female, *noun*
fertilize, *verb*
fetus, *noun*
fever, *noun*
feverish, *adjective*
fiber, *noun*
fin, *noun*
fir, *noun*
fish, *noun*
flipper, *noun*
flower, *noun*
flower, *verb*
flu, *noun*
fly, *noun*
foliage, *noun*
food chain, *noun*
food web, *noun*
fossil, *noun*
fracture, *noun*
fracture, *verb*
fruit, *noun*
fungal, *adjective*
fungus, *noun*
fur, *noun*
gender, *noun*
gene, *noun*
genetic, *adjective*
genetically, *adverb*
genetics, *noun*
germ, *noun*
gill, *noun*
gland, *noun*
grass, *noun*
grow, *verb*
gynecological, *adjective*
gynecologist, *noun*
gynecology, *noun*
habitat, *noun*
hatch, *verb*
heal, *verb*
health, *noun*
healthy, *adjective*
hear, *verb*
hearing, *noun*
heart, *noun*
heart attack, *noun*
heartbeat, *noun*
hepatitis, *noun*
herb, *noun*
herbivore, *noun*
herd, *noun*
heterosexual, *adjective*
hibernate, *verb*
hibernation, *noun*
HIV, *noun*
hormone, *noun*
horn, *noun*
human, *adjective*
human being, *noun*
hybrid, *noun*
hygiene, *noun*
hygienic, *adjective*
illness, *noun*
immune, *adjective*
immune system, *noun*
immunity, *noun*
immunization, *noun*
immunize, *verb*
indigestion, *noun*
inedible, *adjective*
infect, *verb*
infected, *adjective*
infection, *noun*
infectious, *adjective*
inflamed, *verb*
inflammation, *noun*
inhale, *verb*
inherit, *verb*
inheritance, *noun*
inject, *verb*
injection, *noun*
injure, *verb*
injured, *adjective*
injury, *noun*
inner, *adjective*
inoculate, *verb*
inoculation, *noun*
insect, *noun*
insomnia, *noun*
insomniac, *noun*
instinct, *noun*
instinctive, *adjective*
instinctively, *adverb*
insulin, *noun*
intelligence, *noun*
intelligent, *adjective*
intelligently, *adverb*
internal, *adjective*
internally, *adverb*
intestinal, *adjective*
intestine, *noun*
invertebrate, *noun*
involuntarily, *adverb*
involuntary, *adjective*
iron, *noun*
jaw, *noun*
joint, *noun*
kidney, *noun*
larva, *noun*
leaf, *noun*
leukemia, *noun*
life, *noun*
life cycle, *noun*
limb, *noun*
liver, *noun*
lung, *noun*
malaria, *noun*
male, *adjective*
male, *noun*
malnutrition, *noun*
mammal, *noun*
marine, *adjective*
mate, *noun*
mate, *verb*
mature, *adjective*
mature, *verb*
maturity, *noun*
measles, *noun*
medical, *adjective*
medically, *adverb*
medication, *noun*
medicinal, *adjective*
medicine, *noun*
memory, *noun*
menopause, *noun*
menstrual, *adjective*
menstruate, *verb*
menstruation, *noun*
mental, *adjective*
mental illness, *noun*
mentally, *adverb*
mentally ill, *adjective*
metamorphosis, *noun*
microbe, *noun*
microorganism, *noun*
migraine, *noun*
migrate, *verb*
migration, *noun*
migratory, *adjective*
molar, *noun*
mold, *noun*
moldy, *adjective*
molecular, *adjective*
molecule, *noun*
molt, *verb*
multicellular organism, *noun*
nasal, *adjective*
nature, *noun*
nausea, *noun*
nearsighted, *adjective*
nerve, *noun*
nervous, *adjective*
nervously, *adverb*
nervousness, *noun*
nostril, *noun*
nourish, *verb*
nourishing, *adjective*
nourishment, *noun*
nucleus, *noun*
nut, *noun*
nutrient, *noun*
nutrition, *noun*
nutritional, *adjective*
nutritionist, *noun*
nutritious, *adjective*
obese, *adjective*
obesity, *noun*
offspring, *noun*
omnivore, *noun*
operate, *verb*
operation, *noun*
oral, *adjective*
orally, *adverb*
organ, *noun*
organic, *adjective*
organically, *adverb*
organism, *noun*
ovary, *noun*
pack, *noun*
pain, *noun*
palate, *noun*
paralysis, *noun*
paralyze, *verb*
paralyzed, *adjective*
parasite, *noun*
pass, *verb*
passage, *noun*
pelvic, *adjective*
pelvis, *noun*
penicillin, *noun*
period, *noun*
perspiration, *noun*
perspire, *verb*
petal, *noun*
pharmaceutical, *adjective*
pharmaceutical, *noun*
phloem, *noun*
photosynthesis, *noun*
physical, *adjective*
physically, *adverb*
physiology, *noun*

physique, *noun*
plague, *noun*
plankton, *noun*
plant, *noun*
plaque, *noun*
plastic surgery, *noun*
pneumonia, *noun*
pod, *noun*
polio, *noun*
pollen, *noun*
pollinate, *verb*
pollination, *noun*
pouch, *noun*
predator, *noun*
pregnancy, *noun*
pregnant, *adjective*
prey, *noun*
protein, *noun*
protist, *noun*
psychiatrist, *noun*
psychiatry, *noun*
psychological, *adjective*
psychologist, *noun*
psychology, *noun*
puberty, *noun*
pulse, *noun*
pupa, *noun*
pupil, *noun*
pus, *noun*
rash, *noun*
remedy, *noun*
reproduce, *verb*
reproduction, *noun*
reptile, *noun*
respiration, *noun*
retina, *nounv*
revival, *noun*
revive, *verb*
rib, *noun*
rib cage, *noun*
ripe, *adjective*
ripen, *verb*
rodent, *noun*
root, *noun*
rot, *verb*
rotten, *adjective*
saliva, *noun*
sap, *noun*
saturated fat, *noun*
scale, *noun*
scan, *noun*
scar, *noun*
schizophrenia, *noun*
schizophrenic, *adjective*
schizophrenic, *noun*
school, *noun*
sedative, *noun*
seed, *noun*
seizure, *noun*
sense, *noun*
sensitive, *adjective*
sensitively, *adverb*
sensitivity, *noun*
sex, *noun*
sexual, *adjective*
sexually, *adverb*
shed, *verb*
shell, *noun*
shellfish, *noun*
shoal, *noun*
shock, *noun*
shoot, *noun*
shrub, *noun*
shrubbery, *noun*
sick, *adjective*
sickness, *noun*
side effect, *noun*
sight, *noun*
skeleton, *noun*
skin, *noun*
skull, *noun*
smallpox, *noun*
smell, *noun*
snout, *noun*
species, *noun*
sperm, *noun*
spinal, *adjective*
spinal cord, *noun*
spine, *noun*
sprout, *noun*
sprout, *verb*
stalk, *noun*
starch, *noun*
starchy, *adjective*
starve, *verb*
stem, *noun*
sterile, *adjective*
stimulate, *verb*
stimulating, *adjective*
stimulation, *noun*
stimulus, *noun*
sting, *noun*
sting, *verb*
stomach, *noun*
stomachache, *noun*
stroke, *noun*
suffocate, *verb*
suffocation, *noun*
sugar, *noun*
sugary, *adjective*
surgery, *noun*
survival, *noun*
sweat, *noun*
sweat, *verb*
sweaty, *adjective*
symptom, *noun*
tadpole, *noun*
tail, *noun*
tame, *adjective*
taste, *noun*
temperature, *noun*
tentacle, *noun*
test, *noun*
test, *verb*
therapist, *noun*
therapy, *noun*
throat, *noun*
thyroid, *noun*
tissue, *noun*
tongue, *noun*
tooth, *noun*
toothache, *noun*
touch, *noun*
tranquilize, *verb*
tranquilizer, *noun*
transplant, *noun*
transplant, *verb*
transplantation, *noun*
treat, *verb*
treatment, *noun*
tree, *noun*
trunk, *noun*
tuberculosis, *noun*
tumor, *noun*
tusk, *noun*
twin, *noun*
typhoid, *noun*
unborn, *adjective*
unconscious, *adjective*
unconsciousness, *noun*
undernourished, *adjective*
unhealthy, *adjective*
vaccinate, *verb*
vaccination, *noun*
vaccine, *noun*
vacuole, *noun*
vein, *noun*
vertebra, *noun*
vessel, *noun*
viral, *adjective*
virus, *noun*
vitamin, *noun*
voice box, *noun*
warm-blooded, *adjective*
wild, *adjective*
wild, *noun*
wildflower, *noun*
wildlife, *noun*
wing, *noun*
wisdom tooth, *noun*
world, *noun*
wound, *noun*
wound, *verb*
wounded, *adjective*
X-ray, *noun*
X-ray, *verb*
xylem, *noun*
young, *plural noun*
zoology, *noun*

## 3 Business

administrator, *noun*
agency, *noun*
agenda, *noun*
banking, *noun*
bankrupt, *adjective*
bankruptcy, *noun*
blue-collar, *adjective*
board, *noun*
boom, *noun*
branch, *noun*
budget, *noun*
budget, *verb*
capital, *noun*
chain, *noun*
charge card, *noun*
check, *noun*
checkbook, *noun*
client, *noun*
commerce, *noun*
commercial, *adjective*
commercially, *adverb*
company, *noun*
competitor, *noun*
consumer, *noun*
contract, *noun*
corporate, *adjective*
corporation, *noun*
crash, *noun*
deal, *noun*
dealer, *noun*
dealership, *noun*
demand, *noun*
economic, *adjective*
economically, *adverb*
economy, *noun*
empire, *noun*
employ, *verb*
employable, *adjective*
employee, *noun*
employer, *noun*
employment, *noun*
enterprise, *noun*
entrepreneur, *noun*
export, *noun*
export, *verb*
exporter, *noun*
fail, *verb*
fax, *noun*
fax, *verb*
firm, *noun*
free market, *noun*
manage, *verb*
management, *noun*

manager, *noun*
managerial, *adjective*
manufacture, *noun*
manufacture, *verb*
manufacturer, *noun*
memo, *noun*
monopolize, *verb*
monopoly, *noun*
negotiate, *verb*
negotiation, *noun*
negotiator, *noun*
partner, *noun*
partnership, *noun*
patent, *noun*
patent, *verb*
pay, *noun*
pay, *verb*
payable, *adjective*
paycheck, *noun*
payment, *noun*
payroll, *noun*
personnel, *plural noun*
plant, *noun*
practice, *noun*
practice, *verb*
president, *noun*
presidential, *adjective*
price, *noun*
producer, *noun*
product, *noun*
production, *noun*
productive, *adjective*
productively, *adverb*
profession, *noun*
professional, *adjective*
professional, *noun*
professionalism, *noun*
profit, *noun*
profit, *verb*
profitable, *adjective*
profitably, *adverb*
promote, *verb*
promotion, *noun*
proprietor, *noun*
purchase, *noun*
purchase, *verb*
purchaser, *noun*
quarter, *noun*
raise, *noun*
rate, *noun*
real estate, *noun*
realtor, *noun*
rebate, *noun*
receipt, *noun*
recruit, *verb*
recruiter, *noun*
recruitment, *noun*
refund, *noun*
refund, *verb*
rent, *noun*
rent, *verb*
rental, *noun*
renter, *noun*
repay, *verb*
repayment, *noun*
retail, *noun*
retail, *verb*
retailer, *noun*
run, *verb*
salary, *noun*
sale, *noun*
sales clerk, *noun*
salesman, *noun*
salesperson, *noun*
sales representative, *noun*
saleswoman, *noun*
sector, *noun*
self-employed, *adjective*
self-employment, *noun*
sell, *verb*
service, *noun*
share, *noun*
shareholder, *noun*
ship, *verb*
shipment, *noun*
shipping, *noun*
shop, *noun*
shopping mall, *noun*
shut, *verb*
shutdown, *noun*
skilled, *adjective*
sponsor, *noun*
sponsor, *verb*
staff, *noun*
start, *verb*
steel, *noun*
stock, *noun*
stock, *verb*
stockbroker, *noun*
stock exchange, *noun*
store, *noun*
strike, *noun*
strike, *verb*
striker, *noun*
supermarket, *noun*
supplier, *noun*
syndicate, *noun*
tourism, *noun*
trade, *noun*
trade, *verb*
trademark, *noun*
trader, *noun*
trainee, *noun*
transaction, *noun*
underpaid, *adjective*
underpay, *verb*
unprofitable, *adjective*
unskilled, *adjective*
value, *noun*
value, *verb*
venture, *noun*
vice president, *noun*
wage, *noun*
Wall Street, *noun*
warehouse, *noun*
well-paid, *adjective*
white-collar, *adjective*
wholesale, *adjective*
wholesale, *adverb*
wholesaler, *noun*
work, *noun*
work, *verb*
worker, *noun*
workforce, *noun*
working, *adjective*
worth, *noun*
worthless, *adjective*

## 4 Chemistry

absorb, *verb*
absorbent, *adjective*
acid, *noun*
acidic, *adjective*
alloy, *noun*
aluminum, *noun*
antiseptic, *adjective*
antiseptic, *noun*
calcium, *noun*
carbon, *noun*
carbon dioxide, *noun*
carbon monoxide, *noun*
chemical, *adjective*
chemical, *noun*
chemist, *noun*
combine, *verb*
compound, *noun*
copper, *noun*
dilute, *verb*
dilution, *noun*
dissolve, *verb*
distill, *verb*
distillation, *noun*
distilled, *adjective*
element, *noun*
explosive, *adjective*
explosive, *noun*
fat, *noun*
filter, *noun*
filter, *verb*
fuel, *noun*
fuel, *verb*
gas, *noun*
helium, *noun*
hydrogen, *noun*
inflammable, *adjective*
iron, *noun*
lead, *noun*
magnesium, *noun*
mercury, *noun*
metal, *noun*
metallic, *adjective*
metalloid, *noun*
methane, *noun*
molten, *adjective*
narcotic, *adjective*
narcotic, *noun*
neon, *noun*
nickel, *noun*
nitrogen, *noun*
noble gas, *noun*
oil, *noun*
organic, *adjective*
organically, *adverb*
oxygen, *noun*
periodic table, *noun*
petroleum, *noun*
plutonium, *noun*
potassium, *noun*
preservative, *noun*
purification, *noun*
purify, *verb*
radioactive, *adjective*
radioactivity, *noun*
reactant, *noun*
refine, *verb*
residue, *noun*
rust, *noun*
rust, *verb*
semi-metal, *noun*
sodium, *noun*
solubility, *noun*
soluble, *adjective*
solution, *noun*
solvent, *noun*
sublimation, *noun*
substance, *noun*
sulfur, *noun*
tin, *noun*
uranium, *noun*
water vapor, *noun*
zinc, *noun*

## 5 Computers

access, *noun*
access, *verb*
app, *noun*
application, *noun*
attach, *verb*
attachment, *noun*
backup, *noun*
bookmark, *noun*
bookmark, *verb*
boot, *verb*
bug, *noun*
byte, *noun*
checker, *noun*
chip, *noun*
click, *noun*
click, *verb*
computer, *noun*
connect, *verb*
crash, *verb*
cursor, *noun*
cyberspace, *noun*
database, *noun*
default, *noun*
delete, *verb*
deletion, *noun*
desktop computer, *noun*
digital, *adjective*
directory, *noun*
disc, *noun*
disk, *noun*
disk drive, *noun*
down, *adjective*
download, *verb*
drive, *noun*
DVD, *noun*
email, *noun*
email, *verb*
enter, *verb*
erase, *verb*
file, *noun*
folder, *noun*
format, *noun*
gigabyte, *noun*
graphics, *plural noun*
hard disk, *noun*
hardware, *noun*
icon, *noun*
install, *verb*
installation, *noun*
interactive, *adjective*
Internet, *noun*
IT, *noun*
key, *noun*
keyboard, *noun*
kilobyte, *noun*
language, *noun*
laptop, *noun*
load, *verb*
mail, *noun*
mail, *verb*
mailbox, *noun*
mainframe, *noun*
megabyte, *noun*
memory, *noun*
menu, *noun*
message, *noun*
microchip, *noun*
modem, *noun*
monitor, *noun*
mouse, *noun*
mouse pad, *noun*
navigate, *verb*
navigation, *noun*
navigator, *noun*
net, *noun*
network, *noun*
notebook, *noun*
online, *adjective*
online, *adverb*
page, *noun*
paste, *verb*
PC, *noun*
personal computer, *noun*
pointer, *noun*
post, *noun*
processor, *noun*
program, *noun*
program, *verb*
programmer, *noun*
programming, *noun*
reboot, *verb*
run, *verb*
save, *verb*
scan, *verb*
scanner, *noun*
screen, *noun*
screen saver, *noun*
scroll, *verb*
search, *noun*
search engine, *noun*
server, *noun*
shut, *verb*
site, *noun*
software, *noun*
spam, *noun*
store, *verb*
surf, *verb*
surfing, *noun*
tab, *noun*
terminal, *noun*
tutorial, *noun*
upload, *verb*
virtual, *adjective*
virtually, *adverb*
virtual reality, *noun*
virus, *noun*
visit, *verb*
wallpaper, *noun*
web, *noun*
webcam, *noun*
website, *noun*
window, *noun*
word processing, *noun*
word processor, *noun*
World Wide Web, *noun*
WWW, *noun*

## 6 Drama

act, *noun*
act, *verb*
acting, *noun*
actor, *noun*
actress, *noun*
audience, *noun*
audition, *noun*
audition, *verb*
backstage, *adverb*
balcony, *noun*
ballet, *noun*
cast, *noun*
cast, *verb*
choreography, *noun*
comedy, *noun*
co-star, *noun*
co-star, *verb*
costume, *noun*
dialogue, *noun*
director, *noun*
drama, *noun*
dramatic, *adjective*
dramatically, *adverb*
dramatist, *noun*
farce, *noun*
monologue, *noun*
opera, *noun*
part, *noun*
perform, *verb*
performance, *noun*
performer, *noun*
play, *noun*
play, *verb*
playwright, *noun*
portray, *verb*
portrayal, *noun*
produce, *verb*
producer, *noun*
production, *noun*
prop, *noun*
recite, *verb*
rehearsal, *noun*
rehearse, *verb*
role, *noun*
scene, *noun*
scenery, *noun*
screen, *noun*
script, *noun*
series, *noun*
set, *noun*
show business, *noun*
sitcom, *noun*
soap opera, *noun*
stage, *noun*
star, *noun*
star, *verb*
storyboard, *noun*
subtitles, *plural noun*
symbolism, *noun*
theater, *noun*
theatrical, *adjective*
tragedy, *noun*

## 7 General Science

analysis, *noun*
analyze, *verb*
apparatus, *noun*
asteroid, *noun*
barometer, *noun*
biome, *noun*
boiling point, *noun*
C, *abbreviation*
carbon footprint, *noun*
cc, *abbreviation*
centimeter, *noun*
classification, *noun*
classify, *verb*
crude, *noun*
cyclone, *noun*
data, *noun*
decomposer, *noun*
dependent variable, *noun*
diagram, *noun*
discover, *verb*
discovery, *noun*
disprove, *verb*

ecosystem, *noun*
effect, *noun*
El Niño, *noun*
evaluate, *verb*
evaluation, *noun*
evidence, *noun*
evolve, *verb*
experiment, *noun*
experiment, *verb*
experimentation, *noun*
fact, *noun*
factual, *adjective*
false, *adjective*
find, *verb*
flax, *noun*
flow chart, *noun*
fluctuate, *verb*
fluctuation, *noun*
fluid ounce, *noun*
food chain, *noun*
food web, *noun*
foot, *noun*
formula, *noun*
funnel, *noun*
gallon, *noun*
high pressure, *noun*
histogram, *noun*
hybrid, *noun*
hypothesis, *noun*
igneous, *adjective*
inch, *noun*
indicate, *verb*
indicative, *adjective*
indicator, *noun*
instrument, *noun*
invent, *verb*
invention, *noun*
inventive, *adjective*
inventor, *noun*
kilogram, *noun*
kilometer, *noun*
kinetic, *adjective*
laboratory, *noun*
landform, *noun*
line plot, *noun*
liter, *noun*
low pressure, *noun*
magma, *noun*
magnetic field, *noun*
malleable, *adjective*
Mars, *noun*
measurable, *adjective*
measure, *verb*
Mercury, *noun*
metamorphic, *adjective*
meter, *noun*
method, *noun*
methodological, *adjective*
methodology, *noun*
metric, *adjective*
metric system, *noun*
microscope, *noun*
microscopic, *adjective*
mile, *noun*
milligram, *noun*
milliliter, *noun*
millimeter, *noun*
Neptune, *noun*
non-living, *adjective*
nutritious, *adjective*
objective, *adjective*
omnivore, *noun*
ounce, *noun*
outlier, *noun*
parallel circuit, *noun*
phenomenon, *noun*
physical therapy, *noun*
picture graph, *noun*
pie chart, *noun*
pint, *noun*
pound, *noun*
prism, *noun*
property, *noun*
psychoanalyst, *noun*
qualitative observation, *noun*
quantitative observation, *noun*
quart, *noun*
quarter moon, *noun*
repel, *verb*
research, *noun*
rock cycle, *noun*
Saturn, *noun*
science, *noun*
scientific, *adjective*
scientist, *noun*
sea level, *noun*
sediment, *noun*
sedimentary, *adjective*
series circuit, *noun*
silt, *noun*
solar energy, *noun*
solubility, *noun*
specimen, *noun*
static electricity, *noun*
stem and leaf plot, *noun*
study, *noun*
study, *verb*
sublimation, *noun*
technician, *noun*
technological, *adjective*
technology, *noun*
test, *noun*
test, *verb*
test tube, *noun*
theoretical, *adjective*
theoretically, *adverb*
theorist, *noun*
theorize, *verb*
theory, *noun*
thermal conductivity, *noun*
ton, *noun*
tree diagram, *noun*
Venus, *noun*
volume, *noun*
wane, *verb*
water cycle, *noun*
water quality, *noun*
watershed, *noun*
water vapor, *noun*
weathering, *noun*
weigh, *verb*
weight, *noun*
wind vane, *noun*
x-axis, *noun*
yard, *noun*
y-axis, *noun*

## 8 Geography and Earth Science

acid rain, *noun*
adobe, *noun*
African, *adjective*
African, *noun*
African-American, *adjective*
African American, *noun*
agricultural, *adjective*
agriculture, *noun*
air, *noun*
algae, *plural noun*
American, *adjective*
American, *noun*
Antarctic, *noun*
aqueduct, *noun*
Arab, *adjective*
Arab, *noun*
Arctic, *noun*
arid, *adjective*
Asia, *noun*
Asian, *adjective*
Atlantic, *noun*
atlas, *noun*
atmosphere, *noun*
atmospheric, *adjective*
autumn, *noun*
avalanche, *noun*
axis, *noun*
bank, *noun*
barley, *noun*
basin, *noun*
bay, *noun*
beach, *noun*
bean, *noun*
bed, *noun*
biodegradable, *adjective*
blizzard, *noun*
boulder, *noun*
boundary, *noun*
British, *adjective*
British, *noun*
Canadian, *adjective*
Canadian, *noun*
canal, *noun*
canyon, *noun*
cape, *noun*
capital, *noun*
Caribbean, *adjective*
cattle, *plural noun*
cave, *noun*
channel, *noun*
chart, *noun*
Chinese, *adjective*
Chinese, *noun*
city, *noun*
clay, *noun*
cliff, *noun*
climate, *noun*
cloud, *noun*
cloudy, *adjective*
coal, *noun*
coast, *noun*
coastal, *adjective*
coastline, *noun*
compass, *noun*
conservation, *noun*
conserve, *verb*
contaminate, *verb*
contamination, *noun*
continent, *noun*
continental, *adjective*
contour, *noun*
core, *noun*
corn, *noun*
cotton, *noun*
country, *noun*
county, *noun*
crater, *noun*
crevice, *noun*
crop, *noun*
crude, *adjective*
crust, *noun*
cultivate, *verb*
cultivation, *noun*
dairy, *noun*
dam, *noun*
dam, *verb*

Danish, *adjective*
Dane, *noun*
D.C., *abbreviation*
delta, *noun*
depth, *noun*
desert, *noun*
developed, *adjective*
developing, *adjective*
dew, *noun*
dike, *noun*
district, *noun*
ditch, *noun*
drought, *noun*
dune, *noun*
Dutch, *adjective*
earthquake, *noun*
east, *noun*
east, *adjective*
east, *adverb*
eastern, *adjective*
eastward, *adjective*
eastward, *adverb*
ecological, *adjective*
ecologist, *noun*
ecology, *noun*
elevation, *noun*
emissions, *plural noun*
English, *adjective*
environment, *noun*
environmental, *adjective*
environmentally, *adverb*
equator, *noun*
equatorial, *adjective*
equinox, *noun*
erode, *verb*
erosion, *noun*
erupt, *verb*
eruption, *noun*
Europe, *noun*
European, *adjective*
European, *noun*
export, *noun*
export, *verb*
exporter, *noun*
fall, *noun*
fall, *verb*
Far East, *noun*
farm, *noun*
farmer, *noun*
farming, *noun*
farmland, *noun*
fault, *noun*
fertilize, *verb*
fertilizer, *noun*
field, *noun*
flood, *noun*
flood, *verb*
flooding, *noun*
fog, *noun*
foggy, *adjective*
forest, *noun*
formation, *noun*
frost, *noun*
frosty, *adjective*
fumes, *plural noun*
gale, *noun*
geographical, *adjective*
geography, *noun*
geological, *adjective*
geologist, *noun*
geology, *noun*
German, *noun*
glacier, *noun*
global, *adjective*
globally, *adverb*
global warming, *noun*
globe, *noun*
gold, *noun*
gold mine, *noun*
gorge, *noun*
grain, *noun*
granite, *noun*
grassland, *noun*
Greek, *adjective*
Greek, *noun*
greenhouse, *noun*
gulf, *noun*
harvest, *noun*
harvest, *verb*
hemisphere, *noun*
highlands, *plural noun*
high pressure, *noun*
hill, *noun*
hilly, *adjective*
Hispanic, *adjective*
Hispanic, *noun*
humid, *adjective*
humidity, *noun*
hurricane, *noun*
iceberg, *noun*
icicle, *noun*
igneous, *adjective*
Indian, *adjective*
Indian, *noun*
industrial, *adjective*
industrialization, *noun*
industrialized, *adjective*
industry, *noun*
inhabit, *verb*
inhabitant, *noun*
inhabited, *adjective*
inner-city, *adjective*
inner city, *noun*
Inuit, *noun*
Irish, *adjective*
Irish, *noun*
irrigate, *verb*
irrigation, *noun*
island, *noun*
isolated, *adjective*
isthmus, *noun*
Japanese, *adjective*
Japanese, *noun*
jungle, *noun*
Korean, *adjective*
Korean, *noun*
lagoon, *noun*
lake, *noun*
land, *noun*
landform, *noun*
landslide, *noun*
Latin America, *noun*
Latin American, *adjective*
latitude, *noun*
lava, *noun*
levee, *noun*
lightning, *noun*
line, *noun*
livestock, *noun*
local, *adjective*
locally, *adverb*
local time, *noun*
longhouse, *noun*
longitude, *noun*
low pressure, *noun*
low tide, *noun*
magma, *noun*
magnetic field, *noun*
magnitude, *noun*
mainland, *adjective*
mainland, *noun*
manure, *noun*
marble, *noun*
marsh, *noun*
Mediterranean, *noun*
Mediterranean, *adjective*
meridian, *noun*
metamorphic, *adjective*
meteorologist, *noun*
meteorology, *noun*
metropolitan, *adjective*
Mexican, *adjective*
Mexican, *noun*
Middle East, *noun*
Midwest, *noun*
Midwesterner, *noun*
mill, *noun*
mine, *noun*
mineral, *noun*
mining, *noun*
mist, *noun*
misty, *adjective*
monsoon, *noun*
mount, *noun*
mountain, *noun*
mountainous, *adjective*
mountain range, *noun*
mouth, *noun*
nationality, *noun*
nationally, *adverb*
national park, *noun*
native, *adjective*
native, *noun*
Native American, *adjective*
Native American, *noun*
neighbor, *noun*
neighboring, *adjective*
nomad, *noun*
nomadic, *adjective*
north, *adjective*
north, *adverb*
north, *noun*
northeast, *noun*
northeastern, *adjective*
northeast, *adjective*
northeast, *adverb*
northern, *adjective*
northerner, *noun*
Northern Hemisphere, *noun*
North Pole, *noun*
northward, *adjective*
northward, *adverb*
northwest, *adjective*
northwest, *adverb*
northwest, *noun*
northwestern, *adjective*
oasis, *noun*
ocean, *noun*
oceanic, *adjective*
offshore, *adjective*
oil rig, *noun*
ore, *noun*
origin, *noun*
outskirts, *plural noun*
ozone layer, *noun*
Pacific Ocean, *noun*
pasture, *noun*
peak, *noun*
pebble, *noun*
peninsula, *noun*
pest, *noun*
pesticide, *noun*
plain, *noun*
planet, *noun*
planetary, *adjective*
plant, *verb*
plantation, *noun*
plateau, *noun*
plow, *noun*
plow, *verb*
polar, *adjective*
pole, *noun*
Pole, *noun*
Polish, *adjective*
pollutant, *noun*
pollute, *verb*
polluted, *adjective*

pollution, *noun*
pond, *noun*
population, *noun*
populous, *adjective*
port, *noun*
Portuguese, *adjective*
poultry, *noun*
prairie, *noun*
precinct, *noun*
precipitation, *noun*
province, *noun*
provincial, *adjective*
pueblo, *noun*
quake, *noun*
quarry, *noun*
quartz, *noun*
quicksand, *noun*
rain, *noun*
rain, *verb*
rainbow, *noun*
rainfall, *noun*
rainforest, *noun*
rainy, *adjective*
ranch, *noun*
rancher, *noun*
ranching, *noun*
range, *noun*
rapids, *plural noun*
ravine, *noun*
reclaim, *verb*
reclamation, *noun*
reef, *noun*
region, *noun*
regional, *adjective*
relative location, *noun*
reservoir, *noun*
residential, *adjective*
resort, *noun*
rice, *noun*
ridge, *noun*
river, *noun*
rock, *noun*
rock cycle, *noun*
rocky, *adjective*
rugged, *adjective*
rural, *adjective*
Russian, *adjective*
Russian, *noun*
rye, *noun*
sand, *noun*
sandy, *adjective*
sea, *noun*
sea level, *noun*
seashore, *noun*
season, *noun*
seasonal, *adjective*
sediment, *noun*
sedimentary, *adjective*
settlement, *noun*
shore, *noun*
shoreline, *noun*
shower, *noun*
shower, *verb*
silt, *noun*
silver, *noun*
sky, *noun*
sleet, *noun*
smog, *noun*
snow, *noun*
snow, *verb*
snowdrift, *noun*
snowfall, *noun*
snowflake, *noun*
snowstorm, *noun*
snowy, *adjective*
sod, *noun*
soil, *noun*
south, *adjective*
south, *adverb*
south, *noun*
southeast, *adjective*
southeast, *adverb*
southeast, *noun*
southeastern, *adjective*
southern, *adjective*
southerner, *noun*
Southern Hemisphere, *noun*
South Pole, *noun*
southward, *adjective*
southward, *adverb*
southwest, *adjective*
southwest, *adverb*
southwest, *noun*
southwestern, *adjective*
sow, *verb*
Spanish, *adjective*
spring, *noun*
state, *noun*
storm, *noun*
stormy, *adjective*
strait, *noun*
stream, *noun*
suburb, *noun*
suburban, *adjective*
summer, *noun*
summit, *noun*
sun, *noun*
sunlight, *noun*
swamp, *noun*
swampy, *adjective*
Swiss, *adjective*
Swiss, *plural noun*
Taiwanese, *adjective*
Taiwanese, *noun*
temperate, *adjective*
terrain, *noun*
territory, *noun*
thaw, *verb*
thaw, *noun*
Third World, *noun*
thunder, *noun*
thunderstorm, *noun*
tide, *noun*
timber, *noun*
time zone, *noun*
tornado, *noun*
town, *noun*
tractor, *noun*
trade wind, *noun*
transatlantic, *adjective*
transcontinental, *adjective*
transportation, *noun*
tributary, *noun*
tropical, *adjective*
tropics, *plural noun*
tsunami, *noun*
tundra, *noun*
typhoon, *noun*
uninhabited, *adjective*
union, *noun*
unionized, *adjective*
urban, *adjective*
urbanization, *noun*
valley, *noun*
vegetation, *noun*
village, *noun*
vineyard, *noun*
volcanic, *adjective*
volcano, *noun*
waste, *noun*
waste disposal, *noun*
wasteland, *noun*
water, *noun*
water, *verb*
water cycle, *noun*
waterfall, *noun*
waterlogged, *adjective*
water quality, *noun*
watershed, *noun*
waterway, *noun*
wave, *noun*
weather, *noun*
weathered, *adjective*
weather forecast, *noun*
weathering, *noun*
weed, *noun*
well, *noun*
Welsh, *adjective*
west, *adjective*
west, *adverb*
west, *noun*
western, *adjective*
westward, *adjective*
westward, *adverb*
wet, *adjective*
wetland, *noun*
wheat, *noun*
whirlpool, *noun*
whirlwind, *noun*
wilderness, *noun*
wind, *noun*
windchill factor, *noun*
windy, *adjective*
winter, *noun*
wintry, *adjective*
woodland, *noun*
world, *noun*
yield, *noun*

## 9 History, Politics, and Social Studies

abolish, *verb*
abolition, *noun*
abolitionist, *noun*
act, *noun*
administration, *noun*
age, *noun*
air raid, *noun*
alliance, *noun*
ally, *noun*
almanac, *noun*
ambassador, *noun*
amend, *verb*
amendment, *noun*
amnesty, *noun*
ancient, *adjective*
approval, *noun*
approve, *verb*
archaeological, *adjective*
archaeologist, *noun*
archaeology, *noun*
armed forces, *plural noun*
army, *noun*
artifact, *noun*
assassinate, *verb*
assassination, *noun*
assimilate, *verb*
ballot, *noun*
ban, *noun*
ban, *verb*
barter, *noun*
barter, *verb*
battle, *noun*
battleship, *noun*
bill, *noun*
Bill of Rights, *noun*
blockade, *noun*
blockade, *verb*
bloodshed, *noun*

bomb, *noun*
bomb, *verb*
bomber, *noun*
borough, *noun*
boycott, *noun*
boycott, *verb*
brand, *verb*
bureau, *noun*
bureaucracy, *noun*
bureaucratic, *adjective*
cabinet, *noun*
campaign, *noun*
campaign, *verb*
cannon, *noun*
capitalism, *noun*
capitalist, *adjective*
capital punishment, *noun*
capitol, *noun*
cast, *verb*
catastrophe, *noun*
catastrophic, *adjective*
Caucasian, *noun*
Caucasian, *adjective*
cavalry, *noun*
ceasefire, *noun*
censor, *verb*
censorship, *noun*
census, *noun*
century, *noun*
chancellor, *noun*
Chicana, *noun*
Chicano, *noun*
chief, *noun*
chronological, *adjective*
citizen, *noun*
citizenship, *noun*
city hall, *noun*
civic, *adjective*
civilian, *noun*
civilization, *noun*
civilized, *adjective*
civil liberties, *plural noun*
civil rights, *plural noun*
civil war, *noun*
class, *noun*
classical, *adjective*
clergy, *plural noun*
colonial, *adjective*
colonist, *noun*
colonization, *noun*
colonize, *verb*
colony, *noun*
combat, *noun*
command, *verb*
commander, *noun*
commemorate, *verb*
committee, *noun*
communism, *noun*
communist, *adjective*
communist, *noun*
community, *noun*
company, *noun*
Confederacy, *noun*
Confederate, *adjective*
conflict, *noun*
Congress, *noun*
congressman, *noun*
congresswoman, *noun*
conquer, *verb*
conqueror, *noun*
conquest, *noun*
conquistador, *noun*
conservative, *adjective*
conspiracy, *noun*
conspirator, *noun*
constitution, *noun*
constitutional, *adjective*
consul, *noun*
context, *noun*
cotton gin, *noun*
council, *noun*
coup, *noun*
court, *noun*
courthouse, *noun*
court-martial, *noun*
court-martial, *verb*
courtroom, *noun*
creed, *noun*
crime, *noun*
criminal, *adjective*
criminal, *noun*
custom, *noun*
death penalty, *noun*
debate, *verb*
decade, *noun*
decorate, *verb*
decorative, *adjective*
defect, *verb*
defection, *noun*
defector, *noun*
defendant, *noun*
defense, *noun*
defensive, *adjective*
delegation, *noun*
democracy, *noun*
Democrat, *noun*
democratic, *adjective*
democratically, *adverb*
Democratic Party, *noun*
demonstrate, *verb*
demonstration, *noun*
demonstrator, *noun*
department, *noun*
deport, *verb*
deportation, *noun*
depression, *noun*
descend, *verb*
descendant, *noun*
descent, *noun*
deserter, *noun*
destroyer, *noun*
developed, *adjective*
developing, *adjective*
dictator, *noun*
dictatorship, *noun*
disarm, *verb*
disarmament, *noun*
discriminate, *verb*
discrimination, *noun*
discriminatory, *adjective*
dissent, *noun*
dissident, *noun*
district attorney, *noun*
document, *noun*
domestic, *adjective*
domestically, *adverb*
draft, *adjective*
draft, *noun*
draft, *verb*
education, *noun*
educational, *adjective*
elect, *verb*
election, *noun*
electoral, *adjective*
electoral college, *noun*
eligible, *adjective*
eligibility, *noun*
emancipate, *verb*
emancipation, *noun*
embassy, *noun*
emblem, *noun*
emigrate, *verb*
emigration, *noun*
emperor, *noun*
empire, *noun*
empress, *noun*
enact, *verb*
enemy, *noun*
enlist, *verb*
enlistment, *noun*
equal, *adjective*
equality, *noun*
era, *noun*
ethic, *noun*
ethical, *adjective*
ethically, *adverb*
ethnic, *adjective*
ethnicity, *noun*
evidence, *noun*
execute, *verb*
execution, *noun*
exile, *noun*
exile, *verb*
expedition, *noun*
extended family, *noun*
family, *noun*
famine, *noun*
federal, *adjective*
federally, *adverb*
federation, *noun*
felony, *noun*
feminism, *noun*
feminist, *adjective*
feminist, *noun*
first-generation, *adjective*
first lady, *noun*
flag, *noun*
flatboat, *noun*
force, *noun*
forefathers, *plural noun*
fort, *noun*
fortress, *noun*
found, *verb*
foundation, *noun*
founder, *noun*
Fourth of July, *noun*
freedom, *noun*
free market, *noun*
frontier, *noun*
galleon, *noun*
general, *noun*
generation, *noun*
ghetto, *noun*
GNP, *noun*
govern, *verb*
government, *noun*
governmental, *adjective*
governor, *noun*
guilty, *adjective*
hierarchy, *noun*
hieroglyphics, *noun*
historic, *adjective*
historical, *adjective*
history, *noun*
hogan, *noun*
homeland, *noun*
House of Representatives, *noun*
human race, *noun*
human rights, *plural noun*
ideological, *adjective*
ideology, *noun*
igloo, *noun*
illegal, *adjective*
illegally, *adverb*
illiteracy, *noun*
illiterate, *adjective*
immigrant, *noun*
immigrate, *verb*
immigration, *noun*
imperial, *adjective*
imperialism, *noun*
imperialist, *adjective*
inaugural, *adjective*
inaugurate, *verb*
inauguration, *noun*

income tax, *noun*
independence, *noun*
Independence Day, *noun*
independent, *adjective*
independently, *adverb*
indict, *verb*
indictment, *noun*
industrialized, *adjective*
industrialization, *noun*
inequality, *noun*
infantry, *noun*
inflation, *noun*
inflationary, *adjective*
infrastructure, *noun*
injustice, *noun*
innocent, *adjective*
institution, *noun*
institutional, *adjective*
insurance, *noun*
integrate, *verb*
integrated, *adjective*
integration, *noun*
international, *adjective*
internationally, *adverb*
interracial, *adjective*
invade, *verb*
invader, *noun*
invasion, *noun*
investment, *noun*
Ivy League, *adjective*
jail, *noun*
jail, *verb*
judge, *noun*
judgment, *noun*
judicial, *adjective*
judiciary, *noun*
jury, *noun*
justice, *noun*
justice of the peace, *noun*
juvenile, *adjective*
juvenile, *noun*
juvenile delinquent, *noun*
king, *noun*
kingdom, *noun*
knight, *noun*
labor, *noun*
Labor Day, *noun*
labor union, *noun*
landslide, *noun*
law, *noun*
lawsuit, *noun*
lawyer, *noun*
leader, *noun*
leadership, *noun*
league, *noun*
left, *noun*
leftist, *adjective*
left-wing, *adjective*
legal, *adjective*
legality, *noun*
legalize, *verb*
legally, *adverb*
legislate, *verb*
legislation, *noun*
legislative, *adjective*
legislator, *noun*
legislature, *noun*
liberal, *adjective*
liberal, *noun*
liberalism, *noun*
liberty, *noun*
lieutenant, *noun*
longhouse, *noun*
lower-class, *adjective*
lower class, *noun*
magistrate, *noun*
majesty, *noun*
major, *noun*
majority, *noun*
mandatory, *adjective*
march, *noun*
march, *verb*
marine, *noun*
Marine Corps, *noun*
marriage, *noun*
martial, *adjective*
mayor, *noun*
medieval, *adjective*
memorial, *adjective*
memorial, *noun*
middle-class, *adjective*
middle class, *noun*
migrant, *noun*
migrate, *verb*
migration, *noun*
migratory, *adjective*
militant, *adjective*
militant, *noun*
military, *adjective*
military, *noun*
militia, *noun*
minor, *noun*
minority, *noun*
minuteman, *noun*
missile, *noun*
monarch, *noun*
monarchy, *noun*
monument, *noun*
movement, *noun*
nation, *noun*
national, *adjective*
national anthem, *noun*
nationalism, *noun*
nationalist, *noun*
nationalistic, *adjective*
naturalization, *noun*
naturalize, *verb*
naturalized, *adjective*
naval, *adjective*
navy, *noun*
neutral, *adjective*
neutrality, *noun*
nuclear family, *noun*
offender, *noun*
offense, *noun*
office, *noun*
official, *adjective*
official, *noun*
officially, *adverb*
outbreak, *noun*
pacifism, *noun*
pacifist, *noun*
pact, *noun*
palace, *noun*
pan, *verb*
paramilitary, *adjective*
pardon, *noun*
pardon, *verb*
parliament, *noun*
parliamentary, *adjective*
parole, *noun*
parole, *verb*
party, *noun*
pass, *verb*
past, *adjective*
past, *noun*
patriot, *noun*
patriotic, *adjective*
patriotically, *adverb*
patrol, *noun*
peace, *noun*
peaceful, *adjective*
peacefully, *adverb*
peacekeeper, *noun*
peacekeeping, *noun*
peasant, *noun*
penalty, *noun*
penitentiary, *noun*
Pentagon, *noun*
people, *noun*
persecute, *verb*
persecution, *noun*
petition, *noun*
petitioner, *noun*
pictograph, *noun*
pioneer, *noun*
pioneering, *adjective*
pluralism, *noun*
police, *noun*
police force, *noun*
political, *adjective*
politically, *adverb*
politically correct, *adjective*
politician, *noun*
politics, *noun*
power, *noun*
powerful, *adjective*
pre-Columbian, *adjective*
prehistoric, *adjective*
prejudice, *noun*
premier, *noun*
presidency, *noun*
president, *noun*
presidential, *adjective*
prime minister, *noun*
primitive, *adjective*
prince, *noun*
princess, *noun*
prison, *noun*
prisoner, *noun*
prisoner of war, *noun*
progress, *noun*
prohibit, *verb*
prohibition, *noun*
propaganda, *noun*
prosecute, *verb*
prosecutor, *noun*
protest, *noun*
public, *adjective*
public, *noun*
publicly, *adverb*
pueblo, *noun*
queen, *noun*
race, *noun*
racial, *adjective*
racially, *adverb*
racism, *noun*
racist, *adjective*
racist, *noun*
radical, *adjective*
radically, *adverb*
raid, *noun*
rancho, *noun*
rate, *noun*
reactionary, *adjective*
rebel, *noun*
rebel, *verb*
rebellion, *noun*
recession, *noun*
reelect, *verb*
reelection, *noun*
referendum, *noun*
reform, *noun*
reform, *verb*
refugee, *noun*
regime, *noun*
regiment, *noun*
regulate, *verb*
regulation, *noun*
regulatory, *adjective*
reign, *noun*
reign, *verb*
relic, *noun*
remains, *plural noun*
repeal, *noun*
repeal, *verb*
representative, *noun*

reprieve, *noun*
republic, *noun*
Republican, *adjective*
Republican, *noun*
Republican Party, *noun*
restrict, *verb*
restricted, *adjective*
restriction, *noun*
restrictive, *adjective*
retreat, *noun*
retreat, *verb*
revolt, *noun*
revolt, *verb*
revolting, *adjective*
revolution, *noun*
revolutionize, *verb*
right, *noun*
right-wing, *adjective*
riot, *noun*
riot, *verb*
ritual, *noun*
Roman, *adjective*
Roman, *noun*
royal, *adjective*
royalty, *noun*
rule, *noun*
rule, *verb*
ruler, *noun*
run, *verb*
scroll, *noun*
secretary, *noun*
security, *noun*
segregated, *adjective*
segregation, *noun*
self-government, *noun*
senate, *noun*
senator, *noun*
sentence, *noun*
sentence, *verb*
settler, *noun*
sexism, *noun*
sheriff, *noun*
shield, *noun*
shift, *noun*
shooting, *noun*
siege, *noun*
site, *noun*
slave, *noun*
slavery, *noun*
slum, *noun*
social, *adjective*
socialism, *noun*
socialist, *noun*
socially, *adverb*
social science, *noun*
Social Security, *noun*
social work, *noun*
social worker, *noun*
society, *noun*
socioeconomic, *adjective*
sociologist, *noun*
sociology, *noun*
soldier, *noun*
sovereign, *adjective*
spear, *noun*
stagecoach, *noun*
standard of living, *noun*
statehood, *noun*
statesman, *noun*
status, *noun*
status symbol, *noun*
strategic, *adjective*
strike, *noun*
struggle, *noun*
sue, *verb*
suffrage, *noun*
superpower, *noun*
Supreme Court, *noun*
surrender, *noun*
surrender, *verb*
suspect, *noun*
sword, *noun*
tariff, *noun*
tax, *noun*
tax, *verb*
taxable, *adjective*
taxation, *noun*
term, *noun*
terrorism, *noun*
terrorist, *noun*
timeline, *noun*
topical, *adjective*
totalitarian, *adjective*
totalitarianism, *noun*
totem pole, *noun*
town hall, *noun*
tradition, *noun*
traditional, *adjective*
traditionally, *adverb*
traitor, *noun*
treason, *noun*
treaty, *noun*
trend, *noun*
trial, *noun*
tribal, *adjective*
tribe, *noun*
troop, *noun*
truce, *noun*
try, *verb*
tyranny, *noun*
tyrant, *noun*
unconstitutional, *adjective*
underdeveloped, *adjective*
underprivileged, *adjective*
underworld, *noun*
unemployed, *adjective*
unemployment, *noun*
unification, *noun*
unify, *verb*
union, *noun*
unionized, *adjective*
unite, *verb*
united, *adjective*
United Nations, *noun*
unity, *noun*
unlawful, *adjective*
unlawfully, *adverb*
unrest, *noun*
upper-class, *adjective*
upper class, *noun*
uprising, *noun*
utopia, *noun*
utopian, *adjective*
veto, *noun*
veto, *verb*
vice president, *noun*
violate, *verb*
violation, *noun*
violence, *noun*
vote, *noun*
vote, *verb*
voter, *noun*
war, *noun*
warfare, *noun*
warring, *adjective*
warrior, *noun*
water rights, *plural noun*
way of life, *noun*
weapon, *noun*
weaponry, *noun*
welfare, *noun*
westward expansion, *noun*
White House, *noun*
working-class, *adjective*
working class, *noun*
Yankee, *noun*

## 10 Languages and Language Arts

abridged, *adjective*
accent, *noun*
active, *adjective*
adaptation, *noun*
adjective, *noun*
adverb, *noun*
alphabet, *noun*
alphabetical, *adjective*
antonym, *noun*
apostrophe, *noun*
appendix, *noun*
Arabic, *noun*
article, *noun*
asterisk, *noun*
autobiographical, *adjective*
autobiography, *noun*
bilingual, *adjective*
biographer, *noun*
biography, *noun*
book, *noun*
capital, *noun*
capitalize, *verb*
chapter, *noun*
character, *noun*
Chinese, *noun*
citation, *noun*
classic, *noun*
clause, *noun*
cliché, *noun*
closing, *noun*
coherent, *adjective*
coherently, *adverb*
colon, *noun*
comma, *noun*
comparative, *noun*
complete sentence, *noun*
compound, *noun*
compound sentence, *noun*
compound word, *noun*
concise, *adjective*
conclusion, *noun*
conjugate, *verb*
conjunction, *noun*
consonant, *noun*
context, *noun*
contraction, *noun*
contrast, *verb*
Danish, *noun*
dash, *noun*
debate, *noun*
define, *verb*
definite article, *noun*
definition, *noun*
describe, *verb*
description, *noun*
dialect, *noun*
dictation, *noun*
dictionary, *noun*
double negative, *noun*
draft, *noun*
edition, *noun*

EFL, *noun*
ELT, *noun*
emphasis, *noun*
English, *noun*
entry, *noun*
epic, *adjective*
epic, *noun*
ESL, *noun*
essay, *noun*
exclamation point, *noun*
express, *verb*
expression, *noun*
fable, *noun*
fairy tale, *noun*
fantasy, *noun*
fiction, *noun*
figurative, *adjective*
figuratively, *adverb*
first person, *noun*
fluency, *noun*
fluent, *adjective*
fluently, *adverb*
folklore, *noun*
folk tale, *noun*
formal, *adjective*
formally, *adverb*
future, *noun*
future tense, *noun*
gender, *noun*
German, *noun*
glossary, *noun*
grammar, *noun*
grammatical, *adjective*
Greek, *noun*
hardback, *noun*
hero, *noun*
heroine, *noun*
heroism, *noun*
hieroglyphics, *noun*
homograph, *noun*
homophone, *noun*
hyperbole, *noun*
hyphen, *noun*
idiom, *noun*
idiomatic, *adjective*
imperative, *noun*
indefinite article, *noun*
indefinite pronoun, *noun*
index, *noun*
indirect object, *noun*
infinitive, *noun*
informal, *adjective*
informality, *noun*
informally, *adverb*
initial, *noun*
interjection, *noun*
interpret, *verb*
interpreter, *noun*
intransitive, *adjective*
introduction, *noun*
introductory, *adjective*
IPA, *noun*
ironic, *adjective*
irony, *noun*
irregular, *adjective*
Japanese, *noun*
language, *noun*
Latin, *noun*
legend, *noun*
letter, *noun*
line, *noun*
linguistics, *noun*
literal, *adjective*
literary, *adjective*
lowercase, *adjective*
lowercase, *noun*
main clause, *noun*
masculine, *adjective*
mean, *verb*
meaning, *noun*
meaningful, *adjective*
meaningless, *adjective*
metaphor, *noun*
metaphorical, *adjective*
modal verb, *noun*
modification, *noun*
modifier, *noun*
modify, *verb*
monolingual, *adjective*
narrate, *verb*
narration, *noun*
narrative, *noun*
narrator, *noun*
negative, *adjective*
negative, *noun*
negatively, *adverb*
neuter, *adjective*
nonfiction, *adjective*
nonfiction, *noun*
Norse, *noun*
noun, *noun*
novel, *noun*
novelist, *noun*
object, *noun*
oral, *adjective*
orally, *adverb*
paperback, *noun*
paragraph, *noun*
paraphrase, *noun*
paraphrase, *verb*
parentheses, *plural noun*
parody, *noun*
parody, *verb*
participle, *noun*
part of speech, *noun*
passive, *adjective*
passively, *adverb*
passivity, *noun*
past participle, *noun*
past tense, *noun*
pen name, *noun*
period, *noun*
periodical, *noun*
personal pronoun, *noun*
personification, *noun*
phonetic, *adjective*
phonetics, *noun*
phrasal verb, *noun*
phrase, *noun*
pictograph, *noun*
plagiarism, *noun*
plagiarize, *verb*
plot, *noun*
plural, *adjective*
plural, *noun*
poem, *noun*
poet, *noun*
poetic, *adjective*
poetry, *noun*
point, *noun*
Polish, *noun*
Portuguese, *noun*
possessive, *adjective*
possessive, *noun*
predicate, *noun*
preface, *noun*
prefix, *noun*
preposition, *noun*
prepositional, *adjective*
present participle, *noun*
present perfect, *noun*
present tense, *noun*
pronoun, *noun*
pronounce, *verb*
pronunciation, *noun*
proper noun, *noun*
prose, *noun*
proverb, *noun*
publication, *noun*
punctuation, *noun*
punctuation mark, *noun*
put, *verb*
qualifier, *noun*
question mark, *noun*
quotation, *noun*
quotation marks, *plural noun*
quote, *noun*
quote, *verb*
refer, *verb*
reference, *noun*
reference book, *noun*
regular, *adjective*
relative clause, *noun*
relative pronoun, *noun*
reported speech, *noun*
rewrite, *noun*
rewrite, *verb*
rhyme, *noun*
rhyme, *verb*
romance, *noun*
rough draft, *noun*
Russian, *noun*
saga, *noun*
sarcasm, *noun*
sarcastic, *adjective*
sarcastically, *adverb*
satire, *noun*
satirist, *noun*
saying, *noun*
scroll, *noun*
second person, *noun*
semantic, *adjective*
semantics, *noun*
semicolon, *noun*
sense, *noun*
sentence, *noun*
sequel, *noun*
short story, *noun*
simile, *noun*
singular, *adjective*
singular, *noun*
slang, *noun*
slogan, *noun*
sonnet, *noun*
Spanish, *noun*
speech, *noun*
spell, *verb*
spelling, *noun*
statement, *noun*
stereotype, *noun*
stereotype, *verb*
story, *noun*
stress, *noun*
stress, *verb*
stressed, *adjective*
subject, *noun*
subject matter, *noun*
suffix, *noun*
sum, *verb*
summarize, *verb*
summary, *noun*
superlative, *noun*
syllable, *noun*
symbolism, *noun*
synonym, *noun*
syntax, *noun*
table of contents, *noun*
tale, *noun*
tense, *noun*
term, *noun*
term, *verb*
text, *noun*
thematic, *adjective*
thematically, *adverb*
theme, *noun*
thesaurus, *noun*
third person, *noun*

**thriller**, *noun*
**tongue twister**, *noun*
**topic**, *noun*
**topic sentence**, *noun*
**transitive**, *adjective*
**translate**, *verb*
**translation**, *noun*
**translator**, *noun*
**trilogy**, *noun*
**underline**, *verb*
**understatement**, *noun*
**uppercase**, *adjective*
**uppercase**, *noun*
**usage**, *noun*
**verb**, *noun*
**verbal**, *adjective*
**verbally**, *adverb*
**verse**, *noun*
**villain**, *noun*
**vocabulary**, *noun*
**vowel**, *noun*
**Welsh**, *noun*
**word**, *noun*
**write**, *verb*
**writer**, *noun*
**writing**, *noun*

## 11 Math

**absolute value**, *noun*
**add**, *verb*
**addend**, *noun*
**addition**, *noun*
**algebra**, *noun*
**amount**, *verb*
**angle**, *noun*
**arc**, *noun*
**area**, *noun*
**arithmetic**, *noun*
**array**, *noun*
**average**, *adjective*
**average**, *noun*
**average**, *verb*
**axis**, *noun*
**bar graph**, *noun*
**billion**, *number*
**billionth**, *number*
**bisect**, *verb*
**by**, *preposition*
**calculate**, *verb*
**calculation**, *noun*
**calculator**, *noun*
**chart**, *noun*
**circle**, *noun*
**circle graph**, *noun*
**circular**, *adjective*
**circumference**, *noun*
**common denominator**, *noun*
**common factor**, *noun*
**common multiple**, *noun*
**composite number**, *noun*
**cone**, *noun*
**congruent**, *adjective*
**converse**, *noun*
**conversely**, *adverb*
**crescent**, *noun*
**cube**, *noun*
**cubed**, *adjective*
**cubic**, *adjective*
**cylinder**, *noun*
**cylindrical**, *adjective*
**decagon**, *noun*
**decimal**, *adjective*
**decimal**, *noun*
**decimal point**, *noun*
**decimeter**, *noun*
**deduct**, *verb*
**deductible**, *adjective*
**deduction**, *noun*
**degree**, *noun*
**denominator**, *noun*
**diagonal**, *adjective*
**diagonal**, *noun*
**diagonally**, *adverb*
**diameter**, *noun*
**digit**, *noun*
**dimension**, *noun*
**distance**, *noun*
**divide**, *verb*
**dividend**, *noun*
**divisible**, *adjective*
**division**, *noun*
**divisor**, *noun*
**ellipse**, *noun*
**endpoint**, *noun*
**equal**, *adjective*
**equal**, *verb*
**equal sign**, *noun*
**equation**, *noun*
**equilateral**, *adjective*
**equilateral triangle**, *noun*
**even**, *adjective*
**evenly**, *adverb*
**exponent**, *noun*
**fact family**, *noun*
**factor**, *noun*
**figure**, *noun*
**flow chart**, *noun*
**fluid ounce**, *noun*
**foot**, *noun*
**fraction**, *noun*
**fractionally**, *adverb*
**geometric**, *adjective*
**geometry**, *noun*
**gram**, *noun*
**graph**, *noun*
**grid**, *noun*
**height**, *noun*
**heptagon**, *noun*
**heptagonal**, *adjective*
**hexagon**, *noun*
**hexagonal**, *adjective*
**high**, *adjective*
**histogram**, *noun*
**horizontal**, *adjective*
**horizontally**, *adverb*
**hour hand**, *noun*
**hundred thousand**, *number*
**improper fraction**, *noun*
**inequality sign**, *noun*
**integer**, *noun*
**intersect**, *verb*
**isosceles**, *adjective*
**length**, *noun*
**line of symmetry**, *noun*
**line plot**, *noun*
**long**, *adjective*
**make**, *verb*
**mathematical**, *adjective*
**mathematician**, *noun*
**mathematics**, *noun*
**measure**, *verb*
**measurable**, *adjective*
**measurement**, *noun*
**meter**, *noun*
**metric ton**, *noun*
**million**, *number*
**millionth**, *number*
**minus**, *noun*
**minus**, *preposition*
**minus sign**, *noun*
**minute hand**, *noun*
**mixed number**, *noun*
**mode**, *noun*
**multiple**, *noun*
**multiplication**, *noun*
**multiplication sentence**, *noun*
**multiply**, *verb*
**negative integer**, *noun*
**nonagon**, *noun*
**number**, *noun*
**number line**, *noun*
**number sentence**, *noun*
**numerator**, *noun*
**oblong**, *adjective*
**obtuse angle**, *noun*
**obtuse triangle**, *noun*
**odd**, *adjective*
**ordered pair**, *noun*
**organized list**, *noun*
**outlier**, *noun*
**oval**, *adjective*
**oval**, *noun*
**parallel**, *adjective*
**parallelogram**, *noun*
**partial product**, *noun*
**pentagon**, *noun*
**percent**, *noun*
**percentage**, *noun*
**perimeter**, *noun*
**perpendicular**, *adjective*
**pi**, *noun*
**picture graph**, *noun*
**pie chart**, *noun*
**place value**, *noun*
**plane**, *noun*
**plus**, *preposition*
**plus sign**, *noun*
**point**, *noun*
**polygon**, *noun*
**positive integer**, *noun*
**power**, *noun*
**prime factorization**, *noun*
**prime number**, *noun*
**prism**, *noun*
**probability**, *noun*
**problem**, *noun*
**product**, *noun*
**proportion**, *noun*
**proportional**, *adjective*
**protractor**, *noun*
**pyramid**, *noun*
**quadrant**, *noun*
**quadrilateral**, *noun*
**quantify**, *verb*
**quarter-hour**, *noun*
**quarter inch**, *noun*
**quotient**, *noun*
**radius**, *noun*
**range**, *verb*
**ratio**, *noun*
**reciprocal**, *noun*
**rectangle**, *noun*
**rectangular**, *adjective*
**rectangular prism**, *noun*
**rectangular pyramid**, *noun*
**related facts**, *noun*
**relative location**, *noun*
**rhombus**, *noun*
**right angle**, *noun*

right triangle, *noun*
rotation symmetry, *noun*
round, *adjective*
scale, *noun*
scalene triangle, *noun*
semicircle, *noun*
side, *noun*
simplest form, *noun*
size, *noun*
solid figure, *noun*
sphere, *noun*
spherical, *adjective*
square, *adjective*
square, *noun*
square, *verb*
square number, *noun*
square pyramid, *noun*
square root, *noun*
standard form, *noun*
statistic, *noun*
statistical, *adjective*
statistician, *noun*
stem and leaf plot, *noun*
straight, *adjective*
straight angle, *noun*
subtotal, *noun*
subtract, *verb*
subtraction, *noun*
subtraction sign, *noun*
sum, *noun*
table, *noun*
take, *verb*
tall, *adjective*
tally, *noun*
tally chart, *noun*
tally mark, *noun*
ten thousand, *number*
thick, *adjective*
thickness, *noun*
three-dimensional, *adjective*
times, *preposition*
total, *adjective*
total, *noun*
total, *verb*
trapezoid, *noun*
tree diagram, *noun*
triangle, *noun*
triangular, *adjective*
triangular pyramid, *noun*
trigonometry, *noun*
unit, *noun*
unit cost, *noun*
unit fraction, *noun*
unit square, *noun*
vertex, *noun*
wide, *adjective*
width, *noun*
x-axis, *noun*
x-coordinate, *noun*
y-axis, *noun*
y-coordinate, *noun*
zero property, *noun*

## 12 Music

accompany, *verb*
acoustic, *adjective*
anthem, *noun*
band, *noun*
banjo, *noun*
bass, *noun*
bassoon, *noun*
baton, *noun*
beat, *noun*
brass, *noun*
cellist, *noun*
cello, *noun*
choir, *noun*
chord, *noun*
chorus, *noun*
clarinet, *noun*
classical, *adjective*
classical music, *noun*
compose, *verb*
composer, *noun*
concert, *noun*
conduct, *verb*
conductor, *noun*
country music, *noun*
cymbal, *noun*
double bass, *noun*
duet, *noun*
fiddle, *noun*
flat, *adjective*
flat, *adverb*
flatness, *noun*
flute, *noun*
flutist, *noun*
group, *noun*
harmonica, *noun*
harmony, *noun*
harp, *noun*
harpist, *noun*
headphones, *plural noun*
instrument, *noun*
instrumental, *adjective*
jazz, *noun*
key, *noun*
keyboard, *noun*
lyricist, *noun*
lyrics, *plural noun*
major, *adjective*
march, *noun*
melodic, *adjective*
melody, *noun*
minor, *adjective*
musical, *noun*
note, *noun*
oboe, *noun*
orchestra, *noun*
organ, *noun*
organist, *noun*
percussion, *noun*
pianist, *noun*
piano, *noun*
pitch, *noun*
play, *verb*
pop, *noun*
quartet, *noun*
R & B, *noun*
rap, *noun*
rap, *verb*
rapper, *noun*
record, *verb*
reggae, *noun*
rhythm, *noun*
rhythm and blues, *noun*
rhythmic, *adjective*
rock, *noun*
rock 'n' roll, *noun*
salsa, *noun*
saxophone, *noun*
scale, *noun*
sharp, *adjective*
sharpness, *noun*
sing, *verb*
singer, *noun*
single, *noun*
solo, *noun*
soloist, *noun*
sonata, *noun*
song, *noun*
soprano, *noun*
soundtrack, *noun*
string, *noun*
symphony, *noun*
tambourine, *noun*
tempo, *noun*
tenor, *noun*
tone-deaf, *adjective*
tour, *noun*
trio, *noun*
trombone, *noun*
trombonist, *noun*
trumpet, *noun*
trumpeter, *noun*
tuba, *noun*
tune, *noun*
tune, *verb*
viola, *noun*
violin, *noun*
violinist, *noun*
vocal, *adjective*
vocalist, *noun*
vocals, *plural noun*
wind instrument, *noun*
woodwinds, *plural noun*
xylophone, *noun*

## 13 Physics

AC, *noun*
acoustic, *adjective*
amp, *noun*
astronomer, *noun*
astronomy, *noun*
atom, *noun*
atomic, *adjective*
atomic energy, *noun*
battery, *noun*
beam, *noun*
beam, *verb*
boil, *verb*
bubble, *noun*
bubble, *verb*
bulb, *noun*
cable, *noun*
capacity, *noun*
Celsius, *noun*
Centigrade, *noun*
charge, *noun*
charge, *verb*
circuit, *noun*
comet, *noun*
communication, *noun*
condensation, *noun*
condense, *verb*
conductivity, *noun*
constellation, *noun*
consume, *verb*
consumption, *noun*
contract, *verb*
convection, *noun*
current, *noun*
cylinder, *noun*
cylindrical, *adjective*

DC, *noun*
degree, *noun*
density, *noun*
distort, *verb*
distortion, *noun*
echo, *noun*
echo, *verb*
eclipse, *noun*
elastic, *adjective*
elastic, *noun*
electric, *adjective*
electrical, *adjective*
electricity, *noun*
electromagnet, *noun*
electromagnetic, *adjective*
electron, *noun*
electronic, *adjective*
electronically, *adverb*
electronics, *noun*
energy, *noun*
engine, *noun*
evaporate, *verb*
evaporation, *noun*
expand, *verb*
expansion, *noun*
Fahrenheit, *noun*
flexibility, *noun*
flexible, *adjective*
float, *verb*
fluid, *adjective*
fluid, *noun*
force, *noun*
form, *noun*
freeze, *verb*
freezing, *noun*
frequency, *noun*
friction, *noun*
full moon, *noun*
fundamental, *adjective*
fundamentally, *adverb*
fuse, *noun*
fusion, *noun*
galactic, *adjective*
galaxy, *noun*
gaseous, *adjective*
generator, *noun*
gravity, *noun*
harness, *verb*
heat, *noun*
heat, *verb*
hydroelectric, *adjective*
igneous, *adjective*
inaudible, *adjective*
infinite, *adjective*
infinity, *noun*
insulate, *verb*
insulation, *noun*
kilowatt, *noun*
laser, *noun*
lens, *noun*
lever, *noun*
light, *noun*
light year, *noun*
line, *noun*
liquid, *adjective*
liquid, *noun*
lunar, *adjective*
magma, *noun*
magnet, *noun*
magnetic, *adjective*
magnetic field, *noun*
magnetism, *noun*
magnetize, *verb*
magnification, *noun*
magnify, *verb*
magnifying glass, *noun*
mass, *noun*
matter, *noun*
melt, *verb*
metamorphic, *adjective*
meteor, *noun*
meteorite, *noun*
Milky Way, *noun*
momentum, *noun*
moon, *noun*
motion, *noun*
movement, *noun*
nuclear, *adjective*
nuclear energy, *noun*
nuclear weapon, *noun*
nucleus, *noun*
ohm, *noun*
optical, *adjective*
orbit, *noun*
orbit, *verb*
outer space, *noun*
outlet, *noun*
parallel circuit, *noun*
planet, *noun*
planetary, *adjective*
power, *noun*
pressure, *noun*
pressure, *verb*
prism, *noun*
radiation, *noun*
radio, *noun*
ray, *noun*
reflect, *verb*
reflection, *noun*
repel, *verb*
rock cycle, *noun*
series circuit, *noun*
solar, *adjective*
solar energy, *noun*
solar system, *noun*
solid, *noun*
space, *noun*
spectrum, *noun*
speed, *noun*
star, *noun*
static, *noun*
static electricity, *noun*
stress, *noun*
sun, *noun*
supersonic, *adjective*
temperature, *noun*
terminal, *noun*
thermal, *adjective*
thermal conductivity, *noun*
thermometer, *noun*
ultraviolet, *adjective*
vacuum, *noun*
vapor, *noun*
vaporize, *verb*
velocity, *noun*
vibrate, *verb*
vibration, *noun*
volt, *noun*
voltage, *noun*
watt, *noun*
wire, *noun*
wiring, *noun*

## 14 Sports

athlete, *noun*
athletic, *adjective*
backstroke, *noun*
ball, *noun*
ballpark, *noun*
base, *noun*
baseball, *noun*
basketball, *noun*
bat, *noun*
bat, *verb*
baton, *noun*
batter, *noun*
beat, *verb*
birdie, *noun*
body builder, *noun*
body building, *noun*
breaststroke, *noun*
canoe, *noun*
canoeing, *noun*
captain, *noun*
catch, *noun*
center, *noun*
center field, *noun*
champion, *noun*
championship, *noun*
cheerleader, *noun*
compete, *verb*
competition, *noun*
court, *noun*
dash, *noun*
defeat, *noun*
defeat, *verb*
defense, *noun*
diamond, *noun*
dribble, *verb*
dunk, *verb*
exercise, *noun*
field, *noun*
football, *noun*
forward, *noun*
foul, *noun*
foul, *verb*
game, *noun*
goal, *noun*
goalie, *noun*
goalkeeper, *noun*
golf, *noun*
golfer, *noun*
gym, *noun*
gymnasium, *noun*
gymnast, *noun*
gymnastics, *noun*
halftime, *noun*
high jump, *noun*
hockey, *noun*
infield, *noun*
inning, *noun*
intercept, *verb*
interception, *noun*
javelin, *noun*
jog, *noun*
jog, *verb*
jogger, *noun*
jogging, *noun*
judo, *noun*
karate, *noun*
kayak, *noun*
kick, *noun*
kick, *verb*
kickoff, *noun*
kung fu, *noun*
lead, *noun*
lead, *verb*
leader, *noun*
leadership, *noun*
long jump, *noun*
lose, *verb*
loser, *noun*
loss, *noun*
marathon, *noun*
martial arts, *plural noun*
match, *noun*
meet, *noun*
miss, *noun*
mound, *noun*
offense, *noun*
opponent, *noun*

outfield, *noun*
overtime, *noun*
pass, *noun*
pass, *verb*
penalize, *verb*
penalty, *noun*
period, *noun*
pin, *noun*
Ping-Pong, *trademark, noun*
pitch, *noun*
pitch, *verb*
pitcher, *noun*
place, *noun*
play, *noun*
play, *verb*
point, *noun*
pole vault, *noun*
qualifier, *noun*
quarter, *noun*
quarterback, *noun*
race, *noun*
race, *verb*
racehorse, *noun*
racetrack, *noun*
racket, *noun*
racketball, *noun*
relay, *noun*
round, *noun*
run, *noun*
run, *verb*
runner, *noun*
running, *noun*
score, *noun*
score, *verb*
semifinal, *noun*
series, *noun*
set, *noun*
shoot, *verb*
shot, *noun*
ski, *verb*
skiing, *noun*
skydiver, *noun*
skydiving, *noun*
soccer, *noun*
softball, *noun*
spectator, *noun*
sport, *noun*
sportsmanship, *noun*
sprint, *noun*
sprinter, *noun*
stadium, *noun*
surf, *verb*
surfing, *noun*
tackle, *noun*
tackle, *verb*
team, *noun*
teammate, *noun*
tennis, *noun*
tie, *noun*
tie, *verb*
tied, *adjective*
time out, *noun*
touchdown, *noun*
tournament, *noun*
track, *noun*
train, *verb*
trampoline, *noun*
triathlon, *noun*
trophy, *noun*
umpire, *noun*
versus, *preposition*
volleyball, *noun*
warm-up, *adjective*
warm-up, *noun*
water ski, *verb*
water skier, *noun*
water skiing, *noun*
weight-lifter, *noun*
weightlifting, *noun*
windsurf, *verb*
windsurfer, *noun*
windsurfing, *noun*
work out, *verb*
world record, *noun*
World Series, *noun*
wrestle, *verb*
wrestler, *noun*
wrestling, *noun*
yoga, *noun*

## Geographical Names

| Name | Adjective |
| --- | --- |
| Afghanistan | Afghan *or* Afghanistani |
| Africa | African |
| Albania | Albanian |
| Algeria | Algerian |
| America (=the U.S.) | American |
| North America | North American |
| South America | South American |
| Andorra | Andorran |
| Angola | Angolan |
| Antarctic | Antarctic |
| Antigua and Barbuda | Antiguan *and* Barbudan |
| Arctic | Arctic |
| Argentina | Argentinian<br>*person:* Argentinian or Argentine |
| Armenia | Armenian |
| Asia | Asian |
| Atlantic | Atlantic |
| Australia | Australian |
| Austria | Austrian |
| Azerbaijan | Azerbaijani |
| Bahamas, the | Bahamian |
| Bahrain | Bahraini |
| Baltic | Baltic |
| Bangladesh | Bangladeshi |
| Barbados | Barbadian |
| Belarus (Belorussia) | Belorussian |
| Belgium | Belgian |
| Belize | Belizean |
| Benin | Beninese |
| Bermuda | Bermudan |
| Bhutan | Bhutanese |
| Bolivia | Bolivian |
| Bosnia and Herzegovina | Bosnian Herzegovinian |
| Botswana | Botswanan<br>*person:* Motswana<br>*people:* the Batswana |
| Brazil | Brazilian |
| Brunei | Bruneian |
| Bulgaria | Bulgarian |
| Burkina Faso | Burkina *or* Burkinabe |
| Burma (*former name of* Myanmar) | Burmese |
| Burundi | Burundian |
| Cambodia | Cambodian |
| Cameroon | Cameroonian |
| Canada | Canadian |
| Cape Verde | Cape Verdean |
| Caribbean | Caribbean |
| Cayman Islands | Cayman Island<br>*person:* Cayman Islander |
| Central African Republic | Central African |
| Chad | Chadian |
| Chile | Chilean |
| China | Chinese |
| Colombia | Colombian |
| Comoro Islands, the | Comoran |
| Congo, the Democratic | Congolese |
| Costa Rica | Costa Rican |
| Croatia | Croatian |
| Cuba | Cuban |
| Cyprus | Cypriot |
| Czech Republic, the | Czech |
| Denmark | Danish<br>*person:* Dane |

| Name | Adjective |
|---|---|
| Djibouti | Djiboutian |
| Dominica | Dominican |
| Dominican Republic, the | Dominican |
| East Timor | Timorese |
| Ecuador | Ecuadorian |
| Egypt | Egyptian |
| El Salvador | Salvadorian |
| England | English<br>*person:* Englishman, Englishwoman<br>*people:* the English |
| Equatorial Guinea | Equatorial Guinean |
| Eritrea | Eritrean |
| Estonia | Estonian |
| Ethiopia | Ethiopian |
| Europe | European |
| Fiji | Fijian |
| Finland | Finnish<br>*person:* Finn |
| France | French<br>*person:* Frenchman, Frenchwoman<br>*people:* the French |
| Gabon | Gabonese |
| Gambia, the | Gambian |
| Georgia | Georgian |
| Germany | German |
| Ghana | Ghanaian |
| Gibraltar | Gibraltarian |
| Great Britain | British<br>*person:* Briton<br>*people:* the British |
| Greece | Greek |
| Greenland | Greenlandic<br>*person:* Greenlander |
| Grenada | Grenadian |
| Guatemala | Guatemalan |
| Guiana *also* French Guiana | Guianese |
| Guinea | Guinean |
| Guinea-Bissau | Guinea-Bissauan |
| Guyana *also* British Guyana | Guyanese *or* Guyanan |
| Haiti | Haitian |
| Holland (another name for The Netherlands) | Dutch<br>*person:* Dutchman, Dutchwoman<br>*people:* the Dutch |
| Honduras | Honduran |
| Hong Kong | Hong Kong |
| Hungary | Hungarian |
| Iceland | Icelandic<br>*person:* Icelander |
| India | Indian |
| Indonesia | Indonesian |
| Iran | Iranian |
| Iraq | Iraqi |

| Name | Adjective |
|---|---|
| Ireland, Republic of, the | Irish<br>*person:* Irishman, Irishwoman<br>*people:* the Irish |
| Israel | Israeli |
| Italy | Italian |
| Ivory Coast (*former name of* Cote d'Ivoire) | Ivorian |
| Jamaica | Jamaican |
| Japan | Japanese |
| Jordan | Jordanian |
| Kazakhstan | Kazakh |
| Kenya | Kenyan |
| Kiribati | Kiribati |
| Korea, North | North Korean |
| Korea, South | South Korean |
| Kuwait | Kuwaiti |
| Kyrgyzstan | Kyrgyz |
| Laos | Laotian *or* Lao |
| Latvia | Latvian |
| Lebanon | Lebanese |
| Lesotho | Sotho<br>*person:* Mosotho<br>*people:* the Basotho |
| Liberia | Liberian |
| Libya | Libyan |
| Liechtenstein | Liechtenstein<br>*person:* Liechtensteiner |
| Lithuania | Lithuanian |
| Luxemburg | Luxemburg<br>*person:* Luxemburger |
| Macedonia | Macedonian |
| Madagascar | Malagasy |
| Malawi | Malawian |
| Malaysia | Malaysian |
| Maldives, the | Maldivian |
| Mali | Malian |
| Malta | Maltese |
| Marshall Islands, the | Marshallese<br>*person:* Marshall Islander |
| Mauritania | Mauritanian |
| Mauritius | Mauritian |
| Mediterranean | Mediterranean |
| Melanesia | Melanesian |
| Mexico | Mexican |
| Micronesia | Micronesian |
| Moldova | Moldovan |
| Monaco | Monegasque or Monacan |
| Mongolia | Mongolian *or* Mongol |
| Montserrat | Montserratian |
| Morocco | Moroccan |
| Mozambique | Mozambican |
| Myanmar | Burmese |
| Namibia | Namibian |

| Name | Adjective |
|---|---|
| Nauru | Nauruan |
| Nepal | Nepalese<br>*person:* Nepali or Nepalese |
| Netherlands, The | Dutch<br>*person:* Dutchman, Dutchwoman<br>*people:* the Dutch |
| New Zealand | New Zealand<br>*person:* New Zealander |
| Nicaragua | Nicaraguan |
| Niger | Nigerien |
| Nigeria | Nigerian |
| Norway | Norwegian |
| Oman | Omani |
| Pacific | Pacific |
| Pakistan | Pakistani |
| Palestine | Palestinian |
| Panama | Panamanian |
| Papua New Guinea | Papuan *or* Papua New Guinean |
| Paraguay | Paraguayan |
| Persia (*former name of* Iran) | Persian |
| Peru | Peruvian |
| Philippines | Philippine<br>*person:* Filipino |
| Poland | Polish<br>*person:* Pole |
| Polynesia | Polynesian |
| Portugal | Portuguese |
| Puerto Rico | Puerto Rican |
| Qatar | Qatari |
| Romania | Romanian |
| Russia (Russian Federation, the) | Russian |
| Rwanda | Rwandan |
| Saint Kitts & Nevis | Kittitian, Nevisian |
| Saint Lucia | Saint Lucian |
| Saint Vincent and the Grenadines | Vincentian |
| Samoa | Samoan |
| San Marino | Sammarinese San Marinese |
| São Tomé & Principe | São Tomean |
| Saudi Arabia | Saudi Arabian<br>*person:* Saudi |
| Scotland | Scottish<br>*person:* Scot |
| Senegal | Senegalese |
| Seychelles, the | Seychellois |
| Sierra Leone | Sierra Leonean |
| Singapore | Singaporean |
| Slovakia | Slovakian |
| Slovenia | Slovenian *or* Slovene |
| Solomon Islands, the | Soloman Island<br>*person:* Solomon Islander |
| Somalia | Somali |
| South Africa | South African |
| Spain | Spanish<br>*person:* Spaniard<br>*people:* the Spanish |
| Sri Lanka | Sri Lankan |
| Sudan | Sudanese |
| Surinam, Suriname | Surinamese<br>*person:* Surinamer |
| Swaziland | Swazi |
| Sweden | Swedish<br>*person:* Swede |
| Switzerland | Swiss |
| Syria | Syrian |
| Tahiti | Tahitian |
| Taiwan | Taiwanese |
| Tajikistan | Tajik |
| Tanzania | Tanzanian |
| Thailand | Thai |
| Tibet | Tibetan |
| Togo | Togolese |
| Tonga | Tongan |
| Trinidad and Tobago | Trinidadian *or* Tobagonian |
| Tunisia | Tunisian |
| Turkey | Turkish<br>*person:* Turk |
| Turkmenistan | Turkmen |
| Tuvalu | Tuvaluan |
| Uganda | Ugandan |
| Ukraine | Ukrainian |
| United Arab Emirates | Emirati |
| United Kingdom of Great Britain and Northern Ireland, the | British<br>*person:* Briton<br>*people:* the British |
| United States, the | American |
| Uruguay | Uruguayan |
| Uzbekistan | Uzbek |
| Vanuatu | Vanuatuan |
| Venezuela | Venezuelan |
| Vietnam | Vietnamese |
| Wales | Welsh<br>*person:* Welshman, Welshwoman<br>*people:* the Welsh |
| Yemen | Yemen |
| Yugoslavia | Yugoslavian or Yugoslav |
| Zambia | Zambian |
| Zimbabwe | Zimbabwean |

# Weights and Measurements

## U.S. Customary System

### Units of Length

| | | |
|---|---|---|
| 1 inch | | = 2.54 cm |
| 12 inches | = 1 foot | = 0.3048 m |
| 3 feet | = 1 yard | = 0.9144 m |
| 1,760 yards (5,280 feet) | = 1 mile | = 1.609 km |
| 2,025 yards (6,076 feet) | = 1 nautical mile | = 1.852 km |

### Units of Weight

| | | |
|---|---|---|
| 1 ounce | | = 28.35 g |
| 16 ounces | = 1 pound | = 0.4536 kg |
| 2,000 pounds | = 1 ton | = 907.18 kg |
| 2,240 pounds | = 1 long ton | = 1,016.0 kg |

### Units of Volume (Liquid)

| | | |
|---|---|---|
| 1 fluid ounce | | = 29.574 ml |
| 8 fluid ounces | = 1 cup | = 0.2366 l |
| 16 fluid ounces | = 1 pint | = 0.4732 l |
| 2 pints | = 1 quart | = 0.9463 l |
| 4 quarts | = 1 gallon | = 3.7853 l |

### Units of Volume (Dry Measure)

| | | |
|---|---|---|
| 1 peck | | = 8,809.5 $cm^3$ |
| 4 pecks | = 1 bushel | = 35,239 $cm^3$ |

### Units of Area

| | | |
|---|---|---|
| 1 square inch | | = 645.16 $mm^2$ |
| 144 square inches | = 1 square foot | = 0.0929 $m^2$ |
| 9 square feet | = 1 square yard | = 0.8361 $m^2$ |
| 4,840 square yards | = 1 acre | = 4047 $m^2$ |
| 640 acres | = 1 square mile | = 259 ha |

### Temperature

| | |
|---|---|
| degrees Fahrenheit | = (°C x 9/5) + 32 |
| degrees Celsius | = (°F - 32) x 5/9 |

## Metric System

### Units of Length

| | | |
|---|---|---|
| 1 millimeter | | = 0.03937 inch |
| 10 mm | = 1 centimeter | = 0.3937 inch |
| 100 cm | = 1 meter | = 39.37 inches |
| 1,000 m | = 1 kilometer | = 0.6214 mile |

### Units of Weight

| | | |
|---|---|---|
| 1 milligram | | = 0.000035 ounce |
| 1,000 mg | = 1 gram | = 0.035 ounce |
| 1,000 g | = 1 kilogram | = 2.205 pounds |
| 1,000k g | = 1 metric ton | = 2,205 pounds |

### Units of Volume

| | | |
|---|---|---|
| 1 milliliter | | = 0.03 fluid ounce |
| 1,000 ml | = 1 liter | = 1.06 quarts |

### Units of Area

| | | |
|---|---|---|
| 1 square centimeter | | = 0.1550 square inch |
| 10,000 $cm^2$ | = 1 square meter | = 1.196 square yards |
| 10,000 $m^2$ | = 1 hectare | = 2.471 acres |

# Workbook Answer Key

## LESSON 1
### Exercise 1
Group 1: 2, 1, 4, 5, 3
Group 2: 3, 1, 4, 2, 5
Group 3: 4, 3, 5, 2, 1
Group 4: 3, 1, 2, 4, 5
Group 5: 3, 2, 1, 5, 4

### Exercise 2
1 desolate
2 read
3 preoccupation
4 blow
5 every
6 heroic

### Exercise 3
1 fat
2 bright
3 succeed
4 smell
5 hold

## LESSON 2
### Exercise 1
1 beginning
2 excitement
3 different
4 sadden
5 finally
6 library
7 Arctic
8 surprise

### Exercise 2
1 thieves
2 bouncing
3 prettiest
4 supplies
5 daily
6 planned

### Exercise 3
1 chemistry
2 knife
3 seal
4 python
5 wreck
6 giraffe
7 pharmacy
8 hourly

## LESSON 3
### Exercise 1
1 c
2 b
3 a
4 d
5 f
6 e
7 h
8 g

### Exercise 2
1 preposition
2 noun, verb
3 noun, verb
4 noun
5 noun, verb
6 noun, verb
7 noun, verb, adjective
8 noun, adjective

### Exercise 3
1 noun, adjective
2 adjective, noun
3 noun, verb
4 noun, verb
5 verb, noun
6 adjective, adverb
7 noun, verb
8 verb, noun

### Exercise 4
1 verb
2 noun
3 verb
4 noun
5 verb
6 noun
7 adverb
8 adjective
9 noun
10 verb

## LESSON 4
### Exercise 1
1 parameter
2 attention
3 currency
4 penalize
5 scold
6 tolerate

### Exercise 2
1 quick 2
2 certain 3
3 issue 4
4 hook 3
5 pleasant 2
6 flash 5
7 schedule 2
8 term 6

### Exercise 3
1 kind 1
2 guard 1
3 contrast 2
4 fine 5
5 minor 1
6 equal 2

### Exercise 4
1 b
2 a
3 a
4 b
5 b
6 b

## LESSON 5
### Exercise 1
1 wives
2 sheep
3 halves
4 tomatoes
5 geese
6 cacti
7 men
8 oxen

### Exercise 2
1 a) brought, b) brought
2 a) flew, b) flown
3 a) swam, b) swum
4 a) paid, b) paid
5 a) wore, b) worn
6 a) took, b) taken

### Exercise 3
1 buddies
2 bash
3 bug
4 buy
5 dumb
6 weird
7 stomach
8 help

### Exercise 4
1 compensate
2 components
3 outcome
4 restrictions
5 debate
6 aware
7 transfer
8 legislation

## LESSON 6
### Exercise 1
1 run
2 talk
3 back
4 look
5 eat
6 hold

### Exercise 2
1 run into
2 back down
3 look something up
4 talk someone into something
5 eat out
6 hold something against someone

### Exercise 3
1 stand up to
2 drop off
3 taken up
4 pass on
5 run out of
6 go up
7 mixed up
8 turn in

### Exercise 4
1 c
2 e
3 a
4 f
5 b
6 d

### Exercise 5
1 False
2 True
3 False
4 True
5 True
6 False

## LESSON 7
### Exercise 1
1 courage
2 jealousy
3 fever
4 depend
5 library
6 recognize

### Exercise 2

| Nouns | Verbs | Adjectives | Adverbs |
|---|---|---|---|
| 1 defiance | | defiant | defiantly |
| 2 whisper | whisper | | |
| 3 pleasure | | pleasurable | |
| 4 brightness | | bright | brightly |
| 5 father | father | fatherly | |
| 6 recruit | recruit | | |

### Exercise 3

| Nouns | Verbs | Adjectives | Adverbs |
|---|---|---|---|
| fear \| fearlessness | fear | fearful \| fearless | fearfully \| fearlessly |
| delight | delight | delightful \| delighted | delightfully |
| opening \| opener | open | open \| opened | openly |
| weakling \| weakness | weaken | weak | weakly |
| critic | criticize | critical | critically |

### Exercise 4

1 a) inform, b) information, c) informative
2 a) angry, b) anger, c) angrily
3 a) danger, b) dangerous, c) dangerously
4 a) know, b) knowledge, c) known
5 a) confusing b) confusion c) confused

## LESSON 8

### Exercise 1

1 gas station
2 everyone
3 belly button
4 father
5 cougar
6 frying pan
7 perfume
8 cash register

### Exercise 2

1 expensive
2 fall
3 well
4 prison
5 wonderful
6 scream
7 bravery
8 false

### Exercise 3

1 antonym
2 antonym
3 antonym
4 antonym
5 synonym
6 synonym
7 synonym
8 antonym

### Exercise 4

1 a) snack, b) barbecue, c) picnic
2 a) decline, b) said no, c) refused
3 a) perfume, b) aroma, c) odor

### Exercise 5

| List 1 | List 2 |
|---|---|
| 1 hallway | 1 excellent |
| 2 x | 2 hug |
| 3 boring | 3 x |
| 4 lose | 4 worldwide |
| 5 start | 5 scared/frightened |
| 6 x | 6 x |
| 7 symbol | 7 weakness |
| 8 x | 8 help |

## LESSON 9

### Exercise 1

1 Italian
2 Yiddish
3 French
4 Nahuatl
5 Italian
6 Dutch
7 Latin
8 Spanish
9 Malay
10 Greek
11 German
12 Chinese

### Exercise 2

1 c) coffee shop
2 d) bright or beautiful
3 a) a road or racetrack
4 e) home + study
5 f) born into an upper class family
6 b) to owe

### Exercise 3

| English Word | Language Origin | Original word(s) | Original meaning |
|---|---|---|---|
| 1 rank | French | *renc* | line or row |
| 2 biography | Greek | *bios, graphein* | life, to write |
| 3 phobia | Greek | *phobos* | fear |
| 4 mistake | Norse | *mistaka* | to take wrongly |
| 5 reflect | Latin | *reflectere* | to bend back |
| 6 prohibit | Latin | *prohibere* | to hold away or prevent |

### Exercise 4

1 psychology, b) the study of the mind
2 omnivore, f) an animal that eats meat and plants
3 lunatic, a) someone who is crazy or behaves in a very stupid way
4 translation, e) something that has been changed from one language to another
5 centipede, e) a small creature with a long soft body and many small legs
6 minority, d) a small group of people or things that are part of a larger group

### Exercise 5

1 a)
2 a)
3 c)
4 b)

## LESSON 10

### Exercise 1

1 vi–vii
2 A2–A32
3 879–881
4 900
5 882–897
6 A32
7 897–899

### Exercise 2

1 chemistry
2 politics
3 biology
4 computers
5 sports

### Exercise 3

1 froze, page 879
2 gallon, page 900
3 answers may vary, page A16–A17
4 liter, page 900
5 North Carolina, page A32
6 answers may vary, page A9
7 Nepalese, page 899